Ahtahkakoop

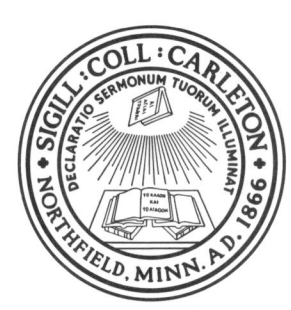

Ahtahkakoop

**The Epic Account of a Plains Cree Head Chief,
His People, and Their Struggle for Survival, 1816-1896**

by Deanna Christensen

— Ahtahkakoop Publishing, 2000 —

Ahtahkakoop Publishing
Box 190
Shell Lake, Saskatchewan S0J 2G0

Canadian Cataloguing in Publication Data

Christensen, Deanna.

   Ahtahkakoop : the epic account of a Plains Cree
Head Chief, his people, and their struggle for survival,
1816-1896

   Includes bibliographical references and index.
   ISBN 0-9687369-0-4

1. Ahtahkakoop, 1816-1896.   2. Cree Indians—
Saskatchewan—History.   I. Ahtahkakoop First Nation.
II. Title.

E99.C88 A38 2000   971.24'004973   C00-920168-8

Printed and bound in Canada by Friesens, Altona, Manitoba

Dedication

*This book is dedicated to Ahtahkakoop by
his descendants today, in thanks*

Contributors

"Let us not think of ourselves but of our children's children."

These profound words were spoken by Chief Ahtahkakoop on August 21st, 1876, at a Chiefs Council prior to their signing of Treaty Six at Fort Carlton, Saskatchewan, on August 23rd, 1876.

Today, Chief Ahtahkakoop would be proud to know that his and his people's children's children have Friends who are Partners, who speak these words with them.

We, the children of Chief Ahtahkakoop and His People, gratefully acknowledge the following Partners for their support in making possible the publication of this book.

Indian and Northern Affairs Canada
Saskatchewan Municipal Affairs Culture and Housing
Saskatchewan Heritage Foundation
SaskPower
SaskEnergy
Weyerhaeuser
Saskatchewan Indian Gaming Authority
Wirtz Corporation – Chicago Blackhawks Hockey Team, Inc.
Northern Grocers Inc.
Crown Life
Saskatchewan Education
Prince Albert Photocopier Ltd.
Heidt Evaluation Services Inc.
Anglican Diocese of Saskatchewan
Hudson's Bay Company

Contents

List of Illustrations, Maps and Photographs

Maps

Photographs

Foreword by Chief Barry L. Ahenakew

We are Nēhiyawak, the Plains Cree. Our ancestors walked this land for thousands of years. Proud and free, they were blessed by the Creator with the Sun Dance, the Prairie Chicken Dance, and the Grass Dance. Millions of buffalo roamed the plains, and life was good.

Then, the white man came, and the world of our people changed. The buffalo vanished. Yet the old people said that the Nēhiyawak could survive—education would be the new buffalo. But the old ways must not be forgotten.

As a child, I witnessed the old ways. I traveled and I saw the Sun Dance, the Prairie Chicken Dance, and the Grass Dance. Many times the shamans, the medicine men, and medicine women stopped by the house to visit with my grandparents, Alice and Andrew Ahenakew. I was proud to be Nēhiyaw. I chose to try and maintain my Indian spirit and my Indian ways. I kept my long hair, I kept my braids, and I was determined to keep my culture. Yet the world of our people was changing again. Many young people were being educated off the reserve, and I saw them being acculturated into white society. It made me think about what lay ahead for the Nēhiyawak, about the welfare of my people.

In time, I was chosen chief of the Ahtahkakoop Band. As a leader, I knew I must do my best to improve the life of the people. And I remembered the wisdom of the elders: "Education is the new buffalo." I resolved that a written history of our people was necessary to restore their pride, through a knowledge of their ancestors, and the old ways.

I met Deanna Christensen, who was interested in our history and in our sacred stories, in 1980. Later it was agreed that she would research and write a history of Chief Ahtahkakoop. What started as a manuscript for developing school curriculum has evolved over 12½ years into this book, *Ahtahkakoop: The Epic Account of a Plains Cree Head Chief, His People, and Their Struggle for Survival, 1816-1896.*

Ahtahkakoop documents the struggle of our great ancestral chief, Ahtahkakoop, and his people, as they made the difficult transition from the days of the buffalo to the days of the plough. They faced oppression, but they persevered. There is still oppression, but this book is witness that, with sober and careful thought, and the courage and perseverance of our ancestors, our people can improve their lives. We can honour and maintain the Sun Dance, the Prairie Chicken Dance, the Grass Dance, and our ceremonies. And we can hold our heads high in the world of today.

The benefits from the *Ahtahkakoop* project are already evident for our people. Our new high school—the first on the reserve—officially opened in 1994, and over 400 students now study on the reserve, learning both the old ways and the new. And the buffalo have returned—a herd now grazes on our land, and our people can see that learning the new ways does not mean abandoning the world of our ancestors.

Ahtahkakoop will help improve the lives of our people. But it will accomplish more than that. The people who read it will come to know and understand the Nēhiyawak. And that is good.

I would like to thank the councils that have supported the Ahtahkakoop History Project throughout the years, and the other people who have been involved in making this book a reality. In addition, I thank the elders who have encouraged me with their patience and love to move ahead on this and other projects. And I especially thank my grandparents, Alice Ahenakew and the late Andrew Ahenakew, and Olive Bird and the late George Bird, for showing me the old ways, and making me proud to be Nēhiyaw.

I would also like to thank Hazel for her encouragement and support, as well as our children, Kishey Pisim, Sikwan Achak, Utin Awasis, Kimowan Kisik, and Mahikan Awasis for being our inspiration, and our grandchildren, Okichitaw Kimaw, Nipawiw Kimaw, and Sakihik Awa, for being our further inspiration.

Barry L. Ahenakew
Chief of the Ahtahkakoop Cree Nation
September 2000

Message from the Bishop of Saskatchewan

Chief Ahtahkakoop was one of a small number of founding fathers of the Diocese of Saskatchewan, and the impact of his spiritual leadership continues to be felt today. His intelligence, insight, and openness to the world around him has been an inspiration to the generations that followed. The history of his gifted and remarkable family is an important part of the history of our Diocese, and I am indebted to Deanna Christensen and the Ahtahkakoop Band for helping us to understand ourselves better.

The Rt. Rev. Anthony Burton
Bishop of Saskatchewan

Saskatchewan Archives Board R-B7063
The Reverend Edward Ahenakew was Ahtahkakoop's great-nephew. He is shown here in 1956.

The People of Ahtahkakoop gratefully acknowledge the generosity of the Reverend Canon Edward Ahenakew Memorial Trust Fund, Diocese of Saskatchewan, Anglican Church of Canada, for contributing to the creation of this book.

Production Team

Barry L. Ahenakew, Chief of the Ahtahkakoop Band and keeper of traditional Plains Cree stories.

Jeff Ahenakew, C.E.O of project.

Willard Ahenakew, art director, illustrator, and project coordinator.

Brian Mlazgar, Canadian Plains Research Center, University of Regina, editing, design and layout.

Donna Achtzehner, Canadian Plains Research Center, University of Regina, technical advice, proofreading.

Diane Bolingbroke, Information Systems Division, Canadian Plains Research Center, University of Regina, cartographer.

Lorena Patino, Information Systems Division, Canadian Plains Research Center, University of Regina, cartographer.

Ed Peekeekoot, illustrator.

Brent Christensen, illustrator.

Ray Christensen, photographer.

Heather Hodgson, Canadian Plains Research Center, University of Regina, indexer.

Corey Kurtz, digital imaging and touchup.

Tuan Nguyen, Central Photo Lab, digital imaging and touchup.

Brian Danchuk, of Brian Danchuk Design, cover design.

Ryan Hildebrand, Friesens Book Division, customer service representative.

Arok Wolvengrey, Department of Indian Languages, Literature and Linguistics, Saskatchewan Indian Federated College, standardization of Cree spelling and translation.

Jean Okimāsis, Department of Indian Languages, Literature and Linguistics, Saskatchewan Indian Federated College, standardization of Cree spelling and translation.

Freda Ahenakew, professor of Cree language and linguistics and translator of sacred stories.

Deanna Christensen, writer, researcher, manuscript conversion coordinator, and book printing liaison.

Preface

On September 10, 1934, towards the end of a season of field work in Saskatchewan, anthropologist David Mandelbaum asked the shaman Fine Day to tell him about the spirit world of the Indian people. Fine Day, who was born in about 1854—some 37 years after Ahtahkakoop's birth—agreed. And so, in an interview that took place on the Sweetgrass Reserve west of present-day Battleford, Fine Day talked about Manitow, the Creator, *ātayohkanak* (the spirit helpers), *pawākanak* (the personal dream spirits), and some of the sacred ceremonies of the Indian people. During his discourse Fine Day cautioned that "these things you ask about today, we should have talked about when we first began because these matters always should come first before all else. That is why I smoked a pipe when we began to talk." He concluded by saying that "in my kindness to man.to* I am telling you this. It is no mistake or sin that we are doing this last. But when you make any history of this, please it would be best to put it first."[1]

In 1994 when we, members of the Ahtahkakoop History Project Committee, reviewed the first draft of *Ahtahkakoop: The Epic Account of a Plains Cree Head Chief, His People, and Their Struggle for Survival 1816–1896*, it was apparent something was missing. Too many questions were arising. Too many understandings were hard to grasp. Very quickly we recognized the wisdom of Fine Day's counsel of 60 years earlier. And so, the pipe was smoked, cloth offerings were made, and it was decided to begin the story of Ahtahkakoop and his people with a section entitled "The World Ahtahkakoop Was Born Into." This was the world of the Nēhiyawak, the Plains Cree. It was a world that had its beginning eons earlier.

We called upon elders and others in the Ahtahkakoop Cree Nation who were versed in oral history to help with this and other parts of the book. All spoke Plains Cree as their first language. Their stories were told in Cree and preserved on audio tapes. Later they were transcribed into Cree, translated into English, and edited. Traditionally, Plains Cree stories are rich in detail, inflection, and cadence. Often they are accompanied by hand movements and other gestures. We have tried to retain the characteristics of Cree story-telling and for that reason editing has been kept to a minimum.

---

* *Manitow* or the Creator.

My task was to incorporate the understandings and interpretations of the elders and others in the Ahtahkakoop Cree Nation with the research gleaned from non-Indian sources. Most of the latter information came from archival and primary sources. These included documents at the Hudson's Bay Company Archives (Provincial Archives of Manitoba), the David Mandelbaum Papers at the Saskatchewan Archives Board, Indian Affairs RG10 and North-West Mounted Police RG18 records, whose primary deposit is at the National Archives of Canada, and books and journals written by newcomers to Saskatchewan River country.

Of particular importance were the writings of Anglican missionary John Hines, who lived with Ahtahkakoop and his people from 1875 to 1888. These included Hines's book *Red Indians of the Plains* and journals, reports and correspondence preserved in the Church of England's Church Missionary Society (CMS) collection; this collection is housed at the National Archives of Canada, the Provincial Archives of Manitoba, and several other locations.

Fortunately, the Anglican Diocese of Saskatchewan made the Asissipi Mission's baptism, marriage, and death registers available for this project. This made it possible to identify women and children by name. In other sources, particularly government documentation, women and children generally remain nameless, and boys are only named when they are old enough to get their own treaty numbers.

There were many challenges. The spelling and translation of Cree names were among the most crucial. Since Cree is traditionally an oral language, white newcomers to the Indian lands recorded names as they heard them, syllable by syllable. The spelling of any particular name often changed from year to year in reports, treaty paylists, and other records, depending on the writer's knowledge of Cree and his ability to record the sounds he heard. To further complicate this situation, the handwriting on the documents was often difficult to read. In order to have some conformity, a group of elders, three Cree language specialists, and others spent many hours interpreting and spelling the names that appeared on the Ahtahkakoop Band's first treaty paylist. The result of this work is a list that includes the names as they appeared on the paylist, their translation, and spellings using Standard Roman Orthography (SRO). This list is contained in the appendices. Additionally, two Cree language specialists in Regina reviewed most of the Cree words in the text and provided standardized spellings. They also created a pronunciation and spelling guide for some of the principal individuals in the book. This, along with a glossary of Cree and English names for geographic areas that were of particular interest to Ahtahkakoop's band, can also be found in the appendices.

Some arbitrary decisions were made during the course of writing the book, particularly when discrepancies were evident. For instance, the dates of births, marriages, and deaths recorded in the journals written by a missionary sometimes differed from the dates in the birth and death mission registers, even though they were kept by the same man. This often made it difficult to determine the age of individuals. Similarly, information on the treaty paylists often varied from year to year or conflicted with the mission records. In these situations, data most consistent with other information was chosen.

The text of *Ahtahkakoop* relies heavily on quotations from primary sources. This was done for two reasons. First, we believe that direct quotations provide a sense of "being there." Second, we wanted to ensure that meanings were not changed through the process of generalizing and paraphrasing. We have not attempted to censure or edit quotations, believing that biased, racist and paternalistic language helps indicate the mind-set of the speaker or writer. Since this is a historical work, some words are used in their historical context. A prime example is the word "half-breed," used in this book as it was used during the 1800s for people of Indian and white ancestry. Today, many of these people call themselves Métis.

As noted elsewhere, this book was conceived as a band history for Ahtahkakoop's descendants. Accordingly, the names of individuals and their family connections are prominent in the book, with many of the names appearing in the genealogy chart on the back endsheet. We hope other readers will find them of interest. It should be noted that Cree family names still being used today are spelt the way families currently spell them.

I would like to thank Chief Barry L. Ahenakew for the wisdom and foresight that enabled the story of Ahtahkakoop and his people to be told. It was due to his practical help, encouragement, and patience that the book was completed. His wife Hazel and their children welcomed my family into their family and they taught me so much. For that I am grateful.

In addition, I thank Jeffrey D. Ahenakew (Ahtahkakoop Education) for his invaluable support, Willard Ahenakew for his enthusiasm, faith, and dedication as project manager, and Clifford Ahenakew and Ruth Ahenakew for their help in keeping the project alive during a period when its continuation was in doubt. I also appreciate Larry Ahenakew's later efforts to keep the book moving ahead. And of course, I want to express my appreciation to the councils that gave me the opportunity to work on *Ahtahkakoop: The Epic Account of a Plains Cree Head Chief, His People, and Their Struggle for Survival 1816–1896* and then supported the project to its completion.

The contribution of the review committee is also acknowledged with thanks. The core committee included Barry Ahenakew, Jeffrey Ahenakew, Willard Ahenakew, Ruth Ahenakew, Freda Ahenakew, Paul Ahenakew, and Deanna Christensen.

Betsy and Murray Burt in Winnipeg deserve special thanks. Because of their extraordinary hospitality, I was able to spend what amounted to many, many months doing research at the Hudson's Bay Company Archives and the Provincial Archives of Manitoba. Another friend, Simon Van Der Heijden, kept my computer and software working and answered many a frantic call, usually just before a deadline.

I am grateful to the elders, including Lawrence Tobacco, George Ponnicappo, and Bill Standingready, along with others who have passed on —Fred Yayahkeekoot, Pius Dustyhorn, Smith Atimoyoo, Alfred McArthur, and Jim Ryder—for their kindness and their teachings. Additionally, I have treasured the friendship of Lizette Ahenakew, Ida Wasacase, Laura Wasacase, Jean Okimāsis, Maria Shepherd, Catherine Lonethunder, Freda Ahenakew, Phyllis Bellegarde, Joan Lavallee, and so many other incredible women. And I thank Joe Naytowhow for his support over many years.

I would also like to acknowledge Sharon Wood, who gave me the opportunity to do a comprehensive report on Fort Carlton for Saskatchewan Parks and Renewable Resources, and Ida Wasacase for getting me involved in the Indian Historic Sites project for the Saskatchewan Indian Federated College. These projects eventually led to my involvement with this book.

There are so many others to thank. Frank Korvemaker and Garth Pugh did the paperwork for a grant from the Saskatchewan Heritage Foundation that was very timely for the continuation of the project. David Meyer kept me informed about things I should know, Tim Jones provided photographs of *mistasiniy*, Margaret Hanna cheerfully answered questions, David Miller shared his copies of the Mandelbaum Papers, and Marian Dinwoodie was always a wealth of information. I am particularly indebted to Stewart Raby for his help and important insights over the years. To all the other people who have helped me in so many ways, thank you.

I would also like to express my appreciation to Freda Ahenakew, Jean

Okimāsis, and Arok Wolvengrey for the many hours they spent working on the spelling and translations of Cree names and words. Freda also transcribed and translated the sacred stories that appear in the book. Stewart Raby and Murray Burt read the manuscript—their suggestions and comments were welcome and invaluable. I also want to acknowledge, with thanks, Blair Stonechild and Bill Brennan's support of the Ahtahkakoop History Project.

The Right Reverend Anthony Burton, Bishop of Saskatchewan, was particularly helpful in making the baptism, marriage, and death registers for the Asissipi Mission (later called Sandy Lake Mission) available to me. Verna Redhead helped make this task easier.

I was delighted to meet Bob and Joan Bens, who put us in touch with the 12th Earl of Southesk in Scotland. And it was exciting that the Earl arranged to have photographs taken of hunting trophies that his great-great grandfather, the 9th Earl of Southesk, acquired during his visit to the North-West in 1859. These are included in Chapter Six.

As always I appreciate the co-operation and help I have received at the archives, libraries, and agencies I have visited over the years. These include the National Archives of Canada, National Library of Canada, Hudson's Bay Company Archives and Provincial Archives of Manitoba, Saskatchewan Archives Board, Saskatchewan Legislative Library, Glenbow Archives and Glenbow Library (Calgary), Claims and Historical Research Centre of Indian and Northern Affairs Canada, Saskatchewan Indian Federated College Library, Office of the Treaty Commissioner (Saskatoon), and Indian Rights and Treaties Research Programme, Federation of Saskatchewan Indian Nations.

I would be remiss if I did not thank the remarkable people—and in particular, Brian Mlazgar—who worked so hard on the technical aspects of this book. A special thank you goes to Brian, who did the editing, design, and layout. Artists Willard Ahenakew, Ed Peekeekoot, and Brent Christensen enhanced the book with their illustrations and paintings. Ray Christensen took the contemporary photographs, Diane Bolingbroke and Lorena Patino created the maps, Heather Hodgson (great-great-great niece of Ahtahkakoop) produced the index and helped in other ways, Corey Kurtz and Tuan Nguyen provided scanning services, and Brian Danchuk designed the dust jacket. And always, Ryan Hildebrand, from Friesens Book Division, smoothed the way. A complete listing of the technical team appears on page xiv of this book.

Additionally permission is gratefully acknowledged to reprint excerpts from the following books: *Buffalo Days and Nights* (Glenbow-Alberta Institute), *Voices of the Plains Cree* (Ruth Buck), and *The Plains Cree* (Canadian Plains Research Center, University of Regina).

And finally, I thank my family for their endurance, patience, and support. I was pleased my son Brent was asked to create three painting for the book, my son Kelly cheerfully took on numerous tasks to help me, and Krista—as usual—was supportive in uncountable ways. But most of all I thank my husband Ray, not only for his photography and technical advice, but for his unselfish day-by-day support that freed me to finish the book.

Deanna Christensen
September 2000

PART ONE

The World
Ahtahkakoop Was Born Into

Illustration by Ed Peekeekoot

CHAPTER ONE

Ahtahkakoop's World

Reverently the old man put down the sacred stone pipe. He adjusted the softly tanned buffalo robe around his shoulders and sat quietly for a moment. A wisp of smoke curled up from the braid of *wihkaskwa** lying in front of him. It floated upward to the opening at the top of the tipi. Then it disappeared, gone to mingle with the stars that sparkled in the heavens above. Gone to take the prayers of the old man to *māmawiwiyohtāwīmaw,* the Creator.[†]

Only then did the old man look around him, around at the children and adults who waited patiently in the flickering light of the fire.

"*Nēhiyawak ōma kiyānaw.* We are the Nēhiyaw. The Nēhiyawak. Exact body. Exact body of people. We are a spiritual people with sacred ceremonies, songs, and language, all gifts of the Creator," he said softly. "It is said our early ancestors came from the east, but we have roamed the prairie for a very long time, much longer than our grandfathers and great-grandfathers can remember. Many people today know us as prairie Cree. We are part of the great Plains Cree nation." The words were not new. Everyone except the very youngest had heard them before. They were part of their teachings. Part of their proud heritage.[‡]

---

* Sweetgrass (*Hierochloe odorata*), a tall fragrant grass that was braided, dried, and used as an incense and purifier.

[†] *Māmawiwiyohtāwīmaw* translates into English as The Father of All Things.

[‡] The following information has been compiled from traditions and oral history related by elders to the younger generations. The elders included Opapēcīw (He Who Is Slow), Kāāyāsitēyahkēkocin (Eagles That Fly In A Downward Cross), Kīsik-awāsis (Sky Child), and Okimawkwanēw (Chief Feather).

"Our people and our relatives from other bands of prairie Cree hunt over a large area," the old man continued. "In the summer we travel onto the plains to hunt buffalo. We gather for religious ceremonies at the sacred place called *mistasiniy*,* where a large rock shaped like a huge buffalo sits in a valley. It is here our people often fast and hold Sun Dances. We go to *manitow-sākahikan*,† where people have been healed for countless years, and to *mikisiwaciya*,‡ one of the many other places sacred to our people."

The old man paused for a moment as he studied the people listening in the tipi, their eyes respectfully turned downward or towards the fire. One boy caught his attention. Big for his age, the child always listened intently, as if he was hearing the story for the first time. He was always eager to learn about the people, and his questions reflected wisdom beyond his years. The old man smiled slightly, and then went on with his story.

"*Nēhiyawak ōma kiyānaw*," he said, his voice growing louder, resonating to the edges of the tipi's circle. "We are Plains Cree. We are buffalo hunters. With the blessing of the Creator we live on *kihcōkāwīmāw*, our Mother Earth.

"During the cold months of the year, when the buffalo seek the shelter of the hills, valleys, and trees of our land, we too choose sheltered places for our camps. *Mihkomin-sākahikan, ayapacināsa, mikisiwaciya, kaskiskawān-atinawa*—all these places are home to our people and to our relatives.§ Here we are safe and secure. With our friends and relatives we build pounds for capturing the buffalo.¹ We hunt elk, moose, and deer, and we trap fur-bearing animals.

"As the days grow warmer and the sun stays with us longer each day, we follow the buffalo onto the plains. We hold our Sun Dance,‖ and then, there on the vast prairie we hunt buffalo and we gather berries, roots, and medicines. We travel south, generally staying between the two branches of

---

* *Mistasiniy* is the Cree word for "big stone."

† Now called Little Manitou Lake, this lake called *manitow-sākahikan* (God's Lake) is situated near present-day Watrous.

‡ *Mikisiwaciya* is the Cree word for the Eagle Hills.

§ The English translations for these locations are: Redberry Lake (*mihkomin-sākahikan*), Moose Woods (*ayapacināsa*), Eagle Hills (*mikisiwaciya*), and Buffalo Hump Hills (*kaskiskawānatinawa*).

‖ In the Cree language, this ceremony is called *nipākwēsimowin*, or All Night Thirst Dance. The term Sun Dance is being used since this is the name that has been used by the Cree People for many years.

the river we call *kā-kisiskāciwan*.* Often we camp near the elbow of the South Branch, but sometimes we go even farther south to *minatināhk*,† many nights from here. Or we go west towards the mountains to visit relatives.

"This is our physical world. It is a good world, a world of plenty for the Nēhiyaw, the Nēhiyawak. Exact body. Exact body of people. It is the physical world in which we live."

The old man grew more serious as he gathered his thoughts together. "The name Nēhiyaw, Nēhiyawak, the names of the places where we live and where we hold our ceremonies, the names we give these places, all these are spiritual. The Creator gave us life. Our land, which we call Mother Earth, nurtures us, gives us growth. The number four is sacred. There are four main spirit helpers, four directions, four seasons, and four stages of life—childhood, young adult, adult, and old age."

"The Sun, which we call *kihc-ōskāpēwis*, is the Great Helper of the Creator," the old man continued. "This spirit helper comes up from the east and it provides us with daylight. If it wasn't for *kihc-ōskāpēwis*, who works for the Creator to give us daylight and warmth, where would the Cree be? In darkness. So we thank the Sun every morning as it comes up for this life-giving. That is the work the Creator gave the Sun. *Kihc-ōskāpēwis* never stops working for the Creator. It never did.

"*Okimāw-piyēsiw*, Chief Thunder that rumbles through the skies in the spring is also sacred. It shakes the ground and shakes the skies. *Piyēsiw* gives people life with life-giving water, the rains that are needed for the body and the things that live on Mother Earth, the rains that are needed for the people. It gives water, which we call the milk of Mother Earth, so that Mother Earth can nurture us. The Creator planned it this way. *Okimāw-piyēsiw*, who is in the south, gives us the water that we need to live.

"*Kisē-nāpēw-yōtin*, Old Man Wind, who lives in the west and comes from the four directions, gives us breath and life for our lungs, it too is sacred. Our lungs circulate the oxygen through our bodies. *Kisē-nāpew-yotin*, it too gives us life.

"The buffalo that roam the prairie by the millions are also put on Mother Earth by the Creator. It was the way of *kisē-nāpēwi-mostos*, Old Man

---

* *Ka-kīsīskāciwan*, which translates as Swift Flowing, is now known as the Saskatchewan River. The Cree called the South Branch of the river *wawaskeiu sipi*, which translates as the Elk, or Red Deer, River.

† Cypress Hills. *Minatināhk* translates as Rolling Hills with Trees.

Buffalo, to feel sorry for the human people. It was this way in the past and it goes on today. *Kisē-nāpēwi-mostos*, in his pity and in his caring, provides so many of the things that we need to survive, like tools, clothing, shelter, and food. He gives his life so we can live. *Kisē-nāpēwi-mostos* is in the north facing south."

The old man waited while one of the boys placed more wood on the fire in the centre of the tipi before continuing.

"And then there is the one we call *okimāwikosisān*, the Chief's Son, the son of the Creator. This spirit is identified in the bear—the four-legged human—because he is so human-like. The Creator gave his Son, this sacred being, the power of healing. He is in charge of healing in our Indian world, and that is why he is so sacred. *Okimāwikosisān* is very sacred. He is the Bear Spirit, and it is to him the Creator gave the power of healing.

"There is also *asināpēwiyiniw*, Old Man Stone. When the Creator was planning how the sky and earth should go on Mother Earth, *okīsikow*, the Sky Spirit,* asked, 'who will speak for the human people when they are put on Mother Earth?'

"All the spirits were sitting around. 'I will, I will speak for the human people,' *asināpēwiyiniw* said. Some of the other spirits sitting around asked Old Man Stone, 'How will you ever speak for them when you sit in one place all the time?'

"'Well,' *asināpēwiyiniw* replied, 'I travel around all over the skies.† I sit all over the world, so from these places I will listen to the human-people. When a person is praying, when he is sounding pitiful to the Creator, when he is thinking about the Creator, I will listen and from there take his prayers to the Creator.'"

"Well, all this is part of our history," the old man said, as he looked at those gathered around him. "It's part of our culture.

"Then there is *mistikonāpēwiyiniw*, Tree Spirit. *Mistikonāpēwiyiniw* is another helper put on Mother Earth to help the human people. He is power-ful. *Mistikonāpēwiyiniw* stands strong. He is the one who is related to peo-ple, he blesses them, he gives strength to the *iyiniwak*, the people.

"And there is *wihkasko-kisēyin*, Old Man Sweet Grass, the spirit of incense and purification. *Wihkasko-kisēyin* purifies the people, their sacred

---

* Sky spirits are like angels.

† Stones in the sky refer to meteorites, asteroids, and other celestial bodies.

belongings such as pipe bowls and pipestems, and the things they use in everyday life. *Wihkaskwa* smoke carries the prayers of the people to the Creator.

"*Nōtokwēw-ātayōhkan* is the Old Woman Spirit, the spirit of comfort. She consoles those who are grieving or unhappy, bringing comfort to them.

"And all the other spirits are also named, like *okimāwāpēs*, the Chief Shell. He is the one who absorbs criticism on behalf of a person or a people. It is for this reason that people sometimes wear shell earrings or decorate their clothing with shells. But even then it is not meant for people to criticize their fellow people."

"We live in a beautiful world," the old man continued, after pausing for only a moment. "The spirit of the Creator, his energy, is part of all things in the world. It is in all our people, in the plants, the animals, birds, water, and fire. In everything. It is a beautiful sacred world. There is nothing else. Yet, it is all things. Everything that exists is part of nature and has a reason and a purpose. The birds are thunderers, and the thunderers are birds. When we pray to the Creator, thanking him for all that has been given and asking his guidance, it is *asināpēwiyiniw*, Old Stone Man, who speaks for us when we cannot rely on ourselves to speak directly to the Creator. It is *mistikonāpēwiyiniw*, Tree Spirit, that gives us strength. The bowl of our sacred pipe is made of stone. The stem is made of wood. Together, Old Stone Man and the Tree Spirit carry our prayers to the Creator. I smudged myself with sweetgrass and smoked the pipe before I started talking to you about these sacred things. I prayed to the Creator. This is what our old men in years long past have always done. It is what I do, for we are Nēhiyaw, Nēhiyawak. Exact body. Exact body of people. We are the Plains Cree people."

The old man sat quietly for a moment as he gazed into the fire. Then he said, "Now I will tell you a sacred story, the Cree story of the first man."*

Another piece of wood was put on the fire. Several of the people in the tipi shifted their positions, and a young mother raised her baby to her breast.

"*Kayās*, a long time ago, at the beginning of the earth," he began, "the

---

* This sacred Cree story, the story of the first man, was told by Barry L. Ahenakew as it was told to him by elders Opapēcīw, Kā-āyāsitēyahkēkocin, Kīsik-awāsis, and Okimāwikwāniyiw. The sacred story was taped in Cree, transcribed in Cree, and then translated into English by Freda Ahenakew. Editing was minimal to retain the characteristics of Cree storytelling.

Creator had workers to help him. I have already told you about some of
these helpers, the Sun Spirit, the Wind Spirit, the Thunder Spirit, and the
Buffalo Spirit. And there was Old Man Stone Spirit, Old Man Sweet Grass
Spirit, Tree Spirit, Old Woman Spirit, and many others, too many to talk
about tonight.

"I have heard old men say there were five kinds of people made when
people were made the world over. It is a long, long time ago that these people were made. There was *osāwasakayak*, the yellow-skinned people.*
There was *kaskitēwiyāsak*, the black-skinned people, the Blacks as we call
them. There was *wāpihkēwak*, the white men, as we call them today.
Mihkwasakayak, that is where we come from, *mihkwasakayak*, the red-
skinned people. And the *wīpasakayak*, the brown-skinned people, they too
used to be. They also were blessed to live on this earth.

"It was back then—before the great flood—that we, the *mihkwasakayak*, were first given this earth to inhabit. It wasn't here where we
now sit on Mother Earth, but on an island to the southeast. The first human
being was called *manitow-iyisin*.† This being was part spirit and part
human. *Manitow-iyisin*, this one was called. It was this God-person who
had started life. It must have been so very, very long ago. It was the descendants of *manitow-iyisin* who strayed away from being a perfect people and
who brought chaos upon themselves. These *manitow*-like people could talk
with animals, and of course the animals were given the ability to communicate, to speak with people. That was what finally gave them trouble.
Pāstāhowin‡ was committed, something so terrible that the Creator was
angry. Something so terrible that I cannot talk about it."

"That was not what the Creator had planned," the old man continued.
"That was not supposed to happen. He had given *manitow-iyisin*'s descendants the freedom to choose, but they began to do things very differently.
That was when the Creator destroyed everything. He had life destroyed. He
destroyed everything he had made up to that time. Even in the sacred stories the sun came up on the other side. So it was, the old people said.

"And again life began. This time the Creator planned that the same thing
would not happen a second time. It was then that he made *asiskīwiyin*,

---

* Oriental people.
† God-like man.
‡ *Pāstāhowin* is something that is so wrong that there are severe consequences.

Earthen Man. *Asiskīwiyin* and the new people were like animals and yet they were humans.

"From here now I will talk about this old man who has died, but who used to have a shaking tent.* *Asiskīwiyin* told how the Earthen Men, their women, and their families lived in caves and along the hillsides. The life of these cave people was very hard and they lived where they could. It was difficult because they hardly had any intelligence, barely enough to survive. Then *iskotēwiyiniw*, Fire Spirit, gave them fire to cook with and to warm themselves. It was so warm when they made a fire! They really respected that. And somehow these people realized that they were not alone. There was a Creator. They were given that.

"And then, from there was Pointed Arrow, *kīnikatos*, as he was called.[2] He was the one who was given *nipwahkēwin*.† *Kīnikatos* invented the bow and arrow. That is why he was given the name Pointed Arrow. *Kīnikatos* learned to make all kinds of tools. From the ribs of the animals he killed, he made knives. From the leg bones he made hide-scrapers. He made pots from clay, baskets from birch bark and willow, and arrow and spearheads from stone. The intelligence that enabled him to do these things was a special gift from the Creator. These tools, weapons, and implements made it easier for the people to hunt the big animals that roamed the land. It was easier to get food for their children and to protect themselves. *Kīnikatos*, Pointed Arrow, was the one given this power to help the people."

"Whatever did it look like at that time?" the old man asked. Then, without waiting for an answer, he continued his story.

"There was an island where all our history took place. This island was towards the southeast. The earth we sit on—the prairie, our Mother—was under water. There was nothing on this land we now sit on, it was all under the water. But on the island there were *iyiniwak*, or people, as they are called. And there were huge animals all over. They were really scary looking animals, big lizard-looking animals. They used to scare and sometimes kill the people."

The old man recollected his thoughts before speaking again. Then he went on with his story of what happened such a long time ago.

---

* The shaking tent, or *kosāpahcikan*, was a lodge that was built where songs were sung to invoke the spirits to enter the lodge and communicate with the people. People sought a shaking tent to get answers to their questions and problems.

† Intelligence.

"It was this *nipwahkēwin*, this power of intelligence that *kīnikatos* possessed, that brought change slowly to the *iyiniwak*. It was the ability to think, the ability to invent with the power of the mind. The Creator thought that all human people should have this power so from *kīnikatos*, intelligence and ingenuity spread.

"Other things were also given. *Asināpēwiyiniw*, Old Man Stone Spirit, with his power felt sorry for the red-skinned people, and he blessed them with both his knowledge and his power."

"It was through *nipwahkēwin* that the people even learned how to fly," the old man explained. "*Asināpēwiyiniw* took them around. It was said that *asiniy*, the Stone Spirit, communicated knowledge of his power to the *iyiniwak* and let the people use his power—his energy—to move their *pimihākana** around. That is how *asināpēwiyiniw*, Old Man Stone Spirit, took them around so they were able to fly.

"The old ones told about giant people from another planet who landed on the red-skins' island. The giant people were big, twice the size of the *iyiniwak*. The red-skins welcomed the giant people and at first the people from the skies treated the red-skins well. But then the giants began to abuse them and made slaves of them. I guess they were smarter and much bigger.

"Many other different things happened. The red-skinned people used their power of stone to fly and they found another island, the one where the *wīpasakayak* lived. They landed their *pimihākana* on this island. At first the red-skins traded, but then they tried to rule the brown-skinned people. The red-skinned people were trying to rule these *wīpasakayak*. This is what got them into trouble. They were using their intelligence to fight these *wīpasakayak* who lived in the west. There was a terrible fight, and life was difficult because of the fighting.

"'It is true, the earth is in terrible shape,' the Creator said to himself. 'This is not what I wanted for the people. They are ruining it by the fighting, using their intelligence the wrong way. Yes! The human people will be punished.'

"Again the human people were punished. The earth shook. The wind blew hard, and volcanoes erupted. Fire swept through the countryside and towns, for these red-skinned people had big towns. The Creator used great force to punish these people and the giant people who had come down from

---

* *Pimihākana* translates into English as "things you fly with," or aeroplanes. *Pimihākan* is the singular form of the word.

a different planet and stayed. It was not right for them to still be there. These *mistiyiniwak* or alien giants had stayed and were trying to rule.

"It was then the earth began to flood. It began to rain and the rivers over-flowed. How it rained! The earth trembled and shook. The water rose and the earth was flooded by the Creator. There were tornadoes. It was flooding. When all this started the giants left the island in their flying machines."

The old man went silent, reflecting on this old story. Some of the people stretched their legs. Then a granddaughter handed a wooden cup filled with muskeg tea to the old man. He sipped the hot liquid slowly, studying the children who had drawn closer to the fire's warmth, and resumed the sacred story.

"The red-skinned people had a stone, a sacred stone given to them by the Creator," the old man said. "It was shiny right through, this sacred stone. It was from this sacred stone that the people's strength came. It was from this stone that they got the power and strength that made it possible for them to do different things, such as fly *pimihākana*.

"The sacred stone was flooded as rains fell and the earth trembled and re-formed itself. The earth was flooded and the sacred stone was under water. It was lost.

"It was before the flooding started and before the stone was lost that one of the red-skinned people was given a vision, the power of seeing into the future. It was then that he was shown how to build a great raft, not even knowing that their island was going to sink. Because of his vision he organized the building of *misi-mitot*, a great raft. It was then that *wīsahkēcāhk*,* as he was called, became sacred.

"*Wīsahkēcāhk* took some of the smaller animals in pairs of males and females and put them on the raft, but he did not take the reptile-like animals, those that were so terribly scary looking. The tornadoes, the earthquakes, and the flood killed them all. *Wīsahkēcāhk* left by raft with the animals as the land disappeared into the flood waters. One of the people on the raft was *omistikōs*,† the first man to be on the new land that we inhabit still to this day.

"All over the earth there was only water to be seen. It was then that *wīsahkēcāhk* floated around with the animals and the *iyiniwak*. They floated

---

* The English translation of *wīsahkēcāhk* is Like a Spirit.

† The English translation of *omistikōs*'s name is Dugout Canoe.

for a long time and *wīsahkēcāhk* began to worry. If he could only find some land, he thought, then they would not starve. Finally, *wīsahkēcāhk* came up with an idea. He would send the loon into the water to find some earth. The loon was gone for a long time, and when the bird returned he did not bring any earth with him. *Wīsahkēcāhk* sent him down for the second time. Again, he came back without anything. And for the third time the loon dived into the water. *Wīsahkēcāhk* waited and waited. Finally *wīsahkēcāhk* saw the bird struggling to reach the raft. He had nearly drowned.

"*Wīsahkēcāhk* then approached the otter. He told the otter how brave and strong he was, and promised him plenty of fish to eat if he would dive into the water and bring up a bit of earth. The otter dived into the water, but he came up without finding any earth. *Wīsahkēcāhk* praised him again, and the otter tried two more times. Again, he came up with nothing. He was so tired he could not try again. *Wīsahkēcāhk* called him a coward, and then he approached the beaver.

"*Wīsahkēcāhk* praised the beaver for his strength and wisdom and promised to make him a fine house for the winter. The beaver dived in two times and found nothing. He was so tired that *wīsahkēcāhk* had to let him rest. Then *wīsahkēcāhk* promised the beaver a wife if he would try one more time. And so the beaver dived deep into the water and stayed for such a long time that he was almost dead when he came back up. *Wīsahkēcāhk* was sad. Then he thought, maybe the muskrat could find some earth.

"So he told the muskrat that the loon, the otter, and the beaver were brave but had failed. He said that if the muskrat went straight down, he would find land. And then he praised the little muskrat and promised him lots of reeds to eat, and rushes and earth to make a house. The muskrat dived in, but when he came up he brought nothing. He went in a second time. This time *wīsahkēcāhk* could smell earth on the muskrat's paws when the small animal returned to the raft. Once again *wīsahkēcāhk* praised the muskrat. This time *wīsahkēcāhk* promised him a wife who would give him many children. The muskrat would be the most numerous animal on Mother Earth. 'Have a brave heart and dive straight down,' *wīsahkēcāhk* told him. The muskrat went into the water for the third time. He was gone so long that *wīsahkēcāhk* feared the animal had drowned. But then he saw some bubbles, and reaching down with his long arm *wīsahkēcāhk* hauled the muskrat onto the raft. The muskrat was almost dead, but in his paws he held a piece of earth."[3]

"The water must have been starting to recede," the old man said. "It was not so deep now, and the muskrat found earth beneath the water. A new island was coming to be seen. It is this earth that we inhabit today. *Wīsahkēcāhk* had found a new island and brought our people here, our ancestral ancestors."

"This was the work of *wīsahkēcāhk*," the old man continued. "*Wīsahkēcāhk* landed his raft on the eastern coast of the new land. It was from this point that the people, the *iyiniwak*—headed by Dugout Canoe—started to multiply and spread out.

"Our relations to the east, the Ojibwa*—like our own Cree people—tell us that when their 'forefathers were living on the great salt water toward the rising sun, the great Megis (sea shell) showed itself above the surface of the great water, and the rays of the sun for a long period were reflected from its glossy back. It gave warmth and light to the An-ish-in-aub-ag (red race). All at once it sank into the deep, and for a time our ancestors were not blessed with its light. It rose to the surface and appeared again on the great river, which drains the water of the Great Lakes, and again for a long time it gave life to our forefathers, and reflected back the rays of the sun. Again it disappeared from sight, and it rose not till it appeared to the eyes of the An-ish-in-aub-ag on the shores of the first great lake. Again it sank from sight, and death daily visited the wigwams of our forefathers, till it showed its back and reflected the rays of the sun once more at Bow-e-ting (Sault Ste Marie.) Here it remained for a long time, but once more, and for the last time, it disappeared, and the An-ish-in-aub-ag was left in darkness and misery, till it floated and once more showed its bright back at Mo-ning-wun-a-kaun-ing (La Pointe Island), where it has ever since reflected back the rays of the sun and blessed our ancestors with life, light, and wisdom. Its rays reach the remotest village of the widespread Ojibways.'"[4]

"The *iyiniwak*—or *anihšināpēk* as the Ojibwa call the red-skinned people—grew greater in numbers," the old man said. "They multiplied and over many years spread west. Our relatives the *sakāwiyiniwak* and the *omaskēkowak*,[†] as well as our own people, the Nēhiyawak, evolved from these people, and we moved even further west. Finally, after countless years, the Nēhiyawak arrived on the prairies. Our language, the Plains Cree language, is similar in many ways to the language spoken by our eastern neighbours the Saulteaux and other peoples who live farther to the east. Some of

---

* Also known as Saulteaux.

† Woods Cree and Swampy Cree.

the words are even the same. And our language is only a little bit different from the languages spoken by the *sakāwiyiniwak* and *omaskēkowak*."[5]

"Now, over there in the southwest," the old man said, motioning with his hand, "the brown-skinned people, they too were punished by the Creator. They were aggressive in taking up for themselves. They fought back against the red-skinned people. Their island earth was also flooded. Those are the ones who live on the west coast now. They are the brown-skinned people, and they are different in appearance from us. They are recognizable. They are descendants of those people who lived on the island in the southwest. All this is part of the huge island we live on today."

"This is a sacred story, how it all began," the old man continued. "It is the story of the first man, Earthen Man, Pointed Arrow, and up to *wīsahkēcāhk*. It is the story of the island we live on today. It is a story passed down through the generations of our people. It all happened such a long time ago, some of it even before the great flood.

"We are Nēhiyaw, Nēhiyawak. Exact body. Exact body of people. Everything in our world is spiritual, from the name of our people and the beings that inhabit Mother Earth to the places we hunt, live, and worship. The Creator, the Great Spirit that we pray to, made the spirits who help Him. They work for Him. How they work for Him!

"*Nēhiyawak ōma kiyānaw.* We are Nēhiyaw, Nēhiyawak. Exact body. Exact body of people. We are Plains Cree."

The light from the fire flickered off the walls of the tipi and brushed the faces of the people who had been listening to the old man's stories. Some of the babies and smaller children now slept. Outside, dogs barked, responding to the far-distant song of the coyotes, and the stars still blazed in the heavens above.

As the old man finished speaking he looked at the boy who had caught his attention earlier. The child with the luminous eyes. The child who already was showing wisdom beyond his years.

It had been on a night such as this, several years earlier, that the boy had been born. It was said the stars blanketed the sky, more numerous and brighter than usual that night. He was given the name Ahtahkakoop, the Cree word for Starblanket, and his mother wrapped him in a blanket decorated with stars. He was born into the race of people called Plains Cree, and this was his world. It was the world Ahtahkakoop was born into.

CHAPTER TWO

Ahtahkakoop's Early Years

Ahtahkakoop was born about 1816[1] within the vast prairie region that was home to his people. Every year in the early summer, his family and other members of the band moved their tipi camp to one of the sacred places on the plains. Here they joined a large encampment of Plains Cree for the annual Sun Dance and other religious ceremonies. After the ceremonies were over they travelled the vast expanses of prairie grasslands hunting buffalo, and they gathered the roots, herbs, and berries that grew on Mother Earth. Summer was also the season when young men organized raids into far-off Blackfoot camps to steal horses. Often the Cree—along with their allies the Assiniboines—were at war with the Blackfoot nations. Then men, women, and children died.

As fall approached, the people separated into smaller family groups and moved into the wooded hills of the parklands—the Thickwood Hills, the Eagle Hills, and the valleys of the Eagle and Battle rivers. Winter came. Now, in addition to building pounds to entrap buffalo, the people killed moose, elk, and deer, and they hunted fur-bearing animals. This was the time for storytelling, the time when dry grass was stuffed between the tipi covers and their liners to insulate the tipis against the cold.

Then, as the days grew longer and the air began to warm, sap started to run in the birch and maple trees. The sap was tapped and made into syrup or sugar. Ducks, geese, and other waterfowl returned from the south, providing a welcome change to the winter diet. Later, the eggs were collected.

It was a good life, the old people have always said. Their spiritual world centred on the Creator and his spirit helpers. In their physical world, life focused on the buffalo. This animal was a powerful spirit helper, a sacred

The buffalo (bison) provided many of the things the people needed to survive, including meat, clothing, tipi covers, blankets, tools, and implements. A full-size bull stands nearly six-and-a-half feet (two metres) tall at the shoulders and weighs about 1,550 pounds (700 kilograms). A cow is smaller, weighing between 775 and 1,025 pounds.

gift placed on Mother Earth for the survival of the Indian people. Its flesh and fat provided food. Its hide was used to make tipi covers, clothing, robes, blankets, mattresses, storage bags, cooking vessels, and such things as ropes, halters, cinches, and thongs. Its paunch was used as a water container. Even dried buffalo dung, called chips, served a useful purpose. It was collected and used to fuel fires on the treeless plains. Practically every other part of the animal also had a use.[2]

Ahtahkakoop saw the ground black with buffalo as far as the eye could see, rolling and undulating, and he felt it tremble as the herds moved. These animals were the gift of the Creator, put on Mother Earth for the survival of the Indian people. As far back as memories went, Ahtahkakoop's family had based its life on the buffalo.

As Ahtahkakoop grew up, he learned the ways of the buffalo hunter and the Plains Cree. Every day was a time of learning. He observed what was going on around him. When old enough, he became active in day-to-day activities and in the sacred ceremonies, learning from first-hand experiences. He listened and he asked questions. Why did people get up when the sun got up? Why did they pray and sing a morning song as the sun rose in the pink and golden sky? What did they learn by watching the sky? These and many other questions intrigued him.

The boy learned the word for the sun, *kīsikāw-pīsim*. From the sacred stories he learned that the Sun was *kihc-ōskāpēwis*, the great spirit helper of the Creator, giver of daylight, growth, warmth and, indeed, life itself.* He also learned that the time between sunrise and sunset was known as "one sun" or the equivalent of one day. From sunset to sunrise was the equivalent of one night, and the distance from one place to another was often measured by the number of nights the people camped during their journey. More precise times were associated with the placement of the sun in the sky. Thus *kīsikāw-pīsim*, the sun, could be used to tell time.

The moon and its phases were also used to measure time. Ahtahkakoop learned that the length of time it took for a new moon to change to a full moon and back again was called "one moon." The new moon, the half moon, the full moon, and all the phases and shapes in between were used as indicators of time within a period of one moon.

There were 13 moons in a lunar year. In determining the beginning of a year, the people observed the most northerly location of the rising sun on the horizon (the summer solstice), and then kept track of the "moons" or lunar months. The "moons" of each year were all identified by seasonal changes. Ahtahkakoop learned, for instance, that the moon when the buds started bursting from the trees was called *sākipakāwi-pīsim*, or "budding moon."† The next moon was called the *opinawēwi-pīsim*, or "egg laying moon," and so it went, with each "moon" or lunar month having its own name.

At night Ahtahkakoop learned to identify the stars. *Atimāpīsim* (Dog Star), known by some as the North Star, was an indicator of direction when travelling. It was sometimes called *ēka kā-ahcīt acāhkos*, or Star That Doesn't Move.[3] The Big Dipper in the sky was called *ocēhkatāhk*. *Otahtwahamāwak*, or the Hair Loosening Stars, were in the southeast.

---

* The Cree word for sun is *kīsikāw-pīsim*. *Kihc-ōskāpēwis* was the Sun Spirit.

† *Sākipakāwi-pīsim* corresponds roughly with the month of May.

Some call these stars Pleiades, or Seven Sisters. And often just as dawn was breaking, before *kīsikāw-pīsim* made its daily appearance, *wāpanatāhk*, or Morning Star,* rose above the eastern horizon.

Ahtahkakoop heard the prayers, drums, and songs that thanked the Creator for all He had given them. And the boy watched the old men of the camp reverently light braids of sweetgrass in hot coals. Cupping the rising smoke in their hands, they spread the smoke over their faces, heads, and bodies to purify themselves. He saw them purify their pipes in the *wihkaskwa* smoke, fill the stone bowls with tobacco, and point the stems in the four directions as they acknowledged the four directions, the sky, and the earth, and the Creator's powerful helpers. Then the men prayed, giving thanks to the Creator and His spirit helpers and asking for guidance and help in their daily life.

Ahtahkakoop already knew about Old Man Stone volunteering to speak for the humans on Mother Earth. "I will listen to the people from where I sit all over the world," *asināpēwiyiniw* had said. "As I sit there I will listen to them, when they are praying to our Creator. Then I will talk to the Creator for them." So it had been said for many years.

"The pipe is made of stone," the old man explained. "Stones and rocks are part of creation, in the heavens, in the earth, and on the earth. The pipe is made from stone. It is the pipe made from stone that speaks for the people, that helps the people. The pipestem is made from the tree. The Tree Spirit is very powerful. 'I will stand for strength,' *mistikonāpēwiyiniw*, the Tree Spirit, had said. So the stem signifies the tree, which is the strength needed during life." The pipestem and the stone bowl together, Ahtahkakoop learned, gave his people strength in their prayers.

"*Wihkasko-kisēyin*, Old Man Sweet Grass, is another spirit helper of the Creator. 'I will speak for the people too,' Sweet Grass had told the Creator. 'I will speak the world over. The pipe speaks world-wide. I will help him.'"

"In the minds of our people," Ahtahkakoop's teacher continued, "the braid of sweetgrass represents the body, the spirit and the mind braided together to form a strong person. A strong Nēhiyaw, strong person, exact people.

"The tobacco in the sacred stone pipe is also a spirit helper. The smoke

---

* Venus.

of the tobacco mixes with the fire in the pipe and disappears into the heavens, to the spirit world. What we see as nothing in the air holds untold energy. This nothingness is full of energy. It is full of the energy that is part of the energy the Creator put in all of His creations. When the smoke mixes with what seems to be nothingness, it is actually communicating with the Creator and his spirit helpers. We were given the sweetgrass and the pipe so we could have a true communication with our Creator. That is what we were given by the Creator."[4]

Another time, when Ahtahkakoop was listening to the old people talk, he learned that there was another dimension to the pipe. "It has been passed down from generation to generation," an old man had said, "that the pipe stands for truth. Sweet Grass Spirit told the Stone Spirit, Tree Spirit, and Tobacco Spirit that 'when a person uses us when praying to our Father, he says the truth. He will fear not to tell the truth. He will not smoke, he will not take us if he does not tell the truth.'

"Truth, this is why we smoke the pipe and use tobacco, sweetgrass, and fire. Purity. There is truth there when he smokes the pipe."

"There is a very special pipestem," the old man said as he continued his teachings. "It is the most Sacred Pipestem. Each Indian nation has one and it is kept in the care of a respected keeper of the pipe. This pipestem is very beautiful. It is longer than most pipestems. The length of it is carved into beautiful designs and decorated with quill work. Feathers hang from the stem, and the quill end of each is wrapped in leather. It is sacred. It is beautiful![5]

"It is these Sacred Pipestems that are unwrapped and brought into the open at special times. If one of these pipestems is brought out during war with our enemies the Blackfoot, the war will end. Each of these pipestems stands for fellowship and good works. In its presence, bad works, hate, and fighting must end. All good things come from there for all people—for those who keep the Sacred Pipestem, and all other peoples in the future— so they can work together and help each other," the old man said.

As soon as he was old enough Ahtahkakoop learned to smudge and purify himself with the smoke from the sweetgrass, and the elders included him and the other boys in some of their pipe ceremonies.

He was also taken into the sweatlodge. In this, a purifying and religious ceremony, the sweatlodge structure itself was important. It was explained to the boys that the sweatlodge was like the womb of Mother Earth, like the womb of a mother with child. The Tree Spirit was represented in the willows that were bent, interwoven, and joined to the ground. A pit was made in the centre to hold the sacred stones, and the frame was covered with hides to make the inside totally dark. The people smudged themselves with sweetgrass. The pipe was smoked. Then a specified number of stones, heated red-hot in a fire outside the sweatlodge to purify them, was carefully put into the pit in the lodge. The hide was let down to cover the doorway. Inside the sweatlodge it was totally dark, without any glimmer of light. It was like the womb.

The spiritual leader splashed water onto the hot rocks to wake up the Stone Spirit. In this way, *asināpēwiyiniw* could hear the prayers said in the lodge and carry them to the Creator. The people prayed. The spiritual leader, he too prayed, and he sang special songs that were given to him by different spirit helpers. The lodge pulsated with the rhythmic sound of his rattle and the ancient songs. "It is like being a child in the woman's womb," the old man said. "The child is clean and innocent. When you emerge from there it is like you are being born again. You are cleansed in the sweatlodge. You are purified."

Often, as part of the sweatlodge and pipe ceremonies, individuals made offerings to the Creator and His spirit helpers. Sometimes it was a sacred object that was offered. Sometimes it was an item that was valued by the individual, such as a special shirt, pair of moccasins, or leggings. Sometimes it was bows and arrows, or sticks in the shape of arrows that were given. With these offerings, the people asked for the blessing of the Creator and his sacred helpers.

Ahtahkakoop learned that there were many different kinds of sweatlodges, including the Bear sweatlodge, the Sun Dance sweatlodge, and the Horse sweatlodge.

The boy was also taught that the world operated under the premise that there was both a physical and a spiritual world, and that they were interconnected. All things on Mother Earth were put there by the Creator, the old people said. Each entity had a spirit or form of energy, and each one had an equal right to live. Every day the people thanked the Creator for all that He had given them—the buffalo and the other animals, the fish, the roots, the berries, the herbs, and the medicines. The pipe was smoked and the people prayed. He saw his relatives make offerings of tobacco before they picked sweetgrass, dug wild turnips, or gathered other gifts from

Mother Earth. And he heard them thank the plant for giving up its life so the Nēhiyawak would live.

In the early summer, after the first berries of the season were picked, Ahtahkakoop's family invited an old man to bless the berries at a ceremonial feast. The sacred pipe was smoked and then the old man, raising the container of berries towards the sky, thanked the Creator for putting the berries on Mother Earth. The Sun, the Creator's main helper, was thanked for ripening the fruit, and Thunder Spirit was thanked for the rain that nourished the berry bush. As the bowl was lowered to the ground, the old man asked Mother Earth to continue growing her fruits for the people to eat.[6] Then the berries were served and eaten. Each family held its own thanksgiving ceremony. A similar ritual was held after a man killed the first duck or goose of the year.

One of the ceremonies of particular significance to Ahtahkakoop and other boys took place after the youngster killed his first game. The animal, no matter how small, was carefully kept until his family had collected enough food to hold a feast. Then friends and relatives were invited to this, a special ceremony. Pipes and offerings were presented to the spirit powers, and in their prayers the people asked that the boy grow up to be a successful hunter so he could provide for his family and relatives. During the ceremony the parents distributed presents to their guests.

Puberty was a special time for the children of the Nēhiyawak. So when Ahtahkakoop was about 14 he was taken to a secluded place in the hills. There, as part of his vision quest, he was left by himself without food or water to fast and pray for a vision.

Ahtahkakoop knew that visions and dreams came from the Creator. Through visions, a person learned which spirit helpers would help him in his journey through life, and he learned what special gifts and abilities had been granted to him by the Creator. It was explained that each individual was born with a spiritual energy or soul. The level of energy within each person varied from one to another. The more a person believed, the stronger that person became. Then the gift from the Creator became even more powerful. So it was told by the old people.

Some people received the gift of healing the sick through their vision quest. Others were given the right to conduct certain ceremonies, to construct a buffalo pound, to lead a war party. In the vision, spirit helpers taught the songs and rituals to go with the special gifts. Men and women, adolescents, and boys and girls could experience visions at any time, not

Illustration by Ed Peekeekoot

Gathering a herd of buffalo together and driving it over a cliff required skill, the co-operation of the entire band, and the help of a man who had been gifted during a vision to conduct the communal hunt. The site where the buffalo went over the cliff was called a buffalo jump. The animals that were not killed by the fall were speared or shot with arrows.

just during rituals and sacred ceremonies. These visions and the spirits that volunteered to help an individual through daily life connected the physical world with the spiritual world.

Ahtahkakoop's sisters and the other girls did not go on a vision quest in the same way the boys did. Instead, they were blessed with visions that often came during a four-day observance that was conducted during their first menstruation. During this rite the girl was secluded with an old woman in a small lodge set up some distance from the camp. She was kept busy during the day chopping firewood, sewing, and preparing hides. At night, the old woman talked to her about a variety of things. She was given very little food to eat during the four days and she cried a great deal. On the fourth night the women of the camp went to the secluded lodge and led the girl to her father's tipi. Two women prayed to their spiritual helpers as the girl entered the tipi, followed by the men and women who had been invited for a ceremonial feast. One of the elderly women, a spiritual leader, offered a pipe to the Creator and her personal spiritual helpers. Then the food was served. Following the feast, the girl's parents gave gifts to their guests.[7]

The girls were taught by their mothers, older sisters, aunts, and grand-mothers. They learned how to dry buffalo meat, pound it into shreds and add melted fat and berries to make *pimīhkān*.* They learned how to cook and prepare a variety of other foods, how to tan furs and hides, how to sew, and how to make and erect tipis. They were shown how to make birch bark baskets and decorate clothing and household articles with quill work. And they were taught how to care for the younger children.

In the woods, valleys, and grasslands, the girls snared game birds, rab-bits, and other small animals, and they learned to identify the various roots, berries, plants, shrubs, and trees that provided food and medicines. They too learned respect for the things placed on Mother Earth, and they gave thanks for all they were given.

As the girls grew older, they learned their roles in the sacred ceremonies of their people, ceremonies such as the Sun Dance, the Prairie Chicken

---

* *Pimīhkān* (pemmican) was a stable food on the plains and in the parklands. Provided it did not become damp, the mixture of dried, shredded buffalo meat and grease kept extremely well. It was made into soup, fried in grease, or eaten just as it came out of the storage bag. Dried berries were sometimes added when the pemmican was mixed.

Dance, the Bear Dance, and the Smoking Tipi ceremony. They learned about the women's ceremonies and how to cook for feasts.*

From an early age, boys were taught the skills of hunting and trapping by their fathers, uncles, and grandfathers. These men were good teachers. Not only were they buffalo hunters of note, but they also knew the ways of the woodland animals with whom they shared Mother Earth. Ahtahkakoop and the other boys learned how to track deer, elk, and moose along almost invisible trails. They learned to identify the footprints and tell-tale signs of other animals. They could tell how large an animal was, when it had made the tracks, and if it was wounded. They learned to make bows and arrows, arrowheads, snares, knife and spear blades, as well as snowshoes. They too became skilled in handling their tools and weapons. The boys learned to respect the animals, and to thank them when they gave up their lives so the Nēhiyawak might live. In this land of plenty, they learned not to kill more than the families could use. To do so was wasteful and disrespectful. The young hunters learned all this, and much more.

Through their travels and the stories told in camp, Ahtahkakoop, his brothers and sisters, and the other children also learned about the Indian nations living within and beyond their immediate world. They knew relatives in other Plains Cree bands, Nēhiyawak who hunted and trapped in the area that became known as Saskatchewan River country. They knew about the *sakāwiyiniwak* (Woods Cree) who hunted and trapped in the northern woodlands, and the *omaskēkowak*† (Swampy Cree) who lived to the east. To the southeast lived Plains Cree who later became known as *kā-tēpwēw-sīpiwiyiniwak* (Calling River People), *wāposwayānak* (Rabbit Skin People), *posākanacīwiyiniwak* (Touchwood People), and the *nēhiyaw-pwātak* (Cree-Sioux) peoples.

The *pwāsīmowak*‡ (Assiniboines) were allies of the Nēhiyawak and co-existed with them in Saskatchewan River country, even though they were distant relatives of the enemy Sioux nations. The *nahkawiyiniwak* (Saulteaux or Plains Ojibwa) lived to the east and were also allied with the Plains Cree. And far to the north lived the *ocīpwayāniwak* (Dene§), who were part of the Athabascan nation.

---

* Except for the sweatlodge ceremonies, women participated in most of the rituals and ceremonies. Women could also become pipe carriers for the Old Women pipes.

† The *omaskēkowak* are also known as the Muskego.

‡ They Talk Similar To The Sioux.

§ The Dene are also known as Chipewayans.

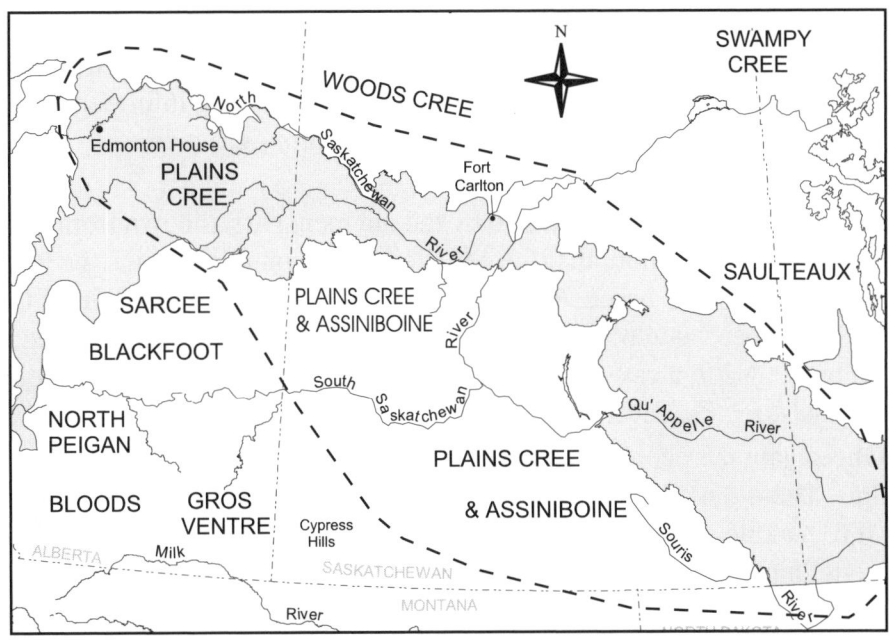

Information Systems Division, Canadian Plains Research Center

The Plains Cree, who were allied with the Assiniboine, spent the winters hunting and trapping in the parklands (see the shaded areas). In the summer they moved onto the plains, sometimes travelling as far as the Missouri River.

The children learned about the enemies of the Plains Cree people. The *kaskitēwayasitak* (Blackfoot) who lived to the southwest. The *mihkoyiniwak* (Bloods), the *pīkāniwiyiniwak* (Peigans), and the *sāsīwak* (Sarcee). All these nations were allies and part of the mighty *ayahciyiniwak*, the Blackfoot Confederacy. These people had not always been enemies, the children were taught, and in earlier years the *ayahciyiniwak* had been their allies.

The children also learned about Indian peoples living in the land far to the south that later became part of the United States of America. One of these groups, the *pāwistikowiyiniwak** (Rapids or Falls People), in not too distant times, had hunted and raided on the northern plains.[8] The youngsters learned about the *pwātak* (Sioux), the *kāhkākiwacēnak* (Raven People or Crow), the *napakistikwānak* (Flatheads), the *kinēpikowiyiniwak* (Snake people or Shoshone), and the *asiskīwikamikowiyiniwak* (the Earthen Lodge People, now known as the Mandans). The people knew of these different tribes, for they journeyed great distances, sometimes travelling as far south

---

* These people were also known as *mistatayak*, or Gros Ventre. *Mistatayak* means "Big Bellies."

as the Mandans' trading villages on the Missouri River. They negotiated trade and peace treaties, and they intermarried. Astute and well-travelled with wide-ranging connections, the Nēhiyawak were well informed about people and activities beyond their traditional hunting grounds.

But it was the sacred stories told by the old men, passed down from generation to generation, that formed the foundation upon which the children's education was based. One of these was the story of the origin of the Cree Sun Dance,* one of the most significant traditional ceremonies honoured by the Nēhiyawak. Many times as he was growing up Ahtahkakoop heard this story. He never forgot the first time.

Once again the people were gathered around the fire in one of the larger tipis. The old man, as he always did, let his gaze fall on each person in the tipi, making everyone feel welcome and part of this special occasion, the re-telling of a sacred story. Then he spoke.

"*Hā!* This one now I call *nipākwēsimow-ātayōhkēwin*, how the first Sun Dance began. This is how the Sun Dance was first given to the Cree. It is a sacred story. This happened a long time ago. The people roamed the prairie then, just as we do now. They travelled about, moving their camps," the old man said.[†]

"There was this one large *ōtēnaw*.[‡] The people lived in tipis and there were many of them. Their children played together all over the place. Sometimes they played far from the *ōtēnaw*. Their parents did not mind because they knew the children always returned back to their tipis, and they knew the bigger children always kept the smaller children and looked after them.

"These children would play like this. Some pretended they were the parents. They had as their children the smaller children. They played with them. They had fun with them. They made houses for them something like

---

* In the Cree language this ceremony is called *nipākwēsimowin*, or All Night Thirst Dance. The term Sun Dance is being used since this is the name that has been used by the Cree people for many years.

† The sacred story of how the Sun Dance was given to the Cree was told by Barry L. Ahenakew, as it was told to him by elders Opapēcīw, Kā-āyāsitēyahkēkocin, Kīsik-awāsis, and Okimāwikwāniyēw. The sacred story was taped in Cree, transcribed in Cree, and then translated into English by Freda Ahenakew. Editing was minimal to retain the characteristics of Cree storytelling.

‡ A Cree town or camp.

the tipis back at their camp, or they made small caves in the soft dirt of the hillsides. It was at these places the children would be playing far from the camp.

"But the parents did not mind. When they were going to move suddenly, they would know where the children were playing, when they were leaving, when they moved camp. When they were preparing to move, they cleaned up and they left. The whole camp moved. They took everything with them. And of course the children who had been playing a distance away would always find them by following tracks. These children were swift and they would catch up to their parents as the camp moved. The children tracked them. The older ones kept watch over the younger ones, and they caught up to the camp. This is always what happened," the old man said.

"Then the same thing happened again, when they camped again. They made a town. The children were playing out at a distance again. The children were having fun. They were all different sizes, some small, some bigger, and some bigger yet. They were playing and having fun.

"Again the leaders knew they were going to move camp. They began preparing. They began tidying up. They took the tipis down, they tied the poles together to make a travois,[9] and they loaded their goods, the very young children, the very old men and women, and others who were unable to walk onto the travois. Then the parents and the others started travelling. When they had been moving for a while they saw dust flying, animals raising dust. A great many buffalo were travelling. They could see the dust made by the buffalo so the parents and their relatives kept travelling.

"And so on they went. And the children who had been playing, they kept on playing. They did not know their parents had moved, that their fathers and mothers were gone. The people were moving faster now to cross before the buffalo reached them, to get out of the way of the buffalo. It was too late to turn back. Now the people were getting ahead of the buffalo. Finally they crossed over. Finally the buffalo travelled by. There was such a great number of buffalo. So many, so great a number of buffalo travelling. And now these buffalo were crossing in front of the children who had strayed away playing. They were crossing between the children and their parents. So many days, so many nights, these buffalo travelled.

"Now these children realized their parents had moved. They followed their parents, they followed them. The buffalo were in the way. They could not do anything. They had been following their parents' tracks. Now the buffalo were crossing in front of them. They could follow no longer.

"The children waited and waited. It so happened there were 40 of them, 40 children. They kept waiting as the great herd of buffalo travelled. Their parents were on the other side. At first the children were not too worried. Then they were quite worried because there were so many buffalo and they were travelling across in front of them.

"Well! Well, now these children were getting anxious. The smaller ones, they were getting anxious. The older children had been taught by their parents, the uncles, and aunts. Their relatives had taught them how to hunt the small animals and the birds. These were the things they hunted now to feed the little ones, and besides they in turn were teaching the young children how to hunt these things.

"When the buffalo had gone by these children could not find the tracks left by their parents and friends. There were only buffalo tracks. All they could see were buffalo tracks. They tried to find their parents, they tried to go in the direction they thought their parents had gone, but they were lost. They were lost wherever they walked.

"Some of the men were sent back to search for the children. They knew where they had left the children but a big storm came upon them. It was really a bad storm. It rained so hard that all the tracks left by the children were erased.

"The children were lost and began to suffer in their travelling. The smaller children were crying often now. The older children were trying to comfort the younger ones. They were trying to tell them not to cry. But the little children were lonely. They were lonely and scared without their parents. The bigger children provided what food they could catch for the young children and for themselves. This is how they survived.

"For a long time the children were lost. They made little shelters here and there. That was how they travelled, barely having enough to eat. They were all going hungry now. Although the parents were searching for them, they could not find them. They were not found."

"It was during this time there came a light that shone in the sky," the old man continued. "It came down and turned into a big light. It shone over where they were. This light shone all over. A voice was heard coming from the light and the children understood. 'You are not to be afraid of the light or when being spoken to,' the voice said. 'You are going to be given something, you are going to be given the power to help yourselves,' these children were told.

"'There are spirits who work for me. There are spirits who will help you. You are not to be afraid of them. There is the one called *okimāwi-kosisān*, the Chief's Son, the chief being the Creator. This is the Bear Spirit. There is the Chief's helper, *kihc-ōskāpēwis*, the Sun. And there is *okimāw-piyēsiw*, Chief Thunderbird. *Kisē-nāpēw-yōtin*, Old Man Wind. *Kisē-nāpēwi-mostos*, Old Man Buffalo. *Asinapēwiyiniw*, Old Man Stone. And *mistikonāpēwiyiniw*, the Tree Spirit. All the spirits you pray to.

"'They will be coming to you,' the children were told. 'You are not to be afraid of them. They are going to help you make a big lodge.

"'You are to be prepared for making a lodge and a Sun Dance. You will be taught songs. You will be taught everything. It will help you. It is for your help, for you to use.

"'First you will have a sweatlodge. You will make a Sun Dance sweat-lodge, that too you will be taught,' the voice told them. So the children were taught to face the lodge to the east, how many willows to use, and how to prepare the offerings that were made from slender sticks shaped like arrows. There will be 40 little sticks, they were told. They did not know why 40, but they made them as they were told.

"'You are also to make a *maskokamik*.* You will be taught how many poles to use and how to make it. That will be the *wēhkātawikān*, the singing lodge that is built before the Sun Dance,' the children were told.

"'You will sing for these little sticks you are giving as offerings, songs that you will be taught,' the voice said. And truly, they were taught. They were taught the Sun songs, Thunderbird songs, Wind songs, Buffalo songs, Stone songs, Bear songs, and songs of the other spirits. They were taught all the songs that are sung before the start of the Sun Dance. Slow sacred songs, *pēkihkātahikana*, these are called, that are sung just before the Sun Dance songs are sung.

"'Not all of you can sing,' the voice told the children. 'Some must dance. When you or someone else promises something, what it is you real-ly want, that is what you will dance for. That is when you make the big lodge. Some of you will sing, some of you will dance. You will all pray. You will be given different things.'

"It was the Thunderbird that gave the *pipikwan*† to these children to

---

* Bear lodge.
† Whistle.

blow on as they danced. They were given different things. 'When you are to make the *wēhkātawikān* you make it four times,' the children were instructed. 'You will have berries that you will offer. All sacred items, such as the 40 stick offerings, are to be there and these are to be incensed and prayed with as offerings by the maker of the Sun Dance. You will also pray and give thanks for the food you have. You will then eat all together. You will make a feast as you pray to the Creator.

"'At that time, when you have sung four times, when you have prepared for it, then you can make the Sun Dance lodge. When you make this big lodge, you will begin by using 12 poles. That will be the first time you make the Sun Dance. The one who has vowed to make the Sun Dance, the leader, must be from one of you.

"'The next time you make a Sun Dance you will add four poles. You will now have 16 poles.[10] The next year, when you have prepared, you will add four more poles. You will then have 20 poles. When you have made a Sun Dance the fourth time you will add four more poles, you will have 24 poles. That will be the number of times you can make a Sun Dance, four times.

"'But if there is so much confidence in the Sun Dance leader that he is asked to make another, and if he agrees—if he prepares again, to make the Sun Dance the fifth time—he will put four more poles. He will have 28 poles now. However, if he makes the Sun Dance five times he will then have to make it three more times.'

"These children, as well as the one who made the Sun Dance, were told that this is the way it was to be done. Then the voice told them that 'When you vow to make a Sun Dance again, which will be the sixth time then, you will add four more poles, and now you will have reached 32 poles. When you make the seventh Sun Dance, you will add four more poles, then you will have put 36 poles. And when you have reached the eighth time the next year, you will add four poles. You will then have 40 poles. That is the most a person should do.'

"They were all taught, and everything went well during the time they were taught. They had enough to eat, they had fun, and for the children who had been crying, it was different now. They were content while they were preparing for their first Sun Dance."

The old man telling the sacred story paused for a moment. He looked around at the children listening intently in the tipi, determining how much they understood. Then he continued. "These spirits were very particular," he told them. "It is true these spirits really had come to them. They taught the children the songs, how to make the big lodge, and how to put things in order.

"It was then they prepared to make *wēhkātawikān*, the singing lodge," the old man said. "The children tried to do exactly as they were told. They all helped. These children no longer cried as much. They were not as lonely. They were laughing more, they were happy, and they had enough to eat. Now everything was turning out well. They began to learn the songs. And then they waited until the moon was as close to being full as possible—just as they had been instructed—to make a *wēhkātawikān*. They made the lodge and sweetgrass braids, and when the time came, they started their singing. How those songs were sung!

"After having a singing lodge four times they made the big Sun Dance lodge. They were told to face the door of the lodge to the south. They selected the *okimāwāhtik*.* They carved a moon on the *okimāwāhtik* and they carved the Thunderbird and the Buffalo. They made a nest for the Thunderbird on top of the pole.[11] Then they pulled Chief Tree up in the centre of the Sun Dance lodge. Stone-being sits there as they smudge Chief Tree and they prepare the Sun Dance lodge and *kahkatēyēhkan*† at the back of the Sun Dance lodge. Kahkatēyēhkan is where they place the buffalo skull. They were taught everything, and they were taught *kīmāskonikēwin*, the secret pipe ceremony.

"They were told to put four people in the places where the spirits would sit. The Sun, the Thunderbird, Old Man Wind, and Old Man Buffalo. There were enough children to put in these places, to sing, to dance, and to do all the things that were needed.

"Now they began the Sun Dance with *ē-pēkihkātahikēt*.‡ The leader of the Sun Dance, he sings and prays. He smudges and does it all.

"And now they began, they were drumming. The whistles were sounding. They had been told how to dance. The boys were on this side, " the old man said, gesturing to his left, "and the girls were on the other side, the right side. The whistles sounded as they were blown in time with the drum.

---

* Chief Tree.

† Altar.

‡ A slow spirit song.

"Now it was quite a long time since the children were lost. Suddenly the parents and grandparents they had been separated from happened to be travelling nearby, to the south of the Sun Dance lodge. They heard something."

The old man cocked his head as he looked around. "What was this they heard?" he asked. "Well, now the scouts went to check. They went over the hill. They crawled up over the hill, and then they saw. They saw a pointed lodge and in front of that a big round lodge with leaves, a lodge made round by leaves with a tree in the centre. Drumming could be heard, and they heard singing. And they could hear the whistles. What was this? It was the first time they ever saw what was before them.

"And now some of the scouts stayed and some were sent back to where the others were waiting. When they ran up to them the scouts told them right away, 'We do not know what kind of people we have found, but we have found people. They are doing something, they are moving about. Whatever they are doing, you must come see them. You must come and see what they are doing. We hear whistles and drumming and they can be heard singing.'

"And so the people who had come from the south went to where they could hear the singing, the drums, the whistles. They climbed over the hill. They could see the big lodge down below, but of course they did not know what it was. From there people who had good eyesight recognized some of the children coming out of the lodge. '*Yohō!* It is that one over there, it is these ones, *yohō!*' They came rushing down the hill, just as fast as they could run. They came. These were their children, these were their grandchildren. They were crying. They were laughing. There was so much happiness as they were joyfully united."

"It was the Creator who had spoken to these children and had given them the big lodge," the old man explained. "This he had given to them to help them. Kinship, love, wellness, all these blessings the Creator gave to the people to celebrate. This is what the Creator had given the children to do for themselves, to do for themselves so their parents could hear. And the parents and grandparents came travelling there, it just so happened they were travelling close by. This blessing was what the Creator had given them.

"'What are you doing,' the parents asked. So then the children began relating their story.

"'This is what happened to us,' the children said. 'There was a big light at night. We were all visible. It was like day. This is what the Creator told us, and he had *okīsikowak** working for Him. In this way he taught us. The spirit helpers taught us songs, how to make whistles, how to dance. They taught us *kīmāskonikēwin,†* as it is called here. We were taught all of this,' the children told their parents.

"It was these children who had been given the Sun Dance. There were 40 of them. There were 40 sticks shaped like arrows that represented the 40 lost children and that was the offering‡ they had given to the Creator, that and their willingness to learn about the preparation of the Sun Dance and the actual Sun Dance."

The old man who was telling the sacred story of the Cree Sun Dance waited for a moment before continuing. Then, he picked up his hand drum. "The songs the children were taught by the Creator and his helpers a long time ago have been handed down through the generations," the old man said. "This song comes from this sacred story, the first Sun Dance. It is this. I will sing a bit."

And so, accompanied by his drum, the old man sang a song from the first Sun Dance.

"Forty poles only we were told," the old man sang, "Forty poles only we were told."

The last beat of the drum faded softly as the old man finished his song. "The children were given this gift by the Creator. They were given the Sun Dance and they taught their parents and relatives how to do this sacred ceremony so the Nēhiyawak would be blessed." Gathering his robe around him, the old man looked at his silent audience, the Sun Dance song still reverberating in the core of their very being. "*Ēkosī!*" he said quietly. "That will be all for now."

Ahtahkakoop remembered and cherished this story. The memories were particularly strong each spring when his relatives began making preparations for their own Sun Dance, for this was part of his heritage. This was the world he was born into.

---

* Sky spirit helpers.

† Secret pipe ceremony.

‡ Contemporary offerings consist of cloth print and ribbons called *wēpināsowina*. The cloth offering is a robe or shawl for the spirits to dance with when the people sing. The ribbons are given to the spirits so they have fancy tassels with which to dance.

CHAPTER THREE

Ahtahkakoop Learns the Story of Buffalo Child

It was June. The Eggs Hatching Moon, *pāskaweho-wipicim*, they called it. Yellow buffalo bean flowers had emerged across the grasslands, replacing the gentle blues of the hardy crocuses that weeks ago had transformed into deceivingly delicate seed-heads that fluttered in the wind. Three moons had passed since the first singing for the Sun Dance. Now the people were packing and getting ready to leave for the ceremonial grounds near the elbow of the South Saskatchewan River.

The women took the tipis down and lashed the poles together to form travois. Tipi covers and household belongings were loaded onto these conveyances. Then, when the camp was ready to leave, the travois were fastened by a series of rawhide thongs to dogs and horses. Babies bundled into moss bags were carried by their mothers, older sisters, or aunts, or sometimes they were tied securely on the travois amongst soft bundles of household goods. Noisily children and unencumbered dogs ran alongside, enjoying the freedom of the prairie. At the front of the procession rode the chief and the leading men. Members of the *okihcihtāw* (Warrior society),* riding the finest horses in the band, flanked the column and formed a rearguard, keeping order, encouraging stragglers, and ensuring the safety of the moving camp.

Their destination—the Sun Dance grounds in a small valley near the elbow of the South Saskatchewan River—was a sacred place. As a boy Ahtahkakoop had been taught about this and other sacred places. But this site, this place by the elbow, was particularly important to the Plains Cree.

---

* Men who had distinguished themselves in warfare and who played a crucial role in the well-being of the camp.

Illustration by Ed Peekeekoot

Ahtahkakoop's family travelling to the Sun Dance grounds.

The story of its sacredness was etched into his mind, a story that became more vivid as the long procession of dog- and horse-drawn travois, people, and horses neared its destination.*

"This happened a long time ago," Ahtahkakoop remembered the old man saying. "A little child had been born and had been lost."

"Our grandfathers and grandmothers were moving their camp long ago," the old man continued. "The baby was tied on one of the travois with thongs of rawhide. They must have come undone as the people were moving. The baby dropped off, and no one noticed because they were happy as they walked and they were talking and visiting. It so happened that his family was at the end of the procession when this child fell off. At first they did not notice as they travelled. It was only much later, for nothing like this had ever happened, nothing like this had ever happened before.

---

* This sacred story was told by Barry L. Ahenakew, as it was told to him by the elders Opapēcīw, Kā-āyāsitēyahkēkocin, Kīsik-awāsis, and Okimāwikwāniyēw. It was taped in Cree, transcribed in Cree, and then translated into English by Freda Ahenakew. Editing was kept to a minimum in order to retain the characteristics of Cree story-telling.

"And so he was left. When this little child fell off he must have been sleeping. He must have been content after breast-feeding. There was nothing, there was no crying right away. There was nothing to worry him. He was full as he slept. He too was happy about his life.

"So his parents continued on their way. They were travelling at the end, behind everyone else. No one was aware of what happened, for stories were told as they travelled.

"And so it happened later now, when he began to get hungry, this little child began to cry and cry. He began crying and crying. He cried when he was hungry."

"The buffalo were travelling not far away, and they heard him," the old man said. "They heard something so they went to check. These animals, when they hear something they don't understand, they search for it. 'Let's see what this noise is,' one of the buffalo said. Some animals are like that. That was how this one buffalo was. It was a female that searched, and some males also looked. These bulls, $h\bar{a}$, they were going to where they heard something. They went and found this little child there on the ground. He was crying.

"'Well, well, what is this we have found,' the buffalo were saying. 'Look! This is a little person, a little one!' 'Look, what is it?' another one asked. These buffalo were using their own language. They were talking to each other. 'Well, I will kill him! I will kill him,' one of the young bulls was saying. I guess he wanted to be a leader, for they too had leaders. The buffalo used to make chiefs of the most powerful one. There was a bull that was a leader for them too, but he was not the one trying to kill this little child. A bull that wanted to be a leader was going to kill this little child. He was going to crush the baby with his head. He was going to use his horns. The others were stopping him.

"'This is a little child, you should not do that to him,' the other buffalo told him. 'This should not be done to him. He does not even know anything. He is not even able to flee. Don't!' The buffalo were trying to tell the young bull not to kill the little child. 'Let him go,' one of the bulls told the young buffalo. 'No, I will kill him,' the young bull said. 'These are the ones who kill us, these human people.'

"'No! no!' some of the buffalo cried out. One of them raced away. He had gone to fetch their leader. Suddenly he came racing back with a big bull. Right away this bull, the leader, raced around. It was there that he raced around this little child. 'He will know what to do,' said the others. This bull, this leader, he raced right around, so that no one would bother the child. The leader was chasing the other buffalo farther and farther away. Then he came to a stop there beside the baby.

"'Yes! What is this? What is this you have found? This one that you have found is alive. Oh my, Oh my, Oh my!' All the while the baby was crying, This little child wanted to suckle.

"'Well, well. It is truly pitiful. It is pitiful this human life that you have found,' the leader said. He felt sorry for him. 'This one over here wanted to kill him' one of the bulls told him. 'Hey! None of that will happen, none of that will happen. Go fetch that one! She is to come and feed this child.' Some of the buffalo left again.

"And now they brought this female and she had lots of milk in her bag. 'That is the one,' the leader told her. 'You are to feed this little child, you are to feed him. Stand on top of him, bend over,' And so she stood over the baby, just exactly where the teats were. She was bent over there. She squatted and fed him.

"And this one, when he found the teat—*āw!* what would the little child know—he began suckling this female buffalo. He got really full with drinking. Well! Well, he was really contented from eating. So then he slept again being so contented from eating.

"By the time his parents and the others realized the child was lost the buffalo had already taken him, for one of them had used *yēskanēwak*[*] to scoop the child up. He scooped him up and carried him like that. This little child was small. The place on top of the bull's head was almost like a bed. It was really soft between the horns where he had been scooped. Now this little child was being carried. There were many buffalo. It was a good thing he had been saved. It's a good thing they fetched the leader right away, this chief buffalo, the king.

"It was then that as soon as the child would cry, if he was not being carried, he would be fed. It was this female who fed him. And in this way the child spent the summer. I guess the buffalo milk was very powerful. This child became so strong, and he soon moved around. He was strong. Very early he began taking steps. The buffalo milk was so good for him, and his parents never found him."

---

[*] The cradle of the horns.

A boy had put some wood on the fire, Ahtahkakoop remembered, and then the old man continued the telling of the sacred story.

"So this was how the buffalo raised him. Finally it was one year, and then two years, three years, four years, and they did not see the Cree very often. Only once in a while! But they would flee right away when they sensed anything like that. They looked after themselves. And the child would be carried, only now he rode on the back of the buffalo. Sometimes he would run. He had so much stamina. He was becoming stronger and bigger. As the boy got older and stronger, his diet changed. Now it was grass, flowers, and leaves that he was eating. He was living on these now.

"He thought himself to be a buffalo, this young man. He was fifteen years old, he was sixteen years old, he was seventeen years old. He continued to grow and he was getting really long and bushy hair. He did not speak, of course. There was no human language, for he never heard the Cree language, just buffalo talk. But, it so happened that one day people startled them. Hey! There was noise and there was dust flying. These people were yelling as they chased the buffalo. Well, he too was fleeing. But he was big now and he ran with the buffalo."

"And these Cree saw him," the old man said. "*Yohō!* They were catching glimpses. They were getting glimpses of this young man. He was running with the buffalo as they disappeared. He was going as fast as the buffalo. Well, well! Some of the Cree were killing the buffalo. They stopped as they spoke to each other.

"'Did you see him? Is that a person we have seen running with the buffalo, or is it a spirit? What is it, what is that we have seen?' Well! Well, they were rather scared. 'Well, well! Okay then, we will take care of the meat,' they said. 'We will bring our wives here to come to take care of this meat.'

"Well, they had decided what they were going to do. So now some of these Crees were telling what they had seen. 'A young man, a boy with long hair, was running with these buffalo. I wonder if we were seeing things if several of us saw him?' they asked among themselves.

"*Hā!* Buffalo Child—as I will call him now—lived with the buffalo. They had run to another place far away and they were crying for their relatives who had been killed, the buffalo that were killed.

"Well, well, now the buffalo were crying, the bulls and the females for their relatives. Buffalo Child was also grieving, although his mother had come through safely, the one who had fed him, and also his father. He knew them as his parents, this mother and the leader, the big bull.

"'*Hā!* That's it, my son,' the leader said. The bull addressed him this way now. The young man understood the buffalo language.

"'Son, look! These people have given us a hard time again. They are the only ones that give us a hard time. Although we too sometimes hurt them, one by one, they still give us a hard time with arrows and they spear us. Well son, you must learn to run from that kind.' The old bull was counselling his child well.

"Buffalo Child had a brother. He had a young brother buffalo, and when they were young they used to fight. They still played together. They pushed each other with their heads, and finally Buffalo Child was getting strong too. Finally the buffalo were getting him strong as they pushed each other around with their heads. He played with them, fought with them. And they ran all the time. They travelled all the time. Buffalo Child, as he grew into a man, became very powerful. He was also good looking. He was getting tall. He was getting older in years. At times the Crees were after them, and they had to run even more.

Buffalo Child was also getting more *nipwahkēt*, more intelligent now. He was getting clever. One day they came to a lake. He was drinking and looking down when he saw his reflection. Never before did he mind his reflection in the water. This time when he was drinking he really saw himself. He looked at the reflections of the others. He saw he was different, he looked different. *Ohōh!* He just let the water out of his mouth, it was dripping there as he looked at these buffalo.

"'Why?' he asked, as he looked at his reflection again in the water. '*Iyaw*, what do I look like? *Yohō!* These people as they are called who chase after us, who are killing us, this is how I look, *yaw!* What do I look like?' Well! Well! He was then bewildered. He went to his father then, this chief, this bull. 'Father! Why do I look like this?'

"'Well son! I knew that some day you would come and ask me this. I will tell you. I will tell you, I will not hide anything from you. It is true you look different, I saved your life, son. You were found and one of the bulls was going to kill you. I stopped it. I felt sorry for you, son, so you wouldn't be killed. These people where you are from, these people the Crees, as they are called, this is where you come from exactly.'

"'I will spare you, I had said at that time, as I felt sorry for you. So then I have raised you. I have cared for you. This is what you know now. You will be worried now. You are not a buffalo my son, you are a person for certain.'

"'Well, well, what will I do, father? What will I do?'

"'You can remain with us. It is all right the way I have raised you. You are like one, a buffalo. You can stay with us.'

"'Father, now I am bewildered. How? How can I stay with you, now that I know I am different of body? I look different. What about my people, my mother and my father? My father is a human, also my mother. How are they? Where are they?'

"'I don't know son, I do not know. I have raised you for a long time.'

"'Well, father, I am going to be quiet, away somewhere. Do not worry when you don't see me right away," the young man said.

"'Well, that is it then, my son. I will see you.' And so Buffalo Child left, only now he knew he was a human. He had no clothes, he had no moccasins. He was naked. He had long hair. He was tall and had a strong body. He was slim when he left to be alone, and he was good looking.

"When he was alone, the young man said to himself, 'I must go home to the people. I greatly appreciate that the buffalo, my father, and also my mother, raised me but now I will look for the people.'"

"And so he left," the old man said. "He walked I wonder for how many days, how many nights, but he was able-bodied. He was strong, stronger than any of the other Crees. He must have been much stronger. He found an *ōtēnaw** with smoke rising from the tipis, so he went towards it.

"Some scouts were on the lookout. They saw this young man come walking. They went to announce his arrival at the Cree camp. 'Someone is coming, a stranger' they said. 'We cannot recognize him, get ready for a stranger is coming!'

"Buffalo Child kept coming. Finally he was getting there. They could not recognize him and he was naked. He did not wear a breechcloth and he was barefoot. Who was this? Now they spoke Cree to him. 'Who are you? Where are you from?' He could not speak to them, he did not understand them.

"'What language are they speaking?' he thought to himself, and he kept walking towards this *ōtēnaw*, to where the tipis were. More and more the tipis were becoming visible. He just went towards these.

"He was not a bit scared. He would leave these people behind anyway

---

* Cree town or encampment.

when in flight running, but he was human, he had to meet his human relatives. He just kept going, and although they talked to him he paid them no attention. Finally he reached where the tipis stood. He was not too pleased with them. These tipis were made of buffalo hides. They were made from hides sewed together. He recognized them, he recognized the smell. It was really buffalo hides. These were his relatives, the buffalo.

"But he was human. Well truly, finally the people and the children were really around him as he walked, walking along with him and talking to him as they walked, 'Who are you? Where are you from? What have you come here for? Why are you naked?' There was so much chattering, the people were chattering.

"After a time Buffalo Child stopped when he thought he was near the centre of the town. There was a big tipi in the centre. He went there. Some people came out, and before he knew it there were many humans around him. They made room for the men coming out of the tipi. These were the chiefs, the councillors, the elders. They were coming towards him, they were not even talking. They were looking at him with his bushy hair. He had long hair—it looked like he never combed his hair—and he was naked. He had no shoes on. Finally one of the men spoke to him. He lifted his hand up for the people to be quiet. '*Ēhā.*' When it was quiet, he asked 'Who are you? Where have you come from? Tell me, tell us your story!'

"How could Buffalo Child respond to him? He did not know. He simply put his head down, finally he looked up. He had thought what to do.

"He did this. He closed his mouth. He simply made signs to talk to them, '*Āw!* He does not speak, he cannot talk!' the people said.

"Well, well. These people began chattering again. Then the chief again spoke. He was making hand signs. 'Come! Come! Come with me!' They took him into the tipi now.

"Only the chiefs, councillors, and some braves were allowed to enter the tipi. They all sat down. At first Buffalo Child kept standing. He saw that they sat upright, cross-legged Cree style. They were all watching him. He looked at how they were sitting, and then slowly he sat down too. He sat like them. He was sitting Cree style, he was sitting up.

"Well, although the men in the tipi talked and asked questions, Buffalo Child could not understand them and he did not know how to talk to them. Finally he simply pointed that he had come from far.

"He did this then. He made signs like horns with his pointing finger, like he had horns, with the *omomatayēw** hanging down. 'Buffalo, *hā*! He is telling about buffalo, where he saw them!' one of the men in the tipi said. Then Buffalo Child pointed to himself with his signs.

"'*Ōh!* You are called Buffalo Child then. Hey! He may be a Blackfoot, maybe a Blackfoot has reached us. But he is in no way dangerous, he does not scare us. '*Hā!* We will watch him,' they said.

"So they watched him.

"'Well now, we will watch him!' And from then on the chief himself watched Buffalo Child, for he liked how the strange young man looked. He was tall, he was of strong body, and he was slim. So now they brought him clothes and a breechcloth was put on him. Moccasins too. They were measuring his feet to make moccasins for him and they combed his hair too. Well, his hair was really tangled everywhere. It took a really long time to comb it. Well, well! But when they braided his hair for him, his braids were thick and very long. Well, well, he looked good! A real Cree.

"Then they began teaching him to speak Cree. He imitated those who were teaching him. They pointed to a tipi and said '*mīkiwāhp*,' and *iyinito-mīkiwāhp*, like a tipi.

"They pointed to the meat rack, *akwāwān*, they told him, and to the *wiyās* hanging on the rack. They were hanging there, strips of buffalo meat spread out on the rack to dry. That was something he didn't like, buffalo meat. It was hanging all over, his relatives. *Wiyās*, meat, he was told.

"'That is why they kill my relatives!' Now he knew. 'They eat the meat, these people eat us.' Well, well. Of course he would not say anything. He didn't know how to tell them anyhow, even though he was being taught to speak Cree, even though they were pointing things out to him every day. Finally he had lived with them for quite a while.

"Then one day, scouts came racing in. 'We have seen buffalo!' they yelled. 'We saw buffalo!' Already he knew what that meant. My relatives have been seen, he said to himself.

"He did not tell anyone about how he had been raised, he kept that quiet. Suddenly buffalo had been seen. They arrived racing. The Cree killed a great many of them. The women took their travois and went to the place where the buffalo had been killed. When they came back the travois were loaded with meat. The women also hauled many hides to their camp. They

---

* A goatee on the chin of a moose or buffalo.

started making dry meat. The women were hanging meat to dry. He watched for a while. His relatives had been killed.

"Buffalo Child was deeply disturbed. At first he thought, 'I will tell them.' Then he said, 'No, I will just leave.'" The old man who was telling the story clapped his hands. "And so in this way Buffalo Child disappeared. It was then that he left the Cree camp.

"Buffalo Child came upon some buffalo as he was travelling, but they wanted to flee when they saw him. The buffalo were scared of a human person, but then he talked to them, '*mmmk mmmki*,' buffalo talk.

"'*Yohō!* What's with this human who knows our language?' the buffalo asked. 'He doesn't want us to be scared of him. He is not going to harm us. And so they stayed, for of course Buffalo Child was speaking to them. And he talked with them. 'I am like you,' he said. They understood each other, and he asked them, 'Where is that one? That one who is my father? He raised me, I am like a buffalo.' He was searching for his father.

"Buffalo Child was thinking, when I was with people they were always chattering. The only time the people were quiet was when they slept. Always there was noise from chattering, dogs barking. Well, well! It is this. It is better to live like this, to live quietly. I would like this much better.

"And then he found his father. Well, well, his father was so pleased that Buffalo Child had come back to them. 'Son! This is my son!' he said. 'My son has arrived! He has come back to us. Thank you, thank you! Well, they celebrated. Then they all came together to hear the young man tell his story. Where did he go? What did he look for? What happened?

"'I will not hide anything from you, father,' Buffalo Child said. 'This body that I have, I am a human. You told me that so I went to live with people. I went looking for them. I went to know them, to see how they lived, to see if I could live with them. Well truly, I even thought about mating with the women. But I did not bother them. I treated them with respect. I respected them, although they really tried to excite me.'

"Already he was talking to them, he was telling them the story. 'But father, I hated it! Always, always when I went out, always there was only buffalo meat hanging on the drying racks. They ate it, they ate us, and they had buffalo skins on the floor. They slept on them. They live in them, *mīkiwāhpa** they called them. They lived in pointed homes, they lived in

_____

* Tipis.

homes made from buffalo hides. Everything is buffalo, simply every-thing is buffalo.'

"'Well son, this is our life,' his father told him. 'This is our life. We were put here on Mother Earth by the Creator. There are so many of us buffalo, but there is one who rules over us, the Creator. Those people you saw, they have the same Creator as we do. They pray, they pray too. It is the same one they pray to. This is our work. We feed the people, we cover them, we keep people warm, and we give people tools, we are made into all kinds of tools. The people live by us. This is our work. That is the reason you saw what you saw.

"'But there is also another law. They cannot over-kill us. They cannot get greedy and kill too much. They can only kill as much as they can use. That is the law. But these Cree must take care, my son. That is the reason you saw what you did. They must treat us with respect, and we too must be good to them. We multiply quickly and there are many of us, but even then we must flee when we see them. That is the way it is my son, so do not mind.'

"'But I do not like what I see father!'

"'*Hā!* but my son, don't mind, forget it! Now, let's travel.' And so Buffalo Child travelled with the buffalo and again, more and more he was getting wiser.

"Well, he ran along with the buffalo. Heh! Now he was content, for this was how he grew up. He was raised this way and he did not think too much about human life.

"Suddenly again they were startled by an attack. The people, the Crees, were yelling as they chased the buffalo. Well, well! The dust was flying! The sounds of hooves could be heard, and the buffalo could be heard as the bulls were being killed.

"Well, well! Buffalo Child was thinking that he hated this. They had to flee more and more often, they were always fleeing to different places."

The old man sat silently for a moment, deep in thought. When he spoke again there was sadness in his voice. "No, Buffalo Child wasn't that old when his father was killed." he said. "This chief bull, his father, was suf-fering when he cried out, 'My son, flee! My son, flee!' He was suffering.

"'No father, I will not flee! I will not flee anymore!'

"'My son, flee! Save your own life!'

"'No father!'

"'Well, well my son! I am so thankful that you came to live with us again. You came home to us. There is a special way that you can roll over while there is still time, before I stop breathing, my son. If you roll over, you will be a buffalo. And if you roll over again, my son, you will be a rock. This is what you can do before I quit breathing if you will flee no more!'

"'Okay father! I will do it, I will do it, I will flee no more. I will flee no more.' It was then that his father's breathing was getting more difficult. Buffalo Child was crying because his father was dying. The buffalo were still being chased, the sound of hooves could still be heard when he rolled over. Buffalo Child was human. He rolled four times. He stood up. He was four-legged, a big bull was standing there. He was a buffalo now.

"He still remembered what his father had told him. 'If you roll over again four times, you will become a rock.' He rolled over again. The Cree were watching him when he changed form, this Buffalo Child. When this buffalo rolled over again he became a rock, but not the same size he had been as a bull. He was much bigger as a rock. He seemed to grow. These Cree hunters were so amazed. The buffalo-shaped rock grew to such a tremendous size. It looked like a buffalo sitting down. It was a buffalo sitting down."

"Of course the Cree told what they had seen," the old man said. "This man called *mostos-awāsis*, Buffalo Child, had the power to change from a man to a buffalo and then to a rock. The rock suddenly became bigger as it sat there in the valley, the people said. They told the story. It was heard all over, how *mostos-awāsis* had lived with the buffalo and how they had seen him change form while they were hunting these buffalo. The Crees started gathering there, they camped there, and they came to see this big rock. They danced, they sang, and they prayed, for of course the buffalo was one of the gifts given by the Creator. And they held their Sun Dances there near the place where the big buffalo rock sat.

"Then a great many people started coming. Saulteaux and Cree came from the east. Cree and Assiniboine from the south, Blackfoot and Cree from the west. And Cree came from the north. They all came.

"This is the big rock, *mistasiniy*,* that we see when we camp near the elbow of the *wāwāskēsiw-sīpiy*† to hold our Sun Dances," Ahtahkakoop

---

* Big Rock.
† Elk or Red Deer River, which is now known as the South Saskatchewan River.

Photograph by Zenon S. Pohorecky, courtesy of the Saskatchewan Archaeological Society

Mistasiniy was situated at the source of the Qu'Appelle Valley near the elbow of the South Saskatchewan River. Weighing 400 tons, it was 26 feet across, stood 14 feet high, and resembled a resting buffalo.

remembered the old man telling his listeners. "It is the big rock that looks like a buffalo sitting. It was there the man called *mostos-awāsis*, Buffalo Child, changed form. He did not want to flee anymore. This is how the story has been passed down from generation to generation. It is a sacred story," the old man had said. "And now, we too come to *mistasiniy* to pray and hold our Sun Dances. For our people, it is a sacred place."*

And so, as the large rock shaped like a sitting buffalo came into view, Ahtahkakoop stood in awe, marvelling at the wonders in the world of the Nēhiyawak. And the boy gave thanks to the Creator, for He was the one who gave them all things.

This was the world into which Ahtahkakoop was born.

---

* On December 1, 1966, engineers from the Canadian government's Prairie Farm Rehabilitation Administration (PFRA) drilled 60 sticks of dynamite into the centre of *mistasiniy* and blasted forty tons off the large boulder. Soon *mistasiniy* and the nearby Sun Dance grounds were flooded as dammed water from the South Saskatchewan River flowed into the upper reaches of the Qu'Appelle Valley, thus creating Lake Diefenbaker. Professor Zenon S. Pohorecky, University of Saskatchewan, who took the above photograph in 1959, was one of the men who led an unsuccessful fight to move the sacred rock before it was flooded. A piece of *mistasiniy* has been placed in a cairn near the town of Elbow in commemoration.

CHAPTER FOUR

Ahtahkakoop Becomes a Man

lthough Ahtahkakoop and the other children were raised as Plains Cree, changes had come to the land of the Nēhiyawak by the time of their birth. The changes had begun slowly at first, beginning with the founding of the Hudson's Bay Company in 1670 and the subsequent construction of York Factory on the shore of Hudson Bay.[1] With a few exceptions, the company's fur traders had been content to sit on the shores of Hudson Bay and wait for Indian trappers, hunters, and middlemen to paddle their fur-laden canoes along the Saskatchewan River and Hayes River system to York Factory. The furs were traded for tobacco, guns, ammunition, knives, hatchets, and other trade goods.[2] Then the men returned to the plains and woodlands of the North-West where they, as "middlemen," traded the European goods with the Indian people living inland. The Plains Cree, allied with the Assiniboines and well armed with single barrel flintlock guns from the traders, became the most powerful Indian nation in the North-West.

In many ways the fur traders had little impact on the Indian people of the plains during the first 90 years of the Hudson's Bay Company's existence. They were far removed from the land of the Nēhiyawak and had little direct influence on daily life. But then, as the years passed, the French—followed by independent British and Scottish traders—pushed into the North-West from Montreal to establish posts in Saskatchewan River country and the northern forests. In 1774, in an effort to combat this competition, the Hudson's Bay Company moved inland and built Cumberland House in the Saskatchewan River delta region. Independent traders from the emerging North West Company leap-frogged up the Saskatchewan and Churchill rivers in attempts to gain an advantage with

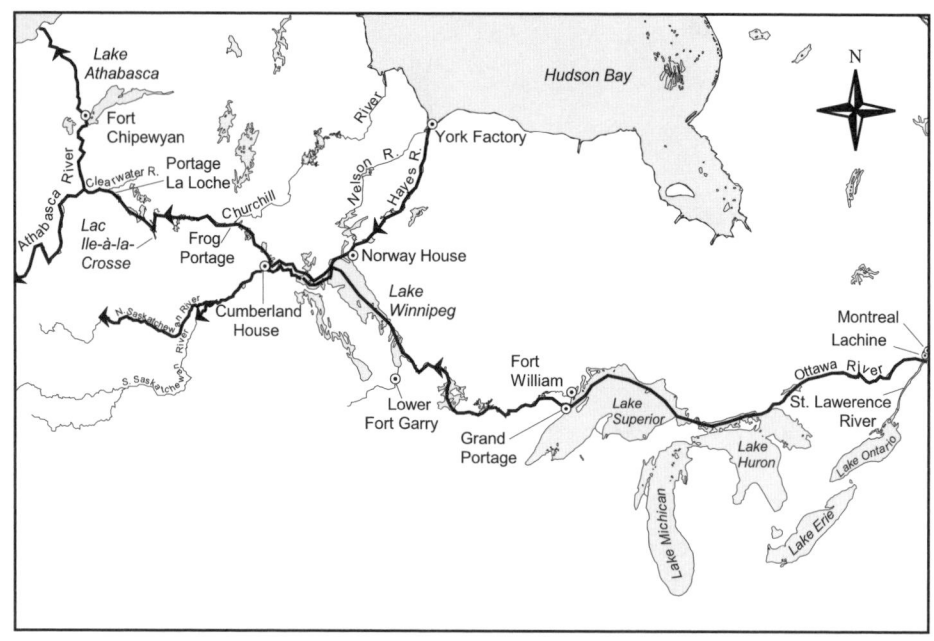

Information Systems Division, Canadian Plains Research Center

The water highways from Montreal and Hudson Bay converged at the northern end of Lake Winnipeg. From there the route led to Cumberland House. From Cumberland House some traders headed north to the Churchill River and the rivers beyond. Others travelled the Saskatchewan River and its branches to the parklands and plains.

the Indian people. The Hudson's Bay Company men, greatly outnumbered, followed as best they could.

During the 1770s and early 1780s a number of competing posts were built on the banks of the North Saskatchewan River well within the travelling range of Ahtahkakoop's family.[3] Then, in the mid-1780s, two posts— one belonging to the North West Company and the other to the Hudson's Bay Company—were established on the South Branch of the Saskatchewan River. Other posts, such as Buckingham House and Manchester House, operated further west along the North Branch.

In 1794 a war party consisting of between 100 and 150 Gros Ventre and Blackfoot warriors attacked the trading houses on the South Branch. The Hudson's Bay Company post was struck first. Three company men, an Indian woman, and two young children were killed. Two other Indian women and the three remaining children were taken prisoner. The North West Company traders situated on the other side of the river, alerted by the attack on the Bay post and better staffed, were able to withstand the assault on their own post when it came. Both companies abandoned the area.[4] The following year, in 1795, new fur trade houses were built on the Saskatchewan River not far from the place where the Chevalier de la Corne had built his French post in 1753.[*] The Hudson's Bay Company called its post Carlton House; this was the first of three fur trade posts in Saskatchewan River country to be given that name. The North West Company post was called Fort St. Louis; it was also known as the Canadians' post, "upper" Nepawi, or "upper" Nippowee.[5]

In 1804 or 1805 the Hudson's Bay and the North West companies returned to the South Branch, building their posts near the river crossing that later became known as the St. Laurent crossing.[6] The Hudson's Bay Company retained the name Carlton House for its post; this trading establishment is often called Carlton House II to distinguish it from its predecessor.

By now the pattern for the fur trade had been set. Most of the fine furs from animals such as beaver, mink, and marten were collected at the northern posts in the forested Churchill and Athabasca river regions. The traders particularly prized beaver pelts. The underhair or fleece was made into strong shiny felt in overseas factories which, in turn, was made into the fashionable beaver hats so popular in Britain and Europe. Indeed, it was the demand for beaver pelts and profit that had ignited and sustained the fur trade.

The Indian people who trapped and hunted on the plains and in the parklands supplied pemmican, dried buffalo meat, grease, leather, and prairie furs such as muskrat, fox, wolf, and a lesser amount of fine furs. Pemmican became the staple food for the boatmen who hauled furs and trade goods along the waterways to and from York Factory and to Grand Portage on the route to Montreal.

Now the fur trade had a more direct impact on the Indian people of Saskatchewan River country. An increasing number of white traders took Indian women as wives. The Cree called the mixed-blood children from these unions *āpihtawikosisānak*, or half-breeds. With traders in their midst, European goods were not only more accessible, but the people had more bargaining power and choice in their trade dealings. There was also a

---

[*] The posts built by the Hudson's Bay Company and the North West Company were situated downstream from the forks on land that is now part of the James Smith Reserve.

Hudson's Bay Company Archives, Provincial Archives of Manitoba, N81-221B

Hunters and trappers traded their harvest of furs and buffalo products for guns, tobacco, blankets, axes and other trade goods.

greater variety and abundance of goods that included metal traps and cooking pots, cloth, tea, beads, and other articles that made life easier. Detrimentally, the use of liquor as an inducement to trade increased, particularly amongst the traders from Montreal. The white fur traders, in addition to trade goods and liquor, also brought new diseases—smallpox, measles, whooping cough, and tuberculosis. The Indian people had little immunity to these diseases, and periodically they raged through the plains, parklands, and woodlands of the North-West. The suffering was horrendous and great numbers of Indian people died.

In 1810, six years before Ahtahkakoop was born, the South Branch houses were abandoned for the last time and the newcomers—the white traders—moved again. This time they chose a flat of land on the south bank of the mighty North Saskatchewan River, some 90 miles upstream from the junction of the North and South branches, for their new posts.* The London-based Hudson's Bay Company once again retained the name

---

* This site was 50 miles upriver from present-day Prince Albert.

Carlton House and manned its post with English and Scottish officers and labouring men called "servants." This post became known as Fort Carlton.[7]

The North West Company had operated a horse station near the site for a number of years. Late each summer, when the first of the company's large "North" canoes reached this place on the bank of the North Branch, senior Nor'Westers left their canoes, "mounted" horses, and travelled onto the plains to get buffalo meat for the canoe brigade. For this reason, the name La Montée was given to the new post.[8] Like other North West Company posts, it was staffed with officers of European ancestry and French-speaking "Canadian" canoemen called "voyageurs." Although the two companies were sometimes in violent competition with each other, the opposing traders feared attacks by Blackfoot, Blood, Peigan, Sarcee, and Gros Ventre warriors and enclosed their posts within a common stockade. The Nēhiyawak called these establishments *wāskahikan*, the Cree word for enclosed buildings or fort.

Ahtahkakoop's family had long been familiar with this flat along the North Saskatchewan River, for it was situated near a natural river crossing on the trail that fur trader Alexander Henry described as the "usual direct route of the Indians between the North and South Branches of the Saskatchewan." The "road is good" he recorded in his journal two years before Carlton House and La Montée were built, "and it is only one day's journey across."[9] The trail Henry spoke of led southeast to the general area where the trading posts on the South Branch had been located. On the north side of the crossing an Indian trail wound through the parkland, forest, and muskeg to Green Lake and the water route to the Churchill River system. Well-established Indian use of the crossing place on the North Saskatchewan River had undoubtedly played a crucial role in the fur traders' decision to build the new posts at this particular site.

The Nor'Westers abandoned La Montée in 1816, only to rebuild three miles upriver from Fort Carlton two years later. The post was closed permanently and the St. Lawrence freight route abandoned in 1821 when the Hudson's Bay Company and the North West Company joined forces to create a new amalgamated Hudson's Bay Company.[10] Ahtahkakoop was five years old when the English company was reorganized.

Under the new arrangement a number of North West Company officers, along with some of their men, were absorbed into the new company. Many employees retired or were discharged. Some of these men returned to the homes of their birth. Others—often with their native families—moved to the Selkirk Settlement, a community that later became known as the Red River Settlement and, still later yet, Winnipeg. Others—particularly the half-breed men—remained in the district, hunting and trapping as "freemen." And some men and their families lived and travelled with Indian bands.

The women who had been living at La Montée had fewer options, particularly if they were of mixed Indian and white ancestry and not Indian. Some women, of course, remained with their husbands. Others found mates amidst the remaining fur trade employees or amongst the freemen. Many returned with their children to the band of their birth. And some women were abandoned to fend for themselves.[11]

With the dismantling of La Montée, chief trader John Peter Pruden was given responsibility for the fur trade in the area that became known as the Carlton District. Pruden was well known among the hunters and trappers of Saskatchewan River country since he had worked at the first Carlton House, been in charge of Carlton House II for two years, and had supervised the construction of Fort Carlton (Carlton House III) on the North Saskatchewan River. With the exception of the 1824-1826 trading seasons, when a temporary replacement was at the post, Pruden had command of Fort Carlton until his retirement in 1837. Like many other fur traders, Pruden was married to an Indian woman according to the custom of the country and they had a number of children.

Pruden kept daily post journals during the years Ahtahkakoop was growing up.[12] The chief trader was very meticulous in his chronicles, recording among other things the arrival of Indian people at the post, how many came, where they were from, and what they brought to trade. Because it was part of his job to know what was going on in the district, the fur trader met with the leaders. He asked about the location of other camps, the whereabouts of the buffalo, and the abundance and condition of game and fur-bearing animals. He also included details on the formation of Cree and Assiniboine war parties, along with accounts of battles and horse-stealing raids. And he noted the arrival of Blackfoot, Blood, Sarcee, Peigan, and Gros Ventre war parties in the district. Warfare was of particular concern to Pruden because hunting and trapping came to a standstill when the nations were at war.

According to Pruden's records, approximately 100 tents of Cree were trading at Fort Carlton during the 1818–19 season. Cree in the district also

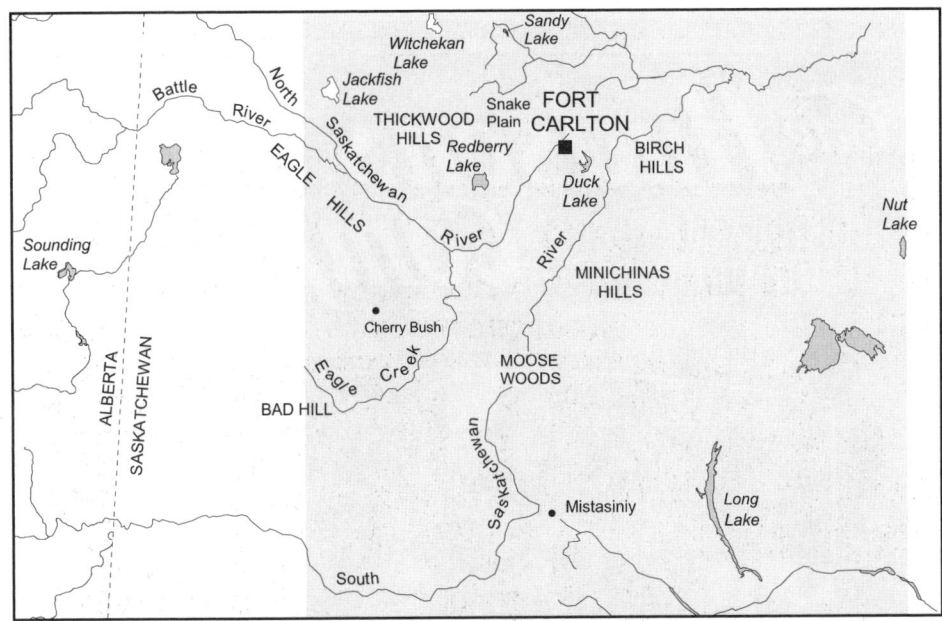

Information Systems Division, Canadian Plains Research Center

The Carlton District, as defined by the shaded area, extended from the elbow of the South Saskatchewan River on the south to Witchekan Lake (Stinking Lake) on the north. Jackfish Lake marked the western boundary, with Nut Lake delineating the eastern limits. (Report of the Carlton District, 1815, HBCA, B. 27/e/1.)

traded at Red River far to the southeast and at the Paint Creek post, which was located near the Vermilion River in what is now east-central Alberta. The Hudson's Bay Company officer reported that although a small number of Cree in the district generally remained in the woods, the greater portion lived on the plains, often in the company of Assiniboines.[13]

Pruden estimated the number of Assiniboine at 300 tents, adding that they always lived on the plains "amongst the buffalo."[14] Sometime prior to 1640 the Assiniboine were a distinct people living east, north, and west of Rainy Lake, separate from the Sioux nation that lived near the headwaters of the Mississippi River. The Assiniboines gradually moved north and west and by the 19th century part of their group was allied with the Plains Cree. The Nēhiyawak and Assinboines often camped together—even though their languages were completely different—and their people intermarried. Together in warfare, they formed a formidable force. Pruden generally called the Plains Cree "Southern," "Southard," or "Southward" Indians, and until 1834 he always referred to the Assiniboines as Stone Indians.[15]

The Fort Carlton journals for the years 1814-1827 show that the Cree were coming to Carlton to trade from places such as the Shell River,

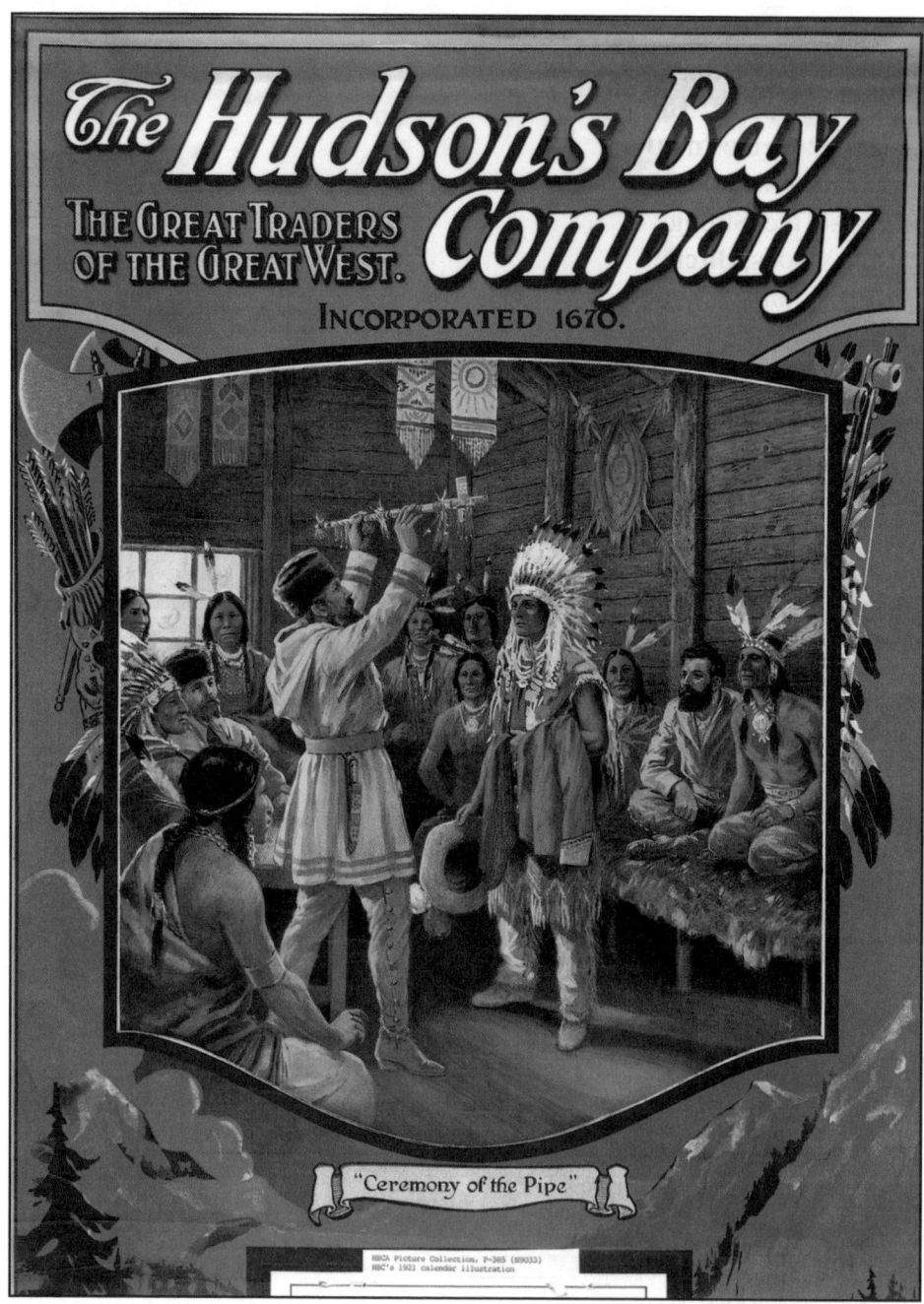

Hudson's Bay Company 1921 calendar illustration by E.N. North,
Hudson's Bay Company Archives, Provincial Archives of Manitoba, N9033

The officers in charge of the Hudson's Bay Company posts participated in traditional Indian ceremonies before meeting to discuss business.

Bloody Berry Lake (Redberry Lake), Fighting River (Battle River), Eagle Hills Creek, Setting River (Sturgeon River), Jack Lake (Jackfish Lake), Thickwood Hills, Birch Hills, Woody Hill, Red Deer Hills, the South Branch, near the "mouth of the branch," "the plains," and the "north side." There were also references to Beaver Hill Cree from the Edmonton House area and the Strongwood Cree. The Assiniboine were coming in from Moose Woods, Birch Hills, Touchwood Hills, Eagle Hills, the area between the North and South branches of the Saskatchewan River, and the "big point" or "long point" of woods near the Minichinas Hills.

By 1823 the concentration of bands in the western part of the Carlton District was large enough that Hudson's Bay Company officials made plans to abandon Fort Carlton and build another post near the mouth of the Battle River. The move was never made, and the Fort Carlton journals in succeeding years made repeated mention of sending company men to the Eagle Hills and the vicinity of the Battle River to trade for buffalo meat and prairie furs.

By the late 1820s the Assiniboine were hunting and camping farther south each year, gradually retreating to land that became part of the United States of America. The Plains Cree, in the meantime, were spending more time in the southern and western parts of their territory. Indicative of this movement, the Fort Carlton journals show that after 1827 an increasing number of Cree camps were located at Moose Woods, on the south side of the South Branch, and in the vicinity of God's Lake (Little Manitou Lake) near present day Watrous.[16]

In 1829, in response to requests from Indian bands living in the middle country between Fort Carlton and Fort Edmonton, the Hudson's Bay Company finally built a post in this region. However, instead of building in the vicinity of the Battle River, company officers built north of present-day Lloydminster on the bank of the North Saskatchewan River. The trading post was named Fort Pitt.[17]

Although Fort Pitt drew some people away from Fort Carlton, many of the hunters and trappers who spent part of their time in the upper regions remained attached to the old post. Accordingly, in addition to frequent references to Moose Woods and God's Lake, the Fort Carlton journals continued to record Cree coming from places such as the Battle River and Jack Lake. There were also the usual references to the South Branch, the Cross Woods, Thickwood Hills, Shell River, Touchwood Hills, Woody Hill, Sliding Hills, and Stinking Lake. The bands camping at these places were

Hudson's Bay Company 1930 calendar illustration by Walter J. Phillips,
Hudson's Bay Company Archives, Provincial Archives of Manitoba, N7811

York boats at Norway House on the northern shore of Lake Winnipeg.

apparently all Plains Cree since the journals also noted Cree "belonging to
the Woods of the north side of the river" as well as general references to
Indians from the "woods" and "from below," meaning downriver from Fort
Carlton. In addition to Woods Cree, there was at least one "Thickwood
band" of Assiniboine, some Saulteaux, the occasional Swampy Cree from
the Cumberland area, and several families of Iroquois. The Iroquois men
had been engaged by the North West Company as voyageurs to help paddle

the large North canoes. Instead of returning to their homes in the east they had remained in the Carlton area.

The arrival of the fur traders added a new component to the annual cycle of activities that were an integral part of Indian life. In late August or early September, hunters, trappers, and their families gathered near Fort Carlton to wait for the York boats loaded with trade goods to arrive from York Factory. After the goods were unloaded and an inventory was taken, the people got their supplies for the fall and winter. Often, if they had nothing to trade, the traders advanced the goods on credit.

During the fall and winter, the men and their families—individually or in groups—returned to the post with their harvest of furs, leather, pemmican, dried meat, and fat. They paid their debts and replenished their supply of trade goods. In the spring, before the ice broke and the boats left for the eastern depot, the people who still had furs and other produce to trade once again came to the post. Then, outfitted for the summer, they left for their hunting grounds. The cycle repeated itself at the end of summer.

Some of the Indian people well known at the post were given seasonal or occasional jobs. Men were hired to hunt buffalo and game animals and to guard horses at Fort Carlton. They served as guides, travelled with company men on their journeys to fetch meat and collect furs, and sometimes were hired to deliver messages. A few were engaged to help man the York boats going to and from York Factory. Occasionally the women were able to obtain extra cooking pots, tea, cloth, beads, thread, or special articles such as combs and looking-glasses by working in the gardens and fields, making moccasins, and helping to make pemmican at the post.

Often the people camped west of Fort Carlton to wait for friends and relatives. They visited relatives living at the post. They prayed and sang during sweatlodge ceremonies, held feasts for departed relatives, and participated in round dances. Frequently the drums could be heard all night as the people danced, gambled, and visited with friends. Sometimes the sick were left at the post to be cared for while the people were hunting, and sometimes the dead were buried there. The people were also fed by the traders when the buffalo were far off and they were starving. For the Plains Cree, Fort Carlton became known as *pēhonānihk*, or the "waiting place."

Despite the changes brought by the fur trade, life for the Nēhiyawak (exact body of people) actually changed very little. Summer was generally a time for Sun Dances, hunting buffalo on horseback, gathering the fruits of Mother Earth, and warfare, either in their home territory or in the lands of the Blackfoot Confederacy and Gros Ventre. From time to time some of the people went south to trade with the Mandans and to visit relatives who had married into southern bands. Occasionally the warriors ventured to the Missouri River and west to the mountains to battle the Sioux nations, the Shoshone, the Cheyenne (*kā-nēhiyawēsicik*, or They Who Speak a Little Cree), the Nez Percé (*payipēyikomak*, or Hole Through the Nose People), and the Flathead.[18] In the winter, the people trapped furs, erected pounds for killing buffalo, and hunted smaller game animals.

Although the trade goods obtained by trading made life easier, the Nēhiyawak could survive without them. It was the buffalo that gave the Plains Cree life, independence, and freedom. Many winters the buffalo were so numerous in the parklands and hills that life—even during the coldest weather—was easy. It was then that buffalo pounds, supervised by men who had been given spiritual help to make them, were built.

Bands who had powerful pound-makers attracted other bands to their camp.* Under the direction of the pound-maker, men and boys cleared an opening in the brush and then cut and hauled logs to make a circular enclosure 30 to 40 feet in diameter. The opening faced east, and a ramp was built leading into the pound. Other men built two curved fences that extended out from the opening like a chute or funnel. Beyond the fences, bundles of brush were placed at intervals for about a mile to extend the widening lines of the funnel.

In a large tipi erected beside the entrance to the pound, the man gifted by the Creator to make the pound sang and prayed, assisted by other men, and they all smoked their pipes as they asked their spirit helpers for continued guidance and a successful hunt. When buffalo were needed to feed the camp, the pound-maker prayed and sang his buffalo songs. He called the buffalo towards the camp and then several young men who had been prepared by the shaman were sent to locate the herd. When the buffalo were found, the animals were guided into the pound where they were killed with arrows as they milled. All the people camped in the vicinity of the pound received their share of the animals, regardless of whether or not they had helped.[19]

---

* One of the noted pound-makers was Sikakwayan (Skunkskin). Of Assiniboine and Cree ancestry, Sikakwayan was married to Mistawasis's sister. He was the father of Poundmaker, a respected Cree chief, and the grandfather of Baptiste Ahenakew's wife, Ellen Ermineskin.

If the pound was successful, other bands pitched their tipis nearby. Then, using that camp as a base, families travelled to their hunting grounds where they trapped and hunted fur-bearing animals and made occasional trips to Fort Carlton to trade for supplies. When the winter was mild and the buffalo stayed on the plains, the people either followed them, or headed in small groups to the woods to hunt elk, moose, and deer. When the animals were scarce, times were hard, but the people always knew that the buffalo and other living things put on earth by the Creator would return.

The first decades of the 19th century were exciting times to be growing up. With buffalo plentiful most years, food was not a concern and the minds of young men were on warfare. In the spring of 1816, the year Ahtahkakoop was born, a large war party of Cree and Assiniboine gathered at the Big Point of Woods near the Minichinas Hills* for an onslaught into Blackfoot country.[20] Many people of the Blackfoot Confederacy died that summer. Two years later the Blackfoot and their allies, along with the Gros Ventre, were in Saskatchewan River country and Cree and Assiniboine people were killed.[21] After several years of bloodshed, warriors from the Blackfoot Confederacy exchanged tobacco with the Cree/Assinboine alliance and peace was made in the spring of 1819. The period of calm was short-lived. War erupted once again across the northern plains during the summer of 1820, culminating in 1821 when several war parties travelled west to fight the Blackfoot.[22]

Raids into enemy camps to steal horses intermingled with the large war parties. And so it went. Season after season of warfare, broken by occasional periods of peace. Sometimes children were officially exchanged between bands in an effort to preserve peace, but the young men sought the excitement and prestige brought by war and horse raids. Peace never lasted for long.

Ahtahkakoop grew up listening to stories about the brave men in his band. He heard how they organized small horse-raiding parties that travelled by foot into Blackfoot country, where horses were numerous and of excellent quality. He heard how these men—often young and daring, sometimes reckless—crept silently into the circle of sleeping tipis. Some deliberately cut the thongs of the finest horses tethered outside the leading men's tipis. Others gathered up the horses hobbled within the vicinity of the camp or confined nearby.

---

* Little Wooded Hills situated 40 miles southeast of Carlton House.

Illustration by Ed Peekeekoot

Young men honed their skills and earned status by stealing the best horses from Blackfoot camps. The greater the risk, the greater the honour.

After the raiders returned home Ahtahkakoop listened to stories of pursuit and battles. He heard how his relatives sang power songs and fought valiantly before they evaded the enemy or were killed. He heard extraordinary stories of escapes, escapes that were assisted by supernatural help. In one story the warriors recounted how they got away from the Blackfoot during a raid into enemy territory. The Blackfoot had chased the Cree into a gully, it was said, and there the Blackfoot surrounded the warriors and made plans to kill them the next day. After darkness fell, the Cree invited the northern lights down.* They came and they told the warriors where to run to reach the river. That was how the Cree escaped. They ran to the river and when the Blackfoot moved in the next day the Cree warriors were gone.[23]

For Ahtahkakoop's people, and other plains people, a display of skill and courage brought honour to a warrior and his family. The bravest, most honoured men were those who had exposed themselves to an unusual

---

* In Cree tradition, the northern lights are the spirits of the departed who are dancing in the night sky.

amount of danger while capturing an enemy's gun, his bow and arrows, war shield, or other equipment of war.

Killing an enemy while under fire brought more honour than killing one from ambush. The taking of a scalp, which consisted of cutting a narrow strip of scalp and hair from the head of an enemy killed by the warrior, was of less value than the way in which the enemy had been killed. Moreover, when the time came for counting coups, the bravery shown by a man while stealing horses was more important than the number of horses he stole.[24] Ahtahkakoop knew, nevertheless, that horses were important beyond the challenges of a raid because they were needed for buffalo hunting, for transportation, for packing goods, for pulling travois, and for gifts. The more horses a family had, the wealthier it was and the more generous it could be. All these were important realities of Indian life.

The boy also knew that large organized war parties were different from horse-raiding parties. They were vengeance parties organized to avenge the death of a relative. It was only on these expeditions that women went along to cook and help maintain the camp. Unlike horse-raids, when the objective was to take horses, vengeance war parties set out to destroy an entire camp belonging to the nation that had been responsible for the death. Men, women, and children all died. When the people heard that such a party was approaching the Fort Carlton district they fled before the attack, seeking shelter in the Thickwood Hills, the northern woodland, or a far-off place.

Success in warfare led to honour and prestige. A man's courage and war exploits determined, to a great extent, his rank within the band. Horses gave him wealth that could be distributed to friends, relatives, visitors, and the needy. A generous warrior was respected. His war feats were told and re-told during his lifetime, and he generally became a leading man in the band. Young men and men who held back during raids and warfare were ridiculed.

For all these reasons, young Ahtahkakoop listened to the war songs and watched with anticipation as the warriors danced and prayed before leaving the camp. After they returned, he sat in awe as war feats were recounted and the bravest were honoured during the victory dances. When a warrior did not come back, he shared the sadness, even though it was acknowledged by the people that the fallen warrior had died as a man should die. Experienced fighters knew the risks when they ventured on a war excursion. Such men were prepared to give up their lives for the glory of war.[25]

As soon as Ahtahkakoop was old enough, he joined the horse raiding parties and the war parties.

Ahtahkakoop was 21 years old when smallpox raged ruthlessly through the plains and parklands of the North-West late in 1837. The dreaded disease had come from the south, where the Sioux nations south of the Missouri had been hard hit the previous summer. Pruden, after hearing rumours of the outbreak in the spring of 1837, started vaccinating Indian and half-breed families who lived and traded at Fort Carlton.[26] Patrick Small, clerk at the trading house, continued this work after Pruden retired at the end of the 1836-37 trading season.

Tragically, the vaccine was defective. By the time this was discovered and new vaccine was obtained from Fort Pelly, it was too late.[27] Assiniboines who had fled north from American territory in an attempt to escape the disease had carried the pestilence with them. Without immunity, the Cree, Assiniboines, Blackfoot and others, including some half-breeds, were ravaged. The sickness began, the chief factor at Edmonton House wrote, "with a dreadful pain in head, Back, neck and bleeding at the Nose, which they say carries them off in two or three days at most."[28] By November, the epidemic was "raging with alarming appearance" in the Fort Carlton area. Many died. The people could do nothing but watch in terror and helplessness.

The Assiniboines were hit the hardest.[29] After the epidemic burned itself out and the remnants of their bands recovered, many of these people retreated south, continuing a trend that had been underway since the 1820s. Some estimate their loss at two-thirds. It is not known how many people amongst Ahtahkakoop's relatives and friends died.

By the late 1830s Ahtahkakoop had grown into a remarkable young man. Six feet, three inches in height, he was strong, extremely well proportioned, and had a deep voice that many years later reminded people of the "deep low sound of a grizzly-bear growl."[30] Because of his physical appearance, some called him *misi-minahik*, or Tall Pine.*

Although Ahtahkakoop drew attention at first sight, those who knew the young man realized that he was impressive intellectually and spiritually as well as physically. Calm and deliberate in both movement and speech, leadership came naturally to him and he was readily accepted by others.[31]

He had learned well from the sacred stories and teachings of his elders. And the Creator and his spirit helpers, through visions and ceremonies, had

---

* *Misi-minahik* translates more correctly as Tall Spruce.

blessed him. He knew the proper procedures and processes of traditional ways. Above all, he was a young man of respect: respectful towards the Creator and the beings in the spiritual world, the buffalo and other living things in the natural world, and his elders, friends, and relatives. All this had been recognized by the old man and by others in the band while Ahtahkakoop was still young. He was given special training, and he learned about spiritual power and healing. He was raised to be a leader.

Acquiring the skills to become a leading man was not always easy. In the words of an old man,

> No matter how brave a man is and no matter how many horses he brings back (from raids), if he has nothing, he can't be a chief. It happened many times that a man would be brave and bring back many horses. But he would trade the horses for clothes and would be too lazy to get hides for a tipi cover and so he could never be a chief. When a young man showed (by his deeds) that he would be a chief some day the old men would go to see him and say, "Now young man, you are climbing higher and higher and are on the way to become a chief. It is for your own good (that we speak). It is not an easy thing to be chief. Look at this chief now. He has to have pity on the poor. When he sees a man in difficulty he must try to help him in whatever way he can. If a person asks for something in his tipi, he must give it to him willingly and without any bad feeling. We are telling you this now because you will meet these things and must have a strong heart.[32]

Ahtahkakoop became a Worthy Young Man, a rank given to young men who had shown bravery, skill and daring during horse raids and battles with the enemy. The Worthy Young Men were among the first warriors to defend the camp when it was attacked and they were the first to pursue the enemy. They were expected to be generous with their belongings and to feed guests and visitors, and it was the Worthy Young Men who protected the women and girls when they were away from the camp.

It was not long until Ahtahkakoop was formally asked to join the *okihcitāw* society (Warrior society). As a Warrior, he was entitled to sit in the Warrior's lodge and take part in the ceremonies and dances. Members of the Warrior society were second in rank to the chief of the band, and their responsibilities included caring for the needy, guarding the column of women, children, old people and their belongings when the camp was being moved, and preparing corpses for burial. One of their most important functions was policing the buffalo hunt, for no man was allowed to hunt individually when the Cree were gathered in a large encampment. To do so might turn the herd or scare it off, and then all the people would suffer.

A Warrior chief, chosen by the members of the society, led the dances and directed the activities carried out by the Warriors. Although this Warrior was not a war chief and had no official functions related to warfare, he was always one of the most courageous and skilled of the fighting men. Because a Warrior—even more than a Worthy Young Man—was expected to be generous, he had to have considerable material wealth to rise within the ranks of the Warrior society.[33]

The chief and recognized leader of a successful, respected band was always an outstanding warrior acclaimed for his courage, skill, and leadership. He was recognized for his abilities as a hunter, trapper, and provider. His generosity and concern for others were well known, and his skills as an orator were demonstrated during councils with his own band members and in larger gatherings involving a number of bands. Often, he was also a man who had powerful spirit helpers.

The prestige and influence of a chief reflected on his people. A successful chief attracted families and individuals from other bands and his camp grew in size. Often these new families had kinship connections with the band. Sometimes they lived in the camp for only a short time, and then joined relatives living elsewhere. Other times they stayed. Always, however, a band had a stable nucleus or core of people who were closely related to the chief and who ordinarily would not leave. Chieftainship was often, but not always, hereditary. If a chief's son was not suitable, a man of high prestige would be chosen instead.[34]

A chief was expected to be more generous than anyone else in day-to-day life and on special occasions. Visitors were housed and fed at his tipi, and gifts were lavishly given. All this required a large tipi, a good supply of horses, buffalo robes, and hides, as well as abundant amounts of buffalo meat, pemmican, berries, root vegetables, and other foodstuffs. Beautifully decorated shirts, moccasins, birch bark baskets, and other such items were also needed for gifts. Male relatives contributed to the expenses and assisted with the responsibilities of the chief, and thus gained prestige in their own right.

The contribution made by the women of the leading men was equally important. They made sure their tipis were a suitable size and well equipped

Illustration by Ed Peekeekoot

During the summer the men hunted buffalo on horseback. A successful chief was always a good provider and respected by other bands.

for guests. They prepared the food, tanned the hides and furs, made the special gifts, and ensured that the chief and his family were appropriately dressed for their position in the band. Because of the workload, the chief and other men of prestige generally had more than one wife. Often the wives were sisters, but not always. Sometimes a second or third wife was the widow of a brother who had died, for a man quite naturally was responsible for the well-being of his dead brother's family. The woman and children would become like his own. Other men in the camp, if they were able, were also expected to care for members of their extended family. In this way, the people looked after the needy, the sick, and the elderly.

Orphans or boys whose relatives were poor often voluntarily came to work and live with the chief or another man of high rank. They looked after his horses, hunted for him, and helped in other ways. In exchange, they were provided with food and clothing, educated in the ways of the people —including skills of hunting and warfare—and treated like members of the family. In a similar way, girls were taken into the chief's tipi to help the women with their work. Other men of rank also welcomed these young people into their homes.

A good camp was an orderly one, where life flowed with the seasons and time cycles determined by nature. The chief and his leading men looked to the spiritual world for guidance in day-to-day life, as well as at special times. Under the guidance of a wise chief and his leading men, the band was governed for the benefit of all its members. A good chief listened carefully when others spoke during council meetings. An outstanding orator, he was able to sway people to his view. As a visionary, he was able to make choices that would ensure survival, and as a realist, he was practical. A strong chief was also able to control the restless young men in his camp. And when a number of bands gathered together, he was among those chosen as spokesmen. In times of war, however, authority was turned over to a war chief who took control of the camp and directed war activities.[35]

The men and women who received special supernatural gifts from the Creator and his spiritual helpers were also important in the life of the Nēhiyawak. From the time he was very young, Ahtahkakoop was aware of this fact. As he grew into manhood his understanding broadened. He knew that some people were given the power to build a buffalo pound. Others were given special abilities to hunt or lead a war party.

Particularly respected were those blessed with extraordinary power to communicate with spirit helpers and those who had the power to heal. They were the shamans or medicine people. Ahtahkakoop learned that medicine men and women had different levels of skill, depending on their knowledge and experience. Men and women with the greatest power and skill received their abilities through visions and dreams. They were also very knowledgeable about the medicinal properties of plants that grew on Mother Earth. They knew how to identify the plants that were made into herbal teas, ointments, and tonics. They knew the best time to collect the roots, barks, leaves, and berries, how to prepare them, and how to determine the correct amount to give a patient.

The healing energy of bear grease, a powerful medicine from *okimaw-kosisan* (the Creator's Son), was used by skilled medicine people, and the people gave thanks that the bear was willing to sacrifice his life so his energy could be used by others in the healing process. Always, the effectiveness of the medicines and procedures depended to a great extent on the energy of the person handling them. These gifts of healing came from the Creator, and a belief in the Creator and the spiritual world were crucial in the healing process. Because of this, prayers were important and offerings were often made to the Creator and his helpers.

Much of the practical information, including how to use the various medicines, was passed on to apprentices or shared with other medicine people. And so the apprentices were taught the treatments for rheumatism, coughs, fevers, kidney and bladder infections, and injuries. They were shown how to make childbirth easier and how to set broken bones. They learned that healing was holistic and that the mind and spirit had to be treated, as well as the body. As these apprentices gained in knowledge, many of them became healers.

The preparation and use of some tonics, treatments, and remedies were common knowledge among band members. For instance, the leaves and flowers of the common plant now called yarrow were used to stop bleeding and to heal wounds. A tea made from the bark of the poplar and willow trees, which contains salicin, was used to relieve pain, reduce fever, and treat inflammation.[36] Dandelion root eased heartburn.

Amongst Ahtahkakoop's people there was another group of powerful spiritual people, those who belonged to the *mitēwiwin* or *mitē* society. The *midēwiwin*, as it was known by the Saulteaux and Ojibwa people, was a secret shamanistic medicine society that had developed from ancient Ojibwa traditions. The Cree people brought the tradition with them as they moved from the east and adapted the society to their own circumstances.[37] Then, during Ahtahkakoop's lifetime, the society was revitalized by the Saulteaux who moved into Saskatchewan River country.

Mitēwiwin was devoted to healing and sacred ceremonies that strengthened communication with the Creator and his helpers and restored life and harmony among the people. Membership required both spiritual power and commitment. Additionally, unlike most of the other societies, *mitēwiwin* was open to women as well as men.

According to the old people there were four main levels of *mitēwiwin*, each one earned through knowledge and shamanistic abilities.[38] The first level was the *wāpaniyiniw*, or morning person. This person had a certain amount of spiritual knowledge and abilities. He had some knowledge of plants, but was a novice in the *mitēwiwin*. He was a beginner.

The *kīsikāwiyiniw*, or day person, had more power, knowledge, and abilities as a spiritual person than the *wāpaniyiniw* did. This person also had more knowledge of plants and the ways of healing, and thus was able to help people.

Next came the *mitēw*, or heart person, who had a vast knowledge of herbs, medicines, and spiritual power. With knowledge that came from the spiritual world, this person had the ability to hurt or to do good. The *kīsikāwiyiniw* and the *wāpaniyiniw* both got much of their knowledge from the *mitēw*.

But there was one other level in the hierarchy of *mitēwiwin*, the old people said. It was the *tipiskāwiyiniw*, or night person. This person never hurt anybody or anything. His knowledge was vast like that of the *mitēw*. He was the only one who could mend, through his knowledge and his spiritual power, the harm a *mitēw* had done to a person or being. He was the only one who could cancel out the wrongdoings of a *mitew*. Despite these exceptional powers and special gifts, the *tipiskāwiyiniw* was humble and unassuming.

The annual *mitēwiwin* gathering included a sharing and exchange of medicines. In this way, *mitēwiwin* was similar to the sacred *pīhtwāwikamik* (Smoking Tipi) ceremony of the Plains Cree when medicines gathered from various parts of the country were exchanged. *Mīniwēk* (bear root) that came from the place now called Idaho or from the southern fringes of present-day Montana. *Apisci-sākwēwaskos* (small shrill-voice herb),[39] that came only from the north country. And *wīhkēs* (rat root), which people from the south had difficulty obtaining. Medicines such as these were exchanged, along with *kāhkākiwikot* (raven's beak) from the mountains and *wāpatow* and *mihkwatow*, a white fungus and a red fungus that also grew in the mountains. The medicines were wrapped in small leather packets and stored in the whole hide of an animal. This hide, which was called *kaskipitākan*, was the badge of *mitēw* membership. It was the shaman's medicine bag.

Stories were told of the wondrous powers of the *mitēw*, the *tipiskawiyiniw*, and the shamans. It was said that these men were so powerful they could make an otter skin dance when it was just a skin and not an animal. One of these stories told of a shaman who, through his special powers, made a medicine bag created from a weasel skin appear to come alive and then run up the shaman's arm to his shoulder. When the weasel was stroked, it became a dry skin once again.[40] These medicine people had so much power they were able to do those things. So it has been said by the old people and those who witnessed such acts of power.

The Creator and his spiritual helpers had blessed Ahtahkakoop with special gifts and knowledge of the past. Because of this, in addition to learning the skills of hunting, warfare, diplomacy, and other attributes of a secular leader, he was instructed in the powerful ways of the *mitēwiwin*. When he was ready, Ahtahkakoop became a member of the *mitēwiwin* and a respected medicine man.

This then was Ahtahkakoop's world. It was a world where the spiritual and physical worlds were closely connected. A world where the Nēhiyawak called upon the Creator and their spiritual helpers to guide and support them in day-to-day life. It was a world where the spiritual world was part of everyday life.

CHAPTER FIVE

Ahtahkakoop and His Family

There were at least five brothers in Ahtahkakoop's family. Masuskapoe (Sitting On Land) was the oldest. Ahtahkakoop (Starblanket) came next, followed by Sasakamoose (One Who Adheres), and Āhāsiw-akohp (Crow Blanket), who later became known as Ahenakew. Nāpēskis, whose name meant "man-like," was the youngest. The names of brothers who died and all the sisters in the family have been lost in time.*

As the years passed Ahtahkakoop, his brothers, and his sisters married and started families of their own.

Masuskapoe died before 1861, leaving descendants to carry on his name.[1] Ahtahkakoop, who was born in about 1816, also married and took several wives according to the custom of his people.

The third brother, Sasakamoose, was a natural leader and a steadfast man of reason. He was born about 1819.[2] Sasakamoose had also been blessed by the Creator. He was a high-ranking member of *mitēwiwin*, and perhaps even more than his brother, a respected shaman. Unlike Ahtahkakoop, however, he was a small man and quick in both speech and

---

* Some people believe that a number of the children may have been descendants of Louis Chastillain, a fur trader from Three Rivers in what is now the Province of Quebec. Chastillain was in charge of the North West Company's post on the South Branch when it was attacked by Gros Ventre and Blackfoot Indians in 1794. The following year he established Fort St. Louis downstream from the junction of the two branches of the Saskatchewan River. He returned to his home in the east after his final contract with the company expired. The name Chastillain is spelled in various ways in archival documentation, including Chattelain, Chatlain, and Chattlin.

Illustration by Willard Ahenakew

Ahenakew was called Āhāsiw-akohp when he was shot in the leg while escaping from a Blackfoot camp.

temper. A beard and a hunched back were his most notable physical features. Sasakamoose had at least three wives. Two of them, in later years, were given the names Mary and Margaret (Maggie).[3]

Ahenakew, the fourth brother, was born around 1823.[4] His first name had been Āhāsiw-akohp, or Crow Blanket. He also had been gifted with supernatural powers and stories were told of his leadership in warfare and his intervention during escapes from enemy warriors. It was during a horse raid against the Blackfoot that Āhāsiw-akohp was given a new name. The raid had been successful, but during their flight Āhāsiw-akohp was shot in the leg. A while later the Cree encountered another party of Blackfoot warriors. Āhāsiw-akohp was going to charge the enemy but then he realized his party was greatly outnumbered. Fighting would be foolhardy. So they raced northeast towards safety. By now, Āhāsiw-akohp's leg was bleeding profusely. As he reached the top of a high hill Āhāsiw-akohp looked back and saw that the Blackfoot were a long distance away.* He dismounted to examine his leg.

"*Ēy ēy, nāh-nakēw!*" the Cree warriors called out when they saw Āhāsiw-akohp stopped on top of the hill. "Oh, no! He stopped!" They rushed to see what was the matter. The wound was looked after, and then the party continued its journey home. Āhāsiw-akohp's wound left him with a permanent limp. People started calling him "*nanahkew*." As the years passed Nanahkew evolved into Crow Blanket's new name, Ahenakew.[5]

Although Ahenakew had at least two wives, only Kīskanakwās (Cut Sleeve) is known by name.[6] Born in 1832 and a widow when she became Ahenakew's wife, Kīskanakwās was from a well-known family in the Battle River and Eagle Hills area. One of her brothers was Piyēwkāmikosit (Red Pheasant), who became the chief of his band. The other known brothers were Wataniy (Wuttunee or Tail Feathers) and Baptiste.

Ahtahkakoop's youngest brother, Nāpēskis (Like A Man), was dashing and handsome. Respected and well liked by people in other bands as well as his own, he was, in the words of Chief Thunderchild, "one of the best in the North West."[7] Perhaps even more than his brothers, he was an "honoured warrior." He was a good hunter and trapper and, while still young, a chief. Fine Day recalled that as a child he saw Nāpēskis being welcomed

---

* The hill where Āhāsiw-akohp stopped is located in what is now southwest Saskatchewan. The hill became known as *ahenakiwin* by the people who hunted and lived in the area.

at Fort Carlton. When Nāpēskis went inside the post, the old man said, the traders

> shot off a lot of guns. The people said "that is the Hudson Bay Company shaking hands with Nāpēskis." …
>
> Nāpēskis brought in a whole bunch of furs. When he came out he wore a chief's coat with gold braid, a pair of red flannel pants, a tall beaver hat and he carried a barrel of whiskey, and powder and shot and other goods. He came to his camp and distributed all the things he had. There were many there who were not really of his band but he gave everything away until he was left only with the new clothes he wore. That was the way of the Hudson Bay Co., they would make the best hunters for chiefs.
>
> Nāpēskis saw that the men were getting very drunk and beginning to make trouble. He gave the barrel of whiskey to one of the Worthy [Young] Men and told him to pass the drinks out only to those who were not too drunk.
>
> We camped there for quite a while and traded for many days. When it was over, Nāpēskis got a good gun and a lot of tobacco and powder from the Hudson Bay Co.[8]

It was Ahtahkakoop, however, who assumed the overall mantle of leadership. He was still a young man when the people noticed his uncanny suggestions on where to camp, or where to find buffalo, and they were impressed with his abilities as a hunter and warrior. They also noted that when Ahtahkakoop led a party of raiders into Blackfoot country many horses were brought home and the warriors generally returned home unscathed. The people knew that Ahtahkakoop was always concerned about the safety of his party.

The accounts of Ahtahkakoop's war feats were legendary and gave witness to the power of his spirit helpers. In one story retold many times around campfires, a party of Blackfoot warriors chased Ahtahkakoop to the edge of a lake in the Beaver Hills.* Trapped and greatly outnumbered, Ahtahkakoop wheeled his horse around. Then, much to the astonishment of the Blackfoot, the Cree warrior charged through their midst unscathed

---

* The Beaver Hills are situated in what is now the Province of Alberta.

and escaped. A few years after this encounter, Ahtahkakoop visited a trading post near present-day Wetaskiwin. Some Blackfoot men at the post recognized him as the Cree who had eluded them in such an astonishing way.
They claimed he must have been blessed, otherwise he could not have
escaped.[9]

All these things the people noticed and by the 1850s—and perhaps even
earlier—Ahtahkakoop was recognized as chief of his band. As was fitting
for a man of his rank, he had at least three wives to maintain his large tipi
and share the workload of band and family responsibilities.[10] One of his
wives was the daughter of Nātowēw.* The identity of the other women—
as in so many other instances—has been lost.

It is unfortunate that little is known about these and the other wives
since they, like Kīskanakwās, had probably come from influential families.
Intermarriage between bands and influential families was not only common but it was an accepted way for families and bands to form and cement
alliances. Ahenakew's union with Kīskanakwās helped further develop the
existing relationship with Red Pheasant's family and band. Similarly, marriages—which were usually arranged by the parents—strengthened connections between other families.

Red Pheasant's band was part of a loosely affiliated group of bands
called *sīpīwiyiniwak* (River People) that had chosen the area between the
North Saskatchewan and the Battle rivers as their home territory. Their
hunting grounds extended west towards present-day Lloydminster and
south to the forks of the South Saskatchewan and Red Deer rivers,† and
beyond.[11]

Plains Cree bands in other areas were similarly affiliated by the middle
part of the 19th century. East and south of Fort Carlton were the
paskohkopāwiyiniwak, the Prairie Willow People.[12] The *natimiwiyiniwak*,
or Upstream People, were the most westerly of the Plains Cree. They traded at Edmonton House and were also known as *amiskwatcīwiyiniwak* or
Beaver Hills People. Closest to the Blackfoot, they were the most avid
horse raiders and bore the brunt of Blackfoot attacks.[13]

Ahtahkakoop's band belonged to the *wāskahikaniyiniwak*, Fort People,
so named because they were closely associated with Fort Carlton. The

---

* *Nātowēw* is the Cree word for Iroquois.
† The Cree knew the South Saskatchewan River (South Branch) as the Red Deer River.

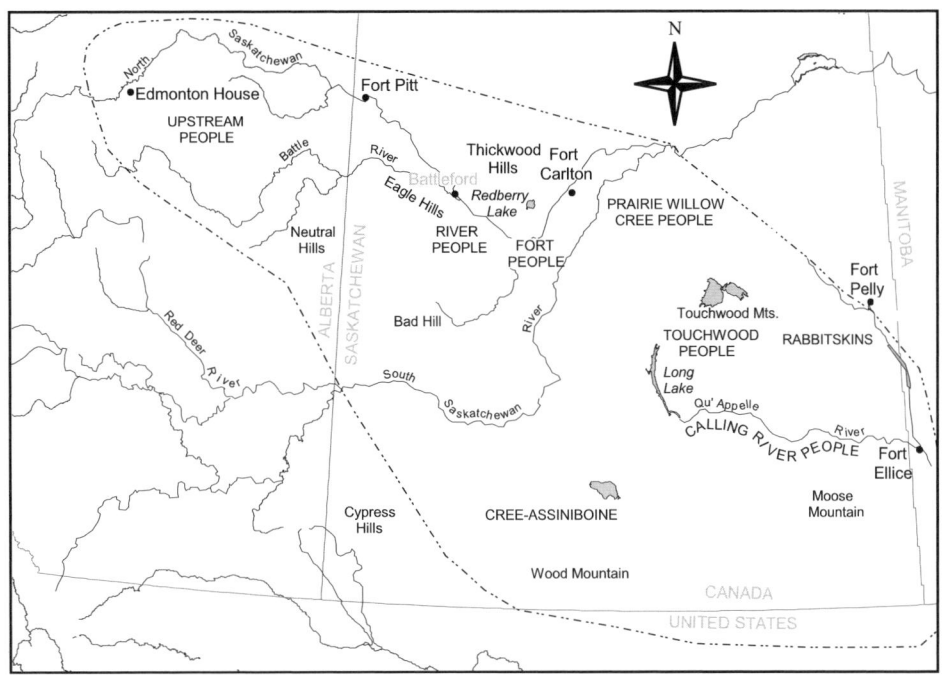

Information Systems Division, Canadian Plains Research Center

Ahtahkakoop's people were part of the wāskahikaniyiniwak, *or Fort People. Their traditional hunting grounds stretched north from Bad Hill to their wintering grounds at Redberry Lake and west to the Eagle Hills and Battle River areas.*

bands of the *wāskahikaniyiniwak* occupied territory north, west, and southwest of Fort Carlton. Ahtahkakoop's traditional hunting grounds stretched north from *maci-waciy* (the Bad Hill) situated northwest of present-day Rosetown to their wintering grounds at *mihkomin-sākahikan* (Redberry Lake). To the west, his band's travels extended to the Eagle Hills and Battle River areas. Their main hunting and camping grounds included *kā-kaskiskawānatinawa* (Buffalo Hump Hills).[14] The range of the other Fort People was within the same territory, with their wintering grounds spread throughout the hills and parklands to optimize their hunting and survival. During warfare and excursions to Blackfoot country, the Missouri River, Cypress Hills, Edmonton House, and the Red River Settlement, the *wāskahikaniyiniwak* of course travelled even further.

Ahtahkakoop became an influential chief of the Fort People. The other main chief was Mistawasis (Big Child), Ahtahkakoop's long-time friend and associate. Mistawasis was known to the Hudson's Bay Company traders as early as 1833 when it was reported in the Carlton House Journal that he had come to the post from "Fighting River" (Battle River) to "take back 2 Horses they had left here in [the] winter."[15] He was likely about 20 years of age at the time. Two years later Mistawasis was hired by chief trader Pruden to help hunt buffalo for the post.[16] Like many other Nēhiyawak, Mistawasis had two names. His second name was Pīwāpisko-mostos, or Iron Buffalo. It was said that once, when Mistawasis was chasing a herd of buffalo, his horse "stumbled and threw him on to the horns of a buffalo bull, which proceeded to throw him up into the air, but he eventually escaped without having sustained any great injury, and when his friends discovered that he was alive and unhurt they gave him the name of 'Iron Buffalo.'"[17]

Although it is not known when their friendship began, as adults and chiefs Ahtahkakoop and Mistawasis were closely allied. They often camped in the same general area, and during the summer their people hunted buffalo together. There were also family connections. Ahtahkakoop's oldest son Kā-miyo-ahcahkwēw (Good Spirit) married Mistawasis's daughter Judique,[18] his daughter Isabella married Mistawasis's oldest son Wēyatōkwapew (Lively Man), and many other band members had similar associations.

As the years passed, Ahtahkakoop, Mistawasis, Nāpēskis, and their people developed a long and significant relationship with Fort Carlton and the Hudson's Bay Company as hunters and trappers. Each year the traders at Fort Carlton collected thousands of pounds of pemmican and then distributed the dried food to boat brigades hauling furs and trade goods back and forth between the inland posts and York Factory. As the traders pushed deeper into the northern forests, pemmican became the lifeline for the fur trade, and its components—dried meat, pounded meat,* and grease—were a necessity. Their procurement depended to a great extent on the co-operation of proficient buffalo hunters like Ahtahkakoop, Mistawasis, and Nāpēskis. Equally valued were the women of their camps who butchered the animals, dried and pounded the meat, rendered the grease, collected and dried the berries, and made the pemmican.

The meat and hides from woodland animals such as elk, moose, and deer were also in demand, but it was furs that provided the profit for the Hudson's Bay Company. So men who trapped fur-bearing animals and

---

* Pounded meat was dried meat that was pounded into shreds with stone hammers.

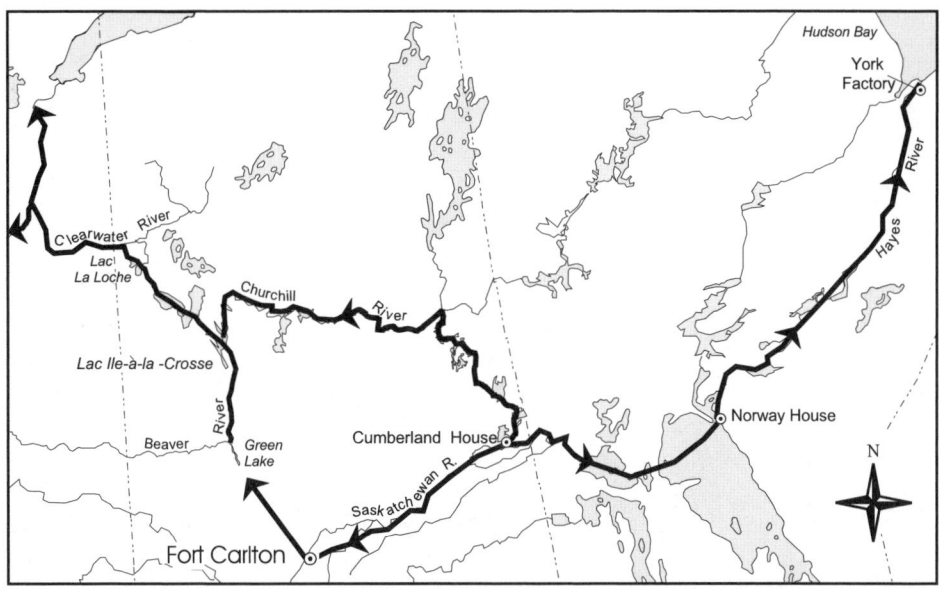

Information Systems Division, Canadian Plains Research Center

Pemmican was sent by boat to Cumberland House to feed the boatmen travelling the eastern and northern waterways. During the winter, dog teams hauled pemmican to Green Lake, where it was forwarded north for the men travelling the northern rivers.

hunted woodland game, along with the women who prepared the pelts and leather, were also important customers at Fort Carlton. Bands that could supply all of these—buffalo produce, meat and skins from game animals, and furs—were especially valued by the traders.

Because of their skills and abilities, Ahtahkakoop and Mistawasis were recognized as leading chiefs of the Carlton district by the Hudson's Bay Company as well as by their own people. The company considered both men to be equal in status[19] but Ahtahkakoop, because he was younger, almost always deferred to Mistawasis. As leading chiefs and important suppliers of pemmican, these two Cree leaders got preferential treatment from the company, including special gifts and gratuities such as flour, tea, sugar, and other trade goods. Like the lesser chief Nāpēskis, they shared these gifts with band members.[20] They were also given coats and high silk hats decorated with a broad gold lace band and three plumes of three different colours called "coloured cocktail feathers." The coat was dark blue, had gold lace on the collar, shoulders, and cuffs, and brass buttons engraved with the letters HBC. These garments were known as chiefs' coats and were a mark of their rank. Lesser chiefs received scarlet coats.[21]

Hudson's Bay Company 1921 calendar illustration, Hudson's Bay Company Archives,
Provincial Archives of Manitoba, HBCA N9032

Before the inland fur trade posts were established, the Indian trappers and hunters from the western plains and forests were greeted with pomp and ceremony when they arrived at York Factory.

With the co-operation of Ahtahkakoop, Mistawasis, and the other chiefs of Saskatchewan country, Fort Carlton became one of the great pemmican posts in the North-West.

In addition to hunting and trapping for the Hudson's Bay Company, Ahtahkakoop was hired for at least two seasons to help man the York boats that made the annual trip to York Factory. Each spring, as soon as the ice was gone from the North Saskatchewan River, the boat brigade left Fort Carlton loaded with bales of furs. These were unloaded at the company's depot on the shores of Hudson Bay, and then the boats returned laden with trade goods for the upcoming season. Ahtahkakoop's great strength no doubt was appreciated, particularly during the return trip when the boat-men had to fight strong currents and rapids and line the boats up the river.* They also had to portage heavy packs at the most difficult and impassable locations.

On one of these trips Ahtahkakoop had to call upon his spirit helpers to save both himself and the people on his boat. According to the story, Ahtahkakoop and the other men from the boats were waiting at York Factory for the ships to arrive from England. Unknown to Ahtahkakoop, there was an old man living at the Bay who had strong spirit helpers. Because the man misused his power he was both disliked and feared by the Indians at York Factory.

"When the ships from England came to Fort York" the story begins,

> no other Indian dared to buy rum until the Old Man had his keg. *Ah-tah-ka-koop* did not know of this custom, and when the others saw him bringing his keg of rum to his camp they were amazed at his hardihood. "The Old Man will never forgive you, and he can harm you," they warned him. "If you have any spirit help that you can trust, make ready for him!"

> *Ah-tah-ka-koop* waited in his camp, and when the Old Man came he said courteously to him, "*Ta-waw*—there is room," and motioned to a place in the tent. But the Old Man would not enter, and said angrily. "I see that you have a keg of rum. It is the custom here that I get the first keg." *Ah-tah-ka-koop* was always a peaceable man, and he answered calmly that he had not known of

---

* In lining or tracking a York boat, the men walked along the shore and pulled the boats up the river using ropes or "lines."

the custom, and offered him a drink. The Old Man refused. "I have come only to warn you. Take care of yourself." And he walked away.

He returned late that night however, and he was drunk. He began to mock the prairie Indians, insulting Ah-tah-ka-koop who was their fur Chief. *Ah-tah-ka-koop* told him to leave, and when he would not, *Ah-tah-ka-koop* seized a smouldering stick from the fire and struck him across the head with it, and left him lying stunned on the ground. When morning came, the Old Man was gone.

As the York boats were leaving with the trade goods for the inland posts, *Ah-tah-ka-koop* received a message. "Watch yourself. I have not forgotten." He knew what that could mean and he said to his men, "Be ready to obey me at once, whenever I give the warning."

The long hard journey began; work for strong men only, poling those heavy boats up river, tracking them over rapids, carrying packs by long portages. Then one day, *Ah-tah-ka-koop* knew that the moment of danger had come, and the men pulled at their oars, tense with waiting. "Down," he shouted suddenly, and as they fell forward, something whirled over their heads to stick quivering in the mast. It was a hatchet, daubed with red. "Take it, anyone who needs an axe," the Chief said. "It is no longer dangerous. But he will try again, for he knows that he has failed this time."

Days later *Ah-tah-ka-koop* had the same foreboding, and gave the same warning. When he shouted, "*Ta-pā-cheek!*" the men dropped, and this time it was a knife, daubed again with red, that flashed past their heads and stuck in the mast. One of the men took it and sheathed it. "He will try again, but not in the same way," *Ah-tah-ka-koop* warned.

They came at last to Lake Winnipeg, and could sail the heavy boat; but the waters became suddenly rough when they were far from shore, and the Chief knew that his enemy had contact with the spirit of the wind. Now, *Ah-tah-ka-koop* was high in the secret society of medicine-men, but he had never had this power. "We are done for," he said to his men, "unless there is one of you who has the protection of the spirit who rules the wind."

Then a great Swampy Cree, whose name was *Omus-skā-ko* said, "I shall try" And he sang a song and chanted words that the others could not understand. After a few minutes, he told them that all would be well, and the force of the wind did abate. They were saved once more. "That was the Old Man's last try," *Ah-tah-ka-koop* said. "The curse that he tried to put upon us will go back now upon himself."

The next year when they made that long journey again to York Factory, the Bay Indians greeted *Ah-tah-ka-koop* with joy. "You have defeated him, friend," they shouted. "He is only skin and bones and must soon die." Before *Ah-tah-ka-koop*'s men had finished making camp, the Old Man's messenger came, imploring the Chief to restore his health, offering him packs of goods as peace offerings. But *Ah-tah-ka-koop*, so the story goes, answered, "I can do nothing for him. His spirit has already gone from him, and the body must die soon." And that is what happened, and the Indians of the Bay rejoiced, for they had been too long enslaved by an Old Man who used the spirit power in a way that was wrong."[22]

When the story was told, it was always emphasized that Ahtahkakoop did not retaliate when the old man at York Factory threatened him because he did not want the curse to come back to his own family, to his children, and grandchildren. What goes around, comes around, the old people said. Ahtahkakoop chose to use his powers to help people, not to hurt them.

Although Ahtahkakoop had more than usual contact with the traders, he maintained the respect of his own people. Excelling as a hunter and trapper, he was rich in horses and carts. He was a good provider, generous and wise, and he possessed all the other qualities needed to be a good chief. As a Nēhiyaw and a member of the highly regarded *mitēwiwin*, he practised his religious beliefs daily and participated in other traditional ceremonies. Both thoughtful and intelligent, Ahtahkakoop not only honoured the past but he looked towards the future, seeking ways to improve the lives of his people and anticipating some of the problems that would assault them as changes increasingly came to Indian lands. In any given situation, Ahtahkakoop carefully weighed the pros and cons before making an important decision. By doing so, he was to say many years later, he "rarely had to regret his actions."[23]

By the late 1850s and early 1860s Masuskapoe, Ahtahkakoop, Sasakamoose, and Ahenakew all had adult children, as well as younger ones. For some of the children, only the Christian names are known, names that were given or chosen when they were baptized according to the rites of a Christian church. Once again, information about their sisters' children and families has been lost.[24]

Masuskapoe's son John Peter would have been in his mid-twenties by 1860. Another son, Macōhōw (Bad Owl), was likely older.

Ahtahkakoop's oldest sons included Kā-miyo-ahcahkwēw (Good Spirit), who was born about 1837 and later given the name Antoine, and Kīsik-awāsis (Sky Child), who was likely about the same age as Kā-miyo-ahcahkwēw. Ahtahkakoop's older daughters included Mary, who was born in 1840,[25] Isabella born in 1842,[26] and Emma, born in 1847. Kā-miyo-astotin (He Who Has A Fine Hat) was born in 1852 and later called Basil. Of the other known children, Joseph was born in 1857, another daughter named Mary was likely born about 1861, Michel was born in 1862,[27] and Philomene's year of birth was 1863.[28]

In Sasakamoose's family, the older children included Seeseequasis (Little Rattlesnake, born in 1851)[29] and Alice, who was likely born in the latter part of the 1850s. Younger children included Joseph, who was born in 1867, Alexander, born in 1868, and Margaret, in 1869.[30]

Ahenakew also had children with wide-ranging ages. Kāh-kāsōw was born in 1846. His name meant He Who Hides; he chose the name Peter Kāh-kāsōw when he was baptized. Wāsēhikot, which means Shiny Nose, was born in 1849. His Christian name was Henry Wāsēhikot. Marie Louise, who apparently was also known as Catherine, was born about 1854,[31] and Baptiste was born in 1858. Three children were born during the sixties: Louis in 1864, Ellen in 1868,[32] and John in 1869. There was one other known son, Antoine, who later took the name Antoine Chatelaine.

Nāpēskis apparently did not have a wife and family.

CHAPTER SIX

Nāpēskis

In mid-July of 1859, Nāpēskis was camped at Cherry Bush south of present-day Biggar with some families who were hunting buffalo for the traders at Fort Carlton.[1] With them was a man by the name of Philip Tate, the half-breed postmaster from Carlton.[2]

The drying racks near the tipis were well-covered with strips of meat from buffalo cows, and women laboured over the hides pegged to the ground, removing fat and tissue that still clung to the skin. Children were scattering saskatoon berries and chokecherries on pieces of leather to dry. Close by, other women and children cleaned the dirt off *mistaskosīmina* (grass berry or Indian turnip) before drying them. Later the stems would be braided together.

On the prairie and hillsides near the camp buffalo continued to graze in great numbers, despite the commotion of the most recent hunt. Occasionally a bull or two or three cows meandered surprisingly near the tipis before rejoining their herd. Berries still hung heavily from the bushes in the ravines, waiting to be picked, and *capri* (antelope) and deer bounded through the bush and across the prairie when disturbed by human activity. In the midst of plenty, Nāpēskis and the others felt blessed by the Creator, and they especially thanked the buffalo for giving up their lives so the Nēhiyawak might live.

Nine or 10 miles away, on the eastern side of a range of hills called the "Roasting Hills," another party of hunters had pitched their tents. This was the camp of the Earl of Southesk, a Scottish adventurer who had come to the North-West via the Red River Settlement to hunt buffalo and grizzly

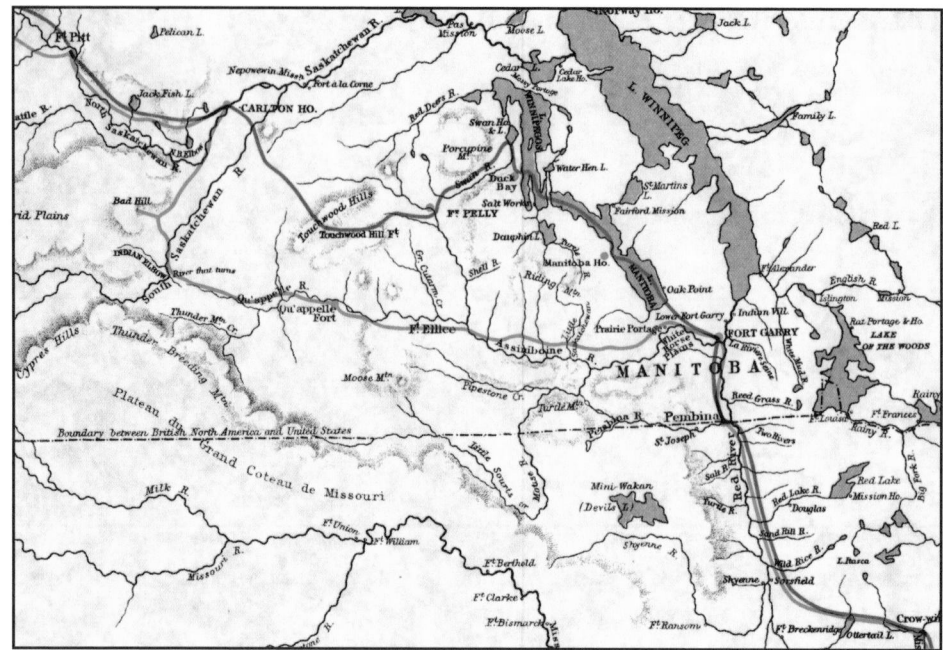

From The Earl of Southesk, *Saskatchewan and the Rocky Mountains*

A portion of Lord Southesk's map illustrating his visit to Saskatchewan River country. His route west is shown in red. The return trip is marked in blue.

bear.[3] The day after crossing the South Branch near its elbow, Southesk saw his first large buffalo herd. "They were on a dry prairie, slightly undulated in character, here and there hilly, and bounded by higher ranges to the west and towards the north," he wrote in his diary. "Immense herds were stringing across the whole face of the country. The deep rolling voice of the mighty multitude came grandly in the air like the booming of a distant ocean."[4]

Southesk also noted that many of the animals were bulls, who were "drawn up in close array; some colossal old fellows stalked about by themselves at the flanks of the columns. The cows were mostly wedged up in the front and centre, while the van kept slowly moving on."

In the description of his first buffalo hunt, as it appeared in his book *Saskatchewan and the Rocky Mountains*, Southesk captured some of the excitement that was a routine part of life for the Nēhiyawak.

When they were within 200 yards of the herd, Southesk wrote that he and the other hunters in his group

> dashed forward; they quickened their pace, but kept their order; we got pretty close to them, the column broke, and the buffaloes cantered off in many separate bands.

Choosing out a small drove of fine-looking cows, M'Kay and I galloped towards them side by side as hard as ever we could go. The harder we pressed, the swifter they ran; they went magnificently, far faster than the bulls; we tried our utmost for a good mile but could not overtake them.

The earl eventually killed a cow as "bands of buffalo were streaming past" him. Then he saw

'an exceedingly fine, sleek, round-barrelled bull, not so large as some of the patriarchs, but with very long, perfect horns, and most

By permission of the 12th Earl of Southesk
The 9th Earl of Southesk.

luxuriant mane and beard.'[6] Hailing this welcome sight, I marked the noble animal for a prey: I remounted in haste, and again stirred up old Bichon [his horse], who, greatly refreshed by the halt, went on as gallantly as before.

Never did bull run more fast and strong. For two miles or more I stuck to him, but by no means could I get within fair shooting-distance. (It was interesting to ride in the midst of that vast black mass of buffaloes, for as I went on, the scattered bands seemed more and more to unite, and I sometimes found myself moving in a sort of triangled enclosure with living walls around me, as the nearer animals strove to edge away on either hand, while the ranks were closed in front, and ever-increasing numbers came thundering in the rear. As long as Bichon kept his footing there was little risk; the buffalo were thinking only of escape, the crowd was not dangerously large or dense, and there was plenty of room, for I was still on a gently undulating plains.)

At last my bull began to slacken his pace. By what strange

instinct did he know that I had chosen him for my own?—the same band was still together, his companions were all with him, not one had yet quitted their ranks, yet with a sudden movement he sprang out from among them, and broke away by himself, rushing off at right angles through an opening in the crowd, and seeming to gather fresh speed as he ran on his separate career.

It was but for a while; he abruptly checked himself, faced round, and stood at bay. I closed on him, trying for a flank shot;—down went his head, onward he came in full charge. Knowing the use-lessness of firing at a buffalo's forehead, I cantered out of his way; he followed me a few yards, then turned and resumed his course.

Another mile—again he slackened, breaking into a trot as he drew near to the top of a gently sloping rise, and there he took up his stand and once more came to bay. I approached till but a few yards were between me and him,—then up went his tail in sign of battle, down went his head for a charge; but this time I was too quick, the Bichon had slipped around him, and before he could make one step, I sent a bullet through his heart. He stopped, stag-gered a few paces, then fell to rise no more.[7]

When Southesk's men came with the cart to get the bull, the earl took only the head and left the rest of the carcass, saying that the meat was "too coarse and tough for human food." Southesk had now achieved two of his objectives. He had "killed a fine cow for eating purposes—the bulls at this season being unfit for food" and he had obtained "a large and perfectly unblemished head to carry home as a trophy." A total of six animals were killed that day in the excitement of the first hunt: the two animals Southesk had killed, a lone bull "in capital condition, with plenty of fat" that wan-dered too close to the camp, and three other bulls.[8]

The next day, July 17, was a Sunday and Southesk took a break from hunt-ing to observe the Christian Sabbath and traditional day of rest. He was relaxing in his tent when, in his own words,

In an instant, without the slightest warning, a storm of noise burst upon us,—bells jingled, whips cracked,—the tramp of galloping horses resounded close at hand. I leapt up to seize my rifle,—it was not there; I hastened out to my men, and found them equally

defenceless, for all guns had been laid aside on account of the
Sunday rest. A strange and unwelcome sight greeted our aston-
ished eyes. Widely apart, extended in a semicircle which completely hemmed us in, a number of armed and mostly naked warriors were rushing down the slope, urging their horses to furious
speed with whip and heel. "The Blackfeet!" said my men, and we
prepared for the worst. The invaders were almost upon us, a few
yards only lay between us and them, when suddenly they checked
their speed, stared at us for a moment, then trotted peacefully up
with smiling faces, offering the most friendly greetings, which my
men heartily reciprocated.

The mystery was soon explained. Our visitors were a party of
Cree Indians and half-breeds from Fort Carlton, who were camping on the other side of the range.… Supposing us to be
Blackfeet, with whom the Crees were just going to war, they
planned to surprise us,—and so indeed they did. Each man had
his mouth full of bullets, ready for action, and most of them were
nearly stark naked; everything had been skilfully planned, some
of the number had been expressly told off [*sic*] to drive away our
horses.[9]

Nāpēskis was one of the mounted warriors.

Startled by the aborted attack and aware of their precarious position in
the event of Blackfoot hostility, Southesk decided to camp near the Cree,
"hunt buffalo in that neighbourhood, and employ the women … to dry a
large store of meat" for his journey to the mountains. Accordingly, the earl
moved his camp to Cherry Bush the next day, passing many herds of buffalo during the 10-mile trek over the shoulder of the Roasting Hills. The
group pitched tents on a sandy knoll about a quarter of a mile from the Cree
encampment. Nāpēskis was with the hunters who came to see Southesk in
his new camp. Although Southesk makes no mention of it, the men
undoubtedly inquired about the purpose of his visit to Indian lands and the
intended length of his stay. Tate, with his six-year-old daughter accompanying him, came over later to see the visitor.

When a large herd of buffalo came over a nearby hill shortly after dinner the hunters "prepared to run them." Nāpēskis, whom the earl described
as a "very bold intelligent young man," asked if he could ride Southesk's
unruly horse named Black. Although Black was a fine-looking animal with

William Armstrong/ National Archives of Canada, C-010500

A prairie Indian camp.

above average speed, the horse had given Southesk considerable trouble during the trip west and practically all references to him included words like unruly, troublesome, impetuous, unmanageable, and violent.[10]

A skillfull horseman, Nāpēskis rode Black easily as he accompanied Southesk to the hollow where the hunters were gathering. Instead of using bows and arrows, the weapons usually preferred for hunting buffalo, he was armed with a muzzleloader.[11] After waiting for half an hour, the signal was given and the men raced towards the buffalo. Nāpēskis, his mouth full of bullets, took the lead, moving quickly to the front of the other hunters. By instinct, honed by years of practice, he kept the muzzle of his gun in an upright position to keep the powder and bullet lying on top of the powder from dislodging.* As he drew alongside a fat cow, the young hunter—in

---

* According to trader Isaac Cowie, flintlock muzzleloaders came in three lengths with 3½ feet being the longest and 2½ feet the shortest. The 2½-foot length was the most common and the Indian warriors generally shortened the barrel even further to make it lighter to carry and easier to conceal. (Cowie, *The Company of Adventurers*, pp. 197-98.)

A buffalo ox skull. The inscription written on the skull says: Buffalo Ox, South branch of the Saskatchewan River, America. Shot 18 July 1859 by Napesskes, a Cree halfbreed with the Earl of Southesk.

one quick smooth motion—tilted the gun downward, aimed, and fired before the bullet and powder had a chance to dislodge. His aim true, the cow dropped to the ground. Nāpēskis threw down a personal article to mark his kill and then he rejoined the chase. Still riding quickly, he reloaded his gun. He poured a "chance handful" of gun powder down the barrel, spit a bullet in on top of the powder, and struck the stock against his heel to send it "all home." Then, keeping the muzzle upright, Nāpēskis went after another cow.[12]

Some of the other hunters likely used bows and arrows because they were easier to use on the run than guns.[13] According to one source, "the arrows were carried in a quiver on the back, in such a position that the bearer, by throwing his right hand just over the left shoulder, could grasp an arrow. The drawing of an arrow, the fitting of the bowstring and the discharging are three movements merged into one, so perfect is their continuity." Skilled hunters often shot an arrow right through the body of the buffalo.[14]

Meanwhile Southesk was left trying to catch up to the other hunters. When he finally closed the gap he found the "buffalo were now running around … in every quarter, the herd for the most part broken into small lots separated by trifling intervals from one another." This fast-paced hunt, conducted by experienced Indian hunters, differed considerably from Southesk's earlier ventures at hunting buffalo for sport. By himself, he had hunted at his own pace, often chasing a herd for several miles before getting a chance to shoot. "No one, til he tried it," Southesk commented later, "can fancy how hard it is to shoot a galloping buffalo from a galloping horse."[15]

Early in the run Southesk had met Nāpēskis, who by now was coming from the opposite direction. Laughingly, Ahtahkakoop's youngest brother

> held up two fingers to show that he had killed a pair of cows. He was very clever at signs. We had previously passed a peculiar-looking skull with slight and much-curved horns, placed by itself on the ground, and no sooner did I notice it, than he made me understand that this was not the head of a bull, but of an ox—a variety of somewhat rare occurrence; that he shot it himself; and that it had stood half as high again as a male of the ordinary description.[16]

The bulls, Southesk said, could have been shot "right and left by dozens," but it was cows they were after. The earl wrote later that he found the cows difficult to distinguish from the young bulls and exceedingly difficult to catch. And so it was only after he had raced after a small herd for more than two miles that the earl finally managed to wound a cow. Bichon tripped. The man and his horse tumbled to the ground, and the cow escaped. In this way, Southesk's hunt ended. Nāpēskis and the others, in the meantime, had completed a successful hunt.

Then the women's work began as they went onto the hunting grounds to butcher the animals. Since each of the hunters had left identifying markers beside the buffalo he had killed, the women and older girls readily found their animals. Skinning and butchering was heavy work, requiring the efforts of more than one person for each animal. With the immense carcass on its back and the head turned sideways to prop the animal up, the women removed the hide from one side. Then they tilted the massive head to the opposite side and skinned the rest of the animal. The meat was cut into manageable pieces and piled on the spread-out hide along with the tongue. Then the women cut off the ribs and dislocated and removed the limbs. They also extracted the long sinews from the backbone and shoulders. The marrowbones were added to the pile of meat before the hide was wrapped around the entire mass. The internal organs were packaged separately. All of this, with considerable effort, was loaded onto carts and then the women and girls moved onto the next animal. What little remained was left for the wolves and dogs.[17]

Still, the work was not done. The weather was hot and the women and girls had to move quickly to preserve the hides and meat after they returned to the camp. Some pegged the heavy hides to the ground and carefully scraped off the fat and tissue. This had to be done as soon as possible after the buffalo was killed. Otherwise the hide would harden and make tanning difficult.

Other women cut the blocks of meat into thin sheets using a spiral motion. The strips of meat were then hung on racks to dry. Women and girls also processed the two kinds of fat that were obtained from the buffalo. Marrow fat came from the large bones. These bones were split, pounded into splinters, and boiled in water until the marrow fat floated to the top. The fat was skimmed off and kept until it was needed. The women rendered the hard fat from the shoulder and rump in metal pots suspended on tripods over the fires.[18] Or sometimes, particularly if there was a shortage of pots, the women and their helpers put large pieces of fat near the fire and collected the drippings in a hide container.

Then some of this harvest from the buffalo was made into pemmican, the nutritious, lightweight food that was so valued by the traders and by their own people. The women and their helpers pounded the dried meat into a shredded mass with stone hammers. Then, with one pouring and the other mixing, the women combined the melted fat with the meat. Sometimes they used marrow fat to produce a fancier type of pemmican. And often, to make it even tastier and more nutritious, handfuls of dried saskatoons or other berries were added. Melted hard fat was used for the rest of the pemmican.

When the women had finished mixing the pemmican, they packed it into rawhide bags. They put leftover rendered hard fat into separate bags. If any marrow fat remained it was stored in buffalo paunches. The rest of the meat, as it was dried, was tied into bales and put into rawhide sacks.[19]

The women chatted and laughed as they worked, thankful that their husbands had more than one wife to share the work. Nearby, joints of buffalo meat roasted on spits over the fires outside the tipis, and under the coals, Indian turnips baked.

Illustration by Ed Peekeekoot

Dressed in the chief's coat supplied by the Hudson's Bay Company, Nāpēskis guided the Earl of Southesk to the Bad Hill to hunt grizzly bear.

The day after the buffalo hunt, Nāpēskis guided Southesk to the Bad Hill to hunt grizzly bears. The earl was obviously impressed with the young Cree, describing him in his journal as "Napesskes, that clever good-looking Indian." He was of Indian and French ancestry by birth, Southesk explained,

> but having always lived with the Indians he completely resembled them in his looks and habits, and nobody much remembered about his European blood. To honour the occasion he had arrayed himself in a new coat,—no less than a superfine blue cloth surtout, with gilt buttons, and a high velvet collar of an anciently fashionable cut; but instead of trowsers he wore leather leggings of the Indian pattern, which reached but a certain way up his limbs, and when the wind blew back his coat skirts there was a strange exhibition of rich mahogany-coloured skin. His long, straight, black hair was twisted into a quantity of tails bound round with coils of brass wire.[20]

The coat was likely a "chief's" coat that had been presented to Nāpēskis by the traders at Fort Carlton, for Ahtahkakoop's youngest brother was said to be "loved" by the Hudson's Bay Company.[21]

The party heading to the Bad Hill was an interesting one: Nāpēskis, a noted Cree warrior and hunter; Southesk, an aristocrat from Scotland; Duncan Robertson, the earl's Scottish gamekeeper and personal assistant; George Kline, a French Canadian who had been hired at the Red River Settlement; and Pierre Nummé, a half-breed engaged as a guide at Fort Ellice.[22] With the exception of Kline, who was driving a lightly loaded horse-drawn cart, the men were mounted on horses supplied by Southesk. Nāpēskis was on a horse named Spot who, in vivid contrast to the buffalo runner Black, was described as a "quiet little" horse.

After leaving the camps at Cherry Bush the men travelled due west for about three miles before veering in a more southwesterly direction. Southesk killed a curious antelope that came too close to the travellers and, shortly thereafter, he reported that the country changed entirely:

> instead of half-dry salt swamps, with here and there a sandy knoll, we now came to a wide arid prairie, level in character but rising occasionally into hills of trifling elevation. Far as the eye could reach these plains were covered with troops of buffalo, thousands and thousands were constantly in sight.[23]

Southesk dismounted and took one or two shots at several cows "without any perceptible result" and the men then travelled another 20 miles or so before the Bad Hill came in sight. Described as a "range of hills, or rather one continuous hill, extending about ten miles in length," the Bad Hill rose a few hundred feet from the surrounding terrain, and its outline was "plain and rounded." Its ravines and coulees, filled with heavy growths of poplar and underbrush, were home to the grizzly bear.

To reach the hill, the men made their way down a gentle slope to a "flat valley of fine level prairie land." Then they travelled two or three miles along the valley floor, soon reaching Eagle Creek at the foot of the Bad Hill. Crossing the creek, they camped in a woody ravine beside a "remarkably fine spring of water." It was at this place only the year before, Nāpēskis told Southesk with Nummé interpreting, that a grizzly bear attacked two Indian men while they were picking berries. One man died, while the other escaped. The "ominous" name of the hills, however, went back many years to the time when "some great misfortune ... befell the Crees or Assiniboines." Nāpēskis was the only one in the party who might have known the story but he apparently chose not to share it. Southesk recorded that "the tradition is lost, or at any rate was unknown to my people."[24]

Before daybreak the next morning Nāpēskis, Southesk, and Nummé went looking for bears. Near the "north-eastern extremity" of the Bad Hill the party saw a large female grizzly and her cub, both of which disappeared before a shot could be fired, and they also caught sight of a large male which was out of range. Then Nāpēskis, who had posted himself as a lookout, saw a grizzly take a swipe at a buffalo bull rushing out of the underbrush. Within a minute or so the grizzly emerged from the bush and, on a small knoll about 100 yards from Southesk, "reared itself on its hind legs, and swayed slowly from side to side, staring at us and trying to get our wind." Southesk missed with his first shot, but "struck it hard and fair with the second shot." Wounded, the bear crashed into the bushes where it thrashed and "raged in his pain" before becoming still. Southesk and Nummé, reluctant to follow, decided to return later to see if the animal was dead. According to Southesk, "Napesskes afterwards said that he would have been willing [to go after the grizzly], but Nummé objected. As the former speaks nothing but Cree, and made no signs, I could not say what might have been the extent of his readiness. To go in appeared to me sheer madness."[25]

After returning to their camp for breakfast, the men spent the rest of the day exploring the valleys and ravines of the Bad Hill. Except for mule deer, the men saw nothing of interest.[26] Then, in the evening, a few buffalo strayed from the main herd to graze near the base of the hills. Nāpēskis and Southesk set off independently to hunt. Crawling "undercover of a little rocky knoll" until he got into range, Southesk finally took aim, fired and hit a "rather good cow" low on the flank. At that instant, he said,

> another shot struck her from the opposite side, the two reports almost mingling in one. It was Napesskes, who having gone forward in search of buffalo some while before, had, by a strange coincidence, stalked and shot at the same cow that I was stalking, neither of us having the least idea as to his fellow-hunter's proceedings.
>
> The wounded cow staggered almost to falling; she had strength, however, to move heavily on. Napesskes went in pursuit,… following the wounded cow down into the plain, and as soon as she arrived there a bull came forward to protect her, keeping constantly at her side, and putting himself always between her and danger's way. For a good while he would not be driven off, and Napesskes, with laudable humanity, refrained from killing him; at length, however, the skilful hunter managed to scare him away, and then very easily secured his companion. We found her to be tolerably fat,—a fortunate circumstance for us, for our provisions were nearly all expended.[27]

The next morning at dawn Nāpēskis accompanied Southesk and three of his men to the place where the grizzly had been shot. They found a young male about three years old lying dead. The animal was skinned and the head removed. Then the group returned to Cherry Bush, once again during their journey seeing "buffalo trooping all over the plains, not in dense enormous herds, but broken into innumerable small straggling bands." Upon their arrival at the Cherry Bush camp, Southesk was "vexed" to learn that Tate, "while riding alone," had shot a full-grown male grizzly bear the day he and Nāpēskis had left for the Bad Hill.

Activity at the Cherry Bush camp had changed little. The hunters were still getting buffalo near the camp—two of Southesk's men had killed nine cows—and the women were busy preparing hides and meat for the traders and for their own families. Southesk hired some women to dry meat and make pemmican from the cows he and his men had killed. Marrow fat and dried berries, both of which were abundant in the camp, were probably used for at least some of Southesk's pemmican. Southesk also arranged for

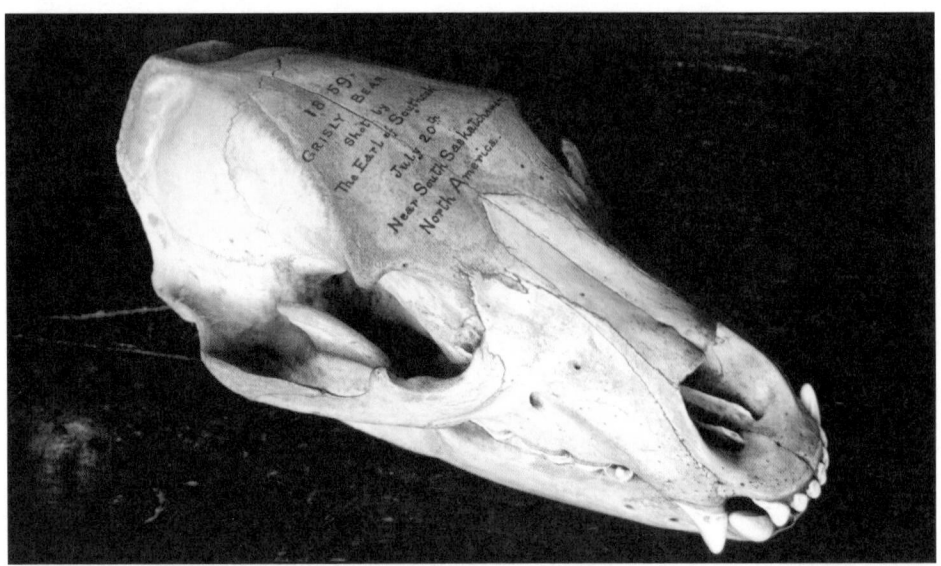

Skull of grizzly bear shot by Southesk while hunting with Nāpēskis. The inscription reads: 1859, Grisly Bear shot by the Earl of Southesk July 20th Near South Saskatchewan, North America.

several of the women to dress the antelope and bear skins, preserve his trophy heads, and sew for him. The earl was pleased with the work, commenting that the skin from the young bear he had shot was "very nicely prepared" and "looked remarkably well." He went on to say that

> These Indian women had been most serviceable to us in dressing skins and heads, drying meat, and mending or making clothes; so, when adding a small present to the mere payment for their work, I was glad to find among my stores a parcel of beads exactly to their taste. It amused me to see that fashion reigned here as imperiously as in more civilised lands; some fine, richly-coloured, oval beads, the size of pigeon's eggs, which I considered my best, and which a year or two before would have been generally admired, were despised and out of date, while the little trashy white ones, no bigger than a pin's head, were highly appreciated. Perhaps the small beads were valued as useful for embroidery, in which the Indian and half-breed women excel, while the larger ones, only serving for necklaces and ornaments, had come to be thought too barbaric by those who lived in the Forts.[28]

Although Southesk implies in this statement that the women were living at the fort, it was likely true only of Tate's wife and perhaps a few others. This was a Cree hunting camp, not a camp of Hudson's Bay Company employees.

While Nāpēskis, Southesk, and the other men were on their trip to the Bad Hill, visitors from a large Cree camp "a day's march away" brought word that Blackfoot war parties "were spread all over the country, and had been trying to entrap them into ambuscades." Not unduly alarmed, for the Cree and Blackfoot were often at war, the hunters had continued their hunt while the women prepared the hides and meat to the stage where they could be safely transported.

Early on July 23 the women dismantled the tipis. Then the personal belongings of their families and the bags of pemmican, dried meat, fat, berries, and turnips, along with the buffalo hides, were packed on the carts and travois. When all was ready the cavalcade of men, women, children, dogs, horses, and carts headed north towards Fort Carlton. Southesk, who had decided to go to Carlton instead of proceeding immediately to Fort Pitt and Edmonton House, accompanied them. After the second day of travelling the group made camp at a wooded creek near the elbow of the North Branch of the Saskatchewan River. They reached the fur trade post during the afternoon of the next day.[29]

When Southesk decided that his horses were too exhausted after the long trip from Fort Garry to continue the journey to the mountains, he went with Tate to the horseguard to select new ones. The choices were made and Tate mounted a young bay horse belonging to the officer in charge of Fort Carlton. Southesk said that "being scarcely broke, it was so violent that he passed it on, after a struggle, to my Indian friend Napesskes, who had just joined us, and under his handling it went quietly enough for the rest of the way."[30]

Back at the post the Scottish earl settled his account and made arrangements to store his trophy heads, skins, heavy goods, and a small supply of liquor until his return from the mountains. He left Fort Carlton on July 27 and was back on November 15 after a trip that took him to Fort Pitt, Edmonton House, and through the Rocky Mountains. Southesk again exchanged horses, this time for the trip to Fort Garry and the first leg of the journey back to Scotland. One of the horses Southesk acquired was the young bay Nāpēskis had successfully ridden in July. It was now "fairly broke in ... a handy, quiet, and very useful animal." It appears Southesk named this horse after his Cree friend, for he later mentioned a horse called "Napesskes."[31] That is the last reference to Nāpēskis in Southesk's book.

Illustration by Willard Ahenakew

Nāpēskis breaking a horse.

Some time in 1859 or early 1860 Nāpēskis went to Ottawa and Montreal with an important unidentified white man. Although the man's name remains unknown, it was not Southesk since the earl travelled to New York City in as direct a route as possible to board a boat for Liverpool. More likely, it was George Simpson,[32] governor of the Hudson's Bay Company. This has not been substantiated but the opportunity was there. Southesk had travelled in the company of Simpson from Lachine (near Montreal) to St. Paul and then Fort Garry via Canadian and American railways, steamboat, and horse and wagon.

When the two men went their separate ways at Fort Garry, Southesk said that the governor "was good enough to leave with me his own canoeman, Toma, one of the trustiest and best of fellows." According to Southesk the Iroquois voyageur "had been constantly employed as Sir George's … [canoe-man] on his previous expeditions to Red River by the usual Canadian [water] route." Toma's duties in Southesk's party included driving the wagon, cooking Southesk's meals, and "along with Duncan, acting as … [his] special attendant."[33] It would have been surprising if Nāpēskis and Toma had not become friends at the Cherry Bush camp and during the trip to Fort Carlton. It would also have been surprising if the two men had not talked about the changes taking place in the land of the Nēhiyawak, the white man's cities in eastern Canada, and the changes in the life of the Iroquois people. Southesk, who considered Simpson to be a friend and Nāpēskis to be an impressive young man, could very well have played a part in arranging Nāpēskis' trip.

Regardless of whether or not Nāpēskis' visit to the east was connected with Toma, Southesk, and Simpson, the trip provided an opportunity for Ahtahkakoop's brother to see first-hand what was happening in American territory to the south and in the lands far to the east. A trip of this magnitude would not have been taken lightly. Instead, it would have been agreed upon after council meetings with Ahtahkakoop, his other brothers, and the leading men of the band. It is said that Nāpēskis went east as a scout, sent to observe a new way of life and to gather information that would be helpful to the Indian people of Saskatchewan River country.

When Nāpēskis returned home more than a year later he brought many gifts with him. Since he was not married, the gifts were distributed amongst his sisters-in-law.[34] During the next weeks and months the men, women, and children spent many hours listening to their friend and relative talk about the different things he had seen and heard. The troubles the

Indian people were having in the American territories as settlers, miners, and soldiers encroached on Indian lands. The railway, and the speed with which people could travel from one place to another. The large towns, with streets and buildings made of wood, stone, and brick. The farms, with their fenced fields and cattle. But most of all Nāpēskis talked about the great number of white people he had seen during his journey, people living on land that had belonged to the Indian nations.

More and more people realized that Nāpēskis was sad, preoccupied, and restless. His brothers' wives talked amongst themselves and wondered if their young brother-in-law had fallen in love with a white girl while he was away and if he was saddened by a hopeless love.[35] Others thought the young warrior was despondent over what he had seen and heard during his journey. And some thought that Nāpēskis feared for the future of the Nēhiyawak, believing that their free way of life would soon be threatened.

Early the next spring Ahtahkakoop's band was camped in the *mikisi-waciya* (Eagle Hills). Instead of brooding, Nāpēskis decided to lead a horse-raiding party into Blackfoot country. At least 20 others joined him, including his nephews Kā-miyo-ahcahkwēw* (Good Spirit) and Macōhōw (Bad Owl). Kā-miyo-ahcahkwēw, who was in his early twenties, was Ahtahkakoop's son; Macōhōw was the son of Nāpēskis' deceased brother Masuskapoe.[36] Others in the raiding party included Ugly Man, Akenaiskak, Ayahtawāsis, Playful One, and Kā-māskāpiwayiskis. There was still snow on the ground so the warriors left on snowshoes. They crossed the prairie to the Red Deer River (the South Saskatchewan River) and then followed it to the mouth of the Old Man River in what is now southern Alberta.

There they stopped to prepare themselves for the mission ahead. Nāpēskis, Bad Owl and some of the others smoked their pipes, sang their songs, and prayed while others scouted ahead.

"If you are careful, you will have horses," Bad Owl told the young men in the group. "One thing goes wrong, its [sic] danger. Our path home looks dark ... Beware, don't make a mistake."[37]

Before long the scouts returned and reported that they had seen Blackfoot hunters going around a bend in the Old Man River, near Poor River. As darkness fell over the land, the raiding party started out. Soon they heard the drums in the Blackfoot camp and, following the sound, came to the camp. They waited patiently as the camp fell silent and slept.

The raid went well. Time after time the Cree warriors crept into the camp

---

* Kā-miyo-ahcahkwēw was later known by some as Antoine.

and led away the best horses. Fearless, Nāpēskis was especially successful. He "was afraid of nothing." As dawn approached, the warriors gathered at a pre-arranged meeting place for the long journey home. Realizing that Kā-miyo-ahcahkwēw was not amongst them, Nāpēskis said he would stay and wait for his nephew. Five men insisted on remaining with him.

By now the Blackfoot had discovered their losses and were pursuing the raiders. Nāpēskis and his friends, still waiting for Kā-miyo-ahcahkwēw, were surrounded. Greatly outnumbered, the Cree fought fiercely in a battle that raged all day and all night. Morning finally came. Playful One, Akenaiskak and the other warriors who had stayed with Nāpēskis all lay dead. The Blackfoot heard Nāpēskis singing. Then he called out, "I could still kill some of you, but why? You have killed all my men and I do not want to live." Nāpēskis then jumped from his hiding place, and standing straight and tall called out, "Shoot, you dogs, shoot." The Blackfoot shot from all around, and the Cree warrior sank slowly to the ground, a dead man.[38] When the Blackfoot told the story later, they said that Nāpēskis "took a long time to kill."

The Blackfoot found a paper of credit on the warrior's body signed by the white man who had taken Nāpēskis to eastern Canada. This credit note authorized Hudson's Bay Company officers to give Nāpēskis goods and supplies on credit at any company post he visited. The Blackfoot showed the paper to a Roman Catholic priest who worked among the Blackfoot nations. He arranged to have the body buried and the grave marked.[39] In telling one version of the story, Thunderchild concluded by saying that there was great sorrow over Nāpēskis' death.[40]

In 1906 Ahenakew's son Kāh-kāsōw visited Fort Macleod and the Blackfoot reserve with his nephew and several other people. Kāh-kāsōw asked questions about the horse raid and the battle in which Nāpēskis was killed. He also asked where his uncle was buried, hoping to visit the grave. The people remembered but it was some distance away and Kāhkāsow was unable to go.[41]

Nāpēskis was apparently killed in 1861, for the Reverend James Settee wrote in his journal in July of that year that a "young half-Cree, half-Saulteau came … he is mourning the death of his uncle Na-pās-kis, who has been killed just lately in battle by the Blackfoot … This Na-pās-kis was a noted Warrior … the bravest of the little plain Fort Chiefs."[42]

Ironically, Nāpēskis' nephew Kā-miyo-ahcahkwēw arrived home unscathed. After stealing several horses from the Blackfoot camp, he had apparently fled to safety instead of waiting for the rest of the war party.

The head of the buffalo bull killed by Southesk in 1859 is on display at Kinnaird Castle in Scotland, the home of the 12th Earl of Southesk. The skull of the buffalo ox killed by Nāpēskis hangs over the back door of the trophy room.

PART TWO

Change

Newcomers arrive to farm.

CHAPTER SEVEN

Newcomers to the Land of the Nēhiyaw

L ate in 1862, a year or so after Nāpēskis was killed, Ahtahkakoop and his two remaining brothers—Sasakamoose and Ahenakew—were wintering in the *kā-mistikwatināk* (Thickwood Hills) with their families. Now 46 years old, Ahtahkakoop was not only a chief recognized by both the Indian people and the Hudson's Bay Company, but he had earned the reputation of being one of the best hunters in the Carlton district. During the summer, when the buffalo were on the plains, the drying racks in his camp were almost always covered with meat. His people were generally well supplied with food and the traders welcomed the buffalo produce and furs that he regularly brought to the post.

The 1862–63 season of snow was to be interesting because Charles A. Messiter built a cabin near Ahtahkakoop's wintering place. Like the Earl of Southesk three years earlier, Messiter had come to hunt buffalo and grizzly bear. There were, however, several significant differences. Southesk, with his Hudson's Bay Company connections, had been well equipped and spent a considerable amount of his time in the North-West travelling with a group of men hired to assist him. Messiter, on the other hand, was an adventurer with "prairie fever" who had travelled by boat from Liverpool, England, in the summer of 1862 with no connections and few resources. Additionally, he intended to spend the winter in the Carlton District instead of travelling. He was one of the growing numbers of visitors coming uninvited to Indian land.

On board the ship that embarked from Liverpool and landed in Quebec, Messiter met two well-to-do Englishmen who also intended to winter in the Fort Carlton area. Their names were Dr. Walter Butler Cheadle and Lord Milton. The three men travelled together to Fort Carlton via Toronto,

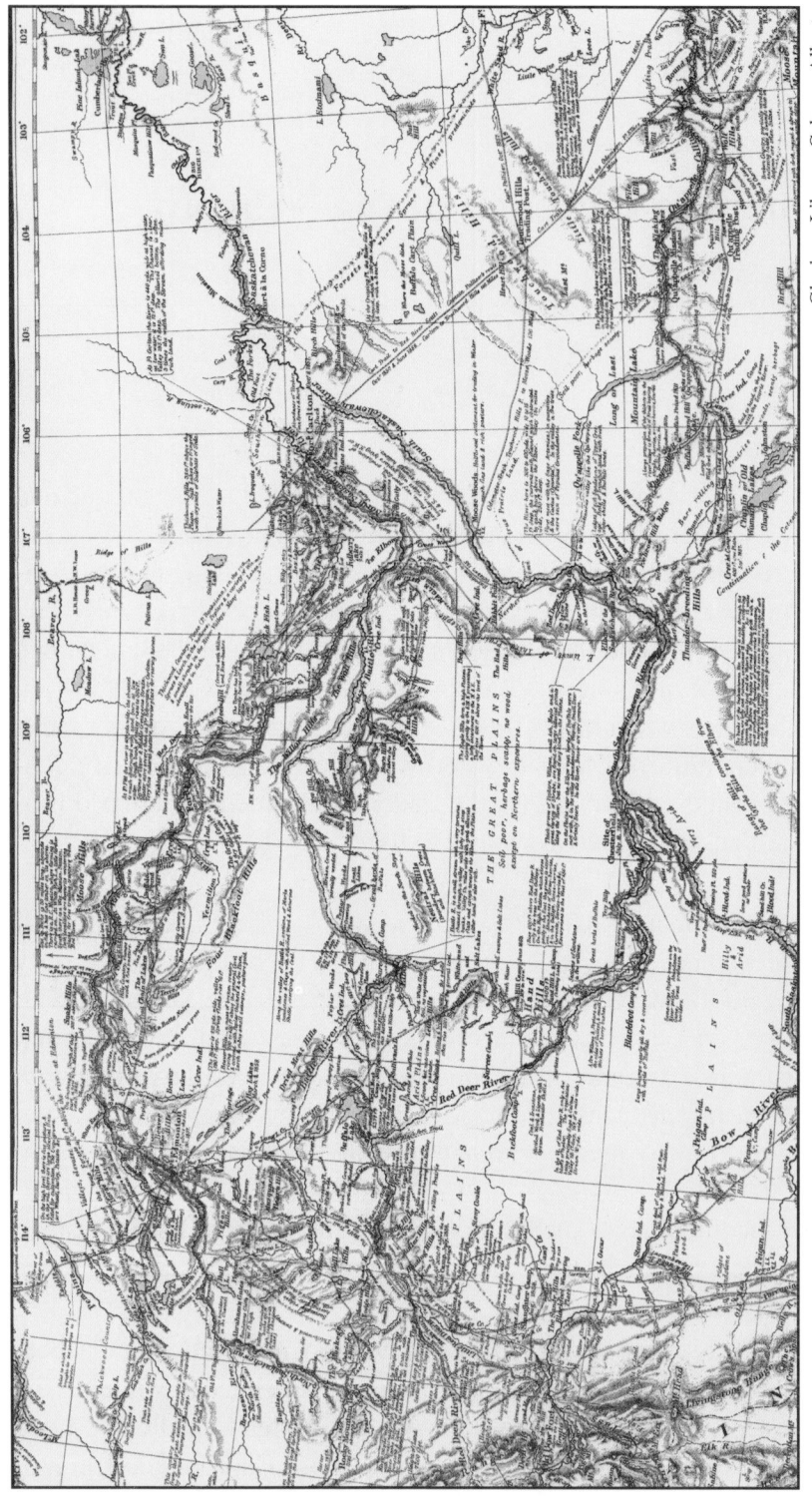

A section of the General Map of the Routes in British North America Explored by the Expedition under Captain Palliser during the years 1857, 1858, 1860.

Detroit, St. Paul, and Fort Garry. They arrived at the fur trade post on the North Saskatchewan River on September 26.[1]

Before choosing a place to spend the winter, Messiter, Cheadle, and Milton spent a number of days hunting buffalo in the country beyond Eagle River. Then, after a successful expedition, they returned to Fort Carlton. Because of continuing conflict between Milton and Messiter, the decision was made to part company. Cheadle and Milton made plans to winter at Whitefish Lake* and left Fort Carlton the evening of October 10. They eventually built their cabin on a "pretty promontory jutting into a lake at 'Jolie Prairie,'" which Cheadle placed nine or 10 miles south of Whitefish Lake.

Left to make his own arrangements, Messiter decided to spend the winter in the Thickwood Hills about 50 miles northwest of Fort Carlton.[3] Game was more abundant and the hills were closer to the plains than the area chosen by Cheadle and Milton. The area had another attraction as well. In Cheadle's words, the Thickwood Hills were "the home of Atahk-akoohp, or 'Star of the Blanket,'† the most noted hunter of the district."[4]

Unlike Southesk, who had left his liquor at Fort Carlton, Messiter, Cheadle, and Milton all took kegs of rum to their wintering places.[5]

Messiter was going to hire one of Ahtahkakoop's sons-in-law at £2 per month to winter with him. When the man—who spoke a little French but no English—asked for all of his pay in advance, Messiter consulted with the officer in charge of Fort Carlton. On his advice, the Englishman instead engaged Badger, a young man married to one of Mistawasis's daughters.[6] Messiter and Badger, along with Badger's wife and child, crossed to the north side of the North Saskatchewan River at the same time as Cheadle and Milton.[7] Messiter's outfit included an ox-drawn cart piled high with winter supplies, a tent, clothing, bedding, and liquor. Two sleds were piled on top of the loaded cart.[8] He also had two teams of sled dogs.

The presence of Southesk, Messiter, Cheadle, and Milton in the Carlton district was an indicator of the seemingly relentless changes coming to Indian lands. For almost a hundred years the fur traders, with a few exceptions, had been the only "newcomers" in Saskatchewan River country.

---

* Whitefish Lake (*atihkamēk sākahikan*) is about 80 miles northwest of present-day Prince Albert.

† The correct translation of Ahtahkakoop is "Star Blanket."

Then, during the 1840s, an increasing number of newcomers with other interests started to appear. The missionaries—Roman Catholic, Methodist (Wesleyan), and Anglican—were among the first to come. For more than two decades they stopped at Indian camps and fur trade posts as they passed through the Carlton district to points further west and north, baptizing the children, the women, and sometimes the men.

There were also non-church visitors to Saskatchewan River country during the 1840s and 1850s. These included Lieutenants Henry J. Warre and M. Vavasour in 1845. Posing as hunters, these men were actually surveying the defensibility of the frontier in response to growing tension between Britain and the United States over boundaries. Artist Paul Kane was at Fort Carlton briefly in both 1846 and 1847; during his 1846 visit he was taken to a buffalo pound and Cree camp about six miles from the post. Some 11 years later a young Englishman by the name of Vidler, who had come west to hunt, was living with Indians in the Carlton district. A visiting missionary reported that when Vidler visited the fur trade post in November, 1857, he was dressed the same as his Indian companions.[9]

Part of John Palliser's exploratory expedition spent the winter of 1857–58 at Fort Carlton,[10] and the next summer two British sportsmen, Captain Brisco of the 11th Hussars and a Mr. Mitchell, were at the post. In 1858, Henry Youle Hind and his party surveyed the South Branch of the Saskatchewan River from north of the elbow to its junction with the Saskatchewan River, and then from the forks to Fort à la Corne. There were other newcomers during the 1850s, including free traders from the Red River Settlement who established a small village at Moose Woods and were successfully challenging Fort Carlton's monopoly on trade.[11] To meet this competition, Carlton traders built an outpost in the village. Unlike the Carlton traders, who tried to keep some controls on the amount of liquor traded, the free traders—many of them half-breeds—distributed liquor in lavish amounts.

Then, in 1859, Southesk arrived. Other visitors that year included three parties of "overlanders" who were passing through Indian lands en route to the Caribou gold fields located in present-day British Columbia.

In July of 1862, the year Messiter, Cheadle, and Milton came, another group of "overlanders" travelling to the gold fields stopped at Fort Carlton. And later in the summer 19-year-old John McDougall came from Norway House on the Hudson's Bay Company boats. He stayed at the post 15 days waiting for his Methodist missionary father, George McDougall, to arrive from the Red River Settlement. After leaving Fort Carlton, the pair visited the church's missions situated farther up the North Saskatchewan River.[12]

Ahtahkakoop, Mistawasis, the other chiefs, and their followers observed the arrival and behaviour of these newcomers with some apprehension. Although most of them did not stay very long, these strangers brought different values to the plains. Some of them looked with disdain at the traditional practices of the Indian people. They talked about the white man's Christian God and this God seemed to be different, depending on who was talking. Other newcomers were taking an unusual interest in the land and in the animals and plants that lived upon Mother Earth. They killed the buffalo, the bear, and other animals for sport. And they asked questions about the Nēhiyawak. How many Cree lived on the prairies? How many lived in the parklands and forests? Where did they live in the winter? How large were their hunting grounds? All these questions were asked, and many more.

Despite their concerns, the Indian people generally treated the visitors with courtesy and assisted when they could. The women cooked, dried meat, sewed, and tanned hides and skins for them. Many times the people invited the newcomers and other visitors into their camp, particularly when the strangers needed help. The Reverend Henry Budd,[13] an Anglican missionary of Swampy Cree ancestry, had been welcomed as a guest in Mistawasis's house at Moose Woods,* and Southesk received help from Nāpēskis and the families in his camp. Sometimes the men even offered to guide and hunt for the newcomers so they could observe the ways of these people and learn more about them.[14]

Faced with these intrusions into their land and their lives, Ahtahkakoop and his leading men had taken advantage of the opportunity to send Nāpēskis to Montreal in late 1859 or early 1860. He went as a scout, to learn what he could about these newcomers, the way they lived, and what changes the Nēhiyawak might expect in the future. In this way, the Nēhiyawak would not be caught off-guard.

Charles Messiter, who had arrived at Fort Carlton in September of 1862 with Dr. Cheadle and Lord Milton, was one of the newcomers who had been treated kindly by the Cree people.

---

* Mistawasis, Ahtahkakoop's long-time friend, was considered the leading man amongst the buffalo hunters who lived and traded in the Moose Woods area in the late 1850s, and sometimes he stayed in a house at the village.

Cheadle recorded the following story in his book. During their hunting trip to Eagle River country, Messiter had wandered off by himself to hunt. It was a cold, windy, and rainy day in early October. When he had not returned by evening, Cheadle fired regular gun shots from the camp, a lighted "brand" was put on top of a pole, and one of the men searched for him. Cheadle said they finally went to bed about midnight, "thanking our stars we are under shelter with good fire & food." Another search party set off at daybreak. Cheadle's journal picks up the account:

> At 8 [a.m.] we saw 5 men on horseback coming towards camp, turned out to be Messiter & 4 Crees. After wandering about half numb with cold until an hour after dark he essayed to light a fire. Matches wet & could not succeed; on again for another hour or so; made for a wood & found there a camp of Crees; taken into Chief's lodge; given his place to sleep in. Things dried. Pipe sent round; large lodge of 15 skins. Meat & muskeg tea. Fat & water as cordial after.... In morning makes them understand he wants to find camp. Go with him; presents them with knives &c. They come into our lodge & breakfast. Pipe went around.... Stay until 1; dine. We make a move then. Chief Junior (rather fine looking fellow, Roman nose, spangled shirt, cap with ribands, medicine bag) gets up & makes oration. Translated by La Ronde; wishes to know what purport of visit to his country, for he had been frightened by the Company's men telling him numbers of white men would soon enter his country & he must beware of them. Told him to hunt, see the country & visit him. He would be glad to see us, & we might go where we wished & hunt as we liked. Thanked him, shook hands, & away they went.[15]

Although Cheadle uses the name Chief Junior in the above account, that was not the spokesman's name. Elsewhere Cheadle refers to him as the "young chief." He also said that an "old chief" shared the tipi where Messiter spent the night. Unfortunately, the old chief was not named. There are no other clues as to the identity of these people. Nevertheless, from the above account it is apparent that the Indian people were beginning to worry about the changes taking place in their territory.

The role of Fort Carlton was also changing. For many years the Cree had called Fort Carlton *pēhonānihk*, "the waiting place," for it was here they often waited for their friends and relatives. Then in 1859—for the first time —a steamboat travelled down the Red River from American territory to

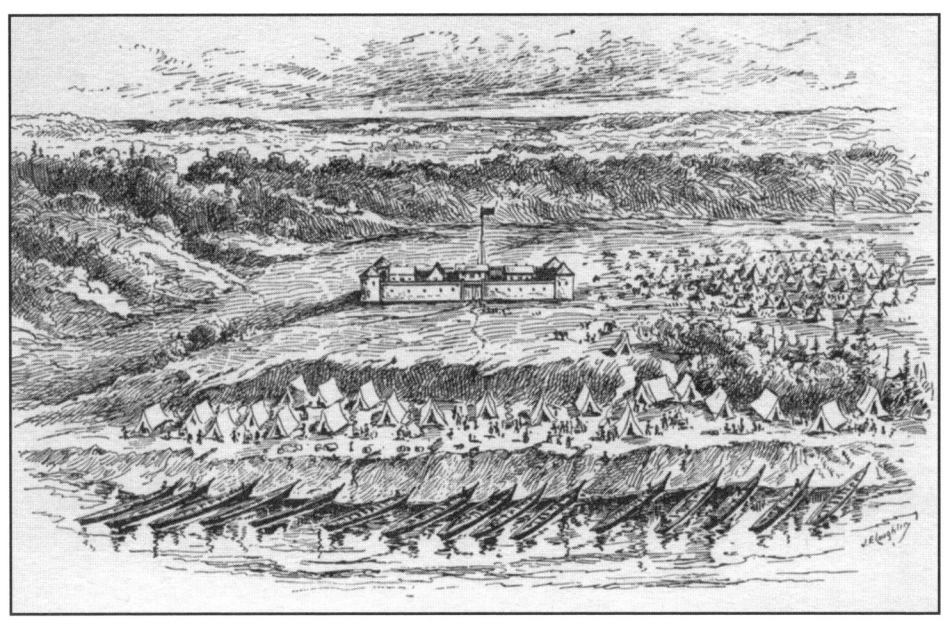

From John McDougall, *Forest, Lake and Prairie*

Fort Carlton, the waiting place, was busy when the boats arrived from York Factory and the Indian people came in to trade. The boat crews camped near the river. The Indian people erected their tipis west of the post.

Fort Garry. Soon afterwards an American railway reached St. Paul. With better access to railways and steamboats and the development of overland cart trails to the Missouri River and the Red River Settlement, visitors coming from the east no longer had to travel the arduous Lake Superior route. Additionally, the Hudson's Bay Company found it easier and cheaper to transport furs, trade goods and supplies to and from the North-West via New York instead of York Factory. And so, with more goods and people coming into Saskatchewan River country via Fort Garry and the American route, Fort Carlton became a waiting place for the newcomers as well as the Indians and half-breeds. The post also become a place to arrange transportation to points further afield, to get supplies, and to hire guides and interpreters.

Young John McDougall described the activity around Fort Carlton when he was there in 1862:

> The old fort and the plain around was a busy scene—our crews
> from the boats, hunters from the plains, parties of Indians in to
> trade, the air full of stories about the southern Indians and the
> tribal wars to and fro, scalps taken and horses stolen, the herds of

buffalo said to be within a hundred miles from the fort, or less than two days out. Buffalo-skin lodges and canvas tents dotted the plain in every direction. Horse-races and foot-races were common occurrences. I championed older Canada against Indians, half-breeds and Hudson's Bay officials and employees, and in the foot-racing and jumping—high, long, and hop, step and jump—"cleaned out the crowd" and made a name for myself and country, and amid such doings spent fifteen days, when father and his party came up and we moved on.[16]

Ahtahkakoop and his band were hunting buffalo on the plains when Messiter and Badger arrived in the Thickwood Hills in mid-October 1862. The two men chose an opening in the trees near a small spring for their cabin and then set about the task of building. The site was about 50 miles northwest of Fort Carlton and 40 miles south of Cheadle and Milton's cabin at *manitow-sākahikan* (God's Lake). The site was likely fairly close to the Green Lake Trail since Milton spent a night at the cabin during a trip from Carlton.[17]

Unaccustomed to construction work—and probably most kinds of physical labour—Messiter found the work difficult. Fortunately for the English adventurer, Badger "was a good hand with an axe." The cabin they erected, unlike most wintering cabins, had gable ends and a double high-pitched roof. This design, Messiter said, was a great deal of trouble to build and

> not any more comfortable than the common form of log house, which is made as follows:—You first put up a frame of logs, notched where they cross one another so as to let them lie close, and of the required dimensions, making the back of the house higher by two logs than the front. Out of this you cut what doors and windows you require. You then make the roof by sloping small straight poles from the lower to the higher side, and cover them with grass and a foot of earth, putting cross poles to keep it all on; and after making your doors and windows your house is finished on the outside, the only things remaining to be done being the chimney and floor, the former of these being always a difficulty.[18]

Messiter and Badger covered the windows of the cabin with parchment made from deer hide. The door, constructed from a portion of Messiter's cart, had a parchment window with a small insert of glass. That single piece of glass, Messiter said, was all he was able to get at Fort Carlton. Since the two men could not find any rocks "about," they made the chimney from mud, grass, and sticks. Built in one of the corners, it had a "large space for a fire, five feet square." Rough stools and a table were made from other parts of the cart, and since they did not have a saw, the floor was made from pine logs, with "each log making one board." Cheadle and Milton's cabin at *manitow-sākahikan* was built the more usual way except that Cheadle dug out two feet of dirt to increase the height from floor to ceiling. Sand and then planking were used on the floor.[19] Although it was not mentioned by either man, mud and moss would have been used to chink spaces between the logs.

The men built a stage for meat and a small storehouse after the cabin was finished, and then they went to visit Ahtahkakoop.[20] According to Messiter, Ahtahkakoop was the "only neighbour within calling distance." The chief was still on his fall hunting trip, but following his return a few days later he and about 20 others went over to see the newcomer. Children were part of the group, but Messiter does not indicate if they were included in his count of 20.

Messiter said that one of the attractions at his cabin was the sugar-bag, "out of which I could not keep the children's fingers." Some of these children were likely Ahtahkakoop's, since Messiter said he had three wives and "no end of children." Later in his account, Messiter said that five or six families were living near Ahtahkakoop.[21]

Soon after this visit Messiter rented two pack ponies from the chief for a trip towards the South Saskatchewan River to hunt buffalo. Messiter's cabin was left under Ahtahkakoop's care while he and Badger were away. After travelling for three days, the hunters reached the place where Mistawasis was wintering. Messiter wrote that:

> Old Mis-ta-wa-sis was also well supplied with wives, having three
> of them, and lived in an immense buffalo-skin lodge, in which
> besides his family, there was room for two of his sons-in-laws and
> their families, and still there was plenty of room for us.[22]

Badger's wife, along with the child, likely travelled with them. Mistawasis was her father and she would not have missed an opportunity to visit her parents. After a stop of two days Messiter and Badger travelled another two days before reaching the South Branch of the Saskatchewan

Illustration by Ed Peekeekoot

The children could not keep their fingers out of the sugar bag in Messiter's cabin.

River. The hunt was successful. Then they returned to Mistawasis's camp before going back to the Thickwood Hills.

Ahtahkakoop, his family, and the others living nearby were invited to Messiter's cabin for Christmas dinner. For the occasion Messiter and a man by the name of Farquharson, who was spending at least part of the winter with him,[23] concocted a "plum" pudding out of the supplies he had purchased and saved for that purpose. Made from flour, a "lot of water," baking powder, suet, sugar, eggs, and a few raisins, currants, and citron-peel, the mixture was put in a bag made from towels and boiled for almost two days. The pudding was rock-hard. Not knowing what else to do, Messiter "sent for A-ta-ka-koup's wife and paid her to boil it all night."

When the guests arrived, Badger served grog made from whiskey and water. On Messiter's prompting, they all "drank to the health of the Queen, the Indians wondering why we stood up as we did it. Then slices of buffalo were handed out on the ends of sticks … these being the fashionable substitutes for forks." The pudding came next. Despite hours of boiling it had remained hard and Messiter was disappointed:

On sticking a knife into it, it was hard work to get it out again, and when it was extracted it brought with it more of the pudding than is usual.

A portion was at last cut for everyone and handed round, but though on most of the slices a plum [raisin] or a currant, and in some cases two or three, were visible, there was not that enthusiasm about it which we had hoped for, everyone eating his or her portion in silence. My piece reminded me of what schoolboys call "turnpike pudding," plums occurring about as often as turnpikes do in travelling.[24]

Ahtahkakoop took Messiter hunting for moose and other game a number of times during the early part of the winter. The chief's skill as a hunter was readily evident. He was a "first rate tracker and a wonderful man on snow-shoes in deep snow," Messiter said, as well as a "good companion." Ahtahkakoop spoke only 20 or 30 words of English and Messiter was limited to the Cree he was able to pick up, so the two men communicated with each other using signs and the few words that both knew.

Messiter described one hunting trip in his book *Sport and Adventures Among the North-American Indians*. He said that he arranged to go hunting with Ahtahkakoop after the Cree leader had found nearby signs of moose. Determined to be as comfortable as possible, Messiter asked one of the women to make an A-tent that was closed at both ends. He explained that he intended to use this on the dog sled instead of the "usual big sheet." He wrote that after

> we had chosen a spot and shovelled away the snow, [and] after laying down a foot of either willows or small fir branches, we put up my tent on its side, the other side forming a slant, and the two ends keeping out all draughts, making us very comfortable. A-ta-ka-koup rather laughed at it when he saw it unpacked.[25]

Messiter estimated the camp to be 10 to 12 miles from his hut. The camp was made "snug," and then they set out

> and soon came on moose-tracks of that morning. A-ta-ka-koup said that they were those of three cows and a bull, and we followed them for more than an hour, by which time we were evidently close to them. The snow was here very deep, as we sank in nearly to our knees with snow-shoes on, and the moose evidently had to jump to get along at all.

Illustration by Ed Peekeekoot

A skilled hunter and tracker, Ahtahkakoop takes aim at a moose cow after a long chase through the snow.

As we were going round a small thicket we heard them start, and almost immediately they broke cover about two hundred yards ahead, going pretty fast. Ata-ka-koup seemed to be confident of coming up with them, and started on the run after them, going at the rate of perhaps six miles an hour, which he could not have kept up for long, and I followed at the rate of five miles. I had had so much snow-shoe travelling that I was in good condition, but I was not such an old hand at it as he was, so that he continued to gain on me, and in half an hour was two hundred yards ahead and gaining still, in spite of all I could do.

I then heard a shot, followed by another, and came up to him standing over a cow, where I left him, as he told me the bull was not far in front, and in a few minutes I saw him, evidently labouring, about a hundred yards off; so I fired, missing with the first barrel and hitting him too far back with the second, on which he increased his speed for a few hundred yards, and then stood at bay. Thinking him weaker than he really was, I went up to within ten yards of him, when down went his head, and in about three tremendous jumps he was almost on me. I fired at his head, and, fortunately perhaps, missing that struck him in the neck, dropping him at once—not three feet from me. He was a splendid fellow, and had a good head, which A-ta-ka-koop carried to camp for me, where we hung it high up on some boughs, intending to fetch it in the spring.

On returning to camp, A-ta-ka-koup took the sleigh and dogs and went to fetch some of the cow meat, the bull being too tough to eat.[26]

Ahtahkakoop had seen a number of lynx tracks, so the following morning he returned home to get some dogs that were "good at treeing lynxes." Messiter remained at the camp, hunting ruffed grouse and a few "willow-grouse" that were plentiful and "capital eating." By the time Ahtahkakoop came back with the dogs, Messiter had cooked the grouse and they were ready to eat.

The following morning the two men started out after lynx. Messiter took his dogs along because it was feared they would make too much noise if left behind. Ahtahkakoop's dogs soon picked up the trail. As they went along, Messiter said Ahtahkakoop

explained the tracks to me, seeming to know what turns they had made and which dogs were leading at the time, and as his dogs were very much smaller than mine, they made a track about half the size.

We had not gone far when we heard them all giving tongue, and knew that the lynx was treed, and soon came to where he had gone up a low fir tree. Ata-ka-koup came up first, and fired, on which the lynx dropped wounded among the dogs. Mine immediately bolted, sleigh-dogs seldom having much pluck; but the two smaller ones went in and killed him good style.[27]

They found two more lynx that day, killing one and losing the other. The following day the men went after white-tailed deer, "but had bad luck … [and] only got one, the reason being that A-ta-ka-koup's dogs behaved badly, by rushing on in front and putting up the deer long before we got near enough to shoot." The two men returned home the fifth day, "having had a most enjoyable hunt."[28]

Messiter also included an account in *Sport and Adventure* of his last hunt with Ahtahkakoop:

> We had followed three deer nearly all day, jumping them once but not getting a shot, when we ascertained that they were in a large thicket about three or four hundred yards ahead of us. A-ta-ka-koup stopped me and lit a small fire, at which he sat down, and lighting his pipe he blew a whiff to the north, south, east, and west, and one upwards. He remained solemnly looking at the fire for nearly an hour, evidently praying, and then declared himself ready, and approached the bushes on one side, placing me on the other; and very soon the deer came out close to me. Having remained so long by such a little fire my fingers were almost frozen and I missed the first; but broke the hind leg of the second, and Ata-ka-koup ran it down, bounding through the deep snow like a deer.[29]

Between the two hunts there had been a shortage of game in both the Thickwood Hills and the Whitefish Lake regions. The buffalo were also scarce. They had not come into the parklands that winter and "reports from all quarters announced their disappearance."[30] Instead of trying to survive on woodland game, Ahtahkakoop and his people left their wintering houses and spent the next two months hunting buffalo on the plains. Messiter did not go with them.[31]

During his stay in the North-West, Messiter also had some dealings with Kihci-mōhkomān (Big Knife), a Cree-Saulteaux who spent the first part of the winter with Ahtahkakoop.[32] Messiter said Kihci-mōhkomān took him deer hunting a number of times but he was "not nearly so good a man in camp as A-ta-ka-koup … being more used to cold than ourselves, we were obliged to get up in the night to replenish the fire." Ahtahkakoop, in contrast, "was always ready to make up the fire at night" and did not shirk work in the hunting camp.[33] Having worked on the Hudson's Bay Company's boat brigades, Ahtahkakoop knew the habits and expectations of the white men when they travelled.

Messiter claimed that Kihci-mōhkomān later took him to Whitefish Lake to visit Cheadle and Milton, claiming that Badger "knew nothing of the country north of the Saskatchewan."[34] Cheadle's journal, which was kept on a daily basis, disputes this story. According to Cheadle's account, Messiter was only in the Whitefish area twice during the winter. The first time, on December 8, 1862, he arrived by dog sled with Badger to compete openly with Hudson's Bay Company traders for furs. His main trade item was liquor, and during the visit Messiter replenished his supply by giving Cheadle 15 marten skins in exchange for a gallon of rum.

Two days later he was back at Cheadle's and Milton's cabin, this time travelling on foot, to get another gallon of rum. Messiter's trading activities were contrary to Hudson's Bay Company policy. In retaliation, the officer at Fort Carlton "seized the train of dogs which he had sold to Messiter & refused any further supplies."[35]

Messiter makes no mention of these activities in his book. He does, however, claim that in March Kihci-mōhkomān took him to a bear's den and assisted in arousing a still-hibernating mother and a "half-grown" male. Messiter killed both of them.[36] Interestingly, he said the den was about 40 miles north of his own cabin, near Kihci-mōhkomān's house. Since a number of other people were camped in the vicinity, Kihci-mōhkomān may have been living for at least part of the winter with or near Okīnomotayēw, the man who became chief of the Stoney Lake Band.[37]

Okīnomotayēw's small wintering house was located near Whitefish Lake, just a few miles north of where Cheadle and Milton had built their cabin. Kēhkēhkowāsis, Okīnomotayēw's father-in-law, was living with them.* In mid-February Okīnomotayēw and his 14-year-old son Maskwamāyow† took Cheadle onto the plains in search of the buffalo. They were fortunate in finding five bulls. Because the purpose of this trip was to get meat, not to participate in "sport," Okīnomotayēw left his son in the camp with Cheadle and stalked and killed one of the buffalo by himself. Kihci-mōhkoman, who had been after the same animals, joined Okīnomotayēw's group. He told Cheadle he had travelled to the plains "via" Ahtahkakoop's place and had not eaten for two days. He succeeded in killing the remaining four bulls, and then went to get his wife and family who were camped, without food, some distance away.

When Kihci-mōhkoman returned, he set his camp up near the place where the buffalo had been killed. Following closely behind him were five other lodges. Cheadle said they "were all in starving condition, not having tasted food for several days, and their prospects for the remainder of the winter were very unpromising, for no buffalo could be found."[38] All of

---

* Okīnamatayo translates into English as "a long goatee," similar to the goatee or tufted chin of a moose. Kēhkēhkowāsis means Hawk Child.

† Bear Tail. Cheadle sometimes referred to Maskwamāyow as Mishoo, or Tail.

these people, with the exception of Kihci-mōhkomān, were likely Woods Cree. Ahtahkakoop and his people, with their closer ties to the buffalo and the prairie, were prepared to follow the buffalo deeper onto the plains in search of food. Kihci-mōhkomān, for some reason, had chosen to remain in the wooded area.

Messiter had not accompanied Ahtahkakoop to the plains, probably for good reason. Cheadle, Milton, and the traders at Fort Carlton had all found Messiter difficult. Ahtahkakoop and his people found him equally irksome. Both Messiter's and Cheadle's written accounts provide details of a violent encounter between Messiter, Ahtahkakoop, and others in his band soon after the Englishman's arrival in the Thickwood Hills. Although the details differ, both accounts indicate that Messiter's supply of liquor was the underlying factor behind the incident. Messiter later claimed that Ahtahkakoop sent one of his sons-in-law back to his father's camp on "the Saskatchewan" to avoid any further confrontation.[39]

So, although Messiter's book gives the impression that he and Ahtahkakoop were on good terms for most of the winter, Messiter actually makes very few references to the chief in his book. This is in sharp contrast to Cheadle's journal, in which he documents regular contact with Okīnomotayēw, his son Maskwamāyow, and Kēhkēhkowāsis. Okīnomotayēw and the others supplied meat to Cheadle and Milton, took them on hunting trips, and generally befriended them.[40] Messiter seems to have been more or less on his own.

Badger left his wife and child with Ahtahkakoop's family "just before spring set in" and took Messiter back to Fort Carlton. The Fort Ellice Journal indicates that Messiter stopped at that post, situated near the junction of the Assiniboine and Qu'Appelle rivers, on April 22, 1863, on his way to the Red River Settlement and England. Cheadle and Milton left their wintering place on April 3, arriving at Fort Carlton on April 6; they left for the Rocky Mountains and the Pacific Ocean on April 10.[41]

CHAPTER EIGHT

Smallpox Kills Hundreds

A htahkakoop and his people, in the meantime, continued to follow their traditional way of life as they honoured the Creator and hunted and trapped to the cycle of the seasons.

For the young men, waging war on the Blackfoot Confederacy continued to be honourable. Nāpēskis and at least five others had been killed by the Blackfoot in 1861. A year or so later, when Messiter was wintering in the Thickwood Hills, one of Ahtahkakoop's sons was among the warriors who joined yet another war party. The warriors found a Blackfoot camp but they were discovered and one of their men killed. Several others were wounded and, according to Messiter's informant, the Cree only escaped because they were better on snowshoes than the Blackfoot.[1] This was only one of many skirmishes during the 1860s as the Cree raided and fought in Blackfoot territory. In retaliation, Blackfoot Confederacy warriors made forays into Saskatchewan River country. Occasionally women were stolen. Often these women were taken as wives and became part of the band. During warfare to avenge the death of a relative, women, children, and the elderly were killed along with the men.[2]

Despite the regularity of warfare, some years peace was made. Fine Day remembered years later that when the Blackfoot wanted to make peace with the Cree they "used to wrap twist tobacco and sweet grass in thick white flannel. They would leave this at the Hudson Bay store [fur trade post] and tell them that they wanted to make peace with a certain tribe. When that tribe came in the bundle was given to them. If they were willing to make peace they make a bundle in turn."[3]

The Cree sometimes made more dramatic overtures. One year a party of

Cree from the Carlton area, led by Mistawasis and Ahtahkakoop, travelled to the "elbow" near present-day Calgary to make peace with the Blackfoot. The Pipestem Bearer carried the sacred pipestem. Before sunrise on the day they were to enter the Blackfoot camp the Cree put on their best clothes. Then the warriors approached the camp. The Pipestem Bearer was at the front. He pointed the unwrapped pipestem towards the tipis as they approached. When the Blackfoot saw the Pipestem Bearer and the warriors they shouted, "The Sacred Stem is coming." During the peace talks the Cree exchanged clothing for horses and they made arrangements for the Blackfoot to come to Saskatchewan River country to formally ratify the peace agreement.[4]

National Archives of Canada, PA-028837

Born before 1854, Fine Day was a noted Cree warrior, hunter, and shaman in Sweetgrass's band. This photograph was taken in 1896.

The large camp the Cree came from extended over half a mile, and when the peace-makers returned home a crier travelled through the camp announcing the coming of the Blackfoot. In the words of an old man whose father had been a member of the peace-making party, the crier

> asked the people to keep the young men from doing any harm....
>
> Some days later the Blackfeet rode up singing and beating drums.... [The Cree] who had been in the advance party came forward and each of them took one Blackfoot into their dwelling for the night. In the morning all the Blackfeet went to the center of the camp and danced there. This dance was the ogihtcitaucimau [*okih-citāwisimowin*, or Warrior Dance]. The advance men then gave presents to the Blackfeet and received gifts in return. After this exchange of gifts the Blackfeet rode off ... escorted by the brave and respected men, onapihgaco wiyiuiwuk [*onāpēkāsowiyiniwak*,

or Brave Warrior People], so they might be protected from the young fellows.[5]

Sometimes, in an effort to maintain peace between the nations, children were exchanged or a leading man in an enemy band adopted a child or young man. Many stories were told of these happenings. For instance, Poundmaker, who later became a noted Cree-Assiniboine chief, was adopted by Crowfoot, a Blackfoot chief. Kayāsaskisin, or Old Moccasin,* was about nine years old when he was given to the Blackfoot in exchange for another boy. He stayed with the Blackfoot four years, and during this time he learned the Blackfoot language and the ways of these people.[6] He was a member of Little Pine's band.

Another story told of Naheyow from One Arrow's band. Naheyow was a young man when he went to Blackfoot country by himself to avenge the death of his father Cīpwastotin, or Pointed Cap. The Blackfoot were so impressed with Naheyow's bravery that he was adopted into one of their bands. The young Cree married a chief's daughter, re-affirmed his courage in battle numerous times, and eventually became a chief. A number of years later Naheyow returned to Cree country to find his mother. He was accompanied by his wife, a herd of 50 "loose" horses, and 25 mounted Blackfoot. When Naheyow found his mother's camp he left the horses and others in his party and—still dressed as a Blackfoot—went in alone. After their initial surprise, the people in the camp greeted him joyfully. Their chief selected 10 men to accompany Naheyow to where the Blackfoot were waiting and the entire group was escorted back to the Cree camp. The next day the 50 horses were distributed amongst the Cree and a peace treaty was made between the two bands.[7]

Other people told of Kā-āyimākohkēw, another Cree with Blackfoot connections. Contrary to his name, which meant Hard to Make Relations, this man spoke both Cree and Blackfoot and he travelled back and forth between Cree and Blackfoot camps, even during times of war.[8]

And then, in what was a highly unusual occurrence during a time of peace, Cree and Blackfoot people met on top of a large hill on what is now the Sweetgrass reserve. For almost two weeks they learned about each other, how they were the same, and how they were different. During the

---

* Kayāsaskisin, who was also known as George Atimoyoo (Dog Tail), was Smith and Lizette Atimoyoo's grandfather.

last two days the people from the two nations spoke about the negative and positive things they saw in each other. The Blackfoot said the Cree would always be poor because they were a jealous people. The Cree were even jealous amongst themselves, the Blackfoot said, and they talked about each other in negative ways. The hill where the Cree and Blackfoot met was called *nakīwaciy*, or Stopping Hill. It was because of what the Blackfoot said, an old man told his grandson, that he always counselled the younger Cree not to listen to gossip and to always be forgiving.[9]

Despite these overtures—and many others—peace seldom lasted long. The young men could not resist the excitement and glory that came from horse raids. With very little provocation, war would once again break out.

For many years the life of a buffalo hunter and his family had been one of independence and freedom. The Cree nation was powerful. Its people were numerous. The land was theirs and they roamed it freely, often travelling over 500 miles during the course of a summer.

Ahtahkakoop's friends and relatives were among the people from Saskatchewan River country who continued to travel to the upper reaches of the Missouri River. There they traded with the Mandans for valuable catlinite pipestone from Minnesota, sea shells from the ocean, chert (flint) from North Dakota, and other articles not readily available at home. Not surprisingly, friendships developed and occasionally the young people found mates during these trading expeditions.

It was a long journey from Saskatchewan River country to the Missouri River. *Pīkāno-sīpiy*,* the Cree called it. Sometimes the people had a hard time as they travelled, particularly if the weather was hot. Wāpasinīwiskwēw (White Stone Woman) told her grandson of such a journey and of how the Creator's helpers came to their aid.†

"Yes, it is true that my grandmother told this story," Lloyd Starblanket, Wāpasinīwiskwēw's grandson, said.[10] "One time Ahtahkakoop and some of the other people were travelling far away, going to the *pīkano-sīpiy*, as that river was called. They were heading south towards the river. It was a very hot day in the summer, and it was this one man who was speaking, 'Well,' he said. 'If I don't reach this river, *pīkano-sīpiy*, soon I will die.'

---

* Muddy River.

† Wāpasinīwiskwēw's story, which Lloyd Starblanket re-told in Cree, was taped and transcribed in Cree and then translated into English by Freda Ahenakew. Editing was minimal to retain the characteristics of Cree storytelling.

Illustration by Ed Peekeekoot.

Slowly a snake emerged from the clouds.

"And so they were travelling, and they were so tired from the heat, it was extremely hot. There was a shortage of water, they could find no water. They were so thirsty. It was noon now, she told us, and the young men had gone on horse-back. They had gone with buffalo paunches and bladders to fetch water, when suddenly they were seen coming exactly at noon. Now the people stopped to rest while they waited for the young men.

"Well, well! Suddenly a great many people were shouting. 'Look at this!' they cried out. There was a small cloud almost directly above but a little back of the people. The people were yelling about it. There was so much yelling! When they looked up, there it was, a little island-like cloud with a snake hanging from it. People were shouting, 'The Thunderbirds are pulling it up! A Thunderbird is pulling it up! The snake will kill us if he drops it.' The men lifted flags, offerings to the Thunderbird, and they pointed their pipes to the Thunderbird.

"This was so surprising to the people. The snake was moving and writhing. The snake was really swinging back and forth, and the cloud would come lower. It seemed the snake was pulling down the Thunderbird that was holding onto him. It was coming so close to the earth, but the Thunderbird was stopping it from coming down any further.

"Suddenly from the west there could be seen a small cloud coming very fast and thunder could be heard. 'It was from there now,' she said, 'it became dark.' There was so much thunder and lightning. The Thunderbirds were fighting this snake, and they were pulling it up into the cloud. Suddenly it started to rain. There was lots of rain, it seemed like pouring rain. And hail started to fall.

"Now there was great rejoicing amongst the people because they had been given so much water, and also ice water. There was great amazement at what they had seen."

"You could have used a ten pound lard pail to measure that snake," Wāpasinīwiskwēw told her grandson many years later. "The snake was that size."

"'Grandchild,' she continued, 'never believe a person who says there are no Thunderbirds. When they say that, do not believe them. There are Thunderbirds, my grandchild, I saw this for myself when the Thunderbirds pulled that snake up into the sky.'

"From that time there was much rejoicing. The people rejoiced at what they had seen and because they had been given so much water during the time that they were dying of thirst."

"'So it was,' Wāpasinīwiskwēw said, 'that no one left the camp for there was a bad storm.' The next morning the storm had quit, and then the people broke camp and travelled still further south. And so they arrived at *pīkano-sīpiy*, as the Missouri River was called.

"And after the time of this story they travelled north, back towards the *kā-kisiskāciwan*, the Saskatchewan River as it is called."

"This is what my deceased grandmother told me," Lloyd Starblanket said. "Wāpasinīwiskwēw, my grandmother was called. She was a really nice old lady, she was good natured, she was kind. This is the one who told me this story.

"Well, this was as far as she told me, this is not a lie."

"That's it."

In another story that has been passed down through the generations, two women and two little boys were returning to Saskatchewan River country from Montana.[11] One of the women had been married down there, the story goes, but the man's family was mean so the women and children were returning home on foot. The group had been travelling for a number of days when they saw a large cloud of dust swirling and rising from the ground. It was buffalo racing towards them. Frightened, the women and children looked for a safe place out of the path of the buffalo. The prairie was flat for miles around and there was no place to go. The women and children knelt on the ground and prayed. The buffalo divided and passed on either side of them, leaving them unhurt.

When these stories were told and re-told during the years that followed, the people gave thanks once again to the Creator and his helpers who guided and protected them.

Although the people continued to travel and live much as they had for generations, Ahtahkakoop and some of the other leaders recognized that changes were coming to their land. When Ahtahkakoop was young, for instance, upwards of 50 million buffalo roamed the plains. Many times the people gazed in wonder at the multitude of beasts spreading from horizon to horizon. For as long as Ahtahkakoop and the people who had come before him could remember, the buffalo—gift of the Creator—had provided food and just about everything else the people needed to survive. Indeed, the buffalo were part of their very being.

The white newcomers who arrived on the plains during the middle years of the 19th century also depended on the buffalo for food, but some of them killed for sport, and sometimes they took only the head. These newcomers also stood in awe when they saw the vast numbers of buffalo on the plains and, in the way of the white man, they recorded their observations in diaries and journals. Their words and images varied little. The Reverend Robert T. Rundle, the first Methodist missionary in Saskatchewan River country, wrote during a journey from Fort Carlton to Edmonton House in August, 1845, that they "passed or saw herds of buffalo more or less for five days. The immense quantity we saw would scarce be credited by an inhabitant of old England. They were in numbers—numberless. The largest herd I ever saw passed near our encampment. They had probably been startled near the river. My guide fired twice during the night to frighten them off from us."[12]

In 1848 artist Paul Kane witnessed buffalo that covered the "plains as far as the eye could reach, and so numerous were they that at times they impeded our progress, filling the air with dust almost to suffocation."[13] John Palliser, head of the exploratory expedition of 1857–1860, wrote that from two miles away the "peculiar grunt [of the buffalo] sounded like the roar of distant rapids in a large river" and there was a vibration "something like a trembling in the ground."[14] And some 10 years later—near the southern reaches of the South Saskatchewan River—it took hunters seven days to pass through a herd.[15]

Stampeding herds like the one encountered by the women and children walking home from the Missouri River were frightening. Often, however, the buffalo almost appeared docile as they parted to let humans pass through their midst. Isaac Cowie, an apprentice clerk at Fort Qu'Appelle, told of one such instance in the summer of 1869 when he "fell in with buffalo innumerable" between Last Mountain Lake and the elbow of the South Saskatchewan River.[16] The buffalo, he said

> blackened the whole country, the compact, moving masses covering it so that not a glimpse of green grass could be seen. Our route took us into the midst of the herd, which opened in front and closed behind the train of carts like water round a ship, but always leaving an open space about the width of the range of an Indian gun in our front, rear and flanks. The earth trembled, day and night, as they moved in billow-like battalions over the undulations of the plain. Every drop of water on our way was foul and yellow with their wallowings and excretions. So we travelled among the multitude for several days, save when we shot a fat cow for food or a bull made a charge and perhaps upset a cart before he was shot down, neither molesting nor molested.[17]

Although it was not immediately apparent to the newcomers, particularly those who were simply passing through Indian land on their journeys of exploration and adventure, the buffalo were dwindling in number and gradually retreating farther west and south. Some years the Indian people of the Carlton area were starving while those of the Fort Pitt and Edmonton House areas lived in plenty. Other years the situation was reversed.

Occasionally the buffalo stayed in the southern regions and did not migrate into the parklands. Such was the situation in 1867. Although both the summer and fall hunts had eventually been successful, the buffalo were "far off" and the hunters had travelled great distances to hunt. The buffalo did not return to the Fort Carlton area that winter. Since the fall hunt "we have not got an animal or seen a plain Indian," the officer in charge of Carlton reported in January of 1868. "The Buffalo are nowhere, and the Indians are starving."[18] To many, it seemed that the buffalo had disappeared from the face of Mother Earth. Of course they returned, but there was reason for concern.

Ahtahkakoop's people were more fortunate than many others, since in recent years they generally wintered in areas where moose, elk, deer, and other game were abundant. They had choices. If the buffalo did not move into their wintering grounds in any particular year, hunting parties were sent in search of the animals. If the buffalo were too far off to make travel practical, they had the option of concentrating on hunting and trapping woodland animals. And unlike the traders at Fort Carlton, who were obliged to remain at their post, Ahtahkakoop and his people were free to move to the most promising hunting grounds.

Changes, nevertheless, were coming. Ahtahkakoop was very much aware of this and he also sensed that the days of the buffalo were numbered. If the buffalo continued to disappear, or if they moved permanently beyond the range of his people, the chief knew that a new way of life would have to be found. This conclusion was based on information drawn from a number of sources. His brother Nāpēskis had travelled through American territory on his journey to Montreal. The young man brought back stories —confirmed from other sources—that Indian people in the American territories were being forced off their lands, and worse yet, were being killed by American soldiers. Nāpēskis also told of large numbers of white people crowded in cities and living on farms, and he told of wondrous things created by these white people.

Ahtahkakoop, too, had a variety of experiences in his own life beyond that of buffalo hunter. He was a trapper, warrior, and member of the *mitēwiwin*. He had rowed, sailed, and tracked York boats along the waterways to and from Hudson Bay in the company of European, French Canadian, half-breed, and Indian boatsmen. At the Hudson's Bay Company's great depot called York Factory he had seen the great body of water that was said to go all the way to England. He had witnessed for himself the large sailing vessels in the harbour and the storehouses overflowing with trade goods that had been unloaded from these ships.

Back in Saskatchewan River country, Ahtahkakoop's contact with the traders at Fort Carlton over a great many years, and even his association with men such as Messiter, provided glimpses of another way of life. Over the years he had listened to many stories about the people living in other parts of the world, and he doubtless was told about their cities, their technological advances, and their wars.

The Cree leader saw the fields of potatoes, turnips, oats, barley, and cabbage that the traders grew at Fort Carlton, and he knew that these foodstuffs were useful when other food supplies failed. It is even likely that some of his people had worked in the gardens at Carlton in exchange for supplies. Ahtahkakoop also knew that many of the traders and newcomers could read and write, and that a whole new world opened up when a boy or girl, man or woman possessed these skills. For the sake of their future, it was a world he was willing to have his children and grandchildren experience.

Along with all this, Ahtahkakoop and his people had been exposed to the white man's religion. In 1838 Roman Catholic priests had stopped at Fort Carlton on their way to Fort Vancouver. Methodist missionary Robert Rundle and two Catholic priests, Father Thibault and Father de Smet, held services and baptized children and adults during brief stops at Fort Carlton during the 1840s, and by the late 1850s the Reverend Henry Budd was travelling from his Anglican Nepowiwin Mission* to Fort Carlton and the traders' village at Moose Woods.[19] Then, in the early 1860s, the Reverend George McDougall established a Methodist mission at Victoria, 84 miles down river from Edmonton House.

As well, for a number of years Roman Catholic priests had been travelling with French-speaking half-breed buffalo hunters from the Red River Settlement. The mixed-blood descendants of French Canadian fur traders and Indian women, these people called themselves Métis.[†] During these expeditions, the priests visited the Indian camps and baptized the children while the men were off hunting or waging war.[20] Several of Ahtahkakoop's children had been baptized in this manner. The chief was to explain later that

> I was away on the warpath when the priest came to my tent and baptised my two children. My wife told me of it on my return. From time to time the priest came to my camp and baptised one after another of my children. I, myself, was never at home when he came."[21]

In telling the story, Ahtahkakoop said the children were never taught anything, and although baptized, they "grew up quite ignorant of Christianity."

Ahtahkakoop and others in his band were puzzled by the missionaries. The Nēhiyawak's daily life was guided by the Creator and his helpers. For them, there was only one God, the Creator or Great Spirit. It sometimes

---

* The Nepowiwin Mission was situated across the river from the Hudson's Bay Company's Fort à la Corne.

[†] The Red River Settlement and the Hudson's Bay Company's Upper Fort Garry formed the nucleus of the community that became Winnipeg.

seemed that each missionary had his own supreme being. Furthermore, each man seemed to think that his God and religion were the best. Often it appeared that the Roman Catholics, Methodists, and Anglicans were fighting with each other as they strived to convert the Nēhiyawak to Christianity.[22]

In about 1863 Ahtahkakoop was at Fort Carlton when the Roman Catholic bishop arrived from the Red River Settlement on a journey to the Catholic mission at Ile-à-la-Crosse. Since no one in the bishop's party knew the way, Ahtahkakoop offered to guide them. The bishop accepted, and the Hudson's Bay Company officer at Fort Carlton hired the chief and his horses to take them as far as Green Lake. The chief said that

> when we camped at night the Bishop asked me to come to
> prayers, I said I knew nothing about it—that I did not know what
> [Christian] prayer meant. The Bishop asked me if I hated religion,
> and I said I knew nothing about it. I asked the Bishop what was
> the use of the priest baptising my children and then teaching them
> nothing. I also said that if the Bishop would send someone to
> teach them I would allow it to be done. The Bishop promised to
> send a priest as a teacher in about a year.[23]

A priest was never sent and Ahtahkakoop and his followers continued to live by hunting.

By the 1860s irreversible changes that had nothing to do with religion were under way. In 1862 James Isbister, the half-breed postmaster at Fort Carlton, retired and established a farm in the vicinity of the North Saskatchewan River some 50 miles downstream from Fort Carlton. This farm became the nucleus of a settlement known as the Isbister settlement.[24] Four years later, in the summer of 1866, the Reverend James Nisbet founded a Presbyterian mission a few miles east of the Isbister settlement. The Hudson's Bay Company built a small post called Fort Albert to serve the settlement and mission, and within a few years the traders developed a farm near the post. The community that developed around the Isbister settlement, the mission, and the Hudson's Bay Company post was given the name Prince Albert.

Meanwhile groups of Métis buffalo hunters from the Red River Settlement started wintering at camps situated along the South Saskatchewan River east of Fort Carlton. These people, for nearly four decades, had driven long trains of ox-drawn carts, horses, and dogs onto

the plains to harvest buffalo products for trade and personal use.
With the buffalo retreating farther
west each year, the distances the
families had to travel increased.
Now some found it easier to winter
along the South Saskatchewan
River and trade at Fort Carlton
instead of returning to their homes.
One of these groups was led by
Gabriel Dumont.[25] By the fall of
1870 a large number of other
Métis, many with farming experience and dissatisfied with life in
the Red River Settlement, moved
west and built log cabins near the
wintering camps along the South
Branch. In response to a request for
a priest to minister to their spiritual
needs, Father Moulin was sent on a
temporary basis from Ile-à-la-
Crosse.

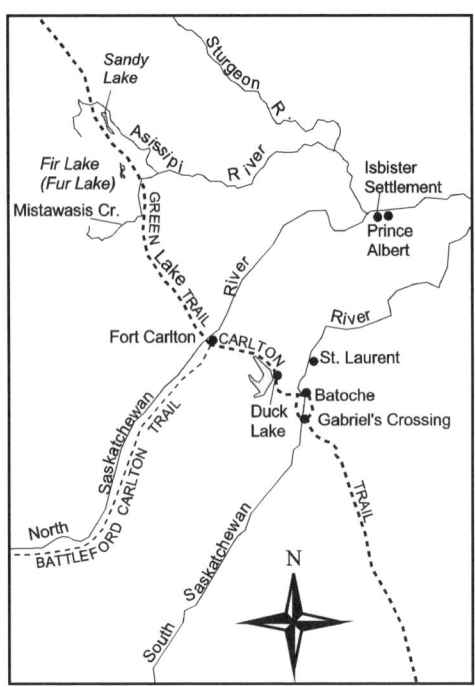

Information Systems Division, Canadian Plains
Research Center

*During the 1860s and 1870s new settle-
ments were established north and east of
Fort Carlton.*

This influx of people to the
Carlton district in 1870 was, in part, closely related to a series of events
unfolding far to the east. It had begun with the passing of the British North
America Act by the British Parliament in 1867. By this act the colonies of
Upper and Lower Canada (Ontario and Quebec), New Brunswick, and
Nova Scotia came together to form "one dominion under the name of
Canada." The new Canadian government almost immediately looked at
ways to expand its land base. To this end, negotiations were started for the
surrender of the Hudson's Bay Company's monopoly over Rupert's Land.
The ensuing discussions involved high-ranking officials of the Hudson's
Bay Company and the British and Canadian governments. The document
that finalized the transfer of Rupert's Land and the North-Western Territory
to Canada acknowledged the existence of aboriginal land claims and
"placed a constitutional obligation on the Canadian government to settle
those claims."[26] The Indian and half-breed peoples occupying these lands
were never consulted.

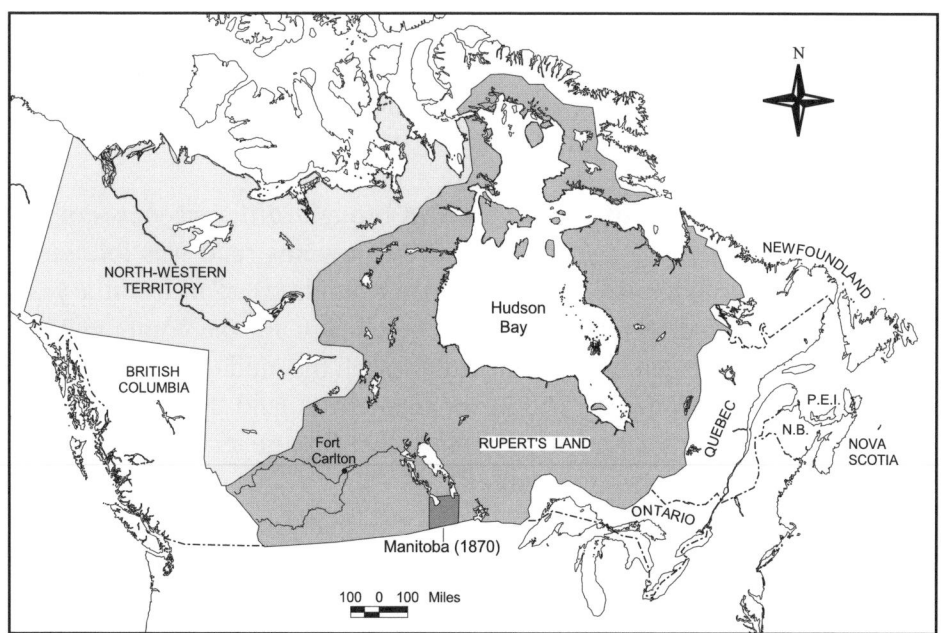

North-Western Territory

Hudson Bay

British Columbia

Newfoundland

Fort Carlton

Rupert's Land

Quebec

P.E.I.

N.B.

Nova Scotia

Ontario

Manitoba (1870)

100 0 100 Miles

Information Systems Division, Canadian Plains Research Center

On July 15, 1870, Rupert's Land and the North-Western Territory officially became part of the Dominion of Canada, followed by British Columbia in 1871, Prince Edward Island in 1873, the Arctic Islands in 1880, and Newfoundland in 1949.

In the Red River Settlement the situation provoked what has been called the Red River Resistance of 1869–70. Although the Métis living in the settlement, under the leadership of Louis Riel, eventually won provincial status, responsible government, and guarantees for land and cultural rights, the victory was hollow.[27] It was soon apparent that preserving their dignity and their way of life would be next to impossible in the new Province of Manitoba.[28] Louis Riel, fearing reprisals for his actions during the resistance, fled to the United States. Many other Métis families moved to the South Branch and other locales in the North-West.

The transfer of the vast lands lying north and west of the Red River Settlement—for the time being at least—went more smoothly for government officials. An order-in-council dated June 23, 1870, formally completed the transfer of jurisdiction, with admission of the North-West Territories to the Dominion of Canada to take effect July 15, 1870. In exchange for surrendering their charter,* the Hudson's Bay Company received one-twentieth

---

* The Hudson's Bay Company's charter had given the company a monopoly of trade in the area drained by rivers flowing into Hudson Bay. The company never "owned" the land, nor did it have political or territorial power over the Indian people.

of the land in the fertile belt, £300,000 cash, and title to all its trading post sites, along with 50,000 acres of land around its posts.[29] The Canadian government appointed Adams G. Archibald as lieutenant-governor to administer affairs in the new Canadian territory.

Canada's acquisition of the North-West brought different views of the world into potential conflict. The idea of owning land was foreign to the Indian people who often travelled many hundreds of miles in a year. The land was sacred, given to them by the Creator for the common good of the Indian people. No one had the right to sell the land. And in any case, the Hudson's Bay Company had never owned the land. How, the people asked, could the company sell something that had never belonged to it? And why had they not been consulted?

At the fur trade posts, Hudson's Bay Company officers found themselves in a situation of ever-declining influence. This was particularly true in the Edmonton district where an influx of white missionaries, gold miners, and free traders was challenging the authority of the Indian nations as well as that of the Hudson's Bay Company. Far to the south, in the Cypress Hills and the vicinity of the Belly, St. Mary, and Oldman rivers, American frontiersmen were building "whiskey posts" and flouting the authority of the new Canadian government. There liquor was being traded in atrocious amounts with tragic results. In the new Province of Manitoba race, religion, status, and wealth were increasingly being used to judge the worthiness of an individual. Because of this attitude, people of Indian and mixed Indian and white ancestry were becoming outsiders in their own land. And in Central Canada, settlers and businessmen were casting their eyes west, looking for a land of golden opportunity.

At Fort Carlton the officer in charge of the Carlton District, Lawrence Clarke, felt that missions and settlements hindered the fur trade. Accordingly, he had discouraged both within his area of jurisdiction. As a result, in 1870 there was only one mission, the newly established Nisbet mission at Prince Albert. The only farming activity, other than that carried out at Fort Carlton, was associated with the Isbister settlement, the Presbyterian mission, and the Hudson's Bay Company's Fort Albert. Because the population of the area had changed little, except for the Métis hunters who were wintering on the South Saskatchewan River and the village of free traders at Moose Woods, the district was not undergoing change as rapidly as the Edmonton region.

Nevertheless, undercurrents of uneasiness were circulating. For years men such as Ahtahkakoop and Mistawasis had experienced a good working relationship with the traders at Fort Carlton. They had worked co-operatively as partners with the Hudson's Bay, procuring pemmican, dried meat, fat, leather, and robes for them. They had hunted for the company, worked as boatmen, guides, and freighters, and assisted in a variety of other ways. In return, the chiefs and their bands had been supplied with tobacco, guns, ammunition, traps, kettles, axes, and other trade goods. This was their land—Indian land. To a great degree, this fact had been respected by the Hudson's Bay Company traders, for they recognized that without the goodwill and assistance of the Indian people the fur trade in the North-West could not have survived, let alone grown. Now this was changing. The Métis hunters living on the South Branch were taking over the role of suppliers of buffalo meat for the company. They were trying to impose their hunting laws on the Indian people, and increasingly they were serving as guides and freighters.

Indian goodwill was still essential because the whites were greatly outnumbered. But the Indian people were no longer as important in the gathering of provisions, and the fur trade was in decline. The balance between the Indian people and the traders that had developed over a great many years was shifting to favour the traders.

The plight of the buffalo was of even more concern. Some years it seemed that the buffalo had vanished from the face of the earth. Many people believed the buffalo would re-appear. Life would return to normal. Others recognized that their people would have to look towards the future and start adapting to the changes, many of which were beyond their control.

And there were other worries. Ahtahkakoop, Mistawasis, and the other chiefs in the North-West of course knew about the transfer of Rupert's Land to the Dominion of Canada. They also knew that the Canadian Government had sent troops to the Red River Settlement to intimidate the Métis and half-breeds and thus ensure the orderly transfer of jurisdiction. From the south they heard stories about broken promises, fighting between American troops and Indian nations throughout the territories of Dakota and Montana and, worse yet, the Americans' policy of extermination.[30]

Closer to home, in their own territory, the Indian leaders were angry about the half-breeds' practice of poisoning wolves and foxes, and they complained that this drastically reduced the number of animals available to trappers. They resented the fact that their dogs died from eating the poisoned meat, and many of the people felt that their horses were perishing from eating grass that had been tainted with strychnine.[31] Moreover, their own people were dying from the rot-gut liquor flowing freely from the traders' camps and from the violence and degradation it provoked. Mistawasis's son was one of the casualties, stabbed during a drinking binge.

Many times Ahtahkakoop and Mistawasis talked into the night about what was happening in their land and beyond. Not only did the chiefs have frequent opportunities to discuss a variety of matters with traders and visitors, but the chiefs both had daughters married to Hudson's Bay men.[32] All this gave them additional insight into the white world and the white way of thinking. It also gave them a perspective of the future that differed from the future envisioned by some of the other Indian leaders. Their position was one of influence, and because of this they were listened to carefully at council meetings with other chiefs and headmen. Indeed, the two chiefs had already taken action. Troubled by the large amount of liquor the free traders were bringing into Indian lands, and well aware of its effect on their people, Ahtahkakoop and Mistawasis had called a council meeting to discuss the situation. As a result of the discussion, a petition was drawn up requesting that the sale of liquor be prohibited in the North-West. This petition, added to the many requests from others for action, was one of the factors that led to the Canadian government's decision to create the North-West Mounted Police.[33]

In 1870 tragedy struck as smallpox raged through the western and northern portions of the North-West. Of necessity, many of the concerns of the Indian leadership were put on hold. The epidemic had been rampant in the Missouri River region the previous summer. News of the disease's approach reached Isaac Cowie, the young clerk at Fort Qu'Appelle, in the fall of 1869. Using small pieces of window glass he took lymph from the arm of a healthy child who had recently been vaccinated at the Red River Settlement. He then undertook his own vaccination program, claiming that he obtained enough lymph to vaccinate "every one requiring it in the fort, from whom the supply was increased sufficiently to vaccinate all the people about the lakes and the Indians visiting them that fall.... those who had been vaccinated at the fort took it [the vaccine] out to the plains and spread it so thoroughly there among the Qu'Appelle and Touchwood Hills Indians that not one single case of smallpox was ever heard of among them."[34]

Even though there had been advance warning that smallpox was sweeping through the American territories, the Indian people and most fur trade posts north and west of Fort Qu'Appelle, for whatever reason, were not adequately prepared for the possibility of an epidemic.[35] By early 1870 some members of the Blackfoot Confederacy were stricken by smallpox through contact with Indians and traders living on the upper reaches of the Missouri River. They carried the pestilence north. In April, 17 Cree warriors "on a raid against the Blackfoot" became infected when they "came upon a Blackfoot camp in a valley." Fine Day said two men from his band were in the war party. According to Fine Day, who was about 15 at the time, the warriors

> saw many crows hovering and the tipis all closed up. They went up, looked into one tipi and saw a corpse all covered with sores. One said, "We'd better go back home." They did, but first [they] cut a piece out of the tipi to cover themselves.

> One of them died before they got home. The other fell sick and was covered with sores. Once they thought he was dead and put him on a travoix before burying him. But he breathed again. They took him off. A second time they thought he was dead and the crier yelled out to prepare the grave. He started to breath again. He died twice in one day. Then he got better but very many Cree caught it from him and died."[36]

The Cree warriors took the disease to their bands. The pestilence then swept down the North Branch of the Saskatchewan River, carried by people trying to escape the terror.[37] By early August 1870, smallpox in one of its most deadly forms reached Fort Carlton. The Indian and half-breed population of Saskatchewan River country was devastated.

At Fort Carlton, 32 of the approximately 70 people living at the post caught the dreaded disease. Women and children were hit the hardest. Twenty-eight people died. Only one of the victims—the clerk at the post— was white.[38] William Traill, who was in temporary charge of Fort Carlton during the summer of 1870, was credited with saving a number of lives. It was said that the young officer "laboured with untiring perseverance in ministering to the necessities of the sick, at whose bedsides he was to be found both day and night, undeterred by the fear of infection, and undismayed by the unusually loathsome nature of the disease."[39] Elsewhere there was anger. At Fort Edmonton some people blamed the traders for causing the epidemic. And at Fort Pitt, it was said that "two hundred Indians died and they brought their dead and threw them against the stockades to try and give the infection to the whites."[40]

William Francis Butler, an official representative of the newly appointed lieutenant-governor of Manitoba, arrived at Fort Carlton early in November, four weeks after the last smallpox victim had been buried. He had been sent to Saskatchewan River country to report on the state of the territories and, in particular, the need for a small force of troops to protect settlements and Hudson's Bay posts. Because of the outbreak of smallpox, Butler's duties were expanded to include inquiring and reporting on the effect of the epidemic. Butler was also to give medicine and written instructions to responsible people in the field, a move that was too late to be of much assistance. In any case, he said "it was found … that many of the bottles had been much injured by frost, and I cannot in any way favourably notice either the composition or general selection of these supplies."[41]

In his official report, written at the completion of the tour of Saskatchewan River country and dated March 10, 1871, Butler wrote that

> To estimate with any thing like accuracy the losses caused among the Indian tribes is a matter of considerable difficulty. Some tribes and portions of tribes suffered much more severely than others. That most competent authority, Père Lacombe, is of opinion that neither the Blood nor Blackfeet Indians had, in proportion to their numbers, as many casualties as the Crees, whose losses may be safely stated at from 600 to 800 persons…. On the other hand, the Assiniboines, or Stonies of the Plains, warned by the memory of the former epidemic [1837], by which they were almost annihilated, fled at the first approach of the disease, and keeping far out in the south-eastern prairies, escaped the infection altogether….
> Altogether, I should be inclined to estimate the entire loss along the North Saskatchewan, not including Blood, Blackfeet, or Peagin Indians, at about 1200 persons.[42]

Butler recognized the difficulty in estimating the number of deaths in such a vast land and his figures are low compared with other sources. For instance missionary John McDougall, who lost two sisters to the disease at the Victoria Mission, stated that "east and west and south, all over the land, the death roll was fearful; fully fifty per cent of the people being carried away."[43] And Ahtahkakoop, six years later, said "the great sickness took half our lodges."[44]

Elsewhere in his report, Butler said that

> the enormous percentage of deaths [was not] very much to be
> wondered at when we consider the circumstances attending this
> epidemic. The people, huddled together in small hordes, were des-
> titute of medical assistance or of even the most ordinary require-
> ments of the hospital. During the period of delirium incidental to
> small-pox, they frequently wandered forth at night into the open
> air, and remained exposed for hours to dew or rain; in the latter
> stages of the disease they took no precautions against cold, and
> frequently died from relapse produced by exposure; on the other
> hand, they appear to have suffered but little pain after the primary
> fever passed away. "I have frequently," says Père André, "asked a
> man in the last stages of small-pox, whose end was close at hand,
> if he was suffering much pain; and the almost invariable reply was,
> 'None whatever.'" They seem also to have died without suffering,
> although the fearfully swollen appearance of the face, upon which
> scarcely a feature was visible, would lead to the supposition that
> such a condition must of necessity be accompanied by great pain.[45]

The death of so many was horrific for Ahtahkakoop and the other sur-
vivors in his band. To make the situation even worse, a vast tract of land
lying west and southwest of Fort Carlton lay burnt in the fall of 1870. The
devastated area began within half a day's travel of Fort Carlton and extended into the Thickwood Hills. Grasses and trees had been destroyed, hills
denuded.[46] The buffalo stayed away and other game fled or died. Deprived
of their traditional wintering grounds, the families in Ahtahkakoop's band
were forced to winter in other locations, probably towards the Battle River
or in the wooded country to the north.

The shortage of buffalo was not confined to the Thickwood Hills and
the immediate vicinity of Fort Carlton. Butler reported that he did not see
"even one solitary" buffalo during the trip from Red River to the Rocky
Mountains[47] and at Fort Carlton

> the few Indians that had come in from the plains brought the same
> tidings of unsuccessful chase—for the buffalo were "far out" on
> the great prairie, and that phrase "far out," applied to buffalo,
> means starvation in the North-west.[48]

It was a devastating time for the Indian bands of the plains and parklands. Physically weakened, emotionally drained, and still mourning the

death of their relatives and friends, the people were forced to pitch camp and travel until they found enough food to survive. Additionally, because of the devastation caused by the epidemic, the people had been unable to make the long trek onto the southern plains to gather a supply of leather, robes, pemmican, dried meat, fat, berries, and roots. It would be a hard and difficult winter.

CHAPTER NINE

Concerns in Indian Country

In November of 1870 Ahtahkakoop and his band were likely part of a
large group of Cree camped upstream from the junction of the Battle
and North Saskatchewan rivers. A small trading house erected by
traders from Fort Carlton stood nearby.[1] Perhaps the Cree had assembled at
the post because they heard that a man sent by the Queen's representative
was coming their way. Or maybe they had gathered for another reason.
Regardless, when Butler heard about the camp he decided to stop there on
his way to Edmonton House. His visit, however it came about, made sense.
The chiefs and leading men were anxious to talk to someone about their concerns, and Butler had been instructed to gather information on the Indian
people living "on the line between Red River and the Rocky Mountains."[2]

A lieutenant in the 69th Regiment, the 32-year-old Butler had been part
of the force sent to the Red River Settlement earlier in the year to ensure a
peaceful transfer of power from the Hudson's Bay Company to the
Dominion of Canada. According to his instructions, confirmed in a letter
dated October 10, 1870,[3] Butler's new duties were directed to four general
areas. In addition to reporting on the effect of the smallpox epidemic, he
was to determine the necessity of sending troops to "assist the local authorities in the maintenance of peace and order." He was asked "to ascertain as
far as in his power, the number of Indians on the line between Red River
and the Rocky Mountains; the different nations and tribes into which they
are divided and the particular locality inhabited, and the language spoken,
and also the names of the principal chiefs of each tribe." In connection with
these inquiries, Butler was instructed to be "careful to obtain the information without in any manner leading the Indians to suppose … [he was] acting under authority, or inducing them to form any expectation based on …
[his] enquiries."

Lastly, Butler was to inquire into certain matters connected with the fur trade, including the number of furs traded, the number and nationality of the people involved in the "Free Trade," and "what portion of the supplies, if any, come from the United States territory, and what portion of the furs are sent thither."

To facilitate his work, Butler was given the "rank and status of Justice of the Peace" and the authority to bestow the same commission on "two gentlemen in the Saskatchewan."[4]

Clad in moccasins, leggings, buffalo "mittaines," and a capote,[5] Butler arrived at the Cree camp near the confluence of the Battle and North Saskatchewan rivers the morning of November 16. The two-and-a-half day journey from Fort Carlton had taken him through the snow-covered tract of burnt land west of the post. Although he found the camp free of smallpox, Butler said "the traces of its effects were to be seen in the seared and disfigured faces around." The half-breed trader living in the small shanty at the camp was also "awfully marked by the terrible scourge."[6] He was one of the four people at Fort Carlton who had been stricken with the disease and survived.

According to Butler, the camp was under the leadership of Mistawasis, whom he described as "a man of small and slight stature, but whose bravery had often been tested in fight against the Blackfeet. He was a man of quiet and dignified manner, a good listener, a fluent speaker, as much at ease and as free from restraint as any lord in Christendom."[7]

Mistawasis headed the delegation of leading men that met with Butler in the traders' small wintering shanty. The other leaders were not named. In the account of the meeting published in his book *The Great Lone Land*, Butler said that he spoke first and explained the purpose of his visit to the North-West. His words were translated by an interpreter. Mistawasis, he said, bent his head in assent after every sentence. There was a pause after the lieutenant finished talking and then Mistawasis spoke.[8]

"He wishes to know if aught can be done against the Blackfeet," the interpreter told Butler. "They are fond of war. He has seen war for many years, and he would wish for peace. It is only the young men, who want scalps and the soft words of the squaws* who desire war."

---

* The word "squaw" is an English derivative of *iskwēw*, the Cree word for "woman." Through use by non-Indian speakers, the word "squaw" has become a derogatory term.

*These photographs of half-breed men posing inside Fort Carlton and an Indian
camp near the post were taken in 1872 by Charles Horetzky, another newcomer.
Horetzky accompanied Sandford Fleming as he surveyed a proposed railway
route across the parklands and northern prairies.*

"The Great Mother wishes her red children to live at peace," Butler responded, "but what is the use? Do they not themselves break the peace when it is made, and is not the war as often commenced by the Crees as by the Blackfeet?"

Butler, in his account, does not give Mistawasis's reply.

Mistawasis spoke again, saying "men have told them that the white man was coming to take their lands, that the white braves were coming to the country, and he wished to know if it was true."

"If the white braves did come," Butler replied, "it would be to protect the red man, and to keep peace amongst all. So dear was the red man to the heart of the chief whom the Great Mother had sent, that the sale of all spirits had been stopped in the Indian country, and henceforth, when he saw any trader bringing whisky or fire-water into the camp, he could tell his young men to go and take the fire-water by force from the trader."

When Mistawasis heard that their petition to prohibit the sale or trade of liquor had been successful he replied: "That is good! That is good!"[9]

After the meeting was over the Indian leaders left the traders' shack. Before long Butler heard loud drumming. Going to the door, he found the young men assembled to perform the "dance of welcome" in his honour. At the conclusion of the dance, Butler "gave an order for tobacco all round."[10]

Butler submitted a report to Lieutenant-Governor Adams G. Archibald after completing his trip through Saskatchewan River country.[11] In it he recorded some of the concerns expressed by the chiefs and headmen during his journey.

The Indians, he said, were understandably worried about the rapid decline in the buffalo and were "not slow to attribute this lessening of ... [their] principal food to the presence of the white and half-breed settlers,* whose active competition for pemmican (valuable as supplying the transport service of the Hudson Bay Company) has led to this all but total extinction of the bison." He went on to say that the Indians also traced

> other grievances—some real, some imaginary—to the same cause. Wherever the half-breed settler or hunter has established himself

---

* Butler uses the term "settler" in a very general sense to include white settlers and French- and English-speaking half-breeds who were not employed by the Hudson's Bay Company.

he has resorted to the use of poison as a means of destroying the wolves and foxes which were numerous on the prairies. This most pernicious practice has had the effect of greatly embittering the Indians against the settler, for not only have large numbers of animals been uselessly destroyed, inasmuch as fully one-half the animals thus killed are lost to the trapper, but also the poison is frequently communicated to the Indian dogs, and thus a very important mode of winter transport is lost to the red man. It is asserted, too, that horses are sometimes poisoned by eating grasses which have become tainted by the presence of strychnine; and although this latter assertion may not be true, yet its effects are the same, as the Indian fully believes it. In consequence of these losses a threat has been made, very generally, by the natives against the half-breeds, to the effect that if the use of poison was persisted in, the horses belonging to the settlers would be shot.[12]

Butler listed six "settlements" in an appendix to his report. All were categorized as "half-breed settlements," and only one (Prince Albert) was on land that is now part of the Province of Saskatchewan. English half-breed settlements had also been established at Victoria and Whitefish Lake in present-day Alberta.[13] French half-breed settlements were located at Lac la Biche, St. Albert, and Lac St. Anne.[14] He made no mention of the Métis wintering camps on the South Branch.

Butler included some words of warning in his report. The policy of the free trader was, he said, "essentially a short-sighted one—he does not care about the future—the continuance and partial well-being of the Indian is of no consequence to him."[15] In regards to the white man he wrote:

To the white man, as a white man, the Indian has no dislike; on the contrary, he is pretty certain to receive him with kindness and friendship, provided always that the new-comer will adopt the native system, join the hunting-camp, and live on the plains; but to the white man as a settler, or hunter on his own account, the Crees and Blackfeet are in direct antagonism. Ownership in any particular portion of the soil by an individual is altogether foreign to men who, in the course of a single summer, roam over 500 miles of prairie.[16]

He noted that the number of "white settlers" in Saskatchewan River country who were not working for the Hudson's Bay Company was "numerically insignificant." Nevertheless, he feared that the discovery of gold on the eastern base of the Rocky Mountains would attract a great number of miners. The result, he suggested, could well be the eruption of open hostility between miners and the Indians "inhabiting the neighbour-hood of such discoveries, or the plains or passes leading to them." He also cautioned that the "Indians and halfbreeds are aware of their strength, and openly speak of it." He added that from his view the situation was more volatile in the Edmonton District and in the vicinity of Victoria and Fort Pitt than on the "lower portions of the river."[17]

Butler said his recommendations to the lieutenant-governor were made "with a view to bringing the regions of the Saskatchewan into a state of order and security, and to establish the authority and jurisdiction of the Dominion Government, as well as to promote the colonization of the coun-try known as the 'Fertile Belt,' and particularly to guard against the deplorable evils arising out of an Indian war." They included the appoint-ment of a civil magistrate or commissioner; this official, he suggested, should live in the "Upper Saskatchewan" and be assisted by civil magis-trates appointed by the Hudson's Bay Company and drawn from the "most influential and respected persons of the French and English half-breed pop-ulations." He also recommended the establishment of a "well-equipped force of from 100 to 150 men, one-third to be mounted" and the establish-ment of two government "stations." The first station, he said, should be near Edmonton House and the other one at the "junction of the North and South Branches of the River Saskatchewan." Then, following the estab-lishment of the government centres, Butler stated that steps should be taken to extinguish "Indian title, within certain limits, to be determined by the geographical features of the locality."[18]

During the months after Butler's visit, the chiefs, headmen, and other leading men met to discuss the rumours circulating through Saskatchewan River country. Talk about their land being "sold" was par-ticularly troublesome. The land was sacred. It belonged to no one man and it could not be sold.

Nevertheless, many of the chiefs knew that more and more newcomers were arriving in their country each year, and that these people would want to divide the land into pieces for farms and towns. Additionally, it was becoming increasingly evident that many of the newcomers showed little respect for the Indian people. The Métis from the Red River Settlement

Illustration by Ed Peekeekoot

The chiefs and leading men met in council to talk about the changes in their land.

were not only beginning to act as if they owned the land, but they were trying to take over the buffalo hunt and enforce their laws on the Indian people. Moreover, half-breed free traders were still trading liquor indiscriminately. Even the officers at the Hudson's Bay Company posts, particularly on the upper reaches of the North Branch of the Saskatchewan River, were losing control and seemed to have little authority. And far to the south, their enemies—the Blackfoot, Peigan, and Bloods—were armed with repeating rifles obtained from American traders.

Still weakened by the smallpox scourge and often hungry, the Indian leaders continued to evaluate their situation. They knew that Indian people in Manitoba were preparing to negotiate treaties with the Queen's representatives, and that people living in other parts of the country had already signed treaties. Most of the chiefs in Saskatchewan River country were willing to share their land, but not until a formal agreement was finalized guaranteeing their rights. They wanted a treaty signed one nation with another. And so discussions continued throughout the winter.

The buffalo remained "far out" on the plains during the winter of 1870-71. Surviving was difficult and by spring 15 bands from the immense Saskatchewan River region were camped at the Hand Hills. These hills lay on the north side of the Red Deer River, far beyond their traditional wintering grounds.*

"In sorrow and in hunger and with many hardships we have gathered here, where we have grass and timber, and since we came, buffalo in the distance, few, though still sufficient to keep us alive," Chief Wihkasko-kiseyin (Sweetgrass) told missionary John McDougall when he visited the camp in late March or early April. "We have grumbled at hunger and disease and long travel through many storms and cold; our hearts have been hard, and we have had bitter thoughts and doubtless said many foolish and bad words.... Your coming has done us good; it has stayed evil and turned our thoughts to better things. We feel today we are not alone."[19]

Once again the chiefs had questions. When McDougall was unable to answer many of them, a party of chiefs representing the Plains Cree travelled to Edmonton House to meet with Chief Factor W.J. Christie. As the officer in charge of the Hudson's Bay Company's Saskatchewan District, Christie was the most influential non-Indian in the North-West Territories.

Sweetgrass, leading chief of the Fort Pitt area, was selected as spokesman when the delegation met with Christie on April 13, 1871. Other chiefs in the group included Kihiwin (The Eagle) and Onataminahos (Little Hunter), who generally wintered in the Saddle Lake region, and Kiskayo (Bob Tail) from the Buffalo Lake area. Their discussion was of such significance that Christie wrote to Lieutenant-Governor Archibald immediately after the meeting. "The object of their visit," Christie reported,

> was to ascertain whether their lands had been sold or not, and what was the intention of the Canadian Government in relation to them. They referred to the epidemic that had raged throughout the past summer, and the subsequent starvation, the poverty of their

---

* The Hand Hills are in present-day Alberta, almost directly south of the elbow of the Battle River.

country, the visible diminution of the buffalo, their sole support, ending by requesting certain presents *at once*, and that I should lay their case before Her Majesty's representative at Fort Garry. Many stories have reached these Indians through various channels, ever since the transfer of the North-West Territories to the Dominion of Canada, and they were most anxious to hear from myself what had taken place.

I told them that the Canadian Government had as yet made no application for their lands or hunting grounds, and when anything was required of them, *most likely Commissioners* would be sent beforehand to treat with them, and that until then they should remain quiet and live at peace with all men. I further stated that Canada, in her treaties with Indians, heretofore, had dealt most liberally with them, and that they were now in settled houses and well off, and that I had no doubt in settling with them the same liberal policy would be followed.

As I was aware that they had heard many exaggerated stories about the troops in Red River, I took the opportunity of telling them why troops had been sent; and if Her Majesty sent troops to the Saskatchewan, it was as much for the protection of the red as the white man, and that they would be for the maintenance of law and order.

They were highly satisfied with the explanations offered, and said they would welcome civilization. As their demands were complied with, and presents given to them, their immediate followers, and for the young men left in camp, they departed well pleased for the present time, with fair promises for the future. At a subsequent interview with the Chiefs alone, they requested that I should write down their words, or messages to their Great Master [the lieutenant-governor] in Red River. I accordingly did so, and have transmitted the messages as delivered.[20]

The petitions delivered by Sweetgrass, Kihīwin, Little Hunter, and Bob Tail were included with Christie's letter. Christie recorded them as follows:

Messages from The Cree Chiefs of The Plains, Saskatchewan, To His Excellency Governor Archibald, our Great Mothers Representative at Fort Garry Red River Settlement.

1. The Chief, Sweet Grass, The Chief of the Country.

GREAT FATHER

I shake hands with you and bid you welcome. We heard our lands were sold and we did not like it, we don't want to sell our lands, it is our property, and no one has a right to sell them.

Our country is getting ruined of fur-bearing animals, hitherto our sole support, and now we are poor and want help—we want you to pity us. We want cattle, tools, agricultural implements, and assistance in everything when we come to settle—our country is no longer able to support us.

Make provision for us against years of starvation. We have had great starvation the past winter, and the small-pox took away many of our people, the old, young, and children.

We want you to stop the Americans from coming to trade on our lands and giving firewater, ammunition and arms to our enemies the Blackfeet.

We made a peace this winter with the Blackfeet. Our young men are foolish, it may not last long.

We invite you to come and see us and to speak with us. If you can't come yourself, send some one in your place.

We send these words by our Master, Mr. Christie in whom we have every confidence.—That is all.

2. Ki.he.win, The Eagle.

GREAT FATHER,—Let us be friendly. We never shed any white man's blood, and have always been friendly with the whites, and want workmen carpenters and farmers to assist us when we settle. I want all my brother Sweetgrass, asks. That is all.

3. The Little Hunter [Onataminahos].

You, my brother, the Great Chief in Red River, treat me as a brother, that is, as a Great Chief.

4. Kis.ki.on, or Short Tail [Kīskāyow, Bob Tail].

My brother, that is coming close, I look upon you as if I saw you; I want you to pity me, and I want help to cultivate the ground for myself and descendants. Come and see us.[21]

Elsewhere in his dispatch to the lieutenant-governor, Christie mentions that copies of the proclamations prohibiting "the traffic in spirituous liquors to Indians or others, and the use of strychnine in the destruction of animal life, have been received, and due publicity given to them." He cautioned, however, that

without any power to enforce these laws, it is almost useless to publish them here; and I take this opportunity of most earnestly soliciting, on behalf of the Company's servants, and settlers in this district, that protection be afforded to life and property here as soon as possible, and that Commissioners be sent to speak with the Indians on behalf of the Canadian Government.[22]

The tone of a memorandum included with Christie's letter differed considerably from the main text. His account of the meetings implied that a friendly exchange had occurred. However, in the memorandum, the Hudson's Bay Company official stated that if he had "not complied with the demands of the Indians—giving them some little presents—and otherwise satisfied them, I have no doubt that they would have proceeded to acts of violence, and once that had commenced, there would have been the beginning of an Indian war, which it is difficult to say when it would have ended."[23] It is very likely that Christie exaggerated the possibility of violence. Most of the spokesmen were generally considered to be friends of the traders and a number of them had converted to Christianity.

Regardless of how he perceived the currents underlying the meeting, Christie recognized the need for the government to act quickly to quell the growing uncertainty and upheaval. He pointed out to the lieutenant-governor that "the buffalo will soon be exterminated, and when starvation comes, these Plain Indian tribes will fall back on the Hudson's Bay Forts and settlements for relief and assistance." Provision must be made to deal with this situation, otherwise he feared violence and bloodshed would result. Christie also expressed the concern that if gold were discovered "in paying quantities" on the eastern slopes of the Rocky Mountains—an event he expected to occur almost any day—a large number of miners would "rush into the Saskatchewan, and, without any form of Government or established laws up there, or force to protect whites or Indians, it is very plain what will be the result." He again stated that the establishment of law and order and "the making of some treaty or settlement with the Indians who inhabit the Saskatchewan District" were of vital importance "to the future of the country and the interest of Canada." Although he did not mention it, Christie no doubt also felt that these steps were crucial to the continued successful operation of the Hudson's Bay Company in the North-West Territories.

In the summer of 1872 Ahtahkakoop and members of his band were living in houses at Fir Lake,* near the trail linking Fort Carlton with Green Lake.[24] Called the Green Lake Trail, this road had been an Indian track until the Hudson's Bay Company started hauling pemmican by dog-sled from Carlton to their post at Green Lake. From Green Lake, the pemmican was transported to Ile-à-la-Crosse, where it was distributed to the boat brigades carrying furs and trade goods along the Churchill River and other northern waterways.

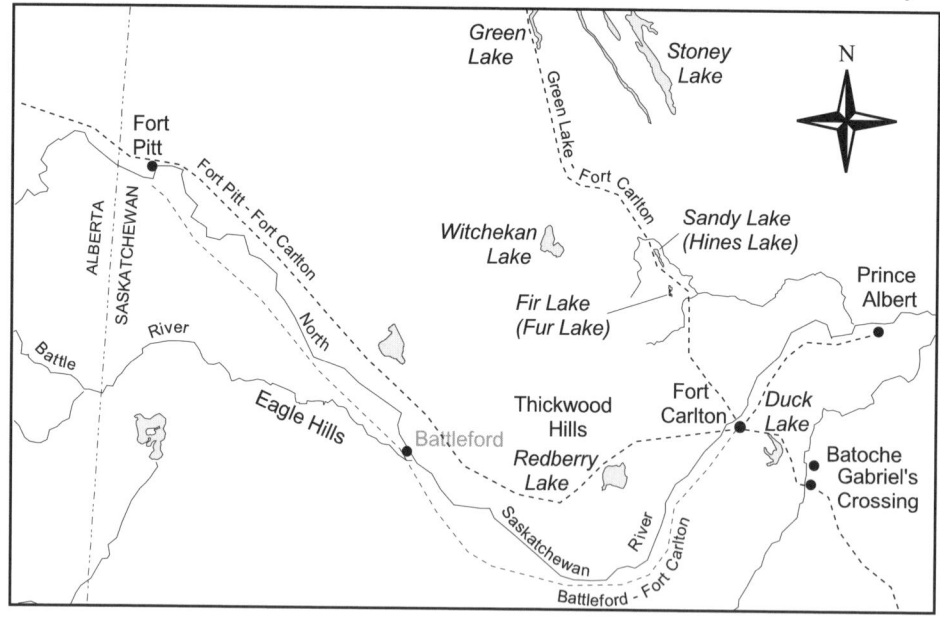

Information Systems Division, Canadian Plains Research Center

By the early 1870s Ahtahkakoop and some of his people had built wintering cabins at oskācakāwikamās, *or Fir Lake, near the Green Lake Trail. Several trails now led from Fort Carlton to the Battle River post, Fort Pitt, and Edmonton House.*

---

* Fir Lake (*oskācakāwikamās*) is located a mile west of present-day Mont Nebo. On current maps this lake is called Fur Lake.

During the 1860s, the Hudson's Bay Company began shipping goods from New York to Fort Garry by rail, steamboat, and ox cart.[25] From Fort Garry, hundreds of ox carts carrying freight to Fort Carlton lumbered across the plains. A faint overland trail soon became a multi-track road etched firmly into the ground. This trail became known as the Carlton Trail. When the carts reached Carlton, they were unloaded, the cargo was sorted and re-packed, and then trade goods and supplies were forwarded to posts situated to the east, west, and north. Freight for the English River (Churchill River) and Athabasca districts was carted via the Green Lake Trail. Fort Carlton became an important distribution and administration centre, with the Green Lake Trail providing an important link to fur-rich lands in the Churchill River region and beyond. Although the old water routes leading to Hudson Bay continued to be used, their importance diminished.

By the early 1870s, when Ahtahkakoop and members of his band built their one-room cabins at Fir Lake, the Hudson's Bay Company's overland system of transport had been in place for almost a decade. Of course these routes were not new. Indian travellers had used the Carlton and Green Lake trails for decades, and some 10 years earlier Southesk, Cheadle, Milton, and other newcomers had travelled inland from eastern points by rail, steamer, horseback, wagon, and buckboard. Nāpēskis had also travelled overland by horseback and train instead of traversing the waterways when he went to Montreal.

By choosing to live near the Green Lake Trail, Ahtahkakoop and his band had taken a crucial step in their adaptation to the changes taking place around them. Instead of following the buffalo onto the distant southern plains, they chose to spend more time near their hunting grounds in and near the parklands. Their cabins became a semi-permanent base from which to hunt buffalo and trap fur-bearing animals. They also undertook their first attempts at cultivating the soil, and in 1872 had planted both a garden and a plot of potatoes. Gardening, however, was not very compatible with buffalo hunting. The people were away from their homes for extended periods and forces of nature, such as heat, drought, hail, grasshoppers, and weeds, all took their toll.

Their nearness to the Green Lake Trail and Fort Carlton opened up new possibilities for men in Ahtahkakoop's band. In earlier years some of the men—including Ahtahkakoop and his brother Masuskapoe—had worked on the York boats travelling to York Factory.[26] Now the men and young men were hired as dog-team and ox-cart drivers, freighters, and guides in the endless task of delivering provisions, trade goods, and fur packs on the overland trails.

There were also numerous opportunities for Ahtahkakoop to learn about events taking place farther afield from travellers who stopped to rest and exchange news. One of the visitors at Fir Lake in the fall of 1872 was W.J. Christie, the Hudson's Bay Company official who had met with Sweetgrass and the other chiefs the previous year. Christie, now an inspecting officer with the company, was on a tour of posts strung out from Fort Garry to Fort Simpson on the Mackenzie River. A man travelling with him was well-known to Ahtahkakoop. He was Daniel Villebrun, who had married Ahenakew's daughter Marie Louise two years earlier.[27]

The journal Christie wrote during his trip included a description of the Green Lake Trail and two stops at Ahtahkakoop's houses at Fir Lake:

> [September] 10th [1872]. Left Carlton at 9 A.M. Horses not being found at once delayed us. Had two carts and two men from Carlton, with buckboard which I drive myself. Daniel Villebrun accompanies me as my servant to and from Fort Simpson. The two men and carts to return from the Green Lake store [storehouse] with furpacks from Athabasca....
>
> Fine open country today, with bluffs of poplar occasionally most beautiful. Country and soil good. Took dinner at lake on left of track. Shortly after dinner on resuming our journey one of the carts got the axle broken, and, having no spare one, had to camp early in order to give them time to come up [with a new axle]. Pine trees now on left of track—the first I have seen since leaving Pine Creek. Met some Crees on their way to Carlton and had a talk with them about lands, trade and debts &tc.
>
> 11th. Breakfasted before sunrise. Left camp at 6 A.M. After leaving camp ground hilly. Plains and at times through woods. The road being new is rather rough for a buckboard. Pines more frequent. Passed At-ah-cu-coop's (Star Blanket) house. Found his wife there—garden full of weeds—potatoes neglected—got kettle full of potatoes from them—have a lake full of whitefish near them but no net, so got no fish from them.
>
> After leaving the houses passed along the shore of lake. Several

lakes on each side of the road—one of them large. The country is
most beautiful in places, rolling prairies and plenty of timber.
Hills to the right. Dinner at Shell River—a fine place for a settlement, soil good. After dinner through hills and woods and came to
a lake abounding in whitefish. One Indian tent here, but having
just come they had no fish. Came on over a side hill and crossed a
river in a canoe, which we got from an Indian. Then Cypress
Hills, with plenty of blue berries. Camped in a fine plain near
Whitefish Lake. Passed several lakes this afternoon. Water fine
everywhere.

12th. Started after an early breakfast. Shortly after the strong
woods commenced and the road became very rough.
Consequently I left my buckboard here, to be taken back by the
Carlton men, and took to the saddle.[28]

Christie reached the south end of Green Lake on September 13, four
days after leaving Fort Carlton. He journeyed by canoe to Portage la Loche
where he crossed the height of land separating two great water systems and
continued his journey by canoe and boat down the Clearwater and
Athabasca rivers to Fort Chipewayan at the western end of Lake Athabasca.
His voyage then took him down the Peace River to Slave River, Great
Slave Lake, and the Mackenzie River. He reached Fort Simpson on the
Mackenzie on October 21.

"Thus terminated this long journey of over 2000 miles from Fort Garry
to Fort Simpson, by land and by water, through lakes and rivers, over
portages, with horses and carts, with boats and canoes, without accident,"
he wrote in his journal. "Time occupied between Fort Garry and Fort
Simpson 61 days, and deducting 15 days for stoppages en route gives 46
days actual time travelling."[29]

Christie spent just over a month at Fort Simpson and then returned to
Fort Carlton by dog sled. On January 27, 1873, he

took dinner at Sandy Lake. Followed on through lakes well wooded
with pine, and camped at Attuckacoop's house, early, on margin
of a lake. Fine clear weather but cold. Found a clean house here
all ready for our reception, with wood cut ready for our chimney
fire. We passed a pleasant evening, everyone pleased with the
prospect of reaching Carlton House tomorrow and getting letters
from the outside.

[January] 28th. Left house, our comfortable hotel of last night, at 4 a.m. Had some difficulty in keeping the track in the dark. After daylight, followed the cart track all the way. We have now left the woods and fine green brush behind us and it is monotonous prairie now all the way, with occasional bluffs of poplar here and there. We took dinner at noon, and, after a tramp of 50 miles arrived at Carlton House in the evening.[30]

Christie made no mention of it in his journal, other than noting that they passed a "pleasant evening" at Fir Lake, but Ahtahkakoop must have asked many questions about the government's intentions and the future confronting the Indian people. The government had taken no action in response to the chiefs' petitions and to the concerns expressed by Christie in 1871. Life in the new North-West Territories continued to be one of uncertainty, rumour, and hardship. The winter of 1872–73 had not been an easy one for the Indian people. Buffalo had been scarce and reports reaching Fort Carlton indicated that the people "were starving all over the plain country, and eating their dogs and horses." Horses were also dying from sickness.

To make the situation even worse, rain had fallen in January, creating a hard crust on the snow. Many of the horses found it impossible to break the crust to reach the grass and were starving to death.[31] Deprived of buffalo, and now their horses, life was becoming increasingly difficult. And in the Moose Woods area, free traders "in dozens" were selling and trading liquor "right and left."[32] There may have been a government proclamation making it illegal to traffic in liquor but, as Christie had feared, it was not worth the paper it was written on.

PART THREE

A New World

Illustration by Ed Peekeekoot

Adapting to a new life.

CHAPTER TEN

The Arrival of John Hines, 1874-1875

It was the summer of 1874 and Ahtahkakoop and his people were travelling to Fort Carlton to get supplies before heading south to hunt buffalo. Ahtahkakoop was on horseback, riding just far enough back to avoid the dust raised by the string of squeaking carts. He had been hunting as they travelled and a few ducks hung across the front of his saddle.[1]

A few miles northwest of Fort Carlton, the band met a party of six men —two of them white—travelling on the Green Lake Trail with 12 ox carts, a wagon, and a buckboard. When Ahtahkakoop got to Carlton, he asked Lawrence Clarke, the factor in charge of the post, about these men. Who were they? What were their intentions, and where were they going?

He was told that the group had been sent by the Church Missionary Society. Administered by a committee in England, this society was responsible for the Church of England's missionary work among native peoples in North America. The leader of the group was Archdeacon Abraham Cowley, an Anglican clergyman from Winnipeg. A half-breed from Winnipeg accompanied him as a servant. Another young man of mixed Indian and white ancestry in the group had just completed his education at St. John's College in Winnipeg. He was en route to the far northern Diocese of Athabasca where he was to serve as a teacher.

John Hines was the fourth man in the party. Twenty-four years old, Hines was the son of an English farmer and a recent graduate of the Church Missionary Society Training Institute in Reading, England. He had been sent by the society to set up an Anglican mission and model farm "for the benefit of the Cree Indians of the great prairie."[2] The committee members apparently were not familiar with the terrain or location of the Indian bands when they issued their instructions, for the young missionary had been told to settle at Green Lake.

Two men accompanied Hines. George McKay, 20, was a half-breed from a respected fur trade family and Lawrence Clarke's new brother-in-law. He was another recent graduate from St. John's College. He spoke fluent Cree and English, and had been engaged by Hines as an interpreter and teacher.[3] The other man was David Stranger, 44, a Swampy Cree from St. Peter's Mission in Manitoba. He had been hired to assist the English missionary "in whatever kind of work" was required. The carts, oxen, and supplies that made up Hines's outfit had been purchased in Winnipeg.

When Ahtahkakoop asked Clarke about the loaded carts, he was told that most of them were hauling supplies for missions in the Athabasca Diocese far to the north. The goods were to be delivered to the Hudson's Bay Company's storehouse at the southern end of Green Lake. From there, they would be forwarded on Hudson's Bay Company boats. The rest of the carts belonged to the young English missionary who was looking for some Indian people to teach.[4]

Clarke likely also told the chief that a troop of red-coated North-West Mounted Police would soon be travelling through the Carlton District on its way to Edmonton House. The act proclaiming the formation of the police force had been passed by the Canadian government in 1873. Now, in 1874, the force was slowly making its way into the North-West Territories. Most of the policemen were being sent to the region west of the Cypress Hills, for it was there that lawlessness and a venomous liquor trade were at their worst. Smaller numbers of police were to be stationed at Swan River near Fort Pelly, where it was proposed to establish the headquarters for the North-West Mounted Police, and at Edmonton House. The message and manner in which the information was given to Ahtahkakoop was not recorded, other than Lieutenant-Governor Alexander Morris[5] had directed Hudson's Bay Company officials to "explain to the Plain Cree Indians the steps taken by the Queen for the preservation of law and order in Her North-West Territories."[6]

Farther to the west William McKay,* the factor at Fort Pitt, was sent onto the plains to inform bands trading at his post about the impending arrival of the police force. The Hudson's Bay Company officer left on his

---

* George McKay's father.

mission August 8 and had to travel seven days before reaching Big Bear's camp of 65 tipis. McKay explained at this camp and the others he visited that

> the object of the Queen in sending a force of Mounted Police into Her Territories was for the preservation of law and order and prevention of aggression on the part of lawless American traders against Her Indians [*sic*] subjects & others of [distributing] intoxicating liquors amongst the Indian tribes. I also requested them to give the Force their good will as coming from Her Majesty the Queen and as being designed to promote peace, harmony, and happiness amongst her people in the North West and that their co-operation was not requested in any action which the Police Force may find it necessary to take nor were they asked to act as allies for any Military purpose. That the Force is sent for the purpose of expressing the good will of the Queen and Her care for Her Indian subjects and are asked therefore to regard the Force with a friendly eye. I also told them it was the wish of the Queen and Her servants to deal friendly and justly by them as she and they have always done in Her Territories and that their welfare is as dear to Her and them as that of Her white subjects.[7]

The chief factor at Edmonton House arranged for missionary John McDougall to deliver a similar message to the Blackfoot and Stoneys in the south-western portion of the territories.

Although Ahtahkakoop welcomed the news that a police force was coming to stop the liquor trade, he was particularly interested in the arrival of John Hines. For 11 years the chief had been waiting for someone to come and teach his children and grandchildren. During this time he and his leading men had carefully observed the clergymen and other newcomers who passed through their country.[8] Additionally, Ahtahkakoop had prayed to the Creator, asking that He send someone who could be trusted, a man who would live with them and be a helper in prayer, farming, and education.[9] After asking Clarke a few questions about John Hines and his plans, the chief got his supplies and left for the plains in search of buffalo. He felt certain he would meet the missionary again.

The archdeacon's party, in the meantime, continued along the Green Lake road. Since the officer at Fort Carlton had raised some questions about the suitability of Green Lake for farming, Hines left his carts and supplies at Whitefish Lake* in the care of David Stranger. Hines, Cowley, and the rest of the men then resumed their journey. John Hines wrote about this trip and his other experiences in the North-West in a book entitled *Red Indians of the Plains* and in a series of journals, letters, and reports.

The young missionary soon saw for himself that the country towards Green Lake was not suitable for his mission. "In the first place," he explained later, "every day's journey from the Saskatchewan River took us that much further from the Plain Cree Indians, for whose welfare I had been sent out." He also noted that although the soil was good, it "was too encumbered with wood to permit of much progress being made in farming, as it would take years of labour and a mint of money to put under cultivation sufficient quantity of land to accommodate the number of Indians I had hoped, in God's appointed time, to collect around me."[10]

Hines and his travelling companions reached the south end of Green Lake on August 13.[11] After depositing the goods for the Diocese of Athabasca in the Hudson's Bay Company's storehouse, Bishop Cowley prepared to return immediately to Whitefish Lake. These plans changed when they met a Roman Catholic priest, "with his own boat [a flat-ended scow] and crew, just on the point of starting for the north end, where the H.B. Company's business establishments are situated." The young Englishman wanted to see more of the area, so arrangements were made for Hines and George McKay to catch a ride with the priest. The two men were soon to regret the decision. After arriving at the post, the priest discovered that Hines was a missionary from a competing denomination. Upset, he used his influence among the Indians and French-speaking half-breeds to discourage anyone from helping the newcomers. When Hines and McKay could not get anyone to ferry them back to the south end of the lake, the trader in charge of the post finally sent them to the opposite side of the lake in a company canoe. From there the two men walked the 20 miles to the south end of the lake, unarmed and without food, through dense bush cut by streams and deep gorges.[12]

It was a miserable trip. A severe thunderstorm struck soon after Hines and McKay left the trading post and it rained for most of the day, soaking

* Now identified on maps as Little Whitefish Lake, this body of water is situated a few miles north of where Cheadle and Milton had wintered in 1862–63.

them to the skin. To make matters worse, Hines's new English knee boots were poorly suited for struggling through bush and muskeg and walking on uneven ground. Before long the young missionary's feet were so sore he was unable to walk. McKay gave his moccasins to Hines and pulled the stiff English boots onto his own feet. The young teacher did not wear them for long and he walked bare-foot the rest of the trip. Hungry and wet, bitten raw by mosquitoes, and sore-footed, Hines and McKay eventually reached the place where Cowley was waiting. Hines reported that he was "more convinced now than ever that Green Lake was not a suitable locality for establishing our new Mission."[13]

The group then separated. The teacher who was travelling to the Athabasca District was reluctant to continue his journey with strangers so McKay, against the wishes of Hines but approved by Cowley, accompanied the young man as far as Ile-à-la-Crosse. Hines, Cowley, and his servant returned to Whitefish Lake where David Stranger had remained with Hines's carts. The archdeacon and his servant then headed back to Winnipeg, leaving the missionary and his helper to fend for themselves. "For the information of those who look upon missionary work as an expensive hobby, and that it pays a man to become a missionary," Hines was to write many years later, "my salary, which was to be £100 per annum, only commenced on the day the Archdeacon left me alone on the banks of White Fish Lake." His personal debt on that date, accumulated in acquiring his outfit and paying other necessary expenses, totalled £80.[14]

John Hines was well suited for the task ahead of him. He had been born on a farm in Cambridgeshire, England, in 1850. As the eldest son, it was expected that he would eventually take over his father's farm. Thus between the ages of 16 and 21 Hines said he worked "daily on the farm like an ordinary labourer." Increasingly, however, the young man became interested in church work and decided that he wanted to become a minister. After upgrading his education, he was accepted by the Church Missionary Society for its 10-month course at Reading. On completion, he embarked for the North-West Territories from Liverpool on May 12, 1874.[15]

Now, some three months later, Hines was left standing beside David Stranger on the shore of Whitefish Lake "without a house or any kind of shelter to protect, either … [himself] or property from the weather."[16] His outfit was piled about him. It included a tent, bedding, clothing, food, and cooking utensils. To assist with the task of building, there were nails, hinges, a pit saw, a grinding stone, and an assortment of carpenter's tools.

His other Winnipeg purchases included a plough, a harrow, "certain kinds of seeds," harness, a light wagon, and several carts. Two horses and three oxen grazed nearby.[17]

The first taste of winter came early that year. Blustering rain turned into a snowstorm, and by September 10 four inches of snow lay on the ground. Hines said he "felt the cold very much indeed, the only shelter we had then, was, three carts forming three sides of a square, and an oilcloth on the top —but the wind & snow came under the cart so furiously that I thought it colder than being exposed & often took a rum to warm myself."[18]

The weather warmed, the snow melted, and Hines and Stranger started preparing for winter. Although the oxen in Hines's possession would be useful once farming activities started, they presented immediate problems for the newcomers. Hines had realized that a store of hay would have to be cut to get them through the winter. He did not, however, anticipate the second problem. The oxen were determined to return home to Winnipeg. At every opportunity they fled the camp, and in one instance the animals reached the banks of the North Saskatchewan River before they were caught by a passing freighter. Hines explained that it was

> the natural instinct of domestic animals in that cold country to remember the place where they were housed and fed the previous winter, and when the autumn comes on, no matter where they may be, if not closely herded, they will go away stealthily and travel hundreds of miles back to their previous winter quarters. And so it was with our cattle.[19]

In between keeping an eye on the oxen and searching for them when they disappeared, Hines and Stranger built a storehouse for their year's supply of food and other goods. Then they started work on a log dwelling house 10 by 14 feet in size. Surprisingly, up until then they had not seen any Indian people in the area. Now this changed.

The two men were cutting trees for their house when about 12 Indians on horseback rode up at a full gallop. They were dressed in buckskin clothing, head-dresses, and feathers. Their faces were decorated with paint and every man in the party carried a gun. One member of the group was Kihci-mōhkomān (Big Knife), the man Messiter, Cheadle and Milton had met during the winter of 1862–63.

Otayapīhkēw (Netmaker) was the leader of the group. He asked Hines who he was and why he was cutting down the trees. With Stranger acting

From John Hines, *Red Indians on the Plains*

Otayapīhkēw led the group that confronted John Hines and David Stranger at Whitefish Lake in the fall of 1874.

as interpreter, Hines explained that he was a missionary looking for a place to settle and some people to teach. Otayapīhkēw quickly replied that they did not want missionaries in their country. He then asked what Hines had brought in his carts, saying that if Hines would trade with them, he could stay. Otherwise, they were "to lose no time in getting out of his country."[20]

Hines said "I explained to him that I was not sure of staying in that place more than one winter, and that as soon as we had prepared our winter quarters and my interpreter had returned, I should travel east, west, north, and south, in search of a place suitable for the work I had in hand, and I named the different places I hoped to visit. But it did not signify what place I named, he declared himself to be the chief of all the people."[21]

Unimpressed by Hines's explanation, Otayapīhkēw demanded payment for the trees that were being cut. In addition, he wanted a weekly supply of food in exchange for use of the ground where Hines was building his winter quarters. The missionary refused, saying they only had enough to feed themselves during the winter. The discussion went on for an hour or so. Hines finally came up with what he thought was a fair compromise. "Let us go on quietly with our work and remain here undisturbed until the winter's snow has melted," he suggested, "and in the meantime try and make yourselves acquainted with our ways and the object of our coming amongst you and then, but not before, say if you still wish us to leave you or not, for it is so unreasonable to say you do not want us, nor anything we have come to do, until you have had an opportunity of proving whether it be good or not."[22]

Hines noted that this proposal seemed to appeal to Otayapīhkēw's followers, since "they thought it was only right to give us a trial." Otayapīhkēw was less certain. Nevertheless, he apparently agreed and asked for some food to make a feast when he got home. "Feeling sure that we had more than held our ground," Hines said he gave the chief a little flour, some tea, sugar, a few dried apples, and a few pieces of tobacco. A man who claimed to be second in command asked for similar presents and received the same items, but in smaller amounts. Otayapīhkēw later demanded money for the hay Hines was cutting but the Englishman refused. Later, however, when Otayapīhkēw's son came and said his wife had just given birth to their first son and "had a longing" for some tea and a little flour, the young missionary "made up a parcel that would do her good." It contained a few pounds of flour, a little piece of butter, some rice, sugar, and a can of condensed milk.[23]

George McKay, Hines's teacher and interpreter, returned from Ile-à-la-Crosse while the hay was being cut. He brought word that the Hudson's Bay Company man in charge of the Green Lake post considered Otayapīhkēw to be an impostor. According to the trader, Otayapīhkēw's followers consisted of his four sons and his son-in-law.[24]

Hines and Stranger discussed the size and type of stable to be built for wintering the cattle. Then the missionary left the construction work to his helper while he and McKay "began to explore" the country. The man who had identified himself as second in command to Otayapīhkēw accompanied them as a guide. They travelled first to Pelican Lake (Chitek Lake), situated about 75 miles northwest of Whitefish Lake. Here they found ten families camped. Hines outlined his plans to build a mission, but "they did not seem inclined to be interested, neither did they care to show us their country."[25] These people also said that since not all of them were present, they would not agree to have their children taught. Hines noted that at least some of the people in the camp wore a cross, or what Hines called the priest's "brand." This, he said, indicated that they had been baptized by Catholic clergymen.[26]

Undaunted by his earlier experiences, Hines then returned to Green Lake. This time a local Indian man agreed to show him some of the country around the north end of the lake. The tour confirmed the missionary's first impression that the area was not suitable for growing grain and raising cattle, and he retraced his steps to Whitefish Lake.

Then, with winter fast approaching, Hines helped Stranger and McKay finish the stable. They caulked the cabin walls to prevent the cold from seeping through the cracks, and pulled nearly 250 whitefish from the lake. Hines said the fish "averaged about three pound each [so] we thought ourselves rich indeed."[27]

Despite this statement, John Hines was troubled. While training in England, he had eagerly looked forward to working with the Indian people of the North-West. Many times he had prayed that "the Lord would be preparing a people for me" and that "His Holy Spirit might be at work upon their hearts, preparing them for the reception of His word."[28] He had now been in the North-West for several months and had met with one discouragement after another.

Determined not to give up, the young missionary left his cabin and travelled south to an area 20 miles from Whitefish Lake. Here he "found a place affording every thing that is required for the establishment of a

Mission … Plains for farming, Wood for building, Lakes for fishing & hay for cattle." Hines liked what he saw and decided that this was the ideal place to establish his mission and farm. There was one drawback. He had not seen any Indian camps in the neighbouring country. And so, taking the initiative, Hines sent McKay to Fort Carlton to talk to "the Chief of the plain Indians whom I heard was staying there for a short time." The interpreter was instructed to tell this chief about Hines's arrival and his desire to see him.[29]

Ahtahkakoop had travelled many miles onto the plains in his search for buffalo. The animals had been butchered where they fell. The meat and fat were processed, the hides scraped, and berries, roots, herbs, and medicines gathered. Then the hunters and their families headed towards Fort Carlton to trade part of their harvest for the supplies required for the coming winter. Although they were bringing back an adequate supply of food, the trip had been unsettling. The herds were small and scattered, alarmingly different from only a few years ago when the buffalo were so numerous that the possibility of their disappearance had been inconceivable.

Ahtahkakoop had thought about the young missionary who was looking for a people to teach during the two months he was on the plains. For a number of years he had realized that irreversible changes were coming to Indian land. Part of being a visionary and a good leader was determining what would happen to his people if he did not do something, if he did not find someone who could teach them how to adapt and survive in the new world.[30]

And so Ahtahkakoop fasted and prayed to the Creator, asking for his guidance and help. The Creator had given the buffalo to the people so they could live. The buffalo had provided almost everything they needed to survive. It was part of their life and their heritage. Now these animals—once so plentiful they were uncountable—were becoming more difficult to find each year. Even though the people prayed and held their ceremonies, still the buffalo much too often did not come or were "far off." And the people asked themselves, had they done something wrong? Had they done something to offend the Creator, the spiritual being who had been an integral part of every day life from time immemorial, the Creator who gave them life?

And other things were happening as well. Sicknesses that could not be cured were striking down the Indian people more frequently than ever before. Only four years earlier the dreaded smallpox had killed half of their people. Increasingly, greater numbers of newcomers were arriving each year. Some were simply passing through Indian territory. Others intended to stay, and it was said that many more were coming. A few of the newcomers preached about a Christian God, baptized the children in the name of this God, and continued their journey to wherever they were going. There was talk of treaty-making. There was also talk that the Hudson's Bay Company had sold Indian lands to the Canadian government.[31] Ominously, pressing down on a people who had lived a free and self-reliant life, was the fear that the buffalo, their livelihood, and their lands were disappearing.

It was a time of self-questioning, introspection, and doubt. Ahtahkakoop and his people prayed, and they fasted and held ceremonies as they looked to the Creator for answers. The people, the Nēhiyawak, knew that whatever road they chose, they would need the blessing of the Creator. Without that, they would fail. Ahtahkakoop acknowledged, nevertheless, that if they were to survive his people needed someone to show them how to farm, teach them how to read and write, and help them expand their knowledge in other ways. Being a spiritual people, they also needed a "praying master" to tell them about the Christian God. If this God was the same spiritual being as the Creator—and they believed He was—there was much more to be learned and understood. They owed that to the Creator and to themselves.

When Ahtahkakoop learned during the summer of 1874 that an English missionary with a plough and oxen had come looking for some Indian people to teach, he believed his prayers had finally been answered. "I consider I have waited long enough," he had told Clarke when he heard of the young Englishman's plans. At first, the chief was going to leave his people and go after Hines. But, as he later explained to the missionary, "when the trading master told me you would not stay at Green Lake, as he felt sure the country would not suit you, and as there seemed a likelihood of seeing you again I went on with my people."[32]

Ahtahkakoop discussed the future many times with his headmen, members of his family, and others in his band while they were on the plains that summer. They decided it was time to act. And so, when his people were within 100 miles of Fort Carlton on their return trip, the chief and one of his younger sons left the main party to look for the missionary.[33] They soon learned that Hines was going to winter at Whitefish Lake. This lessened the urgency of finding him, and Ahtahkakoop decided to stay at Fort Carlton until his people arrived with their buffalo-laden carts.[34]

While he waited, Ahtahkakoop learned what had happened during his absence. Two events were likely of particular interest. On September 5, 1874, almost a month earlier, the *Northcote* sternwheeler had puffed around the bend in the river and docked at Fort Carlton, creating tremendous excitement amongst men, women, and children of all ages. Six days later, after dark on September 11, approximately 20 dishevelled North-West Mounted policemen under the command of Inspector W.D. Jarvis and accompanied by horses, oxen, cows, carts, and wagons struggled up to the gates of Fort Carlton. The men were part of Troop "A" and were en route to their new posting at Fort Edmonton. The early storm that chilled Hines to the bone had played havoc with the policemen and their livestock. Disheartened and in a weakened condition from the wind, rain, bitter cold, and snow, the troop stayed at Fort Carlton almost a week before crossing the river to continue its journey.[35] For the Indian people visiting at Fort Carlton, this was their first glimpse of the force that had been created to preserve law and order in the North-West Territories.

All the excitement was over by the time Ahtahkakoop rode into Fort Carlton, but stories were still being told around the campfires. Once again, there was concrete evidence that life was changing, and that many of these changes were beyond the control of the Indian people.

Ahtahkakoop was still waiting at Fort Carlton for his people to come in from the plains when George McKay arrived with Hines's invitation to come and meet with him.[36]

Hines and Stranger were sitting outside the cabin at Whitefish Lake when Ahtahkakoop, his son, and McKay arrived by horseback on Saturday, October 10. Dismounting, the father and son shook hands with the missionary and his helper. Hines was impressed with Ahtahkakoop from his very first glance and later wrote that he had never seen "a finer built man than the elder of the two. He stood over six feet high, and was well proportioned." Hines added that the son (probably the son later called Joseph) was about sixteen years old.[37]

Shortly after the chief's arrival, Stranger made tea and they all "partook of a frugal meal." Then Ahtahkakoop and Stranger smoked "the pipe of peace in silence." Hines was apparently unaware of the significance of the pipe and did not join them, saying he did not smoke. McKay also refused to take the pipe. When the pipe was empty, Ahtahkakoop reminded Hines of their chance meeting on the Green Lake Trail:

From John Hines, *Red Indians on the Plains*

Ahtahkakoop met John Hines for the first time on October 10, 1874, as David Stranger (left) and Ahtahkakoop's youngest son watch.

I have travelled many miles since I saw you. I never had to go so far before to seek buffalo, and then we only saw a few. The buffalo are getting very scarce and our country is becoming very poor. When I think of the large herds of buffalo and other animals that used to roam about our country, and compare the state of things then with what they are now, my mind gets troubled. The wild animals may last my time out, but when I look into the faces of my children and grandchildren, my heart weeps for them, for I cannot see how they are going to live. I am not like many of my countrymen. I have seen this calamity coming upon us for years past, but some will not believe it even now, and I have had a longing desire to settle down and get my living like the white man, but I have had no one to teach me."[38]

"Mostly every year Ministers are passing through My country," Ahtahkakoop continued. "I always behave kindly to them, and beg of them to stay with me and my people, but no they say, they cannot do this, they were not sent out to Me but to other Indians."[39]

The chief went on to say that he had given up hope of having a minister to teach his people. He felt the loss very much for, as he explained, "I love my children & am anxious that they should know mor [sic] of the God Who Made them, than I their father."[40]

There was a pause, and then Ahtahkakoop told Hines, "I have said enough ... and I will listen to you now."[41]

Hines replied that his

object in leaving the country across the great water, where the great Queen lived, and coming many miles to see his country was that the praying masters over there had heard from one of their Bishops that the Indians in the Saskatchewan country were likely, in the course of a few years, to come face to face with starvation, owing, as he had just said, to the disappearance of the wild animals, and this same Bishop had asked the praying masters to send some one who would live with these Indians and teach them, not only how to cultivate the ground and raise food from it, but also teach them to raise cattle which would to a certain extent take the place of the buffalo, and also teach the Indians how to make grease from the milk of the cow. This, the Bishop said, would attract the Indians around the missionary, and then he could have a school and teach the children to read and understand the white man's language, and so prepare them for the change that was bound to come over their country before the end of the present generation, and he could also teach the old people about "Keche Munnato"* (the Great God) from His own great Book."[42]

"The praying masters in England had kind hearts," Hines continued, "and they were sorry when they heard of the distress of the Saskatchewan Indians, and they had asked me if I would leave my home and friends and go out and live among these strange people, and try to learn their language, and teach them all those things that the good Bishop had suggested; and I said that I would go—believing it to be the will of the 'Keche Munnato' that I should do so, and 'here I am.'"

Ahtahkakoop, who by now had decided that this was the teacher he had been praying for, responded, saying,

> "I am well pleased with what you say. My heart is touched by the kindness of people I never saw, and I believe 'Keche Munnato' wishes us to know all the things you have spoken about, and that is why He made you ready to come, and I promise that I will use my influence to make our new effort a success."[43]

With these basic understandings in place, Ahtahkakoop and his son stayed at Hines's cabin for two nights, thus giving each side a chance to appraise the other. Hines also took the opportunity to start the process of converting Ahtahkakoop to Christianity. The Englishman spoke about "the wisdom and goodness of the Keche Munnato," and he told the chief that he had been praying that God would "prepare a people for me to work amongst, and to-day I realised that He had heard my prayer and granted my request, and I wanted him to believe that God had been preparing him and his people as much as He had me for the great work that was before us." According to Hines, the chief "assented, saying he hoped soon to understand these things better, but at present he was only like a little child in understanding."[44] Hines, nevertheless, was aware that this was an intelligent man sitting and talking with him. He was particularly impressed with the answer "the plains chief" gave when asked "if he thought he was a sinner."

"Among the Indians ... [I am] considered a very good man," Ahtahkakoop had replied, but "I have no doubt 'Muneto' (God) can see things in one that are not pleasing to him & therefore I must consider

---

* Great Spirit.

myself a transgressor." When Hines recorded this response in one of his reports he added, "What simplicity of language yet what wisdom of thought, are displayed in this Simple statement. How many a Man of perfect education is labouring under the impression, that because he cannot see sin in himself, God cannot, thus bringing God on equal with himself."[45]

Before the visit was over, the chief asked Hines where he planned on settling. Hines said he did not know but he was looking for a place with plenty of good land, extensive hay meadows, big trees for building, and a lake or river where the people could catch fish occasionally. "Yes," Ahtahkakoop responded, "all these things will be necessary, and I think I know of such a place." The chief was thinking of *yēkawiskāwikamāw* (Sandy Lake), a place where he and his people had often camped. As it turned out, this was the same area Hines had visited and tentatively selected a week or so earlier. Hines wanted to go and look at the country right away, but Ahtahkakoop said he had to get back to Fort Carlton to meet the carts coming in from the plains. He agreed, however, to see the missionary at Sandy Lake in about two weeks.[46]

Hines read a chapter from the Bible and said evening prayers before they all went to bed. The following morning Ahtahkakoop and his son left to rejoin their relatives and friends at Fort Carlton. From there, the families probably returned to Fir Lake, the place where they had been wintering for a number of years.

Although Ahtahkakoop felt that Sandy Lake was an ideal place to settle, the decision was too important to be taken lightly. So the chief went to look at a number of locations. His first stop was the southern end of Sandy Lake. The old people said that when the chief came out of the bush he heard birds singing and he saw fish jumping from the lake.[47] The lake was so beautiful, they said. Ahtahkakoop crossed the *ēsis-sīpiy* (Asissipi, or Shell River) and went to a place called *nahkawiyinoskāhtik*, or Saulteaux's Forehead. He sat down and "surveyed" the country before going "uphill" to view the land all around. "It was beautiful" as he looked west towards the Asissipi River, the range of hills, and Sandy Lake. Then he travelled north to *manitow-sākahikan*, where Cheadle and Milton had spent the winter of 1862–63. The chief did not like the look of the land there so he went to Big River where some Chipewayan Indians were camped, to *wacīhk* (the hills south of *manitow-sākahikan*), and to *wīhcēkan* (Stinking Lake) farther to the west. "What he saw there at Witchekan Lake pleased his eye," the old people said, and there were fish in the lake.

When he got back to Fir Lake, Ahtahkakoop called his people together and said, "Let the women cook. We'll get together tomorrow."[48] At the feast the following day the pipe was smoked and the people prayed, asking for guidance and the blessing of the Creator as they tackled the important task ahead of them. Ahtahkakoop told them about his trip and the places that he visited. In his opinion, the chief said, there were two places from which to choose, Sandy Lake and Witchekan Lake. The leading men took turns speaking. Sasakamoose, Ahtahkakoop's brother, summed up the general consensus of the band when he said, "ever since we were small we have camped at Sandy Lake. I think it would be good to take this land, Sandy Lake."[49] And so, it was decided. This was the land Ahtahkakoop and his headmen selected for their settlement. Ahtahkakoop's people moved to Sandy Lake almost immediately after the decision was made.*

Hines, not expecting such decisive action, was surprised several weeks later when he went looking for Ahtahkakoop "to refresh his mind" and found the chief and nine other families camped on the margin of the plains at Sandy Lake. The number of people in Ahtahkakoop's camp totalled 62.[50]

The site was well chosen. The lake, called Sandy Lake because of its sandy beaches, was five miles long and varied in width from a quarter to half a mile. It was bounded on both sides by fairly high plateaux and surrounded by hills covered with birch, poplar, spruce, willow, and a few maple trees. To the southwest, poplar, heavy spruce, and tamarack grew in a tract of woodland, and hay marshes skirted the banks of the Asissipi River. The soil varied from light sandy soil on the ridges to rich loam on the flats and extensive meadow lands. The Green Lake Trail ran along the west side of the lake.

With winter fast approaching, Ahtahkakoop and a number of his people erected temporary shacks for the winter. Then, when they were not busy hunting and doing other chores, the men and older boys prepared logs for permanent homes. Hines, Stranger, and McKay, in the meantime, were wintering as planned in their cabin at Whitefish Lake.

Ahtahkakoop wanted his children and grandchildren to "know more of the God Who Made them" than he did, but he also wanted them to be able to read and write. Accordingly, on November 14 Ahtahkakoop took his youngest son Michel to live with Hines so he could begin his schooling. The boy, who was about 12 years old, was one of the children who had

---

* On modern maps Sandy Lake has been renamed Hines Lake.

Ray Christensen

The Asissipi River winds in a south-easterly direction through the land chosen for Ahtahkakoop's reserve.

Ray Christensen

Looking east across Sandy Lake.

Ray Christensen

Marshlands along the Asissipi River.

been baptized by Roman Catholic priests during the early 1860s.[51] Seven weeks later Hines reported that the lad was making "capital progress." He was reading, "his writing was very good," and he knew two prayers in his own language. Hines obviously had been listening to Ahtahkakoop during their brief visit, for the first Christian prayer Michel learned was "O God, teach me to know myself; & to know Thee." The Lord's Prayer was the second prayer taught to the young lad.[52]

"The interest that other Indians take in this boy is very gratifying indeed," Hines wrote in January of 1875, "& leads me to hope that many more will give their children to be taught in like manner." He went on to say that there were 30 children at Sandy Lake waiting to be taught, but he did not have room for them at Whitefish Lake because "my house is a quite full with four of us." Hines told Ahtahkakoop he would send McKay in the spring to begin teaching the other children.[53]

On the morning of January 10, 1875, Ahtahkakoop gathered 30 people together in his house for the first Christian church service held at Sandy Lake. With McKay interpreting, Hines said the entire service was conducted in Cree. In the afternoon the missionary held a class to prepare those in attendance for baptism. Hines later reported to his superiors that he proceeded slowly so he could drive away the superstitious fear of the white man's religion.[54]

This was the beginning of a regular pattern for John Hines and Ahtahkakoop's people. Every second Friday the missionary, accompanied by Stranger or McKay, travelled the 20 miles to Sandy Lake on snowshoes. Hines visited the people in their houses and tipis every chance he got and conducted church services in the chief's house on Sunday. He also held instructional classes to prepare those willing to be baptized.

Then on Monday, Hines and his travelling companion returned to Whitefish Lake, where the number of Indian families camping nearby had grown from three to nine since the missionary's arrival in the fall. There was another family of nine wintering at *manitow-sākahikan* and the missionary sometimes held services for them. All these families, however, were continually going off in twos and threes to hunt muskrats. As a result Hines, McKay, and Stranger were "left almost alone much of the time."

With little missionary work to do, the Englishman was able to devote three days a week to learning the Cree language. On the boat from England Bishop W.C. Bompas, who had a "slight knowledge of several

Indian languages," had taught Hines the Lord's Prayer in Cree. Now, with the help of George McKay, he started to systematically learn how to speak and understand the language. He also learned Cree syllabics, a system of writing that used a set of characters representing combinations of consonants and vowels. Until this system was developed by Methodist missionary James Evans in the 1840s, there was no way of writing or reading in Cree.[55] Syllabics fixed that problem, thus enabling the missionaries and churches to produce hymn books, prayer books,

ᓄᐦᑖᐏᓈᐣ

ᓄᐦᑖᐏᓈᐣ ᑭᐦᒋᑭᔮᐠ ᐁᐢᔭᐣ, ᑕᐟ ᐃᐦ ᑲᐚᐅᔭᐢᑖᑭᐧ ᑭ ᐃᐧᔮᐧᐃ·ᐧᐧ, ᑭ ᐅᐧᐃᔭᐦᐲᑭᐧᐧ ᑕᐟ ᐃᐧ ᐅᐟᐦᕁᕁᐸᕁ, ᐁ ᐊᐃᐧᐦᕁᒐᓚᐧ ᑕᐟ ᐃᐧ ᐅᕁᑫᑌ ᐅᐟ ᐊᐦᐹᕁ, ᐸ ᐊᕁ ᐊᕁᕁ ᑭᐦᑭᔮᐧᕁ. ᒥᑖᕁᐧ ᐊᓄᐦ ᐸ ᑭᕁᕁ ᓇ ᐅᐦᕁ ᐱᒐᕁᕁᕁ, ᒥᓇ ᐊᕁᐅᓚᐧᐧ ᓂ ᒪᕁᕁᑖᓂᐧ, ᐸ ᐊᕁ ᐊᕁᐅᓚᐊᐧᐦᕁᕁ ᐊᕁᐹ ᐸ ᐊᕁᐅᑕᕁᕁᐹᕁ; ᒥᓇ ᐁᐳᐃᐧᕁ ᐊᑐᐦᕁᕁᐊᕁᐧ ᑫᐅᕁᕁᑫᐃᐧᕁᕁ, ᒡᕁ ᒥᕁᕁᑌᑯᓚᐊᐧᐧ ᒪᕁ ᕁᕁᕁ.

ᐊᑫᕁ.

The Lord's Prayer written in Cree syllabics.

and other materials written in the Cree language. Hines, who realized the importance of being able to speak Cree, worked hard, and within six months of his arrival in the North-West could read the Cree prayer book with ease and talk to the people in their own language "with some degree of freedom."[56]

Ahtahkakoop and many members of his band were supportive of the missionary during his bi-monthly visits to Sandy Lake and, in one sense, Hines felt much encouraged. In many ways, however, the support was tentative and cautious. These "were not men that jumped into a new thing as soon as they saw it, but [they] waited a time to see if it turned out well," Hines noted in ones of his reports.[57] Other men, more open in their opposition, gave Hines "much cause for sorrow of heart" and refused to listen to what the missionary called "the word of life."[58]

Some individuals had specific reasons for resisting Hines's teachings. Like other traditional Indian people of the plains, Ahtahkakoop and his people had a good understanding of their religious beliefs. Spirituality was part of their day-to-day life and they were not afraid to discuss religion with Hines. Nor were they afraid to compare beliefs. One of their concerns centred on what happens after death. Or, more to the point, what happens to the spirit or soul when a person dies? In their Cree tradition, heaven was an Indian town or a village of tipis far to the south. This Indian town was a spiritual place where there was no want, no hunger, the grass was always green, and it was always warm.[59] The heaven Hines talked about seemed to be a different heaven. It was a heaven for white people and Christians.

Kichi-mōhkomān, who was one of the men struggling with the acceptance of the new religion, spent many hours talking to Hines. During one of their discussions Kichi-mōhkomān told a story that for him helped illustrate the dilemma he and others were facing. "There was once a man that had been a great conjurer,"* he told Hines,

> but before he died he left off his practice & became a praying man [Christian]. But after this change he soon died & his spirit went on a very long journey. At last it came to two towns, one designed for the Christian white-man, the other for the Heathen. He went up to one hoping to be admitted but a young spirit met him at the gate & told him it was not to that town he was sent, but to the other, so he journeyed on to the other but the reception was the same & they kept him travelling in this way without admittance into either.

> While journeying thus he met several other Spirits in the same position as himself all of which had become praying men before they died. In the Christian Town he saw a great light & heard singing. In the heathen's Town he saw them all feasting & inviting each other to their tents. He being able to see this & not being allowed to join them, was the cause of much grief to the spirit & so he resolved to return back again to his grave. On his arrival there, he saw a fire. This of course made him afraid but being worried with his journey finding no place for ... [his soul], he resolved to jump into his grave & share the same fate as his body. As soon as the spirit touched the body, it began to move the top of the grave, & he then became sensible & found himself alive again and ... with every facility as before. He remembered the place where they talked of going to hunt before he died & went in that direction. His friends were all terrified at his presence & supposed they had seen a spirit, but was soon convinced that it was their departed friend in reality.[60]

---

* A person with spiritual powers that are beyond human explanation.

His friends fed him. Then the conjurer told the people what had happened. Based on his experience, the conjurer said he had concluded "that it is no use for a man that has ever entered the conjuring Tent or joined in any heathen [traditional] practice to become a praying man. If he does they will not have him at either Town; but children that have never been initiated into these practices may become one with the white people & their spirits go with the white man's spirits when they die."[61]

Hines was not sympathetic. He told Kichi-mōhkomān that the conjurer's story was not true. Only God's word was true. He lectured Kichi-mōhkomān about being naked in the sweatlodge. He said the sweatlodge was a device of the devil, and he argued that Kichi-mōhkomān should pray to God to forgive him his sins so he could become a "praying man."[62] Even the words used by Hines caused problems, for had not the Nēhiyawak prayed to the Creator throughout their history? Did they not already know how to pray? Now it seemed that a "praying man" was a Christian. Now those who prayed to the Creator were called heathens and pagans.

Hines's words and attitude were not reassuring, for the possibility of being separated from loved ones after death created a real dilemma for Ahtahkakoop and his people. Converting to Christianity meant adopting a new religion and a new belief system. For Hines and other clergymen, conversion meant making a choice. The old ways were evil, the people were told, and must be set aside. But how could these ancient traditions be evil, the people asked in return. How could they be wrong when the Creator and his helpers had blessed the Indian people for so many years? Still there was a nagging doubt. Each time the Nēhiyawak went after buffalo it was becoming obvious that their old way of life was ending. Perhaps there was a better way of worshipping the Creator. Perhaps the old traditions had forsaken them.

But if change was necessary, what about their ceremonies, sweatlodges, and medicine bundles? What would happen if these were abandoned, they asked. Who would care for their relatives who had died? The questions and fears were real, for Ahtahkakoop and his people had been taught how to give the feast to honour the dead, and throughout the year these feasts were held by different families. "Old Man Spirit is the overseer in the Indian town," their spiritual leader had told them.

> He is the one who takes care of the Indian heaven. After a person dies and the people want to offer food to the departed person—to that departed spirit—they put on a feast. A man with the ability to

communicate with the Creator and the spirit that had departed is asked to help. He offers the pipe to the south first, and asks Old Man Spirit to help them. Old Man Spirit goes to get the spirit in the tipi village—the Indian town—and he brings him back. Old Man Spirit, that's his job.

They have to come back to earth through a doorway that Cipayasiniw-atayokan, Ghost Stone Spirit, looks after. He opens the doorway that they pass through to come to the feast, to partake in that little bit of food that is put aside for them in remembrance of him. Then Nōtokwēw-ātayōhkan, Old Lady Spirit, is invoked to come and console the people who lost the loved one, and also to console the one who had left for the spirit town in the south, and to make sure everything was all right with everybody. Consoling, that is her job.

And then from there they pray to Cāhkāpēw-ātayohkan, the Cold Touch Spirit, the spirit who lives in the moon, and they pray to him to be easy on others. To be easy on everybody. Then the spirits return to the Indian town and the Ghost Stone Spirit opens the door again so they can enter.[63]

If they could not honour their dead and console the living through this, a traditional Cree feast, who would look after them, the people wondered. And what would happen to them and their relatives if, when they died, they were not accepted in either heaven?

The spiritual and emotional anguish was intense. One very old man talked to Hines for a long time in early February. He explained that he liked what the missionary said, but some of his children had died and he wanted to be with them, rather than being alone in the white man's heaven.[64] Kichi-mōhkomān, after many discussions with Hines, finally agreed to "give" two of his children to Hines for instruction. He himself did not want to become a Christian.[65] For Kichi-mōhkomān, the old man, and many other men and women, it was an unsettling time.

Despite the doubts, Ahtahkakoop remained firm in his belief that a new way of life was essential if his people were to survive. If that meant adapting to a new religion, as well learning to cultivate the soil, so be it. It was not a time for half-measures. Ahtahkakoop was determined to set an example and so, according to Hines, the chief and his wife were "the first two to resign their heathen practices & be taught ... [the] word [of God]."[66]

Ahenakew not only agreed with the course Ahtahkakoop was following, but in some ways was one step ahead of him. The chief's brother, along with his wife Kīskanakwās (Cut Sleeve), and younger members of their family, had spent at least part of the winter of 1874–75 in Prince Albert. Hines was introduced to him there, and during one of their discussions Ahenakew said he would be joining Ahtahkakoop at Sandy Lake in the spring. Ahenakew also made arrangements for three children to be baptized by the Right Reverend John McLean, Bishop of Saskatchewan. During the ceremony, which took place at St. Mary's Anglican Church in Prince Albert on March 21, 1875, a seven-year-old girl was given the name Ellen, a five-year-old boy was called John, and a baby was named James. The baby was likely Ahenakew's grandson rather than his son. Hines was named as godfather in the church records.[67]

The children presented to the bishop were the third, fourth, and fifth persons to be recorded in the baptism register at St. Mary's Church in Prince Albert. Hines said that Ahenakew and his wife had not been baptized but they agreed to prepare themselves for baptism after they moved to Sandy Lake.[68]

Kāh-kāsōw (He Who Hides), one of Ahenakew's older sons, was also expressing an interest in Christianity. At a church service at Sandy Lake in April the young man stood up and said that he had never been taught "to pray," but he had been anxious to learn how for about six months. Kāh-kāsow was in his late 20s.[69]

Sasakamoose, Ahtahkakoop's other living brother, was also supportive of Hines's work, but he was faced with a problem that confronted many families during the next few years. Like numerous men in Ahtahkakoop's band—and other bands as well—Sasakamoose had two wives. Under church policy, a man who lived with more than one wife could not be baptized. Realizing that the men had taken two wives before they knew about "the law among Christians," Hines said he encouraged such men to attend church and send their children to school. He added that to the extent he was allowed, he gave them equal privileges.[70] The missionary also noted that since a woman's workload had grown as her husband's status increased, it was "not difficult to understand" why a man had more than one wife. Polygamy reduced the women's workload, he said, and gave them "greater freedom in the tent than they otherwise could have enjoyed."[71]

During one of their discussions, Sasakamoose told Hines that his first and oldest wife wanted to be baptized. Hines explained that the church did not approve of a man having more than one wife. "If he put her away" Hines told the chief's brother, the woman could be instructed and the bishop would baptize her in February if he came to Sandy Lake as expected. Sasakamoose asked what "putting away" meant. When Hines explained that the two of them could no longer live as man and wife, Sasakamoose responded that "he had done [this] a long time ago, although she continued to live with him & his other wife, but he could not turn her out of his house, he loved her too much for that.... She was his first wife. She had been always kind to him & it would be like taking away a part of himself to take *her* away, & especially as she was getting old & destitute of friends." He added that he had not known it was wrong to take a second wife.[72]

Hines said the woman had been "a constant hearer of the word of God when opportunities afforded itself for seven years" and she had a "very Clear knowledge of the fundamental truth of religion." She had wanted to be baptized for some time, but no Protestant would do it because there was a second wife. When the wife became sick and worsened quickly, Hines took pity on her and made the decision that since she had only one husband "the orthodox number" of spouses had not been exceeded. And so, during his bi-monthly visits to Sandy Lake that winter, the missionary prepared the elder wife for baptism.[73]

The woman was baptized on May 5, 1875, and given the name Mary. She died in the evening and was buried the next day, on May 6, near the place where Hines hoped "to have a church before long." She was about 60 when she died.[74] This was Hines's first recorded burial at Sandy Lake.

Hines, McKay, and Stranger had moved to Sandy Lake with their carts, supplies and equipment in late April, a week or so before Mary Sasakamoose died. Ahtahkakoop and most of his band were away hunting. The missionary spent his first week at Sandy Lake planning the settlement and "portioning out the land to the Indians." He also set land aside at the south-eastern end of the lake for the mission. In his report, Hines noted that the "portioning out" of land was not done satisfactorily because the leading men were not present to advise him. Nevertheless, he thought that no changes would be made when they returned.[75]

Ahtahkakoop used his own resources to get seeds for planting that year, likely trading at Fort Carlton or with settlers in the area. His purchases included 12 bushels of potatoes, four bushels of barley, two bushels of wheat, and a variety of garden seeds. A number of other men also bought seed, with several having almost as much as Ahtahkakoop. The chief gave some of his potatoes and barley to five or six of his principal men for sowing. "It is not much," he told Hines, "but it is sufficient for a garden, & they will remember that they have something growing at home when they are out in the Plains, & they will return as soon as possible after their hunt to partake of their fruits." Additionally, Hines had some seed potatoes, barley, wheat, and other seeds.[76]

Ahtahkakoop took the lead in organizing his people for the work that lay ahead. Because of the shortage of time, implements, and oxen, it was decided to plant one large field, with the harvest to be shared. Breaking the land was a community effort. Hines had four oxen, one of which had been recently purchased with his own money, but there was only one plough.[77] The missionary and Stranger took turns ploughing while the stronger men and women chopped the newly ploughed sod into pieces with axes, and then they pounded and pulverised the clumps with the axe heads.[78] Hines broadcast the seeds himself, scattering them by hand. The work was slow, hard, tedious, and involved the labour of many.[79]

Ahtahkakoop's people were not tillers of the soil. They were buffalo hunters, accustomed to the excitement of the chase and the freedom of the land. Yet, they bent their backs to the task at hand with an enthusiasm that impressed Hines. "Everyone is employed," Hines wrote in his report, adding that while the land was being broken, "weaker" members of the band hunted and gathered food so there would be no interruptions searching for something to eat. Ahtahkakoop's leadership and hard work during this new venture was acknowledged by Hines, who referred to the chief as his "right hand."[80]

In the evenings, after a tiring day working in the fields, the families were visited by Hines as he went from tipi to tipi trying to convert them. The young Englishman ended one of his first reports to the Church Missionary Society with the words "The Gospel & the Plough." It was a concept to which he was seriously committed. Ahtahkakoop and many of his leading men were equally committed, and apparently they were supportive when Hines drew up a set of rules that was read publicly to the people gathered at Sandy Lake.[81]

Although Hines had not indicated how many people returned to Sandy Lake with Ahtahkakoop following the April hunt, seven additional tents of people arrived at the settlement during the week of May 9. This group numbered 60. A week later the missionary noted that 14 families had taken

Illustration by Ed Peekeekoot

Men and women prepared the ground while Hines broadcast the seeds.

"claims" and planted a few seeds. People continued to come as word of this new venture spread until, by June 5, a large camp of 30 families, numbering nearly 240 people, was gathered at the fledging settlement.[82]

Mistawasis, accompanied by "not less than ten men," was among the new arrivals. According to Hines, most of the men in his group were ready to "embrace Christianity." Ahtahkakoop's friend and colleague said he had been asked to put in claims for men who would be coming in the fall, and he would leave it to Hines to decide where they should be located. Hines not only agreed, but he planted some seeds for Mistawasis before he left with his people to hunt buffalo on the plains.[83]

While talking to Mistawasis, Hines learned that the chief had two sisters as wives. The youngest of the women was over 50. Much to the missionary's satisfaction, Mistawasis said he would be willing "to put one of them away" in order to be baptized. The older wife, who Hines said was "nearly past doing work of any kind, eventually moved in with her daughters."[84]

Meanwhile McKay, who had been hired as both an interpreter and a teacher, was also hard at work. He had started classes in Ahtahkakoop's house during the first week in May. By mid-month 23 children were attending. Hines noted that if all the children in the settlement—half of whom had been baptized by the Catholics—came, the number would be close to 50. Nevertheless, the number of children at the school was encouraging, for Hines recognized that many of the families had come to Sandy Lake for the farming, not for the word of God. Without the cultivation, the young Englishman commented wryly, he likely would not see most of them again.[85]

Three or four men at the fledging settlement continued to be openly and "thoroughly opposed to Christianity."[86] One of these men was likely Kīsik-awāsis, a headman and one of Ahtahkakoop's older sons. Kīsik-awāsis and these other men resented how the missionary, in the name of his church, was attacking their traditions. They valued their religious beliefs and did not want to renounce them. Hines said they attended church meetings, but only to ridicule what he had to say. In protest and as a further challenge to the missionary, they built their sweatlodge close to where the Christian services were held, in a place where Hines could not help but observe the physical evidence of the traditional praying and purification ceremony. Hines ridiculed the men for roasting themselves and then hanging some of their "property" as an offering to God. He told them it was absurd to dispose of their property this way, and that God did not hear or approve of what they were doing because He did not take the offerings.

The men told the missionary that he had no proof God did not hear them. To this Hines replied that he knew God hears the Christian prayers because his spirit enters the heart and "makes us happy." This, he said, was not the Indians' experience in the sweatlodge.[87]

The people were anxious to go onto the plains to hunt buffalo after the crops were planted. Initially Hines hoped that the children and some family members would be left at the settlement for the summer. "I will try to supply their children with part of their food, that is until their farms are large enough to produce sufficient for their sustenance," he had written in January of 1875, and "those who feel disposed, [could] give one or two bags of pemmican to the Mission for the support of those children that have no parents to provide for them."[88] This proved to be impossible. In the late spring of 1875 the buffalo were said to be 400 miles away and the elk, moose, and other game in the woodlands were scarce.[89] Hines was disappointed, but he realized the people had little to eat and could not stay. Additionally, they needed pemmican and dried meat to trade for ammunition, tobacco, tea, and other trade goods. The people had to go to the plains, and they would be taking the children with them.

Since the hunting camp would be gone for four months, Hines asked the families individually where they wanted to "claim" land for their farms and homes. Then, instead of going with them, the missionary remained behind to build a house for himself, enlarge the mission field, and plough land at the selected sites. He also planned to plough fields for those he hoped would come later.

Two of Ahtahkakoop's married sons were among those who went onto the plains that summer. The chief gave them tobacco and asked his sons to invite others to join them in their new venture. Ahtahkakoop stayed with Hines at Sandy Lake to assist in whatever way he could.[90]

CHAPTER ELEVEN

Challenges, 1875-1876

The summer of 1875 was an eventful one. Hines, with the assistance of Stranger and McKay, enlarged the mission field and started ploughing land at the farm sites selected by the people who had gone onto the plains. They also built a log house for themselves at the south-eastern end of the lake, on land selected for the mission. This one-room building was 16 by 18 feet. Its roof was thatched and the floor was made from boards. When Hines was not working he practised speaking Cree and he studied for the examinations he would have to pass before being ordained a deacon in the Church of England.[1]

Although Ahtahkakoop and some of his family had remained with Hines to provide practical as well as moral support, the chief had other things on his mind besides farming in 1875. During the 1860s Métis buffalo hunters from the Red River Settlement had started wintering on the South Branch of the Saskatchewan River. This move gained momentum after 1870 and during the next few years their first permanent settlement, St. Laurent de Grandin, developed near a crossing on the river. It was not long before these French-speaking Métis were challenging the right of Indian nations to hunt buffalo freely in their own land. The Métis hunting camps were large and under the control of elected captains who regulated the hunt using a military-like organization. The rules of the hunt included stipulations that everyone who joined the camp was subject to its regulations. This meant, among other things, that an individual or group could not leave the camp, lag behind, or go ahead without permission. The laws were enforced by the captains and "soldiers" who were prepared to use force when they felt it was necessary.

The Métis' determination to control the hunt was aptly demonstrated in the spring of 1873. The buffalo had been extremely scarce across the north-western part of the plains that particular spring and the people were starving. Chief Mistahi-muskwa (Big Bear),* who generally traded at Fort Pitt, headed east with a small band of followers upon learning that a large herd was ranging in the Carlton district. When he reached the buffalo the chief found a Métis hunting party camped nearby. Although most of the hunters were from the St. Laurent region, some had come from as far away as the Qu'Appelle Valley and Wood Mountain areas. Three bands of Cree, consisting of about 40 tipis, had already agreed to hunt with the Métis. Big Bear was asked to join the camp but he refused. Instead, he sent some of his young men to cut a few hundred animals from the herd so his people could hunt independently and without interference.

As soon as the Métis suspected what was happening they summoned Big Bear and the three other chiefs to a council meeting. Big Bear side-stepped questions concerning the whereabouts of his young men. Gabriel Dumont, who was in charge of the camp, responded by insulting and humiliating the chief. Angrily Big Bear left the council meeting. The other three chiefs, equally upset, followed. The next day the Métis council, armed with evidence that Big Bear had issued instructions for the herd to be split, seized a horse, a cart, and harness belonging to the chief, and the young men were ordered to drive the scattered animals back into the main herd.[2]

Ahtahkakoop and Mistawasis also had confrontations with Dumont when the Métis living on the South Branch tried to impose their hunting rules on the Indian people. This was their land, the Cree chiefs said, and they would not be told by the Métis when and how they could hunt.[3]

The right-to-hunt issue took a new twist in the spring of 1875 when the St. Laurent Métis interfered with a hunting party made up of Indian and half-breed people. One of the men, a French half-breed by the name of Primeau, had been outfitted by Lawrence Clarke at Fort Carlton and sent onto the plains to get an edge on the hunting. Peter Ballendine was also in the party. An English half-breed, he had been a postmaster at Fort Carlton and the Battle River post during the 1860s.[4] Dumont claimed that the group was hunting in country that belonged to them and he demanded that the

---

* Although Big Bear was the son of a Saulteaux chief named Black Powder, he was, and is, considered to be Cree by the Indian people. In later years government officials also referred to him as Cree.

Hudson's Bay Company party join the St. Laurent hunting camp and be bound by its rules. When Primeau, Ballendine, and the others refused, Dumont and 40 of his followers—armed with repeating rifles—seized their carts and horses. Dumont's men also took the provisions, robes, and other buffalo products that had been collected. The hunters stood their ground, asserting their right to hunt independently. Faced with this opposition, Dumont and the others eventually backed down. Although the confiscated goods were returned, Dumont fined Primeau $25.[5]

Primeau and Ballendine returned to Fort Carlton and told Clarke what had happened. The Hudson's Bay Company officer, in turn, wrote to Lieutenant-Governor Morris complaining that the French half-breeds had "assumed to themselves the right to enact laws, rules and regulations for the government of the [St. Laurent] Colony and adjoining country of a most tyrannical nature, which the minority of the settlers are perforce bound to obey or be treated with criminal severity." He added that the Indian people were becoming hostile and urged that "unless we have a certain protective force stationed at or near Carlton, the ensuing Winter, I cannot answer for the result, serious difficulties will assuredly arise and life and property be endangered."[6] Clarke did not mention he was against any development that threatened the authority of the Hudson's Bay Company, nor did he acknowledge that the Métis were trying to impose their laws on the Indian nations, and that this in part was adding to the peoples' already uncertain situation.

With the events that had taken place at the Red River Settlement several years earlier still fresh in their minds, Canadian government authorities responded to Clarke's complaint by sending 50 North-West Mounted Policemen under the command of Commissioner G.A. French to Fort Carlton to investigate.[7] These men were stationed at Fort Livingstone, a police post that was situated near a small tributary of the Swan River called Snake Creek. The police had arrived at this post, the first headquarters for the North-West Mounted Police, in the fall of 1874.

For Ahtahkakoop, Mistawasis, and the other Indian leaders, the action of the Métis renewed their concerns about the changes taking place in their land without consultation and approval. There had been Canada's acquisition of the land. No one had explained what that meant in terms of day-to-day living, let alone the future. And now the Métis, recently arrived from the Red River region, were interfering with the rights of the Indian people. The Cree leaders understood that the Métis needed rules and laws so their community could function in an orderly manner for the benefit of the majority. It was another matter, however, when they tried to impose their regulations on the Indian nations. This once again raised the crucial question of whose land it was.

Of equal concern was the Canadian government's slowness in making a treaty with the Cree, Assiniboine, and Saulteaux living in Saskatchewan River country. The chiefs knew that in 1874 the Queen's representatives had signed Treaty Four at Fort Qu'Appelle with the Indian people living south and east of the South Branch of the Saskatchewan River. And they knew that plans were being made to sign Treaty 5 with the Saulteaux and Swampy Cree living to the east and northeast. Ahtahkakoop and the other leading men realized there was considerable dissatisfaction with the terms of Treaty Four and the way it was being administered. Nonetheless, by signing treaties the government had acknowledged that the Indian nations occupying those lands had rights that had to be considered before the white man could legally—and morally—assume control. In Saskatchewan River country, the traditional way of life was being threatened from many directions, but there were no signs—other than talk—that the Canadian government was willing to negotiate a treaty. Instead, they sent men to survey the land[8] and red-coated North-West Mounted Police to patrol the plains.

An increasingly intolerable situation was finally brought to crisis point when members of a telegraph construction crew and a government-sponsored geological survey party arrived in the Carlton District in mid-July of 1875. This was about the same time government officials were deciding how to react to Clarke's letter of complaint about the activities of the Métis.

The story of the telegraph crew had actually started much earlier in the year, when the Canadian government awarded a contract to Richard Fuller to erect the telegraph line from Fort Pelly to a point south of Edmonton.[9] The line was to follow the proposed Canadian Pacific Railway route that had been surveyed through the parklands and northern plains in 1872 by Sandford Fleming, engineer-in-chief for the Canadian Pacific Railway.

Fuller was aware that he might have problems fulfilling his contract and, in a letter to Fleming dated April 8, 1875, pointed out that

> most of the territory that the line runs through is unsurrendered and a great deal of it through the country often chosen as the battle ground of various tribes, and, more recently, if I am correctly

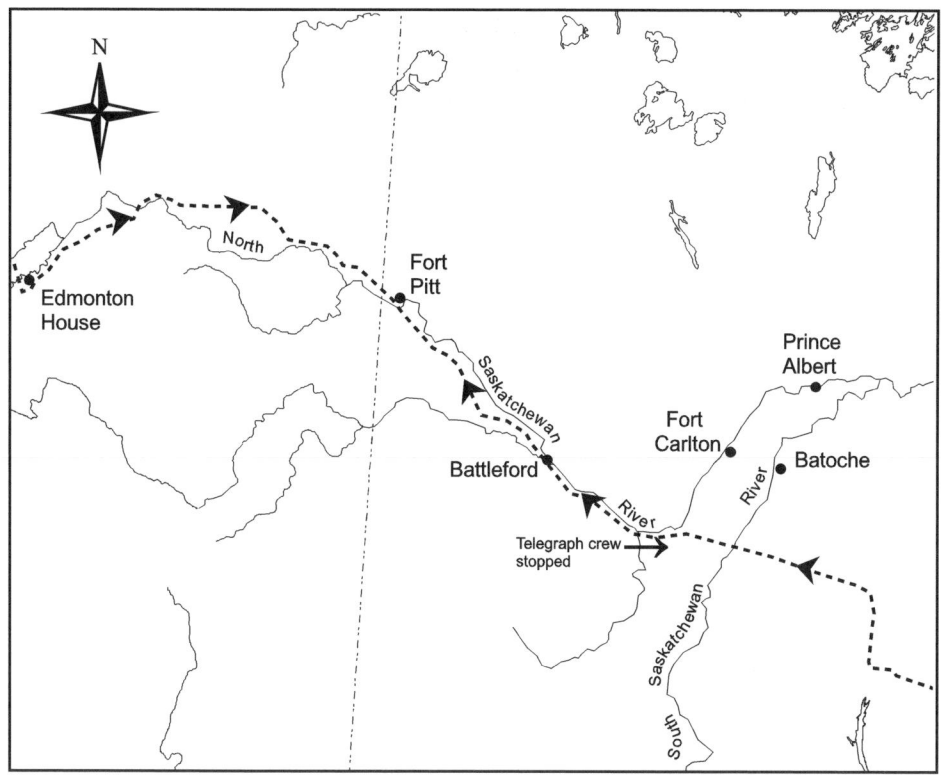

Information Systems Division, Canadian Plains Research Center

The first telegraph crew was instructed to lay the line from Fort Pelly to the elbow of the North Saskatchewan River. The second was to work west from the elbow, while the third crew was expected to run the line east from Edmonton House until it joined up with the line being laid west of the elbow.

informed, disputed hunting grounds between the Half-breeds and their friends of the North Branch and the Indians south. It is not for me to suggest what steps should be taken by the Government to secure the peaceable working of the line, but to call their attention to the facts, and that it would be a source of a great deal of trouble and expense to the Government if my parties should be stopped, or interfered with in their progress.[10]

In another letter dated the same day, he cautioned David Laird, minister of the Interior, that "serious results" could follow any resistance by the Indians and he offered to "deal with the Indians and take the responsibility of satisfying them, until a regular treaty is made."[11]

Fleming replied, telling Fuller that he had been informed by the minister of Public Works that "steps have already been taken to satisfy the Indians along the route of the railway and telegraph lines west of Fort Pelly; but I must warn you that the Government will not be responsible for any imprudence on the part of any of the men under your control."[12]

With this cursory assurance that all was well, Fuller sent three parties into the field to work on the telegraph. The first crew was sent to erect the line from Fort Pelly to the elbow of the North Saskatchewan River, while the second was to work west from the elbow. The third crew was sent to Edmonton House; from there, the line was to be run east until it joined up with the line being laid from the elbow. Knowing there was a good possibility the construction parties would meet opposition as they crossed Indian land, Fuller instructed his workmen that "should you be stopped proceedings [sic] by Indians, you will act civilly to them, and refer them to the officer surveying the line; you will do your best to persuade them to permit you to go on, but on no account whatever will you permit any forcible progress, as it is absolutely imperative that no disturbance should take place with the Indians."[13]

In mid-July the men conducting the geological survey for the Canadian government and the train of ox carts hauling supplies for the construction of the telegraph line arrived in the Carlton district. It was soon evident that Fuller's concerns and instructions had been warranted. Government officials may have made a decision to finally deal with the Indians of the Saskatchewan River region but nobody had told the Indian people about this or any other decision that may have been made. And so, as Ahtahkakoop, Mistawasis and the other Cree leaders watched the procession of surveyors, workmen, horses, ox carts, a hay mower, and a horse-rake enter their territory, their patience grew thin and they decided it was time to force the issue and to assert their rights within Indian land. Ahtahkakoop and Mistawasis stopped the geological survey party near the elbow of the North Saskatchewan River and said it could go no further.[14] Unable to continue their work, the men broke camp and took their freight to Fort Carlton.

The train of ox carts hauling supplies for the construction of the telegraph line, in the meantime, had been allowed to continue on to Carlton. This was the advance party for the crew that had been sent to erect the telegraph line west of the elbow of the North Saskatchewan. Under the supervision of a man by the name of Sinclair, its job was to lay wire, insulators, brackets and other materials and supplies along the route for the telegraph line, cut timber for poles, and cut hay for the oxen.[15]

Illustration by Brent Christensen

In mid-July, 1875, Ahtahkakoop and Mistawasis stopped a geological survey party and a telegraph construction crew at the elbow of the North Saskatchewan River.

Ahtahkakoop and some of his band were waiting at Carlton when the supply train arrived at the post. The chief's message was not long getting to the telegraph crew and it was forwarded to Fuller: "the Indians about the Fort say, and the chief is here, 'Star Blanket' [Ahtahkakoop], that they will not allow a stick to be cut until a treaty is made."[16] This stand was confirmed when a delegation of chiefs and leading men headed by Ahtahkakoop and Mistawasis went to see George Wright, the man in charge of the telegraph work. Peter Ballendine, the former Hudson's Bay Company postmaster, accompanied them as interpreter.[17] The questions were direct. Where was the construction crew going? And did they plan on cutting poles and hay?

Wright replied, saying that the telegraph line was to be built as far as Edmonton. Furthermore, he wanted to cut timber for telegraph poles and hay for wintering the oxen. Wright said the chiefs then

> spoke for some time, repeating their words over and over; they
> said how the Government had promised them a treaty; that they
> had received a letter from Governor Archibald, making them all
> sorts of promises, of which none had never [sic] been fulfilled,
> and now the Government was sending the telegraphs (or speaking
> iron as they called it) through their country without saying any-
> thing to them, or asking their permission; now they wanted their
> rights, they were not going to let the constructing party come any
> farther than the south branch; the government had made a treaty
> with the Indians as far as the south branch, and if Sinclair wanted
> to cut any hay or poles he might cut them on the east of the
> above-mentioned river; and they strictly forbade us cutting any
> hay or poles until a treaty was made with them; and they were not
> going to allow Sinclair to go any farther: but, after a short confab
> amongst themselves, they said we might go on and lay down our
> wire, plant, etc. but cut nothing."[18]

After meeting with the Cree leaders Wright asked Clarke what he should do. Now a government-appointed magistrate as well as the officer in charge of Carlton, Clarke told Wright "not to cut any hay or poles if the Indians had forbidden" it. He added that the telegraph crew would be "perfectly safe" if they continued laying down the wire but it "would not be safe to cut any hay or poles."[19] This effectively stopped construction of the line since little could be done without poles. Moreover, without hay for feeding the cattle, the crew could not work during the winter months.

Wright and Sinclair left the mower and horse-rake at Fort Carlton and then proceeded west to deposit wire and other telegraph supplies along the surveyed route. They were stopped again at Grizzly Bear Coulee just west of the Four Blackfoot Hills,* this time by three Cree men from bands west of Fort Pitt. The spokesman told them that he was

> authorized by his chief ("the little man" as he is called in English)† to stop my Government proceeding until a treaty was made; he said he had never saw wire like that before, and that if they allowed this to be put up it would frighten all their game away; now he wanted the Government to send out a man and tell them what their intentions was, whether the Government hated or liked them, or was they going to make a treaty with them or take their country by force.[20]

Wright explained that a treaty would be made with them but he did not know when. The Cree spokesman responded, saying

> he had been expecting a Commissioner up to speak to them (meaning all of his bands), and when he saw the wire first and heard nothing of the Commissioner, he felt as if something was sticking in his throat. He said that if we insisted on going ahead that they would soon get enough Indians that would make us stop, and that we had only been delayed by him for two days, but they would keep us for weeks; he said all the Indians were of the same mind; when a treaty was made with them all their rights of the land and the country would be the Government's.

The message was clear. Until a treaty was signed, the supply train and telegraph crew could proceed no further. Faced with this determined opposition and fully aware of Fuller's instructions that he was to avoid any dispute with the Indian people, Wright said he "could do nothing but put all the wire, insulators, brackets, etc., etc., in one large pile, protected from fire, and turn the train."[21]

Although Wright believed that the Cree west of Fort Pitt had just learned about the laying down of wire for the telegraph line and were acting independently from the Carlton Indians, this was highly unlikely. The Cree leaders were fully aware of activities in their land and their system for

---

* The Four Blackfoot Hills are southwest of Fort Pitt.
† Sweetgrass's 26-year-old son.

communicating amongst themselves was fast and effective. Many councils had been held since Canada assumed jurisdiction of the North-West Territories to discuss both the intentions of the government and the appropriate Indian response. In a matter as important as the government assuming the right to cut timber and hay in Indian land without permission, co-operative action was inevitable.[22]

The action of the Carlton chiefs, led by Ahtahkakoop and Mistawasis and reinforced by the stoppage at Grizzly Bear Coulee, had the desired affect. By early August, Lieutenant-Governor Alexander Morris* had made arrangements to send the Reverend George McDougall "on a mission to the Indians, informing them that the Dominion Government will send out representatives next summer to make treaties with them at Fort Pitt and Carlton, in the meantime requesting them to let the railway work proceed."[23]

McDougall was the man who had established the Methodist's Victoria mission 70 miles east of Fort Edmonton in the early 1860s. He was also the man who had hauled a large sacred stone known as the "Iron Stone" from a hill near the Battle River to the churchyard of the Victoria mission; the sacred stone was later removed to a Methodist college in Ontario.[24] The clergyman and his wife were in Winnipeg en route to the Bow River in present-day Alberta when the lieutenant-governor asked for help. Upon agreeing to deliver the message to the Indian people, the couple left their travelling companions and headed for Fort Carlton. The appointment of McDougall was one of many instances when government officials and missionaries worked hand-in-hand in their dealings with the Indian people of the North-West.[25]

Meanwhile, on August 5, a column of 50 Mounted Policemen arrived at Fort Carlton to investigate Clarke's complaint against the Métis' hunting practices. After a cursory investigation Commissioner French determined that Clarke had exaggerated the seriousness of the situation. Inspector L.N.F. Crozier and 12 men were left at Fort Carlton to make additional inquiries and French and the rest of the policemen returned to their post at Snake Creek.[26]

McDougall arrived at Fort Carlton a few weeks later and soon found himself thrust into a volatile situation. His first meeting was with a Cree camp consisting of 40 tipis and about 320 people "in the neighbourhood" of Fort Carlton. Although McDougall indicated this was Mistawasis's

* Morris replaced Archibald as lieutenant-governor in 1872.

camp, Ahtahkakoop and several other chiefs were most likely in the assembled group.[27] The missionary read the lieutenant-governor's message to the gathering. It said, in part, that the Great Queen Mother knew that the Indian people had roamed the prairie for centuries and had lived off the buffalo, but now their part of the great country was undergoing change. The buffalo were becoming scarce and an increasing number of white men were coming into the country. To protect the Indians from "undue encroachment" from the newcomers, the Queen would send men to make a treaty with the Indians of Saskatchewan River country the following summer.[28]

"Due notice would be given as to the date and the different places named, when and where meetings would be held," McDougall told the leading Indians. "In the meantime the Indians were to elect their chiefs, decide which chief they would belong to, hold meetings, and come to some understanding among themselves as to the terms of the treaty they would be willing to make with the Queen's servant."[29]

Mistawasis, who was named as head chief of the Carlton Indians, listened carefully. When McDougall finished speaking, Mistawasis turned to the principal chief of the Assiniboines and said, "That is just it, that is all we wanted."[30] The two leading chiefs of the Carlton district—Ahtahkakoop and Mistawasis—had apparently decided to remain in the background at the proceedings since it was the Assiniboine chief who addressed McDougall.

"My heart is full of gratitude," he said. "Foolish men have told us that the Great Chief would send his young men to our country until they outnumbered us, and that then he would laugh at us, but this letter assures us that the Great Chief will act justly towards us."

Then Beardy, chief of the Willow Indians, told McDougall that "if I had heard these words spoken by the Great Queen I could not have believed them with more implicit faith than I do now."[31]

In spite of this apparent initial support, McDougall soon learned that the task of informing the Indian people about the upcoming treaty negotiations was to be much more difficult than he had anticipated. Most of the people were hunting buffalo a considerable distance from Fort Carlton, with many as far away as the "south branch of the Saskatchewan and Red Deer Rivers." But more important, McDougall also discovered that the Cree and "Plain Assiniboines" of the Carlton area were united on two points. They said "they would not receive any presents from Government until a definite time for treaty was stated." Furthermore, although "they deplored the

Glenbow Archives, Calgary, NA 47-26

Sweetgrass was one of the leading chiefs in the Battleford and Fort Pitt areas.

necessity of resorting to extreme measures, yet they were unanimous in their determination to oppose the 'running of lines, or the making of roads through their country,' until a settlement between the Government and them had been effected."[32]

The leading men also told the missionary "that the danger of a collision with the whites was likely to arise from the officious conduct of minor Chiefs who were anxious to make themselves conspicuous, the principal men of the large camps being much more moderate in their demands."[33]

Based on this information, McDougall decided to visit every camp and personally deliver the message from the government. He was accompanied during his travels by John McKay* In all, they visited 21 camps. The largest of these was the combined camp of Big Bear and Sweetgrass, with 100 tipis and about 800 people. Like Ahtahkakoop and Mistawasis, Big Bear refused the presents offered by McDougall. "We want none of the Queens presents," Big Bear told the government's messenger. "When we set a fox trap we scatter pieces of meat all round, but when the fox gets into the trap we knock him on the head, we want no baits, let your Chiefs come like men and talk to us." Sweetgrass was not in the camp but his son and the "principal" men took the presents and asked McDougall to "convey to the Great Chief at Red River their thanks for the presents received and they expressed the greatest loyalty to the government."[34]

---

* An English-speaking half-breed, John McKay was the brother of James McKay, who later served as one of the commissioners at the Treaty Six negotiations at Fort Carlton. He had accompanied the Reverend James Nisbet on his trip west in 1866 to establish a mission in the community that became Prince Albert.

McDougall, despite the refusal of some chiefs to take the presents, was nevertheless generally pleased with the reception he received and in his official report wrote that he "found the Crees reasonable in their demands and anxious to live in peace with the white-man."[35] He also noted that during the councils that invariably followed the reading of the lieutenant-governor's message, the Indian leaders presented some of the subjects and concerns they intended on raising with the treaty commissioners. "Tell the Great Chief," they said,

> 'that we are glad the traders are prohibited bringing spirits into our country; when we see it we want to drink it, and it destroys us; when we do not see it we do not think about it. Ask for us a strong law, prohibiting the free use of poison (strychnine). It has almost exterminated the animals of our country, and often makes us bad friends with our white neighbors. We further request, that a law be made, equally applicable to the Half-breed and Indian, punishing all parties who set fire to our forest or plain. Not many years ago we attributed a prairie fire to malevolence of an enemy, now everyone is reckless in the use of fire, and every year large numbers of valuable animals and birds perish in consequence. We would further ask that our chiefships be established by the Government. Of late years almost every trader sets up his own Chief and the result is we are broken up into little parties, and our best men are no longer respected.'[36]

Then McDougall told the lieutenant-governor about some of the "false reports" he had to combat during his journey that were "all calculated to agitate the native mind":

> In the neighborhood of Carlton an interested party went to considerable trouble to inform the Willow Indians that I had $3,000 for each band, as a present from the Government, and nothing in my long journey gave me greater satisfaction than the manner in which these Indians received my explanation of the contents of my letter of instruction. At the Buffalo Lake I found both Indians and Half-breeds greatly agitated. A gentleman passing through their country had told them that the Mounted Police had received orders to prevent all parties killing buffalo or other animals, except during three months in the year, and these are only samples of the false statements made by parties who would rejoice to witness a conflict of races.[37]

In regards to the stoppage of the telegraph line west of Fort Pitt, the missionary reported that "after carefully investigating the matter and listening to the statements of all parties concerned my opinion is, that an old traveller amongst Indians would have regarded the whole affair as too trivial to be noticed. I have not met with a Chief who would bear with the responsibility of the act."[38]

In a section of McDougall's report that was omitted from the printed version contained in Morris's *The Treaties of Canada with the Indians*,[39] McDougall suggested that Clarke, the officer in charge of Fort Carlton, may have been responsible for some of the agitation in the Carlton area. He wrote that

> I was informed by gentlemen in the vicinity of Carlton that they regarded the Officers of the Hudson Bay Company as somewhat responsible for the present agitated state of the Indians and French Half-Breeds; My observation however would lead to the conclusion that with the exception of their chief official at Carlton who is not very well calculated to treat with Indians or Half-Breeds, there is not a gentlemen in the Service who would not heartily cooperate with the Government in effecting a permanent treaty with the Indians.[40]

This statement may not have been fair to Clarke. Known as a hard-nosed arrogant businessman, Clarke resented the demands put on the company by the missionaries and settlers who were arriving in increasing numbers, and he considered both settlement and missions to be a hindrance to the fur trade. He was in aggressive competition with free traders and merchants at Duck Lake, Moose Woods, and Prince Albert. And undoubtedly he was disliked by a number of people. Nevertheless, he had supported the establishment of a permanent Métis community at St. Laurent—even if it were for business reasons—and apparently was supportive of Ahtahkakoop's desire for his people to be taught how to read, write, and farm. He had lobbied for a police force in the North-West for reasons that included controlling the whiskey-dealing free traders who peddled misery and devastation and protecting the Indians from unscrupulous white men, half-breeds, and Métis. Furthermore, he had advised the telegraph crew to comply with Ahtahkakoop and Mistawasis's warning not to cut hay and wood in their lands. In the view of some, this may have been considered endorsement, and perhaps encouragement, of Indian agitation. More likely, it was the advice of a man with a greater awareness and understanding than

McDougall of the tensions building in Saskatchewan River country.[41] Nevertheless, that does not mean the company officer was always sympathetic to the Indians' cause. In March of 1875, for instance, Clarke had requested that a detachment of 10 Mounted Police be stationed at Fort Carlton to "overawe the Indians" in anticipation of treaty negotiations in 1876.[42]

McDougall, in his report to Lieutenant-Governor Morris, said he delivered the message about the upcoming treaty negotiations to the occupants of 479 lodges. He added that "there may have been a few tents in the forest, and I have heard there are a few Crees at Lesser Slave Lake and Lac la Biche, but the number cannot exceed 20 tents." Based on eight individuals per lodge, the missionary estimated the number of Indians to be "treated with" at Fort Carlton and Fort Pitt in 1876 to be 3,976.[43] If this census of Indian people living in Saskatchewan River country had been made in 1870, when the North-West Territories became part of Canada and before the smallpox epidemic killed many hundreds of men, women, and children, the count would have been dramatically higher.*

The Reverend George McDougall froze to death on the plains north of Calgary in January 1876, less than three months after he completed the task of delivering the lieutenant-governor's message to the Indian people.[44]

Meantime, obviously alarmed by the stand the Indian people had taken against the construction of the telegraph line, the Canadian government followed up McDougall's visit by sending a detachment of North-West Mounted Police to deliver "good-will" presents to the various bands. Consisting of 12 policemen under the command of Inspector L.N.F. Crozier, the detachment arrived at Fort Carlton in early October 1875. Only a few sick and elderly Indian people were at the post. Contrary to his instructions, Crozier went in search of the camps. Word was received later that he was wandering across the prairies in a "deranged state of mind." The officer was eventually taken to Fort Macleod where, after a short leave of absence, he fully recovered.[45]

Most members of Ahtahkakoop's band were off hunting buffalo when McDougall arrived at Sandy Lake late in the summer of 1875, for he found only three tipis and 24 people in the camp.[46] The numbers soon

---

* George McDougall's son John recorded in the book *George Millward McDougall: The Pioneer, Patriot and Missionary*, p. 167, that in 1870 "East and west and south, all over the land, the death roll was fearful; fully fifty per cent of the people being carried away."

increased. The first group of Ahtahkakoop's people, numbering 20, arrived with a good supply of dried meat, fat, and pemmican during the last week of August. Others followed as people responded to Ahtahkakoop's invitation to join him at the fledging settlement. By late October 70 families—including Mistawasis and 15 tipis of his followers—had pitched their lodges in the vicinity of the lake.[47] Some of the new arrivals had helped in the spring with breaking the land and seeding. Others were interested in trying their hand at farming, and some in the large camp, no doubt, had come out of curiosity.

The first farming venture at Sandy Lake was promising, even though the late spring of 1875 had delayed cultivation and seeding until well into May and it was only possible to get one field planted. The small crop of potatoes had flourished. Each family that helped with the planting was able to take about half a bushel home for its personal use. The rest of the potatoes, which the Cree called *askipwāwa*, or "eggs of the earth," were kept as seed for the following spring.[48] The wheat and barley were less successful, producing only 180 bushels. After the grain and potatoes were harvested the families started breaking up the sod in the new fields that had been ploughed by the missionary and David Stranger during the summer months.

Hines continued to help in the fields whenever he could. He also took advantage of every possible opportunity to discuss what he called "the fundamental truth of the Christian religion." He talked to individuals, families, and groups in the evenings and held church services every Sunday. The white man's education remained important and of interest to the parents, and it was not long before 40 of the 50 to 60 children estimated to be at Sandy Lake were attending school classes. Hines, of necessity, served as teacher because George McKay had left Sandy Lake.

The situation annoyed Hines. The young man had been hired as a teacher and interpreter for a three-year term. While visiting friends in Prince Albert during the summer he had run into the new Bishop of Saskatchewan, the Right Reverend John McLean. The bishop had been the warden at St. John's Collegiate School in Winnipeg when George was a student there. Soon after the chance meeting McKay was appointed a catechist* by the bishop and put in charge of the "church people" in Prince Albert. According to Hines, McKay

---

* A lay or secular religious teacher.

Illustration by Ed Peekeekoot

The first crop was cut by hand using scythes supplied by John Hines.

was under an obligation, according to existing rules, to serve in
one or other of the Society's Missions for three years at a uniform
salary and then at the end of that time, if the missionary with
whom he had laboured could report well of his services, he would
be at liberty to return to college and study for the ministry.[49]

McKay's new appointment meant that Hines and Stranger "were left
alone to battle with the work, which was growing apace." An interpreter
and teacher were both needed, Hines complained to church officials in
England, and Stranger, "who was as good a man as I could have for a
native," could not be expected to interpret every night in addition to helping with the farm work. The bishop eventually hired a young English-
speaking half-breed man by the name of Thomas Hourie to replace McKay
as a teacher and interpreter for the mission. According to Hines, he was not
nearly as qualified as McKay.[50]

Gradually, as the weather grew colder, families moved off towards their
winter hunting grounds. By early November those still remaining at Sandy

Lake had split into three groups. Twelve families, including Ahtahkakoop's, stayed at Sandy Lake with Hines. Fifteen families went to Whitefish Lake, while Mistawasis and 13 families returned to houses they had occupied the previous winter at Snake Plain. Situated about 20 miles south of Sandy Lake, these houses were about half-way between Sandy Lake and Fort Carlton. Because of their location, Hines referred to them as the "half-way houses."[51]

At Sandy Lake the winter of 1875–76, in many respects, resembled others of recent years. Most of the families moved into one-room log cabins very similar to those at Fir Lake. The low slanted roofs were made from poles, earth, and grass, and the small windows were covered with scraped hides. A heavy hide hung over the doorway. To cut down on drafts, mud and moss were stuffed into the cracks. Inside, a chimney fireplace similar to the ones built by Cheadle and Messiter in 1862 provided heat and a place for hanging cooking pots. Some of the floors may have been made from logs or boards, but more likely buffalo robes were spread over the ground to make a floor covering and provide warmth.

Beds were made from bundles of long grass covered with buffalo robes and tanned deer and moose hides. Ahtahkakoop and some of the other leading men moved their willow backrests from their tipis into the cabins. Personal belongings, bags and baskets of foodstuffs, equipment for hunting, and weapons for warfare were hung from the walls and ceiling, or stored along the perimeter of the houses. The walls and ceilings of their dwellings were square and the fire was contained in a corner fireplace, but in most other ways the furnishings and division of space were just as they had been in the tipis.

The families at Sandy Lake who had not built cabins remained in their tipis. Most of the dwellings, whether they were tipis or houses, were placed near the southern end of the lake. A communal people, Ahtahkakoop's band members—for now at least—were not willing to live on isolated plots of land.

Throughout the winter the men, often accompanied by their families, spent a good deal of time trapping fur-bearing animals and hunting buffalo, elk, moose, deer, and other game. Often they were gone for two to three weeks at a time. When the people were at home, the horses were looked after, firewood was cut, traps and snowshoes repaired, and the many other tasks that were an essential part of everyday life were carried out. As usual, the women kept busy preparing the meat, furs, and skins. They cooked, sewed, and mended clothing, and looked after the children. They, along with the children, also snared grouse, rabbits, and other small animals and birds. And periodically the people travelled to Fort Carlton to visit and to trade the harvest of their efforts.

Nonetheless, despite the similarities of other years, there was a major difference in the life of Ahtahkakoop's people during the winter of 1875-76. John Hines was living in their midst. His enthusiastic, determined, and persistent efforts to teach about the Christian God, the Bible, and the white man's religion touched many households that year. Hines did not confine his teachings to Sunday services. He held regular school classes for the children in his one-room dwelling. The teachings of the Christian religion were part of their studies, and the children were soon able to recite a number of prayers in their own language.

In the evenings, Hines went from home to home, talking and praying with the people, giving medicine to the sick and distributing clothing that was sent from England. Often he took chalk and a blackboard with him so he could teach Cree syllabics to the young men and women and to anyone else who was interested.[52] Additionally, every alternate Saturday or as often as he could, the missionary travelled to Mistawasis's wintering place at Snake Plain. There he talked and prayed with members of Mistawasis's band and taught syllabics. On Sunday he conducted church services, usually in the chief's house, and then he returned home in the evening so he could be at Sandy Lake for school classes Monday morning.

During trips to Prince Albert, Hines stopped at Fort Carlton. Often members of Ahtahkakoop's band were camped there and he conducted services for whoever was willing to attend. He also visited Beardy's people at Duck Lake, where he was attempting—rather unsuccessfully—to make inroads for the Anglican Church. And of course, wherever he went, the missionary talked about his God and the principles of Christianity in efforts to prepare the adults for baptism. Hines estimated later that he travelled over 1,000 miles that winter "on snowshoes carrying my blanket, kettle, food and axe on my back." Not surprisingly, in the spring he asked the Church Missionary Society to provide him with a train of dogs before the onslaught of the next winter.[53]

Hines tried to get help building a log church at Sandy Lake but most of the men refused, saying they could not spare the time from hunting for food and furs to donate labour. Rather than paying and feeding a work force from his meagre resources, Hines, with Stranger's assistance, decided to do the work himself. The two men cut the wood and had the building partly erected before the project was abandoned for the winter.[54]

Then, with construction work temporarily set aside, Hines concentrated on getting ready for his ordination as Anglican deacon. Thirty men, women, and children gathered for a meal and church service the day before he left for Prince Albert to take his examinations. The young missionary passed and he was ordained deacon on January 9, 1876, by Bishop McLean.[55] Soon after he returned home, the new deacon gave the Anglican mission at Sandy Lake the name Asissipi, presumably after consulting with Ahtahkakoop and his headmen. Asissipi (*ēsis-sīpiy*), which means Shell River, is the Cree name for the picturesque river that flows north and east of the lake. Hines said he chose the name Asissipi, in part, because the word was easy to say and looked good in print.[56]

The new deacon now tackled his work at Sandy Lake in earnest, beginning with the baptism of four children on January 14, 1876. These were the first baptisms conducted by Hines in his new capacity as deacon. The first of these youngsters, the two-week-old granddaughter of Ahtahkakoop and Mistawasis, was given the name Jane. She was the daughter of Ahtahkakoop's son Kā-miyo-ahcahkwēw (Good Spirit) and Mistawasis's daughter Judique.[57] The other children baptized that day included Ann, daughter of Misiwāpak* and his wife Mary,[58] and eight-day-old John, son of Pē-nōsēwēskam (Comes Tracking) and his second wife Tāpwēwiniwok (Truth).[59] The fourth child was also given the name John. Born in 1870, he was the son of Kā-sōhkapiw (Sits Strong) and Owāsēyās (Clear Light).[60]

Some two weeks later Bishop McLean arrived at Sandy Lake in the company of the Reverend John A. Mackay, a half-breed of Swampy Cree ancestry who was posted at Stanley Mission on the Churchill River north of Lac la Ronge. The meeting was a historic one, for it was there in Hines's small one- room house that the three men held the first Church Missionary Society conference west of Winnipeg. It was also the first CMS conference in the Diocese of Saskatchewan. As a result of the discussions that took place, the foundation was laid for the inauguration of "Emmanuel College for the training of native youths for the dual work of teachers and pastors." Following the meeting, a request was forwarded to the Church Missionary Society requesting that Mackay be moved to Prince Albert to teach divinity to the native students at the proposed college.[61]

---

* Misiwāpak was from Mistawasis's band.

By now Hines was teaching the children mornings and afternoons five days a week in the makeshift school in his house. Three evenings a week, in a concentrated effort to prepare adults for baptism, the seemingly tireless missionary conducted "instructional" classes. "One evening after class was over," Hines wrote in his journal, "I asked if they thoroughly understood what they had just been saying. They said they were able now to understand and talk about God's word & his son Jesus: but at first they could not understand it, even though it was in their own language."[62] The missionary therefore felt he was making progress and towards the end of January reported to his superiors that Ahtahkakoop was going to be baptized on January 30. Then, on the "2nd Sunday following [the chief] was to be married according to the rites of the Church of England."[63] Hines either misread Ahtahkakoop's intentions, was overly optimistic, or something happened, for these two events did not take place. Nor does the missionary mention them again for many months.

It was no wonder Ahtahkakoop, his wife, and others were having difficulties. Becoming a Christian did not simply mean accepting a new religion. It meant making a choice. It meant giving up their old religion, for hand-in-hand with Hines's teachings about Christianity was his insistence that the traditional beliefs of the Indian people were not only wrong but they were sinful. During their discussions Hines pressured Ahtahkakoop and his people to destroy their medicine bundles and give up what the missionary called their "heathen ways." He ridiculed the sweatlodge and other ceremonies, and did all he could to persuade his listeners that the Christian path was the only right path to follow.

Ahtahkakoop had not foreseen the demand that he must turn against the traditional ways of his people in order to become a Christian. Thus, even though he had been supportive of Hines in practically every way possible, the implications of formally converting to the white man's religion weighed heavily upon him as a father, husband, and chief. Ahtahkakoop was not going to be rushed into something he might later regret. And so the date of Ahtahkakoop's baptism and marriage remained unresolved as the chief pondered his responsibilities.

Interest in the work of the mission, nevertheless, remained high. For whatever reason, some found it easier than others to make the change. Ahenakew and his family were among those who were particularly receptive to the new religion. Three of their youngest children had been baptized in Prince Albert the previous spring and now, as the chief's brother had promised Hines, other members of his family were taking religious instruction at Sandy Lake. Hines felt that Ahenakew was ready for baptism by the middle of January 1876, but it was his son Kāh-kāsōw (He Who Hides) who came forward first.[64]

Kāh-kāsōw was the man who had told Hines almost a year earlier that he had wanted to learn how "to pray." As a result of this discussion, Kāh-kāsōw was instructed by the missionary and on April 17, 1876, he became the first adult at Sandy Lake to be baptized by Hines after his ordination as a deacon.[65] His two daughters were also presented for baptism. Hines explained in his journal that before baptizing anyone he went over a list of names with the person, or in the case of a child with the parents, and let them select their Christian names. Kāh-kāsōw chose Peter, and on church records thereafter he was referred to as Peter or Peter Kāh-kāsōw. With his own people, the new convert continued to be known by his Cree name. One of Kāh-kāsōw's daughters, who was born in 1873, was given the name Mary; the other girl, born in 1875, was named Nancy.[66] Kāh-kāsōw's wife was Charlotte Hyman (Āyiman, It Is Difficult). A second man, Otacīw (He Loosens Himself), was also baptized the same day. He chose Patrick for his Christian name.[67]

The following Sunday Mistawasis and members of his band arrived from the "half-way houses" where they had passed the winter. They were accompanied by Hourie, the new teacher recruited by the bishop to assist Hines. Hourie had arrived at Sandy Lake in mid-February. After helping Hines for several weeks he was sent to Snake Plain to teach the children in Mistawasis's band. Upon their return to Sandy Lake, Mistawasis, Hourie, and the others pitched their tipis about half a mile from the Asissipi Mission and then went to church. By now, practically all the people who had wintered at Sandy Lake were also living in tipis. The cabins, with their smoky, stagnant air, had been abandoned for the summer.

The day after Mistawasis's arrival Hines sharpened the axes and the people from both bands set to work cutting wood for building houses and fences. "This is work to which the men are very unaccustomed," Hines recorded in his journal, "and they are very tired when night comes." Tired they may have been, but the adult classes that were held three evenings a week continued to be well attended.

While the adults and young men and women worked in the fields and helped gather food, 36 children attended school classes conducted by Hourie.

From John Hines, *Red Indians of the Plains*

John Hines visited from home to home encouraging the parents to attend church and send their children to school.

Interest in mission activities was also reflected in church attendance and baptisms. On April 30, a week after Mistawasis arrived, a woman and two children were baptized. The woman, who was given the name Nancy, was the adult daughter of Misiwāpak; Nancy's younger half-sister Ann had been baptized by Hines on January 14.[68] The two children, Thomas and Mary, were the children of Pē-nōsēwēskam (Comes Tracking) and two of his wives.[69] Their baby brother John had been baptized on January 14.

Fifty-eight people attended the morning service on May 7, with the evening congregation numbering 47. Wāwākimot (Bent Over Coughing), the adult son of Nōtiskwēkasow (He Acts Like He Is After The Girls), was baptized that Sunday; he chose George as his Christian name.[70] The next Sunday, on May 14, the congregation numbered 70 in the morning and 54 in the evening. Hines baptized Emma, another adult daughter of Misiwāpak.[71] Three children were also baptized. The infant son of William Badger and Nancy Mistawasis was given the name Abraham.[72] Ācimākanis (One Who Is Talked About) chose the names James and Ann for his youngsters.[73] These families, along with Misiwāpak's, were all from Mistawasis's band.

Hines, who was making a real effort to learn the language of the people he was living with, conducted his services in Cree or had his words translated so everyone could understand what he was saying. The prayers and hymns were also in Cree. Mistawasis apparently inspired the congregation at every service he attended, for, in Hines's words, the chief

> excelled all the other Indians in his enthusiasm for hymn-singing; he was too old to learn to read, but he had no difficulty in committing the words to memory, and when he sang, he sang unto the Lord, making melody in his heart, and, having said this, I have said all. He had a tremendous voice which got beyond his control several times in each verse, and personally I found it difficult to keep to the tune if he happened to be singing anywhere near me."[74]

Ahtahkakoop, in contrast, had a low deep voice and sang an octave lower than anyone else.[75]

Farming, in the meantime, had not been forgotten. The families started working in the fields as soon as the ground thawed, ploughing and breaking up the lumps of dirt and grasses. Since Hourie had taken over the job of teaching the day school, Hines "was able get about among the people and with practical help and advice assist them in what they were doing."[76] Most of the cultivating was done with Hines's two teams of oxen.

Ahtahkakoop, Mistawasis, and their people did not have any oxen, the missionary explained, and their ponies, unaccustomed to pulling a plough or harrow, "did not take kindly to the work." Planting began the second week of May. While Hines "sowed broadcast" the wheat and barley, the families planted potatoes and a few vegetables on the small plots of land chosen for their homes.[77]

Hines was a good worker and teacher. "I learned the art of stacking and ploughing to perfection [on my father's farm]," he was to write later,

> and I thoroughly understood the management of cattle; and, as a proof of my efficiency in the art of husbandry, let me say that I have competed in an all-England ploughing match, the competition being for the sons of farmers not occupying less than one hundred and fifty acres of land, and no tyro would think of competing in such a match. I did not win the silver cup for the following reasons: I was the only man in the field to use a "swing plough," that is a plough that is guided, both as regards depth and size of furrow, by the eye and arm of the ploughman. The other ploughmen used ploughs with wheels fixed by an iron frame to the beam of the plough—one wheel gauged the depth of the furrow, the other regulated the breadth—and as the ground that year was very dry and hard it was impossible for me to hold my plough steadily and lay my work as evenly as those who used the wheels, but in spite of the odds against me, I was the straightest ploughman in the field."[78]

With an enthusiastic teacher of these capabilities, Ahtahkakoop, his sons, and the other men and young men at Sandy Lake quickly learned the essential skills required to become good farmers.

After the crops were planted the families at Sandy Lake were anxious to go onto the plains to hunt buffalo before the treaty negotiations began. Hines was also looking forward to a trip, but he was going to Winnipeg to get married. He had met his wife-to-be, Emma Moore, on the ship from England. Like Hines, she had travelled with Bishop Bompas and his party as far as Winnipeg. Emma's immediate objectives had been to attend her brother's ordination in Winnipeg, and then she hoped to get a position at a boarding school in Winnipeg for the daughters of Hudson's Bay Company officers. She was successful in both ventures and, by the end of her first year in Manitoba, Emma Moore was the principal and proprietress of the school.[79]

Hines left for Fort Garry on May 17 with a team of ponies, a light wagon, and an Indian guide. David Stranger and Thomas Hourie were left to carry out the work at the mission while he was away. Hines explained that there were

> distinct reasons why I should not take either of my assistants
> away from the place, had I felt myself at liberty to do so, which I
> did not. First, the school, which was an important factor in our
> work, must be kept going, otherwise the children might lose inter-
> est in it, and that branch of our work receive a set-back. Second,
> David's services on the Sunday could not be dispensed with. He
> had acted as my interpreter ever since George was taken from me,
> and now I relied on him to continue the services in my absence.
> Let no one think that the religious part of our duty had been neg-
> lected during our rush of secular work, for such was not the case;
> school had been regularly taught and religious truths instilled in
> the minds of the young, and Sunday services had been regularly
> held in my room, in the open air and from tent to tent.[80]

Stranger, as Hines's "senior partner," was left in charge of the mission. His tasks while Hines was away, in addition to taking the services, includ-ed the construction of an addition to the mission house for himself and the teacher. Hines's hard-working helper was also instructed to continue with the ploughing and to look after the fields and livestock. Stranger and Hourie would not be alone at Sandy Lake. Ahtahkakoop, for the second year in a row, agreed to stay at the settlement instead of taking part in the buffalo hunt.

Ahtahkakoop, Mistawasis, and their followers had much to be proud of in the spring of 1876. For all their lives they had been hunters and trappers, occasionally working for the fur traders and other newcomers, but always depending on the Creator and the buffalo for their livelihood. Now they had taken the first step in adapting to a new way of living. Twenty-five families had selected sites for permanent homes near the shore of Sandy Lake. Five or six houses had been built "by themselves and Stranger" and another 15 were in the process of being erected. A good start had been made at cultivation, and 10 families were still waiting to have their fields ploughed. Ahtahkakoop and Mistawasis's desire to have their children and grandchildren taught had also become a reality as 36 boys and girls began the exciting journey of learning how to read and write.[81]

PART FOUR

Treaty Six

Fort Carlton viewed from the treaty grounds.

CHAPTER TWELVE

Preliminaries to Treaty Six Negotiations

Ahtahkakoop, Mistawasis and their leading men talked about the upcoming treaty negotiations often during the winter of 1875–76 and the subsequent spring. One of their concerns focused on knowing exactly what was being said by all parties during the negotiations. Would the words of Queen Victoria's officials be interpreted accurately to them? And, just as important, would their speeches and the speeches of the other leading men be translated without any change of meaning or intent? Inquiries were made of a number of people. Then, based on the recommendations of Lawrence Clarke at Fort Carlton, Ahtahkakoop and Mistawasis sent couriers to deliver a letter to Peter Erasmus asking him to act as their interpreter during the negotiations.[1]

Erasmus was a half-breed plainsman of Danish and Swampy Cree ancestry who lived with Chief Pakān (The Nut) and his band of Cree at White Fish Lake.* Born in 1833 and raised in the Red River Settlement, Erasmus had studied, somewhat reluctantly, to become an Anglican clergyman. By doing so, he was following in the footsteps of his uncle, the Reverend Henry Budd.[2] In 1855, at the age of 22, he quit his studies to accept a position as interpreter and guide for the Reverend T. Woolsey, the Methodist missionary at Fort Edmonton.[3] Erasmus worked as a guide and interpreter for the Palliser expedition in 1858–59 during its survey of the north-western lands, and then he resumed work with the Methodists, first helping to build a mission at Smoky Lake and later working for George McDougall at the Victoria Mission.[4] In 1865 Erasmus abandoned missionary

---

* This lake is situated in present-day Alberta.

Saskatchewan Archives Board R-A5669

Red Pheasant, the brother of Ahenakew's wife Kīskanakwās.

work and became a free trader, hunter, and trapper. With the permission of Chief Pakān,* he and his new half-breed wife built a house at White Fish Lake, not far from the mission administered by another Methodist, the Reverend H.B. Steinhauer.

The couriers entrusted with the message from Ahtahkakoop and Mistawasis arrived at Erasmus's house early in March of 1876. They told the free hunter that Clarke had recommended him as the "best interpreter in the whole Saskatchewan valley." Erasmus, in his memoirs, *Buffalo Days and Nights*, said he was not personally acquainted with Mistawasis and Ahtahkakoop, but he "knew them by reputation as the two main chiefs of the Prairie Crees."

Erasmus said he would be pleased to act on their behalf. He gave the couriers a letter of consent and asked that a messenger be sent to let him know when he was to be at Fort Carlton.[5]

Several weeks later Mistawasis, his headmen Massan Cardinal and Pierre Cardinal,[†] and others met with Chief Red Pheasant at wintering houses built near the Hudson's Bay Company's trading post at the Battle River. Rumours were circulating that this site, a few miles upstream from the junction of the Battle and North Saskatchewan rivers, had been chosen for the capital of the North-West Territories. A bridge, built on land claimed by the Hudson's Bay Company, provided easy access across the Battle River. East of the bridge, the telegraph crew had erected storehouses and several other buildings on land that became known as Telegraph Flat. Red Pheasant's people had built their houses to the immediate west of the bridge.

---

* Pakān was also known as Sīnam (He Wrings It).

† Also known as Pierre Stone.

Mistawasis and the other men from the Carlton district were still at the houses when Sub-Inspector Frechette of the North-West Mounted Police arrived on March 25 to tentatively claim land for a police post and government buildings. "Judging that it will soon be generally known that this place is to be selected as the seat of government," Commissioner French had explained to Frechette in a confidential letter of instructions, "numerous Squatters are sure to rush in and take up the best sites, thereby putting the police Force to much disadvantage." Frechette therefore was told that after selecting "a location on which no one has at present any claim, you will mark it off with stakes, choosing a natural boundary of Creeks or Rivers, if possible, and you will have several responsible persons to witness the fact of your marking off this ground and to warn Squatters who may hereafter attempt to Squat thereon to the above effect." Thus, even before a treaty had been signed, both the Hudson's Bay Company and the North-West Mounted Police were claiming land for their own use. Mistawasis, Red Pheasant, and the others knew what was happening, for Frechette was told that seven of the eight houses in the wintering settlement were owned by the Indians. He was also told that these Indians were waiting for treaty and would be claiming river lots of 160 acres of land each "at one or the other side of their houses."[6] Their concept of river lots was likely derived from observing the long narrow river lots laid out by the Métis in their settlements along the South Saskatchewan River.[7]

Although Ahtahkakoop's name is not mentioned in the account, it is very likely that he, or at least several of his leading men, were among the visitors. Red Pheasant was Ahenakew's brother-in-law, Mistawasis and his headmen all had strong connections with Ahtahkakoop, and Ahtahkakoop and Mistawasis were the most influential chiefs in the Fort Carlton district. It is also very likely that the men were holding a council to discuss the upcoming treaty and the terms that would be acceptable to them. The lieutenant-governor, through the Reverend George McDougall, had told them the previous summer that they should meet to discuss these matters. This they had been doing for a number of years, and now with the treaty negotiations only a few months away it was crucial that the Indian leaders worked together and were of a common mind. They knew there would be many issues to resolve.

The chiefs apparently had been notified that the treaty negotiations would be held at Fort Carlton in July, and when the time drew near the people gathered at the post to wait for the commissioners. Among the non-Indians who came were the Reverend John McDougall, who was associated with the Victoria and Morleyville missions, and William McKay, the chief factor at the Hudson's Bay Company's Fort Pitt. According to McDougall, word was received the day after their arrival at Carlton that the negotiations had been postponed one month.[8] This was verified almost a week later when Chief Factor Clarke received instructions from Lieutenant-Governor Alexander Morris, via the chief commissioner of the Hudson's Bay Company, to "employ a trusty person to notify the Indians of the dates they should be at Carlton & Fort Pitt for treaty making."[9] The time chosen for the Fort Carlton negotiations was the third week of August. Ahtahkakoop and Mistawasis were apparently able to recall the couriers that had been sent to get Erasmus, for the interpreter said later that when he had not heard from the chiefs by well into August he thought they must have made other arrangements. Instead of waiting any longer, he went buffalo hunting.

Lieutenant-Governor Morris, who headed the Treaty Commission, left Fort Garry for Fort Carlton on July 27, 1876. His travelling group included William J. Christie, one of the treaty commissioners, and A.G. Jackes, a medical doctor who was secretary to the commission. Formerly an officer with the Hudson's Bay Company, Christie was the man who had stayed overnight at Ahtahkakoop's house at Fir Lake during his trip to Fort Simpson in 1872. The third treaty commissioner, James McKay, travelled separately and was to meet Morris near Fort Carlton. McKay was the son of a Scottish boat brigade guide and a half-breed woman. He was a former Hudson's Bay Company employee and a brother-in-law of John Rowand, the man who for 30 years was chief factor of the company's Saskatchewan District. After leaving the employ of the Hudson's Bay Company, McKay gained a reputation as a guide, freighter, businessman, and Manitoba politician.[10] Christie also had Indian blood, but he was the son of Governor Alexander Christie and thus was considered by his associates to be "country-born" rather than a "half-breed."[11] Both Christie and McKay spoke Cree and several other Indian languages.

Sometime during the first week of August, while the treaty commissioners were travelling to Saskatchewan River country, Ahtahkakoop and Mistawasis sent two of their sons to White Fish Lake to get Peter Erasmus. Then the chiefs headed for Fort Carlton to prepare for the negotiations. They chose for their camp a large rolling plain not far from the place where they forded the North Saskatchewan River. This area, along with the flat of

Illustration by Ed Peekeekoot

The sons of Ahtahkakoop and Mistawasis had to travel farther than expected to get Peter Erasmus, the man hired by the chiefs to interpret at the treaty negotiations.

land bordering the river, was the place Ahtahkakoop's people generally camped when they came to Fort Carlton to trade.[12] The post was about two miles to the east, bound by the river on one side and high banks rising to the plains on the other.[13] Not far away the Carlton Trail wound its way from Duck Lake to the fort. And to the west and the north, water glimmered through the trees as the mighty North Saskatchewan swung in a southerly direction. From all directions—and looking north in particular—the view was spectacular.

The site was well chosen. It was large enough for the hundreds of tipis that would soon be pitched. There was plenty of grass and water for the horses, the gentle slope to the flat of land provided easy access to the river, and on the northern edge of the campground a rise of ground provided an excellent location for the commissioners' council tent.

The people arrived, in small and large groups, on horseback and on foot. Behind the tipi of each chief, band members erected their tipis in circle segments to form an impressive camp circle. Soon nearly 2,000 men, women, and children were gathered together, waiting for the arrival of the treaty commissioners. The free traders came too. They set up their tents a short distance from the camp, hoping to get a share of the treaty money that would be distributed to the Indian people at the conclusion of the treaty.

Day and night, the sounds of drums and singing reverberated through the camp, across the rolling parkland to the river bank, and beyond. Some of the songs were sacred, sung to help the people as they prayed for guidance and participated in sweatlodge ceremonies, pipe ceremonies, sacred dances, and feasts. Other songs were secular, sung to accompany gambling games, social dances, and gift-giving.

The people rejoiced in being together in such a large gathering. Games of skill—often involving arrows, sticks, hoops, and balls—and competitions of strength and endurance provided hours of entertainment for young and old. The women cooked for feasts, the children frolicked, young people courted. When the men and women were not involved with sacred ceremonies and games, they visited, and they talked in large and small groups about the momentous event that was about to take place. Farther from camp, men and young men challenged each other on horseback, racing and performing feats of skill, while the best horsemen in the camp practiced for the ceremonies that would precede the treaty negotiations.

Ahtahkakoop and Mistawasis, along with the other chiefs, were still waiting for the commissioners to arrive when they received word that John

Hines and his bride had arrived at Gabriel's Crossing on the South Branch of the Saskatchewan River.[14] Accompanied by a new teacher named A.A.H. Wright, the couple was travelling from Winnipeg to their home at Sandy Lake. The message had been dispatched, Hines wrote later, "by what is known … as Mokissin Telegraphy, that is by native runners. It is quite amazing to the uninitiated, the distance that news is carried by relays of these messengers in an incredibly short time." Because of the advance notice, Hines said

> the Indians were anxiously awaiting our arrival, partly to hear what news we had to give as to the whereabouts of the commissioner, and partly to see ourselves, and after a wonderful amount of handshaking, etc., etc., owing to the fact that I had to hold a sort of reception for my wife, we prepared to continue our journey, as my plans were to take Mrs. H. home to the Mission and leave her there with David, returning by myself to the encampment, and remaining with the Indians until the treaty was completed.[15]

The missionary took Mrs. Hines and Wright, as planned, to Sandy Lake. No one was there but Stranger and Hourie. So, after getting his wife settled, Hines returned to Fort Carlton where he and the Indian people waited "some days" for Lieutenant-Governor Morris and the other treaty commissioners. Hines reported that during the time he was at the post he "had open air services among the Indians at different times."[16]

Ahtahkakoop and Mistawasis received a second message from Dumont's Crossing while they were waiting for Morris's party. This time they were notified that a small group of Saulteaux from the Treaty Four area was planning to stop the lieutenant-governor's party when it reached the crossing. The chiefs reacted quickly, dispatching a small party of men to the South Branch. There the men learned that the Saulteaux had "conceived the idea of forming a combination of the French half-breeds, the Crees, and themselves, to prevent the crossing of the Saskatchewan by the Lieutenant-Governor, and his entrance into the Indian territories." The Saulteaux had talked first to the Métis, who refused to become involved. Then they approached the Cree, who most likely were from the large camp near Fort Carlton. The Cree listened to the Saulteaux in silence. Then "one of them at length arose and pointing to the River Saskatchewan, said, 'Can you stop the flow of that river?' The answer was, 'No,' and the rejoinder was 'No more can you stop the progress of the Queen's Chief.'"[17] The

Saulteaux abandoned their plan, at least temporarily, to stop the commissioners and interfere with the "treaty-making."

When Morris, Christie, and their party finally reached Dumont's Crossing in the afternoon of August 14, a young Cree man came forward with a message from the chiefs welcoming the commissioners and "proffering a safe convoy" to Fort Carlton. He also delivered a letter from Clarke. In this message the chief factor offered the "Commissioners the hospitalities of the fort." Morris sent "replies in advance, thanking the Crees for their action, and accepting the kind offer of Mr. Clarke, to the extent of the use of rooms in the fort."[18]

The carts and effects of a Saulteaux trader by the name of Kissowayis were being ferried across the river by scow when Morris arrived at the crossing. At least 100 carts belonging to other traders and freighters were lined up waiting their turn. Kissowayis, who was from the Portage la Prairie and Yellow Quill bands, "at once came forward and gave up ... his right of crossing" to the Queen's representative. Nevertheless, despite this courtesy, it was late evening before the cavalcade of men, carriages, carts, oxen, and horses crossed the river.[19]

The following day, on August 15, Morris's party and the Cree escort met James McKay* at Duck Lake, about 12 miles from Fort Carlton. Kā-miyēstawēsit (One Who Has A Little Beard, or Beardy), who was camped nearby, was also waiting for the lieutenant-governor. After being introduced, Beardy asked that treaty negotiations be held at the hill near Duck Lake in accordance with a vision that had come to him.[20] Morris replied that after he "reached Carlton, which was the place appointed, ... he would meet the Indians wherever the great body of them desired it." He agreed, nevertheless, to stop at Beardy's camp of Willow Cree on his way to the post. Just as they were leaving for the encampment, a small detachment of North-West Mounted Police rode up under the command of Superintendent James Walker. The police had been sent from Fort Carlton, rather belatedly, to guard the lieutenant-governor "in consequence of the information given by the Crees of the threatened interference with their progress."[21]

The lieutenant-governor was greeted in a friendly manner when he drove into Beardy's camp. The men, he said, "came to my carriage and holding up their right hands to the skies, all joined in an invocation to the

* The third commissioner, who had travelled by a different route.

deity for a blessing on the bright day which had brought the Queen's messenger to see them, and on the messenger and themselves; one of them shook hands with me for the others."[22]

Then Morris's party, accompanied by the Cree and police escorts, continued on to Fort Carlton. Written historical accounts do not record the lieutenant-governor's arrival at the post, but since the road passed near the large camp of 250 tipis, hundreds of men, women, and children must have watched the procession with both excitement and apprehension, wondering what the future held for the Indian people.

Morris, Christie, and Jackes were assigned comfortable rooms at the fur trade post. James McKay declined Clarke's offer and camped about four miles away. Morris immediately made arrangements for a "two days's allowance of provisions" to be issued to the families, almost all of whom had been waiting for a number of days, and perhaps even weeks.[23] In addition to the flour, tea, and other supplies brought by the Queen's representative, a small herd of longhorn cattle had been purchased in Montana and driven across the plains to provide meat for the large gathering. McKay, a massive man weighing more than 350 pounds, shot the cattle from a buggy especially built to accommodate his size. The women in the camp skinned and butchered the animals and the meat was distributed to the bands. That day most of the people tasted beef for the first time. It was later reported that the oxen were so wild and unmanageable that a great number were lost during the trip north, "having returned from whence they came." Eighty-two animals were delivered to Fort Carlton, and another 15 were taken to Fort Pitt for the second round of treaty negotiations.[24]

In the evening, Ahtahkakoop and Mistawasis went to Fort Carlton to pay their respects to the lieutenant-governor and to welcome him "most cordially." Morris acknowledged them as the "two head Chiefs of the Carlton Cree."[25]

The next morning, on August 16, the Cree leaders sent a message to the commissioners saying that they wanted the day "to confer amongst themselves." Additionally, they wanted to try and bring Beardy and the other Willow Cree into the negotiations.[26] There was a third reason for the delay. Ahtahkakoop's and Mistawasis's sons had not yet returned with Peter Erasmus.

The two men had been forced to travel many more miles than anticipated to get the interpreter. Not knowing that the negotiations had been delayed a month, Erasmus assumed when he had not heard from the chiefs "well on

Illustration by Ed Peekeekoot

The chiefs and leading men conferred amongst themselves as they waited for the negotiations to begin.

in August" that they had made other plans. He decided to go after buffalo and joined a large hunting party made up of people from Pakān's and Little Hunter's bands. And so, when the delegation from Fort Carlton arrived at White Fish Lake, Erasmus was not there. The messengers tracked the hunters south and found them about 75 miles away, camped at a lake some 50 miles east and a little south of present-day Vegreville.[27]

A camp guard took the visitors to Little Hunter's tipi.[28] A friend of the Erasmus family, Little Hunter (Onataminahos) was one of the chiefs who had made the representation to Christie at Edmonton House in April of 1871. Little Hunter sent for Erasmus and after talking to the delegation from Ahtahkakoop and Mistawasis, the interpreter returned to his tipi to consult with his wife Charlotte. Then, in his own words, Erasmus said that he

> went back to the men and told them that I would be ready as soon as they wanted to go. "We are ready now," said one man as he rose to his feet from where he was resting. "My father has already started for Carlton and we may be late if we delay."
>
> Packing a few things in a bag for extras, I went with the clothes I was dressed in, hurriedly packed food and cooking utensils on a pack horse and riding Whitey, my buffalo runner, I was ready to start....
>
> Hunter decided to come along with us as he wanted to listen to the treaty negotiations....
>
> We arrived at Carlton the evening of the fifth day of hard riding and long hours, but our horses were all in excellent condition to start with and stood up well to the trip. A large encampment appeared, and separated by a lane were the various tents and canvas shelters that housed the traders. Apparently they had anticipated an agreement on treaty terms and had come prepared to do business with the Indians.
>
> A comfortable teepee had been set up for our use with buffalo robes, new blankets, cooking utensils, and even prepared food. Mr. Hunter was particularly impressed with the care lavished on us for our stay. Certainly it was the best hospitality that could be provided. The camp crier rode among the teepees and announced our arrival. He was riding on a gaily decorated pinto pony. He was telling the people that their interpreter had arrived and that

the chiefs and councillors should get ready for the meeting the next day.

I decided to take a walk around camp and saw Governor Morris walking in front of the Hudson's Bay post. There were over 250 teepees on the Indian section of the grounds. It was an impressive sight. I had never seen so many teepees in one locality before. There were hundreds of horses feeding on the flats, some picketed close by their owner's teepee with the usual assortment of dogs which appeared to have barked themselves to exhaustion as they lay before each teepee.[29]

Sergeant Major Samuel B. Steele, who arrived with a second detachment of police the following evening (August 18), provided another view of the camp:

The lodges or tents were of tanned buffalo hides, many of them large enough to allow 20 or 30 to sit comfortably inside. The fire was built in the centre, the smoke finding its way through an aperture in the top, the proper draught to prevent the occupants from being smoked out being secured by a triangular wing of the tent being held in the right direction by a pole. The skin of the tent was stretched on long spruce poles trimmed quite smooth; these when the Indians were on the move, became part of the means of transport by being passed through the loops of the saddle or back band and trailed along the ground behind the pony; two pieces were lashed across behind to form a sort of hammock-like stretcher, in which were carried the babies, the sick, the wounded, puppies, food, or any camp utensils, etc. On the outside of the lodge the Indians had painted the figures of birds, beasts, or reptiles representing their totems. Like the rest of their race on the plains, the Indians had many thousands of horses, the hills and prairie being covered with them, each family having its own herd and band of ponies. These were driven regularly to water at the Saskatchewan, and on the way back the herders invariably had a quarter-mile race on the level ground from the river to the bench land. The ponies were in first-class condition, and numbers of pinto or piebald ones were to be seen amongst them.[30]

Erasmus recorded a detailed account of the happenings at Fort Carlton, from his point of view, during these important days in his book *Buffalo*

Days and Nights. The skirmishing began even before the official negotiations were under way.

> Peter Ballenden [Ballendine][31] and his brother Sam came to the chiefs and informed them that the Governor desired them to meet … [them] at the fort that evening. I had just returned from my walk when Mista-wa-sis came to my tent and asked me to accompany them.
>
> "I have been told," said the chief, "that the Governor has hired two other interpreters. However, we have decided to pay you ourselves, even if the Governor does not."
>
> The chiefs were dressed in all their finery, feathers, plumes, and ermine-decorated coats. I felt a little out of place among the tribal costumes; and when we came before the assembled officials, they also had quite as great an array of finery as our Indian chiefs. My work clothes, though neat and clean, when compared against all the other finery were indeed inadequate. I wished that I had come better prepared for this situation.
>
> When I saw Peter Ballenden and the Rev. John McKay* seated among the official group, I presumed they were the interpreters the chief had mentioned. I was not too greatly concerned, as I knew both men; their ability as interpreters to a large gathering such as we would be faced with on the morrow would be tested to the limit.
>
> Governor Morris, Hon. James McKay, Clarke, William Christie, now retired from the Hudson's Bay service, and a Dr. Jackes were all seated at the table when we entered. Clarke jumped up and came forward to introduce our party.
>
> I was standing beside Mista-wa-sis, but Clarke paid no attention to my presence while he was conducting the introductions. Although Clarke, Ballenden, Christie, and the Rev. McKay all knew me by name, they did not offer any sign of recognition.
>
> The Governor advanced and shook hands with the chiefs, saying,

---

* This man was John Alexander Mackay, an Anglican clergyman of mixed Swampy Cree and white ancestry. He was not John McKay, the brother of commissioner James McKay.

"I have come to meet you Cree chiefs to make a treaty with you for the surrender of your rights of the land to the government, and further I have two of the most efficient interpreters that could be obtained. There stand Peter Ballenden and the Rev. John McKay."

His words were interpreted by Peter Ballenden.

Big Child [Mistawasis] answered. "We have our own interpreter, Peter Erasmus, and there he is. Mr. Clarke (he pointed directly at Clarke) advised me that Peter Erasmus was a good man to interpret the Cree language. Further than that, he recommended the man as the best interpreter in the whole Saskatchewan valley and plains. Why he did so, only he knows. On Clarke's advice, though I have no acquaintance with the man, I went to a great deal of trouble to fetch him here and though I know nothing of his efficiency, I am prepared to use his services. All our chiefs have agreed."

"Is that correct?" asked Governor Morris of Clarke.

"Peter Erasmus lives several hundred miles from here and I did not know that the chiefs had sent for him; therefore I hired these two other interpreters."

"It was quite unnecessary to send for the man," said the Governor. "We have two interpreters hired by the government and it is up to the government to provide the means of communication."

I had quietly interpreted these side conversations to the chief and he was prepared for an answer.

"Very good," said Mista-wa-sis, "you keep your interpreters and we will keep ours. We will pay our own man and I already see that it will be well for us to do so."

This latter statement by the chief, I interpreted to Morris directly, not waiting for Ballenden to misinterpret the chief's meaning.

"There is no need for you to assume this extra expense for an interpreter when the government is willing to pay for the interpretations," reiterated the Commissioner.

The chief replied rather heatedly, "Our man will interpret as well as yours. I can speak Blackfoot and I know what it takes to interpret.

If you do not want the arrangement, there will be no talks. We did not send for you, you sent for us.

I was quick to translate the conversations before waiting for Ballenden's hesitant and slow interpretations. The Governor's party were huddled at the table in low conversation, none of which I could hear. In the meantime the chiefs gathered together and were about to leave the room when the Governor looked up and saw they were going to leave.

"All right," he said. "You can have your interpreter. My tent will be pitched on the prairie where we will meet."[32]

Ahtahkakoop, Mistawasis, and the other Indian leaders had chosen a site about 400 yards from the Indian camp for the meeting place. The commissioners' council tent was pitched on a piece of "rising ground" facing the camp.

The scene had been set. The next day, the serious work would begin.

CHAPTER THIRTEEN

Treaty Six

T he spiritual men, the chiefs, and their headmen began Friday, August 18, with a pipe ceremony. They gave thanks to the Creator for all that had been given to them, and they prayed for guidance during the Treaty Six negotiations that lay ahead. By mid-morning Ahtahkakoop, Mistawasis, and the other leading men were assembled at the chiefs' tipis waiting for the arrival of the treaty commissioners. On the rise of ground overlooking the Indian camp, stood the canvas council tent. Chairs and a large table for the official government party had been placed inside the tent, and the sides were drawn back to provide a clear view of Queen Victoria's representative, Lieutenant-Governor Alexander Morris, when he arrived.[1] Within the camp circle, men, women, and children gathered in small groups. And beyond the tipis, young men mounted on the best horses in the camp—their faces and bodies painted—practiced intricate manoeuvres or cantered impatiently, waiting.[2]

Beardy and the Willow Cree were not there. The previous day Morris had sent Peter Ballendine to the Duck Lake camp with a message that he would meet them at the "encampment of the Carlton Crees." Beardy refused to come, saying that he had not given Morris "leave to meet the Indians anywhere except at Duck Lake, and that they would only meet [him] there." On the morning of the 18th, as Morris was getting ready to leave for the treaty grounds, a messenger from the Willow Cree requested provisions. The lieutenant-governor refused, stating that provisions would only be issued to those camped at the treaty grounds.[3]

Then the Queen's representative, resplendent in a cocked hat and a dark blue uniform trimmed with gold braid and lace, joined treaty commissioners William J. Christie and James McKay in the carriage that would take them to the council tent. They left Fort Carlton at 10:30, accompanied by an escort of North-West Mounted Police. On their arrival at the treaty grounds the Union Jack* "was hoisted" over the council tent.

In Morris's words, he found the site

> had been most judiciously chosen, being elevated, with abundance of trees, hay marshes and small lakes. The spot which the Indians had left for my council tent overlooked the whole.
>
> The view was very beautiful: the hills and the trees in the distance, and in the foreground the meadow land being dotted with clumps of wood, with the Indian tents clustered here and there to the number of … [250].[5]

Erasmus, who was waiting with the chiefs for the arrival of the treaty commissioners, recalled his impressions of this important day in *Buffalo Days and Nights*:

> The Police, dressed in their smart scarlet uniforms and riding well trained horses, made a big impression with the Indians. In fact the great prestige of the Governor was somewhat overshadowed by the smart appearance of his escort.
>
> Many Indians of that camp were seeing the Mounted Police for the first time. Though small in number, the Police were to be an important factor in establishing in the minds of the tribes the fairness and justice of government for all the people regardless of colour or creed—something they had no concept of in its broader sense.
>
> The Indian's [sic] own rules were handed down from the dim past, their oldest traditions accepted without question. The chiefs and councillors were chosen for outstanding qualities of character. Bravery and ability were the sole measures by which their leaders were qualified to take positions of trust. A son of a chief assumed office following the death of the chief only if he had proved himself qualified under these standards of office.
>
> The Indians recognized and respected the personal qualities of the individuals comprising the Force as being the qualities they

---

* The British flag.

demanded in their own leaders. The administration of impartial justice without regard to colour or creed, and the tenacity of its members in carrying out their duties, soon became a topic of Indian campfire conversation. The small number of this Police Force would have been utterly incapable of handling the thousands of Indians if they had attempted to employ force to compel obedience.

The chief and his councillors administered the laws for their band and the tribe recognized the necessity for rules governing individuals who at times broke the rules set by their leaders for the benefit of the majority. That, in my opinion, is what made possible the successful role that this small Force played in the progress of settlement of our one country.

Our approach to the Governor's tent was delayed by certain ceremonial proceedings that have been far better described than I feel capable of doing. However, let me say that these ceremonial practices had a deep significance to the tribes and can only be explained as a solemn approach to a vital and serious issue for discussion.

Few people realize that those so-called savages were far more deeply affected and influenced by their religious beliefs and convictions than any comparable group of white people, whose lip service to their religion goes no deeper than that. The forms of ceremonial behaviour with which the Indians approached the Governor's tent were based on practices whose actual meaning has long since been lost. The ceremony in the crowning of the kings and queens of England would have little meaning were it not for the benefit of written language.[6]

The narrative of the proceedings written by A.G. Jackes, a medical doctor who served as secretary to the Treaty Commission, provides one of the best descriptions of the sacred ceremonies that preceded the beginning of negotiations. "As soon as the governor and his party arrived," Jackes recorded,

> the Indians who were to take part in the treaty, commenced to assemble near the Chief's [sic] tents, to the sound of beating drums and the discharge of small arms, singing, dancing and loud speaking, going on at the same time.

In about half an hour they were ready to advance and meet the Governor; this they did in a large semi-circle; in their front were about twenty braves on horseback, galloping about in circles, shouting, singing and going through various picturesque perform-ances. The semi-circle steadily advanced until within fifty yards of the Governor's tent, when a halt was made and further peculiar ceremonies commenced, the most remarkable of which was the "dance of the stem." This was commenced by the Chiefs, medi-cine men, councillors, singers and drum-beaters, coming a little to the front and seating themselves on blankets and robes spread for them. The bearer of the [sacred] stem, Wah-wee-kah-nich-kah-oh-tah-mah-hote (the man you strike on the back),* carrying in his hand a large and gorgeously adorned pipe stem, walked slowly along the semi-circle, and advancing to the front, raised the stem to the heavens, then slowly turned to the north, south, east and west, presenting the stem at each point; returning to the seated group he handed the stem to one of the young men, who com-menced a low chant, at the same time performing a ceremonial dance accompanied by the drums and singing of the men and women in the background.

This was all repeated by another of the young men, after which the horsemen again commenced galloping in circles, the whole body slowly advancing. As they approached his tent, the Governor, accompanied by the Hon. W.J. Christie and Hon. Jas. McKay, Commissioners, went forward to meet them and to receive the stem carried by its bearer. It was presented first to the Governor, who in accordance with their customs, stroked it sever-al times, then passed it to the Commissioners who repeated the ceremony.

The significance of this ceremony is that the Governor and Commissioners accepted the friendship of the tribe.[7]

Morris, in his official report, interpreted the pipestem ceremony in a simi-lar manner, stating that "after the stroking had been completed, the Indians sat down in front of the council tent, satisfied that in accordance with their custom we had accepted the friendship of the Cree nation."[8]

---

* A spiritual man, Wāwīkanihk k-ōtāmahoht (He Strikes Him On The Back) was a chief and keeper of the sacred pipestem.

Morris and Jackes had not understood the significance of the sacred pipestem ceremony. The pipestem had been unwrapped and presented to the Treaty Six commissioners. According to Indian traditions, in the presence of the sacred pipestem only the truth could be spoken. Men must put aside their differences and work for good things. Thus, for Ahtahkakoop, Mistawasis, and the other leading men, the promises made during the treaty negotiations at Fort Carlton would be considered as binding as those that appeared in the written document.[9]

Following the sacred pipestem ceremony the chiefs and principal men were presented to the commissioners. They then seated "themselves in regular order in front of the tent."

Erasmus described what happened next in a narrative that is not included in the official accounts recorded by Morris and Jackes[10]:

> We were finally seated on the grass in a large semi-circle in front of the Governor's tent crossed-legged, a position that seems to be the most restful and relaxed manner of listening to a speech. I have seen quite old men rise to their feet to speak from this position without the use of their hands or arms to assist them, all with apparently effortless ease. My own attempts in this regard were never graceful or even easy. I always had to use my hands and arms to assist me. It was a physical feat that I never successfully conquered.
>
> We were patiently awaiting the Commissioner's convenience when the Hon. James McKay came to the front and called Peter Erasmus to come forward to interpret the Governor's speech. I rose to my feet and said, "I object, Sir. It is my impression that I am not employed by the government but am acting only on behalf of the chiefs assembled here. Therefore, I refuse to interpret the Governor's speech; that I consider is the duty of its paid servants." I then faced the Indians and repeated my words in Cree.
>
> McKay again insisted but I just as promptly refused.
>
> Mista-wa-sis turned to me and in an undertone asked me if I thought I was capable of interpreting.
>
> "Certainly I can, or else I would not be here. Let their own men talk first and then you will understand why I refuse to do their bidding."

Big Child and Star Blanket [Mistawasis and Ahtahkakoop] on each side of me nodded their agreement. The former rose to his feet. There was considerable stir among the Indians at the delay. Voices were noticeable from those seated furthest away from the stand. As soon as Big Child stood up there was immediate silence. He was a commanding figure of a man, not tall, but he stood straight and his wide shoulders spoke of strength. He didn't say a word until there was complete silence. Showing his closed fist with index finger protruding, he spoke, "This is number one," indicating "one" with the raising of his hand for all to see. "Already you have broken your word on what you have agreed."

I stood beside him and interpreted word for word as he spoke.

All the Indians rose to their feet and crowded forward behind their chiefs. The Police were kept busy keeping them away from the table. They were like a forest as a gathering storm of words rolled forward. I was thoroughly angered at the manner in which the Governor had been inveigled into this situation.

I had expected neither the strong reaction from the Indians nor McKay's determination to have his own way. I knew that Peter Ballenden had not the education or practice to interpret, and his voice had no carrying quality to make himself heard before all this large assembly. The Rev. McKay [John A. Mackay] had learned his Cree among the Swampy and Saulteaux. While there was a similarity in some words, and I had learned both languages, the Prairie Crees would not understand his Cree. Further, the Prairie Crees looked down on the Swampy and Saulteaux as an inferior race. They would be intolerant at being addressed in Swampy or Saulteaux words. I knew that McKay was not sufficiently versed in the Prairie Cree to confine his interpretations to their own language.

… Both leading chiefs stood without saying a word while all the fuss went on. Finally Big Child was satisfied that the Government party had been sufficiently chastised. He waved to those immediately surrounding him to be seated, and as before, with a few words, restored order.

The Governor was quick to take advantage of the lull after Mistawa-sis had waved his people to silence. You could almost feel the strong tension that still remained. Governor Morris started his address with the Rev. McKay interpreting.[12]

Jackes, in his account of the negotiations, recorded Morris's opening statement thus:

> My Indian brothers, Indians of the plains, I have shaken hands with a few of you, I shake hands with all of you in my heart. God has given us a good day, I trust his eye is upon us, and that what we do will be for the benefit of his children.
>
> What I say and what you say, and what we do, is done openly before the whole people. You are, like me and my friends who are with me, children of the Queen. We are of the same blood, the same God made us and the same Queen rules over us.
>
> I am a Queen's Councillor, I am her Governor of all these territories, and I am here to speak from her to you. I am here now because for many days the Cree nation have been sending word that they wished to see a Queen's messenger face to face. I told the Queen's Councillors your wishes, I sent you word last year by a man who has gone where we will all go by and by,* that a Queen's messenger would meet you this year. I named Forts Carlton and Pitt as the places of meeting, I sent a letter to you saying so, and my heart grew warm when I heard how well you received it.[13]

The lieutenant-governor then talked about some of the arrangements that were made prior to his arrival in the North-West. Included among these was the request for the assistance of McKay and Christie, "two friends and councillors whom I can trust, to help me in the duty."[14]

According to Erasmus, McKay's interpretations

> were mixed with Swampy and Saulteaux words. I mentioned this in English to the table, and the Honourable James angrily shouted, "Stop that, or you will rattle him!"
>
> Mista-wa-sis, after listening for a time, jumped to his feet and said, "We are not Swampy Crees or Saulteaux Indians. We are Plains Crees and demand to be spoken to in our own language."

---

* This is a reference to the Reverend George McDougall, who froze to death on the plains north of Calgary in January 1876.

McKay understood, was confused, and sat down. The Governor turned to me and asked what the chief had said. I explained the chief's words. The Rev. McKay again tried to continue, got mixed up with the Saulteaux words and took his seat.

Ballenden was now called up. I was delighted for I knew the man quite well. He was a good man to interpret personal talks but I knew he would be completely out of his element as an interpreter for such a large meeting, where a man's voice had to carry to reach the men furthest from the stand.

His attitude of the previous evening in not showing me any recognition; and Clarke's conspicuous neglect of a formal introduction, even though he was personally acquainted with me, had fairly made my blood boil. I had no pity for the men who had contributed their share to having me discredited with the Commissioner. Ballenden did exactly as I thought. He made an excellent interpretation of the Governor's words, but in a voice so low that it could not be heard beyond the first ten rows of men seated on the ground. The men in the back rows got to their feet and demanded that he speak in a louder voice; again there was some confusion and the two chiefs beside me got to their feet and ordered the men to be quiet. Ballenden tried to raise his voice, choked, and then sat down. My revenge at that moment was sweet but I could read consternation on the faces of my impolite friends at the table.

The Governor, who I could see was growing exasperated at these frequent interruptions to his talk, said, "All right, Erasmus. Let this be your chance to justify your chiefs' confidence in your work."

I immediately rose to my feet, stepped beside the Governor's table, faced the Crees, and spoke in Cree, reviewing the text of the Governor's speech to them. Then I motioned to the Commissioner to continue his address. I knew my voice had suffered nothing from my heated veins or the exultation that I felt at the complete disposal of the slight so desperately manoeuvred by these men sitting around the table.[15]

Morris, resuming his speech, talked about the treaties he had signed during the previous four years with the Chippewa nation of the "north-west angle of Lake of the Woods," the Cree and Chippewa (Saulteaux) at "Lake Qu'Appelle," and the Swampy Cree at Lake Winnipeg.[16] "And why is all this done?" he asked. "It is because you are the subjects of the Queen as I am. She cares as much for one of you as she does for her white subjects." He also spoke of the friendship between the British and the Indian people of central Canada and the ways in which the Queen's councillors had helped these people.[17]

"We are not here as traders," Lieutenant-Governor Morris told the chiefs and headmen seated before him. "I do not come as to buy or sell horses or goods, I come to you, children of the Queen, to try to help you; when I say yes, I mean it, and when I say no, I mean it too." Then he said:

> I want you to think of my words, I want to tell you that what we talk about is very important. What I trust and hope we will do is not for to-day or to-morrow only; what I will promise, and what I believe and hope you will take, is to last as long as that sun shines and yonder river flows.

> You have to think of those who will come after you, and it will be a remembrance for me as long as I live, if I can go away feeling that I have done well for you. I believe we can understand each other, if not it will be the first occasion on which the Indians have not done so. If you are as anxious for your own welfare as I am, I am certain of what will happen.

> The day is passing. I thank you for the respectful reception you have given me. I will do here as I have done on former occasions. I hope you will speak your minds as fully and as plainly as if I was one of yourselves.

> I wish you to think of what I have said. I wish you to present your Chiefs to me to-day if you are ready, if not then we will wait until to-morrow.[18]

The chiefs requested an adjournment until the next day so they could meet in council. This was granted and the first official meeting was over.

Erasmus picks up the story again:

> The Indians had retired to their teepees or were sitting in groups discussing the treaty terms. Hunter was around somewhere with the other Indians. I was reclining in our tent trying to calm my

ruffled feelings and assess the value of my contribution to the talks when the Governor's cook stuck his head in the tent flaps and said that the Governor wanted to see me. I was about to give the men [*sic*] a curt refusal, thinking that sending the lowest man on their staff to summon me to the great man's presence was another effort to emphasize my status. Then I heard the Hon. James McKay, Christie, and Dr. Jackes questioning the cook, asking if he had found my tent. He answered in the affirmative; then they all came to the tent and said they were to escort me back to the Governor's quarters. Entering, I stood without making any comment, awaiting the gentleman's pleasure. "Well, Mr. Erasmus, I suppose you are slightly exhausted over your labours this forenoon?" I thought I detected a slight hint of sarcasm in his tone and immediately answered, "No, Mr. Morris. Not by the work but by the preliminaries that led up to the work."

He smiled and I heard laughs in the background. Then he came forward to where I was standing and handed me a glass of brandy, which I accepted, for to have refused would have indicated that I was still nursing a grievance in the face of his apparent effort at appeasement.

"Mr. Erasmus, I called you here to congratulate you on your work. You are the first man I ever heard who interpreted to such a large audience without making a mistake. I see you have friends around here, although our first impressions may have discouraged this view."

It was pretty much of an after-dinner speech. Some of the Governor's guests applauded but I noticed that Clarke and Ballenden were not among them. Mr. Morris advised me that, beginning that day, I would be in his pay for the balance of the talks.

"Thank you, Sir. I hope that I may have better co-operation in the next few days. I promise to give you the best I have, and assure you that today's unpleasantness will not be repeated from our side."

I begged to be excused and took my departure without further words.[19]

By this agreement, Erasmus was now working for Morris as well as for Ahtahkakoop, Mistawasis, and the Indian people gathered at Fort Carlton.

Later that evening, at sunset, a detachment of North-West Mounted Police under the command of Colonel W.D. Jarvis arrived from the Swan River barracks. The new contingent included a band, the first to be formed by the North-West Mounted Police. The arrival of this detachment brought the total number of police at Fort Carlton to nearly 100 men and officers.

The Indian people were already assembled at the council tent when the lieutenant-governor and the commissioners arrived by carriage shortly after 10:30 a.m. on August 19. Ahtahkakoop and Mistawasis were seated in the front. Although Erasmus said, "there was not as much pomp and display from the government party" as the previous morning, the officials were accompanied by both the police band and a police escort. Morris spoke briefly to the gathering. Then the major chiefs were introduced. Mistawasis, representing 76 lodges, and Ahtahkakoop, representing "about 70 lodges," were presented first and acknowledged as the "leading chiefs."[20]

Jackes listed the other chiefs who were presented as

> James Smith, of the Fort-a-la-Corne Indians, fifty lodges. John Smith, of the Prince Albert and South Branch Indians, fifty lodges. The Chip-ee-wayan [Ocīpiwayān, Pointed Hood], of the Plain Indians, sixty lodges. Yay-yah-tah-kus-kin-un [Ayahtaskamikinam, Walks In Strange Lands], of the Fishing or Sturgeon Lake Indians, twenty lodges. Pee-yahan-kah-mihk-oo-sit [Pihēw kā-mihkosit, Red Pheasant, who was Ahenakew's brother-in-law], thirty lodges. Wah-wee-kah-nich-kah-oh-tah-mah-hote [Wāwikanihk k-ōtāmahoht, He Strikes Him On The Back] of the River Indians, fifty lodges.[21]

After these leaders were introduced, a messenger from the Indian people under Beardy approached and shook hands with Morris. "I am at a loss at this time what to say," he told Morris, "for the Indians' mind cannot be all the same, that is why I came to tell the Governor the right of it; with a good heart I plead at this time, it is not my own work, I would like to know his mind just now and hear the terms of the treaty."[22] Although the lieutenant-governor refused to disclose the proposed terms, he told the messenger to

---

* Jackes incorrectly identified Ahtahkakoop as a "Wood" Indian. Ahtahkakoop was born and raised as a Plains Cree.

stay, listen, and then "take back my words to his chief." The messenger agreed, and sat with the others.

When Morris was ready to start the day's proceedings, Erasmus was called to interpret. This time he took his place at the end of the table in the council tent without any fuss, and in a deep, clear voice translated the lieutenant-governor's words. "Every word," North-West Mounted Police officer Steele reported, "was distinctly enunciated."[23]

Erasmus's and Jackes's written accounts of the proceedings on that second day differ in several respects. In the version recorded by Jackes, secretary to the commissioners, Morris told the gathered Indian leaders that often when he thought about the future of the people his "heart was sad within" him. The lieutenant-governor said he "saw that the large game was getting scarcer and scarcer," and he feared that "the Indians would melt away like snow in spring before the sun." He wondered "if the Indians of the plains and lakes could not do as their brothers where … [he] came from did." He spoke about his work in other parts of the country, and recalled his visit to the Chippewas and his pleasure in seeing "houses built, gardens planted and wood cut for more houses" on the land they had selected for reserves.

"Understand me," Morris continued,

> I do not want to interfere with your hunting and fishing. I want you to pursue it through the country, as you have heretofore done; but I would like your children to be able to find food for themselves and their children that come after them. Sometimes when you go to hunt you can leave your wives and children at home to take care of your gardens.

> I am glad to know that some of you have already begun to build and to plant; and I would like on behalf of the Queen to give each band that desires it a home of their own; I want to act in this matter while it is time. The country is wide and you are scattered, other people will come in. Now unless the places where you would like to live are secured soon there might be difficulty. The white man might come and settle on the very place where you would like to be. Now what I and my brother Commissioners would like to do is this: we wish to give each band who will accept of it a place where they may live; we wish to give you as much or more land than you need; we wish to send a man that

surveys the land to mark it off, so you will know it is your own, and no one will interfere with you. What I would propose to do is what we have done in other places. For every family of five a reserve to themselves of one square mile. Then, as you may not all have made up your minds where you would like to live, I will tell you how that will be arranged: we would do as has been done with the happiest results at the North-West Angle.* We would send next year a surveyor to agree with you as to the place you would like.

There is one thing I would say about the reserves. The land I name is much more than you will ever be able to farm, and it may be that you would like to do as your brothers where I came from did.

They, when they found they had too much land, asked the Queen to sell it for them; they kept as much as they could want, and the price for which the remainder was sold was put away to increase for them, and many bands now have a yearly income from the land.

But understand me, once the reserve is set aside, it could not be sold unless with the consent of the Queen and the Indians; as long as the Indians wish, it will stand there for their good; no one can take their homes.

Of course, if when a reserve is chosen, a white man had already settled there, his rights must be respected. The rights and interests of the whites and half-breeds are as dear to the Queen as those of the Indians. She deals justly by all, and I am sure my Indian brothers would like to deal with others as they would have others to deal with them. I think you can now understand the questions of homes.

When the Indians settle on a reserve and have a sufficient number of children to be taught, the Queen would maintain a school. Another thing, that affects you all, some of you have temptations as the white men have, and therefore the firewater which does so much harm will not be allowed to be sold or used in the reserve.[24]

---

* The North-West Angle Treaty (Treaty Number Three) was signed in 1873 with the Saulteaux "at the North-West Angle of the Lake of the Woods."

Morris then outlined the tools, implements, livestock, seed, and other items that would be given to assist in the transition from hunter to farmer:

> We would give to every family actually cultivating the soil the following articles, viz., two hoes, one spade, one scythe, one axe, and then to help in breaking the land, one plough and two harrows for every ten families; and to help you to put up houses we give each Chief for his band, one chest of carpenter's tools, one cross-cut saw, five hand saws, one pit saw and files, five augers and one grindstone. Then if a band settles on its reserves the people will require something to aid them in breaking the soil. They could not draw the ploughs themselves, therefore we will give to each Chief for the use of his band one or two yokes of oxen according to the number in the band. In order to encourage the keeping of cattle we would give each band a bull and four cows; having all these things we would give each band enough potatoes, oats, barley and wheat for seed to plant the land actually broken. This would be done once for all to encourage them to grow for themselves.[25]

Additionally, a supply of ammunition and twine would be issued each year.

The lieutenant-governor also talked about the importance of having good chiefs and councillors. "Chiefs ought to be respected, they ought to be looked up to by their people," he told the gathering, adding that the chiefs

> ought to have good Councillors; the Chiefs and Councillors should consult for the good of the people; the Queen expects Indians and whites to obey her laws; she expects them to live at peace with other Indians and with the white men; the Chiefs and Councillors should teach their people so, and once the Queen approves a Chief or Councillor he cannot be removed unless he behaves badly.

> The Chiefs and head men are not to be lightly put aside. When a treaty is made they become servants of the Queen; they are to try and keep order amongst their people. We will try to keep order in the whole country.

> A chief has his braves; you see here the braves of our Queen, and why are they here? To see that no white man does wrong to the Indians. To see that none give liquor to the Indian. To see that the

Indians do no harm to each other. Three years ago some Americans killed some Indians; when the Queen's Councillors heard of it they said, we will send men there to protect the Indians, the Queen's subjects shall not be shot down by the Americans*; now you understand why the police force is in this country, and you should rejoice.[26]

I have said a Chief was to be respected; I wear a uniform because I am an officer of the Queen, the officers of the police wear uniforms as servants of the Queen. So we give to Chiefs and Councillors good and suitable uniform [sic] indicating their office, to wear on these and other great days.

We recognize four headmen to each large band and two to each small one.[27]

The coats presented to the chiefs and headmen, which were to be worn when it was "necessary to show that they are officers of the Queen," would be replaced every three years. Morris also said that each chief was to receive a silver medal and a flag "to put over his lodge to show that he is a chief," and each chief would be paid an annual salary of $25. Headmen, "not exceeding four for each band," would get $15 annually.[28]

Nearing the end of his remarks, Morris told the gathering of leading men that after Treaty Six was signed, he would "make a present to every man, woman and child, of twelve dollars." The money was to be paid "to the head of a family for his wife, and children not married." He also added what he had forgotten to mention earlier: that "if a treaty is made here and at Fort Pitt, we will give every year to the Indians included in it, one thousand five hundred dollars' worth of ammunition and twine."[29]

Then Morris again stressed the permanence of the treaty, stating that what he was promising

was not for to-day or to-morrow only, but should continue as long as the sun shone and the river flowed. My words will pass away and so will yours, so I always write down what I promise, that our children may know what we said and did. Next year I shall send copies of what is written in the treaty, printed on skin, so that it cannot rub out nor be destroyed, and one shall be given to each Chief so that there may be no mistakes.[30]

* This is a reference to the Cypress Hills Massacre of 1873.

Additionally, the lieutenant-governor said, "the Queen will agree to pay yearly five dollars per head for every man, woman and child."[31]

Erasmus, in his account, described an incident that is not mentioned in the official narrative. He said that during the early part of the proceedings, Poundmaker,*

> who was not a chief at the time but just a brave, spoke up and said, "The governor mentions how much land is to be given to us. He says 640 acres, one mile square for each family, he will give us." And in a loud voice he shouted, "This is our land! It isn't a piece of pemmican to be cut off and given in little pieces back to us. It is ours and we will take what we want."
>
> A strong wave of approval came back from the seated Indians at his statement. Some braves in the last row rose to their feet, waved their hands and arms, shouting, "Yes! Yes!" in Cree. Apparently these were Poundmaker's followers. It was some time before the main chiefs could restore order.
>
> The Commissioner was visibly shaken by this demonstration … His assumption had been that the Indians had completely adopted his treaty terms, which by his own words he was not authorized to change in any form. I thought to myself, "A boxer sent into the ring with his hands tied."
>
> The Governor went on to explain that unless certain lands were set aside for the sole use of the Indians, the country would be flooded with white settlers who would not give the Indians any consideration whatever. He made references to other areas where settlement was growing very fast. Morris's speech and explanation were couched in simple terms for the understanding of the Indian people. His manner held a sincerity that was most effective in impressing his audience. Knowing the Indians as I did, I could see that they were receiving the message with a growing understanding of its purpose.

---

* Pitihkwahkēw, or Poundmaker, was a councillor in Red Pheasant's band when Treaty Six was signed. Like many other leading men, Poundmaker had family connections with both Mistawasis's and Ahtahkakoop's bands. In this instance, Mistawasis was Poundmaker's maternal uncle, and within several years, Poundmaker's niece Ellen [daughter of K-ōsihkosiwayāniw (Ermineskin) and Old Woman Lodge] was married to Ahenakew's son Baptiste.

> Standing at the Governor's table I was able to observe the reactions of some of the listeners. I felt that Big Child and Star Blanket were both convinced of the fairness and justice of the terms explained to them by the speaker. I had an increased confidence in my interpretations, my sympathies transferred to the Governor's side, and my early animosity to the party was completely gone. The translations came to my tongue without effort and I seemed inspired to a tension that made my voice heard in the back rows where I had placed Hunter to give me a sign if my voice was not being heard distinctly.[32]

Lieutenant-Governor Morris concluded his speech by thanking the "Indians of the plains" for listening to him:

> I hold out my hand to you full of the Queen's bounty and I hope you will not put it back. We have no object but to discharge our duty to the Queen and towards you. Now that my hand is stretched out to you, it is for you to say whether you will take it and do as I think you ought—act for the good of your people.

> What I have said has been in the face of the people. These things will hold good next year for those that are now away. I have done. What do you say?[33]

When Erasmus finished interpreting Morris's words Mistawasis rose to his feet, came forward, and shook the lieutenant-governor's hand. The chief then responded, saying "We have heard all he has told us, but I want to tell him how it is with us as well; when a thing is thought of quietly, probably that is the best way. I ask this much from him this day that we go and think of his words."[34]

The lieutenant-governor and the other commissioners agreed to the chiefs' request. Since it was Saturday, the meeting was adjourned until Monday at 10 a.m.

On Sunday, August 20, the Reverend John Mackay and the Reverend Constantine Scollen, a Catholic priest who was working with the Blackfoot in what is now southern Alberta, held church services within the stockades at Fort Carlton. In the afternoon, at the request of some of the Indian people, Mackay and Scollen conducted separate services at the camp. More than 200 adults were in attendance at the Anglican service. Hines apparently held at least one service during the days of negotiations, for he said that on one occasion he was "fortunate in securing the services of the commissioner's interpreter." That day he preached from Paul's Epistle to the Philippians, verses 7 and 8.[35]

The Indian leaders did not hold a council on Sunday because, according to Erasmus, the "main chiefs said it was better to let the people have time to talk things over among themselves before calling a meeting."[36] So, instead of a formal meeting, the leading men talked in small groups, pondering the words of the Queen's representative and trying to decide the best course of action. Treaty commissioner James McKay, who had pitched his tent near the Indian camp, met informally with some of the people, listening to their concerns and answering their questions.[37] Little Hunter, who had accompanied Erasmus to Fort Carlton, also talked and listened to people in the camp and kept the interpreter "informed of all the latest developments … in relation to the activities and opinions in regard to treaty talks." Erasmus said that Hunter had "cultivated" a friendship with Ahtahkakoop and Mistawasis, and he suspected his companion "kept them fully informed on all angles of their opposition." Poundmaker and several others also circulated through the camp, but they were trying to rally support against the treaty. And some of the men sought guidance through sweatlodge and other traditional ceremonies.

Beyond the Warrior's lodges and chiefs' tipis, in the main camp and on the playing fields, men, women, young people, and children enjoyed the festivities of the large gathering. One of the main attractions was a game called *ē-pākāhtowēhk* (Playing With A Ball), a team game which resembled field hockey.[38]

When the chiefs requested time on Monday, August 21, to hold a council, Morris said

> I cheerfully granted the delay from the reasonableness of the request; but I was also aware that the head Chiefs were in a position of great difficulty.

> The attitude of the Duck Lake Indians and of the few discontented Saulteaux embarrassed them, while a section of their own people were either averse to make a treaty or desirous of making extravagant demands. The head Chiefs were men of intelligence, and anxious that the people should act unitedly and reasonably.[39]

Ahtahkakoop and Mistawasis asked Erasmus to attend the council. The interpreter's account is the only written record of the meeting:

Illustration by Ed Peekeekoot

The young men raced across the flat and onto the bench after watering their horses at the North Saskatchewan River. Elsewhere, formal races were held and the people played a game resembling field hockey during the break in formal negotiations. Others played games of skill and endurance.

I ... was personally escorted to the meeting by Mista-wa-sis and his ally Star Blanket. They said that I might be called upon to explain the talks, in case of any misunderstanding of my interpretations of the treaty terms. "There are many among us who are trying to confuse and mislead the people; that is why I thought it best to give them lots of time for their bad work. Today they will have to come out in the open and will be forced to show their intentions," said Big Child.

The chiefs were in agreement that it was better to bring about an understanding among their own people before meeting with the Commissioner.

Whether the treaty was actually misunderstood or deliberately misconstrued I know not, but the meeting was hardly underway when Big Child motioned me to disprove any wrong statement by those opposed to the agreement.

There were immediate objections to my taking part in the council but Star Blanket got up and spoke most emphatically. "Mista-wa-sis and I fetched this man here at a great deal of trouble to ourselves because we were told that Peter Erasmus was learned in the language the Governor speaks. You all heard and saw the other men fail to interpret what he tried to say. He, Peter Erasmus, is the people's hired man. He is here to open our eyes and ears to the words that you and I cannot understand. Mista-wa-sis and I have asked him here to keep us right on what was offered in the treaty terms."

Ah-tuk-a-kup's words had the immediate effect of silencing any further attempts to confuse treaty terms. There was then no further need to dispute any statement intended to be misleading by those opposed or trying for better promises under the agreements.

The talks went on all day, only adjourned for a short noon-hour meal. Indian eloquence had full play that day. Many of the council men spoke in addition to the chiefs. There was a Chipewyan Indian* present who argued considerable time away and was supported by Poundmaker and The Badger until a council man rose and objected to his interference.

"This man is not a chief and has no authority to speak for his band. Why should he be allowed to interrupt the council and waste so much of our time?"

There was loud assent from many voices and that silenced the voluble Chipewyan, whom I judged to be the main troublemaker.

Poundmaker and The Badger led the faction who were strong in their objections and refused to grant the possibility of existing by agricultural pursuits. These men had most of their support from those with less than thirty lodges to their count. Late that afternoon, I thought there was little hope of reaching an agreement. I

---

* This man was a Chippewa, not a Chipewyan. Chippewa were also known as Plains Ojibwa and Saulteaux.

was getting tired and about to ask permission to retire when I saw Ah-tuk-a-kup nod to Big Child.

Mista-wa-sis rose to his feet. All afternoon he had sat without taking part in the speeches. All those who were taking part in the previous arguments sat down. There was silence as the man stood and waited for every person to be seated.

"I have heard my brothers speak, complaining of the hardships endured by our people. Some have bewailed the poverty and suffering that has come to Indians because of the destruction of the buffalo as the chief source of our living, the loss of the ancient glory of our forefathers; and with all that I agree, in the silence of my teepee and on the broad prairies where once our fathers could not pass for the great number of those animals that blocked their way; and even in our day, we have had to choose carefully our campground for fear of being trampled in our teepee. With all these things, I think and feel intensely the sorrow my brothers express.

"I speak directly to Poundmaker and The Badger and those others who object to signing this treaty. Have you anything better to offer our people? I ask, again, can you suggest anything that will bring these things back for tomorrow and all the tomorrows that face our people?

"I for one think that the Great White Queen Mother has offered us a way of life when the buffalo are no more. Gone they will be before many snows have come to cover our heads or graves if such should be."

There were loud groans and exclamations of despair at the latter statements from many places among the group. Mista-wa-sis continued after waiting for the murmur to die down.

"I speak the tongue of the Blackfoot. I have been in their lodges. I have seen with my eyes and listened with my ears to the sorrows of that once-proud nation; people whom we have known as our enemies, the Peigan and the Bloods who are their brothers. Pay attention, listen hard to what I am about to say. The Big Knives of the south came into Blackfoot territory as traders; though few in number they have conquered these nations, and that, all the Crees in the days of our fathers and their fathers before them failed to do. How did they do it? Listen closely, my brothers, and you will understand. What was done to them can be done to us if we throw away the hand that is extended to us by this treaty.

"These traders, who were not of our land, with smooth talk and cheap goods persuaded the southern tribes it would be a good thing to have a place to trade products of the hunt, the hides, and the tanned goods. The traders came and built strong forts, and with their long rifles that can kill at twice the distance of our own and the short guns that can spout death six times quicker than you can tell about it, they had the people at their mercy. The Blackfoot soon found out the traders had nothing but whisky to exchange for their skins. Oh, yes! They were generous at first with their rotten whisky, but not for long. The traders demanded pay and got Blackfoot horses, buffalo robes, and all other things they had to offer.

"Those traders laughed at them for fools, and so they were, to sell their heritage for ruin and debauchery. Some of the bravest of the Blackfoot tried to get revenge for the losses but they were shot down like dogs and dragged to the open plains on horses to rot or be eaten by wolves.

"The Great Queen Mother, hearing of the sorrows of her children, sent out the Red Coats. Though these were only of a number you could count on your fingers and toes, yet the cutthroats and criminals who recognized no authority but their guns, who killed each other on the slightest pretence and murdered Indians without fear of reprisal, immediately abandoned their forts, strong as they were, and fled back to their own side of the line. I ask you why those few men could put to flight those bad men who for years have defied the whole of the southern Indian nations?

"Surely these Red Coats are men of flesh and blood as ourselves and a bullet is just as effective on them as on any Blackfoot. Why of course, they are of flesh and blood. They could be killed as easily as any Blackfoot, but ask yourselves why the traders fled in fear from so few men. The southern tribes outnumbered this small

Police Force one hundred to one, but they were helpless in spite of their numbers.

"Let me tell you why these things were so. It was the power that stands behind those few Red Coats that those men feared and wasted no time in getting out when they could; the power that is represented in all the Queen's people, and we the children are counted as important as even the Governor who is her personal speaker.

"The Police are the Queen Mother's agents and have the same laws for whites as they have for the Indians. I have seen these things done and now the Blackfoot welcome these servants of the Queen Mother and invite her Governor for a treaty with them next year.

"I, for one, look to the Queen's law and her Red Coat servants to protect our people against the evils of white man's firewater and to stop the senseless wars among our people, against the Blackfoot, Peigans, and Bloods. We have been in darkness; the Blackfoot and the others are people as we are. They will starve as we will starve when the buffalo are gone. We will be brothers in misery when we could have been brothers in plenty in times when there was no need for any man, woman, or child to be hungry.

"We speak of glory and our memories are all that is left to feed the widows and orphans of those who have died in its attainment. We are few in numbers compared to former times, by wars and the terrible ravages of smallpox. Our people have vanished too. Even if it were possible to gather all the tribes together, to throw away the hand that is offered to help us, we would be too weak to make our demands heard.

"Look to the great Indian nations in the Long Knives' country who have been fighting since the memory of their oldest men. They are being vanquished and swept into the most useless parts of their country. Their days are numbered like those of the buffalo. There is no law or justice for the Indians in Long Knives' country. The Police followed two murderers to Montana and caught them but when they were brought to the Montana court they were turned free because it was not murder to kill an Indian.*

---

* This again is a reference to the Cypress Hills Massacre of 1873.

"The prairies have not been darkened by the blood of our white brothers in our time. Let this always be so. I for one will take the hand that is offered. For my band I have spoken."

There was a deep silence after Mista-wa-sis had taken his seat. No one appeared to have anything to say. Then, finally, Star Blanket rose to his feet and for a long minute stood with his head bowed as if in deep thought or as if he had been profoundly impressed with the former speaker's words.

"Yes," he said finally, "I have carried the dripping scalps of the Blackfoot on my belt and thought it was a great deed of bravery. I thought it was part of the glory of war but I now agree with Mista-wa-sis." Then he raised his voice so that it rang with the power of great conviction, "It is no longer a good thing. If we had been friends we might now be a host of people of all nations and together have power to demand the things some of you foolishly think you can get and insist on now demanding.

"No, that is not the road we took, but killed each other in continuous wars and in horse stealing, all for the glory we all speak of so freely. The great sickness took half our lodges and the dreaded disease (smallpox) fell as heavily on our enemies. We are weak and my brother Mista-wa-sis I think is right that the buffalo will be gone forever before many snows. What then will be left us with which to bargain? With the buffalo gone we will have only the vacant prairie which none of us have learned to use.

"Can we stop the power of the white man from spreading over the land like the grasshoppers that cloud the sky and then fall to consume every blade of grass and every leaf on the trees in their path? I think not. Before this happens let us ponder carefully our choice of roads.

"There are men among you who are trying to blind our eyes, and refuse to see the things that have brought us to this pass. Let us not think of ourselves but of our children's children. We hold our place among the tribes as chiefs and councillors because our people think we have wisdom above others amongst us. Then let us show our wisdom. Let us show our wisdom by choosing the right path now while we yet have a choice.

"We have always lived and received our needs in clothing, shelter,

"Let us not think of ourselves but of our children's children," Ahtahkakoop told the chiefs and leading men during the council. *"Let us show our wisdom by choosing the right path now while we yet have a choice."*

and food from the countless multitudes of buffalo that have been with us since the earliest memory of our people. No-one with open eyes and open minds can doubt that the buffalo will soon be a thing of the past. Will our people live as before when this comes to pass? No! They will die and become just a memory unless we find another way.

"For my part, I think that the Queen Mother has offered us a new way and I have faith in the things my brother Mista-wa-sis has told you. The mother earth has always given us plenty with the grass that fed the buffalo. Surely we Indians can learn the ways of living that made the white man strong and able to vanquish all the great tribes of the southern nations. The white men never had the buffalo but I am told they have cattle in the thousands that are covering the prairie for miles and will replace the buffalo in the Long Knives' country and may even spread over our lands. The white men number their lodges by the thousands, not like us who can only count our tepees by tens. I will accept the Queen's hand for my people. I have spoken."

With the last of his words, the councillors of both main speakers rose to their feet, together held up their hands as a gesture of acceptance, and again took their places. Other chiefs among the assembly spoke a few words in agreement. The greater majority with a few exceptions had accepted the view of the two main chiefs.

Mista-wa-sis adjourned the meetings by saying, "It is good that my brothers go back to their teepees and study these matters with care. We will not be hasty. You will have a chance to ask questions on things you want cleared up. We will have our interpreter mark down the things we think we should have."

To this the Indians agreed. Dismissed, many of the chiefs came up and shook hands with Mista-wa-sis and Ah-tuk-a-kup, thus expressing their unanimous approval of the speeches of the two men that had swung the meeting in favour of treaty terms. I noticed that Poundmaker and The Badger were not among those who came forward to shake hands.

After I had retired to our tent, I lay awake thinking of the things spoken by the two chiefs, and marvelled at the confidence they both felt in the fairness of the justice carried out by this slender arm of the Queen Mother. The statement that the Police had the same laws for the white men and the Indians was true of our country, whereas only the previous year some Americans had committed murder on our side of the line. They had been followed to Montana and arrested but when they were brought before the Montana court, in spite of all the clear evidence of their guilt, the case was dismissed. The men had only killed Indians and that was not considered a crime on that side of the line.[40]

It is not mentioned in the written accounts, but a number of Indian men in the large camp could speak and read some English. These men included William Badger, John Badger (an Anglican missionary), and James Bear, who were headmen in John Smith's band, and Bernard Constant, a headman in James Smith's band. Able to understand both Cree and English, the four headmen no doubt were able to add to the discussions and verify—and perhaps clarify—Erasmus's interpretations of the proceedings.

The third day of the Treaty Six meetings got under way as planned on Tuesday, August 22. Erasmus said the Indian leaders and their followers were slow gathering at the council tent. He blamed the delay on

Poundmaker and The Badger … [who] were trying to gather support for their demands in the matter of treaty terms. Majority opinion had forced them to a grudging consent at the meeting. The Chipewyan [Saulteaux] was again active wherever he could find an audience, and backed by the other two men had regained his former boldness. But I noticed he was having difficulty in getting anyone to listen.[42]

Ahtahkakoop's brother Ahenakew was one of several advisers who remained in a Warrior's lodge to talk amongst themselves and to pray in order to provide guidance for those involved in the negotiations.[43] One of the other advisers was a man from Starblanket's* band in the Treaty Four

---

* This man was a younger brother of Chief Acāhkos k-ōtakohpit, He Who Has Stars For His Blanket, who eventually settled in the Fort Qu'Appelle area. The translation of Acāhkos k-ōtakohpit was shortened to Starblanket. The man remained with Ahtahkakoop's people following the signing of Treaty Six and he became known as *Pwāta* (The Sioux), because he had come from the south where the Sioux lived. He also used the name Starblanket because his brother was called Starblanket.

area. He had come hoping he could help the chiefs at Fort Carlton achieve better treaty terms than those included in Treaty Four.[44] Throughout the treaty negotiations, runners and leading men went back and forth between the Warrior's lodge and the treaty grounds as the leaders consulted and sought advice.

When the Indian people were finally assembled, Morris told the gathering he had talked a great deal and now he was ready to hear the "voices of your principal Chiefs or of those chosen to speak for them."

Poundmaker came forward first, saying that

> We have heard your words that you had to say to us as the representative of the Queen. We were glad to hear what you had to say, and have gathered together in council and thought the words over amongst us, we were glad to hear you tell us how we might live by our own work. When I commence to settle on the lands to make a living for myself and my children, I beg of you to assist me in every way possible—when I am at a loss how to proceed I want the advice and assistance of the Government; the children yet unborn, I wish you to treat them in like manner as they advance in civilization like the white man. This is all I have been told to say now, if I have not said anything in a right manner I wish to be excused; this is the voice of the people.[45]

Morris replied, in part, that "those that come after us in the Government will think of your children as we think of you." He said a chief superintendent of Indian affairs and two or three other men working under him would be sent to look after the Indians and see how they were prospering. Then he added that he could not promise the

> Government will feed and support all the Indians; you are many, and if we were to try to do it, it would take a great deal of money, and some of you would never do anything for yourselves. What I have offered does not take away your living, you will have it then as you have now, and what I offer now is put on top of it. This I can tell you, the Queen's Government will always take a deep interest in your living.[46]

The Badger responded with these words:

> "We want to think of our children; we do not want to be too greedy; when we commence to settle down on the reserves that we select, it is there we want your aid, when we cannot help ourselves and in case of troubles seen and unforeseen in the future.[47]

Sasakamoose, who was Ahtahkakoop's brother and a headman, was one of several leading men who supported The Badger.[48] The brothers, as well as a number of other men, had already started to farm. They knew from experience that there was no time to hunt for food during planting and harvesting, and they had some realization of the time and effort that would be required in making the transition to farming. They also knew first-hand that crops were not always successful. Ahtahkakoop's band had worked hard to plant grain and vegetables that very spring, only to see heavy frost on June 13 cut the young plants to the ground. Frost struck again in July and August, destroying the potatoes and reducing the wheat and barley to fodder.[49] They knew farming would not be easy.

In Erasmus's summary of the discussion, Sasakamoose and others referred

> to portions of the treaty in regard to settlement on reserves, the need for medical help, and guidance in regard to the new project of agriculture. A summary of their remarks meant that they wanted assistance to get established in their new occupation of agriculture, not only financially but also in instruction and management.[50]

Morris sidestepped the issue of additional assistance, saying

> I have told you that the money I have offered you would be paid to you and to your children's children. I know that the sympathy of the Queen, and her assistance, would be given you in any unforeseen circumstances. You must trust to her generosity. Last winter when some of the Indians wanted food because the crops had been destroyed by grasshoppers, although it was not promised in the treaty, nevertheless the Government sent money to buy them food, and in the spring when many of them were sick a man was sent to try and help them. We cannot foresee these things, and all I can promise is that you will be treated kindly, and in that extraordinary circumstances you must trust to the generosity of the Queen.[51]

Then, according to Erasmus,

> the Hon. James McKay, in a somewhat arrogant tone, admonished them in Cree for their demands. "In my experience you always want more than you were promised in the first place and you are never satisfied with what is given you." He made other biting marks detrimental to the character of the Indian.[52]

Jackes's version of McKay's speech is more detailed:

> My friends, I wish to make you a clear explanation of some things
> that it appears you do not understand. It has been said to you by
> your Governor that we did not come here to barter or trade with
> you for the land. You have made demands on the Governor, and
> from the way you have put them a white man would understand
> that you asked for daily provisions, also supplies for your hunt
> and for your pleasure excursions. Now my reasons for explaining
> to you are based on my past experience of treaties, for no sooner
> will the Governor and Commissioners turn their backs on you
> than some of you will say this thing and that thing was promised
> and the promise not fulfilled; that you cannot rely on the Queen's
> representative, that even he will not tell the truth, whilst among
> yourselves are the falsifiers. Now before we rise from here it must
> be understood, and it must be in writing, all that you are promised
> by the Governor and Commissioners, and I hope you will not
> leave until you have thoroughly understood the meaning of every
> word that comes from us. We have not come here to deceive you,
> we have not come here to rob you, we have not come here to take
> away anything that belongs to you, and we are not here to make
> peace as we would to hostile Indians, because you are the children
> of the Great Queen as we are, and there has never been anything
> but peace between us. What you have not understood clearly we
> will do our utmost to make perfectly plain to you.[53]

"In view of my knowledge of what had transpired at their council,"
Erasmus wrote in his account of the proceedings,

> I thought his [McKay's] speech most unfortunate and very harmful.
> His very attitude insulted the intelligence of his listeners. There was
> a distinct murmur of disapproval all over the crowd. McKay had
> hardly taken his seat when The Badger leapt to his feet.

> "I did not say that I wanted to be fed every day. You, I know,
> understand our language and yet you twist my words to suit your
> own meaning. What I did say was that when we settle on the
> ground to work the land, that is when we will need help and that
> is the only way a poor Indian can get along."[54]

"You will remember the promises which I have already made," the
lieutenant-governor replied. "I said you would get seed; you need not

concern yourselves so much about what your grand-children are going to eat; your children will be taught, and then they will be as well able to take care of themselves as the whites around them."[55]

Mistawasis supported The Badger's contention that the commissioners did not understand what the Indian leaders were telling them:

> It is well known that if we had plenty to live on from our gardens we would not still insist on getting more provision, but it is in case of any extremity, and from the ignorance of the Indian in commencing to settle that we thus speak; we are as yet in the dark; this is not a trivial matter for us.
>
> We were glad to hear what the Governor was saying to us and we understood it, but we are not understood, we do not mean to ask for food for every day but only when we commence and in case of famine or calamity. What we speak of and do now will last as long as the sun shines and the river runs, we are looking forward to our children's children, for we are old and have but few days to live.[56]

Ahtahkakoop finally spoke for the first time. He too tried to impress upon the commissioners that their concerns were real and that the chiefs knew what they needed. "The things we have been talking about in our councils," he began,

> I believe are for our own good. I think of the good Councillors of the Queen and of her Commissioners; I was told the Governor was a good man, and now that I see him I believe he is; in coming to see us, and what he has spoken, he has removed almost all obstacles and misunderstandings, and I hope he may remove them all. I have heard the good things you promise us, you have told us of the white man's way of living and mentioned some of the animals by which he gets his living, others you did not. We want food in the spring when we commence to farm; according as the Indian settles down on his reserves, and in proportion as he advances, his wants will increase.[57]

Ahtahkakoop then asked for the rest of the afternoon to consider all the things that had been said. This request was granted, with a "word of warning" from Morris not to "listen to every voice in your camp, listen to your wise men who know something of life, and do not come asking what is unreasonable, it pains me to have to say no, and I tell you again I cannot treat you with more favor than the other Indians." He asked the leading men to be ready to meet the next morning as soon as the Union Jack was raised over the commissioner's council tent.[58]

Despite his evasions, Morris understood what the Indian leaders were telling him. He also understood the implications if he refused to address the question of issuing provisions at seeding time, for he later wrote in his official report that the whole day had been

> occupied with this discussion on the food question, and it was the turning point with regard to the treaty.
>
> The Indians were, as they had been for some time past, full of uneasiness.
>
> They saw the buffalo, the only means of their support, passing away. They were anxious to learn to support themselves by agriculture, but felt too ignorant to do so, and they dreaded that during the transition period they would be swept off by disease or famine—already they have suffered terribly from the ravages of measles, scarlet fever and small-pox.
>
> It was impossible to listen to them without interest, they were not exacting, but they were very apprehensive of their future, and thankful, as one of them put it, "a new life was dawning upon them."[59]

So once again the chiefs and other leading men met in council to discuss their own needs and the terms offered by the Queen's representative. The things they agreed to ask for were written down by Erasmus.

The final day of negotiations took place on Wednesday, August 23. A Saulteaux man interrupted the proceedings almost as soon as they began, but Morris interrupted him, saying that if the "Chippewas want to talk with me I will hear them afterwards. They are a little handful of strangers from the east, I have treated with their whole nation, they are not wiser than their people." Then he urged that the business on hand go ahead: "I hear that the buffalo are near you and you want to be off to your hunt; there are many mouths here to feed and provisions are getting low; now my friends, I am ready to hear you."[60]

Titihkosiw (Kidney), one of the spiritual men in the assembly, rose to his feet. "Listen, my friends," he said. "All of you sitting around here, be patient and listen to what our interpreter has been instructed to tell you. What he will tell you are the things our main chiefs and councillors have decided to ask for and have agreed are for our best interests. There will be no more talk or questions asked of the Governor."[61]

Erasmus then read in Cree

> a list of the things the Indians had agreed in council to ask, viz.:—One ox and cow for each family. Four hoes, two spades, two scythes and a whetstone for each family. Two axes, two hay forks, two reaping hooks, one plough and one harrow for every three families. To each Chief one chest of tools as proposed. Seed of every kind in full to every one actually cultivating the soil. To make some provision for the poor, unfortunate, blind and lame. To supply us with a minister and school teacher of whatever denomination we belong to. To prevent fire-water being sold in the whole Saskatchewan.

> As the tribe advances in civilization, all agricultural implements to be supplied in proportion.

> When timber becomes scarcer on the reserves we select for ourselves, we want to be free to take it anywhere on the common. If our choice of a reserve does not please us before it is surveyed we want to be allowed to select another. We want to be at liberty to hunt on any place as usual. If it should happen that a Government bridge or scow is built on the Saskatchewan at any place, we want passage free. One boar, two sows, one horse, harness and waggon for each Chief. One cooking stove for each Chief. That we be supplied with medicines free of cost. That a hand-mill be given to each band. Lastly in case of war occurring in the country, we do not want to be liable to serve in it.[62]

When Erasmus had finished reading the petition, Titihkosiw spoke directly to the commissioners. "When we look back to the past," he said, "we do not see where the Cree nation has ever watered the ground with the white man's blood, he has always been our friend and we his; trusting to the Giver of all good, to the generosity of the Queen, and to the Governor and his councillors, we hope you will grant us this request."[63]

Wāwikanihk k-ōtāmahoht (He Strikes Him On The Back), chief and keeper of the sacred pipestem, then addressed Morris, McKay and Christie on behalf of the people:

Pity the voice of the Indian, if you grant what we request the sound will echo through the land; open the way; I speak for the children that they may be glad; the land is wide, there is plenty of room. My mouth is full of milk; I am only as a sucking child; I am glad; have compassion on the manner in which I was brought up; let our children be clothed; let us now stand in the light of day to see our way on this earth; long ago it was good when we first were made, I wish the same were back again. But now the law has come, and in that I wish to walk. What God has said, and our mother here (the earth), and these our brethren, let it be so.[64]

A recess was called while Morris consulted with the other commissioners. When the negotiations reconvened Morris told the chiefs and leading men he was ready to answer them "but understand well, it is not to be talked backwards and forwards. I am not going to act like a man bargaining for a horse for you. I have considered well what you have asked for, and my answer will be a final one. I cannot grant everything you ask, but as far as I can go I will, and when done I can only say you will be acting to your own interests if you take my hand."[65]

Morris then went over each section of the petition, giving reasons why certain requests were acceptable or not acceptable:

I will speak of what you asked yesterday and to-day. I told you yesterday that if any great sickness or general famine overtook you, that on the Queen being informed of it by her Indian agent, she in her goodness would give such help as she thought the Indians needed. You asked for help when you settled on your reserves during the time you were planting. You asked very broadly at first. I think the request you make now is reasonable to a certain extent; but help should be given after you settle on the reserve for three years only, for after that time you should have food of your own raising, besides all the things that are given to you; this assistance would only be given to those actually cultivating the soil. Therefore, I would agree to give every spring, for three years, the sum of one thousand dollars to assist you in buying provisions while planting the ground. I do this because you seem anxious to make a living for yourselves, it is more than has been done anywhere else; I must do it on my own responsibility, and trust to the other Queen's councillors to ratify it.[66]

Morris also agreed to give four hoes, two spades, two scythes and whet-stone, two axes, two hay forks, and two reaping hooks for every family "actually cultivating the soil" and a plough and harrow for every three families under the same conditions. He said the carpenter's tools and seed grain had already been promised. He could not "undertake the responsibility of promising provision for the poor, blind and lame." This, the lieutenant-governor said, must be left to the "charity and kind hearts of the people," as it was in white society.

Similarly, although the maintenance of schools had already been promised "when you settled down, and there were enough children," it was up to the "large societies formed for the purpose of sending the gospel to the Indians" to provide ministers. "You see missionaries here on the ground, both Roman Catholic and Protestant," he continued. "They have been in the country for many years. As it has been in the past, so it will be again, you will not be forgotten."

In regards to liquor, he said that "strong laws" had already been passed to prohibit the selling of "fire-water" to the Indians and the police were in the North-West to enforce those laws, as well as those against the use of poison for animals.

Lieutenant-Governor Morris urged the chiefs to select a good place for a reserve from the beginning, but said they would not be held to their choice of reserve before it was surveyed. He acknowledged that the people wanted "to be at liberty to hunt as before." He then went one step further, adding that "I told you we did not want to take that means of living from you, you have it the same as before, only this, if a man, whether Indian or Half-breed, had a good field of grain, you would not destroy it with your hunt."

He went on to say that he did not think the government would be building bridges and scows. That was the responsibility of private enterprise, so free passage was not a question to be considered by the government. And then, responding to the request that the men and young men not be compelled to fight in case of war, the lieutenant-governor said he was sure the Queen "would not ask her Indian children to fight for her unless they wished, but if she did call for them and their wives and children were in danger they are not the men I think them to be, if they did not come forward to their protection."[67]

He agreed to have a clause added to Treaty Six stating that "a medicine chest will be kept at the house of each Indian agent, in case of sickness amongst you." In regards to the number of livestock, the chief commissioner said:

> I offered you to each band, according to size, two or four oxen, also one bull and four cows, and now you ask for an ox and a cow for each family. I suppose in this treaty there will be six hundred families, so it would take very much money to grant these things, and then all the other Indians would want them, so we cannot do it: but that you may see it that we are anxious to have you raise animals of your own we will give you for each band four oxen, one bull, six cows, one boar and two pigs. After a band has settled on a reserve and commenced to raise grain, we will give them a hand-mill.[68]

Morris refused to give a "cooking-stove" to each chief, saying there were too many chiefs to do that. Then he added, "and now, although I fear I am going too far, I will grant the request that each Chief be furnished with a horse, harness, and waggon."[69]

> "I have answered your requests very fully," the lieutenant-governor concluded, "and that there may be no mistake as to what we agree upon, it will be written down, and I will leave a copy with the two principal Chiefs, and as soon as it can be properly printed I will send copies to the Chiefs so that they may know what is written, and there can be no mistake.

> "It now rests with you, my friends, and I ask you without any hesitation to take what I have offered you."[70]

It was Ahtahkakoop who responded to the offer made by the Queen's representative:

> I never sent a letter to the Governor; I was waiting to meet him, and what we have asked we considered would be for the benefit of our children. I am not like some of my friends who have sent their messages down, even stretched out their hands to the Queen asking her to come; I have always said to my people that I would wait to see the Governor arrive, then he would ask what would benefit his children; now I ask my people, those that are in favour of the offer, to say so.[71]

Jackes reported that "they all assented by holding up their hands and shouting."[72] Nevertheless, some were still not satisfied. Poundmaker was among these, and he spoke one more time:

> I do not differ from my people, but I want more explanation. I
> heard what you said yesterday, and I thought that when the law
> was established in this country it would be for our good. From
> what I can hear and see now, I cannot understand that I shall be
> able to clothe my children and feed them as long as the sun shines
> and water runs. With regard to the different Chiefs who are to
> occupy the reserves, I expected they would receive sufficient for
> their support, this is why I speak. In the presence of God and the
> Queen's representative I say this, because I do not know how to
> build a house for myself, you see how naked I am, and if I tried to
> do it my naked body would suffer; again, I do not know how to
> cultivate the ground for myself, at the same time I quite under-
> stand what you have offered to assist us in this.[73]

Then Joseph Thoma, who claimed to be speaking on behalf of Red
Pheasant, said that "some were not present when the list of articles mentioned was made, there are many things overlooked." He then requested
additional assistance, money, and land.[74] The lieutenant-governor was not
pleased and refused to consider the requests. He noted that Red Pheasant
had said nothing when the petition was handed to the treaty commissioners, making him believe that the chief had approved the decisions that had
been made. "What I have offered was thought of long before I saw you,"
Morris continued, and

> it has been accepted by others more in number than you are. I am
> glad that so many are of one mind. I am surprised you are not all.
> I hold out a full hand to you, and it will be a bad day for you and
> your children if I have to return and say that the Indians threw
> away my hand. I cannot accede to the requests of the Red
> Pheasant. I have heard and considered the wants of Mist-ow-asis
> and Ah-tuck-ah-coop, and when the people were spoken to I
> understood they were pleased. As for the little band who are not
> of one mind with the great body, I am quite sure that a week will
> not pass on leaving this before they will regret it."[75]

And, once again, the chief treaty commissioner assured the assembled
people that "I want the Indians to understand that all that has been offered
is a gift, and they still have the same mode of living as before."

After the principal chiefs indicated for the second time that they were
satisfied with the terms outlined by the lieutenant-governor, Red Pheasant

rose to his feet. He repudiated the demands and remarks of Thoma and said the man had spoken on "his own and not by his permission."[76] In Erasmus's words, "that terminated the discussion in the formation of the treaty terms."

Morris thanked the people for their trust, adding, "what we have done has been done before the Great Spirit and in the face of the people." The extra things that had been promised were added to the draft of Treaty Six, and then Morris asked the interpreter to read the entire document to the chiefs and leading men gathered before the council tent.[77] According to Erasmus

> The reading of the treaty took a great deal of time and required the services of all the interpreters but this time there were no fireworks in the matter of words used, nor the objection to Ballenden's voice. Half the Indians were not concerned.

> Mista-wa-sis had called me aside and told me to keep a close watch on the wording to see that it included everything that had been promised. However, the other chiefs appeared satisfied that the Governor would carry out his promises to the letter. I was able to assure Mista-wa-sis that everything promised had been included in the writing.[78]

Before the treaty was signed, however, Mistawasis had one more piece of business to bring before the commissioners. "I wish to speak a word for some Half-breeds who wish to live on the reserves with us, they are as poor as we are and need help," he stated. When asked how many he was referring to, the chief indicated there were about 20. Morris replied that he had heard that

> some Half-breeds want to take lands at Red River and join the Indians here, but they cannot take with both hands. The Half-breeds of the North-West cannot come into the Treaty. The small class of Half-breeds who live as Indians and with the Indians, can be regarded as Indians by the Commissioners, who will judge of each case on its own merits as it comes up, and will report their action to the Queen's Councillors for their approval.[79]

That afternoon, on August 23, 1876, Lieutenant-Governor Morris signed Treaty Six "for the Queen and in her name."* Treaty commissioners

---

* The text of Treaty Six appears in the Appendices.

McKay and Christie placed their signatures on the document. Then Chief Mistawasis and Chief Ahtahkakoop signed, followed by 11 other chiefs and 44 headmen.* The witnesses included Jackes, several North-West Mounted Police and Hudson's Bay Company officers, and a number of half-breed and Métis men from the Carlton district.

The lieutenant-governor presented medals and flags to Mistawasis and Ahtahkakoop at 10 a.m. the next day in front of the council tent. The two head chiefs were also formally presented with the chief's government uniform: a scarlet frock coat braided with gold lace, a top hat of felt with a gold band, pants, shirt, and handkerchief.[80] The other chiefs were given their medals and flags and told that they, along with all the headmen, could get their uniforms at the trading store at Fort Carlton that evening. The uniform for the headmen was similar to that given all the chiefs, except the frock coats were blue instead of red.† According to Erasmus the lieutenant-governor "gave …[the chiefs and headmen] a short discourse on the meaning of the uniforms, which in substance meant that they were now representatives of the Queen Mother and to see that their people should receive justice, and on their part to fulfill the obligations contained in their positions."[81] Morris also arranged for "a present of calicoes, shirts, tobacco, pipes, and other articles" to be given to the Indians.[82]

Morris then announced that he would meet with the Saulteaux who wished to speak to him. When that was done, Christie would start making the treaty payments. The chiefs and councillors were expected to assist with the payments "in every way possible." Additionally, the chiefs who had already selected the location for their reserves were asked to give the information to Christie when they were paid.

"Now, I have only to say farewell," the lieutenant-governor concluded. "We have done a good work; we will never all of us meet again face to face, but I go on to my other work, feeling that I have, in the Queen's hands, been instrumental to your good. I pray God's blessing upon you to make you happy and prosperous, and I bid you farewell."[83]

There was a "general shout of approval" and then, in Erasmus's words, "there was a great deal of hand-shaking and some fine compliments

---

* William Badger, John Badger and James Bear (headmen of John Smith's band) and Bernard Constant (a headman in James Smith's band) signed their names in English on the treaty document. The chiefs and other headmen placed an "x" beside their names.

† In a long-standing tradition, the coats issued to the chiefs by the Hudson's Bay Company were dark blue; the headmen's coats were red. The government ignored this tradition when issuing their coats and reversed the colours.

Illustration by Willard Ahenakew

Chief Ahtahkakoop signing Treaty Six, witnessed by Lieutenant-Governor Alexander Morris, Sergeant Major S.B. Steele, and Commissioner James McKay (seated at end of table).

Ahtahkakoop, Mistawasis, and the other chiefs received their large treaty medals on August 24, 1876. Made of silver, the medal was engraved on both sides.

exchanged on both sides before the Governor took his departure" from the treaty grounds.[84]

Thus, with signatures and marks placed on paper, followed by handshakes, Treaty Six had been sealed, signed, and delivered. The groundwork for change in the Indian lands had been laid.

Ahtahkakoop was relatively pleased with the negotiations. He had foreseen the demise of the buffalo and the increasingly large number of non-Indian people moving onto the plains and into the parkland. His brother Nāpēskis had brought home stories about the large towns in eastern Canada. Ahtahkakoop and many of the other leaders could envision what lay ahead. Justifiably, they were concerned about the future, not so much for themselves but for their children and their children's children. Men of action, they were willing to learn a new way of life and were confident that with adequate help during the transition period they could succeed. Negotiating Treaty Six had been a first step towards this end.

The chiefs and leading men at Fort Carlton believed that they had signed, on behalf of the Indian nations they represented, a treaty to share the land with the settlers and to keep the peace with the government, amongst themselves, and with the newcomers. In exchange, they had negotiated certain rights and guarantees that would "continue as long as the sun shone and river flowed."

They had trusted the lieutenant-governor. His words had been of friendship. He had referred to the men as his Indian brothers. They were, all of them, "children of the Queen," of the same blood, and had been made by the same God. The Queen cared for them, Morris had told the people, and she wanted to help them. Spoken in the presence of the sacred pipe, they believed that the promises made by the lieutenant-governor could not be broken.

Ahtahkakoop, Mistawasis, and the other chiefs had bargained hard, extending the negotiations over several days to obtain as many of their demands as possible. Their understandings were clear. They called the land that would become their reserves *iskonikan*, or "that which is held back." This land was not given to the Crown to be parcelled back to them. It was theirs, and would remain so.[85] The Reverend John McDougall, who attended the negotiations and met in council with the leading men at Fort Pitt in September, held a similar view. "The Indians," he said, "reserved certain areas in the proportion of one section of good land for every five souls. They were to select these reserves, the government was to have them surveyed and to maintain these reserves for the Indians inviolate so long as the grass grows and rivers run. The Cree word Iskomkan means that which is kept back and is the equivalent of the Anglo-Saxon word 'reserves.'"[86]

Ahtahkakoop's band members, who had already started to farm, had identified the land they wanted ploughed in 1875, the year before the treaty was signed. Through discussions with the Reverend John Hines, the chief presumably had some concept of how much land was to be retained under treaty, and he likely believed it would be enough, at least initially. Had not Morris assured the people that the one square mile of land for every family of five, as specified in the treaty, was "much more than you will ever be able to farm"?[87]

As far as the remaining land was concerned, the chiefs and leading men understood that the government wanted to use it for agricultural purposes. Thus, only prairie land to the depth of a plough was surrendered.[88] Time and time again Morris had assured the people that they could hunt and fish as before. Had not Morris said, "I do not want to interfere with your hunting and fishing. I want you to pursue it through the country, as you have heretofore done"?[89] Indeed, the lieutenant-governor's intent was clear, for in his official report he stated that

> I had ascertained that the Indian mind was oppressed with vague fears; they dreaded the treaty; they had been made to believe that they would be compelled to live on the reserves wholly, and abandon their hunting … I accordingly shaped my address, so as to give them confidence in the intentions of the Government, and to quiet their apprehensions. I impressed strongly on them the necessity of changing their present mode of life, and commencing to make homes and gardens for themselves, so as to be prepared for the diminution of the buffalo and other large animals, which is going on so rapidly."[90]

No one had talked about giving the animals, fish, plants, trees, and the minerals lying under the ground to the Queen. So these entities, part of Mother Earth and gifts from the Creator, were not part of Treaty Six. These things were not "given" to the Queen. Along with everything else that was required to make a living, they were "held back" in the vast area where the people had hunted and travelled.[91] If the government or others wanted to use some of the things that were held back, such as trees and minerals, their use would have to be negotiated.

Proud, capable and independent, the chiefs at no time considered relinquishing their authority to the Queen and to her governments. Nor was it the intent of the chiefs and headmen to give up their rights to govern for the common good of their people. That would have been unthinkable.

Some of the leading men, with Ahtahkakoop and Mistawasis at the forefront, nevertheless saw the treaty as an instrument for preparing their children and grandchildren for the future. Ahtahkakoop's band, in particular, had already begun to make the transition to farming. Hopefully, for at least another decade, the buffalo and woodland game would continue to sustain the people as they developed their farms. During this transition, especially in the first years, they would need assistance at planting time. With this knowledge, gained from experience, Ahtahkakoop and the others had asked for provisions and extra assistance in the spring. The lieutenant-governor had seen the reasonableness of the request and agreed.

Aware of the work required to break the ground, plant crops, cut hay, and harvest their crops, the Indian leaders had also successfully negotiated a slight increase in the meagre number of implements, oxen, and cattle that would be provided. Assurances had been given by Morris that seed would be supplied, though he said he refused to include the chiefs' request for instruction in farming as a treaty term. Ahtahkakoop, who had already made arrangements to have John Hines living amongst them, was fully aware of the necessity of this kind of help.

Additionally, Morris had agreed that in times of famine and great sickness, assistance would be forthcoming. And indeed, this aid was not unprecedented. The Hudson's Bay Company had provided similar services for many years to families that traded at the post. The lieutenant-governor had also agreed to place a medicine chest on each reserve. This was deemed necessary by the Indian leaders to combat the diseases new to the Indian people like smallpox, measles, whooping cough, and tuberculosis. For other ailments and sicknesses, many people intended to rely on traditional medicines.

Other concerns about the future had been lessened somewhat when Morris promised that the government would maintain schools. "Your children will be taught, and then they will be as well able to take care of themselves as the whites around them," the lieutenant-governor had said.[92]

And Morris had acknowledged the authority of the chiefs. First and foremost, he had recognized that they were empowered to negotiate and sign Treaty Six on behalf of their bands. He had presented them with uniforms, medals, and flags to identify them as chiefs. Additionally, he had also told the gathering that the chiefs "ought to be respected, they ought to be looked up to by their people.… and the chiefs and head men are not to be lightly put aside."[93]

The lieutenant-governor had also promised that the missionaries would not forget the people, annuity payments would be made each year, the chiefs and headmen would be paid an annual salary, the ban on liquor would continue and—among other things—the men would not have to go to war.

For the Indian people, the things that were promised and talked about during the negotiations were as binding as the words that appeared in the written treaty. These rights and guarantees had been promised in the presence of the sacred pipestem, where only the truth could be spoken.

For the government officials, on the other hand, Treaty Six consisted of printed words which sometimes were in conflict with the Indian people's understanding of what had been promised. The treaty had used words like "cede, release, surrender, and yield up." Except for the reading of the treaty, which included a section on the boundaries of land the Indian nations had "surrendered," there had been little if any discussion on what had actually been given up. Practically all the discussion had centred on what the Indian people would receive as "a gift on top of everything else." And they had been assured that what was offered "is to last as long as that sun shines and yonder river flows," and that the government would not "take away your living, you will have it then as you have now."[94]

The implications of some of Morris's other statements were apparently lost in the flowery words, the symbolism, and perhaps even Erasmus's interpretation of Morris's words. Several times the lieutenant-governor had referred to the leaders as "servants" of the Queen. The proud Plains people were servants to no one. The Indians, as well as the "whites," were expected to obey the Queen's laws, Morris had said. Ahtahkakoop and the others no doubt thought, since no other explanations were given, that this statement referred to the North-West Mounted Police. The people had their own rules and traditions, developed through consensus at band and tribal levels. These had not been part of the negotiations.

Additionally, although the lieutenant-governor had said the chiefs were to be respected and not lightly put aside, he had also stated that "once the Queen approves a Chief or Councillor he cannot be removed unless he behaves badly."[95] In other words the treaty commissioners, on behalf of the Queen and the Canadian government, were claiming the right to approve the appointment of the leading men and to remove a chief or headman from office if he, in the opinion of government officials, "behaves badly." Acknowledged as chiefs and headmen by their band members, these men did not believe that by putting their marks on a piece of paper, they had relinquished their rights to govern themselves and their people. That had not been the intent of the treaty and it was not the understanding of the Indian leadership. Nor was it their intent to give all their land to the Queen, and then have the government give it back in small pieces.

Morris had arrived at Fort Carlton with the terms of Treaty Six already written on paper and limited authority to make changes. As a result of perceptive bargaining, Ahtahkakoop, Mistawasis, and the other leaders had successfully negotiated terms not included in earlier treaties. These included provisions and extra assistance during cultivation and planting, assistance in times of famine and pestilence, and medical care. These terms, considered to be rights and guarantees granted in exchange for sharing the land, were added to the original document before it was signed.

In general the chiefs and other leading men, based on their understanding of the negotiations and treaty terms, were satisfied. The agreement may not have been perfect, and a few men had demanded more. Nonetheless, Ahtahkakoop, Mistawasis, and most of the other leading men realized that a good leader had to be realistic. He had to negotiate for what was obtainable. To do otherwise could mean ending up with less. And so, the Indian leaders and the treaty commissioners signed Treaty Six.

CHAPTER FOURTEEN

The Days After Treaty Six Was
Signed at Fort Carlton

After Treaty Six was signed Morris met with the Saulteaux who had interrupted the final stages of the treaty proceedings. These were the men blamed for trying to stop the lieutenant-governor from crossing the South Saskatchewan River on his way to Fort Carlton. Morris said that the group, which numbered about "half a dozen," included a man who had been paid his treaty money at Fort Qu'Appelle. Most of the others were from Yellow Quill's band.

The lieutenant-governor told the group that they could not receive their treaty money at Fort Carlton because they did not belong there. He restated that the Queen had made treaties with "the whole Chippewa nation except two or three little wandering bands such as you ... I do not think you are any wiser than the Chippewas from the Lake Superior to the North-West Angle." When the spokesman for the group became "insolent," Morris said he "declined to hear them further, and they retired, some stating that they would go to Fort Pitt, which I warned them not to do."[1]

Jackes provided an account of Nus-was-oo-wah-tum's speech, which Morris considered "insolent," along with the confrontation that followed:

> NUS-WAS-OO-WAH-TUM—"When we asked the Cree bands what they intended to do with regard to the treaty they would not come to us; it is true we told them 'do not be in a hurry in giving your assent;' you ought to be detained a little while; all along the prices have been to one side, and we have had no say. He that made us provided everything for our mode of living; I have seen this all along, it has brought me up and I am not tired of it, and

for you, the white man, everything has been made for your maintenance, and now that you come and stand on this our earth
(ground) I do not understand; I see dimly to-day what you are
doing, and I find fault with a portion of it; that is why I stand
back; I would have been glad if every white man of every denomination were now present to hear what I say; through what you
have done you have cheated my kinsmen."

GOVERNOR—"I will not sit here and hear such words from the
Chippewas. Who are you? You come from my country* and you
tell me the Queen has cheated you; it is not so. You say we have
the best of the bargains; you know it is not so. If you have any
requests to make in a respectful manner, I am ready to hear."

CHIPPEWA—"The God that made us and who alone is our master, I am afraid of Him to deviate from his commandment."[2]

The Chippewa refused to discuss the matter further. Ironically, a number of
people in Yellow Quill's band signed an adhesion to Treaty Four at Fort
Pelly about the same time Treaty Six was being negotiated at Fort Carlton.[3]

The Saulteaux left and the registering of the chiefs and headmen who
had signed Treaty Six, along with the men, women, and children in their
bands, began. The leading men assisted with the process, organizing their
people and helping at the table as needed. Christie, with the assistance of
Erasmus and Thomas McKay of Prince Albert, supervised the payment of
money that had been promised: $25 for each chief, $15 for each headman,
and $12 for each man, woman, and child.[4] Every man, beginning with the
chief and the headmen, was listed by name and assigned a treaty number.
The number of women, boys, and girls in his family was recorded, along
with the amount of money paid to the family. The only women named were
those who were alone or considered to be the head of a household. Names
were not given for any of the unmarried children. These payments, Morris
had said, were "presents" or special money to commemorate the signing of
Treaty Six. Payments in all other years were to consist of salaries of $25
for each chief and $15 for each headman (not to exceed four for each
band). Every other person was to be paid an annuity of $5.

---

* As lieutenant-governor of Manitoba and the North-West Territories, Morris resided in
Winnipeg.

1876

			Men	Women	Children Boys	Girls	Amount
		Amt. brought forward					$3795
S.B		Carlton Crees					
		Ah. tah K. ah. Koops band					
Chief	1	Ah. tah K. ah. Koop	1	2	1	2	85
Headman	2	Sah. Sa. Koo. mooi	1	2	2	1	75
do	3	Benjamin / has one arm /	1	1	3	1	75
do	4	Mee. now. ah. chawk. way	1	1	2	3	87
do	5	Kee. sik. ow. as. is	1	1	1	1	57
	6	Pay. nee. sa. was. Kahk.	1	3	3	1	90
	7	Ma. ew. Ka. pew	1	2	5	3	132
	8	Kah. ke. eva. ah. pew. ahk.	1	1	1	1	45
	9	Say. tah. yah. too. way	1	1			24
	10	Koo. ew. Koo. se. wah. yah. new.	1	1		4	72
	11	Na. tah. wee. Kah. pew.	1	1	2	1	60
	12	A. ha. wah. stew.	1	1	5	1	96
	13	Ke. che. moo. Koo. mahn	1	5	3		108
	14	Oo. tah. yah. pee. Kew.	1	1	2	3	84
	15	A. see. nee. wah. pee. wa. yin	1	2	1	1	60
	16	John Saskatchewan	1	1	2		48
	17	Ah. fis. chee. nah. fa. sis	1	1		1	36
	18	Kwahs. Kwa. yah. Kah. sis	1	2	2	1	72
	19	we. che. Kah. pow. us. maw	1	1			24
	20	A. see. nee. we. Kah. pow.	1	1	1	2	60
	21	Kah. Ke. Ka. yahs	1	2			36
	22	Na. see. Kah. sun	1	1	2	2	72
	23	Kah. Kah. Soo	1	1		2	48
	24	Kah. see. yoo. us. too. tew	1	1			24
	25	Chee. pay. ow. ahs. is	1	1	1	2	60
	26	See. yah. fwah. suw	1	1	2		48
	27	Wah. fah. wayo	1	1	3		60
	28	Pee. ya. sees: 1,701.—	1	2	1	1	60
		Amt. Carried forward	28	41	45	34	5594

National Archives of Canada, RG10, vol. 9412

Page one of the first treaty paylist for the Ahtahkakoop Band, 1876. It registered the number of men, women, boys, and girls in the band and documented how much each family was paid.

Even though some of the families left for the plains to hunt buffalo before the treaty registration began, it took two days to complete the registrations and payments. At the end of the second day (August 25), 13 chiefs, 44 headmen, 262 men, 473 women, 473 boys, and 481 girls had been paid, for a total of 1,746. In addition, 41 people from bands that had signed Treaty Four received their payments. It was noted by Jackes that "a large number of the tribe absent at the hunt will be paid next year."[5]

In Ahtahkakoop's band, 53 men, 80 women, 81 boys, and 62 girls, for a total of 276, were paid. These numbers included Ahtahkakoop, who was listed as chief, and the four headmen, Sasakamoose, Wāskitoy (The Thigh),* Kā-miyo-ahcahkwēw, and Kīsik-awāsis.[6] Sasakamoose was Ahtahkakoop's brother, and Kā-miyo-ahcahkwēw and Kīsik-awāsis were his sons. With 53 families paid as part of his band, Ahtahkakoop had the largest number of registered families. Mistawasis, who had 52 families, represented the second largest band.† The other chiefs, with the exception of the Willow Cree who were paid later had between 17 and 23.[7]

The days that followed the signing of Treaty Six were ones of excitement. The people gathered around the traders' tents pitched near the camp as they decided how to spend their treaty money. The concept of money was new for most of them. Until now the hunters, trappers, and their wives had traded the harvest of their work—furs, pemmican, and other country produce—for European goods. They knew the value of their products and were skilled in making a fair deal using the fur trade standard, the "Made Beaver."‡ Now, they had pieces of paper called money with which to barter, and it was difficult to know if prices were fair, if they had given the right amount of money, and if they had received the correct amount of "change." When the people traded at the fur trade posts, they were expected to pay off their debts before new purchases were made. Now they had an assortment of traders and goods to choose from, and the traders had to compete for business.

Tobacco and tea were popular purchases. Supplies for the winter

---

* Wāskitoy was also known as Benjamin Kīskipiton (which translates as Has One Arm Cut Off), and Benjamin One Arm. Hines also referred to him as Benjamin Joyful.

† Dr. A.J. Jackes, secretary to the treaty commissioners, had earlier reported that Ahtahkakoop represented about 70 lodges and Mistawasis represented 76 lodges. Thus, a good number of families apparently went hunting at the completion of the negotiations.

‡ One Made Beaver was the equivalent of one prime beaver skin. The prices for furs, country produce, and trade goods were based on this standard.

included guns, flints, shot, and powder for hunting, and traps, chisels, files, axes, knives and other gear to help with trapping and everyday work. They bought wool blankets, twine for making nets, cloth of various kinds and colours for dresses, leggings, shirts, breechcloths, and other clothing, and coats called capotes. Other purchases included cooking pots, dishes, looking-glasses and combs, beads for decorating clothing, pipe bags, and other items; plumes and fancy feathers for adorning hats; tacks for decorating the stocks of guns; and many other articles. Some people also bought spotted coloured cloth as an offering to Old Woman Spirit and white, yellow, red, blue, and green cloth for offerings to the Creator and his spirit helpers.

Unfortunately for Clarke and the Hudson's Bay Company, the traders at Fort Carlton benefited little from the dealings that took place.[8] The *Northcote* steamboat, loaded with supplies and trading goods that had been picked up at Grand Rapids, was unable to get to Fort Carlton because of low water and boulder-strewn river channels.[*] One hundred tons of freight were unloaded at Cole's Falls, situated some 30 miles downstream from Prince Albert. The steamer then returned to Grand Rapids. Clarke's meagre supply of trade goods at Fort Carlton was soon exhausted and he watched helplessly as his competitors did a profitable business with the hundreds of Indians camped at the treaty grounds.[9]

The people continued to rejoice in being together. They danced and held special ceremonies to help their people. Everywhere, the people talked about the treaty that had just been signed and they hoped, with all their hearts, that the steps just taken would ensure a safe future for their children, their grandchildren, and the ones who would follow. The sound of drums and singing echoed across the Saskatchewan valley day and night as men of all ages, watched by enthusiastic audiences, played gambling games. The young and the agile played field hockey and other games during the day, and on the flat of land by the river, money and rifles changed hands as the best buffalo runners were matched against each other in races that created tremendous excitement.[10] In the camp, the women visited and cooked. And many of the people, for the first time, tasted bannock, an unleavened bread made from flour.[11]

While the treaty payments were being made, Clarke and Morris both sent

---

[*] Grand Rapids is located at the place where the Saskatchewan River empties into Lake Winnipeg.

word to Erasmus that they wished to speak privately with him. The interpreter made the calls later the same day. Erasmus recorded in his memoirs that Clarke apologized for snubbing him on his arrival. "I was in a bad spot after hiring those two men," Clarke explained. "I could not go back on my word." Erasmus responded:

> "Well, as it turned out there was no harm done, but I hope you realize that your actions almost created a riot and could have wrecked the whole business. Trying to pretend you did not know me that first evening I consider a rank insult, and that, my high-minded friend, I do not take without repayment. Further, you should know that you cannot treat men like Mista-wa-sis and Ah-tuk-a-kup as children, and the manner in which the Honourable James spoke during the meeting was equally as stupid."

> "Well, Peter, I hope you hold no grudge. You can understand the position I was in at the time. I hope you will forget the whole miserable business."

> "Certainly, Clarke. The victor is never the man to bear a grudge; it is always the loser, and I hope you bear that in mind."[12]

At a meeting later in the day, Morris complimented Erasmus for the work he had done during the treaty proceedings and said he would be paid "five dollars a day, as you have interpreted for the Indians, as well as the government." Christie interjected that Erasmus had earned the money since he had done "two men's work." He also suggested that the interpreter receive extra pay in recognition of the fact that he had travelled several hundred miles to be there. Morris agreed, and the plainsman was given "fifteen dollars for four days' pay," for a total of 60 dollars.

"This was indeed good news," Erasmus commented, "and the unexpected support from Mr. Christie was, you can believe me, more than ample compensation for my real or imagined slight of the first evening of the talks."

Then Morris hired Erasmus to interpret at the upcoming treaty negotiations at Fort Pitt. His salary was to be $5 per day for both travelling and interpreting.[13]

On the morning of August 26, the day after the treaty payments had been completed, the Indian people crowded inside the stockades at Fort Carlton to pay their farewell visit to the lieutenant-governor. They were led by the chiefs and headmen wearing their new uniforms and treaty medals. The chiefs "came forward in order and shook hands, each one making a few remarks expressive of their gratitude for the benefits received and promised, and of their good will to the white man."[14] Morris replied, saying he was gratified with their co-operation and behaviour, pleased they had taken his advice, and glad they were "determined to go to work and help themselves." He added that "he hoped their Councils would always be wisely conducted, and that they would do everything in their power to maintain peace amongst themselves and with their neighbors." Additionally, he hoped "the Almighty would give them wisdom and prosper them." The Indian people gave three cheers for the Queen, Morris, the North-West Mounted Police, and Clarke, and then they left with a flourish, firing their guns into the air as they went.[15]

Since Morris was reluctant to leave the Fort Carlton area without coming to terms with the Willow Cree, he sent his guide, Pierre Levailler, to deliver a message to the leading men at Duck Lake. In his message the lieutenant-governor told the Willow Cree that if they were willing to accept the terms of the treaty signed by the other chiefs and councillors, he would meet them at James McKay's camp on Monday, August 28. By the time the messenger arrived at Duck Lake, Beardy and the other Willow Cree leaders had already decided to accept the treaty terms, providing Morris came to Duck Lake. Father André, a Catholic priest from the nearby St. Laurent settlement, was asked to write a letter to this effect. Morris's message, however, arrived before André's letter left the camp, so the chiefs decided to go to McKay's camp as requested.

The meeting began with the leading men shaking hands with the Queen's officials. Erasmus interpreted. Seswekos (Cut Nose)* stated that "if it is your intention to honor me with a Chief's clothing, I wish you would give me one that would correspond with the sky above." Cimanaskat (Stump) said "I feel very grateful that I am spared by the Great Spirit to see this day of his, may we be blessed in whatever we do this day."

Then Morris got down to business, outlining his purpose for coming and expressing regret that the Willow Cree would not meet with him at the

---

* Seswekos is also known as Sikiskiwan, which translates as Blood Coming From Cut Nose.

treaty grounds. He refused to grant blue coats to the chiefs, saying that "red is the color all the Queen's Chiefs wear. I wear this coat [dark blue], but it is only worn by those who stand as the Queen's Councillors; her soldiers and her officers wear red, and all the other Chiefs of the Queen wear the coats we have brought, and the good of this is that when the Chief is seen with his uniform and medal everyone knows he is an officer of hers."[16]

Beardy and Cut Nose both expressed concern about the scarcity of the buffalo and asked the government to assist in preserving them. Beardy then informed Morris that although he would accept the terms offered, he wanted to receive assistance when he was "utterly unable to help" himself. He also asked for a blue suit of clothing and requested that the two men* sitting beside him "be Chiefs in our place with me and to have six Councillors (two each) in all."[17]

Morris's response was the same as before: "we cannot support or feed the Indians every day, further than to help them to find the means of doing it for themselves by cultivating the soil. ... You will get your share of the one thousand dollars' worth of provisions when you commence to work on your reserves."[18]

He refused to give blue jackets to the chiefs for the second time, once again going against the Hudson's Bay Company's tradition of giving blue jackets to the "higher" chiefs and scarlet jackets to the "lesser chiefs." He did agree, however, to recognize three chiefs with two councillors to each.

In regards to the preservation of the buffalo, the lieutenant-governor said it was an important topic and would be considered by the North-West Council[†] "to see if a wise law can be passed, one that will be a living law that can be carried out and obeyed." Such a law, he said, would be printed in Cree, as well as French and English. One of the chiefs asked Morris to include the half-breed people in the treaty. Morris replied as before, saying that only "a certain class of Indian Half-breeds who had always lived in the camp with the Indians and were *in fact* Indians, would be recognized."[19]

The chiefs and headmen signed the treaty, and the medals and flags were distributed. When their request that treaty payments be made at Duck Lake was refused, registration and payments were carried out at McKay's camp. Band members were then told to go to Fort Carlton to get their

---

* Sīsīkwanis (Little Rattler) and Kā-pēyakwaskonam (One Arrow).

[†] The governing body for the North-West Territories, whose members were appointed by the Canadian government.

clothing, presents, and the Willow Cree's share of the unused provisions. With this done, the formalities associated with the negotiating and signing of Treaty Six in the Carlton district were complete.

The official party returned to Fort Carlton to settle its accounts and to get ready for the trip to Fort Pitt and the second stage of treaty negotiations.

Ahtahkakoop and Mistawasis visited Erasmus at his tipi early on the day he was getting ready to leave for Fort Pitt. The chiefs told the interpreter that they had not gathered all the money "from their Indians" to pay him. "We were waiting for the Indians to receive all their treaty money," they explained, "before we started collecting your money."

When Erasmus told them he would have to leave for Fort Pitt "today or this evening," Ahtahkakoop replied that they would "start at once and see what we can do. You must wait until we see you later in the day."[20]

As promised, Ahtahkakoop and Mistawasis spent the next few hours collecting money from the families, and in the afternoon they gave Erasmus $230 in payment for his services during the negotiations. "With the sixty I had received from the paymaster Mr. Christie, I felt well paid for my trip," Erasmus said, adding that "I thanked them for the money and told them I was well satisfied with the amount they gave me."

Erasmus, with extra money in his pocket, made a tour of the traders' tents:

> An Indian stopped me while I was making the rounds of the traders' stores and offered to buy Whitey, my buffalo runner horse. "I want a hundred dollars for him without the saddle or bridle," I said.
>
> He accepted at once and handed me a roll of bills for me to count out the money. I called Hunter to witness the counting, as he had been instructed in the use of money. The animal was good value for the price but I mention this incident to show how easily at that time the Indians could have been cheated out of their money.
>
> I bought a good stout cart horse harnessed to a cart for fifty dollars to carry our duffel and the goods we bought. The traders were getting ready to move to the next trading spot at Fort Pitt and were offering some good deals to lighten their loads. I bought a shotgun practically new for about half the asking price from my new brother-in-law,[21] then loaded our carts with staple articles of

food and a stove. This would be the first cooking stove we would have since our marriage.

At our evening stop I took the gun and presented it to John Hunter*; his pleasure was something to see, as he alternately polished the blued steel of the barrel and took aim as if to get used to the feel of the gun. Then I showed him a handsome piece of good print for dresses for his wife and some household utensils as well, but when I showed him all those things his former pleasure evaporated and he looked very grim.

"Peter," he said, "I cannot accept this gun with all the other things that you have bought for us. I never could match such a gift with a return. It is too much. My wife shall have all the things you bought for her but I am sorry you must take the gun back."

"That gun, my friend, is not a gift. It is in payment for all the work looking after the horses and your trouble mixing with the Indians to bring back a report of what was going on in camp. You have earned the price of that gun five times over. Without your help, I could not have prepared my interpretations or made myself familiar with all the things the Governor had to tell the people in that paper the chiefs and councillors signed."

"Yes," said Hunter, "but I was doing those things for my own pleasure and didn't know that it was any help to you. I would have looked after the horses in any case."

"You must not think" I said, "that I would be so ungrateful and selfish as to take all that pay and not give you something for all your wife has done for us and all the kind friendly acts you have done for me personally." Assuming an angry tone, I said, "Throw the gun away if you wish. It is yours to do what you like with it. I do not need another gun as I have one at home just as good."

He was profuse in his apologies. Luckily I had hit on the only theme that could dissolve his ethical beliefs that a gift must always have compensation.

---

* Little Hunter

"You must give those things to my wife as a gift. Do not give her those things as payment for care of your wife, or she will be hurt and refuse them even as a gift." I had not thought of it his way. Such delicate management hadn't occurred to me. To pay his wife for what they considered a friendly service would be putting a price on friendship that would take away the pleasure of doing things for your real friends.[22]

Gradually the scene at Fort Carlton resumed a sense of normalcy. The lieutenant-governor's party, Erasmus, Little Hunter, and many of the traders left for Fort Pitt. Most of the Indian people travelled to the plains to hunt buffalo. And Clarke was left trying to find enough carts and drivers to haul the tons of freight that had been dumped on the banks of the river after the grounding of the *Northcote*.

Meanwhile, the Indian people who traded at Fort Pitt were apparently unsure of the time they were supposed to meet with the treaty commissioners. Morris had been dismayed when he learned on August 18 that Sweetgrass, "the principal Chief of the Plain Crees,* was out hunting and would not be at Fort Pitt." His informant was the Reverend Constantine Scollen, the Catholic priest who had travelled from the Bow River in what is now southern Alberta to attend the treaty negotiations. Sweetgrass, like Ahtahkakoop and Mistawasis, supported the negotiation of a treaty and Scollen believed "that his absence would be a great obstruction" to the treaty-making process.[23]

After consulting with the other commissioners, Morris dispatched John McKay of Prince Albert[24] with a message to Sweetgrass "requesting his presence" at Fort Pitt. McKay must have found the chief, for he and several other leading men were waiting at Fort Pitt when Erasmus and Little Hunter arrived. Sweetgrass had sent his own messengers to other bands, and over the next few days people continued to arrive from the hunting grounds. Most of the Indians gathered at Fort Pitt were either from Sweetgrass's band or from Woods Cree bands.

Erasmus gave an account of the happenings at the fort in his memoirs:

A detachment of Police was already camped on the north side of the river [when we arrived on September 4] and I counted a hundred Indian teepees camped on the flat near the fort.

_____

* Sweetgrass was one of the principal chiefs who traded at Fort Pitt.

Saskatchewan Archives Board, R-A5079

The traders transported their goods in ox carts similar to these.

We crossed the river with a boat that some traders were using to carry their goods across. Although the river was unusually low that fall, crossing goods over safely always gave some concern. By assisting the traders, we got the use of their boat that made the crossing a simple matter.

On the morning of September the fifth, the Governor and his party arrived with a Police escort that had gone out to meet him. All the tribes that were to meet there had not yet arrived but they had sent riders ahead to tell the others of their coming.[25]

The chiefs asked that negotiations be postponed for two days since people were still on the trail. The next morning, on the sixth, Sweetgrass and about 30 leading men paid a welcoming visit to the Queen's representative. The lieutenant-governor reported that "their greeting was cordial, but novel in my experience, as they embraced me in their arms, and kissed me on both cheeks, a reception which they extended also to Mr. Christie and Dr. Jackes."[26] After a short conversation Morris told the assembled group that he "expected them to be ready to meet him at his tent in the morning; time was rapidly passing and he had a long journey yet before him; he trusted their Councils would be wise and the results would be beneficial to them."[27] The Indian leaders had interrupted a buffalo hunt to meet with the commissioners and were also anxious to get moving. They nevertheless wanted to wait until more leading men arrived. Additionally, they welcomed the opportunity to talk to Little Hunter before the proceedings started. The chief had not only sat in on the negotiations at Fort Carlton, but he had spent many hours listening and talking to Ahtahkakoop and Mistawasis, thus gaining a good understanding of the terms and the concerns.

Morris had blamed the delay on the Indians' request for postponement, but James McKay did not arrive until the evening of September 6. Instead of travelling directly to Fort Pitt, the treaty commissioner had gone to the place where the Battle River flowed into the North Saskatchewan River. There he found a group of Saulteaux and Cree from Jackfish Lake who had been camped there for some time.[28] Apparently the commissioners had intended to meet with this and other bands following the proceedings at Fort Pitt. However, the buffalo were near and a good number had already left. There had been about 70 lodges "altogether," McKay explained,

> but as the buffalo were coming near, the poorer ones had started out to hunt, leaving only about ten lodges there. The remaining ones expressed good feeling [*sic*] and said they would like to have waited until the time appointed (September 15th) to meet the Governor and take the treaty, yet as the buffalo hunt was of so much importance to them they could not afford to lose the time, knowing that the Governor had to go to Fort Pitt and return before they could see him, consequently the whole band went out to the plains.[29]

At 10 a.m. on September 7, an escort of police—accompanied by the police band—took the lieutenant-governor and the other commissioners to the council tent. In Morris's words, the tent had been "pitched on the high plateau above the fort, commanding a very fine view, and facing the Indian encampment."[30] About an hour later the Indians started to gather in front of the tent. Erasmus said the delay occurred because

> it was found that there were insufficient young men for the manoeuvres that always preceded a gathering of this kind as at the meeting at Carlton. Finally two young men volunteered their help. They were in training but as yet were not considered fully qualified.
>
> The riders were performing in front of the people who were advancing to the Commissioner's tent when suddenly the two

young men got confused in their movements and crashed their horses into each other. Both men were thrown to the ground, receiving injuries, and the horses were hurt. Fortunately there was a Police doctor on hand who took charge of the injured men. One had a dislocated hip while the other had only minor injuries; as they were taken care of the proceedings went ahead.

To an inexperienced person, viewing it for the first time, the show would appear to be a disorganized undisciplined, crazy display of horsemanship, but this was not true. I had watched them training from a slow walking speed; all movements had an exact timing that was finally speeded up to manoeuvres that were carried out with a speed and intricacy of movement that was most confusing to those watching for the first time.[31]

The chiefs and headmen, followed by the main body of the camp to the "number of between two and three hundred," approached the council tent behind the horsemen. In Jackes's words,

four pipe-stems were carried about and presented to be stroked in token of good feeling and amity (during this performance the band of the Mounted Police played "God save the Queen"), blessings invoked on the whole gathering, the dances performed by the various bands, and finally the pipes of peace smoked by the Governor and Commissioners in turn. The stems, which were finely decorated, were placed with great solemnity on the table in front of the Governor, to be covered for the bearers with blue cloth.[32]

Following the sacred ceremonies, the chiefs and headmen seated themselves cross-legged in front of the council tent and Morris began his address, speaking in words similar to those used near Fort Carlton. He talked about the other treaties that had been signed and what had happened since then. "I see the Queen's Councillors," he elaborated,

taking the Indian by the hand saying we are brothers, we will lift you up, we will teach you if you will learn, the cunning of the white man.… I see gardens growing and houses building; I see them [the Indian people] receiving money from the Queen's commissioners to purchase clothing for their children; at the same time I see them enjoying their hunting and fishing as before, I see them retaining their old mode of living with the Queen's gift in addition."[33]

The lieutenant-governor made several references to the negotiations at Fort Carlton in his speech, acknowledging that the chiefs knew what had happened there. He talked about the dwindling herds of buffalo, the massacre of the Assinboine Indians at Cypress Hills, and the arrival of the North-West Mounted Police. In response to a request from Sweetgrass, he reviewed the terms and promises made at Carlton, and then adjourned the proceedings so the chiefs could meet in council. The following day, September 8, Morris said the leading men asked "for more time to elaborate, which was granted, as we learned that some of them desired to make exorbitant demands, and we wished to let them understand through the avenues by which we had access to them that these would be fruitless."

The Reverend John McDougall was one of the men asked to meet with the chiefs in council on September 8. He said he was introduced by Sweetgrass as a friend and asked to "tell these chiefs what you understood the white Chief to say when we met him yesterday." In response, the missionary went over the notes he had taken the previous day and explained what he had heard. According to McDougall, Sweetgrass asked what, in his view, the chiefs "should do at this time." The missionary, not unexpectedly, advised them "to go before the commissioners on the morrow and signify their acceptance of the proposals brought to them."[34]

Erasmus was also called to the council. He said he was resting when a messenger arrived from Chief Pakān (also known as Sīnam) requesting his presence. "I was questioned at some length," he wrote in his book *Buffalo Days and Nights*,

> about the attitude of the tribes who signed the treaty at Carlton, about details in reference to treaty concessions, and the terms agreed upon, which by that time I had memorized by heart. I gave them a review of the discussions of the council meeting of the chiefs at Carlton, reporting the objections raised by those who opposed the signing, and spoke of the petition that had been drawn up for the Commissioner, with the points agreed to and those refused. I mentioned Poundmaker's and The Badger's efforts at trying to block or misinterpret the terms of the treaty, at which there were some expressions of disgust about their attitude. Then I wound up my talk by a report of the two speeches made by Mista-wa-sis and Ah-tuk-a-kup that had swung the whole opinion of the assembly in favour of the signing.

I could see that the content of these two speeches had a tremendous effect on my audience, as I had reserved the latter for the last before sitting down.

Sweet Grass, who was the most important chief among those gathered in council, rose to his feet to speak to their people.

"Mista-wa-sis and Ah-tuk-a-kup, I consider, are far wiser than I am; therefore if they have accepted this treaty for their people after many days of talk and careful thought, then I am prepared to accept for my people."

Chief Seenum then took his place and spoke. "You have all questioned Peter Erasmus on the things that have taken place at Carlton. He is a stranger to many of you but I am well acquainted with him. I have respect for his words and have confidence in his truthfulness. Mista-wa-sis and Ah-tuk-a-kup both sent their sons all the way from Carlton to where he lives, and he is married to one of our favourite daughters.* He was not at home but they followed him to the prairie where he was hunting buffalo with our people. Little Hunter is a chief and brings back a good report of his work during treaty talks. He would not tell us something that was not for our good. Therefore, as those other chiefs who are in greater numbers than we are have found this treaty good, I and my head man will sign for our people. I have spoken."

Each of the other chiefs with their councillors expressed agreement, each man expressing in his own words ideas that conformed to the general acceptance of treaty terms. They were all willing to sign the treaty and there was not a single dissenting voice.[35]

Despite Erasmus's claim that there were no dissenting voices, Jackes indicated in his account that the Indian leaders were slow in gathering at the council tent the morning of September 9, "as they wished to settle all difficulties and misunderstanding amongst themselves before coming to the treaty tent."[36] Because of the delay, the meeting with the treaty commissioners did not reconvene until 11 a.m.

With everyone finally in place, Lieutenant-Governor Morris told the assembled group he was ready to listen to the leaders.

---

* Charlotte Jackson, the daughter of an Indian woman (presumably a member of Pakān's band) and a European Hudson's Bay Company factor.

There was silence. Erasmus said that Morris "looked puzzled, or rather 'disappointed' might be the better description of his attitude. At other places he had received many objections and a lot of questions." Finally Kihīwin (Eagle) rose, faced the people, and "told them not to be afraid to speak their minds. If there was anything they did not understand or wished to know, this was the place and the time to express their thoughts.[37]

Still there was no response. Morris misinterpreted the silence, thinking that the people were going to reject the treaty. "I had hoped the Indians would have taken me at my word, and taken me as a brother and a friend," he told the people. And he asked, "Why can you not open your hearts to me? I have met many Indians before, but this is the first time I have had all the talking to do myself. Now, cast everything behind your backs, and speak to me face to face. I have offered as we have done to the other Indians. ... I cannot believe it to be possible that you would throw my hand back. Speak and do not be afraid or ashamed."[38] He did not realize that chiefs and leading men had reached a consensus in their council and were prepared to sign the treaty.

Finally Sweetgrass spoke:

> I thank you for this day, and also I thank you for what I have seen and heard, I also thank the Queen for sending you to act for our good. I am glad to have a brother and friend in you, which undoubtedly will raise us above our present condition. I am glad for your offers, and I thank you from my heart. I speak this in the presence of the Divine Being. It is all for our good, I see nothing to be afraid of, I therefore accept of it gladly and take your hand to my heart, may this continue as long as this earth stands and the river flows. The Great King, our Father [the Creator], is now looking upon us this day, He regards all the people equal with one another; He has mercy on the whole earth; He has opened a new world to us. I have pity on all those who have to live by the buffalo. If I am spared until this time next year I want this my brother to commence to act for me, thinking thereby that the buffalo may be protected. It is for that reason I give you my hand. If spared, I shall commence at once to clear a small piece of land for myself, and others of my kinsmen will do the same. We will commence hand in hand to protect the buffalo. When I hold your hand I feel as if the Great Father were looking on us both as brothers. I am thankful. May this earth here never see the white man's blood

spilt on it. I thank God that we stand together, that you all see us; I am thankful that I can raise up my head, and the white man and red man can stand together as long as the sun shines. When I hold your hands and touch your heart, as I do now (suiting his action to the words),* let us be as one. Use your utmost to help me and help my children, so that they may prosper.[39]

The chiefs and leading men expressed their approval with what Morris described as a "guttural sound which takes with them the place of the British cheer."

After a few more words, Morris, Christie, and McKay signed the treaty on behalf of the Queen. Each of the nine chiefs addressed Morris before signing on behalf of their people. Pakān said that Christie, who was then in charge of Edmonton House, had given him a plough "some years ago." Because they had no oxen, he and his brothers "drew the plough themselves, and they pulled up the roots and used them for hoes." The plough was broken now. "I feel my heart sore in the spring when my children want to plough—when they have no implements to use," Pakān told the commissioners. "That is why I am asking ... to have them sent as soon a possible."[40]

Little Hunter, who had left his people on the plains hunting buffalo when he travelled to Fort Carlton with Erasmus, said "I am here alone just now; if I am spared to see next spring, then I will select my Councillors, those that I think worthy I will choose." He added that he was very pleased the treaty had been signed: "When I hear her words that she is going to put to rights this country, it is the help of God that has put it in her heart to come to our assistance. In sending her bounty to us I wish an everlasting grasp of her hand, as long as the sun moves and the river flows.... I am thankful for the children for they will prosper. All the children who are sitting here hope that the Great Spirit will look down upon us as one."[41]

Sekaskōtch (Cut Arm)† said he now recognized that "this that I once dreaded most is coming to my aid and doing for me what I could not do for myself." Tustukeeskwes (Turning Head from Side to Side) stated he was "glad that all his friends and children will not be in want of food hereafter. I am glad that we have everything which we had before still extended to us."

---

* Morris explained that Sweetgrass, "placing one hand over my heart, and the other over his own ... said 'May the white man's blood never be spilt on this earth.'" (See *Treaties*, p. 191.)

† Sekaskōtch translates more correctly as Blood from Cut Arm.

"I need not say anything," Pee-quay-sis stated. "I have been well pleased with all that I have heard, and I need not speak as we are all agreed."

Kinosēw (Fish), who was chief of a small band of Chipewayans, spoke in Cree when he expressed his appreciation to the Queen.[42]

After Chiefs Piyēsiwa kā-wīcekot (Thunderbird Is With Him) and Kihīwin signed Treaty Six, the councillors who were present placed their marks on the document.[43] Then, with the band again playing God Save the Queen, the lieutenant-governor placed the Queen's medal around Sweetgrass's neck. Erasmus noted that the "paying of treaty money and issuing of uniforms took the greater part of two more days."[44] Since a number of chiefs and bands were not at the treaty negotiations, Morris announced that "next year we will send men near to where their bands live, notice will be given, and those who are away now will receive the present of money we are ... [giving] you, the same as if they had been here, and when you go back to the plains I ask you to tell your brothers what we have done."[45]

Big Bear, who led a large band of Plains Cree, arrived from the plains on September 12, too late to take part in the negotiations. The chief explained that "he had been out on the plains hunting the buffalo, and had not heard the time of the meeting; that on hearing of it he had been sent in by the Crees and by the Stonies or Assiniboines to speak for them."[46] Morris agreed to meet with him the next day.

Big Bear was with Sweetgrass and the other leading men when they paid a farewell visit to the treaty commissioners September 13. He took this opportunity to speak to Morris. Since Erasmus had already left for White Fish Lake, the lieutenant-governor had to rely on a less-qualified man to interpret.

Big Bear spoke first:

> I find it difficult to express myself, because some of the bands are not represented. I have come off to speak for the different bands that are out on the plains. It is no small matter we were to consult about. I expected the Chiefs here would have waited until I arrived. The different bands that are out on the plains told me that I should speak in their stead; the Stony Indians as well. The people who have not come, stand as a barrier before what I would have had to say; my mode of living is hard.[47]

Sweetgrass defended his actions and spoke directly to Big Bear:

> My friend, you see the representative of the Queen here, who do you suppose is the maker of it. I think the Great Spirit put it into their hearts to come to our help; I feel as if I saw life when I see the representative of the Queen; let nothing be a barrier between you and him; it is through great difficulty this has been brought to us. Think of our children and those to come after, there is life and succor for them; say yes and take his hand.[48]

"We have all taken it," Pakān added, "and we think it is for our good."

Big Bear was not ready to approve the treaty terms that easily:

> Stop, stop, my friends, I have never seen the Governor before; I have seen Mr. Christie many times. I heard the Governor was to come and I said I shall see him; when I see him I will make a request that he will save me from what I most dread, that is: the rope to be about my neck (hanging), it was not given to us by the Great Spirit that the red man or white man should shed each other's blood."[49]

Big Bear's words were interpreted to mean that he feared being hanged. In an Indian interpretation of what was actually meant, Big Bear is said to be speaking metaphorically. He believed the Indian people should be able to travel freely across the country to support themselves. In his vision of the future, the proposed reserve system appeared to be the same as putting a rope around the neck of the Indian people, choking them and taking away their breath, their life, their livelihood.[50] In his book, *Big Bear*, Hugh Dempsey suggests that the reference to the shedding of blood was a "note of friendship."[51]

Morris, reacting to Big Bear's speech as it was interpreted, thought Big Bear was speaking about capital punishment. "It was given us by the Great Spirit, man should not shed his brother's blood," he retorted, "and it was spoken to us that he who shed his brother's blood, should have his own spilt. No good Indian has the rope about his neck."

"What we want is that we should hear what will make our hearts glad, and all good peoples' hearts glad," Big Bear countered. "There were plenty things left undone, and it does not look well to leave them so."

Morris shot back, "I do not know what has been left undone!"[52]

The exchange obviously frustrated Big Bear. He remained seated until the other leading men had shaken hands with the lieutenant-governor. When they were done, Big Bear rose and taking Morris's hand said,

> I am glad to meet you, I am alone; but if I had known the time, I would have been here with all my people.

> I am not an undutiful child. I do not throw back your hand; but as my people are not here, I do not sign. I will tell them what I have heard, and next year I will come."[53]

The chiefs and headmen then left. About an hour later Big Bear returned to Fort Pitt to see the lieutenant-governor. In Morris's words, the Cree chief feared "I had not fully understood him, and assured me that he accepted the treaty as if he had signed it, and would come next year with all his people and accept it."[54]

Morris and his party pulled out of Fort Pitt that afternoon on the first leg of their journey to Fort Garry.

And so, for now, it was over. At Fort Carlton, Ahtahkakoop and Mistawasis had been able to persuade the other leading men that the best hope for the future lay in signing the treaty and adopting a way of life that would sustain their people once the buffalo were gone. The leading men at Fort Pitt had received an account from Erasmus and Little Hunter of the discussions and terms agreed upon. Influenced by these reports, along with supporting words from the Catholic and Methodist missionaries in their midst,[55] the chiefs and headmen apparently decided to accept the treaty terms with very little discussion outside their councils.

Most of the leaders at Fort Pitt—like Ahtahkakoop and Mistawasis—had a realistic view of the future. Pakān, for instance, had been cultivating the soil for a number of years and knew the value of adequate tools and implements. Many of the leading men at Fort Pitt also accepted that some day the buffalo would be gone and difficult days lay ahead. "Times will be hard for the prairie Indians once the buffalo are gone," Little Hunter had told Erasmus,

> They will have nothing and will not settle on the land until they are nearing starvation. Steinhauer* has often told us that we must

---

* The Reverend Henry Bird Steinhauer, an educated Ojibwa, had been the Methodist missionary at White Fish Lake since 1855.

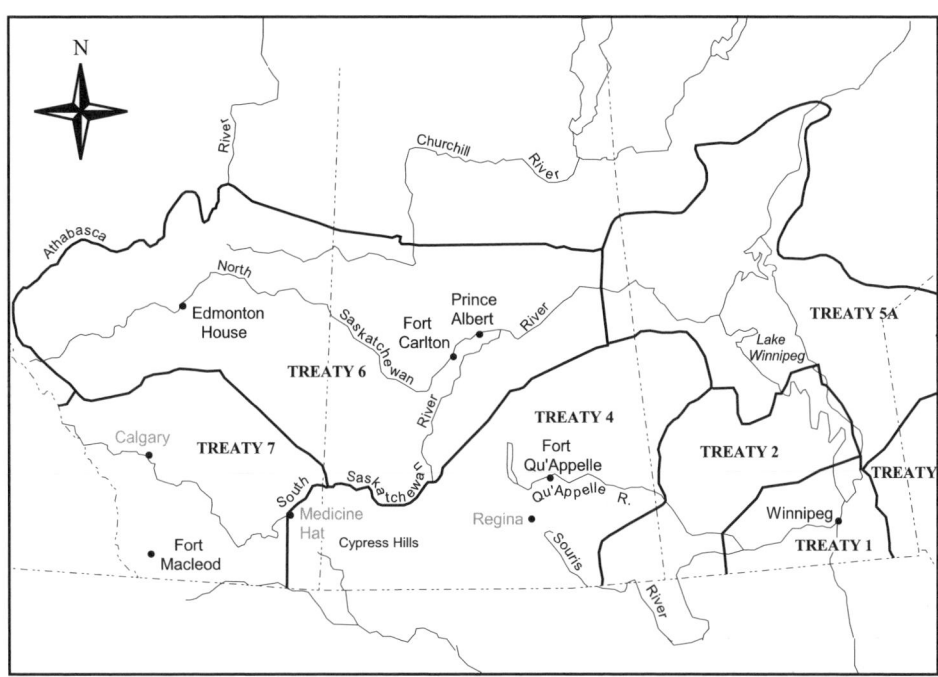

Information Systems Division, Canadian Plains Research Center

Seven treaties were signed by the Indian people of the North-West during the 1870s.

learn to farm and raise animals to support ourselves for the day when the buffalo will be no more. Now I have to believe him. We are lucky that we already know something about raising grain and vegetables, and besides we still have bush game and fish.[56]

Unfortunately, many of the Indian people least prepared to face the inevitable—the buffalo hunters from the Battle River and Fort Pitt districts—were far out on the plains hunting buffalo when the chiefs gathered at Fort Pitt. They did not participate in the treaty-making process, and when they did place their names on an adhesion to Treaty Six, the time for negotiating had passed.

CHAPTER FIFTEEN

Follow-up to the Signing of Treaty Six, 1876

Ahtahkakoop knew where he wanted his reserve to be located and he notified Christie before leaving the treaty grounds. Not surprisingly the chief had selected land on the Green Lake Trail at Sandy Lake, the place where he and his band already had houses and gardens. Ahtahkakoop also told Christie he wanted "his Reserve to join on to that of Mistawasis."[1]

At first Mistawasis said he wanted his reserve "somewhere about the Thickwood Mountain on the [north] Fort Pitt Road about 40 miles from Carlton."[2] By the next year Mistawasis had changed his mind, and he told Sergeant James Walker of the North-West Mounted Police that he wanted his reserve "on Snake Creek from where it empties into Shell River up to the foot of the Thickwood Hills." The Green Lake Trail wound through this area, which included Snake Plain, on its way from Fort Carlton to Ahtahkakoop's reserve. Walker reported that "this reservation joins Ah tah kah coop's,"[3] so the plan to have adjoining reserves had not been abandoned.

Most of the other chiefs who signed Treaty Six had also made up their minds about where they wanted to settle. Cakāstēpēsin (Sun Shine) chose a site on the south side of South Branch of the Saskatchewan River that included Birch Island and a place called Sugar Camp (likely Sugar Island). Beardy and the other two Willow Cree chiefs, One Arrow and Little Rattle, at first indicated that they wanted their reserves at the same place as Cakāstēpēsin, but they later selected land near Duck Lake and Batoche.[4] James Smith reserved land near Fort à la Corne, and Ayahtaskamikinam* favoured land at Sturgeon Lake, north of Prince Albert. John Smith, who

---

* Ayahtaskamikinam was also known as William Twatt.

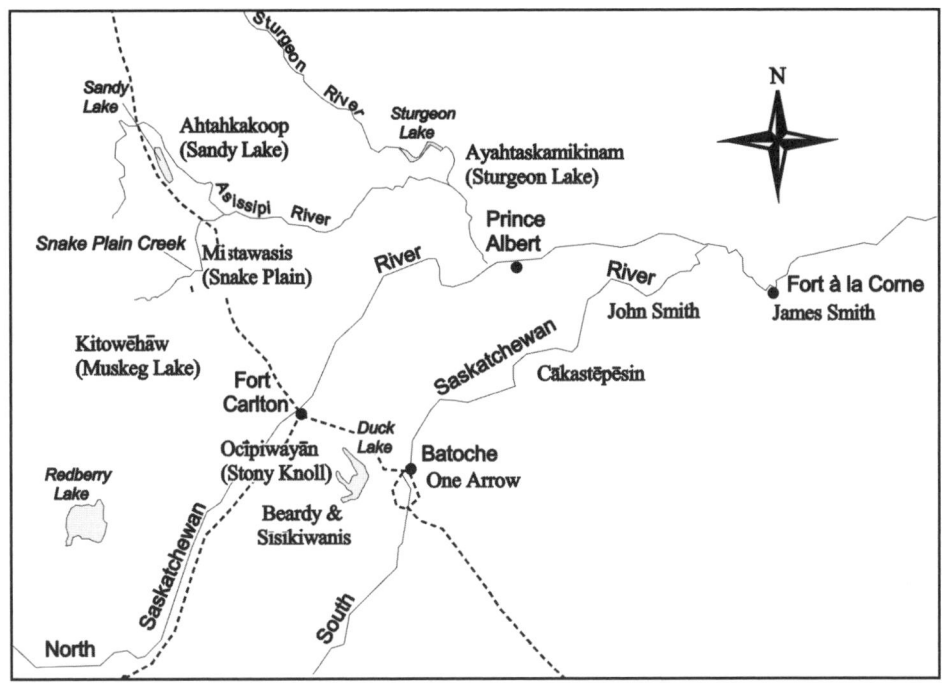

Information Systems Division, Canadian Plains Research Center

Most of the chiefs who signed Treaty Six at Fort Carlton selected land in the Fort Carlton district for their reserves.

was more interested in farming than his brother James, indicated he wanted his reserve on the South Branch below Red Deer Hill. Kitowēhāw (Sound Of Flapping Wings)* and Ocīpiwayan (Pointed Hood) were both undecided, while Red Pheasant and He Strikes Him On The Back expressed their intentions to settle "somewhere near" the Eagle Hills and Battle River, respectively. With only two or three exceptions, these chiefs and their bands already had houses and gardens on the land chosen for their reserves and were anxious to receive agricultural implements and cattle as soon as possible.[5]

"The Early fulfillment of the terms, and the conditions, of the Treaty, to these Indians," Christie recommended to Morris "will facilitate in a great measure the securing the adhesion to the Treaty of those Bands who were absent this Year, and who will have to be dealt with next Year." He concluded that "if the Terms and Conditions of the Treaty are properly attended

---

* John Smith's Reserve became known as Muskoday. Kitowēhāw chose land for the reserve now known as Muskeg Lake.

to and fulfilled, I have no doubt both the Government and the Indians will be greatly benefited thereby."[6]

Before leaving Fort Carlton, Morris complimented Ahtahkakoop and Mistawasis on the "wisdom and reasonableness of their terms," and he later reported that Mistawasis and Ahtahkakoop "shewed sound judgement, and an earnest desire to come to an understanding."[7] He also had praise for the mixed-blood people, both English- and French-speaking, believing that they had used "the influence of their relationship to the Indians in support of our efforts."[8] James McKay, who had camped near the Indian encampment instead of staying at Fort Carlton with the other commissioners, "had the opportunity of meeting them constantly, and learning their views which his familiarity with the Indian dialects enabled him to do."[9] And Erasmus, whom Morris and others described as "a most efficient interpreter," was hired to interpret at Fort Pitt and to assist in other matters relating to Indian affairs.[10]

The treaty negotiations had cost the government $71,217.46.[11] Included in these costs were the medals and flags presented to the chiefs and the uniforms for the chiefs and their headmen. The chief's uniform had consisted of a "chief's coat, hat and trousers," a shirt, a handkerchief, and a belt. Although the headmen were given shirts, handkerchiefs, and belts similar to those given the chiefs, the coats, trousers, and hats were different. Christie was to note later that the coats and hats, and most particularly the pants, were too small. Ahtahkakoop, at well over six feet in height, no doubt was one of many who had trouble fitting their large frames into the new clothing. Accordingly, the treaty commissioner recommended that larger sizes of clothing and hats should be ordered for the chiefs and headmen who were expected to sign adhesions to Treaty Six in 1877. Additionally, there apparently had been a choice of at least two flags, for Christie pointed out for future reference that the Indian leaders preferred the flag with "the *Blue* ground & Crown Union Jack in Corner." He did not mention in his report that some of the chiefs were unhappy with the red colour of their coats. They would have preferred blue.

The lack of attention to details and proper planning was also evident in the packing of the clothing. The large cases were "far too Large and Bulky for the Carts ... and great complaints regarding their size were made by the Freighters." Christie recommended that, in succeeding years, medium-sized cases be used.[12]

Morris, in his official report to the Canadian government, expressed his pleasure that so many of the Cree were willing to start farming and have their children taught.[13] "With few exceptions" he wrote, "they indicated the places [selected for their reserves], in fact most of them have already commenced to settle." The lieutenant-governor endorsed Christie's recommendation that cattle and agricultural implements be "given" to these bands "without delay," and he recommended that "cattle and some implements could be purchased at Prince Albert and thus avoid transportation." Morris added that, although he did not grant the request, he thought the Indian leaders' desire "to be instructed in farming and building, most reasonable, and I would therefore recommend that measures be adopted to provide such instruction for them." Further, he said

> the universal demand for teachers, and by some of the Indians for missionaries, is also encouraging. The former, the Government can supply; for the latter they must rely on the churches ... the field is wide enough for all, and the cry of the Indian for help is a clamant one.[14]

Morris addressed two other concerns in his report: the rapidly disappearing buffalo and the "wandering Half-breeds of the plains." The chiefs and headmen, he wrote, were constantly "pressing on my attention" the urgency of passing laws to preserve the buffalo. He strongly recommended that the North-West Council do this as quickly as possible.[15] In regards to the half-breeds, he said they were

> chiefly of French descent and live the life of the Indians. There are a few who are identified with the Indians, but there is a large class of Metis who live by the hunt of the buffalo, and have no settled homes. I think that a census of the numbers of these should be procured, and while I would not be disposed to recommend their being brought under the treaties, I would suggest that land should be assigned to them, and that on their settling down, if after an examination into their circumstances, it should be found necessary and expedient, some assistance should be given them to enable them to enter upon agricultural operations.[16]

"If the measures suggested by me are adopted, viz., effective regulations with regard to the buffalo, the Indians taught to cultivate the soil, and the erratic Half-breeds encouraged to settle down," Morris concluded, "I believe the solution of all social questions of any present importance in the North-West Territories will have been arrived at."[17]

The submission of his report was one of Morris's last acts before step-ping down as lieutenant-governor of Manitoba and the North-West Territories. In mid-December 1876 he was replaced by David Laird, who resigned as minister of the Interior in Alexander Mackenzie's Liberal gov-ernment to accept the appointment.

Morris's words not only fell on deaf ears, but he was criticized by David Mills, Laird's replacement as minister of the Interior, for agreeing to the additional terms insisted upon by the Carlton chiefs. In an unsigned memorandum to the Privy Council dated January 31, 1877, the new minister stated that, although the treaty contained "the usual provi-sions as regards to schools, annuities, presents of clothing, flags, medals, wagons etc., and the exclusion of intoxicating liquor from the Reserves," he was alarmed about some of the provisions. For example, each chief was to be provided with a set of harness "as soon as convenient," and a hand-mill was to be given to each band "when sufficient grain has been raised to require it." He stated that the "stipulations relating to agricultural imple-ments are somewhat more onerous, too, than in previous Treaties," and he outlined the clause that provided food rations to bands cultivating the soil at seeding time.[18]

However, Mills's greatest difficulty lay with a "wholly new" provision that he quoted almost verbatim:

> that in the event hereafter of the Indians comprised within this Treaty being overtaken by any pestilence, or by a general famine, the Queen, on being satisfied and certified thereof by the Indian agent or agents, will grant to the Indians assistance of such char-acter and such extent as the Chief superintendent of Indian Affairs shall deem necessary and sufficient to relieve the Indians from the calamity that shall have befallen them.[19]

"This stipulation the undersigned regards as extremely objectionable," Mills wrote, "tending, as it will, to predispose the Indians to idleness, since they will regard the provisions as guaranteeing them protection against want, and they will not be inclined to make proper exertions to supply themselves with food and clothing, thereby largely to increase the expen-diture imposed upon the county in the management of its Indian affairs."

"Although the undersigned considers the terms of the Treaty to be very onerous," Mills continued, "some of the provisions being exceedingly objectionable and such as ought not to have been made with any race of savages, he nevertheless thinks it proper to recommend the same for the ratification of Your Excellency, as the mischiefs which might result from refusing to ratify it might produce discontent and dissatisfaction, which in the end would prove more detrimental to the county than the ratification of the objectionable provisions referred to."[20]

Mills's recommendation was accepted and an order-in-council ratifying Treaty Six was issued on February 10, 1877. A toned-down criticism of the clause providing "aid … in case of famine or pestilence" was contained in the minister's annual report. Despite the denunciation, the minister of the Interior nevertheless stated that

> in view of the temper of the Indians of the Saskatchewan during the past season, and of the extravagant demands which they were induced to prefer on certain points, it needed all the temper, tact, judgment [sic] and discretion of which the Commissioners were possessed to bring the negotiations to a satisfactory issue.[21]

Mills restated his criticisms in a "despatch" to Morris dated March 1, 1877. Morris responded with a 16-page letter some three weeks later. After acknowledging receipt of the dispatch, he said "certain observations" were necessary. First, he began,

> I am surprised that, in that dispatch, there is no recognition of the services rendered by the Commissioners, but instead what must be regarded as a censure. In my own case I undertook an arduous and responsible duty, knowing that my connection with the North West was about to cease, because I believed that, from my relations with the Indians, I was more likely to succeed than a stranger and because further I was of opinion from my own experience that it was very undesirable that the new Lieutenant Governor, whoever he might be, should take part in the negotiations of a Treaty which he would be called upon to administer.

> When the Honble Mr. McKenzie invited me to assume the duty, I therefore informed him that if I consented to act, it would be under the influence of these views.

> 2nd I regret to learn that His Excellency finds that in some respects especially in the matter of the distribution of Agricultural implements and the providing of seed grain the terms of this

Treaty are more onerous than those of former Treaties, as I am of
opinion, that though there is a slight increase in these articles
beyond what was conceded at Treaties 3. 4. and 5, yet that
increase was not only justified by the circumstances, but was right
and proper. The Commissioners found the Indians anxious to
make a living by the soil and that they had commenced so to do,
under great difficulties, even, as one of the chiefs stated, dragging
the plough through the ground by their own strength. The
Commissioners believed that it was in the highest degree important to take advantage of their disposition believing it to be alike
in the interest of the Dominion and of the Indians and therefore
they acceded in some measure to the well founded representations
of the Indians, that the Agricultural implements as originally
offered were insufficient in quantity. There was a very slight anal-
ogy between the position of these Indians and the character of the
country they were ceding and that acquired by me and my associates in Treaties 3. 5 and even 4. We were seeking to acquire their
country to make way for settlement, and thus deprive them of
their hunting grounds, and their means of livelihood. The Indians
represented that it would be impossible for them to cultivate the
soil extensively as they intended doing, with so few implements
and the Commissioners co-inciding with them enlarged the grant
and I feel satisfied that in so doing they acted wisely. I may say
further that I have been convinced for sometime that if we are to
succeed in inducing the Indians to cultivate the soil, the provisions of the former Treaties are not sufficiently liberal with regard
to implements and cattle to accomplish the desired end.

3rd I would call your attention to the fact, that in dealing with the
Indian people, the Commissioners away from all opportunity of
obtaining advice must act at times largely on their own responsibility and deal with the emergencies which arise. There is moreover no cast iron form of Treaty which can be imposed on these
people. I have taken the leading part in negotiating Treaties Nos
3. 4. 5 and 6. and in revising Treaties Nos. 1. & 2. and have
encountered on all these occasions difficulties which the
Commissioners overcame, but which they were able to deal with
only by assuming responsibility and at the moment without hesitation making stipulations to obviate the failure of the Treaties.

4th I deeply regret to learn that "His Excellency the Governor General has been advised to express his regret especially to find that the Commissioners felt it necessary to include in the Treaty a novel provision binding the government to come to the assistance of the Indians included in the Treaty in the event of their being visited by any pestilence or famine. It cannot be doubted that this stipulation, as understood by the Indians will have a tendency to predispose them to idleness and to make them less inclined to put forth proper exertions to supply themselves with food and clothing."

I am persuaded that this advise was given without full consideration or knowledge of the position and I regret that before the Privy Council were committed to the step of placing so formal an opinion on record, the courtesy was not extended to me of prior communication with me on so important a subject.

I will now deal with the provision in question which is novel only in so far as that it is embodied in the Treaty, but which is nevertheless as old in practise as the history of civilized Governments.

A. In the first place, I have to remind His Excellency the Governor General in Council of the circumstances which led to the making of this Treaty, the uneasiness of the Indians and the danger of collisions between them and the surveying, telegraph and other parties, which existed, when in 1875, I asked and obtained authority to promise these Indians, a Treaty, with the most tranquillising effect. In the next place, I have to remind you that in the interval, war broke out between the Americans and the Sioux, in a region of the United States, not far distant from our frontier. Our Canadian Indians, are fully aware of all that transpires there, and of the much more liberal terms granted by the American Government to the Indians, when Treaties are made with them, and my only wonder is that the Indians made the Treaty at all.

B. If you refer to my despatch of the 4th December last, you will find it stated, that "the food question was the turning point of the Treaty" and in the record of the proceedings which I transmitted to you, you will find this more fully disclosed.

The Indians demanded progressive assistance as they advanced in civilization, food, and help in time of famine or national calamity. The Commissioners spent a whole day discussing the matter with them, and informed them that the Government would not undertake to feed them, could not take up the difficulties of any single Bands [*sic*] of Indians, but in time of any Tribal general famine, the generosity of the Queen might be looked forward to. In making this last statement the Commissioners felt justified by the whole course of the British Government and of the Canadian, under like circumstances. Such a calamity has ever been regarded as the duty of the state to alleviate. The Commissioners were treating in a region where a trading Company the predecessors of the Canadian Government had promptly acted in this way in the years 1869-1870, and saved the Indians from entire destruction [from smallpox], and they felt that they could rely on the like conduct from the Queen's Government in Canada. They, therefore, assured the Indians, that should a national calamity befal them, they could look for help and in that case only, and they made this assurance, as a counter proposal to the demand for food and general assistance, with the full conviction, that if not given, the Treaty would not be made, and that a failure would lead to consequences of a serious character with regard to the Indian Tribes and entail heavy expenditures on the Government.

The Indians fully understood the effect of the promises of the Commissioners, and its extent, and abandoned their demand for daily food, although they knew that rations were given in the United States. I cannot concur in the advise to His Excellency that this stipulation will predispose the Indians to idleness for on the contrary, I believe it will prove as stimulus to exertion as giving them an assurance, that while endeavouring to gain a new mode of livelihood from the soil, a helping hand would be extended to them by the Crown, if a national tribal famine or pestilence came upon them. I will only add in this connection that after being forced to make the proposal, the Commissioners deliberately inserted the stipulation in the Treaty, in order that there might be no misunderstanding, and that its full scope and effect should be of record.

In the remainder of the 16-page letter to the minister, Morris justified the "publication of the Treaty, amongst the Indians previously treated with," and said he did not think the terms granted to the Cree would affect the upcoming treaty with the Blackfoot since their circumstances were different. He then reminded the minister that the terms granted to the "peaceful section of the Sioux" by the American Government were much more generous and, to the best of his knowledge, included daily rations to the heads of families until they were self-supporting and promises of

> assistance in the way of Schools and instruction in mechanical and agricultural arts and the building for them of houses on allotments to be granted them severally.

> It was the knowledge that similar terms had been previously granted to the American Indians that led to the demands of the Crees for food and clothing, carpenters and blacksmiths, etc. and it is much to their credit that when these demands were refused, they accepted cheerfully, the terms of the Treaty.

After further defence of his actions, Morris concluded by saying that he had sent a copy of the minister's dispatch to James McKay, "one of my associate Commissioners and am authorized, by him to inform you that he concurs in every respect with the representations, in reply thereto, herein contained."[23]

Meanwhile David Laird, during his last year as minister of the Interior, was busy laying the framework for the administration of what the government termed "Indian affairs" in Western Canada. One of his first steps was the creation of four superintendencies that would replace two Boards of Indian Commissioners.* The new superintendencies—the Victoria Superintendency, the Fraser Superintendency, the North-West Superintendency, and the Manitoba Superintendency—were to be administered by superintendents and agents. Of these, the North-West Superintendency was the largest, comprising an area of approximately 206,000 square miles. The Treaty Six area was part of this superintendency.

Laird proposed

> that in each Superintendency, there shall be two or more resident local Agents, who, besides paying the Indians their annuities and

---

* These boards, one for British Columbia and the other for Manitoba and the North-West Territories, had been created in 1873 to advise the government on Indian matters.

distributing the annual presents, may it is hoped be made otherwise useful in instructing the Indians in farming and aiding and
encouraging them in their efforts to help themselves.

The moral and industrial influence which such local agents, if
carefully selected, may exercise on the Bands among whom they
reside it is difficult perhaps to over-estimate.[24]

Laird resigned as minister of the Interior late in 1876 to accept the position of lieutenant-governor of the North-West Territories. For the first time
the position was to be a resident one, with the Queen's representative being
required to live in the Territories. Although Battleford was named the first
capital, the government buildings were not ready. Fort Livingstone* was
designated as the temporary location of the seat of government and the
lieutenant-governor's first residence.[25]

The new lieutenant-governor was at Fort Livingstone when he received
word that he had also been appointed Indian superintendent for the North-
West Superintendency. M.G. Dickieson, who had served as Laird's personal secretary, was appointed assistant Indian superintendent. Dickieson
had served as secretary to the commissioners who negotiated Treaty Four
in 1874, and the following year he assisted with the payment of annuities
at Fort Qu'Appelle.[26]

In March of 1877, Laird informed the government that "for this summer's operation, I think two agents will be sufficient, one for Treaty Four,
and another for Treaty Six."[27] Two months later, government officials in
Ottawa provisionally appointed a military officer by the name of Allan
MacDonald as Indian agent for the Treaty Four area. Instead of hiring
someone to fill the position of agent for Treaty Six, Dickieson was given
the job. This was in addition to his responsibilities as assistant Indian
superintendent.[28] Thus in the Treaty Six area, Dickieson was expected to
pay annuities, issue the annual presents, teach hundreds of Indians how to
farm, and otherwise assist the people in their transition from hunters to
agriculturists. This same man was also expected to carry out the duties of
assistant superintendent for the entire North-West Superintendency.

----

* Fort Livingstone, commonly referred to as the Swan River Barracks, served as the first
headquarters for the North-West Mounted Police.

PART FIVE

The First Years After Treaty Was Signed

Illustration by Ed Peekeekoot

Building a new church.

CHAPTER SIXTEEN

The Transition Begins, 1876-1877

After the signing of Treaty Six and the days of festivities that followed, Ahtahkakoop's band split up. Some of the people went onto the plains to hunt buffalo, while others returned to Sandy Lake to cut hay. There was little, if any, crop to harvest. Heavy frost on June 13 had cut the young plants "to the ground." In July and August, three more frosts hit, destroying the potatoes and reducing the wheat and barley to fodder. Yet Ahtahkakoop's people were not discouraged. "The summer," they said, "had been an exceptional one." Although it was little consolation, Hines noted in his journal that the Prince Albert settlement was also hit by frost and "suffering very much."[1]

The buffalo hunters started returning to the small settlement at Sandy Lake towards the end of October. By then John and Emma Hines had settled into newly married life. During the summer, Stranger—on his own initiative—had partitioned one corner of Hines's single-room house to make a bedroom for the couple. The missionary commented that although this was very thoughtful of Stranger, the house was only 16 by 18 feet in size. The partitioning of the 7- by 10-foot bedroom therefore "made the rest of the room rather small, considering the use it was put to, vis., kitchen, dining- and sitting-room."[2] David Stranger had also erected a small building to serve as living quarters for himself, Hourie, and A.A.H. Wright, the new teacher Hines had brought with him from the Red River Settlement.[3] Sixteen by 18 feet in size, it was situated at one end of the missionary's house.

Hines invited Ahtahkakoop and the four headmen to his home for tea and a meal on October 25. Only the chief, Sasakamoose, and Wāskitoy were able to come because Kā-miyo-ahcahkwēw and Kīsik-awāsis were away. The menu consisted of dried buffalo meat, bread, butter, tea, and preserved pineapple. Bread and butter were not part of their usual fare and the men had never tasted preserved pineapple before, so the meal was another new experience presented by Hines. Although the missionary did not give a full account of their discussion in his journal, he noted that he and the leading men talked about governments and how they obtained their revenue.[4]

Hines also told Ahtahkakoop and his headmen that he would "claim for the mission a square ½ mile, & that this w^d not be expected by the govnmt to be taken out of their Reserve, but w^d be in addition to it."[5] With this point settled, the missionary said he read from the Bible and said prayers before the men returned to their homes.

Ahtahkakoop and Mistawasis had wanted a missionary living with them because they were concerned about their children's and grandchildren's livelihood in the years to come. This remained foremost in their minds, and it is not surprising then that Hines reported to the Church Missionary Society that the two chiefs were "exceedingly anxious for the future education of their children."[6] Mistawasis's decision to choose the Snake Plain area for his reserve complicated Hines's plans for the two bands. The missionary, nevertheless, felt he could not desert Mistawasis's people, particularly since he had two teachers in his employ.

And so, for the winter of 1876–77 Hines tried to maintain two schools. Hourie, the half-breed teacher who had replaced George McKay the previous year, was sent to Snake Plain. In mid-November, 18 children in Mistawasis's band were attending classes even though the chief and half of his men were at their "hunting grounds." By the end of February, food was so scarce at the wintering place that Hourie had to return to Sandy Lake.[7] Meanwhile Wright was put to work teaching at Sandy Lake. The young Englishman could not speak Cree, but Hines hoped he would be useful for "general purposes."[8]

Although Hines's records are incomplete, it is evident that life on Ahtahkakoop's reserve at Sandy Lake continued much as it had the previous winter. Obviously hunting for food and fur-bearing animals, chopping firewood, and other routine responsibilities would have taken a considerable amount of time. The hunting must have been successful, for two traders—one English and the other Scottish—were living in the settlement. Much to Hines's chagrin, neither man would attend church services. The missionary said he was surprised members of Ahtahkakoop's band did not say anything.[9]

In early December, Hines was asked to go to the "fishing lake" with Ahtahkakoop and the others. This lake, called *manitow-sākahikan* (God's Lake), was located about 10 miles to the northwest at the foot of a high hill that could be seen from the mission.* Whitefish Lake, where Hines had spent his first winter in the North-West, was six or seven miles farther north. The temperature approached –45° F the first night Hines was at the fish camp. The cold was so intense the next day that the missionary "was obliged to stand at the further end of the net to keep the water hole from freezing up, in order that the line might pass through while the net was being taken out." Using three nets, the group caught about 41 whitefish averaging five pounds the first day. In two weeks the fishing season was over, for according to Hines, the fish caught the rest of the year did not pay a man for his time. Although Hines had only stayed at the lake several days, he was given 207 fish as his share of the catch.[10]

Early in February most of the men at Sandy Lake were either away hunting for furs and food, or they were on a trading trip to Fort Carlton. Hunting continued through February and into March.[11] As spring settled in, ducks and geese were hunted, and attention turned to collecting and making maple syrup. Some families, including Ahenakew's, left March 28 for groves of maples located 80 to 100 miles from Sandy Lake, possibly near an island in the North Saskatchewan River near Prince Albert.[12] Other families followed the next week. It must have been a leisurely trip for some, with time for visiting with friends and relatives at the "sugar" camp and at Fort Carlton, for Ahenakew and his family did not return to Sandy Lake until May 2.[13]

During the fall and winter of 1876–77, mission activities had continued to dominate Hines's time. The missionary alternated holding Sunday church services at Sandy Lake and Snake Plain. On the Sundays when Hines was with Mistawasis's band, Stranger conducted the services for Ahtahkakoop's people and read sermons written by the missionary. At Sandy Lake, in addition to his church services, Hines regularly visited individual homes where he talked about God and the Bible, and he prayed with the people at every opportunity. The young clergyman even took chalk and a blackboard with him so he could teach Cree syllabics to the young adults and anyone else who was interested.[14] Classes were held to prepare men and women for

---

* Now known as Morin Lake, it is the site of present-day Victoire.

baptism. There were singing classes, Bible classes, and reading and writing classes. By November, six people could read and write Cree syllabics and prayer books were in short supply. The two traders were also drawn under Hines's influence, and by December they were coming to services and helping with the singing.[15]

Christianity and, more specifically, the teachings of the Anglican church were almost inseparable from the task of learning to read and write. Prayer books served as readers and the singing classes were for the sole purpose of teaching Christian hymns. Thirty-one-year-old Kāh-kāsōw (He Who Hides) was one of the most avid learners.[16] Son of Ahenakew and the first adult baptized by Hines at Sandy Lake, Kāh-kāsōw had mastered the syllabic form of writing and the hymns very quickly. He took at least one prayer book with him to the fall hunting camp, and in October wrote a letter to Hines asking for another book so he could continue studying. From the traders he got some loose paper for practising writing. Soon Kāh-kāsōw was teaching others. By spring Hines said that "3 parts of the Indians at the mission who understand syllabics have been taught" by him.[17]

His brothers were among those learning to read. When Hines arrived at Ahenakew's house one evening for lessons, he found the house swept and a stool with a blanket over it waiting for him. Wāsēhikot (Shining Nose)* was sitting with Louis, his younger brother, reading the evening prayers from a church prayer book. The book had been given to Kāh-kāsōw the previous evening.[18] Later Hines saw Baptiste, another of Ahenakew's sons, reading a letter that Louis had written from Fort Carlton. In this new way of communication, Louis reported that the sickness at Battleford was not smallpox but a kind of scurvy, and the seed promised by the government had not arrived.[19] Louis, 13, was one of the students attending Hines's day school.[†]

Both men and women attended singing classes during the winter of 1876–77, with Hines noting in his journal that attendance on January 26 and March 29 numbered 22 and 24 respectively. Although Ahtahkakoop—who had a deep, rumbling voice—went to the classes, he felt uncomfortable until the men started learning to sing bass. That, the chief said, was the "first thing that suited him."[20]

---

* Wāsēhikot took the name Henry when he was baptized.

[†] In 1877, Baptiste was 19 and Wāsēhikot was 27. Ages are approximate and based on information contained in mission records.

The children were also learning the hymns. To offer encouragement, the Scottish trader (a man by the name of Campbell) promised material for a new dress to the girl who made the most progress in singing. The winner was Margaret, Sasakamoose's daughter of "about nine years of age." Upon receiving her prize, which was three yards of print, she was heard to ask very loudly, "I wonder if I had sung louder, would he have given me a little shawl too?"[21]

Most of the leading men and their families made an effort that winter to set an example for other band members by sending their children to school, attending church services, and taking part in the special adult class held by the missionary. Ahenakew's family had been touched as much as any by Hines and his teachings. Adult classes were held at his house, all but one of his children living on the reserve had been baptized, his grown sons had learned to read, 13-year-old Louis was making his mark at school, and Kāh-kāsōw was playing an important role in teaching others. Sasakamoose and Ahtahkakoop's 39-year-old son Kā-miyo-ahcahkwēw[22] were equally supportive. Not everyone, however, was sympathetic. Headman Wāskitoy was in no hurry to adopt Christianity and Ahtahkakoop's son Kīsik-awāsis turned his back on the missionary.

Despite Ahtahkakoop's determination to prepare his children and grand-children for the future, the transition was creating problems and doubts within his own family. His two oldest sons, for instance, were at odds with each other. Kā-miyo-ahcahkwēw, like so many others in his father's band, had been baptized by a Catholic priest. He and his wife Judique had chosen to support Hines and the Anglican mission. Kīsik-awāsis, who was probably in his late 30s or early 40s, would not give up his traditional beliefs and was openly defiant of his father, his brother, and Hines. Ahtahkakoop's wife was also resisting. Her concerns, however, seemed to stem from the fear of being separated from her deceased children after death, rather than a full-fledged denunciation of Christianity.

Ahtahkakoop had some personal doubts of his own and was refusing to be rushed by the missionary into full acceptance of Christianity. "The Chief you have heard so much about is not yet baptised," John Hines had reported to the Church Missionary Society in September of 1876. "I cannot conceive why he does not come forward & offer himself, as he has entirely abandoned all heathen rites, & is a regular attender of the House of God."[23]

On November 21, while having tea with Ahtahkakoop, Hines asked the chief outright why he had not come forward to be baptized. Ahtahkakoop replied that he did not think it would be right to be christened by Hines when his children were baptized by the Roman Catholics, "for in doing so, it w^d convey the idea to his children that he had allowed them to be baptised by a minister in whom he had not sufficient faith."[24] Hines argued "that being baptised by me could not possibly convey that idea now, for both he & his family had practically deserted ... [the Roman Catholic] church by regularly attending our services & by sending their children to our day school, some of whom (his grandchildren) have also been baptised by me." Ahtahkakoop, whom Hines referred to as the "Old Man," responded that he would not desert Hines since he knew the Anglican clergyman cared more about the welfare of the children than the priests.

The subject came up again the next evening, on what Hines called his "happiest evening" since coming to the country, when Ahenakew asked both Hines and Ahtahkakoop to come to his house. Ahenakew told Hines that he and Wāsēhikot, his only son still to be christened, wanted to be baptized. Ahtahkakoop was older, he continued, and they did not want to go before him. The chief apparently had been giving the issue considerable thought and he had probably discussed it with Ahenakew. And so when Ahtahkakoop replied, he said that "he was a man that did nothing in a hurry, consequently he very rarely had to regret his actions." He had put off being baptized to learn more about the religion, the necessity of being baptized, and to prove the religion was the best. Now, Ahtahkakoop stated, he was convinced in his own mind and would likely be baptized before Christmas.[25]

Ahenakew did not wait any longer. Subject to sudden attacks of "illness" and afraid he would die without warning, Ahenakew and his wife were baptized December 17, 1876. Ahenakew chose David as his Christian name. Kīskanakwās (Cut Sleeve) took the name Mary.[26] Ahtahkakoop's baptism did not happen, most likely because his wife refused to be baptized with him.[27]

Wāsēhikot, his wife, and their two-week-old daughter were baptized on February 18, 1877. Wāsēhikot took the name Henry, his wife was given the name Jemima, and the baby was named Sarah. That same day the "second" wife of Mistawasis was also baptized and given the name Ann. She had been living on Ahtahkakoop's reserve with her daughter Judique and Kā-miyo-ahcahkwēw since separating from the Snake Plain chief.[28] This separation was brought about by the church's insistence that men and women with more than one spouse could not be baptized.

While some couples were breaking up, others were considering being married by Hines, for the church taught that living together without going through the ceremony prescribed by the white man's Christian church was as sinful as having two wives. Kā-miyo-ahcahkwēw and Judique were among those thinking about a church marriage. The subject had been raised with Hines for the first time in December following a Bible lesson at Kā-miyo-ahcahkwēw's home on the west side of the lake. Almost three months later Hines met with them again, and this time Ahenakew and his son Kāh-kāsōw were part of the discussion. David and Mary Ahenakew and Antoine and Judique Kā-miyo-ahcahkwēw were "legally" married March 13.[29] They were the first couples to be married by Hines at the Asissipi Mission.

With the coming of spring, Sasakamoose was also ready to be baptized and married. Ahtahkakoop's brother had been in a situation similar to Mistawasis's when Hines first arrived because he too had two wives. Unlike the Snake Plain chief, Ahtahkakoop's brother had refused to "throw away" either wife, saying both had been good to him for many years and he would not desert them. His "first" and eldest wife died in 1875 and now, on Easter Sunday two years later, he was ready to be baptized. Hines had a few nervous moments when the chief's brother was late for the service, but he finally came, explaining that the wind had been blowing "away from his house" and he had not heard the church bell. Sasakamoose, who had chosen Jacob as his Christian name, asked that he and his second wife Margaret be "legally" married following his baptism. This wife, Hines noted, had been baptized much earlier by a Wesleyan clergyman.[30]

It had not been easy for Sasakamoose to convert to Christianity. He had been "one of the great Indian Medicine Men,"[31] a member of *mitēwiwin*, and a leader of Cree traditions. Although he likely believed that the Christian God and the Great Creator were the same deity, the approach was different, and many of the traditional Indian religious ceremonies were considered by Hines and his fellow Christians to be evil. Sasakamoose had told the missionary in the fall that he would be baptized at Easter. Yet doubts prevailed and he spoke to Hines about his inner struggle in early March. Hines could not have understood what was going through the old man's mind. The English missionary had told the people to get rid of evil thoughts and acts, and now in Sasakamoose he perceived what he called the "increasing efforts of the wicked ones to retain his victim." Yet, for

Sasakamoose, it was not the "wicked ones" who tormented him but the power of his traditional beliefs. Hines said that during the last month "the thoughts of his former practices have troubled him much & he feared that after having received Holy Baptism he might be tempted to return to his former practices."[32] For Sasakamoose and many others, rejecting their traditional religion and beliefs was extremely difficult.

Some five weeks after Sasakamoose was baptized and married, Hines conducted a marriage ceremony for Kāh-kāsōw and his wife Charlotte Hyman.[33] They were the third couple on the Ahtahkakoop Reserve to be married by John Hines.

Meanwhile a number of other people had been baptized. These included a three-week-old boy and four daughters of K-ōsihkosiwanāniw (He Who Has An Ermineskin Robe*). The daughters took the names Ellen, Catherine, Mary, and Emma.[34] His wife Chenesis was baptized on April 1, 1877.

The church services and classes to prepare people living on the Mistawasis Reserve for baptism were also bearing fruit. The family of one of Mistawasis's headmen was particularly interested in converting to Christianity. The headman was known as Pierre, Pierre Stone, and Pierre Cardinal. His family later took the name Cardinal. On December 25, 1876, Hines administered the rites of baptism to Pierre's sons John and Thomas and his daughter Mary.[35] Three months later, on March 25, Mistawasis and his wife were baptized. The chief from Snake Plain chose the name Jacob. His wife took the name Mary Jane.[36] After Hines left, David Stranger asked why more people were not coming forward to be baptized. He was told that most felt they were unworthy, or else their lives had been too "bad."

Not everyone was interested in adopting the white man's religion. Some people opposed the missionary openly and vocally. Others, many of whom were "attached to the mission," continued to take part in traditional ceremonies even though they were participating in mission activities. An example of this occurred in early April, a week after Sasakamoose was baptized. By now a number of families were away collecting maple syrup. On April 8, most of those still at the settlement went to a ceremonial feast at Whitefish Lake. The feast was held by the sons of Otayapīhkēw (He Who

---

* The English translation of K-ōsihkosiwanāniw's name was later shortened to Ermineskin.

Webs, or Netmaker), the "old man" who had objected to Hines staying at Whitefish Lake his first year in the country. Hines said he did not think "anything evil" was practised at these feasts. Nevertheless, they were always held on a Sunday, and this of course cut attendance at his services. The missionary was also critical of the practice of giving gifts to wipe out the offences of the year. Unable to appreciate the significance of the traditional ceremony, Hines assured himself that most of the people no longer believed. This was the most trying part of the year, and many of the people were on the point of starvation. "I think," he wrote in his journal, "they go because of the food."[37]

The clash between cultures was evident again two months later when people from Whitefish Lake left some property with Hines and asked for food. Hines retorted that they had some, so he refused. Otayapīhkēw, who was with the group, responded saying that the property of a missionary should be common property since God's gifts were common to all. The Indians looked upon God as their father; the minister taught that he was the father, and all were his children. Therefore, he concluded, Hines's property should also be common. Hines did not record his response. Since he wanted the group to stay for church services the next day, he offered them work— likely in exchange for food—but they refused. The missionary concluded his recording of the exchange with the comment that Otayapīhkēw "was known to be the most headstrong of all the Crees."[38]

Some time afterwards, Ahtahkakoop's son Kīsik-awāsis[39] was also critical of the Anglican missionary. He had come to ask Hines for provisions and matches to go hunting. The missionary said he "changed the subject of conversation to that of religion" and told Kīsik-awāsis "How much better it would be if you sent your children to school." Kīsik-awāsis became excited and said he could not come to the house without Hines talking to him about religion. Ahenakew, who was visiting Hines, "interfered at once & said, 'My nephew, whenever you go into the trader's house does he not ask if you have any furs to sell him. Yes. Well that is his duty. If people went into his store & he never inquired after their furs, he would be neglecting his duty & his master would not be pleased with him. Just so with the minister. If he were to allow you to come in & go out of his house without speaking to you about Xtianity he wd not be doing his duty.'"[40]

The missionary described Kīsik-awāsis as a "conceited, stiff-necked heathen, no one can give him a good word. They speak of him as the man with the stoney heart." Be that as it may, Hines had fallen into the familiar pattern of describing those opposed to him in derogatory terms. Those who were co-operative and receptive to his teachings were described in positive ways. Kā-miyo-ahcahkwēw, for instance, was said by Hines to be one of the "most reliable Indians," and Sasakamoose was a "model for neatness & cleanliness."[41] In contrast, Otayapīhkēw, Kīsik-awāsis, and others who opposed him, were described in uncomplimentary words.

By the beginning of May, Ahtahkakoop and his wife still had not been baptized. According to Hines, Ahenakew "felt grieved" at his brother's delay and blamed the influence of his sister-in-law. Hines apparently felt the same, noting that when Ahtahkakoop was away, his wife rarely attended church or sent their daughter to school.[42] The situation apparently came to a head on or shortly after May 13, a Sunday when everyone who was in the settlement attended church service except Ahtahkakoop's wife and a grandchild.[43] This must have prompted some action by Hines, for the chief agreed to be baptized later in the week. No mention was made of his wife, so Hines and Stranger went to visit her. At first the woman said that when she was baptized, she would follow her children and be baptized by the Catholic priest. Hines argued that this was only an excuse. When she was baptized, she would be giving herself to God, not to a priest. He talked some more, and finally, with tears in her eyes, the woman agreed to follow her husband. Hines noted in his journal that he had rarely noticed tears "in an Indian before." The ceremony took place on May 20, 1877. Ahtahkakoop chose the name John. His wife, daughter of Nātowēw, was given the name Mary.[44]

Even though there was no major outbreak of sickness at Sandy Lake during the winter of 1876–77, bronchitis was a chronic complaint. Hines visited the sick regularly, administering what medicine he had. Ahenakew had frequent bouts of illness and by early February he still was not fully recovered. Others who were ill included Judique, Kā-miyo-ahcahkwēw's wife. Pregnant, she was suffering from a "hurt" received the previous year. Hines was also treating Kā-miyo-ahcahkwēw's mother-in-law for quinsy.* A young man who had stayed in the water too long while hunting ducks was also under his care. Hines explained that he "caught a cold" and had stiffness in his joints.[45]

Judique's son was born at Fort Carlton on April 24. The mother and baby were so weak that Kā-miyo-ahcahkwēw feared they would die. He

---

* Streptococcal tonsillitis.

sent a message to Hines asking him to come and baptize the baby and talk to his wife. By the time the missionary arrived at the post, both Judique and the baby were improving. The child was named Albert when he was baptized on May 6.[46]

Hines, who had health problems of his own, developed a severe headache during the long drive to Fort Carlton and was so sick he was unable to do anything but baptize the baby. Even a request to hold a church service for the people at Fort Carlton was turned down. His pulse had been under 50 for more than a year, the missionary noted in one of his journals. The two doctors he had seen during his visit to the Red River Settlement the previous year had been unable to find any "symptoms of organic disease," so they recommended "great nourishment and a rest." Hines thought the climate might have been to blame for his sickly condition. Whatever the cause, the missionary—despite his apparently busy schedule—said he was often too weak to do very much and without the help of his wife, many things would "go undone."[47]

Preparations for the upcoming agricultural season had not been forgotten amongst all the hunting, trapping, and church activities. On January 13, long before the growing season was upon them, the chief, headmen, and other band members had met at Hines's house to plan the spring planting. Because the crops had been so badly frozen the previous season, collecting seed had been impossible. Thus, the main topic of discussion was how to get grain and other seed for their farms. It was agreed that Mistawasis should be included in the discussion and two men were sent to fetch him. He arrived later in the afternoon. After weighing several alternatives the leading men decided to "petition" the government for help. Hines took down all that was said and prepared the petition. It was read back "to be sure it was as they wished," and then it was given to a Hudson's Bay Company officer who was passing by on his way to Red River.[48] Although government officials agreed to supply a small amount of seed, it did not arrive at Fort Carlton until late April.[49] While they were waiting, the people broke more land with the four oxen that had been given to them under the terms of Treaty Six. Despite the delay, by the end of the month Ahtahkakoop and his band had sown six bushels of wheat, eight bushels of barley, six bushels of potatoes, and some turnips. Mistawasis and his people, who once again put their crops in at Sandy Lake, planted almost as much.[50]

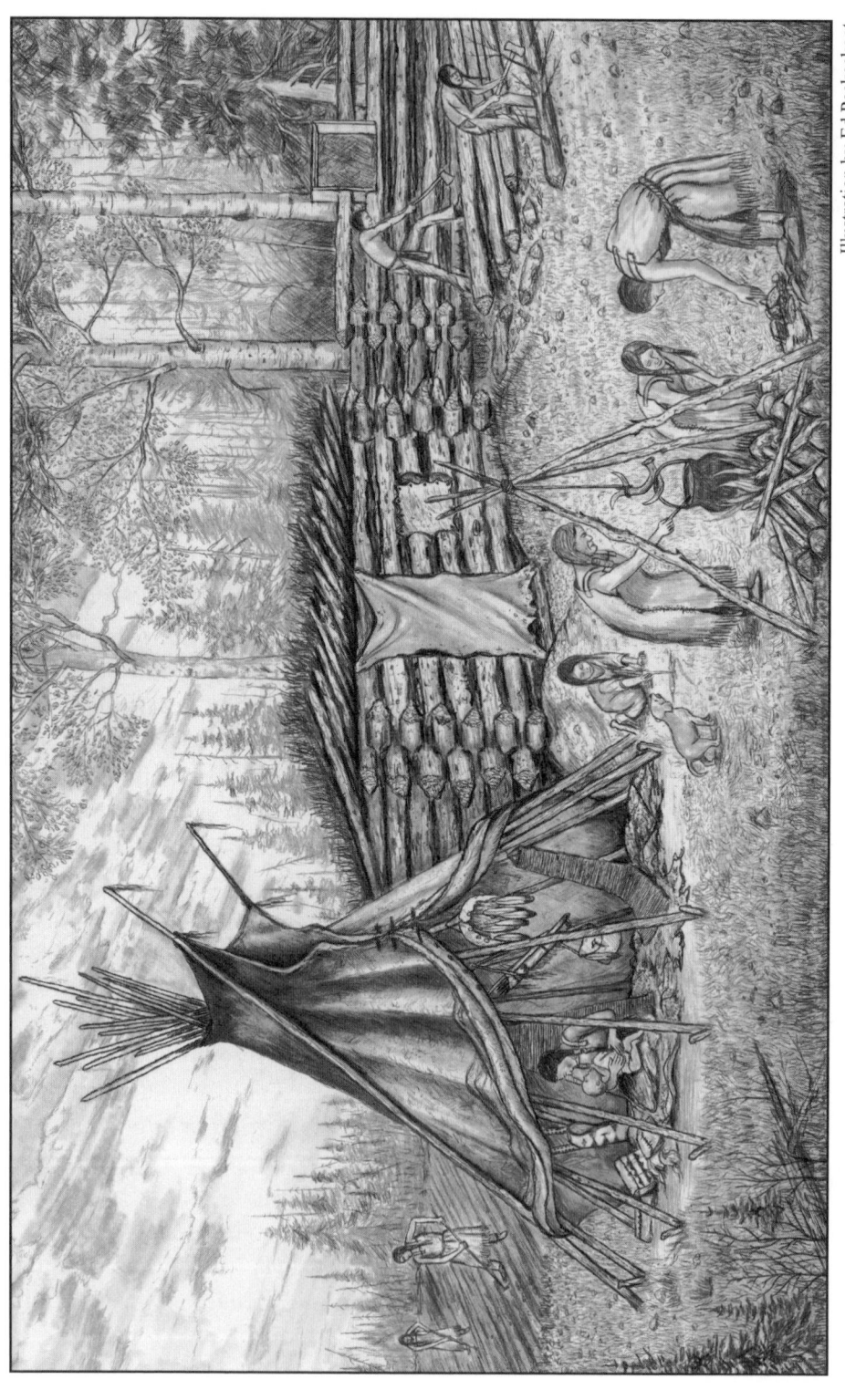

The people moved into tipis when spring came. It was a busy time as the people worked in the fields and started building more substantial houses. Later, they went onto the plains to hunt buffalo.

Illustration by Ed Peekeekoot

A number of houses were under construction that spring to replace those hastily erected during the first season at Sandy Lake. The original buildings, Hines explained, had not been intended as permanent dwellings. He also said that while construction was in progress, attendance at church services and singing classes was low because the young men were working on houses for their parents.[51] One of the houses was for Ahtahkakoop.

With the planting and spring construction work completed, about 50 families left the reserve on May 10. Ahtahkakoop led the large group that travelled to Fort Carlton to get ammunition and supplies for a hunting trip to the plains, while others went to some "fishing lakes." Before leaving, Kāh-kāsōw asked Hines for some books so he could study and teach others while he was on the plains. His 19-year-old brother Baptiste did not go with the hunters. Instead, he returned to the settlement to be with his father and to help look after the fields and the band's small herd of cattle that now consisted of four milking cows, two yoke of oxen (four animals), and six two-year-olds.[52] The cows were milked and, in a new venture, Emma Hines showed the women how to make butter. Most of it was used fairly quickly, but one afternoon Sasakamoose, who had remained at Sandy Lake, brought a birch bark "jar" containing about five pounds of butter to Hines's house. He asked the missionary to store it in his ice cellar, explaining that they "could spare it," and he hoped in mid-summer to get a little flour. Then, Sasakamoose said, they would eat bread and butter.[53]

Hines, in the meantime, had been improving the mission. In March he and his helpers cut posts and pickets for fencing the mission's property and wood for building a new house and a church. By the end of the month, Hines had 5,000 poplar and pine poles cut 12 feet long and 1,700 juniper pickets that were nine feet long.[54] Rather than building the house and church himself with volunteer labour, the missionary arranged for a Prince Albert carpenter to do the work. Hines explained that the people were destitute and he could not "expect them to support a missionary." If they helped build, they could not hunt, and he would have to feed them. It was cheaper in the long run, he said, to pay to have the work done.[55]

A hired carpenter was also necessary, in part at least, because David Stranger had completed his term and was returning to Red River. This left Hines without an interpreter and all-round helper. It appears, however, that Stranger was expected to come back since Hines suggested he be sent to Pelican and Whitefish lakes as a catechist. In Stranger's absence, Benjamin Joyful read prayers and led the singing on at least one occasion. Hines was impressed by Benjamin and hoped that some day he would become an evangelist. "What a work for a man, who two years ago was a heathen & did not know a letter," Hines wrote in his journal. "A man's heart advises his way, but the Lord directs his steps."[56]

The clergyman left for Prince Albert May 24 to get the carpenter and to look after other business. On the way, he stopped at Fort Carlton and held services for some of Ahtahkakoop's people who were still camped there.[57] Shortly after Hines's return to Sandy Lake during the first week of June 1877, sharp frost "almost entirely ruined" the turnips and cut the wheat and barley "almost to the ground." Luckily, the grain recovered.[58]

Ahtahkakoop returned from the hunting grounds with Kāh-kāsōw, who was sick, on June 23. Buffalo had been found about 80 miles from Fort Carlton and 140 miles from Sandy Lake. The animals were very few and scattered, the chief reported, and it was his belief that the buffalo would never collect again.[59] Kāh-kāsōw's teaching venture had been less successful than previously. Only three young men had agreed to be taught. After six weeks of studying, Kāh-kāsōw told Hines, they could read short catechisms.

Like the others still on the reserve, Ahtahkakoop preferred the airiness of a tipi to the stuffy confines of his house, so he pitched his tipi and settled in for the summer. The first year under treaty was nearly complete. Despite the crop failure in 1876, the band had done well. The people's health had been relatively good, the food supply was adequate, and the trapping season profitable. With faith and confidence, Ahtahkakoop and his people were looking optimistically towards the future and a new way of life.

CHAPTER SEVENTEEN

The Last of the Buffalo Hunts, 1877

Most of the families in Ahtahkakoop's band, like other Indian people from Saskatchewan River country, were searching for buffalo on the south side of the North Saskatchewan River when Ahtahkakoop received word on July 3, 1877, that buffalo had been seen within a two-day journey from his reserve. The horses were quickly harnessed, the ox carts readied, and the hunters were off. Ahtahkakoop's hunting party was not well equipped, for the best guns and horses—buffalo runners as well as draught animals—had been sent with the hunters who went onto the plains in May. Additionally, the group was small because only a few people were camped at Sandy Lake. Ahtahkakoop asked Hines to join the hunting party but he turned down the invitation, saying the weather was wet and Mrs. Hines was not feeling very well.

After travelling some distance, the hunters discovered that either their ammunition had dropped off the cart or it had been left behind. Ahtahkakoop, assuming the leadership that came so naturally for him, told the party to continue travelling towards the river while he back-tracked in search of the missing ammunition. Just after 7 a.m. the next morning, when he was about a mile from the mission, the chief met John and Emma Hines travelling in a buckboard. The weather was now "fine" and his wife was feeling better, Hines explained to the chief, so they had decided to join the hunters. Ahtahkakoop, who was on horseback, gave directions, adding that "'I shall most likely overtake you before you get to the place where we shall have to leave the main road.'" The chief eventually found the ammunition lying on the ground "nearly opposite" the Hines's house and, true to his word, joined the couple before they had travelled another six miles. The trio stopped for dinner at Snake Plain and then caught up to the main party opposite the half-way houses. They had been delayed there for four hours because of a thunderstorm.[1]

When the storm was over, Hines wrote in his journal, the hunting party travelled until it reached a "place noted for ducks."[2] Here camp was made for the night. Hines said he had the usual headache "as a matter of course" during the first day of travelling, and Mrs. Hines was "very sick" until he "relieved the pain." The missionary noted that those who "were able to read the Bible & Prayer Book, did so, at every halting place." Prayers were also held in the evening, so the people continued their tradition of asking God's assistance in carrying out a successful hunt. Only a year or two earlier these same men would have smoked the sacred pipe and prayed to the Creator and his spirit helpers for guidance and help.

The following morning everyone was up by 6. Breakfast was made and eaten, prayers said, and the hunters resumed their journey. Ahtahkakoop took the lead, followed by Hines, and then the ox carts. The day quickly became very hot and, at 9 a.m., the chief decided to put the ox carts in front and let them set the pace. While Kāh-kāsōw's wife Charlotte was moving her ox cart forward in the line it hit part of Hines's buckboard. The buckboard turned over and, although no one was hurt, one of its wheels "was slightly broken" and the axle was bent. The whole party stopped and waited for the repairs to be made.[3]

When they came to Muskeg Creek the water was high and the ground soft. To keep the horses and oxen from sinking into the mud, the men and young men cut willows that were growing nearby. Then Ahtahkakoop waded into the water and laid the sticks on the bottom of the creek. With that done, he and his people ate dinner. Hines wrote in his journal that "the Indians have a plan peculiar to themselves which is,—When they get into trouble immediately to sit down & eat to strengthen them for their difficulties." These breaks also provided opportunities for the people to consult amongst themselves, making sure that everyone knew what had to be done. The meal finished, the animals were "speedily harnessed" and the job of crossing the creek began.

Ahtahkakoop entered the water first with his horses and cart. The animals pulled hard and, with a great deal of effort, the cart landed safely on the other side. The oxen-drawn carts went next. All but the last one crossed easily. The ox pulling that cart struggled and churned up the landing, making it much worse than it had been. Hines, who came last, had even more trouble. He drove in without any problem, but the landing was too soft for

Illustration by Ed Peekeekoot

As the horse struggled, two of the young men kept John Hines's buckboard from overturning in Muskeg Creek.

the narrow wheels on the buckboard. The mare got excited, the bolt of the whipple tree broke, and the horse turned partly around and became restless. Three of the young men sprang into the creek to hold the mare down while Ahtahkakoop rushed into the water, retrieved Emma Hines, and carried her on his back to the shore. Then the mare was detached from the buckboard and both were taken to firm land. Once again the buckboard had been damaged.

That night the hunting party camped eight miles west of a high bare hill known as *osāpahcikan-ispatinaw*.*

The following morning Hines rose at 3 o'clock to hunt ducks. He was unsuccessful, and when he returned to camp three hours later Ahtahkakoop

---

* The Last Little Witigo Hill. A *wīhtikow* is a spirit being of the north country. This hill is north of present-day Blaine Lake. It is also known as Crown Hill.

and the others were ready to leave. The missionary held prayers, and then they were off. Instead of breakfast, the missionary and his wife ate pemmican as they travelled. Later in the morning, the group came to a place where buffalo meat had been recently dried. The chief and some of the others refilled their pipes,* and then they resumed their journey. They had not gone very far when "all at once the dogs set off at full speed for a small bluff of poplar trees." Kāh-kāsōw and two others rode quickly after the dogs to see what had attracted them. It was only a badger.

Dinner was delayed that day because the hunters and their families had trouble finding water. After the meal was over Kāh-kāsōw and Michel, the chief's 15-year-old son, rode ahead to search for buffalo tracks. At about four in the afternoon a "jumping deer" (White-tailed Deer) was sighted but Hines said it was too far away for anyone in the main party to get a shot away. Kāh-kāsōw, who was "farther off," was able to get close enough to shoot, but his flintlock misfired "so he got nothing." They continued on, reaching Onion Lake about 7 p.m. Here they made camp for the night. By now provisions were getting low. Hines said he had some food, but only enough for two meals if he had to feed everyone. After what was likely a meagre meal, Ahtahkakoop took Hines's gun, which was of a more modern style than his own, and went for ducks. He came back with only one.

The next morning Hines lent one of his horses to Kāh-kāsōw. Taking a "great turn to the right," Ahenakew's son once again set off in search of buffalo. The rest of the hunting party continued on to the North Saskatchewan River, where they waited for Kāh-kāsōw about 20 miles above the elbow. In the meantime Ahtahkakoop went off to hunt ducks "or anything else eatable." The news was good when Kāh-kāsōw returned, for he had seen fresh buffalo tracks about 15 miles to the west. Hines provided dinner for the camp after the chief returned and then they were on the trail again.

The hunters found tracks along the margin of the river about 6 p.m. Kāh-kāsōw, who once again had been scouting ahead, reported that he thought he had seen four or five buffalo near the river. The group immediately became quiet so the animals would not panic and escape across the water. Mounting their horses, the men went in pursuit. Ahtahkakoop was riding Hines's horse because his own was "old and slow." The missionary

---

* The men smoked a tobacco mixture in clay pipes obtained from the traders. These pipes were different from the handcrafted sacred pipes.

had also loaned him his gun. The Englishman, in the meantime, ran to get his black mare so he could drive his wife to see "the sport." When she refused to go, Hines got on his horse and went by himself.

The hunters found a herd of 100 buffalo "feeding like a band of domestic cattle" near a wooded area. Ahtahkakoop dismounted. Leaving Hines's horse with Baptiste, the chief "crept around" to get into position to fire the first shot. His gun thundered, a buffalo cow fell to the ground, and the rest of the herd started to move. Baptiste let go of Hines's horse to shoot his own gun. Untrained as a buffalo hunter, the horse bolted and ran. The young man abandoned the hunt and took off after the missionary's horse. Then the herd of buffalo split. Half of the animals scattered across the plains, with hunters riding after them. The other half headed towards Hines, who had just arrived on the scene. The clergyman said he rode parallel to the river to keep the animals from crossing. Ahtahkakoop, in the meantime, was too far from the buffalo to shoot without a horse, so he skinned the animal he had just killed. As darkness fell, a guard was posted to keep the wolves and dogs away from the carcasses while the rest of the people made camp and feasted on fresh buffalo meat.[4]

The next morning, July 8, was Sunday. The people rose early, had breakfast, and Hines conducted a short service. Then they went to fetch the meat.* Back at the camp, women and older girls cut the meat into strips and hung it on quickly erected racks to dry. Others staked the buffalo hides to the ground and scraped off the fat and flesh. Hines was philosophical as well as practical about the women and men working on a Sabbath, saying it was more sinful to let the meat spoil. He and his wife, both of whom were likely ill, spent most of the day in their tent.

The camp broke up the following morning and the hunting party headed for home with the hides and meat-laden carts. Although extremely hot weather forced a halt during midday, the group continued its journey after the temperature cooled down, eventually reaching a "pretty place" to camp. Hines said the feed for the cattle was excellent and the water was good.

To get a head start on the intense heat the following day, the people were up by 3 a.m. They had breakfast, prayed, and were on the road by 4:30. Dinner was eaten opposite Redberry Lake, which Hines described as

---

* Hines does not elaborate further, but the process of "fetching the meat" would have involved skinning and butchering the animals.

being nearly round and about eight miles across. The hills surrounding the lake were very high and covered with different kinds of berry trees, but the water was salty, and there were no fish in the lake. They stayed at the halting place four hours, gaining some respite from the heat before continuing their journey. Misfortune again struck Hines when the *pīsākanāpiy* (rawhide rope) that was used to repair the buckboard earlier in the trip broke, the whipple tree fell, and the horse got away. Kāh-kāsōw went after the horse while Ahtahkakoop helped Hines repair the buckboard. Camp that night was made opposite Salt Lake.

On July 11, the second last day of the trip, the camp rose about 5 a.m. and dinner was eaten nearly four miles west of Muskeg Creek. Hines was having more problems with his buckboard. When the hunting party grew tired of waiting, it went ahead, leaving Michel and Joseph Ahtahkakoop to help. The buckboard was soon fixed and Hines and his two "young assistants" overtook the main party before it reached the creek. This time the crossing was made "on its rise." The ground was firmer here, no doubt helped by the hot weather, and the crossing was made without any difficulty. They camped that night with a "mail carrier" for the Hudson's Bay Company opposite the halfway houses. He joined the group for evening prayers after supper.

Departure the next morning was delayed because the horses, knowing they were near home, had set off on their own during the night. Hines noted that Ahtahkakoop's horse was "more faithful" and stayed at the camp. Although the chief left on horseback early in the morning to look for the missing animals, it was 8:30 before he returned with them. Once under way, the remaining 25 miles to Sandy Lake were completed without stopping for lunch.

Hines finished his account of the trip by saying that they had not seen another person other than the mail carrier during the nine-day trip. The other hunters were all on the south side of the North Saskatchewan River.[5]

CHAPTER EIGHTEEN

The Beginning of Hard Times, 1877-1878

The days immediately after the hunting party returned to Ahtahkakoop's reserve were spent making pemmican and tanning hides. Left-over strips of dried meat were tied into neat bundles for later use, and the extra fat was stored in bladders and other containers. Then part of the harvest from the buffalo hunt was put away for later use. The rest was packed into carts and on July 17, 1877, five days after returning from the buffalo hunt, Ahtahkakoop and the others left for Fort Carlton. There they would trade, wait for the families who had gone onto the far plains to hunt buffalo, and prepare for the first annual treaty payments.[1] While he was at the post, Ahtahkakoop also expected to get the tools, implements, and other goods that had been promised under the terms of the treaty.*

There had been questions and concerns about the timing of the treaty payment. Earlier in the year Ahtahkakoop, Mistawasis, and the other leading chiefs had learned that Indian department officials would be too busy securing adhesions to Treaty Six and making treaty annuity payments in the western part of the treaty area to meet with them at a reasonable time. Government officials were also making arrangements to negotiate Treaty Seven with the Blackfoot, Blood, Peigan, Sarcee, Stoney, and other Indian nations in what is now the Province of Alberta.† Since the people needed

---

* Ahtahkakoop had already received some of the livestock, for Hines had reported in May that the band had four oxen, four milking cows, and six two-year-old cows. Since this exceeded the number of animals specified in the treaty, some of these animals must have been privately owned.

† This treaty was signed at Blackfoot Crossing on September 22, 1877.

implements for harvesting their hay, grain, and other crops, the chiefs requested that someone else pay them.[2] Accordingly, arrangements were made for Superintendent James Walker, the North-West Mounted Police officer in charge of Fort Battleford, to go to Carlton in the capacity of acting Indian agent.[3]

The first annuity payments did not go smoothly. When Ahtahkakoop and the others arrived at Fort Carlton they learned that muddy conditions on the Carlton Trail had delayed the train of ox carts hauling implements and other supplies from Winnipeg. In addition to the implements, tools, and other goods promised under the treaty, the carts carried 150 bags of flour weighing 100 pounds each, 800 pounds of tea, 1,600 pounds of sugar, 800 pounds of tobacco, and ammunition valued at $500 for distribution at the payments. Fifty oxen to be killed for beef accompanied the carts. When it was apparent that the ox train would be late arriving at Fort Carlton, Lawrence Clarke was instructed to issue provisions to the people gathered at the treaty grounds from his own warehouses and bill the government.[4]

Everyone was waiting for both the ox train and Walker to arrive when John and Emma Hines drove up to the post on July 21. The couple waited several days, during which time the missionary conducted church services in English at the post and in Cree at the treaty grounds. He visited from tipi to tipi, and baptized two infants. Then, after concluding that the implements "would probably be a long time reaching Carlton owing to wet weather," the couple returned to Sandy Lake, driving eight miserable hours through rain.[5]

Walker finally arrived and the annuity payments were completed at Fort Carlton on August 3. During discussions with the acting Indian agent, Ahtahkakoop again stated that he wanted his reserve "around Sandy Lake and down each side of the Shell River." This reserve, Walker reported, "joins" Mistawasis's reserve.[6] Fifty-two men, 81 women, 84 boys, and 71 girls in Ahtahkakoop's band, for a total of 288, were paid.[7]

Since the "presents" and supplies still had not arrived, Walker said he

> advised the Indians to return to their hunting grounds, and reservations, and to trust in the Government carrying out their part of the treaty as soon as the articles promised were delivered; this they decided to do and told me they had full confidence in the Government, and that they would place their cases in my hands, and do just as I had told them.[8]

Illustration by Ed Peekeekoot

Most of Ahtahkakoop's people hunted buffalo while he waited at Fort Carlton for the implements. The women fleshed the hides, dried the meat, and pounded it to shreds in camps near the hunting grounds. Later, they would make pemmican.

After arranging for Lawrence Clarke to receive the Indian department goods when they arrived, Walker went to Prince Albert to make additional payments before returning to Battleford. Some of the people left for the hunting grounds as suggested. Ahtahkakoop, however, had received word that the carts hauling the goods were getting close to Fort Carlton. Since his people had neither sickles nor scythes for cutting their hay and grain, Ahtahkakoop—along with others—decided to wait.[9]

Ahtahkakoop's information was correct and the carts arrived several days after Walker's departure.[10] The supplies were under the charge of a Mr. McDonald, agent for James McKay.* Neither McDonald nor Clarke had been authorized to distribute the implements and tools. Accordingly,

---

* One of the commissioners at the Treaty Six negotiations.

McDonald told the leading chiefs that he had "sent to Battleford, expressly on their account" for Walker to return to Fort Carlton. This McDonald "did not do," the North-West Mounted Police officer was to report later. He explained that McDonald

> only notified me that the supplies were forwarded and wished me to come down and receive them; but as I had previously arranged with Mr. Clark [*sic*] to receive the supplies at Prince Albert and Carlton and I expected that the Indians had all dispersed, I wrote to Mr. McDonald asking him to deliver the supplies to Mr. Clark.[11]

Assuming that everything was under control, Walker did not take any further action until he received a letter from Clarke on August 19 informing him that "all the Chiefs and a large number of the Indians were still at Carlton" waiting for the implements and other goods to be distributed. The officer immediately left for Fort Carlton where, not unexpectedly, he found trouble brewing. All but two of the chiefs had signed a petition to Governor General Dufferin "wishing to give up the treaty, and complaining of the way they had been treated by the Indian Department."[12] Walker said he responded by holding

> a council with the Chiefs as soon as I could get them together, and after I explained to them why they had not received their presents, they signed a letter addressed to me, a copy of which I enclose and also expressed their fullest satisfaction with the treaty and all parties connected with it. And after I had distributed the presents, and was about to leave them, they collected together and gave three cheers for the Queen, Lt. Gov. Laird and myself. I feel confident that these Indians were influenced by some parties to act as they did, as none of the Chiefs could tell me what was in the petition they had signed to go to Ottawa, but they all said they did not think there was anything against the Government or the Treaty in it.[13]

The letter that was written and delivered to Walker stated:

> We the undersigned chiefs of the Cree Nation who signed the Treaty that was made at Carlton last summer wish you to express to our Good Father, the Governor of this Country, our entire, and complete content and satisfaction with the terms and conditions of that Treaty; and to thank our good Mother the Queen ... for the

generous way in which she has fulfilled the promises that … [she made]. We also request you to tell our Good Father, the Governor that we hope he will forgive us that some of us, by the misrepresentations and false reports that were circulated amongst us, that the Government did not intend to fulfil their part of the Treaty, were led to sign a paper telling that we were not pleased with the manner in which we were being used and were dissatisfied with our Treaty. We now know that these reports are lies and that it was no fault of our Good Mother's Counsellors that we did not receive our presents at the time we were told to assemble together to be paid our yearly money.

We want also to tell you that we are well pleased with the way in which you have dealt with us, for the patience you have borne with our many questions and the kindness you have shown in explaining the articles in the Treaty that we did not quite understand. Also for the trouble you have taken to distribute the Presents so as to enable us to go to our homes with as little further delay as possible. We wish you well.[14]

The letter was signed by "Your Friends," Mistawasis, Ahtahkakoop, Kitowēhāw, Cakāstēpēsin, Wāwikanihk k-ōtāmahoht (He Strikes Him On The Back), Ocīpiwayān's son,* and Kā-pēyakwaskonam (One Arrow). Two other chiefs, John Smith and Ayahtaskamikinam (also known as William Twatt), signed the letter at Prince Albert.

After waiting at Fort Carlton for nearly a month, Ahtahkakoop and his people had finally received some of the tools, implements, and other goods that had been promised under the treaty. The time of delivery for specific items is uncertain although government records indicate that by June, 1878, Ahtahkakoop's band had received: 1 plough, 1 harrow, 1 whipple-tree, 2 sets of whipple-trees, 6 trace chains, 14 scythes, 14 snaiths, 14 hay forks, 18 axes, 20 hoes, 12 spades, 13 sickles, 1 grindstone, 1 cross-cut saw, 1 pit saw, 1 tool chest, 1 set of harness, 9 hand saws, 1 wagon, 1 horse, 10 augers, 6 cross-cut saw files, 6 pit saw files, 12 hand saw files, 1 tiller, and 4 oxen.[15] The tools, implements, and oxen were to be shared by the 52 families in the band. No mention of the milking cows and two-year-old

---

* Although government documentation refers to this man as Young Chipewayan, his name was Ispimihk-kā-kitot (Thunders Above.)

cows referred to by Hines is made in the government's statement of distribution. Mistawasis's band, with an almost identical number of families, was given the same allotment of goods and livestock.

It is doubtful Ahtahkakoop and Mistawasis were as satisfied with the summer's proceedings as the chiefs' letter to Walker indicated. The oxen supplied by the government were obviously wild and in poor condition. The axes were too small to be useful and many of the implements were poorly made. The leading men were also upset with the long wait at Fort Carlton. Their crops had looked extremely good before leaving for Carlton in mid-July. The potatoes were ready to use, and the hay was thriving. Waiting at Carlton, expecting their spades, scythes and other implements to be distributed, had been a waste of time, but without them harvesting would have been difficult. Additionally, some of the men—including Ahtahkakoop—were building new houses and they would now be pressed to complete them before winter.

While Ahtahkakoop waited at Fort Carlton and members of his band searched for buffalo on the plains, Hines carried on with farming activities on the reserve. Some of the hay had been ready to cut soon after the chief left Sandy Lake in July. Stranger had not returned from Manitoba so the missionary tried to hire a man at Fort Carlton to assist him. Unsuccessful, he and school teacher Wright started cutting the hay by hand. The work did not go without difficulty, for the hay marsh was under water and they were "obliged to cut here or there." However, the manual work, combined with less studying and mental work, was good for Hines and the missionary noted in his journal that his health was much better.[16]

Stranger, who was a widower when he started working for John Hines in 1874, arrived back at the mission on August 26 with his two daughters, 20-year-old Elizabeth and 13-year-old Sophia. Travelling in their party from Winnipeg was Hines's newly recruited teacher, Edward K. Matheson.[17] Twenty-two-years old, the young man had been recommended for work in the Saskatchewan Diocese by his cousin, Samuel Pritchard Matheson, who later became the archbishop of Rupert's Land.[18]

On September 3, Ahtahkakoop, Mistawasis, and 15 or 16 families pulled into Sandy Lake with their implements and supplies. Almost immediately they set to work cutting hay, barley, and wheat with their new scythes. Mistawasis left on September 6 to supervise the cutting of hay at Snake Plain, but he was back six days later to help cut the wheat he had planted at Sandy Lake. Finally, on September 20, the harvest was finished. The grain was gathered into sheaves to await threshing and the hay was stacked.* According to Hines, the crops were "tolerably good" despite the frost in early June. The Englishman was pleased with a trial patch of flax, saying that he had proven flax could be grown and ripened in the country. It was one of the most fattening foods for cattle, he noted, and improved the quality of milk and butter; even the manure was better.[19]

The potato crop in 1877 was good, realizing "about 20 fold." The people had been eating potatoes since their arrival back from Fort Carlton, and even then, when their harvest was complete on October 13, they had "amongst them" 180 bushels for winter use. Another 350 bushels were kept as seed potatoes for planting the next spring and stored in Hines's root cellar.[20] No mention was made of turnips and other vegetables, but Walker had reported in August that Ahtahkakoop's band had a "good sized field of turnips." It is likely that some other garden vegetables, such as carrots and onions, had also been planted.

Hines was to maintain his relationship with Mistawasis's band throughout the winter. He assigned Matheson to the Snake Plain school, continued to hold regular services and instructional classes for Mistawasis's people, and supplied medicine to the sick.[21] Work started on a new school in mid-October, with Hines feeding the men who volunteered one day's labour to the project. Stranger finished the school a month later.[22] Matheson did not speak Cree, but Hines noted in March that he had made good progress learning the language. He had been born in the country and had heard Cree spoken since childhood, Hines explained, so the language came naturally to him. Nevertheless, the missionary said the young man was lonely at first because he had no one to talk with in English.[23]

The schools at Snake Plain and Sandy Lake, where Wright continued as teacher, both gave Hines "discouragement." For some of the problems, the missionary blamed the pattern of settlement that had developed, with some houses being three to four miles from the schools. Miserable weather and hunting trips adversely affected attendance. Additionally, some families may have intentionally settled some distance from the schools in an effort to stay beyond the mission's influence. In any case, the number of children

---

* To thresh the wheat, the men, women, and children beat the stalks of grain with sticks. Then the grain was separated from the chaff, often by tossing the mixture into the air and letting the wind blow the chaff away.

attending classes was lower than expected and Hines let Wright go in December. The missionary and his wife took over the teaching duties at Sandy Lake. Emma was well qualified for the work, having been the principal of a girls' school in Winnipeg before her marriage.

In its year-end report for 1878, the Indian Branch of the Department of the Interior gave the enrolment at the Asissipi Mission as 11 boys and 10 girls. According to this report, the average daily attendance was 10. In March 1878, Hines said that on the average 28 of the 45 children on Ahtahkakoop's reserve were going to school. The curriculum included reading, spelling, writing, arithmetic, grammar, and diction. Only three other schools were listed in government documentation for the Treaty Six area for the year ending June 30, 1878.[24]

Mission activities continued to keep Hines busy and, as usual, he devoted more time in his journal to mission work than to the activities of band members. This in part was because he wrote in his journal sporadically. Sometimes the entries were made daily, but more often they were weekly or even less frequent. Understandably Hines's prime interest focused on his own activities and concerns. But the sparseness of information was often because Hines did not know what was happening. A prime example of this occurred on November 10, 1877.

This was the scheduled night for adult classes at Ahenakew's house. The chief and his wife were both absent, so on his way home the missionary stopped at Ahtahkakoop's to find out why the couple had not attended. He discovered that Ahtahkakoop had visitors and they were all in his newly completed house. As soon as Hines was seated, one of Ahtahkakoop's sons brought a kettle of tea and a plate of berry pemmican. "Rather surprised at this unusual treatment," the Englishman asked Stranger what he thought was going on. His helper replied that it was the chief's first night in his new home. Hines told the group how pleased he was that the chief had such a large and durable house, and then suggested they have prayers together. There were 11 people there in all, Hines wrote, and "the visitors all left before we finished supper." Hines presumably had prayers with Ahtahkakoop's family before returning home. It seems, then, that the missionary found out about a noteworthy event quite by accident.[25]

Hines continued through November with his usual schedule of teaching at the school, holding singing and instructional classes at Ahenakew's and Kā-miyo-ahcahkwēw's houses, visiting the sick, and carrying out an assortment of miscellaneous activities. It was not unusual for Ahtahkakoop's wife and daughter to be absent from the classes when the chief was away. This bothered Hines, often resulting in a terse note in his journal, and it obviously disturbed Ahenakew as well. The issue came to a head on November 22 while Ahtahkakoop was away on a 10-day hunting trip. Once again Ahtahkakoop's wife and daughter skipped the class. Ahenakew told Hines he was pleased that because of his lameness, the classes were being held at his house, "but as there were many who found it too far to walk, he hoped I w^d hold the class in his brother's house for the future, as he, though lame w^d would not think that far to go to listen to the 'Word of God.'"[26] The "old man," Hines noted with some satisfaction, "had observed, like myself, the non-attendance of the chief's wife & daughters & w^d therefore rather have the class held at their house so that they might not fail to be present, although it w^d cost him a long walk."

The change was made quickly. A class was held at Ahtahkakoop's house on November 28, while the chief was still away, and again on the 30th following his return.[27] Another class was held at Ahtahkakoop's on December 5. The following day Hines met with people from the west side of the lake at Kā-miyo-ahcahkwēw's house. Hines's work schedule was proving to be too strenuous and, on December 7, the clergyman wrote in his journal that he would have to give up the singing classes. They were too hard on his throat. In their place, he planned to hold two evening classes a week for general discussion, with each get-together beginning and closing with a hymn. The new program would be introduced in late December after the men returned from fishing.[28]

Hines's persistence was paying off. In November, a man who had attended one of the classes at Kā-miyo-ahcahkwēw's home showed up at church services the following Sunday. Until then he had refused to go to church or send his children to school. About the same time, another man made his first appearance at Sunday services, and the next week he brought a friend with him.[29]

Hines was also continuing to win converts at Snake Plain. On December 16, for instance, parents "in great distress" sent a message asking the missionary to come and see their sick child. Five-year-old Alexander Asicahcās (Against The Belly) died soon after Hines saw him, and he was taken to Sandy Lake for burial. The father headed the funeral procession on horseback. Behind him came a horse-drawn sleigh carrying the body, and then family and friends. The boy was buried on the 18th. Hines said they came so soon because the mother was "fretting."[30] A week later, on December 25, nine adults were baptized at Snake Plain. The service was held at Mistawasis's house because the school was too small. The converts included three sons of Pierre Stone and Sasakamoose and two daughters-in-law. Pierre was one of Mistawasis's headmen.[31]

All the men at the Ahtahkakoop Reserve, with the exception of three "invalids," were fishing at *manitow-sākahikan* when the funeral was held for the boy from Mistawasis's band. The men had left December 12. Initially the catch was poor, but on December 27 Hines recorded in his journal that the prospects at the fish camp finally looked "a bit brighter."[32]

Ahtahkakoop went to Fort Carlton at least twice in December of 1877. His first trip early in the month was prompted, in part at least, by the high prices being charged by free traders* who were bartering at Sandy Lake.[33] He returned with trade goods valued at $500 supplied by the Hudson's Bay Company. These goods included provisions, clothes, files, axes, traps, and ammunition.[34] About two weeks later the chief again went to the post, this time to take in the furs he had collected and to receive his annual Christmas presents from the Hudson's Bay Company. Hines, who was in the midst of a four-day visit at Snake Plain when Ahtahkakoop arrived there, explained that Ahtahkakoop and Mistawasis "have always been looked upon by the Co. as the representatives of the Carlton Crees." For this reason, along with the fact that they were "regular customers," the chiefs were given presents each Christmas. These included a bag of flour and a few pounds of sugar, raisins, tea, dried apples, rice, and tobacco.[35] When Ahtahkakoop returned to the reserve, he shared the gifts with others.[36]

On December 29, three men from Snake Plain came to Sandy Lake to thresh their barley. Mistawasis joined them the next day, arriving in time for the second church service. The group left on December 31, with eight bushels of barley and 12 bushels of potatoes.[37]

New Year's Day was a day of festivities, with people visiting from home to home. This year Hines held a short service in the morning. A number of people who had not attended church before were in the congregation, yet the missionary was disappointed. "I am sorry to say," he wrote in his journal, that "many of our professing Indians were absent. They seem

---

* Free traders was a term used for traders not associated with a fur trade company, and in particular, the Hudson's Bay Company.

to care more for the perishable things of earth than for the endurable riches of Eternity."[38] The clergyman was being unfair. He could not expect the people at Sandy Lake to abandon all their old customs overnight. He also overlooked the fact that many of the people associated with the mission were members of leading families in the community and had responsibilities that extended beyond the Asissipi Mission.

Despite Hines's remarks, the people had not abandoned the mission. During the second week of January, when Hines was so sick he could hardly walk, several people came to visit him at his house. Then, following the morning church service on January 13—which Hines said he conducted with great difficulty—Ahtahkakoop and one of his brothers came to dine with him. This, Hines noted, was "a way the Indian has of showing his sympathy."[39] The rest of the month was also encouraging. Attendance at the adult classes reached an all-time high on January 23 when 20 people attended. A month later a large congregation, described by Hines as being "unusually great," gathered for church services. Hines attributed this to the fact that the men had returned from a "hunt."[40]

A number of other milestones were reached during the early months of 1878. Most notable of these occurred on February 26, 1878, when the first communion was conducted at the Asissipi Mission and Ahtahkakoop and his wife Mary were "lawfully married."[41] The Reverend John A. Mackay, the Anglican missionary at Battleford who had previously served at Stanley Mission and The Pas, was in attendance for this special occasion. Mackay was slated to teach at Emmanuel College when it opened in Prince Albert in late 1879.[42] He was also one of the men who had tried to interpret at the Treaty Six negotiations.

On March 11, three other marriages took place. Ahenakew's son Henry Wāsēhikot married his wife Jemima; Simon Apotum (Could Be) married a woman Hines called Martha; and David Stranger remarried, taking a woman by the name of Isabella as his wife.[43]

By now, work was under way on a new house for John and Emma Hines. Because the men on the Ahtahkakoop reserve had been reluctant to help saw wood for the mission house, much of the lumber—as well as the shingles—was purchased in Prince Albert. Hines understood the men's predicament, saying that it was unreasonable to expect men to volunteer their labour when the winter had been "very trying" for them.[44] Food had been scarce, and of necessity the people put all their energies into survival. Moreover, when the men did have extra time, they worked on their own houses. And so, in February he hired a carpenter from Prince Albert. Work started on the house February 18, and with Stranger's help the carpenter erected the frame for a building 22 feet by 16 feet with "upper rooms." Because there was not a shed or building available where the carpenter could prepare the boards and keep his tools and materials dry, a workbench was constructed in the one-room schoolhouse. Thus, the small building now served as a school, church, and carpenter's shop. Hines, who had been teaching since Wright left, said "it was now that I got an insight into the mysteries of carpentry, for, whilst teaching the children, I kept an eye on my mechanic, and learned many things from him which I found useful."[45]

Despite the apparent normalcy of activities, the winter had been a "trying" one. Hines placed part of the blame on the Hudson's Bay Company, for it had "made a new law, viz, To stop giving out goods on credit." From the earliest days of the fur trade, it had been customary for the hunters and trappers to obtain shot, powder, axes, chisels, traps, and other goods on credit. These were paid for later, using the produce from the hunt as payment. When the advances were stopped, Hines said the people "were unable to follow the chase, as they were minus ammunition & traps." Rabbits were scarce during the winter of 1877–78, adding to the hardship. Hines was able to provide a small amount of potatoes, barley, and milk at crucial times, without which, he wrote in his journal, "many, I fear, would have been obliged to leave the mission" to search for food.[46] He added that the "effects of this extremity" were still being felt at Sandy Lake in June. Fort Carlton, on the other hand, was reasonably well stocked with pemmican. Its source was the Métis hunting parties from St. Laurent that had travelled hundreds of miles onto the southern plains during the previous summer. Ironically, they had been outfitted by the Hudson's Bay Company.

Because food was scarce, a significant number of bands that usually wintered in the parklands and northern plains spent the winter of 1877–78 in the Cypress Hills area. There they competed with each other, the Blackfoot, and Sitting Bull's Lakota Sioux for dwindling herds of buffalo.* In the northern parklands, many of the bands that wintered in their traditional hunting grounds were much hungrier than Ahtahkakoop's people. A Hudson's Bay Company official wrote in February, 1878, that "the starvation among the Indians is very sad, and I hope the Government may do

---

* By the spring of 1877, 5,000 Lakota Sioux led by Sitting Bull had sought refuge in Canada after defeating General George Custer's forces at the Little Bighorn in Montana. These Sioux remained in the Wood Mountain area for four-and-a-half years.

A number of bands, including those of Saswēpiw (Sits All Over The Land) and Young Ocīpiwayān from the Fort Carlton district, and Big Bear, Lucky Man, and Little Pine from the Battle River area, spent the winters of the late 1870s and early 1880s hunting buffalo near the border.

whats right to ameliorate their condition."[47] Some tentative steps were taken. For example, Lieutenant-Governor Laird and Indian agent Dickieson, who had moved to Battleford in August of 1877, issued provisions to destitute Indians and delegations that came to the lieutenant-governor's combined office and residence. The government officials also authorized the limited distribution of supplies to the starving people who went to Fort Carlton, Prince Albert, Fort Pitt, and Fort Saskatchewan for help. At Carlton, this assistance amounted to 1,400 pounds of flour, 991 pounds of pemmican, 30 pounds of tea, 30 pounds of tobacco, and 60 pounds of sugar.[48] Similar goods in larger quantities—with the exception of the sugar and the addition of bacon—were distributed by Dickieson and Laird at Battleford.

Dickinson warned officials in Ottawa that during the winter of 1877–78 many Indian people had been "very poorly off, starving in fact" and conditions the following winter would likely be worse.[49] Like Laird, he recognized that without provisions the bands could not take time from hunting to cultivate and plant crops. "A few thousand dollars expended would be

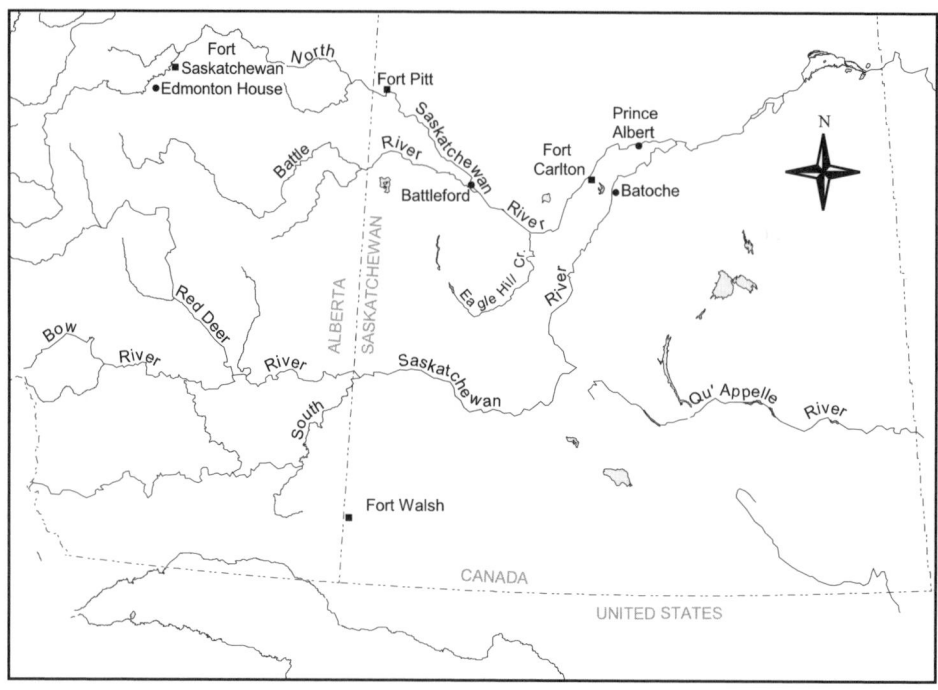

Information Systems Division, Canadian Plains Research Center

Hundreds of Indian people went to Hudson's Bay Company and North-West Mounted Police posts or to Battleford for assistance during the winter of 1877-78.

the means of raising a large quantity of potatoes and grain," he explained. In regard to some of the expenditures that were being recommended, the agent noted that

> It may be said the treaty does not stipulate for ... [these] that is true, but when, as I think, we are on the eve of an Indian outbreak which will be caused principally by starvation, it does not do to scan the lines of a treaty too closely ... I write perhaps a little strongly on these points, but I do so as I believe the Government cannot move too soon in helping the Indians liberally.[50]

Laird by now was finding his duties as Indian superintendent "onerous" and incompatible with his position as lieutenant-governor. He complained about the drudgery of his "disagreeable Indian duties" and he did not think either he or Dickieson was being paid enough.[51] Already feeling over-whelmed, Laird was also annoyed with the requests from Ottawa for statistical information about his superintendency. In November, 1877, he told David Mills, minister of the Interior, that he could not fill up the blanks in the Tabular Statement forwarded by you. It cannot be expected that a Superintendent assisted by two agents whose time, since they entered on their duties in August last, has been taken up entirely in paying the Indians their annuities, could furnish a statement, for instance, of the number of fish caught or quantity of furs taken, or the number of shanties and wigwams, or the bushels of grain raised in a district extending from the boundary line of the United States to the Arctic Ocean, and from Keewatin and Manitoba to British Columbia and Alaska.[52]

"I am treated with scant consideration by my successor in the Department of Interior," Laird told Prime Minister Alexander Mackenzie several months later."[53] And repeatedly the lieutenant-governor found that Mills's tendency to snub him, ignore him, and handle things in Ottawa drastically hindered his work. The minister's apparent ignorance about the vastness of the North-West and the magnitude of the problems facing Laird, Dickieson, and the Indian people was readily evident. In 1876, for instance, Laird had requested $1,000 to "engage competent persons to shew the Indians how to put in their crops." Mills refused, but after at least two more letters from Laird, he reconsidered and in May notified the Indian superintendent that

I have today ordered that $600 be placed at your disposal for that purpose, which I hope may suffice for this year, considering the short time for which the services of the persons employed will be required. I may state in this connection that I regard this work as a part of the duties of the local Indian Agents, at least so far as the localities in which they are stationed are concerned. I presume Mr. Dickieson, who I understand is well acquainted with agriculture, would be very glad to *direct* and *advise* the Indians in their efforts at farming, and I trust you will insist that Mr. Macdonald* shall also give the bands under his supervision the necessary assistance and advice. During the greater portion of the year the ordinary Indian Agents have very little to do, and the amount of compensation is very large in proportion to their work. The ordinary Agent who is either not disposed or not competent to instruct and actively aid the Indians in putting in and taking care of their

* Allan MacDonald, Indian agent for the Treaty Four area.

crops ought not, in my opinion, to be retained in our service. It
seems to me therefore that any other persons who may be
engaged for this purpose ought to be sent to points where the
services of the Agents are not conveniently available and the persons so employed should work with the Indians and take all possible pains to give them practical instruction.[54]

Similarly, Mills at first refused Laird's request for money to purchase
provisions and seeds for the bands that wanted to plant crops in the spring
of 1878. Again Laird objected and some moneys were made available. The
minister, in a letter to Laird, explained his actions saying that

by Treaty No. 6 the stipulation to furnish provisions for the
Indians during the seeding and planting time comes into operation
only after they have been located on their reserves, which have
not yet been selected and laid off. It was for this reason and
because the money could not be made generally available in
accordance with the terms of the Treaty that the item was struck
out of the Estimates which you forwarded to the Department in
December 1876. When the various bands come to settle upon
their reservations, it is believed, they would be found very unwilling to admit that the aid given to a few, before the reserves were
set apart, was a fulfilment of the stipulations of the Treaty. We
have, however, already informed you that $1,000 has been placed
at your disposal for this Season. It may be advantageously given
to aid those bands of Indians who have determined upon the
localities where they wish to have their reserves and who are prepared to commence farming in advance of surveys. It is very
desirable that their crops should be placed upon the lands which
they desire to retain, and this sum, it was thought, would be as
much as the Indians who may be in a position to receive aid
would be entitled to under the Treaty if the various bands had settled down as contemplated.[55]

Mills's decision to issue provisions at seeding time to selected bands,
even though the reserves had not been surveyed, was likely influenced by
the realization that the buffalo were disappearing much quicker than anyone had expected. Commercial hide-hunters south of the border, armed
with repeating Winchester rifles, were devastating the herds, and increased
pressure exerted by Métis hunters and the Indian people congregated in the

Cypress Hills and Wood Mountain area added to the toll. Hines had a third reason for the rapid disappearance of the herds. He blamed this tragedy, in part, on a

> sickness technically called the mange, which made its appearance in the country about the winter of 1877–78, which attacked both the buffalo and the Indian ponies, and as all their hair came off, many of them died from the effects of the cold as well as from the sickness itself.[56]

Whatever the reasons, the herds that had once numbered in the millions were becoming increasingly smaller and more widely scattered every year. Dickieson realized the far-reaching implications. "When the buffalo shall have been exterminated," he wrote to Lawrence Vankoughnet, deputy superintendent general of Indian Affairs, in April of 1878, "the Government will have to maintain for some years nearly all the Indians who now subsist on these animals."[57]

Meanwhile Laird—only two years after Treaty Six was signed—was considering ways to undermine the treaties and the authority of the chiefs and headmen. He questioned the concept of reserves in an official government report, and he wondered if the land on the reserves should be divided into lots and given to individuals, thus breaking up the reserves. Laird went further, recommending that "instead of large Reserves, each Indian head of a family should receive non-transferable script [scrip], or the right to locate on a certain quantity of land in any tract open for settlement." He also denounced the concept of any form of "municipal" government, saying that the Indians were not intelligent enough to administer their own affairs. Just as damning, he struck at the heart of communal living that been the core of Indian society for many generations. "The Indian who makes a laudable effort to provide for the support of his family," he wrote in his report, "seeing that his stores often have to go to feed his starving brethren, then loses heart himself, and drops down to the level of the precarious hand-to-mouth system of the Band generally."[58] With these statements Laird not only displayed a complete lack of understanding of Indian society, tradition, and culture, but he conveniently overlooked the fact that the buffalo had all but disappeared and the farms were still too small to support any one family. If the people did not share what game, furs, and farm produce they were able to harvest, the hardship would be wretched.

CHAPTER NINETEEN

Ahtahkakoop's Reserve Is Surveyed, 1878-1879

The spring of 1878 was the earliest on record in Saskatchewan River country.[1] By late March the snow had melted, the ground had thawed, and the people on Ahtahkakoop's reserve were in their fields, ploughing and preparing soil for the new crop. The chief went to Fort Carlton on April 4 to get the seeds and provisions that would enable his people to plant their crops and break more land.[2] Fortunately Laird had made the appropriate arrangements and Ahtahkakoop took charge of 1,100 pounds of flour, 16 pounds of tea, 12 pounds of sugar, 10 pounds of tobacco, and 700 pounds of pemmican. For seed, he was given 20 bushels of wheat, 25 bushels of barley, and 50 bushels of potatoes.[3] Government officials were to report later that Ahtahkakoop's band—with 40 acres under cultivation—and several other bands had made good use of the seed that was given to them. Others, not surprisingly, "for want of provisions and someone to instruct them did not make good use of the seed or break land."[4]

Although spring had come early in 1878, this land was one of dramatic change and by the end of April cold weather had returned with a vengeance. Severe colds and coughs spread through the district and included Sandy Lake in their sweep. Hines was among those afflicted. The missionary reported in his journal that he had returned home from a trip to Fort Carlton the first week of May chilled to the bone and "quite exhausted from the cold." The wind had cut right through him, even though he was wrapped in a buffalo skin coat and a buffalo robe. Hines explained in his journal that he had been unwell for some time, and felt the cold more than usual. By Sunday, May 5, the missionary was so sick he was unable to conduct or even attend church services. Two weeks later, although not fully recovered, he was back into his routine and held two services on Sunday.[5]

While Hines recuperated, a hunting party was on the plains searching for the elusive buffalo. The hunters were successful, and on May 25 one of Ahtahkakoop's sons returned to the reserve with two cartloads of fresh meat. Since the winter had been one of hardship Hines said the meat was "an agreeable surprise to the settlement." When the man, unidentified other than being the son of Ahtahkakoop, returned to the hunting grounds two days later he took six hymn books, six daily prayer books, and five small catechisms, all in syllabics, with him for distribution.[6] The Indian people of the Asissipi Mission, Hines explained in his journal, had been helpful in "diffusing knowledge among other Indians, who have not had the benefit of a teacher. I tell them always to teach the person to read before giving him a book."[7]

Ahtahkakoop, now 62, had stayed at Sandy Lake to help those looking after the farms instead of going onto the plains with the hunting party. Late in May he and one of his brothers took charge of the fire that was burning limestone into *wāpitanisk** or lime, for Hines's nearly completed house.[8] The powdered lime would later be mixed with varying amounts of water and used to plaster and whitewash the walls. Hines noted in his journal that he paid his helpers because they were "too poor to give their labour."[9]

Hines's "substantial" one-and-a-half storey house aroused the curiosity of three or four of the missionary's "greatest enemies." They asked me, Hines said, "how long I intended to stay among them? I told them, I hoped to remain among them until they could not distinguish my body from the earth. I thought so, said one to the other by his building such a good house."[10] Despite his determination to stay at Sandy Lake, Hines nevertheless was beginning to recognize several drawbacks to the location of the Asissipi mission. Sandy Lake, he said, was 100 miles from the nearest flourmill, 50 miles from the nearest store, 550 miles from the nearest "town," and there were "no white settlers, half-breeds included, nearer than Prince Albert, 100 miles."[†] Furthermore, without competition, the prices at Fort Carlton were high. Provisions were cheaper at Battleford, and even at a place as far away as Lake Athabasca, clothing was less expensive that at Carlton.[11]

At least two groups that visited Hines during 1878 were interested in the

---

* White clay powder.

† During this period, people travelled to Prince Albert via Fort Carlton.

activities of the mission. The first group, consisting of about 30 Indian people from The Pas and the Fort à la Corne regions, were travelling the Green
Lake Trail late in May. Hines reported that 15 people stopped at his house
to visit. When they left, he gave them seven syllabic hymn books, "as about
that number were able to read them."[12] The group also visited
Ahtahkakoop, and since Anglican missions had been established at both
The Pas and Fort à la Corne,[13] experiences were likely shared and compared.

Several weeks later, 10 families from Okīnomotayēw's band paid a
visit. Hines said they were living at "a lake in the woods called Stoney
Lake."* He invited them to church, and a good number came for a short
service before they left. Hines evidently had several conversations with
them about farming and education, for he pointed out that the land around
Stoney Lake was not suitable for agriculture and he suggested they settle
at Whitefish Lake. He also promised to provide a teacher after the band
moved. By now Hines's command of the Cree language was reasonably
good so he decided to send Stranger to Okīnomotayēw's people, saying he
could interpret for himself.[14]

Other visitors left Hines disheartened. These included about 20
freighters, mostly half-breed, who camped near the Asissipi Mission in late
June. They stayed one night and then made preparations to leave, even
though it was a Sunday. The missionary said he was grieved to see them
go, and as they left, he loudly rang the church bell.[15]

The behaviour of certain unidentified people in Ahtahkakoop's band
had also disturbed Hines. On June 2, 1878, after the church service, he
arranged a meeting with the chief and his councillors about "a certain case
of immorality, and as the parties concerned were closely related to them I
said it was their duty as Xtians to put down all vice."[16] No other information was provided. Hines did not identify the people involved, nor did he
indicate the outcome of the discussion. Evidence suggests, however, that
Kīsik-awāsis may have been one of the parties. He had openly opposed
both his father and Hines and he was absent from the reserve when the
annuities were paid later that year, taking his money at Battleford instead
of at his home reserve. Additionally, he was closely related to the chief and
headmen, for he was Ahtahkakoop's son, Kā-miyo-ahcahkwēw's brother,
and Sasakamoose's nephew. If Kīsik-awāsis was one of the parties in this
"case of immorality," religion and changing values were continuing to
deepen the rift between relatives and friends.

---

* Delaronde Lake.

On Wednesday, August 7, 1878, government surveyor Edgar Bray arrived at Sandy Lake with a survey party to lay out the boundaries for the land Ahtahkakoop and his people had retained for their reserve. According to his instructions, Bray was to survey a reserve with "a length North and South, of more than eleven miles and a width of six miles."[17] The north boundary was to be placed one mile north of the lake, with the western boundary about half a mile to the west of the lake.[18] Despite the fact that government documentation stated in 1876 and again in 1877 that Ahtahkakoop wanted his reserve "joining" Mistawasis's reserve, this had not been taken into consideration when Bray's instructions were drawn up. Furthermore, because no one had discussed the details of the survey with Ahtahkakoop, Bray did not realize that Ahtahkakoop had already identified the general area where he wanted his reserve.[19]

Bray met with the chief and leading men on August 8, the day after his arrival, and hired four people to assist him. The surveyor identified them as Joseph, Jacob, Simon, and Kihci-mōhkomān.*

On Friday the surveyor took the instrument readings required to determine the latitude and meridian for the survey, and on Saturday he started the field work by measuring one mile north of the lake, where the northern boundary was to be placed.[20]

On Monday (August 12), with the assistance of the four men from Ahtahkakoop's band and others in his party, Bray "ran" the line for the north boundary of the reserve west about two miles.† When Sasakamoose and Ahtahkakoop realized from talking with Bray that the reserve was not going to be surveyed according to the people's wishes, they protested. In addition to wanting their reserve adjoining Mistawasis's reserve, Ahtahkakoop had always been very definite about *iskonikan*,‡ the land he wanted for his reserve. He wanted an area that would provide a living for his people: good agricultural land, extensive hay meadows, big trees for building, water for fishing—as well as for the people and their livestock—and woodlands for hunting and trapping. He had travelled to several locations before selecting the place where he wanted to settle, even before

---

* Bray only gave the first names for three of the men, but in all likelihood these men were Ahtahkakoop's son Joseph, his brother and headman Jacob Sasakamoose, and Simon Apotum.

† For measuring distances, the men used a device called a chain that was 66 feet in length and made up of 100 links of equal length.

‡ Land that is held back.

Treaty Six negotiations had taken place. Then, after this land at Sandy Lake was chosen, Hines helped him mark the reserve's boundaries and the location of the small farms. Now his wishes were being ignored. If Bray continued the survey according to his instructions, the reserve would not join onto the northern boundary of Mistawasis's reserve. Furthermore, some of the improvements made by band members, as well as some of the woodland, would be outside the boundaries proposed by the government.[21]

Although Bray listened to the complaints, he either did not understand what he was being told or else chose to ignore them. The chief was "not satisfied with direction of lines," Bray wrote in his diary on August 13, but he "consented to have North and South line run at about 1/2 mile from Lake." This line was to mark the western boundary of the reserve. He made no mention of Ahtahkakoop's instructions that he wanted his reserve adjoining Mistawasis's reserve.

Bray stopped work on the north boundary and began to survey the north-south line. By August 17 the survey party had reached the "7 mile post." Three days later, the men had finished another four miles and pounded a post into the ground to mark the 11-mile point. Bray considered this point to be the southwest corner of the reserve.[22]

On August 21, the surveyor moved his camp to the Asissipi River, apparently getting ready to complete the survey despite the dissatisfaction expressed earlier. Ahtahkakoop immediately called a council of his leading men to discuss the issue.[23] The decision was then made to stop the survey until Laird could be asked at the upcoming treaty payments to have the survey changed.[24] Bray "discharged" Kichi-mōhkomān and left the next day with the other men to survey the Mistawasis Reserve. When Sasakamoose became sick on August 24 he was replaced by Ahenakew's son Wāsēhikot. All the men left Bray on August 31 to attend the annuity payments scheduled for September 2 at Fort Carlton.[25]

Ahtahkakoop was not the only chief unhappy with the boundaries of his reserve. His complaints, along with those of the other chiefs, were forwarded to the lieutenant-governor in Battleford, and it was in response to these that Laird had accompanied Inspector Walker to the Carlton district for the payments.[26] Ahtahkakoop's appeal was successful and Bray was instructed to survey the reserve "as desired by a counsel of the head men of the band."[27] Ahtahkakoop had a similar understanding of the meeting, saying later he had been told "that as I wanted the lines laid out, they would be done."[28]

Ahtahkakoop was at Fort Carlton when Bray returned to Sandy Lake to complete the survey on September 19. Apparently unwilling to proceed before talking further with the chief, the surveyor went to the fur trade post, found Ahtahkakoop, and then retraced his steps to the reserve. After measuring Sandy Lake the government representative met with the headmen on September 25. According to Bray, the leading men said they wanted "to have the reserve 7 miles North & South instead of 11 as originally proposed." The reserve would thus be 11 miles by seven miles, with its length being east to west instead of north and south. Ahtahkakoop was to say later that there was a misunderstanding with Laird and the surveyor, because he wanted no less than a mile between his and Mistawasis's reserve to "prevent any large white settlement between them."[29] The survey, as carried out, put an even greater distance between the two reserves than before.

Bray hired five Indian men, including Jacob Sasakamoose,* to assist him.[30] First they completed the north boundary, and then they ran the line for the eastern side of the reserve. With that done, the line was run west to meet up with the western boundary. At each corner temporary posts were dug into the ground to mark the "angles."[31]

Before Bray left Sandy Lake, he surveyed a 160-acre parcel of land at the extreme southeast side of the lake for Hines's Asissipi Mission. This land was within the reserve boundaries laid out by Bray, but it was not part of Ahtahkakoop's reserve. In Hines's words, this land was "in addition" to the reserve land and he wanted the survey done so it would appear on the map.[32] Bray considered Hines to be a "squatter," noting that the clergyman's improvements "cannot be estimated in value at less than 2,000 dollars."[33] The land was registered to Alex J. Hines.[34]

For some unexplained reason and despite instructions from Laird, the reserve of land chained out by Bray between September 26 and October 12, 1878, was 10 miles by seven miles in size, not 11 by 7 miles.[35] Additionally, it was more than seven miles north of Mistawasis's reserve.

There was also a discrepancy in the number of square miles contained in the reserve. Bray, in his Field Notes and Report, noted that the reserve consisted of 69.95 square miles. A lithographed plan and other documentation prepared a number of years later gave the area as 67.2 square miles; this was the area confirmed for the Ahtahkakoop Reserve by the order-in-council of May 17, 1889. It was later explained that Bray's figure of 69.95

---

* Sasakamoose was replaced by Baptiste Ahenakew on October 8.

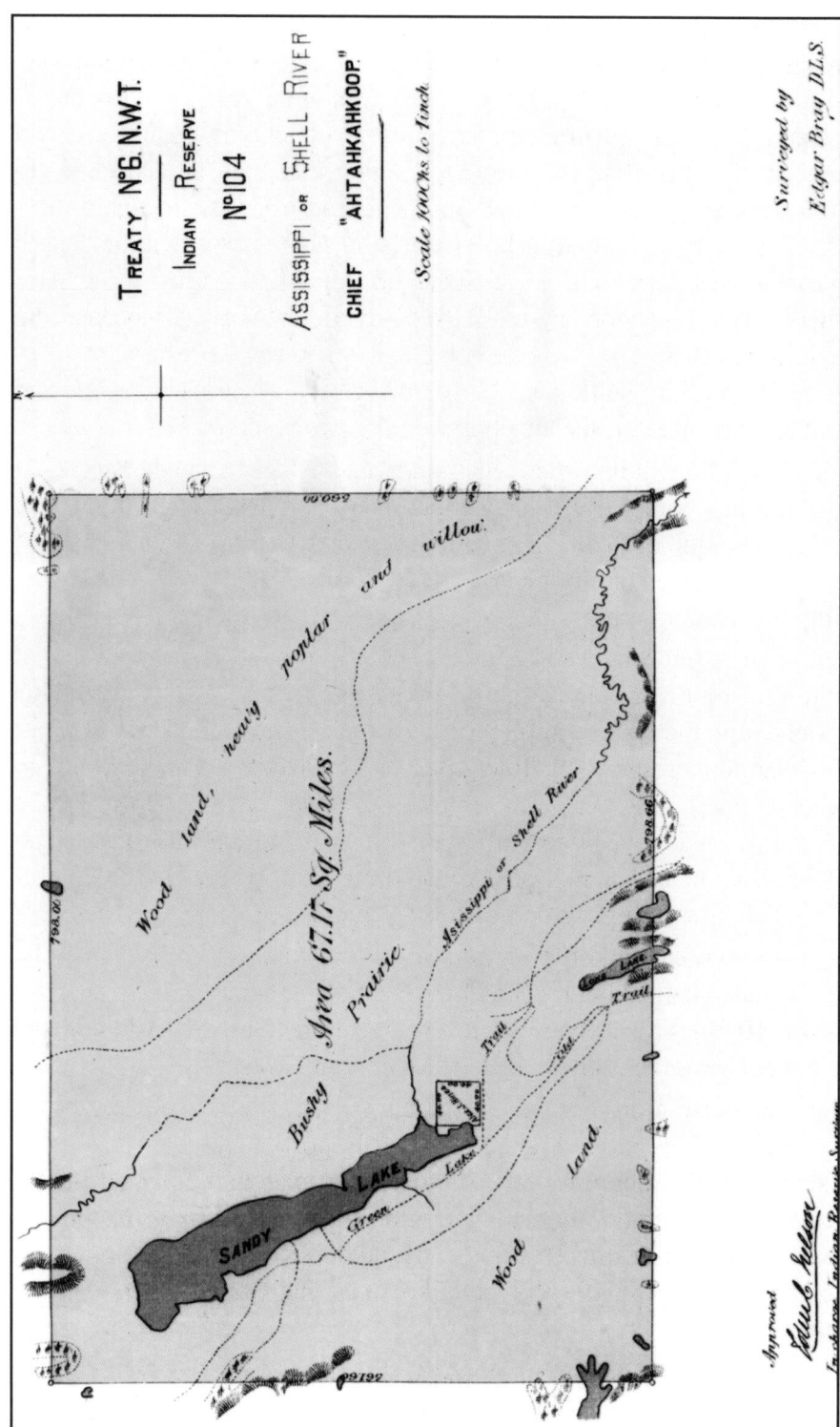

Survey map of the Ahtahkakoop Reserve by Edgar Bray, D.L.S, 1878.

National Library of Canada

square miles included .25 square miles for "Squatters' claims" and 2.53 square miles of water, leaving 67.17 square miles for the reserve. When rounded off, the number became 67.2.[36]

Bray included a description in his field notes of the land that was contained within the 1878 boundaries of the reserve. "About one half the reserve," he wrote,

> is wooded with Poplar, Spruce, Jack Pine, and Tamarac; Poplar being the most abundant and the other timber in proportion as they are written. In size the Poplar is nearly all small and is therefore of not much value.
>
> The Spruce is often of good size and quality, and with the tamarac, is valuable for building purposes. The Jack Pine is mostly short and brushy and appears to be of very little use except where it is small enough for fencing rails.
>
> The prairie lies on each side of the Asissippi River, and is of a brushy nature and is dotted frequently with Poplar bluffs.
>
> The quality of the land in the woods changes with the timber; thus in the north easterly portion of the reserve where the timber is poplar with occasional spruce and tamarac the soil is good, except of course, when the land is wet, whereas in the south westerly section where jack pine is the principal timber the land is chiefly made up of light sandy Knolls and is entirely unfit for cultivation.
>
> Nearly all of the prairie is good land. I should estimate that about two thirds of the reserve is suitable for cultivation.[37]

Later in the same document, he noted that the condition of the Indian people living on the Ahtahkakoop and Mistawasis reserves

> appears to be more satisfactory than that of any others I noticed within the limits comprising treaty No 6. Chief Atakukoops band at Sandy Lake especially may be mentioned as being honestly desirous of improving their condition. This band had, the last season, a considerable area of land sown with grain and a large quantity of potatoes planted.[38]

On September 2, 1878, 283 members of Ahtahkakoop's band received their annuities at Fort Carlton. Twenty-four others were paid elsewhere as "absentees," and their payments added to the Ahtahkakoop Band paylist at a later date, making a total of 307.[39] Surprisingly, Kīsik-awāsis was paid at Battleford as a "straggler."* Since an adjustment does not appear to have been made to the band's paylist, Ahtahkakoop's son and headman, along with his wife and two children, were not included in the total number of people paid in 1878 as part of Ahtahkakoop's band.[40]

Four Woods Cree chiefs, who Laird said represented the "Plain Stony Tribe of Indians," signed an adhesion to Treaty Six at Fort Carlton on September 3. Although Laird said Okīnomotayēw (Long Goatee) and Kā-ohpatawakinam (He Who Makes Dust Fly)† were both from Green Lake, Okīnomotayēw was living in the Stoney Lake (Delaronde Lake) area.[41] Macikwanās (Bad Weed) was from Pelican Lake, and Sēsēweham (He Who Makes It Rattle) was from the Whitefish Lake area north of Sandy Lake.[42]

At Duck Lake, the three chiefs of the Willow Cree refused to accept annuities when Laird rejected their request that "a large supply of provisions might be given them, and that all their presents should be brought to the place of payment." Beardy and his headmen held firm but the other chiefs and most of the Willow Cree took their payments after a three-day wait.[43]

The lieutenant-governor was to report later that the flour given to the Treaty Six bands had been milled by Captain Henry S. Moore of Prince Albert and was of excellent quality, unlike the inferior product issued to the Treaty Four bands.[44] Laird said the cattle supplied to the bands in Treaty Six were apparently tamer than those issued the previous year, and most chiefs (with the notable exception of Beardy) accepted the cattle allotted to them. The other articles distributed to the bands were said to be of "fair quality."[45]

Ahtahkakoop and the other chiefs, in addition to expressing displeasure about the survey of their reserves, raised another issue with the lieutenant-governor while he was at Fort Carlton. In Laird's words,

> the principal subject which they urged upon me was to ask the Government to grant them an increased allowance of provisions at seed time. They said that there are so many Chiefs that when the $1,000 promised to those around Carlton came to be divided there were only two or three days provisions for each band. The Chiefs

---

* Straggler was a term used to describe a person who was entitled to an annuity but who was not listed on a band paylist.

† Kā-ohpatawakinam is more commonly known as Flying Dust.

"Atakacoop" and "Mistawasis," who were the principal speakers
said they knew I had not power to accede to their requests, but
they desired me to lay their prayer before the Government at
Ottawa.[46]

Quite obviously Ahtahkakoop and the other chiefs were tackling a
major problem, one that would drastically hinder the advancement of agriculture and self-sufficiency on the reserves if it was not resolved. Since the
buffalo had disappeared much faster than anyone had anticipated, the
assumption that the Indian people could continue to support themselves
with the buffalo hunt while learning to farm was no longer valid. The
chiefs knew from experience that it took time to cultivate the soil, plant
crops, and take in the harvest. The dramatic shortage of buffalo had made
the search for food a priority. If their families were to be fed, the men had
to hunt. If they were away hunting, they could not work on their farms.
And, if they did not plant crops, there would be nothing to harvest. Laird
listened, and promised to forward the chiefs' request to officials in Ottawa.

Laird was probably more receptive to the Carlton chiefs' request for
additional provisions at seeding time than he might have been a few weeks
earlier. He had just spent several gruelling days at Sounding Lake, where
approximately 1,800 Indian people had gathered to receive their treaty payments. It had been Laird's intent to pay annuities to the bands that had
signed Treaty Six and then convince the other chiefs, including Big Bear,
to sign an adhesion to the treaty. Much to Laird's disappointment Big Bear
had come with only two or three band members, and he had come to negotiate, not to sign. The other chiefs "held back and refused to accept their
annuities until the result of 'Big Bear's' efforts to induce ... better terms
was made known."[47]

The chiefs had met with Laird in a "public conference" on August 15,
16, and 18. Big Bear, who was the main spokesman, asked for better terms
on behalf of the other chiefs and himself, emphasizing that "the Treaty did
not furnish enough for the people to live upon." Laird countered that it was
not the intent of the treaty "to support the Indians entirely, but to assist
them in procuring their own subsistence." In any case, the lieutenant-
governor finally told the assembly, he "had no power to alter the terms of
the Treaty." Big Bear refused to accept the treaty and said instead that he
wanted Laird to "lay his requests, on behalf of himself and the other chiefs,
before those who had authority to change the Treaty."[48] The chief indicated
he would come back next year to get an answer. With discussions ended,

the treaty chiefs and their bands accepted their annuities and two additional chiefs signed adhesions to Treaty Six.

Although Laird recognized several weeks later the reasonableness of Ahtahkakoop's and Mistawasis's request for additional provisions at seeding time, he also realized that by granting their requests the government could refuse to seriously consider Big Bear's. "I am of opinion," Laird reported to the minister of the Interior, that the requests made by Ahtahkakoop and Mistawasis

> should be granted. They are well-disposed Indians, and are making an effort to cultivate the soil. Mr. Dickieson reports that the chiefs towards Edmonton have also asked for more provisions at seed time as well as for instruction in farming. In Treaty No. 4 the same thing is required. In short I believe it would be economy on the part of the Government, to aid for a few years in the spring, all those bands that seem disposed to abandon the chase and become herdsmen and farmers. If something is not done in this way to assist the Indians, I fear their destitution will interfere seriously with the settlement of the Country.

> In regard to "Big Bear's" requests, I would advise to do nothing for one band within the limits of a Treaty that is not done for all. Perhaps the Treaty ought to remain unchanged, and the Government make such additions thereto, in the form of efforts to provide them instructors in agriculture and such aid in provisions for a few years at seed time as may enable them to work upon their reserves for some weeks each spring.[49]

Laird elaborated on his recommendations in a letter to the superintendent general of Indian Affairs dated November 11, 1878. He suggested that 15 farm instructors be appointed. Five of these, he suggested, should be stationed in the Treaty Four area, eight in the Treaty Six area, and two in the Treaty Seven area. He added that if permanent farm instructors were given responsibility for several bands, the position of sub-agent could be abolished. He also advised that the farm instructors would be of little use unless both seeds and provisions were distributed in the spring.[50] The recommendations were approved by Lawrence Vankoughnet, deputy superintendent general of Indian Affairs, and John A. Macdonald, who had regained power for the Conservatives in the 1878 federal election. Macdonald now held the dual positions of prime minister and superintendent generalof Indian Affairs.[51] By approving these measures, the first step in what Vankoughnet saw as "gratuitous assistance" for the Indian people of the North-West had been taken. For the Indian people, the granting of these measures was a matter of survival and an opportunity to succeed.

The growing season of 1878 once again demonstrated to Ahtahkakoop and his people the precariousness of farming in the North-West. The spring had been very dry and the crops at the Ahtahkakoop Reserve shrivelled and burned. Rain brought relief in June but later, during a vicious storm, hail stones as large as hens' eggs pounded the ground. Fortunately, the worst of the storm missed the fields and the crops escaped damage. In the end, all turned out well, and Hines said the planted fields were more productive than in the previous year.[52]

The hunters searching for buffalo were not so fortunate. The large herds had disappeared from the northern plains and the few buffalo that remained were in poor condition with "neither flesh nor grease about them."[53] The men and their families "brought nothing" with them when they returned to Ahtahkakoop's reserve late in the summer. Other bands faced a similar situation, and some of their people remained in the Cypress Hills for the winter instead of returning to their traditional winter hunting grounds in the parklands.

Not surprisingly, the winter of 1878–79 was one of great hardship for Ahtahkakoop and his people. The cattle supplied by the government were not nearly as tame as Laird had indicated. Most died or ran away, even though they were looked after.[54] The crops may have been promising, but the amount of produce harvested was small and not nearly enough to support the community. The buffalo hunt had failed. Game animals were scarce. Moreover, with the exception of a few bears and common foxes, hardly any fur-bearing animals were killed. Without buffalo meat and furs, the people had nothing to exchange for provisions at Fort Carlton. As a result, Hines reported in his annual letter to the Church Missionary Society, there was "a great deal of starvation."[55]

To make a bad situation even worse, the horses were afflicted with mange and many were dying. One of Ahtahkakoop's brothers was the hardest hit, losing all ten of his ponies.[56] The loss of the horses, Hines said, meant that many families "did not possess a horse with which to take their grist to the only mill in the country, which ... was one hundred miles from Sandy Lake."

In other areas there were reports of families eating mice, dogs, and buffalo skins to stay alive. Hundreds of Indian people went to see the

While Indian people in the parklands and northern plains starved, buffalo were being killed indiscriminately on the American side of the border. This is a buffalo hide yard in Dodge City, Kansas, 1878, with baling presses in the background.

government officials at Battleford for assistance.[57] A general impression existed among them, Dickieson reported, that "they had been promised when the Treaty was concluded that they should be fed whenever they were in want." He said he made every effort to correct this "erroneous idea," urging the people to support themselves by hunting and fishing and impressing upon them that "while the Government will not allow them to starve," they must "exert themselves to earn the food given them." Then, in an effort to keep the bands in "their usual places of residence," Dickieson issued instructions for food to be distributed at Fort Carlton, Prince Albert, Fort Pitt, Victoria, Fort Edmonton, and Fort Saskatchewan.[58] Vankoughnet was later to write that the "patience and endurance displayed by the Indians of the North-West Territories … are beyond all praise."[59]

Ahtahkakoop picked up the supplies for his band at Fort Carlton early in February.[60] The Hudson's Bay Company—whose storehouses at Carlton had been completely empty of pemmican in July and August—had obviously obtained a large supply from Métis hunters, for the mixture of fat and dried meat was among the provisions given to Ahtahkakoop.[61] The chief took the provisions back to the reserve and then arranged for his followers to pick up their share at his house. At least part of this distribution took place on February 3, for Hines reported that he found the heads of 18 families gathered at the chief's house when he stopped by for a visit. The people were not accustomed to being dependent on someone else for food and they were discouraged. Many of the young men were angry. They could see their self-sufficiency being threatened by events beyond their control, and they felt helpless and frustrated. It was a difficult time to be a chief. Ahtahkakoop tried to give his followers hope and encouragement. He talked about the old way of living and compared it to the present and the prospects of the future "if his Young Men would persevere."[62]

Hines had not known in advance about the distribution of food at Ahtahkakoop's house. His initial plan had been to visit a number of homes, but on seeing so many gathered together in one place he welcomed the opportunity to speak to them. Later the clergyman wrote in his journal that he had been pleased with the turn of events because he could say "more in the hearing of them all than time would otherwise have permitted." It was contrary to the nature of the Indian, he went on to say, "to interrogate a reply in private, lest they should offend some of their friends." In a group, the people spoke quite freely.[63] Hines was also taking advantage of a manoeuvre used when he visited Snake Plain. Knowing that the people gathered at Mistawasis's house to visit and hear the latest news, the missionary preferred to hold services there, instead of in the school. That way, he said, there was a chance to talk to people who would not attend a regular service if they were asked. Many people, he added, do not have "the audacity to go out, when I make known my intention of holding a service."[64]

Some people, however, did have the "audacity" to leave, for despite Hines's hard work and Ahtahkakoop's support, a large number of families were still resisting his efforts. In December of 1878, Hines noted that more than half of the population on the Ahtahkakoop Reserve (163 people) were non-Christians or, to use Hines's term, "heathens." Of those who had converted to Christianity, 82 had been baptized by Protestant clergymen and 50 by Roman Catholic priests.[65] Nevertheless, the missionary believed he was making inroads. In 1878 he had baptized 16 adults and 21 children, including his six-week-old daughter Henrietta.[66] The number of Indian communicants had increased from nine to 20 in less than a year. This brought the total number of communicants at Sandy Lake to 26, a number that included Hines and his wife Emma, school teacher Matheson, and Stranger. Hines was still travelling to the Mistawasis Reserve every second weekend to conduct services. Here too the number of people presenting themselves for baptism had increased, with 22 adults and 17 children coming forward in 1878.[67]

Early in 1879 the missionary conducted three more marriage ceremonies. Wāwiyēwēskocawēs,* the son of Iskwēsis, married Elizabeth Ironhouse on February 23. Six weeks later David Stranger's daughter Elizabeth married John F. Pritchard, the new teacher hired by Hines to teach at Snake Plain. And early in May, Ahtahkakoop's son Kā-miyo-astotin married Janet Ermineskin.[68]

Hines operated two schools during the winter of 1878-79. When Pritchard, who was Edward Matheson's cousin, took over the school at Snake Plain, Hines moved Matheson to the Asissipi Mission School.[69] Hines apparently taught some classes in addition to his other duties, and two of his talented senior students were helping the younger pupils.[70] One of the student teachers was Ahenakew's son Louis, who was about 15. The other helper was Sasakamoose's 12-year-old son Joseph.[71]

Again, enrolment figures provided by Hines and government documentation differed. In his annual letter to the Church Missionary Society, the missionary said the "native scholars" at the Asissipi school numbered 24 boys and 20 girls. According to government sources, 21 children were enrolled, with an average attendance of 15.[72] The government figure would have been the one used to determine the Asissipi school grant that was requested by the Church of England in December, 1878.[73] This grant, based on $12 per student per year, used the average attendance as the basis for determining the amount of the grant. The upper limit was $300 for 25 students.

Dickieson was to say later in the year that the government could not expect to get good teachers for $300 or less per year.[74] But now, early in 1879, he was caught up in more immediate problems. Laird had submitted his resignation as Indian superintendent of the North-West Superintendency on January 1, 1879; it was accepted, with the resignation being effective March 31. On April 1, Dickieson assumed the role of acting Indian superintendent, a position he was to hold in addition to being assistant Indian superintendent for the superintendency and Indian agent for Treaty Six.[75] Laird remained on as lieutenant-governor of the North-West Territories.

---

* Wāwiyēwēskocawēs, which translates as He Who Has A Little Flame Around Him, was also known as Charles Round Plain. Iskwēsis is the Cree word for girl.

Before resigning, Laird had recognized the impossibility of the superintendency functioning with any degree of competency with a staff of two. His request for 15 farm instructors had already been approved. Then, in a letter dated January 1, 1879, the day his resignation was submitted, Laird asked for two additional Indian agents to be appointed immediately, one for the Prince Albert district and one for the Fort Edmonton district.[76] The Indian agents, Laird wrote, would take care of annuity payments and supervise the farm instructors.

Dickieson received word in February that Laird's request for the Indian agents had been approved, with the notation that they would not arrive in time to help with seeding.[76]

CHAPTER TWENTY

Ahenakew Dies, 1879-1880

The late arrival of the farm instructors in 1879 did not hamper work at Ahtahkakoop's reserve. Thanks to the chief's foresight, his band members already had someone to teach them how to farm. They had a small collection of implements, knew how to use them, and early in the spring had received 80 bushels of seed wheat, 18 bushels of barley, 50 bushels of potatoes, and a few vegetable seeds from government officials. Hines said the amount of seed wheat had been increased from the previous year because both barley and potatoes were hard to get in the Prince Albert district. Not enough hay had been cut in the district to winter cattle, he explained. Consequently, these crops had been used as feed.[1] The men, women, and young people worked hard that spring and the fields were all planted before the end of April.

Ahtahkakoop, Mistawasis, and the other chiefs had again been disheartened when they saw the small amount of provisions issued by the government. The previous year they had requested enough food to get them through the planting season. Officials at the highest level had approved additional quantities and provided an extra $1,000 for this purpose. Dickieson had also distributed foodstuffs left over from the annuity payments, deeming "it better to use these supplies then [in the spring], thus enabling the Indians to put in more seed." Nevertheless, the amount of provisions distributed was small and, as the Indian agent explained,

> even with the largely increased quantity provided there was considerable regret expressed when it came to be divided that more could not be given to each band. This arose from the fact that the Indians understood (or at least now say they did) when the Treaty

was concluded that $1,000 worth of provisions was to be given to each band. They consequently were disappointed when they received their share.[2]

Okīnomotayēw, who had signed an adhesion to Treaty 6 in 1878, was among those interested in farming. The previous year, using pointed sticks, he and his followers had planted potatoes at Stoney Lake and had managed to save 10 bushels for seed. In mid-April Okīnomotayēw told Hines that they planned on settling at *manitow-sākahikan*.* They wanted to farm but they had no grain to plant, no land broken, no oxen or horses, and no plough. Hines wrote a letter to Lawrence Clarke at Fort Carlton asking him to give Okīnomotayēw some seed, and he offered to "lend" the chief some land at the mission. When the men returned from the fort, they brought with them a harrow, a plough, a small amount of potatoes, barley, wheat, and provisions. Stranger ploughed a small field for them at Sandy Lake, and then he helped Okīnomotayēw and the others plant their potatoes and grain before they left for their "old haunt" at Stoney Lake.[3] The missionary told the chief that he and Stranger would hoe the field during the summer. In return, the men gave Hines dried fish and deer meat when they came to the mission, and they worked on the road so Hines could visit them during the summer.[4] So, like Mistawasis's people, Okīnomotayēw's band planted its first field of grain at Sandy Lake.

The month of May was wet and the crops thrived. But the "buffalo are no more," Hines said, and the people were concerned with the future and what they would eat.[5] It was still raining in early June. The wet weather, following a difficult winter, took its toll. Consumption[†] was "very prevalent" and there was "much sickness" throughout the North-West. For a while no one attended church because of illness. Six-year-old John Pē-nōsēwēskam (Comes Tracking), the third person baptized by Hines at the Asissipi Mission, died in April. David Stranger's son, John Edward, died in May. He was four months old. Then Pē-nōsēwēskam, young John's father, went hunting ducks while he was sick. He became wet and chilled, his illness worsened, and he died at Fort Carlton. Hines said Pē-nōsēwēskam was a "heathen" who had offered himself and several of his children for baptism four years earlier. Hines had baptized the children, but refused Pē-nōsēwēskam because he had two wives.[6]

---

* God's Lake, located 10 miles north of the mission.

[†] Pulmonary tuberculosis.

Ahenakew, brother of Ahtahkakoop and Sasakamoose, was the third man to die that spring. He had become sick with what appeared to be a feverish cold at the end of May. Complications set in, and on June 2 Ahenakew gathered his family to him. In Hines's words, "the old man, like the Patriarch Jacob strengthened himself upon his bed & gave as it proved to be his farewell admonition to his sons." He told them not to grieve and to follow his good advice.

Sasakamoose sat with Ahenakew until midnight, and then Ahtahkakoop took over the vigil. As Sasakamoose was leaving, Ahenakew said his good-byes, telling his brothers that "he should not live till morning, he felt certain God was calling him." He died before the sun rose on June 3, 1879.[7] Although Hines was at the mission, he was not called to Ahenakew's bedside.

According to the missionary's records a third man, Kasokaskwet (He Who Has Strong Medicine), died June 8; he was 50 years old.[8]

Spring did not bring the expected relief to the North-West in 1879, and the demands for assistance did not lessen. Dickieson, who was now serving as acting Indian superintendent, reported that most of the Indians frequenting Battleford had gone onto the plains in search of buffalo. When the families found very few animals—if any at all—they came back. The government official said that although he made every effort to get the people to make their living by hunting and fishing,

> the number who remained in the vicinity of the agency remained
> nearly the same from 500 to 900 persons; no sooner had one party
> gone away than another arrived to take its place. I have been visited
> by Crees, Saulteaux, Stonies, Chipewyans, Bloods, Blackfeet,
> Sarcees, Piegans and Sioux. The necessity of attending to so many
> different parties has taken up great part of my time, and left me
> sometimes for days no leisure to attend to correspondence and
> other office work, much less to visit outposts of the agency where
> my presence was almost indispensable, and several matters requir-
> ing attention have consequently been allowed to stand, very much
> against my wish, and with detriment to the Department.[9]

At Battleford, Dickieson initially "employed those able to work in cutting and piling cordwood and had a number [of men] engaged in improving the road and river crossing." There was no demand for the quantity of wood cut, but the official felt it all worthwhile since the men were given some experience "working." Unable to keep the men busy, he set up a small farm some eight miles from Battleford and hired a man to teach people how to cultivate the soil and plant and harvest crops. For those who did not want "to work," the acting superintendent offered to supply ammunition so they could hunt. "A great many," he said, "preferred hunting to working and went away."[10] He concluded with the statement "I have not stinted the supplies to those who were working, or ammunition to those who preferred hunting while I have not been more liberal than I was actually forced to be to those who would neither work nor hunt." The many Indian people who lived in the Treaty Six area beyond easy reach of the agency at Battleford were left to fend for themselves or to seek assistance from officers at the Hudson's Bay Company and North-West Mounted Police posts.

Dickieson had particular praise for Ahtahkakoop, Mistawasis, Little Hunter, Red Pheasant, and their bands in 1879. These people, he wrote in his official report, "have been entirely dependent on the chase up to the last few years and the progress they have made is encouraging, and in another year they ought to raise enough to prevent actual starvation."[11]

He also had kind words for Chief Wapahaska (White Cap) and his band of Dakota Sioux who had decided in 1878 to settle at Moose Woods south of present-day Saskatoon. This band of Sissetonwon had crossed the border into Canada from Minnesota late in 1862 following the "Sioux Uprising." Since then they had been living in the eastern parklands. The band had not been considered eligible to sign the Canadian treaties, but because the Dakota had earned a reputation as good freighters, hunters, trappers, and labourers, White Cap's people were receiving government help to begin farming.[12]

Another band of Dakota Sioux,* consisting of about 20 lodges, also arrived in the Prince Albert area during the summer of 1878. These people were not part of White Cap's group. Instead, they were Wahpetonwon and M'dewakontonwon who had moved west following the "Uprising" of 1862 but had remained on the American side of the international boundary. In 1877, as anger directed against the Lakota Sioux spread following Custer's defeat at the Little Bighorn, they slipped into Canada, heading first for

---

* These people were eventually given land at Round Plain, which is now known as the Wahpeton Reserve.

Portage la Prairie, and then Prince Albert. They began cutting and hauling saw-logs for the Hudson's Bay Company's new lumber mill almost immediately after arriving in the district.[13] Dickieson apparently did not realize there was more than one group of Dakota. Accordingly, when he described White Cap's people in July of 1879 as "well-disposed, peaceable and good workers," he presumably was referring to all three groups.[14] A fourth group of Sioux, consisting of 70 lodges from Sitting Bull's large camp near Wood Mountain, showed up at Prince Albert later in the summer. These people were Tetonwon, a branch of the Lakota Sioux. Their arrival threw the residents of Prince Albert into an unnecessary panic.[15]

By 1879 Dickieson, frustrated with his duties in the North-West Territories, had arranged to exchange jobs with Walter Orde, an employee of the Department of Finance in Ottawa. Under this arrangement, Orde was to take over the position of Indian agent at Battleford and Dickieson would move to Ottawa.[16] It was agreed that Dickieson would not leave for the east until the new agent was in place at Battleford.

Other changes were also being made in the "management" of the Indian people. The position of Indian superintendent was abolished and on May 30, 1879, Edgar Dewdney was appointed Indian commissioner. A Conservative member of Parliament, Dewdney was a personal friend of Prime Minister Macdonald and had represented a British Columbia constituency since 1872.[17] According to Macdonald, in his capacity of minister of the Interior, the position of Indian commissioner was created to deal with the "gravity of the situation as regards the Indians of the great plains of the North-West."[18] The appointment was also part of an over-all plan to "reorganize the system of administering Indian affairs in the North West Territories."[19]

The new Indian commissioner arrived at Fort Walsh* on June 26 via the American route that passed through Bismarck and Fort Benton. He was accompanied by two government farmers who would be assigned postings in the Treaty Seven area. Here at Cypress Hills, in the last stronghold for buffalo on Canadian soil, Dewdney soon discovered for himself that reports about the "scarcity of Buffalo had not been exaggerated." He conferred with Cree, Saulteaux, Assiniboine, and Blackfoot Confederacy chiefs, urging them to select their reserves and begin farming, and he

---

* A North-West Mounted Police fort in the Cypress Hills.

Based on National Archives of Canada, PA-050746

Big Bear's camp at Maple Creek, north of the Cypress Hills. Big Bear, whose band suffered greatly from starvation, did not return to the Fort Pitt area until 1883.

impressed upon his audiences that the "Government expected they should work the same as the white man did." He also warned that those capable of working should not expect to get rations without exerting themselves. At the same time Dewdney realized that, for a while at least, food would have to be distributed since there was nothing for the people to eat.[20]

While at Fort Walsh, Dewdney met with Big Bear and some of the other chiefs who had not yet signed Treaty Six.[21] Big Bear was still insisting on better terms, even though great numbers of his impoverished followers were deserting to other bands. Little Pine and Lucky Man, on the other hand, relented in the face of starvation and signed an adhesion to Treaty Six in Dewdney's presence. Following the councils with the leading men, the commissioner issued a small amount of provisions and the chiefs and their followers went to search for buffalo in the vicinity of the border. Their prospects were not hopeful, Dewdney said, for the story was the same "from one end of the country to the other, the Sioux are preventing the Buffalo from crossing the line."[22]

Dewdney, accompanied by North-West Mounted Police Commissioner James F. Macleod, then travelled further west to visit Blackfoot, Blood, Peigan, and Sarcee camps. At Blackfoot Crossing he found "about 1300 Indians in a very destitute condition, & many on the verge of starvation." Everywhere, except in the vicinity of Morleyville where the Stoneys were less dependent on buffalo, men, women, and children were starving. "If you will drive away the Sioux and make a hole so that the Buffalo may come," Crowfoot, head chief of the Blackfoot, told Dewdney, "we will not trouble you for food, if you don't do that you must feed us or show us how to live."[23] The Indian commissioner distributed food and arranged for the Mounted Police to take over this responsibility once he left.

Dewdney spent three weeks in what is now present-day Alberta conferring at various locales with senior police officers, chiefs, and others. During this time he also settled the two farmers on land selected for the government farms. Then, on August 1, he left for Saskatchewan River country.

Following a brief stop in Edmonton, the Indian commissioner travelled to the Hudson's Bay Company's Fort Victoria where he met with Pakān and other chiefs from the area. Dewdney said they "all had grievances about bad ploughs and spades and wild cattle."[24] He assured them that

> if it was found on examination that they had not received what was promised them by the Treaties, they should be replaced; that agents and instructors were about to be sent to reside among them; that nothing would in future be given them until strictly examined; and that from this out [*sic*] they might depend upon getting what they were entitled to.[25]

Dewdney soon learned that potential problems were brewing at Battleford. Dickieson's replacement, Walter Orde, had not arrived from Ottawa with the money for the treaty payments and there was no word on when to expect him. To meet the government's commitments for the upcoming treaty payments at Sounding Lake, Dewdney had $15,000 worth of cheques printed in denominations ranging from $2 to $50. Taking the cheques with him, the commissioner travelled to Sounding Lake accompanied by eight North-West Mounted Policemen. They arrived at the large camp on August 19. From Dewdney's and the traders' points of view, the issuance of cheques did not appear to present any problems when the annuities were paid. Dewdney, in his report to Macdonald, did not mention the reaction of the chiefs, the leading men, and their band members.[26]

On his return to Battleford, Dewdney took part in a "conference on Indian affairs" authorized by the Department of the Interior and called by Laird. The participants were to be Laird, Dewdney, and Dickieson, plus three members of the North-West Council: Police Commissioner Macleod, stipendiary magistrate Hugh Richardson, and Pascal Breland, a half-breed who spoke French and Cree as well as English.[27] Everyone was available in Battleford for the meeting on August 26 except Breland, whose arrival was uncertain, so the meeting went ahead without him. The plight of the

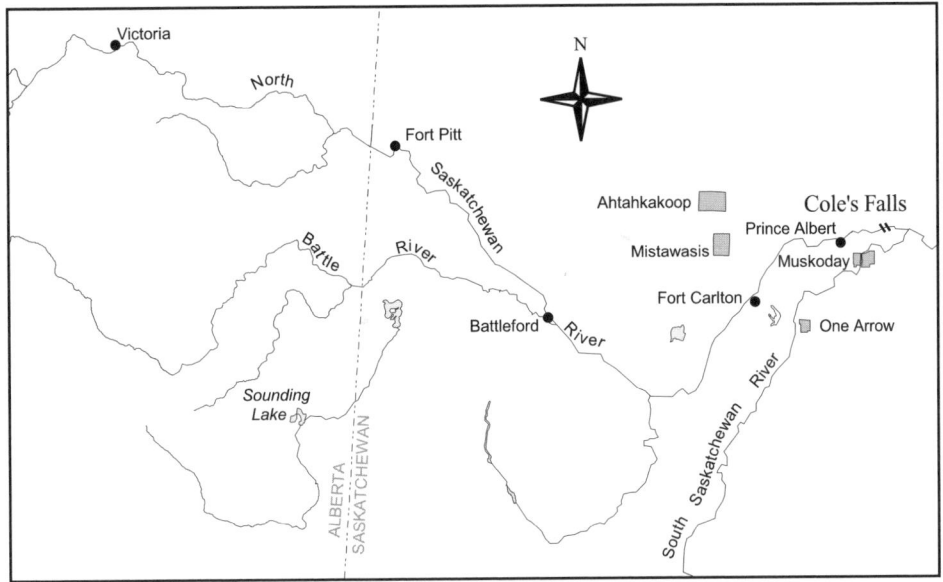

Information Systems Division, Canadian Plains Research Center

In 1879 the grounding of the steamboat Northcote *at Cole's Falls east of Prince Albert complicated the distribution of annuities, tools, supplies, cattle, and horses in the Treaty Six area.*

Indian people was the major topic of discussion when the men met, with their major decisions focusing on the necessity of purchasing food and supplies to get the bands through the winter. Laird refused "to have anything to do with the purchase of the supplies recommended by the conference" and authorized Dewdney to act on his behalf. Dewdney took preliminary steps to purchase flour and then another conference was called to get Breland's input. He told the officials he did not think, in view of the situation, they "had been sufficiently liberal" in their recommendations for supplies. "We determined to support his suggestions," Dewdney reported, "and sent a further requisition to the Government."[28] Later, when these steps to avoid starvation and death were put into place, Vankoughnet issued orders from Ottawa that the agents were to "require labour from able-bodied Indians for any supplies given to them."[29]

Orde finally arrived in Battleford on August 27, just as Dewdney was getting ready to print cheques for the payments that were due farther west. The new agent was late because he, along with farm instructors, cattle, horses, and supplies for the Treaty Six area, had been aboard the *Northcote* on its third voyage that summer up the North Saskatchewan River. The sternwheeler had encountered numerous mishaps due to low water and finally ground to a halt, unable to climb Cole's Falls east of Prince Albert. Orde was hustled overland to Battleford with the annuity money. The money was then forwarded to Victoria and Edmonton, where North-West Mounted Police officers would serve as paymasters, and Dickieson left for the payments at Fort Pitt.[30] In all three instances, the police looked after the distribution of supplies, just as they had at Sounding Lake.

In the meantime Ahtahkakoop and his people had already received their payments. Accompanied by a staff sergeant and two constables, Superintendent Walker had travelled to Carlton earlier in August to perform his duties as paymaster and acting Indian agent. Since the *Northcote* had not yet arrived and the chiefs gathered at Fort Carlton were opposed to accepting cheques, the officer reported that he

> deemed it advisable to put off the payments for a few days, and went down to the forks of the Saskatchewan expecting to meet the steamer conveying Mr. Orde, Indian Agent, with the money, and bring him up overland as quickly as possible. After waiting at the forks two nights and a day and hearing nothing of the steamer or Mr. Orde, I returned to Carlton, and after explaining the situation to the Indians, they consented to take cheques as payments, so I proceeded to make the payments.[31]

A total of 270 persons in Ahtahkakoop's band were paid at Carlton on August 18, with several others receiving their annuities at Battleford.[32] Because the *Northcote* still had not arrived, the people had to wait at Fort Carlton several more days to receive their supplies, tools, and implements. Once again, time that could have been spent hunting, cutting hay, and harvesting crops was wasted.

When word was finally received that the captain of the *Northcote* had decided it would be impossible to climb Cole's Falls,[33] the plans changed. Orde left for Battleford, the 52 head of cattle were unloaded and driven to the Muskoday Reserve,* and the steamboat—after returning to the forks—headed up the South Saskatchewan River to Chief One Arrow's reserve. There Lawrence Clarke took charge of the remaining cargo. The supplies,

---

* Chief John Smith's reserve on the South Saskatchewan River southeast of Prince Albert.

implements, equipment, and other goods were transferred to 100 carts and taken to Fort Carlton.[34] Walker distributed the presents and supplies to the chiefs still waiting at the post, and then most of the people left to hunt or attend their farms.

It had been apparent during the councils and informal discussions held in the large camp during the treaty payments that there was considerable dissatisfaction with the treaty. The people felt the government was not keeping some of the promises that had been made when Treaty Six was negotiated. They were also unhappy with many of the implements, the cattle, and the amount of assistance being given when their people were trying hard to succeed at farming but were still starving. The chiefs had laid their concerns before Laird and other government officials numerous times, but no answers had ever been received. Additionally, Ahtahkakoop, Mistawasis, and Kitowēhāw (Sound of Flapping Wings) were displeased with the survey of Ahtahkakoop's reserve.* Not surprisingly, when Ahtahkakoop and Mistawasis learned that the new Indian commissioner was expected at Fort Carlton in a week or so they decided to wait for him.

Dewdney arrived from Battleford in a York boat the afternoon of September 1. That evening Ahtahkakoop and Mistawasis paid a visit to the commissioner and arranged for an "interview" at 7:30 the next morning. According to a "special correspondent" for the Montreal *Gazette*, who had arrived overland from Winnipeg a day or so before, the early time was agreed on because Dewdney wanted to leave for Prince Albert "about the middle of the day."[35]

The commissioner was ready at the appointed time, but Ahtahkakoop and Mistawasis had sent for Kitowēhāw and he still had not arrived. About 8:30 a.m. the two chiefs left their camp to tell Dewdney that they would wait for Kitowēhāw before beginning the meeting. Mistawasis was wearing his red chief's coat with the gold lace. The silver treaty medal hung around his neck. He was "a man of small stature, with a most benevolent, thoughtful looking face," the correspondent reported, while Ahtahkakoop was "taller and more muscular looking." Ahtahkakoop was apparently wearing his regular clothes, for in all probability the chief's clothing presented to him in 1876 had been too small to wear comfortably and with dignity.

---

* Kitowēhāw was chief at the Muskeg Lake Reserve.

Kitowēhāw, described as a "stout, vigorous looking man," finally arrived and the proceedings commenced.[36]

The "special correspondent" was allowed to attend and report on the meeting. His article was published in the Montreal *Gazette* on September 29, 1879.[37] It was, according to Dewdney, a "very exhaustive report of the interview [and] ... perfectly correct."[38] The meeting, the correspondent wrote,

> took place in one of the offices of the Hudson's Bay Company. The three chiefs, with their councillors, were outside of a bar, the chiefs and two others being seated on a form, and the five other Councillors being squatted on the floor, evidently a favourite attitude. A silence of a few minutes prevailed, and then "Atahakoup" —The Star Blanket—came forward. He shook hands first with Mr. Dewdney, then with the rest of us, and then commenced his statement. There had been some little difficulty about an interpreter, the Indians being specially suspicious on this point, and they had brought one of their own tribe who was reputed to speak good English, to act in the capacity. But he broke down at the very outset; and Mr. Taylor, of the H.B.C's service, acted throughout the conference, the Indian standing by as a sort of check. The statement in the language of the interpreter, was as follows:—

> We waited for you, and we see you now; we wonder if our word met you. We have often been talking of the promises we got and when we saw that they were not carried out in their spirit, we made representations to the Minister, but they were as if they were thrown into the water. We are very glad to meet you now, as you come with full authority to act. We will not touch on anything, but the promises which have not been fulfilled. We are very much pleased with the aid given us, as we hear of starvation on the plains, there being no buffalo. We are only beginning to be able to support ourselves, and it will take time to do so fully. We want what aid Government can give us. We have endeavored to fulfil our part of the treaty. We know the plan of Government to make us self-supporting is a right one; but we have not the knowledge to carry it out. A few of us have stuck manfully to the tilling of the soil, but many have not done so. The seed given to us has been put in the ground, and is producing well, but the crops are

still standing, and until they are harvested we want aid. This is the view of all the chiefs; we want a little help in shape of provisions until harvesting is done. The cattle we got from Government all died; they were brought from Montana, and we protested that they would not do. We saw the keepers of them on horseback. We did not want at the time to annoy the Governor, and we took these cattle. They were like the wild fowl, we saw them here, and then they disappeared; some, when tied in stables, choked themselves; some could not be fed, and to catch them was a fight, so wild were they. They did not take to the food, although the grass was good, and even barley and wheat fed to them in the sheaf had no effect upon them. In taking the treaty, we expected to raise cattle from the six given to us, and we expect and hope Government will replace them. We have two oxen left, and these have been working all summer breaking up land. It is impossible that we can get on with these two oxen, and we want some aid if we can get it from Government; and if this can be done, not only myself but all who want to live by the cultivation of the soil, will be pleased. We think what we ask is not unreasonable, and we hope it will be granted. Another thing we wish to mention is about reserves. I pointed out where I wanted it and it was said a surveyor would be sent to survey it. I told the Commissioners at the Treaty that I had selected the spot I wanted. When the surveyor was sent out I could not get it laid out as I wanted it and that has been troubling me since. I protested at the time, and the surveyor told me he was following out his instructions. I suggested that it would be better to postpone the survey until I had seen the Governor, and he post-poned the survey. I saw the Governor and he told me that as I wanted the lines laid out, they would be done. We wanted the three reserves to have a mile between them There is a long distance between the reserves, and mine is in a part that is swampy and useless. We want it brought further south so as to bring the reserves nearer together, and prevent any large white settlements between them.

MISTAWASES ... then came forward and said: I will tell you, as we understood the treaty made with Governor Morris. We understood from him that he was coming into the country to help us to live, and we were told how we were to get a living, and we put ourselves at work at once to settle down. For every three families we were to get a plough and harrow, and one yoke of oxen was to go with each three families. We have been told since that it is not in the treaty. In … [insisting] on the yoke of oxen for the three families we were not told we were not to get them, and we thought we would have them. As to the cattle, we never expected them to be brought from the Montana quarter, when we were told we were to get milching cows.* What was the use of these cattle being brought so far, when tame cattle could have been had as near as the Prince Albert settlement, or Red River. We expected that we would have had good cattle, but those brought were so poor that it was a mockery of the promises to give us cattle with little else than skin and bone. We had great difficulty in getting the cattle on to our reserves, and we had no provisions given us to support us while driving them home. We put them into stables and did what we could with them. We were told by Governor Laird that they were tame, but I saw the Governor cutting away round from them. It would have been better to have given us some buffalos. Government is too slow in helping the Indians if they are going to help us at all. The fall before we saw Governor Laird, and wished him to give us more ample assistance in the way of farm implements and seeds. He said his powers were limited, but he would write to the Government, and let us know. To all these representations we received no answer. The country is getting so poor that it is for us either death by starvation, and such aid as will enable us to live. The buffalo was our only dependence before the transfer of the country, and this and other wild animals are disappearing, and we must farm to enable us to live. Now, we want to know how we are to live this following winter, what help we can depend upon from Government in the shape of food. We have not come here, except from necessity but we want to know what quantity of food we can depend upon for the winter. True, the Government have pacified the country, we have no longer wars with the Blackfeets, but the buffalo has been driven away

---

* Cows that are raised for their milk, and presumably in this case, for breeding, instead of for beef.

There is no longer war between the tribes; that has been stopped; but we are dependent now upon the Government for food. We are fond of money, but we are compelled to spend our annuity in getting food. This last winter we got a good deal of food from the Government, and we are thankful for it. So far as we can see, the policy of the Government has been directed to its own advantage, and the Indians have not been considered so much. What we have mentioned, we would like the commissioner to consider, and we want a definite answer. When we are asked a question we answer yes or no, and we would like the Government to do the same. I am an old man now and am at peace with everyone; I [am] weak and my dependence for support is centred on the Government. On the transfer of the country we were told that the Queen would do us all the good in the world, and that the Indians would ... [share] her bounty. With this message came presents of tobacco, and I took it at once and I pray now that the bounty then promised may be extended to us.

KETAWAYO [Kitowēhāw] was the next speaker. He said:—I understood the treaty in the same way that the others who have spoken understood it. When we asked for the yoke of oxen for each three families, although we were not told we should get them, we understood we would. If we had been told that we were not to get them, we would not have complained. It was the expectation of them that made us feel that we could live by breaking up ground. Every chief, we understood, was to get four oxen and six cows for himself; and we did not understand that they were to be used for the whole tribe. I think the aid from Government was very slow in coming. With a band of a hundred families it would be perfectly ridiculous that we could get on with four oxen. Every farmer, however poor, at Prince Albert has his yoke of oxen and we have tried and find that we cannot do with so few. We are new at this kind of work, but even white men cannot get on with so few oxen, and I agree with what has been said about the cattle. I was away when my tribe took them, or I would not have accepted them. We are not used to cattle, and when we were promised milk cows we expected they would be tame animals, that could be handled. We know why these Montana cattle were given us; because they were cheaper, and the Government, thinking us a

simple people, thought we would take them. The cattle have all
died. If we had got cattle of the country, and they had died, we
would think it was our fault, and we would not have asked to
have them replaced. We had plenty of hay, but the cattle were so
poor that it did them no good. We were promised pigs and sheep
and chickens, the first were promised in the treaty. We wanted a
copy of the treaty at the time it was made, but did not get one
until the winter before last. I know the pigs are mentioned in the
treaty, but we are not yet in a position to support them, and we
don't want them now. The chickens and the sheep we understood
we would get. We got some flour and ammunition from Major
Walker, and an ox to kill. We do not want to kill the ox, we want
to keep him for work in putting in the crops in the spring. It is a
good ox, trained to work, and I advised the band not to kill him,
as he would be of more use to keep. If it had been one of those
wild Montana cattle I would have killed him. I hear of buffalo on
the plains, and I am going off to see if I can get some food to pass
the winter with. We would like to have some help in the shape of
provisions in the meantime, and we wish to know what we can
depend upon. The help which the Government and the Hudson's
Bay Company have given us has kept us alive until now. Mr.
Clarke always gives us something when we come to the post. We
hear that the Government are sending instructors. They are all
from below, and if I am to have one, I would rather have one from
the country, who understands the language, and with whom I
could speak face to face, without an interpreter. There are not
enough of instructors sent up, and if more are needed, I hope half-
breeds will be selected, as it will help them, too. There are a lot of
half-breeds who want to take the treaty and join the reserves, and
who would be of assistance; but they were told that they could not
come in, as they had white blood in their veins. Some of the families of the half-breeds were in the treaty, and the men would like
to come in. He hoped a favorable view would be taken of their
requests. It is better that we should tell each other what we think.
Hitherto everything we have asked has been promised to be represented to the Government, but we have never got any answer, and
we want now an answer. The chiefs were promised in the treaty a
horse and waggon. I have never got a horse, and I want one.[39]

When Kitowēhāw finished speaking, Ahtahkakoop came forward again, saying that he wanted "to mention a few things more that I forgot before. I object to white men being sent us as instructors," he told Dewdney

> as I would prefer to have had men in the country who understood the language. The men are here, and they cannot be sent back. I am glad instructors are coming; it is a good plan, and will teach us many things we want to know; and if we find them following the instructions of the Government, we will do all we can to follow their teaching. We are pleased with the grant of ammunition given to us, but we think it strange that we do not get gun caps. We mentioned this to Major Walker, and he said he had no instructions on the subject. We have some flint-locks among us yet, and we want some flints. There are fishing lakes where I live, and we got some twine for nets, but not enough for our purpose, and we would like to get an extra supply. The axes brought this year have been small ones, unfit for our use. We want larger ones.

The correspondent left the council meeting just as Petihkwahākēw* (Comes To Us With The Sound of Wings), one of Kitowēhāw's councillors, began to speak. "The statements of the chiefs I have given, as taken down from the interpreter, and I have no doubt those that followed were substantially the same," the correspondent wrote, concluding this section of his report.

Dewdney was impressed by the presentations made by the chiefs. "They were the first Indians that I had met in the North West," he reported to Prime Minister Macdonald, superintendent general of Indians Affairs,

> who appeared to me to have any substantial grievances. They complained in the first place, that they had not been treated fairly in regard to their Reservations, and explained to me that a misunderstanding had occured [sic] between themselves, the surveyors and the Lieutenant Governor. They had been promised what they wanted but the surveyor sent to rectify their boundaries had not done so in accordance with those promises. Their other grievance was in reference to the cattle which had been given them the year previously.
>
> Upon inquiry I found that their statements were perfectly correct —that cattle had been given to them sore-footed, poor and wild;

---

* Petihkwahākēw's name was often spelled Petakwakiw or Petaquakey.

that most of them had died during the winter, although they had taken every possible care they could of them, and I thought it only right that I should on behalf of the Government, promise that these two grievances which appeared to me to be substantial should be redressed. I promised as soon as I could obtain cattle similar to those which were promised them at the Treaty to replace them.

I also stated that I saw no reason why the boundaries of their Reserve should not be altered to suit their wishes.

They were very anxious to know what the Government intended to do for them the coming winter.

They had been always dependent on the Buffalo to a very large extent for the winters food.

They said their crops which they had been taking very great care of, and which they were anxious then to go back to secure would not be sufficient to carry them over the winter and they then had no food with which to harvest them.

I gave them a few sacks of flour, some tobacco, and tea and told them that as soon as the farming Instructors arrived, who were now close at hand, they would receive assistance while working on their reservations as well as during the winter.

I explained to them the policy of the Government, and they expressed themselves much pleased with what I told them and I am satisfied from what I know of these chiefs that they, as well as the Indians under them will be able to make their own living in the course of a very few years. They have had the advantage of having Missionaries who have assisted them in the way of agriculture for some years.[40]

Apparently satisfied with the meeting, Ahtahkakoop, armed with the flour, tobacco, and tea, headed for home. The flour would help ward off hunger pangs but would do little towards meeting the nutritional needs of people accustomed to a diet dependent largely on meat. The chief could only hope that the provisions promised would be enough to sustain his people during the upcoming winter. And hopefully, this time something would be done to fix the boundaries of his reserve.

The *Gazette* correspondent had his own interpretation of what he had seen and heard during his visit at Fort Carlton. His views were contained in the last part of the report dated September 2, 1879. "The burden" of the chiefs and their people he wrote,

> is the same. The disappearance of the buffalo has brought these people face to face with starvation, and they want food. They profess a willingness to work, and as to some of them the profession is an honest one. The two chiefs, first mentioned [Ahtahkakoop and Mistawasis], are already becoming, for Indians, extensive farmers. Their complaint of want of good faith in carrying out the treaties on the part of the Government, is a most serious one. In some cases it is not justified, in others it rests upon too solid a foundation of truth. The complaint that they expected a yoke of oxen for every three families, and have not got them, involved no breach of treaty obligations on the part of the Government. They have got all that was promised them by the terms of the treaties. But it is to be feared that the Indian character was not sufficiently taken into account in dealing with them. That they asked for the oxen is undoubted; that an emphatic understanding that they must not expect them, was not arrived at I fear is also true; and with the Indians any request which he makes, and which is not positively refused, he assumes to be granted. The request in this case certainly does not appear to have been an unreasonable one. If it was intended in good faith to give these oxen as working animals to break up the land, with the view to the Indians becoming tillers of the soil, then certainly a yoke to every three families is not an exorbitant demand. That, however, was not the treaty. What was in it, six milch cows to each band, seems to have been carried out in the most disgraceful way. To fulfil it by sending in wild Montana cattle, was surely a mockery, and there was a tone of bitter irony in the chief's remark that they know why these cattle had been sent to them, because they were cheap. It is an unfortunate impression to get among the Indians that the treaties are made simply as a means of getting peaceable possession of the country, and to be kept with the least regard to their welfare. It would be interesting to know who supplied these cattle, and whether the same American speculators, who have been making a rich harvest out of supplying the wants of the Government in the North-West, had a hand in the matter.

And these Montana cattle are not the only ones in which the poor
Indians have been the sufferers by Government contractors. They
were promised carts, good ones, iron bound, and a horse and waggon for each chief. I saw in the yards of the Hudson's Bay
Company some of the carts and waggons supplied, and which
have been refused by those for whom they were intended. The
carts are the poorest description of Red River carts, which have
been used by freighters up to this point, and are really unfit for
further use; while the waggons are literally falling to pieces. The
Indians refused to take them, and they were right. Whether the
Government have paid for them is another question, but I am
inclined to think it may be answered in the affirmative. So with
the axes which have been obtained for them. They are here, mis-
erably small ones, and have also been refused. It is in these matters that the Government have evidently been wrong, and have
given the Indians the opportunity of accusing them of bad faith.
Whatever may be said of the general policy in relation to the
Indian question, and it is undoubtedly fraught with difficulties,
there should be no question about the importance of a fulfilment
of the obligations imposed by the treaties upon the Government,
in such a manner as to remove all doubt in the minds of the
Indians of their good faith. I believe Mr. Dewdney fully appreci-
ates the importance of this view, but it is necessary that he should
be armed with a large discretion. Much difficulty has arisen from
the limited powers give to Governor Laird. From all I can hear he
has performed the duties of this office faithfully and well, and he
is certainly very popular. But his hands have been tied. Letters to
the Department, while it had the misfortune to be under the
charge of Mr. David Mills, remained unnoticed, until at last disheartened by this treatment he tendered his resignation. He was
induced by Mr. Mackenzie to permit it to remain in abeyance for
a time; but his treatment at the hands of a Minister of his own
party, who succeeded him in the administration of the Department
of the Interior, was anything but creditable. I hope Mr. Dewdney
will have no grounds for similar complaint. If he is fit for the
position, and I believe he is thoroughly fit for it, he should have at
least discretion enough to enable him to meet cases of decided
emergency.

I have referred to the manner in which contracts have been fulfilled, in relation to supplies for the Indians. I saw the evidence at
Carlton that there is not much improvement in this respect. On the
top of the hill leading down to the fort were six Red River carts,
laden with agricultural implements. These, I learned were for the
Government, and were destined for Edmonton. They have been
three months on the road from Winnipeg, are in the charge of a
single man, who complains that he is almost starved, his provisions having given out, and his animals—miserable oxen at the
start—are so utterly broken down that he can go no further. The
implements, intended for use this fall, are due in Edmonton now,
and yet here they are, after three months trailing, only a little
more than half their journey. It is said the contractor for transport
has sub-let his contract to persons evidently unequal to the
responsibility. But whatever the cause, the fact is one which
should challenge the closest enquiry, with a view to the preven-
tion of the recurrence of such disasters in the future. ... It is to be
hoped that the whole system of transport may soon be changed, a
change which, as I propose showing before this series of letters is
brought to a close, may be brought about at comparatively little
expense, if the Government has the foresight to abandon the fuss
and feathers which have left so lamentable a record of waste of
time and money in connection with the development of the North-
West.

Before leaving Fort Carlton, Dewdney decided that the farm instructors
who had arrived on the *Northcote* should take the animals and freight
required for the winter with them to their assigned locations. The remaining
goods would be stored at Fort Carlton until spring, when they would be
shipped west on the first steamboat going up the river. The horses unloaded
from the steamer, the commissioner noted, had arrived in "first class order
and are a fine lot of animals," but the cattle were not as good. Once again
"some of them were very old, some footsore and others small."[41] The commissioner then travelled to Prince Albert to interview other chiefs, meet with
the farm instructors, and arrange with Moore's mill to supply flour for the
Indian agencies. The contract for supplying seed wheat was not let, probably
because of the cost. Undeterred, the commissioner said "I am in the hopes
we will be able to get along with a few hundred bushels for seed."[42]

Three of the farm instructors were placed in the Carlton district. George

Chaffee was to be responsible for the reserves "near Fort Carlton," including the Ahtahkakoop and Mistawasis reserves. John Tompkins was placed "near" Fort Carlton and Duck Lake, and W.A. Loucks was stationed near Prince Albert. The men were instructed to place their farms off the reserves so each instructor could serve a number of bands and any one band could not claim the instructor as its own. Dewdney thought this was particularly important, since he hoped the produce raised on the farms with the help of "assistants and what labor they can obtain from the Indians themselves" could be used to support the instructor and his staff. He also hoped to provide some of the food and seed required for the reserves. In this way, he suggested, the instructor's farm will hopefully "more than repay the Government for the expenditure." He cautioned, however, that for this first year the instructors should not build anything more substantial than necessary until they were sure the location was right. Because of this directive, most of the farm instructors spent the first winter in buildings they could use later as granaries or storehouses.[43]

The farm instructors in the Carlton-Prince Albert area were to be under the supervision of a newly appointed Indian agent, Palmer Clarke. He was to establish his headquarters at Fort Carlton. Although Orde was supposed to replace Dickieson in the dual position of Indian agent for the Battleford area and clerk for the superintendency, Dewdney planned on moving him to the superintendency's permanent headquarters in Regina. This would leave Clarke and J.G. Steward, the agent for the western district, to handle the agents' duties in the Treaty Six area. The commissioner did not consider this a problem. "With the advantage of a navigable river running through the whole length of Treaty 6," Dewdney wrote in his report to Macdonald, "I think Messrs. Clarke and Stewart will have no difficulty in attending to the Indian affairs of the Treaty."[44] Dickieson relinquished his positions of acting Indian superintendent, Indian agent, and superintendency clerk in mid-September and returned to Ottawa.[45]

An inspector of Indian agencies by the name of Thomas P. Wadsworth had also been appointed. His job, as suggested by his title, was to inspect the reserves and report on the state of affairs on each of them. He had helped get the farm instructors established in the Treaty Four area while Dewdney was on the western part of his tour, and then arrived at Fort Carlton the day before Dewdney. Thus Dewdney and Wadsworth both had an opportunity to meet the new agents and instructors before they went their separate ways for the winter.[46]

With his business finished in the Carlton region, Dewdney returned to Battleford, "settled" the farm instructors near the reserves in that area, and returned to Fort Walsh on September 17. There, in the southwestern part of the North-West Superintendency, he spent more than a month making final arrangements for the farm instructors, meeting with Indian delegations, and attending to other "Indian affairs." Then, "when snow had fallen and the winter storms were commencing and the Indians were about taking up their winter quarters," the commissioner left for Ottawa early in November.[47]

The intent of this visit, he informed Macdonald, was "to report to you what I had been doing, to submit to you the Indian grievances and to in person consult with you on matters which the Indians complained they had repeatedly asked to have submitted to the Government and to which they have been unable to obtain any reply." Countering complaints from non-Indians about his absence from the superintendency, Dewdney replied that the Indians "all knew that it was on their business he was visiting Ottawa and understood perfectly the benefits likely to arise from a personal interview with the Government on these matters, many of which they had represented they were unable to obtain an answer to."[48]

In his written report to Macdonald, Dewdney wrote that during his stay in the North-West, he had

> a good opportunity of meeting most of the prominent Indian Chiefs as well as becoming personally acquainted with a large number of our Indians.
>
> From repeated interviews both at regular council and in private, I have formed a very favourable impression of them & I am convinced the new policy of the Government if properly administered will eventually turn out to be most satisfactory.[49]

He noted that the Cree in the Treaty Six area were making some progress in their farming ventures, and

> are all alive to the necessity of making their living out of the soil, and every mail brings me information from the different farmers that the Indians are ready to give their assistance, my only fear is that so many will be anxious to work that we will not be in a position to keep them all going.[50]

Dewdney also included recommendations and observations in his report relevant to the development of farms on the reserves. Ignoring the concerns of Ahtahkakoop and Kitowēhāw, the commissioner said he was

convinced that it will be found that Instructors strangers to the
Indians, with the assistance of Half Breed interpreters will carry
out their duties to the satisfaction of the Indians generally better
than any local man, either white or halfbreed.

I have found that our interpreters have their favourites and it is
most essential that whoever has anything to do with Indians
should be in a position to treat all fairly and alike.[51]

He went on to say that "no one can at once force an Indian to take hold
of the plough and keep steady at work," and suggested that those who had
already started farming would need little help. Others who were anxious to
learn but who had no experience could make themselves "generally useful"
on the reserve, and by farming under the direction of the instructor, they
would soon be able "to work a piece of ground" for their families. "The
idea of taking a few Indians from each Reservation and teaching them as
you would pupils on a Model Farm would not be a success," he said.[52]

Dewdney suggested that, in the future, annuity payments should be paid
on the reserves whenever possible. The people who were not settled on
reserves could get their money directly from the agent during a prescribed
period of time. Any money saved on supplying provisions to large camps
"could be utilized in the purchase of clothing—a necessary which I fear,
the Government to some extent will have to furnish before long."

Several factors had contributed to this recommendation. The Indian
commissioner reported that a number of non-treaty Indians had been
camped at Sounding Lake when the annuities were paid in 1879. He felt
their questions and speeches were disruptive and delayed the payments. He
was also concerned about the "falsehoods" spread by "designing white
men" and "half-breeds" intent on stirring up trouble, and he thought "some
man of authority in whom they have confidence" should be continually circulating among the Indian people to "counteract the impression these representatives make upon them." This presumably would be easier to do if
the payments were made on the reserves. Besides, he added, "it does no
good to get so large a number of Indians together as met at Sounding
Lake." The commissioner also recognized that the off-reserve payments
took people away from their farms and hunting grounds, resulting in "a
good deal of valuable time … [being] lost to them."[53]

Additionally, Dewdney recommended the introduction of tokens or
tickets to "prevent the Indians imposing on the Government."[54] Sometimes

children were "loaned" to increase the amount of the annuity payment,[55] and the government claimed that some people were being paid more than once. The commissioner described how he envisioned the tickets being used:

> Before the rations are issued at the payments the agents will visit the different lodges and satisfy themselves that the man who represents himself as the head of a family has the number [of people] belonging to him that the ticket will show, and he will be paid his annuity for that number. The place where the Indian is paid will also be inserted on the ticket at the time of payment, and the year in which he is paid will be crossed with a pen. This will prevent the same ticket being used twice. No Indian shall be paid, unless he has his ticket, and to receive rations or anything else from the Government, he must understand that he must be in possession of it.[56]

Another recommendation focused on the position of Indian medical superintendent. "During my sojourn in the North West ... had I not seen on opening some medicine chests at Battleford instructions how these medicines were to be used from Dr. Hagarty who I subsequently ascertained was the Medical Superintendent," Dewdney wrote in his report, "I should not have known of the existence of such an officer." He later reviewed the government's estimates and discovered that a large sum of money had been included to cover the man's salary and expenses. Since a number of experienced medical men, including the North-West Mounted Police doctors, were being paid "for the special purpose of attending to the Indians," Dewdney stated that the position of medical superintendent should be abolished.[57]

Vankoughnet, in a memorandum accompanying Dewdney's report, said that he generally agreed with the Indian commissioner's views.[58]

The arrival of the Indian agent and farm instructors in the Carlton district had little if any impact on Ahtahkakoop and his people during the fall of 1879 and the following winter. There nevertheless must have been meetings and consultations, particularly between Indian agent Palmer Clarke and Ahtahkakoop. These more than likely took place during the chief's frequent visits to Fort Carlton. Hines also had some dealings with the government official. In October 1879, for instance, he asked the agent about the availability of a government grant to help defray the cost of erecting a school. Clarke recommended that $100 be given, and this was approved. Hines also asked if there was additional money to help with the salary of teachers working for him, for he had been paying the teachers out of his own pocket.[59]

The children on the Ahtahkakoop Reserve were now being taught by Hines, his wife Emma, and David Stranger. Classes were held two times a day, five days a week. Fifteen-year-old Louis Ahenakew, one of the first students in the school, was a "pupil teacher." John Pritchard was in charge of the school at Mistawasis's reserve, while Edward Matheson, who had taught at Sandy Lake the previous year, was among the first group of students to enroll at Emmanuel College when it opened in Prince Albert on November 1, 1879.[60] Operated by the Anglican Church under the guidance of Bishop John McLean, the school provided training for Indian catechists and a course in theology for those who hoped to be ordained. Later a "collegiate" course was offered to prepare boys and young men for university training. Archdeacon John Mackay served as McLean's assistant and teacher.[61]

The hay, grain, and vegetables growing on Ahtahkakoop's reserve the summer of 1879 were harvested without any help from the new farm instructors and the Indian agent. If anything, the harvest was held up because of the delays at Fort Carlton in distributing the annuities and "presents" and the meeting with the commissioner.

Encouragingly, the crops were the best yet, with some of the potatoes weighing 28 ounces.[62] Hines said the amount of wheat and barley harvested was so great that "we despaired of being able to beat it all out with sticks, so our thoughts went back across the ages to primitive times and people who were similarly situated as ourselves, and we studied their methods of beating out the corn." After some discussion, the missionary and Ahtahkakoop's people decided to tread out the grain,

> but, instead of using the slow dirty ox, we proposed using our sprightly ponies, and instead of making a thrashing-floor on the ground, where a considerable amount of soil must unavoidably become mixed with the grain, we decided to make our floor on the ice, and this is how we made it. We went on to the lake and marked out a circle on the snow about thirty yards in diameter, and we then cut holes through the ice along the circle about fourteen feet apart, and, when these were made, we placed two posts

Illustration by Ed Peekeekoot

Hines (left) and the men from Ahtahkakoop's band cleared the snow from Sandy Lake to make a "threshing floor." Then they erected a corral and used ponies to tread the kernels of wheat from the sheaves.

or pickets in each hole, and, holding these in an upright position, with a block of wood between each two, to keep them a certain distance apart, we scraped the snow and loose ice into the hole with our feet until the pickets would stand alone, and then we went on to the next hole and did likewise.[63]

By next morning the pickets were frozen solid in the lake and "stood as firm as growing trees." The men and older boys then hauled fence posts to the site and

began to build a fence around the circle by placing one end of a pole between one pair of pickets, and the other end between the next pair, and, starting from the ice, we kept on going round and round until the fence was about five feet high. We next set to work to shovel all the snow out of the circle, and swept the ice clean. We also built a small circle leading out of the larger one, but in this case we did not clean out the snow, as this was intended only for the horses to rest in whilst the men attended to the straw and grain. ... Having finished both the "corrals," we hauled the sheaves from the stacks to the thrashing-floor and placed them in position in this way—the butt end of one sheaf we placed against the fence poles, with the ears pointing towards the centre of the circle, and the next sheaf was placed opposite the last, but reversed, that is, with the ears overlapping the ears of the other sheaf, and so we went on, placing the sheaves close together until we had completed the circle, and having cut the bands, the time had arrived for putting our horse-power into action. So we opened the gate which connected the two corrals, and drove in the ponies, eight in all, and having guided their heads in one direction, we began driving them round—the fence on the one side and the slippery ice on the other kept the ponies from leaving the sheaves, and, much quicker than it takes to say how it was done, the horses had become accustomed to their work, and trotted along as though in harness, and about twenty circles sufficed to tread out the grain from the upper part of the sheaves.

The men and boys then drove the horses into the smaller circle to rest while they turned the straw over and shook it. After this was done, the ponies were put back into the large "corral" to finish treading the sheaves. Hines said that in

an incredibly short time all the grain was trodden out. Again the horses were turned into the smaller circle and the men began shaking up the straw with their forks to allow the loose grain to fall out of the straw, and then the straw was thrown over the fence. Then fresh sheaves were brought and placed in position and the same method adopted. It took two large loads of sheaves to make a double course around the circle. When the grain, chaff and short straws got to be about six or eight inches deep, they were all shovelled into a heap in the centre, and in a few hours we had quite a large heap of such mixture in the centre of the floor.

Those who have never tried to thrash grain in this way can scarcely believe how much can be done in one day, but the tedious part of the work still remained to be done, and that was to separate the grain from the chaff, etc. We had no machinery for such a purpose, so we had to do it by the help of the wind, and this necessitated our being exposed to a fifteen or twenty miles an hour wind, blowing across the face of a frozen lake, which, to say the least, was not very agreeable. Well, the next thing to be done was to make a sieve, which we did in this way. We took half a raw hide of a domestic animal which had been killed for the winter supply of meat. An Indian woman removed the hair from the hide and made the skin into thick parchment. We then took some 1 in. by 9 in. boards and nailed them together, thus making a frame 4 feet by 2½ feet; then, having soaked the parchment, we stretched it tightly across the frame, nailing it securely all round, and, as the parchment dried, it became very tight, and, when quite dry, I ruled lines on it lengthwise and cross-wise about 1½ inches apart. I then went to my gun case and took out my wad cutter, and, having placed the sieve on a log with a level top, I proceeded to punch holes through the parchment where the lines I had ruled intersected each other. A sharp decisive blow made a clean cut in the parchment, and the holes were about five-eighths of an inch in diameter. We then nailed a short piece of wood to each side of the frame for handles, and our sieve was complete. We next made a hole in the ice away from the land to ensure our getting not only the full benefit of all the wind there might be at the time, but also to avoid an eddy in the current of air, as often happens near the shore. Having inserted a long pole in a slanting position, we connected the sieve to the top of this pole with a rope, and the machinery for cleaning the grain was complete.

After the wheat was winnowed, or separated from the chaff and dirt using the makeshift sieve, it had to be ground into flour before it was very useful. This, Hines said, meant hauling the grain "one hundred miles … to the nearest grist-mill [a mill for grinding grain], the round journey occupying seven or eight days."[64] This presented a real problem. Although enough healthy horses had been found to thresh the grain, many of the families did not have animals to take their wheat to the Prince Albert mill. And even if they did, Hines said it was more expensive to haul the wheat and get the flour ground than to buy flour at Fort Carlton.[65]

The optimism resulting from the good crops and the innovative way of threshing the grain was short-lived. Winter descended with a vengeance early in the fall of 1879. On October 9, one foot of snow fell, the weather turned cold, and one of the severest winters for years settled in. The buffalo were gone from the northern plains and parklands.[66] Other animals that were hunted for food and pelts were scarce, the fish camp at *manitow-sākahikan* failed, and by December Hines was reporting a considerable amount of illness on Ahtahkakoop's reserve because of the cold and lack of food.[67]

During January only a few people—mainly the elderly and the sick—were on the reserve.[68] The rest were at their "hunting grounds," trying to survive off a land destitute of game. Iskwēsis's son Wāwiyēwēskocawēs (Charles Roundplain), 30, and seven-year-old Pierre Weyatokwapas (Jolly Man) died in January, followed in early February by Andrew Flett, the man hired by Hines to saw lumber for the new church.[69] February, Hines noted in his journal, was a month in which "great sickness" prevailed. One man told Hines that he was striving to be a Christian, but he was always ill. Around him he saw that others who were "striving the hardest to be Xtians were sick & dying." The people adhering to their traditional way of life, on the other hand, were "apparently strong and healthy."[70] He and many others in Ahtahkakoop's band found this hard to understand.

The wheat obtained from the harvest became a mixed blessing during the winter. Those who were able to get their wheat ground into flour made bannock, but eating only dry bread gave them "hot chests" or heartburn. Others roasted whole wheat kernels in frying pans and ate them as "one might eat roasted coffee." The wheat was exceedingly dry, and "not being accustomed to a farinaceous diet, their constitutions suffered." To make the grain more digestible, the missionary said he saw many of the people "take their ponies, dying from the effects of the mange, kill them and boil their bones in order to get a little fat, with which to grease the wheat, when roasting."[71]

The sickness continued into March and April, "ravaging" the settlement. Hines visited the sick and distributed what medicine he had. Ahtahkakoop's nine-year-old grandson, William Kā-miyo-ahcahkwēw, was among the children who were sick. The boy, along with a trader's daughter, was suffering from a "low fever" and "gradually sinking."[72] By March 26 someone was ill in practically every house on the reserve. Hines thought the custom of gathering at the homes of the sick was unwise. With all the people crowded into the houses and with the wood fires burning vigorously, the houses became "like furnaces." It was hard to keep the "proper" temperature, and this he believed was injurious to the person who was sick. William Kā-miyo-ahcahkwēw and the trader's daughter died early in April. Another boy died April 14.[73]

Hines said that William's funeral was "the most affecting & best conducted funeral that has yet taken place at Assissippi." After the church

Illustration by Ed Peekeekoot

When their families were starving and there was nothing else to eat, some of the women roasted kernels of wheat in a frying pan over an open fire.

service the children accompanied the coffin to the graveyard, "marching 2 x 2." The boy's parents (Kā-miyo-ahcahkwēw and Judique Mistawasis) and the others who attended the funeral followed "according to their relationship" to William.[74]

The first geese were sighted two days before the second boy's death, on April 12, bringing hope that the difficult days would soon be over. It was not to be. On April 16 it started snowing again, and within 24 hours a foot of fresh snow lay piled on the ground. "What will become of our poor people is hard to say," Hines wrote in his journal. It had now been six months and eight days since the first snowfall. The people were extremely poor and, in Hines words, "greatly in need of game."[75]

The "feverish cold" continued to "ravage" the little settlement at Sandy Lake. "Every day," Hines wrote on April 23,

> one or other of the children is falling with it. Poor little lambs, they seem to suffer most. Just fancy poor little children suffering from fever & having nothing to eat but parched wheat. It just dries up their very nature at once, & in many cases they get so rapidly weak that before we get to them they are almost too far gone to be benefitted.[76]

As he went from home to home visiting the sick, Hines talked to the people and listened to their troubles. "Many of them counting days since they last partook of food," Hines wrote in his journal. "There is not one house in the whole settlement that I visit that someone or other of its inmates ask me for food."[77] Many a time when starving Indians came to the mission house, Hines said

> my wife and I have felt compelled to share our scanty meal with them and very often these hungry Indians, after taking two or three mouthfuls of food would ask for a piece of paper to wrap the rest in, and when we have remarked they did not eat like hungry people, they replied, 'We are very hungry, but so are our wives and children, and we wish them to have a taste of food too.'[78]

Hines, Emma, and their daughter Henrietta got ill towards the end of April, and although the missionary was back at work within five days, the child continued to suffer from a "kind of choking fit." And many others were still sick. On April 28 Hines visited one his students, 15-year-old Arthur Hyman, who had been suffering from consumption for over a year. That same day he was "fetched over the lake" to see another 15-year-old,

David Cīpay-awāsis (Ghost Child). This boy was the only surviving son in his family.[79] Then, on April 29, the missionary went on a "visiting tour" around the lake. His first call was to see David, and then he stopped at the chief's house before travelling to the north end of the lake. Because he had some "misgivings" about the ice, the missionary went over the hill, "which was very difficult." After administering to the three people he found at home, and learning that the ice was safe, Hines crossed the lake, and went about one-and-a-half miles south to make another call. On reaching the "homeward" end of the lake, he visited a child of two years who was ill "with the fever."[80]

David Cīpay-awāsis, who had been baptized March 29, died April 30. Arthur Hyman, the boy with consumption, died before midnight on May 28.[81]

Sixteen-year-old Sophia Stranger had also been in poor health. David and Isabella were planning to take her to the Red River Settlement but on May 10 the girl's condition worsened. She died May 26, 1880, two days before Arthur. The Strangers, who had lost their infant son John the previous May, cancelled their trip and Stranger enrolled at Emmanuel College in the fall.[82]

Despite the sickness and hardship, interest in Hines's mission remained strong. Ninety-four people had attended morning church services on Easter Sunday. Thirteen adults and 11 children were baptized, and in the afternoon 19 took communion. According to Hines there were now only two whole families on the Ahtahkakoop Reserve who were "heathen," although there were non-Christians in some families. No man had more than one wife, and everyone rested on Sunday.[83] Although Hines does not mention it, a number of women were heading up their own families. At least some of these women had been put aside by their husbands in order to meet the church's policy that the men could only have one wife. Other wives remarried. Masuskapoe,* for example, had more than one wife until approximately 1880 when a woman and boy[84] went to live with Kā-kīsikāwapiw.†

On April 12, two weeks after Easter, Baptiste Ahenakew married 17-year-old Ellen Ermineskin. Ellen was the daughter of K-ōsihkosowayānēw (Ermineskin) and Nōtokwēwāhp (Old Woman's Lodge). She had attended the Asissipi School and at the time of the wedding was working as a maid

---

* John Peter Masuskapoe, son of Ahtahkakoop's brother Masuskapoe.

† Kā-kīsikāwapiw (He Who Sits In A Day) took Levi as his Christian name. Many years later he was known as Levi Turner. Matilda and her son were both dead by 1885.

in the Hines's home. According to the missionary, Baptiste and Ellen were the first "bachelor & spinster" to be married in the church.* All the other couples had been previously married in the traditional way.[85] Hines also celebrated a special day that spring. He completed his studies to become an Anglican priest and was ordained in Prince Albert on March 7, 1880.

Despite the sickness and hardship experienced during the dreadful winter, the people in Ahtahkakoop's band had carried on as best they could. On April 10, just before the last snowfall, Ahtahkakoop and one of his councillors travelled to Fort Carlton to get the seed grain supplied by the government. About the same time, some of the women left for "sugar-making" on the banks of the North Saskatchewan River. The snow melted quickly, and several weeks later most of the people were "off" picking cranberries. These berries, Hines said, hung on the trees all winter and were even better in the spring than in the fall. Meanwhile high water in the creek caused problems when the cow belonging to Ahenakew's widow drowned in the creek behind the mission.[86]

The crops were planted as soon as the fields were dry, and by May 3 some band members were busy ploughing new land. It turned out to be a wet spring. By the middle of the month rain and hail storms were making farm work impossible. Finally "good growing weather" arrived at the end of the month and the fields began to look green.

On May 31 Ahtahkakoop and his people made ready to welcome the new Indian agent—soniyaw kimaw or "money master," as he was called—to their reserve. If Palmer Clarke comes, Hines wrote in his journal, this will be the first government official "of note" to visit the Ahtahkakoop Reserve and see the Asissipi Mission.[87]

Clarke may not have come. Hines's journal ended on June 19 and no further mention of the agent was made. In retrospect, this was not necessarily bad. Most of the Indian people who had agents and farm instructors living in their midst quickly fell under the control of the government officials. The scarcity of food gave the officials a tremendous advantage. To receive "relief," able-bodied Indians were required to work to the satisfaction of the farm instructors. In some instances they were given ammunition to hunt. But, more often, they were required to prepare fence rails, cut and

---

* Ellen's mother, Nōtokwēwāhp, was Chief Poundmaker's sister and Mistawasis's niece.

haul timber out of the bush, and do other work. The widows with children and the old men and women received provisions, although likely not in the amounts required to meet their needs.[88]

The people were also required to help the farm instructors who, according to Indian agent Clarke, had gained the confidence of the Indians. In view of the expectations when Treaty Six was signed and the assurances made by Dewdney only a few months earlier, this opinion likely was not shared by all the chiefs. The Indian agent, nevertheless, was pleased. "The system of rationing and of work on the reserves which I instructed the Farmers to carry out," Palmer Clarke reported in March, "will result I think in nearly every farmer having a house by April next and enough fence rails cut to enclose all the land they can plough this season."[89] His report did not note that families on the Ahtahkakoop Reserve worked without the threat of starvation being held over them, and he did not acknowledge that being forced to work in return for food was demeaning. Nor was there any reference to the concerns of the leading men that few, if any, of the newcomers sent by the government could speak an Indian language.

The officials of the Hudson's Bay Company viewed the situation from yet another perspective. For example, Chief Commissioner Grahame wrote in January 1880 that "it is to be regretted that the policy pursued by the Government Agents should lead the Indians to abandon their hunting habits, for this will not only seriously affect our collection of Furs, but reduce them to wretchedness, while their children will grow up in ignorance of trapping."[90] It was also noted that because of government policy the children would not know how to hunt. Hudson's Bay Company officials could hardly be considered unbiased since the well being of the company and its shareholders depended on a viable fur trade. Nevertheless, it was becoming a known fact that if men had to remain at home to look after the livestock and their farms, they could not be away for extended periods trapping and hunting. If they were not trapping, the people did not have disposable income to buy ammunition, traps, clothing, blankets, food, and other necessities. And if they were not hunting on the grasslands and in the woods, it was difficult to collect the herbs, berries, and roots needed for their medicines. All this complicated their plight, making their lives even more precarious.

Meanwhile, Emma Hines—pregnant with her second child—was having health problems and had arranged to travel to Winnipeg with Bishop McLean. John and Emma Hines made one last visit to the people who were

Illustration by Ed Peekeekoot

Construction of the new church on the Ahtahkakoop Reserve.

sick in late May and then the couple, along with their young daughter, left for Prince Albert. The run-off from the heavy winter snowfall had turned the usually placid streams into torrents. Hines did not go into details, but the horse belonging to the mission drowned while crossing a plank bridge at Snake Creek. This undoubtedly caused delays. Their departure from Sandy Lake may also have been delayed by the deaths of Sophia Stranger and Arthur Hyman and the pending visit of the Indian agent.

For whatever reason, the family was late reaching Prince Albert. Bishop McLean had not waited for them. This put the Asissipi Mission clergyman in a difficult position, for he had expected to get $175 from the bishop to help pay for the construction work at the Asissipi Mission. Without the money from the bishop, Hines was left with a total of $195 for the entire upcoming year. My salary, he wrote in his journal, will not pay my debt for provisions at Fort Carlton. He was particularly upset because he and his wife had been very frugal, spending less than $45 on clothing and furniture combined in the four years since their marriage. Not getting the $175 from the bishop would cause even further hardship.[91] Of more immediate concern, because of the mix-up in Prince Albert Emma Hines did not go to Winnipeg. Their son died at birth in July. Hines blamed the baby's death on "isolation and the absence of medical care."[92]

By now John Hines was frustrated, and slightly bitter. He had seen Ahtahkakoop and his people suffering during the winter, and he had helped as best he could at a heavy personal cost. When starving people ask for food, he wrote in his journal,

> it is hard under present circumstances to deny them. My expenses during the past winter have far exceeded my income. If my Indians are not better off another winter than they have been this, I cannot live among them on my present salary. Let me tell the Society again what everyone in the country admits. Asissipi is situated the farthest from civilization of all our missions in the N.W.T.[93]

He explained that in other regions the Indian people went to the forts for assistance; at the Ahtahkakoop Reserve they went to their hunting grounds and left the poor for the missionary to look after. Although Hines made no mention of it, people in other locations were getting food from the Indian agents and farm instructors, as well as at the forts, and the farm instructor in Prince Albert had set up a soup kitchen.[94] Presumably Ahtahkakoop's band had collected some provisions from the agent, for help had been promised and 78,064 pounds of flour, 8,959 pounds of beef, and 17,263 pounds of bacon were distributed in the Carlton district by government officials between January 1 and July 1, 1880.[95] Regardless, based on Hines's reports, whatever was given had not been enough to prevent the hunger and the sickness that stalk impoverished people.

And so, with the arrival of spring, the seasons had again come full circle at Ahtahkakoop's reserve, beginning and ending with sickness and death. During this time little help had been received from the government.

A New Church Is Built, 1880-1881

The wet spring of 1880 turned into a soggy summer. Storm after storm swept through the reserve during the third week of June. Hail pounded the crops, driving the young plants into the ground, and swarms of mosquitoes, spawned in the dampness, made life outdoors a misery for everyone.[1]

During a break in the rain towards the end of June, Hines managed to get the roof on the new church, nailing with one hand while fighting mosquitoes with the other. Most of the men, in the meantime, were away from the reserve hunting. A few others were freighting.[2]

On July 25 Ahtahkakoop and his people left for Fort Carlton to attend the treaty payments that were scheduled to begin the next day. For the first time since Treaty Six was signed, the Indian agent for the Carlton Agency presided over the event. There was another change as well, although it most likely passed unnoticed: the agent and other government workers were now employees of the Department of Indian Affairs. This new department, created on May 7, 1880, took over the functions that had previously been administered by the Department of the Interior. It was primarily an administrative move, since most of the personnel remained the same. John A. Macdonald retained the title of superintendent in the new department, in addition to being prime minister. Lawrence Vankoughnet continued to serve as deputy superintendent general. Edgar Dewdney was still Indian commissioner, and Palmer Clarke remained on staff as Indian agent for the reserves north of Fort Carlton, including the Ahtahkakoop Reserve.

One hundred and ninety-five people accepted their annuities as part of Ahtahkakoop's band at Fort Carlton in 1880. This was 75 fewer than the previous year's 270. According to government documentation only one child, a girl, had been born during the paylist year.* Eight people had died since the last treaty payment, including the headman Wāskitoy.³ Kihci-mōhkomān was also dead, drowned while canoeing in Sandy Lake. It was a Sunday in the spring, when the lake was still partly covered with ice. The people sitting in the churchyard saw the canoe's prow tip up out of the lake and Kihci-mōhkomān slid into the water. His body and the canoe were never recovered.⁴

According to the 1880 paylist, 11 families (consisting of 11 men, 14 women, 11 boys, and 18 girls for a total of 54 people) had transferred to other bands. Of these families, three went to Mistawasis's band, three went to Okīnomotayēw's, three went to Kitowēhāw's, and two transferred to Kā-ohpatawakinam's (Flying Dust's) band at Meadow Lake.⁵

Seven heads of households who had been paid in 1879 did not receive their annuity payments in 1880. All but one were women, and at least three had children listed on their tickets. Additionally, another 25 people listed on the 1880 paylist—most of whom had families—had not taken their annuity payments in 1879 and were absent again in 1880.⁶

There likely was no single reason why people left. Ahtahkakoop, unhappy with the swampy land that had been included in the survey of his reserve, believed that some left because they did not think they could make a living on the reserve the way it was surveyed.⁷ Several families which transferred from Ahtahkakoop's band joined northern chiefs who did not sign Treaty Six until 1878, and in each case they had strong connections with these bands.⁸ Another family had two children at Mistawasis's reserve, so they joined relatives at Snake Plain. Some of the families and individuals who had not taken their payments for a number of years may have wanted to continue trapping and hunting instead of learning how to farm. They may have joined other bands, or gone off on their own. Others may have rejected Christianity, the restrictive life on the reserve, or the ultimatum to give up one or more of their wives. Some of the women and children—cast off during a family's conversion to Christianity—apparently left, perhaps returning to the band of their birth. A few families and individuals likely chose to give up their treaty Indian status in an attempt to integrate into the white man's world. And some may have died.

---

* The Asissipi Mission baptism and death registers indicate that one boy and three girls were born during this period and all of them lived. The term "paylist year" is being used to identify the time from one treaty payment to the next. Thus, in 1880, the paylist year was from August 18, 1879, to July 26, 1880.

According to the 1880 treaty paylist, not all the changes involved people moving away from the reserve, for there were also transfers into Ahtahkakoop's band. One family of four came from Okīnomotayēw's band, while eight members of another family transferred from Ayahtaskamikinam's Sturgeon Lake Reserve. A woman described on the paylist as a "former wife" of a man in the Mistawasis Band was added to the Ahtahkakoop band list; a girl was registered on the same ticket. Another "former" wife, this time the wife of a man in the Ahtahkakoop Band, was given a new number on the paylist for herself and her daughter; her husband remained on the list with a wife and a boy.

The treaty paylist also gave some indication of happenings in the lives of band members. For example, Ahtahkakoop's son Joseph had married 17-year-old Mary Joyful, the daughter of Benjamin Joyful. Emma Ahtahkakoop and Kā-tāh-twēhototawāt had given their eight-year-old daughter Maria to her grandparents—Ahtahkakoop and his wife—to raise. Kakwēciyaw (Questioning Body), who had gone to Qu'Appelle in 1878, had returned with a wife and three girls, while Wīcikāpawīmēw (He Who Stands With You),[9] who had been at Red River when the treaty money was paid in 1879, had returned, still single.

More significant, there was a change in the leadership of the band. Wāskitoy, the headman who had died the previous year, was replaced by Ahenakew's 30-year-old son Wāsēhikot. Surprisingly, Wāsēhikot—for the first time—was listed under ticket #5, the number previously assigned to Kīsik-awāsis. Son of Ahtahkakoop and one of the original headmen, Kīsik-awāsis's name was inserted under Wāsēhikot's former number, ticket #33. Kīsik-awāsis, in the meantime, had moved to Red Pheasant's reserve with his family where he was paid under ticket #30 in 1880. The following year, he was reported to be at Victoria, situated east of Edmonton, and in 1882 he had gone to Edmonton and his name was taken off the Red Pheasant paylist. Kīsik-awāsis's name and the #33 ticket number were both dropped from Ahtahkakoop's treaty paylist in 1881. No official explanation for Kīsik-awāsis's departure was provided in the government documentation and no one was named to replace Kīsik-awāsis as a headman. As a result of these changes, Ahtahkakoop's headmen were reduced from four to three in number.

The fields of wheat and barley on the Ahtahkakoop Reserve had thrived during the wet summer of 1880 and were in contention for prizes the government was offering for the "best general crop" grown that year. Vying for the honours were farmers from the Ahtahkakoop, Mistawasis, and Muskeg Lake reserves.* The fields at Ahtahkakoop's Reserve were inspected on August 21 and in due course it was announced that Ahtahkakoop had won first prize. The award was a yoke of oxen. One of his councillors came in second, winning a cow.[11]

The exhilaration derived from knowing that their fields had received high marks from the government official was short-lived. Four days after the inspection, on August 25, the crops were hit by a "hard" frost. The wheat was partly destroyed and the potato tops cut down. On the 28th, the temperatures once again dropped substantially below freezing and, according to Hines, the wheat was "spoiled entirely." A month later the missionary wrote that he did not think there was "a single grist" on the reserve "fit for grinding" into flour.[12] So although the fields of grain at the Ahtahkakoop Reserve had been judged excellent, with two of them winning top prizes in the government's competition, the practical results told a different story. The wheat and, to a lesser extent the barley, had been destroyed by the early frost, leaving Ahtahkakoop and his people once again at the mercy of elements over which they had absolutely no control. The situation was similar throughout the Carlton and Prince Albert districts, hitting both Indian and non-Indian farmers alike.

Nevertheless, winning the yoke of oxen and the cow was gratifying, for Ahtahkakoop and his councillor had proved that with a fair break from the weather they could grow grain successfully. Equally important, the prizes had a practical aspect. The oxen supplied by the government had not only been too few in number to meet the practical needs of the bands, but they had gained a well-deserved reputation for being wild and of poor quality. Most had died, even though they had been well looked after. The replacement animals brought west in the summer of 1879 were "not a good lot of cattle" either. There were a few good ones, Dewdney had reported, but still "some of them were very old, some footsore, and others small."[13]

The lack of good oxen had been hurting farming operations on all the reserves, and in August the chiefs and headmen of the Carlton district requested more working cattle. Indian agent Clarke, in passing their

---

* In previous documentation, the Muskeg Lake Reserve had been referred to as Kitowēhāw's reserve. Petihkwahākēw, who had signed Treaty Six as one of Kitowēhāw's headmen, was now chief. Kitowēhāw had left the reserve and was living with his Métis cousins on the South Branch of the Saskatchewan River. He was now known as Alexander Cayen.

request on to higher authorities, said that three or four families had to wait, sometimes for a considerable length of time, to use the same yoke of oxen. The season was short, he reported, the farms were some distance apart, and valuable time was lost.[14] Since this situation existed at the Ahtahkakoop Reserve as well as on the other reserves, the new oxen were not only welcome but they would be put to good use.

Despite the obstacles, the farms on Ahtahkakoop's reserve were developing well. The houses were a good size, and said to be "fairly well kept." The stables were of reasonable proportions and well constructed, and the fences were strong and well built. Most of the people had also dug root cellars for storing potatoes.[15]

John M. Rae, who replaced Palmer Clarke as the Carlton Agency Indian agent in the fall of 1880, made his first visit to Ahtahkakoop's Reserve the week of September 20. He was pleased with the progress of the band. His account of the crops, however, reflected the band's ability to farm rather than the outcome of its efforts. He also conveniently overlooked the shortages that band members were sure to face in the coming winter. He reported that the wheat "which is of very good quality, has been damaged by the frost," and noted that it had been cut and stacked. The potatoes were said to be very good, but each family only had a small patch. And surprisingly, in view of the numerous reports of failed crops, the agent said the barley was good, and it too was all cut and stacked.[16]

Rae recognized that Ahtahkakoop and his leading men were responsible, capable men. They were "evidently trying to do their best," the agent said, and were willing to give the government farmer some seed grain and potatoes for "safe keeping" until spring. He also noted that the amount of land broken was not as great as he would have liked, but he acknowledged that this was due to the "scarcity of work cattle" and the amount of time put into their homes, stables, and other facilities.

Ahtahkakoop and Rae had several discussions during the agent's tour of the reserve. One of the topics evidently centred on the distribution of provisions and the government's "food for work" policy. Rae reported that at the request of the chief, he spoke to the headmen and men who were present. "[I] told them plainly that the provisions we were giving out were for the men who worked only," the agent said, "and that I would visit the reserve frequently and see what work was being done for the provisions I gave them; that as long as I saw that they were really trying to get on, I would help them with tools and provisions when necessary."[17] With that said, the agent left it to Ahtahkakoop and his headmen to supervise the distribution of the provisions as they thought best.

Farm instructor George Chaffee, meanwhile, was getting settled on the "home farm" situated on the Green Lake Trail a few miles north of the Mistawasis Reserve. He had 30 acres of land broken, a house, storehouse, root house, granary, stable, a team of horses, and one-and-a-half yokes of oxen. His staff and helpers included an assistant, an interpreter, and Indian labourers.[18]

Probably because of the distance and the fact that good progress was being made at Sandy Lake under the guidance of the chief, his headmen, and Hines, the farm instructor made very few visits to the Ahtahkakoop Reserve. As a result, the people were left alone to work out the many adjustments required in their new life without interference from a government official.

During 1880 the white man's religion was beginning to drive a wedge between families in the Ahtahkakoop and Mistawasis bands. Mistawasis had, for some time, wanted an ordained missionary living on his reserve. When requests to the Church Missionary Society were ignored, the chief asked the Presbyterians to come, and they accepted.[19]

Hines, who was advised by his superiors to abandon the missionary work at Snake Plain and turn his attention towards two reserves northwest of Prince Albert, was bitter. In his view, the Presbyterians—even after they agreed to send a missionary to Mistawasis's people—made little effort to start work on the reserve. As an example, Hines said that although a man had been hired to build a church and house at Snake Plain, a minister had made only two or three visits to the reserve over a period of many months. Moreover, he stayed only a few hours each time. The Asissipi missionary compared this to his own experiences in 1874, writing that he had been left on the shore of Whitefish Lake on the eve of winter with David Stranger, a few supplies, three oxen, two horses, and no buildings. A site had not been chosen for his mission, the nearest Indians were not friendly, and there were no Indian houses—or any other house for that matter—nearby. It was, he said, a time of great anxiety. To make his predicament even more difficult, Hines said he had problems getting good teachers. He also had to travel back and forth, first between Whitefish and Sandy lakes, and then Sandy Lake and Snake Plain to administer to the needs of the people. The

Anglican missionary did not mention it, but he also had to build his first house and other buildings with logs cut by himself and his helper. Despite his depth of feelings, Hines nevertheless continued to hold services at Snake Plain during 1880. His efforts were appreciated by many and he was called to the reserve to baptize the young and the sick.[20] Hines closed the school on the Mistawasis Reserve at the end of June, 1880. Pritchard, who had taught at Snake Plain since 1878,[21] enrolled at Emmanuel College in Prince Albert.

Hines did not record Ahtahkakoop's reaction to the changes, and he did not indicate if the decision affected the relationship between the two chiefs. Regardless, in the months and years to come, splits developed between relatives and friends.

At Sandy Lake, interest in Christianity and the mission continued to grow throughout 1880. Construction of the church, which was situated 70 yards from the lake, was progressing well with the assistance of a carpenter. In July Hines reported that the men "belonging" to the mission each gave a day's work at the church, and by the end of the month the carpenter had completed his part of the construction. Another tradesman, this time a plasterer from Prince Albert, was at work in September. Hines said he designed the seats himself and "all were made by David and myself."[22]

Disaster threatened on December 4 when a fire broke out in the new church. Louis Ahenakew, along with a man and two women who were at Hines's house, helped carry pails of water from the lake to fight the fire. They successfully put it out, but Hines said the man froze his hands so badly he would "lose a greater part of the winter with his hands." The others also froze their hands, but less severely.[23]

A meeting was held in the school December 24, 1880, to formalize the operation of the new church. Of their own accord, the people decided "that the women folk should occupy the seats on one side of the aisle and the men folk on the other."[24] The people selected Peter Kāh-kasōw and Jacob Sasakamoose to serve as church wardens. Baptiste Ahenakew, described by Hines as "quite a young man, 'son of good old David Ahenakew,'" was chosen as church keeper. It was decided that the offering on Christmas Day would be divided between Hines, the wardens, church keeper, and the Asissipi church fund. And, as they had been doing for the past two winters, Ahtahkakoop's people agreed to keep the church clean and to supply firewood for the school and Sunday services. They also promised to cut fence rails and posts for the church yard.

The offerings on Christmas Day consisted of muskrat skins, cotton handkerchiefs, and household articles such as cups, saucers, and plates. Some people also gave notes written in syllabics saying they would donate tea and flour. Hines estimated the value of the offering at $14.[25]

Fifteen adults and 25 children had been baptized during the year and there were 17 new communicants. According to Hines, 11 people–seven adults and four children–died in 1880. This compares to eight listed in the treaty paylists for the period between treaty payments; Hines's figure covered a different time period and would have included Stranger's daughter and others who were not members of Ahtahkakoop's band.[26]

With Stranger and Pritchard both attending Emmanuel College and the mission growing larger month by month, Hines and his wife set about managing church activities with the assistance of the wardens and the church keeper. Because of the expense, the decision was made not to hire another teacher and the couple, with the assistance of student teacher Louis Ahenakew, took over the teaching duties at the school. Average attendance, according to government records, was 16. The schoolhouse was comfortable, well-built and considered by government officials to be a good one.[27]

In addition to regular classes, Hines organized special events for the children. One such occurrence took place on December 31 when John and Emma Hines invited the children to tea at their home. Then, in the evening, the youngsters gathered at the school with their parents to enjoy "a well hung" Christmas tree, "the gathering of whose fruit was left for the enjoyment of the Scholars. Over 100 prizes were given in this way which consisted of articles of clothing from dear friends in England,—dried apples, peppermints, & sundry other things."[28] This was the first Christmas seen by some of the people, Hines said, and it was enjoyed by both young and old.

Despite the festivities, life was not good. Hines wrote in December of 1880 that "poverty is a weak word to describe the distress of our people."[29] The wheat crops had failed and the harvest from the barley and potato fields was far too small to last the winter. The soup pots, once rich with buffalo meat, were no longer full of nutritious, protein-rich food. Meat from deer, moose, elk, and small animals such as rabbits and muskrats was added to the thin broth when available, but increased hunting pressures were reducing the number of these animals. As a consequence, the amount of meat being eaten was considerably less than the people were accustomed to. And far too often there was no meat.

To add to the problems, muskrats were the only fur-bearing animals killed during the winter of 1880–81. Without money, credit advances, furs, and country produce to trade, the people were unable to purchase the ammunition, traps, and other equipment needed to trap and hunt. Even if they had been available, under the new regime long hunting and trapping trips were discouraged.

Not surprisingly, illness as well as hunger were rampant. *Kiwetin** that came from the south signifying the beginning of the end of winter brought little relief.[30] There were at least five deaths in February and March, and three more in April. One of the dead was the widow of Wāskitoy, the head-man who had died the previous year.[31] The rest were children, five of whom were under seven years of age. Hines wrote in his journal on March 6, 1881, that "for every birth, we have had 3 deaths for the last 3 years."[32]

---

* *Kiwetin* are winds that come from the north, taking over the land and making it winter. As spring approaches, *Kiwetin* head home to the north country.

CHAPTER TWENTY-TWO

Fort Carlton Chiefs Meet With the Marquis of Lorne, 1881-1882

With another disastrous winter behind them, Ahtahkakoop, his people, and John Hines geared up for a memorable occasion, the dedication of the new Anglican church at Sandy Lake. Hines and Stranger had built the church with the help of two workmen from Prince Albert and volunteer labour from band members. Several people had saved it from destruction in a fire on December 4, and a considerable amount of effort—and soul-searching—had been invested in learning a new religion. In naming the church, Hines fulfilled a promise to himself made in 1874 after he landed in North America. He explained that the boat from England

> arrived at New Jersey on a Sunday, in time for morning service, and the Bishop preached in the evening. After the long rough passage it did seem pleasant and I did enjoy the services, so much so that I promised then and there that the first Church I might be privileged to build I would call St. Mark's, after the name of the little church in which we had worshipped that day. This promise I faithfully kept.[1]

And so the little log church overlooking Sandy Lake was called St. Mark's.

The Bishop of Saskatchewan, the Reverend John McLean, left Prince Albert for the Ahtahkakoop Reserve on May 6 to dedicate St. Mark's. He kept a journal of the trip that graphically retells the story of his journey and the events that took place at the Mistawasis and Ahtahkakoop reserves.[2]

> May 6th, 1881.—Started from Prince Albert in company with the Rev. Canon Mackay, C.M.S. Secretary. The same day we crossed

the Saskatchewan at Carlton, and camped about a mile beyond the river.

May 7th.—Continued our journey. About 3 p.m. we reached Snake Plain (Big Child's reserve). It is a very fine section of the country, well wooded and watered, the soil being good and well adapted for farming. We had service in the chief's house—thirty persons present. I addressed them at some length, explaining the work that the C.M.S. had done among their brethren at Red River, Moose, Athabasca, and throughout Rupert's Land generally, and expressing my regret that in their anxiety to have a separate missionary stationed at Snake Plain, the chief and some of the people should have separated themselves from Mr. Hines' Mission, and invited a Presbyterian minister to come amongst them after all he had done for them. The service was conducted in Cree by Canon Mackay. I was much pleased to notice how heartily they joined in.

After service we left for Asisippi [the Asissipi Mission at Sandy Lake] which we reached the same night, and where we were hospitably entertained by Mr. and Mrs. Hines. The country through which we passed was very beautiful, and contains a great deal of good farming land. The reserve at Asisippi is well chosen, and possesses every natural advantage in the way of wood, water, and good soil, to render it a most desirable location for the Indians. The Mission buildings are excellent. The Church is a neat substantial edifice—just what I should call a model Mission Church. It owes much of its neatness to the personal efforts of Mr. Hines, who did a great deal towards it with his own hands. The dwelling house is commodious and comfortable, strongly and neatly built, and likely to last for many years. I cannot help thinking that independently of the comfort of the missionary, it is a great point gained to have a neat and comfortable mission house. It becomes in some sort a model for the Indians. In the neat, tidy appearance of some of their small dwelling houses, I recognised the effect of the excellent example set before them by Mr. Hines.

Sunday, May 8th.—Morning service in the Church (St. Mark's), at 10.30 a.m. The service was conducted in Cree by the Rev. Canon Mackay, and the Rev. Mr. Hines. I was pleased to notice the ease and clearness with which Mr. Hines read the service. He has mastered the language so well that he can now preach in it and converse with the people readily. My sermon was interpreted by the Rev. Canon Mackay. I then confirmed fifty-two persons, including "Star Blanket," the chief of the Asisippi Indians, and two of his councillors.* Of these, eight were from the Snake Plain reserve, one being a councillor. The latter, an old man,† walked the whole distance of twenty-five miles to be present at the service. In the afternoon there was a second service, when Canon Mackay preached, and Holy Communion was administered to twenty-eight persons. I stated that I would be glad to meet the heads of families in the School House on Monday.

May 9th.—A meeting was held of the heads of families in the School House. There was a full attendance. I addressed them with special reference to the progress made at Asisippi, and the state of things at Snake Plain reserve. I pointed out that the fact of eight persons having come all the way from that reserve to Asisippi to be confirmed and to partake of Holy Communion, was a sufficient proof that they valued their connection with the Church of England Mission, and that, therefore, both Mr. Hines and myself felt that it would be his duty to visit and exercise a pastoral charge over these members of the Church, and any others who might prefer remaining in connection with the C.M.S. Mission.

I then invited any of the Indians present to narrate their experiences and give their views. The first who stood up was the councillor from Snake Plain. He said, "I am much rejoiced at the prospect of the Mission being continued at the Snake Plain, I love the Church of England, her services, her teaching, and her Prayer Book. I never miss an opportunity of attending the Church at Asisippi for Holy Communion, though I travel twenty-five miles to do so."

The next speaker was "Star Blanket," the chief of the Asisippi Indians. He is a fine intelligent-looking old man, and has used his

---

* Since Sasakamoose and Wāsēhikot were both there, it appears that Kā-miyo-ahcahk-wēw was absent.

† Pierre Stone, who was also known as Pierre Cardinal.

influence among the Indians in forwarding the work of the Mission. He said, "I am glad to see you. My heart has been full of thankfulness these two days. I was once a poor heathen—ignorant of God. I heard the truth of the Gospel through Mr. Hines. For a time I was unsettled, but now I believe in the Saviour, and never have any desire to return to my old ways. In the old times I have camped on the very spot where the Church is now standing. I was then engaged in hunting or making war. I thank God for what I see to-day. I regard the building of the Mission as God's work, and the coming of the Bishop seems to be the completion of the work. The Indians of my band have the same thankful feelings as myself. With God's help I will give all the aid I can to the Mission as long as I have strength to sit up. I do not claim credit for turning my people to the Christian religion, it was their own work."

"Star Blanket" was followed by his brother, Jacob Susukwumos, a councillor. He said, "I, too, am thankful for what I see today. I almost cried yesterday when I saw the Bishop and two clergymen in our Church. I have been not only a heathen, but a conjuror or medicine man. I knew every heathen superstition; I paid to be taught all the mysteries. God has seen fit to change my mind, and I am now a Christian. The change must have come from God—it could not have come from myself. God showed me that I was in the power of the evil one, and that I could only escape by coming to Jesus. Both I, and the others here, were brought to the Saviour by God's blessing on the teaching of Mr. Hines. I heard in Church yesterday that heathen superstitions were crumbling away, and that Christianity is growing and spreading. I believe this is true. I am thankful to see the Church completed and the mission growing so strong. I remember that in my heathen days I once camped with my wife and child on the very spot where the Church door now is. I felt very lonely—just like a beast, for I knew not God. I little thought then, though no doubt God had ordained it, that in the very place where I sat, the Church would be built, and that my wife would be the first buried there. She was then, like myself, a poor heathen, but before she died she was brought to Jesus, and was a baptised member of His Church. Her favourite hymn during her last illness was:

"Alas! and did my Saviour bleed,
And did my Sovereign die?"

When he had finished Peter Kakasoo (the hider) rose and said, "From the first time I heard the Gospel I believed it and tried to follow it. My constant effort has been to help the progress of the work. I hope we shall receive a supply of Cree prayer books in the syllabic character. They are much wanted in the mission."

On inquiry I found that this Indian was the first man baptised at Asisippi by Mr. Hines; that he then became a Scripture reader to the Indians in the plains, and that he has been a great help to Mr. Hines.

Wāsēhikot, who had replaced Kīsik-awāsis as headman, said he had great confidence in the chief and was glad to follow his example. "I believed from the first time I ever heard," he stated. McLean described Ahenakew's son as a good-looking young man with a "graceful action in speaking."[3]

Then Ahtahkakoop told about his children being baptized by Catholic priests while he was away on the warpath. "From time to time the priest came to my camp, and baptised one after another of my children," Ahtahkakoop recounted. "I, myself, was never at home when he came, and both my wife and myself remained heathen. My children as they grew older were never taught anything by the priest. They grew up quite ignorant of Christianity."[4]

The chief went on to say that when he asked a Roman Catholic bishop to send someone to teach them, the clergyman

promised to send a priest as teacher in about a year from that time, but I waited eleven years and no teacher came. At last Mr. Hines arrived and began to teach from the Bible. I invited him to be our minister. In a short time he established his mission here. Some time after this I again saw the Roman Catholic Bishop. He told me I had done wrong in going to a Protestant minister. I replied that the Roman Catholic priests had done nothing but baptised my children—that they had let them grow up without giving them any instruction, and that he, the Bishop, had not kept his promise to send a priest as teacher. After I invited Mr. Hines to stay with my band, I spoke to the Snake Plain Indians, and they all agreed to join in receiving instruction from him. I, myself, and wife and one of my children have been baptised by Mr. Hines. Four of my children, who were baptised by the Roman Catholic priest, were instructed by Mr. Hines and confirmed yesterday.[5]

Following the meeting in the schoolhouse, another service was held in the church; six more people were confirmed, bringing the total to 58.

Louis Ahenakew was one of those confirmed during the Sunday service. Under the guidance of Hines, and with the encouragement of his family, the boy had learned quickly at school and converted to Christianity at an early age. Now he was ready to take another step in furthering his education, and Hines asked during the bishop's visit that Louis be sent to Emmanuel College. With some pride, the bishop recorded in his journal that Louis was a communicant entirely trained at the mission.[6] The request was approved and arrangements were made for Louis to enroll in the collegiate school at Emmanuel College in the fall.

Farming activities on the reserve had gone well during the spring of 1881. Thirty additional acres were cultivated and wheat, barley, potatoes, and small vegetables sown. In late May the Indian agent reported that both the crops and Ahtahkakoop's people were "doing capitally." He reported, however, that the band did not have enough cattle and at least two more yokes of oxen were needed. The families, he said, intended on breaking another 75 to 100 acres during the summer and "were determined to do their best."[7] Government officials were particularly pleased since Ahtahkakoop's band, at Hines's prompting, had built their houses and planted their gardens and crops on individual, separate plots of land, even before the treaties were signed. This was in line with government policy that encouraged farmers to work individual fields.[8]

What was overlooked—but more likely intentionally disregarded—was the fact that this practice was contrary to the traditional communal way of life. Moreover, it had distinct drawbacks. For Hines, the most obvious were the problems resulting from homes being located some distance from the school and church. Attendance suffered during miserable weather, and trips to visit the sick were often arduous. For band members, the placement of the homes meant unaccustomed isolation from family and friends.

Nevertheless, the people were doing remarkably well in their quest to learn a new way of living. The government, Hines wrote in June, considered the Ahtahkakoop Band to be the "most provident of all the bands in the Saskatchewan District & the most civilized."[9] Church and government officials tended to credit the missionaries for the progress on reserves such as Ahtahkakoop's. Dewdney, for example, had written the previous year that besides teaching the children, the "advice & counsel of experienced missionaries have made the Indians of these reservations more tractable than those that have not had the same advantage."[10] The Indian commissioner ignored the fact that Hines and several of the other missionaries were on the reserves at the request of the chiefs and their leading men. In Ahtahkakoop's case, he had been waiting 11 years for someone to come and teach his children and grandchildren. Once the chief found Hines, he was willing to work with him to build a future for his band in a rapidly changing world. Part of this responsibility was encouraging his people to farm. The work was tiring, particularly since tools and implements were primitive and few in numbers. Each plough and harrow was shared by three families. The wheat and barley were sown by hand, and the grain and hay were hand-cut using scythes. The grain was usually threshed with sticks or flails. Far too often, it was a great deal of work with little to show for the effort.

Early in August, for the first time since Treaty Six was signed, the annuities were paid at the individual reserves instead of at Fort Carlton. Indian agent Rae arrived at Ahtahkakoop's reserve August 5. The chief, two of his headmen (Sasakamoose and Wāsēhikot), and 185 band members received their payments in 1881.[11] Headman Kā-miyo-ahcahkwēw, his wife, and four children were absent. The family was not included in the 1881 total but remained on the paylist.[12] Interestingly, Kīsik-awāsis and his family were removed from the Ahtahkakoop paylist without any written comment by the agent.* The names of 30 other people, along with their dependants, were also deleted from the paylist without comment; these people had not taken their annuities with Ahtahkakoop's band for at least two years. On the positive side, five men with 12 family members and two older women had returned to the reserve after missing the previous year's payment.

The paylist, augmented by Hines's mission records, provides other information. Kāh-kāsōw and Mēmēkwaniwēw (Feather-Voice),[†] for

---

* According to the Red Pheasant paylist, Kīsik-awāsis was at Victoria, near Edmonton, when the treaty payments were made in 1881.

† Mēmēkwaniwēw was the son of Ahtahkakoop's nephew, John Peter Masuskapoe. He chose William as his Christian name; his descendants later took Williams for their surname.

instance, had new sons. And Baptiste Ahenakew, Kā-miyo-ahcahkwēw, Nayneecassum (Glittering), Sōniyaw-āyāwēw (He Has Money), Piyēsīs (Bird), and Kā-tāh-twēhototawāt (Bird Landing On Someone Repeatedly) all had new daughters.*

The treaty paylist for 1881 also indicates that six girls, four boys, and two women had died. The dead included Wāskitoy's widow, a girl in Sasakamoose's family, and one of Ahtahkakoop's grandchildren (the daughter of Mary and Edward Genereux). Additionally, two girls and a woman on Otinikēw's ticket were dead.† One of Otinikēw's sons had died the previous year, so in a two-year period the man lost his wife and three children. On a happier note, Ahtahkakoop's 18-year-old daughter Philomene married Johnny Jimmuk from the Mistawasis Band in May of 1881.[13] Jimmuk was also known as John James Dufraine.

Several weeks after the treaty payments were made, the Marquis of Lorne, governor general of Canada, arrived at Fort Carlton to meet with the chiefs of the district.[14] He was Queen Victoria's son-in-law, as well as her official representative. The governor general's first council in the North-West Territories had been at Fort Qu'Appelle where he met with Treaty Four chiefs, leading men, and Standing Buffalo,[15] a Dakota chief. Standing Buffalo, who had spoken first, expressed his gratitude for being on British soil. He asked for a church, a school, clothing, ammunition, and farm implements so he and his people could live like white men. The governor general said help would be given to build a school and implements and food would be given to those who worked. Spokesmen for the Treaty Four chiefs then told the governor general that "all those here wish to live," but they could not "live by the first Treaty." In order to survive, many had to eat their dogs and horses, and even some of the oxen that had been given to them. The chiefs asked for more implements and oxen, as well as clothing and food. Others added pigs, sheep, horses, buckboards, wagons, guns, threshing machines, needles and thread, and the services of a doctor to the list. If assistance, particularly in the form of food and clothing, was not given for the upcoming winter "plenty of us will die," one chief had told the Queen's representative. The chiefs also had complaints about their

---

* Piyēsīs was married to Ahtahkakoop's second daughter named Mary, while Kā-tāh-twēhototawāt was the husband of the chief's daughter Emma.

† *Otinikēw* translates as Taking Something, i.e., Signing Treaty.

agent and farm instructors and their lack of authority to make decisions. They said that promises made under the treaty were not kept, and they objected to the colour of the red coats that had been given to them.[16]

The Marquis of Lorne was apparently under the impression that the Indian people who were farming in the Carlton area were making a good living. For this reason, perhaps, his initial reaction to the Fort Qu'Appelle chiefs was generally unsympathetic. "I have heard many eloquent speeches. I am quite sure that men who speak so well can work as well as their red brethren in the Sask," he scolded. "Hands were not given by Manitou to fill pipes only but to work. I am sure that red men … [in] the Sask when they work do well and do not starve and I have noticed that the men who talk most and ask most do not work."[17]

Based on Sidney P. Hall, National Archives of Canada, C-012943

Standing Buffalo addressing the Marquis of Lorne, August 18, 1881.

The governor general had assured the Treaty Four chiefs, nevertheless, that he understood "the difficulties they have put before me and I pity and sympathize & know that it is hard to take to new things." The people used to make a living "in the old days in the chase" and now they had to make a living out of the land. He knew their hearts were good, the Marquis of Lorne continued, and agreed it was difficult to work with "too few animals." He said he would see if oxen and implements could be given to those "who shew a disposition to work." Additionally he cautioned them about "breaking treaty for the treaty was made for them and their children's good."

At the conclusion of the meeting the chiefs were given food and "warm & light" clothing to distribute among the women "at their discretion." A medal was also presented to Chief Day Star "because he has worked well on his farm." The Marquis of Lorne noted in his report that "this medal is

Sidney P. Hall, National Library of Canada, NL-17732

The North-West Mounted Police, under the direction of Superintendent W.M. Herchmer and with the help of a single scow, transported 80 horses, 19 wagons, several ambulances, buckboards, and more than 50 men across the South Saskatchewan River at Batoche.

one given to the Chiefs who shew the best disposition to carry out the treaties."

The governor general met with the chiefs and leading men of the Carlton district on August 26, 1881. A sketch drawn by Sidney P. Hall, an English artist who accompanied the Marquis of Lorne on his tour of the North-West, indicates that the council was likely held at the Hudson's Bay Company's Big House, the home and office of Chief Factor Lawrence Clarke.[18] An article written by another member of the government party noted that the Cree at the meeting were dressed like "ordinary mortals," and many of them had short hair.[19] Nevertheless, not everyone was dressed in that fashion. According to another report, the Dakota chief White Cap "wore a beautiful snow-white tunic of fine caribou skin, richly ornamented with porcupine quills, coloured silk, and bead work. From his shoulders hung some twenty or thirty scalps taken in the horrible Minnesota* massacre."[20]

---

* The Dakota Sioux Uprising of 1862.

Sidney P. Hall, National Library of Canada, NL-17725

North-West Mounted Police at the Batoche Crossing driving some of the 80 horses in the Marquis of Lorne's party across the South Saskatchewan River.

The official report of the council stated that Ahtahkakoop and Mistawasis were "the principal Cree Chiefs of the N.W. and represent the Cree Nation of the Woods & on the plains."[21] Although an English translation of the proceedings was recorded in this report, the name of the interpreter was not given.

Chief Mistawasis spoke first. The Snake Plain chief said that although he had no "great complaints," he wanted to say a few words about the poverty of his people. The "kindness" shown to them by the government was good, he said, but it was not enough

> to put us on our feet.... [we] want strength which means help! The white man knows where strength comes from. The Indians see the same. They want animals, that is where strength comes. As crops increase we want more power, and we know not what to do with our present and future crops, unless more strength is given us we shall starve. The Indian cannot lift himself up. If we are successful in bringing in our crops I would ask if there is any way of obtaining a grist mill by which to grind our wheat. I speak not only for myself but for all.[22]

Shouts of agreement rose from the gathered chiefs and leading men, and then Mistawasis continued:

> My gratitude I cannot express when I see the Gov[n] General who has just come in time for me to see him. Many a time I had not provisions, was deprived of them but I was never angry. The agent has been kind to us and was acting to his instructions. I felt there was no use to grumble. Many a time I was very sad when I saw my poor people all starving and I could do nothing for them.

Waiting in the fenced yard in front of the Big House at Fort Carlton, where the meeting took place, August 26, 1881.

We want teachers for schools. I am short of firearms and ammunition and cannot kill what I require. It will be a great help to us in winter. We have tried to carry out all the instructors advice on his farm. I know that cultivating the ground is the only way of living, that I deserve help in this as the animals which gave . . . [us our] living are gone & will not return. I would like to know if the implements & cattle I have asked for will be given me—as I said before it is not for myself for I am becoming old & wish before I leave my children & grandchildren I would like to see them settled & strong.

At the time of Treaties it was mentioned that while the sun rose & set and the water ran, the faith in the treaties was to be kept. I was always peaceful since a child with the whites and am anxious to be friendly with those now coming. There are others to speak. I am glad to hear that the representative of the Queen is here and I hope to get what I ask.[23]

Chief Ahtahkakoop spoke next.

I have reason to be thankful to see His Excellency and since this [treaty] medal was put on my neck from the Great Mother I am thankful—& all my tribe—to see the Great Mother's representative here that I will speak for her as I speak for my children. I am a poor man and now will express my views on this subject, but as I look round I do not see anything I could live by. I see nothing, all that I used to live on has gone. Where I used to get my … [living] was the animal the buffalo, and also I had horses, now the buffalo and the horses have left me. I say with that I am a poor man.

You may have seen the poverty of the land as regards the animal —that was my hunting ground. I used to find them all I wanted. Now it is a solitary wilderness. I find nothing there, when I look at all this I see but one thing left, that is to work the ground. I am too old to work but I think of my children & grandchildren they may learn.

The first thing [we want] is some strength, i.e. farm implements & cattle—these are necessary. If we dont progress faster than in the past years, we shall move very shortly and my Grandchildren will not see it for we walk very slowly now. Why I say this is that the crops we have raised the half was spoilt as sickness came on us and my people could not work. I remember right on the treaty it was said that if any famine or trouble came the Government would see to us and help. My trouble arose from partly starvation and sickness. The remedy I ask for now. We want nets, we want guns. I ask for these only for living. There is another thing we lack. When I take a flail to thrash I lose part of my wheat. I want a thrashing machine. A thrasher and a reaper and the power to work them. There is no end to my losses. I loose [*sic*] in the thrashing. I have miles sometimes to go through the snow to have my grain ground, and I only am able to bring back a handful [of flour]. I make no doubt that His Excellency will sympathize with us, that he will open his heart towards the trouble of his Indian Children. What we want is speedy help on my farms. I have no more to say. I wish to be remembered to the Great Mother & to the Princess and please remember me in the cold winter days & give me covering for my women and children.[24]

There was consensus among the other chiefs that they required additional assistance in order to farm and adapt successfully to their new life.

Chief John Smith said the first thing he wanted was a teacher so he and the children could learn to speak English. He also wanted a "native missionary" who was supported by the government "to preach to them." His other wants were many, but a reaper and implements to work the farms were needed the most. "I try to work. I want help not for myself, for my children," he said. "I have tried to do what the white man has told me and I have done my best." In closing, he said that some of his people who still lived in the north "would like land and would come & live with me."[25]

John Smith's brother, Chief James Smith, told the governor general that his "wants" were the same as the chiefs who had spoken before him. He wanted his reserve surveyed as soon as possible, oxen to replace the ones that were "nearly all gone" or were sick, and a horse, since he "had to come on foot and will have to return some way." Ayahtaskamikinam, the chief from Sturgeon Lake, said "the wants of the other chiefs are mine but this is an addition. The reserve that was laid out for me, I would like to sell the wood." He asked for ammunition and some twine for making nets, in addition to the requests made by his friends. "It is the want of these things & implements that keep us back," he explained. Ayahtaskamikinam also said that he wanted an Indian agent who could speak Cree.[26]

Chief Petihkwahākēw, who had replaced Kitowēhāw as chief of the Muskeg Lake Band, told the governor general that he agreed "with these old men who have spoken," and then he asked for "implements like the white man uses—a thrashing mill and Fanning Mill," as well as oxen. He was also concerned about the survey of his reserve: three houses built by band members had been left outside the boundaries and he wished "they had been left in." In regards to hunger and sickness, he stated that they could not "find anything to give to the sick—nothing fresh that they may require. Its from want of provisions that there is so much sickness." He ended his speech with an interesting question, put forth without any additional comment or clarification: "Who is the master of these animals on our reserve?"

Chief Cakāstēpēsin endorsed what the others had said, adding that he wanted "help besides what was given at the Treaty. Also I would like my reserve to be put right." And Beardy said that "everything that was promised at the Treaty I want fulfilled now," including a yoke of oxen and a cow for "each 3 heads of families." He also asked for "something fresh" to eat for his families, some clothing for the children, and shoes for the men. He concluded by asking that food be given to the people at Fort Carlton for the journey home.

Glenbow Archives, Calgary, NA-1032-5   Based on Sidney P. Hall, National Archives of
                                              Canada, C-012969

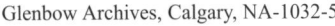

Chief Beardy, shown on the left in earlier days, chose a reserve at Duck Lake. On the right, he is addressing the Marquis of Lorne, Governor General of Canada. The inscription on the lower right reads: "Above is Beardy's signature written by his secretary in Cree characters." The writing on the lower left reads "Aug. 26. The great 'Beardy' making speech at pow-wow, Ft. Carlton."

"I am glad to have heard what has been said through the Chiefs and I shall give the messages to the Queen they have sent ... their homage," the Marquis of Lorne responded. "I shall be able to tell her that I have found them good chiefs and attending to the advice of the Government, and I like to hear that the young chiefs are following the example of old chiefs who have taken to farming."

Then the Marquis of Lorne told the chiefs that he had

> come from the Queen to enquire about you but not to change the treaty. At the same time I have come to give presents to those who will work beyond what treaty has been promised. I am glad to find that govt has done even more than promised by Treaty. You must remember that you are numerous, that it cost the Government much money to help them and that the Queen has to take care of all her children some white men as well as red and I

have heard where the sun rises that the white men complain that too much is given to her red children and not enough to white— therefore Chiefs must understand that however much they may be loved.

Following the governor general's statement, Ahtahkakoop rose for the second time. He had heard several chiefs express concern about the surveys of their reserves and he decided to add his voice to the others. "I keep true to what was told me. I got a reserve & I wish to keep it for my children," he began, but "the wood is of no use on part of my reserve. I don't see that we can get a living off it. I went to the Governor (Mr. Laird) about it. If it is surveyed over again, I would wish to have as much. Some of my people are not with me now but they might come back. I would like to show the Surveyor a paper showing him what I wanted. I would wish for an answer."[27]

When Ahtahkakoop was finished speaking, the two northern chiefs, Okīnomotayēw and Kā-ohpatawakinam, spoke. After endorsing what the other chiefs had said, Okīnomotayēw stated that he would like "the people at the back here to come on to my reserve. I was building my house this spring and I had to leave off for I had nothing to eat. I want help. I am always starving all the way when I come here. I borrowed provisions to bring me here, Flour, Bacon, Tea and Shot." Okīnomotayēw also said he would like some oxen to take him home. Kā-ohpatawakinam, when he spoke, agreed with Ayahtaskamikinam "in all he said." Moreover, he heard his reserve was being surveyed* and he wanted a wagon "like the other chiefs," a "double barrelled gun & some twine for making nets and some oxen," and other animals promised in the treaty.

The last chief to take part in the council was One Arrow, who was too ill to stand. He spoke through a "deputy," saying that he wanted more oxen and another cow, "which is due to me. I would wish to get some clothing for the children to keep them warm, & something to eat today & some food to take home with me and stores for children yet unborn."[28]

With the speeches drawing to a close, the governor general assured the Indian leaders that "the Treaties will be kept … Many present have made very sensible requests and I hope that help will be given by gifts of more implements and oxen to those who try and help themselves. The Government are also endeavouring to make places for schools."

---

* It was surveyed in August, 1881.

Sidney P. Hall, National Archives of Canada, C-12980

The chiefs and leading men from the Battleford and Fort Pitt areas assembled at Battleford to meet the Marquis of Lorne.

Then he told the chiefs that "in memory of this visit a medal is to be given to 2 chiefs who had proved themselves worthy, and that also on this occasion, food, clothing and a suit of clothes for each chief will be given and also some blankets." There were presents for the women, and it was announced that sufficient food would be given for the journey home.[29] The medals, made of silver "with medallion busts of the princess and ... [the Marquis of Lorne]," were presented to Mistawasis and Ahtahkakoop.[30]

Following his meeting with the Carlton chiefs, the governor general boarded the steamboat *Lilly* for the journey to Battleford where he was to meet with chiefs of that area. At the territorial capital, the governor general repeated the message that he had not come "to alter treaties but to ... see how by keeping the treaties I can help them to live." And he told them that the other chiefs were having few difficulties.[31]

The chiefs and headmen at the Battleford council seemed reluctant to speak at first, but when they did, their requests were similar to those at Fort Qu'Appelle and Fort Carlton. They wanted to farm, but to do so they needed more help. There were requests for oxen, small implements, and modern equipment like the white men had, as well as instruction on how to use them. They talked about being hungry, sick, and poorly clothed, and said they had no way of fixing implements when they broke.

The Marquis of Lorne promised that oxen and smaller implements would be "given to the deserving & those recommended by the agents, and through their friend Mr. Dewdney,* whom the government and the Queen trust. That Mr. Dewdney wishes those who work to receive more implements, that they must come and see Mr. Dewdney in regards to their small wants." He told the chiefs they would be given food to take home, and "though not asked for they would have tea, sugar, tobacco, and blankets." Some fresh meat would be distributed, and the chiefs would be given some "prints" (cloth) for the women. The chiefs apparently did not receive suits and other clothing, and medals were not presented. The Marquis of Lorne concluded the council by saying that "We shall do our best in the winter to prevent any from starving. I am very sorry to hear many have been suffering and they must obey the instructions of the agents … the Queen will never allow her children white or red to starve. I hope you all enjoy your food."[32] Although it was not noted in the proceedings, some of the bands from the area were not represented since Big Bear, Lucky Man, Little Pine, and others were still trying to hunt buffalo in American territory. At the completion of the council at Battleford, the governor general and his party travelled to Blackfoot Crossing, the Peigan Reserve, and Fort Macleod to meet with the Treaty Seven chiefs.

In view of what the Marquis of Lorne had seen and heard during his visits to Fort Qu'Appelle and Fort Carlton, it is difficult to understand how he could have told the Battleford leaders that the other chiefs were experiencing no difficulties. He had been told that the animals were gone, the people were starving, often they were too sick to work in their fields, and many did not have enough clothing to see them through the winter. Additionally, none had enough cattle, implements, and land under cultivation to support themselves. And even if they had, hard work and good intentions were not always enough. As Ahtahkakoop had discovered numerous times, the forces of nature were often against them, with late and early frosts, too much or too little rain, and hail and grasshoppers destroying their crops.

The governor general's visit, nevertheless, had several positive repercussions. He affirmed the problems facing the Indian people of the plains and parklands, and he was prepared to report his findings to Queen Victoria and the governments of England and Canada. Most importantly, he assured

---

* Edgar Dewdney was appointed lieutenant-governor in 1881, in addition to his position as Indian commissioner.

the leading men, as her Majesty's representative, that the terms of the treaties would be honoured and that additional help would be given.

This did not go over particularly well with Canadian officials who were trying to cut costs. "It appears from the record of the various interviews had by His Excellency with the Indians," Lawrence Vankoughnet, deputy superintendent general of Indian Affairs wrote to Prime Minister Macdonald, "that His Excellency promised that more Schools should be established among them; that more agricultural implements and cattle should be given them, and provisions to those who work their lands."[33]

Unwilling to wait for the government to supply modern equipment, Ahtahkakoop and Mistawasis asked Indian agent Rae to buy a threshing machine for them. Rae agreed and arrangements were made for the machine "to be paid of by themselves in toll." This seemed like a sensible investment. The crops were better in 1881 than in the previous year, even though some fields were injured by frost. The two bands paid half of the purchase price the following spring.[34]

Louis Ahenakew was one of 30 boys enrolled in the collegiate program at Emmanuel College in the fall of 1881. According to church officials, "Greek, Latin, Mathematics and all the ordinary branches of an English Education … [were] taught" at this school.[35] Louis would not have felt completely alone. David Stranger had returned for his second year of studies to be ordained a deacon, and three teachers who had worked under Hines—A.A.H. Wright, Edward Matheson, and John Pritchard—were taking advanced studies at the college under the direction of Bishop McLean and Canon Mackay.[36] Hines had personally delivered Louis to Prince Albert. The missionary had high expectations for the young man, saying he hoped that Louis, who six years ago "knew next to nothing," would become an ordained minister. Louis more than held his own at the school. Ahenakew's son was "not only an honest and responsible boy," McLean and Mackay reported, "but his mental capacities bring him well into the foreground among those of European descent."[37]

While David Stranger and Louis Ahenakew attended school in Prince Albert, John and Emma Hines carried on with the school and church work at Ahtahkakoop's reserve. In addition to dispensing medicines and helping teach, Emma "held classes for women, at which prayer and the reading of portions of Scripture occupied their right proportion of time." The subjects, Hines said, were "cleanliness" and sewing. During the early part of the winter, Emma started a sewing class for the senior schoolgirls. Their first project was a patchwork quilt made from cloth and thread supplied from friends in England.[38]

The women and children were invited to the Hines's home one afternoon early in January for tea and a "magic lantern show." The men came at 6 p.m. The show made quite an impression and Hines noted in his journal that some who had been conjurers in earlier days were "more convinced than ever that they possessed no power or skill at all in working wonders."[39] The following week he gave the children a "Xmas tree" decorated with clothing and other articles that were distributed among them, giving both enjoyment and "comfort." Then, on January 29, the missionary noted in his journal with some satisfaction that he had baptized Cīpay-awāsis (Ghost-child), the oldest man at the mission. This man, he said, "has been very obstinate for a long time but has at last yielded to the Spirit's influence." He took Isaac as his Christian name.[40]

Even though the crops in 1881 were better than some years, rabbits and muskrats were numerous, and the Queen's son-in-law (The Marquis of Lorne) had promised that provisions would be supplied, food was scarce during the winter of 1881–82. The hunters in Ahtahkakoop's band shared their meat and pelts, and the farmers gave freely of what little produce they had, but it was not enough to ward off hunger. Inadequate food, overheated houses, and a change in lifestyle took their toll. When a three-year-old girl died on Ahtahkakoop's reserve on March 5, Hines wrote that this was only the third death during the winter and the "warm weather perhaps has been the reason of so few deaths." He nevertheless foresaw bleak days ahead, predicting one or two more would die as "the change of the moon has brought with it dull cold weather, & if it lasts the poor half-starved Indians will suffer much." The cold lasted, and it was stormy much of the month. On March 12 Hines noted that the sun had hardly been out since the full moon. Later he said it had been snowing every day and the roads were the worst he had ever seen them.

The people suffered in ways never documented or even acknowledged in government reports. "My wife contrives to make a large kettle of soup every day at noon," Hines wrote in his journal on March 12, and "we have some of the children in to dinner every day. If it were not for this, I think very few would be able to attend regularly. I watch some of them with an aching heart, they look so thin & cold. One poor boy I take in on the sly & give him a meal now & then extra, otherwise he would, I feel sure, break down. Why I take him in on the sly, is, that I may not hurt the feelings of the other children, he is certainly the most in need."[41]

Three-year-old Agnes Roundplain died March 16. Ten days later Hines visited the student who had been getting the extra food. The boy, his mother, and grandmother were all so sick the missionary said "I scarcely know which is nearest the grave." He baptized the grandmother (Maria Mōhkomānawēw*) on March 26 and she died within a day. The woman's three-year-old step-daughter died April 1.[42]

During these days of heartbreak, one event brought excitement into some of the homes. At the Asissipi Mission school the senior girls finished the quilts they had been working on during the winter. Hines said that although they had not been told, he was sure the students suspected the quilts were for them to keep.[43] The girls no doubt had already been taught to sew by their mothers, but the quilts were a new application of their skills. They could justly be proud of their achievement when they took the quilts home.

---

* Mōhkomānawēw translates as Knife Voice.

CHAPTER TWENTY-THREE

Ahtahkakoop Holds a Bear Ceremony, 1882-1883

S ad news from England hit John and Emma Hines relentlessly during the first months of 1882. Emma's father died on January 12. Her mother died a month later, and then the couple received word that Emma's sister, the last member of her family, was sick. Hines wrote the Church Missionary Society requesting permission to return to England for a short visit, but death would not wait and the sister died on April 19. This left the couple "practically alone in the world." Hines's father had died about 15 months after the young missionary left England and Emma's brother died several months after her marriage.[1]

Although it was the "rule of the Society" that missionaries work in the field for 10 years before taking their first furlough, John Hines's request to go to England for a visit was approved because of unusual circumstances. It was agreed that Stranger, who would be ordained a deacon in May, should take charge of the Asissipi Mission and Louis Ahenakew, 18, would temporarily leave his studies at Emmanuel College to manage the school.[2]

Since Emma's sister died before plans were settled, Hines postponed the trip until August and carried out his usual duties until departure time. He did not keep a journal during this period, but from other accounts the spring and summer apparently went well. Hines finally had a bit more money to work with since his request for a school grant from the government had been approved. Interest in the school was remaining constant as the children, encouraged by their parents, learned the skills of the newcomers. All of the students were learning to read, spell, and do arithmetic. Additionally, four were taking classes in writing, six were studying geography, and two were enrolled in music and singing classes. According to government documentation, 18 students were registered in 1882, with an average daily attendance of 14.[3] It is probable that more children were attending school than indicated by the government figures since the officials tended to underestimate the numbers.

In addition to his work on the Ahtahkakoop Reserve, Hines continued to visit at Snake Plain, where he claimed his church services outdrew those conducted by the Presbyterian minister. Hines wrote many years later that the Presbyterian minister,

> not liking this … came to see me and asked me to conduct my services in his Church in the morning, and he would occupy the pulpit in the afternoon, as the people, he said, were too few to be broken up into two congregations. I told him he should have thought of that before he came and settled at the mission, "besides, it would be a waste of Christian time and Christian usefulness to keep you here just for one service a week.[4]

Hines, Emma, and their daughter Henrietta left for England in August, before harvest. Stranger and Louis, as previously arranged, were left in charge of the mission and school.

Band members sowed 111 acres of land to crops and broke another 50 acres during the spring and summer of 1882. According to government documentation, which provided itemized details on farming activities for the first time, 65 acres were planted to wheat, 30 acres to barley, five acres to potatoes, five acres to turnips, one acre to carrots, and several acres to garden vegetables.[5] Indian agent Rae said there was no point having additional land broken in the Carlton Agency unless more oxen were sent. There were barely enough now to handle the work to be done, he reported, and at least another 10 yoke were needed. He recommended that some of the old oxen on the reserves should be killed to supply food for the treaty payments and replaced with younger animals.[6] Ahtahkakoop's band was luckier than some since it had nine oxen, and several families had privately owned stock.

Although there were changes within families and a small decline in population during the 1881–82 treaty paylist year, Ahtahkakoop's band had remained constant during this period. Thirty-one men, 45 women, 50 boys, 53 girls, and six "other persons," for a total of 185, had taken their payments in 1882. Kā-miyo-ahcahkwēw and his family were back. Six people (three girls, two boys, and a woman) had died and a girl and two boys were born. Michel Ahtahkakoop, the chief's youngest son, had married Mary Jane Okimāsis from One Arrow's band and had his own ticket. Wāskitoy's son, Thomas Mahkistikwān (Big Head) had also married; interestingly, and this was not uncommon, the wife was not included on his new ticket on the treaty paylist. In another change, a woman and a boy had transferred from Petihkwahākēw's band.[7]

Although the crops grew well in 1882 the actual outcome depends greatly on which report is used. Indian Commissioner Dewdney, in his year-end report, included Rae's statements that it had been a successful year. On September 11, for instance, the agent noted that the crops in the Carlton District looked good and returns would be double those of the previous year. Prospects were still excellent on October 27 when he reported that threshing was under way on most reserves and the yield of grain was far higher than the year before.[8]

These statements, however, did not tell the entire story. In a report dated December 4, Rae said that it rained heavily in the Carlton district after the grain was stacked and the harvest was not as good as expected. The threshing machines were breaking down, causing delays, and in all of the Prince Albert area, including Duck Lake, only three threshers were in running order.[9] The thresher purchased by Ahtahkakoop and Mistawasis was one of the implements that was broken. With no one to fix it, the machine was useless and all the threshing at Ahtahkakoop's reserve that year was done "with a flail on the ice."[10] The proceeds from the crop, nevertheless, made it possible for Ahtahkakoop and Mistawasis to pay the balance owing on the thresher in the fall of 1882. It had given them only one season of work.[11]

According to government officials, the farmers on the Ahtahkakoop Reserve cut 80 tons of hay in 1882. One thousand bushels of wheat were harvested, along with 400 bushels of barley, 570 bushels of potatoes, 2,800 bushels of turnips, and 50 bushels of carrots. The men and young men had also been busy with construction work, and during the past several years 19 houses and 12 stables had been built.[12]

After the harvest was finished, some of the men who owned oxen broke 50 acres of land for two nearby settlers. They were paid $5 an acre. Other men cut rails and fenced several hundred acres for the farmers.[13] As a result of this work, the families had much needed money to purchase clothing, blankets, food, traps, ice chisels, guns, and ammunition for the upcoming winter. The fields of grain and the gardens may have produced some food, but they did not provide cash for purchasing goods that previously had been obtained by trading at Fort Carlton.

T.P. Wadsworth, who had been appointed inspector of Indian agencies in 1879, was at the reserve in mid-October. It was a Saturday, and not surprisingly the school was not in session and Louis was away. The inspector noted in his report that Ahtahkakoop and Mistawasis had been settled for four years and had made good progress. Despite numerous statements by others that the two bands were doing very well, Wadsworth reported that "They do not show the rapid advancement of some, but it may be solid, the first enthusiasm has worn off, and there is some slight danger of their having reached the height of their ambition (which is not high) unless the supervision is continued." The chiefs, he noted, have no complaints but asked for government assistance for a longer time, saying "the better farmers they became, the less inclination and the less success they have in hunting." He said he "lectured" the farmers for not doing any fall ploughing and told them their crops next year would be late and caught by early frost, but "as the period when they would suffer for the negligence was so far off, they took the matter complacently."[14] Wadsworth then continued on his way. What he failed to note was the fact that a number of the men had been hired by local farmers that fall to work off the reserve. Although this had hampered work on the reserve, it provided cash for buying winter supplies.

The arrogant, paternalistic attitude of government officials like Wadsworth offended a good number of people at Ahtahkakoop's reserve. Chief factor Clarke at Fort Carlton, who was also a man known for arrogance, had to deal with many of the same people as Ahtahkakoop but he was in a better position to challenge them. His actions, nevertheless, drew adverse reaction from the government.

"Mr. Clarke is acting in every way possible against the Government," Indian agent Rae complained to Commissioner Dewdney in August, 1882. "He refuses to take cows, bulls, lumber and shingles on the sternwheelers unless the freight is prepaid, because he says he will not get paid. He even orders the clerks 'not to give postage stamps unless paid in cash.'" Another time Rae complained that Clarke ordered one of the employees to move everything out of the Indian department office at Fort Carlton, threatening to "put us out" if the man did not comply.[15]

Rae went on to accuse the Hudson's Bay Company officer of interfering with the Indians, saying that Clarke prevented Ayahtaskamikinam and

John Smith "from taking their seed wheat this spring," and he told Petihkwahākēw's band

> not to take the supplies I was offering them viz 50 lbs flour and 20 lbs bacon. Clarke then gave them 2 sacks of flour and 100 lbs bacon, some tea, sugar and tobacco. Whether he expects pay or not I cannot pay. The Indians, I believe, expect to get grub from Clarke for haying and harvest. It is a bad principle to establish, and some law should be passed inflicting both a fine and imprisonment on any man interfering injuriously in Indian matters.[16]

Dewdney forwarded a copy of the letter to Hudson's Bay Company headquarters in London. The London Committee reacted by telling Chief Commissioner Grahame in Winnipeg to give Clarke instructions that would "prevent his acting in a similar manner in future." Grahame sent a copy of Rae's letter and the London Committee's directive, along with a request for his version of the incidents, to Clarke.* The letter, dated December 18, 1882, also stated that "The desire of the Committee that our Officers should act cordially with the Agents of the Government must be complied with." Clarke no doubt continued to upset the Indian department officials in minor ways, but he had been officially reprimanded and put in his place.[17]

The settling influence of Hines was missed at the Ahtahkakoop Reserve as a rift developed between David Stranger and members of the Asissipi Mission. Hines did not elaborate, other than explaining that Ahtahkakoop's people had known David as a "Swampy Indian" and a labouring man. Then "as it were by a stroke of magic he was converted by the Bishop into a Minister of the Church of England and set over them as their Pastor. Many of the people here know more than he, Mr. Stranger, does and what makes things worse they know it, hence the little influence he has over them."[18]

Hines considered Ahenakew and Sasakamoose among those who had an excellent understanding of Christianity. For example, the missionary said that between being baptized in 1876 and his death in 1879, Ahenakew "had striven earnestly to fulfil his Xtian duties, he was one of those men rare to

---

* In 1882 the headquarters for the Hudson's Bay Company's Saskatchewan District (formerly the Carlton District) was transferred from Fort Carlton to Prince Albert. As a result of this change, chief factor Lawrence Clarke moved to Prince Albert in October 1882. Fort Carlton was put under the charge of Charles N. Garson, who held the position of clerk.

meet with, always willing to converse about religion & to defend it if he heard it spoken against. And further, he seemed thoroughly to understand in what Xtianity consisted & the duties incumbent on Xtians."[19] Similarly, Sasakamoose, who was known as a "consistent Christian," was said to have "a great grasp of the essential truths of the Gospel." So much so, that after a long conversation with Sasakamoose, Bishop McLean told Hines that "this old man is a regular theologian."[20]

The feelings at Sandy Lake must have run deep and the problems many during the winter of 1882–83. Unlike other years, the women refused to clean the church and the men would not bring firewood unless they were paid. "For the past five years," Hines was to say later, "the Asissipi Indians [had] always supplied the Church & school with fuel, and the women kept the Church washed and dusted,—washed every month and dusted whenever it required it, and all this was done without pay—but as soon as I left they refused to continue their contribution. I asked Stranger if he had told them to bring fuel etc. as usual, he said he had; but not one would listen to him." As a result, not a "single stick of firewood" was supplied to the church during the winter and only one woman eventually volunteered to clean the building.[21] Stranger was not a bad man, Hines said, but a humble Christian man willing to work for his Lord, but he needs to be sent among heathens where he will be respected.[22]

The day school was also affected by the dissension and Louis returned to Emmanuel College ahead of schedule. His cousin Joseph, the sixteen-year-old son of the headman Sasakamoose, went with him. The Ahtahkakoop Band now had two young men enrolled at Emmanuel College.[23] Hines apparently did not know what was happening during his absence. Stranger wrote what he thought would please Emma and Hines, the missionary said, so the news was misleading.

Food was scarce during the winter of 1882–83, despite the relatively good crops, and the men spent a considerable amount of time hunting north of Sandy Lake.[24] The winter was a time of sickness. Since Stranger was not qualified to distribute the medicine Hines had been dispensing, the people in Ahtahkakoop's band went to the Presbyterian minister at Snake Plain for assistance. This, Hines claimed, gave him influence and his competitor drew some of the people to him. Hines claimed that some of the people on Ahtahkakoop's reserve moved to the Mistawasis Reserve,[25] but if they did it was only temporary and no transfers in membership were made.

Illustration by Ed Peekeekoot

A feast held by Ahtahkakoop on behalf of his family during the Bear Ceremony.

Ahtahkakoop and his wife were among those who became very ill. Instead of going to the Presbyterian minister for help, the couple turned to their traditional beliefs and promised the Bear Spirit* they would hold a feast in his honour if their lives were spared. The chief and his wife recovered, and in the spring they fulfilled their promise.[26] By having the feast, they were honouring the Creator and giving thanks for having been healed.

Hines, in the meantime, was having troubles of his own. Several months after arriving in England he received word that the Finance Committee, the governing body of the Diocese of Saskatchewan, had suggested that Stranger be put in charge of the Asissipi Mission per-

Diocese of Saskatchewan Archives, Prince Albert
Portrait of the Hines family, taken during their visit to England.

manently. Hines was told he might be transferred to Blackfoot country. The missionary was upset. He did not want to leave Ahtahkakoop and his people. Moreover, without even knowing about the problems at the Asissipi Mission during his absence, he felt Stranger was not "capable" of taking over the mission and would not be "firm" enough to be successful. Hines thus embarked on a campaign to remain at Sandy Lake. The stress took its toll, and in February he was under the care of a doctor for a medical condition that the doctors could not "grapple, & therefore in all probability I sh[d] never entirely recover—that it was on the nerves of the skin, & w[d] be aggravated by anxiety & excitement. Didn't think climate would affect it so could leave when … [I] wanted to."[27] Emma also became ill, and her doctor recommended she not take on more work or strain than what she faced at the Asissipi Mission. Despite their medical problems, John and Emma were anxious to return to their mission, and they expressed their wish to leave England the first or second week of May.[28]

---

* The Bear Spirit, son of the Creator, was entrusted with healing by the Creator.

By now John and Emma Hines were feeling poorly used by the Church Missionary Society. Hines kept up a torrent of letters to church officials, and even Emma became involved when their proposal to save money was rebuked. She felt much of the society's money was not being well spent, and she outlined what they had done to cut costs. She had prepared the meals for the workmen herself, she noted. They had replaced the mission's horse with their own funds; her husband had done much of the construction work himself; and they had even paid the extra teachers out of the government grants earned by themselves.[29] Hines, in his frustration, hit out at the native clergymen, saying that they were treated much better than the English missionaries.[30]

John and Emma Hines won the immediate struggle, and they were permitted to return to their Asissipi Mission at Sandy Lake. After an absence of nearly 10 months, they arrived at the Ahtahkakoop Reserve, via New York City and Winnipeg, on June 20, 1883.[31]

Good Crops Yet the People Starved,
1883-1884

Ahtahkakoop and his people were well and busy when John and Emma Hines returned to Sandy Lake in June of 1883. The crops had been put in early and apparently were progressing satisfactorily. The families had planted 80 acres to wheat, 50 acres to barley, 18 acres to potatoes, 12 acres to turnips, and two acres to carrots. In addition there were four acres of other garden vegetables and an undetermined acreage of oats.[1] This was a substantial increase over the previous year, contradicting Wadsworth's derogatory statements about the people's interest in farming.

Unaware of the problems between Stranger and Ahtahkakoop's people, Hines was surprised to find the church in a "very dirty state." He asked Stranger "whose turn it was to clean the church, [and] he then for the first time told me that since I left" the women would not clean the church and the men refused to bring firewood.[2] Hines arranged for some women to do the cleaning, and on June 24—four days after his arrival—two services were held. Hines delivered the sermon in the morning and Stranger preached in the afternoon. The Englishman was back teaching in the classroom when inspector Wadsworth and Indian agent Rae came to the reserve on July 1 to examine the reserve, the school, and the students.

In addition to his day-to-day duties Hines also tried to find a new placing for Stranger, believing that his assistant could better serve the Anglican Church by working with people not yet converted to Christianity. He sent Stranger to visit several families living at Whitefish Lake on July 1. Towards the end of the month, the clergyman went to Prince Albert to tell the bishop that Stranger was no longer needed at

Sandy Lake. Hines suggested he go to Sturgeon Lake where 20 families were living, and he actually took David there a week or so later. Bishop McLean vetoed the move. The bishop also refused to allow Stranger to work with the people at Pelican (Chitek) and Whitefish lakes. Instead, he was moved to Prince Albert.[3]

The summer of 1883 was exceptionally wet. Overland routes became impassable because of too much rain and there were reports of streams so swollen that men had to hold their belongings above their heads as they struggled through shoulder-high water. The rain retarded the ripening of the crops. The first day of barley-cutting was August 16, compared to August 1 in 1882. Although the wheat was also slow maturing, it was thick and of such excellent quality that fields at the Ahtahkakoop Reserve— along with several other reserves—were said to be "equal, if not superior, to those of the white settlers in the vicinity."[4] The first wheat was cut on August 21 at the north end of the lake. "It seems strange," Hines wrote in his journal, "that this Man's wheat is always ripe a week earlier than any other wheat in the settlement."[5] Six days later Hines finished stacking the barley and oats in the mission fields and Ahtahkakoop started cutting the wheat in his field.

Harvest continued into September, and this year much of the wheat was cut using a reaping machine loaned by the Indian department. Although the reaper reduced both the manual labour and the time involved in taking the crop off, Hines noted that the government had not sent anyone to show the Indian farmers how to use it. Hines was less than complimentary about this lack of foresight, particularly in view of the breakdown of the thresher bought by Ahtahkakoop and Mistawasis in 1881. "If I had not been there to give instructions and to make minor repairs as needed," Hines wrote in his journal, the reaper "likely would have broken down." Then, he added, the rest of the uncut crops would have been frozen and spoiled before they could be cut.[6] The reaper was kept in working order and the results were substantially better than the previous year: 1,300 bushels of wheat, 400 bushels of oats, 1,000 of barley, 1,600 of potatoes, and 3,000 of turnips.[7] The number of livestock on the reserve was also gradually increasing, with 16 horses and 11 oxen recorded. A total of 225 acres of land was broken and 166 acres were enclosed by fences.

Ahtahkakoop's people were just finishing their harvest when the most important government official to date, Lawrence Vankoughnet, arrived on their reserve on September 12. Deputy superintendent general of Indian

Affairs, he had come with Rae to attend the treaty payments and inspect the reserve. During his tour the official encouraged parents to send their children to school regularly, saying it "would enable them to acquire that knowledge which would enable them when grown up, to hold their own with the white man."[8] This, in part, was likely advance work to promote a new industrial school that was opening in Battleford that fall.

The number of people who received their treaty money in 1883 was 192, an increase of seven from the previous year. Included in this number was Benjamin Wāskitoy (Thigh), a band member who had come from the south. He had only been paid twice before and appeared on the list with a new number.[*] Another man, Mōhkomānawēw, had transferred from Flying Dust's band at Meadow Lake and married one of Pē-nōsēwēskam's[†] widows; before going to Kā-ohpatawakinam's band in 1880 he had been registered in Mistawasis's band.[9] One man, four boys, and two girls had died during the paylist year and nine babies had been born and survived. Kā-miyo-astotin (Ahtahkakoop's son), Joseph Ahtahkakoop, and Mary Ahtahkakoop all had new sons and Kā-miyo-ahcahkwēw had a baby daughter. These babies were Ahtahkakoop's grandchildren: There was also a great-grandson, for Kā-miyo-ahcahkwēw's daughter Mary had married Donald LeBlanc and given birth to twin boys; only one of the babies survived. And a girl—Ahtahkakoop's great-niece—was born to Kāh-kāsōw and his wife Charlotte. Among the dead were Baptiste Ahenakew's only son, one of Mary Ahtahkakoop's sons, and one of two girls still listed under the number assigned to the former headman Wāskitoy.[10] Additionally, Kā-miyo-astotin and his wife Janet Ermineskin were raising a nephew. It is said that family members felt sorry for the couple because they did not have any children born to them, so—as was the custom—they were given a child.

Additionally, another notation on the treaty paylist indicated that Ahenakew's son Wāsēhikot, who had taken over Wāskitoy's headman position, "gives up his councillorship." No explanation was given. The position was not filled, leaving Ahtahkakoop's band with only two headmen, Sasakamoose and Kā-miyo-ahcahkwēw.

Despite the successful harvest of 1883 and a slight increase in population, problems of several kinds were looming and Ahtahkakoop's band was

---

* Wāskitoy was likely the son of the deceased headman Wāskitoy.

† Pē-nōsēwēskam was the man who had become chilled while duck hunting during the 1879–80 paylist year. He died at Fort Carlton.

becoming "somewhat disheartened in their farming operations."[11] In an effort to cut costs, Indian agent Rae had given no more implements than "indispensable" in the spring. As the year progressed, many implements and tools became useless and beyond repair.[12] The distance to the nearest flour mill was also a concern and, finally, the problem was being recognized by government officials. Wadsworth, for instance, in his report of October 9, 1883, told of one man from Ahtahkakoop's band who had been gone 10 days taking a load of wheat to the mill at Prince Albert. According to Hines, this length of time was not unusual because the 200-mile round trip involved eight days of actual travelling.[13] "Could some arrangements be arrived at whereby these Indians could have milling facilities," the inspector wrote, "I feel justified in stating that 1884–85 would find all those north of Carlton self-supporting."

The lack of a market for surplus grain was equally devastating. Without cash or some trading mechanism, the people found it difficult to obtain goods such as tea, tobacco, meat, clothing, ammunition, traps, cloth, and blankets. Hayter Reed, acting assistant Indian commissioner, acknowledged this during a tour of the Saskatchewan region in 1883 and he later suggested that the department buy surplus wheat, "which can be done at a very low figure and turn it into flour."[14] The flour could be distributed to needy bands, he continued, and the proceeds from the wheat would enable farmers to purchase needed articles.

With a successful farming season completed and John and Emma Hines back in their midst, the people looked ahead to winter. There were many uncertainties. What good would their wheat be if they could not sell the grain or get it milled into flour? Would the animals hunted for food and furs be plentiful during the winter? And what about the industrial school? The children had been doing well at the Asissipi Mission school and they were able to live at home. What changes, the people wondered, would the industrial school bring to their settlement and to their lives?

Even the continuing presence of John and Emma Hines was in question, for on October 10 the Church Missionary Society's finance committee in Prince Albert recommended that Hines take over the Anglican mission at The Pas. This was more practical in view of Hines's ability to speak Cree than the earlier proposal to send him to Blackfoot country. Nevertheless, Hines fought back, in all probability backed by Ahtahkakoop. Accusations of disloyalty were levelled at John and Emma

Hines as fiery letters travelled back and forth between Prince Albert and the Asissipi Mission. Because of her health and the couple's reluctance to abandon Ahtahkakoop and his people, Emma offered to stay at the Asissipi mission while her husband went to The Pas. The couple eventually won the battle, which had started the year before while they were in England, and the committee decided to send the Reverend John Settee to The Pas; Stranger was to replace him at a later date.[15]

Louis Ahenakew, instead of continuing classes at Emmanuel College, was sent to teach school at a mission in the Eagle Hills. Louis would likely be disappointed not to be back at Emmanuel College, Mackay wrote to Hines, but he could go another time.[16] The young school teacher left the Ahtahkakoop Reserve on October 22. Presumably, Joseph Sasakamoose had returned to the college in Prince Albert, for it was Ellen Ahenakew, Louis's sister and a former pupil in the mission school, who assisted Hines at the school during the fall of 1883.

Meanwhile the children at the Asissipi Mission school were, in Wadsworth's words, making "creditable progress in reading, spelling, multiplication, and other tables." He also noted that the students were familiar with the map of the world. Eighteen of the 20 students registered at the school were present for his examinations.[17]

Hines believed that his mission was successful in part because he and Emma lived in the community, often working hand-in-hand with the people and "carrying into effect during the week what ... [was taught] on Sunday."[18] He was not just a visitor who dropped by periodically to conduct church services, and he worked hard. The clergyman conducted school classes every morning and afternoon five times a week with Ellen's help. He held two church services in Cree each Sunday, helped with the farming, distributed clothing sent by friends in England, visited the sick, dispensed medicine, gave comfort and advice as best he could, and above all, continually urged the people to be good Christians. Attendance at church was usually good. Even when extremely cold weather, sickness, or hunting trips resulted in what Hines described as a small congregation, about 35 people attended each service.[19]

Hines was also providing practical help for some of the poorest members of his mission, in addition to ministering to their spiritual needs. For example, on November 6 an old blind woman was led to the mission by her granddaughter.* She asked for a little ginger. Hines gave it to her, along

---

* The old blind woman was Iskwēsis's mother and Kā-kīsikāwapiw's grandmother.

with a warm jacket and a chemise. Then he read and explained the 9th chapter of St. John to his visitors.[20] This reading from the Bible tells how Jesus restored the sight of a blind man. The following Sunday Hines wrote in his journal that Emma always made a large pot of soup on Sunday and asked "the poorest of our people after morning service to our kitchen to a soup dinner. Today we had eleven. One the blind woman (a widow) before referred to, 2 other widows, an orphan girl, and [the] rest old women & children. Gave the old women a chemise each." Hines also distributed gifts of clothing sent from England to the school children; each girl received a skirt, jacket, hood, and scarf, and the boys were given a shirt, jacket, cap, and scarf. One boy was given trousers.[21]

In addition to dressing the students in clothes that white children wore, the clothing fulfilled a need that for some families was becoming desperate. Garments and robes were wearing out, and the leather and furs needed for making new ones were becoming increasingly difficult to get. The buffalo that had provided leather, robes, and sinew were gone. Smaller game animals were fewer in number and harder to hunt, particularly since the men were expected to stay on the reserve to look after their farms. Widows and families headed by the women who had been "thrown away" in the process of reducing the number of wives to one per man suffered the most.

The winter started well enough. For the first time government officials arranged for the Carlton Agency's threshing machine to be sent to the various reserves to thresh the grain. Since their own thresher had given only one season of use and flailing the grain by hand was notoriously slow, the people decided they would wait for the government machine. In early November the weather was still good, there was no snow, and the muskrat houses were easily seen, so many of the men went on extended "rat" hunting trips. These tiny animals provided meat, as well as pelts. The Hudson's Bay Company, concerned about free traders in the area, gave Kāh-kāsōw goods valued at £200 to trade for the muskrat and other furs the men harvested. These goods, Hines said, were given "in the Fall without taking any security from him for the same, a proof of his honesty."[22]

After the warm days of early November, snow fell and it turned bitterly cold. Food was scarce for those who remained in the settlement while the men were hunting. On November 12, Hines gave all the children a "soup dinner." On the 13th each student received a large roast potato; two days later the students were given soup, and on the 23rd they had another "potato dinner."[23] Lack of clothing and food was a problem for a number of families, and often the people had to be resourceful in order to survive. Hines told of one such instance. He had asked a "female parishioner" why her children had not been at school for the last five days. She replied that they did not have any shoes. She added that her husband had left for Fort Carlton four days ago. She and her children had killed one of their dogs the day before, and except for dog meat they had eaten nothing but mice since his departure. Fortunately, Hines noted in his journal, these "were very numerous in their house." Before leaving the clergyman gave the woman a skirt and bale covering to tie around their feet.[24]

Tragedy struck Kāh-kāsōw's family in mid-November. On November 17 Charlotte asked Hines to visit their four-year-old son Angus, who had been sick for three months. The house was crowded when the missionary arrived because the child was near death. Hines prayed and told the gathering that children were "only lent to us." God had given five children into Peter and Charlotte's care for a short time. He asked them to bear their loss as Christians. When the boy was still alive the next day, Kāh-kāsōw offered £1 and asked for prayers in the church. The missionary refused the money but he prayed for the boy and his family as requested. The child died on November 20. He was Kāh-kāsōw's only son. Understandably upset by the child's death, Charlotte came to Hines for comfort two days later.[25]

When warm weather returned the first week of December it was accompanied by wet snow. The dampness brought on colds. Emma Hines was one of many who were stricken and Hines had to take time off from his teaching duties to look after her. Ellen Ahenakew took over the school during his absence.[26] Others were affected and when the men returned from the hunting grounds in the middle of December, they found "much sickness" in their homes.

Ahtahkakoop was still away when Sasakamoose told Hines about the chief "relapsing into a semi-state of heathenism" while the missionary and his wife were in England. The clergyman gave no reason for the disclosure. He did, however, ask "several of the Communicants if they had heard of the chief's relapse & they all declared they had."[27]

Ahtahkakoop returned home December 21. Hines said "I went at once to see him but finding I was unable to speak to him ... [I] invited both himself and wife to call on me." Hines said that when confronted with the relapse the next day both Ahtahkakoop and his wife confessed without shame, that they still retained a belief in the efficacy of *bear-worship*. The chief said that both he & his wife were very ill last winter when I was in England, and they remembered that before the white man's religion was brought to them, they used when ill, to promise the bears that if they got well again, that they would give a feast in honour of them. (At these feasts speeches are made to the bear's spirits)—So we promised the bears last winter we would give them a feast in the spring, which we did, & said the chief, "You see we are still alive."[28]

Hines responded by saying how sorry he was to find the couple still possessing such a faith and "showed him how humiliating to himself & how dishonouring to God such a faith was." Then he explained, obviously from his point of view, that God gave man dominion over all living creatures, while the old faith "placed man beneath the animal creation."

The chief fired back that when the Reverend Mackay and the bishop came to speak to them they told the people they should keep their promises, so he did. When Hines tried to lecture the couple about Christianity, he said the chief "got up in a dreadful … [state], and said 'I was to ask Mr. McKay [*sic*]what he said and what he meant' and then he left with his wife, saying as he went out of the house, that he would not come to church again."

The next day was Sunday, and true to his word, Ahtahkakoop and his wife were not at church. Hines said the "principal Indians seem to feel very sorry for the Chief" and prayers were said for him. The afternoon service, uncharacteristically, was cancelled. Hines explained that he was "quite unequal for a second service" because of the effects of an "influenza cold & the trouble about the chief." Nevertheless, there apparently was a meeting to discuss the situation, for Hines wrote in his journal that the headmen "think with me that the best plan to follow, is to send for Arch. D. McKay [*sic*] to give the Chief an explanation of what he said, as there are many at the Mission who might be influenced by him."[29]

Sasakamoose and Kā-miyo-ahcahkwēw must have met with Ahtahkakoop within the next day or so. And perhaps others joined them. The discussion that took place can only be surmised, but one would have to believe that the decision was made to put the collective good of the community above anything else, for the chief and his wife were part of the large congregation that attended services on Christmas morning.

In Hines's account, the missionary did not acknowledge that most of the people in the band had probably attended the Bear Feast given by

Ahtahkakoop and his wife. Moreover, most of these people, within some part of their being and despite their conversion to Christianity, likely still believed in the healing powers of the Bear Spirit. Religious traditions entrenched for countless years could not be set aside as easily as Hines supposed. Nor would Hines's belief that God had given human beings dominion over all living creatures have found easy acceptance. In traditional beliefs, the people lived in harmony with nature and the spirit of the Creator was embodied in all living things. They could no more have dominion over these things than they could own the land and the creatures on it.

The Asissipi clergyman travelled to Prince Albert early in January to speak to Mackay. The archdeacon was unable to return to the Ahtahkakoop Reserve with Hines, but he said he would write a letter to the chief. If that did not work, Mackay agreed to make the trip after classes at Emmanuel College resumed. While in Prince Albert Hines preached at the Sunday morning service in the cathedral. Only 11 were present, including those associated with the college.[30] This was a much smaller number than would have attended a similar service at the Asissipi Mission.

Hines delivered Mackay's letter to Ahtahkakoop on January 15 and the following day the chief came to see him. Although Hines said it was a "friendly interview," Ahtahkakoop was "loath to speak about" the course he had been following for the past year and never "said out plainly that he was convinced of his error."[31] So the difficulties with the new faith continued to haunt Ahtahkakoop's family.

Hines, too, was having difficulties because his European upbringing and Christian ideology clashed with the realities of Indian culture and beliefs. He had dedicated his adult life to teaching the Indian people how to become Christians, how to farm, and how to adapt to the white man's way of living. At one level, he was a hard-working, caring man, but at another level he believed the white man and his values to be far superior. An illustration of this can be found in his entry for December 8, 1883. Hines had gone to visit a three-year-old child sick with aggravated diarrhoea. When he found the boy outside with few clothes on, no hat, and wet feet he admonished the mother. The woman replied that she knew the child should not be out but she could not keep him indoors. In recording the incident in his journal, Hines wrote that

> Indians from their childhood had their own way. They are rarely
> chastised by their parents, the result is, that they grow up self-
> willed and proud giving honour to no one. I have been told by

some of the Indians, "that they look upon the whites as a lot of slaves. They all seem to be under some one else, and no man is his own master. As for us we go when and where we please and return the same." How much better the Indians would be, at least many of them, if placed under similar law, to be exempt of course from being sold or cruelly beaten, but compelled to work and give honour to whom honour is due.[32]

Indian Commissioner Edgar Dewdney,* who was in a position to develop policy based on his personal views, was also making judgements about the Indian way of life. For instance, in a letter dated October 2, 1883, he was critical of the tradition of sharing, saying that the costs of assistance were not going down, in part because Indians who worked gave freely to non-workers on and off the reserve. The commissioner went further, saying that not much we do will have a permanent effect on adults, so we "must take charge of the youth and keep him constantly within the circle of civilization." Believing that the only way to do this was to separate the children from their parents, Dewdney worked with the Anglican Church in founding the Battleford Industrial School.[33]

Officials chose Government House, the former residence and office of Lieutenant-Governor Dewdney, to house the new school. The building had become vacant earlier in the year when Dewdney moved to Regina, the new capital of the North-West Territories.† The new acting assistant Indian commissioner, Hayter Reed, was assigned the task of overseeing repairs and the recruitment of students for the school. The Reverend Thomas Clarke, an Anglican clergyman, was appointed principal.

Reed reported that although the outside walls of the log building were covered with clapboard, and the inside walls were plastered, the building was drafty and cold. "Under the authority to repair it," he said, "I did sufficient I think to make it habitable for the winter by stopping all the drafts inside, putting on double windows, plastering, etc.; at all events the boys will be more comfortable there, than in their teepees or shanties."[34]

---

* Like John A. Macdonald, who held the dual position of superintendent general of Indians Affairs and prime minister of Canada, Dewdney served as both Indian commissioner and lieutenant-governor.

† The abandonment of Battleford as capital had followed the Canadian government's 1881 decision to build the Canadian Pacific Railway (CPR) across the southern plains instead of through the parklands. A point on the map along the proposed route was chosen for the new capital and called Regina, and in March 1883 the seat of government was officially transferred to that small community.

Saskatchewan Archives Board R-A2287

Government House in Battleford, recently vacated by Lieutenant-Governor Dewdney, was converted to a residential industrial school for Indian children in 1883. In later years the building was enlarged.

Reed also reported that in accordance with the commissioner's instructions, he had

> collected 14 boys from the neighborhood of Battleford, between the ages of 6 and 14 years … Each band was allotted its proportionate number to send to this school but it was found that the Indians, except those the most advanced in civilization, would not consent to their Children attending. Numerous reasons being advanced—Among the number, that the parents would lose the Children's Treaty Money, would also be deprived of the work the lads were capable of doing. They would be detained too long and never allowed to be seen by their parents. The Children would be sent to some part of the Country to be taught there. Their Children's hair would be cut short. Again others said they would wait and see what the institution meant, before consigning their boys to it; but all no doubt were actuated in refusing, at all events at first, by the fact of the power laying in their own hands, and they wished to exercise it.[35]

"The Indians in the neighborhood of Pitt would not allow any to go," Reed continued, and "it was doubtful with those at Edmonton." Because their experiences with Hines and with Emmanuel College in Prince Albert had generally been favourable, the people in Ahtahkakoop's Band were more open to the new venture. Thus, two boys—both students from Hines's Asissipi school—were recruited from the Ahtahkakoop Band. They were picked up by Indian agent J. Ansdell Macrae on December 14, 1883, and delivered to the school at Battleford. Four other boys from bands in the Carlton Agency went with them.[36] Macrae had replaced Rae as the agent for the Carlton Agency five weeks earlier, on November 9.

According to Reed, upon their arrival all the children were

> thoroughly washed, cleaned, and dressed in the new cloths [sic] provided for them, before being allowed through the building; this creating a wonderful metamorphosis, in so much that their own friends found it difficult to recognize them.[37]

Indian education had changed. Instead of receiving their lower levels of education on the reserves, children would be taken from their homes and placed in a foreign environment many miles from their parents. Visits home were discouraged, further separating the children from both their families and their culture.

The men had continued to hunt and trap during much of December, still waiting for the thresher to come. According to Hines, the people were finally

> told that they were to thrash about the beginning of the New Year & were told to be in readiness, so that when the machines reached the reserve there would be no delay. Consequently all our people were waiting at home, daily expecting the machine. They dare not leave for the purpose of hunting lest the machinist finding them absent, should take his machine back again. They were kept waiting in a starving condition for one month.[38]

In the middle of January 1884, a few men took a chance and went hunting, while others—including Ahtahkakoop—threshed some grain by hand and took it to Prince Albert to be milled. Later in the month Hines recorded in his journal that "Our poor people are very badly off for food," but they hear there is a "probability" of getting a threshing machine soon. It took another few days, but the thresher finally arrived early in February. Six hundred bushels were threshed by February 9, and 10 days later the job was complete. It had taken 15 days to thresh approximately 2,000 bushels of wheat and barley.[39]

The suffering, however, did not end. The clergyman wrote in his journal:

> As soon as the thrashing was over they all expected to start off at once to the mill, but no, the Government official sent word that they were not to move until he gave the orders, at the same time giving them no idea how long they would have to wait. Here again they were kept in a state of suspense as well as starvation for they dare not leave home to hunt lest the order to march should come whilst they were absent. Finally after waiting 22 days the men started on the 200 mile trip, leaving nothing behind for their families to eat but unground wheat and we do not expect them back again before the 17th or 18th Inst. The poor starving creatures in the meantime are suffering much, especially those who are too ill to eat wheat. No one but ourselves knows what amount of food we are called upon to give away. Today [March 9] we gave a dinner to 15 people, principally old women. Sometimes reports reach you that the Indians are well cared for by their Government & that they are contented and doing well on their farms. These reports must be from people who really know nothing of the true state of the poor Indians but who takes a delight in praising those in authority whether they are deserving of praise or not.[40]

Since Hines's journals were forwarded to the Church Missionary Society's head office in England, he added that "these remarks may seem to some out of place in a journal of this kind but we are living among the Indians & feel very keenly their suffering & therefore we feel bound to write facts relative to our work."

To further emphasize the living conditions of some of the people on the reserve, Hines described his visit to a 70-year-old widow who was sick. It was −45° degrees Fahrenheit the day he went to see her:

> The house is a flat roofed log hut, scarcely high enough for one to stand upright in. It is doorless & floorless, that is, there is a hole on one side where they go in & out, but no door to keep out the cold, & the bare ground is the floor. There is a hole dug in the centre of the hut, where I suppose they have a few potatoes stored away. There are a few sticks placed evenly across to keep one from falling in. They have a little pine brush spread on the ground all around & a little hay spread on the top & this serves them for beds. The house is about 16 feet square. On entering, to the right

is a family of six, a man, wife, & 4 children. These occupying the first corner. The next to this is a widow with one child, & the next is a widow with 2 children. The next to them is the widow whom I went especially to see. She was lying on the bed I have described with but one blanket to cover herself with. The next was a new married couple which completed the third corner. A widow & 7 children occupied the end, & another married couple occupied the 4th corner, which completed the number of occupants, making in all 24 souls.[41]

Government officials, in recording each year the number of houses on the reserve, seldom if ever spoke of the shanties where some people lived. Nor did they refer to living conditions or give more than passing mention to the hardship and poverty suffered under the new regime. Hines, in his description, was struck by the poverty and no doubt applied his own European standards to the home and its occupants. But until the arrival of the white man, the people of Ahtahkakoop's band—like other buffalo hunters—had always lived in family groups in tipis. These, too, were one-room dwellings without "regular" floors. But made from buffalo hides and equipped with insulated linings, buffalo robes for bedding and flooring, and a fire in the middle, a tipi was a versatile, comfortable home.

Now the buffalo were gone. When the tipi coverings, household furnishing, and clothing supplied by the massive animal wore out, there was no way to replace them in the traditional way. People needed money, which was next to impossible to get without working off the reserve or being successful at hunting and trapping. Both of these options depended on men who were able to work and hunt the animals that were becoming increasingly scarce each year. Before the arrival of the missionaries, widows often became the second or third wives of men in the community and thus were looked after. In this household of 24 people visited by Hines, there were only three men, one of them newly married and probably young. Four of the women were widows, with a total of 10 children amongst them. The bedding and clothing were not adequate, the log shanty was drafty and cold, and the people were hungry and sick.

The widow was only one of many who were sick during the winter and spring of 1884. Hines believed that the sickness throughout the band was "brought on … principally by starvation." He went further, writing in his journal that he was "certain our Indians would have been better off today

Sidney P. Hall, National Library of Canada, NL-17738

This drawing of the Hudson's Bay Company's mill in Prince Albert was sketched in 1881 during the Marquis of Lorne's visit. Note the ceremonial arch to the left of the mill. The mill was destroyed by fire in 1884.

if the Government had not taken them under their charge. What the Government has done, has tended to make them less independent, less energetic & less provident, than they were before the treaty."[42]

The "sickness" had started early in the winter, gaining momentum as the weeks passed. Early in February, about the time the thresher arrived, nearly all the people on the reserve were suffering from bad colds. A three-month-old baby became very ill on February 21 and died seven days later. On March 7, a six-month-old girl who had been weak since birth had a severe cough and cold.[43]

It was in the midst of this illness that government officials told the men to take their grain to Prince Albert. They set off on the 200-mile return trip immediately, leaving little or no food for their families. After the men were gone Hines was "obliged to close the day school, children being all ill with colds." The missionary also had a severe cold and was too sick to leave the house for two days after closing the school. The chief and the other men, knowing their families were without food, must have pushed both themselves and the oxen, for they were back on March 16, several days sooner than expected. Hines, whose cold was almost six months old, was able to hold two church services the day of their arrival, but he said his chest was still sore.[44]

Ahtahkakoop brought word from Prince Albert that David Stranger was very ill with a bad cough. He also delivered a letter from Louis and Joseph. Writing in English, the youths said they were tired of studying at Emmanuel College and wanted to come home to help their friends with the farms. They knew their relatives were badly off and felt they were doing nothing to help. "I feel sorry for this," Hines wrote in his journal, adding that he hoped the boys would continue their studies because "once they start teaching, they will have a salary & can help."[45]

Hines, still suffering from a cold and a sore chest, continued visiting the sick and giving medicine. The six-month-old girl grew progressively weaker and died March 19. That same day Hines recorded in his journal that sickness in the settlement was getting worse, no doubt prolonged by continuing cold weather. Indian agent Macrae arrived at the reserve March 21. Ahtahkakoop no doubt discussed the situation with the agent and Hines took him to see some of the sick.

On the evening of March 22, Ahtahkakoop met with some of the leading men to discuss the sickness and poverty on the reserve. It was decided that a relief fund should be started, with Sasakamoose acting as "relieving officer." The next morning Sasakamoose talked to Hines before the church service, asking if an announcement about the relief program could be made in church. Hines, of course, agreed.[46] It is not clear from the documentation, but it appears that the rations would be drawn from a supply of provisions delivered by the Indian agent for the up-coming planting season. It is also possible that the men had been able to trade some of their flour for provisions in Prince Albert. Regardless, the leading men were responsible for delivering the provisions that would lessen some of the suffering.

Towards the end of the month Hines travelled to Prince Albert to see Stranger. Hines explained that his former helper had not been "strong" for some time. Each spring and fall he suffered from the same "complaint," which most likely included a bad cough, and every attack was harder on him. David Stranger was very sick when Hines saw him. He died on April 5.[47] His wife Isabella moved back to the Ahtahkakoop Reserve in July, having lost her husband and two children in the year she had been away from the reserve.[48]

Wāsēhikot's wife Jemima had also been sick. She died April 6, 1884, at the age of 38.[49]

When Hines returned to Sandy Lake after his last visit with Stranger, Louis Ahenakew and Joseph Sasakamoose came with him. Louis was to be sent to Devon,* but until he left the young teacher was put in charge of the Asissipi school. Joseph, who was 17, would assist Hines after Louis left.[50]

The day school "flourished" under the management of Louis Ahenakew. "He is certainly cutout for a School Teacher," Hines wrote in his journal, adding that "He has such a capital way of keeping order. He writes as well on a blackboard as I have ever seen any one write." Thus Louis was making a name for himself in the new order of life. His family, the chief, Hines, and other church officials were exceedingly proud of the young man who had been one of the first students in the Asissipi mission school.[51]

During the days of sickness and hardship, Hines had carried on with other aspects of his mission work. Between 60 and 70 people had attended both church services on March 2, when the men were still waiting to take their grain to the mill at Prince Albert. The missionary also continued to visit and hold services at Mistawasis's reserve on his way to Fort Carlton and Prince Albert. Hines, of necessity, had changed his procedures for baptism. Before the Presbyterian minister moved to the Mistawasis Reserve, the people went "through a course" before being baptized. Now the Anglican clergyman baptized first and gave instruction later.[52] Interest in the Church of England continued, and it was not unusual for people from Mistawasis's band to attend services at St. Mark's Church at Sandy Lake.

Hines also had contact with the family of Macikwanās (Bad Weed), the chief of the Pelican Lake Band. The missionary told of one encounter in his journal. He said that one of Macikwanās's wives was visiting in Prince Albert in about 1874 when a man from Ahtahkakoop's band saw her and fell in love. Hines said the man had "an interview" with Macikwanās, and about a year later he gave the chief —in the traditional way—a dowry of two horses for the woman.[53] In 1875 the couple joined the settlement at Sandy Lake. Two years later both were baptized, along with two children, and for a number of years the woman served as a "washer woman" for Emma Hines. When the 59-year-old woman became very sick early in

---

* Devon, called The Pas by the Hudson's Bay Company, was situated 75 miles downstream from Cumberland House.

Illustration by Ed Peekeekoot

Louis Ahenakew, in John Hines's words, was "certainly cutout for a School Teacher." He taught at the Asissipi Mission school in 1884 before taking over the school at Devon.

1884 her sister, who was one of Macikwanās's wives, came from Pelican Lake to be with her.[54]

Then something very special happened. The woman told Hines during a visit on April 6 that two or three days earlier, while "quite awake," she saw people taking her to the cemetery. The group met Hines and Jesus just as they got to the top of the hill, going up from the lake to the church. The woman said

> Jesus told me that I w^d have to go back for a little while, but not for long. He told me the hour He w^d come for me, but I cannot remember it now, so I thought the procession turned round again to take me home, & this brought me to myself, & I was very sorry when I found He did not want me yet, but He told me it w^d not be for long.[55]

Macikwanās and the woman's sister were both non-Christians who followed the traditional way. After the woman was blessed with the vision, the sister—who had always been indifferent to Christianity and smoked her pipe while the others prayed—started kneeling during prayers at the house. On Sunday morning, Macikwanās entered a church for the first time in his life to attend a Christian service.

The woman died suddenly the night of April 7. Hines said that just before dying she said three times "in a clear & rather loud tone, 'Kwiusk,' (Right on, Good)." Then she "fell asleep … but it was the sleep of death." The funeral was held on April 8.[56]

The following Sunday, April 13, was Easter Sunday. Kihci-mōhkomān's widow and her four children were baptized after almost eight weeks of instruction. Ocīkīskicās (Short Pants) chose the name Jemima for her Christian name. The children, ranging in age from five to 18, were named Thomas, Elizabeth, James, and George. The next day Hines visited members of the congregation who had not attended Easter Sunday services. He asked about their absence and they told him that they thought the people without offerings would not be allowed to stay.[57]

A few days later Hines said that Ahtahkakoop's third son, a young man about 25 years of age, came to the mission. It appears, Hines wrote in his journal, that he was "very anxious about his soul's welfare." The missionary went on to say that the son was not a communicant but wanted to be. He had come to the house at Hines's request to get payment for digging some graves. The young man told Hines he "never anticipated any payment for doing such work. He had understood that those who dug the graves and made the coffins were paid for doing so out of the offertory, but he felt sure that if he dug graves for others without wishing remuneration, when his turn came to die his bones would not be left uncovered."[58]

On April 20 Hines gathered some of the young people together for the first Sunday school class to be held on Ahtahkakoop's reserve. There had not been a need before, the missionary explained, because day school was very much like Sunday school. This class was for the benefit of "scholars" who were too old to attend school and who were needed at home. The following week Hines was particularly pleased when two "heathens" attended. At the conclusion of the class, the young people were given work to do at home.[59] And so the word of God was spreading and becoming more deeply entrenched at the Ahtahkakoop Reserve.

Surprisingly, government records suggest that the winter of 1883–84 was a good one for Ahtahkakoop's people. That obviously was not true. Indian agent Macrae had visited the Ahtahkakoop Reserve at least twice during the winter. The first time was the last week of February, during the period when the people were starving and the men were waiting for permission to take their wheat to the mill in Prince Albert. He was there again the middle of March, so the agent knew about the people's plight—in regards to both sickness and hunger—from first-hand observation. Yet, in his report written several months later Macrae chose to minimize the hardship, to the point of being dishonest. The Ahtahkakoop Band was doing well, he wrote, and he surmised that they had probably "sustained themselves last winter" because Mistawasis had.[60]

This information was picked up and used by Macdonald, superintendent general of Indian Affairs, when he wrote in his annual report that Ahtahkakoop and Mistawasis had been "able to sustain themselves during the winter upon the products of the soil, the fruit of their own labour."[61] They had enough grain for seed, he continued, and flour for food while planting. This last statement may have been true, but it only told a small part of the story. The grain and flour remained because the government thresher had not been sent to their reserve until the first week of February. Then there were further delays when permission to take the grain to the mill was not granted until mid-March. By then winter was over. To make the situation worse, the men were unable to go hunting or take hand-threshed grain into Prince Albert to be milled since they dared not be away when instructions came from the agent. They had benefited very little during the winter from their crops.

Macrae, in a report to his superiors, acknowledged that the band "can do little more to ameliorate their condition until greater facility for milling grain is offered to them." He then minimized the situation and clouded any insight he may have had when he added that "last winter was spent almost entirely in getting their grain ground, entailing a large amount of labor on both men and work oxen."[62] Again, a misrepresentation, since the band had in reality spent the winter waiting for the government thresher and for permission to get the wheat ground into flour.

Ahtahkakoop and his band understandably were discouraged by so much effort, so little return, and the hardship and poverty that seemed to go hand-in-hand with farming and the new way of life. Macrae, not surprisingly, feared their progress would be affected by this feeling.

Other bands were having similar problems. For instance, in the Battleford and Fort Pitt areas, the greatest hardship was amongst "those Indians who are anxious to progress and have reaped good crops as neither a market is found nor a mill in existence to grind the grain."[63] Despite statements such as this, government officials chose to ignore or overlook the people's hardship and the government's mismanagement. For example, Reed had reported the end of January 1884, that there were 2,000 bushels of surplus grain in the Carlton and Duck Lake districts and 500 surplus bushels at Battleford and Pitt.[64] Although his definition of "surplus" was not given, the term was not appropriate. By the end of January the government's machine had not even arrived at Ahtahkakoop's reserve to thresh the grain. Useless would have been a more accurate word for the surplus.

The grain sitting on reserves, nevertheless, had prodded the government to action. Reed recognized in late December that there was no market for any surplus grain that was grown and he recommended that the department buy some of the wheat. This would serve two purposes, he said. The proceeds from the sale of the grain could be used to buy needed articles, and the flour milled from the wheat could be used to assist poorer bands.[65] In February, Ottawa gave approval for Indian agents to purchase some of the "surplus" grain. Macrae reported later that he bought grain at market prices and by "directing the expenditure of the amount paid therefor, secured great benefit to the Indians. An almost entire control of the crop was kept." By keeping "control," the agent said he was able to guard against "unfair dealings" and goods were obtained for the "Indians on advantageous terms."[66] Another source indicated that beginning April 16, bands in the Carlton district milled nearly 1,750 bushels of grain into flour and sold, "under permit from the agent," 356 bushels of wheat and 673 bushels of barley. Half of this amount belonged to Ahtahkakoop and Mistawasis band members.[67]

The word "control," combined with financial restraint, was starting to be more prevalent in the thoughts and actions of government officials, and it appeared in various ways. The most obvious was at the reserves where farm instructors and Indian agents had a strong presence. Despite the already deplorable living conditions, the government cut food rations to a minimum, and the "work for food" policy was vigorously enforced. At a different level of control, all vouchers had to be signed by the Indian commissioner, which meant delays as agents forwarded vouchers to Regina for approval. Additionally, by insisting on more control in Ottawa, senior government officials there were making it impossible for Indian department employees working in the field to act humanely. The "discretionary powers" of agents and farm instructors were slashed. Even the Indian commissioner had his authority greatly reduced.

There were also other examples of control and power. For instance, in November of 1883 Vankoughnet requested that a permit system be implemented to prevent Indian people from going into towns without permission. Although this request was turned down by Macdonald, discretionary powers "as to removal" by the police were approved.[68] And in February, on the recommendation of Reed and Macdonald, Saswēpiw (Sits All Over The Land) was deposed as a chief of the Willow Cree by the Canadian government "in accordance with Section 72 of Indian Act 1880." The document upon which this action was based said that Saswēpiw was deemed "incompetent for the position owing to his wandering habits and that this chief has done all he could to prevent the members of his band from settling upon their Reserve [at Duck Lake] & cultivating the land thereon."[69] Saswēpiw was replaced by Okimāsis, one of his headmen.*

Big Bear, the last chief to sign an adhesion to Treaty Six, could not be dealt with so easily. Because of his resistance to the treaty, the chief had attracted some of the most independent men on the plains, and his camp became the rallying point for the disillusioned and the alienated. When 5,000 hungry Plains Indians were escorted by the North-West Mounted

* The reserve for Beardy's Willow Cree was marked out for them on the trail between Batoche and Fort Carlton in January 1880.

Police towards their reserves in 1882, Big Bear and his followers were not among them. However, by winter Big Bear could hold out no longer and on December 8, 1882, he signed an adhesion to Treaty Six at Fort Walsh. The following summer he and the other chiefs in his camp led their starving destitute people north. Big Bear did not immediately select a reserve since he still wanted better terms. He also wanted to see what was happening on the other reserves. Because he was unwilling to select a reserve, government officials refused to issue rations to his people.[70]

The police and Indian department officials kept a close watch on Big Bear. Reed reported in December that he thought the chief had "some project in view for next spring at Battleford." To counter this, he asked that the number of police be increased and that efforts be made by Indian agents to frustrate any co-operative actions by the leading men. "It is by meeting the Indians at every step and often by anticipating their intentions," he wrote to Indian Commissioner Dewdney, "that one can ever be successful and not wait until their plans are formed for then nothing can stop them."[71]

There were signs that Indian people elsewhere throughout the North-West were becoming frustrated and defiant. Far too often they were treated unfairly by Indian agents, farm instructors, and other Indian Affairs employees and officials. And sometimes they retaliated. Ration houses were broken into, band-owned oxen were killed for food, the authority of the North-West Mounted Police was challenged, and Indian people were leaving their reserves in greater numbers.[72] In a letter dated April 12, 1884, Reed expressed his concerns about the inclination of the Indian people to visit from reserve to reserve in the spring and his fear that they might attempt to gather in large numbers near Indian Head, Broadview, and Battleford. He also warned that the Indians might seize unprotected stores and kill more cattle, particularly if rations were stopped because they left their reserves or refused to work. And he recommended that large gatherings not only be prevented if possible, but the ring leaders should be arrested "if the slightest pretext offers."[73]

In response to signs of unrest, government officials made plans to send a detachment of 50 North-West Mounted Police to Battleford "as soon as the snow leaves" to strengthen the 103 men already posted in Saskatchewan River country. Forty-seven of the policemen in place were stationed at Battleford, 12 of them were at Prince Albert, 19 were at Fort Pitt, and 25 were at Fort Saskatchewan.[74]

Most of the concerns, as evident in the postings of the police, were directed away from the Fort Carlton district where a number of bands were seriously trying to farm. At Sandy Lake, on the Ahtahkakoop Reserve, the chief and members of his band were frustrated, disillusioned, and perhaps angry. But they were also patient. The people had spent a difficult winter, but they had fared better than many other bands. Indian Affairs officials may have been making more frequent trips to the reserve than previously, but because of distance they were not meddling in day-to-day affairs. Furthermore, because it was important to the government that at least some bands were progressing, it is likely that the Ahtahkakoop Band received preferential treatment at the hands of Indian Affairs officials. Nevertheless, there had been too much sickness and hunger. When was it going to get better, they must often have asked themselves during the difficult times. What good was a successful crop when they could not use it?

A Time of Unrest, 1884-1885

Farm instructor George Chaffee had arrived at Ahtahkakoop's reserve in late March 1884, soon after the men returned from the flour mill at Prince Albert. With Hines as interpreter, the instructor spent an entire day inspecting the farms and meeting with the chief and leading men. The families cleaned 80 bushels of wheat for seeding on April 14. Then, despite the weather being so cold that the ice was still "very solid" in the lake, the men started planting their fields. By April 23, about 90 bushels of wheat had been planted. The next day four inches of snow fell.[1] By the time the planting season was over 110 acres of land had been sown to wheat, along with 50 acres to barley, eight acres to potatoes, five acres to turnips, one acre to carrots, and three acres to garden vegetables.[2]

On May 9, heavy smoke filled the air as fires surged towards the settlement. Flames engulfed the pines, poplars, and birch, and during the next days thousands of trees on the reserve were destroyed. The people fought desperately to extinguish the fires, or at least change their course. All the buildings and the livestock were saved, but many families lost the fences around their fields.

The devastation was frightening. "In the past 4 days the Sun has been almost constantly hid from view by the smoke," Hines wrote on May 17. "It is painful to go abt. & see nothing but black ground & charred trees, thousands of rabbits & prairie chickens must have been burned to death. I was through a small pine forest this morning & it was grievous to see the poor birds sitting singly about, as if afraid to move, many of their mates having been burnt up on their nests with their eggs or young as the case may have been."[3]

Ahtahkakoop travelled to Prince Albert to buy lumber and shingles to build a "superior" house for himself after the fires were extinguished. As usual the group, which included the chief's eldest son Kā-miyo-ahcahk-wēw, three of his nephews, and Hines, camped at Snake Plain and Fort Carlton during their journey. Later in the month Ahtahkakoop and Sasakamoose went to Fort Carlton to meet with Dewdney. Acting in his capacity of Indian commissioner, the lieutenant-governor told the chiefs and headmen that "the Govt. Farm instructors would remain with them for 2 years more, & then they'd be left to manage on their own." Hines, in recording the information in his journal, added that was "really what they have been doing all along."[4]

Following the meeting at Fort Carlton, Sasakamoose—who had been trading for the Hudson's Bay Company that spring—headed northwest with a new supply of trade goods. People were gathering at Pelican Lake (Chitek Lake) for the annual *mitēwiwin* ceremonies when he arrived at Macikwanās's reserve early in June. Under the leadership of Macikwanās, this band was one of the most traditional in the area, and each year people came regularly from places such as the Fort Pitt and Battleford areas, Whitefish Lake, Sturgeon Lake, and Stoney Lake to participate in *mitēwiwin*, Sun Dance, and other sacred ceremonies. Knowing that Ahtahkakoop's brother had been a great shaman before his conversion to Christianity, the people asked him to stay. According to Hines, Sasakamoose refused. If anyone else from the Ahtahkakoop Band was at or near Pelican Lake in early June, no one told the missionary.[5]

By the time Sasakamoose returned to Sandy Lake, Ahtahkakoop's sons Kā-miyo-ahcahkwēw, Kā-miyo-astotin, Joseph, and Michel, along with a number of other men, were working on the chief's new house. The rafters were put up on June 17 with Hines's help, and three weeks later the roof was shingled. This was likely the first house on the reserve—besides the missionary's—to have shingles on the roof instead of poles, moss, and sod. At least one other house of similar quality was erected at the same time, but Hines did not give any details about this house or its owner. With the exception of a "gift of a few pounds of nails" from the government, these houses were built entirely with lumber and other materials purchased or otherwise obtained by Ahtahkakoop and the other builder.[6] Combined with construction activities, the farmers replaced the fences that had been destroyed by the fires and did their daily chores.

Hines, in the meantime, kept busy with the school and other mission activities. The farm instructor visited in June and counted all the children old enough to be enrolled. Hines said the count was made, in part, because the government was going to supply a biscuit for the students' dinner.[7]

Dewdney considered the school run by Hines to be the most successful school in the North-West Territories. "It is most surprising," the commissioner reported, "to witness the ability which some of the youngsters under him display, some boys of ten or twelve being much in advance of the average white children of a similar age in arithmetic, spelling, etc." Of all the children sent to the Industrial School in Battleford "who had previously attended any Indian school, those instructed by Mr. Hines were the most advanced." Additionally, the two boys who had enrolled at Emmanuel College and displayed "marked ability"[8] were now working as teachers. Joseph Sasakamoose was assisting Hines at the school at Sandy Lake and Louis Ahenakew was soon to be sent to Devon to take charge of the school and serve as catechist.

Hines's duties, as usual, extended beyond teaching in the school and preaching on Sundays. When children were not at school, for example, the clergyman went to their homes to find out why they were absent. He gave out clothing sent from England so the children would be dressed warmly enough to come to classes. He also called on the sick, distributed medicine, said prayers, and often helped fix ploughs or other implements during his visits. People came to his house for food and to have their hair cut. Hair-cutting, the clergyman wrote in his journal, was a "new feature in my work."[9] For the men, young men, and boys, getting their hair cut was another outward sign that they had adapted Christianity to their lives. Before their conversion, they—like their ancestors before them—had believed that the three sections of hair that made up a braid represented the spirit, mind, and body. Braiding them together represented binding the spirit, mind, and body in order to make a strong person. To cut their hair, other than during times of mourning, was unnatural.

Hines, as usual, worked hard enforcing the rules of the church, so when he was "informed" by church members that a few people had been trading with half-breeds on Sunday, he "applied … [himself] to the case."[10] The missionary was also applying himself to converting more people to Christianity. In one instance he told of a "heathen" man who had expressed a desire to become a Christian. The conversion, however, presented a problem since his wife was determined to leave if he followed this new path. She was "very stiff-necked," the man explained, and "was very rarely made to change her mind." He added that, except for the children, he would not mind too much if she left. The husband asked Hines to go and see his wife.[11]

Hines obliged. He spent one hour talking to the woman, during which time "she never once opened her mouth." Showing a determination, and perhaps a stubbornness equalling that of the wife, Hines wrote in his journal that

> There is a species of granite which refuses to yield to the influence of iron wedges and sledge hammers but which surrenders to the silent influence of wooden wedge steeped in water. Perhaps we can manage her stubborn nature by silent force.[12]

The man and his brother-in-law, who up until now had also followed the traditional ways, were at church the following Sunday.

The growing season of 1884 had started with very little rain and devastating fires. In mid-June, a different kind of burning—the kind that occurs when it does not rain on the prairies and in the parklands of the North-West—consumed the crops. The earth parched, cracks opened, and crops shrivelled. Hines wrote in his journal on June 16 that in all the time he had been in the North-West, he had never seen the ground so dry. Extracts from his journal entries told the story:

> June 16: "The weather has been very dry all this Spring and the growing crops are suffering much from lack of moisture. We had prayers for rain yesterday."

> June 21: "Black clouds have been passing all round us during this past week, & heavy showers must have fallen not far from us, but up to the present, no rain has fallen here. The sun is scorching hot, and the wind feels as if it blew from off the face of a huge fire. All vegetation is dying for want of rain, even the weeds cannot grow. It is the general belief now that we are on the eve of a famine. We have not a single vegetable in our field this year. Peas were the only things that came up & for a time gave us hope, but now they have nearly all disappeared."

> June 22: "All the Indians are very much down in spirits abt. their crops."

> June 29: "Two services, not many present, nearly half of our people being away hunting ducks & whatever else they can catch for

food. Last night it began to rain abt. 7 & continued until 7 this morning. It is impossible to estimate the good it will do, though we fear it has come rather too late for the wheat crops, but what seems impossible to me is possible with God."[13]

Some of the potatoes and vegetables managed to survive the drought. Then, again, disaster struck. On June 30, heavy frost cut down "all the potatoes that had come up." Several days later, on July 5, the "sharpest frost of the summer" hit. As a result, Hines wrote in his journal, "wild berries & vegetation of every kind have suffered very much." The following day was sunny. This would have a bad effect on the frost-bitten plants, the missionary concluded.[14]

For the first time since Ahtahkakoop and his people settled on the reserve at Sandy Lake, there would be no crops to tend during the summer. Seven men went to work on the government farm located north of the Mistawasis Reserve on July 7, where presumably they got rations to feed their families in exchange for labour. Nine days later several more people left the reserve. Hines said they had nothing to eat and no crops to look after, so there was nothing to hold them there. They were not expected back before the first week of August. Even haying was impossible because in mid-July, when the hay was usually cut, the grass was only six inches high.[15]

Life, nevertheless, continued, and on July 21 Louis Ahenakew married 18-year-old Catherine Ermineskin, daughter of K-ōsihkosiwanāniw (He Who Has An Ermineskin Robe). Louis was 20. Although Hines said Catherine was from Battleford, K-ōsihkosiwanāniw had been on the Ahtahkakoop Band paylist from 1876 until the 1883–84 paylist year, when he, his wife Chenisis, and the unmarried children moved to the Battleford area. Interestingly Catherine's sister Ellen was married to Louis's brother, Baptiste Ahenakew. Another sister, Janet, was the wife of Ahtahkakoop's son Kā-miyo-astotin.[16] Hines had announced the banns in church the day before the wedding, noting that he had waited a month before making the announcement because he thought Louis should have stayed single longer. Louis "thought so himself," Hines continued, "but the maternal parents of both were too pressing." Hines objected in particular to the extra costs associated with paying Louis as a married man instead of a single one.[17]

While Ahtahkakoop and his people struggled with their farms and the new way of life, anger and frustration were spreading throughout much of the land that later would became part of the Province of Saskatchewan. By early 1884 the federal government, under the direction of Lawrence Vankoughnet, had launched a program of cost-cutting and financial entrenchment. Despite the hardship and difficulties already facing the Indian people, assistant Indian commissioner Hayter Reed ordered Indian department employees to reduce the meagre rations being issued to the bands. In some instances aid was cut completely.[18] Starvation, inadequate clothing, sickness, and death were all taking their toll, and proud men who had been self-sufficient only a few years earlier were forced to beg for food to feed their hungry families. Moreover, because of government policy, Indian agents and farm instructors were stripped of any discretionary power they may have had and were unable to react reasonably to individual situations. Not surprisingly, hostility surfaced on a number of occasions as desperate men challenged the authority of Indian agents and farm instructors. In several angry incidents, bloodshed was narrowly averted.

For example, at the Crooked Lake Agency in the Qu'Appelle Valley area, a group of 25 armed men demanded an interview with farm instructor Hilton Keith after rations were stopped in February, one of the coldest months of the year. A scuffle followed, during which the instructor claimed to have been knocked down, bruised, and struck with a knife.[19] Keith called the police and charges were laid against four men; one charge was later withdrawn and the other men, who pleaded guilty, were discharged.

At Frog Lake, also in February, Big Bear's father-in-law Yāyākotēwi-wāpas (Turned Up Rabbit Nose) told farm instructor John Delaney that he had been hunting for a long time but had been unable to kill anything. The man said he was hungry and asked for food. In a report of the incident that followed, written by Indian agent John Rae, "Delaney refused to give him anything, according to orders and asked the Indian to go." Yāyākotēwi-wāpas sat down on a pile of frozen fish, saying that he would not leave until he was given some rations. When Delaney grabbed the man by the arm and tried to push him out, Yāyākotēwi-wāpos drew a clasp knife. The farm instructor ran out, locking the door behind him, and called the police. Charges were laid and the man was given two months hard labour for drawing the knife. Thomas Quinn, the acting sub-agent at Frog Lake, reacted with the comment that he hoped the sentence "will have a good effect on Big Bear's band."

Dissent of another kind, combined with the efforts of a number of chiefs to gain better conditions for their people, was also developing in the spring and summer of 1884. In the south, Chief Payipwāt* (Hole In The Sioux)

---

* His name is sometimes spelled Piapot.

had wintered on a reserve chosen for him by government officials—against his wishes—near Indian Head. Forty-two of his people died that winter. With the coming of spring Payipwāt demanded the right to select his own reserve and led his people towards the Qu'Appelle Valley. There he planned to hold a Sun Dance and a council to discuss reserves and treaty terms.

Government officials reacted immediately by sending a force of 54 policemen with a cannon to show Payipwāt that "his power in this country is nothing."[20] A dangerous situation was avoided when the chief agreed to meet with government officials at Fort Qu'Appelle to discuss his grievances. Reed, looking for an opportunity to further restrict the lives of the Indian people, requested that the North-West Mounted Police take steps to keep the Indians from "roaming the country." Their behaviour alarmed the settlers, Reed claimed, and kept the Indians from planting their crops.[21] Reed's superiors refused the request. In the end, Payipwāt was the winner. He successfully held a Sun Dance on the Pasqua Reserve in June and later moved to a reserve of his own choosing in the Qu'Appelle Valley, west of Muscowpetung's reserve.[22] He settled there in August with 37 lodges.

Meanwhile, in Saskatchewan River country, Big Bear had not given up on his plans to forge a united front for dealing with the government. As a first step, planned in consultation with other chiefs from the Battleford area, he decided to hold a Sun Dance followed by a grand council on Poundmaker's reserve. Among the topics to be discussed was the formation of "one big reserve, or one part of the West, for the Indians." After the council, Big Bear intended to meet with Dewdney in Regina before travelling to Ottawa to present the chiefs' grievances to top government officials there.[23]

The response to his invitations for both the Sun Dance and the council, carried by messengers bearing tobacco, was overwhelming. By mid-June, 2,000 people had gathered on the Poundmaker Reserve.[24] Then plans went awry. On June 18—the day before the Sun Dance was to begin—two of Papēwē's* sons asked John Craig, the farm instructor from the neighbouring Little Pine Reserve, for some food. The young men had been receiving rations because they were ill. Craig agreed to give one of the sons, a man by the name of Ayiwinis (The Clothes), some food. He turned down Kā-wīcētwēmāt (He Who Speaks Their Language), claiming that his injuries had healed. Tempers flared and, according to Poundmaker farm instructor

---

* Papēwē translates as Lucky Man.

Sidney P. Hall, National Archives of Canada,
C-013001

Poundmaker, chief of the reserve where the Sun Dance was held.

Robert Jefferson, "Craig lost command of his temper and pushed them out. One of them caught up an axe handle that lay near the door and hit Craig on the arm with it. He was not injured at all, hardly hurt but the insult demanded punishment and his position vindication, so he laid the matter before the police."[25]

The situation was so tense, ready to explode at any moment, that the North-West Mounted Police decided to wait until the Sun Dance was over before trying to arrest the two men. During the confrontations that took place at the conclusion of the ceremony, some of the chiefs made every effort to prevent bloodshed. Big Bear shouted "Peace, Peace," and old men rode through the crowd crying "Do not shoot first" as the angry crowd jostled and taunted the police. Lucky Man's sons were finally arrested and hauled away.[26] No shots were fired and no one was hurt. Superintendent Crozier of the Mounted Police was to report several days later that "It is yet to me incomprehensible how some one did not fire, and it is more than fortunate they did not—Had a shot been fired by either the Police or Indians, I fear it would have been the signal for an engagement, and when that had taken place, it is hard to foretell what the consequences would have been." He also informed Dewdney and his superior officer that a number of Indian people had "complained that Craig the Instructor had used them badly at different times and often."[27]

Crozier, Jefferson, and others all put the blame firmly on Craig for the near tragedy. At the preliminary hearing held on July 4, Crozier—in his capacity of justice of the peace—said that Craig

> in this instance acted indiscreetly, and might easily have tided
> over the difficulty. Prisoner had a reasonable excuse, in being

sick, for asking for rations, and a little discretion would have saved a very great deal of trouble at a most inopportune moment. Of course Craig had his orders, and orders must be obeyed, but the discretion allowed him might have been exercised.[28]

Jefferson agreed, saying the confrontation between Craig and Kā-wīcētwēmāt should not have happened. "The man who cannot exercise patience and forbearance in full measure should never have any dealings with Indians, much less be placed in charge of them," the farm instructor explained.

> In the present case, if the Indian had understood all the Instructor was saying to him, the assault would have taken place sooner. Besides all which, the trouble was all over a few pounds of flour. The game was not worth the candle.[29]

He added that few Hudson's Bay Company men had been assaulted during the long history of the company in the North-West.

Although the judge determined that Craig was largely responsible for the incident, he nevertheless found Kā-wīcētwēmāt guilty when he appeared in a Battleford court a month later. He was sentenced to seven days in the guardhouse at the North-West Mounted Police post. The charges against Ayiwinis were dropped.[30]

The near disaster sent warning signals to government officials. Indian agent Rae wrote that he did not "think that Big Bear or any of the others are going to submit to be starved out, and there is no doubt that these men are particularly hard-up." In regards to the restrictions on the discretionary powers of agents, he said that if he was given "proper power" and supplies to act liberally in certain situations there would be "no more trouble." He warned, however, that if the department continues to enforce the present orders, "full preparations should be made to fight them, as it will sooner or later come to this, if more liberal treatment is not given."[31]

Crozier also supported discretionary power for the agents. "If you will pardon my speaking out on a matter outside my own province, I would most respectfully suggest that the Agent be given discretionary power, to some extent at least, to feed and thereby humour the unsettled Indians, even if they do not do much work for some time, which after all should hardly be expected from a lot of savages at once."[32]

Vankoughnet at last took action to loosen control slightly. "If you concur in Crozier's recommendations," he wired Dewdney, "that the Agent

The town of Prince Albert, which developed on the south side of the North Saskatchewan River, was situated east of the Isbister settlement.

have more discretionary power as regards … [Big Bear] and other new arrivals, [you] may authorize it, provided no loss of prestige by [giving] too many concessions."[33] He cautioned, however, that rations were to be given only to Indians on their reserves and they were to be stopped "under any circumstances unless Indians worked."

For Big Bear, the confrontation on the Poundmaker Reserve had destroyed any possibility of meeting in council with the chiefs and leading men who had come for the Sun Dance.[34] It also ruined Big Bear's plans of going to Regina and then Ottawa to meet with government officials. Some of the chiefs withdrew their support, and the old chief found his control of the young men and more militant members of his camp eroding. As for the government, they stepped up their surveillance of Big Bear, Poundmaker, Lucky Man, Little Poplar, and other leaders they considered trouble-makers.

Unrest and frustration in the Prince Albert area had a wider base. By 1884 Prince Albert had grown from a small mission to a town of 600 people situated in the midst of a developing farming community. There were a number of fine homes, a post office, a hotel, a restaurant, a newspaper, a lumber mill, two grist (flour) mills, and the Hudson's Bay Company store, as well as other stores and places of business. To the south, a community of French-speaking Métis had developed on the South Branch of the Saskatchewan River at Batoche and St. Laurent. And situated in the four directions around Prince Albert were the Indian reserves. As for Fort Carlton, only a skeleton staff remained at the old fur trade post after Lawrence Clarke moved the headquarters of the Hudson's Bay Company Saskatchewan District* to Prince Albert in 1882.

During the early 1880s discontent had grown throughout the entire area. The Indian people were starving and disillusioned. The Métis living on the South Branch had a number of concerns, including the government's delay in surveying the land and issuing scrip. And the white and half-breed settlers had economic and political concerns, many of which had evolved from the diversion of the Canadian Pacific Railway to the southern plains. By a stroke of a pen, the economic base had shifted from Saskatchewan River country to Regina and other towns along the mainline of the railway. There were problems with the way government contracts were let, and farmers everywhere suffered from poor crops. The various groups had sent numerous petitions and letters to Ottawa. All were met with apparent indifference.

Finally, in May of 1884, a general meeting of settlers and Métis was held in Prince Albert to discuss the problems. As a result of this gathering, a delegation was sent to Montana to ask Louis Riel, the Métis leader who had been instrumental in the creation of the Province of Manitoba in 1870, for assistance. One of the men in the delegation was James Isbister, the English-speaking half-breed who had retired from the Hudson's Bay Company in 1862 and founded the Isbister settlement; this settlement was near the site later chosen for Prince Albert. The others were Gabriel Dumont, Moïse Ouellette, and Michel Dumas, all Métis from the South Branch. The men returned from Montana with Riel on July 5. Riel spoke moderately when he met with groups of people in the area and support for a united approach to Ottawa, for a while at least, grew.

The concerns of the Métis were the most volatile as settlers continued to move onto land near their still unsurveyed farms. Initially a good number of white settlers supported the Métis in their struggle for title to their farmland, but as "agitation became rife" during the months that followed Riel's arrival, support lessened. John Hines suspected that some individuals who

---

* The Carlton District had been renamed the Lower Saskatchewan District in 1873 and then the Saskatchewan District in 1874.

continued to support Riel had ulterior motives. "Many of the leading citizens of Prince Albert," he wrote,

> showed great sympathy with the agitation—insomuch that it was difficult for a non-interested party to decide who were most interested, those who considered themselves entitled to scrip, or those who had no such claim, but who hoped ultimately to get possession of it![35]

In late July a number of Indian people attended one of Riel's meetings at Duck Lake. Among other things, the Métis leader was reported to have said that the Indian people had "'rights' as well as the half-breeds, and that he wished to be the means of having them redressed."[36] The concerns of the Métis, despite Riel's talk, were different than those of the Indian people and the chiefs decided to proceed on their own.

Subsequently, Beardy invited the leading men of the Carlton district to a council at Duck Lake. Instead of asking Riel for assistance, he turned to Big Bear. The Cree chief was on his way to Fort Pitt to select a reserve when the messenger found him. He turned around and, accompanied by Lucky Man, headed for Beardy's reserve. On July 31, the "Duck Lake and Battleford Chiefs with considerable number of men" went to the Indian agency office at Fort Carlton to request food for the council. Although their request was turned down by sub-Indian agent Ansdell Macrae, he took "measures to ascertain what was going on at D. Lake."[37] As an added precaution, a member of the North-West Mounted Police force was sent to the small village of Duck Lake to keep a watchful eye on the proceedings.

Nine chiefs from the Carlton and Prince Albert area, including Beardy, Okimāsis, Ahtahkakoop, and Mistawasis, 14 headmen, Big Bear, and Lucky Man were in attendance when the council came to order.[38] Big Bear apparently was one of the first to speak. Unlike the Carlton chiefs, who had been living on their reserves for a number of years, Big Bear was still trying to resolve some of the issues facing the Indian people before he selected and moved onto his reserve. His words mirrored his dissatisfaction with the government:

> Yes, I am willing to speak. Since the leaves have begun to come it is why I have been walking, walking, trying to make myself understood. It is why I have come to Duck Lake. To show you why I have been so anxious, it is because I have been trying to seize the promises which they made to me, I have been grasping

but I cannot find them. What they have promised me straightway I have not yet seen the half of it.

We have all been deceived in the same way. It is the cause of our meeting at Duck Lake. They offered me a spot as a reserve. As I see that they are not going to be honest I am afraid to take a reserve. They have given me to choose between several small reserves but I feel sad to abandon the liberty of my own land when they come to me and offer me small plots to stay there and in return not to get half of what they have promised me.[39]

"When will you have a big meeting?" he asked. "It has come to me as through the bushes that you are not yet all united, take time and become united, and I will speak."

The disillusionment and disappointment of the other leading men were evident as the list of grievances grew. They all found themselves in a distressing situation. Ahtahkakoop and Mistawasis were fully aware of the problems. Their bands were trying to farm with the tools, cattle, and other things promised by the government. They were experiencing some success, in part because of Ahtahkakoop's foresight in having Hines settle with them. The people in their bands, nonetheless, were suffering. Members of bands without their advantages were suffering more.

Most of the grievances had been discussed with the Queen's representatives and government officials many times since the treaty was signed. Their people were hungry, poorly clothed, and often sick, the chiefs said. The implements distributed by the government were of poor quality. The oxen and horses were wild. Their words seemed to have fallen on deaf ears, for very little was ever done about their plight.

In addition to their chronic concerns, the chiefs were unhappy that the Hudson's Bay Company had been paid £300,000 for Indian land.[40] In their view, the great English company was already rich. It was not fair, and they demanded that the Hudson's Bay Company turn the £300,000 over to the Indian people to provide "a basis on which to build new treaties."[41] Moreover, the company had been granted title to land at its trading posts, and it was given one-twentieth of all the land situated in the fertile belt of what had been Indian land. Had the leading men known that the Hudson's Bay Company would eventually receive 3.3 million acres of land in what is now the Province of Saskatchewan, their resentment would have turned to outright rage. The Indian people of Saskatchewan had only been allowed to keep 1.5 million acres.[42]

After meeting for almost a week, Beardy sent two of his men to Fort Carlton on August 6 to ask Macrae a second time for provisions to feed the people attending the council. Again Macrae refused, claiming untruthfully that since "nothing was known of the object of their meeting and that they were holding it on their own account, no food would be supplied to them." This was unacceptable to the chiefs. They decided to request provisions from the agent one more time. If that failed, they would kill an ox. Accordingly, the next day one of the headmen from the James Smith Band delivered a note to Macrae signed by Ahtahkakoop and Mistawasis asking "in respectful" terms for food. This food, the note said, would be distributed at the chiefs' council that was being held to discuss their grievances against the government. Macrae responded saying that "the Government was unaware that they had grievances to consult over (as was stated in their note) but that if, under their head chiefs, they had matter for consultation, and choose to enter upon it in an open manner, i.e., at the Agency, rations to the chiefs and councillors would be provided."[43]

On Saturday, August 9, the chiefs moved to Fort Carlton and erected their tipis near the post. Almost immediately a delegation was sent to demand that an ox be killed for food. Macrae stood his ground and refused. Another request for a "beef ox" was turned down on Monday. At Macrae's request, the "working men" accompanying the chiefs were sent home and rations were issued. Then, in the evening, the chiefs arranged to meet with Macrae the following day, August 11.

The council was held in the "open air" instead of in Macrae's office. Chief after chief stated his concerns and grievances. Most of them were shared by other bands living in the plains and parklands of the North-West Territories. None were new.

Macrae, who said he had secured an "excellent interpreter," took notes, and then summarized the grievances and requests in a report to Dewdney dated August 25, 1884.[44]

According to Macrae's report, the chiefs said they did not have enough oxen to make a living as farmers. Furthermore, the ones they did have were wild and many had died or been killed because they were "intractable." The oxen, they said, should be replaced.

The cows were too wild to be stabled, the chiefs said, and died of exposure during the winter. Many of the horses were also wild. The cows and horses should also be replaced.

Illustration by Brent Christensen

Sub-agent Macrae, with the help of an interpreter, recorded the grievances of the chiefs and leading men at a meeting held inside the stockade at Fort Carlton.

The wagons were poorly made and continually breaking down. As a result, chiefs often had to travel on foot. Since many of them were old men, "means of conveyance" should be given to the chiefs, along with good horses.

They told Macrae that "the promises made to them at the time of their treaty was that when they were destitute, liberal assistance would be given to them. That the crops are now poor, rats [muskrats] are scarce, and other game is likely to be so, and they look forward with the greatest fear to the approaching winter. In view of the above mentioned promise they claim that the Government should give them liberal treatment during the season, for having disposed of all the property that they owned before the treaty, in order to tide over times of distress since, they are now reduced to absolute and complete dependence upon what relief is extended to them. With the present amount of assistance, they cannot work effectively on their reserves, and it should be increased."

The chiefs also told Macrae that Lieutenant-Governor Morris had promised "they should not be short of clothing; yet they never received any, and it is feared that this winter some of them will be unable to leave their houses without freezing to death."

Moreover, schools had not been established as promised. They wanted schoolhouses built and kept in good repair. Medicine chests—also promised—had not been placed on the reserves. They wanted this done, pointing out that "many live among them, or near them who could administer drugs benificially [sic] but as they haven't them, they suffer from complaints that might be cured."

In regards to "machinery," the chiefs said "they were told that they would see how the white man lived, and would be taught to live like him. It is seen that he has threshing mills, mowers, reapers, and rakes. As the Govm^t. pledged itself to put them in the same position as the white man it should give them these things."

They pointed out that many of their people wanted to settle, but they were "forced to wander" as there was "not enough of anything supplied to them to enable all to farm, although a living by agriculture was promised to them." The chiefs asked that "all bad things, implements and tools, as well as stock etc. should be replaced by gifts of better articles." And they wanted harnesses to be supplied with the oxen, maps of their reserves given to them so they would not be robbed of their land, and beef provided at all treaty payments.

The chiefs also issued a warning: "Requests for redress of these griev-ances have been again & again made without effect. They are glad that the young men have not resorted to violent measures to gain it. That it is almost too hard for them to bear the treatment received at the hands of the government, after its 'sweet promises' made in order to get their country from them. They now fear that they are going to be cheated. They will wait until next summer to see if this council has the desired effect, failing which they will take measures to get what they desire." Macrae added that "the 'proposed measures' could not be elicited, but a suggestion of the idea of war was repudiated."

Additionally, the leading men told the agent that they were losing con-fidence in the government. "At the time of making the treaty, they were comparatively well off. ... now [they] are 'full of fear' for they believe that the Government which pretended to be friendly is going to cheat them. ... [had] the Treaty promises been carried out all would have been well, instead of the present feeling existing." The agent added that "they blame not the Queen, but the Government at Ottawa."[45]

Macrae then summarized the comments of two men, Joseph Badger from the South Branch and Big Bear. The agent said that Badger "spoke very plainly on the alleged grievances, and warned the Government that it must redress them, to escape the measures that may be taken."

Big Bear, in his speech, fully supported the council, telling Macrae that the chiefs should be given what they requested. He was obviously pleased with the results of the council, declaring that "a year ago, he stood alone in making these demands; now the whole of the Indians are with him."

Macrae concluded his report to Dewdney with his own warning that "an answer in detail is expected by the Council, which declared itself to be a representative one of the Battleford as well as Carlton Crees. No doubt need be entertained that the Indians regard it as such."

When the council ended, Macrae gave food to the chiefs for the trip home. Big Bear met with Louis Riel in Prince Albert before returning to the Fort Pitt area. Ahtahkakoop and his headmen returned to Sandy Lake and their scorched crops, and the other chiefs who farmed went home to similar situations.

The chiefs' complaints and concerns reflected what was happening in Saskatchewan River country and beyond. When Ahtahkakoop and Mistawasis signed Treaty Six they believed they could support their early farming ventures by hunting and trapping. The change would be gradual and the hardship minimized. The original intent was no longer possible. The buffalo had disappeared much faster than anyone could imagine. Animals of all kinds—moose, elk, deer, fur-bearing animals, small creatures such as rabbits, and even fish—were becoming scarce, reduced in numbers by the increased pressures being put upon them with the disappearance of the buffalo. The Indian peoples' traditional economy had vanished with the animals. Ahtahkakoop and a number of the other chiefs were making a serious effort to farm, but just as they were starting to make some headway, drought, frost, and disintegrating tools dashed their hopes. In 1884 there would be no crops. The chiefs believed that the government had promised to look after their band members. This promise was not being kept, and some of the people were seriously beginning to wonder if they could survive.

Macrae shared some of their concerns. In a report written on August 11, the day before he met with the chiefs, the agent reported to his superiors that the crops were "indifferent," and most of them would not mature before frost. He went on to say that the muskrats, which were a staple food, would be "most scarce" during the upcoming winter, and the "principal dependence will be on rabbits." Destitution was sure to occur, Macrae said, and the Indian people would suffer more than any time since treaty, "for, in former years, some property was owned that could be disposed of for the alleviation of their misery, but this recourse being no longer left to them, they have now only the Government's assistance to depend on."[46]

Then he aimed some veiled criticism at the government, writing that "nothing prevents all of our Indians from being settled on their reserves, except our incapacity to furnish enough material for agriculture. They are all desirous of settling, but have not the wherewithal to enable them to commence farming." The northern reserves, meaning Ahtahkakoop's and Mistawasis's reserves in particular, experienced another year of steady progress, he continued, but they laboured under "some disadvantage" since they were isolated and many miles from a mill. In order to progress further, the agent said, they needed a mill and shops to repair things so they could become self-sufficient.

Macrae also proposed that carpenter and blacksmith shops be established at Snake Plain to serve the Mistawasis, Ahtahkakoop and Muskeg Lake bands. "The natural ingenuity of the Indians renders them so handy with tools," he explained, "that much may be hoped for from practice and experience."[47] This natural talent had long been recognized by Hudson's Bay Company officers, but it was unusual for an Indian department official to speak in such a manner. It was also in sharp contrast to repetitive comments by others about tools and implements broken through misuse.

Although the government seemed unwilling to tackle the problems and concerns of the residents of the Carlton and Prince Albert districts, it was prepared to maintain law and order. Accordingly, when Riel arrived in the St. Laurent area in July, surveillance in Saskatchewan River country increased. The North-West Mounted Police regularly patrolled the Duck Lake, St. Laurent, and Batoche areas, and an unusual number of telegrams and letters kept government and police officials informed about activities in the area. In response to the council at Beardy's reserve, a policeman had been sent to the small village of Duck Lake and on August 12—the day Macrae was meeting with the chiefs—a non-commissioned Mounted Police officer and three men were sent to the village on "detachment duty" to replace the one-man surveillance. Despite this flurry of police action, Sergeant W.A. Brooks noted that the presence of both Riel and Big Bear in Prince Albert during the middle of August "caused very little excitement and people did not seem to pay much attention to them."[48]

The citizens of Prince Albert may not have been unduly concerned, but government officials were and they proceeded to strengthen their position. The names of people who associated themselves with Riel were sent to Prince Albert on August 15; and on August 24, Sergeant Harry Keenan reported that upwards of 250 half-breeds and an even greater number of Indian men in the Carlton area were capable of bearing arms.* With a little more time, he said, it would be possible to conduct a more accurate survey without creating suspicion.[49] Keenan's information was later updated to include 235 Indian men and 165 half-breed men in the "environs of Duck Lake"; included in the Indian total were men from the Beardy, One Arrow, Okimāsis, Mistawasis, Ahtahkakoop, and Muskeg Lake bands. According to the same report, the number of Indian men in the "environs of Prince Albert" totalled 200, consisting of men in the bands of John Smith, James Smith, Cakāstēpēsin, Ayahtaskamikinam, and unnamed bands in the vicinity of Green Lake; there were 300 half-breeds in this same area.[50]

---

* Keenan included the Métis in his figures for half-breeds.

On August 16, a few days after Ahtahkakoop and his headmen returned from the councils at Beardy's reserve and Fort Carlton, a frost "cut down the potatoes and other vegetables" that had managed to survive the drought. The next day, after church services, Hines took a kettle of oatmeal gruel with him when he went to visit the sick. A month and a half later—on October 3—four inches of snow fell and covered the "shocks, what few there are." Two-thirds of the grain was still standing, "as green as it ought to have been in July." Hines said it was only good for livestock fodder.[51] Interestingly, government documentation indicated that 400 bushels of wheat were harvested at the Ahtahkakoop Reserve that year, along with 1,000 bushels of potatoes and 800 of turnips.[52] These figures, based on comments by Hines, were either false or did not take into account the quality of the product, for the missionary reported that the people had to hunt to survive because there "was no grain or potatoes this year."[53]

Asināpēwiyin (Stone Man), who had been very sick for several months, died on October 4, the day after the snowfall.[54] Hines wrote in his journal that he was "busy in getting the grave dug & the coffin made." The next day some of people were "at the house where the corpse … [was] lying" instead of attending Sunday church services. Additionally, others had gone to *manitow-sakahikan* for a traditional ceremony. The number at church was small, but Hines rationalized that people had probably gone to *manitow-sākahikan* "to get something to eat, as nearly all here are hungry." In his opinion they should not have gone because it "will strengthen the heathens in their belief."[55] Obviously, despite the missionary's claims that practically everyone at Sandy Lake had converted to Christianity, Ahtahkakoop's people had not entirely forsaken their traditional ways. Asināpēwiyin was buried the evening of October 5.

Five days later, on October 10, government officials were on the reserve to make treaty payments to 180 people. This figure included Ahtahkakoop, headmen Sasakamoose and Kā-miyo-ahcahkwēw, 32 men, 45 women, 49 boys, 48 girls, and six other persons. Six men and their families, for a total of 22 people, were absent. Although no reason was given on the paylists for their absence, it likely reflected the shortage of food and the necessity of hunting to make a living. These families were not included in the government's total. Had they been, the population of the band would have shown an increase of 10 during the year.

The treaty paylist indicated that five girls and four boys had been born during the 1883–84 paylist year, and one girl and three boys had died. Only two adult deaths were recorded. Wāsēhikot's wife Jemima, 38, had died in April, and Asināpēwiyin died six days before the treaty payments. Kā-miyo-ahcahkwēw's daughter Mary, who had been given her own paylist number in 1883 when she married Donald LeBlanc, had her only child "disallowed" because the boy's father was not a treaty Indian; this child was one of Ahtahkakoop's great-grandsons.* The decision to disallow the boy's treaty status was apparently overruled since his mother received $5 in arrears in 1885; the note on the paylist read "Paid for by me 1883, but Boy not paid for last year."[56] In one of the marriages that took place during the 1883–84 treaty year, Peter Peekeekoot (Hook Nose) married Isabella, daughter of the headman Wāskitoy who had died in 1879. Peekeekoot was the son of John Peter Masuskapoe[†] and nephew of Ahtahkakoop. The newly married couple was listed under Wāskitoy's ticket on the treaty paylist instead of being given a new number. Additionally, a woman from the Mistawasis Reserve married into the band, and Ahtahkakoop's daughter Philomene, who had married Johnny Jimmuk from the Mistawasis Band in 1881, transferred with her husband back to her father's band.[57]

Treaty day in 1884 featured a "football" game (probably soccer) in the afternoon. Hines reported that the "young men came across the Lake" to play. Kāh-kāsōw won 10 pounds of flour and 10 pounds of beef for scoring the first goal. One of Ahtahkakoop's sons received a print shirt for scoring the second goal. The prizes were given by the Indian agent.[58]

Unlike the previous week, when most of the people were either supporting Asināpēwiyin's widow or attending a traditional ceremony at *manitow-sakahikan*, there was a good-sized congregation at both church services on Sunday. Hines noted with pride that two of the young men in his Sunday school class had returned home with their lessons completed after freighting for two weeks.

With treaty payments out of the way, many of the families in Ahtahkakoop's band scattered to eke a living off the land. By October 26, two-thirds of the people were gone. Some were fishing, while others were hunting rabbits and whatever else they could kill. Hines predicted that very few people would be at Sandy Lake during the winter because there had been "no harvest."[59]

---

* Mary Kā-miyo-ahcahkwēw and her son were discharged from treaty in 1889.
[†] John Peter Masuskapoe was the son of Masuskapoe, Ahtahkakoop's deceased brother.

By early November the people from Sandy Lake and Snake Plain were starving, and Ahtahkakoop and Mistawasis were extremely unhappy with way sub-Indian agent Macrae was treating them. Together, the two chiefs went to Fort Carlton, this time to lay their grievances before Indian agent Rae and inspector Wadsworth. The two government officials were not at the post when the chiefs arrived but they were expected November 9. While they waited, Ahtahkakoop and Mistawasis met with their long-time acquaintance, Peter Ballendine. A former employee of the Hudson's Bay Company at Fort Carlton, Ballendine had been hired by the government to circulate amongst the bands. His instructions were to collect information on the various activities of the people and to use his influence in convincing the chiefs to keep the peace during these unsettling times.* At the request of Ahtahkakoop and Mistawasis, Ballendine reported to Reed that the two chiefs were

> much disatisfied [sic] with their agent [Macrae] and Instructor [Chaffee]. Since the payments they say that not more than 40 lbs of Flour has been esued [sic] to them. They say that they think that they are imposed upon being good natured Indians.

> The two Chiefs stated to me today [November 8, 1884] that there is a many a time they are very angry but always hold themselves not to say anything, fering [sic] they may excite their young men and other friends....

> Both the Chiefs demand help as their crops are a ... [failure], and state that they understood from Gov. Morris that in the event their crops failing that they would get help from the Government at the first Treaty.

> I would recommend that the two Chiefs should be assisted better than they have been I am sorry to say that the whole Band are relly [sic] starving. As far as I can see I think they are justified to complain. They both ask me to write you soon as they are in great want and wish to get help. If not there will be some families die [from] want of grub.[60]

---

* Although some sources consider Ballendine to be a "secret agent" hired by the government to spy on the Indian, half-breed, and Métis peoples, Ahtahkakoop, Mistawasis, Poundmaker, and others knew he was reporting to government officials.

Ballendine told Ahtahkakoop and Mistawasis that he believed Rae would help them when he saw that they really were "in great want."

The meeting with Rae and Wadsworth went well. The chiefs' complaints were forwarded to Dewdney, who responded quickly when he heard of the dire conditions under which Ahtahkakoop's and Mistawasis's people were living. These chiefs, he wrote to Macdonald, superintendent general of Indian Affairs, on November 25, "have been two of our best Indians. I think it is the more important that they and their bands should be well cared for now that they have met with misfortune."[61] Provisions, ammunition, and twine for trapping were distributed. Some extra assistance was likely given to other bands as well, for Macdonald was to report later that because of the crop failure, "an abundance of food" was made available in the autumn.[62]

Dewdney believed that the bands of the Carlton and Battleford regions had stated "openly and frankly what they wished the government would do, over and above what it was doing for them—their requests not being great."[63] He had forwarded the petition from the council meeting at Fort Carlton to officials in Ottawa, where it was met with apparent indifference. The Canadian government once again was procrastinating instead of reacting to the critical grievances of the Indian peoples. They did so despite warnings from the North-West Mounted Police, Hudson's Bay Company officers, settlers, and others fully aware of the turmoil that was reaching an ignition point.

Concerned about the lack of response from Ottawa and confronted with rumours that Beardy and Big Bear were planning a Sun Dance at Beardy's reserve in the summer of 1885, Dewdney sent assistant Indian commissioner Hayter Reed to interview the chiefs in the Duck Lake, Prince Albert, and Battleford areas. The chiefs were tired of talking and refused to meet with Reed until a response to their petition was received. In his report, Reed acknowledged the truth in many of the grievances.[64] The bull assigned to Ahtahkakoop died before "the Indians had actual possession of it on the Reserve," he reported to Macdonald, and there was "much truth" in the complaint that many of the cattle were wild and not easily managed. Furthermore the light wagons were useless. In regards to implements, he said the agents only gave the implements they thought the Indians needed. Otherwise, Reed claimed, the tools broke before the Indian farmers learned how to use them.

Instead of recommending immediate action to solve the problems that had been reported every year since 1876, Reed proposed breaking up some of the large Indian agencies and appointing extra agents. This move, he said, might also separate some of the bands from the Indian movement that seemed to be developing to address the grievances.[65]

Ahtahkakoop was also concerned about the state of affairs in the North-West. Riel, still interested in getting the support of chiefs in the Carlton district, sent William Badger to talk to Ahtahkakoop and Mistawasis on his behalf in November, 1884. The two chiefs refused to let Badger speak, telling him that they "did not wish their names [to] appear among people who were trying to make trouble." Ahtahkakoop explained further, saying that "it seems only yesterday that I took the Governors hand as my friend and I cannot think of doing anything contrary."[66]

Riel did not give up easily. According to Hines, one of Riel's agents "spent the early part of the winter among the French half-breeds a few miles north of Sandy Lake and was constantly appealing to the Indians as well as the half-breeds to join issue with them."[67] When this venture was unsuccessful, the "agent" returned to Batoche. Riel sent messengers to other areas as well, trying to win support for his cause. Despite their reluctance to join forces with the Métis, a number of chiefs were still determined to press the government into addressing their grievances. Beardy and Big Bear continued their plans to hold a Sun Dance at Beardy's reserve in 1885. Throughout the fall and winter, their representatives travelled from reserve to reserve delivering tobacco and invitations to bands as far away as Edmonton to the west and the Qu'Appelle Valley in the south.[68] Ahtahkakoop supported the chiefs in their endeavours to have their grievances addressed, but he was concerned about the anger that was becoming increasingly evident, even in his own band. A level-headed, rational man, he was trying to honour his side of the treaty while at the same time working towards the betterment of his people. During the summer of 1884 he had foreseen the trouble that was coming. Ahtahkakoop now looked to the future with apprehension.[69]

These feelings intensified every time Ahtahkakoop went to Fort Carlton. After Riel's arrival at St. Laurent and the chiefs' council at Beardy's reserve, government officials had decided it would be difficult to police the Duck Lake, St. Laurent, and Fort Carlton areas from Prince Albert. To remedy the situation, the North-West Mounted Police arranged to lease a major portion of Fort Carlton. The old fur trade post was a shadow of its former self when the police arrived. Only the northeast and

By 1884 some of the stockades at Fort Carlton had been removed. The Big House on the right served as the home and office of chief factor Lawrence Clarke before he moved to Prince Albert.

southwest bastions were still standing. The stockades on the south and west sides of the fort had been taken down, and many of the buildings were vacant and in poor condition. Despite the post's deterioration, the location was considered ideal for a large detachment of police because it was near Beardy's reserve and the village of Duck Lake, where a telegraph line linked Battleford with Qu'Appelle.

By December, repairs had been made to the old log buildings and two officers, 30 non-commissioned officers, and 20 horses were stationed at Fort Carlton.[70] Now when Ahtahkakoop went to the post he found three different groups there, all with different responsibilities and perspectives. The Hudson's Bay Company, under clerk Charles N. Garson, still traded for furs and operated the store located within the stockades. Sub-Indian agent Macrae supervised the farm instructors, monitored activities on the Indian reserves, handed out rations, and generally enforced the policies of the Indian department. And now the police were there. They took over all the buildings not being used by Garson and Macrae, including the Big House. The red-coated policemen were respected by Ahtahkakoop and his people, but their increased numbers were unsettling.

Ahtahkakoop's people spent most of the winter of 1884–85 on their hunting grounds.[71] Those who remained at home looked after the children, the old, the sick, and the livestock. Hines continued with his mission work as best he could, preaching, teaching, visiting the ill, and travelling to the hunting camps. Kā-kīsikāwapiw's wife Matilda was among those who were sick.* She had had become ill on the hunting grounds and taken a powerful emetic. When her condition grew worse, Kā-kīsikāwapiw brought the woman back to the reserve. Hines said the "retching" that resulted from the emetic must have injured her, and "we fear that nothing can save her." Matilda died on November 8.[72]

The day after Matilda's death, Wāpāsōs (White Skin)—the son-in-law in the only entirely "heathen" family on the Ahtahkakoop Reserve—was baptized.† He took Jesse as his Christian name. This was an "exceedingly stubborn" family, Hines noted in his journal, and the wife and the others tried to prevent the conversion.[73]

Later in November Sasakamoose went with the missionary to visit Okīnomotayēw at Stoney Lake. This chief, as early as 1879, had watched the children working in the classroom at Sandy Lake and commented that "Truly the children are wise."[74] Despite this initial interest, it had taken a year after Hines's return from England for Okīnomotayēw to visit the mission. The Stoney Lake band had no "particular anxiety" to become Christians, Hines had noted in his journal, "but they were equally indifferent to the observances of their heathen friends & neighbours. Their whole time and thoughts seem to be taken up with 'How they shall feed and clothe themselves.'" They wanted to learn how to farm, and although the government said it would help, the promises were continually broken. These people think all white men are inseparable, Hines continued, and so they blamed him as well as government officials for their plight.[75]

Hines, nevertheless, had been interested in working with Okīnomotayēw's band for some time and decided to help. And so, soon after Sasakamoose and Hines returned to the mission, Wāsēhikot was sent to teach the children in Okīnomotayēw's camp.[76]

---

* Kā-kīsikāwapiw (Levi Turner) was the son of Iskwēsis and grandson of the old blind woman Hines ministered to on a regular basis. Matilda, 40, had been married to Ahtahkakoop's nephew Masuskapoe before he was baptized by Hines and had to give up one of his wives.

† This was probably the man who in July had asked Hines to intervene with his wife, whom he described as being "very-stiff necked."

The missionary travelled to Okīnomotayēw's camp again early in January, 1885. Ahtahkakoop's eldest son, Kā-miyo-ahcahkwēw, went with him. During the visit they learned that two of the principal councillors were the most reluctant to become Christians. One of these men was Okīnomotayēw's eldest son. He was married to the daughter of Macikwanās, the Pelican Lake chief, and had promised to take part in traditional ceremonies in the spring. The other councillor was the son of the "late Chief, who died 6 years ago." Despite the opposition of the two councillors, Okīnomotayēw said that "if any of his people refused to embrace Xtianity it would not be his fault." And then the Stoney Lake chief

> pointed out to his people the decayed state of heathenism and the strength & freshness of Xtianity. He went on to say, "My councillor & followers, a long time ago our heathen way of worship spread throughout the length and breadth of this country. I remember when the White mans religion was not known amongst us, heathenism was then like a great tree with many branches & appeared to be healthy, but as soon as this new religion was brought to us, so soon did our old worship begin to die out, and now it is like a sapless tree, there is only one little branch with a few green leaves on it, but it must soon fall off."* ... "What hope have we in this dry tree? When it was apparently healthy and strong, What good did it do us? It kept us ignorant & poor. But look what his new religion has done & is doing. It has changed hundreds of our fellow country men & made them wise, happy, & provident. Look at the one [Wāsēhikot] who had been here with us during the past month. When I compare myself with him, I am inclined to think he is not an Indian, he seems so much superior to us in every way, but he is an Indian not withstanding. It is his religion that has made him what we now see him to be. ... I want you all to understand that I renounce heathenism & am going to give myself up to the Minister to be taught and nothing will please your chief more than for you to do the same. Let us all have the same mind, we are not many, why should we be divided? There is only one God & he has sent us His laws. Let us try to be obedient & follow His will."[77]

---

* According to Hines, this was a reference to the "Pelican Lake band of Indians who are still strongly opposed to Xtianity."

Kā-miyo-ahcahkwēw then spoke "very well." He told the two councillors who wanted to keep their traditional ways that

> he could sympathise with … [them], he knew their feelings, as he
> had experienced the same himself; and so was prepared to give
> them some help in the shape of advice, he knew they were under
> a promise to perform certain heathen rites, but when they made
> that promise they knew of nothing better. The light had not yet
> shined in their midst and shown them what is truth & what is not
> truth, & therefore they were not bound to perform that promise,
> seeing they made it in their ignorance. He exhorted them to fol-
> low the good advice of their chief & not cause a division in their
> band.[78]

Hines, in recording the incident, noted that the Roman Catholic priest had baptized a number of children and young people in Okīnomotayēw's band.

The following month, February 1885, the success of the school at the Ahtahkakoop Reserve was publicly recognized when Dewdney announced that the school had been awarded first prize for the best conducted school in the North-West Territories and Manitoba. Third prize went to White Fish Lake in what is now Alberta, with the second, fourth, and fifth prizes going to schools in Manitoba. In the letter informing Hines of the award, Dewdney said he would like to see some industrial arts taught at the Asissipi Mission school. Hines responded, saying that the boys were generally very small and taken out of school when they were big enough to help with farm work and trapping. However, if the Indian commissioner could suggest a suitable industry, the clergyman said he would do his best to teach some industrial arts classes. He also noted that both he and the agent wanted to see a kindergarten at the school, and his wife—who was already teaching sewing—was interested in showing the girls how to knit.[79]

The prize for running the "best conducted school" was $100. Hines decided to use the money to further his work with Okīnomotayēw's band. By March, presumably in a step to start farming in a more serious way, Okīnomotayēw and his band had made plans to move 12 miles south of their camp at Stoney Lake.[80]

And so the winter passed. Surprisingly, Hines did not mention any unusual hunger or sickness after Ahtahkakoop and Mistawasis met with Rae and Wadsworth in November. It is possible that the extra rations distributed by the government, along with the ammunition and twine given for hunting and trapping, made for a better winter than usual. Their winter experience provided another example of what many of the people already believed. Once again, it seemed that Indian people who followed the traditional way, living in tipis and hunting and gathering their food, were healthier than those who lived in over-crowded, over-heated houses and subsisted on inadequate food.

Meanwhile, based on the report Haytor Reed submitted following his 1884 tour of Saskatchewan River country, the old Carlton Agency was split into two separate agencies. The new Carlton Agency included the Ahtahkakoop, Mistawasis, Muskeg Lake, Okīnomotayēw, and Flying Dust reserves. The Prince Albert Agency consisted of the Beardy, Okimāsis, One Arrow, James Smith, John Smith, Ayahtaskamikinam, and Cakāstēpēsin reserves.

The complaints made by Ahtahkakoop and Mistawasis against Macrae apparently had been heard and the sub-agent was transferred to "another office of duties." Macrae's replacement, former policeman John B. Lash, was appointed Indian agent for the Carlton Agency and would arrive at Fort Carlton on January 22, 1885.[81] Lash had previously been the clerk at the Macleod agency office in Blackfoot country. According to Dewdney, he was acquainted with the work of the Battleford and Carlton agencies and possessed "knowledge of the manner of handling and dealing with Indians." In addition, "his intimacy with proper management of an office" made him well suited for the position.[82] George Chaffee retained responsibility as instructor on the agency farm situated three miles north of the Mistawasis Reserve. Rae was temporarily in charge of both the Prince Albert and Battleford agencies. John Tompkins stayed on as farm instructor at the Duck Lake Agency farm.

In Lash's letter of appointment, Dewdney instructed the agent to communicate directly with the commissioner's office on "all matters pertaining to your duties, inspecting and signing all returns and vouchers previous to their being forwarded." The procedures for handling returns and vouchers were further defined, and then the new agent was advised that during seeding, haying, and harvesting seasons, "you will … spend as much of your time on the different Reserves as will be consistent with your office work, and it must be borne in mind the more personal supervision that can be given working Indians and encouragement shown your subordinates connected with them, the greater will be their advancement."[83]

Dewdney also pointed out that since the bands in the Carlton area were "fairly well advanced little difficulty need be experienced in doing away with the tribal system as regards farming operation among the later arrivals on the Reserves with a view to the encouragement of a more self-reliant spirit than that ordinarily possessed by Indians first going on a Reservation."

In addition to promoting the destruction of the tribal system, Dewdney wanted detailed records kept for each family. He told Lash that:

> You will, apart from such books as you find have been kept in the office, retain a book in which will be entered everything relating to each family in your agency, this will be a history of its progress, showing among other things the cattle, implements, tools as it may have received, the number of workers, help given in the way of provisions generally speaking, the acreage under crop, how the seed was provided, quantity sown and that harvested, how disposed of, and what has been owed to the Department in the way of issues, buildings erected and fences built and whatever else you may deem of importance. This I know will occupy much of your time if carried out. I therefore desire that you do not allow your other duties to fall in arrear in order to carry out the desired end.

Dewdney also asked Lash to impress upon the farm instructors and others that instead of cultivating and seeding a large area of land indifferently, it was

> far preferable to seed a lesser quantity in a husbandlike manner. I cannot instil this fact upon your mind too strongly as I fear much of our past want of success in certain quarters is accountable to the too hurried manner of plowing and seeding and the great desire of showing in the returns that large tracts have been placed under cultivation.

Additionally, he instructed that no expenditures or hiring of men was to be done without prior authority from the commissioner's office.

In regards to rations, Dewdney stated that the amount of rations issued in the Carlton area during the winter had been increased considerably because of the bad crops. After the next "seeding and harvesting," he instructed, "there must be a great reduction in these and they must not range higher than those of the last few years." Additionally, "no labor is to be paid for in provisions, what is meant by this is that over and above an allowance of rations for a good days work no provisions are to be given Indians, and no stores are ever to be issued to any but Indians." Furthermore, the Indian people "where possible must work for the clothing given them."

Lash was also expected to inspect the schools in the agency and report on any matters that he considered significant since "the education of the young is of paramount importance."

Although Lash was to communicate directly with Dewdney in several areas, the commissioner said that when the agent arrived at Fort Carlton it would "be well to confer with Mr Rae, the Agent at Battleford, as to your plans for the ensuing springs work, to whose orders you will be subservient until otherwise informed."

Regarding the policy of rations in exchange for work, Dewdney instructed Lash that

> a perusal of the instructions issued from time to time from this office to your predecessor will guide you in many particulars, but owing to constantly recurring circumstances which cannot be foreseen it is impossible to lay down for agents and others in charge of Indians such rules from which no departure can be taken, you have therefore to rely upon your knowledge of Indian character to direct your course, but the fact must constantly be before you that all Indians, old and young must perform such work as is within their power in return for the aid extended them.[84]

Yet Dewdney was willing to make some exceptions, particularly if it would benefit the government. "I would ask you to remember that you will have under your supervision some of the most reliable Indians in the Territories, such as Mistawasis and Ahtahkakoop," his letter concluded. "Indians of this class will require to be treated with more or less consideration, as their loyalty in time of excitement must not be forgotten."

Gabriel Dumont, leader of the South Branch Métis.

PART SIX

The Uprising and Its Aftermath

National Library of Canada, NL22080

Battle at Batoche.

CHAPTER TWENTY-SIX

The Uprising, 1885

On March 20, 1885, a messenger from Fort Carlton made his way hurriedly to Ahtahkakoop's house. His message was alarming. The Métis on the South Branch had taken a number of men, including Indian agent Lash, as prisoners. They had seized arms and ammunition, taken food from stores in the neighbourhood, and had cut the telegraph line. Lawrence Clarke and Superintendent Crozier wanted Ahtahkakoop to come to Fort Carlton as quickly as possible.

It took only a few minutes for Ahtahkakoop to get ready. He and his travelling companions stopped at Snake Plain to pick up Mistawasis, and then the men proceeded to Fort Carlton. Their talk as they travelled the Green Lake Trail to the newly outfitted North-West Mounted Police post was troubled and full of concern. In the old days, Ahtahkakoop and Mistawasis had been respected warriors. Those days were over and the two men—both nearly 70 years old—were realistic. They knew that violence would be useless.

But even more important, the chiefs had signed a treaty with the Queen. By doing so, they had agreed to "maintain peace and good order between each other, and also between themselves and other tribes of Indians, and between themselves and others of Her Majesty's subjects, whether Indians or whites."[1] Both Ahtahkakoop and Mistawasis were determined to honour the treaty. They were not willing to take up arms against the Queen, and if some of the Indian people joined the Métis, the chiefs "did not want to be compelled to shoot down their own flesh and blood."[2] Throughout the winter Ahtahkakoop had refused to consider the Métis' pleas for support, even in the face of threats. He was determined to remain neutral.

As Ahtahkakoop, Mistawasis, and the rest of their party crossed the frozen North Saskatchewan River, they could see that Fort Carlton had changed. Cordwood was piled high to form a temporary stockade around the open sides of the old fur trade fort. Horses and oxen grazed around the post in larger numbers than had been seen for a number of years. Inside the stockades, the changes were even more substantial. A 7-pound field gun from Fort Battleford sat in the square. And the post was crowded, for Crozier had brought an additional 25 policemen from Battleford with him to strengthen the detachment that was already stationed at Fort Carlton. The chiefs learned that more policemen from Battleford were expected within a few days. Additionally, a detachment of 90 policemen under the command of Commissioner Acheson Gosford Irvine had left Regina and was headed for Saskatchewan River country.[3] But most surprising was the presence of 50 civilian volunteers from Prince Albert. These men, the chiefs were told, had come to help defend Fort Carlton.[4]

During the meeting with officials, Ahtahkakoop and Mistawasis were told that Louis Riel had formed a provisional government at Batoche. Furthermore, the Métis were becoming increasingly militant and frustrated while they waited for a reply to their latest petition to Ottawa. As for Riel, increasingly he was pulling away from the Roman Catholic Church and its priests, and he was calling himself a prophet. On March 19 the Métis, with Gabriel Dumont as their adjutant-general, had taken destiny into their own hands and started securing the Batoche area. A number of prisoners were taken, including Indian agent Lash, his interpreter, and the magistrate at Batoche. At least two stores were raided for ammunition and firearms, and the telegraph line was cut. And now, in their latest move, Riel and Dumont had demanded the surrender of Fort Carlton.

If fighting broke out, Clarke and Crozier asked the chiefs, where did their loyalties lie? Whom would they support? Would they honour the treaties? In Clarke's report of the meeting, the Hudson's Bay Company official said Ahtahkakoop and Mistawasis pledged "to remain quiet and loyal."* If Riel's men came and they were unable "to send them away by force," the chiefs told the officials, "they with their wives, families and cattle would retire to Prince Albert and camp on the North Bank of the river

---

* Clarke had met with John Smith, James Smith, Ayahtaskamikinam, and one of Cakāstēpēsin's councillors before coming to Fort Carlton. These chiefs had assured Clarke that they too would stay "loyal."

opposite the town for their protection." Pleased with the answer, Crozier assured the chiefs that the government would supply food to those who remained neutral. The two officials also promised that the police could provide "ample protection, being situated between them and the rebel camp."[5]

The following day, Chaffee sent men and sleighs from Mistawasis's and Petihkwahākēw's reserves to pick up supplies at Fort Carlton. Ahtahkakoop and Mistawasis arrived soon after the sleighs. They reported that Riel had sent another messenger to persuade them to join the Métis in their fight against the government. Even though threats had been made, the chiefs remained firm. They would "have nothing to do with him or his party." And they once again expressed their loyalty to the Queen and to the treaty.[6]

The messenger who spoke to Ahtahkakoop and Mistawasis after trouble erupted on March 19 was only one of several runners dispatched by Riel. At Petihkwahākēw's Muskeg Lake Reserve, for instance, 10 families were unable to ward off Riel's delegation and they "were driven in by the rebels to their camp & forced to join them."[7]

Back at home, Ahtahkakoop called the people to watch an unusual display of northern lights. "Come my children," he called out late at night. "Come from your homes. See how the spirits of the departed dance. Lo! the lights are red. Prepare to learn of pestilence and trouble in our land, or of the shedding of blood. When the ghost dancer is red, calamity is at hand. So it has been taught by our Old Men."[8]

Despite signs that the Métis were becoming increasingly militant, their open aggression had surprised many people. Even Hines, who was travelling in the Carlton area on the 19th when the uprising began, was caught unaware. The missionary had left Sandy Lake with one of the men from the reserve on March 17 for a leisurely trip to Prince Albert.[9] They stopped at Snake Plain, where the missionary held prayers, called on Mistawasis, and conducted a church service with 12 people in attendance. The men stayed with one of Mistawasis's councillors* the first night away from home.

The second night Hines and his companion camped at Fort Carlton. Some of the policemen were busy getting ready for the extra men who had been ordered from Battleford, while others strengthened the stockades. Despite this activity, Hines wrote later that "not a word was said to me

---

* Probably Pierre Stone.

about any definite action having been taken by the rebels."[10] Had police officers anticipated any immediate problems, they surely would have suggested Hines return home. Nothing was said, so the two men continued their journey. Camp was made the third night at an English-speaking half-breed's house 35 miles east of Fort Carlton. Here Hines spent part of the evening learning to spin wool. The clergyman wrote later that he "was so much taken up with the whole thing that I decided to write & ask the Lieut-Governor to give our Indians some sheep and we would teach them to spin and knit."[11]

Hines and his companion were in for a shock the next day, March 20. Upon their arrival in Prince Albert at about 12 noon they

> noticed a crowd of people standing on the road opposite the only gunsmith's shop there was in the place, having their guns repaired, etc. As soon as I was recognised they wanted to know where I had come from, and when I said from Carlton, they asked me question after question about the rebels, and how I had managed to get past the forks of the road (a road that leaves the Carlton and Prince Albert trail for the French Settlement*) as they understood the French patrols had taken possession of all the thoroughfares in the district, and when I told them that we neither saw nor heard of anyone guarding the roads we passed, neither I nor the Indian believed any of the information they possessed was true. They then asked me where we had passed the previous night, and if we did not hear horsemen riding past us during the night? I asked them if any one had ridden past us during the night and how they knew it. They then told us about the doings of the half-breeds at Duck Lake … and that the police had ridden to the town during the night to ask for volunteers to go to Carlton to assist the police. In a few minutes any doubts we had entertained about the genuineness of their story were removed by the appearance of sleighloads of men, the wealthiest and the pick of Prince Albert, armed to the teeth, on their way to Carlton. It appears that whilst I and my Indian were jogging along as unconcernedly as possible during the afternoon we left Carlton, and sleeping contentedly through the night on the bare ground with only the canopy of heaven above us—the disturbances mentioned above were taking place.[12]

---

* The Métis settlement on the South Branch.

Although Hines was wrong about the volunteers being "armed to the teeth," since two-thirds of them had neither gun nor ammunition, he was right about the make-up of the convoy.[13] Included among the volunteers were men such as Captain Henry Moore, the owner of a grist mill, and Thomas McKay, who was elected mayor of Prince Albert in November. These men were the civilians Ahtahkakoop and Mistawasis had seen at Fort Carlton when they met with Clarke and Crozier on March 21.

Many of the stories Hines heard while he was in Prince Albert were false. For instance, he was told that all the Indians in the area had taken up arms, and Ahtahkakoop had joined the rebels. Hines refuted these stories, convinced that Ahtahkakoop and many others would remain loyal to both the Queen and the treaty.

One of the other rumours evoked considerable controversy. It concerned Lawrence Clarke, who had just returned from a business trip to Ottawa. On March 17, during the last stage of his trip home, the Hudson's Bay Company official stopped to speak to some Métis at the South Branch. They asked if there was any answer to their last petition. It was said that Clarke replied "in a domineering and authoritative manner" that "the government were sending up five hundred men to take Riel."[14] In Hines's words, the "gentleman [who was] well known and, up to that time, trusted by all the half-breeds in the country … spake unadvisedly with his lips, and his words acted like oil on fire, and in a few days the country was all ablaze with anger, fear, and excitement."[15] Clarke vehemently denied saying anything to mobilize the Métis, but the story circulated and the damage was done.[16]

Clarke, nevertheless, was not only in a position to know the government's plans but there was a considerable amount of truth in the statement. He had met with Dewdney before leaving Regina on March 13 to discuss the situation unfolding in Saskatchewan River country.[17] Additionally, he would have been told that Commissioner Irvine was getting ready to take nearly 100 North-West Mounted policemen to the Fort Carlton area.[18] This force left Regina on March 18, the day after Clarke's encounter with the Métis at Batoche.

Dewdney did not think extra reinforcements would be needed. Nevertheless, as he explained in a confidential letter dated March 18 to Joseph Wrigley, the trade commissioner of the Hudson's Bay Company, "I think it is better to have a good force in the north this summer & so show the agitators that the Govt. won't stand any nonsense & it will assist us very materially in handling our Indians."[19]

Because of the troubles along the South Branch and in the Fort Carlton area, Hines and his travelling companion left Prince Albert before finishing their business and headed for home. Instead of travelling by way of Fort Carlton, the two men crossed the North Saskatchewan River and followed a well-defined trail to Sturgeon Lake. Then they cut cross-country, breaking their way with difficulty through "frozen snow" a foot deep. The men reached the Ahtahkakoop Reserve on March 23, where—as expected—the people were carrying on with their daily lives. A large congregation had attended church services during Hines's absence. The prayers and sermon prepared by Hines had been read by schoolmaster Joseph Sasakamoose. Emma Hines had played the harmonium and led the singing.[20]

The people were eager to hear what Hines had learned during his trip to Prince Albert. Although the missionary implied in his journal that they were hearing of the unrest for the first time, Ahtahkakoop had been to Fort Carlton and talked to Clarke and Crozier at least twice during the missionary's absence. Hines, in fact, was only able to tell the people what he had learned during his trip to and from Prince Albert.

At 2 a.m. on Sunday, March 29, another messenger rode into the tiny settlement on the Ahtahkakoop Reserve. Farm instructor George Chaffee had sent him, and the news was not good. Three days earlier, on March 26, the police and volunteers had clashed with the Métis near Duck Lake and been forced to withdraw. One policeman and nine volunteers had died in the skirmish and 14 men were wounded. Two of the wounded policeman died the next day.[21] Four Métis and an old Indian man had been killed, and three Métis were wounded.[22] Fort Carlton had been abandoned in flames, and the police and volunteers had fled to Prince Albert. Since the Green Lake Trail through Ahtahkakoop's and Mistawasis's reserves now lay open, Chaffee advised the people to pack up and move towards Prince Albert as quickly as possible.

Later, the people learned more of the story. Following their defeat at Duck Lake, Crozier had led his battered force of policemen and volunteers back to Fort Carlton. Commissioner Irvine arrived at the post from Prince Albert with a force of 100 policemen within half an hour of Crozier's return.

The North-West Mounted Police commissioner was furious, and presumably his anger grew as he learned more about the activities that led up to the confrontation at Duck Lake. The Métis had strengthened their position in the Batoche area after the volunteers left for Fort Carlton on March 20. They had taken more prisoners, re-cut the telegraph line, and seized additional supplies. The situation took on a new dimension when Riel broke away from the Catholic Church. As tension grew, so did verbal skirmishes and threats.

Then, surprisingly unaware that the Métis had taken possession of Hillyard Mitchell's store at the Duck Lake settlement, a group of civilians and police from Fort Carlton was sent to get more supplies from the merchant.[23] Confronted near the small community by a group of Métis under the leadership of Gabriel Dumont, the Carlton party chose the sensible course. They returned to the fort to report and get further orders.

Crozier knew Irvine would be arriving later that day with 100 policemen. Once he was assured that everyone had returned safely from their misadventure, the officer was prepared to wait for reinforcements before taking any further action. There the matter should have ended, at least for the time being. But a number of leading Prince Albert citizens who were among the volunteers would not let the matter rest. Calling Crozier a coward, they taunted him to go after the rebels "if he were not afraid of them."[24] Irvine was to say later that he was "led to the belief that this officer's better judgement was overruled by the impetuosity displayed by both the police and volunteers."[25] In Hines's opinion, "impatience, and liquor, were the sole cause of the disaster" at Duck Lake.[26] Regardless, after some discussion it was "unanimously contended that a small body of half-breeds could not be allowed to carry a bluff of this kind, and orders were given to move forward."[27] Gabriel Dumont's men did not back down. The result was damning, both in the number of dead and wounded and in the message it presented. The police were not invincible. They could be defeated.

Not only had the police and volunteers been forced to retreat at Duck Lake, but Irvine decided that Fort Carlton was indefensible and his force was not large enough to protect it. Accordingly, he called a "council of war," where it was decided to evacuate the post at 2 a.m. on March 28.[28] Assistant Indian commissioner Hayter Reed, who was among the officials gathered at Fort Carlton, "assumed some of [the] goods and gave them to the Farming Instructor to give to the loyal Indians, saying that it was better for the loyal Indians to get them than the rebels to benefit [from] them."[29] He then ordered Chaffee to bring sleighs and men from the agency farm and Mistawasis's reserve to pick up the flour, tea, tobacco, bacon, and other supplies he had claimed for the department. The men were instructed to deposit the goods halfway between Carlton and Snake Plain and then return for a second load.

The evacuation plans were aborted during the early hours of March 28 when hay in one of the buildings was accidentally pushed too close to a hot stovepipe. A fire erupted. When efforts to put it out failed, the police, Hudson's Bay Company and government officials, volunteers, and others abandoned the post.[30] By the time the men from Mistawasis's reserve returned for a second load of supplies, part of the stockade and a number of buildings lay in smouldering ruin. The rest of the post was destroyed later by fires that were deliberately set.[31]

In their haste to get away, Hudson's Bay Company and Indian department officials had left food at Fort Carlton. Some of it escaped the fire and the men sent by Chaffee were able to re-load their sleighs. These loads, along with the rest of the supplies that had been cached along the road, were hauled to the Mistawasis Reserve. Then preparations began for the move towards Prince Albert.

When Chaffee's messenger arrived at the Ahtahkakoop Reserve shortly after midnight on March 29, there was little hesitation. The leading men met quickly and reconfirmed their earlier decision to leave if there was a possibility Riel's men might come to their settlement. They would remain neutral. And so messengers went quickly from home to home to wake up the people and tell them to pack.

The families worked efficiently. By 6 a.m., before dawn broke, double and single sleighs loaded with women, children, and a few belongings were travelling south on the Green Lake Trail. Behind the caravan of sleighs, the young men and boys drove the cattle.[32] At least three men from Ahtahkakoop's band—Kā-tāh-twēhototawāt,* Kīnikwānāsiw (Flying In A Circle Going Up To A Point), and Wāpāsōs (White Skin)—did not travel with them.

Hines had misunderstood the plans. He thought a meeting was to be held at 6 a.m. to decide what to do. Accordingly, when the messenger sent by Ahtahkakoop arrived at the mission house to see if they were ready to leave, the Englishman and his wife were still in bed.[33] Since Ahtahkakoop's people were already on the road, the couple moved quickly. Hines did what he thought best for the cattle, harnessed the ponies to the sleigh, and loaded some hay and bedding. Emma, in the meantime, dressed their daughter, quickly packed some food, and put one change of clothes for each of them

---

* Kā-tāh-twēhototawāt was married to Ahtahkakoop's daughter Emma.

into a box. These were "stowed away in the sleigh," Hines said, "and we followed after the Indians."

Ahtahkakoop and his people had been travelling almost three hours by the time Hines and his family overtook them. When the group stopped for breakfast Emma discovered she had forgotten to pack dishes, utensils, and a kettle for boiling water. Some of the women offered to loan these necessities, and this immediate problem was looked after. The couple had also forgotten to bring a tent, so they would have to sleep "on the snow under the shelter of a willow bush, with only a cart cover thrown over it to shelter … [them] from the wind."[34]

When Ahtahkakoop's people reached Snake Plain Creek,* they left the well-travelled Green Lake Trail and veered east towards the Asissipi River.[35] A short time later Mistawasis's band, accompanied by Chaffee and some settlers, caught up to them. Some of the sleighs in this cavalcade were heavily laden with the provisions hauled from Fort Carlton. Behind the sleighs, young men and boys herded cattle that had been gathered from the reserve, the agency farm, and the settlers' homesteads. Petihkwahākēw's people were not amongst the new arrivals, for according to Chaffee, this band refused to gather up their stock and leave the reserve.[36] The farm instructor made no mention that at least 10 families from this band had been forced to join the rebels.

It had been a long, difficult day and everyone was tired. As evening approached, Ahtahkakoop and Mistawasis—along with their leading men and Chaffee—decided to set up an overnight camp near the junction of Snake Plain Creek and the Asissipi River. The people were settling down for the night when three men from Petihkwahākēw's band rushed into the camp. They claimed that the rebels had crossed the North Saskatchewan River and were "on their way out in force to compel all the Indians north of the river to join their ranks. Their band, they said, had escaped to the Thickwood mountain to hide, and they themselves had come over to warn us to flee to Prince Albert with all the speed possible."[37]

The leading men roused everyone from their blankets. The oxen and horses were harnessed, the sleighs reloaded, and the weary group of nearly 400 men, women, and children continued their trek through the darkness of the night. It was cold, with nearly 20 degrees of frost, the snow was deep,

---

* Snake Plain Creek is now known as Mistawasis Creek.

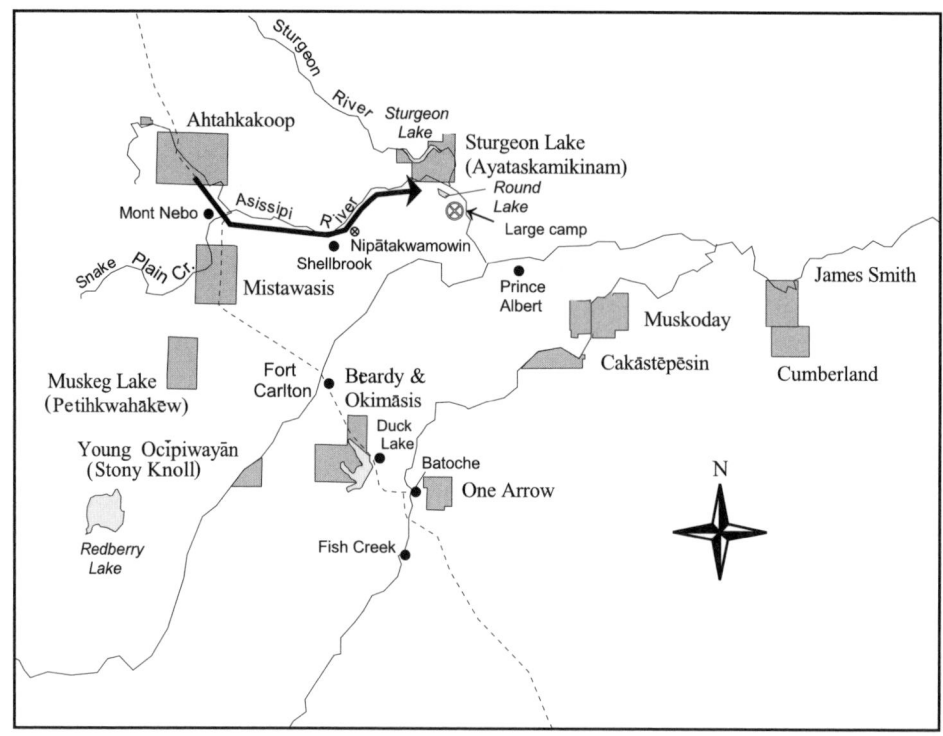

Information Systems Division, Canadian Plains Research Center

Ahtahkakoop and Mistawasis stayed on the north side of the North Saskatchewan River during their journey to Round Plain.

and the trail untrodden.[38] The front animals and sleighs broke trail, often assisted by the men and older boys. Because of the unfavourable conditions and the exhaustion of both the people and the animals, the procession stopped often to rest. Finally, about daybreak, they made camp at a place about halfway between the Ahtahkakoop Reserve and Prince Albert. Located northeast of the present-day town of Shellbrook, this location became known as *nīpā-takwānimowin*, "the place where they fled to during the night."[39] The people discovered later that the message delivered to the camp that first night by the men from Muskeg Lake was not true and the forced march had not been necessary. In Hines's words, the messengers "had been sent by their band to hasten our flight so as to put a wider space between us and the Mission, in order that the course might be clear for them to make a raid on our property left behind, as the rebels referred to, neither then nor afterwards, crossed the North Saskatchewan River."[40]

After a short but much-needed rest, the men, women, and children continued their trek towards Prince Albert. The cavalcade was impressive as more than 60 sleighs forged their way through the snow. Harnesses jangled, men shouted encouragement to their oxen and horses, women and children helped out as best they could, and the boys and young men herded the cattle that, even in the deep snow, tended to stray off in attempts to return home.

Keeping on the north side of the North Saskatchewan River, Ahtahkakoop and the others reached Sturgeon Lake on April 5, seven difficult days after leaving their reserves. Originally there had been talk of going to Prince Albert, but after some discussion it was decided to set up camp at Round Plain* because there was better pasture for the cattle.[41]

Having finally reached their destination, the people erected their tipis and tents to create a large camp the likes of which had not been seen for many years. The following day, April 6, Ahtahkakoop and Mistawasis, along with Hines and his family, Chaffee, the settlers, and several others, crossed the still-frozen North Saskatchewan River and entered Prince Albert. The Indian delegation, accompanied by Hines, first went to see Commissioner Irvine who was entrenched in the town with the police under his command. Then the chiefs made arrangements to get rations for the Indian camp.[42]

During their various meetings, the chiefs learned that the Canadian government had reacted quickly to the Métis' challenge at Duck Lake by raising and dispatching militia units from across Canada to Saskatchewan River country. Even as they talked, Major-General Frederick Dobson Middleton, commander of the Canadian Militia,† had left Troy (Qu'Appelle) with a force of 800 men from the Winnipeg area. They were travelling north towards Saskatchewan River country. Other militia units, from places such as Toronto, Montreal, Quebec, and Halifax, were on their way and would be deployed as needed.

Ahtahkakoop and Mistawasis were anxious to learn more, but they were worried that the ice on the North Saskatchewan would start breaking up, making crossing of the river impossible. Consequently, on April 7 they took their supplies across the river and cached them on the river bank. This

---

* This location was between Ayahtaskamikinam's reserve at Sturgeon Lake and the area where the Wahpetonwon Dakota Sioux were living.

† Middleton had arrived in Winnipeg from Toronto via the American route March 27, the day after the skirmish at Duck Lake. From Winnipeg he took a Canadian Pacific Railway (CPR) train to Troy.

Canadian troops wind their way through the Qu'Appelle Valley on their way to Batoche. The first troops to reach Saskatchewan River country were under the direct command of Major-General Frederick Dobson Middleton, commander of the Canadian Militia.

done, they returned to Prince Albert, where dispatches—and then rumours —from Battleford had the town in turmoil.

The reports were disturbing. Several Stoney (Assiniboine) men from the Eagle Hills 18 miles south of Battleford had killed their farm instructor and a settler.[43] When people from Poundmaker's and Little Pine's bands went to see the Indian agent at Battleford to get food and find out what was happening in the Carlton area, residents of Battleford panicked. They abandoned the town and sought refuge in the North-West Mounted Police post. After Indian agent Rae refused to meet with the gathered Indians, some homes and businesses were robbed of food and clothing and vandalized. Then most of the Indian people either returned to their own camps or— fearing retaliation—joined Poundmaker's camp. Little Pine, who had been sickly for some time, died on the way back to his reserve. Later small groups of half-breeds and Indians, acting on their own initiative, looted more of the vacated homes and stores. Several buildings were burned. Meanwhile the townspeople and settlers from the surrounding district remained in the fort.[44]

Even more agonizing was the report that nine men had been killed at

William R. Rutherford, Glenbow Collection, Calgary, Alberta

The artist wrote that this sketch of Red Pheasant helping farm instructor Applegarth and his wife escape from the Stoney Indians was drawn on the spot May 29, 1885, from details given to him by Red Pheasant. Red Pheasant was Ahenakew's brother-in-law. [See page 823 for full credit.]

Frog Lake by militants in Big Bear's camp on April 2. As a result of this action, the camp was now under the control of Big Bear's war chief, Kāpapāmahcahkwēw (Wandering Spirit)* and Big Bear's son Āyimisīs (Little Difficult One). All the dead men were white except Indian agent Thomas Quinn, whose mother was a half-breed woman. Included among the dead were two Roman Catholic priests. Closer to home, Ahtahkakoop learned from freighters returning from Green Lake that homes at Sandy Lake had been broken into and some cattle had been killed.[45]

With heavy hearts Ahtahkakoop and Mistawasis returned to their neutral camp on April 12. The following day teams were dispatched to pick up the supplies cached on the river bank. Hines had planned to leave his wife and daughter in Prince Albert and return to the camp with the teams. This was not to be. Warm weather brought thawing conditions. The ice in the North Saskatchewan River cracked, rumbled, and then started to break-up before Hines could cross. For the next week, there was no communication between the Indian camp and Prince Albert.

Ahtahkakoop, Mistawasis, Ayahtaskamikinam, and probably leading men from the Dakota at Round Plain arranged for hunting parties to supply

---

* Wandering Spirit was formerly a member of Ocīpiwayān's band.

Saskatchewan Archives Board, R-A27292

Wandering Spirit, who was formerly of Ocīpiwayān's Band, was Big Bear's war chief. This sketch was made by Theresa Gowanlock, one of the white women taken prisoner after her husband was killed at Frog Lake.

fresh meat to the people camped north of Prince Albert. The hunters set up one of their base camps near present-day Canwood. Fortunately it was a relatively good year for elk. The men killed and butchered the animals, stacked the horns in a pile near their camp, and sent the meat and hides to the people gathered at Round Plain. As the days passed the pile of horns grew larger and larger.[46] Back at the camp, the fresh meat was a welcome addition to the rations supplied by the government. For the first time in a number of years, food was not a problem.

Although the people in the large camp appreciated the chance to visit and renew friendships, it was not a time for rejoicing. Uncertainty and worry about their homes and their friends in other parts of the country hung over the camp in an ominous cloud. Boys from Ahtahkakoop's and Mistawasis's bands were at the industrial school in Battleford, and band members had relatives living in the Battleford area.

The Ahenakew family had reason to be particularly concerned. Kīskanakwās (Cut Sleeve), widow of Ahtahkakoop's brother Ahenakew, and her daughter Ellen had left in the fall to spend the winter in the Eagle Hills. Kīskanakwās had three reasons for making the trip. Her brother Chief Red Pheasant was sick, her young son John was attending the industrial school in Battleford, and another son, 27-year-old Antoine, was working for traders in the area.* After the winter was over and the sap was running, Kīskanakwās had planned to make maple sugar during her trip home.[47] Now she, several members of her immediate family, and other relatives were stranded in one of the trouble areas. And no one knew what had happened to them.

---

* Antoine, whose Cree name was Wāpastimos (White Horse), later took Chatelain as his surname.

James Peters, National Archives of Canada, C-017610

Despite the turmoil in Saskatchewan River country, Cree men from the area visited Prince Albert unmolested and even posed for photographs.

On April 20 Ahtahkakoop and Mistawasis, with about 17 band members, were finally able to cross the river into Prince Albert. Hines held a church service for them. They stayed with the missionary overnight, went into the centre of Prince Albert the next day—apparently travelling unmolested despite the agitation in other parts of the country—and re-crossed the river in the evening. During their visit, Ahtahkakoop and Hines discussed the reports of vandalism at Sandy Lake and decided that a few of the young men should go to the reserve to appraise the damage. The missionary loaned one of his horses to Joseph Sasakamoose, and he along with eight or nine other young men returned to the reserve. They discovered that the reports were true. The houses had been broken into and robbed, and Joseph found a few things belonging to the missionary's family, including a valuable sugar basin, lying on the road about a mile from the mission house.[48] Several days after Joseph and his travelling companions returned to the camp on the north side of the river, eight inches of snow fell on the Prince Albert district.[49]

The days passed slowly as news trickled into the camp from the troubled areas. Stores and homes at Lac la Biche, Cold Lake, and Green Lake had been plundered. The war chiefs in Big Bear's band had successfully forced a peaceful evacuation of Fort Pitt, taken more prisoners,* and permitted the North-West Mounted Police detachment to leave by boat. General Middleton's troops had been involved in a skirmish with the Métis under the command of Gabriel Dumont at Fish Creek on April 24; this engagement in a coulee located south of Batoche had ended in a draw, with neither side claiming victory. Two other columns of troops were consolidating their forces further to the west. Lieutenant-Colonel William Otter, with several militia units newly arrived by train from eastern Canada and approximately 50 members of the North-West Mounted Police, arrived at Battleford April 24. Seven days later Otter left for Poundmaker's camp at Cut Knife Hill with a force of about 325 men. In the fight that erupted when Otter attacked the sleeping camp early on May 2, Poundmaker's men —along with the other men in the camp—rallied quickly and turned the troops back. A bloody rout was prevented when Poundmaker stopped his warriors from chasing the retreating soldiers.

Meanwhile Major-General T.B. Strange had left Calgary with a third military column and was travelling towards Fort Pitt and Big Bear's camp. He was accompanied by Major Samuel B. Steele and 50 North-West Mounted Police constables and civilians who became known as Steele's Scouts.

Of more immediate concern to Ahtahkakoop and his people were the happenings in the Prince Albert district. Middleton's troops had finally left their camp at Fish Creek on May 7 and were headed for Batoche. Greatly outnumbered in both men and ammunition, the Métis were defeated on May 12 after four days of fighting. Louis Riel surrendered on May 15. A number of Métis were arrested, while Gabriel Dumont and others fled to the United States.

On May 13, the day after Batoche fell, Hines held two church services in the Indian camp. More than 200 people attended each service.

Five days later, Ahtahkakoop, Mistawasis, Ayahtaskamikinam, Kā-miyo-ahcahkwēw, and three other leading men were invited to attend a

---

* The civilians were given the choice of moving to the Indian camp or fleeing by boat with the North-West Mounted Police. The civilians chose Big Bear's camp.

special meeting of the Church Missionary Society's Saskatchewan Finance Committee. Bishop McLean started the meeting, which was held in Prince Albert, by addressing the chiefs. Hines interpreted "sentence by sentence." According to the minutes of that meeting,[50] the bishop

> expressed his thankfulness to God that while so many Indians had rebelled against the Queen's authority, they had remained faithful. He pointed out the terrible sin the rebels had been guilty of and the grievous punishment that had already fallen on many of them and would doubtless fall on the rest.

> He also stated that his committee would inform the Society of their Good Conduct and that both the Government and the Society would be gratified by it.

Mistawasis responded that

> long ago when they were heathens they would readily have joined the rebellion and would have made very light of it but now that they are Christians they think very differently.

> When they saw that it was coming to actual fighting they knew they would be asked to join the rebels on pain of punishment so they voluntarily left their homes and went a great way off to avoid them, and further that they would rather die on the spot than fight against the Queen. ... during the ... [rebellion and] since they have been in Prince Albert they have been agitated by many contradictory rumors but in the midst of all they have been able to look to God for help and guidance.

Ahtahkakoop, who was introduced as the chief of the Asissipi Indians, spoke next. According to the minutes, he said

> he was glad we had all met together—that he forsaw [sic] this rebellion last summer—that he had confidence in the White people and in the Queen and in Lord Lorne—but chiefly he trusted in God for deliverance.

> He has always tried to promote peace & he believed that God would open up his mind that he might know his duty—that he and his brother chiefs acted in concert & helped each other—that the rebels had reviled him for not joining the rebellion—that Riel the rebel leader had sent them letters asking them to join, but that

they would not even reply to his letters. Their friends, the Indians at Duck Lake who were rebels had also pressed them to join but in vain—that he was sorry for this rebellion as they had very nearly become able to support themselves by their own labour—that they are too late now to sow any wheat this year but they are going back to see what can be done about Garden produce—That they thank the Queen for sending soldiers to put down this rebellion & they hope that God will prevent the like happening again.

Ahtahkakoop and Mistawasis again had spoken on behalf of all those present, even though not all the chiefs were Christians.

Kā-miyo-ahcahkwēw reaffirmed the messages delivered by his father and Mistawasis. "He was glad we were writing down what the chiefs had said and that it would be sent to England," the secretary recorded. "He agreed in what they stated & further he wished to say he believed it was only God's grace that had kept them from falling into the crime of rebellion like the other Indians."

The minutes ended with the notation that they had been read and approved by the Bishop of Saskatchewan.

Two days later, on May 20, General Middleton and his soldiers marched triumphantly into Prince Albert. Ahtahkakoop, Mistawasis, some of their band members, and other loyal chiefs and followers were part of the large crowd that overflowed the streets to witness the arrival of the troops. In acknowledgement of their allegiance to the Queen, assistant Indian commissioner Reed invited the loyal Indians to meet with the general. Hines went with them to interpret. In the missionary's words, "We were all pleased by the kindly way in which we were received by all. The chiefs said that for the past month their minds had been much disturbed by wars and rumours of war."[51] Hines did not name the chiefs who met with Middleton, but in addition to Ahtahkakoop and Mistawasis, they likely included Ayahtaskamikinam, James Smith, Muskoday chief John Smith, and perhaps Cakāstēpēsin.

After finishing their business in Prince Albert, Middleton and some of his troops boarded the sternwheeler *North West*. Although their main destination was Fort Pitt, where the remnants of Big Bear's camp of Plains and Woods Cree were camped, the general stopped at Battleford long enough to formally accept Poundmaker's surrender.

James Peters, National Archives of Canada, C-004593

Poundmaker, in the striped blanket, talks to one of General Middleton's officers through an interpreter after surrendering on May 26.

It was now almost two months since Ahtahkakoop and his people had left their reserve. Anxious to see the damage and get planting underway, an advance party of 20 of Ahtahkakoop's men—accompanied by Hines—left for Sandy Lake on May 23. Others soon followed.[52]

The scene that greeted them was not as bad as expected. The houses, including the mission house, had been broken into and robbed, but with the exception of a few broken windows and doors, no other damage had been done.[53] Hines's animals had not fared as well. His cat had been killed and left on the doorstep, the cows were dry through neglect, the calves had either been killed or starved to death, and the pigs had been slaughtered.

Inside, the intruders had stolen the missionary's barley, wheat, flour, meat, and 150 pounds of sugar. Boxes had been searched, their contents scattered about, and wearing apparel, bed clothing, cutlery, crockery and cooking utensils stolen. Items such as pictures, furniture, and the harmonium had "not been injured." Although Hines estimated his loss at £100 he was "agreeably surprised to find that not a thing in our Church, not even a pane of glass had been injured, and the interior of our house had been treated with the same respect."

This he contrasted to "the treatment meted out to other white people in the affected districts; their pianos, pictures as well as all kinds of furniture were literally smashed to pieces and thrown out of doors."[54] Farm instructor Chaffee, for instance, discovered his house robbed, the household furniture carried off, and his pigs and hens killed. Nevertheless, although a considerable amount of damage had been done, the house and other buildings had not been burned.[55] Hines unfortunately did not describe the losses in the Indian homes on the Ahtahkakoop and Mistawasis reserves.

Members of Petihkwahākēw's band were blamed for much of the plundering at the agency farm and at the Ahtahkakoop and Mistawasis reserves.[56] However, in his account of damages, Hines noted that it was

> only fair to state that some of the Roman Catholic Indian women from the Muskeg Lake reserve, when they heard of our return to the Mission, brought back unrequested many of the articles they had taken out of our house during our absence. Some of the things such as crockery and cutlery we were glad to have, but we refused to accept articles of clothing which had been used by them for several weeks.[57]

Interestingly, Hines noted in his journal that the wife of a man from Mistawasis's band "headed" the women who "did much of the pillaging at our Mission." Her husband, Hines claimed, had joined the rebels and taken part in the fighting at Batoche.[58]

When Hines and several others returned to the neutral camp north of Prince Albert on June 5, they were bearers of news that brought both joy and sorrow. Ahenakew's widow Kīskanakwās had returned home safely from Battleford, but her story was heart rending. After the alarm was sounded that Poundmaker and Little Pine were moving towards Battleford, John and the other students were discharged from the industrial school. Kīskanakwās was separated from both John and Ellen during one of the "scares" that followed the plundering in Battleford, and her son Antoine, who had been scouting and delivering messages for the police, was taken prisoner by "rebel" Indians.[59] Unable to find her two younger children, the 53-year-old woman finally headed for Sandy Lake. Obviously terrified, she walked for 25 days, travelling in the safety of night and hiding during day-

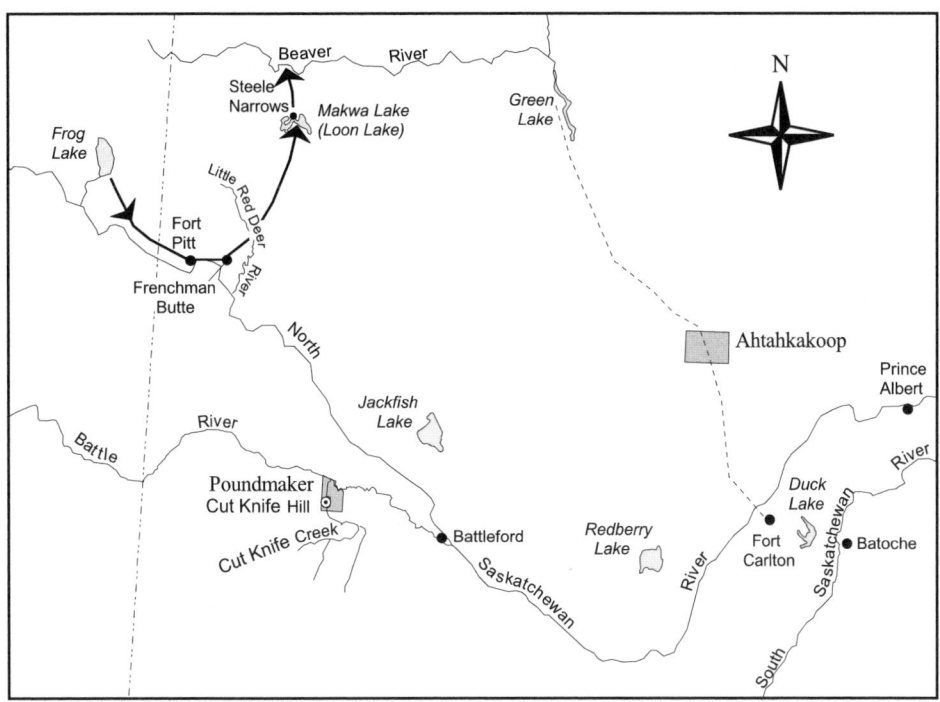

Information Systems Division, Canadian Plains Research Center

The people in Big Bear's camp left Frog Lake and headed for Pipestone Creek near Fort Pitt when they learned the militia was coming. After the skirmish at Frenchman's Butte they fled north towards Makwa Lake.

light hours. She had neither blanket nor fire and kept warm by twisting dry prairie grass into a rope and winding it around her body. By the time Kīskanakwās reached Sandy Lake, her feet were so sore that all the nails had come off. She was hungry, exhausted, did not know what had happened to John and Ellen, and was afraid Antoine had been killed.[60] The people gave thanks for Kīskanakwās's endurance and safe return, and then their thoughts turned to the people whose whereabouts and fate were unknown. These were days of despair, but Ahenakew's three children all survived. Ellen and her youngest brother John returned safely to Sandy Lake. It was later learned that Antoine was also safe.

The neutral camp was astir with its own news when Hines and his travelling companions returned in early June, for the troubles in other parts to the North-West were not over. Within a few days Irvine was taking a force of 120 North-West Mounted Police from Prince Albert to Green Lake to secure that area. The red-coated men with their horses and jangling wagons would pass right by many of their homes.

Events in the Fort Pitt area, however, dominated most discussions in the camp. Following the forced evacuation of Fort Pitt in mid-April, Big Bear's people had returned to Frog Lake with their prisoners. When the people learned some two weeks later that Strange's column of militia and police was heading their way, they re-traced their steps to the fort, setting up camp at Pipestone Creek. They replenished their meagre supplies with flour, bacon, and other goods from Fort Pitt. The buildings that had been used by the police were burned, and then the people moved to Frenchman's Butte east of the fur trade post to hold a Sun Dance. On May 25, before the dance was finished, General Strange reached the remains of Fort Pitt. The sacred ceremony was abandoned and the Plains Cree and Woods Cree, with their prisoners, withdrew to Red Deer Creek. Quickly they made preparations to defend their families. Strange's troops attacked on May 28. After an exchange of fire, the two forces retreated in opposite directions. Big Bear's group of men, women, and children then fled north in heavy rain through marshes, woods, and swamps towards Makwa (Loon) Lake.

The men under Steele's command followed Big Bear while Strange waited at Fort Pitt for General Middleton to arrive. On June 3 Steele's Scouts skirmished with the Cree at a narrow ford at Makwa Lake.* When the Cree were able to keep the scouts from crossing the narrows, Steele withdrew and waited for Middleton and Strange. The large combined force reached Makwa Lake June 7 but its attempt to follow the Cree as they fled north through densely wooded marsh failed. Several days later the Woods Cree and the remaining prisoners slipped away from the Plains Cree and headed north towards the Beaver River. The last of the prisoners were released June 18. Then most of the Plains and Woods Cree, in large and small groups, made their way to Fort Pitt where they surrendered.[61] No one knew what had happened to Big Bear.

On June 16, two days before the Cree released the prisoners north of Makwa Lake, Ahtahkakoop's people in the neutral camp north of Prince Albert took their tipis down. Hines and his family crossed the river and arrived there about noon. They all had dinner and then the group—consisting of about 70 people—headed for Sandy Lake. They arrived on the 18th, still not knowing if it was completely safe to do so. Three days later

---

* This ford between Makwa Lake and Sanderson Bay (formerly Tulibee Lake) later became known as Steele Narrows.

Hines baptized the two new-born babies. One of these was a son born to Baptiste Ahenakew and his wife Ellen Ermineskin on June 10. He was named Edward, and his grandmother Kȋskanakwās had arrived from the Battleford area in time to help with his birth. The other child was a daughter named Betsy, born to Peter Peekeekoot and Bella Joyful* on June 3.[62]

Ahtahkakoop told his people to pitch their tipis close to his house instead of returning to their farms. He explained that some of the Indians who had been arrested would likely escape from the soldiers and police and would travel in large enough bands to cause anxiety. He therefore thought it would be better if the people stayed together. Hines and his family moved into their house about a half mile away, but an alarm was rigged up so the clergyman could alert the others if they were attacked.[63]

At least four brigades of ox-drawn carts rumbled through the reserve during the first weeks following the families' return. These teams were carrying Hudson's Bay Company freight to the post at Green Lake.[64] This was not unusual, since the road had long been used to transport goods and supplies from Fort Carlton to Green Lake. This year, however, the teams were much later than usual, delayed by the ill-fated uprising.

A visitor who pounded on Hines's door at 3 a.m. on June 28 raised considerably more excitement. He was a police messenger on his way to Green Lake with an urgent warning that Big Bear's son, with 20 mounted men, had appeared at Duck Lake. It was feared he was trying to raise an Indian army to attack the policemen who had travelled north to Green Lake.[65] Speculation was short-lived. On July 4, the Mounted Police who had been sent to Green Lake stopped at the reserve on their return to Prince Albert. They reported that Big Bear, accompanied by his young son Horse Child and a headman, had surrendered to three policemen at Fort Carlton during the early hours of July 2. Two days later Irvine arrested a small party of Big Bear's followers in a camp pitched near the ruins of the post.[66] Some said later that Big Bear had evaded three columns of troops to surrender to one of the few militia units not pursuing him.

Ahtahkakoop and his people were to learn more later about the full extent of the tragedy of 1885. The citizens of Prince Albert, fearing an attack by the Métis from the South Branch, had barricaded themselves in the town.

---

* Bella, the daughter of Wāskitoy, was also known as Isabella.

Saskatchewan Archives Board, R-A8812

Big Bear was taken to Prince Albert after he surrendered at Fort Carlton. He is shown here with four members of the North-West Mounted Police.

Dumont's and Riel's forces never made any attempt to attack, not even when Prince Albert was left undefended while the volunteers went to Fort Carlton in late March. Rumours of a general Indian uprising swept through Saskatchewan River country, yet Ahtahkakoop, Mistawasis, and other loyal chiefs in the Prince Albert and Carlton areas—along with some of their followers—made periodic visits to the town. They not only came, but they remained for several days at a time, all without causing alarm. Elsewhere, there were countless stories of friendly exchanges between Indians and whites, even in Poundmaker's and Big Bear's camps at the peak of hostilities. The Woods Cree at Frog Lake—and even Big Bear himself—protected white prisoners taken by the warriors. At Fort Pitt, the Hudson's Bay Company employees, their families, and other civilians had voluntarily gone to Big Bear's camp instead of leaving the fort with the police. And the camp itself had grown impressively in size when many Woods Cree in the area joined because they feared government retaliation.

At Battleford, the settlers and police retained their self-imposed siege for nearly a month, terrified that the Indians would attack. Men from

"Sketches on the Red Pheasant Reserve. Searching the camp for firearms and stolen goods after the surrender of Poundmaker and his forces." [See page 823 for full credit.]

Poundmaker's camp at Cut Knife Hill took a few prisoners at Bresaylor and elsewhere in the neighbourhood. They also seized a freight train and its teamsters,[67] but they never approached Battleford again in large numbers after their initial foray. Many families from other bands moved to Poundmaker's camp, but most came seeking protection from the militia, not to make war. Additionally, the farm instructor at Poundmaker's reserve remained with the band throughout the duration of the troubles.

Many individuals recognized that the isolated outbreaks of violence had been primarily the "outburst of a few young warriors" and "sporadic raids for food."[68] None of these attacks had the approval of the chiefs. With the exception of the massacre at Frog Lake and the murder of the farm instructor and white settler, the Indian people had fought to defend their camps against attacking militia units.

Much was made of the plundering done by groups of Indian people. Later it was learned that members of the government militia units had indiscriminately stolen and "confiscated" personal belongings from Métis homes on the South Branch, from Indian and white settler homes along their routes, from houses and businesses in Battleford, and from buildings at Fort Pitt. Among those named were General Middleton, Captain S.L. Bedson (warden of Stony Mountain Penitentiary), and Captain Arthur "Gattling Gun" Howard.[69] Angus McKay, who had been in charge of Fort Pitt for part of 1884, reported that when the troops were at Fort Pitt "much booty was obtained in the way of Furs, Leather and souvenirs of all kinds —since from the General down to the Lance Corporal and private as well as transport officer, Teamsters and scouts—not even excluding the famous Gattling Gun Howard all were more or less employed in the nefarious art of looting to the extent of outrivaling poor Loo at his own business."[70]

In the attacks launched by government troops against the Indian people, not one resulted in a victory for the militia. Otter would have suffered heavy losses if Poundmaker had not controlled his warriors. At Frenchman's Butte and Makwa Lake against the Plains and Woods Cree in Big Bear's camp, the results were stand-offs. Furthermore, a large government force had even been forced to withdraw at Fish Creek when confronted by the poorly armed Métis.

The outcome could have been different. If Ahtahkakoop and Mistawasis had been willing to join Louis Riel and the Métis, in Hines's words, "Prince Albert would have been taken, as it would then have been attacked from both sides, but instead of helping the rebels, many of them exposed themselves to great danger in order to help the loyalists and they felt equal sorrow with the white population at the trouble thus caused."[71]

To be fair to Dumont and Riel, the Métis never made any move to attack Prince Albert, and repeatedly they did not follow up on any advantage they might have had. The fight at Duck Lake should never have happened. The government should have moved more quickly to deal with the concerns of both the Métis and the Indian people. Clarke should have used more common sense when talking to the Métis at the South Branch, Crozier should have waited for Irvine to arrive at Fort Carlton, and throughout Saskatchewan River country the government should have been more compassionate in issuing food to starving men, women, and children. But after the first shots were fired at Duck Lake, an irreversible chain of events was provoked. If Ahtahkakoop and Mistawasis had taken up arms, their example would likely have ignited violent outbreaks throughout Saskatchewan River country and beyond. Instead, they had remained loyal.

Several individuals who had an association with Ahtahkakoop's band were directly involved in the government side of the uprising. Ahenakew's son Antoine had scouted and carried despatches for the police and Hudson's Bay Company. George McKay, the band's first teacher, had served as a chaplain, scout, and interpreter for troops in the Battleford area. He had also attempted "to open a parley with a white flag" at Makwa Lake during the encounter with the Plains and Woods Cree.[72] Another teacher

Ahenakew's son Antoine was working for merchant James Clinkskill, who owned the Battleford store shown here, in 1885. The following year he took scrip and was removed from the Ahtahkakoop Band Paylist.

who had worked for Hines, Thomas Hourie, was one of the scouts who captured Louis Riel on May 15; he was riding the same horse Joseph Sasakamoose had borrowed nearly four weeks earlier for the reconnaissance trip to the Ahtahkakoop Reserve.[73]

At one level, Dewdney understood the events that had torn Saskatchewan River country apart. In a report to John A. Macdonald, who still held the positions of prime minister and superintendent general of Indian Affairs, the Indian commissioner wrote that in light of what Indians had said before and after the troubles,

> their participation in it sprang, not from universal race hatred,
> from the existence of grievances, discontent or general malignity,
> but rather from a feeling that the action of a few Indian discon-
> tents, who were influenced by the half-breed movement, and of
> their young men, who, when excited by these, lost their heads and
> commenced raiding, committed them to association with the
> rebels in order—after the sources of supply from the Department
> were closed to them, from the causes before described—to gain

the necessities of life and protection against individual white men, which the law at the moment was unable to afford.[74]

However, at another level, Dewdney either did not realize the magnitude of the suffering and the frustration, or he chose to ignore it. He also chose to disregard the fact that many of the raids for food and clothing were made by women and children, not warriors, in order to feed and clothe their families.

Despite conciliatory talk, the government intentionally used the isolated incidents of violence and unrest as opportunities to launch a show of power. Its objective, some say, was "to smash the Cree diplomatic campaign for native unity and revision of the treaties."[75] The clash at Duck Lake and the government's response "effectively killed the Indian cause," while the Indian action at Battleford and Frog Lake "discredited the movement and provided an excuse for using troops against the Indians."[76] The government spent more than $5 million putting down an uprising that had been sparked by Macdonald's unwillingness to spend the money required to address the concerns of the native peoples of the North-West.[77]

Throughout all of the troubles, Ahtahkakoop and most of his people had remained loyal to the treaty, and by doing so had remained neutral.[78] Others tried to take credit for their response. Dewdney reported that farm instructor Chaffee was instrumental in getting Ahtahkakoop and Mistawasis away from the troubled area, while Reed said that it was "owing to his [Chaffee's] conduct that the loyalty of so many Indians was retained." According to Hines, band members remained loyal because of their religion, not because they did not have cause for complaint, and not because they were afraid of the consequences of being rebels.[79] What these government and church officials forgot was the fact that Ahtahkakoop and his people chose to remain loyal of their own accord, for their reasons, and not for anyone else's. Ahtahkakoop had made a pledge on behalf of his people never to take up arms. If he and Mistawasis had chosen to become rebels, no one could have stopped them without a great deal of bloodshed. Dewdney knew this, acknowledging that Ahtahkakoop and Mistawasis "deserve credit for the stand they took, and the manner in which they controlled their bands."[80] Honourable men, the two leaders had lived up to their word, word given when Treaty Six was signed in 1876.

CHAPTER TWENTY-SEVEN

Uprising Aftermath, 1885-1886

Ahtahkakoop and his people tried to resume a normal life after they returned to their homes on the reserve in late May and early June of 1885. It was too late to plant wheat and oats, but they managed to put in 20 acres of barley, 4½ acres of potatoes, and five acres of turnips, for a total of 29½ acres. This compared to 260 acres the previous year. The only other Indian crops planted that year in the Prince Albert, Carlton, and Battleford areas were at Chaffee's agency farm and at the Mistawasis, Beardy, and Okimāsis reserves.[1]

A hot spell hit in mid-June, with the "heat almost unbearable." By the end of the month only a few potatoes were up. Undeterred by the events of the past few months, the rumours and stories still circulating, and the unco-operative weather, the men broke new land, summer-fallowed,* and made what preparations they could for seeding the next spring. The children, in the meantime, were called back to school, and by June 27 about 35 young-sters were attending classes.[2] According to government reports for 1885, there were 23 houses, 18 stables, and two other buildings on the Ahtahkakoop Reserve. The people had 16 oxen that were classified as "treaty" or on loan.† Most of the 17 privately-owned horses were considered by government officials to be ponies and not suitable for work.[3]

On June 29, several days before Big Bear surrendered at Fort Carlton, Margaret Sasakamoose married a "Canadian" by the name of John M.

---

* Summer-fallowed land is land that has been ploughed and left unseeded for a season in order to increase production the following year.

† Treaty oxen were those supplied to the band under the terms of the treaty. Cattle "on loan" were breeding animals that were loaned to the band so it could enlarge its herd more quickly.

Cameron. Hines reported that the man, who was a farmer, trader, and freighter, "appears to be well off and certainly is not uneducated."[4] Margaret, who was 17 when she married, was the daughter of Sasakamoose and a sister to Joseph and Alexander. Cameron was 30.

Other associations with the non-Indian community continued much as they had before the uprising. On July 6, a Hudson's Bay Company officer at Prince Albert sent Kā-miyo-ahcahkwēw to Green Lake.[5] And a week or so later farm instructor Chaffee, his family and servants, and a Mr. Johnstone and family drove more than 13 miles to attend services at the Asissipi Mission.[6] Freighters stopped to exchange news during hauls along the Green Lake Trail and often men from the reserve were hired to help with the wagons and carts. It was during exchanges such as these, and trips to Prince Albert, that the people kept in touch with happenings in the district.

The biggest news during July focused on the wrapping up of the uprising. At Fort Pitt and Battleford the troops boarded the sternwheelers *North West*, *Marquis*, and *Baroness* for the trip to Grand Rapids in the first stage of their journey to Manitoba and Central Canada.

Riel was charged with treason, while his councillors were charged with treason-felony. Big Bear, Poundmaker, and about 20 other Indian men were charged with treason-felony, 12 men were charged with murder, and more than 20 others faced charges ranging from felony, arson, horse-stealing and stealing cattle, to larceny.[7] The Métis and 21 Indians—including Big Bear and Poundmaker—were taken to Regina. The remaining Indian prisoners were locked up at Battleford to await trial in that town.

Almost all the government officials in Saskatchewan River country went to Regina for the trials, apparently forgetting to make arrangements to supply food for the loyal Indians. The people were "literally starving," Hines wrote in his journal on August 3. Many were saying "with truth," he continued, that the disloyal Indians were better off. They were well clad, had no cattle or fields to attend to and could roam in search of game. In contrast, the loyalists had to plough and cut hay "with only dry bread to work upon, & scarcely 3 ozs per head per diem of that, & are also very poorly clothed."[8]

Despite their complaints, Ahtahkakoop's people were to quickly find out that they were considerably better off than many of their relatives, for their band—like other loyal bands—was to "be treated as heretofore." This was not the case with bands and individuals identified by assistant Indian commissioner Hayter Reed as being "disloyal." As part of new government policies that he was promoting, Reed took steps, particularly in the Battleford area, to restrict the movement and activities of the Indian people. "I am

Big Bear (in the striped blanket) and Poundmaker (in the vest) were charged with treason-felony and taken to Regina to await trials. Big Bear's son, Horse Child, sits beside his father.

adopting the system," he wrote to Dewdney on August 16, 1885, "of keeping the Indians on their respective Reserves and not allowing any [to] leave them without passes—I know this is hardly supportable by any legal enactment but we must do many things which can only be supported by common sense and by what may be for the general good. I get the Police to send out daily and send any Indians without passes back to their reserves."

Furthermore, he continued, in order to deprive "the Rebel Indians of their horses I intend having them all collected and branded with the I.D. [Indian Department] Brand and tell the Indians that they must not use them without the permission of the instructor, (that is off the Reserve)."[9] This was being done, even though most of the horses were personally owned by individual Indians.

Other recommendations put forth by Reed during the summer of 1885 included punishing "both Half-breeds & Indians" for "every crime committed by them," abolishing the tribal system "in so far as rebel Indians are concerned by doing away with Chiefs & Councillors, their medals being taken from them," and never again paying treaty money to bands and individuals who had "rebelled." He also recommended breaking up some of the bands and reserves, restricting and monitoring the use of shot guns for hunting, seizing all rifles, and strictly enforcing the policy that the people must work for "every pound of provisions given them."[10]

The restrictions and unsettling times drew several families and individuals to the Ahtahkakoop Reserve in the hope that they would be allowed to settle there.[11] Among them were K-ōsihkosiwanāniw (Ermineskin) and his wife Chenesis. The couple had been put on the Ahtahkakoop paylist in 1876, but they moved to the Battleford area during 1883–84. Three of K-ōsihkosiwanāniw's daughters, however, had married into Ahtahkakoop's band and he now used these connections to return to Sandy Lake.[12] Hines said that several of the other men who wanted to live on the reserve came from Battleford and Duck Lake and had "engaged in the war against the crown in the late rebellion."[13]

Ahtahkakoop and his principal men met at Hines's house late in August to discuss the new arrivals and what should be done about them. Hines did not record any of the discussion, but it was important enough that the minutes were sent to Dewdney through Indian agent Rae.[14] Among other things, the leading men at the Ahtahkakoop Reserve must have requested the renewal of K-ōsihkosiwanāniw's membership in their band, for he was added to the paylist at the treaty payments made in October.

It is likely another concern was also discussed at the meeting. Okīnomotayēw and his Stoney Lake band had not been heard of since the outbreak of hostilities at Duck Lake. When Kā-miyo-ahcahkwēw made enquiries during his trip to Green Lake in July, he was told that Okīnomotayēw was hunting and no one knew where he had gone.[15] Now it was being said by Indian agent Rae in Prince Albert that the chief and his entire band had taken part in the plundering at Green Lake and "like the rest of the rebels, had forfeited their right to any further assistance." This, according to Hines, included £20 for the erection of the school house, as well as the cattle, seed grain, and other items promised during the previous winter.

Sasakamoose was sent to search for Okīnomotayēw. He found the chief, but he and his people were in dire straits. They were starving, and their clothes were in tatters, "literally worn off their backs from contact with the undergrowth in the forest." The chief told a sad story of courage, hunger, deprivation, and cold. When he and his two sons heard about the looting that was taking place in various parts of the country, Okīnomotayēw said that he and the people camping with him "decided to hide away in the thickest part of the forest they could find, many miles from any trail." Some of their own possessions were left behind in order to save the property that had been given to them by the government They carried the farm implements on their backs until they could be hidden in the bush, and the chest of tools given to them at Fort Carlton "was lugged about with them in all their wanderings" during the 10 weeks they were in hiding.[16]

Ahtahkakoop's brother took Okīnomotayēw and his two sons as far as *manitow-sākahikan*. Leaving the men there, he then returned to Sandy Lake where he arranged for clothing and food to be taken to them. The following morning the two men, accompanied by Sasakamoose, continued their journey to the Ahtahkakoop Reserve.

Later in the day Ahtahkakoop, Sasakamoose and Kā-miyo-ahcahkwēw joined Okīnomotayēw and his sons for dinner at Hines's house. The Stoney Lake chief denied taking part in the looting. He explained that he had not been at Green Lake from treaty payment time the previous fall until June of 1885, when the Hudson's Bay Company officer at Green Lake sent for him on "entirely different business." They had been invited to join in the looting, Okīnomotayēw said, but refused. Despite this refusal, he was told that another man had been named chief in his place, and that his name had been "cancelled." Two or three weaker ones in his band, nevertheless, had accepted some of the stolen food when it was offered. Additionally, the week before Sasakamoose found them, one of Okīnomotayēw's sons had seen a few band members wearing new clothes. He told them to return the clothing to the Hudson's Bay Company man. The chief then spread the word that if any of his people had anything stolen in their possession, no matter how small, they were not to come to his camp because it would reflect on everyone.[17]

Ahtahkakoop and Hines decided it would be best to take Okīnomotayēw to Prince Albert where he could tell his story in person to Indian agent Rae. It was a most disillusioning visit. The agent treated Okīnomotayēw and his councillors as if they were "the means of the rebellion, whereas in truth, they knew nothing about it until five battles had been fought," Hines recorded in his journal. "I shall feel it my duty to write to the Lieut. Governor, & state the facts to him." Then the missionary added a damning incrimination, writing that although Okīnomotayēw and his people were "nominally heathen, their lives were far more consistent with Xtian doctrines, than the nominally Xtian Agent, who had treated them so contemptuously. The greatest difficulty is to catch this man sober. So it is in this new country—those whom we expect to be last are often 1st."[18]

Not surprisingly, the summer and fall months of 1885 were troubled ones, full of unease and apprehension. Riel had been found guilty in August and

National Archives of Canada, C-001874

White Cap, a Dakota chief, was the only Indian man acquitted of treason-felony during the trials that followed the uprising. He is shown here still in chains.

sentenced to death in the first of a series of trials. By the end of September, Poundmaker, Big Bear and 18 other Indian men had been found guilty of treason-felony and sentenced to prison terms that generally ranged from two to three years; only White Cap had been acquitted.[19] The charge "treason-felony," in essence, was a charge of designing and intending to levy war against the Queen. Three other Indian men were convicted of felony and given two- and three-year prison sentences.

In Battleford, the Indian men were tried by Judge Charles Rouleau, whose home at Battleford had been burned after he and his family fled to Swift Current at the start of the uprising. He meted out longer sentences for theft-related charges and arson than those being given for treason-felony. One man, for instance, was given 14 years for arson, and two others were sentenced to 10 years for the same offence. Almost all the men convicted of stealing horses and cattle received either four or six years. Rouleau found 11 of the 12 men charged with murder guilty without the benefit of a jury and sentenced them to hang. Three were later reprieved. A twelfth man had his murder charge reduced to manslaughter; he was convicted, and sentenced to 20 years in jail. None of these men had been represented by a lawyer at their trials. And few, if any spoke English.[20]

In comparison, 11 of the Métis charged with treason-felony were sentenced to seven years, three men were given four years, four received a one-year sentence, eight were granted conditional discharges, and four men were discharged before the trials began.[21] Two white men associated with the Métis had also been charged with treason-felony; one was acquitted and the other was found not guilty due to insanity.

Reed told Dewdney that the Indians convicted of murder should be hanged in a public place. "I am desirous of having the Indians witness it," he wrote. "No sound threshing having been given them I think a sight of this sort will cause them to meditate for many a day."[22] The editor of Battleford's newspaper, the *Saskatchewan Herald*, reflected similar thinking, proclaiming that a public execution "would have a wholesome influence on the Indians at large."[23]

Aware of this attitude, an Indian agent who was often drunk, and a judge in Battleford who had been described by Father André at Batoche as a "vindictive man and a servile instrument in the hands of the government,"[24] the Indian people of Saskatchewan River country were becoming discouraged and questioning their future.

Sasakamoose, the wise old man who had once been a high-ranking medicine man, was sensitive to the mood on Ahtahkakoop's reserve and on several occasions spoke to the people, trying to give some renewed faith and direction. On one occasion in mid-September he spoke between church services and preached what Hines said "might be termed an open air sermon, and invited those who were halting between two opinions, to decide for the Lord." He asked them to come to the service the next Sunday, and four "gave in their names."[25]

Soon afterwards, Sasakamoose gave another "long address" to the people when they gathered to get rations. First he told them that the government wanted the farmers to sow some of their wheat in the fall. This, it was felt, might give the grain a better chance of ripening. Sasakamoose encouraged "the young men to do their best to deposit as much grain as possible before the ground was frozen." Then he drew their attention to the unsettling state of many of their Indian neighbours. "Many lost their lives in the conflict," he said, and "the rest are still in terror of the law, expecting every day to be fetched away from their families to receive their punishments. Look around on all sides & see if my words are not true." Sasakamoose urged the people to go to church. He talked about the sense of peace he felt when he went, saying that "the atmosphere seems to belong to another world," and he felt God was looking after them.[26]

The people responded to Sasakamoose's appeal and pulled together in these times of uncertainty and doubt. On October 11 Hines reported that the congregation was the largest since the church was built. There were not enough benches and people had to sit on the floor between the rows of seats.[27]

Some men from Ahtahkakoop's reserve—including Hines—were on the road to Prince Albert to get supplies when they first heard that government officials would be on the reserve October 23 to make the annuity payments. Although they were within a few hours of the town, a number of men turned around immediately and returned home.

One hundred and eighty-two people, including the chief and two head-men, were paid in 1885.[28] Three men, along with 20 family members, were not included. One of these men was Ahtahkakoop's son-in-law, Kā-tāh-twēhototawāt, the husband of Emma. The agent claimed that Kā-tāh-twēhototawāt was a rebel and had killed oxen during the uprising. The two other men, Kinikwānāsiw and Wāpāsōs, were also said to have killed oxen, and the agent claimed they had been with the rebels. None of the 23 was paid in 1885.[29]

Although a notation on the treaty paylist indicated that one of Ahenakew's sons had married an Ermineskin from Battleford, both Louis and his wife Catherine were listed under his deceased father's number as children. Other newcomers, besides Louis's wife and K-ōsihkosi-wanāniw's family, included Jimmy Fraser and David Stranger's widow Isabella and her daughter Annie. Fraser was a single man who had been paid with his mother Nancy as a member of the Mistawasis band in 1883.[30] Isabella, whose husband had died in Prince Albert on April 5, 1884, had taken her annuity payment as a straggler the previous year. Two other women who had been paid as stragglers in 1884 were also added to the paylist; one of them had four daughters. The appeals of the men who had fought at Duck Lake and Cut Knife Hill apparently had failed, for no other individuals or families were added to the band list. One man who had been absent in 1884 was still away. And although Margaret Sasakamoose had married a white man, she was still listed under her father's number.

Five boys and three girls had been born and survived during the treaty year.* One man and three women had died, and for the first time since the treaty was signed, there were no recorded deaths of children on the paylist.[31] The extra rations during the spring, the time spent in the camp north of Prince Albert, and tipi life away from drafty and often overheated

---

* These children included sons born to Michel Ahtahkakoop, Joseph Ahtahkakoop, and Baptiste Ahenakew, and a daughter born to Peekeekoot and Isabella Wāskitoy. Ahtahkakoop also had a new great-granddaughter, a child named Ellen born to Kā-miyo-ahcahkwēw's daughter Mary and Donald LeBlanc; because the father was a non-Indian, the girl was not included on the treaty paylist.

houses may well have contributed to the lower death rate. It is also possible that the sickly and weaker children had died in previous years.

There is no record of what Indian agent Rae told the people during the treaty payments. However, government officials at the highest levels had decided that the Indians who "caused no trouble should be treated in the same manner as before." Those who were especially loyal would be rewarded. Those who were "rebels" would not receive their treaty payments until "all that had been destroyed on the reserves was replaced."[32] It is very likely that Rae passed this information on to Ahtahkakoop and his people.

Additional constraints were also being considered, based on recommendations made by Haytor Reed, assistant Indian commissioner.[33] For example, government officials were considering the introduction of "the pass system" for all Indians. Under this system, Indian people—and particularly those who had been involved in the "rebellion"—would be prevented "from leaving their Reserves without passes signed by an official of the Department." This was to be strictly enforced for "disloyal" bands and efforts were to be made to introduce the pass system to all bands. Vankoughnet noted, however, that a pass "should not be insisted on for loyal Indians." In addition, the policy that "labor should be exacted from each and every Indian for every pound of provisions and for clothing given them" was to be strictly "applied to all able-bodied Indians."[34]

Officials at the highest level were also in agreement that efforts should be made to break up the tribal system as much as possible. Indian agents and farm instructors would be instructed to deal directly with individual Indians instead of acting through the chief. This was to be done carefully, however, so the chief "may not be able to rouse a hostile feeling among their Indians against the Department." It was also agreed that efforts should be made to disarm all Indians "not by compulsion but by persuasion and by keeping ammunition from them."[35] And so it went, as the government used the events of 1885 to clamp down on the Indian people of the North-West, exerting control at every possible level.

It was not intended, at least initially, to impose all of these restrictions on the loyal bands. Ahtahkakoop and Mistawasis, for instance, each received a gun as one of the "rewards" given to "Indians especially distinguished for loyalty during the late rebellion," particularly when their lives were "threatened by rebel half breeds."

Other rewards were forthcoming. In addition to the gun, the government gave Ahtahkakoop 20 sheep, two oxen and $50. The rest of Ahtahkakoop's band received five cows and 20 sheep to share amongst them. Mistawasis received the same gifts as Ahtahkakoop; his people were given 50 cows and 20 sheep. The other loyal bands in the agency received only cows and oxen, and in lesser amounts; their chiefs apparently did not receive the special gifts.[36]

Government officials must have distributed seed at the treaty payments, for Hines reported on October 26, three days after the officials left, that the people were busy planting wheat and onion seeds. Although the fall planting might reap benefits for the following year, it did nothing to alleviate conditions for the upcoming winter. Because of the uprising, only 29½ acres of land had been sown. The barley had apparently failed, and only 310 bushels of potatoes and 300 of turnips were harvested.[37]

Fortunately fur-bearing animals were plentiful in the parklands and woods during the winter of 1885–86. To take advantage of the increase, the Indian department reversed its policy of shutting the Indian people "up on Reserves and giving them barely enough to sustain life."[38] Instead, in many instances the government supplied ammunition and twine and sent the people out to hunt. In Ahtahkakoop's band some of the people looked after the stock and snared and hunted small animals near the reserve. The hunters went into the woods to secure furs and meat. The surplus provided the resources for the people to trade for cloth, pots, traps, and food items to supplement the meagre provisions grudgingly distributed by the government.

Kāh-kāsōw, who had traded for the Hudson's Bay Company officer at Fort Carlton in previous years, was outfitted out of Prince Albert to trade at Snake Plain, Sandy Lake, and nearby camps. He left Prince Albert with his first outfit on November 3. Almost two weeks later it was reported in the Prince Albert journal that "Ka ka soos' man [is] in from Sandy Lake. Furs are plentiful and a good trade expected." On November 16, the man and his companions "crossed" their goods over the North Saskatchewan River. This meant they travelled the northern trail instead of taking the southern route past the ruins of Fort Carlton. Two other men (Dreaver and Johnstone) brought furs in from Sandy Lake on November 18, and Kāh-kāsōw arrived with sleighs heavily loaded with furs on December 9 and December 21.[39] In both instances, Kāh-kāsōw left the post with loads of trading goods.

Then, on December 26, Ahtahkakoop and the other chiefs came into

Prince Albert for their "Christmas gratuities," a tradition that had been followed for many years. Since 1810 this festive occasion had taken place at Fort Carlton. Chiefs, sometimes with members of their bands, had come in their finery to receive gifts of food, clothing, and other supplies. It was a gathering time, with food, speeches, and an exchange of news. Sometimes they stayed for the New Year's dance that had become even more festive during the last decade, when families living near the post and Métis from the South Branch joined in the fun.

However, this time it was different. Prince Albert was a white man's town. Residents were more interested in Christmas concerts, card parties, and English-style socials than in the traditional exchanges between the Hudson's Bay Company and the leading chiefs of the district. An era had ended. Even the road to Prince Albert had changed. Until the spring of 1885 the people had usually travelled to Prince Albert via the Green Lake Trail. They camped at Snake Plain and Fort Carlton on the way, visiting and catching up on the news at both places. Then they headed north-east to Prince Albert. Now there was no reason to stop at Fort Carlton, and with a trail well marked by jangling sleighs and wagons during the uprising, Ahtahkakoop's people often took this shorter route and stayed on the north side of the North Saskatchewan River until they reached Prince Albert.

Back at Sandy Lake, John and Emma Hines did not forget the school children and the sick during the Christmas season. On December 19 the couple gave the youngsters the "usual" presents of clothing that had been collected and sent by friends in England. Three days later Hines rode to the north end of the lake to see two sick women. One had injured her wrist cutting firewood. The other woman, 21-year-old Sara Nātakām,* was very ill with consumption. She died about 10 p.m. on Christmas Day, five hours after taking communion. She was the wife of Nātakām (Mac Knife), son of Kihci-mōhkomān. Earlier on Christmas Day, eight people were "communicated."[40]

The school and its students were continuing to do well. Joseph Sasakamoose had been schoolmaster under Hines's supervision until early November, when he was sent to Stoney Lake to teach syllabics and spread the word of God to Okīnomotayēw's band. After Joseph left, Hines recruited Louis's sister Ellen to help at the Asissipi mission school.[41] And so the tradition of the brightest students helping teach others continued.

---

* Sara was John Peter Mususkapoe's daughter.

The children demonstrated their skills to Ahtahkakoop, the Indian agent, and inspecting officer Herchmer on February 7, 1886. Because it was a Saturday, the men took books and slates to the students' homes. At the conclusion of the testing, Herchmer said "in the presence of the chief and the Government Officials who were present, that the children he had just inspected were much in advance of any other Indian children he had ever inspected in reading, writing & arithmetic."[42] In addition to these subjects, Herchmer reported that one student was learning grammar and 13 were taking geography. Government records indicated that 23 were enrolled at the school, with a daily attendance of 17. Hines considered 35 to be the usual enrolment. At the Asissipi Mission school, and elsewhere in the agency, the Indian department was supplying biscuits for the students. Lash noted that the biscuits "induced many parents to send their children regularly."[43]

Meanwhile Joseph Sasakamoose was doing good work at Okīno-motayēw's wintering place at Stoney Lake. In less than a month, one of the chief's sons was reading syllabics with ease, and others presumably were also mastering the printed word. One of Ahtahkakoop's sons (probably Kā-miyo-ahcahkwēw) accompanied Hines for services at Stoney Lake in mid-December. During that visit, the missionary baptized the old chief, one of his sons, and his only daughter. He also baptized Otasewehas, a man the same age as Okīnomotayēw whom Hines described as being "not a councillor but among the principal men," Otasewehas's daughter of about 16 years of age, and a grandchild.[44] When Hines returned in February, "according to previous arrangement," everyone was away hunting. This, Hines wrote in his journal, is "proof of [the] uncertainty of missionary services among Indians who depend entirely upon hunting for a livelihood."

Louis Ahenakew, during this time, was teaching on a reserve four miles from Devon.* Louis conducted church services at Devon and on the reserve, in addition to being schoolmaster. Bishop McLean was pleased with Louis's work and reported that he was "a young man of excellent character and ability, and has been employed as a catechist in the Mission with good results. He has proved himself an acceptable and faithful missionary as well as a successful teacher." Louis worked under the direction of the bishop, but his salary was paid by the government.[45]

Although Hines had "abandoned" Mistawasis's people after the Presbyterian minister established himself on the reserve at Snake Plain,

---

* The school on the reserve was often referred to as Eddy, or Big Eddy.

some of the people remained loyal to the Anglican church and still attended services at the Asissipi Mission. Hines, in his journal, recounted two stories that illustrated the continuing connections between families at Snake Plain and the Asissipi Mission and the rift these created.

He wrote that the people at Ahtahkakoop's reserve received word in mid-December that Pierre, the old councillor who used to walk from Snake Plain to attend services at the Asissipi Mission, was sick and failing quickly. He said he wanted to be buried in the church yard at Sandy Lake.

On January 2, 1886, Hines received word just as he was going to bed that Pierre was dying and had sent for him. The missionary left about 10 o'clock the next morning. With the road heavy with snow, the wind blowing from the north, and the temperature sitting at -15° F, it took seven hours to travel the 24 miles. He found Pierre lying on the floor in one corner of a bare room 14 feet square. About 20 people, including Hines, were in the room over the next hours. Hines held prayers and stayed until 9 o'clock the following morning. Then he returned home. Facing a wind "dead ahead" and hungry, having eaten only a few mouthfuls of unleavened bread dipped in pork fat, the missionary said he felt the cold very much.[46]

Pierre died on January 6.[47] His sons brought the body to the Ahtahkakoop Reserve the next evening. Their story was a sad one. They told Hines that both Mistawasis and the Presbyterian minister refused to come to the house. The only person they could find to help before death and to prepare the body after death was a widow. The sons had to build the coffin themselves because no one else would do it. In recording their story, Hines explained that there had been a great deal of jealousy and antagonism—which the missionary said bordered on hatred—directed towards the Anglicans after the Presbyterian minister established his church on the Mistawasis Reserve. "This feeling," Hines said, "has been allowed to grow and has at last resulted in what I may term the boycotting of the family in question."

"A more heartless and unChristlike spirit I think never existed among a body of so called Xtians," Hines wrote in his journal. "It is actually worse than heathenism, for my people tell me, that in their heathen state when anyone was sick, even a child, if any were camped near, they always gave what assistance they could before death, & after death, they took the entire charge of the funeral, the friends of the deceased being allowed to remain quiet."

When the time came for burial the old man's body was carried to the grave by Ahtahkakoop, one of his sons, and two nephews.[48]

Several months later an old woman arrived on foot from the Mistawasis Reserve. She was another one of the people who walked about 24 miles to attend church services at the Asissipi Mission. The old woman said she had missed Easter services in the spring because she was too sick to travel. Then she announced that she was going to spend her remaining days at the Ahtahkakoop Reserve "among friends." Hines, in his journal, commented that her son was "heartless."[49]

Ahtahkakoop and his people, because of their loyalty and special standing with the government, were removed from much of the repression and control exerted in Saskatchewan country after the uprising was extinguished. Annuities were withheld from all bands deemed by government officials to be rebels until everything destroyed on the reserves was replaced and a strict work for food policy was enforced. Restrictions were placed on travel, guns, and the use of horses off the reserve. Prime Minister John A. Macdonald, in his capacity as superintendent general of Indian Affairs, directed that Big Bear's band "be broken up and the members distributed among other Bands."[50] Closer to home, Hayter Reed told the superintendent of Indian Affairs that Petihkwahākēw "and his band will be properly dealt with when the time comes as already recommended and approved by the Department" for joining the rebels after the skirmish at Fish Creek.[51] This statement was likely based on farm instructor Chaffee's report of June 30, 1885. The Indians in Petihkwahākēw's band had "broken the Treaty and have been so backward and so lazy in farming," Chaffee had written, that "I would suggest that the chief be broken & the Indians be split up and one half be put under Mistawasis & the other half be put under Starblanket [Ahtahkakoop] & they be forced to work or suffer."[52] This recommendation, for whatever reason, was not put into effect.

In late November, about the time the executions were to take place in Battleford, reports were received that Indian people were assembling at the traditional gathering place at Sounding Lake located southwest of Battleford. Rumours circulated that the Indians were going to rise in rebellion, and settlers living near Battleford once again fled to the North-West Mounted Police barracks.[53] The gathering of people had been misinterpreted and the rumours of another uprising proved to be false.

Regardless, the upcoming executions—imposed by the white man's justice system—no doubt were raising levels of concern, sadness, frustration, and anger amongst the people. And even though Ahtahkakoop's people had remained loyal to the treaty and neutral in the happenings of 1885, many in the band were connected by marriage and friendship to families in the Battleford area. At a personal level, they would not have been untouched by the events unfolding 80 miles southwest of them.

At Battleford, on November 26, a small number of people from the nearby reserves were permitted to camp in the vicinity of the North-West Mounted Police barracks. During the night campfires lit the prairie sky as "comrades" of the warriors to be executed chanted the "death-songs of their tribes."[54] The next morning, 11 days after Riel was hung in Regina, the eight men who were to die sang their own death songs and were executed in public at the barracks. Some of the Indians from the nearby camp, seated on the ground in front of the gallows, were among the large crowd of whites who gathered to witness the deaths. Their presence had been demanded by government officials and many citizens of Battleford who believed a public hanging "would have a wholesome influence on the Indians at large and tend largely to the preservation of peace."[55] The bodies were not released to the relatives and friends who had come to be with the men as they died. Instead, they were buried in a single grave near the barracks and the warriors were denied the traditional ceremonies associated with death.

Two months later, even though the Indian people were said to be "more settled" than before, Hudson's Bay Company officials reported that the government "appears more alive to the importance of preventing alarm and disquiet. They are contemplating sending in the spring General Middleton with a flying column of about 1200 men to pass through the Northwest."[56] This intent was verified in a proclamation issued by Dewdney on February 16, 1886, that stated in part that as

> the Government intends to send a large number of soldiers and police into the country, it will be necessary for any Indian who wishes to hunt off his Reserve, to get permission, from the Agent, to carry firearms.
>
> There is a law, both for whites and Indians, prohibiting them from carrying fire-arms in settled Districts, and as a friend, I wish to notify you that any Indian found with fire-arms, off his Reserve, without permission of the Agent, will be liable to arrest.[57]

Meanwhile, the government had other means for subduing the Indian nations. Not only were its officials enforcing the work for food policy, but they were withholding food as a way of punishing all members of "rebel" bands. At the Beardy and Okimāsis reserves, for instance, half rations were being issued even though they were the only bands other than Ahtahkakoop's and Mistawasis's to plant crops in the spring of 1885. The government's policy was questioned by a Hudson's Bay Company employee at Prince Albert. "They are able to snare a few rabbits when the weather is not too cold and thus manage to exist," George Davison wrote in a confidential letter to a superior officer dated January 11, 1886. "They are also badly off for clothing, especially for the women. Surely the Government cannot be aware of this state of affairs? A small outlay for Print, Blankets, with a more generous issue of provisions would go a long way to make these unfortunate ... [people] contented, and feel well disposed to the Government."[58]

The people in One Arrow's band were considerably worse off. While One Arrow was serving a three-year sentence at the Stony Mountain Penitentiary for treason-felony, government officials decided to "join" his band with either Beardy's or Okimāsis's band. One Arrow's people refused to move and, according to Reed, withholding "provisions was the only means at the disposal of the Agent and Instructor by which they could bring a pressure to bear upon these Indians in the desired direction."[59] Inspector A. Ross Cuthbert, North-West Mounted Police, reported in a confidential letter dated January 20, 1886, that it would be impossible to exaggerate the misery of One Arrow's people. "They have absolutely nothing & have had nothing since last Spring," he wrote,

> owing it is said to their refusal to leave their reserve at the solicitation of Mr. [John] Tompkins, the farm instructor. ... On my asking them why they would not leave their reserve they answered that they had done considerable work on it, built, & fenced, etc. & had received letters from One Arrow* telling them not to leave their reserve for they might get into trouble by doing so. They are miserable beyond description ... & are poorly clothed & huddled in their huts like sheep in a pen. ... Last summer they lived on gophers & this winter on rabbits which they killed with bows & arrows & snared with raw hide, they can't go far for them having no clothes for this severe weather. The rabbits after having been numerous are dying off, their only means of subsistence thereby

* One Arrow took sick while he was in the penitentiary and died on April 25, 1886.

ceasing, & it will certainly become a problem to these Indians how to keep life in their bodies.[60]

Cuthbert's report was forwarded to his superiors, and then to senior officials in the Department of Indian Affairs. His findings were verified by inspecting officer Herchmer, who visited One Arrow's reserve later in January. He reported that he found "several very sick people in need of better food than they could get, and that he was informed that neither the Agent nor the Instructor had been there since the previous winter, and that when the Indians went to Farm 8 [near Duck Lake] to ask for assistance, they got none." He added that the Indians were suffering greatly for want of clothes, and blankets, some poor creatures having none at all and others, one sick in tatters." Eventually the band—and the sick in particular—received some relief.

Later, after a series of letters and reports exchanged hands, Vankoughnet informed Macdonald on June 15, 1886, that even though farm instructor Tompkins had followed the orders of acting Indian agent Lash and agent Rae,

> [his] conduct in this matter was extremely culpable. He was living near this Band and it was clearly his duty to have visited them and to have ascertained for himself what the true condition of matters was. Had he done so there is no doubt that the sick would not have been in such a condition as Mr. Inspector Herchmer and the Police found them in when they visited.[61]

The people at Ahtahkakoop's reserve were more fortunate than those on One Arrow's reserve. Fur-bearing animals and other small game had been plentiful in their area, so hunger and clothing had not been a major problem during the winter of 1885–86. Moreover, because they worked hard, were progressing in a way approved by the white officials, and had remained neutral in 1885, they received special treatment. Band members may not have felt "well disposed" towards the government, but their relationship with government officials, on the surface at least, was relatively cordial. During the troubles of 1885 Ahtahkakoop had been determined to honour the treaty he had signed with the Queen's representative. He had known the hazards of resisting the forces of the white man's civilization. He was also realistic. So, when he and his councillors had tea with Hines on February 26, 1886, to discuss "things relative to the mission, & the rumours which are freely circulated & believed in of another rising among the Indians and half-breeds this Spring," Ahtahkakoop commented during the discussion that he could not believe anyone would be foolish enough to do so.[62]

A Changing Community

One of the first students becomes a teacher.

Ahtahkakoop Goes to Ottawa, 1886-1887

Distanced by miles and philosophy from many of the events that had taken place during 1885, Ahtahkakoop and his people seized the opportunities offered by their loyalty to become more self-reliant. By doing so, they hoped to make a better life for their children, grandchildren, and the generations to follow.

During the winter of 1885–86, the men and boys cut and hauled logs out of the bush for a number of construction projects planned for the summer. The weather co-operated in the early spring of 1886 and Ahtahkakoop started sowing his wheat on April 15, the earliest date yet. Helped by family members, the 70-year-old chief planted 18 acres of wheat, eight acres of barley, one acre of potatoes, and one acre of turnips. His son Kā-miyo-ahcahkwēw, who was now 50, sowed seven acres in wheat and three in barley at his own farm. He also planted half an acre in potatoes and a quarter of an acre in turnips. Kā-miyo-astotin, 34, sowed an amount almost equalling that of his brother. The Ahenakew family, with Baptiste and Kāh-kāsōw listed as the farmers, planted 32¾ and 15½ acres respectively.[1] Baptiste was 28 and his brother Kāh-kāsōw was 40.

This detailed information about the amount of seed sown was recorded by the band's new farm instructor, John Hines. The missionary had been offered this position, in addition to his mission responsibilities, by government officials in March. He had accepted, at an annual salary of £100, after consulting with the bishop and others, rationalizing that "in complying with this request, I am doing nothing more than what I have always been doing, the only difference is, that the Lieut-Governor now recognizes my services." Hines reported to Charles Adams, the new acting Indian agent stationed in Prince Albert, and his government duties—in addition to teaching farming and encouraging Ahtahkakoop's and Okīnomotayēw's people in their various ventures—included preparing monthly reports and distributing rations.[2]

In his report on the amount of land seeded in 1886, the new farm instructor noted that because "in many instances the fathers, sons and son-in-laws farm in the field, I have recorded them as one man. I arrive[d] at the number of acres by the number of bushels sown."[3] In addition to the men in the Ahtahkakoop and Ahenakew families, 14 other farmers were named. These included Peter Masuskapoe who had sown 20¼ acres, Sōniyāw-ayāwēw (He Has Money) who had planted 13¼ acres, and John Masināscēs (Spotted), with 12¼ acres in crop. Sasakamoose's small field consisted of 5½ acres. This field had likely been sown by Joseph and Alexander since their father was trading at Stoney Lake for John Cameron, his new son-in-law, when the crops were planted. A number of other men seeded between six and 10 acres, bringing the total amount of land planted in 1886 to 215 acres. The fields were covered by a foot of wet snow by May 2, but Hines said no severe damage was done. Instead, the extra moisture gave the crops a good start and the growing season was full of promise.[4]

Adams, who had replaced Indian agent Rae in 1886, had been impressed with the Ahtahkakoop Band from the beginning of his term. In May he acknowledged that Ahtahkakoop's people, along with the bands at Snake Plain and Duck Lake, had worked hard to get their grain, potatoes, and gardens planted and were "showing really good work." Later, Adams wrote that "I found the bands of Chiefs Mistawasis and Attackakoop much farther advanced in civilized ways than I had imagined."[5]

Hines's stint as farm instructor was short-lived. After three months, he submitted his resignation in a letter dated June 5, 1886, stating that he did not have the time to do justice to the position. He agreed to "continue in office until" Dewdney appointed a replacement.[6] Although the missionary gave up a salary of £100, he wrote soon afterwards that he continued doing what he had "always been doing," helping the people without the burden of completing government reports and giving out rations.

A large number of the people went hunting for wild duck eggs in early June. Later in the month and into early July, they were on their hunting grounds. By now it was apparent the crops were in trouble. Hot dry weather in June resulted in the barley "bursting into ear" before the end of the month. The wheat was also "very forward," but the growth of both crops was stunted and the stalks were very short. During the first week of July a ferocious hail storm hit the north end of the reserve. Tearing along the Asissipi River it destroyed half of one crop. Although the rest of the fields were spared, Hines wrote on July 16 that it was "fearfully hot & no rain, crops are dying, not ripening." He also reported that the first barley had been cut 77 days after being planted.[7]

The weather, despite its relentless attack on the crops, was favourable for Saskatoon berries and many families set up berry-picking camps in the bush during July. Some families, the missionary reported, were away from the settlement for as long as two weeks and picked five to six bushels.[8] The children helped dry the purplish-red berries in the sun before they were packed into storage bags. Later they would be made into soup or fried in fat.

The biggest project, however, was the construction of a large, two-storey barn. It was 60 feet by 40 feet in size and featured a stable on the lower underground level and a threshing floor on the upper level. By the end of June, the men had sawed 3,900 feet of lumber, squared 20 12-foot logs and hauled them to the saw pit, dug the basement to a depth of six feet, erected the stable walls using peeled logs, placed sleepers* on top of the stable for the barn floor, and erected the walls of the upper level. Fifty logs 20 feet in length had also been prepared for the roof rafters.[9] During the summer the barn floor was completed and the roof was built and covered with shingles supplied by the Indian department. A similar barn was built at the Mistawasis Reserve. These barns, the Indian agent reported the next year, "are the best barns in the North-West, and equal to a great many in Ontario."[10]

Work advanced in other areas as well. By the end of June the farmers had broken 24 acres of new land, ploughed 14 acres of previously broken land, and weeded and "earthed up" the potatoes. In addition, the walls for a new house were put up. "We should have had more breaking done during the past month," Hines noted in his month-end report for June, "had it not been for the lack of breaking ploughs—there being only 2 fit for use on this reserve, & one of these I had to manufacture out of 2 or 3 broken ones." He added that "this report leaves me without a single pound of flour on the reserve & without instructions as to when or where I shall receive the next supply."[11]

---

* Floor beams.

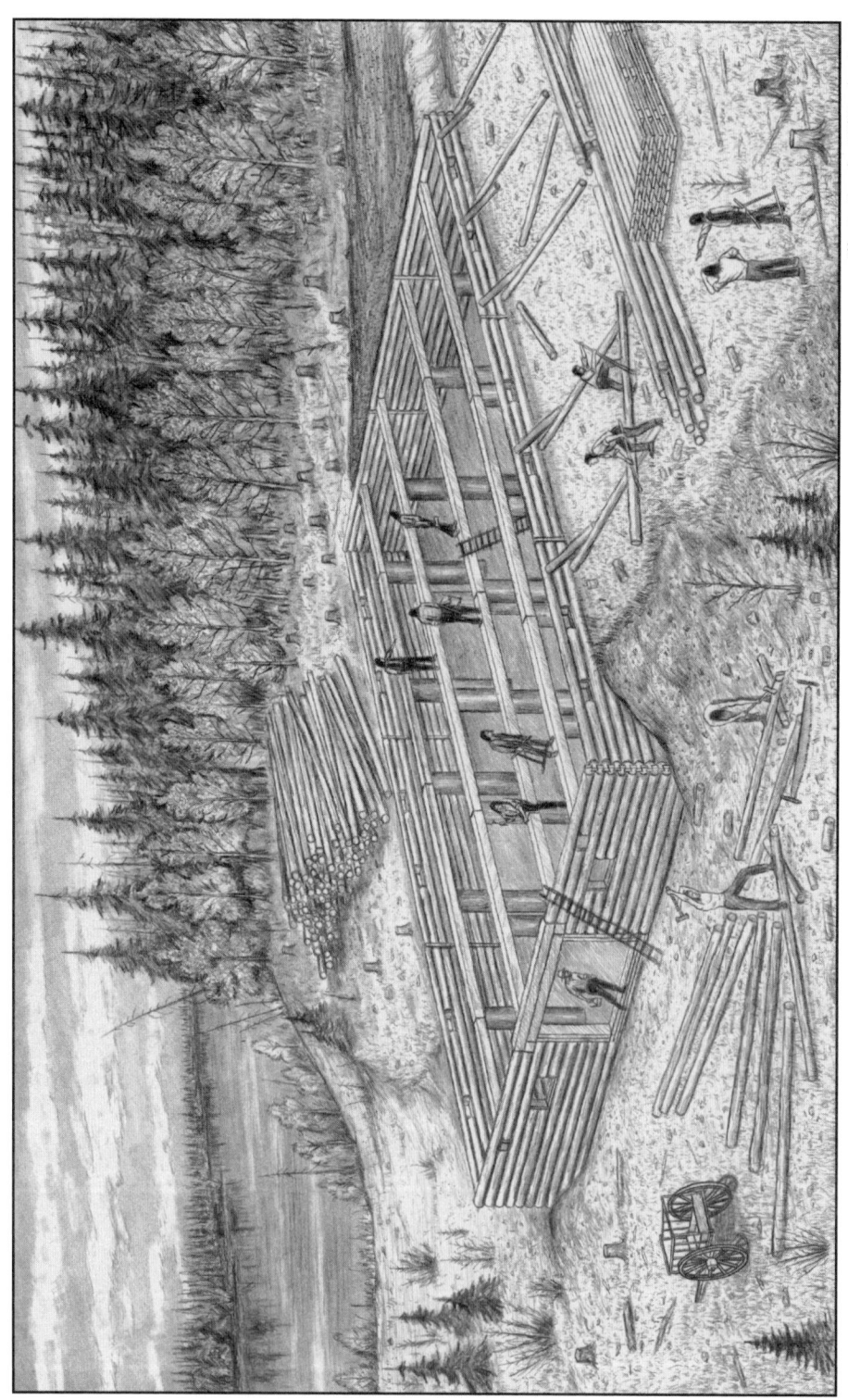

Illustration by Ed Peekeekoot

When completed, the large two-storey barn built during the summer of 1886 was said to be equal to a great many barns in Ontario.

A number of men had also been "employed" making a cart road between Ahtahkakoop's reserve and Stoney Lake. Okīnomotayēw was the first to try it, starting from the Ahtahkakoop Reserve early in July. Cutting through bush and muskeg and crossing creeks not yet bridged, the new road was barely passable. After travelling about half way to Stoney Lake, the chief and his companions decided it would be easier to carry their freight on their backs and walk than struggle with the ox and cart. When Hines tried the road shortly afterwards, his conveyance broke down before he reached the place where Okīnomotayēw had abandoned his cart. The Englishman left most of his belongings beside the road and travelled the rest of the way on horseback.

About 50 people were waiting when Hines arrived at Okīnomotayēw's camp. In addition to holding two services, the missionary made arrangements to build a school at Stoney Lake and send Joseph Sasakamoose as teacher for the upcoming winter. Then, because the people were starving, they "pitched off" to look for food. "It is very hard work teaching starving Indians," Hines was to write in his journal after returning to the Asissipi Mission. "Their whole conversation turns on food. Poor things, it is hard to forget the pangs of hunger."[12]

Amazingly, despite the tremendous amount of work that was done during the spring and summer of 1886, it had been a time of "much sickness." As so often was the case, the sickness began in March. In April an unidentified woman who was dying woke up suddenly and cried out, in a voice much louder than she had been able to use for the previous three weeks, "Lift them up now." Hines said he thought the "Everlasting doors were lifted up at her request." Isabella Wāskitoy, Peekeekoot's 21-year-old wife, died from consumption on May 13. She left behind a young daughter. Several days later, on the evening of May 17, the infant son of Michel Ahtahkakoop (Ahtahkakoop's youngest son) and Mary Jane Okimāsis died. Michel had told Hines the previous October, after the birth of the boy, that he had wished for a child for a long time, and he wanted "to present it to Him [God] as soon as possible." Hines was pleased, but suggested they wait another week or so to have the baby baptized since he was not yet a week old. The chief's grandson was seven months old when he died. Hines said the baby "had suffered very much in that time."[13]

Many more people were sick in June and Iskwēsis's mother, the "poor old blind woman," was dying. Hines wrote in his journal that the woman had "been in a sitting posture night and day for over a year, her arms are spread out & her hands resting on the ground to steady herself. What a mercy it will be, if it pleases the Lord to take her." In mid-June the woman was "insensible" and Hines had prayers in her tent with "the watchers and friends." Less than half an hour after the missionary left to visit Ahtahkakoop the woman was dead. Because of the severe heat, she was buried that evening.[14] Despite his care of the woman for so many years, Hines did not provide either a Cree or Christian name for her in the death register. He referred to her only as the "Blind woman, mother of Iskwasis,* baptized by priests long ago, name not known, age about 90."[15] Masuskapoe's five-year-old son Jeremiah also died in June.[16] And Hines, who was only 36, was once again in poor health, crippled with rheumatic pain in his left hip and knee and unable to walk without the help of one or two sticks.

The sickness on the reserve got worse through July and August. The men who were working on the barn were particularly hard hit. Hines explained that these men drank large amounts of cold water during the extremely hot days of early July while doing the heavy work of sawing boards and cutting building logs. In many instances this brought on severe cases of diarrhoea. Several became very ill.[17] Other people—both adults and children—were stricken with fevers, colds, and unspecified illness throughout the summer. Kā-kīsikāwapiw's infant daughter Maggie died on July 30. A second boy in Masuskapoe's family died on August 2. He was nine.

Hines and his wife continued giving out medicine. Then, not knowing what else to do, the missionary vaccinated the people with vaccine "points" that had been supplied by the Indian agent in May. Although it was not indicated, the vaccine was probably for smallpox.[18] When Hines was too sick to carry out his duties, Joseph Sasakamoose and Emma Hines conducted church services. Emma also took on some of the other mission work, including a visit to Okīnomotayēw and four families camped at Sandy Lake when her husband was house-bound with diarrhoea.

Ahtahkakoop's people were not the only ones struck with unusual summer illnesses. North-West Mounted Police reports indicated that a

---

* Her grandchildren included Wāwiyēwēskocawēs (Charles Roundplain), Kā-kīsikāwapiw (who later took the name Levi Turner), Andrew Apotum, and a woman who married James Campbell in Mistawasis's band.

typho-malarial type of illness had swept through the entire country in 1886. In addition, there were general reports of fevers, rheumatism, furuncular diseases,* colds, diarrhoea and biliousness, most of which fit the symptoms described by Hines in his journals.[19] Contrary to these reports, acting Indian agent Adams stated that although there had been no contagious diseases, there was the "usual ratio of deaths" from scrofula and consumption. These diseases were described by Adams as being the "principal causes of death among our Indians."[20]

Despite the sickness—or perhaps because of it—attendance at church was usually good, providing the people were at the settlement and not ill. Many of the women and girls attended Bible classes regularly. Similar classes for the men and boys were less successful, with Hines writing that although the women's class "keeps up well, that for men & boys does not —why I cannot say."[21]

A few individuals were taking on special responsibilities in the mission. The church wardens and church keeper were members of Ahtahkakoop's band. Louis Ahenakew, who had returned from Devon, and Joseph Sasakamoose both conducted church services in addition to teaching. Kā-miyo-ahcahkwēw frequently accompanied Hines on his visits to Stoney Lake and elsewhere. Ahtahkakoop's brother Sasakamoose was supportive in a special way, encouraging the people to go to church and to carry out their farming duties responsibly as they worked to build a new future. The headman's work extended beyond the Ahtahkakoop Reserve. So, when Sasakamoose was trading at Stoney Lake, he visited the sick, prayed with them, and told them stories from the Bible.[22] Another time Sasakamoose joined Okīnomotayēw and his wife and nine people from Ahtahkakoop's band at the missionary's house. Hines read from the Bible, said prayers, and Sasakamoose—as he had done many times before—spoke to the gathering.[23]

There was considerable overlap in Sasakamoose's roles as a headman in the Ahtahkakoop band and a supporter of the mission. This had been evident when Okīnomotayēw and the nine men visited Hines in June. Two services were held, the first one the evening they arrived and the second one in the garden at Hines's house the following day. When the clergyman said "Let us pray," some of the men did not kneel. Okīnomotayēw "at once told them to do so" and, with the exception of a man who had been baptized by

---

* Conditions characterized by furuncles, or boils.

Illustration by Ed Peekeekoot

Sasakamoose explained to Okīnomotayēw's people the importance of kneeling while they prayed.

a Catholic priest some years ago, they all did. Sasakamoose noticed this and at the end of the service very eloquently expressed his views about the importance of kneeling.

When the minister said "Let us pray," the headman explained,

> "he meant let us all pray. Now, if anyone is in charge of an oar boat & when he gives the word of command to do anything, if all the men put themselves in readiness to do what is required of them, it looks well, but if some of the men refuse to move, it looks bad."

It was the same for praying, he explained:

> "When you wish to make a journey across your lake in your Birch bark canoes, you don't throw your things in anyhow, & get in yourself in the same careless way, & then paddle out into the deep, because a canoe is a difficult thing to manage. It must be

evenly balanced, and you must take your place carefully, so that when you launch out you may devote all your attention to the work of propelling your craft and not be troubled with the unsteadiness with which it rides on the water caused by the careless and uneven way you placed your things inside; besides the canoe will go much faster if evenly balanced. Now, when we pray to God, it is like launching out our thoughts from the shore of this world, & directing them Heavenward. But our minds are just as unsteady as a canoe, & to begin to pray without either warning or preparation, we should find it quite as difficult to keep our thoughts centred upon God, as to keep an unevenly balanced canoe under control. Therefore when the minister says 'Let us pray,' it is a warning to make steady. We kneel 1st In reverence to the Great God to whom we are about to speak. 2nd We kneel because the action is calculated to arouse the attention of the careless to what we are about do & 3rd We kneel because it is an attitude best calculated to exclude from our notice any passing object which might tend to draw away our thoughts from the object of our prayers. So you see kneeling in prayer is like having your canoe evenly balanced."[24]

Beyond the direct references to kneeling before they prayed lay a fundamental philosophy that had enabled a people to put aside their traditional religion in order to adopt a new way of life. This new way of life was necessary because the buffalo had gone, and with these animals went their old life. To make their new venture work, everyone had to pull and work together. It was like rowing a canoe. If the people were not balanced and if they did not work in unison, with one goal in mind, they would not succeed. In Sasakamoose's view, kneeling and praying to the Christian God was one way to keep focused and in balance.

In some ways, the conversion to Christianity was not as difficult as might be supposed. The Indian people, traditionally, were a spiritual people whose religious traditions were part of everyday life. Hines had noted this almost immediately after his arrival in the North-West in 1874. He told of one Indian man, whom he considered to be heathen, lighting a campfire and then offering prayers to the Creator while waiting for the kettle to boil. When the prayer was explained to him by his interpreter, Hines said he "saw how much there was in his prayer that was true and good, and how many thoughts we had in common." He also pointed out that instead of praying while waiting for the kettle to boil, "we Christians could wait patiently until supper was over before saying our prayers."[25]

Prayer and traditional ceremonies were part of everyday life for Indian people. The day began and ended with the people giving thanks to the Creator. When needed, prayers and pipe ceremonies were held during the day. It is not surprising then that the people in Ahtahkakoop's band who became Christians were willing to join Hines in prayers at his home, in their homes, and at evening and morning campfires while travelling. Ahtahkakoop recognized that there were some basic similarities between his traditional beliefs and the Christian religion. Hines recognized this too, explaining that "heathen" Indians believe in "one great & good God, & believe that He is the giver of all good things. They also believe in a future state which will differ in degrees of happiness, according to each individual deserts. They believe also in an evil Spirit which they call a bad God."[26]

More difficult for Ahtahkakoop's people than fundamental Christian beliefs had been the church's insistence that many of the traditional ways, such as honouring a medicine bundle and participating in sweatlodge and other sacred ceremonies, were evil. Medicine bundles were burned. Hair was cut. Wives and mothers who had been part of a family unit were turned out. Just as disturbing, rifts developed within families, among friends, and between bands as denominations competed with each other.

Hines and his message, nevertheless, had struck a chord in the people and they responded, many of them with joy and enthusiasm. For men such as Sasakamoose, his new-found religion brought peace and contentment. For his son Joseph and nephew Louis, the conversion to Christianity opened up a whole new world of opportunity. Others were more practical, Hines said, believing that if they became Christians, the church would feed them, and they would have the claim of a child upon its parent.[27]

The appointment of Charles Adams as acting Indian agent was one of several changes made by the government in Saskatchewan River country in 1886. When Adams started his new job the main office for the Carlton Agency was located in Prince Albert, three miles from the steamboat landing. This was not as suitable as the previous location at Fort Carlton and in May steps were taken to address the management of the reserves in the area. The decision was made to split the agency into two districts. The main office for the northern reserves was to be established at Chaffee's farm a few miles north of the Mistawasis Reserve, with Adams as Indian agent.

Chaffee was to move to Mistawasis's reserve, where "his whole time [could] be devoted to those Indians." A new house and a few outbuildings were to be built at this location. Later it was deemed more practical to put the agent in the new buildings on the Mistawasis Reserve and to divide the farm instructor's time between several reserves.[28] This agency, to be called the Carlton Agency, included the reserves of Ahtahkakoop, Mistawasis, Petihkwahākēw, Ayahtaskamikinam, and Flying Dust.

Instructions were also issued to establish the Duck Lake Agency office on Beardy's reserve. This agency included the Beardy, Okimāsis, One Arrow, James Smith, John Smith (Muskoday), Cakāstēpēsin, and White Cap reserves, as well as a small group of people from the Cumberland House Reserve who had moved to land south of James Smith's reserve in 1883.

Some changes took place immediately and had involved Anglican clergymen with Prince Albert connections. Hines's appointment as farm instructor for the Ahtahkakoop and Stoney Lake bands had been one of these. His appointment, however, lasted only a few months because the missionary felt he did not have time to hold down the position of farm instructor and still carry out his responsibilities at the mission. Archdeacon John A. Mackay, who had been teaching at Emmanuel College, accepted the position of Indian agent in Battleford. Mackay intended to retain his position as archdeacon, Bishop McLean informed the Church Missionary Society, because he felt he could do both jobs without hurting his missionary work. The bishop further explained that this was an emergency situation because the government needed someone in Battleford to keep "these dangerous Indians quiet."[29] Hines vehemently opposed Mackay's intention of holding down both jobs and drawing a salary for each, and during the next year directed very pointed, often racist comments to the bishop and to the London Committee.[30]

The Reverend George McKay took over many of John Mackay's teaching responsibilities at Emmanuel College. This was the man who had come west with Hines in 1874 to serve as the missionary's interpreter and teacher. From a well-known fur trade family, George had done well since leaving Hines's mission. He had been sent to England to study, and after graduating in 1878 from a college in Cambridge was ordained an Anglican deacon. On his return to Canada, McKay worked with the Peigans in what is now Alberta. Later he was appointed a canon of the Saskatchewan Diocese, and he served as a chaplain to the militia during the uprising of

1885. Shortly thereafter George McKay returned to Prince Albert where he was appointed an archdeacon and an instructor in Latin, Greek, and higher mathematics at Emmanuel College.[31]

Although Hines had submitted his letter of resignation as farm instructor in June, he was asked to submit harvest information at the end of the 1886 growing season. He refused, saying he did not want to commit himself "with regard to the number of bushels harvested by each individual." Government documentation indicated the following harvest for the band: 642 bushels of wheat, 200 bushels of barley, 800 bushels of potatoes, 20 bushels of carrots, and two bushels of vegetables grown from garden seeds. In addition, 220 tons of hay were cut.[32]

Despite the construction work and sickness in 1886, most of the grain was threshed during the summer. This was a welcome change from other years, when band members sometimes waited months for the Indian department's implement to arrive. No reason was given for the early threshing but a number of factors were likely involved. The harvest was small, the grain had ripened quickly because of the dry hot summer, and the department's thresher arrived earlier than usual.

In addition to the two-storey barn, four new houses, one stable and 17 root cellars had been built. This brought the total number of houses to 31; there were 22 stables and 17 root cellars.[33] Not only did the head of each family now have a house suitable for winter, but most had a comfortable stable as well as corrals and a yard for stacking hay. Some of the homes were described as being "substantial" and well equipped with a "few comforts" such as cooking stoves, clocks, coal oil lamps, tables, chairs, and bedsteads. Three hundred acres of land were well fenced, and the farming implements and tools were said by government officials to be "of improved pattern."[34] Nevertheless, despite the government statistics, most of the people continued to live in tipis or tents during the warm months and very few used chairs and bedsteads.

The herds of livestock, as well as the number of houses, were also growing. Inspecting officer Wadsworth reported in December, 1886, that livestock supplied under the terms of the treaty or on loan numbered 25 work oxen, 20 cows, two bulls, seven steers, five heifers, 11 calves, and 28 sheep. Thirty horses, one ox, 11 cows, and 15 head of young cattle were privately owned.[35] In his official reports from Ottawa, Macdonald was particularly pleased, stating that "each family occupies a separate holding and the rights of individual property are fully respected."[36]

Alice Kihci-mōhkomān died on September 30. She was the eight-year-old daughter of Kihci-mōhkomān and his widow Ocīkiskicās. Two days later band members received their 1886 treaty payments. According to the paylist, Alice was the second girl in Ocīkiskicās's family to die during the 1885–86 treaty paylist year.[37] The paylist also noted the death of Michel's infant son, two of Masuskapoe's boys, Peekeekoot's wife Isabella, Nātakām's wife Sarah, and the 90-year-old blind woman. Sarah and Isabella were both 21. No men were reported to have died.[38] The paylist did not include the death of Kā-kīsikāwapiw's infant daughter because she had been born and died during the 1885–86 paylist year. In total, according to the government document, three women, three girls, and three boys had died since the 1885 payments.[39]

The only new children included in treaty payments were two girls. One of the babies was a fifth daughter for Kāh-kāsōw. The other girl was born to Thomas, Wāskitoy's son.* And, interestingly, the Ahenakew and Ermineskin families strengthened their family ties when Wāsēhikot, the former headman whose wife had died in 1884, married K-ōsihkosi-wanāniw's 16-year-old daughter Isabella. Three of Ahenakew's sons were now married to Ermineskins.

The treaty paylist for 1886 also indicated that Antoine, son of Ahenakew and Kīskanakwās, took scrip and was discharged from Treaty Six.† Alexander, son of Ahtahkakoop's daughter Mary Genereux, along with Mrs. Mary Pruden and Jimmy Fraser, also took scrip and were discharged.[40]

The totals on the treaty paylist showed that 182 people were paid in 1886. Ahtahkakoop, as specified by treaty, was paid his chief's salary of $25 and the headmen were paid $15 each. The other men, with their wives and dependants, received annuities of $5 each. The three men, with their families, who had been classified as rebels in 1885 were not paid.

A month or so after the treaty payments, Adams was removed from his position of acting Indian agent for issuing provisions contrary to the rules of the Indian department. Wadsworth thought Adams acted from ignorance and "want of judgement," rather than from evil intentions. He noted that the agent "seems" to be related to the Sioux and others, and then he attributed

---

* Thomas was later known as Thomas Bighead.

† Scrip was a certificate issued by the government that could be exchanged for land. Antoine Ahenakew changed his name to Antoine Chatlain and lived in the Battleford and Meadow Lake districts until his death in 1943.

the improper actions to his native ancestry. Half-breeds, he stated, were "constitutionally unfitted for a position requiring" firmness and tact.[41] Wadsworth failed to consider that Adams, although newly arrived in Saskatchewan River country, had been born in the Red River Settlement and had worked for the Hudson's Bay Company in various parts of the North-West before moving as a settler to the Prince Albert district. He was likely acutely aware of the suffering and hardship being endured by the people. Compassion, however, was not a sentiment compatible with government policy.

Wadsworth's statement reflected his general attitude towards Indian people and those considered to be half-breed and Métis. The inspecting officer, like many other Anglo-Saxons and particularly those in positions of power and influence, generally felt superior to non-whites. This attitude was evident in the reports and writings of government officials, newspaper editors, and church officials. Even Hines, although in many ways a compassionate and caring man, considered himself to be above the Indian and half-breed people with whom he worked. In his journals he consistently made reference to "his Indians" and he talked about the "poor things" who were sick and starving. Closer to home, he and Emma apparently gave their daughter private lessons instead of allowing the child to attend classes with the boys and girls from Ahtahkakoop's band. And the couple did not permit her to play with the Indian children. "Our little daughter," Hines wrote in 1886 when the girl was eight, "is often weary & dull with having no companions to play or learn with."[42]

Hines's attitude towards native missionaries had been evident in his relationship with David Stranger. It was further demonstrated in the series of letters written about Archdeacon John A. Mackay's appointment as Indian agent and his rapid climb within the church hierarchy of the Diocese of Saskatchewan. On the surface, Hines's opposition to Mackay's appointment focused on the difficulty of handling missionary work when the job as Indian agent was so time-consuming. He claimed that Mackay gave priority to his government work, and in one instance refused to stay at the Ahtahkakoop Reserve for church services. This, Hines said, had a bad effect on the Indians. He also questioned the cost to the Church Missionary Society.

But Hines's objections were more deeply entrenched. In a letter to Christopher Cyprian Fenn, London secretary of the Church Missionary Society, Hines said the society was very kind to Mackay, "in as much as he being a native, they have allowed him contrary to their printed rules, a salary half as large again as a European."[43] The letter was dated March 22, 1886. Nine months later, when Mackay was still doing both jobs, Hines again wrote to the official complaining about the amount of money the archdeacon was being paid:

> I would not trouble myself Mr. Fenn abt the salaries of the native clergy, if they were paid from a native church fund but when the funds have to be raised in England, I as an English man & an agent of the Society, shall consider it my duty to raise my voice against such cases as the one in question. In fact there have been pounds & pounds of the society's funds spent for which the Society's work has received no benifit [*sic*]—Where are all the CMS Students who have been trained at Emmanuel College at the CMS expense? An honest investigation would reveal much.[44]

Several months later, while raising the same concerns, he complained about Mackay's personal expenses and stated that natives should not be given more positions and responsibilities "than European missionaries until the native church raises at least half the salaries of the native pastors." Many of these men, Hines claimed, are not worth much, and he cited George McKay, whom he said was lazy.[45]

Part of Hines's displeasure was based on frustration. He had built his mission from scratch, worked in the fields alongside Ahtahkakoop's people, fed those who were starving, and cut costs wherever possible—even to the point of paying for many things out of his own pocket. Ahtahkakoop and his people had supported Hines in most mission activities, and the students from his school were among the best in the North-West. Yet the missionary felt he was continually overlooked by church officials. In his opinion, Mackay had been receiving preferential treatment. And now George McKay, who had started his career at Sandy Lake as an interpreter and teacher, had been appointed an archdeacon and was teaching at Emmanuel College.

Hines's distress intensified after Bishop McLean died in the fall of 1886.[46] The bishop had indicated during the summer that he planned to promote Hines to archdeacon and send him to reorganize the Battleford missions. This had been discussed with Hines in the fall. The missionary agreed to move, and in a letter to McLean suggested that a "native brother," the Reverend J.R. Settee,[*] take over the Asissipi mission in the spring. Hines said the bishop died an hour before his letter of acceptance arrived

---

* Son of the Reverend James Settee, John Richard Settee was ordained a deacon in 1885 when he was in charge of the mission at Moose Lake.

in Prince Albert.[47] As a result of the bishop's death, Hines remained at the Asissipi mission.

William Cyprian Pinkham, Archdeacon of Manitoba, was named to replace McLean as Bishop of the Saskatchewan Diocese. He was married to Archdeacon Mackay's sister-in-law. Although Pinkham was not consecrated as bishop until August 7, 1887, he took over management of the diocese as "Bishop Nominate," and at a meeting of the Finance Committee on April 27, 1887, he announced that Archdeacon George McKay was being moved to Battleford. Mackay returned to Prince Albert as secretary of the Finance Committee. Within a few months he was appointed principal of the boarding school associated with Emmanuel College.[48]

And so, as they had many times before, family connections continued to operate in Saskatchewan River country. John A. Mackay was the half-breed son of a Hudson's Bay Company factor at Moose Factory. He had connections in the Red River Settlement and now his brother-in-law was the new Bishop of Saskatchewan. George McKay, who was also of Indian ancestry, was the son of William McKay, the chief factor who had served at Fort Ellice and Fort Pitt. George had additional family connections since he was Lawrence Clarke's brother-in-law. Hines and his wife—who had no family still alive in England, or anywhere else for that matter—were on their own. This no doubt contributed to the missionary's frustration.

Yet despite Hines's occasional pettiness and his paternalistic and colonialist attitude, the Englishman was caring, compassionate, and hard-working. He endured hardship, poor health, and loneliness to do what he considered to be God's work. Ahtahkakoop and his people, for the most part, were grateful John and Emma Hines were in their midst. The couple had opened up new doors and given practical help in farming, health care, and education. The people admired Hines's honesty and integrity, and they had accepted his Christian God as their own. The English missionary, nevertheless, was never really part of their lives. He was on the outside. Often, he did not know what was happening on the reserve or he did not understand. Sometimes his counselling was meddlesome. He was often perplexed by the people he considered to be under his care, while they likely resented the undercurrent of superiority that was common in so many white people and half-breeds.

In early October, after the 1886 treaty payments were made, Ahtahkakoop set off on a great adventure. It all began when a messenger sent by government officials arrived at the reserve about 8:30 p.m. on Sunday October

3. Ahtahkakoop and Mistawasis, along with some other loyal chiefs, had been invited to Ottawa to meet the prime minister and to attend the unveiling of a monument honouring Mohawk chief Joseph Brant.* The chief from the reserve at Sandy Lake was to get ready as quickly as possible because he had to leave with the messenger that night. Mistawasis was already packing and would be ready when they arrived at Snake Plain.[49]

Word travelled quickly and there was great excitement, particularly since advance notice of the trip had not been given. The chief "was on his way to Canada at 10 p.m." Hines, in describing the quick departure, wrote that "perhaps the Chief's family expressed it best when they said to us a day or so after he had gone that the whole affair was so sudden that they had no time to cry until after their father had left."[50] It was reported later in the Toronto *Globe* that the two chiefs thought they would have to walk, so "their young men had all taken off their moccasins, and given them saying: these will last you, fathers, till you return."[51] Although this made a good story, the chiefs knew Nāpēskis had journeyed to Montreal by train some 26 years earlier, and they knew that many others—including hundreds of militia—had travelled to and from the North-West since then. They had some idea of the trip before them.

The Carlton chiefs and their escort travelled to Regina, likely by buckboard or wagon, where they joined Kāh-kīwīstahāw (Flying In A Circle) and Louis O'Soup for the trip to Ottawa. Kāh-kīwīstahāw was the Cree chief of a reserve bearing his name that bordered the Qu'Appelle Valley east of Regina. O'Soup, whose Indian name translated as Back Fat, was Saulteaux and a headman of the Cowessess Band. Cowessess's reserve was at Crooked Lake, adjacent to Kāh-kīwīstahāw's reserve. The other members of the Ottawa party consisted of interpreter Peter Hourie, who was a half-breed from Regina, and Colonel Allan MacDonald, the Indian agent for the Qu'Appelle Agency. They boarded the train in Regina and, in the first of many new experiences, headed east.

Upon their arrival in Ottawa on October 11, Ahtahkakoop and the others were taken to a levee, or formal reception, at City Hall. Here they met a delegation from the Blackfoot Confederacy. Headed by Crowfoot, principal chief of the Blackfoot, these men had arrived in Ottawa in two separate groups. Crowfoot had left his reserve first, accompanied by Father

---

* Known by his people as Thayendanegea, Brant was a Mohawk war chief, Loyalist, and statesman. He had fought for the British during the American Revolution and then led his people to Canada early in 1785. The town of Brantford was named after him.

Blackfoot Confederacy chiefs outside Earnscliffe, Ottawa, the residence of Prime Minister John A. Macdonald, October 1886. Front row, left to right: North Axe (Peigan chief), One Spot (minor Blood chief). Middle row, left to right: Three Bulls (Crowfoot's half-brother), Crowfoot (Blackfoot chief), Red Crow (Blood chief). Back row, left to right: Father Lacombe, Jean L'Heureux, interpreter.

Albert Lacombe, minor Blackfoot chief Three Bulls, and interpreter Jean L'Heureux. While the two chiefs and the priest visited in Montreal and Quebec City, L'Heureux returned west to get the Blood chiefs named Red Crow and One Spot, and North Axe, a Peigan chief.[52]

The Indian leaders from the North-West Territories left for Brantford by train the next day. Crowfoot and Three Bulls were no longer with the group. Tired and suffering the effects of strange food and a foreign environment, the Blackfoot chief had decided to return home with Lacombe instead of going to Brantford. Three Bulls went with them.[53]

The other leading men reached Brantford on October 12. The Toronto *Globe* noted that they "have nearly all their treaty medals hanging by the chains from their necks." Ahtahkakoop, Mistawasis, and Kāh-kīwīstahāw were wearing their chief's coats, which the *Globe* described as "bright scarlet military coats with brass buttons."[54] The western delegation was taken immediately to one of the best hotels in Brantford to rest and prepare for the unveiling of the monument honouring Joseph Brant.

During the next few weeks interpreter Peter Hourie was of great assistance in bridging the gaps between the Indian and white cultures. Described by one reporter as being "genteel and quite capable," Hourie was said to be "willing to answer the millions of questions put to him."[55] Ahtahkakoop and the others would also have had many questions, for by boarding the train in early October, they had entered a bewildering new world.

Shortly after noon on October 13, a parade of dignitaries left the Indian office in Brantford and headed for Victoria Park, where more than 20,000 people had gathered for the unveiling of the Brant Memorial. The procession was led by a 26-piece brass band composed of members of the Six Nations. Representatives from the Brant Memorial Association came next, followed by Six Nations chiefs, Ahtahkakoop, Mistawasis, Red Crow, and the other principal men from the North-West, leading men from the Six Nations, and warriors in traditional outfits. A Chippewa band brought up the rear of the Indian contingent. Then came carriages, interspersed with other bands, bearing guests such as the lieutenant-governor of Ontario, the mayor of Brantford, and General Middleton, the commander of the Canadian militia. In a show of military might, 100 men of the Dufferin Rifles formed the guard of honour and 24 mounted men from the Burford Cavalry Troop served as an escort.[56]

The western Indian leaders were seated with the other dignitaries on

The bronze statue of Joseph Brant and the life-size figures on the pedestal were cast from the melted barrels of cannons supplied by the British government. The figures on the pedestal represent the chiefs of the Six Nations, while the bas-relief on two sides of the base depict Brant addressing chiefs in council and about 15 men performing a war dance. At the request of the Six Nations people, their totems—the bear, the wolf and the tortoise—were included on the memorial.

the platform in front of the covered monument, and for the next two hours they listened as speaker after speaker praised the Mohawk chief who had died 79 years earlier. The president of the Brant Memorial Association, in his address, acknowledged the Indian people on the platform and in the audience.

"It is very gratifying," he said, "to see present so many of our old friends, the chiefs and warriors of the Six Nations Indians, who have associated with them ... leading chiefs from the North West as well as some representatives of the old confederacy from the United States. ... These Indian tribes that you now see before you, are from various parts of America, and are the descendants and living representatives of that great and powerful race which for so many centuries controlled the destinies of the American continent, you see them to-day meeting peaceably with their white brethren who represent the new."[57]

Then came the highlight of the afternoon. The lieutenant-governor of Ontario pulled the cord to unveil a nine-foot bronze statue of Joseph Brant. Standing on top of a covered granite pedestal, Brant was dressed in buckskin and a long flowing robe. A loud cheer rose from the crowd and the war whoops of the western chiefs punctuated the air. Kāh-kīwīstahāw, it was reported in the Toronto *Globe*, was the most enthusiastic. Then the Six Nation Indians, in a diversion from the prepared program, performed a war dance around the base of the statue. At the conclusion of the dance 12 of their leaders cut cords to reveal the rest of the monument. There were more speeches, a memorial song was sung, one of Pauline Johnson's poems was read,* and Onondaga chief John Buck and others spoke to bring an end to the official ceremony.[58]

At 2 p.m. the procession of Indian and non-Indian dignitaries made its way to a park where thousands of people were watching "well-contested" games that included lacrosse and foot races. There were also displays of Indian singing and dancing.[59] Then, in the evening, Ahtahkakoop and the other leading men were invited to a banquet that featured, among other things, oyster soup, veal with Indian corn, macaroni and cheese, wild partridge, mutton, plum pudding, blancmange, and trifle pudding.[60]

Speeches were again part of the festivities, with Red Crow speaking on behalf of the western chiefs; his speech was interpreted by L'Heureux. The

---

* Pauline Johnson was the daughter of Mohawk chief and interpreter H.M. Johnson.

highlight of the evening occurred when Six Nations Chief A.G. Smith rose and addressed the audience in "perfect" English. He had the crowd laughing and applauding, in what a reporter described as "one of the best speeches of the evening."[61] The reporter does not indicate if the speech was interpreted for the benefit of the western visitors. But even if they did not understand what the chief was saying, Ahtahkakoop and the others in his party must have been impressed with Smith's mastery of the English language and his ability to interact with his white audience.

A storm swept through the Brantford area after the chiefs returned to their hotel, with rain and high winds continuing into the next day. Despite the weather, the principal men from the North-West, along with visitors from the United States, toured the Mohawk Institution where 90 boys and girls attended school. The tour began with an assembly in one of the classrooms, where the children sang "Tell Me, Ye Winged Winds" in a welcome to the visitors. Then the chiefs and the headman observed the students at work in the classrooms and industrial departments.[62]

"The Crees were much interested in a knitting machine," a reporter for the Toronto *Globe* observed, likely not realizing that Ahtahkakoop and Mistawasis both had new flocks of sheep. Their interest was genuine as they inspected how the machine worked and speculated on how they could use such a machine at home. They, along with the chiefs from the Blackfoot Confederacy, were each given a pair of mittens made by the students. The reporter also noted that both the "Crees and Blackfeet wondered at the exhibition of work done by the pupils, some of which was being done while they were there."[63] The visitors were informed that two girls were leaving to teach school and two male graduates were working, one as a carpenter and the other as a blacksmith.[64]

The chiefs were then taken to a small Mohawk church where they admired tablets over 100 years old inscribed with the Creed, Ten Commandments, and Lord's Prayer in the Mohawk language.[65] O'Soup was one of the men who spoke during the course of the tour. His address, as translated by Hourie, was reported by the *Globe* as "a fine piece of eloquence worthy, as one of the visitors from the United States said, of [the Seneca orator] Red Jacket."[66]

After visiting the school and church, the western visitors were taken on a tour of buildings and business establishments in Brantford. Then, in the evening, they were special guests at Stratford's opera house, where they watched a special performance featuring choruses, duets, and demonstrations of Mohawk dances. Most of the performers were young Indians.[67]

The next day, Friday, October 15, Ahtahkakoop, Mistawasis, and the other chiefs were taken by carriage to Oahweken on the Six Nations Reserve, where the Iroquois had planned a council to welcome the westerners.[68] Included in the party, in addition to the delegation from the North-West, were a number of government officials, several visitors from New York State, and some newspaper reporters. It was noticed by some that the principal men from the Carlton and Qu'Appelle agencies (generally referred to as "Cree chiefs" in the newspaper reports) and the Blackfoot were uneasy with each other, and there was a detectable coldness between them.

The council house was filled with Iroquois council members and warriors, as well as men, women, and children when the delegation arrived. At about 12:30 in the afternoon the superintendent of the reserve made some opening remarks and introduced the principal men from the North-West. These speeches and all the speeches that followed were interpreted into the Iroquois, Blackfoot, Cree, and English languages.

Chief John Buck, firekeeper of the Six Nations, welcomed the Indian leaders and the men from New York. "It was the will of the Great Spirit," he said,

> that there should be many different languages, so that men could
> not understand each other. It was also the will of the great Spirit
> to allow them all to meet together in one council house. Each of
> them was going to his long home, but were spared to-day to see
> the chiefs from the North-west at their reserve, and they were glad
> to have them in their midst.[69]

He then explained to "his brethren from the North-west and his white friends from the United States ... that it was the custom of the Iroquois when any strangers met with them in their council house to welcome them, shake hands with them, and exchange greetings." The chiefs were asked to stand in a semi-circle at the front of the gathering and the Iroquois chiefs and leading men "walked round in single file shaking hands with each." The warriors, women and children followed, each saying Sako, good day, to each of the visitors.

During the council that followed, the members of the western delegation spoke in turn.[70] When it was time for the Cree leaders to speak, Ahtahkakoop rose first, saying he "was glad they had met to-day, they came to meet their friends, and to see things they had never seen before. The iron trap which brought them was so wonderful that though so far off,

National Archives of Canada, C-019258

The chiefs from the Carlton and Qu'Appelle districts posed for a formal photo-graph in Brantford on October 16, 1886. Ahtahkakoop is seated on the left, beside Kāh-kīwīstahāw. Mistawasis is seated on the right. In the back row, O'Soup is on the left and interpreter Peter Hourie is on the right.

it was not long since he was in his own house. He thanked them for their kindness."

Mistawasis also thanked the government for allowing "them to come there, and hoped God would bless them. He would tell his people what he had seen on his return."

Kāh-kīwīstahāw and O'Soup expressed similar sentiments, thanking God and the government for making the trip possible, adding that they were thankful to meet and shake hands with their friends. O'Soup added that "he was thankful that he had met red and white men together and that here the red men were equal to the white men, and more than that, he was thankful that his children would soon learn to read and write like the white men."

Following the council the western delegation toured a shingle and planing mill and a coffin factory, both of which were owned and operated by the Iroquois. The machinery, especially the jig-saw and moulder, particularly impressed them and the men were all given samples of the work to take home.[71]

The next morning, October 16, Ahtahkakoop and the other leading men visited Brant's tomb near the Mohawk church and then they were photographed in separate groups by a professional photographer. In the afternoon the chiefs and the headman from the North-West Territories were presented with bronze medals to commemorate the unveiling of the Brant Memorial. The medals were made from the same bronze used in the statue; one side featured the likeness of Joseph Brant, while the other was a representation of the monument that had been unveiled on October 13. The Toronto *Globe* reported that at "the close of this ceremony the Blackfeet walked over of their own accord and heartily shook hands and exchanged greetings with their former enemies, the Crees and Sotos [Saulteaux]. This was done spontaneously, and surprised those present, who had observed the coldness between them before this."[72]

Then the Blackfoot Confederacy chiefs and their interpreter returned to Ottawa before heading home. Ahtahkakoop, Mistawasis, Kāh-kīwīstahāw, and O'Soup—along with Indian agent MacDonald and interpreter Hourie —stayed in Brantford to attend the Six Nations Agricultural Society's Fair the following week.

The Cree and Saulteaux men attended services at two different churches on Sunday, October 17. The organ at Brantford's Grace Church particularly intrigued and mystified them. They wondered where the sound came from, and one of the chiefs was heard to comment in his own language that the organ had "the voice of thunder."[73]

So many things were foreign, including the beds in the elegant hotels. Unlike the Blackfoot, the Cree and Saulteaux leaders slept on the floor and would not use the beds. When asked why, it was reported that "they shrugged their shoulders and said the bed was much too white and clean for them to soil. No persuading could induce them to go to bed like white men."[74]

Meals created a bigger problem. The chiefs, according to interpreter L'Heureux, "were not accustomed to eat at stated times and became hungry between meals at the hotel. I was therefore obliged to satisfy their hunger. They were also annoyed at the meals in the regular dining rooms, by being stared at and crowded about."

The strange food and the changes in eating habits, he continued, "together with the use of fruit and iced water in hot weather being liable to disorder them, I was instructed by a medical adviser to give them freely of tonic to their taste, ginger ale being mentioned as suitable I gave it to them as charged."[75] Most, if not all, of the western leading men took a liking to ginger ale and the interpreters kept busy keeping this soft drink, which was reputed to help settle upset stomachs, on hand.

On Monday, October 18, the Cree and Saulteaux leaders were taken to the Council House of the Chippewa, located near Hagersville, to attend a grand council.[76] The Chippewa, who were also known as Ojibwa, were called Saulteaux in the North-West. Since O'Soup was a member of this nation, he in particular would have felt more at home here than with the Iroquois. Ahtahkakoop, Mistawasis, and Kāh-kīwīstahāw likely felt the same. Not only had the Saulteaux and Cree been allies for many years, but Ahtahkakoop, Mistawasis, and Kāh-kīwīstahāw all likely had Saulteaux people as band members. Additionally, since Saulteaux and Cree were both Algonquian languages, many of the words would have been similar, thus making communication easier.

The next day they moved to the Six Nations Reserve for the agricultural show and fair. The Iroquois had been farming in Canada the white man's way for nearly 100 years,* so their progress and experiences would have been of great interest to the visitors.

---

* The agriculture legacy of the Iroquois went back to approximately 1000 AD when their ancestors started planting corn, beans and squash.

Then, on October 21, Ahtahkakoop and the others boarded the train for Toronto. They spent the night at the Palmer house and the following day undertook a busy sightseeing agenda in this, the capital city of the Province of Ontario. At the unveiling of the Brant Memorial a week earlier, Middleton, the Dufferin Rifles, and the Burford Cavalry had been very conspicuous. Now the chiefs and headman were taken to New Fort, where Colonel Otter was in charge. Ahtahkakoop and the others knew, of course, that Otter was the man who had led the attack on Cut Knife Hill the previous year. They were given a tour of the barracks by the colonel and several of his officers. When a big gun was fired for their "edification," it was said that Ahtahkakoop and the others "were much impressed by the noise of the discharge."[77]

The next stop was the zoo where the principal men saw animals they did not even know existed. Like most visitors, the antics of the monkeys particularly delighted the entire group. During the afternoon they visited "Government house." Here the Ontario lieutenant-governor and his wife "made them feel at home" while showing them the conservatory and the beautiful grounds, which they "much admired." Then they were taken along Yonge Street to the university and "many other places including a few private residences." According to the Toronto *Globe*, their reception everywhere was so hearty that Mistawasis told Colonel MacDonald that "he thought he must have been careful in choosing the best-natured people to call upon." The reporter added that the Cree chiefs "were much impressed with the size of the city and the beautiful residences and buildings they saw, but still more with the miles of stores which they passed." That evening Ahtahkakoop and the others boarded the Grand Trunk express train to Ottawa. "Kah-kee-wis-ta-haw," the reporter wrote, "on bidding farewell to those he had seen before during his visit, became so enthusiastic that he performed a dance on the cars."[78]

In Ottawa, the chiefs and O'Soup were booked into the Grand Union Hotel. The first official business in the country's capital city was a visit to Earnscliff, the residence of the prime minister. There Sir John A. Macdonald received them "in good style" as both prime minister and superintendent general of Indian Affairs.

Macdonald was particularly impressed by Ahtahkakoop and during their visit the chief was asked "by the great gentleman to give a Cree name to his daughter." Hines, who recounted the story later, said that

> after thinking for a few seconds, he told them that he would give
> the young Lady half [of] of his own name, saying that Starblanket

National Archives of Canada, C-003340

The Parliament Buildings, street lights, and block after block of impressive build-
ings and stores—such as those on Montreal's St. James Street (below)—were
among the wonders seen during Ahtahkakoop's visit to Central Canada.

National Archives of Canada, C-070926

William James Topley/ National Archives of Canada, PA-008942

The Grand Union Hotel in Ottawa, where Ahtahkakoop, Mistawasis, Kāh-kīwīs-tahāw, and O'Soup stayed during their visit to Ottawa, was bigger and much fancier than any building they had ever seen at home.

was known well, not only in the Saskatchewan country, but in Canada and elsewhere, & he had done nothing to be ashamed of it, but could go boldly where ever his name had gone before. He then named her Ah tah kis kwāo "Star Lady." The great-gentleman, he says, seemed much pleased with the name & said his daughter should always be called by the name he had given her, so she would be a constant reminder of their meeting.[79]

The prime minister's wife also spoke, saying "how pleased she was to have seen & heard the Chiefs, and as they had very far to go home, she would pray to God to give them a safe Journey & bring them back to their families in health & safety." These words, Ahtahkakoop said, "went to his heart—it showed that we were all one family & God was our Father. It made one feel certain that we should reach home safely & find all well."

Before leaving the prime minister's residence, arrangements were made for Ahtahkakoop, Mistawasis, Kāh-kīwīstahāw and O'Soup to meet with Prime Minister Macdonald and the Privy Council in the Parliament Buildings at 3:30 that afternoon. During this meeting, the Ottawa *Free Press* reported, 'the usual pow-wow took place." The chiefs delegated O'Soup to speak on their behalf. The topics discussed were not disclosed in the newspaper account, but it was reported that when asked about their trip, it was "ascertained from the Indians through their interpreter that they were well pleased with what they have seen, and highly delighted with the manner in which they have been entertained by the citizens wherever they have been."[80]

In one home, for instance, Ahtahkakoop and Mistawasis were asked to sing several Cree hymns. The two chiefs—a tall dignified man with a voice as low as a grizzly bear, and the other, much smaller and gifted with a magnificent voice that soared—sang one hymn. Their audience was so fascinated that the chiefs were asked to sing the song again very slowly. One of the men wrote the Cree words down, syllable by syllable. Then a young lady played the tune on the piano and everyone, Indian and non-Indian, sang together.[81]

In addition to visiting private residences, the chiefs were taken to church regularly during their eastern visit. Ahtahkakoop told Hines later that although he could not understand any of the services, it was good to be there and to see so many people attending "God's church and to see how quietly and orderly they behaved." He also said that when he spoke at public meetings and revealed that "he and his people were Xtians," he was applauded. His audiences were even more impressed when the chief said that three of the children in his band—his nephews Louis Ahenakew and Joseph Sasakamoose and his niece Ellen Ahenakew—were able to teach and that the two young men had charge of government schools.[82] For people whose knowledge of the Indian people of the North-West came primarily from stories about the uprising the previous year, these were illuminating encounters.

From Ottawa, the western delegation took the train to Montreal. Here, for the first time since they left home, a reporter arranged a private interview with the chiefs and headman. Indian agent MacDonald was present and Peter Hourie interpreted. The article resulting from this interview appeared in the October 25 issue of the Montreal *Gazette*.

The reporter described the scene when he entered the leading men's "commodious" room at St. Lawrence Hall. Mistawasis, who was described as "a little stooped man about 70 years of age, with a bronzed skin, long, straight, black hair, with occasioned silvered threads, a prominent nose, high cheek bones," was sitting on a lounge. He was dressed "in civilized costume—civilized, if part of the fashion of to-day with an admixture of the cut of garments our great grandfathers wore. His coat is of the most brilliant red cloth, ornamented with brass buttons as large as saucers." The coat, the reporter explained, "was a present the day the treaty was signed." Around his neck hung a large treaty medal and the medal presented by the Marquis of Lorne in 1881. He was also wearing the medal commemorating the unveiling of the Brant Memorial and in the lapel of his jacket was a silver ring that "some white chief had presented to him." All in all, the old chief was said to "look picturesque."

Kāh-kīwīstahāw was wearing trousers and a flannel shirt. He had discarded his jacket, stockings and moccasins and was "squatted in true Indian fashion on the floor. An old newspaper was placed beside him which he utilized as a spittoon to the better preservation of the carpet. He worked at a neat briar root calumet with the intensity of a suction engine." In the reporter's view, Kāh-kīwīstahāw "was the most uncivilized of the four chiefs, and as yet he has not been converted to Christianity. He is a splendid looking typical Indian. His long hair greased and plaited falls down on his back. He has a good humoured smile, but his *tout ensemble* is not such as would inspire confidence in one timid."

Mistawasis, O'Soup, and Ahtahkakoop were also smoking—for, in the reporter's words, "the Indians are inveterate smokers"—and all of them were using their discarded stockings "as a repository for the supply of pipes and tobacco." O'Soup had "stretched himself in an arm chair." Ahtahkakoop was sitting on the edge of the bed. His legs were aching, the chief told the reporter, and he could not sit in a chair. O'Soup and Ahtahkakoop, the reporter asserted "are rather more civilized than the others." No further description was given.

Ahtahkakoop and Mistawasis remained in the background and let Kāh-kīwīstahāw and O'Soup deal with the reporter.

When asked through interpreter Hourie how he liked the home of the white man, Kāh-kīwīstahāw replied that "We have seen what we have come to see and we thank the white man. It gives us great pleasure to see the greatness and every day we travel we see more and more. … When we return we will tell of the wonders of the white man. We are thankful to the Government for bringing us to see what we have seen. I speak the truth."

Ahtahkakoop, Mistawasis, and O'Soup endorsed his statement, saying "*Aha! Aha!*"*

"How do you like riding the train?" the reporter then asked. "Who would not like to ride on such a swift fire horse?" Kāh-kīwīstahāw responded. "It was the first time we travelled on the fire horse. We thought we would not like it at first, but we liked it all at once. We would like to travel as quick on the prairie. We will like the fire horse better if it takes us back safe to our families and young men."

"Do you intend to become a Christian," Kāh-kīwīstahāw was asked next. The chief sidestepped the question, saying that when he returned home he would tell his people "how great are the white men Christians." He would also tell his people that they should become Christians and send their children to school, but he did not think they would listen.[83]

"This ended the moral and social portion of the conversation," the reporter wrote, "and the topic was changed to the political. Mr. Hourie was asked by Lieutenant-Colonel MacDonald to give every word and every complaint made by the Indians."

When asked how his people were treated on the reserve, Kāh-kīwīstahāw made some general comments and then said O'Soup would answer the question. The reporter repeated the question to Ahtahkakoop and Mistawasis, but the two chiefs said "they had selected Back Fat [O'Soup] to speak for them and that he would tell all their grievances. Their lips were sealed except to say thanks."

The reporter turned to O'Soup and asked if the Crees were loyal to the Queen. He replied, "I told the agent again and again that the Crees will never take the warpath against the Great Mother. How many times have I said this? Why am I asked again? I speak the truth." Once again the chiefs indicated their support and approval.

O'Soup, "with many forcible gestures," then outlined the grievances of

---

* *Aha* is a Cree expression of agreement.

the Indian people and touched upon many of the concerns that had been aired so many times before. There was a shortage of ploughs and oxen, he said. They had been trying to get a mill and threshing machine near the reserves in order to help themselves, and they were often treated poorly and unfairly. Moreover, they used to get more ammunition for hunting than they do now. "When the white chief, Morris, made the treaty with the Indians," O'Soup said,

> he stated plainly that every Indian would be treated alike. We feel jealous, and are come to see the great father [Prime Minister Macdonald] to complain because some are treated better than others as it were. Far out west the Blackfeet chiefs have horses and light carts (buggies). We are not so well treated. The Blackfeet are the worst children the Queen has, and we are good and loyal. We try to do everything that the Government wants and we do not get so much. ... I want our chiefs to be treated as other chiefs. ... Here is an old chief (pointing to Big Child) he has to walk when he travels. The white man is great, but when we came away we left our young men and children, and we don't know how they may be treated until we go back.

The reporter interrupted with "a question a little germane to the grievance topic." O'Soup objected, saying "'newsman' asked Indian for his grievances to tell the great white man, but he jumped from one subject to another." The newsman backed down, saying he "thought it better to continue on the grievance discourse."

And so O'Soup continued to speak:

> Now if you saw the state of those poor Indians out there you would feel something in your heart to have pity on the poor. And again there is another thing. We have to live on reserves with people we don't understand. I don't see why they cannot find agents and instructors who live in the country. The reason why I mention this is that it was one cause of the big trouble last year. Some men don't care for the poor Indian. They push him out of the door or give him a blow. They know we don't know anything and they don't take notice of us. We are not like dogs; we are human beings.

The reporter noted that this seemed to bring the interview to an end, but then O'Soup suggested that "the Government should provide the Indian chiefs with tickets on the fire horses to come to Ottawa whenever they had a grievance. He also suggested that the Government should take care of old men and orphans and build homes for them." And Kāh-kīwīstahāw complained that "his farm instructor was driving away his young men." With that statement, the interview was over.[84]

The newspaper article made no reference to the itinerary for the Montreal visit, other than to say that the three Cree chiefs and the Saulteaux headman were leaving the morning of October 25 to shoot the rapids at Lachine.*

Then, the visit finished, the chiefs, headman, Indian agent, and interpreter boarded another train for the trip home. There must have been other stops and visits on the return trip—probably in Winnipeg and Regina—since Ahtahkakoop did not get back to his reserve until the week of November 15.[85]

And what an arrival it must have been! Ahtahkakoop had been gone for nearly six weeks, away in a white man's world where so many things were strange. He had not been completely unprepared for what he saw. Nāpēskis, his youngest brother, had told his relatives about the iron horse and other marvellous things in the white man's world on his return from Central Canada in 1859 or 1860. Moreover, Ahtahkakoop had interacted with people of European ancestry more than most Indian leaders. He had been to York Factory, and often he had questioned Lawrence Clarke, other Hudson's Bay Company men, and visitors to his land about countries and people far away. Then Hines had come, eager to talk about many things. The missionary had taught geography to the adults and talked about events such as the Prussian War. Ahtahkakoop, on a small scale, was even familiar with a white man's house and furnishings since he had been in Hines's sparsely furnished home many times.

Nevertheless, he could not have been prepared for the many wonders seen and heard during his journey. The clanging and puffing of the train—the iron trap, as Ahtahkakoop had called it. The food, the beautiful dishes and table settings, and strange things, like people sitting at tables in large rooms at specific times to eat. Street upon street of stores, gas lamps, massive buildings, manicured lawns, and colourful flowers. Thousands of people living and scurrying about in one place and hundreds of people staring at them. And magnificent things, like the unbelievably large Parliament Buildings and labour-saving agricultural implements and tools.

---

* Lachine, an important fur trade centre, was on the south bank of Montreal Island.

Days and nights filled with talk and questions followed Ahtahkakoop's arrival home. The people must have laughed as their chief described the antics of some of the people he observed and met, and gasped in amazement as story after story unfolded.

Ahtahkakoop "remembered very well indeed all he saw & was told," Hines recorded in his journal after listening to the chief, adding that "on the whole the officials treated them very well." The words of the prime minister's wife had remained in Ahtahkakoop's mind and heart during the journey home. "I have seen the Lady's prayer answered," Ahtahkakoop observed. "We have had good health, fine weather & a safe journey home, and I shall always remember with pleasure my 1st & perhaps my last visit to the white-mans community."[86] Unfortunately, Hines recorded very little of what he heard during the exciting week following the chief's return.

One story not included in the newspaper accounts circulated during the years after the journey east. It related to a visit to the Parliament Buildings. "When the House was in session," it was retold,

> a cannon used to be fired at noon near the door of the old
> Parliament Buildings. Some of the members who wanted to see
> what the chiefs would do, took them to a balcony over the door,
> just before the noon hour. The Chiefs waited calmly, ignorant of
> what was in store. The others, a bit uneasy themselves, kept
> checking the time of their watches, for everyone knows that the
> roar of a cannon is hard on some nervous systems. At twelve
> sharp, the cannon was fired. The chiefs made no movement,
> showed no surprise. It was as though the sound had made no
> impression upon them, for they were long used to hiding their
> feelings, and were trained from early years to show no sign of
> fear. The only one who spoke was Mistawasis, and his voice was
> calm: "*Tapwā so ke ta kwan*," he said. (Verily, the sound is
> loud!)[87]

And so the stories went, passed from person to person as the wonders of the white man's world were recounted.

The people on the Ahtahkakoop Reserve were fully immersed in the fur trade by the time their chief returned home. After several years of shortage, fur-bearing animals were plentiful, and many of the families spent much of the winter on their hunting grounds. Half a dozen traders wintered on or near the reserve,[88] including one outfitted by the Hudson's Bay Company. The furs were "of the best quality," the company's officer in Prince Albert reported, and by the end of the winter the total trade at the outpost at Sandy Lake amounted to $2,212.[89]

In explaining the fluctuation in the number of fur-bearing animals, the Hudson's Bay Company officer in Prince Albert said that

> north of the north bank of the Saskatchewan as in all districts north, certain classes of fur bearing animals fluctuate in numbers. For instance, foxes, lynx, marten, mink, musquash & skunk appear in great numbers for a space of three years and then disappear nearly altogether for the same space of time until at the beginning of the fourth year they are found increasing in numbers and go on increasing rapidly during the two next successive years, and then appear to be almost exterminated. The increase and decrease of this class of fur bearing animals always follow the enormous increase of rabbit and decline ... in three years, with [almost] utter extinction of this little food animal.
>
> Bear, beaver, fisher, otter, wolf and wolverine do not materially vary in numbers in the Country aloof from settlement.[90]

Louis Ahenakew was teaching at the Asissipi school in the fall of 1886.[91] As usual, the school and its students were doing well. Peter Kāh-kasōw's daughter Mary was the "head scholar," the inspector from the Indian department reported after visiting the school in November. She could read the Bible fluently and intelligently, he said, adding that the other children were reading and spelling in the "second book and primer." Five boys and 16 girls were on the November register.[92] Hines pointed out with pride that when he held church services in English, for the benefit of the traders wintering in the vicinity, a number of the young people were able to join in the responses. Others, the missionary said, would also be able to if he had enough books.[93]

Although Hines had planned on sending Joseph Sasakamoose to teach at Stoney Lake during the winter, Louis Ahenakew went instead. However, with so many people away hunting, Louis was soon recalled and in mid-December John Cardinal* was sent in his place to teach syllabics. Hines

---

* John, 22, was also known as John Pierre. He was the son of Pierre, the old councillor from Mistawasis's band. In August, 1887, he married Ahtahkakoop's granddaughter Maria, the daughter of Kā-tāh-twēhototawāt and Emma Ahtahkakoop.

described John as "one of our Indians."[94] A man was hired to build a school, and Hines travelled to this, the beginning of a settlement, to conduct services as often as he could.

Okīnomotayēw, Hines said, "is one of the finest characters I have ever met with among the Indians. His wife is a very good old lady too, in fact all his family, with the exception of his eldest son, are good simple hearted people, & full of faith. The eldest son, however, is as bitter against religion as any man I have met with. The fact is, he has two wives, & both are from the Pelican Lake Band, a bitter set of heathens."[95] Hines did not elaborate on the effect his condemnations against heathens had on Okīnomotayēw's family and band.

When Anglican church statistics were prepared for 1886, the Stoney Lake people were included in the tally of Christian adherents to the Asissipi Mission. According to these figures, there was a total of 190 Christians and 106 non-Christians in the two bands. Hines pointed out that the men, women, and children he had baptized in Mistawasis's band were not included in the count because he had withdrawn from Snake Plain. The clergyman also noted that since the Asissipi Mission was established, he had buried 57 native Christians. Nine of these people had died in 1886.[96]

Meanwhile, the Battleford Industrial School had been repaired and improvements made following Colonel Otter's evacuation of the building the previous summer. The school was reopened in October, 1886, while Ahtahkakoop was in Ottawa. Although the facility was now able to handle 30 boys and 30 girls, only 12 boys and two girls were registered. According to principal Thomas Clarke, some of the boys who joined relatives at the time of the uprising had returned to the school and "surrendered." It was very difficult to get additional students for the school, he reported, "as the Indians have been advised, by parties from whom a different attitude should have been expected, not to send their children to this institution."[97] Faced with this problem, Mackay, who was still the Indian agent for the Battleford Agency, "recruited" boys and girls as he travelled throughout the Battleford and Prince Albert districts.[98] This was obviously part of his job as Indian agent in the Battleford area, but recruiting in the Carlton and Duck Lake areas was an extension of his dual role as archdeacon and Indian agent.

The year 1887 came in with vengeance. The people were sick and the weather was bitterly cold. Church services were cancelled on January 1 because of extreme temperatures. At services the next day, Hines said "It was nearly impossible to *hear myself* speak in church, the noise made by coughing was so great."[99]

A week later a girl was struck by an illness Hines initially called scarlet fever. More likely it was a case of the deadly form of measles that was devastating Okīnomotayēw's band at Stoney Lake.[100] Hines had discovered the extent of the illness during a routine visit in early January. When he arrived at the chief's one-room house the missionary discovered that 17 of the 20 people in the house were down with the fever, and the other three were not well. The story was the same in the other houses and tents at Stoney Lake. The people were starving, desperately sick, and very few of them were strong enough to hunt. In addition to worrying about their own fate, Okīnomotayēw and the others were anxious about friends and relatives who were off hunting and trapping. No one knew how they were faring. John Cardinal, who had been sent to teach syllabics, was healthy. George Robertson, the man building the school, and his wife and two children were also well, but a third child had the "fever." Robertson had given food from his own supplies to Okīnomotayēw's family and Mrs. Robertson had been nursing the sick. Without this help, Hines said many would have died before he arrived.[101] After making arrangements for a trader living nearby to provide food to the families, Hines travelled the 70 miles back to Ahtahkakoop's reserve as quickly as he could.

The people acted without hesitation when they heard the news. Men were sent north with food and medicine, and a messenger was dispatched south to inform government officials of the situation. Farm instructor Chaffee was at Sandy Lake several days later. He visited four houses at Ahtahkakoop's reserve, left some beef, and then either went to Stoney Lake himself, or sent beef, flour, rice, tea, disinfectant, and medicine with some of Ahtahkakoop's men. Towards the end of January, Joseph Sasakamoose took additional medicine to the small camp.[102]

When he returned home on February 3, Joseph reported that 11 people had died at Stoney Lake in 20 days. The sickness, however, was diminishing, with only two considered to be seriously ill. One of these people died a short time later. Among the dead during the terrible sickness was Otasewehas, the old man Hines had baptized with the chief a year earlier. This man, the clergyman said, was a fine old fellow who was loved by all who knew him. His last work on earth had been to help clear the trees and stumps from the land selected for the school at Stoney Lake. Also dead was a man described by Hines as a "heathen but not so bitter against religion as the chief's eldest son."[103]

Hines later estimated that one-quarter of the people in the camp died. Most of the dead were men. The missionary explained that the men would be getting better, but because they had to provide food for their families they ventured into the cold "still in an unfit state." Too weak to walk, they crept "on their hands and knees over the snow as they moved about in the bush setting their snares for rabbits." As a result of the extreme cold and their exertions in an unfit state, the men became sicker and some died.[104]

When Hines returned to Stoney Lake a week or so later he baptized one adult and "legally" married Okīnomotayēw and his wife, the chief's son and his wife, and his daughter and her husband.[105]

Disinfectant was used freely on Ahtahkakoop's reserve, and despite contact with Okīnomotayēw's band, only a few people came down with the "fever." Nevertheless there was much sickness. Part of the blame was put on the extremely low temperatures that lasted from day to day without relief throughout much of the winter. Hines described it as the most "bitter" weather he had seen since his arrival in Saskatchewan River country more than 12 years earlier. Colds, diarrhoea, and other ailments persisted. Two young men who were suffering from consumption were not expected to live very long. One of these men—20-year-old Josiah Asināpēwiyinin (Stone Man)—had been Hines's servant during the first part of the winter, but general weakness forced him to quit. He died on February 2. The other young man, 21-year-old John Masināscēs (Spotted), died on February 15. Five-year-old George Pē-nōsēwēskam (Comes Tracking) died March 28; he was buried the same afternoon. On April 25, the spirit left the body of an old woman who had been sick for a long time; Harriet Numowela was 70.[106] Both Hines and his wife were sick during this time, and on at least one occasion Louis Ahenakew had to conduct church services.

Although Dewdney persisted in claiming that a large percentage of the sickness and death was due to "hereditary" diseases, Thomas White, the new superintendent general of Indian Affairs, acknowledged that the "past year [was] remarkable for the unusual mortality which prevailed in very many of the bands." He attributed this, in part, to the extreme, "protracted" cold weather and poorly ventilated, over-heated and often unduly crowded rooms that were used for all purposes. He recommended that when agents promote the construction of houses, they try to "arrange the interior more in accordance with ordinary hygiene principles."[107]

Sickness of another kind had taken its toll in the Stony Mountain Penitentiary in Manitoba. Prison confinement devastated the Indian men who were put in prison after the uprising. Poundmaker, clearly in poor health, had been released after serving slightly more than six months of his sentence. He died on July 4, 1886, while visiting his adopted father Crowfoot in Blackfoot country. Gradually others were released on "humanitarian" grounds. By January of 1887, even though the jury had recommended clemency, Big Bear was the only Indian connected with the uprising still in prison. He was failing fast and prison officials feared he would die in custody. On January 15, 1887, Ahtahkakoop, Mistawasis, Ayahtaskamikinam, and John Smith sent a petition to Dewdney requesting Big Bear's release.[108] Dewdney and Vankoughnet both opposed releasing Big Bear. They agreed that "it is considered that members of his Band settling down quietly with other Bands, would become disturbed and disorganized and would no doubt desire to leave their present location in order to join him." Before the Indian affairs officials could make their views known, Big Bear was set free on February 4, 1887, "upon grounds of ill health."[109] A sick and broken man, the chief went to Little Pine's reserve where he died almost a year later, on January 17, 1888.

Three Deaths for Every Birth, 1887-1888

The foundation for a new life laid by Ahtahkakoop, Sasakamoose, Ahenakew and the other leading men was readily evident on the Ahtahkakoop Reserve by 1887. The clean, neat houses, each with its own stable and fenced field, were said to look "quite like a settlement." And the large barn with the shingled roof—along with a similar structure at the Mistawasis Reserve—continued to draw attention as a superior barn that "was equal to a great many in Ontario."[1]

The influences of Ahtahkakoop's trip to the Brantford area could also be seen. Upon their return home, Ahtahkakoop and Mistawasis apparently asked for equipment to diversify and make better use of their resources. Their requests, or at least some of them, were approved and both bands were given milk pans, churns for making butter, and similar equipment. Some families became very interested in making butter and a few built "very good milk cellars."

Both bands were also supplied with at least one spinning wheel so they could make better use of the sheep they had received the previous year.[2] Ahtahkakoop's people were already familiar with sheep and working with wool since Hines had imported some Leicestershires a few years earlier. The missionary had taught the men how to shear the animals and some had quickly become efficient at the task. Even before Hines's sheep arrived, Emma had taught the women and older girls how to knit with yarn sent by friends in England, and the government had on at least two occasions supplied yarn and knitting needles. Regardless, the experience with their own flock of sheep was not a good one. Government officials had failed to make arrangements to sell or otherwise dispose of the surplus wool. Under provisions of the Indian Act, the people were unable to sell the fleece on their own. So like the unground wheat that so often sat heaped in useless piles, the fleece lay unused in the barn. Because the people gained very little profit from the wool, government officials reported late in 1887 that there was general indifference to shearing.[3]

There were also problems with the sheep themselves. Indian agent Rae reported in August that the lambs were healthy, but the adult animals had some sort of disease and were not doing very well.[4] Additionally, a number of sheep had wandered off. A government official blamed this on the people, saying that the flies were bad and smudges were not kept going.[5] Hines had another explanation. The clergyman recalled that when he introduced sheep to the reserve several years earlier he chose the long-coated Leicestershire breed. The long wool caught on the underbrush, thus discouraging the sheep from straying. The government, Hines said, supplied

> a flock of Merino sheep, but as this class of sheep was not encumbered with very long wool, they took to wandering and sometimes were found miles from home, and many of them fell a prey to the wolves, etc., whereas the sheep imported by me being of the Leicestershire breed, they were contented to remain near home with the satisfactory result that neither I nor the Indians who shared them with me, lost one, either from wolves or drowning.[6]

The women benefited more directly from the sheep than the men since they were able to spin and card the wool into yarn for knitting mittens and stockings. Already skilled at intricate quill, bead, and leather work, the women applied their talents to sewing with cloth. Many pieces of their work were of such high quality, Hines said, that they

> won prizes at different competitions. We sent one Indian woman's work, which consisted of gloves, stockings, cross-overs and comforters to an exhibition held at Ottawa, two thousand miles from our mission, and her work gained for her about three pounds in prizes, which included knitting needles of all sizes, crochet hooks and tatting shuttles, with several pounds of the finest coloured fingering wool that could be obtained.[7]

So, although the sheep did not bring the benefits that had been hoped for, the women were recognized for their work and were able to add to their families' meagre supply of clothing.

The crops in 1887 were more successful than the sheep. The men had gone into Prince Albert in mid-March to get their supply of food for the

Illustration by Ed Peekeekoot

The community that developed on the Ahtahkakoop Reserve was well known for its hard-working people, neat houses, well-built stables, and fenced fields.

planting season. Band members had saved wheat from the previous year's harvest to use as seed, and perhaps for this reason the amount of wheat sown was less than in 1886. The acreage seeded to barley was also smaller.[8] Despite the reductions, government records indicated that in 1887 the Ahtahkakoop Band had the greatest number of acres sown to crop in the Treaty 6 area.

The routine of hunting, getting firewood, and looking after their fields, stock, and families was broken in early June when "a great number" of the families went fishing. Later in the month Ahtahkakoop and other principal men on the reserve contributed food for a feast to celebrate the "Queen's Jubilee." Hines gave 10 pounds of tea as his share. Why does the government not do anything of this sort, Hines had mused in his journal, adding that it would not cost much and would help "unite the Indians more firmly in their loyalty."[9]

Two weeks later members of Ahtahkakoop's and Okīnomotayēw's bands celebrated the marriages of two couples in what Hines called the first linking of the bands by matrimony since his arrival in the North-West. In the first wedding, which took place July 5, Kate Asināpēwiyin (Tāpwēwiniwok)—the widow of Pē-nōsēwēskam and Asinapēwiyin—married a widower from Stoney Lake. The following day a young man from the Ahtahkakoop Band and a young woman from Okīnomotayēw's band were married. Hines does not identify the couple and they are not included in the mission's marriage register.[10] Okīnomotayēw was among the eight people who came from Stoney Lake for the weddings.

A month later Ahtahkakoop's granddaughter, Maria Kā-tāh-twēho-totawāt, married John Cardinal from Mistawasis's band. The daughter of Emma Ahtahkakoop and Kā-tāh-twēhototawāt, Maria had been raised by Ahtahkakoop and his wife. She remained with her grandparents when her father, mother and the other children left the reserve after the uprising. John Cardinal transferred to Ahtahkakoop's band in 1888.[11]

Usually the hot temperatures of summer broke the cycle of sickness and death that routinely haunted the people during the winter and early spring. This year it was different as rain and cold weather continued into August and the sickness relentlessly persisted. A girl 18 months of age died in June. By mid-July many people had bad colds, and on July 23 a four-month-old boy died.[12] Two other children were very sick. Emily Ayamuskin, 3, was paralyzed on one side and doing poorly, and Wāsēhikot's son James, 12, had been suffering from scrofula for nearly two years and was "half eaten up" by the disease. Scrofula, which was tuberculosis of the neck lymph nodes, predisposed its victims to pulmonary diseases such as consumption* and a premature death. "It is a horrible disease for anyone to have," Hines said, "but it seems to take its worst form among the Indians. Their necks are almost eaten entirely away."[13]

Although the weather took its toll on the people, the rain nurtured the crops. The plants did not shrivel in the heat like the year before and by early August the wheat stalks were full and luxuriant. Hines said he had never seen the crops looking so good, and Indian agent Rae estimated a harvest of at least 25 bushels to the acre. Nevertheless, the people looked skyward. The sun had only been shining an average of two hours a day, and temperatures were so low that the missionary recorded on August 6 that it was cold enough to be November. Everyone worried that the wheat would not ripen before being cut down by a heavy frost. If that happened, another season of hard work would be wasted. A few days later their prayers were

---

* Consumption was tuberculosis of the lungs.

answered and the sun came out. The people started cutting their hay, and on August 14 the missionary wrote in his journal that the people were tired from "hay making."[14] By the time they were done, 230 tons had been cut, making it the largest hay crop to date.

The crops ripened and the frost held off. As a result, the people harvested 1,160 bushels of wheat, their second largest crop on record. Rae, however, had exaggerated the yield since the fields of wheat averaged 10 bushels per acre, not 25. In comparison, the record harvest of 1,300 bushels in 1883 had averaged 16.25 bushels per acre. Nevertheless, it was a good crop, and the people gave thanks. Eight hundred bushels of barley were also produced. The fields of potatoes did particularly well, producing 1,800 bushels, while the turnip harvest amounted to 350 bushels, and the carrots, 50 bushels. Since other vegetables were eaten as they matured, no records were kept. The oats either failed or were used directly off the field as fodder for the cattle since none was apparently harvested. In addition to planting, harvesting, and looking after their stock, the farmers fenced an additional 270 acres of land, bringing the total to 570 acres. They broke 104 acres, increasing their cultivated land from 216 to 320 acres, and did a considerable amount of summer fallowing and fall ploughing.[15]

Meanwhile 24 boys and girls were registered at the Asissipi Mission school on the Ahtahkakoop Reserve and continuing to work well under teacher Joseph Sasakamoose. "As usual," Hines recorded in his journal, we are credited with "having the best Indian school in the territories, i.e., The children are the most advanced both in scriptures & secular knowledge." In addition to diction, which was being taught formally for the first time, the curriculum included the usual subjects of spelling, writing, arithmetic, and geography.[16]

Louis Ahenakew was teaching at Stoney Lake, where he had moved with his wife and infant daughter after the completion of the school building in May. There was considerable interest in the school and many of the adult men attended classes when they were not working and hunting.[17] Hines, despite the establishment of the school, was facing competition from a Catholic priest in the area, and with Okīnomotayēw's and Louis's support, was trying to keep the priest's influence to a minimum.[18] The Englishman was also competing with another force, for Okīnomotayēw's eldest son was still following the traditional ways and resisting Hines, as well as the priests. The son had made one compromise, however: he still refused to attend church services but his children were allowed to go to school.[19]

Since the death of Wāskitoy and the resignation of Wāsēhikot as headman, Ahtahkakoop had been assisted by two headmen rather than the four specified by the treaty. This was remedied in 1887 when band members elected Kā-miyo-astotin, 35, and Kāh-kāsōw, 41, as headmen. Their terms, according to government documentation, was for "life or good behaviour."[20] Kā-miyo-astotin, who was given the name Basil when he was baptized, was Ahtahkakoop's third son.* Kāh-kāsōw, whose Christian name was Peter, was the first adult to be baptized by Hines and the man who had taught syllabics in the buffalo camps during the first years the missionary was living amongst them. He was Ahenakew's son.

In total, 188 people received their annuity payments in 1887. The three men considered to be rebels—along with their families—were not paid. There had been six recorded deaths during the paylist year: a boy, two young men, a girl, a woman, and a man.[21] Five boys and four girls were born.[22]

The 1887 paylist indicated that three women who had married non-Indians, along with their families, were discharged. Margaret Sasakamoose and John Cameron were married in 1885. Ahtahkakoop's daughter Mary, whose son Alexander had been discharged the previous year, had been married to Joe Genereux since 1859. Marie, Masuskapoe's daughter, was the third woman to be discharged. She had married Gabriel Vandall and been given her own ticket in 1879. Additionally, Kā-miyo-ahcahkwēw's daughter Mary, wife of Donald LeBlanc, and her son were commuted.† Thus, in 1887 Sasakamoose's daughter, one of Ahtahkakoop's daughters, a granddaughter, and a great-niece were removed from the Ahtahkakoop Band paylist. And Ahtahkakoop's daughter Emma Kā-tāh-twēhototawāt and her five children were not paid because Kā-tāh-twēhototawāt had been classified as a rebel.

The paylist provides other information.[23] For instance, Louis Ahenakew's sister Ellen, 18, married John Hyman, who was also 18. Until 1897 John's

---

* Kā-miyo-astotin's Christian name was pronounced Ba-seel; he was later known as Basil Starblanket.

† When a person was "commuted," he or she gave up treaty status and received a lump sum of money equivalent to 10 annuity payments. People who were "discharged" generally took scrip, a certificate issued by the government that could be exchanged for land.

name appeared as Lyman on the treaty paylists. He was the son of Nīhtāwikāpawiw-iskwēw (Good Standing Woman) and her deceased husband Āyiman. John's sister Charlotte had been married to Kāh-kāsōw for a number of years. In another marriage of note, Peter Peekeekoot married 16-year-old Ida Kīnikwānāsiw. Peekeekoot's first wife, daughter of the headman Wāskitoy, had died in 1886; she left one daughter.

Only one new entry appeared on the paylist. Greyeyes* (K-ōsihkosi-wayāniw's son), along with his wife, two sons, and a daughter, had come from Battleford and were now listed as band members; it was noted on the paylist that he had been "presented with Cattle" by the Indian commissioner. The paylist also indicated that two men who had been away and not paid for several years were still absent.

The treaty day, as usual, had been a time of excitement as four different traders set out their goods in order "to attract the attention of buyers." Hines said he was told by the traders that soap was selling the "readiest of anything."[24]

A 10-week-old baby died six days after the treaty payments were made. Sasakamoose's only grandson, Duncan Cameron, 14 months, died from bronchitis about a week later. He was Margaret's son. And then at the end of October, Kāh-kāsōw's daughter Betsy—also stricken with bronchitis—died. She was four. When another baby died in early November from bronchitis, Hines wrote in his journal that the death rate was very high, with three deaths for every birth.[25]

During this time of sickness, the government's ineptness was once again evident as the sheaves of wheat from the large crop remained piled in the stack yards waiting for the Indian department's thresher. It eventually arrived in early November. The men threshed their grain for nearly a month, but the machine was in poor condition and progress was slow. Then, although the men were not finished, the machine was sent to Mistawasis's reserve where the people were becoming impatient. There was one positive move, nonetheless. The government, at long last, was realizing the uselessness of excess wheat. Faced with the double-edged prospect of a large crop of wheat and not finishing the threshing until late winter or early spring, inspecting officer Wadsworth gave the Ahtahkakoop

---

* Two of Greyeye's sons, Norbert and Sam, were being raised on the Ahtahkakoop Reserve by their grandfather K-ōsihkosiwanāniw, and four of his sisters had married into the band.

farmers permission to sell two-thirds of their surplus wheat in order to purchase meat.[26]

And so in December, with their threshing partially done, the men took
some of their wheat to Stobart's new grist mill in the village of Duck Lake.
They also sold some of their grain to the Indian department.[27]

Indian agent Joseph A. Finlayson, who had taken over the Carlton Agency
in November, reported the last week of December that after threshing part of
their wheat the people at the Ahtahkakoop Reserve were "doing tolerably
well in hunting and living on the produce of their crops." Five weeks later,
game, rabbits, and fur-bearing animals were all very scarce. Eventually it
was conceded that the hunt during the winter of 1887–88 had failed.[28] Before
they settled on their reserve, Ahtahkakoop's people had broken into small
hunting camps to eke a living off the land when game was scarce. Now,
although thankful for their crops, they were tied to the reserve. They could
no longer travel extensively, spreading themselves through the parklands and
forests to make the best use of the resources that were available.

The perception that the "heathen" Indians were better off than the
Christians continued to plague the people. This was once again
brought to the surface after an old woman who regularly walked 25 miles
from Snake Plain to take Holy Communion at Sandy Lake hanged herself.
Her son told the story to Hines in mid-June. Two of his daughters had died
during the winter, the man explained, and his six-year-old son was very ill.
The man's mother, who lived a short distance away,

> came over to see the little boy one evening. She saw he w^d not
> live long & she complained bitterly at losing so many of her
> grandchildren. Her son rebuked her for this, & told [her] to go
> back to her house as it was getting late. About 4 the next morning
> the little boy died. The father told his wife not to cry and make a
> noise, but to bear the loss bravely and without murmuring. They
> laid out the child in his grave clothes & then the father went out
> for a short walk. He went towards his stable, as he approached it,
> a year old heifer (one he had given to his son some months previ-
> ous) came running to meet him, and began frisking about as
> though it were wishing to be caressed as the little boy used to
> caress it. This so touched the man's heart, that he could no longer
> restrain his grief, & immediately began to cry aloud, the wife
> hearing this went outside and began to cry too. The supposition is,

that the grandmother heard the wailing & judged what had happened & in a fit of insanity, caused by excessive grief, she put an end to herself. ... Her son feels very much distressed, & thinks the hand of God is very heavy upon him & begins to draw comparisons reflecting to the prosperity of his heathen neighbours and also to some Xtians who do nothing to show that they are Xtians but whose lives correspond with that of the heathens. I had a long talk with him & read the 73 Psalm to him, from which he appeared to derive much comfort, & he left me with a desire to trust God more in the future.[29]

This was a story—without the tragic death of the woman—that Hines had heard numerous times from members of the Asissipi Mission who lived on Ahtahkakoop's reserve.

The decision to adopt Christianity, nevertheless, had been made more than 10 years earlier and most people in Ahtahkakoop's band remained loyal to the mission. At Easter in 1887, for instance, 61 people had taken communion. Of these, 22 were married couples and the rest were widows and young people. Two of the largest congregations of the year attended church on July 31, and in September between 50 and 60 people attended two services. The congregation was even larger on October 30 when the new bishop of the Saskatchewan Diocese, William Cyprian Pinkham, was at the Asissipi Mission. Forty-eight of the 63 people who took communion were confirmed church members.[30] The offerings at the service, which Pinkham described as "delightful," amounted to nearly $18 "in money and kind." Hines, in his journal, said he liked the new bishop.[31]

In the afternoon Ahtahkakoop's wife, Mary Nātowēw, and a daughter were among the seven people confirmed at services held at the chief's house.[32] And so, 13 years after Hines's association with the Ahtahkakoop Band began, Mary's outward resistance to the church had finally been overcome. During the early days of the mission, when Ahenakew was still alive, Bible classes had been held at Ahtahkakoop's house in an effort to win her over. She had agonised over being baptized, and over the years her attendance at church had been marginal. The woman's opposition must have caused numerous problems in the chief's household and perhaps explains the surprisingly few references to her children, other than Kā-miyo-ahcahk-wēw, in Hines's church records. Interestingly, Hines makes no mention of the woman's confirmation, perhaps indicating that he considered the long delay to be his failure and one he did not wish to emphasize.

From John Hines, *Red Indians of the Plains*

St. Mark's Church, Ahtahkakoop Reserve (date unknown). Congregations were often large during 1887, and it was not uncommon for 60 people to take communion.

In his report on the visit to the Ahtahkakoop Reserve, Pinkham commented on the "superior intelligence" of the people. Methods that succeed with white people, he commented, would succeed among the Indian people. He also said that a child died while he was on the reserve.[33]

Several weeks later, on November 20, church members elected a new warden, and on December 12 and 13, four new seats were made for the church. Hines explained that "Church work was … thoroughly organized with our churchwardens, vestry-men, and a regular system of offertories, though cash at that time was not in circulation at the Mission." The churchwardens, among other things, were responsible for looking after the offerings. On a Communion Sunday,

> a large table [was placed] near the door, and when the people entered the Church they used to place their offerings upon it. These gifts consisted of packets of tea, sugar, soap, varying in weight, but never under a half-pound, and sometimes they would weigh as much as 2 lbs. each packet, and sugar and soap at that time were 1s. a lb. Others would give reels of sewing cotton,

packets of needles, knives, forks, plates, cups and saucers, tobacco, pieces of print varying in length from 1 to 10 yards in the piece (print at that time was sold in the Saskatchewan from 1s. to 1s. 6d. per yard);* others would give a piece of deerskin made into leather, and sometimes several pairs of moccasins ready made would be placed on the table; some, if they had recently returned with flour from the grist mill, would give from 8 to 20 lbs. of flour; others would bring from five to fifteen boards 10 feet long, 6 inches broad and 1 inch thick. These latter would be left outside the Church door and a note in Cree syllabics would be placed on the table stating the number of boards, and who from; others would give the skins of the fur-bearing animals, such as red fox, mink and musquash [muskrat], and I have often known on a Communion Sunday, when Indians have been leaving the Church and feeling thankful for fresh grace received, deposit on the table a second offertory of such things as they possessed. I have known an Indian to leave behind him that which he prized more than anything else, namely his fire bag. This is a bag made by his wife from deerskin, and is often elaborately ornamented with bead work, and in which is carried a pipe, tobacco, steel, flint, touchwood, and sundry small articles, including a pocket-knife; this bag is a constant companion of every man, and is worn attached to his belt. The reason why it is called a fire bag is, because it contains the means for making fire, namely, flint, steel and touchwood.[34]

On the Monday after the service, the church wardens took the offering to the missionary's house where a value was placed on each item and the total amount was recorded in a book kept especially for this purpose. "After the amount had been duly entered in the book," Hines said, "the articles became my own property, and I was responsible for their value in cash. Then, when diocesan appeals reached us, the churchwardens decided what amount should be sent, and I forwarded my own cheque to the Secretary of the Synod, and the amount was entered in the book, showing how much and for what purpose it had been paid out." Hines said he used the articles "in bartering for fuel or certain kinds of food from the Indians, and for paying labour in my field, etc., etc."[35]

---

* In British currency, a shilling was a 20th of a pound sterling; 1s. 6d was one shilling and six pence, or 1½ shillings.

The influence of Hines and the Asissipi Mission on Ahtahkakoop's reserve had grown over the years. At the school, religious components of the curriculum were as important as reading, writing, and other secular subjects. Joseph took the church service when Hines was sick or away, and Louis Ahenakew conducted church services at Stoney Lake in addition to teaching at the school, further demonstrating the close ties between the school and the church.

Like clergymen and priests elsewhere, Hines was able to exert pressure and influence behaviour. One such occasion had taken place in July when the missionary excommunicated Peekeekoot for what he considered to be immoral behaviour. Hines explained that the young man's wife had died in 1886, leaving him with a daughter to raise. He was now living with Ida Kīnikwānāsiw, a 16-year-old from a heathen family, in an unmarried state. The excommunication had the desired effect and Ida was baptized August 28, 1887. The couple was married eight days later.[36]

The missionary was also being consulted on issues that should have been handled by the chief and his headmen. In one such instance two men asked him to settle a grievance. Hines explained in his journal that one man had "sold" his field to a second party. Soon afterwards the second man died and the field was claimed by the deceased man's father, who sold it to yet another party. The first man came to Hines and said he had only sold the land, not the fence. Accordingly, he was claiming the fence. Hines said no one was present when the deal was made and he did not give any indication on how the situation was settled. Nor did he explain the practice of "selling" fields on the reserve.[37]

In another instance, several years earlier, a widower with several small children had asked the clergyman to help him select a new wife. The man agreed with Hines's suggested choice, a widow who had been showing considerable interest in his children, and then he asked the Englishman to propose for him. Hines agreed, with some misgivings. He explained that after "having obtained my wife's permission, I called on the widow at my earliest convenience and explained matters to her, taking great pains to make her understand I was proposing for the other fellow, and not for myself. ... My mission was successful, and in due course they were lawfully married, and the union proved to be a very happy one."[38]

By the fall of 1887 it was evident that Hines and his wife were not to be with Ahtahkakoop's people much longer. In early September the clergyman had been sent to The Pas to investigate some problems at the Devon Mission and then to report on the "true state of affairs."[39] Six weeks after his return, plans were being made to move him to Devon. The change, however, was not to take effect immediately since Emma Hines wanted to take their 10-year-old daughter to England and place her in the "Children's Home." Emma would then rejoin her husband at Sandy Lake before the move was made. It was recommended that the Reverend John R. Settee take over the Asissipi Mission under the supervision of Archdeacon J.A. Mackay.[40] Louis Ahenakew was to remain at Stoney Lake with Okīnomotayēw's band.

Changes—some administrative and others more drastic—were also underway in the Indian department. Indian agent John Rae was, in the words of Commissioner Dewdney, "relieved of his duties." Joseph A. Finlayson, who spoke Cree as well as English, arrived in November, 1887, to oversee the newly created Carlton Agency. This new agency included all reserves on the north side of the North Saskatchewan River, including Ahtahkakoop's. George Chaffee remained as farm instructor. The Duck Lake Agency was put in charge of W.C. McKenzie, Indian agent. He had two farm instructors, Louis Marion and Justus Wilson. The instructors were to be in charge of the provisions and personally administer them, in addition to overseeing farming operations.[41]

In addition to these administrative changes, the department was forging ahead in its efforts to destroy the communal traditions of the Indian people. One step taken towards this end was the "practice of giving cows to individual Indians as their own property, subject only to the return by them after a reasonable lapse of time of an equally good animal from the progeny raised." This, Dewdney commented, "promises to work admirably."[42] As well, Thomas White, the new superintendent general of Indian Affairs, indicated in his year-end report, that farmers who were working hard to become independent were beginning to appreciate "holding their locations in severalty instead of in common."[43]

The power of many chiefs was being thwarted and, increasingly, the government began pushing vigorously for policies of assimilation. This was particularly evident in White's reports. Impressed with the transformation in appearance and manners of children attending the industrial schools, White questioned the wisdom of allowing the children to follow a trade or occupation on their reserves after they left the residential school. Instead, he urged that every "possible legitimate means" be taken to prevent those getting an education from returning home, for "they are injured" more than they help. He further recommended that "strong inducements" be used to encourage students to establish themselves off their reserve so they can "become amalgamated with the general community."[44]

Pressure was also being exerted to impose white values on the Indian people. The superintendent general was critical of houses with a single room that was used for all purposes which, among other things, meant that people of both sexes slept in the same room. He did not think enough control was exerted over children, he was against the use of blankets as an "article of dress," he deplored long hair on men, and thought there were too many dogs on reserves, particularly if they bothered the sheep or slept in the houses.[45] It was thus becoming evident that the government wanted to become increasingly involved in the daily life of the Indian people and, in some ways, to widen the schism between two different cultures in an attempt to bring about assimilation.

By early December, 1887, Joseph Sasakamoose was sick. Hines wrote in his journal on December 4 that he was afraid the young teacher had consumption. The next few days were trying ones. Joseph's health worsened and on December 7 he was reported to be very ill. To everyone's relief he rallied and by December 10, even though he was suffering "from much pain in his heart," Sasakamoose's son was feeling somewhat better. However, during the next weeks Joseph's health did not improve further, and Hines wrote in his journal on December 22 that "from what I can learn, it will be some time before he recovers." Instead of taking his wife and daughter to Winnipeg on the first stage of their trip to England, Hines took Joseph's place in the classroom. He said he hoped the delay would give the young man a chance to regain his health.[46]

Joseph was only one of many who were sick in December, for Hines reported that once again there was "much sickness" among the people. Extreme cold worsened the situation. On December 18 it was -43°F. Two days later the thermometer dipped to -45°F. Then, perversely, temperatures soared. It not only thawed, but it rained. Hines commented that, with a temperature change of 70 degrees within 24 hours, it was no wonder so much sickness prevailed.

On December 22, Philip Wīcikāpawīmēw (He Who Stands With You), the father of the 10-week-boy who had died in October, was dead. Three days later, on Christmas Day, James Wāsēhikot, 12, died from scrofula. He was buried two days later. With the coming of the new year, Emily

Ayamuskin, suffering from paralysis, was very "debilitated" and not expected to survive. Another child living at the end of the lake was near death, and there were at least three case of consumption, besides Joseph, in the settlement.[47]

An old man who had been "ailing much" during the past six years was one of the people Hines visited when he made his rounds dispensing medicine and comfort. This man, Hines said, "believes he is suffering from the effects of poison, given him secretly by the old heathen, who opposed my staying at Whitefish Lake in the Fall of '74. The heathens in years gone by, did much harm to one another this way."[48]

Although he was still weak in mid-January, Joseph Sasakamoose was well enough to attend church services and he told Hines that he wanted to try teaching again. If the work proved to be too difficult for Joseph, it was decided that Archdeacon Mackay would make other arrangements during the time Hines was away. The young man was back in the classroom by January 19.[49]

With this plan in place Hines quickly prepared for the trip to Winnipeg. He made a special trip to Mistawasis's reserve to see several sick people who still supported the Anglican Church. While there he administered Holy Communion and held a short service. Back at Ahtahkakoop's reserve, two services in Cree were conducted on January 22. The English settlers "for 12 miles around" requested a service in English and this was held in the afternoon. Eight people were present. Hines made a final visit to the sick on the reserve and then he left for Winnipeg with Emma and their daughter Henrietta.

Emily Ayamuskin, now 4, Thomas Chicken, 4 months, and Paul Mēmēmēkwanawēw, 1, died before Hines returned on March 17, 1888. Three babies were born. Joseph had only been able to teach for a month or so before becoming too sick to continue. As a result, the school was closed for a month. Because of the young man's illness, a catechist by the name of Cook and the Reverend I.J. Taylor travelled to the reserve to hold services.[50] General sickness had not lessened, and Hines reported upon his return that everyone had colds. Despite the sickness and death that was taking its toll on the people, Indian agent Finlayson reported in March that the Ahtahkakoop Band was "in good health."[51]

CHAPTER THIRTY

John Hines Leaves, 1888-1889

Joseph Sasakamoose "cannot last long, he is rapidly wasting away," Hines wrote in his journal on April 7, 1888. "He speaks very cheerfully of the future, & is just waiting God's own time for him to depart this life." The young teacher died two days later, "in peace," and was buried April 10. He was 21 years old. Ironically, Joseph's agreement with Hines to teach for three years after being educated at the expense of the Church Missionary Society had expired on March 31.[1]

Sasakamoose, like so many other parents who had lost children, was badly shaken by the death of his son. "The poor old Father bears the blow very well," Hines wrote the day of the funeral. "It is indeed hard for the old couple, their only remaining son [Alexander] is deaf and dumb. Poor Joseph was their sole support. The old man said to-day in reference to this matter that he had faith to believe God would provide for his few remaining days on earth."[2] A week later Sasakamoose came to see Hines, very "sorrowful" but bearing up well "considering the heavy blow he has received." The missionary read a chapter of the Bible to Sasakamoose and they prayed together. "He cried very much as he repeated the Lord's prayer after me," Hines wrote in his journal, "but he said they were not tears of complaint, but tears of gratitude to God for having sent the Gospel of consolation & peace, to cheer & comfort them in their hours of trial." Hines gave some clothing to the "good old Christian" before he left.[3]

In May Sasakamoose and his wife Maggie were living in a tent near the mission house. The old man, who had served faithfully as his brother's senior headman and a warden of the church for so many years, told the missionary that he missed Joseph the most after 2 o'clock in the afternoon. When Hines asked him why, Sasakamoose replied that "each time the school bell rings, I fancy it is my son ringing it, & the sound cheers me up, but as the bell does not ring again after two, I seem to realize my loneliness."[4]

The new teacher ringing the bell was a young Irishman by the name of J.M.R. Neely. Hines had brought him to the mission late in March when it became apparent that Joseph would not be able to teach any more. A "full member of the Church of England," Neely did not speak Cree. Hines knew this would be difficult for the children, but he hoped they would make more of an effort to speak English. To his advantage, Neely was a "practical chemist" and it was anticipated that this background would be of much help with the sick. Many people in Ahtahkakoop's band met the teacher for the first time when he accompanied Hines on his visits the day that Joseph died.[5]

There were other changes at the mission. Following the second church service on April 8, the congregation elected three new church wardens. Each man made a long speech, during which he praised John and Emma Hines for the work they had done during their 14 years with the band. After some discussion the men decided to petition the bishop and ask if there was some way to keep the missionary and his wife at Sandy Lake. Ahtahkakoop and the councillors left the next day to get the agent to write the letter for them. Hines was very touched, saying that "It seems very hard to part with our people, I might say our spiritual children. We have known them for so many years, in fact we seem to know them, if possible, better than they know themselves, & were it not that the work in other parts of the Diocese was suffering for lack of proper supervision, I could not, I think, bear to separate myself from them."[6]

The weather turned miserable in mid-April when six inches of snow fell. It is "lying on the top of the old," Hines wrote in his journal, "& the last three nights have been very cold and everywhere is as wintery in appearance as it was 2 months ago." On April 24 it snowed heavily all day, and when the missionary went to visit Eliza Cipay-awāsis, Joseph Kā-miyo-ahcahkwēw's wife of seven months, he said "the roads were so bad …[that he] scarcely got back without an accident." Eliza, 21, was very sick with consumption and Hines did not think she would recover. Her husband was Ahtahkakoop's grandson, the son of Kā-miyo-ahcahkwēw and Judique. The clergyman said that although Joseph had been baptized and confirmed, he "for some reason or other, never attends church." Hines reported in his journal that before the young woman died on May 10 she asked her husband to take communion but he refused.[7]

The last piles of snow—the remains of a deep drift—finally melted on June 3. The cattle had survived the long winter in excellent condition, and the people had wheat left in the spring for planting because they had not been able to get all of it ground into flour. Understandably, cultivating and planting had been delayed in the spring of 1888 because of the snow and cold. Food was scarce, so the people found various ways to survive. Some of the men got ammunition from Indian agent Finlayson late in the spring for hunting. The agent said he "allowed" some of the men to go to Prince Albert and other places to look for work. In early June, many of the people were away fishing, and then, in the middle of the month, it rained for four days and three nights without stopping, flooding yards, roads, and fields. By now, many of the families were once again "off in search of food." Others took wheat from the 1887 harvest to Prince Albert to be ground. Hines asked the question that had been asked so many times before in various forms, "What would people in England think if they had to take their wheat 200 miles to get it ground?"[8]

Meanwhile, in England, Emma Hines was doing her share of lobbying to allow her family to stay at Sandy Lake. She told the secretary of the Church Missionary Society about the petition and offered to join her husband at Sandy Lake for the winter. Otherwise, Emma said, she would not return to Canada until the following year because her daughter Henrietta was not well and needed a high, dry climate. The efforts of Ahtahkakoop, his headmen, and Emma Hines had little effect, and the move was affirmed. As soon as the Reverend John Settee arrived from Grand Rapids,* Hines would leave for The Pas. Emma decided to live in England for a year and place Henrietta in a day school to bring her up to the level of the other students in the Children's House. She would join her husband at The Pas in 1889.[9]

As the time for Hines's departure drew near, Ahtahkakoop and others continued to show their support. People from the Mistawasis Reserve were part of a large congregation at two church services held at Sandy Lake on May 20. "Our chief came in to spend the evening with me," Hines wrote in his journal, and "he spoke for about 2 hours on religion, & other matters, & we enjoyed the conversation much. I wish the Parent Committee [CMS committee in England] could have heard & understood, all he said. They'd have blessed God & taken courage."[10]

---

* Grand Rapids is in present-day Manitoba near the place where the Saskatchewan River flows into Lake Winnipeg.

Hines made his last visit to Okīnomotayēw's people at Stoney Lake early in June. The families told him they were sorry he was leaving, and said they would adhere to the church and God's word. It was a difficult mission, the missionary noted, since there were two or three Roman Catholic traders nearby who worked hard for their church.[11]

Several days later, on June 9, Lawrence Clarke arrived at the Ahtahkakoop Reserve with three other people. The Hudson's Bay Company officer paid his respects to Ahtahkakoop and the leading men, visited Hines, and then measured the church for a carpet he intended on donating to the church. In Hines's words, Clarke's gift would serve as "a lasting reminder to the Indians of our all having worshipped together in the church, & as a token of his satisfaction with all he saw at the mission." Clarke and the others stayed overnight, and the next day they joined Ahtahkakoop and his people at the morning service. In the afternoon six government officials, in addition to Clarke's party, were in the congregation for a service that was conducted in English.[12]

The following week Hines travelled to Snake Plain to hold the final service for settlers living between the Mistawasis and Ahtahkakoop reserves. Thirty people were present, despite the four-day rain that caused floods "everywhere." Hines recorded in his journal that he hoped Mr. Settee "will be able to keep up the monthly service at Snake Plains in English."[13] Okīnomotayēw and Louis Ahenakew arrived from Stoney Lake later in the week to say good-bye. Louis, whose three years of teaching for Hines had also come to an end, wanted to go to Battleford. Okīnomotayēw, on the other hand, was hoping Archdeacon Mackay would let Louis remain at Stoney Lake. Hines agreed with the chief, in part because he did not want the band to fall into the hands of the Catholic priests. Hines referred to Louis as a catechist in his journal entry.

On July 1, Ahtahkakoop's people attended services in full force. The usual two services were held, but this time communion was taken at both, with 61 communicants present. It was a very impressive service, Hines said, "as this is most likely the last Sunday I shall be here."

Settee arrived the morning of July 4. The next day a farewell service was held. "The chief & Councillors tried to speak," Hines said, "but were so much overcome that they could only say a very few words. The meeting was very touching."[14] These were the last words recorded by the missionary in his journal before departing for The Pas.

Hines left the Ahtahkakoop Reserve July 6, 1888, after serving

Illustration by Ed Peekeekoot

Ahtahkakoop's people gathered in the church yard at Sandy Lake on July 6, 1888, to say goodbye to John Hines.

Ahtahkakoop's people for 14 years. Baptiste Ahenakew's son Edward, who was three years old at the time, recalled many years later that "as in a dream, I remember his departure from Sandy Lake. ... His wagons were loaded, I remember, and the yard was full of kneeling people, while he stood, praying for them. It was a sad day for Sandy Lake, I have often been told."[15]

Nine days later John Hines, 38, loaded his family's worldly belongings onto the steamboat *North West*. He disembarked at The Pas, which earlier had been known as the Devon Mission, and on July 17 the missionary assumed responsibility for The Pas Mission. Hines was also appointed the rural dean of the Cumberland District, of which The Pas was a part; he remained in that position until 1903 when he returned to the Prince Albert District. In poor health, he retired in 1911 at the age of 61. His book *Red Indians of the Plains* was published in 1915. John Hines outlived his wife and spent his last years in St. Vital, Manitoba, where he died, blind, in 1931.[16]

Ahtahkakoop had seen part of his dream fulfilled. In 1874, when John Hines arrived in the North-West as a young man of 24 years, the chief and his people followed the buffalo and hunted and trapped for a living. For a number of years the chief had realized that the old way of life would soon be gone, and he looked for someone to teach his children and grand-children the skills that would be necessary to adapt to the new life. Hines appeared near Fort Carlton, almost like an answer to a prayer. The missionary was asked to settle with the band. John Hines's prayers had also been answered.

With the clergyman's guidance, Ahtahkakoop's people learned how to plough the land, plant and harvest their crops on individual plots of land, fix implements, and look after their livestock. At the mission school estab-lished by the missionary, the children studied reading, spelling and writing, in both Cree syllabics and in English, as well as arithmetic and geography. They learned to speak English, and they learned about the Bible and the Christian God. Emma Hines, who was described by Bishop McLean as a "most devoted" missionary's wife and "quite a model," assisted with the school and church, taught the girls and women how to knit, prepared meals for the hungry, helped looked after the sick, and contributed in many untold ways.[17]

The adults on the reserve attended church services, Bible classes, prayer meetings, and evening school classes. The people's knowledge of the world expanded as Hines exposed them to geography, the rotation of the earth on its axis, and the effect of centrifugal force. They talked about the British Empire and contemporary events like the Turko-Russian War.[18] And on special occasions, like Christmas, Hines delighted children and adults alike with magic lantern shows.

The missionary was a tireless worker—even when ill—as he persistently visited houses and tipis, praying, preaching, dispensing medicines, and distributing clothing to the children and to the needy. Hines even expanded his mission to include—for a short time at least—Mistawasis's band, and then Okīnomotayēw's people. Gradually the people abandoned their traditional religion as they were baptized and confirmed in the Anglican Church, one by one, and in small groups. When Hines left the Asissipi Mission in 1888, at least 61 of the 76 adults in the Ahtahkakoop band were communicants in the church and most of the children had been baptized. Two of his first students had become qualified teachers, and other students excelled at the Battleford Industrial School and Emmanuel College. Equally satisfying, the Asissipi Mission school was considered the best Indian school in the North-West and the children in Ahtahkakoop's band were said to be the brightest and most advanced.

Hines's success was not his alone. Without the support of Ahtahkakoop and the leading men, very little of this would have been possible. Sasakamoose and Ahenakew had been particularly supportive. By working and pulling together—a deliberate action compared by Sasakamoose to the technique required to row a canoe—the people had accomplished a great deal in a short 14 years. Yet it had not been easy. Even within Ahtahkakoop's family the conversion to Christianity caused division, and it was not until the fall of 1887 that the chief's wife became a confirmed member of the Anglican Church. A number of families were torn by religion, and problems developed between bands. For some, the conversion to Christianity was like a veneer, with traditional beliefs and values still strong beneath the surface. And a few of Ahtahkakoop's people—despite the pressure put on them—never abandoned their ancestral beliefs. They prayed in the traditional way, and they continued to attend sacred ceremonies held on other reserves, particularly those at Whitefish and Pelican lakes.

Ahtahkakoop, nonetheless, saw the results of the work pushed forward by the missionary and himself. The children were not only going to school, but they were doing exceptionally well. The farmers on the reserve were considered to be among the best in the North-West. Most of the people had relatively good houses that were clean and neat, each with its own stable and fenced fields of grain. Horses, cattle and sheep grazed on the meadows and, not far from Ahtahkakoop's two-storey house, a small church, school, mission house, teacher's dwelling, and farm overlooked the lake.

The people were not yet able to fully support themselves with the produce from their farming ventures, but they were doing better than most other bands. Men with larger farms used their extra flour, when they had any, to feed the men who helped with the harvest of hay and grain, and sometimes they were able to barter for bacon, tea, and other goods at stores in Prince Albert.[19] Most families did some trapping and hunting when game was available to provide extra food and money, while a select few hunted and trapped extensively so their relatives could concentrate on their farms. The people traded amongst themselves, and in times of need they shared. Some of the young men also earned extra money by freighting or doing occasional work for nearby farmers.

Their progress had been hampered by inadequate supplies of oxen and implements, dependence on the Indian department's thresher, the lack of milling facilities within a reasonable distance, and a procedure for selling surplus grain. There had been much hardship and frustration over the years as crops were destroyed by drought, heavy frost, and hail. There was too much sickness and death, and the traditional bands that hunted and trapped seemed to be better off than the Christian ones that were trying to farm.

Ahtahkakoop and his people, nevertheless, had taken some important first steps on the road to self-sufficiency, and they were adapting admirably to the new world imposed upon them. With Hines's departure, an era in the history of the band had ended. The journals, letters, and reports that provided some insight into life on the Ahtahkakoop Reserve also came to an end. Hines's replacement, the Reverend John Richard Settee, evidently did not forward his journals, if indeed he kept any, to the Church Missionary Society Committee, and he apparently wrote very few letters and reports. Thus, with Hines's departure, a valuable source of information—however limited, biased, and self-serving it may have been—no longer existed.

John R. Settee was the son of James Settee, one of the first native missionaries sponsored by the Church Mission Society. The younger Settee was a graduate of Emmanuel College and at the time of his ordination as deacon in 1885 was in charge of the Anglican mission at Moose Lake.* He was moved to Grand Rapids shortly afterwards, where he stayed until his appointment to the Asissipi Mission in 1888. Bishop McLean, in 1885, had described John Settee as

> a pious man, of good ability. He is most obliging and kindly in his manner, and I should say he is well calculated to gain the good-will of the Indians. I was pleased with the amount of his reading. It was very creditable, considering his few opportunities. I also liked the apparent zest with which he undertook to read the books I prescribed for priest's orders.[20]

The new missionary was supported by Ahtahkakoop and his people when he first arrived at the Asissipi Mission. The church at Ahtahkakoop's reserve had a solid foundation. Three new church wardens had been elected by the congregation just before Hines left, most of the adults and children were baptized, and a large percentage of the adults were confirmed and communicants in the church. Additionally, the school and its students had an excellent reputation, with one of its first graduates teaching at the school at Stoney Lake.

On a wider scope, Ahtahkakoop and Kāh-kāsōw were lay delegates to the synod of the Diocese of Saskatchewan, along with a number of leading men from other bands. The lay delegates took their responsibilities seriously and it was said by church officials that "the number of Indian Chiefs and Councillors who are shewing year by year increased interest in Church work, is a gratifying and significant fact, indicating the wisdom shewn in giving Indian Congregations in the Diocese the same organization and privileges in Church government as their white brethren enjoy."[21] These men, the writer continued, are showing intelligence and interest in all that concerns the true welfare of their children. Ahtahkakoop, not surprisingly, was often the spokesman for the Indian lay delegates at the synod meetings.

Ahtahkakoop was interested in the welfare of the adults, as well as the children, and in 1889 he moved, seconded by Kāh-kāsōw, "that the Synod request the Society to procure the printing of 1,500 copies of the Book of Common Prayer in the Cree syllabics characters." In speaking to the motion, Ahtahkakoop told the delegates he was pleased to be at the meeting, even if he did not understand the language being used to conduct it. He

---

* Moose Lake is situated northwest of Grand Rapids.

said it was important to have the books since they would be useful to those like himself advanced in years who could not attend schools and read English. It was appropriate for Kāh-kāsōw to second the motion, for he had spent many hours teaching syllabics in hunting camps when the buffalo were still on the prairies. Chiefs John Smith and James Smith also spoke briefly in support of the motion.[22]

From John Hines, *Red Indians of the Plains*

John Smith, from the Muskoday Reserve, was one of the lay delegates to the synod of the Diocese of Saskatchewan.

The people went on with their lives after Hines left. Logs for building and rails for fencing were cut. Additional land was cultivated, and the men summer-fallowed their bare fields and built more houses and stables.[23] The livestock were looked after, firewood cut, and gardens and fields tended. The sheep were clipped, some of the wool was carded, and butter was churned. When the families were not busy at these activities, they snared rabbits, hunted whatever other animals they could find, and gathered roots, berries, and other plants for food and medicines.

The mower broke down that summer, delaying the cutting of the hay. The turnips, which were turning out to be a difficult crop to grow, failed. And although the wheat crop was relatively good, the farmers were still faced with the perennial problem of getting their grain threshed and milled into flour.[24]

By the fall of 1889 Hayter Reed, the man known by many as Iron Heart[25] because of his harsh, unfeeling treatment of the Indian people, had replaced Edgar Dewdney as Indian commissioner. Dewdney was now the new minister of the Interior and superintendent general of Indian Affairs in John A. Macdonald's re-elected Conservative government. One of Reed's first moves as commissioner was to tour the reserves in Saskatchewan River country.

When Ahtahkakoop and Mistawasis met with Reed they again told him how difficult it was to get their wheat ground into flour and they offered a solution. Get us a small grist mill, they had said, and we will contribute "a Dollar for each Indian on the Reserves towards the cost." They further suggested that "in the absence of this years pay sheets" those of the last year could be used as a guide. Based on these figures, Ahtahkakoop's band would contribute $165 and Mistawasis's people, $149. The meeting went well, Reed reported later to Dewdney, adding that he was impressed by the "rational way in which these Indians express themselves about matters in general, and with regard to delays in things reaching them, and kindred subjects, having no inclination to grumble or be unreasonable."[26]

Reed supported Ahtahkakoop's and Mistawasis's request for a grist mill in his report to Dewdney, saying what the people had known for many years: the distance they had to haul grist "rendered their wheat of comparatively little value to them." He also noted that with a year or two of good harvests the bands would recoup the cost. Surprisingly, Reed went several steps further. He recommended that a small steam thresher be purchased, in addition to the grist mill. The engine from the mill could be used for threshing, he explained, and the cost of hiring horses would be avoided. To keep costs down, band members could supply the labour to construct the mill. The commissioner had one more suggestion. He noted that since there was a considerable amount of good timber on and adjacent to the reserves, a small saw mill driven by a portable steam engine could also be acquired. Lumber costs could be saved and lumber and flour could be exchanged between the mills.[27]

Indian agent Joseph Finlayson arrived on the reserve October 4 to make the treaty payments for 1888. In total, 162 people received their annuities. This figure does not include the three "rebels" and their families. Ahtahkakoop's son-in-law, Kā-tāh-twēhototawāt, was reported to be at File Hills. Kīnikwānāsiw, one of the other "rebels," was living on the reserve with six members of his family; another son had married into Okīnomotayēw's band. Wāpāsōs was still at Sandy Lake.[28] Commissioner Reed noted in a report dated October 31, 1888, that approximately 10 to 15 percent of the "rebel" Indians living in the North-West were paid their annuities that year. He added that more rebels would be paid the following year.[29] Several months later Reed told farm instructors and agents that if any of the "rebel" Indians had children attending industrial schools, the annuity was to be paid to the principal instead of the parents, "for the benefit of the children themselves."[30]

According to the 1888 Ahtahkakoop annuities paylist, one man, six boys, and three girls had died during the treaty paylist year. Joseph Sasakamoose's death was included in the count for "boys" since he did not have his own ticket. Similarly, Eliza Cīpay-awāsis (Joseph Kā-miyo-ahc-ahkwēw's wife) was among the "girls" who died during the paylist year.[31] Baptiste Ahenakew and his wife Ellen Ermineskin had a new baby boy named Charles, and his sister Ellen, who was married to John Hyman, had given birth to a girl called Maud. The only other baby born during the treaty paylist year was a daughter born to Kate Tapwewiniwok, the widow of Asināpēwiyin who had married a man from Okīnomotayēw's band the previous summer.[32]

There was one new name on the paylist, Kaskitēwistikwān (Blackhead), who was also known as William James Robertson. Twenty-six years old, he had married Cīpay-awāsis's daughter Mary in 1886.[33] It was their daughter Annie who had died from bronchitis in November, 1887. On the 1888 paylist, Mary was still included on her mother's ticket and Blackhead was listed without a number. Although the man was not paid, the notation beside his name stated that he "is generally a good Indian."[34] He transferred from the Moosomin Band to the Ahtahkakoop Band in 1889.

Inspector Wadsworth also came to the reserve sometime during the fall. He, like other government officials, continued to praise the efforts of the Ahtahkakoop Band and reported that the people on the Ahtahkakoop Reserve show "great zeal in their work." Dewdney, in his dual capacity of minister of the Interior and superintendent general of Indian Affairs, echoed the praise in his annual report. Indian agent Finlayson added that "these Indians on the whole are industrious and civilized."[35]

J. Ansdell Macrae, the government's inspector of Protestant industrial schools, was the third government official to visit the reserve in the fall of 1888. Macrae was the Indian agent Ahtahkakoop and Mistawasis had complained about when he was stationed at Fort Carlton in 1884. Following his inspection of the school, Macrae reported that the school at Sandy Lake was in the "same prosperous condition that it has been for some years past; and its general standing is far better than that of any other day-school that I have visited." Neely, Macrae continued, is "showing his ability to keep it

up to the standard of excellence attained by Mr. Hines. All the children of
the reserve that can be expected to attend the school do so."³⁶ Neely's lack
of Cree was probably an asset in Macrae's view since he believed that more
emphasis was needed on English to hasten assimilation.

Twenty-two youngsters were enrolled in the school, with an average
daily attendance of 17. A choir had been formed and "mental arithmetic"
was now part of the curriculum. Surprisingly, despite Macrae's commen-
dation, only three students were studying reading and spelling. One was
learning grammar, five were taking arithmetic, and two were studying
geography.³⁷

Praise from the various officials did nothing to alleviate the hardship of
yet another winter. The people on Ahtahkakoop's reserve waited for the
Indian department threshing machine until the end of November. Once it
arrived the machine not only repeatedly broke down but moving it from
one yard to another was time-consuming and delayed the work. As a result
of these inefficiencies, band members were unable to finish threshing their
wheat before officials came to move the implement to another reserve.³⁸

Grain sat useless, unthreshed and unground. Most of the able-bodied men
went fishing in November, with only fair results. Their efforts to hunt fur-
bearing animals and game met with even less success. The situation worsened as temperatures remained mild with very little snow, making transportation difficult with both sleighs and "wheels." The weather was a "great
drawback" in killing large game, Finlayson reported, and "no moose nor deer
of any kind have been killed by the Indians since fall, and they are completely out of leather for moccasins." By March it was apparent that hunting
and trapping had failed over a wide area, not just around the Ahtahkakoop
Reserve. The Okīnomotayēw, Pelican Lake, Ayahtaskamikinam, and Flying
Dust bands, for instance, were all reported to be in a bad way.³⁹ The Hudson's
Bay Company, in the meantime, had closed its Asissipi River outpost at
"Asissipi" as part of a company plan to cut expenses. Instead of wintering at
Sandy Lake, a trader had made weekly visits to Ahtahkakoop's,
Mistawasis's, and Petihkwahākēw's Muskeg Lake reserves to "gather what
furs the Indians have on hand at the time."⁴⁰

With food so scarce band members presumably received extra provisions
from the government to continue working on their farms. They also cut logs
and rails and tried to transport them out of the bush, but there was only one
month during the entire winter with enough snow to sled the timber out.

Regardless of what assistance the government gave, the people undoubtedly were hungry, sick, and suffering. According to government officials, a "mild form of whooping cough" passed through the Carlton Agency during the early part of the winter. The illness may have been considered mild, but it brought death to six children and persisted into April of 1889. With two exceptions, the children were all under two years of age. Charles, son of Baptiste Ahenakew and Ellen Ermineskin, died in November, 1888. He was eight months. Emma, one year, daughter of Benjamin Wāskitoy and Una Cīpay-awāsis, died in December, followed by Louis Ahenakew's daughter Esther, two months. George Chicken died in March. He was five. In April Benjamin Wāskitoy lost his second child, three-year-old Josiah, to whooping cough.[41] The Asissipi Mission death register included the deaths of two other children from whooping cough, Edward Cardinal, eight months, and Louisa Cardinal, four months. They were grandchildren of the old councillor from Mistawasis's band. Since Hines was no longer on the reserve and Settee does not appear to have written journals, and reports, there was no record of the people who caught the disease and survived. Nor was there a record of the hunger and sickness that prevailed during the winter. The agent—not surprisingly in view of past years—said in various reports that the health of the people was "tolerable" to fairly good.[42]

With the end of winter in sight the thresher finally returned to the Ahtahkakoop Reserve and threshing was finished in the middle of March. The men hauled their grain over bad roads to Prince Albert where it was sold "at a disadvantage" for flour and other necessities.[43] This was particularly frustrating since the wheat produced in 1888 on the Ahtahkakoop and Mistawasis reserves was "pronounced by experienced farmers and millers as first-class." However, because they were not able to get it ground, Finlayson said "it was not of such benefit to them as it would have been if ground into flour for their use." He further concluded after witnessing the ridiculous situation for an entire winter, that the people in the Ahtahkakoop and Mistawasis bands "would be prosperous had they the facility for disposing of their produce, as in other agencies, where grist mills and stores are near at hand."[44]

It was now eight years since the chiefs had formally requested a grist mill. In 1881 Mistawasis had asked the Marquis of Lorne if "there is any way of obtaining a grist mill by which to grind our wheat. I speak not only for myself but for all."[45] Three years later, at the meeting with Macrae at Fort Carlton, the chiefs had again asked for a mill. Macrae supported their request in a report to his superiors, but no action was taken. And now, in 1889, the chiefs—this time supported by Finlayson—were offering to contribute "a Dollar for each Indian on the Reserves towards the cost." Reed apparently was listening and ready to act on the request. Maybe this time, something would happen.

Promises Broken, Feelings of Betrayal

Indian people in the Battleford area, c. 1890s

The Years 1889-1893

By the spring of 1889 Ahtahkakoop was 73. He had witnessed tremendous changes during his life. Some, like the disappearance of the buffalo, the arrival of the newcomers, and the development of towns and settlements were obvious. The results of his people's efforts to make the transition from buffalo hunter to farmer were also unmistakable. Other changes were more difficult to define, and their implications were just starting to be realized. Sweatlodges and medicine bundles, for instance, were no longer readily visible, the men and boys had cut their hair, and the young men laboured in the fields and tended livestock instead of earning their status within the band through warfare and the buffalo hunt.

In this, their first complete year without John Hines to assist them, Ahtahkakoop and his people hoped for a successful growing season. Seeding had started earlier than usual because of the light snowfall during the winter.[1] This early beginning of the spring work was hampered, however, by an influenza epidemic that struck the Prince Albert and Carlton districts just as the seeding was completed.* Characterized by a severe cold accompanied by a fever, the sickness was particularly hard on the old people and those who were suffering from chronic illnesses.[2] As soon as the men and young men recovered their strength, they began the "very tedious" work of hauling the timber out of the bush with wagons. This cumbersome task was necessary because there had not been enough snow during the winter to skid the logs.[3]

That summer of 1889 Wāsēhikot, Greyeyes, and some of the younger farmers—including John Hyman, Piwiyinis,[4] and Thomas Bighead—began

---

* Although no one died during the epidemic, mission records indicated that Cahkāpēw (Cold Touch Spirit) died in June from consumption.

clearing and breaking land on the hillsides and on the bench.* It was hoped that crops planted on the higher ground would mature more quickly and suffer less damage from early frosts.[5] It was also hoped that the virgin land would provide better crops. Until now, the fields had all been on the "bottom" land near Sandy Lake.

The growing season of 1889, like the winter before, was a disaster. Very little rain fell, and it was hot. Then the tinder-dry grass caught fire and during August prairie fires raged through the Carlton Agency. Ahtahkakoop's people spent two weeks trying to keep the flames from devouring their farms and hay fields. They had some success, but a considerable amount of hay burned and fences were destroyed. The fires were not isolated. Grass fires became forest fires and the country burned as far north as Green Lake and northeast to Montreal Lake. The hay that escaped the fire was stunted by continued hot dry weather. By mid-August the families at Sandy Lake were stacking hay and "securing" what grain there was. Encouragingly, the fields on the higher newly cultivated land did better than the old fields. On the bottom lands, some of the fields were "entire failures."[6]

By November, most of the able-bodied men were away hunting and fishing with little success. Fur-bearing animals and larger game animals were all scarce and at the end of the month Indian agent Finlayson reported to his superiors that "I really do not know how they [the people] will pass the winter."

The situation got worse. The winter of 1889–90 was cold and stormy with unusually deep snow. The crops, for the most part, had been destroyed by the drought and game animals continued to be scarce. By mid–January it was conceded that trapping and hunting had also failed. Without furs to trade, Finlayson reported, the Indians "were further impoverished … [and] were unable to supply themselves from their own earnings with sufficient clothing." As a result, many of the children were unable to go to school because they did not have warm clothing.[7] Most other years the families had been able to trade for some of their necessities and Hines had provided the children, the sick, and the destitute with a few articles of clothing and extra food. Now John and Emma Hines were gone and both the crops and the hunt were failures. The government provided a few articles of clothing and some food, but it was not enough.

The weather continued cold. By the end of January, influenza of epidemic proportions, sometimes called "la grippe," had spread from Snake

---

* A level ledge on a hill-slope.

Illustration by Ed Peekeekoot

The men and older boys cut logs and building timber and hauled them out of the woods with ox-drawn sleds when they learned that the request for a portable sawmill had been approved.

Plain to Sandy Lake. Finlayson reported on February 1 that "almost every able-bodied man [at Sandy Lake] is sick." Betsy Masuskapoe, 4, John Peter Sīyāmwaskwēpiw (Sitting With Head Down), 50, and his wife Nancy, about 50, were dead. A fourth victim, 50-year-old Iskwēsis, was dead by the time the agent wrote his report. Practically every other man, woman and child was "prostrated" by the epidemic. Finlayson suspected that since the weather was cold there would be relapses. He requested meat for making broth and told the people not to go outside.[8] The flu epidemic continued its course north, losing its "virulence as it travelled further in that direction." The Ahtahkakoop Reserve had been the hardest hit of all the reserves in the Carlton Agency.

The men, despite the sickness and hardship, accomplished "a good deal of work" during the winter months. Six houses were erected wall high and two stables were built, "all of hewn logs and of respectable dimensions." Some, if not all, of the new houses were built on the hillsides and on the bench where the new fields were located. The people looked after their cattle, did their daily chores, and managed to eke a living off the land. And then, learning that the request for a portable sawmill had been approved, the men, their older sons, and their sons-in-law worked hard in March—before the snow was gone—cutting and hauling 700 "saw logs" and building timber for the construction of more houses and stables.[9]

Ahtahkakoop's and Mistawasis's request for a grist mill had also been approved, and during the winter of 1889–90 the machinery for both the grist mill and the portable sawmill was delivered to the Carlton Agency headquarters on the Mistawasis Reserve. The money to pay for both mills had been deducted from treaty money designated for the Petihkwahākēw and Okīnomotayēw bands, as well as from the Ahtahkakoop and Mistawasis bands.[10] Indian agent Finlayson hired eight men to erect the building on Mistawasis's reserve and to install the machinery for the mill. The Indian farmers were told that they would be expected to give a percentage of their flour and sawn lumber to the Indian Department as a toll, or payment, to offset the cost of using the equipment. This despite the fact that they had purchased both mills through deductions from their treaty payments.

Only four hundred bushels of grain were ground in the new mill, but the quality of the flour was declared "good." At long last the people from Ahtahkakoop's band would no longer have to make the long trip to Prince Albert to get their grist ground into flour. Unfortunately, during this first winter of the mill's operation, the people had very little wheat to grind.[11]

The willingness to assist the Carlton Agency bands in acquiring a grist mill and sawmill had not extended to the acquisition of other labour-saving implements. It was Indian Commissioner Hayter Reed's opinion that Indian families should cultivate "a quantity [of land] which can be worked within its own resources." This meant, in part, that "sufficiently advanced" farmers were "required to make for themselves such articles as land-rollers, harness, fork-handles, hay-racks, etc." Additionally, unlike their white neighbours who were acquiring modern equipment, the reserve farmers were expected to use simple implements like cradles, scythes, and flails. The more efficient, labour-saving equipment, Reed stated, was only justifiable in instances were labour was scarce, otherwise the Indians would be left with "little more to do than to sit and smoke their pipes."[12]

Reed later outlined several of the premises upon which he was formulating government policy. If an Indian farmer confined his farming operation to one acre, the commissioner argued, "he should, in an ordinary year raise, at a moderate computation, some eighteen bushels of wheat (where this can be successfully grown) which, after making all necessary deductions, will give him nearly, if not quite, five bags of flour." If the family planted a portion of a second acre to roots and vegetables, and had a cow or two, the "man has made a long stride to independence."[13]

This was how "peasants" in other countries lived with "no better implements than the hoe, the rake, cradle, sickle and flail," the commissioner rationalized. He then stated that Indian farmers would not acquire and use labour-intensive equipment such as scythes, cradles and rakes if they were "encouraged to contemplate the performance of their work by such labour saving machines as can rarely be obtained and kept in repair entirely from their own resources." Additionally, under Reed's concept of severalty, plots of land would be held and worked by individuals. Similarly, tools and implements would be privately owned, and farmers would not be allowed to combine their resources to communally own larger labour-saving devices such as reapers and mowers.

And so, with this definition of minimal self-sufficiency before them, government officials orchestrated agricultural policies that were designed to not only fail but to keep the people in poverty.[14] To further restrict and control the initiative of bands and individual farmers, governments officials also started to enforce amendments made to the Indian Act in 1881 and 1882 that restricted the sale of produce grown by any Indian or band. Policies were also developed to prevent the barter, sale, or slaughter of livestock without the permission of the Indian agent, thus making many of the animals more or less useless.[15]

The new directives were particularly unfair to bands such as Ahtahkakoop's. His people had been working hard to improve their fields and herds of livestock. Practically all the families were sowing more than one acre of land to wheat, with some planting a significantly larger amount. Equally crucial, Ahtahkakoop's people had never, since the beginning of their farming venture, been able to produce 18 bushels to the acre. Instead their crops since 1882, when records were first kept, averaged 9.26 bushels per acre. In two of these years, returns were less than five bushels per acre and, according to Reed's calculations, would have produced only 1½ bags of flour.[16] Thus one acre of wheat under conditions as they actually existed would be of little help in sustaining the people during the winter. It is unlikely that the other bands—and the settlers, for that matter—were doing any better.

The wretched winter of 1889–90 was followed by a miserable spring. Crops had been so poor the previous year that very few families were able to save seed wheat. The situation was the same in other parts of the district. Seed was scarce and the prices were driven upward. Then, after the farmers finally obtained their seed, unpleasant cold weather delayed planting until well into May.[17]

Because of the problems getting seed and the late start working in the fields, only 92 acres were sown in wheat in 1890, down considerably from other years. Ahtahkakoop's son Kā-miyo-astotin planted the largest amount, 10 acres. The next largest fields of wheat were held by Ahtahkakoop and Sōniyāw-ayāwēw[18] who planted 6 acres each. Wāsēhikot, Greyeyes, and Piwiyinis each had five acres.[19] In total, 158.5 acres were planted to wheat and various other crops, 60 less than the previous year.[20] With the exception of Ahtahkakoop and Kā-miyo-astotin, these farmers were working land on the elevated areas and had abandoned their fields on the bottom land between the river and the bench.[21]

Saskatchewan Archives Board, R-B1650

8th Street East, Prince Albert in the 1890s. Because of provisions in the Indian Act, the Indian people were not able to sell livestock and surplus grain in Prince Albert—or anywhere else—without the permission of the Indian agent.

The crops were held back by cold, dry weather that extended into June. It finally rained in July and then hot weather arrived. The crops grew rapidly, the hay was luxuriant, and many looked forward to a good harvest with estimates ranging up to 26 bushels per acre. Haying started about the third week of July.

Interestingly, despite the government's intent to outlaw labour-saving devices, Ahtahkakoop's people had a new reaper. By mid-August they were beginning to wonder if they would get a chance to use it. The crops had been slow in maturing, an early frost damaged many of the fields, and towards the end of the month heavy rains fell. It was difficult to collect and stack the hay and the ripening of the grain was further retarded. Then, for three consecutive nights in early September, there was a heavy frost. When McGibbon inspected the crops several days later he noted that the grain in the new fields on the bench was likely far enough advanced to be "beyond being much injured by frost." Other farmers were not so fortunate and Ahtahkakoop reported several days later that some of the fields were "completely destroyed by frost." In typical government fashion, inspector Alex McGibbon felt "the damage may not be so bad as he says."[22]

The cattle did better than the crops in 1890. Many of the animals were in the bluffs and difficult to find when McGibbon made his inspection tour. Nevertheless, he saw enough to report that "there is a splendid herd of cattle here." The animals, which included 45 oxen, three bulls, 43 cows, 23 steers, 12 heifers, 16 bull calves and 20 heifer calves, numbered 162. There were also five sheep and one band-owned horse. McGibbon noted that the hay was "cut and stacked at some distance and will be hauled during the winter. Owing to the wet some of the hay cut and in cocks [conical piles of hay] will no doubt be damaged." He also reported that the fences were fair, and there were good stables and corrals near the houses. He noted, however, that some of the fencing "is not so straight and the fields not so square as they might be in some places."

The wet weather continued into the fall. As a result, much of the crop was still standing at the end of September and it was not until October that the people were able to get into their small fields to cut the grain.[23] The final results varied, depending on where the fields were situated. In total, only 523 bushels of wheat were harvested, and they were produced primarily by seven farmers: Sōniyāw-ayāwēw, Wāsēhikot, Greyeyes, John Hyman, Piwiyinis, Peekeekoot, and Thomas Bighead. Their yields ranged from 40 to 90 bushels.[24] Three other men—Mēmēkwaniwēw (Feather

Voice, son of John Peter Masuskapoe), Osāwanāsiw, and Blackhead —had yields ranging between eight and 20 bushels. The 18 other families who had planted wheat that year—including Ahtahkakoop and his sons Kā-miyo-ahcahkwēw, Kā-miyo-astotin, and Michel—ended up with nothing. For those who did take off a crop, the quality of wheat varied. Most of the grain was suitable for seed, but only four farmers had wheat that was rated "good" or "pretty good." Results were more or less the same throughout the district. The wheat in 1890, the Indian agent reported, was generally so damaged that "it produced flour of inferior quality, but by mixing it with good flour it was made eatable and no complaints were made by the Indians of its fitness for consumption."[25]

The farmers who planted barley and oats were generally more success-ful and got some return for their effort with 246 bushels of barley and 180 bushels of oats being harvested. But with these crops, as well as with the wheat, the amount produced differed from family to family. Fortunately the potatoes and turnips were not affected by the frost and did fairly well, resulting in a harvest of 287 bushels of potatoes and 402 bushels of turnips, with individual yields varying from four to 60 bushels. Additionally, all but two families cut and stacked hay, with Kāh-kāsōw, Sōniyāw-ayāwēw, Piwiyinis, and Kīnikwānāsiw having the greatest amounts.[26] And so in this year, as in so many others, the hunters and farmers shared their harvest.

Despite Indian commissioner Reed's contention that the Indian farmers would sit around and smoke their pipes if they had labour-saving devices like reapers, the men had experienced one of their busiest summers ever. The portable sawmill arrived at Sandy Lake the end of May, 1890, just as seeding drew to a close. Band members helped the millwright put the saw in running order and sawing began on June 4. For the next few weeks the people were "mostly employed in assisting the millwright & rafting logs across the lake."[27] By the time the machine was ordered to Onion Lake, 33,000 feet of sawn lumber had been produced. It averaged out to 1,833 feet of lumber for each of the 18 men who had spearheaded their families' efforts to produce the boards. Finlayson pointed out, however, that two or three men had taken out more logs than the others. They thus had a larger amount of lumber for their efforts.[28]

The sawn lumber was hauled to the individual farm sites for completing houses and doing repairs. Then, in addition to ongoing construction, 20 more acres were broken on higher ground and 40 acres of previously cul-tivated land were summer-fallowed.

McGibbon, who had been impressed with the amount of work being done on the reserve, came up with a suggestion for some of the newly-cut lumber during his inspection in September. He had been told that Finlayson planned on keeping the new reaper under cover in Ahtahkakoop's large barn. "With the lumber now on hand," the inspector suggested, "it would be very easy to put up a shed for the special purpose of storing such articles."[29] He does not indicate if the lumber for the shed was to come out of the toll collected as payment for the use of the sawmill, or from the timber that had been hauled and sawn for the families' own use.

The weather was unusually mild in November, and after making the necessary preparations for winter many of the people went hunting and fishing. Because there was very little snow, they caught mainly muskrats, and even these small animals that provided furs and morsels of meat were scarce. Their fishing ventures were also relatively unsuccessful. And so the winter and following spring once again were difficult, made even more so by the knowledge that although a grist mill had finally been erected within a reasonable distance of the reserve, the people had very little wheat suitable for flour.

Three girls and a 30-year-old woman died between November 1, 1890, and January 27, 1891. On March 23 Ahtahkakoop's son Joseph, 28, died. Joseph left his widow, Mary Joyful, with two sons and a daughter; a third son had been born before Christmas but he died in July, four months after his father. By the time the 1891 annuities were paid at least another four people were dead. These included Ahtahkakoop's 18-year-old granddaughter Maria Kā-tāh-twēhototawāt, who had married John Cardinal in 1887, and Mōhkomānawēw's wife Vida Nutukwas, 40.[30]

The summer of 1891 was finally a good one. A warm spring followed a mild winter and the seeding of 208 acres was completed early.[31] This was an increase of 50½ acres over the previous year. For once the rain and hot weather came when needed and the crops thrived. It was ironic that in this of all years, J. McKay, an acting farming instructor hired by the Indian department, was placed on the Ahtahkakoop Reserve. He may have been of some assistance, but Ahtahkakoop's people had earned the reputation of being hard-working, thrifty, and living in "very comfortable circumstances" without the day-by-day intervention of a government official. His supervision may have benefited the summer's operations, or it may have been considered merely interference.

The trend of moving the small farms to "locations on the hillsides and more elevated portions of the reserve, where the land is of a rich quality, and the danger from early frost much lessened"[32] continued during the summer of 1891. New land was broken and older fields and houses abandoned. In fact, so much new ground was cleared and turned that inspector McGibbon was forced to admit that "I think for the Present they have as much land broken as they can well attend to in a Proper manner."[33]

Construction work had also progressed during the summer. The six houses started the previous year were completed and described as being "very good" when McGibbon arrived for his annual visit in September. "Some of the houses are well finished," McGibbon reported, with "shingled roofs, good cellars, lined with boards, little sheds for implements." One of the new houses, described as being "very nice," had been built by Ahtahkakoop's son Michel. The stables on the reserve were also good, with some "very good" ones built within the past year. He also noted that piles of lumber produced by the portable sawmill were on hand for repairs and building new homes.

Harvesting was well under way when McGibbon was on the reserve and he found most of the men working in the fields "securing the grain." The women were assisting.[34] Elsewhere in his report for 1891 the inspector stated that

> The wheat, oats and barley are a fine crop, mostly cut and in stook. The Indians will have flour enough of their own this year.

> Potatoes are very good and there will be plenty of them for the use of the Band.

> Turnips are … very irregular, whether from bad seed or not I cannot say, but in many places the seed did not come up at all, still they will have plenty of turnips.

> Some very good onions and carrots were noticed. The gardens were only fairly weeded and thinned.[35]

Despite the positive accounting, Amédée Forget, who had replaced Reed as assistant Indian commissioner, wrote in the margin of McGibbon's report that the agent would be contacted about the gardens being only fairly weeded and thinned.[36]

In all, 1,724 bushels of wheat were harvested in 1891. Ahtahkakoop and his son Kā-miyo-astotin jointly produced 200 bushels of wheat on 13 acres of land. Some farmers produced more than 100 bushels on smaller fields, including Sōniyāw-ayāwēw, Kāh-kāsōw, Peekeekoot, Kā-miyo-ahcahk-wēw, Wāsēhikot, Greyeyes, and brothers Baptiste and Louis Ahenakew who had farmed together this particular year. In addition to the wheat, the Ahtahkakoop farmers produced 298 bushels of oats, 807 bushels of barley, 668 bushels of potatoes, 320 bushels of turnips, 18 of carrots, and 21 bushels of onions.[37]

Band cattle were also doing well, increasing in number from 162 to 198 during the year. The number of calves was particularly satisfactory. Thirty-seven of the 42 cows had given birth, with several calves still to come after McGibbon's report was written. In addition to the calves, band-owned stock consisted of 49 oxen, 2 bulls, 42 cows, 39 steers, and 29 heifers. The number of animals owned by individuals was also on the increase and included 2 oxen, 10 sheep,[38] 19 cows, and 32 young cattle. In addition to cattle, Ahtahkakoop's youngest son Michel had 5 pigs. And following the trend established years ago, there were 36 privately owned horses. McGibbon did not see all the livestock during his visit. He noted that "there being no flies the cattle wander far away" and he did not want to take the people away from their harvesting to round up the cattle. Nevertheless, he saw enough of the animals to report that they were in "fine condition." McGibbon noted that the prices received for the wool in 1891 had been good, and he hoped this would encourage the people to "take more interest in the raising of sheep." He also commented that the fences "were good and in good repair."[39]

Ahtahkakoop and Mistawasis were on their way home after visiting students at the industrial school in Battleford when McGibbon inspected the reserve at Sandy Lake. Ordinarily Ahtahkakoop would have gone to the agency office to see the inspector when he got back, but he was 75 and the trip to Battleford had been hard on him. Reluctant to travel any further, the chief sent Kā-miyo-astotin with several requests. McGibbon reported that the chief

> would like a small store put up to put provisions in when these were sent to the Reserve. At present the lower part of the barn is used for this purpose and it is not suitable.
>
> He wanted a little help in the way of extra provisions whilst putting up the building.
>
> The Chief also told his son to ask for him a double waggon, as the one he has is nearly used up. He has had it for many years. The

Illustration by Ed Peekeekoot

The number of privately owned and band-owned stock on the Ahtahkakoop Reserve increased dramatically during the early 1890s.

Chief is a most reasonable man and I hope his request will be granted. Both he and his son are Progressive and show a good example to the rest of the Band.[40]

The commissioner's office approved the request for a storehouse with the notation that the sawmill would supply the lumber and the agent could arrange rations for the men erecting the building. In regards to the request for the wagon, Forget noted that the estimates for the Carlton Agency included money for a wagon and the "matter will be referred to the Commissioner."[41]

During the trip to Battlefield, Ahtahkakoop and Mistawasis had seen settlers using reapers and binders to harvest their wheat. The farmers in Mistawasis's band, who had planted 152 acres of land to wheat and produced the best crop in the Carlton Agency, had used scythes and cradles to cut most of their grain in 1891. Worried about losing a portion of their grain, some of the farmers had hired a man with a self-binder for $1 an hour to help with the harvest. Mistawasis knew Ahtahkakoop had acquired a reaper the previous summer. He also knew that the Battleford Indians and John Smith's reserve had reapers.[42] Upset, Mistawasis asked to meet with McGibbon on his return from Battleford. The inspector, who was still on the reserve, agreed.

About 40 members of Mistawasis's band attended the meeting. The chief asked McGibbon why they did not have reapers and self-binders like the settlers. "They were anxious to raise grain enough so as to be independent of the Government for flour," he said, "but ... if they had to cut it with cradles the result would be that they would put less crops in, and of course they would still be dependent on supplies." The inspector told the farmers that "the Policy of the Department was not to supply these implements where there were enough [men] to cut the grain with cradles." McGibbon, nevertheless, recognized the rationale in the chief's comments, and noted in his report that some of the wheat was too ripe and should have been cut earlier. "It is a pity that good wheat should be lost for want of facilities to harvest it, whether by reapers, binders or cradles and that some good grain will be lost this year there is no doubt." McGibbon also informed his superiors that the men on the Mistawasis Reserve asked for a "shingle machine, now that they had a steam engine to run one," and offered to pay for it in instalments.[43]

McGibbon's superiors were not sympathetic. Forget, who took his orders from Indian commissioner Reed, wrote in a marginal note that

The agent will be asked for explanation of this hiring of a self-binder. Difficulties are thrown in the Commissioner's way on every hand in carrying out the Dept's policy to make Indians do their work with the least possible use of labour saving implements.

The agent was told by the Commissioner when he applied for a reaper at this point, that the area under crop as compared with number of working Indians available to handle cradles rendered it out of the question to make any exception to Dept's policy regarding labour saving implements.[44]

In another marginal note the assistant Indian commissioner wrote that

it may be here further remarked that it seems a pity that by consenting to hold such a meeting and discussing the matter, so much importance should have been given to it, as it will now have [to be] answered in the eyes of the Indians.

It appears moreover to be regretted that the Inspector, who is well aware of the Dept's policy having once consented to discuss it, did not defend it much more vigourously than he appears to have done.[45]

In response to McGibbon's report and the marginal notes, Reed took the inspector to task for not fully supporting the government's policy. McGibbon, in reply, claimed that during the meeting he "was at pains to make it clear to the Indians that they were at no disadvantage as compared with others in this respect, although from the stories which had reached them, they had formed the impression that such was the case." He also told Reed that he supported the policy regarding labour-saving implements. It is "a good policy with some exceptions of course," he was quoted as saying, "and I will see that so far as I am concerned, I shall throw no obstacles in the way."[46] In a later communication, Reed instructed agents and inspectors to discourage the use of labour-saving machines and any idea that they had been promised under treaty.[47]

Reed and McGibbon, of course, were mistaken in their comments that the Mistawasis Band was not at a disadvantage.

Ahtahkakoop's people had a new reaper, and that gave them an edge over other bands. Mistawasis and his band members were fully aware of this fact.

On September 26, 1892, after McGibbon left, surveyor A.W. Ponton arrived at Ahtahkakoop's reserve to survey and subdivide the cultivated part of the reserve into forty-acre lots. This new government initiative was a direct result of Reed's statement in 1888 that he had "come to the conclusion that the time has arrived where the Reserves should be divided up, and parcelled into separate Farms."

Ponton hired a number of men in Ahtahkakoop's band to assist him, and although the work progressed slowly because of "unfavourable" weather, he said the men "gave good satisfaction." Ponton noted elsewhere in his report that he wanted to engage Indian labour when it "could be profitably employed." The Sandy Lake men, he said, were the first to offer who were hired.[48] By assisting Ponton, the men not only earned extra money, but they saw first-hand what Ponton was doing and became familiar with the new lay-out of lots.* According to Ponton, the survey was done in accordance with the "legal sub-divisions of the Dominion Lands systems."

Threshing of grain on the Ahtahkakoop Reserve was completed on January 15 and then the men began taking their wheat to the grist mill on the Mistawasis Reserve to be ground into flour. Because the steam engine was fuelled by wood, each of the men did his share of cutting and hauling firewood to keep the boiler going. More grain was taken to the mill towards the end of March. The mill ran well the entire winter, Indian agent Finlayson noted, and turned out good flour.[49] Later he reported that with the exception of widows, orphans, and those disabled by sickness and age, the people of Ahtahkakoop's band "provided themselves with flour for the winter," and in some instances had a little left.[50]

Muskrats were available in larger numbers than usual during the winter of 1891–92, and although bears, fishers, martens, wolverines, and beaver were not plentiful, there was a "fairly good supply" of other animals.[51] Good hunting meant extra meat for the soup pot, as well as furs to trade for tea, tobacco, kettles, traps, knives, cloth, clothing, beads, raisins, soap, and other articles.

As in every other year, the men, women and older children tended the stock, cut firewood, hauled hay and water, hunted, and did chores. A good number of "saw logs" were cut and hauled to the sawmill site on the shore

---

* Ahtahkakoop's people did not recognize or approve these lots, and the rest of the reserve was never surveyed.

of Sandy Lake, and in March, 1892, the people were busy hauling rails for fences and logs to build more houses.

John Cardinal's baby daughter, named Mary, died in November, four months after the death of her mother, Marie Kā-tāh-twēhototawāt. At the end of February, 1892, agent Finlayson reported that many of the people in the Carlton Agency were "ailing from influenza colds." In March he referred to the illness as "La grippe and bad colds." Severe colds with fever continued through April and into May. The Ahtahkakoop Band was hit harder than any of the others in the agency and there was a great deal of suffering.[52] Osāwanāsiw's five-year-old daughter, Mary Cardinal, died March 28 and Sasakamoose's wife Maggie died May 29. She was 50. There were three other deaths that spring, two children and a 50-year-old.[53]

Incessant cold temperatures in April and into May prolonged the sickness of 1892. The stormy weather also delayed seeding, so while they were waiting for the weather to clear, the men went hunting. This venture met "with little success."[54] When seeding finally got under way, Ahtahkakoop decided he was getting old and no longer able to work in the fields. So, for the first time since settling at Sandy Lake, the 76-year-old chief did not have any fields—with the exception of half an acre of potatoes—listed under his own name.[55] Despite the slow start and McGibbon's opinion that additional land should not be put into service, the farmers planted the largest number of acres ever, 256 compared to 208 the previous year. Most of the increase, 50½ acres, was in wheat.[56]

At least part of Ahtahkakoop's land was planted by Kā-miyo-astotin, and it is possible that Kā-miyo-ahcahkwēw and Michel planted on it as well. In any case, in 1892 Kā-miyo-astotin was working the largest farm on the reserve, with 16 acres in wheat, six in oats, 5½ in barley, two in potatoes, half an acre in peas, and a small plot in garden vegetables. Michel Ahtahkakoop, who at 30 was considerably younger than his brothers Kā-miyo-ahcahkwēw and Kā-miyo-astotin, was one of the young men working particularly hard to establish his own farm. He was the first farmer to raise pigs. He had some cattle, and during the spring had increased his planted acreage from 4½ acres the previous year to nearly 15½ acres. Even if a portion of the land had previously been worked under his father's name, it was an impressive increase.

Several others had also increased their holdings substantially, including Kāh-kāsōw and Wāsēhikot. Mēmēkwaniwēw was now working his father's farm and had broken two more acres of land. His brother Jacob Masuskapoe, who had married Piyēsīs and Mary Ahtahkakoop's daughter and transferred to his own ticket, planted four acres of wheat and a small amount of potatoes and garden vegetables. Sasakamoose was another of the older men who did not plant any crops that year, but his son Alexander increased his acreage in crop.[57]

The weather co-operated once May was over and, by the end of June, Finlayson reported that the crops appeared "heavier" than usual. The people started cutting their hay in July and then, weeks later, they took in their bountiful harvest, thankful that all their efforts were being rewarded.[58]

John Cardinal died August 8 at the age of 28, a year after his wife's death and eight months after his daughter died. Two weeks later Isabelle Apotum, 24, wife of Andrew, was dead; a daughter had also died during the year.

Threshing, for a change, began in mid-October and the final result— 2,287 bushels of wheat—was gratifying. Although this was a record for the Ahtahkakoop Reserve, the number was somewhat misleading since yields for the farmers varied from seven bushels an acre to near-bumper crops of 20 bushels per acre. Although no acknowledgement or explanation was given for this diversity, McGibbon had said earlier that the best crops were grown on the elevated land. In any case, not everyone benefited to the same extent. In addition to the wheat, 646 bushels of oats, 738 bushels of barley, and 652 bushels of potatoes were produced. Although 135 bushels of turnips were harvested, McGibbon said they had been eaten by worms.[59]

Regardless, the determination of Ahtahkakoop's people to succeed was finally paying off. They were "industrious and hard-working," McGibbon reported following his visit to the reserve in October, 1892. "In driving along the reserve, no one would think but that he was going through a thriving settlement in Ontario or Quebec." The houses were of a "good class, and are cleanly kept; at every house an improvement of some kind was going on." Nearly 1,000 logs were stacked at the sawmill site waiting to be sawed. Ten acres of new land had been broken—some of it in new fields on the east side of the Asissipi River—and 25 acres were in summer fallow. Much of the fencing had been renewed and repaired, and the inspector had counted more than 70 "stalks [stooks]" of grain at different points.[60]

McGibbon also calculated that 550 tons of hay had been cut and stacked to get the livestock through the winter. Although the number of livestock

Illustration by Ed Peekeekoot

As the supply of flour increased, bannock became a staple food. This bread was cooked in frying pans over open fires and on cooking stoves inside the houses.

had increased, he said the rate of growth was smaller than in other years. On a positive note, permission had been given to kill 10 of the cattle for meat, so at long last the band was receiving some direct benefit from their cattle besides milk and cream. A few of the sheep had also been killed, and the rest had died.[61] Despite these reductions, the herd of band-owned stock had increased from 198 to 241 animals, with privately owned livestock growing from 104 to 111.[62]

There was only one mower on the reserve to cut hay for 352 animals and McGibbon, along with Ahtahkakoop, Kā-miyo-astotin, Kāh-kāsōw, Kā-miyo-ahcahkwēw, and the other leading men, was concerned that a serious situation could develop if the mower broke down. Government officials in Regina did not consider this to be a particular problem. They indicated that another mower was not possible, but more scythes would be sent. In the same document, displeasure was expressed that the increase in the number of animals had been so small, even though the farmers were worried about being able to supply enough hay if the one and only mower broke down.[63] Government officials far from the working fields still did not understand. If the mower broke down and scythes had to be used, in McGibbon's words, "it throws the haying late and interferes with the harvesting when that begins."[64]

True to his vision of creating a different life for his children and his grandchildren, Ahtahkakoop continued to be a strong supporter of the Asissipi school after John Hines left for The Pas. The school had done extremely well under the management of Hines, Louis Ahenakew, and Joseph Sasakamoose. Now all three men were gone. Hines had moved to a new mission, Louis was teaching elsewhere, and Joseph was dead. The transition from one era to another did not go smoothly. J.M.R. Neely, the young Irishman hired in 1888 to replace Joseph, stayed just over a year. His tenure was a difficult one. He could not speak Cree so it was difficult for him to communicate with the children and parents. Additionally, because the crops and animals failed, the band was destitute. Many of the children did not have enough warm clothing to attend school during the winter and enrolment was down.

But there were other problems. Although the first report on Neely's performance had been generally favourable, it soon became apparent that he was not teaching subjects that had always been part of the curriculum. Only three out of 17 students, for instance, were studying reading, spelling and writing and only five were taking arithmetic.[65] J. Ansdell Macrae, inspector of Protestant Indian Schools, was more critical during his second inspection when he reported that the buildings, furnishing, and stock of school materials were all "bad." The report also rated a number of other criteria based on a scale of 1 to 4, with "4" indicating "highest excellence." According to this scale, the management of the school and organization were both rated 3, but a rating of 2 was given in the categories of following the course of studies, cleanliness of pupils, and cleanliness of the school.[66]

Needless to say, the school's dramatic and rapid decline from the days when John Hines, Louis Ahenakew, and Joseph Sasakamoose were in charge created considerable concern on the reserve, as well as among Anglican officials in Prince Albert. Changes to improve the situation were implemented quickly. Alex Seymour, described as a "painstaking, earnest teacher" replaced Neely. Enrolment went back up to 25, with an average attendance of 21, and improvements were made to both the school building and the furniture.

Some of these changes were in place by March, 1890, when Wadsworth reported that the schoolroom was "comfortable." He added that students were registered in Standards I to V. Most of the 17 children present were girls and, with a few exceptions, they were "not very well dressed, but they had clean faces and hands, and their hair [was] neatly combed." The children had recovered quickly from the disruption in their education and the inspector expressed his pleasure with their progress in reading, writing, arithmetic, "spellings, meaning and in speaking English." Seymour, he continued, "takes very great interest in his work; he has an aptitude for teaching Indian children not common to all teachers." Finlayson also acknowledged the excellent progress when he wrote in August of the same year that attendance was "regular and the pupils well behaved and fairly advanced in reading, writing and arithmetic."[67]

School inspector Ansdell Macrae, less charitable, noted that the school, "formerly one of the best in the Territories, had been affected by two changes of teachers." He did acknowledge, however, that changes to the building and furniture had been partially carried out.[68] There was another change as well. In 1890, for the first time, government documentation referred to the school established by John Hines as the Sandy Lake School. In previous years it had been called the Asissipi school.[69]

Because of government and church policies aimed at using residential schools as assimilation tools, the 1890–91 school year was the last time for many years, with one exception, that Standards IV and V were taught on the Ahtahkakoop Reserve.[70] Without the senior grades, enrolment at the Sandy Lake School was reduced from 23 to 15 in 1892. Of the 15 students attending the day school, eight were in Standard I, four were in Standard II, and three were in Standard III. Seymour and his students continued to apply themselves and by 1892 the school was once again one of the best in the North-West Territories, with top marks awarded in all academically related categories. Nonetheless, the building itself still was not in particularly good shape. Repairs had only upgraded its condition from bad to fair in the opinion of Macrae, and the furniture was still considered to be bad. Interestingly, in 1890, 1891, and 1892, inspector McGibbon reported that the school and other mission buildings were either comfortable or in good repair.[71]

In 1893, after teaching three years at the Ahtahkakoop Reserve, Seymour was replaced by William R. Dreaver. The Reverend John Settee—unlike John Hines who had been actively involved in the school during his 14 years at Sandy Lake—apparently had very little to do with the children's education during the years that Neely, Seymour, and Dreaver served as teachers.

Ahtahkakoop, Mistawasis, and the other chiefs in the Carlton and Duck Lake agencies had been disturbed when they learned that Standards IV and V would not be taught at the day schools during the 1891–92 school year.[72] In their quest for education and knowledge, band members wanted their children, grandchildren and generations to come to acquire the skills and knowledge required to support themselves. For some of the children Standard III may have been sufficient, but for many others advanced skills were both needed and wanted.

For these young people the alternatives were minimal. The closest off-reserve school, Prince Albert's Emmanuel College, could only admit a small number of students into its program.* The other alternative, one tenaciously promoted by government and church officials, was the Battleford Industrial School. This school, however, was not only a long distance from

---

* Although Emmanuel College had initially been established to train candidates as priests, teachers, and general mission workers, a nondenominational collegiate school for boys was affiliated with the college in 1881. After 1886, when plans for a university lapsed, the school functioned as an Indian boarding and training school.

home but by the late 1880s restrictive measures had been gradually introduced. Speaking "Indian languages," for instance, was only permitted during certain hours of the day, and during recreation periods "white" games were played and "Indianism" excluded.[73] Additionally, Reed implemented a pass system designed to prevent parents from visiting their children without the agent's permission.[74]

There were complaints about the quality and quantity of food being served, the inadequate care of sick students, the dictatorial behaviour of principal Thomas Clarke, and the practice of sending the girls to white homes on "out service" as servants. Some chiefs expressed concern that they were not able to take their children out of the school. There were also some doubts about the education the children were receiving since there were only two academic teachers for the entire school; other staff consisted of administrative personnel and men and women who provided practical instruction in trades and household skills. And, not surprisingly, many of the children were lonely and unhappy, being so far from home and having their lives regimented by bells. Concerns were not confined to the Indian people, for government officials were beginning to question principal Clarke's management of the school and his drinking habits.[75]

The Indian people responded to the heavy-handed policies being introduced under the auspices of Hayter Reed and supported by his superiors in Ottawa, by refusing to send their children to the Battleford Industrial School. As a result, only one student out of the 300 school-age children in the Carlton Agency was enrolled at the school in 1890. In contrast, 28 of the 40 school-age children on Ahtahkakoop's reserve attended the Sandy Lake day school.[76]

Anxious about the future of their children, the chiefs and leading men of the Carlton and Duck Lake agencies petitioned the government in October, 1890, to establish an industrial school in Prince Albert. Ahtahkakoop, Mistawasis, Okīnomotayēw, John Smith, James Smith, John Badger, Francis Dreavor, Ayahtaskamikinam, Benjamin Joyful, and Kā-tā-piskawāt (One Who Wears It Around His Neck) from Cumberland House were among those who signed the petition. A number of these men, including Ahtahkakoop, were lay delegates to the synod of the Church of England's Diocese of Saskatchewan. The benefits of an industrial school in Prince Albert were obvious. Not only would the students be closer to home, but as lay delegates to the synod, the chiefs and leading men would expect to have some influence on the education of their children. Bishop W. Cyprian

Ahtahkakoop was one of the lay delegates who attended a conference of the Diocese of Saskatchewan on August 5, 1891, to discuss concerns about the Battleford Industrial School. The conference was held at St. Alban's Church, Prince Albert. Ahtahkakoop is seated in the front row, fourth from the left.

Pinkham, who had replaced John McLean as Bishop of Saskatchewan in 1887, supported the petition. He also pointed out that there were approximately 514 "children of school age" in the area.[77]

The government responded to the petition by sending officials from reserve to reserve to "recruit" children. Because of this effort, which often involved taking children from their homes unwillingly, the student population at the Battleford Industrial School grew from 56 to 120 during the course of the 1890–91 school year. A number of the new students had been "procured from the Duck Lake and Carlton agencies" during the winter by Indian Commissioner Hayter Reed, and the principal of the school, the Reverend Thomas Clarke.[78]

Still worried about the children's education and unwilling to give up, Ahtahkakoop and a number of other chiefs and headmen attended a conference of the Diocese of Saskatchewan as lay delegates on August 5, 1891, the day before the synod was to meet. Mistawasis was not part of this group since he was now a Presbyterian, not an Anglican. Ahtahkakoop was one of the spokesmen, and during the course of the meeting he sought the bishop's counsel regarding the administration of affairs at the Battleford Industrial School.[79]

When their request for an industrial school in Prince Albert continued to be ignored, Ahtahkakoop, Mistawasis, and their leading men circulated another petition. It was signed by practically all the men in both bands, plus the Christian Indians in Okīnomotayēw's band at Stoney Lake, and sent to Edgar Dewdney in his capacity as superintendent general of Indian Affairs. The situation was also discussed with a number of people, including those with access to D.H. McDowall, the elected member of Parliament for the Saskatchewan District.* In June, 1891, Indian agent Finlayson had even taken up the cause by writing directly to McDowall, an action the Indian commissioner considered quite irregular. Finlayson pointed out that the men who had signed the latest petition represented 400 Indians. The Indians have been told that McDowall would support them, Finlayson continued, adding that there is no question a school in Prince Albert is needed since Battleford is too far away.[80]

In October 1893 the two old friends, Ahtahkakoop and Mistawasis, travelled to Battleford to visit the industrial school and the students from their reserves.[81] This was a trip that was to be made many times more by parents in the two bands, for when the grant for a new school was finally approved, it went to the Roman Catholic Church for a school at Duck Lake. Since the people in Ahtahkakoop's and Mistawasis's bands were predominantly Protestants during a time when religious lines were firmly drawn, the new school was of little value to them.[82]

By now, speaking an Indian language at the industrial school was forbidden at any time and the pass system that restricted parents from visiting their children was being vigourously enforced.[83] School and government officials took satisfaction in saying that the children who left school were working at the agencies and as servants in private homes, with the balance living in white settlements "and all are self-supporting."[84] This was misleading, if not an outright lie. Government documentation indicated that 19 of the 49 students who had been "discharged" or taken off the student roll at the Battleford Industrial School between 1884 and May of 1893 were

---

* In 1882 the land that had been named the North-West Territories was divided into districts; these included the districts of Saskatchewan, Assiniboia, Alberta, Athabasca, and a much smaller North-West Territories. The boundaries of the District of Keewatin had been defined in 1876.

dead. Twelve had died at school, with consumption being the major cause of death, and six had died after returning home or taking jobs in the white community. Another student died after being transferred to Emmanuel College.

Of the 29 former students who were still alive—or presumed in 1893 to be alive—11 boys had left the school during the uprising and did not return, seven were withdrawn by their parents, and three had "deserted." Only three of the 10 girls who had been "discharged" were still alive in 1893. Five had died at school, one returned home and died, and one was sent to work as a servant in Regina, where she died. Of the remaining three girls, one was the Indian commissioner's servant. The other two had been sent home after only a few days at the school because they were considered too old and "not fit for a pupil." Thus, the "discharged" industrial school students with the best survival rates were the ones who left during the uprising and did not return, along with those who "deserted," were withdrawn by their parents, or rejected by school authorities. These students accounted for 24 of the 29 "discharged" students from various reserves still alive in 1893.[85]

Although Ahtahkakoop was still supporting the concept of a well-run industrial school in the early 1890s, various aspects of the government's policies of control and assimilation were beginning to press upon his people. The restrictions were not as evident on the Ahtahkakoop Reserve as elsewhere, but they were still there. For instance, while other parents complained to officials about the school passes, Ahtahkakoop said that he and his people "had never been refused permission to visit their own children, but had been allowed and assisted to go anytime when their work was done."[86] The document that contained this statement was signed at Ahtahkakoop's house in March, 1892. The chief evidently had said that "distance was no obstacle" in visiting the industrial school in Battleford. This likely was not true since Ahtahkakoop and others in his band had been working hard to have a school built in Prince Albert. Regardless, for a people who had traditionally travelled freely over a vast country, it was degrading and humiliating to have to request permission to visit their own children. It was also time-consuming, for the parents first had to find the agent in order to get the piece of paper they needed to make the trip.

Other restrictions and controls prevented the Indian people from selling any portion of their crops and gardens without permission. They also needed permission to sell or slaughter cattle for meat, even if the animal was privately owned, and Hayter Reed was insisting that modern equipment was only justifiable in instances where manual labour was scarce. Thus farmers had to work with simple implements such as cradles, scythes, and hoes, and were expected to make many of their tools and implements.[87] The concept of making equipment, of course, was not new to the Indian people. Traditionally they had always manufactured their own bows and arrows, projectile points, harness, snowshoes, toboggans, fishing nets, knives, spoons, and whatever else was needed. Nevertheless, this was a change in direction and when enforced in a rough manner did little to enhance relationships between the families and government officials.

By 1892 Hayter Reed had taken a further step against Indian self-sufficiency, stating that labour-saving devices were to be discouraged, even when purchased with the farmers' own money. And the list of equipment to be hand-made by the farmers now included items such as "axe and hay-fork handles, ox collars, milk pans, churns, rope, harness, and bob-sleighs."[88] The agents and farm instructors were expected to impose government policy on the Indian population. Their activities, as well as those of the Indian people, were monitored by Reed and assistant commissioner Forget. Agents were regularly criticized by their superiors, and they were called upon to explain why gardens had weeds, turnip seeds had been broadcast, fences were crooked, and the ratio of calves to cows was down.

Late in 1892 Joseph Finlayson, Indian agent for the Carlton Agency, fell victim to prejudices that had been building against him for a number of years, even though the reserves under his care were progressing and the inspectors' reports had been good. Inspector Wadsworth, for instance, had reported in 1887 that

> Finlayson is getting along nicely with the Indians. He has great influence over them and they all respect him. He is very careful and on the whole has his Agency in very good shape considering that he has had very little assistance in the way of farmers and the former clerk was of little use in the office and none whatever outside.[89]

Two years later, in October of 1891, McGibbon noted that Finlayson "continues to possess the confidence of his Indians and the work seems to go on smoothly. He is very careful of the property under his charge."[90] The following year the inspector reported that the agent was working hard, had almost too much to do, and needed help. The commissioner reacted immediately and adversely, saying additional help was a step backwards and a younger man could cope with the workload.

Despite the inspectors' favourable reports, Reed's biases surfaced when he claimed in 1892 that Finlayson "laboured under the disadvantage of being one of the natives of the country, brought up in the service of the Hudson's Bay Company." He is "too much imbued with Indian ideas to be likely to advance them," the commissioner stated, and since he has a very slip-shod manner of conducting business, the management of the Carlton Agency is "negative rather than positive." The agent's greatest difficulty, he continued, was getting the Indian farmers to cut enough hay and "harvest their crops without the use of such labour saving implements as the Department is opposed to for Indian use."[91]

The commissioner was also critical of what he called the agent's "intemperate habits." Obviously the commissioner had chosen to ignore the drinking habits of many others, including Indian agent John Rae, Finlayson's white predecessor and a man Hines claimed was difficult to find sober. Finlayson was 64 years old, Reed concluded in a memorandum on the agent, and not likely to change. The commissioner suggested he be given retirement, commenting that the man would probably return to his farm near Prince Albert.

Finlayson was removed from his position in the Carlton Agency in November, 1892, but instead of retiring he exchanged places with Hilton Keith, the agent for the Touchwood Hills Agency. Finlayson was eventually fired because he would not make "his Indians provide hay and harvest their crop without the use of labour saving implements as the department is opposed to for Indian use." Keith, who was born in England, had been with the Indian department since the early 1880s. He spoke Cree, and had a reputation for toughness.[92]

The new agent arrived at the agency headquarters on the Mistawasis Reserve in November, a month or so after inspector McGibbon reported that the Ahtahkakoop Band was making steady progress. There was more land in crop than ever before, the inspector had stated. Moreover, the number of livestock was increasing, the houses were continually being improved, and most people lived in relative comfort, supplementing their agricultural endeavours with trapping, hunting, fishing, and freighting.

These observations, of course, were not new, for each year following the signing of Treaty Six government officials had described the Ahtahkakoop Band as being industrious, hard-working, thrifty, and progressive. They considered Ahtahkakoop to be a reasonable man, a good leader, and a good example to the rest of his band.

Although the comments were gratifying, Ahtahkakoop likely found the numerical growth of his band more satisfying. In the old days a successful chief was a wise man, an honoured warrior, and a good hunter. His band grew in size as new families and individuals were attracted by the chief's ability to provide and care for his people. When Treaty Six was signed, a number of families who had connections with other bands were listed on the Ahtahkakoop Band paylist. Gradually, as their own chiefs entered treaty, some of these people returned to their own bands. Others left the reserve because they did not want to become Christian farmers. Some took scrip or were absorbed into nearby communities, and many died. Thus, during the 1880s the population of the band declined.

By the 1890s this was changing. The people of the Ahtahkakoop Band were successfully making the transition from buffalo hunters to farmers. The leadership was strong, and the reserve was relatively free of harassment from government officials. At the 1889 treaty payments, 156 men, women and children had received their annuities. Over the next four years the numbers grew. The most dramatic change occurred on the 1890 paylist when 31 new people were paid, bringing the total to 187. This number increased to 196 in 1891, and by 1892 the band's population had grown to 208. The Ahtahkakoop Band was now the largest band in the Carlton and Duck Lake agencies. In comparison, the population of the Mistawasis Reserve had dropped slightly to 156; all the others were remaining fairly constant at lower numbers.

Part of this growth was because births were finally outnumbering deaths. In 1889, when 156 were paid, seven deaths and nine births were recorded on the treaty paylist. Ten people died and 14 babies were born during the 1889–1890 paylist year, and the following year, when crops were poor and hunting animals scarce, there were 10 deaths and 11 births. The paylist for 1892, following a winter of relative comfort, indicated that five people had died and 13 babies were born.[93]

Although the decline in deaths and an increase in the number of babies were encouraging, the transfer of a number of families from the Mistawasis and Okīnomotayēw bands played a significant role in the growing population. Nine of the newcomers were related to Pierre, the councillor from Snake Plain. His son John Cardinal had transferred from Mistawasis's band in 1888. Two years later John's mother and two brothers, Osāwanāsew and Mac Cardinal, along with their families, were listed on the Ahtahkakoop Band paylist. Another new arrival from the Mistawasis Band was 15-year-old Albert Snake, the grandson of the late Chief Ocīpiwayān; Albert had arrived at the Mistawasis Reserve from the plains with his grandmother, Emma Snake, during the 1884–85 paylist year. His sister was married to one of the Cardinals.[94]

Māyātis and his father Kīnikwānāsiw,* who had transferred to Okīnomotayēw's band in 1888 and 1889 respectively, returned to Ahtahkakoop's band during the 1889–90 treaty paylist year. Each man brought a wife and one child with him. The following year three more sons transferred to the Ahtahkakoop Band.[95] These men had been listed under their own tickets in Okīnomotayēw's band when they went there with their father in 1889. No reasons were given on the paysheets for any of these transfers. Isaac Masuskapoe's new wife, also from Okīnomotayēw's band, was another addition and included on the paylist for the first time.

There were also two transfers from the Poundmaker Band during the early 1890s. Quacha, who was Greyeyes's mother-in-law, transferred to the Ahtahkakoop Band in 1890. Her transfer was accompanied by a letter from the Indian commissioner and a document giving band consent. The next year Pēmwēwēstik (Wind Blowing By), with his wife, and four girls, was listed on the paylist. The notation beside the entry stated that this family has "returned to this, their own band; were pd last year under #21 Poundmaker."[96] This transfer, like Quacha's the previous year, was accompanied by a letter from the commissioner.

Additionally, three people from Petihkwahākēw's band had transferred to an existing ticket, and a number of relatives from other bands were living with some of Ahtahkakoop's people. Surprisingly, Ahtahkakoop's son-in-law Kā-tāh-twēhototawāt was still on the band paylist even though he had not been paid since 1884. Also of interest was a note on the 1892 paylist that one of Kihci-mōhkomān's sons—who was now a member of Flying Dust's band—claimed arrears for the years 1881–1892.[97]

During the years 1889 to 1893 most families in the Ahtahkakoop Band

---

* Kīnikwānāsiw was one of the men who reportedly had killed an ox and been with the "rebels" during the uprising of 1885.

mourned the death of relatives. The early 1890s were particularly tragic for Ahtahkakoop and his wife. Their son Joseph, 28, and his newborn son both died in 1891. That same year the chief's granddaughter Maria Kā-tāh-twēhototawāt and her only child, an infant daughter, died. Maria's husband, John Cardinal, died in 1892. Sasaka-moose's wife was dead. The Ahenakew brothers and the Masus-kapoes all lost children, as did many other people in the band. And Iskwēsis, whom Hines had visited so often, had also died.[98] With Hines gone, none of the suffering was documented, or even mentioned because government reports generally did not deal with that kind of information.

Sidney P. Hall, National Archives of Canada, C-012998

Saskatchewan (alias Johnny Longmore) was on the Ahtahkakoop paylist from 1876 to 1879. He later lived in the Battleford area, and during the Uprising of 1885 delivered messages for the militia. In 1889 his former wife, Julien Favel, married Sasakamoose's son Alexander.

On a happier note, marriages were celebrated as bonds strengthened between families. For instance Thomas Knife, son of Kihci-mōhkomān, married Matilda, daughter of John Peter Masuskapoe. His brother James married Kā-miyo-ahcahkwēw's daughter Jane who, at the age of two weeks, had been the first person at the Asissipi Mission to be baptized by John Hines. Her mother was Judique, the daughter of Mistawasis.

Jacob, another of Masuskapoe's sons, had married Emily Bird, the daughter of Piyēsīs and Mary Ahtahkakoop, and Isaac Masuskapoe married the daughter of Omas-kaway-ka-pew from Okīnomotayēw's band. Sasakamoose's son Alexander married Julien Favel, the former wife of Johnny Saskatchewan. Ahenakew's son John married Eliza, the daughter of Maskwamāyow (Bear Tail), a non-Christian headman from Okīnomotayēw's band, while Albert Snake married Jemima, Michel Ahtahkakoop's daughter. Joseph Kā-miyo-ahcahkwēw, whose first wife had died a few months after their marriage, married Phoebe, the daughter of Kā-yīkowan (The Fog). Wāsēhikot's daughter Sarah married Joseph, son of Okīnomotayēw, and Kāh-kāsōw's daughter Mary married Greyeyes's son Norbert. Additionally, Joseph Ahtahkakoop's widow, Mary Joyful, married Mac Cardinal, brother of John and William.[99]

At least 47 babies were born during the years 1889 to 1893. These included a daughter born to Mary Jane Okimāsis and her husband, Michel Ahtahkakoop. Kāh-kāsōw and his wife Charlotte Hyman finally had a boy to complement their family of five girls, and Kāh-kāsōw's sister, Ellen Ahenakew, who had married John Hyman, delivered their first child, a boy. Wāsēhikot's second wife, Isabella Ermineskin, gave birth to two children, and Baptiste Ahenakew and Ellen Ermineskin had a girl. Alexander Sasakamoose was the father of a son and a daughter, and Kā-miyo-ahc-ahkwēw and Kāh-kāsōw were both grandfathers. Of particular note was a son born to Louis Ahenakew and Catherine Ermineskin on April 3, 1892. Named Allan Ellis Ahenakew, he would serve for much of his adult life as the chief of the Ahtahkakoop Band.[100]

Perhaps it was a sign of the times. As the government cracked down on the Indian people, their interest in the traditional ceremonies renewed and grew. Some bands, despite the government's attempts to prevent them, continued to have Sun Dances. Reed reported, for instance, that although visitors had been sent away, the agent had to allow a Sun Dance to proceed on Payipwāt's reserve in June, 1892, because he had no legal way to stop it.[101] The Cree in the Battleford area, meanwhile, had acquired the right to perform the Sioux Dance. This created consternation among some government officials who feared the spread of the messianic Ghost Dance religion north of the Canadian border.* And to the north and east of the Ahtahkakoop Reserve, the people living at Whitefish Lake, Pelican Lake, and Sturgeon Lake were still holding Sun Dances, Give Away Dances (*matāhitowin*), and other traditional ceremonies. *Matāhitowin*, which translates as "passing off something to each other," was a sacred dance held for *pāhkahkos*, the spirit of famine. The ceremony was held in the fall so there would be good luck and prosperity throughout the winter. The snow would fall and there would be no disease and no sickness. *Pāhkahkos* was also known as Bony Spectre.[102]

---

* In South Dakota, the Ghost Dance of the Dakota Sioux had ultimately led to the massacre at Wounded Knee on December 28, 1890. More than 200 people—most of them women and children— were killed by soldiers in the 7th Cavalry.

This photograph was taken at a Grass Dance on Beardy's reserve during the 1890s. The dance was purchased from the Assiniboines.

Despite the fact that Edgar Dewdney had said in 1884, when he was still Indian commissioner, that he had "never known any trouble brought about by holding" a Sun Dance[103] and some agents said the dances were harmless, government officials were determined to stop the them. They claimed that the ceremonies were not only detrimental to assimilation but they took the families away from their farming responsibilities at inappropriate times. The sacred ceremonies, government and church officials stated, undermined the missionaries' work and they counteracted the training given the students at the residential schools.[104]

There was no provision under the Indian Act to prevent the traditional dances and ceremonies of Indian people living on the plains and in the parklands. As a result, the agents and other government officials had to look elsewhere.[105] So they called upon the powers granted under the Indian Act to prevent people from leaving their reserves. This would at least limit the number of people attending the dances and ceremonies.

Meanwhile, at Ahtahkakoop's reserve the Reverend John Settee was not as rigid and influential in keeping the people separated from their traditional culture as John Hines had been. Some of the young men started participating in Give Away Dances at Sturgeon, Whitefish, and Pelican lakes during the early 1890s. The increased contact with traditional bands led to marriages. Albert Cahkāpēw, a young man in his early twenties who was known as Otitāskonikēw (Person Who Prays With A Pipe), married the daughter of a heathen from Pelican Lake, and John Ahenakew married the daughter of a heathen from Stoney Lake.[106] Additionally, a young man from Pelican Lake was courting one of Mōhkomānawēw's daughters. Kīnikwānāsiw and some of his family were still following the traditional ways, and Peter George Knife (Kihci-mōhkomān's son) was learning how to conduct sacred ceremonies.[107]

Ahtahkakoop had turned to McGibbon for help when the inspector was on the reserve in October of 1892, telling him that Give Away dancing was on the increase. The chief said he would not allow the dances to be held on the reserve, so the young men were holding the dances just outside its boundaries or travelling to other reserves. As a devout Christian and a man who had made a commitment to a new way of life many years earlier, Ahtahkakoop asked McGibbon if the Department of Indian Affairs would help him put an end to the dances. The inspector passed the information on to Reed, who then asked the North-West Mounted Police to patrol the Carlton and Duck Lake agencies "to look after such occurrences."[108]

CHAPTER THIRTY-TWO

Ahtahkakoop's Journey Ends, 1893-1896

The appointment of Hilton Keith as Indian agent for the Carlton Agency late in 1892 was one of many changes in the Department of Indian Affairs that was to directly and indirectly affect Ahtahkakoop and his people during the next four years.* Edgar Dewdney had resigned as minister of the Interior and superintendent general of Indian Affairs in 1892 to become lieutenant-governor of the Province of British Columbia. He was replaced by T.M. Daly. Lawrence Vankoughnet, who had held the position of deputy superintendent general since 1874, retired in October of 1893. Hayter Reed, formerly Indian commissioner, was promoted to deputy superintendent general. Surprisingly the changes ended there. Amédée Forget remained assistant Indian commissioner and the position of Indian commissioner was not filled.

Hilton Keith's replacement of Joseph Finlayson as agent affected the Indian people in the Carlton Agency considerably more than the other changes. Reed considered Finlayson, a former Hudson's Bay Company employee, too sympathetic to the plight of the Indian people to perform well for the government in the Carlton Agency. British-born Keith, on the other hand, had been working for the Indian department since the early 1880s and had earned the reputation of a hard-liner. As a farm instructor for the Crooked Lake Agency, his vigorous enforcement of Reed's directive to cut winter rations had resulted in a violent and near-explosive confrontation

---

* In addition to these changes, John A. Macdonald, prime minister and a former superintendent general of Indian Affairs, had died in 1891. He was followed by a succession of Conservative prime ministers: J.J.C. Abbott (1891–92); J.S.D. Thompson (1892–94); Mackenzie Bowell (1894–96) and Charles Tupper (1896).

Illustration by Ed Peekeekoot

Two band members, Kāh-kāsōw and Osāwanāsiw, served as volunteer farm instructors, helping the farmers and keeping records for the government.

with Yellow Calf's band.[1] And earlier in 1892—the year of his transfer—Keith was the agent who invoked an article in the Indian Act to remove visiting Indians from a Sun Dance held at the Piapot Reserve.

In 1893, still distant from the eyes of government overseers, Ahtahkakoop's people continued to assume more responsibility for their own well-being. For instance, Kāh-kāsōw and Osāwanāsiw, on a volunteer basis and without any remuneration, were now serving as farm instructors and keeping the records required by the Indian agent. Kāh-kāsōw looked after one side of Sandy Lake, with Osāwanāsiw responsible for the other. They did a good job, inspector McGibbon said, noting that they "both keep correct accounts in their own way, and were prepared to give any information that was required. They are careful and reliable men."[2]

The Ahtahkakoop farmers had taken good care of their cattle during the winter of 1892–93 despite extreme cold and heavy snow, and the animals were in good condition when spring arrived. The weather, however, had delayed seeding. As a result, only 201¾ acres were planted, compared to

256 acres the previous year. Of this land, 144 acres were put into wheat. The remaining acres went into oats, barley, potatoes, and peas. Only four men—Sōniyāw-ayāwēw, Mōhkomānawēw, Baptiste Ahenakew, and John Hyman—planted garden vegetables.[3]

The greatest amounts of land were worked by Sōniyāw-ayāwēw and Osāwanāsiw. Ahtahkakoop, whose health had improved since 1892, and his son Michel worked their fields together. Other co-operative ventures, besides Baptiste and his brother-in-law John Hyman, included Thomas Bighead and Andrew Apotum, Kāh-kāsōw and son-in-law Norbert Greyeyes, Wāskitoy and Māyātis, Albert Chakāpēw and Piwiyinis (Little Man), and Nātakām (North, Going Towards The Water, also known as Mac Knife) and Kā-nahahcāpiw (Good With A Bow, also known as Jumper Tate).[4] Interestingly, Michel Ahtahkakoop was listed with his brother Kā-miyo-astotin, as well as with his father. As in so many other years, the crops started off well and were looking good in June. But very little rain fell during the summer, and crops throughout the entire district suffered.[5]

Encouraged by Ahtahkakoop, Kāh-kāsōw, and Osāwanāsiw, some of the men cleared and broke more land during the summer months, cultivated the summer-fallowed fields, and cut 480 tons of hay for the herd of livestock that now numbered 239 head. This total included 56 calves from 73 cows.[6]

In addition to their usual chores, the men helped saw the logs stacked on the shore of the lake. Then they erected the building requested by Ahtahkakoop in 1891 for storing the rations supplied by the government. In making the request, the chief had explained to McGibbon that the provisions were delivered to the reserve in bulk and stored in the lower part of the big barn. The arrangement was not suitable, everyone agreed, since this part of the barn was used as a stable.[7]

Although the chief's intent in 1891 had been to erect a small storehouse for the use of the band, Keith issued orders to make the place suitable for government officials "to stop in when visiting the reserve." The 17 by 15 foot log building that was built had a thatched roof, a chimney, and two windows. A small stable was also erected. Keith then went one step further. He decided that "instead of rations being issued in bulk, as formerly, these will be given weekly, either agent, clerk or the interpreter performing the work." As a result, McGibbon reported that even though Kāh-kāsōw and Osāwanāsiw were "careful and reliable men … the agent having built the storehouse, and having arranged to attend to the issues from the agency, the services of these two men will no longer be required. They receive no remuneration of any kind for their trouble."[8]

Many of the people were continuing to improve their houses and farms. The 77-year-old chief was no exception. With the help of his family, Ahtahkakoop had partitioned his house into rooms. This had made the house more difficult to heat, so during 1892–93 the chief installed an extra stove given to him by the Indian commissioner. His latest improvement was clapboarding the outside of his house, and by late summer the lumber for this job was stacked beside the house.[9] Similar projects were on-going throughout the reserve.

The families were in the fields harvesting their grain when McGibbon arrived on the reserve in September, 1893. The reaper must have been in poor repair, for most of the crop was being hand-cut using cradles. As usual the women, young people and children worked in the fields with the men and helped haul the bundles of grain to the "stack yards."[10]

Ahtahkakoop "was dressed in his best wearing four medals" in honour of the visit when McGibbon stopped at the chief's house. From there the inspector went to every other home and "took an inventory of implements and tools in the hands of the Indians." The chief was particularly proud of Kā-miyo-astotin's farm, and he was waiting at his son's house when McGibbon arrived there for his inspection. McGibbon described the one-and-a-half storey house, situated on the east side of the Asissipi River, as one of the best homes on the reserve. Twenty-two by 27 feet, it had rooms on both levels. The upper floor was dressed with boards and the roof was shingled. Kā-miyo-astotin had done all the work himself, the inspector said, with home-made lumber being "used entirely in the construction, also home-made shingles." An "outside" kitchen under construction also had a shingle roof. Inside, the house was very clean and well furnished with cook and box stoves, bedsteads, tables, and chairs. The walls were covered with pictures from Chatter Box, and there were pretty bark baskets for holding tea.11

McGibbon made no mention of Kā-miyo-astotin's growing family. Because Kā-miyo-astotin, 41, and his wife Janet Ermineskin, 37, did not have children of their own, relatives were willing to share their children. And so, during the 1882–83 paylist year, a nephew called Pacī (James Starblanket) was given to the couple to raise. Nine years later Janet's niece, two-year-old Sophia Ahenakew, moved in with them. The child was the daughter of Janet's sister Ellen and her husband Baptiste Ahenakew. Then, during the 1892–93 paylist year, Kā-miyo-astotin's 11-year-old nephew,

Illustration by Ed Peekeekoot

Kā-miyo-astotin and Janet Ermineskin's house was one of many well-built homes that were furnished with cook stoves, tables, chairs, and beds.

John Robert Ahtahkakoop, joined the family. The boy was Ahtahkakoop's grandson and the eldest son of Kā-miyo-astotin's deceased brother Joseph and his widow Mary Joyful.* The boy took Starblanket as his surname when he entered Emmanuel College in 1894. His younger brother Joseph had moved in with Ahtahkakoop and his wife a year or so earlier.[12] Mary Joyful kept her seven-year-old daughter named Maggie.[†]

Kā-miyo-astotin, the inspector said, was a good farmer and a thrifty, hard-working man. In this growing season, when the amount of land put into crops had been reduced because of the late spring, the chief's son had sown seven acres of wheat, four acres of oats, four acres of barley, half an acre of peas, and half an acre of potatoes. His stables, fences, and corrals were all good. He had wheat and hay left over from the previous winter, his cattle were in good condition, and 19 tons of hay had been put up for the upcoming winter. McGibbon also noted that some summer-fallowing had been done and more land was being broken.[13]

As part of the inspection, McGibbon recorded the tools and implements found at Kā-miyo-astotin's house. They were typical of what was generally found at an Indian homestead, he said, and included a "scythe, snaith, auger, 1½ inch, chisel, grindstone, hoe, plough, set harrows, three sections, set of ox harness, spade, axe, hay fork, two milk pans, milk pail, cart," and similar items. The whole place showed thrift and enterprise, he concluded, and there were many more such places on the reserve.

Following the completion of his inspection, McGibbon reported that he "found the houses of a good class, and in nearly every case cleanly kept. Some of the houses are well-finished and are comfortably furnished." He also noted that a number of the families had privately owned wagons and 900 logs "were piled on the edge of the lake ready to be sawn into lumber."

Despite the inspector's words of praise, Kā-miyo-astotin would have been disappointed with the results of his summer work. His wheat fields only produced 4.3 bushels per acre, for a total of 30 bushels. The rest of his harvest amounted to 30 bushels of oats, 18 bushels of barley, and 50 bushels of potatoes. The peas either failed or were eaten during the course of the summer. With a few exceptions, the other farmers on the reserve had

---

* John Robert's mother, Mary Joyful, married Mac Cardinal October 17, 1892. The son of Pierre and brother to John and Osāwanāsiw, he was sometimes known as Mac Pierre.

† See the genealogy chart on the inside of the back cover for clarification of relationships.

the same results. In the end, only 723 bushels of wheat were harvested, amounting to an average of just over five bushels an acre. Once again the yields varied from field to field. Sōniyāw-ayāwēw's crop was the most successful, producing 11 bushels per acre on 11 acres of land. Two fields failed entirely, with others producing yields of two to three bushels an acre.[14] In Keith's words, the crops did not turn out as well as expected. With results such as these it was impossible to rely solely on farm produce to survive. Even Sōniyāw-ayāwēw's crop of 11 bushels per acre was far below the estimate Reed had used in developing his "peasant" farming policies. The potato crop was also poor, producing only 325 bushels. This was down about 50 percent from the previous two years.

With the crops and hay cut and stored, Ahtahkakoop's sons clapboarded their father's house and other men started work on five new houses and eight stables. Houses were winterized by stuffing moss into cracks between logs and around windows and doors, mudding the exterior of the log houses, and checking the roofs and chimneys. The women sewed and repaired clothing as they and their families prepared for another winter.

Government and church records did not document the winter of 1893–94, but it must have been another difficult one. With the exception of Sōniyāw-ayāwēw's harvest, the crops had been very poor. To survive, men hunted for furs and meat, and the women and children snared rabbits, other small animals, and prairie chickens. The people probably also had beef on several occasions since the government was continuing its policy of "condemning and killing off" some of the old animals for meat and replacing them with young ones.[15]

During the winter the men threshed their wheat. Some of the grain was kept for seed and the rest was hauled to the flour mill on the Mistawasis Reserve. In total the grist ground at the mill produced 17,152 pounds of flour. Although disappointing, this was considerably better than results obtained elsewhere in the Carlton Agency. The wheat taken to the mill by the Mistawasis farmers, for instance, only produced 5,989 pounds of flour, and farmers from Petihkwahākēw's reserve received 415 pounds of flour from their disastrous crop. Interestingly, statistics for 1893–94 indicated that one bushel of wheat was producing about 30 pounds of flour.[16]

Two hundred and thirty-one saw logs were cut during the winter and skidded out of the bush to the sawmill site. Fence rails were cut and taken to the farmsteads, cattle fed, and daily chores done. Yet there was still time for the adults to enjoy each other's company, to joke and tell stories, play cards and other games, participate in games of challenge, and teach the children the ways of the people.

In the evenings, the children gathered around the stoves to listen to the old people tell stories about *wīsahkēcāhk*, the being who—through his adventures and misadventures—taught the children how to behave and show respect. Edward Ahenakew, the son of Baptiste Ahenakew and Ellen Ermineskin, recalled many years later that the children loved to listen to his grandfather K-ōsihkosiwanāniw recount his adventures on the prairies during the days when the people still hunted buffalo and fought the Blackfoot.

"One time, many years ago," K-ōsihkosiwanāniw said, in telling one of his many stories, "we were at war with the Blackfoot. I was riding my favourite horse and chasing a Blackfoot warrior. I rode fast and caught up to him, even though his horse was running as hard as it could. My gun was not loaded, but as I drew close I opened my powder horn and spilled some powder into the bore of my gun. So far so good." Then, as he went through the motions of loading his gun, K-ōsihkosiwanāniw continued his story. "I put a bullet into my mouth to moisten it with saliva. That's the way that men loaded their guns while racing after buffalo. The saliva on the bullet acted as a wad between the powder and bullet. When I got close to the Blackfoot, I aimed the gun at his bare back and pulled the trigger. But no bullet hit. There was only the black mark of the powder on the warrior's skin. The bullet must have rolled out when I raised my gun to shoot." The old man laughed, adding that "I missed the chance to make a great name for myself."[17]

And K-ōsihkosiwanāniw told about the time "he had—secretly, he thought—helped an old Blackfoot couple and a girl escape when the Crees attacked the camp." A number of other women heard of his kindness. They were "afraid for their own lives, [so] they gave themselves up to him, somewhat to his embarrassment." According to Edward Ahenakew, "most of these women were in time taken by single men and they became Crees, married to men who were their hereditary foes."[18]

Many stories were told by the other men, for most of them had been buffalo hunters and all but the youngest had stolen horses and gone to war against the Blackfoot. The women, too, had stories to tell the children, stories of the old days when they roamed the prairies at will, making pemmican and gathering food and medicines from the land. And stories were told of the special spiritual powers possessed—and still possessed—by people in the band.

The winter passed. Fortunately no major epidemics struck the adults and consumption did not claim any victims. The very young were less fortunate, and four children died during the winter and early spring of 1893–94. A 60-year-old woman also died.[19]

In some ways life on the Ahtahkakoop Reserve was similar to that being experienced by the newcomers trying to wrest a living from their homesteads. Many of the white homesteaders had to build their homes and develop their farms with limited resources and they faced many of the same problems faced by Ahtahkakoop's people. Knowledge of good techniques for dry-land farming was limited amongst all farmers, including the farm instructors. The Red Fife wheat that was almost universally planted was slow to mature and thus prone to frost damage. Drought, hail, grasshoppers, and other uncontrollable factors often resulted in failures.

There were, however, many differences. Most of Ahtahkakoop's people were still content to live without the beds, tables, and other furniture used in the white community, and in the summer they moved into tipis pitched near their houses. The food was prepared in much the same way as before, except buffalo meat was no longer obtainable. Moose, elk, deer, small animals, wildfowl, dried berries and roots, when available, and beef when approved by government officials, formed the basis of their meals. A few garden vegetables were generally available in the summer, most people had potatoes for part of the winter, and bannock was made when there was flour. To some extent, the people still lived a communal life. Some men were hunters and trappers. Others devoted most of their time to their farms. Thus, the people were able to share farm produce and wild meat, furs, and hides amongst themselves.

Nevertheless, in times of food shortages the options of the Indian people were limited. They could not sell their farm produce without a permit, there were no nearby stores, and because they were situated a long way from a settlement the opportunities to make extra money were generally limited to freighting, occasionally working for local farmers, and trapping. The government did provide rations in times of dire need, but generally the aid was not sufficient to ward off hunger pangs and it was only given to the sick, the aged, and people who worked in exchange for the food.

The spring of 1894 arrived, and with this season of renewal came the geese and ducks that provided temporary relief from hunger. Some of the men continued working on their houses and stables while they waited for the fields to dry. The houses were cleaned up, the people moved into their tipis and tents, and a new growing season was upon them. In total, 196 acres of land were planted in 1894, almost the same as the previous year's 202 acres.[20]

Osāwanāsiw continued to serve as farm instructor well into 1894. He now worked on his own, without Kāh-kāsōw's assistance, and handled both sides of the lake himself. He also continued to "keep the books in his own way." McGibbon, following an inspection in July, praised him for being "wonderfully correct in knowing all about implements and other property on the reserve." The inspector added that Osāwanāsiw "has a fine house, has good stables and corrals, and his implements are nicely stored away. His children attend school regularly. This man is thrifty and enterprising."[21]

Under Osāwanāsiw's guidance, rubbish had been cleared away from the houses, the potatoes and gardens were well weeded—with the exception of the turnips that had been broadcast instead of being planted in rows—and the fencing was improved. The farmers broke more land, and when McGibbon was on the reserve in July they were ploughing the summer-fallowed fields. McGibbon noted that the "land is good, but it needs preparation in order to ensure a good crop." He therefore recommended that after the fields were ploughed in the early summer they should be harrowed and re-harrowed to kill all the weeds. Later he explained that it was better to "properly fallow ten acres than fifty only half done, which, I regret to say, is too much the case, not only among Indians, but with white people also; hence the country is overrun with weeds."[22]

The herd of cattle, held by 41 families, had increased from 239 to 290 since the last inspection. The cattle were all properly branded and the books properly kept. The band had at least one new Galloway bull,* one of several provided by the government to various bands to improve the herds. Described by McGibbon as "a splendid-looking animal," it was in Kā-miyo-astotin's care. Thirty-two head of cattle and 41 horses were privately owned and a few farmers had some "very good pigs" and poultry, as well as privately owned wagons.[23]

McGibbon also noted that the some of the men were sawing the 231 logs that had been hauled to the sawmill site during the winter. The lumber would be used, he said, to erect a shed on the edge of the lake to house the

* A Scottish breed of cattle, Galloways had black curly hair.

sawmill. This would protect the machinery and provide a place for sawing in wet weather.

The inspector once again found all the houses comfortable, "cleanly and neatly kept," and "good stabling in every case." Ahtahkakoop's house had been clapboarded on the outside, and was not only more comfortable but its appearance was improved. Kā-miyo-astotin's fields of oats and potatoes were good, he had a good garden, new fencing, and a dairy, with "a number of milk pans filled with milk." Ahtahkakoop's reserve, McGibbon reported, was "in good shape—cattle, fences, houses, stables, being all that could reasonably be desired."

Although early rains had given hope for a good crop, drought ravaged the fields later in the summer of 1894. The amount of wheat harvested was only slightly better than the previous year and the quality of the grain was poor. Surprisingly, barley and oats did fairly well, while the crop of potatoes was similar to the previous year; turnips amounted to 530 bushels. The hay harvest met with some success, with 761 tons cut.[24] Kā-miyo-astotin was by far the most successful farmer in 1894. His nine-acre field of wheat produced 112 bushels, compared to the next largest crop, 69 bushels of wheat grown by Baptiste Ahenakew. Kā-miyo-astotin's 226 bushels of oats were more than half of the total for the other farmers combined, and his 40 tons of hay were only three tons less than the 43 tons cut by Greyeyes.[25]

Despite McGibbon's comments about the necessity of bringing the fields into better condition, Keith reported that although the Ahtahkakoop Reserve "suffered severely from drought … better culture here resulted in a crop fifty per cent better than on Mistawasis Reserve." The Ahtahkakoop farmers may have produced the better crop, but the agent made it difficult for them to get the wheat ground into flour. "The crop [throughout the agency] being small," he reported to the superintendent general of Indian Affairs, "I found that it would be less expensive to send those who had grists to the Prince Albert Mill" than operate the mill on Mistawasis's reserve. And so the men from Ahtahkakoop's reserve once again had to make the long trip into Prince Albert to get their wheat milled.[26]

The children, in the meantime, were doing well at school despite three different teachers after the death of Joseph Sasakamoose and the departure of John and Emma Hines. J.M.R. Neely, who had taken over from Joseph, was replaced by Alexander Seymour in 1890. Three years later William R. Dreaver took charge of the school. Because government officials insisted that older children attend the Battleford Industrial School, all the students at the Sandy Lake School after 1891, with the exception of one student in 1893, were enrolled in Standards I to III.

Ahtahkakoop and most of his people, nevertheless, still supported the education of their children and in July of 1894, when McGibbon visited the reserve, 18 of the 23 boys and girls of school age were registered at the day school.[27] Despite continuing problems with the industrial school at Battleford, nine other students—the same number as the previous year— were still at the school in 1894.[28] These students were Albert Kā-miyo-ahc-ahkwēw, son of Kā-miyo-ahcahkwēw and Judique; Agnes Pīwiyinīs, daughter of Pīwiyinīs (Little Man); Charles Nayneecassum, son of Philip Wīcikāpawīmēw (He Who Stands With You) and Caroline Nayneecassum (Glittering);* Annie Stranger, daughter of David and Isabella Stranger; Sasakamoose's granddaughter Louisa; Alexander Nayneecassum, son of Duncan and Maggie Nayneecassum; Phoebe Kāh-kāsōw, daughter of Kāh-kāsōw and Charlotte Hyman; Charles Cahkāpēw, son of Cahkāpēw; and Christie Joyful.† With the exception of Christie Joyful, who died, these students were also registered for the 1894–95 term. There was one new addition, Mac Cardinal's daughter Marie.

Three other students were attending Emmanuel College. William Wāsēhikot, who was also known as William Robinson, had been enrolled since October 6, 1890, and was studying to be a teacher. Joseph Ahtahkakoop's sons John Robert and Joseph entered the boarding school December 12, 1894.[29]

During William Dreaver's term as teacher at the Sandy Lake School, the building was plastered and a three-foot-high wainscoting was installed on the lower part of the walls. The school, McGibbon said, was in good repair, comfortable, and the stationery and furniture were "sufficient." In addition to their regular school subjects, the students were making baskets from bark and a variety of other materials, as well as brooms. The girls were learning how to knit and the boys were gardening. The children, McGibbon noted, were clean and "fairly well clothed, except in foot-gear."[30]

Louis Ahenakew replaced Dreaver as teacher during the latter part of

---

* After Wīcikāpawīmēw died, Caroline married Māyātis, son of Kīnikwānāsiw. The boy later took the name Charles Little.

† Christie was the sister of Mary Joyful, Joseph Ahtahkakoop's widow.

1894. Ahenakew's son had been teaching at Stoney Lake when Hines left Ahtahkakoop's reserve in 1888. The school was closed two years later because Okīnomotayēw's people were often away hunting and attendance was low. Louis then spent four months teaching in a tent on the Little Pine Reserve. From there he returned to Stoney Lake, where he taught for three years. The number of students continued to be small and the school was closed when four children were taken to the school in Battleford. Louis's next move, in 1894, was back to the Ahtahkakoop Reserve.[31]

In a report dated August 12, 1894, McGibbon noted that the church was badly in need of paint. He added that the Reverend John Settee was leaving for the Devon Mission. These brief comments did little to reflect the turmoil that had been affecting the mission since Settee replaced John Hines in 1888. The problems had been developing over a number of years, and in January of 1894 Bishop Pinkham had admitted that Settee "is not quite the man for the post & we have no one more suitable."[32]

There were a number of concerns. The most obvious was the condition of the mission property. Unlike Hines and his wife, who had kept the mission neat and in good order, Settee let the buildings fall into disrepair and the mission house was becoming increasingly dirty and over-run with "vermin." But there was an even more overriding problem. The mission at the Ahtahkakoop Reserve was an important one, the bishop said, and "there are many true Xtians there, some of whom appear to know more than Mr. Settee himself." This was obviously creating a difficult situation. The missionary was not setting a good example, Ahtahkakoop's people had lost their respect for him, and although they continued to have their children baptized, support for the church was declining. Despite the problems, the bishop nevertheless said Settee was an excellent man but better suited to serve elsewhere. Then, apparently unaware of the state of the buildings, he added that the mission house and church were good but needed some repairs.[33]

The bishop made arrangements for Settee to substitute for Hines at the Devon Mission while the missionary was on leave in England. Upon Hines's return, Settee would be sent to Moose Lake, or "some other place." The Reverend G.S. Winter, who had been stationed at York Factory for a number of years, was recruited to take Settee's place at the Sandy Lake Mission.[34] To make the house ready for Winter, Archdeacon John Mackay, a hired man, and a student from Emmanuel College "thoroughly washed and kalsomined* the different rooms, leaving only the kitchen which being a log building, and not plastered, required white-washing with lime."[35]

Winter went to the Sandy Lake Mission "full of hope." He had been told, he wrote in his journal, that the Indians at the Ahtahkakoop Reserve "are a splendid set of people" and the "fruit of Mr. Hines' work is often the subject of conversation among the settlers & other white people in the district." Unable to drive a buckboard or wagon, Winter—with his family—was taken to the Ahtahkakoop Reserve by William Dreaver. They arrived Saturday, September 8, 1894, six months after the appointment had been confirmed. The new missionary had been warned that the buildings needed some repairs, so tools were included with his household goods.[36]

The next day being Sunday, the new missionary held two services for Ahtahkakoop's people. One of the boys from Emmanuel College accompanied the hymns on the harmonium. Winter wrote later that he was "intensely delighted with the people" and Ahtahkakoop "seems a nice man." The chief, in turn, was able to understand the Cree spoken by Winter and his wife, and expressed pleasure that Winter would be able to preach without having to learn the language.[37] In Winter's words, the people "spoke in glowing terms of their former white Praying Chief."

Winter, however, did not find everything to his liking and his stay was short. So short, in fact, that he was gone after three nights. He had found the church dirty with signs of "spitting about, from chewing tobacco in the sacred edifice." But it was the house he found most upsetting, saying it was "everything that was unpleasant & unwholesome." The smell was so terrible his wife threw up, the walls were "black" with vermin, and the children were covered with bites after spending two nights in the house. The Winter family slept outside the third night and then returned to Prince Albert.[38] They were, according to Louis Ahenakew, words, "driven back by the bedbugs and fleese."[39]

Mackay asked the missionary if he would consider the house a "sufficient residence" if it were cleaned thoroughly and outhouses put up, but Winter refused to return to the Sandy Lake Mission. The bishop was to write a few months later, repeating what he had written in January 1894

---

* Kalsomining (also spelt calsomining) is the application of a white or tinted wash that is made from a powdered mixture of glue, whiting or zinc white, and water. It is brushed onto interior plastered walls.

about Settee, that "Mr. Winter is not, I am sorry to say, quite the man for us." He added that much "to my surprise, I found on his arrival he was not able to drive himself … [and] still seems helpless in that respect." A missionary here has to be quite self-sufficient, he concluded. Mackay was equally unimpressed, stating that after the kitchen was rebuilt and the repairs completed the house was in "an excellent state of repair, but I do not think it would satisfy Mr. Winter."[40]

To temporarily fill the void at Sandy Lake, the Reverend John Badger was transferred from the St. James Mission on the Muskoday Reserve (John Smith's reserve) late in 1894.[41] Badger, who was a member of the Muskoday Band and a graduate of Emmanuel College, had begun his church career as a catechist. Following his ordination as a deacon in 1886 he was given charge of the Fort à la Corne Mission and, later, the St. James Mission. At the time of his transfer to the Sandy Lake Mission he was a headman, as well as missionary, on his reserve. Winter was allowed to stay in Prince Albert while he was put in temporary charge of Badger's mission. Later, by his own request, the missionary from York Factory was sent north of Prince Albert to establish a mission for the traditional people living at Sturgeon Lake.[42]

Badger soon discovered that the Church of England was losing its grip on the settlement at Sandy Lake. Participation in traditional ceremonies was growing and exchanges with people still following the old traditional ways had became more common. Soon after his arrival he had to deal with a situation where a young heathen man from the Pelican Lake Band, accompanied by several friends, arrived to take one of Mōhkomānawēw's daughters for his wife. The young woman was a Christian and the clergyman tried to prevent her from leaving. He was unsuccessful and the woman transferred to the Pelican Lake Band.[43]

During his stay at the Sandy Lake Mission, Badger tore down the old log kitchen attached to the mission and built a new one. Other repairs were made, and by the time the fall of 1895 arrived the mission was in "an excellent state of repair." Archdeacon Mackay and Bishop Pinkham both thought Winter should return to the Sandy Lake Mission. Luckily for Ahtahkakoop's people, he refused and insisted on working with Ayahtaskamikinam's "heathen" band at Sturgeon Lake.[44] He arrived there early in October, 1895.

Meanwhile a member of the Church Missionary Society's Finance Committee in Prince Albert, a man by the name of James Taylor, had "offered himself to Indian work." His offer was accepted, and it was agreed to send him to the Sandy Lake Mission. His appointment was effective October 1. Until Taylor was of the "Holy Order," Winter was to go to Sandy Lake once a month for services. And so Badger returned to the Muskoday Reserve and Taylor took charge of the Sandy Lake Mission. Taylor studied during the winter and was ordained the following May.

According to the bishop, Taylor was a "good missionary" who won the respect and confidence of his parishioners. Unfortunately, Taylor did not speak Cree. Normally this would have caused considerable problems, but Louis Ahenakew, who was into his second year of teaching at the school, was pressed into service as an interpreter. "I am sorry," he wrote to Hines in December, 1895, "that I have to do this without anything extra."[45]

Indian agent Hilton Keith, in the meantime, was making some changes of his own in the Carlton Agency and at the Ahtahkakoop Reserve. He had taken over from Joseph Finlayson in November, 1892, not long after McGibbon indicated that Finlayson had too much work and needed help. The commissioner responded by saying that a younger man could handle the job, and Finlayson was moved to Touchwood Hills.

Despite Reed's reluctance to get extra help for Finlayson, Keith hired a half-breed interpreter and teamster, Rupert Pratt, to complement his staff of farm instructor George Chaffee, clerk H.W. Halpin, and W. Giles, miller and blacksmith. He built a new house for the clerk and interpreter at the agency headquarters, improved the building that housed the flour mill, and had a blacksmith shop erected. Then a second farmer, A.J. Coburn, was hired. Chaffee was sent to Touchwood Hills in exchange for Louis Couture. As a result of this exchange, Finlayson and Chaffee were once again working together—this time at Touchwood Hills—and Couture had rejoined Keith at the Carlton Agency.[46] Couture was French and Roman Catholic, a combination that was a concern to church officials in Prince Albert and to Hines in far-away Devon. Couture was placed on Petihkwahākēw's reserve at Muskeg Lake.

The Ahtahkakoop Band had, for many years, been considered one of the most progressive in the North-West Territories. They had earned this reputation by their willingness to make the adaptations necessary to survive with dignity in their changing world, and they had worked hard. Hines had been an influential teacher for 14 years. After the missionary moved to Devon, the agent and farm instructor visited periodically, providing guidance, issuing orders, and levelling criticisms. At least once a year government officials of a higher rank inspected the work of the Indian people, the agent, and his staff. Inspector Wadsworth had set the scene for change in 1890 when he reported that Ahtahkakoop's people farmed extensively but their exertions were "in a measure discounted by the distance the reserve is from the agency, and in consequence the limited attention they can receive in the overseeing of their farm work." This was written, even though in the same report Wadsworth said the band was superior to most others of the same size, with most living comfortably and only a few "in want." He credited the band's success, in part, on "the large number of fine able-bodied men it contains."[47]

Ignoring this statement, Keith took a significant step to restrict the band's autonomy when he issued orders that the storehouse requested by Ahtahkakoop for storing the rations should be expanded into a building suitable for "stopping-over." A stable was also built. Then, in another crucial step, Keith decided that the agent, an instructor, or the interpreter would make weekly trips to the reserve to issue rations. Despite this decision, Osāwanāsiw—for a while at least—had continued to serve as farm instructor.

This came to an end in 1895 when Louis Couture, farm instructor, was sent to live on the Ahtahkakoop Reserve. Instead of erecting new structures, the house and farm buildings vacated by Couture at Petihkwahākēw's reserve were moved to a location on the west side of the lake overlooking the water. The buildings were nearly completed when McGibbon visited the reserve in October. They had a certain "ruggedness," the inspector said, from being pulled down and rebuilt. The inspector does not indicate who had done the work, but if past examples hold true it was the men from the two reserves who worked in exchange for food.[48]

The farm instructor's house was a fair size. The sitting room and dining room were separated by an arch, and there was a summer kitchen as well as the regular kitchen. Two good bedrooms were located upstairs. There was also a small office, a store house, and a good stable. A panel fence with a gate and a turnstile surrounded the premises.

The new farm instructor took his duties seriously. The amount of land sown by each farmer was recorded with numbers in decimals (such as 5.2 acres) instead of rounded-off figures. Of more importance and concern, he visited the houses and stables once or twice a week. Generally he found them clean and neat.

He also followed up on McGibbon's suggestion of the previous year that the land was good, but needed more preparation. Thus he encouraged the men to spend more time bringing "the fields into better condition."[49] In all, 230 acres of land were planted in 1895, an increase of 35 over the previous year. Unlike the Mistawasis and Muskeg reserves, where drought, gophers, and other "uncontrollable circumstances" resulted in a total loss of crop, the Ahtahkakoop farmers harvested 2,320 bushels of wheat.[50] Although this was a substantial increase over the previous year when 869 bushels were harvested, the results again varied from field to field. The wheat planted by Sōniyāw-ayāwēw, one of the better farmers on the reserve, and his step-son John Piyēsīs (Bird) produced the largest harvest, 219 bushels. Sōniyāw-ayāwēw, 45, did not help cut this crop, for he died in June from consumption.[51] Wāsēhikot, with 204 bushels of wheat, had the second largest crop of wheat followed by Thomas Knife, 135 bushels; Alexander Sasakamoose, 125 bushels; Kāh-kāsōw and Norbert Greyeyes, 122 bushels; and Albert Snake, with 108 bushels. Surprisingly, Kā-miyo-astotin's wheat crop amounted to only 50 bushels.[52]

The wheat was stacked in well-fenced corrals throughout the reserve by the time inspector Wadsworth, who had not inspected the reserve for a number of years, visited in October. Some of the wheat, the inspector reported, "showed a good sample, but a good deal of smut among the wheat." The fields were well fenced, the potatoes "were a fair crop, but the only appearance of turnips were some broadcast, and not thinned, consequently they were no good."[53]

Wadsworth did not inspect all the cattle on account of an early snow storm that drove them into the treed areas. He did, however, see one of the Galloway bulls. It had grown into a "very fine animal," he reported. The inspector also "observed one scrub bull,* which is an infringement of the rules." The calves had not done as well as the adult animals. There were only 30 and just a few were black. Moreover, on instructions from Keith, the calves had been tied up to facilitate milking and many were "very poor and in low condition."[54]

Ahtahkakoop and his wife Mary Nātowēw were now living with Kā-miyo-astotin and Janet Ermineskin in their home on the south side of the Asissipi River. The chief was at the house when inspector Wadsworth stopped by for a visit. He was in good health, the government official

---

* A bull of mixed or inferior breeding.

noted, adding that "as is usual with him, he talked very loyally and sensibly of his work, and the work of the Government on his Reserve."[55]

Ahtahkakoop's house near the mission now sat empty. At most of the other houses, good supplies of sawn lumber were on hand for making room partitions and furniture.* Tables, chairs and beds were still novelties for people who had lived comfortably in tipis for so many years. Yet times were changing, and gradually Ahtahkakoop's people changed too. The houses were continually being improved and rooms were being partitioned for sleeping areas. Kā-miyo-astotin was one of the first to have wooden furniture, and Wāskitoy was among those who became furniture-makers during the next year.[56]

Ten boys and nine girls were registered at the day school in 1895, with Louis Ahenakew as teacher. Attendance was generally better in the winter than in the warmer months, and when Wadsworth visited in October, 12 of the 19 children were present. The inspector reported that the youngsters "looked healthy and well, were clean, fairly well dressed and answered questions intelligently they appeared to be well provided with books, slates, etc." He added that the "school house is in fair condition, was clean and reasonably well furnished."

Joseph and John Robert Starblanket were still attending the boarding school at Emmanuel College. William Wāsēhikot, who was not well, had transferred from Emmanuel College to the Battleford Industrial School. There he joined six boys and five girls from Ahtahkakoop's reserve. Two of the boys, Simon Apotum's son Jeremiah and K-ōsihkosiwanāniw's adopted son Joseph MacKay, were enrolled at the Battleford school for the first time.[57]

By now the Battleford Industrial School had undergone several changes. Thomas Clarke had resigned as principal on December 31, 1894, following several years of criticism aimed at his drinking habits and management of the school.[58] He was replaced by the Reverend Edward Matheson, who had started his teaching career under John Hines in 1877. J.M.R. Neely, the teacher who had done so poorly at the Sandy Lake School following Joseph Sasakamoose's death and Hines's departure, was appointed assistant principal. His tenure, not surprisingly, was short-lived.

---

* The band's share of the lumber sawed in 1894–95 had been 47,000 feet after the agent claimed the government's share in toll, or payment, for the use of the saw.

Students dressed in uniforms pose with school staff outside the Battleford Industrial School.

In another new development, as of July 1, 1895, the school was under the direct control of Cyprian Pinkham, the Bishop of Saskatchewan and Calgary. Funding, however, came from the government on a per capita basis, and the bishop pointed out that the school was subject "therefore to the [Indian] department whose inspector pay regular visits and reports fully the condition in which he finds it."[59]

In addition to their classroom work, the boys at the Battleford school were being taught "blacksmithing, carpentering, kalsomining, painting, printing, shoemaking, farming and gardening: while the girls are instructed in baking, cooking, washing, mending and all kinds of general household work."[60] Some of the older girls, including Phoebe Kāh-kāsōw, were "Out Pupils" and worked in local homes, while the boys sometimes helped out on nearby farms. School officials reported that in addition to their schooling, "care is also taken to impress upon the young minds the higher moral and spiritual truths which are so necessary for the pupils' truest welfare. Sunday services, Sunday school, singing practices, morning and evening prayers are conducted regularly, and all the good reading matter we can procure is given to them."

By 1895 Hilton Keith's attitude and his tendency to "work along lines of his own and to act without consulting" the Commissioner's office were creating problems in the Carlton Agency.[61] On his own initiative the agent took extra tolls in lumber if he felt a man had not done his fair share in cutting and sawing the timber at the sawmill. He penalized individuals if he felt they had neglected their farms or livestock,[62] was rigid and often not very diplomatic in his dealings on the reserves, and preferred to dealt directly with individual band members "without the intervention of a Headman." Many people, and particularly those at the Mistawasis Reserve who had almost daily contact with Keith, resented the way they were treated.

Finally, in October of 1895, Mistawasis and his leading men asked to meet with Wadsworth. In his follow-up report the inspector indicated that before closing the meeting, he

> gave the Indians some advice as to their attitude towards the Agent, and it was then and there agreed between the Agent, the Chiefs, and the Indians to be good friends, to let bygones of former disagreements be bygones, and they would start from that day not to lose their temper towards one another.

> I think that it will be deduced from this account of the Indian's [*sic*] grievances that the Agent was treating them, in one sense, too much as children, in not condescending to explain to them their business transactions: his failing to do this left the suspicion in their minds that he was acting dishonestly towards them.

> A little more frankness towards them on his part, will do much to make his relations with them pleasant and tend to the greater prosperity of the Indians, as he cannot be their advisor and director, when they hold antagonistic feelings towards him, for it destroys the influence which he should be able to exert for their advancement.[63]

In a letter to Assistant Indian Commissioner Forget dated February 17, 1896, the agent reacted to Wadsworth's report. He had "taken the greatest pains to explain their business to the Indians and that they have, almost without exception understood these," he stated. "They are not at all the kind of people to be easily deceived in such matters, being naturally over-suspicious."

He then blamed the complaints on one of Mistawasis's headmen who aims at becoming Chief of the Band and is well aware that his selection would not be recommended by the Agent so long as I am in charge here ... As for the rest of the Band, their antagonistic feeling towards me, arise from no want of frankness or even personal kindness on my part but rather from the necessity I have found of attempting to check their laziness and extravagance.[64]

Keith's pre-occupation with butter-making was also causing problems. Almost from the time he arrived in the Carlton Agency, the agent was determined that the women should be milking the cows and making butter. This resulted in a perpetual battle of wills. The women told him they preferred cream to butter. When they did not make butter regularly and in the amounts the agent thought appropriate, he called them lazy. He went even further, saying that the "the laziness of the women, who should give far more attention to butter-making ... has been always a drawback."[65] Even on the Ahtahkakoop Reserve, where a number of women had been making butter for many years, Keith felt the amount being made was too small.[66]

Finally, in order to overcome the problems associated with milking when the calves were running freely, many people—including those on Ahtahkakoop's reserve—started tying them up. This resulted in sickly, poor calves. During his inspection trip of 1895, Wadsworth tried to impress upon Keith that the calves should be allowed to run with their mothers. Keith responded, saying he could not let the calves run with their mothers and still comply with the order to have the cows milked.[67] The agent later said he had been misunderstood and was being accused unjustly: he had only told the people "to milk as many cows as they might do without injuring the stock."[68] Regardless, the calves had not been separated from their mothers and tied up in previous years. And now, all of a sudden, the practice was common on a number of reserves. Wadsworth, in commenting on the situation, said that realistically before milking could be done on any large scale the people needed milking pails and pans, a milk house or dairy, and a calf pasture with access to pure water, shade, and smudges to keep the flies away.[69]

Although it snowed early in the fall of 1895, while Wadsworth was still on the reserve, the winter was not severe. Deer, rabbits, and other animals were numerous throughout the winter, so when the men were not busy hauling hay and tending their stock, they hunted and trapped. Houses continued to be improved, and the ceilings in the farm instructor's house were dressed with lumber. During the last weeks of winter the men, as always, started making preparations for the upcoming construction season by cutting fence rails and timber for boards and shingles. By the time winter was over, 2,000 logs were stacked on the shore of Sandy Lake. When the ducks and geese flew in from the south, they too were plentiful and hunting continued into spring.[70] And so it was a relatively comfortable winter. Many of the farmers had harvested good crops the previous summer, hunting was better than average throughout the winter, a great deal of construction lumber was cut, and the cattle came through the winter in excellent condition.

Still, sickness prevailed. By March of 1896 many people were suffering with coughs, colds, and influenza. Then Charlotte Kāh-kasōw, Kā-miyo-ahcahkwēw, Albert Snake, Pahkwāstihk (Drying Wind, who was also known as James Knife), and several other adults, along with many children, came down with an illness that Keith first suspected to be measles. Later he referred to the ailment as "only fever colds." Sickness and death brought on by scrofula continued to take their toll, with Keith saying that nearly every family in the agency was more or less afflicted. This "dreadful disease, scrofula, so prevalent in the Indian," Hayter Reed wrote in one of his reports as superintendent general of Indian Affairs, "makes him greatly predisposed to pulmonary attacks, and finally carries him to an early grave."[71]

As Hines and so many others had done over the years, Keith also noted that "those who live by hunting and fishing" continued to be healthier than those who lived in houses and farmed. Indians living on reserves often died from diseases fairly healthy white people would easily recover from, Keith stated, adding that the Indians who made their living hunting and who were "much more exposed to the effects of the weather, … manage to rally, even from severe attacks of disease."[72] He made no mention of the sickness and death at the industrial school. And he did not acknowledge that the people who hunted and trapped for a living still followed the traditional ways, eating wild meat and plants and utilizing medicinal herbs and other plants to maintain their health. Keith did, however, suggest that a small hospital with a kitchen was needed since the people who were very sick had "no chance" at home "owing to the noise, heat, and poor nursing."

Eleven people died between March and the end of November 1896. These included seven children under five years of age, two teenagers, a young adult, and one elderly woman. Three had died from influenza, six from consumption, and two from inflammation of the lungs. Among the dead were: Agnes, 1, daughter of Alexander and Betsy Nayneecassum, from influenza; Eliza, 17, daughter of Simon and Martha Apotum, from consumption; Joseph, 4 months, son of John and Ellen Hyman, from inflammation of the lungs; Jessie and Maria Knife, 1, twin daughters of Thomas and Harriet Knife, from influenza; Charlotte, about 70, the mother of Phoebe Kā-miyo-ahcahkwēw (Joseph's wife), from consumption; Josiah, 2, son of James and Jane Knife (Kihci-mōhkomān), from consumption; John, 2, son of Joseph and Elizabeth Piwīyinīs, from consumption; and Abraham, 2, son of Kāh-kāsōw and Charlotte Hyman, from consumption and whooping cough.[73]

In 1896 the government issued a new branding directive for cattle. Previously all animals on the reserve had been marked using the Indian department's brand. Individual farmers were now given the right to brand their privately owned animals with distinctive personal brands. So, early in 1896, the farmers asked the blacksmith at the agency headquarters to forge their brands. Then the cattle on the east side of the lake were rounded up and taken to the corrals on Kā-miyo-astotin's farm to be branded. The remaining animals were taken to a location on the west side.[74]

The people planted 19 more acres of land in the spring of 1896 than in 1895. In other years any increase had gone to enlarge the wheat fields. This year it was different. Government officials, after years of pushing for larger fields of grain, were encouraging the farmers to put more emphasis on root vegetables. In trying to follow this new directive, Ahtahkakoop's people reduced the acreage planted to wheat very slightly from 184 acres the previous year to 179. Root vegetables were sown on 13 acres, an increase of 10 acres, while the potato fields grew from 10 acres to 13 acres. The only other major change was in oats, with 33 acres put into this crop compared to 19 acres in 1895,[75] and there was a field of oats grown for Couture's horses. An additional acre of potatoes was sown for the old people on the reserve and to provide an extra supply of seed potatoes.

Heavy spring rains filled the sloughs, flooded the hay meadows, and nourished the crops during the spring and early summer. By the end of June the hay meadows not covered with water were looking good. An excellent supply of wild fruit was expected, the fields looked "promising," and Keith reported that "the prospects for a good crop is grand, which with the facilities these Indians have over others should place many of them in an independent position."[76]

Despite these optimistic comments, food supplies had run low during the month. In the agent's words, "we had to let many of the Indians go away hunting and digging roots."[77] Other years the people would have decided for themselves when they should look for food. But then, many things had changed after the farm instructor moved onto the reserve.

Indian agent Keith reported in mid-1896 that farmer Couture was "doing very well with 'Ahtahkakoop's' Band who are very good Indians."[78] This apparently did not matter to government officials. In July, 1896, William J. O'Donnell replaced Couture as farm instructor. O'Donnell had been removed from the Edmonton district "in consequence of his drunken habits" after being given a warning that was not heeded. Couture was sent to Edmonton on a straight exchange.[79]

Trouble was not long in erupting. Several weeks after O'Donnell arrived, Nayneecassum and Mōhkomānawēw went to the ration house to get some provisions. Although Nayneecassum had been sick and was weak, O'Donnell refused to help him because he said the man was not working. Mōhkomānawēw had his head down and did not see what happened next, but he heard an oath, and then a blow. Looking up quickly he saw Nayneecassum reeling. The instructor tried to strike Nayneecassum a second time, but missed. Mōhkomānawēw tried to grab O'Donnell by the waist, but he too missed and the instructor ran off.[80]

Nayneecassum's son-in-law, Nātakām (Mac Knife), also witnessed the incident. Nātakām said he had come to the ration house to pick up some flour belonging to another man. His version of the incident was the same as Mōhkomānawēw's, except he actually saw the instructor hit Nayneecassum. Nātakām said Nayneecassum did not strike O'Donnell. He further explained that his father-in-law was a hunter and did not do much farm work. Although strong-looking, he had been sick and was coughing and spitting blood. At the time of the incident, Nayneecassum was supporting his wife and two boys.[81]

O'Donnell's story differed. The farm instructor said he told Nayneecassum and Mōhkomānawēw that he did not have any provisions. Nayneecassum struck him first, so O'Donnell turned and hit him back. Then, according to the instructor, Mōhkomānawēw grabbed him and tried to trip him.[82]

For the time being, the incident ended there. O'Donnell continued to drink and there were a number of reports of drunkenness during the next months. One such incident took place at a threshing on Robert Isbister's farm in the fall of 1896. Several men from the Ahtahkakoop Reserve were among those who witnessed his behaviour,* and there were many other such incidents.[83]

Keith, in the meantime, was having his own problems. The agent continued to deal harshly with people, particularly when he felt they were not working hard enough. He also strictly enforced the government's policy of working for rations. All this resulted in tempestuous dealings.

Other issues implicating Keith and his agency staff were also surfacing. The Indian agent had been seen drunk in the village of Duck Lake, where he used foul language and made a spectacle of himself. He was also drunk at a wedding near the Ahtahkakoop Reserve, as well as on other occasions.[84]

Additionally, Keith was accused of giving a drink of liquor to Ahtahkakoop during a trip to the Battleford Industrial School in 1894. Keith justified his action by saying that the old chief "was tired and starting back on a long trip home." The agent also quoted Ahtahkakoop as saying that "others higher than him in rank had done the same." Kā-miyo-astotin, Kāh-kāsōw, and William Badger from the Mistawasis Reserve all said they were given liquor during the same trip. And there were other stories of Keith drinking and giving liquor to Indian people.[85]

Stories of immorality also circulated. The charges went back as far as 1892—soon after Keith moved to the Carlton Agency—when a women said the agent had given her $5 to have sex with him. The latest reported impropriety took place in the summer of 1896 when another woman complained that the agent had asked her daughter to come to his house and wash dishes. The girl went. She said later that the agent had bargained for sex. Keith denied these and other charges.[86]

The next year a number of formal charges concerning Keith's immorality, drunkenness, and the illegal practice of giving liquor to Indians were laid by the Presbyterian minister on the Mistawasis Reserve, supported by Sandy Lake's missionary James Taylor and T.O. Davis, the local member of parliament. During the investigation that followed, Keith claimed that

---

* It took more than a year but James Taylor, the new missionary at the Sandy Lake Mission, finally laid a complaint against the farm instructor. At the conclusion of the investigation, Acting Commissioner Forget determined that there was sufficient proof of "drunkenness and harsh treatment" to warrant his discharge. He was fired two weeks later. (See document dated December 15, 1897, NA, RG10, vol. 3765, file 32,772. Also see documents dated November 20 and December 29, 1897.)

Davis bore a personal grudge against him and wanted to give the agent's job to someone else. He also blamed Taylor for some of his problems, saying that the missionary had been working against him. The agent thought this was because Taylor "was not permitted to run the District," adding that this would be understood by anyone who knew his record.

In response to complaints made by people in the Mistawasis Band, Keith told the commissioner that "my official reports have shown you that most of the people are lazy, immoral and untrustworthy. These people whom as you are aware, I have had to manage with a firm hand, are always ready to swear to any accusation that might injure me. Yet even so, the better class among them, have refused to listen to Davis's emissaries, and have treated with contempt those who have sworn falsely against me."[87]

Following an investigation by Indian department staff, the commissioner decided that the charges of immorality had not been proven sufficiently, and there had been none of "recent occurrence." He also said that except for giving a drink to Ahtahkakoop, there was little other evidence to support the charge of giving liquor to Indians. Thus he concluded that there was no cause for discipline, other than warning Keith to be careful. No mention was made of his sobriety, or lack of it.[88]

Another member of the Carlton Agency staff was in trouble in 1896. Interpreter Rupert Pratt was arrested for being drunk in public, but when the police realized he was a half-breed and not a treaty Indian he was released without penalty. When this case was investigated by the Department of Indian Affairs, it was decided that a "disciplinary measure" was all that was required.[89]

And so, in a space of just a few years, circumstances for Ahtahkakoop and his people had drastically changed. After Hines left, the people—under Ahtahkakoop's leadership—maintained their reputation as one of the most progressive bands in the North-West while working and living relatively free from outside intervention. Then the government sent a farm instructor into their midst to supervise day-to-day life. This was bad enough for a proud people, many of whom still remembered the days of freedom as warriors, buffalo hunters, and trappers. But the situation was severely aggravated when a farm instructor with a well-known history of drunkenness, a man who did not hesitate to use physical force, was put "in charge" of them. Even the Indian agent was developing a questionable reputation that made him hard to trust, let alone to like. For decades before the Canadian government came on the scene, Ahtahkakoop's successful relationship with the Hudson's Bay Company had been based on co-operation and trust. These two fundamental factors had been the foundation of his dealings with government officials since the signing of Treaty Six in 1876. Even through the times of frustration and hardship, Ahtahkakoop believed that by working together good times would eventually come for his band. Now, in some respects, the foundation was being threatened as the government tightened its reins on the Indian people.

Other changes far beyond the Carlton Agency would soon have direct repercussions on the Indian people of the North-West Territories. On June 23, 1896, the Conservative government in Ottawa was defeated by the Liberals. Wilfrid Laurier became the new prime minister and Clifford Sifton was appointed superintendent general of Indian Affairs. Then, during the next year, Hayter Reed was fired from his position as deputy superintendent general of Indian Affairs and replaced by James A. Smart.

Outwardly Ahtahkakoop's people seemed little affected by these events over which they had no control. In the spring of 1896, like every other spring since settling at Sandy Lake, most families cleaned their houses before closing them and moving into tipis and tents.[90] As soon as the fields were dry they planted 250 acres of land, an increase of 19 acres over the previous year.[91] During the summer new houses were erected and older homes improved.

Some of the new buildings were small cabins built by young men just beginning to farm. The other new dwellings—those built by established farmers—generally had an upstairs and in some cases the lower floor was divided into partitioned rooms. "These Indians," agent Keith reported in 1896, "are very comfortably housed far more so than the settlers around about." He also felt that when the tools and implements the farmers had bought with their own earnings were combined with those supplied by the government, "they are fairly well supplied with implements and tools."[92] These "earnings" came from the sale of cattle, freighting, trapping, and occasionally working for nearby settlers. Additionally, some years surplus grain was sold with the permission of the agent.

By the end of June the herd of cattle, which was held by 39 families, numbered 348 and consisted of five bulls, 57 oxen, 117 cows, 60 steers, 34 heifers, 36 bull calves, and 39 heifer calves. Since the people were now permitted to dispose of some of their cattle, 55 animals had been killed for beef and four steers had been sold since June, 1894. During this same period, five heifers, two heifer calves, one steer, and one cow had died from various causes and one cow, two heifers, and a bull calf had drowned. In 1896, 26 head of cattle and 42 horses were privately owned and there was one band horse. The stock was in "the best of condition," inspector McGibbon reported when he visited the reserve late in July, and the production of calves had been excellent, with 75 calves from 81 cows.[93] He added that the families were farming on individual land holdings, with 349 acres in the hands of the 39 families who had livestock. The fences, corrals, houses, stables and other outbuildings were well constructed and maintained, and most of the gardens were weeded and neat.

Ahtahkakoop and his wife, Mary Nātowēw, were still living with Kā-miyo-astotin when McGibbon arrived for his inspection in 1896. Eighty years old, Ahtahkakoop no longer worked in the fields. He nevertheless set a good example by looking after the garden for his son and, much to the pleasure of government officials, had planted the turnips in drills instead of broadcasting them. The turnips, along with the onions and carrots, were doing well.[94]

Like others on the reserve, Kā-miyo-astotin was continuing to improve his property. This year's project was a lean-to attached to the house. His four-acre field of wheat was the same size as the previous year. He had also planted seven acres of oats and 1½ acres in potatoes and garden vegetables. It is a "fine place," McGibbon said, with a "good house and stables and a new corral where cattle were branded."

"A large quantity of berries were on sheets drying for the winter" when McGibbon stopped at the house, and "a large pot filled with new potatoes and part of a badger was on the outside preparing for the midday meal." The inspector also noted that "butter is made. This is a thrifty comfortable looking place."

The government official visited all the families on the reserve and reported on the number of acres sown and other things he thought worthy of special mention. For instance, Baptiste Ahenakew had a "nice field of about 8 acres of wheat and barley and one acre of garden, all looking well." His brother Kāh-kāsōw had planted wheat on nine acres, in addition to 1½ acres of oats, two of barley, and one of garden vegetables.[95] Jacob Mususkapoe had planted about nine acres in wheat and oats, plus a large garden, and he had collected logs for a new house and sawed boards for his stable roof. Mēmēkwaniwēw, Jacob's brother, had four acres of good wheat, an acre in root vegetables, and well-built fences. Headman

Kā-miyo-ahcahkwēw had a good house and six acres of wheat, while his younger brother Michel was breaking more land and summer-fallowing along the slope. Sasakamoose's son, Alexander, had planted five acres of wheat and one-quarter acre of turnips. Albert Snake had seven acres in wheat, while Peekeekoot had a new house with a shingled roof, four acres of wheat and half an acre of garden vegetables. Peter George Knife (Kihci-mōhkomān) was building a new house and had three acres sown in wheat and one-quarter of an acre in garden vegetables.

Wāsēhikot had a particularly good farmstead, described thus by McGibbon:

> Good new house, shingled roof, gables also shingled, up stairs rooms, and all very clean. Summer kitchen, cook stove, work shop, 3 good stables and a large corral. Two good gardens and a field of 6 acres wheat and 3 of oats, all looking well, good fences, a nice place, milk house, calf pasture. There were 14 pails of milk on the shelves. Has poultry. No open chimney in house. Smudges for the cattle.

Greyeyes's place was "prosperous looking" with a nice house with a lean-to kitchen, storehouse and granary, with planted fields consisting of about 10 acres of wheat, three of oats, 1½ acres of potatoes, as well as turnips and garden vegetables. He also had five new tipis.[96]

At the mission by the lake, the buildings had been improved since McGibbon was last on the reserve, although still not painted. James Taylor had built a new fence that enclosed a "garden which formerly was full of weeds" but was now, according to the inspector, "one of the best to be seen." A panel fence had been built around the church property. Louis Ahenakew had the school in "fair condition, clean and reasonably well furnished."[97] There was one new addition, a bell that had been recently presented to the mission by Clarence C. Chipman, trade commissioner of the Hudson's Bay Company.[98] The 160 acres of land set aside by Hines for the mission was still not part of the reserve. Archdeacon Mackay explained that the land had been surveyed and allotted for use by the mission when the first survey was done, with title being held by occupation before the reserve was surveyed.[99]

McGibbon summarized his inspection, saying that "I never went over a reserve where there was more uniformity in the way fields and gardens were kept, not one good here and there, but all were good." Then the inspector added for public record, "They are a nice lot of people, and are sure to continue to get along well under the active management of Mr. O'Donnell whose long experience peculiarly fits him to deal with a reserve like this." As much as the inspector's compliments may have pleased him, Ahtahkakoop would have been troubled by McGibbon's last comment had he known about it, for it was common knowledge that O'Donnell had a drinking problem.

Ahtahkakoop was proud that the school established by John Hines was now being run by one of its first students. According to McGibbon, Louis Ahenakew was "doing capital work." The students were "clean, fairly well dressed and answered questions intelligently [and] appeared to be well provided with books, slates, etc." Twenty of the 23 school-age children on the reserve were enrolled at the school in 1896, with two more students on the register the following year.[100] Two-thirds of the students in 1896 were in Standard I.

Fewer students than usual, two boys and three girls, were attending the Battleford Industrial School These students were Charles Nayneecassum, Jeremia Apotum, Agnes Pīwiyinīs, Phoebe Kāh-kāsōw, and Marie Cardinal. Ahtahkakoop's grandson, 20-year-old Albert Kā-miyo-ahcahk-wēw, had completed his training at the Battleford school and was now enrolled in the teacher program at Emmanuel College.[101] Annie Stranger had completed five years at the school and been discharged, along with Sasakamoose's granddaughter Louisa. Alexander Nayneecassum was discharged after finishing four years, had his own treaty number, and was farming on the reserve.* Charles Cahkāpēw, Joseph MacKay, and William Wāsēhikot were on sick leave when the treaty payments were made in October.† Charles Cahkāpēw, 20, and Joseph MacKay,‡ 17, were both dead from consumption by the end of 1896. Joseph Ahtahkakoop's sons, John Robert and Joseph,§ were still attending the boarding school at Emmanuel College, where they were joined by Baptiste Ahenakew's 11-year-old son Edward.[102]

---

* Alexander Nayneecassum died during the 1897–98 paylist year.

† Although William returned to school in 1897, he died in 1899 at the age of 22.

‡ Joseph Mackay was the adopted son of K-ōsihkosiwanāniw and his wife Chenesis.

§ Joseph Starblanket, died in 1902 at the age of 18.

Faced with government restrictions and the combined efforts of government officials and missionaries to destroy their culture, many Indian people returned to their traditional beliefs for strength and comfort during the mid-1890s. Attendance at Give Away Dances and other sacred ceremonies grew and increasing numbers of Sun Dances were reported. Still determined to put an end to the ceremonies, but with only limited authority to do so, the Canadian government amended Section 114 of the Indian Act in 1894 to enable the police to arrest and remove visitors from a reserve as trespassers. The following year the government went one step further and passed an amendment stating that:

> Every Indian or other person who engages in, or assists in celebrating or encourages either directly or indirectly another to celebrate, any Indian festival, dance or other ceremony of which the giving away or paying or giving back of money, goods or articles of any sort forms a part, or is a feature, whether such gift of money, goods or articles takes place before, at, or after the celebration of the same, and every Indian or other person who engages or assists in any celebration or dance of which the wounding or mutilation of the dead or living body of any human being or animal forms a part or is a feature, is guilty of an indictable offence and is liable to imprisonment for a term not exceeding six months and less than two months; but nothing in this section shall be construed to prevent the holding of any agricultural show or exhibition or the giving of prizes for exhibits thereat.[103]

Under this legislation, Give Away Dances were illegal because they involved the giving of gifts such as clothing and food. The Sun Dance, the ceremony that received the most publicity because it was open to observers, did not fall under Section 114 providing there was no piercing or mutilation of the body.

In 1895 the newly amended act was used to stop a Sun Dance in progress in the Touchwood Hills Agency and to subsequently arrest a man by the name of Matoose for "inciting the Indians to commit a breach of peace." When Matoose appeared before a justice of the peace he was "bound over to keep the peace for three months, and to find a surety of $200 and failing that to remain in custody until such time as the agent saw fit." He was jailed for five days and then released "on instructions from the agent."[104] The following year Kah-pee-cha-pees from the Qu'Appelle area

Medicine Hat Museum and Art Gallery

In spite of government opposition, the Cree in the Battleford area held a Sun Dance in June, 1895. The Sun Dance lodge can be seen on the left side of the photograph above. The photograph below shows the singers with their drums and some of the Sun Dance participants. The man in the chief's jacket, who has a treaty medal hanging around his neck, is Chief Thunderchild.

RCMP Museum, Regina

was sentenced to two months of hard labour for sponsoring a Sun Dance.[105] In both cases Reed and Forget expressed concern over the actions of over-zealous agents. Reed consequently warned the agents to be careful about the methods they used to prevent the dances.[106] Meanwhile, the traditional ceremonies at Whitefish, Pelican and Sturgeon lakes drew less attention from government officials than those being held in areas closer to agency headquarters and police detachments. It was easier to ignore these ceremonies than try to stop them, so they flourished.

In addition to using legislation to stop traditional ceremonies, government officials took a longer view and turned to the residential schools to rally against all aspects of "Indianism."[107] The mechanism was already in place, for in 1894 the Indian Act had been amended to give justices of the peace and Indian agents the power to commit "children of Indian blood under the age of sixteen years, to such industrial school or boarding school, there to be kept, cared for and educated for a period not extending beyond the time at which such children shall reach the age of eighteen years." Truant children could be arrested and returned to school, and there were provisions for fines or imprisonment, or both, for parents and guardians who refused to have their children attend school.[108]

Reed explained further in his annual report for 1895–96 that

> the policy of the department, as to the retention of pupils, has been that boys should remain at the industrial-schools until they attain an age at which, in addition to their having obtained a rudimentary education and some trade or calling, or at least some knowledge of carpentry, their characters shall have been sufficiently formed as to ensure as much as possible against their returning to the uncivilized mode of life.[109]

As a result of this policy a large number of children spent most of their childhood years at residential boarding schools. There they learned skills and trades that would be helpful in daily life after they left the schools. But to accomplish this, boys and girls were separated from their parents at an ever-decreasing age, with assimilation being firmly entrenched as an objective of the educational system.[110] Infrequent visits home meant that many children grew up barely knowing their parents, grandparents, and relatives. Not only were the children separated from their families, they were separated from their culture. They did not grow up listening in the traditional way to stories about their proud heritage and the achievements of their friends and relatives.

Saskatchewan Archives Board, R-A8223-1   Saskatchewan Archives Board, R-A8223-2

Thomas Moore, as photographed in a traditional outfit and a school uniform following his admittance to the Regina Industrial School in 1896. These photographs were published in the Canadian House of Commons Sessional Papers *(1897, no. 11).*

There were no old men and women to teach about the sacred ways. They did not hear the many stories of *wīsahkēcāhk* and the teachings of the elders, they were not allowed to speak Cree, and they lost their language. Equally devastating, the boys and girls did not learn to respect animals, birds, fish, plants, and all other living things. The boys were not taught how to hunt and trap by their fathers and male relatives. The girls did not learn how to identify, collect, and prepare herbs, medicines, and edible plants, or how to prepare soft fur and hides, snare animals and birds, or how to dry meat. Moreover, the girls and the boys did not learn how to raise the children they would one day have from watching their parents and relatives.

At Sandy Lake the instability of the mission during the early 1890s and increasing government pressures and restrictions took their toll. Christianity had not lived up to the expectations of many people living on the Ahtahkakoop Reserve. And even though government officials continued to praise their efforts and their successes, too many people were sick and dying and too many families were hungry. Men, women, and young people started listening to an inner voice that called them back to their traditional ways. Many of them responded by participating in the ceremonies and dances still being held at Whitefish, Pelican, and Sturgeon lakes. Perhaps by honouring *pāhkahkos*, the spirit of famine, at a Give Away Dance they would be blessed with luck and prosperity. And perhaps, through the Sun Dance, the Prairie Chicken Dance (Little Bear Feast), and other sacred ceremonies they would be blessed with good health and old age with lots of great-grandchildren. Peter George Knife, 21-year-old son of Kihci-mōhkomān, was one of those seeking to renew his cultural roots by participating in ceremonies at nearby reserves, and soon he would be hosting a Sun Dance at Whitefish Lake.[111]

James Taylor, the missionary at the Sandy Lake Mission, confirmed that "giving-away" dances were held frequently on nearby reserves during the winter of 1895–96. He also reported that baptized Indians as well as "heathens" left the reserve at Sandy Lake to attend.[112] Participation in the dances was further verified in February, 1896, when the Reverend Winter was told during a visit to the Ahtahkakoop Reserve that some people "had relapsed or at any rate joined in the dances." According to this missionary, one of Ahtahkakoop's sons was "the ring leader."[113]

Several months later, in June, Winter noted that the "chief councillor" was among those from Ahtahkakoop's band who attended Sturgeon Lake's "heathen spring dance." Urged by his wife, Winter erected a tent at the sacred Sun Dance "encampment" and then made "every effort" to get a large congregation at a Christian service that was held while the dance was in progress. Thirty-one people came, including "Sandy Lake and other so called Christians." Ahtahkakoop's "chief councillor" was among those present. Reminiscent of Hines ringing the church bell when freighters left the Ahtahkakoop Reserve on a Sunday without attending church services, Winter said he "spoke loudly" during the service so the "heathens" could hear. In the background, the drums and singing continued.[114]

Many of the people obviously felt comfortable being Christians and still taking part in the traditional ceremonies. So, when confronted by Winter, they told him that the "heathen acknowledges the same God as the Christians."[115] In their own way, they were reconciling Christianity with their traditional faith.

John Hines, who was still in England, heard about the "relapses" and

Illustration by Ed Peekeekoot

Increasingly, people on Ahtahkakoop's reserve came to believe that they could be Christians and still take part in some of the traditional ceremonies. Gambling games, such as the hand game shown here, were also becoming more popular.

wrote Louis Ahenakew to find out what was happening. The teacher responded, saying that "in regards to the seed you sowed in this Reserve some of it is flourishing and some choked by thorns."[116]

Ahtahkakoop, nevertheless, still believed that conversion to Christianity had been a necessary step in forging a new way of life for his children and his grandchildren. He had made the decision to convert to Christianity after considerable thought, saying that "he was a man that did nothing in a hurry, consequently he very rarely had to regret his actions."[117] Following his baptism according to the rites of the Church of England on May 20, 1877, the chief became a strong supporter of the mission despite opposition from his wife and at least one of his sons. He had encouraged the children to get an education, he served as a lay delegate to the synod of the Diocese of Saskatchewan, and he was elected by that body to the Provincial Synod. Not surprisingly, at a synod meeting in Prince Albert on June 17, 1896, Ahtahkakoop expressed his "deep regret that so many Indians have joined in the heathen dances that are conducted around the reserves." Before sitting down, "the aged chief" thanked the synod for passing a "resolution asking the Indian Department to place the children of non-treaty Indians on the same footing in our Boarding and Industrial Schools as the children of treaty Indians."[118]

Ahtahkakoop apparently did not discuss the renewed interest in the dances and ceremonies with McGibbon when the inspector visited the reserve a month later. He did, however, tell the inspector that some of the younger men "are disposed to do a little more gambling than he would like." Instructor O'Donnell, the inspector reported to his superiors, "will endeavour to stop this in so far as he is able to do so."[119]

When Ahtahkakoop embarked his band on the journey to find a way for their children and grandchildren to survive in a world without buffalo, it is unlikely he realized the pitfalls and the frustrations that lay ahead. His people had faced these challenges and forged on. Births were finally outnumbering deaths and new families were moving to the reserve. As a result, by the mid-1890s Ahtahkakoop's band had become the largest in the Carlton Agency and the only one in the agency showing a steady increase.[120] In 1896 the treaty paylist showed a population of 48 men, 56 women, 54 boys, 51 girls, five male relatives, and five female relatives, for a total of 219.[121] The adults had acquired the skills and knowledge required to live by mixed farming, held back mainly by restrictions imposed by external forces, and many had learned to read and write syllabics. The young men still hunted and trapped when they were not busy at farm work, and some earned extra money by freighting and sometimes working for white neighbours. Men and women—youngsters when the treaties were signed—were raising families of their own and sending their children to school. The students were learning to read, write, and speak English, and some were mastering trades to equip them to live in white communities.

Now, after years of leading their people along the path to a new life, Ahtahkakoop and his brother Sasakamoose were gradually stepping aside. Ahtahkakoop's eldest son, 59-year-old Kā-miyo-ahcahkwēw, was a headman when Treaty Six was signed in 1876 and he still held that position 20 years later. Kāh-kāsōw, 50, was elected to the position of headman in 1887, and he—along with Kā-miyo-ahcahkwēw—had long supported the church and both had worked hard to promote the reserve, mission, and school.* Sasakamoose's son Joseph had his teaching career ended by death while he was still very young, but Louis Ahenakew, 32, was carrying on in a fashion that would have made his father very proud had he still been alive.

However, it was Ahtahkakoop's son Kā-miyo-astotin, 44, later known as Basil Starblanket, who was gradually assuming the leadership of the reserve. His farm and house were among the best on the reserve, one of the first Galloway bulls had been put in his care, and when the system of individual brands was introduced, his corrals were used to brand the cattle east of the river. He had also "supertended" the construction of a "very good bridge" over the Asissipi River when the water became too deep to ford. The work was undertaken and completed in July, 1896, during the days between Couture's departure and O'Donnell's arrival, days when there was no government official on the reserve. McGibbon saw the bridge within days after it was completed and declared that "a good job they made of it."[122]

By August of 1896 Mistawasis, Ahtahkakoop's friend and colleague, was dead. Together the two men had guided their people though the difficult transition from buffalo hunter to farmer. Ahtahkakoop had envisioned a new world for the children and grandchildren of his people. Now this was being extended even further, as a new generation of great-grandchildren came into this world. Ahtahkakoop may have been disappointed,

---

* Kā-miyo-ahcahkwēw's Christian name was Antoine. Kāh-kāsōw, the son of Ahtahkakoop's brother Ahenakew, took Peter as his Christian name when he was baptized.

and perhaps discouraged, when some of his people started looking towards the old traditional ways for renewed spiritual growth. They had learned the white man's ways in order to survive. Now many of them wanted to start a new journey, one leading towards their cultural identity, believing that they could live in two worlds. For others, Christianity and the white man's learning had given them what they wanted, and they searched no longer.[123]

Ahtahkakoop was both a visionary and a realist. A noted buffalo hunter and warrior, Ahtahkakoop had been blessed with special spiritual powers. He had been a member of the *mitēwiwin*. He was a respected chief, and a man known for his intelligence and reasoned

Saskatchewan Archives Board, Based on S-B6136
Chief Ahtahkakoop, August 6, 1891.

mind. Faced with the final destruction of the buffalo and relentless waves of newcomers to the land he shared with the other Plains people, Ahtahkakoop took the steps he believed necessary for the survival of his people.

On December 4, 1896, Chief Ahtahkakoop was walking down a hill with his grandson Pacī (James Starblanket) to attend a feast. He fell, apparently stricken with a heart attack. Pacī ran down the hill for help but it was too late. The old chief was dead, his journey complete. He was said to be about 80 years of age.

A government official ordered black crepe for the inner walls of the church and black carpet for the aisle and the pathway to the gate. Ahtahkakoop was buried in St. Mark's cemetery three days after his death, on December 7, 1896.

Epilogue

The last quarter of the 19th century was an extremely difficult time to be a chief. Only a few years earlier buffalo had roamed the plains and parklands in herds so large that they blackened the ground as far as the eye could see. These animals had given Ahtahkakoop's people, and those who came before them, most of what they needed to survive. Then, almost overnight, the buffalo were gone. Treaties were signed and newcomers arrived in escalating numbers each year. The old life was gone forever.

Realizing that his children and grandchildren would have to adopt a new way of living if they were to survive, Ahtahkakoop asked John Hines to live with them, educate the children, and teach their parents how to farm. Confronted with numerous obstacles, disappointments, and heartbreak, the people persevered in their struggle to create a life without buffalo. What an incredible amount of patience, trust, and belief in a new life Ahtahkakoop must have had to guide his people along their journey!

Within a space of 21 years, Ahtahkakoop and his people had achieved the almost impossible. Men who had been buffalo hunters and warriors now planted crops, cut hay, and tended livestock, only occasionally hunting and trapping game and fur-bearing animals.

Woman who had prepared the harvest from the buffalo—the meat, the hides, and the many side-products—helped in the fields, weeded the gardens, and made butter. Young men and women who still remembered the days of freedom on the plains could read and write, and most of the people had converted to Christianity, exchanging their traditional beliefs for a new religion. As for the younger children, Ahtahkakoop's grandchildren and great-grandchildren, the new way of life was all they knew. The old way of life existed only in the stories and memories of their mothers and fathers, aunts and uncles, grandparents, and the old people. Ahtahkakoop's people, with the encouragement and help of John Hines, had learned how to survive in the world forced upon them by the disappearance of the buffalo and the onslaught of newcomers.

During the 1890s, Canadian government policy became increasingly oppressive. Some of Ahtahkakoop's people, including one of the chief's sons and a headman, began attending traditional sacred ceremonies on other reserves. Perhaps it was a way of saying that they were willing to learn a new way of life, but they did not want to abandon the age-old traditions of their people. Soon the traditional beliefs would be forced underground by government officials.

Regardless, with wisdom and foresight Ahtahkakoop had laid the foundation upon which future generations could build. The chief believed his people could succeed in adopting a new life. His faith and trust were well-founded. Kā-miyo-astotin took over as chief after his father died and he served in that capacity until his own death. Ahtahkakoop's nephew, Louis Ahenakew, became a qualified teacher. A great-nephew, Edward Ahenakew, was ordained priest in the Church of England and in time was made a canon. In addition to his church work, Edward also served as the western Canadian president of the League of Indians of Canada, and he was the author of *Voices of the Plains Cree* and other works. Another great-nephew, Andrew Ahenakew (Edward's cousin), served as Archdeacon of Saskatchewan. And Allan Ahenakew, one of Louis's sons, served as chief of the Ahtahkakoop Band for much of his adult life.

Band members from the next generations continued to excel in areas such as education, farming, Indian politics, professional hockey, policing, and social work.

"Let us not think of ourselves but of our children's children," Ahtahkakoop had told the leading men at the Treaty Six negotiations. "Let us show our wisdom by choosing the right path now while we yet have a choice." The choice to survive with dignity was made. Ahtahkakoop's people, through determination and hard work, made the transition from buffalo hunter and warrior to agriculturist, and from traditional spirituality to Christianity.

One of Ahtahkakoop's visions became reality in 1994 when the first high school on the Ahtahkakoop Reserve was officially opened. A Hall of Achievement recognizing the accomplishments of band members has been incorporated into the building. Ahtahkakoop's legacy continues. Now, as then, the children are the future.

Chief Barry L. Ahenakew
Ahtahkakoop Cree Nation

Ray Christensen

Ribbon cutting ceremony to officially open the Ahtahkakoop High School, September 15, 1994.

Ray Christensen

The new Ahtahkakoop High School features a mosaic of Chief Ahtahkakoop. Part of the elementary school can be seen on the left.

A wall mural on the high school commemorates the wisdom of Chief Ahtahkakoop.

A buffalo herd has been re-established on the reserve but now education—not the buffalo—is the means of survival.

Appendix A:
The Treaty at Forts Carlton and Pitt,
Number Six*

ARTICLES OF A TREATY made and concluded near Carlton, on the twenty-third day of August, and on the twenty-eighth day of said month, respectively, and near Fort Pitt on the ninth day of September, in the year of Our Lord one thousand eight hundred and seventy-six, between Her Most Gracious Majesty the Queen of Great Britain and Ireland, by her Commissioners, the Honourable Alexander Morris, Lieutenant-Governor of the Province of Manitoba and the North-West Territories, and the Honourable James McKay and the Honourable William Joseph Christie, of the one part; and the Plain and the Wood Cree Tribes of Indians, and the other Tribes of Indians, inhabitants of the country within the limits hereinafter defined and described, by their Chiefs, chosen and named as hereinafter mentioned, of the other part.

WHEREAS the Indians inhabiting the said country, have, pursuant to an appointment made by the said Commissioners, been convened at meetings at Fort Carlton, Fort Pitt and Battle River, to deliberate upon certain matters of interest to Her Most Gracious Majesty, of the one part, and the said Indians of the other;

And whereas the said Indians have been notified and informed by Her Majesty's said Commissioners that it is the desire of Her Majesty to open up for settlement, immigration and such other purposes as to her Majesty may seem meet, a tract of country, bounded and described as hereinafter mentioned, and to obtain the consent thereto of her Indian subjects inhabiting the said tract, and to make a treaty and arrange with them, so that there may be peace and good will between them and Her Majesty, and that they may know and be assured of what allowance they are to count upon and receive from her Majesty's bounty and benevolence;

---

* As quoted in Morris, *The Treaties of Canada With the Indians*, 351-57.

And whereas the Indians of the said tract, duly convened in Council as aforesaid, and being requested by Her Majesty's Commissioners to name certain Chiefs and head men, who should be authorized, on their behalf, to conduct such negotiations and sign any treaty to be founded thereon, and to become responsible to Her Majesty for the faithful performance by their respective bands of such obligations as shall be assumed by them, the said Indians have thereupon named for that purpose, that is to say:—representing the Indians who make the treaty at Carlton, the several Chiefs and Councillors who have subscribed hereto, and representing the Indians who make the treaty at Fort Pitt, the several Chiefs and Councillors who have subscribed hereto;

And thereupon, in open council, the different bands having presented their Chiefs to the said Commissioners as the Chiefs and head men, for the purposes aforesaid, of the respective bands of Indians inhabiting the district hereinafter described;

And whereas the said Commissioners then and there received and acknowledged the persons so represented, as Chiefs and head men, for the purposes aforesaid, of the respective bands of Indians inhabiting the said district hereinafter described;

And whereas the said Commissioners have proceeded to negotiate a treaty with the said Indians, and the same has been finally agreed upon and concluded as follows, that is to say:—

The Plain and Wood Cree Tribes of Indians, and all the other Indians inhabiting the district hereinafter described and defined, do hereby cede, release, surrender and yield up to the Government of the Dominion of Canada for Her Majesty the Queen and her successors forever, all their rights, titles and privileges whatsoever, to the lands included within the following limits, that is to say:—

Commencing at the mouth of the river emptying into the north-west angle of Cumberland Lake, thence westerly up the said river to the source, thence on a straight line in a westerly direction to the head of Green Lake, thence northerly to the elbow in the Beaver River, thence down the said river northerly to a point twenty miles from the said elbow; thence in a westerly direction, keeping on a line generally parallel with the said Beaver River (above the elbow), and about twenty miles distance therefrom, to the source of the said river; thence northerly to the north-easterly point of the south shore of Red Deer Lake, continuing westerly along the said shore to the western limit thereof, and thence due west to the Athabaska River, thence up the said river, against the stream, to the Jasper House, in the Rocky Mountains; thence on a course south-eastwardly, following the easterly range of the Mountains, to the source of the main branch of the Red Deer River; thence down the said river, with the stream, to the junction therewith of the outlet of the river, being the outlet of the Buffalo Lake; thence due east twenty miles; thence on a straight line south-eastwardly to the mouth of the said Red Deer River on the South Branch of the Saskatchewan River; thence eastwardly and northwardly, following on the boundaries of the tracts conceded by the several Treaties numbered Four and Five, to the place of beginning;

And also all their rights, titles and privileges whatsoever, to all other lands, wherever situated, in the North-West Territories, or in any other Province or portion of Her Majesty's Dominions, situated and being within the Dominion of Canada;

The tract comprised within the lines above described, embracing an area of one hundred and twenty-one thousand square miles, be the same more or less;

To have and to hold the same to Her Majesty the Queen and her successors forever;

And Her Majesty the Queen hereby agrees and undertakes to lay aside reserves for farming lands, due respect being had to lands at present cultivated by the said Indians, and other reserves for the benefit of the said Indians, to be administered and dealt with for them by Her Majesty's Government of the Dominion of Canada, provided all such reserves shall not exceed in all one square mile for each family of five, or in that proportion for larger or smaller families, in manner following, that is to say;

That the Chief Superintendent of Indian Affairs shall depute and send a suitable person to determine and set apart the reserves for each Band, after consulting with the Indians thereof as to the locality which may be found to be most suitable for them;

Provided, however, that Her Majesty reserves the right to deal with any settlers within the bounds of any lands reserved for any Band as she shall deem fit, and also that the aforesaid reserves of land or any interest therein may be sold or otherwise disposed of by Her Majesty's Government for the use and benefit of the said Indians entitled thereto, with the consent first had and obtained; and with a view to show the satisfaction of Her Majesty with the behaviour and good conduct of her Indians, she hereby, through her Commissioners, makes them a present of twelve dollars for each man, woman and child belonging to the bands here represented, in extinguishment of all claims heretofore preferred;

And further, Her Majesty agrees to maintain schools for instruction in such reserves hereby made, as to her Government of the Dominion of Canada may seem advisable, whenever the Indians of the reserve shall desire it;

Her Majesty further agrees with her said Indians that within the boundary of Indian reserves, until otherwise determined by her Government of the Dominion of Canada, no intoxicating liquor shall be allowed to be introduced or sold, and all laws now in force or hereafter to be enacted to preserve her Indian subjects inhabiting the reserves or living elsewhere within her North-West Territories from the evil influence of the use of intoxicating liquors, shall be strictly enforced;

Her Majesty further agrees with her said Indians that they, the said Indians, shall have right to pursue their avocations of hunting and fishing throughout the tract surrendered as hereinbefore described, subject to such regulations as may from time to time be made by her Government of her Dominion of Canada, and saving and excepting such tracts as may from time to time be required or taken up for settlement, mining, lumbering or other purposes by her said Government of the Dominion of Canada, or by any of the subjects thereof, duly authorized therefor, by the said Government;

It is further agreed between Her Majesty and Her said Indians, that such sections of the reserves above indicated as may at any time be required for public works or buildings of what nature soever, may be appropriated for that purpose by Her Majesty's Government of the Dominion of Canada, due compensation being made for the value of any improvement thereon;

And, further, that Her Majesty's Commissioners shall, as soon as possible, after the execution of this treaty, cause to be taken, an accurate census of all the Indians inhabiting the tract above described, distributing them in families, and shall in every year ensuing the date hereof, at some period in each year, to be duly notified to the Indians, and at a place or places to be appointed for that purpose, within the territories ceded, pay to each Indian person the sum of five dollars per head yearly;

It is further agreed between Her Majesty and the said Indians that the sum of fifteen hundred dollars per annum, shall be yearly and every year expended by Her Majesty in the purchase of ammunition and twine for nets for the use of the said Indians, in manner following, that is to say:—In the reasonable discretion as regards the distribution thereof, among the Indians inhabiting the several reserves, or otherwise included herein, of Her Majesty's Indian Agent having the supervision of this treaty;

It is further agreed between Her Majesty and the said Indians that the following articles shall be supplied to any Band of the said Indians who are now cultivating the soil, or who shall hereafter commence to cultivate the land, that is to say:—Four hoes for every family actually cultivating, also two spades per family as aforesaid; one plough for every three families as aforesaid, one harrow for every three families as aforesaid; two scythes, and one whetstone and two hayforks and two reaping-hooks for every family as aforesaid; and also two axes, and also one cross-cut saw, and also one hand-saw, one pit-saw, the necessary files, one grindstone and one auger for each band; and also for each Chief, for the use of his band, one chest of ordinary carpenter's tools; also for each band, enough of wheat, barley, potatoes and oats to plant the land actually broken up for cultivation by such band; also for each band, four oxen, one bull and six cows, also one boar and two sows, and one handmill when any band shall raise sufficient grain therefor. All the aforesaid articles to be given *once for all* for the encouragement of the practice of agriculture among the Indians;

It is further agreed between Her Majesty and the said Indians, that each Chief, duly recognized as such, shall receive an annual salary of twenty-five dollars per annum; and each subordinate officer, not exceeding four for each band, shall receive fifteen dollars per annum; and each such Chief and subordinate officer as aforesaid, shall also receive, once every three years, a suitable suit of clothing, and each Chief shall receive, in recognition of the closing of the treaty, a suitable flag and medal, and also, as soon as convenient, one horse, harness and waggon;

That in the event hereafter of the Indians comprised within this treaty being overtaken by any pestilence, or by a general famine, the Queen, on being satisfied and certified thereof by her Indian Agent or Agents, will grant to the Indians assistance of such character and to such extent as her Chief Superintendent of Indian Affairs shall deem necessary and sufficient to relieve the Indians from the calamity that shall have befallen them;

That during the next three years, after two or more of the reserves hereby agreed to be set apart to the Indians, shall have been agreed upon and surveyed, there shall be granted to the Indians included under the Chiefs adhering to the treaty at Carlton, each spring, the sum of one thousand dollars to be expended for them by Her Majesty's Indian Agents, in the purchase of provisions for the use of such of the band as are actually settled on the reserves and are engaged in cultivating the soil, to assist them in such cultivation;

That a medicine chest shall be kept at the house of each Indian Agent for the use and benefit of the Indians, at the discretion of such Agent;

That with regard to the Indians included under the Chiefs adhering to the treaty at Fort Pitt, and to those under Chiefs within the treaty limits who may hereafter give their adhesion hereto (exclusively, however, of the Indians of the Carlton Region) there shall, during three years, after two or more reserves shall have been agreed upon and surveyed, be distributed each spring among the bands cultivating the soil on such reserves, by Her Majesty's Chief Indian Agent for this treaty in his discretion, a sum not exceeding one thousand dollars, in the purchase of provisions for the use of such members of the band as are actually settled on the reserves and engaged in the cultivation of the soil, to assist and encourage them in such cultivation;

That, in lieu of waggons, if they desire it, and declare their option to that effect, there shall be given to each of the Chiefs adhering hereto, at Fort Pitt or elsewhere hereafter (exclusively of those in the Carlton District) in recognition of this treaty, so soon as the same can be conveniently transported, two carts, with iron bushings and tires;

And the undersigned Chiefs, on their behalf, and on behalf of all other Indians inhabiting the tract within ceded, do hereby solemnly promise and engage to strictly observe this treaty, and also to conduct and behave themselves as good and loyal subjects of Her Majesty the Queen;

They promise and engage that they will in all respects obey and abide by the law, and they will maintain peace and good order between each other, and also between themselves and other tribes of Indians, and between themselves and others of Her Majesty's subjects, whether Indians or Whites, now inhabiting or hereafter to inhabit any part of the said ceded tracts, and that they will not molest the person or property of any inhabitant of such ceded tracts, or the property of Her Majesty the Queen, or interfere with or trouble any person passing or travelling through the said tracts or any part thereof; and that they will aid and assist the officers of Her Majesty in bringing to justice and punishment any Indian offending against the stipulations of this treaty, or infringing the laws in force in the country so ceded.

IN WITNESS WHEREOF, Her Majesty's said Commissioners and the said Indian Chiefs have hereunto subscribed and set their hands, at or near Fort Carlton, on the day and year aforesaid, and near Fort Pitt on the day above aforesaid.

(Signed) ALEXANDER MORRIS,
Lieut.-Governor, N.-W.T.

JAMES McKAY,
W.J.CHRISTIE,
    Indian Commissioners.
MIST-OW-AS-IS,   His x mark
AH-TUK-UK-KOOP,   "x"
    Head Chiefs of the Carlton Indians
PEE-YAHN-KAH-NIHK-OO-SIT,   "x"
AH-YAH-TUS-KUM-IK-IM-UM,   "x"
KEE-TOO-WA-HAN,   "x"
CHA-KAS-TA-PAY-SIN,   "x"
JOHN SMITH,   "x"
JAMES SMITH,   "x"
CHIP-EE-WAY-AN,   "x"
    Chiefs
MASSAN,   "x"
PIERRE CADIEN,   "x"
OO-YAH-TIK-WAH-PAHN,   "x"
MAHS-KEE-TE-TIM-UN,   "x"
    Councillors of Mist-ow-as-is
SAH-SAH-KOO-MOOS,   "x"
BENJAMIN,   "x"
MEE-NOW-AH-CHAHK-WAY,   "x"
KEE-SIK-OW-ASIS,   "x"
    Councillors of Ah-tuk-uk-koop
PEE-TOOK-AH-HAN-UP-EE-GIN-EW, "x"
PEE-AY-CHEW,   "x"
TAH-WAH-PISK-EE-KAHP-POW,   "x"
AHS-KOOS,   "x"
    Councillors of Pee-yahn-kah-nihk-oo-sit
PET-E-QUA-CAY,   "x"
JEAN BAPTISTE,   "x"
ISIDORE WOLFE,   "x"
KEE-KOO-HOOS,   "x"
    Councillors of Kee-too-wa-han
OO-SAHN-ASKU-NUKIP,   "x"
YAW-YAW-LOO-WAY,   "x"
SOO-SOU-AIM-EE-LUAHN,   "x"

NUS-YOH-YAK-EE-NAH-KOOS,   "x"
  Councillors of Ah-yah-tus-kum-ik-im-um
WILLIAM BADGER,
BENJAMIN JOYFUL,   "x"
JOHN BADGER,
JAMES BEAR,
  Councillors of John Smith
KAH-TIP-IS-KOOR-AHT,   His x mark.
KAH-KEW-EE-KWAHW-AHS-UM, "x"
NAH-PACH,   "x"
MUS-IN-AH-NE-HIM-AHN,   "x"
  Councillors of Cha-kas-ta-pay-sin
BERNARD CONSTANT,
HENRY SMITH,   "x"
MAH-TUA-AHS-TIM-OO-WE-GIN, "x"
JACOB McLEAN,   "x"
  Councillors of James Smith
NAH-POO-CHEE-CHEES,   "x"
NAH-WIS,   "x"
KAH-PAH-PAH-MAH-CHAHK-NAY, "x"
KEE-YEW-AH-KAH-PIM-WAHT, "x"
  Councillors of Chip-ee-way-an
NAH-WEE-KAH-NICK-KAH-OO-TAH-MAH-HOTE
(or Neeh-cha-aw-asis), *Chief*   "x"

Signed by the Chiefs within named in the presence of the following witnesses, the same having been first read and explained by Peter Erasmus,
Peter Ballendine and the Rev. John McKay:

(Signed) A.G. JACKES, M.D.
  JAMES WALKER,
  J.H. McILREE,
   N.-W.M.P.
  PIERRE LEVAILLER.   His x mark.
  ISIDORE DUMOND.   "x"
  JEAN DUMOND.   "x"
  PETER HOURIE.
  FRANÇOIS GINGRAS.
  J.B. MITCHELL,
   Staff Constable, N.-W.M.P.

J.H. PRICE,
  Hospital Steward, N.-W.M.P.
XAVIER LETANGER.   His x mark.
WILLIAM SINCLAIR.
A.R. KENNEDY.
R.J. PRITCHARD.
L. CLARKE.
W. McKAY.
W.D. JARVIS,
  Inspector, N.-W.M.P.

Appendix B:
The First Ahtahkakoop Band Treaty Paylist, 1876

The name that appears on the paylist is given first, followed by standardized spelling using Standard Roman Orthography (SRO), and the English Translation.

1. Ah.tahk.ah.koop, Ahtahkakohp (Star Blanket)
2. Sah.sa.koo.moose, Sasākwamōs (One Who Adheres)
3. Benjamin. Also called Wāskitoy (Thigh)
4. Mee.now.ah.chauk.way, Kā-miyo-ahcahkwēw (Good Spirit)
5. Kee.sik.ow.as.is, Kīsik-awāsis (Sky Child)
6. Pay.nee.sā.wās,kahk, Pē-nōsēwēskam (Comes Tracking)
7. Ma.sus.ka.pew, Mēsaskēpiw (Sits On Land)
8. Kah.ke.nā.ah.pam.aht, Kā-kī-nahāpamāt (He Who Sees Him Clearly)
9. Say.tah.pah.too.way, Kā-tapahtowēt (He Who Has A Low Voice)
10. Koo.see.koo.se.wah.yah.new, K-ōsihkosiwayāniw (He Who Has An Ermineskin Robe)
11. Nā.tah.wee.kah.pow, Nīthāwikāpaw (Stands Well)
12. Ā.hā.nah.kew, Ahenakew, a derivative of ēy ēh, nāh-nakīw (Oh No, He Stopped)
13. Ke.che.moo.koo.mahn, Kihci-mōhkomān (Big Knife)
14. Oo.tah.yah.pee.kew, Otayapīhkēw (Netmaker)
15. Ā.see.nee.wah.pee.wa.yin, Asināpēwiyin (Stone Man)
16. John Saskatchewan, Kisiskāciwan (The River Runs Fast)
17. Ah.pis.chee.nah.pa.sees, Apisci-nāpēsis (Small Boy)
18. Kwahs.kwā.pah.kah.nis, Kwāskwē-pakānis (Little Jumping Nut)
19. We.chi.kah.pow ni.māw, Wīcikāpawimēw (He Who Stands With You)
20. Ā.see.nee.we.kah.pow, Asinīwikāpawiw (Standing Like A Rock)
21. Kah.ke.kā.yahs, Kākikēyās (Always Wind Blowing)
22. Nā.nee.kan.seem, Nēh-nēhkasam (Glittering)
23. Kah.kah.soo, Kāh-kāsōw (He Who Hides)
24. Kah.mee.yoo.us.too.ten, Kā-miyo-astotin (He Who Has A Fine Hat)
25. Chee.pay.ow.ahs.is, Cīpay-awāsis (Ghost-child)
26. See.yah.pwah.seem, Sīyāpwāsam (Sun Shines Through Something)
27. Wah.pah.ways, Wāpawēs (He Who Has White Hair)
28. Pee.yā.sees, Piyēsīs (Bird)
29. Cha.kah.paw, Cahkāpēw (Cold Touch Spirit)

30. Kah.me.yoo.kun.ow.ah.pem.māw, Kā-miyo-kanawāpamēw (He Who Looks On Someone Favourably)
31. Kah.kee.sik.ah.wah.pew, Kākīsikāwapiw (He Who Sits In Day)
32. Tah.twā-hoo.tow.aht, Kā-tāh-twēhototawāt (Bird Landing On Someone Repeatedly)
33. Wah.sah.he.koot, Wāsēhikot (Shiny Nose)
34. Wee.tah.ki.ā.kiw, Wē-tahki-yāhkēw (He Who Glides Before Landing)
35. Wā.me.kouw.oo.way, Mēmēkwanawēw (Feather Voice)
36. Mah.ne.chees, Omānicēs (A Little Stranger)
37. Kā.kā.kwah.ka.am.kwas.oo.wāt, Kēhkēhkwa kā-mēkōsowēt (Training A Hawk)
38. Ah-kahm-us-kee-we-yin, Akāmaskīwiyin (A Man From Across The Land)
39. Wah.we.yā.wās.koo.ta.wa.yahs, Wāwiyēwēskocawēs (He Who Has A Little Flame Around Him)
40. See.yoo.we.yahw.ah.way, Sōniyāw-ayāwēw (He Has Money)
41. Pam.wā.wās.teek, Pēmwēwēstik (Wind Blowing By)
42. Kā.kwā.che.yow, Kakwēciyaw (Questioning Body)
43. See.yahm.us.kwa.pew, Siyāmwaskwēpiw (Sitting With Head Down)
44. Much.ee.kis.a.ye.new, Maci-kisēyiniw (Bad Old Man)
45. Mary (Atak.a.coops daughter)
46. Ah.tah.pis.kis.kum, Aht-āpiskiskam (Changes The Shape Of Stone As He Walks)
47. Noo.too.kwā.up, Nōtokwēwāhp (Old Woman Lodge)
48. Sā.wās.kum.ik.up, Sēwēskanikap (Rattling Horn)
49. Wah.Cask, Wacask (Muskrat)
50. Nā.tah.wee.kah.pow.is.kway, Nahtāwikāpawiw-iskwew (Good Standing Woman)
51. Is.kwā.sis, Iskwēsis (Girl)
52. Moos.kow.e.pus.ee.koo, Maskawi-pasikōw (She Gets Up Strong)
53. Is.kwā.sis No. 2, Iskwēsis (Little Girl)
54. Kis.tah.chik, Kistāhcik (A Highly Thought Of Root/Stick)
55. Kah.yee.Kiw.um, Kāyīkowan (The Fog)
56. Kwā.sā.sis, Kwēsēsis (Little Shell Girl)
57. Kee.wah.see.wisk, Kīwāsēwisk (Dimming Light)
58. Ah.chee.tum, Āhcihtam (He Hears It Differently)
59. Nee.pus.ce.te.yā.wham, Nipasicihcētahwāw (I Slap His/Her Hand)
60. Chee.pā.tick.ok.oo.hoo, Cīpēhtako-ōhōw (Grey Owl)
61. Mah.chee.kwah.nahs, Macikwansās (Bad Weed)
62. Nee.pee.tah.ahs.sew, Nīpin-āhāsiw (Summer Crow)
63. Kah.ke.kā.see.kwan, Kākikē-sīkwan (Forever Spring)
64. Pus.koo.kwah.ow, Paskokwayaw (Bare Neck)
65. Wā.ni.nā.waph, Wāninēwāp (Wandering Eyes)
66. Oo.tee.noo.kao, Otinikēw (He Takes Something)

Appendix C:
Guide to Cree Pronunciation

Many Cree names and words have been included in this text, and their representation often varies between a number of spelling systems. Some names have received a standardized English spelling, such as Ahtahkakoop or Mistawasis. As such, these names are written following English convention (complete with capitalization, lack of diacritics, etc.). Others have not been standardized, but are still cited in the form English recorders have attempted to give them at various times. However, Cree is very different in sound and pattern from English and any adaptation of the English spelling system ultimately fails to accurately represent the Cree language. Fortunately, a Standard Roman Orthography (SRO), based on Cree, rather than English, is in use for writing the Cree language, and an attempt has been made to give the SRO form of most, if not all, Cree names and words in this text. The Cree SRO differs from English spelling conventions in two main respects: the use of diacritics (or macrons) to indicate long vowels and the lack of all capitalization. (In this volume, a concession has been made to the expectations of readers of English in that capitals have been used for Cree names.) It is this Cree spelling system which will be used below in the pronunciation guide. While it is impossible to do justice to the complexities of the language in a simplified summary, it is hoped that the following will give readers a sense of how Plains Cree speakers pronounce the various words found in the text.

There are seven vowels in Plains Cree:

a	as in b*u*t	*ī*	as in b*ea*t
ā	as in f*a*ther	*o*	as in b*oo*k
ē	as in b*ay*	*ō*	as in b*oa*t
i	as in b*i*t		

Both the short and the long "o" exhibit significant variations among dialects and subdialects, and even among individual speakers. Thus, *o* can sometimes sound closer to b*oa*t, though more clipped. Similarly, *ō* often comes across as close to b*oo*t, which accounts for English spellings such as Moosomin and Moose Jaw.

The pronunciation of Cree vowels can be modified when they appear with certain consonants. *h* is an aspirate, as in English, and the brief puff of air it entails changes the vowel sounds as follows:

ah or *āh*	as in f*a*ther, but shorter
ih or *īh*	as in b*ea*t, but shorter
oh or *ōh*	as in b*oa*t, but shorter

w and *y* also alter vowel sounds

aw	as in p*ou*ch
āw	as in n*ow*
ēw	has no equivalent, but sounds like a compressed *ay-oo*
iw	similar to n*ew*, or often sounded like *o*
īw	has no equivalent, but sounds like a compressed *ee-oo*
ow or *ōw*	as in kn*ow*
ay	as in b*i*te
iy	as in *ī*
oy	as in b*oy*

Consonants in Cree are generally pronounced as they are in English, although there are fewer of them (*b, d, f, g, j, l, q, r, u, v,* and *z* have no equivalent in the Cree dialects spoken in Saskatchewan). Exceptions are:

c	as in c*a*ts in Plains Cree, closer to cat*ch* in other dialects
k, p and *t*	these are always unaspirated, or clipped, and sometimes may sound closer to *g, b* and *d* in English
th	as in *th*en (this sound appears only in the Woods Cree dialect)

A very important aspect of any language, and one rarely if ever represented in spelling, is the stress or intonation pattern. The Cree stress pattern differs considerably from that of English and can present many problems for the non-speaker. Although the best source is to hear a fluent speaker of Cree, the following simplified rules may help. (In the examples that follow, the syllables in the Cree word to receive stress will appear in capital letters, with the approximate pronunciations given in brackets. In two syllable words, the final (or ultimate) syllable is typically given the main stress (e.g. *wacask* [wuh TSUSK] "muskrat", *cīpay* [tsee PIE] "ghost"). In words of three or more syllables, the third last (or anti-penultimate) syllable receives the main stress, while the final syllable also receives some stress (e.g. *asiniy* [US sin nee] "stone," *atāhkakohp* [uh TAAH kuh kohp]). This pattern holds even where the second last (or penultimate) syllable is long (e.g. *awāsis* [UH waa sis] "child," *piyēsīs* [PEE yay cease] "bird"). This can be particularly difficult for English speakers to adjust to since stress does not commonly fall on the anti-penultimate in English, and never if the penultimate is long. Thus, pronouncing *piyēsis* as [pee YAY cease] is just as incorrect in Cree as pronouncing "syllable" as [sil LAB bull] in English.

As an additional aid, some of the most important Cree names from the text are given in the following glossary, complete with SRO spellings and approximate pronunciations indicating stress:

Ahenakew (Derivative of ēy ēh, nāh-nakīw (Oh No, He Stopped)—
    a HEN a cue
Ahtahkoop, Ahtahkakohp (Star Blanket)—a TAAH ka kohp
Asināpēwiyin (Stone Man)—us SIN naa PAY we yin
Ayahtaskamikinam (Walks In Strange Land)—EYE yuh TUSS kum MI kin num
Cahkāpēw (Cold Touch Spirit)—TSUHK kaa payo
Cakāstēpēsin (Sunshine)—TSU kaa STAY pay sin
Cīpay-awāsis (Ghost-child)—TSEE pie UH waa sis
Iskwēsis (Girl)—ISS kway sis
Kāh-kāsōw (He Who Hides)—KAAH kaa so
Kāh-kīwīstahāw (Flying In A Circle)—KAAK key WEES tuh how
Kā-miyo-ahcahkwēw (Good Spirit)—KAA me WUH tsuh kwayo
Kā-miyo-astotin (He Who Has A Fine Hat)—kaa ME yo US tote tin
Kā-tāh-twēhototawāt (Bird Landing On Someone Repeatedly)—
    KAA taah TWAY ho TOE tuh watt
Kihci-mōhkomān (Big Knife)—KEYH tsi MOH ko man
Kīskanakwās (Cut Sleeve)—Kees KUN nuh kwaas
Kīnikwānāsiw (Flying In A Circle Going Up To A Point)—
    KEE nick KWAA naa sew
Kīsik-awāsis (Sky Child)—KEE sick KUH waa sis
Kitowēhāw (Sound Of Flapping Wings)—kit TOE way how
K-ōsihkosiwayāniw (He Who Has An Ermineskin Robe)—
    KOE seeh KOH si WHY yaan niw
Macikwanās (Bad Weed)—muh TSI kwun naas
Masuskapoe, Mēsaskēpiw (Sits On Land)—may SUSK kay po
Mēmēkwanawēw (Feather Voice)—MAY may KWUN nuh wayo
Mistawāsis (Big Child)—miss TUH waa sis
Mōhkomānawēw (Knife Voice)—MOH ko MAN nuh wayo
Nāpēskis (Like A Man)—NAA pace kiss
Nātakām (North, Going Towards The Water)—NAA tsuh calm
Nātowēw (Iroquois)—NAA toe wayo
Nayneecassum, Nēh-nēhkasam (Glittering)—nay NAYH kuh sum

Nēhiyaw (Exact body [Plains Cree, singular])—NAY he yow
Nēhiyawak (Exact body of people [Plains Cree, plural])—nay HE yow wuck
Ocīpiwayān (Pointed Hood)—o TSEE pwuh yaan
Okimāsis (Little Chief)—o KIM maa sis
Okīnomotayēw (A Long Goatee)—o KEE noh MOH tuh yayo
Otayapīhkēw (Netmaker)—oh tie YUH peehk kayo
Petihkwahākēw (Comes To Us With The Sound of Wings)—
        PIT teeh KWUH haa kayo
Osāwanāsiw (South Wind)—O saa WUN naa sew
Peekeekoot, Pīkikot (Hook Nose)—PEE ko koot
Pē-nōsēwēskam (Comes Tracking)—PAY no SAY way scum
Sasakamoose, Sasākwamōs (One Who Adheres)—sah SAA kwuh moose
Sōniyāw-ayāwēw (He Has Money)—soo NEE yow-WHY yow wayo
Wāsēhikot (Shiny Nose)—waa SAY hick koot
Wāskitoy (Thigh)—WAAS skit toy

This guide has been revised for its inclusion here. The original was first published in Bill Barry's *People Places* (Regina: Canadian Plains Research Center, 1997). Both versions were prepared by Arok Wolvengrey, Professor of Indian Languages at Saskatchewan Indian Federated College, and were based on his more detailed article, "On the Spelling and Pronunciation of First Nations Languages and Names in Saskatchewan," printed in *Prairie Forum* 23, no 1 (Spring 1998). An even more extensive discussion of Cree will be included in the forthcoming Cree-English dictionary, *nēhiyawēwin: itwēwina*, to be published in 2001 by the Canadian Plains Research Center.

Appendix D:
Glossary of Indian People

AHENAKEW, ANTOINE. The son of David Ahenakew, he changed his name to Antoine Chatelain, took scrip, lived the rest of his life in the Battleford and Meadow Lake districts.

AHENAKEW, BAPTISTE. Ahenakew's son.

AHENAKEW, JOHN. Ahenakew's son.

AHENAKEW, LOUIS. Ahenakew's son. He became a teacher.

AHENAKEW. Ahtahkakoop's brother. This name is derived from Ēy ēh, nāh-nakiw, Oh No, He Stopped. His earlier name was Āhāsiwakohp (Crow Blanket).

AHTAHKAKOOP (STARBLANKET). Chief of the Ahtahkakoop Band.

AHTAHKAKOOP, MICHEL. One of Ahtahkakoop's younger sons.

AYAHTASKAMIKINAM (WALKS IN STRANGE LAND). Chief at Sturgeon Lake. He was also known as William Twatt.

ĀYIMISĪS (LITTLE DIFFICULT ONE). Big Bear's son.

BEARDY. Chief of the Beardy Band.

BIG BEAR. Chief of the Big Bear Band.

BIGHEAD, THOMAS (MAHKISTIKWĀN). Wāskitoy's son.

CAKĀSTĒPĒSIN (SUN SHINE). Chief of the Cakāstēpēsin Band.

CARDINAL, JOHN. Also known as John Pierre. He married Ahtahkakoop's granddaughter, Maria Kā-tāh-twēhototawāt, daughter of Emma Ahtahkakoop and Kā-tāh-twēhototawāt.

CĪPAYAWĀSIS (GHOST-CHILD). He chose David as his Christian name.

GREYEYES. Ermineskin's son and the father of Norbert Greyeyes.

HE STRIKES HIM ON THE BACK. Chief of the He Strikes Him On The Back Band, which later occupied land called the Sweetgrass Reserve.

HYMAN, CHARLOTTE. Hyman is a derivative of āyiman (It Is Difficult). This name was spelt as Iyemun in the mission records and Lyman on some treaty paylists. She was married to Kāh-kāsōw.

ISKWĒSIS (CREE WORD FOR GIRL). Daughter of the old blind woman. Wāwiyēwēskocawēs (He Who Has A Little Flame Around Him, also known as Charles Round Plain) and Kākīsikāwapiw (He Who Sits In Day, known as Levi Turner) were her sons.

ISPIMIHK-KĀ-KITOT (THUNDERS ABOVE). Ocīpiwayān's son. He was also known as Young Chipewayan.

JIMMUK. Also known as John James Dufraine. He married Ahtahkakoop's daughter Philomene in May of 1881.

James Smith. Chief of the James Smith Reserve. He was John Smith's brother.

John Smith. Chief of the John Smith Band (Muskoday Reserve).

Kāh-kāsōw (He Who Hides). Ahenakew's son. He taught people how to read in the buffalo hunting camps.

Kāh-kīwīstahāw (Flying In A Circle). The Cree chief who travelled to Ottawa with Ahtahkakoop, Mistawasis and O'Soup in 1886. His reserve was situated at Round Lake in the Qu'Appelle Valley.

Kākikēyās (Always Wind Blowing). He married Alice Sasakamoose.

Kā-miyo-ahcahkwēw (Good Spirit). Son of Ahtahkakoop. He took Antoine as his given name when he was baptized. He was married to Mistawasis's daughter Judique.

Kā-miyo-ahcahkwēw, Joseph. Son of Kāmiyoahcahkwēw.

Kā-miyo-astotin (He Who Has A Fine Hat). Ahtahkakoop's son. He was given the name Basil when he was baptized.

Kā-nahahcāpīw (Good With A Bow). He was also known as Jumper Tate.

Kā-ohpatawakinam (He Who Makes Dust Fly). A "Green Lake" chief who took his reserve at Meadow Lake. The translation of his name is generally shortened to Flying Dust.

Kā-tāh-twēhototawāt (Bird Landing On Someone Repeatedly). He was married to Ahtahkakoop's daughter Emma. He was considered a "rebel" during the 1885 Uprising and left the Ahtahkakoop reserve.

Kihci-mōhkomān (Big Knife). Drowned in Sandy Lake during the 1879-80 paylist year.

Kīsik-awāsis (Sky Child). Ahtahkakoop's son. He was a headman at the signing of treaty but left the reserve a few years later.

Kīskanakwās (Cut Sleeve). Ahenakew's wife.

Kissowayis. The Saulteaux trader who gave up his right of crossing at Dumont's Crossing to Lieutenant-Governor Morris in 1876.

Kitowēhāw (Sound Of Flapping Wings). Chief who signed Treaty Six and chose a reserve at Muskeg Lake Reserve. Petihkwahākēw took his place when Kitowēhāw joined the Métis at the South Branch, where he was known as Alexander Cayen.

K-ōsihkosiwayāniw (He Who has an Ermineskin Robe). The English translation was later shortened to Ermineskin. Originally from the Bears' Hills south of Edmonton. Three of his daughters married sons of Ahenakew and another married Ahtahkakoop's son Basil.

Little Hunter. One of the chiefs from Saddle Lake.

Lucky Man. A Battleford chief allied with Big Bear.

Macikwansās (Bad Weed). Chief of Pelican Lake Band.

Masuskapoe (Sits On Land). Ahtahkakoop's oldest brother. He died before 1861.

Masuskapoe, John Peter. Masuskapoe's son.

Māyātis (Ugly Man). Son of Kīnikwānāsiw. Charles Little was his step-son.

Mēmēkwanawēw (Feather Voice). The son of Ahtahkakoop's nephew John Peter Masuskapoe. He took William as his Christian name. His family later took Williams as their surname.

MISTAWASIS (BIG CHILD). Chief of the band that settled at Snake Plain. He was Ahtahkakoop's colleague and friend.

MŌHKOMĀNAWĒW (KNIFE VOICE). He transferred from the Flying Dust Band in 1883 and married Pēnōsēwēskam's widow.

NĀPĒSKIS. Ahtahkakoop's youngest brother. He was killed by the Blackfoot in about 1861.

NĀTAKĀM (NORTH, GOING TOWARDS THE WATER). Also known as Mac Knife. He was Kihci-mōhkomān's) son.

NĀTOWĒW. Ahtahkakoop's wife. Natowāo is the Cree word for Iroquois.

NAYNEECASSUM, CHARLES. Charles Nayneecassum was the son of Philip Wāwiyēwēskocawēs and Caroline Nayneecassum. The boy later took the name Charles Little.

O'SOUP, LOUIS. O'Soup, whose Indian name translated as Back Fat, was Saulteaux and a headman of the Cowessess Band living at Round Lake in the Qu'Appelle Valley. He travelled to Ottawa with Ahtahkakoop, Mistawasis, and Kahkewistahaw in 1886.

OCĪPIWAYĀN (POINTED HOOD). Chief of the Ocīpiwayān Band. He died in 1877. His name was also spelt Chipewayan.

OKIMĀSIS (LITTLE CHIEF). Headman of Saswēpiw's Willow Cree. He replaced Saswēpiw as chief in 1884 after Saswēpiw was deposed by the Canadian government.

OKINOMOTAYĒW (A LONG GOATEE, SIMILAR TO THE GOATEE OR TUFTED CHIN OF A MOOSE). He was the chief at Stoney Lake.

OLD BLIND WOMAN. Iskwēsis's mother.

ONE ARROW. Chief of the One Arrow Band.

OSĀWANĀSIW (SOUTH WIND). Also known as William Cardinal and William Pierre, he served as volunteer farm instructor in the early 1890s.

PAKĀN (THE NUT). He was also called, Seenum (Wringing Something). This chief lived on land that is now part of present-day Alberta.

PAYIPWĀT (HOLE IN THE SIOUX). Chief of the Payipwāt Band.

PEEKEEKOOT, PETER (HOOK NOSE). Son of John Peter Masuskapoe. He married Waskitoy's daughter and took his father-in-law's treaty number.

PĒNŌSĒWĒSKAM (COMES TRACKING). He died at Fort Carlton in 1879 after becoming chilled while hunting.

PETIHKWAHĀKĒW (COMES TO US WITH THE SOUND OF WINGS). His name is sometimes spelt as Petaquakey. He signed Treaty Six as Kitowēhēw's councillor and later became chief of the Muskeg Lake Band.

PIERRE. Was known as Peter Pierre and Pierre Stone. He was a councillor in Mistawasis's Band. His family later took the name Cardinal.

PIYĒSĪS (BIRD). He married Ahtahkakoop's daughter Mary, but later deserted her and left the reserve.

POUNDMAKER. Chief of the Poundmaker Band.

RED PHEASANT. Chief of the Red Pheasant Band. He was Ahenakew's brother-in-law.

SASAKAMOOSE (ONE WHO ADHERES). Ahtahkakoop's brother.

SASAKAMOOSE, ALEXANDER. Sasakamoose's son.

Sasakamoose, Joseph. Sasakamoose's son. A teacher, he died in 1888 when he was 21 years old.

Sasakamoose, Maggie. Sasakamoose's wife.

Sasakamoose, Margaret. Sasakamoose's daughter. She married John Cameron and was discharged from treaty in 1887.

Sasakamoose, Mary. Sasakamoose's wife. She was the first person the Reverend John Hines buried at Sandy Lake.

Saswēpiw (Sits All Over The Land). Deposed as one of the chiefs of the Willow Cree by the Canadian government in 1884. He was replaced by Okimāsis.

Sekaskōtch (Blood From Cut Arm). Chief from Onion Lake.

Sīsīkwanis (Little Rattle). He signed Treaty Six as chief with Beardy and One Arrow.

Starblanket, James. Also known as Pacī, he was raised by Kā-miyo-astotin and his wife. He was with Ahtahkakoop when he died.

Stranger, David. From the St. Peter's Band near the Red River Settlement, Stranger was hired by John Hines in 1874 to help him establish a mission in Saskatchewan River country.

Sweetgrass. One of the leading chiefs who traded at Fort Pitt.

Titihkosiw (Kidney). He was one of the spiritual men at the signing of Treaty Six at Fort Carlton.

Wandering Spirit. He signed Treaty Six with Ocīpiwayān's Band, and later became a war chief in Big Bear's band.

Wāsēhikot (Shiny Nose). Son of Ahenakew. He took Henry as his Christian name.

Wāskitoy (Thigh). Also known as Benjamin and Benjamin One Arm. He was listed as a headman when Treaty Six was signed.

Wāskitoy, Benjamin. Son of the headman Wāskitoy and brother of Thomas Bighead.

Appendix E:
Glossary of Non-Indian People

ADAMS, CHARLES. Acting Indian Agent.

ARCHIBALD, ADAMS G. First lieutenant-governor of the North-West Territories. He served in that capacity from 1870 to 1872.

BALLENDINE, PETER. Son of John Ballendine, Hudson's Bay Company (HBC) and an Indian woman named Jane. He was born at Cumberland House in 1836 and educated at St. John's School in Winnipeg. His cousin Sam was married to one of the women in Ahtahkakoop's band.

BARING-GOULD, B. Secretary to Church Missionary Society, 1895-1913.

BUTLER, WILLIAM FRANCIS. Sent by the lieutenant-governor in 1870 to report on the state of the territories.

CHEADLE, WALTER BUTLER. From England, he wintered south of Whitefish Lake in 1862.

CHRISTIE, W.J. The half-breed son of Governor Alexander Christie. He was educated in Aberdeen, Scotland, and rose through the ranks to inspecting officer. He served a short term on the North-West Council and was a commissioner for the Treaty Six negotiations.

CLARKE, LAWRENCE. The HBC officer put in charge of Fort Carlton in 1867.

CLARKE, PALMER. Indian agent.

CLARKE, THOMAS. Appointed principal of the Battleford Industrial School in 1883. He resigned December, 1894.

CROZIER, L.N.F. NWMP commissioned officer.

DEWDNEY, EDGAR. Appointed Indian Commissioner in 1879 and lieutenant-governor in 1881. He later served as minister of the Interior and superintendent general of Indian Affairs.

DICKIESON, M.G. Indian agent and deputy Indian Superintendent.

DUMONT, GABRIEL. Métis leader on the South Branch.

ERASMUS, PETER. Interpreter during the Treaty Six negotiations.

FENN, CHRISTOPHER CYPRIAN. Secretary for the Church Missionary Society (CMS). Based in London, he was responsible for the Canadian missions from 1870-72 and 1881-1983.

FINLAYSON, JOSEPH. Indian agent stationed at Fort Carlton.

FORGET, AMÉDÉE. Born in Marieville, Lower Canada, in 1847 he served as secretary to the Manitoba Half-Breed Commission, and in 1876 became clerk to the Executive Council of the North-West Territories and secretary to both Lieutenant-Governor David Laird and his successor, Edgar Dewdney. Forget was later appointed assistant Indian commissioner, Indian commissioner, and then lieutenant-governor.

GRAHAME, JAMES A. Chief commissioner of the HBC, stationed in Winnipeg.

HINES, EMMA. John Hines's wife.

HINES, JOHN. Born in England in 1850 with a farming background, he became an Anglican missionary. He lived with Ahtahkakoop's people from 1875 to 1888.

HOURIE, PETER. The half-breed interpreter who accompanied Ahtahkakoop, Mistawasis, and O'Soup to Ottawa.

IRVINE, A.G. Commissioner of the North-West Mounted Police (NWMP) in 1885.

ISBISTER, JAMES. The half-breed postmaster at Fort Carlton who retired and established a farm in the vicinity of the North Saskatchewan River some 50 miles downstream from Fort Carlton. This farm became the nucleus of a settlement known as the Isbister settlement, which was the forerunner of Prince Albert.

KEITH, HILTON. Indian agent.

LAIRD, DAVID. First resident lieutenant-governor and Indian superintendent in the North-West Territories.

LASH, JOHN B. Indian agent for the Carlton Agency. He was taken prisoner by Louis Riel during the Uprising of 1885.

LEBLANC, DONALD. He married Kā-miyo-ahcahkwēw's daughter Mary.

MACDONALD, COL. ALLAN. Indian agent for the Qu'Appelle Agency who accompanied Ahtahkakoop, Mistawasis, Kāh-kīwīstahāw, and O'Soup to Ottawa in 1886.

MACDONALD, SIR JOHN A. Conservative prime minister, 1867-73 and 1878-91.

MACKENZIE, ALEXANDER. Liberal prime minister of Canada, 1873-78.

MACRAE, J. ANSDELL. Sub-Indian agent and later inspector of Protestant schools.

MATHESON, EDWARD. A teacher at Sandy Lake, he was the first student to graduate from Emmanuel College. In 1895 he was appointed principal of the Battleford Industrial School

McDOUGALL, GEORGE. A Methodist missionary, he founded the Victoria and Morleyville missions.

McDOUGALL, JOHN. George McDougall's son. He followed in his father's footsteps and became a Methodist missionary.

McGIBBON, ALEX. Inspector of reserves and agencies.

McKAY, GEORGE. The half-breed son of William McKay, the HBC officer stationed at Fort Ellice and then Fort Pitt. In 1874 his sister Catherine married Lawrence Clarke, the factor at Fort Carlton. He was the first teacher at the Asissipi Mission school.

McKAY, JAMES. A half-breed, he served on the Council of Assiniboia from 1868-69, became an influential member of the Manitoba government, and was on the Council of the North-West Territories from 1873 to 1875. He was an advisor for Treaties One, Two, and Three, and a commissioner for Treaties Five and Six.

McKAY, JOHN. Brother of James McKay. He accompanied the Reverend James Nisbet to Prince Albert in 1866, and in 1876 was ordained in the Presbyterian Church.

JOHN A. MACKAY. Son of the chief factor at Moose Factory and his Indian wife, he became a missionary and eventually an archdeacon in the Diocese of Saskatchewan and warden of Emmanuel College. He was hired by the government to interpret at the Treaty Six negotiations.

McLEAN, JOHN. First bishop of Saskatchewan.

MESSITER, CHARLES A. An English adventurer who wintered in the Thickwood Hills near Ahtahkakoop in 1862.

MIDDLETON, MAJOR-GENERAL FREDERICK DOBSON. Commander of the Canadian Militia in 1885.

MILTON, LORD. From England, he wintered south of Whitefish Lake with Dr. Cheadle in 1862.

MORRIS, ALEXANDER. Replaced Archibald as lieutenant-governor of Manitoba and the North-West Territories in December of 1872. He was the chief commissioner at the Treaty Six negotiations.

NEELY, J.M.R. A young Irishman who spoke no Cree, hired to replace Joseph Sasakamoose as teacher.

O'DONNELL, WILLIAM J. Farm instructor on the Ahtahkakoop Reserve in 1896.

PINKAM, CYPRIAN. Replaced McLean as Bishop of Saskatchewan and Calgary.

PRITCHARD, JOHN. Born in the Red River Settlement. He taught at the Asissipi Mission, enrolled at Emmanuel College, and was ordained a deacon and priest.

RAE, J.M. Indian agent.

REED, HAYTOR. Indian agent who rose through the ranks to become Indian commissioner and deputy superintendent general.

RIEL, LOUIS. A founder of the Province of Manitoba and Métis leader during the Uprising of 1885.

SETTEE, JOHN RICHARD. Son of the Reverend James Settee. He replaced Hines as missionary at Sandy Lake in 1888.

SOUTHESK, EARL OF. A Scottish traveller who hunted with Nāpēskis during a tour of the North-West in 1859.

STRANGER, DAVID. A Swampy Cree from St. Peter's Mission in Manitoba. Hines hired him in 1874 as his general helper. He attended Emmanuel College, but died before he completed his studies.

TAYLOR, JAMES. He took charge of the mission at Sandy Lake in 1895.

VANKOUGHNET, LAWRENCE. Deputy superintendent general of Indian Affairs, 1874-93.

VILLEBRUN, DANIEL. Married to Ahenakew's daughter Marie Louis. He was Peter Ballendine's assistant at the Battle River post when it opened in 1868.

WADSWORTH, THOS. P. Inspector of reserves and agencies.

WALKER, JAMES. Officer in charge of NWMP post at Battleford.

WINTER, G.S. Missionary who was at the Sandy Lake Mission in 1894 for less than a week. He later went to Sturgeon Lake.

WRIGHT A.A.H. He taught at the Asissipi Mission school for two years, then enrolled at Emmanuel College and was ordained an Anglican priest. By 1886 he was an independent member of the Church Missionary Society's Finance Committee in Prince Albert.

WRIGLEY, JOSEPH. Hudson's Bay Company trade commissioner in 1885.

Appendix F:
Glossary of Place Names

Asissipi River (Shell River), *ēsis-sīpiy*

Bad Hill, *maci-waciy*

Battle River, *nōtinito-sīpiy*

Buffalo Hump Hills, *kaskiskawānatinawa*

Cherry Bush, *kā-misāskwatōminiskāk* (Chokecherry Bush)

Cypress Hills, *minatināhk* (Rolling Hills With Trees)

Eagle Hills, *mikisiwaciya*

Elk or Red Deer River (South Saskatchewan River), *wāwāskēsiw-sīpiy*

Fir Lake, *oskācakāwikamās*

God's Lake (Morin Lake), *manitow-sākahikan*

Hand Hills, *micihcīyahciya*

Long Lake (Last Mountain Lake), *kinokamak*

Loon Lake (Makwa Lake), *mākwa-sākahikan*

Missouri River (Muddy River), *pīkānosīpiy*

Moose Woods, *ayapacinās*

Na-ka-win-oskatik, or Saulteaux's Forehead, *nahkawiyin oskāhtik*

Nipowiwin, *nīpawiwin*

Redberry Lake, *mihkomin-sākahikan*

Sandy Lake, *yēkawiskāwikamāw*

Saskatchewan River, *kā-kisiskāciwan* (The River Runs Fast)

Stopping Hill, *nakīwaciy*

The Last Little Witigo Hill, *osāpahcikan-ispatinaw*

The place where they fled to during the night, *nipā-takwānimowin*

Thickwood Hills, *kā-mistikwatināk*

Whitefish Lake, *atihkamēk sākahikan*

Witchekan Lake (Stinking Lake), *wīhcēkan*

Notes

Abbreviations

GA   Glenbow Archives, Calgary, Alberta
HBCA   Hudson's Bay Company Archives
NA   National Archives of Canada
PAM   Provincial Archives of Manitoba
SAB   Saskatchewan Archives Board

Preface

1. Fine Day, as told to David Mandelbaum, September 10, 1934, David Mandelbaum Papers, Saskatchewan Archives Board, (hereafter referred to as SAB, R875).

Chapter One: Ahtahkakoop's World

1. A buffalo pound consisted of a chute and corral built from logs to trap buffalo.

2. Chief Thunderchild's version of the story of Pointed Arrow, as recorded by Edward Ahenakew and edited by Ruth Buck, appears in Edward Ahenakew, *Voices of the Plains Cree* (Toronto: McClelland and Stewart Limited, 1973), 67. In the reprint of *Voices of the Plains Cree*, published in 1995 by the Canadian Plains Research Center, the story is on page 45.

3. Several versions of this story exist. The one that appears here is based, in part, on a story told by Peter Knife of the Ahtahkakoop Band. Peter Knife was an elder of the band, a Sun Dance maker, and a pipe keeper. The Cree of the Churchill and Saskatchewan river regions in what is now the province of Saskatchewan told explorer David Thompson a similar story during the latter part of the 1700s, except that narrative did not include the loon. Additionally, unlike the story told by Peter Knife, in which the loon and several of the animals died, none died in the story recorded by Thompson. His version can be found in *David Thompson's Narrative: 1784-1812*, published by the Champlain Society in 1916 and 1962. See the 1962 edition, pages 77-78.

4. John Maclean, *Native Tribes of Canada* (1896; Toronto: Coles Publishing Company Ltd., 1980), 169-70. This story was told by Henry Warren, a "native Ojibway" who related "a tradition which he heard in a speech delivered by one of the native priests wherein their religion is symbolized in the figure of a sea-shell, and the migrations of the people recorded." Maclean cited as his source A.F. Chamberlain, "The Mississaugas"; Winsor's *Critical History of America*, vol. 4, p. 175; *American Antiquarian* 8, p. 388; and the "Annual Report of the Bureau of Ethnology," 1885-86, pp. 150, 183, 184.

5. The Plains Cree language is part of the Algonquian linguistic family. In Canada, Algonquian speakers occupy a vast territory extending from the Maritimes and the Atlantic Ocean to the foothills of the Rocky Mountains. These people include the Cree,

Blackfoot, Blood, Peigan, Saulteaux, and Ojibwa peoples. Although the different peoples speak their own languages and there are numerous dialects, many of the words have remained the same.

Chapter Two: Ahtahkakoop's Early Years

1. According to Anglican Church records, Ahtahkakoop was about 80 years of age when he died on December 4, 1896. (See record #30 in the record of deaths contained in the Diocese of Saskatchewan Parish Register for the Sandy Lake Mission, volume 1.) The first death in this register occurred in November 1894. This register is housed at the Anglican Diocese of Saskatchewan Synod Office in Prince Albert.

2. For further information, see David G. Mandelbaum, *The Plains Cree: An Ethnographic, Historical, and Comparative Study* (Regina: Canadian Plains Research Center, 1979), 59, 60, 92, 93.

3. See ibid., 360.

4. Elder Jim Cannepotao (*Kā-nīpitēhtēw*), interview by the author at Onion Lake, Saskatchewan, January 29, 1984, and information compiled from traditions and oral history related by the elders to the younger generations.

5. For Mandelbaum's description of the Sacred Pipestem and its use, see *The Plains Cree*, 122, 172-74.

6. For Mandelbaum's description of "first event ceremonialism," see ibid., 222-23.

7. Mandelbaum described this puberty observance in *The Plains Cree*, 145.

8. For further information on the *pāwistikowiyiniwak* (Gros Ventre), see Dale R. Russell, *Eighteenth-Century Western Cree and their Neighbours*, Archaeological Survey of Canada, Mercury Series Paper 143 (Hull: Canadian Museum of Civilization, 1991), 200-12.

9. The travois was a transport device that was pulled by horses and dogs. Mandelbaum, *The Plains Cree*, 65, described the horse travois thus: "The horse travois was made by crossing two poles [generally tipi poles] near the ends and binding them together with sinew and thongs. Two sticks were fastened transversely across the arms of the travois and a number of thongs tied across the parallel sticks. The load was borne on this carrier. The travois was fastened to the horse by a rawhide thong girth which passed around the belly just behind the fore legs and was fastened to each arm of the travois where it rested on the horse's back." The travois drawn by a dog was made the same way, except the poles were considerably smaller, the frame was a netted oval, and "the harness consisted of a thong around the neck and another around the belly."

10. Contemporary Sun Dance makers sometimes use 14 poles to construct the Sun Dance lodge and 12 willows to make the Sun Dance sweatlodge. Instead of increasing the number of poles in the Sun Dance lodge, as related in the sacred story, they increase the willows in the Sun Dance sweatlodge by four each year to a maximum of 40.

11. Contemporary Sun Dance makers often wrap cloth offerings around Chief Tree (the centre pole), or hang the offerings from the Thunderbird nest.

Chapter Four: Ahtahkakoop Becomes a Man

1. The company was incorporated by the name the "Governor and Company of Adventurers of England tradeing into Hudson's Bay." Its charter was granted by King Charles II of England on May 2, 1670.

2. Andrew Graham, a senior Hudson's Bay Company officer, wrote in 1775 that these articles were "the principle [*sic*] useful Articles" traded with the Keiskatchewan Indians (Cree) who "are the chief contributors to the Company's Trade." He added that because they had plenty of food "any thing more than is necessary would be Superfluous and Burthesome." See Andrew Graham's Extract from "Observations on Hudson's Bay," Appendix B, *Isham's Observations and Notes, 1743-1749* (London: The Hudson's Bay Record Society, 1949), 309-10.

3. These posts included trading houses near the junction of the North Saskatchewan and Sturgeon rivers (1776-81), Lower and Upper Hudson Houses (1778-89), and a number of posts operated by independent traders from Montreal.

4. John Cornelius Van Driel, letter dated September 18, 1774, York Factory, to John Fish, McTavish Frobisher & Co. Correspondence Inward, Public Archives of Manitoba, Hudson's Bay Company Archives (hereafter referred to as HBCA), F.3/1, fos.195-95d. Van Driel, who survived the attack on the South Branch House, said the "french post … was well fortified with loghouses over each Gateway of the Stockades, with 5 Canadians & 3 Cree Indians to defend the same."

5. The name Carlton House was also used for a Hudson's Bay Company post built on the Assiniboine River in 1795. Other names for the North West Company's Fort St. Louis —"upper" Nepawi or "upper" Nippowee—are derivatives of *nipawiwin*, the Cree word for "standing place." A post operated by a third company, the XY Company (New North West Company), and possibly one other post traded in the vicinity of Carlton House and Fort St. Louis for at least part of the time under discussion.

6. The posts were situated six miles downstream from the South Branch Houses that had been abandoned in 1794.

7. Historical documents sometimes refer to the post on the North Saskatchewan River as Carlton House III to distinguish it from its predecessors.

8. The name La Montée came from the French word *monter*, "to mount." See Arthur S. Morton, *A History of the Canadian West to 1870-71* (1937; Toronto: University of Toronto Press, 1973), 454.

9. Elliott Coues (ed.), *New Light on the Early History of the Greater Northwest: The Manuscript Journals of Alexander Henry and of David Thompson, 1799–1814*, vol. 2 (New York: Francis P. Harper, 1897), 491. The "crossing" was described by Nor'Wester Alexander Henry in his journal entry for September 5, 1808.

10. The St. Lawrence route continued to be used by company officers and others travelling inland from Montreal. Furs, trade goods, supplies, and new recruits were transported to and from England via York Factory and Hudson Bay.

11. The number of people at La Montée affected by the amalgamation of the two companies was significant. During the 1818-1819 season, two years before the union of the two companies, La Montée was staffed by 31 men, most of whom were French Canadians or half-breeds. The Canadians, according to Hudson's Bay Company officer

John Peter Pruden, were "old Standers at this place" and had families. The total population of the post was said to be more than 140 souls. In contrast, there were 17 Europeans—born in either Scotland or England—at Carlton House, most of whom were on short contracts and unmarried. See Report of the Carlton District, 1818-19, Hudson's Bay Company Archives, Provincial Archives of Manitoba (hereafter HBCA, PAM), B.27/e/2, fos. 2d-3.

12. The Carlton House Journals (HBCA, PAM, B.27/4-23) are housed at the Hudson's Bay Company Archives in Winnipeg, Manitoba. With the exception of citations for Hudson's Bay Company Archives documentation and direct quotations, the name Fort Carlton hereafter will be used instead of Carlton House.

13. Report of the Carlton District, 1818-1819, HBCA, PAM, B.27/e/2, fo. 1.

14. Ibid.

15. The names Stone Indians, Stonies, and Stoneys came from an Ojibwa word that described the practice of these people to cook with hot stones. The Cree called the Assiniboine *pwāsimowak*, which means "They Talk Similar to the Sioux."

16. For further information on the movement of the Indian nations, see Dale R. Russell, *Eighteenth-Century Western Cree and their Neighbours*. Also see David Meyer, "Time-Depth of the Western Woods Cree Occupation of Northern Ontario, Manitoba, and Saskatchewan," in William Cowan (ed.), *Papers of the Eighteenth Algonquian Conference* (Ottawa: Carleton University, 1987).

17. Fort Pitt is located upstream from the Red Deer Hills.

18. The Plains Cree sometimes referred to their enemies, and more specifically the Blackfoot, as *awahkānak* or slaves. They also used the term *ayahciyiniwak*, which means different people.

19. This information is drawn from interviews by David Mandelbaum with Fine Day and Musqua (Bear) at the Sweetgrass Reserve in July 1934. These men of the River People were born in the 1850s. Both men were noted warriors during the days of intertribal warfare and both were shamans. See the David Mandelbaum Papers, Saskatchewan Archives Board (hereafter SAB), R875, 8a, folder 2/3, III, pp. 116-39 for Fine Day's information and folder 2/3, II, p. 32 for Musqua's testimony. Mandelbaum's book *The Plains Cree* was based to a considerable degree on information obtained from Fine Day, Musqua, and other informants. For additional information on pounds, see Mandelbaum, *The Plains Cree*, 52-55. The pound described by Fine Day was built under the supervision of Sikakwayan (Skunkskin), the grandfather of Baptiste Ahenakew's wife Ellen Ermineskin. Baptiste, the son of Ahenakew and Kīskanakwās, was Ahtahkakoop's nephew. Ellen was the daughter of Skunkskin's daughter Nōtokwēwāhk (Old Woman Lodge) and K-ōsihkosiwayāniw (He Who Has An Ermineskin Robe).

20. Carlton House Journal, 1815-16, HBCA, PAM, B.27/a/5, fo. 28; and Carlton House Journal, 1816-17, HBCA, PAM, B.27/a/6, fos. 7d, 27d, 31. Also see Deanna Christensen, "A 'Convenient Place': A History of Fort Carlton, 1810-1885," 59, 65 (prepared for the Parks Branch, Saskatchewan Parks and Renewable Resources).

21. Report of the Carlton District, 1818-19, HBCA, PAM, B.27/e/2, fo. 1. Also see Carlton House Journal, 1818-19, HBCA, PAM, B.27/a/8, fo. 3, and Christensen, "Convenient Place," 72-73.

22. Carlton House Journal, 1818-19, HBCA, PAM, B.27/a/8, fos. 3, 28, 34; and the August 6 entry in the Carlton House Journal for 1821-22, HBCA, PAM, B.27/a/11, fo. 9d. Also see the Carlton House Journal for 1820-21, HBCA, PAM, B.27/a/10, fo. 7d.

23. Alex Ahenakew, June 1996 review meeting. Although the year of this escape is uncertain, the story is similar to many of the stories that have been passed down through the generations.

24. Mandelbaum, *The Plains Cree*, 246-47, and Hugh Dempsey, *Red Crow, Warrior Chief* (Saskatoon: Western Producer Prairie Books, 1980), 57.

25. For a fuller discussion of warfare, see Mandelbaum, *The Plains Cree*, 239-58.

26. Carlton House Journal, 1836-37, HBCA, PAM, B.27/a/22, entry for May 13, 1837, fo. 32d.

27. John Rowand to Governor George Simpson, December 28, 1837, HBCA, PAM, D.5/4, fos. 360-360d. Also see Fort Pelly Journal, 1837-38, HBCA, PAM, B.159/a/17, fos. 9, 10d-12.

28. Rowand to Simpson, December 25, 1837, Edmonton House Correspondence, HBCA, PAM, B.60/b/1.

29. Arthur J. Ray, in *Indians in the Fur Trade: Their Role as Hunters, Trappers and Middlemen in the Lands Southwest of Hudson Bay, 1660-1870* (Toronto and Buffalo: University of Toronto Press, 1974), 187, suggests that two-thirds of the Assiniboine died from smallpox. His estimate is based on figures taken from E. Denig's *Five Indian Tribes of the Upper Missouri*, edited by J.C. Ewers (Norman: University of Oklahoma Press, 1961).

30. The Reverend John Hines, upon meeting Ahtahkakoop for the first time, said the chief was more than six feet in height and so well proportioned that "I thought I never saw a finer built man." John Hines, *Red Indians of the Plains: Thirty years' missionary experience in the Saskatchewan* (London: Society for Promoting Christian Knowledge, 1915), 78. Also see Edward Ahenakew, "Genealogical Sketch of My Family," 9, from the American Philosophical Society Library, Philadelphia. Born in 1885, Edward Ahenakew was Ahtahkakoop's nephew and the son of Baptiste Ahenakew and Ellen Ermineskin. He was ordained deacon in the Anglican Church in 1910 and priest in 1912. He served as a general missionary, the clergyman in charge of missions at Onion Lake and the James Smith reserves, and honourary canon of St. Alban's Anglican Church in Prince Albert. Edward Ahenakew also served a long term as a delegate to the General Synod of Canada, co-authored a Cree dictionary with Archdeacon R. Faries, and was awarded the King George Medal and the Queen Elizabeth Coronation Medal. A lake west of Wollaston Lake in northern Saskatchewan has been named in his honour.

31. Edward Ahenakew, "Genealogical Sketch," 9.

32. Fine Day, as quoted in Mandelbaum, *The Plains Cree*, 106.

33. For more information on Worthy Young Men and the Warrior society, see ibid., 110-21.

34. Oral history passed down by elders to the younger generations. Also see ibid., 105-10.

35. Oral history passed down by elders to the younger generations. Also see ibid., 100-10.

36. Salicin is closely related to acetylsalicylic acid (ASA) which is the active ingredient in aspirin and similar modern-day products.

37. Other Indian nations to introduce *midēwiwin* to their people included the Sisseton Sioux and the Poncas. See Karl Schlesier, "Rethinking The Midewiwin and the Plains Ceremonial Called the Sun Dance," *Plains Anthropological Journal of the Plains Anthropological Society* 35, no. 127 (February 1990): 18.

38. Oral history passed down by elders to the younger generations. Also see Karl Schlesier, "Rethinking The Midewiwin," 18; and *People of the Lakes*, The American Indians Series (Alexander, VA: Time Life Books, 1994), 103-4.

39. Some words do not translate adequately into English.

40. Barry L. Ahenakew, as told to him by the elders. Ruth Buck, in *Voices of the Plains Cree*, wrote that in 1913 an old medicine man at Onion Lake gave his medicine bag to her mother, Dr. Elizabeth Matheson, before he died. "It contained or was contained in a weasel skin, which the old man 'brought to life' so convincingly that both the doctor and her driver, James Buller, a well-educated Indian, believed that they saw a live weasel run up the old man's arm to his shoulder, and that when he stroked it, it became a dry skin once more." (See page 188.)

Chapter Five: Ahtahkakoop and His Family

1. See Edward Ahenakew's handwritten notes for "The History of the Ahenakews," (Edward Ahenakew Papers, SAB, R-1, file #5, p. 10) and *Voices of the Plains Cree*, 162. These references indicate that Masuskapoe died prior to 1861, which was the year Nāpēskis was killed.

2. When Sasakamoose died in 1899, he was said to be about 80 years old. This would make his birth year approximately 1819. According to his marriage certificate, Sasakamoose was 50 when he married in 1877, making his birth year 1827. This is one of many instances where discrepancies appear in the records and arbitrary decisions have had to be made. In this instance, the earlier date is being used since it is more consistent with other information. See death record #54 in the Sandy Lake Diocese of Saskatchewan Parish Register: Baptisms, Confirmations, Marriages, Burials, &c. (vol. 1). Also see record #3 in the marriage register contained in the Register of Births, Marriages and Deaths at Asissipi Mission, Diocese of Saskatchewan, North-West Territories of Canada, 1875. These registers are housed at the Anglican Diocese of Saskatchewan Synod Office.

3. Edward Ahenakew Papers, SAB, R-1, file #5, p. 8. Also see "The Story of the Ahenakews," by Edward Ahenakew, edited by Ruth Matheson Buck, *Saskatchewan History* 17, no. 1 (1964): 17. When these women were baptized by the Reverend John Hines during the 1870s, the first and oldest surviving wife was named Mary. The other wife took the name Margaret but was often called Maggie.

4. According to Ahenakew's death certificate he was 56 when he died in 1879, making 1823 the approximate year of his birth. His marriage certificate states his age as 50 when he married in 1877; based on this document he was born in 1827. The birth date of 1823 is being used. (See record #8 in the Asissipi Mission Death Register and record #26 in the Asissipi Mission Marriage Register. These registers are contained in the Church of England's Asissipi Mission Register, Diocese of Saskatchewan, dated 1875.)

5. Paul Ahenakew and Barry L. Ahenakew, June 1996 review meeting. Paul Ahenakew is an elder and former chief of the Ahtahkakoop Band.

6. Edward Ahenakew, "The Story of the Ahenakews," *Saskatchewan History* 17, no. 1 (1964): 18. Ahenakew was named David when he was baptized. His wife Kīskanakwās took the name Mary. The Asissipi Mission Marriage Register indicates that Ahenakew and Kīskanakwās were widower and widow when they married according to the rites of the Church of England in 1877 (Asissipi Mission Register, 1875, Marriage Register record #26).

7. Recollections of Thunderchild, in hand-written notes as recorded by Edward Ahenakew in 1923, Edward Ahenakew Papers, SAB, R-1, file #2, p. 168. Many of the stories Thunderchild told Ahenakew can be found in Edward Ahenakew's *Voices of the Plains Cree*.

8. Fine Day, as told to David Mandelbaum, August 6, 1934, David Mandelbaum Collection, SAB, R-875, folder 8a, 2/3, p. 40. Fine Day was born before 1854. The spelling of Nāpēskis's name has been regularized in this quotation.

9. Lloyd Starblanket, who is an elder in the Ahtahkakoop Band, as told to Barry L. Ahenakew.

10. Charles A. Messiter, *Sport and Adventures among the North American Indians* (London: R. H. Porter, 1890), 32.

11. See Mandelbaum, *The Plains Cree*, 10-11.

12. These people are sometimes known as the Willow or Savannah People.

13. See Mandelbaum, *The Plains Cree*, 9-11.

14. Angus Knife, an elder in the Ahtahkakoop Band, as told to Barry L. Ahenakew.

15. Carlton House Journal, 1832-33, HBCA, PAM,, PAM, B.27/a/19, fo. 20d.

16. Carlton House Journal, 1834-35, HBCA, PAM,, B.27/a/21, May 23, 1835, fo. 30.

17. Hines, *Red Indians of the Plains*, 117.

18. Kā-miyo-ahcahkwēw was given the name Antoine when he was baptized. See Asissipi Mission Marriage Register, record #2. The Asissipi Marriage Register indicates that Kā-miyo-ahcahkwēw was born in 1837. Roman Catholic Church records state that he was born in 1839 and baptized in 1844. (See genealogy report prepared by Alexander Dietz for the Ahtahkakoop Band.) He was given the name Antoine.

19. Hines, *Red Indians of the Plains*, p. 182.

20. Fine Day, as told to David Mandelbaum, August 8, 1934, David Mandelbaum Collection, SAB, R-875, folder 8a, 2/3, p. 41.

21. Editorial notes by Isaac Cowie accompanying the Fort Ellice Journal for 1858-59, National Archives of Canada (NA), Ottawa, MG19, D14, p. 10. Although this is a Fort Ellice Journal, Hudson's Bay Company policy would have been consistent throughout the Northern Department. Fort Ellice was situated near the junction of the Assiniboine and Qu'Appelle rivers. Cowie was stationed at Fort Qu'Appelle and Last Mountain House during the 1860s and 1870s.

22. Edward Ahenakew, *Voices of the Plains Cree*, 142-43.

23. Asissipi Journal, October 25-December 31, 1876, entry dated November 22, 1876, Church Missionary Society records (CMS), NA, MG 17, B.2, Microfilm Reel #A102. The National Archives of Canada (NA) is the main depository for the Church Missionary Society records. CMS records are available at a number of other archives,

including the Provincial Archives of Manitoba, where most of the work for this book was done.

24. These names and birth dates are based primarily on entries in the Asissipi Mission baptism, marriage, and death registers, as well as Treaty Paylists for the Ahtahkakoop Band.

25. Dietz, genealogy report.

26. Ibid.

27. Ibid.

28. Emma married John Kā-tāh-twēhototawāt (Bird Landing On Someone Repeatedly); Mary married Edward Genereux, an employee at Fort Carlton; Isabella married Mistawasis's oldest son Weyatōkwapew; Mary (2) married Peter Piyēsīs (Bird); and Philomene married John Jimmuk, who transferred from the Mistawasis Band to the Ahtahkakoop Band in 1884. Jimmuk was also known as John James Dufraine.

29. Dietz, genealogy report.

30. According to Catholic church records, Alexander was baptized on August 18, 1868. Margaret was born on April 4, 1869 (Church records and newspaper clipping). Alice married Kākikēyās (Always Wind Blowing) and Margaret married John M. Cameron, a freighter and trader who was born in Ontario.

31. Marie Louise married Daniel Villebrun; in the late 1860s Villebrun was working for the Hudson's Bay Company.

32. Ellen married John Hyman. Hyman is derived from *Āyiman* (It Is Difficult). His name appears as Lyman on several treaty paylists.

Chapter Six: Nāpēskis

1. Earl of Southesk, *Saskatchewan and the Rocky Mountains: A Diary and Narrative of Travel, Sport, and Adventure, during a Journey through the Hudson's Bay Company's Territories, in 1859 and 1860* (Toronto: James Campbell and Son, 1875), 99, 104.

2. Some sources, including Southesk, spell Tate's name as Tait.

3. Southesk, 98, 103. Southesk's descriptions of the country, the buffalo, and his experiences with Nāpēskis are taken from his book, *Saskatchewan and the Rocky Mountains*, 92-130, 299, 302. Southesk had travelled from Lachine (near Montreal) to Fort Garry in the company of George Simpson, the Governor of the Hudson's Bay Company. The group had travelled the new route via the American railway and the Red River instead of the traditional water highway leading to the North-West. Toma, an Iroquois voyageurs who had served as one of Simpson's canoe men during previous trips to Fort Garry, accompanied Southesk on his hunting trip.

4. Ibid., 92.

5. M'Kay (John McKay), a half-breed, was Southesk's guide. He was a younger brother of James McKay, a commissioner at the signing of Treaty Six in 1876.

6. In the preface to his book *Saskatchewan and the Rocky Mountains*, Southesk pointed out that when he included a "literal, or almost literal, transcript from ... [his] diary, ... [he marked] *such extracts when they occur, by single inverted commas.*" The italics are Southesk's.

7. Southesk, *Saskatchewan and the Rocky Mountains*, 93-94.

8. Ibid., 92-98.

9. Ibid., 99-100.

10. Southesk had bought the horse from James McKay.

11. See Mandelbaum, *The Plains Cree*, 96, and Ray, *Indians in the Fur Trade*, 75, 78.

12. Adapted from Southesk, *Saskatchewan and the Rocky Mountains*, 125. Also see Robert Jefferson, *Fifty Years on the Saskatchewan*, Canadian North-West Society Publications, vol. 1, no. 5 (Battleford, Saskatchewan), 66. According to Jefferson, neither paper nor wads were used to keep the powder and bullet in place. He went on to say many hands "were maimed, fingers blown off and other mischances by guns bursting owing to the bullet sticking in a dirty barrel."

13. The men generally kept their guns for warfare.

14. Jefferson, *Fifty Years on the Saskatchewan*, 66.

15. Southesk, *Saskatchewan and the Rocky Mountains*, 105.

16. Ibid. Several days later Southesk saw a similar animal in the midst of a small herd of buffalo. In his description of the animal, the earl said it was "towering far above the rest; it was one of those glossy, flat-sided, long-legged oxen already spoken of. They fall into this condition in calf-hood, either from the attacks of wolves, or from measures taken by the Indians." (See p. 118.)

17. See Mandelbaum, *The Plains Cree*, 58, and Jefferson, *Fifty Years on the Saskatchewan*, 67-68.

18. Hard fat is sometimes called tallow fat or grease.

19. See Mandelbaum, *The Plains Cree*, 58-59. Also see Mary Weekes, *The Last Buffalo Hunter: As told to her by Norbert Welsh* (New York: Thomas Nelson and Sons, 1939), 112.

20. Southesk, *Saskatchewan and the Rocky Mountains*, 108.

21. Chief Thunderchild, as told to Edward Ahenakew, Edward Ahenakew Papers, SAB, R-1, file 2, p. 168.

22. Southesk, *Saskatchewan and the Rocky Mountains*, 35, said that in Hudson's Bay account records Kline was sometimes spelt Klyne or Cline. For information about the other men, see pp. 35, 53, and 54.

23. Ibid., 109.

24. Ibid., 109-11.

25. Ibid., 111-13.

26. Ibid., 113, said the Indians called the mule deer "Black-Tailed Cabrees."

27. Ibid., 115.

28. Ibid., 124. Quotations such as this one have been used unedited to illustrate the "mindsets," perceptions, and biases of the various writers. Isaac Cowie, an Orkneyman who served as clerk in the Hudson's Bay Company's Swan River District some 10 years later, noted that "small white beads were predominant in the decoration of Indian dress and moccasins, arranged in square, circular and other geometric patterns, which were much more artistic than many of the embroideries of the Métis in the attempt to copy

flowers and leaves in coloured threads and silk, although some of the latter produced beautiful results. 'Pigeon Egg Beads' were the size of pigeon eggs and, like them, mottled. Beads of the same size and shape were also in red, white, blue, and black.... In the later 1860's they had gone out of fashion and boxes of them remained on hand as dead stock at Fort Qu'Appelle." (See NA, MG19, D14, Editorial notes written by Isaac Cowie to accompany typed copies of Fort Ellice journals for 1858-59, 1860, and 1863-64, p. 11.)

29. Ibid., 119, 125-27.

30. Ibid., 130. Since Carlton House journals for this period do not exist, an account of Southesk's visit does not appear in the post's documentation.

31. Ibid., 299, 302.

32. Simpson was governor of the Hudson's Bay Company from 1821, the year the Hudson's Bay Company and the North West Company joined forces, until his death in Lachine on September 7, 1860. After travelling with Southesk to Fort Garry in 1859, Simpson headed to Norway House.

33. Southesk, *Saskatchewan and the Rocky Mountains*, 5. Toma was also known as Thomas Ariwakenha (see p. 35).

34. Edward Ahenakew, "Story of the Ahenakews," *Saskatchewan History* 17, no. 1: 17.

35. Edward Ahenakew Papers, SAB R-1, file #5. There is duplication of page numbers and some repetition of information in this particular file. The story of Nāpēskis appears on pages numbered 9, 14[b], 15[b], and 16a. An edited version appears in "The Story of the Ahenakews," 17. Also see Edward Ahenakew, "Genealogical Sketch of My Family," from the American Philosophical Society Library, Philadelphia. In the first chapter of a handwritten draft of a novel entitled "Black Hawk," Ahenakew appears to be telling the story of Nāpēskis. In that story the young warrior explains his sadness to his older brother thus:

"'There is trouble that weighs heavy in my heart, my manhood is put to much strain. Two thousand miles is a long way brother.' He took a picture out of his pocket and handed it over. His brother looked at it and it proved to be the picture of a girl, a white girl, with smiling eyes. 'In Ottawa, her horse ran away and I stopped the horse. She was good to me because I saved her life. She gave me her likeness and I came away. My brother will be the only one that will know.'

"The older man sat silently and then handed back the picture. 'Twenty hundreds of miles is far, my brother but that is no obstacle. Something else is more difficult than the mere distance. You are no fool—you know what I mean.'" ("Black Hawk," Edward Ahenakew Papers, SAB R-1, file #7, p. 7.)

36. Edward Ahenakew Papers, SAB, R-1, file #5, p. 10.

37. Thunderchild, Edward Ahenakew Papers, SAB, R-1, file #2, p. 170.

38. See Edward Ahenakew's hand-written notes of the story told by Thunderchild (SAB R-1, file #2, pp. 168 and 170) and a hand-written account by Ahenakew (file #5, p. 10). According to Thunderchild's version of the story, when the Blackfoot recounted the story later they said Nāpēskis left Poor Creek and walked fighting them. He "took a long time to kill" the Blackfoot said.

39. Edward Ahenakew's "Genealogical Sketch of My Family," American Philosophical Society Library, Philadelphia, pp. 16-17.

40. Thunderchild, Edward Ahenakew Papers, SAB, R-1, file #2, p. 168.

41. Edward Ahenakew, "Genealogical Sketch of My Family," 16-17. Ahenakew, in this source, said his "uncle [Kāh-kāsōw] would have liked to have stood silently for a short time, at least, beside the grave but the distance was too great from where he was. His nephew and others who accompanied him wanted to come back, and they overruled him. Kāh-kāsōw took the name Peter Kāh-kāsōw when he was baptized.

42. Cited in *Voices of the Plains Cree*, 162.

Chapter Seven: Newcomers to the Land of the Nēhiyaw

1. [Walter Butler] Cheadle, *Dr. Cheadle's Journal of a Trip Across Canada 1862–63*, Introduction and notes by A.G. Doughty and Gustave Lanctot (Ottawa: Graphic Publishers Ltd., 1931), 66. See NA, MG24, H40, vol. 1, which contains the original manuscript, for further information. Cheadle, a medical doctor, was 27 years old in 1862 (*Journal*, p. 7). Lord Milton (William Fitzwilliam, Viscount Milton) was 23. Also see chapter one in Charles Alston Messiter, *Sport and Adventures*.

2. Cheadle, *Journal*, 70. This lake, called *manitow-sākahikan* (God's Lake), is about 5 miles north of the Ahtahkakoop Reserve. It was sometimes referred to as Spirit Lake or Devil's Lake, and today is known as Morin Lake. In this book the Cree name for the lake, *manitow-sākahikan*, is being used to distinguish it from God's Lake (Manitou Lake) near present-day Watrous. Cheadle said Jolie Prairie was about one-half mile south of River Crochet (Crooked River). In a book credited to Milton and Cheadle but written mainly by Cheadle, *The North-West Passage by Land, being the narrative of an expedition from the Atlantic to the Pacific* (London: Cassell, Petter, and Galpin, fifth edition, [1865]), 72, Cheadle calls the area La Belle Prairie. He described it as a "lovely little spot, a small prairie of perhaps 200 acres, surrounded by low wooded hills, and on one side a lake winding with many an inlet amongst the hills and into the plain, while here and there a tiny promontory, richly clothed with pines and aspens, stretched out into the water."

3. Cheadle used the French name, *Montagne du Bois*, for the Thickwood Hills.

4. Milton and Cheadle, *North-West Passage*, 71.

5. Messiter is given the name Treemiss in Milton and Cheadle's book, *The North-West Passage by Land*.

6. Cheadle, *Journal*, 69.

7. Cheadle, *Journal*, 70, said that an old man Milton had hired to guide them over the mountains in the spring accompanied Messiter to the Thickwood Hills. Messiter does not mention this in his book *Sport and Adventures*. Here, as elsewhere, Cheadle's version is taken over Messiter's since Cheadle kept a daily journal. Messiter's book was written later and in many respects is not accurate; furthermore it was written to present himself in a good light, and often it seems to be at least partially based on information that was written by people such as Cheadle and Southesk. It does, nevertheless, contain information not found elsewhere.

8. Cheadle, *Journal*, 69. Also see Messiter, *Sport and Adventures*, 28.

9. See Christensen, A "Convenient Place," 260-64, 274, 279.

10. Palliser, an Irish sportsman and explorer, headed a three-year scientific exploratory expedition known as the British North American Exploring Expedition of 1857-1860. Its objective was to gather information for the British government about the land south of the North and South Saskatchewan rivers and the southern passes through the Rocky Mountains.

11. The Hudson's Bay Company's monopoly on the trade in the North-West had been broken in 1849 when four Métis in the Red River Settlement were accused of illegally trading furs with Indian trappers. In a case that went to court on May 17, one of the men was found "guilty of Trading Furs," but he was set free and not punished. This ruling, in essence, opened up the North-West to competition.

12. This information was compiled from Christensen, "A Convenient Place," 260-64, 274-75, 279-80, 295. George McDougall, John's father, founded the Victoria mission 70 miles downstream from Edmonton House soon after his trip to Saskatchewan River country.

13. For information on the Reverend Henry Budd's visit to Moose Woods, see his account of a trip to Mistawasis's camp appended to the Nepowewin Mission Journal, June 28, 1857-March 13, 1858, CMS, Microfilm Reel #A84. A Swampy Cree from Norway House, Henry Budd was the first ordained native clergyman in Western Canada. He established the Nepowiwin Mission opposite Fort à la Corne I in 1852; this Hudson's Bay Company post was situated just east of present-day James Smith Reserve. Budd's mission was one of the earliest missions established by the Church of England's Church Missionary Society in the land now called Saskatchewan.

14. Paul Ahenakew, in an interview with the author at the Ahtahkakoop Reserve, October 18, 1995.

15. Cheadle, *Journal*, 64, 66.

16. John McDougall, *Forest, Lake and Prairie: Twenty Years of Frontier Life in Western Canada—1842-62* (Toronto: William Briggs, 1910), 136.

17. Messiter, 29-30, 51. Also see Milton and Cheadle, 118. Messiter incorrectly said that the site was 90 miles northwest of Fort Carlton.

18. Messiter, 30.

19. Ibid., 31. Also see Cheadle, *Journal*, 75.

20. A stage is a raised platform or scaffold built for keeping meat and other items out of the reach of animals.

21. Messiter, *Sport and Adventures,* 32, 59.

22. Ibid., 32.

23. According to Messiter, Farquharson was a painter from Edinburgh who wanted to go to the gold fields in British Columbia. The man was in dire straits at Fort Carlton when Messiter invited him to winter with him in the Thickwood Hills. Poorly suited for life in the North-West, he spent a miserable winter.

24. Messiter, *Sport and Adventures,* 57 -59.

25. Ibid., 45, 46.

26. Ibid., 46-47.

27. Ibid., 48.

28. Ibid., 49.

29. Ibid., 66-67.

30. Milton and Cheadle, *North-West Passage,* 146.

31. Ibid., 146.

32. Cheadle spelt Kihci-mōhkomān's name Gatchi Mohkamarn. Cheadle said Kihci-mōhkomān was Saulteaux; Messiter said he was Cree. See Cheadle's *Journal,* fn. 26, 310; and Messiter, *Sport and Adventures,* 51.

33. Messiter, *Sport and Adventures,* 52-53, 67.

34. Ibid., 51.

35. Cheadle, *Journal,* 92, 93, 95, 97, 112. Clerk A.R. Lillie was in charge of Fort Carlton for the 1862-1864 seasons.

36. Messiter, *Sport and Adventures,* 70, 71.

37. Some 12 years later Kihci-mōhkoman was with Otayapīhkēw (Netmaker) when John Hines was at Whitefish Lake. (See Hines, *Red Indians,* 66.) Also see letter from Hines to the CMS committee, dated November 20, 1874, CMS, Microfilm Reel #A101. Kihci-mōhkomān was a member of Ahtahkakoop's band when Treaty Six was signed in 1876.

38. Cheadle, *Journal,* 111-13. Also see Milton and Cheadle, North-West Passage, 146-47.

39. Cheadle, *Journal,* 92- 93. Also see Messiter, *Sport and Adventures,* 38-42, 54-55.

40. See Cheadle's *Journal,* 71-126 and notes on 309-10.

41. Messiter, *Sport and Adventures,* 79. Also see Cheadle, *Journal,* 126-27, and the Fort Ellice Journal, 1862-63, April 22, 1863, NA, MG19, D14.

Chapter Eight: Smallpox Kills Hundreds

1. Messiter, *Sport and Adventures,* 54. Unfortunately, Messiter does not give the names of Ahtahkakoop's son and his informant.

2. Some of Chief Thunderchild's stories about horse raids and revenge warfare can be found in Edward Ahenakew's *Voices of the Plains Cree.* Thunderchild, whose people at one time were part of Mistawasis's band, told these stories to the Reverend Edward Ahenakew in 1923.

3. Fine Day, as told to Mandelbaum, August 14, 1934, on the Sweetgrass Reserve, SAB, R-875, 8a, file 2/3, p. 77. The practice of using tobacco and the neutrality of a Hudson's Bay Company officer to make offers of peace was noted in the Carlton House journals. For example, on February 12, 1828, the officer in charge of the post passed on to a Cree man "the tobacco sent down from the Slave [Blackfoot] Indians for Peace which he … [took] away with him to present to his country men the Cree Indians, & who is to forward other Tobacco for the same purpose to the Slave Indians to ratify the peace of the contending parties." See the Carlton House Journal for 1827-28, HBCA, PAM, B.27/a/16, 26d.

4. This account is compiled in part from notes taken by Mandelbaum when he interviewed Fine Day on the Sweetgrass Reserve, August 14, 1943 (SAB, R-875, 8a, file 2/3, pp. 76-77); and Thomas Muchahaw (Tapahtowēw, or "Low Voice") and Peter

Dreaver (Kā-kisēyiniw-pimohtēw, or "Walks Like An Old Man"), July 18, 1934, on the Mistawasis Reserve. (See SAB, R-875, 8a, file 1/3, p. 187.)

5. Muchahaw, as told to Mandelbaum, SAB, R-875, 8a, file 1/3, p. 187. Several verb tenses have been changed in the translation.

6. Alexander Ahenakew, review meeting June 1996.

7. This story is recorded in Mary Weekes, *The Last Buffalo Hunter*, 140-49.

8. Barry L. Ahenakew, review meeting November 1996.

9. Peter Peekeekoot (Hook Nose), as told to his grandson, elder Paul Ahenakew. The story was re-told by Paul Ahenakew at a review meeting in June 1996. Peter was the grandson of Ahtahkakoop's brother Masuskapoe.

10. Lloyd Starblanket is an elder in the Ahtahkakoop Band. Wāpasinīwiskwēw (White Stone Woman), who was later known as Mary Jane Okimāsis, was the daughter of Akamasiniy; before marrying Ahtahkakoop's son Michel in 1882 she was a member of the One Arrow Band. Wāpasinīwiskwēw was 19 when Treaty 6 was signed in 1876.

11. Based on a story told by Minnie Fraser to Freda Ahenakew in October 1986. Almost 91 years of age when she told this story, Minnie Fraser was the granddaughter of Ahenakew and the daughter of Louis and Ellen Ahenakew.

12. [Reverend Robert Terrill Rundle], *The Rundle Journals: 1840-1848*, notes and introduction by Gerald M. Hutchinson, edited by Hugh Dempsey (Calgary: Historical Society of Alberta and Glenbow-Alberta Institute, 1977), 189.

13. Paul Kane, *Wanderings of an Artist Among the Indians of North America, 1846-48 from Canada to Vancouver's Island and Oregon through the Hudson's Bay Company's Territory and back again* (London: Longman, Brown, Green, Longmans and Roberts, 1859), 130-31.

14. John Palliser, *The Papers of the Palliser Expedition*, edited with an introduction and notes by Irene M. Spry (Toronto: The Champlain Society, 1968), 258. Palliser said he was more than two miles from the buffalo on July 31, 1858, when he made this observation.

15. Hudson's Bay Company man Andrew McDermott, in Joel A. Allen, *American Bisons, Living and Extinct, Memoirs of the Museum of Comparative Zoology* 14, no. 10 (Cambridge, MA, 1876), 173, as cited in Frank Gilbert Roe, *The North American Buffalo: A critical study of the species in its wild state*, 2nd ed. (Toronto: University of Toronto Press, 1970), 364.

16. Fort Qu'Appelle was a Hudson's Bay Company post situated in the Qu'Appelle Valley at the present site of the town of Fort Qu'Appelle.

17. Isaac Cowie, *The Company of Adventurers: A Narrative of Seven Years in the Service of the Hudson's Bay Company During 1867–1874 on the Great Buffalo Plains* (Toronto: William Briggs, 1913), 373-74.

18. Lawrence Clarke, officer in charge of Fort Carlton, to William McMurray, January 27, 1868, Private letters from the fur trade, compiled by Clifford Wilson (Off-print from papers read before the Historical and Scientific Society of Manitoba, serial 3, no. 5, 1950, p. 40.)

19. For information on Budd, see p. 748, endnote 2.

20. Bishop of Saskatchewan's Journal of a Visit to the Church Missionary Society's

Mission at Asissipi (Asissipi River) in the Diocese of Saskatchewan, May 6, 1881, CMS, Microfilm Reel #110. Also see Hines, *Red Indians*, 79-80.

21. Ibid., Ahtahkakoop told this story at church the day he was confirmed. He told a similar story to Hines the first time he met the missionary. (See Hines, *Red Indians*, 80.)

22. This is based on a conversation between Paul Ahenakew and the author on October 18, 1995, at the Ahtahkakoop Reserve.

23. Bishop of Saskatchewan's Journal, May 6, 1881. Hines records a similar story in his book *Red Indians,* 79-80. In this version, Ahtahkakoop said: "on the way the Bishop spoke to me about religion, and wanted to baptise me; I told him I did not know enough to be baptised, but I promised that if he would send a priest to live among us and teach us I would settle in some suitable place, and collect my followers around me. The Bishop was pleased, and said if I would be at Carlton the next summer about the same time of the year, he would arrange to have a priest there who should remain with us, and I agreed to do so. He tried hard to get me to be baptised before we parted, but I refused, not because I hated religion but because I did not know enough about it. The next summer came and I kept my appointment, and true enough a party of priests arrived from Winnipeg, and I made myself known to them. But they said they had no instructions to remain with any Indians at or near Carlton, but they would be pleased to baptise any children there might be in my camp—in fact any adults too who would submit to be baptised. I was much disappointed at the Bishop forgetting all about me and his promise, and I told them so; however, I said I would wait another year and see what the Bishop would do then, and I refused to let them baptise any of my people until they had first been taught."

24. Isbister's farm was situated about one mile east of the penitentiary at present-day Prince Albert.

25. Born at Red River in December 1837, Gabriel was the son of Métis hunter Isidore Dumont and the grandson of a French-Canadian voyageur by the name of Jean-Baptiste Dumont.

26. Kent McNeil, *Native Claims in Rupert's Land and the North-Western Territory: Canada's Constitutional Obligations*, Studies in Aboriginal Rights, no. 5 (Saskatoon: University of Saskatchewan Native Law Centre, 1982), 1, and elsewhere in his document. Also see Frank J. Tough, "Aboriginal Rights Versus the Deed of Surrender: The Legal Rights of Native Peoples and Canada's Acquisition of the Hudson's Bay Company Territory," *Prairie Forum* 17, no. 2 (Fall 1992).

27. The Manitoba Act was passed May 12, 1870, with the transfer of jurisdiction effective July 15, 1870. Gerald Friesen, in *The Canadian Prairies*, provides a good general overview of the Red River Resistance and the events surrounding the creation of the Province of Manitoba.

28. For example, in a confidential letter written to Prime Minister John A. Macdonald on October 9, 1871, Lieutenant-Governor Adams G. Archibald said that "many of the French half-breeds have been so beaten and outraged by a small but noisy section of the people [mainly English-speaking newcomers from Ontario] … that they feel as if they were living in a state of slavery.… Bitter hatred of these people is a yoke so intolerable that they would gladly escape it by any sacrifice." Cited in Arthur S. Morton, *A History of the Canadian West*, 920.

29. See Tough, "Aboriginal Rights Versus the Deed of Surrender," 238.

30. Lieutenant Butler's Report to Adams G. Archibald, lieutenant-governor of Manitoba, dated March 10, 1871, as contained in William Francis Butler, *The Great Lone Land* (Toronto: The Musson Book Company, Ltd., 1924), 359. This report hereafter is referred to as "Report." Butler said that "This state of hostility has latterly degenerated, on the part of the Americans, into a war of extermination; and the policy of 'clearing out' the red man has now become a recognized portion of Indian warfare. Some of these acts of extermination find their way into the public records, many of them never find publicity." (See *The Great Lone Land*, 359.) Similar statements can be found in other documentation.

31. Butler, "Report," 358-59.

32. Ahtahkakoop's daughter Mary was married to Edward Genereux, who worked at Fort Carlton during the 1860s. (See Ahtahkakoop Treaty Paylists; Saskatchewan Servants Equipment, Outfit 1863, HBCA, PAM, B.60/d/149; and Saskatchewan Servants' Book Debts 1865-65, HBCA, PAM, B.60/d/156, fos. 66-66d. One of Mistawasis's daughters married James Dreaver. From the Orkney Islands, Dreaver was 19 in 1848 when he arrived in the North-West to work at Fort Carlton.

33. Hines, *Red Indians*, 151.

34. Cowie, *Company of Adventurers*, 381-82. The youngster was the grandchild of visitor Pascal Breland. A half-breed, Breland was a member of the Council of Assiniboia and a magistrate for the Red River Settlement.

35. Butler, in his report to Archibald, said that since the last major smallpox epidemic [1837] "the disease appears to have visited some of the tribes at intervals of greater or less duration, but until this and the previous year its ravages were confined to certain localities and did not extend universally throughout the country." According to Butler, several vaccination programs were attempted in 1870. He said that Nisbet vaccinated a number of individuals at his Presbyterian mission in Prince Albert. Then the officer in charge of Fort Pitt used "vaccine matter" obtained from a Saulteaux inoculated by Nisbet to immunize everyone living at Fort Pitt. Apparently none of these people came down with smallpox. Vaccine administered at Fort Edmonton and nearby St. Albert "was of little or no avail to check the spread of the disease." This vaccine, Butler continued, may have been ineffective because it "was of a spurious description, having been brought from Fort Benton, on the Missouri River, by traders during the early summer, and ... it was used when the disease had reached its height, while on the other hand, the vaccination carried on from Mr. Nisbet's Mission appears to have been commenced early in the spring, and also to have been of a genuine description." Butler makes no mention of a vaccination program at Fort Carlton. (See Butler, "Report," 366, 368.)

36. Fine Day, as told to Mandelbaum, August 9, 1943, Mandelbaum Papers, SAB, R-875 8a. folder 2/3 (Part 3), p. 54. Also see Butler who, in a similar story, reported that the Cree warriors carried away clothes and scalps from the infected camp (Butler, "Report," 367). Elsewhere in his report Butler stated that "It is very generally believed in the Saskatchewan that this disease was originally communicated to the [American] Blackfeet tribes by Missouri traders with a view to the accumulation of robes; and this opinion, monstrous though it may appear, has been somewhat verified by the Western press when treating of the epidemic last year." (See Butler, "Report," 359.)

37. Butler, "Report," 367. Also see Cowie, *Company of Adventurers*, 382. W.T. Chartier, another Hudson's Bay Company officer, in a letter to Hudson's Bay Company Governor D.A. Smith dated September 5, 1870, confirmed that the smallpox entered Saskatchewan country via the Blackfoot. Chartier wrote that "The Indians blame the whites [presumably those at Fort Edmonton] for it, although they know they brought it to us themselves from the Blackfeet and Pagan who got it from the Americans in the Missouri." Chartier wrote the letter while camped across the river from Fort Carlton. (Chartier to Smith, September 5, 1870, Archibald Papers, NA, M537.)

38. Butler, "Report," 369. On pages 227-28 of *The Great Lone Land*, Butler says 36 of the 60 people at the post had smallpox and 32 died. Also see Carlton House Inward Correspondence, HBCA, PAM, B.27/c/2, fo. 21a. The white victim was Donald McDonald, clerk at Fort Carlton. Only two other white people in the entire North-West were reported to have died during the epidemic; they were the daughters of Methodist missionary George McDougall who was stationed at the Victoria Mission in what is now eastern Alberta.

39. Ibid., 369.

40. Ibid., 368. Also see Chartier to Smith, September 5, 1870.

41. For further information on the purpose of Butler's trip, see S.W. Hill's letter to Butler dated Fort Garry, October 10, 1870, in the Appendix of Butler's *Lone Land*, 353-54. Hill was private secretary to Archibald. Also see Butler, "Report," 371.

42. Butler, "Report," 369-70.

43. John McDougall, *George Millward McDougall: The Pioneer, Patriot and Missionary* (Toronto: William Briggs, 1888), 167. Also see 157, 161. John McDougall was the son of George McDougall.

44. Peter Erasmus, *Buffalo Days and Nights, as told to Henry Thompson*, introduction by Irene Spry (Calgary: Glenbow-Alberta Institute, 1976), 249. Chartier, in his letter to Smith, dated September 5, 1870, estimated that two-thirds of the Indian population would be wiped out. Although this estimate apparently was high, the results nevertheless were tragic.

45. Butler, "Report," 369. Father André was the newly arrived Catholic priest at the St. Laurent mission on the South Branch of the Saskatchewan River.

46. Butler, *Lone Land*, 235.

47. Butler, "Report," 358.

48. Butler, *Lone Land*, 229. In December of 1870 the clerk at Fort Carlton wrote that the Hudson's Bay Company carts had just arrived from the plains, "having had to go about 3 or 400 miles for their meat." Letter from Henry Hardisty to Roderick MacFarlane, December 1870, NA, MG29, A11, vol. 1, pp. 28-29.

Chapter Nine: Concerns in Indian Country

1. Butler, *Lone Land*, 236, said the camp was "some distance above" the confluence of the Battle and North Saskatchewan rivers.

2. S.W. Hill, private secretary to the lieutenant-governor, to Butler, October 10, 1870, in the Appendix, Butler's *Lone Land*, 354.

3. Ibid., 353-54.

4. Butler, *Lone Land*, 201.

5. A *capote* was a knee-length woollen great coat with a hood attached to the collar.

6. Butler, *Lone Land*, 236-37. The man in charge of the post was likely Peter Ballendine, one of the interpreters when Treaty Six was negotiated at Fort Carlton in 1876. His assistant, Daniel Villebrun, was married to Ahenakew's daughter Marie Louise. Also known as Catherine, she was likely at the trading house with her husband when Butler visited.

7. Ibid., 237.

8. Ibid. Butler does not mention a delegation of leaders, but it is unlikely that Mistawasis would have met Butler by himself. The interpreter was probably Peter Ballendine.

9. Ibid. The material within quotation marks is exactly as Butler wrote it, except for several changes in punctuation.

10. Ibid., 238.

11. A copy of Lieutenant W. F. Butler's report to Lieutenant-Governor Archibald, dated Manitoba, March 10, 1871, is contained in the appendix of Butler's book the *Great Lone Land*, 355-86. Butler's journey had taken 119 days. He covered about 2,700 miles, travelling the Carlton Trail from Fort Garry to Fort Carlton, and then west as far as Rocky Mountain House. Retracing his steps to Fort Carlton, he visited Prince Albert, Fort à la Corne, Cumberland House, and posts in present-day Manitoba on his return trip to Fort Garry.

12. Butler, "Report," 358-59.

13. This White Fish Lake should not be confused with Whitefish Lake near present-day Debden, Saskatchewan.

14. Butler, "Report," 383-84. He said that Victoria, which was near a Wesleyan (Methodist) mission, was situated on the North Branch of the Saskatchewan River 84 miles below [i.e., east of] Edmonton House. The settlement at White Fish Lake, where another Wesleyan Mission was located, was 60 miles northeast of Victoria. The settlement at Lac La Biche (70 miles north-west of Fort Pitt) had a Roman Catholic mission. St. Albert, comprised of "900 French" before the smallpox epidemic, was the largest settlement on the Saskatchewan River and home to Bishop Grandin and his Roman Catholic mission; it was located nine miles north of Edmonton House. The French half-breed settlement at Lac St. Anne, which was also Roman Catholic, was located 50 miles northwest of Edmonton.

15. Ibid., 360.

16. Ibid., 361.

17. Ibid., 363-66.

18. Ibid., 378-79.

19. Cited in Hugh A. Dempsey, *Big Bear: The End of Freedom* (Vancouver/Toronto: Douglas & McIntyre, 1984), 43. John McDougall, son of Methodist missionary George McDougall, was the young man who visited Fort Carlton in 1862. He later took over the Wesleyan mission at Victoria.

20. Letter from W.J. Christie, chief factor in charge of the Hudson's Bay Company's

Saskatchewan District, to Lieutenant-Governor Archibald, dated April 13, 1871, as contained in Alexander Morris, *The Treaties of Canada with the Indians of Manitoba and the North-West Territories* (1880; Coles Publishing Company, Toronto, 1979), 169. The italics are Butler's.

21. Ibid., 170-72.

22. Ibid., 169-70.

23. Ibid., 170.

24. Oral tradition. Also see William Joseph Christie's Journal of a Voyage from Fort Garry to Fort Simpson, MacKenzie River, by Land and Water, and of his Return by Dog-train to Carlton, performed on a tour of inspection of posts, August 22, 1872 to January 28, 1873, entries dated September 11, 1872, and January 27, 1873, NA, MG29, A6, pp. 4, 5, 22. Christie was now inspecting chief factor of the Hudson's Bay Company. The document housed at the National Archives of Canada is a typewritten copy made by retired fur trader Isaac Cowie; the original is in HBCA, PAM, E. 23/1.

25. Fort Garry, where the community of Winnipeg developed, had become the Hudson's Bay Company's administrative centre in the new land during George Simpson's tenure as governor of the company.

26. Masuskapoe was listed as one of the Hudson's Bay Company tripmen in 1855. (See York Factory Tripman Book, Outfit 1855, HBCA, PAM, B.239/d/888, fo. 2.) A tripman was a man hired to work on the York boats for the voyage to and from York Factory.

27. Although a Catholic priest entered the name of Ahenakew's daughter as Catherine when she married in May, 1870, the woman apparently used the name Marie Louise. (See the family's genealogy record in the Denny Collection, M7144, file 5334,000, at the Glenbow Archives, Calgary.)

28. William Joseph Christie (inspecting chief factor of the Hudson's Bay Company), "Journal of a Voyage," 4-5.

29. Ibid., 14.

30. Ibid., 22.

31. Ibid., 22.

32. Lawrence Clarke, officer in charge of Fort Carlton, to Richard Hardisty, officer in charge of the Saskatchewan District, in a letter dated March 26, 1873, Richard Hardisty fonds, Glenbow Archives Calgary, M 5908, file 231, item 1538. Clarke also indicated in this letter that the "Indians and freemen are all starving."

Chapter 10: The Arrival of John Hines, 1874-1875

1. Hines, *Red Indians*, 78. Published in 1915, the book was written 41 years after the missionary's arrival in the North-West. Hines says in his introductory note that he left all his records "behind him in the land of his experiences." Fortunately, much of this documentation (which includes journals, letters, and reports) has been preserved as part of the Church Missionary Society records and is available on microfilm at a number of archives in Canada, including the National Archives of Canada and the Provincial Archives of Manitoba. For this book, the field records have been relied on more extensively than the published work, particularly when discrepancies occur between the two sources.

2. Ibid., 25. The decision to develop a farm in association with the mission was in response to a report presented to the Church Missionary Society committee by the newly consecrated Bishop of Athabasca, the Reverend W.C. Bompas. In his report, Bompas said that buffalo and other large animals were rapidly becoming "exterminated" in the North-West, and he suggested "that if any of their students, besides having other necessary qualifications for the work, had also a knowledge of agriculture, they would do well to occupy this field." He explained that "Indians would be attracted to it [the mission], and owing to the growing scarcity of buffaloes, would turn their attention to agriculture. Then schools could be started for the children, and a regular system of religious instruction could be carried on for all." John Hines, who had just completed his studies, was recruited for this new venture. He travelled with Bompas from England to Winnipeg. From there, Bompas travelled by boat to the Athabasca district and Hines went overland to Saskatchewan River country with Cowley's party. (See Hines, *Red Indians*, 24.)

3. Ibid., 45. In 1874 George's father, William McKay, was the factor at Fort Pitt after having served at the Hudson's Bay Company's Fort Ellice for many years. His mother Mary was the sister of the Reverend Thomas Cook who had a Church Missionary Society mission near Fort Ellice. In 1874 George's sister Catherine married Lawrence Clarke, the factor at Fort Carlton. Thus George McKay was well connected with both the fur trade and the Church of England.

4. See ibid., 53-54, 78.

5. Alexander Morris, who was born in Perth, Upper Canada, in 1826, had replaced Adams G. Archibald as lieutenant-governor of Manitoba and the North-West Territories in December of 1872. Prior to this appointment, Morris had served as a minister in Sir John A. Macdonald's Conservative government from 1869 to July 1872, when he was appointed chief justice of Manitoba. He resigned from the bench in December of 1872 to accept the position of lieutenant-governor.

6. William McKay, letter dated Fort Pitt, August 29, 1874, to Richard Hardisty, Edmonton House, Morris Papers, Provincial Archives of Manitoba (PAM), MG 12, B.1, file 901.

7. Ibid. McKay's tour of Indian camps included Sweetgrass's camp as well as Big Bear's. After delivering his message at each camp, he distributed presents of tea, sugar, tobacco, ammunition, clay pipes, twine, and knives. While McKay was delivering this message to the Indian people who traded at Fort Pitt, McDougall, soon to be associated with the Morleyville Mission near the Bow and Elk (South Saskatchewan) rivers, was carrying a similar message to the Blackfoot and Stoneys of the southwestern plains; he had received his instructions on July 31 while camped between the Bow and Elk rivers. McKay's and McDougall's reports were forwarded to Lieutenant-Governor Alexander Morris. (See file 901 in the Morris Papers, PAM, MG 12, B.1.)

8. Paul Ahenakew, interview October 18, 1995, at the Ahtahkakoop Reserve.

9. Barry L. Ahenakew, at the 1994 review meetings.

10. Hines, *Red Indians*, 53-54.

11. Letter from Hines to the Church Missionary Society (CMS) committee, London, dated November 20, 1874, CMS, NA, MG 17, B.2, Microfilm Reel #A101. In his book, Hines said that Cowley left him on the shore of Whitefish Lake on August 13, after they

returned from Green Lake. The date in the November 20 letter is used here since the book was written some 40 years later without the benefit of notes or journals.

12. Hines, *Red Indians*, 55-58. Also see letter from Hines to the CMS committee, dated November 20, 1874, CMS, Microfilm Reel #A101.

13. Ibid., 58-61.

14. Ibid., 64.

15. Included in Hines's travelling party were the newly consecrated Bishop of Athabasca, the Right Reverend W.C. Bompas, and his bride; Emma Moore, the sister of a missionary working in Manitoba; and several others connected with the Church Missionary Society. They landed at New Jersey, USA, after a 12-day voyage and then went by train as far as the banks of the Red River where Hines and members of his party boarded a riverboat for the trip to Winnipeg. From Winnipeg Hines travelled overland to Saskatchewan River country with ox carts and a horse-drawn wagon. See Hines, *Red Indians*, 9, 15, 25, 29, 30-40.

16. Hines, in a letter to the Reverend Henry Wright, dated January 4, 1875, CMS, Microfilm Reel #A101.

17. In his book, Hines said that Archdeacon Cowley had left his oxen with him, adding to the three he had purchased with his own money. According to his report of January 11, 1875, CMS, Microfilm Reel #A101, Hines had three oxen and later purchased a fourth.

18. Hines, report to the CMS committee dated January 4, 1875, CMS, Microfilm Reel #A101.

19. Hines, *Red Indians*, 65.

20. Ibid., 66. Also see Hines, report dated November 20, 1874, CMS, Microfilm Reel #A101.

21. Ibid.

22. As cited in Hines, *Red Indians*, 68. The words within the quotation marks appear within quotation marks in Hines's book. In order to avoid the awkward construction of double and single quotation marks, this form of citation is being used here and in similar instances throughout this book.

23. Hines, *Red Indians*, 68, 69, 72.

24. Ibid., 71-72.

25. Ibid., 75.

26. Letter from Hines to the CMS committee dated November 20, 1874, CMS, Microfilm Reel #A101.

27. Ibid., *Red Indians*, 76.

28. Letter from Hines to Wright, CMS committee, dated January 4, 1875, CMS, Microfilm Reel #A101.

29. Hines, report to the CMS committee dated November 20, 1874, CMS, Microfilm Reel #101.

30. The following has been compiled from information given by Barry L. Ahenakew, Willard Ahenakew, and others at the review meetings held in 1994.

31. For instance, see Christie to Archibald, April 13, 1871, in Morris, *Treaties*, 169.

32. Hines, *Red Indians*, 78-79.

33. Ibid., 80.

34. In *Red Indians*, 80, Hines implies that Ahtahkakoop went directly to see him upon learning of his whereabouts. In his report to the CMS committee dated November 20, 1874, Hines says he sent George McKay to Fort Carlton to get Ahtahkakoop. The interpreter was back with the chief in eight days. The version that appeared in the report to the CMS committee is used here since it is considered to be more accurate.

35. G.A. French, commissioner of the North-West Mounted Police, Commissioner's Report, 1874, as contained in *Opening up the West, Being the Official Reports to Parliament of the Activities of the Royal North-West Mounted Police Force from 1874–1881* (1874-1881; Coles Publishing Company: Toronto, 1973). Also see Inspector W.O. Jarvis to French, November 2, 1874, p. 68.

36. Hines, report to the CMS committee dated Whitefish Lake, November 20, 1874, CMS, Microfilm Reel #A101.

37. Hines, *Red Indians*, 78. According to the Asissipi Mission Marriage Register, record #19, Joseph was 23 when he married in 1880. His death certificate indicates he was 28 in 1891, so there are discrepancies regarding his age.

38. As cited in Hines, *Red Indians*, 79.

39. Hines, report to Wright, January 4, 1875, CMS, Microfilm Reel #A101.

40. As cited in Hines's report to Wright, January 4, 1875, CMS, Microfilm Reel #A101.

41. As cited in Hines, *Red Indians*, 80.

42. Hines, *Red Indians*, 80-81. The bishop was W.C. Bompas, the newly consecrated Bishop of Athabasca.

43. As cited in *Red Indians*, 81.

44. Ibid., 81-82.

45. As cited in Hines's report to the CMS committee dated November 20, 1874, entry for October 12, CMS, Microfilm Reel #101.

46. Hines, *Red Indians*, 82.

47. Peter Knife, in a transcript of an interview conducted by Austin Ahenakew, pp. 7-8. A copy of the transcript is on file with the Federation of Saskatchewan Indian Nations' Indian Rights and Treaties Research Progamme, Regina. Peter Knife was the grandson of Kichi-mōhkomān (Big Knife) and son of Nātakām (Mac Knife). He said he was told the story of Ahtahkakoop's selection of Sandy Lake by eight "old men": Ahtahkakoop's sons, Kā-miyo-astotin and Michel; Knife's grandfather, Kāh-kāsōw; his son-in-law's father, Louis Ahenakew; his father-in-law, Nīsōtēw (Twin), also known as Jacob and John Scott; Pipanīk (Misty); Siyākāpanos (Old Masuskapoe, Solomon's father); and his father Nātakām.

48. Peter Knife, interview by Austin Ahenakew.

49. Ibid. pp. 8-9.

50. Hines, report to the CMS committee, dated November 20, 1874, CMS, Microfilm Reel #A101, entry for October 12, 1874. In his entry for December 19, Hines indicated that another five families who were camped between Fort Carlton and Sandy Lake had heard about Hines's arrival and planned on moving to Sandy Lake for the winter.

However, the early snow "prevented them from doing so." He also said that in December he talked to some Indian people in Prince Albert who said they would join Ahtahkakoop's group in the spring. This was likely Ahenakew's family.

51. According to Roman Catholic records, Michel was born in 1862 and baptized the following year.

52. Hines, report to the CMS committee dated November 20, 1874, and Wright, January 4, 1875, CMS Microfilm, Reel #A101.

53. Hines to Wright, report dated January 4, 1875, CMS Reel, #A101.

54. Hines, report to the CMS committee beginning January 11, 1875, entry for January 11, 1875, CMS, Microfilm Reel #A101.

55. Although syllabics are still used, particularly by older people, they are gradually being replaced by the Roman alphabet and contemporary orthography.

56. Bishop of Saskatchewan's Journal, January to May 1875, CMS, Microfilm Reel #A101.

57. Hines, report to the CMS committee beginning January 11, 1875, entry for May 17, CMS, Microfilm Reel #A101.

58. Ibid., entry for January 26, 1875, CMS, Microfilm Reel #A101.

59. Barry L. Ahenakew, 1994 review meetings.

60. Hines, report to the CMS committee beginning January 11, 1875, entry for February 20, CMS, Microfilm Reel #101.

61. Ibid. Some minor corrections in spelling and punctuation have been made.

62. Hines, report to the CMS committee beginning January 11, 1875, entry for February 20, CMS, Microfilm Reel #A101.

63. As told by Barry L. Ahenakew at the 1994 review meetings.

64. Hines, report to the CMS committee beginning January 11, 1875, entry for February 8, CMS, Microfilm Reel #A101.

65. Ibid., entry for February 20, CMS, Microfilm Reel #A101. Hines said that he spent more time talking to Kihci-mōhkomān than anyone else.

66. Hines, report to the CMS committee dated January 4, 1875, CMS Microfilm, Reel #A101.

67. In a report to the CMS committee dated November 20, 1874, Hines said he had talked to some Indians in Prince Albert who said they would join Ahtahkakoop in the spring. In March, Hines said he presented the children living with the chief's brother to the bishop for baptism; he also said the parents would be moving to Sandy Lake in the spring. It is therefore assumed that Hines was talking about Ahenakew and his family in the November report. The children's baptism records are contained in the St. Mary's Prince Albert and District Register of Baptisms, 1875-1891 (records #3, #4, and #5). In 1879 a boy, presumably James, was transferred from Ahenakew's treaty paylist ticket to Wāsēhikot's ticket. Wāsēhikot was Ahenakew's son. James Wāsēhikot died in 1887 at the age of 12. (Asissipi Mission Death Register, record #68. This register, along with other Asissipi and Sandy Lake Mission registers and the St. Mary's register, are housed at the Synod Office, Diocese of Saskatchewan, Prince Albert.) Bella Starblanket, the daughter of Ahtahkakoop's son Kā-miyo-astotin, confirmed in an interview that Ahenakew had lived at Prince Albert before moving to Sandy Lake.

68. Hines, report to the CMS committee beginning January 11, 1875, entry for April 20, CMS, Microfilm Reel #A101.

69. Hines, report to the CMS committee beginning January 11, 1875, entry for April 29, CMS, Microfilm Reel #A101. Kāh-kāsōw explained that "6 months ago [when] he was travelling from the North branch of the Saskatchewan to the South Branch ... [he] met a Minister. This Minister stopped him and asked him if he ever said his prayers. He said no, he was never taught to pray. The Minister then pulled his ear & told him he was as bad as an ox." In Hines's words, the clergyman "went on again leaving the man in the same position as he found him." Hines said Kāh-kāsōw was about 25 years old. However, according to the Asissipi Mission Marriage Register (record #4), Kāh-kāsōw was 31 years of age when he was married on May 10, 1877. This would make his birth year about 1846. His age was not recorded in his baptismal record.

70. Hines, report to the CMS committee beginning January 11, 1875, entry for May 17, CMS, Microfilm Reel #A101.

71. Hines, *Red Indians*, 118.

72. Hines, report to the CMS committee beginning January 11, 1875, CMS, Microfilm Reel #A101.

73. Ibid. Also see Hines, *Red Indians*, 157.

74. Hines, report to the CMS committee beginning January 11, 1875, entry for May 17, CMS, Microfilm Reel #A101. The dates used here for her baptism, death, and burial have been taken from the Asissipi Mission Death Register, record #1. In his report to the CMS, Hines said Sasakamoose's wife was baptized on May 5, died that evening and was buried on May 8.

75. Ibid., entry for April 29.

76. Ibid., entries for April 29 and May 17, 1975. Also see Enclosure from Hines to Abraham Cowley, Lisgar, June 5, 1875, dated at the Star Settlement, June 5, 1875, CMS, Microfilm Reel #A101. The Star Settlement was the name Hines had tentatively given to the collection of houses at Sandy Lake; the name was chosen in honour of Ahtahkakoop (Starblanket). Also see Hines, *Red Indians*, 87.

77. Hines, report to the CMS committee beginning January 11, 1875, entry for April 29, CMS, Microfilm Reel #A101. This was the plough Hines had brought with him from Winnipeg.

78. Hines, *Red Indians*, 87.

79. Enclosure from Hines to Cowley, June 5, 1875.

80. Hines, report to the CMS committee beginning January 11, 1875, entry for May 17, CMS, Microfilm Reel #A101.

81. Ibid.

82. Ibid., entry for May 17, 1875. Also see the enclosure from Hines to Abraham Cowley, June 5, 1875, CMS, Microfilm Reel #A101. The figure of 240 is based on eight people per tipi.

83. Ibid.

84. Enclosure from Hines to Abraham Cowley, June 5, 1875, CMS, Microfilm Reel #A101. Also see Hines, *Red Indians*, 158. One of the daughters was Judique, wife of Ahtahkakoop's son Kā-miyo-ahcahkwēw.

85. Hines, report to the CMS committee dated January 4, 1875. Also see report of January 11, entry for May 17, 1875; and enclosure to Cowley, June 5, 1875.

86. Hines, January 11, 1875 report, entry for May 17.

87. Ibid.

88. Hines, report to the CMS committee dated January 4, 1875.

89. Hines, January 11, 1875 report, entry for May 17, CMS, Microfilm Reel #A101.

90. Hines, *Red Indians*, 88. Hines did not name the sons, but one of them most certainly was Kā-miyo-ahcahkwēw, who was a headman. The other was likely Kīsik-awāsis, who was also a headman. Despite his opposition to Hines, Kīsik-awāsis was probably supportive of the farming aspect of activities at Sandy Lake. The next oldest son, Kā-miyo-astotin, 24, was considerably younger and not a headman; he likely would not have been given this responsibility.

Chapter Eleven: Challenges, 1875-1876

1. Hines, *Red Indians*, 90, 129. Also see Hines, letter to the CMS Committee, January 25, 1876, CMS, Microfilm Reel #A101.

2. Dempsey, *Big Bear*, 53, 56. Also see Constance Sissons, *John Kerr* (Toronto: Oxford University Press, 1946), 153-61. From Perth, Ontario, Kerr spent two years during the early 1870s hunting with Gabriel Dumont and the Métis on the South Branch.

3. Barry L. Ahenakew, as passed down through the generations.

4. Peter Ballendine's cousin Sam Ballendine married Kīwāsēwisk (Dimming Light), a women in Ahtahkakoop's band. Kīwāsēwisk was given ticket number 57 on the Ahtahkakoop Band treaty paylist when Treaty Six was signed in 1876. Her name was dropped from the Ahtahkakoop Band treaty paylist in 1880.

5. George F. G. Stanley, "The Half-Breed 'Rising' of 1875," *Canadian Historical Review* (December 1936): 399, 408-09.

6. Ibid., 399. Clarke's letter was dated July 10, 1875. He repeated his request for a protective force two days later.

7. Ibid., 409-10. The police were members of Troop "D."

8. The survey parties included one led by Sandford Fleming, the chief engineer for the Canadian Pacific Railway, who was in the Fort Carlton area in 1872 surveying a proposed railway route across the parklands and northern prairies. That same summer, deputy-surveyor W.S. Gore surveyed the land around each Hudson's Bay Company post, and in 1873 Robert Bell was conducting a survey west of the elbow of the South Saskatchewan River.

9. Fort Pelly was a Hudson's Bay Company post situated on a flat of land near the Assiniboine River in the east-central part of what is now the Province of Saskatchewan.

10. Richard Fuller, telegraph contractor, to Sandford Fleming, engineer-in-chief for the Canadian Pacific Railway, letter dated Hamilton, Ontario, April 8, 1875, Return submitted to the House of Commons by Secretary of State, April 5, 1877, Canada House of Commons (CHC), *Sessional Papers*, 1877 (no. 57), pp. 17, 18.

11. Fuller to David Laird, minister of the Interior, April 8, 1875, CHC, *Sessional Papers*, 1877 (no. 57), p. 18.

12. Fleming to Fuller, April 13, 1875, CHC, *Sessional Papers*, 1877 (no. 57), p. 18.

13. Extract from Letter of Instructions to Men, written by Fuller, in CHC, *Sessional Papers*, 1877 (no. 57), p. 24.

14. Huard D. Mulkins, Carlton House, to Fuller, July 20, 1875 CHC, *Sessional Papers*, 1877 (no. 57), p. 19.

15. See CHC, *Sessional Papers*, 1877 (no. 57), Fuller to Fleming, November 1875, p. 22; George G. Wright, report dated December 22, 1875, p. 23; and Fuller to F. Braun, secretary, Department of Public Works, March 7, 1877, p. 25.

16. Mulkins to Fuller, in a communication dated Carlton House, July 20, 1875, CHC, *Sessional Papers*, 1877 (no. 57), p. 19.

17. This is the man who was in the hunting party that challenged the Métis hunting camp earlier in the year.

18. Wright, letter dated Swan River, December 22, 1875, CHC, *Sessional Papers*, 1877 (no. 57), p. 23. Wright indicated that he was not able to give "any dates of delays or stoppages" since he did not have his memorandum book with him when he wrote his report. He said they arrived at Fort Carlton "in the latter part of July."

19. Ibid.

20. Ibid. Also see Allen Ronaghan, "Three Scouts and the Cart Train," *Alberta History* (Winter 1977): 12-13.

21. Ibid., p. 24.

22. Objections to a survey party cutting poles and hay had also been raised by at least one band east of the South Branch of the Saskatchewan River. Not all bands in this area had signed Treaty Four and in early August a group of people from 25 tipis under the leadership of Yellow Quill stopped a telegraph crew laying supplies near Poplar Plain. The man in charge of the crew reported that the "Indians say that the Government had not paid them for the right of way for road and telegraph line, and say they will stop us unless paid; they also demand fifty cents for each pole used in construction of line and buildings, and unless paid they will cut line as fast as constructed." Fuller received a similar message from one of the chiefs at Fort Pelly. The lieutenant-governor intervened and some presents were issued, bringing an end to that particular incident.

23. Rowan to Fuller, August 11, 1875, CHC, *Sessional Papers*, 1877, (no. 57), p. 22. Also see Alexander Morris, *Treaties*, 171-72.

24. This stone weighed 386 pounds and was said by the Indian people to have been placed on the hill by Nanebozo, the "great spirit of the Ojibwa," after the great flood that, in the sacred stories, had covered the land. See John McDougall's *George Millward McDougall*, 141-42.

25. George McDougall, his wife, and a son had stopped in Winnipeg on their return from a 14-month furlough to Eastern Ontario and England. Upon agreeing to help, McDougall and his wife headed for Fort Carlton instead of continuing their journey to the Bow River, where he had been instructed to establish a mission to administer to the Stoney Indians of the area. The mission, which was situated northwest of present day Calgary near the junction of the Bow and Ghost rivers, became known as Morleyville.

See John McDougall, *Opening the Great West: Experiences of a Missionary in 1875-76* (Calgary: Glenbow-Alberta Institute, 1970), 19-20. Also see McDougall's *George Millward McDougall*, 203-05. John McDougall, ordained in 1874, was George's son.

26. Stanley, "The Half-Breed 'Rising' of 1875," 411. Major-General Sir E. Selby-Smythe, the officer in charge of the Canadian militia, was on an inspection tour of the North-West Mounted Police posts and he accompanied the police to Fort Carlton. He agreed with French's appraisal of the situation. Since Dumont and most of the other Métis were on their summer hunt when the police and Selby-Smythe arrived, Crozier was instructed to arrest Dumont when he returned from the plains. He was then to be brought before Crozier and Clarke, in their capacities as justices of the peace, to explore the matter further. French and the police returned to the Swan River barracks, while Selby-Smythe continued on to the post near Fort Edmonton. On August 20, Clarke and Crozier attended a meeting of Métis at St. Laurent. After the Métis leaders explained the intent of their regulations, Dumont apologized and offered to make any reparation required.

27. Although McDougall did not name Ahtahkakoop, he almost certainly was in attendance. Not only had he been the chief spokesman when the telegraph and survey parties were stopped, but Hines was at Fort Carlton when McDougall was at the post; it is unlikely Hines would have been there and not Ahtahkakoop.

28. Hines, *Red Indians*, 129-30.

29. Ibid., 130.

30. George McDougall to Morris, in a report dated Morleyville, Bow River, Rocky Mountains, October 23, 1875, p. 2, Morris Papers, PAM, MG 12, B1, file 1136. Except for punctuation and the omission of part of one paragraph, as indicated later, this handwritten report is the same as the one that appears in Morris, *Treaties*, 174.

31. Ibid., pp. 2-3.

32. Ibid., pp. 1-2.

33. Ibid., p. 2.

34. McDougall's report, dated October 23, 1875, p. 3, Morris Papers, PAM MG12, B1, file 1136. Also see the attachment to his report.

35. Ibid., p. 3.

36. McDougall's report in Morris, *Treaties*, 174-75.

37. McDougall's report, Morris Papers, pp. 5-6. Also see Morris, *Treaties,* 175.

38. Ibid., p. 6.

39. Ibid., pp. 6-7.

40. Ibid.

41. See Christensen, "A Convenient Place," 325, 367, 369, 370, for indications of Clarke's personality and his responses to the changes in the North-West.

42. James A. Grahame to Clarke, March 24, 1875, Carlton House Inward Correspondence, HBCA, PAM, B.27/c/2, fo. 64d.

43. McDougall's report, Morris Papers, p. 7. McDougall wrote that "Believing it would be satisfactory to your Honor and of service to the Commissioners I have kept the number of all the Tents visited and the names of the places where I met the Indians." The

list was attached to his report as page 8. Some of the statistics most relevant to Ahtahkakoop's band and Fort Carlton follow. The first figure indicates the number of tipis in the camp; McDougall's estimate of people (based on 8 persons per tipis) is enclosed in brackets: Carlton, 10 tipis (80 people); Duck Lake, 30 (240); Fort à la Corne, 25 (200); Pelican Lake, 12 (96); Prince Albert, 10 (80); Spirit Lake [*manitow-sākahikan*], 4 (32); South Branch, 30 (240); Whitefish Lake, 20 (160). He also indicated there were 100 tipis (800 people) in Sweetgrass's camp [this camp included Big Bear and many of his followers, plus others]; and 3 tipis of Cree and 70 tipis of Assiniboine at the mouth of the Red Deer River. McDougall recorded 40 lodges and 320 people in Mistawasis's camp, and three tipis and 24 people at Sandy Lake. Since Mistawasis's camp included other chiefs and their followers and most of Ahtahkakoop's people were either on the plains or in the vicinity of Fort Carlton when McDougall visited, the figures do not accurately reflect the number of people in Ahtahkakoop's band.

44. John McDougall, *Opening the Great West*, 32-33. George McDougall's son John continued his ministry.

45. John Peter Turner, *The North-West Mounted Police 1873-1893*, vol. 1 (Ottawa: King's Printer and Controller of Stationary, 1950), 249. Also see Dempsey, *Big Bear*, 65-66.

46. Attachment to McDougall's report.

47. Hines, report dated January 25, 1876, CMS, Microfilm, Reel #A101. Hines incorrectly dated this letter January 25, 1875.

48. Hines to Cowley, November 4, 1875, CMS, Microfilm, Reel #A101.

49. Hines, *Red Indians*, 91-92. Also see Hines to Cowley, November 4, 1875, CMS, Microfilm, Reel #A101.

50. Ibid., 90-91. Also see Hines to Cowley, November 4, 1875, CMS, Microfilm, Reel #A101; and Hines, Asissipi Journal, January 28-May 15, 1876, CMS, Microfilm Reel #102, entry for February 12.

51. Hines to Cowley, November. 4, 1875, CMS, Microfilm Reel #A101. Also see Hines, Asissipi Journal, January 28-May 15, 1876, entry for January 28; and Hines, *Red Indians*, 132. In his journal, Hines said the houses had been built by some Indians two or three years ago and "as a number of my people are wintering there they make use of them."

52. Hines, *Red Indians*, 153.

53. Hines, report dated January 11, 1875, entry for May 17, CMS, Microfilm, Reel #A101.

54. Hines to CMS Committee, January 25, 187[6], CMS, #A101.

55. Hines to Wright, CMS secretary, January 20, 1876 CMS, Microfilm Reel #A101.

56. Hines, *Red Indians*, 181. The first reference to the name "Asissipi" occurs in the Asissipi Journal covering the period January 28-May 15, 1876.

57. Asissipi Mission Register, Diocese of Saskatchewan, 1875, Baptism Register record #1. Jane's is the first name entered in the register of baptisms for the mission at Sandy Lake. She was born on January 1, 1876. In Hines's record, Kā-miyo-ahcahkwēw's name was spelt as Menowachakwās. Kā-miyo-ahcahkwēw had been given the name Antoine when he was baptized by a Catholic priest in 1844. (Dietz, genealogy report.) The Asissipi Mission Register is housed at the Synod Office, Diocese of Saskatchewan, Prince Albert.

58. Asissipi Mission Baptism Register, record #2. Hines said Ann Misiwāpak was a child but he did not know when she was born.

59. Ibid., record #3. The child was born on January 6, 1876.

60. Ibid., record #4.

61. Hines, *Red Indians*, 91-92, and W.F. Payton, *The Diocese of Saskatchewan of the Anglican Church of Canada: 100 Years 1874–1974 (A Historical Sketch of the Diocese of Saskatchewan of the Anglican Church of Canada)* (n.p.: circa. 1973), 27. The Reverend Payton was Archdeacon Emeritus at the time of writing. Also see Asissipi Journal, January 28, 1876-May 15, 1876, CMS, Microfilm Reel #A102, entry for January 28.

62. Hines, Asissipi Journal, January 28-May 15, 1876, p. 2. CMS, Microfilm Reel #A102.

63. Hines, to the CMS Committee January 25, 187[6], CMS, Microfilm Reel A101, entry for January 30, 1876.

64. Hines, Asissipi Journal, January 28-May 15, 1876, entry for April 17.

65. Hines, report to CMS beginning January 11, 1875, entry for April 29, 1875.

66. Asissipi Mission Baptism Register records #5, #6, and #7. Hyman is derived from Āyiman, which translates as Hard Times.

67. Ibid., record #8.

68. Ibid., record #11. Also see record #2. This family was from Mistawasis's band.

69. Ibid., records #9 and #10. Thomas was the son of Okimāwapiwin (Chief's Sitting Spot), Pē-nōsēwēskam's first wife. Mary's mother, Tāpwēwiniwok (Truth), was Pē-nōsēwēskam's second wife. Both of these children had been born in 1874. Also see record #3.

70. Ibid., record #12.

71. Ibid., record #13.

72. Ibid., record #14. The boy was born in 1876.

73. Ibid., records #15 and #16. James was born in 1873 and Ann was born in 1875. Like many of the other fathers, Acimākanis (One Who Is Talked About) was a trapper.

74. Hines, *Red Indians*, 164.

75. Edward Ahenakew, "Genealogical Sketch of My Family," 10.

76. Hines, *Red Indians*, 132.

77. Some of the seed supplied by Mistawasis and his followers had been obtained from the chief's son-in-law, James (Jimmy) Dreaver. A retired Hudson's Bay Company employee, Dreaver was farming at Lily Plain some 80 miles from Sandy Lake.

78. Hines, *Red Indians*, 15-16. Hines's father bought him a wheel plough for the following year, but John was three months over the age limit. A younger brother entered the next year and won the silver cup in his age class; he was also declared "the second best ploughman in the whole field, which included all classes."

79. Hines to CMS Committee, Feb. 1, 1876, CMS, Microfilm Reel #101. Also see Hines, *Red Indians*, 30. In his letter dated February 1, 1876, in which he requested permission to marry, Hines gave his future wife's name as Mary Anne Moore. However, on their daughter's baptism certificate, her name was given as Emma Marianne. (Asissipi

Mission Baptism Register, record #94.) In her letters, Mrs. Hines signed her name as Emma. Her brother was the Reverend W. Moore, who became seriously ill with consumption within two years of Emma's arrival in Winnipeg.

80. Hines, *Red Indians*, 134.

81. Hines, Asissipi Journal, January 28-May 15, 1876, entry for May 15.

Chapter Twelve: Preliminaries to Treaty Six Negotiations

1. Peter Erasmus, *Buffalo Days and Nights*, 229-30.

2. Henry Budd, a Swampy Cree from Norway House, was orphaned at a young age and educated in the Red River Settlement under the auspices of the Church Missionary Society. He was ordained a deacon in 1850 and served at Cumberland House and The Pas before founding the Nepowiwin Mission across the river from Fort à la Corne. He died in 1875. Budd's ancestors included Hudson's Bay Company trader Matthew Cocking. For more information on Budd see page 732, endnote 13.

3. Erasmus, *Buffalo Days and Nights*, 16-17.

4. *The Canadian Encyclopaedia*, vol. 1 (1985), 589, s.v. "Erasmus, Peter, P." by Hugh A. Dempsey.

5. Erasmus, *Buffalo Days and Nights*, 229-30.

6. Sub-Inspector Frechette of the North-West Mounted Police said that these houses were "owned by Indians Massane Cardinal, P. Cardinal, Mista Wassis, chief, Watima, Red Pheasant & others." A non-Indian owned the eighth house. The Battle River region was part of Red Pheasant's traditional hunting grounds. See Frechette to Commissioner G.A. French, April 4, 1876, and French, in Confidential Instructions to Frechette, March 3, 1876, NA, Royal Canadian Mounted Police Papers, RG18, vol. 10, file 160-76. It is interesting to note in Frechette's report that the names of the Indian men "living" in the houses were added later using a finer pen and perhaps even different handwriting.

7. The 1878 survey of Prince Albert was also based on river lots.

8. McDougall, *Opening the Great West,* 53.

9. James A. Grahame, Hudson's Bay Company chief commissioner, to Clarke, in a letter dated June 13, 1876, Carlton House Inward Correspondence Book, 1872-84, HBCA, PAM, B.27/c/2. fo. 126.

10. McKay, like Erasmus, had been a guide in the Palliser expedition. Part of a powerful family through his marriage to Margaret Rowand, McKay served on the Council of Assiniboia for 1868-69, became an influential member of the Manitoba government, and was on the Council of the North-West Territories from 1873 to 1875. He was an advisor for Treaties One, Two, and Three, and a commissioner for Treaties Five and Six. *The Canadian Encyclopaedia*, vol. 2, 1057, "McKay, James," by Irene Spry.

11. Educated in Aberdeen, Scotland, Christie was employed by the Hudson's Bay Company from 1843 to 1873. He served a short term on the North-West Council and assisted with Treaty Four as well as Treaty Six. (Erasmus, *Buffalo Days and Nights*, 319-20, note 4.)

12. Oral history as passed down through the generations.

13. According to Morris, "the encampment of the Carlton Crees, [was] about two miles from the fort. See *Treaties*, 182. The differences in the mileage between the fort and the camp that appear in various sources apparently depends on whether the distance was measured between Fort Carlton and the council tent, or from the post to the centre of the massive Indian camp.

14. Gabriel's Crossing was situated some 20 miles from Fort Carlton. The ferry was operated by Gabriel Dumont, the leading man among the Métis living on the South Branch. Hines referred to the crossing as Dumont's Crossing.

15. Hines, *Red Indians*, 142-43. Although Hines said the camp was five miles south of Carlton, this distance—based on other evidence—is too great and the direction is wrong. He may have been referring to Commissioner James McKay's camp.

16. Ibid., 144.

17. As recorded in Morris, *Treaties*, 176-77. Also see 181.

18. Ibid., 181, 177.

19. Ibid., 181. Also see 141-42. Kissowayis was a brother of The Gambler, one of the spokesmen at Treaty Four.

20. Ibid., 181, 188. Also see Stan Cuthand, "Beardy (Kamiscowesit)," *Saskatchewan Indian* (January/February 1990): 17.

21. Ibid., 181, 177.

22. Ibid., 182.

23. Ibid., 197.

24. Christie to Morris, October 12, 1876, NA, Indian Affairs Records, RG10, vol. 6694. At Fort Pitt Christie had to buy 28 additional animals from the freighters in order to provide rations for the people gathered there. Also see Sissons, *John Kerr*, 235. Kerr, who was one of the drivers in Morris's party, witnessed the signatures of the Willow Cree chiefs and headmen when they signed Treaty Six on August 28, 1876. He had lived with the Métis at St. Laurent several years earlier.

25. Morris, *Treaties*, 182.

26. Ibid., 182.

27. Erasmus, *Buffalo Days and Nights*, 232, 235.

28. In his book (p. 235), Erasmus said his wife had given birth two days earlier to a boy they called David. A family tree at the back of *Buffalo Days and Nights* indicates that David was born on July 4, 1876. Either the chart is wrong, or Erasmus was embellishing his story.

29. Erasmus, *Buffalo Days and Nights*, 236. Permission to reprint extensive excerpts from the book *Buffalo Days and Nights*, published by Glenbow-Alberta Institute in 1976, is gratefully acknowledged. It should be noted that the spellings of Mistawasis, Ahtahkakoop, Ballendine, and tipi are used as they appeared in the book.

30. S.B. Steele, *Forty Years in Canada* (Toronto: McClelland, Goodchild & Stewart Ltd., 1915), 104.

31. Peter Ballendine was the former Hudson's Bay Company employee referred to earlier.

32. Erasmus, *Buffalo Days and Nights*, 237-38.

33. Steele, *Forty Years in Canada*, 102.

Chapter Thirteen: Treaty Six

1. See Morris, *Treaties*, 182, 197, and Steele, 103. Steele (p. 102) said the council tent was "pitched on an eminence about a quarter of a mile from the Indian camp."

2. Mandelbaum discusses face and body painting on p. 87 of *The Plains Cree*.

3. Morris, *Treaties*, 182.

4. Ibid., 182, 197.

5. Ibid., 182. In this particular quote, Morris said there were 200 tipis. Jackes, in the "narrative of the proceedings" in the same book said there were 250; this is the figure used by Erasmus, Steele, Kerr, and others.

6. Erasmus, *Buffalo Days and Nights*, 239-40.

7. Jackes's narrative in Morris's *Treaties*, 197-98.

8. Morris, *Treaties*, 183. Morris's description of the ceremony differed slightly. He wrote that during the "dance of the pipe-stem, the stem was elevated to the north, south, west and east, a ceremonial dance was then performed by the Chiefs and head men, the Indian men and women shouting the while."

9. John Leonard Taylor explained in *The Spirit of the Alberta Indian Treaties* that "From the point of view of the government officials, the ceremonial was merely a picturesque preliminary favoured by Indian custom. To them, the binding act of making treaty was the signing of the document at the close of the negotiations. This was the mode of affirming agreements among Europeans. On the other hand, 'the only means used by the Indians to finalize an agreement or to ensure a final commitment was by the use of the pipe.'" See John Leonard Taylor, in Richard Price (ed.), "Two Views on the Meaning of Treaties Six and Seven," *The Spirit of the Alberta Indian Treaties* (Toronto: Institute for Research on Public Policy, 1979), 18.

10. The following section on Treaty Six is drawn from three main sources. The first is from Erasmus's recollections as they appeared in *Buffalo Days and Nights*. The two official government accounts consist of Morris's "despatch," dated December 4, 1876, and the day-by-day record of the proceedings written by A.G. Jackes, a medical doctor who was secretary to the Treaty Commission. Morris's report and Jackes's narrative are both included in *The Treaties of Canada with the Indians*.

11. The Plains Cree chiefs expected to be addressed in their own dialect, particularly in this instance when accurate interpretation was so important.

12. Erasmus, *Buffalo Days and Nights*, 240-42.

13. As recorded in Jackes's narrative, *Treaties*, 199.

14. The full account of Morris's speech can be found in Jackes's narrative, *Treaties*, 199-202.

15. Erasmus, *Buffalo Days and Nights*, 242-43. Although Erasmus claimed that "The Governor spoke for an hour or so explaining the purpose of the treaty and its objectives, and describing in some detail the terms," Jackes's narrative indicates that Morris presented the proposed terms the following day. See Jackes's narrative, *Treaties*, 204-08.

16. Indian Commissioner Wemyss M. Simpson and Adams G. Archibald, lieutenant-governor of Manitoba and the North-West Territories, signed Treaty One with Chippewa and Swampy Cree nations at Lower Fort Garry August 3, 1871; this treaty is sometimes called the Stone Fort Treaty. Several weeks later, on August 21, the two government officials signed Treaty Two (Manitoba Post Treaty) with Chippewa nations at Manitoba Post. Lieutenant-Governor Alexander Morris, Archibald's successor, signed the North-West Angle Treaty, Number Three, with Saulteaux nations at Fort Francis October 3, 1873. The following year, on September 15, 1874, Morris and David Laird, Indian commissioner, signed Treaty Four at Fort Qu'Appelle with the Cree and Saulteaux nations and "other Indians, inhabitants of the territory" defined in the treaty. Morris signed the Lake Winnipeg Treaty, Number Five, with Saulteaux and Swampy Cree nations at Berens River and Norway House in September 1875. In addition to a number of adhesions that were signed with various bands in the early to mid-1870s, Treaties One and Two were revised in 1875.

17. As recorded in Jackes's narrative, *Treaties*, 200-01.

18. Ibid., 201-2.

19. Erasmus, *Buffalo Days and Nights*, 243-44.

20. Jackes's narrative, *Treaties*, 203.

21. Ibid., 203.

22. As recorded in ibid., 203.

23. NWMP officer Steele wrote that Erasmus's voice was deep, clear, and mellow. See Steele, *Forty Years in Canada*, 103.

24. As recorded in Jackes's narrative, *Treaties*, 204-6.

25. Ibid., 206.

26. For an excellent account of the Cypress Hills Massacre, see Philip Goldring's "Whisky, Horses and Death: The Cypress Hills Massacre and its Sequel," *Canadian Historic Sites: Occasional Papers in Archaeology and History* #21, published by the National Historic Parks and Sites Branch, 1979.

27. As recorded in Jackes's narrative, *Treaties*, 206-7.

28. Ibid., 208. Also see the copy of Treaty Six, as contained in an appendix of *Treaties*, 354; and Appendix A of this book.

29. Ibid., 207.

30. Ibid., 207-8.

31. Ibid., 208.

32. Erasmus, *Buffalo Days and Nights*, 244-45.

33. As recorded in Jackes's narrative, *Treaties*, 208.

34. Ibid., 208. Erasmus's version of Mistawasis's speech is identical in meaning, with only the words varying slightly.

35. See Morris and Jackes, *Treaties*, 184, 209. Hines said he held "open-air services among the Indians at different times" (see Hines, *Red Indians*, 144).

36. Erasmus, *Buffalo Days and Nights*, 245.

37. Morris, *Treaties*, 195.

38. Austin Ahenakew, as told to Barry L. Ahenakew. Players manoeuvred a hide-covered ball up and down a playing field with curved sticks as they attempted to drive the ball between the opponent's goal markers at the end of the field. The ball, which was about five inches in diameter, was made from buffalo hide and stuffed with buffalo or antelope hair. Mandelbaum describes this and other games in his book *The Plains Cree*, 133.

39. Morris, *Treaties*, 184.

40. Erasmus, *Buffalo Days and Nights*, 245-51. Morris and Jackes made several references in their accounts to a Chippewa who was vocal in his opposition to the treaty, but do not mention a Chipewyan.

41. John Smith and James Smith, whose family had moved west from the Red River region some years previous, were brothers.

42. Erasmus, *Buffalo Days and Nights*, 251.

43. Paul Ahenakew, review meeting, June 18, 1996.

44. Oral history from the elders on the Ahtahkakoop Reserve, as told by Joseph Sasakamoose to his son Jeffrey Sasakamoose; and Edwin Ahenakew to his son Paul Ahenakew and other sons.

45. As recorded in Jackes's narrative, *Treaties*, 210.

46. Ibid., 211.

47. Ibid. Erasmus's version of Badger's speech is a shortened version of Jackes's account (see Erasmus, *Buffalo Days and Nights*, 251).

48. See Jackes's narrative, *Treaties*, 211; and Erasmus, *Buffalo Days and Nights*, 251.

49. Hines, Annual Letter to the CMS, 1876, CMS Reel #A102.

50. Erasmus, *Buffalo Days and Nights*, 251.

51. Morris, *Treaties*, 211.

52. Erasmus, *Buffalo Days and Nights*, 251.

53. As recorded in Jackes's narrative, *Treaties*, 211-12. Erasmus said that McKay's speech was not interpreted. Since the speech is included in Jackes's narrative, Erasmus is either mistaken, McKay provided his version of the speech following the proceedings, or one of the other interpreters provided the information. Morris noted in his report that McKay spoke "with effect in the Cree tongue" (Morris, *Treaties*, 185).

54. Erasmus, *Buffalo Days and Nights*, 251-52. According to Jackes's account, The Badger said: "I do not want you to feed me every day; you must not understand that from what I have said. When we commence to settle down on the ground to make there our own living, it is then we want your help, and that is the only way that I can see how the poor can get along." (See Jackes's narrative, *Treaties*, 212-13.)

55. As recorded in Jackes's narrative, *Treaties*, 213.

56. Ibid., 213. This statement is not included in Erasmus's account.

57. Ibid..

58. Ibid., 214.

59. Morris, *Treaties*, 185.

60. As recorded in Jackes's narrative, *Treaties*, 214.

61. Erasmus, *Buffalo Days and Nights*, 253. Jackes's summation is very similar.

62. As recorded in Jackes's narrative, *Treaties*, 214-15.

63. Ibid., 215.

64. Ibid., 215-16.

65. Ibid., 216.

66. Ibid., 217. Erasmus, 253, said Morris "consented to a grant of one thousand dollars to assist those actually engaged in farming land on the reserves, but this would operate for three years only. This would apply to each band."

67. Ibid., 217-18.

68. Ibid., 218-19.

69. Ibid., 219.

70. Ibid.

71. Ibid.

72. Ibid., and Erasmus, *Buffalo Days and Nights*, 253.

73. As recorded in Jackes's narrative, *Treaties*, 219-20.

74. Thoma's speech is recorded in Jackes's narrative, *Treaties*, 220.

75. As recorded in Jackes's narrative, *Treaties*, 221.

76. Ibid., and Erasmus, *Buffalo Days and Nights*, 253.

77. As recorded in Jackes's narrative, *Treaties*, 221.

78. Erasmus, *Buffalo Days and Nights*, 254.

79. As recorded in Jackes's narrative, *Treaties*, 222.

80. Steele, *Forty Years in Canada*, 105. Also see Jackes's narrative, *Treaties*, 222, and Christie to the deputy minister of the Interior, Feb. 17, 1877, NA RG10, vol., 7570.

81. Erasmus, *Buffalo Days and Nights*, 254.

82. As recorded in Jackes's narrative, *Treaties*, 222.

83. Ibid., 222-23.

84. Erasmus, *Buffalo Days and Nights*, 254.

85. This is the consensus of elders who received the information from their grandparents, many of whom were at the treaty signings. Paul Ahenakew, a great grandson of Ahenakew and a former chief of the Ahtahkakoop Band, explained in June 1994 that "this land was never turned over to the Crown. It was held back for the grandchildren for all time." He went on to say that the old people know this because shortly after the treaty was made, it was apparent that some of the things that had been agreed to were not carried out. The people started teaching the children and grandchildren so they would be aware of what the agreements were. For further information on the elders' interpretation, see "Elders' Interpretation of Treaty 4: A Report on the Treaty Interpretation Project," prepared by the Indian Rights and Treaties Research Program, Federation of Saskatchewan Indians, August 31, 1978. Also see Price, *The Spirit of the Alberta Indian Treaties*, and Delia Opekokew, *The First Nations: Indian Government and the Canadian Confederation* (n.p.: Federation of Saskatchewan Indians, 1980).

86. McDougall, *Opening the Great West*, 60. McDougall, who spoke Cree, had travelled to Fort Carlton in July to attend the treaty negotiations, not knowing that they had been

postponed. He did not return in August, but travelled to Fort Pitt in September where he was asked by Chief Sweetgrass to attend one of the council meetings held during negotiations there. (See pp. 58-60.)

87. As recorded in Jackes's narrative, *Treaties*, 205.

88. For a sampling of this widely held view, see "Elders' Interpretation of Treaty 4," 5-23. Also see *Statement of Treaty Issues: Treaties as a Bridge to the Future* (Saskatoon: Office of the Treaty Commissioner, 1998).

89. As recorded in Jackes's narrative, *Treaties*, 204.

90. Morris, *Treaties*, 183.

91. For a sampling of these widely held views, see "Elders' Interpretation of Treaty 4," 5-23.

92. As recorded in Jackes's narrative, *Treaties*, 213.

93. Ibid., 206.

94. Ibid., 202, 211.

95. Ibid., 206.

Chapter Fourteen:
The Days After Treaty Six Was Signed at Fort Carlton

1. See Morris, *Treaties*, p. 187 and Jackes's narrative, *Treaties*, 223.

2. Jackes's narrative, *Treaties*, 223-24.

3. Morris, *Treaties*, 187.

4. Christie to Morris, October 12, 1876, NA, RG10, vol. 6694.

5. Jackes's narrative, *Treaties*, p. 224.

6. Indian Affairs Treaty Annuity Paylists, Ahtahkakoop Band, 1876, NA, RG 10, vol. 9412. The Ahtahkakoop Treaty Paylists 1876-1897 can be found in volumes 9412-9430 of this collection.

7. Christie's memorandum, October 10, 1876, NA, RG10, vol. 6694.

8. Hudson's Bay Company Chief Commissioner Grahame to Clarke, August 17, 1876, Carlton House Inward Correspondence, 1872-84, HBCA, PAM, B.27/c/2, fos. 143d, 149d.

9. Bruce Peel, *Steamboats on the Saskatchewan* (Saskatoon: Western Producer Prairie Books, 1972), 37. Also see "Excerpt from the Colin Thomson Memoirs," 10 (unpublished manuscript on file at Saskatchewan Parks and Renewable Resources). Thomson had arrived at Fort Carlton on August 4, 1876, to assume duties as an apprentice clerk at the post.

10. In his reminiscences, John Kerr mentions Christie's and Jackes's attendance at a dance performed by some of the women in a large tipi; Kerr said he took part in a pole vaulting competition. See Sissons, *John Kerr*, 239.

11. Fred Yayahkeekoot, in Christensen, "A Convenient Place," 386.

12. Erasmus, *Buffalo Days and Nights*, 254-55.

13. Ibid., 255.

14. As recorded in Jackes's narrative, *Treaties*, 224. Also see Morris, *Treaties*, 187.

15. Jackes, 224-25, and Morris, *Treaties*, 187.

16. As recorded in Jackes's narrative, *Treaties*, 226.

17. Ibid., 227.

18. It was Erasmus's understanding that each band was to get a grant of $1,000, for "three years only," to assist those actually farming. See Erasmus, *Buffalo Days and Nights*, 253.

19. As recorded in Jackes, *Treaties*, 228.

20. As recorded in Erasmus, *Buffalo Days and Nights*, 256.

21. Erasmus's youngest sister was married to a "trader, a big strapping Swede by the name of Pederson." See Erasmus, *Buffalo Days and Nights*, 236.

22. Ibid., 255-57.

23. Morris, *Treaties*, 183. Scollen, who was working with the Blackfoot, had learned about Sweetgrass's whereabouts during his journey from the Bow River to Fort Carlton.

24. This was the John McKay who had accompanied George McDougall on part of the 1875 trip to notify the Indian people about the upcoming treaty.

25. Erasmus, *Buffalo Days and Nights*, 258.

26. Morris, *Treaties*, 189.

27. Jackes's narrative, *Treaties*, 229.

28. Morris said this band was "a mixed one, composed of Crees and Saulteaux from Jack Fish Lake, their Chief being the Yellow Sky." (See *Treaties*, 190.) According to Jackes (p. 229), "this band was composed … of the Saulteaux of Jack Fish Lake and of some Crees under the Yellow Sky Chief … They numbered in all sixty-seven tents."

29. Jackes's narrative, *Treaties*, 229.

30. Morris, *Treaties*, 190.

31. Erasmus, *Buffalo Days and Nights*, 259-60.

32. Jackes's narrative, *Treaties*, 230. Morris, *Treaties*, 190, said the pipestems were "covered with calico and cloth, and returned to their bearers."

33. The complete text of Morris's speech can be found in Jackes's narrative, *Treaties*, 230-31.

34. As recorded in McDougall, *Opening the Great West*, 58-59.

35. Erasmus, *Buffalo Days and Nights*, 258-59. Erasmus's sequence of events, as recorded in *Buffalo Days and Nights*, differs from that recorded in *Treaties* and John McDougall's *Opening the Great West*. According to Erasmus, his meeting with the chiefs took place before the council with the lieutenant-governor began. The accounts of Jackes, Morris, and McDougall state that the council meetings were held mid-way during the proceedings. It is not likely that Sweetgrass, Pakān, and the other chiefs would have agreed to the treaty terms without having met with Morris and without having the terms formally read to them.

36. Jackes's narrative, *Treaties*, 235. Morris, *Treaties*, 190, said that "the Indians were slow of gathering, being still in council, endeavoring to agree amongst themselves."

37. Erasmus, *Buffalo Days and Nights*, 260.

38. As recorded in Jackes's narrative, *Treaties*, 236.

39. Ibid., 236-37. Erasmus, *Buffalo Days and Nights*, 260, indicated this encounter happened on the first day of meetings. In both Morris's and Jackes's accounts, it took place
on September 9, the day following the Indian council. According to Erasmus, Sweetgrass
concluded his speech thus: "I am no wiser than my brothers at Fort Carlton who have
accepted the Queen Mother's hand. I will sign for my people."

40. Jackes's narrative, *Treaties*, 238.

41. As recorded in ibid., *Treaties*, 238.

42. Ibid., 238-39.

43. Jackes's narrative, *Treaties*, 238.

44. Erasmus, *Buffalo Days and Nights*, 261.

45. Jackes's narrative, *Treaties*, 237-38.

46. Morris, *Treaties*, 192.

47. As recorded in Jackes's narrative, *Treaties*, 239.

48. Ibid., 240.

49. Ibid.

50. Barry L. Ahenakew, as cited in Deanna Christensen, "Selected Aspects of Fort Pitt's
History" (Saskatchewan Parks and Renewable Resources, February 29, 1984), 129. In
Big Bear, 74, Hugh Dempsey says that Big Bear "was not talking about a fear of being
hanged ... rather, he was using a common expression on the plains that denoted a per-
son giving up his freedom. It was analogous to a wild horse having a rope placed
around its neck so that it could no longer wander unfettered and free ... Presumably,
Big Bear's interpreter had confused the term *ay-saka-pay-kinit* (lead by the neck) with
ay-hah-kotit (hanged by the neck)." Dempsey suggests that the interpreter was the
Reverend John McKay (John A. Mackay) who had tried, unsatisfactorily, to interpret at
Fort Carlton.

51. Dempsey, *Big Bear*, 74.

52. As recorded in Jackes's narrative, *Treaties*, 240.

53. Ibid., 242.

54. Morris, *Treaties*, 193. Also see Jackes's narrative, *Treaties*, 242.

55. Dempsey, *Big Bear*, 72.

56. Erasmus, *Buffalo Days and Nights*, 257.

Chapter Fifteen: Follow-up to the Signing of Treaty Six, 1876

1. Christie, in a memorandum dated October 10, 1876, NA, RG10, vol. 3656. According
to Hines, Ahtahkakoop and Mistawasis had originally planned on sharing a large
reserve and forming one mission at Sandy Lake. This, however, may have been wish-
ful thinking on Hines's part. Moreover, in view of treaty terms specifying that each
band was to have its own reserve and that in order to qualify for assistance the people
had to be living and farming on the reserve, the shared territory would have been unre-
alistic. See Hines, Asissipi Journal, May 17-September 30, 1876. CMS, Microfilm Reel
#A101, entry for August 17.

2. Christie, October 10, 1876, NA, RG10, vol. 3656.

3. James Walker, memorandum dated August 20, 1877, NA, RG10, vol. 3656, file 9092.

4. See Christie, October 10, 1876, and Walker, August 20, 1877.

5. Christie, October 10, 1876.

6. Christie to Morris, October 12, 1876, pp. 3-4, NA, RG10, vol. 6694.

7. Hines, *Red Indians*, 144, and Morris, *Treaties*, 176.

8. Morris, *Treaties*, 179.

9. Ibid., 195.

10. Ibid., 196, and Erasmus, *Buffalo Days and Nights*, 261.

11. CHC, *Sessional Papers*, 1876 (no. 10), Annual Report of the Department of the Interior, p. 154.

12. Christie to E.A. Meredith, deputy minister of the Interior, February 17, 1877, NA, RG10, vol. 7570.

13. Morris, *Treaties*, 194.

14. Ibid.

15. Morris said that although the buffalo were "fast decreasing in numbers ... I am satisfied that a few simple regulations would preserve the herds for many years. The subject was constantly pressed on my attention by the Indians, and I promised that the matter would be considered by the North-West Council. The council that has governed the territories for the last four years was engaged in maturing a law for this purpose, and had our regime continued we would have passed a statute for their preservation. I commend the matter to the attention of our successors as one of urgent importance." (See Morris, *Treaties*, 195.)

16. Morris, *Treaties*, 195.

17. Ibid.

18. Minister of the Interior to the Privy Council, in a memorandum dated January 31, 1877, NA, RG10, vol. 3636, file 66942, pp. 4-5.

19. Ibid. p. 6.

20. Ibid., pp. 6-8.

21. Morris, *Treaties*, 176. Also see David Mills, CHC, *Sessional Papers*, 1877 (no. 11), pp. x, xi.

22. Morris to the minister of the Interior, letter dated March 27, 1877, NA, RG10, vol. 3636, file 6694-2, pp. 1-12.

23. Ibid, pp. 12-16.

24. David Laird, CHC, *Sessional Papers*, 1876 (no. 9), p. xiv.

25. A North-West Mounted Police post, Fort Livingstone, had been established near the Swan River in 1874 as headquarters for the North-West Mounted Police. Officials soon discovered that the post was too far from the main areas to be policed and the headquarters were moved to Fort Macleod in 1876 and then to Fort Walsh in 1878. The order-in-council designating Battleford as capital was dated October 7, 1876; the subsequent order-in-council naming Fort Livingstone as temporary capital was issued November 14, 1876. The first session of the North-West Council was held at the NWMP post in March, 1877.

26. A.J. Looy, "Saskatchewan's First Indian Agent: M.G. Dickieson," *Saskatchewan History* 32, no. 3 (Autumn, 1979): 104. Laird's and Dickieson's appointments, respectively, as superintendent and assistant superintendent were authorized by an order-in-council dated December 15, 1876.

27. Ibid., 106.

28. Ibid., 107.

Chapter Sixteen: The Transition Begins, 1876-1877

1. Hines, Annual Letter to the CMS, 1876, CMS, Microfilm Reel #A102.

2. Hines, *Red Indians,* 134, 143.

3. Wright taught at the Asissipi school for two years. He enrolled at Emmanuel College during the early 1880s and was ordained an Anglican priest. By 1886, Wright was an independent member of the Church Missionary Society's Finance Committee in Prince Albert.

4. Hines, Asissipi Journal, October 25-December 31, 1876, CMS, Microfilm Reel #A102, entry for October 25.

5. Ibid.

6. Hines to CMS, letter dated January 9, 1877, CMS, Microfilm Reel #A102.

7. Hines, Asissipi Journal, October 25-December 31, 1876, entry for November 27; and Asissipi Journal, January 9-March 30, 1877, CMS, Microfilm Reel #A102, entry for February 24. Hines explained that the men in Mistawasis's band were away hunting, the people at his settlement "were hungry," and he could not afford to help with his meagre resources.

8. Hines, Asissipi Journal, May 17-September 30, 1876, CMS, Microfilm Reel #A102, entry for September 30.

9. Hines, Asissipi Journal, October 25-December 31, 1876, CMS, Microfilm Reel #102, entry for November 12. These traders may have been with Stobart, Eden and Company. (See Christensen, "A Convenient Place" p. 438.)

10. Ibid., entries for December 14, 15, and 27, 1876.

11. Ibid., entry for October 25; Asissipi Journal, January 9-March 30, 1877, entries for February 4, 18, and March 28; and the Asissipi Journal April 1-June 30, 1877, CMS, Microfilm Reel #A102, entry for May 2.

12. Both Manitoba maple and birch trees were tapped. In his book *Red Indians*, 101, Hines tells of a tragic incident where nine people from Sandy Lake were making maple sugar on an island near Prince Albert when the ice in the river broke and jammed. The water rose rapidly, flooding the island and seven of the people drowned. No mention of this accident was found in Hines's incomplete set of journals.

13. Asissipi Journal, January 9-March 30, 1877, entry for March 28; and the Asissipi Journal April 1-June 30, 1877, CMS, Microfilm Reel #A102, entries for April 6 and May 2.

14. Hines, *Red Indians*, 153.

15. Hines, Asissipi Journal, October 25-December 31, 1876, CMS, Microfilm Reel #A102, entries for November 6 and December 17.

16. Kāh-kāsōw's marriage certificate indicates that he was 31 in 1877. (Asissipi Mission Marriage Register, record #4.)

17. Hines, Asissipi Journal, April 1-June 30, 1877, CMS, Microfilm Reel #A102, entries for May 10 and April 12; and Hines, Asissipi Journal, October 25-December 31, 1876, CMS, Microfilm Reel #A102, passim.

18. Hines, Asissipi Journal, January 9-March 30, 1877, CMS, Microfilm Reel #A102, entry for January 24.

19. Hines, Asissipi Journal, April 1-June 30, 1877, CMS, Microfilm Reel #A102, entry for April 11, 1877.

20. Hines, Asissipi Journal, January 9-March 30, 1877, CMS, Microfilm Reel #A102, entry for March 29.

21. Hines, Asissipi Journal, April 1-June 30, 1877, CMS, Microfilm Reel #A102, entry for April 13.

22. Kā-miyo-ahcahkwēw's marriage record indicates that he was 40 in March of 1877; his wife Judique was 34. (Asissipi Mission Marriage Register, record #2.)

23. Hines, Annual Letter to the Church Missionary Society, September 30, 1876, CMS, Microfilm Reel #A102.

24. Hines, Asissipi Journal, October 25-December 31, 1876, CMS, Microfilm Reel #102, entry for November 21. In other statements Ahtahkakoop is reported to have said that he was not in the camp when the priests baptized the children.

25. Hines, Asissipi Journal, October 25-December 31, 1876, entry for November 22, 1876.

26. Hines, Asissipi Journal, January 9-March 30, 1877, CMS, Microfilm Reel #A102, entry for February 11; and Hines, Asissipi Journal, October 25-December 31, 1876, entry for December 17, 1876. Also see Asissipi Mission Baptism Register, records #20 and #21.

27. See Hines, Asissipi Journal, April 1-June 30, 1877, CMS, Microfilm Reel #A102, entry for May 17.

28. Hines, Asissipi Journal, January 9-March 31, 1877, entry for February, 18. Also see Asissipi Mission Baptism Register, records #26, #27, and #28. Wāsēhikot had told Hines that he and his wife wanted to wait until the baby was born before they were baptized.

29. Hines, Asissipi Journal, October 25-December 31, 1876, CMS, Microfilm Reel #A102, entry for December 1. Also see the journal for January 9-March 31, 1877, CMS, Microfilm Reel #A102, entries for February 28 and March 13; and records #2 and #26 in the Asissipi Mission marriage register. In the register, Hines indicated that Ahenakew's marriage should have been entered as #3.

30. Hines, Asissipi Journal, April 1-June 30, 1877, CMS, Microfilm Reel #A102, entry for April 1. For Sasakamoose's baptism and marriage records, see Asissipi Mission Baptism Register, record #36, and Asissipi Mission Marriage Register, record #3. The two ceremonies took place on April 1, 1877.

31. Hines, Asissipi Journal, January 9-March 30, 1877, CMS, Microfilm Reel #A102, entry for March 9.

32. Ibid.

33. Kāh-kāsōw and Charlotte Hyman were married on May 10, 1877. (Asissipi Mission marriage register, record #4.)

34. Infant John was baptized on February 20, 1877; he was the son of a woman identified only as Sasakamoose. (Asissipi Mission Baptism Register, record #30.) K-ōsihkosi-wayāniw's daughters were aged 9 to 15. With the exception of Emma, who was baptized April 1, the girls were christened on March 11, 1877 (Asissipi Mission Baptism Register, records #31, #32, #33, and #37.)

35. Asissipi Mission Baptism Register, records #22, #23, and #24. In 1887 John Pierre (Cardinal) married Ahtahkakoop's granddaughter Maria, daughter of Emma Ahtahkakoop and John Kā-tāh-twēhototawāt (Bird Landing On Someone Repeatedly). When Pierre was baptized, he took the Christian name Peter; his wife Sāwākoomoowusk chose Betsy. Three other sons—Ahkusk (Arrowhead), Osāwanāsiw (South Wind), and Mark— along with the wives of Ahkusk and Osāwanāsiw, were baptized the following Christmas. Mark was more commonly known as Mac. (Asissipi Mission Baptism Register, records #54, #55, #56, #57, and #58.

36. Asissipi Mission Baptism Register, records #34 and #35.

37. Hines, Asissipi Journal, April 1-June 30, 1877, CMS, Microfilm Reel #A102, entry for April 8.

38. Ibid., entry for June 23.

39. Hines does not identify the man, other than saying it was one of Ahenakew's nephews. However, by elimination, it must have been Kīsik-awāsis.

40. Hines, Asissipi Journal, April 1, 1879-February 28, 1880, CMS, Microfilm Reel #A104, undated entry for June. Some changes in punctuation have been made.

41. Hines, Asissipi Journal, October 25-December 30, 1876, entry for December 1; and Asissipi Journal, April 1-June 30, 1877, CMS, Microfilm Reel #A102, entry for April 1.

42. Hines, Asissipi Journal, January 9-March 30, 1877, CMS, Microfilm Reel #A102, entry for February 11.

43. The granddaughter may have been Maria, the daughter of Emma Ahtahkakoop and Kā-tāh-twēhototawāt.

44. Hines, Asissipi Journal, April 1-June 30, 1877, CMS, Microfilm Reel #A102, entries for May 13 and 20. Also see Asissipi Mission Baptism Register, records #39 and #40.

45. Hines, Asissipi Journal, January 9-March 30, 1877, entries for February 4, 11, and 28; and Asissipi Journal, April 1-June 30, CMS, Microfilm Reel #A102, entry for May 2. Hines referred to Judique as Mrs. Kā-miyo-ahcahkwēw.

46. Hines, April 1-June 30, 1877, entry for May 7. Also see Asissipi Mission Baptism Register, record #38.

47. Hines, Asissipi Journal, April 1-June 30, 1877, entry for May 7. Also see Asissipi Journal, January 9-March 30, 1877, CMS, Microfilm Reel #A102, entry for January 14.

48. Hines, Asissipi Journal, January 9-March 30, 1877, CMS, Microfilm Reel #A102, entries for January 13 and 15.

49. Hines, Asissipi Journal, April 1-June 30, 1877, CMS, Microfilm Reel #A102, entries for April 11 and 29.

50. Ibid., entry for April 30, 1877.

51. Ibid., entries for April 4 and 15, 1877.

52. Ibid., entries for May 15, 1877.

53. Ibid., entry for June 26, 1877.

54. Hines, Asissipi Journal, January 9-March 30, 1877, CMS, Microfilm Reel #A102, entry for March 29.

55. Hines to CMS, December 3, 1876, CMS, Microfilm Reel #A102.

56. Hines, Asissipi Journal, April 1-June 30, 1877, CMS, Microfilm Reel #A102, entry for June 23. The identity of this man is uncertain.

57. Ibid., entries for June 1 and 2, 1877.

58. Ibid., entry for June 2, 1877.

59. Ibid., entries for June 20 and 23, 1877.

Chapter Seventeen: The Last of the Buffalo Hunts, 1877

1. Asissipi Journal, July 4-September 30, 1877, CMS, Microfilm Reel #A102, entry for July 4.

2. Hines explained in his journal that when the ducks were moulting, a great number were killed each year at this location.

3. Hines recorded the hunting trip in the July 4-July 12 entries of the Asissipi Journal, July 4-September 30, 1877, CMS, Microfilm Reel #A102.

4. Hines did not indicate how many buffalo were shot.

5. This was in sharp contrast to earlier years when large herds ranged on both sides of the North Saskatchewan River.

Chapter Eighteen: The Beginning of Hard Times, 1877-1878

1. Hines, Asissipi Journal, July 4-September 30, 1877, CMS, Microfilm Reel #A102, entry for July 17.

2. Christie, in an undated "Memoranda regarding places and dates for meeting Indians, Summer of 1877, to secure adhesions to Treaty of 1876 of absent Chiefs and their Bands within Treaty Limits, and for paying the Annuities according to the terms and conditions of Treaty," NA, RG10, vol. 6694-2. The officials planned on being in the Upper Saskatchewan region in July, the Victoria area on August 10, Fort Pitt on September 1, and the Battle River district about September 10.

3. Hines, Asissipi Journal, July 4-September 30, 1877, CMS, Microfilm Reel #A102, entry for July 24. Also see Christie's memorandum, NA, RG10, vol. 6694-2.

4. Christie's memorandum, NA, RG10, 6694-2. Also see Grahame to Clarke, May 12, 1877, HBCA, PAM, B. 27/c/2, fo. 188.

5. Hines, Asissipi Journal, July 4-September 30, 1877, CMS, Microfilm Reel #A102, entry for July 24.

6. Walker, NA, RG10, vol. 3656, file 9092.

7. Ahtahkakoop Band Treaty Paylist for 1877. The previous year, 53 men, 80 women, 81 boys, and 62 girls were paid. Six others were paid elsewhere and their names, without numbers, transferred to the 1877 paylist. Five of these people (a man, woman, and three children) appeared under their own number on the 1878 paylist.

8. James Walker, in a letter to M.G. Dickieson, August 28, 1877, NA, RG10, vol. 3654, file 8855.

9. Hines, Asissipi Journal, July 4-September 30, 1877, CMS, Microfilm Reel #A102, entry for August 11.

10. Walker to Dickieson, August 28, 1877, NA, RG10, vol. 3654, file 8855.

11. Ibid.

12. Ibid. The chiefs who signed the petition were not identified.

13. Ibid..

14. Letter from the chiefs of the Carlton district written at Fort Carlton on August 28, 1877, NA, RG10, vol. 3654, file 8855. William McKay, a clerk with the Hudson's Bay Company, witnessed the signatures at Fort Carlton. Philip Turner was the witness at Prince Albert. The letter was probably dictated to Lawrence Clarke.

15. Statement showing distribution of Implements, Cattle, Seed, Grain, &c., to Indians of Treaty No. 6, up to the 30th June, 1878, CHC, *Sessional Papers*, 1879 (no. 7), pp. 62-63.

16. Hines, Asissipi Journal, CMS, Microfilm Reel #A102, September 30, 1877, entries for July 26 and August 11.

17. [Edward K. Matheson], "The Journal of Edward K. Matheson," intro. by Ruth Buck, *Saskatchewan History* 4 (1951): 107.

18. Payton, *Diocese of Saskatchewan*, 46. Archdeacon Payton wrote the book to commemorate the 100th anniversary of the Diocese of Saskatchewan. No publishing data was provided. Matheson taught for one year at Snake Plain and one year at Sandy Lake.

19. Hines, Asissipi Journal, July 4-September 30, 1877, CMS, Microfilm Reel #A102, entries for September 3, 6, 12, and 20.

20. Hines, Asissipi Journal, October 13 to December 31, 1877, CMS, Microfilm Reel #A103, entry for October 13.

21. Hines, Asissipi Journal, July 4-September 30, 1877, CMS, Microfilm Reel #A102, entry for August 31. Also see Minutes of the Church Missionary Conference, Carlton House, August 29, 1877, CMS, Microfilm Reel #A102.

22. Hines, Asissipi Journal, October 13-December 31, 1877, CMS, Microfilm #A103, entries for October 21 and November 20.

23. Hines, Asissipi Journal, January 1-March 19, 1878, CMS, Microfilm Reel #A103, entry for March 18.

24. Statement of the condition of the various Indian Schools in the Dominion, for the Year ended 30th June, 1878, Annual Report of the Department of the Interior for the Year ended June 30, 1878. CHC, *Sessional Papers*, 1879 (no. 7), pp. 224-25, Also see Hines, Asissipi Journal, January 1-March 28, 1878, entry for March 18.

25. Hines, Asissipi Journal, October 13-December 31, 1877, CMS, Microfilm Reel #A103, entry for November 10.

26. Ibid., entry for November 20.

27. Ibid., entries for November 22, 28, and 30.

28. Ibid., entries for December 5 and 7.

29. Ibid., entries for November 26 and December 2.

30. Ibid., entry for December 16. Also see Asissipi Mission Death Register, record #3.

31. See Asissipi Mission Baptism Register, records #54 to #58. The sons were Ahkusk (Henry), Osāwanāsiw (William), and Mark, who was more commonly called Mac. Some of the sons later took Cardinal as their surname.

32. Hines, Asissipi Journal, October 13-December 31, 1877, CMS, Microfilm Reel #A103, entries for December 12 and 27.

33. In an earlier journal, Hines mentions two traders, one English and the other Scottish, living at Sandy Lake. In the October 13-December 31, 1877 journal, he makes reference to a half-breed trader from Stobart Eden & Company who periodically stopped at Sandy Lake and Snake Plain to trade.

34. Hines, Asissipi Journal, October 13-December 31, 1877, CMS, Microfilm Reel #A103, entry for December 10. Hines noted in his journal that Ahtahkakoop respected the Sabbath and refused to trade with an Indian trapper from Whitefish Lake on Sunday, December 9.

35. Ibid., entry for December 26.

36. Fine Day, as told to Mandelbaum, August 8, 1934, Mandelbaum Papers, SAB, R-875, 8a 2/3.

37. Hines, Asissipi Journal, October 13-December 31, 1877, entries for December 29 and 31.

38. Hines, Asissipi Journal, January 1-March 29, 1878, CMS, Microfilm Reel #A103, entry for January 1, CMS.

39. Ibid., entries for January 7, 9, and 13.

40. Ibid., entries for January 15, 22, and February 24.

41. According to Hines's journal for January 1-March 29, 1878, entry for February 26, and J. A Mackay's journal for January 1-March 29, 1878, entry for February 25 (CMS, Microfilm Reel #A103), Ahtahkakoop and his wife were married February 26. The Asissipi Mission Marriage Register, record #5, gives the date as February 25.

42. Hines, Asissipi Journal, January 1-March 29, 1878, CMS, Microfilm Reel #A103, entry for February 26.

43. Asissipi Mission Marriage Register, Diocese of Saskatchewan, 1875, records #6, #7, and #8. Jemima had been born at Pelican Lake.

44. Hines, Asissipi Journal, April 1-June 30, 1878, CMS, Microfilm Reel #A103, entry for June 1.

45. Hines, *Red Indians*, 171. The first carpenter had accomplished little.

46. Hines, Asissipi Journal, April 1-June 30, 1878, CMS, Microfilm Reel #A103, entry for June 1.

47. Chief Commissioner James A. Grahame to Clarke, February 23, 1878, HBCA, PAM, B.27/c/2, fo. 212.

48. Provisions distributed to destitute Indians & delegations up to June 30, 1878, CHC, *Sessional Papers*, 1879 (no. 7), p. 42. It is assumed that the units were "pounds," since no unit values were given.

49. Dickieson to Lawrence Vankoughnet, deputy superintendent general of Indian Affairs, April 2, 1878, NA, RG10, file 10,3672. Vankoughnet had been appointed deputy super-intendent general of Indian Affairs in 1873; he served in that capacity until 1893.

50. Ibid.

51. Laird to Alexander Mackenzie, April 20, 1878, SAB, Laird Papers, as cited in Looy, "Saskatchewan's First Indian Agent."

52. Laird to Mills, November 18, 1877, CHC, 1878 (no. 10), p. 45.

53. Laird to Mackenzie, April 20, 1878, SAB, Laird Papers. Mills was the minister who had been so critical of Morris and the other treaty commissioners following the signing of Treaty Six. He replaced Laird as minister of the Interior in 1876. Mackenzie, a Liberal, was prime minister from 1873-78.

54. Mills to Laird, letter dated May 22, 1878, pp. 2-4, NA, RG10, vol. 8904.

55. Ibid., pp. 1-2, NA, RG10, vol. 8904.

56. Hines, *Red Indians*, 146. Hines does not mention the mange in his journals or annual letters.

57. Dickieson to Vankoughnet, deputy superintendent general of Indian Affairs, April 2, 1878, NA, RG10, file 10,3672.

58. Extract of a letter written by Laird November 11, 1878, CHC, *Sessional Papers*, 1879 (no. 7), p. 65.

Chapter Nineteen: Ahtahkakoop's Reserve is Surveyed, 1878-1879

1. Hines, Asissipi Journal, January 1-March 30, 1878, CMS, Microfilm #A102, entry for March 29.

2. Hines, Asissipi Journal, April 1-June 30, 1878, CMS, Microfilm #A103, entry for April 4.

3. Provisions distributed to Indians at Seed Time and Statement showing distribution of Implements, Cattle, Seed, Grain, &, to Indians of Treaty No. 6, up to the 30th June, 1878, CHC, *Sessional Papers*, 1879 (no. 7), pp. 59, 62, and 63.

4. Extract of letter from Laird [to superintendent general of Indian Affairs] dated November 11, 1878, CHC, *Sessional Papers*, 1879 (no. 7), p. 64. Also see Laird to superintendent general of Indian Affairs, December 5, 1878, CHC *Sessional Papers*, 1879 (no. 7), p. 57.

5. Hines, Asissipi Journal, April 1-June 30, 1878, CMS, Microfilm Reel #A103, entries for May 4 and 19.

6. Ibid., entry for May 27.

7. Ibid.

8. Hines did not indicate if this was Ahenakew or Sasakamoose.

9. Hines, Asissipi Journal, April 1-June 30, 1878, CMS, Microfilm Reel #A103, entry for June 1.

10. Hines, in his annual letter to the CMS, November 30, 1878, CMS, Microfilm Reel #A103. Hines indicated in the same letter that government surveyor Edgar Bray estimated the value of the house at $2,000 when he was at Sandy Lake during the summer.

11. Hines, Asissipi Journal, April 1-June 30, 1878, CMS, Microfilm Reel #A103, entry for June 1. The flour mill was at Prince Albert, the "store" was at Fort Carlton, and the "town" was likely Winnipeg.

12. Ibid., entry for May 27.

13. The Nepowewin [Nipawiwin (Standing Place)] Mission was located on the north bank of the Saskatchewan River, across from the Hudson's Bay Company's Fort à la Corne and east of the James Smith Reserve.

14. Hines, Asissipi Journal, April 1-June 30, 1878, CMS, Microfilm Reel #A103, entry for June 21. Also see the letter dated February 7, 1879.

15. Ibid, entry for June 30, 1878.

16. Ibid., entry for June 2.

17. Edgar Bray (Dominion Land Surveyor), "Field Notes and Report of the Survey of the Asissippi (Chief Atakukoop) and Snake Plain (Chief Mistowasis) Indian Reserves, Green Lake Road, North West Territory, August 9, 1878 to October 14, 1878," Department of Indian Affairs and Northern Development, Indian Lands Registry, Field Book #725, Microfiche #1381, p. 93. His report was dated January 10, 1879, at Oakville, Ontario.

18. Edgar Bray, "Diary of Work Done in Saskatchewan in TP 49-6-3, TP 50-6-3, TP 50-7-3, TP 51-6-3, TP 51-7-3 [Ahtahkakoop and Mistawasis Reserves], 1878," Department of Indian Affairs and Northern Development, Indian Lands Registry, Field Book #726, Microfiche #203, pp. 11-12.

19. Elder Paul Ahenakew, review meeting in Regina, May 28, 1997. According to Treaty Six, "the Chief Superintendent of Indians Affairs shall depute and send a suitable person to determine and set apart the reserves for each band, after consulting with the Indians thereof as to the locality which may be found to be most suitable for them." See Appendix A.

20. Bray, "Diary," 11.

21. "Chronicles by the Way," dated Prince Albert, September 2, 1879, written by a "special correspondent," Montreal *Gazette*, September 29, 1879. The unidentified correspondent was Tom White, publisher and editor of the *Gazette* and Conservative member of Parliament in Macdonald's government. The article, which was part of a series written by White during a visit to the North-West, contains an account of a meeting between Ahtahkakoop, Mistawasis, and Kitowēhāw and Indian Commissioner Edgar Dewdney on September 2, 1879. Dewdney had been appointed Indian Commissioner in 1879. In a report dated January 2, 1880, Dewdney said that "a very exhaustive report of the interview was published in the Montreal *Gazette* and was perfectly correct." See E[dgar] Dewdney, Report of his proceedings since his arrival at Fort Walsh on 26th June, 1879, NA, RG10, vol. 3740, file 17,858, p. 51. This reference also appears in CHC, *Sessional Papers*, 1880 (no. 4), p. 87. Additionally see Bray's "Diary," 12. During his meeting with Dewdney in 1879, Ahtahkakoop added a third concern, saying that his reserve was "in a part that is swampy and useless."

22. Bray, "Diary," 12.

23. According to Paul Ahenakew, Ahtahkakoop and the leading men would not have objected so strenuously to Bray's survey if they had not already determined where they wanted the boundaries to be placed. (Review meeting in Regina, May 28, 1997.)

24. Laird to the minister of the Interior, November 12, 1878, NA, RG10, vol. 10,771, pp. 5-6.) Also see Bray's "Field Book," 93. Bray reported in his field notes that "upon the Indians seeing the direction and length of this line they expressed much dissatisfaction with the survey and at a meeting of the head men it was decided to have me stop the work until the Lieutenant Governor could … [be] seen and an effort made to have the shape of reserve changed so that all the improvements of the band would lie within the boundaries thereof, which would not be the case if run as was first intended." Also see Bray's "Diary," 13. Bray makes no mention of Ahtahkakoop's and Mistawasis's reserves adjoining each other.

25. Bray, "Diary," 13-14.

26. Laird to the minister of the Interior, November 12, 1878, NA, RG10, vol. 10,771, pp. 5-6.

27. Bray, "Field Book," 94.

28. "Chronicles by the Way," dated Prince Albert, September 2, 1879, Montreal *Gazette*, September 29, 1879.

29. Ibid.

30. Bray, "Field Book," 94, and "Diary," 18. On page 95 of his field notes, Bray said the Ahtahkakoop Reserve, as surveyed, was nearly 10 miles in length, seven miles in width, and contained 69.95 square miles. He also said that it was surveyed for the "Chief Atakukoop band who numbered in 1878, 304 souls." The numbers actually total 307, excluding Kĩsik-awãsis's family of 4.

31. Some ten years later the temporary markers were replaced with "solid iron posts, two inches square and three feet six inches long [that were] driven into the ground to within four inches of the top." Each corner "was further defined by four pits, three feet square and one foot deep, each six feet from the post and arranged at the corners of a square, one of the diagonals being in the direction of the reserve boundary and the other perpendicular thereto." See John C. Nelson (comp.), *Descriptions and Plans of Certain Indian Reserves in the Province of Manitoba and the North-West Territories, 1889* (n.p.: 1889) (compiled from data submitted in 1887). Nelson was in charge of Indian Reserve Surveys. He indicated that in cases where the post could not be driven far enough into the ground, a cairn of stones was erected around it. The information contained in his report was prepared from original records and eventually formed the basis of a submission to the Privy Council that was approved by His Excellency the Governor General in Council on May 17, 1889. This procedure, according to Nelson, officially confirmed the reserves and their boundaries. Nelson said that the descriptions of the boundaries and lithographed plans of the reserves contained in his report were sufficient "in detail to enable a surveyor to re-establish such boundaries should they become obliterated."

32. Hines, Asissipi Journal, October 25-December 31, 1876, CMS, Microfilm Reel #A102, entry for October 25. In this entry, Hines said he had set aside one-half square

mile of land as mission property, which would be 320 acres, not 160 acres. Also see Hines to the deputy minister of the Interior, letter dated April 4, 1910, NA, RG15, Department of the Interior, vol. 1029, file 16,2295; and statutory declarations of Archdeacon John A. Mackay (November 19, 1910), John Hines (May 25, 1911), and Edward K. Matheson, Diocese of Saskatchewan Archives, Box XII, Property Agreements, Sandy Lake 1879-1911.

33. Bray, "Field Book," 96.

34. Hines willed the property to the Anglican Church. See Reserve General Register, Treaty Research Office, Department of Indian and Northern Affairs. Also see Hines to the deputy minister of the Interior, letter dated April 4, 1910, NA, RG15, Department of the Interior, vol. 1029, file 16,2295.

35. Bray, "Field Book," 95. Also see Bray's "Diary," 12, 18-20. According to government documentation compiled in 1887 and based on Bray's survey, the Ahtahkakoop Reserve was bound:

"by a line beginning at a post and mound at its south-east corner, and running north five hundred and sixty chains more or less, to a post; thence west seven hundred and ninety eight chains, more or less, to a post; thence south five hundred and sixty-one chains and sixty links, more or less, to a post; and thence east seven hundred and ninety eight chains and sixty-six links, more or less, to the point of beginning; containing an area of sixty-seven and two-tenths square miles, more or less." (See *Descriptions and Plans of Certain Indian Reserves*, 59.)

36. See Bray's "Field Book," 95, and map and information in *Descriptions and Plans of Certain Indian Reserves*, 59 and the following page. The discrepancy was explained in a memorandum dated August 17, 1908, written by the surveyor general, Topographical Surveys Branch, Department of the Interior (file 10131 S).

37. Bray, "Field Book," 95-96.

38. Ibid., 101.

39. The figure of 307 includes 53 men and 15 women who had their own tickets. Four of the men were listed by themselves. All but three of the women assigned tickets had children listed with them.

40. Ahtahkakoop Band Paylist for 1878. In 1877 Kīsik-awāsis had received payments for himself, his wife, one boy, and one girl.

41. See Hines, Asissipi Journal, April 1-June 30, 1878 entry for June 21. Also see the letter dated February 7, 1879, CMS, Microfilm Reel #A103.

42. See Morris, *Treaties*, 364-65, and Laird, to the minister of the Interior, November 12, 1878, NA, RG10, vol. 3670, file 10,771.

43. Laird, December 30, 1878, to minister of the Interior, NA, RG10, vol. 3670, file 10,379, pp. 7-8.

44. Moore had built a large steam saw and grist mill in Prince Albert in the mid-1870s to replace the wind-driven grist mill that had previously served the district. See G.W.D. Abrams, *Prince Albert, The First Century* (Saskatoon, Modern Press, 1966), 19.

45. Laird, December 30, 1878, NA, RG10, vol. 3670, file 10,379, p. 15. Laird said, however, that the ammunition arrived too late to be distributed at Fort Pitt and the beef was "rather late" for Sounding Lake. The payments were made at Sounding Lake in mid-August and at Fort Pitt towards the end of the month.

46. Laird to the minister of the Interior, November 12, 1878, NA, RG10, vol. 3670, file 10,771, p. 6.

47. Ibid., p. 5.

48. Ibid., p. 4.

49. Ibid., pp. 7-8.

50. Laird [to John A. Macdonald, superintendent general of Indian Affairs], November, 11, 1878, CHC, *Sessional Papers*, 1879 (no. 7), p. 56.

51. Lawrence Vankoughnet to Macdonald, superintendent general of Indian Affairs, December 17, 1878, NA, RG10, vol. 3670, file 10,771. Macdonald's approval was written by hand on the last page of the memorandum. Macdonald's Conservative government had been replaced by Alexander Mackenzie's Liberal government in November of 1873.

52. Hines, Asissipi Journal, April 1-June 30, 1878, CMS, Microfilm Reel #A103, entry for June 11. Also see Hines's annual letter, November 30, 1878, CMS, Microfilm Reel #A103.

53. Hines, annual letter to CMS, November 30, 1878, CMS, Microfilm Reel #A103. Also see Hudson's Bay Company officer Alex Matheson to Roderick MacFarlane, letter dated August 9, 1878, at Fort Carlton, NA, Roderick MacFarlane Correspondence, MG29, A11, vol. 1, p. 711.

54. "Chronicles by the Way," dated Prince Albert, September 2, 1879, Montreal *Gazette*, September 29, 1879.

55. Hines, Annual Letter to the CMS, February 4, 1880, CMS, Microfilm Reel #A104.

56. Hines, *Red Indians*, 146.

57. Dickieson to the minister of the Interior, July 21, 1879, NA, RG10, vol. 15,678, pp. 1-2.

58. Ibid., pp. 1-4.

59. Vankoughnet, CHC, *Sessional Papers*, 1880 (no. 4), p. 13.

60. Hines, letter to CMS, February 7, 1879, CMS, Microfilm Reel #A103.

61. Ibid. Also see Matheson to MacFarlane, NA, MG29, A11, vol. 1, p. 711; and HBCA, PAM, B. 27/c/2, Carlton House Inward Correspondence Book, fos. 239, 262.

62. Ibid.

63. Ibid.

64. Hines, Asissipi Journal, January 1-March 29, 1878, CMS, Microfilm Reel #A103, entry for March 3.

65. Hines, annual letter to CMS, December 7, 1878, CMS, Microfilm Reel #A103. Hines said there were 50 families and 300 "souls" at Sandy Lake. The treaty paylist indicates that 307 were paid annuities in 1878 as members of Ahtahkakoop's band.

66. Henrietta Agnes Ellen Elizabeth Hines, born October 16, 1878, was baptized on December 1, 1878. (Asissipi Mission Baptism Register, record #94.)

67. Hines, annual letter to CMS, November 30, 1878, CMS, Microfilm Reel #A103. Also see Hines, letter to the CMS dated February 7, 1879, CMS, Microfilm Reel #A103. It should be noted that these numbers do not correspond with those in the register.

68. Asissipi Mission Marriage Register, records #12, #13, and #14. Iskwēsis's number on the treaty paylist was #51; a younger woman, who was listed as Iskwāsis No. 2, was given #53.

69. Shewing the Condition of the various Indian Schools in the Dominion, CHC, *Sessional Papers*, 1880 (no. 4), p. 300. Pritchard, like Matheson, was the first cousin of Samuel Pritchard Matheson, the future archbishop of Rupert's Land. He arrived at the Asissipi Mission in the fall of 1878, spent two years teaching under Hines's supervision, and then enrolled at Emmanuel College. See Hines, *Red Indians*, 174; Payton, *Diocese of Saskatchewan*, 16; and Hines, annual letter, November 30, 1878.

70. Hines's annual letter, November 30, 1878, CMS, Microfilm Reel #A103.

71. Copy of the Bishop of Saskatchewan's Journal of a Visit to the CMS's Mission at Asissippi in the Diocese of Saskatchewan, May 6, 1881, CMS, Microfilm Reel #110. According to the Asissipi Marriage Register, record #33, Louis was 20 when he was married on July 21, 1884. This would make his birth year approximately 1864. Since Joseph was 21 when he died on April 9, 1880, he was born about 1867. (See Asissipi Mission Death Register, record #72.)

72. See Hines, November 30, 1878, and CHC, *Sessional Papers*, 1880 (no. 4), p. 300.

73. Laird to Vankoughnet, December 5, 1878, CHC, *Sessional Papers*, 1879 (no. 7), p. 57.

74. Dickieson to minister of the Interior, July 21, 1879, RG10, vol. 3360, file 15,678, p. 8.

75. Looy, "Saskatchewan's First Indian Agent," 107-8. Laird had tried to resign as Indian superintendent in April, 1878, but Prime Minister Alexander Mackenzie refused to accept his resignation. See ibid., 114, n. 14.

76. Laird to the superintendent general of Indian Affairs, January 1, 1879, NA, RG10, 4412.

77. Looy, "Saskatchewan's First Indian Agent," 107.

Chapter Twenty: Ahenakew Dies, 1879-1880

1. Hines, Asissipi Journal, April 1, 1879-February 28, 1880, CMS, Microfilm Reel #A104, entry for April 1. This was supported by Dickieson, who said that "great difficulty was experienced in procuring a sufficient quantity of barley and potatoes, and more would have been planted could seed have been procured." (Dickieson to the minister of the Interior, July 21, 1879, NA, RG10, vol. 3360, file 15,678.)

2. Dickieson to the minister of the Interior, July 21, 1879, NA, RG10, vol. 3360, file 15,678, p. 6.

3. Hines, Asissipi Journal, April 1, 1879-February 28, 1880, CMS, Microfilm Reel #A104, entry for April 1. Hines said Okīnamatayayo's band had received oxen, cows and calves the previous fall; all but one had died during the winter and the remaining animal was in very poor condition.

4. Hines, *Red Indians*, 166. Stranger also helped Mistawasis's people plant their fields that year.

5. Hines, Asissipi Journal, April 1, 1879-February 28, 1880, CMS, Microfilm Reel #104, undated entry for May.

6. Ibid., undated entry for June. Also see Asissipi Mission Death Register, records #5 and #7. Pē-nōsēwēskam had been supporting his mother, as well as two wives and four children at the time of his death.

7. Ibid., undated June entry.

8. Ibid., entries for June. Also see Asissipi Mission Death Register, record #9. Others may also have died that spring, for Hines generally only recorded the deaths of those he buried.

9. Dickieson to the minister of the Interior, July 21, 1879, pp. 1-2, NA, RG10, vol. 3360, file 15,678. Also see report by Vankoughnet, *Sessional Papers*, 1880 (no. 4), p. 13.

10. Dickieson to the minister of the Interior, July 21, 1879, NA, RG10, vol. 3360, file 15,678.

11. Ibid., p. 7.

12. Peter Douglas Elias, *The Dakota of the Canadian Northwest: Lessons for Survival*, (Winnipeg: The University of Manitoba Press, 1988), 167-70. White Cap and his people had been living west of Fort Ellice, north of Fort Qu'Appelle, and east of the South Saskatchewan River since arriving in Canada.

13. Ibid., pp. 202-3.

14. Dickieson, to the minister of the Interior, July 21, 1879, p. 8.

15. Elias, *The Dakota*, 203.

16. Vankoughnet to Dickieson, November 17, 1879, NA, RG10, vol. 4419, as cited in Looy, "Saskatchewan's First Indian Agent," 113.

17. In 1881 Dewdney was appointed lieutenant-governor, a position he held concurrently with that of Indian commissioner until 1888.

18. Macdonald, CHC, *Sessional Papers*, Annual Report of the Department of the Interior, 1880 (no. 4), pp. xi-xii.

19. Indian Commissioner Edgar Dewdney to Macdonald, superintendent general of Indian Affairs, dated January 2, 1880, NA, RG10, vol. 3704, file 17,858, p. 1.

20. Ibid., pp. 2-7.

21. Dewdney, on page 6 of his report, said that he had "not formed such a poor opinion of 'Big Bear' as some appear to have done, he is of a very independent character, self-reliant, and appears to know how to make his living without begging from the Government."

22. Dewdney to Macdonald, in report dated January 2, 1880, NA, RG10, vol. 3704, file 17,858, pp. 12-13.

23. Ibid., pp. 11-12, and elsewhere. The Bloods were expected at Fort Macleod later.

24. The Stoneys had also complained about implements, saying the "spades would double up as soon as used and the ploughs were cross ploughs instead of breaking ploughs." Upon checking, Dewdney said the "price agreed to be given for the spades was so small that no better article could be obtained for the money." He confirmed that the ploughs were cross ploughs, not breaking ploughs. See Dewdney's report pp. 24-34.

25. Dewdney to Macdonald, in report dated January 2, 1880, p. 34. NA, RG10, vol. 3704, file 17,858.

26. Ibid., pp. 35-39.

27. Breland had preceded Laird to Sounding Lake the previous year "to use his influence with the Indians" in persuading some of the non-treaty chiefs to sign an adhesion to Treaty Six.

28. Dewdney to Macdonald, in report dated January 2, 1880, pp. 37-38, 45-55.

29. Vankoughnet, Report of the Deputy Superintendent-General of Indian Affairs, CHC, *Sessional Papers* 1880 (no. 4), pp. 12-13.

30. Dewdney to Macdonald, in report dated January 2, 1880, p. 45, NA, RG10, vol. 3704, file 17,858.

31. Report of Superintendent Walker, contained in Report of the Commissioner, North-West Mounted Police, 1879, *Opening Up the West*, 22.

32. Ahtahkakoop Band Treaty Paylist for 1879.

33. Peel, *Steamboats*, 50-51.

34. Ibid. Also see Dewdney, report to superintendent general of Indian Affairs, January 2, 1880, CHC, *Sessional Papers*, 1880 (no. 4), p. 86. Dewdney stated that Clarke sent 100 carts to haul the cargo; Peel used the figure 150.

35. "Chronicles by the Way," a report by a special correspondent [Tom White] dated Fort Carlton, September 1, 1879, in the Montreal *Gazette*, Saturday, September 27, 1879.

36. Kitowēhāw was also known as Alexander Cayen.

37. "Chronicles by the Way," a report by a special correspondent dated Fort Carlton, September 2, 1879, the Montreal *Gazette*, Monday, September 29, 1879.

38. Dewdney to Macdonald, in report dated January 2, 1880, p. 51, NA, RG10, vol. 3704, file 17,858.

39. The account of this meeting is contained in "Chronicles by the Way," dated Fort Carlton, September 2, 1879.

40. Dewdney, January 2, 1880, NA, RG10, vol. 3704, file 17,858, pp. 51-54(a).

41. Ibid., pp. 48, 50.

42. Ibid., pp. 46-48. Prices of $1.25 and $1.50 a bushel had been quoted.

43. Ibid., pp. 104, 106-7, 110-11.

44. Ibid.

45. Ibid., p. 115. Also see Looy, "Saskatchewan's First Indian Agent," 113.

46. In total, six farm instructors were sent to the Treaty Four area and nine instructors to the Treaty Six area. In the Treaty Seven area, there were two agency farm instructors and two government farmers; the farms were established 30 miles west of Fort Macleod and five miles from Calgary. There was one Indian agent for the Treaty Four area and two (not counting Orde, who was to be moved to Regina) in the Treaty Six area. As of January 2, 1880, no agents had been appointed for Treaty Seven. (See Dewdney to Macdonald, in report dated January 2, 1880, pp. 104-5; and "Chronicles by the Way," Montreal *Gazette*, September 27 and September 30, 1879.)

47. Dewdney to Macdonald, in report dated January 2, 1880, NA, RG10, vol. 3704, file 17,858, pp. 57, 94.

48. Ibid.

49. Ibid., pp. 95-96.

50. Ibid., p. 101.

51. Ibid., p. 107.

52. Ibid., p. 108.

53. Ibid., pp. 43-45.

54. Ibid., p. 113. Dewdney felt that some of the Sarcee Indians at Blackfoot Crossing, and probably people at other places as well, had been paid more than once. According to Dewdney, metal checks with treaty number on them had been issued when "first the Treaties were made." This was said to be a failure since many of the checks were either lost or used as wagers in the gambling games.

55. Paul Ahenakew, November 1996 review meeting. Also see statement by Lazarus Roan, Smallboy's Camp, in *The Spirit of the Alberta Indian Treaties*, 116. Roan, who was 72 when he was interviewed in 1974, was given similar information by men who had been at the first treaty payment.

56. Dewdney to Macdonald, in report dated January 2, 1880, pp. 113-14.

57. Ibid., pp. 117-18.

58. Vankoughnet to Macdonald, January 8, 1880, NA, RG10, vol. 3704, file 17,858.

59. Hines to Palmer Clarke, October 16, 1879, NA, RG10, vol. 3701, file 17,304. Also see Minutes of the Seventh Meeting of the Finance Committee, Diocese of Saskatchewan, Prince Albert, March 31, 1880, CMS, Microfilm Reel #A104; and Dewdney to superintendent general of Indian Affairs, December 31, 1880 CHC, *Sessional Papers*, 1881 (no. 14), p. 90.

60. Minutes of the Seventh Meeting of the Finance Committee, Diocese of Saskatchewan, Prince Albert, March 31, 1880, CMS, Microfilm Reel #A104. Also see Payton, *Diocese of Saskatchewan*, 47-48.

61. Payton, *Diocese of Saskatchewan*, 16-17, 35, 37.

62. Hines, Asissipi Journal, April 1, 1879-February 28, 1880, CMS, Microfilm Reel #A104, undated September entry.

63. The account of treading the grain in contained in Hines's *Red Indians*, 167-70.

64. See ibid., 170.

65. Hines, March 1-June 19, 1880 journal, CMS, Microfilm Reel A#104, entry for April 17. Also see Hines, *Red Indians*, 146.

66. Even in the south the buffalo were almost non-existent, trapped on the American side of the border by fires that prevented them from migrating north. Dewdney explained that in November 1879, "as if by some preconstructed arrangement," fires were lit along the Canadian-American boundary, and the ground was burnt from Wood Mountain west to the Rocky Mountains, and north to the latitude of Qu'Appelle. This action, which he blamed on the Sioux in American territory and Canadian Indians who had crossed the border to hunt, prevented the buffalo from travelling north towards the reserves. See Dewdney, CHC *Sessional Papers* 1881 (no. 14), p. 93.

67. Hines, April 1-February 28, 1880 journal, undated December entry.

68. Ibid., undated January entry.

69. Ibid., entries for January and February and the Asissipi Mission Death Register, records #11, #12, and #13. Charles Roundplain had been married by Hines in February of 1879. Andrew Flett was originally from St. Peter's Mission in Manitoba; Hines journal indicates he died early in February, but the register gives the date, probably incorrectly, as March 20, 1880.

70. Ibid., undated February entry.

71. Hines, annual letter to the CMS dated February 4, 1880, CMS, Microfilm Reel #A104. Also see Hines, *Red Indians*, 146.

72. Hines, Asissipi Journal, March 1-June 19, 1880, CMS, Microfilm Reel #A104, entry for March 21. Also see the Ahtahkakoop Band Treaty Paylist for 1880. Both children lived on the west side of the lake.

73. Ibid., entries for March 26 and April 4. In one of many discrepancies, Hines said in his journal that nine-year-old William died on Saturday, April 3, and was buried on April 4. His death certificate indicates that the boy was eight years old and that he died April 1 and was buried April 2. (See Asissipi Mission Death Register, record #14.)

74. Ibid., entry for April 4.

75. Ibid., entries for April 12 and 17.

76. Ibid., entry for April 23.

77. Ibid., entry for April 18.

78. Hines, *Red Indians*, 146-47.

79. Hines also refers to Arthur as Arthur Crane. He was the son of Nahtāwikāpawiwiskwew (Good Standing Woman) and brother of Kāh-kāsōw's wife Charlotte. David was the son of Cīpay-awāsis (Ghost Child).

80. Hines, March 1-June 19, 1880 journal, entries for April 28 and 29.

81. Ibid., entry for May 28, 29. Also see Asissipi Mission Death Register, records #15 and #18. The death register indicates that Arthur was 17 when he died, not "about 15" as stated by Hines in his journal.

82. Ibid., entry for May 26. Also see Asissipi Mission Death Register, record #17, which states that Sophia was 16 when she died. In his journal entry, Hines said she was nearly 14; this may be a mistake since the missionary said Sophia was 13 when she came to Sandy Lake in 1877.

83. Ibid., entry for March 28, 1880. Also see Hines's annual letter, February 4, 1880, CMS, Microfilm Reel #A104. The numbers of adults and children baptized, as given in Hines's journal, differ from those recorded in the Asissipi Mission Baptism Register. Men, women, and children baptized during the first months of 1880 included: Ahtahkakoop's son-in law Kā-tāh-twēhototawāt (Bird Landing On Someone Repeatedly), who chose the name John; three of Ahtahkakoop's grandchildren (George, Maria, and Susan, children of Emma Ahtahkakoop and Kā-tāh-twēhototawāt); Charles, the adult son of Kā-tāh-twēhototawāt; and Ahtahkakoop's nephew Peter Masuskapoe (Peekeekoot, or Hook Nose) and his wife Annie. Others baptized during the first months of 1880 included K-ōsihkosowayāniw (Ermineskin), who took the name Adam, and Iskwēsis's son Kā-kīsikāwapiw and his wife Sophia. (See Asissipi Mission Baptism Register, records #123 to #138.)

84. Although the treaty paylists do not show the transfer of the woman and boy from Masuskapoe's ticket to Kā-kīsikāwapiw's ticket until 1882, the Asissipi Mission Register, Diocese of Saskatchewan, 1875, marriage record #18, indicates that Kā-kīsikāwapiw married Matilda on October 31, 1880.

85. Hines, March 1-June 19, 1880 journal, entry for April 12, 1880. Baptiste was 22 when he married. Ellen Ermineskin, as well as being Poundmaker's niece, was Mistawasis's great niece. (See "The Story of the Ahenakew's," 18, 20.) The expense of keeping the young woman as a servant was too high, Hines said, because he often had to feed her relatives and friends; she was let go after working for only a few months. (See March 1-June 19, 1880 journal, entry for May 1.)

86. Ibid., entries for April 10 and 25.

87. Ibid., entry for May 31, 1880.

88. Indian agent W. Palmer Clarke to superintendent general of Indian Affairs, September 1, 1880, CHC, *Sessional Papers*, 1881 (no. 14), p. 101.

89. Palmer Clarke to Vankoughnet, March 3, 1880, vol. 3711, file 19,960.

90. Chief Commissioner James A. Grahame to Lawrence Clarke, January 16, 1880, in response to Clarke's report on the condition of the Indian people in the Carlton District, Carlton House Inward Correspondence, 1872-84, HBCA, PAM, B.27/c/2.

91. Hines, March 1-June 19, 1880 journal, entries for May 28, June 3, 4, and 28.

92. Hines, *Red Indians*, p. 227.

93. Hines, March 1-June 19, 1880 journal entry for April 19.

94. See Indian agent Palmer Clarke to Vankoughnet, March 3, 1880, NA, RG10, vol. 3,711, file 19,960.

95. Indian agent J. [John] M. Rae to superintendent general of Indian Affairs, August 4, 1882 [*sic*], CHC, *Sessional Papers*, 1883 (no. 5).

Chapter Twenty-One: A New Church is Built, 1880-1881

1. Hines, Asissipi Journal, March 1-June 19, 1880, CMS, Microfilm Reel #A104, entry for June 19. The microfilm is so damaged it is impossible to read Hines's assessment of the damage and his other comments.

2. Ibid., entries for June 20 and 24.

3. Wāskitoy, as noted earlier, was also known as Benjamin, Benjamin One Arm and Benjamin Has One Arm. Hines referred to him as Benjamin Joyful and Torn by a Bear. See Hines's journals, particularly the journal for February 20-May 9, 1881, CMS, Microfilm Reel #A110, entry for April 25.

4. Paul Ahenakew, November 1996 review meeting. On the 1880 paylist, the wrong family was listed on Kihci-mōhkomān's #13 ticket. His widow, Ocīkiskicās (Short Pants), was listed as #84 along with four girls and four boys.

5. See the Ahtahkakoop Band Treaty Paylists for 1880. In earlier documentation Kā-ohpatawakinam's and Okīnomotayēw's people, were often referred to as the Green Lake Indians.

6. See the Ahtahkakoop Band Treaty Paylists for 1879, 1880, and 1881.

7. Governor General's report of meetings with the Indians, November 4, 1881, NA, RG10, vol. 3768, file 33,642.

8. For instance, Otayapīhkēw (Netmaker), the man who had opposed Hines at Whitefish Lake late in 1874, had registered as a member of Ahtahkakoop's band under ticket #14 when Treaty Six was signed in 1876. He was one of the men who transferred to Okīnomotayēw's band in 1880. Similarly, Kwāskwēpakānis (Little Jumping Nut, #18 on the 1876 Ahtahkakoop paylist) and Geordie Mirasty (#72 on the Ahtahkakoop paylist) both had strong connections with Kā-ohpatawakinam's (Flying Dust's) band; they had traditionally traded at the Hudson's Bay Company's Green Lake post rather than at Fort Carlton. These men transferred to Ka-opahtawakinam's band in 1880, probably in antic-ipation of the 1881 survey of the reserve at Meadow Lake. Although Mirasty had been registered as a member of Ahtahkakoop's band from 1877 to 1879, he was listed as a headman on Ka-opahtawakinam's treaty paylist in 1880, and he collected the annuities for people listed under three different tickets.

9. Kakwēciyaw's (Questioning Body) treaty paylist number was #42. Wīcikāpawimēw's (He Stands With You) paylist number was #94; he was paid at Prince Albert, not Fort Carlton.

10. In 1879 Kīsik-awāsis had been paid as a headman in Ahtahkakoop's band and he col-lected annuities for himself, his wife, two boys, and one girl. The following year Kīsik-awāsis received his annuity payment under ticket #30 in Red Pheasant's band; one woman, one boy, and three girls were included on his ticket. Interestingly, although Kīsik-awāsis was now listed on Red Pheasant's paylist, he was paid as a headman from Ahtahkakoop's band. However, it was noted on the Red Pheasant paylist that Kīsik-awāsis would not be paid as a headman in subsequent years unless he was one of Red Pheasant's headmen. (See the Ahtahkakoop and Red Pheasant treaty paylists.)

11. J.M. Rae, September 25, 1880, CHC, *Sessional Papers*, 1881 (no. 14), p. 82. Rae replaced Palmer Clarke as Indian agent for the Carlton Agency in the fall of 1880.

12. Hines, Asissipi Journal, July 1-December 31, 1880, CMS, Microfilm Reel #A110, entries for August 20, 25, 28, September 30.

13. Dewdney, report of his 1879 tour of the North-West, January 2, 1880, NA, RG10, vol. 3704, file 17,858, pp. 50-52.

14. W. Palmer Clarke, September 1, 1880, CHC, *Sessional Papers*, 1881 (no. 14), p. 102.

15. Rae, CHC, *Sessional Papers*, 1881 (no. 14), p. 82.

16. Ibid.

17. Ibid.

18. Ibid., p. 95.

19. Minutes of the 7th Meeting of the CMS Financial Committee, Prince Albert, March 3, 1880. Also see Hines, Asissipi Journal, March 1-June 19, CMS, Microfilm Reel #A104, entries for May 19, 24, and 31, 1880; and Hines, *Red Indians*, 184.

20. Hines, *Red Indians*, 184. Also see Hines's Asissipi Journal for July 1-December 31, 1880, Microfilm Reel, #A110, entries for August 30, November 8 and December 23, CMS.

21. Pritchard had also held church services in the school house between Hines's regular visits.

22. Hines, *Red Indians*, 175.

23. Hines, Asissipi Journal, July 1-December 31, 1880, Microfilm Reel, #A110, entry for December 4.

24. Hines, *Red Indians*, 175. Hines said that this custom was still practised in 1913, two years before he wrote his book. The women sat on the left side.

25. Hines, Asissipi Journal, July 1-December 31, 1880, Microfilm Reel, #A110, entry for December 24.

26. Ibid., entry for December 26.

27. Dewdney to superintendent general of Indian Affairs, December 31, 1880, CHC, *Sessional Papers*, 1881, (no. 14), p. 90. Also see Hines, *Red Indians*, 187-88.

28. Hines, Asissipi Journal, July 1-December 31, 1880, CMS, Microfilm Reel #A110, in a note dated January 1, 1881, appended to the end of the journal.

29. Ibid., entry for December 26, 1880.

30. See Hines's Asissipi Journal, February 20-May 9, 1881, entry for April 1. Hines wrote in his journal that "the Indians call this [wind] 'Kewatin' the going home wind, meaning that it is the end of winter."

31. Wāskitoy's widow died on April 25, 1881. See Hines's journal for February 20-May 9, 1881, CMS, Microfilm Reel #110, entry for April 25. Her husband had died sometime between the 1879 and 1880 treaty payments. Hines did not record either of their deaths in the Asissipi Mission Death Register.

32. Hines, Asissipi Journal, February 20-May 9, 1881, CMS, Microfilm Reel #A111, entry for March 6, and the Asissipi Mission Death Register. In his journal, which started on February 20, Hines said there were three deaths in March and three more in April. The death register shows five died in February and two in April. These figures do not include the death of Wāskitoy's widow.

Chapter Twenty-Two:
Fort Carlton Chiefs Meet With the Marquis of Lorne, 1881-1882

1. Hines, *Red Indians*, 31, 175. Also see Hines, Asissipi Journal, June 24-November 11, 1883, CMS, Microfilm Reel #A111, entry for October 14.

2. Hines, *Red Indians*, 176-79. Copy of the Bishop of Saskatchewan's Journal of a Visit to the CMS's Mission at Asisippi in the Diocese of Saskatchewan, May 6, 1881, CMS, Microfilm Reel #110.

3. Bishop of Saskatchewan's "Journal of a Visit."

4. Hines, *Red Indians*, 179-80.

5. Ibid.

6. See also, Bishop of Saskatchewan's "Journal of a Visit."

7. Extract of a report from the Indian agent at Fort Carlton [Rae] to superintendent general of Indian Affairs dated May 27, 1881, CHC, *Sessional Papers*, 1882 (no. 6), p. xi.

8. Dewdney, December 31, 1880, CHC, *Sessional Papers*, 1881 (no. 14), p. 79.

9. Hines, Asissipi Journal, June 3-August 18, 1881, Microfilm Reel #A110, entry for June 20, CMS, Microfilm Reel #A110.

10. Dewdney, January 2, 1880, RG10 vol. 3704, file 17,858, pp. 116-17.

11. Ahtahkakoop Band Treaty Paylist for 1881.

12. Kā-miyo-ahcahkwēw, who was closer in age to Kīsik-awāsis than to his other brothers, had apparently been away in May when the new church was dedicated. This, plus his absence at the treaty payments, suggests that Kīsik-awāsis's problems may have been troubling Kā-miyo-ahcahkwēw.

13. Otinikēw (He Takes Something) had one girl and one boy remaining on his ticket. Jimmuk, who was listed under ticket #94 in the Mistawasis Band, transferred to Ahtahkakoop's band in 1884. (See the Ahtahkakoop Band paylists and Asissipi Mission Register, Diocese of Saskatchewan, 1875, marriage resister record #22.)

14. Sir John Douglas Sutherland Campbell, the Marquis of Lorne. See CHC, *Sessional Papers*, 1880 (no. 4), p. vii. He was governor general from 1878-83.

15. The Marquis of Lorne's interviews with the chiefs and leading men in Treaty Four and Six were recorded in Reports of the different councils which His Excellency the Governor General held with the Indians while in the N.W.T., November 4, 1881, NA, RG10, vol. 3768, file 33,642, pp. 1-40.

16. Reports of the different councils which His Excellency the Governor General held with the Indians while in the N.W.T., November 4, 1881, NA, RG10, vol. 3768, file 33,642, pp. 1-13.

17. Report of the Marquis of Lorne's trip, pp. 13-15.

18. Sydney P. Hall, sketch of people outside the Big House at Fort Carlton drawn during the Marquis of Lorne's visit, National Archives photograph C-012965.

19. Lord Lorne's Expedition of the North West, Articles contributed to the *Scotsman* and the *Edinburgh Courant*, August 29, 1881, contained in a scrapbook of newspaper clippings, Glenbow Archives, Calgary (GA), D971.2. M147. It should be noted that there were mistakes in the text of these articles.

20. R.C. Russell, *The Carlton Trail: The Broad Highway into the Saskatchewan Country From the Red River Settlement, 1840–1880* (Saskatoon: Western Producer, 1955), 107. Russell used as his source reports written by W.H. Williams, a special correspondent for the Toronto *Globe*, who accompanied the Marquis of Lorne's party to the North-West.

21. Report of the Marquis of Lorne's trip, p. 19.

22. Ibid., p. 16. Some punctuation marks and capital letters have been added to the quotations taken from this report.

23. Ibid., pp. 16-17.

24. Ibid, pp. 18, 19. Some punctuation and capital letters have been added.

25. The statements of John Smith and the other chiefs can be found in the Report of the Marquis of Lorne's trip, pp. 20-24.

26. Report of the Marquis of Lorne's trip, pp. 21-22. Ayahtaskamikinam, as noted earlier, was also known as William Twatt. The governor general's report incorrectly gave Ayahtaskamikinam's name as William Watt.

27. Ibid., p. 26.

28. The remarks of Okīnomotayēw, Kā-ohpatawakinam, and One Arrow appear on pages 26-27 of ibid.

29. Report of the Marquis of Lorne's trip, pp. 20-28.

30. Ibid, p. 28. Also see Russell, *The Carlton Trail*, 107.

31. Report of the Marquis of Lorne's trip, pp. 30, 39.

32. Ibid., p. 40.

33. Vankoughnet to Macdonald, prime minister and superintendent general of Indian Affairs, November 16, 1881, NA, RG10, vol. 3768, file 33,642. Vankoughnet suggested in the letter that extracts be taken from the interviews "shewing in one column the demands of the Indians and in another the replies of His Excellency, also a blank column for the remarks of the Indian Commissioner for Manitoba and the North West Territories [Dewdney] to whom the same will be forwarded with a request to state in the Column provided for the purpose in which manner the Department can best fulfil the promises made by His Excellency."

34. Rae to superintendent general of Indian Affairs, November 4, 1881, CHC, *Sessional Papers*, 1882, (no. 6), p. 83. Also see Rae, December 4, 1882, CHC, *Sessional Papers*, 1883 (no. #5), p. 225.

35. An Emmanuel College brochure attached to the Proceedings of the Fourth Meeting of the Synod of the Diocese of Saskatchewan, August 28, 1889, CMS, Microfilm Reel #A116. Also see Jean E. Murray, "Early History of Emmanuel College," *Saskatchewan History* 60, no. 3 (1956). Most of the students were the sons of settlers.

36. Hines, Asissipi Journal, January 1-March 31, 1882, CMS, Microfilm Reel #A110. Matheson was ordained deacon in 1880, priest in 1881, and he graduated in divinity in 1882. Pritchard was ordained deacon in August 1882 and priest in 1885. Wright, who had returned to England for a short visit after working for Hines, was taking theology, as well as teaching in Prince Albert. Stranger was studying to be a deacon. (See Payton, *Diocese of Saskatchewan*, 48, 49.)

37. Hines, Asissipi Journal, January 1-March 31, 1882, CMS, Microfilm Reel #A110, entry for March 1.

38. Ibid., entry for March 27.

39. Ibid, entry for January 3, 1882.

40. Ibid., entry for January 29, 1882. Also see Asissipi Mission Baptism Register, record #167.

41. Ibid., entry for March 12, 1882.

42. Ibid., entries for March 26 and 27, 1882. Also see the Asissipi Mission Baptism Register, record #170, and Asissipi Mission Death Register, records #33 and #34.

43. Hines, Asissipi Journal, January 1-March 31, 1882, entry for March 27.

Chapter Twenty-Three:
Ahtahkakoop Holds a Bear Ceremony, 1882-1883

1. The couple was already lonely, for as Hines explained, "we were isolated from white people, our nearest neighbours being fifty miles away." Now England seemed farther away than ever. And these feelings intensified when the last letter written to Emma's mother was returned to them with the word "unknown" written across it. "It is evident,"

Hines said, "that before our letter reached England [she and] all her friends had passed away: that not one of them received a line from us to help soften their dying pillows." (See Hines, *Red Indians*, 194-95.)

2. Hines, *Red Indians*, 195. Also see Hines's letter dated March 20, 1882, CMS, Microfilm Reel #A110. Hines had only been in the field for eight years.

3. Statement Showing the Condition of the various Indian Schools for the Year ended 30th June, 1882, CHC, 1883 (no. 5), pp. 250-51. Hines's salary was paid for by the Church Missionary Society. Previously he had been paying the teachers and many other mission expenses out of his salary, so the money no doubt was appreciated. The government grant was based on $12 per capita per year based on an average daily attendance, with the provision that it was not to exceed $300 for 25 pupils. Schools entirely supported by the government received $300 for the teacher's salary and $12 per annum for each pupil numbering over 25 and up to 42, with the amount not to exceed $504.

4. Hines, *Red Indians*, 183.

5. "Farming Agencies and Indian Reservations," CHC, *Sessional Papers*, 1883 (no. 5), pp. 264-65, 270-71. Also see Wadsworth, October 9, 1883, CHC, *Sessional Papers*, 1884 (no. 4), p.121.

6. Rae, April 12, 1882, NA, RG10, vol. 3600, file 1752.

7. Ahtahkakoop Band Treaty Paylist for 1882; the payments were made at the Ahtahkakoop Reserve on September 22. Also see the Asissipi Mission baptism and marriage registers for the period.

8. Dewdney, December 15, 1882, CHC, *Sessional Papers*, 1883 (no. 5), p. 194.

9. Ibid. Also see Rae, December 4, 1882, in ibid., p. 225.

10. Inspecting officer Wadsworth, October 9, 1883, CHC, *Sessional Papers*, 1884 (no. 4), p. 121.

11. On December 4, 1882, Rae reported that the two chiefs "will have no difficulty in paying the balance this fall." (See Rae, December 4, 1882, CHC, *Sessional Papers*, 1883 (no. 5), p. 225.

12. Farming Agencies and Indian Reservations, CHC, *Sessional Papers*, 1883 (no. 5), pp. 264-65, 270-71.

13. Wadsworth, October 9, 1883, CHC, *Sessional Papers*, 1884 (no. 4), p. 121. The inspector identified the settlers as Driver (more likely Dreaver) and Johnston.

14. Wadsworth, December 9, 1882, CHC, *Sessional Papers*, 1883 (no. 5), p. 186. Although it was Wadsworth who said that several of the men in Ahtahkakoop's band had broken land and fenced for Dreaver and Johnston, he did not report this until the following fall.

15. Rae to Indian commissioner, August 4, 1882, Carlton House Inward Correspondence, 1872-84, HBCA, PAM, B.27/c/2, fo. 392.

16. Ibid.

17. Grahame to Clarke, December 18, 1882, Carlton House Inward Correspondence, 1872-84, HBCA, PAM, B.27/c/2, fo. 391.

18. Hines to Miss Newnham (England), August 21, 1883, CMS, Microfilm Reel #A111. Also see Hines to Christopher Cyprian Fenn, secretary for the CMS, June 30, 1883,

Microfilm Reel #A111. Based in London, Fenn was responsible for the Canadian missions from 1870-72 and 1881-93.

19. Hines, Asissipi Journal, April 1, 1879-February 28, 1880, CMS, Microfilm Reel #104, undated entry for June. Punctuation has been changed.

20. [James Taylor], *The Guide*, published by the Battleford Industrial School, Battleford, February, 1899, vol. vii, no. 2.

21. Hines to Miss Newnham, August 21, 1883, CMS, Microfilm Reel #A111. Also see Hines to Fenn, CMS secretary, June 30, 1882, CMS, Microfilm Reel #A111.

22. Hines to Newnham, August 21, 1883, CMS, Microfilm Reel #A111.

23. Hines to Fenn, January 17, 1883, CMS, Microfilm Reel #111.

24. A census taken by government officials showing the "Number of Indians in the North-West Territories and their whereabouts on the 31st December, 1882," indicated that 29 were "north hunting" and 15 were on the reserve. The "total number of Indians" was given as 185. See CHC, *Sessional Papers*, 1883 (no. 5), p. 201.

25. Hines to the Finance Committee, Prince Albert, October 13, 1883, CMS, Microfilm Reel #A111.

26. Hines, Asissipi Journal, November 12, 1883-January 26, 1884, CMS, Microfilm Reel #A111, entries for December 20 and 22, 1883.

27. Hines to CMS, November 27, 1882. Also see letters dated February 22 and 27, 1883, CMS, Microfilm Reel #A111.

28. Ibid. Also see document from Emma Hines's doctor dated February 26, 1883, CMS, Microfilm Reel #A111.

29. Emma Hines to Fenn, April 1, 1883, CMS, Microfilm Reel, A111.

30. Hines to CMS Committee, April 12, 1883, CMS, Microfilm Reel #A111.

31. Hines, letters to CMS, June 30, 1883, and to Newnham, August 21, 1883, CMS, Microfilm Reel #A111.

Chapter Twenty-Four: Good Crops Yet the People Starved, 1883-1884

1. Tabular Statement on Farming Agencies and Indian Reservations, CHC, *Sessional Papers*, 1884 (no. 4), pp. 192-93. Although the document indicated that oats were not planted, it also showed that 400 bushels of oats were harvested.

2. Hines to Miss Newnham (England), August 21, 1883, CMS, Microfilm Reel A111.

3. Hines, Asissipi Journal, June 24-November 11, 1883, CMS, Microfilm Reel #A111, entries for July 15, 24, and August 3; and Asissipi Journal, January 31-June 30, 1884, CMS, Microfilm Reel #A112, entry for May 2.

4. Macdonald, Annual Report of Indian Affairs for the Year 1883, January 1, 1884, CHC, *Sessional Papers*, 1884 (no. 4), p. xlviii.

5. Hines, Asissipi Journal, June 24-November 11, 1883, CMS, Microfilm Reel #A112, entry for August 21.

6. Ibid., entry for September 8, 1883.

7. Tabular Statement on Farming Agencies and Indian Reservations [for 1883], CHC,

Sessional Papers, 1884. (no. 4), pp. 192-93, 198-99. The report on pages 192-93 indicates that only two bushels of carrots were harvested, whereas the report on pages 198-99 gives the figure as 200. In 1882 the harvest had amounted to 1,000 bushels of wheat, 400 bushels of barley, 2,800 turnips, and 50 bushels of carrots.

8. Hines, Asissipi Journal, June 24-November 11, 1883, CMS, Microfilm Reel #A111, entry for September 12, CMS, Microfilm Reel #A111.

9. Mōhkomānawēw had been registered as #20 in the Flying Dust Band. When he transferred to the Ahtahkakoop Band and married Okimāw waskiwin-nōtikwāw (Chief Root Old Lady), one of Pē-nōsēwēskam's widows, he was issued ticket number #101. Pē-nōsēwēskam's youngest widow, Kate Tapwewiniwok (Truth), had married James Asināpēwiyin (Stone Man) in March 1881.

10. See the Ahtahkakoop Band Treaty Paylist for 1883, RG10, vol. 9416.

11. Inspecting officer Wadsworth, letter dated October 9, 1883, CHC, *Sessional Papers*, 1884 (no. 4), p. 121.

12. Indian agent J. Ansdell Macrae to superintendent general of Indian Affairs, report dated August 11, 1884, CHC, *Sessional Papers*, 1885 (no. 3), p. 78. Macrae replaced Rae as Indian agent in November, 1883.

13. Hines, Asissipi Journal, January 31-June 30, 1884, CMS, Microfilm Reel #A112, entry for February 23.

14. Hayter Reed, acting assistant Indian commissioner, to Indian commissioner in a report dated December 28, 1883, NA, RG10, vol. 3668, file 10,644, p. 4.

15. Minutes of the Finance Committee, Prince Albert, October 10, 1883, CMS, Microfilm Reel #A111. Also see letters written by Hines to the CMS Committee, October 13, 1883, and J.A. Mackay to Hines, October 18, 1883, CMS, Microfilm Reel, #A111. All apparently was forgiven as time healed the rift, and in a letter dated January, 1884, Hines wrote he was happy to know that he had been "acquitted of any disloyalty to the society." (See CMS, Microfilm Reel #A112.)

16. Hines, Asissipi Journal, June 24-November 11, 1883, entry for October 22. Also see Mackay to Hines, letter dated October 15, 1883, CMS, Microfilm Reel #A111.

17. Wadsworth, report dated October 9, 1883, CHC, *Sessional Papers*, 1884 (no 4), p. 121.

18. Hines, Asissipi Journal, June 24-November 11, 1883, entry for September 8, CMS, Microfilm Reel, #A111. Also see entry for October 22.

19. Ibid., entries for October 22 and 29. Also see the November 12, 1883-January 26, 1884 journal, entry for November 25, CMS, Microfilm Reel #A111.

20. Ibid., entry for November 6, 1883.

21. Ibid., entry for October 29.

22. Ibid., January 31-June 30, 1884, entry for June 8, CMS, Microfilm Reel #A112.

23. Ibid., November 12, 1883 to January 26, 1884, entries for November 12, 13, 15, and 23, CMS, Microfilm Reel #A111.

24. Ibid., November 12, 1883-January 26, 1884, entry for November 25, CMS, Microfilm Reel, #A111.

25. Ibid., entries for November 17, 18, 20, and 22, CMS, Microfilm Reel, #A111. Also see

Asissipi Mission Death Register, record #39. In the death record, Hines said the boy was three.

26. Ibid., entries for December 2 and 13, CMS, Microfilm Reel, #A111.

27. Ibid., entry for December 20, CMS, Microfilm Reel, #A111.

28. Ibid., entry for December 22, 1883, CMS, Microfilm Reel, #A111.

29. Ibid., entry for December 22, 1883, CMS, Microfilm Reel, #A111, entries for December 22 and 23.

30. Ibid., entry for January 10, 1884, CMS, Microfilm Reel #A111.

31. Ibid., entries for January 15 and 16, 1884, CMS, Microfilm Reel #A111.

32. Ibid., entry for December 8, CMS, Microfilm Reel #A111.

33. Dewdney to superintendent general of Indian Affairs, letter dated October 2, 1883, CHC, *Sessional Papers*, 1884 (no. #4), pp. 102-4.

34. Hayter Reed, acting assistant commissioner to Indian Commissioner Dewdney, December 28, 1883, NA, RG10, vol. 3668, file 10,644, p. 13.

35. Ibid., pp. 11-12.

36. Hines, Asissipi journal, November 12, 1883-January 26, 1884, entry for December 16.

37. Hayter Reed, acting assistant commissioner to Indian Commissioner Dewdney, December 28, 1883, NA, RG10, vol. 3668, file 10,644, p. 13.

38. Hines, Asissipi Journal, January 31-June 20, 1884, CMS, Microfilm Reel #A112, entry for March 9.

39. Ibid., entries for January 13, February 9, 19 and 23.

40. Ibid., entry for March 9, 1884.

41. Ibid., , entry for February 16.

42. Ibid. entry for March 9.

43. Thomas Sōniyāw-āyāwēw (He Has Money) had been born in November; in his journal, Hines said the baby was two months old when he died. The child's mother was Ahtahkakoop's daughter Mary Piyēsīs (Bird). Although Hines called her Mary in Asissipi baptism record #191, he incorrectly referred to her as Jane in an earlier record (#151). The six-month-old baby was Emma, daughter of Baptiste and Ellen Ahenakew, she died March 19. See Asissipi Mission Death Register, records #40 and #41.

44. Hines, Asissipi Journal, January 31-June 20, 1884, CMS, Microfilm Reel #A112, entries for February 8 and 21, March 7, 12, 15, 16, 19, and April 3.

45. Ibid., entries for March 16 and 19, 1884.

46. Ibid., entry for March 23, 1884.

47. Ibid., entry for May 2.

48. Ibid., entries for March 19, 29, and May 2. Also see the Asissipi Journal for November 12, 1883-January 26, 1884, CMS, Microfilm Reel #A111, entry for January 10; and the Asissipi Journal for July 1, 1884-January 10, 1885, CMS, Microfilm Reel #A112, entry for July 27.

49. Hines, Asissipi Mission Death Register, record #42. Surprisingly, Hines makes no mention of her death in his journal, further illustrating the incompleteness of his records.

50. Hines, Asissipi Journal, January 31-June 30, 1884, CMS, Microfilm Reel #A112, entry for April 3.

51. Ibid., entry for June 6.

52. Various journal entries for 1884. Also see Hines, *Red Indians*, 184.

53. Hines said the dowry was one horse, but according to oral history the man gave two horses to Macikwanās. (Paul Ahenakew, review meeting May 28, 1997.)

54. Hines, Asissipi Journal for January 31-June 30, 1884, CMS, Microfilm Reel #A112, entry for April 6.

55. Ibid.

56. Ibid., April 8.

57. Ibid., entries for February 26 and April 14. Also see Asissipi Mission Baptism Register, records #195–#199. Kihci-mōhkomān had drowned in Sandy Lake some four years earlier.

58. Ibid., entry for April 18. Joseph was the closest in age to the young man described by Hines. However, he was Ahtahkakoop's fourth son. Kā-miyo-astotin, Kīsik-awāsis, and Kā-miyo-ahcahkwēw were all older.

59. Ibid., entries for April 20 and 27.

60. Macrae, Indian agent for the Carlton agency, to superintendent general, August 11, 1884, CHC, *Sessional Papers*, 1885 (no. 3), p. 81. Macrae had arrived at Fort Carlton November 9, 1883, replacing Rae.

61. Macdonald, annual report of Indian Affairs for year ended December 31, 1884, January 1, 1884, CHC, *Sessional Papers*, 1885 (no. 3), p. xlii.

62. Macrae, August 11, 1884, CHC, *Sessional Papers*, 1885, (no. 3), p. 79.

63. Reed to Indian commissioner, December 28, 1883, NA, RG10, vol. 3668, file 10,644, p. 5.

64. Reed to superintendent general of Indian affairs, January 28, 1884, NA, RG10, vol. 3668, file 10,644.

65. Reed to superintendent general of Indian affairs December 28, 1883, NA, RG10, vol. 3668, file 10,644.

66. Macrae, August 11, 1884, CHC, *Sessional Papers*, 1885, (no. 3), p. 78.

67. Wadsworth, report dated December 31, 1885, CHC, *Sessional Papers*, 1886 (no. 4), p. 184.

68. Vankoughnet, November 15, 1883, NA, RG18, vol. 1,009. The main concern seemed to be women, whose families were probably starving, camping near towns with NWMP posts for "improper purposes," i.e., prostitution. Also see Comptroller White, June 6, 1884, NA, RG18, vol. 1,009.

69. A Certified Copy of a Report of the Committee of the Honourable the Privy Council, approved by His Excellency the Governor General in Council on the 25th February, 1884, NA, RG10, vol. 3668, file 10,644. In the same file, also see Macdonald to the Privy Council, January 18, 1884, and Reed to Indian commissioner, December 28, 1883.

70. Rae to Indian commissioner, November 10, 1883, NA, RG10, vol. 311.

71. Reed to Indian Commissioner Dewdney, December 28, 1883, NA, RG10, vol. 3668, file 10,644, pp. 10-11.

72. For further information see Sarah Carter's *Lost Harvests: Prairie Indian Reserve Farmers and Government Policy* (Montreal & Kingston: McGill-Queen's University Press, 1990.)

73. Reed to Macdonald, April 12, 1884, NA, RG10, vol. 3668, file 10,644.

74. Fred White, comptroller, to Vankoughnet, March, 1884 [day of month unreadable], NA, RG10, vol. 3668, file 10,644.

Chapter Twenty-Five: A Time of Unrest, 1884-1885

1. Hines, Asissipi Journal, January 31-June 30, 1884, CMS, Microfilm Reel #A112, entries for March 22, April 14, and 25.

2. Tabular Statement of Farming Agencies and Indian Reservations [for 1884], CHC, *Sessional Papers*, 1885 (no. 3), part 1, pp. 192-93.

3. Hines, Asissipi Journal, January 31-June 30, 1884, CMS, Microfilm Reel #A112, entries for May 9 and 17.

4. Ibid., entry for June 6.

5. Ibid., entry for June 8. Also see Hines, Asissipi Journal, July 1, 1884-January 10, 1885, entry for July 19. Hines said that the Pelican Lake Band formed 'the backbone of heathenism of these parts."

6. Ibid., entry for June 11. Also see ibid., July 10, and a report by J. Ansdell Macrae dated August 11, 1884, CHC, *Sessional Papers*, 1885 (no. 3), p. 82.

7. Ibid., entry for June 9.

8. Dewdney, November 25, 1884, in Annual Report of Indian Affairs for the Year Ended 31st December 1884, CHC, *Sessional Papers*, 1885 (no. 3), p. 161.

9. Hines, Asissipi Journal, July 1, 1884-January 10, 1885, CMS, Microfilm Reel #A112, entry for July 3.

10. Hines, Asissipi Journal, January 31-June 30, 1884, CMS, Microfilm Reel #A112, entry for May 11.

11. Hines, Asissipi Journal, July 1, 1884-January 10, 1885, entry for July 5.

12. Ibid.

13. Hines, Asissipi Journal, January 31-June 30, 1884, entries for June.

14. Hines, Asissipi Journal, July 1, 1884-January 10, 1885, entries for July 1 and 5, 1884.

15. Ibid., entries for July 13 and 17.

16. K-ōsihkosiwanāniw was originally from the Bear Hills south of Edmonton. (Edward Ahenakew, "Story of the Ahenakews," 20.) The family returned to Ahtahkakoop's reserve in 1885 and was given a new treaty number. A note on the paylist stated that Ermineskin was "from B'ford and always known as a good man, he remained here with his relatives." He died during the 1905-06 paylist year. Another man by the name of Ermineskin was chief of the Ermineskin Band, situated in what is now Alberta, from 1879 to 1921.

17. Hines, Asissipi Journal, July 1, 1884-January 10, 1885, entry for July 20. This marriage, like most others of the time, was likely arranged by the parents. Also see Asissipi Mission Marriage Register, record #33.

18. Reed to Vankoughnet, February 27, 1884, NA, RG10, vol. 3666, file 10,181.

19. Inspector Richard Burton Dean, report dated February 28, 1884, NA, RG10, vol. 3666, file 10,181. Also see Carter, *Lost Harvests*, pp. 121-22.

20. Carter, *Lost Harvests*, 124.

21. Macdonald, January 1, 1885, CHC, *Sessional Papers*, 1885 (no. 3), p. x. Also see Reed to Commissioner Acheson Gosford Irvine, North-West Mounted Police, letter dated May 18, 1884, Royal Canadian Mounted Police Papers, NA, RG18, vol. 1015, file 1212; and Carter, *Lost Harvests*, 122-27.

22. Carter, *Lost Harvests*, 125.

23. Fine Day, in "Incidents of the Rebellion," *The Cree Rebellion of '84: Chapters in the North-West History Prior to 1890*, Battleford Historical Society, vol. 1, no. 1, June 1926, p. 13. According to Fine Day, who was among the group gathered at Poundmaker's reserve, the chiefs felt they had become slaves of the government, "doing tasks and receiving bad food, and little of that." This article consists of an interview with Fine Day by Campbell Innes. A copy of *The Cree Rebellion of '84* can be found at the Saskatchewan Archives Board, Regina office. Also see Hugh A. Dempsey, *Big Bear: The End of Freedom* (Vancouver/Toronto: Douglas & McIntyre, 1984), 123.

24. According to Rae, Indians had come "from all the Reserves with the exception of the Stonies, who remained and worked on their Reserves." He does not indicate if he is referring to the reserves in the Battleford area or to a wider area. (See Rae, report dated June 21, 1884, NA, RG10, vol. 3576, file 309, Part B.) Had Ahtahkakoop, Mistawasis, and other chiefs from the Carlton and Prince Albert areas been in attendance, they most likely would have been mentioned in government and North-West Mounted Police reports; no such mention was found in the primary source materials consulted.

25. Robert Jefferson, "Incidents of the Rebellion as Related by Robert Jefferson," in *The Cree Rebellion of '84*, vol. 1, no. 1, June 1926, p. 25.

26. Superintendent L.N.F. Crozier to Dewdney, June 22, 1884, NA, RG10, vol. 3576, file 309, Part B. Also see Fine Day, *The Cree Rebellion of '84*, p. 13, and Rae to Dewdney, June 21, 1884, NA, RG10, vol. 3576, file 309 Part B.

27. Crozier to Dewdney, June 22, 1884, NA, RG10, vol. 3576, file 309, Part B.

28. *Saskatchewan Herald*, Battleford, July 12, 1884.

29. Jefferson, "Incidents of the Rebellion," pp. 25, 35.

30. *Saskatchewan Herald*, July 12, 1884.

31. Rae to Dewdney, June 28, 1884, NA, RG10, vol. 3576, file 309, Part B.

32. Crozier to Dewdney, June 22, 1884, NA, RG10, vol. 3576, file 309, Part B.

33. Vankoughnet to Dewdney, July 7, 1884, NA, RG10, vol. 3580, file 730.

34. According to Fine Day, who helped in the preparations for the Sun Dance and then participated in the sacred ceremony, the council was to be held after the Sun Dance. (See Fine Day, in "Incidents of the Rebellion," 14, 15, 18.)

35. Hines, *Red Indians*, 197.

36. Report of the Commissioner of the North-West Mounted Police Force, 1885, p. 20, in *Settlers and Rebels: Being the Official Reports to Parliament of the Activities of the Royal North-West Mounted Police Force from 1882–1885* (Toronto:Coles Publishing Company, 1973). The report of activity in the Batoche area had come from Crozier.

37. Macrae [to Dewdney], August 25, 1884, NA, RG10, vol. 3697, file 15,423.

38. Constable Joseph MacDermot to the Officer Comanding, North-West Mounted Police, Battleford, August 16, 1884, NA RG18, vol. 12, file 20-1885, vol. 4. Also see Crozier to Irvine, August 9, 1884, NA, RG18, vol. 1015, file folder 1137-1150. The chiefs in attendance, besides Ahtahkakoop, Mistawasis, Beardy, and Okimāsis, likely included Petihkwahākēw from Muskeg Lake; John Smith and One Arrow from the South Branch, James Smith from Fort à la Corne, and Ayahtaskamikinam from Sturgeon Lake. Lucky Man and Big Bear from the Battleford area, were also present.

39. George F.G. Stanley, *The Birth of Western Canada: A History of the Riel Rebellions* (Toronto: University of Toronto Press, 1961), p. 290.

40. *Saskatchewan Herald*, August 9, 1884. Also see Dempsey, *Big Bear*, 138.

41. Ibid.

42. Province of Saskatchewan, *Indian Lands and Canada's Responsibility — The Saskatchewan Position: A Short Survey of Western Indian Treaties and Land Settlement* [c. 1977-1982].

43. Sub-agent Macrae to Dewdney, August 25, 1884, NA, RG10, vol. 3697, file 15,423.

44. The list of grievances presented by the delegation of chiefs and headmen was included in Macrae's report to Dewdney dated August 25, 1884. The order of the grievances out-lined here differs slightly from the original document and some minor changes in punc-tuation have been made. Macrae had written to Dewdney on August 12 giving a brief outline of the meeting and the events leading up to it. Interestingly, in his report dated August 25, Macrae said the more detailed report "was not forwarded by last mail" at the request of Hayter Reed, assistant Indian commissioner.

45. Macrae to Dewdney, August 25, 1884.

46. Macrae, August 11, 1884, CHC, *Sessional Papers*, 1885 (no. 3), p. 79.

47. Ibid., pp. 79-81.

48. Sergeant W.A. Brooks, dated Prince Albert, August 21, 1884, NA, RG18, vol. 1017.

49. Sergeant Harry Keenan, Duck Lake, August 24, 1884, NA, RG18, vol. 1017.

50. "Statement shewing the Number of Indians and Half Breeds in the Environs of Duck Lake and Prince Albert," NA, RG18, vol. 1018, file 2265 (no date).

51. Hines, Asissipi Journal, July 1, 1884-January 10, 1885, CMS, Microfilm Reel #A112, entries for August 17 and October 3.

52. Tabular Statement of Farming Agencies and Indian Reservations [for 1884], CHC, *Sessional Papers*, 1885 (no. 3), part 1, pp. 192-93.

53. Hines, Asissipi Journal, January 16-July 26, 1885, CMS, Microfilm Reel #A113, entry for February 15.

54. At the time of his death Asināpēwiyin, 50, was married to Kate Tāpwēwiniwok, Pē-nōsēwēskam's youngest widow. His death was entered as record #43 in the Asissipi Mission Death Register.

55. Hines, Asissipi Journal, July 1, 1884-January 10, 1885, CMS, Microfilm Reel #A112, entries for October 4 and 5.

56. Robert James was the twin who had been born in 1883 and survived.

57. Ahtahkakoop Band Treaty Paylist for 1884, NA, RG10, vol. 9417.

58. Hines, Asissipi Journal, July 1, 1884-January 10, 1885, CMS, Microfilm Reel #A112, entry for October 10.

59. Ibid., entries for October 24 and 26.

60. Peter Ballendine to Reed, November 8, 1884, NA, RG10, vol. 3582, file 949. Some minor changes in punctuation have been made.

61. Dewdney to superintendent general of Indian Affairs, November 25, 1884, CHC, *Sessional Papers*, 1885 (no. 3), p. 157.

62. Macdonald, Annual Report of Indian Affairs, dated January 1, 1886, CHC, *Sessional Papers*, 1886 (no. 4) , p. xi.

63. Dewdney, CHC, *Sessional Papers*, 1886 (no. 4), p. 140.

64. Reed to superintendent general of Indian Affairs, January 23, 1885, NA, RG10, vol. 3697, file 15,423.

65. Reed to Macdonald, January 23, 1885, NA, RG10, vol. 3697, file 15,423.

66. Peter Ballendine, to Dewdney, November 20, 1884, NA, RG10, vol. 3582, file 949.

67. Hines, *Red Indians*, 197.

68. Ballendine to Dewdney, November 20, 1884, NA, RG10, vol. 3701, file 17,169. Also see NWMP commissioner's report for 1885, *Settlers and Rebels*, p. 21.

69. Minutes of the Meeting of the Saskatchewan Finance Committee of the CMS held at Prince Albert on Monday, May 18, at 4:40 p.m., 1885, Prince Albert Historical Society Archives, 190b.

70. Crozier to Irvine, December 1, 1884, NA, RG18, vol. 1019, file 2422.

71. Hines, Asissipi Journal, July 1, 1884-January 10, 1885, CMS, Microfilm Reel #A112, entry for October 26. Also see Hines, Asissipi Journal, January 16-July 26, 1885, CMS, Microfilm Reel #A113, entry for February 15, 1885.

72. Ibid., entries for November 6 and 8. Also see Asissipi Mission Death Register, record #44.

73. Ibid., entry for November 9.

74. Hines, Asissipi Journal, April 1, 1879-February 28, 1880, CMS, Microfilm Reel #A104, undated September entry.

75. Hines, Asissipi Journal, July 1, 1884-January 10, 1885, CMS, Microfilm Reel #A112, entries for July 15, 26, and November 30.

76. Ibid., entry for November 30 and January 10.

77. Ibid., entry for January 10.

78. Ibid.

79. Copy of a letter from Dewdney to Hines, dated February 21, 1885, CMS, Microfilm Reel #113. Also see Hines to the Indian commissioner, in a letter dated March 12, 1885, on the same microfilm reel.

80. Hines, letter to Dewdney, March 12, 1885, CMS, Microfilm Reel #A113.

81. Dewdney to Lash, letter dated January 9, 1885, NA, RG10, vol. 3704, file 17,799. In this letter, Dewdney told Lash it had "been considered expedient to relieve Mr. Sub-Agent Macrae and transfer him to another office of duties." Also see Lash to superintendent general of Indian Affairs, October 31, 1885, CHC, *Sessional Papers*, 1886 (no. 4), p. 125.

82. Dewdney to superintendent general of Indian Affairs, letter dated January 8, 1885, NA, RG10, vol. 3704, file 17,799.

83. Dewdney to Lash, letter dated January 9, 1885, NA, RG10, vol. 3704, file 17,799.

84. Ibid.

Chapter Twenty-Six: The Uprising, 1885

1. Morris, *Treaties*, 355.

2. Hines, *Red Indians*, 199. Also see Hines to the CMS Committee, July 10, 1885, CMS, Microfilm Reel #A113.

3. Irvine, North-West Mounted Police Annual Report, 1885, *Settlers and Rebels*, 21, 22. Also see Bob Beal and Rod Macleod, *Prairie Fire: The 1885 North-West Rebellion* (1984; Toronto: McClelland & Stewart Inc., paperback edition, 1994), 137-38.

4. Charles Pelham Mulvaney, *The History of the North-West Rebellion of 1885* (Toronto: A.H. Hovey & Company, 1885), 37, 38. Also see confidential letter from Lawrence Clarke to Joseph Wrigley, Hudson's Bay Company trade commissioner, July 6, 1885, HBCA, PAM, B.332/b/1, fo. 103d. The volunteers arrived at 10 p.m. March 20.

5. Lawrence Clarke to Joseph Wrigley, in a confidential letter dated July 6, 1885, HBCA, PAM, B.332/b/1, fos. 96-121d.

6. Clarke to Wrigley, in a confidential letter dated July 6, 1885, HBCA, PAM, B.332/b/1. Also see Hines, letter to the CMS Committee, July 10, 1885, CMS, Microfilm Reel #A113.

7. Clarke to Wrigley, in a confidential letter dated July 6, 1885, HBCA, PAM, B.332/b/1. George Robertson confirmed that people in Petihkwahākēw's band were forced to join the rebels when he said that a man called Wolf and others "from the Muskeg Lake Indians" were taken to Duck Lake "not of their own accord." Robertson's statement can be found in Evidence Before the Rebellion 1886 Claims Commission at Prince Albert, HBCA, PAM, E.9/29. fo. 15.

8. Edward Ahenakew, *Voices of the Plains Cree*, 96.

9. The following account of Hines's trip to Prince Albert is taken from his book *Red Indians*, 199-201. Hines mistakenly recorded that he left for Fort Carlton after Ahtahkakoop returned from his meeting with Crozier and Clarke.

10. Hines, *Red Indians*, 200. Also see Asissipi Journal, January 16-July 26, 1885, CMS, Microfilm Reel #A113, entry for March 24.

11. Hines, Asissipi Journal, January 16-July 26, 1885, CMS, Microfilm Reel #A113, entry for March 24.

12. Hines, *Red Indians*, 200-01.

13. Clarke to Wrigley, July 6, 1885, HBCA, PAM, B.332/b/1, fo. 102.

14. According to the Montreal *Gazette*, May 26, 1885, this information came from the men who were taken prisoner at the start of the uprising. Also see Norman F. Black, *History of Saskatchewan and the North West Territories*, vol. 1 (Regina: Saskatchewan Historical Company, 1913), 267.

15. Hines, *Red Indians*, 198. Hines does not name the "gentleman" but the description fits Clarke and is consistent with other references. Clarke had left for Central Canada in February. Hines, *Red Indians*, 198, said the "gentleman" had taken the Métis' petition with him.

16. Black, in *History of Saskatchewan and the North West Territories*, 267, said that while Clarke's comment to the Métis "has not figured prominently in former English accounts of the rebellion the facts are common property to this day [1913] all through the Batoche, Duck Lake and Prince Albert country."

17. Clarke to Wrigley in a confidential letter dated July 6, 1885, Prince Albert Correspondence Book, 1884-89, HBCA, PAM, B.332/b/1, fo. 96. Also see Beal and Macleod, *Prairie Fire*, 137-38.

18. In North-West Mounted Police documentation, the number of men in Irvine's company varied from 90 to 92, excluding the commissioner.

19. Dewdney to Wrigley, March 18, 1885, GA, Dewdney Papers, 1671-1672, as cited in *Prairie Fire*, 139.

20. Hines, Asissipi Journal, January 16-July 26, 1885, CMS, Microfilm Reel #A113, entry for March 24.

21. The number of policemen and volunteers killed and wounded during the fighting at Duck Lake is taken from Appendix N, North-West Mounted Police Annual Report, 1885, *Settlers and Rebels*, 96-97.

22. Douglas W. Light, *Footprints in the Dust* (North Battleford: Turner-Warwick Publications Inc., 1987), 608. According to Mulvaney, *The North-West Rebellion*, 32, five Métis and the old Indian man died at Duck Lake.

23. The Duck Lake settlement is sometimes called the Stobbart settlement.

24. Black, *History of Saskatchewan and the North West Territories*, 282. Also see Beal and Macleod, *Prairie Fire*, 155.

25. Irvine, Report of the Commissioner of the North-West Mounted Police Force, 1885, *Setters and Rebels*, 25.

26. Hines, *Red Indians*, 199. Daniel Milligan confirmed the use of liquor, saying the Duck Lake fight did not have to happen but there was too much liquor. Milligan was 19 when he came west in 1885 to work on the sternwheelers *Marquis* and *North West* for the Hudson's Bay Company. See Prince Albert Historical Society Archives, file 14C.

27. John Peter Turner, *The North-West Mounted Police: 1873–1893*, vol. 2, (Ottawa: King's Printer, 1950), 106.

28. Clarke to Wrigley, July 6, 1885, Prince Albert Correspondence Book, 1884-89, HBCA, PAM, B.332/b/1, fo.112d.

29. Charles N. Garson, HBC Rebellion Claims, HBCA, PAM, B.332/b/1, fo. 196.

30. Irvine, North-West Mounted Police Annual Report, 1885, *Settlers and Rebels*, 40. Also see Clarke to Wrigley, July 6, 1885, and John G. Donkin, *Trooper and the Redskin in*

the Far Northwest: Recollections of Life in the North-West Mounted Police, Canada, 1884–1888 (London: Sampson Low, Marston, Searle and Rivington Limited, 1889; Facsimile edition published by Coles Publishing Company, Toronto, 1973), 128-29.

31. Edward Spencer, Prince Albert Historical Society, file 68. Spencer was working for Chaffee and helped remove goods from the post. Also see George Robertson, Evidence Before the Rebellion 1886 Claims Commission at Prince Albert, HBCA, PAM, E.9/29, fo. 13. Robertson worked as a labourer and was living about 400 yards from Fort Carlton with his family; they remained in their home following the evacuation of the post but did not take part in the uprising.

32. Hines, *Red Indians*, 202.

33. Ibid. Hines claims in his book that he told Chaffee's messenger to tell the chief that "we would have a public meeting at 6 a.m. to decide what had best be done." Then he and his wife went back to bed. Obviously Ahtahkakoop had decided much earlier what course of action would be taken. In his journal, Hines does not mention that he and his family left three hours after the others.

34. Ibid., 202-3. Also see Hines, Asissipi Journal, January 16-July 26, 1885, CMS, Microfilm Reel #A113, entry for May 27. There are discrepancies in Hines's journal and his book. For instance, in his journal, Hines said he loaded a tent onto the sleigh; according to his book, they forgot the tent.

35. Except when indicated otherwise, the following account is drawn mainly from Hines, *Red Indians,* and Hines's Asissipi Journal, January 16-July 26, 1885, CMS, Microfilm Reel #A113. The entries for April 6 to May 22 were included in Hines's entry for May 27.

36. Chaffee, report dated June 30, 1885, NA, RG10, vol. 3716, file 22,279.

37. Hines, *Red Indians*, 203.

38. Hines, Asissipi Journal, January 16-July 26, 1885, CMS, Microfilm Reel #A113, entry for May 27. Also see Hines, *Red Indians*, 204, and Chaffee, report dated June 30, 1885, NA, RG10, vol. 3716, file 22,279.

39. Barry L. Ahenakew, interview May 28, 1997. Hines referred to this place as Ne-pa-tu-kwa-moo-win, "to signify our arrival through the night in a sleepy condition."

40. Hines, *Red Indians*, 203.

41. Hines, Asissipi Journal, January 16-July 26, 1885, CMS, Microfilm Reel #A113, entry for May 27.

42. Ibid.

43. Farm instructor James Payne and settler Barney Tremont, both of whom were known for their dislike of Indian people, were killed on March 30.

44. For accounts of events relevant to the Uprising of 1885, see Blair Stonechild and Bill Waiser, *Loyal till Death: Indians and the North-West Rebellion* (Calgary: Fifth House Ltd., 1997). Also see Beal and Macleod, *Prairie Fire*; Douglas W. Light, *Footprints in the Dust*; Gerald Friesen, *The Canadian Prairies* (Toronto: University of Toronto Press, 1984): and John L. Tobias, "Canada's Subjugation of the Plains Cree, 1879-1885," *The Canadian Historical Review* 64, no. 4 (1983): 542-44.

45. Hines, Asissipi Journal, January 16-July 26, 1885, CMS, Microfilm Reel #A113, entry for May 27.

46. Paul Ahenakew, review meeting May 28, 1997.

47. Hines, Asissipi Journal, January 16-July 26, 1885, CMS, Microfilm Reel #A113, entry for May 31.

48. Ibid., entry for May 27. The sugar basin had belonged to Emma Hines's mother.

49. Ibid.

50. Minutes of the meeting of the Saskatchewan Finance Committee of the CMS held at (Goshen) Prince Albert on Monday May 18th at 4:30 p.m. (1885), CMS, Microfilm Reel #A113.

51. Hines, Asissipi Journal, January 16-July 26, 1885, CMS, Microfilm Reel #A113, entry for May 27.

52. Ibid.

53. Ibid.

54. Ibid., entries for May 27 and June 27. Also see Hines, *Red Indians*, 212.

55. Chaffee, report dated June 30, 1885, NA, RG10, vol. 3716, file 22,279.

56. Ibid. Also see Hines's *Red Indians*, 204, 212.

57. Hines, *Red Indians*, 212.

58. Hines, Asissipi Journal, August 1,1885-January 4, 1886, CMS, Microfilm Reel #A113, entry for October 24, 1885.

59. There are several versions of Antoine's activities during the uprising. On May 31, Hines recorded in his Asissipi Journal for January 16-July 26, 1885, that Antoine had acted as a scout and carried dispatches for the North-West Mounted Police at Battleford. He was then sent to Fort Pitt where he was captured by some "rebel" Indians. According to his obituary, December 2, 1943, Antoine was taken prisoner by the "Poundmaker Indians, and after his release took despatches from Wm. McKay, of the Hudson's Bay Company, Battleford, to the North West Mounted Police at Prince Albert." Light, *Footprints in the Dust*, 230, said that Antoine was a dispatch rider for the Hudson's Bay Company, and he was later asked by Middleton to deliver a message to Big Bear but he—like everyone else—was unable to find the chief.

60. This story appeared in the May 31 entry of Hines's Asissipi Journal, for January 16-July 26, 1885 (CMS, Microfilm Reel #A113). Kīskanakwās likely arrived within a day or so of that date since Hines makes no mention of her when he and the others arrived at the reserve on May 26. Her grandson, Edward Ahenakew, was born on June 10, more than a week later. The baby's parents were Baptiste Ahenakew and Ellen Ermineskin.

61. Much of this account was taken from W.J. McLean, "Reminiscences of the Tragic Events at Frog Lake and in [the] Fort Pitt District with some of the experiences of the writer and his family during the North West Rebellion of 1885," HBCA, PAM, Copy No. 80. McLean was the Hudson's Bay Company officer in charge of Fort Pitt when the warriors in Big Bear's camp forced the evacuation of the post. He and his family, along with the other civilians at the post, chose to go to Big Bear's camp rather than leave on the scow with the police. McLean and his family remained with the Cree until June 18 when they were released. Also see Stonechild and Waiser, *Loyal till Death*, 182-91; and Beal and Macleod, *Prairie Fire*, 283-90.

62. Asissipi Mission Baptism Register, records #219 and #218.

63. Hines, Asissipi Journal, January 16-July 26, 1885, CMS, Microfilm Reel #A113, entry for June 28.

64. Prince Albert Journal, 1881-86, HBCA, PAM, B.332/a/1, fo. 75d (entries for June 17, 18, 19, 27).

65. Hines, Asissipi Journal, January 16-July 26, 1885, CMS, Microfilm Reel #A113, entry for June 29.

66. Sergeant Smart to Superintendent J. H. McIllree, September 1, 1885, NA, RG18, vol. 1022, file 3094.

67. See Margaret R. Stobie, *The Other Side of Rebellion: The Remarkable Story of Charles Bremner and his Furs* (Edmonton: NeWest Publishers Ltd., 1986), 45-47, 56.

68. Gerald Friesen, *The Canadian Prairies*, 153. In his analysis (pp. 542-43), Friesen refers to Tobias, "Canada's Subjugation of the Plains Cree, 1879-1885."

69. Rudy Wiebe and Bob Beal, *War in the West: Voices of the 1885 Rebellion* (Toronto: McClelland and Stewart Limited, 1985), 109-10 and elsewhere in the book. Also see Stobie, *The Other Side of Rebellion*.

70. Angus McKay, untitled manuscript, SAB, CP948, file 18. Middleton was later charged with stealing furs worth at least $5,364.50 from Charles Bremner at Bresaylor; Bremner was finally reimbursed by the government during the 1899-1900 fiscal year after a House of Commons investigation found Middleton's actions to be illegal. See Stobie, *The Other Side of Rebellion*, 178-79; and Beal and Macleod, *Prairie Fire*, 340.

71. Hines, Asissipi Journal, May 6, 1887-January 22, 1888, CMS, Microfilm Reel #A115, entry for June 20. The index to the CMS collection incorrectly indicates that this journal was written by G.S. Winter.

72. Newspaper clipping containing a letter from Thomas Bland Strange, CMS, Microfilm Reel #A113. Also see Payton, *Diocese of Saskatchewan*, 39.

73. Hines, *Red Indians*, 204, 208. Thomas Hourie participated in the capture of Riel, not Big Bear as stated in Hines's book.

74. Dewdney to superintendent general of Indian Affairs, December 17, 1885, CHC, *Sessional Papers*, 1886 (no. 4), p. 140.

75. Friesen, *Canadian Prairies*, 153. Also see Tobias, "Canada's Subjugation of the Plains Cree."

76. John L. Tobias, "A Brief History of the Ahtahkakoop Band, 1870-1920," 22 (prepared for the Federation of Saskatchewan Indians, 1975). Also see Stonechild and Waiser, *Loyal till Death*.

77. See Friesen, *Canadian Prairies*, 231.

78. According to the paylist for 1885, three men in Ahtahkakoop's band were accused of being rebels. Ahtahkakoop's son-in-law Kā-tāh-twēhototawāt was reputed to have killed oxen, while Kīnikwānāsiw (#85) and Wāpāsōs, #103, were said to have been with the rebels and killed oxen. Their families consisted of 23 people, none of whom received annuity payments in 1885.

79. Dewdney, Annual Report of Indian Affairs, dated January 1, 1886, CHC, *Sessional Papers*, 1886 (no. 4), p. xxxix. Also see Reed to superintendent general, July 22, 1885, NA, RG10, vol. 3716, file 22,279; and Hines, *Red Indians*, 213.

80. Dewdney, January 1, 1886, CHC, *Sessional Papers*, 1886 (no. 4), p. xxxviii.

Chapter Twenty-Seven: Uprising Aftermath, 1885-1886

1. Statistics on agriculture and houses, etc. CHC, *Sessional Papers*, 1886 (no. 4), pp. 202-3, 210-11.

2. Chaffee to Lash, June 30, 1885, NA, RG10, vol. 3716, file 22,279. Also see Hines, Asissipi Journal, January 16, 1885, CMS, Microfilm Reel #A113, entries for May 29, June 27 and 28.

3. Statistics on agriculture and houses, CHC (no. 4), pp. 202-3 and 210-11.

4. Asissipi Journal, January 16-July 26, 1885, CMS, Microfilm Reel #A113, entry for July 5. Also see Asissipi Mission Marriage Register, record #37. Cameron was born in Perth, Canada. Margaret was two years younger than Joseph and one year younger than Alexander, who was known as Alexan.

5. Prince Albert Journal, 1881-86, HBCA, PAM, B. 332/a/1, fo. 76d. The journal referred to him as "young Attakakoop." Hines indicated on July 21 that Kā-miyo-ahcahkwēw, the chief's eldest son, had returned from Green Lake.

6. Asissipi Journal, January 16-July 26, 1885, CMS, Microfilm Reel #A113, entry for July 12.

7. See Stonechild and Waiser, *Loyal till Death*, 192-93 and Appendix 5, pp. 261-63. Also see Beal and Macleod, *Prairie Fire*, 308-9.

8. Asissipi Journal, August 1, 1885-January 4, 1886, CMS, Microfilm Reel #A113, entry for August 3

9. Reed to Dewdney, August 16, 1885, Dewdney Papers, North-West Rebellion, NA, MG.27, pp. 2076-2087, as cited in "Study of Passes for Indians to Leave their Reserves," B. Bennett, Treaties and Historical Research Centre, Department of Indian and Northern Affairs, October, 1974, p. 3.

10. Reed to Dewdney, July 20, 1885, NA, RG10, vol. 3584, file 1130. For additional information on the government's repression, see Stonechild and Waiser, *Loyal till Death*, 227-28, 230-337; and Tobias, "Canada's Subjugation of the Plains Cree, 1879-1885." A copy of Reed's memorandum to Dewdney can be found in *Loyal till Death*, 250-53.

11. Asissipi Journal, August 1, 1885-January 4, 1886, CMS, Microfilm Reel #A113, entry for August 26.

12. Janet Ermineskin was married to Ahtahkakoop's son Kā-miyo-astotin (Basil), Ellen was married to Baptiste Ahenakew, and Catherine was married to Louis Ahenakew.

13. Asissipi Journal, August 1, 1885-January 4, 1886, CMS, Microfilm Reel #A113, entry for August 26. Also see Asissipi Journal, January 16-May 25, 1886, on the same microfilm reel, entry for April 11; in this entry, Hines talks about a "heathen" from Battleford who took part in the rebellion and was among those who fired on Otter at Cut Knife Creek. Hines said he talked to the man several times during the winter, and he wanted to be baptized. He does not name the man.

14. Ibid.

15. Asissipi Journal, January 16-July 26, 1885, CMS, Microfilm Reel #A113, entry for July 21. Hines implies that Kā-miyo-ahcahkwēw's sole reason for going to Green Lake was to carry the message to Okīnomotayēw. He makes no mention of his being sent by the Hudson's Bay Company.

16. Hines, *Red Indians*, 209.

17. Asissipi Journal, August 1, 1885-January 4, 1886, CMS, Microfilm Reel #A113, entry for August 31. Also see Hines, *Red Indians*, 209.

18. Ibid., entry for September 7.

19. Stonechild and Waiser, in *Loyal till Death*, provide a list of Indian convictions in appendix 5, pp. 261-263. This list was taken from CHC, *Sessional Papers*, 1886 (no. 8), appendix O.

20. See Appendix 5, pp. 261-63 in Stonechild and Waiser, *Loyal till Death*.

21. Stonechild and Waiser, *Loyal till Death*, 202.

22. Reed to Dewdney, September 6, 1885, Glenbow Archives, Dewdney Papers, pp. 1240-1249, as cited in *Prairie Fire*, 331.

23. *Saskatchewan Herald*, August 10, 1885.

24. Fr. André to Archbishop Taché, August 20, 1885, SAB, Taché Papers, as cited in Beal and Macleod, *Prairie Fire*.

25. Asissipi Journal, August 1, 1885-January 4, 1886, CMS, Microfilm Reel #A113, entry for September 13.

26. Ibid., entries for September 19.

27. Ibid., entry for October 11.

28. Ahtahkakoop Band Paylist, 1885. There were still only two headmen, Sasakamoose and Kā-miyo-ahcahkwēw. The total number paid consisted of 31 men, 44 women, 51 boys, 54 girls, and two women listed as relatives.

29. Kā-tāh-twēhototawāt never took treaty payments at the Ahtahkakoop Reserve again. He—and presumably Emma and their children—was at File Hills in 1888 and by 1890 he was reported to be living at Turtle Mountain in what is now the Province of Manitoba. In 1898 Kā-tāh-twēhototawāt's name was removed from the Ahtahkakoop Band paylist. Kīnikwānāsiw, who had transferred from the Sturgeon Lake Band to Ahtahkakoop's band in 1880, transferred to Okīnomotayēw's band in 1889; he returned in 1890. Wāpāsōs, who was given ticket #70 in Ahtahkakoop's band in 1877 and who had his number changed to #103 without explanation in 1884, transferred to Mistawasis's band in 1888.

30. Jimmy Fraser's mother was listed as #53 on the Mistawasis Band Paylist. The young man had not been paid in 1884. The paylist spells Isabella Stranger's name as Isabel; her marriage certificate indicates her name was Isabella.

31. See the Asissipi Mission Baptism and Death registers and the Ahtahkakoop Band Treaty Paylist for 1885. The paylist indicates that the child born to Joseph Ahtahkakoop was a girl. Hines's baptism record, which is presumed to be correct, indicates that the baby was a boy named Joseph after his father. One of the women who died was Kā-kīsikāwapiw's wife Matilda.

32. Vankoughnet to Dewdney, October 28, 1885, NA, RG10, vol. 3584, file 1130 Part 1B. Also see Macdonald, Annual Report of the Department of Indian Affairs, January 1, 1887, CHC, 1887 (no. 6), p. ix.

33. Memorandum for the Honourable the Indian Commissioner, dated July 20, 1885, prepared by Haytor Reed, NA, RG10, vol. 3584, file 1130.

34. Vankoughnet to Dewdney, October 28, 1885, NA, RG10, vol. 3584, file 1130, Part 1B. Also see Dewdney in a report dated December 17, 1885, CHC (no. 4, 1886), p. 141. The rationale for this policy of work for rations was elaborated on page 145 of this report, with Dewdney explaining that the intent was "to extract as much work as possible for the food given them; and if our agents issued rations indiscriminately, the object desired, namely, to train them to habits of industry, and eventually, make them self-supporting, could not be gained. On the other hand, when an able bodied Indian knows that he will not be fed in wanton idleness, he usually exerts himself in the direction of our wishes, and some return is made for the outlay."

35. Vankoughnet to Dewdney, October 28, 1885, NA, RG10, vol. 3584, file 1130, Part 1B. Vankoughnet states that the superintendent general of Indian Affairs (Prime Minister John A. Macdonald) concurred with the policy outlined in the letter

36. Memorandum of rewards to Indians especially distinguished for loyalty during the late rebellion, GA, M1951.

37. Grains and Roots Sown and Harvested, year ending December 31, 1885, CHC, *Sessional Papers*, 1886 (no. 4), pp. 202-3 and 210-11.

38. Hudson's Bay Company Commissioner Joseph Wrigley to William Armit, company secretary in London, December 21, 1885, HBCA, PAM, D. 13/7, fo. 313.

39. Prince Albert Journal, 1881-86, HBCA, PAM, B.332/a/1, fos. 82d, 83, and 85.

40. Asissipi Journal, August 1, 1885-January 4, 1886, CMS, Microfilm Reel #A113, entries for November 23, December 23, 25, and January 4. Also see Asissipi Mission Death Register, record #47.

41. Asissipi Journal, August 1, 1885-January 4, 1886, CMS, Microfilm Reel #A113, entry for November 9.

42. Asissipi Journal, January 16-May 25, 1886, CMS, Microfilm Reel #A113, entry for February 6, 1886.

43. Wadsworth, CHC, *Sessional Papers*, 1887 (no. 6), Part I, p. 173; and Lash, October 31, 1885, CHC, 1886 (no. 4), p. 125.

44. Asissipi Journal, August 1, 1885-January 4, 1886, CMS, Microfilm Reel #A113, entry for December 18. Okīnomotayēw took the name John, his son was named Joseph and his daughter Agnes when they were baptized on December 15, 1885. Otasewehas was given the name Jacob; his daughter chose Emma, and the grandson became Peter. (See Asissipi Mission Baptism Register, records #225-#230.) The Asissipi Mission Marriage Register, records #45, #47 and #48 indicate that Okīnomotayēw's son and daughter were married on February 10, 1887, the same day that Okīnomotayēw and his wife Emma married.

45. Bishop McLean, in "A report of a journey to Cumberland House, etc. in 1885," as contained in Payton, *Diocese of Saskatchewan*, 167. The report was originally published by the CMS *Intelligencer* in January, 1886. Also see CHC, 1887 (no. 6), Part 2, p. 170.

46. Asissipi Journal, August 1, 1885-January 4, 1886, CMS, Microfilm Reel #A113, entry for January 4, 1886.

47. Pierre's death certificate indicates that he died on January 8, not January 6. (See Asissipi Mission Death Register, record #48. According to this record, he was buried January 9, 1886. These dates are probably incorrect since some of the information was

contained in a postscript dated January 8 at the end of the Asissipi Journal, August 1, 1885-January 4, 1886.)

48. Asissipi Journal, August 1, 1885-January 4, 1886, CMS, Microfilm Reel #A113, post-script dated January 8.

49. Asissipi Journal, January 16-May 25, 1886, CMS, Microfilm Reel #A113, entry for May 25.

50. Vankoughnet to Dewdney, October 28, 1885, NA, RG10, vol. 3584, file 1130, Part 1B.

51. Reed to Macdonald, July 22, 1885, NA, RG10, vol. 3716, file 22,279. It should be noted that several reports indicated that some families in this band were forced to join the Métis on the South Branch during the early days of hostilities.

52. Chaffee's monthly report to Indian agent Lash, dated June 30, 1885, NA, RG10, vol. 3716, file 22,279.

53. Prince Albert Journal, 1881-1886, HBCA, PAM, B.332/a/1, entries for November 25 and December 2, 1885, fos. 84.

54. Charles A. Boulton, *I Fought Riel: A Military Memoir*, ed. Heather Robertson (Toronto: James Lorimer & Company, 1985), 224. Also see P.G. Laurie, *Saskatchewan Herald*, November 27, 1885.

55. Regina *Leader* supplement, December 3, 1885, as cited in Beal and Macleod, *Prairie Fire*, 338.

56. Wrigley to Armit, January 26, 1886, HBCA, PAM, D.12/7.

57. Dewdney, February 16, 1886, NA, RG10, vol. 1143, as cited in B. Bennett, Study of Passes for Indians to Leave Their Reserves, Treaties and Historical Research Centre, October 1974. The large force of police and soldiers was not sent.

58. George Davison to Wrigley, January 11, 1886, Prince Albert Correspondence Book, 1884-1886, HBCA, PAM, B.332/b/1.

59. Reed to superintendent general of Indian Affairs, June 2, 1886, NA, RG10, vol. 3746, file 29589.

60. Inspector A. Ross Cuthbert, North-West Mounted Police, to Superintendent A. Bowen Perry, commanding officer in Prince Albert, January 20, 1886, NA, RG18, vol. 1038, file 67-68. For One Arrow's death, see Stonechild and Waiser, *Loyal till Death*, 235.

61. Vankoughnet to superintendent general of Indian Affairs, June 15, 1886, NA, RG10, vol. 3746, file 29,589.

62. Asissipi Journal, January 16-May 25, 1886, CMS, Microfilm Reel #A113, entry for February 26, 1886.

Chapter Twenty-Eight: Ahtahkakoop Goes to Ottawa, 1886-1887

1. Return showing Crops sown and harvested by Individual Indians on Prince Albert Agency, 1886, Sandy Lake [Ahtahkakoop] Reserve [No. 104], CHC, *Sessional Papers*, 1887 (no. 6), Part I, p. 278. The Ahtahkakoop Reserve was the only reserve in the Carlton Agency for which this information was given.

2. Hines, Asissipi Journal, January 16-May 25, 1886, CMS, Microfilm Reel #A113, entry for March 26. Also see Hines to Fenn, April 28, 1886, and McLean to the CMS

Committee, June 2, 1886, CMS, Microfilm Reel #113. Adams's appointment as acting Indian agent had been effective in February, 1886. He toured the agency with Rae for a month before assuming full responsibility on April 30.

3. Return showing Crops sown and harvested by Individual Indians on Prince Albert Agency, 1886, Sandy Lake Reserve [No. 104], CHC, *Sessional Papers*, 1887 (no. 6), Part I, p. 278.

4. Hines, Asissipi Journal, January 16-May 25, 1886, CMS, Microfilm Reel #A113, entry for May 2. Also see Hines's report on crops sown on the Ahtahkakoop Reserve, 1886, CHC, *Sessional Papers*, 1887 (no. 6), Part I, p. 278.

5. Charles Adams, acting Indian agent, in a report dated May 21, 1886, NA, RG10, vol. 3752, file 30,407. Also see Adams to superintendent general of Indian Affairs, August 30, 1886, CHC, *Sessional Papers*, 1887 (no. 6), p. 125.

6. Hines to Dewdney, June 5, 1886, CMS, Microfilm Reel #A114.

7. Hines, in his month-end report for June, 1886, NA, RG10, vol. 3758, file 31,668. Also see the Asissipi Journal, June 2-November 15, 1886, CMS, Microfilm Reel #A114, entries for June 13 and 20, and July 5, 6, 16, and 18.

8. Hines, Asissipi Journal, June 2-November 15, 1886, CMS, Microfilm Reel #A114, entry for July 21.

9. Hines, in his farm instructor's report for the month of June, 1886, submitted to acting Indian agent [Charles Adams], NA, RG10, vol. 3758, file 31,668.

10. Rae, in a report dated August 5, 1887, CHC, *Sessional Papers*, 1888 (no. 15), Part I, pp. 90-91. Also see Wadsworth's report dated December 1, 1886, CHC, *Sessional Papers*, 1887 (no. 6), Part I, p. 173. Rae had replaced Adams on a temporary basis late in 1886.

11. Hines, in his month-end report for June, 1886, NA, RG10, vol. 3758, file 31,668. Also see the Farming Agencies and Indian Reservations reports, CHC, *Sessional Papers*, 1886 (no. 4), pp. 210-11, and 1887 (no. 6), pp. 246-47.

12. Hines, Asissipi Journal, June 2-November 15, 1886, CMS, Microfilm Reel #A114, entry for July 17.

13. Hines, Asissipi Journal, January 16-May 25, 1886, CMS, Microfilm Reel #A113, entry for May 18, and Asissipi Journal, August 1, 1885-January 4, 1886, CMS, Microfilm Reel #A113, entry for October 3, 1885. There is a discrepancy in Hines's records regarding the child's name. On his birth record the child's name is given as Angus; on the death record he is named Josiah. (See record #222 in the Asissipi Mission Baptism Register, and record #50 in the death register.)

14. Hines, Asissipi Journal, June 2-November 15, 1886, CMS, Microfilm Reel #A114, entries for June 10, 15, and 17.

15. Asissipi Mission Death Register, record #52.

16. Ibid., record #51.

17. Hines, Asissipi Journal, June 2-November 15, 1886, CMS, Microfilm Reel #A114, entry for July 5.

18. See August and September entries in the Asissipi Journal, June 2-November 15, 1886, CMS, Microfilm Reel #A114. Also see Adams, May 21, 1886, NA, RG10, vol. 3752, file 30,407.

19. Report of the Commissioner of the North-West Mounted Police, 1886, CHC, *Sessional Papers*, 1887 (no. 7), pp. 91 and 92.

20. Adams, in a report dated August 30, 1886, CHC, *Sessional Papers*, 1887 (no. 6), Part I, p. 125.

21. Hines, Asissipi Journal, June 2-November 15, 1886, CMS, Microfilm Reel #A114, entries for June 6 and 13 and July 5. Also see entries for April, Asissipi Journal, January 16-May 25, 1886.

22. Hines, Asissipi Journal, January 16-May 25, 1886, CMS, Microfilm Reel #A113, entry for May 9.

23. Hines, Asissipi Journal, June 2-November 15, 1886, CMS, Microfilm Reel #114, entries for August 8 and 20.

24. Ibid., entries for June 22 and 24.

25. Hines, *Red Indians*, 73-74. The man referred to was with Otayapīhkēw at Whitefish Lake in 1874, and he guided Hines to Pelican Lake that fall.

26. Hines, Asissipi Journal, November 18, 1886-May 5, 1887, CMS, Microfilm Reel #A114, entry for March 5.

27. Hines to McLean, in a letter dated June 29, 1886, CMS, Microfilm Reel A114.

28. Dewdney to Macdonald, May 17, 1886, NA, RG10, vol. 3746, file 29584 Also see Wadsworth, April 30, 1886, NA, RG10, vol. 3746, file 29690-1; and Thos. White, superintendent general, Annual Report for Indian Affairs, CHC, *Sessional Papers*, 1888 (no. 15), p. li.

29. McLean to the CMS Committee in London, March 17, 1886, CMS, Microfilm Reel #A113.

30. For example, see Hines to McLean, June 29, 1885, CMS, Microfilm Reel A114.

31. Payton, *Diocese of Saskatchewan*, 38-39.

32. Approximate Return of Grain and Roots Sown and Harvested, CHC, *Sessional Papers*, 1887 (no. 6), pp. 236-37, 246-47, also see p. 278.

33. Wadsworth, in a report dated December 1, 1886, CHC, *Sessional Papers*, 1887 (no. 6), Part I, p. 173. Also see report on Approximate Return of Grain and Roots Sown and Harvested, CHC, *Sessional Papers*, 1887 (no. 6), pp. 246-47 and 236-37. Some figures in these reports differ.

34. Wadsworth, December 1, 1886, CHC, *Sessional Papers*, 1887 (no. 6), Part I, p. 172. Also see CHC, *Sessional Papers*, 1887 (no. 6), p. xlvii.

35. Wadsworth, in a report dated December 1, 1886, CHC, *Sessional Papers*, 1887 (no. 6), Part I, p. 173.

36. Macdonald, superintendent general of Indian Affairs, in his annual report, CHC, *Sessional Papers*, 1887 (no. 6), p. xlvii.

37. Hines, Asissipi Mission Death Register, record #55. Hines does not include the second girl in his death register.

38. Peekeekoot's wife Isabella was the daughter of Wāskitoy, one of the original headmen. Peekeekoot was John Peter Masuskapoe's son and Ahtahkakoop's great nephew. Nātakām's wife Sara was Masuskapoe's daughter. Nātakām, who was also known as Mac Knife, was Kihci-mōhkomān's son. The old blind woman was Iskwēsis's mother.

39. See Asissipi Mission Death Register, records #47 and #49–#55.

40. Mary Ahtahkakoop had been married for a number of years to Edward Genereux, a non-Indian who worked for the Hudson's Bay Company. Mrs. Mary Pruden had been on the Ahtahkakoop treaty band list since 1879; her husband was likely related to John Peter Pruden, the officer who had been in charge of Fort Carlton almost continuously from 1810 to 1837. Jimmy Fraser was paid with his mother at the Mistawasis Reserve in 1883; he joined the Ahtahkakoop Band in 1885.

41. Wadsworth, November 16, 1886, NA, RG10, vol. 3773, file 35764. Also see Dewdney, December 2, 1886, in the same file.

42. Hines, Asissipi Journal, January 16-May 25, 1886, CMS, Microfilm Reel #A113, entry for January 29, 1886.

43. Hines to Fenn, Church Missionary Society, London, March 22, 1886, CMS, Microfilm Reel #A113.

44. Hines to Fenn, December 14, 1886, CMS, Microfilm Reel #114.

45. Hines to Fenn, March 28, 1887, CMS, Microfilm Reel A114.

46. Bishop McLean died on November 7, 1886. (See Payton, p. 38.)

47. Hines, Asissipi Journal, June 2-November 15, 1886, CMS, Microfilm Reel #A114, entry for November 15. Also see Minutes of the Finance Committee, April 27, 1887, CMS, Microfilm Reel #A114 and McLean, July 12, 1886.

48. See Payton, *Diocese of Saskatchewan*, 35, 37, 41, 43, and Minutes of the Finance Committee, April 27, 1887, CMS, Microfilm Reel #A114.

49. Hines, Asissipi Journal, June 2-November 15, 1886, CMS, Microfilm Reel #A114, in a postscript dated November 20,1886, at the end of the journal. According to the Prince Albert *Times and Saskatchewan Review*, October 8, 1886, Ahtahkakoop and Mistawasis left Prince Albert on October 4.

50. Hines, postscript dated November 20, 1886, added to the Asissipi Journal for June 2-November 15, 1886, CMS, Microfilm Reel #A114.

51. The Toronto *Globe*, October 19, 1886. The story was told by Lieutenant-Colonel MacDonald, the Indian agent from the Qu'Appelle Agency who had accompanied the chiefs to Ottawa.

52. Hugh A. Dempsey, *Red Crow, Warrior Chief* (Saskatoon: Western Producer Prairie Books, 1980), 164. Other chiefs to visit eastern Canada that summer included Stoney chief Jonas Goodstoney and Samson and Pakān from the Edmonton area. They were accompanied by Methodist minister John McDougall.

53. Ottawa *Daily Free Press*, October 19, 1886. Also see Dempsey, *Red Crow*, 165-67; and Macdonald, January 1, 1887, CHC, *Sessional Papers*, 1887 (no. 6), p. x.

54. The Toronto *Globe*, as cited in Dempsey, *Red Crow*, 167. O'Soup was a councillor, not a chief, so his coat would have been blue.

55. Brantford *Daily Expositor*, October 18, 1886.

56. Brantford *Daily Courier*, October 14, 1886. Also see the Toronto *Globe*, October 14, 1886.

57. Brantford *Daily Courier*, October 14, 1886.

58. The Toronto *Globe*, October 14, 1886. Also see the issue for October 13, 1886.

59. The Toronto *Globe*, October 14, 1886.

60. Brantford *Daily Courier*, October 15, 1886. Also see the Toronto *Globe*, October 14, 1886; and Dempsey, *Red Crow*, 169.

61. Brantford *Daily Courier*, October 15, 1886. The reporter from the *Globe* (October 14, 1886) agreed, saying it was "the speech of the evening." Also see Dempsey, *Red Crow*, 169.

62. Dempsey, *Red Crow*, 169. The Toronto *Globe*, October 15, 1886, called this complex the "Mohawk Station of the New England Company."

63. The Toronto *Globe*, October 15, 1886.

64. Dempsey, *Red Crow*, 169.

65. The Toronto *Globe*, October 15, 1886. The church was St. Paul's, Her Majesty's Chapel of the Mohawks; it was said to be the first Protestant Church in Ontario. According to the *Globe*, the church was known as "Her Majesty's Royal Chapel of the Mohawk Nation."

66. The Toronto *Globe*, October 15, 1886. Also see Brantford *Daily Courier*, October, 15, 1886.

67. Brantford *Daily Courier*, October 15, 1886. See the October 14 issue for the program.

68. Oahweken is the spelling used in the Brantford paper; the *Globe* used Ohaweken.

69. The Toronto *Globe*, October 19, 1886.

70. The following account of the council, unless otherwise specified, is taken from the Toronto *Globe*, October 19, 1886.

71. Toronto *Globe*, October 19, 1886, and the Brantford *Daily Courier*, October, 16, 1886.

72. The Toronto *Globe*, October 19, 1886. Also see the Brantford *Daily Courier*, October 16, 1886. An identical medal made from silver was given to interpreter L'Heureux to present to Crowfoot.

73. Brantford *Daily Expositor*, October 18, 1886.

74. Ibid.

75. Jean L'Heureux, undated matter accompanying expense account, Indian Affairs Archives, no. 32864, as cited by Dempsey in *Red Crow*, 167.

76. The Brantford *Weekly Expositor*, October 22, 1886.

77. See the Brantford *Daily Courier*, October 25, 1886; and the Toronto *Globe*, October 23, 1886.

78. The Toronto *Globe*, October 23, 1886.

79. Hines, Asissipi Journal, June 2-November 15, 1886, CMS, Microfilm Reel #A114, in a postscript dated November 20,1886. Hines said that Ahtahkakoop had been at the home of either Macdonald or the Marquis of Lansdowne, governor general of Canada, but Ahtahkakoop could not remember the name of the man. The chiefs' visit with Macdonald is well documented in other sources, whereas no mention was found of a visit with the governor general. Additionally, Edward Ahenakew wrote much later that he was told by Henry McKay, son of the late Hudson's Bay Company chief factor William McKay, that Ahtahkakoop gave the Cree name to Macdonald's daughter. (See "The Story of the Ahenakews," 17.) Henry was George McKay's brother.

80. Ottawa *Free Press*, October 23, 1886.

81. Hines, Asissipi Journal, June 2-November 15, 1886, CMS, Microfilm Reel #A114, in a postscript dated November 20, 1886.

82. Ibid.

83. It had been reported in the Toronto *Globe* on October 23 that "one of the results of the trip will be the establishment of a school on Kah-kee-wis-ta-haw's reserve as soon as he returns. He has always been opposed to schools, but told Col. Macdonald [*sic*] and others that after what he had seen he should not only not oppose them in future, but would see that one was established at once, and that the young people on his reserve attend it."

84. The interview in its entirety can be found in the Montreal *Gazette*, October 25, 1886.

85. Hines recorded in the postscript dated November 20 added to his Asissipi Journal, June 2-November 15, 1886, that Ahtahkakoop arrived home "last week."

86. Hines, Asissipi Journal, June 2-November 15, 1886, postscript dated November 20, 1886.

87. Edward Ahenakew said he was told this story by Henry McKay. It appears in "The Story of the Ahenakews," 15.

88. Prince Albert Report for 1887, HBCA, PAM, B.332/e/1. Also see various entries in Hines's journals.

89. See Hines, Asissipi Journal, November 18, 1886-May 5, 1887, CMS, Microfilm Reel #A114, entry for February 20, and Prince Albert Report for 1887, HBCA, PAM, B.332/e/1, p. 1.

90. Prince Albert Report for 1887, HBCA, PAM, B.332/e/1, pp. 2-3. Some changes in punctuation and spelling have been made.

91. Hines, Asissipi Journal, June 2-November 1886 journal, CMS, Microfilm #114, entry for November 15.

92. Wadsworth, report, dated December 31, 1886, CHC, *Sessional Papers*, 1887 (no. 6), Part I, p. 173. Two students were 15 years of age and four were 13 years old. Of the other children, one was 12 years old, four were 11, two were 10, two were nine, three were eight, and three were six years of age.

93. Hines, Asissipi Journal, November 18, 1886-May 5, 1887, CMS, Microfilm Reel #A114, entry for February 20.

94. Hines, Asissipi Journal, June 2-November 15, 1886, CMS, Microfilm Reel #A114, entry for November 15. Also see Asissipi Journal, November 18, 1886-May 5, 1887, CMS, Microfilm Reel #A114, entry for December 17.

95. Hines, Asissipi Journal, November 18, 1886-May 5, 1887, CMS, Microfilm Reel #A114, entry for February 2.

96. Hines, Asissipi Journal, June 2-November 15, 1886, CMS, Microfilm Reel #114, entry for November 15.

97. Thomas Clarke, principal of the Battleford Industrial School, to superintendent general of Indian Affairs, July 30, 1886, CHC, *Sessional Papers*, 1887 (no. 6), Part I, p. 140. Also see J.A. Macrae, inspector of Protestant schools, to superintendent general of Indian Affairs, October 23, 1888, CHC, *Sessional Papers*, 1889 (no. 16), pp. 145-46.

John Ahenakew was not one of the students picked up, for he had completed Standard IV and was helping his family farm on the reserve.

98. Mackay to Fenn, December 13, 1886, CMS, Microfilm Reel #A114.

99. Hines, Asissipi Journal, November 18, 1886-May 5, 1887, CMS, Microfilm Reel #A114, entries for January 1 and 2.

100. In his journal Hines said the illness was either scarlet fever or measles; in his book, he said the people were stricken with a virulent kind of measles.

101. Hines, Asissipi Journal, November 18, 1886-May 5, 1887, CMS, Microfilm Reel #A114, entry for January 10. Also see Hines, *Red Indians*, 216.

102. Hines, *Red Indians*, p. 216. Also see Asissipi Journal, November 18, 1886-May 5, 1887, CMS, Microfilm Reel #A114, entry for February 3, 1887.

103. See Asissipi Journal, November 18, 1886-May 5, 1887, CMS, Microfilm Reel #A114, entries for January 15, 30, and February 3.

104. Hines, *Red Indians*, 216.

105. See Asissipi Journal, November 18, 1886-May 5, 1887, CMS, Microfilm Reel #A114, entry for February 12. Also see Asissipi Mission Marriage Register, entries #45-#47 and Asissipi Mission Baptism Register, record #244. Okīnomotayēw's daughter married Sēsēweham's son from Whitefish Lake.

106. Hines, Asissipi Journal, November 18, 1886-May 5, 1887, CMS, Microfilm Reel #A114, entries for January 13, February 3, 15, and April 25. Also see Asissipi Mission Death Register, records #56–#59. Harriet Numowela was likely Sōniyāw-ayāwēw's mother.

107. Dewdney, CHC, *Sessional Papers*, 1887 (no. 6), Part I, p. 110. Also see Thomas White, superintendent general of Indian Affairs, December 31, 1887, in his annual report, CHC, *Sessional Papers*, 1888 (no. 15), p. lxxxiv.

108. Petition to the Indian commissioner from Mistawasis, Ahtahkakoop, Twatt (Ayahtaskamikinam), and John Smith dated January 15, 1887, NA, RG10, vol. 3774, file 36,846. Owen Hughes, Lawrence Clarke, and Thomas McKay witnessed the placement of the chiefs' marks beside their names.

109. Reed to Macdonald, January 29, 1887, NA, RG10, vol. 3774, file 36,846. Also see letter from the surgeon at the Stony Mountain Penitentiary January 27, 1887; Vankoughnet to Macdonald, February 5, 1887; and letter from the Stony Mountain Penitentiary to Vankoughnet, February 21, 1887, on the same file.

Chapter Twenty-Nine: Three Deaths for Every Birth, 1887-1888

1. Rae to superintendent general of Indian Affairs, August 5, 1887, CHC, *Sessional Papers*, 1888 (no. 15), part 1, pp. 90-91.

2. Ibid. Also see Wadsworth, report dated December 1, 1887, NA, RG10, vol. 3809, file 53,828-1.

3. Hines, *Red Indians*, 185. Also see report dated December 1, 1887, NA, vol. 3809, file 53,828-1.

4. Rae to superintendent general of Indian Affairs, August 5, 1887, CHC, *Sessional Papers*, 1888 (no. 15), Part 1, p. 90.

5. Wadsworth's report dated December 1, 1887, NA, RG10, vol. 3809, file 53828-1.

6. Hines, *Red Indians*, 186.

7. Ibid., 185.

8. One hundred and sixteen acres of wheat were planted, compared to 136 the previous year; barley was down from 60 to 40 acres. Other crops increased slightly. The figures that follow indicate the amount of land planted in the various crops in 1887, with amounts for 1886 shown in brackets: potatoes, 18 acres (14); turnips, 11 acres (5); and carrots, 3 (1). Four acres were planted to oats. See Approximate Return of Grain and Roots Sowed and Harvested, CHC, *Sessional Papers*, 1888 (no. 15), Part 1, pp. 202-03 and pp. 212-13, and similar records for the previous year.

9. Hines, Asissipi Journal, 1887-January 22, 1888, CMS, Microfilm Reel #A115, entry for June 20. The index to the CMS microfilm collection incorrectly indicates that this journal was kept by the Reverend. G.S. Winter.

10. Hines, Asissipi Journal, May 6, 1887-January 22, 1888, CMS, Microfilm Reel #A115, entries for July 4, 5, and 6. Also see Asissipi Mission Marriage Register, record #49. Kate's son Josiah, 20, had died in February. She married a man listed as #10 on the Okīnomotayēw paylist. The second marriage was likely between Māyātis (Ugly Man), the son of Kīnikwānāsiw (Flying In A Circle Going Up To A Point), and a daughter from ticket #7 in Okīnomotayēw's band.

11. See Asissipi Mission Marriage Register, record #50. John Cardinal, son of the old councillor from the Mistawasis Reserve, was also known as John Pierre. Although John and Maria were married on August 2, 1887, their marriage was not recorded on the treaty paylist until 1888.

12. Asissipi Mission Death Register, records #61 and #62. Also see Asissipi Journal, May 6, 1887-January 22, 1888, CMS, Microfilm Reel #A115, entries for May 29, June 14, and July 23. Hines gave the girl's name as Emily Ayamuskin; this may have been a mistake since a four-year-old girl, also identified as Emily Ayamuskin, died on February 1, 1888. The boy was John Cardinal, son of Osāwanāsiw (South Wind, who was also known as William Cardinal and William Pierre) and his wife Jane (Okimowi-pāmohcēs, Walks Around Quietly). Osāwanāsiw and his family transferred to the Ahtahkakoop Band in 1890.

13. Hines, Asissipi Journal, May 6, 1887-January 22, 1888, CMS, Microfilm Reel #A115, entry for August 26, 1887.

14. Ibid., entries for August 6 and 14.

15. See Approximate Return of Grain and Roots Sowed and Harvested, CHC, *Sessional Papers*, 1888 (no. 15), Part 1, pp. 202-03, 212-13.

16. Hines, Asissipi Journal, May 6, 1887-January 22, 1888, CMS, Microfilm Reel #A115, entry for June 1. Average attendance at the school in 1887 was 19. Twenty-three of the 24 students registered were learning spelling and arithmetic. Ten were also taking writing and geography. Inspector Wadsworth and Indian agent Rae visited the reserve in June 1.

17. Ibid., entry for October 7. His daughter Augusta was born on February 15, 1887.

18. For example, see ibid., entry for June 12.

19. Ibid., entry for October 7.

20. Ahtahkakoop Band Treaty Paylist for 1887, RG10, vol. 9420. Also see CHC, *Sessional Papers*, 1898 (no. 14), p. 465.

21. The dead included George Pē-nōsēwēskam, 5; Josiah Asināpēwiyin, 20; John Masināscēs (Spotted), 21, and his father James, 53; a girl 1½; and Sōniyāw-ayāwēw's mother, Harriet Numowla.

22. The new babies included Charlotte, daughter of Pīwiyinīs (Little Man) and Elizabeth; Maggie, daughter of Joseph Ahtahkakoop and Mary Joyful; Paul, son of Mēmēmēkwanawēw and Emma Okimāsis; Annie, daughter of Blackhead (Kaskitēwistikwān, also known as William James Robertson) and Mary Cīpay-awāsis; Alexander, son of Wāsēhikot and Isabella Ermineskin; Agusta, daughter of Louis Ahenakew and Catherine Ermineskin; John Mark, son of Osāwanāsiw (William Cardinal) and Jane; Isabella, daughter of Mōhkomānawēw and Vida (Nutukwas) Pē-nōsēwēskam; George, son of Kā-kīsikāwapiw and Sophia Masuskapoe; Emma, daughter of Wāskitoy and Una Cahkāpēw; Philip, son of Wīcikāpawīmēw (He Who Stands With You) and Caroline Nayneecassum; and William James, son of Mac Cardinal and Mary. See Asissipi Mission Baptism Register.

23. The paylist list also showed that the last daughter still living in Iskwēsis's home had married James Campbell in the Mistawasis Band. There was no reference to the two marriages that had taken place in July between members of the Ahtahkakoop and Okīnomotayēw bands.

24. Hines, Asissipi Journal, May 6, 1887-January 22, 1888, CMS, Microfilm Reel #A115, entry for October 1. Hines says the treaty payments were made on October 1; the paylist is dated October 2.

25. Ibid., entry for November 6 and Asissipi Mission Death Register, records #63–#66. The 10-week-old boy was Philip Wīcikāpawīmēw. The baby who died in November was 10-month-old Annie Robertson, the daughter of Blackhead and Mary Cīpay-awāsis; Blackhead transferred from the Moosomin Band to Ahtahkakoop's band in 1888.

26. Joseph Finlayson, December 4, 1887, Indian Agent J. Finlayson's Reports on the Carlton Agency, 1887 to 1890, NA, RG10, vol. 3791, file 44732.

27. Ibid., December 26, 1887.

28. Ibid.. Also see ibid., February 3, 1888; and Reed, October 31, 1888, CHC, *Sessional Papers*, 1889 (no. 16), Part 1, p. 124.

29. Hines, Asissipi Journal, May 6, 1887-January 22, 1888, CMS, Microfilm Reel #A115, entry for June 18.

30. A report by J.A. Mackay dated February 20, 1888, CMS, Microfilm Reel #A115, indicated that there were 200 baptized "natives" in the Asissipi Mission, which included Okīnomotayēw's band as well as Ahtahkakoop's. Ninety people in these bands had associations with the Catholic church. Among the Anglicans, 70 took communion. During 1887, 13 adults and 13 children had been baptized, and a total of 15 boys and 25 girls were enrolled at schools at Sandy Lake and Stoney Lake. Indian contributions to the church amounted to $80.

31. Bishop William Cyprian Pinkham to Fenn, CMS Committee, November 9, 1887,

CMS, Microfilm Reel #A114. Also see Hines, Asissipi Journal, May 6, 1887-January 22, 1888, CMS, Microfilm Reel #A115, entry for November 2.

32. Pinkham to Fenn, CMS Committee, November 9, 1887, CMS, Microfilm Reel A#114. Pinkham said one of the other people confirmed on October 30 was a Canadian who farmed in the vicinity, had been brought up as a Baptist, and was married to one of the women from the band.

33. This child was Kāh-kāsōw's daughter Betsy.

34. Hines, *Red Indians*, 190-91.

35. Ibid.

36. Hines, Asissipi Journal, May 6, 1887-January 22, 1888, CMS, Microfilm Reel #A115, entries for July 31 and August 28 and 29. Also see Asissipi Mission Baptism Register, record #262 and Asissipi Mission Marriage Register, record #51.

37. Asissipi Journal, November 18, 1886-May 5, 1887, CMS, Microfilm Reel #A114, entry for April 4.

38. Hines, *Red Indians*, 160-61.

39. Minutes of the CMS Finance Committee, August 29, 1887, CMS, Microfilm Reel #A114.

40. Minutes of the CMS Finance Committee, November 3, 1887, CMS, Microfilm Reel #A114.

41. Wadsworth to superintendent general of Indian Affairs, October 12, 1888, CHC, *Sessional Papers*, 1889 (no. 16), Part 1, pp. 132, 134.

42. Dewdney, December 23, 1887, CHC, *Sessional Papers*, 1888 (no. 15), Part 1, p. 190.

43. Thomas White, superintendent general of Indian Affairs, in the Report of the Department of Indian Affairs for the Year Ending December 31, 1887, CHC, *Sessional Papers*, 1888 (no. 15), p. xiv.

44. Ibid., p. lxxviii.

45. Ibid., p. lxxxi.

46. See Hines, Asissipi Journal, May 6, 1887-January 22, 1888, CMS, Microfilm Reel #A115, entries for December 4, 7, 10, 22, and 30.

47. See Asissipi Mission Death Register, records #67–#69.

48. Hines, Asissipi Journal, March 18-July 27, 1888, CMS, Microfilm Reel #A115, entry for March 20.

49. Hines, Asissipi Journal, May 6, 1887-January 22, 1888, CMS, Microfilm Reel #A115, entry for January 19.

50. Hines, Asissipi Journal, March 18, 1887-July 24, 1888, CMS, Microfilm Reel #A115, entry for March 18. The deaths of the children were recorded in the Asissipi Mission Death Register, records #69–#71. The new babies included Charles, son of Baptiste Ahenakew and Ellen Ermineskin; and Jane Mary, daughter of Donald LeBlanc and Mary Kā-miyo-ahcahkwēw. See Asissipi Mission Baptism Register, records #283 and #284. The third child was not included in the register. The index to the CMS records incorrectly states that this is Hines's The Pas journal for March 18-July 27, 1888.

51. Finlayson, March 6, 1888, NA, RG10, vol. 3791, file 44732.

Chapter Thirty: John Hines Leaves, 1888-1889

1. Hines, Asissipi Journal, March 18-July 27, 1888, CMS, Microfilm Reel #A115, entries for April 7 and 10.
2. Ibid., entry for April 10.
3. Ibid., entry for April 18.
4. Ibid., entry for May 29.
5. Ibid., entries for March 29 and April 2.
6. Ibid., entry for April 8.
7. Ibid., entries for April 17 and 24, and May 10. Also see the Asissipi Mission Marriage Register, Series 2, record #27, and Asissipi Mission Death Register, record #74.
8. Ibid., entries for June 3, 17, and 22. Also see Finlayson, June 8, 1888, NA, RG10, vol. 3791, file 44,732. Government documentation for 1888 did not provide a breakdown on the amount of land planted.
9. Emma Hines to Fenn, secretary of CMS, May 29, 1888, and June 1, 1888, CMS, Microfilm Reel #A115.
10. Hines, Asissipi Journal, March 18-July 27, 1888, CMS, Microfilm Reel #A115, entry for May 20.
11. Ibid., entry for June 8.
12. Ibid., entry for June 10.
13. Ibid., entry for June 23.
14. Ibid., entry for July 5.
15. Edward Ahenakew, who became an Anglican priest and canon, as cited in *Voices of the Plains Cree*, 184. This quotation was taken from a paper prepared by Ahenakew for a church publication in about 1950.
16. See Hines, *Red Indians*, 231-33, 319-20. Also see Edward Ahenakew, *Voices of the Plains Cree*, 184.
17. McLean to the CMS Committee, March 3, 1886, CMS, A113.
18. For example, see Hines, *Red Indians*, 155-66, 162-63.
19. See ibid., 229.
20. "Bishop McLean's report of a journey to Cumberland House, etc. in 1885," in the CMS's *Intelligencer*, January 1886, as cited in Appendix D of Payton's book *Diocese of Saskatchewan*, 170.
21. *The Sower in the West*, Diocese of Saskatchewan and Calgary, vol. 4, October, 1891, CMS, Microfilm Reel #A117.
22. Minutes of the Fourth Meeting of the Synod of the Diocese of Saskatchewan, held in Prince Albert August 28, 1889, CMS, Microfilm Reel #116.
23. Hayter Reed, Indian commissioner, in a report dated October 27, 1888, NA, RG10, vol. 3806, file 52,332. Also see Wadsworth, October 12, 1888, CHC, *Sessional Papers*, 1889 (no. 16), Part 1, p. 135. Reed, previously assistant Indian commissioner, replaced Dewdney as Indian commissioner in 1888. Dewdney, now a member of Parliament in Macdonald's Conservative government, had been appointed superintendent general of Indian Affairs.

24. Reed to Dewdney, superintendent general of Indian Affairs, October 27, 1888, NA, RG10, vol. 3806, file 52,332.

25. Carter, *Lost Harvests*, 120. For an excellent summary of Reed's career, see ibid., 142-46, 238.

26. Reed to Dewdney, October 27, 1888, NA, RG10, vol. 3806, file 52,332.

27. Ibid.

28. Ahtahkakoop Band Paylist for 1888.

29. See Reed to superintendent general of Indian Affairs, October 31, 1888, CHC, *Sessional Papers*, 1889 (no. 16), Part 1, p. 124.

30. Duck Lake Agency Letterbook, Prince Albert Historical Society, #209, entry for January 31, 1889, in which the agent is acknowledging instructions sent by the Indian commissioner in a letter dated January 10, 1889.

31. Ahtahkakoop Band Paylist for 1888. See the Asissipi Mission Marriage Register, Series 2, record #27, and the Asissipi Mission Death Register, record #74 for Eliza's marriage and death. The other dead shown on the 1888 paylist, besides Joseph Sasakamoose and Eliza Kā-miyo-ahcahkwēw, included Wīcikāpawīmēw and his infant son Philip; two of Kīskanakwās's grandchildren, James Wāsēhikot and Betsy Kāh-kāsōw; Apotum's son; Mēmēkwaniwēw's son Paul; a boy and a girl from Nōtokwēwāhp's (Old Woman Lodge) ticket, and Annie Robertson, daughter of Mary Cīpay-awāsis and Blackhead. Hines and Settee, in addition to these deaths, also recorded the deaths of Duncan Cameron, son of Margaret Sasakamoose and John Cameron; Emily Ayamuskin and Thomas Chicken (these may have been the children listed as dead on Nōtokwēwāhp's ticket); Charles Thomas Robertson; and an unnamed 23-year-old who died from consumption. Also see the Asissipi Mission Death Register, records #56–#75.

32. Hines and Settee included the following births in the mission registers: Thomas, son of Chicken and Dinah Kihci-mōhkomān; Joseph Duncan, son of Margaret Sasakamoose and John Cameron; Nancy, daughter of Thomas Ayamuskin and Mary Blackbird; Jane Mary, daughter of Mary Kā-miyo-ahcahkwēw and Donald LeBlanc (Asissipi Mission Baptism Register, records #269, #270, and #283–#287); and Elizabeth, daughter of Osāwanāsiw and Jane Okīmowi-pāmohcēs; Mary, daughter of Kā-kitowē-pimohtēw (He Who Walks Noisily); Betsy, daughter of Joseph Ahtahkakoop and Mary Joyful; Edward, son of Mac Cardinal and Mary; and Betsy, daughter of William James Robson and Mary (Sandy Lake Mission Baptism Register (Book 1), records #290-#293, #297, #299.) Osāwanāsiw and Mac Cardinal were the sons of Pierre, the old councillor from Mistawasis.

33. Asissipi Mission Marriage Register, record #41.

34. On the 1888 paylist, it was stated that Blackhead had come from the Starblanket Reserve in the Qu'Appelle area. The 1889 paylist indicated that he had last been paid in the Moosomin band in 1884. He was not paid arrears.

35. Wadsworth, October 12, 1888 CHC, *Sessional Papers*, 1889 (no. 16), Part 1, p. 135. Also see Dewdney, January 1, 1889, CHC, *Sessional Papers*, 1889 (no. 16), pp. lx-lxi; and Finlayson, August 15, 1888, CHC, *Sessional Papers*, 1889 (no. 16), Part 1, p. 90.

36. Macrae to superintendent general of Indian Affairs, October 23, 1888, CHC, *Sessional Papers*, 1889 (no. 16), Part 1, p. 145.

37. Macrae, CHC, *Sessional Papers*, 1889 (no. 16), Part 1, pp. 300-01.

38. Finlayson, Report on the Carlton District, November 30, 1888, NA, RG10, vol. 3791, file 44,732. The comment about the thresher breaking down and delays resulting from moving from one yard to another appeared in his entry for January 3, 1889, and referred to Mistawasis's reserve. The same conditions would have existed at Ahtahkakoop's reserve.

39. Finlayson, November 30, 1889, January 17 and 26, and March 29, 1890, NA, RG10, vol. 3791, file 44,732.

40. Clarke, Prince Albert Report, 1887, B.332/e/1, fo. 15.

41. See the Ahtahkakoop Band Paylist for 1889 and the Asissipi Mission Death Register, records #76-#82. Benjamin Wāskitoy and Chicken were married to daughters of Chakāpēw (Cold Touch Spirit); Chakāpēw died from consumption on June 22, 1889. The 1883 paylist indicated that Wāskitoy had come from "the south, only paid 3 times formerly Attackacoop's Band." Edward Cardinal was Mac Cardinal's son. Although Louisa was recorded as being the daughter of Joseph and Maria Cardinal, she was more likely the daughter of John Cardinal and Maria Kā-tāh-twēhototawāt. (See Sandy Lake Mission Baptism Register (Book 1), records #293 and #305.

42. Finlayson, January 3 and 26, and March 29, 1889, Reports on the Carlton Agency, 1887 to 1890, NA, RG10, vol. 3791, file 44732.

43. Finlayson, January 3 and March 29, 1889, Reports on the Carlton Agency, 1887 to 1890, NA, RG10, vol. 3791, file 44,732. Finlayson was referring to the Mistawasis band when he talked about the roads, but the situation would have been even worse for Ahtahkakoop's people because of the greater distance to Prince Albert.

44. Finlayson to superintendent general of Indian Affairs, July 2, 1889, CHC, *Sessional Papers*, 1890 (no. 12), Part 1, p. 80.

45. Report of the Marquis of Lorne's trip, 1881, NA, RG10, vol. 3768, file 33,642, p. 16.

Chapter Thirty-One: The Years 1889-1893

1. The government did not include agricultural statistics for the Ahtahkakoop Band in the *Sessional Papers* for 1889.

2. Finlayson, reports dated May 8 and June 1, 1889, Carlton Agency Reports 1887 to 1890, NA, RG10, vol. 3791, file 44,732; and report dated July 2, 1890, CHC, *Sessional Papers*, 1889 (no. 12), Part 1, p. 90. Also see Asissipi Mission Death Register, record #83.

3. Finlayson, July 2, 1889, CHC, *Sessional Papers*, 1890 (no. 12), Part 1, p. 80.

4. Pīwiyinīs (Little Man), 29, was the son of William Cīpay-awāsis and Emily Asināpēwiyin. He married Elizabeth Iron House after the 1880 death of her husband Wāwiyēwēskocawēs. Pīwiyinīs took over Wāwiyēwēskocawēs's paylist number, #39, in 1884. (See Asissipi Mission Baptism Register, record #157, marriage records #11 and #25, and the Ahtahkakoop Band Paylists.)

5. Alex McGibbon, September 3, 1890, NA, RG10, vol. 3843, file 72,695-2, p. 16.

6. Finlayson, August 30, 1889, NA, RG10, vol. 3791, file 44,732. Also see Reed to superintendent general of Indian Affairs, October 31, 1889, NA, RG10, vol. 3791, file

44,732; and Finlayson to superintendent general of Indian Affairs, August 6, 1890, *Sessional Papers*, 1891 (no. 18), p. 57.

7. Finlayson to superintendent general of Indian Affairs, August 6, 1890, CHC, *Sessional Papers*, 1891 (no. 18), p. 57.

8. Finlayson, February 1, 1890, NA, RG10, vol. 3791, file 44,732: and Finlayson, August 6, CHC, *Sessional Papers*, 1891 (no. 18), p. 57. The death records are contained in the Asissipi Mission Death Register, records #88-#91.

9. Finlayson, March 31, 1890, Carlton Agency Reports 1887 to 1890, NA, RG10, vol. 3791, file 44,732.

10. Officer Commanding, North-West Mounted Police, Prince Albert, October 28, 1889, NA, RG18, vol. 1140, file 174.

11. Finlayson, January 17, 1890, Carlton Agency Reports 1887 to 1890, NA, RG10, vol. 3791, file 44,732. Also see Finlayson to superintendent general of Indian Affairs, August 6, 1891, CHC, *Sessional Papers*, 1891 (no.18), p. 57.

12. Reed to superintendent general of Indian Affairs, October 31, 1889, CHC, *Sessional Papers*, 1890 (no. 12), Part 1, p. 162.

13. Reed to superintendent general of Indian Affairs, December 1, 1891, CHC, *Sessional Papers*, 1892 (no. 14), p. 193. In this report, Reed refers to a letter of instruction circulated two years earlier.

14. For an excellent discussion of the "peasant farming" concept, see Carter, *Lost Harvests*, 209-13.

15. Carter, *Lost Harvests*, 156-57, 148-49.

16. See statistics for the various years in the *Sessional Papers*. These figures do not include 1885, when wheat was not planted because of the uprising. The smallest crop was in 1884, with 3.6 bushels to an acre; the largest harvest was in 1883, with 16.25 bushels per acre. Statistics were not available for 1889.

17. Finlayson, April 30 and June 2, 1890, Carlton Agency Reports 1887 to 1890, NA, RG10, vol. 3791, file 44,732.

18. Sōniyāw-ayāwēw was living with Ahtahkakoop's daughter Mary Piyēsīs, who had been deserted by her husband in the early 1880s. According to Hines, the woman waited some time for her husband to return but she had children and was poor, so she moved in with another man who treated her very kindly. They had two more children and wanted to marry but could not legally do so. Hines thought they were better off living together than the man leaving so he did not try to break them up. Sōniyāw-ayāwēw took over Piyēsīs's treaty number, and on some documentation both names—Piyēsīs and Sōniyāw-ayāwēw—are used for this family. (See Hines, Asissipi Journal, July 1, 1884-January 10, 1885, entry for December 14. 1884, CMS, Microfilm Reel A112.)

19. Returns showing the Individual Indians who Sowed and Harvested and the Amount of their Crops in the Year 1890, CHC, *Sessional Papers*, 1891 (no. 18), p. 288.

20. According to inspector McGibbon in his September 10, 1890 report (NA, RG10, vol. 3843, file 72,695-2) 95 acres were planted to wheat, 26 to barley, 15 to oats, 9 to potatoes, 6½ to turnips, and 25 or 26 acres in garden vegetables. These figures differ from those that appeared in the department's annual report.

21. McGibbon, September 10, 1890, NA, RG10, vol. 3843, file 72,695-2, p. 16.

22. Ibid.

23. Finlayson, October 18, 1890, Carlton Agency Reports 1887 to 1890, NA, RG10, vol. 3791, file 44,732.

24. Return showing the Individual Indians who Sowed and Harvested and the Amount of their Crops in the Year 1890, CHC, *Sessional Papers*, 1891 (no. 18), Part 1, p. 288.

25. Finlayson to superintendent general of Indian Affairs, August 1, 1891, CHC, *Sessional Papers*, 1892 (no. 14), Part 1, p. 80.

26. Return showing the Individual Indians who Sowed and Harvested and the Amount of their Crops in the Year 1890, CHC, *Sessional Papers*, 1891 (no. 18), Part 1, p. 288. Kīnikwānāsiw, who had transferred to Okīnomotayēw's band in 1889, rejoined Ahtahkakoop's band in 1890.

27. Finlayson, March 31, June 2, and July 5, 1890, Carlton Agency Reports 1887 to 1890, NA, RG10, vol. 3791, file 44,732.

28. Finlayson, July 5, 1890, Carlton Agency Reports 1887 to 1890, NA, RG10, vol. 3791, file 44,732. Also see Finlayson to superintendent general of Indian Affairs, August 6, 1890, CHC, *Sessional Papers*, 1891 (no. 18), p. 57.

29. McGibbon, September 10, 1890, NA, RG10, vol. 3843, file 72,695-2.

30. See Asissipi Mission Death Register, records #98-#108, and the Ahtahkakoop Band Paylist for 1891.

31. This was an increase of 50½ acres from the previous year when the amount of seeded acreage was less than other years. According to McGibbon, the crops seeded broke down to: wheat, 112 acres; barley, 55 acres; oats, 27 acres; potatoes, 7 acres; peas, 1 acre; turnips, 2 acres, and gardens, 2 acres. See McGibbon, September 19, 1891, NA, RG10, vol. 3860, file 82,319-3.

32. A.W. Ponton, government surveyor, September 1892, CHC, *Sessional Papers*, 1893 (no. 14), p. 223.

33. McGibbon, September 19, NA, RG10, vol. 3860, file 82,319-3.

34. McGibbon, September 9, 1892, CHC, *Sessional Papers*, 1893 (no. 14), p. 96.

35. McGibbon, September 19, 1891, NA, RG10, vol. 3860, file 82,319-3.

36. Amédée Forget was born in Marieville, in present-day Quebec, in 1847 and educated by the Jesuits of Marieville College. A lawyer by profession, he served as secretary to the Manitoba Half-Breed Commission, and in 1876 became clerk to the Executive Council of the North-West Territories and secretary to both Lieutenant-Governor David Laird, and his successor, Edgar Dewdney. Forget was appointed assistant Indian commissioner, in addition to his other duties, in the late 1880s.

37. See Returns showing Crops Sown and Harvested by Individual Indians in Carlton Agency, Season of 1891, CHC, *Sessional Papers*, 1892 (no. 14), Part 1, pp. 339-40. In his report McGibbon stated that the fields on the high lands produced the best results.

38. Elsewhere in the report McGibbon reported that the number of sheep was five, the same as the previous year.

39. McGibbon, September 19, 1891, NA, RG10, vol. 3860, file 82,319-3, p. 6. The new crop of calves consisted of 15 bull calves and 22 heifer calves.

40. Ibid., p. 18.

41. Marginal notes in McGibbon's 1891 report, p. 18.

42. Carter, *Lost Harvests*, 221.

43. McGibbon in his inspection report for 1891 dated September 19, 1891, NA, RG10, Microfilm Reel C-10151, vol. 3860, file 82,319-3.

44. Forget, assistant Indian commissioner, in a hand-written marginal note on page 7 of McGibbon's 1891 report, NA, RG10, vol. 3860, file 82,319-3.

45. Forget, hand-written marginal note on page 16 of McGibbon's 1891 report, NA, RG10, vol. 3860, file 82,319-3.

46. Reed to the deputy superintendent general of Indian Affairs, February 16, 1892, NA, RG10, vol. 3860, file 82,319-3.

47. Reed, February 18, 1892, NA, RG10, vol. 3860, file 82,319-3.

48. Ponton, Indian reserve surveyor, to superintendent general of Indian Affairs, September 12, 1892, CHC, *Sessional Papers*, 1893 (no. 14), pp. 222-23. Also see NA, RG10, vol. 3881, file 94,543.

49. Finlayson, monthly reports dated January 31, February 29, and March 31, 1892, NA, RG10, vol. 3869, file 88,297.

50. Finlayson, June 30, 1892, CHC, *Sessional Papers*, 1893 (no. 14), p. 178.

51. Superintendent John Cotton, "F" Division, North-West Mounted Police annual report, dated November 30, 1892, CHC, *Sessional Papers* (no. 15), p. 28. Cotton was stationed in Prince Albert.

52. Finlayson, February 29, March 3, and May 4, 1892, Carlton Agency Reports 1887 to 1890, NA, RG10, vol. 3869, file 88,297.

53. Asissipi Mission Death Register, records #110 to #114. According to the register, Ellen Robertson, 21 months (daughter of Blackhead), Samuel Partridge (Chicken), three months, and a 50-year-old whose name was illegible in the register also died.

54. Finlayson, May 4, 31, and June 30, 1892, NA, RG10, vol. 3869, file 88,297.

55. See McGibbon's report to superintendent general of Indian Affairs, October 3, 1893, CHC, *Sessional Papers*, 1894 (no. 14) p. 185. The inspector had arrived on the reserve in October, 1892.

56. In his inspection report reprinted in the *Sessional Papers*, McGibbon said 254 acres were planted in 1892, 46 more than the previous year. The figure 256 was taken from the "returns" of individual farmers prepared by the department.

57. See Returns showing Crops Sown and Harvested by Individual Indians in Carlton Agency, Season of 1892, CHC, *Sessional Papers*, p. 371.

58. Finlayson, reports of June 30 and July 31, 1892, NA, RG10, vol. 3869, file 88,297. Also see Agents Monthly Report for October (dated November 4, 1892) prepared by Henry W. Halpin, agency clerk, located in the same file. Halpin was acting agent at the end of November during the exchange of responsibilities between Joseph Finlayson and the newly appointed agent, Hilton Keith.

59. McGibbon, October 5, 1892, NA, RG10, vol. 3894, file 97,015. Also see his report dated October 3, 1893, CHC, *Sessional Papers*, 1894 (no. 14) p. 185.

60. McGibbon, October 3, 1893, CHC, *Sessional Papers*, 1894 (no. 14), p. 185.

61. Although McGibbon indicated in his report of October 5, 1892, that the sheep had either been killed or died, his report dated October 3, 1893, in the CHC, *Sessional Papers*, 1894 (no. 14), indicated there were 10 sheep in private hands.

62. McGibbon, October 5, 1892, NA, RG10, vol. 3894, file 97,015. Figures in the various reports differ somewhat.

63. Ibid.

64. Wadsworth, December 1, 1887, NA, RG10, vol. 3843, file 72,695-2.

65. Report on Schools for year ending June 30, 1888, CHC, *Sessional Papers*, 1889 (no. 16), Part 1, pp. 300-01. The "standard courses of study" can be found in CHC, *Sessional Papers*, 1894 (no. 14), pp. 282-83.

66. Report on Protestant Indian Day Schools in the North-West Territories since October 1889, CHC, *Sessional Papers*, 1891 (no. 18), Part 1, p. 68.

67. Wadsworth to superintendent general of Indian Affairs, October 30, 1890, CHC, *Sessional Papers*, 1891 (no. 18), p. 153. Also see Finlayson, August 6, 1890, CHC, *Sessional Papers*, 1891 (no. 18), p. 57. Wadsworth arrived at the Carlton Agency March 27, 1890.

68. J. Ansdell Macrae, inspector of Protestant Indian Schools to superintendent general of Indian Affairs, August 12, 1890, CHC, *Sessional Papers*, 1891 (no. 18), p. 64.

69. Showing the Conditions of the various Indian Schools for the Year ended June 30, 1888, *Sessional Papers*, 1889 (no. 16), Part 1, pp. 300-01, and 1890 (no. 12), Part 1, p. 260.

70. In 1893 there was one student in Standard IV. See school reports in various *Sessional Papers*.

71. Macrae to superintendent general of Indian Affairs, August 12, 1890, CHC, *Sessional Papers*, 1891 (no. 18), p. 64. His report covered the period from September 1889 to August 12, 1890. Also see Report Showing the Condition of the various Indian Schools for the Year ended June 30, 1892, CHC, *Sessional Papers*, 1893 (no. 14), Part 1, p. 304, and subsequent reports, and McGibbon, October 3, 1893, CHC, *Sessional Papers*, 1894 (no. 14), pp. 181, 217-18.

72. See Bishop Pinkham,NA, RG10, vol. 3844, file 73,320.

73. Macrae, October 23, 1888, in CHC, *Sessional Papers*, 1889 (no. 16), Part 1, pp. 146-47. Also see Thomas Clarke, principal of the Battleford Industrial School, September 9, 1892, CHC, *Sessional Papers*, 1893 (no. 14), p. 210.

74. Forget, Circular letter, March 29, 1889, NA, RG10, vol. 1142.

75. J.R. Miller, *Shingwauk's Vision: A History of Native Residential Schools* (Toronto: University of Toronto Press, 1996), 110-12.

76. Pinkham, dated October 21, 1890, RG10, vol. 3844, file 73,320.

77. See Pinkham, NA, RG10, vol. 3844, file 73,320.

78. Clarke, principal of the Battleford Industrial School, September 29, 1891, CHC, *Sessional Papers*, (no. 14), p. 167.

79. *The Sower in the West*, Diocese of Saskatchewan and Calgary, NWT, vol. 4, October 1891, CMS, Microfilm Reel #A117. The church conference was held the day before the

synod of the Saskatchewan Diocese met. J.R. Miller, in *Shingwauk's Vision*, 345-46, states that Clarke anticipated criticism of the industrial school and "went to considerable trouble to ensure that friends of his school and of the DIA [Department of Indian Affairs] would be in attendance to counter the critics." He cited as his source, T. Clarke to Hayter Reed, July 14, 1891, NA, Hayter Reed Papers, vol. 12, file "Rev. T. Clarke 1891-92," p. 132.

80. Finlayson to D.H. McDowall, June 24, 1891, NA, RG10, vol. 3844, file 73,320.

81. By now the chiefs and the other parents who travelled to Battleford to see their children needed permission to leave the reserves.

82. Records indicate that in 1892 there were 191 Protestants, nine Roman Catholics, and eight "pagans" on the Ahtahkakoop Reserve. [See Census Return of Resident and Nomadic Indians; Denominations to which they belong, etc., CHC, *Sessional Papers*, 1893 (no. 14), p. 319.]

83. Clarke, September 9, 1892, CHC, *Sessional Papers*, 1893 (no. 14), p. 210.

84. Ibid., p. 211.

85. See Report showing status of discharged Pupils from the Battleford Industrial School up to the 30th June, 1893, CHC, *Sessional Papers*, 1894 (no. 14), pp. 102-3. One of the columns in the chart containing this information is headed "Reason for Discharge and History of Pupils since Discharge."

86. From a document dated March 22, 1892, signed by John A. Settee, interpreter, and witnessed by R.S. McKenzie, Indian agent for the Duck Lake Agency, and J.A. Finlayson, Indian agent for the Carlton Agency, NA, RG10, vol. 3844, file 73,320.

87. Reed, October 31, 1889, CHC, *Sessional Papers*, 1890 (no. 12), Part 1, pp. 162.

88. Reed, October 31, 1892, CHC, *Sessional Papers*, 1893 (no. 14), p. 49.

89. Wadsworth, December 1, 1887, NA, RG10, vol. 3843, file 72,6952.

90. McGibbon, September 19, 1891, NA, RG10, vol. 3860, file 82,319-3.

91. Reed, in a Memorandum re: Indian agent Finlayson, July 26, 1894, NA, RG10, vol. 3894, file 97,015.

92. Ibid. Also see document dated November 16, 1892, NA, RG10, vol. 3765, file 32,772.

93. See the Ahtahkakoop Band paylists 1889-1892.

94. Albert Snake transferred from ticket #133 on the Mistawasis Band Paylist. Emma Snake's number was #118. In oral testimony presented February 12, 1955, Alfred Snake, Ocīpiwayān's grandson, stated that his sister was married to a man by the name of Cardinal who lived at Snake Plain. (See "Inquiry into the Claim of the Stoney Knoll Indian Reserve, No. 107," December 1994, Young Chipeewayan Inquiry, Indian Claims Commission, p. 10.)

95. Kīnikwānāsiw had formerly been listed as #85 on the Ahtahkakoop Band Paylist; his new number was #133. Māyātis was given #129; Kanahasantum (Alert, Knowing Person), #135, Mistapēw (Giant Man), #136; and Tāwāpitēwiyiniw (Teeth Missing) #137. Tāwāpitēwiyiniw, who was also known as Big John, became a headman of the Ahtahkakoop Band in 1928.

96. Pēmwēwēstik (Wind Blowing By) had last been paid with Ahtahkakoop's Band in 1883 under ticket #41; his new number was 138.

97. Kihci-mōhkomān had drowned in Sandy Lake during the 1879-80 paylist year.

98. See the Asissipi Mission death records.

99. See the Asissipi Mission Marriage Register (2).

100. Sandy Lake Mission Baptism Register (Book 1). Allan Ahenakew's baptism record is #350.

101. Reed to superintendent general of Indian Affairs, June 21, 1892, vol. 3876, file 91,749.

102. Barry L. Ahenakew, review meeting November 23, 1997. For further information on Give Away Dances, see Katherine Pettipas, *Severing the Ties that Bind: Government Repression of Indigenous Religious Ceremonies on the Prairies*, Manitoba Studies in Native History 7 (Winnipeg: University of Manitoba Press, 1994), 54-56, and Mandelbaum, The *Plains Cree*, 206-7.

103. Dewdney, November 25, 1884, CHC, *Sessional Papers*, 1885 (no. 3), p. 158.

104. For a comprehensive study on the suppression of sacred Indian ceremonies and dances, see Pettipas, *Severing the Ties that Bind*.

105. Until 1895, Section 14 of the Indian Act only extended to the potlatches of the Indian people living on the Northwest Pacific Coast.

106. Asissipi Mission Marriage Register (2), records #42 and 44.

107. Interview with Barry L. Ahenakew.

108. McGibbon, October 1892, NA, RG10, vol. 3894, file 97,015.

Chapter Thirty-Two: Ahtahkakoop's Journey Ends, 1893-1896

1. For more on this incident, which took place in February, 1884, and involved Yellow Calf's band at Crooked Lake, see Carter, *Lost Harvests*, pp. 120-21. Also see Indian commissioner to superintendent general of Indian Affairs, June 21, 1892, NA, RG10, vol. 3876, file 91,749.

2. McGibbon, June 28, 1894, CHC, *Sessional Papers*, 1895 (no. 14), p. 97.

3. Return showing Crops sown and harvested by individual Indians in the Carlton Agency, season of 1893, CHC, *Sessional Papers*, 1894 (no. 14), pp. 338-39. In addition to the 144 acres of wheat, 33 acres of oats, nine acres of barley, 10 acres of potatoes, and half an acre of peas were planted. Also see Keith to superintendent general of Indian Affairs, August 29, 1893, CHC, *Sessional Papers*, 1894 (no. 14), p. 81.

4. Thomas Bighead was the son of Wāskitoy, one of the original headmen; Andrew, the son of Iskwēsis, was married to Simon Apotum's daughter. Wāskitoy (#102 on the treaty paylist) was likely another son of the old headman.

5. Keith, July 31, 1894, CHC, *Sessional Papers*, 1895 (no. 14), p. 76.

6. The farmers who cut more than 20 tons of hay included Sōniyāw-ayāwēw, Baptiste Ahenakew and John Hyman, Kāh-kāsōw and Norbert, Nātakām, Greyeyes, Michel and Ahtahkakoop, Kā-miyo-ahcahkwēw, Isaac Masuskapoe, Osāwanāsiw, and Apotum. See McGibbon, June 28, 1894, CHC, *Sessional Papers*, 1895, (no. 14), p. 97; and the 1893 returns, CHC, *Sessional Papers*, 1894 (14), pp. 338-39.

7. McGibbon, October 30, 1891, NA, RG10, vol. 3860, file 82,319. Also see McGibbon,

June 28, 1894, NA, RG10, vol. 3860, file 82,319-3, p. 18. Partially reprinted in CHC, *Sessional Papers*, 1895 (no. 14), pp. 96-97.

8. McGibbon, June 28, 1894, CHC, *Sessional Papers*, 1895, (no. 14), pp. 96-97. This report referred to an inspection visit to the Ahtahkakoop Reserve in September, 1893.

9. Ibid.

10. Ibid., p. 96.

11. Ibid., p. 97.

12. Ahtahkakoop Band paylists for 1883, 1891, 1892, and 1893. John Robert was born in 1882. His brother Joseph was born in 1884. James Starblanket was incorrectly listed on several treaty paylists as Kā-miyo-astotin's son. Although Joseph Ahtahkakoop's widow married Mac Pierre Cardinal in 1892, the marriage did not last and she was given her own ticket at the 1894 treaty payments. Her two sons remained with Ahtahkakoop and Kā-miyo-astotin. Her daughter transferred to the new ticket with her. Mary Joyful married again during the 1901-02 paylist year, this time to Kā-nahahcāpiw (Jumper Tate).

13. McGibbon, June 28, 1894, CHC, *Sessional Papers*, 1895 (no. 14), pp. 96-97.

14. See Return showing Crops sown and harvested by individual Indians in the Carlton Agency, season of 1893, CHC, *Sessional Papers*, 1893 (no. 14), pp. 338-39.

15. Keith, July 31, 1894, CHC, *Sessional Papers*, 1895 (no. 14), p. 76.

16. McGibbon, August 12, 1895, CHC, *Sessional Papers*, 1896 (no. 14), p. 213. McGibbon had arrived in the Carlton Agency July 9, 1884. Also see Keith, July 31, 1894, CHC, *Sessional Papers*, 1895 (no. 14), p.76; and July 23, 1895, CHC, *Sessional Papers*, 1896 (no. 14), p. 173. If 1 pound of flour equals three cups of flour, one bushel of wheat would produce 90 cups of flour. To take this one step further, if 8 cups of flour are used to make one large bannock, one bushel of wheat would make 11 recipes of bannock. (Today's wheat averages 60 pounds of flour per bushel.)

17. This story is based on a story told by Edward Ahenakew in "The Story of the Ahenakews," 20-21.

18. Ibid., 21.

19. Asissipi Mission Death Register, records #125-#129.

20. Return showing Crops sown and harvested by individual Indians in the Carlton Agency, season of 1894, CHC, *Sessional Papers*, 1895 (no. 14), pp. 346-47. According to inspector McGibbon, the amount of land planted in 1894 was reduced by 18 acres from the previous year to 196 acres. See McGibbon, August 12, 1894, CHC, *Sessional Papers*, 1896, (no. 14), p. 212.

21. McGibbon to superintendent general of Indian Affairs, August 12, 1894, CHC, *Sessional Papers*, 1896 (no. 14), p. 212. McGibbon arrived at the Carlton Agency head-quarters on July 9, almost two months earlier than other years.

22. Ibid. Keith, in his report dated July 23, 1895, for the year ending June 30, 1895, indicated that new fencing had been erected around 75 acres, 71 acres were summer-fallowed, 43 acres were broken, and 65 acres were ploughed in the fall. See Keith to superintendent general of Indian Affairs, July 23, 1895, CHC, *Sessional Papers*, 1896 (no. 14), p. 173.

23. Ibid.

24. Only 869 bushels of grain were obtained from the 136 acres planted to wheat. See Return showing crops sown and harvested by individual Indians in the Carlton Agency, season of 1894, CHC, *Sessional Papers*, 1895 (no. 14), pp. 346-47. Although the return indicates that Sōniyāw-ayāwēw harvested 50 bushels of carrots, the amount of land sown to this root vegetable was left blank, for him as well as all of the other farmers. Also see Keith, July 31, 1894, CHC, *Sessional Papers*, 1895 (no. 14), p. 76.

25. See Return showing Crops sown and harvested by individual Indians in the Carlton Agency, season of 1894, CHC, *Sessional Papers*, 1895 (no. 14), pp. 346-47. Kā-miyo-astotin harvested 226 bushels of oats; the rest of the farmers produced a total of 178 bushels.

26. Keith to superintendent general of Indian Affairs, July 23, 1895, CHC, *Sessional Papers*, 1896 (no. 14), pp. 173-74.

27. McGibbon to superintendent general of Indian Affairs, October 8, 1894, CHC, *Sessional Papers*, 1895 (no. 14), p. 179.

28. Although McGibbon stated that six students were at the Battleford Industrial School in 1893, the 1893 paylist indicated that nine were enrolled.

29. William, who was raised by Wāsēhikot, was registered as William Robinson. The boy was 13 or 14 when he was given his own treaty number in October 1890 and admitted to Emmanuel College. See the treaty paylists and Report of Training & Industrial School at Emmanuel College, Prince Albert, quarter ended December 31, 1894, CMS, Microfilm Reel #118.

30. McGibbon to superintendent general of Indian Affairs, October 8, 1894, CHC, *Sessional Papers*, 1895 (no. 14), p. 179, and October 3, 1893, CHC, *Sessional Papers*, 1894 (no. 14), p. 217.

31. Louis Ahenakew to Hines, December 23, 1895, CMS, Microfilm Reel #A119.

32. Pinkham, January 18, 1894, CMS, Microfilm Reel #A118.

33. Ibid.

34. Minutes of Saskatchewan CMS Finance Committee held in Prince Albert March 30, 1894, and J.A. Mackay to the CMS, March 12, 1894, CMS, Microfilm Reel #A118. Although Winter's move to the Asissipi Mission was confirmed in March, the missionary did not arrive until September.

35. Mackay to Pinkham, March 16, 1896, CMS, Microfilm Reel #119.

36. G.S. Winter to Edward Higgens, CMS acting secretary, September 12, 1894, CMS, Microfilm Reel #118. Also see letters to Higgens dated October 15 and December 16, 1894; and Winter's Prince Albert Journal, December 1894, CMS, Microfilm Reel #118, pp. 4-7.

37. Winter, Prince Albert Journal, December 1894, CMS, Microfilm Reel #118, pp. 5-6.

38. Ibid., pp. 5-7. Also see Winter to Higgens, CMS, September 12, 1894.

39. Louis Ahenakew to Hines, December 23, 1895, CMS, Microfilm Reel #119.

40. See Pinkham to the CMS Committee, March 12, 1895, CMS, Microfilm Reel #119; and J.A. Mackay to Pinkham, March 16, 1896, CMS, Microfilm Reel #A119. Hines, when consulted in England, wrote that the house at Sandy Lake must still be "in a good

state of presentation" and should be for a number of years. The kitchen, which was the first building erected, was "under another roof" and should be pulled down. He also suggested that in addition to applying a new coat of plaster on the walls of the dwelling house, the woodwork should be painted and a new kitchen with a room over top should be built. See Hines to B.B. Gould, CMS, March 30, 1895, CMS, Microfilm Reel #A118.

41. Minutes of Saskatchewan CMS Finance Committee meeting held in Prince Albert October 20, 1894, CMS Microfilm Reel #118.

42. Minutes of Saskatchewan Finance Committee Meeting held at Prince Albert, July 25, 1895, CMS, Microfilm Reel #119. Also see McLean, April 27, 1886, CMS, Microfilm Reel #113.

43. Winter, Prince Albert Journal, December 2, 1894-February 24, 1895, CMS, Microfilm Reel #118, entry for December 12, 1894. Also see Ahtahkakoop Treaty Paylist for 1895. The Pelican Lake Band had signed an adhesion to Treaty 6 in 1890.

44. Minutes of Saskatchewan Finance Committee Meeting held at Prince Albert July 25 and October 30, 1895. Also see Mackay to Pinkham, March 16, 1896, and Mackay, April 7, 1896, Microfilm Reel #A119. Church officials tried to close the mission at Sturgeon Lake in the summer of 1896, but failed when Winter appealed to the CMS parent committee in London and offered to work at half salary or to try and live on the children's allowance and assistance from friends. Those who have seen "the horror of heathenism as we have (such as we never contemplated)," he explained, would feel that they too would make any sacrifice." See Winter to the CMS Parent Committee, June, 1896, CMS, Microfilm Reel #A119.

45. Minutes of the Finance Committee, July 25, 1895, and May 20, 1896; and Pinkham, May 18, 1896, CMS, Microfilm Reel #A119. Also see Louis Ahenakew to Hines, December 23, 1895, CMS, Microfilm Reel #A119.

46. Keith to superintendent general of Indian Affairs, August 29, 1893, CHC, 1894 (no. 14), p. 82; July 31, 1894, CHC, Sessional Papers, 1895 (no. 14), p. 76; and July 23, 1895, CHC, Sessional Papers, 1896 (no. 14,), p. 175. Also see McGibbon, August 12, 1895, CHC, Sessional Papers, 1896 (no. 14), p. 211.

47. Wadsworth, October 30, 1890, CHC, Sessional Papers, 1891 (no. 18), p. 152. He was on the reserve in March of the same year.

48. McGibbon, August 6, 1896, NA, RG10, vol. 3894, file 97,015. Also see McGibbon to superintendent general of Indian Affairs, September 21, 1896, CHC, Sessional Papers, 1897 (no. 14), p. 240. Although McGibbon, who had arrived at the Carlton Agency July 25, 1896, said the farm instructor's house was on the north side of the lake, it was more likely situated on the west side.

49. McGibbon to superintendent general of Indian Affairs, August 12, 1895, CHC, Sessional Papers, 1896 (no. 14), p. 212.

50. Chief inspector Wadsworth wrote in October, 1895, that he was "grieved at the desolation shewn in the appearance of the grain fields [at the Mistawasis and Muskeg Lake reserves], caused by the total loss of crop from drought and other uncontrollable circumstances, in consequence, the Indians are very poor and despondent, having no ready and available resources, excepting hunting, and the Department." Wadsworth, October 25, 1895, NA, RG10, vol. 3894, file 97,015.

51. Sandy Lake Mission Death Register (1), record #6. John Piyēsīs was the son of Piyēsīs and Ahtahkakoop's daughter Mary.

52. Return showing crops sown and harvested by individual Indians in Carlton Agency, season of 1895, CHC, *Sessional Papers*, 1896 (no. 14), p. 478.

53. Wadsworth, October 25, 1895, NA, RG10, vol. 3894, file 97,015. Only six farmers had planted turnips.

54. Ibid. Also see Keith to superintendent general of Indian Affairs, February 17, 1896, NA, RG10, vol. 3894, file 97,015.

55. Ibid.

56. Ibid. Also see Keith, month-end report dated March 31, 1896, NA, RG10, vol. 1619. According to Keith, Wāskitoy had made "a bedstead & tables instead of sleeping and feeding on the floor." Also see Keith to superintendent general of Indian Affairs, July 23, 1895, CHC, *Sessional Papers*, 1896 (no. 14), p. 76.

57. See Ahtahkakoop Band paylists.

58. See Miller, *Shingwauk's Vision*, 110-12.

59. *The Guide*, July 1895, vol. 4, no. 1, and July, 1896, vol. 4, no. 1. *The Guide* was published monthly by the Indian Industrial School, Battleford. According to information in the paper, "all the mechanical work in connection with *The Guide* … [was] performed by our pupils."

60. See *The Guide*, July 1895, vol. 4, no. 1, and July, 1896, vol. 5, no. 1. Also see E. Matheson, principal of the Indian Industrial School, Battleford, to superintendent general of Indian Affairs, July 31, 1895, CHC, *Sessional Papers*, 1896 (no. 14), pp. 49-50. Matheson, who had begun his teaching career working for John Hines, took over as principal on April 1, 1895. Thomas Clarke had resigned December 31, 1894.

61. Forget's marginal note on a letter dated February 17, 1896, written by Keith to refute some of complaints made against him in October of 1895, NA, RG10, vol. 3894, file 97,015.

62. Keith, February 17, 1896, NA, RG10, vol. 3894, file 97,015.

63. Wadsworth, memorandum [and inspection report], October 25, 1895, NA, RG10, vol. 3894, file 97,015, p. 21.

64. Keith, February 17, 1896, NA, RG10, vol. 3894, file 97,015, pp. 14-15.

65. Keith, July 31, 1894, CHC, *Sessional Papers*, 1895 (no. 14), p. 76; and July 23, 1895, CHC, *Sessional Papers*, 1896 (no. 14), p. 173.

66. Keith to superintendent general of Indian Affairs, July 23, 1895, CHC, *Sessional Papers*, 1896 (no. 14), p. 173.

67. Wadsworth, memorandum and report, October 25, 1895, NA, RG10, vol. 3894, file 97,015.

68. Keith to Forget, February 17, 1896, vol. 3894, file 97,015.

69. Wadsworth, in a memorandum and report dated October 25, 1895, RG10, vol. 3894, file 97,015.

70. See Keith, March 31, 1896, NA, RG10, vol. 1619; and James Taylor, *The Guide*, July 1896, vol. 5, no. 1.

71. Reed, Annual Report for Indian Affairs, CHC, *Sessional Papers*, 1897 (no. 14), p. xxxviii.

72. Keith, monthly report dated March 31, 1896, NA, RG10, vol. 1619; and year-end report dated July 28, 1896, CHC, *Sessional Papers*, 1897 (no. 14), p. 161. Also see Keith to superintendent general of Indian Affairs, August 29, 1893, CHC, *Sessional Papers*, 1894 (no. 14), p. 82.

73. See Sandy Lake Mission Death Register, records #16–#29.

74. Keith, monthly reports dated March 31, 1896, and June 30, 1896, NA, RG10, vol. 1619. Also see Wadsworth, October 25, 1895, NA, RG10, vol. 3894, file 97,015, pp. 32 and 37.

75. McGibbon to superintendent general of Indian Affairs, September 21, 1896, CHC, *Sessional Papers*, 1897 (no. 14), p. 240.

76. Keith, monthly report dated June 30, NA, RG10, vol. 1619.

77. Ibid.

78. Ibid.

79. Forget, December 15, 1897, NA, RG10, vol. 3765, file 32,772.

80. Investigation against William J. O'Donnell, which started October 9, 1897, NA, RG10, vol. 3765, file 32,772.

81. Ibid.

82. Ibid.

83. Ibid.

84. Inspector W. J. Chisholm, Oct. 12, 1897, and various other letters, reports and telegrams in NA, RG10, vol. 3765, file 32,772. Chisholm had been appointed inspector of reserves for the Prince Albert and Battleford areas following the Liberal government's re-organization of the Indian Department.

85. Investigation against Keith, July 9, 1897; William J. Chisholm, October 12, 1897, and Keith, October 27, 1897, NA, RG10, vol. 3765, file 32,772.

86. Investigation against Keith, July 9, 1897; Chisholm, October 12, 1897, and Keith, October 27, 1897, NA, RG10, vol. 3765, file 32,772.

87. Ibid.

88. Chisholm, December 15, 1897, vol. 3765, file 32772.

89. Chisholm, November 20, 1897, NA, RG10, vol. 3765, file 32,772.

90. McGibbon, report dated August 6, 1896, NA, RG10, vol. 3894, file 97,015, pp. 34, 37. This report covered the period July 1, 1894 to June 30, 1896. The inspector noted that most of the houses were closed up but they "had been thoroughly cleaned up in and around." Also see Reed, October 1890, CHC, *Sessional Papers*, 1891 (no. 18), part 1, p. 135.

91. McGibbon, August 6, 1896, NA, RG10, vol. 3894, file 97,015, p. 31. The acreage sown to wheat, 179 acres, was a decrease of 5 acres from the previous year. The largest increase was oats, with 33 acres being planted compared to 19 in 1895. The acreage of other crops planted in 1896, with the figures for 1895 in brackets were: barley, 12 (15); potatoes, 13 (10); and root vegetables, 12 (3).

92. Keith, monthly report dated March 31, 1896, NA, RG10, vol. 1619. Also see Keith, July 28, 1896, CHC, *Sessional Papers*, 1893 (no. 14), p. 162.

93. McGibbon, August 6, 1896, NA, RG10, vol. 3894, file 97,015, and September 21, 1896, CHC, *Sessional Papers*, 1897 (no. 14), p. 240. McGibbon's report of August 6 gives statistics for receipt of new animals and the disposal of animals between 1894 and 1896. This includes a breakdown of the 55 animals that were killed for beef.

94. McGibbon's report on the houses, fields, etc. was contained in the report dated August 6, 1896, NA, RG10, vol. 3894, file 97,015.

95. McGibbon entered Baptiste's name twice, with different figures. In the first reference he said Baptiste had planted eight acres of wheat and barley and one acre of garden, all of which looked "well." In the second reference, he said Baptiste had "a good field of 7 acres wheat, 3 of oats and one of garden, good crop."

96. McGibbon, August 6, 1896, NA, RG10, vol. 3894, file 97,015.

97. Ibid.

98. Ibid.

99. Mackay, in a memorandum following his letter dated May 23, 1896, CMS, Microfilm Reel #A119. The same situation existed at the Red Pheasant and Battleford missions. On other reserves the society was allowed to use six acres of land while it was occupied by a mission, but the society did not have title to the land.

100. McGibbon to superintendent general of Indian Affairs, CHC, *Sessional Papers*, 1897 (no. 14), p. 372.

101. *The Guide*, July, 1896, vol. 5, no. 1.

102. This information was compiled primarily from the treaty paylists.

103. Section 114 of the Indian Act as amended in 1895. See *Indian Acts and Amendments, 1868-1950* (Ottawa: Treaties and Historical Research Centre, Department of Indian and Northern Affairs, 1981.)

104. Superintendent A. Bowen Perry to commissioner of the North-West Mounted Police (Annual Report for 1895), December 1, 1895, CHC, *Sessional Papers*, 1896 (no. 15), p. 64.

105. Reed to Forget, July 9, 1895, NA, RG10, vol. 3,852, file 60,511-1.

106. For example, see Reed to Forget, June 26, 1895, NA, vol. 3,852, file 60,511-1 and Forget, September 29, 1895, CHC, *Sessional Papers*, 1896 (no. 14), p. 199. Also see documents dated June 27, 1894, June 15, 22 and 26, 1895, and June 6, 1896, NA, RG10, vol. 3825, file 60,511-1.

107. F.H. Paget (commissioner's office), June 9, 1896, NA, RG10, vol. 3,825, file 60,511-1. Also see amendment to Section 114 of the Indian Act, *Indian Acts and Amendments, 1868-1950.*

108. See sections 137 to 138 of the Indian Act as amended in 1894, *Indian Acts and Amendments, 1868-1950.*

109. Reed, Annual Report for Indian Affairs, CHC, *Sessional Papers*, no. 14, 1897, p. xxxviii.

110. For an excellent study of residential schools, see Miller, *Shingwauk's Vision.*

111. Barry L. Ahenakew, review meeting November 23, 1997.

112. James Taylor, *The Guide*, Battleford, Saskatchewan, July 1896, vol. 5, no. 1. According to Taylor, these dances, "have been a great hindrance to both Christianity and civilisation."

113. Winter, Sturgeon Lake Journal, December 1, 1895-February 29, 1896, CMS, Microfilm Reel #119, entries for December 29, 1895, February 23, 1896, and elsewhere. Winter did not identify the son he considered to be the "ring-leader."

114. Winter, Sturgeon Lake Journal May 31-August 20, 1896, CMS, Microfilm Reel #119, entries for June 5-8, 1896.

115. Ibid., entry for June 6, 1896, CMS, Microfilm Reel #119. Also see ibid., September 4, 1896-November 29, 1896, entry for September 19, 1896.

116. Louis Ahenakew to Hines, December 23, 1895, CMS, Microfilm Reel #119.

117. Hines, Asissipi Journal, October 25-December 31, 1876, CMS, Microfilm Reel #A102, entry for November 22.

118. *The Guide*, Battleford, Saskatchewan, January, 1897, vol. 5, no. 7.

119. McGibbon, September 21, 1896, CHC, *Sessional Papers* 1897 (no. 14), p. 241.

120. For example in 1895 McGibbon indicated that during the past year the population of the Ahtahkakoop Band was 213. In comparison, the populations on the other reserves in the Carlton Agency were: Mistawasis, 146; Ayahtaskamikinam, 141 ; Okīnomotayēw, 99; Petihkwahākēw, 74; Flying Dust, 63; and Pelican Lake, 41. (See McGibbon, August 12, 1895, CHC, *Sessional Papers* 1896 (no. 14), p. 214.) The Ahtahkakoop Paylist for 1896 indicated that the population at Sandy Lake had grown to 219.

121. Ahtahkakoop Paylist for 1896. Interestingly, Ahtahkakoop's son-in-law Kā-tāh-twēhototawāt was still on the paylist although he had not been paid since 1884.

122. McGibbon, August 6, 1896. NA, RG10, vol. 3894, file 97,015. Also see McGibbon, September 21, 1896, CHC, *Sessional Papers*, no. 14, 1897, p. 241.

123. Myrtle Doucette (Nīkwēsis), taped in Cree by Freda Ahenakew, May 1994, on the Ahtahkakoop Reserve. Nīkwēsis was over 90 years of age at the time of the interview.

The images which appear on pages 511 (Catalogue Number R133.46, "Searching the Camp for Firearms and Stolen Goods," Collection of Glenbow Museum. Gift of the Devonian Foundation, 1979. Production date 1885, Rutherford, Robert William, 10.5 x 24.6 cm. Watercolor and Pencil on Paper) and 523 (Catalogue Number R133.41, "Escape of Applegarth, the Farm Instructor, and His Wife," Collection of Glenbow Museum. Gift of the Devonian Foundation, 1979. Production date 1885, Rutherford, Robert William [z RUT20773]d, 13.4 x 25.0 cm. Watercolor and Pencil on Paper) were provided by the Glenbow Museum.

Selected Bibliography

Archives

Hudson's Bay Company Archives (HBCA), Provincial Archives of Manitoba (PAM)

Carlton House Post Journals, Correspondence Books, Account Books, and District Reports
London Inward Correspondence from York Factory
Prince Albert Journals, Correspondence Books and Reports

National Archives of Canada (NA)

Church Missionary Society Papers (CMS, MG17, B2)

Department of Indian Affairs Papers (RG10, Black Series)

Royal Canadian Mounted Police Papers (RG18)

[Walter Butler] Cheadle, original of *Dr. Cheadle's Journal of a Trip Across Canada 1862-63* (MG24, H40, vol. 1)

William Joseph Christie's Journal of a Voyage from Fort Garry to Fort Simpson, MacKenzie River, by Land and Water, and of his Return by Dog-train to Carlton, performed on a tour of inspection of posts, August 22, 1872 to January 28, 1873 (MG29, A6)

Public Archives of Manitoba (PAM)

Church Missionary Society Papers (CMS, MG17, B2)
Morris Papers (MG12, B1)

Saskatchewan Archives Board (SAB)

David Mandelbaum Papers (SAB, R-875)
Edward Ahenakew Papers (SAB, R-1)

Anglican Diocese of Saskatchewan Archives, Prince Albert, Saskatchewan

Register of Births, Marriages and Deaths at Asissipi Mission, Diocese of Saskatchewan, North-West Territories of Canada, 1875

Sandy Lake Diocese of Saskatchewan Parish Register: Baptisms, Confirmations, Marriages, Burials, &c Mission Register [vol. 1]

Other Research Collections

Canada, Department of Indian Affairs and Northern Development, Treaties and Historical Research Centre, Ottawa

Office of the Treaty Commissioner, Saskatoon, Saskatchewan
Prince Albert Historical Society Archives
Saskatchewan Indian Federated College Library, Regina, Saskatchewan

Interviews and Oral History

Alexander Ahenakew

Alice Ahenakew

Angus Knife

Barry L. Ahenakew

Bella Starblanket

George Starblanket

Jim Kā-Nīpitēhtēw

Lance Ahenakew

Lloyd Starblanket

Marie Smallboy, Wolf Walker (Dan Minde) Resource Centre, Hobbema

Olive and Richard Robinson (Saskatoon)

Opapēcīw, Kā-āyāsitēyahkēkocin, and Kīsik-awāsis, who told some of the sacred stories
   to the younger generations

Paul Ahenakew

Willard Ahenakew

Working Teams

Core members of the review committee include: Chief Barry L. Ahenakew, Jeffrey D.
   Ahenakew, Willard Ahenakew, Ruth Ahenakew, Freda Ahenakew, Paul Ahenakew, and
   Deanna Christensen. Freda Ahenakew, Jean Okimāsis, and Arok Wolvengrey assisted
   with translations and spellings of Cree words.

Published and Unpublished Primary Sources

Boulton, Charles A. *I Fought Riel: A Military Memoir*, ed. Heather Robertson. Toronto:
   James Lorimer & Company, 1985.

Bray, Edgar. Diary of Work Done in Saskatchewan in TP 49-6-3, TP 50-6-3, TP 50-7-3,
   TP 51-6-3, TP 51-7-3 [Ahtahkakoop and Mistawasis Reserves], 1878, Department of
   Indian Affairs and Northern Development, Indian Lands Registry, Field Book #726,
   Microfiche #203.

Bray, Edgar. Field Notes and Report of the Survey of the Asissippi (Chief Atakukoop) and
   Snake Plain (Chief Mistowasis) Indian Reserves, Green Lake Road, North West
   Territory, August 9, 1878 to October 14, 1878, Department of Indian Affairs and
   Northern Development, Indian Lands Registry, Field Book #725, Microfiche #1381.
   The report was dated January 10, 1879, at Oakville, Ontario.

Cameron, William Bleasdell. *Blood Red the Sun*. Edmonton: Hurtig, 1977.

Canada. House of Commons. *Sessional Papers*.

Canada. *Descriptions and Plans of Certain Indian Reserves in the Province of Manitoba and the North-West Territories, 1889*, compiled by John C. Nelson, 1887.

Cheadle, [Walter Butler]. *Dr. Cheadle's Journal of a Trip Across Canada 1862-63*. Introduction and notes by A.G. Doughty and Gustave Lanctot. Ottawa: Graphic Publishers Ltd., 1931.

Coues, Elliott, ed. *New Light on the Early History of the Greater Northwest: The Manuscript Journals of Alexander Henry and of David Thompson, 1799–1814*, vol. 2. New York: Francis P. Harper, 1897.

Cowie, Isaac. *The Company of Adventurers: A Narrative of Seven Years in the Service of the Hudson's Bay Company During 1867–1874 on the Great Buffalo Plains*. Toronto: William Briggs, 1913.

Earl of Southesk. *Saskatchewan and the Rocky Mountains: A Diary and Narrative of Travel, Sport, and Adventure, during a Journey through the Hudson's Bay Company's Territories, in 1859 and 1860*. Toronto: James Campbell and Son, 1875.

Erasmus, Peter. *Buffalo Days and Nights*, as told to Henry Thompson, intro. Irene Spry. Calgary: Glenbow-Alberta Institute, 1976.

Federation of Saskatchewan Indians. "Elders' Interpretation of Treaty 4: A Report on the Treaty Interpretation Project," Regina: Indian Rights and Treaties Research Programme, August 31, 1978.

Fine Day. "Incidents of the Rebellion," in *The Cree Rebellion of '84: Chapters in the North-West History Prior to 1890*, Battleford Historical Society, vol. 1, no. 1, June 1926.

Franklin, John. *Narrative of a Journey to the Shore of the Polar Sea in the Years 1819, 20, 21, and 22*, vol. 1, second edition. London: John Murray, Albemarle-Street, 1824.

Hines, John. *The Red Indians of the Plains: Thirty Years' Missionary Experience in the Saskatchewan*. London: Society for Promoting Christian Knowledge, 1915.

Jefferson, Robert. *Fifty Years on the Saskatchewan*, Canadian North-West Society Publications, vol. 1, no. 5, 1929, Battleford, Saskatchewan.

Kane, Paul. *Wanderings of An Artist Among the Indians of North America from Canada to Vancouver's Island and Oregon Through the Hudson's Bay Company's Territory and Back Again*. London: Longman, Brown, Green, Longmans, and Roberts, 1859.

McDougall, John. *Opening the Great West: Experiences of a Missionary in 1875–76*. Calgary: Glenbow-Alberta Institute, 1970.

McLean W.J. "Reminiscences of the Tragic Events at Frog Lake and in [the] Fort Pitt District with some of the experiences of the writer and his family during the North West Rebellion of 1885." HBCA Copy No. 80.

Messiter, Charles Alston. *Sport and Adventures among the North American Indians*. London: R.H. Porter, 1890.

Milton, Viscount and Cheadle, W.B. *The North-West Passage by Land, being the narrative of an Expedition from the Atlantic to the Pacific*. London: Cassell, Petter, and Galpin, 1865.

Morris, Alexander. *The Treaties of Canada with the Indians of Manitoba and the North-*

West Territories, Including the Negotiations on Which They were Based, and Other Information Relating Thereto. Toronto: Belfords, Clarke & Co., 1880. Facsimile edition published by Coles, Toronto, 1979.

North-West Mounted Police. *Opening up the West, being the Official Reports to Parliament of the Activities of the Royal North-West Mounted Police Force from 1874-1881 by the Commissioners of the Royal North-West Mounted Police*. Introduction by Commissioner W.L. Higgitt. Facsimile edition published by Coles, Toronto, 1973.

North-West Mounted Police. *Settlers and Rebels: Being the Official Reports to Parliament of the Activities of the Royal North-West Mounted Police Force from 1882–1885*. Introduction by Commissioner W.L. Higgitt. Facsimile edition published by Coles, Toronto, 1973.

North-West Mounted Police. *The New West: Being the Official Reports to Parliament of the Activities of the Royal North-West Mounted Police Force from 1888–1889*. Introduction by Commissioner W.L. Higgitt. Facsimile edition published by Coles, Toronto, 1973.

Palliser, John. *The Papers of the Palliser Expedition*, edited with an introduction and notes by Irene M. Spry. Toronto: The Champlain Society, 1968.

Steele, S.B. *Forty Years in Canada*. Toronto: McClelland, Goodchild & Stewart, 1915.

Thompson, David. *David Thompson's Narrative: 1784–1812*, Publications of the Champlain Society. Toronto: The Champlain Society, 1962.

Weekes, Mary. *The Last Buffalo Hunter: As told to her by Norbert Welsh*. New York: Thomas Nelson and Sons, 1939.

Published and Unpublished Secondary Sources

[Ahenakew, Edward]. "Story of the Ahenakews," ed. Ruth Matheson Buck, *Saskatchewan History*, vol. 17, no. 1, 1964.

[Rundle, Robert Terrill]. *The Rundle Journals: 1840–1848*, with introduction and notes by Gerald M. Hutchinson, edited by Hugh Dempsey. Calgary: Historical Society of Alberta and Glenbow-Alberta Institute, 1977.

Abrams, G.W.D. *Prince Albert, The First Century*. Saskatoon: Modern Press, 1966.

Ahenakew, Edward. "Genealogical Sketch of My Family," written April 27, 1948. American Philosophical Society Library.

Ahenakew, Edward. *Voices of the Plains Cree*, ed. Ruth Buck. Toronto: McClelland and Stewart Limited, 1973. Reprinted by Canadian Plains Research Center, 1995.

Archer, John H. *Saskatchewan: A History*. Saskatoon: Western Producer Prairie Books, 1980

Beal, Bob, and Macleod, Rod. *Prairie Fire: The 1885 North-West Rebellion*. Edmonton: Hurtig, 1984. Edition cited: Toronto: McClelland & Stewart Inc., 1994.

Black, Norman F. *History of Saskatchewan and the North West Territories*, vol. 1. Regina: Saskatchewan Historical Company, 1913.

Carter, Sarah. *Lost Harvests: Prairie Indian Reserve Farmers and Government*. Montreal & Kingston: McGill-Queen's University Press, 1990.

Charlebois, Peter. *The Life of Louis Riel.* Toronto: NC Press, 1975.

Christensen, Deanna. "Selected Aspects of Fort Pitt's History." Saskatchewan Parks and Renewable Resources, February 29, 1984.

Christensen, Deanna. "A 'Convenient Place': A History of Fort Carlton, 1810–1885." Saskatchewan Parks and Renewable Resources, 1985.

Christensen, Deanna, and Fieguth, Menno. *Historic Saskatchewan.* Toronto: Oxford University Press, 1986.

Dempsey, Hugh A. *Big Bear: The End of Freedom.* Vancouver/Toronto: Douglas & McIntyre, 1984.

Dempsey, Hugh A. *Red Crow, Warrior Chief.* Saskatoon: Western Producer Prairie Books, 1980.

Dietz, Alexander. Ahtahkakoop Genealogy Report prepared for the Ahtahkakoop Band, 1999.

Elias, Peter Douglas. *The Dakota of the Canadian Northwest: Lessons for Survival,* Manitoba Studies in Native History 5. Winnipeg: University of Manitoba Press, 1988.

Epp, Henry T. *Long Ago Today: The Story of Saskatchewan's Earliest Peoples.* Saskatoon: Saskatchewan Archaeological Society, 1991.

Friesen, Gerald. *The Canadian Prairies: A History.* Toronto: University of Toronto Press, 1984.

Fung, Ka-Iu, ed. *Atlas of Saskatchewan.* Saskatoon: University of Saskatchewan, 1999.

Goldring, Philip. "Whisky, Horses and Death: The Cypress Hills Massacre and its Sequel," *Canadian Historic Sites: Occasional Papers in Archaeology and History #21,* published by the National Historic Parks and Sites Branch, 1979.

Government of Saskatchewan. *Indian Lands and Canada's Responsibility—The Saskatchewan Position,* n. d.

Hildebrandt, Walter. *Views from Fort Battleford: Constructed Visions of an Anglo-Canadian West.* Regina: Canadian Plains Research Center, 1994.

Landes, Ruth. *Ojibwa Religion and the Midēwiwin.* Madison, Wisconsin: The University of Wisconsin Press, 1968.

Light, Douglas W. *Footprints in the Dust.* North Battleford, Saskatchewan: Turner-Warwick, 1987.

Looy, A.J. "Saskatchewan's First Indian Agent: M.G. Dickieson," *Saskatchewan History,* vol. 32, no. 3, Autumn, 1979.

Maclean, John. *Native Tribes of Canada.* Toronto: William Briggs, 1896. Facsimile edition published by Coles, Toronto, 1980.

Mandelbaum, David G. *The Plains Cree: An Ethnographic, Historical, and Comparative Study.* Regina: Canadian Plains Research Center, 1979.

McDougall, John. *George Millward McDougall: The Pioneer, Patriot and Missionary.* Toronto: William Briggs, 1888.

McNeil, Kent. *Native Claims in Rupert's Land and the North-Western Territory: Canada's Constitutional Obligations,* Studies in Aboriginal Rights, no. 5, University of Saskatchewan, Native Law Centre, 1982.

Meyer, David. "Time-Depth of the Western Woods Cree Occupation of Northern Ontario, Manitoba, and Saskatchewan," *Papers of the Eighteenth Algonquian Conference*, ed. William Cowan. Ottawa: Carleton University, 1987.

Miller, J.R. *Shingwauk's Vision: A History of Native Residential Schools.* Toronto: University of Toronto Press, 1996.

Morton, Arthur S. *A History of the Canadian West to 1870–71*, second edition edited by Lewis G. Thomas. Published in co-operation with the University of Saskatchewan by the University of Toronto Press, 1973.

Mulvaney, Charles Pelham. *The History of the North-West Rebellion of 1885.* Toronto: A.H. Hovey & Company, 1885.

Murray, Jean E. "Early History of Emmanuel College," *Saskatchewan History*, vol. 60, no. 3, 1956.

Opekokew, Delia. *The First Nations: Indian Government and the Canadian Confederation.* Saskatoon: Federation of Saskatchewan Indians, 1980.

Payton, W.F. *The Diocese of Saskatchewan of the Anglican Church of Canada: 100 Years 1874–1974 (A Historical Sketch of the Diocese of Saskatchewan of the Anglican Church of Canada)* [circa 1973].

Peel, Bruce. *Steamboats on the Saskatchewan.* Saskatoon: Prairie Books, The Western Producer, 1972.

Pettipas, Katherine. *Severing the Ties that Bind: Government Repression of Indigenous Religious Ceremonies on the Prairies*, Manitoba Studies in Native History VII, University of Manitoba Press, 1994.

Price, Richard, ed. *The Spirit of the Alberta Indian Treaties.* Montreal: Institute for Research on Public Policy [in partnership with the Indian Association of Alberta], 1979.

Ray, Arthur J. *Indians in the Fur Trade: Their Role as Hunters, Trappers and Middlemen in the Lands Southwest of Hudson Bay, 1660–1870.* Toronto: University of Toronto Press, 1974.

Richards, J. Howard, ed. *Atlas of Saskatchewan.* Saskatoon: University of Saskatchewan, 1969.

Roe, Frank Gilbert. *The North American Buffalo: A critical study of the species in its wild state*, 2nd ed. Toronto: University of Toronto Press, 1970.

Ronaghan, Allen. "Three Scouts and the Cart Train," *Alberta History*, Winter 1977.

Russell, Dale R. "The Ethnographic and Demographic Context of Central Saskatchewan to 1800," *Nipawin Reservoir Heritage Study, vol. 3: Regional Overview and Research Considerations*, David Burley and David Meyer, eds. Saskatchewan Research Council Report No. C-805-25-E-82, Saskatoon, 1982.

Russell, Dale R. *Eighteenth-Century Western Cree and Their Neighbours*, Archaeological Survey of Canada, Mercury Series Paper 143. Hull, Quebec: Canadian Museum of Civilization, 1991.

Russell, R.C. *The Carlton Trail: The Broad Highway into the Saskatchewan Country From the Red River Settlement, 1840–1880.* Saskatoon: Prairie Books, The Western Producer, 1971.

Schlesier, Karl. "Rethinking The Midewiwin And The Plains Ceremonial Called The Sun Dance," *Plains Anthropological Journal of the Plains Anthropological Society*, vol. 35, number 127, February 1990.

Sissons, Constance. *John Kerr*. Toronto: Oxford University Press, 1946.

Stanley, George F.G. "The Half-Breed 'Rising' of 1875," *Canadian Historical Review*, December, 1936.

Stanley, George F.G. *The Birth of Western Canada: a History of the Riel Rebellions*. London: Longmans, Green and Co. Ltd., 1936. Second edition with unaltered text published by the University of Toronto Press, 1961.

Stobie, Margaret R. *The Other Side of Rebellion: The Remarkable Story of Charles Bremner and his Furs*. Edmonton: NeWest, 1986.

Stonechild, Blair, and Bill Waiser. *Loyal till Death: Indians and the North-West Rebellion*. Calgary: Fifth House, 1997.

Tobias, John L. "A Brief History of the Ahtahkakoop Band, 1870–1920" (manuscript, Federation of Saskatchewan Indians), 1975.

Tobias, John L. "Canada's Subjugation of the Plains Cree, 1879–1885, *The Canadian Historical Review* 64, no. 4, 1983.

Tough, Frank J. "Aboriginal Rights Versus the Deed of Surrender: The Legal Rights of Native Peoples and Canada's Acquisition of the Hudson's Bay Company Territory," *Prairie Forum*, Special Issue: Native Studies, vol. 17, no. 2, Fall 1992.

Wiebe, Rudy and Bob Beal. *War in the West: Voices of the 1885 Rebellion*. Toronto: McClelland and Stewart, 1885.

Wilson, Clifford. Off-print from papers read before the Historical and Scientific Society of Manitoba, serial 3, no. 5, 1950.

Newspapers

Brantford *Daily Courier*

Brantford *Daily Expositor*

Brantford *Weekly Expositor*

Illustrated War News

Montreal *Gazette*

Ottawa *Free Press*

Prince Albert *Times*

Saskatchewan Herald, Battleford

The Globe, Toronto

The Guide, Battleford Indian Industrial School

Index

The Descendants of Ahtahkakoop and His Brothers

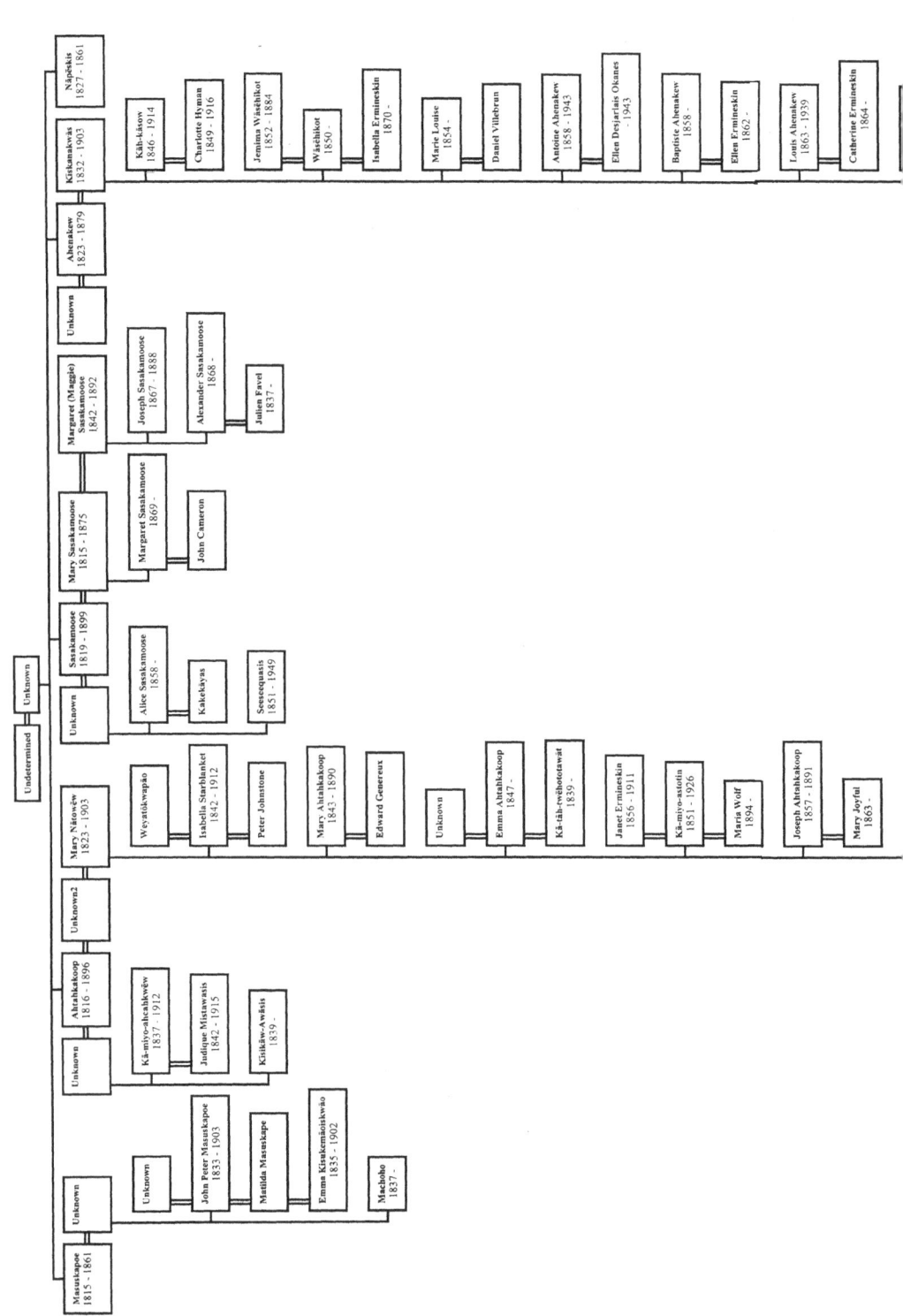

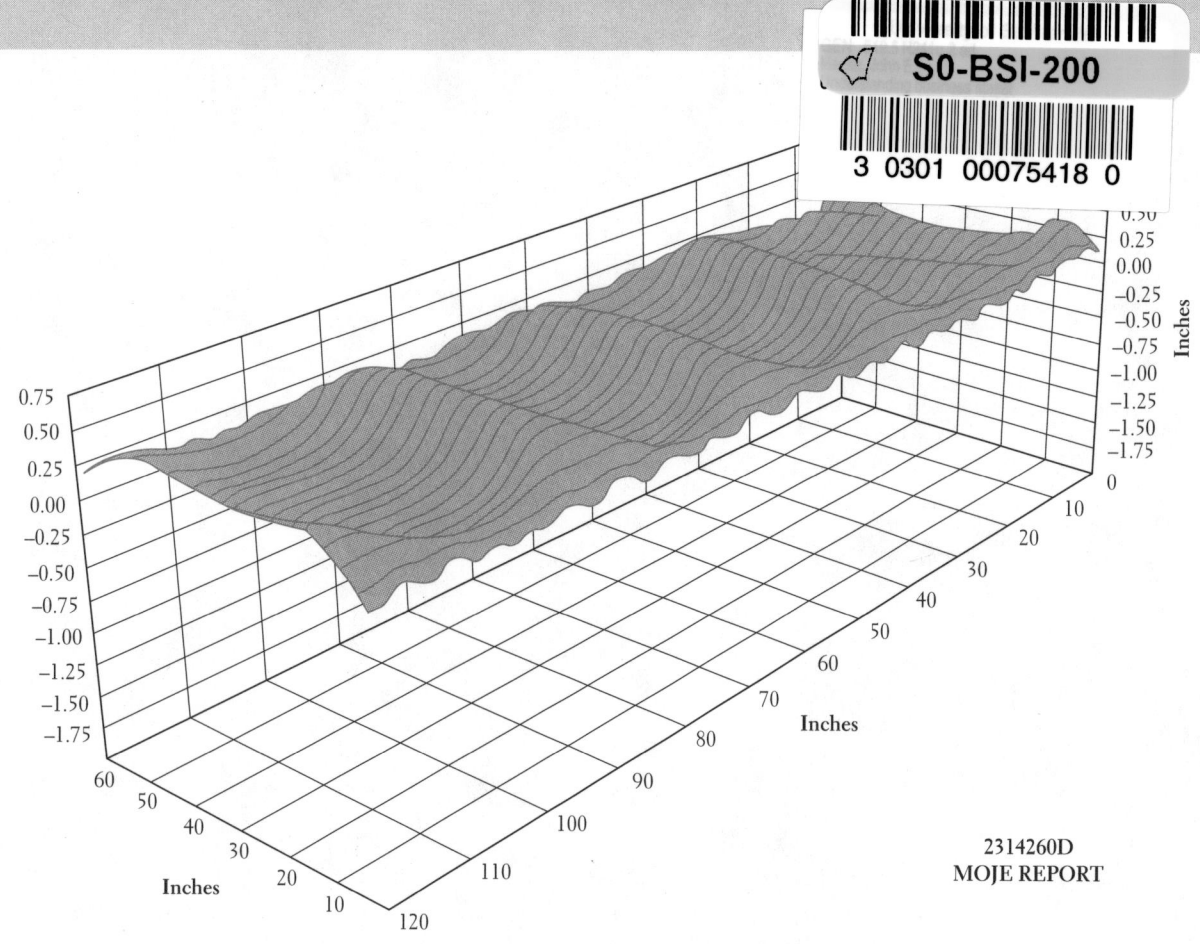

2314260D
MOJE REPORT

This is an exaggerated profile of a large aluminum sheet made from x-ray measurements. Quality engineers use this plot to monitor the flatness of each sheet, an essential characteristic to control for high quality. The idea of constantly improving quality by controlling variation is of vital importance and relies on a strong statistical foundation.

UNDERSTANDING BUSINESS STATISTICS

THE IRWIN SERIES IN PRODUCTION OPERATIONS MANAGEMENT

Aquilano and Chase
Fundamentals of Operations Management
First Edition

Chase and Aquilano
Production and Operations Management
Sixth Edition

Berry et al.
ITEK, Inc.
First Edition

Hill
Manufacturing Strategy: Text & Cases
Second Edition

Klein
Revitalizing Manufacturing: Text & Cases
First Edition

Lambert and Stock
Strategic Logistics Management
Third Edition

Leenders, Fearon, and England
Purchasing and Materials Management
Ninth Edition

Lotfi and Pegels
Decision Support Systems for Production & Operations Management for Use with IBM PC
Second Edition

Nahmias
Production and Operations Analysis
Second Edition

Niebel
Motion and Time Study
Eighth Edition

Sasser, Clark, Garvin, Graham, Jaikumar, and Maister
Cases in Operations Management: Analysis & Action
First Edition

Schonberger and Knod
Operations Management: Continuous Improvement
Fifth Edition

Stevenson
Production/Operations Management
Fourth Edition

Vollmann, Berry, and Whybark
Manufacturing Planning & Control Systems
Third Edition

Whybark
International Operations Management: A Selection of Imede Cases
First Edition

THE IRWIN SERIES IN STATISTICS

Aczel
Complete Business Statistics
Second Edition

Duncan
Quality Control & Industrial Statistics
Fifth Edition

Emory and Cooper
Business Research Methods
Fourth Edition

Gitlow, Gitlow, Oppenheim, and Oppenheim
Tools and Methods for the Improvement of Quality
First Edition

Hall and Adelman
Computerized Business Statistics
Second Edition

Hanke and Reitsch
Understanding Business Statistics
Second Edition

Mason and Lind
Statistical Techniques in Business and Economics
Eighth Edition

Neter, Wasserman, and Kutner
Applied Linear Statistical Models
Third Edition

Neter, Wasserman, and Kutner
Applied Linear Regression Models
Second Edition

Siegel
Practical Business Statistics
Second Edition

Webster
Applied Statistics for Business and Economics
First Edition

Wilson and Keating
Business Forecasting
Second Edition

THE IRWIN SERIES IN QUANTITATIVE METHODS AND MANAGEMENT SCIENCE

Bierman, Bonini, and Hausman
Quantitative Analysis for Business Decisions
Eighth Edition

Knowles
Management Science: Building and Using Models
First Edition

Lotfi and Pegels
Decision Support Systems for Management Science & Operations Research
Second Edition

Stevenson
Introduction to Management Science
Second Edition

Turban and Meredith
Fundamentals of Management Science
Sixth Edition

© RICHARD D. IRWIN, INC., 1991 and 1994

Senior sponsoring editor:	Richard T. Hercher, Jr.
Developmental editor:	Gail Korosa
Marketing manager:	Robb Linsky
Project editor:	Stephanie M. Britt
Production manager:	Ann Cassady
Art coordinator:	Mark Malloy
Compositor:	Weimer Graphics, Inc.
Typeface:	10/12 Electra
Printer:	R. R. Donnelley & Sons Company

Library of Congress Cataloging-in-Publication Data

Hanke, John E.,
   Understanding business statistics / John E. Hanke, Arthur G. Reitsch.—2nd ed.
      p.   cm.
   ISBN 0-256-11219-3 (acid-paper)   0-256-14505-9 (Instructor's Edition)
   1. Industrial management—Statistical methods.   I. Reitsch, Arthur G.,   II. Title.
   HD30.215.H36   1994
   650'.01'5195—dc20   93–16827

Printed in the United States of America
   3 4 5 6 7 8 9 0   DOC   0 9 8 7 6 5 4

UNDERSTANDING BUSINESS STATISTICS

Second Edition

· ·

John E. Hanke
Arthur G. Reitsch

Both of Eastern Washington University

IRWIN

Burr Ridge, Illinois
Boston, Massachusetts
Sydney, Australia

To produce a mighty book, you must choose a mighty theme.
No great and enduring volume can ever be written on the flea,
though many there be that have tried—Herman Melville, *Moby Dick*

. . . .

Dedicated to Geri, Harry, Irene, and Jack (who don't need to read it);
Judy and Judy (who have and might, respectively);
Jill, Amy, Julie, Katrina, and Kevin (who should, but probably never will);
and especially all of our students (who had better).

PREFACE

· ·

But to go to school in a summer morn,
Oh, it drives all joy away!
Under a cruel eye outworn,
The little ones spend the day—
In sighing and dismay.

Blake, *The Schoolboy*

We have written this book in order to bridge the gap between the theoretical foundations of statistics and the need for business managers to extract useful decision-making information from data collections. We understand that a study of statistics may, at first, not seem to be a very exciting endeavor. We also know that once the techniques become familiar, exciting results often follow, results that provide assistance and insight to the difficult task of making decisions.

ACKNOWLEDGMENTS

We wish to thank several thousand previous students for their guidance in developing our writing style, and in particular to those students who helped us with the manuscript during class testing. We are particularly indebted to Judy Johnson, a rate analyst at Washington Water Power, who ran our SAS programs and provided data sets for both examples and exercises. A special thanks to Leonard Presby of William Paterson College for his help in problem checking. We also thank adopters and colleagues across the country (listed below) who reviewed the text and manuscript for this second edition and helped greatly in its refinement. We made an effort to respond to every suggestion. Nevertheless, we take responsibility for the final product and trust it will be pleasing to teach and learn from.

Michael Broida, *Miami University of Ohio*
Thomas MacFarland, *Nova University*
Anil Gulati, *Western New England College*
Elzbieta Trybus, *California State University, Northridge*
Walter Johnston, *Southwest Texas State University*
Mark Bomball, *Eastern Illinois University*

Nagraj Balakrishnan, *Tulane University*

Choonsan Kim, *Western Illinois University*

Robert Hull, *Western Illinois University*

Barbara McKinney, *Western Michigan University*

Steve Rigdon, *Southern Illinois University at Edwardsville*

Gayne Clifford, *North Idaho College*

Sandra Strasser, *Valparaiso University*

We would like to thank again the individuals who aided in developing the first edition of *Understanding Business Statistics*. We extend our sincere thanks to: Mary Jo Boehms, Jackson State Community College; John Briscoe, Indiana State University, Southeast; Alice Griswold, University of Dubuque; J. Morgan Jones, University of North Carolina, Chapel Hill; Someswar Kesh, University of Texas, Arlington; David D. Drueger, St. Cloud State University; Steven W. Lamb, Indiana State University; Frank Leroi, College of San Mateo; Mickey McCormick, Spokane Falls Community College; Peter Phung, El Paso Community College; John Shannon, Suffolk University; Lois Shufeldt, Southwest Missouri State; Scott Stevens, James Madison University; Paul A. Thompson, Ohio State University; Charles E. Tychsen, Northern Virginia Community College; George E. Vlahos, University of Dayton; Min-Chiang Wang, Washington State University; Ray Whitman, University of the District of Columbia; and Mark Wilson, University of Charleston.

Finally, we thank the makers of modern word processors, without whom we might have given up or settled for an inferior product. We also extend thanks to all the people at Irwin for their support. It was a pleasure to work with such a special group of professionals, especially, Dick Hercher, Gail Korosa, and Stephanie Britt. Portions of this text, particularly several data sets, are adapted from those that appeared in our *Business Forecasting* text published by Allyn & Bacon, whom we credit for this reuse.

To the students who attack the subject of business statistics with this book, we sincerely hope you gain an appreciation of the power of these techniques to assist business managers in their most important task: making decisions in the face of uncertainty.

John E. Hanke
Arthur G. Reitsch

NOTE TO THE STUDENT

As you begin your study of business statistics you should know that this material is not here to weed out the faint of heart. Every quality business school requires a sound background in this subject because so many business decisions today are based on a proper analysis of collected data.

We have attempted to present the material, both the easy concepts and the more difficult ones, in an easy-to-understand way. There are numerous examples throughout the text, along with both solved and unsolved exercises. Be sure to check the back of the book for check figures on most of the odd-numbered exercises.

In order for you to master the subjects in this book it is necessary for you to read the material, work some of the exercises and attend class regularly. This is not a subject you can learn by cramming the night before an exam. You may find the video lectures that accompany this text to be useful in understanding the material. They cover the basic topics in Chapters 1 through 10 and are available through your instructor. There is also a Student Solutions Manual and a Study Guide available for additional help.

When you complete your study of statistics, you can be sure you are well prepared for the data analysis tasks that lie ahead in your business career. The topics in this book constitute a wide variety of ways to extract useful information from the data that exist, and that are constantly being collected, in every organization.

We hope your "bag of tricks" will serve you well during your career. Although you will forget some specific details of procedures that are not constantly used, our consulting experience has shown that business school graduates *do* retain the basic premise of statistics: If you know the right methods, almost any data collection can yield fruitful information.

We imagine a meeting sometime in the future attended by the leaders of your company and yourself. A thorny problem is being discussed when the company president turns to you and says, "You studied business in college; how do you see the situation?" We sincerely hope this book and your course have prepared you for this moment, as you begin: "My analysis of the data indicates that . . ."

CONTENTS

. . . .

Introduction to Statistics

There are three kinds of lies: lies, damned lies, and statistics.

B. Disraeli

Objectives

When you have completed this chapter, you will be able to:

Explain the role of statistics in the decision-making process.

Explain the role of the computer in statistics.

Perform computations using summation notation.

 N ational spending on health care rose 11% between 1990 and 1991, the fifth consecutive year of double-digit increases. This trend, reported in *American Demographics* (April 1992, p. 19), is projected to continue through 1996. Health care accounted for 14% of the total output of goods and services in the United States in 1992, up from 12% in 1990. That's $817 billion a year spent on getting or staying well.

This chapter discusses topics essential to your study of business statistics. This book should aid your development as a business manager by improving your ability to make timely, efficient decisions. The authors sincerely hope that it will help you in your business career.

WHY STATISTICS IS IMPORTANT TO MANAGERS

Many entry-level business positions require a working knowledge of statistics. Many other beginning jobs require familiarity with data collection and analysis, or the analysis of reports and studies based on statistics. Knowledge of statistical principles is essential in such jobs. Midlevel and senior managers are also increasingly involved in statistical analysis, especially with personal computers and statistical software. One business leader recently told us, "The day of the seat-of-the-pants manager is almost gone."

The situation described at this chapter's beginning shows the need for a sound statistical background. It is a serious matter that health costs are increasing at a double-digit rate. But how was this information obtained? Was a sample of hospitals and/or doctors taken? If so, how many were sampled? Which hospitals and/or doctors were surveyed? Was the sample large enough to justify the reported increase? You'll deal with many such questions in this book.

THE PURPOSE OF STATISTICS

Every day people are bombarded by data. "Statistics" are associated with numbers generated in news reports, advertising claims, baseball earned run averages, opinion polls, and public debates. Modern organizations have millions of data items in their paper and computer records. Hundreds or thousands of data values are added to this total daily. Some of these additions come about through the normal course of business recordkeeping; others result from special studies and research efforts.

Without statistical procedures, an organization could never make sense of the mountain of data[1] that its business generates. The purpose of the statistical analyses you'll study in this text is to manipulate, summarize, and investigate data to obtain useful decision-making information.

---

[1]Throughout this book the term *data* is treated as a plural term. (The singular form of this word is *datum*.)

Purpose of Statistics

> Statistical analysis is used to manipulate, summarize, and investigate data to obtain useful decision-making information.

Since the collection and study of data are important in many professions, a statistics background is valuable for a variety of careers. Government statistical offices release new numerical information on inflation and unemployment monthly. Forecasters, economists, financial advisors, and policymakers in business and government study these data to make informed decisions. To treat their patients effectively, dentists, doctors, and hospital personnel must understand statistics in research studies reported in medical journals. Elected officials use public opinion polls to gauge what legislation their constituents want. Businesses base decisions on market research studies of consumer buying patterns. Ranchers and farmers record data to study new feeds and crop varieties. Quality control engineers gather data on the reliability of manufactured parts and products. (Chapter 13 provides several examples.)

In the authors' experience, virtually every business manager needs a background in statistical analysis. Many jobs, especially in large companies, require extensive use of statistics. Such jobs often advertise for applicants with sound statistical or quantitative skills.

Although many other jobs don't require a statistical background, such a background may become increasingly important as a person achieves higher positions in management. In our consulting work we've helped managers in personnel, marketing, advertising, production, finance, computer applications, and public relations with their statistical problems. Just as the writing skills you began developing in grade school are vital in your college career, so will the statistical skills you develop through studying this book aid your business career.

STUDENT DATA BASE

Throughout this book are problems relating to the "student data base." These problems ask you to use the statistical techniques you've studied to analyze data generated in your own class. After each class member fills out the questionnaire in Table 1.1, the resulting data can be used in the end-of-chapter problems.

USING COMPUTERS WITH THIS TEXT

As you'll soon discover, statistical manipulation of data requires considerable arithmetic. For this reason, modern computers are essential for most statistical tasks.

This text will provide numerous examples of computer output. Typical data analysis packages have been chosen for these demonstrations. Keep in mind that literally hundreds of data analysis computer programs now available perform similar functions. During your career you may not use the packages in this text, but the ones you'll use will be similar in function and printed output.

TABLE 1.1 Student Questionnaire for Class Data Base

1. My class standing is currently:
   _____ Freshman   _____ Sophomore   _____ Junior
   _____ Senior   _____ Grad Student   _____ Other
2. I am: _____ Female   _____ Male
3. High school grade point average: _____
4. My age is: _____
5. I smoke cigarettes: _____ Regularly _____ Sometimes _____ Never

Please circle one of the following numbers to indicate your level of agreement with each of the statements below:

> 1—Strongly agree
> 2—Agree
> 3—Neutral or no opinion
> 4—Disagree
> 5—Strongly disagree

	SA	A	N	D	SD
6. A knowledge of statistics will be an important part of my working life after I leave college.	1	2	3	4	5
7. It would be a good idea to impose more stringent admission requirements for the business administration program.	1	2	3	4	5
8. Given the nature of statistics, I would prefer to have a quiz each week.	1	2	3	4	5
9. I usually do well in math classes.	1	2	3	4	5
10. In my business career, ethical considerations will be as important to me as making a profit.	1	2	3	4	5
11. Companies should have special programs and policies to help employees starting families.	1	2	3	4	5

Two of the best-known mainframe computer packages for statistical applications are MINITAB (MINITAB Project, University Park, Pennsylvania), and SAS (Statistical Analysis System, SAS Institute, Cary, North Carolina).

MINITAB

This book uses MINITAB since it's one of the easiest of the commonly available statistical packages and it can be employed on both mainframes and microcomputers. We aren't suggesting that you should use MINITAB during your career. Rather, we're showing how easily you can solve statistical applications using the computer. MINITAB instructions and examples are provided throughout the body and at the end of most chapters. Available in most university bookstores, *The Student Edition of MINITAB* is a helpful guide for using MINITAB.

SAS

More powerful than MINITAB, SAS is used more frequently in business applications. SAS instructions and examples appear at the end of selected chapters. The *SAS Guide for Use with Understanding Business Statistics* has been developed specifically for use with this textbook.

COMPUTERIZED BUSINESS STATISTICS

The microcomputer package *Computerized Business Statistics* (CBS), a statistical software package designed specifically for use with this textbook, runs on IBM and IBM-compatible microcomputers. It consists of an instructional text and either a 5.25-inch or 3.5-inch diskette. An overview of each statistical model plus illustrative examples appear at the end of most chapters in this text.

DATA SETS

Appendix C includes a data base of 200 company employees with nine variables so realistic assignments can be made that simulate real-world situations. A data disk with these data and over 50 data sets is also available.

STUDY GUIDE

The *Study Guide for Use with Understanding Business Statistics* available with this text contains input instructions for sample problems using MINITAB and CBS.

APPROACH OF THIS BOOK

This book begins by discussing ways to collect data in the business setting (Chapter 2) and presents easy-to-use graphical summaries of these values (Chapter 3). Numerical summary methods (Chapter 4) are then covered before the discussion moves on to certain important theoretical data distributions (Chapters 5, 6, and 7). The book's first part finishes with the important subjects of estimating unknown statistical values (Chapter 8) and testing the validity of statements made about these values (Chapters 9 and 10).

The second part of the book begins with a technique for determining the relationship between two qualitative variables (Chapter 11) and a variance ratio test (Chapter 12). The important topic of quality control, which uses most of the techniques learned in Chapters 1 through 12, appears in Chapter 13.

The final part of the book deals with sophisticated methods to examine relationships among two or more quantitative variables. All these methods are widely used in business today. Computer use is emphasized throughout these chapters since these procedures require complex arithmetic.

Each chapter contains numerous examples illustrating the concepts under discussion. In addition, Chapters 5 and 9 pose "situations" early in the discussion and resolve them after presenting the statistical technique. These situations realistically depict problems an organization can solve using the right statistical procedure.

A summary near the end of each chapter is followed by "Applications of Statistical Concepts in the Business World." A glossary of key terms, a list of key formulas, several solved exercises, and many unsolved exercises come next. By working through these brief problems, you should be able to master each chapter's topic before moving to the next. Three or four Extended Exercises (minicases) illustrating important chapter concepts follow the Exercises section. Some Extended Exercises are worked through or "solved"; others invite you to find the correct technique and apply it to a practical situation.

Finally, most chapters discuss using Computerized Business Statistics (CBS), MINITAB, or SAS to solve statistical problems. Detailed instructions will help computer novices use the computer to solve statistical problems.

SUMMATION NOTATION

Many statistical procedures call for the addition of several terms or factors. These addition procedures use a shorthand notation called *summation notation*. This method of indicating a sum will be used throughout this book, so you must understand this notation. If you already know summation notation, skip this section.

Summation Sign

The capital Greek letter sigma (Σ) is the **summation sign.** It instructs you to add all the terms that follow it. The key point is that all quantities covered by the summation sign must first be calculated, *then* added together. For example, the notation Σx means to identify all the values designated by x and add them together. The notation $\Sigma (x - y)$ means, first, to find the differences between each x and y pair and then add these differences. The following examples illustrate this concept.

EXAMPLE 1.1   Several data values have been collected and designated by the symbol x. Table 1.2 shows these values and their squared values. The table's columns are then added to form the totals shown.

TABLE 1.2   Data Values and Sums for Example 1.1

Value	x	x^2
x_1	3	9
x_2	5	25
x_3	-6	36
x_4	2	4
x_5	-9	81
Sums:	-5	155

Note that the summation notation presented in this section is a shorthand version. Complete summation notation uses an index of summation, often designated with the letter i. When several x values are to be added, the complete notation would designate the sum as

$$\sum_{i=1}^{n} x_i \tag{1.1}$$

This notation calls for the following sum. First, x_1 is identified, since the notation under the summation sign ($i = 1$) indicates that x_1 is the first term. In Example 1.1,

x_1 equals 3. Next, x_2 is identified (x_2 equals 5 in Example 1.1) and added to x_1. The index i is increased by one unit each time. This process is continued until x_n is added to the sum. In Example 1.1, n equals 5. Therefore, 5 will appear at the top of the summation sign, and x_5 will be the last term in the sum. Thus, the preceding notation calls for adding n values of x together, beginning with x_1 and continuing through x_n.

This book will employ the complete summation notation using a summation index when the computations are complex enough to require it for clarity. Otherwise, the simpler notation will be used.

EXAMPLE 1.2   Based on the sums in Table 1.2, the following summation notation is appropriate:

$$\Sigma x = -5 \qquad \Sigma x^2 = 155 \qquad (\Sigma x)^2 = -5^2 = 25$$

Note that for the sum of squared x values (Σx^2), each x must first be squared, *then* added; this sum is 155. Also note that the sum of x values squared, $(\Sigma x)^2$, produces a different sum, 25.

EXAMPLE 1.3   Two variables are measured for several objects. Table 1.3 shows these values, designated x and y, along with several values computed from them and their sums.

Based on the totals in Table 1.3, the following summation notation is used to summarize the calculations:

$$\Sigma x = 42 \qquad \Sigma y = 46 \qquad \Sigma(x - y) = -4$$
$$\Sigma(x - y)^2 = 62 \qquad \Sigma(x - 3)^2 = 243$$

TABLE 1.3   Data Values and Sums for Example 1.2

Value	x	y	$x - y$	$(x - y)^2$	$(x - 3)^2$
1	5	3	2	4	4
2	2	7	−5	25	1
3	12	8	4	16	81
4	9	10	−1	1	36
5	14	18	−4	16	121
Sums:	42	46	−4	62	243

EXAMPLE 1.4   In March 1992, U.S. industrial production rose to 107.2% of the 1987 average, according to a front-page graph in the April 16, 1992, *Wall Street Journal*. Suppose you wanted to investigate the relationship between industrial production and another economic variable such as the unemployment rate or personal disposable income.

Several data sums are needed to investigate the relationship between two such variables. Chapters 14 and 15 present techniques that require such sums. Table 1.4 presents the x–y data pairs that might result from a study of industrial production and a related variable, along with further necessary calculations and sums. Based on the values calculated in Table 1.4, the following statements can be made using summation notation:

$$\Sigma x = 66 \qquad \Sigma y = 48 \qquad \Sigma xy = -106$$
$$\Sigma x^2 = 3,390 \qquad \Sigma y^2 = 1,040$$

Based on Table 1.4, you should be able to verify the inequality

$$\Sigma x^2 \neq (\Sigma x)^2$$

TABLE 1.4 $x - y$ Data Values and Sums for Example 1.4

Value	x	y	xy	x^2	y^2
1	2	3	6	4	9
2	-4	10	-40	16	100
3	11	9	99	121	81
4	0	29	0	0	841
5	57	-3	-171	3,249	9
Sums:	66	48	-106	3,390	1,040

SUMMARY

This chapter has introduced some basic concepts of business statistics. Keep in mind as you study that the purpose of all statistical procedures, no matter how complex, is to extract useful information from available data. The purpose of this book, and of your business statistics course, is to improve your ability to perform this important function.

Summation notation was reviewed in this chapter. You should be familiar with this notation and its purpose. The exercises that follow will help you to master this simple concept.

Finally, this chapter covers some basic computer concepts used throughout the book. The section at the end of this chapter shows you how to use basic computer packages demonstrated at the end of most chapters.

APPLICATIONS OF STATISTICAL CONCEPTS IN THE BUSINESS WORLD

Following each chapter's Summary is a section called "Applications of Statistical Concepts in the Business World." Its purpose is to provide examples of how concepts discussed in the chapter are applied in the practical business world. There's not enough material in Chapter 1 to illustrate this approach, but you'll find this section useful in other chapters.

Any of the topics in this book could be used in a particular application, but the following chapter topics are quite widely used in the applications indicated.

Accounting: Data collection (Chapter 2), estimation (Chapter 8), hypothesis testing (Chapters 9 and 10).

Finance: Correlation and regression (Chapters 14 and 15), index numbers and time series analysis (Chapter 16).

General management: Data presentation (Chapter 3), business forecasting (Chapter 17), decision making (Chapter 18).

Management information systems: Data collection (Chapter 2), business forecasting (Chapter 17).

Marketing: Hypothesis testing (Chapters 9 and 10), chi-square tests (Chapter 11), analysis of variance (Chapter 12), nonparametric statistics (Chapter 19).

Operations management: Estimation (Chapter 8), hypothesis testing (Chapters 9 and 10), analysis of variance (Chapter 12), index numbers and time series analysis (Chapter 16).

Personnel: Hypothesis testing (Chapters 9 and 10), chi-square tests (Chapter 11), multiple regression (Chapter 15), nonparametric tests (Chapter 19).

Quality control: Data presentation (Chapter 3), descriptive statistics (Chapter 4), estimation (Chapter 8), quality control applications (Chapter 13).

GLOSSARY

Statistical analysis Used to manipulate, summarize, and investigate data to obtain useful decision-making information.

KEY FORMULAS

Summation notation

$$\sum_{i=1}^{n} x_i \qquad (1.1)$$

EXERCISES

1. Design a data collection of 10 values and use them to show that Σx^2 doesn't equal $(\Sigma x)^2$.

2. Consider the following x–y data values:

Value	x	y
1	5	4
2	7	9
3	3	8
4	0	5
5	10	3
6	2	9

a. Find the following sums: Σx, Σy, Σxy.

b. Show that Σx^2 isn't equal to $(\Sigma x)^2$.

3. Using the data collection

Value	x	y	z
1	−3	4	5
2	0	−12	14
3	15	7	−5
4	9	18	11
5	4	0	8

a. Find the following sums: Σx, Σy, Σxy, $\Sigma(x - y + 2z)$.

b. Show that Σy^2 isn't equal to $(\Sigma y)^2$.

4. For a certain data collection, the sum of the x's is 29, the sum of the y's is 48, the sum of their cross products is 357, and the sum of the x's after they're squared is 138. Summarize these results using summation notation.

INTRODUCTION TO THE MICROCOMPUTER PACKAGE

The microcomputer package *Computerized Business Statistics* (CBS) is a statistical software package designed specifically for use with this textbook. The package runs on IBM and IBM-compatible microcomputers and consists of an instructional text and either a 5.25-inch or 3.5-inch diskette. This package can be used to solve most statistical techniques in this text. The end of most chapters gives instructions for solving one or two problems involving statistical techniques available on the CBS package.

To access the package, type **CBS** after you receive the A> prompt on your screen. Your OPTIONS are C = configuration menu, M = main menu, and N = next page. You must choose the configuration menu the first time through to set up the package on your machine. Under the configuration (INPUT/OUTPUT SET UP MENU) your options are: Number of Disk Drives: ?, Program Disk Drive: ?, and Data Disk Drive: ?. After you make the appropriate choices for your machine, you can access the MAIN MENU. This menu lists all statistical techniques that you can run on CBS.

INTRODUCTION TO THE MINITAB COMPUTER PACKAGE

One popular software package used for statistical analysis is MINITAB. Available for both mainframes and microcomputers, MINITAB is one of the computer packages referred to throughout this book. For each MINITAB example in this text, assume that MINITAB has been executed. The MTB> prompt appears on the screen when the call up has been successful. The prompt at the left-most side of your screen tells you what kind of information MINITAB expects you to type.

MINITAB has long been recognized for its straightforward command structure, which will be presented throughout the text. But note that to further enhance ease of use, MINITAB has a new version called Release 8 for micros. It introduces menus and dialog boxes, with the command language retained for added flexibility and speed.

Understanding the MINITAB worksheet is the key to using this program. The worksheet contains columns (variables) and rows (observations). Columns are referred to by number, such as C1 and C2. Columns can also be assigned variable names, such as "Sales," "Price," or "Weight." The example commands discussed next refer to a typical worksheet shown below.

		Columns or variables				
		C1	C2	C3	C4	C5	C6

Rows or Observations

1
2
3
4
5
6
.
.
.

As an example, MINITAB commands are presented to solve Exercise 2.

```
MTB > OUTFILE 'EXAMPLE.PRN'
MTB > SET C1
DATA> 5 7 3 0 10 2
DATA> END
MTB > SET C2
DATA> 4 9 8 5 3 9
DATA> END
MTB > LET C3 = C1*C2
MTB > PRINT C1-C3

 ROW    C1   C2    C3

   1     5    4    20
   2     7    9    63
   3     3    8    24
   4     0    5     0
   5    10    3    30
   6     2    9    18
MTB > LET K1 = SUM (C1)
MTB > LET K2 = SUM (C2)
MTB > LET K3 = SUM (C3)
MTB > PRINT K1-K3
K1      27.0000
K2      38.0000
K3      155.000

MTB > WRITE 'EXAMPLE.DAT' C1-C3
MTB > STOP
```

The **OUTFILE** command is used to save all the commands and output shown on the screen in the file specified "EXAMPLE.PRN" until the MINITAB session is ended with the command **STOP**.

The **SET** command is used to enter data into column 1 (C1) on the worksheet. The **DATA** subcommand is used to enter the data allowing at least one space between data values. The **END** subcommand is used to show that data entry is complete for column 1.

The **LET** command is used to do arithmetic using algebraic expressions such as multiplying C1 times C2 and storing the result in C3.

The **PRINT** command is used to print the contents of columns 1 through 3.

The **LET** command is used to sum the C1 column and store the result in row K1.

The **WRITE** command saves the data in a worksheet called EXAMPLE.DAT. For future use the worksheet can always be accessed by the command **READ 'EXAMPLE.DAT' C1–C3.**

INTRODUCTION TO THE SAS COMPUTER PACKAGE

The Statistical Analysis System (SAS) is one of the most versatile and popular software packages for statistical analysis in business and industry. Available for both mainframes and microcomputers, it's one of the packages referred to throughout this book.

To solve a statistical problem with SAS, we first define the data and then specify the statistical procedures (PROCS) to be used. Certain rules must be observed when running SAS programs:

1. SAS statements always end with a semicolon (;).

2. SAS names must start with a letter and must be eight characters or less.

3. SAS statements end in column 72. Longer statements are continued on the next line.

4. Data must be defined before a procedure can be run. Lines that contain data don't end with a semicolon. However, it's a good idea to include a semicolon at the end of the last line of data.

5. Several procedures can be performed by adding multiple procedure statements.

6. The decimal point must be included when entering data that contain a decimal (for example, 1.89).

7. Job Control Language (JCL) statements must be included with a SAS program. These statements are specific to a particular system and allow the SAS program to execute properly.

The SAS commands to solve Exercise 2 are:

```
$ SAS
OPTIONS PAGESIZE=60 LINESIZE=80;
TITLE "SAS SOLUTION TO EXERCISE 2";
DATA EXAMPLE;
 INPUT X Y;
    XY=X*Y;
CARDS;
5    4
7    9
3    8
0    5
10   3
2    9
PROC PRINT DATA=EXAMPLE;
 SUM X Y XY;
ENDSAS;
```

The OPTIONS statement indicates that the output page size will be 60 lines and that each line will contain 80 spaces.

The TITLE statement names the SAS program.

The DATA statement provides a filename for the data.

The INPUT statement names the variables and provides the correct order for the different fields on the data lines. Note that two variables will be read (X and Y) and a new variable will be created by multiplying ($XY = X*Y$).

The CARDS statement indicates to SAS that the input data follow.

The next six lines contain the data values.

The PROC PRINT statement produces a listing of the data in the file EXAMPLE.

The SUM statement specifies variables to be totaled. The first line is a JCL statement. Table 1.5 shows the output for this SAS run.

TABLE 1.5   SAS Output for Exercise 2

```
SAS SOLUTION TO EXERCISE 2
OBS         X          Y          XY
 1          5          4          20
 2          7          9          63
 3          3          8          24
 4          0          5           0
 5         10          3          30
 6          2          9          18
          ___        ___         ___
           27         38         155
```

DATA COLLECTION

*Those who wish
to succeed must
ask the right
preliminary
questions.*
Aristotle,
Metaphysics II

Objectives

When you have completed this chapter, you will be able to:

Identify the various types of data that analysts collect.

Distinguish between nominal, ordinal, interval, and ratio levels of measurement.

Describe and know when to use various sampling techniques.

Describe the strengths and weaknesses of the more commonly used methods of data collection.

A cover story in the April 10, 1992, *Wall Street Journal* described the opening of Euro Disney, the new Disney theme park in France. The park and its adjoining resort complex cost $3.9 billion to construct.

Chapter 1 introduced the basic ideas of statistics to be presented in this book. In particular it stressed that the purpose of statistical analysis is to convert raw data into useful decision-making information.

WHY DATA COLLECTION PROCEDURES ARE IMPORTANT TO MANAGERS

Before data collections can be processed for decision-making purposes, the analyst must find relevant data. This chapter discusses data collection methods and illustrates the applications of the method. The collection of data that are relevant to the problem being studied is commonly the most difficult, expensive, and time-consuming part of the entire research project. Great care and skill must be exercised in the collection process; unfortunately, such care isn't always taken.

Euro Disney involved a multibillion-dollar gamble by Disney and the French government, which supplied a majority of the financing. This gamble was presumably based on sound research about the market potential for such a venture. Many data-gathering techniques discussed in this chapter were used to provide input into the decision-making process.

TYPES OF DATA

Variable

Statistical data are usually obtained by counting or measuring items. Examples of statistical data measures are the daily Dow Jones Average, unemployment rate, monthly sales of the Bay Point Corporation, and number of women executives at IBM. These data items are called **variables** because they can take on many different values.

Suppose a company wants to survey worker salaries in a particular industry. The company might also decide to compare salaries with other worker characteristics such as age, race, education level, and sex. In this instance the five characteristics—salary, age, race, education level, and sex—are variables in the survey. A variable has no fixed numerical value, whereas a **constant** does have a fixed value.

Constant

> A **variable** is an item of interest that can take on many different numerical values.
> A **constant** has a fixed numerical value.

Quantitative

Qualitative

Variables can be classified as quantitative or qualitative. A **quantitative variable** is one whose values are expressible as numerical quantities, such as measurements or counts. Weight (a measurement) and number of customers (a count) are examples of quantitative variables. A **qualitative variable** is not quantitative and can only be classified, but not measured. Qualitative variables can only be classified. A measurement taken on a qualitative variable conveys information regarding a characteristic (for example, classifying items on an assembly line as defective or not defective). As an example of a qualitative variable, Table 2.1 shows the number of firms classified by industry. It is important to recognize these two classifications when analyzing variables since different statistical techniques apply to different types of variables.

The type of data being analyzed is also important. Throughout this book, the type of data being treated will be identified using one of the data classification schemes discussed in the next section.

TABLE 2.1   Number of Firms by Industry, Spokane County, Washington, 1989

e.g.
qualitative

Services	3,059
Retail trade	2,058
Construction	874
Finance, insurance, and real estate	827
Wholesale trade	792
Unclassified	610
Manufacturing	505
Transportation and public utilities	327
Agriculture and mining	144
Total	9,196

Source: *County Business Patterns*, 1989.

A **quantitative variable** is one whose values can be expressed as numerical quantities, such as measurements or counts. A **qualitative variable** is not quantitative and can only be classified, but not measured.

To prepare data for analysis, you must be familiar with a hierarchy of four numerical scales of measurement: *nominal, ordinal, interval,* and *ratio*. The higher the position of the data type in this hierarchy, the more information the data contain. Thus, data measured on a ratio scale contain more information than data measured on an interval scale, which contain more information than data on an ordinal scale, which in turn contain more information than data on a nominal scale.

Nominal Data   Data measured on a **nominal** scale represent the lowest level in the hierarchy and consist of categories in each of which the number of observations is recorded. Furthermore, the categories are in no logical order and have no particular relationship. The categories are said to be **mutually exclusive** since an individual, object, or measurement can be included in only one of them. The result is qualitative data usually measured by counting. The information in Table 2.1 is measured on a nominal scale: the number of firms has been counted for each industry. If a firm is counted as construction, for example, it cannot be counted as being in any other industry.

> Categories are **mutually exclusive** if an individual, object, or measurement can be included in only one of them.

People's favorite colors are another example of nominal data. If three colors are involved, the categories might be listed in order of preference as red, yellow, green or as green, yellow, red. Furthermore, if a color is red, it cannot be yellow or green. Since the order in which the categories are listed doesn't matter and the categories are mutually exclusive, the data are classified as nominal. Other examples of nominal data categories are male/female, Washington/Oregon/Idaho, urban/rural, train/bus/plane, and the college majors business/history/English/psychology/chemistry. In each of these situations, the categories could be arranged in any order.

> A **nominal** scale consists of mutually exclusive categories in which no logical order is implied.

Ordinal Data

Many data collections consist of qualitative categories where there is a progression or order. This type of data is referred to as **ordinal.** The information in Table 2.2 is measured on an ordinal scale. A rating of "excellent" is higher than a rating of "good," and so on; that is, order exists in the categories.

TABLE 2.2   Employee Ratings of Their Supervisor

Rating	Number of ratings
Excellent	4
Good	15
Fair	10
Poor	2
Total	31

> An **ordinal** scale consists of distinct categories in which order is implied.

Data measured on an ordinal scale contain more information than data measured on a nominal scale because the categories are ordered: values in one category are larger or smaller than values in other categories. Another example of data on an ordinal scale is the education categories on many questionnaires.

_____ Some high school
_____ High school graduate
_____ Some college
_____ College graduate
_____ Graduate school

This is an ordinal scale because each category indicates a higher level of education than the previous one. If the number of persons falling into each of these categories was recorded for a group being studied, ordinal data would result. The data are qualitative or categorical in nature, and the categories progress from little education to much education. Other examples of ordinal data categories are:

_____ Poor	_____ Dislike	_____ Strongly agree
_____ Average	_____ Neutral	_____ Agree
_____ Good	_____ Like	_____ Neutral
_____ Superior		_____ Disagree
		_____ Strongly disagree

In each of these classification schemes, the occurrences in each category are counted, and the categories ascend or descend in some manner.

Interval Data

The next two types of scales involve quantitative data. The first type, the **interval** scale, results when numerical measurements are made on items and the intervals between measurements can be precisely determined. The Table 2.3 data are measured on an interval scale; the distance between any two temperature units is of a known, constant size.

TABLE 2.3   Temperature Desired by Factory Workers

65, 65, 65, 66, 66, 66
67, 67, 67, 67, 67, 67, 67, 67, 67, 68, 68, 68, 68, 68
69, 69, 69, 69, 69, 69, 69, 69, 69, 69, 69, 69, 70, 70, 70, 70, 70, 70, 70, 70, 70, 70,
   70, 70, 70, 70, 70
71, 71, 71, 71, 71, 71, 71, 71, 71, 71, 71, 71, 72, 72, 72, 72, 72, 72, 72, 72, 72, 72
73, 73, 73, 73, 74, 74

Temperature	Number of respondents
65–66	6
67–68	14
69–70	27
71–72	22
73–74	6
Total	75

Note in Table 2.3 that the data collection has been summarized at the bottom of the table, where the number of occurrences in each category is shown. For this summary, the interval-scaled data have been converted to an ordinal scale (i.e., the categories are in ascending order). Such a data summary is called a *frequency distribution* and will be discussed in Chapter 3.

The interval scale is a stronger form of measurement than the ordinal or nominal scale because it allows you to discern not only which observed value is the largest, but also by how much. This is because there is a way of measuring the width of the interval between two values, rather than just ranking them. As an example, the interval cold/hot constitutes an ordinal scale while the interval 65°F/70°F is based on an interval scale. This is the key distinction between interval data and ordinal data: in ordinal data, distances between categories cannot be measured, whereas in interval data they can.

> The **interval** scale is a set of numerical values in which the distance between successive numbers is of measurable constant size.

By implication, data measured on an interval scale have an arbitrary zero point. That is, the person designing the scale arbitrarily decides where to locate the zero point. To qualify as an interval scale, the distance between numerical values needs only be definable. For example, in the consumer price index, if the base year is 1982, the price level during 1982 will be set at 100. Although this is an equal-interval measurement scale, the zero point is arbitrary.

A classic example of interval data is temperature measured in degrees Fahrenheit (Table 2.3). We can compute the amount of heat necessary to raise a room's temperature from 40°F to 60°F. The data values, 40 and 60, aren't arbitrary labels for categories. They are precisely defined numerical values, and the distance between them can also be precisely defined. Moreover, there's an arbitrary zero point for the Fahrenheit scale; the Celsius temperature scale uses a different zero point. Each of these scales constitutes an interval scale since the distance between any two numerical values can be precisely specified, and each scale has an arbitrary point defined to be zero.

Ratio Data

By contrast, data measured on a **ratio** scale have a fixed or nonarbitrary zero point. Such data are scaled using precisely defined intervals like interval-scaled data but have a fixed zero point as well. Data measured on a ratio scale constitute the highest level of measurement. The age data in Table 2.4 are measured on a ratio scale.

TABLE 2.4   Voter Opinion Survey: Age of Respondents

18, 19, 19, 19, 20, 20, 21, 21, 22, 25, 25, 28, 28, 29, 30, 32, 32,
33, 33, 35, 37, 37, 39, 41, 41, 42, 45, 45, 48, 48, 49, 49, 49, 50,
55, 55, 57, 60, 62, 65, 71, 72
Mean = 38.7

Note in Table 2.4 that the data values have been summarized by their average, or *mean*. This and similar ways to describe numerical collections using summary values are described in Chapter 4.

> The **ratio scale** consists of numerical measurements where the distances between numbers are of a known, constant size, and where the ratio of numbers has some meaning; in addition, there is a fixed, nonarbitrary zero point.

Most numerical measurements in practical situations result in data measured on a ratio scale. An example is the lifetime of a television picture tube. The difference between 500 days and 250 days is a measurable difference. Also, we could say that the 500-day tube lasted twice as long as the 250-day tube. By comparison, we wouldn't say that a 60° day is twice as warm as a 30° day. For interval data, the ratio of two numbers isn't appropriate. In addition, a true zero point exists for a ratio scale: zero lifetime means the tube didn't work at all; this zero value is clearly understood by everyone. Other examples of ratio-scaled data include automobile weights, annual salaries, elapsed times, shipping distances, and interest rates.

Before data are analyzed, it's important to first determine whether quantitative or qualitative data have been collected. In other words, it's vital whether (*a*) nominal- or ordinal-scaled data or (*b*) interval- or ratio-scaled data have been collected. Different statistical techniques are used for the two basic types of scales, and erroneous results can be expected if an inappropriate technique is applied.

Most statistical techniques in this book are for use with quantitative data. A few techniques discussed in later chapters are designed for nominal or ordinal data, and these will be clearly identified when they are presented. These techniques (sometimes referred to as *nonparametric techniques*) have entire books devoted to them. Chapters 11 and 19 of this book discuss several nonparametric data analysis procedures.

One final point should be made. It is possible, and sometimes desirable, to drop down the hierarchy scale. Suppose, for example, you've collected ratio-scaled data on people's ages. The numerical ages have been measured, and a fixed zero point is obvious; therefore, a ratio data scale exists. Converting these ratio-scaled ages to categories may be useful. For example, each age could be placed into one of the following categories:

———— Below 20
———— 20 to below 40
———— 40 to below 60
———— 60 to below 80
———— 80 to below 100

The result is data measured on an ordinal scale. However, suppose you had originally collected the age data in these categories. You couldn't convert these data into people's actual ages because the actual age of a person in the category "20 to below 40," for example, isn't known. In other words, it's possible to go down the hierarchy of data but not up.

One exception to this one-way rule is frequently employed in practical situations. The data collected to measure the performance of a department supervisor in Table 2.2 uses the following scale:

1. Excellent.
2. Good.
3. Fair.
4. Poor.

These are ordinal-scaled data since the frequencies in each category have been recorded and the categories are in order. Thus, the data would normally be analyzed using techniques designed for qualitative data (specifically, for ordinal-scaled data). But it's tempting to average the class responses by arbitrarily assigning numerical values to the categories as just shown. Averaging is a technique reserved for quantitative data, either interval or ratio, so it's not strictly appropriate for the ordinal data of Table 2.2.

However, it might be argued that the intervals between the categories are all equal. In other words, the same difference in performance exists between excellent and good as between good and fair as between fair and poor. If this argument is correct, the definition of interval-scaled data has been met; there are equal, measurable distances between successive data values. Therefore, numerical techniques such as averaging would be appropriate. These methods could only be used after numbers (1, 2, 3, . . .) have been assigned to the categories.

Analysts frequently use numerical techniques on ordinal data without addressing the issue of whether equal intervals exist between the categories. This can lead to serious error if unequal intervals actually exist and are ignored in the desire to use common numerical techniques. If the interval equality isn't addressed, the data analysis is suspect since qualitative data may have been converted to quantitative data without proper justification. Figure 2.1 summarizes the characteristics of the four measurement scales.

FIGURE 2.1   Characteristics of Levels of Measurement

Measurement scale	Characteristics	Appropriate statistics	
Nominal	Unique classifications	Mode	MORE INFORMATION ↓
Ordinal	Ranking or rating	Median, percentiles	
Interval	Known difference between any two points	Mean, standard deviation	
Ratio	Known difference between any two points Unique or true zero	Mean, standard deviation	

EXERCISES

1. Explain the difference between a variable and a constant.

2. Explain the differences between qualitative and quantitative data.
3. State whether the following variables are qualitative or quantitative:
   a. The life of a light bulb.
   b. The brand of a light bulb.
   c. The rating of a particular stock.
   d. The expected return on investment for a particular stock.
   e. Number of accidents per week at a manufacturing plant.
   f. The types of accidents that occur at a manufacturing plant.
   g. Number of people who report to work per day at a manufacturing plant.
4. Explain the difference between a nominal scale and an ordinal scale.
5. Explain the difference between an ordinal scale and an interval scale.
6. Explain the difference between an interval scale and a ratio scale.
7. Why are data measured on an interval or ratio scale preferred by statisticians?
8. The following information is included in John Johnson's personnel record:
   a. Sex: male.
   b. Marital status: single.
   c. Education completed: college.
   d. Height: six feet.
   e. Weight: 200 pounds.
   f. Amount of experience: seven years.
   g. Job: machine operator.
   h. Salary: $25,000 per year.

   Classify each of the personnel record items by type of data and method of measurement.

TYPES OF DATA SOURCES

Secondary Data

Primary Data

The data needed for a statistical analysis either are readily available or must be collected. Data that are already available are known as **secondary data,** and data that must be collected are known as **primary data.**

Primary data are collected specifically for the analysis desired. **Secondary data** have already been compiled and are available for statistical analysis.

There are many sources of secondary data. Libraries are perhaps the most obvious example. Very powerful secondary data sources on the business scene include such computer networks as Compuserve, The Source, Dow Jones News Retrieval Service, Standard & Poor's Compustat, and Value Line. Subscribers to these services can access vast amounts of secondary data using the telephone and their own microcomputer.

The federal government generates large quantities of data each year. Published monthly, the *Survey of Current Business* covers many economic indicators. Published annually, the *Statistical Abstract of the United States* contains annual indicators of economic and other national activities. Anyone engaged in business or economic research should become familiar with these easily available sources of vast data on American life. Table 2.5 lists some other sources of data compiled by the federal government and other agencies.

TABLE 2.5   Selected Sources of Secondary Data

Data source	Subjects
American Statistics Index	Guide to sources of government data
Business Conditions Digest	Leading economic indicators
CIS/Index to Publications of the U.S. Government	Congressional publications
County and City Data Book	Data by city and county
Economic Report of the President	Various economic indicators of the United States
Federal Reserve Bulletin	Banks, financial markets, economic conditions
Handbook of Labor Statistics	Historical economic series
Statistics of Income Bulletin	Income and expense data

Data of interest to businesspeople can also be found in private publications and professional journals. The *Business Periodicals Index*, found in most libraries, lists published articles by subject area. People seeking sources of secondary data often consult it.

Secondary data are also available from commercial companies specializing in data services. Examples are the A. C. Nielsen Company, Market Facts, Inc., Market Research Corporation of America, and the J. Walter Thompson Company.

The advantage of using secondary data for a research or statistical investigation is that the data are already available and need not be collected for a specific project. Even purchasing the data from a commercial firm is usually less expensive than collecting primary data. The disadvantage of secondary data is that the specific needs of the analysis aren't always met by these sources. For this reason, many investigations require the collection of data directed specifically toward the matter being researched. The rest of this chapter concerns collecting such primary data.

EXERCISES

9. What are the advantages of primary data over secondary data?
10. Indicate a good secondary data source for each of the following types of information:
    a. Population information for the Pacific Northwest.
    b. A map of Lake County, Illinois.
    c. The birthrate in the United States.
    d. Annual sales of the top three airlines.
    e. Brands of diet cola recently introduced in the United States.

11. The Solomon Development Corporation asked a local research firm to conduct a market feasibility study to determine market factors that might affect the success of an athletic club in the Southwood Shopping Center in Lakeland, North Carolina. The research will require analysis of data on demographics, traffic flow, perceived image of competitors, area resident interest, and potential area growth.

    a. What secondary data sources could be used for this study?

    b. What primary data sources might be needed to complete this study?

DATA-GATHERING TECHNIQUES

The primary data-gathering techniques discussed in this section are widely used throughout business to collect information needed for analysis and decision making. It requires some practice and skill to determine which technique, or combination of techniques, best suits a specific task. The skilled researcher understands each data collection method and can use them to best advantage. The ability to perform good research is based largely on the analyst's skill in choosing among techniques.

Focus Groups

Focus groups are frequently used as a preliminary data-gathering method. These groups involve a small number of people in an informal discussion of items pertinent to the research. A skilled moderator conducts the sessions and leads the discussion into the areas of interest. Sessions last from one to two hours and are usually attended by 8 to 12 people. Since only a small number participate in a focus group, the results are used to direct further research.

It is important to select participants who match the larger group being studied. For example, if you wanted opinions on the adequacy of Medicare, it might be appropriate to choose for the focus group only participants over age 65. It might also be important to choose approximately equal numbers of men and women and to select participants from different areas of the region being studied. The key point is to try to get a fairly representative profile in the focus group so that their comments may be taken as reliable indicators of the opinions of the entire population being studied.

Usually it's wise to have at least three focus groups for each subject of interest. Each focus group will have its own character depending on its membership, and only after two or three sessions will the common themes begin to emerge. A single focus group could be misleading, especially if people with strong opinions dominate the session.

Telephone

Telephone interviewing is another popular technique for gathering information from residents. The advantages of this method are that it's fast, inexpensive, and relatively easy, and it provides a fairly high response rate. The disadvantages are that only simple questions can be asked, the survey must be short, and some people consider such telephone calls an invasion of their privacy and so won't answer.

Mail Questionnaires

Mailed questionnaires are frequently used to gather data when a mailing list exists or when respondents are scattered over a wide area. Detailed questions can be asked since people have time to reread questions and think about their answers. On the other hand, if the questionnaire is too long, people won't take the time to fill it out. The biggest problem with mail questionnaires is getting people to fill them out and return them. When a large group of people don't respond, the analyst faces the difficult problem of determining whether there's a difference between the respondents and nonrespondents. Working with a club or other tightly knit organization helps to minimize this problem. When the general population is surveyed, return rates are commonly very low, and this may lead to erroneous results.

Door-to-Door

The **door-to-door survey** is widely used because it is relatively easy to conduct and it generates high response rates. Care must be taken in selecting and training interviewers and ensuring that the questions are easy to understand. Also, the survey shouldn't be too lengthy. It is possible to cover a wide geographic area using this method and it's easy to obtain a good distribution of incomes of the respondents since people's incomes are usually reflected in their type of housing.

Mall Intercept

The **mall intercept** method is frequently used by market researchers interested in obtaining shoppers' opinions. Interviewers station themselves in heavily traveled shopping areas and invite selected people to answer a few questions. Visuals and other aids can be used in these interviews. People could be asked to taste a new product and comment on it, or people could be shown a new package and asked their opinions.

Registrations

Data are sometimes collected by **new product registrations.** Consumers are often asked to fill out survey forms when they "register" the product for warranty coverage. The obvious problem with the information is that not everyone returns the form. A bias may be introduced that could mislead the company collecting the data.

Observation

Sometimes data for business applications are collected by **observation.** Many such efforts involve the design of an *experiment* where conditions are carefully controlled so that the effects of introduced changes can be observed and analyzed. Experiments aren't as common in business as in science, but they're still used on occasion.

Interviews

The **personal interview** is used when the researcher needs to determine in-depth opinions and attitudes. Although this approach provides quality data, the cost and amount of time required to schedule and conduct personal interviews limit its usefulness.

The previous data-gathering methods all elicit the opinions or attitudes of people. However, many business problems concern the measurement of objects, such as television tubes, logs, or welded assemblies. Measuring objects avoids the problems of interacting and communicating with people, but involves questions of sample size and other considerations discussed in Chapter 8. Figure 2.2 summarizes advantages and disadvantages of each technique.

Experiments

Data sets of interest to the business community are often generated by experimental research. Experiments differ from other data-gathering techniques in terms of degree of control over the research situation. In an **experiment** one variable is manipulated and its effect on another variable is measured, while all other variables are controlled. Examples of business experiments include determining whether a customer prefers one of two brands of cola, whether presentation of unit price information changes average unit price paid, and whether a pay hike increases production. Experimental design is considered an integral part of quality-control operations.

EXERCISES

12. What are the advantages and disadvantages of the following data-gathering techniques?

    a. Focus groups.

    b. Telephone interviews.

    c. Mail questionnaires.

FIGURE 2.2   Advantages and Disadvantages of Data-Gathering Techniques

Data-gathering technique	Advantages	Disadvantages
Focus group	Good preliminary technique	Small sample Cannot project results
Telephone survey	Fast, inexpensive Easy to conduct, high response rate Interviewer flexibility	Simple questions must be asked Survey must be short
Mail survey	Can cover a wide geographical area Inexpensive, standardized questions	Low return rates Time-consuming
Door-to-door	Can cover a wide geographical area Easy to conduct, high return rates	Time-consuming Expensive
Mall intercept	Fast, inexpensive Easy to conduct, visual aids can be used Interviewer flexibility	Cannot project results Survey must be short
Personal interviews	Visual aids can be used Interviewer flexibility Answers can be probed	Expensive Time-consuming Small samples result

    d. Mall intercept.

    e. Door-to-door interviews.

    f. Personal interviews.

13. The New York League of Credit Unions has decided to survey all credit unions in the state to determine how the league can improve service to its members. What type of data-gathering instrument should the league develop?

14. The Metro Association wants to determine voters' feelings about a county bond issue to be voted on next month. The issue involves replacing the present coliseum. Metro needs to determine who is most likely to vote for the proposal and who is most likely to vote against it. Once Metro has this information, it can create a target audience for its advertising. What type of data-gathering approach should Metro develop?

POPULATIONS AND SAMPLES

Population

In statistical studies it's crucial to identify the **population** (the group of subjects or items being studied).

> A **population** is the entire set of individuals or items of interest.

There are times when you can measure or examine each item in the population. Each member of your statistics class, for example, might have filled out the questionnaire in Chapter 1 (Table 1.1). If 35 students are in your class, and if information is desired about only this class, the members constitute a population, and each member can be measured by his or her responses to the questionnaire. When an attempt to measure all members of a population of interest is made, a **census** results.

A **census** is an attempt to measure every item in the population of interest.

You can sometimes conduct a census when population items reside in a computer file. Even if the population is quite large, a computer can measure each item quickly and accurately. An example of this kind of census is the measurement of some variable for all employees in a firm. Records of 5,000 or more employees may be held in a computer file, so it could be easy and fast to obtain information on each if the files had data of interest such as time with the company, age, and performance rating.

In most statistical investigations, a census is difficult, costly, or even impossible. It would be difficult and very time-consuming to measure variables such as age and performance rating for a large company's employees, for instance, if these data were contained in file folders rather than on a computer. It would be impossible to survey each member of a large community since their telephone numbers aren't readily available and personal contact with such a large number couldn't be achieved even with several months' effort. Under such conditions, it's necessary to choose a **sample,** which is a population subset selected for analysis.

A **sample** is a subset selected from the population.

Choosing *representative samples* is a key problem in statistical investigations. Unless it's easy and cost-effective to measure each population item through a census, the investigator faces the problem of how to select a representative sample from the larger population. A representative sample may provide useful insights into the nature of the population being studied, whereas an unrepresentative sample could suggest totally incorrect conclusions about the population.

EXAMPLE 2.1 A September 29, 1989, *Wall Street Journal* story indicated that the Gillette Company seeks to improve its share in the high-tech men's razor market. Suppose a market researcher is responsible for selecting a sample of men to interview about razors. Since it's not possible to contact all men in all selected cities, the researcher decides to sample men in several downtown areas and give them a short series of questions to answer. Interviewers query men during the busy afternoon hours Monday through Friday of a selected week.

The problem with this sample selection method is that many men don't shop during weekday afternoons. Those who work during the day away from downtown locations can't be selected during those hours. The researchers should have scheduled interviews weekends and evenings as well, along with interview areas away from downtown.

EXAMPLE 2.2   The Joe Dear Company, a manufacturer of farm tractors, receives component parts from several suppliers. To check incoming parts' quality, a few are selected for quality-control tests as they arrive in rail cars. For three days, boxcars are opened, and a few parts are removed for testing.

The time period for the test may be too short in this case. Perhaps only two suppliers had shipments due during the three-day test period. A longer sampling period could have ensured that all suppliers were being tested. Also, it might be misleading to select only parts that are easy to access when cars are opened. Suppliers might deliberately put parts known to be good at this location, disguising the real quality level of the entire boxcar load.

The key point in sampling is to be sure that the sampled items represent the population as closely as possible. This task is usually more difficult than it appears. Often we must devote much time and thought to this selection process since after the sample items are measured, it will be assumed that the sample is representative of the population. For example, analysts sampling 100 items from a population of 100,000 items must be sure they used a proper sampling plan before judging the condition of this large population. The rest of this chapter discusses methods of ensuring that a representative sample is drawn from the population of interest.

EXERCISES

15. What is the difference between a population and a sample?

16. What is the difference between a census and a sample?

17. When is a sample preferable to a complete census?

18. Is a census ever preferable to a sample? Give an example.

SIMPLE RANDOM SAMPLING

Random and Nonrandom Samples

There are two basic methods for selecting items from a population. If each item in the population has the same chance of being selected, this constitutes a **random sample.** In a random sample, each possible sample of n items has the same chance of being selected for analysis. If some population items have a greater chance of selection than others, this constitutes a **nonrandom sample.** These two sampling methods are sometimes referred to as *probability* samples (random) and *nonprobability* samples (nonrandom).

There are many different types of random samples. A simple random sample (the most frequently employed) results when n elements are selected from a population in such a way that every possible combination of n elements in the population has an equal probability of being selected.

Simple Random Sampling

> A **simple random sample** results when n elements are selected from a population in such a way that every possible combination of n elements in the population has an equal probability of being selected.

A simple random sample can be thought of as some variation of drawing names from a hat. A method is devised to reach into the population and randomly draw a single item. This procedure is repeated until the desired sample size is reached.

In this sampling procedure, along with the others discussed in this chapter, it is assumed that the sampling is done **without replacement.** That is, an item selected for the sample isn't returned to the population for possible reselection. There are other circumstances when sampling is conducted **with replacement.** In these cases, each sampled item is returned to the population before the next selection takes place.

When sampling is conducted **without replacement,** an item selected for the sample isn't returned to the population for possible reselection. When sampling is conducted **with replacement,** each sampled item is returned to the population before the next selection takes place.

EXAMPLE 2.3   A United Way committee of 10 people needs a three-person subcommittee to write its final report. Committee chair Jennifer Dahl decides to randomly select these people, so committee members write their names on pieces of paper and place them in a jar. Jennifer then selects three of them. The three names selected form the subcommittee. This procedure constitutes a simple random sample selected without replacement.

EXAMPLE 2.4   ACME TV just received an order for 150 TV sets. Fred Ward, owner of ACME, is concerned about the sets' quality. He decides to sample 10 sets and subject them to various tests. Each box containing a set is numbered, from 1 to 150. Then 150 pieces of paper are prepared, each with a number, covering the 1–150 number range. These pieces of paper are put into a jar, and 10 are randomly drawn. The 10 TV sets corresponding to these 10 numbers constitute a simple random sample selected without replacement.

The advantage of any random sample, including the simple random sample, is that it stands a better chance of providing a representative look at the population than does a nonrandom sample. This is because no population item is excluded from fair consideration for inclusion in the sample. In addition, a random sample is defensible. Critics of the sampling results can't fault the method of selection for bias in determining results. By contrast, nonrandom samples are subject to attack even if their results happen to be very representative of the population.

Writing names or numbers on pieces of paper and randomly drawing them is a valid simple random sampling method. However, this method can prove time-consuming if the number of population items is large. The **random number table** provides a quick, easy method of randomly selecting population item numbers.

The **random number table** provides lists of numbers that are randomly generated and can be used to select random samples.

Most computer software packages generate lists of random numbers for use in selecting random samples. One such package is MINITAB. The MINITAB commands to generate and print random numbers for selection of a sample of size 20 from a population of 200 observations are:

```
MTB> RANDOM 20 C1;
SUBC> INTEGER 1 200.
MTB> PRINT C1
C1

    32   135   165   140    73   198     8
   197   151    57    21    13   184    42
    77    99   108   114   128    37
MTB> STOP
```

These MINITAB commands are explained in the MINITAB Computer Package section at the end of this chapter.

Another example of a computerized random number generator (CBS) is presented at the end of this chapter. Appendix E.1 contains a table of random numbers generated with this program.

To use the table in Appendix E.1, choose an arbitrary starting point. Then choose a systematic way of picking numbers from the table. One way is to move from left to right along the arbitrarily chosen row. Another way is to go from top to bottom beginning in the arbitrarily chosen column. By preselecting the method of movement through the table, you remove any chance of bias and the randomness of the sampling procedure is ensured.

To use a random number table, follow these steps:

1. Obtain a list of the population, and consecutively number the items.
2. Identify the number of digits for the last item in the population. If the population contains 675 items, for example, you need three-digit random numbers.
3. Enter the random number table at some arbitrary point, and select numbers from the table in a predetermined way.
4. Determine whether sampling is to be done with or without replacement.
5. Omit any numbers that don't correspond to numbers on the list or that were previously selected from the table (if sampling is done without replacement). Continue until the desired number of items has been selected.
6. Include in the sample the items that correspond to the numbers selected.

EXAMPLE 2.5 Clipper Express Company's delivery fleet contains 80 trucks. Clipper's management is interested in their trucks' average miles per gallon. Clipper assigns the problem to analyst Jodi Lake, who decides to randomly select five trucks to undergo mileage tests during the next two weeks. Jodi would like to select a simple random sample. Rather than write 80 numbers on pieces of paper and randomly draw 5 of them, she decides to use a random number table.

Jodi obtains a list that identifies each truck by a number on the hood. Since there are fewer than 100 trucks in the fleet, two-digit random numbers are used to select the sample of trucks. Table 2.6 contains a portion of the random number table in Appendix E.1. Beginning at an arbitrarily chosen point, say, the upper left corner, and moving left to right, five random numbers are selected:

45, 72, 53, 84, 00

TABLE 2.6   Partial Random Number Table

45725	38400	89452	31237	46598	31246	31002	32650	56421	89078
12457	32650	98740	56426	98451	02300	98450	59874	99544	56122
45112	00221	56446	23554	89710	56478	57410	00123	66658	45488
12450	56451	98451	98457	19457	32659	54201	00215	05579	65127
01245	61548	89700	23305	65704	65490	89567	32150	56401	66457
45618	23015	95781	65190	65734	56427	02455	54667	56102	65480
45611	23359	60058	67544	94567	88461	23346	56754	31216	64572
40015	50998	67723	33751	21334	56112	02240	97645	31278	56481
45002	21137	23199	89764	65722	34556	56420	12341	23498	88945
45500	65722	64977	65895	33348	56000	64559	56734	56779	56487

The first three numbers are valid, so Jodi includes their counterpart trucks in the sample. The next two numbers can't be used; no trucks are numbered 84 or 00. The next random numbers in the table are:

89, 45, 23, 12, 37

There's no truck number 89, and truck number 45 has already been selected (sampling is being done without replacement). Truck numbers 23 and 12 are valid numbers, and this completes the selection process. Jodi uses the trucks with the following numbers for mileage tests:

45, 72, 53, 23, 12

Jodi identifies the five trucks corresponding to the selected numbers and begins the mileage tests Monday morning. The selection process was completely random, and no charge of bias can be leveled at Jodi no matter what the mileage tests reveal. She has selected a simple random sample using a random number table.

EXAMPLE 2.6   From the general membership of the Postal Workers Union, 25 members are to be selected to constitute a committee to meet with management on labor issues. Since there are strong opinions throughout the union on these issues, it's important that union leadership use a completely random and defensible selection method. Union secretary Max Learner is to select the committee.

Max decides to use an existing list of union members, with the first person being number 1, the second number 2, and so on. Max produces a random number table and asks an objective witness to select a starting point on one page. Max has already explained to his witness that he intends to move left to right in picking numbers. Since there are 7,452 members in the union, four-digit numbers are used. After discarding duplicate numbers and those greater than 7,452, 25 valid numbers are selected. Persons corresponding to these numbers on the membership list constitute the committee.

EXERCISES

19. Explain the term *random sample*.
20. Describe some methods for selecting a random sample.
21. What is the difference between a random sample and a nonrandom sample?
22. Describe the steps necessary to use a table of random numbers.
23. A manufacturing association wants to develop a questionnaire to send all 8,250 members. The association decides to survey 30 members and requests assistance in finalizing the questionnaire. What type of sampling technique should be employed?
24. (This question refers to Exercise 23.) Describe the steps necessary to use a table of random numbers for selecting the sample of 30 members.

OTHER SAMPLING TECHNIQUES

If a simple random sample is possible and convenient, this is usually the best method. It is easy to perform, it's easy to understand, and no sampling bias can be charged after the selections are made. However, it's not always possible to take a simple random sample. For this method to be used, a list of the population must be available. If a store wanted to sample its credit card holders, for example, such a list would be available. But if it wanted to sample shoppers in its service area, there would be no list and it wouldn't be possible to match random numbers with shoppers.

Simple random sampling can be difficult if the population is quite large. It might be difficult, for example, to go through 50,000 personnel folders looking for those that correspond to 50 randomly selected numbers. Nevertheless, random samples are still desirable since they provide the best insurance against sample selection bias. This section discusses sampling methods other than simple random sampling.

Researchers have methods to ensure the randomness of sampled items that offer more convenience or lower cost than simple random sampling. In one such technique, **systematic sampling,** population items are arranged in a random sequence and every *n*th item is selected for the sample.

Systematic Sample

A **systematic sample** is one in which every *n*th item in the population sequence is selected.

If systematic sampling is to be used, the population must be arranged in some random line or sequence. If N is the population size and *n* is the sample size, then N/*n* is the gap between successive sampled items. For example, if there are 1,000 items in a population and 100 items are to be sampled, then every 10th item (1,000/100) is selected. If 250 items are to be systematically selected from a population of 5,850 items, then every 23d item (5,850/250) is selected. In the latter example, as in most real-world situations, the calculation N/n doesn't produce a whole number for the sample interval. Since $5,850/250 = 23.4$, the sample interval is rounded to 23. Note that if you round up, you'll run out of population items, so it's a good idea to always round down.

The starting point for sample selection is randomly determined from the first N/n items in the population. For example, if every 10th item is to be selected from a population, then a random starting point among the first 10 population items is selected using a random number table. If the random number 8 is selected, the items for the sample are numbers 8, 18, 28, 38, and so on.

EXAMPLE 2.7 A machine fills aluminum cans with soft drink, producing a line of cans that are then boxed and shipped. Zane Griffey, quality-control manager, wants to determine the line's average fill volume. This figure is an important measure of line quality since too much fill will cost the company money, while too little might create bad publicity if a consumer group detects the underfilling.

Zane decides to take a systematic sample of the can line since the can population is in a moving line and can be thought of as infinite in length. He decides to approach the line at an arbitrary time tomorrow and to take every 50th can as it passes the selection point. He'll repeat this procedure several times during various days and various shifts over the next two weeks. By measuring each sampled can's fill volume, Zane will have a good idea of how the machine is performing. He'll then use the lot acceptance procedures of Chapter 13 ("Quality-Control Applications") to decide if the line-filling volume is acceptable.

EXAMPLE 2.8 Ken Greenwood is personnel director for Waterworks Sprinkler Company, which produces commercial sprinkler systems. Ken wants to study his company's labor force. Specifically, he seeks information on overtime per week, on employees' age distribution, and on their education level. The personnel officer's employee file folders contain all these data. Since the company employs about 12,500 people and records aren't currently stored on a computer, some kind of sampling procedure must be employed. Ken wants to be sure that his sampling procedure will result in sample results that are representative of the entire labor force.

Ken decides to sample 350 personnel file folders from his company's total of 12,500 folders. Instead of taking a time-consuming simple random sample, Ken tells his staff to take a systematic sample since the file folders are arranged in alphabetical order. With population size of 12,500 and sample size of 350, the sample interval for a systematic sample is $12,500/350 = 35.7$, rounded to 35.

Ken enters a random number table for a two-digit number and gets 18. He then computes all 350 of his random numbers as 18, 53 (18 + 35), 88 (18 + 35 + 35), and so on. Personnel files corresponding to these numbers are then pulled so Ken can record employee variables of overtime per week, age, and education level. He knows his sample will be representative of his company's total work force since he has a random sample.

Another method analysts frequently employ is the **stratified random sample.** Here, the population is broken into subgroups, or strata, and each group is individually sampled.

In a **stratified random sample,** the population is broken into meaningful strata or subgroups and each group is randomly sampled.

Stratification is frequently performed on such demographic variables as gender, age, and income. For example, a city's residents might be stratified by income. Since residents' income level is reflected in housing type, separate samples could be taken for small houses, large houses, mobile homes, apartments, and so on. Age could also be used as a stratifying variable. Such a survey could include visits to a retirement community and a high school plus door-to-door interviews in a middle-income neighborhood.

It's important to stratify a population using variables that are relevant to the study. If the survey involves voting preference, stratifying based on age, income, and gender would make sense. Stratifying the population by height or eye color would not since these variables have no logical relationship with voting preference.

The advantage of stratifying a population prior to sampling is that the sample size—and hence the cost—can be reduced without sacrificing accuracy. If simple random sampling were used in a city study, you might have to sample 1,000 residents to ensure that the correct proportions of males and females, young and old, and wealthy and poor were included. If the population were first stratified according to age, income, and sex, the sample size might be reduced considerably, with attendant reductions in the time and cost needed for the study.

EXAMPLE 2.9   Cominco Electronics wants to sample electronic assemblies from its inventory as part of its continuing quality control efforts (Chapter 13 details quality control). Cominco supplies parts to the U.S. Navy. Management is concerned about a *U.S. Naval Institute Proceedings* article (May 1989, p. 205) outlining Congress's budgetary concerns and suggesting navy fleet size may be reduced. Such a cut would affect Cominco's business considerably, so management wants to carefully assess the quality of the assemblies it sends the Navy.

Cominco's president is also aware of Lockheed Corp.'s efforts to move more of its business from military to civilian work, as described in a February 10, 1992, *Wall Street Journal* front-page story. Cominco may have to consider a major effort to build its civilian business in the future. In the meantime, its electronic assemblies' quality is of primary concern.

Since three different companies supply parts to Cominco, the population of parts in inventory is first stratified by supplier. Past records indicate that 20% of the parts are supplied by supplier A, 70% by supplier B, and the other 10% by supplier C. Management has decided on a total sample size of 850 parts, which will reflect the proportions in the population. That is, 20% of the sample will be parts from supplier A, and so on. This results in the following sample sizes for the three strata:

Supplier A: (.20)(850) = 170
Supplier B: (.70)(850) = 595
Supplier C: (.10)(850) =   85
     Total sample size   = 850

Now that the strata and their sample sizes have been determined, a simple random sample of parts is selected from each supplier. The sampling method used in this example is stratified sampling followed by simple random sampling within each stratum.

EXAMPLE 2.10   Michelle Sutcliffe, analyst for Professional Investment Group, is investigating earnings of large service companies. Once a year, *Fortune* magazine lists the largest service companies in the United States. This list (called the Fortune Service 500) is organized by six major industry groups (Table 2.7). Since collecting data for all 500 corporations would be extremely time-consuming, Michelle selects a random sample of 50 firms. She believes that firms in the same industry group share common earnings characteristics so she treats each group as a separate stratum. Table 2.7 shows how Michelle computed the appropriate number of companies to randomly select from each service group. For example, since 150 of the 500 companies, or 30%, are financial, she selects a simple random sample of 50 × .30 = 15 from this group.

TABLE 2.7   Fortune Service 500 Companies (Example 2.10)

Group	Number of companies	Percentage of population	Sample size
Financial	150	150/500 = .30	15*
Diversified	100	100/500 = .20	10
Commercial banking	100	100/500 = .20	10
Retailing	50	50/500 = .10	5
Transportation	50	50/500 = .10	5
Utilities	50	50/500 = .10	5
	500	1.00	50

*Thirty percent of 50 equals 15 financial service companies to be included in the final sample.

Cluster Sample

The final random sampling technique discussed in this section is the **cluster sample**. In this method, instead of individual items, groups or clusters of items are selected to be in the sample.

Cluster sampling involves randomly selecting groups or clusters of items for inclusion in the sample.

For this technique, the population must be grouped so that a random process can be used to select the sample groups. Once a group or cluster has been randomly picked, each item in the group is included in the sample. If the cluster groups are quite large, a simple random sample can be selected from each.

EXAMPLE 2.11   Forest Resources, a lumber company, wants to randomly sample logs to measure for moisture content and number of board-feet. Since the logs are in piles in the lumberyard, and since each pile contains similar logs, it's decided to regard the piles as clusters and randomly choose among them. There are 58 log piles, so two-digit random numbers are chosen. Log piles are prenumbered so piles corresponding to the random numbers can be identified. Each log in the chosen piles is then measured.

EXAMPLE 2.12   Panorex, Inc., uses a city map to randomly survey residents regarding their preferences for local TV news programs. Each city block is numbered for a total of 758 blocks. Twenty 3-digit random numbers are chosen, and blocks corresponding to these numbers are used in the sample. Interviewers are sent to interview each residence on the selected blocks. Several trips are needed to secure these interviews since many people aren't home on the first call. This interview process results in a cluster sample that's random.

Three nonrandom sampling procedures are frequently used in practical situations. First, in a **judgment** sample, items selected for inclusion in the sample are chosen using the sampler's judgment. Second, the **convenience** sample is so named because the most convenient population items are selected. The third is a **quota** sample, selected on the basis of specific guidelines about which items and/or how many should be drawn.

EXAMPLE 2.13   Fidelity Associates' board of directors has decided to sample opinions of other companies around the country regarding the economic forecast for next year. Company president Sean Bradford chooses those persons to be interviewed by telephone. This is a judgment sample because the specific individuals to be called aren't selected randomly; rather, Bradford's judgment is used in the selection process. If the company president is experienced and personally selects a representative group to sample—a good sample should result. On the other hand, if Sean talks only to friends who aren't in a good position to assess economic conditions, a misleading picture of the company's operating environment could result. This is the danger of a judgment sample: the sampler must use good judgment in choosing items to be sampled. In addition, a judgment sample can be difficult to defend, especially when the results displease someone.

EXAMPLE 2.14   A market research class has decided to sample student opinion on several subjects for a class project. The team leader assigns each student a sample of 10 people and requests that interviews be completed in one week. This could be called a quota sample because each student's quota is a sample of 10, or it could be called a convenience sample because each student will presumably sample the 10 most convenient people in the absence of any other instructions. A poor sample will likely result. No thought has been given to the nature of the population or to whether the sampling team will be contacting students of various ages, majors, places of residence, and so on. If results of this sample are extended to the entire student population, inaccurate conclusions are quite possible.

EXAMPLE 2.15   A September 19, 1989, *Wall Street Journal* lead story stated, "In the Soviet Union, the newly elected are besieged by problems." Soviet politicians may discover the usefulness of a technique used for years by American politicians: the political poll. If such survey work were to be undertaken in the Soviet Union, identifying a representative sample would be crucial. Selecting such a sample would probably incorporate stratification and cluster sampling and would likely require a good bit of judgment as well.

Two conflicting objectives must be balanced in sampling from a population: accuracy and cost. If accuracy were the only objective, large, totally random samples would always be taken using methods that are fully defensible. If cost were the only objective, small samples would be selected using the fastest, most convenient method. Only when these two objectives are balanced through good judgment can a sampling procedure be determined that truly meets the researcher's needs.

In any sampling procedure, errors in estimating population characteristics are inevitable. Good sampling procedures keep these errors at an acceptably low level. Poor sampling procedures may generate misleading or erroneous results. Later this book will deal with recognition and measurement of these errors.

DATA FILE CONSTRUCTION

This chapter's emphasis is on recognizing the type of data to be collected in a research study, and on designing a plan to produce a representative sample of the population. Since data analysis is only as good as the data collected, this is a key concept and one sometimes overlooked in the haste to begin the analysis.

Of equal importance in ensuring that the final data analysis results are accurate is the careful coding of data and file construction after data have been collected. In our consulting work we sometimes see situations where careful collection of data is followed by careless, even sloppy keying of data into the computer and setting up of the data file. Subsequent analysis is then conducted on misleading or erroneous data, leading to improper conclusions.

The important point is to be sure that a carefully monitored process is involved in transferring data from the source documents to the computer file in a format that can be used by the data analysis software. It often helps to visualize the final data file as a rectangular block of numbers in the computer. There is a row for each respondent or entity measured, and a column for each variable recorded. Example 2.16 shows part of such a data block.

EXAMPLE 2.16 Table 1.1 in the previous chapter showed a student questionnaire used to generate a class data base. Table 2.8 shows a small portion of the data base we generated in a recent statistics class. Only 10 lines are shown, representing 10 student responses. Coding for the column variables was as follows (question numbers refer to the questions in Table 1.1):

1. 1 = Freshman, 2 = Sophomore, 3 = Junior, 4 = Senior, 5 = Grad, 6 = Other.
2. 1 = Female, 2 = Male.
3. GPA recorded with one decimal point (e.g., 3.1).
4. Age recorded with two digits.
5. Smoking recorded as 1 = Regularly, 2 = Sometimes, 3 = Never.
6 through 11. Responses recorded with response digit, 1 = Strongly agree,
      2 = Agree, 3 = Neutral, 4 = Disagree, 5 = Strongly disagree.

Note: A nonresponse for any question is recorded as a zero.

TABLE 2.8 Student Questionnaire Data Block (Example 2.16)

2	1	3.1	22	3	1	3	2	4	5	2	
2	1	2.9	21	3	1	4	2	3	5	4	
3	2	3.0	25	3	5	2	3	4	2	3	
2	2	2.2	29	1	3	3	3	2	2	3	
3	2	3.5	23	3	2	4	3	3	4	5	
2	1	2.7	35	3	2	1	1	2	1	2	
2	1	3.8	21	3	2	4	2	4	3	5	
3	2	2.5	20	2	2	1	3	3	3	3	
3	1	2.4	24	3	4	4	5	5	3	4	
3	1	3.3	23	3	3	2	2	2	2	2	

EXERCISES

25. What are the advantages of each of the following sampling techniques?
    a. Simple random sample.
    b. Cluster sample.
    c. Convenience sample.
    d. Stratified random sample.
    e. Systematic sample.
    f. Judgment sample.

26. Which of the sampling methods listed in Exercise 25 are random sampling techniques?

27. What is the danger of using a judgment sample?

28. The Illinois League of Credit Unions has decided to survey all credit unions in the state. The survey's purpose will be to determine how the league can improve service to its members. What type of sampling plan should the league use?

29. A large church wants to investigate its members' attitudes regarding level of financial support, desirability of building a new church, and popularity of the present pastor. A sum of

money has been allocated to research these matters, but the church leadership doesn't know how to proceed. What kind of research package would you recommend?

30. (This question refers to Exercise 29.) What variables should the research address so that the church's research objectives are reached?

SUMMARY

This chapter began by outlining the various kinds of data collected and analyzed in business studies. Sources of secondary data were then introduced along with methods used to collect primary data. Table 2.9 summarizes the sampling methods discussed.

TABLE 2.9   Sampling Methods

Method	Procedure
Random	
Simple	Items are randomly chosen one at a time.
Systematic	Every nth item is chosen from population sequence.
Stratified	The population is separated into meaningful subgroups prior to sampling.
Cluster	Groups or clusters of population items are selected for the sample.
Nonrandom	
Judgment	The researcher's judgment is used to decide which population items will be included in the sample.
Convenience	The most convenient items are selected for the sample.
Quota	Those choosing sampled items are given a quota.

The objective in any sampling method is to select sample items that are representative of the population. Each sampled item can represent hundreds or thousands of population items that weren't selected and won't be measured. For this reason, skilled researchers always strive to select a sound sampling plan. Random sampling provides the necessary assurance that the samples are representative.

APPLICATIONS OF STATISTICAL CONCEPTS IN THE BUSINESS WORLD

THE J & H RESEARCH SERVICE FEASIBILITY STUDY[1]

The applications of this chapter's data-gathering concepts are demonstrated in the activities of most successful organizations. Collecting data relevant to the problem being studied is often the most difficult, expensive, and time-consuming part of the entire research procedure. Let's look at J & H Research Service's approach to collecting reliable data for a feasibility study.

Metropolitan Mortgage donated land to a local university's College of Business. The land is located close to an interstate highway near the MeadowWood Industrial Park. The university decided to develop this property so as to encourage the community's

---

[1]"Physical Fitness Facility Market Analysis." *Decision Science Institute Proceedings*, San Francisco, 1992.

economic growth. The university contracted with J & H Research to determine whether a fitness facility was feasible. J & H agreed to accomplish the following objectives:

1. Determine whether MeadowWood Industrial Park employees are interested in a fitness facility. Determine potential use, reasonable costs, and what employees would pay to use a fitness facility.

2. Determine if the industrial park's employer's personnel office/management groups would be interested in a fitness facility.

3. Determine whether current residents of the surrounding area are interested in such facilities.

4. Define the primary market area and determine whether it would support a fitness facility.

5. Determine whether it's feasible to operate a fitness center at a profit.

J & H Research used the following data-gathering techniques to determine the fitness facility's feasibility:

Objective 1: Each of the seven firms in the industrial park administered a questionnaire to its employees (primary data). A 23% response rate was achieved.

Objective 2: Personal interviews were conducted with appropriate management personnel of each firm (primary data).

Objective 3: A door-to-door survey was conducted for residents of the surrounding area (primary data). A 63.4% response rate was achieved.

Objective 4: Census data were acquired for communities within a 10-mile radius of the proposed site (secondary data). A list of all fitness clubs in the area was compiled using both primary (telephone interviews) and secondary (*Journal of Business* articles) data sources. The list included size, staffing, type of programs offered, and physical facilities. A County Engineer's report was used to describe the site and determine access (secondary data). Articles in local business publications provided data on local business and residential development (secondary data). Observation and personal interviews were used to determine traffic flow (primary data).

Objective 5: An appraisal report was used to determine land and building costs for the area (secondary data). Telephone interviews were conducted to determine building and equipment costs (primary data).

OTHER APPLICATIONS

Much information has already been collected and is available in libraries and computer data bases. Businesses of all types frequently use these sources rather than spend time and money to collect new data. *The Wall Street Journal,* read by many businesspeople daily, is a continuing source of secondary data.

Collecting primary data through sampling is common in the business world. Whenever information on a large population is desired, some kind of sampling is usually employed. Here are a few situations that call for sampling:

The accounting department wants to know the status of its accounts receivable.

A manufacturer of aluminum panels is interested in the quality level of its manufacturing process.

A car manufacturer needs to know a new model's average miles per gallon for advertising purposes.

The number of overtime hours per week in a large plant needs to be monitored on a monthly basis.

Company management needs to determine its large work force's opinion of a proposed union.

A large health care service must consider its clients' attitudes so that service may be improved.

Credit union customers need to be surveyed about their satisfaction with current service and interest in new services.

Supplier performance regarding the number of defective units shipped to a plant must be evaluated by a company's quality-control department.

A bank with over 10,000 customers wants to develop a profile of a highly profitable customer.

A restaurant is facing declining revenues each month and wants to know what customers think of their dining experience.

A university is interested in determining its graduates' attitudes toward a proposed fund-raising campaign.

Glossary

Variable An item of interest that can take on many different numerical values.

Constant An item with a fixed numerical value.

Quantitative variable A variable whose values are expressible as numerical quantities, such as measurements or counts.

Qualitative variable A variable that isn't quantitative and can only be classified, but not measured.

Mutually exclusive Categories, only one of which can include a given individual, object, or measurement.

Nominal scale A scale consisting of mutually exclusive categories in which no logical order is implied.

Ordinal scale A scale consisting of distinct categories in which order is implied.

Interval scale A scale consisting of numerical values in which the distance between successive numbers is of measurable constant size.

Ratio scale A scale consisting of numerical measurements where the distances between numbers are of a known, constant size, and where the ratio of numbers has some meaning; in addition, there is a fixed, nonarbitrary zero point.

Primary data Data collected specifically for the analysis desired.

Secondary data Data already collected and available for statistical analysis.

Population The entire set of individuals or items of interest.

Census An attempt to measure every item in the population of interest.

Sample A subset selected from the population.

Simple random sample A sample that results when n elements are selected from a population in such a way that every possible combination of n elements in the population has an equal probability of being selected.

Sampling without replacement Sampling in which an item selected isn't returned to the population for possible reselection.

Sampling with replacement Sampling in which each selected item is returned to the population before the next selection takes place.

Random number table A table used to provide lists of numbers that are randomly generated and can be used to select random samples.

Systematic sample A sample in which every nth item in the population sequence is selected.

Stratified random sample A sample in which the population is broken into meaningful strata or subgroups, and each group is randomly sampled.

Cluster sample A sample in which groups or clusters of items are randomly selected for inclusion.

SOLVED EXERCISES

1. LEVELS OF MEASUREMENT
Refer to the student questionnaire presented in Table 1.1. For each of the first six questions, identify the level of measurement.

Solution:

(1) ordinal, (2) nominal, (3) ratio, (4) ratio, (5) ordinal, (6) ordinal.

2. SECONDARY AND PRIMARY DATA
Garfield Bay Marina, located on Lake Pend Oreille, was acquired by Westland Mortgage Service Company through repossession. The marina hasn't been producing revenue because it lacks a floating breakwater to protect it against high waves. To build the floating breakwater, Westland Mortgage must obtain permission from the Idaho Land Use Commission. Westland must convince the commission that the marina is needed. To do this, Westland must analyze competitive marinas on the lake, demonstrate that Garfield Bay can support the marina, and determine demand in the competitive market area for covered and uncovered boat slips.

a. What secondary data sources might be used to complete this study?

b. What primary data sources might be used to complete this study?

Solution:

a. Census data should be gathered to establish the market area's demographics. Boater registration data should be gathered from state government sources to help determine boat slip demand.

b. Marina operators and dealers should be interviewed. A physical survey of the number of occupied and vacant boat slips on Lake Pend Oreille should be completed.

3. SAMPLES
(This question refers to Solved Exercise 2.) What kind of sampling plan should be used to determine the number of occupied and vacant boat slips on Lake Pend Oreille?

Solution:

A census of all the marinas located on Lake Pend Oreille should be completed.

EXERCISES

31. Specify whether each of the following variables is qualitative or quantitative. For each variable, identify its type of measurement scale.

    a. Gasoline mileage.

    b. Gasoline brand.

    c. A person's temperature.

    d. A test score.

    e. A worker's job performance rating.

    f. A worker's job classification.

    g. A football team's ranking.

32. Discuss the adequacy of each of the following sampling approaches:

    a. A radio disk jockey wishes to determine the most popular song in her city. She asks listeners to call and indicate their preference.

    b. A citizens' group interested in generating public and financial support for a waste-to-energy garbage-burning plant prints a questionnaire in a local newspaper. Readers are asked to return the questionnaires by mail.

    c. A drugstore wishes to examine whether it's losing or gaining customers. The manager chooses a sample from the store's list of credit card holders by selecting every 25th name.

    d. A research company obtains a sample for a focus group by randomly calling households and including every third respondent who's willing to participate.

    e. A research company obtains a sample for a focus group by selecting respondents through organized groups (church groups, clubs, and charitable organizations). The organizations are paid for securing a respondent, but no individual is directly compensated.

33. Uptown Radiology is developing a medical imaging center more complete and technologically advanced than any other currently located in the New England area. Uptown Radiology asked PMA Research to evaluate the market and project revenues for five years. The study's objectives are to:

Identify market areas for each type of procedure the new facility will offer.

Gather and analyze existing data on market area revenue for each such procedure.

Identify health care industry trends that will positively or negatively affect revenue from these procedures.

    a. What secondary data sources might be used to complete this study?

    b. What primary data sources might be used to complete this study?

34. The Bay Area Rapid Transit (BART) wants to gather information from transit users and nonusers that it can use in developing marketing programs for maintaining present riders and attracting new riders. BART isn't sure what questions to ask, so it decides to do some preliminary research. Would focus groups be useful for this purpose? What method should be used to recruit participants?

35. A rental car company wants to estimate its fleet's average odometer mileage. Over 12,000 cars are in the fleet, so a sampling plan is needed. After analyzing the potential errors involved in sampling, the company decides on a sample size of 1,200 cars. A stratification on car size is also decided on, based on the following proportions of cars in the fleet.

Large cars	20%
Medium-sized cars	35
Small cars	20
Compact cars	25

    a. How many cars should be sampled from each size category?

    b. Are there any other stratifications that should be made before the sample is taken?

    c. How should the sample be taken from each stratum?

36. The Northtown Shopping Mall Association wants to develop a data base on kinds of people who shop at the mall. The association decides to conduct a study of people who shop there. What type of data-gathering approach should it use? What method should it use to recruit participants?

37. (This question refers to Exercise 36.) The interviewer asked each survey participant about the average amount spent per mall visit. The array of these amounts for the 100 people interviewed is

1. 10	21. 13	41. 15	61. 22	81. 62
2. 83	22. 10	42. 5	62. 7	82. 22
3. 71	23. 62	43. 59	63. 55	83. 9
4. 14	24. 10	44. 12	64. 92	84. 15
5. 82	25. 41	45. 52	65. 63	85. 95
6. 11	26. 22	46. 21	66. 55	86. 44
7. 47	27. 58	47. 13	67. 39	87. 15
8. 0	28. 45	48. 25	68. 89	88. 14
9. 25	29. 36	49. 54	69. 87	89. 25
10. 20	30. 65	50. 65	70. 25	90. 45
11. 95	31. 87	51. 74	71. 82	91. 35
12. 62	32. 41	52. 26	72. 29	92. 49
13. 36	33. 0	53. 32	73. 10	93. 4
14. 24	34. 48	54. 69	74. 75	94. 84
15. 42	35. 30	55. 80	75. 17	95. 15
16. 56	36. 50	56. 90	76. 96	96. 45
17. 55	37. 60	57. 84	77. 5	97. 66
18. 85	38. 70	58. 8	78. 36	98. 33
19. 99	39. 54	59. 24	79. 44	99. 18
20. 15	40. 82	60. 27	80. 22	100. 77

Use a table of random numbers to select a simple random sample of 30 dollar amounts, then compute the average of these values. Sampling should be done with replacement.

38. Identify whether each variable in the company data base found in Appendix C is qualitative or quantitative. For each variable, identify its type of measurement scale.

EXTENDED EXERCISES

39. DEER PARK CREDIT UNION

The Deer Park Credit Union wants to improve its services to maintain its market share and possibly add members. It decides on a market research project consisting of two parts. First, names are randomly selected from its mailing list, and these people are invited to participate in a focus group. They're offered $25 to attend a one-hour session which is tape-recorded for review by management. A number of corrective-action ideas emerge from these meetings.

    Next, a mail questionnaire is developed and mailed to a random sample of 350 persons selected from the credit union's membership list. This four-page questionnaire covers present usage of services, asks for a list of additional services desired, and contains a number of rating questions for evaluating the credit union's performance. About 75% of these questionnaires are returned within two weeks, and they're entered on the credit union's computer for analysis.

A final report is prepared that summarizes the focus group discussions and the tabulation of the questionnaires. A staff meeting is called to evaluate these results and to decide on actions to improve services, add new ones, and increase membership.

a. What is the advantage of holding the focus group meetings before the questionnaire is finalized?

b. Do you think the 75% return rate for the questionnaire is adequate? What might have been done to increase the return rate?

c. Do you think the credit union will learn what it wants to after reviewing this two-stage research?

40. THE SPOKANE INDIAN TRIBE FEASIBILITY STUDY[2]

The Spokane Indian Reservation in Eastern Washington is approximately 50 miles northwest of Spokane. The reservation's western and southern boundaries are comprised of 36 miles of Lake Roosevelt shoreline.

For the past two years, the tribe has investigated the potential for developing a recreational site at the confluence of the Spokane and Columbia Rivers on Lake Roosevelt. Plans include the possibility of building an RV park, motel (lodging and meeting rooms), marina (dock and rental slips), houseboat rental operation, grocery/fishing tackle store, picnic area, beach and swimming area, cultural center with gift shop, casino, and golf course. The Spokane Tribe has invited bids for a market analysis and feasibility study of these businesses. Before preparing your bid, do the following:

a. List primary sources of data that you would use to develop the market analysis. Explain how you would use each source.

b. List secondary sources of data that you would use. Explain how each would be used.

41. METROPOLITAN HOLDING COMPANY

The Metropolitan Holding Company has four subsidiaries, all in different cities. Top management, led by company president Wendy Watts, wants to determine company employees' attitudes toward the parent company and their subsidiary company. She decided to undertake this research after reading "The Champion of the Modern Corner Store," an article in *Working Woman* (September 1989). This article described the winning managerial formula of the woman who's president of her company, and Wendy wants to assess employees' attitudes in her own company as a first step in modifying her management style.

Wendy specifically wants to learn about employee loyalty to the holding company and to the employees' subsidiary company. If there's strong loyalty toward the subsidiary company and little loyalty toward the parent company, top management would hesitate to implement further plans for centralizing control of the firm.

Top management has developed a number of ideas to assess loyalty among the many employees. It is recognized that there are many different types of employees, including male and female, union and nonunion, short-term and long-term, and those from different subsidiary companies.

---

[2]"The Spokane Indian Tribe Feasibility Study." *Decision Science Institute Proceedings*, New Orleans, 1991.

A mail questionnaire has been suggested to measure employee attitudes, and a tentative set of questions has been developed.

a. Would you favor using a mail questionnaire in this case?

b. Would it be useful to stratify the population prior to the research? If so, how?

c. If you were to design this research, what methods would you employ?

MICROCOMPUTER PACKAGE

You can use the micro package *Computerized Business Statistics* to generate random numbers. In Exercise 37 you used a table of random numbers to select a simple random sample of 30 average dollar amounts from a population of 100 items.

Computer Solution

On the main menu of *Computerized Business Statistics*, a 7 is selected, which indicates Sampling and Estimation.

```
        Sampling and Estimation
        PROGRAM OPTIONS MENU
0. CBS Configuration
1. Generate Random Numbers
2. Central Limit Theorem Demonstration
3. Compute Sample Size
4. Interval Estimation
5. Quick Reviews
6. Exit to Main Menu
7. Exit to Operating System
Press ↵ to select option under hi-lite bar. Press number or up/down arrow keys to
move hi-lite bar.
```

This program generates random numbers, demonstrates the central limit theorem, determines sample sizes, and computes interval estimates.

Since the problem involves the generation of random numbers, 1 is selected.

```
Enter number of random numbers (10–1250) and press ↵ 30
```

The screen will now show a partial table of random numbers.

```
Send copy to the printer? Y/N press ↵ Y
```

```
Store random numbers in a data file? (Y/N, press ↵): Y
```

These features allow you to print out a copy of the random numbers and store them for future use.

MINITAB COMPUTER PACKAGE

The MINITAB commands to generate random numbers to solve Exercise 37 are:

```
MTB>   RANDOM 30 VALUES INTO C1;
SUBC>  INTEGER 1 TO 100.
MTB>   PRINT C1
C1
40    20    90    8    67    47    65    12    85    26    28    80
27    56    61    1    12    81    1     43    7     58    14    84
61    78    33    8    22    85

MTB> STOP
```

The **RANDOM** command selects 30 values and stores them in column 1 of the worksheet (C1). The semicolon at the end of line 1 requests a subcommand prompt.

The **INTEGER** subcommand indicates that the 30 random numbers are to be integers from 1 to 100. A period must be placed at the end of the last subcommand line.

The **PRINT** command is used to print the 30 random numbers.

Chapter

3

Data Presentation

"The question
is," said Alice,
"whether you
can make words
mean so many
different
things."

"The question
is," said Humpty
Dumpty, "which
is to be master—
that's all."

Lewis Carroll,
*Through the
Looking-Glass*

Objectives

When you have completed this chapter, you will be able to:

Organize a data collection into a frequency distribution.

Determine the most effective method for presenting a data collection.

Construct various charts and graphs, such as pie charts, bar charts, histograms, frequency polygons, and ogives.

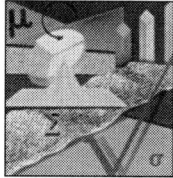

On Friday, April 17, 1992, *The Wall Street Journal* reported that the U.S. trade deficit had narrowed in February 1992 to a seasonally adjusted $3.38 billion from a revised $5.95 billion in January. These figures were obtained from the U.S. Department of Commerce.

Chapter 2 covered various ways of collecting data for decision making. It stressed the importance of carefully identifying needed data and ensuring that these data values are properly selected from the population under study.

WHY DATA PRESENTATION METHODS ARE IMPORTANT TO MANAGERS

Once data have been collected, they must be processed in some way so that any important patterns become apparent. The rest of this book discusses ways to convert raw data into the kinds of information decision makers need. Some of the most basic and most widely used techniques for summarizing important data collections appear in this chapter. These techniques are important for both qualitative data (nominal and ordinal) and quantitative data (interval and ratio). Additional methods for summarizing quantitative data collections are discussed in Chapter 4.

The U.S. trade deficit is an economic indicator business and government leaders watch closely. Charts and graphs are effective ways to track this important value over time. *The Wall Street Journal* uses graphs to show readers the history of important economic variables (Figure 3.1) and most issues have graphs on the front page to accompany lead stories. This chapter will show methods to construct effective charts and graphs.

FIGURE 3.1   U.S. Trade Deficit, 1989–92 (in billions of dollars)

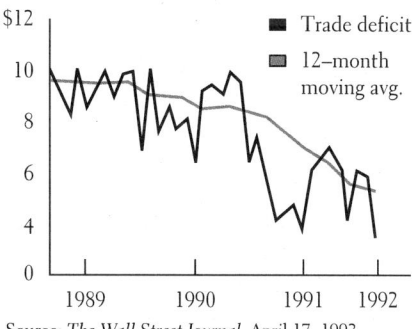

Source: *The Wall Street Journal*, April 17, 1992.

FREQUENCY DISTRIBUTIONS

The concept of a **distribution** is important in statistics. This is the term statisticians use to represent a collection, array, or group of numerical values.

> A **distribution** is a collection, array, or group of numerical values.

Frequency Distribution

A common, very helpful way to summarize data collections is through the **frequency distribution.** This data display method shows the frequency (number of occurrences) in each of several categories. Frequency distributions can summarize large volumes of data values so decision makers can extract useful information directly from the collection.

> A **frequency distribution** is a list of data classes or categories along with the number of values that fall into each.

EXAMPLE 3.1   The Brite Paint Company asked several people to indicate their favorite color. Tabulation of the results (Table 3.1) shows that 12 people indicated red as their favorite color, 8 chose green, 8 selected blue, and 4 picked yellow (nominal data). This tabulation represents a frequency distribution because various categories (colors) are listed along with the number of times (frequency) each was chosen. Unless some predetermined order exists, categories are listed in order of magnitude, the category with the largest frequency is listed first, and so forth.

TABLE 3.1   Favorite Colors (Example 3.1)

Color	Frequency
Red	12
Green	8
Blue	8
Yellow	4
	32

EXAMPLE 3.2   A sample of 86 shoppers was asked to what extent they agree with the statement, "Trudy's Apparel sells high-quality clothing." The frequency distribution in Table 3.2 summarizes the results (ordinal data). The table indicates fairly strong support for the statement. This frequency distribution concisely and clearly shows the reactions of the sample of shoppers to this statement.

Note that Tables 3.1 and 3.2 both summarize qualitative data.

When the raw data are measured on a quantitative scale, either interval or ratio, categories or classes must be designed for the data values before a frequency distribu-

TABLE 3.2 Reaction to the Statement, "Trudy's Apparel Sells High-Quality Clothing" (Example 3.2)

Reaction	Frequency
Strongly agree	12
Agree	35
Neutral or no opinion	27
Disagree	10
Strongly disagree	2
	86

tion can be formulated. No firm rule exists for determining the appropriate number of classes for a particular frequency distribution, but this number is usually between 5 and 15. If there are too few classes, the results may be too general to permit detection of underlying tendencies in the data. On the other hand, too many classes defeat the purpose of the frequency distribution, which is to summarize a large data collection so it can be easily understood and used in decision making.

The technical process of generating a frequency distribution is quite tedious and time-consuming. Therefore, a less rigorous approach will be suggested in the next section. Note that this approach uses several rules of thumb.

The first step in constructing a frequency distribution for quantitative data is to decide on the number of classes (usually 5 to 15). If there are a large number of items or observations (more than 1,000) in the data set, a relatively large number of classes (11 or more) is generally used. If the data set is small (say, fewer than 60 observations), a small number of classes (5 or 6) is used. Table 3.3 provides guidelines for selecting the number of classes.

The second step is to determine the size of each class. Frequency distributions are usually constructed using equal class widths. The exception occurs when it's necessary to leave the last class open-ended. Class width can be determined by finding the difference between the largest value in the data set and the smallest value and dividing

TABLE 3.3 Guidelines for Number of Classes in a Frequency Distribution

Number of observations	Number of classes
Fewer than 30	5
30 to fewer than 60	6
60 to fewer than 130	7
130 to fewer than 250	8
250 to fewer than 500	9
500 to fewer than 1,000	10
1,000 to fewer than 2,000	11
2,000 to fewer than 4,000	12
4,000 to fewer than 8,000	13
8,000 and over	14

it by the number of classes desired. Since people tend to be 5- and 10-oriented, class widths of these sizes are desirable and are used whenever possible.

The third step is to tally the number of values in each class. This involves listing the classes and then going through the data set, placing a tally mark by the appropriate class. Classes are organized so that their limits don't overlap (i.e., the classes are mutually exclusive).

The last step is to prepare a table of the distribution. It is common to show frequencies both as actual counts and as percentages, or relative frequencies. (The concept of relative frequencies will be explained in the next section.)

Constructing a Frequency Distribution

Steps for constructing a frequency distribution
1. Determine the number of classes, usually 5 to 15 (see Table 3.3).
2. Determine the size of each class. Class size is determined by finding the difference between the largest value in the data set and the smallest value and dividing it by the number of classes desired.
3. Determine the starting point for the first class.
4. Tally the number of values that occur in each class.
5. Prepare a table of the distribution using actual counts and/or percentages (relative frequencies).

(*Note*: These steps should only be considered as rules of thumb and not as a rigorous process for constructing a frequency distribution.)

EXAMPLE 3.3   The frequency distribution in Table 3.4 summarizes Sunrunner Corporation executives' incomes. Table 3.3 shows that with 97 observations, the frequency distribution should contain seven income classes. Notice that the choice of a convenient income class width, $10,000, makes the data summary easy to follow.

Table 3.4 illustrates the concept of mutually exclusive categories or classes. The class limits, such as "20,000 to less than 30,000," make it impossible for a person to

TABLE 3.4   Executive Incomes for the Sunrunner Corporation (Example 3.3)

Annual income ($)	Frequency
20,000 to less than 30,000	5
30,000 to less than 40,000	17
40,000 to less than 50,000	22
50,000 to less than 60,000	28
60,000 to less than 70,000	14
70,000 to less than 80,000	8
80,000 to less than 90,000	3
	97

belong to more than one income category since each begins where the previous one left off. This table is an example of a frequency distribution that neatly summarizes many raw data values.

EXAMPLE 3.4   Management of Atlas Contractors closely follows the number of trucks produced in the United States because demand for transmissions is closely related to this variable. The *New York Times* for September 10, 1989, indicated 66,427 trucks were produced for the most recent week.

While Atlas is excited about the recent truck volume, it is having trouble with its quality control. The company has had difficulty meeting demand this year because of the number of errors per shift (Table 3.5).

TABLE 3.5   Errors per Shift (Example 3.4)

Number of errors	Frequency (number of days)
0–4	11
5–9	22
10–14	13
15–19	8
20–24	3
25–29	2
	59

This table has six classes. It is easy to read, and it summarizes error occurrences in the manufacturing process. Note that the classes have an equal width, five units. Classes of unequal width (for example, 0–4, 5–10, 11–18, 19–25, and 26 or more) would make the underlying data more difficult to interpret. Also note that the variable, number of errors per shift, is measured in whole numbers. Thus, the classes (0–4, 5–9, etc.) are mutually exclusive.

When there are many observations or objects to classify in a frequency distribution, it may be more helpful to study the *percentage* of items falling into each class rather than the actual frequencies. It might be more meaningful, for example, to observe that 12% of a college's students are business majors than to know that there are 942 business majors.

Relative Frequencies   **Relative frequencies,** or percentages, are calculated for a frequency distribution by dividing the actual frequency for each class by the total number of objects classified. Table 3.6 does this for the Sunrunner Corporation executive incomes in Table 3.4. Note that in Table 3.6, each frequency is divided by 97, the total number of executives, to form the percentages in the last column. This column of percentages should total 1.000. (If calculation is done by hand, this sum may not precisely equal 1 due to rounding errors.)

TABLE 3.6 Relative Frequencies for Executive Incomes (Example 3.3)

Annual income ($)	Frequency	Relative frequency
20,000 to less than 30,000	5	5/97 = .052
30,000 to less than 40,000	17	17/97 = .175
40,000 to less than 50,000	22	22/97 = .227
50,000 to less than 60,000	28	28/97 = .289
60,000 to less than 70,000	14	14/97 = .144
70,000 to less than 80,000	8	8/97 = .082
80,000 to less than 90,000	3	3/97 = .031
	97	1.000

Relative frequencies such as those in Table 3.6 can be very useful in summarizing large data collections.

> **Relative frequencies** are percentages calculated by dividing the actual frequency for each class by the total number of observations being classified.

EXAMPLE 3.5   Kyle Chang owns The Wash Tub, a dry cleaners. He wants to know the number of customer orders processed per day. A random sample of days is selected for study using sampling methods discussed in Chapter 2. Table 3.7 shows the resulting data. Kyle wants to use these data to understand the pattern of his customer load, but it's difficult to deal with so much raw data. Kyle knows a frequency distribution can summarize these values. He hopes the patterns that underlie the data will become more apparent and aid him in planning for future customer service.

TABLE 3.7 Customers per Day for The Wash Tub (Example 3.5)

65	23	26	45	12	45	56	35	26	45	25
56	45	32	12	56	53	23	24	45	36	35
15	45	19	05	56	53	26	53	56	54	52
25	26	34	35	36	31	23	26	25	46	45
56	52	51	53	26	64	23	24	21	29	28
65	39	38	26	37	24	28	25	35	67	38
16	18	46	23	35	38	32	57	48	49	53
34	31	37	28	29	37	34	31	26	25	43

Table 3.7 gives the raw data. Kyle follows the steps presented earlier in the chapter:

1. Table 3.3 shows that with 88 observations, Kyle should use about seven classes.
2. Class width is determined by finding the difference between the largest value in the data set (67) and the smallest value (5) and dividing it by the number of

classes desired $[(67 - 5)/7 = 8.9]$. A class width of 9 will provide approximately seven classes. However, people tend to think in terms of 5s and 10s, so Kyle decides that a class width of 10 will provide a frequency distribution that's easier to understand.

3. Next, Kyle organizes the classes so they don't overlap. He can now tally the number of values in each class (Table 3.8). Since the smallest value in the data is 5, he decides that a reasonable starting class is 0 to 9.

TABLE 3.8 Tally Sheet for Wash Tub Customers (Example 3.5)

Number of customers	Tallies	Count	Relative frequency
0–9	I	1	.011
10–19	Ⅲ I	6	.068
20–29	Ⅲ Ⅲ Ⅲ Ⅲ Ⅲ II	27	.307
30–39	Ⅲ Ⅲ Ⅲ Ⅲ II	22	.250
40–49	Ⅲ Ⅲ II	12	.136
50–59	Ⅲ Ⅲ Ⅲ I	16	.182
60–69	IIII	4	.046
		88	1.000

4. Finally, Kyle constructs the distribution using actual counts and percentages (relative frequencies) (Table 3.8).

The basic frequency distribution of Table 3.8 helps Kyle evaluate his business's customer load. For instance, on 30.7% of the days studied, The Wash Tub had between 20 and 29 customers.

EXERCISES

1. Why are data collections organized into frequency distributions?

2. What is the difference between a frequency distribution and a relative frequency distribution?

3. Describe the steps necessary to convert a frequency distribution into a relative frequency distribution.

4. If a data collection has 80 values, approximately how many classes should be included in its frequency distribution?

5. If a data collection has 880 values, approximately how many classes should be included in its frequency distribution?

6. A data collection contains 400 observations. The lowest value is 23, and the highest value is 60. What would be a good lower limit for the first class in a frequency distribution?

7. Jacob Palmer, the production manager of a food-processing plant, has recorded the number of batches rejected daily for the past 50 days. The lowest was 2 and the highest 36. Jacob wants to construct a frequency distribution for this series. How should he determine the following?

     a. Approximate number of classes.

     b. Class width.

     c. Limits for the first class.

8. Football is still the most televised sport, but the summer Olympic Games are a quadrennial contender. Convert this frequency distribution into a relative frequency distribution.

Sport category	Hours aired, 1988
Football	423
Olympics	270
Basketball	263
Golf	218
Baseball	184
Tennis	90
Bowling	36
Other	110
Total	1,594

Source: Nielsen Media Research.

9. SAE Airlines has applied to the Civil Aeronautics Board (CAB) for a new route between Minneapolis and Billings. Carol Hart, company analyst, is estimating when the CAB is most likely to rule on the company's application. She assembles the waiting times for applications filed during the past year, acquiring observations for 120 filings. The data are stated in days from the date of application until a CAB ruling.

52	63	72	95	99	77	65	43	58	67
64	54	78	98	82	84	75	77	69	49
58	57	69	71	80	90	85	96	87	44
42	73	82	65	79	67	85	73	88	77
84	44	98	58	82	64	95	67	99	69
98	47	79	41	90	50	45	56	47	54
54	67	78	95	94	75	69	41	52	65
65	54	79	98	86	85	78	71	63	44
56	58	67	71	81	95	85	92	84	42
48	70	84	65	70	66	87	74	86	75
89	42	90	58	87	67	96	63	90	68
97	49	77	40	98	54	46	59	48	59

     a. Construct a frequency distribution for this data collection.

     b. Construct a relative frequency distribution for this data collection.

10. Westland Investments is interested in purchasing Moreland Realty. As a part of the prepurchase negotiations, Jim Moreland, president of Moreland Realty, collects selling prices for 80 homes in the surrounding market area (prices are recorded in thousands of dollars):

35	110	37	58	72	102	39	125	31	48
64	54	108	98	82	84	75	77	69	49
42	73	32	65	109	67	85	73	88	77
98	47	79	41	90	30	45	56	47	114

54	67	78	95	94	75	69	41	122	65
89	42	90	58	87	27	96	63	90	68
36	58	27	71	81	95	85	92	84	42
48	70	104	65	70	66	87	34	86	75

a. Construct a frequency distribution for this data collection.

b. Construct a relative frequency distribution for this data collection.

CUMULATIVE FREQUENCY DISTRIBUTIONS

Cumulative Frequencies

The frequency distributions of Tables 3.1, 3.2, 3.4, 3.5, 3.6, and 3.8 show the number of items, or frequency, in each of several classes or categories. Sometimes it's useful to show the total number of occurrences above or below certain key values. The **cumulative frequency distribution** provides this kind of data summary.

> The **cumulative frequency distribution** shows the total number of occurrences that lie above or below certain key values.

Examples 3.6 and 3.7 show how to construct a cumulative frequency distribution.

EXAMPLE 3.6   The data of Table 3.4 are to be used to form a cumulative frequency distribution for Sunrunner Corporation executive incomes. As shown in Table 3.9, the cumulative frequency for each class is the sum of the frequencies for that class and all lower classes. For example, the cumulative frequency for the "$50,000 to less than $60,000" class is 72, which is the frequency of that class (28) plus the frequencies of all lower classes (5 + 17 + 22 + 28).

This type of cumulative frequency distribution is sometimes referred to as a *less-than* distribution because it enables one to readily see how many data values are less than some value. For instance, 72 of Sunrunner Corporation's executives earn less than

TABLE 3.9   Less-than Cumulative Frequency Distribution of Executive Incomes (Example 3.6)

Annual income ($)	Frequency	Cumulative frequency	Relative frequency	Cumulative relative frequency
20,000 to less than 30,000	5	5	.052	.052
30,000 to less than 40,000	17	22	.175	.227
40,000 to less than 50,000	22	44	.227	.454
50,000 to less than 60,000	28	72	.289	.743
60,000 to less than 70,000	14	86	.144	.887
70,000 to less than 80,000	8	94	.082	.969
80,000 to less than 90,000	3	97	.031	1.000
	97		1.000	

$60,000. Note that the last value in the cumulative column (97) is equal to the total number of observations (the summation of the frequency column).

Similarly, the cumulative relative frequency (.743) for the $50,000–$60,000 class is computed by taking the relative frequency for the "$50,000 to less than $60,000" class (.289) and adding it to the relative frequencies of all the lower classes (.052 + .175 + .227 + .289 = .743). This means that 74.3% of Sunrunner's executives earn less than $60,000. Note that the last value in the cumulative relative frequency column is equal to 1.000, or 100%. This column will always sum to 1.000.

Sometimes a *more-than* cumulative frequency distribution is useful. Such a cumulative distribution shows the number and/or percentage of items in the data collection that are greater than certain key values as is shown in Example 3.7.

EXAMPLE 3.7   In Example 3.5, Kyle wanted to determine how frequently the customer load becomes unmanageable. A more-than cumulative frequency distribution will help identify the magnitude of this problem.

Table 3.10 is formed from the frequency distribution in Table 3.8. Kyle has determined that when 30 or more customers arrive in a single day, customers aren't helped in a timely manner and he loses business. Table 3.10 shows that there were 54 days when 30 or more customers arrived. In fact, the table shows that on 61.4% of the days 30 or more customers showed up. Kyle also knows that when 40 or more customers arrive in a single day, he must turn some of them away. Table 3.10 shows that this occurred on 32 days, or 36.4% of the time. These facts indicate to Kyle that he needs additional staff.

TABLE 3.10   The Wash Tub Customers per Day: More-than Cumulative Frequency Distribution (Example 3.7)

Customers per day	Frequency	More-than frequency	Relative frequency	More-than relative frequency
0–9	1	88	.011	1.000
10–19	6	87	.068	.989
20–29	27	81	.307	.921
30–39	22	54	.250	.614
40–49	12	32	.136	.364
50–59	16	20	.182	.228
60–69	4	4	.046	.046
	88		1.000	

EXERCISES

11. Why are data collections organized into cumulative frequency distributions?

12. What is the difference between a less-than cumulative frequency distribution and a more-than cumulative frequency distribution?

13. In a less-than cumulative frequency distribution, what percentage of the total frequencies fall below the upper limit of the highest class?

14. Alliance Pacific, Inc., conducted a voter opinion survey to provide input regarding a proposed waste-to-energy facility for the area. The following frequency distribution shows survey participants' family income levels.

Income level	Frequency
Under $15,000	296
$15,000 to less than $30,000	631
$30,000 to less than $50,000	404
$50,000 and over	130
Total	1,461

Source: "Waste-to-Energy Facility Voter Opinion Survey."
Spokane: Alliance Pacific, Inc., August 1985.

a. How many classes should have been used to construct this frequency distribution?

b. Construct a relative frequency distribution for this data collection.

c. Construct a cumulative relative frequency distribution indicating the percentage of respondents with a family income less than $30,000.

15. An independent research firm surveyed households with residents age 55 or older. The following frequency distribution shows how respondents answered the question, "How many driving minutes from a hospital is the farthest that you would consider living during your retirement?"

Driving minutes	Frequency
5 minutes or less	47
6 to 10 minutes	150
11 to 15 minutes	128
16 to 20 minutes	67
21 minutes or more	94
Total	486

Source: "Surveys of Older Homeowners Concerning Retirement Attitudes." Spokane: Decision Science Associates, June 1986.

a. How could you improve this frequency distribution?

b. Construct a relative frequency distribution for this data collection.

c. Construct a cumulative relative frequency distribution.

16. Answerphone Service, Inc., wants to do a better job of billing customers for services rendered. Owner Sloan Spalding decides that he needs to know how long it takes to complete various incoming calls. The following data collection includes 150 random calls that were monitored and timed (calls are rounded to the nearest minute):

1	2	4	8	12	9	10	30	45	6
5	11	8	9	8	7	9	5	1	2
6	7	4	2	1	3	15	7	4	3
8	4	3	5	1	1	5	2	4	8
17	5	8	22	13	5	5	8	7	6
40	2	7	31	27	21	4	9	10	11

11	5	7	18	16	19	3	3	15	16
15	14	18	9	5	6	9	4	7	3
4	7	4	12	4	3	18	5	6	5
5	6	13	6	7	2	7	2	4	8
27	6	9	20	16	2	6	8	3	7
10	2	9	30	37	22	5	19	14	11
7	15	4	5	3	6	7	3	7	9
10	2	5	35	7	31	14	9	30	19
1	15	7	16	6	9	3	13	5	6

a. Construct a frequency distribution for this data collection.

b. Construct a relative frequency distribution for this data collection.

c. Construct a cumulative relative frequency distribution showing the likelihood that an incoming call will last less than 10 minutes.

d. What is the likelihood that an incoming call will last less than 25 minutes?

17. Terry Anderson, analyst for Apple One Advertising, needs to develop a meaningful presentation for the following list of one-year advertising expenditures of a sample of 72 firms in the industry (expenditures are reported in thousands of dollars).

223	258	312	452	365	400	279	264	311
325	188	200	192	425	512	289	367	214
300	250	350	375	425	475	512	487	175
248	269	357	290	248	325	444	412	520
154	160	260	340	430	510	490	230	380
303	350	250	175	325	375	212	387	125
348	289	387	190	248	323	344	312	420
254	165	210	440	330	210	430	260	390

a. Construct a cumulative relative frequency distribution showing the likelihood that a firm will have expenditures less than $300,000.

b. Construct a cumulative relative frequency distribution showing the likelihood that a firm will have expenditures more than $400,000.

CHARTS AND GRAPHS

Frequency distributions are a good way to present the essential aspects of a data collections in concise, understandable terms. But pictures can be even more effective in displaying large data collections. This section presents various methods of using pictures to summarize a data collection.

The simplest charts and graphs to construct are for nominal and ordinal data. Because the data constitute categories, the classes are readily apparent and easily described graphically.

Pie Chart

The **pie chart** is an effective way of displaying the percentage breakdown of data by category. This type of chart is particularly useful if the relative sizes of the data components are to be emphasized. Budgets and other economic information are frequently depicted using pie charts. A complete circle, 360°, represents the total number of observations. Sizes of the slices are proportional to each category's relative frequency. For example, if a category's relative frequency is .25, that category's slice is 25% of 360°, or 90° (one fourth of the circle).

Table 3.1 showed 32 people's favorite colors. If the total number of people is divided into the number of people who selected each color, relative frequencies result: 12/32 = .375, 8/32 = .25, 8/32 = .25, and 4/32 = .125. Note that the relative frequencies sum to 1.000, or 100% (.375 + .25 + .25 + .125 = 1.000). Since 37.5 percent of the customers selected red, the slice assigned to this category is 37.5% of 360° [(.375)(360) = 135°]. Other arcs' lengths are calculated similarly (Figure 3.2—percentages are rounded).

Pie charts can also effectively present ratio- or interval-scaled data after they have been organized into categories.

EXAMPLE 3.8   The Washington Water Power Company's *1991 Annual Report* reveals total operating revenues were $566.8 million in 1991: $411.8 million from electric revenues, $73.3 million from natural gas revenues, and $81.7 million from nonutility revenues. One way to show where the company dollar came from is a pie chart. Total revenue is divided into each part: 411.8/566.8 = .727, 73.3/566.8 = .129, and 81.7/566.8 = .144 (Figure 3.3).

EXAMPLE 3.9   "Retailers' cash registers are ringing merrily," said *Barrons* magazine, August 28, 1989. Suppose the Itrex Company wants to expand its facilities to take advantage of these rising sales.

Itrex is to make a presentation to a group of bankers in preparation for a loan request. Itrex management wants to concisely indicate how company funds were expended during the past fiscal year. A pie chart is chosen for the purpose (Figure 3.4).

Figure 3.4 illustrates the advantage of the pie chart; it's easy to achieve a quick and fairly accurate picture of the numbers being represented. If greater details are needed, use some other method of summarizing raw data, such as a frequency distribution.

Bar Chart

The **bar chart** is another common method for graphically presenting nominal- and ordinal-scaled data. One bar represents the frequency for each category. The height of

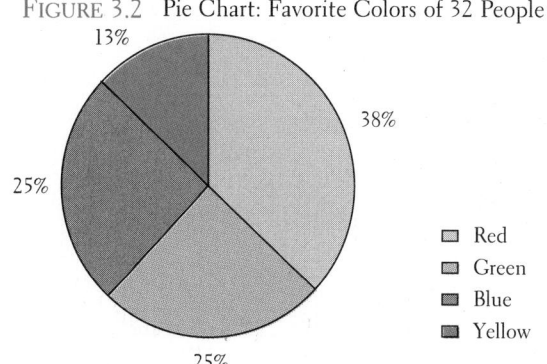

FIGURE 3.2   Pie Chart: Favorite Colors of 32 People

□ Red
□ Green
□ Blue
□ Yellow

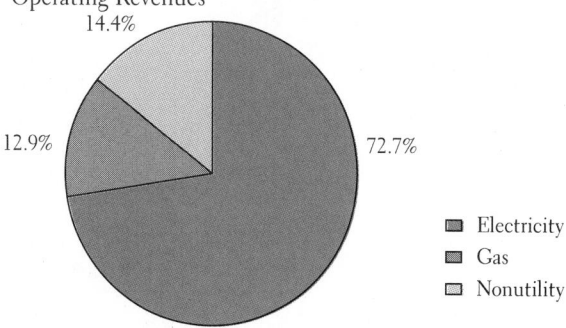

FIGURE 3.3   Pie Chart Showing Washington Water Power Operating Revenues

□ Electricity
□ Gas
□ Nonutility

Source: Washington Water Power Co., 1991 Annual Report.

FIGURE 3.4 Pie Chart: Itrex Company Expenditures

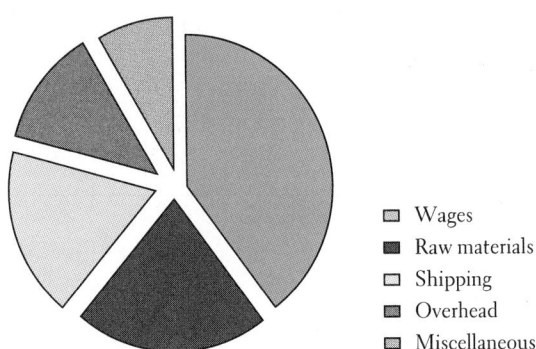

- ▨ Wages
- ▨ Raw materials
- ▨ Shipping
- ▨ Overhead
- ▨ Miscellaneous

FIGURE 3.5 Bar Chart: Favorite Colors of 32 People

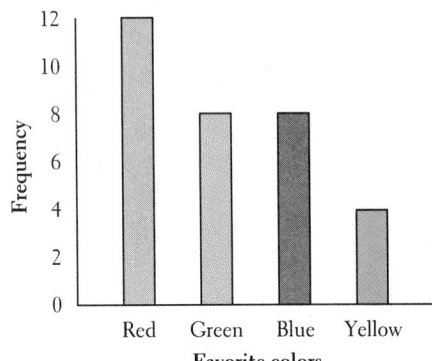

the bar is proportional to the number of items in its category. Bars are usually positioned vertically with their bases located on the horizontal axis of the graph. The bars are separated, and this is why such a graph is frequently used for nominal and ordinal data: the separations emphasize the plotting of frequencies for distinct categories.

Figure 3.2, a pie chart, showed 32 people's favorite colors. Figure 3.5 presents these data in a bar chart.

EXAMPLE 3.10 Bar charts are frequently used to compare a variable's values from one time period to another. Figure 3.6 shows U.S. raw steel production by month from 1989 until March 1992. It is easy to see the production trend by looking at this graph.

FIGURE 3.6 Bar Chart: Steel Production, 1989–92 (in millions of tons)

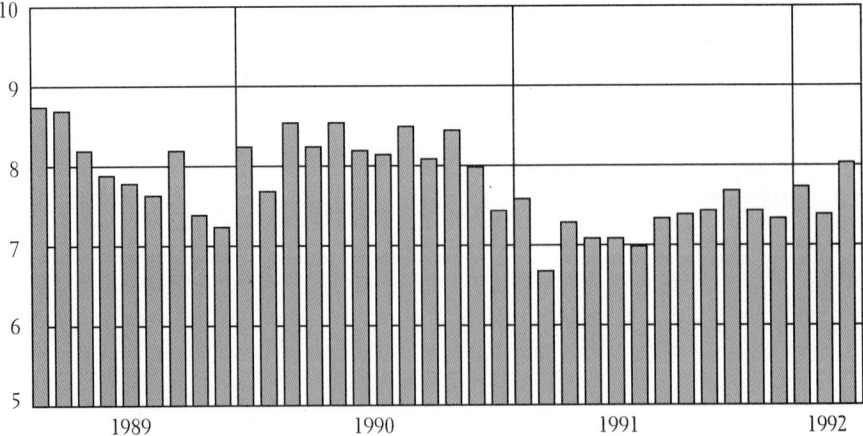

Source: *The Wall Street Journal*, April 27, 1992, p. 1.

Note from Figure 3.6 that the vertical scale begins at 5, not 0. This could possibly lead to problems of interpretation or a false picture of the original data. Watch for the possible distortion effects of such labeling in other graphs. This topic will be discussed further in a later section.

Bars are sometimes placed side by side to compare two different variables or a single variable for two different time periods (Figure 3.7). This bar chart reports how 1,997 adults responded to two questions concerning government regulation of airlines. Most bar charts are organized with the bars in a vertical position. Sometimes, however, for space reasons, the bars are in a horizontal position.

FIGURE 3.7   An Example of a Multiple Bar Chart

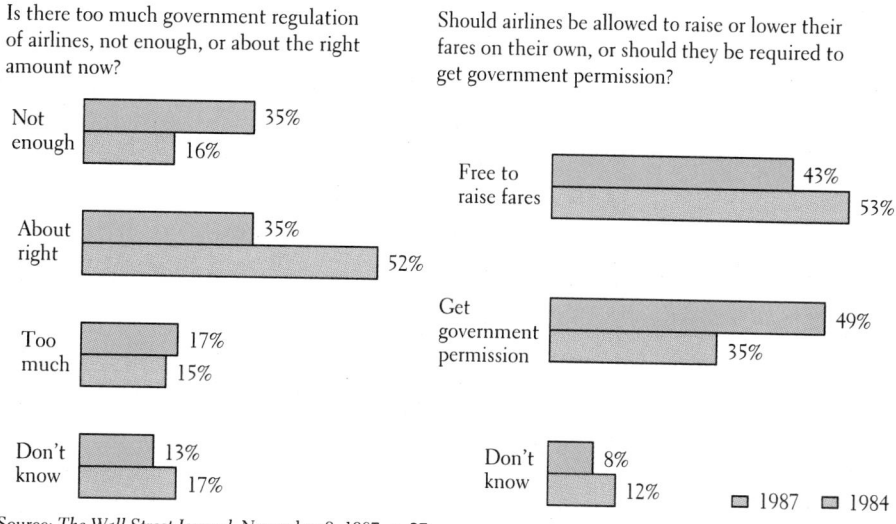

Source: *The Wall Street Journal,* November 9, 1987, p. 27.

THE PARETO CHART

Pareto Chart

The **Pareto chart** is a special case of the bar chart, which is frequently used in quality control. This type of chart consists of bars that describe components of a production or assembly line. Its purpose is to identify key causes of unacceptable quality. Each bar's height represents the number of occurrences of each problem, so the chart shows the degree of the quality problem for each variable measured. Figure 3.8 shows bar heights arranged in descending order of height.

The **Pareto chart** is a bar chart used to identify and prioritize problems.

The Pareto chart may also include a second scale showing the cumulative percentages of the variables being measured across the bar chart's categories. The right vertical axis is scaled to accommodate percentages from 0 to 100. Figure 3.8 demonstrates both of these features.

EXAMPLE 3.11   Susan Delano is quality control manager for a small job shop making special truck seats to order. Her job includes tracking major quality problems in the shop, and she decides to construct a Pareto chart for the past month. Susan determines the major quality problems on the seat line and finds out how many of each type of problem occurred. Figure 3.8 shows these occurrences along with the cumulative percentages scaled on the right axis. Susan's chart will highlight the factory's quality problems during a meeting with top management.

FIGURE 3.8   Pareto Chart: Truck Seats

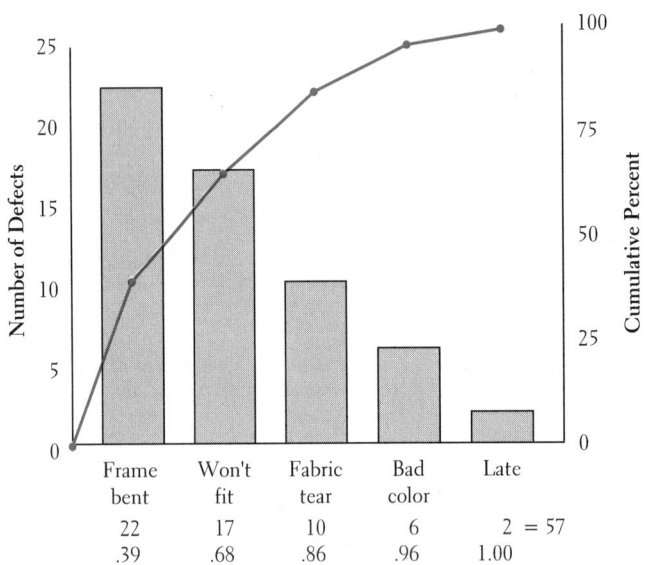

	Frame bent	Won't fit	Fabric tear	Bad color	Late	
	22	17	10	6	2	= 57
	.39	.68	.86	.96	1.00	

Histogram

The **histogram** is frequently used to graphically present interval and ratio data. In this graphing method, categories or classes are plotted along the horizontal axis of the graph, and numerical values of each class are represented by vertical bars. A histogram is like a bar chart except that there's no space between the bars. This is why the histogram is often used for interval and ratio data: the adjacent bars indicate that a numerical range is being summarized by indicating the frequencies in arbitrarily chosen classes.

EXAMPLE 3.12   The executive incomes in Table 3.4 are to be presented in a chart or graph. The histogram is chosen as an effective method (Figure 3.9). The seven income categories appear on the horizontal axis, and the frequencies appear as vertical bars.

FIGURE 3.9   Histogram: Executive Incomes for the Sunrunner Corporation

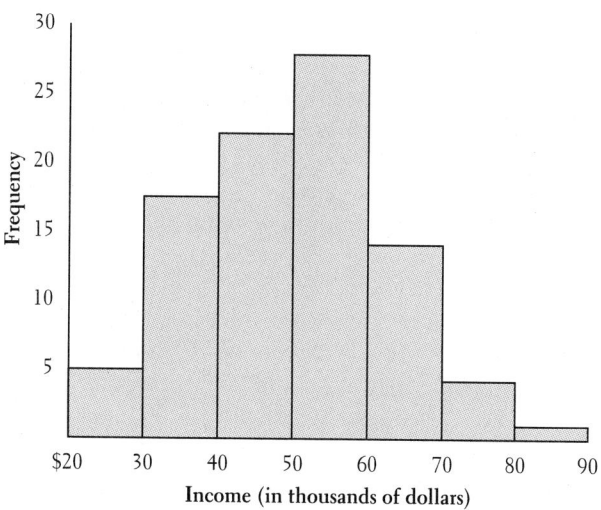

Stem-and-Leaf Plot

A **stem-and-leaf plot** is an alternative way to show data. This approach is similar to the histogram except that the actual data are displayed instead of bars. Example 3.13 illustrates the stem-and-leaf plot.

EXAMPLE 3.13   Consider the data for number of customers per day for The Wash Tub (Table 3.7). To form a stem-and-leaf plot for these values, treat the first digit (the 10s place) as the stem. Next, treat the second digit (the 1s place) as the leaf. The first number in Table 3.7 is 65. Thus, the 5, which is in the 1s place, will be located in row 6 (the row corresponding to the stem, 6):

Stem	
0	
1	
2	
3	
4	
5	
6	5

When the values are placed in order, the stem-and-leaf plot looks like this:

Stem	Leaf
0	5
1	225689
2	1333334444555556666666688899
3	11122444555556677778889
4	355555556689
5	1223333346666667
6	4557

Note that the stem-and-leaf plot provides more information than a histogram because the actual digits are shown instead of bars.

Frequency Polygon

The **frequency polygon** is another common method for graphically presenting interval and ratio data. To construct a frequency polygon, mark the frequencies on the vertical axis and the values of the variable being measured on the horizontal axis, as with the histogram. Next, plot each class frequency by placing a dot above the class midpoint, and connect successive dots with straight lines to form a polygon. Two new classes with frequencies of zero are added at the ends of the horizontal scale. This allows the polygon to reach the horizontal axis at both ends of the distribution (Example 3.14).

EXAMPLE 3.14   A frequency polygon can be drawn for the executive incomes (Table 3.4) by plotting the income category on the horizontal axis, putting a dot above each midpoint to indicate frequency, and connecting the dots. Figure 3.10 shows that the polygon touches the horizontal axis at $15,000 and $95,000. These values represent the midpoints of the two new classes containing zero frequencies, which are added to the ends of the horizontal scale.

FIGURE 3.10   Frequency Polygon: Executive Incomes

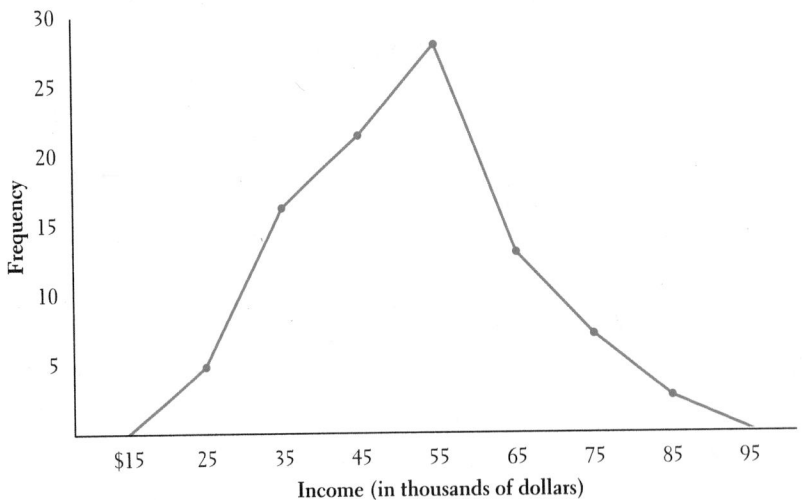

The frequency polygon of Table 3.10 outlines the data pattern clearly. If the purpose of presenting these executive incomes is to compare them with other distributions, the frequency polygon summarizes the data well.

Ogive

A graph of a cumulative frequency distribution is called an **ogive**. An ogive is used to determine how many observations lie above or below a certain value in a distribution. A *less-than* ogive tells how many items in the distribution have a value less than the upper limit of each class. First, a cumulative frequency distribution is constructed. Next, the cumulative frequencies are plotted at the upper class limit of each category. Finally, the points are connected with straight lines to form the ogive curve (Example 3.15).

A less-than ogive can also be constructed for a relative frequency distribution. The only difference involves the vertical scale. For a relative frequency distribution, this scale will range from 0 to 100%, indicating the fraction of the total number of observations that fall into or below each class. This approach is also demonstrated in Example 3.15.

EXAMPLE 3.15   Recall the less-than cumulative frequency distribution for Sunrunner Corporation executive incomes (Table 3.9). The cumulative frequency for each class is the sum of the frequencies for that class and for all lower classes. The less-than ogive curve is constructed by plotting these cumulative frequencies at the upper limit of each class. Figure 3.11 can be used to answer questions such as, "How many Sunrunner executives have incomes less than $60,000?" The answer is 72.

FIGURE 3.11   Ogive: Executive Incomes (frequencies)

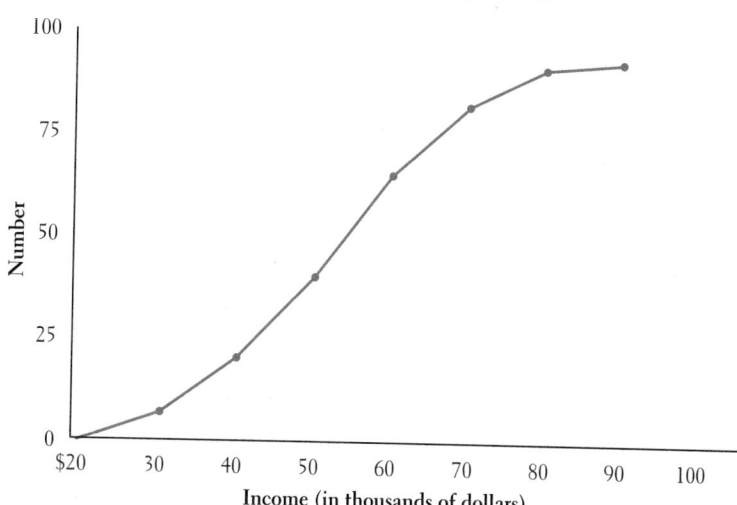

Similarly, Figure 3.12 shows the less-than ogive curve for *relative* frequencies. This curve can be used to answer questions such as, "What percentage of Sunrunner executives have incomes less than $60,000?" The answer is 74.3%.

A *more-than* ogive shows how many items in the distribution have a value greater than or equal to the lower limit of a particular class. This type of curve can also be developed for either a cumulative frequency distribution or a cumulative relative frequency distribution.

The **time series graph** portrays data measured over time. The graph's horizontal axis represents time periods, and the vertical axis shows the numerical values corresponding to these time periods.

FIGURE 3.12   Ogive: Executive Incomes (relative frequencies)

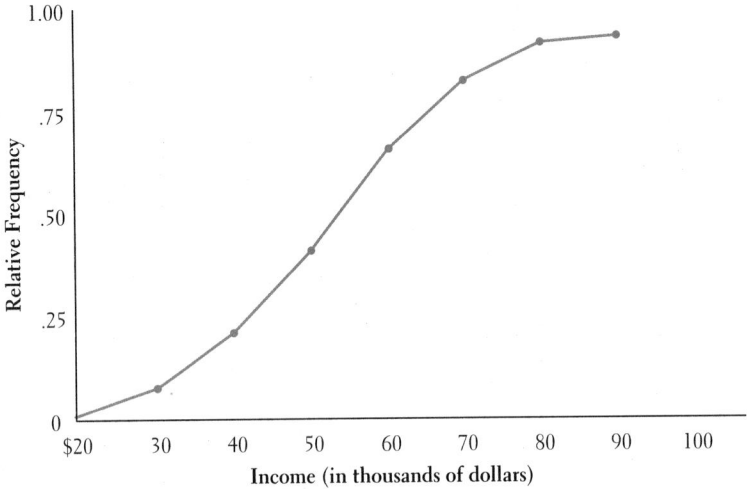

EXAMPLE 3.16   The Washington Water Power Company wants to show its average residential revenue per kilowatt-hour for the past six years in the *1991 Annual Report*. A time series graph is used for this purpose (Figure 3.13).

FIGURE 3.13   Time Series Graph: Average Residential Revenue per Kilowatt-Hour (WWP)

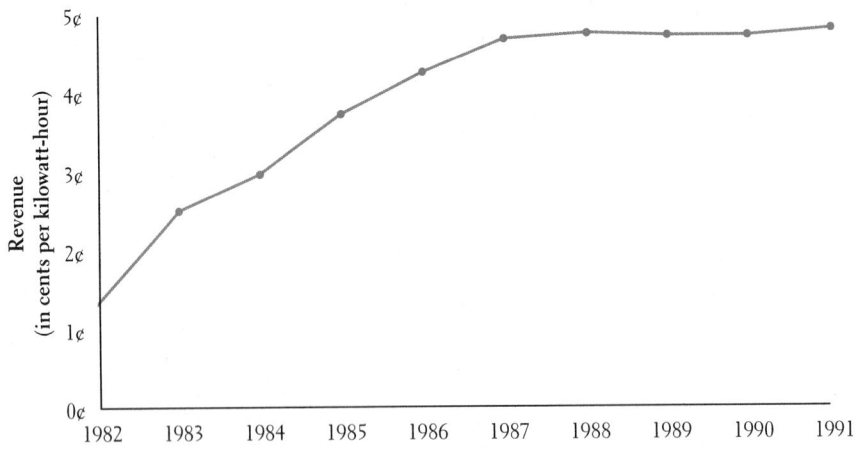

The advantage of the time series graph is that the rise or fall over time is usually obvious. It is apparent from Figure 3.13 that average residential revenue per kilowatt-hour for WWP has been increasing from 1982 to 1991. Time series data are important to almost all businesses, and will be covered thoroughly in Chapters 16 and 17.

It is important to note that many modern software packages for personal computers have graphing features. Small computers and the availability of data analysis programs have put sophisticated graphing capabilities within the reach of the smallest business and so choosing the most effective and accurate graphing method is increasingly important.

The MINITAB commands to generate a stem-and-leaf plot such as in Example 3.13 are:

```
MTB>  SET INTO C1
DATA> 65 23 26 . . . . . . . 26 25 43
DATA> END
MTB > STEM AND LEAF DISPLAY OF C1

Stem-and-leaf of C1        N = 88
Leaf Unit = 1.0

0           5
1           22
1           5689
2           133333444
2           555556666666688899
3           11122444
3           55555667778889
4           3
4           55555556689
5           122333334
5           6666667
6           4
6           557

MTB > STOP
```

Note that the MINITAB stem-and-leaf plot splits each 10s group into two groups to show more of the distribution of the number of customers per day. For example, the first 1 stem represents numbers from 10 to 14 and indicates that there were two days with 12 customers. The second 1 stem represents numbers from 15 to 19 and reveals that there was one day of 15 customers, one day of 16 customers, one day of 18 customers, and one day of 19 customers.

HOW TO LIE WITH STATISTICS

As a final note regarding creating and interpreting different kinds of graphs, be careful to avoid distortions. It is easy to deliberately distort a graph to give a misleading picture of the facts. A delightful little book, *How to Lie with Statistics*, exposes many graphing pitfalls that lead to distortions of original data.[1]

An example of such a distortion appears in Extended Exercise 44, " Kane's Chemicals." Can you see why the original data values were distorted as you look from the first barrel to the second?

---

[1]Darrell Huff, *How to Lie with Statistics* (New York: W. W. Norton, 1954).

As a second example of how two very different impressions can be developed from the same data, consider Figure 3.14 that appeared in *The Wall Street Journal* (July 29, 1992). This time series graph shows the Dow Jones Industrial Average's movement during one day's trading.

Note from Figure 3.14 that the Dow Jones was just under 3285 at the start of the day, and about 3335 at the end. With the vertical axis scaled as shown, this increase appears as a very significant growth. However, if the vertical axis is scaled over a wider range, the increase is difficult to detect (Figure 3.15). So which graph is correct? Both, or neither, depending on the graph's use. An investor that follows the market closely on a minute-to-minute basis would be interested in the market's sharp upturn shown in Figure 3.14. An investor looking at a portfolio's long-term growth probably wouldn't be interested in a daily graph at all, knowing in advance that it probably looks like Figure 3.15.

FIGURE 3.14   The Dow's Performance (DJIA at five-minute intervals yesterday)

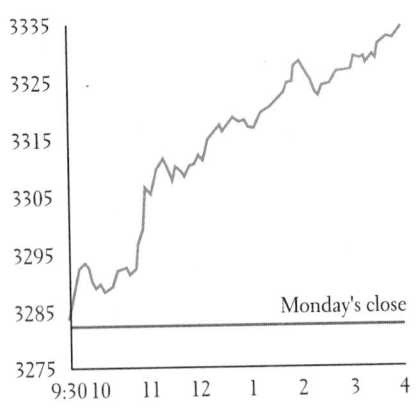

FIGURE 3.15   The Dow's Performance

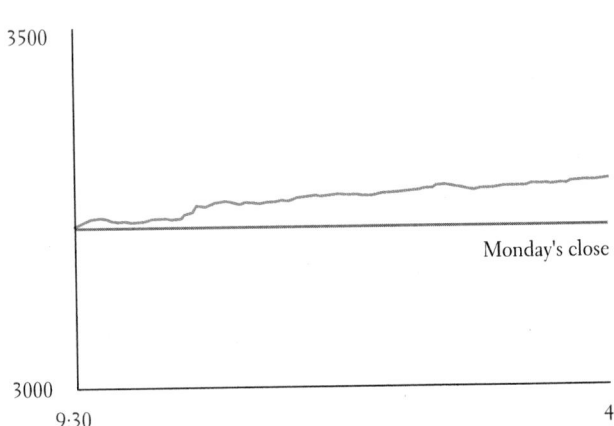

Figures 3.14 and 3.15 illustrate the point that great care must be taken in constructing a graph to ensure that it gives an accurate, appropriate impression of the original data.

As mentioned earlier, charts and graphs are widely used in almost all business publications because of the need to summarize important data collections. Figures 3.16 through 3.20 are examples of actual charts and graphs in national publications. Evaluate each figure, and indicate whether it does a fair job of displaying the data or whether it presents a distorted picture.

EXERCISES

18. What is the difference between a pie chart and a bar chart?

19. What is the difference between a histogram and a bar chart?

20. What is the difference between a histogram and a frequency polygon?

21. What are the advantages of a frequency polygon over a histogram?

FIGURE 3.16   Bar Chart: VCR Families

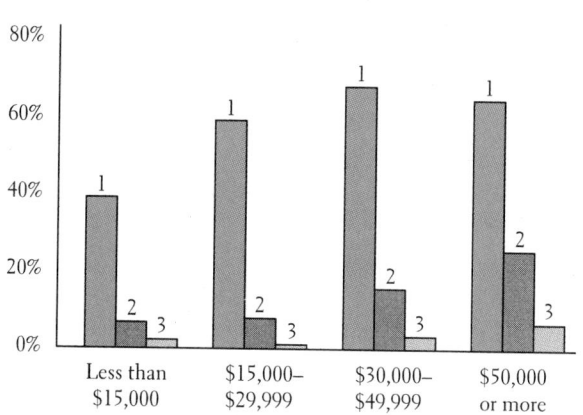

Source: The Roper Organization

FIGURE 3.17   Bar Chart: Class Standing for Questionnaire

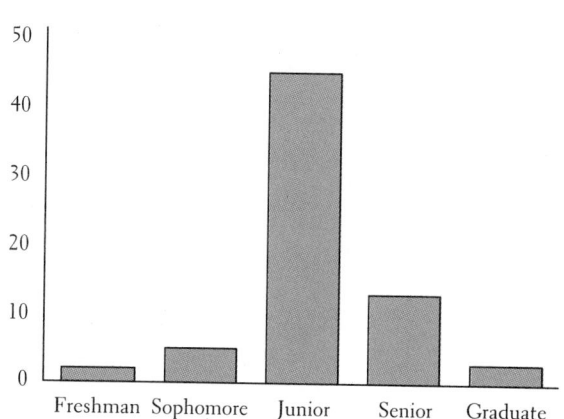

Source: Data was gathered from the questionnaire (Table 1.1) administered to one of the author's classes.

FIGURE 3.18   Pie Charts: Budget Breakdown

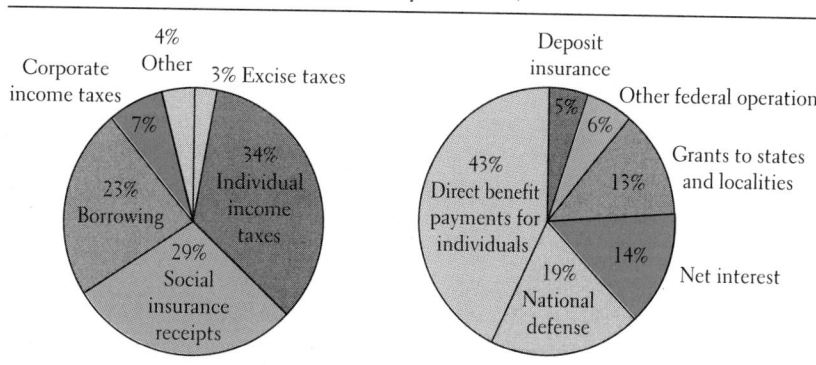

Source: *Spokesman-Review*, January 30, 1992, p. 1.

22. When should a less-than ogive be constructed?

23. How are time series graphs used?

24. A small-town PTA conducted a survey about drinking and driving via 166 telephone interviews. The following data reflect responses to the question, "Do you think the drinking driver problem has increased or decreased since 1988?"

Increased	96
Decreased	34
About the same	36
Total	166

FIGURE 3.19   Pictogram: Bungee Jumps, 1990–91

Estimated Number of Jumps

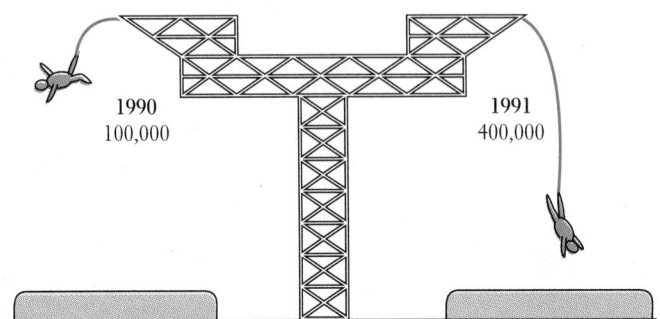

Source: North American Bungee Association

FIGURE 3.20   Time Series Graph: Shrinking Market, 1984–87

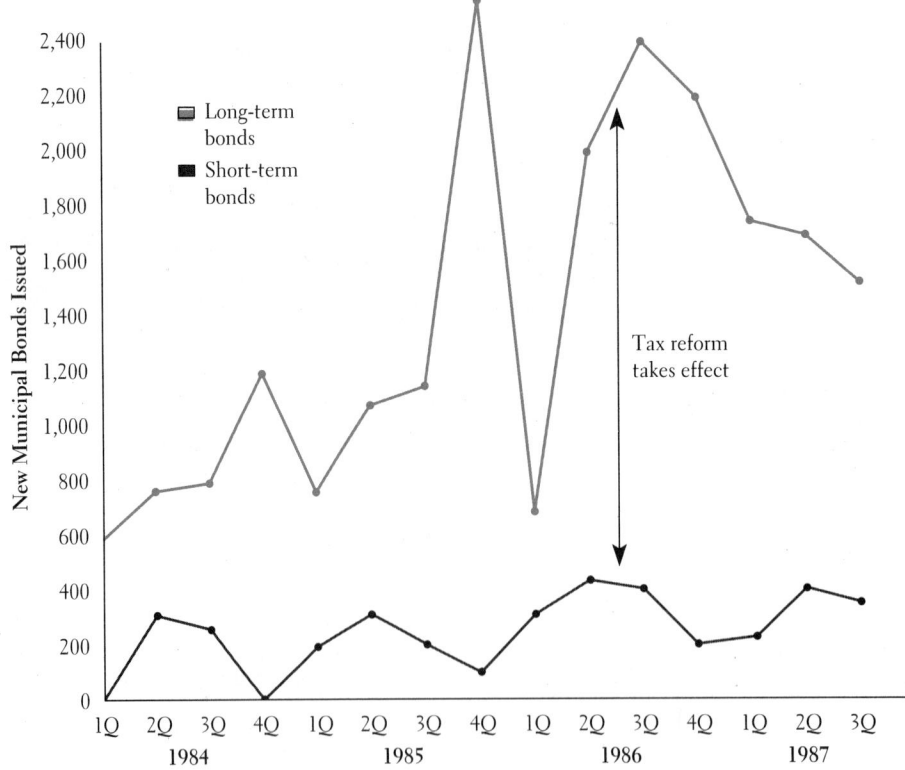

Source: *U.S. News & World Report*, October 26, 1987, p. 43.

a. Develop a pie chart.

b. Develop a bar chart.

c. Which chart is the better way to report these data?

25. During a pro football game's third quarter, a chart is to be presented to TV viewers to break down one team's scoring during the season. The data are:

Receivers	58%
Kickers	25
Running backs	11
Defense	6
Total	100%

a. What kind of chart should be used to present these data?

b. Construct this chart.

26. Finch Construction Company is negotiating with a local union and needs to present a chart of average hourly earnings in the construction industry from 1976 to 1985. What kind of chart would you recommend to Finch for the distribution that follows? Construct the appropriate chart.

Year	Hourly earnings
1976	$ 7.71
1977	8.10
1978	8.66
1979	9.27
1980	9.94
1981	10.82
1982	11.63
1983	11.92
1984	12.03
1985	12.20

Source: U.S. Dept. of Labor Monthly Labor Review.

27. An independent research firm surveyed households with residents 55 years of age or older. The following frequency distribution shows how respondents answered the question, "How many driving minutes from a hospital is the furthest that you would consider living during your retirement?"

Driving minutes	Frequency
5 minutes or less	47
6 to 10 minutes	150
11 to 15 minutes	128
16 to 20 minutes	67
21 minutes or more	94
Total	486

Source: "Surveys of Older Homeowners Concerning Retirement Attitudes." Spokane: Decision Science Associates, June 1986.

a. Construct a histogram.

b. Construct a frequency polygon.

c. Which type of graph would best show each separate class in the distribution?

d. Which type of graph shows the data pattern most clearly?

e. Construct a less-than ogive for the cumulative frequency distribution.

f. How many respondents would not consider living more than 20 minutes from a hospital?

28. Answerphone Service, Inc., wants to do a better job of billing customers for services rendered. Owner Sloan Spalding needs to know how long it takes to complete various incoming calls. For data collection, 150 random calls were monitored and timed, as shown in Exercise 16. Use the frequency distributions you constructed in Exercise 16 to:

a. Construct a histogram.

b. Construct a frequency polygon.

c. Construct a more-than ogive for the cumulative relative frequency distribution.

d. What percentage of the incoming calls will last more than 10 minutes?

SUMMARY

This chapter has presented important ways of summarizing data collections so that their important features can be quickly and easily understood and used in the decision-making process. These methods are especially important for qualitative data. Data measured on a nominal or ordinal scale are frequently summarized using the techniques of this chapter. Since such data often occur in practical situations, these techniques are prevalent in most business applications.

Frequency distributions were discussed as a way to present a data collection's essential features. Steps to be followed in preparing a frequency distribution were presented along with a discussion of relative frequencies and cumulative frequency distributions. Graphing methods to visually summarize collected data were shown. The purpose of charts and graphs is to briefly show the essential aspects of data arrays so the decision maker can understand and use their important information.

APPLICATIONS OF STATISTICAL CONCEPTS IN THE BUSINESS WORLD

KAISER ALUMINUM COMPANY'S USE OF CHARTS AND GRAPHS

Kaiser Aluminum Company's elaborate quality assurance system in the Trentwood plant has helped make it one of the world's leading aluminum suppliers. The applications section of Chapter 13 ("Quality-Control Applications") details this system.

Kaiser's computerized quality-control system generates huge amounts of raw data. These data values must somehow be displayed to those responsible for the operation of the aluminum production process. Charts and graphs are widely used for this purpose. Figures 3.21 through 3.23 (a pie chart, a bar chart, and a time series graph) were taken from quality-control reports Kaiser's system generated. These figures are rou-

FIGURE 3.21   Kaiser Aluminum Start
Weight Breakdown   FIGURE 3.22   Kaiser Aluminum Recovery Distribution

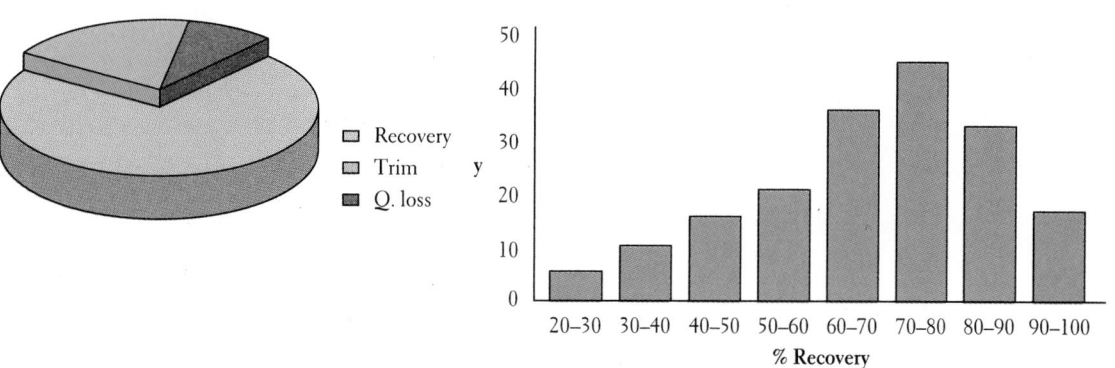

FIGURE 3.23   Kaiser Aluminum Recovery Defect Trends, Time Series Graph

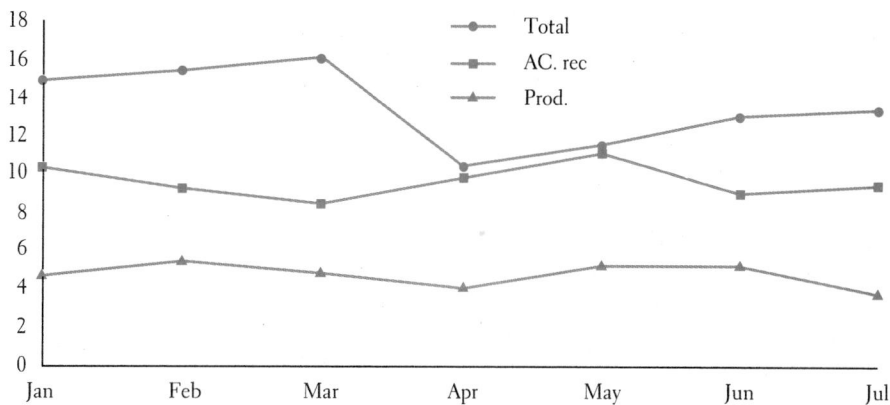

tinely reviewed by quality-control engineers and managers. As you see, Kaiser depends on graphical representations to ensure its products' quality.

OTHER APPLICATIONS

Here are additional areas where this chapter's techniques might prove useful. Data collection is described on the left; a possible summary technique is on the right.

Data collection	Possible summary technique
Ages of customers by category	Frequency distribution
Annual expenditures of company funds	Pie chart
Sales of wine by winery	Bar chart
Hourly wages of factory workers	Cumulative frequency distribution
Annual sales, 1979 to present	Time series graph
County government sources of revenue	Pie chart
Accounts receivable by store	Bar chart

Data collection	Possible summary technique
Credit card holders by state	Bar chart
Incomes of city residents	Cumulative frequency distribution
U.S. annual trade deficit	Time series graph
Monthly prime interest rate	Time series graph
U.S. population years of education	Frequency distribution
Annual sales of eight sales agents	Bar chart
Monthly sales by department	Bar chart
Average stock price per week	Time series graph
Dow Jones average, daily	Time series graph
State expenditures by department	Pie chart
VISA credit card purchase amounts	Cumulative frequency distribution
Company employee job rating scores	Histogram
Units shipped from factory monthly	Time series graph
Smokers per 100,000 by age category	Histogram
Annual sales of new cars	Time series graph
Scores on medical school exam	Cumulative frequency distribution
Graduating seniors' grade point averages	Frequency distribution
Percentage of defective parts by supplier	Pie chart
Quality control: bad units per week	Time series graph

GLOSSARY

Distribution A collection, array, or group of numerical values.

Frequency distribution A list of several data classes or categories along with the number of values that fall into each.

Relative frequencies Percentages calculated by dividing the actual frequency for each class by the total number of observations being classified.

Cumulative frequency distribution A distribution showing the total number of occurrences that lie above or below certain key values.

Pie chart A method of presenting qualitative data summaries in which a circle is divided into sectors corresponding to the relative frequency for each class.

Bar chart A method of graphically presenting nominal and ordinal data in which one bar is used to represent the frequency for each category.

Pareto chart A bar chart used to identify and prioritize problems.

Histogram Used to graphically present interval and ratio data. The categories or classes are plotted along the graph's horizontal axis. Numerical values of each class are represented by vertical bars.

Stem and leaf Similar to histogram except that actual data are displayed instead of bars.

Frequency polygon Used to graphically present interval and ratio data. Formed by connecting the points corresponding to each class midpoint and frequency with straight lines.

Ogive A graph of a cumulative frequency distribution or cumulative relative frequency distribution.

Time series graph A graph of data values measured over time.

SOLVED EXERCISES

1. FREQUENCY DISTRIBUTION

Art Martinez, owner of a small jewelry store, has recorded the number of customers for each of the past 500 days. The smallest number was 7 and the largest 62. Art wants to construct a frequency distribution for this series. How should he set up the following?

a. Approximate number of classes.

b. Class width.

c. Limits for the first class.

Solution:

a. Table 3.3 shows that for 500 observations, about 10 classes should be used.

b. Class width is determined by subtracting the smallest value from the largest value and dividing the result by the appropriate number of classes: $(62 - 7)/10 = 5.5$. Thus, the class width should be 5 or 6. Since people are 5- and 10-oriented, a class width of 5 is chosen.

c. The first class must include the lowest value, 7. Since the variable (number of customers) is measured in whole numbers, the first class is 5–9.

2. RELATIVE AND CUMULATIVE FREQUENCY DISTRIBUTIONS

A voter opinion survey conducted by Alliance Pacific, Inc., provided voter input regarding a proposed waste-to-energy facility for the area. The following frequency distribution shows survey participants' age groups:

Age category	Frequency
18 to under 30	255
30 to under 45	510
45 to under 60	427
60 and over	405
Total	1,597

Source: *Waste-to-Energy Facility Voter Opinion Survey.*
Spokane: Alliance Pacific, Inc., August 1985.

a. How could you improve this frequency distribution?

b. Construct a relative frequency distribution for this data collection.

c. Construct a cumulative relative frequency distribution indicating the percentage of respondents who are less than 45.

Solution:

a. Table 3.3 shows that around 11 classes should be used for n equal to 1,597.

b.

Age category	Frequency	Relative frequency	Cumulative frequency
18 to under 30	255	.160	.160
30 to under 45	510	.319	.479
45 to under 60	427	.267	.746
60 and over	405	.254	1.000
Total	1,597	1.000	

c. The cumulative relative frequency distribution shows that 47.9% of the respondents were less than 45 years old.

3. PIE AND BAR CHARTS

The December 14, 1987, edition of *U.S. News & World Report* reported the following values for the number of contact lenses worn by Americans:

Kind of contact lens	Number of Americans (millions)
Soft, daily wear	11.5
Rigid, gas-permeable	4.0
Soft, extended wear	3.5
Hard	1.5
Total	20.5

a. Construct a pie chart.

b. Construct a bar chart.

Solution:

a. The total number of Americans who have contact lenses is divided according to each different kind: $11.5/20.5 = .561$, $4.0/20.5 = .195$, $3.5/20.5 = .171$, and $1.5/20.5 = .073$. Figure
3.24 shows a pie chart for these data.

b. Figure 3.25 shows a bar chart for this distribution.

FIGURE 3.24   Pie Chart: Contact Lenses by Type in United States

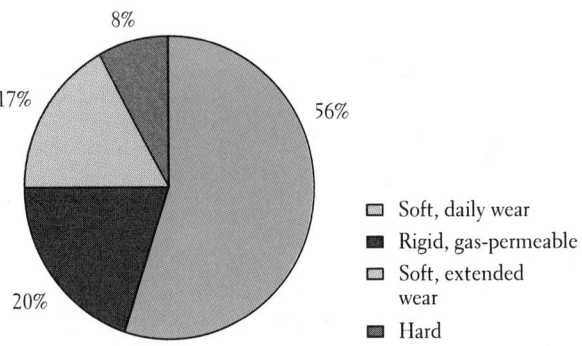

FIGURE 3.25   Bar Chart: Contact Lenses by Type in United States

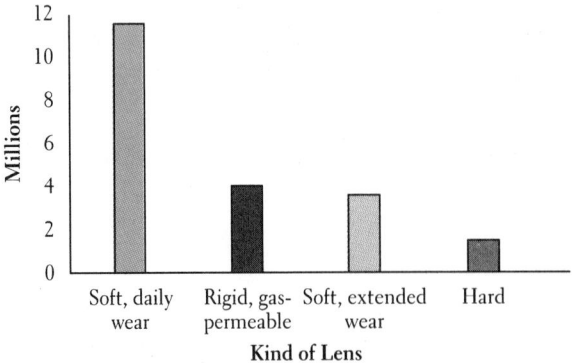

EXERCISES

29. Bo Bosworth, statistician for the Omar Corporation, is preparing a frequency distribution that allows a person to determine the number of employees producing less than specified outputs. What kind of frequency distribution should Bo prepare?

30. April Marshall, manager of the university bookstore, has recorded the charge purchases made by students in one day. Of a total of 140 charges, the smallest was $40.58 and the largest $97.52. She wants to construct a frequency distribution for this series. How should she set up the following?

    a. Approximate number of classes.

    b. Class width.

    c. Limits for the first class.

31. Decision Science Associates conducted a survey of health care consumers to assess buying patterns and perceptions in the Missoula, Montana, market. The following frequency distribution shows who provided the respondents' health insurance coverage:

Coverage	Frequency
Employer	246
Spouse	150
Both	93
Total	489

Source: *Survey of Missoula Health Care Consumers with Employer-Paid Insurance.* Missoula: Decision Science Associates, February 1987.

    a. Construct a relative frequency distribution for this data collection.

    b. Construct a pie chart.

    c. Construct a bar chart.

32. The survey in Exercise 31 asked respondents, "How many people live in your household (including yourself)?" The following distribution classifies the responses:

Number of people	Frequency
1	52
2	147
3	102
4	116
5 to 7	66
8 or more	2
Total	485

Source: *Survey of Missoula Health Care Consumers with Employer-Paid Insurance.* Missoula: Decision Science Associates, February 1987.

    a. How could you improve this frequency distribution?

    b. Construct a relative frequency distribution for this data collection.

    c. Construct a less-than cumulative relative frequency distribution.

    d. Construct a more-than cumulative relative frequency distribution.

    e. What percentage of the households had five or more occupants?

33. Prior to putting a new tire on the market, Goodwheel Tire Company conducts tread life tests on a random sample of 150 tires. The following frequency distribution shows the results:

Number of miles (thousands)	Frequency
20 to under 25	7
25 to under 30	14
30 to under 35	28
35 to under 40	45
40 to under 45	30
45 to under 50	15
50 to under 55	11
Total	150

    a. Construct a relative frequency distribution for this data collection.

    b. Construct a cumulative relative frequency distribution that will indicate the percentage of tires that lasted more than 40,000 miles.

    c. Construct a frequency polygon.

    d. Construct a less-than ogive for the cumulative relative frequency distribution.

    e. What percentage of the tires lasted less than 40,000 miles?

34. In a feasibility study to determine whether to build a destination resort, Mark Craze analyzes the following data series on the number of visitors at the Coulee Dam Visitor Center.

Year	Visitors
1969	250,265
1970	250,929
1971	321,333
1972	342,269
1973	268,528
1974	468,136
1975	390,129
1976	300,140
1977	271,140
1978	282,752
1979	244,006
1980	161,524
1981	277,134
1982	382,343
1983	617,737
1984	453,881

Source: *Market Feasibility Study for a Proposed Resort Development at Crescent Bay on Lake Roosevelt.* Grand Coulee: Decision Science Associates, February 1985.

a. What type of chart or graph should Mark construct?

b. Construct the appropriate graph for this data series.

35. For the market feasibility study in Exercise 34, Mark needs to present the following projected occupancy percentages:

Month	Percentage
January	10
February	15
March	30
April	45
May	70
June	90
July	100
August	100
September	80
October	60
November	25
December	15

Source: *Market Feasibility Study for a Proposed Resort Development at Crescent Bay on Lake Roosevelt*. Grand Coulee: Decision Science Associates, February 1985.

a. What type of chart or graph should Mark construct?

b. Construct the appropriate chart for this data series.

36. Gene Madlock needs to display the following data of the top nine geographical distributions of 1983 capital commitments for independent private firms: California, $424.9 million; Connecticut, $4.3 million; Georgia, $43 million; Massachusetts, $322.5 million; Michigan, $18 million; New York, $215.1 million; Rhode Island, $30.4 million; Texas, $5 million; and Washington, $104 million (Source: *Venture Capital Journal*, July 1983).

a. What type of chart or graph should Gene construct?

b. Construct the appropriate chart or graph for this data series.

37. The following data collection shows the normal daily mean temperatures of 70 selected cities:

67.5	40.0	71.2	61.9	62.6	60.6	56.6	50.3
49.8	54.0	57.5	68.0	75.6	61.2	77.0	51.1
49.2	50.4	52.1	49.7	56.4	56.2	68.2	45.0
55.1	51.5	48.6	39.7	38.2	44.7	64.6	54.1
55.4	44.7	51.1	49.4	45.3	53.1	56.2	47.3
47.6	54.5	60.0	59.0	41.3	54.5	49.6	51.7
59.9	53.0	54.3	50.3	50.3	63.3	45.3	61.8
59.2	66.0	63.4	66.3	51.7	44.1	59.5	57.7
51.4	47.2	54.8	46.1	45.7	79.7		

Source: *1987 Statistical Abstract of the United States.*

a. Construct a frequency distribution.

b. Construct a histogram.

c. Construct a chart to show the number of cities that have a normal daily mean temperature less than 50°.

38. The following data collection shows net income as a percentage of equity for a sample of 209 companies from the 1992 Fortune 500 survey:

17	17	3	23	19	21	16	39	11	16	27
23	15	22	6	21	35	13	4	17	18	11
22	25	11	21	18	20	14	3	11	12	19
18	18	18	9	9	18	8	10	22	11	12
8	12	2	23	14	28	12	7	16	0	22
7	20	18	7	2	17	6	15	11	10	3
12	7	14	14	20	15	15	16	12	9	14
2	5	11	25	17	9	10	12	11	12	14
49	11	36	12	11	12	22	13	9	22	7
14	0	16	12	16	5	19	12	11	18	18
14	22	7	8	13	10	16	11	13	44	11
36	14	14	11	12	14	4	18	0	4	1
16	10	12	5	22	1	20	10	12	3	3
7	14	14	18	16	17	18	13	3	17	17
3	19	10	13	7	14	2	7	9	12	8
8	8	8	14	6	14	3	13	9	8	7
10	12	20	9	14	14	20	12	13	16	5
11	13	13	16	10	6	7	14	27	7	19
20	21	8	2	1	22	15	8	1	16	22

a. Construct a frequency distribution.

b. Construct both a histogram and a frequency polygon.

c. Construct a chart to show the number of companies whose net income as a percentage of equity is greater than 20.

39. Referring to the company data base in Appendix C, select a random sample of 100 employees and:

a. Construct a frequency distribution for variable x_1, number of years with the company.

b. Construct a chart or graph to display this data series.

40. Referring to the company data base in Appendix C, select a random sample of 75 employees and:

a. Construct a frequency distribution for variable x_2, number of overtime hours worked during the past six months.

b. Construct a chart or graph to display this data series.

41. Referring to the company data base in Appendix C, use the population of employees and:

a. Construct a frequency distribution for variable x_8, annual base salary.

b. Construct a chart or graph to display this data series.

42. Referring to the company data base in Appendix C, select the first 150 employees and:

a. Construct a frequency distribution for variable x_9, employee age.

b. Construct a chart or graph to display this data series.

EXTENDED EXERCISES

43. AMSBURY GLASS SHOWERS

For five years, Amsbury Glass Company has been making and delivering fiberglass shower stalls, which have recently become its biggest revenue producer. Ron Murphy, president of Amsbury, has decided that this product's sales history justifies increasing plant manufacturing capacity, which will require additional financing. Ron is considering how best to state his case to the area banks.

The increase in unit sales of shower stalls has been particularly dramatic during the past fiscal year. Ron decides to focus on this increase in presenting his case. The numbers of units delivered during each of the past 12 months are 348, 412, 643, 658, 942, 789, 1,135, 1,247, 1,254, 1,562, 1,503, 1,829.

Ron confers with production manager Pete Roper. They agree that these sales levels justify additional plant capacity and that they want to display the current need in dramatic fashion. Ron decides to prepare a time series graph of these data (Figure 3.26) as a key component of management's presentation to the banks.

FIGURE 3.26   Time Series Graph: Sales of Amsbury Shower Stalls

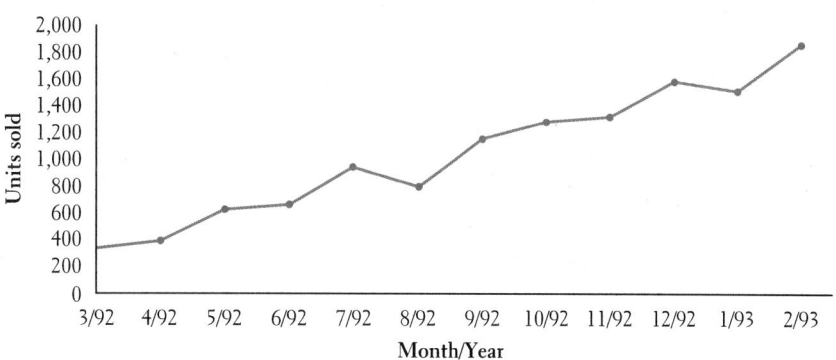

a. How effective do you think the graph will be in persuading the banks to grant additional loans?

b. What other graphing methods might have been used to show sales history?

44. KANE'S CHEMICALS

Kane's Chemicals makes film products, using crude oil in its manufacturing process. During last year's stockholders' meeting, management was severely criticized for using an excessive amount of foreign oil as opposed to domestic oil. Efforts to reduce foreign imports and increase domestic usage during the past year have resulted in a 50% reduction in the number of barrels of foreign oil used.

John Kane, company president, plans to continue reducing the company's imports of foreign oil. He's encouraged by a *Wall Street Journal* article (October 27, 1989) indicating that domestic oil activity is increasing. The journal stated that "fear is finally leaving the oil patch."

Mr. Kane decides to highlight the past year's reduction during his presentation to stockholders at the upcoming annual meeting. He wants to make sure stockholders understand the progress that has been made since the previous meeting. He decides to use a graph (Figure 3.27) to dramatize the reduction in foreign oil consumption.

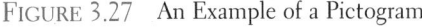

FIGURE 3.27   An Example of a Pictogram

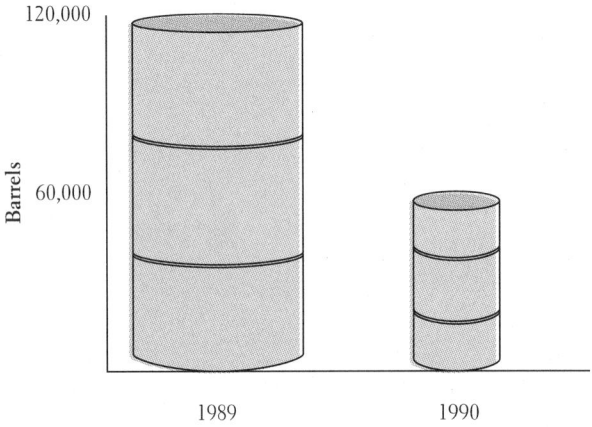

a. How effective do you think Figure 3.27's graph will be in convincing stockholders that dependence on foreign oil has been reduced?

b. Is the graph misleading in any way?

c. What do you think is the best way to visually depict the past year's import reduction?

45. WILCO VACUUM CENTER

Wilco Vacuum Center, a vacuum cleaner retailer, has recorded the number of units sold per day during the past several months. After assembling the raw data for the most recent month, store owner Mary Rose decides that the data represent a typical month and should be highlighted in an upcoming review with store employees. Unit sales per day for the past month are:

```
56,   89,   64,   23,   45,   65,   21,   78,   67,   59,   85,   63,
54,   21,   46,   49,   78,   86,   91,   65,   34,   64,   67,   56,
54,   23,   46,   34,   37,   38,   49
```

Mary wants to use both a tabular presentation and a graph for these values. It's important to show the data in an unbiased but effective manner. Mary assigns you the task of creating a frequency distribution for these data values and then determining what type of chart or graph will most effectively present them.

MICROCOMPUTER PACKAGE

You can use the micro package *Computerized Business Statistics* to construct a frequency distribution.

Kyle Chang wants to learn more about the number of customer orders processed per day in his retail operation. Table 3.7 showed a random sample of orders. Kyle wants to construct a frequency distribution for this data collection.

Computer Solution

On the main menu of *Computerized Business Statistics* a **3** is selected: Descriptive Statistics.

Since the data for this problem need to be entered on the keyboard a **1** is selected.

```
Descriptive Statistics - Define New Problem
 Raw or Group Data: Enter R/G, press ↵ R
```

Since the data are in raw form and not grouped, **R** is selected.

```
Population or Sample Data: Enter P/S, press ↵ P
```

The data will be treated as a population, so a **P** is selected.

```
Number of Data Points: Enter 1 - 125, press ↵ 88
```

Since the data collection consists of 88 customer counts, 88 is the correct entry.

```
Variable Name: Enter 0-5 char., press ↵ PRICE
```

The answer is **PRICE**.

```
Problem definition correct? Enter Y/N/Q, press ↵ Y
```

If the problem has been set up correctly, the answer is **Y**.

Next, the program provides spaces for the raw data to be entered. The data values are numbered from 1 to 88. The cursor allows you to replace the 0s on the screen with the actual data values.

```
Table Commands Enter Raw Data    File: None
              Price
1.              65
2.              23
3.              26
4.              45
5.              12
  .              .
  .              .
  .              .
88.             43
Press F when Finished
```

When the data have been entered and **F** pressed, the program asks:

```
Save data? Enter Y/N, press ↵ N
```

Now the program options menu reappears and you are instructed:

```
Enter number (1-9) for your selection from the menu & press ↵ 7
```

You are now ready to run the problem, so enter a 7. You will be asked:

```
Convert raw data to group data? Y/N & press ↵ Y
```

Since this problem involves the construction of a frequency distribution, the answer is **Y**. The lowest and highest values of the data collection appear on the screen, and you are asked to enter the number of groups.

```
Lowest Data Value:                          5
Highest Data Value:                        67
Enter Number of Groups (2–10) & press ↵ 7
```

Since $n = 88$, seven groups are desired. Next, the program asks:

```
Enter Value for Lower Limit & press ↵ 0
```

Since the class width will be 10, the first class should start with 0. The program summarizes the situation:

```
Lowest Data Value:                 5
Highest Data Value:               67
Number of Groups:                  7
Lower Limit:                       0

Interval 10
```

The program computes the class width, or interval, and asks:

```
Is computed interval okay? Y/N & press ↵ Y
```

The program divides the data into seven groups of class width 10 (see Table 3.8) and calculates the mean, median, mode, range, variance, and standard deviation of the data (these concepts will be covered in Chapter 4). It then offers you the option of computing a relative frequency table (see Table 3.8). You may choose to save the solved problem on disk, print it, or merely view it on the screen.

```
S = Screen Output
P = Printer (hard copy)
D = Data Disk (text file)
R = Return to Descriptive Statistics Menu
Select Output Option: Enter letter and press ↵ P
```

Since a hard copy of the results is needed, **P,** or printer, is selected.

MINITAB COMPUTER PACKAGE

The MINITAB commands to generate charts for Kyle Chang's data (Table 3.7) are:

```
MTB > READ 'CHANG.DAT' C1
      88 ROWS READ

C1
  65 23 26 45 · · ·

MTB > HISTOGRAM C1;
SUBC> INCREMENT = 10;
SUBC> START AT 0.

Histogram of C1 N = 88
```

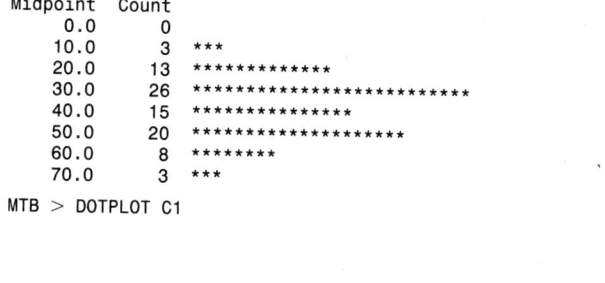

```
Midpoint  Count
    0.0     0
   10.0     3   ***
   20.0    13   *************
   30.0    26   **************************
   40.0    15   ***************
   50.0    20   ********************
   60.0     8   ********
   70.0     3   ***
MTB > DOTPLOT C1
```

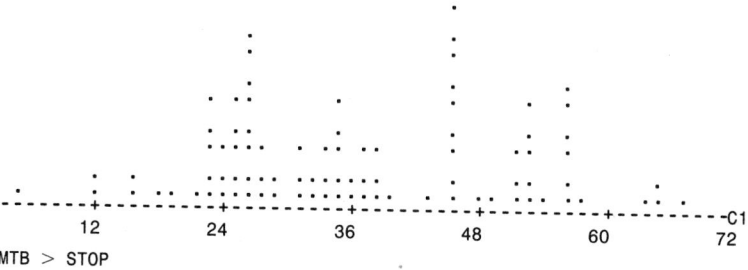

```
                                      .
                        .                       .
                        .                       .
                    .  ..                       .           .  .
                    .  ..                       .           .  .
                    ......    .   . ..  ..      .  .      .:   .
      .      .   :     ......  .......  .  . .  .    ..  ..   .
    . .    . : .   . ..:.......:.. .. .:.  . .:. ..: .:.  .:. .
  ----------+---------+---------+---------+---------+---------+---C1
           12        24        36        48        60        72
MTB > STOP
```

The **READ** command is used to read the customers per day data file called CHANG.DAT into column 1 (C1).

The **HISTOGRAM** command breaks the data range down into a reasonable set of intervals and assigns each datum to the midpoint of the interval within which it falls. The semicolon at the end of line 1 requests a subcommand prompt.

The **INCREMENT** subcommand allows you to choose the width of each interval, in this case 10.

The **START** subcommand specifies the midpoint for the first interval, in this case 0.

The **DOTPLOT** command generates a horizontal display similar to a histogram. The dotplot's bars are vertical, arrayed across what looks like a continuous range. However, the dotplot is broken down into intervals just like the histogram.

SAS COMPUTER PACKAGE

The SAS commands to generate a histogram for Kyle Chang's data (Table 3.7) are:

```
TITLE ''SAS COMMANDS FOR THE WASH TUB DATA'';
DATA WASH;
 INFILE 'WASH.DAT';
 INPUT CUST 1-2;
PROC CHART;
 VBAR CUST;
```

The **TITLE** statement names the SAS program.

The **DATA** statement provides a filename for the data.

The **INFILE** statement identifies an external file that you want to read with an INPUT statement.

The **INPUT** statement names the variable CUST and indicates that it is located in columns 1–2.

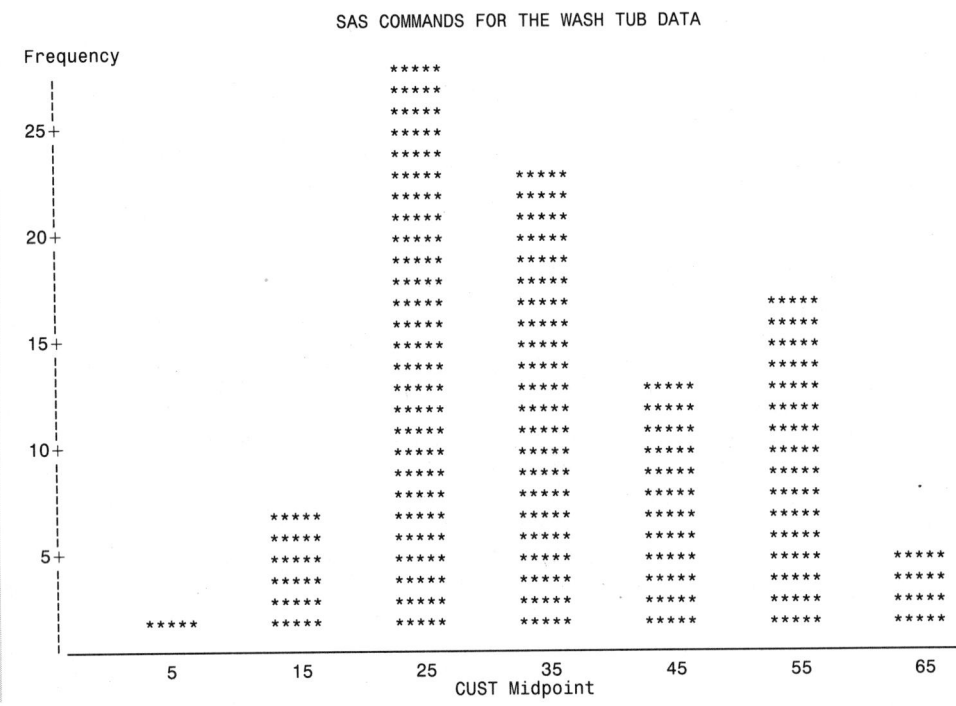

The **PROC CHART** statement produces vertical and horizontal bar charts (also called histograms).

The **VBAR** statement lists the variables for which you want vertical bar charts. At the bottom of each bar, **CHART** prints a name or value. For qualitative variables, the category label is printed below each bar. For quantitative variables, the value is the midpoint of the interval represented by the bar.

The SAS output is shown in Table 3.11.

TABLE 3.11   SAS Histogram for The Washtub Data

SAS COMMANDS FOR THE WASH TUB DATA

Frequency

DESCRIPTIVE STATISTICS

*Figures won't
lie, but liars will
figure.*
Gen. C. H.
Grosvenor

Objectives

When you have completed this chapter, you will be able to:

Compute the following measures of central tendency: mean, median, mode, and weighted mean.

Explain the advantages and disadvantages of each measure of central tendency.

Compute the following measures of variability: variance, standard deviation, and coefficient of variation.

Explain the advantages and disadvantages of using each measure of variability.

 *Financial Executive* for May/June 1989 contained an article entitled, "Are Performance Fees Justified?" The *Yes* portion of this article argued that financial advisors should be paid based on the performance of their clients' portfolio accounts. The *No* position argued that advisors should be paid for their best efforts since portfolio performance depends on many factors other than the quality of advice.

The previous two chapters described various ways of collecting data and displaying them. Frequency distributions and graphs are important for showing the essential properties of data collections to assist in the decision-making process. These methods are especially important if the collected data are qualitative, that is, measured on either a nominal or an ordinal scale.

WHY DESCRIPTIVE STATISTICS IS IMPORTANT TO MANAGERS

The methods for collecting and graphically presenting data discussed in Chapters 2 and 3 provide a starting point for data analysis. But managers also need to be acquainted with numerical descriptive measures that provide brief, easy-to-understand summaries of a data collection. These measures fall into two broad categories: measures of central tendency and measures of variability. Measures of central tendency describe the central location in a set of numerical observations. Measures of variability describe the spread or dispersion of the data values.

A possible way to resolve the issue posed by the *Financial Executive* article is to collect data on the performance of many different portfolio accounts, both those involving financial advisors and those not. These data values would need to be summarized in some way so that their essential characteristics become obvious. Important numerical methods of summarizing data collections are discussed in this chapter.

MEASURES OF CENTRAL TENDENCY

In calculating summary values for a data collection, the first consideration is to find a central, or typical value for the data. This section presents four important measures of central tendency: mean, median, mode, and weighted mean.

Mean

The **arithmetic mean**, or simply the **mean**, is a summary value calculated by summing the numerical data values and dividing by the number of values.

> The **arithmetic mean** of a collection of numerical values is the sum of these values divided by the number of values. The symbol for the population mean is the Greek letter μ (mu), and the symbol for a sample mean is $\bar{x}$(x-bar).

Measurements of a data set are often denoted

$$x_1, x_2, x_3, \ldots, x_N$$

where x_1 is the first measurement in the data set, x_2 is the second measurement, and so on up to x_N, the last or Nth measurement in the data set. For four measurements, 3, 6, 4, and 9, the data set is

$$x_1 = 3, x_2 = 6, x_3 = 4, x_4 = 9$$

In any statistical study, there are usually two different data collections of interest: the population and the sample. Equation 4.1 is the formula for computing the mean of a population:

$$\mu = \frac{\Sigma x}{N} \tag{4.1}$$

where μ = Population mean
Σx = Sum of all population data values
N = Population size

To simplify the computations in this text, some shorthand notation is used. In the simplified notation for summing all x values, Σx, the summations are understood to extend from 1 to N. A more formal and complete notation system for this procedure is

$$\sum_{i=1}^{N} x_i$$

where the subscript i varies from its initial value of 1 to N in increments of 1. Since almost all sums run from 1 to N, the starting ($i = 1$) and ending (N) indices will be suppressed, and the simpler notation will be used except where the more complete notation is needed for clarity.

Any measurable characteristic of a population, for example, the population mean (μ) is called a **parameter.**

A population **parameter** is any measurable characteristic of a population.

Equation 4.2 is used to compute the mean of a sample:

$$\bar{x} = \frac{\Sigma x}{n} \tag{4.2}$$

where $\bar{x}$ = Sample mean
Σx = Sum of all sample data values
n = sample size

Any measurable characteristic of a sample, for example, the sample mean ($\bar{x}$), is called a **statistic**. A sample statistic is frequently used to estimate a population parameter.

A sample **statistic** is any measurable characteristic of a sample.

Characteristics of the arithmetic mean
1. Every data set measured on an interval or ratio level has a mean.
2. The mean has valuable mathematical properties that make it convenient to use in further computations.
3. The mean is sensitive to extreme values.
4. The sum of the deviations of the numbers in a data set from the mean is zero: $\Sigma(x - \mu) = 0$ and $\Sigma(x - \bar{x}) = 0$.
5. The sum of the squared deviations of the numbers in a data set from the mean is a minimum value: $\Sigma(x - \mu)^2$ is a minimum value, and $\Sigma(x - \bar{x})^2$ is a minimum value.

EXAMPLE 4.1 An instructor is interested in computing the mean age of the five people in a small class. Since the only people of interest are those in the class, this group constitutes a population, so Equation 4.1 is used to calculate the mean. Their ages are 21, 19, 25, 19, and 23. Their mean is calculated as

$$\mu = \frac{\Sigma x}{N} = \frac{21 + 19 + 25 + 19 + 23}{5} = 21.4$$

The mean or average age of the students in the class is 21.4 years. Note that the sum of deviations from the mean, $\Sigma(x - \mu)$, equals 0: $[(21 - 21.4) + (19 - 21.4) + (25 - 21.4) + (19 - 21.4) + (23 - 21.4)] = 0$.

EXAMPLE 4.2 The Atlas Welding & Sharpening Shop has 10 employees. Personnel records give the number of sick days each employee used during the past month. Equation 4.1 is used to calculate their mean. The data values and the mean calculation are

$$\mu = \frac{\Sigma x}{N} = \frac{3 + 0 + 5 + 6 + 1 + 0 + 11 + 8 + 0 + 4}{10} = 3.8$$

The computation reveals that an average of 3.8 sick days per hourly employee were taken during the past month.

Note that the sum of the squared deviations from the mean is equal to 127.6:
$\Sigma(x - \mu)^2 = [(3 - 3.8)^2 + (0 - 3.8)^2 + (5 - 3.8)^2 + (6 - 3.8)^2 + (1 - 3.8)^2 + (0 - 3.8)^2 + (11 - 3.8)^2 + (8 - 3.8)^2 + (0 - 3.8)^2 + (4 - 3.8)^2] = 127.6$.

This is a minimum value because the population mean is the mathematical center of the distribution of 10 population values. If any value other than 3.8 is subtracted from the data values and the resulting deviations are squared and summed, the result will be a number larger than 127.6. Note that the results will be exactly the same if the data collection is treated as a sample.

The advantage of the arithmetic mean is that it's easy to compute, is understood by almost everyone, and is a good central value to use in summarizing a data collection, no matter how many values the collection contains. The disadvantage of the mean is that extreme values distort it. For this reason, the mean isn't the best summary statistic for all data collections.

EXAMPLE 4.3   Table 4.1 shows sales of the six largest restaurant chains. A mean sales amount of $5,280 million is computed using Equation 4.2:

$$\bar{x} = \frac{\Sigma x}{n} = \frac{14,110 + 5,590 + 3,700 + 3,030 + 2,800 + 2,450}{6} = 5,280$$

Note that this mean has been distorted upward by McDonald's sales of $14,110 million.

TABLE 4.1   Sales for the Six Largest Restaurant Chains, 1987 (Example 4.3)

Company	Sales ($ millions)
McDonald's	14,110
Burger King	5,590
Kentucky Fried Chicken	3,700
Hardee's	3,030
Wendy's	2,800
Pizza Hut	2,450

Source: C. Bovee and W. Arens, *Contemporary Advertising*. (Homewood, Ill.: Richard D. Irwin, 1989).

EXAMPLE 4.4   The journal *Accountancy* (July 1991, p. 78) reported on a study that computed the average (mean) monthly cost of leasing a car for employees of the major accounting firms in England. These costs ranged from a low of 284 pounds per month for the Volkswagen Golf, to a high of 1148 pounds per month for the Jaguar Sovereign. If the mean was also used to summarize the cost of all cars, it would be distorted upward by the high cost of the Jaguar.

Median

In cases where you want a typical, central value that doesn't suffer the distorting effects of extreme values, use the **median** to summarize the data. Approximately half the data values in a set are less than the median, and approximately half are greater.

> The **median** of a data collection is the middle item in a set of observations that are arranged in order of magnitude.

Equation 4.3 is used to compute the *item number* of the median in a data set that is arranged in ascending or descending order:

$$\text{Median item number} = \frac{n + 1}{2} \qquad\qquad (4.3)$$

Characteristics of the median
1. Every ordinal-level, interval-level, and ratio-level data set has a median.
2. The median is not sensitive to extreme values.
3. The median does not have certain valuable mathematical properties for use in further computations.

EXAMPLE 4.5   Table 4.2 shows 1989 sales for a random sample of 11 of the top 50 retail chains. Clint Stone wants to compute a summary value to show the average sales for Table 4.2. The sample's mean, using Equation 4.2, is $8,383.5 million. This is considered a misleading summary statistic because it's distorted upward by two or three large values in the data collection.

TABLE 4.2   Sales for 11 of Top 50 Retail Chains, 1989 (Example 4.5)

Retail chain	Sales ($ millions)
Sears	$31,599
J.C. Penney	16,103
A & P	11,148
Albertsons	7,423
Walgreen	5,380
Toys "Я" Us	4,788
Tandy	4,181
Circle K	3,493
Costco	2,943
Nordstrom	2,671
Revco	2,490

Source: *Industry Surveys*, May 2, 1991, p. R80.

The median is the middle item in a set of observations. When data values are arrayed from highest to lowest as in Table 4.2, the median can be easily found. In this data collection, the median is $4,788 since half the values are greater than $4,788 and half are less. The median item can also be computed using Equation 4.3:

$$\text{Median item value} = \frac{n + 1}{2} = \frac{11 + 1}{2} = \text{6th item}$$

The median, $4,788, is the sixth item in the array. The value $4,788 is a central summary value that isn't distorted by Sears and J.C. Penney's comparatively high sales, which are now values that are only counted as ones in the analysis.

EXAMPLE 4.6 The median number of people treated daily at St. Luke's Hospital's emergency room must be determined from the following data for the past six days:

25, 26, 45, 52, 65, 78

Since the number of values is even, the two values in the center are used to compute the median; their average (mean) represents the median of the collection. The calculated average (mean) of the two central values, 45 and 52, is 48.5, so this is the median. Half of the values in the data array are less than 48.5, and half are greater. The median item can also be computed using Equation 4.3:

$$\text{Median item number} = \frac{n + 1}{2} = \frac{6 + 1}{2} = 3.5$$

Since the median is item 3.5 in the array, the third and fourth elements need to be averaged: $(45 + 52)/2 = 48.5$. Therefore, 48.5 is the median number of patients treated in St. Luke's emergency room during the six-day period.

The median separates a data array into two equal sections. If each section is subdivided by a new median, the result is four equal sections. Each of the three separating values is called a *quartile*; the middle quartile is the original median. An extension of this idea, which is often used on very large data arrays, is to separate the data into 100 sections, each with the same number of data elements. The separating values are then called *percentiles*.

It is sometimes important to know the most prevalent value in a data collection. The value that occurs most frequently is known as the **mode**.

Mode

The **mode** of a data collection is the value that occurs most frequently.

> **Characteristics of the mode**
> 1. Some data sets do not have a mode.
> 2. Some data collections have more than one mode.
> 3. The mode does not have certain valuable mathematical properties for use in further computations.

EXAMPLE 4.7   A data collection consists of the values 2, 3, 3, 5, 6, 4, 3, 6, 7, 9, 3, 2, and 6. The mode of this collection is 3, since there are more 3s (four of them) than any other number.

EXAMPLE 4.8   The mode is to be determined for the following data values:

12, 14, 15, 16, 15, 18, 19, 20, 14

In this data array, two values (14 and 15) occur with a frequency of two. Therefore, the collection can be said to be bimodal, with modes 14 and 15. If no value appeared more than once, the data collection would have no mode.

Table 4.3 compares advantages and disadvantages of the mean, median, and mode.

TABLE 4.3   A Comparison of the Mean, Median, and Mode

Average	Advantages	Disadvantages
Mean	Reflects the value of every data point Easy to compute and understand Has valuable mathematical properties; useful for further computations	Unduly influenced by extreme values
Median	Not distorted by extreme values	Lacking certain mathematical properties
Mode	Value that appears most frequently	Lacking certain mathematical properties Some data sets have no mode

In Chapter 3 frequency distributions were graphed as rectangles (histograms) or smooth curves (frequency polygons). A frequency polygon with many classes approaches a smooth curve (see Figure 4.1) with the frequency recorded on the *y*-axis and the class scale on the *x*-axis.

Analysts are frequently concerned about how data values are distributed, that is, how values in the data collection are spread out between the extremes. Differences among the mean, median, and mode can be easily seen from graphs of **symmetrical** and **skewed distributions**. Figure 4.1 shows three curves: one that is symmetrical (curve *a*) and two that are skewed (curves *b* and *c*). Curve *a* depicts a symmetrical distribution because a vertical line drawn from the peak of the curve to the horizontal axis will divide the area of the curve into two equal, symmetrical parts. Note that the mean, median, and mode are all located at the peak value of curve *a*.

FIGURE 4.1 Symmetrical and Skewed Distributions

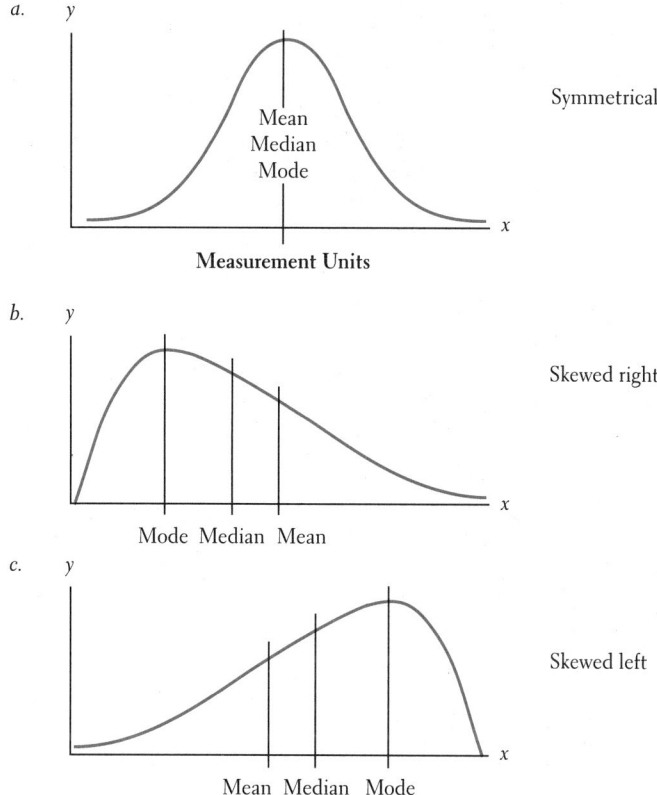

A **symmetrical distribution** is represented by a curve that can be divided by a vertical line into two parts that are mirror images.

Curves *b* and *c* in Figure 4.1 are referred to as skewed curves because they lack symmetry. Values in such distributions are concentrated at either the low end or the high end of the scale along the horizontal axis. Curve *b* is skewed to the right, or the high end of the scale (such a distribution is sometimes referred to as *positively skewed*). The mean is drawn away from the highest point of the curve toward the skewed end. This is because the mean is sensitive to a few extreme values at that end of the curve. The mode (the value that occurs most frequently) is the *x* value corresponding to the highest point of the curve, and the median (the most typical value) is located between the mean and mode.

When the distribution is skewed to the left (curve *c* of Figure 4.1), the mean is pulled away from the highest point of the curve toward the low end of the scale. The median is pulled down, but not as much, and the mode remains at the highest point on the curve.

A skewed **distribution** is represented by a curve that lacks symmetry.

Figure 4.1 illustrates the effects of skewness on the three averages discussed in this section. In particular, this figure demonstrates the importance of determining the extent of skewness of a distribution before choosing among the averaging methods for a summary value. The median is generally the best measure of central tendency to use when a distribution is skewed.

Weighted Mean   The final measure of central tendency to be discussed in this chapter is the **weighted mean,** so named because in its calculation some data values are given more weight than others.

The **weighted mean** assigns more weight to some data values than to others.

In calculating the arithmetic mean of a data array using Equation 4.1 or 4.2, it's implicitly assumed that each data value carries the same weight. If, for some reason, certain data values are more important than others, different weights can be assigned to the values in calculating the mean.

Equation 4.4 is used to calculate the weighted mean for either a population or a sample:

$$\bar{x}_w = \frac{\sum\limits_{i=1}^{n} w_i x_i}{\sum\limits_{i=1}^{n} w_i} \tag{4.4}$$

where $\bar{x}_w$ = Weighted mean
x_i = Data values to be averaged
w_i = Weights applied to the *x* values

Note from Equation 4.4 that each selected weight is multiplied by the corresponding data value. Next these weighted values are summed. Finally, this summation of weighted values is divided by the summation of the weights. The result is the computation of a mean to which some data values contribute more than others.

EXAMPLE 4.9   Professor Chin gives three regular exams, a midterm, and a final exam in his statistics class each semester. These exam grades are averaged to determine each class member's final grade. The three regular exams each account for 15% of the grade, the midterm accounts for 25%, and the final accounts for 30%. Thus, the five exams' weights are .15, .15, .15, .25, .30. One class member achieves scores of 75, 82, 84, 79, and 91 during the quarter. Her final average score using the weighted mean is

$$\bar{x}_w = \frac{w_1 x_1 + w_2 x_2 + w_3 x_3 + w_4 x_4 + w_5 x_5}{w_1 + w_2 + w_3 + w_4 + w_5}$$

$$= \frac{(.15)75 + (.15)82 + (.15)84 + (.25)79 + (.30)91}{.15 + .15 + .15 + .25 + .30}$$

$$= \frac{83.2}{1} = 83.2$$

EXAMPLE 4.10   Table 4.4 shows the percentage of the civilian labor force unemployed in three counties of Eastern Washington. Barbara McWilliams must make a presentation to the Spokane Economic Development Council showing the region's unemployment rate. Table 4.4 gives unemployment rates and labor force sizes for the three counties. She calculates the mean percentage unemployed for the three counties to be $(15.1 + 13.4 + 7.8)/3 = 12.1\%$. However, since Spokane County is much larger than the other two counties, Barbara feels that this figure doesn't truly reflect the region's unemployment rate. She decides that a weighted mean is more appropriate and calculates it using each county's civilian labor force as the weights:

$$\bar{x}_w = \frac{(.151)(7,360) + (.134)(3,670) + (.078)(162,300)}{7,360 + 3,670 + 162,300}$$

$$= \frac{14,263}{173,330} = .082$$

The weighted average of the percentage of the labor force unemployed for the region is 8.2%. This value is much more representative of the region because it properly reflects the size of each county's labor force.

TABLE 4.4   Civilian Labor Force (Example 4.10)

County	Percentage unemployed	Civilian labor force
Adams	15.1	7,360
Pend Oreille	13.4	3,670
Spokane	7.8	162,300

Source: Washington State Employment Security Department, Labor Market and Economic Analysis Branch, July 1986.

The analyst must carefully choose which of the four methods of summarizing central tendency is most appropriate for a given data collection. The mean is commonly used but may not be appropriate if there are extreme values in the collection. In these cases, the median may provide a more accurate summary statistic. The mode is used when the value that occurs most frequently is desired. Its disadvantage is that this value may not accurately represent the entire collection. The weighted mean is used when certain data values are more important than others.

EXERCISES

1. Which measure of central tendency (mean, median, mode) is most sensitive to extreme values?

2. Which measure of central tendency is used to indicate the value with the greatest frequency?

3. Which measure of central tendency places differing amounts of importance on the values in a data collection?

4. When a data collection contains extreme values, which measure of central tendency should be used?

5. Which measure of central tendency takes into account the value of every item in a data collection in its computation?

6. Which measure of central tendency is useful for performing statistical procedures such as comparing central tendencies of several data sets?

7. Which measure of central tendency has mathematical properties that enable it to be easily used in further computations?

8. Which measure of central tendency allows different weights to be assigned to the values being averaged?

9. Which measure of central tendency would be a good choice for an average for a collection containing many small values and one very large value?

10. If one of the values slightly larger than the mean in a data collection is replaced by a very large value, does the mean go up, go down, or stay the same? How does this replacement affect the median?

11. If you wanted an average to be proportional to a community's total income, which measure of central tendency would you use?

12. If you wanted an average to represent income received by the most people in a community, which measure of central tendency would you use?

13. If you wanted an average to represent incomes of a community, in the sense that it would differ as little as possible from those incomes, which measure of central tendency would you use?

14. If you were to manufacture a new aluminum window screen and wished to produce only one size, which measure of central tendency would you use to assess market demand?

15. What is the difference between a sample statistic and a population parameter?

16. What is the difference between a symmetrical distribution and a skewed distribution?

17. Indicate whether the distribution for each of the following variables is symmetrical, skewed right, or skewed left:

    a. Annual household income.

    b. Lengths of rolls of wallpaper.

    c. Scores on a very easy statistics exam.

    d. Family size.

    e. Mileages of tires before wearout.

18. Indicate where the mean, median, and mode are located on each of the following types of distribution:

    a. Skewed right.

    b. Symmetrical.

    c. Skewed left.

    d. Values concentrated at the upper end of the scale.

    e. Symmetry lacking in the upper end.

19. What is the shape of the distribution described by the following measures of central tendency: mean = 46, median = 42, mode = 39?

20. What is the shape of the distribution described by the following measures of central tendency: mean = 3.1, median = 3.1, mode = 3.1?

21. What is the shape of the distribution described by the following measures of central tendency: mean = 105, median = 110, mode = 115?

22. The following data show a population consisting of the number of Snickers candy bars purchased from a cafeteria vending machine on the first 10 days of operation: 7, 3, 0, 5, 8, 6, 7, 10, 1, 3.

    a. Calculate the mode, median, and mean for this data collection.

    b. Which measure of central tendency would you use to estimate monthly sales of Snickers from this vending machine?

    c. Compute the sum of the deviations from the mean: $\Sigma(x - \mu)$.

    d. Compute the sum of the squared deviations from the mean: $\Sigma(x - \mu)^2$. Is it possible to obtain a smaller sum of squared deviations by using any number other than the mean?

23. Ten bear markets shown here have ravaged investors since the 1940s. In the rate of their descent, none of these declining markets rivaled what occurred in the fall of 1987. The most important question at that time was how long it would last.

Bear market	Months long
1948–1949	8
1953	8
1957	3
1960	10
1961–1962	7
1966	8
1968–1970	18
1973–1974	21
1976–1978	17
1981–1982	16

Source: "The Months Ahead," *Changing Times*, December 1987.

    a. What is the modal length of the bear market?

    b. Which value divides the data collection into two equal parts?

    c. Calculate the mean for this data collection.

    d. Which of these measures of central tendency would you use to estimate the duration of the 1987 bear market?

24. Ted Mitchell, manager of Ted's Corner Grocery, investigates the average amount consumers spend on groceries during a one-week period. The following data represent the amounts spent last week by a randomly selected sample of 12 customers:

$ 65	$ 75	$ 85
153	250	99
80	191	55
131	93	182

    a. Calculate the mode, median, and mean for this data collection.

    b. Which measure of central tendency would you use to indicate the typical amount of groceries purchased?

25. In 1989, franchise restaurant chains were expected to have U.S. sales of $70.4 billion, up 11.5% from the year before, according to an analysis prepared by *Restaurant Business* magazine and the consulting firm Technomic Inc. On a per-unit basis, 1989 sales for franchise chain outlets were expected to average $737,000. Here are data for the five leading chains based on total sales.

Restaurant chain	1989 sales (millions)	Number of units
McDonald's	$12,012	8,270
Burger King	5,110	5,361
Pizza Hut	3,100	6,050
Hardee's	3,040	3,327
Kentucky Fried Chicken	3,000	4,997

Source: *Industry Surveys*, March 15, 1990, p. L42.

    a. Calculate the median, and mean for both the 1989 sales and the number of franchises.

    b. Compute the average per outlet for the five leading chains. Compare this value to what was expected from the consulting report.

26. Anderson Motors sold 53 Honda Civics in 1992 for the regular price of $8,250 (standard price, with options costing extra). In October, when the new models arrived, the 1993 standard price was reduced to $7,350. Anderson sold 15 Civics at this reduced price. In a December closeout sale Anderson sold 7 Civics for $6,650. What was the average price that Anderson received for Honda Civics in 1992 (not including cost of optional extras)?

27. Burt Distribution Corporation has a main office in Madison, Wisconsin, and a branch office in Cleveland. Branch manager Julie Pearson is concerned about the amount of money being spent on sending one- to two-pound packages to the main office. The following quantities indicate volumes of packages sent at different postal rates for the past year.

Type of mailing	Number of packages	Rate
Fourth class	2,023	$2.13
Third class	5,478	1.38
First class	8,457	2.40
Special delivery	1,023	2.95
Registered	423	3.60

What was the average cost of sending one- to two-pounds packages to the main office?

28. Perfection Tire Company wants to determine average mileage for a particular tire before wearout so it can establish a warranty policy. A sample is selected, and the following mileages are recorded to the nearest thousand miles:

33 41 55 47 38 45 47 46 48 39 40 40 41 42
38 48 50 49 36 44 44 45 42 35 46 43 47 47

a. Calculate the mode, median, and mean for this data collection.
b. Is the data collection symmetrical or skewed?
c. Which measure of central tendency would you use to help determine the warranty policy?

29. Alton's Traction Headquarters sells four types of Goodyear tires, The following table lists the volume and price for each type of tire sold during a recent month:

Type of tire	Number sold	Price
F-32 radial	288	$49.95
Tiempo radial	940	29.95
Arriva radial	348	39.95
Vector radial	456	44.95

What was Alton's average revenue per Goodyear tire sold?

30. Jim Donaldson, marketing director of Clear Soft Drink Company, wants to determine the average selling price (in cents) for eight-ounce cans of soft drinks in Chicago supermarkets. He samples 44 brands and finds the following prices:

55 52 62 78 41 45 45 65 72 49 55
65 54 55 77 54 65 45 48 70 60 50
40 42 56 81 49 61 63 66 69 48 42
67 50 59 70 59 68 41 41 77 65 54

a. Calculate the mode, median, and mean for this data collection.
b. Is the data collection symmetrical or skewed?
c. Which measure of central tendency should Jim Donaldson use if he's interested in determining the typical price of an eight-ounce can of pop?

MEASURES OF VARIABILITY

Computing a measure of central tendency for a data collection is a valuable way to summarize the numerical values, especially if there are a large number of them. There's another measurement of equal importance, however. We often need to know the extent of variability of the numbers in a data collection or distribution. The best descriptions of variability concern the deviations of the data values from some measure of central tendency, although other methods are also commonly used. This section presents three common measures of dispersion or variation: the range, variance, and standard deviation.

While measures of dispersion or variability are important in a variety of applications, there's probably no more important application area than quality control. It has been said that variability is the chief enemy of good quality. This is because consistency of output in a manufacturing operation is generally a sign of good quality, while extreme variability is generally a sign of poor quality. Chapter 13 ("Quality-Control Applications") explores variability and its relationship to the main job of business everywhere: achieving and maintaining good quality.

Range

The simplest measure of variability is the **range** (the difference between the highest and lowest values in a data set). Texaco's stock price varied from $51 to $54 in 1992, whereas Chevron's stock price varied from $60 to $78. Texaco's price range is $54 − $51 = $3, while Chevron's is $78 − $60 = $18. Comparison of ranges tells the analyst that Chevron's price was much more variable than Texaco's.

The **range** is the difference between the highest and lowest values in a data set.

The range isn't always a good measure of variability. Whenever an extreme value is present in a distribution, the range will indicate excessive variation. For example, in Table 4.2 the range for retail chain sales is $31,599 − $2,490 = $29,109. Sears' extremely large sales total has too much influence on the range.

The best descriptions of variability deal with deviations of the data values from some measure of central tendency. Since the mean has nice mathematical properties, it's a commonly used measure of central tendency. Next we'll look at two important measures of variability: variance and standard deviation.

Variance

The population **variance** is the average of the squared differences between the data values and the mean. It has certain mathematical properties that make it useful in other statistical applications; some of these uses will be presented in later chapters. However, interpreting the variance as the average of the squared differences isn't useful as a descriptive measure. Equation 4.5 shows how the variance for a population of data values is computed:

$$\sigma^2 = \frac{\Sigma(x - \mu)^2}{N} \tag{4.5}$$

where σ^2 = Population variance
 x = Population values
 μ = Population mean
 N = Number of observations in the population

The **variance** is the average of the squared differences between the data values and the mean.

EXAMPLE 4.11   Table 4.5 presents a population of five ages. The mean of this data array is found by summing the values and dividing by N, so $\mu = 200/5 = 40$. The mean age of 40 accurately describes the central tendency of the data collection. But what about variability? To what extent do the data values differ from their mean? Column 2 of Table 4.5 calculates and sums the deviations from the mean. However, taking the average of these deviations provides no indication of variability. The summation equals 0 since the mean is at the mathematical center of the array, and the negative values cancel out the positive values. Example 4.1 illustrated this concept.

TABLE 4.5   Data Collection of Ages (Examples 4.11 and 4.12)

x	$x - \mu$	$(x - \mu)^2$
20	−20	400
30	−10	100
40	0	0
50	10	100
60	20	400
Sums: 200	0	1,000

$\Sigma x = 200; \Sigma(x - \mu) = 0$
$\Sigma(x - \mu)^2 = 1,000$
Mean $= \mu = 200/5 = 40$
Variance $= \sigma^2 = 1,000/5 = 200$
Standard deviation $= \sigma = \sqrt{200} = 14.1$

One mathematical approach to eliminating the minus signs is to square each deviation (column 3 of Table 4.5). After squaring the deviations, Equation 4.5 is applied and the variance of ages is computed:

$$\sigma^2 = \frac{\Sigma(x - \mu)^2}{N} = \frac{1,000}{5} = 200$$

Unfortunately, knowing that the average squared deviation in Example 4.11 equals 200 isn't very meaningful. One solution to this problem is to return to the original units of measure by taking the square root of the variance. Equation 4.6 shows how

Standard Deviation   the square root of the variance, called the population **standard deviation,** is computed.

The standard deviation is the standard amount by which the values in a data collection differ from the mean:

$$\sigma = \sqrt{\frac{\Sigma(x - \mu)^2}{N}}$$

(4.6)

The **standard deviation** measures the standard amount by which the values in a data collection differ from the mean.

EXAMPLE 4.12   The last column of Table 4.5 shows values for use in Equation 4.6 to compute the standard deviation of the population data. This column shows the squared difference between each data value and the mean of the distribution, 40. The sum of these squared deviations is 1,000, and their average is 200. The square root of 200 is 14.1, so this is the standard deviation of the data array. The data values have a mean of 40 and a standard deviation of 14.1. This means that the standard amount by which the values in the array differ from their mean (40) is about 14.1.

The standard deviation is commonly used to describe the extent to which a collection of data values is dispersed around its mean. A small standard deviation means that the values tend to be close to their mean. A large standard deviation means that the values are widely scattered about their mean.

The data of Table 4.5 were defined to be a population and Equations 4.5 and 4.6 were used to calculate population variance and standard deviation. If the measured data constitute a sample, the calculation differs slightly and Equation 4.7 is used to calculate the sample variance. Also, the sample standard deviation is computed by taking the square root of the sample variance ($s = \sqrt{s^2}$). Note in Equation 4.7 that the denominator is 1 less than the sample size ($n - 1$) rather than the entire population size (N) used in Equations 4.5 and 4.6. Note also that while the Greek letter σ (sigma) was used to represent the population parameter, the letter s is used to represent the sample statistic:

Sample variance

$$s^2 = \frac{\Sigma(x - \bar{x})^2}{n - 1}$$

(4.7)

where s^2 = Sample variance
s = Sample standard deviation
x = The sample values
$\bar{x}$ = Sample mean
n = Number of observations in the sample

Degrees of Freedom

The denominator in Equation 4.7, ($n - 1$), represents **degrees of freedom**. This term appears frequently in statistical applications and refers to the number of data values in the sample that are free of each other in the sense that they carry unique information.

Degrees of freedom refers to the number of data elements that are free to vary.

The sample standard deviation calculation of Equation 4.7 uses the sample mean ($\bar{x}$) as an estimate of the population mean (μ). If the sum of the squared deviations in Equation 4.7's numerator were divided by the sample size, n, a biased variance would result. That is, the value of s^2, which is an estimate of the unknown population variance (σ^2), would tend, over many trials, to be slightly too small. This is because the $\Sigma(x - \bar{x})^2$ computation provides a minimum value, as Example 4.2 illustrated. Had the actual population mean been used in Equation 4.7, the numerator would probably have been slightly larger.

Mathematicians have discovered that the small-size bias of Equation 4.7's numerator is compensated for by reducing the denominator as well. By using $(n - 1)$ in the denominator of the sample variance calculation, the bias is removed and an unbiased estimate of the unknown population variance results.

In general, a piece of sample information is lost each time a sample statistic is used to estimate an unknown population parameter in an equation. In Equation 4.7, it would be preferable to measure the sampled items' variability around the true population mean, but since this value isn't known, an estimate—the sample mean—is used in its place.

A shortcut formula has been derived for calculating the sample variance and standard deviation. This is handy when the data being evaluated number more than a few items. Equation 4.8 is the shortcut formula to compute the sample variance. The sample standard deviation is computed by taking the square root of this variance:

$$s^2 = \frac{\Sigma x^2 - \dfrac{(\Sigma x)^2}{n}}{n - 1} \tag{4.8}$$

Both the sum of the sample x values and the sum of their squared values are needed for the calculation. Note that Σx^2 does not equal $(\Sigma x)^2$, as Chapter 1 pointed out.

It is easy to become confused by all the equations used to compute the variance and standard deviation. However, Equation 4.8 can be used in most cases since real-world situations usually involve samples.

EXAMPLE 4.13   Table 4.6 shows a data collection representing the number of units sold per day in a random sample of selling days for Jarms, an appliance dealer. As shown, the mean of the sample is 7.08 units. Since the data represent a sample,

TABLE 4.6   Jarms Appliances Sold (Example 4.13)

4	5	12	9	10	8
7	4	5	3	0	1
8	2	15	7	9	11
9	8	7	8	6	12

$n = 24$
$\Sigma x = 170$
$\bar{x} = 170/24 = 7.08$
$\Sigma x^2 = 1,512$

Equation 4.8 can be used to calculate the standard deviation. The x^2 values used to compute this sum are:

16	25	144	81	100	64
49	16	25	9	0	1
64	4	225	49	81	121
81	64	49	64	36	144

The variance can now be computed using Equation 4.8:

$$s^2 = \frac{\Sigma x^2 - \frac{(\Sigma x)^2}{n}}{n - 1} = \frac{1,512 - \frac{(170)^2}{24}}{24 - 1} = \frac{307.8}{23} = 13.38$$

The square root of the variance is the standard deviation:

$$s = \sqrt{13.38} = 3.66$$

Jarms Appliances sells an average (mean) of 7.08 units per day. Typical variation in these sales is 3.66 units from the mean of 7.08.

Many handheld calculators automatically figure the mean and standard deviation. In calculating standard deviation, we must know whether the data constitute a population or a sample so that the proper denominator can be used. Calculators commonly have two keys for this purpose: the N key for populations and the $(n - 1)$ key for samples.

In addition, most data analysis programs for either mainframe or personal computers include the mean and standard deviation as summary measures of data collections. The MINITAB commands for computing descriptive statistics for the Jarms Appliance Store example are:

```
MTB>  SET INTO C1
DATA> 4 5 12 9 10  8 7 4 5 3 0 1 8 2 15 7 9 11 9
DATA> 8 7 8 6 12
DATA> END
MTB>  DESCRIBE C1

            N       MEAN     MEDIAN    TRMEAN     STDEV    SEMEAN
C1         24      7.083      7.500     7.045     3.658     0.747

          MIN        MAX         Q1        Q3
C1      0.000     15.000      4.250     9.000

MTB > STOP
```

The "MINITAB Computer Package" section at the end of this chapter explains these MINITAB commands and the output.

Figure 4.2 shows the variability of the mean and standard deviation for different data distributions. In part *a*, three distributions appear. Since they all have the same shape, these three symmetrical distributions clearly have the same standard deviation. That is, data values in all three distributions are approximately the same distance from their respective means. However, their means are different; each is at a different point on the horizontal axis.

FIGURE 4.2 Data Distributions

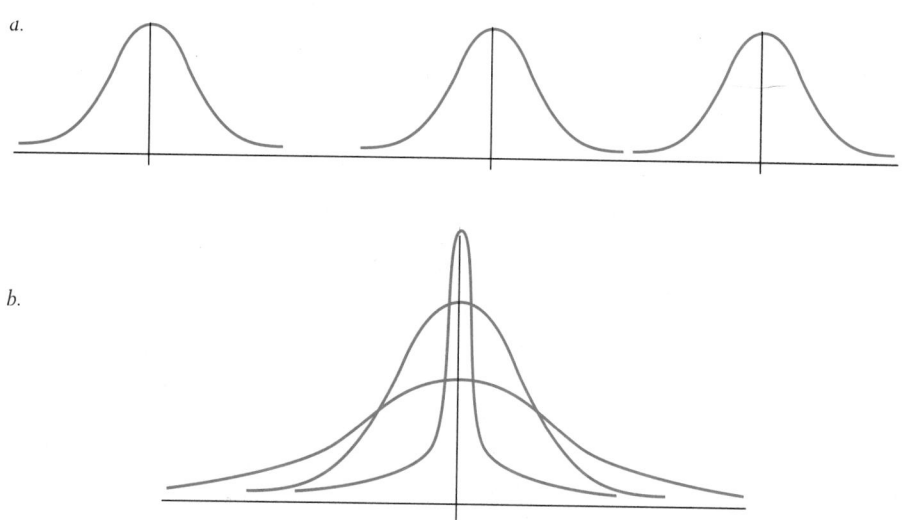

By contrast, the three symmetrical curves of part *b* all have the same mean. However, their standard deviations are different. The widest curves' data values are typically far from the mean compared with the middle curve's, and the inner-curve data values are even more tightly packed about the mean. Figure 4.2 illustrates the importance of knowing both the mean and standard deviation of a data distribution for an accurate summary of the distribution.

Coefficient of Variation Another method sometimes used to measure the variability of a population or sample of data values is the **coefficient of variation**. This statistic specifies the size of the standard deviation as a percentage of the mean. It is calculated by dividing the standard deviation by the mean. The coefficient of variation indicates the *relative* amount of variability in a distribution.

> The **coefficient of variation** for a data collection expresses the standard deviation as a percentage of the mean.

Equation 4.9 is used to calculate the coefficient of variation for a sample. The abbreviation CV is used for this statistic:

$$CV = \frac{s}{\bar{x}}(100) \tag{4.9}$$

Note that for a population, s in the numerator would be replaced by σ, and $\bar{x}$ in the denominator would be replaced by μ.

Decision makers use the coefficient of variation to: (1) determine how reliable the mean is as a measure of central tendency, (2) assess whether the standard deviation is large, small, or somewhere in between, or (3) compare two or more distributions' variability.

EXAMPLE 4.14   The president of First Federal Bank was nervous about an attempted takeover of the bank, especially after reading a *Wall Street Journal* article (April 15, 1992) about Banc One's plans to buy Valley National Bank of Arizona, reportedly for around $1.23 billion. Although there had been no specific threat against First Federal Bank, the president and bank board wanted certain facts and figures about the bank right away.

Kim Horns, a new analyst for the bank, was asked to collect a number of statistics for presentation to the bank board. She was to compare the average account balances at the downtown and suburban branches. A random sample of savings account balances was drawn from both locations. For the main office, the mean account balance was $1,248.50 with standard deviation of $537.93. At the branch, the mean was $743.84 with standard deviation of $325.10. Kim saw that the suburban branch had a lower average account balance, but she found it difficult to compare the variability of the two branches due to the difference in means. For this reason, Kim decided to compute the coefficient of variation for each branch:

Main office:
$$CV = \frac{s}{\bar{x}}(100) = \frac{537.93}{1,248.50}(100) = 43.1\%$$

Suburban office:
$$CV = \frac{s}{\bar{x}}(100) = \frac{325.10}{743.84}(100) = 43.7\%$$

Clearly, both the mean and standard deviation of account balances at the suburban branch are smaller than at the main office. However, as a percentage of their means, the two offices' standard deviations are about equal. In this sense, the variability of account balances at the two locations is relatively the same.

MEASURES OF POSITION

Suppose that a person feels he is drastically underpaid compared with other people with similar experience and background. One way to demonstrate this condition is to obtain these other employees' salaries and show the discrepancy. A measure of position

Percentile

or relative standing can be used to evaluate an individual salary compared with the entire group. One measure of the position of a particular observation is its **percentile ranking.** The pth percentile is the value of x such that p percent of the observations fall below the pth percentile and $(100 - p)$ percent lie above it.

> The pth **percentile** is the value of x such that $p\%$ of the observations fall below the pth percentile and $(100 - p)\%$ lie above it.

For example, the person who felt underpaid discovered that he was in the 20th percentile. This means that 20% of all employees with similar experience and background have salaries below his and 80% have higher salaries.

Percentiles divide observations into 100 parts of equal size. The procedure for obtaining a particular percentile is similar to the computation of the median. In fact, the median describes the 50th percentile. Deciles divide observations into 10 parts of equal size. Quartiles divide observations into four parts of equal size.

Another measure of position is a **standard score.** Like a percentile, a standard score determines the relative position of any particular data value, x. The standard score indicates the number of standard deviations by which a particular value lies above or below the mean. Standard scores are discussed in detail in Chapter 6.

Since the standard deviation is a measure of standard distance from the mean, knowing the mean and standard deviation provides the analyst with great insight about the data from which they were computed. Two important statistical concepts are often used in this process: Chebyshev's theorem and the empirical rule.

Chebyshev's Theorem

Chebyshev's theorem (sometimes referred to as *Tchebysheff's theorem*), credited to Russian mathematician P. L. Chebyshev, states that no matter what the shape of a distribution, at least 75% of the values will fall within ± 2 standard deviations of the mean of the distribution, and at least 89% of the values will lie within ± 3 standard deviations of the mean. Chebyshev's theorem will be discussed in detail in Chapter 6.

Empirical Rule

A popular rule of thumb in statistics, the **empirical rule,** involves a collection of data values that is symmetrical about its mean with most values close to the mean. Figure 4.3 shows a bell-shaped distribution with the following characteristics:

1. Approximately 68% of the values are within one standard deviation of the mean.
2. Approximately 95% of the values are within two standard deviations of the mean.
3. Approximately 99.7% of the values are within three standard deviations of the mean.

Note that Chebyshev's theorem is extremely conservative compared to the empirical rule (75% of the values instead of 95% lie within two standard deviations). The reason is that Chebyshev's theorem applies to any population or sample, without regard to the shape of the distribution. The empirical rule is also discussed in depth in Chapter 6.

Finally, it should be noted that the data used in this chapter to illustrate key concepts are **raw data,** that is, they consist of individual measurements. Table 4.6 is an

FIGURE 4.3   Bell-Shaped Distribution

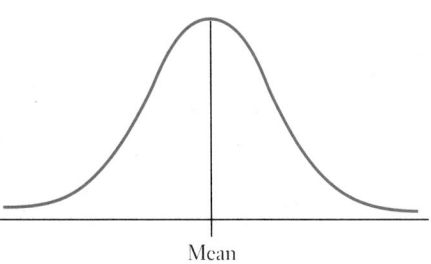

Mean

example of raw data. By contrast, many data sets are presented in **grouped data** form. The frequency distribution described in Chapter 3 is presenting grouped data (see Table 3.5).

Sometimes summary statistics must be calculated such as mean and standard deviation from grouped data. When this is necessary, each data value is assumed to have the value of the midpoint of its data category, since specific data values aren't given. After making this conversion, the formulas presented in this chapter can be used. Example 4.15 shows how the grouped data from a frequency distribution are converted to estimated raw data values so that formulas such as Equations 4.2 and 4.8 can be used.

EXAMPLE 4.15   The following frequency distribution has been constructed to show a data collection.

Class	Frequency
5–9	2
10–14	3
15–19	4

To calculate the estimated mean and standard deviation of the original data set, each value is assumed to take on the value of the middle or midpoint of its class. That is, each value in the 5–9 class is assumed to equal 7; values in the 10–14 class are all assumed to be 12; and values in the 15–19 range are assumed to be 17. This conversion results in the estimated original data set

7 7 12 12 12 17 17 17 17

We can now use the raw data formulas (Equations 4.2 and 4.8).

EXERCISES

31. What is the difference between a measure of central tendency and a measure of variability?
32. What is the difference between standard deviation and variance?
33. What is the difference between absolute variation and relative variation?

34. Why are deviations from the mean *squared* in computing standard deviation?

35. In the formula for sample standard deviation, why is the sum of squared deviations divided by $(n - 1)$ instead of by n?

36. Why is the concept of degrees of freedom important?

37. Suppose you live in an area where the standard deviation for the average weekly amount of rainfall is zero. Describe your climate.

38. Jim Perez, customer service manager for National Tune-up Corporation, collected the following data representing the number of complaints his department received on each of eight randomly selected days:

    10, 12, 8, 5, 11, 10, 9, 14

    a. Compute the range.

    b. Compute the standard deviation.

    c. Compute the variance.

    d. Compute the coefficient of variation.

    e. Interpret each of these measures of variability.

39. Phoenix Body & Frame employs eight workers. The following data collection shows each worker's years of experience: 1, 7, 9, 15, 9, 1, 7, 15. Treat this data collection as a population.

    a. Compute the standard deviation.

    b. If a worker with 8 years of experience is added, how will this affect the standard deviation?

    c. If a worker with 15 years of experience replaces a worker with 7 years of experience, how will this affect the standard deviation?

    d. If a worker with no years of experience replaces a worker with 7 years of experience, how will this affect the standard deviation?

40. As a manufacturer of some product requiring great uniformity (interchangeability of parts), would you be interested in a product whose pertinent characteristics included a large or small standard deviation?

41. The ages of some people in an office are 23, 25, 34, 35, 37, 41, 42, and 56. Treat this data collection as a sample.

    a. Compute the range.

    b. Compute the standard deviation.

    c. Compute the variance.

    d. Compute the coefficient of variation.

42. Last year at this time, personal loan data at Farmers and Merchants Bank showed a mean of $650 and a standard deviation of $300. Recently the mean was calculated to be $1,000 and the standard deviation $350. Did loans last year show more or less relative variation than recent loans?

43. Michelle Wang wants to determine the variability of the amounts of checks she writes during a typical month. The following data collection represents 11 checks randomly selected from last month's personal checking account: $8.63, $102.36, $45.00, $50.12,

$75.65, $9.87, $224.56, $78.95, $78.98, $15.62, $20.00. What is the average amount per check? What is the standard amount of variability per check?

44. The annual salaries of Lake City Transmission's seven workers are $15,000, $22,000, $25,000, $17,500, $14,500, $32,500, and $13,250. A competitor, Transmission Exchange Company, pays workers a mean annual salary of $21,000 with standard deviation of $3,000. Compare the two companies' means and relative variability.

45. Dick Hoover, owner of Modern Office Equipment, is concerned about freight costs and clerical costs incurred on small orders. To reduce expenditures in this area, he'll introduce a discount policy for orders over $40 to encourage customers to consolidate a number of small orders into large orders. The mean amounts per transaction for a sample of 28 customers are

10, 15, 20, 25, 15, 17, 41, 50, 5, 9, 12, 14, 35, 18,
19, 17, 28, 29, 11, 11, 43, 54, 7, 8, 16, 13, 37, 18

   a. Compute the variance.
   b. Compute the standard deviation.
   c. Compute the coefficient of variation.
   d. Is the distribution symmetrical, positively skewed, or negatively skewed?
   e. If the policy is successful, will the mean of the distribution increase, decrease, or remain the same?
   f. If the policy is successful, will the standard deviation of the distribution increase, decrease, or remain the same?

46. Describe what the standard deviation measures.

SUMMARY

This chapter has presented various quantitative measurements to summarize essential characteristics of data collections. It described methods to measure and summarize the two key elements of a data collection: central tendency and variability.

The mean, median, mode, and weighted mean were presented as methods of indicating a central summary value for a data collection. The range, variance, standard deviation, and coefficient of variation were presented as methods to indicate the degree of variability. The analyst must carefully choose among these methods in computing summary statistics so that they fairly and accurately summarize the underlying data collection.

APPLICATIONS OF STATISTICAL CONCEPTS IN THE BUSINESS WORLD

A HOSPITAL'S USE OF STANDARD DEVIATION

Bill Fisher is the chief financial officer at a hospital in Spokane, Washington. Several years ago he took two statistics classes from the authors while earning his bachelor's degree in business administration.

The federal government pays Bill's hospital in accordance with established dollar values for various procedures. The government recognizes that there is variability in the actual amount hospitals spend for various treatments, but makes a standard payment for each, with one exception. If the amount of the treatment exceeds three standard deviations above the mean, the government will make a special payment to the hospital to cover this procedure but only after careful review.

Bill keeps continuous track of the mean and standard deviation of each procedure covered by government reimbursement, and he compares the cost of each patient treatment with the three-standard-deviation upper limit. When the hospital's cost for a treatment exceeds the mean plus three standard deviations, he requests an additional payment.

During the previous year, one patient alone exceeded the three-standard-deviation upper limit by almost $300,000. By knowing the mean plus three-standard-deviation limit, Bill was able to claim this extra amount from Medicare for the hospital.

OTHER APPLICATIONS

The two essential components of any data collection, measures of central tendency and variability, are commonly used as summary values. Accountants, for example, constantly deal with numerical values and employ summary figures to describe various accounts' current condition and to make comparisons over time.

Financial data abound in the business world and are routinely summarized so their essential properties can be analyzed and used by decision makers. Production or manufacturing functions in businesses measure such things as output, temperature, and pressure. These data values must be briefly described using summary statistics if they are to be useful to managers.

Personnel records contain many quantitative variables (overtime hours per week, years of education, months with the company, and hourly rate of pay, for example) that must be summarized for use in intelligent decision making.

Although several measurements made in marketing result in categorical data, many quantitative measurements are used too. Examples are units sold per day, dollar volume per day for each department in a retail store, number of credit card uses per month by customers, and number of units sold for each type and style of product.

A key aspect of any business in this highly competitive age is quality control. Summary measures such as those discussed in this chapter are commonly used to measure such indications of quality as defective units per batch, variability of a manufacturing process, and sizes and weights of parts.

GLOSSARY

Arithmetic mean The sum of the numerical values in a collection divided by the number of values. The symbol for the population mean is the Greek letter μ (mu). The symbol for a sample mean is $\bar{x}$ (x-bar).

Parameter Any measurable characteristic of a population.

Statistic Any measurable characteristic of a sample.

Median The middle item in a set of observations that are arranged in order of magnitude.

Mode The value that occurs most frequently in a data collection.

Symmetrical distribution A curve that can be divided by a vertical line into two parts that are mirror images.

Skewed distribution A curve that lacks symmetry.

Weighted mean A mean computation in which some data values are assigned more weight than others.

Range The difference between the highest and lowest values in a data set.

Variance The average of the squared differences between the data values and the mean.

Standard deviation A measure of the standard amount by which the values in a data collection differ from the mean.

Degrees of freedom The number of data elements that are free to vary.

Coefficient of variation The standard deviation expressed as a percentage of the mean.

Percentile A value of x such that p% of the observations fall below the pth percentile and $(100 - p)$% lie above it.

KEY FORMULAS

Arithmetic mean—population

$$\mu = \frac{\Sigma x}{N} \tag{4.1}$$

Arithmetic mean—sample

$$\bar{x} = \frac{\Sigma x}{n} \tag{4.2}$$

Median

$$\text{Median item number} = \frac{n + 1}{2} \tag{4.3}$$

Weighted mean

$$\bar{x}_w = \frac{\sum\limits_{i=1}^{n} w_i x_i}{\sum\limits_{i=1}^{n} w_i} \tag{4.4}$$

Variance—population

$$\sigma^2 = \frac{\Sigma (x - \mu)^2}{N} \tag{4.5}$$

Standard deviation—population

$$\sigma = \sqrt{\frac{\Sigma (x - \mu)^2}{N}} \tag{4.6}$$

Variance—sample

$$s^2 = \frac{\Sigma (x - \bar{x})^2}{n - 1} \tag{4.7}$$

Variance—sample

$$s^2 = \frac{\Sigma x^2 - \frac{(\Sigma x)^2}{n}}{n-1} \qquad (4.8)$$

Coefficient of variation

$$CV = \frac{s}{\bar{x}}(100) \qquad (4.9)$$

SOLVED EXERCISES

1. CHOOSING AMONG THE MEAN, MEDIAN, MODE, AND WEIGHTED MEAN

Which measure of central tendency should be used in each of the following situations?

a. You want to determine the average annual percentage rate of net profit to sales for the General Electric Company for the past seven years.

b. You want to determine the average amount each worker receives per month to ensure a fair distribution in a profit-sharing plan.

c. You want to determine a representative wage value for use in arbitration for Precision Landscape Systems. The company employs 200 workers, including several highly paid specialists.

Solution:

a. The weighted mean should be used to weight the profit rates by the sales values for each year.

b. The mean should be used to divide the total profits to be shared by workers.

c. The median should be used so that the highly paid specialists' salaries don't distort the representative wage value.

2. COMPUTATION OF MEAN, MEDIAN, AND MODE

June Shapiro is thinking about starting an advertising agency and is interested in analyzing firms that operate in the Little Rock area. The following data collection shows a sample of the local agencies, 1992 total billings, and the number of full-time employees.

Agency	Billings ($ millions)	Employees
Wendt Advertising	7.4	29
Clark, White & Associates	5.0	31
Coons, Corker & Associates	3.5	10
Elgee Corporation	2.1	3
Pierce-Stuart & Associates	1.5	8
Robideaux & Associates	1.2	15
Pacific Advertising	1.0	4
Bright Ideas, Inc.	1.0	5
Creative Consultants	.4	1
Degerness & Associates	.3	3
Rasor & Associates	.2	4

a. Compare the mean, median, and mode for 1992 billings per agency.

b. Which measure of central tendency should June use if she wants the typical amount of 1992 billings?

c. Compute the mean, median, and mode for the number of employees per agency.

d. Which measure of central tendency should June use if she wants to measure variability as well?

Solution:

x	x^2	y	y^2
7.4	54.76	29	841
5.0	25.00	31	961
3.5	12.25	10	100
2.1	4.41	3	9
1.5	2.25	8	64
1.2	1.44	15	225
1.0	1.00	4	16
1.0	1.00	5	25
.4	.16	1	1
.3	.09	3	9
.2	.04	4	16
23.6	102.40	113	2,267

a. Mean $= \bar{x} = \dfrac{\Sigma x}{n} = \dfrac{23.6}{11} = 2.1455$

Median item number $= \dfrac{n+1}{2} = \dfrac{11+1}{2} = \dfrac{12}{2} = 6$

Median $= 1.2$
Mode $= 1.0$

b. June should use the median, 1.2, if she wants the typical amount. This value is not unduly influenced by the billings of $7.4 million for Wendt Advertising.

c. Mean $= \bar{x} = \dfrac{\Sigma x}{n} = \dfrac{113}{11} = 10.273$

Median item number $= \dfrac{n+1}{2} = \dfrac{11+1}{2} = \dfrac{12}{2} = 6$

Median $= 5$
Mode $= 3, 4$

d. Since June wants to perform further computations, such as finding the standard deviation, she should use the mean, 10.273.

3. COMPUTATION OF VARIANCE AND STANDARD DEVIATION

Refer to the data June Shapiro collected in Solved Exercise 2.

a. Compute the variance and standard deviation for billings per agency.

b. Compute the variance and standard deviation for number of employees per agency.

Solution:

a. Variance:

$$s^2 = \frac{\Sigma x^2 - \frac{(\Sigma x)^2}{n}}{n-1} = \frac{102.4 - \frac{(23.6)^2}{11}}{11-1} = \frac{51.77}{10} = 5.18$$

Standard deviation:

$$s = 2.276$$

b. Variance:

$$s^2 = \frac{\Sigma x^2 - \frac{(\Sigma x)^2}{n}}{n-1} = \frac{2{,}267 - \frac{(113)^2}{11}}{11-1} = \frac{1{,}106}{10} = 110.6$$

Standard deviation:

$$s = 10.52$$

4. COMPUTATION OF THE COEFFICIENT OF VARIATION

Refer to the data June Shapiro collected in Solved Exercise 2.

a. Compute the coefficient of variation for billings per agency.

b. Compute the coefficient of variation for number of employees per agency.

Solution:

a. $CV = \frac{s}{\bar{x}}(100) = \frac{2.276}{2.1455}(100) = 106\%$

b. $CV = \frac{s}{\bar{x}}(100) = \frac{10.52}{10.273}(100) = 102.4\%$

EXERCISES

47. Which measure of central tendency is a good choice for an average if further computations are needed?

48. For a certain operation, a factory supervisor is told to set a standard time that "differs as little as possible from the time now taken by all the employees in the shop." The supervisor should use which measure of central tendency?

49. Adams Tractor Company employs six workers aged 21, 27, 19, 35, 31, and 29. Treat this data collection as a population.

   a. Compute the mean and median.

   b. Compute the standard deviation.

   c. If a new worker of age 27 is added, how will this affect the standard deviation?

   d. (This question refers to the original six workers.) If a worker of age 20 replaces the worker who's 35, how will this affect the mean and standard deviation?

   e. (This question refers to the original six workers.) If a worker of age 38 replaces the worker who's 27, how will this affect the standard deviation?

50. The largest 12 U.S. daily newspapers have daily circulations as listed below (as of March 31, 1988). Treat this data collection as a population. Compute the mean and median.

Newspaper	Circulation
The Wall Street Journal	2,025,176
USA Today	1,345,271
New York Daily News	1,283,302
Los Angeles Times	1,132,920
New York Times	1,078,443
Washington Post	810,011
Chicago Tribune	774,045
Detroit News	688,218
Newsday	665,218
Detroit Free Press	647,763
Chicago Sun Times	625,035
San Francisco Chronicle	569,185

Source: Audit Bureau of Circulation.

51. The following data collection shows the current number of enrollees, the number of companies or groups served, and the number of primary physicians for the top Spokane-area health care plans. Treat this data collection as a sample.

Organization	Enrollees	Companies	Physicians
HMOs:			
HMO Washington	161	14	46
Foundation Health Plan	3,569	139	145
Group Health Northwest	30,000	350	26
HealthPlus	10,500	125	47
Maxicare Washington	173	11	12
PPOs:			
United Northwest Services	50,000	10	170
Inland Health Associates	29,000	9	86
Medical Services Corp.	17,373	580	541
First Choice Health Plan	3,836	291	43
Blue Cross Prudent Buyer	3,128	33	114

Source: "Hospitals Health Care & Insurance," *Journal of Business*, Nov. 25–Dec. 9, 1987.

a. Compute the mean and standard deviation of the number of enrollees in the 10 health plans.

b. Compute the mean and standard deviation of the number of companies or groups served by the 10 health plans.

c. Compute the mean and standard deviation of the number of primary physicians used by the 10 health plans.

d. Compute the median number of enrollees in the 10 health plans.

e. Compute the median number of companies or groups served by the 10 health plans.

f. Compute the median number of primary physicians used by the 10 health plans.

g. Is there any application for the weighted mean in this data collection?

h. Which average would you choose (mean or median) for each data collection if you wanted to describe the typical health care plan?

i. Compute the coefficient of variation for the five HMOs and the five preferred provider organizations (PPOs) for each of the three data collections. Compare the relative variability of the two types of health care plans.

52. The Hord Automobile Manufacturing Company is considering two brands of batteries for its latest model. The Telco battery has a mean lifetime of 55 months with a standard deviation of 5 months. The Long-Life battery has a mean lifetime of 45 months with a standard deviation of 3 months.

a. If the decision criterion for selecting a brand of battery is maximum lifetime, which brand should be selected?

b. Which brand should be selected if consistency of service is the decision criterion?

53. The following data represent net income as a percentage of sales (rounded to the nearest full percentage during 1992 for a random sample of 70 of the 500 largest industrial corporations:

5	6	8	10	4	9	7
9	6	4	9	10	9	8
3	9	5	9	9	8	7
10	2	7	4	8	5	10
9	6	8	8	8	7	8
6	11	9	11	7	7	11
10	8	8	5	9	8	8
8	9	10	7	7	7	5
8	7	9	9	8	6	9
5	8	8	7	9	13	8

Compute summary measures for this distribution. Write a memo to management comparing your company's percentage, which is 9, to this distribution.

54. Before deciding on purchasing stock in the Electronic Research & Development Corporation, the management of Fidelity Investments, a mutual fund, wants data on price movements of the firm's stock during the past year. Thirty-five days of the past year were randomly selected, and the closing price (to the nearest dollar) was recorded for each day:

43	29	42	35	32	28	22
52	34	35	32	28	50	33
34	37	29	30	28	29	24
39	27	40	43	48	33	48
29	28	39	36	49	26	47

$n = 35$

a. Fidelity decides not to purchase the stock unless the mean closing price for last year is $34 or more. Is further analysis of these data necessary?

b. Fidelity is also interested in this stock's variability. They won't invest in it if the usual variation from the mean price is more than $10. Would they be interested?

c. Finally, Fidelity needs to compare Electronic Research & Development Corporation stock to that of Innovative Technology Systems. Fidelity is satisfied with both stocks and will purchase the one with less relative variability in price. If Innovative Technology Systems stock has a mean price of $61 and standard deviation of $12, which stock should Fidelity purchase?

55. Demand for both covered and open boat slips on Lake Pend Oreille in Idaho is:

Marina	Covered		Open		Total
	Occupied	Vacant	Occupied	Vacant	
The Captn's Table	0	0	22	3	25
Lee Peters Moorage	44	0	19	2	65
Sunset Resort	0	0	18	10	28
Bottle Bay Resort	0	0	20	2	22
Sandpoint Marina	26	0	109	0	135
Windbag Marina	0	0	60	0	60
Holiday Shores	0	0	33	2	35
Ellisport Marina	0	0	75	0	75
Pend Oreille Shores	0	0	33	32	65
Unknown name	0	0	63	7	70
Scenic Bay Marina	58	0	116	3	177
Vista Bay Resort	30	0	36	4	70
Bitter End Marina	0	0	103	2	105
Bayview Marina	65	0	13	2	80
Boileau's	119	1	20	4	144
McDonald's Hudson Bay Resort	90	0	90	0	180
Totals	432	1	830	73	1,336

Source: *Development Plan for Harbor View Marina in Garfield Bay on Lake Pend Oreille.* J & H Research Service, November 1987.

Metropolitan Mortgage & Securities Company has repossessed a vacant marina and is trying to decide how many slips to develop. Write a memo to Metropolitan summarizing the number of covered, open, and total boat slips presently on the lake, along with the percent vacant of each.

56. The *merchandise trade balance* is computed by finding the difference between merchandise exported and merchandise imported (exports minus imports). In 1980, the United States exported merchandise worth $221 billion and imported merchandise valued at $245 billion for a trade balance of negative $24 billion. In 1990, the United States exported merchandise worth $394 billion and imported merchandise valued at $495 billion for a trade balance of negative $101 billion. U.S. exports to and imports from a sample of nine countries in 1980 and 1990 (in millions of dollars) were:

Country	1980		1990	
	Exports	Imports	Exports	Imports
Austria	$ 447	$ 389	$ 873	$ 1,316
Bolivia	172	182	139	203
France	7,485	5,265	13,652	13,124
Japan	20,790	18,672	48,585	89,655
Mexico	15,145	12,580	28,378	30,172
Norway	843	2,632	1,281	1,848
Saudi Arabia	5,768	12,648	4,035	9,974
South Africa	2,463	3,321	1,732	1,701
Venezuela	4,573	5,321	3,107	9,447

Source: *Statistical Abstract of the United States* 1991, pp. 806–9.

a. Compute the merchandise trade balance in both 1980 and 1990 for the sample of nine countries.

b. Compute the 50th percentile for imports in 1990.

57. A wave of consolidation in 1986–88 changed the major airlines substantially. Several large mergers and acquisitions concentrated the industry. Market shares for the largest airlines in 1985 and 1988 were:

	1985	1988
American	13.2%	15.2%
United	12.5	15.1
Delta	9.0	13.2
Continental	4.9	9.9
Northwest	NA	9.1
TWA	9.6	8.4
Eastern	10.0	7.0
Pan Am	8.1	6.7
USAir	NA	4.2
Piedmont	NA	3.3
NWA	6.7	NA
People Express	3.3	NA
Republic	3.2	NA

Source: *Industry Surveys*, May 4, 1991, p. A17.

a. Compute the mean and standard deviation for the 10 largest airlines in 1985 and 1988.

b. Write a paragraph discussing your findings.

58. This exercise refers to the company data base in Appendix C. Select a sample of 10 workers.

a. Compute the mean and standard deviation for each of the following variables.

x_1 = Number of years with the company

x_2 = Number of overtime hours worked during the past six months

x_4 = Number of continuing education courses completed

x_5 = Number of sick days taken during the past six months

x_6 = Score on company aptitude test

x_8 = Annual base salary

x_9 = Employee age

b. Indicate whether each variable is symmetrical, positively skewed, or negatively skewed.

EXTENDED EXERCISES

59. WORDAN WINE BOTTLING

Mike Wordan, a grape grower, is considering buying a wine-bottling plant and producing a line of quality table wines. Mike wants to know the bottling plant's capacity and works out an arrangement with Rick Roig, the current owner, to sample a number of production days. The number of bottles produced per day by the current process will be recorded. These data will help Mike decide if a purchase is feasible.

Test days are randomly selected during the busy bottling season. For each of the 25 days selected for the sample, the production line is observed, and the number of bottles produced is recorded. Since a backlog of wine awaits bottling, Mike believes that the output is a function of the capabilities of the process, not of raw material availability.

After sample values are recorded, the following statistics are calculated:

$$n = 25 \text{ days} \qquad \bar{x} = 584 \text{ bottles} \qquad s = 253 \text{ bottles}$$

Mike has not yet determined an appropriate price for the bottling facility and hasn't yet talked with bankers about financing. But Mike thinks the sample statistics will help him judge the purchase's feasibility.

a. What can Mike conclude after considering the statistics from the sampled days?

b. Was the sample size sufficiently large to make the statistics useful?

c. Are any problem areas revealed by the sample?

60. PIERONE'S CLOTHING COMPANY

Pierone's, a men's clothing company, sends salespeople to small retail establishments around the country. Every two years the company buys a large number of cars for salespeople to use in their travels. Bob Pierone, the owner, read an article in *Fortune* (September 25, 1989) indicating that automakers are trying to develop cars that run on methanol. Such a car would be much cleaner and would accelerate faster. Bob is interested in this concept, but meanwhile he must replace his current fleet.

The company has narrowed the choice of car to two models. Since the price and estimated upkeep costs for each are about the same, Bob must determine the miles per gallon of each car. If one car has substantially better mileage than the other, the choice will be made in its favor.

Pierone's arranges to test-drive a number of cars of each model for one week. Each car will be driven about 1,000 miles to produce a fair estimate of mileage. Sample statistics from this test are:

Model 1	Model 2
$\bar{x} = 19.4$ mpg	$\bar{x} = 20.1$ mpg
$s = 1.7$ mpg	$s = 5.3$ mpg
$n = 12$ cars	$n = 15$ cars

The company will use these data in deciding which model to buy. They'll be purchasing 500 to 600 cars.

a. What do you think about the sample sizes used for this test?

b. The standard deviation for model 2 is much larger than for model 1. In view of the number of cars to be purchased, is this a problem?

c. Overall, what direction do the sample results give Pierone's Clothing Company?

61. SECOND AVENUE CAR STEREOS

Second Avenue Radio produces car stereos. It is concerned about the number of units produced during the past several weeks. Owner Sally Dempsey decides to select a random sample of observation times. The number of units produced during each selected hour will be recorded.

Numbers recorded for the sample are:

5	6	8	4	5	9	7	5	8	4	9	8	7	6	8
4	6	5	7	5	7	6	8	9	3	4	8	2	9	5
5	1	5	6	8	6	6	9	5	9	0	5	7	8	6

a. What useful statistics can be calculated from the sample data?

b. Summarize the results of the sampling effort in a memo to Dempsey.

62. OUR LADY OF LOURDES HOSPITAL

One variable recorded for Our Lady of Lourdes Hospital employees is family size. Benefits director Curtis Huff asks you to quickly estimate the average family size per employee. Family sizes for the population of 200 employees are:

(1) 3	(35) 1	(69) 2	(102) 1	(135) 5	(168) 6
(2) 2	(36) 2	(70) 4	(103) 2	(136) 2	(169) 3
(3) 7	(37) 4	(71) 3	(104) 5	(137) 1	(170) 2
(4) 3	(38) 1	(72) 7	(105) 3	(138) 4	(171) 3
(5) 4	(39) 4	(73) 2	(106) 2	(139) 2	(172) 4
(6) 2	(40) 2	(74) 6	(107) 1	(140) 4	(173) 2
(7) 3	(41) 1	(75) 2	(108) 2	(141) 1	(174) 2
(8) 1	(42) 3	(76) 7	(109) 2	(142) 2	(175) 1
(9) 5	(43) 5	(77) 3	(110) 1	(143) 4	(176) 5
(10) 3	(44) 2	(78) 6	(111) 4	(144) 1	(177) 3
(11) 2	(45) 1	(79) 4	(112) 1	(145) 2	(178) 2
(12) 3	(46) 4	(80) 2	(113) 1	(146) 2	(179) 4
(13) 4	(47) 3	(81) 3	(114) 2	(147) 5	(180) 3
(14) 1	(48) 5	(82) 5	(115) 2	(148) 3	(181) 5
(15) 2	(49) 2	(83) 2	(116) 1	(149) 1	(182) 3
(16) 2	(50) 4	(84) 1	(117) 4	(150) 2	(183) 1
(17) 4	(51) 1	(85) 3	(118) 2	(151) 6	(184) 2
(18) 4	(52) 6	(86) 3	(119) 1	(152) 2	(185) 4
(19) 3	(53) 2	(87) 2	(120) 3	(153) 5	(186) 3
(20) 2	(54) 5	(88) 4	(121) 5	(154) 1	(187) 2
(21) 1	(55) 4	(89) 1	(122) 1	(155) 2	(188) 5
(22) 5	(56) 1	(90) 2	(123) 2	(156) 1	(189) 3
(23) 2	(57) 2	(91) 3	(124) 3	(157) 4	(190) 4
(24) 1	(58) 1	(92) 3	(125) 4	(158) 2	(191) 3
(25) 4	(59) 5	(93) 2	(126) 3	(159) 2	(192) 2
(26) 3	(60) 2	(94) 4	(127) 2	(160) 7	(193) 3
(27) 2	(61) 7	(95) 1	(128) 1	(161) 4	(194) 2
(28) 3	(62) 1	(96) 2	(129) 6	(162) 2	(195) 5
(29) 6	(63) 2	(97) 4	(130) 1	(163) 1	(196) 3
(30) 1	(64) 6	(98) 3	(131) 2	(164) 7	(197) 3
(31) 2	(65) 4	(99) 2	(132) 5	(165) 2	(198) 2
(32) 4	(66) 1	(100) 6	(133) 2	(166) 7	(199) 5
(33) 3	(67) 2	(101) 4	(134) 1	(167) 4	(200) 1
(34) 2	(68) 1				

a. Select a simple random sample of 30 family sizes and compute the mean. (See MINITAB section at the end of this chapter for instructions.)

b. You've decided to supply Curtis with additional information, so also compute the sample standard deviation. (Save these answers, since they'll be used in future exercises.)

MICROCOMPUTER PACKAGE
. . . .

You can use the micro package *Computerized Business Statistics* to compute measures of central tendency and variability.

In Exercise 54, you analyzed price movements of Electronic Research & Development Corporation stock for 35 days. Computation of both mean and standard deviation of this data collection was necessary.

Computer Solution:

On the main menu of *Computerized Business Statistics*, a **3** is selected, indicating Descriptive Statistics.

Since the data for this problem need to be entered on the keyboard, **1** is selected.

```
Descriptive Statistics–Define New Problem
Raw or Group Data: Enter R/G, press ↵ R
```

Since the data are in raw form and haven't been grouped, **R** is selected.

```
Population or Sample Data: Enter P/S, press ↵ S
```

Since the data constitute a sample, choose **S**.

```
Number of Data Points: Enter 1 – 25, press ↵ 35
```

Since the data collection consists of 35 closing stock prices, **35** is the correct entry.

```
Variable Name Enter 0–5 Char. Press ↵ Price
```

The variable name used in this problem is **Price**.

```
Problem Definition Correct? Enter Y/N/Q, press ↵ Y
```

If the problem has been set up correctly, the answer is **Y**.

Next, the program provides spaces for the raw data to be entered. Data values are numbered from 1 to 35. The cursor allows you to replace the 0.0s on the screen with the actual data values.

```
Table Commands     Enter Raw Data     File: None
                Price
1.                 43
2.                 29
3.                 42
4.                 35
5.                 32
  .                 .
  .                 .
  .                 .
35.                47

Press F when Finished
```

After the data are entered and **F** pressed, you are asked:

```
Save data? Enter Y/N & press ↵ N
```

If you want to save these data in a disk file, answer **Y**; otherwise enter **N**.

The program options menu then reappears, and you are instructed to:

```
Enter number (1 – 9) for your selection from the menu & press ⏎ 7
```

You are now ready to run the problem, so enter 7.

```
Convert raw data to group data? Y/N & press ⏎ N
```

If you want to convert these raw data to group data, answer **Y**; otherwise answer **N**. Next, you are given output selections. Since a hard copy of the results is needed, **P**, or printer, is selected.

MINITAB COMPUTER PACKAGE

The MINITAB commands to solve Extended Exercise 62 are:

```
MTB > RANDOM 30 C1;
SUBC> INTEGERS 1:200.
MTB > PRINT C1
C1
    173     138     180      76      69     141     130     140      84
     53     159      28     194     156      43     150      63     192
    173     171      83     109     158     106     189     160     104
     88      94      49
MTB > SET INTO C2
DATA> 2 4 3 7 2 1 1 4 1 2 3 2 1 5 2 2 2 2 3 2 2 2 3 7 5 4 4 2
MTB > END
MTB > DESCRIBE C2

                  N     MEAN    MEDIAN    TRMEAN     STDEV    SEMEAN
C2               30    2.800     2.000     2.615     1.584     0.289

                MIN      MAX        Q1        Q3
C2            1.000    7.000     2.000     4.000
MTB > BOXPLOT C2

                       -------------------
          --------(+)                    I-----------------------------
                       -------------------
          ----+---------+---------+---------+---------+---------+--C1
            1.2       2.4       3.6       4.8       6.0       7.2
MTB > WRITE 'CH4EX62.DAT' C2
MTB > STOP
```

The **RANDOM** command and **INTEGERS** subcommand are used to generate 30 random numbers between 1 and 200. The **PRINT** command is used to list the random numbers stored in C1. The family sizes for each random number are included in the sample and entered into C2 with the **SET** command. The **END** command is used when the data entry is complete.

Next, the **DESCRIBE** command is used to obtain descriptive statistics for C2. The output includes the sample size (**N**), the mean (**MEAN**), a mean for the remaining values after removing the smallest 5% and the largest 5% (**TRMEAN**), the median (**MEDIAN**), the standard deviation (**STDEV**), the standard error of the mean (**SEMEAN**) (which will be discussed in Chapter 7), the smallest number (**MIN**), the largest number (**MAX**), first quartile or 25th percentile (**Q1**), and third quartile or 75th percentile (**Q3**).

The **BOXPLOT** command generates a box plot (sometimes referred to as a box-and-whisker plot) that provides another way of looking at a data set in an effort to determine its central tendency, variability, and the existence of unusually large or small values. The box plot consists of five summary measures: median, lower quartile, upper quartile, smallest observation, and largest observation.

The rectangular box represents the middle half of the data, along with dashed lines extending to either side, indicating the data's variability. The median value, 2.0 in this case, is marked with a tick mark (+) inside the box. The box's left and right ends represent the data's first and third quartiles. In this example, the first quartile equals 2.0 and the third quartile equals 4.0.

Finally, the **WRITE** command is used to store the contents of column 2 in a file called CH4EX62.DAT for future use.

SAS Computer Package

A data file called COURSE.DAT was created (see Table 2.8) to analyze data compiled from the class questionnaire (Table 1.1) for one of the authors' classes. SAS commands to provide descriptive statistics for the quantitative variables are:

```
TITLE ''STUDENT QUESTIONNAIRE RESULTS'';
DATA QUEST;
 INFILE 'COURSE.DAT';
 INPUT GPA 5–7 AGE 9–10;
PROC MEANS;
 VAR GPA AGE;
```

The **TITLE** statement names the SAS program.

The **DATA** statement provides a filename for the data.

The **INFILE** statement identifies an external file, COURSE.DAT, to be read with an **INPUT** statement.

The **INPUT** statement names the variable GPA and indicates that it is located in columns 5–7. The variable **AGE** is located in columns 9–10.

The **PROC MEANS** statement produces simple descriptive statistics for the variables listed on the VAR statement. In this example descriptive statistics will be printed for the variables GPA and AGE. Table 4.7 shows the SAS output.

TABLE 4.7   Student Questionnaire Results

Variable	N	Mean	Std Dev	Minimum	Maximum
GPA	75	2.9733333	0.5176175	1.8000000	4.0000000
AGE	75	30.0533333	8.9335283	19.0000000	46.0000000

BASIC PROBABILITY AND DISCRETE PROBABILITY DISTRIBUTIONS

*And now sits
Expectation in
the air.*

Shakespeare,

Henry V

Objectives

When you have completed this chapter, you will be able to:

Explain the differences among the relative frequency, subjective, and classical approaches to probability.

Explain and use the basic rules of probability.

Construct discrete probability distributions—the binomial, hypergeometric, and Poisson distributions in particular.

Find the probabilities associated with particular outcomes for the binomial, hypergeometric, and Poisson distributions.

Compute the mean and standard deviation for discrete probability distributions.

On January 12, 1992, the *New York Times* had a front-page article, "How to Sell More U.S. Cars: Japanese Drivers Offer Hints." With 33% of cars bought in the United States coming from Japan, U.S. automakers were very concerned about their companies' futures.

Previous chapters covered methods of collecting data and summarizing or presenting these numerical values. We saw how charts, graphs, averages, and measures of variability effectively summarize large data collections. Such summary methods bring out the key points of data collections for use in the decision-making process.

WHY DISCRETE PROBABILITY DISTRIBUTIONS ARE IMPORTANT TO MANAGERS

This chapter begins by introducing probability concepts. Entire textbooks have been written on this subject. You'll be studying simple probability principles needed to illustrate important concepts introduced later in this and the following chapters. If you've studied probability recently, you can skip this section. If you need some review on this subject, the material here will help you. If you're new to probability, study this section in depth.

Following the discussion of probability, important statistical background material will be introduced followed by three theoretical but very useful statistical distributions: the binomial, the hypergeometric, and the Poisson. Because these theoretical formulations are closely related to many real situations in the business world, they have great practical value.

Regarding the *New York Times* article just mentioned, one of the distributions discussed in this chapter might be of use in analyzing and forecasting U.S. auto sales patterns. Although these distributions are theoretical, one or more of them might model certain aspects of auto sales quite closely, and could therefore provide valuable information to an auto company's management.

BASIC PROBABILITY DEFINITIONS AND RULES

Probability

This section reviews basic probability definitions and rules. A **probability** indicates the likelihood that a future event will occur. Probability values vary between 0 and 1, reflecting the range of likelihood from impossible to totally certain.

> A **probability** is a measure of likelihood that a future event will occur; it can assume any value between 0 and 1, inclusive.

An easily understood probability is the likelihood of heads appearing on the flip of a fair coin. This probability is one half, or .50. This value means that there's a 50% chance of heads appearing on any flip.

Most business decisions have several possible outcomes. A **sample space** is the collection of all possible outcomes that can result from a business decision. Any process that generates well-defined outcomes is an **experiment**. Examples of experiments are the selection of a part for inspection, an investment decision, the choice of a plant location, and the completion of a sales call. The individual outcomes from an experiment are called **events**. Thus, an experiment's sample space consists of all the events that the experiment can produce. For example, the sample space for the selection and testing of a factory part might consist of the events *part okay,* and *part defective.*

> A **sample space** is the collection of all possible outcomes for an experiment. An **experiment** is any process that generates well-defined outcomes. An **event** is a possible outcome of an experiment.

There are three different ways to assign probabilities to events using relative frequencies, subjective probabilities, and classical probabilities. When probabilities are assigned to experimental outcomes, two basic requirements must be satisfied: (1) the probability values assigned to each event must be between 0 and 1, and (2) the probabilities of all events must add to 1.

Relative Frequency

The **relative frequency** method of assigning probabilities is based on experimentation or historical data. This type of probability is defined as the number of times an event occurs divided by the total number of times the experiment is performed. For example, if a consulting firm submits 100 proposals and 20 are accepted, the probability of a future successful proposal can be estimated as 20/100 or .20.

Subjective Probability

A **subjective probability** reflects feelings or opinions regarding the likelihood that an outcome will occur. If a management team think there's a .35 probability of a new product's success in the marketplace, this constitutes a subjective probability. The value .35 is an opinion rather than a value based on objective evidence.

Classical Probability

In the **classical probability** method, the assumption is the events of an experiment are equally likely. This method is most frequently used with games of chance. Since classical probability is not directly applicable to most business decision-making situations, it won't be discussed further.

> **Relative frequency** probabilities are defined as the number of times an event occurs divided by the total number of times the experiment is performed. **Subjective probabilities** reflect feelings or opinions concerning the likelihood that a particular outcome will occur.

Several terms are used in discussing probabilities and their applications. Some of the most important ones are defined in the following box and illustrated in Figure 5.1.

FIGURE 5.1 Probability Concepts: Venn Diagrams

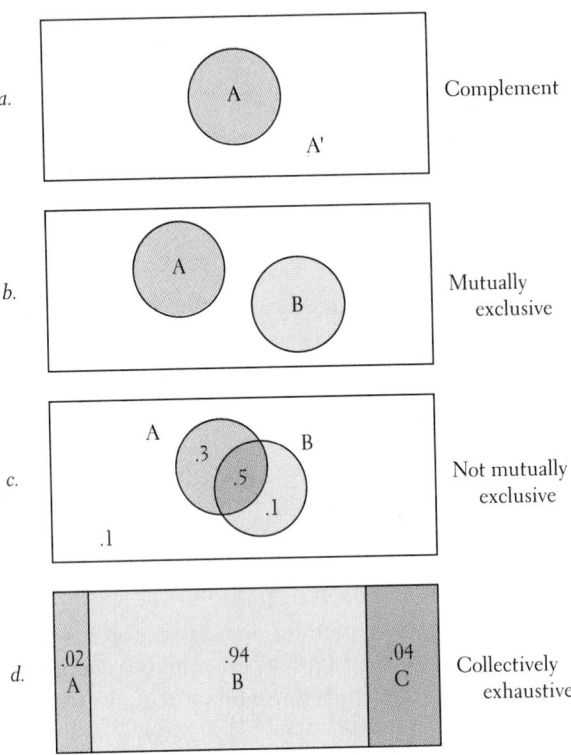

a. — Complement

b. — Mutually exclusive

c. — Not mutually exclusive

d. — Collectively exhaustive

The **complement** of any event is the collection of outcomes that are not contained in that event.

A list of events is **collectively exhaustive** if it includes every possible event that can occur.

Events are **mutually exclusive** if the occurrence of one precludes the occurrence of any other.

Figure 5.1*a* shows event A and its complement, event A′. The complement of event A is the collection of outcomes not contained in event A.

Figure 5.1*b* shows two events, A and B, that are mutually exclusive. If A occurs, for example, B has not occurred, by definition.

Parts *c* and *d* of Figure 5.1 are explained in Examples 5.1 and 5.2, respectively.

Various probability rules help us find the likelihood of future events. To use these rules, you must understand the two different types of event combinations that can occur in business applications. Suppose that two events, A and B, have been identified in a sample space. Some situations require determination of the probability $P(A \text{ or } B)$,

Addition Rule

which is the probability that *either* event A *or* event B occurs. Other problems require determination of the probability that *both* events will occur, P(A and B).

For computing the probability that *either* event A or event B occurs, the **addition rule** is used. To use this rule, you must determine whether the events of interest are mutually exclusive.

Addition rule

For events that are *not* mutually exclusive,

$$P(A \text{ or } B) = P(A) + P(B) - P(A \text{ and } B).$$

For mutually exclusive events,

$$P(A \text{ or } B) = P(A) + P(B) \qquad [\text{since } P(A \text{ and } B) = 0]$$

In many probability situations, the outcome of interest can occur in more than one way. The addition rule requires that all such ways be identified and their probabilities computed. If these ways are mutually exclusive, their probabilities are added to determine the overall probability of the desired outcome.

EXAMPLE 5.1   Fairchild Credit Union records indicate that of a total of 1,000 customers, 800 have checking accounts, 600 have savings accounts, and 500 have both. What is the probability that a customer selected at random will have either a checking or a savings account?

Figure 5.1c illustrates this situation. The events *have a checking account* (denoted A) and *have a savings account* (denoted B) are *not* mutually exclusive because customers can have both types of accounts. Therefore, the computation is

$$P(A \text{ or } B) = P(A) + P(B) - P(A \text{ and } B)$$
$$= .8 + .6 - .5$$
$$= .9$$

Note in Figure 5.1c that 30% of the customers have a checking account only, 10% have a savings account only, 50% have both, and 10% have neither.

EXAMPLE 5.2   Diet Right Cola Company has an automatic machine that fills bottles with 16 ounces of the firm's beverage. Most bottles are filled properly; however, some are overfilled or underfilled. A random sample of 1,000 bottles tested showed:

Event	Ounces	Number of bottles	Probability
A	<16	20	.02
B	16	940	.94
C	>16	40	.04
		1,000	1.00

What is the probability that a particular bottle will be *either* underfilled or overfilled?

Figure 5.1*d* shows that the events are mutually exclusive and collectively exhaustive. Therefore, $P(A \text{ or } B \text{ or } C) = 1.00$. Applying the addition rule for mutually exclusive events,

$$P(A \text{ or } C) = P(A) + P(C)$$
$$= .02 + .04$$
$$= .06$$

The probability that a particular bottle will be either underfilled or overfilled is .06.

Multiplication Rule

If you have to compute the probability that *both* event A and event B will occur, use the **multiplication rule.** To use this rule, you must determine whether the events are independent or dependent.

Independent

A formal mathematical definition of the terms that must be met for two events to be considered **independent** can be found in mathematical statistics textbooks. For practical purposes this formal definition states that two events are independent if one's occurrence in no way affects the likelihood that the second will occur. For example, when flipping a fair coin in a fair way, the event "heads appears on first flip" doesn't change the probability of observing heads on the second flip; this probability remains .50. In this case, the two events are independent.

> Events A and B are **independent** if the occurrence of one in no way affects the likelihood that the second will occur.

Dependent

Events A and B are **dependent** if one's occurrence alters the likelihood that the second will occur. For example, the event "person smokes" changes the probability of getting lung cancer since a medical connection between these two events has been established. In this case the two events (smoking and lung cancer) are considered dependent events with regard to probability assessment.

> Events A and B are **dependent** if the occurrence of one alters the likelihood that the second will occur.

For independent events, the probabilities of successive events are multiplied together to get the probability of that sequence. For dependent events, the idea is the same, but care must be taken to ascertain the events' exact probabilities since they may change depending on which events have previously occurred. The multiplication rules for independent and dependent events follow, along with several examples.

Multiplication rule

For events that are independent,

$$P(A \text{ and } B) = P(A) \times P(B)$$

For events that are dependent (the general multiplication rule),

$$P(A \text{ and } B) = P(A) \times P(B|A)$$

(Note: The vertical line means *given*.)

EXAMPLE 5.3   A company is considering introducing two new products to a local market. Management believes that the chance of success is about 50% for the first and 75% for the second. What is the probability that both products will be successful? Both probabilities are subjective because they're based on management opinion (expert though it might be) rather than on documented facts. If the assumption is that the two opinions are independent of each other, the multiplication rule for independent events calls for multiplying the two probabilities of success to find the desired probability:

$$
\begin{aligned}
P(A \text{ and } B) &= P(A) \times P(B) \\
&= .50 \times .75 \\
&= .375
\end{aligned}
$$

There's about a 37.5% chance that both products will be successful.

EXAMPLE 5.4   According to the Roper Organization, *American Demographics* (February 1993, p. 12), one in six customers who receive mail-ordered items indicate that delivery takes too long. The manager of a mail-order catalog distributor wants to determine the probability that all 10 of the orders sent out during a 12-hour period will be delivered in a timely fashion. The probability .167 is assigned to the event *delivery took too long*. Since this value is based on past experience, it's considered a relative frequency probability.

First the probability of the complement of *delivery took too long* needs to be calculated. Since the probability of delivery took too long is .167, the probability of a timely delivery is $(1 - .167) = .833$. If the status of each delivery is independent of every other delivery, the probability of all 10 deliveries being completed in a timely manner is computed using the multiplication rule for independent events:

$$.833^{10} = .161$$

There's about a 16% chance that all ten of the deliveries during the 12-hour period were delivered in a timely fashion.

EXAMPLE 5.5   A supervisor takes three feed bags from a filling machine and carefully weighs their contents. From past records she knows that the machine overfills the bags 10% of the time, so the probability .10 is assigned to the event *bag overfilled.* It is also known that such defective bags occur randomly, so one bag's status is independent of all others. What is the probability that no more than one bag in the sample of three is overfilled?

Both the addition rule and multiplication rule for independent events are used to answer this question. There's more than one way to properly fill two or three bags. Using C to represent a correctly filled bag and O to indicate an overfilled bag, the multiplication and addition rules can be employed to calculate the desired probability:

Qualifying events:
CCC, CCO, COC, OCC
Probability:
$(.9)(.9)(.9) + (.9)(.9)(.1) + (.9)(.1)(.9) + (.1)(.9)(.9) = .972$

It's quite likely (about a 97% chance) that no more than one overfilled bag will be found in the three bags sampled.

EXAMPLE 5.6   It is known that 25% of the persons taking the CPA exam in a certain city took a CPA review course from a local university. Of those who took the course, 60% passed the exam. What is the probability that a randomly selected person took the course and passed the exam?

The general multiplication rule for dependent events is used to calculate the answer. The probability of taking the course is $P(B) = .25\%$, followed by the probability of passing *given* the course was taken: $P(A|B) = 60\%$. So the correct probability is

$$P(A \text{ and } B) = P(B) \times P(A|B) = (.25)(.60) = .15$$

EXAMPLE 5.7   Past history shows that 15% of a laundromat's washers need a new motor during the first two years of operation. Of those needing new motors, 80% also need new drive belts during the same period. What is the probability that a machine will need both a new motor and new drive belts during its first two years?

The probability of needing a new motor, $P(B)$, is 15% and the probability of needing new belts is $P(A|B) = 80\%$ *given* a new motor is needed, so the probability is

$$P(A \text{ and } B) = P(B) \times P(A|B) = (.15)(.80) = .12$$

Chapter 18 provides additional material involving dependent events and their probabilities.

EXERCISES

1. Explain the concept of probability.

2. Why must a probability be a number between 0 and 1?

3. When is the multiplication rule of probability useful?

4. When is the addition rule of probability useful?

5. A local department store has collected data on TV sales for the past 50 days:

Number of TVs sold	Number of days
0	10
1	15
2	12
3	8
4 or more	5

  a. Based on this history, how many outcomes are possible?

  b. Assign probabilities to the various outcomes.

  c. What is the probability that no TVs will be sold tomorrow?

  d. What is the probability that more than two TVs will be sold tomorrow?

  e. What is the probability that four or more TVs will be sold on each of the next two days?

6. Almost one in three Americans is a sports fan, according to a 1990 survey by Lieberman Research for *Sports Illustrated*. About 30% of American adults say they are very interested in sports. Around 43% are fairly interested, while 27% aren't interested in sports. Based on the study's results, what is the probability that:

  a. An adult interviewed at random will be very or fairly interested in sports?

  b. The next three adults interviewed will be sports fans?

  c. Two of the next three adults interviewed will be nonfans?

7. Jill Sharp likes to play pool after school. She especially enjoys playing the Pigon brothers, Bob and Bill. Jill feels that she has a 90% chance of beating either brother on any given afternoon and that her second game isn't affected by an earlier win or loss. Find the probability that:

  a. Jill will beat both Pigon brothers this afternoon.

  b. Jill will beat one brother and lose to the other this afternoon.

  c. Jill will beat Bob and lose to Bill this afternoon.

  d. Jill will lose to Bob Pigon two afternoons in a row.

8. You own a small business and have contracted to supply your product at a fixed price of $20 per unit. You like the security provided by a guaranteed contract, but you're worried about either of two possible catastrophes: (*a*) the Federal Reserve will engineer a tight-money "credit crunch" that dries up the financing you need to buy raw materials and manufacture your product, or (*b*) the Fed will permit an easy-money inflation that increases your material and labor costs and prevents you from making a profit at a price of $20 per unit. You believe that the probability of tight money is .2 and the probability of easy money is .1. If tight money and easy money are mutually exclusive, what is the probability of one or the other?

9. S. Ward reported in "Children's Reactions to Commercials" (*Journal of Advertising Research*, April 1972) that children often have a very low understanding of commercials, even those designed to appeal to them. Ward's studies showed that only 45% of 5-to-7-

year-olds understand commercials. An advertising agent shows a TV commercial to three children randomly selected from this age group. Find the probability that:

  a. The commercial's message is understood by all three children.

  b. The commercial's message isn't understood by any of the three children.

  c. The commercial's message is understood by one of the three children.

10. Mike May, owner of Mike's Conoco, estimates that 90% of the motorists stopping at the station purchase gas. He also estimates that of those who buy gas, 20% also purchase oil. Find the probability that a customer entering the station will purchase both gas and oil.

11. On Wall Street, tradition has it that if an NFC team or one of the old NFL teams now in the AFC (Indianapolis Colts, Cleveland Browns, and Pittsburgh Steelers) wins the Super Bowl, stock prices will be higher a year later. If an AFC team wins, the market will stumble ("An Examination of the Super Bowl Stock Market Predictor," *Decision Science Institute Proceedings*, November 21–23, 1988, p. 317). A *USA Today* article (January 23, 1992) indicates that it has worked 22 of 25 times. Suppose the probability in 1993 that the Dallas Cowboys of the NFC would win the game was .75. Find the probability that stock prices will increase in 1993.

RANDOM VARIABLES

Random Variable

An important concept in many statistical applications is the random variable. Experiments and their individual outcomes called *events* were discussed earlier in the chapter. Experiments result in simple events that correspond to values of some numerical variable. A **random variable** is defined by assigning one numerical value to each simple event of an experiment that yields random outcomes.

A **random variable** is defined by assigning one numerical value to each simple event of an experiment that yields random outcomes.

An example of a random variable is the number of courses taken during a specific term by any of 100 college students. The number of courses varies from one to five from student to student. Other examples of random variables are the number of children per family, number of telephone calls to a mail order company per minute, and number of successful bids per month by a contractor.

Discrete Random Variable

In each of these situations, the random variable is measured by counting the number of *successes* that occur. Such variables are called **discrete random variables** because only certain values for the variable are possible. In each of the preceding examples, only integer values—0, 1, 2, 3, and so on—are possible.

> A **discrete random variable** is a variable that can assume only values from a predetermined set.

There are other random variables for which any value within some range is possible, such as a person's weight or a car's mileage. Known as *continuous random variables*, they will be discussed in the next chapter.

EXERCISES

12. What is a random variable?

13. Four students have employment interviews scheduled at Keytronic, Inc. Each applicant will either get the job or be turned down.

    a. List the possible outcomes in terms of the results of the four interviews.

    b. Define a random variable that represents the number of offers made.

    c. Show what value the random variable will assume for each possible outcome.

14. Identify which of the following random variables can be classified as discrete.

    a. How long it took you to travel to school today.

    b. The number of students in this class.

    c. The number of questions you answered correctly on your first statistics test.

    d. The number of people in a sample of 50 who prefer a certain light beer over a competitor's brand.

    e. The length of time between tenants for a particular apartment.

    f. The number of finance majors in this class.

    g. The time of arrival of a bus.

    h. The amount of natural gas used per month to heat a hospital.

    i. The exact amount of diet pop in a can.

15. Which of the variables listed in the company data base from Appendix C are discrete variables?

■ SITUATION 5.1 Central Motors sells new and used cars in a large city. Its owners are worried because their sales have been trending downward for the past three years. After one owner reads a March 12, 1992, *Wall Street Journal* front-page story about difficulties connected with sales and car salespeople, they do a serious study of their sales picture.

After some discussion, they focus on several key matters. One problem involves examining the number of cars sold per day in an effort to anticipate future stocking requirements. Management believes important decision-making information resides in data it collected on the number of cars sold over the past few months. The investigating team notices that sales per day seem to be random. That is, the number of sales one day doesn't seem to affect the number of sales the next day. In a recent team meeting, it was agreed that as much as possible needs to be learned from the collected data. (This situation will be solved at the end of this section.) ■

PROBABILITY DISTRIBUTIONS

Probability Distribution

Rather than consider the probability that a single, identified event will occur, it's often of interest to consider all the different values that a random variable can assume along with the probability of each. A listing of the possible values that a discrete random variable can assume along with their associated probabilities is called a **probability distribution.**

> A **probability distribution** is a listing of the possible values that a random variable can assume along with their probabilities.

Table 5.1 is an example of a probability distribution. Used in Example 5.8, it lists the values, *x*'s, that the variable can assume along with the observed frequency of each. Figure 5.2 graphs this probability distribution.

TABLE 5.1 Probability Distribution of Absent Employees (Example 5.8)

Employees absent per day, x	Number of days, f	Probability, P(x)
1	18	.085
2	25	.118
3	39	.184
4	46	.217
5	27	.127
6	25	.118
7	22	.104
8	10	.047
	212	1.000

EXAMPLE 5.8 In Table 5.1, *x* represents the number of absent employees per day observed over the past 212 days, and *f* represents the number of times each *x* value was observed. For example, there were 18 days when only one employee was absent, and 25 days when two employees were absent. The first two columns constitute a frequency distribution of past employee absences.

Each frequency in Table 5.1 is divided by the total frequency, 212, to produce the relative frequencies in the third column (for example 18/212 = .085). The first and third columns constitute the probability distribution for future employees' absences. Inherent in these relative frequencies is the assumption that the future will reflect the conditions that prevailed in the past. In other words, a frequency distribution is a

FIGURE 5.2   Graph of Probability Distribution

Number of days, x

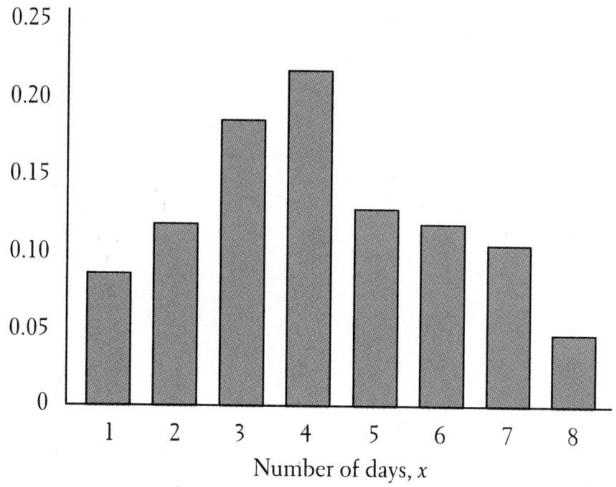

summary of what happened in the past, and a probability distribution is a summary of what might happen in the future.

Note in Table 5.1 that the sum of the relative frequencies is 1.00, or 100%. This is always the case for a probability distribution (disregarding rounding errors). The probability distribution must contain all possible values that the random variable can assume. Therefore, the sum of the probabilities must be 1.00.

■ SITUATION 5.1—RESOLVED   The data in Table 5.2 were collected from company records and represent the cars Central Motors sold per day for the past 100 days. The company now has better information about unit sales per day, which will help in managing its business. The probability distribution in Table 5.2 is a good summary of the anticipated sales levels for the future. This table shows that the probability of selling 13 cars on any day is .23, for example.

TABLE 5.2   Probability Distribution of Cars Sold (Situation 5.1)

Cars sold per day, x	Number of days, f	Probability, $P(x)$
10	8	.08
11	12	.12
12	19	.19
13	23	.23
14	18	.18
15	20	.20
	100	1.00

Chapter 3 described how to construct a cumulative relative frequency distribution. Table 5.3 applies this technique to the Table 5.2 car sales data. Now management can see at a glance that the probability of selling 13 or fewer cars on a given day is .62.

TABLE 5.3   Cumulative Probability Distribution of Cars Sold (Situation 5.1)

Cars sold per day, x	Number of days, f	Probability, P(x)	Less than or equal cumulative probability	More than or equal cumulative probability
10	8	.08	.08	1.00
11	12	.12	.20	.92
12	19	.19	.39	.80
13	23	.23	.62	.61
14	18	.18	.80	.38
15	20	.20	1.00	.20
	100	1.00		

EXERCISES

16. What is a probability distribution?

17. What is the difference between a frequency distribution and a probability distribution?

18. Mr. Sands is considering making an offer to purchase a new home. He was inspired to find a home in the country after reading the article "Peaceable Kingdom for a Weekend Farmer" in the February 1989 issue of *Home Beautiful.*

    After looking at several homes for sale, he subjectively assessed this distribution for the purchase price:

Purchase price	P(x)
$80,000	.20
85,000	.50
90,000	.30

    a. Is this a frequency distribution or a probability distribution?

    b. What is the probability that the home will cost Mr. Sands no more than $85,000?

    c. Why do the probabilities sum to 1?

19. Let x represent the number of days in which accidents occurred in the Kaypra plant during the past year.

Number of accidents	Number of days
0	185
1	102
2	55
3	12
4	11

    a. Is this a frequency distribution or a probability distribution?

    b. Construct a probability distribution.

    c. Graph the probability distribution.

    d. What is the probability of two accidents tomorrow?

    e. What is the probability of less than two accidents tomorrow?

20. Let x represent the number of defective units produced by an assembly line during a typical day.

Number of defectives	P(x)
0	.40
1	.30
2	.15
3	.10
4	.05

a. Is this a frequency distribution or a probability distribution?

b. Graph the probability distribution.

c. What is the probability of no defectives tomorrow?

d. What is the probability of more than two defectives tomorrow?

e. What is the probability of no defectives in the next two days?

21. Construct a probability distribution for the variable for number of company courses completed in the company data base in Appendix C.

■ SITUATION 5.2   Central Motors management is trying to decide whether to take out an insurance policy on its repair shop, which is separated from the main building complex. Central has evaluated the possible risks of fire loss on its building (Table 5.4). Although many dollar loss amounts are possible, Central has summarized possible losses in terms of the key values in Table 5.4. The possible losses and the corresponding probabilities estimated by management constitute a discrete probability distribution.

TABLE 5.4   Insurance Loss Probability Distribution (Situation 5.2)

x (loss)	P(x)	x · P(x)
$ 0	.925	0
5,000	.010	50
15,000	.010	150
30,000	.020	600
75,000	.020	1,500
100,000	.010	1,000
250,000	.005	1,250
	1.000	$4,550 ■

EXPECTED VALUE

It is often helpful to summarize a probability distribution by specifying the average, or mean, value of the distribution. In statistics, this average or mean is known as the **expected value.**

Expected Value

The **expected value** of a discrete random variable is the average value that the random variable assumes over a large number of observations.

EXAMPLE 5.9   The expected value of a discrete probability distribution, such as the one in Table 5.1, is found by multiplying each value of x by its probability of occurrence and adding these products.

Table 5.5 repeats Table 5.1's probability distribution with the expected value calculated in the third column. The final column is the product of each x value in the distribution and its probability. The sum of these products is approximately 4.2. This is the average number of absent employees per day over the time of the collected data; it's the expected value of the probability distribution. (Of course, we wouldn't expect to find 4.2 employees absent during any particular day, because only integer values (0, 1, 2, 3, 4, etc.) can be assumed by the discrete variable *number of people.*)

TABLE 5.5   Expected Value for Absent Employees Distribution (Example 5.9)

x	$P(x)$	$x \cdot P(x)$
1	.085	.085
2	.118	.236
3	.184	.552
4	.217	.868
5	.127	.635
6	.118	.708
7	.104	.728
8	.047	.376
	1.000	$E(x) = 4.188$

The formula for computing the expected value from a discrete probability distribution is

$$E(x) = \Sigma[x \cdot P(x)] \tag{5.1}$$

where $E(x)$ = Expected value
                x = Each value of the distribution
            $P(x)$ = Probability of each x occurring

The computation of an expected value is actually an application of the weighted mean concept discussed in Chapter 4. The difference is that when the expected value is computed, the x's are weighted by probabilities that add to 1. Since the weights add to 1, the summation doesn't need to be divided by the total of the weights. Thus, the summation itself is the expected value.

Chapter 4 noted that an analyst should specify both the mean and standard deviation to adequately describe a population or sample. This is also true for probability distributions. The expected value is used to measure the central tendency of a probability distribution and the standard deviation is used to measure the variability.

The procedure for computing a probability distribution's standard deviation is similar to the one shown in Chapter 4. First, we compute the population variance:

$$\sigma^2 = \Sigma(x - \mu)^2 P(x) \tag{5.2}$$

The standard deviation of x is then computed by taking the square root of the variance. Example 5.10 demonstrates the computations.

EXAMPLE 5.10   The expected value for the absent employees probability distribution (see Table 5.1) computed in Example 5.9 was 4.2. We use Equation 5.2 to compute the variance for this distribution:

$$
\begin{aligned}
\sigma^2 &= \Sigma(x - \mu)^2 P(x) \\
&= (1 - 4.2)^2(.085) + (2 - 4.2)^2(.118) + \\
&\quad (3 - 4.2)^2(.184) + (4 - 4.2)^2(.217) + \\
&\quad (5 - 4.2)^2(.127) + (6 - 4.2)^2(.118) + \\
&\quad (7 - 4.2)^2(.104) + (8 - 4.2)^2(.047) \\
&= .870 + .571 + .265 + .009 + .081 + .382 + .815 + .679 \\
&= 3.67
\end{aligned}
$$

The standard deviation is

$$
\sigma = \sqrt{\sigma^2} = \sqrt{3.67} = 1.92
$$

The mean (4.2) and the standard deviation (1.92) can be used to describe the probability distribution in the same way that $\bar{x}$ and s were used to describe a relative frequency distribution in Chapter 4. The average number of absent employees per day over time is expected to be near 4.2. Similarly, $\sigma = 1.92$ measures the spread or variability of the probability distribution.

■ SITUATION 5.2—RESOLVED   In forming the probability distribution of Table 5.4, Central Motors estimated key loss values along with their probabilities.

Central's analyst noticed that the sum of the probabilities of some type of loss equaled .075. This means that the probability of no loss must be .925 $(1 - .075)$.

The third column of Table 5.4 shows the multiplication of each x times its probability. These products sum to $4,550, the expected value of the distribution. Central's management can now evaluate bids from insurance companies with the reasoning that this expected loss value should be covered by the face value of the insurance. Central's analyst realizes that in figuring its bid, an insurance company must add overhead and profit to this expected loss value. But $4,550, the expected annual loss due to fire, is a benchmark value that will help Central Motors decide which bid to accept. ■

EXERCISES

22. What is an expected value?

23. Mr. Sands is considering purchasing a new home. He subjectively determined a distribution for the purchase price:

Purchase price	$P(x)$
$80,000	.20
85,000	.50
90,000	.30

Compute the expected value and standard deviation for this probability distribution.

24. According to the March 1989 issue of *Electronics* magazine, the United States is attempting to develop a high-density television technology and reenter the consumer electronics market. A primary concern to Electo, a company hoping to enter this market, is the defective rate of its computer chip line.

Let x represent the number of defective units produced by this line during a typical day.

Number of defectives	$P(x)$
0	.40
1	.30
2	.15
3	.10
4 or more	.05

Compute the expected value and standard deviation for this probability distribution.

25. Demand for computer keyboards for the ISC Corporation varies greatly from month to month. The following probability distribution shows monthly demand for keyboards during the past two years. Find the expected value of demand for next month.

Monthly demand	$P(x)$
40	.15
45	.25
50	.45
55	.15

26. Compute the expected value and standard deviation for the variable *number of continuing education courses completed* (variable x_4) found in the company data base in Appendix C.

■ SITUATION 5.3 Central Motors is continuing to evaluate its daily sales volume. In particular, management wants to define a profitable day for the business. After talking with the dealership accountant, they decide that any day on which 13 or more cars are sold is profitable. Management now wishes to evaluate sales days based on this definition. ■

THE BINOMIAL DISTRIBUTION

Mathematicians have defined numerous theoretical distributions of numerical values. Some are of particular interest to businesspeople because they correspond closely to real-world events. One widely used probability distribution for a discrete random variable is the **binomial distribution.**

The **binomial distribution** is a discrete probability distribution involving the likelihood of x successes in n trials of a binomial experiment.

The binomial distribution describes a situation that produces one of two possible outcomes on each trial. In addition, the probabilities of these outcomes must remain constant from trial to trial, and the trials must be independent. The binomial distribution is useful when the real situation being modeled meets the following criteria:

Essential characteristics of the binomial distribution

1. There are *n* identical trials that lead to one of two outcomes: success or failure.
2. The probability of each outcome remains constant from trial to trial. The probability of one of these outcomes, called *success*, is designated *p*.
3. The trials are independent.

A good example of a binomial experiment is flipping a fair coin several times. There are only two possible outcomes for each trial, or flip (heads and tails); the probability of heads or tails remains constant from flip to flip (.50 each); and the flips are independent of each other.

EXAMPLE 5.11   A fair coin is to be flipped three times. What is the probability of obtaining exactly two heads?

One method of calculating probability in such a situation is to use a *tree diagram*, so called because it shows the various possible outcomes of an experiment in a drawing that looks like the branches of a tree. The tree diagram for the coin-flipping situation appears in Figure 5.3.

FIGURE 5.3   Coin-Flip Tree Diagram

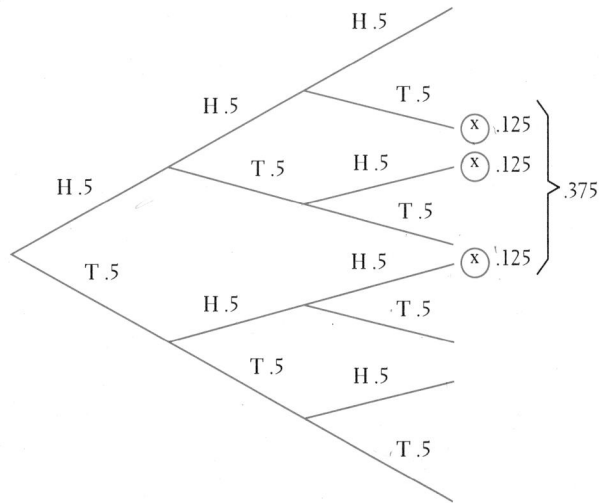

Each branch in Figure 5.3 represents a coin flip. The multiplication rule is used to compute the probability of every independent way in which two heads can result. Note that each way of getting two heads has the same probability, .125. The addition rule is then used to compute the final probability of getting two heads; this probability is .375.

To find the overall probability of two heads, first calculate the probability of achieving two heads in each of the several possible ways. Next, multiply this value by the number of possible ways of attaining this result. Thus, the final probability is

$$3 \times (.5 \times .5 \times .5) = .375$$

The first part of this calculation indicates the number of ways (3) in which the desired outcome (two heads) can occur. The second calculation (.5 × .5 × .5 = .125) indicates the probability of achieving this result using one of the possible paths in the diagram. The final result (.375) is the probability of flipping a fair coin three times and obtaining exactly two heads.

Now Example 5.11 is modeled using the binomial distribution, already established as a good model of this situation. This calculation requires the binomial formula:

$$P(x) = \binom{n}{x} p^x (1 - p)^{n-x} \tag{5.3}$$

where $P(x)$ = Probability of x successes in n trials

n = Number of trials

$\binom{n}{x}$ = Number of ways of getting exactly x successes in n trials

p = Probability of success on any one trial

$(1 - p)$ = Probability of failure on any one trial.

Combination

The first term in Equation 5.3 is called "the combination of n things taken x at a time." A **combination** represents the number of ways we could reach into a collection of n items and choose x of them. For the coin-flipping example, it represents the number of different ways two heads can result from three coin flips.

> A **combination** represents the number of possible ways of choosing x things out of n things when the order of choosing isn't important.

Equation 5.4 is used to evaluate combinations:

$$\binom{n}{x} = \frac{n!}{x!(n-x)!} \tag{5.4}$$

The exclamation point (!) in Equation 5.4 means *factorial*. To calculate a factorial, multiply the value preceding the factorial sign by 1 less, by 1 less than that, and so on down to 1. For example, 4! means 4 × 3 × 2 × 1 = 24. To calculate 6!, find the product 6 × 5 × 4 × 3 × 2 × 1, which is 720. Mathematicians define 0! to be equal to 1 because there is only one way to choose 0 things. Some additional factorial expressions are solved in Example 5.12.

Example 5.12
$$5! = (5)(4)(3)(2)(1) = 120$$
$$3! = (3)(2)(1) = 6$$
$$8! = (8)(7)(6)(5)(4)(3)(2)(1) = 40{,}320$$

Factorial expressions such as these are employed in computing combinations using Equation 5.4.

Example 5.13 How many ways can we select a committee of three from a group of five people? This represents the combination $\binom{5}{3}$ and is evaluated

$$\binom{n}{x} = \frac{n!}{x!(n-x)!} = \frac{5!}{3!(5-3)!} = \frac{(5)(4)(3)(2)(1)}{(3)(2)(1)(2)(1)} = 10$$

There are 10 different ways to select a committee of three from a group of five.

In evaluating combinations, make sure that the order in which the items are selected doesn't matter. A committee consisting of Sue, Bill, and Joe is the same as a committee of Bill, Joe, and Sue; the order in which the names are listed isn't important.

Example 5.14 Returning to the coin flip situation in Example 5.11, the problem can be solved using the binomial formula (Equation 5.3). There are three ways in which two heads can occur out of three flips of the fair coin:

$$\binom{n}{x} = \frac{n!}{x!(n-x)!} = \frac{3!}{2!(3-2)!} = \frac{(3)(2)(1)}{(2)(1)(1)} = 3$$

The probability of one of these three ways of obtaining two heads is

$$p^x(1-p)^{n-x} = (.5)^2(1-.5)^{3-2} = (.5)^2(.5)^1 = .125$$

Therefore, the probability of obtaining two heads on three flips of a fair coin is

$$P(x = 2) = \binom{n}{x} p^x(1-p)^{n-x} = (3)(.5)^2(1-.5)^{3-2} = .375$$

This is the same probability calculated using the tree diagram of Figure 5.3.

Figure 5.4 charts the binomial distribution for the coin-flipping example just discussed. The horizontal axis indicates all possible numbers of heads that can occur, and the vertical axis lists the probability of each x occurring. The probability of two heads is highlighted in Figure 5.4 by the shaded bar for that event. As shown, this probability is .375. Note that the probabilities of the outcomes add to 1.0.

FIGURE 5.4 Binomial Distribution for Coin Flip ($n = 3$, $p = .5$)

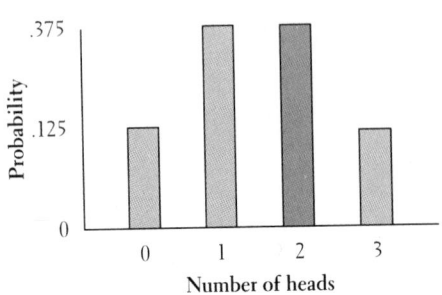

■ SITUATION 5.3—RESOLVED Central Motors' management team wants to use the binomial distribution to model the probabilities of profitable sales days and defines a profitable day as one in which 13 or more cars are sold. In conjunction with the established probability distribution for number of cars sold per day (Table 5.2), the probability of a profitable day can be computed using the addition rule. This is done by adding the probabilities of a 13-sale day (.23), 14-sale day (.18), and 15-sale day (.20). The total is .61. Central Motors concludes that there's about a 61% chance of profitable sales on any given day.

Deciding to use the binomial distribution in this situation was premature. All three criteria for this distribution need to be addressed for accurate results to be expected. Central's management considers these criteria with the following results:

1. The situation results in one of two possible outcomes each day: a profitable day or an unprofitable day.
2. Does the probability of a profitable day (.61) remain constant from day to day? This is management's critical question. If the probability changes due to the day of the week or as a result of changing economic conditions, the binomial distribution won't accurately model the situation. However, as suggested earlier, management believes that the number of cars sold is a random event, so the probability of a good day remains constant; one day's sales level doesn't seem to affect the next day's. Management decides that the criterion of constant probability is met.
3. Based on the preceding conclusion, management decides that the third criterion of the binomial distribution is also met: daily sales levels are indeed independent of each other. ■

EXERCISES

27. Describe a situation that would suggest use of the binomial distribution.
28. What are the essential properties of the binomial distribution?
29. Explain how combinations are useful.
30. Which of the following situations might be modeled by the binomial distribution assuming a large population?
    a. The number of trucks in a fleet that will need a major overhaul next year.
    b. The number of calls to a police dispatcher within an hour.

    c. The length of time necessary to handle customer telephone inquiries.

    d. The number of defective units per shipment.

    e. The number of defective forks in a production run of 1,000.

31. A TV picture tube may be purchased from one of seven suppliers. In how many ways can two suppliers be chosen from the seven?

Assume statistical independence for Exercises 32–34.

32. It is known that 30% of MasterCharge accounts in a local bank have balances over $2,000. Suppose four accounts are selected at random.

    a. What is the probability that the first account selected is over $2,000 and the next three aren't?

    b. What is the probability that the first three accounts selected are under $2,000 and the last account is over $2,000?

    c. In how many different ways can a person select one account over $2,000 and three accounts under $2,000?

    d. What is the probability of selecting one account over $2,000 and three accounts under $2,000?

33. Suppose it's determined that 30% of the people in Houston, Texas, read the evening paper. If three people are selected at random, what is the probability:

    a. Of selecting exactly two people who read the evening paper?

    b. That none reads the evening paper?

    c. That at least one person reads the evening paper?

34. According to a declassified IRS audit manual, it's not just the items that appear on your tax return that can produce an audit. The absence of certain items can raise the DIF (Discriminate Function) number and cause your return to be targeted for examination. This DIF number indicates the likelihood that an audit of the return will result in an additional tax assessment. The DIF program is also highly effective in singling out incorrectly completed tax returns. Only about 17% of audits of taxpayers in the $25,000–$50,000 income category result in no change in the amount of tax due (*Tax Guide for College Teachers*, Academic Information Service, Inc., 1992).

    a. What is the probability that if the IRS audits a taxpayer with income of $45,000 it will produce no change in the tax due?

    b. What is the probability that if the IRS audits a taxpayer with income of $30,000 it will produce some change in the tax due?

    c. If the IRS randomly audits four taxpayers with income between $25,000 and $50,000, what is the probability that two or more audits will produce no change in the tax due?

■ SITUATION 5.4 Central Motors is examining the probabilities of different numbers of profitable days now that the binomial process has been deemed an appropriate model.

1. What is the probability that all six days in a work week will be profitable?

2. What is the probability of at least four profitable days in a work week?

3. What is the probability of no profitable days in a work week?

4. What is the probability of at least 10 profitable days in a 15-day period?

Answering these questions requires solving the binomial formula, Equation 5.3, several times. If Central's management wants answers to even more *what if* questions, the number of calculations will increase. Fortunately, statisticians have anticipated this situation and solved the binomial formula for hundreds of different problems. These computations appear in the binomial table in Appendix E.2, which is discussed in the next section. ∎

THE BINOMIAL TABLE

Binomial Table

Before the binomial table can be used, the values of n, p, and x must be known. The number of trials in a binomial experiment is represented by n, the probability of success for each trial by p, and the number of successes for which the probability is desired by x. The following four examples illustrate the binomial table's use:

1. $n = 6$, $p = .40$, $x = 6$
2. $n = 8$, $p = .50$, $x \geq 4$
3. $n = 9$, $p = .30$, $x = 0$
4. $n = 15$, $p = .20$, $x \leq 3$

The binomial table is divided into blocks by n, the number of trials. The answer to the first problem is found in the block for $n = 6$. Find this section in the binomial table in Appendix E.2. The column headings represent values of p, so the desired column is the one headed .40. Now look at the left edge of the table. The row labels represent values of x. Reading probabilities using the appropriate x row and p column avoids the necessity of solving the binomial formula.

EXAMPLE 5.15   Find the probability that $x = 6$ if $n = 6$ and $p = .40$. The probability is .004, which is read directly from the intersection of the row $x = 6$ and the column $p = .40$ in the block for $n = 6$.

EXAMPLE 5.16   Find the probability that $x \geq 4$ if $n = 8$ and $p = .50$. This value is found by adding the individual probabilities for $x = 4$ through $x = 8$ in the $p = .50$ column of the $n = 8$ block; the sum is $.273 + .219 + .109 + .031 + .004 = .636$.

EXAMPLE 5.17   Find the probability that $x = 0$ if $n = 9$ and $p = .30$. The probability is .040, which is read directly from the intersection of the row $x = 0$ and the column $p = .30$ in the $n = 9$ block.

EXAMPLE 5.18   Find the probability that $x \leq 3$ if $n = 15$ and $p = .20$. The individual probabilities for $x = 0$ through $x = 3$ in the $n = 15$ block, $p = .20$ column, are added: $.035 + .132 + .231 + .250 = .648$.

Figure 5.5 plots the binomial distribution for Example 5.18. The number of possible successes is between 0 and 15 inclusive, and these values are shown on the horizontal

FIGURE 5.5   Binomial Distribution for Example 5.18 ($n = 15, p = .20$)

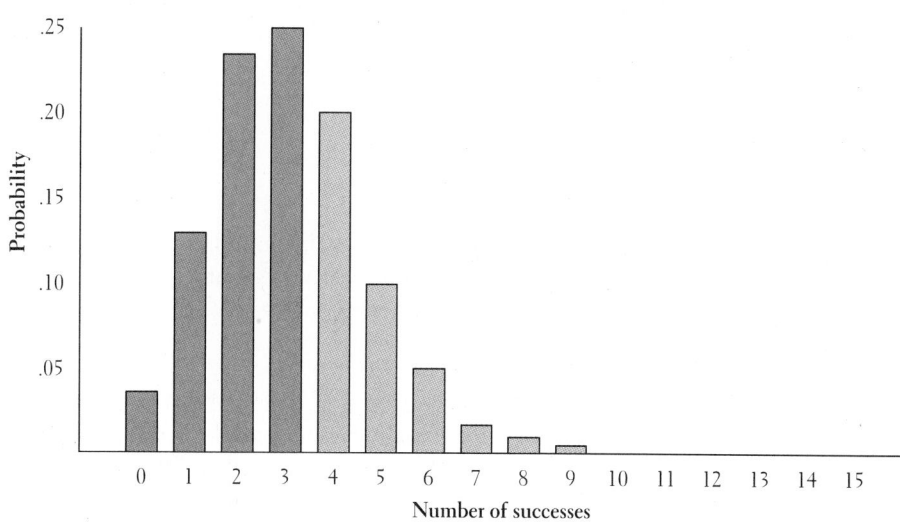

axis. Probabilities are scaled on the vertical axis. Figure 5.5 shades the appropriate probabilities, which add to .648.

In summary, the binomial table reflects the results of solving the binomial formula hundreds of times. It can be used to answer binomial problems if three values are known: the number of trials in the experiment (n), the probability of success on each trial (p), and the number of successes (x) for which the probability is to be computed. Remember that this process is only valid once it has been established that the binomial distribution is a good model of reality. That is, all three conditions that define the binomial distribution must be met.

The widespread use of microcomputers and software packages such as MINITAB may make tables like Appendix E.2's binomial table obsolete. Computer programs calculate binomial probabilities precisely. The MINITAB commands for computing the binomial probability for Example 5.17 are:

```
MTB> SET C1
DATA> 0
DATA> END
MTB> PDF C1;
SUBC> BINOMIAL 9 .3.
      K              P(X = K)
     0.00            0.0404
MTB> STOP
```

The PDF command calculates the probability for the specified value. In this case, the data value was set at $x = 0$ and the binomial subcommand was used to solve for $n = 9$ and $p = .3$.

The MINITAB commands for computing the binomial probability for Example 5.18 are:

```
MTB> SET C1
DATA> 0:3
DATA> END
MTB> CDF C1;
SUBC> BINOMIAL 15 .2.
        K          P(X LESS OR = K)
       0.00              0.0352
       1.00              0.1671
       2.00              0.3980
       3.00              0.6482
MTB> STOP
```

The CDF command computes the cumulative probability of a value less than or equal to x. In this case, the data value was set at $x = 0$ to $x = 3$ and the binomial subcommand used to solve for $n = 15$ and $p = .2$.

■ SITUATION 5.4—PARTIALLY RESOLVED Central Motors is now in a position to use the information from the binomial distribution in its decision-making process. The four desired probabilities must first be restated in appropriate terms. The probability of a profitable day (.61) is rounded to .60 for use in the binomial table. Table 5.6 shows the computations used to construct the binomial table for $n = 6$ and $p = .60$. Management's questions can easily be answered by referring to the binomial table in Appendix E.2.

1. $n = 6, p = .60, x = 6$: from the table, $P(x = 6) = .047$
2. $n = 6, p = .60, x \geq 4$: from the table,
   $P(x \geq 4) = .311 + .187 + .047 = .545$
3. $n = 6, p = .60, x = 0$; from the table, $P(x = 0) = .004$
4. $n = 15, p = .60, x \geq 10$; from the table,
   $P(x \geq 10) = .186 + .127 + .063 + .022 + .005 + .000 = .403$

TABLE 5.6 Probability Distribution for the Number of Profitable Days, Where $n = 6$ and $p = .60$ (Situation 5.4)

x		$P(x)$
0	$\dfrac{6!}{0!6!}(.60)^0 \ (.40)^6 =$	.0041
1	$\dfrac{6!}{1!5!}(.60)^1 \ (.40)^5 =$	.0369
2	$\dfrac{6!}{2!4!}(.60)^2 \ (.40)^4 =$	.1382
3	$\dfrac{6!}{3!3!}(.60)^3 \ (.40)^3 =$	.2765
4	$\dfrac{6!}{4!2!}(.60)^4 \ (.40)^2 =$	.3110
5	$\dfrac{6!}{5!1!}(.60)^5 \ (.40)^1 =$	.1866
6	$\dfrac{6!}{6!0!}(.60)^6 \ (.40)^0 =$	.0467
		1.0000

From this analysis, management can see that it's almost impossible for each day of the week to be profitable (.047, from solution 1). Given the current probability of a good sales day, this level of weekly profit is extremely unlikely. The probability of four or more profitable days is slightly greater than 50% (.545, from solution 2).

On the other hand, Central is quite unlikely to have a bad week, that is, one with no profitable days (.004, from solution 3). Finally, there's less than an even chance (.403, from solution 4) of 10 or more profitable days out of 15.

Management must increase the probability of a profitable day to a larger value to obtain a more encouraging profit picture. It must emphasize salesperson training, increased advertising, and customer incentives if business is to improve. Modeling the sales volume situation with the binomial distribution helps management focus on its unsatisfactory profit picture. The end of the next section further analyzes Central's profit picture. ■

EXERCISES

For the following exercises, assume statistical independence.

35. For a binomial distribution with $n = 8$ and $p = .10$, find:
    a. $P(x = 4)$.
    b. $P(x \leq 3)$.
    c. $P(x \geq 7)$.
    d. $P(x \leq 2)$.

36. For a binomial distribution with $n = 20$ and $p = .50$, find:
    a. $P(x = 14)$.
    b. $P(x \leq 13)$.
    c. $P(x \geq 7)$.
    d. $P(x \geq 2)$.

37. A lawyer who specializes in drug violations and litigation estimates that she wins 70% of her cases that go to court. She has just read "Drugs: The Case for Legalization" in the October 3, 1989, issue of *Financial World* and wants to use some of the article's arguments in her own trial work.

    Based on her estimated probability of success, if she presently represents five defendants in different cases, what is the probability that she'll win at least three cases?

38. A film manufacturer advertises that 90 out of 100 prints will develop. Suppose you buy a roll of 20 prints but 5 don't develop. If the manufacturer's claim is true, what is the probability that 5 prints won't develop? Find the probability that 5 or more prints won't develop.

39. In the past, Phil Anderson has made mistakes on 5% of the tax returns he prepares. What is the probability that he'll make no mistakes on the first seven returns he prepares for the current tax year?

40. A project manager has determined that a subcontractor fails to deliver standard orders on schedule about 20% of the time. The project manager has six orders that this subcontractor has agreed to deliver. Calculate the probability that:

    a. The subcontractor will deliver all of the orders.

    b. The subcontractor will deliver at least four of the orders.

    c. The subcontractor will deliver exactly five orders.

41. On Wall Street tradition says that if an NFC team or one of the old NFL teams now in the AFC (Indianapolis Colts, Cleveland Browns, and Pittsburgh Steelers) wins the Super Bowl, stock prices will be higher a year later. If an AFC team wins, the market will stumble ("An Examination of the Super Bowl Stock Market Predictor," *Decision Science Institute Proceedings*, November 21–23, 1988, p. 317). A *USA Today* article (January 23, 1992) indicates that it has worked 22 of 25 times. Suppose that the game outcome and stock price increases are unrelated. Find the probability of the game predicting increases in stock prices 22 times out of 25. Use a computer program.

42. If 40% of the employees in the company data base (see Appendix C) are females, and 10 employees are randomly chosen to serve on a committee, what is the probability that:

    a. Four women will be selected?

    b. No women will be selected?

    c. No more than four women will be selected?

MEAN AND STANDARD DEVIATION OF THE BINOMIAL DISTRIBUTION

Mean and Standard Deviation of Binomial

As demonstrated in Chapter 4, the mean and standard deviation are frequently used to summarize data collections. If possible outcomes of a binomial experiment are viewed as a data collection, the mean and standard deviation thus constitute good summary measures. The formulas for the mean (μ) and standard deviation (σ) of a binomial distribution are

$$\mu = np \tag{5.5}$$
$$\sigma = \sqrt{np(1 - p)} \tag{5.6}$$

■ SITUATION 5.4—RESOLVED   Central Motors can use Equations 5.5 and 5.6 to find the mean and standard deviation of the number of profitable days per six-day work week. Since each day has a 61% chance of being profitable, $n = 6$ and $p = .61$. The mean and standard deviation are

$$\mu = np = (6)(.61) = 3.66$$
$$\sigma = \sqrt{np(1 - p)} = \sqrt{(6)(.61)(.39)} = 1.19$$

Central Motors now knows that if sales over a long period of time are studied, an average of 3.66 profitable days can be expected per week. The standard deviation of profitable days per week is 1.19. In other words, the number of profitable days per week typically varies from the mean by approximately 1.19 days. The low average number of profitable days isn't considered satisfactory, and management attention focuses on ways to improve profitability. Attention is directed specifically toward raising the probability of a profitable day, which now stands at only 61%. ■

EXERCISES

For the following exercises, assume statistical independence.

43. If four customers are asked whether they like a product, and the probability of any of them answering yes is .25, would you expect, on the average, about one yes from the four customers? If you keep asking samples of four customers if they like the product, what would you expect the variability in yes answers to be?

44. For a binomial distribution with $n = 9$ and $p = .20$, find the mean and standard deviation.

45. For a binomial distribution with $n = 20$ and $p = .50$, find the mean and standard deviation.

46. Fifty percent of the residents of Lake County are registered to vote. If 10 people are selected at random:

    a. Determine the average of this probability distribution.

    b. Determine the variability of this probability distribution.

47. A project manager has determined that a subcontractor delivers standard orders on schedule about 90% of the time. The manager has placed 10 orders that this subcontractor has agreed to deliver.

    a. What is the probability that the subcontractor will deliver all of the orders on schedule?

    b. What is the mean of this probability distribution?

    c. What is the standard deviation of this probability distribution?

48. A salesperson has a 20% chance of making a sale to any customer called upon. If five calls are made:

    a. What is the probability that fewer than three sales will be made?

    b. What is the probability of no sales made?

    c. What is the average number of sales?

    d. What is the variability in the number of sales for each five calls made?

    e. Is the binomial distribution a good model of this situation?

49. Forty percent of the employees in the company data base (see Appendix C) are female. What are the mean and standard deviation of the number of females if random samples of 50 employees are taken?

■ SITUATION 5.5 On Monday morning, Central Motors management discovered that a batch containing bad parts may have been sent to a customer over the weekend. A bin containing 15 fuel pumps was used to select 5 pumps to be shipped to fill an order. It was discovered later that the 15 fuel pumps in the bin had been tested, and only 10 were in satisfactory condition. Management hopes that there were no defective pumps in the order. The Central analyst must determine the probability that all 5 of them are okay. ■

THE HYPERGEOMETRIC DISTRIBUTION

The binomial distribution assumes that the population from which the sample is drawn is infinitely large. For this reason, the probability of success doesn't change with each trial. In the coin-flipping example, the number of "available" heads doesn't decrease as head flips occur. The "supply" of heads can be viewed as infinitely large so that the probability of flipping a head remains at .50 no matter how many are flipped.

When the population cannot be assumed to be infinitely large, or even very large, the binomial distribution isn't appropriate. This is because each time an item is selected from the population, the population size is reduced and the probability of success on the next trial changes. The *hypergeometric distribution* is used to model such situations.

An example of such a situation is the determination of the probability of forming a committee of all women if three persons are randomly chosen from a group of five women and four men. The binomial distribution doesn't model this situation because the probability of getting a female member changes each time a selection is made.

Another example is the determination of the probability of obtaining two good parts out of an inventory bin that contains four good parts and eight bad ones. Again, the probabilities keep changing with each draw so that the constant probability requirement of the binomial distribution is violated.

Hypergeometric Distribution

The **hypergeometric distribution** is used to model finite-population situations where samples are taken without replacement. The formula for this distribution is

$$P(x) = \frac{C_{n-x}^{N-r} C_x^r}{C_n^N} \quad (5.7)$$

where N = Population size
n = Sample size
r = Number of successes in population
x = Number of successes in sample for which a probability is desired
C = Combination

Note: C_x^n is an alternative way of expressing a combination.

> The **hypergeometric distribution** is used to model finite-population situations where sampling is done without replacement and where the probability of a certain number of successes is to be calculated.

EXAMPLE 5.19   In a room containing eight people there are four members of a union. A random sample of three is selected for a committee. What is the probability that exactly one of them is a union member? Since the population is quite small (N = 8) and the sampling must be done without replacement, the binomial distribution isn't appropriate; the probability of selecting a union member changes each time a person is chosen. The hypergeometric distribution should be used with the following parameters:

$$N = 8 \qquad r = 4 \qquad n = 3 \qquad x = 1$$

The solution is

$$P(x = 1) = \frac{C_{3-1}^{8-4} \, C_1^4}{C_3^8} = \frac{\dfrac{4!}{2!2!} \, \dfrac{4!}{1!3!}}{\dfrac{8!}{3!5!}} = \frac{\dfrac{(4)(3)(2)(1)(4)(3)(2)(1)}{(2)(1)(2)(1)(1)(3)(2)(1)}}{\dfrac{(8)(7)(6)(5)(4)(3)(2)(1)}{(3)(2)(1)(5)(4)(3)(2)(1)}}$$

$$= \frac{24}{56} = .429$$

EXAMPLE 5.20   An auditor randomly selects 3 accounts from a group of 10 for careful examination. The company being audited knows that 4 of the tax accounts contain errors. What is the probability that all 3 of the accounts selected are error-free? Here $N = 10$, $n = 3$, $r = 6$ (the number of good accounts in the population), and $x = 3$ (the number of good accounts in the sample). The solution is

$$P(x = 3) = \frac{C_{3-3}^{10-6} \, C_3^6}{C_3^{10}} = \frac{\dfrac{4!}{0!4!} \, \dfrac{6!}{3!3!}}{\dfrac{10!}{3!7!}}$$

$$= \frac{\dfrac{(4)(3)(2)(1)(6)(5)(4)(3)(2)(1)}{(1)(4)(3)(2)(1)(3)(2)(1)(3)(2)(1)}}{\dfrac{(10)(9)(8)(7)(6)(5)(4)(3)(2)(1)}{(3)(2)(1)(7)(6)(5)(4)(3)(2)(1)}} = \frac{20}{120} = .167$$

- SITUATION 5.5—RESOLVED   The fuel pump problem can be modeled with the hypergeometric distribution but not the binomial. When the first pump is selected for shipment, the probability of getting a good one is 10 chances out of 15, or .67. But the chance of getting a good pump on the second try changes. Now there are only 14 pumps in the population and either 9 or 10 good ones, depending on whether the first one was good or bad. Although each pump drawn is either good or bad, this situation cannot be modeled with the binomial distribution because the small population size (15) results in a different probability of success each time a trial takes place.

The values required for the hypergeometric distribution formula are

$N = 15$ (the number of pumps in the population)
$n = 5$ (the number of pumps in the sample)
$r = 10$ (the number of good pumps in the population)
$x = 5$ (the number of good pumps in the sample for which the probability is to be determined)

Placing these values into Equation 5.7 produces the probability of a completely good shipment:

$$P(5) = \frac{C_{5-5}^{15-10} \, C_5^{10}}{C_5^{15}} = \frac{\dfrac{5!}{0!5!} \cdot \dfrac{10!}{5!5!}}{\dfrac{15!}{5!10!}} = \frac{(1)(252)}{3{,}003} = .0839$$

It is apparent that there's a very low probability (.0839) of a defect-free shipment. Management should contact the buyer and arrange to test the shipment and replace the defective pumps. ∎

EXERCISES

50. Explain the similarities between the binomial distribution and the hypergeometric distribution.

51. Explain the differences between the binomial distribution and the hypergeometric distribution.

52. Given $N = 10$, $n = 4$, $r = 5$, and $x = 3$, solve this hypergeometric problem.

53. A tire store has 20 identical grade A tires in stock. Five of these tires are slightly damaged. A customer purchases a set of four tires. Compute the probability distribution for the number of undamaged tires obtained by the customer.

54. The Kingston Bank has 15 accounts receivable with open balances in its RV loan department. The bank president wants to modify the bank's business after reading a *Bankers Monthly* article entitled, "Banks that Make Money without Lending It" (February 1989, p. 58). He decides to sample some of the RV loans and study their profitability.
    Of the outstanding loans, six have balances above $1,000. The president selects at random five accounts receivable for study. Find the probability that exactly two of these audited accounts will have balances over $1,000.

55. Local 429 has 25 members. Fifteen are in favor of a strike, and 10 are not. Find the probability that a random sample of 6 workers contains 3 who favor the strike and 3 who oppose it.

56. A government agency is checking label specifications for a product. Suppose that in a particular crate, 6 out of 24 cans' contents don't meet their label specifications. The agency chooses 6 cans from a crate. What is the probability that the agency will find no mislabeled cans?

∎ SITUATION 5.6 Another problem Central Motors management faces concerns the main office's telephone switchboard. The number of people answering the switchboard varies considerably during the day even though the number of incoming calls is steady over the entire working day. Management believes that analysis of this situation could provide useful information for deciding how many people to assign to the switchboard. ∎

The Poisson Distribution

Poisson Distribution

The Poisson distribution is another useful theoretical distribution for modeling certain real situations. Probabilities can be found without lengthy and costly observations of the real world.

The **Poisson distribution** is used to model situations where the number of trials is very large and the number of successes is very small. The key issue to address before using the Poisson distribution involves the concept of randomness. That is, the arrival of the events in question mustn't follow any pattern. If the arrivals are truly random, the Poisson distribution can provide useful decision-making information.

> The **Poisson distribution** is used to model situations where there are random arrivals of events per unit of space or time, and where the probability of a specific number of successes is desired. It can be shown mathematically that a binomial distribution for which n becomes very large and p becomes very small approaches the Poisson distribution.

The formula for the Poisson distribution is

$$P(x) = \frac{\mu^x e^{-\mu}}{x!} \tag{5.8}$$

where μ = Mean number of arrivals per unit of time or space
x = Number of arrivals for which the probability is desired
e = Base of the natural logarithms, a mathematical constant approximately equal to 2.71828

Equation 5.8 shows that the Poisson distribution describes a discrete random variable that may assume any value in an infinite sequence ($x = 0, 1, 2, 3, \ldots$). Note that we need only one measure to compute the probability of a given x value: the mean number of arrivals per unit of time or space (μ). Examples 5.21 and 5.22 illustrate Equation 5.8's use.

EXAMPLE 5.21   A mail-order house switchboard receives an average of 3.5 orders per hour. These arrivals appear to be random; that is, there's no discernible pattern during the day or from day to day. What is the probability of exactly four calls arriving in a given hour? Since $\mu = 3.5$ and $x = 4$, the probability is

$$P(x = 4) = \frac{3.5^4 (2.71828)^{-3.5}}{4!} = \frac{150.0625}{4 \cdot 3 \cdot 2 \cdot 1 \, (2.71828)^{3.5}} = .189$$

Example 5.22 *The American Statistician* (November 1992, pp. 246–53) reported on a study, "A Bayesian Analysis of a Poisson Random Effects Model for Home Run Hitters," that showed how the Poisson distribution could be used to estimate a hitter's ability to hit home runs. The statistic used for measuring a player's home run hitting ability is the observed rate, which divides the total number of home runs in a career by the total number of official at-bats. In baseball statistics books[1] this home run rate statistic is usually expressed as the number of at-bats for each home run hit. Babe Ruth was the greatest home run hitter with 714 career home runs in 8,389 career at-bats: a rate of .085. Using the Poisson distribution with an average rate of .085, what is the probability of Babe Ruth hitting no home runs in his next 10 at-bats? The rate is .085 for 1 at-bat or .85 for 10 at-bats. Hence $\mu = .85$ and $x = 0$. The probability is

$$P(x = 0) = \frac{.85^0 (2.71828)^{-.85}}{0!} = \frac{1}{(2.71828)^{.85}} = .427$$

■　Situation 5.6—Partially Resolved　After addressing the randomness issue, Central Motors management decides that phone calls are indeed random. There don't appear to be certain times of day when more calls arrive compared to others, and there doesn't seem to be any pattern. So they model the telephone situation using the Poisson process.

Management decides on a five-minute interval as the unit of time to evaluate. To use the Poisson distribution, Central's analyst must compute the mean, or average, number of arrivals per five-minute interval during the work day. Several five-minute intervals are selected at random during the next week. It is determined that the mean number of calls during these intervals is 4.8. This value is the mean of the Poisson distribution used to calculate probabilities.

Table 5.7 presents the probability distribution for the number of arrivals per five-minute interval. Figure 5.6 graphs this probability distribution. To find the probabilities to complete Table 5.7, we solve the Poisson formula (Equation 5.8) several times. Fortunately, statisticians have anticipated this situation and have solved the Poisson formula for hundreds of different problems. (Results of these computations, the Poisson Table in Appendix E.4, are discussed in the next section.) ■

Exercises

57. Explain the difference between the binomial distribution and the Poisson distribution.

58. Given $\mu = 1, x = 1$, solve this Poisson problem.

59. The Medical Lake fire station receives an average of two calls per day. Construct a probability distribution for the number of calls, assuming the Poisson distribution is an appropriate model.

60. In the past, trucks have randomly arrived at a loading dock at the rate of one per hour. What is the probability that no trucks will arrive in the next hour?

[1]S. Siwoff, S. Hirdt, T. Hirdt, and P. Hirdt, *The 1991 Elias Baseball Analyst* (New York: Fireside, 1991).

TABLE 5.7   Probability Distribution for the Arrival of Telephone Calls (Situation 5.6)

x		$P(x)$
0	$\dfrac{4.8^0\ 2.71828^{-4.8}}{0!} =$	.0082
1	$\dfrac{4.8^1\ 2.71828^{-4.8}}{1!} =$	.0395
2	$\dfrac{4.8^2\ 2.71828^{-4.8}}{2!} =$	.0948
3	$\dfrac{4.8^3\ 2.71828^{-4.8}}{3!} =$	.1517
4	$\dfrac{4.8^4\ 2.71828^{-4.8}}{4!} =$	.1820
5	$\dfrac{4.8^5\ 2.71828^{-4.8}}{5!} =$	.1747
6	$\dfrac{4.8^6\ 2.71828^{-4.8}}{6!} =$	.1398
7	$\dfrac{4.8^7\ 2.71828^{-4.8}}{7!} =$	.0959
8	$\dfrac{4.8^8\ 2.71828^{-4.8}}{8!} =$	.0575
9	$\dfrac{4.8^9\ 2.71828^{-4.8}}{9!} =$	.0307

FIGURE 5.6   Graphical Representation for the Probability Distribution of Telephone Call Arrivals

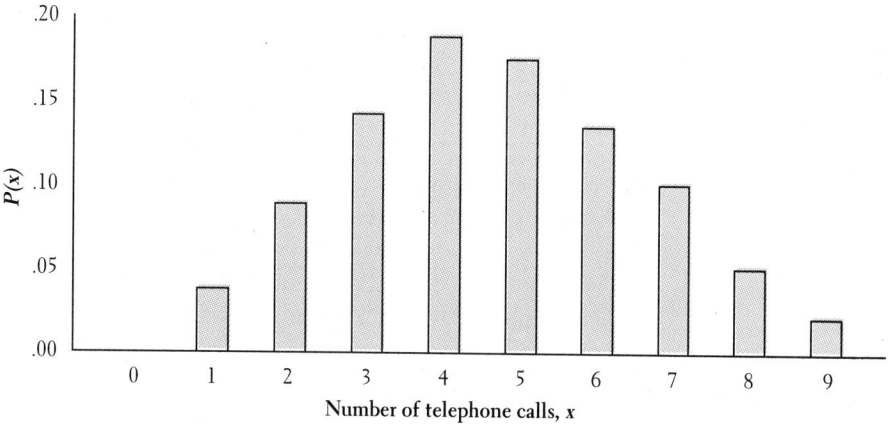

61. The Cheney Federal Credit Union receives, on the average, 2.2 applications for home improvement loans per week. What is the probability that it will receive two applications this week?

62. Inland Empire Telephone observes that 3.2 calls per minute come in on a certain line, on the average. What is the probability that five calls will come in on that line during the next minute?

63. The Pannell Corporation deposits cash reserves into its sick-leave fund on the assumption that its employees will require sick-leave pay for a total of 1.5 days, on the average, each month. What is the probability that no employees will call in sick this month?

POISSON DISTRIBUTION TABLE

Poisson Table

The Poisson distribution of Equation 5.8 has been solved for hundreds of values and compiled in a table (see Appendix E.4) for convenient use. The blocks of probabilities are headed by various values of μ, the mean or average number of occurrences per unit of time or space. Using the appropriate column, we can read the probabilities of the x values appearing on the left edge of the table.

EXAMPLE 5.23   From 1983 through 1987, the average number of fatal accidents for certificated route air carriers was 2.8 (*Statistical Abstract of the United States: 1989*, p. 611). Assume that the number of fatal accidents per year among certificated route air carriers can be adequately described by a Poisson probability distribution with mean 2.8. What is the probability of 3 or more fatal accidents in 1988? Look in the Poisson table in the column for $\mu = 2.8$. The probabilities of 0 through 2 accidents from this column are added: $P(x = 0) + P(x = 1) + P(x = 2) = .0608 + .1703 + .2384 = .4695$. The probability of 3 or more equals .5305 $(1 - .4695)$.

EXAMPLE 5.24   If the mean value of a Poisson process is .90, what is the probability the x will be either 0 or 1? From the Poisson table for $\mu = .90$, the probabilities of 0 and 1 can be added: $P(x = 0) + P(x = 1) = .4066 + .3659 = .7725$.

EXAMPLE 5.25   According to *Fortune*, July 3, 1989, Westinghouse has been trying to make quality "the company religion," especially in the manufacturing processes.

Suppose a key process at Westinghouse generates errors at an average rate of 5.7 per hour. Errors arrive randomly, and the probability of 3 or fewer errors in a given hour is to be determined. This process can be modeled with the Poisson distribution. In the $\mu = 5.7$ column of the Poisson table, probabilities of 0 through 3 are added: $P(x = 0) + P(x = 1) + P(x = 2) + P(x = 3) = .0033 + .0191 + .0544 + .1033 = .1801$.

Figure 5.7 shows the Poisson distribution for Example 5.25. The number of occurrences is plotted on the horizontal axis, and probabilities are plotted vertically. The probability of 3 or fewer errors is shaded. This total area is the correct answer to the problem, .1801.

A software package such as MINITAB may be used in place of the Poisson table in Appendix E.4. MINITAB commands for computing Table 5.7's Poisson probability distribution are:

```
MTB> PDF;
SUBC> POISSON 4.8.
      K          P(X = K)
      0          0.0082
      SEE TABLE 5.7 FOR REST OF PROBABILITIES
MTB> STOP
```

FIGURE 5.7   Poisson Distribution for Example 5.25 ($\mu = 5.7$)

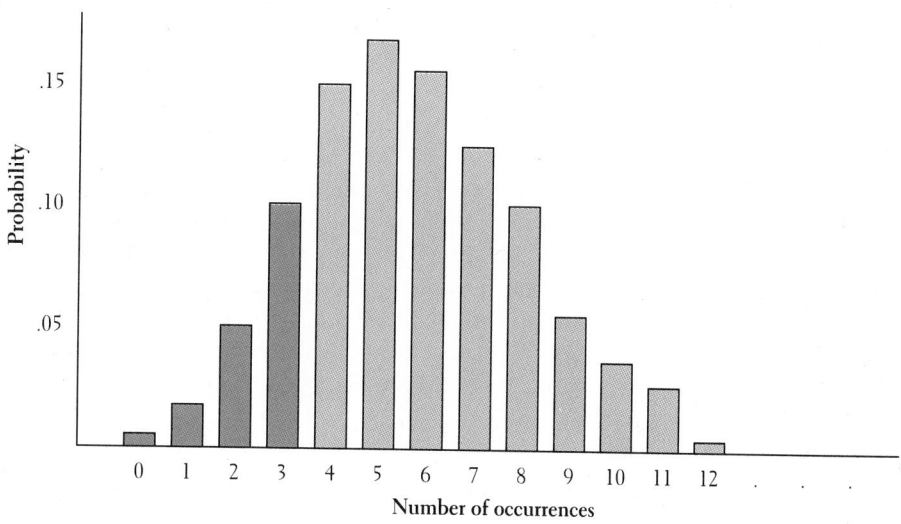

The PDF command calculates individual probabilities for the Poisson distribution with a mean of 4.8.

The MINITAB commands for computing the Poisson probability for Example 5.25 are:

```
MTB> SET C1
DATA> 0:3
DATA> END
MTB> CDF C1;
SUBC> POISSON 5.7.
        K          P(X LESS OR = K)
        0.00          0.0033
        1.00          0.0224
        2.00          0.0768
        3.00          0.1800
MTB> STOP
```

The CDF command computes the cumulative probability of a value less than or equal to x. In this case, the DATA command was used to specify the range $x = 0$ to $x = 3$, and the Poisson subcommand solved for a Poisson distribution with a mean of 5.7.

The definition of the Poisson distribution states that the mean number of arrivals per unit of time or space must be determined. The telephone example used a length of time as the measurement unit, namely, a five-minute period. The Poisson distribution can also be used to model the random arrivals of items per unit of space.

EXAMPLE 5.26   Suppose an aluminum sheet roll manufacturer wants to compute the probability of a defect-free roll. A roll of aluminum sheet is the unit of space to be modeled. To use the Poisson distribution, the mean number of defects that "arrive" on each roll must be known.

The aluminum sheet production process is watched over a period of several days, and it's decided that defects do occur on a random basis and the mean number of defects per roll is observed to be .30. The Poisson table can now be used to find the probability of a defect-free roll. Turn to this table and find the column headed by a μ of .30. The probability that x (number of defects on any given roll) equals 0 is the first number in the column: $P(x = 0) = .7408$.

If the mean number of defects per roll is .30 and these defects arrive randomly, the manager of the aluminum sheet process knows that there's a 74% chance of the process producing a defect-free roll. A decision can now be made as to whether this level of quality is satisfactory. With only a 74% chance of a defect-free roll, the manager decides that corrective action must be taken. A training process for operators is started, and the machine manufacturer is contacted about necessary improvements.

■ SITUATION 5.6—RESOLVED   In Appendix E.4's Poisson table, locate the column corresponding to a mean (μ) of 4.8. This column indicates that the probability that x will be 0 is .0082, the probability that x will be 1 is .0395, and so on. These same values appear in Table 5.7.

Management can now determine the probabilities pertinent to the switchboard staffing problem. Remember that the time period being used is five minutes and that the mean number of phone calls during this interval is 4.8. Management seeks probabilities of the following events: no calls, three or fewer calls, and five or fewer calls.

The probabilities associated with these events are found in the Poisson table's $\mu = 4.8$ column. The first probability, for $x = 0$, is read directly from the table: .0082. The second probability is the sum of the probabilities for x values 0 through 3; the third is the sum of the probabilities for x values 0 through 5. The three desired probabilities are

$$P(x = 0) = .0082$$
$$P(x \leq 3) = .2942$$
$$P(x \leq 5) = .6509$$

Management is surprised at these low probabilities. It had hoped to use only one operator to staff the switchboard, but apparently many incoming calls can be expected.

The next key question is how long it takes an operator to service each call. If each call can be answered and processed in a few seconds, one operator might be enough. However, if each call averages one minute or more, additional operators will be needed. ■

EXERCISES

64. Given $\mu = 4.6$, $x = 3$, solve this Poisson problem.

65. Given $\mu = 5.3$, $x \geq 4$, solve this Poisson problem.

66. Customers arrive at the Country Counter supermarket at the rate of two every three minutes. What is the probability that five customers will arrive within the next six minutes?

67. The Bon Department Store has determined that demand for a certain model of camera is Poisson-distributed with a mean of two per week. The camera department manager wants

to study current camera demand to see if it justifies offering photography classes. She has just read "Into the Landscape" in *American Photographer* (August 1989, p. 34) and thinks such a class would be effective.

  a. Determine the probability distribution of weekly demand for the camera.

  b. If the store stocks four of these cameras in a particular week, what is the probability that demand will exceed supply?

68. Cars arrive at the ZZ Car Wash at the average rate of 9 per hour. If arrivals per hour follow the Poisson distribution, find the probability of 15 or more arrivals during any given hour of operation.

69. Customer arrivals at the Federal Credit Union are Poisson-distributed and average 2.5 per minute.

  a. What is the probability of exactly three arrivals in a one-minute period?

  b. What is the probability of fewer than three arrivals in a one-minute period?

  c. What is the probability of more than three arrivals in a one-minute period?

  d. What is the probability of exactly three arrivals in a two-minute period?

70. It is estimated that the number of taxis waiting to pick up customers in front of the JFK Terminal is Poisson-distributed with a mean of 5.5 cabs.

  a. Find the probability that on random observation, exactly 6 cabs will be waiting.

  b. Find the probability that on random observation, more than 10 cabs will be waiting.

  c. Find the probability that on random observation, no cabs will be waiting.

■ SITUATION 5.7 Central Motors' final problem involves inventory of a key part, engine spark plugs. Their large inventory has been supplied by a single manufacturer, which has recently informed them that some plugs may be defective. The supplier has found that about 2% of the plugs delivered during the past three years won't function properly. Since spark plugs will be randomly drawn from inventory, and since a plug either works properly or doesn't, Central decides that this situation can be modeled using the binomial distribution.

The problem would be simple if a tune-up for only one car were being considered. In that case, n, the number of plugs drawn from inventory, would be 4, 6, or 8, depending on the engine size. The binomial table could then be used to find, for example, the probability of no defective plugs used in a tune-up.

But Central is interested in the larger picture. Each week it draws approximately 100 plugs from inventory. They wish to model this situation with the binomial distribution; that is, management wants to know the probability of having no defective spark plugs drawn from inventory during a week. It also wants to know the probability of drawing five or fewer defective spark plugs. This problem can be characterized as follows:

$$n = 100 \qquad p = .02 \qquad \begin{array}{l} P(x = 0) = ? \\ P(x \le 5) = ? \end{array}$$

The binomial formula can be used to find the probabilities for various numbers of defective plugs in each 100-plug batch. This would be very time-consuming, however, since the number of "trials" (100) is so large. Moreover, a binomial table rarely contains entries for n larger than 20. Thus, even though this situation is eligible for modeling with the binomial distribution, there doesn't seem to be a handy way to find the desired probabilities. ∎

POISSON APPROXIMATION TO THE BINOMIAL

Poisson Approximation to the Binomial

In binomial distribution problems where n is large and where the probability of success (p) is either quite small or quite large, probabilities can be approximated using the Poisson distribution. In this method, the "arrivals" of successes of the binomial are presumed to follow a Poisson process. Although probabilities computed using this approximation aren't precise, they're quite close to the true binomial probabilities.

> The Poisson distribution provides a close approximation to the binomial distribution when n is large and p is either quite small or quite large. As a rule of thumb, use of the approximation is appropriate when $n > 20$ and $np \leq 5$ or $n(1 - p) \leq 5$.

Figure 5.8 summarizes methods to find binomial probabilities. The vertical axis represents n, the number of independent trials in the binomial experiment. If n is small enough, the binomial table can be used to find the correct probability of the desired outcome. If n is larger than 20 (the maximum size of most binomial tables), the binomial probability must be approximated. If the rule of thumb holds ($np \leq 5$ or $n[1 - p] \leq 5$), this approximation can be made using the Poisson distribution. If this

FIGURE 5.8   Methods of Solving Binomial Problems

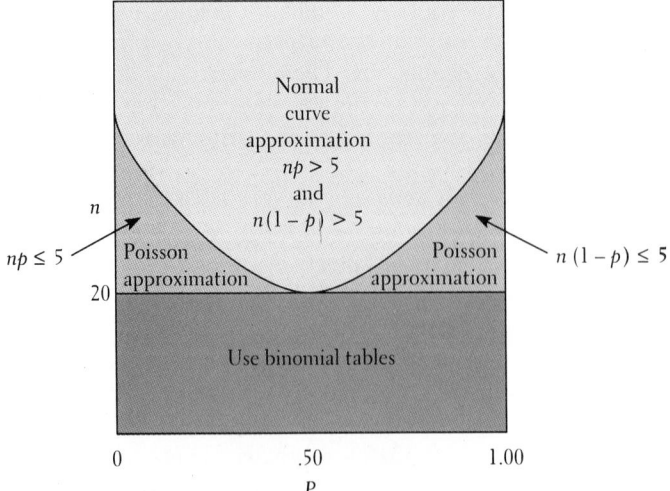

rule of thumb doesn't hold, the approximation is made using the normal distribution, which we will describe in Chapter 6.

EXAMPLE 5.27   One percent of the employees in a large factory are absent each day. If 70 employee names are randomly selected, what is the probability that no more than one is absent? Since n is quite large and $np \leq 5$ ($np = .7$), this binomial problem can be solved using the Poisson approximation. The mean number of absent employees calculated using Equation 5.5 is used to enter the Poisson table:

$$\mu = np = (70)(.01) = .7$$

The Poisson table column for $\mu = .7$ is used:

$$P(x = 0) + P(x = 1) = .4966 + .3476 = .8442$$

EXAMPLE 5.28   A sample of 116 parts is randomly drawn from inventory to be shipped to a customer. We know that the process that produced the parts generates 2.5% defective parts over time. What is the probability that the shipment contains exactly three defectives? Again, the large n and small p call for approximating the binomial probability using the Poisson distribution ($np = 2.9$):

$$\mu = np = (116)(.025) = 2.9$$

Referring to the Poisson table column for $\mu = 2.9$,

$$P(x = 3) = .2237$$

Note that software packages such as MINITAB make binomial approximations unnecessary. MINITAB commands for computing the binomial probability for Example 5.28 are:

```
MTB> SET C1
DATA> 3
DATA> END
MTB> PDF C1;
SUBC> BINOMIAL 116 .025.
       K            P(X = K)
     3.00           0.2266
MTB> STOP
```

Note how close the Poisson approximation .2237 is to the correct binomial probability, .2266.

■ SITUATION 5.7—RESOLVED   In Central Motors' spark plug problem, n is large (100) and p is quite small (.02). Therefore, the Poisson distribution is used as an approximation of the true binomial distribution to find the probability that all the spark plugs used in a week are defect-free. The first step is to calculate the mean of this binomial situation:

$$\mu = np = (100)(.02) = 2 \quad \text{(verifying that } np \leq 5)$$

The average number of faulty plugs in each week's supply of 100 is 2, so the Poisson table is entered using the column for a mean of 2. The reasoning is that defective plugs arrive at an average rate of 2 in each lot of 100.

Turn to the Poisson table in Appendix E.4 and find the column for a mean of 2. This column contains the probabilities of several occurrences of x, the number of defective plugs in each 100-plug batch. The first entry is for $x = 0$, the value desired by Central Motors. $P(x = 0) = .1353$, indicating a small probability that the plugs selected for the week will be defect-free. Central needs to work with its supplier to replace all the plugs in inventory or to establish a testing procedure for each plug prior to using it in a tune-up.

What is the probability that there will be 4 bad plugs in each week's 100-unit lot? The probability entry for $x = 4$ from the Poisson table is .0902.

The alternative would be to use the binomial formula:

$$P(x = 4) = \binom{100}{4}(.02)^4(.98)^{100-4} = .090208$$

Note how close the Poisson approximation is to the true binomial probability.

What is the probability of 5 or fewer bad plugs in each week's 100-unit lot? The answer is approximated by adding the probabilities for 0 through 5 in the $\mu = 2$ column in the Poisson table:

$$P(x \leq 5) = .1353 + .2707 + .2707 + .1804 + .0902 + .0361$$
$$= .9834$$

There's about a 98% chance that the week's supply of 100 spark plugs will contain 5 or fewer defective units. ∎

EXERCISES

71. When is the Poisson distribution a good approximation of the binomial distribution?

72. Why is the Poisson distribution used as an approximation of the binomial distribution?

73. *a.* Given $n = 25$, $p = .02$, $x = 1$, solve this binomial problem.

    b. Given $n = 40$, $p = .97$, $x = 4$, solve this binomial problem.

74. Three percent of the hand calculators of a particular model fail within the first month of operation. F-Mart has just received a batch of 100.

    a. What is the expected number of calculators that will fail in the first month of operation?

    b. Find the probability that no calculators will fail.

    c. Find the probability that more than three calculators will fail.

    d. Find the probability that fewer than two calculators will fail.

75. The Articulate Corporation has come to expect that 99% of its accounts receivable balances are error-free. A sample of 200 accounts has been selected for audit.

    a. What is the probability that none of the accounts will have errors?

    b. What is the probability that five of the accounts will have errors?

    c. What is the probability that more than five of the accounts will have errors?

76. TAB University has determined that 4% of newly accepted graduate students don't register for classes. Next fall's class list has 100 newly admitted graduate students. Find the probability that at least 90 will register for classes.

SUMMARY

. . . .

This chapter has covered some basic ideas of probability and introduced the concepts of random variables and probability distributions. These concepts are necessary for the statistical procedures in the remainder of this book.

In addition, this chapter explained three important theoretical distributions and their applications to real-world business problems: the binomial, the hypergeometric, and the Poisson distributions. When a practical problem fits the specifications of one of these distributions, valuable decision-making information can be gained without doing expensive, time-consuming manipulations and real-world observations.

APPLICATIONS OF STATISTICAL CONCEPTS IN THE BUSINESS WORLD

. . . .

This chapter's procedures enjoy increasing practice in the business world. Their use in providing decision makers with reliable information is becoming more and more apparent as growing numbers of college students enter the business world armed with knowledge of these techniques. The concepts of probability, random variables, and probability distributions help decision makers assess the future with some degree of confidence. Indeed, an ability to deal with the uncertain future is vital for a modern business executive.

The concept of expected value is quite useful for establishing a baseline for assessing an opportunity's monetary aspects. Expected loss due to fire or theft can be used to determine the appropriate level of insurance payments, for example. The average number of defective units per shift can assist in a company's quality-control efforts. If a discrete probability distribution can be formed based on past history, then the expected value (or average value of this distribution) can provide management with valuable baseline performance information.

The binomial distribution is widely applicable in business because so many situations involve the concept of success versus failure. The key point, as this chapter stressed, is to make sure the trials are independent before using the binomial distribution as a model. Examples of situations that can be modeled with the binomial distribution, assuming this independence assumption is met, are:

1. Manufactured or purchased parts either meet quality-control specifications or don't.

2. A customer buying a major appliance either returns for another purchase or goes elsewhere.

3. A bid for a contract job either is successful or results in failure.

4. An employee hired using the company's screening process either proves to be satisfactory or does not work out.

5. An account payable either results in the company being paid or becomes a bad-debt expense.

6. As a result of an intensive advertising campaign, a company's market share either increases or does not increase.

The Poisson distribution is widely applicable in business because many situations involve random arrivals. The key point, as stressed in this chapter, is to be sure the occurrences are random before using the Poisson distribution as a model. A few examples of situations that might be modeled with the Poisson, if this randomness assumption is met, are:

1. The arrivals of cars at a tollbooth, customers at a bank or checkout counter, or trucks at a weighing station.
2. The arrivals of telephone calls at a switchboard.
3. The number of defects per mile of underground cable.
4. The number of blemishes per panel.

GLOSSARY

Probability A measure of the likelihood that a future event will occur; it can assume any value between 0 and 1, inclusive.

Sample space The collection of all possible outcomes for an experiment.

Experiment Any process that generates well-defined outcomes.

Event A possible outcome of an experiment.

Relative frequency A probability defined as the number of times an event occurs divided by the total number of times an experiment is performed.

Subjective probability A probability value that reflects the feelings or opinions concerning the likelihood that a particular outcome will occur.

Complement The collection of outcomes that aren't contained in a given event.

Collectively exhaustive Refers to a list containing every possible event that can occur.

Mutually exclusive Refers to events where the occurrence of one precludes the occurrence of any other.

Addition rule A rule used when it's necessary to compute the probability that *either* event A or event B occurs.

Independence A condition involving two events where one event's occurrence in no way influences the likelihood of the other's occurrence.

Dependence A condition involving two events where one event's occurrence alters the likelihood of the other's occurrence.

Multiplication rule A rule used when it's necessary to compute the probability that *both* event A and event B occur.

Random variable A variable defined by assigning one numerical value to each simple event of an experiment that yields random outcomes.

Discrete random variable A variable that can assume only values from a predetermined set.

Probability distribution A listing of the possible values that a random variable can assume along with their probabilities.

Expected value The average value assumed by a random variable over a large number of observations.

Binomial distribution A discrete probability distribution involving the likelihood of x successes in n trials of a binomial experiment.

Combination The number of ways in which x things can be chosen from a collection of n things when the order of choosing isn't important.

Hypergeometric distribution A distribution used to model finite-population situations where sampling is done without replacement and where the probability of a certain number of successes is to be calculated.

Poisson distribution A distribution used to model situations where the arrivals of events per unit of space or time are random and where the probability of a specific number of successes is to be determined.

KEY FORMULAS

· ·

Expected value of a discrete random variable

$$E(x) = \Sigma[x \cdot P(x)] \tag{5.1}$$

Variance of a discrete random variable

$$\sigma^2 = \Sigma(x - \mu)^2 P(x) \tag{5.2}$$

Binomial probability distribution

$$P(x) = \binom{n}{x} p^x (1 - p)^{n-x} \tag{5.3}$$

Combination formula

$$\binom{n}{x} = \frac{n!}{x! \, (n - x)!} \tag{5.4}$$

Expected value (mean) for a binomial probability distribution

$$\mu = np \tag{5.5}$$

Standard deviation for a binomial probability distribution

$$\sigma = \sqrt{np \, (1 - p)} \tag{5.6}$$

The hypergeometric probability distribution

$$P(x) = \frac{C_{n-x}^{N-r} C_x^r}{C_n^N} \tag{5.7}$$

The Poisson probability distribution

$$P(x) = \frac{\mu^x e^{-\mu}}{x!} \tag{5.8}$$

SOLVED EXERCISES

· ·

1. MULTIPLICATION AND ADDITION RULES

A motel keeps two vehicles ready for picking up patrons at the airport and railway station. Due to demand and chance of mechanical failure, the probability that a specific vehicle will be available when needed is .6. One vehicle's availability is independent of the other's.

a. In the event of two arrivals calling at the same time (one from the airport and one from the railway station) what is the probability that both vehicles will be available?

b. Find the probability that neither will be available.

c. If one call is placed from the airport, what is the probability that a vehicle is available?

Solution

a. The probability that one vehicle will be available is .6. The probability that both vehicles will be available is .6 × .6 = .36.

b. The probability that one vehicle won't be available is (1 − .6) = .4. The probability that both vehicles won't be available is .4 × .4 = .16.

c. There are three ways that at least one of the two vehicles will be available. Either only the first vehicle is available, only the second vehicle is available, or both vehicles are available. The probability that both are available is .36. The probability of just one vehicle being available is .6 × .4 = .24, and this can occur in two different ways. Therefore, the probability of at least one of the vehicles being available is .36 + .24 + .24 = .84. An alternative solution would be to compute the complement of neither vehicle being available: 1 − .16 = .84.

2. RANDOM VARIABLES

Identify which of the following random variables can be classified as discrete.

a. The number of people arriving at a checkout counter.

b. The number of ounces in a bottle of cola.

c. Tomorrow's temperature.

d. The number of sales made by a car salesperson today.

e. The weight of a roast bought at the supermarket.

f. The number of offers received on a house for sale.

Solution:

a. The number of people is a discrete variable.

b. The number of ounces is a continuous variable.

c. Temperature is a continuous variable.

d. The number of sales is a discrete variable.

e. Weight is a continuous variable.

f. The number of offers is a discrete variable.

3. PROBABILITY DISTRIBUTION

Hanson Construction Company is having a problem with broken tools. A probability distribution of the number of broken tools each day for the past three months is:

Number of broken tools	$P(x)$
0	.30
1	.25
2	.15
3	.20
4 or more	.10

a. Find the probability of three broken tools tomorrow.

b. Find the probability of more than one broken tool tomorrow.

c. Find the probability of no broken tools in the next two days.

Solution:

a. P(3) = .20.

b. P(2) + P(3) + P(4) = .15 + .20 + .10 = .45.

c. P(0) × P(0) = .30 × .30 = .09.

4. EXPECTED VALUE

The Nutra Company has determined that if a new line of sweetener is marketed, the following probability distribution will describe its contribution to the firm's profits during the next three months:

Profit contribution	P(Profit contribution)
−$ 3,000	.2
$ 5,000	.5
$20,000	.3

Nutra has decided it should market the new sweetener if expected contribution to profit for the next three months is over $10,000. Based on the probability distribution, will it market the new sweetener?

Solution:

$$(.2 \times -3,000) + (.5 \times 5,000) + (.3 \times 20,000) = \$7,900$$

The company shouldn't market the new sweetener.

5. COMBINATIONS

Mary Livingston, president of the Maxell Corporation in Chicago, must prepare an itinerary for visiting three of the company's six plants. The trip's cost will depend on which plants she chooses to visit. How many different itineraries are possible?

Solution:

$$\binom{6}{3} = \frac{6!}{3!(6-3)!} = \frac{(6)\,(5)\,(4)\,(3)\,(2)\,(1)}{(3)\,(2)\,(1)\,(3)\,(2)\,(1)} = 20$$

6. BINOMIAL DISTRIBUTION

Large shipments of incoming parts at the Drummond Manufacturing plant are inspected for defective items using a random sampling scheme. Five items are to be examined; a lot is rejected if one or more defective items are observed. If the lot contains 5% defectives, what is the probability that it will be accepted? Rejected?

Solution:

The shipment will be accepted only when there are zero defectives. This can only happen one way:

$$\binom{5}{0} = \frac{5!}{0!(5-0)!} = \frac{(5)\,(4)\,(3)\,(2)\,(1)}{(1)\,(5)\,(4)\,(3)\,(2)\,(1)} = 1$$

Therefore, the probability of accepting the shipment is

$$P(0) = \binom{5}{0} p^0 (1-p)^{5-0} = (1).05^0 (1-.05)^5 = .7738$$

The probability of rejecting the shipment is

$$(1 - .7738) = .2262$$

7. BINOMIAL DISTRIBUTION

Sixty percent of the residents of King County are registered to vote. If 10 people who are old enough to vote are selected at random, find the probability of obtaining:

a. Ten registered voters.

b. Exactly five registered voters.

c. No registered voters.

Solution:

a. $n = 10, p = .60, x = 10$: from the table, $P(x = 10) = .006$.

b. $n = 10, p = .60, x = 5$: from the table, $P(x = 5) = .201$.

c. $n = 10, p = .60, x = 0$: from the table, $P(x = 0) = .000$.

8. BINOMIAL DISTRIBUTION

Colorado Power Company provides lower rates to customers who agree to use energy mainly at off-peak hours. Thirty percent of its customers take advantage of these savings. The consumer affairs department has randomly selected 12 customers to participate in a focus group discussing when people use the most energy. The department supervisor is concerned that the group will contain a large proportion of off-peak users.

a. What is the probability of obtaining fewer than three off-peak users in the focus group?

b. What is the probability of obtaining more than four off-peak users in the focus group?

c. What is the probability of obtaining fewer than eight regular customers in the focus group?

d. Compute the mean and the standard deviation of off-peak users in the focus group.

Solution:

a. $n = 12, p = .30, x < 3$: from the table, $P(x < 3) = .253$.

b. $n = 12, p = .30, x > 4$: from the table, $P(x > 4) = (1 - .724) = .276$.

c. $n = 12, p = .70, x < 8$: from the table, $P(x < 8) = .275$.

d. $\mu = np = 12(.30) = 3.6$
    $\sigma = \sqrt{np(1-p)} = \sqrt{12(.30)(.70)} = 1.59$.

9. HYPERGEOMETRIC DISTRIBUTION

Mr. Heath is responsible for purchasing cases of wine for the Casa Blanca restaurant. Periodically, he selects a test case (12 bottles per case) to determine the adequacy of the sealing process.

For this test, he randomly selects and tests four bottles in the case. If a case contains two spoiled bottles of wine, find the probability that exactly one of them will appear in Mr. Heath's sample.

Solution

$$P(x = 1) = \frac{C_{n-x}^{N-r} C_x^r}{C_n^N} = \frac{\dfrac{10!}{3!7!} \dfrac{2!}{1!1!}}{\dfrac{12!}{4!8!}}$$

$$= \frac{\dfrac{(10)\ (9)\ (8)\ (7)\ (6)\ (5)\ (4)\ (3)\ (2)\ (1)\ (2)\ (1)}{(3)\ (2)\ (1)\ (7)\ (6)\ (5)\ (4)\ (3)\ (2)\ (1)\ (1)\ (1)}}{\dfrac{(12)\ (11)\ (10)\ (9)\ (8)\ (7)\ (6)\ (5)\ (4)\ (3)\ (2)\ (1)}{(4)\ (3)\ (2)\ (1)\ (8)\ (7)\ (6)\ (5)\ (4)\ (3)\ (2)\ (1)}} = \frac{240}{495} = .485$$

10. POISSON DISTRIBUTION

The Knoxville Economic Development Council has determined that the number of small businesses that declare bankruptcy per month has a Poisson distribution with a mean of 2.6. Find the probability of:

a. No bankruptcies occurring next month.

b. Three bankruptcies occurring next month.

c. Fewer than three bankruptcies occurring next month.

d. One or more bankruptcies occurring next month.

e. Two bankruptcies occurring within the next two months.

Solution:

a. $P(x = 0) = .0743$.

b. $P(x = 3) = .2176$.

c. $P(x < 3) = .5184$.

d. $P(x \geq 1) = 1 - P(x = 0) = 1 - .0743 = .9257$.

e. $\mu = 5.2$ for a two-month period.
$P(x = 2) = .0746$.

11. POISSON APPROXIMATION OF THE BINOMIAL DISTRIBUTION

The Citizen Company prides itself in meeting shipping deadlines. Jim Marshall, the president, boasts that out of every 100 orders, 98 are filled by the deadline. During a one-week period, 80 orders were processed. Assuming Marshall's claim is true, what is the probability that:

a. Exactly two orders weren't shipped on time?

b. Fewer than three orders weren't shipped on time?

c. Six or more orders weren't shipped on time?

Solution:

$$p = x/n = 2/100 = .02 \qquad np = 80(.02) = 1.6$$

a. $P(x = 2) = .2584$.

b. $P(x < 3) = .7833$.

c. $P(x \geq 6) = (1 - .9940) = .0060$.

EXERCISES

77. State whether the following random variables are discrete or continuous.

    a. Number of errors found in an audit of a company's financial records.

    b. Length of time a customer waits for service at a supermarket checkout counter.

    c. Number of cars recalled by General Motors next year.

    d. Actual number of ounces of beer in a 12-ounce can.

78. Which of the following situations should be modeled with the binomial distribution? Which should be modeled with the Poisson distribution?

    a. Telephone calls to a police department switchboard.

    b. Successive tosses of a coin weighted 70/30 in favor of heads.

    c. Items coming off a production line are classified as good or bad. The overall proportion of good items remains constant over time, and each successive item's quality is independent of the others'.

    d. Workers coming to a tool crib to check out an expensive tool.

    e. Orders lining up at a drill press for processing.

    f. Successive single births at a hospital, classified by gender.

    g. Each successive computer terminal entry made by an operator and classified as either correct or incorrect; the operator's accuracy is improving over time.

    h. Percent of parts produced on the night shift that are defective.

79. A major computer manufacturing company receives silicon chips in standard batches from a subcontractor. The plant manager has read an article on Intel's i486 processor in *Personal Computing* (July 1989, p. 25) and realizes that product quality is a primary ingredient of company success. He decides to examine recent batches of chips.

    Suppose there's an average of six defective chips per batch shipped by the subcontractor. What proportion of batches contains three or more defective chips?

80. A plan for reorganizing a corporation must be approved by 80% of the directors. If 15 directors are on the board, and if the probability that any of them will approve is .70, find the probability of the plan being approved by the board. Assume statistical independence.

81. The average number of customers per minute at a certain bank's window is 1. What is the probability that during a given minute three or fewer customers will appear?

82. A shoe store has room for three pairs of boots in a window display and has seven styles from which to choose. How many different arrangements are possible, assuming the order of the shoe arrangement doesn't matter?

83. An automatic machine produces washers, 4% of which are defective. If a sample of 50 washers is drawn at random from the machine's production what is the probability of observing at least one defective?

84. A traveling salesperson makes a sale to 30% of potential customers. What is the probability that he gets at least one sale in the next five customer contacts?

85. The two primary problems with a bottle-filling machine are overfilling and underfilling. If the machine overfills 3% of the time and underfills 3% of the time, find the probability that the next bottle will be filled properly.

86. The Vis-a-Vis firm hires two new employees from a total of eight applicants (five men and three women). Both new employees are men. Find the probability that if the new employees were chosen randomly, neither would be a woman.

87. For promotional consideration, Chet's Flower Shop provides fresh plants each day for Channel 3's "Noon Show." If six plants are on hand at the shop on a particular day, in how many ways can five be selected for delivery?

88. Dr. Moyer is considering investing a fixed sum of money in each of three business ventures. Assume that the probability distribution for the number of successful ventures out of the three is:

x	P(x)
0	.024
1	.178
2	.432
3	.366

Find the expected value of x. Find the probability that Dr. Moyer will enjoy:

a. At least two successful ventures.

b. No successful ventures.

c. Fewer than two successful ventures.

89. J. & H. Research was asked to conduct a market feasibility study ("Market Analysis for Harbor Marina," J & H Research, August 1987) of the proposed redevelopment of the Harbor View Marina for Metropolitan Mortgage. Analysis of the three options Metropolitan faces was complicated by each option's range of possible selling prices. J. & H. Research decided that an accurate analysis would involve converting the range of selling prices and other costs under each option to a single dollar amount. The following price probabilities for the first option were estimated by commercial property brokers who knew the marina and the competitive market area:

Price	Probability
$400,000	.4
500,000	.4
600,000	.2

Compute a single dollar amount for this option.

90. Pam Stanley, personnel director for Portland Kleenex, has 10 people going through a communication skills training program. The company president has selected four of them to meet with him as a committee to discuss their current training. Pam is certain that two of the trainees are unhappy about the program. Find the probability that:

a. No unhappy person will be on the committee.

b. One unhappy person will be on the committee.

91. Scott Ford has determined that a new car buyer will order factory-installed air condition-
ing about 30% of the time. Find the probability that:

    a. The next four buyers will all order factory air conditioning.

    b. None of the next three buyers will order factory air conditioning.

    c. Two out of the next four buyers will order factory air conditioning.

92. The Family Hospital emergency room is concerned about the increasing number of head
injuries it treats. Emergency room chief physician Judy Sample has just received her October 27, 1989, issue of the *Journal of the American Medical Association* and reads an article
on head injuries (p. 2251). She decides to study the problem of head injuries more closely.

    Judy determines that the emergency room can handle a maximum of five head injuries
per shift. She finds that the number of patients with head injuries averages 1.5 per shift.
Find the probability that more than five head injuries will arrive during a given shift.

93. The probability of Allyn and Allyn Publishers binding a book upside-down is .008. If a run
of 600 books is bound, what is the probability that at least one book will be bound upside-
down?

94. An average of three misprints appear per issue in the *Denver Review* newspaper. If it's assumed that the number of misprints is Poisson-distributed and there are 60 pages in the
average issue, find the probability that a randomly selected page has no misprints.

95. Anderson Manufacturing produces wallpaper. On the average, three rolls out of 1,000 have
serious defects. If a retail store orders 500 rolls of wallpaper, what is the probability that
two or more of them will have a serious defect?

96. The La Junta city council has five members. Two are local contractors. If two members are
selected at random to fill vacancies on the zoning committee, what is the probability that
both contractors will be selected?

EXTENDED EXERCISES

· ·

97. ACE CUSTOM RACING TIRES

The Ace Corporation, a manufacturer of custom racing tires, is evaluating the market for a new
line of tires. The proposed new tire will be test-marketed for one year only. If the tire is successful, it will be modified and incorporated into the company's regular line. For this reason, the
company is considering costs and profits for the next year only.

After carefully analyzing the market, Ace estimates the following profits, along with the probability of obtaining each. Although the company recognizes that many other actual profits are
possible, Ace considers these to be a good representation of the profit picture.

Profit	Probability
$ 5,000	.05
10,000	.20
20,000	.25
30,000	.25
40,000	.15
50,000	.10

Ace has determined that the fixed cost of producing the tire for a year is $20,000. Based on
these figures, it decides to go ahead and manufacture the new tire. Ace's reasoning is that the

expected value (expected profit) from the probability distribution is $25,750, whereas the cost of achieving this expected profit is only $20,000. This leaves an expected net profit of $5,750.

a. Are the figures in the company's analysis correct?

b. What factors other than those considered by the company are relevant to this decision?

98. ALPHA MACHINE COMPANY

The Alpha Machine Company is developing a new device to fill small cardboard boxes with carefully measured quantities of material. The most interested client is a large breakfast cereal company and acquiring this account would mean considerable new business for Alpha.

The cereal company's quality-control standards are high—a matter receiving great attention at Alpha. Specifically, almost all boxes filled with cereal must be within a rather tight tolerance in terms of fill weight. The cereal company wants assurances that these standards will be met before it signs a contract.

Alpha decides to determine what percentage of the boxes filled in a trial run will fall outside the specified weight interval. Alpha estimates around 10%, based on tests of the filling machine, but it needs more definitive data on which to base the sales effort. Since the acceptable fill interval is specified, Alpha knows that this situation can be modeled by the binomial distribution: each box's fill weight either falls within this interval or doesn't, and repeated testing of the machine reveals no pattern to defective fills. In other words, misfilled boxes seem to appear randomly, and the trial independence requirement of the binomial definition is met.

In a trial run of 500 boxes, eight boxes are found to fall outside the acceptable fill interval. This represents a defective percentage of 8/500 = .016. Alpha management now believes it can model the box-filling situation with the binomial distribution, where the probability of a defective unit is estimated to be .016.

Alpha's attention now turns to the basic unit of delivery used by the cereal company: a 250-box carton. Alpha decides that if it can show the cereal company the kind of quality performance the machine will provide on such cartons, Alpha might make a large sale. Alpha realizes that modeling this situation with the binomial distribution will require using the Poisson approximation to the binomial, because n is quite large ($n = 250$) and p is quite small ($p = .016$).

a. Is it a valid assumption that the binomial distribution is a good model for this situation?

b. Is the Poisson approximation appropriate here?

c. Construct a probability distribution for the number of defective boxes per 250-box carton. Does the quality level inherent in this distribution appear acceptable? Do you think the cereal company will be satisfied with the quality level reflected by this distribution?

99. INFRASTRUCTURE PROBLEMS

Suppose a major inner city problem in a large West coast city is an elevated roadway. Due to the heavy volume of truck traffic over this roadway, its bridge supports might fail. The city's Urban Commission considers restricting the number of trucks that may use the bridge during the day while it seeks funding for repairing the bridge. But local trucking firms exert pressure once this possibility becomes known. The commission wants to conduct an intense study of truck traffic but is uncertain about how to proceed.

Staff analysts suggest using the Poisson distribution to model truck traffic. They point out that trucks arrive randomly during the working day (a fact established in recent studies at the bridge) and that the Poisson distribution can provide probabilities of various numbers of truck arrivals. By looking at these probabilities, and by changing the mean arrival rate and examining other scenarios, the analysts think they can effectively model the situation and develop an approach that can counter local trucking firms' arguments. The current arrival rate of trucks is known to be four per minute.

a. Under the current conditions, what is the probability of more than three trucks arriving in any one minute?

b. Suppose the commission wants to reduce the probability of more than three trucks per minute to 20%. What would the mean arrival rate have to be reduced to in order to achieve this figure?

MICROCOMPUTER PACKAGE
. . . .

You can use the micro package *Computerized Business Statistics* to solve binomial and Poisson problems.

In Situation 5.4, Central Motors needed to find the probability that a 15-day period will include at least 10 profitable days. Management determined that the probability of a profitable day was .61.

Computer Solution:

From the main menu of *Computerized Business Statistics*, a 5 is selected, which indicates Probability Distributions. The probability distributions menu appears on the screen:

```
Probability Distributions—PROGRAM OPTIONS MENU
          OPTIONS                  ----FUNCTIONS----

 1. Binomial                  P(x ≥ a)    P(x = a)          P(a ≤ x ≤ b)
 2. Poisson                   P(x ≥ a)    P(x = a)          P(a ≤ x ≤ b)
 3. Hypergeometric            P(x ≥ a)    P(x = a)          P(a ≤ x ≤ b)
 4. Normal                    P(x ≥ a)    P(mean ≤ x ≤ a)   P(a ≤ x ≤ b)
 5. t                         P(x ≥ a)    P(mean ≤ x ≤ a)   P(a ≤ x ≤ b)
 6. F                         P(x ≥ a)
 7. Chi-Square                P(x ≥ a)
 8. Quick Reviews
 9. Return to Main Menu
10. Exit to Operating System
Use arrow keys to move hi-lite to desired selection and press ↵
```

Central wants to know the probability of at least 10 profitable days, $P(x \geq 10)$, so the $P(x \geq a)$ function for the binomial is chosen. Instructions appear on the screen and the appropriate values are entered:

```
Enter Number of Trials (2 - 30000) and press ↵          15
Enter Probability of an Occurrence (0-1) and press ↵    .61
Enter Number of Occurrences (0-15) and press ↵          10
```

Next, the screen shows the probability distribution for $n = 15$, $p = .61$. The correct answer for $P(x \geq 10)$ is .4346.

In Situation 5.6, Central Motors needed to determine the probability that five or fewer calls will arrive at the telephone switchboard within a five-minute period. Central's analyst used a Poisson probability distribution with a mean of 4.8.

Computer Solution:

From the main menu of *Computerized Business Statistics*, a 5 is again selected. The probability distribution menu is then shown on the screen.

Central wants to know the probability of five or fewer calls $P(0 \leq x \leq 5)$, so Poisson– $P(a \leq x \leq b)$ is chosen.

```
Enter Average Number of Occurrences    (.1 - 25) and press ↵  4.8
Enter Lower Limit                      (0 - 24) and press ↵   0
Enter Upper Limit                      (.1 - 24) and press ↵  5
```

The probability distribution for $\mu = 4.8$ is then shown on the screen. The correct answer for $P(0 \leq x \leq 5)$ is .6510.

MINITAB COMPUTER PACKAGE

Many common statistical distributions are available in MINITAB. All that's needed is an indication of the type of distribution (binomial or Poisson) and the value(s) of the parameter(s) that describe it (n and p for the binomial and μ for the Poisson). MINITAB also allows for the determination of both individual and cumulative probabilities. The **PDF** command calculates individual probabilities for discrete distributions. The **CDF** command calculates probabilities for the cumulative distribution function.

The MINITAB commands to solve Situation 5.4's Central Motors problem are shown next. First, find the probability that a 15-day period will include at least 10 profitable days if the probability of a profitable day is .61:

```
MTB > SET C1
DATA> 10:15
DATA> END
MTB > PDF C1;
SUBC> BINOMIAL 15 .61.
      K          P(X = K)
    10.00          0.1933
    11.00          0.1374
    12.00          0.0716
    13.00          0.0259
    14.00          0.0058
    15.00          0.0006
```

The **SET** command is used to indicate the required outcomes, 10 through 15.

The **PDF** command generates a probability density function. The **BINOMIAL** subcommand is used to generate the probability function for a binomial distribution with $n = 15$ and $p = .61$. This problem could also be solved using the commands:

```
MTB > SET C2
DATA> 5
DATA> END
MTB > CDF C2
SUBC> BINOMIAL 15 .39.
       K  P(X LESS OR = K)
     5.00            0.4346
```

Central Motors also wants to know the probability of five or fewer calls. The MINITAB commands are:

```
MTB > SET C3
DATA> 5
MTB > END
MTB > CDF C3;
SUBC> POISSON 4.8.
       K  P(X LESS OR = K)
     5.00             0.6510
MTB > STOP
```

Again the **SET** command is used to indicate the required outcome, 5.

The **CDF** command generates a cumulative probability density function. The **POISSON** subcommand is used to generate the probability function for a Poisson distribution with $\mu = 4.8$.

Chapter

6

CONTINUOUS PROBABILITY DISTRIBUTIONS

This weighty business will not brook delay.
Shakespeare,
Henry VI

Objectives

When you have completed this chapter, you will be able to:

Explain and apply the uniform distribution.

List the important properties of the normal probability distribution.

Determine the probability, using the standard normal distribution, that an observation will lie between two points or will be above or below some specified value.

Use the normal distribution as an approximation of the binomial.

The second section of *The Wall Street Journal*, April 20, 1992, reported on the average length of leisure trips taken by upscale Americans. These travelers were classified as either "adventure enthusiasts" or members of the "country club set."

Chapter 5 discussed discrete probability distributions, where random variables assume only specific designated values. In contrast, continuous probability distributions involve random variables that can assume any value within a specified range. These variables are called *continuous random variables*. This chapter examines two special continuous variables of particular importance to managers.

WHY MANAGERS NEED TO KNOW ABOUT CONTINUOUS PROBABILITY DISTRIBUTIONS

Many real-world observations can be modeled using the key distribution discussed in this chapter: the normal distribution. If the actual situation meets the conditions of this important model, valuable answers can be found without expensive, time-consuming observations. In addition, the normal distribution is the key to understanding the most important concept in statistics—the sampling distribution—the subject of Chapter 7.

In the just-mentioned article, the average length of leisure trips could be modeled by the most important distribution in statistics: the normal curve. If this theoretical distribution provided a good model, several important questions might be answered about the probabilities of the lengths of trips—valuable information to a leisure travel business.

CONTINUOUS RANDOM VARIABLES

Continuous Random Variable

Chapter 5 introduced the concept of a discrete random variable, one that can assume only certain predetermined values. A variable that can assume any value within some range is called a **continuous random variable**. Such a variable is measured on a numerical scale, that is, it constitutes either interval or ratio data.

> A **continuous random variable** is measured on a numerical scale. Each observation of the random variable can assume any value within some specified range.

There are numerous examples of continuous random variables, since most measurements made in business applications are of this type. The average number of miles per gallon of gas consumed by a car is one example. A small car might average between 25 and 30 miles per gallon, but its average mileage would be unlikely to *exactly* equal some specified value. A claimed mileage of 28 miles per gallon, for example, is commonly understood to mean *approximately* 28. In fact, it's almost impossible for this car to average *precisely* 28 miles per gallon, since that implies an average mileage of 28.0000 . . . , out to an infinite number of decimal places. Since there's only one value of interest, 28, out of an infinite number of possible values, the probability is equal to 1/∞, or approximately zero.

When dealing with a continuous random variable, the probability that the variable will fall within a specified range is sought, instead of the probability that the variable will assume a specific value. The following two questions illustrate the difference between discrete and continuous random variables:

1. What is the probability that the number of people arriving at the checkout counter in the next 30 seconds will be exactly two?
2. What is the probability that the lifetime of an electronic switch will be between four and six years?

The first question suggests the use of a discrete probability distribution. There can only be a discrete number of persons appearing at the checkout counter, such as zero, one, or two. In fact, if arrivals occur randomly and the average arrival rate is known, this answer can be computed using the Poisson distribution.

The second question suggests a continuous probability distribution. *Any* lifetime is possible within some reasonable range. A value between 4.385 and 4.587 years is possible, as is a value between 5 7/8 and 5 15/16 years. The probability that the observed lifetime will fall into a particular range is properly requested, since the probability of the lifetime precisely equaling some particular value is approximately zero.

THE UNIFORM DISTRIBUTION

Uniform Distribution

There are specific theoretical probability distributions for continuous random variables, just as there are for discrete random variables. The binomial and Poisson distributions, discussed in Chapter 5, are examples of the latter. The **uniform distribution** is sometimes appropriate when continuous random variables are being observed and where the outcome of an observation is equally likely to occur within any given segment of equal size in the specified range.

> The **uniform distribution** describes a random variable that is as likely to occur in one segment of a given size within a specified range as another.

Figure 6.1 shows a uniform distribution. The range within which the random variable can appear is specified by the values *a* and *b*. The probability "curve" is of uniform height at all points between *a* and *b*, which suggests equal probabilities of the random variable appearing within any segment of a given width in this range. Probability is equal to the area under the density curve. The area or probability of the rectangle equals 1.00, or 100%.

Figure 6.1   Uniform Distribution

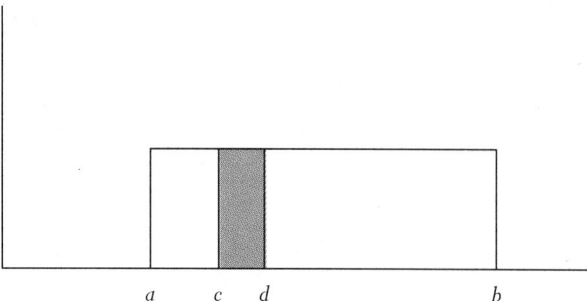

$$a \qquad c \quad d \qquad\qquad\qquad b$$

Furthermore, the probability of the variable falling between any two points c and d (see Figure 6.1) is equal to the percentage of the total range included between c and d.

$$P(c \leq x \leq d) = \frac{d - c}{b - a} \tag{6.1}$$

Note that since the probability of a value x being precisely equal to any specified value is approximately zero, the equality sign may or may not be included in the specification of a range. That is,

$$P(c < x < d) = P(c \leq x \leq d)$$

This applies to Equation 6.1 and to any other interval specification for a continuous variable.

Example 6.1   Ernie Longnecker, foreman at Trentwood Aluminum, knows that weights of cast aluminum blocks are uniformly distributed within a range of 350 to 450 pounds. If Ernie selects a block at random, what is the probability that it weighs between 375 and 380 pounds? Since the random variable, block weight, is known to be uniformly distributed, a particular block weight has the same probability of appearing in any segment of specified width in the range 350 to 450. To answer the question, Ernie needs to compute the percentage of the desired range relative to the total possible range (see Figure 6.2):

$$P(c \leq x \leq d) = \frac{d - c}{b - a} = \frac{380 - 375}{450 - 350} = \frac{5}{100} = .05$$

So, five percent of the blocks fall in the interval or Ernie can say there's a 5% chance that any randomly selected block will have a weight in this interval.

Example 6.2   Marilyn Horner knows that the years of company experience for Pacific Western Industries factory workers form a uniform distribution with a minimum of 0 and a maximum of 12.5 years. She wants to select an employee randomly and

FIGURE 6.2   Uniform Distribution

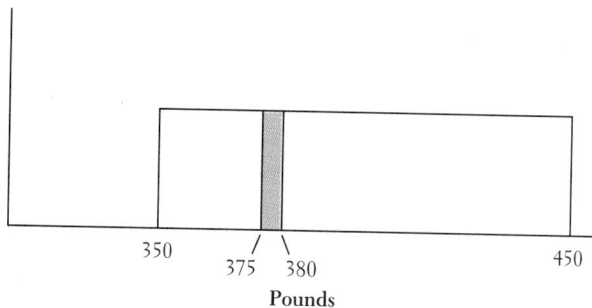

350   375   380   450

Pounds

determine the probability that this person has between 2.5 and 7.4 years of experience with the company. This question can be reworded: What percentage of the total range, 0 to 12.5, is the interval 2.5 to 7.4? The answer is

$$P(c \le x \le d) = \frac{d-c}{b-a} = \frac{7.4 - 2.5}{12.5 - 0} = \frac{4.9}{12.5} = .392$$

There's about a 39% chance that an employee's time with Pacific Western Industries falls in the range 2.5 to 7.4 years.

Mean and Standard Deviation of Uniform

The mean and standard deviation of a uniform distribution are sometimes of interest. The average value of a random variable that follows a uniform distribution falls halfway between the range extremes. In other words, the mean is simply the average of the range boundaries (Equation 6.2). Equation 6.3 measures the standard deviation of a uniform distribution.

$$\text{Mean of uniform distribution} = \frac{a+b}{2} \tag{6.2}$$

$$\text{Standard deviation of uniform distribution} = \sqrt{\frac{(b-a)^2}{12}} \tag{6.3}$$

where a = Lower limit of range
         b = Upper limit of range

EXAMPLE 6.3   Tamsen Stone, accountant for High-Performance Yard Care Tools Company, has determined that the ages of accounts receivable are uniformly distributed within a range of 4.7 weeks to 29.4 weeks. Tamsen needs to describe these account ages. The mean and standard deviation of these values provide easily understood summaries of the account age data. These values are calculated using Equations 6.2 and 6.3:

$$\text{Mean} = \frac{4.7 + 29.4}{2} = 17.05$$

$$\text{Standard deviation} = \sqrt{\frac{(29.4 - 4.7)^2}{12}} = 7.13$$

The distribution of account receivable ages has a mean of 17.05 weeks and a standard deviation of 7.13 weeks. Tamsen knows that the average account receivable is 17.05 weeks old and that the ages deviate from their mean by a standard amount of 7.13 weeks.

The MINITAB computer software package can be used to compute uniform probabilities. MINITAB commands for computing the probability for Example 6.2 are:

```
MTB> SET C1
DATA> 2.5
DATA> 7.4
DATA> END
MTB> CDF C1;
SUBC> UNIFORM  0  12.5.
      2.5              0.2000
      7.4              0.5920
MTB> STOP
```

The CDF command is used to compute the cumulative probability of a value less than or equal to x. In this case, the data values were set at $x = 2.5$ and $x = 7.4$. The UNIFORM subcommand is used to solve for the probability of an item falling below 2.5 (.2000) and the probability of an item falling below 7.4 (.5920). Therefore, the probability of an item falling between 2.5 and 7.4 is $(.5920 - .2000) = .3920$.

EXAMPLE 6.4   Joe Price, superintendent of the Justus Bag Company, wants to check the weight of grain bags filled by a machine that bags wheat. Joe knows that the correct weight for each bag is 125 pounds and that there's room for variability in this weight. A preliminary sample shows that bag weights are evenly distributed between 115 and 135 pounds. The range of tolerance for fill weight for shipping purposes has been determined as + or − five pounds. Mr. Price wants to know what percentage of the bags fall into this tolerance range.

Since he's observed that weights are equally distributed between 115 and 135 pounds, the uniform distribution can be used as a model. Joe needs to determine what percentage of the total range is constituted by the desired range using Equation 6.1:

$$P(c \le x \le d) = \frac{d - c}{b - a} = \frac{130 - 120}{135 - 115} = \frac{10}{20} = .50$$

Fifty percent of the bags will fall within five pounds of the desired weight of 125 pounds. Joe can now decide whether this is an acceptable quality level.

The mean and standard deviation of bag weight might also be relevant to Joe's decision. Using Equations 6.2 and 6.3, these summary values are

$$\text{Mean} = \frac{115 + 135}{2} = 125 \text{ pounds}$$

$$\text{Standard deviation} = \sqrt{\frac{(135 - 115)^2}{12}} = 5.77 \text{ pounds}$$

This is an example of a quality-control concern, a subject discussed at length in Chapter 13.

EXERCISES

1. Explain the difference between the uniform distribution and the Poisson distribution.

2. If you were to graph a uniform distribution, what would it look like?

3. What continuous random variables are of interest to a credit union studying daily customer transactions?

4. Which of the following random variables can be classified as continuous?

   a. The number of people arriving at a toll gate.

   b. The number of ounces in a bottle of milk.

   c. Tomorrow's temperature.

   d. The number of sales a real estate agent made this month.

   e. The weight of a steak bought at the supermarket.

   f. The number of offers received on a car for sale.

   g. Number of errors found in a company's accounts receivable records.

   h. Length of time a patient waits for a doctor.

   i. How long it took you to travel to school today.

5. Which of the variables listed in the company data base in Appendix C are continuous variables?

6. A West Coast commuter airline's manager of air operations has just read an article in *The Wall Street Journal* (November 6, 1989) indicating that air service between the United States and Japan is to be greatly expanded. She's concerned about flight time between San Diego and Los Angeles, as that route is a key link to the Orient flights. Flight time between Los Angeles and San Diego is known to be uniformly distributed between 80 and 100 minutes.

   a. What is the average flight time between the two cities?

   b. What is the standard variation in flight time between the two cities?

   c. What percentage of flights can be expected to take between 85 and 95 minutes?

   d. Find the probability that a flight will take more than 96 minutes.

   e. Determine the probability that a flight will take less than 80 minutes.

7. General Equipment Manufacturing believes that one of its rolling machines is producing aluminum sheets of varying thickness. The machine typically produces sheets between 75 and 150 millimeters thick. It is known that this random variable is uniformly distributed. Sheets less than 100 millimeters thick are unacceptable to buyers and must be scrapped.

   a. Find the average thickness of the aluminum sheets produced by this machine.

   b. What is the standard variation in thickness of the aluminum sheets produced by this machine?

   c. Find the probability that a sheet produced by this machine will have to be scrapped.

8. In a brick laying class the times students take to construct a standard two-by-three–foot test wall fall on a uniform distribution with a mean of 200 seconds. The difference between the longest and shortest time observed is 100 seconds. Find the probability that a student will take between 160 and 190 seconds to construct the wall.

9. A traffic light is set to switch from red to green according to a uniform distribution with a mean of 45 seconds. The difference between the smallest and largest number of seconds it takes the light to switch is eight seconds.

   a. Compute the standard deviation of this distribution.

   b. Find the probability that the light will take at least 43 seconds to switch.

   c. What is the probability that the light will take less than 43 seconds to switch?

NORMAL DISTRIBUTION

In the 18th century, astronomers observed that repeated measurements of the same value (such as the mass of an object) tended to vary. When a large number of such observations were recorded, organized into a frequency distribution, and plotted on a graph, the recurring result was the shape in Figure 6.3. It was subsequently discovered that this distribution could be closely approximated with a continuous distribution sometimes referred to as the *normal distribution*. This distribution is also referred to as the *bell-shaped curve* or the *Gaussian curve*.

FIGURE 6.3   Normal Distribution

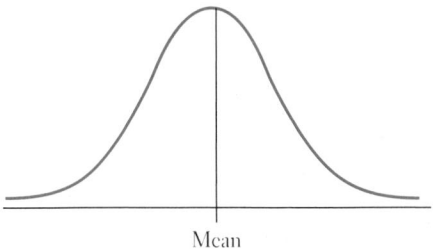

Mean

There are three reasons why the normal distribution is the most important theoretical distribution in business statistics:

1. The normal distribution approximates the observed frequency distributions of many natural and physical measurements, such as IQs, weights, heights, sales, product lifetimes, and variability of human and machine outputs.

2. The normal distribution can often be used to estimate binomial probabilities when *n* is greater than 20.

3. The normal distribution is a good approximation of distributions of both sample means and sample proportions of large samples ($n \geq 30$). Chapter 7 examines this concept in depth.

Normal Distribution

Many variables in nature and business have numerical observations that tend to cluster around their mean. In other words, it's more likely that an observation will be close to the mean of the data collection than far away. When this condition holds, the **normal distribution** will provide a good model of the data collection.

The **normal distribution** is a continuous distribution that has a bell shape and is determined by its mean and standard deviation.

Figure 6.3 shows the shape of a typical normal curve. Note that the curve is symmetrical: half the area of the curve lies above the mean and half below it, and these halves are mirror images. Also note that away from the mean toward either of the tails, the height of the curve decreases. This corresponds to a decreasing probability of finding a value the further we move from the mean.

The theoretical normal distribution approaches infinity at the positive and negative ends of the curve. In practice this aspect is ignored since the probability of an observation occurring is very small as the distance from the mean increases. A discussion of the mathematical equation for the normal curve is beyond the scope of this text, but the formula is presented here to show its dependence on two key parameters: the mean and standard deviation of the distribution. The so-called probability density function for the normal distribution is

$$f(x) = \frac{1}{\sigma\sqrt{2\pi}}e^{-(1/2)\,[(x-\mu)/\sigma]^2} \tag{6.4}$$

where
x = Any value of the continuous random variable
μ = Mean of the normal random variable
σ = Standard deviation of the normal random variable
e = 2.71828 . . . (natural log base)
π = 3.1416 . . . (used to find the circumference of a circle)

Note that there are two unspecified values in the equation: the mean of the distribution (μ) and the standard deviation (σ). Both e and π are constants with known values. If the mean and standard deviation are known, then a specific normal curve has been identified, and probabilities can be found.

Figure 6.4 shows three normal curves, each with a different mean. However, the three distributions have the same standard deviation. This can be seen by the identical shape or dispersion of each curve.

Figure 6.5 shows three normal curves, all with the same mean. However, the extent of their variability is different. Curve A has a larger standard deviation than curve B, and curve C has the smallest standard deviation of all.

Figures 6.4 and 6.5 show that both the mean and the standard deviation must be known before a specific normal curve can be identified out of the infinite number of curves available.

FIGURE 6.4 Normal Curves with Different Means but the Same Standard Deviation

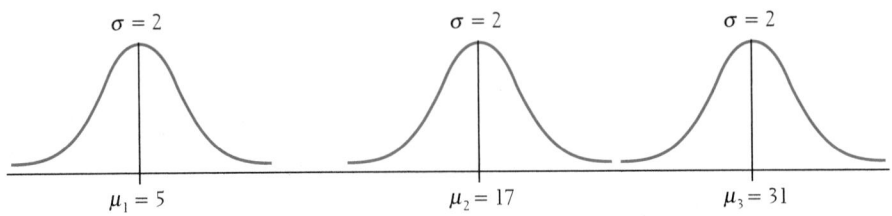

FIGURE 6.5 Normal Curves with the Same Mean but Different Standard Deviations

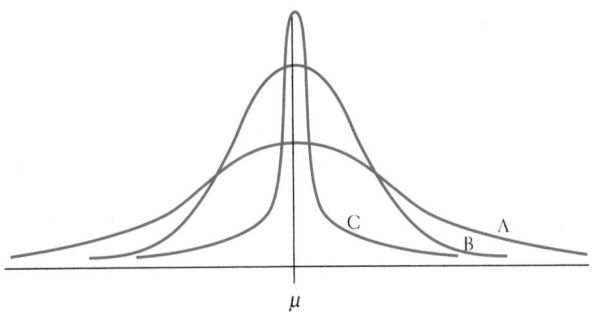

Characteristics of the normal distribution

1. The normal distribution has a bell shape and is symmetrical about its mean.
2. Knowledge of the mean and standard deviation is necessary to identify a specific normal distribution.
3. Each combination of mean and standard deviation specifies a unique normal distribution.
4. The normal distribution extends indefinitely in either direction from the mean.
5. The normal distribution is measured on a continuous scale, and the probability of obtaining a precise value is approximately zero.
6. The total area under the curve is equal to 1.0, or 100%. Fifty percent of the area is above the mean, and 50% is below the mean.
7. The probability that a random variable will have a value between any two points is equal to the area under the curve between those points. This area can be determined using either calculus or the standard normal table in Appendix E.6.

EXERCISES

10. Explain the difference between the uniform distribution and the normal distribution.

11. Explain the difference between the binomial distribution and the normal distribution.

12. If you were to graph a normal distribution, what would it look like?

13. Which of the following are characteristics of the normal distribution?

   a. The normal distribution is skewed.

   b. Knowledge of the median and standard deviation is necessary to construct a specific normal distribution.

   c. Each combination of mean and standard deviation defines a unique normal distribution.

   d. The normal distribution extends indefinitely in either direction from the mean.

   e. The normal distribution is measured on a discrete scale.

   f. The total area under the curve is equal to 1.0 or 100%.

   g. The probability that a random variable will have a value between any two points is equal to the area under the curve between those points.

14. Why is the normal distribution the most important theoretical distribution in business statistics?

FINDING NORMAL CURVE AREAS

To find normal curve areas, we must use integral calculus along with Equation 6.4, and the computations are complex. For this reason, it would be convenient if a table for normal curve areas were available, as they are for the binomial and Poisson distributions. Unfortunately, more than one table would be necessary. Figures 6.4 and 6.5 show that the normal distribution is actually an infinitely large family of distributions, one for each possible combination of mean and standard deviation. The number of normal distributions is therefore unlimited, and providing a table of probabilities for each combination of mean and standard deviation wouldn't be practical.

Fortunately, the problem of dealing with an infinite family of normal distributions can be solved by transforming all normal distributions to the **standard normal distribution,** which has a mean of 0 and a standard deviation of 1.

Standard Normal Distribution

> The **standard normal distribution** has a mean of 0 and a standard deviation of 1.

z Value

Any normal distribution can be converted to the standard normal distribution by standardizing each of its observations in terms of **z values.** The z value measures the distance in standard deviations between the mean of the normal curve and the x value of interest.

The **z value** is a measure of the number of standard deviations between the mean or center of a normal curve and the value of interest.

Equation 6.5 shows how the observations from any normal distribution can be standardized by forming a standard normal distribution of z values:

$$z = \frac{x - \mu}{\sigma} \tag{6.5}$$

where z = Number of standard deviations from mean
   x = Value of interest
   μ = Mean of distribution
   σ = Standard deviation of distribution

Examples 6.5 and 6.6 illustrate applications of Equation 6.5.

Normal Curve Areas   EXAMPLE 6.5   A normal curve has a mean of 500 and standard deviation of 25. An analyst wants to find the normal curve areas both above and below the value 535.
   What is the correct z value for 535? From Equation 6.5, the z value is

$$z = \frac{x - \mu}{\sigma} = \frac{535 - 500}{25} = 1.40$$

Figure 6.6 shows both the actual scale of this normal distribution and the standardized scale for the standard normal distribution. Note that the standard normal distribution is created by converting the actual values to z values.

FIGURE 6.6   Normal Curve for Example 6.5

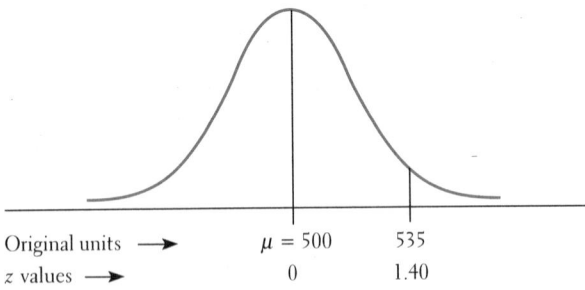

Original units ⟶ $\mu = 500$ 535
z values ⟶   0   1.40

EXAMPLE 6.6   Coffee prices recently tumbled to a 14-year low of 76.5 cents a pound, according to *The Wall Street Journal* (October 4, 1989). Suppose a small importer in Florida watches these prices closely, as they're directly related to profits.
   The importer averages 2,700 pounds per month with a standard deviation of 130 pounds. What is the z value for 2,200 pounds on this distribution?

$$z = \frac{2200 - 2700}{130} = -3.85$$

After the z value is calculated for the standard normal distribution, the next step is to use the standard normal table to look up the corresponding area under the curve. The standard normal table (Appendix E.6) is designed to be read in units of z, the number of standard deviations from the mean. The table shows the area under the curve between the mean and selected values of z. Remember that this table specifies the area between the *center* of the curve and the point specified by the z value.

Since the normal distribution is symmetrical about its mean, the left half of the curve is a mirror image of the right half. Because of this symmetry, the standard normal table provides only the right half (i.e., positive z values) of the distribution. If the z value of interest is negative, the minus sign is ignored, and the area is obtained in the same manner as if the z value were positive. For example, the area under the curve between the mean and $+2$ standard deviations is exactly equal to the area under the curve between the mean and -2 standard deviations.

Examples 6.7 through 6.14 illustrate applications of the standard normal table.

EXAMPLE 6.7   A normal distribution has a mean of 5 and standard deviation of 2.1. What is the probability that a numerical value randomly drawn from this distribution will lie between 5 and 6? In this example, the question is phrased properly because the normal distribution represents a continuous random variable, and probabilities must be stated for a range, not a specific value. Figure 6.7 shows the desired area. Using Equation 6.5, the z value is: $z = (6 - 5)/2.1 = 0.48$.

FIGURE 6.7   Normal Curve Area for Example 6.6

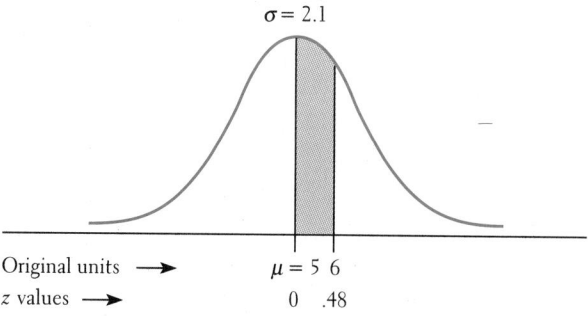

Original units $\longrightarrow$ $\mu = 5$ 6
z values $\longrightarrow$ 0   .48

Since the area desired extends from the mean of the curve (5) to a point of interest, $x(6)$, the desired area can be read directly from the standard normal table using the calculated z value. Note the graph at the top of the table in Appendix E.6, which suggests that the areas under the curve are measured from the center of the curve to the point of interest.

The left column of the standard normal table lists the z value with only one digit on each side of the decimal point. Since the z value for this example is 0.48, the 0.4 row is used. The values across the top of the table give the second digit to the right of the decimal point. Since this digit is 8 in this example, the .08 column is used. At the intersection of the 0.4 row and the .08 column of the table is the value .1844. This is the percentage of the total area under the curve found between the center of the distribution and a point 0.48 standard deviations away. There's about an 18% chance of drawing a value from this normal distribution that lies between 5 and 6.

Now the reason for the empirical rule in Chapter 4 can be explained. Using the standard normal table, we can find the percentages of items on a standard normal distribution that will fall within 1, 2, and 3 standard deviations of the mean. Example 6.8 calculates these values.

EXAMPLE 6.8   What percentage of the values on a normal curve can be expected to fall within 1, 2, and 3 standard deviations of the mean? The standard normal table is entered with $z = 1$, $z = 2$, and $z = 3$, and the areas are determined using the process explained in Example 6.7. These areas are then doubled to account for values both above and below the mean:

$$z = 1: \quad (.3413)(2) = .6826$$
$$z = 2: \quad (.4772)(2) = .9544$$
$$z = 3: \quad (.4987)(2) = .9974$$

These values establish the empirical rule presented in Chapter 4: about 68% of the values are within one standard deviation of the mean, about 95.5% are within two standard deviations, and over 99.7% are within three standard deviations. Figure 6.8 shows these areas.

FIGURE 6.8   Normal Curve Areas for Example 6.7

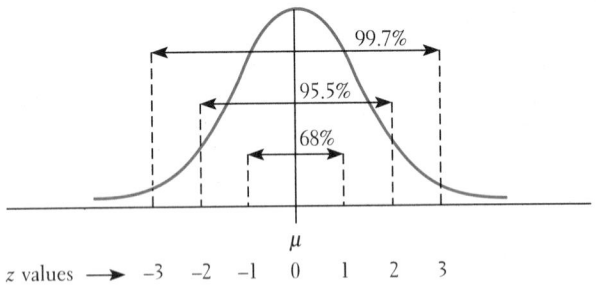

EXAMPLE 6.9   Fund managers noted that mutual fund sales nationally rose 4.2 billion in August 1989 to the highest value in two years (*The Wall Street Journal*, October 2, 1989). A study showed that the number of mutual fund shares traded on a local exchange was normally distributed with a mean of 250 and standard deviation of 12. Fund analyst Sherry Showalter needs to determine the probability that a share value

randomly selected from this distribution will fall between 225 and 250. The z value is $(225 - 250)/12 = -2.08$.

The negative sign of the z value indicates that the x value of interest (225) is less than the mean of the distribution (250); the negative sign is ignored when the z value is looked up in the standard normal table. As in Example 6.8, since this area is measured from the mean of the curve to some point, the desired area or probability can be read directly from the table. The 2.0 row of the table is used along with the .08 column, and the desired area is read from the table as .4812. Thus, there's about a 48% chance that a randomly selected item from this distribution will fall in the interval 225 to 250.

Examples 6.8 and 6.9 both involved areas measured from the mean or center of the normal curve to a point of interest. As a result, the normal curve area could be read directly from the table. Three other kinds of normal curve areas might also be of interest:

1. An area that lies at one end of the curve (see Example 6.10).
2. An area that spans the curve mean; that is, some of the area is above the mean, and some is below (see Example 6.11).
3. An area that is either above the mean or below it but does not include the mean (see Example 6.12).

EXAMPLE 6.10   A normal distribution has a mean of 4.9 and standard deviation of 1.2. What percentage of the area under this curve lies above 6? This question can be rephrased: What is the probability that an item randomly selected from this distribution will have a value above 6? Figure 6.9 shows the desired area.

FIGURE 6.9   Normal Curve Area for Example 6.10

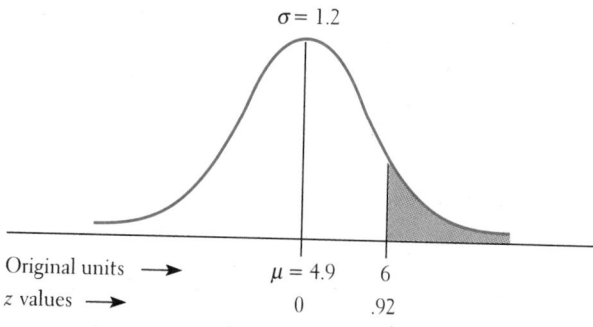

To solve this problem, we must first find the area from the mean of the curve (4.9) to the x value of interest (6). This area is found by calculating the z value and referring to the standard normal table. The z value is $(6 - 4.9)/1.2 = 0.92$.

The area from the standard normal table corresponding to a z value of 0.92 is .3212 (found at the intersection of the 0.9 row and the .02 column). To find the desired area, remember that exactly 50% of a normal curve lies above the mean and 50% lies below it. If half the normal curve area lies above the mean of 4.9, and if the area .3212 lies between 4.9 and 6, then the remaining portion of the half must lie above 6. Therefore, the desired area is .5000 − .3212 = .1788. There's about an 18% chance that a randomly selected item will have a value greater than 6 since about 18% of the curve area lies above this value.

EXAMPLE 6.11   What is the probability that an item drawn from an inventory of television tubes will have a shelf life between 2 and 10 weeks? The ages are known to follow a normal distribution with a mean of 5 weeks and standard deviation of 4 weeks. Figure 6.10 shows the desired area.

   This problem actually involves two normal curve areas, each measured from the center of the curve, that must be determined separately. The two areas are added together to find the desired value. The two z values and their areas are

$$z = (2 - 5)/4 = -0.75 \rightarrow .2734 \quad \text{(area between 2 and 5)}$$
$$z = (10 - 5)/4 = 1.25 \rightarrow \underline{.3944} \quad \text{(area between 5 and 10)}$$
$$\text{Sum} = .6678 \quad \text{(area between 2 and 10)}$$

There's about a 67% chance that a randomly selected television tube will have a lifetime between 2 and 10 weeks.

FIGURE 6.10   Normal Curve Area for Example 6.11

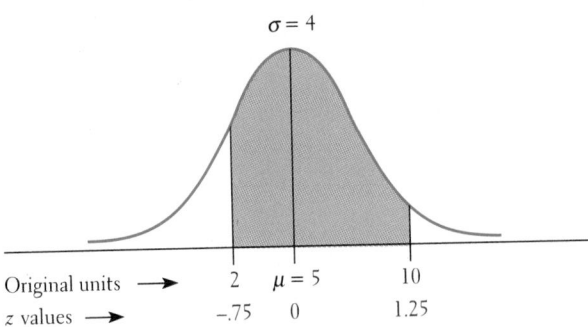

EXAMPLE 6.12   Years of company experience of a pool of first-line supervisors at Future Business Products, Inc., are known to follow a normal distribution with a mean of 7.8 years and standard deviation of 1.5 years. This information came to light when the company president investigated the firm's retention problem after reading an article (*Inc.* magazine, May 1989, p. 132) about the advantages of bonus and incentive systems for employees. Find the probability that a randomly selected supervisor has between 8 and 10 years of experience. Figure 6.11 shows the area to be determined.

   To solve this problem, first find the area between the mean of the curve, 7.8, and 10, the upper value of interest. The area between 7.8 and 8 will then be subtracted

FIGURE 6.11   Normal Curve Area for Example 6.12

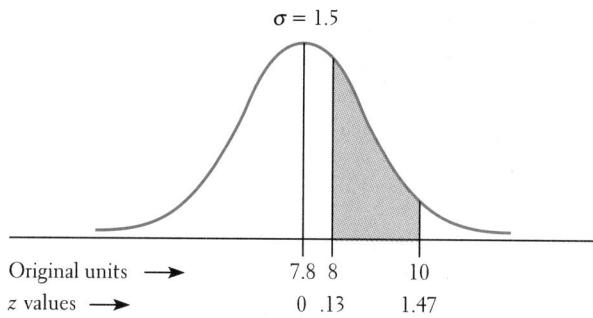

from it. The result is the area lying between 8 and 10. The two z values and their areas from the standard normal table are

$$z = (10 - 7.8)/1.5 = 1.47 \rightarrow .4292 \quad \text{(area between 7.8 and 10)}$$
$$z = (8 - 7.8)/1.5 = 0.13 \rightarrow \underline{.0517} \quad \text{(area between 7.8 and 8)}$$
$$\text{Difference} = .3775 \quad \text{(area between 8 and 10)}$$

There's about a 38% chance that a selected supervisor will have between 8 and 10 years of experience with Future Business Products, Inc.

Sometimes an analyst knows the area under the curve and must find an actual value or a z value. Example 6.13 illustrates this situation.

EXAMPLE 6.13   Alpine Tire Company has determined from road tests that the mean mileage of its main product is 50,000 miles with a standard deviation of 5,000 miles, and that the collected data are normally distributed. Alpine wishes to offer a warranty providing free replacement for any new tire that fails before the guaranteed mileage. If Alpine wishes to replace no more than 10% of the tires, what should the guaranteed mileage be?

Figure 6.12 shades the area of interest. To solve this problem, reverse the procedure for using the standard normal table. That is, instead of looking up the area for a par-

FIGURE 6.12   Normal Curve Area for Example 6.13

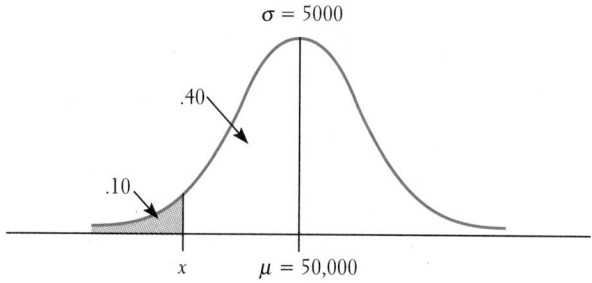

ticular *z* value, the analyst looks for the *z* value that coincides with the area of interest under the curve. This area equals 10%, but to find the appropriate *z* value in the table, the analyst must subtract 10% from 50% (see Figure 6.12). The area closest to .4000 is .3997, which is found at the intersection of the 1.2 row and the .08 column. The *z* value is thus −1.28 (the negative sign indicates that the *z* value is below the mean). To find the appropriate mileage for the guarantee, a *z* value of −1.28 is substituted into Equation 6.5:

$$z = \frac{x - \mu}{\sigma}$$

$$-1.28 = \frac{x - 50{,}000}{5{,}000}$$

$$x - 50{,}000 = -1.28(5{,}000)$$
$$x - 50{,}000 = -6{,}400$$
$$x = 43{,}600$$

Alpine should set its guarantee at about 43,600 miles since only 10% of failures will occur before that mileage has been reached.

As implied by the preceding example, Equation 6.5 can be manipulated so that *x* can be solved for directly: $x = \mu + z\sigma$.

EXAMPLE 6.14   A study reported in *Educational and Psychological Measurement*[1] used the Stanford-Binet Fourth Edition to measure a Composite Standard Age Score (CAS) for a sample of 5,013 subjects. Each of the four content areas had a mean SAS of 100 and a standard deviation of 16. If a person scores higher than 92% of the people who took the exam on the Quantitative Reasoning content area, what score did this person get if the scores are assumed to be normally distributed? With 92% of the scores below this *x* value, 42% of the scores must lie between the mean of 100 and *x* (see Figure 6.13). In the standard normal table, an area of .4207 is closest to the de-

FIGURE 6.13   Normal Curve Area for Example 6.14

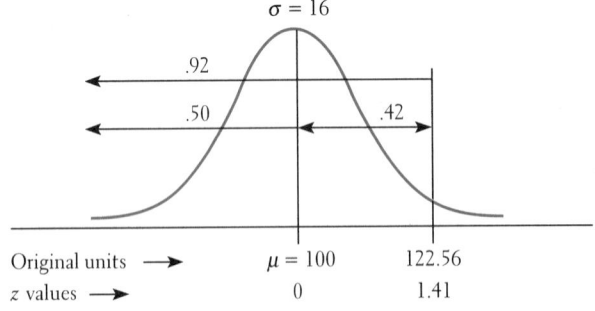

[1]V. E. Glaub and R. W. Kamphaus, "Construction of a nonverbal adaptation of the Stanford-Binet Fourth Edition," *Educational and Psychological Measurement*, Vol. 51, pp. 231–41.

sired value of .42. The z value for this area is 1.41, so x is 1.41 standard deviations above the mean:

$$x = \mu + z\sigma$$
$$x = 100 + (1.41)(16) = 122.56$$

Ninety-two percent of the people scored below 122.56 on Quantitative Reasoning.

The MINITAB computer software package can be used to compute normal curve probabilities. The MINITAB commands for computing the normal probability for Example 6.9 are:

```
MTB> SET C1
DATA> 225
DATA> 250
DATA> END
MTB> CDF C1;
SUBC> NORMAL 250 12.
  225    0.0186
  250    0.5000
MTB> STOP
```

The CDF command is used to compute the cumulative probability of a value less than or equal to x. In this case, the data values were set at $x = 225$ and $x = 250$. The NORMAL subcommand is used to solve for the probability of an item falling below 225 (.0186) and the probability of an item falling below 250 (.5000). Therefore, the probability of an item falling between 225 and 250 is $(.5000 - .0186) = .4814$.

Example 6.8 provided areas for the empirical rule, which applies only if the distribution in question follows a normal curve or can be closely approximated with one. For distributions that don't follow a normal curve, areas can be estimated through the use of **Chebyshev's theorem,** which was briefly mentioned in Chapter 4. This theorem states that regardless of how the data values are distributed, at least a certain percentage will lie within a specified range around the mean.

Chebyshev's Theorem

Chebyshev's theorem

Regardless of how the data values are distributed, at least $(1 - 1/k^2)$ of the values will lie within k standard deviations of the mean (for $k \geq 1$).

EXAMPLE 6.15   The distribution of ages in a factory do not follow a normal distribution but have a mean of 44.8 with a standard deviation of 9.7. Using Chebyshev's theorem, a lower bound for the percentage of ages within two standard deviations of the mean can be calculated:

$$(1 - 1/k^2) = 1 - 1/2^2 = 1 - 1/4 = .75$$

Thus, at least 75% of the ages in the factory are within two standard deviations of the mean. In other words, the ages of at least 75% of the employees range from $44.8 - (2)(9.7)$ to $44.8 + (2)(9.7)$, or from 25.4 to 64.2 years.

EXERCISES

15. In using the standard normal table to look up a z value, what point is used consistently as the reference point?

16. Why doesn't the standard normal table contain areas above .5000?

17. Why are x values converted to z values?

18. Draw a normal curve and shade the area under the curve for each of the following:

    a. The area between the mean and $z = 0.75$.

    b. The area between the mean and $z = -1.75$.

    c. The area between $z = -1.25$ and $z = 0.25$.

    d. The area between $z = 0.30$ and $z = 2.00$.

    e. The area above $z = 1.00$.

    f. The area below $z = -3.00$.

19. Find the probability of an item falling into each of the shaded intervals drawn in Exercise 18.

20. Find the z value that corresponds to each of the areas described:

    a. Seventy percent of the items lie above this z value.

    b. Twenty percent of the items lie below this z value.

    c. Ten percent of the items lie above this z value.

    d. Sixty percent of the items lie above this z value.

21. Home loan applications are normally distributed with mean of $100,000 and standard deviation of $25,000 at the Rainier State Bank. Bank policy requires that applications involving loan amounts in the lowest 5% be submitted to a vice president in charge of authorizing low-income housing loans. What size home loan requests are submitted to this vice president?

22. Street lights in the residential areas served by Utah Power & Electric are constructed to have a mean lifetime of 500 days with standard deviation of 50 days. If it can be assumed that street light lifetimes are normally distributed, what percentage of the lamps:

    a. Last longer than two years?

    b. Last between 400 and 625 days?

    c. Last longer than 600 days?

    d. Last between 350 and 450 days?

23. Fuel consumption of a fleet of 1,000 trucks is normally distributed with a mean of 12 miles per gallon and standard deviation of 2 miles per gallon.

    a. How many trucks will average 11 miles or more per gallon?

    b. How many trucks will average less than 10 miles per gallon?

    c. How many trucks will average between 9.5 and 14 miles per gallon?

    d. How many trucks will average between 9 and 11 miles per gallon?

    e. Find the probability that a truck selected at random will average over 13.5 miles per gallon.

    f. Seventy percent of the trucks average more than what mileage?

    g. Ten percent of the trucks average less than what mileage?

24. Horace Gainey, analyst for Splice Soft Drink Corporation, is setting the fill level for the company's new soft drink dispensers. If the ounces of fill are normally distributed with a mean of μ and standard deviation of 0.2 ounces, what should Horace set μ at so that eight-ounce cups will overflow only one time in a thousand?

25. Brooks Publishing Company has discovered that the number of words contained in new manuscripts in excess of the number specified in the author's contract is normally distributed with a mean of 40,000 words and standard deviation of 10,000 words. If Brooks wants to be 90% certain that a new manuscript will be less than 250,000 words, how many words should be specified in the author's contract?

26. Workers' hourly wage at a state correctional institution is normally distributed with a mean of $9.10 and a standard deviation of $0.90.

   a. Determine the probability that a worker's hourly wage exceeds $10.00.

   b. Find the probability that a worker's hourly rate is between $7.70 and $11.50.

   c. What proportion of the workers earn less than $8.50?

   d. Half the workers earn more than what amount?

Normal Approximation to the Binomial

Chapter 5 presented the binomial distribution and various methods of solving binomial problems. As Figure 5.8 shows, if the number of trials (*n*) is 20 or less, the correct binomial probabilities can be found in the binomial tables of Appendix E.2. If *n* is greater than 20 and the probability of success, *p*, is either very small or very large, the Poisson distribution can provide a good approximation using the method discussed in Chapter 5.

Suppose a binomial problem involves an *n* value larger than 20 (so that the binomial tables cannot be used) and a proportion that's neither very small nor very large. In such a case, the Poisson approximation isn't appropriate, and another method of solving the problem must be found.

As suggested by Figure 5.8, the normal curve provides a good approximation to the binomial distribution under these conditions. The approximation is made that the discrete binomial distribution follows the continuous normal distribution. This approximation introduces an error into the probability calculations, but this error has been found to be quite small.

When the normal approximation is used, the mean and standard deviation of the binomial distribution must be found so that they can be used to compute normal curve probabilities.

Normal Approximation to the Binomial

> The normal distribution provides a close approximation to the binomial distribution when *n* is large and *p* is close to .5. As a rule of thumb, this approximation is appropriate when $np > 5$ and $n(1 - p) > 5$.

Both the Poisson and binomial distributions are discrete, whereas the normal curve is continuous. Since discrete variables involve only specified values, intervals will have to be assigned to the continuous normal distribution to represent binomial values. For example, continuous values in the range 4.5 to 5.5 correspond to the discrete value 5. This addition and subtraction of .5 to the x value is commonly referred to as the **continuity correction factor.**

To find the binomial probability of exactly 5 successes, the normal curve approximation is used based on the probability (i.e., the area under the normal curve) between 4.5 and 5.5. If the desired binomial probability is for 15 or more successes, the normal curve area from 14.5 to ∞ is found. If the binomial probability of interest involves 4 or fewer successes, the appropriate normal curve area is from 4.5 to $-\infty$.

Since the number of trials, or sample size, is usually large in practical situations where the normal distribution is used to approximate the binomial, the continuity correction factor typically has a negligible effect. However, this correction is made in the examples and exercises that follow.

Figure 6.14 shows how the normal curve can be used to give binomial probability approximations. The bars represent binomial probabilities for the distribution of x successes in 100 trials where the probability of success is .5. The normal curve superimposed over the binomial histogram has a mean and standard deviation equal to (from Equations 5.5 and 5.6):

$$\mu = np = (100)(.50) = 50$$
$$\sigma = \sqrt{np(1 - p)} = \sqrt{(100)(.50)(.50)} = 5$$

Figure 6.14 shows that the area in any set of bars (the binomial probability) approximately equals the corresponding area under the curve (the normal probability).

FIGURE 6.14   Normal Approximation to the Binomial

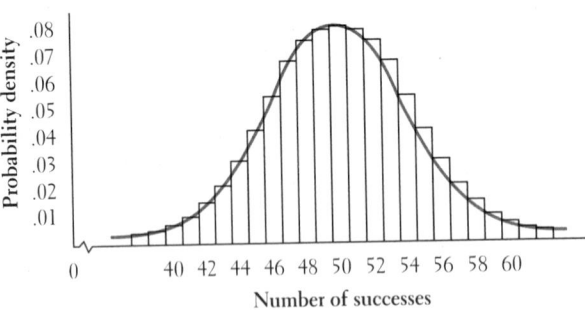

Figure 6.15 also shows how the binomial distribution can be approximated by the normal distribution. In Figure 6.15 three binomial probability distributions have been plotted for $p = .5$: $n = 5$, $n = 10$, and $n = 20$. Normal distributions with means of np and standard deviations of $\sqrt{np(1 - p)}$ have been superimposed on the binomial

FIGURE 6.15   Normal Approximation to the Binomial

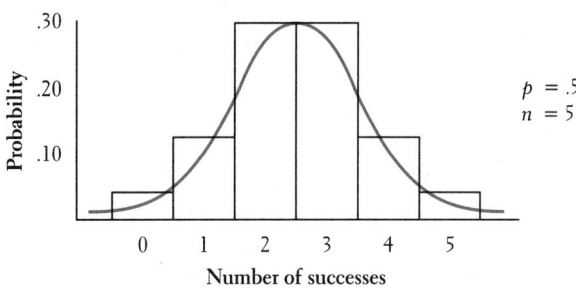

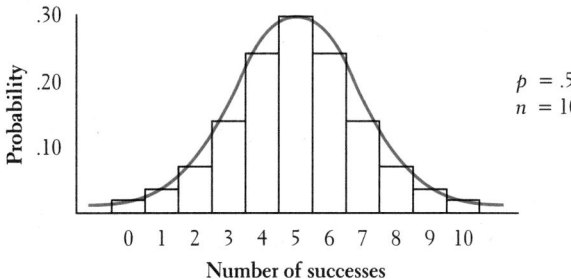

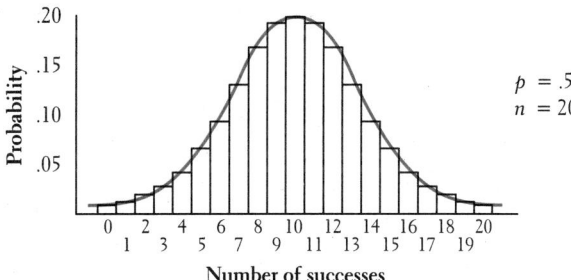

distributions. Figure 6.15 indicates that as *n* increases, the normal distribution more closely approximates the binomial distribution.

EXAMPLE 6.16   The librarian of the John Kennedy Library, Don Lake, randomly selects 100 books from the shelves and inspects their physical condition. In his last inspection, 40% of the books were in unsatisfactory condition. Assuming this percentage still holds, what is the probability that Don will find at least 50% of the sampled books unsatisfactory?

This is a binomial situation, since a book is either in good condition or not and since independence between selections is ensured due to random sampling. The binomial problem can be stated

$$n = 100 \qquad p = .40 \qquad P(x \geq 50) = ?$$

The normal curve can provide an approximation to the correct binomial answer, since n is too large for the binomial tables and the proportion (.40) precludes use of the Poisson approximation ($np = 40$). The mean and standard deviation of the binomial situation are found first:

$$\mu = np = (100)(.40) = 40$$
$$\sigma = \sqrt{np(1 - p)} = \sqrt{(100)(.40)(.60)} = 4.9$$

Figure 6.16 shows the area that needs to be computed from the standard normal table. Note that the continuity correction factor is used. The desired area to be found in the standard normal table is from 40 to 49.5. The z value for the desired area is

$$z = (49.5 - 40)/4.9 = 1.94$$

The standard normal table indicates an area of .4738 for a z value of 1.94. There is only a small chance ($.5000 - .4738 = .0262$) or 2.62%, that 50 or more of the sampled books will be unsatisfactory.

FIGURE 6.16 Normal Approximation to Binomial

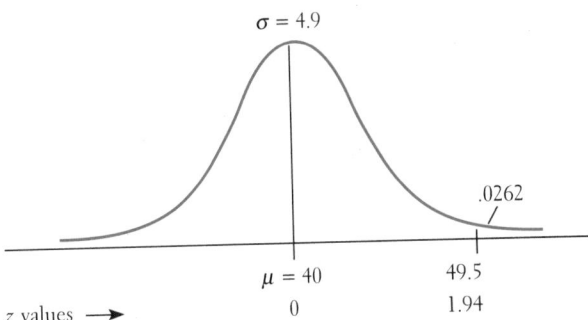

EXERCISES
27. When is the Poisson distribution a good approximation for the binomial distribution?
28. When is the normal distribution a good approximation for the binomial distribution?
29. What problem occurs when the normal distribution is used to approximate the binomial distribution? (*Hint:* This problem doesn't occur when the Poisson distribution is used.)
30. Explain the concept behind the continuity correction factor.
31. For a binomial distribution with $n = 50$ and $p = .40$, find:
    a. $P(x \geq 20)$.
    b. $P(x \leq 15)$.
    c. $P(x \geq 17)$.
    d. $P(x \leq 24)$.

32. In the past, Sue Megard has made mistakes on 10% of the tax returns she's prepared. Find the probability that she'll make mistakes on fewer than 5 of the 70 returns she prepares for 1993. Assume statistical independence.

33. A salesperson has a 30% chance of making a sale to any customer called upon. If 110 calls are made during a particular month, determine the probability that:

    a. At least 30 sales are made.

    b. Forty or fewer sales are made.

34. Four percent of the washers an automatic machine produces are defective. If a sample of 300 washers is drawn at random from the machine's production, what is the probability of observing at least 10 defectives?

35. As of 1989, according to the *Statistical Abstract of the United States: 1991*, 13.5% of the country's 92.8 million households were classified as one-person households. If 1,500 households are randomly selected to participate in an Arbitron survey to determine TV ratings, find the probability that no more than 195 of these are one-person households.

36. Boulevard Restaurant's management has been studying whether new customers return within a month. The collected data reveal that 60% of the new customers have returned. If 90 new customers dine at the Boulevard Restaurant this month, find the probability that at least 50 will return next month.

SUMMARY

This chapter has presented two continuous probability distributions that are useful models of many practical business situations: the uniform distribution and the normal distribution. The normal curve in particular is used frequently in business applications because so many business variables have values corresponding to the two key attributes of the normal curve: the values are symmetrically clustered around their mean, and there are more values close to the mean than far from it.

We must understand how to compute normal curve probabilities given the mean and standard deviation of the distribution because of the many situations that can be modeled with the normal curve. The next chapter gives an even more important reason for understanding normal curve areas. The normal curve underlies the inferential process that is the basis of all statistics: the process of reaching conclusions about populations based on sample evidence.

Finally, the normal approximation to the binomial distribution was presented. Along with the binomial procedures of Chapter 5, four methods of solving a binomial problem have been introduced: the binomial formula, the binomial tables, the Poisson approximation, and the normal approximation.

APPLICATIONS OF STATISTICAL CONCEPTS IN THE BUSINESS WORLD

Many numerical data arrays in the business world closely resemble a uniform distribution and can be modeled as discussed in this chapter. Also, at times the normal approximation is useful for computing binomial probabilities. But the greatest application of these concepts involves the many data collections found in the business world that approximate the shape of a normal curve.

When such a data array is found, percentages or probabilities can be easily determined using z values and the standard normal table. In fact, this method is so easy that it's frequently used even before the data distribution has been verified to resemble a normal curve. Obviously, it's important to verify the normality assumption if the results are to be accurate. Here are examples of variables that might follow a normal distribution and for which this chapter's techniques are useful.

Accounting: accounts receivable, accounts payable, cash balance, value of inventory, bad debt expense.

Manufacturing: dollar value of inventory, number of days to receive shipment, number of overtime hours per week, hours of labor per unit, weights of manufactured parts, lengths of parts.

Finance: interest rate paid as deviation from prime rate, company's stock price as percentage of Dow Jones, ratio of annual dividends to earnings, several companies' price/earnings ratios.

Marketing: ages of credit card holders, numerical ratings of store performance by customers, monthly market share, miles traveled by customers to store.

Personnel: time with company, years of education, score on company entrance test, job performance rating, number of dependents, annual salary, sick days taken per year.

Quality control: time between defects, defective items per shift, time until part failure, time until defective condition detected.

GLOSSARY

Continuous random variable A random variable that can assume any value within some specified range.

Uniform distribution A distribution describing a random variable that is as likely to occur in one segment of a given size within a specified range as another.

Normal distribution A continuous distribution that has a bell shape and is determined by its mean and standard deviation.

Standard normal distribution A normal distribution that has a mean of 0 and a standard deviation of 1.

z value A measure of the number of standard deviations between the mean or center of a normal curve and the value of interest.

Chebyshev's theorem A rule stating that regardless of how the data values are distributed, at least $(1 - 1/k^2)$ of the values will lie within k standard deviations of the mean (for $k \geq 1$).

KEY FORMULAS

Uniform probabilities

$$P(c \leq x \leq d) = \frac{d - c}{b - a} \tag{6.1}$$

Mean of uniform distribution

$$\mu = \frac{a + b}{2} \tag{6.2}$$

Standard deviation of uniform distribution

$$\sigma = \sqrt{\frac{(b-a)^2}{12}} \tag{6.3}$$

Normal distribution probability density function

$$f(x) = \frac{1}{\sigma\sqrt{2\pi}} e^{-(1/2)\ [(x\ -\ \mu)/\sigma]^2} \tag{6.4}$$

z value or standardized value

$$z = \frac{x - \mu}{\sigma} \tag{6.5}$$

SOLVED EXERCISES
. . . .

1. UNIFORM DISTRIBUTION

The Latah Creek Winery produces between 200 and 300 gallons of wine each day. The uniform distribution best describes this process.

a. On average, how much wine is produced each day?

b. What is the amount of variability in the number of gallons of wine produced from day to day?

c. In what percentage of days can production be expected to fall between 220 and 270 gallons?

d. What is the probability that production will be more than 280 gallons tomorrow?

Solution:

a. Mean $= \dfrac{200 + 300}{2} = 250$

b. Standard deviation $= \sqrt{\dfrac{(300 - 200)^2}{12}} = 28.9$

c. $P(220 \leq x \leq 270) = \dfrac{270 - 220}{300 - 200} = \dfrac{50}{100} = .50$

d. $P(280 \leq x \leq 300) = \dfrac{300 - 280}{300 - 200} = \dfrac{20}{100} = .20$

2. NORMAL DISTRIBUTION

American Carpets has 2,000 accounts receivable. The mean and standard deviation are $300 and $50, respectively. Assume that the accounts are normally distributed.

a. How many accounts exceed $400?

b. How many accounts are below $250?

c. What is the probability that an account selected at random will be between $200 and $350?

d. What percentage of the accounts are between $325 and $375?

e. Forty percent of the accounts exceed what dollar amount? (*Hint:* Fifty percent of the accounts are for more than $300.)

f. Twenty percent of the accounts are below what dollar amount?

Solution:

a. $z = (400 - 300)/50 = 2.0 \rightarrow .4772$ (area between 300 and 400)
$(.5000 - .4772) = .0228$ (area above 400)
$2,000 \times .0228 = 45.6$, or approximately 46 accounts

b. $z = (250 - 300)/50 = -1.0 \rightarrow .3413$ (area between 250 and 300)
$(.5000 - .3413) = .1587$ (area below 250)
$2,000 \times .1587 = 317.4$, or approximately 317 accounts

c. $z = (200 - 300)/50 = -2.0 \rightarrow .4772$ (area between 200 and 300)
$z = (350 - 300)/50 = 1.0 \quad \rightarrow .3413$ (area between 300 and 350)
$\qquad\qquad\qquad$ Sum $= \overline{.8185}$ (area between 200 and 350)
The probability is approximately .82.

d. $z = (375 - 300)/50 = 1.5 \rightarrow .4332$ (area between 300 and 375)
$z = (325 - 300)/50 = 0.5 \rightarrow \underline{.1915}$ (area between 300 and 325)
$\qquad\qquad\qquad$ Difference $= \overline{.2417}$ (area between 325 and 375)
The percentage is approximately 24%.

e. $(.5000 - .4000) = .1000 \rightarrow z = 0.25$
$x = \mu + z\sigma = 300 + 0.25(50) = 312.5$
Forty percent of the accounts are worth more than $312.50.

f $(.5000 - .2000) = .3000 \rightarrow z = -0.84$
$x = \mu + z\sigma = 300 + (-0.84)(50) = 258$
Twenty percent of the accounts are worth less than $258.

3. NORMAL APPROXIMATION TO THE BINOMIAL DISTRIBUTION

New Jersey Power Company provides lower rates to customers who agree to use energy mainly at off-peak hours. Thirty percent of their customers take advantage of these savings. The consumer affairs department has conducted a focus group and is preparing to conduct a random telephone survey of 500 customers. The department supervisor wants to make sure that the group will contain a sufficient proportion of off-peak users.

a. What is the probability of obtaining fewer than 150 off-peak users in the telephone survey?

b. What is the smallest number of off-peak users likely to be included in this sample? (*Hint:* Use three standard deviations below the mean, which will include .9987 of the area under the curve.)

Solution:

a. $\mu = np = 500(.30) = 150$
Since 50% of a normal curve lies below the mean, the probability of obtaining fewer than 150 customers is 50%.

b. $\sigma = \sqrt{np(1 - p)} = \sqrt{500(.30)(.70)} = 10.25$
$x = \mu + z\sigma = 150 + (-3.0)(10.25) = 119.25$
The probability of fewer than 119 off-peak users in the sample is .0013.

EXERCISES

37. Draw a normal curve and shade in the area under the curve for each of the following:
    a. The area between the mean and $z = 2.50$.
    b. The area between the mean and $z = -0.75$.
    c. The area between $z = -1.55$ and $z = 0.89$.
    d. The area between $z = -0.38$ and $z = -2.18$.
    e. The area above $z = 2.68$.
    f. The area below $z = -1.15$.

38. Find the probability that an item would fall in each of the shaded intervals drawn in Exercise 37.

39. Find the z value that corresponds to each of the areas described:
    a. Fifty percent of the items lie above this z value.
    b. Thirty percent of the items lie below this z value.
    c. The chances are 1 in 10 that an item selected at random will deviate from the mean by more than this z value.
    d. Five percent of the items will lie more than this distance (measured in terms of a z value) from the mean.

40. The total time needed to process a mortgage loan application at Bancshares Mortgage Company is uniformly distributed between five and nine days.
    a. What is the average loan processing time?
    b. What is the variability in the loan processing time?
    c. What percentage of loans are processed within eight days?
    d. Find the probability that a loan will take more than six days to be processed.

41. Mary Walsh is studying the records of the Valley Appliance Company to determine the adequacy of the present warranty policy for refrigerators. She finds that the length of time Valley Appliance refrigerators operate before requiring repairs is normally distributed with mean 5.7 years and standard deviation 2.1 years. The company presently repairs free any machine that fails to work properly within a two-year period after purchase. What percentage of Valley Appliance refrigerators require these free repairs?

42. The Barcellos' Tum Tum Resort staff tracks the number of days each guest stays. They've discovered that this variable is normally distributed with a mean of 9 and a standard deviation of 3. The forecast for next month indicates that 500 guests are expected.
    a. How many guests are expected to stay fewer than 5 days?
    b. How many guests are expected to stay more than 15 days?
    c. How many guests are expected to stay between 6 and 12 days?
    d. Fifteen percent of the guests leave after how many days?
    e. Seventy-five percent of the guests stay longer than how many days?

43. The label on Spic and Clean laundry detergent boxes indicates net weight of 27 ounces. A machine fills these boxes in a uniformly distributed manner, with the smallest box con-

taining 26 ounces and the largest 28 ounces. Quality control accepts boxes filled within 0.9 ounces of the amount stated on the box.

  a. How much variability is there in the amount put in the boxes?

  b. What is the probability that a box will be filled with between 26.8 and 27.5 ounces?

  c. What is the probability that a box will fail to meet the quality-control standard?

44. A large L-Mart discount store's maintenance department has been instructed to replace all light bulbs at the same time. Past experience indicates that light bulbs' life is normally distributed with a mean life of 750 hours and standard deviation of 40 hours. When should the lights be replaced so that no more than 7% burn out?

45. Forrest Paint Company accountant, Dan Joyner, has a history of making errors on 6% of the invoices he processes. Forrest Paint processed 400 invoices last month.

  a. How many invoices would you expect to have errors?

  b. Determine the probability that Don made fewer than 20 errors.

  c. Determine the probability that Don made more than 30 errors.

46. Jake runs the concession stand for a Chicago-area minor league baseball team. He knows that hot dog sales are normally distributed with an average of 600 hot dogs per day and standard deviation of 45. Jake reconsiders how much to stock in his business after reading an article in *Sport* magazine (March 1989) about Chicago-area baseball. This article predicted good crowds for Chicago teams, which Jake thinks will affect his business.

   Jake wants to make sure that he doesn't run out of hot dogs. How many hot dogs should he order so that the probability of running out is less than 1% each day?

47. A swimming pool is filled at a rate between 32 and 39 gallons per minute. (Assume a uniform distribution.)

  a. Find the average rate at which the pool is filled.

  b. Find the probability that the rate at any one time is below 35 gallons per minute.

48. Automobile inspectors in New Mexico have determined that 11% of all cars coming in for annual inspection fail. What is the probability that 20 or more cars out of the next 130 cars tested will fail the inspection?

49. An automobile machine produces bearings, 2% of which are defective. If a sample of 600 bearings is drawn at random, what is the probability of observing six or fewer defectives?

50. The personnel director of Kershaw's, Inc., Kelly Moreland, needs to administer an aptitude test to 30 job applicants. Kelly has just read an article about how managers cope with labor shortages (*Personnel Management*, May 1989). This article made Kelly think about how to improve the selection process for hirees, and she has bought an aptitude exam from a national company for use at Kershaw's.

   The booklet for the test informs her that the average length of time required to complete the exam is 120 minutes with standard deviation of 25 minutes. When should she end the test if she wishes to allow sufficient time for 80% of the applicants to finish? (Assume that test times are normally distributed.)

51. Associated Investment Advisors sells annuities based on annual payout during the lifetimes of the participants in the plan. They've determined that participants' lifetimes are approximately normally distributed with a mean of 72 years and standard deviation of 4.7 years.

a. What is the probability that a plan participant will receive payments beyond age 65? Beyond age 70? Beyond age 75? Beyond age 80?

b. Sixty percent of the plan participants are beyond what age?

52. City planner Terry Novak knows that mean family income is $28,000 with a standard deviation of $9,000 in Bonners Ferry, Kentucky, a community of 20,000 households. He also knows that family income isn't a normally distributed variable. Terry is applying for a grant and must answer the following question: At least what percentage of incomes lie within $10,000 of the mean income?

53. Innovative Technology Systems manufactures electronic cables for computers. Innovative has found from past experience that 97% of the cables shipped are acceptable. It ships most of its cables to Compaq Computers. *The Wall Street Journal* (November 3, 1989) has just said that Compaq's stock plunged after it reported lower-than-expected fourth-quarter profits. This has Innovative concerned about the quality of its cables because Compaq has indicated it must cut production costs and may examine its commitment to Innovative.

   A shipment of 400 cables has just been sent to Compaq. Innovative's contract calls for at least 380 acceptable cables. What is the probability that this shipment will fulfill the contract conditions?

54. You've worked part-time at Ranch Thrift, a large supermarket, for the past three years. Your boss knows that you're completing your business degree and asks you to study the average customer expenditure per visit. You sample 500 customer expenditures and determine that this variable is normally distributed with an average expenditure of $31.28 and standard deviation of $7.29. Write your boss a memo analyzing the average customer expenditure per visit.

EXTENDED EXERCISES

55. IRS REFUNDS

An IRS regional office plots a large sample of tax refund amounts, finding that they form a bell-shaped curve with refunds fairly close to this center value, suggesting a normal distribution. The average refund is $748 with standard deviation of $124. Since the data plot is so close to a normal curve, they decide that probability or percentage questions can be answered using the standard normal table.

A refund greater than $1,000 is considered "large" and the office manager wants to know what percentage of current refunds, based on the normal distribution, exceed this amount.

A second question involves new withholding guidelines for taxpayers. It is estimated that the average refund amount will rise by $150 after these guidelines go into effect. The office wonders how the percentage of large refunds will be affected.

The office wants to find the percentage of refunds over $1,000 that might be expected based on current guidelines. The z value is calculated, and the resulting area is subtracted from .50 to determine the area in the standard normal upper tail:

$$z = (1,000 - 748)/124 = 2.03 \rightarrow .4788 \quad \text{(area between 748 and 1,000)}$$
$$.5000 - .4788 = .0212 \quad \text{(area above 1,000)}$$

About 2% of the refunds under the current withholding guidelines can be expected to exceed $1,000.

With the new guidelines in effect, a \$150 increase to \$898, in the average refund can be expected. The office has assumed that the standard deviation of refund balances will remain the same, \$124, even though the mean has shifted. Under this assumption, the percentage of the normal curve above \$1,000 can be found using the z value and the standard normal table:

$$z = (1,000 - 898)/124 = 0.82 \rightarrow .2939 \quad \text{(area between 898 and 1,000)}$$
$$.5000 - .2939 = .2061 \quad \text{(area above 1,000)}$$

The increase in average refund raises the percentage of refunds of over \$1,000 to about 21%. This increase from 2% to 21% is important to the IRS office for planning auditing time and clerical duties.

a. What would happen to the percentage of refunds over \$1,000 if the average refund amount actually dropped \$75?

b. After the 2% figure has been computed under the current withholding policy, how could the assumption of a normal distribution be checked?

56. RANCH LIFE INSURANCE COMPANY OF FLORIDA

Kim Carter, statistician for Ranch Life Insurance Company of Florida, notices that monthly premium receipts appear to follow a normal distribution. After plotting receipts for a typical month and observing their distribution, Kim decides that the normality assumption is reasonable.

Ranch wants to determine the percentage of monthly receipts that fall into the range \$125 to \$175, since such amounts are difficult to handle. They aren't large enough to warrant investment attention, unless there are many of them, nor are they small enough to ignore by putting them into the cash account.

To find the percentage of accounts in this range, Kim computes the mean and standard deviation of monthly premium receipts. She determines these values to be \$100 and \$38, respectively.

a. What percentage of monthly receipts can be expected to fall into the range \$125 to \$175?

b. Kim predicts that within two years the average monthly premium will rise to \$150. Assuming the standard deviation remains the same, how would this change the answer to Question *a*?

c. Describe how the assumption of normality might be verified in this case.

57. SPECIFIC ELECTRIC

Jess Franklin of Specific Electric Appliance Manufacturing Company's finance department has been studying interest rates on its short-term loans from the company's banks. For comparison purposes, he's been following the T-bill rate for several months. The most recent yield, as reported in *The Wall Street Journal* (February 23, 1990), is 7.80%. He has also been watching the rate Specific's bank charges.

Jess assumes that his bank rate, which varies from day to day, can be described by a normal curve and he uses normal curve procedures to compute various probabilities. These probabilities are used in preparing for market rate shifts under an acceptable level of risk.

In presenting his work to the firm's top management, Jess mentions the normality assumption and then shows the computations for market rate probabilities and the preparations based on these probabilities. Company president Mary Montana interrupts, saying, "I don't know about your assumption of a normal distribution for daily interest rates. It seems to me the assumption isn't valid, since rates often seem to be on a long-term increase or decrease. If that's true, the assumption of a normal distribution may be valid, but not the assumption of an un-changing average."

a. What are the strengths in Mary's statement?

b. What are the weaknesses in Mary's statement?

c. Is there any way Mary's concern about a shifting mean could be incorporated into Jess's calculations?

58. GMAT SCORES FOR CITY UNIVERSITY

Professors Williams, Ross, Stanley, and Richards are serving on the MBA Committee at City University. The committee is to set a cutoff level for admitting students into the MBA program using the GMAT (Graduate Management Admissions Test). Currently, the mean test score nationally is 475 with standard deviation of 75. Scores are thought to be approximately normally distributed.

Professor Ross suggests analyzing City's 100 most recent MBA applicants' scores to see if they resemble GMAT scores nationwide. If the sample is similar, Professor Ross proposes that a score be chosen that would permit 25% of the applicants to be admitted to the program. The 100 GMAT scores are:

568	395	489	288	396	442	672	492	465	523	494	513	486
606	486	514	497	399	562	507	457	449	553	492	330	375
365	415	575	432	378	403	518	476	355	470	512	527	366
422	506	542	452	579	400	429	383	569	381	514	465	439
505	429	564	438	350	595	476	469	462	446	565	450	
600	568	450	580	450	423	598	458	494	582	623	401	
461	564	519	375	553	543	480	322	490	436	446	465	
412	483	452	389	611	569	368	469	348	522	479	473	

a. Are City University applicants similar to the national average?

b. If Professor Ross's proposal is accepted, what cutoff score should be used for admittance?

c. Professor Richards feels that one third of the applicants should be admitted. What cutoff score would he propose?

59. EUREKA DAIRY

Jim Black is in charge of quality control at Eureka Dairy in Deer Park, Georgia. Jim is concerned about grade A milk's bacteria count per cubic centimeter. On July 15 the bacteria count was 31,000. Jim's problem is to determine whether something is wrong with the production process. Eureka Dairy over a long period of time has regulated its processing to achieve a mean bacteria count of 21,000 with standard deviation of 3,000. A distribution plotted from the bacteria counts over a long period of time is normal in form. Each day the count is plotted on a chart similar to Figure 6.17. Jim needs to determine whether this chart is useful.

a. What are the chances in 1,000 that the bacteria count will exceed 30,000 if the day-to-day variation in Figure 6.17 is purely random?

b. Determine the probability of a bacteria count of 31,000 or more.

c. Which is the more reasonable assumption: that a bacteria count of 31,000 might reasonably be expected, or that something is wrong? Explain your answer.

d. Is the charting device in Figure 6.17 helpful in maintaining high quality? Explain your answer.

e. Why would it be important for this dairy to find the mean value of these bacteria counts every month?

FIGURE 6.17   Bacteria Counts in Grade A Milk

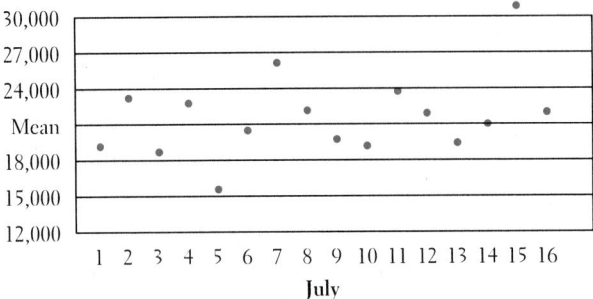

MICROCOMPUTER PACKAGE

The micro package *Computerized Business Statistics* can be used to solve normal curve problems. Suppose Applied Business Systems, Inc., needs to know what percentage of its orders exceeded 135 miles. Applied's analyst knows that shipping distances are normally distributed with a mean of 125 miles and standard deviation of 28 miles.

Computer Solution:

From the main menu of *Computerized Business Statistics*, a **5** is selected, indicating Probability Distributions. This menu appeared at the end of Chapter 5.

This problem involves the normal distribution. Since Applied needs to know what percentage of its orders exceeded 135 miles, the arrow is moved to normal $P(X \geq a)$.

```
Enter Mean and Press ↵ 125
Enter Standard Deviation and Press ↵ 28
Enter A and Press ↵ 135
```

The normal probability distribution for $\mu = 125$ and $\sigma = 28$ is shown on the screen. The correct answer for $P(x \geq 135)$ is .3601.

MINITAB COMPUTER PACKAGE

Two discrete statistical distributions (binomial and Poisson) were demonstrated at the end of Chapter 5. This section covers the MINITAB for two continuous statistical distributions: uniform and normal. All we need is to indicate the type of distribution and the value(s) of the parameter(s) that describe it (a to b for the uniform and μ and σ for the normal). The **CDF** command is used to calculate probabilities for the cumulative distribution function.

The **CDF** for any value x is the probability that a random variable with the specified distribution has a value less than or equal to x.

The MINITAB commands for Solved Exercise 1.*c* are shown to find the percentage of days that production can be expected to fall between 220 and 270 gallons for a uniform distribution with a range of 200 to 300.

```
MTB> SET C1
MTB> 220
MTB> 270
MTB> END
MTB> CDF C1;
SUBC> UNIFORM 200 300.
   220.0000      0.2000
   270.0000      0.7000
```

The **SET** command is used to identify the interval of interest. The **CDF** command is used to generate a cumulative probability density function. The **UNIFORM** subcommand is used to generate the probability function for a uniform distribution from 200 to 300. The percentage is $(.7 - .2 = .5)$ or 50%.

The MINITAB commands for Solved Exercise 2.*a* to determine the probability that an account exceeds $400 if the accounts receivable are normally distributed with mean $300 and standard deviation $50 are:

```
MTB> SET C2
MTB> 400
MTB> END
MTB> CDF C2;
SUBC> NORMAL 300 50.
   400.0000      0.9772
```

The **SET** command is used to identify the interval of interest. The **CDF** command is used again to generate a cumulative probability density function. The **NORMAL** subcommand is used to generate the probability function for a normal distribution with a mean of $300 and standard deviation of $50. The probability is $(1 - .9772) = .0228$.

SAMPLING DISTRIBUTIONS

*To see the world
in a grain of
sand.*
Blake, *Auguries
of Innocence*

Objectives

When you have completed this chapter, you will be able to:

Explain the concept of sampling distributions.

Construct a sampling distribution of sample means.

Construct a sampling distribution of sample proportions.

Explain why the central limit theorem is important to statistical decision making.

In May 1989, *Business Month* featured an article entitled "Quest for Quality" describing quality-improvement efforts of Hewlett-Packard. The company had trimmed its defective rate on connections to 1,800 per million and was startled to find that a similar Japanese company had a rate of only 4 per million. Hewlett-Packard vowed to improve its defective rate.

The preceding chapter introduced the normal distribution and some of its applications. This chapter covers more important uses for this theoretical distribution and establishes the most important concept in statistics: the sampling distribution.

WHY MANAGERS NEED TO KNOW ABOUT SAMPLING DISTRIBUTIONS

Most statistical applications involve sampling items from the population being studied. Chapter 2 discussed ways to make the sample selection to ensure that a representative group of items is collected and measured. This selection process is important because the sample's characteristics are inferred to hold for the entire population, even though only a very small part of the population is actually sampled and measured.

This chapter deals with the accuracy of this inference process. Once the inference is made that the population possesses the same characteristics as the sample, the analyst must determine the extent of possible error involved in this process. Since sampling is commonplace in most organizations, knowing how to measure and understand this inherent error is vital to every manager. Assessing possible error involves a thorough understanding of statistics' most important concept: the sampling distribution.

Hewlett-Packard's attempts to reduce the defective rate must be closely monitored. A real quality improvement must be distinguished from a random fluctuation in the defective rate. The concept of sampling distributions is the key to understanding the difference.

SAMPLING ERROR

A sample mean isn't likely to equal the mean of the population from which the sample was selected. Nor is a sample standard deviation or other sample measure likely to exactly equal its corresponding population value. Some difference between a sample statistic and its corresponding population parameter is to be expected. This difference, called the **sampling error,** is due purely to chance.

> **Sampling error** is the difference between a sample statistic and its corresponding population parameter.

EXAMPLE 7.1   Jarms Hardware's five workers have worked at the store for 2, 4, 5, 8, and 11 years, respectively, for an average (mean) of 6 years. If a sample of two workers with 5 and 11 years of experience is selected at random from this population, a sample mean of 8 results. The sampling error is 2, the difference between the sample statistic (8) and the corresponding population parameter (6) ($\bar{x} - \mu = 8 - 6 = 2$). If a second sample of two workers is selected at random from this population, and these workers have 2 and 8 years of experience, a sample mean of 5 results. In this case, the sampling error is -1, the difference between the sample statistic (5) and the corresponding population parameter (6) ($\bar{x} - \mu = 5 - 6 = -1$). Different combinations of two workers provide different sample means. How can analysts use sample means to estimate population means when there's almost always an error? To deal with the question of sample accuracy, we must understand the concept of sampling distributions.

DISTRIBUTION OF SAMPLING MEANS

Sampling Distribution

Chapters 5 and 6 presented the binomial and normal distributions as models of certain realistic situations. This chapter's key concept involves a distribution of sample statistics. When a sample is taken from a population, a numerical sample statistic results. This statistic should be viewed *as if it were selected from the distribution of all possible values of that sample statistic*. This theoretical distribution of the sample statistic is called the **sampling distribution**.

> A **sampling distribution** includes all possible values that a statistic, such as a sample mean, can assume for a given sample size.

Because population and sample sizes in practical situations are usually quite large, it's not feasible to actually formulate the array of possible sample results from which the statistic is drawn. There are countless ways to reach into a large population and select a sample and, hence, countless sample means from which to choose.

Even though in most real-life situations it's not possible to list all possible sample statistics, a limited-population example can be used to illustrate this concept.

EXAMPLE 7.2   A population consists of ages 10, 20, 30, 40, and 50. A random sample of two is to be selected from this population and the sample mean computed. The sampling distribution consists of every possible sample mean. Since both N and n are quite small, we can find all possible samples and compute their means. Sampling for this example is done with replacement. That is, after the first population item is selected for the sample, it's returned to the population for possible selection again. In nearly all practical situations, the population size is sufficiently large that this replacement isn't necessary to ensure randomness.

Table 7.1 shows every possible sample pair that can be drawn from this population. Since $N = 5$ and $n = 2$, there are 25 possible sample pairs. The second column shows the mean value of each sample pair (the sample statistic); this column constitutes the sampling distribution for this example. Table 7.2 summarizes this sampling distribution, where duplicate sample means are combined to form a probability distribution. Figure 7.1 shows the probability distribution's shape.

TABLE 7.1   Sampling Distribution of Means (Example 7.2)

Sampled ages	Sample means	$(\bar{x} - \mu_{\bar{x}})$	$(\bar{x} - \mu_{\bar{x}})^2$
10, 10	10	−20	400
10, 20	15	−15	225
10, 30	20	−10	100
10, 40	25	−5	25
10, 50	30	0	0
20, 10	15	−15	225
20, 20	20	−10	100
20, 30	25	−5	25
20, 40	30	0	0
20, 50	35	5	25
30, 10	20	−10	100
30, 20	25	−5	25
30, 30	30	0	0
30, 40	35	5	25
30, 50	40	10	100
40, 10	25	−5	25
40, 20	30	0	0
40, 30	35	5	25
40, 40	40	10	100
40, 50	45	15	225
50, 10	30	0	0
50, 20	35	5	25
50, 30	40	10	100
50, 40	45	15	225
50, 50	50	20	400
	Sum = 750		2,500

TABLE 7.2   Probability Distribution of Means (Example 7.2)

Sample mean	Frequency	Probability
10	1	.04
15	2	.08
20	3	.12
25	4	.16
30	5	.20
35	4	.16
40	3	.12
45	2	.08
50	1	.04
		1.00

If a random sample of two ages is taken from the population (10, 20, 30, 40, 50) with replacement and the sample mean computed, it's *as if* this sample mean had been randomly selected from Table 7.1's sampling distribution. The sampling distribution underlies the inferential process in all statistical sampling situations, and you must have a mental image of this distribution. Chapters 8, 9, and 10, in particular, rely on

FIGURE 7.1 Distribution of Sample Means

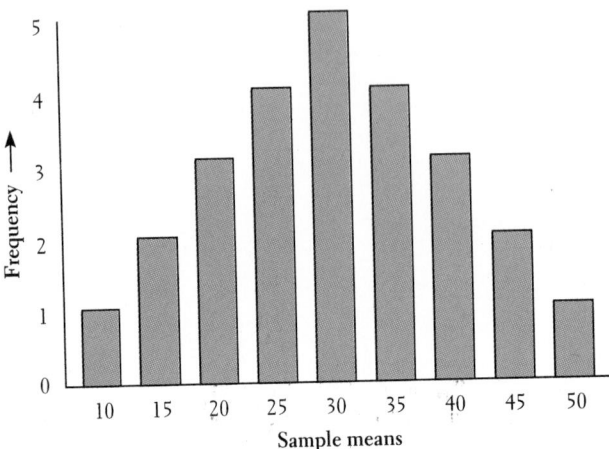

the concept of a sampling distribution in developing procedures for estimation and hypothesis testing.

Note the shape of Figure 7.1. The sample means seem to cluster about a central value, 30 (which happens to be the population mean). The distribution is also symmetrical, with as many values above 30 as below it. This description sounds like a normal distribution; in fact, this appearance isn't accidental, as will be discussed in the next section.

The population in Example 7.2 consists of ages 10, 20, 30, 40, and 50. From Equation 4.1, the population mean age is

$$\mu = \frac{\Sigma x}{N} = \frac{150}{5} = 30$$

The mean of the sampling distribution in Table 7.1 is also calculated using Equation 4.1:

$$\mu_{\bar{x}} = \frac{\Sigma \bar{x}}{n} = \frac{750}{25} = 30$$

The two means are the same. As specified by Equation 7.1, the mean of the population and mean of the sampling distribution are equal:

$$\mu_x = \mu_{\bar{x}} \tag{7.1}$$

where μ_x = Population mean
$\mu_{\bar{x}}$ = Mean of the sampling distribution

This is true for any sample or population size. This fact is intuitively appealing since we would expect sample means to cluster around the population mean. The frequency distribution of Table 7.2 shows this symmetrical clustering of sample means around the population mean value of 30.

From Equation 4.6, the standard deviation for the population ages 10, 20, 30, 40, and 50 can be computed.

$$\sigma = \sqrt{\frac{\Sigma(x - \mu)^2}{N}} = \sqrt{\frac{1,000}{5}} = \sqrt{200} = 14.1$$

The standard deviation of the sampling distribution is

$$\sigma_{\bar{x}} = \sqrt{\frac{\Sigma(\bar{x} - \mu_{\bar{x}})^2}{n}} = \sqrt{\frac{2,500}{25}} = \sqrt{100} = 10$$

Note that the standard deviation of the sampling distribution is less than the standard deviation of the population. This relationship is also intuitively appealing. It is reasonable to assume that the means of samples of two population values would tend to be closer to the population mean than would the individual population values themselves. Why the sampling distribution standard deviation happens to be 10 isn't intuitively obvious.

Equation 7.2 shows how to compute the standard deviation of the sampling distribution of means without requiring a listing of all the possible sample means:

$$\sigma_{\bar{x}} = \frac{\sigma}{\sqrt{n}} \tag{7.2}$$

where $\sigma_{\bar{x}}$ = Standard deviation of the sampling distribution (called the
        standard error of the mean)
        σ = Population standard deviation
        n = Sample size

Standard Error of the Mean

The term *standard error* is frequently used to identify the standard deviation of a sampling distribution. More precisely, the **standard error of the mean** is the standard deviation of the sampling distribution of sample means.

> The **standard error of the mean** is the standard deviation of the sampling distribution of sample means.

The standard error of the mean for Example 7.2 is

$$\sigma_{\bar{x}} = \frac{\sigma}{\sqrt{n}} = \frac{14.1}{\sqrt{2}} = \frac{14.1}{1.41} = 10$$

The value of the standard error of the mean depends on two factors:

1. The variability of the population as measured by its standard deviation (σ).
2. The sample size used (n).

EXAMPLE 7.3   A random sample of 50 Deaconess Medical Center employees is selected to determine the average amount of time since the last promotion. This action was prompted by an article on the increasing complexity of succession, reported in *Personnel Management* (January 1990). The president is concerned that time in rank, rather than competence, determines who'll be promoted.

The data values on time since promotion are collected from personnel files using a systematic sampling plan (covered in Chapter 2). Average (mean) time is computed to be 4.78 years. Analyst Pam Shore recognizes that if sampling were repeated and different people were selected by the random process, a different sample mean would result. It is as if 4.78 had been randomly drawn from the sampling distribution of means.

If the population standard deviation is known to be 1.2 years, the standard error of the mean for sample size 50 is

$$\sigma_{\bar{x}} = \frac{\sigma}{\sqrt{n}} = \frac{1.2}{\sqrt{50}} = \frac{1.2}{7.07} = 0.17$$

Note how the standard error of the mean is affected by both the variability of the population and the sample size selected. If the variability of the population is smaller, say, one year, then the standard error decreases:

$$\sigma_{\bar{x}} = \frac{\sigma}{\sqrt{n}} = \frac{1.0}{\sqrt{50}} = \frac{1.0}{7.07} = 0.14$$

If a larger sample size is used—say, 400—the standard error also decreases:

$$\sigma_{\bar{x}} = \frac{\sigma}{\sqrt{n}} = \frac{1.2}{\sqrt{400}} = \frac{1.2}{20} = 0.06$$

Having σ in the numerator makes sense, since we'd expect populations with high variability to have a more variable sampling distribution than populations with little variability. Placing the sample size, n, in the denominator seems reasonable also. This suggests that using a larger sample size decreases the variability (standard error) of the sampling distribution and results in sample means that are closer to the population mean than we'd get using a small sample size.

Central Limit Theorem   The population and sampling distributions in Example 7.2 illustrate the essential features of the **central limit theorem,** another important concept in statistics. This famous theorem states that the bell-shaped appearance of the sampling distribution of Table 7.2 and Figure 7.1 is no accident. The central limit theorem states that if a population is normally distributed, the distribution of sample means drawn from that population is also normally distributed. More important, if the population isn't normal, the distribution of sample means will be approximately normal if the sample is sufficiently large.

> The **central limit theorem** states that if a sufficiently large random sample of n observations is selected from any population, the sampling distribution of sample means will be approximately a normal distribution. The larger the sample size, n, the better will be the normal approximation to the sampling distribution of sample means.

The central limit theorem states that the distribution of sample means "approaches" a normal curve as the sample size increases. Table 7.1 shows the sampling distribution of means for a sample size of two. This distribution isn't perfectly normal since it is, in fact, a discrete distribution with only the specified values possible. In contrast, the normal distribution is a continuous distribution, as discussed in Chapter 6. However, had a sample size of 50 been used, the sampling distribution, although still not perfectly smooth, would be close to a smooth normal curve. And if a sample of 500 had been used, the resulting discrete distribution would be almost indistinguishable from the continuous normal curve. That's what is meant by the definition of the central limit theorem: the larger the sample size used, the closer the sampling distribution is to the normal curve.

The key feature of the central limit theorem is that the distribution of sample means approaches a normal curve *regardless of the population shape* if the sample is sufficiently large. This makes the central limit theorem valuable in statistical applications because analysts can use normal curve probability techniques for a sampling distribution even if there is no knowledge of the population's shape. Figure 7.2 illustrates this key feature of the central limit theorem.

Each population in Figure 7.2 has a different shape. Population a is skewed to the high side; population b is skewed to the lower end. Population c's shape is even more nonnormal, while population d is the opposite of normal: data values are concentrated in the high and low regions with almost none in the middle. But when large enough samples are taken from each population and the mean is computed for each, these sample means approximate normal distributions, as the curves on the right side of Figure 7.2 show.

Probabilities can be computed for these normally distributed sampling distributions using the normal curve procedures of Chapter 6.

The central limit theorem provides the basic definition for the sampling distribution of sample means. If the sample size is reasonably large, these values form a normal curve with a mean equal to μ and standard error equal to $\sigma/\sqrt{n}$. As a rule of thumb, a sample size of 30 is the minimum needed to ensure the approximate normal shape of the sampling distribution. For smaller sample sizes, the shape of the population distribution must be known. If it's close to a normal distribution, the sampling distribution of means can still be assumed to be normal. If the population is nonnormal, and a small sample size is used, the sampling distribution may fail to follow a normal curve, and procedures discussed in Chapter 19 must be used.

FIGURE 7.2   Populations and Sampling Distributions

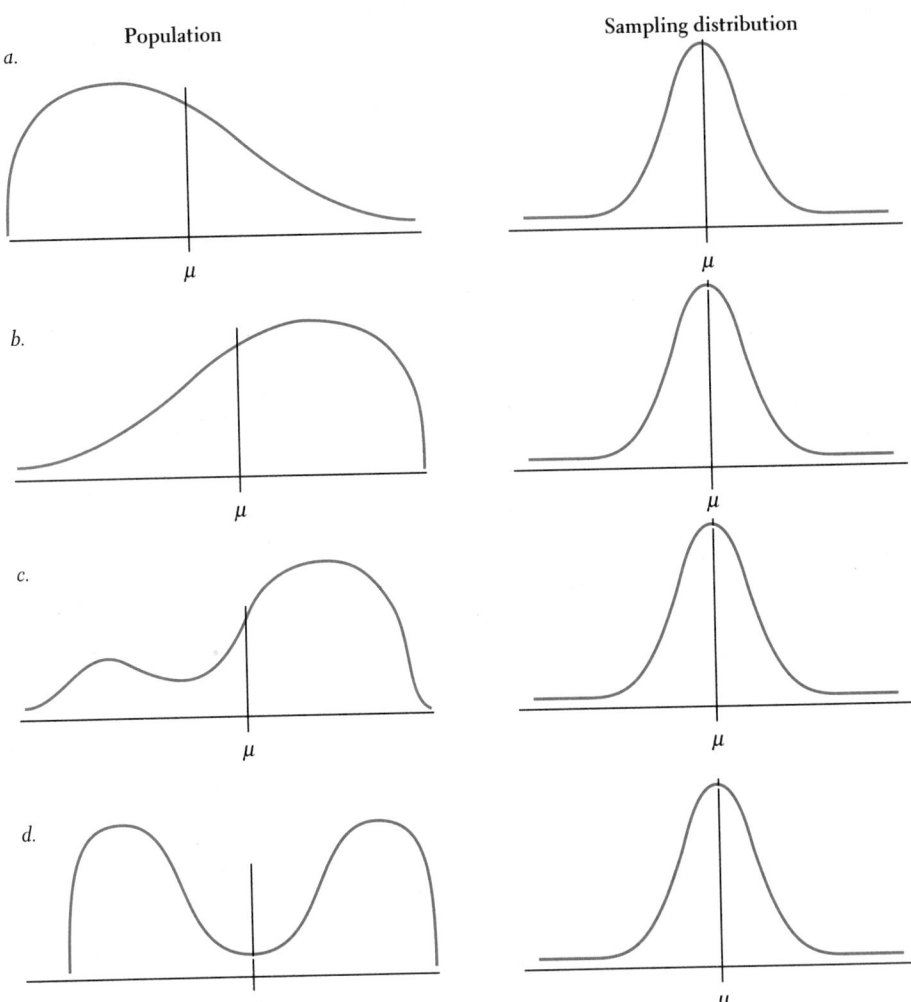

Sampling Distribution of Means

Properties of the sampling distribution of means
1. The mean of the sampling distribution of means equals the population mean: $\mu_x = \mu_{\bar{x}}$.
2. The standard deviation of the sampling distribution of means (standard error) equals the population standard deviation divided by the square root of the sample size: $\sigma_{\bar{x}} = \sigma/\sqrt{n}$.
3. The sampling distribution of means is approximately normal for sufficiently large sample sizes ($n \geq 30$).

EXAMPLE 7.4 A population has a mean of 5.7 and standard deviation of 1.9. A sample of 50 items is randomly selected from this population. Find the probability that the sample mean lies between 5.5 and 5.8.

Two areas are found from the normal sampling distribution and added to determine the correct answer. Figure 7.3 shows the desired area.

FIGURE 7.3 Sampling Distribution of Means for Example 7.4

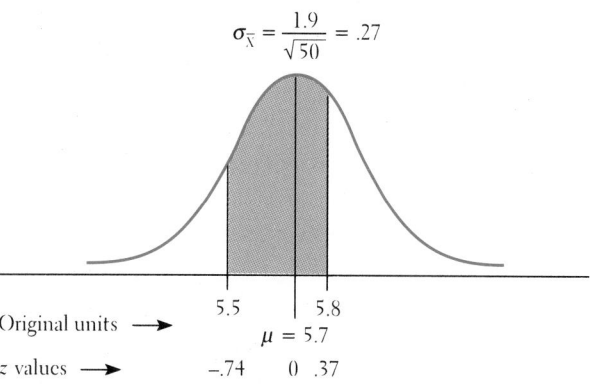

$$\sigma_{\bar{x}} = \frac{1.9}{\sqrt{50}} = .27$$

Original units → 5.5   5.8
$\mu = 5.7$

z values →   −.74   0 .37

The calculations are

$$\sigma_{\bar{x}} = \frac{\sigma}{\sqrt{n}} = \frac{1.9}{\sqrt{50}} = \frac{1.9}{7.07} = 0.27$$

$$z = \frac{\bar{x} - \mu}{\sigma_{\bar{x}}} = \frac{5.5 - 5.7}{0.27} = -0.74 \rightarrow .2704 \text{ (area between 5.5 and 5.7)}$$

$$z = \frac{\bar{x} - \mu}{\sigma_{\bar{x}}} = \frac{5.8 - 5.7}{0.27} = 0.37 \quad \rightarrow \underline{.1443} \text{ (area between 5.7 and 5.8)}$$

$$\text{Sum} = \quad .4147 \text{ (area between 5.5 and 5.8)}$$

There's a 41.47% chance that the sample mean will fall between 5.5 and 5.8 if a sample size of 50 is used.

In real-life business situations, the population standard deviation is usually unknown. In such cases, the sample standard deviation, s, is used as an unbiased estimate of the population standard deviation, σ (i.e., s replaces σ in Equation 7.2). Whenever s is used, the t distribution, rather than the normal, is the theoretically correct distribution. (Chapter 8 discusses this concept.) However, whenever the sample size is sufficiently large (30 or greater) or the population is normally distributed, the central limit theorem indicates that the sampling distribution of means will be approximately normal.

EXAMPLE 7.5   A population is known to have a mean of 100. If a sample of 75 items is selected from this population, what is the probability that the sample mean will fall between 100 and 102 if the sample standard deviation is 10?

Since the sample size is greater than 30, a normal sampling distribution can be assumed. The mean of the sampling distribution, in accordance with Equation 7.1, is the population mean, 100. The standard error of the mean can't be calculated exactly because the standard deviation of the population isn't known. However, the sample standard deviation, $s = 10$, can be used as an estimate. In practical applications, this estimation process is typically used since only sample information is available.

The standard error of the mean, in accordance with Equation 7.2, is estimated as

$$s_{\bar{x}} = \frac{s}{\sqrt{n}} = \frac{10}{\sqrt{75}} = \frac{10}{8.66} = 1.15$$

These values are shown on the sampling distribution of Figure 7.4.

FIGURE 7.4   Sampling Distribution of Means for Example 7.5

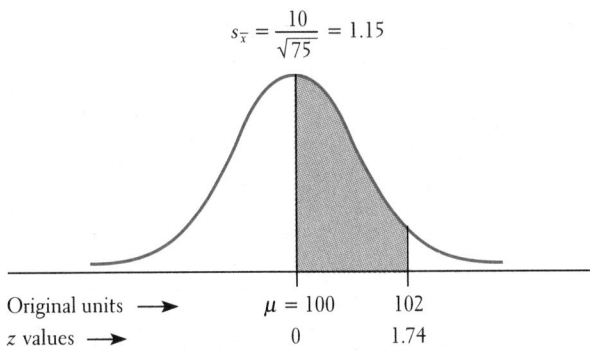

$$s_{\bar{x}} = \frac{10}{\sqrt{75}} = 1.15$$

| Original units $\longrightarrow$ | $\mu = 100$ | 102 |
| z values $\longrightarrow$ | 0 | 1.74 |

The desired area can be found by computing the z value as demonstrated in Figure 7.3. This calculation and the resulting area in the right side of the curve are

$$z = \frac{102 - 100}{1.15} = 1.74 \rightarrow .4591 \text{ (area between 100 and 102)}$$

There's about a 46% chance that the sample mean will lie between 100 and 102 when a sample size of 75 is used.

A good way to understand the concept of the sampling distribution of a statistic is to use MINITAB for simulating the sampling process. The MINITAB Computer Package section at this chapter's end gives an example.

EXERCISES

1. What is sampling error?
2. What is meant by the statement "Sampling error is due to chance"?
3. What is a sampling distribution?

4. Why are sampling distributions important?

5. What thought should the term *standard error* bring to mind?

6. Why is the central limit theorem important?

7. Why is it important for a statistician to assume that a sampling distribution is normally distributed?

8. What effect does each of the following changes have on the variability of a sampling distribution of means?

   a. The population standard deviation is increased.

   b. The sample size is increased.

   c. The population mean is decreased.

9. Describe the shape of the sampling distribution of means when:

   a. The population is normally distributed.

   b. The population is not normally distributed, but the sample size is small (less than 30).

   c. The population is not normally distributed, but the sample size is large (30 or greater).

10. Distinguish the following measures: population mean (μ), sample mean (x), and sampling distribution mean ($\mu_{\bar{x}}$). How do these means compare in size for a specific case?

11. Distinguish the following measures: population standard deviation (σ), sample standard deviation (s), and standard error of the mean ($\sigma_{\bar{x}}$). How do these standard deviations compare in size for a specific case?

12. A normally distributed variable has a mean of 100 and standard deviation of 15. What is the probability that:

   a. A value selected at random will be less than 110?

   b. A value selected at random will be between 85 and 95?

   c. A sample of 20 items will have a mean less than 95?

   d. A sample of 200 items will have a mean less than 95?

   e. A sample of 500 items will have a mean less than 95?

13. A sample of 36 employees has a mean education level of 14 years with a standard deviation of 2 years. What is the standard deviation of the sampling distribution of sample means?

14. A sample of 100 batteries has been selected from a production line that yields batteries with a mean lifetime of 40 months and standard deviation of 10 months. If a different sample of 400 is taken from the same population, will the standard error of the mean be larger, the same, or smaller? Calculate the new standard error of the mean.

15. Suppose an analyst wants to use the information on commodity prices introduced in an article "Commodity-Indexed Debt" (*Columbia Journal of World Business*, Winter, 1988, p. 57). Under the assumption that these prices are normally distributed with a mean of 75 cents and a standard deviation of 9 cents, a random sample of 81 commodity prices is selected. What is the probability that:

   a. The first price selected at random from the population will be larger than 84 cents?

   b. The mean of the sample will be larger than 84 cents?

   c. The mean of the sample will be between 74 and 76 cents?

   d. The mean of the sample will be smaller than 73.5 cents?

16. An automatic machine used to fill cans of soup has mean filling weight of 16 ounces and $\sigma = 0.5$.
    a. What is the probability of obtaining a sample of 49 cans with a mean larger than 16.1 ounces?
    b. Find the probability that the sample mean will be within 0.05 ounces of the population mean, 16 ounces.

17. If all possible samples of size 64 are selected from a population whose mean is 100 and whose standard deviation is 20, between what limits would the middle 80% of the sample means be expected to fall?

18. Family income distribution in St. Paul, Minnesota, is skewed to the right. The latest census reveals mean family income of $24,000 with standard deviation of $4,000. In a simple random sample of 75 families, find the probability that the sample mean family income will differ from St. Paul's mean income by more than $500.

19. A random sample of 40 computer chips is drawn from a population and the weight of each recorded. A previous study showed that the population mean weight was 0.8 ounces with a standard deviation of 0.1 ounces.
    This action is being taken in response to an article on a new PC, the Compaq Systempro (*PC Magazine*, February 27, 1990). The subject of this article has direct application to a chip supplier that now wants to investigate chip weight, a key aspect of a new system involving computer graphics.
    a. What is the probability that the sample has a mean weight between 0.75 and 0.90 ounces?
    b. Determine the probability that the sample has a mean weight less than 0.5 ounces.
    c. How would the sampling distribution of sample means change if the sample size were increased from 40 to 400?

20. A population consists of the following units produced today by four workers:

Worker	Units produced
A	5
B	3
C	7
D	8

   a. Compute the population mean and standard deviation.
   b. Develop a table showing every possible sample of size two (sample with replacement).
   c. Compute the mean of each of the samples of size two.
   d. Compute the mean of this sampling distribution. Does this mean equal the population mean?
   e. Compute the standard error of the mean for this sampling distribution using Equation 7.2.
   f. Compute the standard deviation of the sampling distribution of means. Does this standard deviation equal the standard error of the mean?
   g. Which distribution has less variability: the population distribution or the sampling distribution of sample means?

SAMPLING DISTRIBUTION OF SAMPLE PROPORTIONS

The binomial distribution (Chapter 5) involves finding the probabilities of different numbers of "successes" in a binomial experiment. The binomial distribution is a discrete probability distribution showing the probability of x successes in n trials of a binomial experiment, where each trial results in either success or failure. It is frequently relevant to inquire about the proportion of successes rather than the actual number. Equation 7.3 shows that for a sample of n trials of a binomial experiment, the proportion of successes, the statistic $\bar{p}$, is computed by dividing the number of successes, x, by the number of trials, n:

$$\bar{p} = \frac{x}{n} \tag{7.3}$$

EXAMPLE 7.6   Table 7.3 shows a population of five employees that includes two college graduates. Using Equation 7.3, the proportion of college graduates is

$$p = \frac{2}{5} = .40$$

Forty percent of the workers are college graduates.

TABLE 7.3   Population of Workers (Example 7.6)

Worker	College graduate
A	Yes
B	No
C	No
D	Yes
E	No

EXAMPLE 7.7   Example 7.6 involved a population of five employees including two college graduates. A random sample of two employees is to be selected from this population and the sample proportion of college graduates computed. Several different samples could be selected.

Table 7.4 shows every possible sample pair that can be drawn from the population when sampling is done with replacement. Since $N = 5$ and $n = 2$, there are 25 possible sample pairs. The third column of Table 7.4 shows the proportion of college graduates for each sample pair (the sample statistic). This column constitutes the sampling distribution of proportions for this example. The probability distribution of Table 7.5 summarizes the sampling distribution's values.

Now the mean proportion of the sampling distribution for a sample size of two is calculated:

$$\mu_{\bar{p}} = \frac{10.0}{25} = .40$$

TABLE 7.4 Sampling Distribution of Proportions (Example 7.6)

Sampled workers	Sample characteristics	Sample proportion of college graduates	$(\bar{p} - \mu_{\bar{p}})$	$(\bar{p} - \mu_{\bar{p}})^2$
A, A	Y, Y	1.00	.60	.36
A, B	Y, N	.50	.10	.01
A, C	Y, N	.50	.10	.01
A, D	Y, Y	1.00	.60	.36
A, E	Y, N	.50	.10	.01
B, A	N, Y	.50	.10	.01
B, B	N, N	.00	−.40	.16
B, C	N, N	.00	−.40	.16
B, D	N, Y	.50	.10	.01
B, E	N, N	.00	−.40	.16
C, A	N, Y	.50	.10	.01
C, B	N, N	.00	−.40	.16
C, C	N, N	.00	−.40	.16
C, D	N, Y	.50	.10	.01
C, E	N, N	.00	−.40	.16
D, A	Y, Y	1.00	.60	.36
D, B	Y, N	.50	.10	.01
D, C	Y, N	.50	.10	.01
D, D	Y, Y	1.00	.60	.36
D, E	Y, N	.50	.10	.01
E, A	N, Y	.50	.10	.01
E, B	N, N	.00	−.40	.16
E, C	N, N	.00	−.40	.16
E, D	N, Y	.50	.10	.01
E, E	N, N	.00	−.40	.16
		$\Sigma\bar{p} = 10.00$		3.00

TABLE 7.5 Probability Distribution of Proportions

$\bar{p}$	Frequency	Probability
.00	9	.36
.50	12	.48
1.00	4	.16

Note in the preceding example that the two mean proportions are the same. Equation 7.4 shows that the true population proportion and the mean of the sampling distribution of proportions are equal:

$$p = \mu_{\bar{p}} \tag{7.4}$$

where p = Population proportion
$\mu_{\bar{p}}$ = Mean of the sampling distribution of proportions

When the population is infinite or very large, or when sampling is conducted with replacement, the standard deviation of the sampling distribution of proportions is computed as

$$\sigma_{\bar{p}} = \sqrt{\frac{p(1-p)}{n}} \qquad\qquad (7.5)$$

where $\sigma_{\bar{p}}$ = Standard deviation of the sampling distribution (the standard error
               of the proportion)
         p = Population proportion
         n = Sample size

Remember that the term *standard error* is frequently used to identify the standard deviation of a sampling distribution. In the same way, the standard deviation of the sampling distribution of sample proportions is referred to as the **standard error of the proportion.**

Standard Error of the
Proportion

> The **standard error of the proportion** is the standard deviation of the sampling distribution of sample proportions.

EXAMPLE 7.8   The standard error of the proportion for Example 7.7 is

$$\sigma_{\bar{p}} = \sqrt{\frac{p(1-p)}{n}} = \sqrt{\frac{.40(1-.40)}{2}} = \sqrt{.12} = .3464$$

Computation of the standard deviation for Table 7.4's sampling distribution confirms that the standard error of the proportion is the standard deviation of the sampling distribution of proportions:

$$\sigma_{\bar{p}} = \sqrt{\frac{\Sigma(\bar{p} - \mu_{\bar{p}})^2}{n}} = \sqrt{\frac{3.00}{25}} = \sqrt{.12} = .3464$$

We can show that the proportion of successes in a binomial experiment approaches a normal distribution as the number of trials, n, increases. Chapter 6 emphasized that the normal distribution provides a close approximation to the binomial distribution when n is large and p is neither small nor large. Specifically, to use the normal curve for proportion problems, both np and $n(1 - p)$ should be 5 or greater. Since most real-life business situations that involve the binomial distribution require fairly large sample sizes, the normal approximation to the binomial distribution is frequently used.

EXAMPLE 7.9   Five percent of the cathode ray tubes the Jaypro Company makes for PC monitors are returned by the monitor manufacturer as defective. This is of great concern to Jaypro, especially after a March 1992 article in *PC World*, "Buyer's Guide: Super VGA Monitors" (page 178). Jaypro considers it essential to improve its quality performance if it's to continue supplying tubes to the industry.

After a quality-improvement program, Jaypro will sample its cathode ray tubes to see if quality has risen. A random sample of 125 tubes will be pulled from inventory during the next few days. What is the probability that more than 8% of them will be defective, assuming that the overall defective rate is still 5 percent? Figure 7.5 shows the desired area.

FIGURE 7.5   Sampling Distribution of Proportions for Example 7.9

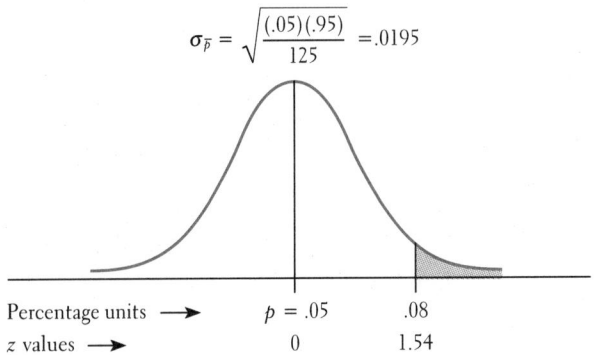

$$\sigma_{\bar{p}} = \sqrt{\frac{(.05)(.95)}{125}} = .0195$$

Percentage units ⟶ $p = .05$ .08
z values ⟶   0   1.54

The calculations for the desired area are

$$\sigma_{\bar{p}} = \sqrt{\frac{p(1-p)}{n}} = \sqrt{\frac{.05(1-.05)}{125}} = \sqrt{.00038} = .0195$$

$$z = \frac{\bar{p}-p}{\sigma_{\bar{p}}} = \frac{.08 - .05}{.0195} = 1.54 \rightarrow .4382 \text{ (area between .05 and .08)}$$

$$.5000 - .4382 = .0618 \text{ (area above .08)}$$

There's approximately a .0618 chance that 8% or more of the tubes will be defective, assuming a population defective rate of 5%.

EXAMPLE 7.10   The following quote appeared in *The Spokesman-Review* on October 30, 1989:

> City Councilwoman Sheri Bernard appears to be riding a wave of anti-incinerator sentiment into the Spokane mayor's office. A survey, conducted Oct. 19–25 for *The Spokesman-Review* and *Spokane Chronicle*, shows Bernard far ahead of her campaign rival and fellow councilman, Rob Higgins. Of the 200 city voters selected at random and surveyed by Market Trends Inc. of Spokane, 46% said they would vote for Bernard if the election were held tomorrow. . . . Another 19% were undecided when the survey was taken, some two weeks before the election.

Sheri's campaign manager, counting on about half of the undecided voters, feels confident that 55% of the population of voters will choose Sheri Bernard.

On November 6, one day before the election, a random sample of 35 voters is taken to assess voting preference. What is the probability that this sample will indicate that Sheri will lose (i.e., that fewer than 50% of the sampled voters prefer her) if in fact, she has a population preference of 55%? Figure 7.6 shows the area to be found.

FIGURE 7.6   Sampling Distribution of Proportions for Example 7.10

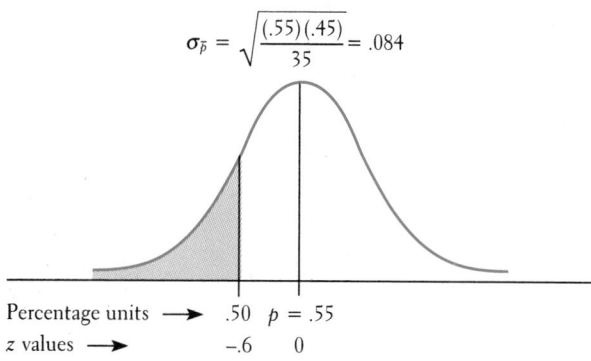

$$\sigma_{\bar{p}} = \sqrt{\frac{(.55)(.45)}{35}} = .084$$

Percentage units $\longrightarrow$ .50 $p = .55$
z values $\longrightarrow$ $-.6$ 0

The calculations for the desired area are

$$\sigma_{\bar{p}} = \sqrt{\frac{p(1-p)}{n}} = \sqrt{\frac{.55(1-.55)}{35}} = \sqrt{.007} = .084$$

$$z = \frac{\bar{p}-p}{\sigma_{\bar{p}}} = \frac{.50-.55}{.084} = -0.60 \rightarrow .2257 \text{ (area between .50 and .55)}$$

$$.5000 - .2257 = .2743 \text{ (area below .50)}$$

There's about a 27% chance that the sample of 35 will mislead Sheri's campaign manager into thinking she'll lose when, in fact, she has a 55% population voter preference. A larger sample size would reduce this probability of error.

EXAMPLE 7.11   How would a sample size of 150 alter the risk of error in Example 7.10 if Sheri is still assumed to have a population voter preference of 55%? Figure 7.7 shows the area to be found.

FIGURE 7.7   Sampling Distribution of Proportions for Example 7.11

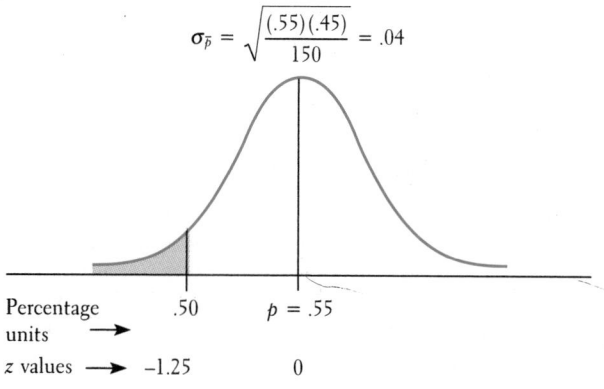

$$\sigma_{\bar{p}} = \sqrt{\frac{(.55)(.45)}{150}} = .04$$

Percentage units $\longrightarrow$ .50 $p = .55$
z values $\longrightarrow$ -1.25 0

The calculations for the desired area are

$$\sigma_{\bar{p}} = \sqrt{\frac{p(1-p)}{n}} = \sqrt{\frac{.55(1-.55)}{150}} = \sqrt{.00165} = .04$$

$$z = \frac{\bar{p} - p}{\sigma_{\bar{p}}} = \frac{.50 - .55}{.04} = -1.25 \rightarrow .3944 \text{ (area between .50 and .55)}$$

$$.5000 - .3944 = .1056 \text{ (area below .50)}$$

The increased sample size reduces the probability of misleading results from 27.43% to 10.56%.

EXERCISES

21. Explain the difference between the number of successes in a binomial experiment and the percentage of successes.

22. If you took a statistics quiz and answered 16 out of the 20 questions correctly, what percentage of the questions did you get right?

23. What effect does increasing the sample size have on the variability of a sampling distribution of proportions?

24. When is it appropriate to use the normal approximation for the sampling distribution of proportions?

25. Seventy percent of a population of employees are male. In a sample of 10 employees, what are the mean and standard deviation of the sampling distribution for the proportion of males selected?

26. (This question refers to Exercise 25.) How will increasing the sample size to 100 affect the mean and standard deviation of the sampling distribution? Calculate the new standard error of the proportion.

27. Approximately 20% of the independent grocery stores in Bonner County offer trading stamps. If a sample of 50 stores is selected, find the probability that:

    a. The first store selected at random from the population will offer trading stamps.

    b. The proportion of stores offering trading stamps will be greater than 25%.

    c. The proportion of stores offering trading stamps will be less than 22%.

    d. The proportion of stores offering trading stamps will be between 17% and 23%.

28. Seventeen percent of the people who file tax returns in the state of Georgia have gross taxable incomes of more than $50,000. If a sample of 400 Georgia returns is randomly selected, what is the probability that more than 20% of these people have gross taxable incomes in excess of $50,000?

29. Doyle's Wholesale Toys' marketing manager is interested in computer-assisted toys after reading an article about them in *PC Computing* ("PCs in Toyland," August 1989, p. 90). She wants to investigate entry into this market and thinks the extent of repeat customers for her company will play a key role in such a venture's success.

    She believes that 60% of her firm's orders come from repeat customers. A simple random sample of 80 orders will be used to verify this assumption. Assuming that her belief is correct, find the probability that the sample percentage will be less than 50%.

30. Last year 75% of Hart Department Store's credit card purchases were for less than $150. In a random sample of 200 credit card purchases, what is the probability that purchases less than $150 amount to:

    a. Between 70% and 80%?

    b. More than 80%?

    c. More than 20%?

31. A population consists of the following six units produced today. One unit is defective.

Item	Condition
A	OK
B	Defective
C	OK
D	OK
E	OK
F	OK

    a. Compute the population proportion for defective units.

    b. Develop a table showing every possible sample of size two (sample with replacement).

    c. Compute the proportion defective of each of the samples of size two shown in part b.

    d. Compute the mean of this sampling distribution of sample proportions. Does this mean proportion equal the population proportion?

    e. Compute the standard error of the proportion for this sampling distribution.

    f. Compute the standard deviation of the sampling distribution of proportions. Does this standard deviation equal the standard error of the proportion?

THE FINITE-POPULATION MULTIPLIER

Many populations that decision makers examine are limited in size (finite). However, Equation 7.2 is based on a population that's infinite or very large. This is why analysts frequently sample from finite populations with replacement (each item selected for inclusion in a sample is immediately put back into the population so that it might be chosen again). But sometimes we can't sample with replacement, as when items are destroyed in the sampling process. For example, if TV picture tube lifetimes are tested to determine the time until failure, sampling without replacement is mandatory.

For reasons of cost and convenience, sampling is frequently done without replacement. As long as the sample size is small relative to the population, sampling without replacement yields essentially the same results as sampling with replacement. However, as a rule of thumb, if the sample size is more than 5% of the population, the results of sampling with and without replacement will differ. This occurs because the probabilities change significantly from selection to selection when sampling without replacement from a small population. Chapter 5 stated that the hypergeometric distribution is appropriate for determining sample probabilities in this situation. Fortunately, the hypergeometric modification can be reduced to the simple form known as the **finite-population multiplier:**

$$\text{Finite-population multiplier} = \sqrt{\frac{N - n}{N - 1}} \qquad (7.6)$$

where N = Population size
    n = Sample size

Equation 7.6 is used to modify the standard error formula to reflect changing probabilities when the sample size exceeds 5% of the population ($n/N > .05$). The standard error is simply multiplied by the finite-population multiplier.

> The **finite-population multiplier** is used to modify a standard error formula to reflect changing probabilities, when sampling is done without replacement from a finite population and the sample size exceeds 5% of the population ($n/N > .05$).

EXAMPLE 7.12   In Example 7.6, Table 7.3 showed a population of five employees including two college graduates. Table 7.4 showed the 25 possible samples of two that could be selected using sampling with replacement. Table 7.6 shows the 10 possible samples of two that can be selected using sampling without replacement.

TABLE 7.6 Sampling Distribution of Proportions for Example 7.6 without Replacement (Example 7.12)

Sampled workers	Sample characteristics	Sample proportion of college graduates
A, B	Y, N	.50
A, C	Y, N	.50
A, D	Y, Y	1.00
A, E	Y, N	.50
B, C	N, N	.00
B, D	N, Y	.50
B, E	N, N	.00
C, D	N, Y	.50
C, E	N, N	.00
D, E	Y, N	.50
	$\Sigma\bar{p} =$	$\overline{4.00}$

Since the sample represents over 5% of the population ($n/N = \frac{2}{5}$, or 40%, of the population), the standard error of the proportion should be modified using the finite-population multiplier:

$$\sigma_{\bar{p}} = \sqrt{\frac{p(1-p)}{n}}\sqrt{\frac{N-n}{N-1}} = \sqrt{\frac{.40(1-.40)}{2}}\sqrt{\frac{5-2}{5-1}} = \sqrt{.12}\sqrt{.75} = .30$$

You can compute the standard deviation for the sampling distribution in Table 7.6 and confirm that the standard error of the proportion modified by the finite-population multiplier is the standard deviation of the sampling distribution of proportions.

EXAMPLE 7.13 In Example 7.2 all possible samples of two ages were selected with replacement from the population of five ages: 10, 20, 30, 40, and 50. Table 7.1 gave the resulting sampling distribution of 25 sample means. The mean of this sampling distribution was 30 and the standard deviation was

$$\sigma_{\bar{x}} = \sigma/\sqrt{n} = 14.1/\sqrt{2} = 10$$

What if the samples of two ages were selected without replacement? Table 7.7 shows the resulting sampling distribution of 10 sample means. The mean of this sampling distribution is still 30. However, the standard deviation must be calculated using the finite-population multiplier because the sample size exceeds 5% of the population $[(n/N = {}^2/_5 = .4)$. The standard deviation of this sampling distribution is

$$\sigma_{\bar{x}} = \frac{\sigma}{\sqrt{n}}\sqrt{\frac{N-n}{N-1}} = \frac{14.1}{\sqrt{2}}\sqrt{\frac{5-2}{5-1}} = 10\sqrt{.75} = 8.66$$

You can compute the standard deviation for the sampling distribution of Table 7.7 and confirm that the standard error of the mean modified by the finite-population multiplier is the standard deviation of the sampling distribution of means.

TABLE 7.7 Sampling Distribution of Sample Means for Example 7.2 without Replacement (Example 7.13)

Sampled ages	Sample means
10, 20	15
10, 30	20
10, 40	25
10, 50	30
20, 30	25
20, 40	30
20, 50	35
30, 40	35
30, 50	40
40, 50	45
	$\Sigma\bar{x} = 300$

EXERCISES

32. Explain the difference between sampling with replacement and sampling without replacement.

33. Why is it necessary to use the finite-population multiplier?

34. When is it necessary to use the finite-population multiplier?

35. For a normally distributed population of $N = 750$ with a mean of 20 and standard deviation of 2, find the standard error of the mean for sampling distributions based on the following sample sizes (sampling is done without replacement):

   a. 25.

   b. 60.

   c. 100.

36. The mean of a normally distributed population of 500 items is 175, and the standard deviation is 19. A sample of 81 items is selected without replacement from this population. What is the probability that:

   a. The first item selected at random from the population will be greater than 184?

   b. The mean of the sample will be greater than 180?

   c. The mean of the sample will be between 173 and 177?

   d. The mean of the sample will be smaller than 172?

37. Approximately 20% of the 200 independent grocery stores in Alameda offer trading stamps. In a sample of 50 stores selected without replacement, what is the probability that:

   a. The percentage of stores offering trading stamps will be greater than 27%?

   b. The percentage of stores offering trading stamps will be less than 14%?

   c. The percentage of stores offering trading stamps will be between 15% and 19%?

38. After reading that "premature deaths cost American industry more than $25 billion and 132 million workdays of lost production each year" (*World Traveler*, May 1992, p. 30), Mary Upton, president of SCI Corporation, is considering implementing a physical fitness program for her 800 employees. A simple random sample of 100 employees selected without replacement is taken to estimate what percentage would participate. Mary will implement the program if at least 50% of her employees would participate. If 400 out of 800 is the true population proportion, what is the probability that fewer than 45 out of the 100 people surveyed will show a desire to participate in the program?

39. This question refers to the population in Exercise 20:

Worker	Units produced
A	5
B	3
C	7
D	8

   a. Develop a table showing every possible sample of size two (sample without replacement).

   b. Compute the mean of each of the samples in part *a*.

   c. Compute the mean of this sampling distribution. Does this mean equal the population mean?

   d. Compute the standard error of the mean for this sampling distribution (remember the correction factor).

    e. Compute the standard deviation of the sampling distribution of means. Does this standard deviation equal the standard error of the mean?

40. This question refers to the population in Exercise 31:

Item	Condition
A	OK
B	Defective
C	OK
D	OK
E	OK
F	OK

    a. Develop a table showing every possible sample of size two (sample without replacement).

    b. Compute the proportion of each of the samples in part *a.*

    c. Compute the mean proportion of this sampling distribution of sample proportions. Does this mean proportion equal the population proportion?

    d. Compute the standard error of the proportion for this sampling distribution.

    e. Compute the standard deviation of the sampling distribution of proportions. Is this standard deviation equal to the standard error of the proportion?

SUMMARY

This chapter presented the most important concept in statistics, the sampling distribution. Whenever a sample is taken from the population being studied, a statistic computed from this sample should be viewed as being drawn from the distribution of all possible sample statistics. This key concept of statistical inference will be used throughout the rest of this book.

This chapter discussed two sampling distributions: the sampling distribution of means and the sampling distribution of proportions. More sampling distributions appear in later chapters. Both distributions discussed here are used in the next two chapters when procedures for estimation and hypothesis testing are developed.

It is vital that you understand the basic concept of the sampling distribution. Spend as much time as necessary with this chapter to gain this understanding. If you have a firm grasp of the idea of a sampling distribution, you'll find the rest of the text much easier to understand.

APPLICATIONS OF STATISTICAL CONCEPTS IN THE BUSINESS WORLD

Whenever the variability of sample results is called into question, the concept of the sampling distribution is applicable. Here are some sample statistics that may or may not signal an important shift, depending on the position in the sampling distribution.

1. A new manager in a branch bank reports an increase of $125 in the average savings account balance after one month on the job.

2. Accounts receivable has a new average balance "significantly" below the previous level due to a new campaign to reduce receivables.
3. The percentage of customers returning merchandise, based on a random sample of buyers, falls after a new "be a friend" campaign is started at the returns desk.
4. A small loan office manager notices that the average amount requested by loan customers has increased a bit during the past two weeks.
5. The personnel department of a large company is proud of its "pride in excellence" program, which, it claims, has reduced the absenteeism rate during the past six months. The claim is based on a sample of workers over a two-week period.
6. The average number of times a store's credit card is used per customer has dropped below the average of a year ago.
7. A quality-control manager points with pride to a reduction in nonfunctioning units from 5.8% to 4.3%. The latter figure is based on a random sample of 35.

GLOSSARY

Sampling error The difference between a sample statistic and its corresponding population parameter.

Sampling distribution A distribution that includes all possible values a statistic, such as a sample mean, can assume for a given sample size.

Standard error of the mean The standard deviation of the sampling distribution of sample means.

Central limit theorem A theorem stating that if a sufficiently large random sample of n observations is selected from any population, the sampling distribution of sample means will be approximately a normal distribution.

Standard error of the proportion The standard deviation of the sampling distribution of sample proportions.

Finite-population multiplier A factor used to modify standard error formulas to reflect changing probabilities if sampling is done without replacement from a finite population and the sample constitutes more than 5% of the population ($n/N > .05$).

KEY FORMULAS

Mean of the sampling distribution of means

$$\mu_x = \mu_{\bar{x}} \tag{7.1}$$

Standard error of the mean

$$\sigma_{\bar{x}} = \frac{\sigma}{\sqrt{n}} \tag{7.2}$$

Percentage or proportion of successes

$$\bar{p} = \frac{x}{n} \tag{7.3}$$

Mean of the sampling distribution of proportions

$$p = \mu_{\bar{p}}$$

Standard error of the proportion

$$\sigma_{\bar{p}} = \sqrt{\frac{p(1 - p)}{n}}$$
(7.5)

Finite-population multiplier

$$\sqrt{\frac{N - n}{N - 1}}$$
(7.6)

SOLVED EXERCISES
· ·

1. SAMPLING DISTRIBUTION OF MEANS

The Timeless Battery Company claims that its batteries have a mean life of 60 months and standard deviation of 9 months. A consumer group testing this claim purchases 36 batteries and determines the mean lifetime.

a. Compute the standard error of the mean.

b. Assuming that Timeless's claim is true, what is the probability that the sample's mean life is less than 58?

c. Determine the probability that the mean life of the sample is between 57 and 63.

d. Assume that the actual population mean lifetime for Timeless batteries is 55 months. Find the probability that the mean life of the sample is at least 60.

e. If the consumer group's sample mean is 55, what would you conclude if you were its analyst?

Solution:

a. $\sigma_{\bar{x}} = \dfrac{\sigma}{\sqrt{n}} = \dfrac{9}{\sqrt{36}} = \dfrac{9}{6} = 1.5$

b. $z = \dfrac{\bar{x} - \mu}{\sigma_{\bar{x}}} = \dfrac{58 - 60}{1.5} = -1.33 \rightarrow$ .4082 (area between 58 and 60)

$.5000 - .4082 = .0918$ (area below 58)

The probability is about 9%.

c. $z = \dfrac{\bar{x} - \mu}{\sigma_{\bar{x}}} = \dfrac{63 - 60}{1.5} = 2.00 \rightarrow$ .4772 (area between 60 and 63)

$.4772 + .4772 = .9544$ (area betwen 57 and 63)

The probability is about 95%.

d. $z = \dfrac{\bar{x} - \mu}{\sigma_{\bar{x}}} = \dfrac{60 - 55}{1.5} = 3.33 \rightarrow$ almost .5000 (area between 55 and 60)

$.5000 - .5000 = .0000$ (area above 60)

The probability is approximately zero.

e. You should conclude that Timeless's claim is false. It is almost impossible to get a sample mean of 55 from a population with a mean of 60 using a sample size of 36.

2. SAMPLING DISTRIBUTION OF PROPORTIONS

Laser Dynamics Corporation is considering advertising on the TV show, "Roseanne." The A.C. Nielsen ratings in *U.S.A. Today* (July 1, 1992) showed that "Roseanne" had a rating share (shares are the percentage of sets in use) of 25 on June 23, 1992. Vicki Laser, public relations director, suspects that the actual percentage is less than 25%. Vicki hires an independent research agency to take a random sample of 750 viewers watching TV at 9 P.M. Tuesday, June 30, 1992. The agency finds that 175 were watching "Roseanne." Do these data present sufficient evidence to contradict the A.C. Nielsen ratings?

Solution:

$$\bar{p} = \frac{x}{n} = \frac{175}{750} = .233$$

$$\sigma_{\bar{p}} = \sqrt{\frac{p(1-p)}{n}} = \sqrt{\frac{.25(1-.25)}{750}} = \sqrt{.00025} = .0158$$

$$z = \frac{\bar{p} - p}{\sigma_{\bar{p}}} = \frac{.233 - .25}{.0158} = -1.08 \to .3599 \quad \text{(area between .25 and .233)}$$

$$.5000 - .3599 = .1401 \quad \text{(area below .233)}$$

The probability of finding 175 or fewer viewers watching "Roseanne" out of a sample of 750 is approximately .14 (14%) if the true population percentage is 25%.

3. FINITE-POPULATION MULTIPLIER

The hourly wages for the Hem Iron Works plant's 500 workers average (mean) $8.50 with standard deviation of $2.20. What is the probability that the mean wage of a sample of 100 workers will be:

a. More than $9?

b. Between $8.15 and $8.40?

Solution:

a. $$\sigma_{\bar{x}} = \frac{\sigma}{\sqrt{n}} \sqrt{\frac{N-n}{N-1}} = \frac{2.20}{\sqrt{100}} \sqrt{\frac{500-100}{500-1}} = 0.22(.8953) = 0.197$$

$$z = \frac{\bar{x} - \mu}{\sigma_{\bar{x}}} = \frac{9 - 8.5}{0.197} = 2.54 \to .4945 \quad \text{(area between 8.50 and 9.00)}$$

$$.5000 - .4945 = .0055 \quad \text{(area above 9)}$$

The probability is about .55%.

b. $$z = \frac{\bar{x} - \mu}{\sigma_{\bar{x}}} = \frac{8.4 - 8.5}{0.197} = -0.51 \to .1950 \quad \text{(area between 8.40 and 8.50)}$$

$$.5000 - .1950 = .3050 \quad \text{(area below 8.4)}$$

$$z = \frac{\bar{x} - \mu}{\sigma_{\bar{x}}} = \frac{8.15 - 8.5}{0.197} = -1.78 \to .4625 \quad \text{(area between 8.15 and 8.50)}$$

$$.5000 - .4625 = .0375 \quad \text{(area below 8.15)}$$

$$.3050 - .0375 = .2675 \quad \text{(area between 8.15 and 8.40)}$$

The probability is almost 27%.

EXERCISES

. . . .

41. "College Mergers: An Emerging Alternative," *Community, Technical and Junior College Journal*, (August/September 1988, p. 37) interests Niagara Falls and Niagara Central Community College officials, who are considering a merger. One question critical to a merger is the number of credit hours students have completed at each institution. If total credit hours per student at Niagara Falls Community College are normally distributed with a mean of 50 and a standard deviation of 5, what is the probability that:

    a. A student at random will have more than 55 credit hours?

    b. A student at random will have between 55 and 60 credit hours?

    c. A sample of 10 students will have a mean less than 49 hours?

    d. A sample of 100 students will have a mean less than 49 hours?

    e. A sample of 400 students will have a mean less than 49 hours?

42. A variable representing the probability that a person entering a shop will buy something follows a binomial distribution and has a population proportion equal to .25. What is the probability that:

    a. A person entering the shop will buy something?

    b. At least 1 person out of a sample of 5 people entering the shop will buy something?

    c. More than 30 people out of a sample of 100 entering the shop will buy something?

    d. More than 120 people out of a sample of 400 entering the shop will buy something?

43. For a normally distributed population of $N = 250$ with a mean of 60 and standard deviation of 5, find the standard error of the mean for sampling distributions based on the following sample sizes, if sampling is done without replacement:

    a. 10.

    b. 50.

    c. 100.

44. California had 9.5% unemployment in June 1992 (*The Spokane-Review*, July 3, 1992). Find the probability that the percentage of unemployed in a random sample of 600 people is over 10%.

45. Bill Barkley believes that 25% of all persons with incomes above $75,000 will be audited by the IRS on a random basis at least once in a 10-year period.

    a. What is the probability that of a sample of 150 people with incomes over $75,000, at least 45 will have been audited at least once in the past 10 years?

    b. If a random sample of 300 is selected, what is the probability that the proportion of the sample who were audited at least once is between 20% and 30%?

46. The number of column inches of classified advertisements appearing on Fridays in the *Tampa Bay Chronicle* is roughly normally distributed with mean 427 and standard deviation 44 inches. Assume that results for the past 20 consecutive Fridays can be regarded as a random sample ($n = 20$).

    a. What is the probability that the number of column inches appearing last Friday was more than 450?

    b. Find the mean and standard error of the total number of column inches of classified advertisements for a sampling distribution of 20 Fridays.

c. Find the probability that the average number of column inches per Friday will be between 400 and 500.

47. There are about 1,400 automobile dealers in the Chicago area with average (mean) dollar sales per dealer around $750,000. A random sample of 250 dealers is selected, and the mean and standard deviation are computed. If the standard deviation is $95,000, what is the probability that the sample mean is between $740,000 and $765,000?

48. Linda Rice, Western Life Insurance Company analyst, is concerned with whether insurance applications provide complete information. From past experience, Linda has found that 80% of the applications provide complete information. If the next 100 applications are considered a random sample, what is the probability that the proportion of completed applications will fall within 5 percentage points of the population percentage?

49. A tax analyst wishes to sample a population of 5,000 tax returns after reading an article in *Accountancy* (June 1989, p. 27) on tax planning for the year 1992. In this population of returns, the proportion of people who authorized $1 for support of political parties is 60%. If the analyst randomly selects a sample of 500 returns, find the probability that the sample percentage authorizing $1 of support will be between 55% and 65%.

50. A consumer magazine reported that families in the Southwest spend an average of $23.54 for eating out each week. An economist checks this value for the Midwest. He selects a random sample of 121 families and calculates a mean weekly expenditure for eating out of $25.34 with standard deviation of $4.62. Would you say that families in the Midwest spend more eating out, or is the difference in mean expenditures due to chance sampling error?

51. A mortgage company knows that 8% of its home loan recipients default within the first five years. What is the probability that out of 350 loan recipients, fewer than 25 will default within the next five years?

52. A population of high school students has a mean grade point average (GPA) of 2.98 with standard deviation of 0.39. Suppose federal education auditors conduct a random sample of students to determine whether their mean GPA meets certain federal guidelines. They take a random sample of 75 students and calculate the sample GPA.

    a. Find the probability that the sample GPA is less than 2.98.

    b. Find the probability that the sample GPA is greater than 3.00.

    c. Find the probability that the sample GPA is between 2.9 and 3.1.

53. Touch, a well-known cold remedy, is advertised to relieve cold symptoms for an average (mean) of 12 hours with standard deviation of 3 hours. Assuming this claim is true, if a sample of 50 patients with colds are given this medicine, what is the probability that the average relief will last:

    a. Between 11.5 and 12.5 hours?

    b. More than 13 hours?

    c. Less than 10 hours?

54. In a population of 900 business majors at a large midwestern university, mean GPA is 3.0 with standard deviation of 0.3. If a random sample of 75 students is selected, find the probability that the sample mean GPA will differ from the population mean GPA by more than 0.05.

55. The following data show how many computers each of four Computer Korner salespeople sold last week and whether each salesperson had previous computer sales experience before working at Computer Korner.

Salesperson	Sales	Experience
A	5	Y
B	4	Y
C	2	Y
D	1	N

a. Compute the population mean and standard deviation for the number of sales last week.

b. Develop a table showing every possible sample of two (sample without replacement).

c. Compute the mean of each of the samples in part b.

d. Compute the mean of this sampling distribution. Does this mean equal the population mean?

e. Compute the standard error of the mean for this sampling distribution.

f. Compute the standard deviation of the sampling distribution of means. Does this standard deviation equal the standard error of the mean?

56. This question refers to Exercise 55.

a. Compute the population proportion for the percentage of salespeople who have previous experience.

b. Develop a table showing every possible sample of two (sample without replacement).

c. Compute the proportion of each of the samples in part b.

d. Compute the mean proportion of this sampling distribution of sample proportions. Does this mean proportion equal the population proportion?

e. Compute the standard error of the proportion for this sampling distribution.

f. Compute the standard deviation of the sampling distribution of proportions. Does this standard deviation equal the standard error of the proportion?

EXTENDED EXERCISES

57. THE WICKLAND CORPORATION

This exercise is a class project. The Wickland Corporation has examined the number of sales for the past 200 days, which are listed below. Past experience has shown the variable to be normally distributed with a mean of 100 and standard deviation of 10. Select a random sample of 30 sales values (sample with replacement). Each class member should select his or her own individual random sample. For each sample, calculate the sample mean and standard deviation. These values should then be assembled for the class.

100	89	95	103	82	77	97	109	99	100
99	105	99	109	108	96	104	111	90	99

96	100	88	103	99	112	88	101	102	99
100	91	112	96	107	106	82	90	96	84
105	85	99	91	109	85	107	99	80	94
99	92	83	111	104	110	80	127	118	110
117	85	114	105	96	89	105	87	98	96
109	80	98	94	102	98	93	103	102	97
107	98	96	107	101	104	88	109	87	93
92	104	111	91	106	94	80	102	104	81
121	90	87	95	85	111	98	110	121	90
118	120	99	115	105	117	99	101	84	103
112	107	92	87	109	110	105	98	99	104
101	115	97	120	113	110	96	100	126	95
107	114	114	93	86	100	93	105	121	112
93	120	84	95	77	89	96	105	115	109
111	89	84	94	104	105	86	92	98	109
102	103	99	114	99	101	104	110	97	96
90	100	105	107	95	100	97	85	96	105
104	98	104	101	111	107	95	98	87	90

a. How do your sample mean and standard deviation compare with the population parameters?

b. The class as a whole should construct a sampling distribution of sample means and compute the mean and standard deviation.

c. Does the sampling distribution of sample means appear to approximate a normal distribution?

d. Are the mean and standard error of the class sampling distribution close to the values expected from the population data?

58. GADY ELECTRONICS

Gady Electronics, Inc., makes keyboards for use in personal computers. One small chip whose operation is critical in the keyboard is made by a supplier in California. The supplier has had quality-control problems, but Gady is reluctant to switch to another supplier because of the chip's unique capabilities.

The problem is acute since Al Gady, the company's quality-control officer, read an article about Microsoft bringing stereo sound and synchronized audio/video to some of its software. These changes underline the importance of properly operating keyboards in the future.

In a meeting with the supplier two weeks ago, Al pointed out that about 10% of the chips arriving at the Gady plant were defective. This caused Gady many problems such as the expense of inspection and replacement of defective units. The supplier assured Al that measures would be taken to improve the quality.

Al decided to inspect a random sample of the chips that arrived at the plant a week after this meeting. A random sampling plan was designed for selecting chips from various shipments over a week's time. A total of 50 chips were selected and subjected to tests. Of the 50 chips in the sample, 4, or 8%, were found to be defective.

Al complained to the supplier about the lack of significant progress in reducing the defective percentage of the chips. The manager of the chip operation replied, "A defective rate of

8% shows significant progress in improving the quality level of the chips; after all, 8% is less than 10%."

a. What is the probability of getting a sample percentage of 8% or less if the true population defective percentage is 10%?

b. By using correct statistical procedures, determine who is right.

c. Based on the answers to the preceding questions, what should Al tell the supplier?

59. BOARDSTROM DEPARTMENT STORE

Julie Elway (manager of Boardstrom Department Store in Tulsa, Oklahoma) and her management team are considering allowing the store to issue its own credit card to customers. First, Julie wants to know whether Boardstrom customers' average dollar purchase is the same as the national average for such stores, $73. The standard deviation for this population of stores is $8. The team formulates a plan to take a random sample of customer purchase amounts. Each department in the store is to be sampled during a three-week period, and various days of the week and times of day will be used in collecting the data.

The management team isn't sure how to use the data once it's collected. They recognize that even if the population average purchase amount for the store is $73, a sample average might differ from this amount. The team has discussed the variability of sample means from sample to sample and wonders how the results should be interpreted after the sampling process is completed.

A random sampling plan of purchase amounts is developed, but management is concerned about the variability of sample means. Store manager Elway decides to sample 100 purchase amounts taken from various departments of the store at various times of the day and days of the week. After the sample is taken, a mean of $70 is computed.

Next, it is assumed that the store's average purchase amount is $73, the national average. Figure 7.8 shows the sampling distribution that applies when the population standard deviation of $8 is used to calculate the standard error of the mean:

$$\sigma_{\bar{x}} = \frac{\sigma}{\sqrt{n}} = \frac{8}{\sqrt{100}} = \frac{8}{10} = 0.8$$

FIGURE 7.8   Sampling Distribution of Means for Exercise 59

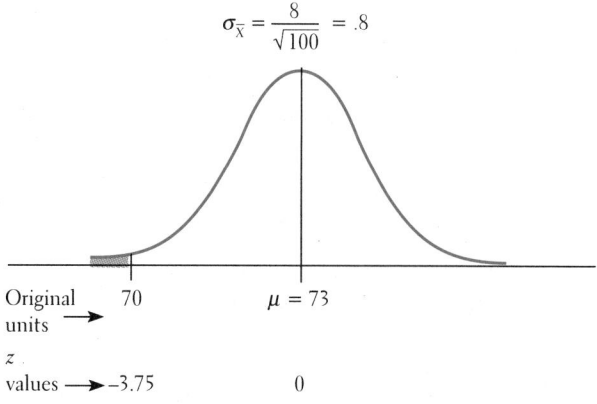

If the population standard deviation were unknown, the sample standard deviation could have been used to estimate it.

Store management can now evaluate the $70 sample mean. How likely is it that this value was drawn from Figure 7.8's sampling distribution? The answer to this question will help Julie's team decide how likely it is that the population mean for the store equals the national average. Write a memo to management on this subject.

60. OUR LADY OF LOURDES HOSPITAL

Chapter 4 presented family sizes for a population of 200 Our Lady of Lourdes Hospital employees. You were asked to select a random sample of size 30 and compute the mean and standard deviation. Assume that the population mean is 2.9.

a. By how much does your sample mean differ from the population mean? Explain this difference.

b. The class as a whole should construct a sampling distribution of sample means and compute its mean and standard deviation.

c. Does the sampling distribution of sample means appear to approximate a normal distribution?

MICROCOMPUTER PACKAGE
. . . .

The micro package *Computerized Business Statistics* may be used to solve sampling distribution problems based on the normal curve.

In Exercise 59, Julie Elway, Boardstrom Department Store manager, wanted to know whether Boardstrom customers' average dollar purchase matched the national average for such stores, $73.

Computer Solution

From the main menu of *Computerized Business Statistics* a **5** is selected, indicating Probability Distributions.

This problem involves the normal distribution. Since Julie wanted to know whether the Boardstrom average dollar purchase, $70, differed significantly from the national average for such stores, $73, the arrow is moved to normal $P(\text{Mean} \leq x \leq a)$.

```
Enter Mean and Press ↵ 73
Enter Standard Deviation and Press ↵ .8
Enter A and Press ↵ 76
```

The normal probability distribution for $\mu = 73$ and $\sigma = 0.8$ is then shown on the screen. Note that the area between 76 and 73 is the same as the area between 70 and 73.

The correct answer for $P(70 \leq x \leq 73)$ is .4987. The probability of obtaining a sample mean of $70 from a population with a mean of $73 is practically zero $(.5000 - .4987 = .0013)$.

MINITAB COMPUTER PACKAGE
. . . .

The MINITAB package can be used to generate a sampling distribution. Suppose you want to simulate 100 random samples of size $n = 40$ drawn from a population including the integer numbers 1 to 100. The MINITAB commands necessary to accomplish this task are:

```
MTB> RANDOM 100 C1-C40;
SUBC> INTEGER 1 100.
MTB> ADD C1-C40, PUT SUM IN C41
MTB> DIVIDE C41 BY 40, PUT SAMPLE AVERAGES IN C42
MTB> DESCRIBE C42
C42  N        MEAN    MEDIAN    STDEV
     100     50.498   50.288   3.860

C42  MIN      MAX      Q1       Q3
    41.525   60.250  47.806   53.225
MRB> STOP
```

The RANDOM and INTEGER commands generate 40 samples of size 100. Each sample consists of numbers in the range 1 to 100. The ADD command adds the values in each row across the 40 columns and places the sums in column C41. The DIVIDE command divides each sum by 40, thus calculating the sample mean. At this point, the columns C1, . . . , C40, C41, and C42 look like:

```
ROW    C1   . . .    C40       C41        C42
 1     52            48      2145.542    53.639
 2     40            62      1934.678    48.367
 .      .             .         .           .
 .      .             .         .           .
 .      .             .         .           .
100    72            31      2047.112    51.178
```

Column C42 contains the 100 sample means. The DESCRIBE command calculates the mean, standard deviation, minimum, and maximum for these 100 sample means. The mean of the sampling distribution is 50.5 (the population mean is also 50.5), and the standard deviation of the sampling distribution is 3.86 (the standard deviation of *all* possible sample means of sample size 40 is $\sigma/\sqrt{n} = 29/\sqrt{40} = 4.59$).

The HISTOGRAM command produces:

```
MTB> HISTOGRAM C42

Histogram of C42  N = 100

Midpoint  Count
      42      1  /
      44      5  /////
      46     13  /////////////
      48     14  //////////////
      50     23  ///////////////////////
      52     17  /////////////////
      54     14  //////////////
      56      8  ////////
      58      3  ///
      60      2  //
MTB>STOP
```

The central limit theorem indicates that the sampling distribution should be a normal distribution (with a mean of 50.5 and a standard deviation of 4.59). The histogram does look very much like a normal distribution.

Chapter

8

ESTIMATION

Errors, like straws, upon the surface flow; he who would search for pearls must dive below.
Dryden, "All for Love"

Objectives

When you have completed this chapter, you will be able to:

Describe the mean and proportion of a population using point and interval estimates.

Construct interval estimates for a population mean and a population proportion.

Determine the impact of sample size on an interval estimate.

Compute the required sample size for an estimation problem involving a population mean and a population proportion.

Compute the maximum tolerable error for a specific sample size.

A front-page April 30, 1992, *Wall Street Journal* story covered Ross Perot's independent bid for the U.S. presidency. His bid was based on the belief that many voters preferred his brand of leadership.

Chapter 7 covered sampling distributions. It mentioned that sampling distributions provide the foundation for two important statistical concepts: estimation and hypothesis testing. This chapter concerns estimation. Chapters 9 and 10 examine hypothesis testing.

WHY MANAGERS NEED TO KNOW ABOUT ESTIMATION

Decision makers frequently investigate certain characteristics of populations of data values. As you've already learned, usually it is necessary to sample such populations and infer that the characteristics of the sample apply to the population as well. This chapter examines the inferential process with emphasis on the amount of error that is inherent. Understanding the concepts of this chapter is vital to any sampling procedure.

Regarding *The Wall Street Journal*'s article on Ross Perot, any candidate must estimate the voters' inclinations on a constant basis. The estimation procedures in this chapter are commonly used in political polls and many other places.

POINT AND INTERVAL ESTIMATES OF A POPULATION MEAN

Point Estimate

A **point estimate** is a single value measured from a sample and used as an estimate of the corresponding population value (parameter). Although there are many population parameters of potential interest to a decision maker, the two most important are the population mean and population proportion.

> A **point estimate** is a single value that is measured from a sample and used as an estimate of the corresponding population parameter.

When a point estimate of the population mean is desired, the sample mean is used. When the population proportion is of interest, the sample proportion is used as a point estimate.

EXAMPLE 8.1   Espinoza Construction, a building contractor, needs to estimate the average (mean) weight of a certain structural steel beam used in large buildings. A sampling plan is devised to select such beams over the next two months from the three firms that make them. This process produces a sample of 150 beams, that are weighed at the manufacturers' sites. Their average weight is calculated to be 125.7 tons; this is the point estimate of the mean weight of all such beams.

EXAMPLE 8.2   A study designed to answer these questions was reported in *The Accounting Review*: Are government contractors more profitable than other firms, and do such contractors shift some of the overhead and pension costs of their commercial operations to the government?[1] The results of the study were based on a large sample of government contractors who also have commercial business. The author, Lichtenberg, concluded these contractors have a profit rate (return on assets) that is 68 to 82 percent higher than other companies. This conclusion required the inference that the sample contractor profit rate (a percentage) could be inferred or projected to all such firms.

The problem with a point estimate is that it conveys no sense of accuracy. For example, the statement, "The sample mean, an estimate of the population mean, is 150 pounds," doesn't reflect the sample size or the extent of the population's variability. This point estimate might be very accurate or very misleading depending on these two factors.

Interval Estimate

An **interval estimate** indicates the sample estimate accuracy. The interval estimate specifies an interval within which the true population parameter is quite likely to lie and a **confidence coefficient** is used to indicate the likelihood that the population parameter lies within that interval. The confidence coefficient can be expressed as a

Confidence Level

percentage and called a **confidence level.**

An **interval estimate** establishes an interval within which it's quite likely that the population parameter lies. A **confidence coefficient** is used to indicate the likelihood that an interval estimate contains the population parameter. A **confidence level** is the confidence coefficient expressed as a percentage.

Interval estimates are based on the theory developed in Chapter 7. The normal sampling distribution, as established by the central limit theorem, is used to construct interval estimates. Figure 8.1 illustrates this process.

Suppose that the mean, μ, of a population is known, and the sampling distribution, consisting of all possible sample means for a certain sample size, has been constructed. Such a distribution appears in Figure 8.1. The interval *a–b* is constructed such that *a* and *b* are equally distant from the mean of the curve, μ, and include 95% of the sample means.

Next, suppose a person takes a random sample and computes the mean as if this mean were selected from the sampling distribution of means in Figure 8.1. Suppose the value obtained is the sample mean $\bar{x}_1$. The person is now instructed to calculate an interval of width *a–b* and place the chosen sample mean in the middle of this interval. The resulting interval is shown below the curve in Figure 8.1. This sampler

---

[1]Frank P. Lichtenberg, "A Perspective on Accounting for Defense Contracts," *The Accounting Review* (October 1992), pp. 741–52.

FIGURE 8.1 Sampling Distribution of Means

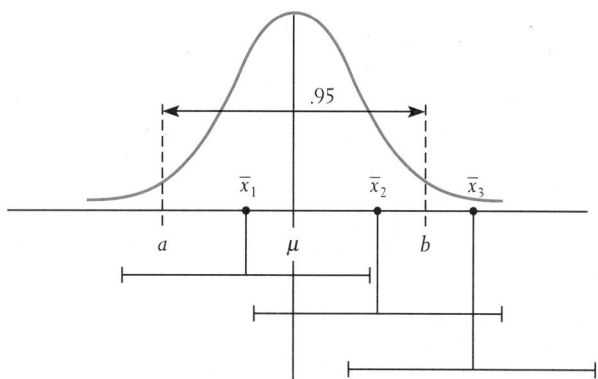

would be pleased to be told that this interval contains the true population mean, μ, even though he or she wouldn't know where in the interval μ is.

Now a second sampler approaches the sampling distribution, selects sample mean $\bar{x}_2$, and constructs an interval of the same width a–b, centering it on the sample mean. This interval is shown in Figure 8.1 and also contains the population mean, μ.

Finally, a third person randomly selects a sample mean from Figure 8.1's sampling distribution, calculates the mean $\bar{x}_3$, and constructs the a–b interval around it. Unfortunately, this interval does not contain the population mean. This happened to sampler 3, not because of errors in the sampling process, but because of the randomness of sample results. Actually, sampler 3 had only a 5% chance of having such bad luck since only 5% of the sample means in Figure 8.1 lead to intervals that don't contain the population mean.

An analyst cannot see the sampling distribution from which the sample mean is drawn. However, the process of constructing an interval around the point estimate $\bar{x}$ is undertaken with the understanding that there's a high probability, but not a certainty, that the resulting interval will contain the population mean. The formula used to construct an interval estimate for the population mean is

Interval Estimate for Means

$$\bar{x} \pm z \frac{\sigma}{\sqrt{n}} \tag{8.1}$$

where $\bar{x}$ = Sample mean
z = Value from standard normal table reflecting confidence level
σ = Population standard deviation
n = Sample size

This equation is used whenever the population standard deviation is known.

Note that four values must be known before an interval estimate for the population mean can be constructed. First, the sample mean, $\bar{x}$, must be known. This value is computed from the sample values.

Next, the degree of confidence in the interval estimate must be established. This leads to the selection of a *z* value. In Figure 8.1, 95% of the curve is included in the width of the *a–b* interval. This translates to 95% confidence that the resulting interval contains the population mean. To find the correct *z* value, this percentage is divided in half since one half of the 95% lies on either side of the normal curve mean. Half of .95 is .4750, and in the standard normal table in Appendix E.6, this area is found in the 1.9 row and the .06 column. Thus, the correct *z* value is 1.96. In other words, a distance of 1.96 standard deviations on either side of the mean of any normal curve defines an area that includes 95% of the curve's values. You can use the standard normal table to verify the confidence levels and corresponding *z* values in Table 8.1. These are values commonly used for interval estimates.

TABLE 8.1   Interval Estimate *z* Values

Confidence level	*z* value
.90	1.645
.95	1.96
.98	2.33
.99	2.575

Equation 8.1 indicates that the population standard deviation, σ, must also be known. In practice, this usually isn't possible; the only way to identify σ without error is to conduct a census. Instead, an estimate of σ is used to construct the interval estimate. The sample standard deviation, *s*, provides an unbiased estimate of the unknown σ and is substituted in Equation 8.1 to construct the interval. This introduces a certain amount of error, but this error is usually quite small, especially if large samples are used.

When the sample value *s* is used, the *t* distribution rather than the *z* distribution is theoretically correct; this distribution will be discussed in depth later in this chapter. The *t* value replaces the *z* value in Equation 8.1. If the sample size is 30 or greater, however, the *z* value is quite close to *t*, and its use introduces only minor error. Equation 8.2 is used to compute the interval estimate for means when both of the following conditions apply: the population standard deviation (σ) is estimated using the sample standard deviation (*s*), and the sample size is 30 or greater:

$$\bar{x} \pm z \frac{s}{\sqrt{n}} \tag{8.2}$$

where $\bar{x}$ = Sample mean
z = Value from standard normal table reflecting confidence level
s = Sample standard deviation
n = Sample size

Remember that if the sample size constitutes more than 5% of a finite population, the standard error of the mean must be modified by the finite-population multiplier.

Finally, Equation 8.1 or 8.2 requires that the sample size, n, be known. Note that the equation for an interval estimate specifies an area z standard errors around the sample mean. In Equation 8.1, the standard error is the standard deviation of the sampling distribution of means, $\sigma/\sqrt{n}$. An estimate of this standard error, $s/\sqrt{n}$, is used in Equation 8.2.

As Equations 8.1 and 8.2 show and as common sense suggests, three factors determine the interval estimate's width and, hence, its accuracy. First, the z value is multiplied by the standard error of the mean to create the interval estimate. This suggests that a higher confidence level (going from a 95% level to a 99% level, for example) requires the use of a larger z value, which leads to a wider interval.

Second, note that σ (or its estimator, s) is in the numerator of the standard error of the mean. As discussed in Chapter 7, populations with high variability have a larger standard error of the mean. Therefore, the more variable the population, as measured by σ, the wider the interval. Remember that wider intervals mean less accurate interval estimates.

Third, the sample size, n, is in the denominator of the standard error of the mean. As discussed in Chapter 7, larger sample sizes produce smaller standard errors and, thus, narrower or more accurate interval estimates. This is intuitively appealing since we would expect larger samples to yield better estimates of population values than smaller samples. The larger the sample, the more information from the population is contained in the sample.

The normal curve is the appropriate distribution for constructing an interval estimate when:

1. The population standard deviation is known, or
2. The population standard deviation is unknown and the sample size is 30 or greater.

EXAMPLE 8.3   A random sample of 500 shoppers is selected from Northgate Shopping Center to determine the average distance customers travel to the mall. An analysis of the sample results reveal $\bar{x} = 23.5$ miles and $s = 10.4$ miles.

The point estimate for the unknown population mean of all shoppers at the mall is 23.5 miles, the sample mean. The interval estimate for μ, using 95% confidence and Equation 8.2, is

$$\bar{x} \pm z\frac{s}{\sqrt{n}} = 23.5 \pm 1.96\frac{10.4}{\sqrt{500}}$$
$$= 23.5 \pm 1.96(0.465)$$
$$= 23.5 \pm 0.91$$
$$= 22.6 \text{ to } 24.4$$

It can be stated with 95% confidence that the average distance traveled to the mall by the population of shoppers is somewhere between 22.6 and 24.4 miles. More precisely, a statistician would state that if 100 samples of size 500 were selected, their means and standard deviations computed, and interval estimates constructed, 95 out of the 100 intervals would be expected to contain the population mean.

EXAMPLE 8.4   Suppose the sample results in Example 8.3 had been misstated. The sample measurements were correct, but the sample size was actually 50, not 500. What would happen to the interval estimate? The new calculations are

$$23.5 \pm 1.96 \frac{10.4}{\sqrt{50}} = 23.5 \pm 1.96(1.47)$$
$$= 23.5 \pm 2.88$$
$$= 20.6 \text{ to } 26.4$$

The population standard deviation is still estimated at 10.4 miles, and the confidence level for the interval is still 95%. But because the sample size is smaller, the interval is wider and hence less accurate. For this case, it can be said with 95% confidence that the unknown population mean is somewhere in the interval 20.6–26.4 miles.

In Example 8.4 an interval estimate was computed based on a sample size of 50. This interval estimate could also be constructed using the MINITAB software package. The MINITAB commands are:

```
MTB> RANDOM 50 C1;
SUBC> NORMAL 23.5 10.4.
MTB> DESCRIBE C1

C1    N    MEAN    MEDIAN    STDEV
      50   25.45   26.63     11.76

C1    MIN    MAX     Q1      Q3
      1.85   42.97   15.45   35.41

MTB> ZINTERVAL 95 PERCENT CONFIDENCE ASSUMED SIGMA 11.76 FOR C1
  N    MEAN    STDEV   SE MEAN   95.0 PERCENT C.I.
  50   25.45   11.76   1.66      (22.19, 28.72)

MTB> STOP
```

The RANDOM command is used to generate a sample of 50 observations and the NORMAL subcommand generates these 50 observations from a normal population with a mean of 23.5 and standard deviation of 10.4. The ZINTERVAL command is used to compute a 95% interval estimate for the data stored in C1 using the sample standard deviation, 11.76, as an estimate of the population standard deviation. Note that the ZINTERVAL command consists of the confidence level, assumed sigma, and column where the data are located.

EXAMPLE 8.5   A large automobile retailer, Avanti Southwest, studies the 1,300 customers who've taken delivery on new cars during the past year. Brad Peterson, sales manager, is attempting to measure customer satisfaction. He designs a systematic sampling plan for use with company records on the past year's customers. The selected individuals are called and asked to rate satisfaction with their car on a 1–10 scale, with 1 being the worst and 10 the best rating. Brad recognizes that this scale constitutes ordinal data, as discussed in Chapter 2, but because he believes equal intervals exist between successive rating numbers, he decides to treat the data as interval-scaled. He samples 375 customers, computes the sample mean and standard deviation, and develops an interval estimate of the population average customer rating. He recognizes that he should use the finite-population multiplier because he is sampling without replacement and the sample size exceeds 5% of the population (n/N = 375/1,300 = .288). The sample measures are $\bar{x}$ = 7.81, s = 2.3.

Brad chooses the 95% confidence level and calculates the interval estimate:

$$7.81 \pm 1.96\frac{2.3}{\sqrt{375}}\sqrt{\frac{1,300 - 375}{1,300 - 1}} = 7.81 \pm 1.96(0.119)\sqrt{0.712}$$
$$= 7.81 \pm 1.96(0.119)(0.844)$$
$$= 7.81 \pm 0.197$$
$$= 7.61 \text{ to } 8.01$$

Brad can say with 95% confidence that if a census were taken of all the firm's customers from the past year, the average satisfaction rating would be somewhere between 7.61 and 8.01 on a 1–10 scale.

EXERCISES

1. Explain the difference between a point estimate and an interval estimate.
2. What advantage does an interval estimate provide an analyst compared with a point estimate?
3. How does a reduced sample size affect an interval estimate?
4. How does decreasing the level of confidence affect an interval estimate?
5. How does decreased population variability affect an interval estimate?
6. What is the appropriate z value for the following confidence levels?
   a. 80%.
   b. 88%.
   c. 94%.
   d. 98%.
7. The Fresh-Juice Company packages frozen lemonade in cans claimed to have a mean weight of 16 ounces. The population standard deviation is known to be 0.1. Determine a point estimate for the population mean if a random sample of 12 cans have the following weights, in ounces:

15.94	16.04	16.26	15.87	16.03	16.01
16.14	15.95	15.98	16.07	15.83	15.90

8. Determine interval estimates for each of the following:

	Sample mean	σ	Sample size	Confidence level
a.	100	15	75	95%
b.	24.8	4.5	45	99
c.	7.5	1.4	300	90
d.	0.8	0.2	100	98

9. The average amount of gas purchased is recorded for a sample of 50 customers at Gary's Union Service Station. If the sample mean is 12 gallons and standard deviation is 3 gallons, compute the 95% interval estimate of the mean number of gallons purchased per customer.

10. (This question refers to Exercise 9.) Compute the 95% interval estimate of the mean number of gallons purchased per customer.

    a. If the sample of customers was actually 100.

    b. If the sample size was actually 36.

    c. Explain what effect sample size has on the width of the interval estimate.

11. (This question refers to Exercise 9.) Compute the interval estimate of the mean number of gallons purchased by the 50 customers using:

    a. A 99% confidence level.

    b. A 90% confidence level.

    c. Explain what effect the confidence level has on the width of the interval estimate.

12. (This question refers to Exercise 9.) Compute the 95% interval estimate of the mean number of gallons purchased by the 50 customers using:

    a. A sample standard deviation of 4.

    b. A sample standard deviation of 2.

    c. Explain what effect population variability has on the width of the interval estimate.

 13. The First Federal Credit Union wants to estimate the mean amount of outstanding automobile loans. Past experience reveals that the standard deviation is $250. Determine a 98% interval estimate for the population mean if a random sample of size 100 has a sample mean of $1,950. Interpret the meaning of this interval.

 14. The length of time between billing and receipt of payment was recorded for a random sample of 50 clients (of a total of 950) of the legal firm of Schwan, Schwan, and Waldo. The sample mean and standard deviation for the 50 accounts were 29.6 days and 11.8 days, respectively. Calculate an 88% confidence interval estimate for the mean time between billing and receipt of payment for all of the firm's accounts. Describe the meaning of the interval.

15. New Horizons Airlines wants to estimate the mean number of unoccupied seats per flight to Germany over the past year. New Horizons is looking for increased business with the two Germanies after the liberalizing political events of November 1989 in East Germany, and after studying the technical progress in East Germany as described in the *GDR Review* (April 1989 issue).

    To accomplish this investigation, records of 400 flights are randomly selected from the files, and the number of unoccupied seats is noted for each flight. The sample mean and standard deviation are 8.1 seats and 5.7 seats, respectively. Estimate the mean number of unoccupied seats per flight during the past year using a 95% interval estimate. Interpret this interval's meaning.

16. This exercise refers to variable x_1, number of years with the company, in Appendix C's company data base. Assume that the population standard deviation is 5. Select a simple random sample of 36 employees and construct a 95% interval estimate for the average number of years with the company. Write a memo summarizing the results.

POINT AND INTERVAL ESTIMATES OF POPULATION PROPORTIONS

Chapter 6 demonstrated that the normal distribution provides a good approximation for the binomial distribution when $np > 5$ and $n(1 - p) > 5$. Since most proportion situations meet these criteria, the normal distribution is usually used to create interval estimates for population proportions.

Once the sample proportion has been computed as a point estimate of the population proportion, an interval is formed around this sample value, and this becomes the interval estimate for the unknown population parameter. Equation 8.3 uses the formula for the standard error of the proportion established in Chapter 7 to compute the interval estimate for a population proportion:

Interval Estimate for Proportions

$$\bar{p} \pm z \sqrt{\frac{p(1 - p)}{n}} \tag{8.3}$$

where $\bar{p}$ = Sample proportion
       z = Value from standard normal table reflecting confidence level
       n = Sample size
       p = Population proportion

Equation 8.3 presents the same difficulty as Equation 8.2 for the population mean interval estimate. A population parameter, in this case p, must be known before the interval can be computed. The solution to this problem is the same as for means: a sample estimate is used in place of the population value to form the interval. The sample proportion, $\bar{p}$, is used as an estimate of the unknown population proportion, p. This substitution leads to a small amount of error in the estimation process.

Remember that if the sample makes up more than 5% of a finite population, the standard error of the proportion must be modified by the finite-population multiplier.

EXAMPLE 8.6 Example 7:10 referred to a newspaper article in *The Spokesman-Review* (October 30, 1989) with the quote:

A survey, conducted Oct. 19–25 for *The Spokesman-Review* and *Spokane Chronicle,* shows Bernard far ahead of her campaign rival and fellow councilman, Rob Higgins. Of the 200 city voters selected at random and surveyed by Market Trends Inc. of Spokane, 46% said they would vote for Bernard if the election were held tomorrow; 26.5% said they would vote for Higgins. Another 19% were undecided when the survey was taken, some two weeks before the election. Market Trends vice president William Robinson, project manager for the survey, said that he believes a turnaround is extremely unlikely at this point in the campaign. Even giving Higgins the most favorable break under the sample's 7% margin of error—in which he would gain 7% and Bernard would lose 7%—and allowing him an even split of the undecided voters, Bernard is still leading, Robinson explained.

The point estimate of the population preference for Sheri Bernard is .46, the sample proportion. A 95% interval estimate is computed by substituting $\bar{p}$ for p in Equation 8.3:

$$\bar{p} \pm z \sqrt{\frac{p(1-p)}{n}} = .46 \pm 1.96 \sqrt{\frac{(.46)(.54)}{200}}$$
$$= .46 \pm 1.96\sqrt{.0012}$$
$$= .46 \pm 1.96(.035)$$
$$= .46 \pm .069$$
$$= .391 \text{ to } .529$$

Note that, as the article stated, the margin of error is 7% (.069). It can be said with 95% confidence that if the vote were held at this time, between 39.1% and 52.9% of the voting public would vote for Sheri Bernard. This is the procedure pollsters and the news media use prior to an election. These results might have been reported as, "Forty-six percent of the registered voters prefer Sheri Bernard, with a margin of error of 7%."

EXAMPLE 8.7 The Kenless Corporation has been getting complaints about the toaster it markets in the eastern part of the country. To deal with this problem, the company first wants to know the percentage of the toasters sold that have problems. A rebate program has been in effect for six months, so the company decides to use the names on the rebate list as a population from which to sample. A random sample of 1,800 names is chosen from this list, and a brief questionnaire is mailed to these people along with an additional $5 gift certificate. A total of 1,675 questionnaires came back, which represents a good return rate, 93% [(1,675/1,800)100]. The company is satisfied that a representative sample has been obtained.

Twelve percent of the respondents said they experienced problems. The interval estimate is computed at the 99% confidence level. To find the correct z value for 99% confidence, this percentage is divided in half, producing a standard normal table area of .4950. In Appendix E.6, the z value is found in the 2.5 row halfway between the .07 and .08 columns. Thus, the z value is approximately 2.575. The interval estimate is

$$.12 \pm 2.575 \sqrt{\frac{(.12)(.88)}{1,675}} = .12 \pm 2.575\sqrt{.000063}$$
$$= .12 \pm 2.575(.0079)$$
$$= .12 \pm .02$$
$$= .10 \text{ to } .14$$

Kenless can state with 99% confidence that the percentage of buyers who have had problems with the toaster is between 10% and 14%. This quality level is considered unsatisfactory by company management, and a quality improvement program is initiated. (Chapter 13 discusses relevant procedures for ensuring good quality.)

EXERCISES

17. Why is the normal curve used in most problems requiring an interval estimate for a proportion?

18. Determine confidence intervals for each of the following:

	Sample proportion	Sample size	Confidence level
a.	.30	55	95%
b.	.50	35	99
c.	.75	200	90
d.	.10	400	98

19. The Target Corporation personnel director wants to estimate the number of employees within one year of retirement. A simple random sample of 80 employee records is selected, and four people are found to be within one year of retirement. Formulate a 98% interval estimate for the true proportion of employees within one year of retirement in the entire corporation.

20. (This question refers to Exercise 19.) Compute the 98% interval estimate of the proportion of employees within one year of retirement (with $\bar{p}$ still .05):

   a. For a sample of 200 employees.

   b. For a sample size of 40.

   c. Explain what effect sample size has on the width of the interval estimate.

21. (This question refers to Exercise 19.) Compute the interval estimate of the proportion of employees within one year of retirement for a sample of 80 using:

   a. A 99% confidence level.

   b. A 90% confidence level.

   c. Explain what effect the confidence level has on the width of the interval estimate.

22. (This question refers to Exercise 19.) Compute the 98% interval estimate of the proportion of employees within one year of retirement for a sample of 80 using:

   a. A population proportion of .10.

   b. A population proportion of .01.

23. The IRS is estimating the total number of tax accountants who had their own tax returns audited last year. If a random sample of 100 returns showed that 16 were audited, develop a 90% interval estimate for the true proportion of tax accountants whose returns were audited last year. Interpret the meaning of this interval.

24. Taco Now is studying its market penetration in Tampa. Taco Now's analyst asks 900 randomly selected residents whether they've been to Taco Now in the past month. Of those surveyed, 300 responded yes. Compute a 99% interval estimate for the true percentage of city residents who've been to Taco Now in the past month. Describe the meaning of this interval.

25. Radio Castle tests a sample of 200 transistors and finds that 8 are defective. Calculate a 98% interval estimate for p, the true proportion of defectives. Interpret the meaning of this interval.

26. The *Spokane Chronicle* randomly sampled 500 registered voters to determine if they would vote for the annexation of Spokane Valley, a small adjoining community. Find a 90% inter-

val estimate for the proportion of the population favoring annexation if 200 of the sampled voters said they would vote favorably. Interpret the meaning of this interval.

27. In a market research study, a sample of 320 individuals are asked if they're aware of a soft drink product. If 180 of the respondents indicate awareness, develop a 95% interval estimate for the proportion of individuals in the population who are aware of the product. What does this interval suggest?

28. This exercise refers to variable x_3, gender, in Appendix C's company data base. Select a simple random sample of 50 employees and construct a 95% interval estimate for the proportion of females with the company. Interpret this interval's meaning.

SMALL-SAMPLE ESTIMATION

So far in this chapter the examples have involved rather large sample sizes. As a rule of thumb, large samples are considered to be those with 30 or more observations. In most practical situations, you can acquire a large sample, in which case these procedures will apply.

Small-Sample Estimation for Means

There are times, however, when it is practical to use a small sample. For example, some sampled items must be destroyed to be measured, and if these items are expensive, a small sample size is almost mandatory. Other samples consist of historical evidence, and if only a few measurements are available, you can't go back and collect more.

Small samples are rarely used to estimate population proportions because this causes very wide (i.e., inaccurate) intervals. For example, if 5 out of 25 people prefer a particular product, the 95% interval estimate for the population proportion, using Equation 8.3, is

$$.20 \pm 1.96 \sqrt{\frac{(.20)(.80)}{25}} = .20 \pm 1.96\sqrt{.0064}$$
$$= .20 \pm 1.96(.08)$$
$$= .20 \pm .1568$$
$$= .043 \text{ to } .357$$

This interval is too wide to be useful. Management judgment alone could probably produce a much tighter interval estimate.

Using small samples to estimate the population mean can produce useful intervals if the population standard deviation isn't too large, and if it can be assumed that the population is approximately normally distributed. In these cases, the t distribution is used to form the interval estimate. Again, as a rule of thumb, a sample size less than 30 suggests use of the t distribution. Also, as stated earlier in this chapter, the t distribution is appropriate whenever the sample statistic s is used to estimate the population parameter σ.

t Distribution

The t distribution is a theoretical distribution that has many applications in statistics. It was first developed by W. S. Gosset, a scientist in the Guiness brewery in Ireland, who published his discovery in 1908 under the pen name Student. Gosset discovered that when sampling from a normal distribution, the t statistic has a sampling distribution much like the z statistic. The primary difference between the t and z sampling distributions is that the t statistic is more variable than the z. This is because the t statistic contains two random quantities ($\bar{x}$ and s) while the z statistic contains only one ($\bar{x}$).

The t distribution is a family of distributions similar to the standard normal distribution. There's a specific t distribution for each number of degrees of freedom, $n - 1$. There's a unique t distribution for 2 degrees of freedom, for 7 degrees of freedom, for 15 degrees of freedom, and so forth. Figure 8.2 shows the standard normal distribution (z distribution) and its relationship to t distributions with 12 and 25 degrees of freedom.

FIGURE 8.2 Normal Distribution and t Distributions

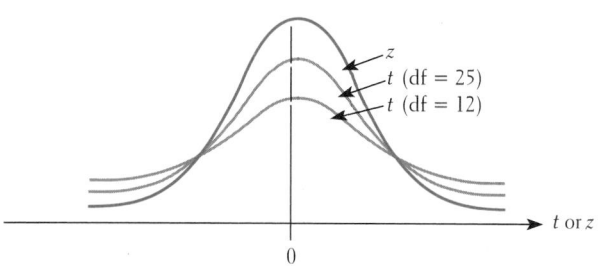

Note that the increased variability in the sampling distribution of t depends on the sample size, n. If n is small, the sampling distribution of t is more variable. You can see in Figure 8.2 that the increased variability of the t statistic means that the t value that locates the area in the lower or upper tail will be larger than the corresponding value of z, especially for small sample sizes.

Equation 8.4 forms an interval estimate for the population mean when the sample size is small and σ is unknown. This equation also requires that the population values be approximately normally distributed. The small-sample interval estimate is

$$\bar{x} \pm t \frac{s}{\sqrt{n}} \tag{8.4}$$

where $\bar{x}$ = Sample mean
 t = Value from t distribution reflecting confidence level
 s = Sample standard deviation
 n = Sample size

Note the similarity between Equations 8.2 and 8.4. The only difference is that the t distribution, instead of the normal curve, is used to reflect the confidence level. The flowchart of Figure 8.3 summarizes the steps for determining when the t distribution is appropriate.

Use of the t table in Appendix E.7 requires that the area in the curve's lower and upper tails be known, as suggested by the shaded graph at the top of the table. Sup-

Figure 8.3   Sampling Distribution for Test of Population Mean

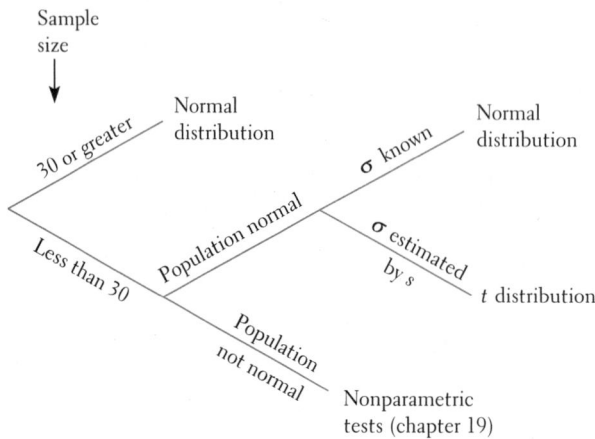

pose a 95% confidence level is desired for an interval estimate. With 95% of the curve inside the interval, there must be 5% outside it, or 2.5% in each tail.

The second value required for the *t* table is the number of degrees of freedom (a concept discussed in Chapter 4). We stated there that a piece of sample information is lost each time a sample statistic is used to estimate an unknown population parameter in an equation. Thus, when the sample standard deviation (*s*) is used as an estimate of the population standard deviation (σ) for computing the standard error of the mean, the degrees of freedom equal $n - 1$. If a sample of 10 has been selected, the degrees of freedom total $n - 1 = 9$.

> The ***t* distribution** is the appropriate distribution for constructing an interval estimate when the population is approximately normally distributed, the population standard deviation is unknown, and the sample size is less than 30.

Once again, remember that if the sample constitutes more than 5% of a finite population, the standard error of the mean must be modified by the finite-population multiplier.

EXAMPLE 8.8   An interval estimate is to be formed around a sample mean. A sample of eight has been selected, and a 98% confidence level is chosen. What is the correct *t* value?

A 98% confidence level implies an area of .01 in each tail of the *t* distribution, and the number of degrees of freedom is 7 (8 − 1). Therefore, the *t* table is entered using row 7 and column .02 for a two-tailed area. The correct *t* value from the table is 2.998.

EXAMPLE 8.9 Jean Simmons, a health store owner in Dallas, Texas, has just read an article entitled "The Cholesterol Myth" in *The Atlantic Monthly*, September 1989. It prompted Jean to estimate the average fat content per pound of hamburger sold in Dallas stores. For her sample, she purchased one pound of hamburger from each of nine randomly selected stores. She cooked the hamburger, poured off the fat, and weighed it. The results for each of the stores, in ounces of fat, are

3.3   4.8   5.1   4.5   4.0   3.9   4.7   5.0   3.6

Jean now wants to compute a 90% interval estimate for the average fat content per pound of hamburger. The mean and standard deviation for the sample are $\bar{x} = 4.322$, $s = 0.644$. The interval estimate is

$$4.322 \pm 1.86 \frac{0.644}{\sqrt{9}} = 4.322 \pm 1.86(0.2147)$$
$$= 4.322 \pm 0.3993$$
$$= 3.923 \text{ to } 4.721$$

Using a very small sample size (nine), it can be stated with 90% confidence that the average fat content per pound of hamburger is between 3.923 and 4.721 ounces.

An interval estimate using the t distribution can also be computed using the MINITAB software package. The MINITAB commands for estimating the interval in Example 8.9 are:

```
MTB> SET INTO C1
DATA> 3.3 4.8 5.1 4.5 4.0 3.9 4.7 5.0 3.6
DATA> END
MTB> DESCRIBE C1

C1       N        MEAN      MEDIAN      STDEV
         9        4.322     4.500       0.644

C1       MIN      MAX       Q1          Q3
         3.30     5.100     3.750       4.9400

MTB> TINTERVAL 90 PERCENT CONFIDENCE FOR C1
    N        MEAN       STDEV      SE MEAN      90.0 PERCENT C.I.
    9        4.322      0.644      0.215        (3.923, 4.721)

MTB> STOP
```

The TINTERVAL command is used to compute a 90% interval estimate for the data stored in C1 using the sample standard deviation as an estimate of the population standard deviation. Note that the TINTERVAL command consists of the confidence level and column where the data are located. The population standard deviation is estimated from the sample data located in the column indicated.

EXERCISES

For exercises 32 through 40, assume you're sampling from a normal population.

29. When is it appropriate to use the t distribution?

30. Explain the differences between the normal curve and the t distribution.

31. Why is $n - 1$ the number of degrees of freedom used to construct an interval estimate using the *t* distribution?

32. Find the appropriate *t* value for each of the following situations:

    a. 95% interval estimate for 8 degrees of freedom.

    b. 99% interval estimate for 14 degrees of freedom.

    c. 90% interval estimate for a sample size of 12.

    d. 90% interval estimate for a sample size of 27.

33. In each of the following cases, should the normal distribution or the *t* distribution be used to form an interval estimate?

	Sample mean	*s*	Sample size	Interval estimate
a.	10	2	25	95%
b.	30	5.5	55	99
c.	50	9.4	10	90
d.	1	0.2	100	98

34. Determine an interval estimate for each of the cases in Exercise 33.

35. Quality Foods' regional manager wants to determine the average fat content per pound of steak sold in Portland, Maine. She's considering quitting her job and starting a cattle ranch after reading the article "Queen of the Range" in the January 1989 issue of *Successful Farming*. Her ranch would produce low-fat beef for sale to upscale consumers. Her interest is increased by an article in *Successful Farming* (February 1990), in which columnist Bill Helming discussed the critical factor of beef demand in the market of the 1990s.

    She purchases one steak from each of the 20 stores in the area and determines average fat content per pound:

    2.1   3.2   2.8   3.0   2.5   3.2   2.7   2.6   4.1   2.9
    2.4   3.7   3.8   2.9   3.3   3.5   2.8   2.2   2.7   2.7

    Construct a 90% interval estimate for the average fat content of steaks in the region. Interpret this interval's meaning.

36. A dentist wishes to improve appointment scheduling. He tracks the average (mean) time he spends with each patient over a one-week period. The sample of 25 patients results in a mean time of 35 minutes with standard deviation of 10 minutes. Construct a 95% interval estimate for the mean time spent per patient. Interpret this interval's meaning.

37. The Microspace Corporation produces an electronic component used in microcomputers. To fulfill government regulations, Microspace must estimate this component's average lifetime, in hours, before failure. A random sample of 22 components are found to last an average (mean) of 2,487 hours with standard deviation of 73 hours. Construct a 99% interval estimate for this component's mean lifetime before failure. Write a brief statement describing the interval.

38. The United Paint Company tests a new brand of paint for square feet of coverage per gallon, a measure to be specified on the can label. A sample of 15 different gallons are tested, with average (mean) coverage of 197 square feet and standard deviation of 11.2

square feet. Construct a 98% interval estimate for the mean square feet of coverage per gallon. Interpret this interval's meaning.

39. *The Wall Street Journal* (November 10, 1989) listed the leading mutual funds. A fund called Colonial Income Plus led the list with a 12-month return of 13.42%. Suppose an investor compared this figure with the average return of mutual funds currently available to investors.

    A random sample of 30 mutual funds with assets of at least $100 million were selected and the mean and standard deviation of yield computed. The sample was selected from a population of 250 money market mutual funds with assets of at least $100 million. The mean was 9.43%, and the standard deviation was 2.79%. Construct a 90% interval estimate for the average yield of the 250 funds. What is the interval?

40. This exercise refers to variable x_9, employee age, in Appendix C's company data base. It is known that the population is normally distributed. Select a simple random sample of 16 employees and construct a 95% interval estimate for the average employee age. Interpret the meaning of this interval.

SAMPLE SIZE AND ESTIMATION ERROR

One frequently asked question in statistics is: How large a sample should be taken? It is a difficult question, and a clear understanding of the concept of sampling distributions is necessary to answer it.

Three factors affect the determination of sample size for estimating a population mean: (1) the confidence level, (2) the maximum tolerable error, and (3) the population variation. Note that none of these factors has any direct relationship to the population's size.

Maximum Tolerable Error   The **maximum tolerable error** is a concept that refers to the maximum amount by which the sample statistic (the estimate) differs from the population parameter, for a specified confidence level.

> The **maximum tolerable error** is the maximum amount by which the sample statistic (the estimate) differs from the population parameter for a specified confidence level.

If the sample statistic is normally distributed in accordance with the central limit theorem, sample size can be estimated by using the following four steps.

Sample Size for Means   **Step 1** Determine the confidence level, usually .90, .95, or .99. A higher confidence level requires a larger sample size. The appropriate z value is then found, just as in the procedure for interval estimates.

Step 2 Determine how much error, E, is tolerable. The magnitude of error will depend on how critical an accurate estimate is. A smaller tolerable error requires a larger sample size. The value of E calls for a subjective decision by the analyst.

Step 3 Determine the population standard deviation, or, if it's unknown, estimate it. This can be done by using a standard deviation based on past experience with similar analyses. Another possibility is to conduct a pilot study, taking a small sample and using the sample standard deviation, s, to estimate the population standard deviation, σ.

Step 4 Use the information gathered in Steps 1 through 3 in Equation 8.5,

$$n = \frac{z^2\sigma^2}{E^2} \qquad (8.5)$$

where n = Sample size
        z = Value from standard normal table reflecting confidence level
        σ = Population standard deviation
        E = Maximum tolerable error

EXAMPLE 8.10   What if the Northgate Shopping Center manager (see Example 8.4) decides that the interval estimate is too wide? Instead of accepting an error of 2.9 on either side of the mean ($23.5 - 20.6 = 2.9$), he states, "I want a 95% chance that the mean obtained from the random sample is no more than one mile from the true population mean. I'd like it to be even closer, but one mile is the maximum error I can tolerate."

The manager is essentially saying, "Based on a sample size of n, if the estimate of the population mean is computed to be 23.5 miles, I want to be confident that the population mean falls in the interval 22.5 to 24.5 miles."

Figure 8.4 shows the sampling distribution for this example and indicates that the maximum tolerable error, E, is $z(\sigma/\sqrt{n})$:

$$E = z\frac{\sigma}{\sqrt{n}} \qquad (8.6)$$

Equation 8.6 can be rearranged so that n, the sample size, is the value to be solved for. This is how Equation 8.5 was derived.

FIGURE 8.4   Sampling Distribution of Means

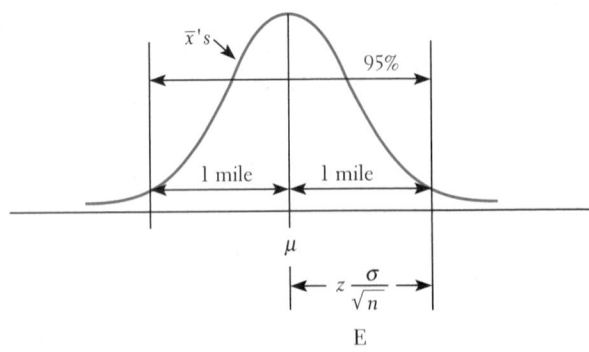

In general, if an analyst requires more precision, the sample size must be increased. The maximum tolerable error is proportional to $1/\sqrt{n}$, so to decrease the maximum tolerable error by half, four times as many observations are needed in the sample ($1/\sqrt{n} = 1/\sqrt{4} = 1/2$). To reduce the error to one-fourth its original value, 16 times as many observations are needed in the sample.

EXAMPLE 8.11   As stated in Example 8.10, the manager wants a sample large enough that the maximum tolerable error is one mile. The sample size, from Equation 8.6, is

$$1 = 1.96 \frac{10.4}{\sqrt{n}}$$
$$\sqrt{n} = 1.96(10.4)$$
$$\sqrt{n} = 20.384$$
$$n = 20.384^2$$
$$n = 415.5, \text{ rounded to } 416$$

The manager needs a sample of at least 416 shoppers. (*Note:* The sample size figure is always rounded upward. This ensures that the criteria for maximum tolerable error are met.) Equation 8.5 produces the same result:

$$n = \frac{z^2 \, \sigma^2}{E^2} = \frac{1.96^2 (10.4)^2}{1^2} = 415.5$$

EXAMPLE 8.12   Herb Kau wants to estimate the mean weight of cartons shipped from a plant. The sample mean is to be no more than 2 pounds from the population mean with 95% confidence. The population standard deviation is estimated to be 10 pounds. How large a sample is needed? Using Equation 8.5, the calculations are

$$n = \frac{z^2 \, \sigma^2}{E^2} = \frac{1.96^2 (10)^2}{2^2} = 96.04, \text{ rounded to } 97$$

A sample size of 97 cartons will give 95% assurance that the sample mean is no more than 2 pounds from the population mean.

EXAMPLE 8.13   (Refer to Example 8.12.) Herb Kau decides that his budget will permit a sample size of 200 cartons. Using this sample size, what is the maximum tolerable error? Equation 8.6 is used to solve for E:

$$E = z \frac{\sigma}{\sqrt{n}}$$
$$= 1.96 \frac{10}{\sqrt{200}}$$
$$= 1.4$$

With the larger sample size of 200, there's a 95% chance that the sample mean will be no more than 1.4 pounds from the population mean.

The procedure for determining the appropriate sample size for estimating a proportion is similar to the one used for sample means. Steps 1 and 2 are essentially the same. Steps 3 and 4 are revised as follows:

Step 3 Determine the population proportion or, if it's unknown, estimate it. If information is available on the population proportion (p), possibly from a previous study, use this value. Another method is to take a small preliminary sample and use the sample proportion, $\bar{p}$, as an estimate of p.

Step 4 Use the information gathered in steps 1 through 3 in Equation 8.7:

$$n = \frac{z^2\, p(1 - p)}{E^2} \tag{8.7}$$

where n = Sample size
   z = Value from standard normal table reflecting confidence level
   p = Population proportion
   E = Maximum tolerable error

The maximum tolerable error is computed using Equation 8.8:

$$E = z\sqrt{\frac{p(1 - p)}{n}} \tag{8.8}$$

Equation 8.8 can be rearranged so that n, the sample size, is the value to be solved for. This is how Equation 8.7 was derived.

The z value for Equation 8.7 is found in the standard normal table after the confidence level has been chosen. For a confidence level of 95%, a z value of 1.96 is used. If n is to be solved for, the decision maker must specify the maximum tolerable error, E. If E is to be solved for, the sample size, n, and the value p must be estimated and inserted in Equation 8.8.

EXAMPLE 8.14   A study published (July 31, 1992) in the *Annals of Surgery* says the use of positron emission tomography could help women detect breast tumors earlier. The study, funded by the U.S. Energy Department and the Revlon Group, looked at 14 women and correctly determined the status of the women's tumors in 12 cases. John Glaspy, an assistant professor of medicine at the University of California, Los Angeles, cautioned in *The Wall Street Journal* (July 31, 1992) that such a small study cannot be deemed statistically significant. A much larger sample of cases would be needed to show what promise, if any, the technology holds for breast cancer patients. If the percentage of successful determinations is around 85% and it is convenient for a sample of 196 women to be tested, what is the maximum tolerable error at the 95% confidence level? The value E is computed using Equation 8.8:

$$E = z\sqrt{\frac{p(1 - p)}{n}}$$

$$= 1.96\sqrt{\frac{(.85)(.15)}{196}}$$

$$= 1.96\ (.0255)$$
$$= .05$$

There is a 95% chance that the sample percentage of successful determinations, based on a sample size of 196, is within 5% of the true population percentage.

The estimated population proportion affects the width of the interval estimate. The width is greatest when p is .5, and it decreases as p gets larger or smaller. This can be seen by multiplying p by $(1 - p)$ in the numerator of the standard error of the proportion in Equation 8.8. If p equals .5, $p(1 - p)$ equals .25. If p is larger or smaller, $p(1 - p)$ is smaller than .25. Because of this, when p is not known or cannot be estimated, it is assumed to be .5. This is a conservative approach since using .5 results in the largest sample size possible.

Steps for computing sample size
1. Determine the confidence level.
2. Determine how much error, E, is tolerable.
3. Determine the population standard deviation or proportion. If it is unknown, estimate it.
4. Compute the sample size using either Equation 8.5 or Equation 8.7.

EXAMPLE 8.15 Suppose Dr. John Glaspy is unhappy with the 5.0% value for E (see Example 8.14); it is too large. When asked about the maximum error that would be acceptable, he decides on 2.5%. If this value of E is used, what sample size is necessary? Equation 8.7 is solved:

$$n = \frac{z^2\ p(1 - p)}{E^2} = \frac{1.96^2\ (.85)(.15)}{.025^2} = 783.7, \text{ rounded to } 784$$

The sample size must be increased from 196 to 784 to reduce the maximum tolerable error from 5% to 2.5%. Note that to cut the maximum tolerable error in half, the sample size had to be multiplied by 4.

EXAMPLE 8.16 Jenna Webster is manager of Easy-Quit, a program that has helped thousands of people stop smoking. She wants a rough idea of the proportion of previous clients who still are not smoking. She has just read an article in *Health* (March 1989) about the effects of air pollutants, including tobacco smoke. Because of the increased emphasis on quality air, Jenna believes her program could expand considerably if it's truly effective.

How large a sample of previous clients should she take to test the program's effectiveness? Jenna wants to be quite sure (99% confident) that the sample estimate is no more than .03 from the true population proportion. Easy-Quit has no idea what proportion of its past clients still aren't smoking. Equation 8.7 is used to solve for sample size, using .5 as the estimate of the population proportion:

$$n = \frac{z^2\, p(1-p)}{E^2} = \frac{2.575^2(.5)(.5)}{.03^2} = 1,841.8, \text{ rounded to } 1,842$$

A sample size of 1,842 will provide 99% confidence that the sample proportion of those still not smoking will be within 3 percentage points of the true population value.

EXAMPLE 8.17   (Refer to Example 8.16.) Jenna decides Easy-Quit cannot afford to take a sample of 1,842. What would happen to E if the sample size were reduced to 1,000? Equation 8.8 is used to answer this question:

$$E = 2.575 \sqrt{\frac{(.5)(.5)}{1,000}}$$
$$= 2.575(.0158)$$
$$= .0407$$

Reducing the sample size to 1,000 increases the maximum tolerable error slightly. Easy-Quit now has a maximum error of about .04, which is considered acceptable.

EXERCISES

41. What is maximum tolerable error?

42. Explain the relationship between maximum tolerable error and the width of an interval estimate.

43. Joey August, a local beer distributor, is aware that weather conditions influence the volume of beer sold. Joey would like to know with 98% certainty the true mean daily precipitation in his region within 0.08 inch. Past experience indicates that the standard deviation can be assumed to be 0.20 inch.

 a. How many observations of daily precipitation are required?

 b. What sample size is required to reduce the maximum tolerable error to 0.05 inch?

 c. Compute the maximum tolerable error for a sample of 100 observations.

44. Chet Lemon is interested in opening a health spa for smokers. His interest was intensified after reading the cover story on health spas in the April 1989 issue of *Health*. He thinks there might be a market for such a service, since many people want to improve their health but are having difficulty quitting smoking.

 To accurately forecast the demand for such a service, Chet needs to estimate the percentage of smokers in the neighborhood he's considering for his spa. Chet has decided to select a sample of 400 people and construct a 95% interval estimate for the proportion of smokers. Chet estimates that 25% of the target population smokes.

 a. Compute the maximum tolerable error.

 b. Compute the maximum tolerable error for a sample size of 1,000.

 c. How many people need to be interviewed for the sample percentage to be no more than 6% from the population percentage?

45. A national research firm wants to estimate the proportion of TV households that will watch a "Cheers" rerun next week. The research director decides to select a random sample and ask viewers whether they'll watch the show. The A.C. Nielsen ratings reported in USA *Today*, July 1, 1992, showed "Cheers" with a market share of 23% on June 25, 1992. (Market share comprises the percentage of sets in use that watched "Cheers.") How many viewers should be randomly selected to produce a 98% interval estimate for the true proportion of viewers if a maximum tolerable error of 3 percentage points is desired?

46. The Davis Real Estate Appraisers Agency has a client who wishes to know the average value of one-acre lots in Bend County. The client requires Davis to be 99% confident that its estimate is within $2,000 of the correct value. From past data, the standard deviation is believed to be $8,000.

    a. How many estimates are required?

    b. What sample size is needed to reduce the maximum tolerable error to $1,000?

    c. Compute the maximum tolerable error for a sample of 50 estimates.

47. The Mountain View Treatment Center would like to estimate the mean time a counselor spends with each patient. If the population standard deviation is estimated to be 35 minutes, how large should the sample be for a maximum tolerable error of 5 minutes? Use a confidence level of 95%.

48. The Cameron Advertising Agency wants to measure the proportion of the population that responds favorably to a new commercial for Safe Band-Aids. The agency seeks to estimate the proportion of favorable responses within .04 at the 90% confidence level. What sample size should be used if the agency has no idea what the population proportion is?

49. This exercise refers to variable x_8, annual base salary, found in Appendix C's company data base. Assume that the population standard deviation is $6,500 and that a maximum tolerable error of $3,000 is desired. How large should the sample be for a 95% interval estimate of average annual base salary?

50. This exercise refers to variable x_2, number of overtime hours worked during the past six months, found in Appendix C's company data base. Assume that the population standard deviation is 30. If a sample of 25 is selected, compute the maximum tolerable error for a 95% interval estimate for average number of overtime hours worked during the past six months.

SUMMARY

This chapter developed one of the primary uses of the sampling distribution. The estimation process for the population mean and the population proportion was covered, with emphasis on formulating interval estimates. An interval estimate provides the decision maker with a sense of the estimate's accuracy, which a point estimate does not.

An adjunct of the interval estimation process is using the sampling distribution to determine the needed sample size or the maximum tolerable error in estimating a population mean or proportion. This process is extremely useful, since almost every sampling situation requires decisions on how many items or persons to sample and how much accuracy attends the estimation process.

APPLICATIONS OF STATISTICAL CONCEPTS IN THE BUSINESS WORLD

SPOKANE TEACHERS CREDIT UNION

Steve Dahlstrom is president of Spokane Teachers Credit Union. The credit union regularly conducts a mail survey to determine members' attitudes toward its services. Among the demographic questions in each survey is whether a member is a teacher in the local area, since persons other than teachers can belong.

The credit union has been tracking the percentage of members who are teachers for several years. Each survey produces an estimate of this percentage, namely, the sample percentage. However, Steve recognizes that this point estimate can vary from survey to survey, even if the overall population percentage doesn't change. For this reason, an interval estimate is constructed around the point estimate each time a survey is taken. If this interval includes the historical percentage, the credit union assumes the population value hasn't shifted. Alternatively, when the interval estimate doesn't include this historical value, a shift is assumed to have occurred.

The credit union's marketing program assumes a high percentage of teachers in its membership, so a shift away from the historical percentage would affect the credit union's operations.

OTHER APPLICATIONS

The typical business estimates unknown population parameters daily. Speculation, guessing, and forecasting are common in modern business, whether done intuitively or more formally. Because of the need to continually assess the condition of a population of interest, estimating key population parameters is an ongoing management concern.

For this reason, the formal estimating procedures in this chapter are important. This is especially true for the procedures for risk assessment, since risk is often difficult to determine intuitively. Determining sample size is also a constant problem in any business where samples are used to estimate population parameters. Examples of population parameters whose values might be of great interest to a business include:

Average savings account balance in a branch bank

Average number of sick days taken per year

Percentage of the market that will be captured by a new product

Average lifetime of TV sets (quality control department)

Percentage of population that recognizes an advertising theme

Mean number of products returned for service each week

Average shipping distance for mail-order customers

Average delay, in days, between ordering and receiving parts

Percentage of the work force absent any given day

Average inventory turnover, in days, for a company's products

Percentage of cartons incorrectly filled in a packing plant (for quality-control records)

Average income per household

Average days per stay in a hospital

GLOSSARY

Point estimate A single value that is measured from a sample and used as an estimate of the corresponding population parameter.

Interval estimate An interval within which the population parameter quite likely lies.

Confidence coefficient A coefficient used to indicate the likelihood that an interval estimate contains the population parameter.

Confidence level A confidence coefficient expressed as a percentage.

t distribution A distribution used to construct an interval estimate when the population is approximately normally distributed, the population standard deviation is unknown, and the sample size is less than 30.

Maximum tolerable error The maximum amount by which the sample statistic (the estimate) differs from the population parameter for a specified confidence level.

KEY FORMULAS

Interval estimate for sample mean—population standard deviation known

$$\bar{x} \pm z \frac{\sigma}{\sqrt{n}} \tag{8.1}$$

Interval estimate for sample mean—population standard deviation unknown

$$\bar{x} \pm z \frac{s}{\sqrt{n}} \tag{8.2}$$

Interval estimate for population proportion

$$\bar{p} \pm z \sqrt{\frac{p(1-p)}{n}} \tag{8.3}$$

Interval estimate for sample means—small samples

$$\bar{x} \pm t \frac{s}{\sqrt{n}} \tag{8.4}$$

Sample size determination—mean

$$n = \frac{z^2 \sigma^2}{E^2} \tag{8.5}$$

Maximum tolerable error—mean

$$E = z \frac{\sigma}{\sqrt{n}} \tag{8.6}$$

Sample size determination—proportion

$$n = \frac{z^2 p(1-p)}{E^2} \tag{8.7}$$

Maximum tolerable error—proportion

$$E = z\sqrt{\frac{p(1-p)}{n}}$$ (8.8)

SOLVED EXERCISES

1. INTERVAL ESTIMATION OF A POPULATION MEAN—LARGE SAMPLE

Gattos Pizza specializes in home delivery and is considering a special two-for-one deal designed to increase the size of customer orders. To determine if the deal works, Gattos estimates the average size of customer orders at this time. A sample of 36 orders is selected, and the mean amount is $14.37 with standard deviation of $4.02.

a. Construct a 95% interval estimate. Interpret the meaning of this interval.

b. If the population standard deviation is known to be $3.50, construct a 90% interval estimate. Interpret the meaning of this interval.

Solution:

a. $\bar{x} \pm z\dfrac{s}{\sqrt{n}} = 14.37 \pm 1.96\dfrac{4.02}{\sqrt{36}}$

$\qquad = 14.37 \pm 1.96(0.67)$

$\qquad = 14.37 \pm 1.31$

$\qquad = \$13.06 \text{ to } \$15.68$

Gattos can say with 95% confidence that the average amount of a customer order is between $13.06 and $15.68.

b. $\bar{x} \pm z\dfrac{\sigma}{\sqrt{n}} = 14.37 \pm 1.645\dfrac{3.50}{\sqrt{36}}$

$\qquad = 14.37 \pm 1.645(0.58)$

$\qquad = 14.37 \pm 0.96$

$\qquad = \$13.41 \text{ to } \$15.33$

Gattos can say with 90% confidence that the average amount of a customer order is between $13.41 and $15.33.

2. INTERVAL ESTIMATION OF A POPULATION PROPORTION

A new cheese spread is tested in five local supermarkets. A sample of 600 shoppers try the product, and 348 indicate that they like it. Construct a 98% interval estimate for the percentage of shoppers who like the new cheese spread, and interpret this interval's meaning.

Solution:

$$\bar{p} \pm z\sqrt{\frac{p(1-p)}{n}} = .58 \pm 2.33\sqrt{\frac{(.58)(.42)}{600}}$$

$\qquad\qquad = .58 \pm 2.33\sqrt{.0004}$

$\qquad\qquad = .58 \pm 2.33(.02)$

$\qquad\qquad = .58 \pm .047$

$\qquad\qquad = .533 \text{ to } .627$

It can be said with 98% confidence that the percentage of the population of shoppers who like the new cheese spread is between 53.3% and 62.7%.

3. INTERVAL ESTIMATION OF A POPULATION MEAN—SMALL SAMPLE, σ UNKNOWN

The Mass Bay Transit Authority (MBTA) must estimate the average number of passenger miles traveled per person per route for a federal agency. MBTA employee Trudy Monk rides the streetcar each day and calculates the number of passenger miles per person per route. Trudy has ridden the Beacon Street route 22 times this year and computed an average number of passenger miles of 3.2 with a standard deviation of 0.6. Construct a 99% interval estimate for average passenger miles traveled per person on the Beacon Street route, and interpret this interval's meaning. It is known that passenger miles closely follow a normal distribution.

Solution:

$$\bar{x} \pm t\frac{s}{\sqrt{n}} = 3.2 \pm 2.831\frac{0.6}{\sqrt{22}}$$
$$= 3.2 \pm 2.831(0.128)$$
$$= 3.2 \pm 0.36$$
$$= 2.84 \text{ to } 3.56$$

The MBTA can now report to the federal agency, with 99% confidence, that the average number of passenger miles traveled per person on the Beacon Street route last year was between 2.84 and 3.56.

4. SAMPLE SIZE FOR INTERVAL ESTIMATE OF A POPULATION MEAN

A gift shop is interested in the charges made by credit card customers. The owner wants an estimate of the mean purchase amount for credit card customers that's within $1.00 of the actual population mean. For a 90% confidence level, how large a sample is necessary if the population standard deviation is estimated at $4.75?

Solution:

$$n = \frac{z^2\sigma^2}{E^2} = \frac{1.645^2(4.75^2)}{1.00^2} = 61$$

5. MAXIMUM TOLERABLE ERROR FOR INTERVAL ESTIMATE OF A POPULATION MEAN

If the gift shop owner in Solved Exercise 4 uses a sample of 100 credit card customers, what is the maximum tolerable error?

Solution:

$$E = z\frac{\sigma}{\sqrt{n}}$$
$$= 1.645\frac{4.75}{\sqrt{100}}$$
$$= \$0.78$$

6. SAMPLE SIZE FOR INTERVAL ESTIMATE OF A POPULATION PROPORTION

The California Institute for Tourism plans to survey out-of-state visitors to determine if they plan to stay in the state more than one week. It would like to be 95% confident of its estimate.

How many tourists should be sampled if the institute wants the sample proportion of visitors staying longer than one week to be within .03 of the true proportion?

Solution:

$$n = \frac{z^2 p(1-p)}{E^2} = \frac{1.96^2(.5)(.5)}{.03^2} = 1,067.1, \text{ rounded to } 1,068$$

7. MAXIMUM TOLERABLE ERROR FOR INTERVAL ESTIMATE OF A POPULATION PROPORTION

If the California Institute for Tourism (see Solved Exercise 6) uses a sample of 400 credit card customers, what is the maximum tolerable error?

Solution:

$$E = z\sqrt{\frac{p(1-p)}{n}}$$

$$= 1.96\sqrt{\frac{(.5)(.5)}{400}}$$

$$= 1.96(.025)$$

$$= .049$$

EXERCISES

51. Construct an interval estimate for each of the following situations:
    a. $\bar{x} = 14$, $\sigma = 2$, $n = 25$, 90% confidence level.
    b. $\bar{x} = 128$, $s = 24$, $n = 80$, 95% confidence level.
    c. $\bar{p} = .62$, $n = 125$, 99% confidence level.
    d. $\bar{x} = 1.8$, $s = 0.02$, $n = 25$, 80% confidence level.

52. Find the appropriate sample size for each of the following situations:
    a. $\bar{x} = 147$, $\sigma = 11$, $E = 2$, 95% confidence level.
    b. $\bar{p} = .24$, $E = .05$ (5%), 90% confidence level.
    c. $E = .07$ (7%), 98% confidence level.

53. Decision Science Associates, an independent research firm, employs people to call households weekday evenings, 5 to 9 P.M., to conduct telephone interviews. President Paul Dawson needs to estimate how many people to hire to complete a job requiring 2,000 interviews. His preliminary test of 36 calls reveals that they require an average of 16.8 minutes with standard deviation of 4.2 minutes. Calculate a 99% interval estimate for the true mean length of all 2,000 interviews.

54. A random sample of 50 workers on a shopping mall construction project indicated that 3 weren't wearing hard hats. The project's population is 500 workers. Construct a 90% interval estimate for the proportion of workers not wearing hard hats.

55. A quality-control engineer conducted a test of the tensile strength of 15 aluminum wires and found a mean tensile strength of 95 with a standard deviation of 7.6. Construct a 98% interval estimate for the average tensile strength of aluminum wires.

56. The Mutual Insurance Company needs to study the annual health insurance claims for men between the ages of 40 and 50 to determine the necessity of a rate increase. A random sample of 450 claims produced a sample mean of $742 and sample standard deviation of $53. Find the 98% interval estimate for the population mean claim.

57. The Klassic Design Corporation would like to compare its employees' annual salaries with those of similar companies in the industry. Klassic hasn't been using an employment agency for its staffing needs but is considering doing so after reading the article "Employing a Private Employment Firm" in the *Personnel Journal* (September 1989 issue).

    In a random sample of 18 companies, average salary is found to be $31,780 with standard deviation of $5,450. Find the 95% interval estimate for the mean salary of companies in the industry.

58. The auditors of Litho-Art Printers want to know the proportion of accurate accounts receivable based on an audit verification letter sent to customers. On the basis of the letter, 180 out of 200 responses were verified as accurate. Find the 99% interval estimate for the true proportion of accurate accounts receivable.

59. The Specific Tire Corporation wants to be sure that its estimate of a new brand's average mileage is no more than 525 miles off the true average. It is known that the standard deviation for this type of tire is about 2,500 miles. If Specific wants to be 90% certain that the sample mean is within the desired interval, how many tires should be tested? If Specific wants to be 99% certain, how many tires should be tested?

60. Inland Market Research conducts telephone interviews to test advertising recall. Swanson's has just developed a new advertising campaign and has asked Inland to bid on a contract to test people's recall. Swanson's wants to be 98% confident that the sample percentage is within 7% of the actual population percentage of individuals who recall the new advertising slogan. How many telephone interviews should Inland plan?

61. Using the sample size determined for the 98% interval estimate in Exercise 60, Inland Market Research completed the telephone interviews and found that 90 respondents recalled the new advertising slogan. Find the 98% interval estimate.

62. A 1989 study by Jones at the Massachusetts Institute of Technology compared world auto manufacturers, finding that the average European large-volume car plant took 36.2 hours to build a car (*Business Week*, January 15, 1992). Compute a 90% interval estimate for this study if the standard deviation was 2.6 and sample size was 27 plants.

63. In his book, *Customers for Life*, Dallas Cadillac dealer Carl Sewell figures a lifetime customer will spend a total of $332,000 at one of his 10 dealerships. Nissan Motors luxury Infiniti brand was founded with the idea that superior customer service by its dealers would distinguish it from other brands. General Manager William R. Bruce decides to determine the proportion of Infiniti owners who rate Nissan's customer service as superior. If he can tolerate a maximum error of 4%, how large a sample should he select for a 90% interval estimate?

64. This exercise refers to variable x_6, score on company aptitude test, found in Appendix C's company data base. Select a simple random sample of 40 employees (sample with replacement) and construct a 90% interval estimate for the average score on the company aptitude test. Interpret the meaning of this interval.

65. The following data consist of the prime interest rates for 100 randomly chosen weeks. Select a random sample of 20 weeks (sample without replacement), and construct a 95% inter-

val estimate. Assume this population is normally distributed, and remember the finite-population correction factor.

1 10.9	11.6	14.0	7.7	10.0	11.3	8.7	13.1
9 10.3	11.9	12.0	11.7	6.7	9.3	8.8	10.7
17 11.8	9.5	13.0	11.6	7.1	10.6	8.0	9.8
25 11.6	8.6	9.5	8.2	10.8	11.6	8.6	10.8
33 12.7	12.8	6.9	9.0	11.9	11.7	10.5	8.9
41 7.6	7.3	9.9	8.5	14.0	10.2	10.3	6.5
49 11.5	12.2	7.8	10.5	12.9	10.5	8.0	9.7
57 7.3	13.5	11.1	9.8	13.3	11.5	6.3	11.4
65 7.1	12.1	8.0	10.6	12.1	8.6	11.6	6.8
73 8.3	12.6	8.9	9.9	9.1	9.8	12.9	8.3
81 10.1	11.9	9.9	10.2	7.5	9.1	12.0	10.1
89 11.5	10.6	5.9	11.8	8.7	12.1	6.1	8.9
97 9.4	11.0	7.8	8.3				

EXTENDED EXERCISES

66. TENTH KEY MAIL ORDERS

Tenth Key, a mail-order company with a small retail store, does most of its business through the mail. Customer satisfaction is important in the company's philosophy, and questionnaires are frequently used to assess customers' satisfaction with the firm's products.

A major aspect of customer satisfaction has just come to light as a result of an open-ended question on a recent mail survey. When asked what single thing would most improve the company's service, many people indicated faster service. Company president Grace Slick would like to know the average time between a customer's mailing or calling in an order and the company's filling the order.

Grace decides to conduct a telephone survey of current customers since there's only one key question to be asked. A random sample of customers can easily be selected from recent customer orders using a systematic sampling plan. The remaining issue is how many customers to call.

Equation 8.5 is used to compute sample size. Grace decides the margin of error for time between ordering and receipt of goods should be 1.5 days. A 95% confidence level will be used. The standard deviation of times is unknown, and there are many guesses about this value.

Grace takes a preliminary sample to estimate the variability in receipt times. Fifty names are randomly selected from the current customer list and called. Each person is asked how long it took for their most recent order to arrive, from the time of order placement. The average time for the sample of 50 wasn't of interest, but the standard deviation of 2.7 days was used as an estimate of the population standard deviation.

Once the values needed for Equation 8.5 were determined, the necessary sample size was computed:

$$n = \frac{z^2 \, \sigma^2}{E^2} = \frac{1.96^2(2.7^2)}{1.5^2} = 12.45$$

Rounded to $n = 13$, this seemed a very small sample size. It was apparent that the degree of accuracy Grace requested had already been exceeded by the preliminary sample of 50. Based on the time needed to call the 50 people, she estimated that a sample of 500 would be quickly and easily accomplished. The maximum tolerable error for a sample of this size was computed using Equation 8.6:

$$E = 1.96\frac{2.7}{\sqrt{500}}$$
$$= 1.96(0.12)$$
$$= 0.24$$

a. Summarize the accuracy for a sample size of 500 in one statement.

b. Suppose the maximum tolerable error of 0.24 day is considered more accurate than necessary. What should the sample size be if this error were changed to one day?

c. The assumption that the population standard deviation is 2.7 days was based on a sample of 50. How could this be checked as the sample continues to be taken?

67. CEA PENSION FUND

The CEA (a state teachers association) has invested a considerable portion of its pension fund in the stock market. The total portfolio value is constantly monitored by CEA officials and by their investment advisors. The holdings' yield or dividend payout hasn't been followed in the past, and the association would like to know its approximate average value.

CEA's portfolio contains several thousand stocks, each with a different yield. The yield is calculated as the annual dividend divided by the current stock price. As each stock's price fluctuates on a day-to-day basis, the yield changes also. To sample yields, we must not only sample different stocks in the portfolio, but also check them at different points in time. A sampling plan is needed to select the stock yields, which will be averaged and used to estimate the total portfolio yield over time.

It will take time to select the stocks and the points in time to use in the sample, which argues for a small sample size. On the other hand, CEA would like a fairly accurate average yield figure to report to its membership. More accuracy suggests a larger sample. Therefore, a sample size that balances cost against accuracy must be determined.

Key association officials differ in their opinions of a tolerable margin of error. The maximum tolerable error ranges from .5% to 2% among these officials. It is assumed that the yield of the total holdings is around 5%.

a. Construct a table that shows several maximum tolerable errors and their associated sample sizes.

b. How long a period should be used to define the population of yields from which the sample will be taken?

c. Based on the table constructed for question *a*, what sample size would you choose if you were the association president, considering both accuracy and the implied cost of sampling?

68. WHITFIELD UNIVERSITY BASKETBALL

Bobby Day, basketball coach for Whitfield University, is curious about male high school seniors' heights, especially after reading an article in *Coach* (August 1989) that described a new zone defense. Bobby thinks player height is the key to its success. It seems to him that senior males' average height has been increasing sharply over the past five years. Bobby wants to know the average height of graduating high school males in the five-state area that supplies most of Whitfield's basketball players.

Bobby has two things to consider in selecting a sample of high school graduating seniors. First, how will the sample be taken? There are hundreds of high schools in the five-state area and hundreds of students in each school. Some method of randomly sampling these students will have to be devised.

Second, how many students should be sampled? Bobby wants a certain amount of accuracy, but understands that accuracy must be paid for with increased sample size.

a. How should students be sampled from the high schools in the five-state area?

b. Write a statement that the coach can understand and that, complete with information supplied by the coach, will provide the information necessary to compute sample size.

c. Suppose that after questions *a* and *b* are answered and a survey is designed, the cost of estimating high school males' average height is found to be $1,500. Do you think the coach will ask the university administration for the money to conduct this study?

69. Park and Fly Car Rental

Park and Fly Car Rental has a 150-car fleet. Manager Shawn Birch is concerned about his cars' average miles per gallon of gas since he needs to determine how much to charge customers per mile for usage of the automobiles. Shawn selects and tests a sample of 20 cars.

You work for Park and Fly and are assigned to estimate the average mileage per auto. Actual mileages for the entire fleet of 150 cars (rounded to the nearest whole number) are:

27	24	22	23	25	30	26	24	23	23	26
22	21	27	28	27	27	27	24	21	26	18
27	20	23	30	25	25	21	24	25	27	24
26	24	26	23	31	25	22	23	31	25	26
21	28	27	23	23	23	29	25	24	24	20
26	25	29	18	20	17	28	22	26	22	21
25	25	25	25	21	21	28	29	24	23	26
22	20	30	24	22	23	22	22	23	23	20
26	21	28	28	27	24	22	23	33	20	21
24	24	21	29	29	26	24	28	26	21	22
25	23	25	25	24	23	25	23	27	23	20
20	28	20	22	20	24	25	23	24	25	25
26	23	28	22	23	23	24	21	25	25	25
24	23	23	18	16	24	22				

a. Select a random sample of 20 mileages (sample with replacement) and construct a 95% interval estimate. *put item back in population*

b. If you're told that the maximum tolerable error is one mile per gallon, what sample size would you recommend?

c. What is the maximum tolerable error if a sample size of 40 is used?

70. Our Lady of Lourdes Hospital

Chapter 4 presented family sizes for a population of 200 Our Lady of Lourdes Hospital employees. Customer benefits director Curtis Huff has asked you to quickly estimate average family size per employee. You've computed the mean and presented it to the director as a point estimate of the population mean. Mr. Huff isn't satisfied with your work. He wants to know how accurate your estimate is.

a. Develop 90%, 95%, and 99% interval estimates for the mean.

b. Discuss whether the finite-population multiplier should be used in this situation.

c. If the sample size were increased to 50, what effect would this have on your interval?

d. Write a memo to Mr. Huff summarizing your results.

MICROCOMPUTER PACKAGE

The micro package *Computerized Business Statistics* can be used to compute sample size.

Suppose you wanted to find the sample size needed to estimate the average annual billing amount for your clients. The population standard deviation of annual billing amounts is estimated to be about $2,500. A confidence level of 95% is chosen, and sample sizes are to be computed for maximum tolerable errors of $200, $300, and $500.

Computer Solution:

From the main menu of *Computerized Business Statistics*, a 7 is selected, indicating Sampling and Estimation. The sampling and estimation menu is then shown on the screen. This menu was presented at the end of Chapter 2.

Since the problem involves the determination of sample size, **Compute Sample Size** is selected.

```
SAMPLE SIZE ANALYSIS
1. Sample Size from Alpha/Beta Error
2. Sample Size from Sampling Error
      Enter Option (1-2) and press ↵ 2
```

Alpha/beta error has not been discussed, so the correct response is **2**, "sample size from sampling error."

```
Enter Standard Deviation and press ↵ 2500
```

The estimated population standard deviation for this exercise is $2,500.

```
Enter Alpha error: 1 = .1, 2 = .05, 3 = .025, 4 = .01, 5 = .005, 6 = Other
Select Alpha: Enter 1–6 and press ↵ 3
```

The concept of alpha error hasn't been covered yet. Alpha error refers to the area in one tail. For a confidence level of 95%, the alpha error is $(1 - .95)/2 = .025$, and a **3** is entered.

```
Critical Z for Alpha = .025 and press ↵ 1.96
```

The correct z value for a 95% confidence level is 1.96.

```
Enter the Sampling Error and press ↵ 200
```

Sampling error is the same as maximum tolerable error. The maximum tolerable error for this exercise is $200.

Finally, the program provides the answer:

```
Sample Size = 600
```

This process can be repeated for maximum tolerable errors of $300 and $500.

MINITAB COMPUTER PACKAGE

The following commands show how the MINITAB package is used to solve the Our Lady of Lourdes Hospital exercise (Extended Exercise 70).

First, the program is used to generate 30 random numbers.

```
MTB> RANDOM 30 C1;
SUBC> INTEGER 1 200.
MTB> PRINT C1
C1
     78    106    75    68    104    41     2    73
     53     53    24   101     42   189    57    42
    155     19    15    88    161    93   111    35
     57    193   106    94     23   182
```

Next, the family sizes that correspond to the random numbers are entered as data, and the mean and standard deviation are computed:

```
MTB> SET INTO C2
DATA> 6 2 2 1 5 1 2 2 2 2 1 4 3 3 2 3 2 3 2 4 4 2
DATA> 4 1 2 3 2 4 2 3
DATA> END
MTB> DESCRIBE C2
   C2        N     MEAN    MEDIAN    STDEV
            30    2.633    2.0000    1.217
   C2      MIN      MAX        Q1       Q3
         1.000    6.000     2.000    3.250
```

Finally, a 95% interval estimate is computed using the sample standard deviation, 1.217, as an estimate of the population standard deviation.

```
MTB> ZINTERVAL 95 1.217 C2
    N     MEAN    STDEV    SE MEAN    95.0 PERCENT C.I.
   30    2.633    1.217       .222     (2.197, 3.069)
MTB> STOP
```

The ZINTERVAL command is used to compute a 95% interval estimate for the data stored in C2 using the sample standard deviation, 1.217, as an estimate of the population standard deviation. Note that the ZINTERVAL command consists of the confidence level, assumed σ, and column where the data are located. If 100 students develop interval estimates using the population in Extended Exercise 62 in Chapter 4, 95 of the intervals will contain the actual population mean. The interval estimate developed in this example, 2.197 to 3.069, does include the actual population mean, which is 2.9.

HYPOTHESIS TESTING

*Say not, "This is
the truth," but
"So it seems
to me to be
as I now see
the things I
think I see."*
Inscription
above a doorway
at the German
Naval Officers
School in Kiel

Objectives

When you have completed this chapter, you will be able to:

Describe the difference between estimation and hypothesis
testing.

Use the four-step hypothesis-testing procedure to solve
practical business problems.

Identify the two forms of potential error in the hypothesis-
testing procedure and understand their consequences.

Develop decision rules.

Conduct tests of hypotheses about population means and
population proportions.

Develop the operating characteristic curve and power curve for
each decision rule.

According to *The Wall Street Journal*, February 27, 1990, Waldenbooks is launching a new membership program. Frequent book buyers will receive benefits including discounts on future purchases.

The preceding chapters have set the stage for one of the most important statistical applications: hypothesis testing. Most real-world statistical analyses to assist the decision-making process involve this important concept. This chapter and the next cover this topic, that is based on the sampling distribution ideas of Chapter 7. If you can't fully understand this chapter's concepts, a review of Chapter 7 may prove helpful.

WHY MANAGERS NEED TO KNOW ABOUT HYPOTHESIS TESTING

Managers receive data signals each day from various aspects of their businesses. Some of these might be called false signals because they simply reflect chance or random fluctuations in daily operations. Other changes signal significant shifts in important measures of company health. This chapter concerns understanding the difference between random and significant changes.

For the Waldenbooks program management of the chain must carefully monitor sales to detect the effect. They must distinguish between a significant sales upturn and a temporary increase due to random effects. This chapter deals with how to do this.

INTRODUCTION

It is important at the outset to understand the difference between hypothesis testing (the subject of this chapter) and estimation (the subject of Chapter 8). Both procedures involve the use of sampling distributions. The major difference is whether a predetermined notion of the state of the population being sampled has been established. If nothing is known about the population, estimation is used to provide point and interval estimates about population parameters of interest. If information about the population is claimed or suspected, **hypothesis testing** is used to determine the feasibility of this information.

Estimation versus Hypothesis Testing

> **Estimation** involves using sample evidence to estimate the unknown characteristics of a population. **Hypothesis testing** involves using sample evidence to assess the likelihood that an assumption about some characteristic of a population is true.

The difference between estimation and hypothesis testing may be easier to understand by determining which of these two questions is relevant to a particular statistical study:

1. What is the state of the population? Since no information about it exists, a random sample will be selected, appropriate statistics computed, and inferences about population parameters made. The likelihood of error in this estimation process is recognized and measured.

2. Does the population possess the characteristics that are claimed, suggested, or hypothesized? The claim being made about the population is in doubt, so a random sample from this population is selected, appropriate statistics computed, and, once these sample results are examined, the decision of whether to reject the claim about the population is made. The likelihood of error in this hypothesis-testing process is then assessed.

■ SITUATION 9.1   Five months ago Sue and Bill Johnson took over a chemical manufacturing company started by Bill's parents. The company supplies a variety of basic chemicals to many firms, including the Anderson Corporation. One of the Johnson's big accounts with Anderson involves a chemical that Anderson uses in making a medication that helps control high cholesterol.

In their early contacts, Anderson's purchasing manager suggested that Bill and Sue read a study that appeared in *The Journal of the American Medical Association*.[1] Among other things, it indicated that of those persons seeing a doctor about high cholesterol, 19.2% were given a prescription for medication. Anderson's product is often prescribed for these people.

Anderson has developed a test for incoming shipments of Johnson's chemical that combines measures of acidity and potency. According to the contract between them, this measure is supposed to be at least 425 units. In checking their own records from the factory floor, Bill and Sue find the following information:

1. A total of 55 batches have been tested using the Anderson acidity/potency measure during the past three years. This sample of 55 batches was randomly selected from the several hundred batches produced.

2. The average measurement for the sample batches was 415 acidity/potency units with a standard deviation of 30.

When first confronted with this sample evidence, Sue and Bill conclude that their process is not meeting specification. On second thought, however, they are not so sure. Perhaps the process is performing as specified and the 415 figure is due to random variability inherent in sampling. Also, they note that Anderson has never indicated

---

[1]W. H. Giles, R. F. Anda, D. H. Jones, M. K. Serdula, R. K. Merritt, and F. DeStefano, "Recent Trends in the Identification and Treatment of High Blood Cholesterol by Physicians," *The Journal of the American Medical Association* (March 3, 1993), pp. 1133–38.

displeasure with the quality of their product. Sue realizes from her experience in a college statistics course that the 10-unit deficit (425–415) could be due to randomness, but she and Bill decide the matter must be investigated. ■

HYPOTHESIS-TESTING STEPS AND PROCEDURES

The following steps constitute the procedure for testing a hypothesis about the state of a population. The specific calculations vary from test to test.

Hypothesis-Testing Steps   **Step 1** State the null and alternative hypotheses (these terms will be explained in depth later in this section).

The first step in the hypothesis-testing procedure is to state the null, or no-change, hypothesis. The null hypothesis states that the difference between a sample statistic and the corresponding claimed population parameter is due to the chance variation involved in sampling. The alternative hypothesis is the opposite statement about the population, which must be true if the null hypothesis is false.

Step 2 Assume the null hypothesis is true, and determine the appropriate sampling distribution for this assumption.

The null hypothesis stands on trial much as a person charged with a crime: innocence is assumed unless sufficient evidence is produced to indicate guilt. That is, the null hypothesis is assumed to be true unless sample evidence can be produced to indicate that this assumption is extremely unlikely, in which case the null hypothesis will be judged "guilty" or false.

Under the assumption that the null hypothesis is true, a sampling distribution is developed from which the calculated test statistic will be drawn. The specific sampling distribution will vary from test to test.

Step 3 Take a random sample from the population under investigation and compute the appropriate test statistic from the collected data.

Random samples are required to ensure that the sample is representative of the population. After the sample has been selected, the appropriate statistic, a single numerical value, is calculated from the data. This statistic is commonly the sample mean or sample proportion.

Step 4 Assess the likelihood of selecting the test statistic from the assumed sampling distribution.

If it seems quite unlikely that the computed test statistic could be drawn from the sampling distribution, the null hypothesis is rejected. The testing process assumes that the null hypothesis is true, and if an extremely unlikely occurrence accompanies this assumption, the assumption must be abandoned.

On the other hand, if the test statistic seems likely to have come from the assumed sampling distribution, the null hypothesis isn't rejected. In this case the sample hasn't produced evidence strong enough to suggest that the null hypothesis is false.

EXAMPLE 9.1   A sales brochure for a new light bulb claims that such bulbs' average lifetime is 1,000 hours. A random sample of 250 bulbs is taken from inventory, and each is tested until failure. These test bulbs' average lifetime is computed and used to test the null hypothesis that all such bulbs' average lifetime is 1,000 hours. Suppose one of the following test results occurs:

1. The sample average (mean) lifetime is 999 hours. This sample average is less than the claimed 1,000-hour average for the population of light bulbs; however, it seems quite reasonable that if the population averages 1,000 hours, the sample could average 999 hours. The sample evidence doesn't seem to contradict the null hypothesis, so the null hypothesis isn't rejected.
2. The sample average (mean) lifetime is 700 hours. This sample evidence seems incompatible with the claimed population average of 1,000 hours. Observing such a low sample average seems extremely unlikely if the null hypothesis is true, especially since such a large sample was used (250). The null hypothesis is rejected.

The two hypothesis-testing outcomes in the preceding example are intuitively obvious. It isn't necessary to understand hypothesis-testing procedures to arrive at the correct conclusion if the sample evidence is this clear. Most situations, however, are not intuitively obvious. One must usually follow the four hypothesis-testing steps to correctly assess the probability that the null hypothesis is true.

The hypothesis to be tested about a population can come about in any of several ways. Someone may claim that the population of interest has certain characteristics. A salesperson, for example, might claim that a new machine averages nine months between breakdowns. A sales brochure might claim that no more than 5% of the electronic components ordered from a company will prove defective when installed in larger assemblies.

Other hypothesis-testing applications involve hypotheses or claims that aren't as apparent. The following four situations relevant to a business setting illustrate this point.

EXAMPLE 9.2   A study conducted to determine the annual salaries of company trainers around the United States found that the average (mean) salary was $63,627 ("Honey, They Shrunk My Paycheck," *Training*, November 1992, p. 21). The study pointed out that salaries differed by several demographic characteristics including location, number of company employees, gross sales/assets of company, industry, sex, education level, age, and years of experience. An analyst wants to determine whether the average salary of company trainers in New York state is similar to the national average. The appropriate hypothesis is that the average salary is $63,627. A random sample of salaries will be acquired, and if the sample mean is different enough, it will be concluded that company trainers are paid differently in the state of New York.

EXAMPLE 9.3   The management team at a bank wonders whether the average savings account balances for two of its branches are the same or different. One branch has just had its interior remodeled, an action that management took based on an article in *The Banker*, "Putting on the Ritz" (February 1989 issue). This article pointed out the profit advantages of making a bank's interior appealing to customers.

The appropriate hypothesis is that the average balances are equal. Sample accounts will be selected from each branch and, if there's a large enough difference between them, it will be concluded that the population of account balances at the two branches have different averages.

EXAMPLE 9.4   A state government agency is concerned about unemployment rates in the state's two major cities. Random samples are selected from each city and the sample unemployment rates determined. The appropriate hypothesis is that the two population unemployment rates are equal. If the sample rates are very close, it will be concluded that the cities have the same unemployment rate. If the sample rates are quite different, it will be concluded that they have different unemployment rates.

EXAMPLE 9.5   A new machine purchased by the Sun Company to fill containers with orange juice is supposed to have an average fill volume of 16 ounces. Before using the machine in the production process, the company decides to sample its output volumes to see if the claim is true. The appropriate hypothesis is that the machine does indeed average 16 ounces of fill. Several containers are filled under production conditions, and the sample mean volume is computed. If this sample average is close to 16 ounces, it will be concluded that the claimed machine average is correct. If the sample average volume isn't close to 16 ounces, the company that sold the machine will be called to adjust or replace it.

Each of the previous examples involves the testing of a single hypothesis or claim about the state of the population of interest. In statistics, these claims are tested in the form of null hypotheses.

Step 1 in the hypothesis-testing procedure calls for stating the null and alternative hypotheses. The **null hypothesis** states that the difference between a sample statistic and its assumed population parameter is due to the chance variation inherent in sampling.

Null Hypothesis

> The **null hypothesis** is the assumption about the population that is tested using sample evidence. It states that the difference between a sample statistic and the assumed population parameter is due to chance variation in sampling. The symbol for the null hypothesis is H_0.

Analysts usually design their tests based on the assumption that there has been no change in the population of interest. Why not state the hypothesis in a positive form? Why not claim that a difference exists between the sample statistic and the population parameter, due to some cause? Unfortunately, this type of hypothesis cannot be tested definitively. Evidence that's consistent with a hypothesis stated in a positive form can almost never be taken as conclusive grounds for accepting the hypothesis. A finding that is consistent with such a hypothesis might be consistent with other hypotheses too and, thus, doesn't establish the truth of the given hypothesis. Example 9.6 illustrates this point.

EXAMPLE 9.6 Suppose a coin is suspected of being biased in favor of tails. The coin is flipped 100 times, and the outcome is 53 tails. It would *not* be correct to jump to the conclusion that the coin is biased simply because more than the expected number of tails (50) resulted. In fact, a total of 53 tails is consistent with the hypothesis that the coin is fair. It wouldn't be surprising to flip a fair coin 100 times and observe 53 tails. On the other hand, 85 or 90 tails in 100 flips would seen to contradict the hypothesis of a fair coin. In this event, there would be a strong case for a biased coin.

Alternative Hypothesis

Suppose the null hypothesis being tested is false. In hypothesis testing, an **alternative hypothesis** is stated that holds true if the null hypothesis is false. The objective of a hypothesis test is to use sample evidence to choose between these two statements about the state of the population of interest.

> The **alternative hypothesis** in a hypothesis test is the statement about the population that must be true if the null hypothesis is false. The symbol for the alternative hypothesis is H_1.

An alternative hypothesis may indicate a change from the null hypothesis in a particular direction, or it may indicate a change without specifying direction. In Example 9.5, the machine was claimed to fill containers with 16 ounces each; thus, the null hypothesis is $H_0: \mu = 16$. This hypothesis would be rejected if the sample mean was found to be either too large or too small; so the alternative hypothesis is $H_1: \mu \neq 16$. Because no direction is specified in the alternative hypothesis (the sample mean could be greater than or less than 16 ounces), this is called a **two-tailed test**.

Frequently, the analyst is concerned with only one alternative. For example a manager wonders if a quality improvement program has reduced the percentage of defective units produced below the previous rate of 15%; thus, the null hypothesis is $H_0: p \geq .15$. This hypothesis would be rejected if the sample defective rate was found to be reduced; so the alternative hypothesis is $H_1: p < .15$. If the analyst is concerned only with an alternative in a single direction, this is called a **one-tailed test**.

One- and Two-Tailed Tests

> A **one-tailed test** is one in which the alternative hypothesis indicates a direction (either greater or less than); a **two-tailed test** is one in which the alternative hypothesis does not specify direction.

■ SITUATION 9.1—PARTIALLY RESOLVED Sue and Bill Johnson have records from a sample of 55 chemical batches showing an average acidity/potency measurement of 415 units. Since their contract with Anderson specifies a mean of 425 units, they are concerned about maintaining a good relationship with Anderson. Since a mean below 425 is of concern, their hypothesis test will be one-tailed. The null and alternative hypotheses are:

$$H_0: \mu \geq 425$$
$$H_1: \mu < 425$$

An alternative hypothesis uses one of three signs: the unequal sign ($\neq$), the less-than sign ($<$), or the greater-than sign ($>$). The Johnsons have chosen among three possible situations and specified the alternative hypothesis accordingly:

1. If the population mean isn't 425, it would be either less than or greater than 425. The alternative hypothesis is two-tailed and uses the unequal sign ($H_1: \mu \neq 425$).
2. If the population mean isn't greater than or equal to 425, it's less than 425. The less-than sign is used in the alternative hypothesis ($H_1: \mu < 425$); this is a one-tailed test.
3. If the population mean isn't less than or equal to 425, it's greater than 425. The alternative hypothesis utilizes the greater-than sign ($H_1: \mu > 425$); this is also a one-tailed test.

Because their sole concern is deterioration in the chemical process, the Johnsons chose alternative 2. They'll examine the sample evidence to decide between the null hypothesis (population mean greater than or equal to 425) and the alternative hypothesis (population mean less than 425).

For any hypothesis test, one of the three alternative hypothesis types must be chosen. The choice depends on the state of the population that's believed to exist if the null hypothesis is false. ■

EXERCISES

1. Explain the similarities and differences between hypothesis testing and estimation.
2. Why do analysts test the null hypothesis?

3. What are the steps used in hypothesis testing?
4. Why is it necessary to assume that the null hypothesis is true?
5. Jim Young is considering running for mayor. He would like to have some idea of the possibility of winning. He wants you as a consultant to tell him how to get information to help him make a decision. In the context of hypothesis testing, what would you recommend to Jim?

6. Explain the difference between the null hypothesis and the alternative hypothesis.
7. Explain the difference between a one-tailed test and a two-tailed test.
8. What are the two possible conclusions in a test of a hypothesis?
9. State the appropriate null hypothesis and alternative hypothesis to test the following statements:
    a. A supplier of plastic strips has agreed to send a manufacturing firm shipments containing no more than 2% defectives.

   b. The average time for delivery of Leading Edge Computers is seven days.

   c. A manufacturer claims that the average life of a transistor battery is at least 600 hours.

   d. The average age of Tech University students is 21 years.

   e. The Headache Pharmaceutical Company claims that the average time for a pain reliever to take effect is five minutes.

   f. A random sample of accounts receivable were checked to determine whether the proportion that were delinquent has changed from 10%.

ERRORS IN HYPOTHESIS TESTING

As discussed in Chapter 8, an important aspect of estimation is determining the possibility of error. Error assessment is an integral part of estimating population characteristics using sample evidence. Likewise, in testing a hypothesis the analyst must assess the likelihood that the conclusion reached is wrong.

EXAMPLE 9.7   A company is testing the claim that the average weight of parts produced by a new machine is 2 pounds. The null hypothesis is H_0: $\mu = 2$, and the alternative hypothesis is H_1: $\mu \neq 2$. A random sample of parts is selected from the output of the new machine and their average weight determined. Now the company must decide whether to reject the null hypothesis that the population average weight is 2 pounds.

Two types of errors might occur in this situation:

1. If the company decides to reject the 2-pound claim, it could be making a mistake. Perhaps the machine actually produces parts with an average weight of exactly 2 pounds. An erroneous conclusion might be reached because the sample average was misleading.

2. If the company fails to reject the 2-pound claim, it could also be making a mistake. The machine might actually be producing parts that average 1 or 3 pounds, and if the sample average is close to 2 pounds, the company might erroneously fail to reject the null hypothesis.

In hypothesis testing, one of the two types of error just described is always a possibility. The sample, although selected randomly, could lead to an incorrect rejection of the null hypothesis or an incorrect acceptance of the null hypothesis. These two types

Type I and Type II Errors of hypothesis-testing errors are known as **type I** and **type II errors,** respectively.

In hypothesis testing, rejecting a true null hypothesis is known as a **type I error;** the probability of committing such an error is denoted alpha (α). Failing to reject a false null hypothesis is known as a **type II error;** the probability of committing this error is denoted beta (β).

Table 9.1 summarizes the risks inherent in testing any null hypothesis. Note that the table's rows represent the world's true state, or the actual condition (true versus false) of the null hypothesis being tested. Unfortunately, we can't determine which state of the world is true without some risk of error if sample evidence is used to make the decision. In terms of time and money we can rarely conduct a complete census of the population and thus arrive at an error-free conclusion regarding the null hypothesis. Instead, a sample is selected from the population and, based on this sample's characteristics, the null hypothesis is either rejected or not rejected. Since this decision is based on examination of a sample that forms only part of the population, an erroneous conclusion is always possible.

TABLE 9.1   Type I and Type II Errors

True state of the world	Conclusion based on sample evidence	
	Fail to reject null hypothesis	Reject null hypothesis
Null hypothesis true	Correct decision	Type I error
Null hypothesis false	Type II error	Correct decision

As Table 9.1 shows, there are four possible outcomes to a hypothesis test. This is because there are two possible states of the world (null hypothesis true, null hypothesis false) and two possible conclusions based on the sample evidence (fail to reject null hypothesis, reject null hypothesis). Two of the four possible outcomes represent correct conclusions: failing to reject a true null hypothesis and rejecting a false null hypothesis. Note that if a decision maker reaches the correct conclusion, this will probably not be known until some future time.

Table 9.1 also indicates the two possible ways to commit an error in reaching a conclusion about a population on the basis of sample information. A null hypothesis that turns out to be correct might be rejected on the basis of the sample evidence; this is a type I error. On the other hand, a null hypothesis that turns out to be false might not be rejected based on the sample evidence; this is a type II error. Again, note that, at the moment of decision, there's no way of knowing whether the decision is correct. This will become evident later and, if the conclusion is incorrect, there's usually a price or penalty to be paid.

> A **type I error** is only possible if the null hypothesis is rejected, while a **type II error** is only possible if the null hypothesis is not rejected.

The penalties associated with committing type I and type II errors concern decision makers. If there's no penalty for an incorrect decision, there's no need to spend time and money collecting sample information in an attempt to make the correct decision.

Businesspeople, however, strive to make correct decisions, usually based on sample, or incomplete, information about the true state of the world. It is particularly important in hypothesis testing to balance the penalties of type I and type II errors against each other before reaching a conclusion. This important subject is discussed later in this chapter.

EXERCISES

10. Explain the difference between a type I error and a type II error.

11. Which type of error is it more important to control: type I or type II?

12. When does an analyst risk making a type II error?

13. When does an analyst risk making a type I error?

14. If the null hypothesis is true, what type of error might be made?

15. If the null hypothesis is false, what type of error might be made?

16. Coffee Delight claims on their labels that each can contains 2 pounds of coffee. If an experiment is conducted and the null hypothesis rejected, what kind of error could be made? Explain the implications of such an error. If the null hypothesis is not rejected, what kind of error could be made? Explain the implications of such an error.

17. State the null and alternative hypotheses for testing the claim that the average salary of the employees listed in the Appendix C company data base is $34,000. If a study is conducted and the null hypothesis rejected, what kind of error could be made? Explain the implications of such an error. If the null hypothesis is not rejected, what kind of error could be made? Explain the implications of such an error.

18. The American Management Association surveyed 1,005 firms in December 1988, discovering that polygraph testing is declining in U.S. firms (*Personnel*, May 1989, p. 39). The article "Lie Detectors Can Make a Liar of You" (*Discover*, June 1986, p. 7) may explain this decline. The article indicates that if 1,000 people took a polygraph test and 500 told the truth and 500 lied, the polygraph would indicate that approximately 185 of the people who told the truth were liars and 120 of the liars told the truth.

    a. The null hypothesis is that a person is telling the truth and the alternative hypothesis is that a person is lying. In this context, describe type I and type II errors.

    b. Based on the survey results, what is the approximate probability that a polygraph test will result in a type I error?

DEVELOPING DECISION RULES

Step 2 in the hypothesis-testing procedure calls for determining the appropriate sampling distribution, assuming the null hypothesis is true. The central limit theorem (Chapter 7) indicates that the sampling distribution of means is a normal distribution for sample sizes that are sufficiently large (30 or greater).

Step 3 of the hypothesis-testing procedure involves computing a statistic from the sample. For testing a hypothesis about a population mean, this statistic will be the sample mean. However, to complete Step 4 (determining the probability of getting the sample statistic from the assumed sampling distribution), a significance level must be chosen.

We hope that the correct decision concerning the null hypothesis will be reached based on sample evidence, but there's always a possibility of rejecting a true H_0 or failing to reject a false H_0. The probabilities of these events are known as alpha (α) and beta (β), respectively. The probability of rejecting a null hypothesis that's true is called the **level of significance** of a hypothesis test. It is fairly common to designate a particular significance level—usually .01, .02, .05, or .10—without any thought as to why this value is chosen. In real decision-making situations, the analyst must choose the significance level by asking: What probability of rejecting a true null hypothesis am I willing to accept? We must understand that a low probability of committing a type I or alpha error generates a higher probability of committing a type II or beta error, and vice versa, for any given sample size.

> The **level of significance** of a hypothesis test is the probability of rejecting a null hypothesis that is true. It is designated by the symbol α (alpha).

How does an analyst choose an appropriate value for alpha? The answer depends on the relative penalties associated with type I and type II errors. If rejecting a true H_0 is more costly than failing to reject a false H_0, a small alpha should be chosen. If failing to reject a false H_0 is more costly than rejecting a true H_0, a larger alpha should be chosen.

A **decision rule** indicates the conditions under which the null hypothesis will be rejected. This rule specifies the action to be taken for each possible sample outcome.

> A hypothesis-testing **decision rule** specifies the action to be taken for each possible sample outcome.

Figure 9.1 illustrates the development of the decision rule in a hypothesis test for a population mean. If the null hypothesis is assumed true, the sampling distribution in Figure 9.1 is the appropriate distribution from which to draw the sample mean.

Note that two numerical values, *a* and *b*, appear on the ends of the curve. These are the decision rule critical values. They represent the points beyond which a sample mean drawn from this distribution may be viewed as unlikely. In general terms, using Figure 9.1, the decision rule for this example might be stated:

If the mean computed from the sample data is between *a* and *b*, fail to reject the null hypothesis, since such a result is compatible with the assumed sampling distribution. If the sample mean is less than *a* or greater than *b*, reject the null hypothesis, since such extreme values are unlikely to have been drawn from this sampling distribution.

Rather than state the decision rule and test statistic in units of measurement (such as hours, dollars, or seconds), the usual method is to specify these two important val-

FIGURE 9.1   Sampling Distribution of Means

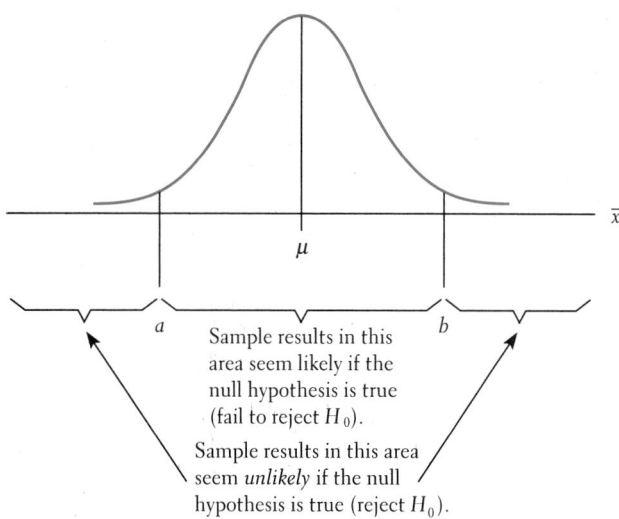

ues in terms of standardized z scores. In this approach (discussed in Chapter 6), the sample statistic is expressed in terms of the number of standard deviations between it and its mean; that value is then compared with a table value of z. In Equation 9.1, z is computed as the difference between the observed sample value and the hypothesized or assumed population value, divided by the standard error of the appropriate sampling distribution:

$$z = \frac{\text{Observed value} - \text{Assumed value}}{\text{Standard error of sampling distribution}} \qquad (9.1)$$

Equation 9.1 is used throughout this chapter to compute the sample test statistic. The standardized method is the common way of using sample data to determine the likelihood that the null hypothesis is true.

EXERCISES

19. In a hypothesis test, is it necessary to assume that the population is approximately normally distributed? Why or why not?

20. What is meant by a significance level of .05?

21. What is the difference between a significance level and an alpha level?

22. An analyst decides to change the significance level from .05 to .10. What happens to beta when this change is made?

23. Alpha has been set at .01 in a hypothesis test. It is determined that the cost of a type I error is relatively low compared with the cost of a type II error. Is the significance level appropriate for this test?

24. Comment on the statement: The risks in a hypothesis test can be minimized by using a very low significance level.

HYPOTHESIS TESTS ABOUT A POPULATION MEAN: LARGE SAMPLES

This chapter has provided the background material necessary to test a hypothesis about a population mean. Recall the hypothesis-testing steps established early in the chapter. First, the null and alternative hypotheses are stated. Second, the null hypothesis is assumed true and the appropriate sampling distribution under this assumption identified. Third, a random sample is taken and the appropriate test statistic computed. Finally, the likelihood that the test statistic came from the assumed sampling distribution is computed, and this leads to acceptance or rejection of the null hypothesis.

EXAMPLE 9.8   The American work force's average age is decreasing according to an article in *Personnel Management* (August 1989). Honeycutt, Inc., wants to determine if its shareholders' average age is also dropping. In 1985 a study showed that its shareholders' mean age was 55.

Since the question involves a downward change only, a one-tailed test is in order. The null and alternative hypotheses are

$$H_0: \mu \geq 55$$
$$H_1: \mu < 55$$

If the null hypothesis is assumed true, the sampling distribution from which the sample mean will be drawn is normal with a mean of 55 years. A random sample of 250 stockholders is drawn from the company's stockholder list and contacted about their ages. The standard deviation of ages in the population of stockholders is assumed to be 12 years, the value established in the 1985 study. Based on these values, the assumed sampling distribution is developed as shown in Figure 9.2.

FIGURE 9.2   Sampling Distribution of Means for Example 9.8

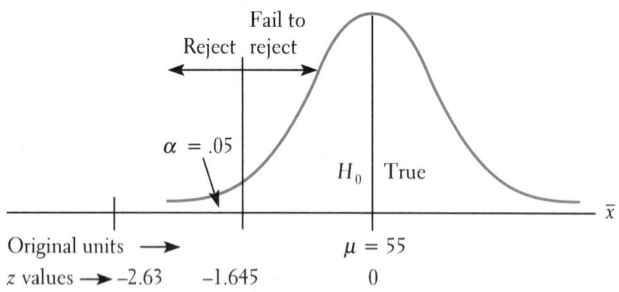

The sampling distribution in Figure 9.2 is based on the assumption that H_0 is true. The sampling distribution has a mean of 55 and standard error of 0.76, based on the known standard deviation of the population and the chosen sample size. A significance level of .05 is chosen, as shown in the figure. With 5% of the curve on the lower end, 45% must lie between the curve mean and the critical value. From the standard normal table, this area corresponds to a z value of 1.645, which is negative since the area lies below the mean.

The decision rule for this hypothesis test is

If the sample mean lies more than 1.645 standard errors below the mean of 55 years, reject the null hypothesis; otherwise fail to reject it (if $z < -1.645$ reject H_0).

We must now compute the sample mean and find how many standard errors below the curve mean it lies. Suppose the sample reveals a mean of 53 years. The sample z value is computed using Equation 9.1. This equation states the necessary calculations in general terms, whereas Equation 9.2 is used specifically to test a hypothesis about a population mean:

$$z = \frac{\bar{x} - \mu}{\sigma_{\bar{x}}} \tag{9.2}$$

where $\bar{x}$ = Sample mean
      μ = Hypothesized population mean
      $\sigma_{\bar{x}}$ = Standard error of mean

The standard deviation of the sampling distribution (the standard error of the mean) is

$$\sigma_{\bar{x}} = \frac{\sigma}{\sqrt{n}} = \frac{12}{\sqrt{250}} = 0.76$$

$$z = \frac{\bar{x} - \mu}{\sigma_{\bar{x}}} = \frac{53 - 55}{0.76} = -2.63$$

The computed z value (-2.63) is below the critical z value from the standard normal table (-1.645). The decision rule calls for rejection of the null hypothesis. The reasoning is that such a low sample mean is quite unlikely to have come from a sampling distribution with a mean of 55. There is a small chance of error in rejecting the null hypothesis.

EXAMPLE 9.9   Has the average time between telephone orders changed from 3.8 minutes, the mean of two years ago? This is the question facing a telephone mailorder company that has just started selling items based on special promotional materials. Company management is familiar with an article discussing the reasons for reduced business after such an action ("An Alternative Explanation for Lower Repeat Rates after Promotion Purchases," *Journal of Marketing Research*, May 1989, p. 205) and wants to follow repeat business carefully.

A random sample of 100 telephone orders reveals a sample mean of 4 minutes with a standard deviation of 0.5 minutes. A significance level of .02 is chosen for this hypothesis test. Since the question involves a change in either direction from the previous average, the alternative hypothesis will be stated as a two-tailed test. The null and alternative hypotheses are

H_0: $\mu = 3.8$
H_1: $\mu \neq 3.8$

The population standard deviation is unknown but will be estimated using the sample standard deviation, $s = 0.5$. Figure 9.3 shows the appropriate sampling distribution, assuming the null hypothesis is true.

FIGURE 9.3   Sampling Distribution of Means for Example 9.9

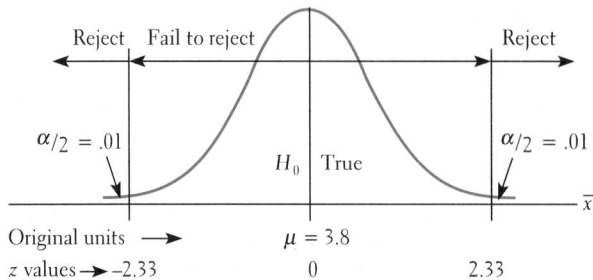

Reject Fail to reject   Reject

$\alpha/2 = .01$ $\alpha/2 = .01$

H_0 | True

Original units ⟶
z values ⟶ −2.33 $\mu = 3.8$
                                           0   2.33

Note in Figure 9.3 that alpha (.02) has been split between the two ends of the curve. Since the alternative hypothesis is nondirectional, a sample mean that's either too large or too small will result in rejection of the null hypothesis. The two critical z values are 2.33 and −2.33, as shown.

The decision rule for this hypothesis test is

If the sample mean lies more than 2.33 standard errors below or above the mean of 3.8 minutes, reject the null hypothesis; otherwise, fail to reject it (if $z < -2.33$ or $z > 2.33$ reject H_0).

The test z value is calculated from the sample and used to make the decision:

$$s_{\bar{x}} = \frac{s}{\sqrt{n}} = \frac{0.5}{\sqrt{100}} = 0.05$$

$$z = \frac{\bar{x} - \mu}{s_{\bar{x}}} = \frac{4 - 3.8}{0.05} = 4.00$$

Since the test value for z (4.00) is greater than the upper limit ($z = 2.33$), the null hypothesis is rejected. There is, as always, a possibility that a type I error has been committed (the rejected null hypothesis might actually be true).

EXAMPLE 9.10   Human Affairs, a company that markets a motivational training program, claims that the performance ratings of factory workers will rise after completion of the course. To test this claim, the Eastland Corporation, which is considering buying the program, randomly samples 75 employees from the Prentice Hill Corporation, which recently used the program. The average worker rating for Prentice Hill was 75 before the training program; no follow-up study was conducted after completion of the program. The sample evidence is

$$\bar{x} = 77 \qquad s = 13 \qquad n = 75$$

The null and alternative hypotheses for this test are

$$H_0: \mu \le 75$$
$$H_1: \mu > 75$$

If the null hypothesis is assumed true, the sample mean will be drawn from the sampling distribution of Figure 9.4.

FIGURE 9.4   Sampling Distribution of Means for Example 9.10

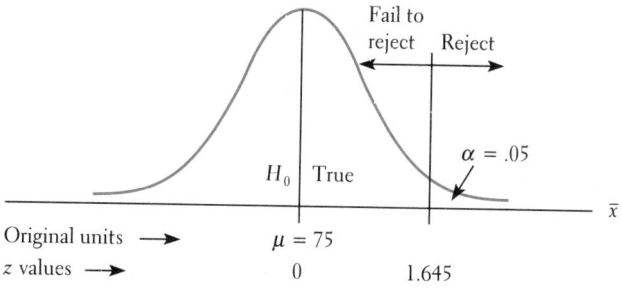

A significance level of .05 is chosen for the test, resulting in the decision rule:

If the sample mean is more than 1.645 standard errors above the assumed population mean of 75, reject the null hypothesis. Otherwise, fail to reject it (if $z > 1.645$ reject H_0).

The z value from the sample data is then calculated:

$$s_{\bar{x}} = \frac{s}{\sqrt{n}} = \frac{13}{\sqrt{75}} = 1.5$$

$$z = \frac{\bar{x} - \mu}{s_{\bar{x}}} = \frac{77 - 75}{1.5} = 1.33$$

Since the calculated z value (1.33) is less than the critical z value (1.645), the null hypothesis is not rejected. There's not enough sample evidence to reject the hypothesis that the population mean is still 75 following completion of the training program. Of course, there's some chance of a type II error, since the null hypothesis might actually be false.

p-VALUES AND HYPOTHESIS TESTING

According to the statistical test procedure illustrated in Examples 9.8 through 9.10, the conclusion is stated in terms of rejecting or not rejecting the null hypothesis based on a reject region (alpha) selected prior to conducting the test. A second method of presenting the results of a statistical test reports the extent to which the test statistic disagrees with the null hypothesis. This method has become popular because analysts want to know what percentage of the sampling distribution lies beyond the sample statistic on the curve, and most statistical computer programs report this result in terms of a p-value (probability value). The p-value is the probability of observing a sample value as extreme as, or more extreme than, the value observed, given that H_0 is true. This area represents the probability of a type I error if the null hypothesis is rejected. The p-value is compared to the alpha value, and, on this basis, the null hypothesis is either rejected or not rejected. If p is less than alpha, the null hypothesis is rejected (if $p < \alpha$, reject H_0). If p is greater than or equal to alpha, the null hypothesis is not rejected (if $p \geq \alpha$, don't reject H_0).

p-Value

> The **p-value** is the probability of observing a sample value as extreme as, or more extreme than, the value actually observed, given that H_0 is true.

Statistical data analysis programs commonly compute the p-value during the execution of a hypothesis test. The following examples illustrate the way to interpret p-values.

EXAMPLE 9.11   Gene Rice, an assistant coach in the NFL, is preparing for the college draft and wants to test the hypothesis that NFL linemen's mean weight is at least 270 pounds, as reported in a 1992 *Sporting News* article. Gene feels that the mean weight is more than 270 pounds and decides to use the .05 significance level to test the null and alternative hypotheses:

$$H_0: \mu \leq 270$$
$$H_1: \mu > 270$$

Figure 9.5 shows the sampling distribution based on the assumption that the population mean is really 270. The decision rule for this hypothesis test is

If the sample mean is more than 1.645 standard errors above the assumed population mean of 270 pounds, reject the null hypothesis. Otherwise, fail to reject it (if $z > 1.645$ reject H_0).

A random sample of 50 players yields

$$\bar{x} = 281 \qquad s = 35$$

FIGURE 9.5   *p*-Value Computation for Example 9.11

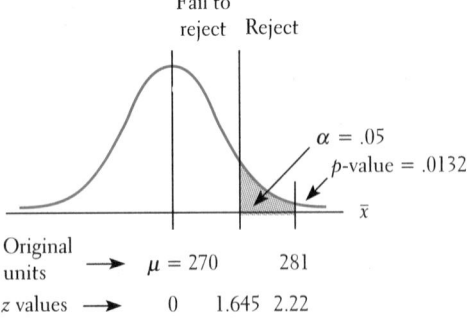

Fail to
reject   Reject

$\alpha = .05$
p-value = .0132

$\bar{x}$

Original
units $\longrightarrow$ $\mu = 270$ 281

z values $\longrightarrow$ 0   1.645   2.22

The estimated standard deviation of this sampling distribution is

$$s_{\bar{x}} = \frac{s}{\sqrt{n}} = \frac{35}{\sqrt{50}} = 4.95$$

The z value is

$$z = \frac{281 - 270}{4.95} = 2.22$$

The p-value is determined using the standard normal table. The area between the mean and a z value of 2.22 is .4868. The p-value is the area above the z value (.5000 − .4868 = .0132). The probability of observing a z value at least as large as 2.22 is only .0132 if the null hypothesis is true.

This small p-value represents the risk of rejecting a true null hypothesis. The decision rule is

If p-value $< \alpha$, reject H_0.

If p-value $\geq \alpha$, fail to reject H_0.

Since the p-value is less than the significance level (.0132 < .05), the null hypothesis is rejected. Gene has concluded that the mean weight for linemen is more than 270 pounds. The probability that this conclusion is wrong is .0132. Note that if Gene had chosen a .01 significance level, his conclusion would have been to fail to reject. The significance level choice clearly plays a critical part in the hypothesis-testing procedure.

The MINITAB commands to perform the hypothesis test for Example 9.11 are:

```
MTB> ZTEST OF MU=270, ASSUMING SIGMA=35, ON C1;
SUBC> ALTERNATIVE +1.
```

The output for this test is:

```
TEST OF MU = 270 VS MU G.T. 270
THE ASSUMED SIGMA = 35

      N  MEAN  STDEV  SE MEAN    Z   P VALUE
C1   50   281     35     4.95  2.22    .0132

MTB> STOP
```

The ZTEST command is used to test the null hypothesis that $\mu = 270$. The standard deviation of 35 is assumed based on the sample data stored in C1. The ALTERNATIVE +1 subcommand tests the null against the alternative hypothesis that $\mu >$ 270. Note that the ALTERNATIVE +1 subcommand tells the program to do a one-tailed test above the mean. ALTERNATIVE −1 means to test one-tailed below the mean. If there is no ALTERNATIVE subcommand, a two-tailed test is performed.

The p-values for Examples 9.8 through 9.10 are now computed. When Example 9.8 is run on a computer program, a p-value of .0043 results. Since this p-value is less than the significance level (.0043 < .05), the null hypothesis is rejected.

A z value of -2.63, from the standard normal table, represents an area of .4957 below the mean. Since the area on the lower end of the curve below the z value is wanted, .4957 is subtracted from .5000. Thus, the p-value is

$$p\text{-value} = .5000 - .4957 = .0043 \text{ (area below a } z \text{ value of } -2.63)$$

When Example 9.9 is run on a computer program, the result is a p-value of .00006. Since the p-value is less than the significance level (.00006 < .02), the null hypothesis is rejected. Note that for a two-tailed test the p-value is determined by doubling the area above the z value.

A z value of 4.00, from the standard normal table, includes an area of .49997 above the mean. Since the area on the upper end of the curve above the z value is wanted, .49997 is subtracted from .5000. The p-value is

$$p\text{-value} = 2(.5000 - .49997) = 2(.00003) = .00006$$

When Example 9.10 is run on a computer program, the result is a p-value of .0918. Since the p-value is greater than the significance level (.0918 > .05), the null hypothesis is not rejected.

A z value of 1.33, from the standard normal table, includes an area of .4082 above the mean. Since the area above the z value of 1.33 is wanted, .4082 is subtracted from .5000:

$$p\text{-value} = .5000 - .4082 = .0918 \text{ (area above a } z \text{ value of } 1.33)$$

Steps for computing p-values:

1. Determine the value of the test statistic (z or t) computed using the sample data.
2a. If the test is one-tailed, the p-value is equal to the area beyond the z or t.
2b. If the test is two-tailed, the p-value equals twice the area beyond the observed z or t.

■ SITUATION 9.1—RESOLVED The hypothesis test formulated by the Johnsons can now be executed. The sample data are

$$\bar{x} = 415 \qquad s = 30 \qquad n = 55$$

The null and alternative hypotheses are

$$H_0: \mu \geq 425$$
$$H_1: \mu < 425$$

Since the sample size is greater than 30, the sampling distribution of means can be assumed normal without knowledge of the shape of the population distribution. The sampling distribution has a mean of 425, assuming the null hypothesis is true.

Figure 9.6 shows the sampling distribution and the decision rule z value based on a significance level of .05. The decision rule is

> If the sample mean is more than 1.645 standard errors below the assumed population mean of 425 hours, reject the null hypothesis; otherwise, fail to reject it (if $z < -1.645$ reject H_0).

FIGURE 9.6   Sampling Distribution of Means for Situation 9.1

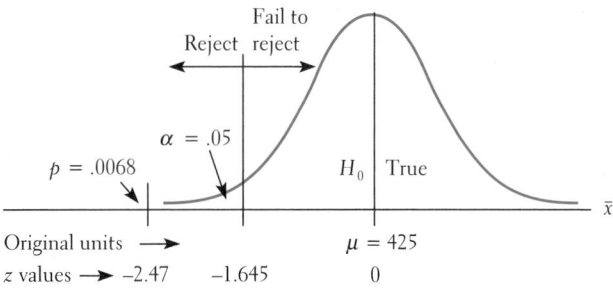

The sample z value is now calculated and compared with the table z value of -1.645. The calculation is

$$s_{\bar{x}} = \frac{s}{\sqrt{n}} = \frac{30}{\sqrt{55}} = 4.05$$

$$z = \frac{\bar{x} - \mu}{s_{\bar{x}}} = \frac{415 - 425}{4.05} = -2.47$$

Since the calculated z value (-2.47) is less than the critical value of z (-1.645), the null hypothesis is rejected. The possibility of a type I error must be considered; however, the chance of this error is quite low. In fact, there is only a 5% chance that the Johnsons could reject a true null hypothesis since 5% was the significance level, or alpha, chosen at the start of the test.

When Situation 9.1 is run on a computer program, the result is a p-value of .0068. Since the p-value is less than the significance level (.0068 < .05), the null hypothesis is rejected.

A z value of -2.47, from the standard normal table, includes an area of .4932 below the mean, as shown in Figure 9.6. Since the area on the lower end of the curve beyond the z value is wanted, .4932 is subtracted from .5000:

$$p\text{-value} = .5000 - .4932 = .0068 \text{ (area below a } z \text{ value of } -2.47)$$

The probability of observing a sample mean as extreme as 415, given that the population mean is actually 425, is .0068. ∎

EXERCISES

25. Under what conditions is it necessary to assume that the population being sampled is approximately normal?

26. Bill Ford, manager of the Bon Resort Hotel, believes that the average guest bill is at least $400. The population is normally distributed with a standard deviation of $60. State the decision rule for a significance level of .15 if a sample of 49 guest bills are surveyed. If the sample mean is $375, what should Bill's conclusion be? Explain what type of error might have been made. Compute the *p*-value.

27. A manufacturing assembly line operation has a scheduled mean completion time of 30 minutes. The population has a standard deviation of 4 minutes. State the decision rule for a sample of 64 observations tested at the .01 significance level. For a one-tail test state the appropriate conclusion if the sample mean is 35 minutes. Explain what type of error might have been made. Compute the *p*-value.

28. The Howell Manufacturing Company produces bearings. Past experience shows that the production process is normally distributed and produces bearings with an average diameter of 2.1 inches and standard deviation of 0.12 inch. Nineteen bearings are randomly selected from the production process and have a mean diameter of 1.9 inches. What would you conclude if you tested at the .05 significance level? Compute the *p*-value.

29. A university statistics professor has been asked to develop a way of determining profitable bank customers. The bank hired the professor after management read "Teaching Old Bankers New Tricks," in *Bankers Monthly* (February 1990, p. 58). This article discusses ways of improving bankers' performance and generating higher profits. Management wants a good description of a profitable customer, and the professor begins studying profitability.

    Five years ago a study was conducted that showed an average service charge for checking accounts of $3.20 with standard deviation of $0.40. The professor is interested in detecting a situation for which the average service charge is either greater than or less than $3.20. What should she conclude at the .01 significance level if a sample of 100 accounts has a mean service charge of $3.50?

HYPOTHESIS TESTS ABOUT A POPULATION MEAN: SMALL SAMPLES

Small-Sample Mean Test

When the sample size is small (less than 30), the distribution of the population from which the sample was selected must be assumed to be approximately normal. If this assumption can be made and the population standard deviation is known, the sampling distribution of sample means can be assumed to be normally distributed. If the population standard deviation is unknown, the sampling distribution of sample means is described by the *t* distribution. The test statistic is computed using Equation 9.3:

$$t = \frac{\bar{x} - \mu}{s_{\bar{x}}} \tag{9.3}$$

where $\bar{x}$ = Sample mean
        μ = Hypothesized population mean
        $s_{\bar{x}}$ = Estimated standard error of the mean $\left(\dfrac{s}{\sqrt{n}}\right)$

When the sample size is small and the population is nonnormal, nonparametric tests such as those discussed in Chapter 19 are used. Figure 8.3 summarized the procedure for determining the appropriate sampling distribution of sample means for hypothesis tests about a population mean.

EXAMPLE 9.12   The Tapico Corporation is concerned about the breaking strength of the steel cables made in its plant. A major buyer is interested in purchasing a large number of cables and has stated that the average breaking point must not be less than one ton. Tapico thinks that one ton is the approximate breaking point of the cables, but decides to test the hypothesis that the average (mean) breaking strength is one ton against the alternative that it is less.

This situation suggests a very small sample size. The cables to be tested will each be broken and the weight at breakage recorded. The average of these breaking points will then be used to test the null hypothesis. A small sample size is appropriate because each sampled item is destroyed in the process. A large sample would be too costly.

The null and alternative hypotheses are

$$H_0: \mu \geq 1$$
$$H_1: \mu < 1$$

Tapico decides it can afford to break 10 cables and designs a process to do so. A significance level of .05 is chosen for the test. The sample results are

$$\bar{x} = 0.96 \text{ tons} \qquad s = 0.15 \text{ tons} \qquad n = 10$$

This hypothesis test involves a different sampling distribution. When there's a small sample size (usually considered less than 30) and the population standard deviation is unknown (and estimated by the sample standard deviation, s), the t distribution is the correct sampling distribution if the population is assumed to be normal. After reviewing its cables' breaking points, the company decides that these weights are probably distributed in a bell-shaped manner about their mean, and that a normal distribution is an appropriate assumption. Figure 9.7 summarizes the test.

FIGURE 9.7 t Distribution Hypothesis Test for Example 9.12

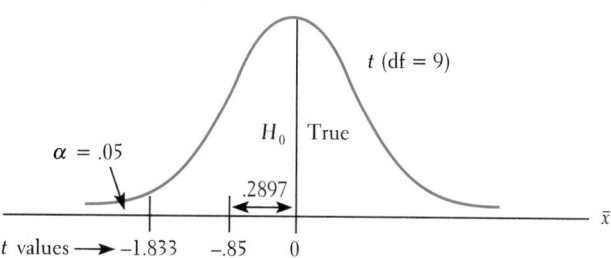

The critical value for the test is found in the t table in Appendix E.7. As demonstrated in Chapter 8, to use this table, you must know the area on one end of the curve. Since this is a one-tailed test and alpha is .05, this area is .05. Thus, the .05 column at the bottom of the t table is used to find the critical value.

You must also know the degrees of freedom $(n - 1)$ for the test. For a sample size of 10, the number of degrees of freedom is 9 $(10 - 1)$. The critical value observed from the *t* table is 1.833. Since this value is below the curve mean, it's negative (−1.833), as Figure 9.7 shows.

The decision rule is

> If the sample mean is more than 1.833 standard errors below the assumed population mean of one ton, reject the null hypothesis; otherwise, fail to reject it (if $t < -1.833$ reject H_0).

For this test, using Equation 9.3

$$s_{\bar{x}} = \frac{s}{\sqrt{n}} = \frac{0.15}{\sqrt{10}} = 0.047$$

$$t = \frac{\bar{x} - \mu}{s_{\bar{x}}} = \frac{0.96 - 1}{0.047} = -0.85$$

Since the test *t* value (−0.85) isn't below the critical value (−1.833), the null hypothesis is not rejected. According to this hypothesis test, the company is justified in advertising an average breaking weight of one ton. However, a type II error is possible. If the average breaking weight is less than one ton, a type II error could be very costly. Perhaps the expense of a larger sample should be incurred to ensure that customer problems don't arise later.

When Example 9.12 is run on a computer program, the result is a *p*-value of approximately .2087. Since the *p*-value is greater than the significance level (.2087 > .05), the null hypothesis is not rejected.

The MINITAB commands to find the *p*-value for Example 9.12 are

```
MTB> CDE -.85;
SUBC> +.9.
-.85    .2087
```

EXAMPLE 9.13   In Example 8.9, Jean Simmons, a Dallas health store owner, decided to test the average fat content per pound of hamburger sold in Dallas stores. To do so, she purchased one pound of hamburger from each of nine randomly selected stores. She cooked the hamburger, poured off the fat, and weighed it. The results for each of the stores, in ounces of fat, were

3.3   4.8   5.1   4.5   4.0   3.9   4.7   5.0   3.6

Jean wants to test the null hypothesis that the average fat level is 4.0 ounces using the .05 significance level and a two-tailed test. She assumes that the population is normally distributed.

Since the sample size is only 9 and the population standard deviation isn't known, the *t* test based on 8 degrees of freedom is appropriate. The decision rule is

> If the sample mean is more than 2.306 standard errors below or above the assumed population mean of 4.0 ounces, reject the null hypothesis; otherwise, fail to reject it (if $t < -2.306$ or $t > 2.306$ reject H_0).

For this test, using Equation 9.3

$$s_{\bar{x}} = \frac{s}{\sqrt{n}} = \frac{0.644}{\sqrt{9}} = 0.215$$

$$t = \frac{\bar{x} - \mu}{s_{\bar{x}}} = \frac{(4.322 - 4.0)}{0.215} = 1.5$$

Since the test t value (1.5) is not greater than the critical value (2.306), the null hypothesis is not rejected. According to this hypothesis test, Jean can't reject the premise that the average fat content of the hamburger is 4.0 ounces. The p-value, .17, shown in the MINITAB output, gives the probability of observing a sample mean as extreme as 4.322, if the population mean is actually 4.0.

The MINITAB software package can be used for hypothesis testing. The MINITAB commands to solve Example 9.13 are:

```
MTB> SET INTO C1
DATA> 3.3 4.8 5.1 4.5 4.0 3.9 4.7 5.0 3.6
DATA> END
MTB> DESCRIBE C1

C1    N     MEAN     MEDIAN    STDEV
      9     4.322    4.500     0.644

C1    MIN     MAX     Q1       Q3
      3.30    5.100   3.750    4.9400

MTB> TTEST OF MU = 4.0 ON C1

TEST OF MU = 4.0 VS MU N.E. 4.0

  N     MEAN    STDEV    SE MEAN      T    P VALUE
  9     4.322   0.644    0.215      1.5    .17

MTB> STOP
```

The TTEST command is used to test the null hypothesis that $\mu = 4$. Since there's no ALTERNATIVE subcommand, the alternative hypothesis is two-tailed, H_1: $\mu \neq 4$. This t test will use the standard deviation of the sample data stored in C1.

EXERCISES

30. When should the t distribution be used?

31. Steel Wheel Tires claims that its tires have a mean tread life of at least 45,000 miles. Suppose a test yielded results of $n = 22$, $\bar{x} = 43,000$, $s = 3,000$.

    a. State the null and alternative hypotheses.

    b. State the decision rule if the hypothesis is tested at the 1% significance level.

    c. State the appropriate conclusion.

    d. What type of error might be made?

    e. Estimate the p-value.

32. The employees' union claims that average seniority is at least 12 years for the TCA Corporation. In a random sample of 49 employees, average seniority is found to be 11.5 years with standard deviation of 1 year. Test the union's claim at the .02 significance level.

33. The Canon Toy Company buys batteries for its electric toys. The supplier guarantees that the batteries will last an average of 19 hours. After receiving customer complaints, Canon randomly selects 10 batteries from its stock and measures their duration. The results are

1	18.0
2	18.4
3	19.0
4	20.2
5	19.6
6	18.6
7	19.4
8	19.2
·9	17.0
10	18.5

Assuming that these batteries' lifetimes are normally distributed, test the supplier's guarantee at the .10 significance level.

HYPOTHESIS TESTS ABOUT A POPULATION PROPORTION

So far, this chapter has presented situations where the average (mean) value of a population is tested (e.g., the average time between machine breakdowns, the average age of stockholders, and the average breaking strength of steel cables).

Analysts are also interested in the percentage of items in a population that meet certain specifications. Politicians are concerned with the percentage of voters who favor a particular issue, government agencies want to know about the percentage of people unemployed, and business managers are interested in the percentage of parts produced or purchased that are defective.

As with the population mean, if the population percentage is unknown and information about its value is desired, a random sample is drawn from the population, the sample percentage computed, and this value used as an estimate of the unknown population value. (Chapter 8 discussed this estimation process.) On the other hand, if a claim about the population percentage has been made sample evidence can be used to reject or fail to reject this claim. This hypothesis-testing procedure for proportions is discussed next.

The testing methodology depends on whether a small sample or a large sample is used. For small samples ($n \leq 20$) the binomial distribution is used. For large samples ($n > 20$) the normal distribution is acceptable if $np > 5$ and $n(1 - p) > 5$. Since most proportion analyses involve large samples, only the large-sample test is discussed here.

Test for a Population Proportion

Large-sample tests of means and proportions are very similar, since the sampling distribution for each is the normal distribution. As Equation 9.4 shows, the difference between the sample proportion and the hypothesized or claimed population proportion is divided by the standard error of the sampling distribution of proportions to produce the test statistic:

$$z = \frac{x/n - p}{\sigma_{\bar{p}}} \tag{9.4}$$

where x = Number of sample successes
n = Sample size
p = Hypothesized population proportion
$\sigma_{\bar{p}}$ = Standard error of the proportion

Remember from Equation 7.3 that x/n is equal to the sample proportion, $\bar{p}$.

■ SITUATION 9.2   Sue and Bill Johnson turn their attention to the quality of another product their company makes: an acidic compound used in making an over-the-counter pain relief product. According to their own quality-control standards, no more than 3% of the 200-pound batches produced in the factory can fail a very thorough and time-consuming series of chemical analysis tests. A failure means that the product is not acceptable to Johnson's customers.

The null hypothesis to be tested is that the percentage of failed batches over a long period of time is 3% or less, against the alternative that it is more than 3%. Thus, the one-tailed test involves the following two hypotheses:

H_0: $p \leq .03$
H_1: $p > .03$

As discussed in Chapter 8, the appropriate sampling distribution for large-sample proportions is the normal distribution. The mean of this distribution is the population proportion, and the standard error of the distribution is $\sigma_{\bar{p}} = \sqrt{p(1 - p)/n}$. ■

EXAMPLE 9.14   Kawneer Architectural Products is checking the production of steel cable conduits in its main plant. Since these components are usually enclosed in walls and other structures, the quality level must be quite high. A quality improvement program has been underway on the conduit line for the past six months, and the foreman claims that the previous defective rate of 2% has been reduced. Kawneer's management decides to test this claim.

Since the foreman claims a difference on the down side, a one-tailed test is appropriate. Thus, the hypotheses are

H_0: $p \geq .02$
H_1: $p < .02$

A random sample of conduits is selected over the next two weeks. A total of 358 are chosen, and, of these, 4 are found to be defective. The sample evidence is

$n = 358$ $\bar{p} = 4/358 = .0112$

Kawneer Architectural Products decides to take a 10% chance of rejecting the null hypothesis if it's true. Since the test is one-tailed, an area of .4000 (.5000 − .1000) is looked up in the standard normal table. This results in a critical z value of -1.28 (negative because it's below the curve mean). Figure 9.8 summarizes the hypothesis test.

FIGURE 9.8   Sampling Distribution of $\bar{p}$ for Example 9.14

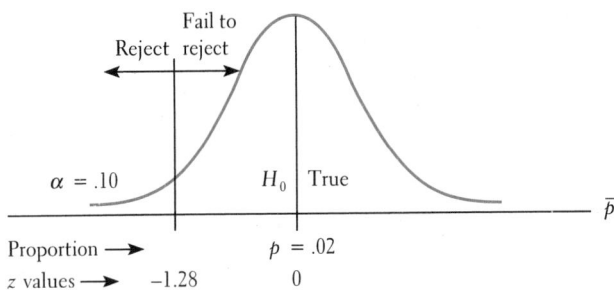

The decision rule for this hypothesis test is

If the sample proportion lies more than 1.28 standard errors below the proportion of .02 defectives, reject the null hypothesis; otherwise, fail to reject it (if $z < -1.28$ reject H_0).

The test value of z is computed:

$$\sigma_{\bar{p}} = \sqrt{\frac{p(1-p)}{n}} = \sqrt{\frac{.02(1-.02)}{358}} = .0074$$

$$z = \frac{\bar{p} - p}{\sigma_{\bar{p}}} = \frac{.0112 - .02}{.0074} = \frac{-.0088}{.0074} = -1.19$$

Since the test value of z (-1.19) isn't below the critical value of z (-1.28), the null hypothesis is not rejected. At the .10 significance level, the conduit foreman is *not* justified in claiming improved quality. Based on the sample evidence, Kawneer can't conclude that their conduit production line's quality improvement program has been successful.

When Example 9.14 is run on a computer program, the result is a p-value of .1170. Since the p-value is greater than the significance level (.1170 > .10), the null hypothesis is not rejected.

A z value of -1.19, from the standard normal table, includes an area of .3830 below the mean. Since the area on the lower end of the curve beyond the z value is wanted, .3830 is subtracted from .5000. The p-value is

$$p\text{-value} = .5000 - .3830 = .1170 \text{ (area below a } z \text{ value of } -1.19)$$

EXAMPLE 9.15   An article in the *Free China Review* (May 1992, page 26) discusses the severe competition from newly opened banks, forcing existing financial institutions to improve their products and services. Stockton International, such an institution, is trying to improve its accounts receivable levels in Taiwan.

For several years, the percentage of accounts receivable that are past due each month has been around 6%. The accounting department thinks it has evidence that economic conditions have caused this percentage to increase. A hypothesis test seems in order.

During the past month, Stockton issued invoices to 478 suppliers. Of these, 42 are past due. The sample evidence is

$$n = 478 \qquad \bar{p} = 42/478 = .0879$$

The accounting department points to the past-due rate of nearly 9% as an indication that measures need to be taken to ensure prompt payment on the part of all suppliers. Stockton management isn't sure the sample size justifies this action. The null and alternative hypotheses are formulated:

$$H_0: p \leq .06$$
$$H_1: p > .06$$

Stockton chooses a significance level of 5%, resulting in the hypothesis test diagram in Figure 9.9.

FIGURE 9.9   Sampling Distribution of $\bar{p}$ for Example 9.15

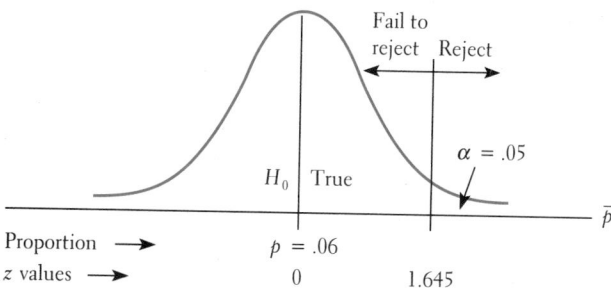

The decision rule for this hypothesis test is

If the sample proportion lies more than 1.645 standard errors above the proportion .06, reject the null hypothesis; otherwise, fail to reject it (if $z > 1.645$ reject H_0).

The test z value is computed:

$$\sigma_{\bar{p}} = \sqrt{\frac{p(1-p)}{n}} = \sqrt{\frac{.06(1-.06)}{478}} = .011$$
$$z = \frac{\bar{p} - p}{\sigma_{\bar{p}}} = \frac{.0879 - .06}{.011} = \frac{.0279}{.011} = 2.54$$

The large test z value results in rejection of the null hypothesis (since $2.54 > 1.645$). It appears that the accounting department is right: there seems to have been an increase in the percentage of past-due accounts receivable, and corrective action is required.

When Example 9.15 is run on a computer program, the result is a *p*-value of .0055. Since the *p*-value is less than the significance level (.0055 < .05), the null hypothesis is rejected. The probability of observing a sample proportion as extreme as .0879, given that the population proportion is actually .06, is .0055.

The *p*-value was computed by looking up a *z* value of 2.54, from the standard normal table, which includes an area of .4945 above the mean. Since the area on the upper end of the curve beyond the *z* value is wanted, .4945 is subtracted from .5000:

$$p\text{-value} = .5000 - .4945 = .0055 \text{ (area above a } z \text{ value of 2.54)}$$

■ SITUATION 9.2—RESOLVED   The Johnsons wish to test the hypothesis that substandard batches still amount to 3% of total production against the alternative that this percentage has increased. A significance level of .02 is chosen for this one-tailed test, resulting in the sampling distribution in Figure 9.10.

FIGURE 9.10   Sampling Distribution of $\bar{p}$ for Situation 9.2

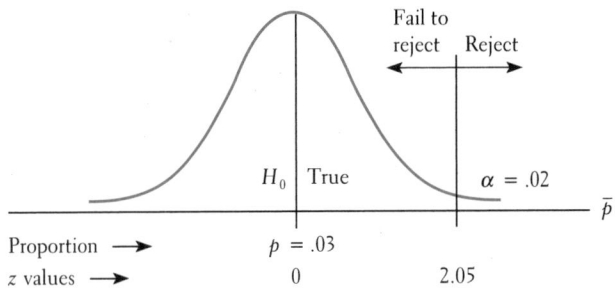

The decision rule for this hypothesis test is

If the sample proportion lies more than 2.05 standard errors above the proportion of .03 defectives, reject the null hypothesis; otherwise, fail to reject it (if *z* > 2.05 reject H_0).

A random sample of batches is drawn from various shifts over the next month. Each batch is closely inspected to determine whether it is substandard. At the end of the month, it's found that of the 180 batches inspected, 8 are substandard. The sample evidence can be stated as

$$n = 180 \qquad \bar{p} = 8/180 = .0444$$

The sample proportion (.0444) is above the acceptable population proportion specified in the null hypothesis (.03). Does the sample size of 180 provide enough sample evidence to reject the null hypothesis?

The test value for *z* is computed based on the sample proportion of .0444 and the sample size of 180:

$$\sigma_{\bar{p}} = \sqrt{\frac{p(1-p)}{n}} = \sqrt{\frac{.03(1-.03)}{180}} = .0127$$

$$z = \frac{\bar{p} - p}{\sigma_{\bar{p}}} = \frac{.0444 - .03}{.0127} = 1.13$$

The computed z value (1.13) is less than the critical z value from the standard normal table (2.05). The null hypothesis that the substandard rate for the batches is still 3% is not rejected. Since the null hypothesis has not been rejected, there's some chance that a type II error has occurred.

Running Situation 9.2 on a computer program results in a p-value of .1292. Since the p-value is greater than the significance level (.1292 > .02), the null hypothesis is not rejected.

A z value of 1.13, from the standard normal table, represents an area of .3708 above the mean. Since the area on the upper end of the curve beyond the z value is wanted, .3708 is subtracted from .5000:

$$p\text{-value} = .5000 - .3708 = .1292 \text{ (area above a } z \text{ value of 1.13) } \blacksquare$$

EXERCISES

34. What are the similarities and differences between the test procedure for means and the test procedure for proportions?

35. What sampling distribution is appropriate for tests of proportions when the sample size is small? When the sample size is large?

36. Steve Peel is considering purchasing a business. The business has stated that no more than 25% of its accounts receivable are more than 30 days past due. In a sample of 50 accounts, the sample proportion is tested at the .05 significance level. State the null and alternative hypotheses and the appropriate decision rule. State the conclusion if the sample proportion, $\bar{p}$, is .29. Explain what type of error might have been made.

37. Jack Knive knows from past experience that 12% of the recipients of auto loans from the Community Credit Union default within the first year. Jack feels that the default rate is increasing. If he obtains evidence that the percentage of customers who default is now greater than 12%, the credit union will revise its guidelines for granting auto loans. A random sample of 150 customers who received loans a year ago indicates that 23 have since defaulted. State the null and alternative hypotheses and the appropriate decision rule. State your conclusion and explain what type of error might have been made.

38. The Neptune Automobile Company advertises that 90% of the owners of new Neptunes are satisfied with their purchase. Center Neptune in Green Bay, Wisconsin, wants to determine if this is true for its own customers. Of 40 customers contacted, 35 indicate they're satisfied. Is the percentage of all Center Neptune customers that are satisfied as high as the advertisement indicates? Test at the .01 significance level.

39. According to The Wall Street Journal (May 25, 1988), the percentage of 10-to-19 year-olds who drink coffee was 8.9% in 1984. In 1988, a sample of 742 young people showed that 5.3% drank coffee. Is the conclusion that a lower percentage of young people were drinking coffee in 1988 justified using a .01 significance level?

40. Four years ago the proportion of college graduates in Appendix C's company data base was .25. You feel that this proportion has increased. State the null and alternative hypotheses. Select a simple random sample of 25 observations from the data base and test your hypothesis at the .15 significance level.

TYPE II ERRORS, OPERATING CHARACTERISTIC CURVES, AND POWER CURVES

So far in this chapter, attention has been directed toward assessing the probability of a type I error. Each figure summarizing a hypothesis test reflects the necessary assumption that the null hypothesis is true. But what if it's false? A type II error occurs when a false null hypothesis is not rejected.

Under the assumption that the null hypothesis is true, a single value for the population parameter under test is specified. For example, in Situation 9.1 the Johnsons tested the hypothesis that the mean acidity/potency measurement of batches sent to Anderson was 425 units. If this hypothesis is assumed true, the correct sampling distribution is the one with a population mean of 425 (see Figure 9.11a). Figure 9.11a also shows the probability of the sample results leading to an incorrect decision. This error is the incorrect rejection of a true null hypothesis—a type I error—and the probability of it occurring is alpha.

However, suppose the null hypothesis is false. If the true population mean isn't 425, what is it? There are many—in fact, an infinite number of—values that the population mean could be if it's not 425. For this reason, asking for the probability of a type II error in a hypothesis test isn't a fair question. The probability of a type II error can be determined only if the population mean is specified.

Referring to the Johnson's batch problem (Situation 9.1), the Johnsons decide to assess the probability of a type II error. They're satisfied with the type I error probability chosen ($\alpha = .05$), but are now concerned about the chances of failing to reject the null hypothesis if it is false. The situation summarized is

$$H_0: \mu \geq 425$$
$$H_1: \mu < 425$$
$$n = 55 \qquad s = 30 \qquad \alpha = .05$$

Note that these specifications don't include the sample mean. The present concern is with assessing the probabilities of error, not with failing to reject or rejecting the null hypothesis, so the sample mean isn't needed.

In the selection of alpha (the probability of a type I error), the Johnsons must think about the penalty associated with such an error and decide on the acceptable probability of incurring this penalty. They have decided that a 5% chance of rejecting a true null hypothesis is acceptable.

Determining the chance of a type II error is more difficult. Since there are many values that the population mean could be, if it's not as specified in the null hypothesis, several representative values of the mean must be chosen. For each of these, the probability of a type II error (beta) is computed. The Johnsons pick three possible values for the population mean, other than the null hypothesis value of 425, and then compute the probability of a type II error for each. The chosen values are 421, 418, and

FIGURE 9.11 Type II Error

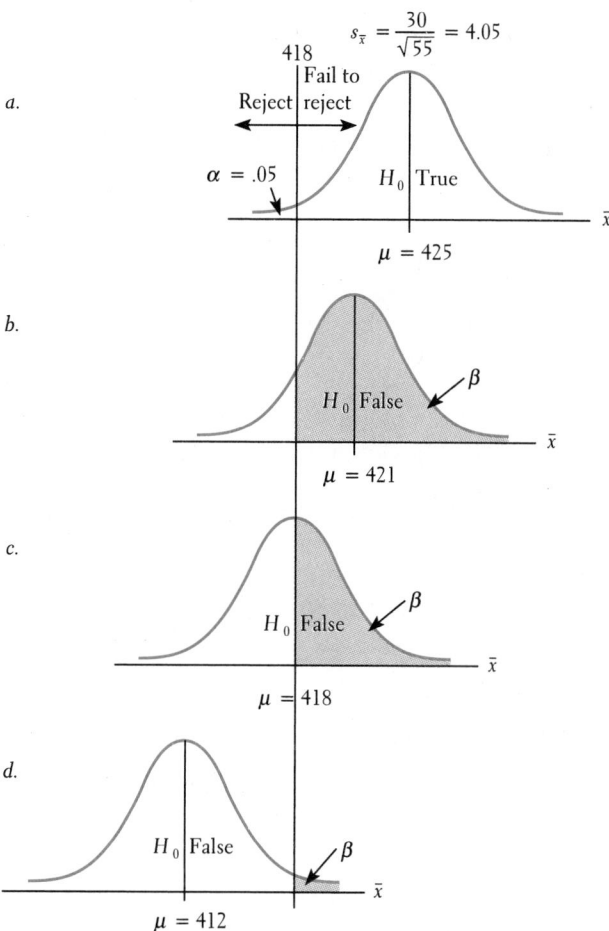

412 units. The Johnsons believe that knowing the probabilities of accepting the false null hypothesis for each of these three values will enable them to assess the level of accuracy for their chosen sample size. In other words, they wish to complete the entries in Table 9.2.

TABLE 9.2 Type II Errors

Population mean (μ)	Probability of accepting a false null hypothesis (β)
421	?
418	?
412	?

By choosing several representative values for the unknown population mean, they can assess the risks associated with failing to reject a false null hypothesis. The three values in Table 9.2 will give the Johnsons an idea of how risky their hypothesis test is with regard to a type II error. Since they already know the probability of a type I error, this will put them in a good position to decide if the risk level is acceptable.

The probability of committing a type II error must be computed for each of the three representative values for the population mean in Table 9.2. Figure 9.11a shows the sampling distribution associated with the null hypothesis being true, along with the probability of rejecting it (alpha). Figure 9.11 also shows three other sampling distributions—b, c, and d—each reflecting one of the chosen alternative population mean values of Table 9.2. The probability that the false null hypothesis won't be rejected (beta) is shown as the shaded area in each diagram.

After each of Figure 9.11's shaded areas is determined and the values for Table 9.2 computed, a picture of the potential for a type II error emerges. Each shaded area in Figure 9.11 is part of a normal distribution. To use a normal curve to find areas, we must know two things: the mean and the standard deviation (standard error). Table 9.2 lists the means of the three distributions in Figure 9.11. The standard error for each is assumed to be 4.05. This assumption is based on the idea that even if the population mean is slightly different from 425, the standard deviation of the population will still be about 30, the sample standard deviation. If this is true, then the same standard error should exist for all the sampling distributions being considered, since n = 55 for each. The shaded areas for each of the alternative hypothesis curves in Figure 9.11 are now found.

The critical value for rejection of the null hypothesis is the point on the curve that is z standard errors below the assumed population mean of 425, or

$$425 - 1.645(4.05) = 418.34 \text{ (rounded to 418)}$$

Figure 9.11a shows this value.

If the population mean is actually 421, the probability of failing to reject a false null hypothesis (making a type II error) is shown as the shaded region in Figure 9.11b. The computations for this area are

$$z = \frac{418 - 421}{4.05} = -0.74 \rightarrow .2704 \text{ (area between 418 and 421 in Figure 9.11b)}$$

$$\beta = .5000 + .2704 = .7704 \quad \text{(area above 418 in Figure 9.11b)}$$

If the population mean is actually 418, the probability of making a type II error is shown in Figure 9.11c. In this case, $\beta = .5000$, since half of the curve is above 418.

If the population mean is actually 412, the probability of making a type II error is shown in Figure 9.11d. The computations are

$$z = \frac{418 - 412}{4.05} = 1.48 \rightarrow .4306 \text{ (area between 412 and 418 in Figure 9.11d)}$$

$$\beta = .5000 - .4306 = .0694 \quad \text{(area above 418 in Figure 9.11d)}$$

OC Curve

The three beta values are entered beside their respective population mean values in Table 9.3. When these values are plotted, the result is called the **operating characteristic curve** (OC curve) for the hypothesis test (see Figure 9.12). Note that the curve has been hand-fitted to the three calculated values.

TABLE 9.3   Operating Characteristic Curve Values

Population mean (μ)	β (error)
421	.77
418	.50
412	.07

FIGURE 9.12   Operating Characteristic Curve

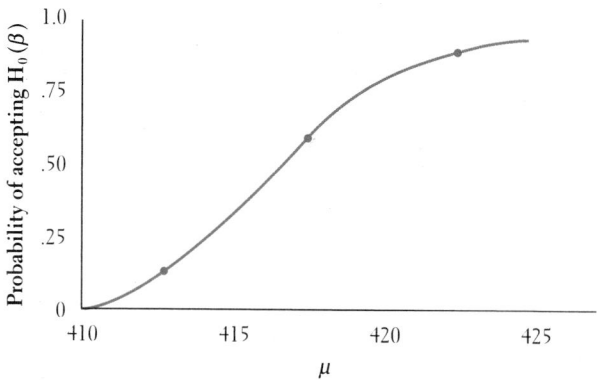

We can also designate the probability of correctly rejecting a false null hypothesis $(1 - \beta)$. Table 9.4 gives these values for the selected population means. A curve plotted through these values is called the **power curve** of the test and appears in Figure 9.13.

Power Curve

TABLE 9.4   Power Curve Values

Population mean (μ)	$1 - \beta$ (correct decision)
421	.23
418	.50
412	.93

Table 9.3 and Figure 9.12 show the probabilities of committing a type II error under three different population mean alternatives. Table 9.4 and Figure 9.13 show the likelihood of reaching the correct conclusion under these same conditions. The operating characteristic curve shows the probability of making a type II error, and the power

FIGURE 9.13   Power Curve

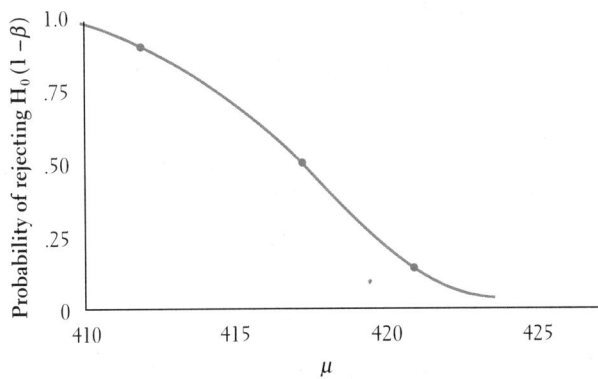

curve shows the probability of correctly rejecting a false null hypothesis. The power curve is used more frequently because it indicates the power of the test to correctly detect a false null hypothesis.

> The **operating characteristic curve** for a hypothesis test shows the probability of failing to reject a false null hypothesis for each possible value of the true population parameter. The **power curve** shows the probability of rejecting a false null hypothesis for each possible value of the true population parameter.

This "power" to detect a false null hypothesis is often the key to maintaining high quality, among other applications. The maintenance and improvement of quality are examined in Chapter 13—hypothesis testing is a vital part of this process.

The Johnsons can now assess the risks associated with their hypothesis test. The probability of incorrectly rejecting a true null hypothesis is 5% (alpha). The probabilities of incorrectly failing to reject a false null hypothesis, or of correctly rejecting a false null hypothesis, are summarized by the operating characteristic curve and the power curve, respectively. The Johnsons can now use their management judgment to decide if their chosen sample size ($n = 55$) has produced acceptable levels of risk.

EXERCISES

41.   When can a type II error occur?

42.   If a population mean is unspecified, can the probability of a type II error be determined?

43.   If the probability of making a type I error is decreased, how does this affect the probability of making a type II error?

44. If the probability of making a type II error is decreased, how does this affect the probability of making a type I error?

45. Which is more important to control: type I error or type II error?

46. When does an analyst risk making a type I error?

47. Explain the difference between an operating characteristic curve and a power curve.

48. A French auto manufacturer claims that a new company model will average at least 50 miles per gallon of gas. The population has a standard deviation of 5 miles per gallon. State the decision rule for a sample of 50 cars tested at the .02 significance level.

   a. What is the probability of committing a type II error if actual mileage is 50 miles per gallon?

   b. What is the probability of committing a type II error if actual mileage is 47 miles per gallon?

   c. What is the probability of committing a type II error if actual mileage is 48 miles per gallon?

   d. State the appropriate conclusion if the sample mean, $\bar{x}$, is 48 miles per gallon.

49. Draw the operating characteristic curve for Exercise 48.

50. Draw the power curve for Exercise 48.

51. Each week the Florida State Patrol intercepts an average of $56 million worth of drugs being transported north on Interstate 95. Over 36 randomly chosen weeks in 1992, the patrol intercepted an average of $60 million in drugs per week with a standard deviation of $20 million. Does this sample evidence indicate increasing movement of drugs through Florida? Test at the .05 significance level. Compute the probability of a type II error if the population mean is actually $59 million.

52. Draw the operating characteristic curve for Exercise 51.

53. Draw the power curve for Exercise 51.

54. Bill Ford, Bon Resort Hotel manager, believes that the average guest bill is at least $400. The population is normally distributed with standard deviation of $60. In Exercise 26 you were asked to state the decision rule for a significance level of .15 using a sample of 49 guest bills. You were also asked "if the sample mean is $375, what should Bill's conclusion be?" What is the probability of a type II error if the population average guest bill is actually $375?

55. Jack Knive knows from past experience that 12% of Community Credit Union's auto loan recipients default within the first year. Jack feels that the default rate is increasing. If he obtains evidence that the percentage of customers who default is now greater than 12%, the credit union will revise its guidelines for granting auto loans. In a random sample of 150 customers who received loans one year ago, 23 have since defaulted. Find the probability of a type II error if the population percentage is actually 15%.

56. Four years ago the percentage of college graduates in Appendix C's company data base was 25%. You feel that this percentage has increased. In Exercise 40 you were asked to select a simple random sample of 25 observations from the data base and test a hypothesis at the .15 significance level. Find the probability of a type II error if the population percentage of college graduates is actually 30%.

COMPUTING SAMPLE SIZE FOR A HYPOTHESIS TEST

Chapter 8 discussed how sample size decisions are made for interval estimation problems once the analyst has specified the desired degree of precision. This section shows how sample size decisions are made for hypothesis-testing problems once the analyst has specified allowable probabilities for type I and type II errors.

After considering the situation for their hypothesis test, the Johnsons decide the risk level is too high. They're comfortable with the type I error probability, since they set it at 5%, but they find too much risk associated with the power curve in Figure 9.13. The power of the test to detect a drop in mean chemical batch to 421 units is rather low (23%). A drop to this level would signal a significant deterioration in acidity/potency performance, and they decide to increase the power of the test to detect such a drop. To do this, they need to increase the sample size.

To determine sample size in a hypothesis-testing situation, three things must be known or estimated. First, the population standard deviation, or an estimate of it, must be specified. The Johnsons' initial sample of 55 revealed a sample standard deviation of 30 units; this will be used as the estimate of the population standard deviation.

Next, the risks of both type I and type II errors must be specified. The alpha level has already been established: $\alpha = .05$. Specifying the beta risk requires that a value for the population mean also be specified. In other words, the Johnsons must complete the following statement:

Beta equals _____ when the population mean equals _____.

Completing this statement indicates not only the tolerable probability of failing to reject a false null hypothesis but also the population mean value for which this risk is appropriate. Suppose the value .02 is chosen for beta. The statement for acceptable type II error can then be reworded:

If the population mean has dropped from 425 to _____, we want only a 2% chance of failing to reject the false claim that the population mean is still 425.

By filling in the blank in this statement, the Johnsons will have all the information they need to solve for the appropriate sample size. This sample size will guarantee that the desired risk levels for both type I and type II errors are met.

The Johnsons decide the population mean value for the beta specification should be 415. They reason that if the population mean has dropped as low as 415, they want to be almost certain that the hypothesis test will detect this fact and that the false null hypothesis will be rejected. They want to take only a 2% chance that the test will fail to detect this shift, leading to acceptance of the false null hypothesis.

The sample size needed in this hypothesis test can now be found. Figure 9.14 summarizes this situation. The top curve is the sampling distribution that applies if the null hypothesis is true. The mean of the curve is 425, and the probability of rejecting the true null hypothesis (alpha) is shown on the left end of the curve. The lower curve indicates that the population mean is in fact 415. The probability of failing to reject the false null hypothesis is shown on the upper end of this curve (beta). Note that the critical z value for the upper curve is -1.645 (since 5% of the curve is excluded on

FIGURE 9.14 Hypothesis Test

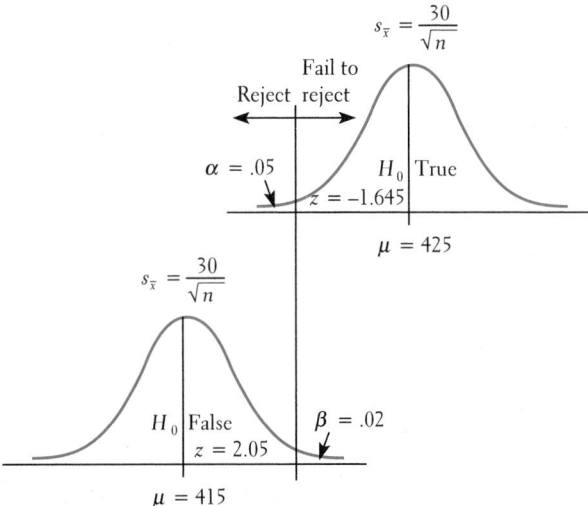

the lower end), and for the lower curve it is $z = 2.05$ (since 2% of the curve is excluded on the upper end).

The vertical line extending through both the curves of Figure 9.14 is the decision rule critical value. A sample mean above this value will lead to a failure to reject the null hypothesis, and a sample mean below this value will lead to rejection. This value can be specified using both curves. The following calculation states the decision rule value on the left using the upper curve and on the right using the lower curve. These two specifications are for the same value, as reflected by the equal sign between them. The result is one equation with one unknown: the sample size, n. The equation can thus be solved for the appropriate sample size:

$$425 - 1.645(30/\sqrt{n}) = 415 + 2.05(30/\sqrt{n})$$
$$10 = 49.35/\sqrt{n} + 61.5/\sqrt{n}$$
$$\sqrt{n} = 110.85/10$$
$$\sqrt{n} = 11.085$$
$$n = 122.9, \text{ rounded to } 123$$

The Johnsons should increase their sample size from the original value of 55 to 123 batches. This larger sample size, although costing more time and money, will yield the desired risk levels they specified.

EXERCISES

57. Is it possible to control the probabilities of both a type I and a type II error in a particular hypothesis test? If so, how is this accomplished?

58. If the sample size is increased in a hypothesis test after the acceptable type I and type II errors have been specified, increasing accuracy will result. Would this accuracy be

reflected in a lower alpha, would beta be decreased, or could both alpha and beta be decreased?

59. How could an analyst decrease the probabilities of both a type I error and a type II error in a hypothesis test?

60. What three things must an analyst know to determine the appropriate sample size for a hypothesis test?

61. Swingline Products produces bags of charcoal with a mean weight of 5 pounds and standard deviation of 1 pound. Quality Control samples the production process to determine whether standards are being met. A hypothesis test is conducted at the 5% significance level. The firm wants to guard against failing to reject the null hypothesis if the true mean is 5.4 pounds at a level of .10. What sample size should be selected for a one-tailed test?

62. The Genesis Company produces bearings. Past experience shows that the process produces bearings with an average diameter of 4 inches and standard deviation of 0.2 inch. An alpha level of .10 is desired. If the population mean isn't 4 inches but has dropped to 3.8 inches, Genesis wants only a 5% chance of accepting the false notion that the population mean is still 4 inches. What sample size should Genesis select?

63. The Neptune Automobile Company advertised in *Business Week* that 90% of the owners of new Neptunes are satisfied with their purchase. It wants to check whether this percentage has dropped. An alpha level of .01 is desired for the hypothesis test. If the population percentage has dropped to 85%, Neptune wants only a 10% chance of accepting the false notion that the population percentage is actually 90%. What sample size should Neptune select?

Choosing the Significance Level in Hypothesis Testing

Choosing Alpha

Some final thoughts are in order regarding the selection of a significance level in a hypothesis test. Throughout this chapter the significance level has been set arbitrarily or has been based on "consideration of the costs of a type I error." In practice, too often, little thought is given to the choice of alpha. The most common significance level in use is 5% and in fact, the authors have encountered situations where the choice of a significance level other than 5% was deemed "incorrect." Not considering the significance level might be expensive.

Some business leaders indicate that students are incorrectly taught to always select low significance levels in their business classes. The automatic selection of a low significance level, or a low chance of committing a type I error, might reflect the point of view: I'll continue to believe that the conditions of the past are unchanged; unless I see overwhelming evidence to the contrary, I'll continue to accept the status quo.

Such a statement can be regarded as extremely conservative. Most businesspeople need to take more risk in their decisions if they're to discover new opportunities and remain competitive. In addition, analysts must recognize that for a given amount of evidence (a given sample size), reducing the probability of a type I error increases the probability of a type II error. In other words, having too much faith in the status quo can lead to failure to detect a change in conditions.

The key point is that the costs associated with type I and type II errors need to be weighed in the choice of alpha. If the cost of a type I error is low compared with the cost of a type II error, then alpha should be relatively high. If committing a type I error is quite costly and a type II error is inexpensive, then a very low value of alpha should be chosen. By considering the costs of an error in a hypothesis test, the decision maker is in a better position to set the proper level of risk exposure.

SUMMARY

This chapter has covered one of statistics' most important topics: hypothesis testing. It may seem, at first glance, that estimation (Chapter 8) is more widely used, but, in fact, hypothesis testing is very common in business applications of all kinds.

Hypothesis tests of both a population mean and a population proportion were discussed. These two population parameters are involved in many practical applications; numerous examples follow.

This chapter also discussed the risk of a type II error. These risks are summarized by the operating characteristic curve or the power curve and, along with the chosen alpha value, show the analyst to what extent the chosen sample size creates exposure to risk. As always in statistical applications, the analyst must choose between a large expensive sample size with low risk, and a small inexpensive sample size with much risk.

Finally, the chapter addressed how to answer the most popular question in statistics: How large a sample should be used? As shown, the answer basically depends on how much risk of error the analyst is willing to take.

APPLICATIONS OF STATISTICAL CONCEPTS IN THE BUSINESS WORLD

THE KAISER ALUMINUM COMPANY'S USE OF HYPOTHESIS TESTING

Kaiser Aluminum is a supplier of aluminum stock to many industries around the world. Its award-winning quality improvement program is detailed in Chapter 13, "Quality-Control Applications." One of Kaiser's quality practices is to take a sample from each batch of aluminum stock and subject it to a number of tests.

Lori Anderson (a recent business graduate) is an accountant at Kaiser. Part of her job is to help design sampling plans for the aluminum-producing factory. She recently explained one of the tests to us: the "ultimate" test. Several dog-bone–shaped segments are cut from samples of aluminum stock and subjected to a pull test. The number of pounds required to break the dog bone is recorded for each test, and the average of these values becomes the sample statistic, measured in pounds.

The sample mean breaking point is used in a hypothesis test to see if the specification breaking point hypothesis can be rejected. If not, the batch is judged to be of high quality on the strength factor. If the null hypothesis is rejected because of a low average breaking point, the batch is suspect and an investigation is launched. Lori uses her business statistics courses regularly in her involvement in Kaiser's sampling process.

OTHER APPLICATIONS

Hypothesis testing is widely used in accounting, finance, production, marketing, personnel, quality control, and all other areas involving measuring items of interest. Questions that suggest that the test of a population mean is in order include:

1. Has the average value of a company's accounts receivable balance changed during the past year?
2. Has the average lifetime of an electronics part decreased since a new supplier of components began deliveries?
3. Has the average age of employees changed since the company began hiring significant numbers of women three years ago?
4. Has the average interest rate a company paid on its many loans changed over the past six months?
5. The average number of defectives per truckload, as measured by a company's quality-control department, has been 4.5 for several months. Has it decreased as a result of the QC department's improvement efforts?

Hypothesis tests involving a population percentage are also common. Again, all functional areas of business are candidates for this kind of hypothesis test since the percentage of items in the total population that are in a particular condition is frequently of interest. Questions that might arise regarding a population percentage include:

1. Has the percentage of minorities in a large company work force, previously known to be 12%, increased as a result of affirmative action efforts?
2. Has the percentage of accounts receivable that result in bad-debt expense increased as a result of depressed economic conditions?
3. Has the percentage of manufactured components that are defective responded to a recent quality-control effort?
4. Has the percentage of loan applications accepted by all branches of the bank changed during the past year?
5. In a taste test a year ago, only 35% of a consumer panel rated our soft drink superior to that of our competitor. A new-formula drink has been developed, and the taste test will again be tried. Will there be an improvement?

GLOSSARY

Hypothesis testing Using sample evidence to assess the likelihood that an assumption about some characteristic of a population is true.

Null hypothesis (H_0) The assumption about the population that is tested using sample evidence. It states that any difference between a sample statistic and its assumed population parameter is due to chance variation in sampling.

Alternative hypothesis (H_1) The statement about the population that must be true if the null hypothesis is false.

One-tailed test A hypothesis test in which the alternative hypothesis indicates direction (either greater or less than).

Two-tailed test A hypothesis test in which the alternative hypothesis does not specify direction.

Type I error Rejection of a true null hypothesis.

Type II error Failure to reject a false null hypothesis.

Level of significance The probability of rejecting a null hypothesis that is true. It is designated by the symbol α (alpha).

Decision rule A hypothesis test rule that specifies the action to be taken for each possible sample outcome.

_p_-value The probability of observing a sample value as extreme as, or more extreme than, the value actually observed, given that H_0 is true.

Operating characteristic curve A curve that shows the probability of failing to reject a false null hypothesis for each possible value of the true population parameter.

Power curve A curve that shows the probability of rejecting a false null hypothesis for each possible value of the true population parameter.

KEY FORMULAS

Standardized test statistic

$$z = \frac{\text{Observed value} - \text{Assumed value}}{\text{Standard error of sampling distribution}} \tag{9.1}$$

Standardized test statistic—population mean (large-sample case)

$$z = \frac{\bar{x} - \mu}{\sigma_{\bar{x}}} \tag{9.2}$$

Standardized test statistic—population mean (small-sample case)

$$t = \frac{\bar{x} - \mu}{s_{\bar{x}}} \tag{9.3}$$

Standardized test statistic—population proportion

$$z = \frac{x/n - p}{\sigma_{\bar{p}}} \tag{9.4}$$

SOLVED EXERCISES

1. ONE-SAMPLE HYPOTHESIS TEST FOR MEANS—LARGE SAMPLE

A company claims that the rubber belts it manufactures have a mean service life of at least 800 hours. A simple random sample of 36 belts from a large shipment reveals a mean life of 780 hours and standard deviation of 90 hours.

a. What is the appropriate conclusion of a hypothesis test done at the .05 significance level?

b. If a computer program is used for this problem, what *p*-value would it compute?

Solution:

a. The null and alternative hypotheses are

H_0: $\mu \geq 800$
H_1: $\mu < 800$

The decision rule is:

If the sample mean lies more than 1.645 standard errors below the assumed population mean of 800 hours, reject the null hypothesis; otherwise, fail to reject it (reject H_0 if $z < -1.645$).

$$s_{\bar{x}} = \frac{s}{\sqrt{n}} = \frac{90}{\sqrt{36}} = 15$$

$$z = \frac{\bar{x} - \mu}{s_{\bar{x}}} = \frac{780 - 800}{15} = -1.33$$

Since the test value for z (-1.33) is larger than the critical value ($z = -1.645$), the null hypothesis is not rejected. There's insufficient evidence to dispute the company's claim. There's a possibility that a type II error has been committed, since the accepted null hypothesis might actually be false.

b. Look up the z value of -1.33 in the standard normal table. The area between the mean and a z value of -1.33 is .4082. Therefore, the p-value is (.5000 $-$ .4082), or .0918.

2. One-Sample Hypothesis Test for Means—Small Sample

The maker of a certain car model claims that the car averages 31 miles per gallon of unleaded gas. A random sample of nine cars is selected, and each car is driven on a supply of one gallon of unleaded gas.

a. State the decision rule in terms of mileage if an alpha of .01 is used and the sample standard deviation equals three miles per gallon.

b. What is the appropriate conclusion if the nine cars average 29.5 miles per gallon?

Solution:

a. The null and alternative hypotheses are

$$H_0: \mu \geq 31$$
$$H_1: \mu < 31$$

Degrees of freedom equal $(n - 1) = (9 - 1) = 8$. The decision rule is to reject the null hypothesis if the test value for t is less than -2.896 (reject H_0 if $t < -2.896$).

b. $$s_{\bar{x}} = \frac{s}{\sqrt{n}} = \frac{3}{\sqrt{9}} = 1$$

$$t = \frac{\bar{x} - \mu}{s_{\bar{x}}} = \frac{29.5 - 31}{1} = -1.50$$

Since the test value for t (-1.50) is larger than the critical value ($t = -2.896$), the null hypothesis is not rejected. The car maker's claim appears to be true. Of course, a type II error may have been committed.

3. One-Sample Hypothesis Test for Proportions

A certain manufacturing process turns out 20% defective items. The manufacturer will continue the process as long as the percentage of defective items isn't significantly larger than the norm of 20%. A random sample of 100 items is selected and tested. If 30 items are defective, what is the correct decision at the .02 significance level?

Solution:

The null and alternative hypotheses are

$$H_0: p \leq .20$$
$$H_1: p > .20$$

The decision rule is:

> If the sample proportion of defectives lies more than 2.05 standard errors above the assumed population percentage of 20%, reject the null hypothesis; otherwise, fail to reject it (reject H_0 if $z > 2.05$).

$$\sigma_{\bar{p}} = \sqrt{\frac{p(1-p)}{n}} = \sqrt{\frac{.20(1-.20)}{100}} = .04$$

$$z = \frac{(x/n - p)}{\sigma_{\bar{p}}} = \frac{(30/100 - .20)}{.04} = \frac{.10}{.04} = 2.5$$

Since the test value of z (2.5) is greater than z's critical value (2.05), the null hypothesis is rejected. The percentage of defective items is significantly larger than the normal 20%. There's a possibility that a type I error has been committed.

4. TYPE II ERROR

The hypothesis-testing procedure in Solved Exercise 1 led to the conclusion that the null hypothesis should not be rejected. The possibility of a type II error was mentioned. Calculate the probability of a type II error if it's assumed that the rubber belts have a mean service life of 780 hours.

Solution:

Figure 9.15 illustrates the solution. The decision rule was to reject the null hypothesis if the computed z value is less than -1.645. If this z value is converted to hours, the null hypothesis will be rejected if the sample has an average service life less than 775.3 hours:

$$-1.645 = \frac{\bar{x} - 800}{15}$$
$$-24.7 = \bar{x} - 800$$
$$\bar{x} = 775.3$$

If the population mean is actually 780, the probability of obtaining a sample mean greater than 775.3 by chance is $(.5000 + .1217) = .6217$. This is the probability of a type II error.

$$z = \frac{\bar{x} - \mu}{s_{\bar{x}}} = \frac{775.3 - 780}{15} = -0.31 \rightarrow .1217 \text{ (area between 775.3 and 780)}$$

5. SAMPLE SIZE FOR A HYPOTHESIS TEST

Manufacturers' advertising claims are sometimes tested by the Federal Trade Commission (FTC) to verify their accuracy. The makers of Venetian Spaghetti Sauce have advertised that their 32-ounce jar is always filled to the top. Management is concerned that the FTC will test this claim and find it untrue. Venetian wants to determine the appropriate sample size for a test of its own. The population standard deviation is 0.5 ounce. A significance level of .05 is desired. If the population mean isn't 32 ounces, but has dropped to 31.8 ounces, Venetian wants only a

FIGURE 9.15   Type II Error Calculation

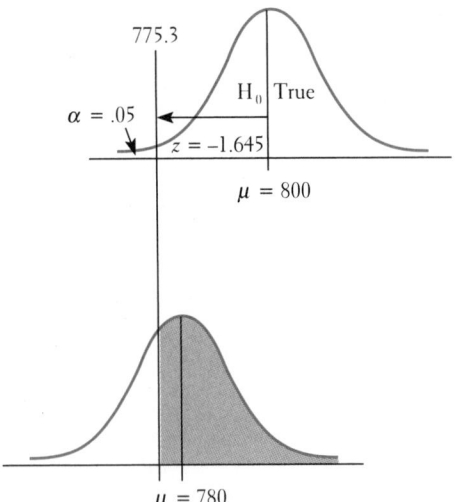

10% chance of accepting the false notion that the population mean is still 32 ounces. What sample size should Venetian select?

Solution:

A significance level, or alpha, of .05 is equivalent to the value

$$32 - 1.645(0.5/\sqrt{n})$$

If the population mean has dropped to 31.8 ounces, Venetian wants only a 10% chance of failing to reject the false notion that the population mean is still 32 ounces. This corresponds to a value of

$$31.8 + 1.28(0.5/\sqrt{n})$$

The appropriate sample size is computed by equating these two expressions and solving for *n*:

$$32 - 1.645(0.5/\sqrt{n}) = 31.8 + 1.28(0.5/\sqrt{n})$$
$$0.2 = 0.8225/\sqrt{n} + 0.64/\sqrt{n}$$
$$\sqrt{n} = 1.4625/0.2$$
$$\sqrt{n} = 7.3125$$
$$n = 53.5$$

Venetian should use a sample size of 54.

EXERCISES

64. How do hypothesis-testing procedures differ when the population standard deviation is unknown?

65. Does rejecting a null hypothesis disprove it? Why or why not?

66. Does a sample result that is inconsistent with the null hypothesis lead to its rejection? Why or why not?

67. What is meant when a null hypothesis is rejected on the basis of sample information?

68. Explain why no single level of probability is used to reject or accept a hypothesis.

69. If a hypothesized value is rejected because it differs from a sample statistic by two or more standard deviation units, what is the likelihood that a true hypothesis has been rejected?

70. If minimum load-bearing capacity of New Mexico's bridges is 20 tons, state the null and alternative hypotheses to test a sample of bridges.

71. State the appropriate sampling distribution for each of the following hypothesis tests. Also state the necessary assumptions.
    a. $H_0: \mu = 40; \sigma = 3; n = 25$. *p.31. for small samples & t*
    b. $H_0: \mu = 70; s = 8; n = 25$.
    c. $H_0: \mu = 20, s = 4; n = 25$.
    d. $H_0: p = .10; n = 58$.
    e. $H_0: p = .05; n = 39$.

72. The null hypothesis is that the old tire manufacturing process is as good as the new one. What kind of cost would a type I error create in this situation?

73. The null hypothesis is that a television tube manufacturing process is producing no more than the maximum allowable rate of defective tubes. What kind of cost would a type II error create in this situation?

74. Which of the following statements about the probabilities of type I and type II errors are *not* correct?
    a. A type I error can never occur if H_0 is false.
    b. A type II error can never occur if H_0 is true.
    c. If H_0 is true, it is possible to make a type I error or make a correct decision.
    d. If H_0 is false, it is possible to make a type II error or make a correct decision.
    e. It's not possible to specify the probabilities of both type I and type II errors in the same hypothesis test because only one or the other can occur.

75. For a sample of 35, the sample mean is 96 and the standard deviation is 3. Using the .02 level of significance, test the hypothesis that the population mean is 100.

76. For a sample of 18, the sample mean is 6 and the standard deviation is 0.5. Using the .05 level of significance, test that the sample mean is greater than the hypothesized population mean of 5.

77. For a sample of 50, the sample proportion is .85. Using the .01 level of significance, test the hypothesis that the population proportion is .80.

78. A company has purchased a large quantity of steel wire. The supplier claims that the wire has a mean tensile strength of 80 pounds or more. The company tests a sample of 13 pieces of the wire and finds a mean of 78.64 and standard deviation of 4 pounds. Should the company dispute the claimed mean tensile strength on the basis of this evidence at the .05 significance level?

79. The May 5, 1988, *Wall Street Journal* reported an increase in the percentage of taxpayers who used professional preparers from 45% in 1986 to 47% in 1987. In a 1988 study to see

if a significant increase in the usage of professional preparers had occurred, of a random sample of 1,000 taxpayers, 494 indicated they used a professional preparer. Using the 10% significance level, can it be concluded that there has been an increase since 1987?

80. A package-filling device is set to fill cereal boxes with a mean weight of 20 ounces of cereal per box. The standard deviation of the amount actually put into the boxes is 0.5 ounces. A random sample of 25 filled boxes is weighed, yielding a mean weight of 20.27 ounces. Test at the .05 significance level to determine whether the device is working properly.

81. Under a standard manufacturing process, the breaking strength of nylon thread is normally distributed, with mean of 100 and standard deviation of 5. A new, cheaper process is tested, and a sample of 25 threads is drawn, with the results $\bar{x} = 98.4$, $s = 5.5$. Your assistant has noted, "Since the sample mean isn't significantly less than 100 at alpha .05, we have strong justification for installing the new process." Do you agree?

82. A manufacturer claims that a customer will find no more than 8% defective knee braces in a large shipment. A customer decides to test this claim after reading an article in the *American Journal of Sports Medicine* (July/August 1989, p. 535). This article discusses the forces exerted on a knee brace used for injured athletes and convinces the customer that high quality is essential.

   A random sample of 200 braces is selected from the shipment, and 28 defectives are found. Should the manufacturer's claim be disputed at the .01 significance level?

83. Investigators for the National Transportation Safety Board (NTSB) stopped 1,500 heavy trucks by surprise in five states and ordered 46.1% off the road because their brakes were out of adjustment, the *Detroit News* reported (*The Spokesman-Review*, July 20, 1992). About 10% of the trucks inspected had other serious brake problems, the newspaper said. The state patrol in another state decides to stop a random sample of 200 trucks to determine whether the problem is as widespread as reported and finds 88 of the trucks with brakes out of adjustment. Does this provide evidence that the actual percentage of 46.1% reported by the NTSB is too high? (Test using the .01 significance level.)

84. The manufacturer of Cola Pop is in the process of producing 12-ounce cans. The automated pouring device needs frequent checking to verify that it's actually putting 12 ounces in each can. Cans' weights are known to be normally distributed with a standard deviation of 0.2 ounce. State the null and alternative hypotheses. State the decision rule if the hypothesis is to be tested at the 5% significance level for a sample of 36 cans. State the appropriate conclusion if the sample mean is 12.5 ounces. Explain what type of error might be made.

85. According to a survey of family travel plans conducted by the U.S. Travel Data Center for *Better Homes and Gardens*, 49% of the family vacationers intending to travel with children in 1992 planned to visit a theme park (*The Wall Street Journal*, April 15, 1992). Brandon Kim, president of Wild Kingdom, is interested in building a theme park in Madison, Wisconsin. He decides to survey 700 families in the surrounding area and determine whether at least 49% intend to visit a theme park on their vacation. If 325 respondents indicate they intend to do so, what should Brandon conclude? (Use the .01 significance level.)

86. In a certain year, the mean interest rate on loans to all large retailers was 6%, and the standard deviation was 0.2 percentage points. Two years later, a simple random sample of 100 loans to large retailers yielded a mean interest rate of 6.015%. Assume you're willing to run a 1% risk of concluding a change has occurred when in fact there has been no change. Would you conclude that there has been a change in the average level of interest

rates for large retailers? If, in fact, the average interest rate for all large retailers was 6.015%, would the conclusion that a change has occurred in the average interest rate for large retailers result in a correct decision, a type I error, or a type II error?

87. The Slick Corporation manufactures razor blades and wishes to test if men appreciate its new extra-sharp blade. The company hires a research firm to recruit people to test the new blade. The research firm randomly selects 50 men to use the blade for a one-week trial period. At the end of the experiment, participants are asked if they would purchase the new blade. When this experiment was done last year, 50% of the respondents indicated that they would buy the blade. Slick wants to charge more for the new blade, so it hopes that the percentage will increase. Of the 50 men, 30 say they would buy the new blade. Testing at the .01 significance level, is there a significant increase in the proportion of men who say they'll purchase the new blade?

88. A photographic processing stage is supposed to last an average of 30 seconds. If the process takes more or less than 30 seconds, the picture's quality will suffer. This is especially true for certain high-quality film used for professional purposes. The Sanders Company is expecting a rush of such film after reading a notice in *American Photographer* about Ilford's new XPI film. Sanders knows that professional photographers expect perfection and is concerned about its processing times.

Sanders decides to select 25 pieces of film and run them through the process. If the sample mean is 33 seconds and sample standard deviation is 3 seconds, what should Sanders conclude if it tests at the .05 significance level? Assume that the process is normally distributed.

89. The California Power Company wants to determine whether mean residential electricity usage per household increased during January. Past experience indicates that usage is normally distributed with a mean of 700 kwh and standard deviation of 50 kwh. A simple random sample of 50 households was selected for January, and mean usage was found to be 715 kwh. Test at the .02 significance level whether mean residential electricity usage per household has increased for the month of January.

90. Western, Inc., manufactures men's sports shirts carried in 24% of the men's clothing stores on the West Coast. Western recently sampled 60 men's clothing stores on the East Coast and found that 12 stores carried its brand. At the .10 significance level, is there evidence that Western has poorer distribution on the East Coast?

91. A coin-operated coffee machine was designed to discharge at least 8 ounces of beverage per cup, with standard deviation .9 ounce. An analyst selects a random sample of 36 cupfuls for a consumer-testing service and is willing to have an alpha risk of 10%. Compute the test's power and the probability of a type II error if the population average amount dispensed is:

a. 7.8 ounces.

b. 7.85 ounces.

92. (This question refers to Exercise 91.) If the analyst wants 98% power to detect a shift in the population mean from 8 ounces to 7.9 ounces, what sample size must be selected?

93. (This question refers to Exercise 91.) If the analyst wishes an alpha risk of 5%, compute the test's power and the probability of a type II error if the population average amount dispensed is:

a. 7.8 ounces.

b. 7.85 ounces.

94. Using Appendix C's company data base, test the null hypothesis that the mean number of years with the company for the 200 employees is 12.6. Use the .02 significance level for a simple random sample of 40 employees selected with replacement.

95. Using Appendix C's company data base, test the null hypothesis that the proportions of males and females employed by the company are equal. Use the .01 significance level for a simple random sample of 35 employees selected with replacement.

EXTENDED EXERCISES

96. RICH HEALTH PRODUCTS

The Rich Health Products Company wants to know if its six-month effort to reduce absenteeism has produced results. The campaign resulted from a study that revealed an average of 2.9 sick days taken per employee in the company's main manufacturing plant. Concern over this matter increased after the personnel manager read an article about absenteeism in the nursing profession ("Absenteeism among Hospital Nurses: An Idiographic-Longitudinal Analysis," *Academy of Management Journal*, June 1989).

A random sample of 50 employee records will be used to determine any improvement. The company decides to test the null hypothesis that the average number of sick days taken per month is still 2.9 against the alternative that the average has decreased. Rich management considers the penalty associated with a type I error, which would mean concluding that the absentee rate has declined when in fact it hasn't. This would divert management attention away from a continuing absentee problem. In view of this undesirable situation, management decides on a significance level of 2%: they will accept only a 2% chance of thinking there has been an improvement when there really hasn't.

The hypothesis test is summarized as follows:

$$H_0: \mu \geq 2.9 \qquad n = 50$$
$$H_1: \mu < 2.9 \qquad \alpha = .02$$

The sample mean and sample standard deviation are computed to be 2.75 and 0.83 days per month, respectively. The personnel director is anxious to conclude that the absentee reduction campaign has been a success, but other members of management aren't sure the sample results are significant. They decide to continue with the hypothesis test.

The critical z value is the one that yields an area of .48 on a normal curve, since this is a one-tailed test and $\alpha = .02$. This z value is -2.05, which leads to the decision rule:

If the sample mean is more than 2.05 standard errors below the assumed population mean of 2.9, reject the null hypothesis; otherwise, fail to reject it (reject if $z < -2.05$).

The test value for z is computed next. The unknown population standard deviation is estimated using the sample standard deviation, $s = 0.83$:

$$z = \frac{2.75 - 2.9}{0.83/\sqrt{50}} = \frac{-0.15}{0.117} = -1.28$$

The test value of z, -1.28, isn't low enough to fall into the rejection range ($z < -2.05$), so the null hypothesis cannot be rejected. The personnel director insists that the absentee reduction program has been successful and can't understand why a reduced sample average doesn't bear this out. A colleague points out that the combination of sample mean, the variability of absent days (as measured by s) and, most important, the sample size ($n = 50$) don't constitute enough evidence to claim that a reduction has taken place among all of Rich's employees. The personnel director is determined to establish the reduction campaign's validity and asks what it would take to do so. It is agreed that if the 2.75 average is shown to hold up over a larger sample size, the null hypothesis of no change can be rejected. The personnel director decides to sample more worker records to build the sample size.

a. What considerations are important in selecting persons to be in the sample from all of Rich's employees?

b. What is the minimum sample size that would result in rejection of the null hypothesis, under the assumption that the sample mean again turned out to be 2.75?

c. What does a type II error mean in this situation?

97. CHERRY LANE APPLE ORCHARD

Cherry Lane Orchards grows and processes apples. Its share of the applesauce market has been around 30% for several years. Recently its other apple products have been losing ground, and management has decided to try to increase the applesauce market share in an attempt to maintain plant capacity.

A marketing firm was retained to develop a campaign for the firm's applesauce. When the campaign was first presented to management, it was rejected as offbeat and possibly even offensive. The marketing firm, pointing out the success of similar approaches in other markets, finally convinced Cherry Lane to try the campaign. After the deal was signed, management stated they would watch the results closely to determine whether the company's market share was still around 30%. Since the new campaign was so different, it was agreed that the market share could change in either direction. That is, the new campaign might either increase or decrease the present share.

A method of randomly sampling consumers across many geographical markets was designed, with sampling to begin shortly after initiation of the new advertising campaign. A sample size of 1,000 consumers was planned, and the sample distribution convinced management that the sample was random and representative. The percentage of applesauce buyers in this sample who chose the Cherry Lane brand would be used to determine the new campaign's effectiveness.

a. What are the null and alternative hypotheses?

b. In view of the risks involved, what is an appropriate significance level for the test?

c. What is the decision rule for this test?

d. How far from 30% can the sample percentage be before the null hypothesis is rejected?

98. MILGARD ALUMINUM

Milgard Manufacturing, an aluminum processing company, decides to check the weights of the large rolls of aluminum foil one of its processing plants produces. Rolls are supposed to average 950 pounds, but increased raw material costs have led management to suspect that this average has increased. If so, valuable aluminum is being lost. Corrective action could save the company many dollars over a year's time.

Milgard wants to test the hypothesis that the rolls' average weight is 950 pounds against the alternative that it is actually greater. A total of 250 rolls are to be randomly sampled and weighed to test the null hypothesis. A preliminary sample indicates a sample standard deviation of 5.8 pounds. Since this is similar to standard deviation figures of past studies, it's used as an estimate of the population standard deviation.

Milgard's management is familiar with hypothesis testing and the risks that must be assumed. After considering the consequences of rejecting a true null hypothesis (believing that the average has increased beyond 950 pounds when it hasn't), they decide on a significance level of 5%.

a. What are the null and alternative hypotheses?

b. What is the decision rule?

c. What does a type II error mean in this situation?

d. Choose three values for the average weight of the aluminum rolls, other than 950 pounds, and compute the probabilities of failing to reject and of rejecting the null hypothesis for each. Summarize these calculations by forming the operating characteristic curve and the power curve.

e. After reviewing the risk situation, as indicated by the significance level and the power curve, along with the cost of individually weighing 250 aluminum rolls, management decides that they've allowed for more test accuracy than they're willing to pay for. After thinking carefully about the risks they're willing to take, they formulate the following risk specifications:

$$\alpha = .05$$
$$\beta = .05 \text{ if } \mu = 952$$

f. What sample size will meet these risk specifications, assuming that the population standard deviation is 5.8 pounds?

99. WHITFIELD UNIVERSITY BASKETBALL

Bobby Day, basketball coach for Whitfield University, has just been fired, and the administration is attempting to hire a new coach. President Fredrickson must determine the new coach's salary. He feels that a coach's average salary for a school the size of Whitfield is $100,000. The president orders his assistant, Ken Dolan, to study this issue. Ken decides to sample 54 schools and test the president's hypothesis. The 54 salaries are:

99,541	88,946	95,292	102,677	82,200	77,331
96,805	108,830	98,584	100,358	99,326	105,207
98,957	108,827	108,239	95,867	104,182	111,255
90,446	99,483	96,166	99,956	88,452	103,121
98,897	111,854	88,209	100,381	102,281	99,076
99,892	91,353	111,597	96,003	106,994	105,967
82,139	89,856	96,377	84,055	104,997	85,154
99,206	90,775	109,276	85,210	106,501	98,986
80,008	93,535	99,388	92,242	82,518	111,352

a. What significance level should Ken use?

b. What is Ken's conclusion concerning the president's hypothesis?

c. What kind of error might Ken be making?

100. OUR LADY OF LOURDES HOSPITAL

Chapter 4 gave family sizes for a population of 200 Our Lady of Lourdes Hospital employees. Customer benefits director Curtis Huff believes that the average family size has decreased since the last time this variable was studied, five years ago. At that time, family size averaged 2.9.

a. Develop the null and alternative hypotheses to test Mr. Huff's belief.

b. Use the .02 significance level to test the null hypothesis. Use the sample results you computed in Chapter 4. p 125 #62

c. In Chapter 8, a new random sample was generated. The new sample's descriptive statistics using MINITAB are:

```
MTB> DESCRIBE C2
C2      N      MEAN    MEDIAN    STDEV
       30     2.633    2.0000    1.217

C2     MIN     MAX      Q1        Q3
      1.000   6.000    2.000     3.250
```

Test the hypothesis developed in part *a* using the results presented on the MINITAB output. What is your conclusion using the .05 significance level? The MINITAB commands to perform this hypothesis test appear in the "MINITAB Computer Package" section.

MICROCOMPUTER PACKAGE

The micro package *Computerized Business Statistics* may be used to solve hypothesis-testing problems.

Sue and Bill Johnson (Situation 9.1) have records from the past three years showing that the acidity/potency measure is 415 units. The Johnsons are worried that the process is not meeting specification. Sue and Bill decide that a hypothesis test is in order.

Computer Solution:

From the main menu of *Computerized Business Statistics* an 8 is selected, which indicates Hypothesis Testing. Since the problem involves entering data from the keyboard, a 1 is selected. The following choices appear on the screen:

```
Data Type: (R) Raw (S) Summary                                          S
Data Form: (M) Means (P) Proportion                                     M
Proportion data consists of values from 0 to 1
Population: (1) One Population (2) Two Populations                      1
Variance: (P) Population (S) Sample                                     S
Testing: (1) One Sided (2) Two Sided                                    1
         (L) Lower Limit (U) Upper Limit                                L
Hypothesis Value:                                                     425
Enter F when finished  Instructions for each option are provided here.
```

The choices are

$$S = \text{Summary}$$
$$M = \text{Means}$$
$$1 = \text{One Population}$$
$$S = \text{Sample}$$
$$1 = \text{One Sided}$$
$$L = \text{Lower Limit}$$
$$425 = \text{Hypothesized population mean } (\mu)$$

F is entered to indicate that you are finished with this menu.

```
Sample Size:                                                55
Sample Mean:                                               415
Standard Deviation (S):                                     30
Enter F when finished   Instructions for each option
                        are provided here.
```

The choices are

$$n = 55$$
$$\bar{x} = 415$$
$$s = 30$$

Next, the screen shows:

```
Alpha Error 1 = 0.1, 2 = 0.05, 3 = 0.025, 4 = 0.01, 5 = 0.005,
        6 = Other
Select Alpha: enter 1–6 and press ↵ 2
```

A 2 is entered for the .05 significance level and the screen shows:

```
Degrees of Freedom: 54
Critical Z (Test Statistic)................... 1.645
```

Next, the hypothesis-testing program options menu reappears. A 7 is entered so that the problem can be run. The hypothesis-testing output menu then appears. The choice in this case is **P** for printer.

MINITAB COMPUTER PACKAGE

The MINITAB commands to perform the hypothesis test for Extended Exercise 100 are

```
MTB> ZTEST OF MU=2.9, ASSUMING SIGMA=1.217, ON C2;
SUBC> ALTERNATIVE −1.
```

The output of this test is

```
TEST OF MU = 2.9 VS MU L.T. 2.9
THE ASSUMED SIGMA = 1.22

        N      MEAN    STDEV   SE MEAN     Z      P VALUE
C2     30     2.633    1.217     .22     −1.20    .1200
MTB> STOP
```

The ZTEST command is used to test the null hypothesis that $\mu \geq 2.9$. The standard deviation of 1.217 is assumed based on the sample data stored in C2. The ALTERNATIVE −1 subcommand tests the null against the alternative hypothesis that $\mu < 2.9$. Note that the ALTERNATIVE +1 subcommand tells the program to do a one-tailed test above the mean. If there is no ALTERNATIVE subcommand, a two-tailed test is performed.

Chapter

10

Two-Population Hypothesis Tests

Some circumstantial evidence is very strong, as when you find a trout in the milk.

Thoreau,

Journal

Objectives

When you have completed this chapter, you will be able to:

Conduct two-population hypothesis tests for population means.

Conduct two-population hypothesis tests for population proportions.

Recognize business applications in which two-population hypothesis testing can be applied.

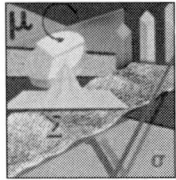

In its February 1989 issue, *Personnel Management* featured an article comparing on-the-job training and training through off-site courses and seminars. On-the-job training was recognized as more expensive, but the relative effectiveness of the two methods was in question.

Chapter 9 developed two very useful hypothesis-testing procedures: the test of a single population mean and the test of a single population proportion. Comparison of two populations of interest frequently occurs in practice. This chapter covers these important hypothesis tests.

WHY MANAGERS NEED TO KNOW ABOUT HYPOTHESIS TESTING FOR TWO POPULATIONS

We sometimes want to compare two populations to see whether they can be regarded as the same or different. Two-sample tests are used to evaluate claims about the equality of the means or proportions of two populations. Occasionally, the analyst's objective is to evaluate a claim about a specific difference between the means or proportions of two populations. For example, a claim may be that the means of two populations are equal, or a claim may be that the mean of one population is greater (or less) than the mean of another population.

At the completion of this chapter, you'll have examined one-sample tests for both means and proportions, discussed in Chapter 9, and the two-sample tests introduced in this chapter. All these hypothesis tests use the four basic steps presented early in Chapter 9. These steps apply to all other hypothesis tests as well.

Regarding the *Personnel Management* article, specific measures of worker productivity need to be developed and recorded for two samples of trainees, one for each training method. The two methods can then be compared and observed differences tested.

HYPOTHESIS TESTS ABOUT THE DIFFERENCE BETWEEN TWO POPULATION MEANS: LARGE SAMPLES

When testing two populations for equality of means, the null hypothesis under test is that the two population means are equal. This hypothesis won't be rejected unless sufficient evidence is gathered to reject it with small chance of error. The alternative hypothesis can use the unequal sign, the greater-than sign, or the less-than sign. This choice depends on the claim being made about the populations of interest. For a two-tailed test, the null and alternative hypotheses are

$$H_0: \mu_1 - \mu_2 = 0$$
$$H_1: \mu_1 - \mu_2 \neq 0$$

For a one-tailed test the null and alternative hypotheses are either

$$H_0: \mu_1 - \mu_2 \leq 0 \qquad \text{or} \qquad H_0: \mu_1 - \mu_2 \geq 0$$
$$H_1: \mu_1 - \mu_2 > 0 \qquad\qquad\qquad H_1: \mu_1 - \mu_2 < 0$$

Note that 0 could be replaced in these hypotheses with any value of interest. For example, the null and alternative hypotheses might be

$$H_0: \mu_1 - \mu_2 = 5$$
$$H_1: \mu_1 - \mu_2 \neq 5$$

Independent samples are selected from two populations, and the observations making up one sample are chosen independently of the observations making up the other sample. After random samples are taken from each of the two populations, the sample means are computed and the difference between them calculated. This difference is the test statistic used to reject or fail to reject the null hypothesis. If this difference is large, the null hypothesis is rejected. If this difference is small, the null hypothesis isn't rejected. To determine whether the sample mean difference is large or small, the sampling distribution for this statistic is consulted. The specifications for this distribution depend on the two sample sizes and their population variances. Since the population variances are usually unknown, sample variances are generally used to approximate them.

The sampling distribution for sample mean differences for large samples (each 30 or larger) is the normal distribution. This distribution has a mean of 0, which is intuitively obvious based on this reasoning. If the null hypothesis is true (no difference between the population means), we would expect sample mean differences to cluster around the difference between the population means, which is 0. There would be as many sample mean differences above 0 as below, and they would tend to be close to 0 rather than far away.

The sampling distribution for sample mean differences appears in Figure 10.1. Note that the sample mean differences are clustered around 0. If the difference between the sample means is close to 0, which is likely if the two populations have the same mean, the null hypothesis is not rejected. If a large difference is found, the null hypothesis is rejected.

FIGURE 10.1   Sampling Distribution of Sample Mean Differences

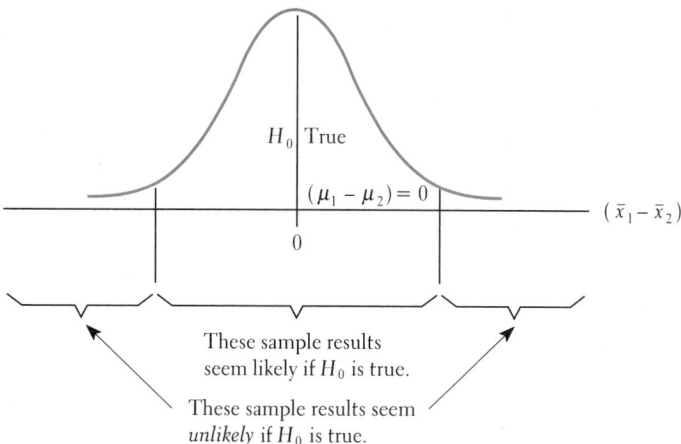

The test statistic for the two-population mean test is a *z* value since the sampling distribution is normally distributed. The *z* value measures the number of standard errors between 0, the mean of the curve, and the difference between the two sample means. The use of the normal distribution is based on the assumptions:

1. The observations in the two samples are independent.
2. The sample sizes are each 30 or larger.

If sample sizes less than 30 are used, we must assume that the populations are normally distributed.

Equation 10.1 shows the calculation for the **standard error of the difference between population means,** $\sigma_{\bar{x}_1 - \bar{x}_2}$:

$$\sigma_{\bar{x}_1 - \bar{x}_2} = \sqrt{\frac{\sigma_1^2}{n_1} + \frac{\sigma_2^2}{n_2}}$$ (10.1)

where $\sigma_{\bar{x}_1 - \bar{x}_2}$ = Standard error of the difference between population means
σ_1^2 = Variance of population 1
σ_2^2 = Variance of population 2
n_1 = Size of sample 1
n_2 = Size of sample 2

Note that to solve Equation 10.1 the variances of the populations under test must be known. In practice, the sample variances are usually used to estimate the unknown population parameters:

$$s_{\bar{x}_1 - \bar{x}_2} = \sqrt{\frac{s_1^2}{n_1} + \frac{s_2^2}{n_2}}$$ (10.2)

where $s_{\bar{x}_1 - \bar{x}_2}$ = Estimated standard error of the difference between population means
s_1^2 = Variance of sample 1
s_2^2 = Variance of sample 2
n_1 = Size of sample 1
n_2 = Size of sample 2

> The **standard error of the difference between population means** is the standard deviation of the sampling distribution of differences between all possible sample means of given sample sizes.

The standard error of the difference between population means calculated using Equation 10.1 or 10.2 is the standard deviation of the sampling distribution shown in Figure 10.1. This standard error is the denominator in the equation used to calculate the standardized difference between the sample means and the hypothesized population means:

$$z = \frac{(\bar{x}_1 - \bar{x}_2) - (\mu_1 - \mu_2)}{\sigma_{\bar{x}_1 - \bar{x}_2}}$$

Since we hypothesized that the difference between the population means is 0, Equation 10.3 omits the $(\mu_1 - \mu_2)$ term:

$$z = \frac{(\bar{x}_1 - \bar{x}_2)}{\sigma_{\bar{x}_1 - \bar{x}_2}} \qquad (10.3)$$

where $\sigma_{\bar{x}_1 - \bar{x}_2}$ = Standard error of the difference between population means
$\bar{x}_1$ = Mean from sample 1
$\bar{x}_2$ = Mean from sample 2

The following three examples illustrate the hypothesis test for two population means.

EXAMPLE 10.1   In preparing for upcoming union negotiations, Debbie Rush, chief labor negotiator for the Belmont Company, wants to know if there is more absenteeism among the company's unionized employees than among its nonunion employees. She has just read an article in *The Wall Street Journal* (May 19, 1992) describing a problem with disability claims in Ohio. Such claims accounted for almost 12% of employment discrimination cases in that state between 1985 and 1990. This article convinces Debbie that she must learn all she can about health problems in her company's work force, and she decides to start with absenteeism based on claimed health problems.

The null hypothesis she wants to test is that the average number of absent days per year is the same for both union and nonunion groups. Since Debbie is interested only in knowing if union absenteeism is higher, a one-tailed test is appropriate.

A random sample of workers is taken from each of the two groups: union and nonunion. The mean and standard deviation of absent days are calculated for each group:

$\bar{x}_1 = 9.3$ days $s_1 = 3.1$ days $n_1 = 50$ (Union)
$\bar{x}_2 = 8.7$ days $s_2 = 2.3$ days $n_2 = 45$ (Nonunion)

Debbie is tempted to cite the sample means as evidence in upcoming discussions with the union, but she realizes that the difference in sample means could be due to chance sampling error. The null and alternative hypotheses she decides to test are

$H_0: (\mu_1 - \mu_2) \leq 0$
$H_1: (\mu_1 - \mu_2) > 0$

If the null hypothesis is assumed true, the difference between the two sample means will be drawn from the sampling distribution in Figure 10.2.

Debbie decides to use a significance level of .05 for the test, which results in the following decision rule:

FIGURE 10.2   Sampling Distribution of Sample Mean Differences for Example 10.1

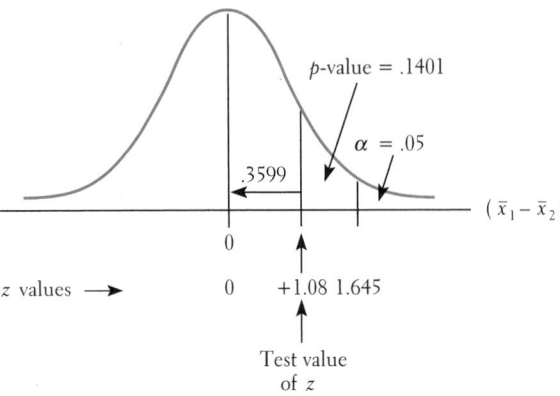

If the difference between the two sample means is more than 1.645 standard errors above the assumed mean (0) of the sampling distribution, reject the null hypothesis; otherwise, fail to reject it (reject H_0 if $z > 1.645$).

The estimate of the standard error of the difference between population means is calculated using Equation 10.2. Note that the sample standard deviations have been squared to produce the sample variances used as estimates of the unknown population variances:

$$s_{\bar{x}_1 - \bar{x}_2} = \sqrt{\frac{s_1^2}{n_1} + \frac{s_2^2}{n_2}}$$

$$= \sqrt{\frac{3.1^2}{50} + \frac{2.3^2}{45}} = \sqrt{0.1922 + 0.1176} = \sqrt{0.3098}$$

$$= 0.557$$

Since n_1 and n_2 are each 30 or greater, the samples are considered large and the z test can be used for the test of significance. The selection process must also meet another criterion underlying the use of the z test: sample independence. This means that the selection of one employee doesn't affect the selection of any other employee. The z value is calculated using the standard error of 0.557 as the denominator.

$$z = \frac{\bar{x}_1 - \bar{x}_2}{s_{\bar{x}_1 - \bar{x}_2}} = \frac{9.3 - 8.7}{0.557} = 1.08$$

The calculated z value is 1.08, indicating that the difference between the two sample means is 1.08 standard errors above 0, the mean of the assumed sampling distribution. Since the test value of z (1.08) isn't larger than the critical value of z from the standard normal table (1.645), the null hypothesis cannot be rejected. Debbie's evidence isn't strong enough for her to say that union employees have more absent days per year than nonunion employees. Although this is probably the correct conclusion, a type II error is possible.

When this example is run on a computer program, the result is a *p*-value of .1401. Since the *p*-value is greater than the significance level (.1401 > .05), the null hypothesis is not rejected.

A *z* value of 1.08, from the standard normal table, includes an area of .3599 above the mean as shown in Figure 10.2. Since the area on the upper end of the curve beyond the *z* value is wanted, .3599 is subtracted from .5000. The *p*-value is:

$$p\text{-value} = .5000 - .3599 = .1401 \text{ (area above a } z \text{ value of 1.08)}$$

EXAMPLE 10.2   Gene Marsh, the manager of a large mall, is very interested in the results of a study published in *The Journal of Social Psychology*.[1] The study tested whether fat customers experience longer response times from salespersons than their thinner counterparts. Observations were collected during 15-minute intervals on four consecutive Saturday afternoons in an urban shopping mall at two separate shoe stores. A total of 181 customers were classified as either fat or nonfat and the average time it took the salesperson to wait on them recorded. The mean response time to the nonfat group was 16.6 seconds while the mean response time to the fat group was 29.7 seconds. The null and alternative hypotheses are

$$H_0: \mu_1 - \mu_2 \geq 0$$
$$H_1: \mu_1 - \mu_2 < 0$$

A .10 significance level is chosen for this one-tailed test. The decision rule is

If the difference between the two sample means is more than 1.28 standard errors below the assumed mean (0) of the sampling distribution, reject the null hypothesis; otherwise, fail to reject it (reject H_0 if $z < -1.28$).

Suppose the sample results are:

$\bar{x}_1 = 16.6$ seconds	$s_1 = 11.6$ seconds	$n_1 = 106$
$\bar{x}_2 = 29.7$ seconds	$s_2 = 18.6$ seconds	$n_2 = 75$

The estimate of the standard error of the difference between population means is calculated using Equation 10.2:

$$s_{\bar{x}_1 - \bar{x}_2} = \sqrt{\frac{11.6^2}{106} + \frac{18.6^2}{75}} = \sqrt{1.269 + 4.613} = \sqrt{5.882}$$
$$s_{\bar{x}_1 - \bar{x}_2} = 2.425$$

The *z* value is then calculated using the standard error of 2.425 as the denominator:

$$z = \frac{16.6 - 29.7}{2.425} = \frac{-13.1}{2.425} = -5.4$$

---

[1] L. L. Pauley, "Customer Weight as a Variable in Salespersons' Response Time." *The Journal of Social Psychology* (1989), pp. 713–14.

Since the calculated value for z (-5.4) is lower than the critical value (-1.28), the hypothesis is rejected. Fat customers experienced longer response times from salespersons than nonfat customers. While this is probably the correct conclusion, a type I error is possible.

When Example 10.2 is run on a computer program, the result is a *p*-value of .0000. Since the *p*-value is less than the significance level (.0000 < .10), the null hypothesis is rejected.

A z value of -5.4, from the standard normal table, includes an area of approximately .5000 below the mean. Since the area on the lower end of the curve beyond the z value is wanted, .5000 is subtracted from .5000: *p*-value = .5000 − .5000 = .0000 (area below a z value of -5.4).

The probability of observing a difference in sample means as extreme as 13.1, given that the population mean difference is actually 0, is approximately .0000.

EXAMPLE 10.3   Colleen Heaton, a college grants writer, wants to know if the average age of students at her university is greater than the average for other universities in Alabama. If it is, this would strengthen the chances of a favorable response to her application for funds for adult education programs. At a conference, Colleen participates in a panel discussion involving on-the-job training's importance as an extension of college study. Each panel member is required to read an article about the value of learning in developing competitive improvements in a company (*Training and Development*, February 7, 1992, p. 33). Colleen takes a random sample of student records from her own university (population 1) and devises a method to randomly select student ages from the other three universities in the state (population 2). She chooses a significance level of .02 for this one-tailed test.

The hypotheses under test are

$$H_0: (\mu_1 - \mu_2) \leq 0$$
$$H_1: (\mu_1 - \mu_2) > 0$$

The decision rule is

If the difference between the two sample means is more than 2.05 standard errors above the assumed mean (0) of the sampling distribution, reject the null hypothesis (reject H_0 if $z > 2.05$).

The samples are selected and provide the following results:

$$\bar{x}_1 = 28.7 \text{ years} \qquad s_1 = 5.1 \text{ years} \qquad n_1 = 125$$
$$\bar{x}_2 = 24.9 \text{ years} \qquad s_2 = 3.5 \text{ years} \qquad n_2 = 250$$

The estimate of the standard error of the difference between population means is calculated using Equation 10.2:

$$s_{\bar{x}_1 - \bar{x}_2} = \sqrt{\frac{5.1^2}{125} + \frac{3.5^2}{250}} = \sqrt{0.208 + 0.049} = \sqrt{0.257}$$
$$= 0.507$$

The z value is calculated using the standard error of 0.507 as the denominator in Equation 10.3:

$$z = \frac{28.7 - 24.9}{0.507} = \frac{3.8}{0.507} = 7.50$$

Since the calculated z value is greater than the critical z value (7.50 > 2.05), the null hypothesis is rejected with small chance of error. Colleen is justified in claiming that the average age of students at her university is greater than the average for the other universities in the state.

When a computer program is used to test the three null hypotheses in this section, p-values appear in the printout. Recall from Chapter 9 that a p-value represents the area under the sampling distribution curve that lies beyond the z value calculated from the sample data. It thus constitutes the risk of a type I error that must be assumed if the null hypothesis is rejected. Table 10.1 shows the p-values for this chapter's hypothesis tests.

TABLE 10.1   Hypothesis Test p-Values

Example	Test z or t value	p-value (alpha for rejection)	Test conclusion
Example 10.1	1.08	.1401	Don't reject H_0
Example 10.2	−5.4	.0000	Reject H_0
Example 10.3	7.50	.0000	Reject H_0
Example 10.4	2.49	.0128*	Reject H_0
Example 10.5	2.19	.0561*	Reject H_0
Example 10.6	−1.11	.1335	Don't reject H_0
Example 10.7	−2.40	.0082	Reject H_0

*Computed using the CBS computer package.

EXERCISES

1. What is the difference between a one-sample test and a two-sample test?
2. When a two-sample test for the difference in population means is performed, what is the null hypothesis?
3. What is the test statistic for Exercise 2?
4. What does the sampling distribution for the difference between two population means depend on?
5. What do we call the standard deviation for the sampling distribution of the difference between two population means?
6. What is the mean of the sampling distribution of differences in population means?
7. What is the appropriate sampling distribution for a two-sample test when each of the sample sizes is 30 or greater?
8. What assumptions are made when the sampling distribution for Exercise 7 is used?

For the rest of the exercises in this section, assume that the observations in the two samples are independent.

9. Ted Gibbons, analyst for the National Painter's Union, is evaluating the mean drying times of two types of paint. The results of his experiment are

$$\bar{x}_1 = 320 \text{ minutes} \qquad s_1 = 25 \text{ minutes} \qquad n_1 = 32$$
$$\bar{x}_2 = 350 \text{ minutes} \qquad s_2 = 29 \text{ minutes} \qquad n_2 = 37$$

a. Does Ted have to assume equal variances?

b. Does Ted have to assume independent samples?

c. Does Ted have to assume normal populations?

d. Is the appropriate sampling distribution the normal curve?

e. Compute the standard error of the difference.

f. State the decision rule.

g. Using the .05 significance level, test to determine whether there is a difference between the mean drying times of the two types of paints.

h. What is Ted's conclusion?

10. For the past 10 years, Payless Rental Agency has been purchasing tires from the Union Tire Company to mount on its fleet of rental cars. A representative of the Goodwheel Tire Corporation claims that its brand gets better mileage. Payless decides to test the Goodwheel claim. Each company is asked to submit a random sample of 36 tires for a simulated road-wear test to determine the average time until wearout. The results are

$$\bar{x}_1 = 44,000 \text{ miles} \qquad s_1 = 3,500 \text{ miles} \qquad n_1 = 36 \text{ (Goodwheel)}$$
$$\bar{x}_2 = 41,000 \text{ miles} \qquad s_2 = 4,000 \text{ miles} \qquad n_2 = 36 \text{ (Union)}$$

Payless decides to test the Goodwheel claim at the .02 significance level.

a. State the alternative hypothesis.

b. Is the appropriate sampling distribution the normal curve or the t distribution?

c. State the decision rule.

d. Test to determine whether the Goodwheel claim is valid.

e. What should Payless conclude?

11. Chris Todd, personnel director of the Macro Corporation, has been instructed to determine if wage discrimination exists between the company's male and female employees. Chris decides to test a random sample of hourly wages for company employees. The results are

$$\bar{x}_1 = \$8.10 \qquad s_1 = \$0.95 \qquad n_1 = 75 \text{ (females)}$$
$$\bar{x}_2 = \$8.90 \qquad s_2 = \$1.10 \qquad n_2 = 75 \text{ (males)}$$

Chris tests at the .10 significance level to determine whether females have lower hourly wages than males. What is Chris's conclusion?

12. The Hewlet-Desoto Corporation is planning on locating a new plant in either Waukegan, Illinois, or Madison, Wisconsin. If the cost of new homes is significantly lower in either city relative to the other, the plant will be located there. A study is conducted to deter-

mine whether the average cost of new homes is significantly lower in Waukegan or Madison. The random sample results are

$$\bar{x}_1 = \$82,000 \qquad s_1 = \$10,525 \qquad n_1 = 60 \text{ (Waukegan)}$$
$$\bar{x}_2 = \$77,500 \qquad s_2 = \$9,830 \qquad n_2 = 60 \text{ (Madison)}$$

If the Hewlet-Desoto Corporation tests at the .01 significance level, will it find a difference in the cost of new homes between the two cities?

13. The Environmental Protection Agency (EPA) conducts studies designed to estimate cars' gas mileages. The EPA has been asked to compare highway mileages for cars using supreme unleaded versus regular unleaded gasoline. The EPA selects 80 cars and tests the number of miles per gallon obtained for each of 40 cars using supreme unleaded gasoline and each of 40 cars using regular unleaded gasoline. The results are

$$\bar{x}_1 = 29.3 \text{ mpg} \qquad s_1 = 1.9 \text{ mpg} \qquad n_1 = 40 \text{ (supreme unleaded)}$$
$$\bar{x}_2 = 28.9 \text{ mpg} \qquad s_2 = 1.7 \text{ mpg} \qquad n_2 = 40 \text{ (regular unleaded)}$$

What should the EPA conclude if the test is conducted using the .01 significance level?

14. According to *The Wall Street Journal* (May 16, 1988), the average annual hours per worker in the United States total 1,898; in Japan, this figure is 2,152. Suppose these values are based on random samples of 800 U.S. workers and 500 Japanese workers. The standard deviations of annual hours are 153 for the U.S. workers and 187 for the Japanese. Do Japanese workers spend more hours on the job than American workers? Use a significance level of .05.

HYPOTHESIS TESTING ABOUT THE DIFFERENCE BETWEEN TWO POPULATION MEANS: SMALL SAMPLES

Analysts must sometimes test for a difference between two population means using small samples. This test is used when sampling items means destroying them, when sampling is very expensive, or when only a few historical values can be obtained.

The test is the same as the two-population mean test for large samples, except that the t distribution is used instead of the normal curve. The t test is considered appropriate when either sample size is less than 30. Use of the t distribution assumes:

1. The observations in the two samples are independent.
2. The two populations are approximately normal.
3. The two populations have equal variances.

Equation 10.1 showed that the standard error of the difference between two population means equals the square root of the sum of the two population variances, which are adjusted for sample size. Since it's assumed that the two populations have equal variances ($\sigma_1^2 = \sigma_2^2$), Equation 10.1 can be rewritten as

$$\sigma_{\bar{x}_1 - \bar{x}_2} = \sigma\sqrt{\frac{1}{n_1} + \frac{1}{n_2}} \qquad\qquad (10.4)$$

If the variance, σ^2, is unknown, the two sample variances can be used to compute a **pooled estimate of the variance.** Equation 10.5 is used to solve for the square root of this pooled estimate of the variance:

$$s_{pooled} = \sqrt{\frac{s_1^2 (n_1 - 1) + s_2^2 (n_2 - 1)}{n_1 + n_2 - 2}} \tag{10.5}$$

> **A pooled estimate of the variance** of a population is based on the combination of two or more sample variances and is appropriate whenever the variances of two or more populations are assumed equal.

If the square root of the pooled estimate of the variance (s) is substituted for σ in Equation 10.4, the result is the estimate of the standard deviation of the sampling distribution (called the standard error of the difference):

$$s_{\bar{x}_1 - \bar{x}_2} = s_{pooled} \sqrt{\frac{1}{n_1} + \frac{1}{n_2}} \tag{10.6}$$

The standard error of the difference between population means forms the denominator in Equation 10.7, which is used to calculate the test t value.

$$t = \frac{\bar{x}_1 - \bar{x}_2}{s_{\bar{x}_1 - \bar{x}_2}} \tag{10.7}$$

where $s_{\bar{x}_1 - \bar{x}_2}$ = Standard error of the difference between population means

$\bar{x}_1$ = Mean from sample 1

$\bar{x}_2$ = Mean from sample 2

The null hypothesis to be tested is that the two populations from which the samples were taken have the same mean. Under the assumption that this hypothesis is true, the sample statistic is computed using Equation 10.7. A significance level is then chosen, and the t table is consulted for the critical test value, where the correct number of degrees of freedom is $(n_1 - 1) + (n_2 - 1)$, or $(n_1 + n_2 - 2)$. Two degrees of freedom are lost because two sample statistics (the sample variances) are used as estimates of population parameters in the computation of the pooled variance. If the test statistic is less than this critical value, the null hypothesis is not rejected. If it is greater than the critical value, the null hypothesis is rejected at the chosen significance level.

EXAMPLE 10.4 The Bates Company has come up with a new manufacturing process for making the tubing used in high-quality bicycle frames. Because strength is such an important element in the design of a bicycle frame, a few of the frames made with the new tubing are to be stress-tested and the failure points compared with those of the conventional frames made by the company. Because the frames are quite expensive in terms of both materials and labor, it's decided to stress-test eight new frames and seven old ones; each frame will be subjected to an increasing load force until failure. The company will use a machine that gives a combined stress reading as it increases the stress load.

The null and alternative hypotheses are

$$H_0: (\mu_1 - \mu_2) \leq 0$$
$$H_1: (\mu_1 - \mu_2) > 0$$

If the null hypothesis is assumed true, the difference between the two sample means will be drawn from the sampling distribution in Figure 10.3. A significance level of .05 is chosen for the test. The t table is consulted using df $= (8 + 7 - 2) = 13$. The critical t value for a one-tailed test, found in the .05 column of the t table, is 1.771. The decision rule is

If the difference between the two sample means is more than 1.771 standard errors above the assumed mean (0) of the sampling distributions, reject the null hypothesis (reject H_0 if $t > 1.771$).

The samples are selected and provide the following results:

New frames	Old frames
$\bar{x}_1 = 27.8$ units	$\bar{x}_2 = 23.7$ units
$n_1 = 8$	$n_2 = 7$
$s_1 = 3.4$ units	$s_2 = 2.9$ units

The square root of the pooled estimate of the variance is computed using Equation 10.5:

$$s_{\text{pooled}} = \sqrt{\frac{s_1^2(n_1 - 1) + s_2^2(n_2 - 1)}{n_1 + n_2 - 2}}$$

FIGURE 10.3 Sampling Distribution of Sample Mean Differences for Example 10.4

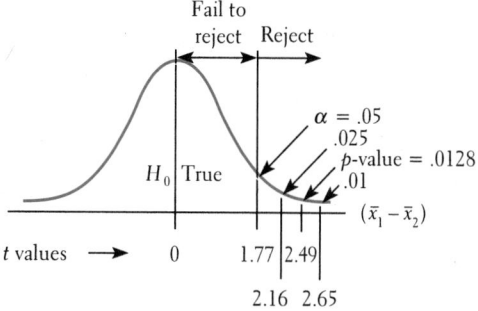

$$= \sqrt{\frac{3.4^2(8-1) + 2.9^2(7-1)}{8+7-2}}$$
$$= \sqrt{10.106}$$
$$= 3.18$$

This value, 3.18, is substituted into Equation 10.6 to compute the standard error of the difference.

$$s_{\bar{x}_1 - \bar{x}_2} = 3.18 \sqrt{\frac{1}{8} + \frac{1}{7}} = 3.18(0.518) = 1.647$$

The standard error of the difference between population means, calculated using Equation 10.6, forms the denominator of Equation 10.7, which is used to calculate the t value:

$$t = \frac{\bar{x}_1 - \bar{x}_2}{s_{\bar{x}_1 - \bar{x}_2}} = \frac{27.8 - 23.7}{1.647} = \frac{4.1}{1.647} = 2.49$$

Since the test value for t (2.49) is larger than the critical t value (1.771), the null hypothesis is rejected at the .05 significance level. Bates concludes, based on its small sample, that the new frames do exceed the old frames in terms of strength. Bates believes it may have made a breakthrough in bicycle frame construction. However, the company would feel much better about this conclusion if a larger sample had been used.

When this example is run on a computer program, the result is a *p*-value of .0128. Since the *p*-value is less than the significance level (.0128 < .05), the null hypothesis is rejected.

A t value of 2.49 lies between 2.160 and 2.650 in the t table for 13 degrees of freedom. Figure 10.3 shows that .025 represents the area above the t value of 2.16, and .01 represents the area above the t value of 2.65. The CBS computer program provides a *p*-value of .0128 shown as the area above 2.49 in Figure 10.3.

EXERCISES

15. What is the appropriate sampling distribution for a two-sample test when sample sizes are smaller than 30?

16. What assumptions are required when the appropriate sampling distribution for Exercise 15 is used?

17. Two shipments of nylon cord have just arrived from different suppliers. The company analyst decides to test for any difference in tensile strength. The results of the test, in pounds per square inch, are:

Supplier A	Supplier B
37	41
39	42
41	38

Supplier A	Supplier B
35	45
36	40
34	39
38	

a. Does the analyst have to assume equal variances?

b. Does the analyst have to assume independence?

c. Does the analyst have to assume normal populations?

d. Is the appropriate sampling distribution the normal curve or the t distribution?

e. Compute the square root of the pooled estimate of the variance for the two samples.

f. Compute the appropriate number of degrees of freedom.

g. Compute the standard error of the difference.

h. State the decision rule.

i. Using the .05 significance level, test to determine whether the two suppliers' nylon cords have the same mean tensile strength.

For the rest of the exercises in this section, assume that the observations in the two samples are independent, the two populations are approximately normal, and the populations have equal variances.

18. The Eastern Publishing Company hires college students to sell books during the summer. The company wants to evaluate the effectiveness of the new training program. To measure its efficiency, a company representative randomly selects a group of salespeople, records for each person the number of sales consummated during the past summer, and indicates whether the salesperson participated in the new training program. The results are

$$\bar{x}_1 = 482 \text{ books} \qquad s_1 = 43 \text{ books} \qquad n_1 = 22 \text{ (training)}$$
$$\bar{x}_2 = 465 \text{ books} \qquad s_2 = 39 \text{ books} \qquad n_2 = 27 \text{ (no training)}$$

a. State the null and alternative hypotheses.

b. Is the appropriate sampling distribution the normal curve or the t distribution?

c. State the decision rule.

d. Do these data present sufficient evidence to indicate a difference in the average number of books sold at the .05 significance level?   – No

19. Exercise 13 discussed EPA studies designed to estimate auto gas mileage. Suppose the EPA is comparing city mileages for station wagons versus four-door sedans. The EPA selects 24 station wagons and 22 sedans and determines the miles per gallon rating (mpg) for each. The results are

$$\bar{x}_1 = 28.2 \text{ mpg} \qquad s_1 = 1.9 \text{ mpg} \qquad n_1 = 24 \text{ (wagons)}$$
$$\bar{x}_2 = 31.5 \text{ mpg} \qquad s_2 = 2.1 \text{ mpg} \qquad n_2 = 22 \text{ (sedans)}$$

a. State the null and alternative hypotheses.

b. Is the appropriate sampling distribution the normal curve or the t distribution?

c. State the decision rule.

d. What should the EPA conclude if the test is conducted at the .05 significance level?

20. The Tendy Corporation wants to determine if productivity will be increased by instituting a bonus plan. The corporation decides to use the bonus plan in 13 randomly selected plants and compare the results with 15 plants that operate on the usual salary basis. The number of units produced per day is

$$\bar{x}_1 = 45 \text{ units} \qquad s_1 = 7 \text{ units} \qquad n_1 = 13 \text{ (bonus)}$$
$$\bar{x}_2 = 43 \text{ units} \qquad s_2 = 6 \text{ units} \qquad n_2 = 15 \text{ (salary)}$$

   a. State the null and alternative hypotheses.

   b. What should the Tendy Corporation conclude if the test is conducted at the .01 significance level?

21. The General Automobile Company is considering the purchase of batteries in bulk from two suppliers. A sample of 15 batteries is randomly selected from each supplier and tested. The mean lifetimes are

$$\bar{x}_1 = 1{,}345 \text{ hours} \qquad s_1 = 31 \text{ hours} \qquad n_1 = 15 \text{ (A)}$$
$$\bar{x}_2 = 1{,}310 \text{ hours} \qquad s_2 = 28 \text{ hours} \qquad n_2 = 15 \text{ (B)}$$

   a. State the null and alternative hypotheses.

   b. What should General Automobile conclude if the test is conducted at the .05 significance level?

HYPOTHESIS TESTING FOR MEANS: DEPENDENT SAMPLES

In Exercise 13 of this chapter, the Environmental Protection Agency compared highway mileages for automobiles using supreme unleaded versus regular unleaded gasoline. A total of 80 cars were tested: 40 used supreme unleaded gas, and the other 40 used regular unleaded gas. Different samples were used because one of the underlying assumptions of the two-sample mean test is independence of samples.

What if the EPA had tested the same 40 cars using supreme unleaded gas in one trial and regular unleaded gas in another? This would eliminate the possibility of one sample containing a large number of cars that normally get excellent gas mileage. Unlike the test in Exercise 13, which involved independent samples, the EPA could have

Matched Pairs

used **matched pairs,** so called because two sets of measurements are taken for each automobile: one for supreme unleaded gas and a second for regular unleaded gas. The same number of cars with excellent gas mileage would be contained in both the supreme unleaded and the regular unleaded groups. In the matched-pairs test, there's no need to assume that the two underlying populations have equal variances. The only assumption necessary is that the population of differences is normal.

Note that it is difficult to design a matched-pairs experiment. One criterion for this type of test is that the treatment doesn't change the subjects or objects being examined.

> **Matched pairs** result when each data value in one sample is matched with a corresponding data value in the other sample.

The matched-pair t test focuses on the differences in paired observations. It involves computing the mean and standard deviation of the differences. Equation 10.8 simply substitutes the difference (d) for x in Equation 4.1 to compute the mean:

$$\bar{d} = \frac{\Sigma d}{n} \tag{10.8}$$

where $\bar{d}$ = Average difference between the paired observations
  d = Difference
  n = Number of differences

Equation 10.9 substitutes the difference (d) for x in Equation 4.8 and takes the square root to compute the standard deviation of the differences:

$$s_d = \sqrt{\frac{\Sigma d^2 - \dfrac{(\Sigma d)^2}{n}}{n - 1}} \tag{10.9}$$

The standard deviation of the sampling distribution is the sample standard deviation, computed using Equation 10.9, divided by the square root of the sample size. Equation 10.10 shows this standard deviation as the denominator of the formula for the matched-pairs t test for dependent samples:

$$t = \frac{\bar{d}}{s_d / \sqrt{n}} \tag{10.10}$$

where s_d = Standard deviation of the differences
  $\bar{d}$ = Average difference between the paired observations
  n = Number of differences

EXAMPLE 10.5 The EPA selects a sample of 10 cars to determine if there's a significant difference in mileage between supreme unleaded gas and regular unleaded gas. The null and alternative hypotheses are

H_0: $(\mu_1 - \mu_2) = 0$
H_1: $(\mu_1 - \mu_2) \neq 0$

A significance level of .10 is chosen for the test. The number of degrees of freedom for the matched-pairs t test is $n - 1$, so the t table is consulted for df = $(10 - 1) = 9$. The critical t value for a two-tailed test is found in the .10 column of the t table, indicating a critical value of 1.833. The decision rule is

If the average difference between the paired observations is more than 1.833 standard errors above or below the assumed mean (0) of the sampling distribution, reject the null hypothesis (reject H_0 if $t < -1.833$ or $t > 1.833$).

The results of the EPA test are:

Automobile	Supreme unleaded	Regular unleaded	Difference (d)	Squared difference (d^2)
1	28.2	27.4	0.8	0.64
2	30.1	29.0	1.1	1.21
3	32.8	29.4	3.4	11.56
4	30.0	28.0	2.0	4.00
5	28.9	31.0	-2.1	4.41
6	31.0	29.6	1.4	1.96
7	32.3	28.3	4.0	16.00
8	30.4	29.6	0.8	0.64
9	27.0	27.0	0.0	0.00
10	28.5	28.0	0.5	0.25
			11.9	40.67

From Equation 10.8, the average difference between the paired observations is

$$\bar{d} = \frac{\Sigma d}{n} = \frac{11.9}{10} = 1.19$$

From Equation 10.9, the standard deviation of the differences is

$$s_d = \sqrt{\frac{\Sigma d^2 - \frac{(\Sigma d)^2}{n}}{n - 1}} = \sqrt{\frac{40.67 - \frac{(11.9)^2}{10}}{10 - 1}}$$

$$= \sqrt{\frac{40.67 - 14.16}{9}} = \sqrt{\frac{26.51}{9}} = \sqrt{2.95} = 1.72$$

The matched-pairs t statistic is

$$t = \frac{\bar{d}}{s_d/\sqrt{n}} = \frac{1.19}{1.72/\sqrt{10}} = \frac{1.19}{0.544} = 2.19$$

Since the test value for t (2.19) is larger than the critical t value of 1.833, the null hypothesis is rejected at the .10 significance level. The EPA concludes, based on its small sample, that the supreme unleaded gas gave significantly better mileage than the regular unleaded gas. Although this is probably the correct conclusion, a type I error, which would occur if the mileage is the same for the two types of gasoline, is possible.

EXERCISES

22. Explain the difference between dependent and independent samples.

23. Burgans Furniture has asked the Create America Advertising Agency to develop a new advertising campaign. Burgans' marketing manager, Megan Hubble, decides to evaluate the

campaign's effectiveness. Megan collects data on monthly sales before and during the campaign for eight regional stores. The results are:

Store	Average sales before	Average sales during
1	$63,458	$65,496
2	48,510	52,462
3	51,203	50,864
4	75,241	79,520
5	60,123	71,145
6	55,555	55,600
7	45,456	48,654
8	57,438	60,897

a. State the null and alternative hypotheses.

b. Is the appropriate sampling distribution the normal curve or the t distribution?

c. State the decision rule.

d. Using the .05 significance level, test to determine if the advertising campaign was effective.

e. What should Megan conclude?

24. Pam Soltaro teaches typing and word processing at City Community College. Pam feels that students type faster on computer-based word processors than on electronic typewriters. She decides to test this hypothesis on nine advanced students. The results, in words per minute, are:

Student	Word processor	Electronic typewriter
1	55	51
2	69	65
3	70	70
4	75	76
5	82	80
6	65	62
7	60	57
8	73	71
9	77	72

a. State the null and alternative hypotheses.

b. Is the appropriate sampling distribution the normal curve or the t distribution?

c. State the decision rule.

d. Using the .025 significance level, test to determine if students type faster on word processors.

e. What should Pam conclude?

25. The Gilbert Research Company is testing two commercials for the Detroit Edison Electric Company. Both commercials were shown to 12 customers, who were asked to rate the commercials on a dial with a scale from 1 to 100. The results are:

Customer	Value received commercial	Electric card commercial
1	95	87
2	59	65
3	73	80
4	65	73
5	32	45
6	45	39
7	60	57
8	83	81
9	27	33
10	50	40
11	63	66
12	95	93

a. State the null and alternative hypotheses.

b. Is the appropriate sampling distribution the normal curve or the *t* distribution?

c. State the decision rule.

d. Using the .10 significance level, test to determine whether customers liked one campaign better than the other.

e. What should Gilbert Research conclude?

26. Jim Dyke, owner of the Westside Bowling Alley, wants to offer a special promotion. Jim would like to advertise bowling lessons that are guaranteed to improve a person's score. Before offering a money-back guarantee, Jim decides to test the claim on a sample of 15 people. Jim records participant scores for three games bowled before the lessons and compares them with scores from three games bowled after the lessons are completed. The results are:

Participant	Before lessons	After lessons
1	270	300
2	300	325
3	175	280
4	243	298
5	305	291
6	330	356
7	350	382
8	274	273
9	297	361
10	306	326
11	385	412
12	411	458
13	241	287
14	258	264
15	308	342

a. State the null and alternative hypotheses.

b. State the decision rule using the .05 significance level.

c. Test to determine whether participants improved after the bowling lessons.

d. What should Jim conclude?

HYPOTHESIS TESTING FOR PROPORTIONS FROM TWO POPULATIONS

An analyst may wish to compare two populations on the basis of the proportion or percentage of their members that meet certain conditions. The four hypothesis-testing steps from Chapter 9 are used for this test.

To test for the difference between two population proportions, a random sample from each population is taken and the sample proportion calculated for each. The difference between the sample proportions is the test statistic, and its sampling distribution is the normal distribution. The null hypothesis under test is that the two populations have the same proportion. This hypothesis will not be rejected unless sufficient evidence is gathered to reject it with small chance of error. For a two-tailed test, the null and alternative hypotheses are

$$H_0: p_1 - p_2 = 0$$
$$H_1: p_1 - p_2 \neq 0$$

For a one-tailed test, the null and alternative hypotheses are either

$$H_0: p_1 - p_2 \leq 0 \quad \text{or} \quad H_0: p_1 - p_2 \geq 0$$
$$H_1: p_1 - p_2 > 0 \qquad\qquad H_1: p_1 - p_2 < 0$$

Note that 0 could be replaced in these hypotheses with any value of interest. For example, the null and alternative hypotheses might be

$$H_0: p_1 - p_2 = .20$$
$$H_1: p_1 - p_2 \neq .20$$

If the null hypothesis is assumed true, the sampling distribution will have a mean of 0, the difference between the population proportions. Sample proportion differences are thus arrayed about the mean of 0 on a normal curve, as shown in Figure 10.4.

As suggested by Figure 10.4, if the difference between the sample proportions is close to 0, this supports the null hypothesis that the populations have the same

FIGURE 10.4 Sampling Distribution of Sample Proportion Differences

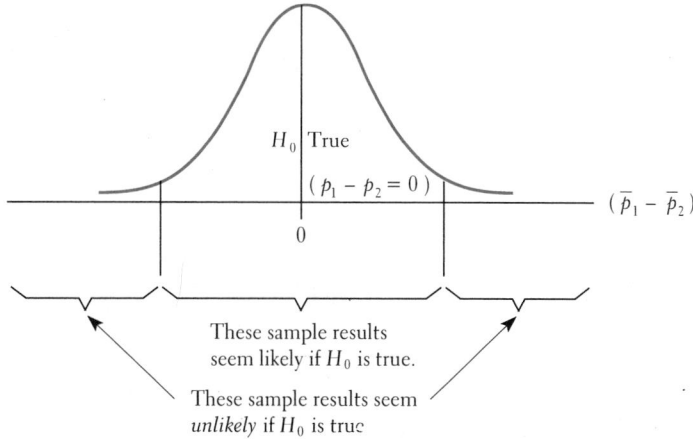

These sample results seem likely if H_0 is true.

These sample results seem *unlikely* if H_0 is true

proportion. In this case, the null hypothesis will not be rejected. If the samples have very different proportions, the null hypothesis will be rejected.

In the two-sample test for proportions, the pooled estimate of the population proportion ($\hat{p}$) is computed by averaging the two sample proportions:

$$\hat{p} = \frac{x_1 + x_2}{n_1 + n_2} \qquad (10.11)$$

where x_1 = Number of successes in sample 1
        x_2 = Number of successes in sample 2
        n_1 = Size of sample 1
        n_2 = Size of sample 2

Note that if the population proportions are equal ($p_1 = p_2$), then the two samples came from the same population. If each sample proportion is viewed as an estimate of the same population proportion, combining the two samples, as is done in Equation 10.11, should provide an improved estimate of the true value of the population proportion.

The pooled estimate of the population proportion ($\hat{p}$) is used in Equation 10.12 to compute the standard deviation of the sampling distribution of the differences (called the **standard error of the difference between population proportions**):

$$\sigma_{\bar{p}_1 - \bar{p}_2} = \sqrt{\hat{p}(1 - \hat{p})\left(\frac{1}{n_1} + \frac{1}{n_2}\right)} \qquad (10.12)$$

where $\sigma_{\bar{p}_1 - \bar{p}_2}$ = Estimate of the standard error of the difference between
                          population proportions
        $\hat{p}$ = Pooled estimate of the population proportion
        n_1 = Size of sample 1
        n_2 = Size of sample 2

> The **standard error of the difference between population proportions** is the standard deviation of the sampling distribution of differences between all possible sample proportions for given sample sizes.

The standard error calculated using Equation 10.12 constitutes the denominator in the equation that analyzes the difference between the sample proportions and the hypothesized population proportions:

$$z = \frac{(\bar{p}_1 - \bar{p}_2) - (p_1 - p_2)}{\sigma_{\bar{p}_1 - \bar{p}_2}}$$

Since it's hypothesized that the difference between the population proportions is 0, Equation 10.13 is developed without the $(p_1 - p_2)$ term:

$$z = \frac{\bar{p}_1 - \bar{p}_2}{\sigma_{\bar{p}_1 - \bar{p}_2}}$$ (10.13)

where $\sigma_{\bar{p}_1 - \bar{p}_2}$ = Standard error of the difference between population proportions
$\bar{p}_1$ = Proportion of successes for sample 1
$\bar{p}_2$ = Proportion of successes for sample 2

The null hypothesis being tested is that the two populations from which the samples were taken have the same proportion. Under the assumption that this hypothesis is true, the sample statistic is computed using Equation 10.13. A significance level is then chosen, and the z table is consulted for the critical test value. If the test statistic is less than this critical value, the null hypothesis is not rejected. If it's greater than the critical value, the null hypothesis is rejected at the chosen significance level.

It is usually not helpful to compare two population proportions using small samples. This test is not sensitive enough to detect a difference when small samples are used; therefore, the normal distribution will be used along with large sample sizes in the following examples.

EXAMPLE 10.6   Joseph Conrad, an economic analyst for the state of West Virginia, wants to determine whether the unemployment rate is the same or different for two towns in the state's coal mining region. The null and alternative hypotheses are

H_0: $(p_1 - p_2) = 0$
H_1: $(p_1 - p_2) \neq 0$

Joseph decides to use a significance level of .05 for the test, resulting in the following decision rule:

If the difference between the two sample proportions is more than 1.96 standard errors below or above the assumed mean (0) of the sampling distribution, reject the null hypothesis (reject H_0 if $z < -1.96$ or $z > 1.96$).

Joseph selects random samples of people from each town and computes these results:

$x_1 = 55$ people unemployed $n_1 = 550$ people
$x_2 = 90$ people unemployed $n_2 = 750$ people

The pooled estimate of the population proportion ($\hat{p}$) is computed by averaging the two sample proportions using Equation 10.11:

$$\hat{p} = \frac{x_1 + x_2}{n_1 + n_2} = \frac{55 + 90}{550 + 750} = \frac{145}{1,300} = .1115$$

The standard deviation of the sampling distribution of the differences between proportions (the standard error of the difference) is computed by inserting the pooled estimate of the population proportion (.1115) into Equation 10.12:

$$\sigma_{\bar{p}_1 - \bar{p}_2} = \sqrt{\hat{p}(1 - \hat{p})\left(\frac{1}{n_1} + \frac{1}{n_2}\right)} = \sqrt{.1115(.8885)\left(\frac{1}{550} + \frac{1}{750}\right)}$$

$$= \sqrt{(.099)(.0032)} = \sqrt{.000317} = .018$$

The z value is calculated using the standard error of .018 as the denominator in Equation 10.13:

$$z = \frac{\bar{p}_1 - \bar{p}_2}{\sigma_{\bar{p}_1 - \bar{p}_2}} = \frac{.10 - .12}{.018} = -1.11$$

The calculated z value is -1.11, indicating that the difference between the two sample proportions is 1.11 standard errors below 0, the mean of the assumed sampling distribution. Since the test value of z (-1.11) isn't lower than the critical value of z from the standard normal table (-1.96), the null hypothesis cannot be rejected. The sample evidence isn't strong enough to reject the hypothesis that the two towns have the same unemployment rate. Although this is probably the correct conclusion, a type II error is possible.

EXAMPLE 10.7 A union suspects that more men than women work over 40 hours per week in a large plant. The union complains to management about discrimination toward women in assigning overtime. The union and the company agree to use a random sample of worker records from the past year to decide this issue. Since the suspicion is that the population of women working overtime is less than that of men, a one-tailed test is suggested. The null and alternative hypotheses, along with the sample evidence resulting from a large random sample of employee records, are

$$H_0{:}(p_1 - p_2) \geq 0$$
$$H_1{:}(p_1 - p_2) < 0$$

where p_1 = Population proportion of women
p_2 = Population proportion of men
x_1 = 114 women worked overtime n_1 = 875 women
x_2 = 162 men worked overtime n_2 = 950 men

The union and management analysts agree to use a significance level of .05 for the test, leading to the following decision rule:

If the difference between the two sample proportions is more than 1.645 standard errors below the assumed mean (0) of the sampling distribution, reject the null hypothesis (reject H_0 if $z < -1.645$).

The pooled estimate of the population proportion ($\hat{p}$) is computed by averaging the two sample proportions using Equation 10.11:

$$\hat{p} = \frac{114 + 162}{875 + 950} = \frac{276}{1,825} = .15$$

The standard error of the difference is computed by using the pooled estimate of the population proportion (.15) in Equation 10.12:

$$\sigma_{\bar{p}_1 - \bar{p}_2} = \sqrt{(.15)(.85)\left(\frac{1}{875} + \frac{1}{950}\right)} = .0167$$

The z value is calculated using the standard error of .0167 as the denominator in Equation 10.13:

$$z = \frac{\bar{p}_1 - \bar{p}_2}{\sigma_{\bar{p}_1 - \bar{p}_2}} = \frac{.13 - .17}{.0167} = -2.40$$

Since the z value from the sample exceeds the critical z value from the standard normal table ($-2.40 < -1.645$), the null hypothesis is rejected. It is concluded that women workers are putting in less overtime than men. Company management can argue that the sample results are misleading, that discrimination in overtime doesn't really exist. In effect, they would be arguing that a type I error has been committed. However, since there's only a 5% chance of such an error, the company would be wise to modify its overtime policy rather than fight the sample findings.

Table 10.1 lists the calculated z values for the tests of this section along with the computed p-values.

EXERCISES

27. For a two-sample test for the difference in population proportions, what is the null hypothesis?

28. What is the test statistic for Exercise 27?

29. What assumptions does the sampling distribution for the difference between two population proportions depend on?

30. What is the standard deviation of the sampling distribution for the difference between two population proportions called?

31. What is the mean of the sampling distribution of differences in population proportions?

32. According to a *USA Today*/CNN Gallup poll of 755 registered voters conducted on July 17–18, 1992 (*USA Today*), 56% supported Bill Clinton. *Newsweek* (July 27, 1992) reported a survey that indicated 59% favored Clinton. Suppose the *Newsweek* survey was based on a sample of 1,032 voters. If the two samples were randomly selected from the same population, what is the pooled estimate of the variance for the percentage of voters who favor Clinton? If tested at the .05 significance level, do the data provide sufficient evidence to indicate that the two samples were selected from different populations?

33. The Latah Creek Winery presently markets in the state of Oregon. The winery is considering expansion to Idaho and must determine if a new marketing strategy is needed for this market. One of its best white wines is taste-tested in both regions, and the proportions of wine drinkers who liked the wine are recorded:

$$x_1 = 372 \text{ liked the wine} \qquad n_1 = 600 \text{ (Idaho)}$$
$$x_2 = 544 \text{ liked the wine} \qquad n_2 = 800 \text{ (Oregon)}$$

a. State the null and alternative hypotheses.

b. Is the appropriate sampling distribution the normal curve or the *t* distribution?

c. Compute the standard error of the difference.

d. State the decision rule.

e. Using the .01 significance level, test to determine whether there's a difference between the proportions of wine drinkers who liked the wine.

f. What should the Latah Creek Winery conclude?

34. In Exercise 25, the Gilbert Research Company agreed to test two advertising campaigns for the Detroit Edison Electric Company. Two TV commercials were developed and shown in the company's market area on the three local channels over a three-day period. The following week Gilbert Research conducted a telephone survey to identify people who had seen the commercials. People who had seen only one commercial were asked to state its primary message. The results are

$x_1 = 72$ recalled primary message $n_1 = 152$ (value received commercial)
$x_2 = 74$ recalled primary message $n_2 = 171$ (electric card commercial)

a. State the null and alternative hypotheses.

b. Is the appropriate sampling distribution the normal curve or the *t* distribution?

c. Compute the standard error of the difference.

d. State the decision rule.

e. Using the .10 significance level, test to determine whether there's a difference between the proportions of people who recalled the primary message of each commercial.

f. What should Gilbert Research conclude?

35. *The Wall Street Journal*, May 23, 1988, reported the percentage of fatal accidents involving car rollovers to be different for small cars and large cars. For the former, the percentage was 26%; for the latter, it was 21%. If these results were based on samples of 150 from each group, would you conclude that large cars are safer?

SUMMARY
. . . .

You have now been exposed to several kinds of hypothesis tests widely used in the business world. Each of these tests follows the same four steps discussed early in Chapter 9:

1. The null and alternative hypotheses are stated.

2. The null hypothesis is assumed true, and the sampling distribution for the test is identified based on this assumption.

3. A random sample is taken from the population(s) under study and the appropriate sample statistic computed.

4. The likelihood that the sample statistic could have been drawn from the assumed sampling distribution is assessed. If this probability is high, the null hypothesis is not rejected. If this probability is low, the null hypothesis is rejected.

Table 10.2 summarizes the hypothesis tests that have been presented. The null hypothesis to be tested appears in the first column. The second column provides the appropriate sample statistic to be computed from the sample data. The third column shows the sampling distribution for the test, and the fourth column shows the parameters of that distribution under the assumption that the null hypothesis is true.

TABLE 10.2   Hypothesis Test Summary

H_0	Test statistic	Sampling distribution	Parameters of sampling distribution
$\mu = 150^*$	$\bar{x}$	Normal or t	μ and $\sigma/\sqrt{n}$
$p = .75^*$	$\bar{p}$	Normal	p and $\sqrt{\dfrac{p(1-p)}{n}}$
$(\mu_1 - \mu_2) = 0$	$\bar{x}_1 - \bar{x}_2$	Normal or t	0 and $\sqrt{\dfrac{\sigma_1^2}{n_1} + \dfrac{\sigma_2^2}{n_2}}$
$(p_1 - p_2) = 0$	$\bar{p}_1 - \bar{p}_2$	Normal	0 and $\sqrt{p(1-p)\left(\dfrac{1}{n_1} + \dfrac{1}{n_2}\right)}$

*Example value

By referring to Table 10.2, you should be able to conduct any of the hypothesis tests discussed so far. Also, additional hypothesis tests that you'll encounter in this text and in the business world should be easy for you to conduct. The same four steps are followed in every hypothesis test; you need only know the correct sample statistic to compute, the correct sampling distribution to consult, and the parameters of that distribution.

APPLICATIONS OF STATISTICAL CONCEPTS IN THE BUSINESS WORLD
. . . .

THE SPOKANE TRANSIT AUTHORITY'S USE OF HYPOTHESIS TESTING

Christine Fueston is planning manager for the Spokane Transit Authority (STA). One of her responsibilities is ensuring that the data reported to the Urban Mass Transit Authority (UMTA) are collected in accordance with the Uniform System of Accounts and Records and Reporting System requirements. She must report fixed-route motorbus passenger mile data along with van pool ridership and mileage data.

Christine has developed a sampling plan that's in compliance with the sampling procedures for obtaining fixed-route bus operating data. Using this plan, she sends surveyors out to ride the buses and collect the appropriate information. Statistical issues that concern her are sample size, precision, and confidence levels. Christine frequently must test hypotheses about population parameters using sample statistics. Since bus routes change from year to year, she must sometimes perform a two-population hypothesis test to determine whether the statistical base has shifted from year to year. If so, funding relationships with the federal government could change.

   After Christine has completed her analysis each year, she is required to hire an independent statistician to verify and validate her work.

OTHER APPLICATIONS

As mentioned in Chapter 9, hypothesis tests are widely employed in practical situations to test claims or suspicions about populations using sample data. The hypothesis tests covered in this chapter are two-population tests for means and proportions. Here are examples of questions that might be answered by one of the hypothesis tests presented in this chapter.

   How do two alcoholic treatment centers compare on the percentage of clients who are alcohol-free one year after treatment?

   Is the average price of a basket of food the same or different between Safeway and Dominick's food stores?

   Are the percentages of defective parts from two suppliers the same or different?

   Is the percentage of clients over age 65 the same or different for Blue Cross compared with Group Health?

GLOSSARY

Standard error of the difference between population means The standard deviation of the sampling distribution of differences between all possible sample means for given sample sizes.

Pooled estimate of the variance The combination of two or more sample variances, which is appropriate whenever the variances of two or more populations are assumed equal.

Matched pairs The matching of each data value in one sample with a corresponding data value in the other sample.

Standard error of the difference between population proportions The standard deviation of the sampling distribution of differences between all possible sample proportions for given sample sizes.

KEY FORMULAS

Standard error of the difference between two population means

$$\sigma_{\bar{x}_1 - \bar{x}_2} = \sqrt{\frac{\sigma_1^2}{n_1} + \frac{\sigma_2^2}{n_2}} \tag{10.1}$$

Estimated standard error of the difference between two population means

$$s_{\bar{x}_1 - \bar{x}_2} = \sqrt{\frac{s_1^2}{n_1} + \frac{s_2^2}{n_2}} \tag{10.2}$$

Two-sample mean z test statistic

$$z = \frac{\bar{x}_1 - \bar{x}_2}{\sigma_{\bar{x}_1 - \bar{x}_2}} \tag{10.3}$$

Standard error of the difference between two population means when the variances are equal

$$\sigma_{\bar{x}_1 - \bar{x}_2} = \sigma \sqrt{\frac{1}{n_1} + \frac{1}{n_2}} \qquad (10.4)$$

Pooled variance estimate

$$s_{\text{pooled}} = \sqrt{\frac{s_1^2 (n_1 - 1) + s_2^2 (n_2 - 1)}{n_1 + n_2 - 2}} \qquad (10.5)$$

Estimated standard error of the difference between two population means when the variances are equal

$$s_{\bar{x}_1 - \bar{x}_2} = s \sqrt{\frac{1}{n_1} + \frac{1}{n_2}} \qquad (10.6)$$

Two-sample mean t test statistic

$$t = \frac{\bar{x}_1 - \bar{x}_2}{s_{\bar{x}_1 - \bar{x}_2}} \qquad (10.7)$$

Sample mean—matched samples

$$\bar{d} = \frac{\Sigma d}{n} \qquad (10.8)$$

Sample standard deviation—matched samples

$$s_d = \sqrt{\frac{\Sigma d^2 - \frac{(\Sigma d)^2}{n}}{n - 1}} \qquad (10.9)$$

Matched-pairs t test statistic

$$t = \frac{\bar{d}}{s_d / \sqrt{n}} \qquad (10.10)$$

Pooled estimator of the population proportion

$$\hat{p} = \frac{x_1 + x_2}{n_1 + n_2} \qquad (10.11)$$

Estimated standard error of the difference between two population proportions

$$\sigma_{\bar{p}_1 - \bar{p}_2} = \sqrt{\hat{p}(1 - \hat{p}) \left(\frac{1}{n_1} + \frac{1}{n_2} \right)} \qquad (10.12)$$

Two-sample z test statistic for proportions

$$z = \frac{\bar{p}_1 - \bar{p}_2}{\sigma_{\bar{p}_1 - \bar{p}_2}}$$

(10.13)

SOLVED EXERCISES

1. TWO POPULATION MEANS—LARGE SAMPLES

"Greater Reliance on Foreign Oil Feared as U.S. Output Tumbles," reported the *New York Times* on its front page, January 18, 1990. The Puget Power Company wonders if higher oil prices might result, which, in turn, could cause higher electrical usage for home heating. To measure changes over the past year, a simple random sample of 40 households was selected for January 1989 and compared with a sample of 50 households for January 1990. The sample results are

$$\bar{x}_1 = 1{,}645 \text{ kwh} \qquad s_1 = 298 \text{ kwh} \qquad n_1 = 40 \text{ (1989)}$$
$$\bar{x}_2 = 1{,}803 \text{ kwh} \qquad s_2 = 305 \text{ kwh} \qquad n_2 = 50 \text{ (1990)}$$

Test at the .10 significance level if the average residential electricity usage per household has changed for the month of January.

a. State the null and alternative hypotheses.

b. Is the appropriate sampling distribution the normal curve or the t distribution?

c. State the decision rule.

d. What should Puget Power conclude?

Solution:

a. The null and alternative hypotheses are

$$H_0\text{:}(\mu_1 - \mu_2) = 0$$
$$H_1\text{:}(\mu_1 - \mu_2) \neq 0$$

b. The sampling distribution for sample mean differences in the two-sample mean test for large samples (30 or larger) is the normal distribution.

c. This is a two-tailed test at the .10 significance level using the z value. Divide the significance level in half: $.10/2 = .05$. Look up $(.5000 - .0500) = .4500$ in the body of the standard normal table. The appropriate z value is 1.645. Therefore, the decision rule is

> If the difference between the two sample means is more than 1.645 standard errors above or below the assumed mean (0) of the sampling distribution, reject the null hypothesis (reject H_0 if $z < -1.645$ or $z > 1.645$).

d. $s_{\bar{x}_1 - \bar{x}_2} = \sqrt{\dfrac{s_1^2}{n_1} + \dfrac{s_2^2}{n_2}} = \sqrt{\dfrac{298^2}{40} + \dfrac{305^2}{50}} = 63.88$

$$z = \frac{\bar{x}_1 - \bar{x}_2}{s_{\bar{x}_1 - \bar{x}_2}} = \frac{1{,}645 - 1{,}803}{63.88} = -2.47$$

Since the computed z value (-2.47) is below the critical z value (-1.645), reject the null hypothesis and conclude that the average residential electricity usage per household has changed for the month of January.

2. Two Population Means—Small Samples

Gale Marrs, personnel manager of the Baxter Richfield Company, suspects that older workers miss more days per year due to illness than younger workers. Gale decides to test this hypothesis and randomly samples the records of 10 older (40 years or over) and 10 younger (under 40 years old) employees. Gale feels that the populations are normally distributed. The results are:

Older	Younger
37	24
19	42
21	18
35	15
16	0
4	9
0	10
12	20
63	22
25	13

a. State the null and alternative hypotheses.

b. Is the appropriate sampling distribution the normal curve or the t distribution?

c. State the decision rule if Gale tests at the .05 significance level.

d. What should Gale Marrs conclude?

Solution:

a. The null and alternative hypotheses are

$$H_0:(\mu_1 - \mu_2) \leq 0$$
$$H_1:(\mu_1 - \mu_2) > 0$$

b. The t test is considered appropriate when either sample size is less than 30 and the populations from which they are selected are normally distributed.

c. This is a one-tailed test at the .05 significance level using the t value. The number of degrees of freedom for this t test is df $= (n_1 + n_2 - 2) = (10 + 10 - 2) = 18$. Look up the value in the t table for 18 degrees of freedom in the .05 significance column. The appropriate t value is 1.734. Therefore, the decision rule is

> If the difference between the two sample means is more than 1.734 standard errors above the assumed mean (0) of the sampling distribution, reject the null hypothesis (reject H_0 if $t > 1.734$).

d. $\bar{x}_1 = 23.2 \quad s_1 = 18.3 \quad n_1 = 10$
$\bar{x}_2 = 17.3 \quad s_2 = 11.2 \quad n_2 = 10$

$$s_{\text{pooled}} = \sqrt{\frac{s_1^2(n_1 - 1) + s_2^2(n_2 - 1)}{n_1 + n_2 - 2}}$$

$$= \sqrt{\frac{18.3^2(10 - 1) + 11.2^2(10 - 1)}{10 + 10 - 2}} = 15.17$$

$$s_{\bar{x}_1 - \bar{x}_2} = 15.17 \sqrt{\frac{1}{10} + \frac{1}{10}} = 6.78$$

$$t = \frac{\bar{x}_1 - \bar{x}_2}{s_{\bar{x}_1 - \bar{x}_2}} = \frac{23.2 - 17.3}{6.78} = 0.87$$

Since 0.87 does not exceed the critical t value (1.734), fail to reject the null hypothesis. Based on the sample evidence, Gale cannot conclude that older workers miss more days due to illness per year than younger workers.

3. Two Population Means—Dependent Samples

Katrina Bell, analyst for the Hexaco Oil Company, has been assigned to investigate the claim that Hexaco dealers charge more for unleaded gas than independent dealers. Katrina is afraid that if she chooses two independent random samples of stations for each type of dealer, the variability in price due to geographic location might be a factor. To eliminate this source of variability, she chooses a pair of stations—one independent and one Hexaco—in close geographic proximity. The results of Katrina's sampling are:

Region	Hexaco	Independent	Difference (d)	Squared difference (d^2)
1	90.5	89.9	0.6	0.36
2	91.9	90.9	1.0	1.00
3	92.7	90.9	1.8	3.24
4	91.9	90.9	1.0	1.00
5	93.6	91.8	1.8	3.24
6	89.9	90.9	−1.0	1.00
7	90.9	90.9	0.0	0.00
8	89.8	88.9	0.9	0.81
9	88.7	88.9	−0.2	0.04
10	87.9	88.6	−0.7	0.49
11	92.7	91.9	0.8	0.64
			6.0	11.82

a. State the null and alternative hypotheses.

b. State the decision rule if Katrina tests at the .01 significance level.

c. What should Katrina conclude?

Solution:

a. The null and alternative hypotheses are

$$H_0: (\mu_1 - \mu_2) \leq 0$$
$$H_1: (\mu_1 - \mu_2) > 0$$

b. This is a one-tailed test at the .01 significance level using the t value. The degrees of freedom for this t test total $(n - 1) = (11 - 1) = 10$. Look up the value in the t table for 10 degrees of freedom in the .01 significance column. The appropriate t value is 2.764. Therefore, the decision rule is

If the difference between the two sample means is more than 2.764 standard errors above the assumed mean (0) of the sampling distribution, reject the null hypothesis (reject H_0 if $t > 2.764$).

c. $\bar{d} = \dfrac{\Sigma d}{n} = \dfrac{6}{11} = 0.545$

$$s_d = \sqrt{\dfrac{\Sigma d^2 - \dfrac{(\Sigma d)^2}{n}}{n - 1}} = \sqrt{\dfrac{11.82 - \dfrac{(6.0)^2}{11}}{11 - 1}}$$

$$= \sqrt{\dfrac{11.82 - 3.27}{10}} = \sqrt{\dfrac{8.55}{10}} = \sqrt{0.855} = 0.925$$

$$t = \dfrac{\bar{d}}{s_d / \sqrt{n}} = \dfrac{0.545}{0.925 / \sqrt{11}} = \dfrac{0.545}{0.279} = 1.95$$

Since the test value for t (1.95) is smaller than the critical t value (2.764), the null hypothesis is not rejected. Katrina concludes that she does not have sufficient evidence to support the claim that Hexaco dealers charge more than independent dealers.

4. Two Population Proportions

Pacific Northwest Electric, a major gas and electric company, is attempting to take over a smaller concern, Idaho Light and Power. Pacific's securities consultant reports that a larger proportion of male Idaho shareholders support the takeover bid than female shareholders. Kim Gamble, Pacific's president, has asked Eddie Kennedy, Pacific's statistician, to conduct a telephone survey of a random sample of shareholders to confirm this report. Eddie samples 1,000 shareholders (400 male and 600 female) and finds that 220 males and 320 females support the takeover bid.

a. State the null and alternative hypotheses.

b. State the decision rule if Eddie tests at the .05 significance level.

c. What should Eddie conclude?

Solution:

a. The null and alternative hypotheses are

$$H_0:(p_1 - p_2) \leq 0$$
$$H_1:(p_1 - p_2) > 0$$

b. This is a one-tailed test at the .05 significance level using the z value. Look up $(.5000 - .0500) = .4500$ in the body of the standard normal table. The appropriate z value is 1.645. Therefore, the decision rule is

If the difference between the two sample means is more than 1.645 standard errors above the assumed mean (0) of the sampling distribution, reject the null hypothesis (reject H_0 if $z > 1.645$).

c. $\hat{p} = \dfrac{x_1 + x_2}{n_1 + n_2} = \dfrac{220 + 320}{400 + 600} = \dfrac{540}{1,000} = .54$

$$\sigma_{\bar{p}_1 - \bar{p}_2} = \sqrt{\hat{p}(1 - \hat{p})\left(\dfrac{1}{n_1} + \dfrac{1}{n_2}\right)} = \sqrt{.54(.46)\left(\dfrac{1}{400} + \dfrac{1}{600}\right)}$$

$$\sigma_{\bar{p}_1 - \bar{p}_2} = \sqrt{(.2484)(.0042)} = \sqrt{.001} = .032$$

$$z = \dfrac{\bar{p}_1 - \bar{p}_2}{\sigma_{\bar{p}_1 - \bar{p}_2}} = \dfrac{.55 - .533}{.032} = 0.53$$

Since the test value for z (0.53) is smaller than the critical z value of 1.645, the null hypothesis is not rejected. Eddie concludes that he doesn't have sufficient evidence to support the securities consultant's report.

EXERCISES

36. Why are two-sample tests performed?

37. State the three types of claims that can be made about means or proportions in a two-sample test.

38. Explain when the t distribution instead of the normal curve is used to test a hypothesis.

39. Cary Richey, a history student, wants to compare the average height of ancient Romans and Greeks. After considerable reading, she can find only a few references to height, and those for men only. Based on the following data, where heights are recorded in inches, can she conclude that the Greek and Roman populations had different average heights if she tests at the .10 significance level?

$$\bar{x}_1 = 61.4 \text{ inches} \quad s_1 = 3.7 \text{ inches} \quad n_1 = 32 \text{ (Greeks)}$$
$$\bar{x}_2 = 63.8 \text{ inches} \quad s_2 = 2.9 \text{ inches} \quad n_2 = 32 \text{ (Romans)}$$

40. On May 5, 1988, *The Wall Street Journal* reported that the average age of the industrial base in Japan was 10 years and that in the United States was 17 years. The implication is that Japan has a more modern industrial base than the United States. Suppose the stated averages were based on a survey of 75 Japanese firms and 80 U.S. firms, and the standard deviations of equipment age were 4.9 years for Japanese firms and 5.1 years for U.S. firms. At the .05 significance level, what conclusion can be reached?

41. A car company wants to test the collision characteristics of two of its car designs. Dummies are to be the "drivers" for these cars and are designed to record impact forces on the head and chest. Cars equipped with these dummies are then crashed into a solid wall at a speed of 30 miles per hour. The company hopes that its new L car will show a lower impact force than its conventional car. Since each car is destroyed by the test, only a few cars are tested. Based on the following sample evidence, can the company conclude that the new L car is safer if the test is done at the .05 significance level? (The variable recorded is a combined measurement of the head and chest forces on impact.)

$$n_1 = 5 \quad \bar{x}_1 = 129.7 \quad s_1 = 5.3 \text{ (old car)}$$
$$n_2 = 7 \quad \bar{x}_2 = 113.8 \quad s_2 = 4.3 \text{ (L car)}$$

42. *The Miami Herald* surveyed a number of subscribers to determine who was reading its Sunday edition. Of 400 men surveyed, 78% read it, and 85% of the 300 surveyed women read it. Is there a significant difference at the .10 significance level?

43. After a fire, a company can find only a few of its records. The accounting department was about to test the difference between the average sales per customer for two of the company's stores. The recovered records, consisting of only a few customer accounts, produced the following results. Based on this small sample, and using a .05 significance level, is one store selling more per customer than the other?

$$n_1 = 38 \quad \bar{x}_1 = \$53.87 \quad s_1 = \$10.43 \text{ (store 1)}$$
$$n_2 = 42 \quad \bar{x}_2 = \$68.13 \quad s_2 = \$11.94 \text{ (store 2)}$$

44. A Harris poll reported in *Newsweek* (March 28, 1988) revealed a decrease in Americans' average number of leisure hours per week. In 1980 there were 19 hours per week, but in

1987 only 17. This conclusion was based on a sample of 1,500 adults in each poll. If the standard deviation was 2.5 in 1980 and 2.1 in 1987, can we conclude at the .01 significance level that there has been a decrease in Americans' average number of weekly leisure hours?

45. In each of the following situations, test to see whether one group has a larger average (mean) value than the other. For each test, use a significance level of .05.

a. $n_1 = 5$ $\bar{x}_1 = 12,569$ $s_1 = 2,439$
   $n_2 = 7$ $\bar{x}_2 = 22,736$ $s_2 = 3,981$

b. $n_1 = 26$ $\bar{x}_1 = 34.7$ $s_1 = 3.9$
   $n_2 = 19$ $\bar{x}_2 = 24.1$ $s_2 = 3.2$

c. $n_1 = 18$ $\bar{x}_1 = 235.8$ $s_1 = 34.9$
   $n_2 = 13$ $\bar{x}_2 = 199.3$ $s_2 = 21.5$

46. *Playboy* magazine (July 1988) reported that the distance of an average commute in Southern California is 10.7 miles each way. Assume this conclusion is based on a random sample of 350 commuters. Suppose the average commute in Illinois is 5 miles, based on the same sample size. Use the .02 significance level to determine if the evidence supports the conclusion that commuters in California drive farther than those in Illinois, if both standard deviations are 2.7 miles.

47. According to the *Statistical Bulletin* (October–December 1982), the average number of deaths per 1,000 troops was 1.20 for the Army and 1.57 for the Marine Corps. Is this difference significant at the .10 level? Assume that the figures are based on random samples of 5,000 from each service. (*Note:* Since each sampled person either did or did not die, this should be treated as a proportion problem.)

48. On May 25, 1988, *The Wall Street Journal* reported a difference in the prison return rate between inmates who had a furlough and those who didn't. The former had a return rate of 12%, and the latter had a return rate of 31%. Assuming that this conclusion is based on random samples of 225 inmates from each of the two populations, can you conclude that furloughs reduce the return rate at the .05 significance level?

49. In 1992, the National League of Cities conducted a survey of 620 cities and towns. It found that 54% have negative balance sheets, up from 52% in 1991 (*USA Today*, July 9, 1992). The 1991 sample consisted of 580 cities and towns. Test at the .10 significance level to determine whether the percentage of cities and towns with negative balance sheets has changed significantly since 1991.

50. A study reported in *Industrial Quality Control* provided two analysts' 16 independent determinations of hydroquinone's melting point.

Analyst I	Analyst II
174.0	173.0
173.5	173.0
173.0	172.0
173.5	173.0
171.5	171.0
172.5	172.0
173.5	171.0
173.5	172.0

Source: *Quality Control and Industrial Statistics* (Homewood, IL: Irwin, 1986).

Is there enough evidence to conclude at the .05 significance level that there's a tendency for one analyst to get higher results than the other?

51. Baseball fans like to argue about which league is better: the National or the American. American League fans claim that because of the designated hitter, there's more offense in American League games. To test this claim, data were gathered on the number of runs scored by each team in the 1991 season (*The Sporting News 1992 Yearbook*). The results are:

American	Runs		National	Runs
Boston	731		New York	640
Milwaukee	799		Cincinnati	689
Seattle	702		Montreal	579
Detroit	817		Pittsburgh	768
Toronto	684		Chicago	695
Texas	829		St. Louis	651
Cleveland	576		San Diego	636
Kansas City	727		San Francisco	649
New York	674		Atlanta	749
Minnesota	776		Philadelphia	629
Oakland	760		Houston	605
Baltimore	686		Los Angeles	665
Chicago	758			
California	653			

Test at the .025 significance level the claim that there are typically more runs scored per team in the American League.

EXTENDED EXERCISES
. . . .

52. BRICE COMPANY

The Brice Company needs to replace a machine that produces bolts of various sizes from steel stock. Two machines are being considered for purchase, and research to date has revealed that they cost about the same, have about the same lifetime, and have comparable warranties. Tom Brice, the owner's son and a recent college graduate, has just joined the company. His first job is to make a recommendation to his father about which machine to buy.

Tom calls several other companies around the country, locating five that are using one of the machines and four that are using the other. He discusses his problem with their manufacturing managers, and two of them agree to let him visit their facilities to sample the bolt production line. Tom conducts the visits and, over the course of several days, obtains what he thinks are good random samples of each machine's output. Measurements are made to determine the number of bolts in each sample that fall outside specifications, as well as the variability in diameter, the key factor in a precision bolt. Here are the data Tony collects:

Machine 1: $n = 25$ bolts, percentage outside specifications = 4%
              Standard deviation of diameter = 0.02 inch
Machine 2: $n = 31$ bolts, percentage outside specifications = 3.2%
              Standard deviation of diameter = 0.08 inch

Tom thinks he has enough data to decide which machine to buy. He tests the hypothesis that the two machines produce the same percentage of bolts outside specifications:

$$H_0: \quad (p_1 - p_2) = 0$$
$$H_1: \quad (p_1 - p_2) \neq 0$$

Tom computes a test value of 1.14, that is smaller than the critical values of z found in the standard normal table for small values of alpha. Tom thus fails to reject the null hypothesis of equal rates for the two machines with small chance of error.

a Has Tom conducted the hypothesis test correctly?

b. Has the test statistic of 1.14 been computed correctly?

c. Are there any factors that should be considered in the machine purchase decision that Tom has not addressed?

d. How would you react to the statement: "Machine 2 has a lower percentage of out-of-tolerance parts than Machine 1 (3.2% compared to 4.0%) and is therefore superior"?

e. If machine 1 costs less, what should Tom recommend to his father?

53. SUBURBAN REGIONAL UNIVERSITY

Suburban Regional University is competing with Downtown University for funding from the state legislature and has been accused of lowering its admission standards to attract more students. Tom Douglas, an outside consultant, is hired to see if this is true. He decides to randomly select student files to collect high school grade point averages and SAT scores.

Both universities agree to the process, and the results are to be made available to both. Mr. Douglas is familiar with the situation described in *The Wall Street Journal* (September 12, 1989) regarding a general decline in college entrance test scores during the past school year. He knows his analysis must take this decline into account.

Mr. Douglas conducts his test with 250 student files randomly selected from each university. The results are:

	Suburban	Downtown
High school GPA:		
Mean	2.63	2.94
Standard deviation	0.38	0.41
SAT score:		
Mean	985	935
Standard deviation	21	105

a. Test the hypothesis that the two universities have the same quality of student as measured by high school grade point average.

b. Test for quality of student by using the two universities' SAT scores.

c. What are your conclusions about student quality based on these two hypothesis tests?

d. What does the large difference between the SAT score standard deviations suggest?

54. OLYMPIC MANUFACTURING

The Olympic Manufacturing Company uses both ABC and XYZ placement companies to recruit management talent. The two companies' service levels appear to be about equal, but ABC has just raised its rates. ABC claims that more of the people it places are still on the job after one year, and that this is due to its superior screening procedures.

As personnel director for Olympic, it's your job to decide if ABC is worth the higher rate. You're aware of the many other placement agencies available, having just seen several of their ads in *The Wall Street Journal* section "The Mart" (June 17, 1992, pp. B13–B15). The performance of the two agencies currently being used is thus of great importance.

A sample of employees placed by each agency is easily obtained, so getting a reasonable sample size is no problem. Files on all employees are available in the personnel office.

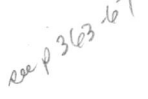
see p 363 b7

a. How would you take a random sample in this case?

b. Suppose 85% of XYZ's placements are still on the job after one year, a value obtained from a sample of 300 employees from this placement agency. At the .05 significance level, how high would ABC's retention rate have to be for the null hypothesis of equal population retention rates to be rejected?

c. What other factors besides retention rate might you consider in evaluating ABC's new, higher cost?

MICROCOMPUTER PACKAGE

The micro package *Computerized Business Statistics* can be used to solve two-population hypothesis-testing problems.

The Puget Power Company (see Solved Exercise 1) wants to determine whether the average electricity usage per household has changed for the month of January. A simple random sample of 40 households was selected for January 1989 and compared with a sample of 50 households for January 1990. A two-population hypothesis test was conducted to determine whether the average has changed.

Computer Solution:

From the main menu of *Computerized Business Statistics* an 8 is selected, which indicates hypothesis testing. The hypothesis-testing menu appears on the screen.

Since the problem involves entering data from the keyboard, a 1 is selected.

```
Data Type:    (R) Row      (S) Summary                              S
Data Form:    (M) Means    (P) Proportion                          M
Proportion data consists of values from 0 to 1

Population:   (1) One Population (2) Two Populations                2
              (U) Unmatched Samples  (M) Matched Samples            U
Variance:  (P) Population    (S) Sample                             S
Testing:   (1) One Sided     (2) Two Sided                          2
Hypothesis Value:                                                   0
Enter F when finished       Instructions for each option
                            are provided here
```

The choices are

S = Summary
M = Means
2 = Two populations
U = Unmatched

S = Sample
2 = Two-sided
0 = Hypothesized population mean $(\mu_1 - \mu_2) = 0$

F is entered to indicate that you are finished with this menu.

```
Sample Size for Group 1:                                  40
Sample Size for Group 2                                   50
Sample Mean for Group 1:                                  1645
Sample Mean for Group 2:                                  1803
Standard Deviation for Group 1:                           298
Standard Deviation for Group 2:                           305
```

The choices are

$$n_1 = 40$$
$$n_2 = 50$$
$$\bar{x}_1 = 1{,}645$$
$$\bar{x}_2 = 1{,}803$$
$$s_1 = 298$$
$$s_2 = 305$$

```
Alpha Error:    1 = 0.2, 2 = 0.1, 3 = 0.05, 4 = 0.02,
                5 = 0.01, 6 = Other
Select Alpha:   enter 1-6 and press ⏎ 2
```

A **2** is entered for the .10 significance level and the screen shows:

```
Degrees of Freedom:   88
Critical Z (Test Statistic)  .................................1.645
```

Next, the hypothesis-testing program options menu reappears. A **7** is entered so that the problem can be run. The hypothesis-testing output menu then appears. The choice in this case is **P** for printer.

MINITAB COMPUTER PACKAGE

· ·

The MINITAB commands to perform the hypothesis test for Solved Exercise 2 are

```
MTB> SET OLDER INTO C1
DATA> 37 19 21 35 16 4 0 12 63 25
DATA> END
MTB> SET YOUNGER INTO C2
DATA> 24 42 18 15 0 9 10 20 22 13
DATA> END
MTB> TWOSAMPLE T .95 FOR C1 VS C2;
SUBC> ALTERNATIVE +1;
SUBC> POOLED.

TWOSAMPLE T FOR C1 VS C2
       N       MEAN    STDEV    SE MEAN
C1    10       23.2    18.3     5.80
C2    10       17.3    11.2     3.54
```

```
95 PCT CI FOR MU C1 - MU C2: (-8.4, 20.2)
TTEST MU C1 - MU C2 (VS GT): T = .87 P = .20 DF = 18
POOLED STDEV = 15.2
MTB> STOP
```

The TWOSAMPLE T command is used to test the null hypothesis that $\mu_1 - \mu_2 \leq 0$. The command calculates a $K\%$ confidence interval for $\mu_1 - \mu_2$. The ALTERNATIVE +1 subcommand tests the null against the alternative hypothesis that $\mu_1 - \mu_2 > 0$. If there is no ALTERNATIVE subcommand, a two-tailed test is performed. The POOLED subcommand assumes the two populations have equal variances and that the common variance is estimated by the pooled variance.

CHI-SQUARE TESTS

*Ye shall know
the truth, and
the truth shall
make you free.*

St. John 8:32

Objectives

When you have completed this chapter, you will be able to:

Explain the difference between the test of independence and the goodness-of-fit test.

Compute expected frequencies and the chi-square statistic.

Apply the contingency table in a decision-making application.

Apply the goodness-of-fit test in a decision-making application.

M en are losing their grip on the labor force, according to an *American Demographics* article, "Workers in 2000" (March 1990, p. 36). The increasing impact of American women on the labor force is predicted for the 1990s.

Chapters 8 through 10 introduced estimation and hypothesis testing. Hypothesis tests about a population mean or proportion were constructed for one and two samples. For these tests it was assumed that the populations being sampled were normally distributed. These tests dealt with data that were at least interval-scaled, such as heights, ages, and incomes. There are some situations where the data aren't interval or ratio, but are nominal or ordinal. In these situations, no assumptions can be made about the population's shape. This chapter will introduce chi-square tests, which cover some of these situations.

WHY MANAGERS NEED TO KNOW ABOUT CHI-SQUARE TESTS

This chapter discusses two hypothesis tests for which the chi-square distribution is the appropriate sampling distribution. Because of the frequency with which nominal and ordinal data are collected in practical situations, these techniques are particularly useful in business. Additional hypothesis tests of this type for qualitative data are covered in Chapter 19.

Regarding the *American Demographics* article, the changing nature of the work force could be monitored year by year by recording the numbers of men and women in such job categories as executive, professional, sales, service, and laborer. The techniques in this chapter could be used to detect significant changes.

CONTINGENCY TABLE TEST

Contingency Table Test
The **contingency table test** is designed to determine whether two categorical variables are related. It is sometimes called the *test of independence* since the null hypothesis being tested states that the two categorical variables are *independent*. This test is quite useful because the analyst is often interested in finding whether one categorical variable is related to another.

> The **contingency table test** determines whether two categorical variables are related to each other.

The data necessary for the contingency table test consist of sample measurements on two categorical variables (nominal- or ordinal-scaled). These data values are arrayed in tabular form, which enables the analyst to see a *display* of the collected data. This type of table is sometimes referred to as a *cross-classification table* (*crosstabs* for short).

The null and alternative hypotheses that the analyst must choose between after examining the sample data are

H_0: The row and column variables are independent.

H_1: The row and column variables are dependent.

The contingency table test is often used to analyze important aspects of survey data. Surveys typically contain questions designed to measure certain demographic characteristics of the sample (for instance, age category, sex, income level, marital status, and educational level). Another type of question frequently found in a survey instrument elicits respondents' attitudes and opinions. Many contingency table tests contrast a demographic variable with an attitude variable. For example, the male/female variable might be cross-tabulated with a rating on store prices, or age categories might be cross-tabulated with the response to a statement about a presidential candidate. The purpose of such tests is to determine if different population types, as distinguished by the demographic questions, have different attitudes regarding the subjects investigated by the survey. "Applications of Statistical Concepts in the Business World" at this chapter's end gives additional examples of contingency table applications.

EXAMPLE 11.1   Jim Moore, marketing director for Bell Manufacturing Corporation, wants to know if there's a difference in brand awareness between men and women concerning the company's environmental control system. Jim randomly surveyed 100 people. Table 11.1 gives the results. The column totals show that 60 men and 40 women were surveyed. The row totals show that of the 100 respondents, 70 were aware of the company's environmental control system and 30 were unaware. These row and column totals are the result of random sampling.

TABLE 11.1   Contingency Table for Gender and Brand Awareness (Example 11.1)

Brand awareness	Gender		Totals
	Male	Female	
Aware	36	34	70
Unaware	24	6	30
Totals	60	40	100

As stated in Chapter 9, the first step in the hypothesis-testing procedure is to state the null and alternative hypotheses. The null hypothesis for this contingency table test is that the two categorical variables are independent of each other. This hypothesis states that a person's gender in no way indicates whether the person is aware of Bell's environmental control system. In other words, knowledge of which column a person is in, is of no value in trying to guess in which row that person falls. In the case of Table 11.1, if all females were aware of the control system and all males were unaware, it would be obvious that males and females differed in their awareness level. The null hypothesis would obviously be false under these conditions.

Table 11.1 is typical of most contingency tables in that it is not immediately obvious from the table whether the null hypothesis is true or false. A statistical test is needed to determine whether there's a relationship between the row and column variables.

The null and alternative hypotheses for this situation are

H_0: Gender and brand awareness are independent.

H_1: Gender and brand awareness are dependent.

The second step in the hypothesis-testing procedure is to assume that the null hypothesis is true. For Example 11.1, if gender and brand awareness are assumed to be independent, how many observations would be expected to fall in each cell of Table 11.1? Example 11.2 demonstrates the computation of the expected number of observations in each cell.

EXAMPLE 11.2   The probability that a person is aware of the Bell environmental control system in Example 11.1 is found by noting that there are 70 aware persons out of the 100 people sampled:

$$\bar{p} = x/n = 70/100 = .70$$

If gender and brand awareness are independent, as stated in the null hypothesis, Jim would expect 70% of the 60 males to be aware of the Bell system. In other words, he expects that 42 males ($.70 \times 60 = 42$) would be aware of the company's product. Likewise, Jim would expect 70% of the 40 females, or 28, to be aware of the Bell system. Note that the expected frequencies for the "aware" row must sum to the total observed frequencies: $42 + 28 = 70$. The upper right corner of each cell in Table 11.2 shows the expected frequencies.

TABLE 11.2   Expected Frequencies for Example 11.2

Brand awareness	Gender		Totals
	Male	Female	
Aware	36 [42]	34 [28]	70
Unaware	24 [18]	6 [12]	30
Totals	60	40	100

Equation 11.1 provides an easy method for computing expected frequencies. Chapter 5 showed that independence of events A and B implies that $P(A \text{ and } B) = P(A) \times P(B)$. Similarly, in the contingency table analysis, if the categories are independent, the probability that an item is classified in any particular cell of the table is the product of the corresponding marginal probabilities. To calculate the expected frequency for a particular cell, multiply the row total by the column total and then divide this product by the total sample size:

$$f_e = \frac{(\text{Row total})(\text{Column total})}{\text{Sample size}} \tag{11.1}$$

The expected frequency for the male-unaware cell of Table 11.2 is

$$f_e = \frac{(\text{Row total})(\text{Column total})}{\text{Sample size}} = \frac{(30)(60)}{100} = 18$$

A widely used rule of thumb for this test states that each expected frequency in a contingency table must be five or greater ($f_e \geq 5$) for the test to be accurate.

A test statistic is now needed that compares the observed and expected frequencies for each cell of Table 11.2. If the observed frequencies are quite close to the expected frequencies, the statistic should indicate a failure to reject the null hypothesis of independence. This is the appropriate conclusion because the expected frequencies are computed under the assumption that the two categorical variables are independent. If the observed and expected frequencies are quite different, the test statistic should lead to rejection of the null hypothesis.

Equation 11.2 is used for the cell-by-cell comparisons. The computed value is called a *chi-square* (χ^2) *statistic*. If the null hypothesis is true, the distribution of this computed value is approximately a chi-square distribution. Actually, the chi-square is a family of probability distributions. As with the t distribution, the χ^2 probability distribution is characterized by a single parameter, the degrees of freedom. Figure 11.1 shows the chi-square distribution for selected df values. The distribution is skewed positively, but as df increases, it approaches the shape of the normal distribution:

$$\chi^2 = \sum \frac{(f_o - f_e)^2}{f_e} \tag{11.2}$$

where: f_o = Observed frequency
         f_e = Expected frequency

FIGURE 11.1   Chi-Square Distributions for Various df

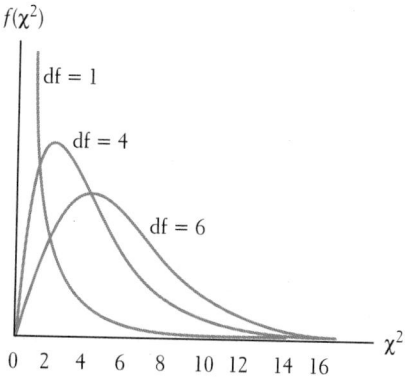

Note that the comparison between the observed and expected frequencies for each cell is being made in the numerator. If large differences exist from cell to cell, a large statistic results; small differences produce a small statistic. The contingency table hypothesis test is therefore a one-tailed test to the right. As Figure 11.2 shows, a large test statistic leads to a rejection of the null hypothesis while a small statistic leads to a failure to reject.

If the null hypothesis is true, the test value is drawn from the chi-square distribution. To determine the specific distribution from which it is drawn, we must calculate the degrees of freedom using Equation 11.3:

$$\text{df} = (r - 1)(c - 1) \tag{11.3}$$

where: r = Number of rows
c = Number of columns

Examples 11.3 and 11.4 illustrate these concepts.

EXAMPLE 11.3 Table 11.3 shows chi-square calculations from the cell values in Table 11.2. Note in Equation 11.2 that each value of the fraction following the summation sign is calculated; then these are added together. Since there are two rows and two columns in Table 11.2, there are four terms to calculate and sum using Equation 11.2.

Table 11.3 shows that the test statistic computed from the sample data is 7.143. If this calculated value is judged to be small, it's because the observed values in the cells are close to those that would be expected if the null hypothesis is true. If the test statistic turns out to be large, it's because the observed and expected frequencies are not close.

TABLE 11.3 Chi-Square Computations for Example 11.3

f_o	f_e	$(f_o - f_e)$	$(f_o - f_e)^2$	$(f_o - f_e)^2/f_e$
36	42	−6	36	36/42 = 0.857
34	28	6	36	36/28 = 1.286
24	18	6	36	36/18 = 2.000
6	12	−6	36	36/12 = 3.000
				χ^2 = 7.143

The null hypothesis for Example 11.1 is now tested at the 5% significance level. From Equation 11.3, the degrees of freedom are

$$\text{df} = (r - 1)(c - 1) = (2 - 1)(2 - 1) = (1)(1) = 1$$

The rationale for this degree of freedom value is as follows: Of the four cells in Table 11.2, how many are free to vary, given that the row and column totals must be maintained? The answer is one. If a value for one cell is known, the rest of the cell values are determined by the row and column totals. If the expected frequency for the male-aware cell is known to be 42, then the expected frequency for the female-aware cell must be 28 because the expected frequencies for the awareness row must add to 70. Likewise, if the expected frequency for the male-aware cell is 42, the expected frequency for the male-unaware cell must be 18 because the expected frequencies for the male column must add to 60.

Use Appendix E.8's chi-square table to find the critical chi-square value. As this table shows, the critical value for a chi-square distribution with one degree of freedom at the .05 significance level is 3.841. The decision rule is

If the calculated chi-square statistic is larger than 3.841, reject the null hypothesis; otherwise, fail to reject it (reject H_0 if $\chi^2 > 3.841$).

The chi-square statistic of 7.143 exceeds the critical value. This statistic's large value is due to the large differences between the observed and expected frequencies in the four cells of the contingency table. The null hypothesis is rejected with small chance of error (5%). These sample data reveal a dependence between gender and brand awareness.

Table 11.2 illuminates the dependency between gender and brand awareness now that it has been supported statistically. The table shows that although 28 females were expected to be aware of Bell's environmental control system, 34 females were actually aware. Evidently, females are more likely to be aware of this system than males.

Figure 11.2 summarizes this situation. If the null hypothesis is true, the test statistic is drawn from this distribution. However, since the test value is larger than the critical value, this seems quite unlikely, so the null hypothesis is rejected.

FIGURE 11.2   Chi-Square Distribution (Example 11.3)

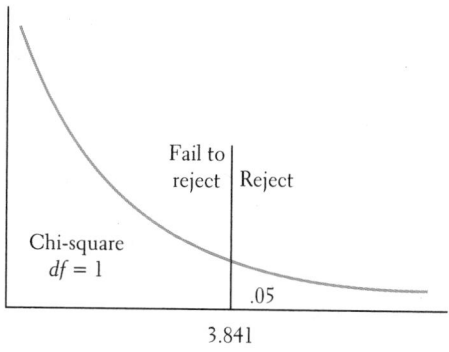

The chi-square contingency table test can be performed using MINITAB. The appropriate commands to solve Example 11.3 are:

```
MTB > READ C1 C2
DATA> 36 34
DATA> 24 6
DATA> END
      2 ROWS READ
MTB > NAME C1 'MALE' C2 'FEMALE'
MTB > CHISQUARE C1 C2
```

```
Expected counts are printed below observed counts

            MALE      FEMALE     Total
     1        36         34         70
           42.00      28.00

     2        24          6         30
           18.00      12.00

  Total       60         40        100

ChiSq = 0.857 + 1.286 +
        2.000 + 3.000 = 7.143
df = 1

MTB > CDF 7.143;
SUBC> CHISQUARE WITH DF = 1.
    7.1430    0.9925
MTB > STOP
```

Note that the READ command is used to input the data instead of the SET command. The READ command puts 36 and 24 into C1 and 34 and 6 into C2. The NAME command is used to name the columns of the table. The CHISQUARE command performs the analysis. The output produces a table that contains both the observed frequencies and the expected frequencies.

The CDF command is used to generate a cumulative probability density function. The CHISQUARE subcommand is used to generate the probability function for a chi-square distribution with one degree of freedom. Note that the p-value (.0075) is computed by subtracting .9925 from 1 ($1.0000 - .9925 = .0075$).

EXAMPLE 11.4   Are baby boomers (25- to 44-year-olds) more likely to be employed than other age groups? A custom telephone survey of 4,000 respondents completed by Bruskin/Goldring Research indicates that of Americans 18 years of age or older: 63% are currently employed full-time, or are part-time employees not looking for full-time employment; 10% are unemployed or employed looking for full-time work, and 27% are unemployed and not looking.[1]

Table 11.4 shows the data classified by employment status and age. Do the data present sufficient evidence to indicate that employment status varies according to age group? The null and alternative hypotheses are

H_0: Employment status and age group are independent.

H_1: Employment status and age group are dependent.

Table 11.4 shows the observed frequencies. The expected frequencies, under the assumption that the null hypothesis is true, are calculated using Equation 11.1. For example, the expected frequency for the new workers-employed cell in the contingency table is

$$f_e = \frac{(2,520)(560)}{4,000} = 352.8$$

---

[1] "Where Workers Live," *American Demographics Desk Reference Series: American Workers*, Dow-Jones, Inc. December 1992, pp. 2–3.

TABLE 11.4 Contingency Table for Employment Status and Age Group (Example 11.4)

Age group	Employment status			Totals
	Employed	Looking	Not looking	
New Workers (18–24)	360	120	80	560
Boomers (25–44)	1440	160	200	1800
Peak Earners (45–54)	440	40	80	560
Seniors (55–64)	200	40	200	440
Retires (65 +)	80	40	520	640
Totals	2520	400	1080	4000

Source: Adapted from American Workers, a supplement to *American Demographics*, December 1992,
pp. 2–3.

The expected frequencies, along with the calculation of the chi-square statistic, appear in Table 11.5. The calculations begin in the upper left corner of the table and move from left to right.

TABLE 11.5 Chi-Square Computations for Example 11.4

f_o	f_e	$\dfrac{(f_o - f_e)^2}{f_e}$
360	352.8	.147
120	56.0	73.143
80	151.2	33.528
1440	1134.0	82.571
160	180.0	2.222
200	486.0	168.305
440	352.8	21.553
40	56.0	4.571
80	151.2	33.528
200	277.2	21.500
40	44.0	0.364
200	118.8	55.500
80	403.2	259.073
40	64.0	9.000
520	172.8	697.615
	Sum:	1462.620

The test statistic, as shown in Table 11.5, is 1462.62. This value reflects the large differences between the observed frequencies and the expected frequencies if the null hypothesis of independence is true. The number of degrees of freedom for the test is

$$df = (5 - 1)(3 - 1) = (4)(2) = 8$$

Table 11.6 shows the rationale for computing the degrees of freedom for the contingency table (Table 11.4). Of the 15 cells, how many are free to vary when the expected frequencies are computed? The answer is eight. If eight expected frequencies are specified, the rest are determined by the row and column totals. For instance, if the eight

TABLE 11.6   Illustration of Degrees of Freedom for Table 11.4

Age group	Employment status			Totals
	Employed	Looking	Not looking	
New Workers (18–24)	f_e	f_e		560
Boomers (25–44)	f_e	f_e		1800
Peak Earners (45–54)	f_e	f_e		560
Seniors (55–64)	f_e	f_e		440
Retires (65+)				640
Totals	2520	400	1080	4000

values represented by f_e in Table 11.6 are known, the remaining values can be computed. Thus, there are $(r - 1)(c - 1)$ degrees of freedom in this table and in all contingency tables.

The critical chi-square value (from the table) for 8 degrees of freedom is 20.09 for a significance level of .01. The decision rule is

If the calculated chi-square statistic is larger than 20.09, reject the null hypothesis (reject H_0 if $\chi^2 > 20.09$).

The null hypothesis is rejected since the test value (1462.62) is larger than the critical value (20.09). The sample data lead to the conclusion that employment status and age group are dependent. Tables 11.4 and 11.5 show that baby boomers are more likely to be employed than other age groups.

EXERCISES

1. What kind of data are used for the chi-square contingency table test?
2. Why is the chi-square contingency table test useful in business applications?
3. What is the goal of the contingency table test?
4. State the null and alternative hypotheses for a contingency table test.
5. How are the expected frequencies computed for a contingency table test?
6. If a contingency table has four columns and three rows, how many degrees of freedom are there for the chi-square contingency table test?
7. Core-Mark Distributors classifies its accounts receivable as either paid on time or overdue. Core-Mark also classifies the accounts as local or national. The data from the past few weeks are:

Proximity	Payment status	
	Paid	Overdue
Local	75	95
National	60	110

  a. State the null and alternative hypotheses.
  b. Compute the degrees of freedom.
  c. State the decision rule using the .02 significance level.
  d. Test whether the proximity of the debtor has any bearing on payment status.

8. Pacific Advertising researches the relationship between favorite type of advertising message and income level for a sample of customers. The data are:

Income	Favorite advertisement		
	A	B	C
Low	25	40	70
Medium	30	30	30
High	45	20	10

a. State the null and alternative hypotheses.
b. Compute the degrees of freedom.
c. State the decision rule using the .05 significance level.
d. Test whether income level is related to advertising preference.

9. The Computervision Corporation researches whether part quality is independent of production shift. The data on numbers of good versus defective parts are:

Shift	Part quality	
	Defective	Good
Day	67	726
Swing	33	575
Night	61	363

a. State the null and alternative hypotheses.
b. Compute the degrees of freedom.
c. State the decision rule using the .05 significance level.
d. Test whether part quality is independent of production shift.

10. The A. D. Nickel Department Store sells gift certificates during the Christmas season. Sales manager Leo Henneman wants to determine if the value of a certificate has anything to do with what a customer purchases with it. The data collected from a sample of customers are:

Department	Certificate value		
	$10	$50	$100+
Appliances	22	26	54
Clothing	33	31	22
Hardware	41	43	19

a. State the null and alternative hypotheses.
b. Compute the degrees of freedom.
c. State the decision rule using the .01 significance level.
d. Test whether certificate value has anything to do with what a customer purchases.

11. The Metropolitan Improvement Association is planning to build a new coliseum in Pueblo, Colorado. The group undertook a market research study for Southern Colorado to

determine sports preferences of males in various age groups. A random sample of 680 males provided these results:

Sport	Age group			
	18–30	31–45	46–60	61+
Hockey	25	50	75	100
Basketball	100	80	30	10
Football	5	25	25	30
Soccer	20	30	40	35

a. State the null and alternative hypotheses.
b. Compute the degrees of freedom.
c. State the decision rule using the .10 significance level.
d. Is age related to sport preference?

GOODNESS-OF-FIT TEST

Goodness-of-Fit Test

The contingency table measures the "fit" of observed category frequencies to those frequencies expected under the assumption that the null hypothesis is true. A more general application of this procedure is the **goodness-of-fit test,** which determines whether frequencies observed for some categorical variable could have been drawn from a hypothesized population distribution.

The null and alternative hypotheses that the analyst must choose between after examining the sample data are

H_0: The sample is from the specified population.
H_1: The sample is not from the specified population.

> The **goodness-of-fit test** determines the likelihood that the frequencies observed for a categorical variable could have been drawn from a hypothesized population.

As stated in the definition of this test, only one categorical variable is involved. In contrast, the contingency table test covered earlier in this chapter involved the comparison of *two* categorical variables. The exercises at the end of this chapter will help distinguish between these two chi-square tests.

Equation 11.2 is used to calculate the chi-square test value for the goodness-of-fit test just as for the contingency table test. If the numbers of observed and expected frequencies among the categories are quite close, the resulting statistic will be small and the null hypothesis not rejected. If large differences exist among categories, a large statistic results and the null hypothesis will be rejected. Thus, like the contingency table test, the goodness-of-fit test is a one-tailed test to the right.

In using the chi-square table to find the critical value, we must determine the degrees of freedom. For the goodness-of-fit test, this number is calculated using Equation 11.4. Note that one degree of freedom is always lost because the expected frequencies must sum to the total number of observed frequencies. Additional degrees of freedom are lost whenever sample statistics are used to estimate population parameters in the computations for the expected frequencies:

$$df = k - 1 - c \tag{11.4}$$

where k = Number of categories
        c = Number of unknown population parameters estimated by sample statistics

EXAMPLE 11.5   Equinox Food Exchange, an international food distributor, wants to know if there has been a shift in the size of shipments exported to Poland since that country began moving away from a state-controlled economy. An article in *Financial World* (March 3, 1992, p. 38) intensified Equinox's interest. If the export pattern has shifted, Equinox must adjust its purchasing pattern.

A random sample of shipments exported within the past five months, one from each month, was selected and the size (measured in 1,000 pounds) recorded:

Type:	A	B	C	D	E	Total
Number of shipments:	12	15	21	9	11	68

These numbers constitute the observed frequencies for the five shipments. The null and alternative hypotheses are

H_0: The populations of sizes of shipments are equal ($p = .20$).
H_1: At least one p_i is not equal to .20.

Under the assumption that the null hypothesis of equal type preference is true, how many shipments are expected to fall into each of the five categories? The answer is one fifth (20%) of the total sample size. Since $n = 68$, the null hypothesis implies that $(68 \times .20) = 13.6$ shipments would, on the average, be sent for each month. The value 13.6 is the expected frequency for each category. The observed and expected frequencies are displayed together:

Brand:	A	B	C	D	E	Total
Observed frequency:	12	15	21	9	11	68
Expected frequency:	13.6	13.6	13.6	13.6	13.6	68

The chi-square statistic calculated from Equation 11.2 is 6.411, as Table 11.7 shows.

In this example, there are five categories ($k = 5$), and there are no unknown population parameters to be estimated with sample statistics ($c = 0$). Thus, degrees of freedom is $5 - 1 - 0 = 4$. Figure 11.3 shows several significance levels and critical

TABLE 11.7   Chi-Square Computations for Example 11.5

f_o	f_e	$(f_o - f_e)^2 / f_e$
12	13.6	0.188
15	13.6	0.144
21	13.6	4.026
9	13.6	1.556
11	13.6	0.497
		$\chi^2 = 6.411$

FIGURE 11.3   Chi-Square Distribution for Four df (Example 11.5)

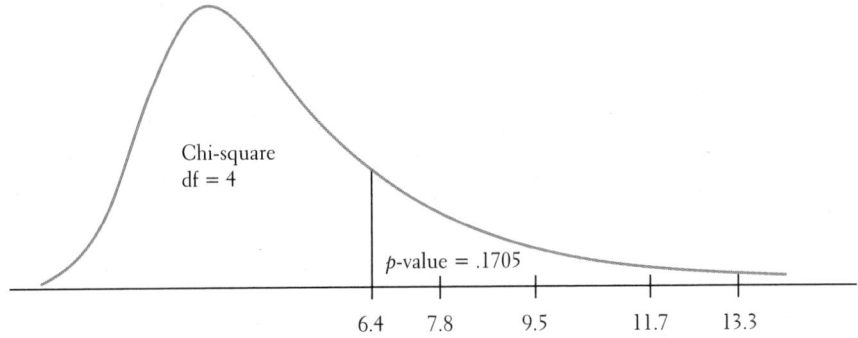

values selected from Appendix E.8's chi-square table for the distribution based on four degrees of freedom:

Alpha	.10	.05	.02	.01
Chi-square:	7.779	9.488	11.668	13.277

The computed test value ($\chi^2 = 6.411$) is smaller than any of the critical values shown in Figure 11.3. The exact probability of rejecting a true null hypothesis is the *p*-value, .1705. The null hypothesis should not be rejected. There doesn't appear to be any difference among the five sizes of shipments Equinox Food Exchange exported to Poland.

EXAMPLE 11.6   *Shopping Journal* reported a recent study indicating that the breakdown of mall shoppers by age in a large city was:

Age category:	<21	21–35	36–50	51–65	66+
Percentage:	10%	32%	31%	16%	11%

In a random sample of shoppers in the Marshall Department Store's main branch, shoppers were asked to indicate their age categories. The following observed frequencies resulted:

Age category:	< 21	21–35	36–50	51–65	66+
Observed frequency:	18	51	42	89	50

Do the ages found in the Marshall study correspond to the age distribution reported by *Shopping Journal?*

The null and alternative hypotheses are

H_0: $p_1 = .10$, $p_2 = .32$, $p_3 = .31$, $p_4 = .16$, $p_5 = .11$.

H_1: The population proportions are not $p_1 = .10$, $p_2 = .32$, $p_3 = .31$, $p_4 = .16$, $p_5 = .11$.

The expected frequencies were calculated by taking the percentages from the *Shopping Journal* study and multiplying them by the sample size, 250. For example, the expected frequency for shoppers under age 21 is 25 (.10 × 250). The expected and observed frequencies are:

Age category:	< 21	21–35	36–50	51–65	66+
Observed frequency:	18	51	42	89	50
Expected frequency:	25.0	80.0	77.5	40.0	27.5

Equation 11.2 is used to compute the chi-square test statistic and determine how well the age distribution obtained in the department store fits the age statistics of the large city. Table 11.8 shows the chi-square value for the test.

TABLE 11.8   Chi-Square Computations for Example 11.6

f_o	f_e	$(f_o - f_e)^2 / f_e$
18	25.0	2.0
51	80.0	10.5
42	77.5	16.3
89	40.0	60.0
50	27.5	18.4
		$\chi^2 = 107.2$

The test value of 107.2 is compared with the table value of chi-square, again using the distribution for four degrees of freedom ($k = 5$, $c = 0$). At the .01 significance level, the decision rule is

If the calculated chi-square statistic is larger than 13.277, reject the null hypothesis (reject H_0 if $\chi^2 > 13.277$).

Since the sample chi-square statistic (107.2) is larger than the critical value (13.277), the null hypothesis is rejected. Marshall Department Store shoppers don't appear to conform to the large city's age distribution reported by *Shopping Journal*.

RULE OF FIVE

The test statistic used to compare the relative sizes of expected and observed frequencies has an approximate chi-square distribution. The distribution of this test statistic is actually discrete, but it can be approximated by using a continuous chi-square distribution when sample size n is large. This is the approach used in Chapter 6 to approximate the discrete binomial distribution using the normal distribution. The discrete distribution of the test statistic χ^2 is approximated using the continuous chi-square distribution. To assure that n is large enough, the conservative rule is to require that the expected frequency for each cell be at least 5. If a cell's expected frequency is less than 5, cells should be combined in such a way that meaningful categories result. Example 11.7 illustrates the use of the rule of five.

EXAMPLE 11.7 Lilah Novak, factory manager for a transmissions manufacturer, wants to use a simulation computer program to model the movement of goods on the factory floor. She's interested in improving the factory's efficiency, especially after reading an editorial in *Management Accounting* (August 1989), which described the increasing pressure on U.S. manufacturing from overseas competition. She also read a front-page *Wall Street Journal* (March 2, 1990) article describing the rapid expansion of Korean car companies.

A key assumption of the program is that the arrival of finished goods off the assembly line follow a Poisson distribution. Since Lilah has no idea whether this assumption is valid, she selects a random sample of factory hours and records the arrivals per hour (Table 11.9).

TABLE 11.9   Shipment Arrivals per Hour (Example 11.7)

Arrivals/hour	Frequency
0	3
1	15
2	23
3	20
4	12
5	10
6	7
7 or more	5
	$n = 95$

The null hypothesis under test is that the sample data were drawn from a population that follows a Poisson distribution:

H_0: The population is Poisson-distributed.

H_1: The population is not Poisson-distributed.

Under the assumption that the null hypothesis is true, Table 11.9's observed frequencies are compared with the expected frequencies based on the appropriate Poisson distribution. The chi-square statistic for the test is then calculated using Equation 11.2.

To find the expected frequencies, Lilah must know the mean number of population arrivals so that the correct column of the Poisson table can be consulted. However, the population mean is not known, so the sample mean from Table 11.9 must be calculated and used as an estimate. This is the same as the process for computing a weighted mean, which was introduced in Chapter 4. Each value in the first column of Table 11.9 is multiplied by the frequency (second column), and these products are added. This sum is divided by the total number of sample hours (95) to produce the sample mean:

$$\bar{x}_w = \frac{\Sigma wx}{\Sigma w}$$
$$= \frac{(0\times3) + (1\times15) + (2\times23) + (3\times20) + (4\times12) + (5\times10) + (6\times7) + (7\times5)}{3 + 15 + 23 + 20 + 12 + 10 + 7 + 5}$$
$$= \frac{296}{95} = 3.1$$

The average number of arrivals per hour for the sample, 3.1, is used as an estimate of the unknown population mean.

We now consult the Poisson table in Appendix E.4 to find the expected frequencies, under the assumption that the population is Poisson-distributed. The probabilities from the $\mu = 3.1$ column of the Poisson table are shown in Table 11.10. These probabilities are multiplied by 95, the number of sampled hours, to form the expected frequencies. Table 11.10 shows these values as well.

TABLE 11.10   Expected Frequencies for Example 11.7

Frequency	Poisson probability ($\mu = 3.1$)	f_e (probability × 95)
0	.0450	4.275*
1	.1397	13.272
2	.2165	20.568
3	.2237	21.252
4	.1734	16.473
5	.1075	10.213
6	.0555	5.273
7 or more	.0387	3.677

*95 × .0450 = 4.275

Based on the rule of five, none of the expected frequencies in Table 11.10's f_e column should be less than five. However, the first category, the one for 0 arrivals per hour, has an expected frequency of 4.275. Also, the last category, the one for 7 or more arrivals per hour, has an expected frequency of 3.677. These values violate the rule of five. Lilah must combine the "0" and "1" categories and also the "6" and "7 or more" categories so that none of the expected frequencies is less than 5. This reduces the number of categories, and the degrees of freedom, but results in a valid test. Once these categories have been combined in Table 11.11, the expected frequency of the "0 and 1" category is 17.547, and its observed frequency equals 18. The expected frequency of the "6 or more" category is 8.949, and the observed frequency now equals 12.

TABLE 11.11   Goodness-of-Fit Test for Example 11.7

Frequency	Poisson prob. for $\mu = 3.1$	f_e (prob. × 95)	f_o	$\dfrac{(f_o - f_e)^2}{f_e}$
0 or 1	.1847	17.547*	18	.012
2	.2165	20.568	23	.288
3	.2237	21.252	20	.074
4	.1734	16.473	12	1.215
5	.1075	10.213	10	.004
6 or more	.0942	8.949	12	1.040
			Sum: 95	2.633

*95 × .1847 = 17.547

After the expected frequencies are computed, they're compared with the observed frequencies, and the chi-square statistic is calculated. As shown in Table 11.11, this test value is 2.633. For this equation, there are six categories ($k = 6$). One population parameter, the mean, wasn't known and was estimated using a sample statistic, so $c = 1$. Finally, the expected frequencies must sum to 95, so one more degree of freedom is lost. Thus, the degrees of freedom is

$$\text{df} = k - 1 - c = 6 - 1 - 1 = 4$$

In the chi-square table for four degrees of freedom, the critical value for $\alpha = .10$ is 7.779. Smaller significance levels have even larger critical values. At the .10 significance level, the decision rule is

If the calculated chi-square statistic is larger than 7.779, reject the null hypothesis (reject H_0 if $\chi^2 > 7.779$).

Since the test statistic (2.633) is smaller than the critical value (7.779), the null hypothesis is not rejected. The sample data support the assumption that the population is Poisson-distributed, and Lilah can use the computer simulation program based on this assumption.

Figure 11.4 shows the test statistic compared to the critical or table chi-square value. Note that the p-value is .6220. This means that Lilah must assume a .6220 risk of making a type I error if she rejects the null hypothesis.

FIGURE 11.4   Chi-Square Distribution for Four df (Example 11.7)

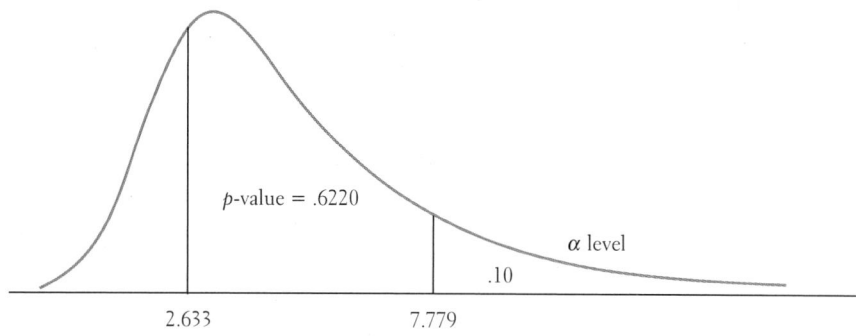

p-value = .6220

α level

.10

2.633   7.779

EXERCISES

12. What kind of data are used in the chi-square goodness-of-fit test?

13. Why is the chi-square goodness-of-fit test useful in business applications?

14. What is the goal of the goodness-of-fit test?

15. State the null and alternative hypotheses for a goodness-of-fit test.

16. How are the expected frequencies computed for a goodness-of-fit test?

17. If a goodness-of-fit test to investigate equal brand preference has four categories, how many degrees of freedom are involved in the test?

18. If a goodness-of-fit test to investigate whether a variable is normally distributed has eight categories, how many degrees of freedom are involved in the test?

19. How do the contingency table test and the goodness-of-fit test differ?

20. The Shaga Soft Drink Company is about to enter the diet cola market and wants to know if consumers prefer a certain brand in a blind taste test. Two hundred diet cola drinkers are offered four different beverages in identical containers and asked to indicate their favorite. The results are:

Favorite diet cola			
A	B	C	D
60	43	46	51

  a. State the null and alternative hypotheses.

  b. Compute the degrees of freedom.

  c. State the decision rule using the .01 significance level.

  d. Test if people prefer one brand over another.

21. Kay Bright, accounting supervisor for Westman Corporation, wants to know if the company's accounting process can be simulated using the Poisson distribution to describe the

incidence of error. Kay takes a random sample of 400 accounts from the firm's accounting records and summarizes the number of errors found in each account. The results are:

Number of errors	Number of accounts
0	102
1	140
2	75
3	52
4 or more	31
	400

a. State the null and alternative hypotheses.

b. Compute the degrees of freedom.

c. State the decision rule using the .05 significance level.

d. Test whether the Poisson distribution describes the incidence of error in the firm's accounting records.

22. The First Intercounty Bank surveyed the number of business failures in those counties where it has branches. Vice President Cal Worship is trying to obtain data to help him decide how to distribute the bank's staff of commercial loan officers specially trained to handle bankruptcies. The results of the sampling are:

County:	A	B	C	D	E	Sum
Observed failures:	17	23	25	12	23	100

a. State the null and alternative hypotheses.

b. Compute the degrees of freedom.

c. State the decision rule using the .10 significance level.

d. Determine whether or not it's reasonable for Cal to make loan officer assignments under the assumption that all five counties have the same number of problem businesses.

23. Past records indicate that the average number of service calls received at the Magna service facility is four per one-hour interval. A random sample of 200 hour intervals is taken and the frequencies of service calls recorded. The results are:

Number of calls	Number of 200 hour intervals
0	45
1	99
2	32
3	19
4 or more	5
	Sum = 200

Use the .05 significance level to test whether the Poisson distribution describes the number of service calls received at the Magna service facility.

FINAL NOTES ON CHI-SQUARE TESTS

Several important things should be noted about the use of the chi-square tests discussed in this chapter. First, the expected frequencies should, as a rule of thumb, all be 5 or greater. If expected frequencies are lower, the test may be invalidated since the chi-square distribution may not represent the true sampling distribution.

Most data analysis computer programs can conduct the contingency table test, and some are capable of the goodness-of-fit test. These analyses' results usually include a display of the data along with the computed chi-square value and the p-value. The analyst can make a rational decision to reject or fail to reject the null hypothesis based on knowledge of the p-value.

When the null hypothesis is rejected for the contingency table test, the conclusion is that there is a dependence between the row and column variables. The analyst's next task is to determine the nature of this dependence. That is, after the hypothesis of independence is rejected, the analyst's interest shifts to finding which rows tend to influence which columns. This task is most easily accomplished by an inspection of the contingency table.

Likewise, a rejection in a goodness-of-fit test leads to an investigation of the ways in which the sample data fail to conform to the hypothesized population distribution. Those categories with more than the expected number of items are contrasted with categories that have less than the expected number. Insights into the nature of the population are thus gained.

Quantitative data, either interval or ratio, are frequently collected in statistical analyses. Since the chi-square tests discussed in this chapter are used only with categorical data, it's often desirable to convert quantitative data to categorical data so that these tests may be employed. For example, ages of sampled people from a night college program might be collected along with a variable measuring graduate/undergraduate status. If the analyst wants to investigate the relationship between age and status using a contingency table, it's necessary to first convert the ratio-scaled age data to ordinal data. Several age categories can be established and each person placed into one of them; this type of problem is illustrated in Exercise 34. Each person is also classified as a graduate or undergraduate.

EXERCISES

24. What is the rule of thumb regarding the number of expected frequencies necessary to conduct a valid chi-square test?

25. How is the p-value helpful to an analyst conducting a chi-square test?

26. After rejecting a null hypothesis in a contingency table test, what should the analyst do?

27. Alliance Pacific, Inc., conducted a voter opinion survey to elicit input from area voters regarding a proposed aquifer protection area. People were asked how they would vote on the ballot, and this variable was tested against income level, in thousands. The results are:

Income level ($000)	Voter preference		
	Yes	No	Undecided
Under 15	155	55	35
15 to under 30	409	110	30
30 to under 50	269	45	26
50 and over	84	11	9

Source: "Spokane Aquifer Protection Area Voter Opinion Survey," Spokane: Alliance Pacific, Inc., August 1985.

a. State the null and alternative hypotheses.

b. Compute the degrees of freedom.

c. State the decision rule using the .05 significance level.

d. Test whether income level is related to a person's vote on the aquifer protection area.

28. In the survey in Exercise 27, the variable *educational level* was also tested against how people plan to vote on the ballot measure. The results are:

Educational level	Voter preference		
	Yes	No	Undecided
High school	303	65	30
Some college	282	70	40
College graduate	332	86	30

Source: "Spokane Aquifer Protection Area Voter Opinion Survey," Spokane: Alliance Pacific, Inc., August 1985.

a. State the null and alternative hypotheses.

b. Compute the degrees of freedom.

c. State the decision rule using the .01 significance level.

d. Test whether educational level is related to whether a person voted yes for the aquifer protection area.

29. The Dayton Corporation is trying to decide how to allot its advertising budget. Harold Ellis, company analyst, suggests that the company study how effective other firms have been with different types of advertising. He obtains the following data:

Type of advertisement	Number of stores		
	Increased sales	Stable sales	Decreased sales
Newspaper	18	12	4
Radio	12	16	3
TV	14	16	2

a. State the null and alternative hypotheses.

b. Compute the degrees of freedom.

c. State the decision rule using the .10 significance level.

d. Test whether type of advertising affects sales.

SUMMARY

This chapter presented two important statistical tests designed for qualitative or categorical data. These tests are widely used in business because many business applications involve measurements on people rather than things. Surveying people's attitudes usually results in categorical data, and investigating the relationships involved in such data requires the use of qualitative data techniques such as the tests discussed in this chapter. Additional methods of analyzing qualitative data appear in Chapter 19.

The contingency table test is designed to examine the relationship between two categorical variables. One of the variables is arrayed in the rows of the contingency table, and the other appears in the columns. The chi-square statistic is then computed. This statistic measures the degree of conformity between the observed frequencies in each cell of the table and the frequencies that are expected under the assumption of independence between the two variables.

The goodness-of-fit test measures the extent to which the frequencies observed in each category of a single variable conform to the frequencies that are expected for a hypothesized population. The nature of the population under test must be specified before the test is conducted. Under the assumption that the sample conforms to this hypothesized population, the expected frequencies are determined and compared with the observed frequencies using the chi-square statistic. The population condition specified in the null hypothesis is then either rejected or not rejected.

APPLICATIONS OF STATISTICAL CONCEPTS IN THE BUSINESS WORLD

ALLIANCE PACIFIC'S USE OF CHI-SQUARE TESTS

Jack Geraghty is president of Alliance Pacific, Inc. (API), a public relations and public affairs firm that specializes in crisis management and community awareness campaigns. API has determined public opinion on such issues as recycling, the police and fire departments staffing, electrical magnetic fields, sewers, whether to build a coliseum, and whether to build a waste-to-energy plant. The firm also specializes in helping local school districts obtain voter approval of bond levies.

Jack frequently conducts public opinion surveys. In each survey, one section asks respondents for demographic data to be used for statistical analysis. Jack uses the chi-square test of independence (crosstabs) to determine the relationship between each demographic variable and respondents' attitudes on various issues. For example, Jack uses crosstabs to determine the demographics (gender, education, age, income, etc.) of the type of person who will vote yes on a particular bond issue.

OTHER APPLICATIONS

The contingency table test is widely used in business because market research often involves collecting categorical data. Here are examples of cross-tabulations that might appear in a business setting. The demographic variables in the left column would be compared with any one of the opinion variables in the right column through the use of a contingency table test.

Demographic variables	Opinion variables
Age category	Automobile preference
Sex	Favorite department store
Marital status	Health care provider
Educational level	Opinion on social security
Area of residence	Preferred presidential candidate
Occupation	Rating on 1-to-5 scale of:
Type of residence	Prices
Number in household	Service
Income level	Value
Years in community	Safety of funds invested
Employment status	Quality of management
Own home versus rent	Career satisfaction

The goodness-of-fit test is not as widely used as the contingency table test but still has many business applications. Following are several variables that might be examined and compared with the indicated population distribution.

Variable	Hypothetical population
Age	Age distribution from different state
Local candidate preference	National candidate preference
Telephone call arrivals	Poisson distribution
Time of completion	Normal distribution
Weight of parts	Normal distribution
Time of delivery	Normal distribution
Product preference	Equal preference
TV show preference	Equal preference
Defectives by plant	Equal defective rates

GLOSSARY

Contingency table test A test to determine whether two categorical variables are related to each other.

Goodness-of-fit test A test to determine the likelihood that the frequencies observed for a categorical variable could have been drawn from a hypothesized population.

KEY FORMULAS

Expected frequencies

$$f_e = \frac{(\text{Row total})(\text{Column total})}{\text{Sample size}} \tag{11.1}$$

Chi-square statistic

$$\chi^2 = \sum \frac{(f_o - f_e)^2}{f_e} \tag{11.2}$$

Contingency table test degrees of freedom

$$df = (r - 1)(c - 1) \tag{11.3}$$

Goodness-of-fit test degrees of freedom

$$df = k - 1 - c \tag{11.4}$$

SOLVED EXERCISES

· ·

1. CONTINGENCY TABLE TEST

Decision Science Associates conducted a telephone survey to assess older homeowners' attitudes toward retirement. People 55 years of age or older were asked, "How important to you is 24-hour community security in deciding where to live during your retirement?" Respondents indicated this factor was either "important" or "not important." This variable was tested against gender to determine if males and females answered the question differently. The results are:

Gender	Important	Not important
Male	140	60
Female	180	20

Source: "Survey of Older Homeowners Concerning Retirement Attitudes,"
Spokane: Decision Science Associates, June 1986.

a. State the null and alternative hypotheses.

b. Compute the degrees of freedom.

c. State the decision rule using the .05 significance level.

d. Test if gender is related to whether a person feels 24-hour security is important in determining where to live during retirement.

Solution:

a. H_0: Gender and the importance of 24-hour security are independent.

   H_1: Gender and the importance of 24-hour security are dependent.

b. $df = (r - 1)(c - 1) = (2 - 1)(2 - 1) = 1$.

c. If the calculated chi-square statistic is larger than 3.841, reject the null hypothesis (reject H_0 if $\chi^2 > 3.841$).

d. The computations for the expected frequencies are

$$(200)(320)/400 = 160$$
$$(200)(80)/400 = 40$$
$$(200)(320)/400 = 160$$
$$(200)(80)/400 = 40$$

The observed and expected frequencies are shown in Table 11.12.

The chi-square computations are shown in Table 11.13. Since the calculated chi-square statistic (25) is larger than the critical value at the .05 significance level (3.841), reject the null hypothesis and conclude that gender and the importance of 24-hour security are dependent. Inspection of the table shows that females are more likely than males to want 24-hour security.

TABLE 11.12   Expected Frequencies for Solved Exercise 11.1

Gender	Important		Not important		
Male	140	160	60	40	200
Female	180	160	20	40	200
Totals	320		80		400

TABLE 11.13   Chi-Square Computations for Solved Exercise 11.1

f_o	f_e	$(f_o - f_e)^2 / f_e$
140	160	2.5
60	40	10.0
180	160	2.5
20	40	10.0
		$\chi^2 = 25.0$

2. GOODNESS-OF-FIT TEST—NORMAL DISTRIBUTION

The Hewlet-Desoto Corporation has several thousand hourly workers. Company analyst Peggy Flaherty wants to determine if a normal distribution can be used to describe the firm's hourly wage scale. She selects a random sample of hourly workers and records their wage rates. Peggy finds that the sample mean and standard deviation are $8.00 and $0.78, respectively. She develops a frequency distribution of hourly workers (Table 11.14) and tests at the .05 significance level to see whether the hourly wage scale for the company is normally distributed.

TABLE 11.14   Data for Solved Exercise 11.2

Hourly wage ($)	Number of workers
6.00 to under 6.50	12
6.50 to under 7.00	38
7.00 to under 7.50	104
7.50 to under 8.00	131
8.00 to under 8.50	117
8.50 to under 9.00	98
9.00 to under 9.50	47
9.50 to under 10.00	13
	560

a. State the null and alternative hypotheses.

b. Compute the degrees of freedom.

c. State the decision rule using the .05 significance level.

d. Test whether the company's hourly wage scale is normally distributed.

Solution:

a. H_0: The population of hourly wages is normally distributed.

   H_1: The population of hourly wages is not normally distributed.

b. df $= k - 1 - c = 8 - 1 - 2 = 5$. $c = 2$ because two sample statistics (the sample mean and standard deviation) are used to estimate population parameters (the population mean and standard deviation).

c. If the calculated chi-square statistic is larger than 11.07, reject the null hypothesis at the .05 significance level (reject H_0 if $\chi^2 > 11.07$).

d. The null hypothesis is assumed to be true, so the sample mean and standard deviation are used to develop a theoretical distribution that is assumed to be normal. The computations for the expected frequencies are presented in Table 11.15.

TABLE 11.15   Expected Frequencies for Solved Exercise 11.2

Hourly wage ($)	$\bar{x}$	z	Area	f_e
6.00 to under 6.50	6.50	−1.92	.0274	15*
6.50 to under 7.00	7.00	−1.28	.0729	41
7.00 to under 7.50	7.50	−0.64	.1608	90
7.50 to under 8.00	8.00	0.00	.2389	134
8.00 to under 8.50	8.50	0.64	.2389	134
8.50 to under 9.00	9.00	1.28	.1608	90
9.00 to under 9.50	9.50	1.92	.0729	41
9.50 to under 10.00	10.00	2.56	.0274	15
			1.0000	560

*$560 \times .0274 = 15$

Since a normally distributed variable theoretically ranges from $-\infty$ to $+\infty$, the area between the mean of the distribution (8.00) and the lower limit of the first class (6.00) is .5000 (the area from $-\infty$ to the mean).

The next step is to compute z values for the upper boundaries of each class. The upper boundary for the first class is 6.50. The z value for 6.50 is

$$z = \frac{x - \bar{x}}{s} = \frac{6.50 - 8.00}{0.78} = -1.92$$

From Appendix E.6's standard normal table, the area between a z value of -1.92 and the mean is .4726. If this area is subtracted from the area between the mean and $-\infty$ (.5000), the area of the class "6.00 to under 6.50" is .0274 (.5000 − .4726).

The z value for the upper boundary of the second class is

$$z = \frac{x - \bar{x}}{s} = \frac{7.00 - 8.00}{0.78} = -1.28$$

The standard normal table shows that the area between a z value of -1.28 and the mean is .3997. If this area is subtracted from the area between the mean and -1.92, the area of the class "6.50 to under 7.00" is .0729 (.4726 − .3997). Table 11.15 shows similar computations for the other class intervals.

· Finally, Table 11.16 shows the differences between the observed and expected frequencies along with the chi-square computation.

TABLE 11.16   Chi-Square Computations for Solved Exercise 11.2

Hourly wage ($)	f_o	f_e	$(f_o - f_e)^2/f_e$
6.00 to under 6.50	12	15	0.60
6.50 to under 7.00	38	41	0.22
7.00 to under 7.50	104	90	2.18
7.50 to under 8.00	131	134	0.07
8.00 to under 8.50	117	134	2.16
8.50 to under 9.00	98	90	0.71
9.00 to under 9.50	47	41	0.88
9.50 to under 10.00	13	15	0.27
		560	$\chi^2 = 7.09$

Since the calculated chi-square statistic (7.09) is smaller than the critical value (11.07), Peggy fails to reject the null hypothesis and concludes that the hourly wage scale is normally distributed.

EXERCISES
. . . .

30. When the chi-square test is used, is it necessary to assume that the population is normally distributed?

31. What are the similarities between the chi-square distribution and the *t* distribution? What are the differences?

32. Why is the alternative hypothesis one-tailed for chi-square tests?

33. Janis Yee, Financial Fleet Corporation director of marketing, conducts an experiment to determine if the type of postage used on the envelope containing a questionnaire affects whether a respondent returns it. Janis mails out 4,000 questionnaires, half using a postage meter and half using a regular stamp. The results are:

	Type of postage	
	Meter	Stamp
Response	750	775
No response	1,250	1,225

a. State the null and alternative hypotheses.

b. Compute the degrees of freedom.

c. State the decision rule using the .01 significance level.

d. Test if the response rate varies with the type of postage used.

34. Tony Greenwell, Wise Insurance Company analyst, believes younger drivers have more auto accidents and should be charged more for car insurance. To test this hypothesis, Tony gathers statistical evidence on claim rates for various age groups over a five-year period:

Age group	Claim	No claim
16 to under 21	50	175
21 to under 35	45	225
35 to under 50	38	375
50 and over	34	225

    a. State the null and alternative hypotheses.

    b. Compute the degrees of freedom.

    c. State the decision rule using the .05 significance level.

    d. Test if the number of claims is dependent on age.

35. Holly Largent, vice president of computing at Northern University, has collected data on the number of times service to users was interrupted per day over the past year. Holly wants to determine the appropriate probability distribution for this variable so that she can create a simulation process. The data are:

Interruptions per day	Number of days
0	117
1	128
2	63
3	30
4	13
5 or more	14
	365

What should Holly conclude?

36. Bif Peanut Butter Company is worried that consumers prefer other brands to Bif. It hires an independent research firm to conduct a telephone survey in a market test area. The research firm calls 400 households and obtains the following brand preferences:

Brand A	Bif	Brand C	Brand D	Brand E
75	65	90	82	88

Write a brief memo for the research firm summarizing the results.

37. Diane Morton, marketing director of the Spokane Transit Authority, has hired Decision Science Associates to conduct a marketing research study. Diane wants to determine if riders live closer to a bus stop than nonriders. DSA surveys 1,201 Spokane County residents. The results are:

Proximity to bus stop	Riders	Nonriders	
Less than 1 block	200	234	434
1 or 2 blocks	170	221	391
3 or 4 blocks	55	112	167
5 or more blocks	52	117	169
Don't know	12	28	40
Totals	489	712	1,201

Source: "1984 Market Survey for Spokane Transit Authority," Spokane: Decision Science Associates, April 1984.

Write a memo to Diane explaining the results of this study.

38. Berry Wise has written a computer program to generate single-digit random numbers and wants to make sure it works properly. His friend, Michelle Conrath, is taking a statistics course and agrees to test the program. Michelle uses the program to generate 1,000 numbers.

Numbers	Frequency
0	90
1	85
2	115
3	101
4	92
5	107
6	85
7	112
8	113
9	100
	$n = \overline{1,000}$

What should Michelle tell Berry about the program?

39. Carla Parrish believes demand for jelly doughnuts on weekends at the Strick's Doughnut Company is normally distributed. If she's correct, the inventory problem of how many doughnuts to produce on Friday can be solved. Carla gathers data for the past 100 weekends:

```
40  45  34  35  40  37  36  44  42  39  39  42
45  39  38  37  42  37  35  42  40  41  40  36
42  42  33  33  34  39  38  37  36  39  36  31
41  39  45  43  30  40  38  39  42  38  38  37
34  36  40  42  45  31  47  35  37  39  43  45
35  43  40  40  33  39  44  37  49  45  45  39
47  40  38  44  38  39  31  37  36  41  36  44
37  37  48  50  45  43  42  35  37  40  37  42
31  42  40  41
```

If Carla uses the .05 significance level, what should she conclude?

40. "Videophiles," an *American Demographics* (July 1992) article, reports demographics of media users. Once a year, Simmons Market Research Bureau asks nearly 20,000 Americans to give a detailed picture of their buying behavior, media use, demographics, and attitudes. The survey asks about most forms of media use, including magazine and newspaper reading, movie going, radio listening, TV viewing, videotape renting, and the buying of books, video games, and compact discs. Simmons identified seven types of media users, each with distinct demographic characteristics. A total of 2,800 respondents were identified as either videophiles or CD buyers; the accompanying table breaks down the results by household income categories.

Household income	Videophiles	CD buyers	Total
Less than $15,000	208	84	292
$15,000 to under $35,000	512	300	812
$35,000 to under $60,000	560	384	944
$60,000 or more	320	432	752
	1,600	1,200	2,800

Todd Corlett is interested in opening a store for videophiles (heavy users of videotapes, video games, and cable TV) and wants to know whether CD buyers are prevalent in the same household income categories as videophiles. This information will help him determine where to locate his new store.

Should Todd conclude that people's classification as either videophiles or CD buyers is independent of household income categories?

41. Robinson Research conducts a market segmentation study for the Atlanta area. Company president Bill Robinson identified seven types of media users, each with distinct demographic characteristics. To determine whether these findings are consistent with the entire U.S. population, Robinson compared his results with those reported by Simmons Market Research Bureau (*American Demographics*, July 1992). Simmons' percentages for each segmentation group were: TV fans (22%), radio listeners (22%), newspaper readers (20%), movie goers (12%), book buyers (10%), videophiles (8%), and CD buyers (6%). When Robinson classified its 500 sampled people, the results were: TV fans (100), radio listeners (120), newspaper readers (80), movie goers (80), book buyers (35), videophiles (60), and CD buyers (25). Are Bill Robinson's findings distributed the same as those reported by Simmons Market Research Bureau?

42. This question refers to Appendix C's company data base. Test the null hypothesis that the proportion of males and females (variable x_3) employed by the company is independent of amount of education (variable x_7). Use the .05 significance level and a sample size of 50.

43. This question refers to Appendix C's company data base. Test to determine whether the number of sick days taken during the past six months (variable x_5) is a Poisson-distributed variable. Use the .10 significance level and a sample size of 35.

44. This question refers to Appendix C's company data base. Test to determine whether employee age (variable x_9) is a normally distributed variable. Use the .05 significance level and a sample of 100.

EXTENDED EXERCISES

45. BABBET ELECTRONICS

Joe Burt is quality-control manager for the Babbet Electronics Company factory that produces compact discs (CDs). His boss, the plant manager, recently told a meeting of company executives that he'd read an article in *Gramophone* magazine (August 1989) about CD sales in the Japanese market. The manager stated that the quality of units produced by Babbet had slipped during the past year, making the company ineffective in this market.

Joe replied that quality had not gone down, but he had no data to back him up. He decided to seek sound evidence that would either confirm or contradict the plant manager's statement.

Company records prior to a year ago were obtained to get an idea of the quality level at that time. Then a random sample of quality reports for 224 CDs was taken from records for the past six months. Five categories were established for the CDs' condition (Table 11.17). The historical

TABLE 11.17 Data for Extended Exercise 45

		Product quality			
	OK	Slight rework	Major rework	Sell at discount	Discard
Then	163	37	10	8	6
Now	125	56	12	15	16

percentages were multiplied by 224, the sample size, to produce the expected frequencies. These were then compared with the observed frequencies in each category so a goodness-of-fit test could be conducted. The null hypothesis under test is that quality had not changed during the past few months.

Using Table 11.17's data, Joe calculates a test value of 41.82 for the goodness-of-fit test. He considers this a very large test value and realizes that his boss is right: the CD line's quality has deteriorated during the past year, and something must be done about it.

a. Did Joe calculate the test statistic correctly?

b. What are the critical table values for chi-square for several significance levels?

c. Is Joe's final conclusion correct?

46. SHELTY OIL COMPANY

For many years, Shelty Oil Company (a national retailer of gasoline and other car products) has offered its own credit card. Maintaining this service is expensive, and Shelty management wonders if the card should be dropped. There's a feeling that general credit cards, so popular in recent years, are preferred by customers over cards that can be used only with one company.

A consultant hired by the company designs a survey to be sent to a random sample of 1,383 holders. One of the demographic questions asks respondents whether they're heavy, medium, or light users of the Shelty card. Another question uses a 1-to-7 point scale to determine the respondent's opinion about the desirability of continuing the Shelty card. Table 11.18 shows the resulting data.

a. What is the null hypothesis in this situation?

b. What is the test statistic, the number of degrees of freedom for the test, and the critical value for a significance level of .05?

c. Using the .05 significance level, state the result of this test in simple terms.

TABLE 11.18   Data for Extended Exercise 46

Card use	Not desirable					Quite desirable	
	1	2	3	4	5	6	7
Heavy	56	79	87	93	128	59	21
Medium	67	89	94	132	32	21	16
Light	87	128	90	64	21	10	9

47. VALLEY HOSPITAL[2]

Lane Samson, chief administrator for a small hospital in western Washington, has hired a consultant to conduct a research study in his hospital's service area. A series of focus groups is conducted, along with a door-to-door survey. Among the matters of interest to Lane is the survey response to the following statement:

For most health problems, I would be comfortable being treated at Valley Hospital.

[2]This exercise is based on a study completed in May 1988 for a small hospital located in western Washington.

Survey respondents were asked to react to this statement with one of the following responses:

Strongly disagree, Disagree, Neutral or no opinion, Agree, Strongly agree.

Lane has seen the tabulation of responses for the entire sample, but he wants to compare responses by two key geographic areas. The first (area 1) is the area in the immediate vicinity of the hospital (within four miles). The second area (area 2) consists of the county the hospital is in, outside the four-mile area.

The data have been run on the SPSS computer program, version x. Here are the SPSS commands to generate a cross-tabulation of area by statement response:

```
CROSSTABS TABLES=VAR5 BY VAR14
STATISTICS 1
```

When the data were being keyed into the computer, the area number (1 or 2) was the fifth variable, so this variable received the name VAR5. Responses to the statement of interest to Lane were keyed in as variable 14, so that variable received the name VAR14. The second command line shown asks the program to compute the chi-square value and the p-value for the data.

After the computer run was completed, the following output was produced and printed:

		VAR 14				
		SD	D	N	A	SA
VAR5	1	9	30	53	65	17
	2	21	45	42	15	11

Chi-Square = 36.97   P = .0000

Lane interprets the output as follows. The cross-tabulation shows the number of responses in each of the 10 possible response categories. The total number of responses is 308, the door-to-door sample size.

The chi-square statistic, 36.97, was computed using Equation 11.2. Lane computes the degrees of freedom to be 4, leading to a table value of 13.277 at the .01 significance level. He thus rejects the null hypothesis of independence between rows and columns and concludes that the two areas react differently to being treated at Valley Hospital. In analyzing the cross-tabulation, Lane finds that people in area 1 (near the hospital) are more comfortable with being treated at Valley Hospital than those living farther away. Lane decides that an advertising campaign might improve this situation.

a. Did Lane reach the correct conclusion based on the computer output?

b. Did he use the correct degrees of freedom value and the correct value from the chi-square table?

c. Lane didn't know how to interpret the p-value printed on the computer output. Write a brief paragraph that explains this value to him.

MICROCOMPUTER PACKAGE
. . . .

The micro package *Computerized Business Statistics* can be used to solve chi-square problems.

In Solved Exercise 11.1, Decision Science Associates attempted to determine if there was dependence between gender and whether people 55 years of age or older felt 24-hour security was important in deciding where they live during retirement.

Computer Solution:

From the main menu of *Computerized Business Statistics* a **12** is selected, indicating chi-square analysis. Since the problem involves entering data from the keyboard, a **1** is selected.

```
Chi-Square Analysis—Define New Problem
OPTIONS          1 = Goodness of Fit
                 2 = Test for Independence
Select Test: Enter 1/2, Press ↵ 2
```

Since a contingency table test, or test for independence, is needed, a **2** is selected.

```
Number of Columns: Enter 2-10, Press ↵ 2
Number of Rows: Enter 2-10, Press ↵ 2
```

Solved Exercise 11.1 involves a contingency table with 2 columns and 2 rows.

```
Alpha Error 1 = 0.1, 2 = 0.05, 3 = 0.025, 4 = 0.01, 5 = Other
Select Alpha: Enter 1-5, Press ↵ 2
```

The significance level selected for this exercise is .05.

```
Degrees of Freedom:  ................................ 1
Critical Chi-Square: ............................ 3.84

Chi-Square Analysis—Enter Column Labels
            Column 1   X1
            Column 2   X2
Press end when Finished
```

Variable 1 is entered as **IMP** and variable 2 as **SEX**, and end is pressed.

```
Problem definition correct? Enter Y/N/Q, Press ↵ Y
```

Following the **Y** response, the program is ready for the data to be entered.

```
Enter Observations
       IMP  SEX
    1   0    0
    2   0    0
```

After the data have been entered, the screen shows:

```
    IMP  SEX
1   140   60
2   180   20
```

F is entered to indicate that you are finished with this menu.

```
Save Data? Enter Y/N, Press ↵ N
```

Next, the chi-square analysis program options menu reappears.

A 7 is entered so that the problem can be run, and the chi-square analysis output menu appears. The choice in this case was **P** for printer.

Now, the program asks:

```
Want Graphic?
Enter Y/N and press enter: Y
```

The choice in this case was **Y** for yes. The resulting graph is shown in Figure 11.5.

FIGURE 11.5 Computer Output

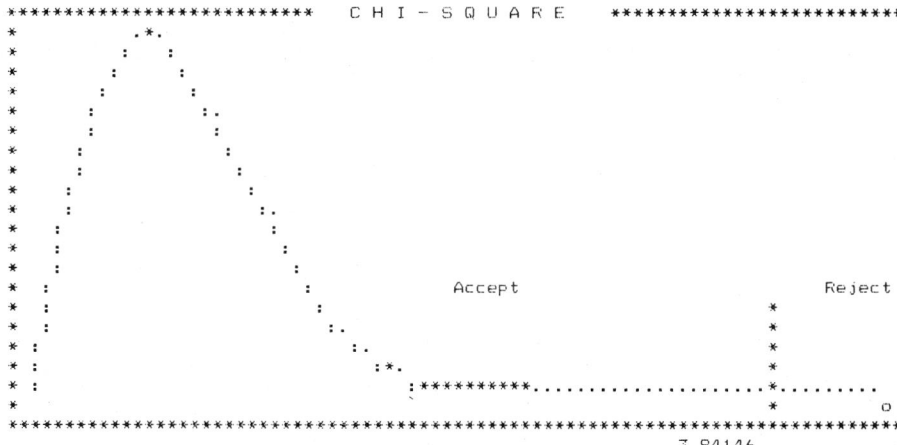

MINITAB COMPUTER PACKAGE

The MINITAB commands to perform the chi-square test of independence for Exercise 28 are:

```
MTB > READ C1–C3
DATA> 303 65 30
DATA> 282 70 40
DATA> 332 86 30
DATA> END
     3 ROWS READ

MTB > NAME C1 'YES' C2 'NO' C3 'UNDECID'
MTB > CHISQUARE FOR TABLE IN C1-C3
```

Expected counts are printed below observed counts

	YES	NO	UNDECID	Total
1	303	65	30	398
	294.80	71.05	32.15	
2	282	70	40	392
	290.36	69.98	31.66	
3	332	86	30	448
	331.84	79.97	36.19	
Total	917	221	100	1238

```
ChiSq = 0.228 + 0.515 + 0.144 +
        0.241 + 0.000 + 2.195 +
        0.000 + 0.454 + 1.058 = 4.834
df = 4

MTB > CDF 4.834;
SUBC> CHISQUARE FOR DF = 4.
    4.8340    0.6952
MTB > STOP
```

The READ command is used to input the data instead of the SET command. The READ command puts 303, 282, and 332 into C1; 65, 70, and 86 into C2; and 30, 40, and 30 into C3. The NAME command is used to name the columns of the table. The CHISQUARE command performs the analysis. The output produces a table that contains both the observed frequencies and the expected frequencies.

The CDF command is used to generate a cumulative probability density function. The CHISQUARE subcommand is used to generate the probability function for a chi-square distribution with four degrees of freedom. Note that the p-value (.3048) is computed by subtracting .6952 from 1 (1.0000 − .6952 = .3048). Since the p-value is greater than the significance level, .3048 > .01, the null hypothesis is not rejected.

SAS Computer Package

```
TITLE ''CHI-SQUARE TEST FOR EXAMPLE 11-4'';
DATA DEFECTS;
INPUT COMPANY $ DEFECT $ COUNT@@;
CARDS;
A MINOR 14 A MAJOR 25 A REPLACE 18
B MINOR 5 B MAJOR 16 B REPLACE 10
PROC PRINT;
PROC FREQ;
 WEIGHT COUNT;
 TABLES COMPANY*DEFECT/CHISQ;
```

The TITLE command names the SAS run. The DATA command gives the data a name. The INPUT command names and orders the different fields on the data lines. The $ indicates that both COMPANY and DEFECT are character data. The @@ indicates that each card image contains two additional sets of data, and the CARDS command is a message that the input data will follow. The next line specifies that 14 defects from supplier A were minor, 25 were major, and 18 required replacement. The next line summarizes the defects for supplier B. The PROC PRINT command directs SAS to list the data. The PROC FREQ command and WEIGHT COUNT subcommand specify that the values of the variable COUNT are relative weights for the observations. The TABLES subcommand directs SAS to produce a contingency table of the variables COMPANY and DEFECT. Finally, the CHISQ command produces the chi-square statistic. The results are presented in Table 11.19.

TABLE 11.19   SAS Output for Example 11.4

```
              CHI-SQUARE TEST FOR EXAMPLE 11-4

                TABLE OF COMPANY BY DEFECT

COMPANY        DEFECT

Frequency |
Percent   |
Row Pct   |
Col Pct   | MAJOR   | MINOR   | REPLACE |  Total
--------- + -------+--------+--------+
A         |    25 |    14 |    18 |     57
          | 28.41 | 15.91 | 20.45 |  64.77
          | 43.86 | 24.56 | 31.58 |
          | 60.98 | 73.68 | 64.29 |
--------- + -------+--------+--------+
B         |    16 |     5 |    10 |     31
          | 18.18 |  5.68 | 11.36 |  35.23
          | 51.61 | 16.13 | 32.26 |
          | 39.02 | 26.32 | 35.71 |
--------- + -------+--------+--------+
Total          41      19      28      88
            46.59   21.59   31.82  100.00
```

STATISTICS FOR TABLE OF COMPANY BY DEFECT

Statistic	DF	Value	Prob
Chi-Square	2	0.923	0.630
Likelihood Ratio Chi-Square	2	0.951	0.622
Mantel-Haenszel Chi-Square	1	0.130	0.718
Phi Coefficient		0.102	
Contingency Coefficient		0.102	
Cramer's V		0.102	

Sample Size = 88

VARIABILITY HYPOTHESIS TESTS AND ANALYSIS OF VARIANCE

Strange! All this difference should be 'twixt Tweedledum and Tweedledee.

John Byron

Objectives

When you have completed this chapter, you will be able to:

Apply the single-population variance test to a business situation.

Apply the hypothesis test for the difference between two population variances to a business situation.

Estimate variance using both the *within* method and the *between* method.

Describe the *F* distribution and apply it to an analysis of variance.

Perform an analysis of variance for a one-way design.

Perform an analysis of variance for a two-way design.

List the assumptions behind the analysis of variance.

An April 1992 *Personnel Journal* article, "An Incentive Pay Success Story," described how a new incentive pay system at Viking Freight Company raised worker productivity.

Chapter 9 showed how to evaluate claims about the means and proportions of a population. Chapter 10 discussed how to evaluate claims about the equality of the means and proportions of two populations. This chapter will explain how to evaluate claims about the variance of a population and claims about the equality of the variances of two populations. Most important, you'll learn how to test the null hypothesis that the means of several populations are equal.

WHY MANAGERS NEED TO KNOW ABOUT ANALYSIS OF VARIANCE

One hypothesis test covered in Chapter 10 was the two-population mean test. In this test, the equality of two population means was tested using sample evidence taken from each population. An important subject of Chapter 12 is the hypothesis test for three or more population means. Even though population *means* are being compared, this test is conducted by focusing on the variances of these populations. For this reason, the test is called *analysis of variance,* usually abbreviated ANOVA.

Judging by the *Personnel Journal* article, a freight company might be very interested in investigating several incentive pay systems involving hourly employees. A method of measuring worker productivity would be determined and various freight firms sampled that use a variety of incentive plans. The sample results would be analyzed using the ANOVA procedures described in this chapter to determine if the plans were the same or different with regard to raising productivity.

SINGLE-POPULATION VARIANCE TEST

One-Population Variance Test

Analysts are sometimes interested in investigating the variability of a population rather than its mean or proportion. This is because uniformity of output is often critical in industrial applications. In fact, excessive variability is considered the number one enemy of high quality, as discussed at length in Chapter 13. The hypothesis test discussed in this section is designed to determine whether a population's variance equals some predetermined value.

The standard deviation of a data collection is used to describe the variability in that collection. As discussed in Chapter 4, the standard deviation can be thought of as the standard difference between the items in a data collection and their mean. Chapter 4 also defined the variance of a data set as the square of its standard deviation. The sample variance, although not particularly useful as a descriptive measure, is used to test the null hypothesis involving variability and is useful in understanding the procedure for analysis of variance.

The null hypothesis for the variance test is that the population variance is equal to some prespecified value. Since the usual issue of interest is whether the population variance is greater than this value, a one-tailed test is generally performed.

To test the null hypothesis, a random sample of items is taken from the population under investigation and a test statistic computed from these data. Equation 12.1 is used to compute the test statistic:

$$\chi^2 = \frac{(n-1)s^2}{\sigma^2} \tag{12.1}$$

where $n - 1$ = Degrees of freedom for the test where n is the sample size
s^2 = Sample variance
σ^2 = Population variance, assuming the null hypothesis is true

Note that the appropriate sampling distribution for this test is the chi-square distribution. In other words, if the null hypothesis is true, the test statistic computed using Equation 12.1 is taken from the chi-square distribution. In Chapter 11 you learned that a particular chi-square distribution is specified by a single parameter, its degrees of freedom. For this test, the degrees of freedom is one less than the sample size $(n - 1)$.

EXAMPLE 12.1   Ellie Gordan, an analyst with the Economic Development Council, wants to know if the variability of ages in a local community is the same or greater than that of the entire state. The standard deviation of state ages, known from a recent study, is 12 years. Ellie plans to take a random sample of 25 people from the community and determine their ages. She'll then calculate the sample variance and use Equation 12.1 to produce the sample statistic. The null and alternative hypotheses are

$H_0: \sigma^2 \leq 144$
$H_1: \sigma^2 > 144$

The sample is taken and results in a sample standard deviation of 15 years. The sample variance is thus 225, and the sample chi-square statistic is

$$\chi^2 = \frac{(n-1)s^2}{\sigma^2} = \frac{(25-1)(15)^2}{12^2} = 37.5$$

If the null hypothesis is true, the sample statistic of 37.5 is drawn from the theoretical chi-square distribution—specifically, the distribution with 24 degrees of freedom $(25 - 1 = 24)$. Note from Equation 12.1 that the larger the sample variance is compared to the hypothesized population variance, the larger the test statistic produced. Thus, a large sample statistic leads to rejection of the null hypothesis, and a small statistic results in failure to reject. The chi-square table (Appendix E.8) is used to determine whether it's likely or unlikely for the value 37.5 to be drawn from the assumed chi-square sampling distribution.

Suppose this test is to be conducted at the .02 significance level. From the .02 column of the chi-square table and the 24 row, the critical value is found to be 40.27. The decision rule is

If $\chi^2 > 40.27$, reject the null hypothesis that the population variance is 144 (reject H_0 if $\chi^2 > 40.27$).

Since the calculated test statistic is 37.5, the null hypothesis is not rejected (at the risk of a type II error). Note from the chi-square table that if an alpha of .05 had been chosen, the critical table value would be 36.415, and the null hypothesis would have been rejected (37.5 > 36.415). This example illustrates the importance of thinking carefully about the appropriate risk of a type I error in a hypothesis test.

Figure 12.1 summarizes Example 12.1. The null hypothesis is assumed true, leading to the drawing of a sample statistic from a chi-square distribution with 24 degrees of freedom. The test statistic along with three critical values are shown in Figure 12.1.

FIGURE 12.1   Chi-Square Test

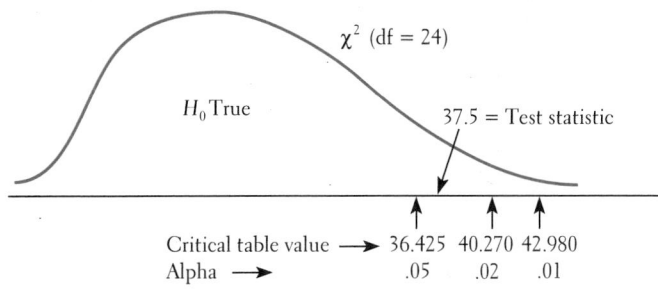

EXERCISES

1. Why is the variance test useful in business applications?

2. State the null and alternative hypotheses for a single-population variance test of your choice.

3. Alan Roberts, production manager of the Mountain Tire Company, believes there is too much variability in the life of tires produced by the night shift. If the process is working properly, Mountain Tires should last an average of 45,000 miles with a standard deviation of 4,000 miles. Alan decides to test to determine if the variability of tire mileages produced by the night shift is greater than 4,000 miles. He selects a sample of 12 tires and computes a sample standard deviation of 4,112 miles.

   a. State the null and alternative hypotheses.

   b. Compute the degrees of freedom.

   c. State the decision rule using the .02 significance level.

   d. Test whether the standard deviation of tires produced by the night shift is greater than 4,000 miles.

4. Chris Karst, owner of a large chain of pet kennels, would like to determine the feasibility of providing a dental insurance plan for her employees. She's concerned about both the average cost and whether the standard deviation exceeds $200. A random sample of eight employees reveals the following dental expenses, in dollars, for the previous year:

342   425   625   975   141   52   342   459

    a. Using a 95% confidence interval, estimate the average cost of providing dental insurance.

    b. If Chris uses the .05 significance level, is there evidence that the population standard deviation of dental expenses is above $200?

TWO-POPULATION VARIANCE TEST

Two-Population Variance Test

Sometimes it's of interest to compare two populations to see if one is more variable in some important measurement than the other. The null hypothesis is that the two populations have the same variance, and the alternative hypothesis is that one has a greater variance than the other. Random samples are taken from each population and the sample variances computed. These values are then used in Equation 12.2 to compute the sample statistic:

F-ratio

$$F = \frac{s_1^2}{s_2^2} \tag{12.2}$$

where s_1^2 = Variance of sample 1
             s_2^2 = Variance of sample 2

    Note: for convenience in finding F values, the largest sample variance is usually placed in the numerator.

    The test statistic for Equation 12.2 is called the *F ratio*. If the null hypothesis of equal population variances is true, the ratio of sample variances is drawn from the theoretical F distribution. By consulting the F table in Appendix E.9, we can assess the likelihood of this event. If it seems likely that the F ratio could have come from the assumed sampling distribution, the null hypothesis is not rejected. If it's quite unlikely the F ratio could be drawn from the assumed distribution, the null hypothesis is rejected.

    The particular F distribution that applies to a specific test is determined by two parameters: the degrees of freedom for the numerator and the degrees of freedom for the denominator. Each of these values is $n - 1$. If these values are known and a value for alpha chosen, the critical F value can be found from the F table.

EXAMPLE 12.2   Wanda Flikke, president of Fidelity Mutual, wants to know if the hourly wage variability is the same at two of her branches, or if the variability of the Highland Branch (branch 1) is greater than that of the Oakwood Branch (branch 2). Her interest in salaries at Fidelity increased after she read an article in *Dollars & Sense* (May 1989) on significant income inequality in the United States. Comparing the income variability of the two branches is the first step of a complete income study.

    Random samples are taken of hourly wages from each branch to determine the sample variances. Wanda chooses the .05 significance level. The null and alternative hypotheses are

$$H_0: \sigma_1^2 - \sigma_2^2 \leq 0$$
$$H_1: \sigma_1^2 - \sigma_2^2 > 0$$

The sample results are

$$s_1 = \$3.79 \qquad s_1^2 = 14.3641 \qquad n_1 = 21 \text{ (branch 1)}$$
$$s_2 = \$2.48 \qquad s_2^2 = 6.1504 \qquad n_2 = 25 \text{ (branch 2)}$$

The F statistic is calculated using Equation 12.2:

$$F = \frac{s_1^2}{s_2^2} = \frac{14.3641}{6.1504} = 2.34$$

The F ratio indicates that the sample variance from population 1 is 2.34 times the sample variance from population 2. However, given the sample sizes, is this enough evidence to reject the hypothesis that the two populations have the same variance? The critical F value is needed to answer this question. First, the degrees of freedom for the numerator and denominator are calculated:

$$\text{df (numerator)} = (n_1 - 1) = (21 - 1) = 20$$
$$\text{df (denominator)} = (n_2 - 1) = (25 - 1) = 24$$

The F table in Appendix E.9 is used to find the critical value. There are two F values in the table: one for the .05 significance level and one for the .01 level. Since this is a one-tailed test, as suggested by the alternative hypothesis, the entire .05 or .01 area will lie on the upper end of the curve.

The columns of the F table represent the numerator degrees of freedom, so column 20 is selected. The row labels correspond to denominator degrees of freedom, so row 24 is selected. The critical F value at the .05 significance level for 20 degrees of freedom in the numerator and 24 degrees of freedom in the denominator is 2.02.

The F ratio calculated from the sample data is 2.34. Based on this test value, the null hypothesis is rejected (2.34 > 2.02). If a 5% risk of a type I error is acceptable, Wanda can conclude that the populations don't have the same variance.

EXAMPLE 12.3   Are the variances of two populations of inventory part ages the same or does population 2 have a greater variance? To answer this question, random samples of 53 parts are taken from each of these inventory populations and the sample variances calculated. The test is to be conducted at the .01 significance level. The null and alternative hypotheses are

$$H_0\colon \sigma_2^2 - \sigma_1^2 \le 0$$
$$H_1\colon \sigma_2^2 - \sigma_1^2 > 0$$

The numerator and denominator degrees of freedom are each 52 (53 − 1). In the abbreviated F table in Appendix E.9, the 50 row and the 50 column are used as approximations of the degrees of freedom. The decision rule is

If the calculated F ratio is larger than 1.94, reject the null hypothesis (reject H_0 if $F > 1.94$).

The sample results are

$$s_1^2 = 489 \qquad n_1 = 53 \text{ (inventory 1)}$$
$$s_2^2 = 1{,}370 \qquad n_2 = 53 \text{ (inventory 2)}$$

The *F* statistic is calculated using Equation 12.2:

$$F = \frac{s_2^2}{s_1^2} = \frac{1{,}370}{489} = 2.8$$

One of the sample variances is 2.8 times as large as the other. The null hypothesis is rejected since the test statistic (2.8) exceeds the critical value (1.94) from the *F* table. It is safe to conclude that inventory 2 has more variability in age than inventory 1.

EXERCISES

5. Why is the larger sample variance placed in the numerator in the equation for the *F* statistic?

6. Explain how the *F* test helps to determine whether two sample variances are equal or different.

7. State the null and alternative hypotheses for a two-population variance test of your choice.

8. How many parameters determine the particular *F* distribution that applies to a specific test?

9. The Vantage Company uses two machines to produce ball bearings used in wheel assemblies. It is essential that the diameter of these bearings not vary significantly from the specification of 0.3 inch. Production Manager Pedro Hernandez is afraid that one of the machines is producing bearings that vary from specifications by an excessive amount, and he decides to compare the two machines. He selects a random sample of 20 bearings from each machine's production lot and computes the standard deviation of the diameters:

   $$s_1 = 0.002 \qquad n_1 = 20 \text{ (machine 1)}$$
   $$s_2 = 0.0015 \qquad n_2 = 20 \text{ (machine 2)}$$

   a. State the null and alternative hypotheses.

   b. Compute the degrees of freedom.

   c. State the decision rule using the .05 significance level.

   d. Test if the variability of ball bearing diameters differs for the two machines.

10. The American Car Association is conducting an experiment to refute the claim that foreign automobiles get better gas mileage than American-made cars. Sue Wainwright, president of the association, feels that the variance in gas mileage obtained by foreign-made models is greater than for American-made models. A mileage test is conducted on 16 vehicles. The results, in miles per gallon, are:

| American | 35.3 | 32.6 | 37.1 | 34.1 | 31.9 | 36.4 | 35.7 | 33.3 |
| Foreign | 41.3 | 36.8 | 37.8 | 37.1 | 35.0 | 37.9 | 34.8 | 31.3 |

   a. Write a memo to Sue reporting the results of the test that foreign cars get better mileage.

   b. Write a memo to Sue reporting the results of the test of her belief that the variance in gas mileage obtained by foreign models is greater than for American models.

ANOVA BASICS

Analysis of Variance

The **analysis of variance,** or **ANOVA,** procedure uses a single numerical variable measured on the sample items to test the null hypothesis of equal population means. This variable can be either interval- or ratio-scaled. It must be, in other words, a quantitative rather than a qualitative variable. This variable is sometimes called the *dependent variable*, especially in computer programs that perform ANOVA.

The null hypothesis under test in ANOVA is that all the populations being studied (at least three) have the same mean value for the dependent variable. The null and alternative hypotheses in ANOVA are

H_0: $\mu_1 = \mu_2 = \mu_3 = \cdots = \mu_c$.
H_1: Not all populations have the same mean.

> **Analysis of variance (ANOVA)** is a statistical procedure for determining whether the means of three or more populations are equal.

In the ANOVA test, sample evidence is gathered from each of the populations under study, and these data are used to compute a sample statistic. The appropriate sampling distribution is then consulted to see if the sample statistic contradicts the assumption that the null hypothesis is true. If so, it's rejected; otherwise, it's not rejected. This hypothesis test uses the same steps outlined at the beginning of Chapter 9.

Recall for the two-population variance test that the ratio of the sample variances is computed and checked against the F distribution. This procedure is also used in ANOVA to test the null hypothesis.

In analysis of variance we assume that all the populations being studied have the same variance, regardless of whether their means are equal. That is, whether the populations have equal or unequal means, the variability of items around their respective means is the same. If this assumption is sound, the null hypothesis of equal population means can be tested using the F distribution.

Under this key assumption, it becomes important to be able to estimate what the variance is and we will describe two methods here. The first method produces a valid estimate of the unknown common variance of the populations *regardless* of whether the populations have equal means. This method is known as the ***within*** **method** of variance estimation. The second method produces a valid estimate of the variance of the populations *only if* the null hypothesis of equal population means is true. This method is known as the ***between*** **method.**

Within Method

Between Method

> The ***within*** **method** of estimating the variance of the populations produces a valid estimate whether or not the null hypothesis is true. The ***between*** **method** produces a valid estimate only if the null hypothesis is true.

The final step in ANOVA involves calculating a ratio with the *between* method estimate in the numerator and the *within* method estimate in the denominator. If the null hypothesis that the populations have the same mean is true, this ratio consists of two separate estimates of the same population variance and is thus drawn from the *F* distribution. However, if the population means are not equal, the estimate in the numerator will be inflated, resulting in a very large ratio. It will be obvious upon consulting the *F* distribution that such a large ratio isn't likely to have been drawn from this distribution, and the null hypothesis will be rejected. The hypothesis test in ANOVA is one-tailed: a large *F* statistic will lead to rejection of the null hypothesis, and a small value will lead to failure to reject.

EXERCISES

11. What is the purpose of analysis of variance?
12. What kinds of data are used with analysis of variance?
13. State the null and alternative hypotheses for an analysis of variance.
14. What is the difference between the *within* method estimate and the *between* method estimate of the variance?

WITHIN METHOD

The *within* method of variance estimation will produce a valid estimate regardless of whether the null hypothesis of equal population means is true. This is because the variability of sample values is determined by comparing each data item with its own sample mean. Each sample value drawn from population A is compared with sample mean A, each item drawn from population B is compared with sample mean B, and so on. Equation 12.3 is used to compute the variance estimate using the *within* method:

$$s_w^2 = \frac{\sum_j \sum_i (x_{ij} - \bar{x}_j)^2}{c(n-1)} \qquad (12.3)$$

where s_w^2 = Estimate of the sample variance using *within* method
   x_{ij} = *i*th data item in group *j*
   $\bar{x}_j$ = Mean of group *j*
   c = Number of groups
   n = Number of sample items in each group

The double summation signs in Equation 12.3 call for first summing the values indicated by the right summation sign, and then summing the values indicated by the left one. First, the differences between each *x* value and its group mean are found, squared, and summed. Then, these sums for each group are added. The result is the sum of the squared deviations between each sample measurement and its group mean. This value is frequently called the *sum of squares within* (SS_w). This sum is then divided by the appropriate degrees of freedom to produce an estimate of the unknown population variance.

The appropriate number of degrees of freedom for the *within* method is computed as $c(n - 1)$ if the number of observations in each group is equal. Since the mean of each group is subtracted from each item in that group, only $(n - 1)$ items within each group are free to vary. And since there are c groups, c is multiplied by $(n - 1)$ to obtain the *within* method degrees of freedom.

Equation 12.3's key point is that each sample measurement is compared to the mean of its *own* group. Example 12.4 illustrates this concept.

EXAMPLE 12.4 The fill weights of four packages of frozen spinach are sampled from each of three crates. The question is whether the average weights of the packages are the same or different among the three crates. Here are the sampled weights (in ounces), group means, grand mean, and estimate of the *within* method variance using Equation 12.3:

	Group 1	Group 2	Group 3	
	12.4	11.9	10.3	
	13.7	9.3	12.4	
	11.5	12.1	11.9	
	10.3	10.6	10.2	
Mean:	12.0	11.0	11.2	Grand mean: 11.4

$$\Sigma(x_i - \bar{x}_1)^2 = (12.4 - 12)^2 + (13.7 - 12)^2 + (11.5 - 12)^2$$
$$+ (10.3 - 12)^2 = 6.19$$
$$\Sigma(x_i - \bar{x}_2)^2 = (11.9 - 11)^2 + (9.3 - 11)^2 + (12.1 - 11)^2$$
$$+ (10.6 - 11)^2 = 5.07$$
$$\Sigma(x_i - \bar{x}_3)^2 = (10.3 - 11.2)^2 + (12.4 - 11.2)^2 + (11.9 - 11.2)^2$$
$$+ (10.2 - 11.2)^2 = 3.74$$

$$s_w^2 = \frac{\Sigma(x_{ij} - \bar{x}_j)^2}{c(n - 1)} = \frac{6.19 + 5.07 + 3.74}{3(4 - 1)} = \frac{15}{9} = 1.67$$

Note that each x value in the sample is compared with the mean of its own group. These differences are then squared and summed in accordance with Equation 12.3. The resulting values are added and divided by the degrees of freedom. The result, 1.67, is an estimate of the common variance of the three populations. The s_w^2 term is frequently referred to as the *mean square error (MSE)*.

The reason the *within* method produces a valid estimate of the unknown population variance, regardless of the status of H_0, appears in Figure 12.2. Figure 12.2*a* shows a situation for which the null hypothesis is true: the sample values drawn from each of the three populations, although not precisely equal, are nearly equal, so the three sample means are very close.

By contrast, Figure 12.2*b* reflects a situation where the null hypothesis is obviously false. The sampled items from each population have very different values, resulting in very different sample means. However, using the *within* method, the *same* variance

FIGURE 12.2   Variance Estimation

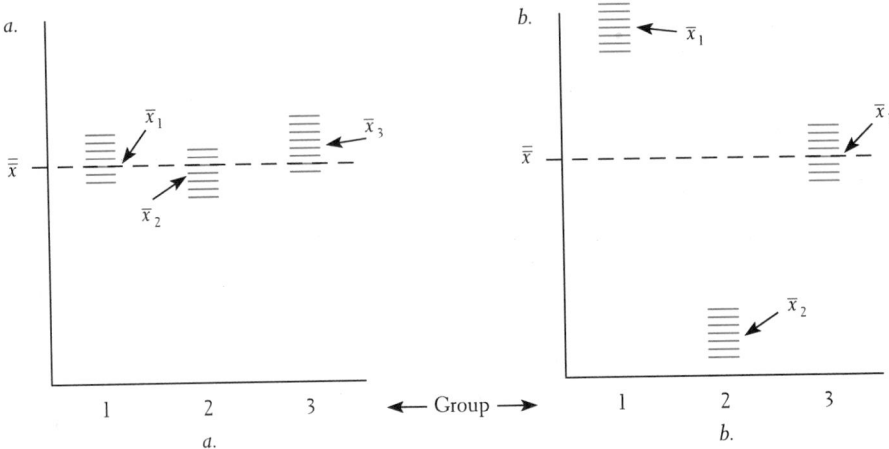

estimate will result for part *b* as for part *a*. This is because each item in each sample is compared with its own group mean. The fact that the group means are all quite different is not reflected in the calculation of Equation 12.3. Note that the assumption of equal population variances appears to be true for both plots: the scatter of data values around their means is the same for each group.

EXERCISES

15. What assumption must be valid for the *within* method to be used to estimate the variance?

16. Explain why the number of degrees of freedom for the *within* method is $c(n - 1)$.

17. How is the sum of squares within (SS_w) computed?

18. Four persons who drink a particular brand of coffee were asked to record the number of cups consumed during a day. The same was done for drinkers of three other brands. The results are shown below. Estimate the common population variance using the *within* method.

	Brand A	Brand B	Brand C	Brand D	
	3	5	2	3	
	2	1	10	6	
	5	4	5	4	
	6	6	7	5	
Mean	4	4	6	4.5	$\bar{\bar{x}} = 4.625$

BETWEEN METHOD

The second method of estimating the common variance of the populations produces a valid estimate only if the null hypothesis is true. To understand the *between* method, recall the central limit theorem presented in Chapter 7. This key theorem in statistics states that the distribution of sample means tends toward a normal distribution as the sample size increases, with a mean of μ and a standard error of $\sigma/\sqrt{n}$. If the standard error of the mean is $\sigma/\sqrt{n}$, then the variance of the distribution equals the standard error squared, σ^2/n.

This variance is a measure of the differences between all sample means that could be drawn from the distribution and the mean of the population. The square root of this variance is the standard error of the mean, the standard difference between a sample mean and the population mean. The standard error was described in Chapter 7.

In ANOVA, to estimate the variance of the sampling distribution of means, we must first estimate the population mean. The mean of all sample values provides such an estimate. Next, the difference between each group mean and this estimated population mean is determined, and these differences are squared and summed. This value is frequently called the *sum of squares between* (SS_b). This sum is then divided by the appropriate number of degrees of freedom to produce the estimate of the sampling distribution variance. Equation 12.4 shows the computation of the estimate of the variance of the sampling distribution of means:

$$s_{\bar{x}}^2 = \frac{\sum_j (\bar{x}_j - \bar{\bar{x}})^2}{c - 1} \tag{12.4}$$

where $s_{\bar{x}}^2 =$ Estimate of the variance of the sampling distribution of means
   $\bar{x}_j =$ Mean of group j
   $\bar{\bar{x}} =$ Grand mean (mean of all data values), used as an estimate of μ
   $c =$ Number of groups

Remember from the sampling distribution of sample means that $\sigma_{\bar{x}}^2 = \sigma^2/n$, where n is the sample size, or number of items in each group. Evaluating this equation for an estimate of the variance (σ^2) produces

$$\sigma_{\bar{x}}^2 = \frac{\sigma^2}{n}$$
$$n\sigma_{\bar{x}}^2 = \sigma^2$$
$$\sigma^2 = n\sigma_{\bar{x}}^2$$

Therefore, an estimate of σ^2 can be computed by multiplying n by the estimate of $\sigma_{\bar{x}}^2$, or

$$s^2 = ns_{\bar{x}}^2$$

Thus, the *between* method estimate of the variance can be computed by substituting Equation 12.4 for $s_{\bar{x}}^2$:

$$s_b^2 = \frac{n\sum_j (\bar{x}_j - \bar{\bar{x}})^2}{c - 1} \tag{12.5}$$

where $s_b^2 =$ *Between* method estimate of the common population variance
   $\bar{x}_j =$ Mean of group j
   $\bar{\bar{x}} =$ Grand mean (mean of all data values), used as estimate of μ

c = Number of groups

n = Number of sample items in each group if the number of observations in each group is equal

The appropriate degrees of freedom value for the *between* method is $c - 1$. Since the grand mean is subtracted from the mean of each group, only $(c - 1)$ means are free to vary. Note that Equation 12.5 assumes that the number of observations in each group, n, is equal.

EXAMPLE 12.5   In Example 12.4 the fill weights of four packages of frozen spinach were sampled from each of three crates and an estimate of the unknown population variance was calculated using the *within* method. In this example the unknown population variance will be estimated using the *between* method:

$$(12.0 - 11.4)^2 + (11.0 - 11.4)^2 + (11.2 - 11.4)^2 = 0.56$$

$$s_b^2 = \frac{n \sum_i (\bar{x}_i - \bar{\bar{x}})^2}{c - 1} = \frac{4(0.56)}{3 - 1} = \frac{2.24}{2} = 1.12$$

The estimate of the population variance computed using the *between* method is 1.12.

Figure 12.2 illustrates why this "estimate" is valid only if the null hypothesis is true. In part *a* of Figure 12.2, the null hypothesis appears to be true, and the variability of the three sample means around the grand mean ($\bar{\bar{x}}$) can be measured and used as a reliable estimate. In part *b* the situation is different. Because the null hypothesis is obviously false (that is, the populations have different means), the squared differences between the three sample means and the grand mean are quite large. The result is an inflated estimate of the population variance, not a true estimate. Figure 12.2 shows why the *between* method works only if the null hypothesis is true. In the next section we will introduce a statistical test to determine whether the *between* method has produced an inflated estimate.

EXERCISES

19. When is the *between* method of estimating the variance a valid approach?

20. Explain why df for the *between* method equals $c - 1$.

21. How is the sum of squares between (SS_b) computed?

22. Four persons who drink a particular brand of coffee were asked to record the number of cups consumed during a day. The same was done for drinkers of three other brands. The results are shown below. Estimate the population variance using the *between* method.

Brand A	Brand B	Brand C	Brand D
3	5	2	3
2	1	10	6
5	4	5	4
6	6	7	5

ANOVA F TEST AND TABLE

After the *within* and *between* methods have been used to estimate the unknown variance of the populations, a ratio is formed from these two estimates:

$$F = \frac{s_b^2 \ (\textit{Between} \text{ method estimate of } \sigma^2)}{s_w^2 \ (\textit{Within} \text{ method estimate of } \sigma^2)} \qquad (12.6)$$

If the null hypothesis is true, both the numerator and denominator of Equation 12.6 are valid estimates of the common variance of the populations being studied. This ratio will thus conform to the F distribution. However, if the null hypothesis is false, Equation 12.6's numerator is actually an inflated estimate of σ^2; the denominator will remain a valid estimate. Under this condition, the F value will be very large, and we conclude that the null hypothesis is false. Figure 12.3 shows the sampling distribution for the ANOVA test along with the acceptance and rejection regions.

Figure 12.3 illustrates the final step in the ANOVA hypothesis test. If the null hypothesis of equal population means is true, the calculated F statistic was drawn from this distribution. As the figure indicates, this appears reasonable as long as the F value is not too large. If a large F value results from the sample data, we conclude that unequal population means have caused the numerator in the F calculation to become inflated, and the null hypothesis is rejected. Note in Figure 12.3 that alpha (α), the probability of a type I error, is indicated in the upper (right-hand) tail. If the null hypothesis is actually true, there's some chance that it will be erroneously declared false. The chance of this occurring is equal to alpha, or the significance level of the test.

FIGURE 12.3 F Distribution

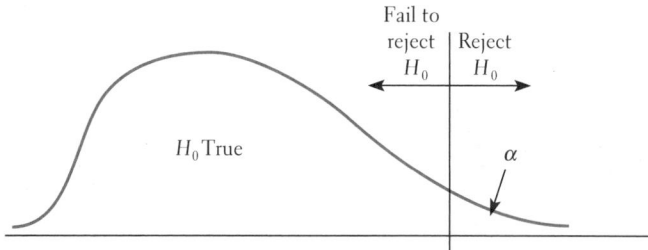

The results of an analysis of variance are usually displayed in an ANOVA table that summarizes the key values for the test. This table has a standard format that is used in most textbooks and computer programs that perform ANOVA. Table 12.1 shows the general form of the ANOVA table.

Table 12.1 summarizes the calculations needed to test the equality of several population means using analysis of variance. First, the *within* method is used to estimate σ^2. Each data value is compared with its own group mean, and the sum of squared differences is divided by the degrees of freedom, $c(n - 1)$.

TABLE 12.1   ANOVA Table

Source of variation	SS	df	Estimate of σ^2	F ratio
Between groups	$n\sum_j (\bar{x}_j - \bar{\bar{x}})^2$	$c - 1$	SS_b/df_b	s_b^2/s_w^2
Within groups	$\sum_j \sum_i (x_{ij} - \bar{x}_j)^2$	$c(n - 1)$	SS_w/df_w	
Total	$\sum_j \sum_i (x_{ij} - \bar{\bar{x}})^2$	$nc - 1$		

j = Column number

i = Row number

c = Number of columns (groups)

n = Number of items in each group (sample size)

Next, the *between* method is used to estimate the common but unknown variance of the populations. As shown in the sum of squares (SS) column of Table 12.1, the sample mean for each group is compared with $\bar{\bar{x}}$, the estimate of the common population mean. This sum is multiplied by n, the number of items in each group. The sum of squares is then divided by the appropriate degrees of freedom, $(c - 1)$. This "estimate" of σ^2 is used in the numerator of the F ratio calculation. Finally, the *between* method estimate is divided by the *within* method estimate. The result is the computed F ratio for the test.

Note that Table 12.1 also shows the total sum of squares and the total degrees of freedom. These values, typically included in a computer printout for ANOVA, are simply the sum of the *between* and *within* values for SS and df.

> The **ANOVA table** contains columns showing the sources of variation, the sums of squares, the degrees of freedom, the estimates of the variance, and the F value for the analysis of variance procedure.

An example will illustrate the test calculations needed to complete an ANOVA table. If you understand the calculations in this example, you'll understand the numerous calculations performed by computer programs that compute analysis of variance and produce an ANOVA table in the final printout.

EXAMPLE 12.6   Joanne Herr, an analyst for the Best Foods grocery chain, wants to know if three stores have the same average dollar amount per purchase. A random sample of six purchases is chosen from each store. Table 12.2 presents the data collected from this sample along with the sample mean for each store and the grand mean of all the sample data. Joanne will test at the .01 significance level.

The null hypothesis under test is that all three populations from which the sample data were drawn have the same mean. The alternative hypothesis is that the popula-

Table 12.2   ANOVA Sample Data (in Dollars) for Example 12.6

	Store 1	Store 2	Store 3
	12.05	15.17	9.48
	23.94	18.52	6.92
	14.63	19.57	10.47
	25.78	21.40	7.63
	17.52	13.59	11.90
	18.45	20.57	5.92
Mean:	18.73	18.14	8.72

Grand mean = $\overline{\overline{x}}$ = 15.20, $c = 3$, $n = 6$

tions don't have the same mean. The first two sample means in Table 12.2 suggest that the null hypothesis is true, since they're very close. However, the third sample mean, 8.72, is considerably smaller than the other two. But is this difference due to chance sampling or to the fact that the populations have different means? This is the question addressed in the ANOVA procedure.

Both the *within* and *between* methods are used to estimate the variance of the three populations. Remember the key assumption behind ANOVA: all populations have the same variance regardless of whether they have the same mean. Table 12.3 shows the calculations for the *within* method, and Table 12.4 shows calculations for the *between* method.

Table 12.3   *Within* Method Calculation for Example 12.6

Store 1:

$(12.05 - 18.73)^2 + (23.94 - 18.73)^2 + (14.63 - 18.73)^2 + (25.78 - 18.73)^2 + (17.52 - 18.73)^2 + (18.45 - 18.73)^2 = 139.82$

Store 2:

$(15.17 - 18.14)^2 + (18.52 - 18.14)^2 + (19.57 - 18.14)^2 + (21.40 - 18.14)^2 + (13.59 - 18.14)^2 + (20.57 - 18.14)^2 = 48.25$

Store 3:

$(9.48 - 8.72)^2 + (6.92 - 8.72)^2 + (10.47 - 8.72)^2 + (7.63 - 8.72)^2 + (11.90 - 8.72)^2 + (5.92 - 8.72)^2 = 26.02$

Sum of squares within $(SS_w) = 139.82 + 48.25 + 26.02$
$= 214.09$

Table 12.4   *Between* Method Calculation for Example 12.6

$(18.73 - 15.20)^2 + (18.14 - 15.20)^2 + (8.72 - 15.20)^2 = 63.09$

Sum of squares between $(SS_b) = 6(63.09) = 378.54$

The values calculated in Tables 12.3 and 12.4 are used to complete the ANOVA table. Since there are three populations being tested, $c = 3$. A sample of six values was drawn from each population, so $n = 6$. Table 12.5 shows the ANOVA table for this example.

TABLE 12.5 ANOVA Table for Example 12.6

Source of variation	SS	df	Estimate of σ^2	F ratio
Between groups	378.54	2	189.27	13.26
Within groups	214.09	15	14.27	
Total	592.63	17		

Note: The degrees of freedom were calculated as follows:

$$c - 1 = 3 - 1 = 2 \quad \text{(between groups)}$$
$$c(n - 1) = 3(6 - 1) = 15 \quad \text{(within groups)}$$

As shown in Table 12.5, the *between* method of estimating σ^2 produces a value of 189.27, whereas the *within* method estimate is 14.27. The F ratio indicates that the *between* method estimate is 13.26 times the *within* method value. Is this difference due to chance sampling error, or is it due to the fact that the null hypothesis is false? To answer this question, the F table is consulted and a critical value determined.

Two degrees of freedom are associated with the numerator of the F ratio, and 15 degrees of freedom are associated with the denominator. From the F table in Appendix E.9, the critical value is 6.36 for these degrees of freedom at the .01 level. The calculated F value of 13.26 is larger than the critical value, which means there is enough sample evidence to reject the null hypothesis of equal population means.

When a computer program is used to solve this example, as will be discussed next, a p-value of .0005 results. The p-value indicates that the probability of obtaining an F value greater than 13.26 by chance alone is .0005, if H_0 is true.

Since one of the group means is smaller than the others, Joanne concludes that although stores 1 and 2 might have equal average purchase amounts, store 3 appears to be below the average of the other two. This conclusion is not based on an intuitive inspection of the data shown in Table 12.2, but on a statistical rejection of the null hypothesis of equal means. Joanne has used the ANOVA procedure to conclude that corrective action is needed to bring store 3 up to the average of the other two stores.

The MINITAB commands to perform analysis of variance for Example 12.6 are:

```
MTB > SET C1
DATA> 12.05 23.94 14.63 25.78 17.52 18.45
DATA> 15.17 18.52 19.57 21.40 13.59 20.57
DATA>  9.48  6.92 10.47  7.63 11.90  5.92
MTB > END
MTB > SET C2
DATA> 1 1 1 1 1 1 2 2 2 2 2 2 3 3 3 3 3 3
MTB > END
MTB > NAME C1 'AMOUNT' C2 'STORES'
MTB > ONEWAY C1 C2

ANALYSIS OF VARIANCE ON AMOUNT
SOURCE     DF      SS      MS       F        P
STORES      2    378.4   189.2   13.26   0.0005
ERROR      15    214.1    14.3
TOTAL      17    592.5
```

```
                                      INDIVIDUAL 95 PCT CI'S FOR MEAN
                                      BASED ON POOLED STDEV
    LEVEL       N       MEAN   STDEV  ----------+---------+---------+-------
        1       6     18.728   5.288                          (-----*------)
        2       6     18.137   3.106                          (-----*------)
        3       6      8.720   2.281   (-----*------)
                                      ----------+---------+---------+-------
    POOLED STDEV =     3.778                   10.0      15.0      20.0
```

The SET command is used to enter the average dollar amount per purchase into C1, and to identify in which store the purchase was made in C2. The ONEWAY command performs the one-way analysis of variance. The output produces an ANOVA table and also analyzes the differences between the group means.

Note that $3.778^2 = 14.3$, the value listed in the sum of squares column for the ERROR row. Thus, the mean square error is equivalent to the pooled estimate of σ^2.

Note also that the MINITAB output includes a 95% confidence interval for the population mean corresponding to each group. Each of these confidence intervals is calculated using the POOLED STDEV = 3.778 and the t distribution based on the degrees of freedom for the error mean square. The confidence interval for the mean of store (level) 1 is

$$
\begin{aligned}
\bar{x}_1 \pm t\frac{s_p}{\sqrt{n}} &= 18.728 \pm 2.131\frac{3.778}{\sqrt{6}} \\
&= 18.728 \pm 2.131(1.542) \\
&= 18.728 \pm 3.286 \\
&= 15.442 \text{ to } 22.014
\end{aligned}
$$

A few comments are in order regarding the analysis of variance procedure discussed in this chapter. First, the examples have implicitly assumed that the same sample size is used for each of the populations under test. In the ANOVA table, this sample size is denoted n, the number of items in each group. More complex versions of the ANOVA procedure can accommodate different sample sizes for the different groups. The simple procedure presented here, which assumes equal sample sizes, is the preferable method if equal samples are possible and convenient.

As mentioned in earlier chapters for other hypothesis tests, computer programs often print the p-value for the test along with the test statistic. In ANOVA, the p-value represents the area of the F distribution that lies above the calculated F value. As with other tests, this p-value is the risk of a type I error that must be assumed if the null hypothesis is rejected.

The key assumption in ANOVA is that the populations have the same variance regardless of whether they have the same means. This assumption can be checked after the sample data have been collected. The sample variances can be examined to see if they are about the same. Pairwise comparisons between sample variances can also be made using the two-population variance test discussed earlier in this chapter. If the null hypotheses of equal population variances are not rejected for all possible pairs, the assumption of equal variances necessary for ANOVA can be made with confidence.

Finally, if the populations don't have the same mean, then which populations have unequal means? The quickest and easiest way to answer this question is to inspect the sample means to see if any are either much higher or much lower than the others. In Example 12.6, it was concluded that store 3, with a mean of 8.72, had a lower average purchase amount than the other two stores. More formal procedures exist for finding the significant sample mean differences once the null hypothesis has been rejected. More advanced texts on analysis of variance describe these procedures.

EXERCISES

23. What is an F ratio?

24. What is an ANOVA table?

25. Four persons who drink a particular brand of coffee were asked to record the number of cups consumed during a day. The same was done for drinkers of three other brands. The results are shown below. (Exercises 18 and 22 asked you to estimate the variance using the *within* and *between* methods for these data.) Construct an ANOVA table to test if there's a difference in the average number of cups consumed for each brand.

Brand A	Brand B	Brand C	Brand D
3	5	2	3
2	1	10	6
5	4	5	4
6	6	7	5

26. The Economy Fuel Company delivers home-heating oil in a four-city area. Owner Jill Grover is interested in determining the speed with which bills are paid in the four cities. Random samples of six accounts are selected in each area, and the numbers of days between delivery and payment of the bill are recorded. The results are partially summarized below:

Source of variation	SS	df	Estimate of σ^2	F ratio
Between groups	128.14	3		
Within groups	864.35	20		
Total				

a. State the null and alternative hypotheses.

b. State the decision rule if the null hypothesis is tested at the .05 significance level.

c. Complete the ANOVA table.

d. What should Jill conclude?

27. The Harrington Corporation manufactures VCRs. Tom Roberts, production manager, has a choice of three subcontractors from which to buy parts. Tom purchases five batches from each subcontractor, with the same number of items in each batch. The number of defectives per batch is determined, and an analysis of variance is run on the computer.

The results are partially summarized below:

Source of variation	SS	df	Estimate of σ^2	F ratio
Between groups	496.54			
Within groups	333.20			
Total		14		

a. State the null and alternative hypotheses.

b. Compute the appropriate degrees of freedom values.

c. State the decision rule if the null hypothesis is tested at the .01 significance level.

d. Complete the ANOVA table.

e. What should Tom conclude?

f. Can Tom determine which subcontractor is best by examining the ANOVA table?

28. The Bandy Corporation, an electronics firm, has sent a number of employees to four educational institutions for technical training. This action was initiated by an article on assessing training needs in the *Training and Development Journal* (April 1989, p. 61). The company hoped that the training would improve employee productivity and product quality.

At the end of the program, Bandy tested the 40 graduates. The scores are:

Program A	Program B	Program C	Program D
95	92	85	98
88	88	81	65
90	80	86	74
99	75	91	82
89	67	78	90
93	78	81	62
95	92	86	75
97	80	90	85
85	77	75	70
90	69	83	82

| Mean | 92.1 | 79.8 | 83.6 | 78.3 | $\bar{\bar{x}} = 83.45$ |

a. State the null and alternative hypotheses.

b. Compute the degrees of freedom.

c. State the decision rule if the null hypothesis is tested at the .05 significance level.

d. What should Bandy conclude?

e. Can Bandy determine which program is best by examining the data presented?

TWO-WAY ANALYSIS OF VARIANCE

The ANOVA discussion and examples to this point have taken into account only one source for the variability in the dependent variable: the groups identified in the populations under test. In Example 12.6, only the different stores could explain differences in average purchase amount. This situation is an example of a *one-way* ANOVA because there is only one factor identified to explain the sample mean differences.

It is sometimes desirable to identify *two* possible causes for differences in the dependent variable. In such a case, a *two-way* ANOVA is conducted. In this procedure, two possible causes for the variability in the dependent variable are identified. Random samples are taken from the populations of interest, and the sample results are used to test the relevant null hypotheses.

To conduct a two-way ANOVA, we must measure the dependent variable for every combination of the two factors being considered. Examples 12.7 and 12.8 illustrate a two-way design.

EXAMPLE 12.7   In Example 12.6, Joanne Herr sought to determine if there was a difference in the average dollar amount per purchase among three stores. What if she also wishes to determine if there's a difference in the average dollar amount per purchase due to the effects of two different advertising campaigns?

The data in Table 12.2 are rearranged so that they can be examined using two-way analysis of variance. As Table 12.6 shows, there are three groups in factor 1 (store) and two groups in factor 2 (advertising campaign). A sample of three items ($n = 3$) were taken and measured for each of the six cells of the table ($3 \times 2 = 6$).

TABLE 12.6   ANOVA Sample Data (Dollars) for Example 12.7

Advertising campaign	Store 1	Store 2	Store 3	Means
A	(16.87) 12.05 23.94 14.63	(17.75) 15.17 18.52 19.57	(8.96) 9.48 6.92 10.47	14.53
B	(20.58) 25.78 17.52 18.45	(18.52) 21.40 13.59 20.57	(8.48) 7.63 11.90 5.92	15.86
Mean:	18.73	18.14	8.72	15.20

Grand mean = 15.20, $r = 2$, $c = 3$, $n = 3$
Store 1 mean = 18.73
Store 2 mean = 18.14
Store 3 mean = 8.72
Advertising campaign A mean = 14.53
Advertising campaign B mean = 15.86
Store 1 and advertising campaign A mean = 16.87
Store 2 and advertising campaign A mean = 17.75
Store 3 and advertising campaign A mean = 8.96
Store 1 and advertising campaign B mean = 20.58
Store 2 and advertising campaign B mean = 18.52
Store 3 and advertising campaign B mean = 8.48

EXAMPLE 12.8   Ginny Nash, a professor at Midwestern University, has received a grant to study effects of different types of fertilizers and different types of soils. In her grant application, she quoted extensively from an article in *The Futurist* (July–August 1989) discussing drought-reduced harvests around the world and the need for increased efficiency in farming.

Ginny decides to investigate four different fertilizers (classified A, B, C, and D) on several acres planted in soybeans. Ginny plants the soybeans in five different soil types labeled 1, 2, 3, 4, and 5. At the end of the growing season, certain acres will be sampled and carefully measured for soybean yield. She hopes that this experiment will reveal fertilizer and soil combinations that produce heavy yields. The data will be collected by measuring the yield for every possible combination of fertilizer and soil type. A sample of n plots of land will be used for each of these 20 combinations, and a two-way ANOVA will be performed.

The two-way analysis of variance procedure will be used to test for differences in the dependent variable that are produced by the column variable. The null hypothesis being tested is that the various levels of the column variable all have the same population mean; this is the same test that was performed for the one-way analysis of variance. Likewise, another null hypothesis will state that the various levels of the row variable have the same average value in the population. These two null hypotheses could be tested separately, which would involve two one-way ANOVAs utilizing the procedure described earlier in this chapter. However, it's more convenient and time-efficient to test the row and column variables at the same time. This results in two null hypotheses under test: one for the rows and one for the columns.

A more important reason for using two-way ANOVA is that it enables a third hypothesis to be tested. Since every combination of the row and column variables will be sampled, we can examine the **interaction** effect of these variables. In Example 12.8, some unexpected result might occur when a particular fertilizer is used with a particular soil type. If so, interaction is present. The following two situations illustrate the concept of interaction for Example 12.8.

Interaction

1. The average yield of fertilizer A is 100 units per acre. The average yield of soil type 1 is 98 units per acre. When fertilizer A is used with soil type 1, an average of 99 units per acre is produced. Since nothing unexpected has happened when fertilizer A is used with soil type 1, no interaction is present.
2. Fertilizer B averages 110 units per acre, and soil type 1 averages 98. When the two are used together, the average yield is 150 units per acre. Apparently, something unusual is occurring when fertilizer B is used on soil type 1. Interaction is present.

Interaction occurs when the levels of one factor interrelate significantly with the levels of the second factor in influencing the dependent variable.

In a two-way ANOVA, the first null hypothesis under test concerns the presence of interaction:

H_0: There is no interaction between the row and column factors in the populations under test.

If interaction is found, the analyst usually turns next to determining why certain levels of one factor interact with certain levels of the second factor. This is done by examining the various cell means. Interaction is found infrequently; however, when it is found, the analyst may not be interested in testing other hypotheses.

If no interaction is found, the row and column variables are examined for differences in the dependent variable. The null hypotheses under test are

H_0: There is no difference in the average value of the dependent variable for the row populations.

H_0: There is no difference in the average value of the dependent variable for the column populations.

EXAMPLE 12.9 William McGonigle, a personnel analyst, wants to conduct a two-way analysis of variance to see if the variable *time with company* is affected by either of two factors: the employee's location in the company's work areas and the employee's pay status. Each employee is assigned to one of four company work areas in various parts of the city. There are three types of employee in terms of method of payment: hourly, monthly, and annual. The data collection consists of samples from every possible combination of company location and payment method. This will result in a data table with 12 cells (four locations times three payment types). The null hypotheses to be tested are:

H_0: There is no interaction between work location and payment method.

H_0: There is no difference in time with company by work location.

H_0: There is no difference in time with company by payment method.

EXAMPLE 12.10 A study reported in the *Journal of Marketing Research* investigated the effects of price, brand, and store information on buyers' product evaluations.[1] Suppose the dependent variable was the buyer's perception of product quality as measured by a numerical value. Two of the factors studied were price and brand. There were five prices for handheld calculators ($17, $28, $39, $50, and the absence of a price) and three brands (Hewlett Packard, Royal, and Sony). The data collection consisted of samples from every possible combination of price and brand. This resulted in a data table with 15 cells. The null hypotheses to be tested are:

H_0: There is no interaction between price and brand.

H_0: There is no difference in perception of product quality for the different price levels.

H_0: There is no difference in perception of product quality for the different brands.

[1]Dodds, W. B., K. B. Monroe, and D. Grewal, "Effects of Price, Brand, and Store Information on Buyers' Product Evaluations," *Journal of Marketing Research*, August 1991, pp. 307–19.

The calculations involved in a two-way analysis of variance are considerable. The wide availability of computer programs that perform ANOVA has virtually eliminated hand calculations for this technique. As with all computer data analysis programs, however, knowing what's being done with the data is important for proper interpretation and understanding. The specific calculations for two-way ANOVA won't be presented here, but we will describe the general nature of the analysis and interpret the computer output.

The key assumption behind two-way ANOVA is the same as for one-way ANOVA: all populations under test are assumed to have the same variance. If there are three rows in the data table and five columns, there are 15 cells and 15 separate populations from which to sample. Regardless of whether the means of these 15 populations are the same, it must be assumed that they vary to the same extent. They must all have the same variance if the ANOVA procedure is to work properly.

There are four ways of estimating the unknown common variance of the populations in the two-way ANOVA procedure. One of these ways, the *within* method, produces a reliable estimate of this variance regardless of whether any of the three null hypotheses are true. As with one-way ANOVA, the *within* method measures the variability of each sample value around its *own cell mean*. Even if several of the cells in the data table have very different means, this won't influence the calculation of the variance estimate using the *within* method. Computing the sum of squares using the *within* method calls for comparing the first data value to the mean of the cell it's in. This difference is squared and added to the squared differences between all the other sample data measurements and their own cell means. The resulting value is divided by the appropriate number of degrees of freedom, $rc(n - 1)$. Since the cell mean is subtracted from each of the n items in the cell, one of these items is not free to vary. Each cell thus has $(n - 1)$ degrees of freedom, and there are r (the number of rows) times c (the number of columns) cells. This *within* estimate of the variance is the denominator of each of the F ratios.

The second method of estimating the variance is valid only if there is no interaction among the populations. If there is interaction, this method produces an inflated estimate. The df value is computed in the same manner as for the contingency table test: $(r - 1)(c - 1)$.

The third method of estimating the variance produces a valid estimate only if the null hypothesis about column mean equality is true. If this hypothesis is false, an inflated estimate will result. This is the same as using the *between* method to estimate the variance in one-way ANOVA. The degrees of freedom equal the number of columns minus 1 $(c - 1)$.

Likewise, the final method of estimating the variance is valid only if the null hypothesis about row mean equality is true. If it is not, an inflated estimate results. Again, the procedure is similar to the *between* method estimate of the variance in one-way ANOVA. The degrees of freedom equal the number of rows minus 1 $(r - 1)$. Table 12.7 shows the formulas for two-way ANOVA.

The final result of a two-way ANOVA is the calculation of three F ratios. As just mentioned, the denominator for each of these ratios is the *within* method estimate of the unknown variance of the populations. The numerators of the ratios are the

TABLE 12.7   Two-Way Analysis of Variance Table

Source of variation	SS	df	Estimate of σ^2	F ratio
Rows	$cn\sum_i (\bar{x}_{ri} - \bar{\bar{x}})^2$	$r - 1$	SS_r/df_r	s_r^2/s_w^2
Columns	$m\sum_j (\bar{x}_{cj} - \bar{\bar{x}})^2$	$c - 1$	SS_c/df_c	s_c^2/s_w^2
Interactions	$n[\sum_i\sum_j (\bar{x}_{ij} - \bar{x}_{ri} - \bar{x}_{cj} + \bar{\bar{x}})^2]$	$(r - 1)(c - 1)$	SS_i/df_i	s_i^2/s_w^2
Within groups	$\sum_i\sum_j\sum_k (x_{ijk} - \bar{x}_{ij})^2$	$rc(n - 1)$	SS_w/df_w	
Total	$\sum_i\sum_j\sum_k (x_{ijk} - \bar{\bar{x}})^2$	$nrc - 1$		

j = Column number
i = Row number
k = Observation number within a cell
r = Number of rows
c = Number of columns
n = Number of observations in each cell

[handwritten annotations: $(3 \times 4)(4-1)$; $12(3)$; 36; $= DF$]

"estimates" produced under the assumption that each of the three null hypotheses is true. Each F ratio is examined to see if it's unusually large. Any F ratio that's larger than the table value for F results in rejection of the corresponding null hypothesis. The general form of each of the three final F ratios is

$$F = \frac{s_i^2 \ (\textit{Interaction} \text{ estimate of } \sigma^2)}{s_w^2 \ (\textit{Within} \text{ method estimate of } \sigma^2)} \quad \text{(Interaction)}$$

$$F = \frac{s_c^2 \ (\textit{Between column} \text{ method estimate of } \sigma^2)}{s_w^2 \ (\textit{Within} \text{ method estimate of } \sigma^2)} \quad \text{(Columns)}$$

$$F = \frac{s_r^2 \ (\textit{Between row} \text{ method estimate of } \sigma^2)}{s_w^2 \ (\textit{Within} \text{ method estimate of } \sigma^2)} \quad \text{(Rows)}$$

If all three null hypotheses are true, the numerators and denominators of these F ratio calculations will all be valid estimates of the same unknown population variance. As you have seen, such a ratio is drawn from the F distribution. However, if any of the three null hypotheses are false, the numerator in the corresponding ratio will be inflated and a large F value will result leading to a rejection of the null hypothesis.

EXAMPLE 12.11   Table 12.8 presents the two-way ANOVA table for Example 12.7. Four "estimates" of the common variance of all populations have been calculated. However, only the *within* method produces a valid estimate regardless of the status of any null hypothesis. The sample evidence has produced the value 16.019 as the *within* method estimate of σ^2.

TABLE 12.8   ANOVA Table for Example 12.11

Source of variation	SS	df	Estimate of σ^2	F ratio
Rows	8.013	1	8.013	0.50
Columns	378.381	2	189.190	11.81
Interaction	13.851	2	6.925	0.43
Within	192.223	12	16.019	
Total	592.468	17		

The three null hypotheses under test in Table 12.8 are:

H_0: There is no interaction between store and advertising campaign in the population.

H_0: The row populations (advertising campaigns) both have the same mean.

H_0: The column populations (stores) all have the same mean.

Note that in Example 12.6 Joanne Herr has already tested the null hypothesis that the column populations, or stores, all have the same mean.

The F ratios of Table 12.8 are calculated by dividing each of the three "estimates" of σ^2 corresponding to the three null hypotheses by 16.019, the valid estimate of σ^2. These calculations are:

F ratio	Degrees of freedom	Critical F (.05)
8.013/16.019 = 0.500	1, 12	4.75
189.190/16.019 = 11.810	2, 12	3.88
6.925/16.019 = 0.432	2, 12	3.88

Note that the *within* estimate of σ^2 ($s_w^2 = 16.019$) is used in each of the denominators. Also shown are the degrees of freedom for the numerator and denominator for each hypothesis test. These values appear in Table 12.8 for each row of the table. Note that the sum of squares (378.381) and the degrees of freedom (2) for the columns from Table 12.8 match (subject to rounding errors) the *between groups* row of Table 12.5. In both cases, the difference between store means is being tested.

The critical ratios from the F table are found for the .05 significance level and compared to the calculated F ratios. The calculated F value for interaction (0.432) is less than the critical value (3.88), so the null hypothesis is not rejected. The calculated F value for rows (0.500) is less than the critical value (4.75), so the null hypothesis for rows is not rejected. The calculated F value for columns (11.810) is larger than the critical value (3.88), so the null hypothesis for columns is rejected.

The conclusions for the two-way analysis of variance are:

1. There is no interaction between the stores and advertising campaigns in the population.
2. The advertising campaigns both have the same mean.
3. The stores have different means.

For the first two conclusions, the possibility of a type II error exists. In either case, the null hypothesis might actually be false. For the last conclusion, there's a chance that the rejected null hypothesis might actually be true. An assessment of the risks of error and the associated penalties is an important final step in any hypothesis test.

The third conclusion states that the different stores do not have the same mean in the population. This is the same conclusion reached following the analysis in Example 12.6.

Some final comments are in order regarding both one-way and two-way analysis of variance procedures. As has been mentioned several times in this chapter, the key assumption of ANOVA is that all populations have the same variance. Actually, there are three assumptions that must hold for the ANOVA procedure to work properly:

1. All populations under test must have the same variance for the dependent variable.
2. All populations under test must be normally distributed for the dependent variable.
3. The samples taken from the populations under test must be drawn randomly.

These three assumptions should be verified to ensure a valid analysis of variance. These assumptions are sometimes ignored, especially since computer programs that perform ANOVA don't ask the analyst if the assumptions have been addressed. The analyst should at least have some intuitive assurance that the first two assumptions are met and that random samples are being used.

EXERCISES

29. What is the difference between a one-way and a two-way analysis of variance test?
30. What causes interaction in a two-way analysis of variance test?
31. What are the three hypotheses tested in a two-way analysis of variance test?
32. Empire Television Repair Service decided to study the effect of television brand and service center type on set repair time, measured in minutes. Four television brands (A, B, C, D) and four service centers were selected for analysis. Each service center was assigned three television sets of each brand for repair. The results are partially summarized below. The columns refer to television brands, and the rows refer to service centers. Test at the .01 significance level.

Source of variation	SS	df	Estimate of σ^2	F ratio
Rows	3,200	3		
Columns	300	3		
Interaction	800	9		
Within	300	32		
Total	4,600	47		

a. State the null and alternative hypotheses.
b. Is there interaction between service center and television brand?
c. Is there a difference in brands?
d. Is there a difference in service centers?

33. The accompanying table shows a partially completed ANOVA table for a two-way analysis of variance test.

Source of variation	SS	df	Estimate of σ^2	F ratio
Rows	5.1	3		
Columns	18.1	2		
Interaction			2.9	
Within	37.6			
Total		47		

a. Complete the ANOVA table.

b. How many rows were in the original data table?

c. How many columns were in the original data table?

d. How many items were found in each cell in the original data table?

e. If you test at the .01 significance level, what are your conclusions concerning the three hypotheses tested?

34. Jeff Norton, manager of Coldpoint Appliances (a large appliance retailer), feels that the number of units sold depends both on a salesperson's ability and on the brand being sold. For the six most recent monthly periods, he recorded the number of units sold in the downtown store:

Brand sold	Salesperson			
	A	B	C	D
1	4 5 6	3 5 7	8 9 10	2 0 1
	8 3 5	3 4 2	12 9 13	5 1 3
2	5 7 7	9 9 9	8 7 9	3 2 5
	8 6 4	7 5 8	10 8 6	4 1 6

a. State the null and alternative hypotheses.

b. Use a computer program to produce an ANOVA table.

c. Test all of the relevant hypotheses at the .05 significance level.

d. Write Jeff a short memo summarizing your conclusions.

35. Tim Russell, production manager of the Tetronic Corporation, feels that the variation in the number of units produced per hour might be related to both the operator and the machine used to produce the units. This matter is of particular concern to Tim after he read a *Wall Street Journal* article (November 27, 1989) on the Fed's attempt to reverse a manufacturing slump by driving down interest rates. He thinks that this is a good time to study the production issue.

Three Tetronic operators (A, B, C) are observed using each of three different machines (1, 2, 3) for two separate hours:

Machine	Operator		
	A	B	C
1	12 15	17 23	10 14
2	9 12	20 25	12 12
3	8 11	19 22	13 11

    a. State the null and alternative hypotheses.

    b. Use a computer program to produce an ANOVA table.

    c. Test all of the relevant hypotheses at the .01 significance level.

    d. Write Tim a short memo summarizing your conclusions.

OTHER ANOVA DESIGNS

The one-way and two-way designs described in this chapter are the basic ANOVA procedures used in most applications. Modifications to these procedures are sometimes employed in examining the effects of different factors on a variable of interest. Four of the more common variations are described in this section.

1. As mentioned earlier, the basic ANOVA designs assume that sample sizes are equal. For one-way ANOVA, the same sample size is used for each of the treatments. For the two-way design, the same sample size is used in each cell of the data table. More complex designs can accommodate unequal sample sizes. This might be desirable if there were different proportions of items in the populations and the analyst wanted to reflect these differences in the sample. For a two-way ANOVA involving machines and operators, for example, if a particular machine group accounted for 75% of the output, the analyst might want to oversample that group and undersample the others.

   Sometimes it's not possible to obtain the same sample size per treatment or cell. If historical records are being used to generate the sample measurements, for instance, the unavailability of data may lead to unequal sample sizes.

2. In the designs described in this chapter, all populations of interest were sampled. Suppose, for the machine and operator example, there were 3 operators and 5 machines. Since all operators use all machines, there are 15 different populations, one for every combination of machine and operator. In a basic two-way ANOVA, all 15 of these combinations are sampled. Now suppose there are 10 machine groups and 50 operators. A basic design would involve a huge sample size if all 500 populations were sampled. An alternative ANOVA design randomly chooses those populations to be sampled and extends the results to all populations.

3. The basic ANOVA procedure can be broadened to cover three or more factors. In the machine/operator example, a third factor that might affect hourly output is the factory shift during which production took place. If there are 3 shifts, 3 operators, and 5 machine groups, a total of 45 different combinations or populations are involved. In a basic ANOVA design, all 45 combinations would be sampled. An alternative is to randomly choose the operators, machines, and shifts to be sampled and extend the ANOVA results to all of the populations.

   The two-way factorial ANOVA study mentioned in Example 12.10, "Effects of Price, Brand, and Store Information on Buyers' Product Evaluations," (*Journal of Marketing Research*, August 1991) investigated the effects of price, brand, and store information on buyers' perception of product quality. This three-way factorial design actually sampled five price levels, three brand names, and three store names.

4. In the basic one-way ANOVA design, subjects are randomly assigned to treatments. This random assignment provides some assurance that the subjects in each treatment are more or less the same, eliminating the effects of differing subjects. If the subjects are people subjected to differing TV ads, for example, the analyst hopes, through random assignment, that not all the young people end up watching one ad and all the older people end up watching another.

The *randomized block design* removes the effect of differences among treatment subjects by subjecting each subject to all treatments. For example, suppose there are 12 supermarkets in the experiment along with three different display methods for a new product. A simple random ANOVA design would randomly assign display methods to stores, but each store would only use one display type. In a randomized block design, each store uses all three display methods over a period of time, thus eliminating the possible effect of different store types. The order of assigning display methods to stores is done randomly; assignments might appear as follows:

	Store (blocks)											
	1	2	3	4	5	6	7	8	9	10	11	12
	1	2	3	1	2	3	1	2	3	1	2	3
Method	2	3	1	2	3	1	2	3	1	2	3	1
	3	1	2	3	1	2	3	1	2	3	1	2

The different methods of conducting the analysis of variance procedure are sometimes referred to as *experimental designs*. The term *experiment* suggests a scientific application more than a business application, and this is generally true. Business applications often involve observation rather than the manipulation of variables, so the advanced experimental design procedures are not widely used. However, there are certainly times when business situations can be controlled so that the effect of different factors on the variable of interest can be examined. In these cases, the more advanced procedures of experimental design can be quite useful and in fact quality control and research into the design of products are two such important areas.

SUMMARY

In addition to means and proportions, the variabilities of populations are frequently of interest. This chapter has presented methods to test the variability of a single population and to compare the variabilities of two populations.

This chapter has also presented ways to examine the effects of different factors on a variable of interest (the dependent variable). In the one-way analysis of variance, measurements on the dependent variable are made for each level of the single factor believed to affect this variable. Two relevant factors can be examined simultaneously in the two-way ANOVA procedure, and the effects of three or more factors on the dependent variable can be examined through the use of more advanced procedures.

Analysis of variance is a good example of a statistical technique that has become practical due to widespread use of computers. The volume of calculations is such that a design of any useful size is very difficult to perform using hand calculations. Computer programs that perform ANOVA are widely available for personal computers as well as mainframe computers. These programs typically perform both one-way and two-way analyses, and more advanced techniques are sometimes available. An example of the use of a microcomputer program is demonstrated at the end of this chapter.

APPLICATIONS OF STATISTICAL CONCEPTS IN THE BUSINESS WORLD

There are many business applications of the ANOVA techniques discussed in this chapter. When the average value of some variable is compared across three or more populations, the conclusions that result from an ANOVA study can be very useful to management. Often production variables are varied to see which combination yields the optimum manufacturing process. Here are examples of dependent variables whose means for different population groups might be of interest.

Dependent variable	Populations under study
Overtime hours per month	Employees: union hourly, nonunion hourly, salaried
Shipping time	Size of container: small, medium, large
Time to repay loan	Age of customer: under 30, 31–45, 46–65, over 65
Units produced per hour	Shift: 1, 2, 3 Plant: A, B, C, D
Savings account balance	Account holders' age: under 35, 36–50, 51+ Age of account: under 5 years, 5–10 years, over 10 years
Defective units produced	Shift, material supplier, foreman
College GPA	Class: freshman, sophomore, junior, senior Major: business, liberal arts, health sciences Age: under 22, 22–30, 31+
Annual cost of repair for ordered parts	Supplier: A, B, C, D Part cost: under $25, $25–$100, over $100
Points scored by NFL team	Day played: Sunday, Monday, other Opponent: same division, same conference, other
Employee time with company	Plant: 1, 2, 3 Education: high school, some college, college graduate
Age of account receivable	Public corporation, private corporation, partnership
Monthly cash balance	Busy season, moderate season, slow season
Interest rate paid on short-term loan	Bank: A, B, C Season: summer, fall, winter, spring Bull market, bear market, neutral market
Sales per customer	Catalog sale, store sale, discount store sale
Customer rating of store employees	Downtown store, valley store, north store
Time in hospital	Age: under 45, 45–65, 66+ Medical insurance, no medical insurance, Medicare
Complaints per 1,000 customers	Store: 1, 2, 3 Value of item: under $25, $25–$250, over $250
Monthly sales per salesperson	Company car, lease car, own car

GLOSSARY

Analysis of variance (ANOVA) A statistical procedure for determining whether the means of three or more populations are equal.

Within **method** A method of estimating the variance of populations that produces a valid estimate whether or not the null hypothesis is true.

***Between* method** A method of estimating the variance of populations that produces a valid estimate only if the null hypothesis is true.

ANOVA table A table that contains columns showing the sources of variation, the sums of squares, the degrees of freedom, the estimates of the variance, and the F value for the analysis of variance procedure.

Interaction A significant interrelationship between the levels of one factor and the levels of a second factor in influencing the dependent variable.

KEY FORMULAS

Chi-square variance test

$$\chi^2 = \frac{(n-1)s^2}{\sigma^2} \tag{12.1}$$

F ratio for two-population variance test

$$F = \frac{s_1^2}{s_2^2} \tag{12.2}$$

Within method estimate of σ^2

$$s_w^2 = \frac{\sum_j \sum_i (x_{ij} - \bar{x}_j)^2}{c(n-1)} \tag{12.3}$$

Estimate of the sampling distribution variance

$$s_{\bar{x}}^2 = \frac{\sum_j (\bar{x}_j - \bar{\bar{x}})^2}{c-1} \tag{12.4}$$

Between method estimate of σ^2

$$s_b^2 = \frac{n\sum_j (\bar{x}_j - \bar{\bar{x}})^2}{c-1} \tag{12.5}$$

F ratio for ANOVA

$$F = \frac{s_b^2 \ (\textit{Between} \text{ method estimate of } \sigma^2)}{s_w^2 \ (\textit{Within} \text{ method estimate of } \sigma^2)} \tag{12.6}$$

Two-way ANOVA formulas

Estimate of the variance between columns

$$s_c^2 = \frac{rn\sum_j (\bar{x}_{cj} - \bar{\bar{x}})^2}{c-1}$$

Estimate of the variance between rows

$$s_r^2 = \frac{cn\sum_i (\bar{x}_{ri} - \bar{\bar{x}})^2}{r-1}$$

Estimate of the variance for interaction

$$s_i^2 = \frac{n\left[\sum_i \sum_j (\bar{x}_{ij} - \bar{x}_{ri} - \bar{x}_{cj} + \bar{\bar{x}})^2\right]}{(r-1)(c-1)}$$

Estimate of the variance for *within*

$$s_w^2 = \frac{\sum_i \sum_j \sum_k (x_{ijk} - \bar{x}_{ij})}{rc(n-1)}$$

SOLVED EXERCISES

1. ONE-POPULATION VARIANCE TEST

Scientific measuring instruments such as an aircraft altimeter must provide unbiased readings with a small measurement error. The production manager for Hulk Aircraft, Fred Sterling, is concerned about the amount of variation in the readings produced by his company's altimeters. The altimeters are designed to have a standard deviation of 200 feet. Fred decides to test whether the variability of altimeters is greater than 200 feet. He selects a sample of seven altimeters and computes a sample standard deviation of 250 feet.

a. State the null and alternative hypotheses.

b. Compute the degrees of freedom.

c. State the decision rule using the .05 significance level.

d. Test if the variability of the company's altimeters is greater than 200 feet.

Solution:

a. The null and alternative hypotheses are

$$H_0: \sigma^2 \leq 40,000$$
$$H_1: \sigma^2 > 40,000$$

b. df $= (n - 1) = (7 - 1) = 6$

c. The decision rule is

If $\chi^2 > 12.59$, reject the null hypothesis that the population variance is 40,000 (reject H_0 if $\chi^2 > 12.59$).

d. $\chi^2 = \dfrac{(n-1)s^2}{\sigma^2} = \dfrac{(7-1)(250)^2}{200^2} = 9.375$

Since the calculated test statistic (9.375) is lower than the critical table value (12.59), the null hypothesis can't be rejected at the .05 significance level. There isn't sufficient sample evidence to conclude that the population standard deviation is more than 200 feet.

2. TWO-POPULATION VARIANCE TEST

Carla Mitchell, analyst for Abbott Laboratories, a national drug manufacturer, is concerned about the quality of one of its products. Abbott purchases a particular material used to manufacture the product of concern from two different suppliers. The level of defects in the raw material is approximately the same between the two suppliers, but Carla is concerned about the variability from shipment to shipment. If the level of defects tends to vary excessively for either supplier, the quality of the drug product could be affected. To compare the relative variation of the two suppliers, Carla selects 11 shipments from each supplier and measures the percentage of defects in the raw material for each shipment, along with the standard deviations. The results are

$$s_1 = 0.61 \qquad n_1 = 11 \text{ (supplier 1)}$$
$$s_2 = 0.29 \qquad n_2 = 11 \text{ (supplier 2)}$$

a. State the null and alternative hypotheses.

b. Compute the degrees of freedom.

c. State the decision rule using the .05 significance level.

d. Test whether the variability of the shipment defect levels for supplier 1 is greater than for supplier 2.

Solution:

a. The null and alternative hypotheses are

$$H_0: \sigma_1^2 - \sigma_2^2 \le 0$$
$$H_1: \sigma_1^2 - \sigma_2^2 > 0$$

b. $df_1 = (n_1 - 1) = (11 - 1) = 10$
$df_2 = (n_2 - 1) = (11 - 1) = 10$

c. The critical F value is 2.97. The decision rule is

If the calculated F ratio is larger than 2.97, reject H_0 (reject H_0 if $F > 2.97$).

d. $F = \dfrac{s_1^2}{s_2^2} = \dfrac{(0.61)^2}{(0.29)^2} = 4.42$

One of the sample variances is 4.42 times the other. The null hypothesis is rejected since the test statistic (4.42) exceeds the critical value (2.97). Carla should conclude that the variability of shipment defect levels for supplier 1 is greater than for supplier 2.

3. One-Way Analysis of Variance

Color Paint Corporation owner Marlene Perez decides to replace several paint sprayers. After researching the situation, she concludes that four brands appear to be comparable in terms of cost and projected lifetime. Marlene determines that the deciding factor among the four brands is the amount of paint used in normal operation. She measures paint thickness, in millimeters, for several paint tests, with the following results:

	Sprayer A	Sprayer B	Sprayer C	Sprayer D
	5.4	6.1	8.2	7.2
	5.9	5.9	8.5	6.5
	6.2	6.3	6.9	6.8
	7.0	6.5	9.4	7.1
	5.1	7.2	7.9	7.4
	5.5	6.9	8.6	6.7
Mean =	5.85	6.48	8.25	6.95

Grand mean = $\bar{\bar{x}} = 6.88$

a. State the null and alternative hypotheses.

b. Compute the degrees of freedom.

c. State the decision rule if the null hypothesis is tested at the .01 significance level.

d. What should Marlene conclude?

Solution:

a. The null and alternative hypotheses are

H_0: $\mu_1 = \mu_2 = \mu_3 = \mu_4$.
H_1: Not all populations have the same mean.

b. $df_w = c(n - 1) = 4(6 - 1) = 20$
$df_b = (c - 1) = (4 - 1) = 3$

c. Find the F table entry for column 3 and row 20. At the .01 significance level, this critical value is 4.94. The decision rule is

If the calculated F ratio is larger than 4.94, reject the null hypothesis (reject H_0 if $F > 4.94$).

d. Table 12.9 shows the ANOVA table for this problem.

TABLE 12.9   ANOVA Table for Solved Exercise 3

Source of variation	SS	df	Estimate of σ^2	F ratio
Between groups	18.61	3	6.203	16.37
Within groups	7.57	20	0.379	
Total	26.18	23		

The sums of squares in this table are:

$(5.4 - 5.85)^2 + (5.9 - 5.85)^2 + (6.2 - 5.85)^2 +$
$(7.0 - 5.85)^2 + (5.1 - 5.85)^2 + (5.5 - 5.85)^2 +$
$(6.1 - 6.48)^2 + (5.9 - 6.48)^2 + (6.3 - 6.48)^2 +$
$(6.5 - 6.48)^2 + (7.2 - 6.48)^2 + (6.9 - 6.48)^2 +$
$(8.2 - 8.25)^2 + (8.5 - 8.25)^2 + (6.9 - 8.25)^2 +$
$(9.4 - 8.25)^2 + (7.9 - 8.25)^2 + (8.6 - 8.25)^2 +$
$(7.2 - 6.95)^2 + (6.5 - 6.95)^2 + (6.8 - 6.95)^2 +$
$(7.1 - 6.95)^2 + (7.4 - 6.95)^2 + (6.7 - 6.95)^2 =$
$SS_w = 7.57$

$(5.85 - 6.88)^2 + (6.48 - 6.88)^2 + (8.25 - 6.88)^2 +$
$(6.95 - 6.88)^2 = 3.1$

$SS_b = 6(3.1) = 18.6$

$$F = \frac{s_b^2/df_b}{s_w^2/df_w} = \frac{(18.6/3)}{(7.57/20)} = \frac{6.2}{0.379} = 16.36$$

The null hypothesis is rejected since the test statistic (16.36) is larger than the critical value (4.94). Marlene should conclude that paint thickness differs among these four brands of sprayers.

4. TWO-WAY ANALYSIS OF VARIANCE

Julie Barnes, analyst for the marketing research firm Professional Marketing Associates, is conducting research for a client to determine if age and level of education affect income. Table 12.10 shows the results of Julie's data collection. What should Julie conclude if she tests the hypotheses at the .05 significance level?

TABLE 12.10   Income Data for Solved Exercise 4

Age group	High school	Some college	College graduate
18 to <30	$25,000	$36,250	$42,500
	31,450	39,400	46,000
	27,500	35,450	47,250
30 to <50	28,000	46,250	52,600
	30,950	44,400	56,700
	26,250	48,450	57,750
50 +	35,000	46,250	62,800
	38,250	49,400	66,700
	37,700	55,450	70,250

Solution:

The data are run on a microcomputer program demonstrated at the end of this chapter. Table 12.11 shows the results.

TABLE 12.11   Computer Output for Solved Exercise 4

```
                        Information Entered
Number of Variables:              2
Number of Rows:                   3
Number of Columns:                3
Alpha Error:                     .05
GP 1    A       B       C      GP 3    G       H       I
1 =  25,000  36,250  42,500    1 =  35,000  46,250  62,800
2 =  31,450  39,400  46,000    2 =  38,250  49,400  66,700
3 =  27,500  35,450  47,250    3 =  37,700  55,450  70,250

GP 2    D       E       F
1 =  28,000  46,250  52,600
2 =  30,950  44,400  56,700
3 =  26,250  48,450  57,750
```

Results

Source of variation	SS	df	Estimate of σ^2	F ratio
Rows	955,230.9	2	477,601.9	55.87
Columns	2,756,481.8	2	1,378,240.9	161.24
Interaction	163,307.8	4	40,826.9	4.78
Error	153,861.7	18	8,547.9	
Total	4,028,855	26		

```
Critical F-Value (Row):3.55
Critical F-Value (Int):2.93              Reject Null Hypothesis
Critical F-Value (Col):3.55              Reject Null Hypothesis
                                         Reject Null Hypothesis
```

The calculated F ratios are compared with the critical F values:

df	Critical F ($\alpha = .05$)	Calculated F test statistic
2, 18	3.55	55.87
2, 18	3.55	161.24
4, 18	2.93	4.78

Based on the appropriate critical values and the calculated F ratios in Table 12.11, all three null hypotheses are rejected. On this basis, Julie concludes:

1. There is interaction between age and education level. There seem to be unexpected differences when certain age groups are compared to certain education levels. A rejection of the null hypothesis of no interaction sends Julie back to the sample data to search for the age/education level combinations that produced unexpected results.

2. The age groups have different income levels.

3. The educational groups have different income levels.

EXERCISES

36. What is the key assumption that must hold for the analysis of variance procedure to work properly?

37. How is the F distribution similar to the t distribution? How do the distributions differ?

38. What does the term *sum of squares* refer to?

39. Suppose there are 4 degrees of freedom for a chi-square test at the .05 significance level. How would you interpret a chi-square test statistic of 8.4?

40. Suppose the degrees of freedom for an F test are 2 for the numerator and 6 for the denominator. At the .05 significance level, how would you interpret a test statistic of 8.4?

41. Here is a partially completed ANOVA table.

Source of variation	SS	df	Estimate of σ^2	F ratio
Between groups	14,398	3		
Within groups				
Total	19,654	23		

   a. Complete the ANOVA table.
   b. How many groups are being compared?
   c. What is the appropriate critical value if the null hypothesis is tested at the .05 significance level?
   d. Compute the test statistic (F ratio).
   e. Would you reject or fail to reject the null hypothesis?

42. The Hullpak Manufacturing Company produces a part for the aluminum industry that has a critical outside diameter of 2.2 inches. Production manager Albert Moore knows that the standard deviation should not exceed 0.032 inch. Albert knows that cutting is on a

timed basis, which means that the longer the same cutting tool is used, the greater the amount of play. As a result, the average diameter remains relatively constant, but the variability can increase. Albert has inspected a recent sample of 20 parts and determined a sample standard deviation of 0.047 inch. Can Albert conclude at the .05 significance level that the cutting tool should be changed?

43. Stock analyst Robin Booth wants to compare the risks associated with two different stocks. She decides to measure the risk of a given stock on the basis of the variation in daily price changes. Robin selects a random sample of 30 daily price changes for each stock. The results are

$$s_1 = 0.93 \qquad n_1 = 30 \text{ (stock A)}$$
$$s_2 = 0.68 \qquad n_2 = 30 \text{ (stock B)}$$

Robin compares the risks associated with the two stocks in a test at the .05 significance level. What is her conclusion?

44. *Consumer Digest* wants to determine if any differences in average (mean) life exist among five different brands of TV picture tubes. Random samples of three picture tubes of each brand were tested. The results (in hours) are:

Brand A	Brand B	Brand C	Brand D	Brand E
3,520	4,025	4,520	3,987	3,620
3,631	3,901	4,325	4,123	3,358
3,954	3,756	4,189	3,852	3,428

At the .05 significance level, is there evidence of a difference in average life among these five brands of tubes?

45. Here is a partially completed ANOVA table.

Source of variation	SS	df	Estimate of σ^2	F ratio
Between groups		2		
Within groups	129.6	—	5.4	
Total	825.4			

a. Complete the ANOVA table.

b. How many groups are being compared?

c. What is the appropriate critical value if the null hypothesis is tested at the .01 significance level?

d. Compute the test statistic (F ratio).

e. Would you reject the null hypothesis?

46. Here is a partially completed ANOVA table.

see p. 444-5   imp 445

Source of variation	SS	df	Estimate of σ^2	F ratio
Rows	1,488	2		
Columns	48	2		
Interaction	32	4		
Within	520	9		
Total	2,088	17		

see notes p 3-1

a. Complete the ANOVA table.

b. How many rows are being compared?

c. How many columns are being compared?

d. What is the appropriate critical value to test for interaction if the null hypothesis is tested at the .01 significance level?

e. What is the appropriate critical value to test for the difference between columns if the null hypothesis is tested at the .01 significance level?

f. Compute the test statistic (F ratio) for each hypothesis.

g. Would you reject each of the null hypotheses?

h. State your conclusions for this exercise.

47. Fred Burks, manager of the Monty Card Department Store, wonders if his customers are charging more on their Monty Card credit cards than on MasterCharge or VISA. Fred decides to examine nine randomly chosen charges from sales using each of the three cards. The results are:

Monty Card	MasterCharge	VISA
$103	$ 71	$ 98
91	102	111
62	83	72
47	21	9
85	15	24
175	49	39
23	36	64
80	58	71
121	68	40

Can Fred conclude there is a difference in the mean amount charged among the three credit cards? Test at the .05 significance level.

48. Trudy Runge, a government analyst, has conducted a study to determine corporation executives' attitudes toward government economic policy. Trudy wants to find out if attitudes differ for different corporation sizes. Executives of 24 corporations are interviewed, and their scores on several rating scales are averaged. The results (where highest average score represents most favorable attitude) are:

Small	Medium	Large
45	61	68
51	58	70
62	73	72
47	81	59
35	45	74
55	49	69
23	46	64
50	59	71

Can Trudy conclude there is a difference in the average executive attitude toward government economic policy based on corporation size? Test at the .01 significance level.

49. Charles Tortorelli, manager of an assembly line at a vacuum cleaner manufacturing plant, believes that the rate of defective units produced in an eight-hour shift on one of the conveyor belts is affected by which shift is operating the belt. He decides to test this hypothesis by sampling the belt six times for each eight-hour shift and counting the defective units. The results are:

Day	Swing	Night
14	11	28
12	15	27
12	17	17
17	18	25
15	25	24
10	13	26

At the .01 significance level, do the three shifts produce the same mean rate of defective units?

50. Following is a partially completed ANOVA table.

Source of variation	SS	df	Estimate of σ^2	F ratio
Rows	15.4	3		
Columns			6.40	
Interaction	17.1	6		
Within		24		
Total	192.8	35		

a. Complete the ANOVA table.

b. What is the appropriate critical value to test for interaction if the null hypothesis is tested at the .01 significance level?

c. What is the appropriate critical value to test for a difference between columns if the null hypothesis is tested at the .01 significance level?

d. State your conclusions for this exercise.

51. The Sweet Treat Ice Cream Company is planning a test of three new flavors: brandy, peach, and apricot. Cathy Gant, company analyst, also wishes to measure the effects of four different retail price levels: $1.09, $1.19, $1.29, and $1.39 per pint. For test sites Cathy selected 12 geographically separated stores with similar levels of ice cream sales. Cathy arranged to have the new flavors delivered to the stores each week and to see to the proper displaying and pricing of the ice cream in all stores throughout a three-week period. At the end of each week, pints sold of each flavor were recorded for each price level.

Price	Brandy			Peach			Apricot		
1.09	17	18	15	17	15	14	10	12	13
1.19	16	16	13	17	14	12	9	10	11
1.29	14	11	10	14	14	14	8	9	7
1.39	8	9	6	10	9	11	5	7	10

Run the data on a computer program, and write a memo to Cathy summarizing the results.

52. Darlene Spooner (manager of a large discount chain) must choose where to place a popular battery display. Darlene is concerned with both the level and the variability of sales. She's considering placing the display either in the hardware department or next to the checkout counter. Darlene locates the display at the checkout counter in five stores and in the hardware section in four other stores. The results, in number of batteries sold per week, are:

Checkout counter	Hardware department
205	185
185	191
170	178
240	200
201	

Based on the appropriate statistical test, does one location produce better average sales than the other? Based on the appropriate statistical test, does one location show less variability than the other? Use the .01 significance level to reach your decisions.

53. Debbie Majors (Stoneway Corporation training director) is experimenting with three different training methods to determine if there's a difference in their effectiveness. Debbie has a group of 12 new trainees, and is concerned that trainees with previous experience may react to the training methods differently. Therefore, she divides the trainees into two groups: *no experience* and *experienced*. She then exposes two trainees from each group to one of three training methods. Once the training is completed, each trainee is given a test designed to measure the effectiveness of the training. The resulting test scores are:

	Training method		
	A	B	C
No experience	72 78	75 79	81 74
Experienced	82 76	73 78	80 72

Run the data on a computer program, and write a memo to Debbie summarizing the results.

EXTENDED EXERCISES

54. BEST BUY STORES

Stu Owens, president of the Best Buy retail bookstore chain, is planning a major study to find reasons for the variability in sales per customer throughout its store system. Stu has just read a *Wall Street Journal* article (November 21, 1989) describing how book publishers face a painful future austerity. He's concerned about how this might affect his stores' sales and profits.

There are a number of factors that Stu considers relevant to purchase amount. After discussing these matters at several management meetings, he focuses on the following factors of interest:

Male/female customers

Downtown store, valley store, northside store, southside store

Active credit card user, light card user, no card

His attention now turns to designing a study to investigate the effects of these three factors on the key variable of interest to the store: sales amount per customer transaction.

a. How would you design a study to investigate the areas of interest to Best Buy?

b. Design the data table to be used to collect data for the study.

c. Describe how a representative sample could be taken to ensure that Best Buy's objectives are met.

55. CURTIS MYERS COMPANY

The Curtis Myers Company makes TV sets and has recently begun using production teams in an attempt to build morale and improve quality. After a six-month trial period, this effort appears to be successful, based on the company's usual means of measuring the quality of its products. Now the company's attention turns to ways of assessing differences from team to team and from shift to shift. This information is needed so that the company can follow through on its pledge to award bonus payments to teams with superior quality records.

At first glance, the four teams involved seem to have different quality levels as measured by the number of units returned under warranty per week. However, the differences may be due to random error, especially given the limited period of measurement. Curtis Myers' management decides that an analysis of variance would be useful, in which the dependent variable is the weekly number of units returned under warranty. A two-way ANOVA is planned: one factor will be the production team, and the other will be the shift. The three shifts will be used as the row factor, and the four production teams will be used as the column factor.

A random sample of five weeks is used for each of the 12 combinations of team and shift. The resulting data are keyed into the company's small computer, which performs analysis of variance. The ANOVA table in Table 12.12 is produced by this program.

TABLE 12.12   ANOVA Table for Extended Exercise 55

Source of variation	SS	df	Estimate of σ^2	F ratio	F table
Rows *(3 shifts)*	205	2	102.5	6.83	3.19
Columns *(4 prod teams)*	51	3	17.0	1.13	2.80
Interaction	98	6	16.3	1.09	2.29
Within	720	48	15.0		
Total	1,074	59			

a. State the null and alternative hypotheses being tested.

b. State, in the simplest language possible, the conclusions of interest to Curtis Myers' management.

56. CONSUMERS AUTOMOBILE INSURANCE

The Consumer Automobile Insurance Company examines its policy of hiring mostly college graduates for its sales force. Some of its salespeople have a high school education, some have limited college education, and some have a college diploma. It would be fairly easy to randomly select a sample from each group and measure the key variable of interest to the company: annual sales of auto insurance. A one-way analysis of variance is planned.

The company decides to randomly sample four persons from each of the three categories of education and measure annual sales, in thousands of dollars. If education doesn't seem to make a difference in annual sales, the company will abandon its policy of seeking college graduates for its sales force and use lower-cost high school graduates. On the other hand, if a college degree makes a significant difference in sales level, Consumer's current policy will be continued.

Here are annual sales levels, in thousands of dollars, for the sample:

High school	Some college	College graduate
125	98	137
110	115	122
101	103	118
114	112	132

After looking at the sample data, personnel manager Linda Bell states, "College graduates are obviously outperforming those with less education. The policy of seeking college grads should continue."

a. What is your immediate response to Linda Bell's statement?

b. Perform a one-way analysis of variance and produce the appropriate ANOVA table.

c. Now what is your reaction to the personnel manager's statement?

MICROCOMPUTER PACKAGE
. . . .

The micro package *Computerized Business Statistics* can be used to solve two-way ANOVA problems.

In Solved Exercise 4, Julie Barnes, analyst for the marketing research firm Professional Marketing Associates, conducted research for a client to determine whether age and level of education have an effect on income.

Computer Solution:

From the main menu of *Computerized Business Statistics* a **13** is selected, indicating analysis of variance. The analysis of variance menu is shown on the screen.

Since the problem involves entering data from the keyboard, a **1** is selected.

```
Analysis of Variance—Define New Problem
 Number of Variables: Enter 1–2, Press ⏎ 2
```

Since two variables (age and level of education) are to be analyzed, a **2** is selected.

```
Variable #1 (Rows)
Number of Groups: Enter 2–5, Press ⏎ 3
Variable #2 (Columns)
Number of Groups: Enter 2–5, Press ⏎ 3
Alpha Error: Enter 0–1, Press ⏎ .05
```

There are three age categories (rows) and three education levels (columns). The significance level for this exercise is .05.

```
Analysis of Variance—Enter Number of Data Points

          Column 1      Column 2      Column 3
Row 1      - 3 -         - 3 -         - 3 -
Row 2      - 3 -         - 3 -         - 3 -
Row 3      - 3 -         - 3 -         - 3 -
Press F when Finished
```

There are three data points in each cell. **F** is entered once the blanks have been completed.

```
Analysis of Variance—Enter Variable Labels

           Column 1     Column 2     Column 3
Row 1         X1           X2           X3
Row 2         X4           X5           X6
Row 3         X7           X8           X9
Press end when Finished
```

The cells are named A, B, C, D, E, F, G, H, and I. **END** is pressed once the X's have been replaced.

Next, the program asks:

```
Problem definition correct Y/N/Q, Press ⏎ Y
```

After a **Y** response, the program is ready for the data to be entered:

```
Enter Data Values Group 1
        A       B       C

1  =  0        0       0
2  =  0        0       0
3  =  0        0       0
```

After the data have been entered, the screen shows:

```
        A        B        C

1  =  25000    36250    42500
2  =  31450    39400    46000
3  =  27500    35450    47250
```

Next, the screen asks you to enter data values for Group 2. After you've finished, the screen shows:

```
        D        E        F

1  =  28000    46250    52600
2  =  30950    44400    56700
3  =  26250    48450    57750
```

This process is repeated for the third group. **F** is pressed when you're finished. Next, you're asked:

```
Save data? Y/N, Press ⏎ N
```

The analysis of variance menu reappears.

A 7 is entered so that the problem can be run.

The computer responds with the output menu. The choice in this case is **P** for printer. The results are shown in Table 12.11.

MINITAB Computer Package

The two-way analysis of variance can be performed using MINITAB. The appropriate commands to solve Example 12.11 are:

```
MTB> SET C1
DATA> 12.05 23.94 14.63 25.78 17.52 18.45
```

```
DATA> 15.17 18.52 19.57 21.4 13.59 20.57
DATA> 9.48 6.92 10.47 7.63 11.9 5.92
DATA> END
MTB> SET C2
DATA> 1 1 1 1 1 1 2 2 2 2 2 2 3 3 3 3 3 3
DATA> END
MTB> SET C3
DATA> 1 1 1 2 2 2 1 1 1 2 2 2 1 1 1 2 2 2
DATA> END
MTB> NAME C1 'AMOUNT' C2 'COLUMNS' C3 'ROWS'
MTB> TWOWAY C1 C2 C3

ANALYSIS OF VARIANCE AMOUNT
```

SOURCE	DF	SS	MS
COLUMNS	2	378.4	189.2
ROWS	1	8.0	8.0
INTERACTION	2	13.9	6.9
ERROR	12	192.2	16.0
TOTAL	17	592.5	

```
MTB > LET C4=6.9/16
MTB > LET C5=8/16
MTB > LET C6=189.2/16
MTB > PRINT C4-C6
```

ROW	C4	C5	C6
1	0.43125	0.5	11.825

```
MTB > CDF .43125;
SUBC> F DF NUMERATOR = 2, DF DENOMINATOR = 12.
    0.4313    0.3406
MTB > CDF .5;
SUBC> F DF = 1, DF = 12.
    0.5000    0.5070
MTB > CDF 11.825;
SUBC> F DF = 2, DF = 12.
   11.8250    0.9985
MTB > STOP
```

Note that the amounts are entered in a single column, C1, using the SET command. A code is developed (1 = store 1, 2 = store 2, and 3 = store 3) to identify each column or store in C2. A code is also developed (1 = campaign A and 2 = campaign B) to identify each row or advertising campaign in C3. The NAME command is used to name the rows of the table. The TWOWAY command performs the analysis. The computer output produces a table similar to Table 12.8.

The LET command is used to divide the estimate of the variance for the interaction term (6.9) by the estimate of the variance for the *within* (labeled ERROR on the output) term (16). The result is stored in C4. The PRINT command shows the resulting F ratios.

The CDF command is used to generate a cumulative probability density function. The F subcommand is used to generate the probability function for an F distribution with 2 degrees of freedom in the numerator and 12 degrees of freedom in the denominator for the interaction F ratio of .4313. Note that the p-value (.6594) is computed by subtracting .3406 from 1 (1.0000 − .3406 = .6594). Since the p-value is greater than the significance level (.6594 > .01), the null hypothesis is not rejected.

SAS COMPUTER PACKAGE

The SAS computer package can be used to solve ANOVA problems. The SAS commands to solve Example 12.6 are as follows.

```
TITLE ''ANOVA ANALYSIS FOR EXAMPLE 12-6'':;
DATA STORES;
INPUT STORE DOLLARS;
CARDS;
1   12.05
1   23.94
1   14.63
1   25.78
1   17.52
1   18.45
2   15.17
2   18.52
2   19.57
2   21.40
2   13.59
2   20.57
3   9.48
3   6.92
3   10.47
3   7.63
3   11.90
3   5.92
PROC PRINT;
PROC ANOVA;
  CLASS STORE;
  MODEL DOLLARS=STORE;
  MEANS STORE;
```

The title command names the SAS run. The data command gives the data a name. The next 18 lines are card images that represent the stores and average purchase amounts. The PROC PRINT command directs SAS to list the data. The PROC ANOVA command performs analysis of variance. The CLASS subcommand identifies STORE as the variable to be classified. The MODEL subcommand indicates that the average purchase amount is the dependent variable and the type of store is the independent variable. The MEANS subcommand indicates that means are printed for each level of the variable STORE. Table 12.13, on the next page, shows the computer output for this SAS run. This output provides a p-value equal to .0005 (represented as PR > F on the output).

TABLE 12.13   SAS Output for Example 12–6

```
                      ANOVA ANALYSIS FOR EXAMPLE 12-6
                       Analysis of Variance Procedure

Dependent Variable: DOLLARS
                              Sum of            Mean
Source             DF         Squares          Square     F Value    Pr > F

Model               2      378.38083333    189.19041667     13.26     0.0005
Error              15      214.08721667     14.27248111
Corrected Total    17      592.46805000

          R-Square              C.V.          Root MSE       DOLLARS MEAN

          0.638652          24.86274        3.7778937          15.195000

Source             DF        Anova SS      Mean Square     F Value    Pr > F

STORE               2      378.38083333    189.19041667     13.26     0.0005

        Analysis of Variance Procedure

Level of          ----------DOLLARS----------
STORE      N        Mean             SD

1          6     18.7283333      5.28812790
2          6     18.1366667      3.10628825
3          6      8.7200000      2.28125404
```

QUALITY-CONTROL APPLICATIONS

*Come, give us a
taste of your
quality.*
Shakespeare,
"Hamlet"

*Good things
cost less than
bad ones.*
Italian proverb

Objectives

When you have completed this chapter, you will be able to:

Define the quality of a product or service.

Identify and differentiate between assignable and chance variation.

Explain the concept of statistical quality control.

Construct and interpret process control charts.

Describe the basic terms, procedures, and purposes of acceptance sampling.

On February 26, 1992, Kaiser Aluminum Company received Miller Brewing Company's Aluminum Supplier of the Year Award for the second year in a row. This award is based on the quality of material shipped to Miller.

WHY MANAGERS NEED TO KNOW ABOUT QUALITY CONTROL

The importance of producing high-quality products has increased dramatically in recent years. A primary reason for this increase has been foreign competition, particularly from Japan.

Consider what a special edition of *Business Week* said about quality:

> In 40 years, a focus on quality has turned Japan from a maker of knick-knacks into an economic powerhouse—and U.S. and European companies are being forced to respond. The result: a global revolution affecting every facet of business. As it becomes clear that higher quality means lower costs, products will improve, and so will services. For the 1990s and far beyond, quality must remain the priority for business.[1]

Many procedures designed to ensure high-quality production operations rely on a strong statistical foundation with particular attention to understanding variability. This chapter presents statistical concepts and techniques to provide good process control and, thus, high-quality products.

The just-mentioned award to Kaiser Aluminum was due, in the opinion of Kaiser management, to its intensive Total Quality Improvement program. Aspects of this impressive program are discussed at the end of this chapter in the "Applications" section.

BACKGROUND

The concepts of statistical quality control were first developed during the 1920s, primarily through the work of Dr. Walter A. Shewhart of Bell Telephone Laboratories. Dr. Shewhart introduced the idea of controlling production quality rather than inspecting it into each part.

At the end of World War II, the United States enjoyed a tremendous competitive advantage as the only major power with its industrial base left intact. Demand for consumer products kept increasing. Management's number one priority was to make production more efficient. Little attention was paid to controlling product quality.

After the war, Japan faced the difficult task of rebuilding its economy. The country was devoid of abundant natural resources, so redevelopment of industry was based on a management approach that took advantage of its only real resource, the labor force. With the assistance of managerial expertise exported to Japan from the United States

---

[1]*Business Week*, bonus issue, January 15, 1992.

(individuals like W. Edwards Deming, Joseph Juran, and A. V. Feigenbaum), a new managerial approach was developed that emphasized continuous improvement of product quality. This management style, called *management by process*, has helped Japan become the major threat to U.S. industrial superiority. In management by process, the industrial effort's goal is to constantly work on methods for improving the product or service. This approach utilizes new technology, focuses on the customer, and reacts to change quickly.

QUALITY—GENERAL CONSIDERATIONS

Quality

Before various tools and methods for measuring quality can be developed, the term must be defined. The **quality** of a product or service is determined by the extent to which it satisfies all the needs and preferences of its users.

> The **quality** of a product or service is the extent to which it satisfies its users' needs and preferences.

It is important, of course, to have good product designs. But in the production process itself, the key concern is often centered around process variability. It might be said that quality is the absence of variation and that variation is the firm's constant threat. If the variability of parts and assemblies is controlled, higher quality will result in almost any process.

The basic notion of monitoring product quality involves distinguishing between random and caused variability. In fact, it could be said that variability is the key concern in quality-control efforts. All processes produce results that vary from unit to unit. If this variability is slight and of consistent magnitude, good quality is generally indicated. If units are highly variable from one to another, or if the variability pattern is suddenly altered, poor quality is usually indicated.

EXAMPLE 13.1   Suppose the key quality factor for steel ingots is their weight. Each ingot has a different weight than the one produced before or after it. If the process is "in control," this weight variability is said to be randomly determined. That is, the observed variability of weights is presumed to be satisfactory for a process that's producing ingots of acceptable weight quality. By contrast, if the process shifts out of control, one or more ingot weights are judged to be outside the established range of acceptability. In this case, the observed variability is caused by something, namely, a process that's out of control and requires corrective action.

Figure 13.1 graphically demonstrates variability. Imagine a gun shot several times at a target. Plot *a* of Figure 13.1 shows excessive variability, even though the shots are centered on the target. In plot *b*, the variability is acceptable (a tight pattern), but it's centered off the target. In plot *c*, both the variability (scatter) and the center point are acceptable; in this case, the quality, in terms of variability, is acceptable.

FIGURE 13.1 Variability

a.

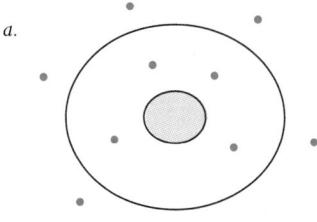

b.

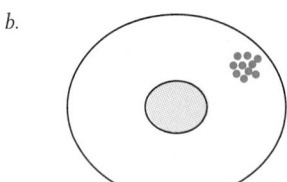

c.

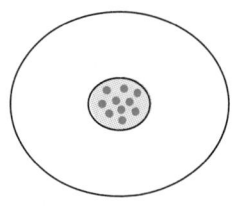

Deming

Before looking at specific quality-control procedures, a few additional comments on the general quality picture are appropriate. W. Edwards Deming, an American statistician, helped to establish effective quality-control methods in Japan in the 1950s, and subsequently helped firms around the world with their quality-improvement efforts. Among his accomplishments was the establishment of 14 key points for managing a quality-improvement and -maintenance program. Deming indicated that following the 14 guidelines creates an organizational climate in which process-management efforts can flourish. For a more complete discussion of these points, see Deming (1986)[2] or Gitlow, Gitlow, Oppenheim, and Oppenheim (1989).[3] The 14 points are:

1. Create constancy of purpose toward improving product and service.
2. Adopt a new philosophy based on the new economic age of high quality, not delays, mistakes, and defective products.

---

[2]W. E. Deming. *Out of the Crisis.* Cambridge, Mass.: M.I.T. Center for Advanced Engineering Study, 1986.
[3]H. Gitlow, S. Gitlow, A. Oppenheim, and R. Oppenheim. . . . *Tools and Methods for the Improvement of Quality.* Homewood, Ill.: Irwin, 1989.

3. Cease dependence on inspection to achieve quality. Instead, build quality into the product in the first place.
4. End the practice of awarding business on the basis of price alone. Instead, minimize total cost by recognizing the hidden cost of buying poor quality.
5. Improve constantly and forever the system of production and service to improve quality and productivity.
6. Institute training on the job.
7. Institute supervision designed to help people and machines produce a better product.
8. Drive out fear so that everyone can concentrate on quality work.
9. Break down barriers between departments so that the entire production team, from design to final delivery, pulls together in the quality effort.
10. Eliminate slogans, exhortations, and targets for the work force that ask for zero defects and new levels of productivity. Such exhortations only create adversarial relationships.
11. Eliminate work standards that prescribe numerical quotas for the day.
12. Remove the barriers that rob the hourly worker of the right to pride of workmanship.
13. Institute a vigorous program of education and training.
14. Put everybody in the company to work to accomplish the transformation.

These 14 points lay the groundwork for a fundamental change in old-style American business methods that involved production and cost objectives without proper attention to quality goals. As such, the 14 points represent the new philosophy business firms need if they're to maintain and improve their sales, profits, and reputations, and remain in business into the next century.

Juran and Deming are two names familiar to all those who've studied quality control. These two pioneers have increased their followings as the importance of improving the quality of U.S. products has become critical. Japan's 40-year-old Deming Prize for quality is Japanese industry's most coveted award.

Deming Prize

Baldrige Award

A more recent development is the Malcolm Baldrige National Quality Award started in 1987. A 1991 *Harvard Business Review* article describes its progress:

> In just four years, the Malcolm Baldrige National Quality Award has become the most important catalyst for transforming American business. More than any other initiative, public or private, it has reshaped managers' thinking and behavior. The Baldrige Award provides companies with a comprehensive framework for assessing their progress toward the new paradigm of management and such commonly acknowledged goals as customer satisfaction and increased employee involvement.[4]

The Baldrige examiners look for the following, to be outlined in no more than 75 pages by the applying firm:

---

[4]David A. Garvin, "How the Baldrige Award Really Works," *Harvard Business Review*, November 1991, pp. 80–93.

Top executives incorporate quality values into day-to-day management.

Its products are as good as or better than those of its competitors.

It is working with suppliers to improve the quality of their products or services.

Customer needs and wants are being met—and customer satisfaction ratings are as good as or better than competitors'.

The company trains workers in quality techniques and has systems in place to ensure that products are high quality.

The quality system yields concrete results, such as gains in market share and reduction in product-cycle time.

Consider these additional points regarding efforts to improve U.S. quality:

Eastman Kodak has all managers attend a four-month course in quality control. *Total Quality Management*(TQM) is the new watchword for many firms. This slogan reflects efforts at every level of the organization to make improvements.

The move toward better quality is considered by enthusiastic companies to be a culture-transforming approach.

Many firms have reached the conclusion that most quality problems are the fault of management, not workers.

It is increasingly recognized that workers themselves are in the best position to find and correct quality problems.

The "perfect factory" is being designed. Under this concept, a part is measured, then the part that it must fit is designed around that measurement. In this way, each final product becomes a made-to-order assembly.

The term *fourth-generation management* is being used to describe the new emphasis on total quality.

Quality efforts are increasing in the service sector as well as the manufacturing sector. Examples are mail and product carriers, airlines, the finance industry, insurance companies, and retailing.

The quest for quality has focused attention on research and development efforts. Specific contributions to product quality are demanded of R&D expenditures.

Quality is designed into the product, instead of inspected in. This is accomplished through design and analysis of appropriate experiments.

Once a company adopts the new quality philosophy, many changes in operations and management approaches may be needed. One slogan of the new quality effort is "Design quality into the product, don't inspect it in." Even so, traditional statistical quality-control methods are still needed to assess the process. This chapter addresses these statistical procedures.

EXERCISES

1. What is quality?
2. Why is quality important?

3. Explain why the management style called management by process has become a major challenge to U.S. industrial competitiveness.

4. Who is Dr. Walter A. Shewhart? What is his contribution to the concept of quality control?

5. Who is W. Edwards Deming? What is his contribution to the concept of quality control?

6. What is the Malcolm Baldrige National Quality Award?

STATISTICAL PROCESS CONTROL

Statistical Process Control

Among managers concerned with quality control, one fundamental goal is to identify out-of-control processes and to bring and keep them in statistical control. The series of activities used to attain this goal is referred to as **statistical process control** (SPC).

> **Statistical process control** (SPC) is the series of actions used to monitor and eliminate variation in order to keep a process in a state of statistical control.

One key to statistical process control is use of a control chart (a time series graph with the *x*-axis scaled in hours, days, weeks, months, years, and so on). The purpose of the chart is to track process variability—the key component in quality control. The time series graph was discussed in Chapter 3.

The control chart's vertical axis is scaled to accommodate the variable being tracked. This variable is the key indicator of quality in the process being monitored. For each time period, this key variable is measured and plotted on the control chart, forming a time series graph as time passes.

In addition to providing a visual display of a process, the control chart separates assignable causes of variation from chance causes of variation.

Assignable Causes

Assignable causes of variation are fluctuations in variation due to events or actions that aren't part of the process design. Examples of assignable causes of variation include dust getting into the air and interfering with microchip production, a worker accidentally setting a machine's controls improperly, or a supplier shipping a batch of defective raw materials to the process. Assignable variation is usually nonrandom in nature and can be eliminated or reduced without modifying the process.

Chance Causes

Chance causes of variation are attributable to design of the process. Examples include the small amount of variation in liquid from one soft drink can to another and the variability in the miles per gallon of a fleet of autos. Chance variation is usually random in nature and can be eliminated or reduced only by changing the process.

> **Assignable causes** of variation are fluctuations in variation due to events or actions that aren't part of the process design. **Chance causes** of variation are attributable to the design of the process.

The most typical format for a control chart will set control limits within ±3 standard deviations of the statistical measure of interest (average, proportion, or range). These limits are called the upper control limit (UCL) and lower control limit (LCL). Recall that in Chapter 6, you learned that for a normal distribution, the mean ±3 standard deviations included almost all (99.74%) of the observations. The 3 standard deviation limits also reduce the likelihood of tampering with the process. Once these control limits are set, the control chart is evaluated from the perspective of (1) discerning any pattern that might exist in the values over time and (2) determining whether any points fall outside the control limits.

Figure 13.2 illustrates several different control charts. The process in plot A is said to be stable because no points fall outside the 3 standard deviation control limits and there doesn't appear to be any pattern in the ordering of values over time.

FIGURE 13.2   Control Chart Patterns of Variation

Plot A: Chance variation, process in control

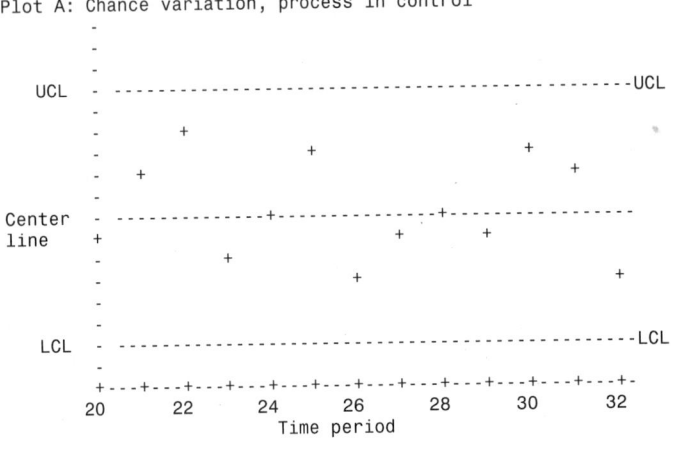

Plot B: Assignable cause variation

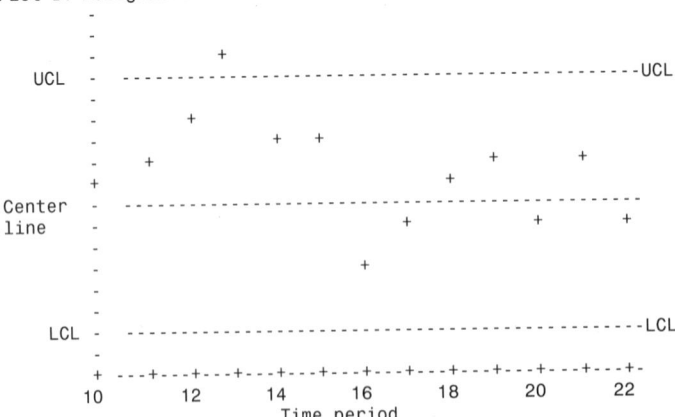

FIGURE 13.2 *continued*

Plot C: Upward trend

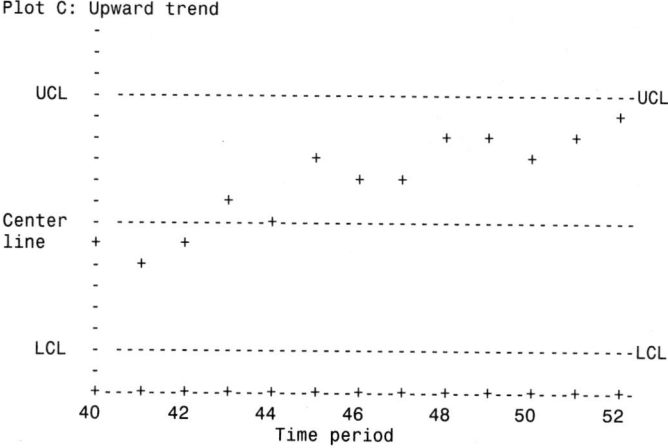

Plot D: Downward trend

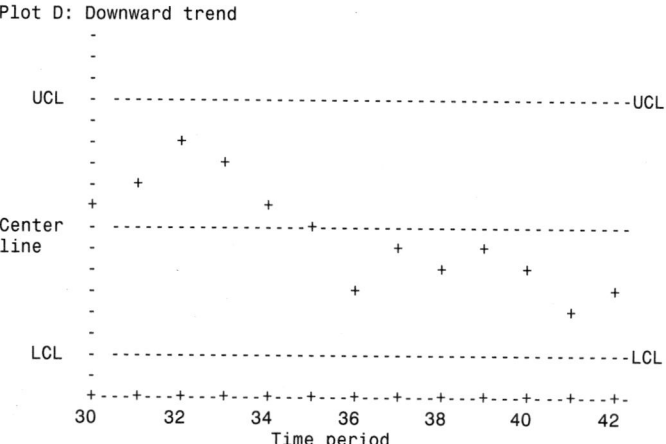

Plot E: Increasing variance

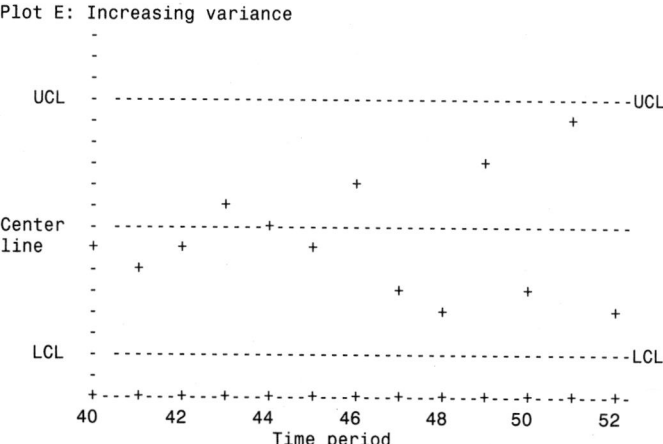

FIGURE 13.2 *continued*

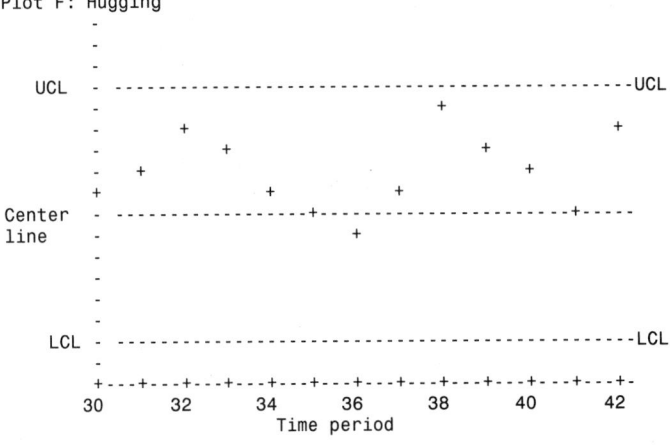

Plot F: Hugging

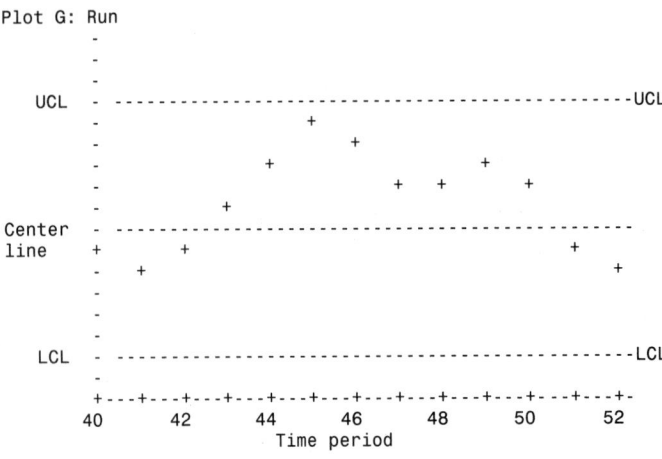

Plot G: Run

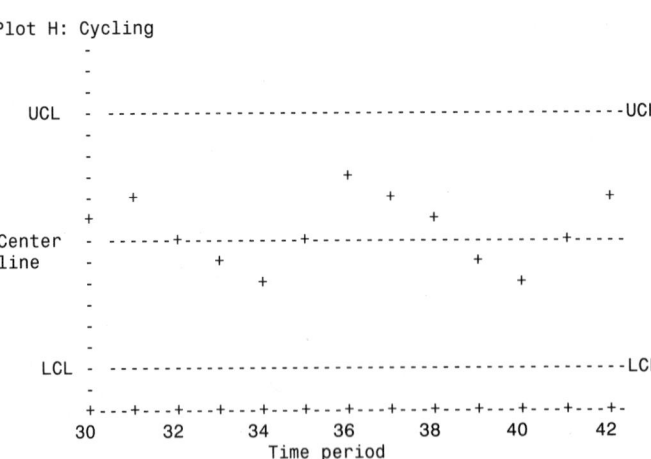

Plot H: Cycling

FIGURE 13.2 *concluded* .

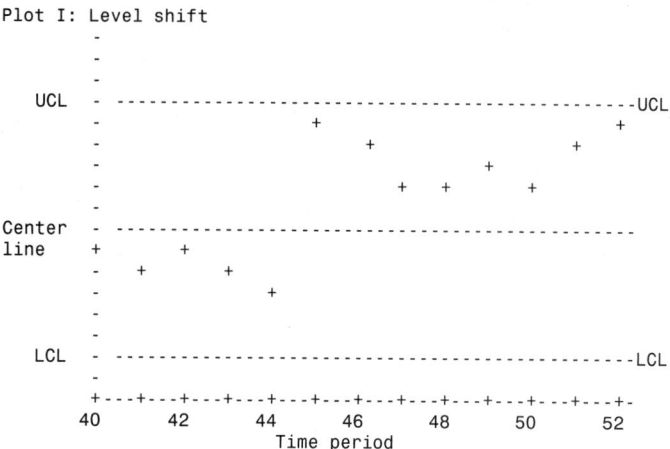

Plot I: Level shift

The process in plot B may or may not be in control since an unusually high measurement appears. One point falls above the 3 standard deviation control limit. The process for this unusually high observation may be in control with a randomly high measurement, or it may be out of control. Management attention is directed toward the process in this time period. This point will have to be further investigated to determine any assignable causes that could have influenced the result.

Plot C shows an upward-trending plot. Plot D shows a downward-trending plot. These processes seem to be in control since each measurement is within the control limits. However, they are obviously drifting out of control. The upward-trending plot can be characterized as resulting from a process whose mean is gradually shifting upward over time. Gradual shifts like these are common in manufacturing processes as machines wear out over time. The downward-trending plot can be characterized as resulting from a process whose mean is gradually shifting downward over time.

Plot E shows a process that's in control but for which the amount of variability is increasing. This results from a process whose mean remains constant but whose variance increases over time. This type of deterioration in a process sometimes results from worker fatigue. Workers pay close attention to every item that they process at the beginning of a shift. However, toward the end of a shift, concentration wanes and workers become careless and/or easily distracted. As a result, some items receive more attention than other items, causing the variance of workers' output to gradually increase.

Plot F shows a process that's in control but with most or all measurements above (or below) the desired process mean. Such a process could be costing money or reflect a quality level that, while satisfactory, could be improved. Also, only a slight shift in process quality could drive the process outside the control limits. Management attention is called for to discover the reasons for the condition and make improvements.

Plot G shows a run of several plots either above or below the desired process average. While all data values are within the control limits, management attention might uncover an undesirable element in the process. Perhaps a particular machine is drifting in and out of tolerance causing the plot pattern.

Plot H illustrates a cycling process. Again, each data plot is within the control limits, but something other than randomness is obviously affecting the output. Management attention might determine the problem and improve the process.

Plot I shows a process with a sudden shift in the level of measurements. This results from a process whose mean suddenly increases but whose variance remains constant. Introducing a new operator, new machine, or different-quality raw materials into the process can cause such a shift.

The rest of this chapter introduces you to statistical methods used in statistical process control. The next section describes how to use control charts to determine whether a particular process is in control.

EXERCISES

7. What term is used to describe a series of actions used to monitor and eliminate variation in order to keep a process in control?

8. What is a control chart? For what purpose is it used?

9. Describe the difference between assignable causes of variation and chance causes of variation. Give examples.

10. Figure 13.3 shows several quality-control plots. Which are in control? If a plot isn't in control, what type of problem exists?

FIGURE 13.3   Control Chart Patterns of Variation (Exercise 10)

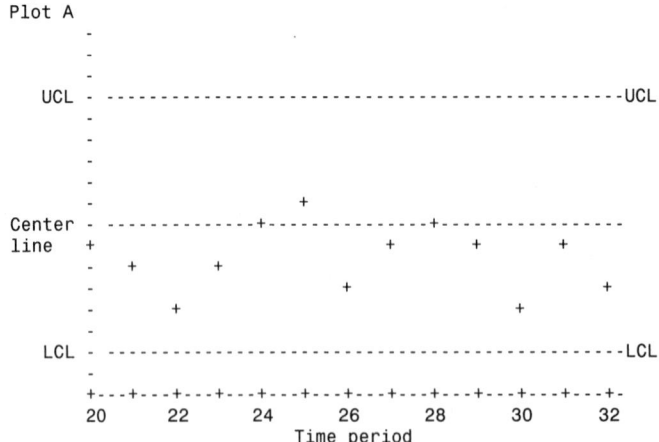

FIGURE 13.3   *continued*

Plot B

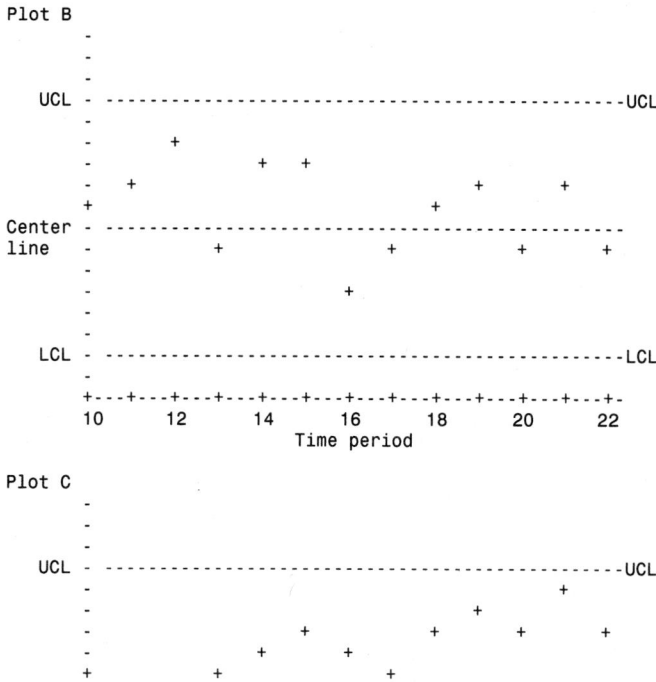

Plot C

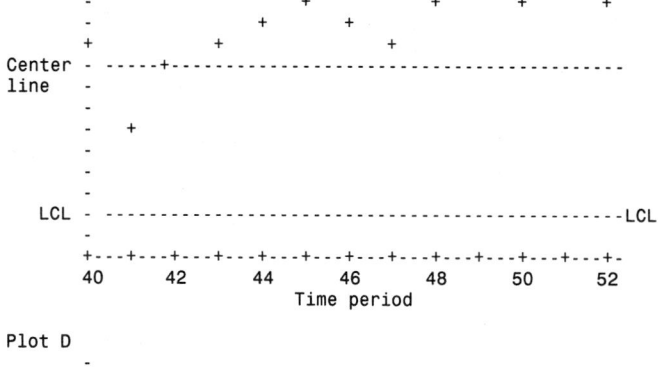

Plot D

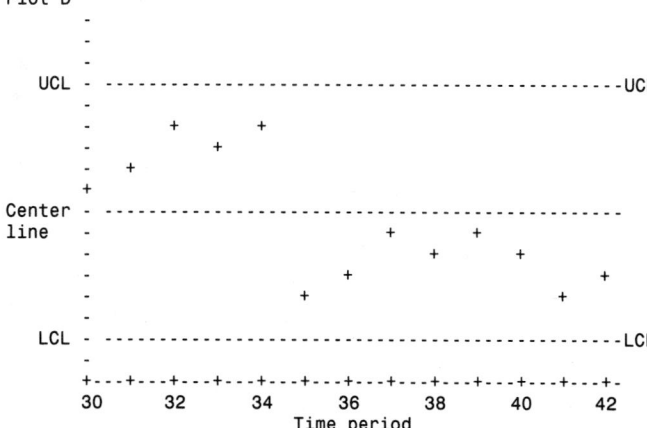

FIGURE 13.3 *continued*

Plot E

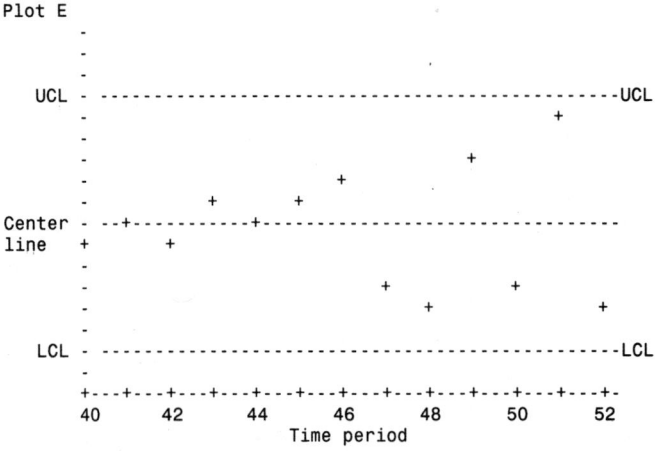

Plot F

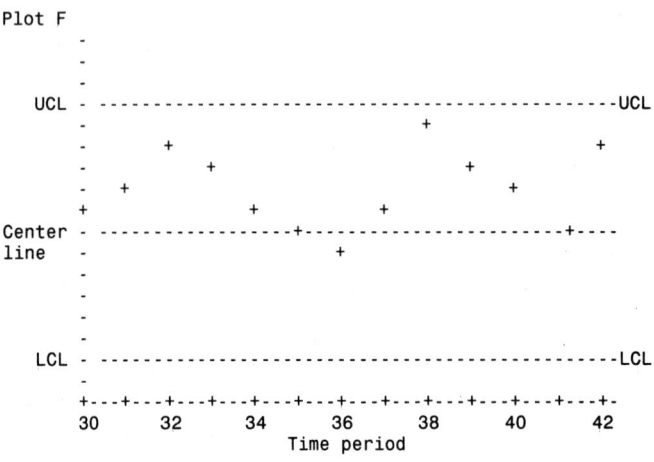

Plot G

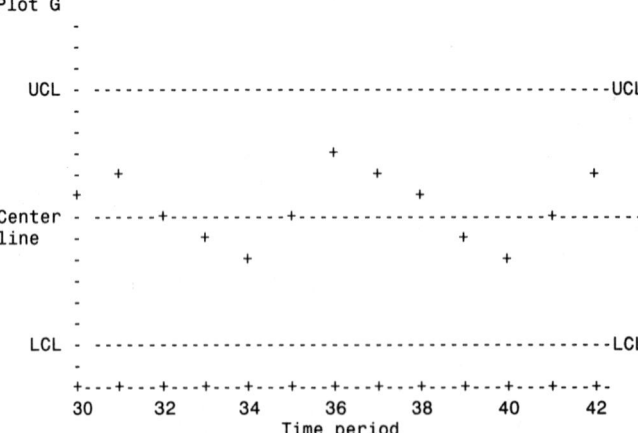

FIGURE 13.3 *concluded*

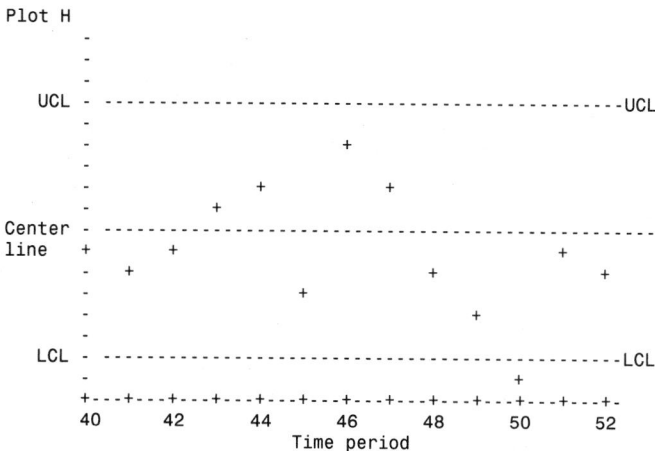

CONTROL CHARTS

Control Charts

The **control chart** is a time series graph that tracks a key variable of interest in the quality effort. Control charts are useful for evaluating a process's past performance as well as for monitoring its current performance. As the previous section indicated, in addition to providing a visual display of a process, the major function of the control chart is to separate assignable causes of variation from chance causes of variation.

> The **control chart** is a time series graph that tracks a key variable of interest in the quality effort.

Figure 13.4 presents an example of an individual measurement control chart. Note that the upper control and lower control limits are positioned (3 standard deviations above and below the mean) so that when the process is in control, the probability of an individual value of the variable of interest falling outside the control limits is small ($.0026 = 1 - .9974$). Note also the assumption that the variable of interest is normally distributed. This assumption is made after examining a plot of this variable and determining that the values approximate a normal distribution. Better yet, a goodness-of-fit test that assumes that the population from which the sample was taken is normally distributed can be conducted. Solved Exercise 11.2 showed this procedure.

The basic idea behind this normality assumption is that when the process is in control, or acceptable, the measured variable is likely to be close to the process mean rather than far away: it's assumed, in fact, that a normal distribution generates the value in each time period. An acceptable region is defined within which each value of

FIGURE 13.4   Individual Measurement Control Chart Showing the Normality Assumption

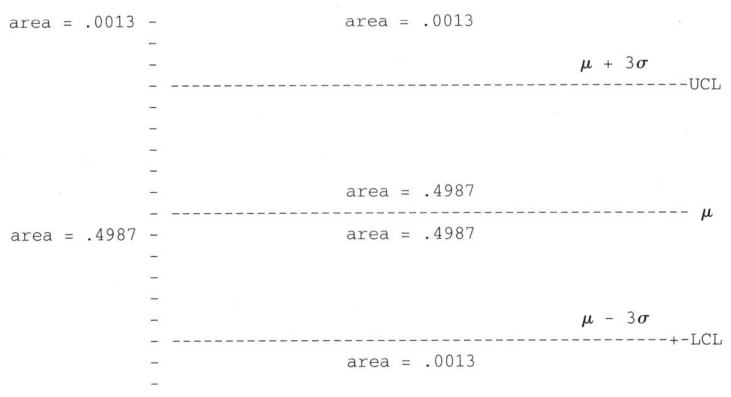

the variable is considered to be acceptable, and outside of which a problem in the process is being signaled.

Under the normality assumption, the acceptable interval can be established by knowing the process mean, the process standard deviation, and the confidence level for the interval. This notion is similar to the range established for the acceptance of a null hypothesis (Chapter 9). Attention is focused on making an inference about a process rather than a specific population of items, so the null and alternative hypotheses are

H_0: The process is in control.
H_1: The process is not in control.

A two-tailed hypothesis test is conducted with the control limits operating as the critical values. Each time a new point is plotted, a decision is made to fail to reject the null hypothesis (the point is within the control limits) or reject it (the point is outside the control limits). Anytime we reject the null hypothesis and conclude that the process isn't in control, we run the risk of making a type I error. Anytime the null hypothesis is not rejected and it's concluded that the process is in control, we run the risk of making a type II error. Example 13.2 illustrates the acceptance or rejection problem in statistical process control.

EXAMPLE 13.2   A large assembly line produces over 10,000 fuel pumps each week. Most of the line is automated, including high technology equipment that measures the volume of output for each pump as assembly is completed. This volume is the key indicator of part quality and is of vital concern to the car manufacturer using the pumps.

Management decides to plot each pump's output volume since the automated machinery is making this measurement. Past experience with the data has shown that pump volume will average .10 gallons per minute with standard deviation of .01 gallons per minute. For control chart purposes, these values are multiplied by 100 for a mean of 10 and standard deviation of 1.

Three standard deviations are used around the mean to form the control chart upper and lower limits. While a lower limit is needed to signal an inadequate pump, the upper limit is also established; while a pump that has "excessive" pump volume isn't a quality problem at first glance, management wants to know why such a measurement happens. The upper and lower control limits, with 99.74% confidence, are

$$\mu \pm 3\sigma = 10 \pm (3)(1) = 7 \text{ to } 13$$

Large rolls of paper with these limits printed on them are loaded into a printer electronically attached to the pump measurement machine. Each pump's volume is plotted on this paper as the completed pump is measured. Each hour, an assembly line worker scans several feet of this paper to observe the volume pattern of completed pumps. Since control limits are printed on the paper, it's very easy to spot out-of-control measurements and look for patterns. Figure 13.5 shows five minutes of this control chart. Most pumps produced during these five minutes are in control, that is, acceptable for shipment to the car manufacturer. However, pump number 25 has a low volume. Since this is the only such pump, the floor supervisor decides that there's no problem with the process; the pump is removed from the line and scrapped.

FIGURE 13.5 Individual Chart for Volume Developed Using MINITAB (Example 13.2)

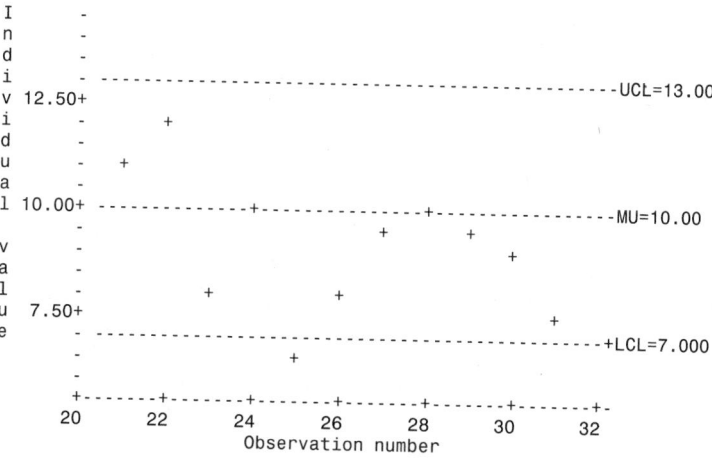

A second problem is revealed by pumps 28 through 32. While all these pumps are within the established control limits, the process seems to drift downward. The automatic machinery may be slipping or deteriorating, resulting in pumps that will soon be below standard. The floor supervisor immediately visits the production line and is prepared to stop the line and determine the reason for the apparent deterioration in quality.

The MINITAB Computer Package section at the end of this chapter gives the MINITAB commands to develop Figure 13.5.

In Example 13.2, the key quality variable being tracked is the volume of output for each pump used by a car manufacturer. In other applications, other variables are deemed to be of key importance in the quality-control effort. Here's a brief description of some quality variables typically tracked on a control chart.

Individual measurements: For very large or expensive assemblies, careful measurement of each unit is sometimes appropriate. These measurements are plotted individually over time, not averaged and plotted. An example is the measured electrical output of large industrial generators. Example 13.2 illustrated a situation where individual pump measurements were monitored. Figure 13.5 showed an individual control chart.

Process mean: This is the average value of the process for each time period. If a small number of items is produced, the entire batch is measured and this population mean is recorded on the chart. More often, a random sample of items is taken and their sample mean is used to estimate the mean of the entire time period's output; then this sample value is plotted on the control chart. Examples 13.3 and 13.4 illustrate situations where process quality is monitored using sample means. Figure 13.6 presents a mean control chart.

Range of measured values: This variable tracks the process variability. In almost all processes, the less variability, the better, as noted earlier. Tracking the difference between the largest and smallest value (the range) is a way of monitoring variability. If the range becomes too great, corrective action is called for as illustrated in Example 13.5. A range control chart appears in Figure 13.11.

Standard deviation: This would seem to be a better way of tracking variability than using the range. The range can be distorted by even a single very large or small value. The standard deviation tends to be less affected by extreme values; however, practitioners use the range much more widely, primarily because it's easier to calculate and interpret than the standard deviation.

Proportion defective: The number of defective units in each time period is calculated (a census) or estimated (a sample) and divided by the total number of items measured. The result is the proportion defective and this value is recorded on the control chart for each time period. This measurement is used when attention is focused on the correct functioning of units as a whole: either one works or it doesn't. Example 13.6 illustrates a situation where the proportion of defective units is monitored. Figure 13.14 shows a proportion control chart.

Number of defects per unit: In large assemblies, the number of nonconforming items per unit is often the focus. For each time period, this value is averaged for the units tested and plotted on the control chart. Examples 13.7 and 13.8 illustrate situations where the number of defects per unit are monitored. The appropriate control charts appear in Figures 13.15 and 13.17.

Number of nonconforming units: Instead of tracking the proportion defective, the total number of nonconforming units is measured for each time period. This variable is appropriate when the batch size remains relatively constant.

EXERCISES

11. Describe how a control chart is used.

12. Where are the upper and lower control limits set for a control chart?

13. When a process is in control, what is the probability of an individual value of the variable of interest falling outside the control limits? Explain how you computed this value.

SM 14. Explain the basic idea behind the normality assumption.

15. Albert Hughes (quality-control engineer for Dillon Aircraft) understands that viscosity of an aircraft primer paint is an important quality characteristic. Since the product is produced in batches and each batch takes several hours to produce, the production rate is slow and an individual control chart is necessary for quality monitoring. Past experience indicates that the average paint viscosity will be 30 units with a standard deviation of 1.2.

   a. Viscosity readings for 18 observations are shown below (sample 1). Albert instructs you to construct a control chart for individual measures and test to determine whether the process is in control. You're to write Albert a report indicating whether the process is in control and, if not, what type of pattern you've observed.

   b. One week later, Albert asks you to take another sample (sample 2) and develop a new control chart. Write Albert a second report.

	Viscosity	
Batch number	Sample 1	Sample 2
1	30.11	30.02
2	30.03	29.79
3	29.89	32.11
4	31.11	29.03
5	29.00	29.59
6	29.54	31.04
7	30.04	29.95
8	29.95	30.26
9	30.26	30.74
10	30.74	32.24
11	31.24	32.02
12	31.02	26.87
13	30.87	27.99
14	29.99	28.57
15	29.57	28.55
16	30.55	29.00
17	30.25	27.81
18	29.81	28.43

CONSTRUCTING A CHART TO MONITOR THE MEAN OF A PROCESS: THE $\bar{x}$ CHART

$\bar{x}$ Chart

Example 13.2 focused on using a control chart to measure the variation in individual observations of a process to determine whether the process was in control. In this section the $\bar{x}$ **chart** is used to detect changes in the process mean by monitoring the variation in the means of samples drawn from the process. Instead of plotting individual observations on the control chart, the analyst plots sample means. (Each sample mean is computed from a sample of n individual observations.) As a rule of thumb, many analysts obtain at least 20 samples of n observations each (where $n > 2$). Since sample means involve more observations, the $\bar{x}$ chart is more sensitive than the individual measurement chart for detecting shifts in the process mean.

> The $\bar{x}$ **chart (mean chart)** is used to detect changes in a process mean by monitoring the variation in the means of samples drawn from the process.

To determine the centerline and control limits for the $\bar{x}$ chart, the analyst must understand the sampling distribution of $\bar{x}$'s. A quick review of the properties of this sampling distribution of means will be helpful.

> Properties of the **sampling distribution of means:**
> 1. The mean of the sampling distribution of means equals the population mean:
>
> $$\mu_{\bar{x}} = \mu_x$$
>
> 2. The standard deviation of the sampling distribution of means (standard error) equals the population standard deviation divided by the square root of the sample size:
>
> $$\sigma_{\bar{x}} = \sigma/\sqrt{n}$$
>
> 3. The sampling distribution of means is approximately normal for sufficiently large sample sizes ($n \geq 30$).

The process mean (μ) may either be known from past experience with the process or be estimated on the basis of sample data. The usual case in industry is to estimate the process mean using the available sample means. The $\bar{x}$ chart centerline, which represents the mean of the process, is computed by averaging the sample means. This mean of the sample means is denoted by $\bar{\bar{x}}$:

$$\bar{\bar{x}} = \frac{\bar{x}_1 + \bar{x}_2 + \bar{x}_3 + \cdots + \bar{x}_k}{k} \tag{13.1}$$

where $\bar{\bar{x}}$ = Estimate of the process mean (chart centerline)
$\bar{x}_i$ = Mean of each sample
k = Number of samples of size n

The process standard deviation (σ) may also either be known from past experience with the process or be estimated using sample data. If the process standard deviation is known, the relevant standard deviation is the standard error of the mean, $\sigma/\sqrt{n}$. This is because the chart is tracking sample means rather than individual observations.

The $\bar{x}$ chart's control limits are determined from the sampling distribution of the means, not the distribution of individual x's. Since the control limits are usually set at three standard deviations, the standard deviation of the sampling distribution is multiplied by 3:

$$\text{LCL} = \bar{\bar{x}} - 3(\sigma/\sqrt{n})$$
$$\text{UCL} = \bar{\bar{x}} + 3(\sigma/\sqrt{n})$$

(13.2)

where $\bar{\bar{x}}$ = Estimate of the process mean (centerline)
σ = Process standard deviation
n = Size of each sample

The resulting control limits are referred to as the 3-sigma control limits. Note that the value 3 can be changed to reflect the quality requirements of the process. Using the value 3 produces control limits that will be exceeded approximately 26 times in 10,000 (.0026) by chance if the process mean and variation remain stable. A value of 2 would produce control limits exceeded approximately 4.6 times in 1,000 (.0456).

Example 13.3 shows how lower and upper control limits are constructed when the population standard deviation is known.

EXAMPLE 13.3   A machine produces cylinders used as the center for 3½-inch computer disks. A total of 25 samples have been selected. Each sample contains nine cylinders ($n = 9$). The average of the sample means is a diameter of $\bar{\bar{x}} = 2.5$ centimeters. Based on past experience, the process standard deviation is known to be $\sigma = 0.003$ centimeters. Quality-control analyst Evelyn Black must develop upper and lower control limits for determining whether the process is in control. She uses Equation 13.2 to compute them:

$$\text{LCL} = \bar{\bar{x}} - 3(\sigma/\sqrt{n})$$
$$= 2.5 - 3(.003/\sqrt{9}) = 2.5 - 3(.001) = 2.497$$
$$\text{UCL} = \bar{\bar{x}} + 3(\sigma/\sqrt{n})$$
$$= 2.5 + 3(.003/\sqrt{9}) = 2.5 + 3(.001) = 2.503$$

Whenever a sample of nine cylinders produces a mean between 2.497 and 2.503, Evelyn concludes that the process is in control. Whenever a sample mean falls outside these limits, she concludes that the process is not in control. If the process is in control, the probability of obtaining a sample mean outside the control limits (making a type I error) is $2(.5000 - .4987) = .0026$.

The process standard deviation is usually unknown and must be estimated from sample data. The most effective approach (and the one used most frequently in industry, especially when small samples are used) is to utilize the ranges of the k samples as an estimate of the process variability. Recall from Chapter 4 that the range, R, of a sample is the difference between the maximum and minimum observations in a data set. The process standard deviation is estimated using Equation 13.3:

$$\hat{\sigma} = \frac{\bar{R}}{d_2}$$

(13.3)

where $\hat{\sigma}$ = Estimate of the process standard deviation
        $\bar{R}$ = Average of the sample ranges
        d_2 = Value selected from the control chart constants table (Table 13.1)

The estimate of the process standard deviation is substituted into Equation 13.2 forming Equation 13.4:

$$\text{LCL} = \bar{\bar{x}} - 3(\hat{\sigma}/\sqrt{n})$$
$$\text{UCL} = \bar{\bar{x}} + 3(\hat{\sigma}/\sqrt{n})$$

(13.4)

The steps for construction of an $\bar{x}$ chart are:

Steps for constructing an $\bar{x}$ chart:
1. Select k samples of data, each of size n.
2. Compute the mean of each sample.
3. Estimate the process mean ($\bar{\bar{x}}$) by averaging the sample means. Use this process mean as the centerline of the chart.
4. Estimate the population standard deviation using $\hat{\sigma} = \bar{R}/d_2$. ($d_2$ is found in Table 13.1.)
5. Compute the 3-sigma control limits:

$$\text{LCL} = \bar{\bar{x}} - 3(\hat{\sigma}/\sqrt{n})$$
$$\text{UCL} = \bar{\bar{x}} + 3(\hat{\sigma}/\sqrt{n})$$

Example 13.4 illustrates the procedure for constructing lower and upper control limits when the population standard deviation is unknown.

EXAMPLE 13.4   Management of the Mead Corporation is considering entering the European market. However, the company controller has recently read an article in *Management Accounting* (July 1992) that points out that even if the company makes good products, if its quality system does not conform to ISO 9000 standards Europeans will not buy.[5] Jeff Frost, Quality Engineer, has been informed that the company's quality system must conform to ISO 9000 standards in order for the company to sell products or services in Europe. Jeff has been told that the quality system described in the ISO 9000 series is the only one that meets European Economic Area (EEA) directives requiring sellers to have quality systems.

Jeff decides to improve the quality of the tensile strength of a textile fiber produced by the company. He selects 16 samples from the first eight hours of a production run.

---

[5]A. F. Borthick and H. P. Roth, "Will Europeans Buy Your Company's Products" *Management Accounting,* July 1992, p. 28.

TABLE 13.1 Control Chart Constants

Number of observations in subgroup, n	A_2	A_3	d_2	d_3	D_3	D_4
2	1.880	2.659	1.128	0.853	0.000	3.267
3	1.023	1.954	1.693	0.888	0.000	2.574
4	0.729	1.628	2.059	0.880	0.000	2.282
5	0.577	1.427	2.326	0.864	0.000	2.114
6	0.483	1.287	2.534	0.848	0.000	2.004
7	0.419	1.182	2.704	0.833	0.076	1.924
8	0.373	1.099	2.847	0.820	0.136	1.864
9	0.337	1.032	2.970	0.808	0.184	1.816
10	0.308	0.975	3.078	0.797	0.223	1.777
11	0.285	0.927	3.173	0.787	0.256	1.744
12	0.266	0.886	3.258	0.778	0.283	1.717
13	0.249	0.850	3.336	0.770	0.307	1.693
14	0.235	0.817	3.407	0.762	0.328	1.672
15	0.223	0.789	3.472	0.755	0.347	1.653
16	0.212	0.763	3.532	0.749	0.363	1.637
17	0.203	0.739	3.588	0.743	0.378	1.622
18	0.194	0.718	3.640	0.738	0.391	1.608
19	0.187	0.698	3.689	0.733	0.403	1.597
20	0.180	0.680	3.735	0.729	0.415	1.585
21	0.173	0.663	3.778	0.724	0.425	1.575
22	0.167	0.647	3.819	0.720	0.434	1.566
23	0.162	0.633	3.858	0.716	0.443	1.557
24	0.157	0.619	3.895	0.712	0.451	1.548
25	0.153	0.606	3.931	0.709	0.459	1.541
Over 25	$3/\sqrt{n}$					

Source: Adapted from *Tools and Methods for the Improvement of Quality*, H. Gitlow, S. Gitlow, A. Oppenheim, and R. Oppenheim (Homewood, IL: Richard D. Irwin, 1989).

Samples are taken at 30-minute intervals. Each sample consists of $n = 4$ fiber specimens.

Table 13.2 summarizes the results. As it shows, the mean of the 16 sample means is $\bar{\bar{x}} = 120$. Since the process standard deviation isn't known, it's estimated using Equation 13.3. The average range and the appropriate d_2 value from Table 13.1 are used to estimate the standard deviation. Each sample's range is computed in the R column in Table 13.2. For example, the range or difference between the largest and smallest fiber strengths for sample number 1 is $(120.85 - 119.50) = 1.35$. At the bottom of Table 13.2, the average range for these samples is computed: $\bar{R} = .92375$. Referring to Table 13.1 for a sample of $n = 4$ fibers, the appropriate d_2 value is 2.059. Using Equation 13.3, the estimate of σ is:

$$\hat{\sigma} = \frac{\bar{R}}{d_2} = \frac{.92375}{2.059} = .449$$

TABLE 13.2   Sixteen Samples of Size 4 from the Tensile Strength Process of Example 13.4

Sample number	Strength of fiber				$\bar{x}$	Range R
	1	2	3	4		
1	120.15	119.50	120.85	119.95	120.11	1.35
2	119.89	119.40	120.45	119.87	119.90	1.05
3	119.62	120.03	120.74	120.13	120.13	1.12
4	120.47	119.89	120.24	120.15	120.19	0.58
5	120.00	119.21	119.68	120.24	119.78	1.03
6	119.99	119.87	119.85	119.84	119.89	0.15
7	120.11	120.01	120.42	119.93	120.12	0.49
8	119.75	120.25	120.14	119.86	120.00	0.50
9	120.18	119.87	119.81	119.77	119.91	0.41
10	120.87	120.57	119.24	120.09	120.19	1.63
11	119.86	119.20	120.30	119.72	119.70	1.10
12	118.86	120.41	119.87	120.53	119.92	1.67
13	119.90	121.12	119.54	120.07	120.16	1.58
14	119.99	120.18	120.06	119.88	120.03	0.30
15	120.03	120.05	120.14	119.33	119.89	0.81
16	119.55	120.56	120.17	119.64	119.98	1.01
					1,919.99	14.78

$$\bar{\bar{x}} = \frac{1,919.99}{16} = 120 \qquad \bar{R} = \frac{14.78}{16} = .92375$$

Equation 13.4 is used to calculate the control limits:

$$\text{LCL} = \bar{\bar{x}} - 3(\hat{\sigma}/\sqrt{n})$$
$$= 120 - 3(.449/\sqrt{4}) = 119.327$$
$$\text{UCL} = \bar{\bar{x}} + 3(\hat{\sigma}/\sqrt{n})$$
$$= 120 + 3(.449/\sqrt{4}) = 120.674$$

Figure 13.6 shows these lower and upper control limits along with the centerline and 16 sample means plotted in sequence. The sample means are all within the control limits so Jeff concludes that the process is in control.

The MINITAB computer package can be used to develop Figure 13.6. The MINITAB commands are:

```
MTB> SET C1
DATA> 120.15   119.50   120.85   119.95
DATA> 119.89   119.40   120.45   119.87
DATA> 119.62   120.03   120.74   120.13
DATA> 120.47   119.89   120.24   120.15
DATA> 120.00   119.21   119.68   120.24
DATA> 119.99   119.87   119.85   119.84
DATA> 120.11   120.01   120.42   119.93
DATA> 119.75   120.25   120.14   119.86
DATA> 120.18   119.87   119.81   119.77
DATA> 120.87   120.57   119.24   120.09
DATA> 119.86   119.20   120.30   119.72
```

FIGURE 13.6 $\bar{x}$ Chart for Strength Developed Using MINITAB (Example 13.4)

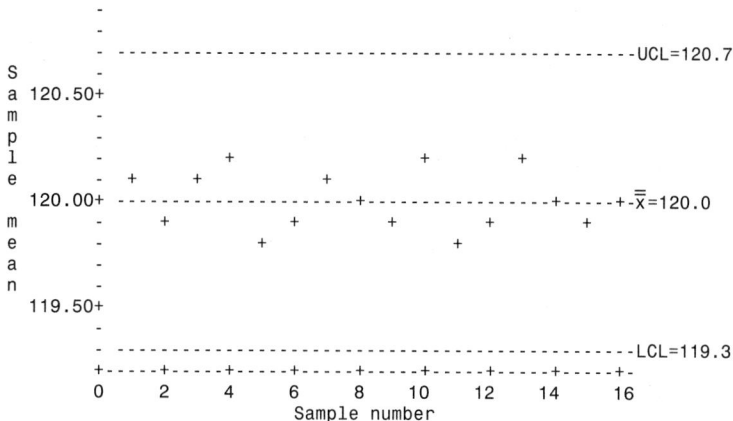

```
DATA>  118.86    120.41    119.87    120.53
DATA>  119.90    121.12    119.54    120.07
DATA>  119.99    120.18    120.06    119.88
DATA>  120.03    120.05    120.14    119.33
DATA>  119.55    120.56    120.17    119.64
DATA>  END
MTB>  NAME C1 'STRENGTH'
MTB>  XBARCHART FOR DATA IN C1, SAMPLE SIZE 4
      OUTPUT SHOWN AS FIGURE 13.6

MTB>  WRITE 'FIBER.DAT' C1
MTB>  STOP
```

The data are entered in sequence into C1. The XBARCHART command plots sample means of size $n = 4$ on an $\bar{x}$ chart (Figure 13.6). The WRITE command is used to save the data located in C1 in a file called FIBER.DAT.

Up to this point, the discussion has focused on determining that a process is not in control by identifying values beyond the control limits on the $\bar{x}$ chart. A closer look at the pattern of all control chart values may also reveal a process that's not in control. This is true even though all of the values may be within the control limits. For example, six points in a row, all increasing or decreasing, indicate that a process is not in control, possibly due to operator fatigue. The process can probably be improved by identifying and eliminating this source of variation. Assorted plot patterns appeared in Figure 13.2.

Analysts use pattern analysis to recognize systematic patterns in an $\bar{x}$ control chart and to identify the source of such process variation. To help detect systematic patterns in $\bar{x}$ charts, each chart is divided into three zones (Figure 13.7). Zone A is defined as the area between 2 and 3 standard deviation units above and below the centerline. Zone B is defined as the area between 1 and 2 standard deviation units above and below the centerline. Zone C is defined as the area between the centerline and ± 1 standard deviation unit.

FIGURE 13.7 $\bar{x}$ Chart Using Zones A, B, and C

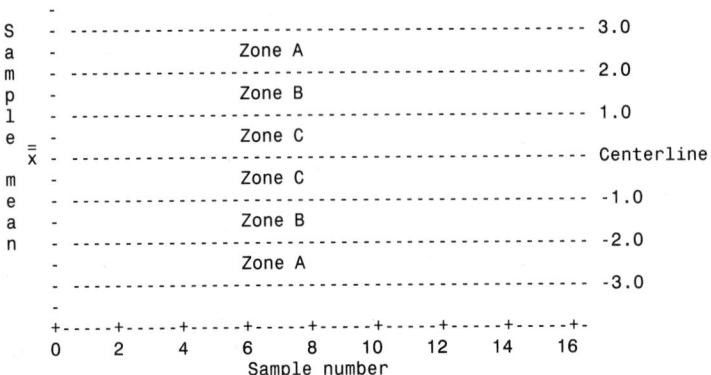

Analysts don't agree about the specific systematic patterns that indicate nonrandom variation. The following specific patterns are used by the MINITAB computer program.[6] Each pattern is illustrated in Figure 13.8.

PATTERN	DESCRIPTION
1	One point beyond zone A (the out-of-control pattern discussed previously).
2	Nine points in a row in zone C or beyond, all on one side of centerline.
3	Six points in a row, all increasing or all decreasing.
4	Fourteen points in a row, alternating up and down.
5	Two out of three points in a row in zone A or beyond.
6	Four out of five points in a row in zone B or beyond (on one side of centerline).
7	Fifteen points in a row in zone C (above or below centerline).
8	Eight points in a row beyond zone C (above or below centerline).

FIGURE 13.8   Eight Patterns Tested for by MINITAB

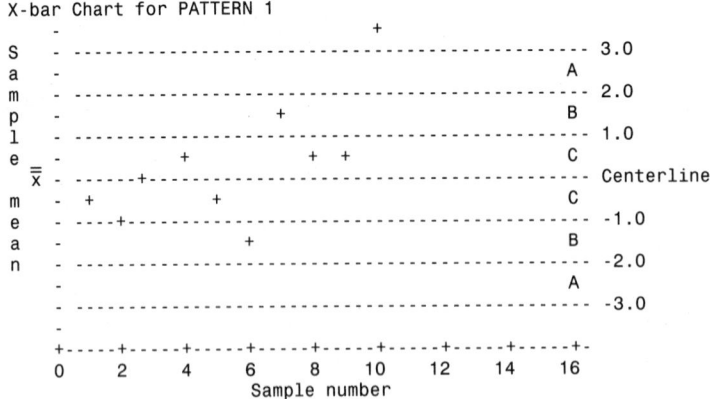

[6]*MINITAB Reference Manual Release 8 PC Version*, State College, PA: MINITAB Statistical Software, 1991.

FIGURE 13.8 *continued*

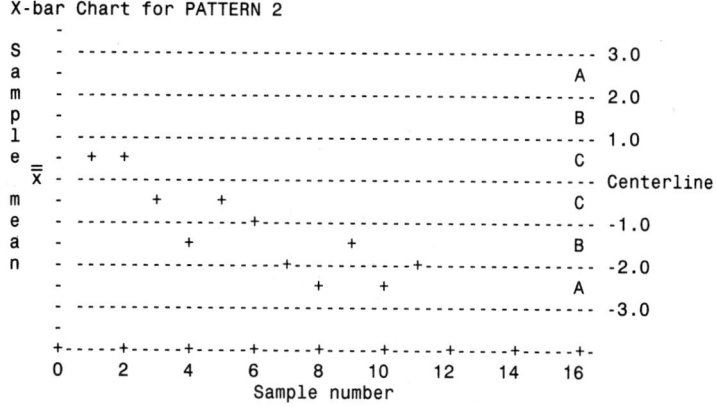

X-bar Chart for PATTERN 2

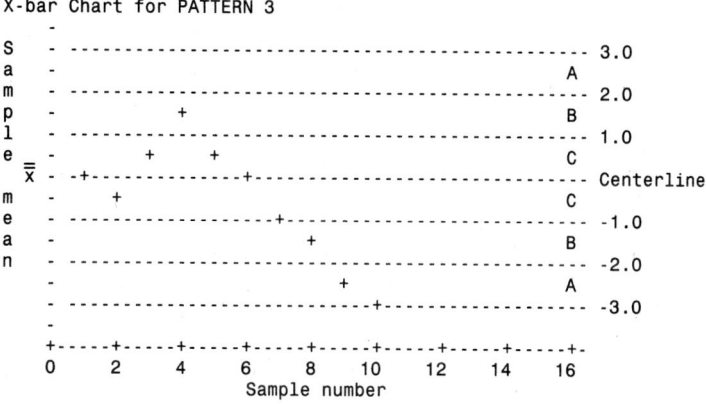

X-bar Chart for PATTERN 3

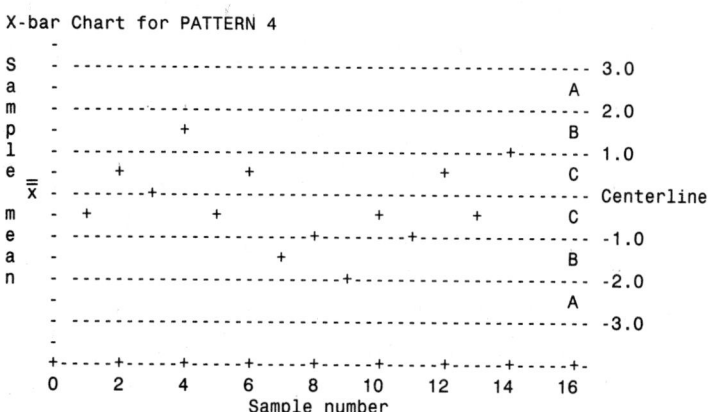

X-bar Chart for PATTERN 4

FIGURE 13.8 *continued*

X-bar Chart for PATTERN 5

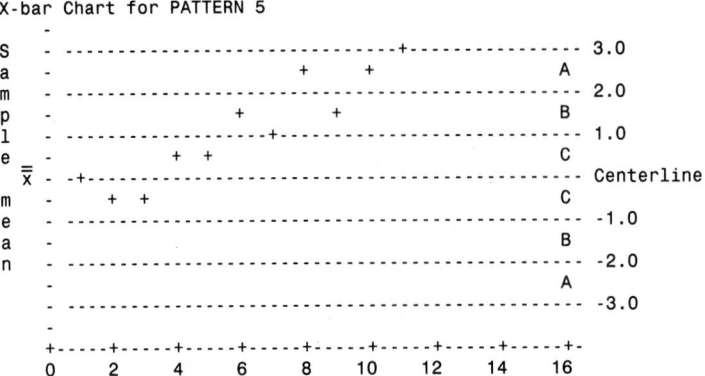

X-bar Chart for PATTERN 6

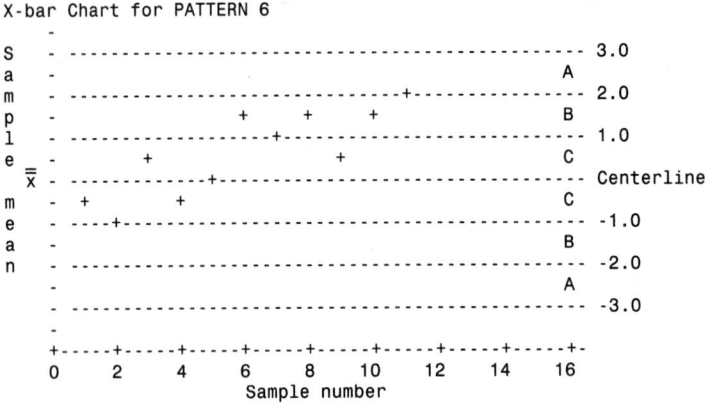

X-bar Chart for PATTERN 7

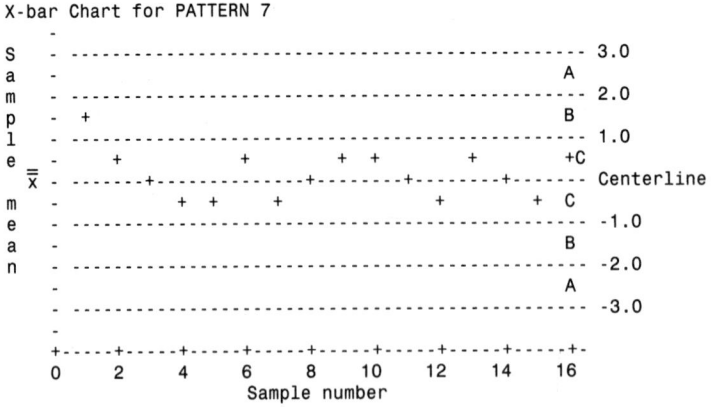

FIGURE 13.8 *concluded*

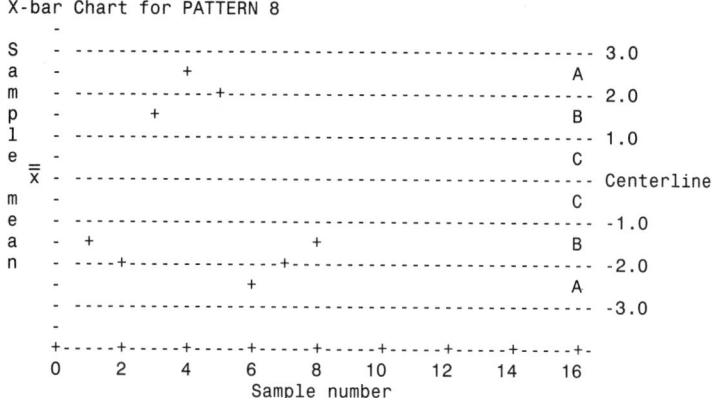

X-bar Chart for PATTERN 8

After examining Figure 13.8, it should be obvious that there's more to control chart inspection than looking for values outside the control limits. In actual practice, analysts need a great deal of knowledge and experience to interpret the particular pattern or assignable causes. Several good textbooks are available if more information on pattern interpretation is needed.

The MINITAB computer package can be used to develop zones A, B, and C for Example 13.4. The MINITAB commands are:

```
MTB >   READ 'FIBER.DAT' C1
        64 ROWS READ

C1
  120.15    119.50    120.85    119.95 . . .

MTB > NAME C1 'STRENGTH'
MTB > XBARCHART FOR DATA IN C1, SAMPLE SIZE 4;
SUBC> SIGMA = .449;
SUBC> SLIMITS 1 2 3;
SUBC> TEST 1:8.
      OUTPUT SHOWN AS FIGURE 13.9
MTB > STOP
```

The READ command is used to read the data from the file FIBER.DAT into C1. The XBARCHART command plots sample means of size $n = 4$ on an $\bar{x}$ chart. Equation 13.3 is used to estimate the process standard deviation. The subcommand SIGMA = .449 is used to provide this information. Zones A, B, and C are included using subcommand SLIMITS 1 2 3, and MINITAB is instructed to search for patterns 1 through 8 using subcommand TEST 1:8. Figure 13.9 shows that no patterns were identified. If MINITAB does detect a pattern, the sample at which the pattern is completed is flagged by placing a value (1 for pattern 1, 2 for pattern 2, and so forth) above or below the plotted value.

FIGURE 13.9 $\bar{x}$ Chart for Strength with Zones A, B, and C (Example 13.4)

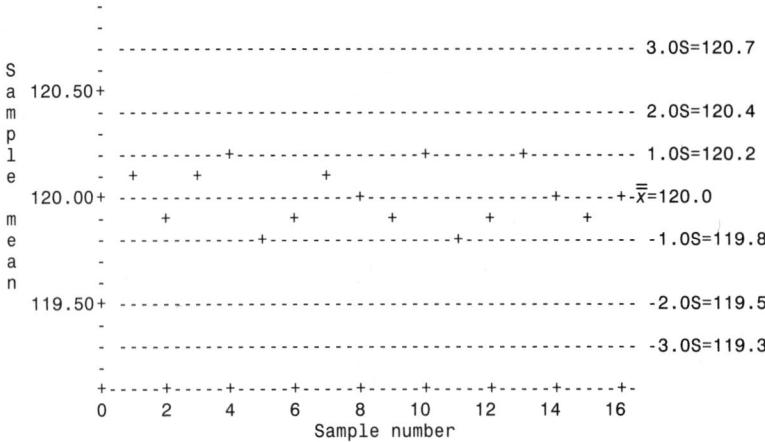

In practice, the $\bar{x}$ chart is typically used in conjunction with a range chart (R chart) that monitors the variation of the process. Used together, these two charts make it possible to determine whether a process is in control.

You've just learned how to determine when a process is not in control because of a shift in the mean. In the next section, you'll learn how to determine whether a variation change indicates an out-of-control process.

EXERCISES

16. The individual measurement chart's control limits are determined from the sampling distribution of individual x's. How are the control limits of an $\bar{x}$ chart determined?

17. Explain how the properties of the sampling distribution of sample means are used to construct an $\bar{x}$ chart.

18. Even if all the values on an $\bar{x}$ chart fall between the control limits, the process may not be in control. Explain.

19. Use pattern analysis to determine which of the processes plotted in the six $\bar{x}$ charts in Figure 13.10 are in control.

FIGURE 13.10   Plots to Be Analyzed Using Pattern Analysis (Exercise 19)

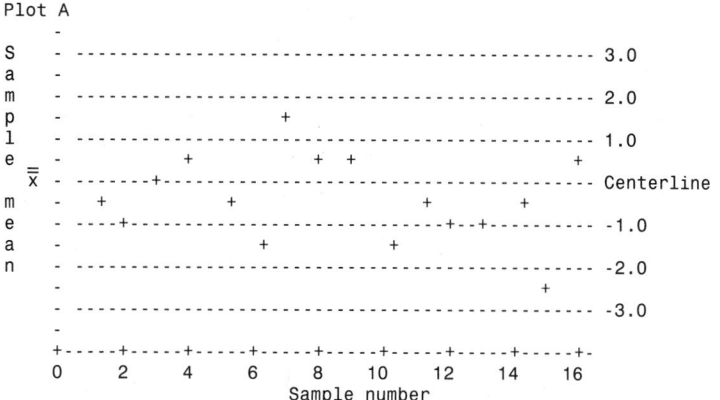

Plot A

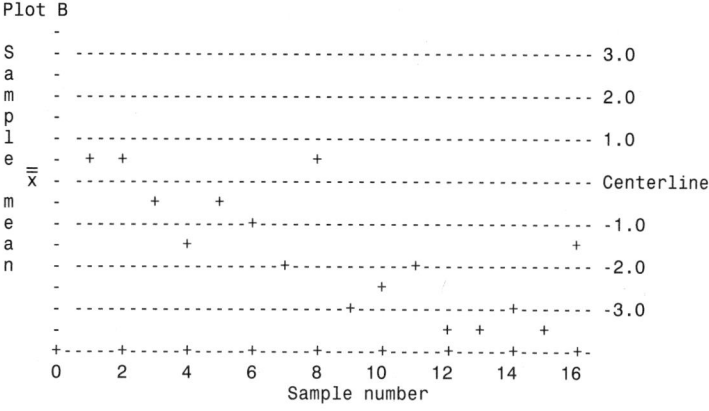

Plot B

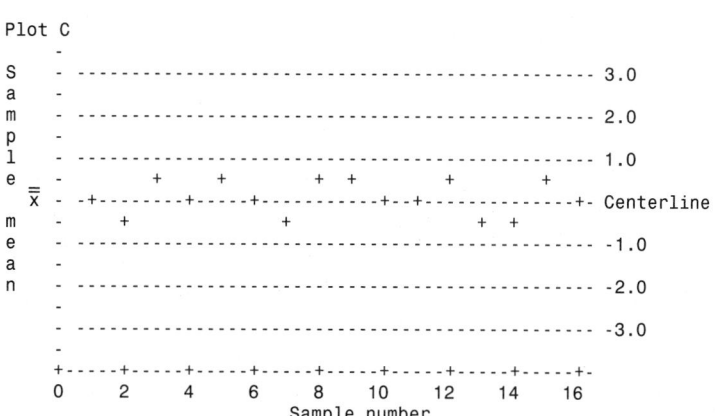

Plot C

FIGURE 13.10   *concluded*

Plot D

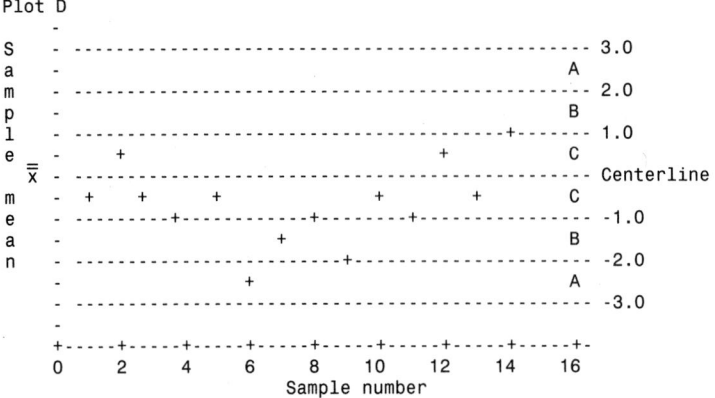

Plot E

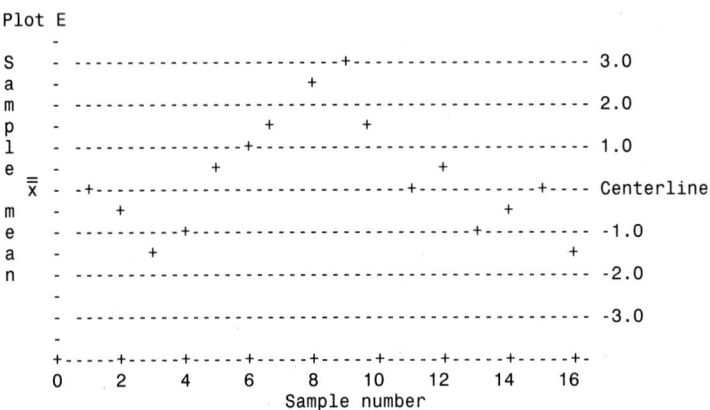

Plot F

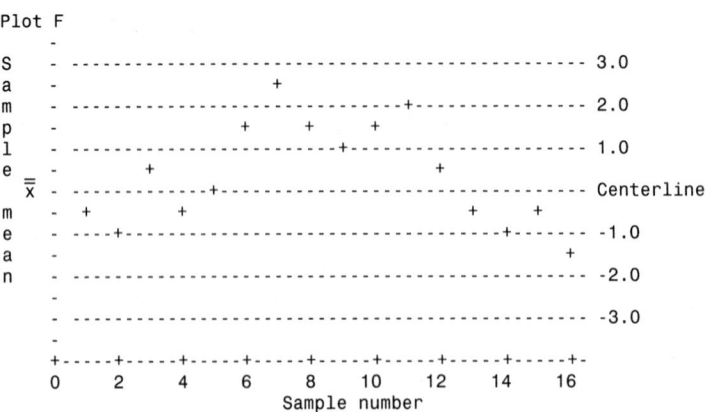

20. Natural gas cylinders are produced by a robot welder to have an average burst strength of 4,000 psi, with standard deviation of 120 psi. Determine upper and lower control limits for a 3-sigma mean control chart in which each sample consists of five cylinders.

21. (Refer to Exercise 20.) Determine whether the process is in control given the following nine sample means:

Mean Burst Strengths								
4005	4058	3995	3854	4001	3897	4112	4067	4012

22. Taft Manufacturing produces softballs that historically have a circumference averaging 12 inches with standard deviation of .04 inches. Determine upper and lower control limits for a 3-sigma mean control chart in which each sample consists of seven softballs.

23. (Refer to Exercise 22.) Determine whether the process is in control given the following eight sample mean circumferences: 12.051, 11.966, 11.981, 11.945, 12.072, 11.998, 12.008, 12.033.

24. Chuck Jackson, manager of the Chariot Inn, monitors the swimming pool's pH level by taking readings every two hours from 9 A.M. to 9 P.M. daily. The past two weeks' results are:

Day 1	Average pH	Range
1	8.21	.17
2	8.26	.15
3	8.08	.19
4	8.26	.22
5	8.19	.18
6	8.14	.13
7	8.09	.10
8	8.21	.16
9	8.20	.21
10	8.09	.12
11	8.16	.21
12	8.09	.08
13	8.24	.16
14	8.19	.19

a. Develop the centerline and upper and lower control limits for a 3-sigma $\bar{x}$ chart.

b. Compute the limits of the six zones (A, B, C).

c. Plot the means and test to determine whether the process is in control.

25. The Wearing Corporation manufactures precision parts such as bolts used in helicopters. Charlene Richards is in charge of quality control. She samples six bolts each hour and measures them using a computerized precision measuring instrument. The data for the past 22 hours are:

Hour	Bolt lengths (centimeters)					
1	21.02	23.41	22.01	24.12	23.88	22.87
2	22.01	22.45	21.21	23.82	24.08	22.37
3	21.54	21.99	23.56	22.35	23.12	23.93
4	24.12	23.83	22.76	24.54	23.21	22.34
5	22.32	22.44	24.31	22.22	23.23	21.89

Hour	Bolt lengths (centimeters)					
6	22.35	23.56	22.87	23.35	25.11	22.27
7	21.92	23.51	24.31	22.52	23.56	21.74
8	21.32	21.41	22.41	21.92	21.86	23.81
9	22.21	22.45	21.31	22.82	22.06	22.35
10	21.44	23.99	23.16	23.75	23.16	22.94
11	22.12	24.83	22.26	24.55	24.26	21.34
12	22.34	21.44	24.41	21.23	24.23	23.85
13	21.35	23.43	22.57	24.36	23.18	24.47
14	23.92	21.51	23.31	22.57	22.56	24.44
15	21.32	22.41	22.31	24.15	21.89	23.87
16	22.31	23.45	23.41	23.82	21.98	21.38
17	21.67	20.99	23.54	22.35	22.12	22.96
18	24.09	22.83	21.76	24.54	23.21	23.34
19	22.34	21.44	24.31	23.62	24.83	24.59
20	21.35	24.56	23.84	23.65	23.18	24.27
21	22.96	22.51	21.31	22.55	22.56	23.44
22	23.95	21.51	24.33	21.32	21.26	22.34

a. Construct the appropriate control chart to monitor this process.

b. Is the process in control?

c. Give an example of an assignable cause that could potentially affect this process.

26. The Circuit Corporation manufactures circuit boards for new personal computers. Board length is very important since they're eventually slipped into slots in a chassis. Company quality analyst Phil Conrath is in charge of stabilizing the length dimension. Boards are cut from large sheets of material by a single rotary cutter continuously fed from a hopper. Phil develops a control chart for the length of the circuit boards produced by the process. The circuit boards' mean length is supposed to be 6 inches with a standard deviation of .08 inch. Phil decides to select five units every hour from the production process. The accompanying table shows the resulting lengths for a two-day period.

Sample number	Cut circuit board lengths				
	1	2	3	4	5
Day 1					
7 A.M.	5.83	6.09	5.91	6.18	5.91
8	6.13	5.99	5.76	6.12	6.19
9	5.94	5.81	6.11	6.28	6.00
10	6.03	5.89	6.01	6.08	6.10
11	5.93	5.99	6.01	6.19	6.11
12 P.M.	6.11	6.01	5.96	5.92	6.09
1	5.84	5.91	6.13	6.28	5.99
2	6.13	6.10	6.01	6.00	6.10
3	6.03	6.19	5.93	5.89	5.91
4	6.14	6.19	5.86	6.17	6.04
5	5.94	5.91	6.01	6.07	6.04
6	6.13	5.88	6.14	6.18	6.14
Day 2					
7 A.M.	6.15	5.95	5.78	6.18	6.10
8	5.94	5.91	6.01	6.20	6.13

Sample number	Cut circuit board lengths				
	1	2	3	4	5
9	5.83	5.88	6.08	6.12	6.11
10	5.97	6.19	5.81	6.08	5.91
11	6.13	5.87	5.77	6.16	6.29
12 P.M.	5.94	5.91	6.21	6.08	6.03
1	6.04	5.93	6.04	6.18	6.13
2	6.13	6.09	5.92	6.08	5.95
3	6.03	5.89	5.97	6.14	6.13
4	5.94	5.83	6.13	6.11	5.90
5	6.01	5.81	6.02	6.03	6.14
6	5.85	6.06	5.97	6.19	5.81

a. Construct the appropriate control chart to monitor this process.

b. Is the process in control?

c. Assume that the population standard deviation is known to be .1 inch. Now is the process in control?

d. Assume that the population standard deviation is unknown and must be estimated. Now is the process in control?

CONSTRUCTING A CHART TO MONITOR THE VARIATION OF A PROCESS: THE R CHART

R Chart

Figure 13.2 demonstrated that a process may be out of statistical control because the mean or variance or both are changing over time. The last section focused on using the $\bar{x}$ chart to detect changes in the process mean by monitoring the variation in the means of samples drawn from the process. In this section, the **range chart (R chart)** is used to detect changes in the process variation by monitoring sample ranges. As a rule of thumb, many analysts obtain at least 20 samples of n observations each (where $n > 2$).

> The **R chart (range chart)** is used to detect changes in the process variation by monitoring sample ranges drawn from the process.

To determine the centerline and control limits for the R chart, we need to understand the sampling distribution for R. The centerline of the $\bar{x}$ chart represented the process mean and was computed by averaging the sample means. Similarly, the centerline of the R chart is the average of the sample ranges (denoted by $\bar{R}$):

$$\bar{R} = \frac{R_1 + R_2 + R_3 + \cdots + R_k}{k} \tag{13.5}$$

where $\bar{R}$ = Average range for the samples (centerline)
  R_i = Range of each sample
  k = Number of samples of size n

To construct the control limits, a measure of the variability of the sampling distribution of R is needed. The estimated standard deviation is denoted s_R. Values d_2 and d_3 are taken from the control chart constants table (Table 13.1) and used to estimate s_R:

$$s_R = \overline{R}\,\frac{d_3}{d_2} \tag{13.6}$$

The control limits for the R chart are constructed in the same way as for the $\overline{x}$ chart. $\overline{R}$ and s_R are substituted for $\overline{x}$ and $\sigma_{\overline{x}}$ in Equation 13.4, forming

$$\text{Control limits} = \overline{R} \pm 3 s_R$$

After substituting $\overline{R}(d_3/d_2)$ for s_R, the equation becomes

$$\overline{R} \pm 3\overline{R}\frac{d_3}{d_2} = \overline{R}\left(1 \pm 3\frac{d_3}{d_2}\right)$$

To simplify the computations, the values D_3 and D_4 are defined as

$$D_3 = 1 - 3\frac{d_3}{d_2}$$

$$D_4 = 1 + 3\frac{d_3}{d_2}$$

and found using Table 13.1. The R chart control limits are constructed using Equation 13.7:

$$\text{LCL} = D_3\overline{R} \tag{13.7}$$
$$\text{UCL} = D_4\overline{R}$$

Steps for constructing an *R* chart:

1. Select k samples of data, each of size n.
2. Compute the range for each sample.
3. Compute the average range $(\overline{R})$. Use the average range as the centerline of the chart.
4. Compute the 3-sigma control limits:

   $\text{LCL} = D_3\overline{R}$ (D_3 and D_4 are found in Table 13.1)
   $\text{UCL} = D_4\overline{R}$

Example 13.5 shows how an R chart is developed.

EXAMPLE 13.5   In Example 13.4, Jeff Frost was monitoring the process mean for textile fibers and discovered that the mean of the process is in control. Now he needs to find out about the process variation.

Each sample's ranges are computed (Table 13.2). So is the average range for these samples ($\overline{R} = .92375$), which will be the centerline for the control chart. Referring to Table 13.1 for a sample of $n = 4$ fibers, the appropriate D_3 value is 0 and the appropriate D_4 value is 2.282. Equation 13.7 is used to calculate the control limits:

$$LCL = D_3\overline{R} = 0(.924) = 0$$
$$UCL = D_4\overline{R} = 2.282(.92375) = 2.108$$

Figure 13.11 shows these lower and upper control limits along with the centerline and the 16 average sample ranges plotted in sequence. The average sample ranges are all within the control limits so the process is deemed to be in control.

FIGURE 13.11   R Chart for Strength Developed Using MINITAB (Example 13.5)

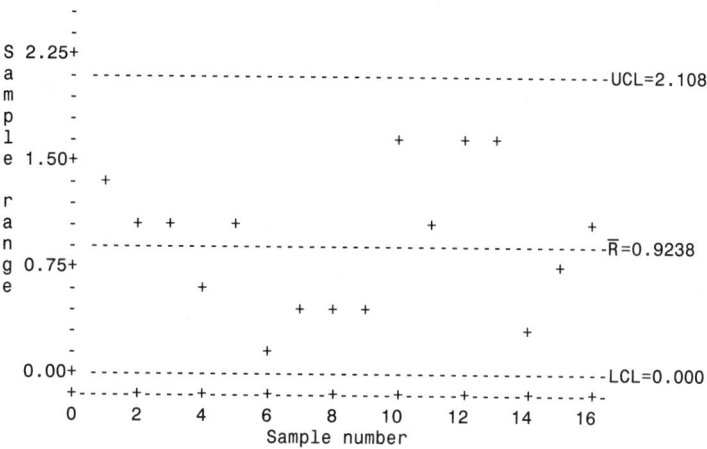

The MINITAB computer package can be used to develop Figure 13.11, The MINITAB commands are:

```
MTB > READ 'FIBER.DAT' C1
    64 ROWS READ

C1
   120.15    119.50    120.85 119.95 . . .

MTB > NAME C1 'STRENGTH'
MTB > RCHART FOR DATA IN C1, SAMPLE SIZE 4
    OUTPUT IS SHOWN IN FIGURE 13.11

MTB > STOP
```

The READ command is used to read the data from the file FIBER.DAT into C1. The RCHART command plots the average sample ranges of samples of size $n = 4$ on an R chart as shown in Figure 13.11

As mentioned earlier, the $\bar{x}$ chart and R charts are usually used together to monitor the mean and variation of a process. Actually, the appropriate procedure is to first construct the *R* chart. If we conclude that the process variation is in control, then it makes sense to construct an $\bar{x}$ chart. Remember, the $\bar{x}$ chart's control limits are dependent on the variation of the process. Thus, if the process variation is out of control, the $\bar{x}$ control limits are not correct either. In other words, if the process variation is changing, any single estimate of the variation won't be representative of the process.

In Figure 13.12, the sample ranges are within their control limits, but the means have drifted downward and the process is no longer in control. In Figure 13.13, the sample means remain within the control limits while the variability of the process has shifted upward and out of control.

A process that's not in control can also be identified by a lone sample value that falls outside the control limits. When this happens, an investigation is usually conducted to determine whether there's an assignable cause.

FIGURE 13.12 $\bar{x}$ and *R* Charts Showing the Mean Out of Control

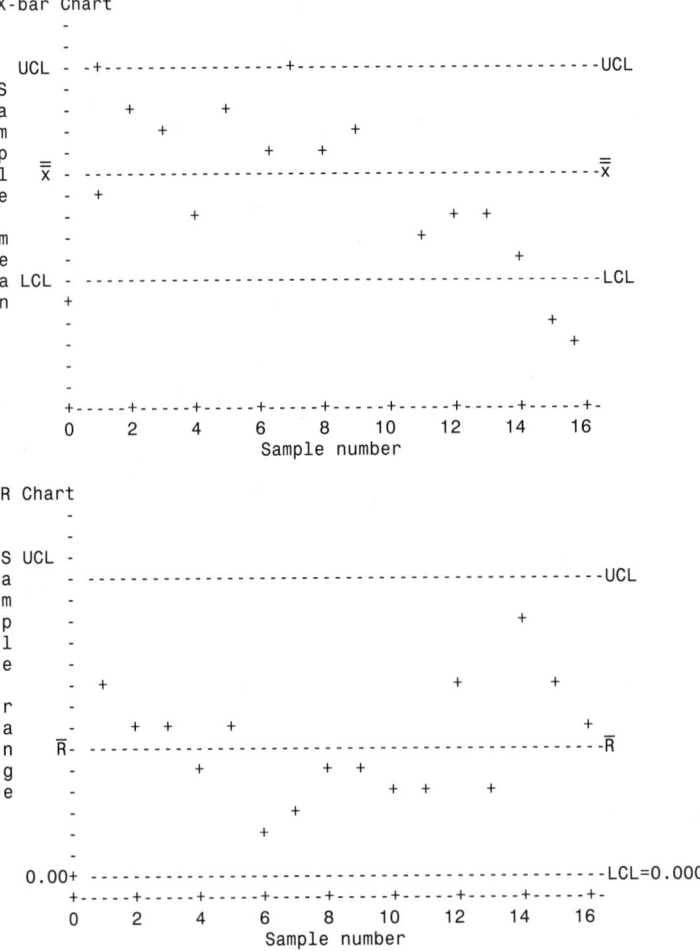

FIGURE 13.13 $\bar{x}$ and R Charts Showing the Variation Out of Control

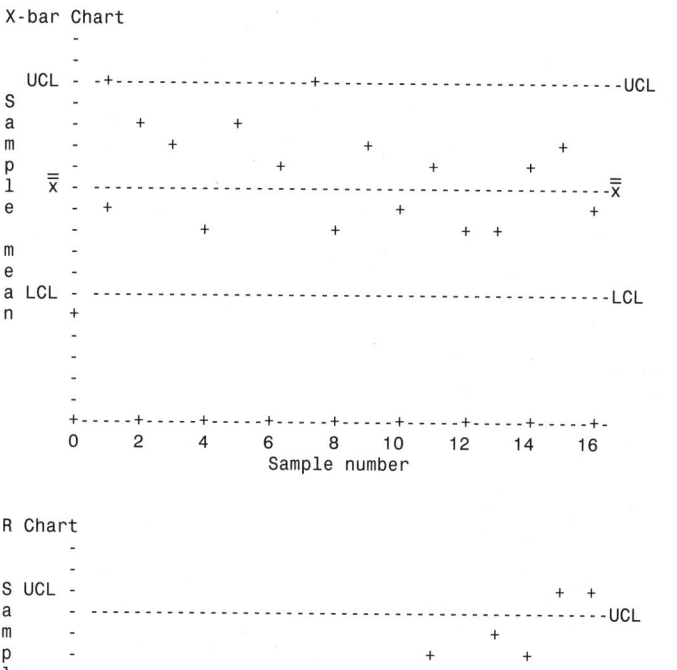

EXERCISES

27. How are the control limits of an R chart determined?

28. What characteristic of a process is an R chart used to monitor?

29. Why is an R chart used in conjunction with an $\bar{x}$ chart? Which chart should be analyzed first? Why?

30. (Refer to Exercise 22.) Taft Manufacturing produces softballs that historically have a circumference averaging 12 inches. Estimate s_R if the average of the sample ranges is .13 inches. Determine upper and lower control limits for a 3-sigma mean control chart in which each sample consists of seven softballs.

31. (Refer to Exercise 30.) Determine whether the process is in control given the following eight sample ranges: .141, .102, .163, .215, .047, .111, .138, .211.

32. (Refer to Exercise 20.) Natural gas cylinders are produced by a robot welder to have an average burst strength of 4,000 psi. The average of the sample ranges is 300 psi. Determine upper and lower control limits for a 3-sigma range control chart in which each sample consists of five cylinders.

33. (Refer to Exercise 32.) Determine whether the process is in control given the following nine sample ranges: 300, 245, 741, 100, 458, 641, 406, 401, 258.

34. (Refer to Exercise 24.) The Chariot Inn manager monitors the swimming pool's pH level by taking readings every two hours from 9 A.M. to 9 P.M. daily. The past two weeks' results are:

Day 1	Average pH	Range
1	8.21	.17
2	8.26	.15
3	8.08	.19
4	8.26	.22
5	8.19	.18
6	8.14	.13
7	8.09	.10
8	8.21	.16
9	8.20	.21
10	8.09	.12
11	8.16	.21
12	8.09	.08
13	8.24	.16
14	8.19	.19

a. Develop the centerline and upper and lower control limits for a 3-sigma R chart.

b. Compute the limits of the six zones.

c. Plot the ranges and test to determine whether the process is in control.

d. In exercise 24, the manager computed an $\bar{x}$ chart. Now that he has both an R chart and an $\bar{x}$ chart, what is his conclusion?

35. (Refer to Exercise 25.) The Wearing Corporation manufactures precision parts such as bolts used in helicopters. Six bolts are sampled each hour and measured using a computerized precision measuring instrument. The data for the past 22 hours are:

Hour	Bolt lengths (centimeters)					
1	21.02	23.41	22.01	24.12	23.88	22.87
2	22.01	22.45	21.21	23.82	24.08	22.37
3	21.54	21.99	23.56	22.35	23.12	23.93
4	24.12	23.83	22.76	24.54	23.21	22.34
5	22.32	22.44	24.31	22.22	23.23	21.89
6	22.35	23.56	22.87	23.35	25.11	22.27
7	21.92	23.51	24.31	22.52	23.56	21.74
8	21.32	21.41	22.41	21.92	21.86	23.81
9	22.21	22.45	21.31	22.82	22.06	22.35
10	21.44	23.99	23.16	23.75	23.16	22.94

Hour	Bolt lengths (centimeters)					
11	22.12	24.83	22.26	24.55	24.26	21.34
12	22.34	21.44	24.41	21.23	24.23	23.85
13	21.35	23.43	22.57	24.36	23.18	24.47
14	23.92	21.51	23.31	22.57	22.56	24.44
15	21.32	22.41	22.31	24.15	21.89	23.87
16	22.31	23.45	23.41	23.82	21.98	21.38
17	21.67	20.99	23.54	22.35	22.12	22.96
18	24.09	22.83	21.76	24.54	23.21	23.34
19	22.34	21.44	24.31	23.62	24.83	24.59
20	21.35	24.56	23.84	23.65	23.18	24.27
21	22.96	22.51	21.31	22.55	22.56	23.44
22	23.95	21.51	24.33	21.32	21.26	22.34

a. Construct the appropriate control chart to monitor the variation of this process.

b. Is the process variation in control?

c. Give an example of an assignable cause that could potentially affect this process variation.

d. In Exercise 25, an $\bar{x}$ chart was constructed. Now that you've examined both an R chart and an $\bar{x}$ chart, what is your conclusion?

36. The Slim-rite Company produces several diet cola drinks. Lynn Stephens, quality-control inspector, monitors the amount of cola injected into 12-ounce cans by one of the filling heads on the automated process. She decides to sample five cans of diet cola each half hour beginning at 6 A.M.. The data for 25 consecutive half-hour periods are:

Hour	Ounces per can				
1	12.0000	12.0225	11.9858	12.0075	12.0180
2	12.0225	12.0150	11.9775	11.9963	11.9850
3	11.9850	12.0045	12.0225	12.0300	11.9955
4	12.0000	12.0225	12.0173	11.9850	11.9850
5	11.9782	11.9925	12.0225	12.0075	12.0367
6	12.0075	12.0225	12.0300	11.9797	11.9955
7	12.0300	12.0420	11.9775	11.9700	12.0000
8	12.0210	12.0375	12.0225	11.9775	11.9850
9	11.9775	11.9992	12.0150	12.0225	11.9625
10	12.0000	12.0120	11.9625	12.0300	12.0488
11	11.9625	12.0338	12.0525	11.9528	12.0225
12	11.9910	12.0525	11.9618	12.0600	12.0150
13	11.9700	12.0000	12.0120	12.0000	11.9850
14	11.9850	12.0075	12.0173	11.9925	11.9925
15	11.9932	12.0225	12.0000	11.9880	12.0075
16	12.0188	12.0150	12.0120	11.9835	12.0000
17	12.0075	12.0443	11.9925	11.9978	12.0225
18	11.9880	12.0225	12.0300	11.9850	12.0075
19	11.9797	11.9700	11.9925	11.9955	12.0075
20	12.0233	12.0075	12.0300	11.9700	11.9925
21	11.9932	12.0225	11.9805	12.0413	12.0225
22	11.9850	11.9677	12.0525	12.0075	12.0300
23	11.9925	12.0450	11.9663	12.0225	12.0525
24	12.0000	12.0075	12.0600	11.9565	11.9475
25	12.0525	12.0150	12.0225	11.9400	11.9580

a. Construct the appropriate control chart to monitor the variation of this process.

b. Is the process variation in control?

c. Give an example of an assignable cause that could potentially affect this process variation.

d. Should an $\bar{x}$ chart be constructed to monitor the process mean?

CONSTRUCTING A CHART TO MONITOR THE PROPORTION OF DEFECTIVES IN A PROCESS: THE p CHART

p Chart

The $\bar{x}$ and R charts are used most often to monitor quantitative variables (height, weight, length, etc.). The chart used to monitor qualitative or categorical variables (successful or unsuccessful, defective or nondefective, conforming or nonconforming) is called the **p chart**. This chart is used to monitor the proportion of defective or nonconforming units produced by a process.

> The **p chart** is used to monitor the proportion of defective or nonconforming units produced by a process.

A p chart is constructed in the same way as the $\bar{x}$ chart. A collection of samples (usually 20 to 30) is obtained while the process is believed to be in control. The p chart is based on the assumption that the number of defectives observed in each sample is a binomial random variable. The process proportion is actually the binomial probability, p (discussed in Chapter 5). When the process is in a state of statistical control, p remains constant over time.

To determine the p chart centerline and control limits, the analyst needs to know the sampling distribution of p. A quick review of the properties of this sampling distribution of proportions will be helpful.

> Properties of the **sampling distribution of proportions**:
> 1. The mean of the sampling distribution of proportions equals the population proportion: $\mu_{\bar{p}} = p$.
> 2. The standard deviation of the sampling distribution of proportions (standard error) equals $\sigma_{\bar{p}} = \sqrt{p(1 - p)/n}$.
> 3. The proportion of successes in a binomial experiment approaches a normal distribution as the number of trials, n, increases.

The process proportion (p) may either be known from past experience with the process or be estimated on the basis of sample data. Using sample data, the p chart centerline is computed by averaging the sample proportions. This is done by letting x_i be the number of defective units in each sample, and n be the sample size. This results in Equation 13.8, which is used to compute the proportion of defective units in each sample:

$$\bar{p}_i = \frac{x_i}{n} \tag{13.8}$$

where $\bar{p}_i$ = Proportion of defective units in sample i
x_i = Number of defective units in sample i
n = Sample size

The appropriate estimator $\hat{p}$ is computed by dividing the total number of defective units in all of the samples by the total number of units sampled:

$$\hat{p} = \frac{\text{Total number of defective units in all } k \text{ samples}}{\text{Total number of units sampled}} \tag{13.9}$$

where $\hat{p}$ = Estimate of the process proportion.

Equation 13.10 is used to compute the 3-sigma control limits. Note that $\hat{p}$ is substituted for p when the process proportion is unknown.

$$\text{LCL} = \hat{p} - 3\sqrt{\frac{\hat{p}(1 - \hat{p})}{n}}$$
$$\text{UCL} = \hat{p} + 3\sqrt{\frac{\hat{p}(1 - \hat{p})}{n}} \tag{13.10}$$

When constructing a p chart, the sample size must be much larger than for $\bar{x}$ and R charts. A large sample size is needed because most processes monitored in industry have relatively small process proportions (often lower than 5%). Samples drawn using small sample sizes would likely not contain any defective items. As a result, most sample proportions would equal 0. Montgomery (1991) provides a formula that computes a sample size large enough to give an analyst a 50% chance of detecting a process shift of some specified proportion.[7]

---

[7]D. C. Montgomery, *Introduction to Statistical Quality Control*, 2nd ed. New York: Wiley, 1991.

Steps for constructing a *p* chart:

1. Select some number of samples of data, each of size *n*. Select a large sample size (*n*), especially if the process proportion is small.
2. Compute the proportion of defective units in each sample: $p_i = x_i/n$.
3. If the process proportion isn't known, estimate it:

$$\hat{p} = \frac{\text{Total number of defective units in all samples}}{\text{Total number of units sampled}}$$

4. Compute the 3-sigma control limits:

$$\text{LCL} = \hat{p} - 3\sqrt{\hat{p}(1-\hat{p})/n}$$
$$\text{UCL} = \hat{p} + 3\sqrt{\hat{p}(1-\hat{p})/n}$$

Example 13.6 shows how a *p* chart is developed.

EXAMPLE 13.6   The Goodlight Headlight Company wants to monitor the filament integrity of headlights coming off the manufacturing line. Quality Vice President Ruth Chang is responsible for determining when assignable causes are affecting the process. Headlights coming off the manufacturing line are sampled and subjected to a voltage 25% higher than that for which they're rated. Each sample consists of 100 bulbs. A bulb is categorized as defective if it burns out during a three-second exposure to this higher voltage. Table 13.3 covers 20 samples from last week's production run.

The proportion of defective units in each sample is computed using Equation 13.8. For sample 1, the proportion of defectives is

$$\hat{p}_1 = \frac{x_1}{n} = \frac{18}{100} = .18$$

The process proportion is estimated using Equation 13.9:

$$\hat{p} = \frac{408}{20(100)} = .204$$

Note that this estimate can also be computed by adding up the sample proportions and dividing by the number of samples (4.08/20 = .204).

Equation 13.10 is used to compute the 3-sigma control limits:

$$\text{LCL} = \hat{p} - 3\sqrt{\frac{\hat{p}(1-\hat{p})}{n}}$$
$$= .204 - 3\sqrt{\frac{.204(1-.204)}{100}}$$
$$= .204 - 3(.04025) = .08325$$

TABLE 13.3   Twenty Samples of Size 100 from a Headlight Production Run (Example 13.6)

Sample number	Number of defectives	Proportion defective
1	18	.18
2	15	.15
3	26	.26
4	15	.15
5	28	.28
6	12	.12
7	24	.24
8	15	.15
9	23	.23
10	41	.41
11	16	.16
12	18	.18
13	24	.24
14	14	.14
15	16	.16
16	18	.18
17	25	.25
18	19	.19
19	15	.15
20	26	.26
	408	4.08

$$\text{UCL} = \hat{p} + 3\sqrt{\frac{\hat{p}(1 - \hat{p})}{n}}$$

$$= .204 + 3\sqrt{\frac{.204(1 - .204)}{100}}$$

$$= .204 + 3(.04025) = .32475$$

Figure 13.14 shows these lower and upper control limits along with the centerline and the 20 sample proportions plotted in sequence. The high proportion of defectives in sample 10 places this sample outside the control limits. Ruth decides to conduct an investigation to determine why so many defectives occurred in sample 10.

The MINITAB computer package can be used to develop Figure 13.14. The MINITAB commands are:

```
MTB > SET C1
DATA> 18 15 26 15 28 12 24 15 23 41
DATA> 16 18 24 14 16 18 25 19 15 26
DATA> END
MTB > NAME C1 'DEFECTS'
MTB > PCHART USING DATA IN C1, SAMPLE SIZE 100
      OUTPUT SHOWN AS FIGURE 13.14
MTB > STOP
```

The data are entered in sequence into C1. The PCHART command plots sample proportions for samples of size 100.

FIGURE 13.14   *p* Chart for Defects Developed Using MINITAB (Example 13.6)

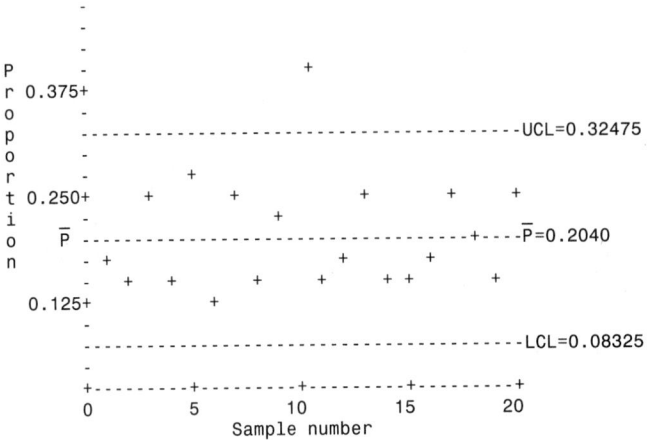

EXERCISES

37. Explain how the properties of the sampling distribution of proportions are used to construct a *p* chart.

38. How are the control limits of a *p* chart determined?

39. What characteristic of a process is a *p* chart used to monitor?

40. When a production process is operating properly, the proportion of defectives is .02. Compute lower and upper control limits for a *p* chart if each sample consists of 200 observations.

41. The Willow Springs Hotel chain is studying the percentage of guest rooms that weren't ready when guests attempted to check in. Assume that from previous research, the population percentage is estimated to be 3%.

   a. What are the control limits if samples of 50 are selected?

   b. What are the control limits if samples of 150 are selected?

   c. What are the control limits if samples of 300 are selected?

   d. How does sample size affect *p* chart control limits?

42. The Bing Corporation uses an injection molding process to provide a bracket used on aircraft passenger seats. Sue Darling, who's in charge of quality, is especially concerned with examining each bracket for cracks, splits, or other imperfections. Daily samples of 100 have been examined for 20 days.

Date		Sample size	Number defective
March	1	100	2
	2	100	3
	3	100	4
	4	100	8

Date	Sample size	Number defective
5	100	4
6	100	3
7	100	6
8	100	1
9	100	3
10	100	4
11	100	1
12	100	8
13	100	4
14	100	2
15	100	5
16	100	4
17	100	6
18	100	4
19	100	3
20	100	5

a. Calculate the proportion defective in each sample.

b. Develop the centerline and upper and lower control limits for a 3-sigma p chart.

c. Compute the limits of the six zones (A, B, C).

d. Plot the proportions and determine whether the process is in control.

43. The Empire Company produces floppy disks for microcomputers. President Larry Williams has recently received several complaints concerning quality. Retailers have indicated that customers keep returning disks containing bad sectors. Larry implements a quality-control program to correct this problem. He instructs his production manager to select a sample of 300 disks from each production run. Here are the proportion of disks with bad sectors taken from 12 production runs:

Sample	Proportion defective
1	.06
2	.08
3	.05
4	.10
5	.03
6	.04
7	.09
8	.12
9	.07
10	.06
11	.09
12	.05

a. Develop a centerline and upper and lower control limits for a 3-sigma p chart.

b. Compute the limits of the six zones.

c. Plot the proportions and test to determine whether the process is in control.

CONSTRUCTING A CHART TO MONITOR THE NUMBER OF DEFECTIVES PER UNIT: THE *c* CHART

c Chart

The *p* chart was used to monitor the proportion of defective units in a sample of *n* units. The *c* chart is used to monitor the number of defects per unit. The *c* chart is used to control a single type of defect or to control all types of defects without distinguishing between types. *c* charts are used to monitor such variables as the number of blemishes on aluminum panels, number of scratches on a CRT screen, or number of defects in a length of wire.

The **c chart** is used to monitor the number of defects per unit.

A *c* chart is constructed in the same way as the *p* chart. A collection of samples (usually 20 to 30) is selected where each sample is obtained by observing a single unit. The *c* chart is appropriate when the sample size per unit is very large and the probability of a defect in any part of the unit is very small. Recall that the situation just described fits the assumption behind the Poisson process discussed in Chapter 5.

The average number of defects ($\bar{c}$) may either be known from past experience with the process or be estimated on the basis of sample data. If the system is stable, an estimate may be available for the average number of defects per unit. If no prior estimate is available, the average number of defects is estimated from the sample data:

$$\bar{c} = \frac{\sum c_i}{n} \tag{13.11}$$

where $\bar{c}$ = Estimate of the average number of defects per unit
  c_i = Number of defects in unit *i*
  n = Number of units sampled

An important property of the Poisson random variable is that the mean and variance are equal. Therefore, the standard deviation equals the square root of the mean. Using this information, Equation 13.12 is developed to compute the 3-sigma control limits:

$$\begin{aligned} \text{LCL} &= \bar{c} - 3\sqrt{\bar{c}} \\ \text{UCL} &= \bar{c} + 3\sqrt{\bar{c}} \end{aligned} \tag{13.12}$$

> **Steps for constructing a c chart:**
> 1. Select some number of samples of data (20 to 30 units), where each sample is obtained by observing a single unit.
> 2. Determine the number of defects for each unit (c_i).
> 3. Estimate the average number of defects per unit, $\bar{c} = \dfrac{\Sigma c_i}{n}$.
> 4. Compute the 3-sigma control limits.
>
> $$\text{LCL} = \bar{c} - 3\sqrt{\bar{c}}$$
> $$\text{UCL} = \bar{c} + 3\sqrt{\bar{c}}$$

Example 13.7 shows how a c chart is developed.

EXAMPLE 13.7   According to an American Management Association Human Resource publication, *HR Focus* (May 1992), Handy HRM Corporation, a New York management consulting firm, surveyed 78 of the largest U.S. corporations and found that 92 percent said they are beginning to measure and base employee remuneration on quality satisfaction from a customer's perspective.[8] Customers of the Mars Automobile Company have recently complained about dirt specks and poor alignment of door panels. Quality engineer Faye Sandberg has been assigned the task of implementing a program to base employee pay on whether the assembly process for these door panels can be kept in control. Cars are randomly selected for a close examination for fit-and-finish defects. Each week, 20 cars are inspected. Table 13.4 shows the results from last week's inspection.

The average number of defects for the sample of 20 vehicles is computed using Equation 13.11:

$$\bar{c} = \frac{\Sigma c_i}{n} = \frac{36}{20} = 1.8$$

Equation 13.12 is used to compute the 3-sigma control limits:

$$\text{LCL} = \bar{c} - 3\sqrt{\bar{c}}$$
$$= 1.8 - 3\sqrt{1.8} = 1.8 - 4.02 = -2.22$$
$$\text{UCL} = \bar{c} + 3\sqrt{\bar{c}}$$
$$= 1.8 + 3\sqrt{1.8} = 1.8 + 4.02 = 5.82$$

---

[8]"Quality Movement Grows, Influences More Paychecks." *HR Focus: American Management Association Human Resources Publication.* May 1992, 69:18.

TABLE 13.4   Number of Defects from the Inspection of Twenty Automobiles (Example 13.7)

Vehicle number	Number of defects
1	0
2	1
3	2
4	3
5	0
6	5
7	2
8	0
9	1
10	2
11	1
12	7
13	1
14	0
15	2
16	4
17	1
18	0
19	1
20	3
	36

Since it's impossible to have a negative number of defects, the lower control limit, -2.22, is replaced by 0. Figure 13.15 shows these lower and upper control limits along with the centerline and the 20 c values plotted in sequence. The control chart shows vehicle 12's c value falling outside the control limits so Faye investigates why vehicle 12 had so many defects.

FIGURE 13.15 c Chart for Defects Developed Using MINITAB (Example 13.7)

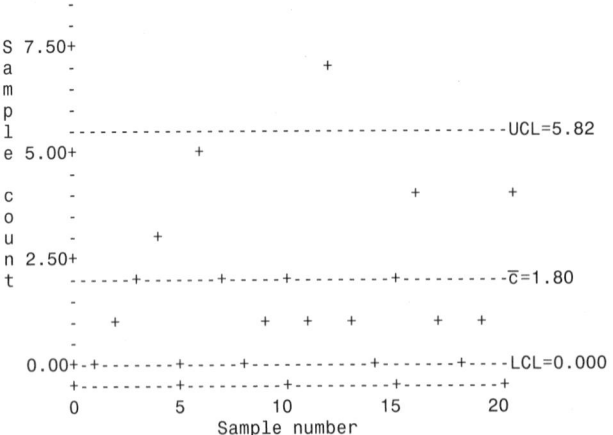

The MINITAB computer package can be used to develop Figure 13.15. The MINI-
TAB commands are:

```
MTB > SET C1
DATA> 0 1 2 3 0 5 2 0 1 2 1 7 1 0 2 4 1 0 1 3
DATA> END
MTB > NAME C1 'DEFECTS'
MTB > CCHART USING DATA IN C1
     OUTPUT SHOWN AS FIGURE 13.15
MTB > STOP
```

The data are entered in sequence into C1. The CCHART command plots the c
values for the 20 vehicles.

EXAMPLE 13.8   Sam Gangee has just been appointed quality-control manager for
Clinton Lawnmowers, which manufactures power mowers. Quality-control manager is
a new position for the company, reflecting management's growing concern about quality's importance in the competitive marketplace. Sam decides to take a look at the
factory quality records as a first step.

Talking with factory supervisors, he finds two major problems. First, the number of
defects for each component in lawnmowers varies from one part to the next. It seems
that chassis problems are most severe, while painting quality problems are least severe.

Second, the key variable sometimes monitored on the factory floor is total number
of defects per lawnmower. Sam agrees that this is the key variable of interest, but he's
distressed to find that this variable hasn't always been recorded. In fact, historical records are spotty. Sam decides that his first job is to begin a systematic program of
sampling the lawnmower line to measure defects per machine. He then wonders about
how to display this variable over time.

After carefully examining the quality of mowers over several weeks, he constructs a
Pareto chart (Figure 13.16). (The Pareto chart was discussed in Chapter 3.) It shows
that the chassis line is causing the most serious quality problem, that is, it's responsible
for the highest number of defects per mower. The next most serious component is the
engine; the least serious is painting. Sam plots the cumulative percentage of defects
against the right axis of the Pareto chart.

Next, Sam tackles the lawnmower line's key quality-control problem, number of
defects per machine. For each lawnmower he has his new inspection team determine
the number of defects as the machine nears the end of the final assembly line. Sam
records the defect measurements on a c chart for the first 18 lawnmowers inspected,
(Figure 13.17). It shows the average number of defects for the sample of 18 lawnmowers is 1.667. The control limits are computed using Equation 13.11:

$$\begin{aligned}
\text{LCL} &= \bar{c} - 3\sqrt{\bar{c}} \\
&= 1.667 - 3\sqrt{1.667} = 1.667 - 3.87 = -2.2 \\
\text{UCL} &= \bar{c} + 3\sqrt{\bar{c}} \\
&= 1.667 + 3\sqrt{1.667} = 1.667 + 3.87 = 5.537
\end{aligned}$$

Sam reached several conclusions after studying his control chart. First, he didn't see
a trend in the defect numbers, either up or down. Next, he noted an out-of-control

FIGURE 13.16   Pareto Chart: Defectives per Mower (Example 13.8)

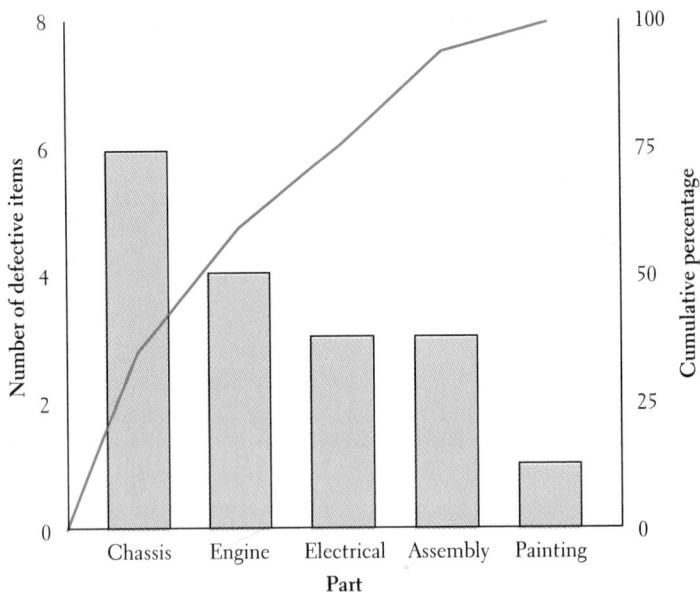

FIGURE 13.17   *c* Chart for Defects Developed Using MINITAB (Example 13.8)

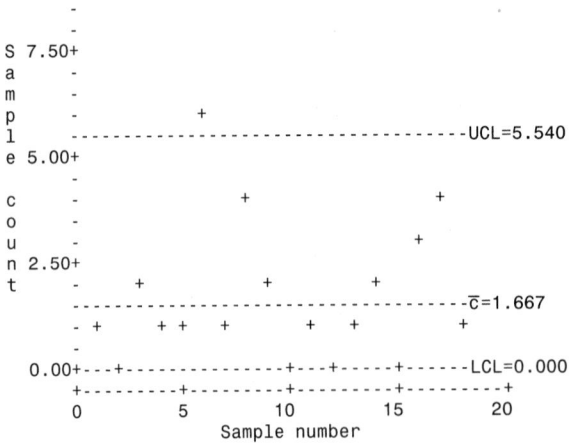

value of six defects for machine 6. At the time, he and his floor supervisors visited the line and determined that there wasn't a problem. He was pleased to see that this high defect rate didn't continue during subsequent lawnmowers.

Finally, Sam noted the estimated mean number of defects per machine (1.667) and decided to take some corrective action regarding this value. Although the control chart indicates that the production process is stabilized around this value, he considers it too high. Sam thinks his first big challenge will be to reduce the average number of defects per lawnmower to a more acceptable figure.

EXERCISES

44. What is the difference between the c chart and the p chart? Indicate the circumstances in which each would be the most appropriate chart.

45. For the following list of variables, indicate whether a c chart or p chart would be most appropriate.

    a. The number of late arrivals out of 325 trains that are scheduled to arrive at a particular station each week.

    b. Periodic samples consisting of 25-foot lengths examined during the production of continuous sheet steel to determine the number of surface scratches, blemishes, or other flaws.

    c. The number of defective switches in samples of 400.

    d. The number of cracks in an engine block.

    e. The number of defects per unit on the final assembly line of a personal computer manufacturer.

46. Jane Lot is vice president of quality for Outdoor Paper Company. The paper is produced so that it appears at the end of a web and is rolled onto a reel. Every reel is examined for imperfections. Results for the past 24 reels are:

Reel	Blemishes	Reel	Blemishes
1	6	13	12
2	9	14	8
3	7	15	7
4	4	16	6
5	8	17	2
6	4	18	5
7	2	19	6
8	11	20	4
9	6	21	6
10	1	22	9
11	2	23	5
12	10	24	4

    a. Develop the centerline and upper and lower control limits for a 3-sigma c chart.

    b. Compute the limits of the six zones.

    c. Plot the number of blemishes and test to determine whether the process is in control.

47. The Richard Irving Publishing Company counts the number of errors that make their way into 18 finished books of approximately equal pages.

Book	Errors	Book	Errors
1	31	4	42
2	25	5	55
3	73	6	88

Book	Errors		Book	Errors
7	41		13	18
8	49		14	92
9	60		15	39
10	65		16	71
11	50		17	51
12	78		18	68

a. Develop the centerline and upper and lower control limits for a 3-sigma *c* chart.

b. Compute the limits of the six zones.

c. Plot the number of errors and test to determine whether the process is in control.

LOT ACCEPTANCE

Lot acceptance and process control are the two primary settings for the application of effective quality-control techniques. In lot acceptance, a sample from a batch or lot of items is inspected to determine the quality level of the entire batch. This batch might be produced by our factory and bound for customers, might be our own lot to be sent forward to another segment of our company, or might be an incoming lot from a supplier. In all these cases, statistical procedures are used to select a sample of items, measure their quality, and reach a decision about the whole lot.

Acceptance Sampling

Acceptance sampling involves risks for both the manufacturer and the consumer of a particular shipment. These risks are comparable to the type I and type II errors discussed in hypotheses testing (Chapter 9). The acceptance procedure is of great importance due to the possibility of these errors and their attendant costs. Only rarely is it possible and cost effective to conduct a census of the entire lot. This is done only when there are few items which are high-priced or of vital importance in later assemblies. For the most part, sampling is the basis for the decision regarding the lot of items, but, as always, when conclusions are reached about all the items after examining only some of them, errors are possible.

The null hypothesis tested in lot acceptance sampling is that the lot has the acceptable level of quality. If the sample quality results seem reasonable against this hypothesis, the hypothesis is not rejected and the entire lot is deemed to have sufficient quality. The danger here is that a false null hypothesis may not be rejected (i.e., a type II error could be committed). The type II error represents the failure to reject a lot that should have been rejected. This is referred to as the **consumer's risk,** since the consumer is incurring the risk of the manufacturer failing to reject a lot that should have been rejected. The penalty for such an error is the acceptance into the next production phase of parts that don't meet specified quality standards, or the delivery of substandard parts to customers.

Consumer's Risk

Alternatively, if the sample results seem unlikely when compared with the null hypothesis, it's rejected. This means that the entire lot will be returned to the manufacturer (either our own company's manufacturing process or a supplier's). The danger here is that a type I error may be committed (i.e., a lot with acceptable quality is

Producer's Risk   erroneously rejected). This is referred to as the **producer's risk,** since the producer is incurring the risk that an acceptable lot will be returned. The cost of such an error is the discarding or "fixing" of a lot that was acceptable in the first place.

Consumer's risk (β) is the probability of failing to reject a product of unacceptable quality. **Producer's risk** (α) is the probability of rejecting a product of acceptable quality.

The basic steps in lot acceptance sampling are covered in Chapter 9. Specifically, the steps are:

1. The null and alternative hypotheses are developed:

    H_0: The lot is of acceptable quality.
    H_1: The lot is not of acceptable quality.

2. The null hypothesis regarding the quality of the population (the entire lot) is assumed true and the appropriate sampling distribution for this assumption is identified.

3. A sample of items is selected from the lot. (See Chapter 2 for sampling methods.) The key quality variable is measured for the sample of items and the sample statistic is computed. This statistic is usually a mean or proportion.

4. If it's likely that the sample statistic could have come from the sampling distribution, the null hypothesis is not rejected (lot acceptance). If it's unlikely that the sample statistic could have come from the sampling distribution, the null hypothesis is rejected (lot rejection).

Example 13.9 illustrates this procedure.

EXAMPLE 13.9 Jenny Fife is responsible for lot acceptance sampling in the receiving area of a company that makes motorized hydraulic pumps. Engines for this product are received in lots of 1,000 every two or three weeks from the engine supplier.

Each time a lot arrives, Jenny randomly selects 50 engines for extensive testing by numbering the engines as they're removed from the packing crate. Next, 50 random numbers are drawn from a random number table and the engines corresponding to these numbers make up the sample. The statistic determined from the sample of engines is the proportion that do not meet specified quality standards for her company, that is, are deemed defective. If this sample proportion is too high, the entire lot of engines is repacked and returned to the supplier for corrective action.

The contract with the supplier specifies that no more than 4% of the engines it ships will be defective. For the most recent shipment, Jenny finds four of the engines in her sample to be defective. Her sample proportion, $4/50 = .08$, is in excess of the permitted defective rate for the entire lot. But this high proportion could be due to random variation in sampling, or the lot could be unacceptable. Jenny's task is to determine which.

The null and alternative hypotheses and the sample results are

$$H_0: p \le .04 \qquad n = 50$$
$$H_1: p > .04 \qquad \bar{p} = .08$$

Jenny chooses the .01 significance level due to the importance of minimizing the probability of a type I error and its associated cost. At this significance level, for a one-tailed test (see the standard normal table), the critical z value is 2.33. The decision rule is

If $z > 2.33$, reject that the process proportion is .04.

The computed z value (see Equation 9.4) is

$$z = \frac{x/n - p}{\sigma_{\bar{p}}} = \frac{.08 - .04}{.0277} = 1.444$$

Since $z = 1.444$, the null hypothesis isn't rejected and the entire lot of 1,000 engines is deemed to have sufficient quality ($1.444 < 2.33$). Jenny allows the engines to enter the factory floor for assembly in hydraulic pumps.

Since Jenny conducts this test several times a month, she develops the following chart to use in summarizing the actions to be taken under several sample outcomes for a sampling plan for $n = 50$:

Number defective	z	Conclusion
4	1.44	Accept lot
5	2.16	Accept lot
6	2.88	Reject lot

Based on these calculations, Jenny issues sampling instructions to her quality-control staff:

Each time a lot of 1,000 engines comes in, take a random sample of 50 engines using the random number table. If five or fewer are defective, accept the lot of engines and enter them into the production process. If six or more are defective, the lot is deemed unacceptable so call me at once.

Jenny reasons that with this set of instructions, she need not be present when each batch arrives. Her staff will inform her if an unacceptable batch is discovered.

Note that most companies are moving away from acceptance sampling. Since acceptance sampling looks at units that have already been produced, the effect on improving quality is minimal. Most companies now rely on using fewer suppliers and making sure that the suppliers they do use demonstrate a capable process that remains in control.

POWER AND OPERATING CHARACTERISTIC (OC) CURVES

A key aspect of any acceptance sampling plan is that it should offer protection, both to the consumer (who doesn't want to accept a bad lot) and to the producer (who doesn't want a good lot rejected).

Power of a Hypothesis Test

The power of any hypothesis test is its ability to detect a false null hypothesis. Chapter 9 defined the power of a test as

$$\text{Power} = 1 - \beta$$

where β is the probability of a type II error. The power of a test is increased by using a larger sample size. In the case of lot acceptance or process control, the higher the power of the test, the better one can detect a quality level below specification. In other words, the larger the sample size, the lower is the probability of a type II error, holding the significance level (probability of a type I error) constant.

As is usually the case in statistical applications, the analyst is torn between little power (at low cost) and high power (at high cost). These factors must be balanced against each other in choosing the desired sample size with its attendant cost and risk.

The alpha or significance level indicates the probability of making a type I error (producer's risk). In considering the type II error, an analyst can choose between using either a power curve showing the probability of rejecting a false null hypothesis or an operating characteristic curve showing the probability of accepting a false null hypothesis (consumer's risk). The power curve plots the probability of rejecting a lot versus a range of possible values that could reflect the shipment's actual quality. The operating characteristic curve plots the probability of accepting a lot versus a range of possible values that could reflect the shipment's actual quality. Procedures for computing these curves were covered late in Chapter 9.

Power Curve

OC Curve

OTHER QUALITY-CONTROL TECHNIQUES

Although the control chart and the lot and process control hypothesis tests are most commonly used in quality control, other statistical techniques can be used as well. As discussed in Chapter 12, analysis of variance tests the hypothesis that several populations have the same mean. In quality control, these populations might represent five different suppliers where the average number of defectives per lot might be compared. For a production line, the three shifts producing parts might be the populations being compared. In general, whenever three or more populations have means that are to be compared, analysis of variance should come to mind.

The contingency table test (Chapter 11) can be used to compare one variable with another, if both variables are measured on a categorical scale (nominal or ordinal data). An example is the comparison of males and females against their quality-control rating (good, average, poor). Or, the different shifts (day, evening, graveyard) might be compared with the quality of output (high, OK, poor). As long as the two variables being compared are both categorical variables, the contingency table test can determine if they're dependent or independent.

Chapter 11 also describes the goodness-of-fit test. This statistical test determines the goodness of fit between the number of observations in each category and the number expected under a specified population. An example is comparing the number of monthly defects per supplier against the same distribution from a year ago. If there has been no change, a good fit will result. If the fit is poor, changes in the defect pattern have occurred among the suppliers. The goodness-of-fit procedure can also be used to check the shape of a distribution against a hypothesized population distribution such as the normal.

In more general terms, many statistical techniques are candidates for inclusion in quality-control efforts. Experimental design has become an especially important aspect of designing quality into products. Imaginative use of any technique in this text might result in an effective quality-control effort. It is even possible that two or more techniques might be combined in certain circumstances to allow management to measure the quality of a firm's efforts.

Exercises

48. What is the difference between lot acceptance and process control?

49. What is meant by the term *producer's risk*?

50. What is meant by the term *consumer's risk*?

51. Briefly summarize the basic steps in lot acceptance sampling.

52. How does the power of a test affect a lot acceptance situation?

53. What function does an operating characteristic curve serve in a lot acceptance situation?

54. Clark Equipment, a wholesaler, has received a shipment of 6,000 can openers. Royce Clayton, vice president of quality, considers a 1% defective rate to be an acceptable quality level. He selects a random sample of 200 can openers and tests to determine whether they work properly. What should Royce conclude if seven of the sampled can openers are defective?

55. (Refer to Exercise 54.) Royce wishes to avoid shipments whose percentage of defectives is as high as 3%. He implements a sampling plan that will select 200 can openers from each shipment. Royce accepts the shipment if the number of defectives in the sample is no more than six. Construct the operating characteristic curve for this acceptance sampling plan.

Summary

. . . .

This chapter began with an overview of the quality-control and improvement process. No greater challenge faces corporate America today than the continual improvement of its products and services. The former chairman of Ford Motor Company, Donald Peterson, has stated that firms unable or unwilling to adopt this attitude won't be around in the next century.

Next we presented the concept of control charts, detailing construction and use of four widely used charts: the $\bar{x}$ chart, range chart (R chart), p chart, and c chart.

Statistical quality-control procedures were discussed next. They are generally applicable in two areas: process control and lot acceptance. In both areas, the focus is on the amount of variability in the key measurements being made.

In process control, a continuous production process is checked on a regular basis. The objective is to assure that the quality level meets or exceeds specifications. An example of such a process is an assembly line that produces small engines. This line runs continuously during working hours, and will continue to do so for the foreseeable future. To assure adequate quality, this process needs to be sampled and measured on a routine basis. Many quality-control procedures are directed toward this end.

By contrast, lot acceptance procedures are designed for batches of products. These batches, or lots, might be purchased from an outside supplier. In this case, sampling procedures are designed either to accept the lot as having sufficient quality, or to reject the entire lot on the basis of the sample quality. Other lots might be produced by a company's own factory, but constitute a batch or lot rather than a continuous stream of products. An example is a batch of small engines to be shipped to a customer. Or, the batch of engines just produced might be sent to another branch of the same company for inclusion in a larger product such as garden tractors. After the lot is manufactured, the production process will shift to another product. In all such cases, the question becomes whether the lot is of sufficient quality to be sent on. This decision is made on the basis of examining the quality of a sample of items taken from the lot.

APPLICATIONS OF STATISTICAL CONCEPTS IN THE BUSINESS WORLD

KAISER ALUMINUM COMPANY'S USE OF QUALITY CONTROL

Successful implementation of quality principles is illustrated by the Total Quality Improvement program at Kaiser Aluminum Company's Trentwood plant in Spokane, Washington. As mentioned at the start of this chapter, Kaiser received the Aluminum Supplier of the Year Award from Miller Brewing Company for the second year in a row in early 1992. Kaiser also received the Ball Corporation Packaging Product Group's first Aluminum Supplier of the Year Award in 1992. These awards reflect Kaiser's commitment to the constant improvement of quality since 1981.

Kaiser's Trentwood plant makes aluminum sheeting and plate with thickness between .008 and 3 inches. In the smaller sizes, enormous rolling mills successively reduce the aluminum stock's thickness. This rolling process is constantly monitored by X-ray and beta-ray sensors in the rolling mills that measure, among other things, thickness of the sheets moving at speeds of up to a mile a minute. These sensors are accurate enough to enable control of the aluminum sheet thickness to within .0002 inch (1/20 the diameter of a human hair)—the tolerance currently deemed necessary for acceptable quality. However, as one of the quality-control engineers told us, Kaiser's efforts are devoted to constantly reducing this figure, resulting in even tighter standards. Many other measurements are constantly made on the aluminum sheet stock, such as speed of the sheet, sheet flatness, and process temperature.

Measurements made on the moving aluminum sheet are fed into a series of computers that analyze the data. If problems are detected or if a trend is apparent that will lead to problems later, the computer makes adjustments in the ongoing process. If these adjustments still don't correct the problem or trend, the operator's control console is signaled so that corrective action can be taken. Such action sometimes involves shutting the line down to avoid producing unacceptable product.

The basic concepts discussed throughout this chapter are utilized in this monitoring process. At Kaiser, however, measurements and analyses are made by sophisticated measuring devices and high-speed computers, not by hand.

Figure 13.18 shows a flow diagram of the Kaiser computer control process.

FIGURE 13.18   Kaiser's Computer Control Process

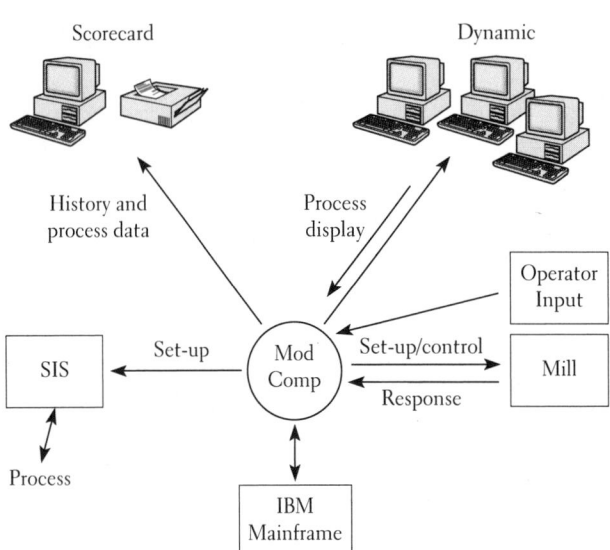

The minicomputer that controls the data collection and analysis is called "Mod-Comp," while "SIS" stands for surface inspection system. The mainframe computer stores vast amounts of historical data and performs some of the more sophisticated data analyses. The system is designed to provide almost instant adjustments to the process and to provide control information to the line operator. A vast data base for analysis by Kaiser's engineers is also generated.

Figure 13.19 shows one of the key reports produced by Kaiser's computerized quality system. This "scorecard" report includes summary information at the top of the page along with several key measurements for each roll of stock: sheet gauge thickness measured by the beta gage and X-ray sensors, the speed of the sheet through the rolling mill, and flatness.

Note that these plots, with the exception of the speed plot, have horizontal lines around the actual measurements. These lines are the tolerance limits. Should a measurement exceed these limits at any time, the green light at the operator's console turns either yellow or red, depending on the problem's severity. This procedure is fol-

FIGURE 13.19   A Report from Kaiser's Computerized Quality System

#1 COLD MILL

WIDTH 52.6	LOT NUMBER= 281491 F	DATE: 9/5/1992
SCHED ENTRY .1500	3-SIGMA 582	GOOD FT 2443.4
CALC ENTRY .1532	MAX SPEED 1016.0	BAD FT 110.2
EXIT THK .0620	GOOD LBS 9562.8	GOOD JEVELS 178.2
TARGET OFFSET – STAND 2	LIGHT HEAD (BETA)	BAD JEVELS 8.0
	AI	REWIND TENSION 9245

TIME: 14:34:27
AVG FLAT 34.2
PEAK FLAT 70.1

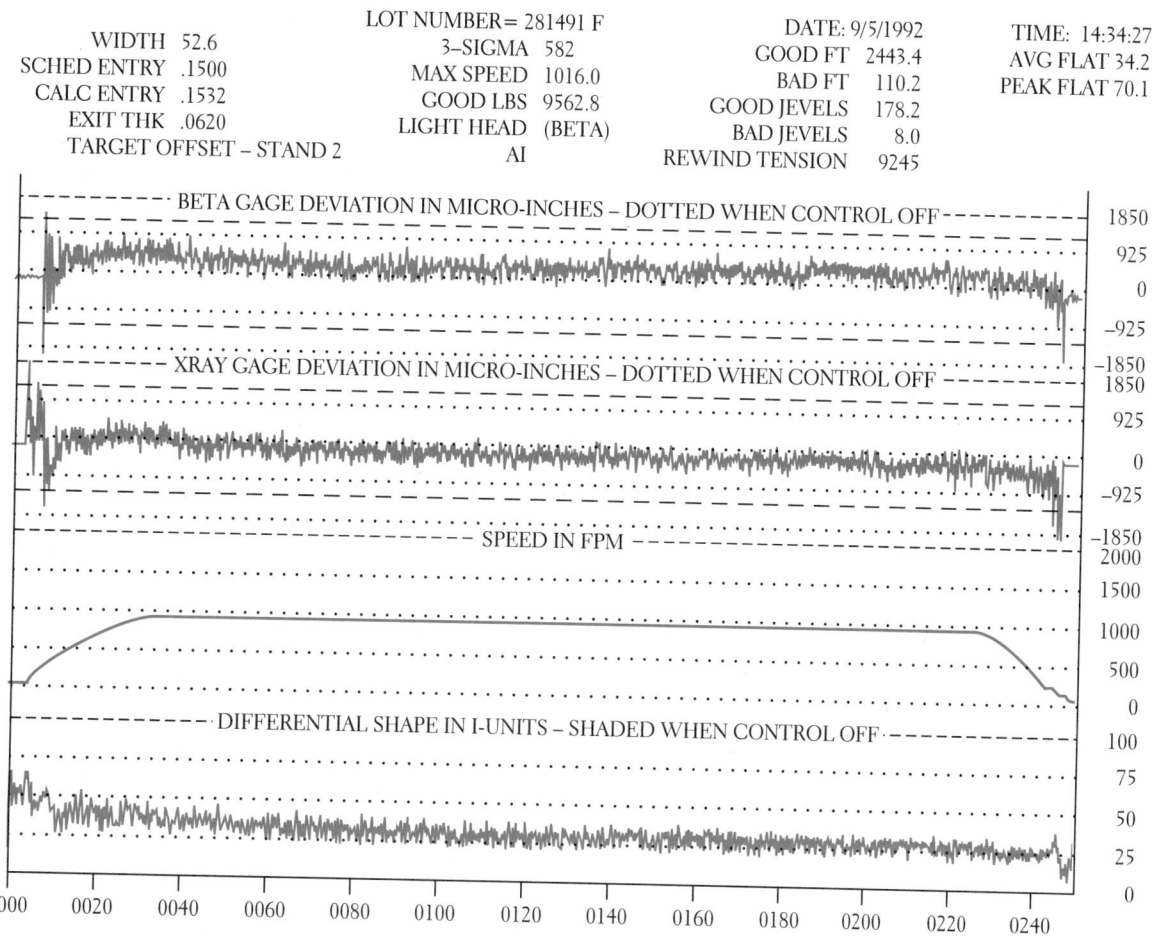

lowed so that the operator can easily and quickly detect a problem and take corrective action, rather than wait until the damage is done and the problem is found through inspection. As a Kaiser engineer told us, "The operators and first-line supervisors have neither the time nor the inclination to wade through columns and rows of numbers."

Figure 13.20 shows an exaggerated profile of a large aluminum sheet made from the X-ray measurements. Quality engineers use this plot to monitor the flatness of each sheet of stock, an essential feature for controlling high quality.

Figures 13.21 through 13.23 show additional charts and graphs generated by Kaiser's computerized data collection and analysis system (chart types discussed in Chapter 3, "Data Presentation"). Among them you'll find the bar chart, pie chart, and time series graph. These charts, along with supporting data, appear in reports generated in various

FIGURE 13.20   Aluminum Sheet Profile at Kaiser

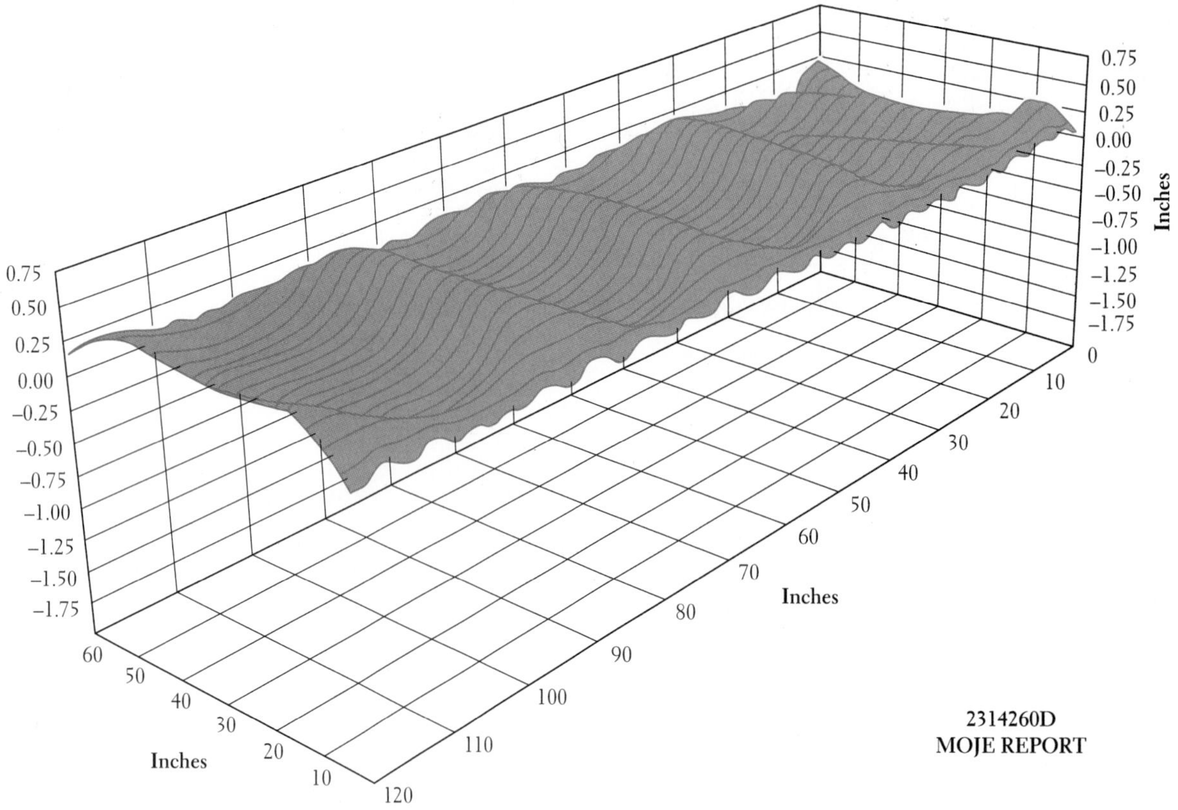

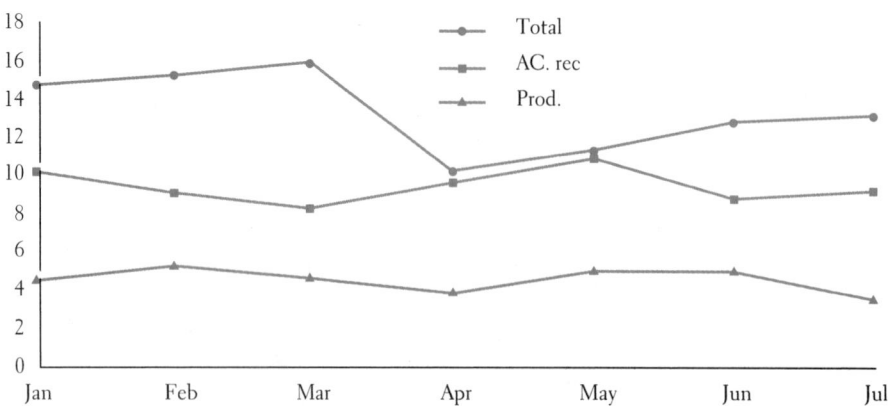

2314260D
MOJE REPORT

FIGURE 13.21   Kaiser Aluminum Recovery Defect Trends, Time Series Graph

FIGURE 13.22 Recovery Trend

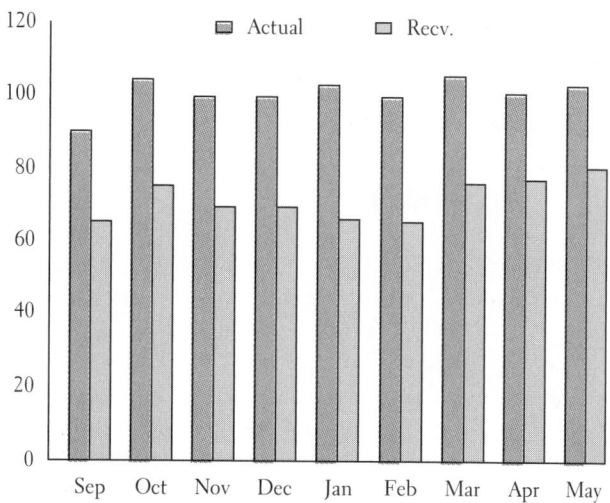

FIGURE 13.23 Start Weight Breakdown

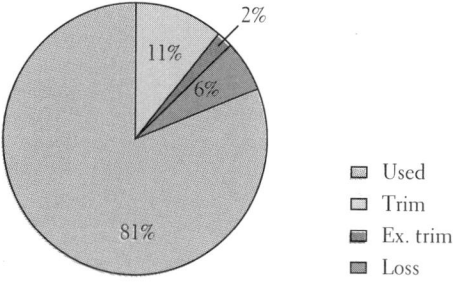

Used
Trim
Ex. trim
Loss

combinations for first-line supervisors, midlevel managers, quality-control engineers, and top management.

Kaiser Aluminum's Total Quality Improvement system is a good example of what is going right in American industry today. The idea of constantly improving quality by controlling variation is a pervasive theme at Kaiser, and all employees from the production line to top management are aware of its vital importance. No more important lesson can be learned by today's business students than the necessity of constantly improving the quality of American goods and services.

OTHER APPLICATIONS

Applications of quality concepts are everywhere in business. As mentioned before, many observers have argued that constant improvement of quality is the most important task facing business in this country. But improving quality isn't easy. According to

Newsweek (September 7, 1992), numerous firms are dropping their Total Quality Management (TQM) programs. In many cases, expectations exceeded results, especially when firms faced layoffs and other labor problems. The key concepts, said *Newsweek*, are patience and labor peace. "Managements expect it to be instant gratification, and that is one of the key reasons for failure." By contrast, companies that use TQM over the long haul have experienced success.

GLOSSARY

Quality The extent to which a product or service satisfies its users' needs and preferences.

Statistical process control (SPC) A series of actions used to monitor and eliminate variation in order to keep a process in a state of statistical control.

Assignable causes Fluctuations in variation due to events or actions that aren't part of the process design.

Chance causes Causes of variation that are attributable to the design of the process.

Control chart A time series graph that tracks a key variable of interest in the quality effort.

$\bar{x}$ chart (mean chart) Chart used to detect changes in the process mean by monitoring the variation in the means of samples drawn from the process.

R chart (range chart) Chart used to detect changes in the process variation by monitoring the ranges of samples drawn from the process.

p chart Chart used to monitor the proportion of defective or nonconforming units produced by a process.

c chart Chart used to monitor the number of defects per unit.

Consumer's risk (β) The probability of failing to reject a product of unacceptable quality.

Producer's risk (α) The probability of rejecting a product of acceptable quality.

KEY FORMULAS

$\bar{x}$ chart centerline

$$\bar{\bar{x}} = \frac{\bar{x}_1 + \bar{x}_2 + \bar{x}_3 + \cdots + \bar{x}_k}{k} \tag{13.1}$$

$\bar{x}$ chart upper and lower control limits (population standard deviation known)

$$\text{LCL} = \bar{\bar{x}} - 3(\sigma/\sqrt{n}) \tag{13.2}$$
$$\text{UCL} = \bar{\bar{x}} + 3(\sigma/\sqrt{n})$$

Estimate of the process standard deviation

$$\hat{\sigma} = \frac{\bar{R}}{d_2} \tag{13.3}$$

$\bar{x}$ chart upper and lower control limits (population standard deviation unknown)

$$\text{LCL} = \bar{\bar{x}} - 3(\hat{\sigma}/\sqrt{n}) \tag{13.4}$$
$$\text{UCL} = \bar{\bar{x}} + 3(\hat{\sigma}/\sqrt{n})$$

Average range

$$\bar{R} = \frac{R_1 + R_2 + R_3 + \cdots + R_k}{k} \tag{13.5}$$

Estimate of standard error of the average ranges

$$s_R = \bar{R}\frac{d_3}{d_2} \tag{13.6}$$

R chart upper and lower control limits

$$\text{LCL} = D_3\bar{R}$$
$$\text{UCL} = D_4\bar{R} \tag{13.7}$$

Proportion of defective units for each sample

$$p_i = \frac{x_i}{n} \tag{13.8}$$

Estimate of the process proportion

$$\hat{p} = \frac{\text{Total number of defective units in all } k \text{ samples}}{\text{Total number of units sampled}} \tag{13.9}$$

p chart upper and lower control limits

$$\text{LCL} = \hat{p} - 3\sqrt{\frac{\hat{p}(1 - \hat{p})}{n}}$$

$$\text{UCL} = \hat{p} + 3\sqrt{\frac{\hat{p}(1 - \hat{p})}{n}} \tag{13.10}$$

Estimate of the average number of defects per unit

$$\bar{c} = \frac{\sum c_i}{n} \tag{13.11}$$

c chart upper and lower control limits

$$\text{LCL} = \bar{c} - 3\sqrt{\bar{c}}$$
$$\text{UCL} = \bar{c} + 3\sqrt{\bar{c}} \tag{13.12}$$

SOLVED EXERCISES
. . . .

1. $\bar{X}$ CHART

The Circuit Corporation manufactures circuit boards for personal computers. The overall length of boards is important since boards are eventually slipped into slots in a chassis. Company quality analyst Phil Sheppard is in charge of stabilizing the length dimension. Boards are cut from large sheets of material by a single rotary cutter continuously fed from a hopper. Phil decides to develop a control chart for the length of the circuit boards produced by the process. The control chart is to be based on five units selected each hour. The accompanying table shows the resulting lengths for a two-day period.

Sample number	Cut circuit board lengths						
	1	2	3	4	5	$\bar{x}$	Range R
Day 1							
7 A.M.	5.83	6.09	5.91	6.18	5.91	5.984	0.35
8	6.13	5.99	5.76	6.12	6.19	6.038	0.43
9	5.94	5.81	6.11	6.28	6.00	6.028	0.47
10	6.03	5.89	6.01	6.08	6.10	6.022	0.21
11	5.93	5.99	6.01	6.19	6.11	6.046	0.26
12 P.M.	6.11	6.01	5.96	5.92	6.09	6.018	0.19
1	5.84	5.91	6.13	6.28	5.99	6.030	0.44
2	6.13	6.10	6.01	6.00	6.10	6.068	0.13
3	6.03	6.19	5.93	5.89	5.91	5.990	0.30
4	6.14	6.19	5.86	6.17	6.04	6.080	0.33
5	5.94	5.91	6.01	6.07	6.04	5.994	0.16
6	6.13	5.88	6.14	6.18	6.14	6.094	0.30
Day 2							
7 A.M.	6.15	5.95	5.78	6.18	6.10	6.032	0.40
8	5.94	5.91	6.01	6.20	6.13	6.038	0.29
9	5.83	5.88	6.08	6.12	6.11	6.004	0.29
10	5.97	6.19	5.81	6.08	5.91	5.992	0.38
11	6.13	5.87	5.77	6.16	6.29	6.044	0.52
12 P.M.	5.94	5.91	6.21	6.08	6.03	6.034	0.30
1	6.04	5.93	6.04	6.18	6.13	6.064	0.25
2	6.13	6.09	5.92	6.08	5.95	6.034	0.21
3	6.03	5.89	5.97	6.14	6.13	6.032	0.25
4	5.94	5.83	6.13	6.11	5.90	5.982	0.30
5	6.01	5.81	6.02	6.03	6.14	6.002	0.33
6	5.85	6.06	5.97	6.19	5.81	5.976	0.38
						144.626	7.47

a. Construct an $\bar{x}$ chart to monitor this process.

b. Is the process in control?

Solution:

a. The mean for the first sample is

$$\bar{x} = \frac{5.83 + 6.09 + 5.91 + 6.18 + 5.91}{5} = 5.984$$

The process mean is estimated

$$\bar{\bar{x}} = \frac{\bar{x}_1 + \bar{x}_2 + \cdots + \bar{x}_k}{k} = \frac{5.984 + 6.038 + \cdots + 5.976}{24}$$

$$= \frac{144.626}{24} = 6.026$$

The range for the first sample is

$$R = 6.18 - 5.83 = 0.35$$

The average of the ranges is

$$\overline{R} = \frac{R_1 + R_2 + \cdots + R_k}{k} = \frac{0.35 + 0.43 + \cdots + 0.38}{24} = \frac{7.47}{24}$$
$$= .3113$$

The process standard deviation is estimated

$$\hat{\sigma} = \frac{\overline{R}}{d_2} = \frac{.3113}{2.326} = 0.1338$$

The control limits are

$$\text{LCL} = \overline{\overline{x}} - 3(\hat{\sigma}/\sqrt{n})$$
$$= 6.026 - 3(.1338/\sqrt{5}) = 5.846$$
$$\text{UCL} = \overline{\overline{x}} + 3(\hat{\sigma}/\sqrt{n})$$
$$= 6.026 + 3(.1338/\sqrt{5}) = 6.205$$

b. Figure 13.24 shows these lower and upper control limits along with the centerline and the 24 sample means plotted in sequence. The sample means are all within the control limits so Phil concludes that the process is in control.

FIGURE 13.24 $\bar{x}$ Chart for Lengths (Solved Exercise 1)

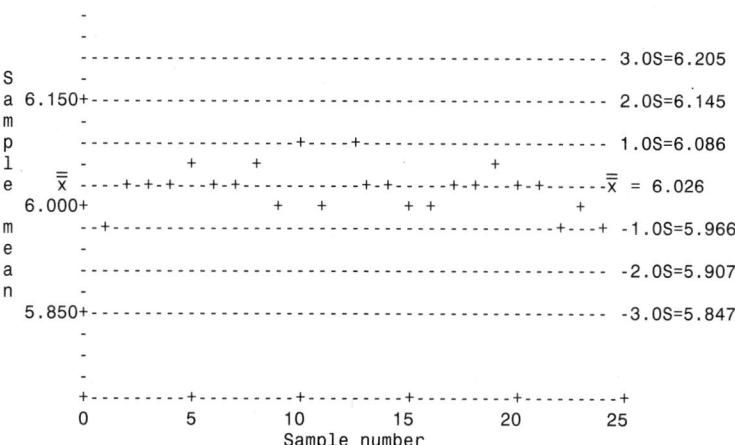

2. RANGE CHART

Refer to Solved Exercise 1.

a. Construct the appropriate control chart to monitor the variation of this process.

b. Is the process variation in control?

c. In Solved Exercise 1, Phil constructed an $\bar{x}$ chart. Now that he has both an R chart and an $\bar{x}$ chart, what is his conclusion?

Solution:

a. The appropriate control chart is the R chart.

b. The average of the ranges is computed in Solved Exercise 1, $\overline{R} = .3113$. This will be the centerline for the control chart.

Referring to Table 13.1 for a sample of $n = 5$ lengths, the appropriate D_3 and D_4 values are 0 and 2.114. Equation 13.7 is used to calculate the control limits:

$$LCL = D_3\overline{R} = 0(.3113) = 0$$
$$UCL = D_4\overline{R} = 2.114(.3113) = .658$$

c. Figure 13.25 shows these lower and upper control limits along with the centerline and the 24 average sample ranges plotted in sequence. The average sample ranges are all within the control limits so the process is concluded to be in control.

FIGURE 13.25   R Chart for Lengths (Solved Exercise 1)

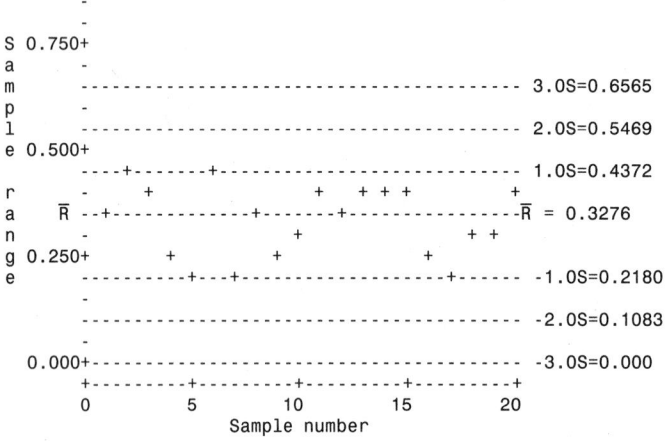

3. *p* CHART

The Sunshine Fruit Juice Company produces frozen juice concentrate packed in 12-ounce cardboard cans. These cans are formed on a machine by spinning them from cardboard stock and attaching metal top and bottom panels. A plastic strip is attached around the can's top. When this strip is pulled, the cardboard tears and the top of the can comes open. Unfortunately, quality-control inspector Clare King has been informed that a large percentage of strips don't open the can when pulled. She must implement an inspection procedure to monitor this process. Clare selects samples of 200 for 22 days and determines the number of defective cans:

Date	Sample size	Number defective	Proportion defective
April 1	200	4	.020
2	200	6	.030
3	200	10	.050
4	200	21	.105
5	200	5	.025

Date	Sample size	Number defective	Proportion defective
6	200	15	.075
7	200	19	.095
8	200	16	.080
9	200	11	.055
10	200	14	.070
11	200	13	.065
12	200	15	.075
13	200	7	.035
14	200	12	.060
15	200	9	.045
16	200	13	.065
17	200	12	.060
18	200	15	.075
19	200	3	.015
20	200	11	.055
21	200	6	.030
22	200	8	.040

a. Show how the proportion defective for sample 1 was computed.

b. Develop the centerline and upper and lower control limits for a 3-sigma p chart.

c. Compute the limits of the six zones.

d. Plot the proportions and test to determine whether the process is in control.

Solution:

a. For sample 1, the proportion of defectives is

$$p_1 = \frac{x_1}{n} = \frac{4}{200} = .02$$

The proportion for each sample is shown above.

b. The process proportion estimate is

$$\hat{p} = \frac{245}{22(200)} = .0557$$

The 3-sigma control limits are

$$\text{LCL} = \hat{p} - 3\sqrt{\frac{\hat{p}(1 - \hat{p})}{n}}$$

$$= .0557 - 3\sqrt{\frac{.0557(1 - .0557)}{200}}$$

$$= .0557 - 3(.0162) = .0071$$

$$\text{UCL} = \hat{p} + 3\sqrt{\frac{\hat{p}(1 - \hat{p})}{n}}$$

$$= .0557 + 3\sqrt{\frac{.0557(1 - .0557)}{200}}$$

$$= .0557 + 3(.0162) = .1043$$

c. Zone C: .0557 − .0162 = .0395
             .0557 + .0162 = .0719
             (.0395 to .0719)
   Zone B: (.0233 to .0395) and (.0719 to .0881)
   Zone A: (.0071 to .0233) and (.0881 to .1043)

d. Figure 13.26 shows these lower and upper control limits along with the centerline and the 22 sample proportions plotted in sequence. The high proportion of defectives in day 4 places this sample outside the control limits. Clare investigates why so many defectives occurred during day 4.

FIGURE 13.26 *p* Chart for Defects (Solved Exercise 3)

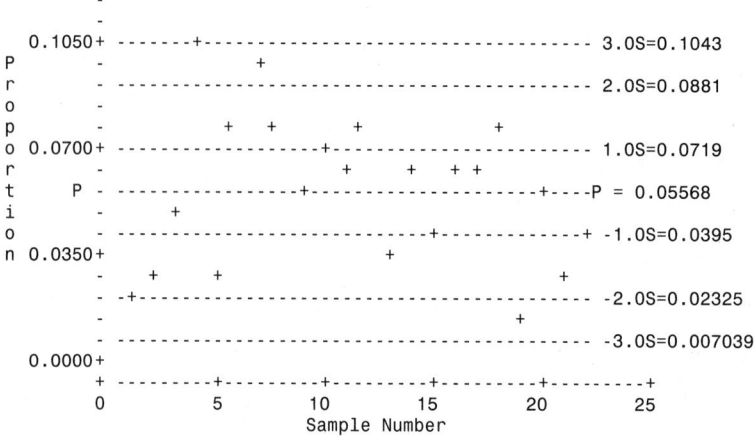

4. *c* CHART

The Neptune Motors Company builds compact cars. Frank Nelson inspects dashboard assemblies and records the number of total assembly defects. Here are the results for 20 dashboards:

Dashboard	Defects	Dashboard	Defects
1	5	11	2
2	4	12	7
3	7	13	4
4	3	14	6
5	8	15	8
6	6	16	3
7	5	17	10
8	6	18	7
9	10	19	4
10	9	20	5

a. Develop the centerline and upper and lower control limits for a 3-sigma *c* chart.

b. Compute the limits of the six zones.

c. Plot the number of defects and test to determine whether the process is in control.

Solution:

a. The average number of defects is

$$\bar{c} = \frac{\sum c_i}{n} = \frac{119}{20} = 5.95$$

The 3-sigma control limits are

$$LCL = \bar{c} - 3\sqrt{\bar{c}}$$
$$= 5.95 - 3\sqrt{5.95} = 5.95 - 3(2.44) = -1.37$$
$$UCL = \bar{c} + 3\sqrt{\bar{c}}$$
$$= 5.95 + 3\sqrt{5.95} = 5.95 + 3(2.44) = 13.27$$

b. Zone C: 5.95 − 2.44 = 3.51
      5.95 + 2.44 = 8.39
      (3.51 to 8.39)
   Zone B: (1.07 to 3.51) and (8.39 to 10.83)
   Zone A: (0 to 1.07) and (10.83 to 13.27)

c. Figure 13.27 shows these lower and upper control limits along with the centerline and the number of defects plotted in sequence. The number of defects is all within the control limits so Frank concludes that the process is in control.

FIGURE 13.27   *c* Chart for Defects (Solved Exercise 4)

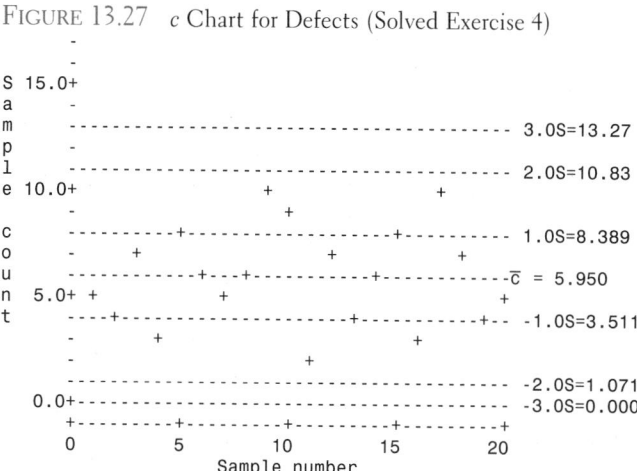

5. LOT ACCEPTANCE

Carlene Foss is in charge of final buyoff for lots of 10,000 transistors manufactured by her company. She judges each lot's quality and either passes it on to the shipping department or junks the entire lot due to poor quality. Management has decided that a lot with 2% or fewer defective transistors is acceptable.

Determine a sampling plan for Carlene to use in accepting or rejecting a lot, given management's definition of a good lot.

Solution:

Carlene decides to sample 100 transistors from each lot and use the sample results to determine the lot's fate. She calculates the probabilities of various sample outcomes, assuming the lot has 2% defectives, as follows:

$$H_0: p \le .02, \qquad n = 100$$
$$H_1: p > .02$$
$$\sigma_{\bar{p}} = \sqrt{\frac{.02(.98)}{100}} = .014$$

Sample results, number of defectives	Sample results, % defective	Probability if H_0 is true
3	.03	.2389
4	.04	.0764
5	.05	.0162
6	.06	.0021

The values in the last column were calculated using normal curve procedures (Chapter 6). For example, the first z value is $(.03 - .02)/.014 = .71$. The normal curve table indicates an area of .2611 for this z value, leaving $.5 - .2611 = .2389$ on the end of the curve. This latter value is the probability of getting a value as large, or larger, than .03 from the sampling distribution, assuming H_0 is true ($p = .02$). Carlene's worksheet for calculating the values in the final column is:

	Assuming H_0 is true:		
Sample value	z	Area	$.5 -$ Area
.03	.71	.2611	.2389
.04	1.43	.4236	.0764
.05	2.14	.4838	.0162
.06	2.86	.4979	.0021

Based on the preceding table, Carlene tells her inspection staff, "When each lot is completed, take a random sample of 100 transistors and have the lab people test them thoroughly. From this sample, record the number that don't work properly. If this number is four or less, send the entire lot to shipping. If the number of defectives is five or more, call me at once—the lot will be rejected and we need to find out what went wrong."

Carlene's reasoning is that if a lot is acceptable ($p = .02$), there's only a .0162 probability of erroneously rejecting it since that's the probability of getting five or more defectives from a sample taken from a good lot.

6. OPERATING CHARACTERISTIC CURVE

In Solved Exercise 5, Carlene Foss developed a sampling plan for accepting or rejecting lots of 10,000 transistors. She's satisfied with her type I error since there's only a .0162 probability of erroneously rejecting a good lot ($\alpha = .0162$). She considers this an acceptably low probability for the producer's risk. She now wonders about the consumer's risk, that is, whether her sampling plan offers sufficient protection for her company's transistor customers.

Develop the operating characteristic (OC) curve for Carlene's sampling plan and evaluate the risks of the plan.

Solution:

Carlene's predetermined decison rule point, from Solved Exercise 5, is five defectives or 5% defective. She decides to calculate the probabilities of failing to reject the false null hypothesis that $p = .02$ for each of three population defective percentages. These values and their corresponding beta values are:

p	Beta
.03	.9236
.05	.5000
.07	.0764

Carlene calculated these beta values using normal curve procedures. If $p = .05$, then exactly half the curve lies below the decision rule point (which is .05). A value in this region would lead to erroneous acceptance of the null hypothesis.

If $p = .03$, the calculated z value is $(.03 - .05)/.014 = -1.43$, and the standard normal area for this z value is .4236. Half the standard normal area must be added to this value since most of the sampling distribution lies below the decision rule point of .05 if $p = .03$. So $\beta = .5000 + .4236 = .9236$.

If $p = .07$, the calculated z value is $(.07 - .05)/.014 = 1.43$ and the standard normal area is .4236. This value must be subtracted from .5000 since only a small part of the sampling distribution lies below .05 if $p = .07$. So $\beta = .5000 - .4236 = .0764$.

Carlene plots her three values on graph paper and draws a smooth line through these points to produce her OC curve (Figure 13.28).

FIGURE 13.28   Operating Characteristic Curve

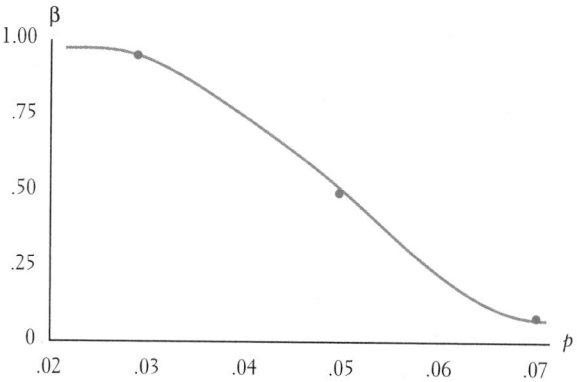

EXERCISES

56. Improving quality is often cited as the most important challenge facing American business today. Define what is meant by *quality* in this regard.

57. Your boss has just read about using control charts to improve quality in a manufacturing operation and asks how to do this. Write a brief memo explaining how the correct use of control charts can help in the quality improvement effort.

58. How are the upper and lower control limits on a control chart established?

59. There are two possible explanations for a measurement on a control chart exceeding the control limits. Explain.

60. Sketch a control chart with several observations for each of the following situations:

    a. Process in control, a single out-of-control observation.

    b. Process in control but drifting upward.

    c. Process in control but drifting downward.

    d. Process in control with strings of measurements above centerline.

    e. Process in control but cycling.

61. Consider a manufacturing operation such as Kaiser Aluminum's Trentwood aluminum factory. (See the "Applications" section for a description of this operation.) Describe an application for each of the following types of control chart for this operation: individual measurements, $\bar{x}$, R, p, and c.

62. Consider a service operation such as a credit union. Describe an application for each of the following types of control chart for this business: individual measurements, $\bar{x}$, R, p, and c.

63. Theory X and Theory Y are discussed in management classes as two different ways of viewing workers and dealing with them in the workplace. Discuss W. Edwards Deming's teachings with regard to these two opposing theories.

64. The Beamer Company makes ball bearings for high-quality bicycle components that demand very close tolerances. Beamer randomly selects 10 ball bearings every hour. Past experience shows the average (mean) diameter to be .37 with an average range of .04 ($\bar{R}$ = .04).

    a. Set up the $\bar{x}$ control chart.

    b. Set up an R chart.

65. (Refer to Exercise 64.) The results of the past five samples are:

Mean	Range
.3691	.020
.3705	.063
.3722	.040
.3699	.057
.3702	.088

    a. Plot the means on the $\bar{x}$ chart.

    b. Plot the ranges on the R chart.

    c. Write a memo to Beamer management indicating the results of your study.

66. A light truck factory has 128 key indicators of quality for completed trucks. During final inspection, each indicator is inspected and either performs properly or does not. Costly rework is necessary for items that don't perform properly, so management wants to track the percentage of nonconforming items per truck. During a trial period, the following percentages were recorded; the period was considered by management to be "normal."

Truck number	% nonconforming
1	3
2	6
3	0
4	7
5	2
6	4
7	0
8	0
9	1
10	4

    a. Set up a *c* chart using the preceding data and plot these values.

    b. Write a brief memo to management indicating the purpose of the *c* chart, how data are to be recorded on it for each completed truck, and how to interpret the results.

67. Boxes of apples received at a processing plant are supposed to have an average weight of 20 pounds. The standard deviation of weights is believed to be 2 pounds. Each boxcar load of boxes is sampled randomly, with 30 boxes being selected and weighed. The receiving inspection plan calls for a one-tailed test (down) and a significance level of .05.

    a. State the null and alternative hypotheses.

    b. State the decision rule for the test.

    c. Pick three key values below 20 pounds and indicate both β and $1 - \beta$ for these values.

    d. Plot the values found in part *c* to form the OC and power curves.

    e. What should be done with a boxcar load of apples whose sampled boxes' mean weight is 19 pounds?

    f. Based on your decision in part *e*, what type of error might have been committed? If this error has been made, what is the nature of the penalty and who will pay it?

68. Johnson and Dumas's article "How to Improve Quality If You're NOT in Manufacturing" (*Training*, November 1992) listed several steps to follow in improving a service firm's quality and hence its market share and profits. Steps range from establishing customer needs to implementing the plan. Suppose you own a formal wear rental shop and you face increased competition. Describe some steps you would take to improve your quality image with your market.

69. "America's Best Plants" (*Industry Week*, October 19, 1992) identified one of the best companies as Air Products and Chemicals, Inc. This company makes polymer emulsion products such as paint and paper coatings. "Foot soldiers run the show" at this company where employees are involved in every aspect of the plant's activities.

    A highlight of the article on Air Products and Chemicals was the 97.9% first-pass yield on its production line. This figure strongly suggests the use of a percentage control chart (*p* chart). Such a chart is also used by Kaiser Aluminum. (See this chapter's "Applications" section.)

    Construct a *p* chart for Air Products and Chemicals using fictitious values. Indicate the time values you choose for the *x*-axis.

542

Chapter Thirteen

70. A manager begins a control chart for the mean weight of steel ingots. She measures the average weights of the 24 ingots produced this week and then forms a control chart. Upon posting it, she says, "It makes no sense to measure quality against the standard established last week. Maybe the process was way out of control then." Evaluate this statement, and either refute it or indicate how to meet the objection it raises.

71. A company intends to use an acceptance sampling plan to monitor the average time between power-up and proper current readings for an electronic component it makes for electronic camera controls. Components are made in batches of 500. Among other things, the company wants to know how many components it must sample and test from each batch. A preliminary sample indicates a sample standard deviation of 1.5 seconds.

    When asked about how accurate the sampling plan should be, the plant manager finally subscribes to the following statements:

    1. If the actual time in the entire batch meets specification (5 seconds), I want only a 2% chance of concluding that this time is more than 5 seconds.

    2. If the actual time in the entire batch is really 6 seconds, I want only a 5% chance of thinking it's 5 seconds.

    a. How big a sample should be taken from each batch?
    b. Select three key values for the key time variable and compute both β and $1 - \beta$ for each.
    c. Plot the values found in part b to form the OC and power curves for this test.

72. The Concave Computer Company is enjoying a considerable increase in business volume. As a result, the accounting department now needs more than the normal 30-day period to process check requests. Unfortunately, the company is no longer getting the discounts its suppliers give for timely payment. Chip Weeks analyzes the amount of time it takes for a check request to flow through the accounting department. Six completed check requests are selected each day, and $\bar{x}$ and R charts are developed for the flow time variable. Flow time data for the past 20 days are:

Day	Days required to process a check request					
1	31	34	25	28	29	31
2	29	32	28	34	30	33
3	24	27	29	31	35	31
4	30	27	29	34	32	38
5	39	37	34	29	30	31
6	32	34	35	38	29	34
7	25	29	32	35	31	32
8	24	33	39	31	34	32
9	26	29	33	35	33	32
10	26	35	33	28	32	30
11	27	34	25	38	39	35
12	29	31	28	32	27	34
13	28	27	26	27	35	31
14	33	27	28	34	32	38
15	31	31	32	29	33	31
16	31	34	35	38	29	34

Day	Days required to process a check request					
17	29	29	32	35	31	32
18	28	33	35	31	34	32
19	36	29	28	35	33	32
20	34	35	32	28	32	30

    a. Construct the appropriate control charts to monitor the mean and variation of this process.

    b. Is the process in control?

    c. Write a report to Chip Weeks that explains the current flow time situation.

73. The Precision Manufacturing Company (which makes needlelike operating instruments for hospital operating rooms) implements statistical process control procedures in its production operation. The company collects one sample of 150 randomly selected manufactured instruments each day for 15 days.

Day	Sample size	Defectives
1	150	5
2	150	7
3	150	3
4	150	2
5	150	4
6	150	5
7	150	8
8	150	6
9	150	3
10	150	1
11	150	2
12	150	6
13	150	7
14	150	14
15	150	5

    a. Construct the appropriate control chart to monitor this process.

    b. Is the process in control?

    c. Write a memo to management that explains the defective instrument situation.

74. In a large chain that sells washers and dryers, the service department decides to improve the effectiveness of its repair work. Maintenance requests that require a second call to complete the repair are monitored for 16 months. Eighty requests are randomly selected for each month.

Month	Total requests	Second visits
1	80	1
2	80	0
3	80	2
4	80	5

Month	Total requests	Second visits
5	80	4
6	80	2
7	80	3
8	80	3
9	80	0
10	80	1
11	80	2
12	80	4
13	80	1
14	80	0
15	80	3
16	80	2

a. Construct the appropriate control chart to monitor this process.

b. Is the process in control? Is the service department's objective of improving the effectiveness of its repair work accomplished?

c. Write a memo to management that explains the repair work's present status. Propose a plan for determining whether the effectiveness of repair work has improved.

75. A production line assembles electric clocks. Clocks are periodically examined for imperfections. Results for the past 20 clocks examined are:

Clock	Defects	Clock	Defects
1	0	11	2
2	1	12	0
3	2	13	0
4	0	14	1
5	1	15	2
6	3	16	2
7	0	17	0
8	1	18	4
9	2	19	1
10	7	20	2

a. Construct the appropriate control chart to monitor this process.

b. Is the process in control?

c. Write a memo to management that summarizes the stability of the process.

EXTENDED EXERCISES

. . . .

76. VALLEY ELECTRONICS

Valley Electronics makes components for commercial electronics assemblies such as oscilloscopes and circuit testers. A large manufacturer of these items has contracted with Valley to make thousands of chassis assemblies, one of Valley's specialties. Each chassis requires certain dimensions and must have two holes drilled in precise locations; a complex electronic component is then attached in these holes.

At Valley's weekly management council meeting, Susan Boyer, who recently joined the company because of her expertise in quality control, suggested tracking the key dimension (distance between holes) and recording values for a sample of chassis components. She planned to construct $\bar{x}$ and R charts whose purposes she then explained to the council.

According to contract specifications, the chassis measurement between mounting holes is 7.6 inches, measured from the edges nearest to each other.

Susan began taking samples of 25 chassis components from the line until she had 10 such samples. After calculating the mean between-hole measurement for each of the 10 samples, she averaged them and found a mean for all sampled chassis of 7.61 inches. The 10 samples' average range was .05 inches. Using a d_2 value from Table 13.1 of 3.931, she estimated the standard deviation for the between-hole measurement to be .0127 inches. Susan called the buyer of the chassis assemblies and, after reporting these values, was assured that they were satisfactory, that is, met the terms of the contract.

a. Check Susan's estimate of the process standard deviation using Table 13.1.

b. Construct $\bar{x}$ and R charts for Susan.

c. Susan wants to show the management council example plots to watch out for as the chassis line continues operations. Use both charts, along with fictitious plot values, to illustrate key future dangers for the chassis line.

77. VALLEY ELECTRONICS #2

(See Extended Exercise 76.) Susan Boyer of Valley Electronics is concerned about the defective rate for Valley's best profit producer, a programmable control for home electronics products. A few customer complaints have raised concerns about the possibility of deteriorating quality.

Susan designs a sampling plan for these components and pulls them from the assembly line over a period of three weeks. She samples them from all shifts, various days of the week, and various times of the day for a total of 20 samplings. Her sample size for each is 25 controllers. Although it takes a lot of time to individually test all aspects of each unit, she's convinced that this is very important for the company's reputation and long-term profitability.

For each sample of 500 controllers, Susan computes the percentage that don't perform properly. After averaging these defective rates, she has an estimate of the defective rate for the entire process, 3.7%. Since the company produces thousands of these units each year, this defective rate means that hundreds of defective units are being sold by the company. Valley's management council agrees with her that this rate is too high so steps are begun to lower it.

At Susan's urging, these attempts are designed around Deming's 14 points for quality improvement discussed earlier in this chapter. The management council agrees that this effort constitutes a change of corporate culture at Valley, but they recognize that the electronic controller isn't the only component facing quality problems and competitive challenges. They agree to hire an outside consultant to help Susan create the necessary changes.

In the meantime, Susan decides to construct a p chart to track the defective rate. She hopes that she'll be able to spot the hoped-for improving trend, as well as watch for any deterioration in the process that may need direct corrective action. Her sampling plan involves sampling from each shift every other day; samples of 500 controllers will be used.

a. Construct the p chart for Susan.

b. Prepare several plots on this chart for Susan to use in her next management council meeting. She wants to show the management team how various plots that might result can help them take appropriate corrective action.

78. CLINTON LAWNMOWERS

Sam Gangee of Example 13.8 has turned to a key quality-control problem in his lawnmower factory, the quality of incoming carburetors received from a supplier. The volume of gasoline that carburetors hold at rest is an important factor in how long it takes to start a lawnmower when cold.

After discussions with design engineers, it's agreed that an average of two cubic inches of gas per carburetor (or less) will constitute the definition of an acceptable lot. A volume greater than two cubic inches can create problems on a cold start. Carburetors arrive in lots of 500 units.

Sam uses a systematic sample (Chapter 2) to randomly select those carburetors that will constitute the sample and be subjected to several quality tests. In each arriving truckload, the sequence of carburetors for sampling purposes is determined by the order in which they're unloaded.

He chooses a sample size of 25, so every 20th item will be sampled (500/25 = 20). For each batch, a random number is chosen between 1 and 20, which is the item number for the first sampled carburetor as it's unloaded. Each 20th item thereafter is also chosen. In his most recent sampling effort, the random number 11 was chosen, so carburetors 11, 31, 51, 71, and so on were marked with special paint as they were unloaded from the truck. These 25 items were then taken to the test lab and measured for gas volume. If the entire lot passed inspection on the basis of sample results, it would be sent to final assembly. If the lot failed due to poor quality in the sample, each of the 500 carburetors would be returned to the supplier. On Wednesday, Sam received the following information from his quality-control staff:

Lot number 275: $n = 25$
$\bar{x}$ (average gas volume per carburetor) $= 4.7$
s (standard deviation of carburetor volume) $= 1.4$

Sam decided to use the normal curve in his hypothesis test since he judged the sample size (25) to be sufficiently large. He made this decision after looking at both the t and normal curve tables and noting how close the values are for samples of 25. The hypotheses under test are:

$H_0: \mu \leq 2$
$H_1: \mu > 2$

He computed the test z value from the sample data contained in his report. (See Chapter 9.)

$$z = \frac{4.7 - 2}{1.4/\sqrt{25}} = 9.64$$

From the standard normal table, Sam found the table critical value to be 2.05, using a significance level of .02 for a one-tail test. Since $9.64 > 2.05$, the null hypothesis was rejected. The sample results ($\bar{x} = 4.7$) don't seem reasonable when compared with the null hypothesis ($\mu \leq 2$).

Sam decided that it's necessary to return the entire lot to the carburetor supplier. In addition, he'll visit the supplier's plant to try to learn what has gone wrong, and to impress on the supplier's management the importance of correct gas volume. He hopes he isn't wasting his time with this effort. (He hopes that he hasn't made a type I error.) Such an error would be embarrassing and might create future problems with the supplier. In addition, lawnmower assembly time would be lost without justification.

Sam next wants to determine the power of this test for $n = 25$ and decide whether he has chosen an adequate sample size. Here are the facts Sam needs to accomplish this task:

$$H_0: \mu \leq 2 \qquad n = 25$$
$$H_1: \mu > 2 \qquad s = 1.4$$
$$s_{\bar{x}} = s/\sqrt{n} \qquad = 1.4/\sqrt{25} = .28$$

Sam previously established a critical z value of 2.05 for a one-tailed hypothesis test using a significance level of .02. In units of gasoline volume, this number of standard errors is 2.574 cubic inches $(2 + 2.05[.28] = 2.574)$. Figure 13.29 shows three areas Sam chooses to calculate beta (probability of type II error) for three different possible values of the population mean.

FIGURE 13.29 Normal Curve Areas

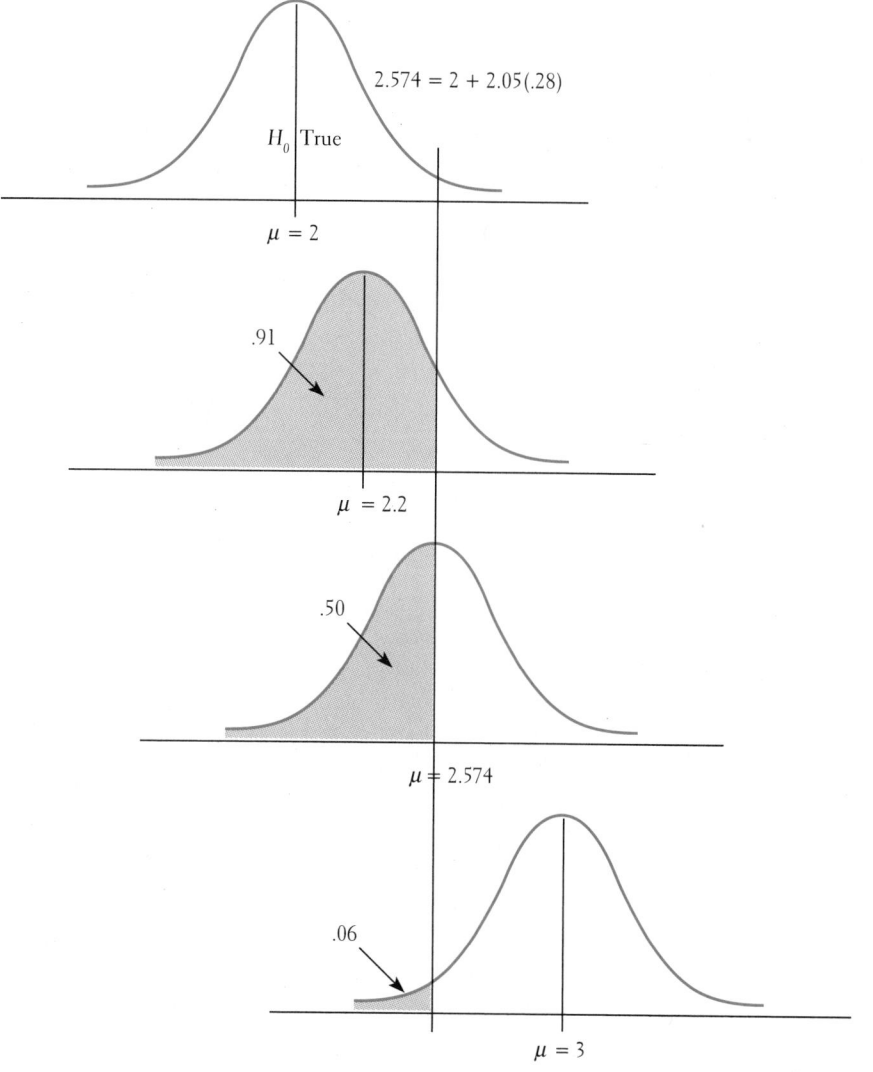

By subtracting the beta values in Figure 13.29 from 1, he computes the power of the test for the three designated population mean values. He summarizes these as follows and plots them on a power curve (Figure 13.30).

Population mean	Power $(1 - \beta)$
2.200	.09
2.574	.50
3.000	.94

FIGURE 13.30   Power Curve

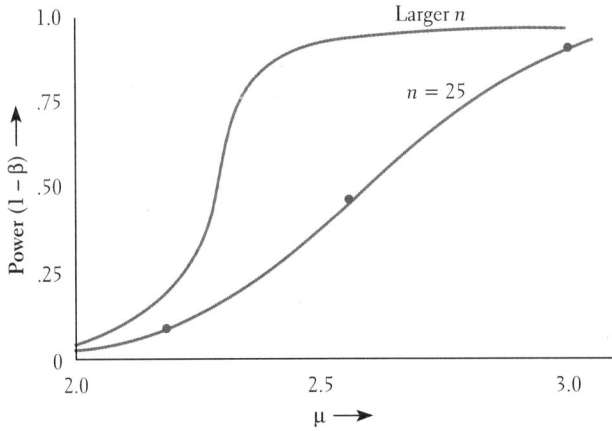

Using Figure 13.30, Sam can find the power of his statistical test to correctly reject the null hypothesis that $\mu \le 2$. He has connected the three points on his graph with a curved line to obtain this power curve. After studying this curve, Sam decides that perhaps his chosen sample size ($n = 25$) isn't powerful enough. He can increase the test power by increasing the sample size. Although this will be more costly, Sam considers it a good investment.

Notice that in Figure 13.30, another power curve has been plotted, one for a larger n. Increasing the sample size above 25 will move the power curve to the left in Figure 13.30, providing greater power to detect a false null hypothesis. After thinking about this matter, Sam plots a family of several power curves using Figure 13.30's format; each curve represents a different sample size. Sam thinks that by studying the test's power for several sample sizes and by considering the cost of using these sample sizes, he can choose the sample size that best meets his needs.

a. Sam's boss indicates that sampling is inexpensive and wonders how the test's power would be affected by increasing the sample size. She suggests trying a sample of 50 and another of 75. Perform the calculations necessary to form new power curves for each.

b. Plot all three power curves on a single graph. Based on these curves, write a brief memo to Sam's boss indicating your choice and the reasons for it.

MINITAB COMPUTER PACKAGE

MINITAB was used to generate the individual chart for average pump volume in Figure 13.5.

```
MTB> SET C1
DATA> 12.1 11 9.7 8.4 10.2 10.4 11 12.6 13 8.8
DATA> 9 7.7 10 11.2 12.2 13 12.1 10.2 10.3 9.7
DATA> 11 12 8 10.2 6.8 8 9.5 10.2 9.4 8.9 7.3 7.2
DATA> END
MTB > NAME C1 'VOLUME'
MTB > ICHART C1;
SUBC> MU=10;
SUBC> SIGMA= 1;
SUBC> XSTART at 21 END 32.
      OUTPUT SHOWN AS FIGURE 13.5
MTB> STOP
```

The data are entered in sequence into C1. The ICHART command plots the pump volumes on an individual chart. The MU and SIGMA subcommands indicate that the mean and standard deviation for this chart should be 10 and 1, respectively. The XSTART subcommand indicates that the chart should begin with pump 21 and end with pump 32.

MINITAB can produce the following statistical process control charts:

XBARCHART produces a chart of sample means.

RCHART produces a chart of sample ranges.

SCHART produces a chart of sample standard deviations.

ICHART produces a chart of individual observations.

MACHART produces a chart of moving averages.

EWMACHART produces a chart of exponentially weighted moving averages.

MRCHART produces a chart of moving ranges.

PCHART produces a chart for proportion of nonconformities.

NCHART produces a chart for number of nonconformities.

CCHART produces a chart for Poisson counts.

UCHART produces a chart for Poisson counts per unit.

14

CORRELATION AND SIMPLE REGRESSION

*There's some
difference
between Peter
and Peter.
Cervantes,
Don Quixote*

Objectives

When you have completed this chapter, you will be able to:

Construct and interpret scatter diagrams.

Calculate the correlation coefficient between two variables.

Develop a regression equation using the least squares
procedure.

Interpret the slope (regression coefficient) and *y*-intercept.

Compute and interpret the standard error of estimate and
develop prediction interval estimates.

Explain the underlying assumptions of regression analysis.

Compute and interpret the simple coefficient of
determination.

Test a hypothesis to determine if two variables are linearly
related.

 An extensive article in *Financial World* (July 7, 1992) discussed the financial health of professional baseball, football, basketball, and hockey franchises. It included a two-page summary of major financial statistics for all teams (pp. 50–51).

Chapter 11 discussed methods of determining the relationship between two categorical variables. Either nominal or ordinal data were needed for these techniques. This chapter explores the relationship between two continuous or quantitative variables. Since so many variables in the business setting are measured on an interval or ratio scale, correlation and regression techniques are widely used to assist the decision-making process.

Why Managers Need to Know about Correlation and Regression Analysis

The basic notions of regression and correlation are examined in this chapter. Extensions of these techniques to situations involving more than two variables appear in Chapter 15. Since regression analysis requires a great many calculations, computer applications for the techniques discussed are emphasized.

This chapter and the next cover regression, one of the most popular techniques in data analysis. Every manager encounters the procedures of correlation and regression in his or her career, and understanding them is essential. Since numerical data abound in the business world, there's a frequent need to examine the relationships among different variables.

Regarding the *Financial World* article just mentioned, it might be of interest to focus on one financial statistic such as "value of franchise" and attempt to find other variables that are highly related. Candidates in the article's financial data were total revenue, player costs, operating income, and media revenue. The procedures this chapter describes can be used to search for important relationships.

Scatter Diagrams

In both correlation and regression analysis, the linear relationship between two continuous variables, designated x and y, is investigated. A sample of items is measured for both x and y, with the focus on the extent to which these two variables are related or correlated.

One useful way of examining the x-y relationship is to view the data using a graph. An x-y plotting system is used for this purpose. The x axis is scaled to accommodate the range of values needed for the x variable, and the y axis is scaled to accommodate the y values. The data pairs are then plotted in two-dimensional space. This x-y plot is called a **scatter diagram**.

Scatter Diagram

> A **scatter diagram** plots a series of x-y data pairs in two-dimensional space.

EXAMPLE 14.1   Five cars are randomly selected from a rental fleet. Each car is weighed and then driven 100 miles to determine its mileage per gallon. The results are:

Car	Weight (pounds)	Miles per gallon
1	2,743	21.4
2	3,518	15.2
3	1,855	38.9
4	5,214	12.7
5	4,341	17.8

The five *x-y* data points can be plotted in two-dimensional space to form a scatter diagram of the data. Weight is chosen to be the *x* variable, so the *x* axis is scaled from 0 to 6,000 pounds. Miles per gallon is the *y* variable, so the *y* axis is scaled from 0 to 40. Each of the five data points is plotted using this *x-y* system (Figure 14.1).

FIGURE 14.1   Weight-Mileage Scatter Diagram

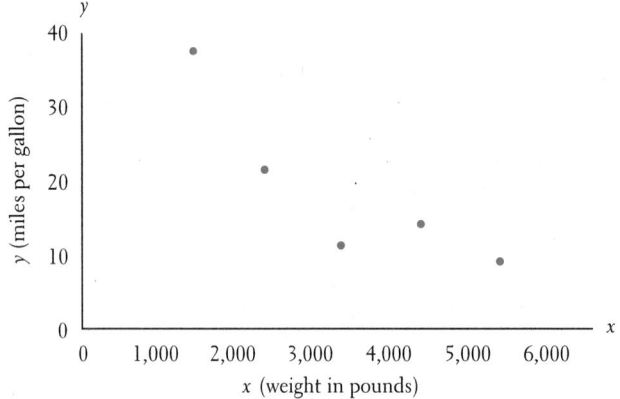

The advantage of the scatter diagram is that it enables one to visualize the relationship between *x* and *y*. Figure 14.1 shows that as a car's weight increases, its mileage tends to decrease. Based on the small sample of five cars, a relationship between weight and mileage seems to exist. It would be preferable to select a much larger sample before drawing any conclusions, of course, and also to measure the extent of the *x-y* relationship.

MINITAB can be used to develop a scatter diagram. The appropriate commands to plot the data from Example 14.1 are:

```
MTB> SET C1
DATA> 21.4 15.2 38.9 12.7 17.8
DATA> END
MTB> SET C2
DATA> 2743 3518 1855 5214 4341
```

```
DATA> END
MTB> NAME C1 'MPG' C2 'WEIGHT'
MTB> PLOT C1 VS C2
    OUTPUT WILL BE SHOWN HERE
MTB> STOP
```

The output for this MINITAB run is similar to the scatter diagram in Figure 14.1.

Figure 14.2 shows some important scatter diagram patterns that should be looked for when examining a particular x-y relationship. (The number of data points has been deliberately kept small in these examples. Plots of real data usually involve many more data points.)

FIGURE 14.2 Scatter Diagrams

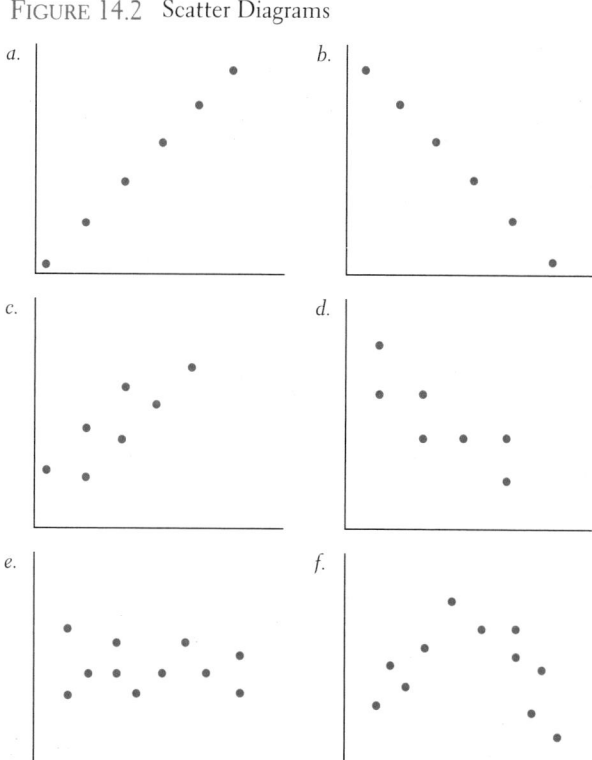

Plot *a* in Figure 14.2 illustrates a perfect positive linear relationship. It is linear because the plotted points lie on a straight line. It is positive because as x increases, y increases also. And it's perfect because the plotted x-y points all lie on this line. Plot *b* shows a perfect negative linear relationship. The relationship is negative because as x increases, y decreases. Plots such as *a* and *b* are rarely seen in practical situations; they're included here to illustrate the extreme cases of linear x-y relationships.

Plots *c* and *d* in Figure 14.2 illustrate relationships typically seen in real-life scatter diagrams. The points in plot *c* represent a positive linear relationship, but not a perfect relationship, since the points don't all lie precisely on a straight line. Plot *d* is similar, except that an imperfect negative relationship is shown. Most scatter diagrams encountered in practical situations are variations of plots *c* and *d*.

Plot *e* illustrates a complete lack of relationship between *x* and *y*. Knowledge of the *x* variable provides no useful information about the *y* variable. This lack of linear relationship is an important concept in hypothesis testing, which is discussed later in this chapter.

Finally, plot *f* illustrates a curved relationship between *x* and *y*. Note that although plot *f* shows a relationship between *x* and *y*, it's not a linear relationship.

CORRELATION COEFFICIENT

The advantage of the scatter diagram is that it enables the analyst to *see* the relationship between the two variables of interest. It is particularly valuable for revealing the presence of curved relationships, which can be missed when numerical measurements of linear correlation are computed.

Correlation Coefficient

It is usually desirable to measure the extent of the relationship between *x* and *y* as well as observe it in a scatter diagram. The measurement used for this purpose is the **correlation coefficient,** which is a numerical value in the range -1 to $+1$ that measures the strength of the linear relationship between two quantitative variables.

> The **correlation coefficient** is a value between -1 and $+1$ that indicates the strength of the linear relationship between two quantitative variables.

Correlation coefficients exist for a population of data values and for each sample selected from it. The symbol for the population correlation coefficient is ρ, the Greek letter rho. For the sample, the correlation coefficient is represented by the letter *r*. As Table 14.1 shows, both ρ and *r* range between -1 and $+1$. As usual, the sample statistic is used to estimate the population parameter. This process will be examined in depth in the next section.

TABLE 14.1   Correlation Coefficients

Data collection	Correlation coefficient	Range of values
Population	ρ	$-1 \leq \rho \leq +1$
Sample	r	$-1 \leq r \leq +1$

For both ρ and *r*:

-1: Perfect negative linear relationship
   0: No linear relationship
$+1$: Perfect positive linear relationship

As Table 14.1 states, a correlation coefficient of $+1$ indicates a perfect positive linear relationship, a value of 0 indicates no relationship, and a value of -1 indicates a perfect negative linear relationship. These values are rarely encountered in real situations, but they're good benchmarks for evaluating the correlation coefficient of any data collection.

Equation 14.1 is used to calculate the sample correlation coefficient. For the population correlation coefficient, the same equation is used, except the population size, N, is substituted for the sample size, n:

$$r = \frac{n\Sigma xy - (\Sigma x)(\Sigma y)}{\sqrt{n\Sigma x^2 - (\Sigma x)^2}\sqrt{n\Sigma y^2 - (\Sigma y)^2}} \tag{14.1}$$

where

Σx = Sum of the x values
Σy = Sum of the y values
Σx^2 = Sum of the squared x values
Σy^2 = Sum of the squared y values
$(\Sigma x)^2$ = Sum of the x values squared
$(\Sigma y)^2$ = Sum of the y values squared
Σxy = Sum of the product of x and y for each paired observation
n = Number of x-y observations

Equation 14.1 is used only for quantitative data and is known as the *Pearson product-moment correlation coefficient.*

EXAMPLE 14.2   A calculator should be used to form a data table of the various sums required for computing r using Equation 14.1. The data in Example 14.1 will be used to form such a table so that the correlation coefficient between car weight and mileage for the sample of five cars can be found. The data, along with the calculations of the necessary sums, appear in Table 14.2.

The values calculated in Table 14.2 are used in Equation 14.1 to calculate the sample correlation coefficient for the sample of five cars:

$$r = \frac{n\Sigma xy - (\Sigma x)(\Sigma y)}{\sqrt{n\Sigma x^2 - (\Sigma x)^2}\sqrt{n\Sigma y^2 - (\Sigma y)^2}}$$

$$= \frac{5(327,820.9) - (17,671)(106)}{\sqrt{5(69,371,475) - (17,671)^2}\sqrt{5(2,680.34) - (106)^2}}$$

$$= \frac{-234,021.5}{273,494.4} = -.855 \text{ rounded to } -.86$$

The correlation coefficient for the sample of five data points is $r = -.86$. This indicates a rather strong negative linear relationship between car weight and miles per gallon in the sample. The correlation coefficient verifies what was apparent in Figure 14.1's scatter diagram.

While both the scatter diagram and the sample correlation coefficient suggest a strong relationship between weight and mileage: (on a scale of 0 to -1, $r = -.86$) the sample size is extremely small and may not provide the analyst with enough

TABLE 14.2   Correlation Coefficient Calculations for Example 14.2

	x	y	xy	x^2	y^2
	2,743	21.4	58,700.2	7,524,049	457.96
	3,518	15.2	53,473.6	12,376,324	231.04
	1,855	38.9	72,159.5	3,441,025	1,513.21
	5,214	12.7	66,217.8	27,185,796	161.29
	4,341	17.8	77,269.8	18,844,281	316.84
Sums:	17,671	106.0	327,820.9	69,371,475	2,680.34

information to infer a significant relationship in the population. A statistical hypothesis test will be developed in the next section to allow us to determine whether a sample relationship can be extended to the population.

MINITAB can be used to compute a correlation coefficient. The appropriate command to compute the correlation coefficient for Example 14.2 is:

```
MTB> CORR C1 C2
Correlation of MPG AND WEIGHT = -0.855
MTB> STOP
```

EXAMPLE 14.3   Queen Hardware Store manager Robin Nash conducts exit interviews of 150 shoppers. She requests several statistics, including number of miles driven to the store (x) and dollar amount of purchase in the store (y). Wanting to know the relationship between these two variables, she keys the x-y pairs into a computer using a program that calculates the correlation coefficient. This program computes r to be .09. Robin concludes that the extremely weak linear relationship between miles driven and purchase amount does not warrant further examination.

The correlation coefficients for the scatter diagrams in Figure 14.2 can be estimated based on the apparent relationships between x and y. In Figure 14.2a, the correlation coefficient is $+1$, since a perfect positive linear relationship is apparent. In plot b, the correlation coefficient is -1. Figure 14.2 c and d show relationships that are not perfect; values for r might be estimated at about $+.75$ for plot c and about $-.75$ for plot d. In plot e, $r = 0$ since there appears to be no x-y relationship. In plot f, r also is approximately 0. This means that there's no *linear* relationship, although the scatter diagram of plot f clearly shows that a nonlinear relationship exists.

HYPOTHESIS TESTING IN CORRELATION ANALYSIS

A statistical question should always be asked when a sample is taken and measurements are made on the sample items: Can the sample results be assumed to hold for the entire population of interest?

The specific concern in correlation analysis is whether it can be concluded, based on sample evidence, that a linear relationship exists between the two continuous variables in the population. The null hypothesis under test states that no correlation exists in the population, that is, $\rho = 0$. The null and two-tailed alternative hypotheses for a correlation analysis are

$$H_0: \rho = 0$$
$$H_1: \rho \neq 0$$

A two-tailed alternative is used when the analyst is testing to determine if any linear relationship exists in the population. A one-tailed alternative is used when the analyst's goal is to determine if either a positive ($H_1: \rho > 0$) or a negative ($H_1: \rho < 0$) relationship exists.

After a sample of x-y pairs has been randomly drawn from the population, the sample correlation coefficient is computed using Equation 14.1. The value of r along with the sample size n are then used to compute the sample statistic for the test. If this statistic is close to 0, the null hypothesis is not rejected. If the statistic is far from 0, the null hypothesis is rejected.

If samples of the same size (n) are selected from a population, and if the r values computed from each sample are distributed normally around $\rho = 0$, only the standard error of r need be known for the usual test involving the normal distribution to be performed, as introduced in Chapter 9:

$$z = \frac{\text{Observed value} - \text{Assumed or hypothesized value}}{\text{Standard error of sampling distribution}}$$

Unfortunately, r values aren't normally distributed, so the normal curve can't be used. However, if the null hypothesis is true, then the appropriate sampling distribution for this test is the t distribution with $n - 2$ degrees of freedom. Two degrees of freedom are lost because two population parameters (μ_x and μ_y) are estimated using sample statistics ($\bar{x}$ and $\bar{y}$). The value for the estimated standard error of r is computed using Equation 14.2:

$$s_r = \sqrt{\frac{1 - r^2}{n - 2}} \tag{14.2}$$

where s_r = Standard error of the correlation coefficient
   r = Sample correlation coefficient
   n = Number of paired observations

Equation 14.3 shows the appropriate test statistic:

$$t = \frac{(r - \rho)}{s_r} \tag{14.3}$$

where r = Sample correlation coefficient
   ρ = Hypothesized population correlation coefficient
   s_r = Standard error of the correlation coefficient
      (computed using Equation 14.2)

EXAMPLE 14.4   An article in *The Academy of Management Review* reports the results of a study examining the roles organization design and culture play in the varying levels of success experienced by advanced manufacturing technologies in organizations.[1] The study conducted by Zammuto and Krakower (1991) examined the relationship between organizations' competing values profiles and a number of organizational characteristics. The study surveyed 332 colleges and universities. One of several hypotheses tested was that a hierarchical value system, reflecting the values and norms associated with bureaucracy, is correlated with the organizational characteristic of formalization.[2] The correlation between the hierarchical value score and the formalization score for the sampled organization was $r = .42$.

The null and a two-tailed alternative hypothesis for this correlation analysis are

$$H_0: \rho = 0$$
$$H_1: \rho \neq 0$$

If the null hypothesis is assumed true, the sampling distribution from which the ratio r/s_r will be drawn is the t distribution with a mean of 0. There are 330 degrees of freedom associated with this test ($n - 2 = 332 - 2 = 330$). If the .05 significance level is chosen, the t table in Appendix E.7 is used to find the critical t value. A choice must be made between the 120 or infinity row. The conservative approach is to select the row providing the highest critical t value. At the intersection of the 120 row and the .05 column (read from the top of the table) is the value 1.98. Since this is a two-tailed test, ± 1.98 are the critical values for the test. The decision rule is:

If the sample t statistic lies more than 1.98 standard errors below or above the assumed mean (0) of the sampling distribution, reject the null hypothesis (reject H_0 if $t < -1.98$ or $t > 1.98$).

The test statistic is calculated using Equations 14.2 and 14.3. The standard error of r is

$$s_r = \sqrt{\frac{1 - r^2}{n - 2}} = \sqrt{\frac{1 - (.42)^2}{330}} = .05$$

The t statistic is

$$t = \frac{r - \rho}{s_r} = \frac{.42 - 0}{.05} = 8.4$$

The appropriate sampling distribution, assuming the null hypothesis is true, appears in Figure 14.3. The calculated t statistic (8.4) is in the rejection area specified by the decision rule ($t < 1.98$), so the null hypothesis is rejected. Zammuto and Krakower conclude that there is a correlation between a hierarchical value system and the organizational characteristic of formalization.

---

[1] R. F. Zammuto and J. Y. Krakower, "Quantitative and Qualitative Studies in Organizational Culture," *Research in Organizational Change and Development* 5 (1991), p. 95.

FIGURE 14.3   Sampling Distribution of $\dfrac{r}{s_r}$ for Example 14.4

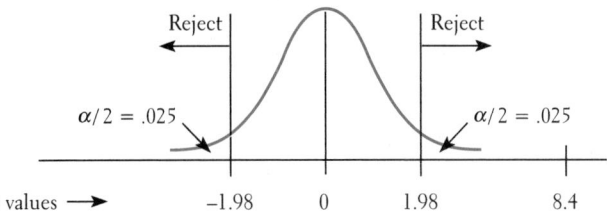

A couple of words of caution about correlation should be mentioned. A correlation between two variables doesn't necessarily mean that one variable causes the other one. Correlation analysis can't be used to directly determine causality. Furthermore, two variables being correlated in a statistical sense doesn't necessarily mean that they're correlated in any direct, meaningful way. For example, we might determine statistically that church attendance and alcohol consumption are highly correlated in a certain large city. However, it might not be possible to determine which is the dependent and which is the independent variable. Whenever population-related variables increase together, it is often a reflection of a general increase in population rather than any direct connection between the two variables.

The next section will consider the problem of finding the best-fitting line for a given set of data. This line will provide a regression equation, a term first used by English scientist Francis Galton (1822–1911) in describing certain relationships in the theory of heredity.[2]

EXERCISES

1. What is a scatter diagram?

2. Why are scatter diagrams important?

3. Why are the magnitude and sign of a correlation coefficient important?

4. What does $r = 0$ imply?

5. What does it mean when r is shown not to be significant?

6. Interpret each of the following correlation coefficients.

    a. $r = -1.00$

    b. $r = 0$

    c. $r = .85$

    d. $r = -.20$

7. Using five data points, show what each relationship in Exercise 6 would look like if plotted on a scatter diagram.

---

[2]W. H. Kruskal, J. M. Tanur, eds., *International Encyclopedia of Statistics* (New York: The Free Press, 1968), Vol. 1, p. 524.

8. Director of Research and Development Donna Pico must defend her budget request for increased funding. Sampling eight pharmaceutical companies, she collects the following data:

Company	Annual profit ($ millions), y	Research and development ($ millions), x
1	$25	$ 5
2	30	7
3	20	4
4	50	10
5	40	8
6	60	12
7	50	6
8	35	11

   a. Plot a scatter diagram.

   b. What kind of relationship exists between these two variables?

   c. Estimate the correlation coefficient.

   d. Compute the correlation coefficient.

   e. Test the correlation coefficient at the .05 significance level.

   f. Write a short memo summarizing the results of this analysis for Donna.

9. Suppose that $n = 400$ and $r = .38$ in a correlation analysis. What is your conclusion concerning the population correlation at the .05 significance level?

10. Ralph Ludwigson, Danielson Tool & Die Corporation personnel director, feels that there's a relationship between the ages of the firm's computer operators and the number of days they were absent from work last month. After reading "Will the New Software Deliver What It Promises?" in *Today's Office* (June 1989, p. 27), he's thinking about the absentee-ism problem since his company's computer operators are using the kind of software the article describes. Ralph selects a random sample of 10 workers and collects the following data:

Worker	Days absent, y	Age, x
1	5	25
2	0	30
3	1	62
4	7	33
5	8	45
6	12	27
7	6	55
8	11	41
9	2	22
10	3	58

   a. Plot a scatter diagram.

   b. What kind of relationship exists between these two variables?

   c. Estimate the correlation coefficient.

    d. Compute the correlation coefficient.

    e. Test the correlation coefficient at the .01 significance level.

    f. What should Ralph conclude?

11. Keith Mikelson, president of the Northeast Siding Company, feels that the amount of time a salesperson spends with a client should be positively related to the size of that client's account. To see if this relationship exists, Keith gathers the following sample data:

Client	Account size, y	Minutes spent, x
1	$1,056	108
2	825	132
3	651	62
4	748	95
5	894	58
6	1,242	134
7	1,058	87
8	1,112	78
9	1,259	120

    a. Plot a scatter diagram.

    b. What kind of relationship exists between these two variables?

    c. Compute the correlation coefficient.

    d. Test the correlation coefficient at the .05 significance level.

    e. What should Keith conclude?

12. Consider the 200 observations in the accompanying table. The dependent variable, y, is the population of the number of shares of Golden Mining stock traded on the Denver exchange each day. The independent variable, x, is the high temperature of Denver, Colorado, for each day. Randomly select observations for 15 days.

    a. Compute the coefficient of correlation for your sample.

    b. Test the hypothesis that there is no relationship between high temperature and shares of stock traded at the .05 significance level.

Observation	y	x	Observation	y	x	Observation	y	x	Observation	y	x
(1)	50	37	(14)	97	46	(27)	42	64	(40)	84	53
(2)	90	77	(15)	69	88	(28)	60	24	(41)	56	61
(3)	46	55	(16)	87	87	(29)	22	29	(42)	48	18
(4)	47	27	(17)	52	82	(30)	91	40	(43)	0	45
(5)	12	49	(18)	52	56	(31)	68	35	(44)	58	4
(6)	23	23	(19)	15	22	(32)	36	37	(45)	27	23
(7)	65	18	(20)	85	49	(33)	22	28	(46)	78	68
(8)	37	1	(21)	41	44	(34)	92	56	(47)	78	79
(9)	87	41	(22)	82	33	(35)	34	33	(48)	72	66
(10)	83	73	(23)	98	77	(36)	34	82	(49)	21	80
(11)	87	61	(24)	99	87	(37)	63	89	(50)	73	99
(12)	39	85	(25)	23	54	(38)	30	78	(51)	54	86
(13)	28	16	(26)	77	8	(39)	31	24	(52)	76	48

Observation	y	x	Observation	y	x	Observation	y	x	Observation	y	x
(53)	55	48	(90)	55	71	(127)	73	44	(164)	69	78
(54)	12	15	(91)	13	53	(128)	13	63	(165)	62	93
(55)	5	70	(92)	50	13	(129)	18	74	(166)	0	51
(56)	2	9	(93)	60	12	(130)	70	40	(167)	8	68
(57)	77	52	(94)	61	30	(131)	9	53	(168)	47	30
(58)	6	71	(95)	73	57	(132)	93	79	(169)	7	81
(59)	67	38	(96)	20	66	(133)	41	9	(170)	48	30
(60)	30	69	(97)	36	27	(134)	17	52	(171)	59	46
(61)	3	13	(98)	85	41	(135)	10	82	(172)	76	99
(62)	6	63	(99)	49	20	(136)	69	37	(173)	54	98
(63)	70	65	(100)	83	66	(137)	5	57	(174)	95	11
(64)	33	87	(101)	22	43	(138)	18	62	(175)	7	6
(65)	13	18	(102)	32	5	(139)	88	21	(176)	24	83
(66)	10	4	(103)	24	13	(140)	99	94	(177)	55	49
(67)	21	29	(104)	63	3	(141)	86	99	(178)	41	39
(68)	56	21	(105)	16	58	(142)	95	45	(179)	14	16
(69)	74	9	(106)	4	13	(143)	78	19	(180)	24	13
(70)	47	8	(107)	79	18	(144)	3	76	(181)	36	31
(71)	34	18	(108)	5	5	(145)	38	81	(182)	62	44
(72)	38	84	(109)	59	26	(146)	57	95	(183)	77	11
(73)	75	64	(110)	99	9	(147)	77	30	(184)	32	60
(74)	0	81	(111)	76	96	(148)	25	59	(185)	12	82
(75)	51	98	(112)	15	94	(149)	99	93	(186)	85	7
(76)	47	55	(113)	10	30	(150)	9	28	(187)	90	68
(77)	63	40	(114)	20	41	(151)	79	85	(188)	78	10
(78)	7	14	(115)	37	1	(152)	79	27	(189)	60	27
(79)	6	11	(116)	56	27	(153)	48	61	(190)	96	90
(80)	68	42	(117)	6	73	(154)	5	7	(191)	51	6
(81)	72	43	(118)	86	19	(155)	24	79	(192)	9	62
(82)	95	73	(119)	27	94	(156)	47	49	(193)	93	78
(83)	82	45	(120)	67	5	(157)	65	71	(194)	61	22
(84)	91	16	(121)	22	31	(158)	56	27	(195)	5	99
(85)	83	21	(122)	32	13	(159)	52	15	(196)	88	51
(86)	27	85	(123)	90	11	(160)	17	88	(197)	45	44
(87)	13	37	(124)	88	50	(161)	45	38	(198)	34	86
(88)	6	89	(125)	35	40	(162)	45	31	(199)	28	47
(89)	76	76	(126)	57	80	(163)	90	35	(200)	44	49

LINEAR EQUATIONS

Dependent and Predictor Variables

When two variables are examined for their correlation, it's usually for the purpose of using one to predict the other. Most correlation and regression studies are initiated based on the desire to examine and explain the changing value of this variable, which, in regression analysis, is called the *dependent variable*. The symbol chosen for the dependent variable is y. A second variable is identified that is believed to be associated with y and is called the *independent* or *predictor variable*; its symbol is x.

When only one predictor variable is identified, the analysis is called *simple regression*. When there are two or more predictor variables, a *multiple regression* analysis is being conducted (as Chapter 15 discusses).

The scatter diagram displays the *x-y* relationship in graphic terms. After the strength of this relationship has been measured with the correlation coefficient, the next step is to draw a straight line through the data points of the scatter diagram so that knowledge of the *x* variable can be used to predict the *y* variable.

Equation 14.4 is used to construct the straight line. The symbols β_0 (beta zero) and β_1 (beta one) represent the line's parameters; once they're specified, the line is fixed. The first parameter, β_0, is the *y*-intercept, or the point where the line crosses the *y* axis, the value of *y* when *x* is 0. The second parameter, β_1, is the slope of the line, or the amount by which *y* changes when *x* increases by one unit:

$$y = \beta_0 + \beta_1 x \tag{14.4}$$

where β_0 = *y*-intercept
          β_1 = Slope of the line

EXAMPLE 14.5   Suppose that $\beta_0 = 8$ and $\beta_1 = 3$. Using Equation 14.4, the linear equation is

$$y = \beta_0 + \beta_1 x$$
$$= 8 + 3x$$

If $x = 0$, then $y = 8$, which is the *y*-intercept (β_0):

$$y = 8 + 3(0) = 8$$

Note that as the value of *x* is increased by 1, the value of *y* increases by 3, which is the slope of the line (β_1):

$$y = 8 + 3(1) = 11 \qquad x = 1$$
$$y = 8 + 3(2) = 14 \qquad x = 2$$
$$y = 8 + 3(3) = 17 \qquad x = 3$$

FUNCTIONAL AND STATISTICAL MODELS

The *x-y* points determined by Equation 14.4 all lie on a straight line. This is considered a *functional* relationship. In plots *c* and *d* in Figure 14.2, the points don't all lie on a straight line. Such relationships are considered *statistical* relationships.

An important question in regression analysis is: Does a perfect relationship exist between the independent (*x*) and dependent (*y*) variables? For example, can the exact value of sales revenue (*y*) be predicted if price per unit (*x*) is specified? This is probably not possible, for several reasons. Sales depend on many variables other than price per unit—such as advertising expense, time of year, state of the economy, etc. In most cases, there's also some variation due strictly to chance or random error, which can't be modeled or explained.

Functional Model   If a model is constructed that hypothesizes an exact relationship between variables, it's called a **functional** or **deterministic model.** Consider the relation between dollar sales (y) of a particular book and number of units sold (x). If the selling price is \$8 per book, the relationship is

$$y = 0 + 8x$$

This equation represents a functional relationship between the variables *dollar sales* (y) and *units sold* (x). A perfect relationship exists. If 10 books are sold, sales revenue equals exactly \$80.

Based on the recognition that most real-world variables can't be predicted exactly, a model is constructed that hypothesizes a relationship between variables allowing for random error. Equation 14.5 is called a **statistical** or **probabilistic model**:

Statistical Model

$$y = \beta_0 + \beta_1 x + \varepsilon \tag{14.5}$$

where β_0 = y-intercept
        β_1 = Slope of the line
        ε = Error

In Equation 14.5, ε (the Greek letter epsilon) represents the error involved when an independent variable is used to predict the dependent variable. This error term accounts for independent variables that affect y but are not included in the model. It also accounts for chance, or random, variability. Thus, ε encompasses two kinds of error: model error (which means that all relevant independent variables aren't included) and chance or random error.

> A **functional model** hypothesizes an exact relationship between variables. A **statistical model** hypothesizes a functional relationship plus some random error.

The probability distribution of ε determines how well the regression model describes the relationship between the independent and dependent variables. Four key assumptions about the general form of the probability distribution of ε underlie the regression analysis procedures discussed in this chapter:

1. The probability distribution of ε is normal.
2. The variance of the probability distribution of ε is constant for all values of x.
3. The mean of the probability distribution of ε is 0. This assumption implies that the mean value of y for a given value of x is $E(y) = \beta_0 + \beta_1 x$.
4. The values of ε are independent of each other. This assumption implies that a random sample of objects has been selected from the population for measurement.

Figure 14.4 shows distributions of errors for three specific values of x. Note that the relative frequency distributions of the errors are normal, with a mean of 0 and a constant variance. The straight line in Figure 14.4 shows the means. It indicates the mean value $E(y)$ for a given value of x and is given by the equation $E(y) = \beta_0 + \beta_1 x$.

FIGURE 14.4 The Probability Distribution of ε

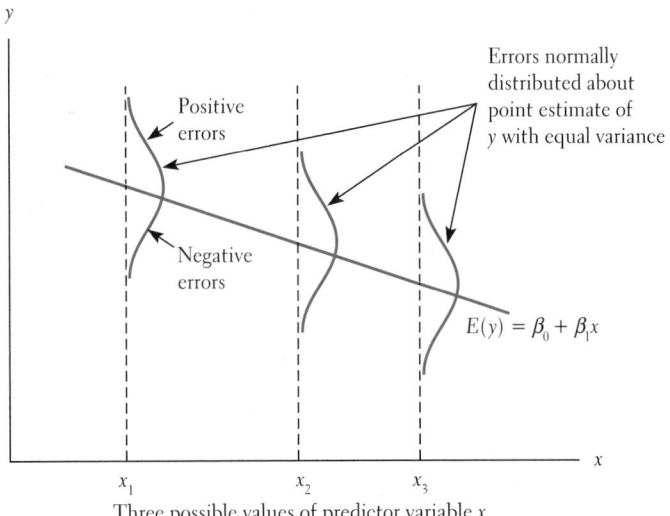

Three possible values of predictor variable x

The four assumptions make it possible for analysts to develop measures of reliability for the least squares estimators. Chapter 15 discusses techniques for checking the validity of these assumptions along with remedies to be applied when they appear to be invalid.

EXAMPLE 14.6 Suppose a bookstore conducts a 12-week experiment to determine the effect of advertising on sales revenue. The relationship between sales revenue (y) and advertising expenditure (x) is expressed as a statistical model:

$$y = \beta_0 + \beta_1(x) + \varepsilon$$
$$= 0 + 20(x) + \varepsilon$$

Note that the functional component ($20x$) of the model indicates that if $10 is spent on advertising, sales revenue will equal $200. However, the statistical model indicates that sales revenue isn't exactly related to advertising expenditure. That is, the random error component (ε) indicates that sales revenue may depend on variables other than advertising expenditure.

SAMPLE REGRESSION LINE

Sample Regression Line

Normally, the exact values of the regression parameters β_0, β_1, and ε are never actually known. From the sample data, estimates of these parameters are found, and the straight line that best fits the set of data points, called the **sample regression line,** is determined. Equation 14.6 uses b_0 and b_1 to estimate β_0 and β_1:

$$\hat{y} = b_0 + b_1 x \tag{14.6}$$

where $\hat{y}$ = Predicted value of the dependent variable
          x = Independent variable
          b_0 = Estimate of the population y-intercept
          b_1 = Estimate of the population line slope

The line determined by Equation 14.6 should pass through the data points so that the y value for a given value of x can be predicted. Note that $\hat{y}$, the predicted value of the dependent variable, is actually the mean y value for the given x value. Also note that for any specified x value in the sample, there are two corresponding y values: the actual, observed value of y corresponding to the observed x, and the predicted mean of y for this x. Therefore, (x, y) is a point on the scatter diagram, and $(x, \hat{y})$ is a point on the regression line $\hat{y} = b_0 + b_1 x$. The difference $(y - \hat{y})$ measures the error involved in predicting the dependent variable, and is discussed in the next section. Note that the line will always pass through a point determined by the means, $(\bar{x}, \bar{y})$.

> The **sample regression line** is a straight line that best fits a set of sample x-y data points.

The definition of the regression line isn't really adequate. The term *best fits* could be interpreted in different ways. Specifically, the method used to fit a straight line to the collected x-y data values needs to be defined.

Method of Least Squares   The method commonly used to determine the sample regression line for a collection of x-y pairs is called the **method of least squares.** This is a mathematical procedure to find the equation for the straight line that minimizes the sum of the squared distances between the line and the data points, as measured in the vertical (y) direction.

> The **method of least squares** determines the equation for the straight line that minimizes the sum of the squared vertical distances between the data points and the line.

The derivation of the equations needed to find the y-intercept and slope of a regression line using the method of least squares requires the use of calculus. This derivation is found in Appendix B; only the results are presented here. Equations 14.7 and 14.8 are used in regression analysis to find the slope and y-intercept of the sample regression line:

$$b_1 = \frac{n\Sigma xy - (\Sigma x)(\Sigma y)}{n\Sigma x^2 - (\Sigma x)^2} \tag{14.7}$$

where Σx = Sum of the x values
         Σy = Sum of the y values
         Σx^2 = Sum of the squared x values
         $(\Sigma x)^2$ = Sum of the x values squared
         Σxy = Sum of the product of x and y for each paired observation
         n = Number of x-y observations

$$b_0 = \frac{\Sigma y}{n} - \frac{b_1 \Sigma x}{n} \tag{14.8}$$

where Σx = Sum of the x values
         Σy = Sum of the y values
         b_1 = Slope of the line computed using Equation 14.7
         n = Number of x-y observations

It should be noted that Equation 14.8 is frequently written as $b_0 = \bar{y} - b_1\bar{x}$.

Equations 14.7 and 14.8 call for several familiar sums. If you've already calculated the correlation coefficient, these sums are available. Almost all data analysis computer packages calculate both the correlation coefficient and the regression equation. Many handheld calculators can calculate the slope and intercept of the regression equation along with the correlation coefficient. (Note that the term *regression coefficient* is synonymous with slope and will be used throughout the rest of the text.)

EXAMPLE 14.7   Amy Green, Green Garden Company president, wants to see if her company's weekly sales volume is related to some other variable. Her company sells garden supplies through its store in a city's suburbs. "1990 Buyers Guide" in *Organic Gardening* (March 1990) got her thinking about how to increase sales.

Amy randomly selects eight weeks from the past two years and records weekly sales volume in thousands of dollars. After reviewing the situation, she decides that the number of TV ads for the store run per week might be correlated with sales; so she also records this variable for each selected week. Table 14.3 presents the collected sample data along with the sums necessary for further calculations.

TABLE 14.3   Regression Analysis Calculations for Example 14.7

	y	x	xy	x^2	y^2
	125	3	375	9	15,625
	152	5	760	25	23,104
	131	4	524	16	17,161
	133	4	532	16	17,689
	142	5	710	25	20,164
	116	3	348	9	13,456
	127	3	381	9	16,129
	163	6	978	36	26,569
Sums:	1,089	33	4,608	145	149,897

$n = 8$
$\bar{y} = 1{,}089/8 = 136.125$
$\bar{x} = 33/8 = 4.125$

The sums in Table 14.3 are used in Equations 14.1, 14.2, 14.3, 14.7, and 14.8 to examine the correlation between x and y and to calculate the sample regression line. First, the correlation coefficient and t value are calculated:

$$r = \frac{8(4{,}608) - (33)(1{,}089)}{\sqrt{8(145) - (33)^2}\,\sqrt{8(149{,}897) - (1{,}089)^2}} = .956$$

There appears to be a strong positive correlation between x and y since r = .956. However, a sample of only eight data points has been examined. Can it be said that the correlation in the population differs from 0 based on such a small sample? To answer this question, a hypothesis test is conducted at the .01 significance level.

The standard error of r is

$$s_r = \sqrt{\frac{1 - (.956)^2}{8 - 2}} = .12$$

The t value is

$$t = \frac{r - \rho}{s_r} = \frac{.956 - 0}{.12} = 7.97$$

The critical t value from the t table for 6 (n − 2 = 8 − 2 = 6) degrees of freedom in the .01 column is 3.707. Since the calculated t value (7.97) exceeds this value, the null hypothesis of no population correlation is rejected at the .01 significance level.

Next, the sample regression line is calculated using the method of least squares:

$$b_1 = \frac{n\Sigma xy - (\Sigma x)(\Sigma y)}{n\Sigma x^2 - (\Sigma x)^2} = \frac{8(4{,}608) - (33)(1{,}089)}{8(145) - (33)^2} = 13.056$$

$$b_0 = \frac{\Sigma y}{n} - \frac{b_1 \Sigma x}{n} = \frac{1{,}089}{8} - \frac{13.056(33)}{8} = 82.268$$

$$\hat{y} = 82.268 + 13.056x$$

Amy can now interpret the values in the sample regression equation. The y-intercept, 82.268, is the expected value of y if x = 0. Since Green Garden runs TV ads each week, this is a case where the interpretation of the y-intercept isn't useful. Most situations are like this, but there are some where useful information can be gained from knowing the expected y value if x is 0.

The interpretation of the slope of the regression line usually produces useful information. From the regression equation, Amy can see that for each increase of one unit in x, the y value is expected to increase by an average of 13.056. In practical terms, the regression equation suggests that for each additional TV ad run by Green Garden, an average of 13.056 additional sales dollars (in thousands) can be expected. This information may be useful to Amy Green in planning next year's advertising budget.

MINITAB can be used to run regression analysis problems. The MINITAB commands to solve Example 14.7 are:

```
MTB > READ C1-C2
DATA> 125 3
```

```
DATA> 152 5
DATA> 131 4
DATA> 133 4
DATA> 142 5
DATA> 116 3
DATA> 127 3
DATA> 163 6
DATA> END
      8 ROWS READ

MTB > NAME C1 'SALES' C2 'ADS'
MTB > CORR C1 C2

Correlation of SALES and ADS = 0.956

MTB > REGRESS C1 ON 1 PREDICTOR C2

The regression equation is
SALES = 82.3 + 13.1 ADS

Predictor        Coef      Stdev      t ratio        p
Constant       82.268      7.000        11.75    0.000
ADS            13.056      1.644         7.94    0.000

s = 4.899    R-sq = 91.3%    R-sq(adj) = 89.9%

Analysis of Variance

SOURCE         DF          SS          MS         F        P
Regression      1      1512.9      1512.9     63.05    0.000
Error           6       144.0        24.0
Total           7      1656.9

MTB > WRITE 'CH14EX8.DAT' C1-C2
MTB > STOP
```

Note that the READ command is used to input the data instead of the SET command. The READ command puts the sales variable into C1 and the TV ads variable into C2. The NAME command is used to name the columns. The CORR command provides the correlation coefficient for these two variables. The REGRESS command is used to develop a regression analysis with sales as the dependent (y) variable (C1) and TV ads as the independent (x) variable (C2). Finally, the WRITE command is used to store the contents of columns C1 and C2 in a file called CH14EX8.DAT.

EXERCISES

13. What is the difference between an independent variable and a dependent variable?

14. What is the difference between a functional model and a statistical model?

15. If $r = 0$, what is the slope for the regression equation?

16. Which of the following situations is inconsistent?

    a. $\hat{y} = 500 + 0.01x$ and $r = .75$

    b. $\hat{y} = 200 + 0.8x$ and $r = -.80$

    c. $\hat{y} = -10 + 2x$ and $r = .50$

    d. $\hat{y} = -8 - 3x$ and $r = -.95$

17. (This question refers to Exercise 8.) Would it be appropriate for Donna to develop a regression equation to predict annual profits based on the amount she has requested for her department? If so, compute the regression equation.

18. (This question refers to Exercise 10.) Would it be appropriate for Ralph to develop a regression equation to predict the number of absent days based on an employee's age? If so, compute the regression equation.

19. AT&T (American Telephone and Telegraph) earnings per share are estimated using GNP (gross national product). The regression equation is $\hat{y} = 0.058 + 0.05x$, where GNP is measured in billions of dollars.

    a. Interpret the slope.

    b. Interpret the y-intercept.

20. James Dobbins, Atlanta Transit Authority maintenance supervisor, must determine whether there's a positive relationship between a bus's annual maintenance cost and its age. If such a relationship exists, James feels that he can do a better job of predicting the annual bus maintenance budget. He collects the following data:

Bus	Maintenance cost ($), y	Age (years), x
1	859	8
2	682	5
3	471	3
4	708	9
5	1,094	11
6	224	2
7	320	1
8	651	8
9	1,049	12

    a. Plot a scatter diagram.

    b. What kind of relationship exists between these two variables?

    c. Compute the correlation coefficient.

    d. Test the correlation coefficient at the .05 significance level.

    e. Should James use regression analysis to predict the annual bus maintenance budget?

    f. Determine the sample regression analysis equation.

    g. Estimate the annual maintenance cost for a five-year-old bus.

21. Anna Sheehan (manager of the Spendwise supermarket chain) would like to be able to predict paperback book sales per week based on the amount of shelf display space (in feet) provided. Anna gathers a sample of 11 weeks:

Week	Number of books sold, y	Feet of shelf space, x
1	275	6.8
2	142	3.3
3	168	4.1
4	197	4.2
5	215	4.8
6	188	3.9
7	241	4.9
8	295	7.7

Week	Number of books sold, y	Feet of shelf space, x
9	125	3.1
10	266	5.9
11	200	5.0

   a. Plot a scatter diagram.

   b. What kind of relationship exists between these two variables?

   c. Compute the correlation coefficient.

   d. Test the correlation coefficient at the .10 significance level.

   e. Should Anna use regression analysis to predict paperback book sales?

   f. Determine the sample regression equation.

   g. Estimate paperback book sales for a week in which four feet of shelf space are provided.

RESIDUALS

Residuals

The difference between an observed y and the mean of y predicted from the sample regression equation, $\hat{y}$, is called a **residual**. Equation 14.9 is used to compute a residual:

$$e = y - \hat{y} \tag{14.9}$$

where e = Residual
          y = Actual value of y
          $\hat{y}$ = Estimated value of the dependent variable using the sample
                regression equation

It should be emphasized that the residual is the vertical deviation of the observed y from the sample regression line, which is known. The residual is different from the model error term, ε, which is the vertical deviation of y from the *unknown* population regression line and, hence, is unknown.

> A **residual** is the difference between an actual y and the value, $\hat{y}$, predicted using the sample regression equation.

EXAMPLE 14.8 Figure 14.5 presents a scatter diagram for the data used in this example (introduced in Example 14.7). The regression equation that best fits these data points is

$$\hat{y} = 82.268 + 13.056x$$

The first two columns in Table 14.4 show the original x-y data points. The $\hat{y}$ value predicted using the x value for each data pair and the regression equation are shown

FIGURE 14.5 Residuals for Example 14.8

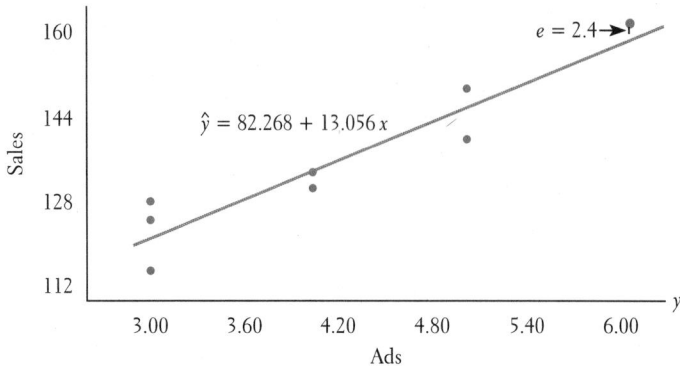

TABLE 14.4 Standard Error of Estimate Calculation for Example 14.9

y	x	$\hat{y}$	$(y - \hat{y})$	$(y - \hat{y})^2$
125	3	121.4	3.6	12.96
152	5	147.6	4.4	19.36
131	4	134.5	−3.5	12.25
133	4	134.5	−1.5	2.25
142	5	147.6	−5.6	31.36
116	3	121.4	−5.4	29.16
127	3	121.4	5.6	31.36
163	6	160.6	2.4	5.30

Sum: 144.0

$$\hat{y} = 82.268 + 13.056x$$

$$s_{y \cdot x} = \sqrt{\frac{\Sigma(y - \hat{y})^2}{n - 2}} = \sqrt{\frac{144.0}{6}} = 4.9$$

in column 3. For example, the last $\hat{y}$ value is calculated from the regression equation using the sample x value 6:

$$\hat{y} = 82.268 + 13.056(6) = 160.604$$

The residual for each pair of observations is in Table 14.4's fourth column. The residual for the last pair of observations (163,6) is

$$e = y - \hat{y}$$
$$= 163.0 - 160.6 = 2.4 \text{ (see Figure 14.5)}$$

STANDARD ERROR OF ESTIMATE

Standard Error of Estimate

The standard deviation of a simple data collection is used to measure the variability, or scatter of data values, about their mean. The **standard error of estimate** is used to measure the variability, or scatter, of the observed sample y values around the sample regression line. It measures the standard or typical difference between the values predicted by the regression equation and the actual y values. This can be seen by the formula for the standard error of estimate:

$$s_{y \cdot x} = \sqrt{\frac{\Sigma(y - \hat{y})^2}{n - 2}}$$ (14.10)

where $s_{y \cdot x}$ = Standard error of estimate
y = Sample y values
$\hat{y}$ = Values of y calculated from the regression equation
n = Sample size

> The **standard error of estimate** is a measure of the variability, or scatter, of the observed sample y values around the regression line.

The $\hat{y}$ values are calculated by substituting the x value of each data pair into the regression equation. The differences between these regression equation estimates and the actual y values (i.e., the residuals) are squared, added, and divided by the degrees of freedom $(n - 2)$. The square root of this value is the standard error of estimate. The value $(n - 2)$ represents the number of degrees of freedom around the fitted regression line. Two degrees of freedom are lost because b_0 and b_1 are used as estimates of β_0 and β_1 in the sample regression equation.

EXAMPLE 14.9 The data used in this example were introduced in Example 14.7. The fourth column of Table 14.4 shows the residuals for each pair of observations. The last column shows the sum of squared residuals (sum of squares error) between the $\hat{y}$ values calculated from the regression equation and the actual y values. Incidentally, this is the value that is minimized by the least squares procedure. If any y-intercept and slope values other than 82.268 and 13.056 were used, the resulting sum of squared residuals would be larger than 144.

When the sum of squared residuals (sum of squares error) is divided by the degrees of freedom and the square root taken, the result is the standard error of estimate. As Table 14.4 shows, for this example the standard error is 4.9. It can be said that the typical or standard difference between the sample y values and their regression line estimates is 4.9 (in thousands of dollars).

EXAMPLE 14.10 According to an article by Adel Novin (1992) in *Management Accounting*, regression analysis is one of the few quantitative techniques available for determining and analyzing the extent of the relationship between overhead costs and various cost drivers.[3] Adel collected data from 12 consecutive months on overhead

---

[3]A. M. Novin, "Applying Overhead: How to Find the Right Bases and Rates," *Management Accounting*, March 1992, pp. 40–43.

costs and machine hours. He used a Lotus 1-2-3 worksheet to develop a regression equation that used machine hours to estimate monthly overhead costs.

$$\hat{y} = 72{,}794 + 74.72x$$
$$s_{y \cdot x} = 9{,}799$$
$$n = 12$$
$$r = .877$$

The y-intercept ($72,794) is an estimate of total monthly fixed overhead costs. The slope of the regression equation ($74.72) is the rate for the application of variable overhead costs (i.e., $74.72 per machine hour). For each additional machine hour (x), monthly overhead costs (y) can be expected to increase by an average of $74.72.

Adel plans to use the regression equation to forecast monthly overhead costs using machine hours. First, however, he notes the size of the standard error of estimate: $9,799. He interprets this to mean since the sample y values (overhead costs) typically differ from this regression estimate by this amount, he can expect his future forecast values of y to have a similar error. The size of this standard error of estimate troubles him since accurate overhead cost forecasts are needed.

PREDICTION AND CONFIDENCE INTERVALS

The sample regression equation is frequently used to make forecasts for y. If a given value of x is substituted in the regression equation, the expected value of y can be found. This y value is similar to the point estimate of the mean discussed in Chapter 8. That is, a single numerical estimate of y is produced without any indication of its accuracy.

A point estimate provides no sense of how far off it may be from the population parameter. To determine that information, a prediction or confidence interval is developed. In fact, analysts can choose between two types of intervals: the **prediction interval** (for a particular value of y) or the **confidence interval** estimate (for the expected value of y). Prediction intervals are used to predict a particular y value for a given value of x. Confidence intervals are used to estimate the mean value of y for a specific value of x.

Prediction Interval

Confidence Interval

Whenever we want to predict one particular value of the dependent variable, given a specific value of the independent variable, we calculate a prediction interval:

$$\hat{y} \pm t\, s_{\hat{y} \cdot x} \tag{14.11}$$

where $\hat{y}$ = Sample regression estimate of y
   t = Value from t distribution based on $n - 2$ degrees of freedom for a given prediction level
   $s_{\hat{y} \cdot x}$ = Estimated standard error of the prediction

The estimated standard error of the prediction $s_{\hat{y} \cdot x}$ is an estimate of the standard deviation of the sampling distribution for the estimator y:

$$s_{\hat{y} \cdot x} = s_{y \cdot x} \sqrt{1 + \frac{1}{n} + \frac{(x_p - \bar{x})^2}{\Sigma(x_i - \bar{x})^2}} \tag{14.12}$$

where $s_{\hat{y}\cdot x}$ = Estimated standard error of the prediction

$s_{y\cdot x}$ = Standard error of estimate

x_p = The given value of x

$\bar{x}$ = The mean of x

$\Sigma(x_i - \bar{x})^2$ = The sum of squares total for the x variable

The sum of squares total for the x variable is computed using

$$\Sigma(x_i - \bar{x})^2 = \Sigma x_i^2 - \frac{(\Sigma x_i)^2}{n}$$

The standard error of estimate $(s_{y\cdot x})$ in Equation 14.12 measures the dispersion of sample data points around the sample regression line. The two terms after the 1 under the square-root sign [$1/n$ and $(x_p - \bar{x})^2/\Sigma(x_i - \bar{x})^2$] measure the dispersion of many sample regression lines around the true population regression line. Example 14.11 illustrates the use of a prediction interval.

EXAMPLE 14.11 Amy Green, Green Garden Company president, wants to estimate sales for next week if she were to run six TV ads. Using the data and the regression equation computed in Example 14.7, she develops a point estimate for next week's sales: $y = 82.268 + 13.056(6) = 160.604$. But Amy isn't satisfied with her prediction. She doesn't know anything about this estimate's accuracy so she uses Equations 14.11 and 14.12 to develop a 95% prediction interval to predict next week's sales if six TV ads are run.

The standard error of the prediction is

$$s_{\hat{y}\cdot x} = s_{y\cdot x}\sqrt{1 + \frac{1}{n} + \frac{(x_p - \bar{x})^2}{\Sigma(x_i - \bar{x})^2}}$$

$$= (4.9)\sqrt{1 + \frac{1}{8} + \frac{(6 - 4.125)^2}{8.875}}$$

$$= (4.9)\sqrt{1 + .125 + .396}$$

$$= (4.9)(1.233)$$

$$= 6.042$$

The computation for the sum of squares total for the x variable is

$$\Sigma(x_i - \bar{x})^2 = \Sigma x_i^2 - \frac{(\Sigma x_i)^2}{n} = 145 - \frac{33^2}{8} = 8.875$$

The prediction interval is

$\hat{y} \pm t\, s_{\hat{y}\cdot x}$

$160.604 \pm 2.447\,(6.042)$

160.604 ± 14.788

145.816 to 175.392

Amy predicts with 95% confidence that weekly sales next week will fall in the interval $145,816 to $175,392 if six TV ads are run.

Instead of trying to predict the outcome of a single experiment at the given x value, an analyst may want to attempt to estimate the mean result of a very large number of experiments at the given x value. The same value is used to predict the y value for a given x value. Equation 14.13 is used to develop a confidence interval:

$$\hat{y} \pm t\, s_{\hat{\mu} \cdot x} \tag{14.13}$$

For the confidence interval, the estimated standard error of estimate, $s_{\hat{\mu} \cdot x}$, is used as the estimate of the standard deviation of the sampling distribution for the estimator y. Amy computes the standard deviation of estimate as

$$s_{\hat{\mu} \cdot x} = s_{y \cdot x} \sqrt{\frac{1}{n} + \frac{(x_p - \bar{x})^2}{\Sigma (x_i - \bar{x})^2}} \tag{14.14}$$

Unlike Equation 14.12, Equation 14.14 doesn't include the 1 under the square root sign. As a result, it produces an interval that's narrower than the prediction interval. This is reasonable, given that predicting a single value is more difficult than estimating the average of a population of values. Figure 14.6 illustrates the difference between prediction intervals and confidence intervals.

Example 14.12 shows the use of a confidence interval.

FIGURE 14.6   Prediction Intervals for Individual Values and Confidence Intervals for Mean Values

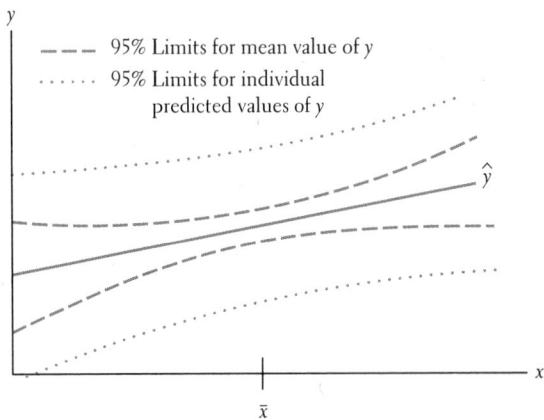

Prediction intervals are used to predict a particular y value for a given value of x. **Confidence intervals** are used to estimate the mean value of y for a specific value of x.

EXAMPLE 14.12 This example is a continuation of Example 14.12. Amy Green decides that it might be more informative to develop a 95% confidence interval for mean weekly sales when six TV ads are run.

The estimated standard error of estimate is

$$s_{\hat{\mu}\cdot x} = s_{y\cdot x}\sqrt{\frac{1}{n} + \frac{(x_p - \bar{x})^2}{\Sigma(x_i - \bar{x})^2}}$$

$$= (4.9)\sqrt{\frac{1}{8} + \frac{(6 - 4.125)^2}{8.875}}$$

$$= (4.9)\sqrt{.125 + .396}$$

$$= (4.9)(0.722)$$

$$= 3.538$$

The confidence interval is

$$\hat{y} \pm t\, s_{\hat{\mu}\cdot x}$$

$$160.604 \pm 2.447\,(3.538)$$

$$160.604 \pm 8.654$$

$$151.950 \text{ to } 169.258$$

Amy is 95% confident that the interval from $151,950 to $169,258 contains the mean sales revenue for a week when six TV ads are run. One reason why the intervals are so large is the small number of data points used to fit the least squares line. The width of the prediction interval could be reduced by using a larger number of data points.

Note that the prediction interval for an individual value of y will always be wider than the confidence interval for a mean value of y. The error in estimating the mean value of y, for a given value of x, is the distance between the least squares line and the true line of means. In contrast, the error in predicting some future value of y is the sum of two errors: the error of estimating the mean value of y plus the random error that's a component of the value of y to be predicted. Note that in Equations 14.12 and 14.14, both the error of prediction and error of estimation take their smallest values when $x_p = \bar{x}$. The further x_p lies from $\bar{x}$, the larger will be the errors of prediction and estimation. This concept is seen in Figure 14.6, which shows prediction intervals for individual values and confidence intervals for mean values.

Also note that the standard normal z value can be used in place of t in Equations 14.11 and 14.13 for sample sizes of 30 or more.

The MINITAB commands to solve Examples 14.8, 14.9, 14.11, and 14.12 are shown in the MINITAB Computer package section. Note that the data were stored in a file called CH14EX8.DAT at the end of Example 14.7.

Exercises

22. What does a residual measure?

23. What is the difference between a residual and the model error term?

24. What does the standard error of estimate measure?

25. If two variables have a correlation coefficient (r) of 1, what is the standard error of estimate $(s_{y \cdot x})$?

26. Can the standard error of estimate $(s_{y \cdot x})$ ever exceed the standard deviation of the dependent variable (s_y)? Can the standard error of estimate $(s_{y \cdot x})$ ever equal the standard deviation of the dependent variable (s_y)? Explain your answers.

27. What is the difference between a prediction interval and a confidence interval?

28. This question refers to Exercise 20. Compute the residual for each bus. Compute the standard error of the estimate. Interpret $s_{y \cdot x}$ in terms of the variables used in this exercise.

29. This question refers to Exercise 20. Develop both a 95% prediction interval and a 95% confidence interval for a 10-year-old bus.

30. Mario Padilla (an accountant for Palmer Furniture Corporation) must determine whether overhead can be estimated based on the number of chairs produced. Mario collects the following monthly data on overhead expenses and chairs produced at seven different plants:

Plant	Overhead expenses y	Number of chairs x
1	$576	112
2	497	122
3	789	147
4	862	173
5	361	94
6	688	151
7	532	109

a. Plot the data on a scatter diagram.

b. Determine the sample regression equation.

c. When an extra chair is produced, what is the average increase in overhead expense?

d. Compute the residual for plant 1.

e. Compute the standard error of estimate.

f. Interpret $s_{y \cdot x}$ in terms of the variables used in this exercise.

g. Compute a point estimate of the overhead expense if 150 chairs are produced.

h. Compute a 95% prediction interval for your prediction for part g.

i. Compute a 95% confidence interval for your prediction for part g.

j. What should Mario conclude?

31. Anna Sheehan, manager of the Spendwise supermarket chain, would like to determine whether a relationship exists between the time it takes to check out a customer and the amount the person purchases. Anna wants to study current purchase amounts before trying such new techniques in future advertising. She collects data for a sample of 12 customers:

Customer	Checkout time (minutes) y	Purchases (rounded to nearest dollar) x
1	3.1	$ 35
2	1.1	14
3	.4	4
4	6.4	78
5	5.8	81
6	8.4	106
7	4.9	61
8	7.9	66
9	2.1	22
10	5.9	54
11	.8	12
12	1.3	19

a. Plot the data on a scatter diagram.

b. Determine the sample regression equation.

c. Compute the residual for customer 12.

d. Compute the standard error of estimate.

e. Interpret $s_{y \cdot x}$ in terms of the variables used in this exercise.

f. Compute a point estimate of the checkout time for a $75 purchase.

g. Compute a 90% prediction interval for your prediction for part f.

h. Compute a 90% confidence interval for your prediction for part f.

i. What should Anna conclude?

COEFFICIENT OF SIMPLE DETERMINATION

Coefficient of Determination

A statistic consulted frequently in regression analysis is the **coefficient of simple determination** (r^2). It is useful because it measures the percentage of the variability in the dependent variable, y, that can be explained by the predictor variable, x.

> The **coefficient of simple determination**, r^2, measures the percentage of the variability in y that can be explained by the predictor variable, x.

It is not a coincidence that the same symbol is used for the coefficient of simple determination (r^2) and the correlation coefficient (r). In fact, the correlation coefficient squared equals the coefficient of simple determination. If the correlation coefficient between two variables is .80, for example, then $r^2 = .64$ or 64% $(.80^2 = .64)$.

To calculate r^2, simply square the correlation coefficient, r. However, to understand why r^2 measures the percentage of the variability in y explained by x, we must understand the formula defining r^2. First, a few terms need to be explained.

The amount of total deviation in the dependent variable is called the *sum of squares total* (SST). This value measures the variability of y *without* taking into consideration the predictor variable, x. The SST is the sum of the squared differences between the sample y values and their mean, as shown by Equation 14.15. If this sum is divided by the appropriate number of degrees of freedom $(n - 1)$, the variance of y results. If the square root of this variance is computed, the standard deviation of y results. These computations are defined by the equations for the standard deviation of a single variable in Chapter 4.

$$\text{SST} = \sum_{i=1}^{n} (y_i - \bar{y})^2 \tag{14.15}$$

where   SST = Sum of squares total
y_i = *i*th value of the dependent variable
$\bar{y}$ = Mean of the dependent variable

EXAMPLE 14.13   The data used in this example were introduced in Example 14.7. The sum of squares total (SST) is computed in Table 14.5, where the mean of y, 136.125, is subtracted from each y value, and the difference is squared. These squared differences are then summed. The sum of squares total (SST) is 1,656.877. Therefore, the standard deviation of the y variable (s_y) is

$$s_y = \sqrt{\frac{\Sigma(y - \bar{y})^2}{n - 1}} = \sqrt{\frac{1{,}656.877}{8 - 1}} = 15.4$$

TABLE 14.5   Sum of Squares Total Calculation for Example 14.14

y	$\bar{y}$	$(y - \bar{y})$	$(y - \bar{y})^2$
125	136.125	−11.125	123.765
152	136.125	15.875	252.016
131	136.125	−5.125	26.266
133	136.125	−3.125	9.766
142	136.125	5.875	34.516
116	136.125	−20.125	405.016
127	136.125	−9.125	83.266
163	136.125	26.875	722.266
	Sums:	0.000	1,656.877

Figure 14.7*a* plots the data in Table 14.4 on a scatter diagram. Figure 14.7*b* shows the case where x contributes no information and the mean of y is used to predict y $(\bar{y} = \hat{y})$. Figure 14.7*c* shows the case where knowledge of x is used to predict y using the regression equation $\hat{y} = b_0 + b_1x$.

The least squares regression line minimizes the *sum of squares error* (SSE). The SSE measures the variability of the sample y values around $\hat{y}$. It represents the amount of deviation in the dependent variable that is *not* explained by the regression equation. If

FIGURE 14.7   Measuring the Sum of Squares Error for Two Cases

a. Scatter diagram of data presented in Table 14.4

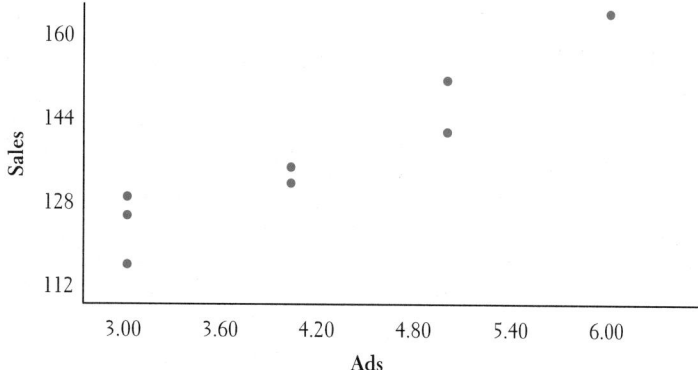

b. Case when *x* contributes no information for predicting y, $\bar{y} = \hat{y}$.

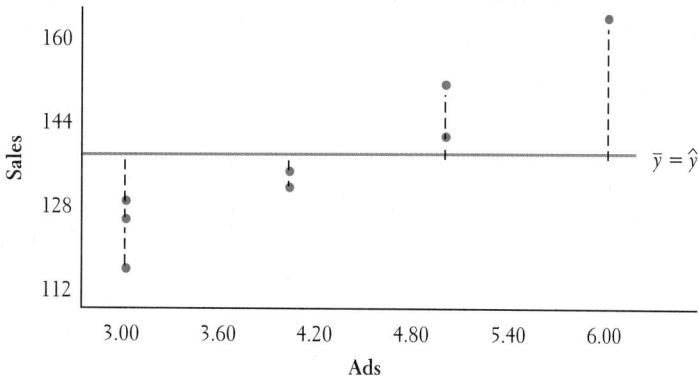

c. Case when knowledge of *x* contributes to predicting y, $\hat{y} = b_0 + b_1 x$.

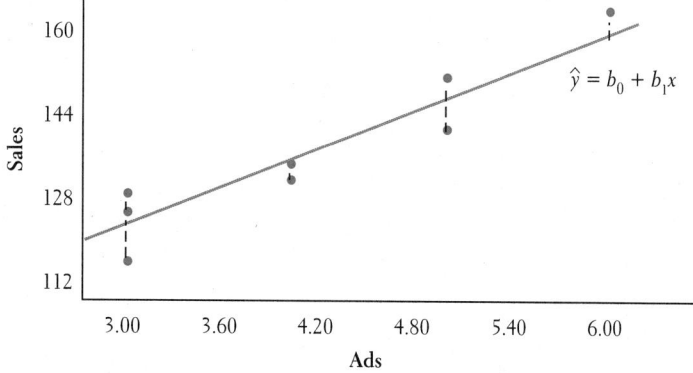

this sum is divided by the appropriate number of degrees of freedom $(n - 2)$, the unexplained variance of y results. The square root of this unexplained variance is the standard error of estimate:

$$\text{SSE} = \sum_{i=1}^{n} (y_i - \hat{y})^2 \tag{14.16}$$

where   SSE = Sum of squares error
        y_i = ith value of the dependent variable
        $\hat{y}$ = Estimated y value for each given x value

The amount of deviation in the dependent variable explained by the regression equation is called the *sum of squares regression* (SSR).

$$\text{SSR} = \text{SST} - \text{SSE} \tag{14.17}$$

where   SSR = Sum of squares regression
        SST = Sum of squares total
        SSE = Sum of squares error

The equation for r^2, the percentage of the variability in the dependent variable, y, that can be explained by the predictor variable, x, can now be defined.

$$r^2 = 1 - \frac{\Sigma(y - \hat{y})^2}{\Sigma(y - \bar{y})^2} \tag{14.18}$$

or

$$r^2 = 1 - \frac{\text{SSE}}{\text{SST}}$$

The ratio following the minus sign represents the percentage of the variability of y that is still unexplained by the regression equation. Since this ratio is the percentage that is *unexplained* by x and the regression equation, 1 minus this value is the percentage that is *explained*. The coefficient of simple determination, r^2, thus measures the percentage of variability in y that is explained when x is used to predict y.

EXAMPLE 14.14   The data used in this example were introduced in Example 14.7. The summations in Tables 14.4 and 14.5 can be inserted in Equation 14.18 to calculate r^2. From Table 14.4, the sum of the squared differences (residuals) between the y values and their regression equation predictions, SSE, is 144 (the numerator of the ratio in Equation 14.18). The denominator computed in Example 14.14, SST = 1,656.88, measures the total extent of variability of y. As shown in Table 14.5, it is the sum of the squared differences between the sample y values and their own mean. Amy then calculates r^2:

$$r^2 = 1 - \frac{\text{SSE}}{\text{SST}} = 1 - \frac{144}{1,656.88} = 1 - .09 = .91$$

When y is predicted using only knowledge of its mean (Figure 14.7b), the total sum of squares or unexplained deviation is 1,656.88. When y is predicted using knowledge of the linear relationship between x and y ($r = .956$) (Figure 14.7c), the sum of squares error or unexplained deviation is reduced to 144. If the ratio of these two values is expressed as a percentage, we can say that only 9% (144/1,656.88) of the variability of y remains unexplained after information on the linear relationship between x and y has been introduced. Therefore, the other 91% ($1 - .09 = .91$) is explained by knowledge of the linear relationship between x and y ($r = .956$). These calculations illustrate the previous definition of r^2.

Since r^2 is the correlation coefficient squared, that is, a number between -1 and $+1$ squared, it must be a number between 0 and $+1$. This is true for all percentages expressed in decimal form and is why r^2 is interpreted as the *percentage* of the variability of y that is explained by x; r^2 is one of the most frequently consulted statistics in regression analysis because it so briefly and accurately reflects the ability of the chosen predictor variable, x, to explain the variability of y.

Figure 14.8 illustrates the coefficient of simple determination, r^2. This figure shows a particular x value along with the average value of y ($\bar{y}$), the regression prediction value for y ($\hat{y}$), and the actual value of y (y). Without knowledge of x, we predict an unknown y value to equal the mean of y. That is, $\bar{y}$ is the best estimate of any unknown value of y. However, if a linear relationship between x and y has been specified, the sample regression equation can be used to predict y. Thus, for any specific value of x, we use $\hat{y}$ rather than $\bar{y}$. Knowledge of the linear relationship between x and y generally produces more accurate predictions of y.

Figure 14.8 also shows how the deviation is explained for a specific x, y data point that lies above the mean. If the linear relationship between x and y is unknown, the mean of y is used to predict y. The total deviation to be explained is the difference

FIGURE 14.8 Explained and Unexplained Variation of y

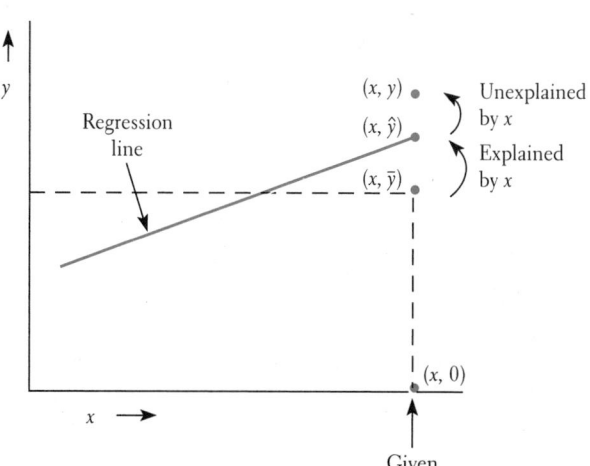

between the actual value of y and its mean $(y - \bar{y})$. Some of this difference is explained by the fact that x is a fairly large value. Since the regression line has a positive slope, a large value of x is associated with a large value of y. The difference, $\hat{y} - \bar{y}$ is explained by the linear relationship between the given x value and y ($r = .956$).

However, y isn't equal to $\hat{y}$; it lies above this value. The distance $y - \hat{y}$ is *not* explained by the linear relationship between x and y. If it were, the x-y value would lie on the regression equation line. This difference is explained by independent variables that affect y, but aren't included in the model, and also by chance, or random, variability, which can't be explained. Of course, the analyst isn't interested in a single data point, but in all the sample data. Equation 14.16 sums the differences for all the data points.

EXAMPLE 14.15 Consider the last data point listed, ($x = 6$, $y = 163$). If the linear relationship between x and y was not known, the best estimate of y would be its mean (136.1). The distance between the actual value of y and its mean is

$$(y - \bar{y}) = (163.0 - 136.1) = 26.9$$

In Example 14.7, a high positive linear relationship ($r = .956$) was found between the number of television ads run per week (x) and weekly sales (y). This correlation implies that if a large number of ads are run next week, sales will be higher than the weekly average ($\bar{y} = 136.1$).

Table 14.4 used the sample regression line to estimate y for each week based on knowledge of the number of TV ads run that week. Six ads were run during the last week, so sales were predicted to be $160,604 (see Example 14.9). The high positive linear relationship between x and y has allowed the analyst to explain a large amount of the variation in the prediction of y (i.e., it has reduced the unexplained deviation from 26.9 to 2.4):

$$(y - \hat{y}) = 163.0 - 160.6 = 2.4$$

The r^2 value of .914 ($.956^2$) indicates that 91.4% of the variance in the weekly sales variable can be explained by the strong linear relationship with the number of TV ads run during the week.

EXERCISES

32. What does the coefficient of simple determination measure?

33. Why is it useful to know both r and r^2?

34. What correlation between x and y is required for the assertion that 85% of the variance of y can be explained by knowledge of x?

35. Mary Union owns a gas station in Cleveland, Ohio. Mary has developed the following regression equation based on the weekly sales of unleaded gas:

$$\hat{y} = 100 - 5x, \qquad n = 64$$

where $\hat{y}$ = Estimate of volume of unleaded gas sold (thousands of gallons)
  x = Price of unleaded gas

a. Interpret the regression coefficient.

b. Compute a point estimate of the weekly sales volume of unleaded gas if the price is 95 cents.

36. Ed Bogdanski, owner of the American Precast Company, has hired you as a part-time analyst. Ed was extremely pleased when you uncovered a positive relationship between the number of building permits issued and the amount of work available to his company. Now he wonders if it's possible to use knowledge of interest rates on first mortgages to predict the number of building permits that will be issued each month. You collect a random sample of data covering nine months:

Month	Building permits, y	Interest rate, x
1	786	10.2%
2	494	12.6
3	289	13.5
4	892	9.7
5	343	10.8
6	888	9.5
7	509	10.9
8	987	9.2
9	187	14.2

a. Plot the data on a scatter diagram.

b. Compute the correlation coefficient.

c. Test the correlation coefficient at the .05 significance level.

d. Determine the sample regression equation.

e. When the interest rate increases by 1%, what is the average decrease in the number of building permits issued?

f. Compute the coefficient of simple determination.

g. Write a sentence to Ed, in simple language, interpreting the r^2 value computed in part f.

h. Write Ed a memo explaining the results of your analysis.

37. Ginny Peters has the following data on a mail order business for 10 cities:

City	Number of mail orders received (thousands), y	Number of catalogs distributed (thousands), x
1	23	7
2	17	3
3	23	5
4	14	2
5	31	10
6	24	8
7	37	14
8	19	4
9	15	1
10	33	12

a. Plot the data on a scatter diagram.

b. Compute the correlation coefficient.

c. Test the correlation coefficient at the .05 significance level.

d. Determine the sample regression equation.

e. When the number of catalogs issued increases by one, what is the effect on the number of mail orders received?

f. Compute the coefficient of simple determination.

g. Write a sentence that Ginny can understand interpreting the r^2 value computed in part f.

h. Write Ginny a memo explaining the results of your analysis.

HYPOTHESIS TESTING IN REGRESSION ANALYSIS

Another key statistic is the t value, which is used to test the null hypothesis that the slope of the regression equation in the population is 0. If a regression equation has 0 slope, a change in x doesn't affect y. In other words, x and y have no correlation in the population. The symbol for the slope in the population regression equation is β_1. The null hypothesis and two-tailed alternative hypothesis for testing the slope are

Hypothesis Test for Slope

$$H_0: \beta_1 = 0$$
$$H_1: \beta_1 \neq 0$$

A two-tailed alternative is used when the goal is to determine whether the slope of the regression equation in the population is not 0. A one-tailed alternative is used when testing to determine whether the slope is positive (H_1: $\beta_1 > 0$) or negative (H_1: $\beta_1 < 0$).

As with the correlation coefficient hypothesis test, we can show that if the null hypothesis (the population slope is 0) is true, then the appropriate sampling distribution for this test is the t distribution with $(n - 2)$ degrees of freedom. Two degrees of freedom are lost because two population parameters (β_0 and β_1) are estimated using sample statistics (b_0 and b_1). The value for the estimated standard error of b_1 (s_b) is computed using Equation 14.19:

$$s_b = \frac{s_{y \cdot x}}{\sqrt{\Sigma(x - \bar{x})^2}} \tag{14.19}$$

where s_b = Standard error of the regression coefficient

$s_{y \cdot x}$ = Standard error of estimate

$\Sigma(x - \bar{x})^2$ = Sum of the squared differences between each observed x and the mean of x

Equation 14.20 shows the appropriate test statistic:

$$t = \frac{b_1 - \beta_1}{s_b} \tag{14.20}$$

where b_1 = Sample regression coefficient

β_1 = Hypothesized population regression coefficient

s_b = Standard error of the regression coefficient

EXAMPLE 14.16   The data in Table 14.4 are used to calculate the t statistic to test the null hypothesis that $\beta_1 = 0$. The null and two-tailed alternative hypotheses for testing the slope are

$H_0: \beta_1 = 0$

$H_1: \beta_1 \neq 0$

There are 6 degrees of freedom associated with this test: $(n - 2) = (8 - 2) = 6$. The .01 significance level is chosen. The t table in Appendix E.7 is used to find the critical t value. In the 6 row and the .01 column is the value 3.707. Since this is a two-tailed test, 3.707 and -3.707 are the critical values. The decision rule is

If the sample t statistic lies more than 3.707 standard errors below or above the assumed mean (0) of the sampling distribution, reject the null hypothesis (reject H_0 if $t < -3.707$ or $t > 3.707$).

Table 14.4 shows the $s_{y \cdot x}$ computation (4.9). This is one of the values needed to calculate the standard error of the regression coefficient using Equation 14.19. We also need the sum of the squared differences between x and its mean. This sum is calculated in Example 14.11: 8.875.

The values necessary to calculate the t statistic using Equation 14.20 are now available. Computation of the standard error of b using Equation 14.19 produces

$$s_b = \frac{s_{y \cdot x}}{\sqrt{\Sigma(x - \bar{x})^2}} = \frac{4.9}{\sqrt{8.875}} = 1.645$$

The sample regression line slope of 13.056 from Example 14.7 is used in Equation 14.20 to compute the test statistic:

$$t = \frac{b_1 - \beta_1}{s_b} = \frac{13.056 - 0}{1.645} = 7.94$$

The computed t (7.94) is larger than the critical t (3.707). Therefore, the null hypothesis is rejected. We conclude that the population regression line does *not* have a slope of 0. There is some linear relationship between x and y in the population.

Incidentally, the hypothesis test just discussed is the same as the test of the hypothesis that the population correlation coefficient is 0. That is, the following two null hypotheses describe the same situation:

$H_0: \rho = 0$ $H_0: \beta_1 = 0$

The first hypothesis states that there's no correlation between x and y. The second states that if a regression line is fitted to the population data, this line will be horizontal; that is, it will have a slope of 0. If one of these hypotheses is true, the other is also.

F *Test*

In fact, if these two null hypotheses are tested separately, the same *t* statistic and test conclusion will result. The reason for learning both tests is that each has its own real-world applications. You can conduct a hypothesis test for the correlation coefficient of Example 14.7 and confirm that the test statistic is also approximately 7.94.

Another key statistic in regression analysis, the *F* statistic, is used to test the null hypothesis that the sample regression equation does not explain a significant percentage of the *y* variable's variance. The null and alternative hypotheses are

$$H_0: \rho^2 = 0$$
$$H_1: \rho^2 > 0$$

At first glance, it appears that this null hypothesis and the null hypothesis tested by the *t* statistic are the same: they both claim that the sample results can't be assumed to hold for the population. These two null hypotheses are indeed similar for a simple regression analysis, but for multiple regression, to be discussed in the next chapter, they serve two different purposes. For this reason, both approaches are presented.

The test statistic for the null hypothesis just stated is drawn from the theoretical *F* distribution if the null hypothesis is true. This is a one-tailed test since ρ^2 can only be 0 or greater. A large *F* statistic will result in rejection of the null hypothesis; a small statistic won't. The *F* statistic is calculated by most regression computer programs and found in the "analysis of variance for the regression" section of the computer output.

Table 14.6 shows a typical ANOVA table for the regression. First, the portion concerning degrees of freedom is explained. You've already learned that the total degrees of freedom equal $n - 1$: one degree of freedom is lost when the mean of *y* is used to predict *y*. You've also learned that when a sample regression equation is used to predict *y*, the degrees of freedom equal $n - 2$ because β_0 and β_1 are estimated using b_0 and b_1 in the equation. This leaves one degree of freedom for the regression. Thus, in simple regression, the number of degrees of freedom for regression will always be 1.

TABLE 14.6 Analysis of Variance for the Regression

Source of variation	df	Sum of squares	Estimate of σ^2	F ratio
Regression	$k - 1$	SSR	SSR/$(k - 1)$	Eq. 14.21
Error or residual	$n - k$	SSE	SSE/$(n - k)$	
Total	$n - 1$	SST		

There are three sources of variation in regression analysis: the total variation, the explained variation (due to regression), and the unexplained variation (error or residual). Note in Table 14.6 that the sum of squares for the total variation is SST. The sum of squares for the unexplained variation is SSE. The estimate of the unexplained variance is computed by dividing this sum of squares by the appropriate degrees of freedom: SSE/$(n - k)$. The sum of squares for the explained variation is SSR. The estimate of the explained variance is also computed by dividing this sum of squares by the appropriate degrees of freedom: SSR/$(k - 1)$. The ratio of these two estimates, the estimate of the variance that is explained divided by the estimate of the variance that is unexplained, provides the F ratio:

$$F = \frac{SSR/(k-1)}{SSE/(n-k)} \tag{14.21}$$

where SSR = Sum of squares regression
       SSE = Sum of squares error
         k = Number of linearly independent parameters to be estimated
           (the number of bs in the equation, unless the predictor variables
           are linearly dependent)
         n = Sample size

Thus, the F test can be used to determine the existence of a linear relationship between x and y. In simple linear regression, this test is equivalent to the t test. In the next chapter, on multiple regression, the F test is used to determine whether a particular equation explains a significant percentage of the variance in the dependent variable; separate t tests are then used to evaluate the significance of each predictor variable. For simple linear regression, you may conduct either an F test or a t test. The results lead to the same conclusion.

EXAMPLE 14.17 Table 14.7 is the regression ANOVA table for the data of Table 14.4. An explanation of the values in this table follows.

TABLE 14.7 ANOVA Regression Table for Example 14.18

Source of variation	df	Sum of squares	Estimate of σ^2*	F ratio
Regression	1	1,512.88	1,512.898	63.0
Error or residual	6	144.00	24.0	
Total	7	1,656.88		

*The estimate of σ^2 is frequently referred to as *mean square*.

The value 1,656.88, which represents SST, is the sum of the squared differences between the y values and their mean. It is a measure of the variability of y before the x-y linear relationship is introduced:

$$SST = \Sigma(y - \bar{y})^2 = 1,656.88$$

The value 144 in Table 14.7 is the sum of the squared differences between the y values and their estimates based on x and the regression equation:

$$SSE = \Sigma(y - \hat{y})^2 = 144$$

The SSR value, 1,512.88, is the sum of squared differences "explained" with the introduction of x. It is the difference between the measure of the total of y variability (1,656.88) and the sum of squares error using x as a predictor (144):

$$SSR = SST - SSE = 1,656.88 - 144 = 1,512.88$$

The appropriate number of degrees of freedom associated with the regression sum of squares equals the number of independent variables. In simple linear regression, the degrees of freedom always equal 1. Table 14.7 shows one degree of freedom for the "regression" source of variation.

The degrees of freedom for the sum of squares error equal $(n - k)$, the sample size n, minus the number of regression coefficients estimated in the regression equation. In simple regression, β_0 and β_1 are the only regression coefficients estimated, so the degrees of freedom always equal $(n - 2)$. Table 14.7 shows six degrees of freedom $(n - k = 8 - 2 = 6)$ for the "residual" source of variation.

The loss of one degree of freedom for the total is due to the estimate of the population mean of y using the sample mean. Table 14.7 indicates a total of seven degrees of freedom $(n - 1 = 8 - 1 = 7)$.

The two sums of squares are divided by their degrees of freedom to produce the estimates of the unknown population variance listed in the fourth column of Table 14.7. The value 24.0 is a valid estimate of this variance regardless of the state of the null hypothesis. However, the estimate in the first row (1,512.88) is valid only if the null hypothesis is true. As shown in Chapter 12 (ANOVA), the ratio of these two "estimates" is drawn from the F distribution if the null hypothesis is true. This ratio (63.0) is computed using Equation 14.21 and is shown in the last column:

$$F = \frac{SSR/(k - 1)}{SSE/(n - k)} = \frac{1,512.88/(2 - 1)}{144/(8 - 2)} = 63.0$$

To determine whether an F value of 63.0 is "large," consult the F table in Appendix E.9. The df reference values for the table are 1 for the numerator and 6 for the denominator. For these degrees of freedom and a significance level of .05, the F table indicates a critical value of 5.99. The decision rule is

If the calculated F value is greater than 5.99, reject the null hypothesis (reject H_0 if $F > 5.99$).

Therefore, reject the null hypothesis with small chance of error. We conclude that the sample regression equation explains a significant percentage of the y variance.

EXAMPLE 14.18   In Table 14.2, the variable of interest is car mileage per gallon, so this is the dependent variable, y. A variable that may be associated with y is car weight; this is the predictor variable, x. These data values were keyed into a computer program that performs regression analysis, SPSS-PC (Statistical Package for the Social Sciences, PC version). Table 14.8 displays the key regression values produced by this program.

The regression constant (b_0) and the regression coefficient (b_1) for the predictor variable are combined to form the regression equation,

$$\hat{y} = 45.109 - .00676x$$

TABLE 14.8   SPSS-PC Computer Output for Example 14.18

r-Squared: .73101   Standard Error: 6.23192

Variables in the Equation

Variable	B	t	Sig t
Weight	−.00676	−2.855	.0648
Constant	45.109	5.111	.0145

Analysis of Variance

	df	Sum of Squares	Mean Square
Regression	1	316.62967	316.62967
Residual	3	116.51033	38.83678

F = 8.15283   Sig F = .0648

The following symbols may help you read this computer output.

$r^2 = .73101$

$s_{y \cdot x} = 6.23192$

$b_1 = -.00676$

$b_0 = 45.109$

SSR = 316.62967

SSE = 116.51033

The regression slope means that for each increase in car weight of one pound, the mileage may be expected to decrease by an average of 0.00676 miles per gallon.

The t value for the equation slope is -2.855. The p-value for this statistic (.0648) indicates the probability of a type I error. To reject the hypothesis that $\beta_1 = 0$ and conclude that there's a nonzero slope in the population, we must risk about a 6% chance of being wrong.

The regression equation has caused a reduction in the sum of squares error. The null hypothesis stating that the sample regression equation doesn't explain a significant percentage of the y variance is tested by the F statistic. The null hypothesis may be rejected if a .0648 risk is acceptable (Sig F = .0648). Note that this is the same p-value computed for the t statistic. This is always true for a simple regression analysis.

Overall, we can conclude that this regression equation is rather weak, even though the r^2 value (73%) might appear promising. The small sample size (5) has produced a regression equation that can be used to predict in the population only if a somewhat high degree of risk is assumed (6.48%). If this were a real-world situation, a much larger sample size would be needed.

EXAMPLE 14.19   Washington Water Power rate analyst Tony Perez wants to study the relationship between temperature and the amount of electricity used by small commercial customers. He needs to determine how sensitive usage is to temperature. Tony uses "cooling degree days" to measure how cold a day is (the higher this value, the colder the day). He has taken a random sample of 22 months and computed the average value of this index, along with the average kilowatt-hours per small commercial customer. Tony runs his data using the SAS computer package. The SAS commands are shown at the end of this chapter. (*Note:* The actual data on usage and cooling degree days were collected for Washington Water Power for a sample of months selected from 1988 through 1989.)

Table 14.9 presents the SAS output. The analyst concludes that temperature is a fairly good predictor of the number of kilowatt-hours consumed by small commercial customers. With large t and F values, the regression equation is significant and can be used in the future to forecast power needs ($t = 7.62$, $F = 58.13$). He's somewhat disappointed, however, that only about 74% of the power consumption variance is explained by temperature. Tony had hoped for a larger r^2 value and wonders if additional predictor variables would explain a higher percentage of the variance.

TABLE 14.9   SAS Computer Output for Example 14.19

```
PEARSON CORRELATION COEFFICIENTS/PROB > :R: UNDER HO = RHO = O/N = 22
            X              Y
X     1.00000        .86256
Y      .86256       1.00000

DEPENDENT VARIABLE: Y
SOURCE      DF    SUM OF SQUARES     MEAN SQUARE     F VALUE    PR > F    R-SQUARE
MODEL        1        1029495.82     1029495.82       58.13     .0001       .744
ERROR       20         354219.50       17710.97            ROOT MSE        Y-MEAN
TOTAL       21        1383715.32                          133.0826          1399.6
SOURCE      DF    TYPE I SS   F VALUE   PR > F   DF   TYPE III SS   F VALUE   PR > F
X            1    1029495.82    58.13    .0001    1   1029495.82     58.13    .0001
                                T FOR HO =                    STD ERROR OF  ESTIMATE
PARAMETER           ESTIMATE    PARAMETER = 0    PR > [T]
INTERCEPT        1135.613175
X                   0.491662        7.62            .0001                      0.06449
                 SUM OF RESIDUALS                                             0.00
                 SUM OF SQUARED RESIDUALS                                 354219.50
```

The following symbols may help you read this computer output:
SSR = 1,029,495.82 $\bar{y}$ = 1,399.6
SSE = 354,219.50 b_0 = 1,135.613175
SST = 1,383,715.32 b_1 = .491662
  r^2 = .744

USING THE REGRESSION EQUATION

The first step in evaluating a sample regression equation is to check the key values in the computer output. The r^2 value must be sufficiently high to encourage the analysis to continue. The t value must be high enough to reject the null hypotheses of zero population slope. Once a regression equation passes these tests, the analyst can use the equation for the intended purposes.

There are generally two purposes for a regression equation once it has been formed from the sample data and deemed significant. The first purpose is to gain insights into the effect of the predictor variable on the dependent variable. In Example 14.19, Tony found that electricity use by small commercial customers is significantly related to temperature. This relationship may prove quite valuable to both the power company and the customer in projecting power needs for the near future. In multiple regression (discussed in Chapter 15), there will be many more opportunities to explore the relationships between predictor variables and the dependent variable, since there are many potential predictor variables to examine.

The second important use of the sample regression equation is to make predictions for y given specified values for x.

EXAMPLE 14.20 Shop owner Carol Hartman is interested in examining the most important variable identified with shop success: number of customers who enter the shop per week. Carol believes that one variable that might be correlated with weekly visits is the county unemployment rate. She selects a random sample of 60 weeks from shop records for the past two years and records the relevant information for the two variables of interest. The data are keyed into the shop's small computer, that has a regression analysis package. Table 14.10 presents the key elements of the computer output.

TABLE 14.10 Computer Output for Example 14.20

r-Squared: .893   Standard Error: 2.1

Variables in the Equation

Variable	B	t	Sig t
V1	−53.8	10.4	.000
Constant	1147.9	9.7	.000

Analysis of Variance

	df	Sum of Squares	Mean Square
Regression	1	112,842	112,842
Residual	58	101,628	1,752.2

F = 64.4   Sig F = .000

Note the significant t statistic in Table 14.10. There's a very small risk (less than .001) of committing a type I error if the null hypothesis is rejected. It can be safely concluded that the slope of the population regression equation is not 0 (based on the large t value). The sample regression equation can be used in conjunction with the population of shop weeks. This regression equation is

$$\hat{y} = 1{,}147.9 - 53.8x$$

where x is the unemployment rate for the county and $\hat{y}$ is the expected value of y given the value of x. The slope of this equation can be interpreted to mean that for each increase of 1 percentage point in the unemployment rate, an average loss of 53.8 customers per week is expected. The r^2 of 89% means that most of the variability in shop visits can be explained by the linear relationship between visits and the unemployment rate.

Carol has judged the regression equation significant and can use it to estimate the number of visits per week given various values for x, the county unemployment rate. The county has issued its unemployment forecast for the next three months, predicting rates of 5.2%, 5.8%, and 7.0%. Based on these forecasts, the regression equation can be used to predict the expected number of shop visits per week for the next three months.

$$\hat{y} = 1147.9 - 53.8(5.2) = 868$$
$$\hat{y} = 1147.9 - 53.8(5.8) = 836$$
$$\hat{y} = 1147.9 - 53.8(7.0) = 771$$

Carol can use these predictions to plan shop operations, especially if she has information on profit per shop visit.

EXERCISES

38. What does it mean when b_1 is shown not to be significant?

39. What is the F statistic used for in regression analysis? What is the t statistic used for in regression analysis?

40. What is the meaning of the statement, "A percentage of the y variance can be explained by x?"

41. Can the number of games a major league baseball team wins be explained by the number of home runs the team hits? The following data come from the *Sporting News 1992 Baseball Yearbook:*

Team	Wins y	Home runs x
Pittsburgh	98	126
Atlanta	94	141
Los Angeles	93	108
San Diego	84	121
St. Louis	84	68
Philadelphia	78	111
Chicago Cubs	77	159
New York Mets	77	117
San Francisco	75	141
Cincinnati	74	164
Montreal	71	95
Houston	65	79
	970	1430

a. Plot the data on a scatter diagram.

p566 b. Develop a regression equation.

c. Compute the residuals.

d. Compute the sum of squares error (SSE).

580 e. Compute the total sum of squares (SST).

f. What percentage of the variance in games won can be explained by the number of home runs the team hit?

g. Test to determine whether the regression equation explains a significant percentage of the variance in the dependent variable.

42. Jane Davis, manager of Quantum Realty, Inc., wants to determine if a home's selling price can be explained by its size. She's familiar with a 1980 study by Cho and Reichert that

used regression analysis to predict house price using a number of predictor variables.[4] They found that size of living space was the most significant factor, and Jane wants to use this finding in her own area. Jane has collected the following data:

Home	Selling price ($000), y	Number of rooms, x
1	90.4	8
2	127.3	9
3	109.6	8
4	131.2	12
5	81.3	6
6	107.9	10
7	135.8	11
8	97.8	7
9	116.7	10
10	164.8	14
11	88.8	7
12	120.5	11
13	109.8	10

a. Plot the data on a scatter diagram.

b. Develop a regression equation.

c. Compute the residuals.

d. Compute the sum of squares error (SSE).

e. Compute the total sum of squares (SST).

f. What percentage of the selling price variance can be explained by the number of rooms?

g. Test to determine whether the regression equation explains a significant percentage of the variance in selling price.

h. Write Jane a memo explaining the results of your analysis.

SUMMARY

This chapter has presented the basic concepts of correlation and simple regression analysis. Correlation is used to measure the extent of the linear relationship between two continuous variables. In regression analysis, a dependent variable is identified along with a predictor or explanatory variable. Using the method of least squares, a regression equation is calculated along with other summary statistics, such as r^2, the t statistic, and the F statistic.

It is important in regression analysis to test the relevant hypotheses before using the regression equation for prediction. Either the t statistic or the F value should be examined and used to determine if the sample regression results can be extended to the

---

[4]C. C. Cho and A. Reichert, "An Application of Multiple Regression Analysis for Appraising Single-family Housing Values," *Business Economics* 15 (January 1980), pp. 47–52.

population from which the sample came. Analysts often make the mistake of looking only at r^2 when evaluating the results of a regression, and this can lead to erroneous conclusions, especially if a small sample size is involved.

The concepts presented in this chapter provide the background necessary for consideration of the more common case in regression analysis: the use of multiple predictor variables—the subject of the next chapter.

APPLICATIONS OF STATISTICAL CONCEPTS IN THE BUSINESS WORLD

As mentioned early in this chapter, regression and correlation analysis are common methods of analyzing data to produce useful decision-making information. There are many numerical variables to consider in the business setting, and often managers want to understand the relationships among them. Correlation analysis is used when knowledge of the relationship between two variables is desired. Regression analysis is used when one variable (y) is to be predicted based on knowledge of another variable (x). Here are several examples of variables that might be of interest in a correlation and regression analysis. The manager would probably want to first see the correlation coefficient between the two variables, and then study the regression equation and determine its ability to produce accurate estimates.

Dependent variable	Predictor variable
Defectives per shift	Temperature of factory
Cost of goods sold/month	Number of employees/month
Number of overtime hours	Average temperature
Employee hourly wage	Employee age
Years with company	High school GPA
Number of defectives per factory branch	Wage rate per branch
Company dividends per share	Earnings per share
Number of shares outstanding	Annual sales
Seconds per computer transaction	Size of computer memory
Student GPA	Age of student
Student rating of professor	Student's class grade
Company cost of capital	Prime interest rate
Time until machine breakdown	Cost of monthly machine maintenance
Cost of rental car per day	Size of rental car company
Salesperson's monthly gross	Number of miles driven
Lifetime of TV picture tube	Temperature of operating space
Pounds of oats per bag	Time since filling machine adjustment
Viscosity of truck oil	Temperature of engine

GLOSSARY

Scatter diagram A plot of *x-y* data pairs in two-dimensional space.

Correlation coefficient A value between -1 and $+1$ that indicates the strength of the linear relationship between two quantitative variables.

Functional model A model that hypothesizes an exact relationship between variables.

Statistical model A model that hypothesizes a functional relationship plus some random error.

Sample regression line The straight line that best fits a set of sample x-y data points.

Method of least squares A method that determines the equation of the straight line that minimizes the sum of the squared vertical distances between the line and the data points.

Residual The difference between an actual y and the value, $\hat{y}$, predicted using the sample regression equation.

Standard error of estimate A measure of the variability, or scatter, of the observed sample y values around the regression line.

Prediction interval An interval used to predict a particular y value for a given value of x.

Confidence interval An interval used to estimate the mean value of y for a specific value of x.

Coefficient of simple determination A measure of the percentage of the variability in y that can be explained by the predictor variable, x.

KEY FORMULAS

Pearson product-moment correlation coefficient

$$r = \frac{n\Sigma xy - (\Sigma x)(\Sigma y)}{\sqrt{n\Sigma x^2 - (\Sigma x)^2}\sqrt{n\Sigma y^2 - (\Sigma y)^2}} \tag{14.1}$$

Standard error of r

$$s_r = \sqrt{\frac{1 - r^2}{n - 2}} \tag{14.2}$$

t statistic for testing if the correlation coefficient differs from 0

$$t = \frac{(r - \rho)}{s_r} \tag{14.3}$$

Functional model for a straight line

$$y = \beta_0 + \beta_1 x \tag{14.4}$$

Statistical model for a straight line

$$y = \beta_0 + \beta_1 x + \varepsilon \tag{14.5}$$

Sample regression equation

$$\hat{y} = b_0 + b_1 x \tag{14.6}$$

Slope or regression coefficient formula

$$b_1 = \frac{n\Sigma xy - (\Sigma x)(\Sigma y)}{n\Sigma x^2 - (\Sigma x)^2} \tag{14.7}$$

y-intercept formula

$$b_0 = \frac{\Sigma y}{n} - \frac{b_1 \Sigma x}{n} \tag{14.8}$$

Residual

$$e = y - \hat{y} \tag{14.9}$$

Standard error of estimate

$$s_{y \cdot x} = \sqrt{\frac{\Sigma(y - \hat{y})^2}{n - 2}} \tag{14.10}$$

Prediction interval

$$\hat{y} \pm t \, s_{\hat{y} \cdot x} \tag{14.11}$$

Standard error of the prediction

$$s_{\hat{y} \cdot x} = s_{y \cdot x} \sqrt{1 + \frac{1}{n} + \frac{(x_p - \bar{x})^2}{\Sigma(x_i - \bar{x})^2}} \tag{14.12}$$

Confidence interval

$$\hat{y} \pm t \, s_{\hat{\mu} \cdot x} \tag{14.13}$$

Estimated standard error of estimate

$$s_{\hat{\mu} \cdot x} = s_{y \cdot x} \sqrt{\frac{1}{n} + \frac{(x_p - \bar{x})^2}{\Sigma(x_i - \bar{x})^2}} \tag{14.14}$$

Sum of squares total

$$SST = \sum_{i=1}^{n} (y_i - \bar{y})^2 \tag{14.15}$$

Sum of squares error

$$SSE = \sum_{i=1}^{n} (y_i - \hat{y})^2 \tag{14.16}$$

Sum of squares regression

$$SSR = SST - SSE \tag{14.17}$$

Coefficient of simple determination

$$r^2 = 1 - \frac{\Sigma(y - \hat{y})^2}{\Sigma(y - \bar{y})^2} \tag{14.18}$$

or

$$r^2 = 1 - \frac{SSE}{SST}$$

Standard error of the regression coefficient, b_1

$$s_b = \frac{s_{y \cdot x}}{\sqrt{\Sigma(x - \bar{x})^2}}$$
(14.19)

t statistic for testing if a regression coefficient differs from 0

$$t = \frac{b_1 - \beta_1}{s_b}$$
(14.20)

F statistic

$$F = \frac{SSR/(k - 1)}{SSE/(n - k)}$$
(14.21)

SOLVED EXERCISES
. . . .

1. CORRELATION ANALYSIS

Carlene Larsen owns several ice cream stands in San Pedro, Texas. She's trying to find some variable that's positively related to daily sales and decides to investigate average temperature. She collects the following data for a random sample of 10 days:

Day	Daily sales (gallons), y	Average temperature (°F), x
1	110	72
2	127	79
3	140	85
4	151	90
5	89	66
6	187	95
7	205	100
8	190	98
9	136	82
10	165	91

a. Compute the correlation coefficient.

b. Test the correlation coefficient at the .025 significance level to determine if there's a positive relationship.

Solution:

a.

Day	y	x	y^2	x^2	xy
1	110	72	12,100	5,184	7,920
2	127	79	16,129	6,241	10,033
3	140	85	19,600	7,225	11,900
4	151	90	22,801	8,100	13,590

Day	y	x	y^2	x^2	xy
5	89	66	7,921	4,356	5,874
6	187	95	34,969	9,025	17,765
7	205	100	42,025	10,000	20,500
8	190	98	36,100	9,604	18,620
9	136	82	18,496	6,724	11,152
10	165	91	27,225	8,281	15,015
Sums:	1,500	858	237,366	74,740	132,369

$$r = \frac{n\Sigma xy - (\Sigma x)(\Sigma y)}{\sqrt{n\Sigma x^2 - (\Sigma x)^2}\sqrt{n\Sigma y^2 - (\Sigma y)^2}}$$

$$= \frac{10(132,369) - (858)(1,500)}{\sqrt{10(74,740) - (858)^2}\sqrt{10(237,366) - (1,500)^2}}$$

$$= \frac{36,690}{\sqrt{11,236}\sqrt{123,660}} = \frac{36,690}{37,275} = .984$$

b. The null and alternative hypotheses are

$H_0: \rho \leq 0$
$H_1: \rho > 0$
$df = (n - 2) = (10 - 2) = 8$

The decision rule is

If the sample t statistic is greater than 2.306, reject the null hypothesis (reject H_0 if $t > 2.306$).

The standard error of r is

$$s_r = \sqrt{\frac{1 - r^2}{n - 2}} = \sqrt{\frac{1 - (.984)^2}{8}} = .063$$

The t statistic is

$$t = \frac{r - \rho}{s_r} = \frac{.984 - 0}{.063} = 15.6$$

The calculated t statistic (15.6) is greater than the t value (2.306), so the null hypothesis is rejected. Carlene concludes that there is a positive linear relationship between average temperature and daily ice cream sales.

2. REGRESSION ANALYSIS

Since Carlene found a positive relationship between the two variables, she would like to use knowledge of average temperature to predict daily ice cream sales.

a. Compute the sample regression equation.

b. Interpret the slope or regression coefficient.

c. Compute the residual for the first day.

d. Compute the standard error of estimate.

e. Test the regression coefficient at the .025 significance level. Use a one-tailed test.

f. Compute the coefficient of simple determination.

g. Compute a 95% prediction interval for a day when the temperature is 90°.

h. Compute a 95% confidence interval for a day when the temperature is 90°.

Solution:

a.
$$b_1 = \frac{n\Sigma xy - (\Sigma x)(\Sigma y)}{n\Sigma x^2 - (\Sigma x)^2}$$

$$= \frac{10(132,369) - (858)(1,500)}{10(74,740) - (858)^2} = \frac{36,690}{11,236} = 3.265$$

$$b_0 = \frac{\Sigma y}{n} - \frac{b_1\Sigma x}{n} = \frac{1,500}{10} - \frac{3.265(858)}{10} = -130.14$$

$$\hat{y} = -130.14 + 3.265x$$

b. If the average temperature increases 1°, daily ice cream sales will increase, on the average, 3.265 gallons.

c. $\hat{y} = -130.14 + 3.265(72) = 104.94$

$e = y - \hat{y} = 110 - 104.94 = 5.06$

d.

Day	y	$\hat{y}$	$y - \hat{y}$	$(y - \hat{y})^2$
1	110	104.94	5.06	25.60
2	127	127.79	-0.80	0.64
3	140	147.39	-7.39	54.61
4	151	163.71	-12.71	161.54
5	89	85.35	3.65	13.32
6	187	180.04	6.96	48.44
7	205	196.37	8.63	74.48
8	190	189.84	0.16	0.03
9	136	137.59	-1.59	2.53
10	165	166.98	-1.98	3.92
			0.00	385.26

$$s_{y\cdot x} = \sqrt{\frac{\Sigma(y - \hat{y})^2}{n - 2}} = \sqrt{\frac{385.26}{8}} = 6.94$$

e. The null and alternative hypotheses are

$H_0: \beta_1 \leq 0$

$H_1: \beta_1 > 0$

$df = (n - 2) = (10 - 2) = 8$

The decision rule is

If the sample t statistic is greater than 2.306, reject the null hypothesis.

The standard error of b_1 is

$$s_b = \frac{s_{y\cdot x}}{\sqrt{\Sigma(x - \bar{x})^2}} = \frac{6.94}{\sqrt{1,123.6}} = .207$$

where

$$\Sigma(x - \bar{x})^2 = \Sigma x^2 - \frac{(\Sigma x)^2}{n} = 74{,}740 - \frac{(858)^2}{10} = 1{,}123.6$$

The t statistic is

$$t = \frac{b_1 - \beta_1}{s_b} = \frac{3.265 - 0}{.207} = 15.8$$

This is the same result obtained when the correlation coefficient was tested. Carlene concludes that there's a positive linear relationship between average temperature and daily ice cream sales. The slope of the regression line is significantly different from 0.

f. $\Sigma(y - \hat{y})^2 = 385.26, \qquad \Sigma(y - \bar{y})^2 = 12{,}366$

$$r^2 = 1 - \frac{\Sigma(y - \hat{y})^2}{\Sigma(y - \bar{y})^2} = 1 - \frac{385.26}{12{,}366} = 1 - .031 = .969$$

g. $\hat{y} = -130.14 + 3.265(90) = 163.71$

$$\hat{y} \pm t\, s_{y \cdot x} \sqrt{1 + \frac{1}{n} + \frac{(x_p - \bar{x})^2}{\Sigma(x_i - \bar{x})^2}}$$

$$163.71 \pm 2.306(6.94) \sqrt{1 + \frac{1}{10} + \frac{(90 - 85.8)^2}{1{,}123.6}}$$

$$163.71 \pm 2.306(6.94)\sqrt{1.1157}$$

$$163.71 \pm 2.306(6.94)\,(1.056)$$

$$163.71 \pm 16.9$$

$$146.81 \text{ to } 180.61$$

h. $\hat{y} \pm t\, s_{y \cdot x} \sqrt{\dfrac{1}{n} + \dfrac{(x_p - \bar{x})^2}{\Sigma(x_1 - \bar{x})^2}}$

$$163.71 \pm 2.306(6.94) \sqrt{\frac{1}{10} + \frac{(90 - 85.8)^2}{1{,}123.6}}$$

$$163.71 \pm 2.306(6.94)\sqrt{.1157}$$

$$163.71 \pm 2.306(6.94)(.34)$$

$$163.71 \pm 5.44$$

$$158.27 \text{ to } 169.15$$

Note that since the sample size is less than 30, the t distribution is consulted for 6 degrees of freedom ($10 - 2 = 8$). Carlene is 95% confident that ice cream sales in gallons will fall in the interval from 146.81 to 180.61 for a day of 90° temperature. She's also 95% confident that the interval from 158.27 to 169.15 encloses the mean sales of ice cream in gallons when a prediction is made for a day of 90° temperature.

EXERCISES

43. What is a sample regression? How is it used?

44. What is the difference between correlation analysis and regression analysis?

45. If two variables have a correlation coefficient (r) equal to 0, what is the value of the standard error of estimate ($s_{y \cdot x}$)?

46. What are two ways in which the slope or regression coefficient can be tested for significance?

47. What is the difference between testing that the population correlation coefficient is 0 and testing that the population regression coefficient is 0?

48. What null hypothesis is tested using the F statistic in simple regression analysis?

49. For the following set of data:

y:	10	15	20	25	30	35	40
x:	6	8	10	12	14	16	18

   a. Plot the data on a scatter diagram.

   b. Compute the correlation coefficient.

50. For the following set of data:

y:	90	80	70	60	50	40	30
x:	20	24	28	32	36	40	44

   a. Plot the data on a scatter diagram.

   b. Compute the sample regression equation.

51. For the following set of data:

y:	12	17	18	22	16	11	21	26
x:	5	8	8	9	6	6	10	12

   a. Plot the data on a scatter diagram.

   b. Compute the sample regression equation.

   c. Compute a point estimate for an x value of 10.

52. A sample correlation coefficient of $r = .60$ was calculated based on a sample of size $n = 40$. Test at the .01 significance level the hypothesis H_0: $\rho = 0$ versus the alternative H_1: $\rho \neq 0$.

53. Test at the .05 significance level the hypothesis H_0: $\beta_1 \geq 0$ versus the alternative H_1: $\beta_1 < 0$, given that a simple linear regression based on a sample of size $n = 26$ produced the sample regression equation $\hat{y} = -2.5 - .6x$, with $s_b = 2.3$.

54. Given the following summary measures:

$$n = 20, \quad \Sigma x = 154.2, \quad \Sigma x^2 = 2,281.3,$$
$$\Sigma xy = 4,002.8, \quad \Sigma y = 613.4, \quad \Sigma y^2 = 19,418.9$$

   a. Compute the correlation coefficient.

   b. Test the correlation coefficient at the .10 significance level. Use a two-tailed test.

   c. Compute the sample regression equation.

55. City Parcel Delivery Service accountant Jean Foster has been asked to compute a new rate schedule for local deliveries. Jean already has data on the average cost per mile of delivery

truck operation, but she needs to determine the average amount of time needed per mile to make a delivery. She collects data on the next 13 runs:

Delivery	Minutes, y	Miles, x
1	28	11
2	27	10
3	35	15
4	15	7
5	8	2
6	14	5
7	20	8
8	29	9
9	13	4
10	16	3
11	40	14
12	9	3
13	31	12

a. Plot the data on a scatter diagram.

b. Compute the correlation coefficient.

c. Test the correlation coefficient at the .05 significance level. Use a two-tailed test.

d. Determine the sample regression equation.

e. What is the average amount of time needed per mile to make a delivery?

f. Compute the coefficient of simple determination.

g. Write a sentence that Jean can understand interpreting the r^2 value computed in part f.

h. Compute the residuals.

i. Compute the sum of squares error (SSE).

j. Compute the sum of squares total (SST).

k. Test to determine whether the regression equation explains a significant percentage of the dependent variable variance. Use the .05 significance level.

l. Predict how long it will take to deliver a package to a business 10 miles away.

m. Develop a 90% prediction interval for part l.

n. Construct a regression ANOVA table.

56. Jim Larkin owns a service station in an area where a large construction project is planned. Jim feels that his gasoline sales are dependent on traffic flow along the street where his station is located. *The Wall Street Journal*, March 2, 1990, predicted that world crude oil prices would rise because of cutbacks in North Sea production. Jim is concerned that this may lead to higher gas prices, which could hurt his business.

   As well, Jim fears that sales will decrease significantly once the construction project begins. Jeff Brunner, a part-time employee and full-time business student, disagrees with Jim. Jeff feels that the station's success is based on customer loyalty and not on traffic flow. Jeff and another student are assigned to do a project in their statistics course. Jeff obtains permission from Jim to study the relationship between gas sales and traffic count and collects a sample of eight days of data:

Day	Total gallons sold (thousands), y	Traffic count (hundreds), x
1	284	9
2	381	13
3	271	11
4	287	9
5	452	17
6	192	5
7	204	7
8	158	4

Write a report for Jeff and his classmate to turn in to their professor. Write a second report for Jeff to give to Jim Larkin.

57. Brian Bosley, a rate analyst for Northeast Power, was asked to determine if there's a linear relationship between electricity consumption and the number of rooms in a single-family dwelling. Because electricity consumption varies from month to month, Brian decided to study usage during January. He collected the following data:

House	Kilowatt-hours (thousands), y	Number of rooms, x
1	8	13
2	6	10
3	9	15
4	5	7
5	8	9
6	5	5
7	7	8
8	9	9
9	3	4
10	6	6
11	8	14
12	6	5

Write a report for Brian's supervisor that analyzes the relationship between these variables.

58. The Dillon Investment Company bids on investments offered by various firms that desire additional financing. Martin Hughes, manager of Dillon, wonders if there's a relationship between Dillon's bid and the bid of Dillon's major competitor, Amfco Securities. He feels that Dillon might be using the same rationale in preparing bids as Amfco. In other words, could Dillon's bid be used to predict Amfco's bid? Martin has tabulated data on the past 12 issues bid on, in terms of the bid's percentage of par value, for both firms:

Issue	Amfco, y	Dillon, x
1	101.5	101.9
2	98.9	99.1
3	100.3	101.1
4	105.9	106.8
5	102.0	102.1
6	97.4	97.1
7	99.3	99.5
8	98.8	99.4

Issue	Amfco, y	Dillon, x
9	103.6	104.1
10	100.1	99.7
11	98.5	99.0
12	100.1	100.3

a. To what extent are the two firms using the same rationale in preparing bids?

b. Develop a regression equation for Mr. Hughes.

c. Predict Amfco's bid if Dillon bids 102% of par value.

d. For the prediction made in part c, what is the probability of Dillon winning this particular bid (if lowest bid wins)?

e. What should Martin bid if he wants a 50% probability of winning the bid? A 75% probability of winning the bid?

59. An investor is considering putting funds into a mutual fund managed by Fidelity—specifically, its Blue Chip fund. She collects a small sample of issues in *The Wall Street Journal* and records the fund's selling price per share (y) along with that day's Dow Jones Industrial Average (x):

Date	y	x
Nov. 8	13.61	2597.13
Dec. 1	14.14	2706.27
Oct. 19	14.02	2643.65
Oct. 11	14.55	2785.33
Oct. 3	14.18	2713.72
Oct. 6	14.50	2773.56
Oct. 24	14.21	2662.91

Values are from *The Wall Street Journal* of the dates shown, all 1989.

a. What is the correlation between x and y?

b. Is the correlation found in part *a* significant?

c. How would you interpret your findings?

d. What is the sample regression equation?

e. What would you recommend to this investor?

60. This exercise refers to the company data base in Appendix C. Select a random sample of 10 workers. Determine if there's a significant relationship between the number of years with the company (x_1) and the number of overtime hours worked during the past six months (x_2).

61. This exercise refers to the company data base in Appendix C. Select a random sample of 15 workers. Develop a regression equation using employee age (x_9) to predict annual base salary (x_8). Use the .05 significance level to determine if this equation explains a significant percentage of the variance in the dependent variable.

62. This exercise refers to the company data base in Appendix C. Select a random sample of 12 workers. Develop a regression equation using employee age (x_9) to predict the number of sick days taken during the past six months (x_5). Use the .10 significance level to determine if the regression coefficient is significantly different from 0.

EXTENDED EXERCISES

63. MURFORD ELECTRONICS

Susan and Charles Murford own a company that retails various kinds of electronic equipment such as TV sets, VCRs, stereo equipment, and video cameras. A variable of great concern to them is their monthly gross sales. Since they have records for this variable over the past five years, it's easy to take a random sample of months to use in a regression analysis.

After thinking about variables that might be related to their extreme variability in monthly sales, the Murfords decide that occupancy rate of the largest hotel in town might correlate well. They base this conclusion on a recent newspaper article that noted the unusually high correlation between this variable and other indicators of local economic activity.

The Murfords randomly select the 10 months for their sample and record their gross sales, in dollars, for each month. They then obtain hotel occupancy rates for these same months from the local chamber of commerce. Table 14.11 shows the data they collected along with the summary statistics generated by a computer program that performs simple regression analysis.

TABLE 14.11 Data and Regression Computer Results for Extended Exercise 63

x (hotel occupancy rate, %)	y (monthly sales, $000)
63 independent	85.2 dependent
79	88.4
55	79.7
88	91.3
85	89.9
42	74.3
54	79.8
60	81.4
78	85.6
62	82.7

```
r-Squared: .94780            Standard Error: 1.27683
               Variables in the Equation
```

Variable	B	t	Sig t
Rate V1	.33934	12.052	.0000
Constant	61.22992	31.920	.0000

Analysis of Variance

	df	Sum of Squares	Mean Square
Regression	1	236.79865	236.79865
Residual	8	13.04235	1.63029

```
     F = 145.24912    Sig F = .0000
```

a. Can these results be extended to the population of all months? Explain.

b. What is the regression equation? If the current occupancy rate is 75%, what is the expected sales level for Murford Electronics?

c. About how far off would you expect the prediction made in part b to be?

64. THE SHIVES INVESTMENT SEMINAR

Cindy Shives has been conducting investment seminars for about three years in a large city. She has heard favorable comments from a number of former attendees and would like to gather some evidence regarding personal attributes that affect success in the investment world. She thinks this knowledge would contribute greatly to her seminars. A *Financial Executive* article, "Corporate Investments—Do You Play the Loser's Game?" (May/June 1989), makes her think carefully about the approach she's using in her seminars.

She randomly chooses 28 former attendees from her files, and they agree to fill out a brief, anonymous questionnaire. She asks them to estimate the percentage increase in their net asset worth during the 12-month period following their attending her seminar. She'll use this variable as the dependent variable in a regression analysis.

Cindy then considers variables that might be related to investment success as measured by the dependent variable. Her files contain the questionnaires that participants filled out at the beginning of her seminar. After looking over these forms, she decides to test two variables (age and number of years of investment experience) against the dependent variable. She matches these data values for each person in the sample with the dependent variable and keys the resulting data into a regression analysis computer program. After the program has run, she tries to interpret the results but can't.

a. Provide some general advice to Cindy Shives about what to look for on the regression output.

b. Describe how Cindy can tell which of her two predictor variables is better.

c. Give some specific benchmark values that Cindy can use in studying the statistics on her computer printout.

65. PLATEN PRINTING

Consider the population of 140 observations in the table below. The Platen Printing Company wishes to determine the relationship between the number of copies produced by an offset printing technique (x) and the associated direct labor cost (y). Select a random sample of 25 observations.

a. Use the .05 significance level to determine if there is a significant relationship.

b. If there is a significant relationship, develop a sample regression equation and use it to predict the direct labor cost for a job involving 275 copies.

c. Develop a 95% prediction interval for your prediction in part *b*.

d. Develop a 95% confidence interval for your prediction in part *b*.

e. How accurate is your regression equation?

Observation	y	x	Observation	y	x	Observation	y	x
(1)	1.0	10	(10)	1.4	40	(19)	1.5	70
(2)	0.9	10	(11)	1.2	40	(20)	2.0	70
(3)	0.8	10	(12)	1.7	50	(21)	0.8	80
(4)	1.3	20	(13)	0.9	50	(22)	0.6	80
(5)	0.9	20	(14)	1.2	50	(23)	1.8	80
(6)	0.6	30	(15)	1.3	50	(24)	1.0	90
(7)	1.1	30	(16)	0.7	60	(25)	2.0	100
(8)	1.0	30	(17)	1.0	60	(26)	0.5	100
(9)	1.4	40	(18)	1.3	70	(27)	1.5	100

Observation	y	x	Observation	y	x	Observation	y	x
(28)	1.3	110	(66)	1.4	240	(104)	3.1	360
(29)	1.7	110	(67)	1.6	240	(105)	2.5	370
(30)	1.2	110	(68)	1.7	240	(106)	2.9	370
(31)	0.8	110	(69)	1.5	250	(107)	2.6	370
(32)	1.0	120	(70)	2.2	250	(108)	3.0	380
(33)	1.8	120	(71)	2.5	250	(109)	3.2	380
(34)	2.1	120	(72)	2.4	260	(110)	2.9	390
(35)	1.5	130	(73)	2.0	260	(111)	2.6	390
(36)	1.9	130	(74)	2.7	260	(112)	2.5	390
(37)	1.7	140	(75)	2.0	270	(113)	2.7	400
(38)	1.2	150	(76)	2.2	270	(114)	3.1	400
(39)	1.4	150	(77)	2.4	270	(115)	2.4	400
(40)	2.1	150	(78)	1.8	280	(116)	3.0	400
(41)	0.9	160	(79)	2.8	290	(117)	3.4	420
(42)	1.1	160	(80)	2.2	290	(118)	3.5	420
(43)	1.7	160	(81)	2.4	290	(119)	3.1	420
(44)	2.0	160	(82)	2.1	290	(120)	2.9	420
(45)	1.6	170	(83)	1.9	290	(121)	2.8	430
(46)	1.9	170	(84)	2.4	300	(122)	3.3	430
(47)	1.7	170	(85)	2.5	300	(123)	2.5	440
(48)	2.2	180	(86)	2.9	300	(124)	2.8	440
(49)	2.4	180	(87)	2.0	300	(125)	2.4	450
(50)	1.6	180	(88)	1.9	310	(126)	2.6	450
(51)	1.8	190	(89)	2.5	310	(127)	3.0	450
(52)	4.1	190	(90)	2.6	310	(128)	3.4	460
(53)	2.0	190	(91)	3.2	320	(129)	3.0	460
(54)	1.5	200	(92)	2.8	320	(130)	3.3	470
(55)	2.1	200	(93)	2.4	320	(131)	3.4	470
(56)	2.5	200	(94)	2.5	320	(132)	3.1	470
(57)	1.7	220	(95)	2.0	330	(133)	3.6	480
(58)	2.0	220	(96)	2.4	340	(134)	3.0	480
(59)	2.3	220	(97)	2.2	340	(135)	2.9	480
(60)	1.8	220	(98)	2.0	340	(136)	3.2	480
(61)	1.3	230	(99)	2.5	350	(137)	2.6	490
(62)	1.6	230	(100)	2.8	350	(138)	3.8	490
(63)	2.8	230	(101)	2.3	350	(139)	3.3	490
(64)	2.2	230	(102)	2.7	350	(140)	2.9	500
(65)	2.6	230	(103)	2.8	360			

MICROCOMPUTER PACKAGE

· ·

The micro package *Computerized Business Statistics* can be used to solve correlation and regression analysis problems.

In Solved Exercises 1 and 2, Carlene Larsen is trying to find some variable that's positively related to daily sales. She investigates average temperature, which she'd like to use to predict daily ice cream sales.

Computer Solution:

From the main menu of *Computerized Business Statistics* a **9** is selected, which indicates Simple Correlation and Regression. The simple correlation and regression menu appears on the screen.

Since the problem involves entering data from the keyboard, a **1** is selected.

```
Simple Correlation and Regression-Define New Problem
Number of Data Points: Enter 4-125, Press ↵ 10
```

Since 10 days were sampled, **10** is selected.

```
Alpha Error 1 = 0.2, 2 = 0.1, 3 = 0.05, 4 = 0.02, 5 = 0.01, 6 = Other
Select Alpha: Enter 1-6, Press ↵ 3
Degrees of Freedom  ............................................... 8
Critical t (Alpha/2)  ........................................ 2.306
Simple Correlation and Regression-Enter Variable Labels
                    Independent Variable X1
                    Dependent Variable    Y

Press END when Finished
```

The variable names are *x* for average temperature and *y* for ice cream sales. **END** is pressed once the blanks have been completed.

Next, the program asks:

```
Problem definition correct Y/N/Q, Press ↵ Y
```

After a **Y** response, the program is ready for the data to be entered:

```
Enter Data Values
        x    y
 1 = 0    0
 2 = 0    0
 3 = 0    0
 4 = 0    0
 5 = 0    0
 6 = 0    0
 7 = 0    0
 8 = 0    0
 9 = 0    0
10 = 0    0

Press F when Finished
```

There are 10 pairs of data points. An **F** is entered once the blanks have been filled.

After the data have been entered, the screen shows:

```
        x    y
 1 =   72  110
 2 =   79  127
 3 =   85  140
 4 =   90  151
 5 =   66   89
 6 =   95  187
 7 =  100  205
 8 =   98  190
 9 =   82  136
10 =   91  165
```

You are asked:

```
Save Data? Y/N, Press ↵ N
```

The simple correlation and regression menu then reappears.

A 7 is entered so that the problem can be run, and the screen shows the output menu. The choice in this case is **P** for printer.

```
Residual analysis?
Enter Y/N, Press ↵ Y

Forecast, Interval analysis?
Enter Y/N, Press ↵ Y
```

Finally, the program asks:

```
Graphics?
Enter Y/N, Press ↵ Y
```

MINITAB COMPUTER PACKAGE
. . . .

The MINITAB commands to solve Examples 14.9, 14.10, 14.12, and 14.13 are:

```
MTB > READ 'CH14EX8.DAT' C1-C2
MTB > BRIEF 3
MTB > REGRESS C1 ON 1 PREDICTOR C2;
SUBC> PREDICT 6.

The regression equation is
SALES = 82.3 + 13.1 ADS

Predictor       Coef      Stdev     t ratio       P
Constant      82.268      7.000       11.75   0.000
ADS           13.056      1.644        7.94   0.000

s = 4.899      R-sq = 91.3%      R-sq(adj) = 89.9%

Analysis of Variance

SOURCE         DF         SS         MS        F        P
Regression      1     1512.9     1512.9    63.05    0.000
Error           6      144.0       24.0
Total           7     1656.9

    Fit   Stdev.Fit        95% C.I.           95% P.I.
 160.61        3.54   (151.95, 169.26)   (145.82, 175.39)

Obs.    ADS      SALES      Fit   Stdev.Fit   Residual   St.Resid
  1    3.00     125.00   121.44       2.53       3.56       0.85
  2    5.00     152.00   147.55       2.25       4.45       1.02
  3    4.00     131.00   134.49       1.74      -3.49      -0.76
  4    4.00     133.00   134.49       1.74      -1.49      -0.33
  5    5.00     142.00   147.55       2.25      -5.55      -1.28
  6    3.00     116.00   121.44       2.53      -5.44      -1.30
  7    3.00     127.00   121.44       2.53       5.56       1.33
  8    6.00     163.00   160.61       3.54       2.39       0.71

MTB > STOP
```

The BRIEF 3 command is used to provide an output that includes a table of residuals. The REGRESS command is used again to develop a regression analysis with sales as the dependent (*y*) variable and TV ads as the independent (*x*) variable. The PREDICT subcommand is used to compute a point estimate, a confidence interval estimate, and a prediction interval for a week when six ads are planned.

SAS Computer Package

· ·

The SAS computer package can be used to run regression analysis problems. The SAS commands to solve Example 14.19 are:

```
TITLE ''REGRESSION ANALYSIS FOR EXAMPLE 14.19'';
DATA USAGE;
INPUT Y X;
CARDS;
1174  246
1202  124
1283   26
1220   61
1182  253
1177  370
1150  634
1812 1069
1887 1225
1762 1212
1641 1066
1292  547
1213  242
1231   67
1443   20
1296  109
1205  272
1201  414
1308  631
1573  774
1684 1066
1855 1384
PROC PRINT;
PROC CORR;
PROC REG;
 MODEL Y=X;
```

Table 14.9 shows the SAS output for this run.

The TITLE command names the SAS run. The DATA command gives the data a name. The INPUT command names and specifies the order for the two data fields. The next 22 lines are card images that represent the y variable (average kilowatt-hours used per small commercial customer for the month) and the x variable (average cooling degree days for the month). The PROC PRINT command directs SAS to list the data. The PROC CORR command indicates that a correlation matrix is desired. The PROC REG command and MODEL subcommand indicate that y and x are the regression variables, with y being the dependent variable and x the independent variable.

MULTIPLE REGRESSION

*Once upon a
midnight dreary,
while I
pondered, weak
and weary, . . .*
Poe, "The
Raven"

Objectives

When you have completed this chapter, you will be able to:

Select good predictor variables.

Interpret a correlation matrix.

Test hypotheses to determine the significance of a multiple regression model and the independent variables in the model.

Recognize potential problems in using multiple regression analysis, especially the problem of multicollinearity.

Develop curvilinear models.

Incorporate qualitative variables into the multiple regression model.

Apply the stepwise regression approach.

Analyze computer output for a multiple regression model.

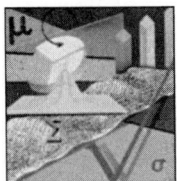

The June 16, 1992, *PC Magazine* compared the 486–50 PC chips' increased speed to its predecessors. It reported that machines with this chip are the most powerful on the market.

Chapter 14 covered simple regression analysis, where one independent variable is used to predict a dependent variable. When there are two or more predictor variables, the analysis is called *multiple regression,* the subject of this chapter.

WHY MANAGERS NEED TO KNOW ABOUT MULTIPLE REGRESSION ANALYSIS

The same logic applies in multiple regression as in simple regression. A single dependent variable is identified whose movements or variance the analyst wishes to explain. The analyst then identifies two or more potential predictor variables that may be correlated with the dependent variable. A random sample of items is selected from the population being studied, and an attempt is made to find a combination of predictor variables that produces a good prediction or regression equation for y.

Since there are many instances in business where movement of a quantitative variable is of great interest, multiple regression is one of the most widely used techniques in practical applications.

Regarding the 486–50 chip in the *PC Magazine* article, it might be interesting to study the effect of various factors on PC chip speed over the past few years. A number of variables that might possibly be related to chip speed could be identified, measured, and analyzed to observe their correlations with chip speed. The ultimate objective might be to find a good prediction equation for chip speed, and possibly extend the equation past current data to predict future speeds.

SELECTING PREDICTOR VARIABLES

Correlation Matrix

In a multiple regression analysis, the first step is to identify the dependent and predictor variables to be included in the prediction model. Next, a random sample is taken, and all the variables are recorded for each sampled item. The third step is to identify the relationships between the dependent and the predictor variables, and also among the predictor variables. This is done by analyzing the data using a computer program that produces a **correlation matrix** for the variables. This matrix is sized in accordance with the number of variables being investigated. If three variables are being analyzed, the correlation matrix will be 3×3 (three rows by three columns). If there are 10 variables, the correlation matrix will be 10×10.

A correlation coefficient for each combination of two variables appears at the intersection of every row and column of the correlation matrix. The two variables being measured are designated by the row number and the column number. Table 15.1 is an example of a correlation matrix for four variables (4×4). The correlation coefficient that indicates the linear relationship between variables 2 and 3 is represented as $r_{2,3}$. Note that the first subscript refers to the row and the second subscript refers to the column. Also note that the relationship between variables 2 and 3 ($r_{2,3}$) is exactly the

TABLE 15.1   Correlation Matrix

Variables	1	2	3	4
1	$r_{1,1}$	$r_{1,2}$	$r_{1,3}$	$r_{1,4}$
2	$r_{2,1}$	$r_{2,2}$	$r_{2,3}$	$r_{2,4}$
3	$r_{3,1}$	$r_{3,2}$	$r_{3,3}$	$r_{3,4}$
4	$r_{4,1}$	$r_{4,2}$	$r_{4,3}$	$r_{4,4}$

same as that between variables 3 and 2 ($r_{3,2}$). Finally, the coefficients along the primary diagonal ($r_{1,1}$, $r_{2,2}$, $r_{3,3}$, $r_{4,4}$) will always be 1 since a variable is always related to itself in a perfect positive way.

A correlation matrix displays the correlation coefficients for every possible pair of variables in the analysis.

For the sake of consistency, and to make it easy to read a typical computer output in this text, the y variable will be entered first and represented as variable 1, or x_1. This means that the first predictor variable will be represented as variable 2, or x_2.

EXAMPLE 15.1   An analyst has identified the dependent variable *job evaluation rating* for hourly employees of a large factory. He also identifies four possible predictor variables: age, entry test score, number of dependents, and years with the company. A random sample of 200 workers is selected from company files, and these four variables are recorded. A correlation matrix is calculated so that the strength of the association between the dependent variable and each predictor variable can be examined (Table 15.2).

The program numbers the variables keyed into the computer from left to right, beginning with number 1. Since the analyst chose to enter y first, the dependent variable in Table 15.2 is variable 1. Row 1 (or column 1) in the correlation matrix should be examined first to determine the correlations between y and the various predictor variables.

TABLE 15.2   Correlation Matrix for Example 15.1

	1	2	3	4	5
1	1	−.27	.78	−.83	.65
2	−.27	1	−.63	.47	−.46
3	.78	−.63	1	−.89	.17
4	−.83	.47	−.89	1	−.21
5	.65	−.46	.17	−.21	1

Inspection of Table 15.2 indicates that variable 2 isn't highly related to variable 1 ($r_{1,2} = -.27$), so it won't be a good predictor of *y*. Variables 3 and 4 have good potential as predictor variables since their correlations are fairly high: $r_{1,3} = .78$ and $r_{1,4} = -.83$. Variable 5 has only fair potential: $r_{1,5} = .65$. The purpose of this analysis is to find the strength of the associations between the dependent variable and the variables chosen as potential predictor variables. In this case, two good potential predictor variables have been found (entry test score and number of dependents), along with a predictor with fair potential (years with company).

There are two guidelines for selecting predictor variables for a multiple regression equation. The first of these is illustrated in Example 15.1. A predictor variable should be strongly correlated with the dependent variable. This is the same logic used in Chapter 14 for identifying a single predictor variable in a simple regression. In multiple regression, however, there's a second guideline that should be followed in selecting predictor variables.

Multicollinearity

If any two predictor variables in a multiple regression are too highly correlated, they interfere with each other by explaining the same variance in the dependent variable. This condition of high correlation between predictor variables is called **multicollinearity**. Multicollinearity is undesirable because it suggests that the predictor variables are not independent, and, as a consequence, it's difficult to say how much of the observed effect is due to an individual predictor variable. In other words, if two variables are highly correlated, they supply almost the same predictive information.

When two predictor variables are highly correlated, the sample regression coefficient estimators, $b_0, b_2, b_3, \ldots, b_k$ of the population regression coefficient parameters, $\beta_0, \beta_2, \beta_3, \ldots, \beta_k$ are undependable. The estimate b_2 of β_2 may not even be close to the true value of β_2 due to the high variability in the sampling distribution of β_2. In extreme cases, b_2 might even be negative when it should be positive. This phenomenon will be illustrated in Example 15.15. Since two variables that are highly correlated add little to the explanation of the dependent variable variance and create undependable regression coefficients, one of them should be dropped from the model.

> **Multicollinearity** results when predictor variables are too highly correlated among themselves.

The ideal in multiple regression analysis is to have uncorrelated predictor variables so that each explains a separate portion of the variation in the dependent variable. Figure 15.1 illustrates this concept. The pie chart represents the total variation of the dependent variable, *y*. The *x*s are separate pieces of the pie labeled A and B, and each explains a separate portion of the variability of *y*. Area C indicates the overlap (that portion of the *y* variance being explained by both predictor variables). Area D represents the unexplained portion of *y*'s variability.

FIGURE 15.1   Multicollinearity

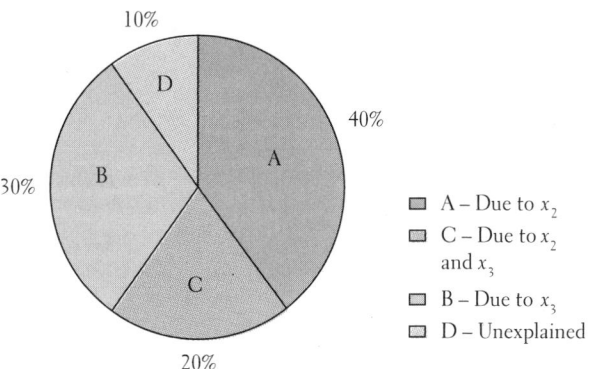

Predictor Variable Selection

The following two rules summarize the considerations that should prevail in selecting predictor variables in a multiple regression.

Rules for selecting predictor variables in a multiple regression:
1. A predictor variable should have a strong correlation with the dependent variable.
2. A predictor variable should not be too highly correlated with any other predictor variable.

EXAMPLE 15.2   In Example 14.7, Amy Green, Green Garden Company president, developed a simple regression model that used the number of TV ads run per week to predict weekly sales of garden supplies. She was able to explain 91.3% of the variance in sales through her knowledge of the linear relationship ($r = .956$) between the number of TV ads and sales. Amy wants to find another predictor variable to explain the remaining 8.7%.

Amy decides that the average temperature during a week should be related to weekly sales of garden supplies. Table 15.3 shows the data and the correlation matrix that result from running the analysis on a multiple regression program.

Both x variables are highly related to the dependent variable ($r_{1,2} = .956$ and $r_{1,3} = .921$) and thus have potential for being good predictor variables. However, the two predictor variables are highly related to each other ($r_{2,3} = .805$), so multicollinearity might be a problem.

EXAMPLE 15.3   The analyst in Example 15.1 can study Table 15.2 further to conduct a multiple regression analysis. The dependent variable (job evaluation rating) is

TABLE 15.3   Data and Correlation Matrix for Example 15.2

y	x_2	x_3
125	3	41
152	5	86
131	4	33
133	4	47
142	5	64
116	3	22
127	3	55
163	6	84

	Variables		
	1	2	3
1	1	.956	.921
2	.956	1	.805
3	.921	.805	1

variable one! Based on the correlation matrix and the two selection rules, the following predictor variable combinations are considered:

1. $y(x_1)$ should be predicted by x_4. *Reason:* x_4 has the highest correlation with the dependent variable of all the predictor variables collected ($r_{1,4} = -.83$) and will explain 69% ($-.83^2$) of the y variance. It is often of interest to run a simple regression analysis using the best single predictor.

2. y shouldn't be predicted by x_3 and x_4 together. *Reason:* Although both x_3 and x_4 have good correlations with the dependent variable ($r_{1,3} = .78$ and $r_{1,4} = -.83$), they are too highly correlated with each other ($r_{3,4} = -.89$). Multicollinearity is quite likely, as these two variables will be explaining the same y variance. When analysts examine correlations for multicollinearity, they use the following rule of thumb: The correlation between the two predictor variables should be well below the lower of the two correlations between the predictor variables and the dependent variable. This rule applies only to the magnitude of the correlation coefficients and ignores their signs. In this case, the correlation between predictor variables ($r_{3,4} = -.89$) *exceeds* the smaller of the dependent-predictor variable correlations ($r_{1,3} = .78$), ignoring the sign, so multicollinearity is likely.

3. y should be predicted by x_4 and x_5 together. *Reason:* x_4 has a good correlation with the dependent variable ($r_{1,4} = -.83$), and x_5 has a fair correlation ($r_{1,5} = .65$). However, the correlation between x_4 and x_5 is low ($r_{4,5} = -.21$), so multicollinearity won't be a problem. This combination should be examined since each predictor variable will explain a separate portion of the y variable variance, and a good prediction equation is likely to result.

4. y should be predicted by x_3 and x_5 together. *Reason:* x_3 and x_5 both have reasonable correlations with y ($r_{1,3} = .78$ and $r_{1,5} = .65$) and a low correlation with each other ($r_{3,5} = .17$). This combination should also produce a good prediction equation with no multicollinearity.

Note that none of these predictor variable combinations involves x_2. This variable has a low correlation with y $(r_{1,2} = -.27)$ and so would not be used alone or in any combination.

The three promising predictor variable combinations identified should be run using a computer program that performs multiple regression. The resulting regressions can then be analyzed to find the best sample prediction equation. Finally, the best sample equation can be evaluated to see if its predictive power for y is strong enough to use in the population.

EXAMPLE 15.4   Example 14.10 developed a regression equation to predict monthly overhead costs using machine hours. However, in a complex manufacturing environment, variable overhead costs may be driven by several equally important factors. Under such circumstances, using more than one base for applying variable overhead costs to products and jobs results in a more accurate cost estimate.[1]

As reported in *Management Accounting*, Nevin (1992) developed a multiple regression equation to forecast monthly overhead costs using direct labor hours, machine hours, and number of setups, as predictor variables. The data and a correlation matrix are presented in Table 15.4. Row 1 of the correlation matrix indicates variable x_3, machine hours, has the best potential $(r_{13} = .878)$ as a predictor variable. Variables x_2 and x_4, direct labor hours and number of setups, both have only fair potential $(r_{12} = .535)$

TABLE 15.4   Data and Correlation Matrix (Example 15.4)

FOH costs	Direct labor hours	Machine hours	Number of setups
155,000	985	1,060	200
160,000	1,068	1,080	225
170,000	1,095	1,100	250
165,000	1,105	1,200	202
185,000	1,200	1,600	210
135,000	1,160	1,100	150
145,000	1,145	1,080	165
150,000	1,025	1,090	180
180,000	1,115	1,300	204
175,000	1,136	1,400	206
190,000	1,185	1,500	208
200,000	1,220	1,700	212

	1 Costs	2 Labor	3 Machine	4 Setups
Costs	1	.535	.878	.627
Labor	.535	1	.768	-.047
Machine	.878	.768	1	.251
Setups	.627	-.047	.251	1

[1]A. M. Novin, "Applying Overhead: How to Find the Right Bases and Rates," *Management Accounting*, March 1992, pp. 40–43.

and ($r_{14} = .627$). The first rule for selecting predictor variables has indicated all three predictor variables have some potential since they are correlated with the dependent variable. Using both rules for selecting predictor variables, the following combinations are considered:

1. A simple regression using machine hours, x_3, as the predictor variable for y should be run. Reason: x_3 has the highest correlation with the dependent variable of all the predictor variables collected ($r_{13} = .878$) and will explain 77.1 percent $(.878)^2$ of the monthly overhead cost variance.
2. The combination of x_2 and x_3 should not be run. Reason: Although x_2 and x_3 are good potential predictor variables (correlations of .535 and .878 with y), they are also highly correlated with each other ($r_{23} = .768$). The correlation of .768 exceeds the smaller of the dependent-predictor variable correlations ($r_{12} = .535$), so multicollinearity is likely. The detection of multicollinearity in a multiple regression will be discussed later in this chapter.
3. The combination of x_3 and x_4 should be used together. Reason: x_3 is the best single predictor and x_4 is a fair predictor (correlation with y is .627). Their correlation with each other ($r_{34} = .251$) is lower than the two correlations with y. The run should be made so the outcome can be assessed.
4. There is no combination of three predictor variables that should be tried. Reason: The correlation matrix does not reveal any combination of three predictor variables that have good correlations with y and low correlations with each other.

Adel can now instruct a computer program to run the desired regressions. The result is presented in Example 15.7.

NOTES ON MULTICOLLINEARITY

When multicollinearity is present, how severe is the problem? Actually, if the analyst only wishes to use the regression model for prediction purposes, multicollinearity may not cause any serious difficulties. The adverse consequences of multicollinearity are:

1. Estimates of the regression coefficients fluctuate markedly from sample to sample.
2. An independent variable that's positively related to the dependent variable can produce a negative regression coefficient if it's highly correlated to another independent variable.
3. Multiple regression is often used as an interpretative tool to evaluate the relative importance of various independent variables. When predictor variables are intercorrelated, they explain the same variance in the prediction of the dependent variable. For this reason, it's difficult to separate the individual influences of each of the independent variables when multicollinearity is present.

It was mentioned earlier that the presence of multicollinearity may not be serious for applications where the analyst only wants to use the regression model for prediction purposes. In this case, the effects of unstable regression coefficients may cancel each other out, resulting in an accurate prediction of y. One example might be a site location study, such as where to locate a new McDonalds or Taco Time. Several highly related independent variables such as traffic count, traffic flow, population density, number of households, and number of registered drivers may be used to predict potential sales volume. Since the model is only being used to predict the best location (potential sales volume), the presence of multicollinearity may not be a severe problem.

EXERCISES

1. Explain the difference between a simple regression model and a multiple regression model.
2. Why does a correlation matrix contain 1s down the primary diagonal?
3. What is multicollinearity? How can it be prevented?
4. What are the characteristics of a good predictor variable?
5. In the following correlation matrix, variable 1 is the dependent variable.

	1	2	3	4
1	1	−.87	.78	.23
2	−.87	1	−.43	−.07
3	.78	−.43	1	.09
4	.23	−.07	.09	1

   a. Are variables 2, 3, and 4 good potential predictor variables?
   b. Will multicollinearity be a problem for any combination? Explain your answer.
   c. Which variable(s) will be included in the final model?

6. This exercise refers to the following correlation matrix where variable 1 is the dependent variable.

	1	2	3	4
1	1	.77	.84	.92
2	.77	1	.75	.81
3	.84	.75	1	.21
4	.92	.81	.21	1

   a. Are variables 2, 3, and 4 good potential predictor variables?
   b. Will multicollinearity be a problem for any combination? Explain your answer.
   c. Which variable(s) will be included in the final model?

7. In the following correlation matrix, variable 1 is the dependent variable.

	1	2	3	4	5	6
1	1	.571	.098	−.539	.810	.764
2		1	.258	−.112	.387	.418
3			1	−.007	.245	.187
4				1	−.419	−.158
5					1	.755
6						1

a. Why is half of the matrix below the primary diagonal blank?

b. Which predictor variables are related to the dependent variable?

c. What kind of relationship exists between variables 1 and 4?

d. Which predictor variable will explain the largest portion of the dependent variable's variance? What percentage will it explain?

e. Is there any evidence of multicollinearity?

f. Which combination or combinations of variables should be investigated further?

THE MULTIPLE REGRESSION EQUATION

Equation 15.1 shows how the population multiple regression model is written:

$$y = \beta_0 + \beta_2 x_2 + \beta_3 x_3 + \cdots + \beta_k x_k + \varepsilon \tag{15.1}$$

where
$$\begin{aligned}
y &= \text{Dependent variable} \\
x_2, x_3, \ldots, x_k &= \text{Predictor variables} \\
\beta_0, \beta_2, \beta_3, \ldots, \beta_k &= \text{Parameters in the population model} \\
\varepsilon &= \text{Random error component}
\end{aligned}$$

Regression Assumptions   The assumptions of the multiple regression model are similar to those for the simple linear regression model:

1. The probability distribution of ε is normal.

2. The variance of the probability distribution of ε is constant for all values of x.

3. The mean of the probability distribution of ε is 0. This assumption implies that the mean value of y for a given value of x is $E(y) = \beta_0 + \beta_2 x_2 + \beta_3 x_3 + \cdots + \beta_k x_k$.

4. The values of ε are independent of each other. This assumption implies that a random sample of objects has been selected from the population for measurement.

The least squares method produced the best-fitting straight line for two variables in Chapter 14. When three variables are analyzed, the least squares method produces a plane (Figure 15.2). When more than three variables are analyzed, the multiple regression model forms a hyperplane (or response surface) through multidimensional space. Note that whenever the term *plane* is used throughout the rest of the text, it will refer to a plane in three-dimensional space or a hyperplane in multidimensional space.

The multiple regression equation minimizes the sum of the squared vertical distances between the actual y values and their estimates based on the regression plane. In other words, in developing the multiple regression equation, $\Sigma(y - \hat{y})^2$ is minimized by the least squares procedure. This is the same quantity minimized in simple regression, as explained in Chapter 14. The difference in multiple regression is that the $\hat{y}$ values are calculated using more than one predictor variable. In other words, two or more predictor variable values are used in the prediction equation to calculate each $\hat{y}$.

Normally, the exact values of the regression parameters $\beta_0, \beta_2, \beta_3, \ldots, \beta_k$, and ε of Equation 15.1 aren't actually known but must be estimated from sample data. From

FIGURE 15.2   Multiple Regression Plane

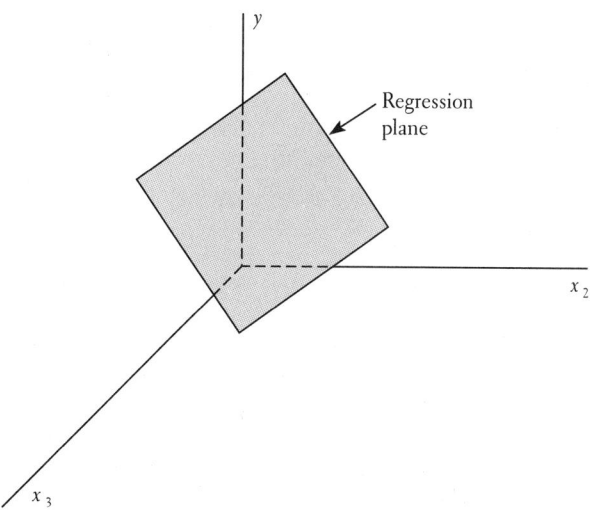

the sample data, estimates of the parameters are found, and the hyperplane that best fits the set of data points, called the *sample regression hyperplane*, is determined. Equation 15.2 uses b_0, b_2, b_3, . . ., and b_k to estimate β_0, β_2, β_3, . . ., and β_k:

Sample Regression Equation

$$\hat{y} = b_0 + b_2 x_2 + b_3 x_3 + \cdots + b_k x_k \tag{15.2}$$

where $\qquad \hat{y}$ = Estimated value of the dependent variable
$x_2, x_3, . . ., x_k$ = Predictor variables
$b_0, b_2, b_3, . . ., b_k$ = Sample estimates of $\beta_0, \beta_2, \beta_3, . . ., \beta_k$

As in the case of the simple regression model, the sample estimates b_0, b_2, b_3, . . ., b_k are obtained as solutions to a set of simultaneous linear equations. These are difficult to solve without the use of a computer program. For this reason, computer programs will be used to solve multiple regression exercises throughout the rest of this text.

If two predictor variables are used in multiple regression, the equation will have a y-intercept and two regression coefficients, one for each predictor (x). As in simple regression, the value b_0 is the y-intercept. If both x_2 and x_3 are 0, the regression equation value for $\hat{y}$ is b_0, the y-intercept. If it's possible for both x_2 and x_3 to approach 0, this interpretation might prove useful. In most cases, however, the two predictor variables are such that they can't be near 0. As in simple regression, the y-intercept rarely has a useful interpretation.

Estimated Regression Coefficient

The b_2, b_3, . . ., b_k values are referred to as **estimated regression coefficients.** Each coefficient measures the average change in y per unit change in the relevant predictor variable. However, since the simultaneous influence of all predictor variables on y is being measured, the net effect of x_2 (or any other x) must be measured apart from any influence of other predictor variables. Therefore, we say that b_2 measures the average change in y per unit increase in x_2, *holding the other predictor variables constant.*

A particular **estimated regression coefficient** measures the average change in the dependent variable for a one-unit increase in the relevant predictor variable, holding the other predictor variables constant.

EXAMPLE 15.5 In Example 15.2, Amy Green used the number of TV ads and average temperature to predict weekly sales. She used MINITAB to produce the following multiple regression equation:

$$\hat{y} = 86.255 + 8.324x_2 + 0.2877x_3$$

The regression coefficients in the equation are interpreted as follows:

1. If the number of ads run per week increases by one, and average daily high temperature during the week is held constant, weekly sales are expected to increase by an average of 8.324 (thousand dollars).
2. If average daily temperature during the week increases by 1°, and the number of ads run per week is held constant, weekly sales are expected to increase by an average of 0.2877 (thousand dollars).

After interpreting the regression coefficients, the analyst can develop point estimates or predictions for y using the regression equation. Values for the predictor variables are substituted into the regression equation, and the $\hat{y}$ value is computed. This is the most common application for multiple regression analysis in the business world, since forecasts of important dependent variables are often desired.

EXAMPLE 15.6 Amy can now use the multiple regression equation in Example 15.5 to predict weekly sales if the number of ads and the average temperature are specified. Suppose these values are known to be

$$x_2 = 4 \text{ (Number of ads)}$$
$$x_3 = 70 \text{ (Average weekly temperature)}$$

The prediction of weekly sales is

$$\begin{aligned} \hat{y} &= 86.255 + 8.324(4) + 0.2877(70) \\ &= 86.255 + 33.296 + 20.160 \\ &= 139.688 \text{ (thousand dollars)} \end{aligned}$$

The predicted weekly sales based on the sample multiple regression equation and the specified values of the predictor variables is $139,688. Now Amy wants to interpret the values in the equation.

How would an increase of one ad per week affect sales if average temperature is held constant?

$$\hat{y} = 86.255 + 8.324(5) + 0.2877(70)$$
$$= 148.012$$

Note that sales have increased by \$8,324 (148,012 − 139,688).

What is the effect on sales of an increase of 1° in the average temperature if the number of ads is held constant?

$$\hat{y} = 86.255 + 8.324(4) + 0.2877(71)$$
$$= 139.976$$

Note that sales have increased by \$288 (139,976 − 139,688).

MINITAB can be used to run multiple regression problems. The MINITAB commands to solve Examples 15.5 and 15.6 are:

```
MTB > READ C1-C3
DATA> 125 3 41
DATA> 152 5 86
DATA> 131 4 33
DATA> 133 4 47
DATA> 142 5 64
DATA> 116 3 22
DATA> 127 3 55
DATA> 163 6 84
DATA> END
      8 ROWS READ

MTB > NAME C1 'SALES' C2 'ADS' C3 'TEMP'
MTB > CORR C1-C3

            SALES       ADS
ADS         0.956
TEMP        0.921     0.805

MTB > REGRESS C1 ON 2 PREDICTORS C2 C3;
SUBC> PREDICT 4 70;
SUBC> PREDICT 5 70;
SUBC> PREDICT 4 71.
```

The regression equation is

```
SALES = 86.3 + 8.32 ADS + 0.288 TEMP
    Fit    Stdev.Fit        95% C.I.               95% P.I.
139.688      1.643    (135.463, 143.912)    (131.608, 147.767)
148.011      1.237    (144.831, 151.191)    (140.426, 155.597)
139.975      1.704    (135.594, 144.357)    (131.813, 148.138)
```

The rest of the regression output is shown in Table 15.6.

```
MTB > STOP
```

Note that the READ command is used to input the data instead of the SET command. The READ command puts the sales variable into C1, the TV ads variable into C2, and the average temperature variable in C3. The NAME command is used to name the table's columns. The CORR command provides the correlation matrix for these three variables. The REGRESS command is used to develop a regression analysis with sales as the dependent (*y*) variable and TV ads and average temperature as the independent (*x*) variables. The first PREDICT subcommand is used to compute both a point and 95% interval estimate for a week when four TV ads are planned and average temperature will be 70°. Note that the output is only partially shown here. Table 15.6 shows complete output.

EXAMPLE 15.7   In Example 15.4, Adel Nevin developed a multiple regression equation to forecast monthly overhead costs. He was able to explain 94.7 percent of the dependent variable variance using machine hours and number of setups as predictor variables.[2] He found:

$$y = 19{,}796.43 + 65.44(MH) + 322.21(NS)$$

where   *y* = Estimated monthly overhead costs
   MH = Machine hours
   NS = Number of setups

Adel can use this equation to predict monthly overhead costs if he specifies the values of the predictor variables. Suppose he wants to predict the monthly overhead costs for next month. He plans on 1,400 machine hours and 205 setups. The predicted value *y* is

$$y = 19{,}796.43 + 65.44(MH) + 322.21(NS)$$
$$y = 19{,}796.43 + 65.44(1400) + 322.21(205) = 177{,}465.48$$

The multiple regression equation predicts that monthly overhead costs will be $177,465.48 next month. Adel wonders about this prediction's accuracy.

STANDARD ERROR OF ESTIMATE

Standard Error of Estimate

In simple regression, as discussed in Chapter 14, the standard error of estimate is used to measure the variability, or scatter, of the observed sample *y* values around the sample regression line. In multiple regression, the **standard error of estimate** measures the variability, or scatter, of the observed sample *y* values around the regression plane. Equation 15.3 shows how the standard error of estimate is computed in multiple regression. This equation is identical to Equation 14.10 except for the computation of the degrees of freedom in the denominator:

$$s_{y \cdot x's} = \sqrt{\frac{\Sigma(y - \hat{y})^2}{n - k}} \tag{15.3}$$

where $s_{y \cdot x's}$ = Standard error of estimate
     y = Sample *y* values
     $\hat{y}$ = Values of *y* calculated from the regression plane or hyperplane
     k = Number of linearly independent parameters to be estimated (the

---

[2]A. M. Novin, "Applying Overhead: How to Find the Right Bases and Rates," *Management Accounting*, March 1992, pp. 40–43.

number of bs in the equation assuming the predictor variables are
linearly independent)

n = Sample size

The **standard error of estimate** measures the variability, or scatter, of the observed sample y values around the regression plane.

EXAMPLE 15.8   Joyce Miller, financial analyst for Edwall Chemical Corporation
(a fertilizer company), wants to predict the weekly interest rate Edwall pays for short-
term funds. The company president has ordered an intensive study of Edwall's financial and sales position after reading a *Wall Street Journal* article (November 2, 1989,
p. C16) indicating that U.S. farmers set an income record in 1988. The president can't
understand why Edwall's 1988 profits were so low.

Joyce randomly selects 100 weeks from the company files and records the interest
paid for each week (the dependent variable), along with several other variables that
she thinks will correlate well. After examining the correlation matrix produced by her
regression computer program, she finds a good predictor combination:

$$\hat{y} = -0.05 + 0.55x_4 - 0.42x_6$$

Joyce analyzes the following summary values

t value for x_4 = 4.79
t value for x_6 = -5.83
R^2 = .91 F = 89.44
$s_{y \cdot x's}$ = 0.004

She decides that the t values, F value, and R^2 all indicate that the regression equation
will do a good job of predicting the weekly interest Edwall paid. But how close will the
predictions based on this regression equation be? The standard error of estimate indicates that for the sample of 100 weeks, $\hat{y}$ typically differs from the actual value of y by
0.004. Joyce considers this typical error to be quite acceptable and is pleased with the
accuracy of the equation. It is easy to measure the two predictor variables, x_4 and x_6,
at the beginning of each week, so she can now make accurate predictions.

PREDICTION AND CONFIDENCE INTERVALS

The sample multiple regression equation is frequently used to make forecasts for y. If
a given set of x values are substituted in the regression equation, the expected value of
y can be found. This y value is called a *point estimate*. However, as stated in Chapter
14, this point estimate doesn't provide any knowledge about the degree of accuracy of
the forecast.

Chapter 14's prediction interval and confidence interval concepts can also be applied to multiple regression analysis. Equation 15.4 is used to compute a prediction
interval for y:

$$\hat{y} \pm t \, s_{\hat{y} \cdot x's}$$ (15.4)

where $\hat{y}$ = Regression equation prediction of y
        t = Value from t distribution based on $n - k$ degrees of freedom
             for a given prediction level
     $s_{\hat{y}\cdot x's}$ = Estimated standard error of the prediction

Equation 15.5 is used to compute a confidence interval for y:

$$\hat{y} \pm t\, s_{\hat{\mu}\cdot x's} \tag{15.5}$$

where $s_{\hat{\mu}\cdot x's}$ = Estimated standard error of the estimate

The assumptions made when we use Equations 15.4 and 15.5 to compute prediction and confidence intervals for y were introduced in Chapter 14 and restated earlier in this chapter. For multiple regression models, the formulas for the standard deviation of the sampling distributions for the estimator y, $s_{\hat{y}\cdot x's}$ and $s_{\hat{\mu}\cdot x's}$, are rather complex and won't be discussed in this text. Those who use regression computer packages will usually be provided both prediction and confidence intervals.

EXAMPLE 15.9   In Example 15.6, Amy Green wants to determine the accuracy of her prediction of $139,688. She decides to develop 95% prediction and confidence intervals. First, she checks the MINITAB computer output and finds the prediction interval is 131.608 to 147.767. Using Equation 15.4 to compute this prediction interval, she gets

$$\hat{y} \pm t\, s_{\hat{y}\cdot x's}$$
$$139.688 \pm 2.571(3.143)$$
$$139.688 \pm 8.080$$
$$131.608 \text{ to } 147.767$$

The t value for five degrees of freedom (df $= n - k = 8 - 3 = 5$) is used. If Amy runs four TV ads and average temperature is 70° next week, she's 95% confident that sales will be between $131,608 and $147,767.

Next, Amy checks the MINITAB computer output and finds the confidence interval is 135.463 to 143.912. Using Equation 15.5 to compute this confidence interval, she gets

$$\hat{y} \pm t\, s_{\hat{\mu}\cdot x's}$$
$$139.688 \pm 2.571(1.643)$$
$$139.688 \pm 4.225$$
$$135.463 \text{ to } 143.912$$

Amy is 95% confident that the mean of the subpopulation of y for a week when she runs four TV ads and average temperature is 70° is between $135,463 and $143,912.

EXAMPLE 15.10   In Example 15.7, Adel Nevin wondered about the accuracy of his prediction of $177,465.48 for the monthly overhead costs for next month. He notices on his computer output that the standard error of fit is 1,670. Adel decides to develop a 90% confidence interval. He substitutes the appropriate values into Equation 15.5:

$$\hat{y} \pm t\, s_{\hat{\mu}\cdot x's}$$
$$177,\!465.48 \pm 1.833(1670)$$
$$177,\!465.48 \pm 3061.11$$
$$174,\!404.37 \text{ to } \$180,\!526.59$$

Note that since the sample size is 12, the t value for 9 degrees of freedom is used. Adel is 90% confident that the interval from $174,404.37 to $180,526.59 contains the mean variable overhead costs for next month if 1,400 machine hours and 205 set-ups are used.

EXERCISES

8. What assumptions underlie the multiple regression model?

9. What is minimized when the least squares method is used to develop a multiple regression equation?

10. What does the estimated regression coefficient measure in multiple regression?

11. What does a residual measure?

12. What does the standard error of estimate measure in multiple regression?

13. Your multiple regression equation is $\hat{y} = 4.72 + 13x_2 - 4.2x_3$. Make a point estimate given $x_2 = 40$ and $x_3 = 20$.

14. Develop a 90% prediction interval for Exercise 13 if $s_{\hat{y}\cdot x's} = 2.8$. Compute this interval for a sample size of 25. Develop a 90% confidence interval for Exercise 13 if $s_{\hat{\mu}\cdot x's} = 1.5$ and the sample size is 43.

15. Mario Padilla (an accountant for the Palmer Furniture Corporation) wants to determine if overhead can be estimated based on the number of chairs and tables produced. Mario collects the following data on overhead expenses for chairs and tables produced at seven different plants:

Plant	Overhead expenses, y	Number of chairs, x_2	Number of tables, x_3
1	$576	112	95
2	497	122	84
3	789	147	102
4	862	173	108
5	361	94	75
6	688	151	99
7	532	109	91

a. Determine the sample multiple regression equation.

b. When an extra chair is produced, what is the average increase in overhead expense?

c. Compute the residual for plant 1.

d. Compute the standard error of estimate.

e. Interpret $s_{y\cdot x's}$ in terms of the variables used in this exercise.

f. Compute a point estimate of the overhead expense if 150 chairs and 100 tables are produced.

g. Calculate a 95% prediction interval for part f.

h. Calculate a 95% confidence interval for part *f*.

i. What should Mario conclude?

16. Spendwise supermarket chain manager Anna Sheehan wants to know if a relationship exists between the time it takes to check out a customer and the amount the person purchases. She chooses two predictor variables: the amount a person purchases and the number of purchased items. Anna collects data for a sample of 12 customers:

Customer	Checkout time (minutes), y	Purchase amount (dollars), x_2	Number of items, x_3
1	3.1	35	8
2	1.1	14	6
3	0.4	4	2
4	6.4	78	13
5	5.8	81	12
6	8.4	106	18
7	4.9	61	11
8	7.9	66	12
9	2.1	22	6
10	5.9	54	12
11	0.8	12	3
12	1.3	19	9

a. Determine the sample multiple regression equation.

b. When an extra item is purchased, what is the average increase in the checkout time?

c. Compute the residual for customer 12.

d. Compute the standard error of estimate.

e. Interpret $s_{y \cdot x's}$ in terms of the variables used in this exercise.

f. Compute a point estimate of the checkout time if a customer purchases 15 items that amount to $75.

g. Calculate a 90% prediction interval for part *f*.

h. Calculate a 90% confidence interval for part *f*.

i. Write a memo to Anna summarizing the results.

HYPOTHESIS TESTING IN MULTIPLE REGRESSION ANALYSIS

After the random sample has been collected, the variables measured, and the correlation matrix examined to find those predictor variable combinations that are of interest, the models with the best potential are analyzed. The objective is to find the best equation for predicting y and to then determine whether this equation meets the analyst's accuracy needs.

The criteria in Chapter 14 for evaluating a simple regression equation are used for multiple regression as well. Specifically, three key statistics should be examined in considering the quality of any regression equation, whether it has one predictor variable or many.

One statistic consulted frequently in multiple regression analysis is the **coefficient of multiple determination,** represented by the symbol R^2. It is useful for measuring the percentage of the variability in the dependent variable, y, that can be explained by the predictor variables.

The **coefficient of multiple determination,** R^2, measures the percentage of the variability in y that can be explained by the predictor variables.

An R^2 value close to 1 means that the equation is very accurate because a large portion of the variability of y is being explained. Equation 15.6 is used to calculate R^2 in a multiple regression. Note that this equation is similar to Equation 14.18 except that the calculations for $\hat{y}$ involve two or more predictor variables; this is denoted by capitalizing the symbol R^2:

$$R^2 = 1 - \frac{\Sigma(y - \hat{y})^2}{\Sigma(y - \bar{y})^2} \tag{15.6}$$

Note that the numerator of the ratio is the sum of squares error (SSE), which is used to measure how well the regression plane fits a set of sample data points. As SSE is reduced by adding new predictor variables to the model, R^2 increases. If a regression plane fits a set of sample data points perfectly, SSE equals 0 and R^2 equals 1.

EXAMPLE 15.11   Amy Green's data were introduced in Example 15.2. When the mean of y was used to predict weekly sales in Example 14.13, the sum of squares total (SST) was 1,656.88 and r^2 was 0:

$$r^2 = 1 - \frac{\text{SSE}}{\text{SST}} = 1 - \frac{1,656.88}{1,656.88} = 1 - 1 = 0$$

In Example 14.14, when knowledge of the relationship between the number of TV ads and weekly sales ($r = .956$) was used to predict the dependent variable, the sum of squares error (SSE) was reduced to 144, and r^2 increased to .913:

$$r^2 = 1 - \frac{\text{SSE}}{\text{SST}} = 1 - \frac{144}{1,656.88} = 1 - .087 = .913$$

Table 15.5 shows the residuals for the data in Example 15.2. The computation of the residual for week 1 (three TV ads were run, and average high temperature for the week was 41°) is

$$\hat{y} = 86.255 + 8.324(3) + 0.2877(41) = 123.021$$
$$e = y - \hat{y} = 125 - 123.021 = 1.979$$

TABLE 15.5   Sum of Squares Error Calculation for Example 15.11

y	x_2	x_3	$\hat{y}$	$(y - \hat{y})$	$(y - \hat{y})^2$
125	3	41	123.021	1.979	3.916
152	5	86	152.614	−0.614	0.377
131	4	33	129.043	1.957	3.830
133	4	47	133.071	−0.071	0.005
142	5	64	146.285	−4.285	18.361
116	3	22	117.555	−1.555	2.418
127	3	55	127.049	−0.049	0.002
163	6	84	160.363	2.638	6.959
			Sums:	0.00	35.868

$$\hat{y} = 86.255 + 8.324x_2 + 0.2877x_3$$

When the residual column is squared and summed, SSE falls to 35.868. R^2 increases to .978:

$$R^2 = 1 - \frac{SSE}{SST} = 1 - \frac{35.868}{1,656.88} = 1 - .022 = .978$$

The information collected up to this point is summarized:

Variables used to explain variance of y	R^2	SSE
None	0	1,656.88
Number of TV ads	.913	144.00
Number of TV ads and average high temperature	.978	35.87

Analysts often make the mistake of looking only at R^2 in evaluating a regression equation. This can lead to problems since R^2 reflects only the reduction in the sum of squares error, as shown in Equation 15.6. The contributions of individual predictor variables should be analyzed and hypotheses tested to see if the sample results can be extrapolated to the population. For these reasons, the t and F statistics in the regression output should also be examined.

The t values in the regression analysis test the hypotheses that the population regression coefficients equal 0. Suppose the following regression equation has been calculated:

$$\hat{y} = 14 - 7x_2 + 5x_3$$

The sample regression coefficient for predictor variable 2 is −7. This can be interpreted to mean that for each increase of one unit in x_2, holding x_3 constant, y can be expected to decrease by an average of seven units. But can this statement be made about the population? This question is answered by examining the t value for the regression coefficient for x_2.

The null hypothesis being tested is

$$H_0: \beta_2 = 0$$

Regression t Test

This null hypothesis states that in the population, regardless of the sample results, when x_2 increases by one, y is unaffected by this increase and assumes a random value. In other words, x_2 is contributing nothing to the predictive ability of the regression equation. If this null hypothesis is true, the test value for t is drawn from the t distribution with $(n - k)$ degrees of freedom (where n is the sample size and k is the number of linearly independent parameters, or βs, estimated in the analysis). A large t value ($t > 3$ or $t < -3$) will usually lead to rejection of the null hypothesis, and a t value close to 0 won't. The analyst therefore hopes for a large t value, either positive or negative, so that the sample regression coefficient can be generalized to the population.

We must also test the null hypothesis that $\beta_3 = 0$. The sample regression coefficient for x_3, which is 5, can't be generalized to the population until this null hypothesis is rejected. Before using the regression equation, we must be sure that all t values in the computer printout are larger than the critical values from the t table for the appropriate degrees of freedom at the significance level being tested.

The computed t values are of particular importance in a multiple regression because they constitute the primary way to detect multicollinearity. If the analyst is unsure about including two variables in the same regression because of their high relationship to each other, the regression is run and the t values are checked. If they are sufficiently large, the correlation between the two predictor variables isn't a problem. If one or both t values fall below the table value for t, multicollinearity is present, rendering the regression coefficients unreliable. The following examples show the use of the t test.

EXAMPLE 15.12 In Example 15.2, Amy Green, Green Garden Company president, developed a multiple regression model that used the number of TV ads run per week and the average temperature for the week to predict weekly sales of garden supplies. When she examined the correlation matrix in Table 15.3, she became concerned about the problem of multicollinearity. Amy decides to test the regression coefficients to make sure that each predictor variable is contributing to the prediction of the dependent variable. First, she tests the number of TV ads run per week (x_2) at the .05 significance level:

$$H_0: \beta_2 = 0$$
$$H_1: \beta_2 \neq 0$$

The decision rule based on 5 degrees of freedom $(n - k) = (8 - 3) = 5$ is

If the calculated t value is less than -2.571 or greater than 2.571, reject the null hypothesis (reject H_0 if $t < -2.571$ or $t > 2.571$).

Table 15.6 presents the results of a multiple regression computer analysis. The computed t value for the number of ads is 5.5. Since the computed t value is greater than the critical t value (2.571), the null hypothesis is rejected. The regression coefficient for the number of ads variable is significantly different from 0.

The same hypothesis test is performed for the regression coefficient for the variable representing average temperature. Table 15.6 shows that the computed t value for this variable is 3.88. Therefore, the regression coefficient for average high temperature is

TABLE 15.6 Computer Output for Examples 15.5, 15.6, and 15.12

```
The regression equation is
SALES = 86.3 + 8.32 ADS + 0.288 TEMP
Predictor        Coef        Stdev      t ratio        p
Constant       86.255        3.963        21.77     0.000
ADS             8.324        1.515         5.50     0.003
TEMP          0.28769      0.07411         3.88     0.012

s = 2.678     R-sq = 97.8%     R-sq (adj) = 97.0%

Analysis of Variance

SOURCE         DF          SS         MS         F         P
Regression      2     1621.01     810.50    112.99     0.000
Error           5       35.87       7.17
Total           7     1656.88

SOURCE         DF      SEQ SS
ADS             1     1512.90
TEMP            1      108.11

Obs.   ADS    SALES      Fit  Stdev.Fit  Residual  St.Resid
1     3.00  125.000  123.021      1.444     1.979      0.88
2     5.00  152.000  152.614      1.794    -0.614     -0.31
3     4.00  131.000  129.043      1.697     1.957      0.94
4     4.00  133.000  133.071      1.022    -0.071     -0.03
5     5.00  142.000  146.285      1.273    -4.285     -1.82
6     3.00  116.000  117.555      1.709    -1.555     -0.75
7     3.00  127.000  127.049      2.002    -0.049     -0.03
8     6.00  163.000  160.363      1.934     2.637      1.42
```

The following symbols may help you read this computer output.

$b_0 = 86.255$	$R^2 = 97.8\%$
$b_2 = 8.324$	$SSR = 1621.01$
$b_3 = .28769$	$SSE = 35.87$
$s_{y \cdot x} = 2.678$	$SST = 1656.88$

also significantly different from 0. Evidently, both variables explain some of the sales variance, so multicollinearity isn't a problem.

The F value is another statistic checked before the regression equation is used to explain the variability in y or to predict y. Just as in a simple regression, the F value tests the null hypothesis that the sample regression equation doesn't explain a significant percent of the y variance. This null hypothesis is

$$H_0: \rho^2 = 0 \text{ (The sample regression equation does not explain a significant percent of the variance in } y.)$$

Regression F Test

This hypothesis is rejected if the F statistic computed from the sample data is larger than the value from the F table.

Proper consideration of the three key factors in evaluating a regression analysis requires some practice and judgment. The following examples illustrate the process that the analyst follows in identifying the best prediction equation for y once those predictor combinations of interest have been determined from the correlation matrix and run on a computer program.

EXAMPLE 15.13   Continuing from Example 15.12, Amy Green tests the F value for her multiple regression equation at the .05 significance level. The null and alternative hypotheses are

$$H_0: \rho^2 = 0$$
$$H_1: \rho^2 > 0$$

Correct values for the degrees of freedom are 2 for the numerator and 5 for the denominator (see Table 15.6). The appropriate number of degrees of freedom associated with the regression sum of squares is the number of independent variables. Since the multiple regression equation in this example has two independent (x) variables, there are 2 degrees of freedom, as Table 15.6 shows for the "regression" source of variation.

Similarly, the degrees of freedom for the "residual" source of variation equal $(n - k)$, the sample size, n, minus the number of coefficients estimated in the regression equation (β_0, β_2, and β_3). Therefore, Table 15.6 shows 5 degrees of freedom $(n - k) = (8 - 3) = 5$ for this source of variation.

Finally, the loss of the degree of freedom for the total is due to the estimate of the population mean of y using the sample mean. Thus, Table 15.6 shows 7 degrees of freedom $(n - 1) = (8 - 1) = 7$ for the "total" row in the ANOVA table.

For 2 and 5 degrees of freedom, Appendix E.9's F table indicates a critical F value of 5.79 for the .05 significance level. The decision rule is

If the calculated F value is greater than 5.79, reject the null hypothesis.

The following sums of squares are found in Table 15.6: SSR = 1,621.01, SSE = 35.87, and SST = 1,656.88. The sums of squares are divided by the appropriate degrees of freedom to produce the estimates of the unknown population variance, referred to as the mean square values (MS) on the computer output. The mean square for the "regression" row is $1,621.01/2 = 810.5$. The mean square for the "residual" row is $35.87/5 = 7.17$. The F value is the ratio of these two estimates of the variance and is computed using Equation 14.21:

$$F = \frac{SSR/(k - 1)}{SSE/(n - k)} = \frac{1,621.01/(3 - 1)}{35.87/(8 - 3)} = \frac{810.5}{7.17} = 113$$

Since the computed F value (113) is larger than the critical F value (5.79), the null hypothesis is rejected. The sample regression equation is explaining a significant percentage of the y variance.

EXAMPLE 15.14   Bank of San Francisco analyst Shane Bahoney seeks a way to accurately predict a customer's profitability. He discovers a measure called the *profitability index* in "Case Study: Old Regional Bank" in *Statistical Decision Models for Management* by Hanke and Reitsch (Allyn & Bacon, 1985). This index is based on the activities of customers, including provisions for loans, savings accounts, and checking accounts.

Shane identifies two potential variables that might correlate well with the profitability index (y): monthly checking account charge and number of checks written per month. He hopes that these two variables will enable the bank to explain the index's variability and to predict customer profitability.

A random sample of 10 customers is selected, and the three numerical measurements are made on each. Table 15.7 shows the resulting data along with the correlation matrix computed from them.

TABLE 15.7   Data and Correlation Matrix for Example 15.14

Profitability index (y)	Monthly checking charge (x_2)	Checks per month (x_3)
31	2.65	35
18	4.08	29
16	3.59	22
37	3.03	55
30	3.41	61
44	2.51	52
15	3.18	25
35	2.75	38
51	2.10	58
59	2.14	83

| | Variables | | |
	1	2	3
1	1	−.867	.885
2	−.867	1	−.630
3	.885	−.630	1

Examination of the correlation matrix in Table 15.7 indicates two potentially good predictor variables. Both x_2 and x_3 have good correlations with the dependent variable ($r_{1,2} = -.867$ and $r_{1,3} = .885$). The best single predictor variable is x_3 because it has the highest correlation with y ($r_{1,3} = .885$) and would explain 78.3% of its variance ($.885^2 = .783$) if used in a simple regression equation.

The F test is used to determine whether the multiple regression equation explains a significant percent of the y variance. The null and alternative hypotheses are

$$H_0: \rho^2 = 0$$
$$H_1: \rho^2 > 0$$

The instructions to run these data on the SAS program are shown at the end of this chapter. Table 15.8 gives the results for this multiple regression run.

There are 2 degrees of freedom for the numerator and 7 for the denominator, as Table 15.8 shows. For the regression row, referred to as "model" on the SAS computer output, df $= (k - 1) = (3 - 1) = 2$. For the residual row, referred to as "error" on the SAS computer output, df $= (n - k) = (10 - 3) = 7$. Finally, for the "total" row, df $= (n - 1) = (10 - 1) = 9$.

For 2 and 7 degrees of freedom, the F table in Appendix E.9 indicates a critical value of 4.74 for the .05 significance level. The decision rule is

If the calculated F value is greater than 4.74, reject the null hypothesis.

The following sums of squares are found in Table 15.8: SSR = 1,874.57, SSE = 113.82, and SST = 1,988.40. The mean square for the "model" row is 1,874.57/2 = 937.29. The mean square for the "error" row is 113.82/7 = 16.26. The F value is

$$F = \frac{SSR/(k-1)}{SSE/(n-k)} = \frac{1,874.57/(3-1)}{113.82/(10-3)} = \frac{937.29}{16.26} = 57.6$$

Since the calculated F value (57.6) is considerably larger than the critical value (4.74), the null hypothesis is rejected with small chance of error. Shane concludes that the sample regression equation explains a significant percentage of the y variance ($\rho^2 > 0$).

The p value provided by the SAS program in Table 15.8 leads to the same conclusion. The p-value for the F statistic is .0001, meaning that the probability of obtaining an R^2 value as large as .943 by chance alone is very small (.0001). The analyst should

TABLE 15.8   SAS Computer Output for Example 15.14

DEPENDENT VARIABLE: INDEX

SOURCE	DF	SUM OF SQUARES	MEAN SQUARE	F VALUE	PR > F	R-SQUARE	
MODEL	2	1874.57	937.29	57.6	.0001	.943	
ERROR	7	113.82	16.26		ROOT MSE		Y-MEAN
TOTAL	9	1988.40			4.0325		33.6

SOURCE	DF	TYPE I SS	F VALUE	PR > F	DF	TYPE III SS	F VALUE	PR > F
X2	1	1496.24	92.01	.0001	1	316.41	19.46	.0031
X3	1	378.33	23.27	.0019	1	378.33	23.27	.0019

PARAMETER	ESTIMATE	T FOR HO = PARAMETER = 0	PR > [T]	STD ERROR OF ESTIMATE
INTERCEPT	49.02			
X2	−11.97	−4.41	.0031	2.71
X3	0.43	4.82	.0019	0.09

OBSERVATION	OBSERVED VALUE	PREDICTED VALUE	RESIDUAL
1	31	32.44	−1.44
2	18	12.72	5.28
3	16	15.56	0.44
4	37	36.55	0.45
5	30	34.60	−4.60
6	44	41.48	2.52
7	15	21.77	−6.77
8	35	32.55	2.45
9	51	48.99	2.01
10	59	59.33	−0.33

SUM OF RESIDUALS	0.00
SUM OF SQUARED RESIDUALS	113.82

The following symbols may help you read this computer output. Some items have been left out of the output to make it easier to read.

SSR = 1,874.57	b_0 = 49.02
SSE = 113.82	b_2 = −11.97
SST = 1,988.40	b_3 = 0.43
R^2 = .943	$(y - \hat{y})$ = −1.44 (Obs. 1)
$\bar{y}$ = 33.6	

conclude that R^2 is significantly different from 0. The multiple regression equation explains a significant percentage of the dependent variable variance.

Attention now turns to the question of whether using x_2 and x_3 together in a multiple regression equation is a good idea. Since both have strong correlations with y, they pass the first test for good predictor variables. But what about the correlation between them? The correlation matrix in Table 15.7 indicates this correlation ($r_{2,3}$) to be $-.63$. Although this value is below both correlations with y ($-.867$ and $.855$), it's still high enough to cause concern about multicollinearity.

The regression should be run and the t values tested to see if multicollinearity is a problem. There are 7 degrees of freedom for the t test, as shown in the "df" column and "error" row. This value is calculated as $(n - k)$, where k is the number of βs, or linearly independent parameters to be estimated in the analysis. Since three parameters are involved (β_0, β_2, and β_3), the degrees of freedom is $(10 - 3) = 7$. For 7 degrees of freedom, the t table indicates a critical value of 2.365 for a two-tailed test at an alpha level of .05. The decision rule is

If the calculated t value is less than -2.365 or greater than 2.365, reject the null hypothesis.

Since both t values (-4.41 and 4.82) are significant, both null hypotheses are rejected. Both regression coefficients are significant, and the regression equation is used to estimate values in the population. The correlation between x_2 and x_3 ($r_{2,3} = -.63$) has not led to multicollinearity.

The p-values provided by the SAS program lead to the same conclusion. The p-values for the t statistics are .0031 and .0019, indicating that probabilities of obtaining regression coefficients as large as -11.97 and .43 by chance alone are very small. The analyst should therefore conclude that the regression coefficients are significantly different from 0. Both predictor variables explain a significant portion of the variance.

Table 15.8's multiple regression equation

$$\hat{y} = 49.02 - 11.97x_2 + 0.43x_3$$

can be interpreted for the population of bank customers as follows: Holding x_3 constant, a \$1 increase in monthly checking charge (x_2) will decrease the profitability index by an average of about 12 units (-11.97). With x_2 held constant, an increase of one check per month (x_3) will increase the profitability index by an average of 0.43 units. Bank management can use these values to evaluate the effects of these two key variables on the important profitability index.

In addition, the multiple regression equation can be used to predict the profitability index for a customer if both x_2 and x_3 are known. For example, a customer who incurs a monthly checking charge of \$1.25 and writes 62 checks is predicted to have a profitability index of 60.72:

$$\hat{y} = 49.02 - 11.97x_2 + 0.43x_3$$
$$= 49.02 - 11.97(1.25) + 0.43(62) = 60.72$$

EXAMPLE 15.15   Rashid Al-Qamra, vice president of a manufacturing firm, wants to promote physical fitness for his company's employees. He first became interested in this idea after reading an article on the rewards of having fit employees, "Let's Get Physical" (*Business Monthly*, March 1990).

While flying to a board of directors meeting, Rashid read in Northwest Airlines' *World Traveler* that "premature deaths cost American industry more than $25 billion and 132 million workdays of lost production each year." Rashid asks statistician Sue Ableson to analyze the effectiveness of the company's fitness center. Sue collects data on several employees for y, the score on a fitness rating scale; x_2, the perceived level of exertion during exercise at the fitness center; and x_3, the average number of visits to the fitness center per week.

Table 15.9 displays the variables along with the correlation matrix generated by a computer program.

TABLE 15.9   Data and Correlation Matrix for Example 15.15

y	x_2	x_3
36	9.6	5.5
12	2.6	1.8
24	3.5	0.9
27	6.1	2.8
36	7.8	4.6
34	6.9	3.7
17	4.4	1.9
23	6.1	1.8
31	7.0	2.7
30	6.8	2.0

		Variables	
	1	2	3
1	1	.896	.748
2	.896	1	.842
3	.748	.842	

After studying the correlation matrix, Sue is pleased to find that both x variables correlate well with y: $r_{1,2} = .896$ and $r_{1,3} = .748$. She decides to run two regressions. First, y will be explained by x_2 alone; she observes that x_2 is the single best predictor, since it has the higher correlation with y. Second, y will be predicted by x_2 and x_3 together; Sue reasons that these two potentially good predictor variables should produce a strong prediction equation when used together. Tables 15.10 and 15.11 show the MINITAB computer results from these two regressions.

Sue notes that R^2 for the multiple regression equation is the same as r^2 using x_2 alone (80.3%), and she decides to use both variables to predict y. The equation, from Table 15.11, is

$$\hat{y} = 5.79 + 3.54x_2 - 0.115x_3$$

She gives this equation to her boss and indicates that it will produce fairly accurate predictions for y, based on the R^2 of about 80%.

TABLE 15.10   MINITAB Computer Output for Example 15.15

```
The regression equation is
Y = 5.88 + 3.48X2

Predictor      Coef        Stdev       t ratio
Constant       5.880
X2             3.480       1.206       5.70

s = 3.802      R-sq = 80.3%

Analysis of Variance

SOURCE         DF          SS          MS
Regression     1           470.37      470.37
Error          8           115.63      14.45
Total          9           586.00
```

TABLE 15.11   MINITAB Computer Output for Example 15.15

```
The regression equation is
Y = 5.79 + 3.54 X2 - 0.11 X3

Predictor      Coef        Stdev       t ratio
Constant       5.793
X2             3.540       1.206       2.94
X3            -0.115       1.755      -0.07

s = 4.063      R-sq = 80.3%

Analysis of Variance

SOURCE         DF          SS          MS
Regression     2           470.44      235.22
Error          7           115.56
Total          9           586.00

SOURCE         DF          SEQ SS
X2             1           470.37
X3             1           0.07
```

The following symbols may help you read this computer output:

b_0 = 5.793		R^2 = 80.3%	
b_2 = 3.540		SSR = 470.44	
b_3 = -0.115		SSE = 115.56	
$s_{y \cdot x's}$ = 4.063		SST = 586.00	

Unfortunately, Sue hasn't guarded against multicollinearity. Table 15.9's correlation matrix indicates that x_2 and x_3 should *not* be used in the same regression equation since the correlation between them is too high ($r_{2,3}$ = .842). This correlation is nearly as high as the correlation between x_2 and y (.896) and higher than the correlation between x_3 and y (.748). For this reason, multicollinearity is sure to result.

Table 15.11 shows symptoms of multicollinearity. The t value for x_2 has dropped from what it was when x_2 was used alone (2.94 compared with 5.70). Worse, the t value for x_3 (-0.07) is not significant. Based on this t value, x_3 shouldn't be used in conjunction with x_2. This conclusion renders the regression equation useless in the population for which it's intended.

There's an even more serious problem caused by multicollinearity: the sign on the regression coefficient for x_3 is the opposite of what it should be. There's a *positive* correlation between x_3 and y ($r_{1,3}$ = .748) but a *negative* regression coefficient

$(b_3 = -0.115)$. The latter value is interpreted to mean that when x_3 increases, holding x_2 constant, y *decreases* by an average of 0.115 units. This regression coefficient doesn't make sense since x_3 and y are positively correlated.

The basic problem caused by multicollinearity is that the sample regression coefficients vary excessively from sample to sample. One sample may produce a small positive value, another may produce a large negative value, the next may produce a large positive value, and so on. As Table 15.11 shows, this particular sample has produced a regression coefficient for x_3 that has varied so much that it's negative instead of positive. If this equation is used, the results are sure to be erroneous. Sue would be much better off using the simple regression equation in Table 15.10, which has an r^2 of 80% along with a valid t value.

EXERCISES

17. What does the coefficient of multiple determination measure?

18. Gary Texaco owns a gas station in Cleveland, Ohio. Gary has developed the following multiple regression equation based on weekly sales of unleaded gas:

$$\hat{y} = 100 - 50x_2 + 4x_3 \qquad s_y = 20 \qquad s_{\hat{\mu} \cdot x's} = 6 \qquad n = 36$$

where $\hat{y}$ = Estimated sales of unleaded gasoline (gallons)
         x_2 = Price of unleaded gasoline (cents)
         x_3 = Traffic count

   a. Interpret the estimated regression coefficients.

   b. Compute a point estimate of weekly sales of unleaded gas if price is .95 and traffic count is 4,456 cars.

   c. Compute a 95% confidence interval for your prediction for part b.

19. Rob Higgens, a real estate broker, wants to develop a regression equation to predict the sale price of homes (in thousands of dollars) in Flint, Michigan. Rob read "An Application of Multiple Regression Analysis for Appraising Single-Family Housing Values" in *Business Economics* (January 1980, pp. 47–52), indicating predictor variables that could be utilized in predicting price (including total living area, number of rooms, number of baths, and age of property). Rob decided to use age of house (x_2), square feet of living space (x_3), measured in hundreds, and number of rooms (x_4) as predictor variables. He collected data for 22 houses and gives it to you to perform an analysis on a microcomputer. A portion of the analysis of variance table follows:

ANALYSIS OF VARIANCE

SOURCE OF VARIATION	DEGREES OF FREEDOM	SUM OF SQUARES
ATTRIBUTABLE TO REGRESSION	3	2448.65
DEVIATION FROM REGRESSION	18	424.81
TOTAL	21	2873.46

   a. Calculate R^2.

   b. Show how the degrees of freedom for the "deviation from regression" was computed.

   c. Should Rob use this multiple regression equation? Why or why not?

20. In Exercise 19, the computer output for housing value appraisal also contained the following information:

VARIABLE NO.	REGRESSION COEFFICIENT	STD. ERROR OF REG COEF.	COMPUTED T VALUE
2	3.15241	0.92010	3.426
3	1.52483	0.39568	3.854
4	2.52752	2.68925	0.940

a. Which variables are contributing significantly to the prediction of sales price at the .01 significance level (one-tailed test)?

b. Interpret the estimated regression coefficients.

c. Is multicollinearity a problem in this analysis?

d. Write a short memo to Rob summarizing your conclusions.

21. Fast Service Food Mart owner Sue McGinty wants to predict the number of quart bottles of pop (y) sold each day. She decides to investigate using the number of people on the street (x_2) and the predicted high temperature (x_3) as predictor variables. A random sample of 30 (nonconsecutive) days is selected. A partial computer output shows the following results:

CORRELATION MATRIX: 3 BY 3

	1	2	3
1	1	.792	.826
2	.792	1	.653
3	.826	.653	1

VARIABLE NO.	MEAN	STANDARD DEVIATION	REGRESSION COEFFICIENT	STD. ERROR OF REG COEF.	COMPUTED T VALUE
2	985.28	240.850	0.13589	0.04855	_____
3	65.87	21.48	0.81245	0.19568	_____
DEPENDENT					
1	62.20	25.90			

INTERCEPT   −31.85

STD. ERROR OF ESTIMATE _____   R-Squared _____

ANALYSIS OF VARIANCE

SOURCE OF VARIATION	DEGREES OF FREEDOM	SUM OF SQUARES	MEAN SQUARES	F VALUE
ATTRIBUTABLE TO REGRESSION	2	12145.54	_____	_____
DEVIATION FROM REGRESSION	_____	3125.61	_____	
TOTAL		15271.15		

a. Analyze the correlation matrix.

b. Test the significance of the estimated regression coefficients at the .05 significance level (one-tailed).

c. Explain how pop sales are affected by an increase of 1° in predicted high temperature.

d. Estimate the number of quart bottles that will be sold tomorrow if the traffic count is 900 people and the high temperature is predicted to be 70°.

e. Calculate the standard error of estimate.

f. Calculate R^2 and interpret its meaning.

g. Calculate the F value and test to determine if the multiple regression equation has increased R^2 significantly. Use the .01 significance level.

h. Is multicollinearity a problem?

i. What should Sue McGinty conclude?

22. A large manufacturing firm's personnel department interviewed and tested a random sample of 21 workers. On the basis of the test results, the following variables were investigated:

$x_2 =$ Dexterity score
$x_3 =$ Aptitude score
$x_4 =$ Anxiety score

Subsequently, the workers were observed to determine the average number of units of work completed (y) in a given time period for each worker. Regression analysis yielded

$$\hat{y} = -212 + 2.12x_2 + 1.80x_3 - 0.45x_4$$
$$\phantom{\hat{y} = -212 + } (.070) \quad (.050) \quad (0.30)$$

The quantities in parentheses are the standard errors of the regression coefficients. Also, $s_{y \cdot x's} = 4.2$ and $s_y = 15.4$.

a. Which variables are making significant contributions to the prediction of work units completed at the .05 significance level (two-tailed test)?

b. Interpret the estimated regression coefficient for the aptitude score variable.

c. Estimate the number of work units completed for a worker with a dexterity score of 100, an aptitude score of 80, and an anxiety score of 10.

d. Calculate the sum of squares error (SSE).

e. Calculate the sum of squares total (SST).

f. Calculate R^2 and interpret its meaning.

23. Stan Birch, owner of Komputer Korner, needs to predict the number of Leading Edge computers he'll sell next month. He collects data on the selling price and amount spent on advertising for 10 randomly selected months:

Month	Sales, y	Selling price, x_2	Advertising expenditures, x_3
1	10	1,300	900
2	6	2,000	700
3	5	1,700	500
4	12	1,500	1,400
5	10	1,600	1,500
6	15	1,200	1,200
7	5	1,600	600
8	12	1,400	1,000
9	17	1,000	1,500
10	20	1,100	2,100

Run the data on a multiple regression program.

a. Analyze the correlation matrix.

b. Which variables are making significant contributions to the prediction of sales at the .05 significance level (two-tailed test)?

c. What is the prediction equation?

d. Interpret the estimated regression coefficients.

e. What percentage of the sales variance can be explained with this equation?

   f. Is multicollinearity a problem in this analysis?

   g. Predict sales for next month if the selling price is $1,500 and $1,000 is spent on advertising.

MODEL BUILDING

The major function of regression analysis is to test several possible models, each based on a sound economic and scientific foundation. When this approach is followed, the regression tests simply serve to determine which model is best.

Model building is the key to the success or failure of regression analysis. If the regression model doesn't represent the true nature of the relationship between the dependent variable and independent variables, the modeling effort will usually be unproductive. Model building involves developing a model that will provide a good fit to a set of data not only mathematically but also intuitively. The process should lead to adopting a model that gives good estimates of the mean value of *y* and good predictions of future values of *y* for given values of *x*.

Model building is the development of a regression equation that will provide a good fit to a particular set of data.

In regression analysis, the two primary activities in model building are determining the form of the model and selecting the variables to be included in the model. The form of the model may be linear, curvilinear, or nonlinear.

So far you've learned that a linear model is a model that's linear in the regression coefficients and the error term. Sometimes the data of interest don't exhibit a linear relationship. When this is the case, some way must be found to deal with a relationship that can't be approximated with a linear model. There are two basic approaches for dealing with curvilinear and nonlinear relationships. The first approach is to fit the data with a curved model. The second approach is to convert one or more variables to another form so that the resulting relationship with *y* is linear. Once the data are plotted, it's often evident that a transformation of the data (such as taking logarithms, square roots, or reciprocals) will produce relatively linear patterns, so that a straight line may be adequate.

A model that's linear in the regression coefficients and the error term may be nonlinear with respect to the independent variables. Such a model is referred to as a *curvilinear model*.

CURVILINEAR MODELS

One important type of curvilinear response model is the polynomial regression model:

$$y = \beta_0 + \beta_1 x + \beta_2 x^2 + \cdots + \beta_k x^k + \varepsilon \tag{15.7}$$

In this model, k is the order of the equation. The value of the highest power of an independent variable in a model is referred to as *order of the model*. For example, the simple linear regression model presented in Equation 14.5

$$y = \beta_0 + \beta_1 x + \varepsilon$$

is a first-order model.

The second-order model is

$$y = \beta_0 + \beta_1 x + \beta_2 x^2 + \varepsilon \qquad (15.8)$$

where y = Dependent variable
x = Independent variable
β_0 = y-intercept
β_1 = Parabola shifter
β_2 = Curvature coefficient
ε = Random error component

This equation provides a curve shaped like a parabola. The β_0 coefficient still represents the intercept where the curve intersects the y axis. The value of β_1 shifts the parabola to the right or left. If $\beta_1 = 0$, for example, the parabola is symmetrical and centered at $y = 0$. Increasing the value of β_1 causes the parabola to shift to the left. The β_2 coefficient describes the curvature. If $\beta_2 = 0$, there's no curvature. If $\beta_2 > 0$, the equation opens upward or is convex (Figure 15.3a). If $\beta_2 < 0$, the equation opens downward or is concave (Figure 15.3b).

The third-order model is

$$y = \beta_0 + \beta_1 x + \beta_2 x^2 + \beta_3 x^3 + \varepsilon \qquad (15.9)$$

where β_3 = Controls the rate of reversal of curvature for the curve

This equation provides a model that contains one reversal in curvature and one peak and one trough (Figure 15.4). Reversals in curvature aren't common, but such relationships can be modeled by third- and higher-order polynomials. Example 15.16 illustrates a second-order model.

EXAMPLE 15.16 Gilbert Garcia owns a chain of hardware stores in Chicago. He wants to predict monthly sales using knowledge of the corresponding monthly advertising expenditures. Gil suspects that sales will increase as the amount spent on advertising increases. However, he also believes that at a certain point, sales will begin to increase at a slower rate. Gil feels that he'll reach a point where there will be little to gain in sales by spending a larger amount on advertising.

Gil selected a random sample of 14 weeks of data from company records (Table 15.12). Figure 15.5 shows a scatter diagram of the data. He notes that sales do appear to level off after a certain amount is spent on advertising. A curvilinear relationship seems to exist between sales and advertising expense.

FIGURE 15.3   Second-Order Models

a. Model with $\beta_2 > 0$ (convex)

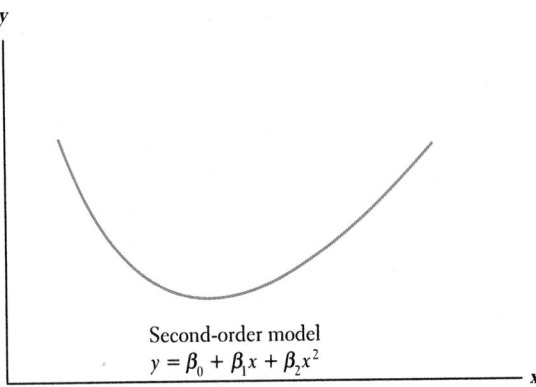

Second-order model
$$y = \beta_0 + \beta_1 x + \beta_2 x^2$$

b. Model with $\beta_2 < 0$ (concave)

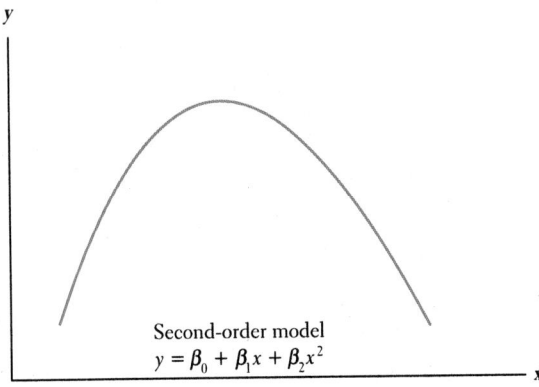

Second-order model
$$y = \beta_0 + \beta_1 x + \beta_2 x^2$$

Gil uses the following MINITAB commands to run a curvilinear model:

```
MTB> SET C1
DATA> 1.1 1.7 2.6 2.4 2.3 2.9 .4 3.2 3.3 3.1 3.2
DATA> 3.0 3.7 3.3
DATA> END
MTB> SET C2
DATA> 3.9 4.9 7.6 6.8 5.9 9.1 3.4 11.6 14.1 14.9
DATA> 10.5 9.9 17.1 12.4
DATA> END
MTB> MULT C2 BY C2 PUT INTO C3
MTB> NAME C1 'SALES' C2 'EXP' C3 'EXPSQR'
MTB> REGRESS C1 ON 1 PREDICTOR C2
     OUTPUT IS SHOWN IN TABLE 15.13
MTB> REGRESS C1 ON 2 PREDICTORS C2 C3
     OUTPUT IS SHOWN IN TABLE 15.14
MTB> STOP
```

FIGURE 15.4   Third-Order Models

a. Model with $\beta_3 > 0$

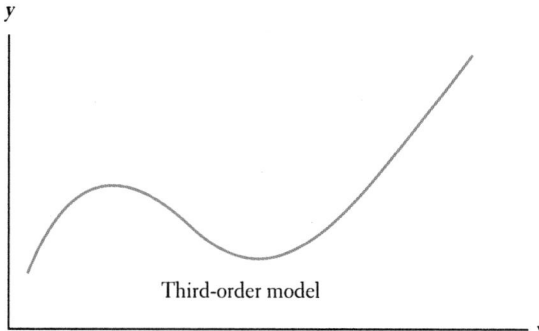

Third-order model

b. Model with $\beta_3 < 0$

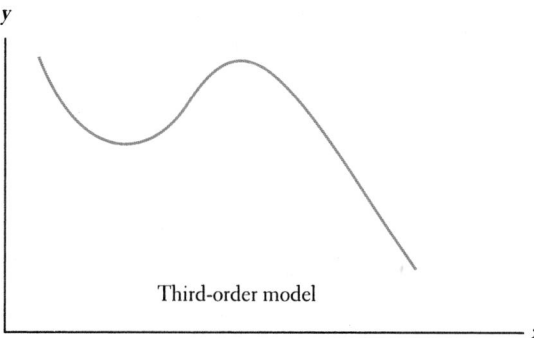

Third-order model

TABLE 15.12   Data for Example 15.16

Week	Sales ($000)	Advertising expenditures ($00)
1	1.1	3.9
2	1.7	4.9
3	2.6	7.6
4	2.4	6.8
5	2.3	5.9
6	2.9	9.1
7	0.4	3.4
8	3.2	11.6
9	3.3	14.1
10	3.1	14.9
11	3.2	10.5
12	3.0	9.9
13	3.7	17.1
14	3.3	12.4

FIGURE 15.5   Data Plot for Example 15.16

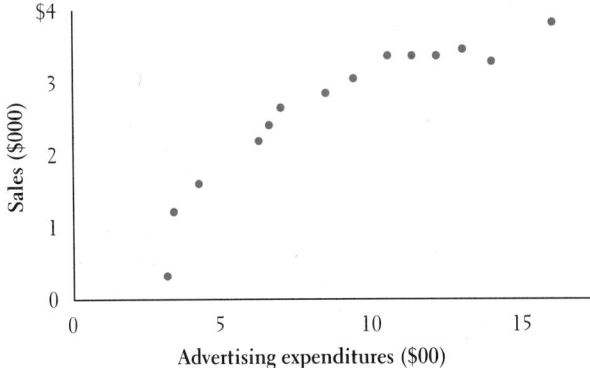

Table 15.13 presents the output for a simple linear regression equation. The linear regression equation, $\hat{y} = 0.754 + 0.194x$, explains 77.7% of the variance in the dependent variable.

Next, Gil instructs the program to square the x_2 variable, thus generating a new variable, x_3 ($x_2^2 = x_3$), which will model the curvilinear effect. Table 15.14 shows the MINITAB output. The multiple regression equation $\hat{y} = -1.01 + 0.627x_2 - 0.022x_3$, explains 93.2% of the variance in y. This equation explains an additional 15.5% of the variance; therefore, if the regression coefficients are both significant, Gil should use it.

The appropriate hypotheses to test the β_1 coefficient are

$$H_0: \beta_1 = 0$$
$$H_1: \beta_1 \neq 0$$

The appropriate degrees of freedom to test this hypothesis is df $= (n - k) = (14 - 3) = 11$. The decision rule if the hypothesis is tested at the .05 significance level is

If the calculated t statistic is less than -2.201 or greater than 2.201, reject the null hypothesis (reject H_0 if $t < -2.201$ or $t > 2.201$).

TABLE 15.13   MINITAB Computer Output for Example 15.16

```
The regression equation is
SALES = 0.754 + 0.194 EXP

Predictor     Coef    Stdev    t ratio
Constant      0.754
EXP           0.194   0.030     6.44

s = 0.461    R-sq = 77.7%

Analysis of Variance

SOURCE        DF      SS        MS
Regression     1      8.89      8.89
Error         12      2.55      0.21
Total         13     11.44
```

TABLE 15.14 MINITAB Computer Output for Example 15.16

```
The regression equation is
SALES = -1.01 + 0.627 EXP - 0.022 EXPSQR

Predictor       Coef      Stdev     t ratio
Constant      -1.009
EXP            0.627      0.088        7.14
EXPSQR        -0.022      0.004       -5.03
s = 0.265    R-sq = 93.2%

Analysis of Variance
SOURCE           DF         SS          MS
Regression        2      10.66        5.33
Error            11       0.77        0.07
Total            13      11.43

SOURCE           DF     SEQ SS
X2                1       8.89
X3                1       1.78
```

The null hypothesis is rejected ($7.14 > 2.201$) and Gil should conclude that the β_1 coefficient is significantly different from 0. The appropriate hypotheses to test the β_2 coefficient are

$$H_0: \beta_2 = 0$$
$$H_1: \beta_2 \neq 0$$

The decision rule is the same as when β_1 was tested.

Table 15.14 shows that the computed t value is -5.03. The null hypothesis is rejected ($-5.03 < -2.201$) and Gil should conclude that the β_2 coefficient is also significantly different from 0. Gil should use the second-order model to predict monthly sales.

If the β_2 coefficient had been significant but the β_1 coefficient not significant, Gil could have tried a model that included only the rate of curvature coefficient (β_2). Equation 15.10 presents this type of quadratic model:

$$y = \beta_0 + \beta_2 x^2 + \varepsilon \tag{15.10}$$

One of the assumptions of regression analysis is that a linear relationship exists between y and each predictor variable. However, the multiple regression model can be generalized to handle curvilinear relationships involving some or all of the predictor variables. A linear model is a model that's linear in the unknown βs. As long as a model is linear in the βs (β^x is not present), the linear statistical model can be used to model curvilinear relationships between the dependent and predictor variables.

Here are examples of curvilinear models. Equation 15.11 shows a reciprocal model:

$$y = \beta_0 + \beta_1(1/x) + \varepsilon \tag{15.11}$$

This is a simple linear regression model because it's linear in the unknown parameters (βs). Equation 15.11, unlike Equations 15.9 and 15.10, involves a transformation of the predictor variable, x. By substituting a transformed x ($1/x$), the analyst can simplify the relationship to one that's linear in its transformation. Unfortunately, the choice of an appropriate transformation is not easy. Analysts often need to study data plots to gain insight into which transformation will be successful. Equations 15.12 and 15.13 show two of the more common transformations. Equation 15.12 shows a square-root transformation:

$$y = \beta_0 + \beta_1 \sqrt{x} + \varepsilon \qquad (15.12)$$

Equation 15.13 shows an exponential model:

$$y = \beta_0 \left[e(\beta_1 x) \right] \varepsilon \qquad (15.13)$$

that is nonlinear in the parameters β_0 and β_1. This model can be transformed into the linear form by using the logarithmic transformation:

$$\text{Log}_e y = \text{Log}_e \beta_0 + \beta_1 \text{Log}_e x + \log_e \varepsilon \qquad (15.14)$$

Figure 15.6 shows the shape of the exponential model. The MINITAB program can be used to perform transformations. The MINITAB Computer Package section at the end of this chapter demonstrates the commands to accomplish this task.

FIGURE 15.6   Exponential Models

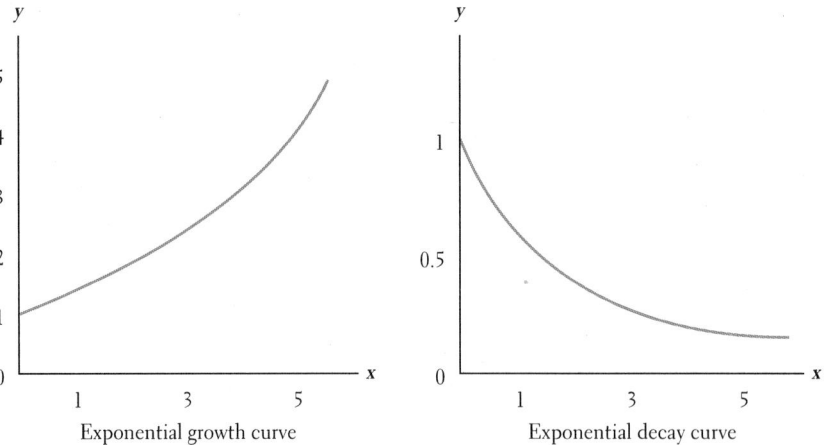

Exponential growth curve   Exponential decay curve

NONLINEAR MODELS

The term *nonlinear regression model* is used to designate any regression model that's not linear in the parameters (β^x is present) and can't be made so by transformation. For example, the exponential model of Equation 15.13 with an additive error term is nonlinear.

Here are examples of nonlinear models:

A logistic growth curve:

$$y = \beta_0 / (1 + \beta_1 \rho^x) + \varepsilon \qquad (15.15)$$

An asymptotic regression curve:

$$y = \beta_0 - \beta_1 \rho^x + \varepsilon$$

(15.16)

Figure 15.7 shows the shapes of these nonlinear curves.

FIGURE 15.7 Nonlinear Models

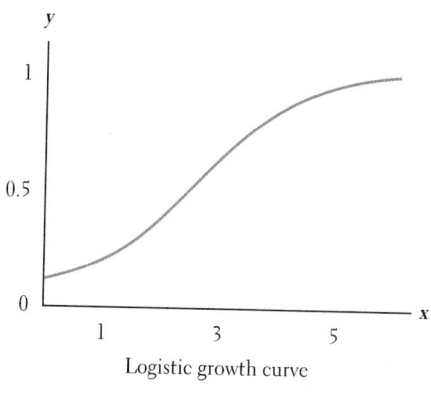

Logistic growth curve

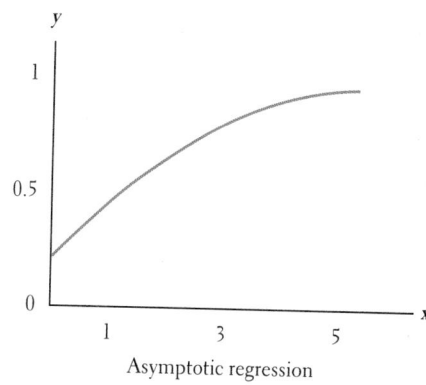

Asymptotic regression

EXERCISES

24. Explain the concept of model building.

25. Explain the differences between linear, curvilinear, and nonlinear models.

26. Briefly sketch the following models:
    a. Parabola.
    b. Third-order.
    c. Second-order.
    d. Exponential model.
    e. Logistic growth curve.

27. Jeff Paco, an analyst at Inland Power & Electric, has been assigned the task of predicting the maximum amount of power that must be generated each day to meet demand during summer. Jeff decides to investigate the relationship between average temperature and demand, measured in megawatts. He knows that demand will increase as the average temperature increases. However, Jeff suspects that as the average temperature rises, demand for electricity will grow at an increasing rate. He's interested in investigating a curvilinear model, so he obtains a random sample of 30 summer days and runs the data on a computer program. The results of running the $\hat{y} = b_0 + b_1 x + b_2 x^2$ model are:

VARIABLE NO.	REGRESSION COEFFICIENT	STD. ERROR OF REG COEF.	COMPUTED T VALUE
X	−10.35489	1.52145	−6.806
X2	0.07012	0.00854	8.211

INTERCEPT   403.68501
R SQUARED   0.962

    a. Test the curvilinear model using the .01 significance level.

    b. Predict the demand in megawatts for a day with average temperature of 92°.

    c. Write a very brief memo summarizing the results.

28. Shelly Daniels is a quality-control engineer for Specific Electric Corporation, which manufactures electric motors. In one step of the manufacturing process, an automatic milling machine produces slots in the motors' shafts. Each batch of shafts is tested, and all shafts that don't meet dimensional tolerances are discarded. The milling machine must be readjusted at the beginning of each new batch because its cutter head wears slightly during production. Shelly must determine how a batch's size affects the number of defective shafts in the batch so that she can select the best batch size. She collects the following data for the average batch size of 13 batches and asks you to analyze it.

Batch	Number of defectives, y	Batch size, x
1	4	25
2	8	50
3	6	75
4	16	100
5	22	125
6	27	150
7	36	175
8	49	200
9	53	225
10	70	250
11	82	275
12	95	300
13	109	325

    a. Plot the data on a scatter diagram.

    b. Develop a first-order model.

    c. Develop a second-order model.

    d. Find the best model.

    e. Predict the number of defectives for a batch size of 300 using the better model.

    f. Write Harry a memo summarizing your results.

QUALITATIVE VARIABLES IN MULTIPLE REGRESSION

Throughout the discussion of regression analysis in this chapter and Chapter 14, we've assumed that all variables in the analysis are quantitative, that is, measured on either an interval or a ratio scale. However, many real-world variables are qualitative, measured on an ordinal or nominal scale. For this reason, a technique has been developed for using qualitative variables in multiple regression equations.

Sometimes a variable of interest in a regression can't possibly be considered quantitative. An example is the variable *gender* (female/male). Although it may be important in predicting a quantitative dependent variable, it's obviously a nominally scaled variable. The best course of action in such a case is to take separate samples of males and females and conduct two separate regression analyses. The result for males can be compared with the results for females to see if the same predictor variables and the same regression coefficients result. Valuable insights can be gained from such a process.

Dummy Variable

If a large sample size isn't possible or is cost-prohibitive, a **dummy variable** can be employed to introduce a qualitative variable into the analysis. For example, a male could be designated with the code 0 and a female could be coded as 1. Each person sampled could then be measured as either a 0 or a 1 for the variable *gender*, and this variable, along with the quantitative variables for these persons, could be entered into a multiple regression program and analyzed.

A **dummy variable** in a regression analysis is a qualitative or categorical variable that is used as a predictor.

EXAMPLE 15.17   A sample of 15 hourly workers in a factory is selected for analysis. The dependent variable is the company's annual job performance rating. Management believes that the company's aptitude test score might be well correlated with the dependent variable, so they record this test score for each person in the sample. Management also thinks that a person's union affiliation might affect job performance rating. All hourly workers belong to either union A or union B. Members of union A are coded as 0s and members of union B as 1s. This is an arbitrary choice—the coding could have been reversed (union A as 1s and union B as 0s). Data for the regression analysis appear in Table 15.15.

TABLE 15.15   Data for Example 15.17

Worker	Job performance rating	Aptitude test score	Union membership
1	5	60	0
2	4	55	0
3	3	35	0
4	10	96	0
5	2	35	0
6	7	81	0
7	6	65	0
8	9	85	0
9	9	99	1
10	2	43	1
11	8	98	1
12	6	91	1
13	7	95	1
14	3	70	1
15	6	85	1

The data in Table 15.15 are keyed into a computer program that performs regression analysis. The dependent variable is numbered 1; the predictor variables are variables 2 and 3. Table 15.16 shows the results.

TABLE 15.16   Computer Output for Example 15.17

VARIABLE NO.	MEAN	STANDARD DEVIATION	CORRELATION X VS Y	REGRESSION COEFFICIENT	STD. ERROR OF REG COEF.	COMPUTED T VALUE
2	76.87	22.90	0.876	0.12041	0.01015	11.86
3	0.47	0.52	0.021	−2.18072	0.45035	−4.84

DEPENDENT		
1	5.80	2.60

INTERCEPT	−1.95646	MULTIPLE CORRELATION	0.96
STD. ERROR OF ESTIMATE	0.78627	R SQUARED	0.92

ANALYSIS OF VARIANCE

SOURCE OF VARIATION	DEGREES OF FREEDOM	SUM OF SQUARES	MEAN SQUARES	F VALUE
ATTRIBUTABLE TO REGRESSION	2	86.981	43.491	70.349
DEVIATION FROM REGRESSION	12	7.419	0.618	
TOTAL	14	94.400		

The following symbols may help you read this computer output:

$s_{x2} = 22.9$	$b_3 = -2.18072$	$s_{y \cdot x} = 0.78627$
$s_{x3} = 0.52$	$s_{b2} = 0.01015$	$R^2 = .92$
$r_{1,2} = .876$	$s_{b3} = 0.45035$	SSR = 86.981
$r_{1,3} = .021$	$s_y = 2.6$	SSE = 7.419
$b_2 = 0.12041$	$b_0 = -1.95646$	SST = 94.400

The multiple regression equation is

$$\hat{y} = -1.96 + 0.12x_2 - 2.18x_3$$

The two t values, the F value, and R^2 all indicate that the regression equation will do a good job of predicting the job performance ratings of all hourly workers in the factory. Now we can interpret the values in the regression equation. The regression coefficient for x_3 is particularly interesting.

Union membership (variable 3) is coded as either a 0 or a 1. If a worker is a member of union A (code 0), the last term in the regression equation drops out (since $x_3 = 0$). If a worker belongs to union B, x_3 equals 1, so the third term in the equation is -2.18. This leads to two separate regression equations: one for members of union A and another for members of union B:

$$\hat{y} = -1.96 + 0.12x_2 \qquad \text{(union A)}$$
$$\hat{y} = -1.96 + 0.12x_2 - 2.18(1)$$
$$= -4.14 + 0.12x_2 \qquad \text{(union B)}$$

In effect, membership in union B reduces a worker's job performance rating by an average of 2.18 points on the average. For both unions' workers, each increase of 1 point in the company's aptitude test score increases the job performance rating by an average of 0.12 points. However, union membership has a definite effect on job performance rating. If two workers, one from each union, each scored 87 on the aptitude test, the regression equation would predict the following job performance ratings for these two employees:

$$\hat{y} = -1.96 + 0.12(87) = 8.48 \qquad \text{(union A)}$$
$$\hat{y} = -4.14 + 0.12(87) = 6.30 \qquad \text{(union B)}$$

Company management may be able to use this information to advantage, although a larger sample size would greatly strengthen the conclusions' validity.

Remember that the choice of coding for this example could have been reversed. If this had been the case, the sign for the regression coefficient for the union membership variable would have been reversed (b_3 would have been 2.18 instead of -2.18).

Example 15.18 illustrates the use of dummy variables in a multiple regression equation as an alternative approach to solving analysis of variance problems.

EXAMPLE 15.18   In Example 12.6, Joanne Herr, analyst for the Best Foods grocery chain, wanted to know whether three stores have the same average dollar amount per purchase. Stores can be thought of as a single qualitative variable set at three levels: A, B, and C. Note that with a qualitative or dummy predictor variable, Joanne cannot attach a quantitative meaning to a given level; all she can do is describe it.

A model can be set up to predict the mean dollar amount per purchase:

$$\hat{y} = \beta_0 + \beta_2 x_2 + \beta_3 x_3$$

where $\hat{y}$ = Expected dollar amount per purchase

$$x_2 = \begin{cases} 1 \text{ if the purchase is made in store A} \\ 0 \text{ if the purchase is not made in store A} \end{cases}$$

$$x_3 = \begin{cases} 1 \text{ if the purchase is made in store B} \\ 0 \text{ if the purchase is not made in store B} \end{cases}$$

Table 15.17 presents the data.

x_2 and x_3 are dummy variables representing purchases in store A or store B, respectively. Note that the three levels of the qualitative variable have been described with only two dummy variables. This is because the mean of store C is accounted for by the intercept β_0. If both x_2 and x_3 equal 0, the purchase must have been made in store C and is represented by the mean purchase for that store. The mean value of y when the purchase is made in store C is

$$\mu_c = \beta_0 + \beta_2(0) + \beta_3(0)$$
$$= \beta_0$$

In Chapter 12, on analysis of variance, the null hypothesis under test was that all three populations from which the sample data were drawn have the same mean. If the three stores have the same average dollar amount per purchase, this hypothesis won't be rejected. However, if a multiple regression model can be developed that allows the

TABLE 15.17   Sample Data for Example 15.18

Purchase (dollars), y	Store A, x_2	Store B, x_3
12.05	1	0
23.94	1	0
14.63	1	0
25.78	1	0
17.52	1	0
18.45	1	0
15.17	0	1
18.52	0	1
19.57	0	1
21.40	0	1
13.59	0	1
20.57	0	1
9.48	0	0
6.92	0	0
10.47	0	0
7.63	0	0
11.90	0	0
5.92	0	0

analyst to predict the average dollar amount per purchase based on knowledge of which store the purchase was made in, this hypothesis can be rejected.

Table 15.18 shows the results of running the data in Table 15.17 on a multiple regression computer program. The regression equation $\hat{y} = 8.72 + 10.01x_2 + 9.42x_3$ explains 64% of the variance in average dollar amount per purchase. Note that the mean purchase for store C, $8.72, equals β_0. The table shows that 8.72 is the predicted value for each person who purchased in store C. Also note that the regression coefficient for x_2, 10.01, equals β_0 subtracted from the mean purchase for store A (18.73 − 8.72). The table of residuals shows that the mean for store A (18.73) is the predicted value for each person who purchased in store A. Finally, the regression coefficient for x_3, 9.42, equals β_0 subtracted from the mean purchase for store B (18.14 − 8.72). The table shows that the mean for store B (18.14) is the predicted value for each person who purchased in store B. Obviously, the multiple regression uses the store means to predict the average dollar amount of purchase for each person.

Note that the "analysis of variance" section of the output is identical to Table 12.5. Using multiple regression, Joanne comes to the same conclusion as she did using analysis of variance.

EXERCISES

29. What is a dummy variable?

30. Why are dummy variables used in multiple regression analysis?

31. The values 0 and 1 are frequently used to create dummy variables. Could 1 and 2 be used instead?

TABLE 15.18 Computer Output for Example 15.18

VARIABLE NO.	MEAN	STANDARD DEVIATION	REGRESSION COEFFICIENT	STD. ERROR OF REG COEF.	COMPUTED T VALUE
2	0.33	0.485	10.008	0.822	4.59
3	0.33	0.485	9.417	0.774	4.32

DEPENDENT

1	15.20	5.90			

INTERCEPT 8.72 MULTIPLE CORRELATION 0.80
STD. ERROR OF ESTIMATE 3.7779 R SQUARED 0.64

ANALYSIS OF VARIANCE

SOURCE OF VARIATION	DEGREES OF FREEDOM	SUM OF SQUARES	MEAN SQUARES	F VALUE
ATTRIBUTABLE TO REGRESSION	2	378.54	189.27	13.26
DEVIATION FROM REGRESSION	15	214.06	14.27	
TOTAL	17	592.60		

OBSERVATION	OBSERVED VALUE	PREDICTED VALUE	RESIDUAL
1	12.05	18.73	−6.68
2	23.94	18.73	5.21
3	14.63	18.73	−4.10
4	25.78	18.73	7.05
5	17.52	18.73	−1.21
6	18.45	18.73	−0.28
7	15.17	18.14	−2.97
8	18.52	18.14	0.38
9	19.57	18.14	1.43
10	21.40	18.14	3.26
11	13.59	18.14	−4.55
12	20.57	18.14	2.43
13	9.48	8.72	0.76
14	6.92	8.72	−1.80
15	10.47	8.72	1.75
16	7.63	8.72	−1.09
17	11.90	8.72	3.18
18	5.92	8.72	−2.80

32. Ellie Burks is personnel director for the JVC Corporation. Presently, JVC hires prospective salespeople and trains them using an expensive program. Ellie has decided to administer an aptitude test to predict which applicants will be most successful on the job. Ellie also wonders if college graduates become better salespeople than do nongraduates. She decides to test the next 15 applicants. She determines whether they're college graduates and codes each person 1 if he or she graduated from college and 0 if not. The 15 prospective salespeople are trained in the program and placed on the job. After one month, their total sales are recorded, and the following data result:

Applicant	Sales, y	Test score, x_2	College graduate, x_3
1	345	52	1
2	405	46	1
3	475	60	1
4	205	20	1
5	355	38	1

Applicant	Sales, y	Test score, x_2	College graduate, x_3
6	300	44	1
7	133	14	0
8	280	28	0
9	165	30	0
10	145	18	0
11	165	32	0
12	340	50	0
13	140	22	0
14	215	30	0
15	145	20	0

a. Plot the data on a scatter diagram. Use 1s for college graduates and 0s for nongraduates.

b. Is test score a good predictor variable?

c. Is knowledge of whether a person is a college graduate a good predictor variable?

d. Indicate the regression equation Ellie should use to predict successful salespeople.

e. Interpret the estimated regression coefficients.

f. Estimate the first month's sales for a college graduate who scored 50 on the test.

g. Estimate the first month's sales for an applicant who didn't graduate from college and who scored 50 on the test.

h. Write a memo to Ellie summarizing your conclusions concerning this situation.

33. Color Paint Corporation owner Marlene Perez is replacing several paint sprayers. After researching the situation, she concludes that four brands appear to be comparable in terms of cost and projected lifetime. Marlene determines that the deciding factor among the four brands will be the amount of paint used in normal operation. She measures the paints' thickness in millimeters, for several tests, with the following results:

	Sprayer A	Sprayer B	Sprayer C	Sprayer D
	5.4	6.1	8.2	7.2
	5.9	5.9	8.5	6.5
	6.2	6.3	6.9	6.8
	7.0	6.5	9.4	7.1
	5.1	7.2	7.9	7.4
	5.5	6.9	8.6	6.7
Means:	5.85	6.48	8.25	6.95

Solve this ANOVA problem using multiple regression. Compare your results to those obtained in Solved Exercise 3 in Chapter 12.

34. *Consumer Digest* wants to determine if any differences in average life exist for five brands of TV picture tubes. Random samples of three tubes of each brand were tested. The results (in hours) are:

Brand A	Brand B	Brand C	Brand D	Brand E
3,520	4,025	4,520	3,987	3,620
3,631	3,901	4,325	4,123	3,358
3,954	3,756	4,189	3,852	3,428

At the .05 significance level, is there evidence of a difference in average life among these five brands of tubes? Solve this analysis of variance problem using multiple regression. Compare your answer to that for Exercise 44 in Chapter 12.

35. Rosanna Staben is studying bus drivers' average hourly wages in three northeastern states to determine if there are significant differences. She collects the following hourly wage data:

	State		
Observation	New York	New Hampshire	New Jersey
1	10	7	8
2	11	6	11
3	9	9	9
4	12	10	9
5	8	8	10
6	13	8	11

a. Develop the appropriate regression model, $\hat{y} = \beta_0 + \beta_2 x_2 + \beta_3 x_3$, to determine whether there are differences in average wages.

b. Predict the average wage for New York bus drivers.

c. Predict the average wage for New Hampshire bus drivers.

d. Predict the average wage for New Jersey bus drivers.

e. Test for significant differences at the .05 significance level.

STEPWISE REGRESSION

Stepwise Regression

A popular multiple regression technique called **stepwise regression analysis** introduces predictor variables into the regression equation one at a time until all potential predictor variables have been analyzed.

> The **stepwise regression analysis** technique enters variables into the regression equation one at a time until all have been analyzed.

Almost all computer programs for stepwise analysis begin by running a simple regression equation using the predictor variable that has the highest correlation with y. This variable is entered first because it explains the largest percentage of y's variance. Next, the stepwise program adds a new variable that's related to the dependent variable but not too highly correlated to the predictor variable already entered into the model. At each subsequent step, a new variable is entered that explains the largest percentage of the variance in y left unexplained by the variables already in the equation.

The stepwise process works as follows. The analyst provides the stepwise computer package with a dependent variable (y) and several potentially important independent variables (x's).

Step 1 The computer fits all possible simple regression models of the form

$$y = \beta_0 + \beta_1 x_1 + \varepsilon$$

The independent variable that produces the largest (absolute) t value is used as the best predictor of y and identified as x_1. Note that at Step 1 the computer will always choose the independent variable with the highest (absolute) correlation with the dependent variable.

Step 2 The computer fits all possible two-variable models that contain x_1. Each of the other independent variables is run in combination with x_1 to form

$$y = \beta_0 + \beta_1 x_1 + \beta_2 x_2 + \varepsilon$$

The new independent variable that produces the largest (absolute) t value is retained and used to predict y in conjunction with x_1. This new predictor is identified as x_2. Note that while x_2 will be correlated to y, it won't be too highly correlated to x_1.

Note that x_1 and x_2 will probably be correlated to some degree and the inclusion of x_2 changes the value of β_1 and its t statistic. Some of the better computer programs recheck β_1 to ensure that it remains sufficiently useful to remain in the model. If it doesn't, the computer searches for the best replacement variable.

Step 3 The computer fits all possible three-variable models that contain x_1 and x_2. Each other independent variable is run in combination with x_1 and x_2 to form

$$y = \beta_0 + \beta_1 x_1 + \beta_2 x_2 + \beta_3 x_3 + \varepsilon$$

The independent variable that produces the largest (absolute) t value is retained and used to predict y in conjunction with x_1 and x_2. This new predictor is identified as x_3. Note that while x_3 will be correlated to y, it won't be too highly correlated to x_1 or x_2.

The stepwise process continues until the step is reached where none of the remaining variables has a β coefficient significantly different from 0 at some specified alpha level. At this point, the computer can't add a new variable that will contribute to the prediction of y. Hence, the result of the stepwise procedure is a model that contains only independent variables with t values that are significant at the specified significance level. Example 15.19 illustrates the stepwise procedure.

EXAMPLE 15.19 Betty Butler, personnel director for Executive Choice, wants to predict whether a particular applicant will become a good secretary. Her interest in this matter increased after she read "Employee Training: Hands On Pays Off" in *The Office* (October 1989, p. 32), which gave Betty some new ideas about training in the workplace.

After her applicants successfully complete a six-month training program, they're placed on a new job, and their performance is rated at the end of the first month. Betty decides to use this performance rating as the dependent variable. Next, she chooses to investigate the following predictor variables:

x_2 = Motivation test score
x_3 = Aptitude test score

$$x_4 = \text{Anxiety test score}$$
$$x_5 = \text{Keyboarding speed and accuracy score}$$
$$x_6 = \text{Computer test score}$$

Betty gathers data on 30 applicants and inputs their scores and first-month performance rating into a data file called BUTLER.DAT.

The MINITAB commands to enter the data and run a correlation matrix for Example 15.19 are:

```
MTB > READ 'BUTLER.DAT' C1–C6
    30 ROWS READ

  ROW   C1    C2    C3    C4   C5    C6
   1    44   22.1   10   4.9   0    2.4
   2    47   22.5   19   3.0   1    2.6
   3    60   23.1   27   1.5   0    2.8
   4    71   24.0   31   0.6   3    2.7
    .   .   .

MTB > NAME C1 'RATING' C2 'APTITUDE' C3 'MOTIVATE' C4 'ANXIETY'
MTB > NAME C5 'KEYBOARD' C6 'COMPUTER'
MTB > CORR C1–C6

                C1        C2        C3        C4       C5
              RATING   APTITUDE  MOTIVATE   ANXIETY  KEYBOARD
C2 APTITUDE   0.798
C3 MOTIVATE   0.676     0.228
C4 ANXIETY   -0.296    -0.287    -0.222
C5 KEYBOARD   0.550     0.540     0.350   -0.279
C6 COMPUTER   0.622     0.695     0.318   -0.244    0.312
```

The READ command is used to read a file called BUTLER.DAT into the MINITAB worksheet. The NAME command is used to identify each variable. The CORR command provides a correlation matrix for the six variables.

Betty examines the correlation matrix and decides that when she runs the stepwise analysis, the aptitude test score will enter the model first because it has the largest correlation with performance rating ($r_{1,2} = .798$) and will explain 63.68% ($.798^2$) of the performance rating variable variance.

She notes that the motivation test score will enter the model second because it's strongly related to performance rating ($r_{1,3} = .676$) but not highly related to the aptitude test score ($r_{2,3} = .228$) already in the model.

Betty also notices that the other variables don't qualify as good predictor variables. The anxiety test score won't be a good predictor because it's not well related to performance rating ($r_{1,4} = -.296$). The keyboarding speed and computer test score variables have potential as good predictor variables ($r_{1,5} = .550$, $r_{1,6} = .622$). However, both of these predictor variables have a multicollinearity problem with the aptitude test score ($r_{2,5} = .540$, $r_{2,6} = .695$).

The MINITAB commands to run a stepwise regression analysis for Example 15.19 are:

```
MTB > STEP C1–C6;
SUBC> FENTER 4.2.

STEPWISE REGRESSION OF RATING ON 5 PREDICTORS, WITH N = 30
```

```
      STEP        1        2
  CONSTANT   -100.85   -86.79

  APTITUDE      6.97     5.93
  T RATIO       7.01    10.60

  MOTIVATE               0.200
  T RATIO                 8.13

  S             6.85     3.75
  R-SQ         63.70    89.48
   MORE? (YES, NO, SUBCOMMAND, OR HELP)
  SUBC> NO
  MTB > STOP
```

The STEP command runs a stepwise analysis using C1 as the dependent variable and C2 through C6 as the independent variables. The FENTER subcommand indicates that the criterion for allowing a new variable to enter the model is $F = 4.2$. If no FENTER subcommand is used, the default is $F = 4$.

Although the printout for MINITAB's stepwise procedure contains t statistics, MINITAB actually uses the F statistic to decide whether a variable should be added to the model. But note that there's a mathematical relationship between the t and F statistics ($t^2 = F$). At each step, the MINITAB program calculates an F statistic for each of the variables not in the model. The variable with the largest F statistic is added, provided its F statistic is larger than the specified cutoff value; FENTER = 4.2 in this example ($F = 4$ is used unless some other value is specified). MINITAB's stepwise procedure does check to make sure that variables entered into the model on an earlier step are still valid.

The stepwise analysis proceeds in the following manner:

Step 1 The model after step one is

$$RATING = -100.85 + 6.97(APTITUDE)$$

This model explains 63.70% of the performance rating variable variance. This model had the largest F statistic, $F = 49.14$. Since 49.14 is greater than 4.2, APTITUDE is added to the model.

If the analysis is performed using the t statistic from the printout, the null and alternative hypotheses to determine whether the aptitude test score's regression coefficient is significantly different from 0 are

$$H_0: \beta_2 = 0$$
$$H_1: \beta_2 \neq 0$$

If the test is conducted at the .05 significance level, the critical t statistic based on 28 ($n - k = 30 - 2$) degrees of freedom is 2.048. The decision rule is

If the calculated t statistic is greater than 2.048 or less than -2.048, reject the null hypothesis (reject H_0 if $t > 2.048$ or $t < -2.048$).

Since the computed t ratio found on the MINITAB output, 7.01 ($t^2 = F = 49.13$), is greater than the critical value ($7.01 > 2.048$), the null hypothesis is rejected. The APTITUDE variable's regression coefficient is significantly different from 0. This result means that the aptitude test score is a good variable and the procedure now moves on to Step 2.

Step 2 The model after Step 2 is

$$RATING = -86.79 + 5.93(APTITUDE) + 0.200(MOTIVATE)$$

This model explains 89.48% of the performance rating variable variance. The null and alternative hypotheses to determine whether the motivation test score's regression coefficient is significantly different from 0 are

$$H_0: \beta_3 = 0$$
$$H_1: \beta_3 \neq 0$$

If the test is conducted at the .05 significance level, the critical t statistic based on 27 ($n - k = 30 - 3$) degrees of freedom is 2.052. The decision rule is

If the calculated t statistic is greater than 2.052 or less than -2.052, reject the null hypothesis (reject H_0 if $t > 2.052$ or $t < -2.052$).

Since the computed t ratio found on the MINITAB output is 8.13, the null hypothesis is rejected. The MOTIVATE variable's regression coefficient is significantly different from 0. This result means that motivation test score is a good variable when used in conjunction with aptitude test score. Note that the t ratio for the APTITUDE variable's regression coefficient, 10.6, is still significant. The procedure now moves on to Step 3.

Step 3 The computer fits all possible three-variable models that contain x_1 and x_2. None of the other independent variables is significant when run in combination with x_1 and x_2 so the stepwise procedure is completed.

Actually, the best three-variable model is developed and discarded because all of the t ratios aren't significant. The best three-variable model is

$$RATING = -89.42 + 6.12(APTITUDE) + 0.202(MOTIVATE) - .592(COMPUTER)$$

This model explains 89.50% of the performance rating variable variance. The null and alternative hypotheses to determine whether the computer test score's regression coefficient is significantly different from 0 are

$$H_0: \beta_6 = 0$$
$$H_1: \beta_6 \neq 0$$

If the test is conducted at the .05 significance level, the critical t statistic based on 26 ($n - k = 30 - 4$) degrees of freedom is 2.056. The decision rule is

If the calculated t statistic is greater than 2.056 or less than -2.056, reject the null hypothesis (reject H_0 if $t > 2.056$ or $t < -2.056$).

If this run is made, the computed t ratio on the MINITAB output is $-.36$. The null hypothesis isn't rejected. The COMPUTER variable's regression coefficient isn't significantly different from 0. This result means that the computer test score isn't a good variable when used in conjunction with the aptitude and motivation test scores.

FINAL NOTES ON STEPWISE REGRESSION

The stepwise regression technique is extremely easy to use. Unfortunately, it's also extremely easy to misuse. Analysts developing a regression model often produce a large set of potential independent variables and then let the stepwise procedure determine which are significant. The problem is that when a large set of independent variables are analyzed, many t tests are performed, and a type I error will likely result. For this reason, the final model might contain some variable that's not linearly related to the dependent variable but entered the model just by chance.

A second problem involves initial selection of potential independent variables. When these variables are selected, high-order terms (curvilinear, nonlinear, and interaction) are often omitted to keep the number of variables manageable. Consequently, several important variables may be initially omitted from the model. Obviously, an analyst's intuitive choice of the initial independent variables is critical to the development of a successful regression model.

EXERCISES

36. Why is stepwise regression used? When should stepwise regression be used?

37. Examine the following correlation matrix, where variable 1 is the dependent variable.

	1	2	3	4
1	1	−.87	.78	.23
2	−.87	1	−.43	−.07
3	.78	−.43	1	.09
4	.23	−.07	.09	1

  a. Which variable would enter the model first? Why?

  b. Which variable would enter the model second? Why?

  c. Which variable or variables would be included in the best prediction equation?

38. Examine the following correlation matrix, where variable 1 is the dependent variable.

	1	2	3	4	5	6
1	1	.571	.098	−.539	.810	.764
2		1	.258	−.112	.387	.418
3			1	−.007	.245	.187
4				1	−.419	−.158
5					1	.755
6						1

  a. Which variable would enter the model first? Why?

  b. Which variable would enter the model second? Why?

  c. Which variable or variables would be included in the best prediction equation?

39. Real estate broker Marilyn Roig wishes to estimate the importance of four factors in determining the price of lots. She runs data for 60 lots on a multiple regression program. Examine the following correlation matrix, where price is the dependent variable.

	Price	View	Slope	Elevation	Area
Price	1	.86	.66	.62	.57
View	.86	1	.65	.73	.38
Slope	.66	.65	1	.09	.61
Elevation	.62	.73	.09	1	.11
Area	.57	.38	.61	.11	1

    a. Which variable would enter the model first? Why?

    b. Which variable would enter the model second? Why?

    c. Which variable or variables would be included in the best prediction equation?

40. Cindy Lawson just bought a major league baseball team. She has been receiving a lot of advice on how to create a winning ballclub. Cindy asks you to study this problem. You decide to use multiple regression analysis to determine which statistics are important in developing a winning team (measured by number of games won during the 1991 season). You gather the following statistics from *The Sporting News 1992 Baseball Yearbook* and run them on a stepwise regression program. Write Cindy a report. Make sure you discuss any multicollinearity problems and provide her with a final regression equation.

Team	Wins	ERA	SO	BA	Runs	HR	SB
Giants	75	4.03	905	.246	649	141	95
Mets	77	3.56	1028	.244	640	117	153
Cubs	77	4.03	927	.253	695	159	123
Reds	74	3.83	997	.258	689	164	124
Pirates	98	3.44	919	.263	768	126	124
Cardinals	84	3.69	822	.255	651	68	202
Phillies	78	3.86	988	.241	629	111	92
Astros	65	4.00	1033	.244	605	79	125
Dodgers	93	3.06	1028	.253	665	108	126
Expos	71	3.64	909	.246	579	95	221
Braves	94	3.49	969	.258	749	141	165
Padres	84	3.57	921	.244	636	121	101
Red Sox	84	4.01	999	.269	731	126	59
White Sox	87	3.79	923	.262	758	139	134
Yankees	71	4.42	936	.256	674	147	109
Tigers	84	4.51	739	.247	817	209	109
Orioles	67	4.59	868	.254	686	170	50
Brewers	83	4.14	859	.271	799	116	106
Indians	57	4.23	862	.254	576	79	84
Blue Jays	91	3.50	971	.257	684	133	148
Mariners	83	3.79	1003	.255	702	126	97
Rangers	85	4.47	1022	.270	829	177	102
Athletics	84	4.57	892	.248	760	159	151
Royals	82	3.92	1004	.264	727	117	119
Angels	81	3.69	990	.255	653	115	94
Twins	95	3.69	876	.280	776	140	107

RESIDUAL ANALYSIS

Model building has been defined as the general process of finding a regression equation that fits the sample data well. A valid model will provide good predictions of *y* for given values of *x*. Choosing the appropriate model is the key to successfully implementing regression analysis.

In Chapter 14, we used Equation 14.9 to compute the residual, or the difference between an actual observed *y* value and the predicted value, $\hat{y}$:

$$e = y - \hat{y}$$

Residual Analysis

Note that the mean of the residuals equals 0: $\Sigma(y - \hat{y}) = 0$. Also, the standard deviation of the residuals equals the standard error of estimate: $s_{y \cdot x's} = \sqrt{\Sigma(y - \hat{y})^2/(n - k)}$.

Examination of a table of residuals or a residual plot can help determine whether a particular regression equation fits the sample data properly. The MINITAB commands to develop a residual plot for Example 15.15 are:

```
MTB> SET C1
DATA> 36 12 24 27 36 34 17 23 31 30
DATA> END
MTB> SET C2
DATA> 9.6 2.6 3.5 6.1 7.8 6.9 4.4 6.1 7.0 6.8
DATA> END
MTB> SET C3
DATA> 5.5 1.8 0.9 2.8 4.6 3.7 1.9 1.8 2.7 2.0
DATA> END

MTB> NAME C1 'Y' C2 'X2' C3 'X3'
MTB> REGRESS C1 ON 2 PREDICTORS C2 C3;
SUBC> RESIDS C4.
     THE REGRESSION OUTPUT IS SHOWN IN TABLE 15.11

MTB> NAME C4 'RESIDUAL' C5 'STAND'

MTB> PLOT C4 VS C1
     THE RESIDUAL PLOT IS SHOWN IN FIGURE 15.8
MTB> STOP
```

Note that the residuals were computed and stored in column C4 by the RESIDS subcommand. The PLOT command shows the residuals (C4) scaled on the *y* axis and plotted against the *y* values (C1) scaled on the *x* axis.

FIGURE 15.8   The Residuals Plotted against *y* for Example 15.15

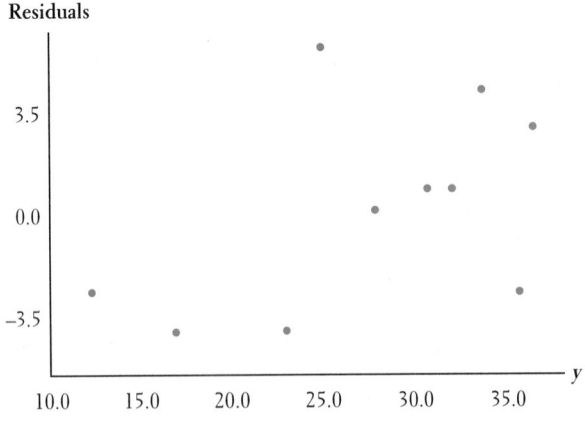

   Residuals can also be standardized and plotted for examination. There are several ways to do this. However, the computations are complex, and computer analysis is essential. A description of the computational procedures is left to more advanced texts. The MINITAB commands to generate and plot standardized residuals for Example 15.15 are:

```
MTB> REGRESS C1 ON 2 PREDICTORS C2 C3;
SUBC> TRESIDS C5.
    THE REGRESSION OUTPUT IS SHOWN IN TABLE 15.11
MTB> PRINT C1-C5

ROW     Y      X2     X3      RESID        STAND
  1     36     9.6    5.5    -3.14846    -1.12525
  2     12     2.6    1.8    -2.79083    -1.12587
  3     24     3.5    0.9     5.91932     2.13424
  4     27     6.1    2.8    -0.06736    -0.01618
  5     36     7.8    4.6     3.12084     0.91071
  6     34     6.9    3.7     4.20376     1.15225
  7     17     4.4    1.9    -4.15210    -1.15032
  8     23     6.1    1.8    -4.18232    -1.26348
  9     31     7.0    2.7     0.73476     0.18649
 10     30     6.8    2.0     0.36238     0.10461


MTB> PLOT C5 VS C1
    THE RESIDUAL PLOT IS SHOWN IN FIGURE 15.9
MTB> STOP
```

FIGURE 15.9   The Standardized Residuals Plotted against y for Example 15.15

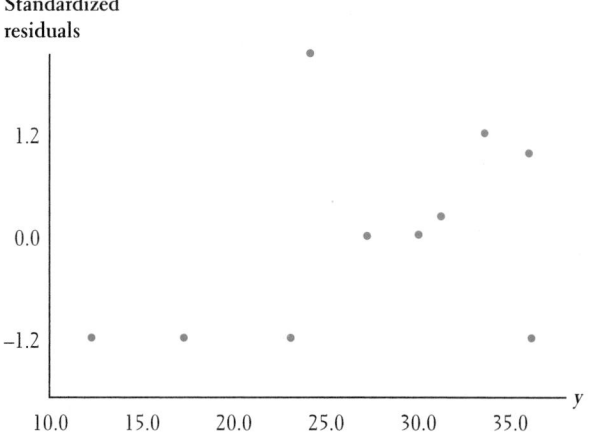

   The standardized residuals were computed and stored in column C5 by the TRESIDS subcommand. The PRINT command shows what has been stored in columns C1 through C5. The PLOT command shows the standardized residuals (C5) scaled on the y axis and plotted against the y values (C1) scaled on the x axis.

FIGURE 15.10 Valid Model

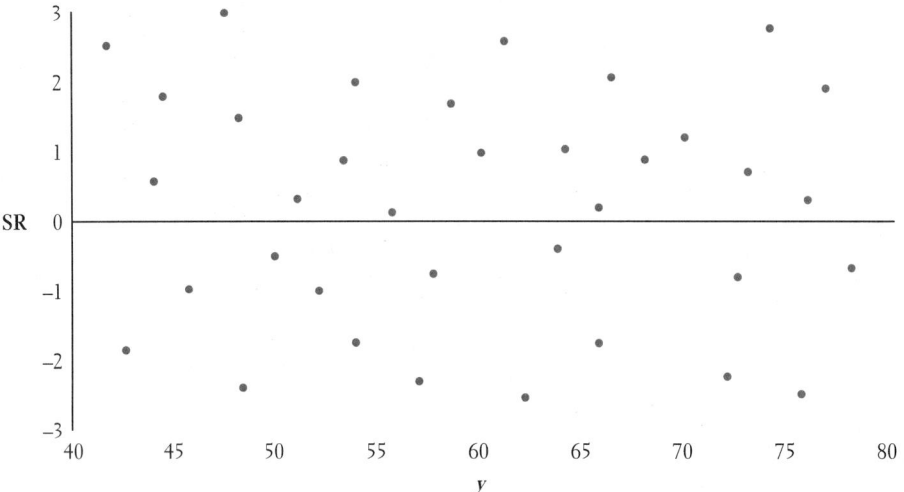

The residuals should satisfy the regression model assumption: they should be normally distributed, uncorrelated, and have the same variance. Figure 15.10 shows a residual plot that appears to meet these assumptions. Characteristics of a good residual plot include:

1. The numbers of positive and negative residuals are approximately equal.
2. When the residuals are standardized, about 68% of them should lie within 1 standard deviation ($s_{y \cdot x's}$) of the regression line or plane, about 95% of them should lie within 2 standard deviations, and about 99% of them should lie within 3 standard deviations.
3. The variability of the residuals should be approximately constant for all values of $\hat{y}$.

When analysts examine a residual plot, they look for obvious indications that the assumptions have been violated. The next section addresses residual plots that clearly indicate violation of at least one assumption.

One assumption for regression analysis is that the population distribution of ε is normal. Small departures from normality don't create serious problems. However, major departures should be of concern. This assumption can be checked by visually inspecting a histogram of the standardized residuals. As just stated, approximately 68% of these residuals should lie within 1 standard deviation, and about 95% of them should lie within 2 standard deviations. Also, if the residuals are normally distributed, the positive and negative residuals should be approximately equal in number. Figure 15.11 shows a distribution that's seriously skewed toward the positive residuals. Since the normal distribution is symmetric, Figure 15.11 suggests that the residuals aren't normally distributed.

FIGURE 15.11   Nonnormality

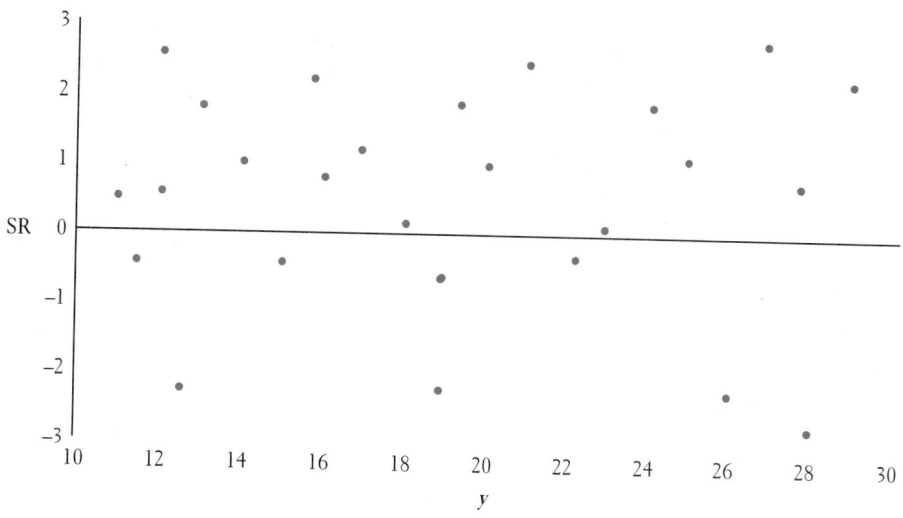

The MINITAB HISTOGRAM command, introduced in Chapter 3, can be used to check the assumption of normality for Example 15.15.

```
MTB> HISTOGRAM C5

Histogram of C5     N = 10

Midpoint    Count
   -1.5        1     *
   -1.0        3     ***
   -0.5        0
    0.0        3     ***
    0.5        0
    1.0        2     **
    1.5        0
    2.0        1     *
MTB> STOP
```

A second assumption of regression analysis is that the dispersion of errors around the regression line or plane is constant. Figure 15.10 showed how the residuals should be dispersed. Figure 15.12 illustrates a residual plot where the error variance increases with x. We may also encounter plots where the error variance decreases as x increases.

A third assumption of regression analysis is that the mean of the probability distribution of the residuals is 0. This assumption implies that the mean value of y for a given value of x is $E(y) = \beta_0 + \beta_2 x_2 + \beta_3 x_3 + \cdots + \beta_k x_k$. Examining a scatter diagram of the relationship between each predictor variable and the dependent variable can help determine whether this assumption has been violated. Figure 15.13 illustrates a parabolic relationship.

A fourth assumption of regression analysis is that the values of the residuals are independent of each other, implying a random sample. Such residuals should

FIGURE 15.12   Unequal Variance

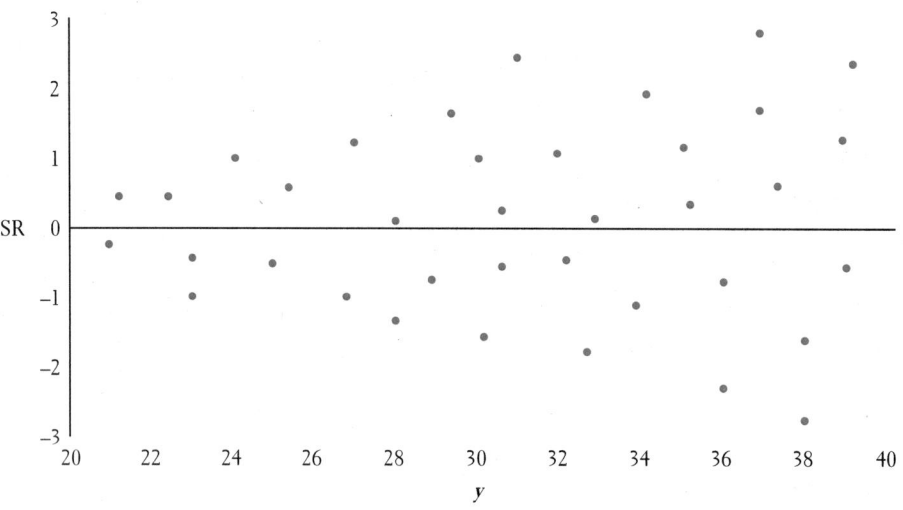

FIGURE 15.13   Nonlinearity

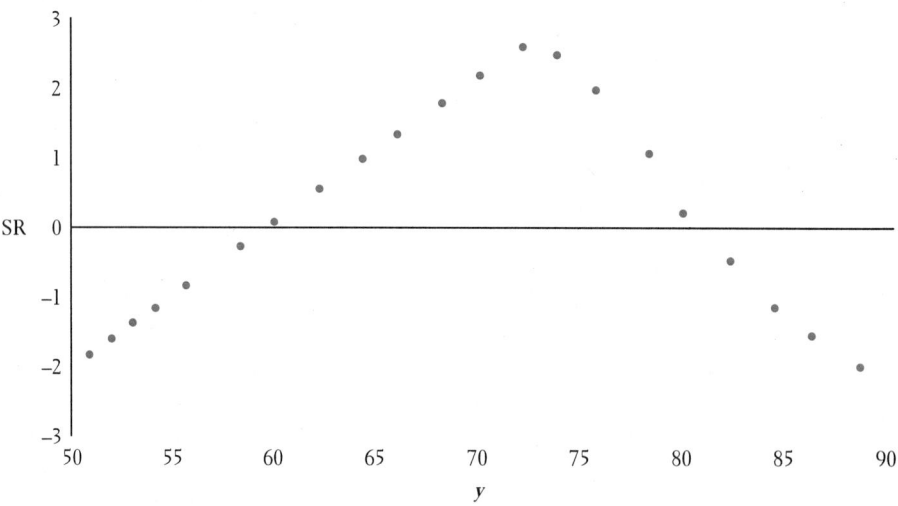

fluctuate in a random pattern around the baseline, 0. If the residuals are uncorrelated, then there should be no patterns in the residual plot. Figure 15.14 illustrates a residual plot with correlated error terms. Whenever data are obtained in a time sequence, there's the potential that the residuals are correlated over time, as discussed in Chapter 17.

FIGURE 15.14 Correlated Residuals

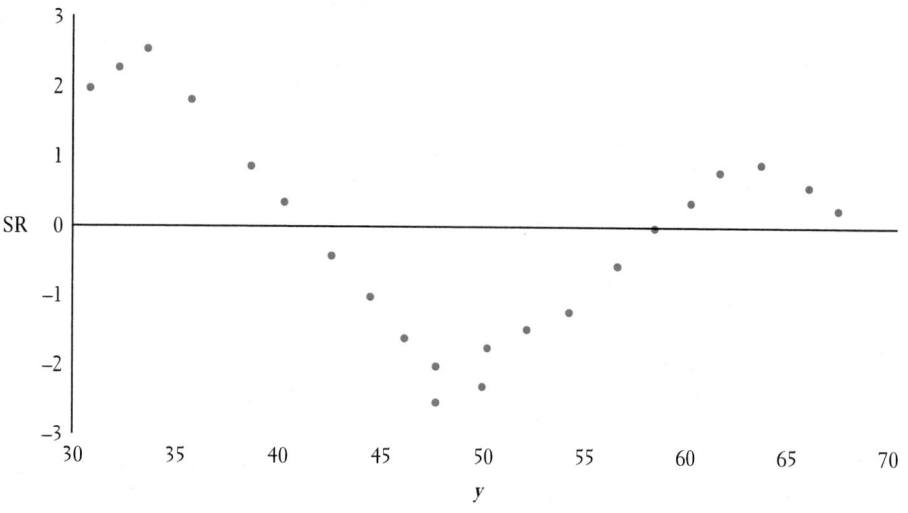

Figure 15.15 shows the presence of an *outlier* (a point that lies far beyond the scatter of the remaining residuals). Outliers can lead to violation of one or both assumptions of equal variance and normality. They can create many problems for the analyst. The reason that an outlier occurred in the first place frequently dictates how it should

FIGURE 15.15 Outlier Plot

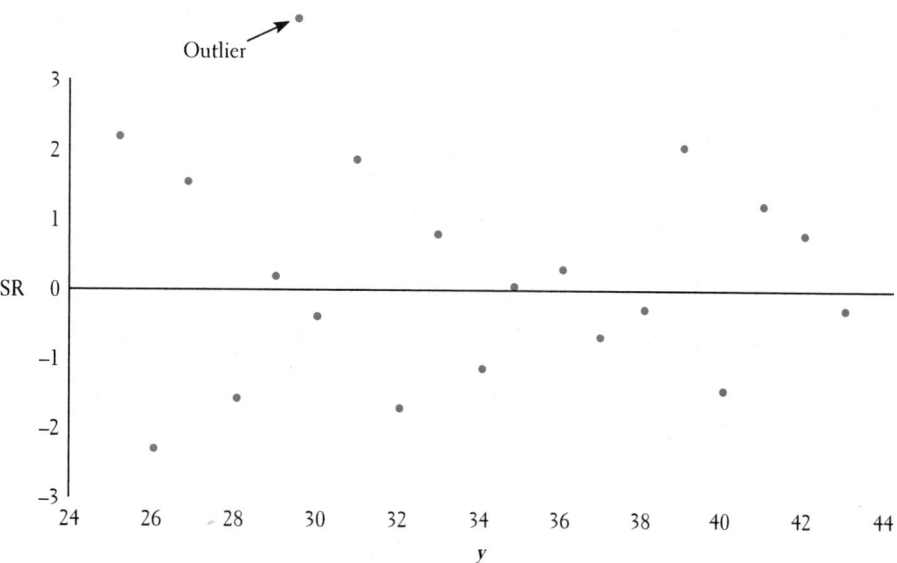

be treated. Alternatives include discarding the point, using mean values in its place, or leaving it in the analysis.

An **outlier** is a point that lies far beyond the scatter of the remaining residuals.

Refer to Extended Exercise 65 for an additional example of how the regression assumptions are checked.

EXERCISES

41. What is the difference between residuals and standardized residuals?

42. List the characteristics of a good residual plot.

43. Whenever data are obtained in a time sequence, there is the potential that the error terms are correlated over time. In this case, which assumption of regression has been violated? How can an analyst determine whether this assumption has been violated?

44. If the numbers of positive and negative residuals aren't approximately equal, which assumption of regression has been violated? How can an analyst determine whether this assumption has been violated?

45. If a residual plot shows that the error variance is increasing as x increases, which assumption of regression has been violated?

46. What is meant when a point is referred to as an outlier?

47. This exercise uses Appendix C's Company Data Base. Select a random sample of 30 employees and develop a multiple regression equation to predict annual base salary (x_8). Examine a residual plot to determine whether your regression equation fits the sample data properly. Write a memo to the company president summarizing results of this analysis.

SUMMARY
. . . .

This chapter has extended the basic regression and correlation concepts of Chapter 14 to situations involving two or more predictor variables. The objective in a regression analysis is to identify as many variables as possible that might be correlated with the dependent variable of interest. The correlation matrix is then examined to find those predictor variables that correlate well with the dependent variable but not with each other. Next, predictor variable combinations are formed and tested using a multiple regression computer program. Finally, the quality of each regression equation is determined by checking R^2, the t values, and the F value. The best prediction equation can then be used, if it's found to be of sufficient quality, to explain the variability of y and to make predictions for y.

In multiple regression, we must guard against multicollinearity. This condition, caused by correlations between predictor variables that are too high, leads to unreliable regression coefficients.

The basic assumptions for simple regression analysis, stated near the end of Chapter 14, hold for multiple regression as well:

1. The probability distribution of ε is normal.
2. The variance of the probability distribution of ε is constant for all values of x.
3. The mean of the probability distribution of ε is 0. This assumption implies that the mean value of y for a given value of x is $E(y) = \beta_0 + \beta_1 x_1 + \beta_2 x_2 + \cdots + \beta_k x_k$.
4. The values of ε are independent of each other. This assumption implies that a random sample of objects has been selected from the population for measurement.

Assumption 4 is of particular importance in business applications. Many business situations involve data measured over months, quarters, or years. When the dependent and predictor variables are measured for these time periods, assumption 4 is often violated because the sampled time periods are in sequence, not randomly selected. Ways to solve this problem are covered in Chapter 17.

APPLICATIONS OF STATISTICAL CONCEPTS IN THE BUSINESS WORLD

Regression analysis is a popular technique in most areas of science and social science, including business. The problem isn't that this powerful technique is underutilized, but that it's used on inappropriate data and that analysts aren't skilled in interpreting the results. This danger has become increasingly acute since the advent of powerful personal computers, which enable almost anyone to perform sophisticated regression analyses.

Here are some areas for which the application of regression analysis might prove fruitful. The dependent variable is listed along with some potential predictor variables. Note that all variables are quantitative.

Dependent variable	Predictor variables
Employee job rating	Age, years with company, number of dependents, years of education
Annual cost of goods sold	Annual measurements of unemployment rate, GNP, total sales dollars, wholesale price index
Product's market share	Advertising budget, number of company employees, length of time product has been on market, time since last product "improvement"
Defects per shift	Number of workers on shift, average age of workers, number of floor supervisors
Employee turnover rate	Percentage of company wages compared with competitor average, average employee age
Local TV news rating	Station power in watts, percentage of newscast commercial time, time since last change of on-camera personnel
Hardness of steel batch	Temperature of process, humidity, time of process
Quality-control index	Hours of overtime, employees per shift

GLOSSARY

Correlation matrix A display of the correlation coefficients for every possible pair of variables in the analysis.

Multicollinearity A condition that results when predictor variables are too highly correlated among themselves.

Estimated regression coefficient A measure of the average change in the dependent variable for a one-unit increase in the relevant predictor variable, holding the other predictor variables constant.

Standard error of estimate A measure of the variability, or scatter, of the observed sample y values around the regression plane.

Coefficient of multiple determination A measure of the percentage of the variability in y that can be explained by the predictor variables.

Model building The development of a regression equation that will provide a good fit to a particular set of data.

Dummy variable A qualitative or categorical variable used as a predictor.

Stepwise regression analysis A technique that enters variables into the regression equation one at a time until all have been analyzed.

Outlier A point that lies far beyond the scatter of the remaining residuals.

KEY FORMULAS

Population multiple regression model

$$y = \beta_0 + \beta_2 x_2 + \beta_3 x_3 + \cdots + \beta_k x_k + \varepsilon \qquad (15.1)$$

Sample multiple regression model

$$\hat{y} = b_0 + b_2 x_2 + b_3 x_3 + \cdots + b_k x_k \qquad (15.2)$$

Standard error of estimate for multiple regression

$$s_{y \cdot x's} = \sqrt{\frac{\Sigma(y - \hat{y})^2}{n - k}} \qquad (15.3)$$

Prediction interval

$$\hat{y} \pm t\, s_{\hat{y} \cdot x's} \qquad (15.4)$$

Confidence interval

$$\hat{y} \pm t\, s_{\hat{\mu} \cdot x's} \qquad (15.5)$$

Coefficient of multiple determination

$$R^2 = 1 - \frac{\Sigma(y - \hat{y})^2}{\Sigma(y - \bar{y})^2} \qquad (15.6)$$

Polynomial model

$$y = \beta_0 + \beta_1 x + \beta_2 x^2 + \cdots + \beta_k x^k + \varepsilon \qquad (15.7)$$

Second-order model

$$y = \beta_0 + \beta_1 x + \beta_2 x^2 + \varepsilon \qquad (15.8)$$

Third-order model

$$y = \beta_0 + \beta_1 x + \beta_2 x^2 + \beta_3 x^3 + \varepsilon \qquad (15.9)$$

Quadratic model

$$y = \beta_0 + \beta_2 x^2 + \varepsilon \qquad (15.10)$$

Reciprocal model

$$y = \beta_0 + \beta_1(1/x) + \varepsilon \qquad (15.11)$$

Square-root transformation

$$y = \beta_0 + \beta_1\sqrt{x} + \varepsilon \qquad (15.12)$$

Exponential model

$$y = \beta_0[e(\beta_1 x)]\varepsilon \qquad (15.13)$$

Logarithmic transformation

$$\text{Log}_e\, y = \text{Log}_e\, \beta_0 + \beta_1 \text{Log}_e\, x + \text{Log}_e\, \varepsilon \qquad (15.14)$$

Logistic growth curve

$$y = \beta_0/(1 + \beta_1 \rho^x) + \varepsilon \qquad (15.15)$$

Asymptotic regression curve

$$y = \beta_0 - \beta_1 \rho^x + \varepsilon \qquad (15.16)$$

SOLVED EXERCISE

. . . .

1. MULTICOLLINEARITY

Herb Hancock, sales manager of the NAPE Company (a large automotive parts distributor), wants to develop a model to predict total annual sales for a region as early as April. If regional sales can be predicted, then total company sales can be estimated. The number of retail outlets in the region that stock the company's parts and the number of cars registered for each region as of April 1 are the two predictor variables Herb wants to investigate. Herb collects the following data:

Region	Sales (millions), y	Number of retail outlets, x_2	Number of cars registered (millions), x_3
1	52.3	2,011	24.6
2	26.0	2,850	22.1
3	20.2	650	7.9
4	16.0	480	12.5
5	30.0	1,694	9.0
6	46.2	2,302	11.5
7	35.0	2,214	20.5
8	3.5	125	4.1
9	33.1	1,840	8.9
10	25.2	1,233	6.1
11	38.2	1,699	9.5

a. Analyze the correlation matrix.

b. Are the regression coefficients valid?

c. How much error is involved in the prediction for region 1?

d. Show how the standard error of estimate was computed.

e. How can this regression equation be improved?

The data are run on a multiple regression program. Table 15.19 shows the computer output.

TABLE 15.19   Computer Output for Solved Exercise 1

```
                       CORRELATION MATRIX: 3 BY 3
                       VAR.    1      2      3

                         1   1.000  0.739  0.548
                         2   0.739  1.000  0.670
                         3   0.548  0.670  1.000

                 STANDARD   REGRESSION   STD. ERROR   COMPUTED
VARIABLE  MEAN   DEVIATION  COEFFICIENT  OF REG COEF. T VALUE
NO.
   2    1554.36  843.91     0.01099      0.00520      2.11
   3      12.43    6.86     0.19466      0.63984      0.30
DEPENDENT
1         29.61   13.76

INTERCEPT                10.109   MULTIPLE CORRELATION   0.74
STD. ERROR OF ESTIMATE   10.305   R SQUARED              0.55

                     ANALYSIS OF VARIANCE
                       DEGREES     SUM OF   MEAN
SOURCE OF VARIATION    OF FREEDOM  SQUARES  SQUARES  F VALUE

ATTRIBUTABLE TO REGRESSION   2     1043.66  521.83   4.91
DEVIATION FROM REGRESSION    8      849.56  106.20
   TOTAL                     10    1893.23

                     TABLE OF RESIDUALS

OBSERVATION      OBSERVED      PREDICTED         RESIDUAL
                 VALUE         VALUE

    1             52.30        36.99657          15.30343
    2             26.00        45.72960         -19.72960
    3             20.20        18.78986           1.41014
    4             16.00        17.81718          -1.81718
    5             30.00        30.47639          -0.47639
    6             46.20        37.64429           8.55571
    7             35.00        38.42921          -3.42921
    8              3.50        12.28098          -8.78098
    9             33.10        32.06130           1.03870
   10             25.20        24.84600           0.35400
   11             38.20        30.62867           7.57133
```

Solution:

a. The number of retail outlets is related to annual sales ($r_{1,2} = .739$) and is potentially a good predictor variable. Number of cars registered is moderately related to annual sales ($r_{1,3} = .548$) and, because of multicollinearity ($r_{2,3} = .670$), won't be a good predictor variable in conjunction with number of retail outlets.

b. No. Multicollinearity is present, causing the regression coefficients to be undependable.

c. $\hat{y} = 10.109 + 0.01099(2{,}011) + 0.19466(24.6)$
   $= 36.997$ million

   $e = (y - \hat{y}) = 52.300 - 36.997 = 15.303$

d. $s_{y \cdot x} = \sqrt{\dfrac{\Sigma(y - \hat{y})^2}{n - k}} = \sqrt{\dfrac{849.56}{11 - 3}} = \sqrt{106.195} = 10.3$

e. New predictor variables should be tried.

Herb decides to investigate a new predictor variable, personal income by region. The data for this new variable are:

Region	Personal income (billions)
1	98.5
2	31.1
3	34.8
4	32.7
5	68.8
6	94.7
7	67.6
8	19.7
9	67.9
10	61.4
11	85.6

The data are run on a multiple regression program. Table 15.20 presents the computer output.

TABLE 15.20 Computer Output for Solved Exercise 1

```
                        CORRELATION MATRIX: 4 BY 4
                        VAR.    1       2       3       4
                         1    1.000   0.739   0.548   0.936
                         2    0.739   1.000   0.670   0.556
                         3    0.548   0.670   1.000   0.281
                         4    0.936   0.556   0.281   1.000

RUN NUMBER 1

VARIABLE            STANDARD    REGRESSION   STD. ERROR    COMPUTED
NO.         MEAN    DEVIATION   COEFFICIENT  OF REG. COEF. T VALUE

  2       1554.36    843.91      0.00238       0.00157      1.52
  3         12.43      6.86      0.45743       0.16750      2.73
  4         60.25     27.17      0.40058       0.03779     10.60

DEPENDENT

  1         29.61     13.76

INTERCEPT                      -3.91771    MULTIPLE CORRELATION    0.987

STD. ERROR OF ESTIMATE          2.668     R SQUARED               0.974

                         ANALYSIS OF VARIANCE

                         DEGREES     SUM OF    MEAN
SOURCE OF VARIATION      OF FREEDOM  SQUARES   SQUARES   F VALUE

ATTRIBUTABLE TO REGRESSION    3      1843.40   614.47     86.33
DEVIATION FROM REGRESSION     7        49.83     7.12
       TOTAL                 10      1893.23

END RUN NO. 1
```

TABLE 15.20   *concluded*

RUN NUMBER 2

VARIABLE NO.	MEAN	STANDARD DEVIATION	REGRESSION COEFFICIENT	STD. ERROR OF REG COEF.	COMPUTED T VALUE
3	12.43	6.86	0.62092	0.13821	4.49
4	60.25	27.17	0.43017	0.03489	12.33

DEPENDENT

1	29.61	13.76			

INTERCEPT   −4.02690   MULTIPLE CORRELATION   0.982

STD. ERROR OF ESTIMATE   2.877   R SQUARED   0.965

ANALYSIS OF VARIANCE

SOURCE OF VARIATION	DEGREES OF FREEDOM	SUM OF SQUARES	MEAN SQUARES	F VALUE
ATTRIBUTABLE TO REGRESSION	2	1827.03	913.52	110.41
DEVIATION FROM REGRESSION	8	66.20	8.27	
TOTAL	10	1893.23		

END RUN NO. 2

RUN NUMBER 3

VARIABLE NO.	MEAN	STANDARD DEVIATION	REGRESSION COEFFICIENT	STD. ERROR OF REG COEF.	COMPUTED T VALUE
2	1554.36	843.91	0.00515	0.00162	3.18
4	60.25	27.17	0.38530	0.05024	7.67

DEPENDENT

1	29.61	13.76			

INTERCEPT   −1.60819   MULTIPLE CORRELATION 0.972

STD. ERROR OF ESTIMATE   3.587   R SQUARED   0.946

ANALYSIS OF VARIANCE

SOURCE OF VARIATION	DEGREES OF FREEDOM	SUM OF SQUARES	MEAN SQUARES	F VALUE
ATTRIBUTABLE TO REGRESSION	2	1790.32	895.16	69.59
DEVIATION FROM REGRESSION	8	102.91	12.86	
TOTAL	10	1893.23		

END RUN NO. 3

f. Is personal income by region a good potential predictor variable?

g. What percentage of the variance in sales will be explained by using only personal income as a predictor variable?

h. What percentage of the variance in sales will be explained by using all three predictor variables?

i. Is the prediction equation in run 1 explaining a significant percentage of the sales variance? Test at the .05 significance level.

j. Test at the .05 significance level to determine if each of the three predictor variables should be used to predict sales.

k. Test at the .05 significance level to determine if personal income and number of retail outlets (x_2 and x_4) should be used to predict sales.

l. Test at the .05 significance level to determine if personal income and number of registered automobiles (x_3 and x_4) should be used to predict sales.

m. Which model should Herb use?

n. Interpret the estimated regression coefficients for the equation in part *j*.

o. Are these regression coefficients valid?

p. Discuss the accuracy of this model.

Solution:

f. Yes. Personal income is highly related to annual sales ($r_{1,4}$ = .936).

g. $(.936)^2 = .876$

h. $R^2 = .974$

i. The null and alternative hypotheses are

$$H_0: \rho^2 = 0$$
$$H_1: \rho^2 > 0$$

The decision rule is

Reject the null hypothesis if the computed F statistic is greater than 4.35.

The following sums of squares are found in Table 15.20: SSR = 1,843.40, SSE = 49.83, and SST = 1,893.23. The sums of squares are divided by the appropriate degrees of freedom to produce the estimates of the unknown population variance, referred to as the mean square values on the computer output. The mean square for the "attributable to regression" row is 1,843.40/3 = 614.47. The mean square for the "error" row is 49.83/7 = 7.12. The F value is the ratio of these two estimates of the variance:

$$F = \frac{\text{SSR}/(k-1)}{\text{SSE}/(n-k)} = \frac{1{,}843.40/(4-1)}{49.83/(11-4)} = \frac{614.47}{7.12} = 86.33$$

Since the calculated F value (86.33) is considerably larger than the critical value (4.35), the null hypothesis is rejected. Herb concludes that the sample regression equation is explaining a significant percentage of the sales variance.

j. The appropriate hypotheses are

$$H_0: \beta_2 = 0, \quad \beta_3 = 0, \quad \beta_4 = 0$$
$$H_1: \beta_2 \neq 0, \quad \beta_3 \neq 0, \quad \beta_4 \neq 0$$

The decision rule is based on $(n - k) = (11 - 4) = 7$ degrees of freedom:

Reject the null hypothesis if the computed t statistic is smaller than -2.365 or greater than 2.365.

Personal income is a significant variable (10.6 > 2.365), as is number of registrations (2.73 > 2.365). However, sales isn't a significant variable (1.52 < 2.365).

k. The variables to be tested are in run 3. The appropriate hypotheses are

$$H_0: \beta_2 = 0, \quad \beta_4 = 0$$
$$H_1: \beta_2 \neq 0, \quad \beta_4 \neq 0$$

The decision rule is based on $(n - k) = (11 - 3) = 8$ degrees of freedom:

> Reject the null hypothesis if the computed t statistic is smaller than -2.306 or greater than 2.306.

Since the computed t statistics for both number of retail outlets, 3.18, and personal income, 7.67, are greater than 2.306, the null hypotheses are rejected. Herb concludes that the variables both explain a significant portion of the sales variance.

l. The variables to be tested are in run 2. The appropriate hypotheses are

$$H_0: \beta_3 = 0, \quad \beta_4 = 0$$
$$H_1: \beta_3 \neq 0, \quad \beta_4 \neq 0$$

The decision rule is based on $(n - k) = (11 - 3) = 8$ degrees of freedom:

> Reject the null hypothesis if the computed t statistic is smaller than -2.306 or greater than 2.306.

Since the computed t statistics for both number of registered automobiles, 4.49, and personal income, 12.33, are greater than 2.306, the null hypotheses are rejected. Herb concludes that the variables both explain a significant portion of the sales variance.

m. Herb should choose the model containing registered autos and personal income (x_3 and x_4) because it explains a higher percentage of the variance ($R^2 = .965$).

n. The equation is $\hat{y} = -4.0269 + 0.62092x_3 + 0.43017x_4$. If the number of registered cars in the region increases by 1 million while personal income remains constant, sales will increase by an average of 620,920. If personal income increases by \$1 billion while the number of cars registered remains constant, sales will increase by an average of 430,170.

o. The regression coefficients should be valid since variables 3 and 4 aren't too highly related to each other ($r_{3,4} = .281$) so multicollinearity isn't a problem.

p. The model explains 96.5% of the sales variance and should be fairly accurate. Each prediction is typically off by about 2.877 million (the value of the standard error of estimate).

EXERCISES

48. Explain each of the following concepts:
    a. Correlation matrix.
    b. Estimated regression coefficient.
    c. R^2.
    d. Coefficient of multiple determination.
    e. Multicollinearity.
    f. Residual.
    g. Dummy variable.
    h. Stepwise regression.
49. Your multiple regression equation is $\hat{y} = 7.81 + 1.5x_2 - 8.46x_3 + 10.68x_4$. Make a point estimate given $x_2 = 2$, $x_3 = 1.4$, $x_4 = 3.5$.

50. Make a 98% confidence interval for Exercise 49 if $s_{\hat{\mu} \cdot x's} = 2.3$. Compute this interval for a sample size of 45.

51. Jack Raines works for a government regulatory agency that wants to determine what miles per gallon (mpg) rating new cars should achieve. Jack builds a multiple regression model using engine size (x_2), car weight (x_3), and rear axle ratio (x_4) to predict miles per gallon (y). He takes a random sample of 14 new cars, records the data for the three potential predictor variables, and determines mpg. The computer output containing the analysis of variance is:

ANALYSIS OF VARIANCE

SOURCE OF VARIATION	DEGREES OF FREEDOM	SUM OF SQUARES	MEAN SQUARES	F-VALUE
ATTRIBUTABLE TO REGRESSION	3	567.12	189.04	
DEVIATION FROM REGRESSION	10	37.89	3.79	
TOTAL	13	605.01		

Test the regression equation at the .05 significance level. State the appropriate hypotheses, decision rule, and conclusion.

52. Government economist Tracy Wilder is trying to predict the demand function for passenger car fuel in the United States. Tracy developed a model that used the actual price of a gallon of regular gas to predict fuel consumption per year. She could only explain 72.8% of the variance with this model. Tracy has decided to add a variable representing the population of the United States to the model. The data are:

Year	Fuel consumed by cars (billions of gallons), y	Price of gasoline, x_2	U.S. population (millions), x_3
1973	78.8	0.39	211.9
1974	75.1	0.53	213.9
1975	76.4	0.57	216.0
1976	79.7	0.59	218.0
1977	80.4	0.62	220.2
1978	81.7	0.63	222.6
1979	77.1	0.86	225.1
1980	71.9	1.19	227.7
1981	71.0	1.31	230.1
1982	70.1	1.22	232.5
1983	69.9	1.16	234.8
1984	68.7	1.13	237.0
1985	69.3	1.12	239.3

Source: *Statistical Abstract of the United States,* various years.

Run the data on a multiple regression program. Write a memo to Tracy summarizing the results of adding the population variable to the model. Recommend to Tracy what she should do next.

53. Ralph Ludwigson, personnel director for Danielson Tool & Die Corporation, feels that there's a relationship between ages of the firm's employees and number of days they were

absent from work last month. He selects a random sample of 10 workers and collects the following data:

Worker	Days absent, y	Age, x
1	5	25
2	0	30
3	1	62
4	7	33
5	8	45
6	12	27
7	6	55
8	11	41
9	2	22
10	3	58

a. Plot the data on a scatter diagram.

b. Develop a linear model.

c. Test this model at the .05 significance level.

d. Develop a curvilinear model.

e. Test this model using the .05 significance level.

f. If you've found a valid model, predict the number of absent days for a 30-year-old employee.

54. This exercise refers to the following correlation matrix, where variable 1 is the dependent variable.

	1	2	3	4
1	1	.77	.84	.92
2	.77	1	.75	.81
3	.84	.75	1	.21
4	.92	.81	.21	1

a. Which variable would enter the model first? Why?

b. Which variable would enter the model second? Why?

c. Which variable or variables would be included in the best prediction equation?

55. Monty Card Department Store manager Fred Burks wonders if his customers are charging more on their Monty Card credit cards than on MasterCharge and VISA. Fred examines nine randomly chosen charges from sales using each of the three cards:

Monty Card	MasterCharge	VISA
$103	$ 71	$ 98
91	102	111
62	83	72
47	21	9
85	15	24
175	49	39
23	36	64
80	58	71
121	68	40

Construct the ANOVA table using multiple regression. Compare your results to the ANOVA table for Exercise 47 in Chapter 12.

56. Decision Science Associates has been asked to do a feasibility study for a proposed destination resort one half mile from the Grand Coulee Dam. Mark Craze isn't happy with the regression model that used the price of a gallon of regular gas to predict the number of visitors to the Grand Coulee Dam Visitors Center. After plotting the data on a scatter diagram, Mark decides to use a dummy variable to represent significant celebrations in the general area. Mark uses a 1 to represent a celebration and a 0 to represent no celebration. In the following table, note that the 1 for 1974 represents the Expo '74 World's Fair in Spokane, Washington, and the 1 for 1983 represents the celebration of the 50th anniversary of the Grand Coulee Dam's construction. Mark also decides to use time as a predictor variable.

Year	Number of visitors, y	Time, x_2	Price of gasoline, x_3	Celebration, x_4
1973	268,528	1	0.39	0
1974	468,136	2	0.53	1
1975	390,129	3	0.57	0
1976	300,140	4	0.59	0
1977	271,140	5	0.62	0
1978	282,752	6	0.63	0
1979	244,006	7	0.86	0
1980	161,524	8	1.19	0
1981	277,134	9	1.31	0
1982	382,343	10	1.22	0
1983	617,737	11	1.16	1
1984	453,881	12	1.13	0

Source: Grand Coulee Dam Visitors Center and *Statistical Abstract of the United States, 1988.*

a. Run a model that utilizes all three predictor variables. Test the t values to determine which predictor variables are significance at the .20 significance level. Use a two-tailed test.

b. Determine the best model and predict the number of visitors for 1986 if the price of gasoline is estimated to be 86 cents and the World's Fair is to be celebrated in Vancouver, Canada, within a day's drive of Grand Coulee Dam.

c. How accurate is the model that you used in part b?

d. Write a report for Mark to present to his boss. Indicate what additional information would be important in deciding whether to recommend that the destination resort be built.

57. Washington Water Power Company rate analyst Judy Johnson is preparing for a rate case and needs to estimate electric residential revenue for 1992. Judy investigates three potential predictor variables: residential use per kilowatt-hour (kwh), residential charge per kwh (cents/kwh), and number of residential electric customers. She collects data from 1968 to 1991:

Year	Revenue (millions of $) y	Use per kwh x_2	Charge (cents/kwh) x_3	Number of customers x_4
1968	19.3	10,413	1.33	139,881
1969	20.4	11,129	1.29	142,806

Year	Revenue (millions of $) y	Use per kwh x_2	Charge (cents/kwh) x_3	Number of customers x_4
1970	20.9	11,361	1.25	146,616
1971	21.9	11,960	1.21	151,640
1972	23.4	12,498	1.19	157,205
1973	24.5	12,667	1.19	162,328
1974	25.8	12,857	1.21	166,558
1975	30.5	13,843	1.29	170,317
1976	33.3	14,223	1.33	175,536
1977	37.2	14,427	1.42	181,553
1978	42.5	14,878	1.52	188,325
1979	48.8	15,763	1.59	194,237
1980	55.4	15,130	1.84	198,847
1981	64.3	14,697	2.17	201,465
1982	78.9	15,221	2.55	203,444
1983	86.5	14,166	2.97	205,533
1984	114.6	14,854	3.70	208,574
1985	129.7	14,997	4.10	210,811
1986	126.1	13,674	4.34	212,865
1987	132.0	13,062	4.71	214,479
1988	138.1	13,284	4.82	215,610
1989	141.2	13,531	4.81	217,164
1990	143.7	13,589	4.81	219,968
1991	149.2	13,800	4.84	223,364

Source: "Financial and Operating Supplement," *Washington Water Power Annual Report*, 1978, 1986, 1991.

a. Develop a good model for Judy to use.

b. Use the model selected in part *a* to predict 1992 revenue given the following estimates: residential use per kwh, 14,000; residential charge per kwh, 4.50; and number of residential electric customers, 215,000.

c. How accurate is the model selected in part *a*?

d. Write documentation supporting your choice so that Judy can testify before the rate commission.

58. Jeff Hawkins, an economist, is studying how important an area's economics are in influencing people's choices of where to live. He feels that people will change jobs and even careers if the money is right. Based on these beliefs, Jeff feels that economics play an important role in determining which cities are rated as the best places to live. He gathers data from Rand McNally & Company, *Places Rated Almanac*, 1981; Moody's Investors Service, *Bond Rating Guide*, 1981; the Bureau of Economic Analysis, "County and Metropolitan Area Personal Income," *Survey of Current Business*, 1981; Commerce Clearing House, *State Tax Handbook*, 1981; and Bureau of Labor Statistics, "State and Metropolitan Area Unemployment," *News*, March 1981. Jeff selects a systematic sample of 31 cities and records data on five variables: overall rank (y), Moody's bond rating (x_2), average household income (x_3), average household taxes (x_4), and local unemployment rate (x_5). Jeff coded the Moody's bond rating as a dummy variable, with 1 representing a rating of AAA, AA, A1 or A. Zero was used to represent any other bond rating, such as BAA1.

Metro area	Ranking, y	Moody's rating, x_2	Average income ($), x_3	Average taxes ($), x_4	Unemployment rate (%), x_5
Amarillo, TX	84	1	28,388	214	4.4
Atlanta, GA	1	1	27,051	1,721	5.5
Billings, MT	125	1	26,943	1,954	4.1
Bridgeport, CT	92	1	33,518	420	6.0
Charleston, WV	52	1	26,738	1,306	7.4
Cleveland, OH	14	0	28,677	716	8.1
Detroit, MI	43	0	30,243	1,541	13.0
Erie, PA	55	0	24,125	740	9.3
Gadsden, AL	244	0	20,928	991	8.7
Greeley, CO	270	1	23,325	1,535	6.4
Jackson, MS	68	1	24,929	1,046	5.0
Kenosha, WI	190	1	26,568	2,593	8.4
Las Vegas, NV	172	0	30,526	194	7.4
Lincoln, NE	79	1	26,922	997	3.5
Los Angeles, CA	47	1	29,792	2,716	8.1
Memphis, TN	66	1	23,614	299	5.9
Miami, FL	20	1	28,042	222	5.2
Modesto, CA	258	1	26,819	2,372	11.8
Monroe, LA	206	0	20,920	567	8.5
Nashua, NH	197	1	25,456	000	4.5
New York, NY	26	0	26,938	2,773	7.6
Peoria, IL	206	1	30,563	1,051	8.4
Phoenix, AZ	45	1	27,975	2,089	6.0
Portland, ME	108	1	23,906	1,572	6.3
Richmond, VA	29	1	28,671	1,605	3.6
St. Louis, MO	24	0	26,136	1,631	7.9
Salem, OR	97	1	23,231	1,943	7.4
Seattle, WA	5	1	30,802	324	6.3
Topeka, KA	140	1	25,620	1,880	5.8
Waterbury, CT	266	0	25,393	341	6.8
Wilmington, DE	109	1	27,232	2,411	6.9

a. Develop a model to predict a city's overall ranking.

b. Test Jeff's theory that economics play an important role in determining which cities are rated as the best places to live.

c. What variables would you add to improve the prediction model? Look in the *Places Rated Almanac* if you need help.

d. Could the Moody's rating variable be coded differently?

e. Use the best model to predict a city's rating if the following information is available: Moody's rating is 1, average income is $30,000, average taxes are $1,000, and unemployment rate is 8%.

59. Professional Investment Group analyst Michelle Sutcliffe is investigating earnings per share for large corporations. Michelle collects data from *Fortune 500*, which ranks the 500 largest industrial corporations by sales. Her random sample of 30 corporations covers the following potential predictor variables: sales, profits, assets, and stockholders' equity.

Corporation	Earnings per share, y	Sales (millions), x_2	Assets (millions), x_3	Stockholders' equity (millions), x_4	Profits as percentage of equity (%), x_5
IBM	8.72	54,217	63,688	38,263	13.7
Boeing	3.10	15,355	12,566	4,987	9.6
Unisys	3.15	9,713	9,958	4,545	12.7
Coca-Cola	2.43	7,658	8,356	3,224	28.4
Northrop	2.01	6,053	3,124	948	9.9
Pfizer	4.08	4,920	6,923	3,882	17.8
Time, Inc.	4.18	4,194	4,424	1,248	20.0
United Brands	3.86	3,268	1,116	419	14.2
Hercules	14.74	2,693	3,492	2,190	37.5
Paccar	6.26	2,424	1,300	801	14.0
Squibb	3.42	2,157	2,782	1,526	23.5
Maytag	1.91	1,909	855	415	36.8
Trinova	2.20	1,682	1,320	631	11.9
Amdahl	2.82	1,505	1,508	766	19.1
Holly Farms	4.31	1,407	685	343	20.9
Dow Jones	2.10	1,314	1,943	848	24.0
Timken	0.78	1,230	1,467	923	1.1
Clorox	1.96	1,126	933	616	17.0
Ball	2.80	1,054	795	397	16.7
Potlatch	3.13	992	1,307	638	13.7
Ferro	2.30	871	532	260	12.2
Telex	5.24	822	618	3,541	22.0
Sealed Power	2.12	774	562	288	9.1
Roper	2.12	714	250	81	24.5
Ametek	0.94	620	538	253	16.3
Coleman	2.72	599	404	184	10.4
Shaklee	1.77	572	414	252	9.3
Carlisle	2.25	543	309	186	10.1
Lukens	3.87	503	323	152	14.3
Russell	1.17	480	445	280	16.6

a. Discuss the potential of each predictor variable.

b. Is multicollinearity a problem with this set of predictor variables?

c. Write a report to Michelle discussing your findings concerning the prediction of earnings per share for large corporations.

60. Spendwise supermarket chain manager Anna Sheehan wants to predict paperback book sales (books per week) based on the amount of shelf display space (in feet) provided. Anna gathers data for a sample of 11 weeks:

Week	Number of books sold, y	Feet of shelf space, x
1	275	6.8
2	142	3.3
3	168	4.1
4	197	4.2
5	215	4.8
6	188	3.9
7	241	4.9

Week	Number of books sold, y	Feet of shelf space, x
8	295	7.7
9	125	3.1
10	266	5.9
11	200	5.0

a. Plot the data on a scatter diagram.

b. Develop a linear model.

c. Develop a curvilinear model.

d. Test both models using the .05 significance level.

e. Use the best model to predict paperback book sales for a week in which five feet of shelf space is provided.

61. Tom Dukich, analyst for Burgan Furniture Company, decides that production scheduling can be improved if an accurate method for predicting quarterly sales can be developed. He investigates the relationship between housing construction permits and furniture sales in the store's market area. Tom feels that permits will lead sales by two quarters. In addition, he wonders if quarterly sales are seasonal. After examining 1988–92 data, Tom decides to create a dummy variable. He uses a 0 to represent first- or second-quarter sales and a 1 to represent third- or fourth-quarter sales. Sales data are recorded in thousands of dollars.

Year	Quarter	Sales	Permits
1988	3	—	20
	4	—	4
1989	1	119	33
	2	77	9
	3	409	13
	4	198	18
1990	1	77	29
	2	121	9
	3	281	11
	4	160	22
1991	1	115	69
	2	145	28
	3	654	21
	4	269	14
1992	1	196	76
	2	276	39
	3	789	19
	4	318	13

a. Develop a simple regression model using housing construction permits as the predictor variable.

b. Develop a multiple regression model by adding the dummy variable.

c. Which model should Tom use?

d. Estimate quarterly sales for 1993 for Burgan Furniture Company.

e. Does this model violate any of the assumptions of multiple regression?

EXTENDED EXERCISES

62. MURPHY TRANSPORT

Charles Murphy is president of Murphy Transport, which hauls and stores household goods in the Midwest. He has been concerned lately about his fleet of trucks, specifically, about the annual cost of maintaining them. He decides to try to find variables that correlate well with this key variable. Mr. Murphy uses a random selection method to choose a sample of 39 trucks.

In addition to the dependent variable (annual truck maintenance cost), four potential predictor variables are selected:

x_2 = Age of truck, in years
x_3 = Weight of truck when empty
x_4 = Average number of trips taken per year
x_5 = Current odometer reading, in miles

He selects the random sample, makes five measurements, and analyzes the data on his personal computer using a statistical program that performs multiple regression. Table 15.21 presents the correlation matrix.

TABLE 15.21 Correlation Matrix for Extended Exercise 62

	1	2	3	4	5
1	1	.795	.338	.811	.949
2	.795	1	.490	.651	.754
3	.338	.490	1	.261	.238
4	.811	.651	.261	1	.780
5	.949	.754	.238	.780	1

After considering this correlation matrix, where the dependent variable is number 1, Mr. Murphy decides he would like to see the following regression runs:

Dependent variable: y
Predictor variables: x_5

x_4, x_5 — MC
x_2, x_5 — MC
x_2, x_4 — MC
x_2, x_3, x_4, x_5
No

The computer program performs these runs and generates the results. The program Mr. Murphy is using prepares a summary of the regression runs (Table 15.22). Mr. Murphy sits down in his office at the end of the day, closes the door, and begins to study these results.

a. Comment on the choices Mr. Murphy made for regressions he would like to see.

b. Based on the correlation matrix and the summary of the regression runs in Table 15.22, which variable(s) do you think should be used to predict annual maintenance cost?

c. Based on your answer to part b, how good a prediction equation will Mr. Murphy have?

TABLE 15.22 Regression Analysis Summary for Extended Exercise 62

Predictor variables	R^2	t values	F value
x_5	.90118	18.37	337.4
x_4, x_5	.91411	2.33	191.6
		10.35	
x_2, x_5	.91572	2.49	195.58
		11.00	
x_2, x_4	.78212	4.52	64.62
		4.97	
x_2, x_3, x_4, x_5	.92866	1.37	110.64
		1.32	
		2.03	
		8.34	

63. SILOS ELECTRONICS

Silos Electronics Company retails various electronic components for businesses, including telephones, paging systems, intercoms, and shortwave radios. Silos has collected a great deal of data over its five years in business, and its president wonders if there's any way to predict dollar amount per sale. This question has become more acute since the company began considering a substantial modification of its product line to include personal computers. "The Data Deluge," an article in the *Washington Post* business section (September 24, 1989), addressed this matter.

The president and his staff begin thinking about other variables from company records that might correlate with dollar amount per sale. The following candidates are finally selected, and a plan is finalized to randomly sample 100 sales over the company's history:

x_2 = Number of employees in purchasing company
x_3 = Distance, in miles, between Silos and purchasing company
x_4 = Size of purchasing company, in annual dollar sales
x_5 = Nature of purchasing company; retail (coded 1), wholesale (coded 2), or both (coded 3)
x_6 = Number of past orders placed by purchasing company

The dependent variable, dollar amount per sale, is designated y. The random sample of measurements for all six variables yields the correlation matrix in Table 15.23.

a. What do you think of the predictor variables selected by Silos?

b. Based on the correlation matrix, which predictor variable combinations would you run?

TABLE 15.23 Correlation Matrix for Extended Exercise 63

	1	2	3	4	5	6
1	1	.23	−.84	.79	−.37	.71
2	.23	1	−.17	.22	−.25	.31
3	−.84	−.17	1	−.81	.33	−.72
4	.79	.22	−.81	1	−.29	.22
5	−.37	−.25	.33	−.29	1	−.83
6	.71	.31	−.72	.22	−.83	1

c. Which combination indicated in part *b* would be best? How good a prediction equation
    would it produce?

64. SOUTHERN HAWAIIAN UNIVERSITY

Ralph Ty is registrar for Southern Hawaiian University, which is experiencing excessive enrollment. The university administration has decided to restrict the number of entering freshmen
using "some reasonable criteria." It is Ralph's job to find a way to do this.

Ralph decides that a person's college grade point average would be a good measure of success
in college. He chooses this as the dependent variable and plans a multiple regression analysis in
an attempt to find a good prediction equation. He thinks that if he can do this, he can make a
good case to the Southern Hawaiian administration that a fair and impartial method has been
found for admitting freshmen to the university.

Ralph thinks about other quantitative variables that might correlate well with college grade
point average. He's not worried about having too many variables or too big a sample size, since
he has access to work study students who can key the data into the university's computer. It
would be easy for him to use the computer's statistical analysis package to perform the multiple
regression.

Ralph has access to all university records in his attempts to find useful predictor variables.
Also, he has the freedom to modify the university's application form if he determines that some
variable not now being collected would be of use.

a. List as many variables as you can that you think would correlate well with Ralph's depen-
    dent variable.

b. Which of these variables do you think are recorded in the university's data system?

c. Which of the variables identified in part *a* would require special collecting? How might this
    be done?

65. MEDIAN FAMILY INCOME

In this exercise, your objective is to build a model to forecast median family income. The variables are

y = Median family income
x_2 = Wages (in millions of dollars) for production workers in manufacturing industries
x_3 = Median gross rent
x_4 = Nonwhite population (percentage)
x_5 = Percentage of occupied households (with more than one person per room)

The population of 200 standard metropolitan statistical areas presented in the accompanying
table was obtained from the *Statistical Abstract*, 1986. Choose a random sample of 40 areas and
develop a good regression model to estimate median income.

Area	Median family income	Wages	Median rent	Nonwhite population (%)	Percentage of occupied households
001	19294	13400	233	20.30	05.2
002	18619	09688	251	18.23	05.7
003	19451	17261	263	17.70	06.0
004	20142	17402	221	04.84	01.9
005	20704	21331	216	11.00	01.9
006	18269	13107	251	35.56	07.6

Area	Median family income	Wages	Median rent	Nonwhite population (%)	Percentage of occupied households
007	23123	20983	246	01.96	01.8
008	18652	16909	239	12.16	06.1
009	20514	19605	231	06.43	02.1
010	23554	13303	315	66.89	15.5
011	20773	17780	260	02.87	02.0
012	21864	17607	222	08.98	02.2
013	21751	19805	228	14.43	02.9
014	22386	20275	252	05.67	02.1
015	18813	18388	193	04.46	03.8
016	19386	20807	232	34.61	06.9
017	21791	18774	244	27.10	03.0
018	20789	22500	223	11.26	02.2
019	24519	18339	252	04.95	02.0
020	18971	15743	232	01.11	04.0
021	18129	14146	224	41.78	07.3
022	15284	13505	165	02.33	02.8
023	21754	19186	226	18.17	04.0
024	17399	14770	203	02.60	02.5
025	20744	18259	231	04.16	02.2
026	21381	15289	231	04.14	01.4
027	21029	17326	301	15.58	05.0
028	18469	13306	256	16.43	03.0
029	19246	12027	215	20.98	04.3
030	17389	10797	191	08.65	03.8
031	21109	17000	232	02.15	02.4
032	18307	15125	216	04.64	01.9
033	21639	19848	212	11.91	03.6
034	22389	19851	238	16.60	02.1
035	20829	19086	227	12.20	02.3
036	20802	21010	222	13.54	02.1
037	21604	22035	238	12.83	02.1
038	19981	16944	238	14.43	03.3
039	20532	19131	237	14.26	03.0
040	19481	18908	253	03.86	02.6
041	17795	17848	253	03.29	03.6
042	21941	17711	270	06.67	02.3
043	19276	14081	244	05.40	02.9
044	21271	16419	232	03.04	01.5
045	20754	15750	233	07.42	01.7
046	20566	15215	229	04.16	02.2
047	21319	17245	251	20.95	02.8
048	21112	21565	223	08.21	02.2
049	20474	15544	219	03.42	01.9
050	19426	12643	219	05.29	02.6
051	17587	12753	181	17.57	04.7
052	17519	16043	237	32.66	05.3
053	19389	13573	240	30.11	04.1
054	20535	18517	220	01.94	01.7
055	17642	14381	216	14.56	04.0
056	18017	15400	201	40.71	06.4
057	19654	14466	237	16.95	03.6

Area	Median family income	Wages	Median rent	Nonwhite population (%)	Percentage of occupied households
058	14779	12277	222	24.12	04.4
059	17723	12975	228	13.70	04.9
060	20217	16819	223	10.52	04.1
061	20562	13006	262	20.29	05.4
062	21671	23232	236	23.82	04.9
063	12931	11500	186	23.04	23.4
064	18996	20351	231	18.12	11.1
065	21946	16110	261	20.45	04.9
066	22244	15179	262	22.24	05.2
067	21416	17757	253	15.82	04.3
068	15366	10485	194	41.44	13.0
069	24314	21193	278	27.20	06.7
070	24351	20687	279	28.17	06.7
071	14651	12222	220	25.96	06.0
072	17249	12405	214	18.87	09.1
073	19246	15912	236	24.33	04.7
074	16983	13602	204	20.99	04.8
075	20857	20917	250	18.92	08.0
076	17768	17535	213	05.37	09.1
077	21009	14946	244	03.11	04.5
078	20699	15633	259	01.39	02.4
079	19369	13163	279	16.11	03.3
080	16386	13272	166	30.32	04.7
081	18472	14321	207	21.02	03.3
082	19923	21654	246	05.44	02.6
083	21456	13600	246	07.62	02.6
084	21152	18864	259	05.58	02.7
085	24471	20803	301	07.85	04.3
086	23667	21202	273	10.61	02.5
087	24804	21371	284	10.10	02.3
088	20311	20169	239	12.29	03.0
089	19428	19267	224	04.57	02.1
090	17571	16453	214	17.08	06.9
091	20319	23468	221	05.80	03.0
092	19611	19015	190	02.59	02.7
093	21569	18478	219	01.55	02.2
094	18464	18738	219	00.91	02.6
095	21622	20431	223	02.31	02.5
096	21822	21425	230	04.34	02.0
097	19668	17362	227	00.99	02.0
098	23024	17178	246	03.81	01.7
099	23659	19701	251	12.73	02.5
100	23637	19936	252	13.02	02.5
101	23836	17772	243	11.35	02.7
102	25693	20000	327	03.43	03.0
103	16131	12215	185	18.74	04.4
104	18339	15697	208	27.64	04.3
105	15833	19093	180	43.32	06.9
106	15504	10875	197	22.48	05.0
107	17617	19157	194	12.94	03.6

Area	Median family income	Wages	Median rent	Nonwhite population (%)	Percentage of occupied households
108	16275	20759	169	13.83	03.5
109	19350	15913	223	21.58	03.9
110	17269	17929	202	29.54	05.7
111	17959	13569	195	35.35	05.9
112	17166	16426	197	27.78	05.0
113	30730	18111	374	14.78	04.0
114	20478	16615	288	13.36	05.2
115	19000	14736	246	16.66	05.8
116	18696	17163	224	11.05	04.3
117	18503	29447	201	15.08	03.9
118	15780	10932	213	03.25	03.8
119	15342	13336	188	08.86	04.8
120	18174	14794	218	20.26	04.1
121	18780	18276	240	23.25	07.9
122	16301	14441	228	06.83	03.5
123	18396	15125	236	26.30	08.3
124	21744	16582	288	26.50	09.4
125	25918	16742	358	13.63	05.6
126	21125	16491	277	32.15	11.2
127	23602	16437	317	19.56	07.5
128	17024	20281	240	04.34	04.3
129	20922	17400	247	16.49	03.5
130	20001	14932	289	31.13	10.2
131	20304	16953	281	18.68	05.5
132	24586	18581	297	24.34	04.9
133	24304	20593	273	27.62	04.1
134	25119	16853	309	28.83	05.7
135	26659	18556	334	21.41	05.3
136	20730	14048	303	12.45	06.0
137	21269	16260	289	07.24	03.3
138	21846	20268	254	20.74	04.1
139	21630	13865	300	17.07	06.0
140	19116	18578	223	23.98	06.3
141	16166	14683	226	26.72	09.9
142	16004	15231	206	16.79	05.9
143	18729	15407	225	12.67	02.6
144	23584	16655	264	13.15	02.4
145	17169	12280	260	04.88	02.0
146	23372	17349	252	10.30	02.5
147	21668	15013	258	11.49	02.7
148	20534	18290	249	05.96	02.4
149	16191	14949	261	10.27	03.3
150	15088	13107	241	12.15	03.1
151	16757	10926	278	09.65	03.8
152	16814	15060	259	17.29	05.1
153	16955	11636	224	11.67	03.0
154	16724	13367	244	21.25	04.6
155	17914	16389	240	23.15	04.3
156	16512	15414	219	17.03	05.0
157	19388	16672	259	10.06	02.9

Area	Median family income	Wages	Median rent	Nonwhite population (%)	Percentage of occupied households
158	19046	11788	282	18.52	08.0
159	19592	13771	312	12.39	03.9
160	18642	11055	272	22.36	12.1
161	19174	13167	264	13.16	05.9
162	13440	12000	216	17.27	04.9
163	18289	13491	255	15.02	04.2
164	15374	14700	212	14.27	04.1
165	16624	18487	223	19.21	04.1
166	17786	11625	285	06.20	02.1
167	16346	13177	240	10.63	03.1
168	19817	16132	279	15.49	04.5
169	17849	18893	205	41.62	08.8
170	16419	10855	202	19.14	04.1
171	21074	15204	252	25.64	03.7
172	17211	15836	202	32.54	05.2
173	15207	12477	182	37.36	05.3
174	18207	16597	186	34.36	05.6
175	17201	18550	204	37.80	05.1
176	23165	16818	240	05.26	01.7
177	21303	17735	241	11.85	02.5
178	24514	18558	252	25.85	05.0
179	25234	17023	275	09.04	03.9
180	24134	17380	251	29.34	05.3
181	24476	26376	239	23.43	04.9
182	25619	20748	260	12.05	03.3
183	23161	25158	236	04.28	02.9
184	28045	17150	285	10.31	03.3
185	21726	21485	238	11.17	02.5
186	20151	19151	239	15.72	03.9
187	23214	20746	262	07.04	02.4
188	22964	18341	238	09.51	02.6
189	22029	18789	241	06.98	02.2
190	20788	24483	208	07.48	02.7
191	18523	16062	215	05.38	03.0
192	19872	15016	223	05.36	02.4
193	21821	24590	225	05.09	02.2
194	20554	20219	227	03.93	03.0
195	20628	19848	223	10.57	02.1
196	18894	17281	227	11.83	03.5
197	18524	18434	197	05.64	03.2
198	23194	19575	248	03.64	01.8
199	23189	22903	253	06.59	02.5
200	22484	21838	224	00.78	03.0

The authors have selected a sample of 80 data points and analyzed these data using the MINITAB package. Please remember that your solution will be different from ours.

A random sample of 80 data points were selected and stored in a file called MEDIAN.DAT. An example of the data file is:

```
008 23194 19575 248 03.64 01.8
```

```
112 23189 22903 253 06.59 02.5
187 22484 21838 224 00.78 03.0
```

The MINITAB commands to read the file and run a regression analysis are:

```
MTB > READ 'MEDIAN.DAT' C1—C6
      80 ROWS READ

ROW    C1     C2      C3     C4     C5     C6

  1   117   18503  29447   201   15.08   3.9
  2   195   20628  19848   223   10.57   2.1
  3    72   17249  12405   214   18.87   9.1
  4    11   20773  17780   260    2.87   2.0
  . . .

MTB > NAME C2 'INCOME' C3 'WAGES' C4 'RENT' C5 'NONWHITE' C6 'HLDS'
MTB > CORR C2—C6

           INCOME    WAGES     RENT  NONWHITE
WAGES       0.562
RENT        0.677    0.131
NONWHITE   -0.230   -0.305   -0.141
HSLD       -0.319   -0.290   -0.115     0.524

MTB > STEP C2—C6;
SUBC> FENTER = 4.

STEPWISE REGRESSION OF INCOME ON 4 PREDICTORS, WITH N = 80

       STEP      1       2
CONSTANT      6432    1114

RENT          55.3    50.1
T RATIO       8.12    9.52

WAGES                 0.393
T RATIO                7.47

S             2153    1650
R-SQ         45.80   68.58
 MORE? (YES, NO, SUBCOMMAND, OR HELP)
SUBC> NO

MTB > REGRESS C2 2 PREDICTORS C3 C4, STORE TRES IN C7

The regression equation is
INCOME = 1114 + 0.393 WAGES + 50.1 RENT

Predictor     Coef    Stdev   t ratio      p
Constant      1114     1445     0.77   0.443
WAGES      0.39310  0.05262     7.47   0.000
RENT        50.137    5.264     9.52   0.000

s = 1650    R-sq = 68.6%    R-sq (adj) = 67.8%

Analysis of Variance

SOURCE       DF        SS           MS       F       P
Regression    2  457258048   228629024   84.02   0.000
Error        77  209523920     2721090
Total        79  666781952

SOURCE       DF      SEQ SS
WAGES         1   210388880
RENT          1   246869184

Unusual Observations
Obs.     WAGES    INCOME      Fit   Stdev.Fit   Residual   St.Resid
  1      29447    18503     22767       749       -4264     -2.90RX
 42      17772    23836     20283       194        3553      2.17R
 63      14949    16191     20076       243       -3885     -2.38R
 74      18558    24514     21044       218        3470      2.12R

R denotes an obs. with a large st. resid.
X denotes an obs. whose X value gives it large influence.
```

```
MTB > HISTOGRAM C7

Histogram of C7  N = 80

MIDPOINT     COUNT
    -3.0         1    *
    -2.5         1    *
    -2.0         2    **
    -1.5         6    ******
    -1.0         7    *******
    -0.5        12    ************
     0.0        18    ******************
     0.5        15    ***************
     1.0        11    ***********
     1.5         5    *****
     2.0         2    **

MTB > NAME C7 'STDRES'
MTB > PLOT C7 VS C2
```

```
         -
         -
         -
   2.0+                                       *     *
         -                  *        *       **
STDRES  -          *     *      *   * * *  *         *
         -              *            * *   *    *  *
         -        *   ** * **   2 *  * * * *      *
   0.0+              3 * ****   **  *            *
         -        *      2 *2 *2   ** **
         -            *    *    * *     **
         -     *       **    *  * *  *
         -        2        *        *
  -2.0+     *              *
         -              *
         -                  *
         -
         -
        ---+---------+---------+---------+---------+---------+----INCOME
         12000     15000     18000     21000     24000     27000
```

```
MTB > STOP
```

Stepwise regression is used to identify the best variables to be used in the model: WAGES and RENT. These variables are then run so that the standardized residuals can be stored in C7. A histogram is run so that the normality assumption can be checked. A plot of standardized residuals is also run so that the rest of the regression assumptions can be checked.

Microcomputer Package

The micro package *Computerized Business Statistics* can be used to solve multiple regression problems.

In Exercise 40, Cindy Lawson bought a major league baseball team. Cindy asks you to write a report on how to develop a winning ball club. You decide to use stepwise multiple regression analysis to determine which statistics are important in creating a winning team.

Computer Solution:

From the main menu of *Computerized Business Statistics*, 10 is selected, indicating Multiple Regression Analysis. The multiple regression analysis menu is shown on the screen.

Since the problem involves entering data from the keyboard, a 1 is selected.

```
Multiple Regression Analysis-Define New Problem
Raw or Correlation Data: Enter R/C, Press ↵ R
Number of Variables: Enter 2-10, Press ↵ 7
```

Since the problem involves one dependent variable (WINS) and six predictor variables (ERA, SO, BA, RUNS, HR, and SB), a 7 is entered.

```
Number of Data Points: Enter 9-125, Press ↵ 26
```

Since there are 26 major league baseball teams, 26 is selected.
    Next, the program asks for the variable names:

```
Multiple Variable Regression-Enter Variable Labels
        Variable 1 X1
        Variable 2 X2
        Variable 3 X3
        Variable 4 X4
        Variable 5 X5
        Variable 6 X6
        Variable Y
Press end when Finished
```

The variable names are ERA, SO, BA, RUNS, HR, SB, and WINS. **END** is pressed once the blanks have been completed.

```
Problem definition correct Y/N/Q, Press ↵ Y
```

After a **Y** response, the program is ready for the data to be entered. There are 26 observations for each of the seven variables. An **F** is entered once the blanks have been completed.

```
Select Dependent Variable: Enter 1-7, Press ↵ 7
```

Since variable 7, WINS, is the dependent variable, a 7 is entered. The screen then shows:

```
Regression Type: F = Full
                 S = Self Stepwise
                 A = Auto Stepwise
Select Type: Enter Letter and Press ↵ A
```

Since a stepwise regression is to be performed, **A** is entered.
    Next, the computer asks:

```
Alpha Error 1 = 0.2, 2 = 0.1, 3 = 0.05, 4 = 0.025, 5 = 0.02, 6 = 0.01, 7 = Other
Select Alpha: Enter 1-7, Press ↵ 3
```

The screen shows:

```
Degrees of Freedom  ................19
    Critical t  ................. 2.093
dof (Numerator, Regression) = 6/ dof (Denominator, Error) = 19
    Critical F  ................. 2.63
```

Next, you are asked:

```
Save Data? Enter Y/N, Press ↵ Y
```

A 7 is entered so that the problem can be run. The screen then shows the output menu. The choice in this case is **P**, for printer.

The program also provides the following alternatives for the user:

```
Multiple Regression Analysis-Optional Results
    R = Residual Analysis              (No)
    C = Correlation Coefficients       (No)
    F = Forecasting                    (No)
Select Optional Results: Enter either (C, F, R) to toggle Option On/Off
Press P to Proceed . . . ?
```

MINITAB COMPUTER PACKAGE

The MINITAB commands to solve Example 15.16 are:

```
MTB > READ 'CH15EX16.DAT' C1 C2
      14 ROWS READ


ROW    C1     C2
  1    1.1    3.9
  2    1.7    4.9
  3    2.6    7.6
  4    2.4    6.8
MTB > NAME C1 'SALES' C2 'EXP'
MTB > LOGE OF C2, PUT INTO C3
MTB > SQRT OF C2, PUT INTO C4
MTB > LET C5 = 1/C2
MTB > NAME C3 'LOGS' C4 'SQRT' C5 '1/EXP'
MTB > PRINT C1-C5
```

ROW	SALES	EXP	LOGS	SQRT	1/EXP
1	1.1	3.9	1.36098	1.97484	0.256410
2	1.7	4.9	1.58924	2.21359	0.204082
3	2.6	7.6	2.02815	2.75681	0.131579
4	2.4	6.8	1.91692	2.60768	0.147059
5	2.3	5.9	1.77495	2.42899	0.169492
6	2.9	9.1	2.20827	3.01662	0.109890
7	0.4	3.4	1.22378	1.84391	0.294118
8	3.2	11.6	2.45101	3.40588	0.086207
9	3.3	14.1	2.64617	3.75500	0.070922
10	3.1	14.9	2.70136	3.86005	0.067114
11	3.2	10.5	2.35138	3.24037	0.095238
12	3.0	9.9	2.29253	3.14643	0.101010
13	3.7	17.1	2.83908	4.13521	0.058480
14	3.3	12.4	2.51770	3.52136	0.080645

The LOGE command is used to calculate logarithms to base e (natural logarithms) for the data in C2 and store them in column C3. The SQRT command is used to calculate square roots for the data in C2 and store them in column C4. The LET command is used to compute the reciprocals for the data in C2 and store them in column C5. The PRINT command is used to show the data stored in columns C1 through C5 of the worksheet.

```
MTB > PLOT C1 VS C2
```

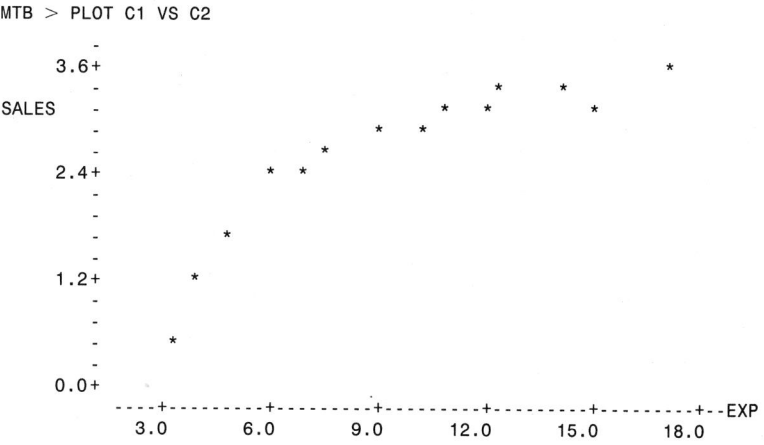

The original data are plotted with sales as the y variable and advertising expenditures as the x variable.

```
MTB > PLOT C1 VS C3
```

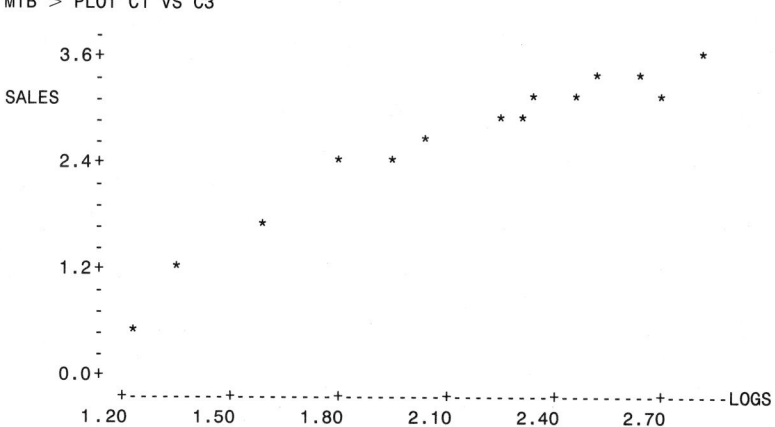

These data are plotted with sales as the *y* variable and the advertising expenditure variable transformed to natural logarithms as the *x* variable. Note that a straight line doesn't fit these data any better than the original data.

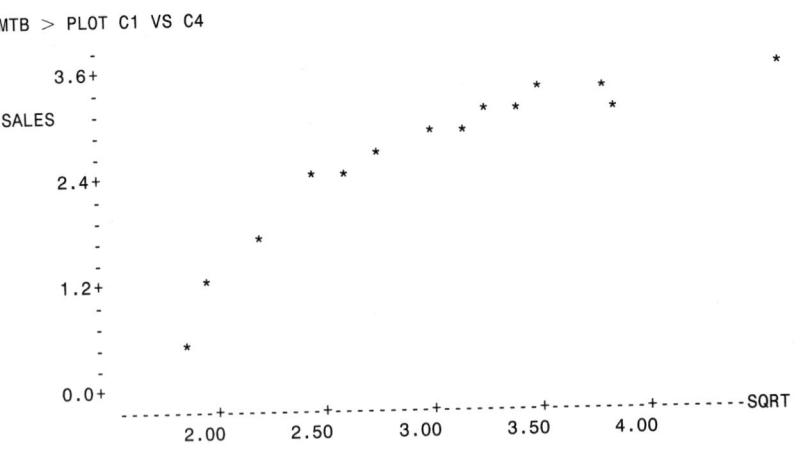

```
MTB > PLOT C1 VS C4
          -
  3.6+                                                                    *
          -
 SALES    -                                               *      *
          -                                         *  *       *
          -                                   *  *
  2.4+                                *  *
          -
          -                     *
          -
  1.2+               *
          -
          -        *
          -
  0.0+    ---------+---------+---------+---------+---------+-------SQRT
            2.00      2.50      3.00      3.50      4.00
```

These data are plotted with sales as the *y* variable and the advertising expenditure variable transformed to square roots as the *x* variable. Note that a straight line should fit these data slightly better than the original data.

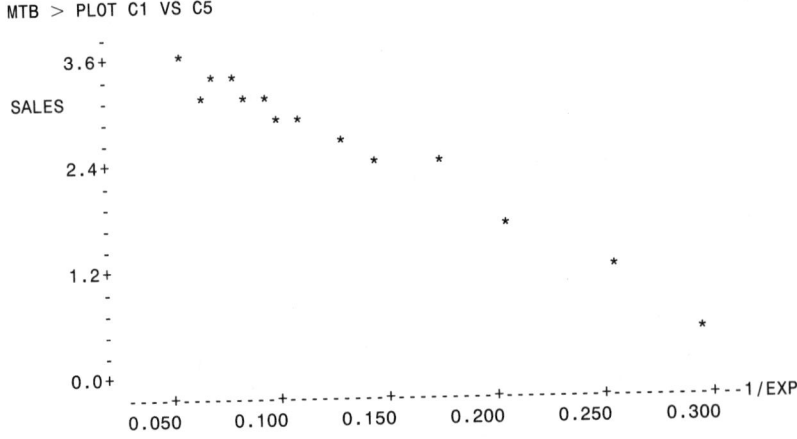

```
MTB > PLOT C1 VS C5
          -
  3.6+        *
          -       *  *
 SALES    -     *   *  *
          -         *  *
          -            *
  2.4+              *      *
          -
          -                   *
          -
  1.2+                           *
          -
          -                          *
          -
  0.0+  ----+---------+---------+---------+---------+---------+--1/EXP
          0.050     0.100     0.150     0.200     0.250     0.300
```

These data are plotted with sales as the y variable and the advertising expenditure variable transformed to reciprocals as the x variable. Note that a straight line should fit these data much better than the original data.

```
MTB > BRIEF 1
MTB > REGRESS C1 1 PREDICTOR C5

The regression equation is
SALES = 4.29 - 12.7 1/EXP

Predictor          Coef        Stdev       t ratio         p
Constant        4.28587      0.07695        55.69       0.000
1/EXP          -12.7132       0.5092       -24.97       0.000

s = 0.1342     R-sq = 98.1%     R-sq (adj) = 98.0%

Analysis of Variance

SOURCE          DF        SS          MS          F          P
Regression       1    11.221      11.221     623.44      0.000
Error           12     0.216       0.018
Total           13    11.437


MTB > STOP
```

The REGRESS command may be preceded by the BRIEF K command where K can equal 1, 2, or 3. Generally, $K = 1$ will produce enough statistics for most applications and will be assumed if the BRIEF command isn't used. When $K = 3$, a table of residuals is added to the basic output. The REGRESS command is used to run a simple regression with sales as the dependent variable and the advertising expenditure variable transformed to reciprocals as the x variable. This model explains 98.1% of the sales variable variance and seems to do a better job than the second-order model of Example 15.16.

SAS COMPUTER PACKAGE

The SAS computer package can be used to run stepwise regression analysis problems. The SAS commands to analyze Solved Exercise 1 are:

```
TITLE 'STEPWISE ANALYSIS FOR SOLVED EXERCISE 1';
DATA SALES;
INPUT SALES OUTLETS AUTOS INCOME;
CARDS;
52.3 2011 24.6 98.5
26.0 2850 22.1 31.1
20.2 650   7.9 34.8
16.0 480  12.5 32.7
30.0 1694  9.0 68.8
46.2 2302 11.5 94.7
35.0 2214 20.5 67.6
 3.5 125   4.1 19.7
33.1 1840  8.9 67.9
25.2 1233  6.1 61.4
38.2 1699  9.5 85.6
PROC STEPWISE;
 MODEL SALES = OUTLETS AUTOS INCOME/
        SLENTRY=.05;
```

The TITLE command names the SAS run. The DATA command gives the data a name. The INPUT command names and specifies the order for the four fields on the data lines. The 11 lines following the CARDS command represent the *y* variable and three *x* variables. The PROC STEPWISE command and MODEL subcommand indicate that the independent variables OUTLETS, AUTOS, and INCOME are to be entered in a regression equation to predict the dependent variable SALES. The SLENTRY = .05 statement specifies the significance level for entering a variable into the final regression model. Table 15.24 presents the output.

TABLE 15.24   SAS Output for Solved Exercise 1

STEPWISE ANALYSIS FOR SOLVED EXERCISE 1

Stepwise Procedure for Dependent Variable SALES

Step 1   Variable INCOME Entered   R-square = 0.87682179   C(p) = 25.76209947

	DF	Sum of Squares	Mean Square	F	Prob>F
Regression	1	1660.02452235	1660.02452235	64.06	0.0001
Error	9	233.20456856	25.91161873		
Total	10	1893.22909091			

Variable	Parameter Estimate	Standard Error	Type II Sum of Squares	F	Prob>F
INTERCEP	1.03230539	3.88620209	1.82835352	0.07	0.7965
INCOME	0.47426771	0.05925344	1660.02452235	64.06	0.0001

Bounds on condition number: 1,   1
. . . .

Step 2   Variable AUTOS Entered   R-square = 0.96503519   C(p) = 4.29970153

	DF	Sum of Squares	Mean Square	F	Prob>F
Regression	2	1827.03269576	913.51634788	110.40	0.0001
Error	8	66.19639515	8.27454939		
Total	10	1893.22909091			

Variable	Parameter Estimate	Standard Error	Type II Sum of Squares	F	Prob>F
INTERCEP	−4.02689773	2.46798811	22.02923556	2.66	0.1414
AUTOS	0.62092180	0.13821024	167.00817341	20.18	0.0020
INCOME	0.43016878	0.03489322	1257.59286751	151.98	0.0001

Bounds on condition number: 1.085938,   4.343753
. . . .

All variables left in the model are significant at the 0.1500 level.
No other variable met the 0.0500 significance level for entry into the model.

Summary of Stepwise Procedure for Dependent Variable SALES

Step	Variable Entered Removed	Number In	Partial R**2	Model R**2	C(p)	F	Prob>F
1	INCOME	1	0.8768	0.8768	25.7621	65.0649	0.0001
2	AUTOS	2	0.0882	0.9650	4.2997	20.1834	0.0020

Chapter

16

INDEX NUMBERS AND TIME SERIES ANALYSIS

*The penguin
flies backwards
because he
doesn't care to
see where he's
going, but wants
to see where
he's been.*

Fred Allen

Objectives

When you have completed this chapter, you will be able to:

Explain how and why index numbers are used.

Compute price, quantity, and value indexes.

Develop a composite index.

Deflate a time series and change its base period.

Identify the component factors that influence a time series.

Explain what causes the trend in a time series and develop an equation to model it.

Compute the cyclical component in a time series and identify what causes this variation.

Identify the seasonal variation in a time series and compute seasonal indexes to describe it.

Isolate irregular or random variation in a time series.

Deseasonalize data.

Develop short-term and long-term series decomposition forecasting models.

The three-month T-bill rate was 3.64% on June 17, 1992, according to that day's *Wall Street Journal*, which also noted that the rate one year earlier was 5.62%.

Previous chapters' discussion of regression analysis and other techniques rests on the assumption that a random sample of items is selected for study, and measured. However, many variables are measured every week, month, quarter, or year. These variables, called *time series* variables, are usually important in business decisions. For this reason, observing and analyzing them carefully is vital in managing any organization.

WHY MANAGERS NEED TO KNOW ABOUT INDEX NUMBERS AND TIME SERIES ANALYSIS

Thousands of index numbers are generated monthly by the federal government. These widely distributed indexes are designed to summarize one or several business time series values in a single, easy-to-understand number.

Companies typically follow many indexes closely, basing their decisions in part on the upward and downward movement of indexes they've decided are key *indicators*. Because of index numbers' widespread use, every manager must understand how they're computed and how they can be used.

This is the first of two chapters concerning analysis and forecasting of time series variables. This chapter presents the decomposition method of analyzing these variables. This approach identifies the component elements that influence each value in a series. Each component is identified so that the series can be projected into the future. The next chapter introduces other ways of accomplishing one of the manager's most important roles: forecasting.

Regarding three-month T-bill rate's sharp drop reported in *The Wall Street Journal*, many firms might want to track the T-bill rate over time. Some firms choose to watch this rate in its percentage form, while others prefer an index number based on a selected period in the past. Such index numbers are one of this chapter's subjects.

PURPOSE OF INDEX NUMBERS

Time Series

Observations of data are frequently made over time. Any variable that consists of data collected, recorded, or observed over successive increments of time is called a **time series**.

> A **time series** consists of data that are collected, recorded, or observed over successive increments of time.

Index Numbers

Index numbers show the movement of values in a time series by converting the actual measured quantities to index, or *relative*, form. Index numbers are specified relative to a base period, usually designated as 100 or 100%. For example, if an index of factory wages has a base period of January 1993 and is currently at a level of 128, the analyst knows that wages are 28% higher now than in January 1993. If a unit production index for a jet airplane factory was based on the first quarter of 1993, an index of 95 in the current quarter would mean that production is 95% of what it was in the base quarter.

Index numbers measure the movement of time series values relative to a base period; the index in the base period equals 100.

CONSTRUCTING AN INDEX

The first consideration in constructing an index is to choose an appropriate base period. The objective is to find a time period that's "normal" in the sense that it represents neither extremely good times nor extremely bad times.

The federal government has judged 1982 to be a "normal" year and has chosen it as the base year for many of its statistical indexes. Other indexes use different years as the base period. From time to time an index is updated by moving its base period forward to a more recent period. Conversion of an index to a new time period is covered later in this chapter.

EXAMPLE 16.1 The Worthrite Company has been keeping an index of its total monthly dollar sales for several years. When the index was started, January 1990 was chosen as the base period. For that month, the sales index was 100. In the latest month, Worthrite management computes the dollar sales index at 178. This means that sales for that month have increased 78% over what they were in the base period, January 1990.

EXAMPLE 16.2 The consumer price index (CPI), prepared by the federal government, consists of many items typically purchased by American consumers. The base period for this index is 1982–84. In March 1992, this index's value was 137. This value indicates that consumer prices in that month were 137% of what they were in the base period, 1982–84.

The usual reason for using index numbers is to summarize the values of a large number of items as a single value that can be monitored over time. For example, the CPI contains values of over 400 items. It would be difficult to assess the state of prices each month by studying all these items' prices, but it's easy to monitor a single value.

Even for a single variable, it's sometimes more convenient to follow an index than to track the variable in its original units. Company monthly sales, for example, might be monitored as an index number rather than in dollars. A company might use a unit production index or a defective item index rather than follow these important variables in their actual units of measurement.

A modification often considered by an analyst is the conversion of time series values measured in dollars to values in constant, or deflated, dollars. An appropriate index number is identified and used in this deflation process.

Index numbers are often of interest because they measure the changes in various economic conditions over time. They're commonly used to measure inflation's effects in various industries and to relate changes in quantities and values to a base period. The explanation and examples that follow show how different kinds of index numbers are computed and used.

TYPES OF INDEXES

Price Index

The basic type of index, and the one most commonly used, is the **price index.** This index measures changes in prices of selected goods and services over time.

A **price index** measures changes in the prices of goods and services over time.

Equation 16.1 is used to calculate a price index. In this formula, PI represents the price index of the items being included. The idea is to calculate these items' current total price and compare it to the same calculation for the base period:

$$PI = \frac{\Sigma P_t}{\Sigma P_b}(100) \tag{16.1}$$

where   PI = Price index
        P_t = Price in period t
        P_b = Price in the base period

The numerator in Equation 16.1 sums the prices of all the items selected for the index in the current period. This total cost is divided by the sum of the prices of these same goods in the base period. The resulting value multiplied by 100 is the price index for that period. These steps are repeated for each period. If only one item is used for the index, the summation signs are ignored. The index in this case is the price of the item in the current period divided by the price of the item in the base period (times 100).

EXAMPLE 16.3   Oil's price per gallon is monitored by a refinery in Anacortes, Washington. The refinery manager read a *New York Times* article (October 24, 1989) stating that oil companies' earnings had slipped—specifically, that Exxon and Phillips Petroleum reported lower third-quarter earnings in 1989. The manager then began a price index for oil so that prices could be more easily monitored.

The base period chosen for the price index was July 1985, when price per barrel was $18. In January 1990, price per barrel was $22. The price index for that month is calculated using Equation 16.1, with only a single item used in the index:

$$PI = \frac{P_t}{P_b}(100) = \frac{22}{18}(100) = 122$$

The refinery can conclude that oil's price per barrel is 22% higher in January 1990 than it was in the base period.

EXAMPLE 16.4 The Daly Manufacturing Company in Chico, California, makes electronic components that are shipped to assembly plants throughout the state. Ruth Kembel, personnel director, has been having trouble hiring qualified people and moving them to California. She has decided to keep track of the monthly cost of living for Chico. Ruth hopes to attract people on the basis of the town's low cost of living compared to other cities in California.

Ruth has defined a "market basket" of typical monthly purchases, including food, fuel, rent, clothing, and entertainment. Since 1982, the cost of this package of goods and services has been carefully measured (Table 16.1).

TABLE 16.1 Calculation of the Price Index for Example 16.4

Year	Monthly cost of market basket	Price index
1982	$435.78	100.00
1983	461.42	105.88
1984	478.83	109.88
1985	485.90	111.50
1986	491.82	112.86
1987	489.40	112.30
1988	495.71	113.75
1989	496.41	113.91
1990	501.14	115.00
1991	503.18	115.47
1992	505.27	115.95

Ruth thinks that the first year of the cost-of-living measurement, 1982, was a typical year, and she decides to use it as the base year in calculating the index. The cost of the package in 1982, $435.78, is divided into the cost of the same package for each year, using Equation 16.1. After moving the decimal point two places to the right to convert decimals to percentages, the cost-of-living indexes in the last column of Table 16.1 result. The index of 100.00 for 1982 indicates that it's the base year. Other years' indexes indicate the price of the market basket for those years relative to 1982. For example, the 1992 index is 505.27/435.78 = 1.1595, or 115.95%.

As these price indexes show, the cost of the defined packages of goods and services has grown steadily since 1982. In 1992, the package cost 115.95% of its price in 1982. In other words, there has been an inflationary effect of about 16% between 1982 and 1992. Ruth believes she can use this series of indexes in her recruiting efforts around the country to show that prices in Chico have risen less than in the rest of the country since 1982.

Quantity Index

Another important index, the **quantity index,** measures changes in quantities of selected goods over time.

A **quantity index** measures changes in the quantities of goods over time.

Equation 16.2, used to calculate a quantity index, follows the same procedure as Equation 16.1 except that quantities of the selected items are used rather than prices. If only one item is tracked, the summation signs in Equation 16.2 are ignored and only the quantities for the single item are used:

$$QI = \frac{\Sigma Q_t}{\Sigma Q_b}(100)$$
(16.2)

where   QI = Quantity index
         Q_t = Quantity in period t
         Q_b = Quantity in the base period

EXAMPLE 16.5   The Carmate Tire Company makes automobile tires and distributes them to wholesalers in a three-state area. Company analyst Calvin Shield has kept track of the number of tires shipped on a monthly basis for several years and has decided to convert these data to a quantity index. He begins the index in June 1991, but he chooses January 1992 as the index's base period (Table 16.2).

TABLE 16.2   Calculation of Quantity Index for Example 16.5

	Month	Number of units shipped	Quantity index
1991	June	149	80.5
	July	135	73.0
	Aug.	163	88.1
	Sept.	160	86.5
	Oct.	175	94.6
	Nov.	142	76.8
	Dec.	163	88.1
1992	Jan.	185	100.0
	Feb.	179	96.8
	Mar.	190	102.7
	Apr.	188	101.6
	May	204	110.3
	June	162	87.6
	July	210	113.5
	Aug.	208	112.4
	Sept.	185	100.0
	Oct.	192	103.8
	Nov.	205	110.8
	Dec.	207	111.9

Each quantity in Table 16.2 is divided by 185 (the number of tires shipped in the base month, January 1992). Equation 16.2 is used for this computation, with the summation signs omitted since there's only one item. Multiplication by 100 produces the quantity indexes in the table's last column. For example, the index for June 1991 is 149/185 = .805, or 80.5%; the December 1992 index is 207/185 = 1.119, or 111.9%.

Calvin believes this quantity index will make managing the company easier since the number of tires shipped is now in index form relative to the base period.

Value Index

A third type of index, the **value index,** measures the dollar value of a group of goods or services.

A **value index** measures the total dollar value of a group of goods or services.

Equation 16.3 is used to calculate a value index. It calls for computing the value of each item in the selected mix. Each item's price is multiplied by its quantity, and these values are added for the current period. The same calculation is made for the base period, and the ratio is formed and multiplied by 100, resulting in the value index:

$$VI = \frac{\sum P_t Q_t}{\sum P_b Q_b}(100) \tag{16.3}$$

where VI = Value index
P_t = Price in period t
P_b = Price in the base period
Q_t = Quantity in period t
Q_b = Quantity in the base period

To calculate a value index for only one item, ignore the summation signs in Equation 16.3.

EXAMPLE 16.6 The Boss Company wants to compare the value of the goods it produced last month with the value of its production in January 1991. Management considers January 1991 to be a "normal" month and wants to compare subsequent months with this period. Using Equation 16.3, the company analyst computes number of units produced for the current month, then multiplies this value by the total direct cost per unit. The result is the value of goods produced, excluding profit and overhead: $43,528. For January 1991, the same calculation produces a value of $29,743. Thus, the value index for Boss's most recent month is (43,528/29,743)100 = 146.35.

The Boss Company's management concludes that there has been a 46% increase in the value of its monthly production between January 1991 and the current month.

Aggregate Index

When an index is used to summarize several items, it's called an *aggregate index* because the prices, quantities, or values of several chosen goods or services are summed in its computation. The summation signs in Equations 16.1, 16.2, and 16.3 indicate the addition of the values for several items in each time period. If the price, quantity, or value history of only a single item is to be followed, the equations are simplified, using a single term in the numerator and denominator instead of the sum of several terms. Such indexes are called *simple indexes* (for example, the monthly price index of

Simple Index

wheat or the quantity index of trucks sold by a manufacturer). Example 16.3 illustrates a simple index.

Implicit in the concept of a "market basket" of goods is the *weighting* of the measured items in accordance with their frequency of use in the area being studied. The consumer price index, for example, doesn't include in its market basket one pound of butter, one car, one house, or one tube of toothpaste. Rather, items are weighted in the construction of the price index to reflect the fact that many tubes of toothpaste are purchased during a year, but a car is purchased only once every several years. This weighting of the items being studied is typically done when the index is constructed.

CONSUMER PRICE INDEX

The most commonly used aggregate index is the **consumer price index,** prepared monthly by the U.S. Dept. of Commerce. This index is widely followed by economists and business leaders as a measure of the prices U.S. consumers are paying for the products and services they commonly buy. Actually, beginning in 1978, the Bureau of Labor Statistics began publishing two consumer price indexes: one for wage earners and clerical workers (CPI-W) and another for all-urban consumers (CPI-U). Both of these important indexes price a market basket of goods and services believed to constitute an American worker's typical purchases. The CPI allows consumers to determine the degree to which price increases are eroding their purchasing power. The CPI has become a yardstick for revising pensions, wages, and other income payments that must keep pace with inflation.

Table 16.3 shows several recent values of the consumer price index (CPI-W). The base period chosen by the U.S. Dept. of Commerce is 1982–84. The index includes prices of about 400 items, such as milk, diapers, beer, bread, pop, gasoline, haircuts, interest rates, doctor fees, and taxes. As the table shows, the CPI-W's value was 136 in January 1992. This reflects an inflation rate of 36% between the base period and that month.

TABLE 16.3   Consumer Price Index and Purchasing Power of the Dollar

Month (1992)	Consumer price index (CPI-W)	Purchasing power (100/CPI-W)
January	136.0	.735
February	136.4	.733
March	137.0	.730

Source: *Survey of Current Business,* April 1992.

The **consumer price index** measures the prices that U.S. consumers pay for the products and services they commonly buy.

In addition to measuring the change in prices of goods and services, the CPI is also used to deflate sales, to determine real disposable income, to find the purchasing power of the dollar, and to establish cost-of-living increases.

Table 16.3 also shows the purchasing power of the dollar for each period. The purchasing power varies inversely with the price index, since a rising price index means that a dollar purchases less. Equation 16.4 shows how purchasing power is computed:

$$\text{Current purchasing power of } \$1 = \frac{100}{\text{Current consumer price index}} \quad (16.4)$$

Table 16.3 shows that in March 1992, the purchasing power was .73. This means that a dollar was worth only 73 cents in terms of its purchasing power relative to the base period.

EXERCISES

1. What is the purpose of calculating a price, quantity, or value index instead of using the original data values?

2. What is the advantage of using an index of the purchasing power of the dollar instead of a price index?

3. What is the advantage of a value index over either a price index or a quantity index?

4. The Data Company has recorded the average cost paid for one of its key computer components each month for several months. Compute a price index based on September using the following data:

Jan.	$123
Feb.	125
Mar.	132
Apr.	131
May	134
June	139
July	140
Aug.	138
Sept.	139
Oct.	142
Nov.	143
Dec.	143

5. In the June 1993 base period, the price of a selected quantity of goods was $1,289.73. In the most recent month, the price index for these goods was 284.7. How much would the selected goods cost if purchased in the most recent month?

6. A canning company buys aluminum in bulk for its operations. In addition to recording the number of pounds of aluminum it purchases each month, the company would like to form a quantity index. Construct such an index using the first month as the base period. The data are:

Pounds of aluminum

278
329

Pounds of aluminum
183
252
287
429
312

7. The Beyer Company wants to know the value of the sick leave benefits it gives its employees each operating quarter. The company records the number of sick days taken each quarter along with an estimate of such day's cost to the company. This value changes from quarter to quarter. Formulate a value index for Beyer based on the last quarter of data. The data are:

Quarter	Number of sick days	Cost per day ($)
1	198	125
2	258	112
3	178	132
4	205	122

8. Here are the price indexes for the purchase of an important commodity in the food business. Convert these values to represent purchasing power of the dollar for each period.

98.7
103.9
112.7
110.4
117.9
129.5

9. Here are figures for total U.S. personal income, in billions, for several months of 1992 and 1993. Convert these dollar values to an index based on January 1993.

1992	June	3,747.1
	July	3,778.6
	Aug.	3,803.7
	Sept.	3,820.8
	Oct.	3,897.2
	Nov.	3,884.1
	Dec.	3,939.0
1993	Jan.	3,921.8
	Feb.	3,946.7
	Mar.	3,985.9
	April	3,999.3
	May	4,020.6
	June	4,046.0
	July	4,071.2

10. According to the *Survey of Current Business*, the industrial production index for March 1988 was 134.1. This index has a base period of 1977. Suppose a company produces and ships 350,000 tons of aluminum during March. If this company is assumed to be in step

with the state of national production used to compute the industrial production index, what would its shipments have been during a typical month in 1977?

11. The BeeWye Company wants a value index for the refrigerators it ships to customers. Here are the number of refrigerators it shipped along with average price charged, by month. Calculate a value index for the company using January 1993 as the base period.

	Month	Number of refrigerators shipped	Average price ($)
1993	Jan.	123	358
	Feb.	89	342
	Mar.	111	360
	Apr.	120	365
	May	114	371
	June	110	368

COMPOSITE INDEX

If a published index is available that accurately reflects the business or industry under study, the time and expense needed to calculate a new index can be avoided. The federal government publishes many indexes each month, each quarter, and each year, and these are widely used throughout business to study the overall economy or specific portions of it.

There may be no single published index that adequately matches the business for which an index is desired. Nevertheless, it may still be possible to avoid the large expense of forming a new index and updating it each time period. Two or more published indexes can be combined to form a new index that meets the analyst's specifications. A weighted average of the indexes being combined is calculated for each time period, and the analyst uses the resulting *composite index*.

Composite Index

EXAMPLE 16.7   Joe Fields wants to use a price index to study the annual dollar sales volume for his furniture business. Eighty percent of his business is retail; the other 20% is involved with wholesale trade. Joe can find separate government indexes for retail and for wholesale furniture prices and wants to combine these into a more accurate index. Table 16.4 shows the indexes Joe found along with the composite index he calculated by combining them.

Each composite index in Table 16.4 was calculated by multiplying the retail index by .80 and adding this value to the wholesale index multiplied by .20. In this way, Joe calculated a single index that reflects his store's sales split: 80% retail and 20% wholesale. For example, the index for 1992 was calculated as $(139.3)(.80) + (167.3)(.20) = 144.9$.

By using the composite index, Joe believes he has an accurate picture of the inflationary tendencies of the furniture business.

TABLE 16.4   Composite Index for Example 16.7

Period	Retail index	Wholesale index	Composite index
1982	123.7	156.9	130.3
1983	124.6	157.4	131.2
1984	127.8	160.2	134.3
1985	129.3	161.2	135.7
1986	130.7	162.5	137.1
1987	132.4	164.0	138.7
1988	133.1	164.7	139.4
1989	135.7	166.4	141.8
1990	136.8	165.1	142.5
1991	138.2	166.7	143.9
1992	139.3	167.3	144.9

DEFLATING A TIME SERIES

A primary reason for finding or calculating a good index number is to *deflate* a time series that's measured in dollars. The analyst often wants to remove the effects of price or value inflation before subjecting the series to further analysis. The first step in such price deflation is to find an appropriate price index, such as found in the federal government's *Survey of Current Business*. Alternatively, two or more published indexes can be combined to form a composite index, as in Example 16.7.

After the appropriate price index has been found or calculated, the decimal point in the index is moved two places to the left. The next step is to divide each dollar value in the time series by the price index for that period. Example 16.8 demonstrates this procedure.

EXAMPLE 16.8   Dollar sales volume for the Wing Company was $35,758 in February; the price index is 243.9 for that month. Deflated dollar sales for the company are

$$\frac{\$35,758}{2.439} = \$14,661$$

Had there been no inflation since the price index's base period, the company's February sales volume would have been only $14,661, not $35,758. The difference between these two values reflects the amount of inflation since the price index base period.

The purpose of deflating a dollar time series is to enable the series to be examined with the effects of inflation removed. A dollar series that appears to be healthy because of its upward trend may actually show downward movement if inflationary effects are removed. A time series analysis (described later in this chapter) is often performed on a dollar time series after such an adjustment is made.

Deflating a Time Series

Steps for deflating a time series measured in dollars:

Step 1 Find an appropriate price index.

Step 2 Move the decimal point in the price index two places to the left.

Step 3 Divide each of the values in the time series by the price index for that period.

EXAMPLE 16.9 The Bentley Rug Company wants to examine its monthly dollar sales volume over the past three years. Because there has been some inflation over this period, chief accountant Sue Chen decides to deflate this time series before examining it. Sue decided to watch sales more closely after reading a *Wall Street Journal* article (October 23, 1989) showing that consumer installment debt is rising faster than GNP. Since Bentley finances almost all purchases, a drop in consumer willingness to incur debt would affect its sales.

Sue finds a price index published by the government that she thinks closely mirrors the rug business, and she records this index for the 12 months of her data. Table 16.5 shows this index, Bentley's actual dollar sales volume each month, and the deflated time series values. These deflated values were calculated by dividing each dollar value by the price index for the month, after moving the decimal point two places to the left. For example, the deflated dollar value for the last month was calculated as $24,793/1.187 = $20,887.

TABLE 16.5 Bentley Company Sales Deflation (Example 16.9)

Month number	Dollar sales	Price index	Deflated sales
1	15,428	110.7	13,937
2	13,538	111.2	12,174
3	16,479	111.0	14,846
4	19,421	112.5	17,263
5	21,937	113.2	19,379
6	18,233	113.9	16,008
7	22,751	115.7	19,664
8	21,840	114.2	19,124
9	25,841	115.0	22,470
10	22,556	116.7	19,328
11	20,779	118.0	17,609
12	24,793	118.7	20,887

Sue thinks that Table 16.5's final column (Bentley's deflated dollar sales volumes) contains figures that are much more meaningful than the unadjusted values. Since the effects of inflation have been removed, the company's performance independent of inflation can now be examined.

CHANGING THE BASE PERIOD

Changing the Base Period

It is sometimes desirable to move the base period for an index forward in time. This adjustment is made when the original base period is many time periods in the past, and an index that better reflects a recent time period is needed. Care must be taken in choosing the new base period, just as for the original base period. A time period should be chosen that's as close as possible to "normal" in that neither extremely good nor extremely bad economic times were experienced in that period.

EXAMPLE 16.10   Abby Smith, president and chief forecaster for the Abby Corporation, wants to update the base period for her company's price index. This index was formed five years ago, when a base period of January 1988 was chosen. She decides to update the base period to January 1992, which she considers to be an average operating month. Table 16.6 shows the old price indexes and the new price indexes for recent months.

TABLE 16.6   Change of Base Period for Example 16.10

	Month	Old price index	New price index
1991	Jan.	123.7	92.87
	Feb.	124.8	93.69
	Mar.	125.3	94.07
	Apr.	126.9	95.27
	May	127.4	95.65
	June	127.2	95.50
	July	128.0	96.10
	Aug.	128.2	96.25
	Sept.	129.7	97.37
	Oct.	130.5	97.97
	Nov.	131.5	98.72
	Dec.	132.9	99.77
1992	Jan.	133.2	100.00
	Feb.	133.8	100.45
	Mar.	134.4	100.90
	Apr.	134.9	101.28
	May	135.8	101.95
	June	135.6	101.80

For the new base period, January 1992, the old index value is 133.2. To compute the new price index for each month in Table 16.6, the old index is divided by 1.332 (the old index for January 1992 with the decimal moved two places left). The result is an index with a base period of January 1992. For example, the new index values for January 1991, January 1992, and June 1992 are

January 1991: 123.7/1.332 =   92.87
January 1992: 133.2/1.332 = 100.00
June 1992: 135.6/1.332 = 101.80

Abby has calculated a price index based on a recent time period, January 1992. She can now compare prices each month using the new price index.

EXERCISES

12. What is the advantage of a composite index over the indexes that might be found in a government publication?

13. What is the purpose of deflating a time series measured in dollars?

14. Which time series variable would yield the most information to the decision maker: raw dollars or deflated dollars?

15. What arithmetic operation is performed to deflate a dollar time series?

16. Why is it that only a time series measured in dollars is a candidate for deflating?

17. The Extra Company is involved equally with producing paper products and with printing newspapers. The company wants to find an index of production that closely matches its operations but is unable to do so. However, two relevant indexes are available: one for paper and related products, and one for printing and publishing. Assuming the company devotes 50% of its efforts to each endeavor, combine the two indexes to form a composite index.

		Paper and products index (1982 = 100)	Printing and publishing index (1982 = 100)
1992	Jan.	133.3	115.2
	Feb.	133.7	114.7
	Mar.	134.4	112.5
	Apr.	134.5	111.7

Source: *Survey of Current Business*, May 1992.

18. The Bluto Company wants to form a composite index for the cost of its workers, who are 80% blue-collar and 20% white-collar workers. Combine the following cost indexes to form such an index.

	Blue-collar workers index	White-collar workers index
Dec. 1983	77.9	74.5
Dec. 1984	82.3	79.6
Dec. 1985	86.7	84.2
Dec. 1986	91.2	88.7
Dec. 1987	94.3	92.8
Dec. 1988	97.5	98.3
Dec. 1989	103.7	104.7

June 1989 = 100

Source: *Statistical Abstract of the United States*, 1991.

19. Deflate the following dollar sales volumes using the commodity price indexes shown. These indexes are for all commodities.

		Sales volume (dollars)	Commodity price index (1982 = 100)
1992	Jan.	358,235	127.2
	Feb.	297,485	127.6
	Mar.	360,321	128.4
	Apr.	378,904	128.4

Source: *Survey of Current Business,* May 1992.

20. An analyst decides to deflate the variable of interest, total manufacturing and trade sales, in millions of dollars, using the consumer price index (CPI-W). Here are values for this time series, as found in the *Survey of Current Business.*

   a. Calculate the deflated values for dollar sales.

   b. Is it appropriate to use the CPI-W for deflating total sales dollars?

   c. As shown, dollar sales are tending upward. How would you characterize deflated dollar sales?

		Sales	CPI-W (1982–84 = 100)
1992	Jan.	423,137	136.0
	Feb.	450,610	136.4
	Mar.	499,134	137.0

21. An analyst decides to study the dollar amounts of home mortgages insured or guaranteed by the Federal Housing Administration. A possible price index to use in deflating these dollar values is the consumer price index for all-urban consumers.

   a. Deflate the dollar series using the CPI-U index.

   b. How appropriate is the CPI-U for deflating this series?

   c. How would you characterize the trend of FHA mortgages before and after deflation?

		FHA mortgages ($ millions)	CPI-U (1982–84 = 100)
1991	Nov.	4,452.92	137.8
	Dec.	3,350.77	137.9
1992	Jan.	2,926.84	138.1
	Feb.	2,508.44	138.6
	Mar.	3,545.40	139.3
	Apr.	3,006.04	139.5

Source: *Survey of Current Business,* May 1992.

DECOMPOSITION OF A TIME SERIES

Decomposition

Earlier in this chapter a time series was defined as data values that are collected, recorded, or observed over successive increments of time. When a time series variable is recorded and observed, it's often difficult or impossible to visualize its various components. The purpose of *decomposing* a time series variable is to observe each of its various elements in isolation. By doing so, we can gain insight into the causes of the series' variability. A second important reason for isolating time series components is to facilitate the forecasting process. If we understand the movements of the various components of a series, forecasting it into the future is much easier.

To understand the elements in a time series, we must consider the mathematical relationships among the various components. The most widely used model for time series decomposition is the *multiplicative model*, in which the series is analyzed as the product of its components:

$$Y = T \times C \times S \times I \tag{16.5}$$

where Y = Actual value of the variable of interest
T = Secular trend
C = Cyclical component
S = Seasonal component
I = Irregular component

In Equation 16.5, Y is the product of four elements acting in combination to produce the series. The multiplicative model is well suited to a wide variety of economic data in which percentage changes best represent the movement in the series. Additive models are also used occasionally and will be described in Chapter 17.

Trend   The **secular trend** of a time series is the long-term component that represents the series' growth or decline over an extended period of time. The basic forces responsible for a series' trend are population growth, price inflation, technological change, and productivity increases. Figure 16.1 shows that annual registration of new passenger cars in the United States from 1960 to 1991 has been increasing by a fairly constant amount, indicating a rising trend.

FIGURE 16.1   New Passenger Car Registrations, 1960–1991

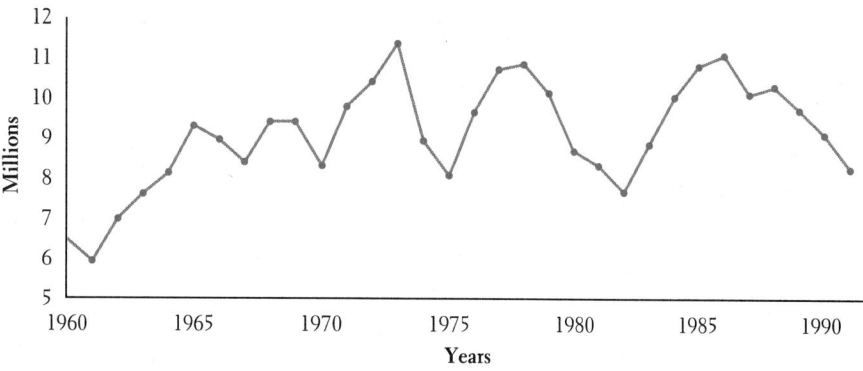

The **secular trend** is the long-term component that represents the growth or decline in the time series over an extended period of time.

Cyclical Component

The **cyclical component** is the wavelike fluctuation around the trend. Any regular pattern of observations above or below the trend line is attributable to the cyclical component of the time series. Figure 16.2 shows a trend line fitted to the data for annual registration of new passenger cars in the United States for 1960 to 1991. The peaks and valleys above and below the trend line represent the cyclical component. Cyclical fluctuations are usually influenced by changing economic conditions.

FIGURE 16.2   Trend for New Passenger Car Registrations, 1960–1991

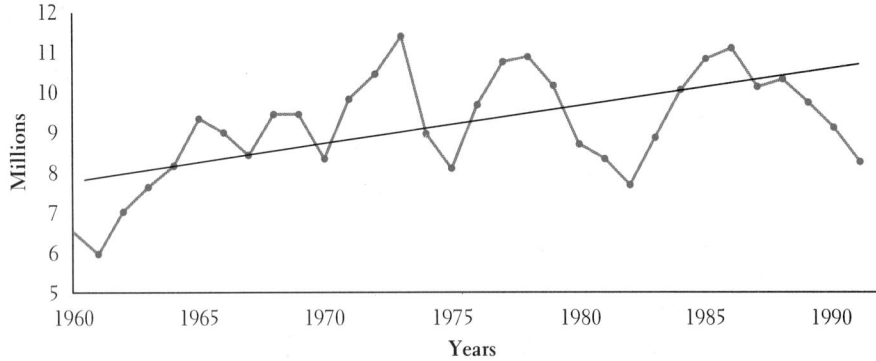

> The **cyclical component** is the wavelike fluctuation around the trend.

Seasonal Component

The **seasonal component** refers to a pattern of change that repeats itself year after year. For a monthly series, the seasonal component measures the variability of the series each January, each February, and so on. For a quarterly series, there are four seasonal measurements, one for each quarter. Seasonal variation may reflect weather conditions, holidays, or varying lengths of calendar months.

> The **seasonal component** is a pattern of change in quarterly or monthly data that repeats itself year to year.

Irregular Component

The **irregular component** is a measure of the remaining variability of the time series after the other components have been removed. It accounts for the random variability in a time series caused by unanticipated and nonrecurring factors. Most of the irregular component is made up of random variability. However, sometimes unpredictable events such as strikes, weather changes (droughts, floods, or earthquakes), election results, armed conflicts, or the passage of legislative bills cause irregularities in a variable.

> The **irregular component** measures the variability of the time series after the other components have been removed.

TREND

Trend Line

The multiplicative model $Y = TC$ is used to analyze annual time series data.

The first component of interest in an annual time series is the secular trend. When an annual time series is observed over a very long time, say, 50 to 100 years, a curvilinear trend pattern is often seen. However, most annual time series are studied over a much shorter period, usually from 10 to 20 years. During such a period, either a typical series reveals a straight-line trend, or a straight line can be used as a close approximation to a slight curvilinear trend. Throughout this chapter, straight-line trends are usually used, although more advanced treatments of time series analyze curvilinear relationships as well. Two curvilinear models appear later in this chapter.

The least squares procedure is used to find the straight line that best fits the observed time series data. Equation 16.6 describes this linear trend function. This is the same procedure used to minimize $\text{SSE} = \Sigma(y - \hat{y})^2$ in regression analysis. For time series analysis, Y is the variable being analyzed, and X is a coded value used to represent the year, quarter, or month.

$$\hat{Y} = b_0 + b_1 X \tag{16.6}$$

where $\hat{Y}$ = Forecast trend value of Y for selected coded time period X
b_0 = Constant or value of Y when X is coded as 0
b_1 = Slope of the trend line
X = Value of time selected

EXAMPLE 16.11 Annual registration of new passenger cars in the United States from 1960 to 1991 is shown in Table 16.7. Figure 16.1 plots these values as the Y variable; years are coded as the independent variable, X, with 1960 as 1, 1961 as 2, and so on. Equations 14.7 and 14.8 use the least squares procedure to compute the trend equation,

$$\hat{Y} = 7.902 + .076X$$

According to the MINITAB computer output, the trend equation explains 27.3% ($r^2 = .273$) of the variance for the new passenger car registration variable. The 1960 estimate for registrations based on the trend equation is 7.978 million (7.902 + .076). Each year, this trend estimate is expected to increase by an average of .076 million or 76,000 (rounded from 76,123) new passenger car registrations. This pattern of constant long-term growth might be attributed to the increase in the driving-age population for this time period. Figure 16.2 fits the trend equation to the actual data.

TABLE 16.7   Registration of New Passenger Cars in the United States, 1960–1991

Year	Registrations (millions) Y	X	Ŷ	Cyclical
1960	6.577	1	7.9780	82.439
1961	5.855	2	8.0542	72.695
1962	6.939	3	8.1303	85.348
1963	7.557	4	8.2064	92.087
1964	8.065	5	8.2825	97.374
1965	9.314	6	8.3586	111.430
1966	9.009	7	8.4348	106.808
1967	8.357	8	8.5109	98.192
1968	9.404	9	8.5870	109.514
1969	9.447	10	8.6631	109.048
1970	8.388	11	8.7393	95.981
1971	9.831	12	8.8154	111.521
1972	10.409	13	8.8915	117.067
1973	11.351	14	8.9676	126.577
1974	8.701	15	9.0438	96.210
1975	8.168	16	9.1199	89.563
1976	9.752	17	9.1960	106.046
1977	10.826	18	9.2721	116.759
1978	10.946	19	9.3482	117.091
1979	10.357	20	9.4244	109.896
1980	8.761	21	9.5005	92.216
1981	8.444	22	9.5766	88.173
1982	7.754	23	9.6527	80.330
1983	8.924	24	9.7289	91.727
1984	10.118	25	9.8050	103.192
1985	10.889	26	9.8811	110.200
1986	11.140	27	9.9572	111.879
1987	10.183	28	10.0333	101.492
1988	10.398	29	10.1095	102.854
1989	9.853	30	10.1856	96.735
1990	9.103	31	10.2617	88.708
1991	8.234	32	10.3378	79.649

Source: U.S. Dept. of Commerce, *Survey of Current Business*, various years.

The MINITAB computer package can be used to compute the trend equation. The MINITAB commands to solve Example 16.11 are:

```
MTB > SET C1
DATA> 6.577 5.855 6.939 7.557 8.065 9.314 9.009 8.357
DATA> 9.404 9.447 8.388 9.831 10.409 11.351 8.701
DATA> 8.168 9.752 10.826 10.946 10.357 8.761 8.444
DATA> 7.754 8.924 10.118 10.889 11.140 10.183 10.398 9.853 9.103 8.234
DATA> END
MTB > SET C2
DATA> 1:32
DATA> END
MTB > NAME C1 'REG' C2 'TIME'
MTB > REGRESS C1 1 PREDICTOR C2
```

```
The regression equation is
REG = 7.90 + 0.0761 TIME

Predictor      Coef       Stdev      t ratio      p
Constant     7.90190    0.42903      18.42     0.000
TIME         0.076123   0.02269       3.36     0.002


s = 1.185    R-sq = 27.3%    R-sq (adj) = 24.9%

Analysis of Variance

SOURCE         DF        SS         MS        F       P
Regression      1     15.808     15.808    11.26    0.002
Error          30     42.124      1.404
Total          31     57.932

Unusual Observations
Obs.    TIME      REG      Fit    Stdev.Fit    Residual    St.Resid
 14     14.0    11.351    8.968     0.217        2.383       2.05R

R denotes an obs. with a large st. resid.
```

Note that the DATA command 1:32 generates the time variable: integers 1 through 32.

Although the linear trend model is used more frequently than any other to describe long-term growth or decline of a time series, the use of curvilinear trends is sometimes necessary. Two of the more useful curvilinear trend models are described next.

Curvilinear and nonlinear trends are appropriate for describing growth patterns of new products, companies, or industries, especially over long periods of time. Figure 16.3 shows the life cycle of a typical new product, company, or industry. This growth pattern is divided into four stages: introduction, growth, maturity, and saturation. Time (represented on the horizontal axis) can vary from days to weeks to months to years, depending on the nature of the market. A linear model won't fit a typical life cycle pattern because the growth of most new products, companies, and industries increases at a *constant rate* (exponential model) instead of a *constant amount* (linear model).

FIGURE 16.3   Life Cycle of a Typical New Product

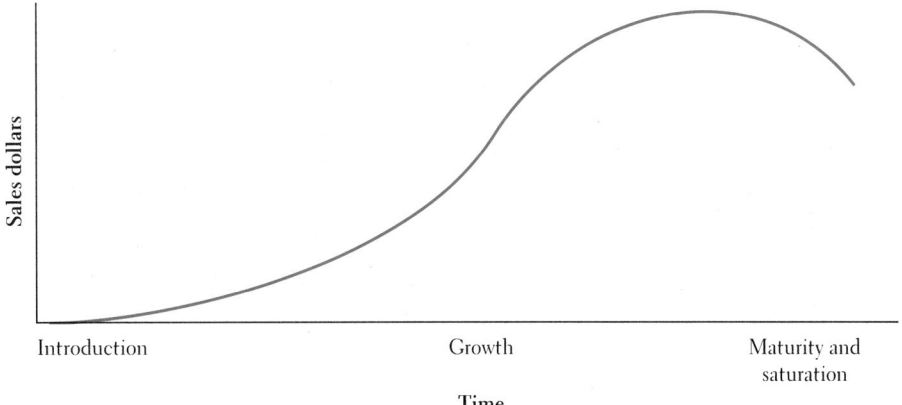

An exponential trend model should be fitted for a product that starts slowly (introduction stage, Figure 16.3) and then increases at a growing rate (growth stage, Figure 16.3) such that the percentage difference from observation to observation is constant. The number of handheld computers sold (Figure 16.4) reflects growth at a constant percentage rate instead of a constant amount. A linear trend might indicate an average growth of 800 computers per year. An exponential fit might indicate an average growth of 32% per year for the figure's data. If the exponential model estimated sales of 7,000 handheld computers for 1988, the increase estimated for 1989 would be 2,240 (7,000 × .32) instead of 800. Computations for various exponential models are complex, so use of appropriate computer programs is recommended.

FIGURE 16.4   Exponential Trend for Handheld Computers

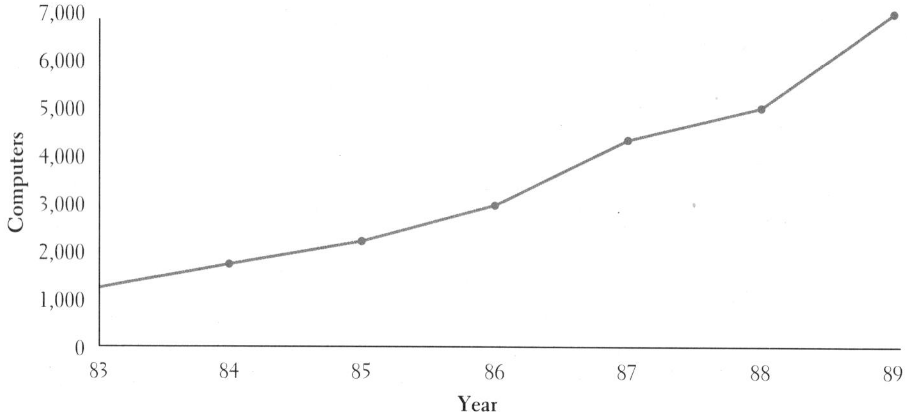

If the analyst isn't careful, the exponential trend model will provide an estimate that's higher than the actual growth of the variable. Note in Figure 16.4 that the exponential model would always forecast an increasing number of handheld computers sold. What happens when market maturity and saturation take place, and the growth rate slows down? The next section discusses growth curves that model this type of situation.

Growth curves of the Gompertz or logistic type represent the tendency of many industries and product lines to grow at a declining rate as they mature (the maturity and saturation stage of Figure 16.3). If product sales begin low, then catch on as sales "boom," and finally ease off as market saturation is reached, the Gompertz curve might be the appropriate trend model. Figure 16.5 shows the general shape of a Gompertz growth curve. Computations for various growth curve models are also complex; again, using appropriate computer programs is recommended.

When an analyst is deciding which trend model to use, the purpose for computing the trend should be carefully identified. If the purpose is to estimate demand for a

FIGURE 16.5   Gompertz Growth Curve

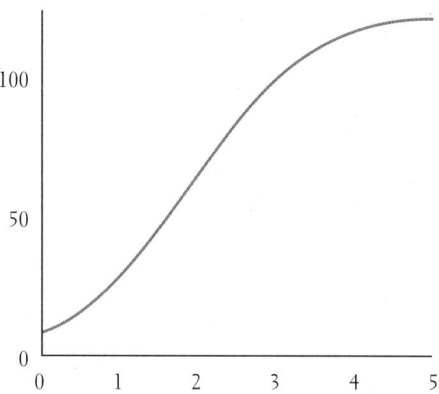

future quarter, you need to know the basic forces affecting long-term demand growth. Choice of the proper trend model is a matter of judgment so an analyst requires experience and common sense. The line or curve that best fits a set of data points might not make sense when projected as the future trend.

EXAMPLE 16.12   Decision Science Associates is doing a feasibility study for a proposed destination resort to be built within one half mile of the Grand Coulee Dam. Paul Nobisch, company president, feels that the large number of tourists who visit the dam each year might be a significant factor in determining whether the resort should be constructed. He assigns one of his employees, Mark Craze, to gather data and develop the appropriate trend model.

Visitors are counted by tour guides as they enter the visitors center. Table 16.8 shows that the number of visitors varied from a low of 161,524 in 1980 to a high of 617,737 in 1983.

Mark plotted the data (Figure 16.6) and decided that a linear trend would fit best. He computed the trend equation $\hat{Y} = 259{,}055 + 8{,}363X$. The correlation between the number of visitors and time is .358, so knowledge of time allows Mark to explain only 12.8% ($.358^2$) of the variance in the number of visitors. The regression equation indicates that the estimated number of visitors for 1969, based on the trend line, is 267,418 (259,055 + 8,363) and that the number has increased by an average of 8,363 persons per year.

The increasing trend for the *number of visitors* variable seems to be based mostly on population growth. The number of visitors increased an average of approximately 2–3% per year from 1969 to 1984. The population of the state of Washington also increased by approximately 2% per year from 1970 to 1984. Since time isn't highly related to the number of visitors, Mark decides that the cyclical component is extremely important.

TABLE 16.8   Number of Visitors Counted at the Grand Coulee Dam Visitors Center, 1969–1984 (Example 16.12)

Year	Visitors	Cyclical
1969	250,265	93.6
1970	250,929	91.0
1971	321,333	113.1
1972	342,269	117.0
1973	268,528	89.3
1974	468,136	151.4
1975	390,129	123.8
1976	300,140	92.1
1977	271,140	81.1
1978	282,752	83.5
1979	244,006	70.5
1980	161,524	44.9
1981	277,134	75.4
1982	382,343	101.7
1983	617,737	160.7
1984	453,881	115.5

Source: *Market Feasibility Study for a Proposed Development at Crescent Bay on Lake Roosevelt,* Spokane: Decision Science Associates, January–February 1985.

FIGURE 16.6   Grand Coulee Dam Visitors, 1969–1984 (Example 16.12)

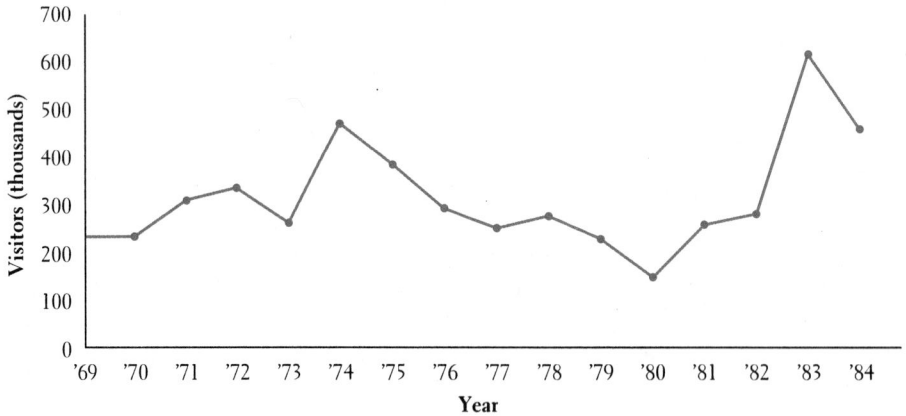

EXERCISES

22. What is a time series?

23. Explain the concept of decomposing a time series.

24. In the decomposition of an annual time series, what components are analyzed?

25. Describe each of the four components in the decomposition of a seasonal time series.

26. Describe the secular trend component.

27. List the basic forces that affect the secular trend of most variables.

28. What kind of trend model should be used in each of the following cases?

    a. The variable is increasing at a constant rate.

    b. The variable increases at a constant rate until it reaches saturation and levels out.

    c. The variable is increasing by a constant amount.

29. If

$$\hat{Y} = 1,600 + 85X$$
$$Y = \text{Annual sales, in units}$$
$$X = 1 \text{ unit/year } (X = 0 \text{ represents July 1, 1972})$$

    a. What were the expected sales based on the trend equation for 1972?

    b. What is the average increase in sales per year?

    c. Estimate the trend value for sales in 1993.

30. Triton Energy Corporation explores for and produces oil and gas. Company analyst Peter Feehan is studying the trend of the company's sales per share.

Year	Sales per share	Year	Sales per share
1972	0.39	1983	7.16
1973	0.81	1984	1.93
1974	0.93	1985	5.17
1975	1.35	1986	7.72
1976	1.48	1987	5.33
1977	2.36	1988	8.12
1978	2.45	1989	10.65
1979	2.52	1990	12.06
1980	2.81	1991	11.63
1981	3.82	1992	5.85*
1982	5.54	1993	6.40*

*Value Line Estimates.
Source: *The Value Line Investment Survey* (New York: Value Line, 1988, 1989, 1991), p. 1844.

    a. Plot the data.

    b. Determine the appropriate trend model. (Use 1972–91.)

    c. If the appropriate model is linear, compute the straight-line trend model.

    d. How well does the linear trend equation fit the data?

    e. What has been the average increase in sales per share per year since 1972?

    f. Estimate the trend value for sales in 1992 and 1993. Compare your trend estimates to *Value Line's.*

31. *Value Line's* estimates of sales and earnings growth for individual companies are derived by correlating sales, earnings, and dividends to appropriate components or subcomponents of the national income accounts, such as capital spending. *Value Line* employee Lynn Wallace examines the trend of capital spending from 1977 to 1993.

Year	($ billions)	Year	($ billions)
1977	214	1986	437
1978	259	1987	443
1979	303	1988	545
1980	323	1989	571
1981	369	1990	587
1982	367	1991	550
1983	357	1992	566*
1984	416	1993	623*
1985	443		

Value Line estimates.
Source: *The Value Line Investment Survey* (New York: Value Line, 1988, 1989, 1991), p. 1750.

a. Plot the data.

b. Determine the appropriate trend model for the years 1977–91.

c. If the appropriate model is linear, compute the straight-line trend model for the years 1977–91.

d. What has the average increase in capital spending per year been since 1977?

e. Estimate the trend value for capital spending in 1992 and 1993.

f. Compare your trend estimate with *Value Line's.*

g. What factor(s) influence the trend of capital spending?

32. The Graphic Scanning Corporation provides telecommunications services. Company analyst Roy Coumbs must determine the appropriate trend model for Graphic's sales per share.

Year	Sales per share	Year	Sales per share
1972	0.23	1981	2.09
1973	0.25	1982	2.32
1974	0.21	1983	2.85
1975	0.36	1984	3.89
1976	0.56	1985	3.29
1977	0.60	1986	3.03
1978	0.77	1987	3.20
1979	1.04	1988	3.51
1980	1.55	1989	2.78

Source: *The Value Line Investment Survey* (New York: Value Line, 1988, 1989), p. 781.

Write a memo describing the appropriate trend model for Graphic's sales per share.

CYCLICAL

Data collected annually obviously can't have a seasonal component. However, annual data can reveal certain cyclical effects. The cyclical component was defined as the wavelike fluctuation around the trend. In Example 16.11, the trend equation explained only 27.3% of the variance in new passenger car registrations. The peaks and valleys above and below the trend line in Figure 16.2 represents cyclical fluctuations in the number of annual registrations of new passenger cars in the United States from 1960 to 1991. These cyclical fluctuations are influenced by changing economic conditions such as interest rates, money supply, consumer demand, inventory levels, and market conditions. Equation 16.7 calculates the cyclical component for annual data:

Cyclical Index

$$C = \frac{Y}{\hat{Y}}(100) \qquad\qquad (16.7)$$

where   C = Cyclical component
        Y = Actual value of the variable of interest
        $\hat{Y}$ = Forecast trend value of Y for selected time period

EXAMPLE 16.13   Table 16.7 provides 1960–91 cyclical indexes for annual registrations of new passenger cars in the United States. Each cyclical relative is computed by dividing the actual number of registrations for each year (Y) by the expected number of registrations ($\hat{Y}$) based on the trend equation $\hat{Y} = 7.902 + .076X$. This ratio is then multiplied by 100 to put it in percentage or index number form.

For example, the first and last cyclical values in Table 16.7 are calculated as follows. (Disregard rounding errors.) The trend estimate for 1960 is

$$\hat{Y} = 7.902 + .076(1) = 7.978$$

The cyclical value in 1960 is

$$C = \frac{6.577}{7.978}(100) = 82.44$$

The trend estimate for 1991 is

$$\hat{Y} = 7.902 + .076123(32) = 10.338$$

The cyclical value for 1991 is

$$C = \frac{8.234}{10.338}(100) = 79.65$$

As Equation 16.7 shows, the cyclical indexes indicate the position of each Y value *relative* to the trend line. This position is indicated by a percentage. For example, in 1960, the Y value was 82.44% of the trend line. In 1965, Y was 111.43% of the trend line. Since the cyclical values are shown as percentages of the trend line, the trend is removed from the series, leaving only the cyclical component for evaluation. In 1960, new car passenger registrations were approximately 17–18% below what was expected based on the trend estimate. In 1965, new passenger car registrations were approximately 11–12% above what was expected based on the trend estimate.

The MINITAB computer package can also be used to compute cyclical relatives. The commands to enter the data and name the variables were given when Example 16.11 was solved. The MINITAB commands to solve Example 16.13 are:

```
MTB > REGRESS C1 1 PREDICTOR C2, TRESIDS IN C3, DHATS IN C4
MTB > LET C5 = (C1/C4)*100
MTB > PRINT C1-C5
```

ROW	REG	TIME	C3	C4	C5
1	6.577	1	−1.25990	7.9780	82.439
2	5.855	2	−1.96539	8.0542	72.695
3	6.939	3	−1.05857	8.1303	85.348
4	7.557	4	−0.57404	8.2064	92.087
5	8.065	5	−0.19136	8.2825	97.374
6	9.314	6	0.83677	8.3586	111.430
7	9.009	7	0.50098	8.4348	106.808
8	8.357	8	−0.13379	8.5109	98.192
9	9.404	9	0.70807	8.5870	109.514
10	9.447	10	0.67753	8.6631	109.048
11	8.388	11	−0.30292	8.7393	95.981
12	9.831	12	0.87416	8.8154	111.521
13	10.409	13	1.30415	8.8915	117.067
14	11.351	14	2.04596	8.9676	126.577
15	8.701	15	−0.29401	9.0438	96.210
16	8.168	16	−0.81619	9.1199	89.563
17	9.752	17	0.47675	9.1960	106.046
18	10.826	18	1.33289	9.2721	116.759
19	10.946	19	1.37156	9.3482	117.091
20	10.357	20	0.80151	9.4244	109.896
21	8.761	21	−0.63649	9.5005	92.216
22	8.444	22	−0.97672	9.5766	88.173
23	7.754	23	−1.64118	9.6527	80.330
24	8.924	24	−0.69756	9.7289	91.727
25	10.118	25	0.27213	9.8050	103.192
26	10.889	26	0.87933	9.8811	110.200
27	11.140	27	1.03597	9.9572	111.879
28	10.183	28	0.13165	10.0333	101.492
29	10.398	29	0.25504	10.1095	102.854
30	9.853	30	−0.29555	10.1856	96.735
31	9.103	31	−1.03555	10.2617	88.708
32	8.234	32	−1.89191	10.3378	79.649

```
MTB > STOP
```

The REGRESS command is producing standardized residuals (TRESIDS) and the predicted Y values (DHATS) and storing them in C3 and C4. The LET command is used so that the actual values, C1, can be divided by the predicted values, C4. The results are multiplied by 100 to create index numbers that are stored in C5.

Cyclical Chart

A cyclical chart, such as Figure 16.7, is developed to help analyze the cyclical component. The cyclical chart shows the trend equation as the base line, represented as 100%. Cyclical patterns are easier to see on a cyclical chart. This type of graph also allows the analyst to compare the variable of interest with the cyclical patterns for other variables and/or business indicators.

The following questions are answered by the cyclical indexes for any time series:

1. Is the series cyclical?
2. If so, how extreme is the cycle?
3. Does the series follow the general state of the economy (business cycle)?

FIGURE 16.7   Cyclical Chart for New Car Registrations, 1960–1991

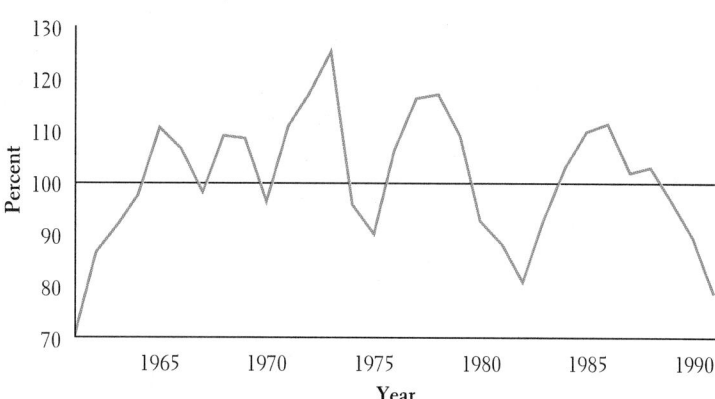

EXAMPLE 16.14   Questions concerning the cyclical pattern for new passenger car registrations are answered in Figure 16.7. The series bottomed out in 1961 (72.7) and then gradually rose until it peaked in 1965 (111.4). Good times generally prevailed for the years 1966–79 (with the exception of 1974 and 1975), followed by a four-year slump in registrations in the early 1980s. In 1985 and 1986, the cyclical was above the trend line, indicating good times for registrations. The series has consistently decreased since 1988, reaching a low of 79.6 in 1991.

The cyclical pattern seems to indicate that new passenger car registrations are influenced to some extent by economic conditions. However, other factors also seem to be affecting the cyclical pattern of this variable.

A variable that might help explain the variability of the cyclical pattern for new passenger car registrations is the new-car price index. When prices are low, registrations should be higher than normal, and when prices are high, registrations should be down. The new-car price index must be adjusted for trend to eliminate effects of inflation. Figure 16.8 compares the cyclical index for new car prices with the cyclicals for registrations. These cyclical indexes are inversely related. Therefore, knowledge of proposed pricing policies should help an analyst forecast the cyclical pattern for new passenger car registrations.

Once a time series has been found to be cyclical and the locations of the peaks and valleys have been determined, the next concern is how much the cycle of the series matches other well-known cycle indicators. The federal government maintains a list of economic indicators (Table 16.9) that assist in this process.

The national economic indicators are divided into three groups. The *coincident indicators* define the economy's basic well-being. When these indicators are up and unemployment rate is down, the economy enjoys good times. When the reverse is true, the economy is depressed or in a recession.

The *leading indicators* in Table 16.9 tend to begin rising before a recession is over and to begin falling prior to the onset of a recession. *Lagging indicators* lag behind the ups and downs of the economy. By comparing the cycle of a company's time series to the behavior of the indicators, it may be possible to tie the series to one or more of

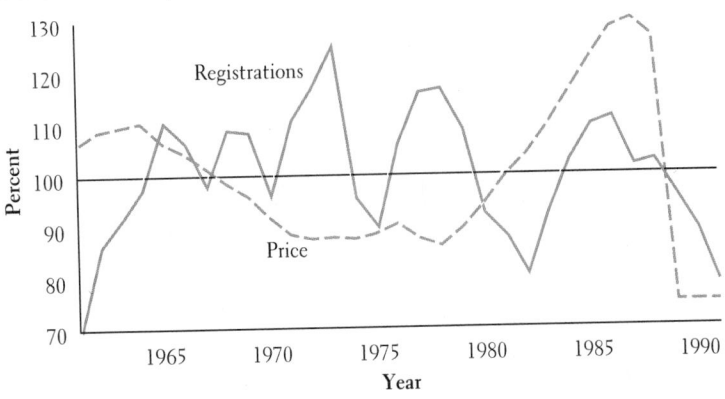

FIGURE 16.8 Cyclical Chart for New Car Registrations and Price Indexes, 1960–1991

TABLE 16.9 Cyclical Indicators (NBER Short List)

Leading indicators	Roughly coincident indicators	Lagging indicators
Average hourly workweek, production workers, manufacturing	GNP in current dollars	Unemployment rate, persons unemployed 15 weeks or over
Average weekly initial claims, state unemployment insurance	GNP in 1972 dollars	Business expenditures, new plant and equipment
Index of net business formation	Index of industrial production	Book value, manufacturing and trade inventories
New orders, durable goods industries	Personal income	Index of labor cost per unit of output in manufacturing
Contracts and orders, plant and equipment	Manufacturing and trade sales	Commercial and industrial loans outstanding in large commercial banks
Index of new building permits, private-housing units	Sales of retail stores	Bank rates on short-term business loans
Change in book value, manufacturing and trade inventories	Employees on nonagricultural payrolls	
Index of industrial materials prices	Unemployment rate, total	
Index of stock prices, 500 common stocks		
Corporate profits after taxes (quarterly)		
Index: ratio, price to unit labor cost, manufacturing		
Change in consumer installment debt		

Source: U.S. Dept. of Commerce.

these national series. The cyclical component of the company series can then be estimated using predictions made by government officials and other experts. In addition,
insights into the company series might be gained if it's demonstrated to be cycling in
harmony with a national series.

Annual time series can be projected into the future using time series printouts such
as those in Table 16.7 and Figure 16.7. The components used in such forecasts depend

on the distance into the future for which the forecast is desired. For relatively short-term forecasts (say, one to two years), we can combine the trend and cyclical projections to calculate the forecast. For longer-term forecasts, only the trend estimate is used since it's not possible to anticipate the state of the economy with any precision more than one or two years into the future.

EXAMPLE 16.15   The multiplicative model is used to forecast new passenger car registrations for 1992. The trend estimate is computed using Equation 16.6. The appropriate value for X in 1992 is 33 (Table 16.7). This value is substituted into the equation, and the trend estimate for 1992 is

$$\hat{Y}(1992) = b_0 + b_1X$$
$$= 7.902 + .076(33) = 10.410$$

Next, all the information that has been gathered concerning the cyclical pattern of new passenger car registrations is analyzed. Registrations have decreased consistently since 1988 (Figure 16.8). Will this pattern continue or will registrations level out or even turn upward again? How will the economy perform? What do the experts forecast for the business cycle? What are the proposed new-car pricing policies for 1992? Do election year politics affect new passenger car registrations? Once these questions are answered, we can choose an estimate for the cyclical relative for 1992. The most important aspect of the cyclical estimate process is to forecast the direction correctly. If the analyst successfully predicts whether a particular variable's cyclical pattern will continue to increase or decrease, level off, or turn upward or downward, the forecast will be fairly accurate. The actual value used for the estimate is not as important as the analyst's correct assessment of the direction.

Economic indicators point to the economy leveling off in 1992 since it's an election year. Therefore, we decided to forecast that the cyclical relative will also level off. The C for 1991 is 79.65 (Table 16.7). The cyclical for 1992 is estimated to be 78 and the forecast using Equation 16.6 is

$$Y(1992) = T \times C = 10.410(.78) = 8.120$$

Note that $\hat{Y}$ is used to estimate T (the trend) in this model.

The relative importance of the individual components of the multiplicative model dictates the accuracy of its forecasts. How well does the trend equation describe the long-term growth? If the trend equation does a good job of explaining a variable, a five-year projection into the future is reasonable. If the trend equation doesn't fit the data, the cyclical component is more important. Since it's extremely difficult to estimate the cyclical index for more than a year or two into the future, long-term forecasts are risky, at best.

EXAMPLE 16.16   In Example 16.12, Mark Craze developed a trend model for the number of visitors to Grand Coulee Dam. Now, he intends to analyze the cyclical so that he can forecast 1986.

Cyclical indexes are calculated in Table 16.8. Next Mark developed a cyclical chart (Figure 16.9) so that he could compare the cyclical indexes for the number of visitors

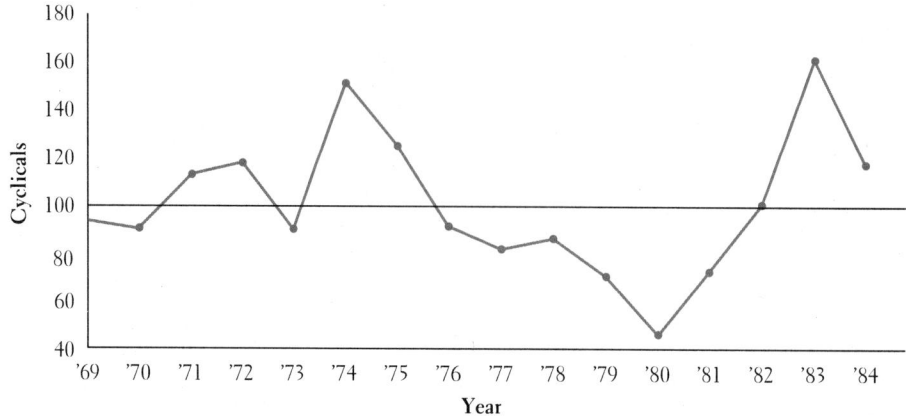

FIGURE 16.9   Visitors—Cyclical

with other factors. He observed that the peak years for visits were 1974 and 1983, and that other above-average years were 1971, 1972, 1975, and 1984. The lowest year was 1980. Other below-average years were 1977, 1978, 1979, and 1981.

Mark compared the cyclical pattern in Figure 16.9 to economic indicators such as gross national product (GNP) and disposable personal income. He concluded that there was no relationship between the business cycle and the number of visitors. Next, he attempted to identify why peaks and troughs occurred for his variable. After a thorough investigation, Mark decided that the major reason 1983 was a good year was that it was the 50th anniversary of the Grand Coulee Dam. A well-advertised celebration during the summer months was extremely well attended. The primary reason 1974 was a good year was the World's Fair in Spokane, Washington, approximately 90 miles from Grand Coulee Dam. (A visit to the dam provided an excellent side trip for visitors to the fair.) Mark speculated that 1980 showed poor attendance because Mount St. Helens erupted in late May of that year.

Next, Mark decided to investigate the relationship between the price of gas and the number of visitors. Gas prices, as reported by the Independent Petroleum Association of America, are shown in Table 16.10. Mark computed the cyclical indexes (also shown in Table 16.10) and developed the cyclical chart in Figure 16.10 to compare them with the cyclical pattern for the number of visitors. This chart indicates an inverse relationship between the price of gas and the number of visitors. When gas prices are high, the number of visitors is generally low; when gas prices are down, the number of visitors is up.

Mark used the multiplicative model $Y = TC$ to estimate the number of people who would visit Grand Coulee Dam in 1986. The trend is estimated by substituting an X coded value of 18 into the regression equation:

$$\hat{Y} = 259{,}055 + 8{,}363X$$
$$= 259{,}055 + 8{,}363(18) = 409{,}589$$

TABLE 16.10   Average National Gas Prices, 1969–1984 (Example 16.16)

Year	Average gas price	Cyclical
1969	34.8	179.3
1970	35.7	134.1
1971	36.5	107.9
1972	36.1	88.0
1973	38.8	80.4
1974	53.2	95.9
1975	56.7	90.5
1976	59.0	84.4
1977	62.2	80.7
1978	62.6	74.2
1979	85.7	93.6
1980	123.8	125.4
1981	131.7	124.3
1982	125.2	110.6
1983	117.0	97.2
1984	117.0	91.7

FIGURE 16.10   Gas Prices and Visitors—Cyclical Chart, 1969–84

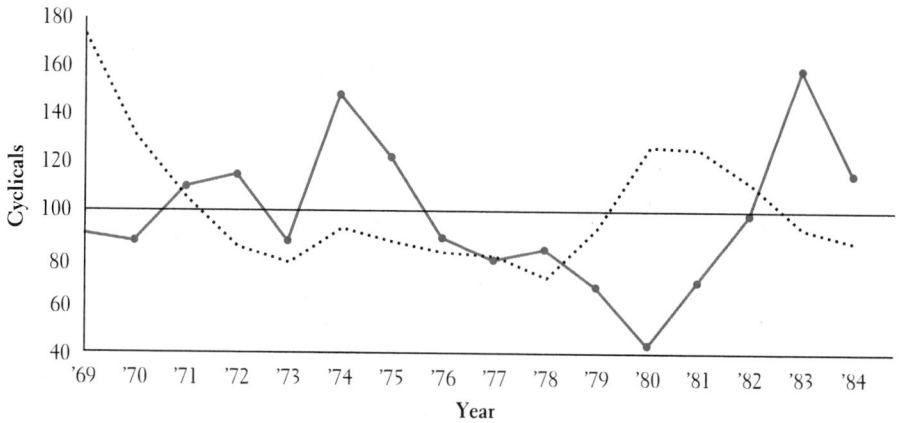

This equation seems appropriate because the population of Washington State is estimated to increase by an average of 2% annually through 1990.

Next, Mark estimated the cyclical index. The price of gasoline was forecast to be
4% less in 1985 and slightly lower in 1986. Vancouver, B.C., was to host Expo '86' in
1986, and 10 million visitors were expected to travel through Washington State. Since
Grand Coulee Dam is approximately a day's drive southeast of Vancouver, many
World's Fair visitors might include this attraction on their itinerary. Mark noted that
large celebrations have had a very positive effect on the number of visitors in the past,
so he chose a cyclical index of 193. The forecast for 1986 is

$$Y(1986) = TC = 409,589(1.93) = 790,507$$

EXERCISES

33. Describe the cyclical component.

34. An analyst has decomposed an annual time series and is ready to forecast future values. Describe the process.

35. What is the basic force that affects the cyclical component of most variables?

36. Describe each of these time series established by the U.S. Dept. of Commerce: leading series, coincident series, lagging series.

37. (This question refers to Exercise 30.) Analyze the cyclical component for Triton sales per share.

    a. Does the economy affect the cyclical component?

    b. Which component is more important: trend or cyclical?

    c. Forecast Triton sales per share for 1992. Use the cyclical relative for 1991 as the estimate for 1992.

38. (This question refers to Exercise 31.) Analyze the cyclical component for the *capital spending* variable.

    a. Does the economy affect the cyclical component?

    b. Which component is more important: trend or cyclical?

    c. Forecast capital spending for 1992 and 1993.

39. A large company's president read "Business Videos—Today's Hot Sales Weapon" in *Industry Week* (October 2, 1989, p. 38). As a result, the company is considering cutting back on TV advertising in favor of giving business videos to its customers. But before taking this action, the president wants to investigate the history of TV advertising in this country, especially the cyclical effect.

    Here are the total dollars spent on U.S. television advertising (in millions) from 1980 to 1989. Calculate cyclical indexes for this annual time series.

Year	Y	Ŷ
1980	11,424	11,456.4
1981	12,811	13,252.7
1982	14,566	15,049.0
1983	16,542	16,845.3
1984	19,670	18,641.6
1985	21,022	20,437.8
1986	22,881	22,234.1
1987	23,904	24,030.4
1988	25,686	25,826.7
1989	26,891	27,623.0

Source: *Statistical Abstract of the United States*, 1988, 1991.

    Analyze the peaks and bottoms of the cyclical component in U.S. TV advertising dollars. Forecast this variable for 1990.

40. The following annual data measure quantity of fish caught in millions of pounds from 1980 to 1989. The trend equation for this series appears also. Calculate the cyclical indicators for this annual series.

Year	Y	$\hat{Y}$
1980	6,482	5,902.25
1981	5,977	6,069.38
1982	6,367	6,236.50
1983	6,439	6,403.62
1984	6,438	6,570.74
1985	6,258	6,737.86
1986	6,031	6,904.98
1987	6,896	7,072.10
1988	7,192	7,239.22
1989	8,463	7,406.35

$\hat{Y} = 5735.1 + 167.12X$

Source: *Statistical Abstract of the United States*, 1988, 1991.

Based on the trend equation and the calculated cyclical indicators, summarize this time series with a brief statement about both the trend and cyclical components. Forecast the quantity of fish caught measured in millions of pounds for 1990.

SEASONAL DATA

Monthly or quarterly time series data are common because businesses generally use accounting techniques based on months or quarters. Projections of monthly and/or quarterly time series into the future are regular exercises for most organizations.

Decomposition of a monthly or quarterly time series can reveal the seasonal and irregular components, in addition to the trend and cyclical components. Examining each of these four components in isolation can reveal interesting and useful information and enables the analyst to combine these elements to produce a good forecast. Forecasts using monthly or quarterly time series are typically made for 1 to 12 months or 1 to 4 quarters into the future. The analyst should have from 4 to 7 years of monthly or quarterly data to perform the calculations necessary for a seasonal analysis.

The first component to be isolated in a monthly or quarterly time series is the seasonal component. An index for each of the 12 months or 4 quarters of the year is required; time series analysis computer programs are used to compute these indexes. Here's a description of the procedure typically used by such programs for monthly data.

The basic idea in calculating a monthly seasonal index is to compare the actual value of the variable (Y) with a 12-month average for the variable. In this way, we can determine whether the Y value is above or below the yearly average and by how much. If quarterly data are analyzed, a four-quarter average is computed for the comparison.

In computing a yearly average for the monthly comparison, an average should be used that is *centered* on the month being examined. Unfortunately, when 12 months are averaged, the center of the average isn't at the center of a month, but rather at the point where one month ends and another begins. For this reason, the following steps are used to center a 12-month average for Y on the month being examined. (These four steps assume that the data start in January.)

Step 1 Compute the 12-month moving total for January through December for the first year's data and place it opposite July 1. Compute the next 12-month moving total by removing January of the first year and adding January of the second year. This is the 12-month moving total from February of the first year through January of the second year; it's placed opposite August 1.

Step 2 Compute a two-year moving total by adding the 12-month moving totals opposite July 1 and August 1. The two-year total includes data for 24 months (January of the first year once, February through December twice, and January of the second year once). This total is centered opposite July 15.

Step 3 Divide the two-year moving total by 24 to obtain the 12-month average centered on July 15.

Seasonal Index

Step 4 The seasonal index for each month is calculated by dividing the actual value for each month by the 12-month centered average and multiplying by 100 so that the ratio is an index number. Equation 16.8 shows how this computation is performed:

$$S = \frac{TSCI}{TCI}(100) \tag{16.8}$$

where S = Seasonal index
$TSCI$ = Actual value of Y
TCI = 12-month centered average

Example 16.17 demonstrates the process of summarizing and computing the final adjusted seasonal indexes for each month.

EXAMPLE 16.17   Table 16.11 shows monthly 1985–86 data for new passenger car registrations. To illustrate the computation of monthly seasonal indexes, the four-step procedure is applied to these data. Each step is demonstrated in Table 16.11 and numbered to coincide with the following discussion:

Step 1 Registrations are summed for January through December 1985: 781 + 790 + 927 + 936 + 912 + 923 + 949 + 926 + 1105 + 973 + 828 + 849 = 10,899. This value is placed opposite July 1, 1985. The next 12-month moving total is computed by removing registrations for January 1985 and adding registrations for January 1986: 10,899 − 781 + 913 = 11,031.

Step 2 The two-year moving total is computed: 10,899 + 11,031 = 21,930.

Step 3 The 12-month centered moving average is computed: 21,930/24 = 913.75.

Step 4 The monthly seasonal index is computed using Equation 16.8:

$$S = \frac{TSCI}{TCI}(100) = \frac{949}{913.75}(100) = 103.86$$

The seasonal index of 103.86 for July 1985 indicates that registrations for this month were approximately 3 to 4% above normal.

The procedure just described is applied for each month, January 1985 to December 1991. Each of the monthly seasonal indexes is shown in Table 16.12. Note that the

TABLE 16.11 Registration of New Passenger Cars by Month, in Thousands, 1985–1986 (Example 16.17)

Period	Registrations	12-month moving total	2-year moving total	12-month centered moving average	Seasonal index
1985	-+				
Jan.	781				
Feb.	790				
March	927				
April	936				
May	912				
June	923	-+			
		10,899	-+		-+
July	949	2	21,930 3	913.75	103.86 4
		11,031	-+		-+
Aug.	926 1	-+	22,094	920.58	100.59
		11,063			
Sept.	1,105		22,047	918.63	120.29
		10,984			
Oct.	973		21,938	914.08	106.45
		10,954			
Nov.	828		21,914	913.08	90.68
		10,960			
Dec.	849		22,009	917.04	92.58
	-+	11,049			
1986					
Jan.	913		22,083	920.13	99.23
		11,034			
Feb.	822		22,036	918.17	89.53
		11,002			
March	848		22,048	918.67	92.31
		11,046			
April	906		22,067	919.46	98.54
		11,021			
May	918		21,933	913.88	100.45
		10,912			
June	1,012		21,877	911.54	111.02
		10,965			
July	934				
Aug.	894				
Sept.	1149				
Oct.	948				
Nov.	719				
Dec.	902				

TABLE 16.12   Summary of the Monthly Seasonal Indexes for Example 16.17

Month	1985	1986	1987	1988	1989	1990	1991	Modified monthly mean	Adjusted seasonal index mean (1.000324)
Jan.		99.23	91.29	89.33	86.85	80.06	83.67	87.79	87.8
Feb.		89.53	76.66	93.57	85.86	85.69	83.02	86.03	86.1
March		92.31	95.55	106.26	99.07	102.12	95.20	97.99	98.0
April		98.54	104.79	98.66	100.20	100.01	97.10	99.35	99.4
May		100.45	97.80	101.04	105.75	109.04	108.12	103.84	103.9
June		111.02	113.48	113.19	115.23	114.19	115.99	114.02	114.1
July	103.86	102.75	106.08	102.11	102.31	103.86		103.19	103.2
Aug.	100.59	99.55	105.96	104.84	109.48	104.09		103.87	103.9
Sept.	120.29	128.96	110.82	109.96	119.71	111.59		115.60	115.6
Oct.	106.45	106.55	94.82	95.14	100.98	107.54		102.28	102.3
Nov.	90.68	81.19	83.13	90.06	84.77	94.14		87.16	87.2
Dec.	92.58	102.51	104.00	105.73	89.08	94.91		98.50	98.5
								1,199.61	1,200.0

months of January–June 1985 don't have seasonal indexes. This is because July 1985 is the first month for which the previous six months of data are available. Likewise, the last six months of 1991 won't have seasonal indexes because when the analyst prepared the data, 1992 values weren't available.

Six seasonal indexes have been calculated for each month in Table 16.12. For January, these values are 99.23, 91.29, 89.33, 86.85, 80.06, and 83.67. We now want to combine these values into a single index for January. This might be done by adding them and dividing by 6 to create an average for the six values. But the usual procedure (and the one followed here) is to remove the highest and lowest of the calculated values and then average the rest. The lowest January index is 80.06 and the highest is 99.23. These are removed to eliminate any distortion that might result from extreme values, and the remaining four indexes are averaged:

$$(91.29 + 89.33 + 86.85 + 83.67)/4 = 87.79$$

This is the value in the "modified monthly mean" column in Table 16.12. The same procedure is followed for the other 11 months: the highest and lowest monthly indexes are removed and the other four are averaged to produce the modified monthly mean.

The modified monthly means just calculated add to 1,199.61 (Table 16.12). It would be convenient if they added to exactly 1,200 since their average would then be exactly 100, or 100%. This adjustment is easy to make since each modified mean can be increased slightly. If the adjusted seasonal indexes then add to exactly 1,200, the interpretation will be straightforward since each monthly index can be compared to their average of 100. The adjustment is made by dividing 1,200 by the sum of the modified monthly means and multiplying this ratio by each monthly index. For Table 16.12's January index, this ratio is

$$\frac{1,200}{1,199.61}(87.79) = 87.8$$

The "adjusted seasonal indexes" column is shown in Table 16.12. Following the adjustment, these values add to exactly 1,200 so their average is exactly 100.

The adjusted seasonal indexes in Table 16.12's last column are interpreted as the seasonal component of new passenger car registrations. Seasonal peaks occur in June and September; seasonal lows occur in January, February, and November. Weather is obviously important in explaining this variable's seasonal pattern. New passenger car registrations tend to be up in good-weather months and down in bad-weather months. September is generally a good month because of new models' introduction for the next year. Results of this analysis can be used to evaluate current sales, to schedule production and shipments, to plan personnel and financing, and to forecast monthly sales.

EXAMPLE 16.18 Julie Ruth is registrar of a midsized university in a Southern city. Among her responsibilities is planning for future enrollments. To do this, she needs some way to forecast the number of students for each quarter of the year.

Julie has quarterly records on the total student count over many years. She decides to use the past five years as an appropriate period to analyze in preparing forecasts for future quarters. Since the budget and facilities planning process is based to a considerable extent on these forecasts, she wants to use as accurate a process as possible in deriving predicted values. Julie knows that enrollments have been stable over the past five years. For this reason, she decides to base her forecasts strictly on the seasonal component.

Julie keys her enrollment data into the university's computer, using a program that will perform a time series decomposition. Part of the computer printout that results from this analysis is shown in Table 16.13.

The seasonal indexes indicate that fall is the most heavily enrolled quarter, followed by winter and then spring. The summer quarter has less than half the enrollment of the other quarters, with a seasonal index of 43.7. Julie can use these seasonal indexes to summarize quarterly enrollment loads and predict staffing and facility needs.

TABLE 16.13 Summary of the Quarterly Seasonal Indexes for Example 16.18

Quarter	1988	1989	1990	1991	1992	Modified qt. mean	Adjusted seasonal index
Fall		129.22	129.81	122.99	123.70	126.50	126.0
Winter		114.43	117.64	120.28	121.64	118.96	118.5
Spring	111.99	112.86	110.11	112.43		112.21	111.8
Summer	44.44	42.86	44.01	43.84		43.92	43.7
						401.59	400.0

Once the seasonal component has been identified, the next step is to compute a monthly or quarterly trend equation (seasonal trend equation). Recall that secular trend was defined as the *long-term* growth or decline in a time series. In conjunction with this definition, the trend of a monthly or quarterly series must be consistent with its long-term behavior. The trend for seasonal data can be computed using one of the following approaches:

1. If monthly or quarterly data are available for the entire annual series (all 10 to 20 years), the seasonal trend equation is computed using all of these values.
2. If the long-term trend equation has already been computed, it can be converted to be used with the seasonal data.
3. If the trend for the time period covered by the seasonal data appears to be similar to the pattern described by the long-term equation, the seasonal trend can be computed directly from the seasonal data.
4. If no long-term data are available, the seasonal trend must be computed directly from the seasonal data.

EXAMPLE 16.19   Figure 16.2 shows the long-term trend equation for the new passenger car registration series from 1960 to 1991. The simplest approach for developing a seasonal trend equation is to use the least squares procedure on the monthly data for 1985 through 1991. This is a reasonable solution if the resulting monthly trend equation accurately reflects the long-term growth pattern. According to Figure 16.2, the slope of a monthly trend equation developed from the monthly data for 1985 through 1991 would have a negative slope. Since the direction of the long-term trend has already been established as positive, the long-term trend equation will have to be converted for use with the seasonal data. This conversion process is demonstrated in Appendix B.

Monthly data for this series, measured in thousands, appear in the first column of Table 16.14 and are used as the Y variable. If the actual data were used to develop the trend equation, the months would represent the independent variable (X) with January 1985 as 1, February 1985 as 2, and so on. Equation 16.6 would then be used to compute the seasonal trend equation.

For this example, the long-term trend equation was converted to a seasonal equation (see Appendix B):

$$\hat{Y} = 819.990 + .5286X$$

Using the seasonal equation, the trend estimate for December 1984 (when X = 0) is 819,990. The resulting trend values using this equation are shown in column 2 of Table 16.14. Note that the trend estimate for January 1985 is 820,519 (819,990 + 529). Also note that the average increase each month is approximately 529 registrations.

Seasonally Adjusted Data

Economic indicators are published in several sources, such as the *Survey of Current Business*. These indicators are frequently adjusted for seasonal influences to enable users to see patterns that are independent of seasonal variations. **Seasonally adjusted data** result when the monthly or quarterly values of a time series are divided by their corresponding seasonal indexes. Removal of the seasonal variation helps clarify basic strengths or weaknesses of the other components in the series. Equation 16.9 shows

TABLE 16.14 Calculations for the Short-Term Components for Examples 16.19–16.23

PERIOD		DATA Y	REGRESSION T	SEAS. ADJ. TCI	CI	C	I
1985	JAN	781.00	820.52	889.39	108.39		
	FEB	790.00	821.05	918.04	111.81		
	MAR	927.00	821.58	945.75	115.11	111.32	103.41
	APR	936.00	822.10	941.81	114.56	109.31	104.81
	MAY	912.00	822.63	878.00	106.73	109.27	97.68
	JUN	923.00	823.16	809.23	98.31	107.87	91.14
	JUL	949.00	823.69	919.34	111.61	108.13	103.22
	AUG	926.00	824.22	891.21	108.13	109.83	98.45
	SEP	1105.00	824.75	955.56	115.86	113.17	102.38
	OCT	973.00	825.28	951.01	115.24	111.70	103.17
	NOV	828.00	825.80	949.67	115.00	115.22	99.81
	DEC	849.00	826.33	861.65	104.27	115.14	90.56
1986	JAN	913.00	826.86	1039.70	125.74	112.99	111.28
	FEB	822.00	827.39	955.22	115.45	112.00	103.08
	MAR	848.00	827.92	865.15	104.50	112.47	92.91
	APR	906.00	828.45	911.62	110.04	108.71	101.22
	MAY	918.00	828.98	883.77	106.61	107.42	99.24
	JUN	1012.00	829.50	887.26	106.96	107.24	99.74
	JUL	934.00	830.03	904.81	109.01	109.15	99.87
	AUG	894.00	830.56	860.42	103.59	110.11	94.08
	SEP	1149.00	831.09	993.60	119.55	108.54	110.15
	OCT	948.00	831.62	926.57	111.42	108.72	102.48
	NOV	719.00	832.15	824.65	99.10	109.87	90.20
	DEC	902.00	832.68	915.44	109.94	104.66	105.04
1987	JAN	800.00	833.21	911.02	109.34	102.66	106.51
	FEB	671.00	833.73	779.75	93.53	104.41	89.57
	MAR	829.00	834.26	845.77	101.38	101.56	99.83
	APR	895.00	834.79	900.56	107.88	99.89	108.00
	MAY	830.00	835.32	799.05	95.66	102.01	93.77
	JUN	963.00	835.85	844.30	101.01	102.50	98.54
	JUL	899.00	836.38	870.91	104.13	100.65	103.45
	AUG	903.00	836.91	869.08	103.84	100.63	103.20
	SEP	955.00	837.43	825.84	98.62	100.07	98.55
	OCT	819.00	837.96	800.49	95.53	101.04	94.55
	NOV	718.00	838.49	823.51	98.21	101.27	96.98
	DEC	901.00	839.02	914.42	108.99	103.95	104.84
1988	JAN	774.00	839.55	881.41	104.99	107.15	97.98
	FEB	810.00	840.08	941.28	112.05	107.90	103.85
	MAR	919.00	840.61	937.59	111.54	106.09	105.13
	APR	852.00	841.13	857.29	101.92	105.52	96.59
	MAY	874.00	841.66	841.41	99.97	103.41	96.67
	JUN	981.00	842.19	860.08	102.12	101.67	100.45
	JUL	883.00	842.72	855.41	101.51	100.49	101.01
	AUG	901.00	843.25	867.15	102.83	99.18	103.68
	SEP	937.00	843.78	810.28	96.03	99.50	96.51
	OCT	807.00	844.31	788.76	93.42	100.71	92.76
	NOV	764.00	844.84	876.27	103.72	99.88	103.84
	DEC	896.00	845.36	909.35	107.57	100.50	107.03
1989	JAN	733.00	845.89	834.72	98.68	101.89	96.85
	FEB	722.00	846.42	839.02	99.13	101.16	97.99
	MAR	833.00	846.95	849.85	100.34	99.74	100.60
	APR	843.00	847.48	848.23	100.09	99.64	100.45
	MAY	885.00	848.01	852.00	100.47	98.75	101.74
	JUN	950.00	848.54	832.90	98.16	98.62	99.53
	JUL	830.00	849.06	804.06	94.70	98.05	96.58
	AUG	880.00	849.59	846.94	99.69	96.34	103.47
	SEP	956.00	850.12	826.71	97.25	94.66	102.73
	OCT	800.00	850.65	781.92	91.92	92.26	99.63
	NOV	666.00	851.18	763.87	89.74	88.86	100.99
	DEC	694.00	851.71	704.34	82.70	87.32	94.71

TABLE 16.14 *concluded*

PERIOD		DATA Y	REGRESSION T	SEAS. ADJ. TCI	CI	C	I
1990	JAN	619.00	852.24	704.90	82.71	87.42	94.61
	FEB	657.00	852.76	763.48	89.53	87.17	102.70
	MAR	773.00	853.29	788.64	92.42	89.09	103.74
	APR	751.00	853.82	755.66	88.50	90.15	98.18
	MAY	819.00	854.35	788.46	92.29	89.89	102.67
	JUN	858.00	854.88	752.24	87.99	88.88	99.01
	JUL	779.00	855.41	754.66	88.22	87.83	100.44
	AUG	777.00	855.94	747.81	87.37	87.33	100.05
	SEP	825.00	856.47	713.42	83.30	88.00	94.66
	OCT	787.00	856.99	769.21	89.76	86.51	103.75
	NOV	683.00	857.52	783.36	91.35	84.93	107.56
	DEC	683.00	858.05	693.17	80.78	84.23	95.91
1991	JAN	599.00	858.58	682.13	79.45	82.16	96.70
	FEB	590.00	859.11	685.62	79.81	79.68	100.16
	MAR	669.00	859.64	682.53	79.40	80.17	99.04
	APR	675.00	860.17	679.19	78.96	80.40	98.21
	MAY	744.00	860.69	716.26	83.22	81.42	102.21
	JUN	792.00	861.22	694.38	80.63	80.60	100.03
	JUL	755.00	861.75	731.41	84.87	79.59	106.65
	AUG	675.00	862.28	649.64	75.34	78.61	95.84
	SEP	737.00	862.81	637.33	73.87	78.68	93.88
	OCT	692.00	863.34	676.36	78.34	76.45	102.47
	NOV	610.00	863.87	699.64	80.99		
	DEC	628.00	864.39	637.35	73.73		
1992	JAN		864.92				
	FEB		865.45				
	MAR		865.98				
	APR		866.51				
	MAY		867.04				
	JUN		867.57				
	JUL		868.09				
	AUG		868.62				
	SEP		869.15				
	OCT		869.68				
	NOV		870.21				
	DEC		870.74				

that seasonally adjusted values include the effects of trend, cyclical, and irregular components once the seasonal component has been eliminated:

$$TCI = \frac{TSCI}{S} \tag{16.9}$$

where TCI = Seasonally adjusted data value
        $TSCI$ = Original Y value
           S = Seasonal index

The unemployment rate, for example, is often seasonally adjusted so that the underlying pattern of this important index can be followed without the distorting effects of seasonal variations. Retail sales are often seasonally adjusted also, especially during the Christmas buying season.

> **Seasonally adjusted data** result when the original monthly or quarterly values of a time series are divided by their corresponding seasonal indexes.

EXAMPLE 16.20   The third column of Table 16.14 (*TCI*) shows seasonally adjusted data for new passenger car registrations. These values were calculated by dividing the actual monthly values in column 1 by the seasonal indexes of Table 16.13 and multiplying the result by 100. The seasonally adjusted value for January 1985, for example, was computed using Equation 16.9:

$$TCI = \frac{TSCI}{S} = \frac{781}{.878} = 889.52$$

(Note: The computer carries more decimal places and produces slightly different values.)

Due to the seasonal component, January registrations typically are down by about 12.2% ($S = 87.8$). The seasonally adjusted value of 889.52 indicates what registrations would have been without the effect of the seasonal component.

Once the seasonal component has been removed for each month in the data, the *TCI* column shows that the number of new passenger car registrations for June (a high-registration month) of each year aren't higher than for January (a low-registration month). In fact, the seasonally adjusted data column shows that January was the best month of 1986. Seasonally adjusted data in Table 16.14 include only the effects of the trend, cyclical, and irregular components.

Next, the short-term cyclical component is computed. Since the data have already been seasonally adjusted, the cyclical and irregular components are isolated by dividing *TCI* by the trend (*T*):

$$CI = \frac{TCI}{T}(100) \qquad\qquad (16.10)$$

where CI = Cyclical-irregular index
TCI = Seasonally adjusted data
T = Trend value

The resulting values appear in the *CI* column. After the data have been adjusted for seasonal and trend influences, the cyclical and irregular components are separated. A moving average is developed to smooth out the irregularities of the *CI* column. This approach is similar to the analysis of the seasonal component, where a 12-month moving average is used to smooth out the trend, cyclical, and irregular influences. Recall that in the computation of the 12-month moving average, a centering problem occurred. Whenever an even number of time periods is used to compute a moving average, centering is a problem. For this reason, an odd number of time periods, such as 5,

7, 9, or 11, is usually used to smooth out irregularities. This approach is demonstrated in Example 16.21.

EXAMPLE 16.21   The CI column in Table 16.14 shows the cyclical-irregular indexes for new passenger car registrations. These values were calculated by dividing the seasonally adjusted data (*TCI*) by the trend estimates (*T*) and multiplying the result by 100. The cyclical-irregular index for January 1985, for example, is

$$CI = \frac{TCI}{T}(100) = \frac{889.39}{820.52}(100) = 108.39$$

The cyclical component is separated from the irregular component by using a five-month moving average. Table 16.15 shows the computations.

Compare the cyclical column (*C*) with the cyclical-irregular column (*CI*). Note that the five-month moving average has smoothed out the CI column's irregularities. The cyclical component rises and falls in a consistent manner, and the cycle is easier to identify. The cyclical index began at 111 in March 1985 and mostly stayed between 100 and 110 through 1988. From this point the cycle of new passenger car registrations dropped to a low of 76.45 in October 1991. This short-term cyclical index should parallel the long-term cyclical analyzed in Figure 16.7. If the short-term cyclical effect is radically different from the long-term cyclical, the monthly trend should be developed by either using all the monthly data or converting the long-term trend equation so that it can be used with the monthly data.

TABLE 16.15   Computational Procedure for Five-Month Moving Average for New Passenger Car Registration Data

Time period (1985)	CI	Five-month moving total	C
January	108.39		
February	111.81		
March	115.11	556.59	111.32
April	114.56	546.51	109.30
May	106.73	546.31	109.26
June	98.31		
July	111.61		

The final step in the decomposition of a seasonal time series is identification of the irregular component. We do this by dividing the *CI* column of Table 16.14 by the *C* column and multiplying the result by 100:

$$I = \frac{CI}{C}(100) \qquad (16.11)$$

where   *I* = Irregular index
   CI = Cyclical-irregular index
   C = Smoothed cyclical index

The irregular component measures the variability of the time series after the other components have been removed. Most of the irregular component is made up of random variability. However, sometimes unpredictable events cause irregularities in a variable.

EXAMPLE 16.22   The last column (I) in Table 16.14 shows the irregular indexes for new passenger car registrations. These values were calculated by dividing the cyclical-irregular indexes by the cyclical indexes and multiplying the result by 100. The irregular index for March 1985, for example, is

$$I = \frac{CI}{C}(100) = \frac{115.11}{111.32}(100) = 103.40$$

Sometimes the irregular variations in a time series can be explained. Examination of the irregular column in Table 16.14 shows that irregularities occurred in September (110.15) and November (90.20) of 1986. These irregularities were caused by wage and strike problems in the auto industry.

One of the key purposes of decomposing a time series is to examine the components of the series in isolation. Once the analyst can look at the trend, seasonal, cyclical, and irregular components of a monthly time series one at a time, valuable insights into the patterns hidden in the original data values may be gained and used to better manage the variable of interest. In addition, identifying the individual components will make it easier to forecast the series.

In forecasting a monthly time series, the decomposition process is reversed. Instead of separating the series into its individual components for examination, the components are recombined to form the forecasts. The trend, seasonal, cyclical, and irregular components are identified for each future period for which a forecast is desired, and the multiplicative model $Y = TSCI$ is used to develop the forecast.

Any monthly or quarterly time series can be used to project (forecast) future periods. This is often the sole objective in collecting time series data and subjecting them to the decomposition process. Since there are many time series values of vital importance to the future health of an organization, forecasting such variables is important in every manager's job, and the time series decomposition process is frequently used to produce accurate forecasts.

EXAMPLE 16.23   This example demonstrates the development of the short-term forecast for January 1992 for new passenger car registrations using Tables 16.12 and 16.14. The example illustrates how each individual component is computed.

1. *Trend.* The monthly trend equation is used to estimate the trend value for January 1992. Since January 1985 was represented by $X = 1$, January 1992 is represented by $X = 85$ in the trend equation. The trend estimate is 864.92:

$$\begin{aligned} \hat{Y} &= 819.990 + .5286X \\ &= 819.990 + .5286(85) \\ &= 864.92 \end{aligned}$$

2. *Seasonal.* Table 16.12 gives the adjusted seasonal index for January, 87.8.

3. *Cyclical.* The cyclical index is estimated using all of the information gathered on the cyclical pattern. The analyst must answer the following questions: Was the cyclical pattern in Table 16.14 increasing or decreasing for the last few months of 1991? Have any leading indicators been identified? What is the economic forecast for 1992? To demonstrate the completion of this example, a cyclical index of 75 is estimated.

4. *Irregular.* Since most irregular fluctuations are random variations, an estimate of 100% or 1.0 is commonly used. Occasionally, an analyst can identify future irregularities. If an irregular event can be anticipated (such as a contract coming due along with a probable strike), the impact can be estimated by using a different irregular index. In this example, an irregular index of 100 is appropriate since no unusual events are foreseen. The forecast for January 1992 is

$$
\begin{aligned}
Y(\text{January 1992}) &= TSCI \\
&= (864.92)(.878)(.75)(1.00) \\
&= 569.55
\end{aligned}
$$

EXERCISES

41. What components are analyzed in the decomposition of a seasonal (monthly or quarterly) time series?

42. For a seasonal time series, what method is used to isolate the trend component?

43. To compute a seasonal index for each month or quarter, the actual Y value is compared with an average. How many periods are averaged for monthly and quarterly data, and what is the center point for these averages?

44. How are the original data values deseasonalized? What arithmetic operation is used to generate the *CI* column in a monthly or quarterly time series printout?

45. How is the C column generated from the *CI* column in the printout? How is the *I* column computed for a monthly or quarterly time series analysis?

46. Do you agree with the statement, "A moving average is a smoothing technique"? Why or why not?

47. What is the purpose of having the monthly seasonal indexes add to exactly 1,200 and the quarterly seasonal indexes add to exactly 400?

48. What model is used to forecast a seasonal time series?

49. Assume the following specific seasonal indexes for January, based on the ratio-to-moving-average method:

    88.2   85.9   64.3   92.4   80.1   82.4

    What is the seasonal index for January using the modified mean method?

50. The expected trend value for September is $900. Assuming a September seasonal index of 91, what would be the forecast for September?

51. The following specific seasonal indexes are given for October:

    65.4   76.8   66.9   72.6   70.0

If the adjustment is 0.98, if the modified mean is used, and if the expected trend for October is $800, what is the forecast for October?

52. A large resort near Williamsburg, Virginia, has been tracking its quarterly sales for several years but has never analyzed these data. The resort manager has read an article in *Travel & Leisure* (July 1989, p. 100) on vacation opportunities in Williamsburg and wants to investigate his resort's sales history. She computes the seasonal indexes for quarterly sales. Which of the following statements about the index are correct?

    a. The sum of the four quarterly index numbers should be 400.

    b. An index of 75 for the first quarter indicates that sales were 25% lower than the average quarterly sales.

    c. An index of 110 for the second quarter indicates that sales were 10% above the average quarterly sales.

    d. The index for any quarter must be between 0 and 200.

    e. The average index for each of the four quarters will be 100.

53. In computing a seasonal index, the specific seasonals were tabulated and the extremes eliminated for each month. The averages for the 12 months were obtained and summed. If the mean for June was 96.9 and the sum for all 12 months is 1,195, what is the adjusted seasonal index for June?

54. Your report for Jim Rogers, Kona Department Store manager, includes the following statistics from last year's sales. Mr. Rogers says, "This report confirms what I've been telling you; business is getting better and better." Is this statement accurate? Why?

Month	Sales (thousands)	Adjusted seasonal index
Jan.	225	52
Feb.	213	49
Mar.	289	85
Apr.	301	92
May	306	93
June	341	98
July	330	95
Aug.	345	90
Sept.	371	100
Oct.	391	118
Nov.	420	129
Dec.	519	199

Source: Kona Department Store records.

55. John Managan, manager of Hallet Confections, is attempting to forecast sales for next year. He has the following adjusted seasonal indexes for sales based on the past four years. John has decided that no trend exists for his sales variable.

Month	Adjusted seasonal index	Month	Adjusted seasonal index
Jan.	60	July	72
Feb.	75	Aug.	78

Month	Adjusted seasonal index	Month	Adjusted seasonal index
Mar.	95	Sept.	105
Apr.	110	Oct.	116
May	107	Nov.	129
June	101	Dec.	152

Source: Hallet Confections records.

    a. John forecasts that sales for the coming year will total $60,000. On the basis of this forecast of total sales, make a forecast of sales for each month.

    b. January sales were $3,500. If this is the prevailing level of sales for the remaining 11 months and the adjusted seasonal indexes are accurate, what will be the total annual sales for this year?

    c. On the basis of January sales and the adjusted seasonal indexes, forecast sales for the second quarter.

56. The adjusted seasonal indexes in the accompanying table reflect the changing volume of business of the Mt. Spokane Resort Hotel, which caters to the family tourist in summer and the skiing enthusiast during winter. No sharp cyclical variations are expected during 1993.

Month	Adjusted seasonal index	Month	Adjusted seasonal index
Jan.	120	July	153
Feb.	137	Aug.	151
Mar.	100	Sept.	95
Apr.	33	Oct.	60
May	47	Nov.	82
June	125	Dec.	97

Source: Mt. Spokane Resort Hotel records.

    a. If 600 tourists visited the resort in January 1993, what is a reasonable estimate for February?

    b. The monthly trend equation is $\hat{Y} = 135 + 5X$, where $X = 1$ represents January 15, 1987. What is the forecast for each month of 1993?

    c. What is the average number of new tourists per month?

57. Goodyear Tire's quarterly sales appear below. Does there appear to be a significant seasonal effect in sales levels? Analyze this time series to get the four seasonal indexes and determine the extent of the seasonal component in Goodyear's sales.

Quarter:	1	2	3	4
1985	2292	2450	2363	2477
1986	2063	2358	2316	2366
1987	2268	2533	2479	2625
1988	2616	2793	2656	2746
1989	2643	2811	2679	2736

Quarter:	1	2	3	4
1990	2692	2871	2900	2810
1991	2497	2791	2838	2781

Source: *The Value Line Investment Survey* (New York: Value Line, 1988, 1989, 1991), p. 127.

58. The following data values represent monthly sales of all retail stores in the United States in billions of dollars. Analyze this series including comments on all four components of the series.

Year:	1985	1986	1987	1988	1989	1990	1991
Jan.	98.8	105.6	106.4	113.6	122.5	132.6	130.9
Feb.	95.6	99.7	105.8	115.0	118.9	127.3	128.6
March	110.2	114.2	120.4	131.6	139.7	148.3	149.3
April	113.1	115.7	125.4	130.9	137.9	145.0	148.5
May	120.3	125.4	129.1	136.0	148.2	154.1	159.8
June	115.0	120.4	129.0	137.5	147.1	153.5	153.9
July	115.5	120.7	129.3	134.1	142.6	148.9	154.6
Aug.	121.1	124.1	131.5	138.7	150.9	157.4	159.9
Sept.	113.8	124.4	124.5	131.9	142.1	145.6	146.7
Oct.	115.8	123.8	128.3	133.8	142.3	151.5	152.1
Nov.	118.1	121.4	126.9	140.2	148.8	156.1	155.6
Dec.	138.6	152.1	157.2	171.0	176.5	179.7	181.0

Source: *Survey of Current Business*, 1989, 1992.

SUMMARY

Price, quantity, and value indexes are widely used in business and government to monitor important economic and business conditions. It is frequently more useful to monitor these conditions using index numbers, which represent percentages of a base-period value, rather than use the original units of measurement. The basic calculations for the three major indexes have been demonstrated in this chapter, along with the calculations necessary to change a base period and to deflate a dollar time series.

Many businesses develop their own indexes to monitor important time series variables, such as sales levels, output quantities, and other monthly and quarterly variables. Almost all businesses take advantage of the hundreds of index numbers maintained by the federal government and by private organizations. The next section lists a few of these widely used indexes.

This chapter has presented a widely used technique for evaluating time series data. In the analysis of annual data, the trend and cyclical components are isolated, studied, and then employed in the forecasting process.

Next, the decomposition analysis for monthly data was presented. In addition to the trend and cyclical components, the seasonal and irregular components are examined in this analysis. The purpose is to study these components in isolation, and thus gain knowledge about the series, and to then recombine the components to forecast the future.

A final note is in order regarding the time horizon for forecasting. If a long-term forecast is needed, annual data are typically collected and analyzed. If the forecast is for one or two years ahead, we can anticipate the cyclical component and use it along with the projected trend to form the forecast. For forecasts three or more years into the future, the cyclical component isn't useful, and the forecast is based primarily on the trend projection.

Short-term forecasts are formed using monthly or quarterly data. Four to seven years of data are usually used to form these forecasts. After the decomposition process, forecasts of up to 12 months or four quarters are made. Forecasts for longer periods of time aren't usually made with monthly or quarterly data, since the data have been collected for too short a period, and since the trend and cyclical components may be considered suspect when used for forecasting far into the future.

APPLICATIONS OF STATISTICAL CONCEPTS IN THE BUSINESS WORLD
. . . .

The United States government and several private agencies maintain national and regional indexes used to monitor various aspects of the economy. Here are some of these indexes. They can be found in any issue of the *Survey of Current Business*, and some are found in the *Statistical Abstract of the United States*.

Consumer Price Index—Wage Earners and Clerical Workers (CPI-W)

Consumer Price Index—All-Urban Consumers (CPI-U)

Industrial Product Index

Producer Price Index (Wholesale Price Index)

Industrial Production—Nondurable Manufactures

Producer Prices—Farm Products

Producer Products—Textile Products and Apparel

Construction Cost Index

Employment Cost Index—Civilian Workers

Employment Cost Index—Blue-Collar Workers

Dow Jones Industrial Average

Standard & Poor's 500 Stock Index

NASDAQ Over-the-Counter Stock Price Index

Price indexes are frequently used to convert dollar time series to constant dollars, that is, to remove the effects of inflation. Here are some of the time series monitored by the federal government in both real dollars and constant dollars. The latter values are calculated by dividing each dollar value by an appropriate price index for the period.

Gross national product
Auto output
Government purchases of goods and services
Personal consumption expenditures by major type of product
National defense purchases of goods and services
Exports and imports of goods and services
Change in business inventories by industry
New plant and equipment expenditures by business

As mentioned earlier in this chapter, many variables are measured each year, quarter, or month that are vital to the successful operation of a business. Time series analysis is a valuable source of information on current operations and often provides the basis for successful forecasting.

Here are variables that might be analyzed by time series decomposition. These are only examples; many businesses have hundreds of time series variables that are carefully watched by managers in various departments and various management levels. Some variables are measured on an annual basis, although most are monitored each month or quarter.

Production:
Labor hours by product
Overtime hours
Product defects

Finance:
Return on investment
Dividends paid
Income per share

Personnel:
Number of employees
Sick days taken
Average hourly wage
Number of employees leaving company

Computer Department:
Number of CPU hours consumed
Number of network transactions

Marketing:
Share of market
Minutes of advertising on television

Accounting:
Cash balance
Accounts receivable
Accounts payable

Quality Control:
Defects per shift
Percentage defective by product line
Item deviation from specification

GLOSSARY

Time series Data that are collected, recorded, or observed over successive increments of time.

Index number A value that measures the movement of time series values relative to a base period; the index in the base period equals 100.

Price index An index that measures changes in the prices of goods and services over time.

Quantity index An index that measures changes in the quantities of goods over time.

Value index An index that measures the total dollar value of a group of goods or services.

Consumer price index An index that measures the prices that U.S. consumers pay for the products and services they commonly buy.

Secular trend The long-term component that represents the growth or decline in a time series over an extended period of time.

Cyclical component The wavelike fluctuation around the trend.

Seasonal component A pattern of change in quarterly or monthly data that repeats itself from year to year.

Irregular component A measure of the variability of the time series after the other components have been removed.

Seasonally adjusted data The data that result when the original monthly or quarterly values of a time series are divided by their corresponding seasonal indexes.

KEY FORMULAS

Price index

$$PI = \frac{\Sigma P_t}{\Sigma P_b}(100) \tag{16.1}$$

Quantity index

$$QI = \frac{\Sigma Q_t}{\Sigma Q_b}(100) \tag{16.2}$$

Value index

$$VI = \frac{\Sigma P_t Q_t}{\Sigma P_b Q_b}(100) \tag{16.3}$$

Purchasing power of the dollar

$$\text{Current purchasing power of } \$1 = \frac{100}{\text{Current consumer price index}} \tag{16.4}$$

Time series decomposition model

$$Y = T \times C \times S \times I \tag{16.5}$$

Trend equation

$$\hat{Y} = b_0 + b_1 X \tag{16.6}$$

Cyclical component (annual data)

$$C = \frac{Y}{\hat{Y}}(100) \tag{16.7}$$

Seasonal component

$$S = \frac{TSCI}{TCI}(100) \tag{16.8}$$

Seasonally adjusted data

$$TCI = \frac{TSCI}{S} \tag{16.9}$$

Cyclical component (seasonal data)

$$CI = \frac{TCI}{T}(100) \tag{16.10}$$

Irregular component

$$I = \frac{CI}{C}(100) \tag{16.11}$$

SOLVED EXERCISES
. . . .

1. FORMING A PRICE INDEX AND CHANGING THE BASE PERIOD
The Bayliner Corporation has decided to expand its manufacturing capacity. Company analyst Steve Donaldson is comparing the cost of housing in various sections of the country. The following data represent median purchase prices (in thousands of dollars) of existing one-family houses in the western region of the United States.

Year	Y
1980	89.3
1981	96.2
1982	98.9
1983	94.9
1984	95.8
1985	95.4
1986	100.9
1987	113.2
1988	124.9
1989	139.9

Source: National Association of Realtors.

a. Form a price index for Steve using 1980 as the base period.

b. Use the indexes from part *a* to change the base period to 1989.

Solution:

a. The price for each year is divided by the price in the base year, 1980, and multiplied by 100. The resulting values are the price indexes for the series with 1980 = 100.

$$1980: (89.3/89.3)100 = 100.0$$
$$1981: (96.2/89.3)100 = 107.7$$
$$1982: (98.9/89.3)100 = 110.8$$
$$1983: (94.9/89.3)100 = 106.3$$
$$1984: (95.8/89.3)100 = 107.3$$
$$1985: (95.4/89.3)100 = 106.8$$
$$1986: (100.9/89.3)100 = 113.0$$
$$1987: (113.2/89.3)100 = 126.8$$
$$1988: (124.9/89.3)100 = 139.9$$
$$1989: (139.9/89.3)100 = 156.7$$

b. The base period can be changed from 1980 to 1989 by using the indexes just calculated. Each index is divided by the index for the new base period, 156.7, and multiplied by 100. This changes the base period to 1989 where the new index is now 100.

$$1980: 100.0/156.7(100) = 63.8$$
$$1981: 107.7/156.7(100) = 68.7$$
$$1982: 110.8/156.7(100) = 70.7$$
$$1983: 106.3/156.7(100) = 67.8$$
$$1984: 107.3/156.7(100) = 68.5$$
$$1985: 106.8/156.7(100) = 68.2$$
$$1986: 113.0/156.7(100) = 72.1$$
$$1987: 126.8/156.7(100) = 80.9$$
$$1988: 139.9/156.7(100) = 89.3$$
$$1989: 156.7/156.7(100) = 100.0$$

2. DEFLATING A TIME SERIES

Susan Meyer, sales manager for a cosmetics company, is concerned with the expense account totals turned in by her salespeople around the country. She computes the average amount her people spent on food and beverages per month over the past several years and sees that this amount has indeed gone up. However, she realizes that there has been inflation during the period of measurement and decides to deflate the actual dollar amounts. Here are the average monthly amounts for food and beverages during the measured years, along with the consumer price index for food and beverages found in the *Statistical Abstract of the United States.*

Year	Average monthly cost	CPI–Food and Beverages (1982–84 = 100)
1983	697	99.5
1984	721	103.2
1985	753	105.6
1986	761	109.1
1987	778	113.5
1988	784	118.2
1989	792	124.9
1990	811	132.1

a. Compute the dollar time series in deflated dollars using the food and beverage index.

b. What conclusion can be reached regarding the trend of salespeople's monthly food and beverage cost over the measured years?

Solution:

a. The dollar values are divided by the price index after moving the decimal on each index two places to the left. The result is the original time series in deflated dollars:

$$1983: \ 697/ \ .995 = 700.5$$
$$1984: \ 721/1.032 = 698.6$$
$$1985: \ 753/1.056 = 713.1$$
$$1986: \ 761/1.091 = 697.5$$
$$1987: \ 778/1.135 = 685.5$$
$$1988: \ 784/1.182 = 663.3$$
$$1989: \ 792/1.249 = 634.1$$
$$1990: \ 811/1.321 = 613.9$$

b. Susan is surprised to see that in terms of 1982–84 dollars, there has actually been a decrease in her salespeople's monthly food and beverage cost from 1983 to 1990. She decides that trying to reduce these expenditures isn't appropriate. In fact, she decides to compliment her sales staff at next month's sales meeting.

3. TREND

In Solved Exercise 1, the Bayliner Corporation has decided to expand its manufacturing capacity by building a new plant. Analyst Steve Donaldson needs to determine the long-term growth of the median purchase price of existing one-family houses in the western region of the United States, in thousands of dollars.

Year	Y
1980	89.3
1981	96.2
1982	98.9
1983	94.9
1984	95.8
1985	95.4
1986	100.9
1987	113.2
1988	124.9
1989	139.9

Source: National Association of Realtors.

a. Compute a linear trend equation.

b. Estimate the trend for 1990.

Solution:

a. Code time as the X variable with $X = 1$ representing 1980.

Year	Y	X	X²	XY
1980	89.3	1	1	89.3
1981	96.2	2	4	192.4
1982	98.9	3	9	296.7
1983	94.9	4	16	379.6
1984	95.8	5	25	479.0
1985	95.4	6	36	572.4
1986	100.9	7	49	706.3
1987	113.2	8	64	905.6
1988	124.9	9	81	1124.1
1989	139.9	10	100	1399.0
Sums:	1,049.4	55	385	6,144.4

The slope, b_1, is computed using Equation 14.7:

$$b_1 = \frac{n\,\Sigma XY - (\Sigma X)(\Sigma Y)}{n\,\Sigma X^2 - (\Sigma X)^2} = \frac{10(6,144.4) - 55(1,049.4)}{10(385) - (55)^2}$$

$$= \frac{61,444 - 57,717}{3,850 - 3,025} = \frac{3,727}{825} = 4.5176$$

The constant b_0 (the value of the trend when X is 0) is computed using Equation 14.8:

$$b_0 = \frac{\Sigma Y}{n} - \frac{b_1\,\Sigma X}{n} = \frac{1,049.4}{10} - \frac{4.5176(55)}{10}$$

$$= 104.94 - 24.85 = 80.09$$

The trend equation is $\hat{Y} = 80.09 + 4.5176X$.

b. The trend estimate for 1990 is

$$\hat{Y} = 80.09 + 4.5176X$$
$$= 80.09 + 4.5176(11) = 129.784$$

4. CYCLICAL COMPONENT

This question refers to Solved Exercise 3.

a. Compute the cyclical component.

b. Forecast the median purchase price of existing one-family houses in the West for 1990. Use a cyclical estimate of 112.

Solution:

a. The cyclical for 1980 is

$$C = \frac{Y}{\hat{Y}}(100) = \frac{89.3}{84.6}(100) = 105.55$$

The cyclical components for each year are:

Year	Y	$\hat{Y}$	C
1980	89.3	84.611	105.54
1981	96.2	89.128	107.73

Year	Y	Ŷ	C
1982	98.9	93.646	105.61
1983	94.9	98.164	96.68
1984	95.8	102.681	93.30
1985	95.4	107.199	88.99
1986	100.9	111.716	90.32
1987	113.2	116.234	97.39
1988	124.9	120.752	103.44
1989	139.9	125.269	111.68

b. $Y(1990) = TC$
$$= 129.784(1.12) = 145,358$$

5. SEASONAL COMPONENT

The Consolidated Edison Company sells electricity and steam in New York City. Betty Springer, company analyst, must determine whether a seasonal pattern exists in the company's quarterly revenues. She collects the following data on quarterly revenues (in millions of dollars):

Year	Mar. 31	June 30	Sept. 30	Dec. 31
1985	1,441	1,209	1,526	1,321
1986	1,414	1,187	1,411	1,185
1987	1,284	1,125	1,493	1,192
1988	1,327	1,102	1,469	1,213

Source: *The Value Line Investment Survey* (New York: Value Line, 1988, 1989), p. 174.

a. Compute the quarterly seasonal indexes.

b. Compute the adjusted quarterly seasonal indexes.

c. Analyze the seasonal pattern for revenues.

Solution:

a. The seasonal variation analysis involves four steps, as Table 16.16 demonstrates.

Step 1 Revenues are summed for the four quarters of 1985:
1,411 + 1,209 + 1,526 + 1,321 = 5,497. This value is placed opposite July 1, 1985. The next four-quarter moving total is computed by removing first-quarter 1985 revenue and adding revenue for the first quarter of 1986:
5497 − 1,441 + 1,414 = 5,470.

Step 2 The two-year moving total is computed: 5,497 + 5,470 = 10,967.

Step 3 The four-quarter centered moving average is computed: 10,967/8 = 1,370.88.

Step 4 The quarterly seasonal index is computed using Equation 16.8:

$$S = \frac{TSCI}{TCI}(100) = \frac{1,526}{1,370.88}(100) = 111.32$$

The seasonal index of 111.32 for the third quarter of 1985 indicates that revenues for this quarter were approximately 11% to 12% above normal.

TABLE 16.16 Quarterly Revenues for the Consolidated Edison Corporation ($ millions), 1985–1988 (Solved Exercise 5)

Quarter	Revenue	Four-quarter moving total	Two-year moving total	Four-quarter centered moving average	Seasonal index
1985					
1st	1,441				
2d	1,209				
		5,497			
3d	1,526		10,967	1,370.88	111.32
		5,470			
4th	1,321		10,918	1,364.75	96.79
1986		5,448			
1st	1,414		10,781	1,347.63	104.93
		5,333			
2d	1,187		10,530	1,316.25	90.18
		5,197			
3d	1,411		10,264	1,283.00	109.98
		5,067			
4th	1,185		10,072	1,259.00	94.12
1987		5,005			
1st	1,284		10,092	1,261.50	101.78
		5,087			
2d	1,125		10,181	1,272.63	88.40
		5,094			
3d	1,493		10,231	1,278.88	116.74
		5,137			
4th	1,192		10,251	1,281.38	93.03
1988		5,114			
1st	1,327		10,204	1,275.50	104.04
		5,090			
2d	1,102		10,201	1,275.13	86.42
		5,111			
3d	1,469				
4th	1,213				

b. Table 16.17 shows each of the quarterly seasonal indexes. Three seasonal indexes have been calculated for each quarter. For the first quarter, these values are 104.93, 101.78, and 104.04. The lowest first-quarter index is 101.78 and the highest is 104.93. These are removed to eliminate any distortion that might result from extreme values, so the remaining index is 104.04 (the value shown in Table 16.17 in the "modified quarterly mean" column). The modified quarterly means add to 397.88; however, they should add up to 400, or an average of 100 for each of the four quarters. The adjustment is made by dividing 400 by the sum of the modified quarterly means and multiplying this ratio by each quarterly index. For the first-quarter index in the table, this ratio is

$$\frac{400}{397.88}(104.04) = 104.6$$

TABLE 16.17 Summary of the Quarterly Seasonal Indexes for Solved Exercise 5

Quarter	1985	1986	1987	1988	Modified quarterly mean	Adjusted seasonal index
1st		104.93	101.78	104.04	104.04	104.6
2d		90.18	88.40	86.42	88.40	88.9
3d	111.32	109.98	116.74		111.32	111.9
4th	96.79	94.12	93.03		94.12	94.6
					397.88	400.0

c. The adjusted seasonal indexes in the last column of Table 16.17 are interpreted as the seasonal component of the revenue variable. A seasonal peak occurs in the third quarter, and the seasonal low occurs in the second quarter.

EXERCISES

59. Describe the differences and similarities among price, quantity, and value indexes.

60. Describe three time series variables (recorded in dollars), one for each of the following:

    a. The series should be analyzed in original raw dollar form.

    b. The series should be deflated with an appropriate price index before analysis.

    c. The series should be analyzed both in raw dollars and in deflated dollars.

61. Describe the basic motivation for deflating a time series in dollars.

62. For which of the following time series variables would the analyst consider deflation, using an appropriate price index?

    a. Number of units produced per month.

    b. Number of overtime hours worked per week.

    c. Monthly dollar volume of spare parts received.

    d. Annual gross profit before taxes.

    e. Average weekly temperature of process.

    f. Dividends paid per quarter.

    g. Monthly cash balance.

    h. Miles driven per month by salespeople.

63. What are the criteria for choosing a base period in calculating any kind of index?

64. What are the advantages of updating the base period in an index? What are the disadvantages?

65. A market basket of goods is defined and priced in forming a price index. Over time, the market mix in the company or country will probably change. Discuss how to deal with this problem, recognizing both the advantages and disadvantages of changing the market basket at a later time.

66. Here is a composite price index developed by a company for use in deflating its annual net profit. The company now wishes to update the series to a more recent period, 1992. Calculate the new index values using this new base period.

Year	Composite price index
1982	246.7
1983	251.4
1984	260.8
1985	259.0
1986	262.2
1987	265.7
1988	270.9
1989	268.6
1990	272.4
1991	275.1
1992	277.8

67. Here are several values of the industrial production index. The series' base period is 1987. Calculate the new values of this series if the new base period is January 1992.

	Period	Industrial production index (1987 = 100)
1991	Sept.	111.4
	Oct.	109.8
	Nov.	107.5
	Dec.	105.2
1992	Jan.	104.7
	Feb.	107.3
	Mar.	106.7

Source: *Survey of Current Business.*

68. Here are the number of marriages in the United States for selected years. Form an index for this time series using 1980 as the base year.

Year	Marriages (in thousands)
1980	2,390
1985	2,425
1986	2,400
1987	2,403
1988	2,389
1989	2,404

Source: *Statistical Abstract of the United States,* 1988, 1989, 1991.

69. The number of divorces in the United States for selected years are shown. Form an index for this time series using 1989 as the base period.

Year	Divorces (in thousands)
1980	1,189
1985	1,187
1986	1,159
1987	1,166

Year	Divorces (in thousands)
1988	1,183
1989	1,163

Source: *Statistical Abstract of the United States,*
1988, 1991.

70. Here are price indexes for prescription drugs and physicians' services. Form a composite index from these two indexes using weights of 20% for drugs and 80% for physicians' services.

Year	Prescription drugs	Physicians' services
1983	213.8	352.3
1984	234.3	376.8
1985	256.5	398.8
1986	278.6	427.7

Source: *Statistical Abstract of the United States, 1988.*

71. Here are consumer price indexes for all urban consumers by the four major regions in the United States for all items. Write a paragraph summarizing the price comparisons for these regions.

Region	CPI-U (Dec. 1977 = 100)			
	1983	1984	1985	1986
Northeast	157.1	164.5	170.7	175.0
Midwest	162.6	168.6	173.7	175.8
South	161.7	168.4	173.8	176.6
West	160.0	167.4	174.5	178.6

Source: *Statistical Abstract of the United States, 1988.*

72. Seasonal indexes of the sales for the CAM Corporation are:

Jan.	120	April	108	July	105	Oct.	100
Feb.	90	May	102	Aug.	90	Nov.	110
Mar.	100	June	110	Sept.	85	Dec.	80

a. Total 1994 sales for the CAM corporation are forecasted to be $60,000. Based on the seasonal indexes, what should sales in the first three months of 1994 total?

b. December 1993 CAM Corporation sales totaled $5,000. Give a reasonable estimate of sales for January 1994 based on the seasonal indexes.

c. CAM Corporation sales amounted to $5,500 in November 1993. Calculate November 1993 sales after adjustment for seasonal variation with the indexes just given.

73. What level of management would tend to be interested in a long-range forecast of annual data? Which level would be most interested in a monthly forecast for the next three months?

74. When would the cyclical component of a time series not be used in making a forecast?

75. What is wrong with this statement? "As president of the company, I want to plan our future plant capacity and so would like to see a monthly forecast of sales dollars including all four components. Prepare a forecast for the next two years."

76. What is wrong with this statement? "As a supervisor of the landing gear assembly line for 737s, I would like to see a forecast of demand for this aircraft. Prepare an annual forecast for 737s for the next 15 years."

77. Here are dollar values (in millions) spent on magazine advertising for beer, wine, and liquor in the United States.

Year	Y	$\hat{Y}$
1980	239	247.5
1981	252	245.1
1982	258	242.6
1983	243	240.2
1984	230	237.7
1985	240	235.3
1986	225	232.8
1987	208	230.4
1988	213	227.9
1989	257	225.5

Source: *Statistical Abstract of the United States*, 1988, 1991.

a. Calculate the cyclical indicators for this series.

b. What is the trend equation for this series?

c. Calculate the average decrease per year in magazine advertising since 1980.

d. What factor(s) affect the trend of this variable?

e. Develop a cyclical chart.

f. What can be said about the cyclical component in this series?

g. Does the economy affect this cyclical component?

h. Which component is more important: trend or cyclical?

i. Forecast the amount to be spent on magazine advertising for beer, wine, and liquor in the United States for 1990. Use the cyclical for 1989.

78. Many firms watch the number of new housing starts in the United States as an indicator of the general level of economic prosperity in the country. The following data values are the monthly number of new housing starts in this country, in thousands.

	1982	1983	1984	1985	1986	1987
Jan.	47.6	92.9	109.2	105.4	115.7	105.1
Feb.	52.0	96.7	130.4	95.8	107.2	102.8
Mar.	78.7	135.8	138.1	145.2	151.0	141.3
Apr.	85.1	136.4	170.9	176.0	188.2	159.6
May	99.2	175.5	182.2	170.5	186.7	158.3
June	91.9	173.8	184.3	163.4	183.6	163.2
July	107.2	162.0	163.1	161.0	172.2	152.8
Aug.	97.2	177.7	147.8	161.1	163.8	143.8

	1982	1983	1984	1985	1986	1987
Sept.	108.4	156.8	149.6	148.6	153.2	152.3
Oct.	111.5	159.9	152.7	173.2	154.9	139.1
Nov.	110.0	136.4	126.5	124.1	115.7	118.9
Dec.	83.4	108.5	99.0	120.5	113.1	85.4

Source: *Survey of Current Business*, 1988.

a. Analyze this series, describing the trend, cyclical, seasonal, and irregular factors.

b. Forecast this series for the next four months by recombining the factors identified in the decomposition process.

79. Here are dollar sales per share for selected bituminous coal firms. Calculate the trend equation for these data and the cyclical indicators. Briefly describe the series using these two components.

Year	Y
1980	904.13
1981	998.00
1982	1,086.22
1983	769.85
1984	827.31
1985	836.07
1986	799.43
1987	687.57
1988	781.77
1989	962.93
1990	1,058.02

Source: *Standard & Poor's Industry Surveys*, October 1988, 1991.

80. Here are quarterly earnings per share for the Kmart Corporation. Analyze this quarterly time series to determine the effects of the trend, cyclical, seasonal, and irregular components.

Quarter:	1	2	3	4
1985	.31	.41	.43	1.27
1986	.47	.59	.44	1.34
1987	.57	.71	.54	1.58
1988	.60	.81	.63	1.96
1989	.24	.37	.27	.98
1990	.25	.37	.27	1.00
1991	.27	.41	.25	1.06

Source: *The Value Line Investment Survey* (New York: Value Line, 1988, 1989, 1991), p. 1638.

81. A company that makes potato chips and other salty snack foods is interested in the time series of monthly liquor store retail sales. It finds the following sales levels (in millions of dollars) in the local library.

Year:	1985	1986	1987	1988	1989	1990	1991
Jan.	1636	1503	1592	1589	1623	1663	1826
Feb.	1575	1489	1628	1578	1614	1701	1819
March	1601	1520	1600	1586	1619	1716	1833
April	1625	1493	1620	1616	1633	1706	1783
May	1596	1497	1638	1634	1648	1678	1769
June	1592	1519	1593	1626	1641	1715	1760
July	1607	1499	1597	1606	1655	1731	1794
Aug.	1598	1464	1591	1585	1649	1761	1822
Sept.	1598	1443	1593	1561	1656	1755	1774
Oct.	1465	1635	1588	1555	1673	1772	1788
Nov.	1482	1600	1550	1571	1663	1778	1781
Dec.	1495	1585	1561	1590	1630	1785	1642

Source: *Survey of Current Business*, 1988, 1992.

 a. Analyze this series, commenting on all four components.

 b. How useful do you think your analysis would be to the snack food company?

82. The following values represent the average annual three-month Treasury bill rate, in percentages for the years 1977 through 1988, found in *The Value Line Investment Survey* (New York: Value Line, 1988). Analyze this time series, indicating the trend of the series and the extent of the cyclical effect. Also, estimate the rate for 1989 and compare your estimate with *Value Line*'s estimate of 8.1.

   5.3, 7.2, 10.1, 11.4, 14.0, 10.6, 8.6, 9.5, 7.5, 6.0, 5.8, 6.7

83. After reading a *Financial World* article (November 14, 1989, p. 38) on how to increase technological development efforts to compete with Japan, a consulting company collects the following data to help it decide on a marketing strategy for its services. Data values represent monthly exports to China in millions of dollars.

Year:	1988	1989	1990	1991
Jan.	350.7	385.9	359.4	411.0
Feb.	375.2	499.2	516.7	486.3
March	401.6	581.8	356.4	472.9
April	348.9	355.2	499.8	505.8
May	401.0	471.0	381.4	630.9
June	348.9	355.2	499.8	505.8
July	399.7	644.7	385.7	538.5
Aug.	409.1	703.7	422.7	560.1
Sept.	406.5	456.2	354.8	470.8
Oct.	412.9	542.4	452.7	570.9
Nov.	449.3	305.0	329.9	621.5
Dec.	533.9	424.4	372.8	580.6

Source: *Survey of Current Business*, 1992.

 a. Analyze this monthly series including comments on all four components of the series.

 b. What do you think are the most significant factors in your analysis as far as the consulting firm is concerned?

 c. Do you think your analysis would help the consulting firm in its marketing efforts?

 d. Forecast this series for the next two months.

84. Describe the conditions under which the original units of measurement of a time series would be of more interest to the analyst than an index computed from these values.

85. Suppose you were president of a medium-sized company. If you could have any three indexes computed for you from company data and presented in a monthly report, which three would you choose?

86. If you were president of a company, which three dollar values would you like to see each month? Would you prefer that these values be in original dollars or deflated dollars?

87. Suppose your company is considering moving its operations to Kansas City. Before making a decision, what indexes would you like to see that summarize conditions in that city?

88. Locate *Value Line* in your library. Find a stock of interest to you and record the quarterly sales volume of this corporation. Analyze this time series to determine the trend, cyclical, seasonal, and irregular components. Summarize your findings in a brief memo, including the extent of your interest in investing your own money in this stock.

89. Locate the *Survey of Current Business* in your library. Find a monthly time series in this publication and record its values for five to seven years. Analyze this time series and report on the four components of the series.

90. Locate a copy of the *Statistical Abstract of the United States* in your library. Record the values of both an annual and a monthly time series from this publication and analyze each. Report your findings with reference to the major components of each series.

EXTENDED EXERCISES
. . . .

91. GARRY PRODUCTS, INC.

Garry Products produces heat shields used on rocket motors and is under contract with NASA to provide shields for the next five years. The company's chief accountant, Barry Mano, has been trying to find a way to monitor the company's cost of producing these shields. The company is under constant pressure from NASA to justify the price of its shields, since its contract with NASA is of the "cost-plus" type. Barry would like to find a way to quickly and easily show how the cost of parts used in the manufacture of the shields increases.

In a current issue of the *Survey of Current Business*, Barry finds the producer price index prepared by the federal government. He decides that this measure of wholesale price inflation would be useful in showing how most or all of the price increases result from material and labor price increases rather than higher company profit margins.

Barry measures the costs of materials and hourly labor for shields produced during the past nine months (Table 16.18). He also records the producer price index for these same months. He hopes that after the shield costs are deflated using this index, a more favorable cost picture will emerge, and NASA's pressure on the company will decline.

a. Use Table 16.18's information to prepare a deflated shield cost for June 1991 through March 1992.

b. Do you think the Garry Company will be successful in reducing NASA's concerns regarding the cost of heat shields?

92. MOOREHOUSE DRY GOODS COMPANY

Sally Moorehouse is president of a company founded by her parents. It currently makes and imports various garments for the wholesale trade on the East Coast and has enjoyed increasing

TABLE 16.18   Garry Company Costs and Producer Price Index (Extended Exercise 91)

Time period	Average shield cost (in $)	Producer price index (1987 = 100)
1991		
June	105,328	116.4
July	104,935	116.1
Aug.	106,833	116.2
Sept.	106,462	116.1
Oct.	107,631	116.4
Nov.	108,003	116.4
Dec.	108,414	115.9
1992		
Jan.	108,286	115.6
Feb.	109,141	116.1
March	109,354	116.1

Source: *Survey of Current Business*, April 1992.

sales levels for the past several years. Sally's main job is to monitor its overall performance and plan for the future.

Sally has just read "Faking It—When You Want the Style But Not the Price" in *Glamour* (October 1989). This article has given her some ideas about the company's clothing line, and she's considering some changes. First, she would like an accurate picture of past sales levels.

During the past 10 years, annual sales, measured in dollars, have increased dramatically. However, profits haven't shown the same increase, which puzzles Sally. She suspects that inflation during these years has caused at least some of the increase in annual dollar sales, and she would like to see the sales picture with inflation removed. She suspects that the picture won't look so rosy if this is done, which might affect her view of the company's past history and her plans for the future.

a. Locate the most current issue of the *Survey of Current Business* in your library.

b. Find the best price index for deflating the Moorehouse Company's annual sales, and record its value for the past 10 years.

c. Based on the index values you found, do you think Sally's concern about inflation during the past 10 years is justified? Explain.

93. CONE LUMBER COMPANY

Mildred Cone, an elderly widow, owns Cone Lumber Company. Her grandson, Robert Thomas, has just graduated from a local business school and, at his grandmother's urging, has decided to manage the business.

One of the first problems Robert faces as he learns his new job is trying to predict monthly company sales volume. Robert decides he should first investigate the company's monthly sales so he knows where he stands.

Monthly sales seem to have a seasonal pattern, with winter being slowest and spring and summer being best. Robert would like to find a way of forecasting the next 12 months' sales volumes at the beginning of each year so rational methods of ordering materials and scheduling the work can be used.

Here are the monthly sales levels, in thousands of dollars, for the past several months. Robert found these data values in the company's records.

	1989	1990	1991	1992
Jan.	29.7	28.4	30.7	31.2
Feb.	21.3	25.7	25.9	29.2
Mar.	30.1	29.9	32.5	30.5
Apr.	35.8	34.6	38.7	37.0
May	42.9	40.2	44.5	45.5
June	44.6	48.9	50.1	51.3
July	50.6	51.4	52.7	54.4
Aug.	48.5	52.9	50.1	50.7
Sept.	51.0	48.8	46.3	44.8
Oct.	44.5	47.2	42.3	43.8
Nov.	40.0	39.2	41.6	40.9
Dec.	32.5	35.4	29.7	30.1

a. Using a time series decomposition computer program, perform the decomposition analysis and summarize what you find about the four components in the series.

b. Forecast the first three months of 1993.

MICROCOMPUTER PACKAGE

The micro package *Computerized Business Statistics* can be used to solve time series analysis problems.

In Solved Exercise 1, Steve Donaldson needs to determine the long-term growth of median purchase prices of existing one-family houses in the West.

Computer Solution:

From the main menu of *Computerized Business Statistics* an 11 is selected, indicating Time Series and Forecasting. The time series and forecasting menu is shown on the screen. Since the problem involves entering data from the keyboard, a 1 is selected.

```
Time Series and Forecasting-Define New Problem
OPTIONS:  1 = Least Squares
          2 = Moving Averages
          3 = Simple Exponential Smoothing
          4 = Smoothing with Trend Factoring
          5 = Trend and Seasonal Smoothing
          6 = Seasonal Indices
Select Model: Enter 1-6, press ↵ 1
```

Since the least squares trend line is desired, a 1 is selected.

```
Linear or Logarithmic Trend: L/O, Press ↵ L
```

Since a linear model is desired, an L is selected.

```
Number of Data Points: Enter 4-125, Press ↵ 10
```

The history period involves 10 years of data.

```
Enter Variable Name (0-5 Char.), Press ↵ Price
```

The variable is entered as **Price**.

```
Problem Definition Correct: Y/N/Q, Press ↵ Y
```

After a **Y** response, the program is ready for the data to be entered.
    After the data have been entered the screen shows:

```
       Price
 1 =   89.3
 2 =   96.2
 3 =   98.9
 4 =   94.9
 5 =   95.8
 6 =   95.4
 7 =  100.9
 8 =  113.2
 9 =  124.9
10 =  139.9
Press F when Finished
```

There are 10 data points. An **F** is entered once the blanks have been filled in.

```
Save data? Enter Y/N, press ↵ N
```

The time series analysis menu reappears. A **7** is entered so that the problem can be run. The screen then displays the output menu. The choice in this case is **P** for printer.
    In Solved Exercise 5, the Consolidated Edison Company sells electricity and steam in New York City. Betty Springer is trying to determine if a seasonal pattern exists in the company's quarter revenues.

Computer Solution

The steps are the same as for the previous example until the Time Series and Forecasting Options Menu reappears. This time the Seasonal Indexes option is chosen.

```
Select Model: Enter 1–6, & Press ↵ 6
Number of Years: Enter 2–10 & Press ↵ 4
```

The history period involves four years of data.

```
Enter Variable Name (0–5 Char.) & Press ↵ Rev
```

The variable is entered as **Rev**.

```
Problem Definition Correct: Y/N/Q, Press ↵ Y
```

After a **Y** response, the program is ready for the data to be entered. There are 16 data points. An **F** is entered once the blanks have been filled in.
    After the data have been entered, the screen shows:

```
      Rev
1 = 1441
2 = 1209
3 = 1526
4 = 1321
5 = 1414
6 = 1187
7 = 1411
8 = 1185
9 = 1284
```

```
10 = 1125
11 = 1493
12 = 1192
13 = 1327
14 = 1102
15 = 1469
16 = 1213
Press F when Finished
```

There are 16 data points. An **F** is entered once the blanks have been filled in.

```
Save data? Enter Y/N, press ↵ N
```

The time series analysis menu then reappears. A **7** is entered so that the problem can be run. Next, the screen shows the output menu. The choice in this case is **P** for printer.

MINITAB COMPUTER PACKAGE

MINITAB can be used to analyze seasonal time series data. The MINITAB commands to analyze Solved Exercise 5 are:

```
MTB > SET C1
DATA> 1441 1209 1526 1321 1414 1187 1411 1185
DATA> 1284 1125 1493 1192 1327 1102 1469 1213
DATA> END
MTB > LET C2 = C1
MTB > LET C3 = C1
MTB > LET C4 = C1
MTB > DELETE 1 C2
MTB > DELETE 1:2 C3
MTB > DELETE 1:3 C4
MTB > LET C5 = C1+C2+C3+C4
MTB > PRINT C1-C5
```

ROW	C1	C2	C3	C4	C5
1	1441	1209	1526	1321	5497
2	1209	1526	1321	1414	5470
3	1526	1321	1414	1187	5448
4	1321	1414	1187	1411	5333
5	1414	1187	1411	1185	5197
6	1187	1411	1185	1284	5067
7	1411	1185	1284	1125	5005
8	1185	1284	1125	1493	5087
9	1284	1125	1493	1192	5094
10	1125	1493	1192	1327	5137
11	1493	1192	1327	1102	5114
12	1192	1327	1102	1469	5090
13	1327	1102	1469	1213	5111
14	1102	1469	1213		
15	1469	1213			
16	1213				

The first step is to compute a four-quarter moving total. The data are copied into columns 2, 3, and 4. Next, the DELETE command is used to delete the first observation in column 2, the first two observations in column 3, and the first three observations in column 4. The LET command is then used to add columns 1 through 4 and store the resulting four-quarter moving total in C5. Next, the same type of process is used to compute a two-year moving total and eventually the quarterly seasonal indexes.

```
MTB > LET C6 = C5
MTB > DELETE 1 C6
MTB > LET C7 = C5+C6
MTB > PRINT C1-C7
 ROW     C1      C2      C3      C4      C5      C6      C7
   1   1441    1209    1526    1321    5497    5470   10967
   2   1209    1526    1321    1414    5470    5448   10918
   3   1526    1321    1414    1187    5448    5333   10781
   4   1321    1414    1187    1411    5333    5197   10530
   5   1414    1187    1411    1185    5197    5067   10264
   6   1187    1411    1185    1284    5067    5005   10072
   7   1411    1185    1284    1125    5005    5087   10092
   8   1185    1284    1125    1493    5087    5094   10181
   9   1284    1125    1493    1192    5094    5137   10231
  10   1125    1493    1192    1327    5137    5114   10251
  11   1493    1192    1327    1102    5114    5090   10204
  12   1192    1327    1102    1469    5090    5111   10201
  13   1327    1102    1469    1213    5111
  14   1102    1469    1213
  15   1469    1213
  16   1213

MTB > LET C8 = C7/8
MTB > LET C9 = (C3/C8)*100
MTB > PRINT C9
C9
  111.316    96.794   104.925    90.180   109.977    94.122
  101.784    88.400   116.743    93.025   104.038    86.423
```

The four-quarter centered moving average (C8) is computed by dividing the two-year moving total (C7) stored in column 7 by 8. Each quarterly seasonal index is computed by dividing the actual value for each quarter (C3) by the four-quarter centered average for that quarter and multiplying by 100 so the result is an index number. The next commands are used to compute the medians for each quarter.

```
MTB > SET C10
DATA> 3 4 1 2 3 4 1 2 3 4 1 2
DATA> END
MTB > DESCRIBE C9;
SUBC> BY C10.
            C10      N    MEDIAN
C9           1       3    104.04
             2       3     88.40
             3       3    111.32
             4       3     94.12

MTB > STOP
```

The SET command is used to identify each quarter. The DESCRIBE command and the BY subcommand are used to compute several statistics of C9 for each value of C10. Only the relevant portion of the output is shown here. The last step, not shown here, is to adjust these values so that they sum to 400.

BUSINESS FORECASTING

Objectives

When you have completed this chapter, you will be able to:

Choose the appropriate forecasting technique for a particular real-world situation.

Measure the errors generated by a forecasting procedure.

Use naive, moving average, and exponential smoothing techniques to create a forecast.

Compute an autocorrelation coefficient.

Construct a correlogram.

Identify whether data are random, nonstationary, or seasonal.

Detect serial correlation in a time series.

Discuss potential solutions to the problem of serial correlation.

Use autoregressive and regression models to forecast.

The chart on the front page of *The Wall Street Journal*, June 15, 1992, showed consumer price index values for the past several quarters. A downward trend was evident.

This chapter could be titled "More Business Forecasting" because the past three chapters have discussed aspects of this subject. In Chapter 14, regression analysis used knowledge of *one* predictor variable to forecast a dependent variable. In Chapter 15, multiple regression analysis used knowledge of *two or more* predictor variables to forecast a dependent variable. In Chapter 16, decomposition of a time series was used to study the components of a series in isolation, and this knowledge was used to make forecasts.

WHY MANAGERS NEED TO KNOW ABOUT BUSINESS FORECASTING

This chapter describes additional techniques to generate forecasts of future values of a time series. The objective is to examine the pattern of the variable in past time periods and to use this pattern to extend values of the variable into the uncertain future. Methods of measuring forecast errors will be introduced, and the various forecasting methods discussed in this text will be summarized. As mentioned before, forecasting is one of a manager's most important tasks. This chapter concludes coverage of this critical topic.

Regarding *The Wall Street Journal* chart, many businesses closely watch the consumer price index as a measure of inflation. Forecasting this important indicator is of great interest to them. Many techniques in this chapter are commonly used to forecast such a series.

CHOOSING THE APPROPRIATE FORECASTING TECHNIQUE

Choosing a Forecasting Model

Forecasting involves extending past experiences into the future. The assumption is that the conditions that generated the historical data are indistinguishable from future conditions, except for those variables explicitly recognized by the forecasting model. To the extent that this assumption is not met, a forecast will be inaccurate unless modified by the judgment of the forecaster.

Recognition that forecasting techniques operate on data generated by historical events leads to identifying the following steps in the forecasting process:

1. Data collection and reduction.
2. Model building.
3. Model evaluation.
4. The forecast.

Often, the most challenging part of the forecasting process is obtaining the proper data and making sure they are correct. If the data are inappropriate or incorrect, the forecast will be inaccurate.

Model building means finding the appropriate model to use with the collected data. The simpler the model, the better the chances that the forecasting process will gain acceptance by managers who must make decisions. Often a balance must be struck between a sophisticated forecasting approach that offers slightly more accuracy and a simple approach that is easily understood by company decision makers.

A typical strategy for evaluating various forecasting methods involves the following steps:

Step 1 A forecasting method is chosen based on the analyst's examination of the pattern of past data.

Step 2 The data set is divided into two sections: an initialization part and a test part.

Step 3 The chosen forecasting method is used to develop fitted values from the initialization part of the data.

Step 4 The model is used to forecast the test part of the data, and the forecasting errors are computed and evaluated. (Measurement error will be discussed in the next section.)

Step 5 A decision about the model is made. The decision might be to use the model in its present form, to modify the model, to develop a forecast using another model and compare the results, or to discard the model and try something else.

The final step is using the selected model to forecast future values of the variable of interest. The actual forecast should be both quantitative and qualitative. The forecasting model provides the quantitative value, and the analyst's judgment provides any qualitative adjustments.

Several methods have been devised to measure the errors generated by a particular forecasting procedure. These methods basically consist of generating forecasts for past periods and comparing these forecasts to the actual values of the forecast variable. The difference between the forecast or estimated value and the observed value is similar to the residual in regression analysis. Equation 17.1 is used to compute the error for each forecast period:

Forecast Error Measurement

$$e_t = Y_t - F_t \tag{17.1}$$

where e_t = Forecast error in time period t
        Y_t = Actual value in time period t
        F_t = Forecast value for time period t

One method for evaluating a forecasting technique uses the summation of the absolute errors. The *mean absolute deviation* (MAD) is the average of the absolute values of the errors:

$$\text{MAD} = \frac{\Sigma |e_t|}{n} \tag{17.2}$$

The *mean squared error* (MSE) method can also be used to evaluate a forecasting technique. Each error is squared and summed and then divided by the number of observations. This approach involves a penalty for large forecasting errors because each error is squared:

$$MSE = \frac{\Sigma e_t^2}{n} \tag{17.3}$$

Sometimes it's useful to compute the forecasting errors in terms of percentages rather than amounts. The *mean absolute percentage error* (MAPE) is computed by finding the absolute error in each period, dividing this by the value actually observed for that period, and then averaging these absolute percentage errors. This approach is useful when the magnitude of the forecast variable is important in evaluating the accuracy of the forecast:

$$MAPE = \frac{\Sigma \frac{|e_t|}{Y_t}}{n} \tag{17.4}$$

Finally, it is sometimes necessary to determine whether a forecasting method is biased (consistently forecasting high or low). The *mean percentage error* (MPE) is computed by finding the error in each period, dividing this by the observed value for that period, and then averaging these percentage errors. If the forecasting approach is unbiased, Equation 17.5 will produce a percentage close to 0. If the result is a large positive percentage, the forecasting method is consistently underestimating. If the result is a large negative percentage, the forecasting method is consistently overestimating.

$$MPE = \frac{\Sigma \frac{e_t}{Y_t}}{n} \tag{17.5}$$

Example 17.1 illustrates how each of these error measurements is computed.

EXAMPLE 17.1   Table 17.1 shows Cosmos Perfume Company's demand (in cases), Y_t, and a forecast of these data, F_t. The forecasting technique used the previous period's demand to derive the forecast for the current period. This simple model will be discussed in the next section. Table 17.1 shows the computations for evaluating this model using MAD, MSE, MAPE, and MPE.

$$MAD = \frac{\Sigma |e_t|}{n} = \frac{39}{9} = 4.3$$

$$MSE = \frac{\Sigma e_t^2}{n} = \frac{213}{9} = 23.7$$

$$MAPE = \frac{\Sigma \frac{|e_t|}{Y_t}}{n} = \frac{64.2\%}{9} = 7.1\%$$

$$MPE = \frac{\Sigma \frac{e_t}{Y_t}}{n} = \frac{24.8\%}{9} = 2.8\%$$

TABLE 17.1   Computations for Forecast Evaluation Methods (Example 17.1)

Time, t	Demand (number of cases), Y_t	Forecast, F_t	Error, e_t	$\lvert e_t \rvert$	e_{t^2}	$\dfrac{\lvert e_t \rvert}{Y_t}$ (%)	$\dfrac{e_t}{Y_t}$ (%)
1	53	—	—	—	—	—	—
2	58	53	5	5	25	8.6	8.6
3	54	58	−4	4	16	7.4	−7.4
4	60	54	6	6	36	10.0	10.0
5	55	60	−5	5	25	9.1	−9.1
6	62	55	7	7	49	11.3	11.3
7	62	62	0	0	0	0.0	0.0
8	65	62	3	3	9	4.6	4.6
9	63	65	−2	2	4	3.2	−3.2
10	70	63	7	7	49	10.0	10.0
		Sums:	17	39	213	64.2	24.8

MAD indicates that each forecast deviated from the actual data by an average of 4.3 cases. The MSE of 23.7 and the MAPE of 7.1% can be compared to the MSE and MAPE for any other method used to forecast these data. Finally, the small MPE of 2.8% indicates that the model is not biased: since this value is close to 0, the model doesn't consistently over- or underestimate demand.

SIMPLE FORECASTING METHODS

Naive Forecasting Method   The easiest methods for forecasting a time series variable, **naive methods,** are intuitively appealing and are widely used by managers, either consciously or subconsciously. The simplest naive method uses the value for the current period as the forecast for the next period:

$$F_{t+1} = Y_t \qquad (17.6)$$

where F_{t+1} = Forecast for time period $t + 1$
Y_t = Y value for time period t

> **Naive methods** are very simple approaches to forecasting, such as using the value from the current period as the estimate for the next period.

This method is demonstrated in Example 17.2.

EXAMPLE 17.2   The Cosmos Perfume Company used the naive approach to forecast demand for cases in Table 17.1. The forecast for period 2 using Equation 17.6 is

$$F_{t+1} = Y_t$$
$$F_{1+1} = Y_1$$
$$F = 53$$

The forecast for period 11 is

$$F_{10+1} = Y_{10}$$
$$F_{11} = 70$$

The problem with this simple model is that it does not take trend or seasonality of the data into consideration. However, if the data have a trend, a naive model can be developed that takes into consideration the increase or decrease from one period to another. Also, if the data are seasonal, a model can be developed that forecasts, for example, this year's sales for June as the June sales from last year.

If a firm has been in business less than three years, the large amounts of data required for advanced forecasting models might not be available. Naive models are frequently used in situations where a new business hasn't had time to develop a useful historical data base.

Moving Averages

The **moving average** model uses the average of several past time periods as the forecast for the next period. In practice, the analyst must decide how many past periods to average. A trial-and-error process is often used to find the number of periods that would be best in minimizing the error; this process amounts to comparing the model's predictions against the known values of recent periods. The term *moving average* implies that as each new observation becomes available, a new mean is computed by dropping the oldest value used in the average and adding the newest one. This new mean is the forecast for the next period. Equation 17.7 is used to compute moving average forecasts:

Moving Average Method

$$F_{t+1} = \frac{Y_t + Y_{t-1} + Y_{t-2} + \cdots + Y_{t-m+1}}{m} \tag{17.7}$$

where F_{t+1} = Forecast for time period $t + 1$
      Y_t = Y value for time period t
      m = Number of terms in the moving average

> The **moving average** model uses the average of several past time periods as the forecast for the next period.

Example 17.3   The moving average method can be used with the data of Table 17.2 to produce a forecast for March (period 15). Suppose the analyst decides to use five periods in the averaging process. The forecast for June (period 6) is the average value of the variable for the five previous time periods, 132.4:

$$F_{t+1} = \frac{Y_t + Y_{t-1} + Y_{t-2} + \cdots + Y_{t-m+1}}{m}$$

TABLE 17.2 Moving Average Forecast for Example 17.3

t	Month	Cost of goods sold ($000s)	Five-month moving total	Five-month moving average	e_t
	1992				
1	Jan	125.7			
2	Feb	129.4			
3	Mar	131.7			
4	Apr	135.0			
5	May	140.2			
6	Jun	141.7	662.0	132.4	9.3
7	Jul	138.4	678.0	135.6	2.8
8	Aug	135.3	687.0	137.4	−2.1
9	Sep	130.9	690.6	138.1	−7.2
10	Oct	130.2	686.5	137.3	−7.1
11	Nov	131.8	676.5	135.3	−3.5
12	Dec	128.2	666.6	133.3	−5.1
	1993				
13	Jan	127.3	656.4	131.3	−4.0
14	Feb	129.3	646.8	129.4	−0.4

```
MEAN SQUARED ERROR (MSE)          =    28.41
MEAN ABSOLUTE PC ERROR (MAPE)     =     3.46%
MEAN PC ERROR (MPE) OR BIAS       =    −1.56%

PERIOD              FORECAST
  15                 129.36
```

$$F_{5+1} = \frac{Y_5 + Y_{5-1} + Y_{5-2} + \cdots + Y_{5-5+1}}{5}$$

$$F_6 = \frac{140.2 + 135.0 + 131.7 + 129.4 + 125.7}{5} = 132.4$$

This average is called "moving" because when the actual value for June becomes known, the averaging process will "move" down one month, dropping January's value and picking up the new June value. This process is repeated each month as a new data value becomes known. Finally, the forecast for period 15 (March) is 129.4:

$$F_{14+1} = \frac{Y_{14} + Y_{14-1} + Y_{14-2} + \cdots + Y_{14-5+1}}{m}$$

$$F_{15} = \frac{129.3 + 127.3 + 128.2 + 131.8 + 130.2}{5} = 129.4$$

EXPONENTIAL SMOOTHING

The disadvantage of the moving average process is that, regardless of how many time periods are used, every value is assumed to contribute equally to the forecast. In most actual situations, this isn't a realistic assumption. Rather, the forecast should usually rely most heavily on the most recent value, less on the value before that, even less on the value before that, and so on. The **exponential smoothing** technique uses a weighted average of past time series values to arrive at a smoothed forecast.

Exponential smoothing is so named because the weights attached to past time periods in forming the forecast decline exponentially. That is, the weights decrease rapidly at first and then less and less so as the time period becomes older. The weight attached to a particular value approaches, but never quite reaches, 0. This method generates accurate forecasts for many time series variables, recognizing the decreasing impact of past time periods as they fade further into the past. The weights used are α for the most recent observation, $\alpha(1 - \alpha)$ for the next most recent, $\alpha(1 - \alpha)^2$ for the next, and so forth. α (alpha) is a constant between 0 and 1. An exponential smoothing forecast is formulated using Equation 17.8:

$$F_{t+1} = \alpha Y_t + (1 - \alpha)F_t \qquad (17.8)$$

where F_{t+1} = Forecast for time period $t + 1$
Y_t = Y value for time period t
α = Smoothing constant, a value between 0 and 1
F_t = Average experience of the series smoothed to period t, or forecast value for period t

Equation 17.8 calls for combining two values in preparing the forecast: the most recent value for the time series (Y_t) and the average experience of the series smoothed to period t (F_t). The forecast is a weighted average of these two values. The smoothing constant, α, is the weight attached to the most recent observation in the series. When α is close to 1, the new forecast will be greatly affected by the most recent observation. When α is close to 0, the new forecast will be very similar to the old one.

> The **exponential smoothing** technique uses a weighted average of past time series values to arrive at smoothed forecasts.

The smoothing constant, α, is the key to the use of exponential smoothing. If forecasts need to be stable and random variations smoothed, a small α is required. If a rapid response to a real change in the pattern of observations is desired, a larger value of α is appropriate. Most exponential smoothing computer packages find the optimal smoothing constant by minimizing the sum of squares error: SSE $= \Sigma e_t^2$.

EXAMPLE 17.4   Jill Tilson owns a small art shop and is attempting to forecast her monthly sales based on past history. She specializes in abstract art and got some new ideas after reading "Exhibiting Abstract Painting in the Era of Its Belatedness" in *Arts Magazine* (March 1992, p. 60). She thinks it's essential to have a good forecast of future sales before initiating any changes suggested by the article.

In December, her forecast for January sales is $12,703. At the end of January, actual sales turn out to be $13,037. Exponential smoothing is being used to generate forecasts, and past experience has shown that a smoothing constant of .25 produces the most accurate forecast. Using Equation 17.8, the forecast prepared at the end of January for the month of February is

$$F_{t+1} = \alpha Y_t + (1 - \alpha)F_t$$
$$= (.25)(13,037) + (.75)(12,703) = 12,787$$

The forecast for February, $12,787, is a weighted average of past time series values (the previous forecast, $12,703) and the actual value of the time series in January ($13,037). The reasoning behind this process is that the same basic forecast is made each month, with some modification based on the actual time series value for that month. In this example, the weighting constant of .25 recognizes a significant, but not overpowering, contribution of the current time series value to the forecast for the next month.

Example 17.4 used a smoothing or weighting constant of .25. In practice, small smoothing constants are generally used because more accurate forecasts are generated if each forecast is modified only slightly by the current value of the variable. The previous forecast, using the exponential smoothing formula, is based on many past values of the variable and should usually be modified only slightly by the current value.

EXAMPLE 17.5 The time series data of Table 17.2 can be forecast using exponential smoothing. A good place to start is January 1992. For this month, the actual value of the time series variable is 125.7. Suppose a smoothing constant of .20 is chosen. Equation 17.8 calls for these two values, along with the value of the previous forecast. Since this is the first data value, an arbitrary value for the previous forecast is chosen. This value should be in the same range as the actual values of the time series, and the actual value of the first period is usually used. In fact, the value chosen for the previous forecast is not critical, because after several forecasts are prepared for future time periods, the influence of this value will have died away exponentially and will not substantially affect the forecast. Using Equation 17.8, the forecast for February (time period 2) is

$$F_{t+1} = \alpha Y_t + (1 - \alpha)F_t$$
$$F_{1+1} = \alpha Y_1 + (1 - \alpha)F_1$$
$$F_2 = (.20)(125.7) + (.80)(125.7) = 125.7$$

Table 17.3 shows the forecast values. The next three forecasts are computed below. Note that for each forecast, the previous forecast is used as the second term in the averaging process.

$$F_3 = (.20)(129.4) + (.80)(125.7) = 126.44$$
$$F_4 = (.20)(131.7) + (.80)(126.44) = 127.49$$
$$F_5 = (.20)(135.0) + (.80)(127.49) = 128.99$$

TABLE 17.3 Exponential Smoothing Forecast for Example 17.5

t		Y_t	F_t	e_t
	1992			
1	Jan	125.7	----	----
2	Feb	129.4	125.70	3.70
3	Mar	131.7	126.44	5.26
4	Apr	135.0	127.49	7.51
5	May	140.2	128.99	11.21
6	Jun	141.7	131.23	10.47
7	Jul	138.4	133.33	5.07
8	Aug	135.3	134.34	0.96
9	Sep	130.9	134.53	−3.63
10	Oct	130.2	133.81	−3.61
11	Nov	131.8	133.09	−1.29
12	Dec	128.2	132.83	−4.63
	1993			
13	Jan	127.3	131.90	−4.60
14	Feb	129.3	130.98	−1.68

```
MEAN SQUARED ERROR (MSE)          =      33.29
MEAN ABSOLUTE PC ERROR (MAPE)     =       3.63%
MEAN PC ERROR (MPE) OR BIAS       =       1.32%

PERIOD            FORECAST
  15              130.65
```

This process is continued until the forecast for March 1993 (period 15) is prepared:

$$F_{15} = (.20)(129.3) + (.80)(130.98) = 130.64$$

Note that the MSE for the smoothing constant of .2 is 33.29, the MAPE is 3.63%, and the MPE is 1.32%. If a smoothing constant of .6 is used, the MSE is reduced to 15.35, the MAPE is reduced to 2.6%, and the MPE is 0.26%. Knowledge of the cost of goods sold this month is evidently very important in forecasting for next month.

Actually, the optimal smoothing constant for these data is close to 1. This means that the naive forecasting model using Equation 17.6 would be appropriate.

The most basic exponential smoothing technique has just been presented. This forecasting method is often used in inventory control systems, where numerous items are to be forecast and low cost is a primary concern. Many statistical computer packages contain exponential smoothing procedures.

In addition to the basic method just described, extensions and modifications to this procedure are widely used. Details of these procedures can be found in more advanced texts on forecasting,[1] but the essential features of these methods are outlined here. Some of the more popular extensions of basic exponential smoothing include:

1. **Trend modifications.** When the time series experiences a trend over time, basic exponential smoothing will consistently underestimate a rising series and over-estimate a falling one. This problem can be solved by adding or subtracting an

---

[1]Recommended is John E. Hanke and Arthur G. Reitsch, *Business Forecasting*, 4th ed. (Boston: Allyn & Bacon, 1992).

amount to each forecast reflecting the trend. The degree of adjustment is constantly upgraded based on the most recent trend indication. A procedure known as *Holt's two-parameter linear exponential smoothing* allows the analyst to estimate separately the smoothed value for the time series and the average trend change at each point in time. The resulting smoothed values will track time series values more accurately for a series containing a trend.

2. **Trend and seasonal modifications.** In addition to a trend adjustment, some time series forecasts benefit from recognition of a seasonal factor. In a monthly or quarterly time series, certain adjustments for the month or quarter being forecast may produce a more accurate prediction. In a monthly series, a seasonal adjustment factor is established for January, one for February, and so on. In a quarterly series, modifications for the first, second, third, and fourth quarters are developed and modified as new data become available. A procedure known as *Winter's linear and seasonal exponential smoothing* allows the analyst to estimate separately the smoothed value of the time series, the average trend gain at each point in time, and a seasonality factor for each time period.

3. **Adaptive filtering.** The adaptive filtering procedure is aimed at finding the best set of weights to use in combining past periods to develop the forecast. A program is used that tests various sets of weights leading to lower and lower measurements of error in forecasting past periods until the optimal weights have been determined. These weights are then used in the forecasting equation for future periods.

EXERCISES

1. Identify the basic steps used in the forecasting process.
2. Describe the typical strategy for evaluating various forecasting methods.
3. Explain the difference between the MAD and the MSE methods for evaluating a forecasting technique.
4. Which method for evaluating a forecasting technique should be used in each of the following situations?
   a. The analyst needs to penalize large forecasting errors.
   b. The analyst feels that the magnitude of the forecast variable is important in evaluating the forecast's accuracy.
   c. The analyst needs to determine whether a forecasting method is biased.

5. Which of the following statements are true concerning the methods used to evaluate forecasts?
   a. The MSE penalizes large errors.
   b. The MAPE takes into consideration the magnitude of the values being forecast.
   c. The advantage of the MAD method is that it relates the size of error to the actual observation.
   d. The MPE is used to determine whether a model is systematically predicting too high or too low.
6. Which forecasting model assumes that the pattern exhibited by the historical observations can best be represented by an arithmetic mean of those observations?

7. Which forecasting model continually revises an estimate in light of more recent experiences?

8. Which forecasting model identifies the component factors that influence each of the values in a series?

9. Which forecasting method uses the value for the current period as the forecast for the next period?

10. Given the following series:

Time period	Y_t	F_t	e_t
1	100	100	—
2	110		
3	115		
4	116		
5	119		
6	120		
7	125		

a. Using a five-month moving average, what is the forecast for period 7?

b. If a smoothing constant of .3 is used, what is the exponentially smoothed forecast for period 4?

c. Continuing part b, what is the forecast error for time period 4?

11. Columbia Mutual Fund invests primarily in technology stocks. The net asset value of the fund at the end of each month of 1992 is as follows:

Month	Mutual fund price
Jan.	9.39
Feb.	8.96
Mar.	8.20
Apr.	7.89
May	8.43
June	9.98
July	9.51
Aug.	10.63
Sept.	9.78
Oct.	11.25
Nov.	11.18
Dec.	12.14

a. Find the forecast value of the mutual fund for each month, starting with February, by using the naive model.

b. Evaluate this forecasting method using MAD.

c. Evaluate this forecasting method using MSE.

d. Evaluate this forecasting method using MAPE.

e. Evaluate this forecasting method using MPE.

f. Forecast the mutual fund price for January 1993.

g. Write a memo summarizing your findings.

12. (This question refers to Exercise 11.) Use a five-month moving average to forecast the mutual fund price for January 1993. Is this forecast better than the forecast made using the naive model? Explain.

13. The yield on a general obligation bond for a small city fluctuates with the market. Monthly quotations for 1992 are:

Month	Yield
Jan.	9.27
Feb.	9.96
Mar.	10.06
Apr.	10.28
May	10.63
June	11.08
July	11.51
Aug.	10.99
Sept.	10.78
Oct.	10.55
Nov.	10.82
Dec.	9.96

a. Find the forecast value of the yield for the obligation bonds for each month, starting with June, by using a five-month moving average.

b. Find the forecast value of the yield for the obligation bonds for each month, starting with April, by using a three-month moving average.

c. Evaluate these forecasting methods using MAD.

d. Evaluate these forecasting methods using MSE.

e. Evaluate these forecasting methods using MAPE.

f. Evaluate these forecasting methods using MPE.

g. Forecast the yield for January 1993 using the best model.

h. Write a memo summarizing your findings.

14. (This question refers to Exercise 13.) Use exponential smoothing, with a smoothing constant of .3 and an initial value of 9.27, to forecast the yield for January 1993. Is this forecast better than the forecast made using the moving average model? Explain.

15. The Hughes Supply Company uses an inventory management method to determine monthly demands for various products. Demand values for the past 12 months for each product have been recorded and are available for future forecasting. Demand values for the past 12 months of 1992 for one electrical fixture are:

Month	Demand
Jan.	205
Feb.	251
Mar.	304
Apr.	284
May	352
June	300

Month	Demand
July	241
Aug.	284
Sept.	312
Oct.	289
Nov.	385
Dec.	256

Source: Hughes Supply Company records.

Use exponential smoothing with a smoothing constant of .2 and an initial value of 205 to forecast demand for January 1993.

16. Hugh Miller, analyst for Southdown Inc. (the nation's second largest cement producer) is attempting to forecast the company's quarterly revenues. The data in millions of dollars are:

Quarter:	1	2	3	4
1986	77.4	88.8	92.1	79.8
1987	77.5	89.1	92.4	80.1
1988	74.7	185.2	162.4	178.1
1989	129.1	158.4	160.6	138.7
1990	127.2	149.8	151.7	132.9
1991	103.0	136.8	141.3	123.5

Source: *Southdown Incorporated Annual Report*, various years.

a. Use exponential smoothing with a smoothing constant of .1 and an initial value of 77.4 to forecast earnings per share for first quarter 1992.

b. Use a smoothing constant of .6 and an initial value of 77.4 to forecast earnings per share for the first quarter of 1992.

c. Evaluate the two smoothing constants if actual quarterly revenue for first quarter 1992 is 107.6.

d. Estimate the smoothing constant that will provide the best forecast.

17. General American Investors Co., a closed-end regulated investment management company, invests primarily in medium- and high-quality stocks. Heather Campbell is studying the asset value per share for this company and would like to forecast this variable for first quarter 1992. The data are:

Quarter:	1	2	3	4
1985	16.98	18.47	17.63	20.63
1986	21.95	23.85	20.44	19.29
1987	22.75	23.94	24.84	16.70
1988	18.04	19.19	18.97	17.03
1989	18.23	19.80	22.89	21.41
1990	21.50	25.05	20.33	20.60
1991	25.33	26.06	28.89	30.60

Source: *General American Investors Company Annual Report*, various years.

Evaluate the asset value per share variable using the following forecasting methods: naive, moving average, and exponential smoothing. Note that actual asset value per share for first quarter 1992 was 27.45. Write a report for Heather indicating which method she should use and why.

Forecasting Using Regression

Econometric Model

In Chapters 14 and 15, regression analysis used knowledge of one or more predictor variables to forecast the variable of interest. In Chapter 16, a special case of regression analysis used time as the predictor variable to forecast the trend of the variable of interest. The use of a predictor variable allows the analyst to forecast the value of a dependent variable when there's a significant linear relationship between the dependent and predictor variables. When the dependent variable is in a time series, the regression analysis is known as an *econometric model*.

In Chapter 16, new passenger car registrations were analyzed using the time series decomposition technique. In that example, the cyclical component seemed to be affected by economic conditions. If this is true, an econometric model might be used to predict new passenger car registrations. If the analyst knows that demand for automobiles (and hence new passenger car registrations) closely follows the pattern of overall economic activity as measured by GNP, then it's possible to derive a prediction equation for new passenger car registrations as a function of the GNP.

For the prediction equation to be useful in forecasting a future value of new passenger car registrations, the analyst must obtain an estimate of the value of the predictor variable, GNP, for the same period in the future. If the value for GNP is unknown and can't be estimated for next year, it cannot be used to forecast new passenger car registrations. This general principle holds true for the predictor variable in any linear regression model used to forecast some future value of the dependent variable.

The essence of econometric model building using regression analysis is the identification and specification of causative factors to be used in a prediction equation. However, recall from Chapter 14 that use of statistical analysis does not allow the analyst to claim cause and effect. In econometric model building, the analyst develops a model based on the theory that the predictor variables influence the behavior of the dependent variable in ways that can be explained on a commonsense basis.

Large-scale econometric models are being used today to model specific firms within an industry, selected industries within the economy, and the total economy. Econometric models include any number of simultaneous multiple linear regression equations. Thus, econometric models are systems of simultaneous equations involving several predictor variables. Further examination of econometric model building is beyond the scope of this text, but many source books are available.

EXAMPLE 17.6 Fred Robnett, economist for Divico Appliance Corporation, must develop a prediction equation to be used during June for forecasting quarterly sales of air conditioners. Fred decides to use as predictor variables disposable personal income, the typical price of an air conditioner unit, and the number of housing starts, lagged one quarter. His rationale for including the last variable is that air conditioners are one of the last items added to the house, so there is a two-quarter lag between a housing start and an air conditioner purchase. The model he develops is

$$\hat{Y} = b_0 + b_1 X_1 + b_2 X_2 + b_3 X_3$$

where $\hat{Y}$ = Forecast of air conditioner sales for next quarter
   X_1 = Estimate of disposable personal income for next quarter
   X_2 = Housing starts last quarter
   X_3 = Price of a typical air conditioner unit this quarter

To forecast air conditioner sales for the third quarter, Fred must obtain the following information: an estimate of disposable personal income for the third quarter, usually supplied by government agencies; the number of housing starts in the first quarter; and the price charged during the present (second) quarter. Fred has the potential for developing a good model. He has to estimate only one of the predictor variables, disposable personal income. Fred will have actual data on both the second-quarter price of a typical air conditioner and the number of housing starts during the first quarter.

In Chapter 16, a *multiplicative* time series model was described, in which the seasonal fluctuation is proportional to the trend level for each observation. This section introduces an *additive* time series model, in which a constant amount is added to the time series trend estimate corresponding to the expected increase in the value of the dependent variable due to seasonal factors. In the multiplicative model, the trend estimate is multiplied by a fixed percentage. In the additive model, a constant amount is *added* to the trend estimate. Equation 17.9 is used to regress quarterly data using this method:

$$\hat{Y}_t = b_0 + b_1 S_1 + b_2 S_2 + b_3 S_3 \tag{17.9}$$

where $\hat{Y}$ = The forecast Y value
   S_1 = 1 if first quarter of the year; 0 otherwise
   S_2 = 1 if second quarter of the year; 0 otherwise
   S_3 = 1 if third quarter of the year; 0 otherwise
   b_0 = Constant
 b_1, b_2, b_3 = Regression coefficients

The variables S_1, S_2, and S_3 are dummy variables representing the first, second, and third quarter, respectively. Note that the four levels of the qualitative variable have been described with only three dummy variables. This is because the fourth quarter's mean will be accounted for by the intercept b_0. If S_1, S_2, and S_3 are all 0, the fourth quarter is represented by b_0.

EXAMPLE 17.7   Washington Water Power Company forecaster Dana Byrnes is trying to forecast electrical usage for residential customers for the third and fourth quarters of 1992. She knows that the data are seasonal and decides to use Equation 17.9 to develop a seasonal regression model. She gathers quarterly data from 1980 through the first two quarters of 1992. Table 17.4 shows electrical usage measured in millions of kilowatt-hours.

TABLE 17.4   Electrical Usage for Washington Water Power Company, 1980–1992
(Example 17.7)

Year	Quarter	Kilowatts (millions)	Year	Quarter	Kilowatts (millions)
1980	1	1,071	1987	1	933
	2	648		2	582
	3	480		3	490
	4	746		4	708
1981	1	965	1988	1	953
	2	661		2	604
	3	501		3	508
	4	768		4	758
1982	1	1,065	1989	1	1,054
	2	667		2	635
	3	486		3	538
	4	780		4	752
1983	1	926	1990	1	969
	2	618		2	655
	3	483		3	568
	4	757		4	752
1984	1	1,047	1991	1	1,085
	2	667		2	692
	3	495		3	568
	4	794		4	783
1985	1	1,068	1992	1	928
	2	625		2	655
	3	499		3	
	4	850		4	
1986	1	975			
	2	623			
	3	496			
	4	728			

Source: *Washington Water Power Annual Report*, various years.

Dana creates dummy variables S_1, S_2, and S_3, representing the first, second, and third quarters, respectively. She stores the data in a file called USAGE.DAT. The data for the four quarters of 1980 are:

Y_t	S_1	S_2	S_3
1071	1	0	0
648	0	1	0
480	0	0	1
746	0	0	0

Dana uses the following MINITAB commands to develop her regression equation and forecast the third and fourth quarters of 1992:

```
MTB > READ 'USAGE.DAT' C1-C4

    ROW     C1      C2     C3     C4
     1     1071      1      0      0
     2      648      0      1      0
     3      480      0      0      1
     4      746      0      0      0
     .      .
     .      .

MTB > NAME C1 'USAGE' C2 'S1' C3 'S2' C4 'S3'
MTB > REGRESS C1 3 PREDICTORS C2-C4;
SUBC> PREDICT 0 0 1;
SUBC> PREDICT 0 0 0.
       THE OUTPUT IS SHOWN IN TABLE 17.5
MTB > STOP
```

TABLE 17.5 MINITAB Output for Seasonal Regression Model for WWP (Example 17.7)

```
The regression equation is
USAGE = 765 + 238 S1 - 124 S2 - 255 S3

Predictor      Coef     Stdev    t ratio        P
Constant     764.67     12.18      62.79    0.000
S1           238.33     16.89      14.11    0.000
S2          -123.74     16.89      -7.33    0.000
S3          -255.33     17.22     -14.82    0.000

s = 42.19    R-sq = 95.3%    R-sq(adj) = 95.0%

Analysis of Variance

SOURCE         DF         SS         MS         F        P
Regression      3    1670269     556756    312.81    0.000
Error          46      81872       1780
Total          49    1752141

SOURCE         DF     SEQ SS
S1              1    1278969
S2              1        130
S3              1     391171

Unusual Observations
Obs.    S1      USAGE       Fit    Stdev.Fit    Residual    St.Resid
 24    0.00    850.00    764.67       12.18       85.33        2.11R
 45    1.00   1085.00   1003.00       11.70       82.00        2.02R

R denotes an obs. with a large st. resid.

Fit      Stdev.Fit       95% C.I.              95% P.I.
509.33     12.18     (484.81, 533.85)    (420.93, 597.74)

764.67     12.18     (740.15, 789.19)    (676.26, 853.07)
```

The seasonal regression model is

$$\hat{Y} = b_0 + b_1 S_1 + b_1 S_2 + b_3 S_3$$

```
USAGE = 764.67 + 238.33 S1 - 123.74 S2 - 255.33 S3
```

Dana notes that this model explains 95.3% of the dependent variable. The third- and fourth-quarter predictions are

```
USAGE = 764.67 + 238.33(0) - 123.74(0) - 255.33(1) (Third quarter)  = 509.34
USAGE = 764.67 + 238.33(0) - 123.74(0) - 255.33(0) (Fourth quarter) = 764.67
```

Note that the constant, 764.67, is the forecast for the fourth quarter. This value is also the average or mean of fourth-quarter electrical usage.

EXERCISES

18. Describe how econometric models are developed and give an example.

19. Explain the difference between a multiplicative model and an additive model.

20. Explain how dummy variables are used in a regression model to represent seasonality.

21. The following multiple regression equation was used to forecast quarterly sales data measured in thousands of units:

$$\hat{Y}_t = 1.2 + 2.1t + 4S_1 - 2S_2 + 0.8S_3$$

where $\hat{Y}_t$ = Forecast Y value for time period t
t = Time or trend effect
S_1 = 1 if first quarter of the year; 0 otherwise
S_2 = 1 if second quarter of the year; 0 otherwise
S_3 = 1 if third quarter of the year; 0 otherwise

a. What is the average growth in sales each quarter if seasonal effects are held constant?

b. What is the forecast for the fourth quarter if the value for the trend is 0?

c. How much are first-quarter sales ahead of fourth-quarter sales on average if the trend effect is held constant?

d. Forecast sales for period 20 (a second quarter).

e. Forecast sales for period 22 (a fourth quarter).

22. Dibrell Brothers, Inc., one of the top three U.S. tobacco dealers, purchases and processes leaf tobacco worldwide for sale to cigarette manufacturers. Hershel Roberts has the task of predicting 1993 sales. Quarterly 1985–92 data in millions of dollars are:

Quarter:	1	2	3	4
1985	59.2	182.0	70.6	69.9
1986	58.7	131.4	85.3	66.8
1987	56.7	125.4	75.7	50.3
1988	93.2	192.1	163.8	105.9
1989	103.2	234.1	184.7	163.0
1990	132.0	220.4	242.4	170.6
1991	161.7	301.6	313.6	226.1
1992	219.3	299.9	264.4	

Source: *Dibrell Brothers Incorporated Annual Report,* various years.

a. Develop a regression model that uses time or the trend to predict sales. Evaluate the model's accuracy. Forecast fourth-quarter sales.

b. Develop a multiple regression model that uses dummy variables to model the seasonal effect. Evaluate the model's accuracy. Forecast fourth-quarter sales.

c. Develop a multiple regression model that uses both trend and seasonality. Evaluate the model's accuracy. Forecast fourth-quarter sales.

d. Forecast sales for each quarter of 1993 using the best model.

23. National Presto manufactures small electrical appliances and housewares. It appears that there's a strong seasonal effect in its business. Develop a multiple regression model using dummy variables to forecast sales for the second, third, and fourth quarters of 1992. Write a report summarizing your results. Quarterly sales (in millions of dollars) are:

Quarter	1	2	3	4
1985	16.3	17.7	28.1	34.3
1986	17.3	16.7	32.2	42.3
1987	17.4	16.9	30.9	36.5
1988	17.5	16.5	28.6	45.5
1989	24.3	24.2	33.8	45.2
1990	20.6	18.7	28.1	59.6
1991	19.5	22.5	38.3	81.2
1992	24.9			

Source: *The Value Line Investment Survey* (New York: Value Line, 1988, 1989, 1992), p. 133.

AUTOCORRELATION

Recall that one underlying assumption of a regression model is that error terms are independent. With time series data, as discussed in Chapter 16, this assumption is questionable. When a variable is measured over time, it is frequently correlated with *itself*, when "lagged" one or more periods. This correlation between time series residuals is measured using the **autocorrelation** coefficient. Correlation between successive residuals is called *first-order autocorrelation*.

Autocorrelation Coefficient

> **Autocorrelation** is the correlation between a variable, lagged one or more periods, and itself.

Autocorrelation is illustrated by Table 17.6. Note that variables Y_{t-1} and Y_{t-2} are actually the Y values lagged by one and two periods, respectively. Y_t values for March (shown on the row for time period 3) are: March sales, $Y_t = 67$; February sales, $Y_{t-1} = 62$; and January sales, $Y_{t-2} = 54$.

Equation 17.10 is commonly used to compute the first-order autocorrelation coefficient, r_1 (the correlation between Y_t and Y_{t-1}):

$$r_1 = \frac{\sum_{t=1}^{n-1} (Y_t - \bar{Y})(Y_{t-1} - \bar{Y})}{\sum_{t=1}^{n} (Y_t - \bar{Y})^2} \tag{17.10}$$

TABLE 17.6 Wagner Florist Shop Monthly Sales (Example 17.8)

Time, t	Month	Original data, Y_t	Y lagged one period, Y_{t-1}	Y lagged two periods, Y_{t-2}
1	January	54	—	—
2	February	62	54	—
3	March	67	62	54
4	April	69	67	62
5	May	73	69	67
6	June	73	73	69
7	July	78	73	73
8	August	81	78	73
9	September	84	81	78
10	October	87	84	81
11	November	91	87	84
12	December	93	91	87

where r_1 = First-order autocorrelation coefficient
$\bar{Y}$ = Mean of the values of the series
Y_t = Observation at time period t
Y_{t-1} = Observation one time period earlier, or at time period $t-1$

Equation 17.11 is the formula for computing the order k autocorrelation coefficient, r_k, between observations that are k periods apart: Y_t and Y_{t-k}:

$$r_k = \frac{\sum_{t=1}^{n-k} (Y_t - \bar{Y})(Y_{t-k} - \bar{Y})}{\sum_{t=1}^{n} (Y_t - \bar{Y})^2} \qquad (17.11)$$

where r_k = Autocorrelation coefficient for a lag of k periods
$\bar{Y}$ = Mean of the values of the series
Y_t = Observation at time period t
Y_{t-k} = Observation k time periods earlier, or at time period $t-k$

EXAMPLE 17.8 Clara Wagner has collected monthly sales data for the last year for Wagner's Florist Shop (Table 17.6). Table 17.7 shows the computations that lead to the use of Equation 17.10.

The first-order autocorrelation coefficient, r_1 (the correlation between Y_t and Y_{t-1}) is computed using the summations from Table 17.7:

$$r_1 = \frac{\sum_{t=1}^{n-1} (Y_t - \bar{Y})(Y_{t-1} - \bar{Y})}{\sum_{t=1}^{n} (Y_t - \bar{Y})^2}$$

$$= \frac{1,079}{1,556} = .69$$

TABLE 17.7 Computations for the First-Order Autocorrelation (Example 17.8)

t	Y_t	Y_{t-1}	$(Y_t - \bar{Y})$	$(Y_{t-1} - \bar{Y})$	$(Y_t - \bar{Y})^2$	$(Y_t - \bar{Y})(Y_{t-1} - \bar{Y})$
1	54	—	-22	—	484	—
2	62	54	-14	-22	196	308
3	67	62	-9	-14	81	126
4	69	67	-7	-9	49	63
5	73	69	-3	-7	9	21
6	73	73	-3	-3	9	9
7	78	73	2	-3	4	-6
8	81	78	5	2	25	10
9	84	81	8	5	64	40
10	87	84	11	8	121	88
11	91	87	15	11	225	165
12	93	91	17	15	289	255
Sums:	912		0		1,556	1,079

$$\bar{Y} = \frac{912}{12} = 76$$

It appears that some autocorrelation exists in this time series lagged one time period. The correlation between Y_t and Y_{t-1} (the autocorrelation for lag 1) is .69. This means that the successive residuals for the monthly sales variable are somewhat correlated with each other. This information may give Clara valuable insights about her time series, may suggest use of an advanced forecasting method, and can warn her about using regression analysis with her data. The last situation will be discussed later in the chapter.

The second-order autocorrelation coefficient, r_2, or the correlation between Y_t and Y_{t-2}, is computed using Equation 17.11. The computations are shown in Table 17.8.

TABLE 17.8 Computations for the Second-Order Autocorrelation (Example 17.8)

t	Y_t	Y_{t-2}	$(Y_t - \bar{Y})$	$(Y_{t-2} - \bar{Y})$	$(Y_t - \bar{Y})^2$	$(Y_t - \bar{Y})(Y_{t-2} - \bar{Y})$
1	54	—	-22	—	484	—
2	62	—	-14	—	196	—
3	67	54	-9	-22	81	198
4	69	62	-7	-14	49	98
5	73	67	-3	-9	9	27
6	73	69	-3	-7	9	21
7	78	73	2	-3	4	-6
8	81	73	5	-3	25	-15
9	84	78	8	2	64	16
10	87	81	11	5	121	55
11	91	84	15	8	225	120
12	93	87	17	11	289	187
Sums:	912		0		1,556	701

$$r_2 = \frac{\sum\limits_{t=1}^{n-2} (Y_t - \bar{Y})(Y_{t-2} - \bar{Y})}{\sum\limits_{t=1}^{n} (Y_t - \bar{Y})^2}$$

$$= \frac{701}{1,556} = .45$$

It appears that moderate autocorrelation exists in this time series lagged two time periods. The correlation between Y_t and Y_{t-2} (the autocorrelation for lag 2) is .45. Note that the autocorrelation coefficient at lag 2 (.45) is less than the autocorrelation coefficient at lag 1 (.69). The denominator is the same for both computations; however, one fewer term is included in the numerator when the autocorrelation for lag 2 is computed. Generally, as the number of time lags, k, increases, the autocorrelation coefficient decreases.

Correlogram

Figure 17.1 shows a correlogram for the Wagner data in Example 17.8. The **correlogram** is a useful graphical tool for displaying autocorrelations for various lags of a time series. The vertical scale on the left shows the number of lagged time periods. The vertical scale on the right shows the autocorrelation coefficients (the correlations between Y_t and Y_{t-k}) corresponding to the number of lagged periods on the left. The horizontal scale at the bottom shows the possible range for an autocorrelation coefficient, -1 to $+1$. The autocorrelation coefficient for a particular time lag is shown relative to this horizontal scale. A vertical line is placed above 0 in the middle of the correlogram. Patterns in a correlogram are used to analyze patterns in the data. This concept is demonstrated in the next section.

FIGURE 17.1   Autocorrelations for Example 17.8

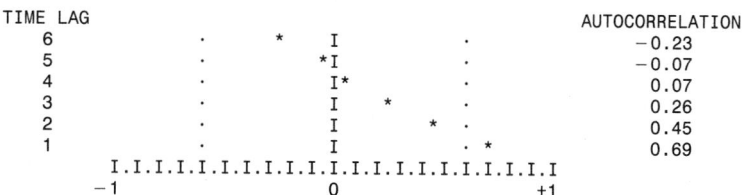

```
TIME LAG                                              AUTOCORRELATION
   6           .      *    I           .                  -0.23
   5           .          *I           .                  -0.07
   4           .           I*          .                   0.07
   3           .           I    *      .                   0.26
   2           .           I        *  .                   0.45
   1       .I.I.I.I.I.I.I.I.I.I.I.I.I.I.I.I.I.I                0.69
          -1                0                +1
```

The **correlogram** is a graphical tool for displaying the autocorrelations for various lags of a time series.

The MINITAB computer package can be used to compute autocorrelations and draw correlograms. The MINITAB commands to solve Example 17.8 are:

```
MTB > SET C1
DATA> 54 62 67 69 73 73 78 81 84 87 91 93
DATA> END
MTB > ACF C1


           -1.0  -0.8  -0.6  -0.4  -0.2   0.0   0.2   0.4   0.6   0.8   1.0
    1    0.693                               XXXXXXXXXXXXXXXXXX
    2    0.451                               XXXXXXXXXXXXX
    3    0.259                               XXXXXXX
    4    0.073                               XXX
    5   -0.069                            XXX
    6   -0.231                         XXXXXXX
    7   -0.307                        XXXXXXXXX
    8   -0.375                        XXXXXXXXXX
    9   -0.389                        XXXXXXXXXXX
   10   -0.365                        XXXXXXXXXX
   11   -0.240                         XXXXXXX
MTB> STOP
```

Note that the MINITAB correlogram differs from Figure 17.1. The autocorrelation scale is shown on the top of the graph instead of at the bottom. The number of lags and their autocorrelation coefficients appear on the left.

Chapter 16 showed how to decompose a time series into its components, including trend, cyclical, seasonal, and irregular. Now data patterns, including some of these components, will be studied using the autocorrelation analysis approach. Autocorrelation coefficients for different time lags of a variable will be used to answer the following questions about a time series data collection:

1. Are the data random?
2. Do the data have a trend (i.e., are they nonstationary)?
3. Are the data seasonal?

If a series is random, the correlation between Y_t and Y_{t-1} is close to 0, indicating that the successive values of a time series are not related to each other.

If a series has a trend, Y_t and Y_{t-1} will be highly correlated; the autocorrelation coefficients will typically differ significantly from 0 for the first several time lags and then gradually drop toward 0 as the number of time lags increases. The autocorrelation coefficient for time lag 1 will be quite large (close to 1). The autocorrelation coefficient for time lag 2 will also be large. However, it won't be as large as for time lag 1 because one fewer term is used to calculate its numerator.

If a series has a seasonal pattern, a significant autocorrelation coefficient will occur at the appropriate time lag, which is 4 for quarterly data and 12 for monthly data.

Table 17.9 shows a time series of 40 three-digit random numbers selected from a random number table. The autocorrelations computed from these data should theoretically equal 0. Of course, the 40 values in Table 17.9 constitute only one of a large number of possible samples of size 40, each of which will produce a different autocorrelation coefficient. Most of these samples will produce autocorrelation coefficients

TABLE 17.9 Time Series with 40 Selected Random Numbers (Example 17.9)

t	Y_t	t	Y_t
1	269	21	465
2	219	22	675
3	058	23	950
4	030	24	013
5	554	25	617
6	221	26	536
7	264	27	767
8	903	28	591
9	082	29	357
10	172	30	961
11	333	31	860
12	602	32	155
13	466	33	491
14	875	34	268
15	119	35	556
16	869	36	183
17	446	37	018
18	505	38	865
19	484	39	191
20	632	40	713

close to 0. But a sample could produce an autocorrelation coefficient significantly different from 0 just by chance.

How does an analyst determine whether an autocorrelation coefficient for the data of Table 17.9 is significantly different from 0? A sampling distribution of autocorrelation coefficients could theoretically be developed by taking an infinite number of samples of 40 random numbers.

Quenouille[2] and others have demonstrated that the autocorrelation coefficients of random data have a sampling distribution that can be approximated by a normal curve with a mean of 0 and standard deviation of $1/\sqrt{n}$. Knowing this, the analyst can compare the sample autocorrelation coefficients with this theoretical sampling distribution and determine if they come from a population whose mean is 0 at particular time lags.

Autocorrelation Hypothesis Test

Actually, the autocorrelation coefficients for all time lags can be tested simultaneously. If the series is truly random, most of the sample autocorrelation coefficients should lie within the range specified by 0 plus or minus a certain number of standard errors. At a specified confidence level, a series can be considered random if the calculated autocorrelation coefficients are all within the interval produced by Equation 17.12:

$$0 \pm z(1/\sqrt{n}) \tag{17.12}$$

[2]M. H. Quenouille, "The Joint Distribution of Serial Correlation Coefficients," *Annuals of Mathematical Statistics* 20 (1949), pp. 561–71.

where z = Standard normal value for a given confidence level
             n = Number of observations in the data series

This procedure is illustrated in Example 17.9.

EXAMPLE 17.9   A hypothesis test is developed to determine whether the series presented in Table 17.9 is random. The null and alternative hypotheses to test if the autocorrelation coefficient for a particular time lag is significantly different from 0 are

$$H_0: \rho_k = 0$$
$$H_1: \rho_k \neq 0$$

Since $n = 40$, the standard error (standard deviation of the sampling distribution of autocorrelation coefficients) is $1/\sqrt{40} = .158$. If the null hypothesis is tested at the .05 significance level, the correct standard normal z value is 1.96, and the critical value is $1.96(.158) = .310$. The decision rule is

If an autocorrelation coefficient is less than $-.310$ or greater than .310, reject the null hypothesis (reject H_0 if $r_k < -.310$ or $r_k > .310$).

The autocorrelation coefficients for the data of Table 17.9 are plotted on a correlogram (Figure 17.2). The two dotted lines parallel to the vertical axis are the 95% confidence limits ($-.310$ and .310). Twenty time lags are checked, and all autocorrelation coefficients lie within these limits. The analyst concludes that this series is random.

If a series has a trend, a significant relationship exists between successive time series values. The autocorrelation coefficients typically differ significantly from 0 for the first several time lags and then gradually drop toward 0 as the number of periods increases.

FIGURE 17.2   Autocorrelations for Random Data (Example 17.9)

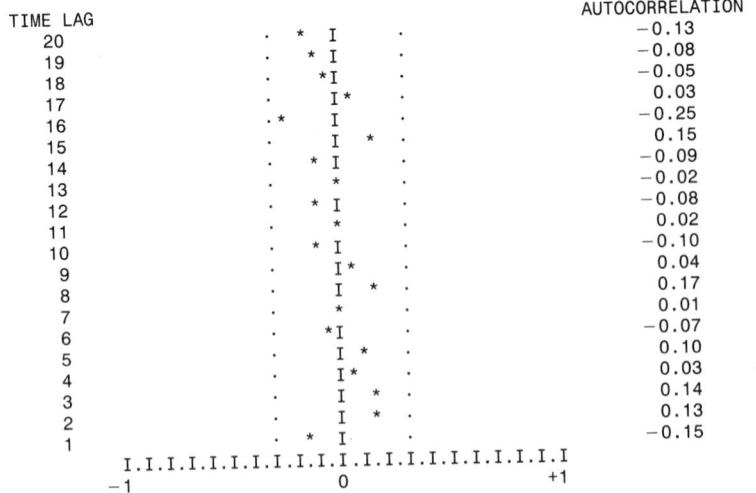

TIME LAG		AUTOCORRELATION
20	`.    *  I    .`	−0.13
19	`.   *  I    .`	−0.08
18	`.     *I    .`	−0.05
17	`.      I *  .`	0.03
16	`.  *   I    .`	−0.25
15	`.      I  *  .`	0.15
14	`.    *  I    .`	−0.09
13	`.      *    .`	−0.02
12	`.    *  I    .`	−0.08
11	`.      *    .`	0.02
10	`.    *  I    .`	−0.10
9	`.      I*   .`	0.04
8	`.      I  *  .`	0.17
7	`.      *    .`	0.01
6	`.     *I    .`	−0.07
5	`.      I *  .`	0.10
4	`.      I*   .`	0.03
3	`.      I  * .`	0.14
2	`.      I  * .`	0.13
1	`.    *  I.   .`	−0.15

```
I.I.I.I.I.I.I.I.I.I.I.I.I.I.I.I.I.I.I.I.I
-1              0              +1
```

Stationary Series

Some advanced forecasting models, such as the Box-Jenkins models, are designed for use with stationary time series. A **stationary series** is one whose basic statistical properties, such as the mean and the variance, remain constant over time. A series that contains no growth or decline is said to be stationary. A series that contains a trend is said to be nonstationary. The autocorrelation coefficients of stationary data drop to 0 after the second or third time lag, whereas for a nonstationary series they differ significantly from 0 for several time periods. In a nonstationary series, the trend must be removed before any further analysis is undertaken, such as analyzing the series with the Box-Jenkins procedures.

A **stationary series** is one whose mean and variance do not change over time.

Differencing

A method called *differencing* is used to remove the trend from a nonstationary series. Y_{t-1} is subtracted from Y_t, Y_{t-2} is subtracted from Y_{t-1}, and so forth, thus creating a new series. This process is illustrated in Table 17.10. The differenced series in Table 17.10 has transformed the original series to a new form. In this new form, the mean and variance remain constant over time; in other words, the series is stationary.

TABLE 17.10 Time Series Illustrating Differenced Data

t	Y_t	Y_{t-1}	$Y_t' = Y_t - Y_{t-1}$
1	21		—
2	24	21	3
3	29	24	5
4	38	29	9
5	40	38	2
6	39	40	−1
7	45	39	6
8	50	45	5
9	60	50	10
10	63	60	3
11	70	63	7
12	71	70	1

The MINITAB computer package can be used to difference data. The MINITAB commands to difference the data in Table 17.10 are:

```
MTB > SET C1
DATA> 21 24 29 38 40 39 45 50 60 63 70 71
MTB > END
MTB > DIFFERENCES 1 FOR C1, STORE IN C2
MTB > PRINT C1-C2
```

```
ROW   C1   C2
  1   21
  2   24    3
  3   29    5
  4   38    9
  5   40    2
  6   39   -1
  7   45    6
  8   50    5
  9   60   10
 10   63    3
 11   70    7
 12   71    1

MTB > STOP
```

The data in column C1 are differenced and stored in column C2. The PRINT command shows the result, which is the same as for Table 17.10.

EXAMPLE 17.10   Jenny Jefferies, a Wall Street analyst, is forecasting the transportation index. She gathers data for a 24-day period from the *Survey of Current Business*. First, Jenny computes a 95% confidence interval for the autocorrelation coefficients:

$$0 \pm 1.96(1/\sqrt{24}) = 0 \pm .40$$

Next, she uses a computer program to compute the autocorrelation coefficients presented in the correlogram in Figure 17.3.

FIGURE 17.3   Autocorrelations for Trend Data (Example 17.10)

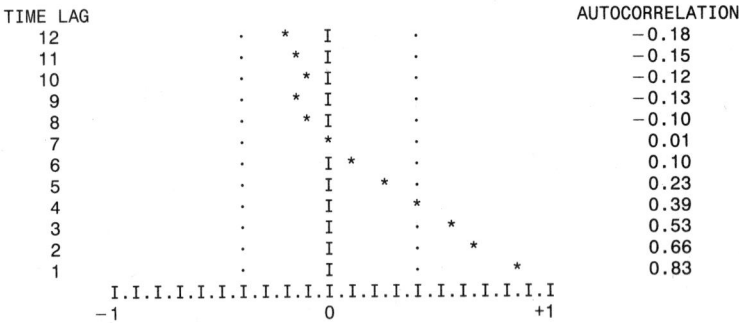

Examining the correlogram, she notices that the autocorrelations for the first three time lags differ significantly from 0: .83, .66, and .53. The values then drop gradually toward 0 rather than dropping exponentially. She decides that a trend exists in the data.

Jenny discovers that the advanced forecasting model she wants to experiment with requires that the series be stationary. She differences the data and uses a computer program to compute the autocorrelation coefficients for the differenced data. The correlogram shown in Figure 17.4 presents the results.

FIGURE 17.4 Autocorrelations for Trend Data Differenced (Example 17.10)

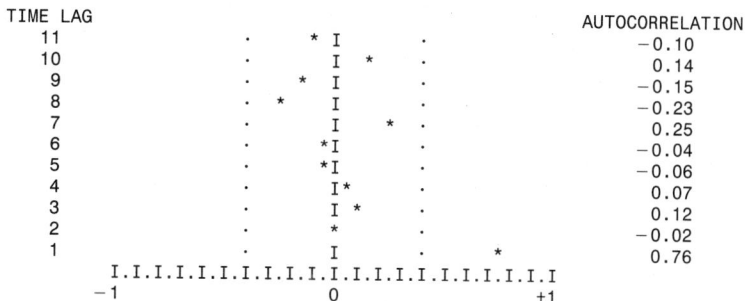

```
TIME LAG                                                      AUTOCORRELATION
  11                    .      * I        .                       -0.10
  10                    .        I   *    .                        0.14
   9                    .    *   I        .                       -0.15
   8                    .  *     I        .                       -0.23
   7                    .        I   *    .                        0.25
   6                    .       *I        .                       -0.04
   5                    .       *I        .                       -0.06
   4                    .        I*        .                       0.07
   3                    .        I *      .                        0.12
   2                    .       *          .                      -0.02
   1                    .        I      .        *                 0.76
         I.I.I.I.I.I.I.I.I.I.I.I.I.I.I.I.I.I.I.I.I
         -1                      0                 +1
```

Jenny is pleased because the autocorrelations for the differenced data are stationary and show that some pattern exists. (The first correlation coefficient equals .76; the autocorrelations then drop off to 0.) She can now use an appropriate advanced forecasting procedure.

If a series is seasonal, a pattern in the data repeats itself regularly during a particular interval of time (usually a year), and a significant autocorrelation coefficient will occur at the appropriate time lag. If quarterly data are analyzed, a significant autocorrelation coefficient will appear at time lag 4. If monthly data are analyzed, a significant autocorrelation coefficient will appear at time lag 12. That is, Januarys will correlate with other Januarys, Februarys with other Februarys, and so on. Example 17.11 illustrates a series that is seasonal.

EXAMPLE 17.11 Cordella Roberts (analyst for the Outboard Marine Corporation) long felt that sales were seasonal, but her company's absorption of six boat builders between 1986 and 1988 (*The Value Line Investment Survey*, 1988) makes her question this assumption. Cordella gathers 1984–92 quarterly sales data on Outboard Marine Corporation (Table 17.11) and computes a 95% confidence interval for the autocorrelation coefficients:

$$0 \pm 1.96 \; 1/\sqrt{34}$$
$$0 \pm .336$$

Next, she uses a computer program to compute the autocorrelation coefficients presented in the correlogram shown in Figure 17.5.

Cordella notes that the autocorrelation coefficient at time lag 4 is significantly different from 0 (.73 > .336). She concludes that Outboard Marine sales are seasonal on a quarterly basis.

If the autocorrelation coefficients of stationary data drop to 0 after the second or third time lag, the series may have a pattern that can be modeled by advanced forecasting techniques, such as the Box-Jenkins models. Example 17.12 illustrates a series with a pattern that might be forecast using such techniques.

TABLE 17.11   Quarterly Sales for Outboard Marine, 1984–1992 (Example 17.11)

Fiscal year ends	Dec. 31	Mar. 31	June 30	Sept. 30
1984	147.6	251.8	273.1	249.1
1985	139.3	221.2	260.2	259.5
1986	140.5	245.5	298.8	287.0
1987	168.8	322.6	393.5	404.3
1988	259.7	401.1	464.6	479.7
1989	264.4	402.6	411.3	385.9
1990	232.7	309.2	310.7	293.0
1991	205.1	234.4	285.4	258.7
1992	193.2	263.7		

Source: *The Value Line Investment Survey* (New York: Value Line, 1988, 1992), p. 1768.

FIGURE 17.5   Autocorrelations for Seasonal Data (Example 17.11)

```
TIME LAG                                                      AUTOCORRELATION
   9                      .    *  I    .                           -0.21
   8                      .       I    *.                           0.28
   7                      .      *I    .                           -0.06
   6                      .    *  I    .                           -0.12
   5                      .   \   I  *  .                           0.17
   4                      .       I    .           *               0.73
   3                      .       I       *                        0.34
   2                      .       I    * .                         0.22
   1                      .       I     .*                         0.45
          I.I.I.I.I.I.I.I.I.I.I.I.I.I.I.I.I.I.I.I.I.I.I
         -1                      0                   +1
```

EXAMPLE 17.12   Evelyn Dunning of Central Chemical Corporation is responsible for anticipating the readings of a particular chemical process. Evelyn has gathered the past 75 readings for the process (Table 17.12) and wonders if there's some pattern to the data. First, she computes a 95% confidence interval for the autocorrelation coefficients:

$$0 \pm 1.96(1/\sqrt{75}) = 0 \pm .226$$

TABLE 17.12   Readings for the Cenex Chemical Process (in Sequence by Columns) (Example 17.12)

60	99	75	79	62	89	72	90
81	26	78	65	81	51	66	78
72	93	66	99	76	85	74	87
78	75	97	72	84	59	66	99
62	57	60	78	57	90	73	72
78	88	98	63	84	60	104	
57	77	61	66	74	78	60	
84	82	96	84	78	66	81	
82	72	80	66	49	97	87	
67	77	72	87	78	65	73	

Next, Evelyn uses a computer program to compute the autocorrelation coefficients (the correlogram in Figure 17.6).

FIGURE 17.6   Autocorrelations for Data with a Pattern (Example 17.12)

```
TIME LAG                                              AUTOCORRELATION
  20             .     I   *.                              0.18
  19            .*     I    .                             -0.18
  18             .     I *  .                              0.10
  17             .    *I    .                             -0.07
  16            . *    I    .                             -0.13
  15             .     I    *                              0.24
  14            *      I    .                             -0.24
  13             .     I  *.                               0.19
  12            .*     I    .                             -0.18
  11             .     I *  .                              0.16
  10            . *    I    .                             -0.16
   9             .     I *  .                              0.08
   8             .    *I    .                             -0.04
   7             .     I *  .                              0.16
   6            . *    I    .                             -0.15
   5             .     I *  .                              0.14
   4             .     *    .                              0.01
   3             .    *I    .                             -0.07
   2             .     I  .*                               0.28
   1      *      .     I    .                             -0.53
        I.I.I.I.I.I.I.I.I.I.I.I.I.I.I.I.I.I.I.I.I
        -1                  0                  +1
```

Evelyn notes that the first two autocorrelation coefficients, −.53 for time lag 1 and .28 for time lag 2, are significantly different from 0, and the autocorrelations then drop close to 0. She concludes that the data do have a pattern that might be modeled by an advanced forecasting technique.

EXAMPLE 17.13   Stu Miller (forecaster for Sears, Roebuck) is attempting to forecast 1992 operating revenue. He collects the data shown in Table 17.13 for the years 1955 through 1991. Stu considers regression analysis, but isn't sure that he can find the proper variables to explain the variability in Sears' sales. Instead, Stu decides to use autocorrelation analysis to study the patterns of his variable. Stu runs these data on a computer program that performs autocorrelation analysis (Figure 17.7).

Stu notes that a 95% confidence interval has been computed and is shown in Figure 17.7 by the dotted lines. Computations for the dotted lines are

$$0 \pm 1.96(1/\sqrt{37})$$
$$0 \pm .322$$

Stu examines the correlogram, noticing that the autocorrelations for the first seven time lags are significantly different from 0 (.92, .83, .73, .64, .55, .46, and .37) and the values then gradually drop to 0. He decides that the data have a trend.

Stu first differences the data and uses his computer program to calculate the autocorrelation coefficients in Figure 17.8. He notes that the autocorrelation coefficient at time lag 3, .65, is significantly different from 0 and that the first two autocorrelation

TABLE 17.13   Operating Revenue for Sears, Roebuck and Disposable Personal Income, 1955–1991 (Example 17.13)

Year	Sears sales Y_t	Disposable personal income X_t	Sears sales lagged one period Y_{t-1}
1955	3,307	273.4	—
1956	3,556	291.3	3,307
1957	3,601	306.9	3,556
1958	3,721	317.1	3,601
1959	4,036	336.1	3,721
1960	4,134	349.4	4,036
1961	4,268	362.9	4,134
1962	4,578	383.9	4,268
1963	5,093	402.8	4,578
1964	5,716	437.0	5,093
1965	6,357	472.2	5,716
1966	6,769	510.4	6,357
1967	7,296	544.5	6,769
1968	8,178	588.1	7,296
1969	8,844	630.4	8,178
1970	9,251	685.9	8,844
1971	10,006	776.8	9,251
1972	10,991	839.6	10,006
1973	12,306	949.8	10,991
1974	13,101	1,038.4	12,306
1975	13,639	1,142.8	13,101
1976	14,950	1,252.6	13,639
1977	17,224	1,379.3	14,950
1978	17,946	1,551.2	17,224
1979	17,514	1,729.3	17,946
1980	25,195	1,918.0	17,514
1981	27,357	2,127.6	25,195
1982	30,020	2,261.4	27,357
1983	35,883	2,428.1	30,020
1984	38,828	2,670.6	35,883
1985	40,715	2,841.1	38,828
1986	44,282	3,022.1	40.715
1987	48,440	3,205.9	44,282
1988	50,251	3,477.8	48.440
1989	53,794	3,725.5	50,251
1990	55,972	4,058.8	53,794
1991	57,242	4,218.4	55,972

Sources: Sears Operating Revenue: *Industry Surveys.* Disposable personal income: *Survey of Current Business,* various years.

coefficients and the fourth are close to being significant. After time lag 3, the pattern appears to drop to 0. Stu wonders whether there is some pattern in these data that can be modeled by one of the more advanced forecasting techniques.

EXERCISES

24. Explain the concept of autocorrelation.

FIGURE 17.7 Autocorrelations for Sears, Roebuck Sales (Example 17.13)

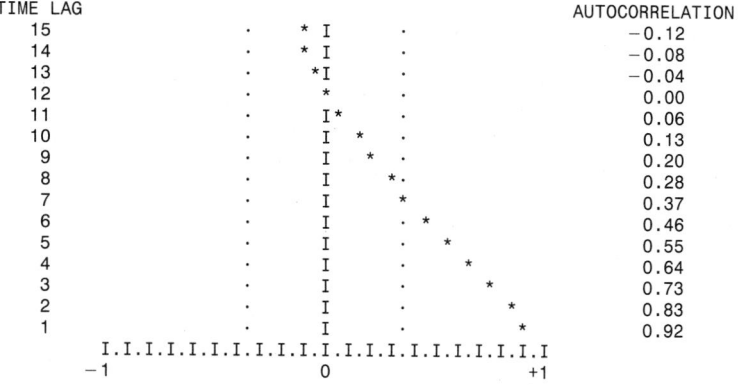

```
TIME LAG                                                    AUTOCORRELATION
   15              .      *  I        .                          −0.12
   14              .      *  I        .                          −0.08
   13              .        *I        .                          −0.04
   12              .         *         .                          0.00
   11              .        I*         .                          0.06
   10              .        I    *    .                           0.13
    9              .        I      *  .                           0.20
    8              .        I        *.                           0.28
    7              .        I        *                            0.37
    6              .        I        .  *                         0.46
    5              .        I        .    *                       0.55
    4              .        I        .        *                   0.64
    3              .        I        .            *               0.73
    2              .        I        .                *           0.83
    1              .        I        .                    *       0.92
       I.I.I.I.I.I.I.I.I.I.I.I.I.I.I.I.I.I.I.I.I
      −1                   0                     +1
```

FIGURE 17.8 Autocorrelations for Sears, Roebuck Sales First Differenced (Example 17.13)

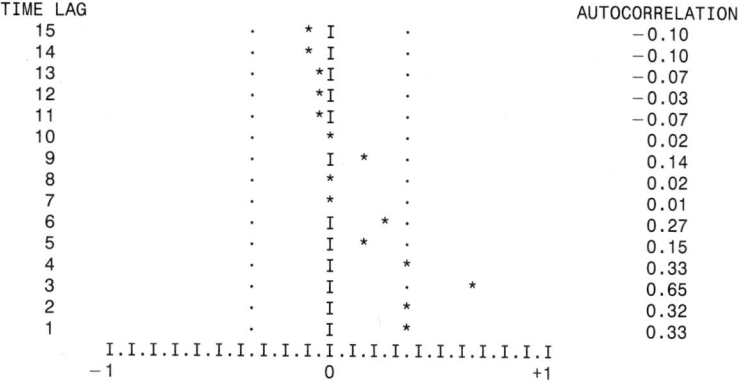

```
TIME LAG                                                    AUTOCORRELATION
   15              .      *  I        .                          −0.10
   14              .      *  I        .                          −0.10
   13              .        *I        .                          −0.07
   12              .        *I        .                          −0.03
   11              .        *I        .                          −0.07
   10              .         *         .                          0.02
    9              .        I  *      .                           0.14
    8              .         *         .                          0.02
    7              .         *         .                          0.01
    6              .        I      *  .                           0.27
    5              .        I  *      .                           0.15
    4              .        I      *                              0.33
    3              .        I        .    *                       0.65
    2              .        I      *                              0.32
    1              .        I      *                              0.33
       I.I.I.I.I.I.I.I.I.I.I.I.I.I.I.I.I.I.I.I.I
      −1                   0                     +1
```

25. What does an autocorrelation coefficient measure?

26. Name and describe the graphical tool analysts use to display the autocorrelations for various lags of a time series.

27. Each of the following statements describes either a stationary or nonstationary series. Indicate which.

    a. A series whose mean and variance remain constant over time.

    b. A series that contains no growth or decline.

    c. A series that has a trend.

    d. A series whose average value is changing over time.

28. How does an analyst determine whether an autocorrelation coefficient is significantly different from 0?

29. Each of the following statements describes a series that either is random, has a trend, or is seasonal. Identify which.

a. A high relationship exists between each successive value.

b. Successive values of a time series are not related to each other.

c. A significant autocorrelation coefficient appears at time lag 12.

d. The autocorrelation coefficients are typically significantly different from 0 for the first several time lags, and then gradually drop to 0 as the number of periods increases.

30. The number of stores owned by Sears has been recorded from 1978 to 1991. Compute the first differences for these data.

Year	Sears stores
1978	862
1979	866
1980	864
1981	851
1982	831
1983	813
1984	798
1985	799
1986	1,047
1987	1,100
1988	1,649
1989	1,731
1990	1,765
1991	1,800

Source: *Statistical Abstract of the United States,* 1988, 1992.

31. Dominion Bank's chief loan officer wants to analyze the bank's loan portfolio from 1984 to 1991. The quarterly data (in millions of dollars) are:

Year	Mar. 31	June 30	Sept. 30	Dec. 31
1984	2313	2495	2609	2792
1985	2860	3099	3202	3161
1986	3399	3471	3545	3851
1987	4458	4850	5093	5318
1988	5756	6013	6158	6289
1989	6369	6568	6646	6861
1990	6836	6918	6782	6680
1991	6424	6283	6130	5939

Source: *The Value Line Investment Survey* (New York: Value Line, 1988, 1992), p. 2017.

a. Compute the autocorrelations for time lags 1 and 2. Test to determine whether these autocorrelation coefficients are significantly different from 0 at the .05 significance level.

b. First difference the bank's quarterly loan data. Now compute the autocorrelation for time lag 1 using the first differenced data.

32. Analyze the autocorrelation coefficients for the series in Figures 17.9, 17.10, and 17.11. Briefly describe each series.

FIGURE 17.9   Autocorrelations for Exercise 32

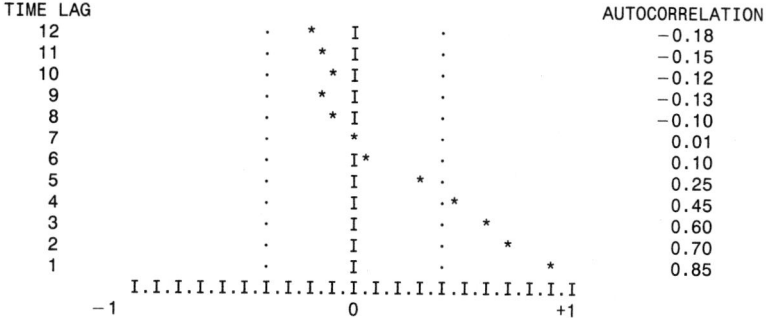

```
TIME LAG                                                    AUTOCORRELATION
  12                    .    *   I       .                     -0.18
  11                    .      *  I      .                     -0.15
  10                    .       *  I     .                     -0.12
   9                    .       *  I     .                     -0.13
   8                    .       *  I     .                     -0.10
   7                    .          *     .                      0.01
   6                    .          I*    .                      0.10
   5                    .          I   * .                      0.25
   4                    .          I       .*                   0.45
   3                    .          I       .    *              0.60
   2                    .          I       .       *           0.70
   1                    .          I       .           *       0.85
      I.I.I.I.I.I.I.I.I.I.I.I.I.I.I.I.I.I.I.I.I.I.I
      -1                          0                    +1
```

FIGURE 17.10   Autocorrelations for Exercise 32

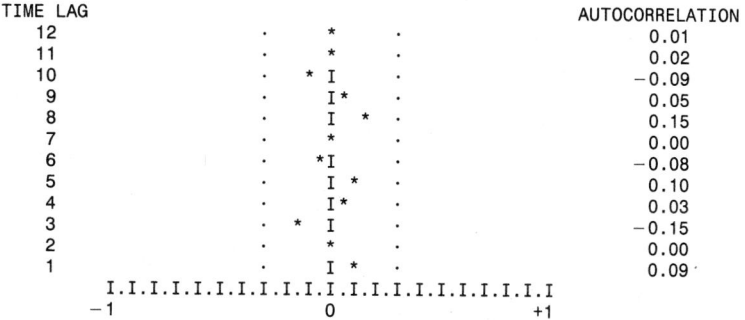

```
TIME LAG                                                    AUTOCORRELATION
  12                    .          *     .                      0.01
  11                    .          *     .                      0.02
  10                    .       *  I     .                     -0.09
   9                    .          I*    .                      0.05
   8                    .          I  *  .                      0.15
   7                    .          *     .                      0.00
   6                    .         *I     .                     -0.08
   5                    .          I *   .                      0.10
   4                    .          I*    .                      0.03
   3                    .       *  I     .                     -0.15
   2                    .          *     .                      0.00
   1                    .          I *   .                      0.09
      I.I.I.I.I.I.I.I.I.I.I.I.I.I.I.I.I.I.I.I.I.I.I
      -1                          0                    +1
```

FIGURE 17.11   Autocorrelations for Exercise 32

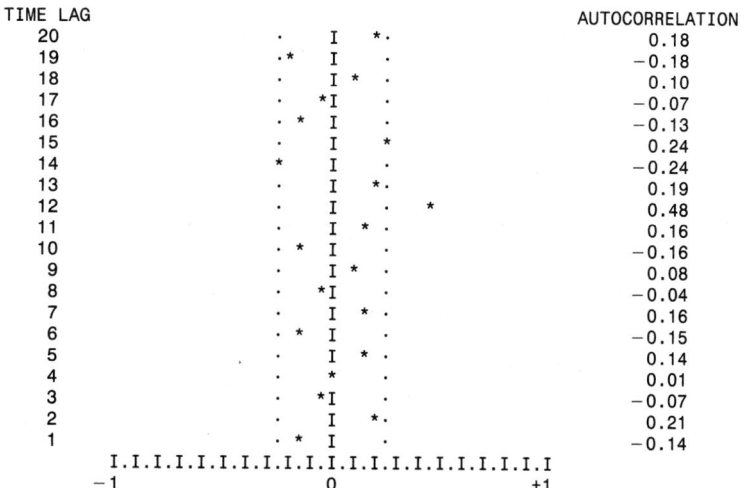

```
TIME LAG                                                    AUTOCORRELATION
  20                    .       I    *.                         0.18
  19                   .*       I       .                      -0.18
  18                    .       I  *    .                       0.10
  17                    .      *I       .                      -0.07
  16                    . *     I       .                      -0.13
  15                    .       I    *                          0.24
  14                   *        I       .                      -0.24
  13                    .       I    *.                         0.19
  12                    .       I       .     *                 0.48
  11                    .       I  * .                          0.16
  10                    . *     I       .                      -0.16
   9                    .       I *     .                       0.08
   8                    .      *I       .                      -0.04
   7                    .       I  * .                          0.16
   6                    . *     I       .                      -0.15
   5                    .       I  * .                          0.14
   4                    .       *       .                       0.01
   3                    .      *I       .                      -0.07
   2                    .       I    *.                         0.21
   1                    . *     I       .                      -0.14
      I.I.I.I.I.I.I.I.I.I.I.I.I.I.I.I.I.I.I.I.I.I.I
      -1                          0                    +1
```

33. Compute the 95% confidence interval for the autocorrelation coefficients for a series of 100 items.

34. Compute the 99% confidence interval for the autocorrelation coefficients for a series of 80 items.

35. The Springtime Catering Corporation wants to expand to cater weddings. James Sloan, company analyst, is to analyze the pattern for the number of marriages for the past 20 years. He has 1965–89 data for the number of marriages (in thousands):

Year	Marriages	Year	Marriages
1965	1,800	1978	2,282
1966	1,857	1979	2,342
1967	1,927	1980	2,390
1968	2,069	1981	2,422
1969	2,145	1982	2,456
1970	2,159	1983	2,446
1971	2,190	1984	2,477
1972	2,282	1985	2,413
1973	2,284	1986	2,407
1974	2,230	1987	2,403
1975	2,153	1988	2,389
1976	2,155	1989	2,404
1977	2,178		

Source: U.S. Dept. of Health and Human Services, National Center for Health Statistics, and *Statistical Abstract of the United States.*

a. Compute the autocorrelations through lag 12 and construct a correlogram.

b. Are the data stationary? If not, compute the first differences for these data.

c. Are the first differences random or is there a pattern?

THE PROBLEM OF AUTOCORRELATION IN REGRESSING TIME SERIES DATA

In Chapters 14 and 15, regression analysis procedures used knowledge of linear relationships to predict the dependent variable of interest. In Chapter 16, a special case of regression analysis used time as a predictor variable to forecast the trend of the variable of interest. One of the underlying assumptions of the regression technique is that the error terms are independent of each other, which implies that a random sample has been selected from the population.

When time series variables are analyzed, this assumption of independence is frequently violated because time series are not randomly chosen samples. In most time series, there's some relationship between the value of the dependent variable in one time period and its value in the next. High sales in one month, for example, usually lead to high sales in the next month. A low unemployment rate in one quarter usually is followed by a low rate in the next quarter. For this reason, correlated error terms are likely whenever regression analysis is used to predict a time series variable.

Serial Correlation

Serial correlation is the term used to describe the situation in which each error term is a function of the previous time period's error term. The autocorrelation coefficient is used to measure serial correlation. Recall Equation 14.5: $y_t = \beta_0 + \beta_1 x_t + \varepsilon_t$. This equation indicates that the error term (ε_t) is the difference between an actual population y value and its value as predicted by the population regression line. As mentioned, one of the underlying assumptions of regression analysis is that the error terms are independent. This assumption can be evaluated using Equation 17.13:

$$\varepsilon_t = \rho_1 \varepsilon_{t-1} + v_t \qquad (17.13)$$

where ε_t = Error term at time period t
$\qquad \varepsilon_{t-1}$ = Error term at time period $t - 1$
$\qquad \rho_1$ = First-order autocorrelation coefficient measuring
$\qquad\qquad$ the correlation between successive error terms
$\qquad v_t$ = Normally distributed independent disturbance term

For serial correlation to exist, all that's needed is for the level of the error term ε_{t-1} to directly affect the level of the next error term, ε_t. The magnitude of the first-order autocorrelation coefficient, ρ_1, indicates the strength of the serial correlation between successive error terms. If $\rho_1 = 0$, the error terms are independent ($\varepsilon_t = v_t$), and there's no serial correlation.

Serial correlation exists when successive observations over time are related to each other.

It should be reemphasized that the residual is the observed vertical deviation of y from the sample regression line and so is known. This residual is different from the model error term, ε_t. The error term is the vertical deviation of y from the unknown population regression line; hence it is unknown.

A major cause of autocorrelated residuals is a specification error, such as an omitted variable or an incorrect functional form. When the time-sequenced effects of a missing variable are positively related, the residuals tend to be positively autocorrelated because the effects of the missing variable are explained by time.

EXAMPLE 17.14 Chapter 16 forecast the number of new passenger car registrations using the decomposition approach. A linear trend line was fitted to the data, and the two variables (new passenger car registrations and time) were shown to be linearly related. In a technical sense, the number of new passenger cars registered can be thought of as unrelated to time. Instead, time is used as a substitute for variables that the registrations variable is actually related to, but that are ignored, unknown, difficult to measure, or too costly to measure.

The model using a linear trend might appear to be a good one, explaining a large portion of the variance in new passenger car registrations. Unfortunately, serial correlation is a potential problem. The model specification might have left out an important variable, such as the driving-age population, that might have a direct impact on auto registrations. If so, the time variable is explaining variance in new passenger car registrations that should be explained by driving-age population. If there's a shift in the direction of the driving-age population variable, the model using time may provide inaccurate forecasts.

Serial correlation in a time series, since it violates one of the key assumptions in regression analysis (a random sample), creates serious problems. Basically, the entire regression analysis must be considered suspect when autocorrelated residuals are present. More specifically, the following problems can result from regressing an autocorrelated series:

1. The regression coefficients in the regression equation are unreliable; that is, they tend to vary widely from one sample to the next. Interpretations based on the regression coefficients may therefore be misleading.
2. The standard error of estimate may be seriously understated, making R^2 spuriously high. The result is that the regression equation may appear to have much greater predictive power in the population than it really does.
3. Confidence intervals and tests employing the t and F distributions can be misleading. These tests rest on the assumption that a random sample has been taken. When this isn't the case, they may lead to erroneous conclusions about the population.

Because of these potential problems, it is always important to check for autocorrelated residuals when a time series variable is subjected to regression analysis. The following examples examine the possibility of serial correlation.

EXAMPLE 17.15   A study called "Using Segmentation to Improve Sales Forecasts Based on Purchase Intent: Which Intenders Actually Buy" (*Journal of Marketing Research*, November 1992) used segments (a stratification sampling as discussed in Chapter 2) to generate improved forecasts.[3] A sample of 12,116 persons indicated the intensity of their intention to buy cars and personal computers along with demographic characteristics such as income. The purpose of the study was improving the ability of forecasters to determine whether a person who intends to buy a product actually does so. Since the data were collected randomly during a short time period, serial correlation is not a problem.

EXAMPLE 17.16   Y. H. Kim and Fay D. Cobb (1992) investigated the accuracy of different models for forecasting corporate earnings.[4] They collected data on quarterly earnings per share from the first quarter 1981 through the fourth quarter 1991 from the *Industrial Compustat Data File* for 40 firms. Suppose a regression model for quarterly earnings per share for Abbott Laboratories and net profit after taxes pro-

---

[3]V. Morwitz and D. Schmittlein, "Using Segmentation to Improve Sales Forecasts Based on Purchase Intent: Which Intenders Actually Buy," *Journal of Marketing Research*, (November 1992), p. 291.

[4]Y. H. Kim and F. D. Cobb, "Forecasting Quarterly Earnings Per Share with Time-Series Methods" 1992 Proceedings Decision Sciences Institute, San Francisco, Vol. 3, p. 1145.

duced an r^2 of 97 percent. This value must be regarded as suspect because the dependent variable is a time series and so serial correlation is possible.

DETECTION OF SERIAL CORRELATION

Serial correlation is the condition in which successive values of the dependent variable in a time series are correlated. Another way of stating this condition is that the residuals, $Y - \hat{Y}$, are correlated from one time period to the next. In such a situation, the assumption of a random sample underlying the regression analysis procedure is violated.

Examination of the table of residuals may reveal the correlation, especially if it's strong. When autocorrelated residuals are present, the differences between the Y values and the regression line estimates, $\hat{Y}$, tend to be similar from one time period to the next, and strings of residuals with the same sign appear.

EXAMPLE 17.17 Birch Corporation analyst Arthur MacKelvie wants to predict yearly dollar sales of the company using regression analysis. The company is considering borrowing money to enter the water-selling market, and this projection is part of preparations for a meeting with Birch's banker. This market is of great interest to Birch management after an article on profits from selling water appeared in the *Los Angeles Times* business section, September 10, 1989.

Arthur is using disposable personal income as the predictor variable. Table 17.14 shows the results of this regression run. Arthur is happy with these results. R^2 equals .995, and the computed t value is 56.9. The model looks good until Arthur examines the table of residuals. Correlation exists between successive values of the dependent variable: the residuals are not randomly distributed but follow a definite pattern. The first five residuals are negative, followed by a string of seven positive residuals. The model starts out consistently overestimating Y, and then, beginning with period 6, it consistently underestimates Y.

The serial correlation in Table 17.14 is easily detected because it is an extreme example. Many cases aren't so obvious, so a statistical test has been developed. The **Durbin-Watson test** is used to determine whether residuals are autocorrelated. The differences between successive residuals are used to calculate the test statistic. The Durbin-Watson statistic is an important feature of most regression analysis programs.

Durbin-Watson Test

The **Durbin-Watson test** detects the presence of autocorrelated residuals (serial correlation) in the regression of a time series.

$$\text{DW} = \frac{\sum\limits_{t=2}^{n} (e_t - e_{t-1})^2}{\sum\limits_{t=1}^{n} e_t^2}$$

(17.14)

TABLE 17.14   Table of Residuals for Birch Corporation (Example 17.17)

VARIABLE NO.	MEAN	STANDARD DEVIATION	CORRELATION X VS Y	REGRESSION COEFFICIENT	STD. ERROR OF REG COEF.	COMPUTED T VALUE
2	600.65	232.36	0.998	0.029	0.00051	56.9
DEPENDENT						
1	16.03	6.80				
INTERCEPT			−1.505	R SQUARED		0.9954
STD. ERROR OF ESTIMATE			0.47665	DURBIN-WATSON STATISTIC		0.7218

TABLE OF RESIDUALS

OBSERVATION	OBSERVED VALUE	PREDICTED VALUE	RESIDUAL
1	8.0	8.30671	−0.30671
2	8.2	8.69495	−0.49495
3	8.5	9.08904	−0.58904
4	9.2	9.08904	−0.50206
5	10.2	10.25378	−0.05378
6	11.4	11.25214	0.14786
7	12.8	12.27968	0.52032
8	13.6	13.39480	0.20520
9	14.6	14.39023	0.20977
10	16.4	15.66298	0.73701
11	17.8	16.89778	0.90222
12	18.6	18.51791	0.08209
13	20.0	20.17892	−0.17892
14	21.9	21.88663	0.01337
15	24.9	24.85834	0.04166
16	27.3	27.20825	0.09175
17	29.1	29.92599	−0.82599

where   DW = Durbin-Watson statistic
e_t = Residual in current time period
e_{t-1} = Residual in preceding time period

Examining Equation 17.14, we see that if the residuals are autocorrelated, they'll be close to each other from one time period to the next. In this case, a small Durbin-Watson statistic will result since the numerator measures the error differences between adjacent time periods. On the other hand, if the residuals are not autocorrelated, a large Durbin-Watson statistic will result. This is because the error terms tend to vary widely from one time period to the next, resulting in a large numerator.

Appendix E.10 contains the Durbin-Watson table and is consulted once the Durbin-Watson statistic has been computed to see whether autocorrelated residuals are present. Note that there are two tables in Appendix E.10: one for the .05 significance level and one for the .01 level. Additional table listings would be necessary for other significance levels.

The column labeled k in the Durbin-Watson table indicates the number of predictor variables used in the regression. Note that there are two columns of Durbin-Watson values under each k. These values represent the lower limit (d_L) and upper limit (d_U) for the test. Sample size dictates which row to use. The Durbin-Watson statistic is interpreted as follows:

1. If the Durbin-Watson statistic computed from the data is below the lower limit, the residuals are positively autocorrelated.

2. If the test statistic is above the upper limit, the residuals are randomly distributed (no autocorrelation).

3. If the test statistic is between the lower and upper limits, the test is inconclusive. A larger sample is needed to determine whether the residuals are autocorrelated.

EXAMPLE 17.18 Continuing Example 17.17, Birch Corporation analyst Arthur MacKelvie is fairly sure that his residuals were autocorrelated. However, he decides to perform the appropriate hypothesis test.

The null and alternative hypotheses are

$$H_0: \quad \rho_1 \leq 0$$
$$H_1: \quad \rho_1 > 0$$

Arthur decides to use the .05 significance level and consults the Durbin-Watson table in Appendix E.10. Since he uses one predictor variable with a sample size of 17, the critical values are $d_L = 1.13$ and $d_U = 1.38$. The decision rule for the .05 significance level is

> Reject the null hypothesis if the calculated Durbin-Watson statistic is less than 1.13. Fail to reject the null hypothesis if the calculated Durbin-Watson statistic is greater than 1.38. If the calculated Durbin-Watson statistic lies between 1.13 and 1.38, the test is inconclusive.

Since the test statistic computed from the sample data (see Table 17.14) is below the critical value from the table ($0.72 < 1.13$), the null hypothesis is rejected. Arthur concludes that the residuals for Birch Corporation's yearly dollar sales volume are positively autocorrelated. He needs to take steps to correct this problem before a regression equation can be used for forecasting.

EXAMPLE 17.19 Parkins Company analyst Linda Lancaster wants to predict monthly cost of goods sold using regression analysis. She has identified four other variables measured each month as possible predictor variables. A combination of two predictor variables appears to produce an accurate prediction equation, with significant t, F, and R^2 values. The Durbin-Watson test statistic is computed to be 1.08 for the sample of 24 months.

Linda decides to use the .01 significance level and consults the Durbin-Watson table in Appendix E.10. For two predictor variables with a sample size of 24, the critical values are $d_L = 0.96$ and $d_U = 1.30$. The decision rule for the .01 significance level is

> Reject the null hypothesis if the calculated Durbin-Watson statistic is less than 0.96. Fail to reject the null hypothesis if the calculated Durbin-Watson statistic is greater than 1.30. If the calculated Durbin-Watson statistic lies between 0.96 and 1.30, the test is inconclusive.

Since the test statistic computed from the sample data is between the critical values from the table, $0.96 < 1.08 < 1.30$, the test is inconclusive. Linda must now consider the risks associated with having serial correlation in her regression equation. She decides that she can't trust the equation to produce accurate predictions using the present data.

Linda knows that if she can obtain data for three years instead of just two, the Durbin-Watson test might be more conclusive. However, only 24 months of data are available. Linda must find some other solution to her problem of serial correlation.

SOLUTIONS TO THE PROBLEM OF SERIAL CORRELATION

Analysts usually check for positively autocorrelated residuals when a regression analysis is performed on time series data. If positively autocorrelated residuals are revealed by the Durbin-Watson test, this situation must be corrected before evaluating the regression equation's effectiveness. The appropriate method for removing autocorrelated residuals depends on what caused them in the first place. Serial correlation can be caused by a specification error (such as an omitted variable), or the independent residuals may be correlated in a correctly specified equation.

The solution to the problem of serial correlation begins with an evaluation of the model specification. Is the model's functional form correct? Were any key variables omitted? Are there specification errors with some pattern over time that might have introduced correlation into the residuals? Since a major cause of positively autocorrelated residuals in business is the omission of a key variable, the best approach is to identify this missing variable. Unfortunately, it's not always possible to improve the model specification. The missing variable, even if known, may not be quantifiable.

EXAMPLE 17.20   Nancy Anderson, analyst for the New England Financial Corporation, has found autocorrelated residuals in several of her regression models. She suspects that business investment in future periods is related to the attitudes of potential investors. However, Nancy has found it extremely difficult to quantify these attitudes. She knows that, whenever possible, her models should be specified in accordance with theoretically sound insight. She also knows that the problem of serial correlation won't be solved by applying any corrective technique to a theoretically unsound model. Nancy must look for another approach to eliminating autocorrelated residuals.

Only after the specification of a time series regression equation has been carefully reviewed should the possibility of some statistical adjustment be considered. Some possible techniques for eliminating serial correlation are:

1. **Autoregressive model.** The creation of an autoregressive model generates a new predictor variable by using the Y variable lagged one or more periods. The knowledge that successive time periods are correlated is incorporated into the model. The autoregressive model is discussed in depth in the next section.
2. **Differences.** Differencing generates new variables that use the actual differences in Y (increase or decrease) from period to period. This approach assumes that the relationship between the error terms as measured by the autocorrelation coefficient equals 1 ($\rho_1 = 1$ in Equation 17.13).
3. **Iterative approach.** The iterative approach also generates new variables that use the actual differences (increase or decrease) from period to period. Where the differencing approach assumes that the relationship between the error terms equals

1, the iterative approach actually estimates the value of the autocorrelation coefficient, ρ_1, in Equation 17.13. This approach has become very popular with the advent of the computer.

AUTOREGRESSIVE MODELS

Autoregressive Model

The creation of an **autoregressive model** generates a new predictor variable by using the Y variable lagged one or more periods. The knowledge that successive time periods are correlated is thus introduced into the model. Equation 17.15 expresses a kth-order autoregressive forecasting model.

An **autoregressive model** generates a new predictor variable by using the Y variable lagged one or more periods.

$$Y_t = \beta_0 + \beta_1 Y_{t-1} + \cdots + \beta_k Y_{t-k} + \varepsilon_t \qquad (17.15)$$

where Y_t = Forecast Y value for time period t
Y_{t-1} = Y value for time period t lagged one period
Y_{t-k} = Y value for time period t lagged k periods
β_0 = Constant
β_1, β_k = Regression coefficients
ε_t = Random component at time t

A first-order autoregressive time series forecast is made using Equation 17.16:

$$\hat{Y}_t = b_0 + b_1 Y_{t-1} \qquad (17.16)$$

where $\hat{Y}_t$ = Forecast Y for time period t
Y_{t-1} = Y for time period t lagged one period
b_0, b_1 = Point estimates of β_0 and β_1

EXAMPLE 17.21   In Example 17.11, Outboard Marine Corporation analyst Cordella Roberts determined that sales were seasonal. Back in 1989, Cordella had decided to try a fourth-order autoregressive model to predict Outboard's quarterly sales. Cordella noted that a trend was present and included the variable time in her model. Her autoregressive equation was

$$\hat{Y}_t = b_0 + b_1 t + b_2 Y_{t-4}$$

where $\hat{Y}_t$ = Forecast Y for time period t
t = Time as measured by period number
Y_{t-4} = Y lagged four periods
b_0, b_1, b_2 = Point estimates of β_0, β_1, and β_2

When Cordella examined the SAS output in Table 17.15 she found that R^2 for the model was 92.7%. She tested the t values for both variables—both were significantly different from 0. However, the Durbin-Watson statistic of 1.13 was inconclusive at the .01 significance level $(.74 < 1.13 < 1.25)$. She knew that a larger sample size was needed. Despite the potential serial correlation problem, Cordella decided to try the fourth-order autoregressive model. Her forecast for the first quarter of 1989 was

$$\hat{Y}_t = b_0 + b_1 t + b_2 Y_{t-4}$$
$$Y_{21} = -26.89 + 8.323 t_{21} + .848 Y_{21-4}$$
$$= -26.89 + 8.323(21) + .848(2590.7)$$
$$= 368.1$$

TABLE 17.15 SAS Computer Output for Autoregressive Forecast of Quarterly Sales for Outboard Marine, 1989 (Example 17.21)

```
                        SEASONAL AUTOREGRESSIVE MODEL

Model: MODEL 1
Dependent Variable: YT      SALES
                          Analysis of Variance

                            Sum of          Mean
Source          DF         Squares        Square      F Value    Prob>F

Model            2     140536.84715    70268.42358     82.946    0.0001
Error           13      11013.10285      847.16176
C Total         15     151549.95000

        Root MSE           29.10604      R-square      0.9273
        Dep Mean          292.57500      Adj R-sq      0.9162
        C.V.                9.94823


                          Parameter Estimates
                        Parameter       Standard    T for H0:
Variable    DF          Estimate          Error     Parameter=0    Prob > |T|

INTERCEP     1        -26.892104     25.88135856       -1.039        0.3177
YT4          1          0.848400      0.11656553        7.278        0.0001
XT           1          8.322962      1.95951922        4.247        0.0010

DURBIN-WATSON D              1.128
(For Number of Obs.)           16
1st Order Autocorrelation   0.286
```

Outboard Marine sales were actually 264.4 for first quarter 1989, showing a forecasting error of 103.7. Cordella was disappointed and decided to use another model.

In 1992, Cordella has a large enough sample (Table 17.16) to give the model another try. She runs the data on SAS. (The instructions appear at the end of this chapter.)

Cordella examines the SAS output, shown in Table 17.17, noting that the model's R^2 is only 64.2%. She tests the t values and finds that the t value (-1.699) for the time variable coefficient isn't significantly different from 0. She also notes that serial correlation is still a problem since the Durbin-Watson statistic, 0.41, is significant at the .01 significance level $(0.41 < 1.07)$. Cordella concludes that this fourth-order autoregressive model won't work for her data.

TABLE 17.16 Quarterly Sales for Outboard Marine, 1984–1992 (Example 17.21)

Year	Quarter	Time	Sales	Sales lagged 4 periods
1984	1	1	147.6	——
	2	2	251.8	——
	3	3	273.1	——
	4	4	249.1	——
1985	1	5	139.3	147.6
	2	6	221.2	251.8
	3	7	260.2	273.1
	4	8	259.5	249.1
1986	1	9	140.5	139.3
	2	10	245.5	221.2
	3	11	298.8	260.2
	4	12	287.0	259.5
1987	1	13	168.8	140.5
	2	14	322.6	245.5
	3	15	393.5	298.8
	4	16	404.3	287.0
1988	1	17	259.7	168.8
	2	18	401.1	322.6
	3	19	464.6	393.5
	4	20	479.7	404.3
1989	1	21	264.4	259.7
	2	22	402.6	401.1
	3	23	411.3	464.6
	4	24	385.9	479.7
1990	1	25	232.7	264.4
	2	26	309.2	402.6
	3	27	310.7	411.3
	4	28	293.0	385.9
1991	1	29	205.1	232.7
	2	30	234.4	309.2
	3	31	285.4	310.7
	4	32	258.7	293.0
1992	1	33	193.2	205.1
	2	34	263.7	234.4
	3			
	4			

Source: *The Value Line Investment Survey* (New York: Value Line, 1988, 1992), p. 1768.

EXAMPLE 17.22 Sears forecaster Stu Miller is still attempting to forecast yearly sales for 1992. He tried several sophisticated forecasting techniques, but couldn't find one that produced accurate forecasts. Stu has decided that regression analysis might be his best approach. He has chosen disposable personal income (Table 17.13) as his predictor variable and uses MINITAB to develop a regression analysis using disposable personal income to predict operation revenue:

TABLE 17.17 SAS Computer Output for Autoregressive Forecast of Outboard
Marine's Quarterly Sales, 1992 (Example 17.21)

```
                    SEASONAL AUTOREGRESSIVE MODEL
Model: MODEL1
Dependent Variable: YT      SALES
                      Analysis of Variance

                        Sum of          Mean
Source          DF      Squares        Square     F Value    Prob>F

Model            2   151160.00562   75580.00281    24.246    0.0001
Error           27    84165.78238    3117.25120
C Total         29   235325.78800

     Root MSE          55.83235      R-square     0.6423
     Dep Mean         293.22000      Adj R-sq     0.6159
     C.V.              19.04111

                               Parameter Estimates

                    Parameter     Standard     T for HO:
Variable    DF       Estimate        Error    Parameter=0    Prob > |T|

INTERCEP     1      91.832977   35.81219998       2.564       0.0162
YT4          1       0.839530    0.12219363       6.870       0.0001
XT           1      -2.182468    1.28425647      -1.699       0.1007

Durbin-Watson D            0.410
(For Number of Obs.)          30
1st Order Autocorrelation  0.755
```

Minitab commands to solve Example 17.22 are:

```
MTB > READ 'SEARS.DAT' C1-C2
     37 ROWS READ

  ROW     C1       C2

   1      3307     273.4
   2      3556     291.3
   3      3601     306.9
   4      3721     317.1
  . . .

MTB > NAME C1 'REVENUE' C2 'INCOME'
MTB > REGRESS C1 1 PREDICTOR C2;
SUBC> RESIDS C3;
SUBC> DW.

The regression equation is
REVENUE = -1201 + 14.4 INCOME

Predictor      Coef     Stdev    t ratio       P
Constant     -1201.0     444.8      -2.70   0.011
INCOME       14.3681    0.2366      60.72   0.000

s = 1729    R-sq = 99.1%    R-sq(adj) = 99.0%

Analysis of Variance

SOURCE        DF            SS             MS         F       P
Regression     1    11018152960    11018152960   3687.22   0.000
Error         35      104587136        2988204
Total         36    11122740224
```

```
Unusual Observations

Obs.      INCOME      REVENUE        Fit     Stdev.Fit     Residual      St.Resid
  25        1729        17514      23646          292        -6132        -3.60R
  33        3206        48440      44862          504         3578         2.16R
  37        4218        57242      59409          715        -2167        -1.38 X
```

R denotes an obs. with a large st. resid.
X denotes an obs. whose X-value gives it large influence.

Durbin-Watson statistic = 0.65

```
MTB > NAME C3 'RESIDUAL'
MTB > PRINT C1-C3

ROW     REVENUE      INCOME       RESIDUAL
  1        3307       273.4         579.77
  2        3556       291.3         571.58
  3        3601       306.9         392.44
  4        3721       317.1         365.89
  5        4036       336.1         407.89
  6        4134       349.4         314.80
  7        4268       362.9         254.83
  8        4578       383.9         263.10
  9        5093       402.8         506.54
 10        5716       437.0         638.16
 11        6357       472.2         773.40
 12        6769       510.4         636.54
 13        7296       544.5         673.59
 14        8178       588.1         929.14
 15        8844       630.4         987.37
 16        9251       685.9         596.94
 17       10006       776.8          45.89
 18       10991       839.6         128.57
 19       12306       949.8        -139.79
 20       13101      1038.4        -617.80
 21       13639      1142.8       -1579.83
 22       14950      1252.6       -1846.44
 23       17224      1379.3       -1392.88
 24       17946      1551.2       -3140.75
 25       17514      1729.3       -6131.70
 26       25195      1918.0       -1161.96
 27       27357      2127.6       -2011.51
 28       30020      2261.4       -1270.95
 29       35883      2428.1        2196.89
 30       38828      2670.6        1657.63
 31       40715      2841.1        1094.88
 32       44282      3022.1        2061.25
 33       48440      3205.9        3578.41
 34       50251      3477.8        1482.73
 35       53794      3725.5        1466.75
 36       55972      4058.8       -1144.13
 37       57242      4218.4       -2167.27
```

The data to run this analysis were stored in a data file called SEARS.DAT. The READ command is used to enter the data into the worksheet. The RESIDS subcommand is used to store the residuals in C3. The DW subcommand is used to compute the Durbin-Watson statistic.

Stu is pleased when he examines the results. R^2 is high (99.1 percent) and the t and F values are both significant. However, Stu notices that the first 18 residuals in the printout of residuals are positive, followed by a string of 10 negative residuals. He decides to test for serial correlation.

The null and alternative hypotheses are

$$H_0: \rho_1 \leq 0$$
$$H_1: \rho_1 > 0$$

Stu decides to use the .01 significance level and consults the Durbin-Watson table in Appendix E.10. For one predictor variable with a sample size of 37, the critical values are $d_L = 1.22$ and $d_U = 1.32$. The decision rule is

Reject the null hypothesis if the calculated Durbin-Watson statistic is less than 1.22. Fail to reject the null hypothesis if the calculated Durbin-Watson statistic is greater than 1.32. If the calculated Durbin-Watson statistic lies between 1.22 and 1.32, the test is inconclusive.

Stu examines the computer output and finds that the Durbin-Watson statistic computed from the sample data is below the critical value from the table, .65 < 1.22. He rejects the null hypothesis and concludes that the residuals for Sears' operating revenue predicted by disposable personal income are positively autocorrelated.

Stu decides to develop an autoregressive model using disposable personal income and Sears sales lagged one period (Table 17.13). The MINITAB commands to lag the operating revenue variable and run the regression analysis are:

```
MTB > LAG 1 DATA IN C1, PUT IN C4
MTB > NAME C4 'REVLAG'
MTB > REGRESS C1 2 PREDICTORS C2 C4;
SUBC> RESIDS C3;
SUBC> DW.

The regression equation is
REVENUE = -256 + 5.58 INCOME + 0.650 REVLAG

36 cases used 1 cases contain missing values

Predictor      Coef      Stdev    t ratio        P
Constant     -256.2      378.4      -0.68    0.503
INCOME        5.579      1.576       3.54    0.001
REVLAG       0.6495     0.1155       5.62    0.000

s = 1270      R-sq = 99.5%  R-sq(adj) = 99.5%


Analysis of Variance

SOURCE          DF            SS           MS         F        P
Regression       2   10797421568   5398710784   3346.19    0.000
Error           33      53241960      1613393
Total           35   10850663424

SOURCE          DF        SEQ SS
INCOME           1   10746431488
REVLAG           1      50990308


Unusual Observations
Obs.    INCOME    REVENUE     Fit   Stdev.Fit   Residual   St.Resid
25        1729      17514   21047         508      -3533     -3.04R
26        1918      25195   21819         836       3376      3.53RX
29        2428      35883   32788         313       3095      2.51R
37        4218      57242   59631         528      -2389     -2.07R

R denotes an obs. with a large st. resid.
X denotes an obs. whose X-value gives it large influence.

Durbin-Watson statistic = 1.93
```

```
MTB > PRINT C1 C2 C4 C3

ROW     REVENUE     INCOME      REVLAG      RESIDUAL
  1        3307      273.4          *             *
  2        3556      291.3        3307         39.22
  3        3601      306.9        3556       -164.54
  4        3721      317.1        3601       -130.67
  5        4036      336.1        3721          0.39
  6        4134      349.4        4036       -180.40
  7        4268      362.9        4134       -185.36
  8        4578      383.9        4268        -79.55
  9        5093      402.8        4578        128.66
 10        5716      437.0        5093        226.37
 11        6357      472.2        5716        266.35
 12        6769      510.4        6357         48.91
 13        7296      544.5        6769        118.08
 14        8178      588.1        7296        414.55
 15        8844      630.4        8178        271.70
 16        9251      685.9        8844        -63.49
 17       10006      776.8        9251        -79.94
 18       10991      839.6       10006         64.34
 19       12306      949.8       10991        124.80
 20       13101     1038.4       12306       -428.58
 21       13639     1142.8       13101       -989.35
 22       14950     1252.6       13639       -640.32
 23       17224     1379.3       14950         75.36
 24       17946     1551.2       17224      -1638.61
 25       17514     1729.3       17946      -3533.10
 26       25195     1918.0       17514       3375.83
 27       27357     2127.6       25195       -620.44
 28       30020     2261.4       27357       -108.12
 29       35883     2428.1       30020       3095.25
 30       38828     2670.6       35883        879.29
 31       40715     2841.1       38828        -97.70
 32       44282     3022.1       40715       1233.93
 33       48440     3205.9       44282       2049.74
 34       50251     3477.8       48440       -356.79
 35       53794     3725.5       50251        628.12
 36       55972     4058.8       53794      -1354.47
 37       57242     4218.4       55972      -2389.46

MTB > STOP
```

The LAG command is used to lag the data in C1 one time period and store it in C4. The PRINT command shows the new variable in C4.

Results of the computer run show that the R^2 is high (99.5 percent) and the t and F values are all significant. Stu examines the table of residuals and doesn't find a correlated pattern. Next, he tests the Durbin-Watson statistic. The critical values taken from the table for two predictor variables and a sample size of 36 are $d_L = 1.15$ and $d_U = 1.38$ ($\alpha = .01$). Since the calculated Durbin-Watson is 1.93, the null hypothesis is not rejected, and Stu concludes that the residuals are not autocorrelated.

ARIMA MODELS

Box-Jenkins Methods

An approach widely known as the **Box-Jenkins methodology** uses both the autoregressive and moving average techniques for forecasting. This methodology doesn't assume the presence of a particular pattern in the historical data of the series to be forecast. Instead, the Box-Jenkins technique, credited to George Box and Gwilym Jenkins, uses an iterative approach of identifying a potentially useful model from a general class of models. The selected model is then checked against the historical data to see if it accurately predicts the series. The model fits well if the residuals between the forecast values and the historical data points are small, randomly distributed, and independent. If the specified model is not satisfactory, the process is repeated using another model designed to improve on the original one. This process is repeated until a satisfactory model is found. Figure 17.12 shows the steps for the Box-Jenkins methodology.

> The **Box-Jenkins methodology** uses both the autoregressive and the moving average techniques for forecasting.

FIGURE 17.12   Flow Diagram of Box-Jenkins Method

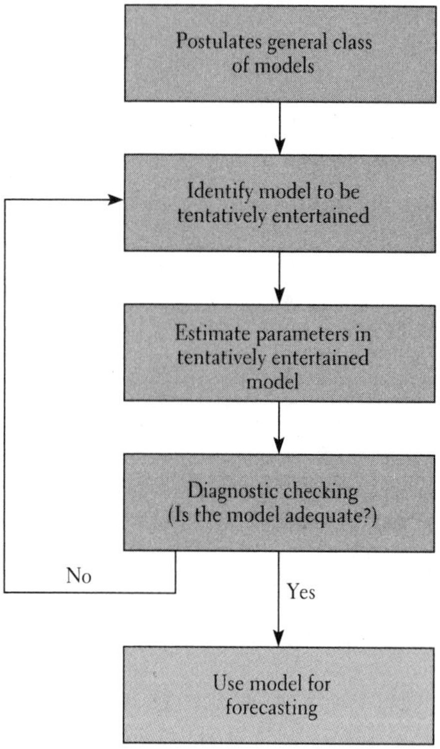

Source: G. P. Box and G. M. Jenkins, *Time Series Analysis Forecasting and Control* (San Francisco: Holden-Day, 1970), p. 19. Reprinted with permission.

To use the Box-Jenkins methodology, the time series of interest must be stationary. Earlier you learned that a stationary series is one whose basic statistical properties, the mean and variance, remain constant over time. You also learned that differencing a nonstationary series frequently produces a stationary series. Once a stationary series has been produced, the Box-Jenkins methodology can be applied. The degree of differencing is denoted by d in the Box-Jenkins model, which is more generally denoted by the expression ARIMA(p,d,q).

Several possible ARIMA models are:

ARIMA(1,0,0): First-order autoregressive model—original data
ARIMA (2,0,0): Second-order autoregressive model—original data
ARIMA(0,0,1): First-order moving average model—original data
ARIMA(0,0,2): Second-order moving average model—original data
ARIMA(1,1,0): First-order autoregressive model—differenced data
ARIMA(2,1,0): Second-order autoregressive model—differenced data
ARIMA(0,1,1): First-order moving average model—differenced data
ARIMA(0,1,2): Second-order moving average model—differenced data
ARIMA(1,0,1): First-order autoregressive moving average model—original data
ARIMA(1,1,1): First-order autoregressive moving average model—differenced data

Once a series has been identified as being stationary, the appropriate form of the ARIMA model is identified by examining a correlogram containing the sample autocorrelation coefficients. Sample partial autocorrelation coefficients are also used to identify the appropriate ARIMA model. Once the model has been selected, a computer program uses a nonlinear least squares procedure to estimate the model coefficients. A discussion of this process is beyond the scope of this introductory textbook.

As a final step in the model selection process, diagnostic checking of the residuals takes place to determine whether the model is appropriate. This is accomplished through examining a correlogram containing the sample autocorrelations of the residuals. If none of the autocorrelations is significantly different from 0, it is assumed that the sample residuals are independent with mean 0, and the model is deemed adequate.

The Box-Jenkins methodology is a powerful tool for providing accurate short-range forecasts. However, it's quite complex, requiring extensive computer analyses to perform the numerous computations required for identifying the model, estimating the parameters, and verifying that the model is adequate. To build a satisfactory model requires a great investment in terms of the analyst's time and computer resources. Also, the analyst should always remember that the more complicated the forecasting model, the less likely its results are to be understood and accepted by management and used in the decision-making process.

EXERCISES

36. Why are autocorrelated residuals a problem in the analysis of time series data?
37. What is the major cause of autocorrelated residuals?
38. When time series variables are analyzed, which underlying assumption is frequently violated?
39. How are autocorrelated residuals detected?

40. If the residuals in a regression equation are positively autocorrelated, which of the following statements are true when the least squares procedure is used?

    a. The standard error of the regression coefficient underestimates the variability.

    b. Confidence intervals are no longer strictly applicable.

    c. The t and F distributions are no longer strictly applicable.

    d. The regression coefficient or coefficients are unreliable.

    e. The standard error of estimate seriously overestimates the variability of the error terms.

    f. R^2 is spuriously low.

41. You test a series of 26 observations with two independent variables at the .05 significance level, and the calculated Durbin-Watson statistic is 1.2. What is your conclusion?

42. You test a series of 57 observations with one independent variable at the .01 significance level, and the calculated Durbin-Watson statistic is 1.4. What is your conclusion?

43. How is the problem of autocorrelated residuals eliminated?

44. Explain the concept of an autoregressive model.

45. How do the differencing and iterative techniques for solving autocorrelated residuals differ?

46. Examine the computer output presented in the accompanying table. Write a memo to your boss evaluating this model.

VARIABLE NO.	MEAN	STAN-DARD DEVIA-TION	CORRELA-TION X VS Y	REGRES-SION COEFFI-CIENT	STD. ERROR OF REG COEF.	COMPUTED T-VALUE
2	542.85	241.16	0.975	4.22517	0.31627	13.45
DEPENDENT						
1	1517.90	1078.70				
INTERCEPT		−792		R SQUARED		0.951
STD. ERROR OF ESTIMATE 341.1				DURBIN-WATSON STATISTIC ____		

TABLE OF RESIDUALS

OBSERVATION	OBSERVED VALUE	PREDICTED VALUE	RESIDUAL
1	295	371.36	−76.36
2	400	447.53	−47.53
3	390	513.91	−123.91
4	425	557.32	−132.32
5	547	638.16	−91.16
6	555	694.76	−139.76
7	620	752.20	−132.20
8	720	841.56	−121.56
9	880	921.98	−41.98
10	1050	1067.51	−17.51
11	1290	1217.29	72.71
12	1528	1379.84	148.16
13	1586	1524.94	61.06
14	1960	1710.47	249.53
15	2118	1890.46	227.54
16	2116	2126.62	−10.62
17	2477	2368.74	108.26
18	2199	2617.67	581.33
19	3702	3050.84	651.16
20	3316	3393.38	−77.38
21	2702	3789.54	−1087.54

47. (This question refers to Exercise 46.) The Durbin-Watson statistic, which was left out of the computer output, is 0.87. Test at the .01 significance level to determine if the residuals are autocorrelated.

48. A study attempts to relate personal savings and personal income (in billions of dollars) for the years 1935–54.

Year	Personal savings	Personal income
1935	2	60
1936	4	69
1937	4	74
1938	1	68
1939	3	73
1940	4	78
1941	11	96
1942	28	123
1943	33	151
1944	37	165
1945	30	171
1946	15	179
1947	7	191
1948	13	210
1949	9	207
1950	13	279
1951	18	257
1952	19	273
1953	20	288
1954	19	290

a. Evaluate the simple regression model in which personal income is used to predict personal savings. Specifically: (1) Test the regression coefficient for significance ($\alpha = .01$). (2) Test the contribution of personal income to the prediction of personal savings, using the t or F test ($\alpha = .01$). (3) Test for serial correlation. How can the model be improved?

b. Develop a dummy variable X_3, representing war years. Let $X_3 = 0$ for peacetime and $X_3 = 1$ for wartime. Consider the war years to be 1941–45. Evaluate this multiple regression model. Specifically: (1) Test to determine if knowledge of the war years variable contributes to the prediction of personal savings ($\alpha = .01$). (2) Test for serial correlation. Is the multiple regression model better than the simple regression model?

SUMMARY

This chapter has presented several ways of forecasting a time series variable. Along with the methods discussed in Chapter 16, these methods are valuable techniques for one of the most important jobs of every manager: predicting future values of variables of importance to the firm.

In terms of collecting data, performing the calculations, and explaining the results to others, simple methods are always preferable to elaborate ones. In addition, they sometimes produce the most accurate forecasts. Only when a more complicated and elaborate method substantially increases forecasting accuracy should such a method be considered. The danger is that the data needed for such techniques may be difficult to acquire or inaccurate, or that others in the organization won't understand and accept such techniques.

Here is a summary of the forecasting methods presented in recent chapters. All these techniques are widely used by forecasters in businesses of all kinds, utilizing the organization's past history to predict future values of important variables. Causal forecasting models include regression and multiple regression analysis. Time series forecasting models include the decomposition method, naive methods, moving averages, exponential smoothing, autoregression, and Box-Jenkins methods.

Regression analysis Regression analysis uses one or more related variables to form a prediction equation for y. Multicollinearity, a high correlation between predictor variables, is sometimes a problem. The necessity of obtaining accurate measurements for the predictor variables must be considered in deciding which variables to use. In developing a linear regression model for forecasting, the analyst should be aware that to predict some future value of the dependent variable, the future value of the predictor variable(s) must be known.

Decomposition method The decomposition method uses only past values of the time series variable to form forecasts. The series is decomposed into its components, which are then analyzed and recombined to form the forecast. Annual time series are decomposed into the secular trend and the cyclical component. Series measured by month or quarter use these two components along with the seasonal and irregular components. Forecasts are generated using the computed trend and seasonal values, along with the analyst's judgment of the values of the cyclical and irregular components.

Naive methods Very simple forecasting methods are often used by beginning forecasters, by businesses that are just starting, or by firms that are introducing a new product. Using the most recent value of Y as the forecast value for the next period is the simplest example of a naive method.

Moving averages The moving average method uses an average of recent periods to form the forecast for the next period. The analyst must decide how many past periods to use, a decision that is often made by trying different numbers of periods and finding the number that produces the most accurate forecasts for recent values of Y.

Exponential smoothing Exponential smoothing uses past periods to form the forecast for Y but assigns ever-decreasing weights to historical periods as they become older. This technique assumes that recent periods are more relevant to the forecast than are older ones. The basic exponential smoothing technique can be expanded to incorporate an adjustment for a trend in the series and/or a seasonal pattern in Y.

Autoregressive models The autoregressive technique takes advantage of the fact that Y values are often correlated with each other from one time period to the next.

"Predictor" variables are formed that are actually historical Y values lagged in time by one or more periods.

Box-Jenkins technique This sophisticated method doesn't assume that there's any particular pattern in the historical data of the series to be forecast. Instead, the technique uses both past values of Y and past error terms in the forecasting process to produce the model. The terms to be used and the weights assigned to past values are found through an iterative process.

Forecasting is widespread in every organization. It has always been performed on an informal, intuitive basis, and the use of more formal methods is constantly growing. The methods you've studied in these chapters, along with the availability of a computer and appropriate software, prepare you to utilize a wide range of formal forecasting methods in your career.

APPLICATIONS OF STATISTICAL CONCEPTS IN THE BUSINESS WORLD

Applications of the forecasting techniques discussed in this chapter are common in organizations of all sizes and types. These methods are widely used in business today, and their use is increasing as more and more business school graduates enter the work force with knowledge of these techniques.

The time series variables listed in the "Applications" section of Chapter 16 are candidates for the forecasting techniques that have just been summarized. It is worthwhile to review these applications and, armed with knowledge of many forecasting techniques, to consider how to approach forecasting each of these variables. Keep in mind that the analyst must seek a balance between a costly, time-consuming, and very accurate technique and a method that's fast, inexpensive, and easily understood by the firm's decision makers. Because of this dilemma, effective forecasting is as much an art as a science.

A summary of applications for the data analysis techniques discussed in these chapters follows.

Regression analysis Regression analysis is used for short- and medium-range forecasting of existing products and services, marketing strategies, production, personnel hiring, and facility planning.

Decomposition method Time series decomposition is used to make long-range forecasts for new plant and equipment planning, financing, new product development, and new methods of assembly. This technique is also used for short-range forecasting for personnel, advertising, inventory, financing, and production planning. It can be used in quality-control efforts to track and study such variables as defective rates over time.

Naive methods Naive methods are used to create short-range forecasts for sales and operations such as inventory, scheduling, and control measurements. This technique is especially useful for a new product or service.

Moving averages Moving average methods are used to make short-range forecasts for operations such as inventory, scheduling, control, pricing, and timing special promotions.

Exponential smoothing Exponential smoothing methods are used to create short-range forecasts of all types for operations such as inventory levels, scheduling of production, pricing decisions, and accounting balances. This technique is often used when a large number of forecasts are required and computer capabilities are available.

Autoregressive models Autoregressive methods are used for short- and medium-range forecasting for economic data ordered in a time series, such as prices, inventory, production, stock prices, and sales.

Box-Jenkins technique Box-Jenkins methods are used for short-range forecasting for such variables as earnings per share, stock prices, day-to-day demand, and inventory control.

GLOSSARY

Naive methods Very simple approaches to forecasting, such as using the value from the current period as the estimate for the next period.

Moving average A model that uses the average of several past time periods as the forecast for the next period.

Exponential smoothing A technique that uses a weighted average of past time series values to arrive at smoothed forecasts.

Autocorrelation The correlation between a variable, lagged one or more periods, and itself.

Correlogram A graphical tool for displaying the autocorrelations for various lags of a time series.

Stationary series A series whose mean and variance do not change over time.

Serial correlation A condition that exists when successive observations over time are related to each other.

Durbin-Watson test A test that detects the presence of autocorrelated residuals (serial correlation) in the regression of a time series.

Autoregressive model A model that generates a new predictor variable by using the Y variable lagged one or more periods.

Box-Jenkins method A methodology that uses both the autoregressive and the moving average techniques for forecasting.

KEY FORMULAS

Forecast error

$$e_t = Y_t - F_t \tag{17.1}$$

Mean absolute deviation

$$\text{MAD} = \frac{\Sigma |e_t|}{n} \tag{17.2}$$

Mean squared error

$$MSE = \frac{\Sigma e_t^2}{n} \tag{17.3}$$

Mean absolute percentage error

$$MAPE = \frac{\Sigma \frac{|e_t|}{Y_t}}{n} \tag{17.4}$$

Mean percentage error (BIAS)

$$MPE = \frac{\Sigma \frac{e_t}{Y_t}}{n} \tag{17.5}$$

Naive model

$$F_{t+1} = Y_t \tag{17.6}$$

Moving average model

$$F_{t+1} = \frac{Y_t + Y_{t-1} + Y_{t-2} + \cdots + Y_{t-m+1}}{m} \tag{17.7}$$

Exponential smoothing model

$$F_{t+1} = \alpha Y_t + (1 - \alpha)F_t \tag{17.8}$$

Seasonal regression model for quarterly data

$$\hat{Y}_t = b_0 + b_1 S_1 + b_2 S_2 + b_3 S_3 \tag{17.9}$$

First order autocorrelation coefficient

$$r_1 = \frac{\sum_{t=1}^{n-1} (Y_t - \bar{Y})(Y_{t-1} - \bar{Y})}{\sum_{t=1}^{n} (Y_t - \bar{Y})^2} \tag{17.10}$$

kth order autocorrelation coefficient

$$r_k = \frac{\sum_{t=1}^{n-k} (Y_t - \bar{Y})(Y_{t-k} - \bar{Y})}{\sum_{t=1}^{n} (Y_t - \bar{Y})^2} \tag{17.11}$$

Autocorrelation coefficient confidence interval

$$0 \pm z \, 1/\sqrt{n} \tag{17.12}$$

First-order serial correlation

$$\varepsilon_t = \rho_1 \varepsilon_{t-1} + v_t \tag{17.13}$$

Durbin-Watson statistic

$$DW = \frac{\sum\limits_{t=2}^{n} (e_t - e_{t-1})^2}{\sum\limits_{t=1}^{n} e_t^2} \tag{17.14}$$

kth-order autoregressive model

$$Y_t = \beta_0 + \beta_1 Y_{t-1} + \cdots + \beta_k Y_{t-k} + \varepsilon_t \tag{17.15}$$

First-order autoregressive model

$$\hat{Y}_t = b_0 + b_1 Y_{t-1} \tag{17.16}$$

SOLVED EXERCISES
. . . .

1. MOVING AVERAGE

Brunswick Corporation is the largest U.S. manufacturer of leisure and recreational products. Sid Foster has been assigned the job of forecasting sales for 1987. He has gathered the data (in millions of dollars) from 1978 to 1986: 1,126, 1,257, 1,200, 1,085, 1,068, 1,216, 1,468, 1,539, 1,717. (Source: *Brunswick Corporation Annual Report*, various years.)

a. Find the forecast value of sales for each year, starting with 1981, by using a three-year moving average.
b. Evaluate this forecasting method using MAD.
c. Evaluate this forecasting method using MSE.
d. Evaluate this forecasting method using MAPE.
e. Evaluate this forecasting method using MPE.
f. Summarize your evaluations of the forecasting errors.
g. Forecast sales for 1987.

Solution:

a. The moving average computations are shown in Table 17.18.
b. The error computations are shown in Table 17.19.

$$MAD = \frac{\Sigma |e_t|}{n} = \frac{1{,}262}{6} = 210.3$$

c. $$MSE = \frac{\Sigma e_t^2}{n} = \frac{331{,}704}{6} = 55{,}284$$

d. $$MAPE = \frac{\Sigma \dfrac{|e_t|}{Y_t}}{n} = \frac{88.9\%}{6} = 14.8\%$$

TABLE 17.18 Moving Average Forecast for Brunswick Sales (Solved Exercise 1)

t	Year	Sales ($ millions)	Three-year moving total	Three-year moving average	e_t
1	1978	1,126			
2	1979	1,257			
3	1980	1,200			
4	1981	1,085	3,583	1,194	− 109
5	1982	1,068	3,542	1,181	− 113
6	1983	1,216	3,353	1,118	98
7	1984	1,468	3,369	1,123	345
8	1985	1,539	3,752	1,251	288
9	1986	1,717	4,223	1,408	309

TABLE 17.19 Computations for Forecast Evaluation Methods (Solved Exercise 1)

Time, t	Sales, Y_t	Forecast, F_t	Error, e_t	$|e_t|$	e_t	$\frac{|e_t|}{Y_t}$ (%)	$\frac{e_t}{Y_t}$ (%)
1	1,126						
2	1,257						
3	1,200						
4	1,085	1,194	− 109	109	11,881	10.0	− 10.0
5	1,068	1,181	− 113	113	12,769	10.6	− 10.6
6	1,216	1,118	98	98	9,604	8.1	8.1
7	1,468	1,123	345	345	119,025	23.5	23.5
8	1,539	1,251	288	288	82,944	18.7	18.7
9	1,717	1,408	309	309	95,481	18.0	18.0
Sums:				1,262	331,704	88.9	47.7

e.
$$\text{MPE} = \frac{\sum \frac{e_t}{Y_t}}{n} = \frac{47.7\%}{6} = 8.0\%$$

f. The forecasting error averages about 210 for each forecast. The MPE or bias is fairly large, 8%. This means that the model is typically predicting on the low side, or underestimating. This might be caused by a trend in the data.

g. The forecast for 1987 is

$$F_{9+1} = \frac{Y_9 + Y_{9-1} + Y_{9-2}}{3}$$

$$F_{10} = \frac{1,717 + 1,539 + 1,468}{3} = \frac{4,724}{3} = 1,574.7 \text{ or } 1,575$$

2. EXPONENTIAL SMOOTHING

Forecast Brunswick Corporation sales using exponential smoothing.

a. Find the forecast value of sales for each year using a smoothing constant of .3 and an initial value of 1,126.

b. Evaluate this forecasting method using MAD.

c. Evaluate this forecasting method using MSE.

d. Evaluate this forecasting method using MAPE.

e. Evaluate this forecasting method using MPE.

f. Compare the smoothing model with the moving average model used in Solved Exercise 1.

g. Forecast sales for 1987.

Solution:

a. The exponential smoothing computations are shown in Table 17.20.

TABLE 17.20   Exponential Smoothing Forecast Computations for Brunswick Sales (Solved Exercise 2)

t	Year	Sales ($ millions)	F_t	e_t
1	1978	1,126	—	—
2	1979	1,257	1,126.0	131.0
3	1980	1,200	1,165.3	34.7
4	1981	1,085	1,175.7	−90.7
5	1982	1,068	1,148.5	−80.5
6	1983	1,216	1,124.4	91.6
7	1984	1,468	1,151.9	316.1
8	1985	1,539	1,246.7	292.3
9	1986	1,717	1,334.4	382.6

b. The error computations are shown in Table 17.21.

$$\text{MAD} = \frac{\Sigma |e_t|}{n} = \frac{1,421}{8} = 177.6$$

c.
$$\text{MSE} = \frac{\Sigma e_t^2}{n} = \frac{373,501}{8} = 46,687.6$$

d.
$$\text{MAPE} = \frac{\Sigma \frac{|e_t|}{Y_t}}{n} = \frac{99.7\%}{8} = 12.5\%$$

e.
$$\text{MPE} = \frac{\Sigma \frac{e_t}{Y_t}}{n} = \frac{67.7\%}{8} = 8.5\%$$

f. MAD, MSE, and MAPE are lower for the exponential smoothing model. If avoiding large forecasting errors is important, the MSE should be used for comparison purposes. The MPE is still too large.

TABLE 17.21 Computations for Forecast Evaluation Methods (Solved Exercise 2)

Time, t	Sales, Y_t	Forecast, F_t	Error, e_t	$|e_t|$	e_t	$\dfrac{|e_t|}{Y_t}$ (%)	$\dfrac{e_t}{Y_t}$ (%)
1	1,126						
2	1,257	1,126	131	131	17,161	10.4	10.4
3	1,200	1,165	35	35	1,225	2.9	2.9
4	1,085	1,176	−91	91	8,281	8.4	−8.4
5	1,068	1,149	−81	81	6,561	7.6	−7.6
6	1,216	1,124	92	92	8,464	7.6	7.6
7	1,468	1,152	316	316	99,856	21.5	21.5
8	1,539	1,247	292	292	85,264	19.0	19.0
9	1,717	1,334	383	383	146,689	22.3	22.3
Sums:				1,421	373,501	99.7	67.7

g. The forecast for 1987 is

$$F_{t+1} = \alpha Y_t + (1 - \alpha)F_t$$
$$F_{10} = \alpha Y_9 + (1 - \alpha)F_9$$
$$= (.3)(1,717) + (.7)(1,334.4) = 1,449.2 \text{ or } 1,449$$

3. AUTOCORRELATION COEFFICIENT COMPUTATION

Gail Robinson, analyst for Etta Life, is studying the amount of life premiums offered from 1982 through 1992 (Table 17.22). She decides to compute the autocorrelations to determine the data's pattern. Compute the autocorrelation coefficient for time lag 1.

TABLE 17.22 Etta Life Yearly Life Premiums (Solved Exercise 3)

Time, t	Year	Original data ($ millions), Y_t	Y lagged one period ($ millions), Y_{t-1}
1	1982	4,509	—
2	1983	5,439	4,509
3	1984	6,286	5,439
4	1985	6,669	6,286
5	1986	6,404	6,669
6	1987	6,169	6,404
7	1988	6,557	6,169
8	1989	8,029	6,557
9	1990	8,214	8,029
10	1991	9,161	8,214
11	1992	10,825	9,161

Source: Etta Company records.

Solution:

The summations to be used in the autocorrelation formula are presented in Table 17.23.

TABLE 17.23   Computations for Life Premiums (Solved Exercise 3)

t	Y_t	Y_{t-1}	$(Y_t - \bar{Y})$	$(Y_{t-1} - \bar{Y})$	$(Y_t - \bar{Y})^2$	$(Y_t - \bar{Y})(Y_{t-1} - \bar{Y})$
1	4,509	—	−2,606	—	6,791,236	—
2	5,439	4,509	−1,676	−2,606	2,808,976	4,367,656
3	6,286	5,439	−829	−1,676	687,241	1,389,404
4	6,669	6,286	−446	−829	198,916	369,734
5	6,404	6,669	−711	−446	505,521	317,106
6	6,169	6,404	−946	−711	894,916	672,606
7	6,557	6,169	−558	−946	311,364	527,868
8	8,029	6,557	914	−558	835,396	−510,012
9	8,214	8,029	1,099	914	1,207,801	1,004,486
10	9,161	8,214	2,046	1,099	4,186,116	2,248,554
11	10,825	9,161	3,710	2,046	13,764,100	7,590,660
Sums:	78,262		0		32,191,583	17,978,062

$$\bar{Y} = \frac{78,262}{11} = 7,115$$

$$r_1 = \frac{\sum\limits_{t=1}^{n-1} (Y_t - \bar{Y})(Y_{t-1} - \bar{Y})}{\sum\limits_{t=1}^{n} (Y_t - \bar{Y})^2}$$

$$= \frac{17,978,062}{32,191,583} = .56$$

It appears that moderate autocorrelation exists in this time series lagged one period. The correlation between Y_t and Y_{t-1}, or the autocorrelation for lag 1, is .56. However, a very small sample was used, so this autocorrelation coefficient should be tested to determine if it is significantly different from 0.

4. AUTOCORRELATION COEFFICIENT TEST OF SIGNIFICANCE

Gail Robinson, analyst for Etta Life, needs to determine whether the autocorrelation coefficient she computed is significantly different from 0.

Solution:

The null and alternative hypotheses to test whether the autocorrelation coefficient for time lag 1 is significantly different from 0 are

$$H_0: \rho_1 = 0$$
$$H_1: \rho_1 \neq 0$$

Since $n = 11$, the standard error (standard deviation of the sampling distribution of autocorrelation coefficients) is $1/\sqrt{11} = .302$. If the null hypothesis is tested at the .05 significance level, the critical value is $1.96(.302) = .592$, and the decision rule is

If the autocorrelation coefficient is less than $-.592$ or greater than $.592$, reject the null hypothesis (reject H_0 if $r_1 < -.592$ or $r_1 > .592$).

Gail concludes, based on her sample, that the data are not autocorrelated at time lag 1 ($.56 < .592$). However, she realizes that 11 time periods don't constitute a very large sample to test.

5. AUTOCORRELATION ANALYSIS

Eastman Kodak statistician Ron Wilson must estimate the company's operating revenue for 1991. He decides to analyze 1969–90 data (Table 17.24).

TABLE 17.24   Yearly Operating Revenue for Eastman Kodak and Disposable Personal Income, 1969–1990 (Solved Exercise 5)

Year	Operating revenue Y_t	Disposable income X_t	Operating revenue lagged one period Y_{t-1}
1969	2,747	630.4	—
1970	2,785	685.9	2,747
1971	2,976	776.8	2,785
1972	3,478	839.6	2,976
1973	4,036	949.8	3,478
1974	4,584	1,038.4	4,036
1975	4,959	1,142.8	4,584
1976	5,438	1,252.6	4,959
1977	5,967	1,379.3	5,438
1978	7,013	1,551.2	5,967
1979	8,028	1,729.3	7,013
1980	9,734	1,918.0	8,028
1981	10,337	2,127.6	9,734
1982	10,815	2,261.4	10,337
1983	10,170	2,428.1	10,815
1984	10,600	2,670.6	10,170
1985	10,631	2,841.1	10,600
1986	11,550	3,022.1	10,631
1987	13,305	3,205.9	11,550
1988	17,034	3,477.8	13,305
1989	18,398	3,725.5	17,034
1990	18,908	4,058.8	18,398

Sources: Eastman Kodak Operating Revenue: *Industry Surveys.* Disposable Personal Income: *Survey of Current Business,* various years.

Solution:

Ron runs an autocorrelation analysis of these data using the MINITAB computer program. The instructions are shown at the end of the chapter. Figure 17.13 shows the results.

The 95% confidence interval is

$$0 \pm 1.96 \, (1/\sqrt{22})$$
$$0 \pm .418$$

FIGURE 17.13   Autocorrelations for Solved Exercise 5

```
ACF of REV
           -1.0 -0.8 -0.6 -0.4 -0.2  0.0  0.2  0.4  0.6  0.8  1.0
            +----+----+----+----+----+----+----+----+----+----+
  1  0.840                             XXXXXXXXXXXXXXXXXXXXXX
  2  0.652                             XXXXXXXXXXXXXXXX
  3  0.468                             XXXXXXXXXXXX
  4  0.352                             XXXXXXXXX
  5  0.267                             XXXXXXX
  6  0.203                             XXXXX
  7  0.131                             XXXX
  8  0.057                             XX
  9 -0.047                           XX
 10 -0.147                         XXXXX
 11 -0.239                        XXXXXX
 12 -0.288                        XXXXXXX
 13 -0.318                       XXXXXXXX
 14 -0.330                       XXXXXXXX
```

Ron examines this correlogram and notices that the autocorrelations for the first three time lags (.84, .65, and .46) are significantly different from 0. The pattern then drops to 0 gradually rather than suddenly. He decides that the data have a trend.

Ron differences the data and uses MINITAB to compute the autocorrelation coefficients in Figure 17.14. Only the first autocorrelation coefficient (.44) is significantly different from 0 so Ron concludes that the first differenced data have some pattern that can be forecast.

FIGURE 17.14   Autocorrelations for Differenced Data for Solved Exercise 5

```
ACF of REVDIFF
           -1.0 -0.8 -0.6 -0.4 -0.2  0.0  0.2  0.4  0.6  0.8  1.0
            +----+----+----+----+----+----+----+----+----+----+
  1  0.443                             XXXXXXXXXXX
  2  0.084                             XXX
  3 -0.260                          XXXXXXX
  4 -0.223                          XXXXXX
  5 -0.361                        XXXXXXXXXX
  6 -0.092                           XXX
  7  0.056                             XX
  8  0.220                             XXXXXX
  9  0.105                             XXXX
 10  0.039                             XX
 11 -0.003                            X
 12 -0.014                            X
 13 -0.006                            X
 14 -0.025                           XX
```

6. SERIAL CORRELATION

Next, Ron develops a regression analysis using disposable personal income to predict yearly operating revenue. Ron employs MINITAB to do his regression analysis using the data in Table 17.24. The MINITAB commands are shown at the end of the chapter.

Ron is pleased when he examines the output (Table 17.25). R^2 is high, 96.2 percent, and the t and F values are both significant. But Ron knows that a test is needed to determine whether serial correlation is a problem.

TABLE 17.25   MINITAB Output for Solved Exercise 6, Disposable Income Used as the Predictor Variable

```
The regression equation is
REV = -313 + 4.58 INCOME

Predictor       Coef     Stdev     t ratio       P
Constant       -313.3     459.6      -0.68     0.503
INCOME          4.5841    0.2050     22.36     0.000

s = 999.0    R-sq = 96.2%    R-sq(adj) = 96.0%

Analysis of Variance

SOURCE        DF           SS           MS         F        P
Regression     1     499156352    499156352    500.14    0.000
Error         20      19960700       998035
Total         21     519117056

Unusual Observations
Obs.    INCOME      REV      Fit    Stdev.Fit    Residual    St.Resid
17        2841    10631    12711          276       -2080       -2.17R
18        3022    11550    13540          301       -1990       -2.09R

R denotes an obs. with a large st. resid.

Durbin-Watson statistic = 0.61
```

Solution:

The null and alternative hypotheses are

$$H_0: \rho_1 \le 0$$
$$H_1: \rho_1 > 0$$

Ron decides to use the .01 significance level and consults the Durbin-Watson table in Appendix E.10. Since he used one predictor variable with a sample size of 22, the critical values are $d_L = 1.00$ and $d_U = 1.17$. The decision rule is

Reject the null hypothesis if the calculated Durbin-Watson statistic is less than 1.00. Fail to reject the null hypothesis if the calculated Durbin-Watson statistic is greater than 1.17. If the calculated Durbin-Watson statistic lies between 1.00 and 1.17, the test is inconclusive.

Ron examines Table 17.25 and finds that the Durbin-Watson statistic computed from the sample data is below the critical value from the table, .61 < 1.00. He rejects the null hypothesis and concludes that the residuals for Eastman Kodak operating revenue predicted by disposable personal income are positively autocorrelated.

Ron decides to develop an autoregressive model using disposable personal income and Eastman Kodak operating revenue lagged one period. The MINITAB commands are shown at the end of the chapter. Table 17.26 shows the output for the autoregressive model.

Ron notices that the R^2 is high, 97.7 percent. However, the t value (1.95) for the disposable personal income variable is not significant at the .01 level. Ron checks the correlation matrix at the bottom of Table 17.26 and determines that multicollinearity is the reason why the disposable personal income variable is not significant. Next, Ron tests the Durbin-Watson statistic. The critical values taken from the table for two predictor variables and a sample size of 21 are $d_L = 0.89$ and $d_U = 1.27$ ($\alpha = .01$). Since the calculated Durbin-Watson is 1.14, the test is inconclusive.

Ron decides to eliminate disposable personal income and runs Eastman Kodak operating revenue lagged one period as the only predictor variable (Table 17.27).

TABLE 17.26 MINITAB Output for Solved Exercise 6, Disposable Income and Revenue Lagged One Period Used as the Predictor Variables

```
The regression equation is
REV = -56 + 1.59 INCOME + 0.706 REVLAG

21 cases used 1 cases contain missing values

Predictor     Coef      Stdev    t ratio       P
Constant     -56.0      394.4     -0.14     0.889
INCOME      1.5938     0.8189      1.95     0.067
REVLAG      0.7060     0.1885      3.75     0.001

s = 788.8    R-sq = 97.7%   R-sq (adj) = 97.4%

Analysis of Variance

Source        DF          SS            MS        F        P
Regression     2    469596448     234798224   377.40    0.000
Error         18     11198757        622153
Total         20    480795200

SOURCE        DF       SEQ SS
INCOME         1    460867648
REVLAG         1      8728800

Unusual Observations
Obs.    INCOME      REV      Fit    Stdev.Fit    Residual    St.Resid
20        3478    17034    14880          358        2154        3.07R

R denotes an obs. with a large st. resid.

Durbin-Watson statistic = 1.14

              REV     INCOME
INCOME      0.981
REVLAG      0.986      0.979
```

TABLE 17.27 MINITAB Output for Solved Exercise 6, Revenue Lagged One Period Used as the Predictor Variable

```
The regression equation is
REV = 230 + 1.06 REVLAG

Predictor     Coef      Stdev    t ratio       P
Constant     229.5      392.0      0.59     0.565
REVLAG     1.06496    0.04161     25.59     0.000

s = 844.7    R-sq = 97.2%   R-sq(adj.) = 97.0%

Analysis of Variance

SOURCE        DF          SS            MS        F        P
Regression     1    467239840     467239840   654.91    0.000
Error         19     13555361        713440
Total         20    480795200

Unusual Observations
Obs.    REVLAG      REV      Fit    Stdev.Fit    Residual    St.Resid
20       13305    17034    14399          278        2635        3.30R
22       18398    18908    19823          458        -915       -1.29 X

R denotes an obs. with a large st. resid.
X denotes an obs. whose X-value gives it large influence.

Durbin-Watson statistic = 1.30
```

Again, the r^2 is high (97.2 percent) and this model has a significant t value (25.6). Ron tests the Durbin-Watson statistic. The critical values taken from the table for one predictor variable and a sample size of 21 are $d_L = 0.97$ and $d_U = 1.16$ ($\alpha = .01$). Since the calculated Durbin-Watson is 1.30, the null hypothesis is not rejected and Ron concludes that the residuals are not autocorrelated. He thinks he has found a good prediction equation for Eastman's operating revenue.

EXERCISES

49. What are the advantages and disadvantages of the naive forecasting model?

50. What are the advantages and disadvantages of the moving average forecasting model?

51. What are the advantages and disadvantages of the exponential smoothing forecasting model?

52. If large forecasting errors are considered disastrous, which evaluation method should be used to compare forecasting models?

53. If the MPE is a large negative value, what should the analyst conclude about the forecasting model?

54. Which forecasting model generates a new predictor variable by using the dependent variable lagged one or more periods?

55. Which forecasting model uses both the autoregressive and moving average techniques for forecasting?

56. Which forecasting model does not assume the presence of any particular pattern in the historical data of the series to be forecast?

57. What are the disadvantages of using Box-Jenkins techniques to forecast?

58. What is a correlogram? How is it used?

59. How should the correlogram look for each of the following situations?

    a. A random series.

    b. A stationary series.

    c. A seasonal series.

60. What is serial correlation?

61. What problems arise when serial correlation is present in a regression equation?

62. Compute the 90% confidence interval for the autocorrelation coefficients for a series that contains 75 items.

63. A series of 43 observations with two independent variables is tested at the .05 significance level, and the calculated Durbin-Watson statistic is 1.0. What is your conclusion?

64. The AVX Corporation manufactures multilayer ceramic capacitors. Pam Williams has been assigned the job of forecasting book value per share for 1990. She has gathered the data from 1975 to 1989: 2.27, 2.59, 2.71, 3.17, 3.73, 5.90, 7.04, 9.64, 9.01, 9.38, 11.05, 12.24, 11.72, 11.81, 14.26. (Source: AVX *Corporation Annual Report*, various years.)

    a. Forecast book value per share for each year, starting with 1980, using a five-year moving average.

b. Evaluate this forecasting method using MAD.

c. Evaluate this forecasting method using MSE.

d. Evaluate this forecasting method using MAPE.

e. Evaluate this forecasting method using MPE.

f. Summarize your evaluation of the forecasting errors.

g. Forecast book value per share for 1990.

65. (This question refers to Exercise 64.) Forecast the AVX Corporation's book value per share using exponential smoothing.

a. Forecast book value per share for each year using a smoothing constant of .6 and an initial value of 2.27.

b. Evaluate this forecasting method using MAD.

c. Evaluate this forecasting method using MSE.

d. Evaluate this forecasting method using MAPE.

e. Evaluate this forecasting method using MPE.

f. Compare the smoothing model with the moving average model used in Exercise 64.

g. Forecast book value per share for 1990.

66. (This question refers to Exercise 64.) Forecast the AVX Corporation's book value per share using an autoregressive model.

a. Evaluate this forecasting method using MSE.

b. Compare the autoregressive model with the models used in Exercises 64 and 65.

c. Forecast book value per share for 1990.

67. Analyze the autocorrelation coefficients for each of the series shown in Figures 17.15, 17.16, and 17.17. Briefly describe each series.

FIGURE 17.15 Autocorrelations for Exercise 67

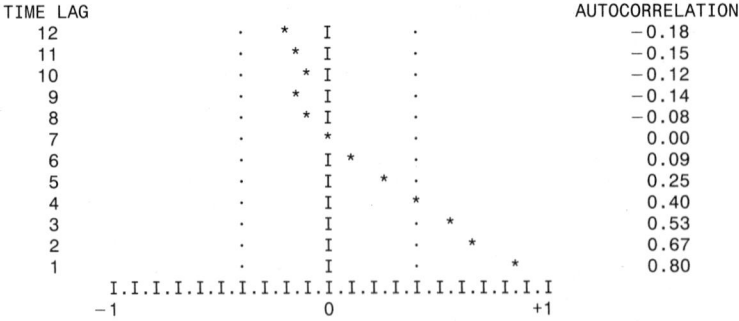

```
TIME LAG                                              AUTOCORRELATION
   12            .    *   I       .                        -0.18
   11            .      * I       .                        -0.15
   10            .       *I       .                        -0.12
    9            .      * I       .                        -0.14
    8            .       *I       .                        -0.08
    7            .         *       .                        0.00
    6            .        I *      .                        0.09
    5            .        I    *   .                        0.25
    4            .        I       *                         0.40
    3            .        I    .   *                        0.53
    2            .        I    .      *                     0.67
    1            .        I    .         *                  0.80
          I.I.I.I.I.I.I.I.I.I.I.I.I.I.I.I.I.I.I.I.I
          -1                0                +1
```

FIGURE 17.16 Autocorrelations for Exercise 67

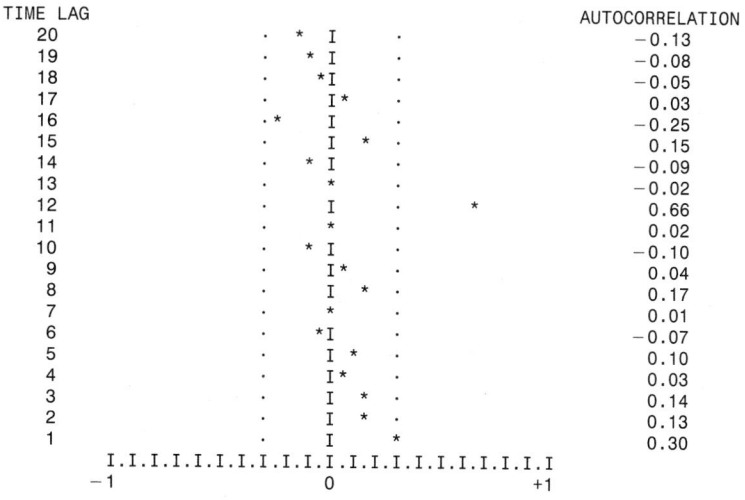

```
TIME LAG                                              AUTOCORRELATION
   20              ·    *   I        ·                     -0.13
   19              ·    *   I        ·                     -0.08
   18              ·       *I        ·                     -0.05
   17              ·        I*       ·                      0.03
   16              · *      I        ·                     -0.25
   15              ·        I    *   ·                      0.15
   14              ·    *   I        ·                     -0.09
   13              ·        *        ·                     -0.02
   12              ·        I        ·        *             0.66
   11              ·        *        ·                      0.02
   10              ·    *   I        ·                     -0.10
    9              ·        I*       ·                      0.04
    8              ·        I   *    ·                      0.17
    7              ·        *        ·                      0.01
    6              ·       *I        ·                     -0.07
    5              ·        I   *    ·                      0.10
    4              ·        I*       ·                      0.03
    3              ·        I    *   ·                      0.14
    2              ·        I    *   ·                      0.13
    1              ·        I        *                      0.30
      I.I.I.I.I.I.I.I.I.I.I.I.I.I.I.I.I.I.I.I.I
          -1                0                +1
```

FIGURE 17.17 Autocorrelations for Exercise 67

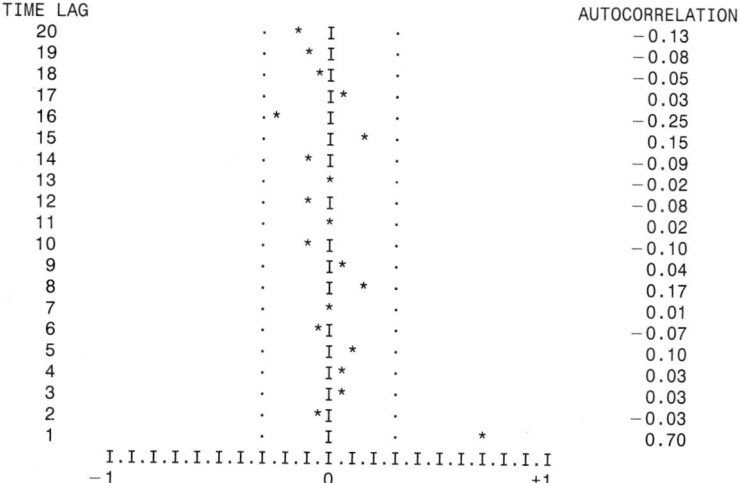

```
TIME LAG                                              AUTOCORRELATION
   20              ·    *   I        ·                     -0.13
   19              ·    *   I        ·                     -0.08
   18              ·       *I        ·                     -0.05
   17              ·        I*       ·                      0.03
   16              · *      I        ·                     -0.25
   15              ·        I    *   ·                      0.15
   14              ·    *   I        ·                     -0.09
   13              ·        *        ·                     -0.02
   12              ·    *   I        ·                     -0.08
   11              ·        *        ·                      0.02
   10              ·    *   I        ·                     -0.10
    9              ·        I*       ·                      0.04
    8              ·        I   *    ·                      0.17
    7              ·        *        ·                      0.01
    6              ·       *I        ·                     -0.07
    5              ·        I  *     ·                      0.10
    4              ·        I*       ·                      0.03
    3              ·        I*       ·                      0.03
    2              ·       *I        ·                     -0.03
    1              ·        I        ·        *             0.70
      I.I.I.I.I.I.I.I.I.I.I.I.I.I.I.I.I.I.I.I.I
          -1                0                +1
```

68. Sid Wynd, analyst for the Rockwell Clinic, must develop a model to predict the number of patients who will receive blood tests during a week. Sid has collected the following data on the number of patients receiving blood tests for the past 25 weeks.

Week	Number of patients	Week	Number of patients
1	249	14	300
2	255	15	298
3	248	16	306
4	258	17	308
5	254	18	308
6	268	19	313
7	260	20	320
8	270	21	323
9	265	22	323
10	287	23	337
11	298	24	340
12	291	25	342
13	291		

Source: Rockwell Clinic records.

    a. Construct a correlogram for these data.

    b. Based on the results of the correlogram, develop an autoregressive model.

    c. Use the model you developed to forecast period 26.

    d. Use an exponential smoothing model.

    e. Compare your results.

69. (This question refers to Exercise 22.) Dibrell Brothers, Inc., purchases and processes leaf tobacco worldwide, for sale to cigarette manufacturers. Hershel Roberts has the task of predicting sales for 1993. Exercise 22 presents 1985–92 quarterly data.

    a. Forecast sales using a naive model. Evaluate the accuracy of this model.

    b. Forecast sales using a moving average model. Evaluate the accuracy of this model.

    c. Forecast sales using an exponential smoothing model. Evaluate the accuracy of this model.

    d. Write a report for Hershel that summarizes your findings and includes a forecast for 1993.

70. Burgan Furniture Company analyst Tom Dukich has decided that production scheduling can be improved by developing an accurate method for predicting quarterly sales. He investigated the relationship between housing construction permits and furniture sales in the store's market area in Exercise 61 in Chapter 15. In addition, he developed a model that used a 0 to represent first- or second-quarter sales and a 1 to represent third- or fourth-quarter sales. The sales data, recorded in thousands of dollars, are:

Year	Quarter	Sales	Year	Quarter	Sales
1989	1	119	1991	1	115
	2	77		2	145
	3	409		3	654
	4	198		4	269
1990	1	77	1992	1	196
	2	121		2	276
	3	281		3	789
	4	160		4	318

Source: Burgan Furniture Company records.

a. Construct a correlogram for these data.

b. Based on the results of the correlogram, develop an autoregressive model.

c. Use the model you developed to forecast sales for the first quarter of 1993.

d. Develop a multiple regression model that uses dummy variables to model the seasonal effect.

e. Write a report indicating which model Tom should use.

71. Harvey Magnuson owns several large construction firms and is considering an investment project in the aerospace/defense industry. He hires you as a consultant to analyze capital expenditures for that industry. In the library you find the following data measured in billions of dollars:

Year	Expenditures
1979	32.65
1980	29.96
1981	26.81
1982	29.50
1983	27.20
1984	31.34
1985	38.99
1986	39.98
1987	39.57
1988	41.56
1989	41.87
1990	42.96

Source: Standard & Poor's *Industry Surveys*, 1988, 1992.

Analyze this series using any of the techniques covered in this text. Write a report for Mr. Magnuson including a 1991 forecast, an explanation of why you used the forecasting method, and an evaluation of that method's accuracy.

72. Harvey Magnuson liked the report that you wrote for him in Exercise 71 and hires you to analyze and forecast U.S. cement consumption for 1992. Again you go to the library and find the following data measured in thousands of short tons:

Year	Consumption
1972	84,559
1973	90,271
1974	82,415
1975	69,985
1976	74,282
1977	80,819
1978	87,284
1979	86,953
1980	77,258
1981	72,717
1982	65,496
1983	72,394
1984	83,784
1985	86,746

Year	Consumption
1986	91,191
1987	92,729
1988	92,379
1989	91,636
1990	88,863
1991	91,756

Source: Standard & Poor's, *Industry Surveys*, 1988, 1992.

Analyze this series using any of the techniques covered in this text. Write a report for Mr. Magnuson including a forecast for 1992, an explanation of why you used the forecasting method, and an evaluation of the forecasting method's accuracy.

73. Gilbert Sheely, analyst for the FCC, must predict the number of TV stations that will change hands in 1991. The data are:

Year	Number	Year	Number
1954	27	1973	25
1955	29	1974	24
1956	21	1975	22
1957	38	1976	32
1958	23	1977	25
1959	21	1978	51
1960	21	1979	47
1961	24	1980	35
1962	16	1981	24
1963	16	1982	30
1964	36	1983	61
1965	32	1984	82
1966	31	1985	99
1967	30	1986	128
1968	20	1987	59
1969	32	1988	70
1970	19	1989	84
1971	27	1990	75
1972	37		

Source: *Broadcasting Magazine*, 1991.

Analyze this series using any of the techniques covered in this text. Write a report for Mr. Sheely including a 1991 forecast, an explanation of why you used the forecasting method, and an evaluation of that method's accuracy.

74. Tracy Wilder, an economist working for the government, is trying to determine the demand function for passenger car motor fuel in the United States. Tracy developed a model using the variables actual price of a gallon of regular gasoline and U.S. population to predict motor fuel consumed per year. Her model explained 83.5% of the variance. Run the data on a regression program and determine whether serial correlation is a problem.

Year	Motor fuel consumed (billions of gallons) Y	Gas price x_2	U.S. population (millions) x_3
1973	78.8	.39	211.9
1974	75.1	.53	213.9
1975	76.4	.57	216.0
1976	79.7	.59	218.0
1977	80.4	.62	220.2
1978	81.7	.63	222.6
1979	77.1	.85	225.1
1980	71.9	1.19	227.7
1981	71.0	1.33	230.1
1982	70.1	1.26	232.5
1983	69.9	1.22	234.8
1984	68.7	1.21	236.3
1985	69.3	1.16	238.5
1986	71.4	.92	240.7
1987	70.6	.95	242.8
1988	71.7	.95	245.1

Source: *Statistical Abstract of the United States* and *Industry Surveys*, various years.

75. (This question refers to Exercise 57 in Chapter 15.) Judy Johnson decided to investigate three potential predictor variables: residential use per kilowatt-hour (kwh), residential charge per kwh (cents/kwh), and number of residential electric customers. You were asked to write a report so that Judy could testify before the Rate Commission. The commission asked her if serial correlation was a problem. She has asked you to write a response to the commission's question.

76. You did an excellent job for Judy Johnson with the Rate Commission testimony in Exercise 75 so she recommended you to work on a problem for the company's president, Paul Chapman. Paul is worried about the possibility of a takeover attempt and the fact that the number of common shareholders has been decreasing since 1983. He instructs you to study the number of common shareholders since 1968 and forecast for 1992. You decide to investigate three potential predictor variables: earnings per share (common), dividends per share (common), and payout ratio. You collect the following data from 1968 to 1991.

Year	Common shareholders Y	Earnings per share X_2	Dividends per share X_3	Payout ratio X_4
1968	26,472	1.68	1.21	72
1969	28,770	1.70	1.28	73
1970	29,681	1.80	1.32	73
1971	30,481	1.86	1.36	72
1972	30,111	1.96	1.39	71
1973	31,052	2.02	1.44	71
1974	30,845	2.11	1.49	71
1975	32,012	2.42	1.53	63
1976	32,846	2.79	1.65	55

Year	Common shareholders Y	Earnings per share X_2	Dividends per share X_3	Payout ratio X_4
1977	32,909	2.38	1.76	74
1978	34,593	2.95	1.94	61
1979	34,359	2.78	2.08	75
1980	36,161	2.33	2.16	93
1981	39,474	3.29	2.28	69
1982	46,278	3.17	2.40	76
1983	47,672	3.02	2.48	82
1984	45,462	2.46	2.48	101
1985	43,313	3.03	2.48	82
1986	41,368	2.06	2.48	120
1987	38,686	2.31	2.48	107
1988	37,072	2.54	2.48	98
1989	36,968	2.70	2.48	92
1990	34,348	2.87	2.48	86
1991	34,058	2.61	2.48	95

Source: "Financial and Operating Supplement," *Washington Water Power Annual Report*, 1978, 1986, 1991.

a. Run these data on the computer and find the best prediction model.

b. Is serial correlation a problem in this model?

c. If serial correlation is a problem, write a memo to Paul that discusses various solutions to the autocorrelation problem and includes your final recommendation.

EXTENDED EXERCISES

77. BUSINESS ACTIVITY INDEX

Dr. Shik Chun Young, professor of economics at Eastern Washington University, is attempting to develop a business activity index for Spokane County.[5] At the county level, personal income is judged as the best available indicator of local business conditions. Personal income is defined as the total income received by households before personal taxes are paid. Unfortunately, personal income data at the county level are estimated by the U.S. Dept. of Commerce on an annual basis and are released 16 months too late.

From Young's knowledge of the Spokane economy, he selects the following 10 series to try as predictor variables:

X_2 = Total employment

X_3 = Manufacturing employment

X_4 = Construction employment

---

[5]John E. Hanke and Arthur G. Reitsch, *Business Forecasting*, 4th ed. (Boston: Allyn & Bacon, 1992).

X_5 = Wholesale and retail trade employment
X_6 = Service employment
X_7 = Bank debits
X_8 = Bank demand deposits
X_9 = Building permits issued
X_{10} = Real estate mortgages
X_{11} = Commercial and industrial electricity consumption

Shik runs a regression model that includes all 10 predictor variables, and the variables are found to explain 96% of the variance. However, other regression statistics indicate several problems. First, of these 10 predictor variables, only 3 have computed t values which are significant at the .05 level. Second, the correlation matrix shows a high degree of interdependence among several of the independent variables—the problem of multicollinearity. For example, the variables for total employment and bank debits have a correlation coefficient of .88; total electricity consumption and bank demand deposits, .76; and building permits issued and real estate mortgages, .68. Finally, the Durbin-Watson statistic, 0.91, indicates a serial correlation problem.

a. Which problem should Dr. Young solve first: multicollinearity or serial correlation? Why?

b. How should Dr. Young attempt to eliminate the problem of serial correlation?

78. PROJECT

As mentioned throughout this chapter, many variables vital to a firm's health are measured every year, quarter, or month. For each of these, there may be several other variables that are highly correlated and that might provide valuable insights and forecasting power.

For this exercise, you are to simulate the identification of an important time series variable for a company of your choice and then analyze the patterns in the data using autocorrelation analysis. In addition, you can use a regression analysis computer program to see if a good prediction equation can be found.

a. Identify a company or organization that interests you. The company can be local, or it can be a national company that has published records including the measurement of time series variables.

b. Identify a key variable for your chosen company and record its values for several years, quarters, or months.

c. Either by hand or with a computer, calculate several autocorrelation coefficients and plot them on a correlogram.

d. Based on the correlogram pattern, describe the patterns in your time series.

e. Compute first differences for your data. Then compute the autocorrelation coefficients, plot them on a correlogram, and describe the resulting patterns.

f. Identify several potential predictor variables that you think might be correlated with the dependent variable. You can use company records along with other data sources in this process.

g. Run the data on a regression analysis computer program and obtain a correlation matrix. Assemble several predictor variable combinations that you think might be successful and run a regression analysis for each. See if you can find a good prediction equation for your dependent variable.

h. Check your model to make sure that serial correlation is not a problem.

79. HYRUM BREWERY

Ralph Hyrum and his brother Claude have decided to open a brewery in a small New England town. They chose a town outside Manchester-Nashua, New Hampshire, after reading that this area is the fastest growing business area in the country (*Inc.* Magazine, March 1992).

To obtain financing for their brewery, the Hyrum brothers are told by their banker that they must have a method of forecasting demand, and hence production. After discussing this matter with the banker, and after the banker tastes some Hyrum beer that evening, they decide a general forecast of beer sales for the region will suffice. The banker is convinced that the Hyrum brothers have a good product and agrees that their sales can be projected as a percentage of overall demand for beer in the region.

This leaves the Hyrum brothers with the task of forecasting overall beer consumption for their part of the region. They hire you as a consultant to provide such a forecast. You begin by assembling the following figures for total beer sales in the region, in hundreds of kegs, which are to be used to develop a forecast for the next two years.

	1989	1990	1991	1992
Jan.	123	132	133	137
Feb.	124	129	131	135
Mar.	138	142	140	147
Apr.	135	151	155	159
May	145	153	158	162
June	179	183	192	188
July	180	193	204	211
Aug.	211	208	225	223
Sept.	187	200	192	199
Oct.	175	177	184	173
Nov.	139	144	148	151
Dec.	127	129	132	135

Forecast using the following methods:

1. Naive method

2. Moving average

3. Simple exponential smoothing

4. Regression analysis

5. Autoregressive model

    a. Are the data stationary? If not, do the data have a trend? Are the data seasonal?

    b. Discuss the pros and cons of each method. Keep in mind the need for collecting more data, the necessity of a computer program, and the need to choose parameters for some of the methods. Also remember that the method chosen must be as accurate as possible and must be understandable to the banker and the Hyrum brothers so they can use it to generate the forecasts they need.

c. Write a report for the Hyrum brothers. Compare each forecasting method using mean absolute percentage error (MAPE). Include a forecast for each month of 1993.

MICROCOMPUTER PACKAGE

The micro package *Computerized Business Statistics* can be used to solve moving average and exponential smoothing problems.

Sid Foster has been assigned the job of forecasting sales for the Brunswick Corporation for 1987 (Solved Exercise 1). He has gathered 1978–86 sales data (in millions of dollars). Sid would like to use the computer program to develop a moving average forecast.

Computer Solution

From the main menu of *Computerized Business Statistics* an 11 is selected, indicating Time Series and Forecasting. Since the problem involves entering data from the keyboard, a 1 is selected.

```
Time Series and Forecasting—Define New Problem
OPTIONS:  1 = Least Squares
          2 = Moving Averages
          3 = Simple Exponential Smoothing
          4 = Smoothing with Trend Factoring
          5 = Trend and Seasonal Smoothing
          6 = Seasonal Indices
Select Model: enter 1–6, press ↵ 2
```

Since a moving average is desired, a 2 is selected.

```
Simple or Weighted Averages: enter S/W, press ↵ S
Number of Data Points: enter 4–125, press ↵ 9
Number of Periods in Average: enter 2–9, press ↵ 3
Variable Name: enter 0–5 char., press ↵ Sales
```

The answers to this series of questions are: a simple average, **S**, is desired, for **9** data points, using a **3**-month moving average, and the variable is entered as **Sales.**

```
Problem definition correct Y/N, press ↵ Y
```

After a **Y** response, the program is ready for the data to be entered. There are nine data points. An **F** is entered once the blanks have been completed.

After the data have been entered the screen shows:

```
    Sales
1 = 1126
2 = 1257
3 = 1200
4 = 1085
5 = 1068
6 = 1216
7 = 1468
8 = 1539
9 = 1717

Save data? Y/N, press ↵ N
```

MINITAB COMPUTER PACKAGE
. . . .

The MINITAB commands to analyze Solved Exercises 5 and 6 are:

```
MTB > READ 'KODAK.DAT' C1-C2
      22 ROWS READ

ROW     C1       C2
  1    2747    630.4
  2    2785    685.9
  3    2976    776.8
  4    3478    839.6
 . . .

MTB > NAME C1 'REV' C2 'INCOME'
MTB > ACF C1
MTB > DIFFERENCES 1 FOR C1, PUT IN C3
MTB > ACF C3
```

The READ command is used to import the KODAK.DAT file into columns 1 and 2. The ACF command is used to compute autocorrelations for the data in C1. The DIFFERENCES command is used to compute the differences for the data in C1 and store these differences in C3.

```
MTB > REGRESS C1 1 PREDICTOR C2;
SUBC> RESIDS C4;
SUBC> DW.
MTB > NAME C4 'RESIDUAL'
MTB > PRINT C1 C2 C4

ROW     REV     INCOME    RESIDUAL

  1    2747     630.4      170.49
  2    2785     685.9      -45.93
  3    2976     776.8     -271.62
  4    3478     839.6      -57.51
  5    4036     949.8       -4.68
  6    4584    1038.4      137.17
  7    4959    1142.8       33.58
  8    5438    1252.6        9.25
  9    5967    1379.3      -42.57
 10    7013    1551.2      215.42
 11    8028    1729.3      413.99
 12    9734    1918.0     1254.96
 13   10337    2127.6      897.12
 14   10815    2261.4      761.77
 15   10170    2428.1     -647.41
 16   10600    2670.6    -1329.06
 17   10631    2841.1    -2079.66
 18   11550    3022.1    -1990.38
 19   13305    3205.9    -1077.95
 20   17034    3477.8     1404.63
 21   18398    3725.5     1633.13
 22   18908    4058.8      615.24
```

The REGRESS command is used to run a regression analysis using disposable income to predict operating revenue. The RESIDS subcommand is used to store the residuals in C4. The DW subcommand is used to compute the Durbin-Watson statistic.

```
MTB > LAG 1 DATA IN C1, PUT IN C5
MTB > NAME C5 'REVLAG'
MTB > REGRESS C1 2 PREDICTORS C2 C5;
SUBC> RESIDS C4;
SUBC> DW.
MTB > CORR C1 C2 C5
```

The LAG command is used to lag the data in C1 one period and store the lagged data in C5. The REGRESS command is used to run a regression analysis using disposable income and operating revenue lagged one period to predict operating revenue. The CORR command is used to compute a correlation matrix for the variables operating revenue, disposable income, and operating revenue lagged one period.

```
MTB > REGRESS C1 1 PREDICTOR C5;
SUBC> RESIDS C4;
SUBC> DW.
```

SAS COMPUTER PACKAGE

The SAS computer package can be used to develop autoregressive models. The SAS commands to analyze Example 17.21 are:

```
TITLE "SEASONAL AUTOREGRESSIVE MODEL";
DATA OUTBOARD;
 INPUT YT XT;
 LABEL YT=SALES
       YT4=LAGSALES
       XT=TIME;
 YT4=LAG4(YT);
CARDS;
147.6 1
251.8 2
273.1 3
249.1 4
139.3 5
221.2 6
260.2 7
259.5 8
140.5 9
245.5 10
298.8 11
287.0 12
168.8 13
322.6 14
393.5 15
404.3 16
259.7 17
401.1 18
464.6 19
479.7 20
264.4 21
402.6 22
411.3 23
385.9 24
232.7 25
309.2 26
310.7 27
293.0 28
205.1 29
234.4 30
285.4 31
258.7 32
193.2 33
263.7 34
PROC REG;
 MODEL YT=YT4 XT/ DW;
ENDSAS;
```

The TITLE command names the SAS run. The DATA command gives the data a name. The INPUT command names and gives the correct order for the two data fields. The YT4= LAG4(YT) command provides YT4 with the value of YT lagged four periods. For example, the value of YT in case 1 is 147.6. Therefore, the value of YT4 in case 5 is also 147.6. The next 20 lines are card images that represent the YT variable (sales) and the XT variable (time). The PROC REG command and MODEL subcommand indicate that YT is the dependent variable and the predictor variables are XT and YT4. The DW subcommand computes the Durbin-Watson statistic.

The SAS computer package can also be used to determine significant autocorrelation coefficients. The SAS commands to analyze Solved Exercises 3 and 4 are:

```
TITLE "SAS ARIMA EXAMPLE";
DATA PREMIUMS;
INPUT Y;
CARDS;
4509
5439
6286
6669
6404
6169
6557
8029
8214
9161
10825
PROC ARIMA;
 IDENTIFY VAR=Y;
```

The TITLE command names the SAS run. The DATA command gives the data a name. The 11 lines of numbers are card images that represent the amount of life premiums offered from 1982 through 1992. The PROC ARIMA command determines the significant autocorrelations among the given lag periods. Table 17.28 shows the computer output for this SAS run.

TABLE 17.28 SAS Output for Solved Exercises 3 and 4

"SAS ARIMA EXAMPLE"

ARIMA PROCEDURE

NAME OF VARIABLE = Y

MEAN OF WORKING SERIES= 7114.73
STANDARD DEVIATION = 1710.7
NUMBER OF OBSERVATIONS= 11

AUTOCORRELATIONS

LAG	COVARIANCE	CORRELATION	-1 9 8 7 6 5 4 3 2 1 0 1 2 3 4 5 6 7 8 9 1	STD
0	2926507	1.00000	|********************|	0
1	1634342	0.55846	|***********● |	0.301511
2	798635	0.27290	|***** |	0.384206
3	358755	0.12259	|** |	0.401441
4	-117672	-0.04021	*| |	0.40483
5	-255636	-0.08735	**| |	0.405193

TABLE 17.28   SAS Output for Solved Exercises 3 and 4

6	−412623	−0.14100	|	•	***|		•	|	0.406901
7	−688545	−0.23528	|	•	*****|		•	|	0.411319
8	−851655	−0.29101	|	•	******|		•	|	0.423377
9	−1049949	−0.35877	|	•	*******|		•	|	0.441187
10	−878905	−0.30033	|	•	******|		•	|	0.466957

|•• MARKS TWO STANDARD ERRORS

INVERSE AUTOCORRELATIONS

LAG	CORRELATION	−1 9 8 7 6 5 4 3 2 1 0 1 2 3 4 5 6 7 8 9 1
1	−0.46311	| • *********| • |
2	0.07776	| • |** • |
3	−0.10922	| • **| • |
4	0.09891	| • |** • |
5	−0.00004	| • | • |

PARTIAL AUTOCORRELATIONS

LAG	CORRELATION	−1 9 8 7 6 5 4 3 2 1 0 1 2 3 4 5 6 7 8 9 1
1	0.55846	| • |***********• |
2	−0.05665	| • *| • |
3	−0.00993	| • | • |
4	−0.13571	| • ***| • |
5	0.00005	| • | • |
6	−0.09434	| • **| • |
7	−0.15075	| • ***| • |
8	−0.13016	| • ***| • |
9	−0.18591	| • ****| • |
10	−0.02254	| • | • |

AUTOCORRELATION CHECK FOR WHITE NOISE

TO LAG	CHI SQUARE	DF	PROB	AUTOCORRELATIONS
6	6.70	6	0.350	0.558 0.273 0.123 −0.040 −0.087 −0.141

Decision Making under Uncertainty

Yong Chu, weeping at the crossroads, said, "Isn't it here that you take a half step wrong and wake up a thousand miles astray?"

the Confucian Hsun-tzu

Objectives

When you have completed this chapter, you will be able to:

Use different criteria to make a decision by means of a payoff table.

Determine the value of perfect information in a complex decision.

Develop a tree diagram.

Make a decision by revising prior probabilities based on additional experimental or sample information.

Explain the concept of utility theory.

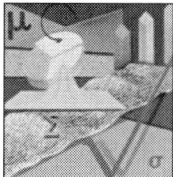

On September 21, 1989, *The Wall Street Journal* reported on the activities of The Procter & Gamble Co. The article indicated that this large company's decision-making process is complex and time-consuming, with every package redesign decision traveling through half a dozen management layers.

The title of this chapter is a good working definition of the management process. The concepts of this text are all designed to prepare the manager to make effective and timely decisions. This chapter examines the uncertainty that attends every business decision.

WHY MANAGERS NEED TO KNOW ABOUT DECISION MAKING

Managers are paid to make decisions for their organizations without all the information they might like. Those who become skilled in the decision-making process move up in the organization and are called on to make even more important decisions.

Since decision making under uncertainty is a daily part of a manager's job, it's only natural that a branch of study in business concentrates exclusively on this aspect of management. This chapter discusses techniques and approaches developed to assist the decision maker. Many of these techniques are commonly used in the automatic thought processes of every manager. Others are not so obvious, and a knowledge of them can help the manager make better decisions.

Procter & Gamble, as reported in *The Wall Street Journal*, saw its earnings rise by 18% in 1989. This achievement suggests an effective decision-making apparatus in spite of its complexity. Perhaps this successful company uses some of the formal decision-making techniques discussed in this chapter.

DECISION CRITERIA AND THE PAYOFF TABLE

All decision makers are faced with alternatives and states of nature. An *alternative* is a course of action or a strategy that may be chosen by a decision maker (for example, not wearing a coat tomorrow). A *state of nature* (or the world) is a situation over which the decision maker has little or no control (for example, tomorrow's weather). To present the decision alternatives, the analyst can develop either *payoff tables* or *tree diagrams*.

Payoff Table

In this section, different decision criteria are represented using the **payoff table.** This method of structuring a complex decision displays the financial consequences of every possible decision against every state of nature that could subsequently develop. In this table, the possible actions to be taken are listed in the columns, and the various states of the world are shown in the rows. By studying the payoff table, the decision maker can assess the financial consequences of different decisions as they relate to the state of the world.

The **payoff table** shows the payoff for every combination of decision and state of the world.

EXAMPLE 18.1 Jenny Hebert, manager of the Ward Department Store, must determine the number of units of a particular product to stock each day. From past experience she knows that the number of units that will be demanded on a given day is between one and six, so these are the stock units that will be considered. Depending on the number of units stocked and the number demanded, a different profit will result. These various profits are summarized in the payoff table in Table 18.1.

As the payoff table shows, there are 36 possible profits each day. Jenny must decide how many units to stock, or which column of the table to choose. The row, representing the true state of the world for the day, is unknown at the time the stocking decision is made and will be determined by the market. As indicated, profits can range anywhere from $25 to $150 each day.

Table 18.1 implies that each unit sold produces a profit of $25. If one unit is stocked and one is demanded, the payoff, as indicated by the upper left value in the table, is $25; this represents the profit generated by selling that unit. Beneath this value are other daily profits of $25, indicating that the only possible profit for the day is the $25 from selling the one unit in stock, regardless of how many additional units are demanded. Other matching values below the diagonal similarly indicate that profits won't rise after the total number of units in stock have been sold.

To the right of each profit along the diagonal, a $10 reduction in daily profit is indicated for each additional unsold unit. For example, the profit of $15 in the first row and second column indicates that if two units are stocked and only one is sold, net profit is $25 for the unit sold, minus $10 lost on the unsold unit. Thus, Table 18.1 indicates a $10 reduction in profit for each additional unsold unit.

TABLE 18.1   Payoff Table for Example 18.1 (Profits in Dollars)

Number demanded	Decision: number of units to stock					
	1	2	3	4	5	6
1	25	15	5	−5	−15	−25
2	25	50	40	30	20	10
3	25	50	75	65	55	45
4	25	50	75	100	90	80
5	25	50	75	100	125	115
6	25	50	75	100	125	150

The payoff table enables the decision maker to view each possible combination of decision and subsequent development. In real situations, the payoff table may be quite large, incorporating many possible decisions and states of the world.

To complete the evaluation of a complex situation, the probabilities of the various events or states of the world identified in the payoff table must be estimated. The picture is then complete: the possible decisions have been identified, the states of the world that might develop have been specified, and the likelihood of each of these developments has been assessed. A rational decision that meets the decision maker's criteria can then be made.

Once the probabilities of the various events have been estimated, the expected monetary value (EMV) of each action or decision can be computed. Recall the concept of expected value discussed in Chapter 5. When the values of a discrete random variable have been identified along with their probabilities of occurring, the average value of this variable over many trials can be computed; this is known as the *expected value of the variable*. Equation 5.1 summarizes this computation of expected value.

Expected Monetary Value

The **expected monetary value** is the average profit that would result if a decision were repeated many times and the decision maker chose the same alternative each time. It is the expected profit for a decision, even though the decision is to be made only once. The EMV of each decision is found by multiplying each event's payoff by the probability of its occurrence and adding these products. This computation is illustrated in Example 18.2.

> The **expected monetary value** is the average profit that would result if a decision were repeated many times and each time the decision maker chose the same alternative.

EXAMPLE 18.2   In Example 18.1, Jenny Hebert needed to decide the number of units of a product to stock each day. From past experience she knows the probabilities of various numbers of units being demanded each day. (See Table 18.2, which indicates that the probability of three units being demanded is .40, for example.) The EMV is computed by multiplying each event's payoff by the probability of its occurrence. Thus, the expected monetary value for the decision to stock four units is

$$EMV = -5(.05) + 30(.15) + 65(.40) + 100(.25) + 100(.10) + 100(.05) = 70.25$$

TABLE 18.2   Payoff Table for Example 18.2: Expected Monetary Value

Probability	Demand	Decision: number of units to stock					
		1	2	3	4	5	6
.05	1	25	15	5	−5	−15	−25
.15	2	25	50	40	30	20	10
.40	3	25	50	75	65	55	45
.25	4	25	50	75	100	90	80
.10	5	25	50	75	100	125	115
.05	6	25	50	75	100	125	150
	EMV:	25	48.25	66.25	70.25	65.50	57.25

The EMV for each decision is shown in the last row of Table 18.2. Jenny can see from examining this row that the decision to stock four units will provide the highest expected profit (highest EMV).

Note that the payoff tables in this chapter use discrete decision levels and demand levels. For example, only certain demands such as 1, 2, 3, 4, 5, or 6 are considered. A more general treatment of the subject would permit any value for demand within some specified range. Such continuous distributions for demand are an extension of the basic ideas presented in this chapter and are covered in texts that discuss decision making under uncertainty in more detail.

EXAMPLE 18.3   King Hardware Store manager Joyce Cary must decide how many lawnmowers to order for summer. It is difficult to order additional units after the season has started, but then there is a cost associated with having more units on hand than can be sold. A lawnmower costs an average of $150 and sells for $200, resulting in a $50 profit. Units that are unsold at the end of the season are sold to a cut-rate mail order house for $25, resulting in a $125 loss per unit. Joyce needs a probability distribution for the season's demand so she can decide how many units to order. The situation is simplified because Joyce can place an order only in hundreds; thus, she knows that she must order either 300, 400, 500, 600, or 700 units.

After going over records from past years and projecting demand for the coming season, she formulates demand probabilities for each stock level. She then calculates the profits for each possible combination of stock level and demand. The result is a payoff table (Table 18.3).

TABLE 18.3   Payoff Table for Example 18.3 (Profits in Thousands of Dollars)

Probability	Demand	Stock level: number of lawnmowers				
		300	400	500	600	700
.10	300	15	2.5	−10	−22.5	−35
.20	400	15	20	7.5	−5	−17.5
.30	500	15	20	25	12.5	0
.25	600	15	20	25	30	17.5
.15	700	15	20	25	30	35
1.00						

The table shows a $15,000 profit for stocking and selling 300 lawnmowers, regardless of how many are demanded. For each additional 100 units stocked and sold, there's an additional $5,000 profit. These values appear along the diagonal of the payoff table and represent profits when the number of units stocked exactly equals the number demanded.

Beneath each profit along the primary diagonal is the same profit, since units demanded in excess of units stocked don't generate additional profits. To the right of each profit along the diagonal is a reduction of $12,500, representing the loss of 100 unsold units.

Joyce can now consider her decision criteria as she contemplates Table 18.3's payoffs. She must decide how many units to stock for the coming season; that is, she must decide which column of the table to use. To make this decision, she must first decide on her financial objective.

One objective is to aim for the highest possible profit. This very aggressive strategy would be implemented by stocking 700 units, since the 700 column contains the largest profit in the table: $35,000. This stock level would also be chosen if Joyce's objective were to meet all customer demand, regardless of profits.

Another objective might be to assume the worst will happen and stock accordingly. If the lowest profit in each column is identified, the maximum of these values is $15,000, found in the first column. Therefore, a very conservative decision maker might choose to stock 300 units: even under the worst conditions (only 300 units demanded), a profit of $15,000 is guaranteed. Another objective that would be met by stocking 300 units is to ensure that no inventory is left over at the end of the season.

Another approach is to stock the number of units that would generate the highest profits, while avoiding any possibility of a loss. This is a popular philosophy in business, sometimes known as the "cover your number" decision criterion. The best choice for this objective is to stock 400 units since the likely profit (90% chance) is $20,000, and no loss is possible.

Another possible objective is to choose that course of action that maximizes the expected profit for the season. To determine the stock level for this objective, calculate the expected monetary value (EMV) for each of the five stock levels, choosing the stock level with the highest EMV.

Here are the expected values for each column of the table. For each stock level, each payoff is multiplied by the probability of that row, and these products are added:

$$
\begin{array}{ll}
\text{Stock 300:} & (1.00)(15) = 15 \\
\text{Stock 400:} & (.10)(2.5) + (.90)(20) = 18.25 \\
\text{Stock 500:} & (.10)(-10) + (.20)(7.5) + (.70)(25) = 18.00 \\
\text{Stock 600:} & (.10)(-22.5) + (.20)(-5) + (.30)(12.5) + (.40)(30) = 12.50 \\
\text{Stock 700:} & (.10)(-35) + (.20)(-17.5) + (.30)(0) + (.25)(17.5) + \\
& (.15)(35) = 2.63
\end{array}
$$

The highest possible expected payoff results from stocking 400 units. The $18,250 payoff results from a combination of the probabilities of various demand levels, from the amount of profit for a unit sold, and from the loss suffered if a stocked unit is unsold. Joyce summarizes the situation as follows:

Decision	Rationale
Stock 300.	Find the highest profit if the worst situation develops.
	Do not have stock on hand at the end of the season.
Stock 400.	Maximize profits but avoid the possibility of a loss.
	Maximize expected profits.
Stock 700.	Try for the highest possible profit.
	Satisfy all possible demand.

Based on this summary, Joyce decides to stock 400 units.

EXPECTED VALUE OF PERFECT INFORMATION

It is often of value to consider what perfect information in a complex decision situation is worth. Although perfect information is seldom available to the decision maker, its value can be used as a benchmark to evaluate the benefit of acquiring additional information. If reliable information costs $1,000 to acquire, but the value of perfect information in the situation is only $500, the additional information is obviously not worth paying for. On the other hand, if the value of perfect information is $10,000 for the same situation, the decision maker might be willing to pay $1,000 to get additional information that would lead to a better decision.

Expected Value of Perfect Information

The **expected value of perfect information** (EVPI) is the difference between the expected payoff with perfect information and the expected payoff under uncertainty. If perfect information produces a profit of $50,000, for example, and the best the decision maker could do under uncertainty is $35,000, then the value of perfect information—should it exist—is the difference, $15,000.

The **expected value of perfect information** is the difference between the payoff that would result with perfect information and the payoff that would result under uncertainty.

EXAMPLE 18.4 Joyce Cary has decided to stock 400 lawnmowers for the season, reasoning that this stock level will maximize the expected payoff at $18,250. She then begins thinking about an offer she received from a forecasting agency to provide her with a forecast of seasonal demand for lawnmowers in her area. She could use this forecast to predict her own sales level. The cost of this forecast is $9,000, and Joyce wonders if such an expenditure is justified.

Joyce decides to calculate the value (to her) of perfect information regarding sales for the upcoming season. She can then compare this value with the cost of the good, but imperfect, information she's being offered.

If Joyce could foresee the season's demand with total accuracy, she'd realize one of the profits along the primary diagonal in Table 18.3. There's a 10% chance that she would correctly foresee a demand of 300 units, stock that number of lawnmowers, and make $15,000. Likewise, there's a 20% chance that she would correctly predict sales of 400 units and make $20,000, and so on. Under these conditions, she would experience the following expected profits for the season. This value is called *the expected profit under certainty:*

$$(.10)(15) + (.20)(20) + (.30)(25) + (.25)(30) + (.15)(35) = 25.75$$

Joyce can now calculate the expected value of perfect information. If she had perfect information, her expected seasonal profit would be $25,750. As things stand, without knowledge of demand, she has calculated expected profit of $18,250. This is the highest expected value she can choose and results from stocking 400 units. The difference between these two values is the expected value of perfect information.

> Expected value of perfect information = Expected payoff with perfect information − Payoff resulting under uncertainty
>
> EVPI = $25,750 − $18,250 = $7,500

Since *perfect* information about the season's demand is worth only $7,500, Joyce is not willing to pay $9,000 for a forecast of demand, even if it is very accurate. She turns down the offer.

EXERCISES

1. Why does an analyst construct a payoff table?
2. Why is it desirable to choose the action in a payoff table that results in the highest expected monetary value (EMV)?
3. Explain the concept of expected profit under certainty.
4. What is meant by the term *expected value of perfect information*? Why is it important to know the EVPI?
5. A year's supply of shoes of a certain popular type must be ordered in advance by a large department store. Each pair costs $30, sells for $60, and can be sold to a discounter for $15 if unsold at the end of the year. Stock levels being considered are 20, 30, 40, and 50 pairs. Construct a payoff table for the following demand levels: 20, 25, 30, 35, 40, 45, 50.
6. (This question refers to Exercise 5.) How many pairs of shoes should be ordered if expected profits are to be maximized? The demand levels, along with their associated probabilities, are:

Dozen	Probability
20	.20
25	.25
30	.20
35	.15
40	.10
45	.05
50	.05

7. Consider the following payoff table (where payoffs are in thousands of dollars):

				Stock level		
Probability	Sales	100	200	300	400	500
.25	100	5	3	1	−1	−3
.35	200	5	10	8	6	4
.25	300	5	10	15	13	11
.10	400	5	10	15	20	18
.05	500	5	10	15	20	25

a. What is the profit on a unit sold?

b. What is the loss on a unit unsold?

    c. What is the expected monetary value if 300 units are stocked?

    d. What is the optimal stocking level if expected profits are to be maximized?

    e. What is the expected value of perfect information?

8. Barnes Tractor and Implement, a farm implement dealer, needs to decide how many large combines to order for the coming year. The matter is complicated by John Deere's new Maximizer combine, a machine featured in *Successful Farming* (February 1989, p. 26). It is the first new combine design by Deere in 20 years, and Barnes is uncertain how its appearance on the market will affect sales of conventional units.

    The choice of how many to order has been narrowed to 10, 20, 30, 40, or 50. The company believes the probabilities associated with selling these numbers of tractors are .15, .15, .20, .25, and .25, respectively. The profit to the dealer of selling a unit is $5,000; the loss associated with failing to sell a stocked unit is $1,000.

    a. Develop the payoff table.

    b. What is the expected monetary value if 50 units are ordered?

    c. What is the optimal stocking level, using the criterion of maximizing expected profit?

    d. What is the expected value of perfect information in this situation?

    e. What criteria would lead to stocking decisions other than the one identified in part *b*?

9. The Evergreen Corporation is trying to decide what size of can opener plant to build in the Cleveland area. Three alternatives are being considered: plants with capacities of 25,000, 40,000, and 55,000 can openers per year. Demand for Evergreen's can openers is uncertain, but management has assigned the following probabilities to five levels of demand. The payoff table also shows the profit, in millions of dollars, for each alternative and each possible level of demand. What size plant should Evergreen build?

		Action: Build plant with capacity of:		
Probability	Demand	25,000	40,000	55,000
.20	20,000	−3	−5	−7
.35	30,000	0	−2	−4
.25	40,000	1	4	5
.10	50,000	2	5	8
.10	60,000	2	6	10

TREE DIAGRAM ANALYSIS

Tree Diagrams

Decision makers frequently use **tree diagrams** to summarize complex situations so that their essential elements can be identified and used to make rational decisions. A valuable visual aid, the tree diagram, allows a complex situation to be easily understood by any manager. Two symbols are generally used in constructing a tree diagram:

1. A box is used to represent a *decision node* from which one of several alternatives may be selected.

2. A circle is used to represent a *state-of-nature node* out of which a particular state of nature will develop.

Example 18.5 and Figure 18.1 illustrate the use of these symbols.

FIGURE 18.1 Decision Tree Diagram for Example 18.5

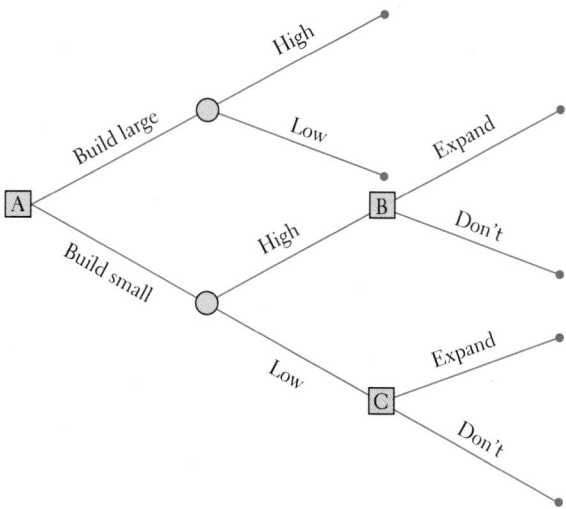

Tree diagrams are charts used by decision makers to summarize complex situations so that their essential elements can be identified.

EXAMPLE 18.5 The King Manufacturing Company must decide whether to build a small plant or a large plant to produce panels for a new product to be introduced next year. After the plant is built and the product produced, market demand will become known (market demand will be either high or low). If a small plant is built, it can be expanded once high market demand has occurred.

Gwynn Luvello, vice president of planning, constructs the tree diagram in Figure 18.1 to help make this decision. The box labeled A on the left side is a decision node. King must decide whether to build a small plant or a large plant. Since there are two alternatives, the tree diagram has two branches labeled *build small* and *build large*. Each branch leads to a circle. The circles are state-of-nature nodes, from which one of two states of nature will result: market demand will be either high or low.

After market demand has been determined, a small plant may or may not be expanded. Boxes B and C represent these decision nodes. The decision is to either expand the small plant or not to expand. Figure 18.1 summarizes the King Company's decision-making situation.

The tree diagram is useful for visualizing the King Company's problem, but by itself it isn't a complete decision-making tool. The next step is to assign cash flows to each tree segment to arrive at a cash value for each branch. These final cash values represent the payoffs.

Organizational decisions such as the ones in these examples are significant because they involve the possibility of more or less profit for the company. At the conclusion of each set of possible outcomes, or branches in a tree diagram, there is some payoff. There are also costs involved with certain branches that must be identified too. Along with the probability and decision branches in the tree diagram, the identification of the costs and payoffs for various possibilities enables the decision maker to assess the situation.

The next step in the process is to assign probabilities to the states of nature. This is usually done subjectively. (Subjective probabilities were discussed in Chapter 5.) Example 18.6 and Figure 18.2 illustrate the idea of assigning payoffs and subjective probabilities to a tree diagram.

FIGURE 18.2   Decision Tree Diagram for Example 18.6

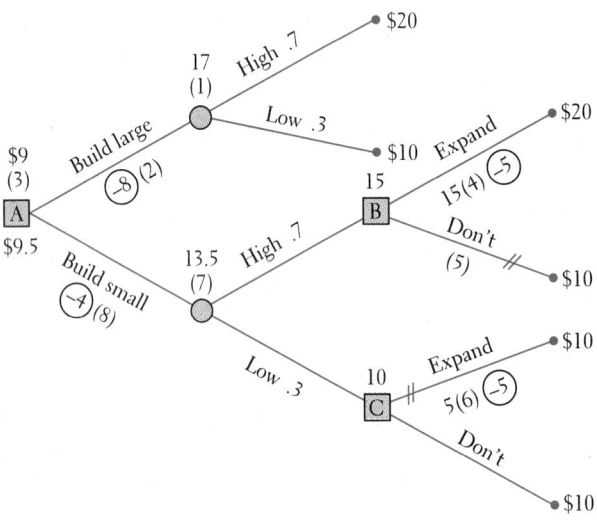

EXAMPLE 18.6   Gwynn Luvello decides to determine the cash flow for the tree diagram in Figure 18.1. Her analyst provides the following cost and payoff estimates:

Costs

Cost of building a large plant: $8 million

Cost of building a small plant: $4 million

Cost of expansion: $5 million

Payoffs

Revenue from high demand for a large or expanded plant: $20 million

Revenue from high demand for a small plant: $10 million

Revenue from low demand: $10 million

Next, Gwynn has the marketing department provide her with estimates for high and low market demand for the new product. The marketing department feels that there is a .7 probability of high demand for the new product and a .3 probability of low demand. Armed with knowledge of the payoffs and probabilities, Gwynn develops Figure 18.2.

With the payoffs and probabilities indicated on the tree diagram, the final step is to find the best decision branch. The best decision usually amounts to the alternative with the highest expected monetary value (EMV). Identifying this alternative requires that the analyst work backward along the tree diagram, starting at the right-hand side of the tree and moving to the left until the first decision node is reached. There are two rules for working backward on a tree diagram:

1. For each state-of-nature node, find the EMV.
2. For each decision node, pick the alternative with the largest EMV.

Example 18.7 illustrates the implementation of these rules.

EXAMPLE 18.7 Gwynn is now ready to make a decision. She begins by computing the EMV for the *build large* decision branch. The analysis is done from right to left. The payoff for high market demand is $20 million, and the probability of it occurring is .7. The payoff for low market demand is $10 million, and the probability of it occurring is .3. Therefore, the EMV is $17 million, as shown:

$$EMV = .7(20) + .3(10) = 17.0$$

Since the cost of building the large plant is $8 million, as indicated by -8 in the circle coded (2) in Figure 18.2, the expected monetary value for this branch is actually $9 million ($17 − $8), as indicated at the point of the figure coded (3).

Next, Gwynn analyzes the *build small* decision branch. Again, the analysis is done from right to left. Payoff for the *high demand–expand* branch is $20 million. However, the cost of expansion is $5 million, as indicated by -5 in the circle, so the EMV is $15 million, the value coded (4), for this branch. This value is larger than the EMV for the *high demand–don't expand* branch ($10 million), so she eliminates the *don't expand* branch by drawing two hashmarks, coded (5), through it.

The payoff for the *low demand–expand* branch is $10 million. Since the cost of expansion is $5 million, the EMV for this branch coded (6), is $5 million. This value is smaller than that for the *low demand–don't expand* branch ($10 million), so Gwynn eliminates the *low demand–expand* branch by drawing two hashmarks through it.

Now Gwynn knows that if a small plant is built and demand is high, she should expand, for an EMV of $15 million. She also knows that if a small plant is built and demand is low, she should not expand, in which case the EMV is estimated to be $10 million.

Next, Gwynn computes an EMV of $13.5 million, coded (7), for the *high/low demand* state-of-nature node:

$$EMV = .7(15) + .3(10) = 13.5$$

Since the cost of building the small plant is $4 million, shown as −4 in the circle coded (8), the expected monetary value for this branch is actually $9.5 million ($13.5 − $4).

Based on the EMV criterion, Gwynn recommends that a small plant be built, and if market demand is high, the plant should be expanded.

BAYES' THEOREM

Bayes' Theorem

Bayes' theorem is designed to modify probability assessments on the basis of additional information. Such modification is a process that takes place in the minds of decision makers every day.

> **Bayes' theorem** involves the process of revising prior probabilities based on additional experimental or sample information.

In the 1700s, the Reverend Thomas Bayes, an English Presbyterian minister and mathematician, developed a formal procedure for using additional information to revise probabilities. This theorem is quite useful in the decision-making process since additional information is often obtained prior to an important decision. Recall the discussion of the expected value of perfect information earlier in this chapter. Although the information gathered from a sample or test market is not perfect, Bayes' theorem provides a way of modifying the decision maker's view of an uncertain world.

In utilizing Bayes' theorem, the tree diagram method will be used. In addition, the two basic rules of probability discussed in Chapter 5 need to be reviewed. Examples 18.8 and 18.9 demonstrate these rules.

EXAMPLE 18.8 The multiplication law of probability states that to determine the probability of a sequence of independent events occurring, the individual probabilities of the events are multiplied together. The multiplication law can also be used for dependent events as long as the sequence is known. The key concept is that if a sequence of events is specified along with their individual probabilities, the multiplication rule can be used to find the probability of that sequence.

Suppose there's a 45% chance that our competitor will reduce the price of a key product. If that happens, there will be an 80% chance that our own sales will be negatively affected. The probability that our sales will drop can be found using the multiplication rule, even though the two events are not independent:

$$P(\text{sales drop}) = (.45)(.80) = .36$$

We have a 36% chance that our sales will drop.

EXAMPLE 18.9   The addition rule states that to find the probability of an event that has more than one way of occurring, the probability of each possible way must be computed, and all these probabilities are then added together. Suppose a television set production line produces a perfect set only 50% of the time, and that the appearance of such a set is random. What is the probability of getting exactly two perfect sets in a random testing of four sets? There are several ways in which this can happen; therefore, each way must be identified, the probability computed, and the resulting probabilities added. Here are the different ways to get two perfect TV sets in a testing of four sets, where G represents good and N represents not good. The probability of each way is computed using the multiplication rule, and the sum of these probabilities is the correct answer:

$$
\begin{aligned}
P(GGNN) &= .5 \times .5 \times .5 \times .5 = .0625 \\
P(GNNG) &= .5 \times .5 \times .5 \times .5 = .0625 \\
P(NNGG) &= .5 \times .5 \times .5 \times .5 = .0625 \\
P(GNGN) &= .5 \times .5 \times .5 \times .5 = .0625 \\
P(NGNG) &= .5 \times .5 \times .5 \times .5 = .0625 \\
P(NGGN) &= .5 \times .5 \times .5 \times .5 = \underline{.0625} \\
&\qquad\qquad\qquad\qquad\qquad\quad .3750
\end{aligned}
$$

There's a 37.5% chance that we could select four TV sets at random and find that exactly two of them are good.

Bayes' theorem appears as Equation 18.1. This equation is actually a shortened version of the full mathematical expression for Bayes' theorem,[1] but the theorem will be used here in this form:

$$P(A|B) = \frac{P(A \text{ and } B)}{P(B)} \tag{18.1}$$

where $P(A|B)$ = Probability of event A occurring given that event B has occurred
   $P(A \text{ and } B)$ = Joint probability of events A and B happening in succession, under conditions of statistical dependence
   $P(B)$ = Probability that event B has occurred

EXAMPLE 18.10   Don Karger, production manager of the MacDonald Manufacturing Corporation, is trying to improve the efficiency of one of his assembly lines. Each Monday morning a machine that produces a key part is set up for the week. Setting up this particular machine is difficult and time-consuming. Don has studied past

---

[1] The general statement of Bayes' theorem for n events $A_1, A_2, \ldots, A_n$ is

$$P(A_1|B) = \frac{P(A_1)P(B|A_1)}{P(A_1)P(B|A_1) + P(A_2)P(B|A_2) + \cdots + P(A_n)P(B|A_n)}$$

records and discovered that the machine is set up correctly only 70% of the time. He also determined that if the machine is set up correctly, it will produce good parts 95% of the time, but if set up incorrectly, will produce good parts only 40% of the time.

Don decides to start the machine and produce one part before he begins the production run. The first part produced is tested and found to be good. What is the revised probability of proper machine setup given this sample evidence?

The application of Bayes' theorem is demonstrated using the tree diagram in Figure 18.3. The first branch shows the two mutually exclusive possibilities for the state of the machine once it's set up Monday morning: the machine is set up either correctly or incorrectly. Past experience indicates that the machine is set up correctly 70% of the time $[P(C) = .7]$. Since the probabilities of a mutually exclusive event must add to 1.0, the probability that the machine is set up incorrectly is .30 $(1.0 - .7 = .3)$.

The secondary branches are based on whether the machine is set up correctly. Past experience indicates that if the machine is set up correctly, the probability that it will produce a good part is .95; incorrect setup reduces this probability to .40.

The numerator of the equation for Bayes' theorem for this example is found by using the multiplication rule in conjunction with Figure 18.3. The probability of a good setup followed by the production of a good part, the numerator is

$$(.70)(.95) = .665$$

FIGURE 18.3   Bayes' Theorem Tree Diagram for Example 18.10

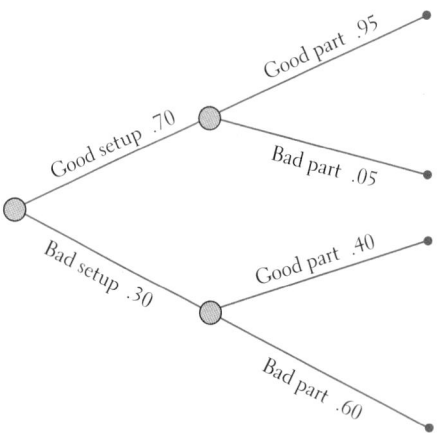

The denominator for Bayes' theorem represents the probability of the given event occurring; in this case, the appearance of a good part. One way to get a good part is following a correct setup, as just shown. The other way is to produce a good part following a bad setup. The denominator of Bayes' theorem is the sum of these two probabilities:

$$(.70)(.95) + (.30)(.40) = .665 + .12 = .785$$

The revised probability that the machine is set up correctly, given that it has produced a good part, is now computed using Equation 18.1.

$$P(A|B) = \frac{P(A \text{ and } B)}{P(B)}$$

$$P(C|GP) \frac{P(C \text{ and } GP)}{P(GP)} = \frac{.665}{.785} = .85$$

When the machine was set up Monday morning, the probability that it was set up correctly was .70. Now that the machine has produced a good part, Don knows that the revised probability of a correct setup is .85. If he wants more assurance, Don can test additional parts.

EXAMPLE 18.11 Loretta Lister, market researcher for the St. Ives Corporation, is using a test market to estimate the national market for her firm's new software product. An article in *The Futurist* (July–August 1992, p. 10) claims that advances in computer technology and information services may soon lead to a global web of networks capable of managing international problems.

She estimates demand for her new software product as either high (40% chance), medium (30% chance), or low (30% chance). St. Ives decides to test-market the product in a midwestern city it has used in the past to estimate national success. Loretta knows that the test market isn't infallible, however, and that it may mislead the company regarding public acceptance of a new product. Specifically, she calculates the following probabilities based on past experience with this test market:

1. For a product that later experiences high national sales, there is a 90% chance that the test market will indicate a successful product.

2. For a product that later experiences a medium national market, there is a 50% chance that the test market will indicate a successful product.

3. For a product that later experiences a low national market, there is a 20% chance that the test market will indicate a successful product.

St. Ives introduces the software product into the test market for a three-month trial period. At the end of this time, the product proves successful in this market. Loretta now wonders what the probability of national success is for this new product.

The initial probabilities of product success are shown in Figure 18.4, along with the probabilities based on the reaction of the test market.

The test market conclusion is that a good product has been developed. Given this result, what is the probability that the product will have high sales nationally? Bayes' theorem is used to compute this revised probability:

$$P(\text{high}|\text{good}) = \frac{P(\text{high and good})}{P(\text{good})}$$

$$= \frac{(.40)(.90)}{(.40)(.90) + (.30)(.50) + (.30)(.20)}$$

$$= \frac{.36}{.36 + .15 + .06} = .63$$

FIGURE 18.4   Test Market Tree Diagram for Example 18.11

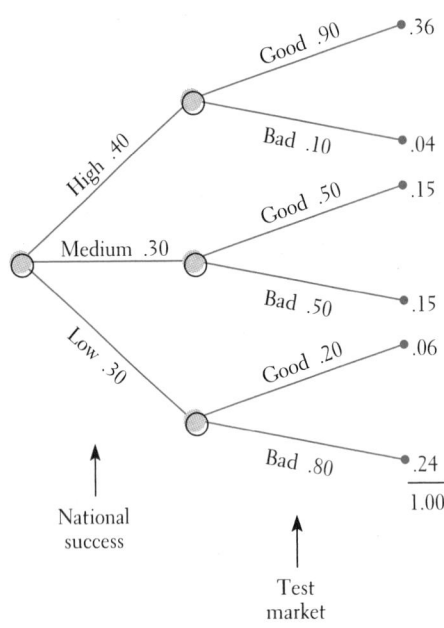

There's a 63% chance that the new product will be successful nationally, given that it has shown a good response in the test market. This is higher than the original probability of a national success (40%) and enables the company to make a more rational decision about committing the millions of dollars necessary to launch the product nationally.

UTILITY CONSIDERATIONS

Utility Theory

The use of the EMV decision criterion is oversimplified in that it assumes indifference among various dollar amounts on the part of the decision maker. In fact, due to their varying asset bases, different companies have different utility functions. Furthermore, individual company managers may have different views of the impact of various sums of money on their organizations. A formal recognition of this matter is sometimes referred to as **utility theory,** because it reflects the usefulness (utility) of various payoffs to the firm.

> **Utility theory** reflects the usefulness (utility) of various payoffs to the firm.

Suppose you were given the choice between taking $500 or risking the money on a double-or-nothing investment (a .5 chance of a payoff of $1,000 and a .5 chance of no payoff). The expected value of the gamble is also $500 (.50 × $1,000 + .50 × 0). Since the expected value of the gamble exactly equals the expected value of the certain payoff, the EMV criterion would result in indifference between these two choices.

Now suppose you are guaranteed $5 million after taxes, and you may choose to risk the money on a double-or-nothing investment (a .5 chance of a payoff of $10 million and a .5 chance of no payoff). The expected value approach again leads to indifference between these two choices, since the expected payoff is $5 million. A very large corporation might actually be indifferent between these two choices, given identical expected values. As individuals, however, we would all choose the sure $5 million rather than take a chance on getting nothing. The reason, based on utility theory, is that the first $5 million has considerable utility (usefulness) in our lives, but the addition of a second $5 million does not. That is, an additional $5 million wouldn't appreciably alter our lives.

EXAMPLE 18.12   A company faces a choice between two propositions, or ventures. For each, the future is uncertain; however, probabilities of the possible outcomes can be estimated, and the payoffs for various alternatives are known. These two ventures are summarized in Figure 18.5.

FIGURE 18.5   Tree Diagrams for Example 18.12 (Millions of Dollars)

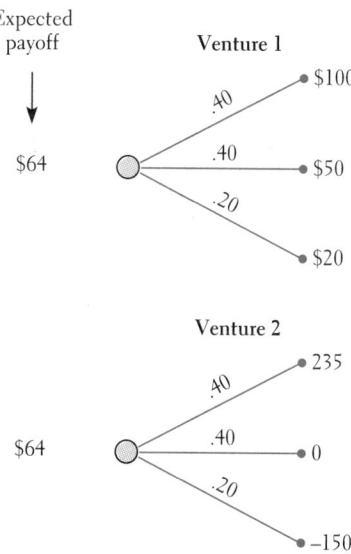

For each venture the expected payoff is $64 million. These values were calculated by multiplying each payoff by its probability of occurring and adding these products. Using EMV reasoning, the two ventures are exactly the same, and the choice between them would result in indifference.

However, when payoffs are examined more closely, there appears to be a big difference between the two ventures. Venture 1 would appeal to a more conservative decision maker since there's no probability of a loss, a profit is guaranteed, and the largest payoff ($100 million) can be regarded as large enough. A more bold or aggressive decision maker might prefer Venture 2. The possibility of a $235 million payoff might be very attractive to the bold manager, and the possibility of no profits or a loss of $150 million might not be viewed as a strong negative factor.

The key point here is that different amounts of money are viewed differently from firm to firm and from one decision maker to another. Utility theory explicitly recognizes these viewpoints and incorporates them into the decision process. More advanced texts on decision making contain discussions about how utility theory is formally incorporated into complex decision-making situations.

EXERCISES

10. How are tree diagrams used by decision makers?

11. Explain how each of the following terms is used in reference to a tree diagram:

    a. State of nature

    b. Decision node

    c. Payoff

12. Bayes' theorem is designed to revise probabilities. What is the basis for such revision?

13. What is the disadvantage of collecting information to use in revising probabilities based on Bayes' theorem?

14. Explain how utility considerations might affect your decision regarding buying car insurance.

15. Explain how utility considerations might affect the Boeing Company's deliberations about designing and building a new commercial aircraft.

16. The national market for a new type of fishing reel is believed to be either strong, medium, or weak, with probabilities .45, .35, and .20, respectively. Probabilities for test market results (based on past experience with the chosen test market) are:

Test market results	National market		
	Strong	Medium	Weak
Good	.85	.50	.25
Bad	.15	.50	.75

    a. Draw the tree diagram that summarizes this situation.

    b. Compute the probabilities of a good test market result and a bad test market result.

    c. Suppose a test market study results in a good test. Compute the revised probabilities of strong, medium, and weak national markets.

17. About 70% of the finished goods produced by a factory are sent to chain store customers, and the remainder go to independent stores. There's a 10% chance that a chain store invoice will remain unpaid at the end of the billing period. For independent stores, this

probability is 50%. What is the probability that an unpaid account is for an independent store?

18. You think there's an 80% chance that you'll be offered a promotion during the next month. This probability is based on your own performance and on rumors of poor appraisals given some of your peers. "Poor Performance Appraisals," a September 1989 *Personnel Journal* article, leads you to believe your company's appraisal system is fair, since there are legal problems associated with a faulty system.

   From watching previous prepromotion activity, you know 90% of people about to be promoted receive an invitation to the executive dining room during the month preceding promotion. A person not about to be promoted has only a 25% chance of receiving such an invitation. If you receive an invitation to the executive dining room, what is the revised probability that you are about to be promoted?

19. Here is a summary of the situation faced by a large construction company regarding the possibility of building a new, large office building, building a smaller office building, or expanding the present building. The key factor is whether business during the next five years will be much greater, somewhat greater, the same, or smaller; the agreed-upon probabilities for these events are .35, .25, .20, and .20, respectively. Gross revenues to the company for each of these events are, in millions, $53, $35, $20, and $15, respectively.

   Cost of building a large building is $10 million. A smaller building could be built for $8 million, but if business turns out to be much larger, it would have to be enlarged at a cost of $4 million. Expanding the present building would cost $4 million and would be adequate to accommodate either the same or a smaller level of business. If business is somewhat greater, a $5 million expansion would be needed; and if business is much greater, a new site would have to be found and built on at a cost of $7 million.

   a. Draw a tree diagram that summarizes this situation.

   b. Compute the expected monetary values for each of three construction possibilities.

   c. Based on expected monetary values only, what is the rational decision sequence for the company?

   d. What utility considerations would enter into the construction decision?

SUMMARY

This chapter has outlined some considerations that attend most decisions in modern organizations, where all the information necessary is usually not available at the time the decision must be made. Rather, estimates, probabilities, and expected values must be used to reach the best decision under conditions of uncertainty.

The payoff table is a way to show the payoffs that result from each combination of decision choice and state of the world. The expected value of perfect information constitutes the maximum amount the decision maker would pay for information that would improve the decision.

Tree diagrams are a way of focusing attention on the key elements in a decision. Tree diagrams incorporate uncertainty branches, decision choices, and final payoffs. Expected monetary value (EMV) calculations are used to evaluate each decision point and identify the best decision.

Finally, utility considerations are a means of recognizing the differences with which assorted firms and decision makers regard various payoffs. The purpose of utility theory is to formally incorporate these different viewpoints into the decision process.

APPLICATIONS OF STATISTICAL CONCEPTS IN THE BUSINESS WORLD

Since decision making in the face of uncertainty is a common element of every manager's role, the concepts discussed in this chapter are used daily by every management decision maker. Unfortunately, these concepts are practiced only at the intuitive level by many managers. The decision process would be improved in many organizations if such concepts and tools as tree diagrams, expected monetary value, payoff tables, and utility theory were more formally incorporated into the process of evaluating complex situations.

Here are a number of hypothetical situations where formal use of the concepts in this chapter might prove helpful. In each situation, the decision is complex and involves many factors, including decision points, probabilities regarding the unknown future, costs of alternatives, final payoffs, and utility theory.

A company must decide whether to introduce a new laundry product or to modify a current product and introduce it as "new and improved."

A major car company is considering several design changes in its lineup. Top managers have spent a lot of time considering the future demands of American consumers as well as the costs and potential profits of various alternatives.

A quality-control manager is involved in the decision about which of five machines to install in a tire factory. The prices are all different, as are the production rates, maintenance costs, and quality of output. The labor needed to run and maintain the machines also varies.

An airplane manufacturer considers developing and introducing a new aircraft type. Because of the enormous cost of such an activity, only one of several contemplated designs can be chosen.

A company that makes computer chips is being wooed by several cities around the country. Management of the company must decide where to locate a new plant; staying in its present location is an alternative also.

Because of a drop in demand, a company that makes and distributes training films must change its way of doing business. Several alternative business activities have been considered along with simply maintaining the present business at a reduced level.

Leaders of a large city are trying to decide some policy matters regarding the city's future direction. Among the alternatives are attempting to expand "smokestack" industries, persuading modern-technology companies to relocate there, and planning a reduction in economic activity with an increase in the "quality of life."

A company is facing increased demand for its products and must decide how to expand operations. It is considering expanding on its present location, expanding to other U.S. locations, and locating some of its operations in other countries. The last consideration entails choosing from amongst several countries.

GLOSSARY

Payoff table A table showing the payoff for every combination of decision and state of the world.

Expected monetary value The average profit that would result if a decision were repeated many times and each time the decision maker chose the same alternative.

Expected value of perfect information The difference between the payoff that would result with perfect information and the payoff that would result under uncertainty.

Tree diagrams Charts used by decision makers to summarize complex situations so that their essential elements can be identified.

Bayes' theorem A theorem that involves the process of revising prior probabilities based on additional experimental or sample information.

Utility theory A concept that reflects the usefulness (utility) of various payoffs to the firm.

KEY FORMULA

Bayes' theorem

$$P(A|B) = \frac{P(A \text{ and } B)}{P(B)} \tag{18.1}$$

SOLVED EXERCISES

1. PAYOFF TABLE

Pat's Pies, a small shop, specializes in baking fancy pies. Pies are baked each morning, and any not sold the same day must be given away. Owner Pat Otten knows from past experience that she can always sell between 8 and 12 apple pies. However, Pat doesn't know how many to bake each day to maximize profits. Records from the past 100 business days show the following demand pattern:

Number of pies sold	Days
8	15
9	25
10	30
11	20
12	10

Each apple pie is sold for $7. The cost to bake an apple pie is $3. Develop a payoff table.

Solution:

Pat can choose one of five alternative decisions: baking 8, 9, 10, 11, or 12 pies, as shown across the top of Table 18.4. Actual demand for any particular day will also be for 8, 9, 10, 11, or 12 pies, as shown in the table's first column.

Note the last column of the first row, where the profit is $20. Twelve pies are baked, but only eight are sold. Profit for each pie sold is $4 ($7 − $3), so the profit for selling eight pies is $32

TABLE 18.4   Payoff Table for Solved Exercises 1 and 2 (Profits in Dollars)

Number demanded	Decision: number of pies to bake				
	8	9	10	11	12
8	32	29	26	23	20
9	32	36	33	30	27
10	32	36	40	37	34
11	32	36	40	44	41
12	32	36	40	44	48
EMV:	32	34.95	36.15	35.25	32.95

($4 × 8). However, four pies were baked and not sold, so the cost for the number of pies baked that exceeded demand is $12 ($3 × 4). Therefore, the payoff for baking 12 pies when demand is for only 8 is $20 ($32 − $12). For the last column of the last row, profit is $48. Twelve pies are baked, and all 12 are sold. Profit for selling 12 pies is $48 ($4 × 12).

Other entries in the payoff table are computed in a similar fashion.

2. EXPECTED MONETARY VALUE

For the situation in Solved Exercise 1, compute the expected monetary value if Pat decides to bake 11 pies. How many pies should Pat bake each day?

Solution:

The probability distribution for demand can be computed from the records in Solved Exercise 1. On 15 out of the 100 days observed, there was demand for eight pies. Therefore, on any given day the probability is .15 (15/100) that demand will be eight pies. Other entries in the following table were computed in the same fashion.

Demand	Days	Probability, $P(x)$
8	15	.15
9	25	.25
10	30	.30
11	20	.20
12	10	.10

The payoff for baking 11 pies when demand is for 8 pies is $23. Since Pat expects this to occur 15% of the time, the expected profit is $3.45 ($23 × .15) Expected profit for each possible demand is computed below in the last column. The expected monetary value for baking 11 pies is $35.25, the summation of the last column.

Demand, x	Probability, $P(x)$	Profit, z	EMV $z \times P(x)$
8	.15	$23	3.45
9	.25	30	7.50
10	.30	37	11.10
11	.20	44	8.80
12	.10	44	4.40
		EMV of baking 11 pies =	35.25

The bottom row of Table 18.4 shows the EMV for each possible action. Pat should bake 10 pies each day to maximize profits. The EMV for this course of action is $36.15.

3. EXPECTED VALUE OF PERFECT INFORMATION

Compute the expected value of perfect information for Solved Exercise 2.

Solution:

If Pat knows that demand is going to be for eight pies, that's the number she'll bake, and her payoff will be $32. With perfect information, the payoff for 9 pies is $36, for 10 pies $40, for 11 pies $44, and for 12 pies $48. The maximum payoff is:

Demand, x	Probability, P(x)	Profit, z	EMV z × P(x)
8	.15	$32	4.80
9	.25	36	9.00
10	.30	40	12.00
11	.20	44	8.80
12	.10	48	4.80
			39.40

The EVPI is $3.25. This is the difference between the maximum payoff ($39.40) and expected monetary value of the best decision ($36.15).

4. TREE DIAGRAM ANALYSIS

Metropolitan Mortgage has just repossessed property on which a marina stands. The marina failed because there was no breakwater to prevent large waves from damaging the boat slips. Paul Sandifer, president of Metropolitan, feels that the company has three options:

1. The property can be sold in its present condition for $400,000.

2. The docks can be renovated, a breakwater built at a cost of $200,000, and the property sold. If the breakwater works, the property should sell for $800,000. If the breakwater doesn't work, the property can be sold for only $300,000. The probability that the breakwater will work is estimated at .9.

3. The docks can be renovated and a breakwater built at a cost of $200,000. Again, the breakwater might not work, in which case the property would have to be sold for $300,000. If the breakwater works, the marina will be operated for five years at a cost of $300,000.

Demand for boat slips will be either high, medium, or low. If demand is high (probability estimated at .1), the property can be sold for $1,300,000. If demand is medium (probability estimated at .5), the property can be sold for $1,100,000. If demand is low (probability estimated at .4), the property can be sold for $900,000. Develop a tree diagram.[2]

Solution:

Figure 18.6 is a tree diagram for this situation. The numbers at the end of each branch are the payoffs. (These payoffs don't include subtraction of the costs involved.) The numbers in rectangles are the EMVs for the decision branches. The tree is analyzed from right to left. The

---

[2]This exercise was adapted from a study by J. E. Hanke, M. Craze, and A. B. Cameron, "A Financial Institution's Dilemma Repossessed Property," *Management Accounting* (May 1991), pp. 44–49.

Figure 18.6   Tree Diagram for Solved Exercise 4

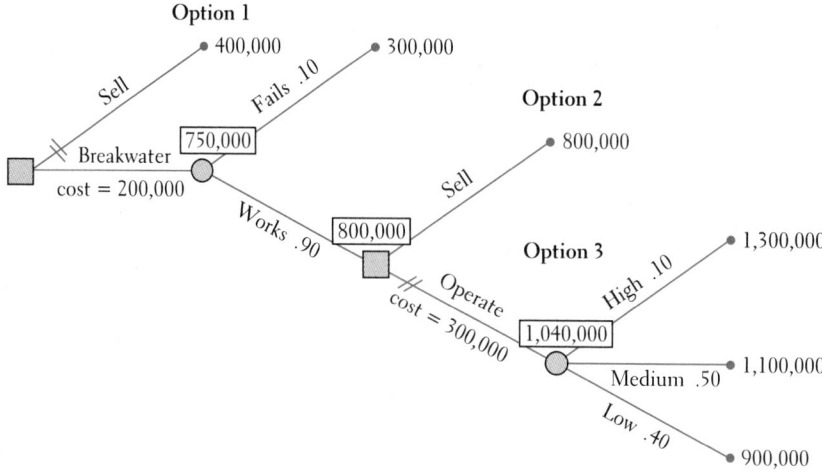

expected monetary value for option 3, the decision branch that involves operating the marina for five years, is about $1 million:

$$\text{EMV} = .1(1,300,000) + .5(1,100,000) + .4(900,000)$$
$$= 1,040,000$$

Since the cost of this decision is $300,000, the expected value for operating the marina for five years is $740,000 ($1,040,000 − $300,000). Therefore, this branch is eliminated because option 2, *build breakwater and sell*, has a higher value, $800,000. Next, the expected monetary value for option 2 is computed to be $750,000:

$$\text{EMV} = .1(300,000) + .9(800,000) = 750,000$$

Option 2 is now compared to option 1. Since the cost of renovating the docks and building the breakwater is $200,000, the expected payoff for option 2 is $550,000 ($750,000 − $200,000). Since this is a better expected payoff than simply selling the property for $400,000, option 2 is the best decision.

5. Bayes' Theorem

First Federal Savings Bank records show that 70% of its car loans are completely repaid. Analysis of the unpaid loans shows that 80% were made to applicants who had been employed at their present jobs for less than two years. Of the repaid loans, 30% were made to applicants who had been employed at their present jobs for less than two years.

a.   What is the probability that a particular loan applicant will have been employed at his or her present job for less than two years?

b.   Given that a particular loan applicant has spent only one year on the present job, what is the revised probability that this person will repay the loan?

c.   Given that a particular loan applicant has spent five years on the present job, what is the revised probability that this person will repay the loan?

Solution:

a. Let R represent repaid loans, U represent unpaid loans, L represent less than two years on the job, and M represent more than two years on the job. The tree diagram for this problem (Figure 18.7) shows the probability that a particular loan applicant will have been employed at the present job for less than two years and repay a loan is .21:

$$P(R \text{ and } L) = P(R) \times P(L|R) = .7 \times .3 = .21$$
$$P(U \text{ and } L) = P(U) \times P(L|U) = .3 \times .8 = \underline{.24}$$
$$P(L) = .45$$

The probability that a particular loan applicant will have been employed on the present job for less than two years is .45.

b. $P(R|L) = \dfrac{P(R \text{ and } L)}{P(L)} = \dfrac{.21}{.45} = .47$

c. $P(R|M) = \dfrac{P(R \text{ and } M)}{P(M)} = \dfrac{.49}{.55} = .89$

FIGURE 18.7   Tree Diagram for Solved Exercise 5

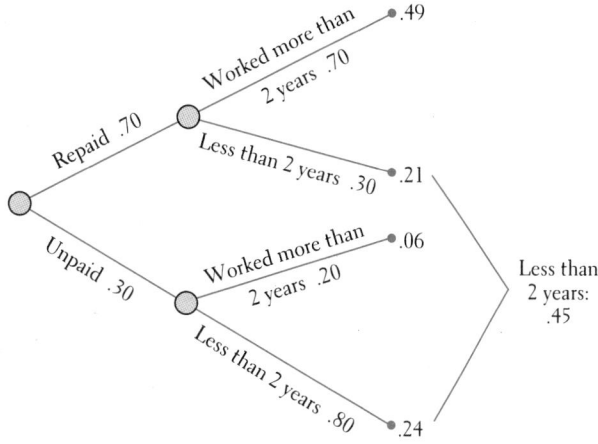

EXERCISES

20. Why is it sometimes useful to revise probabilities?

21. The Skil Corporation is trying to decide whether to introduce a new type of saw. The marketing department has supplied the following estimates:

Demand level	Probability	Expected payoff
Low	.1	− $400,000
Medium	.5	200,000
High	.4	800,000

a. The Skil Corporation must decide the best course of action (*introduce* or *don't introduce*). Develop a payoff table.

b. Compute the expected monetary value for the *introduce* option.

c. Write a memo summarizing the results and recommending a course of action.

22. Your company is developing a new product for the coming year and is concerned about the possibility of its major competitor developing a similar product. Since new products are common in your business, you've experienced similar situations in the past. The competitor is 50% likely to be developing a similar new product, based on the consensus of several of your company's executives.

The annual new product convention can provide a clue as to whether you'll face competition. If the competitor is developing a competing product, there's an 80% chance it will send Sue Smith to the convention. If not the probability of Sue being there is only 40%. Suppose you attend the new product convention and see Sue Smith at a display booth. Find the revised probability that your major competitor is also developing a new competing product.

23. The Programming Institute is in the business of training computer programmers. It guarantees finding each new graduate a job within one week or else will refund the entire cost of training. For every graduate successfully placed, it makes a profit of $1,000. If the cost of training must be refunded, it loses $2,000. From past experience and by watching the want ads, the institute managers have determined demand for programmers during a typical one-week period to be:

Demand level	Probability
10	.10
11	.10
12	.20
13	.25
14	.30
15	.05

a. Develop a payoff table.

b. How large a class should the institute graduate at any one time?

c. Compute the EVPI.

24. Each steering assembly in a car manufacturer's inventory comes from either supplier A, supplier B, or supplier C, with probabilities .25, .45, and .30, respectively. The percentages defective, according to quality-control records, are:

Supplier A: 5%
Supplier B: 4%
Supplier C: 2%

a. What is the probability that the next steering assembly randomly selected from inventory will be defective?

b. If the next assembly is found to be defective, what is the probability that it came from supplier B?

c. If the next assembly is found to operate properly, what is the probability that it came from supplier A?

25. A small community theater applies for many grants to supplement annual revenue. Over time, it has been awarded 40% of the grants it has applied for. By keeping careful records, the theater has noted that for grants that are subsequently awarded, there's a 75% chance that a person from the granting agency will call for clarification; for unsuccessful applications, this probability drops to 30%.

    a. The theater has just received a call from an agency requesting additional information about a grant request. What is the revised probability that the grant will be funded?

    b. Summarize the probability revision process and its results in a brief paragraph.

26. A retailer of airplanes makes $2,000 on a sale of its most popular model and loses $500 if the plane remains unsold at the end of the season. This loss is due to a lower selling price the next year, along with financing and storage costs. An article in *Flying*, "An Invitation to Fly" (June 1989, p. 56), leads the retailer to believe that business will increase during the coming year. This makes the inventory decision more difficult.

    Here are the probabilities of selling the various order units that the retailer is considering for the next year:

Amount	Probability
50	.20
75	.25
100	.30
125	.15
150	.10

    a. Construct a payoff table for this situation.

    b. What is the optimal stocking level if the objective is to maximize expected profits?

    c. What is the EVPI?

    d. State a rational reason for choosing a stocking level other than that identified in part *b.*

    e. What utility considerations might enter into the stocking decision?

27. A snowblower manufacturer must decide how many gasoline engines to order well before its plant begins production. Each engine produces a $250 profit for the company, and each unused engine results in a $50 loss due to financing and storage costs. The company must choose one of the following order levels; the corresponding probabilities for sales are also shown.

Number of engines	Probability of sales
500	.15
750	.25
1,000	.25
1,250	.20
1,500	.10
1,750	.05

    a. Construct a payoff table for this situation.

    b. What is the optimal stocking level for engines if the objective is to maximize expected profits?

    c. What is the expected value of perfect information?

    d. How would the optimal stocking level in part *b* change if the loss per engine unsold were $200?

    e. .How would the optimal stocking level in part *b* change if the profit per engine sold were $350?

28. Describe a marketing situation where a company would be willing to pay to get additional information for the purpose of revising a probability using Bayes' theorem.

29. Describe a situation where a manufacturing company would be willing to pay for additional information about its assembly line in order to revise a key probability using Bayes' theorem.

30. Describe the rationale behind the calculation of the expected value of perfect information.

31. Suppose a tree diagram has been devised that reflects a company's decision nodes, the probability branches of the situation, the costs associated with each branch, and the payoffs at the end of each branch. Describe the rationale used in computing the expected monetary value of the first decision the company must make.

32. Describe the philosophies of two companies that would be at opposite extremes in terms of utility considerations.

33. A company is considering entering one of two ventures described in the following table. Only one of these ventures can be undertaken due to limited company resources.

Venture A		Venture B	
Payoff	Probability	Payoff	Probability
$5,000	.20	−$10,000	.30
7,000	.25	−5,000	.30
10,000	.30	0	.20
15,000	.25	70,000	.20

    a. Compute the EMV for each venture. Which venture would be preferred on the basis of maximizing expected profit?

    b. Describe the kind of company that would strongly prefer venture A. Describe the kind of company that would strongly prefer venture B.

    c. If you could borrow the money to enter one of these two ventures upon graduation, which would you prefer? Why?

34. As manager of a Las Vegas casino, you are confronted with an unusual game designed by one of your employees. The gambler pays a sum of money to play the game, which goes like this:

A fair coin is flipped.
    If heads appear, a pair of dice is thrown.
        If the gambler throws two pairs in a row, the payoff is $1,000.
        Otherwise, the coin is flipped again; heads pays $10, and tails pays nothing.
    If tails appears on the first flip, the gambler throws a pair of dice.
        If a pair is thrown, the gambler wins $50.
        If not, the coin is again thrown; heads pays $20, and tails pays $2.

    a. What is the EMV of the game?

    b. If the casino wants a 5% average payoff on this game, how much should each gambler be required to pay in order to play?

35. A company must choose either venture A, venture B, or venture C. Venture A has a 50% chance of returning $1 million, a 30% chance of returning $2 million, and a 20% chance of requiring a decision. If a certain branch of this decision point is taken, the payoff is $5 million. The other branch will return $10 million with a 30% chance, $8 million with a 40% chance, or nothing with a 30% chance.

    Venture B immediately requires a decision. Branch 1 returns $10 million. Branch 2 has a 40% chance of returning $25 million and a 60% chance of returning $8 million. Branch 3 will return $50 million with a 5% chance, $5 million with a 75% chance, and −$5 million with a 20% chance.

    Venture C either returns $50 million with a 10% chance or requires a decision. Branch 1 of this decision point produces either $10 million or $6 million with equal probability. Branch 2 requires another decision. The first brach returns either $5 million (60% chance) or $9 million (40% chance). The other branch results in either nothing (35% chance), −$10 million (35% chance), or $35 million (30% chance).

    a. Construct a tree diagram for this situation.

    b. What are the optimal decisions at each decision point?

    c. What is the EMV, using the decisions identified in part *b*?

    d. What utility considerations might modify the preceding analysis?

36. Based on several years of experience, a contractor knows there's a 40% chance that he will land any job he bids on. A consultant is willing to survey the market, including the contractor's competitors, to improve the contractor's ability to know in advance if the contract bid will be successful. Upon calling the consultant's references, the contractor finds that when the consultant evaluated bids that subsequently proved successful, she correctly identified a bid as successful 80% of the time. For bids that turned out to be unsuccessful, she incorrectly identified a bid as successful only 15% of the time.

    a. The consultant is hired and, after doing her research, reports that the upcoming bid will be successful. What is the revised probability of a successful bid?

    b. What is the probability of an unsuccessful bid if the consultant predicts the bid to be unsuccessful?

37. You have just won $1,000 in a game of chance at a casino. The casino offers to flip you for double or nothing using a fair coin and an impartial coin flipper.

    a. Would you flip for double or nothing?

    b. In utility terms, justify the answer you gave in part *a*.

38. Your company president makes the following statement to you:

> We are evaluating a consultant's offer to conduct a market survey for us regarding our new breakfast cereal. We developed a payoff table for the various outcomes and have attached probabilities to each possible outcome. The people in the analysis section tell me that the expected value of perfect information is $48,000 and that this should help us reach a rational decision about the consultant's services. How do I use the $48,000 figure in reaching my decision? What does it mean, anyway?

Write a memo to the president, answering her questions.

39. The utility considerations of the local water or electrical power company are probably quite different from a small firm that has just been organized to manufacture and sell computer software.

   a. Describe a venture that would be considered quite risky and describe how each company would probably react to it.

   b. Describe a venture that would be considered quite conservative and describe how each company would probably react to it.

   c. Which company would you prefer to work for in your first job? Does your choice reflect your own attitudes toward monetary utility?

EXTENDED EXERCISES

40. MARSHALL DRY GOODS COMPANY

The Marshall Dry Goods Company has been in the department store business for over 100 years and faces a major decision involving expansion of its operations in its major location, Atlanta, Georgia. Betty Bend is on Marshall's board of directors and is heading a committee of board members considering the matter.

A key element in the expansion decision is whether Marshall's major competitor will respond with an expansion of its own. The company believes there's a 60% chance that such competition will develop.

If the expansion is not followed by increased competition, Marshall believes profits will increase by $50 million per year. If the major competitor expands also, Betty and her committee believe this could take one of three forms: strong expansion, medium expansion, or weak expansion. The committee estimates the probabilities of these three outcomes at .30, .60, and .10, respectively.

For each of these alternatives, Marshall could respond by either increasing its advertising budget or not. Under certain conditions, the competitor might increase its advertising also, and Marshall would then be faced with another advertising budget decision. The situation as developed by Betty and her committee appears in Figure 18.8.

Each probability branch of the tree diagram shows the probabilities estimated by Betty's committee. For each decision branch, Marshall must decide which choice to make. The costs of taking certain branches are shown on the diagram. Finally, the estimated increases in annual profit are shown for each possible final outcome.

   a. What is the optimal decision at each decision node, using the criterion of maximizing expected value?

   b. If Marshall expands in Atlanta, what is the expected annual increase in profits, using the best decision at each decision node?

   c. What utility factors should Betty Bend and her committee consider?

41. MURPHY BROTHERS

Jim Murphy, president of Murphy Brothers, is trying to decide whether to enter a fax machine market with a major company commitment, enter the market with a smaller commitment, or wait and see how the market develops before making a commitment. Jim has read an article about the fax market, "Challenge Is on for Fax Vendors" in The Office (September 1989). He understands that this will become an exciting market and thinks his company can be part of it.

FIGURE 18.8   Marshall Company Tree Diagram for Extended Exercise 40

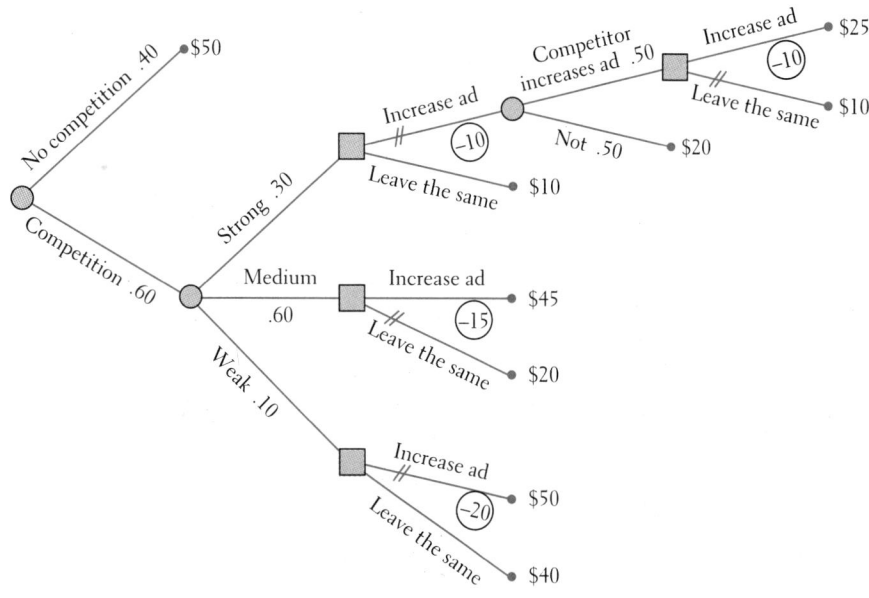

The following factors must be considered in his decision:

1. Entering the market in a major way would cost $60 million.
2. Entering the market on a smaller scale would cost $25 million. If a major market developed, it would cost money to expand the plant and sales staff to accommodate this market.
3. Waiting would cost the company $15 million in lost sales but would enable it to assess the market before making a commitment.

Jim wants to develop a rational way of weighing all the factors that bear on this important decision. He considers using a tree diagram to summarize the situation and to enable the company to find the best course of action. The decision is complicated by the fact that the market's size is unknown at the time the choice must be made. Figure 18.9 reveals the situation's complexity.

The first junction in the tree diagram is a decision node; hence, there are no probabilities attached to the three branches. Murphy Brothers may choose the *major entry* branch, the *small entry* branch, or the *wait* branch. If Jim chooses the *major entry* branch, a negative $60 million will be incurred—the cost of major entry into the market. The payoffs depend on the size of the market that develops. As shown, this market is either high, medium, or low with payoffs of $100, $70, and $30 million, respectively. The expected monetary value in this upper probability fan is $68.5 million, coded (1) in Figure 18.9. The calculation for this EMV is

$$EMV = (.35)(100) + (.35)(70) + (.30)(30) = 68.5$$

When the $60 million cost of major entry is subtracted from this EMV, the result is $8.5 million, coded (2); this is the EMV for choosing the *major entry* option. Jim Murphy will compare this

FIGURE 18.9 Decision Tree Diagram for Extended Exercise 41

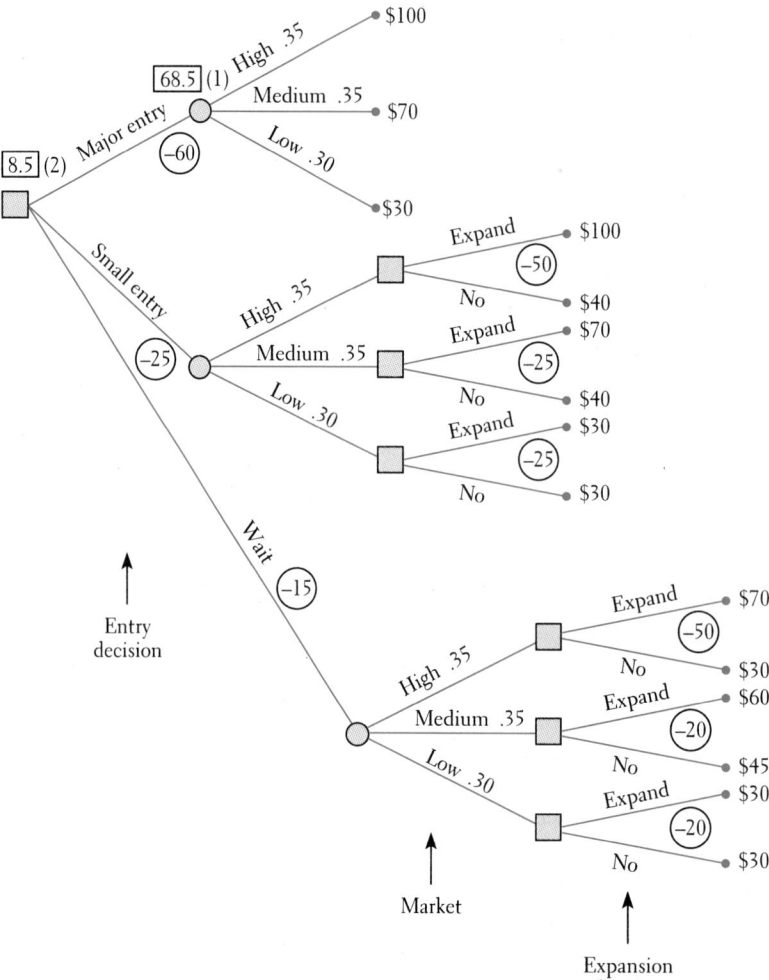

EMV with the expected monetary values of the other two options so that he can make the right decision regarding market entry.

a. Compute the EMV for the *small entry* branch of the tree diagram.

b. Compute the EMV for the *wait* branch of the figure's tree diagram.

c. What should Jim Murphy do?

Microcomputer Package

The micro package *Computerized Business Statistics* can be used to compute posterior and marginal probabilities using prior probabilities and a conditional probability table.

In Solved Exercise 5, the First Federal Savings Bank records show that 70% of its auto loans are completely repaid. An analysis of the unpaid loans shows that 80% were made to applicants who had been at their present jobs for less than two years. Of the repaid loans, 30% were made to applicants who had been employed at their present jobs for less than two years. First Federal wants to answer the following questions:

1. Given that a particular loan applicant has been employed for only one year at the present job, what is the revised probability that this person will repay the loan?

2. Given that a particular loan applicant has been employed for five years at the present job, what is the revised probability that this person will repay the loan?

Computer Solution

On the main menu of *Computerized Business Statistics* a **4** is selected, which indicates Probability Theory.

```
Probability Theory—Program Options Menu

0. CBS Configuration
1. Counting Rules
2. Probability Laws
3. Bayesian Analysis
4. Quick Reviews
5. Exit to Main Menu
6. Exit to Operating System
Press ⏎ to select option under hi-lite bar. Press number or up/down arrow keys to
move hi-light bar.
```

A **3** is selected for Bayesian Analysis.

Since the problem involves entering data from the keyboard, a **1** is selected.

```
Number of States of Nature: Enter 2–10, Press ⏎ 2
```

Since a loan is either unpaid or paid, two states exist.

```
Number of Indicators: Enter 2–10, Press ⏎ 2
```

Since probabilities are given for loans being paid off by applicants employed at their present jobs for more than two years and for less than two years, two indicators are needed.

Next, the indicators are named:

```
Bayesian Analysis - Enter Indicator Labels
      Indicator 1      P1
      Indicator 2      P2
```

Indicator 1 is labeled **P1** and indicator 2 **P2**.

```
Problem definition correct? Enter Y/N/Q, Press ⏎ Y
```

After a **Y** response, the program is ready for the data to be entered:

```
Table Commands Enter State Probabilities
      S1     0
      S2     0
Press F when Finished
```

An **F** is entered once the table has been completed.
   After the table is completed, the screen shows:

```
      S1     .7
      S2     .3
Table Commands Enter Conditional Probabilities
             P1     P2
      S1      0      0
      S2      0      0
Press F when Finished
```

An **F** is entered once the table has been completed.
   After the table has been completed, the screen shows:

```
             P1     P2
      S1     .7     .3
      S2     .2     .8
```

Note that each row must add to 1.0. Row 1 or (S1) gives the probabilities that the loan will be repaid. Row 2 or (S2) gives the probabilities that the loan will not be repaid. Column 1 or (P1) gives the probabilities that an applicant who has been employed on the present job for more than two years will repay the loan. Column 2 or (P2) gives the probabilities that an applicant who has been employed on the present job for less than two years will repay the loan.

   The Bayesian Statistics menu reappears. A 7 is entered so that the problem can run. The screen shows the output menu. The choice in this case was **P** for printer.

   Table 18.5 presents the results. The revised probability that a person who has been employed for only one year on the present job will repay the loan is .47. The revised probability that a person who has been employed for five years on the present job will repay the loan is .89.

TABLE 18.5   Bayesian Analysis Computer Output for Solved Exercise 5

```
                      Information Entered
   Number of States of Nature:      2
   Number of Indicators:            2
   State
1 = 0.7
2 = 0.3
   Conditional Probabilities
     p1     p2
1 = 0.7    0.3
2 = 0.2    0.8
                        Results
   Revised Conditional Table
     p1     p2
1 = 0.891  0.467
2 = 0.109  0.533
   Marginal Probabilities
     p1     p2
1 = 0.55   0.45
```

NONPARAMETRIC STATISTICS

To par or to nonpar, that is the question. Whether t'is nobler in the mind to suffer the slings and arrows of outraged reviewers, or to breach the chasm of unfounded assumptions and light upon the ethereal shores of nonparameters.

Peter Vern Raven, "To Nonparametrics: a Poem"

Objectives

When you have completed this chapter, you will be able to:

Determine whether to use a nonparametric or a parametric test in a decision-making setting.

Apply the following nonparametric tests in decision-making situations: one-sample sign test, one-sample runs tests, Mann-Whitney U test, and Spearman rank correlation test.

The *New York Times* (July 31, 1992, p. C3) reported on *Field and Stream's* and *Outdoor Life's* efforts to improve their image with potential advertisers.

Most statistical techniques in this book make assumptions about the underlying form of the population data. Common assumptions are that the population is normally distributed, that several populations have equal variance, and that the data are measured on an interval or ratio scale. This chapter will discuss a group of techniques called *nonparametric tests* that are useful when these assumptions cannot be made.

Why Managers Need to Know about Nonparametric Statistics

The chi-square tests discussed in Chapter 11 are nonparametric tests. Both the contingency table test and the goodness-of-fit test analyze either nominal or ordinal data, that is, data collected in categories. These tests, especially the contingency table test, are widely used in business applications, which demonstrates the importance of the ability to deal with categorical or ranked data as well as quantitative data (interval or ratio scaled data).

There are many other statistical tests designed for situations where critical assumptions can't be met or where qualitative or categorical data are involved. Analysts who deal with such data should become familiar with books that focus on such tests, generally known as *nonparametric statistical tests*. A few of the more popular nonparametric tests are presented here.

Regarding the efforts of *Field and Stream* and *Outdoor Life*, these magazines might consider surveying their subscribers to determine their interests, life-styles, and income levels among other things. Such a survey would generate a lot of mostly nominal- or ordinal-scaled data. The statistical procedures in this chapter are designed to analyze such data.

Nonparametric versus Parametric Tests

Nonparametric Tests

Nonparametric tests do not require assumptions about the underlying form of the population data. Nonparametric tests are commonly used:

1. When the assumptions required of other popular techniques, usually called *parametric tests*, are not met.

2. When it is necessary to use a small sample size and it is not possible to verify that certain key assumptions are met.

3. When it is necessary to convert qualitative data (nominal or ordinal data) into useful decision-making information.

There are many cases, especially in business situations, where data measured on either a nominal or ordinal scale are collected. Many business applications involve opinions or feelings, and such data are usually in qualitative form.

Nonparametric tests have several advantages over parametric tests. Nonparametric tests:

1. Are generally easy to use and understand.
2. Eliminate the need for the restrictive assumptions of parametric tests.
3. Can be used with small samples.
4. Can be used with qualitative data (nominal or ordinal data).

Unfortunately, nonparametric tests also have disadvantages. Nonparametric tests:

1. Sometimes ignore, waste, or lose information.
2. Are not as efficient as parametric tests.
3. Lead to a greater probability of not rejecting a false null hypothesis (committing a type II error).

Nonparametric tests are statistical tests that do not make assumptions about the underlying form of the population data.

Parametric tests are generally more powerful than nonparametric tests and should be used whenever possible. Also, it's important to note that although nonparametric tests don't make assumptions about the underlying distribution of the population being sampled, they often rely on sampling distributions such as the normal or the chi-square.

ONE-SAMPLE SIGN TEST

The one-sample mean test was discussed in Chapter 9. This test required that the population being sampled follow a normal distribution for a sample size less than 30. The flowchart in Figure 9.7 showed that when the assumption of a normal population is not met for such a small sample, a nonparametric test should be used. The one-sample sign test can be used with small samples where the normality assumption can't be made. However, it's not as discriminating as the one-sample mean test it replaces. The one-sample sign test requires that the population be symmetrical; that is, roughly half of the sample observations are expected to fall on either side of the true mean. If the population is not symmetrical, the null hypothesis should use the median rather than the mean.

The null hypothesis specifies an assumed mean. The test involves assigning each sample observation a plus or minus sign. If a sample value is greater than the assumed mean, a plus is assigned. If the value is less than the assumed mean, a minus is assigned. Values exactly equal to the assumed mean are ignored.

Sign Test

The sign test is virtually identical to a one-sample test for proportions. The cumulative binomial table is used for samples of 20 or less. The normal or Poisson approximation to the binomial is used for sample sizes 21 to 30. The z test for means (Figure

9.7) is used for samples of 30 or more. Example 19.1 illustrates the sign test for a sample of 20 or less.

EXAMPLE 19.1   Beverly Lundquist has just been hired to manage the Sandwich Garden Restaurant in the downtown shopping district of a large southern city. The restaurant gets a lot of lunch business during the noon hour, and people are usually asked to wait for a table. Beverly has been told that the mean time a customer waits between entering the restaurant and being served is 30 minutes. She's afraid that the mean time patrons must wait is more than 30 minutes, so she decides to time a random sample of 18 customers during the next week. Beverly tests at the .05 significance level. The results, measured in minutes, are

```
32  30  25  34  36  29  31  27  32
33  37  32  28  42  40  31  31  32
```

The null and alternative hypotheses are

$$H_0: \mu \le 30$$
$$H_1: \mu > 30$$

Since Beverly doesn't think population waiting times follow a normal distribution, and since she has a small sample size, she chooses the sign test instead of the *t* test of Chapter 9. The first step is to determine whether each sample observation is less than, equal to, or greater than the claimed mean of 30 minutes. A plus sign is assigned to each sample value greater than 30 and a minus sign is assigned to each value less than 30. The next step is to count the plus signs and the minus signs: there are 13 plus signs and 4 minus signs. (Note that one value has been ignored because it equals the claimed mean of 30.)

The decision rule for this hypothesis test is

If the chance of obtaining four or fewer minus signs is less than .05, reject the null hypothesis.

If the null hypothesis is true, the probability of a customer waiting less than 30 minutes is .5. The cumulative binomial table (Appendix E.3) is consulted using $n = 17$ and $p = .5$. The probability of obtaining four or fewer minus signs is .0245. Since this probability is less than .05, the null hypothesis is rejected. Beverly concludes that it takes more than 30 minutes, on average, for customers to receive service.

For samples between 21 and 30, Equation 19.1, for the normal approximation to the binomial, is used, as long as the probability of success is neither quite large nor quite small. (If it is, the Poisson approximation to the binomial is used.)

$$z = \frac{x - (n/2)}{(1/2)\sqrt{n}} \tag{19.1}$$

where x = Number of plus signs or minus signs of interest
n = Total number of plus signs and minus signs

Example 19.2 illustrates the sign test for a sample size of 21 to 30.

EXAMPLE 19.2   After completing the experiment in Example 19.1, Beverly realized that one of her cooks and two of her waitresses were new. She was afraid that this may have caused the average waiting time to be more than 30 minutes. So Beverly repeats the study using a new sample after the new people are properly experienced. She decides to sample 27 customers and test at the .05 significance level. The sample results, measured in minutes, are

```
22  33  25  34  36  29  30  27  31
23  30  32  28  32  40  29  31  35
26  34  33  26  27  37  38  32  34
```

The null and alternative hypotheses are

$$H_0: \mu \leq 30$$
$$H_1: \mu > 30$$

Again, the number of plus signs and minus signs is determined: there are 15 plus signs and 10 minus signs. (Note that two values have been ignored because they equal the claimed mean of 30.)

The decision rule for this hypothesis test is

If the computed z value is larger than 1.645, reject the null hypothesis.

The z value is computed using Equation 19.1:

$$z = \frac{x - (n/2)}{(1/2)\sqrt{n}} = \frac{15 - (25/2)}{(1/2)\sqrt{25}} = \frac{2.5}{2.5} = 1.0$$

Since the calculated z (1.0) is smaller than the critical z (1.645), the null hypothesis is not rejected. Beverly concludes that there's not enough evidence to reject the claimed average waiting time of 30 minutes.

EXERCISES

1. What is the essential difference between parametric statistical methods and nonparametric methods?

2. What is the disadvantage of converting numerical data, such as data measured on a ratio scale, to categorical data, such as those measured on an ordinal scale, in order to analyze the data using a nonparametric method?

3. List several reasons why a nonparametric method would be chosen to analyze sample data.

4. What are the advantages of using nonparametric tests instead of parametric tests? What are the disadvantages?

5. Which tests, parametric or nonparametric, are more powerful?

6. When is the one-sample sign test used?

7. What parametric test is similar to the one-sample sign test?

8. Here are indications of whether a sample of bridge girders are too long or too short, relative to specifications. Do these data suggest a bias toward either long or short girders at the .05 significance level? Girders too long are designated with an L, and those too short with an S.

L, L, S, S, L, S, S, L, S, S, L, L, S
S, S, S, L, L, S, L, L, S, L, L, L, S

9. A bicycle racing team coach randomly determines tire pressures for his team's bikes before each race. If the pressure is not correct, she records it either as too low (L) or too high (H). The data follow. Use the correct statistical test to determine, at the .10 significance level, if the tires tend to be either too high or too low, or whether the occurrence of highs and lows can be considered equal.

H, H, L, L, L, H, H, L, L, L, L, H, H, L, L, L

ONE-SAMPLE RUNS TEST

The one-sample runs test is designed to see if a string of occurrences of two possible types is generated by a random process. A series of heads and tails resulting from coin flips could be tested for randomness, for example, as could a sequence of successes versus failures of some type. If there are only two possible outcomes for each trial and the objective is to determine if the sequence is randomly generated, the runs test can be used.

Special tables for the runs test using small samples can be found in texts devoted to nonparametric methods. If the number of occurrences of either type in the sequence is greater than 20, a normal curve approximation can be used. This is the procedure presented here.

Runs Test

The procedure for the runs test is to examine the sequence of observed events and count the number of runs. A *run* is an uninterrupted series of one of the outcomes. If a coin is flipped six times, for example, where H represents heads and T represents tails, the following sequences result in the number of runs indicated:

1. HHTTHH: There are three runs (two heads, followed by two tails, followed by two heads).
2. HHHTTT: There are two runs (three heads followed by three tails).
3. HTHTHT: There are six runs.

Once the number of runs in the sequence is known, the total number of outcomes of one type is determined (n_1), as is the number of outcomes of the other type (n_2). The test consists of finding if the number of runs can be considered to come from a normal curve with mean (Equation 19.2) and standard deviation (Equation 19.3), provided either n_1 or n_2 is greater than 20.

$$\mu_r = \frac{2n_1n_2}{n_1 + n_2} + 1 \tag{19.2}$$

$$\sigma_r = \sqrt{\frac{2n_1n_2(2n_1n_2 - n_1 - n_2)}{(n_1 + n_2)^2(n_1 + n_2 - 1)}} \tag{19.3}$$

where μ_r = Mean
       σ_r = Standard deviation
       n_1 = Number of occurrences of one kind
       n_2 = Number of occurrences of the other kind

If it's unlikely that the observed number of runs could have come from the normal distribution, the null hypothesis of a random process is rejected. If the observed number of runs seems likely, the null hypothesis of a random process is not rejected.

The z value is calculated using Equation 19.4:

$$z = \frac{r - \mu_r}{\sigma_r} \qquad\qquad (19.4)$$

where μ_r = Mean

         σ_r = Standard deviation

         r = Number of runs

EXAMPLE 19.3   Joe Short flew to Las Vegas and lost $150 playing roulette. He thought he had a foolproof system for playing red versus black, a system he developed at home using a small roulette wheel. After losing his money, he became suspicious about the fairness of the wheel and decided to record the occurrences of red and black for several minutes before hitchhiking back home.

Here is the string of reds and blacks he recorded, where R represents red and B represents black. (Zeros and double zeros were ignored.) The runs are underlined.

B B B R R B R B R R R B B R B R B R R B B B B R R R
B B B R B B B R R R R R B R B R R B B B B R R R

As shown, the number of runs Joe observed was 24. The number of reds was 27 (n_1 = 27), and the number of blacks was 25 (n_2 = 25). The normal distribution is used to test the null hypothesis that the process that generated this sequence is random. The mean and standard deviation of the normal distribution for this test are given by Equations 19.2 and 19.3:

$$\mu_r = \frac{2n_1 n_2}{n_1 + n_2} + 1$$

$$= \frac{2(27)(25)}{27 + 25} + 1 = 26.96$$

$$\sigma_r = \sqrt{\frac{2n_1 n_2 (2n_1 n_2 - n_1 - n_2)}{(n_1 + n_2)^2 (n_1 + n_2 - 1)}}$$

$$= \sqrt{\frac{2(27)(25)[2(27)(25) - 27 - 25]}{(27 + 25)^2 (27 + 25 - 1)}} = 3.56$$

Joe can now complete the randomness test by seeing if the number of runs he observed (24) can be considered unlikely to have come from a normal distribution with the mean and standard deviation shown. He decides to test for randomness at the .05 significance level.

The decision rule for this hypothesis test is

If the computed z value is less than -1.96 or larger than 1.96, reject the null hypothesis.

The z value is

$$z = \frac{r - \mu_r}{\sigma_r} = \frac{24 - 26.96}{3.56} = -0.83$$

Since the calculated z (-0.83) isn't less than the critical z (-1.96), the null hypothesis is not rejected. Joe concludes that the roulette wheel was generating reds and blacks in a random fashion, and that his gambling system was the cause of his losing money.

Figure 19.1 summarizes the test. As shown, an r value of 24 is only 0.83 standard deviations below the mean of 26.96. The standard normal table indicates that approximately 20.33% of the curve lies below a z value of -0.83. Since a two-tailed test was used, the p-value equals .4066 ($2 \times .2033$).

FIGURE 19.1   Runs Test Sampling Distribution for Example 19.3

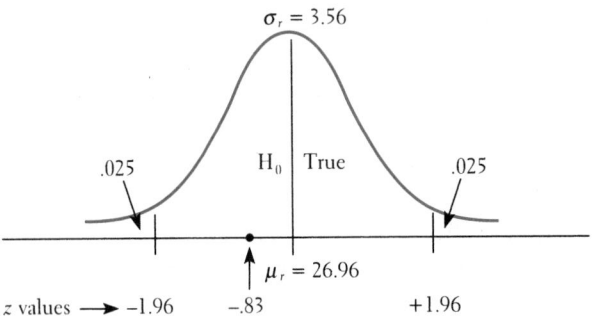

MINITAB can be used to perform a one-sample runs test. The MINITAB commands and output for Example 19.3 are:

```
MTB > SET C1
DATA> +1 +1 +1 -1 -1 +1 -1 +1 -1 -1 -1 +1 +1 -1 +1 -1 +1
DATA> -1 -1 +1 +1 +1 +1 -1 -1 -1 +1 +1 +1 -1 +1 +1 +1 -1
DATA> -1 -1 -1 -1 -1 +1 -1 +1 -1 -1 -1 +1 +1 +1 +1 -1 -1 -1
DATA> END
MTB > RUNS 0, USING C1

    C1

    K =      0.0000

    THE OBSERVED NO. OF RUNS = 24
    THE EXPECTED NO. OF RUNS = 26.9615
    25 OBSERVATIONS ABOVE K 27 BELOW
              THE TEST IS SIGNIFICANT AT 0.4063
              CANNOT REJECT AT ALPHA = 0.05

MTB > STOP
```

The black/red sequence is specified using $+1$ for black and -1 for red. Note that the solution contains the number of runs (24), the mean of the runs statistic if H_0 is true (26.96), and the p-value (.4063). The p-value is the probability of making a type I error if H_0 is rejected.

The runs test can also be used to examine the residuals from a regression analysis. In Chapter 14, you learned that one of the underlying assumptions of regression analysis is that the residuals are independent. This means that the analyst should observe a random pattern in the sample residuals. However, as discussed in Chapter 17, when observations are recorded across time (say, over consecutive months), the residuals are frequently correlated (autocorrelation). When this occurs, the Durbin-Watson statistic is computed to measure autocorrelation.

Use of the Durbin-Watson statistic assumes that the residuals follow a normal distribution. The nonparametric runs test can be used to examine the residuals when the normality assumption is questionable. This is done by recording the sign ($+$ or $-$) of each residual and counting the number of runs. This test is valid regardless of the distribution of the residuals and can be used for any model that assumes that residuals are independent.

EXAMPLE 19.4   In Example 17.22, Stu Miller developed a regression model that used disposable personal income to predict yearly sales for Sears Roebuck. Stu could have used MINITAB to perform the runs test for this situation. The MINITAB commands and results are:

```
MTB > READ 'SEARS.DAT' INTO C1-C2
MTB > REGRESS C1 1 PREDICTOR C2;
SUBC> RESIDS C3.
     COMPUTER OUTPUT WOULD BE SHOWN HERE
MTB > PRINT C3

C3
   378.60    379.25    207.81    186.29    237.68    151.15     97.84
   116.48    369.25    517.75    670.37    552.37    606.25    883.33
   962.44    599.41     93.23    206.92     -7.04   -441.32  -1351.80
 -1564.21  -1048.10  -2711.11  -5614.14   -551.24  -1297.32  - 490.71
  3059.43   2639.88   2161.30

MTB> RUNS ABOVE AND BELOW 0, USING C3

    C3

    K =      0.0000

    THE OBSERVED NO. OF RUNS =   3
    THE EXPECTED NO. OF RUNS = 14.5484
    21 OBSERVATIONS ABOVE K    10 BELOW
            THE TEST IS SIGNIFICANT AT 0.0000

MTB> STOP
```

Note that the solution shows the number of runs, as well as the mean of the runs statistic if the null hypothesis is true. The p-value for this test is .0000. Because this value is smaller than both the .05 and .01 significance levels, H_0 is rejected. Stu concludes that the residuals are autocorrelated.

EXERCISES

10. When is the one-sample runs test used?

11. What parametric test is similar to the one-sample runs test?

SM

12. A production line is believed to generate good and bad assemblies in a random fashion. Data are recorded indicating whether the assembly produced is good (G) or defective in some way (D). The following string of devices was observed at a randomly chosen time. Does this string suggest a random process? Test at the .02 significance level.

> G, G, D, D, G, D, D, D, G, G, D, G, G, D, G, D,
> G, D, D, G, D, D, G, G, G, G, D, D, G, D, D, G

13. A random number generator written for a company's computer is supposed to generate positive and negative numbers randomly. After checking the first series of numbers, the computer analyst thinks the series looks random but decides a statistical test should be undertaken before the program is widely used throughout the company. Here is the observed series of numbers, where P represents a positive number and N represents a negative number. Does the program appear to be random? Test at the .05 significance level.

> P, P, N, N, P, P, P, P, N, N, P, P, P, N, N, P,
> N, P, P, N, P, P, N, P, P, N, N, N, P, P, P, P

MANN-WHITNEY U TEST

Mann-Whitney U *Test*

The Mann-Whitney U test is designed to determine if two sample groups have been drawn from the same population. This test is used as an alternative to the small-sample t test for means described in Chapter 10. The Mann-Whitney U test is used to find whether two independent samples have come from symmetrical populations that have equal means or medians. The test is used when the assumption of two normal populations with equal variances cannot be verified. The data must be measured on at least an ordinal scale, making this test quite useful for ordinal, or ranked, data.

The procedure is to rank the data as if the values in both samples all belong to a single group. The lowest value is assigned a rank of 1, the next lowest a rank of 2, and so on, without regard to which sample the item came from. If the means of the two populations are equal, low and high ranks should be fairly evenly distributed between the two samples. If the means are not equal, one sample will tend to have more high or more low ranks than the other sample. The analysis focuses on the sum of ranks of one of the samples by comparing it with the sum of ranks that would be expected if the population means are equal.

For a combined sample size of 20 or less, special tables for testing the null hypothesis for the two groups are used; such tables are found in books dealing exclusively with nonparametric methods. If the combined sample size is greater than 20, the normal curve has been shown to be a good approximation of the sampling distribution. This normal curve has the parameters shown in Equations 19.6 and 19.7. The Mann-Whitney U statistic is computed using Equation 19.5:

$$U = n_1 n_2 + \frac{n_1(n_1 + 1)}{2} - R_1 \tag{19.5}$$

where U = Mann-Whitney statistic
n_1 = Number of items in sample 1

n_2 = Number of items in sample 2

R_1 = Sum of the ranks in sample 1 (if ties in the rankings occur, average the rankings involved)

If the two samples are of unequal size, let sample 1 represent the sample with the lower number of observations to save computational time.

Standard normal curve procedures are employed to determine if the statistic U could reasonably have been drawn from a normal distribution with the specified parameters. If so, the null hypothesis that the samples came from symmetrical populations with equal means is not rejected. If it's quite unlikely that U could have come from this distribution, the null hypothesis is rejected.

If the null hypothesis is true, then the U statistic has a sampling distribution with the following mean and standard deviation (assuming sufficient sample sizes):

$$\mu_U = \frac{n_1 n_2}{2} \tag{19.6}$$

$$\sigma_U = \sqrt{\frac{n_1 n_2 (n_1 + n_2 + 1)}{12}} \tag{19.7}$$

where n_1 = Number of items in sample 1
         n_2 = Number of items in sample 2

The z value is

$$z = \frac{U - \mu_U}{\sigma_U} \tag{19.8}$$

EXAMPLE 19.5 Two clerks, A and B, are employed in a children's clothing and toy store. The store manager is considering expansion to other locations after reading an article in *Marketing News* (October 1989) on the growing popularity of kid's stores. Comparing the two clerks' sales seems like a good way to determine if one of them could manage a new store. The null and alternative hypotheses are

$$H_0: \mu_1 - \mu_2 = 0$$
$$H_1: \mu_1 - \mu_2 \neq 0$$

If the .05 significance level is used, the decision rule for this hypothesis test is

If the computed z value is less than -1.96 or larger than 1.96, reject the null hypothesis.

The manager records weekly sales amounts for the two clerks for a sample of weeks and wants to know if they can be considered equal. The Mann-Whitney U test will be used to test the hypothesis that the two clerks are the same in this regard, since the sample size is small and since there is evidence that the population of sales amounts is not normal. Table 19.1 lists sales amounts for each clerk along with their rankings.

The U statistic is calculated using Equation 19.5. In this equation, n_1 equals 16 (the number of weeks clerk A was observed), $n_2 = 25$ (the number of weeks clerk B was

TABLE 19.1   Ranked Sales for Mann-Whitney U Test (Example 19.5)

Clerk A		Clerk B	
Sales	Rank	Sales	Rank
197	1	190	3
194	2	180	7
188	4	175	8
185	5	172	10
182	6	167	13
173	9	166	14
169	11	160	17
169	12	157	18
164	15	155	19
161	16	150	21
154	20	146	23
149	22	145	24
142	26	143	25
139	28	140	27
137	29	135	30
130	35	135	31
		134	32
		133	33
		131	34
		122	36
		120	37
		118	38
		109	39
		98	40
		95	41

observed), and $R_1 = 241$. This last value was calculated by summing all the ranks for clerk A. The calculation for U is

$$U = n_1 n_2 + \frac{n_1(n_1 + 1)}{2} - R_1$$

$$= (16)(25) + \frac{16(16 + 1)}{2} - 241$$

$$= 295$$

The parameters of the normal sampling distribution must now be determined to see if a U value of 295 can be considered unusual. Using Equations 19.6 and 19.7, the mean and standard deviation of the normal sampling distribution are calculated:

$$\mu_U = \frac{n_1 n_2}{2} = \frac{(16)(25)}{2} = 200$$

$$\sigma_U = \sqrt{\frac{n_1 n_2 (n_1 + n_2 + 1)}{12}}$$

$$= \sqrt{\frac{(16)(25)(16 + 25 + 1)}{12}} = 37.4$$

The z value for the sample statistic is computed using Equation 19.8:

$$z = \frac{U - \mu_U}{\sigma_U} = \frac{295 - 200}{37.4} = 2.54$$

The sample statistic (295) is 2.54 standard deviations above the curve mean of 200 if the null hypothesis of equal populations is true. This is an unlikely value for this curve, since this z value covers .4945 of the area under the curve, leaving only .0055 on the upper end. The store manager is justified in rejecting the hypothesis that the two clerks are equal in their ability to generate sales. The risk of a type I error in this rejection is only .011 (2 × .0055).

The MINITAB program can be used to conduct the Mann-Whitney U test. MINI-TAB commands to solve Example 19.5 and the test results are:

```
MTB> SET C1
DATA> 1 2 4 5 6 9 11 12 15 16 20 22 26 28 29 35
DATA> END
MTB> SET C2
DATA> 3 7 8 10 13 14 17 18 19 21 23 24 25 27 30 31 32
DATA> 33 34 36 37 38 39 40 41
DATA> END
MTB> MANN-WHITNEY USING C1 AND C2

Mann-Whitney Confidence Interval and Test

C1          N = 16     Median =         13.50
C2          N = 25     Median =         25.00
Point estimate for ETA1-ETA2 is     -10.00
95.1 pct c.i. for ETA1-ETA2 is (-18.00, -3.00)
W = 241.0
Test of ETA1 = ETA2 vs. ETA1 n.e. ETA2 is significant at 0.011

MTB> STOP
```

Note that W on the computer output is the same as R_1 for Example 19.5, 241. The statement "ETA1 n.e. ETA2 is significant at 0.011" indicates that for a two-tailed test the p-value is .011. If the original data had been used instead of the rankings, the value of W would be different; however, the p-value would still equal .011.

EXERCISES

14. When is the Mann-Whitney U test used?

15. What parametric test is similar to the Mann-Whitney U test?

16. The amounts of money won or lost by a husband (H) and wife (W) at Las Vegas are recorded for several trips and ranked from high to low. Here are the data:

    W, W, H, H, H, W, W, H, W, H, W, H, H, H, W, W,
    W, H, H, H, H, H, W, W, W, W, H, W, W, W, H, H

    Can we conclude that the two gamblers have equal ability? Test using the .10 significance level.

17. The numbers of video games sold per week for several weeks are arranged in sequence from low to high and designated A or B, representing the two key company salespeople. The video wholesaler is interested in comparing their efforts, especially after reading an

article in *Marketing and Media Decisions* (November 1989, p. 35) describing two high-power contenders entering the video game market to take on Nintendo, the industry leader. Since the wholesaler features Nintendo games, the owner is nervous about sales volume.

Can the two sellers be considered equally effective? Test using the .05 significance level. The data are

A, A, B, A, A, B, B, A, A, A, A, B, B, A, A, B,
A, B, A, B, B, B, A, B, A, B, B, B, A, B, B, B

SPEARMAN RANK CORRELATION

The Pearson product-moment correlation coefficient, discussed in Chapter 14, is designed to measure the strength of the association between two quantitative variables. That is, the two variables being compared must be measured on either an interval or a ratio scale.

Rank Correlation

There is also a nonparametric counterpart to this measurement known as the *Spearman rank correlation coefficient*. This coefficient measures the extent of association between two variables each measured on an ordinal scale. As such, it's a valuable addition to the analyst's arsenal since many measurements in the business world are made on an ordinal scale.

The data for the Spearman rank correlation coefficient consist of two sets of rankings on the same subjects. The strength of the association between these two rankings is measured by the coefficient. This statistic ranges from -1 (perfect negative correlation) to $+1$ (perfect positive correlation), just as the Pearson coefficient does.

The procedure for calculating the Spearman correlation coefficient is to compare the rankings for the objects under study. The difference between each pair of ranks is denoted d. These differences are squared and added and then used to calculate the correlation coefficient:

$$r_s = 1 - \frac{6\Sigma d^2}{n^3 - n} \tag{19.9}$$

where r_s = Spearman rank correlation coefficient
d^2 = Squared differences between the two ranks
n = Number of objects being compared

The significance of the Spearman rank correlation coefficient is tested in the same way as for the Pearson correlation coefficient. Equation 14.3 is used to compute the test statistic, which has a t distribution based on $(n - 2)$ degrees of freedom. Example 19.6 illustrates this procedure.

EXAMPLE 19.6   Jack Richer wants to see how good a leading sports magazine is at predicting the Big Nine football teams' final standings before the season. For each of the nine teams ranked prior to the season start, Jack records the magazine ranking and checks it against the actual ranking at the end of the season (Table 19.2).

TABLE 19.2 Ranking Data for Spearman Correlation Coefficient (Example 19.6)

Team	Preseason rank	Postseason rank	d	d^2
A	1	4	-3	9
B	2	2	0	0
C	3	5	-2	4
D	4	1	3	9
E	5	7	-2	4
F	6	3	3	9
G	7	9	-2	4
H	8	8	0	0
I	9	6	3	9
				$\overline{48}$

Table 19.2 shows the difference between each preseason and postseason ranking, along with the squared differences. The sum of these squared differences for the nine teams is 48. Equation 19.9 is used to calculate the Spearman correlation coefficient:

$$r_s = 1 - \frac{6\Sigma d^2}{n^3 - n} = 1 - \frac{6(48)}{9^3 - 9} = 1 - .4 = .60$$

For the test of significance, the null and alternative hypotheses are

$$H_0: \rho_s \leq 0$$
$$H_1: \rho_s > 0$$

At the .01 significance level for 7 degrees of freedom (df = $n - 2 = 9 - 2 = 7$), the decision rule is

If the sample t statistic is greater than 2.998, reject the null hypothesis.

The standard error of r is computed using Equation 14.2:

$$s_r = \sqrt{\frac{1 - r^2}{n - 2}} = \sqrt{\frac{1 - (.60)^2}{7}} = .3$$

The t statistic is computed using Equation 14.3:

$$t = \frac{r_s - \rho_s}{s_r} = \frac{.60 - 0}{.3} = 2.0$$

Since the calculated t statistic (2.0) is less than the critical t value (2.998), the null hypothesis is not rejected. The correlation between the sports magazine's preseason rankings and the actual postseason rankings is not significant. Jack considered .60 to be a weak correlation for the "experts" on the magazine's staff and finds that, indeed, such a correlation cannot be generalized to the population of all the magazine's rankings. He immediately writes a letter to the magazine editor explaining his findings and hopes to see his letter published in an upcoming issue.

The MINITAB program can be used to compute the Spearman rank correlation coefficient. The MINITAB commands to solve Example 19.6 are:

```
MTB> SET C1
DATA> 1  2  3  4  5  6  7  8  9
DATA> END
MTB> SET C2
DATA> 4  2  5  1  7  3  9  8  6
DATA> END
MTB> CORRELATION BETWEEN C1 AND C2

Correlation of C1 and C2 = 0.600

MTB> STOP
```

If the original data were unranked, the following commands would be used to develop rankings:

```
MTB> RANK C1, PUT INTO C3
MTB> RANK C2, PUT INTO C4
```

EXERCISES

18. When is the Spearman rank test used?

19. What parametric test is similar to the Spearman rank test?

20. The personnel department of a small company ranks its employees in terms of the number of sick days taken during the year, from highest to lowest. Near the end of this year a series of meetings is held with those who took the most sick days to correct the absentee problem. At the end of the next year, the ranking is again determined to see if the "pep talk" did any good. Here are the two rankings. Was there a significant change during the year if the rankings are tested at the .05 significance level?

Employee	First ranking	Second ranking
A	1	3
B	2	5
C	3	7
D	4	2
E	5	10
F	6	1
G	7	4
H	8	9
I	9	8
J	10	6

21. How similar are the following two rankings? Compute the Spearman rank correlation coefficient to answer this question. Test at the .01 significance level.

Rank 1	Rank 2
1	5
2	3
3	4
4	7
5	1

Rank 1	Rank 2
6	8
7	2
8	6

SUMMARY

This chapter has presented four statistical methods typically used to extract useful information from nominal or ordinal data. These methods are also employed when the underlying assumptions of more powerful parametric methods can't be met. The nonparametric methods are covered more fully in books devoted exclusively to this subject. Such books contain many statistical techniques designed for qualitative data.

The one-sample sign test was presented first as a nonparametric way of testing a claimed population mean. The runs test was presented as a method for determining if a sequence of A/B events is randomly generated. Next, the Mann-Whitney U test was discussed. This technique is designed to detect if two measurements made on an ordinal scale are drawn from the same population. Finally, the Spearman rank correlation coefficient was shown as a method for determining the strength of the relationship between two rankings on the same objects.

APPLICATIONS OF STATISTICAL CONCEPTS IN THE BUSINESS WORLD

Nonparametric methods are not as widely used as they perhaps should be for business applications. It is true that much business data—perhaps most—are quantitative in nature and are therefore properly analyzed using the methods that constitute most of this book. But in many cases, data are collected in categories. Marketing studies are especially involved with such data since these studies commonly measure attitudes.

Here are several questions that might arise in a business setting. For each, the collected data would likely fall in categories.

How do shoppers rank the three major department stores in the downtown area?

As a preliminary step to painting the office areas, what are our employees' favorite colors? Does color choice depend on age, sex, or department?

How do our customers rate the following characteristics of our store?
a. Prices.
b. Service.
c. Convenience.
d. Quality.

The amount by which the length of a manufactured part misses specification is measured for each part. Is there any difference between shifts 1 and 2 regarding these amounts?

Have the sales rankings of our salespeople changed during the past year?

What is the similarity between the rankings of our employees provided by the union's personnel committee and those of shop supervisors?

What is the relationship between the male/female variable and the ratings given the following factors in a recent employee survey?
a. Quality of company management.
b. Fairness of pay level.
c. Opportunity for advancement.

Last year the quality-control department ranked the company's 28 suppliers from best to worst. Rankings have again been made this year. How well do the two rankings correlate?

GLOSSARY

Nonparametric tests Statistical tests that do not make assumptions about the underlying form of the population data.

KEY FORMULAS

Normal approximation to the binomial

$$z = \frac{x - (n/2)}{(1/2)\sqrt{n}} \tag{19.1}$$

Mean for one-sample runs test

$$\mu_r = \frac{2n_1 n_2}{n_1 + n_2} + 1 \tag{19.2}$$

Standard deviation for one-sample runs test

$$\sigma_r = \sqrt{\frac{2n_1 n_2(2n_1 n_2 - n_1 - n_2)}{(n_1 + n_2)^2(n_1 + n_2 - 1)}} \tag{19.3}$$

z value for one-sample runs test

$$z = \frac{r - \mu_r}{\sigma_r} \tag{19.4}$$

Mann-Whitney U statistic

$$U = n_1 n_2 + \frac{n_1(n_1 + 1)}{2} - R_1 \tag{19.5}$$

Mean for Mann-Whitney U test

$$\mu_U = \frac{n_1 n_2}{2} \tag{19.6}$$

Standard deviation for Mann-Whitney U test

$$\sigma_U = \sqrt{\frac{n_1 n_2 (n_1 + n_2 + 1)}{12}} \qquad (19.7)$$

z value for Mann-Whitney U test

$$z = \frac{U - \mu_U}{\sigma_U} \qquad (19.8)$$

Spearman rank correlation coefficient

$$r_s = 1 - \frac{6\Sigma d^2}{n^3 - n} \qquad (19.9)$$

SOLVED EXERCISES

1. ONE-SAMPLE SIGN TEST

A taste test is conducted to determine whether people prefer cherry diet cola or grape. A panel of 40 tasters is asked to rank each drink on a five-point scale. Table 19.3 shows the results. Use the .10 significance level to determine if the tasters indicate a significant difference between the two types of soft drink.

TABLE 19.3 Ranked Scores Assigned to Two Kinds of Diet Soft Drinks (Solved Exercise 1)

Taster	Score Cherry	Score Grape	Sign of difference	Taster	Score Cherry	Score Grape	Sign of difference
1	4	2	+	21	3	5	−
2	1	3	−	22	4	4	0
3	2	2	0	23	1	5	−
4	5	3	+	24	1	3	−
5	3	1	+	25	4	3	+
6	3	2	+	26	5	2	+
7	4	4	0	27	3	5	−
8	1	5	−	28	3	1	+
9	5	4	+	29	2	2	0
10	4	2	+	30	2	5	−
11	3	2	+	31	5	4	+
12	4	1	+	32	5	4	+
13	2	3	−	33	4	3	+
14	1	4	−	34	3	3	0
15	5	4	+	35	1	5	−
16	4	3	+	36	2	5	−
17	5	3	+	37	3	2	+
18	2	4	−	38	4	4	0
19	4	2	+	39	4	2	+
20	5	5	0	40	5	3	+

A 5 denotes the best score; a 1 denotes the worst score. + indicates that cherry was preferred; − indicates that grape was preferred.

Solution:

The null and alternative hypotheses are

$$H_0: p = .50$$
$$H_1: p \neq .50$$

   The first step is to determine the number of plus signs and minus signs. A plus sign is as-signed to each taster who ranked cherry diet cola higher than grape. A minus sign is assigned to each taster who ranked grape higher than cherry. The next step is to count the plus signs and minus signs. There are 21 plus signs and 12 minus signs. (Note that seven values have been ignored because the tasters gave the two beverages the same score.)
   The normal-curve approximation to the binomial distribution is used. In terms of propor-tions, the mean and the standard deviation of the sampling distribution are

$$\mu_p = p = .50$$

$$\sigma_p = \sqrt{\frac{p(1 - p)}{n}} = \sqrt{\frac{.50(.50)}{33}} = \sqrt{.0076} = .087$$

The decision rule for this hypothesis test is

   If the computed z value is less than -1.645 or larger than 1.645, reject the null hypothesis.

The observed proportion of plus signs is

$$\bar{p} = \frac{x}{n} = \frac{21}{33} = .636$$

The z value is

$$z = \frac{\bar{p} - p}{\sigma_p} = \frac{.636 - .50}{.087} = 1.56$$

Since the calculated z (1.56) is less than the critical z (1.645), the null hypothesis is not rejected. There is *not* a significant difference in the number of tasters who preferred one beverage over the other.

2. ONE-SAMPLE RUNS TEST

Chris Belmont has written a computer program to generate random numbers. He decides to test sequences of numbers to look for runs of numbers above and below the median value of 4.5. Consider the following string of 50 digits taken from the random number generator. Perform a one-sample runs test on this series at the .05 significance level.

07904675507234869595534089270867110682607982091123

Solution:

The first step is to identify the number of runs (r), the number of digits less than 4.5 (n_1), and the number of digits larger than 4.5 (n_2).

$$\underline{0}\ \overline{79}\ \underline{04}\ \overline{6755}\ \underline{0}\ \overline{7}\ \underline{234}\ \overline{8695955}\ \underline{340}\ \overline{89}\ \underline{2}\ \overline{7}\ \underline{0}\ \overline{867}\ \overline{110}$$
$$\underline{68}\ \overline{2}\ \underline{6}\ \underline{0}\ \overline{798}\ \underline{20}\ \overline{9}\ \underline{1123}$$

$$r = 23, \quad n_1 = 23, \quad n_2 = 27$$

$$\mu_r = \frac{2n_1 n_2}{n_1 + n_2} + 1$$

$$= \frac{2(23)(27)}{23 + 27} + 1 = 25.84$$

$$\sigma_r = \sqrt{\frac{2n_1 n_2(2n_1 n_2 - n_1 - n_2)}{(n_1 + n_2)^2(n_1 + n_2 - 1)}}$$

$$= \sqrt{\frac{2(23)(27)[2(23)(27) - 23 - 27]}{(23 + 27)^2 (23 + 27 - 1)}} = 3.48$$

The decision rule for this hypothesis test is

If the computed z value is less than -1.96 or larger than 1.96, reject the null hypothesis.

The z value is

$$z = \frac{r - \mu_r}{\sigma_r} = \frac{23 - 25.84}{3.48} = -0.82$$

Since the calculated z (-0.82) is not less than the critical z (-1.96), the null hypothesis is not rejected. The number of runs in the row of numbers is random.

3. MANN-WHITNEY U TEST

Dr. Tom Whitfield of Deaconess Hospital is testing the effectiveness of a new drug in treating paranoia. He records the lengths of hospital stays for paranoid patients treated with an old drug and those for similar patients treated with the new drug. A rank of 1 is assigned to the shortest hospital stay. Dr. Whitfield obtains the following ranks for the lengths of hospital stays for 25 patients:

Old drug	New drug
5	1
9	2
12	3
14	4
15	6
16	7
17	8
20	10
21	11
22	13
23	18
24	19
25	

Is the new drug more effective? Test at the .01 significance level.

Solution:

The null and alternative hypotheses are

$$H_0: \mu_1 - \mu_2 \leq 0$$
$$H_1: \mu_1 - \mu_2 > 0$$

The U statistic is calculated using Equation 19.5. In this equation, $n_1 = 12$ (the number of patients using the new drug), $n_2 = 13$ (the number of patients using the old drug), and $R_1 = 102$. The last value was calculated by summing all the ranks for the new drug. The calculation for U is

$$U = n_1 n_2 + \frac{n_1(n_1 + 1)}{2} - R_1$$

$$= (12)(13) + \frac{12(12 + 1)}{2} - 102$$

$$= 132$$

The U statistic computed from the sample data is 132.

Using Equations 19.6 and 19.7, the mean and standard deviation of the normal sampling distribution are

$$\mu_U = \frac{n_1 n_2}{2} = \frac{(12)(13)}{2} = 78$$

$$\sigma_U = \sqrt{\frac{n_1 n_2 (n_1 + n_2 + 1)}{12}}$$

$$= \sqrt{\frac{(12)(13)(12 + 13 + 1)}{12}} = 18.4$$

The decision rule for this hypothesis test is

If the computed z value is larger than 2.33, reject the null hypothesis.

The z value for the sample statistic is

$$z = \frac{U - \mu_U}{\sigma_U} = \frac{132 - 78}{18.4} = 2.93$$

The calculated z (2.93) is greater than the critical z (2.33); therefore, the null hypothesis is rejected. Dr. Whitfield concludes that patients who used the new drug had a shorter hospital stay than patients who used the old drug.

4. SPEARMAN RANK CORRELATION

Lester Roenfeldt, president of the Crescent Department Store chain, wants to measure the effect of a new incentive system on consumer preferences for various branches of the chain. On the basis of a marketing survey taken last year, 11 stores were ranked according to consumer preferences. This year, the same research was undertaken, with somewhat different rankings (Table 19.4). Lester wants to determine whether there's a significant change in preference rankings during the past year. Test at the .05 significance level.

Solution:

Table 19.4 shows the differences between rankings for each store, along with the squared differences. The sum of these squared differences is 67, and the total number of stores being ranked is 11. These values are used in Equation 19.9 to calculate the Spearman correlation coefficient:

$$r_s = 1 - \frac{6\Sigma d^2}{n^3 - n} = 1 - \frac{6(67)}{11^3 - 11} = 1 - .305 = .695$$

TABLE 19.4   Ranking Data for Solved Exercise 4

Branch	Last year's rank	This year's rank	d	d^2
A	1	5	−4	16
B	2	4	−2	4
C	3	1	2	4
D	4	2	2	4
E	5	9	−4	16
F	6	7	−1	1
G	7	3	4	16
H	8	8	0	0
I	9	11	−2	4
J	10	9	1	1
K	11	10	1	1
				67

For the test of significance, the null and alternative hypotheses are

$$H_0: \rho_s = 0$$
$$H_1: \rho_s \neq 0$$

At the .05 significance level, the decision rule is

If the sample t statistic is less than -2.262 or greater than 2.262, reject the null hypothesis.

The standard error of r is computed using Equation 14.2:

$$s_r = \sqrt{\frac{1 - r^2}{n - 2}} = \sqrt{\frac{1 - (.695)^2}{9}} = .24$$

The t statistic is computed using Equation 14.3:

$$t = \frac{r_s - \rho_s}{s_r} = \frac{.695 - 0}{.24} = 2.90$$

Since the calculated t statistic (2.90) is greater than the critical t value (2.262), the null hypothesis is rejected. Lester concludes that there's a significant similarity between the rankings last year and this year. Apparently the new incentive system has not been particularly effective.

EXERCISES

22. What is the disadvantage of converting quantitative data, such as those measured on a ratio scale, to categorical data, such as those measured on an ordinal scale, in order to analyze the data using a nonparametric method?

23. Here are sample observations for the weights of a new breakfast cereal fed into boxes by a filling machine. Since the sample size is small, and since there's evidence to suggest that the population of weights is not normal, a nonparametric test is in order. Can we conclude that the occurrences of overfills (O) and underfills (U) in the population are equal?

U, U, O, O, O, U, O, O, O, U, U, O, O,
U, O, O, U, U, O, O, O, O, U, U, O, O

24. The number of bad parts found in a PC company's subassemblies is recorded for each order. Also recorded is whether the shipment of parts came from supplier A or supplier B. The plant manager is interested in the quality of units shipped, especially after reading "Five Hot 286 Bargains" in *PC Computing* (February 1989, p. 86). This article described five competitors' products and brought the subassemblies' quality level into sharp focus.

    The shipments are arranged in ascending order, with the lowest number of bad parts appearing first, the next lowest second, and so on to the highest number of bad parts. Here is the ascending list denoted by supplier: A or B. Can the plant manager conclude at the .05 significance level that the two suppliers are supplying part batches of equal quality?

    A, A, A, B, B, A, B, A, A, B, B, A, A, B, A,
    A, B, B, B, A, B, A, A, B, B, B, A, B, B, B

25. Determine the Spearman rank correlation coefficient for the following data. Describe the extent of similarity between the two ranks.

Rank 1	Rank 2
1	6
2	2
3	7
4	1
5	9
6	3
7	10
8	4
9	12
10	5
11	11
12	8

26. Howard Hindman, quality-control engineer for Spartan Manufacturing Company, needs to see if the production process for a particular part is in control. He examines a sample of 30 consecutive parts emerging from the production line and classifies each as either defective or nondefective. Howard wants to test at the .05 significance level if the process generates defective and nondefective parts randomly. Howard classifies the sequence as A = defective and B = nondefective:

    A, A, A, B, B, A, B, A, A, B, B, A, A, B, A,
    A, B, B, B, A, B, A, A, B, B, B, A, B, B, B

27. Evergreen Soft Drink Company President Julie Zappone has asked statistician Ben Showalter to analyze the effectiveness of free samples. Ben conducts an experiment by comparing sales of Evergreen soft drinks on regular days with sales on days when free samples are provided. The results, in sales units, are:

Regular days:	40	50	44	58	39	27	41	46	53	35	31	33
Free-sample days:	42	51	68	71	45	55	60	64	39	68	58	49

Test at the .05 significance level if free samples increase sales.

28. Art Lysone, foreman of the Amoca Plant, wants to know if the number of overtime hours worked is related to age. He records data for overtime hours and age for 12 employees:

Age:	58	47	35	24	60	29	38	42	22	54	28	39
Hours:	5	5	10	13	9	23	0	3	6	18	11	21

Test at the .02 significance level whether the number of hours worked overtime is related to age, using a nonparametric test.

29. Eunice Stern, Dodge Corporation personnel director, analyzes the problem of employee absenteeism. Eunice carefully checks the records of employees with an unusually large number of absences. She wants to determine whether absences are random or occur for some reason. Here's the 42-day attendance record of Larry Wiley, one of these employees. A represents *absent* and P represents *present*.

PPPPPAAAPPAPPPPPAPPAAAPPPPPAPPAPPAPPPAAAA

Test at the .05 significance level to determine whether Larry's absences have occurred randomly.

30. Marian Campbell, a stockbroker for Weber-Payne, observes the behavior of the Dow Jones Industrial Average on the New York Stock Exchange for 60 market days. She wonders if day-to-day changes are random. Marian classifies market behavior each day, using I for *increase* and D for *decrease*:

DIDIIIIDIDDDIIDIIIIDDDDIDIIIDDDIIDIIIDDDIIIIDIDIIIDDDDIIIDIDI

Test at the .01 significance level to determine if stock market ups and downs can be considered random.

31. Sunkiss Vineyards tests its new grape juice, Purple-Power, against the leading seller, Grape-Wonderful. In a study of consumer preferences, 18 people were given unmarked samples of each brand and asked which they liked better. The brand each person tasted first was randomly selected. The results are:

Person	Brand preference	Sign
1	Purple-Power	+
2	Grape-Wonderful	−
3	Purple-Power	+
4	Purple-Power	+
5	Purple-Power	+
6	Grape-Wonderful	−
7	Purple-Power	+
8	Grape-Wonderful	−
9	Purple-Power	+
10	Purple-Power	+
11	Grape-Wonderful	−
12	Purple-Power	+
13	Purple-Power	+
14	Purple-Power	+
15	Purple-Power	+
16	Purple-Power	+
17	Grape-Wonderful	−
18	Purple-Power	+

Test at the .10 significance level whether people prefer Purple-Power.

32. Consider the following set of rankings:

Rank 1	Rank 2
1	8
2	7
3	6
4	5
5	4
6	3
7	2
8	1

   a. What value would you expect for the Spearman rank correlation coefficient?

   b. Compute the Spearman rank correlation coefficient.

33. The Corker-White Advertising Agency decided to test eight different commercials on a group of men and women to determine if there's a relationship between the two groups' rankings. This study was requested by the agency president, who read an article on women in the workplace in *Training and Development Journal* (November 1989, p. 21). She believes men and women could react differently to the commercials.

Commercial	Ranked by women	Ranked by men
A	3	1
B	4	3
C	1	6
D	8	5
E	7	8
F	5	2
G	2	7
H	6	4

   Test at the .10 significance level to determine if there is a significant difference between the way men and women rank the commercials.

34. The Mayor of Deer Park, Tom Truelove, has just read a report stating that median income for his city is $13,329. This figure seems too low to Tom. He decides to take a random sample of 15 families and determine their median income. The results are

$14,100	$15,100	$12,789	$13,500	$14,010
$14,321	$13,560	$13,789	$20,900	$34,010
$12,150	$13,780	$14,189	$21,784	$68,543

   Test at the .05 significance level to determine if the population median is higher than $13,329. Use a nonparametric test.

35. A consumer-testing group wishes to compare tires with five-year guarantees offered by two large mail order department stores. The group selects a random sample of 20 tires from store A and 20 tires from store B and tests them under similar conditions. The tire lives are ranked (the tire that lasted the longest is ranked number 1), and the summation of

the ranks for department store A is 354. Test at the .10 significance level to determine whether there's a significant difference in the lifetimes of the two stores' tires.

36. From 1950 through 1989, National League baseball teams won the World Series 19 times, and American League teams won 21 times. The year-to-year results (with N representing the National League and A representing the American League) are

AAAANNANANNAANNNANANANAAANNAANNNNAAANAN

Test at the .01 significance level to determine if World Series victories have occurred randomly between the two leagues.

37. Frank Kasson, president of Zable Corporation, wants to know if an "Investment in Excellence" program will have a positive impact on potential for advancement within the company. Nine employees are rated as to their promotion potential on a 10-point scale, both before experiencing the program and after. The results are:

Employee	Before	After
A	7	9
B	4	3
C	4	6
D	8	10
E	7	7
F	5	2
G	2	8
H	3	9
I	6	8

Test at the .10 significance level to determine if the program has an impact on advancement potential.

38. The ROTC unit on campus has decided to test two methods of training cadets to break down and reassemble an automatic weapon. The results for the two groups are:

Time	Group	Rank
4.5	1	6
4.3	2	5
5.6	2	12
3.9	2	2
4.0	1	3.5
4.5	1	13
4.6	1	7
4.8	2	8
3.8	2	1
4.0	1	3.5
5.0	1	9
5.2	2	10.5
5.2	2	10.5

Test at the .05 significance level to determine if there is a significant difference between the two methods of training. Use a nonparametric method.

39. Donald Barfield wants to test the relationship between his sales manager's ratings of sales-people and their years of experience.

Salesperson	Years of service	Rating
A	8	4
B	4	3
C	5	6
D	8	10
E	5	7
F	1	2
G	2	8
H	3	9
I	12	1
J	10	5

Test at the .05 significance level to determine if there is a significant relationship between the sales manager's ratings of salespeople and their years of experience. Use a nonparametric method.

40. Flip a coin 100 times and record the sequence of heads and tails. Is the sequence random if tested at the .10 significance level?

EXTENDED EXERCISES

41. THE FAIR COIN

An unpleasant fight with the company union is taking up a great deal of management time at the Bartlett Company. Irene Bartlett, company president, finally reaches an agreement with the union about the final point of contention in the new contract. They decide that the question of whether full disability pay will continue for six or nine months after injury will be resolved by a coin flip.

A local church minister has agreed to flip the coin at a meeting of the company's board of directors and the union leadership. Irene is stunned to learn that the union has now raised the question of which coin will be used and wants some assurance that the coin will be fair.

Irene realizes the union is trying to tax her patience but decides to let the minister select a coin and flip it many times. The outcomes will be recorded and given to a statistics professor, who will then use "some statistical test" to determine if the sequence of heads and tails can be regarded as randomly generated. Here are the test results, where H represents a head and T represents a tail:

H T H T T H H T H H T T T T H H T H T H H T T H T H
T T H H H T T H T H T T H T H H H T T H T T H H T T

Irene counts the number of runs in this sequence as 32, with 25 heads and 27 tails. The statistics professor leaves her a memo before he leaves on spring break: "The mean of the normal sampling distribution for the runs test is 27.0 with a standard deviation of 3.6."

a. Does the sequence of heads and tails appear to be randomly generated?

b. Use the runs test to determine if the claim of a random sequence can be statistically justi-fied using the values Irene's analyst gave her.

c. What should Irene tell the union about the fairness of the coin?

42. THE SALES MOTIVATION PROGRAM

Charlie Fields became sales manager for a national life insurance company a year ago. At that time, he instituted a sales motivation program that he had used successfully in another com-pany. Now, a year later, he wants to assess the impact on his key salespeople's performance. His interest increases after he reads "Productivity Improvement Begins Today" in *Management So-lutions* (June 1988).

When he took the job, Charlie obtained a ranking of the 10 key salespeople in the company. A current ranking has just been issued by top management. These company rankings combine total dollar sales volume and other factors, such as number of new accounts, size of largest account, and total number of accounts.

Here are the key salespeople for the company along with their ratings, both one year ago and currently. After studying these rankings, Charlie isn't sure he has enough evidence to show top management that his first year on the job has paid big dividends to the company. He's especially concerned because company bonus time is only two weeks away.

Salesperson	Rating last year	Rating this year
Campion	1	3
Chapman	2	1
Lopez	3	5
Shapiro	4	2
Zurenko	5	6
Cameron	6	4
Bump	7	9
Kuo	8	8
Hartman	9	10
Faulkner	10	7

a. What is your opinion of Charlie's motivation program after looking at the two rankings?

b. Use the Spearman rank correlation procedure to determine the correlation between last year's rankings and this year's.

c. Based on the correlation coefficient, how effective has the program been?

43. BURNSIDE MANUFACTURING

Burnside Manufacturing Company produces small engines used in rototillers and garden trac-tors. The company has a contract with two companies that supply it with the pistons used in these engines. A continuing problem is out-of-tolerance pistons, which must be returned to the supplier. Recent meetings at Burnside have raised the question of whether the two suppliers are contributing equally to this problem.

To investigate this matter, records are kept for several days on the amount by which pistons are out of tolerance. These error amounts are then ranked from low to high, and the supplier is indicated for each. Burnside thinks it can determine if one supplier is worse than the other by examining these rankings. Obviously, if one supplier has most of the low rankings and the other has most of the high rankings, the higher-ranked supplier is creating most of the problem.

Here are the ranks for out-of-tolerance piston amounts, from low to high; R represents one supplier and S represents the other.

```
R R S R R R S S R R S R S R R S R R S S R S S S S S R
S S S R S R R S S S S S R S S R S S S S R S S S S S S
```

a.   Do the sample results provide any clues about the quality comparison of the two suppliers?

b.   Use the Mann-Whitney U test to determine if a quality difference can be supported statistically.

c.   Assume the role of statistical analyst and write a paragraph summarizing your findings.

MICROCOMPUTER PACKAGE

The micro package *Computerized Business Statistics* can be used to solve nonparametric problems.

In Exercise 27, Ben Showalter analyzed the effectiveness of the policy of free samples. Ben conducted an experiment comparing sales of Evergreen soft drinks on regular days with sales on days when free samples are provided. The results, in sales units, are:

Regular days:	40	50	44	58	39	27	41	46	53	35	31	33
Free-sample days:	42	51	68	71	45	55	60	64	39	68	58	49

Test at the .05 significance level to determine if free samples increase sales.

Computer Solution

From the main menu of *Computerized Business Statistics* a **14** is selected, indicating Nonparametric Methods. The nonparametric methods menu is shown on the screen.

Since the problem involves entering data from the keyboard, a **1** is selected.

```
Nonparametric Methods - Define New Problem
Options:        1 = Wilcoxon Rank-Sum Test
                2 = Mann-Whitney Test
                3 = Wilcoxon Signed-Rank Test
                4 = Spearman Rank Correlation
                5 = Kruskal-Wallis Test
Select Method: Enter 1-5, press ↵ 2
```

Since the Mann-Whitney test is needed to solve Exercise 27, a **2** is selected.

```
Alpha Error: Enter 0-1, press ↵ .05
```

The significance level for this exercise is **.05**.

```
Nonparametric Methods - Enter Number of Data Points
            Population 1      __ 12 __
            Population 2      __ 12 __
Press F when Finished
```

Since each population had 12 observations, a **12** is entered in each blank space.

```
Nonparametric Methods - Enter Population Labels
       Population 1      __ free
       Population 2      __ reg __
Press end when Finished
```

Population 1 is entered as **free**, and population 2 is entered as **reg**.

```
Problem definition correct Y/N/Q, Press ⤶ Y
```

After a **Y** response, the program is ready for the data to be entered. There are 12 data points. An **F** is entered once the blanks have been completed.

After the data have been entered the screen shows:

```
            free      reg
   1 =        42       40
   2 =        51       50
   3 =        68       44
   4 =        71       58
   5 =        45       39
   6 =        55       27
   7 =        60       41
   8 =        64       46
   9 =        39       53
  10 =        68       35
  11 =        58       31
  12 =        49       33
```

Next, the program asks:

```
Save data? Y/N, Press ⤶ N
```

The nonparametric statistics menu reappears. A **7** is entered so that the problem can be run.

```
One or Two Tailed Test? Enter a '1' or a '2' and press ⤶ 1
Lower or Upper Limit? Enter a 'L' or a 'U' and press ⤶ U
```

Since the test involves determining whether the free samples increase sales, a one-tailed test at the upper limit is used. The screen shows the output menu. The choice in this case was **P** for printer.

MINITAB COMPUTER PACKAGE

MINITAB can be used to solve several nonparametric procedures. The MINITAB commands to solve the one-sample sign test for Example 19.1 are:

```
MTB > SET C1
DATA> 32 30 25 34 36 29 31 27 32 33 37 32 28 42 40 31 31 32
DATA> END
MTB > STEST 30 C1;
SUBC> ALTERNATIVE = +1.

SIGN TEST OF MEDIAN = 30.00 VERSUS G.T. 30.00
              N     BELOW    EQUAL    ABOVE    P-VALUE    MEDIAN
C1           18         4        1       13     0.0245     32.00
```

The data are entered into C1 using the SET command. The STEST command is used to compute a sign test for a hypothesized median of 30. The alternative subcommand is used for a one-sided test where the alternative hypothesis is greater than. Note that the p-value, .0245, is exactly the same as the probability of obtaining four or fewer successes from the cumulative binomial table.

Other nonparametric commands demonstrated in this chapter include RUNS (to test data to determine if the order is random), MANN-WHITNEY (to determine the difference between two population medians), and RANK and CORR (to compute the Spearman rank correlation for ordinal data).

Nonparametric commands not demonstrated in this chapter include WTEST (which performs a one-sample Wilcoxon signed-rank test), KRUSKAL WALLIS (which offers a nonparametric alternative to one-way analysis of variance), and FRIEDMAN (which performs a nonparametric analysis of a randomized block experiment).

SAS COMPUTER PACKAGE

The SAS computer package can be used to solve nonparametric models. The SAS commands to analyze Exercise 39 are:

```
TITLE "SPEARMAN RANK FOR EXERCISE 39";
DATA SALESPEOPLE;
 INPUT YEARS RATING;
 LABEL YEARS ='YEARS OF EXPERIENCE'
       RATING ='RATING OF SALESPERSON';
CARDS;
8    4
4    3
5    6
8    10
5    7
1    2
2    8
3    9
12   1
10   5
PROC CORR NOSIMPLE SPEARMAN;
 VAR YEARS RATING;
```

The TITLE command names the SAS run. The DATA command gives the data a name. The INPUT command names and gives the correct order for the two data fields. The next 10 lines are card images that represent the years and rating variables. The PROC CORR NOSIMPLE SPEARMAN command calculates the Spearman rank correlation coefficient between the variables "years of experience" and "rating" indicated on the VAR subcommand. Figure 19.2 shows the results.

Other nonparametric techniques that can be analyzed in SAS using the PROC NPAR1WAY command are the Wilcoxon rank sum test, the Wilcoxon signed rank test, and the Kruskal-Wallis test.

FIGURE 19.2   SAS Output for Exercise 39

```
                              SPEARMAN RANK FOR EXERCISE 39

                                  Correlation Analysis

                            2 'VAR' Variables:  YEARS    RATING
          Spearman Correlation Coefficients/ Prob > |R| under H₀: Rho=0 / N = 10
```

$$\text{Spearman Correlation Coefficients/ Prob} > |R| \text{ under } H_0: Rho=0 / N = 10$$

```
                                     YEARS      RATING
          YEARS                     1.00000    -0.17073
          YEARS OF EXPERIENCE        0.0        0.6372


          RATING                    -0.17073    1.00000
          RATING OF SALESPERSON      0.6372     0.0
```

Appendixes

APPENDIX A EFFECTIVE COMMUNICATIONS

Many of the exercises throughout this text have asked you to "prepare a memo for management explaining the results of your analysis." These assignments reflect our view that good communication is essential if research results are to be used in a firm's decision making. This is especially true when the analysis involves manipulating data and/or using a computer, the subjects of this text. We've seen many cases where a good analysis is ignored because of poor communications.

There are three essential steps to effectively communicating the results of a quantitative study. First, you must really *understand* these results. One purpose of studying statistics, and studying this text, is to develop your understanding of what happens when a computer performs an analysis on data.

Second, you need to *organize* the results before you begin any writing or verbal presentation. The importance of such organization seems obvious, but, again, it's easy to find instances where a presentation is sloppy and difficult to follow.

Third, in the actual written or verbal report, good presenters *practice* their techniques. Many good verbal models are available for you to study, such as TV newscasts and some political speeches. Good writing skills can be developed with practice as well. We can't overestimate the importance of good writing ability in a business career. The rest of this appendix is devoted to preparing written reports. Practice often!

Here are some guidelines to help you develop an effective communication style:

Think about your readers. What is their background? Why would they be interested? How much detail do they want? Do they just want the analysis, or do they want conclusions and recommendations as well? What is their connection to the firm's decision-making process, and what is the best way to get them to use your results?

Be as concise yet complete as you can. Once you've carefully considered your audience, how can you present the pertinent aspects of your research with just the right amount of detail?

Be prepared to present conclusions about your research as well as the results. What effect should your results have on the firm? How can the firm do its business better as a result of your efforts? What change in direction is suggested by your results?

Here is a sample memo written for a fictitious situation similar to those in this text's examples and exercises. The writer has decided that the length and amount of detail are appropriate for the intended audience. For other audiences, a much shorter memo might be appropriate, such as: "Bob/Judy: Average is up to $40.25. Recommend we buy." Another audience (for example, the company's board of directors or bank loan officer) might require a much longer written document.

MEMO

To: Bob and Judy, VPs

From: Art Hank, Analyst

Date: January 18, 1993

Subj.:   Pamco Company Sales

Following your request of January 9, I conducted a study of the average dollar sales of the Pamco Company in conjunction with our proposed acquisition of Pamco during the next six months. Recall that in our last set of figures from Pamco, the average sales amount per customer visit was $37.59.

During the past three months, Pamco has initiated an intense advertising campaign designed to increase customers' average purchase amount. Pamco management has permitted me to take random samples of purchases during the past three weeks, and I've collected a total of 750 transactions during that time. I've used three trained interviewers for this purpose and have sampled during every day of the week at many different times of the day. As a result, I have a very representative view of Pamco's current performance.

The average purchase amount is $40.25, an increase of $2.66 over the previous reported average. With a sample standard deviation of $5.90, this results in a test z value of 12.3 and p-value of .0000. This means that we can make a virtually error-free statement that the average purchase amount at Pamco has increased.

In the face of this significant increase over a short period of time, I believe our faith in Pamco's potential has been justified. Subject to the financial considerations in this matter, I recommend that we move forward to purchase Pamco.

In determining the proper length of your report, remember that this memo is only an example. It would be good practice for you to take one of the exercises in this text that requires a written memo and write three different memos: a short one of two or three sentences, another of about the length of the one just presented, and a longer one of three or four pages.

The organization of a memo or report may vary just as the length, depending on the audience. The following sample outline is for reference in preparing any written report.[1] The topics are only suggestions since a given report might contain many more, or fewer, headings.

I.   Title page
II.   Table of contents

---

[1]From W. Dillon, T. Madden, and N. Firtle, *Marketing Research in a Marketing Environment* (St. Louis: Times Mirror/ Mosby College Publishing, 1987), p. 718.

III.   Introduction
 A.   Background and objectives
 B.   Methodology
  1.   Sample
  2.   Procedure
  3.   Questionnaire
IV.   Management summary
 A.   Key findings
 B.   Conclusions
 C.   Marketing implications and recommendations
V.   Detailed findings
 A.   Evaluation measures
 B.   Diagnostic measures
 C.   Profile composites
VI.   Appendixes
 A.   Questionnaire
 B.   Field materials
 C.   Statistical output

Two additional sample memos are shown next for your reference. Each is a solution to a text exercise. These will help you when your professor assigns a "memo" exercise.

Exercise 53, Chapter 4:

MEMO

To: Al

From: Bob

Date: January 24, 1993

Subj.:   Income as a Percentage of Sales

Following your instructions, I've sampled 70 firms from the 500 largest industrial corporations in the United States and have recorded net income as a percentage of sales for each. In analyzing these data values, I find that the mean is 7.7%, the median is 8%, and the mode is also 8%. We can thus conclude that the mean return on sales is 7.7%, with half the returns being more than 8% and the other half less.

The standard deviation of returns is 2.0098, which tells us the typical amount by which the 70 returns differ from the mean of 7.7%.

Our own figure, according to last year's annual report, is 9%. This places us above the average for the nation, as indicated by my sample figures. I hope this analysis helps you with your upcoming presentation to the board.

Exercise 51, Chapter 12:

MEMO

To: Cindy Bane

From: Cathy Gant

Date: March 11, 1993

Subj.:   ANOVA on Flavor and Price

I have completed the analysis of variance on flavor and price for our new ice cream flavors. This analysis is based on sampling sales volumes from 12 stores in the region. Here is a summary of the F test values I obtained, along with the critical values of F from the table using a .01 significance level:

Effect	Calculated F	Table $F(.01)$
Price	24.12*	4.68
Flavor	22.31*	5.57
Interaction	2.69	3.63

*Significant

The above results show that price has a definite effect on volume sold, as the null hypothesis of equal volume is rejected. Examination of the data indicates that lower prices result in higher volumes sold, as expected.

The null hypothesis of equal volume by flavor is also rejected. The data indicate that brandy and peach are about equal in terms of volume sold, but apricot lags behind.

The null hypothesis of no interaction has not been rejected. This means that unusual sales do not result when certain prices are attached to certain flavors.

On the basis of my analysis, I recommend that we seek to establish as low a price as possible in order to maximize sales, and that we drop the apricot flavor from our new line.

APPENDIX B   DERIVATIONS

CORRELATION DERIVATION

$$r = \frac{\Sigma z_x z_y}{N} = \Sigma \frac{[(x - \mu_x)/\sigma_x][(y - \mu_y)/\sigma_y]}{N}$$

$$= \frac{\Sigma(x - \mu_x)(y - \mu_y)}{\sqrt{(\Sigma x^2/N) - (\Sigma x/N)^2}\sqrt{[(\Sigma y^2/N) - (\Sigma y/N)^2]/N}}$$

$$= \frac{\Sigma(x - \mu_x)(y - \mu_y)}{\sqrt{[N\Sigma x^2 - (\Sigma x)^2]/N^2}\sqrt{[N\Sigma y^2 - (\Sigma y)^2]/(N^2/N)}}$$

$$= \frac{N\Sigma(x - \mu_x)(y - \mu_y)}{\sqrt{N\Sigma x^2 - (\Sigma x)^2}\sqrt{N\Sigma y^2 - (\Sigma y)^2}}$$

$$= \frac{N\Sigma(xy - y\mu_x - x\mu_y + \mu_x\mu_y)}{\sqrt{N\Sigma x^2 - (\Sigma x)^2}\sqrt{N\Sigma y^2 - (\Sigma y)^2}}$$

$$= \frac{N[\Sigma xy - (\Sigma x\Sigma y/N) - (\Sigma x\Sigma y/N) + N(\Sigma x/N)(\Sigma y/N)]}{\sqrt{N\Sigma x^2 - (\Sigma x)^2}\sqrt{N\Sigma y^2 - (\Sigma y)^2}}$$

$$= \frac{N[\Sigma xy - (\Sigma x\Sigma y/N) - (\Sigma x\Sigma y/N) + (\Sigma x\Sigma y/N)]}{\sqrt{N\Sigma x^2 - (\Sigma x)^2}\sqrt{N\Sigma y^2 - (\Sigma y)^2}}$$

$$= \frac{N[\Sigma xy - (\Sigma x\Sigma y)/N]}{\sqrt{N\Sigma x^2 - (\Sigma x)^2}\sqrt{N\Sigma y^2 - (\Sigma y)^2}}$$

$$= \frac{N\Sigma xy - \Sigma x\Sigma y}{\sqrt{N\Sigma x^2 - (\Sigma x)^2}\sqrt{N\Sigma y^2 - (\Sigma y)^2}}$$

LEAST SQUARES DERIVATION

$$d = y - \hat{y}$$
$$= y - (b_0 + b_1 x)$$
$$d^2 = [y - (b_0 + b_1 x)]^2$$
$$\Sigma d^2 = \Sigma[y - (b_0 + b_1 x)]^2$$
$$= \Sigma(y - b_0 \; b_1 x)^2$$

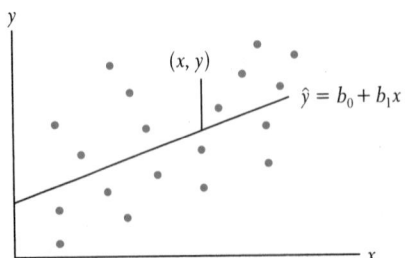

Partial Derivatives

$$\frac{\delta\Sigma}{\delta b_1} = 2\Sigma(y - b_1 x - b_0)(-x) \qquad\qquad \frac{\delta\Sigma}{\delta b_0} = 2\Sigma(y - b_1 x - b_0)(-1)$$

$$= 2\Sigma(-xy + b_1 x^2 + b_0 x) \qquad\qquad = 2\Sigma(-y + b_1 x + b_0)$$

To Obtain Minimums, Set Partials $= 0$

$$\frac{\delta\Sigma}{\delta b_1} = 0: 2\Sigma(-xy + b_1 x^2 + b_0 x) = 0 \qquad \frac{\delta\Sigma}{\delta b_0} = 0: 2\Sigma(-y + b_1 x + b_0) = 0$$

$$\Sigma(-xy + b_1 x^2 + b_0 x) = 0 \qquad\qquad \Sigma(-y + b_1 x + b_0) = 0$$

$$-\Sigma xy + b_0\Sigma x + b_1 x^2 = 0 \qquad\qquad -\Sigma y + Nb_0 + b_1\Sigma x = 0$$

Find a b_0 and b_1 Such That $\Sigma\, d^2$ Is a Minimum

$$b_0\Sigma x + b_1\Sigma x^2 = \Sigma xy \qquad \times N$$
$$Nb_0 + b_1\Sigma x = \Sigma y \qquad \times \Sigma x$$
$$Nb_0\Sigma x + Nb_1\Sigma x^2 = N\Sigma xy$$
$$\underline{Nb_0\Sigma x + b_1(\Sigma x)^2 = \Sigma x\Sigma y} \qquad\qquad \text{subtract}$$
$$Nb\Sigma x^2 - b_1(\Sigma x)^2 = N\Sigma xy - \Sigma x\Sigma y$$
$$b_1[N\Sigma x^2 - (\Sigma x)^2] = N\Sigma xy - \Sigma x\Sigma y$$
$$b_1 = \frac{N\Sigma xy - \Sigma x\Sigma y}{N\Sigma x^2 - (\Sigma x)^2} \qquad \text{slope formula}$$

$$Nb_0 + b_1\Sigma x = \Sigma y$$
$$Nb_0 = \Sigma y - b_1\Sigma x$$
$$b_0 = \frac{\Sigma y}{N} - \frac{b_1\Sigma x}{N} = \bar{\bar{y}} - b\bar{x} \qquad \text{y-intercept formula}$$

Converting Yearly Trend Values to Monthly

Steps for converting the trend equation from annual to monthly:

1. The slope and constant must be converted from annual values to monthly values. To do so, divide b_0 and b_1 by 12. When the data are cumulative or when the annual figures are averages, this step is omitted. In other words, the monthly data must add to the annual totals in order for this step to apply. The annual equation for the new-car registration data is

$$\hat{Y} = 7.901912 + .076123X$$

where 1 unit of x represents 1 year and $x = 0$ represents July 1, 1959.

$$\hat{Y} = 7.901912/12 + .076123/12(X)$$
$$\hat{Y} = .658493 + .0063436X$$

2. The annual and monthly data must be recorded in the same type of units. If they are, skip this step. If they are not, convert the annual to monthly by moving the decimal point accordingly. Since the annual data are recorded in millions of

registrations and the monthly data in thousands, move the decimal point to the right three places.

$$\hat{Y} = 658.493 + 6.3436X$$

3. The x value must be converted from annual to monthly by dividing by 12. The x in the equation refers to units in terms of years. Convert x so that it represents months by dividing it by 12.

$$\hat{Y} = 658.493 + 6.3436/12(X)$$
$$\hat{Y} = 658.493 + .528633X$$

4. The origin must be shifted to the middle of the first month of data, usually January 15. To move forward from July 1, 1959 to January 15, 1985, one must add 305.5 months to the x-coded value. The final monthly equation is

$$\hat{Y} = 658.493 + .528633 (X + 305.5)$$
$$\hat{Y} = 658.493 + .528633X + 161,497$$
$$\hat{Y} = 819.990 + .528633X$$

where $\hat{Y}$ = expected monthly trend values
          X = monthly values with 0 located at January 15, 1985

APPENDIX C   COMPANY DATA BASE

The following data base contains nine variables measured on N = 200 fictitious company employees. Each row represents the values of the nine variables for a single employee. The number in the first column (1–200) is the employee number. Each subsequent column represents the values of one variable for all 200 employees.

The nine variables are defined as follows:

x_1 = Number of years with the company
x_2 = Number of overtime hours worked during the past six months
x_3 = Gender: 1 = Female, 2 = Male
x_4 = Number of continuing education courses completed
x_5 = Number of sick days taken during the past six months
x_6 = Score on company aptitude test
x_7 = Amount of education: 0 = High school diploma, 1 = Some college,
         2 = College degree, 3 = Postgraduate education
x_8 = Annual base salary
x_9 = Employee age

n	x_1	x_2	x_3	x_4	x_5	x_6	x_7	x_8	x_9
1	11	125	1	4	9	121.89	2	23065	44
2	24	225	2	2	2	114.20	1	27180	50
3	17	115	2	3	5	134.11	1	34875	48
4	9	117	1	1	1	113.95	1	23685	53
5	15	26	1	2	0	151.41	2	33550	62
6	6	43	1	4	3	96.65	1	22635	45
7	4	124	2	2	4	98.43	2	19575	26
8	2	71	2	1	1	110.06	1	20430	28
9	17	166	2	2	5	101.98	1	18955	33
10	17	158	1	3	2	101.01	1	25595	40
11	15	182	2	4	4	103.42	2	34975	63
12	21	81	2	3	6	106.88	2	26800	55
13	4	58	1	2	5	99.36	2	22400	50
14	12	203	1	2	3	105.66	2	31200	33
15	23	144	1	2	4	100.91	1	24750	41
16	20	179	1	3	5	73.76	2	30495	53
17	19	96	2	1	5	83.39	0	33965	58
18	12	96	2	4	7	88.41	1	30440	51
19	5	157	2	4	8	98.19	1	25545	39
20	11	27	2	2	4	101.72	1	23960	30
21	11	88	1	0	6	92.63	1	30630	45
22	8	177	2	4	6	92.59	1	38790	61
23	20	211	1	3	1	110.34	2	41705	68
24	1	125	1	0	9	102.91	2	19775	30
25	6	58	2	0	7	110.39	2	37600	57

(continued)

n	x_1	x_2	x_3	x_4	x_5	x_6	x_7	x_8	x_9
26	18	178	1	4	3	124.50	1	34250	49
27	21	166	1	3	5	116.35	1	36195	48
28	7	155	1	3	4	118.64	2	28090	31
29	21	45	2	2	6	115.64	2	35600	60
30	27	157	2	2	5	113.16	2	39975	67
31	20	99	2	0	4	96.92	2	37100	57
32	11	140	1	5	7	94.82	0	27500	32
33	11	101	1	3	9	102.62	1	24450	27
34	3	22	1	4	4	78.89	1	23150	37
35	16	93	1	3	5	83.88	1	35000	37
36	2	3	2	2	5	78.42	0	22025	25
37	12	142	1	4	9	98.67	1	26500	32
38	16	11	2	3	0	86.52	1	36475	53
39	9	124	2	1	5	87.65	2	27200	27
40	15	55	2	3	5	81.40	1	33975	37
41	3	6	2	9	3	107.87	2	19000	23
42	17	12	1	1	6	106.60	1	28650	35
43	17	112	1	3	0	117.57	1	38500	41
44	23	71	2	3	7	96.15	2	40400	63
45	6	28	2	1	3	107.97	1	38900	54
46	1	20	2	5	4	104.72	2	27050	31
47	7	43	1	3	3	85.54	0	26275	33
48	4	113	1	2	4	123.67	1	30000	40
49	22	77	2	5	4	80.55	0	40900	63
50	18	152	2	3	5	91.02	1	37000	54
51	22	0	1	1	4	105.08	1	42250	62
52	25	112	2	3	7	116.61	1	47300	63
53	15	103	1	2	1	120.90	1	30500	39
54	24	215	1	0	7	95.35	0	26180	41
55	15	50	1	3	6	95.94	0	27940	39
56	2	169	2	1	9	118.40	1	15625	26
57	17	92	2	1	3	82.45	0	23650	42
58	7	132	2	1	7	99.18	1	41910	41
59	8	48	1	1	7	107.17	1	38950	56
60	11	200	2	4	9	97.10	0	43650	70
61	10	149	2	4	4	92.41	0	31450	39
62	10	79	1	0	5	101.16	1	24650	40
63	8	48	1	1	8	93.92	0	26250	37
64	15	202	1	1	8	103.45	1	37225	57
65	8	74	1	1	3	103.89	1	23100	29
66	23	74	2	5	4	110.25	1	40370	65
67	24	138	2	5	4	103.60	1	42450	63
68	22	66	1	3	3	109.10	2	38300	65
69	6	68	1	2	5	87.58	1	39500	57
70	3	184	1	1	7	96.21	0	31400	29
71	16	123	2	1	4	101.75	1	32670	39
72	4	105	2	3	7	110.08	2	33110	47

n	x_1	x_2	x_3	x_4	x_5	x_6	x_7	x_8	x_9
73	12	0	2	6	8	104.85	1	35850	61
74	23	52	1	3	4	93.91	0	47100	61
75	13	121	2	4	8	103.45	1	41600	46
76	11	90	2	5	2	101.69	2	40700	42
77	4	31	2	0	3	110.25	1	28750	29
78	3	52	2	3	1	103.51	1	35200	35
79	9	79	2	3	4	109.97	1	38500	45
80	12	136	2	5	4	113.17	2	41800	42
81	3	169	2	2	3	118.46	1	23600	28
82	16	70	2	2	8	126.34	1	42000	46
83	23	26	2	2	7	108.45	1	43175	54
84	2	187	2	3	4	121.46	2	25150	29
85	18	198	2	2	5	106.49	1	37300	42
86	3	171	2	2	9	102.15	2	25100	27
87	7	132	2	5	7	126.34	1	28215	31
88	25	211	2	2	9	106.38	1	47025	65
89	2	112	1	2	1	102.35	2	40500	44
90	17	118	2	1	3	98.12	0	40425	45
91	22	204	2	3	2	96.82	0	42850	51
92	6	24	2	0	3	100.03	1	27500	20
93	27	11	1	3	2	112.69	1	45100	65
94	14	193	1	3	4	121.96	1	42450	57
95	12	100	1	3	8	93.77	0	41900	49
96	24	74	2	0	6	99.70	1	45375	68
97	14	61	1	1	3	93.21	0	34550	39
98	14	96	2	2	1	117.27	1	36100	38
99	11	138	2	3	7	103.46	1	27950	34
100	4	15	2	2	1	106.38	1	24525	28
101	3	13	2	0	7	102.35	1	27175	26
102	12	149	2	2	3	98.12	0	32775	38
103	12	158	2	2	5	122.27	1	35875	46
104	19	209	1	3	5	123.64	1	41800	52
105	12	180	2	0	4	134.53	1	41575	55
106	4	200	1	2	3	100.87	2	32350	31
107	5	182	2	1	7	124.09	1	34900	35
108	23	59	2	4	5	109.13	1	47950	66
109	9	28	1	3	8	102.32	1	23600	31
110	24	112	2	1	4	119.55	1	34875	47
111	21	169	1	1	4	113.04	1	32000	49
112	19	121	2	2	0	103.75	2	35000	46
113	14	28	1	2	8	103.89	1	33000	41
114	3	111	1	3	7	110.25	1	30600	38
115	3	132	2	4	1	93.18	1	27600	25
116	8	24	2	0	9	109.11	2	29900	36
117	15	160	1	4	7	87.58	2	37200	41
118	18	44	1	5	5	96.20	1	36200	51

(continued)

n	x_1	x_2	x_3	x_4	x_5	x_6	x_7	x_8	x_9
119	7	79	2	2	8	89.71	1	32000	34
120	11	187	2	4	0	108.64	1	35200	49
121	5	107	1	0	9	113.15	2	24650	28
122	18	182	1	5	8	104.37	1	36100	46
123	12	48	1	4	3	111.36	1	28150	35
124	2	217	1	2	0	123.07	1	34550	31
125	26	167	1	2	9	99.70	2	45375	67
126	26	33	1	3	2	93.21	0	41600	63
127	11	22	2	1	6	106.27	2	39500	47
128	11	44	2	3	4	102.83	1	37600	44
129	0	81	2	3	7	104.18	1	33900	31
130	7	123	1	0	2	107.48	2	34325	31
131	19	13	1	5	3	119.13	2	38300	40
132	5	189	2	4	0	92.42	0	39500	44
133	26	59	2	0	6	101.15	1	26500	58
134	1	147	2	2	5	93.91	0	26500	28
135	8	50	2	3	8	78.26	0	29000	35
136	3	70	2	1	2	97.98	0	27500	28
137	3	198	1	1	9	100.03	1	25100	25
138	14	193	1	1	3	120.54	1	32000	38
139	11	77	1	0	3	120.93	1	37750	45
140	22	125	2	4	5	125.95	2	44000	56
141	12	160	1	1	5	100.73	1	37750	44
142	17	28	2	0	3	105.08	2	37675	42
143	20	39	2	5	2	123.37	1	43945	62
144	11	154	1	0	1	119.53	3	43800	44
145	14	129	1	1	9	116.61	1	38170	40
146	22	204	2	2	7	119.69	1	40500	49
147	2	90	1	5	6	103.46	1	23325	25
148	14	37	2	4	3	106.38	2	31625	32
149	5	173	2	2	4	110.17	1	34325	35
150	19	6	1	2	4	105.01	1	40500	50
151	22	83	2	1	9	100.02	2	39275	52
152	26	125	1	1	9	135.22	1	43850	58
153	8	169	1	5	4	87.79	2	31625	34
154	16	55	2	4	3	103.14	1	39375	41
155	25	217	2	2	7	112.55	2	47200	66
156	7	19	1	1	1	109.11	1	28150	33
157	23	173	2	0	3	87.58	0	46900	63
158	7	173	2	4	4	92.91	0	29100	28
159	16	105	1	2	5	89.73	1	39400	41
160	2	11	1	1	8	108.57	1	23100	25
161	22	52	2	1	9	113.15	2	41650	46
162	13	103	2	0	5	104.36	1	35850	40
163	19	143	2	1	4	111.00	1	37350	41
164	7	123	2	4	2	111.00	1	31575	34
165	4	114	1	1	9	87.71	0	27350	28

n	x_1	x_2	x_3	x_4	x_5	x_6	x_7	x_8	x_9
166	24	37	1	5	4	99.12	1	47125	64
167	11	100	2	2	7	128.72	1	43675	55
168	8	100	2	2	6	107.85	2	40000	41
169	9	198	2	5	3	107.85	1	31570	44
170	22	198	1	1	9	122.66	0	41750	40
171	25	136	2	0	4	93.35	0	43780	52
172	14	0	2	4	2	115.46	1	43650	38
173	18	17	2	3	8	125.59	1	39750	44
174	8	103	2	0	9	92.37	0	29500	30
175	22	15	1	1	3	99.17	1	41150	44
176	8	107	2	0	3	102.84	1	33000	35
177	13	129	1	5	4	104.18	1	38300	38
178	27	167	2	0	8	107.75	1	46100	69
179	27	118	2	0	8	119.13	2	44000	66
180	3	209	2	5	3	92.42	0	23600	22
181	2	125	2	4	4	101.16	1	24850	29
182	23	22	1	2	5	91.35	1	45000	62
183	9	151	1	1	5	96.82	0	43850	52
184	15	11	2	4	2	96.82	0	40050	47
185	17	39	2	4	1	89.03	1	43800	58
186	5	193	2	0	5	112.67	2	35300	35
187	26	217	2	2	5	121.96	1	46550	68
188	27	189	1	3	7	104.50	2	45800	69
189	12	209	2	2	3	117.48	1	31450	34
190	1	70	2	5	4	96.38	0	20000	20
191	3	52	2	1	6	107.32	1	27300	29
192	0	138	2	0	4	121.36	1	20000	21
193	16	35	2	3	4	94.02	0	34850	47
194	3	9	1	1	3	129.13	1	41800	41
195	5	173	2	2	8	122.14	2	29000	29
196	1	11	2	1	4	93.86	3	30200	30
197	7	129	2	3	6	104.59	1	34450	35
198	2	162	1	3	3	107.85	1	23550	25
199	2	5	2	1	1	101.68	1	22000	26
200	5	74	2	3	6	111.00	1	33000	34

APPENDIX D   ANSWERS TO SELECTED ODD-NUMBERED EXERCISES

We've selected several odd-numbered exercises in each chapter and present the final answers here so you can check your work. Your exact answer depends on the rounding used by you, your hand calculator, or your computer. If your answer is close, you probably did the exercise correctly.

CHAPTER 1

3a. $\Sigma x = 25$, $\Sigma y = 17$, $\Sigma xy = 255$, $\Sigma(x - y + 2z) = 74$ *b.* $\Sigma y^2 = 533$, $\Sigma(y)^2 = 289$

CHAPTER 2

3. *a, c, d, e,* and *g* are quantitative; *b* and *f* are qualitative.
13. Mail survey
29. Focus group and mail survey
31. *a, c, d,* and *e* are quantitative; *b, f,* and *g* are qualitative.
35a. Large: $(.20)(1,200) = 240$
     Medium: $(.35)(1,200) = 420$
     Small: $(.20)(1,200) = 240$
     Compact: $(.25)(1,200) = 300$

CHAPTER 3

5. Ten
9. Using six classes,

Class	Freq.	Rel. freq.
40–49	18	.1500
50–59	18	.1500
60–69	22	.1833
70–79	22	.1833
80–89	20	.1667
90–99	20	.1667
	120	1.0000

13. All (100%)
15. With 486 observations, 9 classes would be better.

Class	Freq.	Rel. freq.	Cum. rel. freq.
5 or fewer	47	.0967	.0967
6–10	150	.3086	.4053
11–15	128	.2634	.6687
16–20	67	.1379	.8066
20 or more	94	.1934	1.0000
	486	1.000	

17.

Class	Freq.	Rel. freq.	Cum. freq. less	Dist. more
100–199	9	.1250	.1250	1.0000
200–299	22	.3056	.4306	.8751
300–399	24	.3333	.7639	.5695
400–499	13	.1806	.9445	.2362
500 and up	4	.0556	1.0000	.0556
	72	1.0000		

31. The pie chart and bar chart instructions are designed to give you practice in graphing. The relative frequency distribution is

Class	Relative frequency
Emp.	.5031
Spouse	.3067
Both	.1902
	1.0000

33a. The frequency distributions that can be used to construct the charts follow.

Class	Rel. FD	Cum less	Cum. more
20 < 25	.0467	.0467	1.0000
25 < 30	.0933	.1400	.9533
30 < 35	.1867	.3267	.8600
35 < 40	.3000	.6267	.6733
40 < 45	.2000	.8267	.3733
45 < 50	.1000	.9267	.1733
50 < 55	.0733	1.0000	.0733
	1.0000		

b. 37.33%
c. 67.33%

35a. Bar chart

37. The frequency distribution to be used in constructing the graphs is

Class	f
35 < 40	2
40 < 45	5
45 < 50	14
50 < 55	19
55 < 60	11
60 < 65	10
65 < 70	5
70 < 75	1
75 < 80	3
	70

CHAPTER 4

1. Mean
3. Weighted mean
5. Mean
7. Mean
9. Median
11. Mean
13. Median
17a. Right   b. Symmetrical   c. Left   d. Right   e. Symmetrical
19. Right
21. Left
23a. 8   b. 9   c. 11.6   d. The median (9)
25a. Median sales $3,100 million, median units 5,361, mean sales $5,252.4 million,
     mean units 5,601.   b. $937,761
27. Weighted mean = 2.11
29. Weighted mean = $37.86
39a. $\sigma = 5$ b. Reduce it   c. Increase it   d. Increase it
41. Assuming a sample:
     a. Range = 33   b. s = 10.38   c. s^2 = 107.74   d. CV = 28.3%
43. Mean = $64.52, s = $62.18
45a. s^2 = $178.76   b. s = $13.37   c. CV = 62.7%
     d. Mean is 21.32, median is 17.5, mode is more than one, so distribution appears
        to be skewed right.
     e. Increase   f. Decrease
47. Mean.
49a. Mean = 27. Median = 28   b. σ = 5.54   c. Decreases
     d. Both decrease   e. Increases
51a. Mean = 14,774, s = 16,692   b. Mean = 156.2, s = 193.3
     c. Mean = 123, s = 155.9   d. Median = 7,168   e. Median = 79
     f. Median = 66.5   g. No   h. Median
53a. Mean = 7.7   b. Median = 8   c. Mode = 8   d. s = 2.01
57a. 1985: Mean = 8.05%, s = 3.52%
     1988: Mean = 9.21%, s = 4.2%

CHAPTER 5

5a. Five outcomes are possible.   b. 0: .20; 1: .30; 2: .24; 3: .16; 4+: .10
    c. .20   d. .26   e. (.10)(.10) = .01
7a. (.90)(.90) = .81   b. (.90)(.10) + (.90)(.10) = .18
    c. (.90)(.10) = .09   d. (.10)(.10) = .01
9a. (.45)(.45)(.45) = .091   b. (.55)(.55)(.55) = .166
    c. 3(.45)(.55)(.55) = .408
11. .66
19a. A frequency distribution

b.

Number	Probability
0	.5068
1	.2795
2	.1507
3	.0329
4+	.0301

23. $E(X) = \$85,500$
25. $E(X) = 48$
31. 21
33a. .189   b. .343   c. .657
35a. .005   b. .995   c. .000   d. .962
37. .8369
39. .6983
41. .0001
43. Yes
45. Mean = 10, SD = 2.24
47a. .9 to the 10th power = .349   b. Mean = 9   c. .95
49. Mean = 20, SD = 3.46
55. .308
61. .2681
63. .2231
65. .7745
67b. .0526
69a. .2138   b. .5438   c. .2424   d. .1404
73a. .3033   b. .0000
75a. .1353   b. .0361   c. .0166
77a. Discrete   b. Continuous
   c. Discrete   d. Continuous
79. .9380
81. .9810
83. .8647
85. .9400
87. 6
89. $480,000
91a. .0081   b. .3430   c. .2646
93. .9918
95. .4422

CHAPTER 6

5. x_1, x_2, x_6, x_8, x_9
7a. Mean = 112.5   b. SD = 21.7   c. 25/75 = 33%
9a. SD = 2.3   b. 6/8 = 75%   c. 2/8 = 25%

13*a*. No   *b*. No   *c*. Yes   *d*. Yes
   e. No   *f*. Yes   *g*. Yes
15. Mean
19. Using the normal table and the z values calculated in Exercise 18:
   a. .2734   *b*. .4599   *c*. .4931
   d. .3593   *e*. .1587   *f*. .0013
21. $100,000 - (1.645)(25,000) = \$58,875$ and below.
23*a*. 692   *b*. 159   *c*. 736   *d*. 242
   e. .2266   *f*. 10.96   *g*. 9.44
25. $x + 40,000 + 1.28(10,000) = 250,000, x = 197,200$
31*a*. .5557   *b*. .0968   *c*. .8438   *d*. .9032
33*a*. .7673   *b*. .9115
35. .2843
39*a*. $z = 0$ *b*. $z = -.52$
   c. $z = \pm1.645$ *d*. $z = \pm1.96$
41. 3.92%
43*a*. $s = .58$ *b*. 35%   *c*. 10%
45*a*. 24   *b*. .1711   *c*. .0853
47*a*. Mean $= 35.5$ *b*. 3/7 $= 42.9\%$
49. .0548
51*a*. .9319, .6664, .2611, .0446   *b*. 70.8 years
53. .9936

CHAPTER 7

9*a*. Normal   *b*. Not normal   *c*. Normal
13. $2/6 = .33$
15*a*. .1587   *b*. About 0   *c*. .6826   *d*. .0668
17. 96.8 to 103.2
19*a*. .9992   *b*. About 0   *c*. Variability would decrease
23. Decreases
25. Mean $= .70, s = .145$
27*a*. .20   *b*. .1894   *c*. .6368   *d*. .4038
29. .0336
31*a*. $1/6 = .17$
   b. With replacement, there will be $6^2 = 36$ different samples, with either an OK
      or a defective unit on the first draw, and likewise on the second.
   c. Twenty-five pairs will be OK, OK ($p = 1.00$). Ten pairs will be one OK and one
      defective ($p = .50$). One pair will be both defective ($p = .00$)
   d. .17; yes, the same
   e. .266
   f. .266, yes, the same
   g. Sampling distribution
35*a*. .40   *b*. .248   *c*. .186
37*a*. .0764   *b*. .1112   *c*. .2668

39a. Mean = 5.75, s = 1.92   c. Mean = 5.75, yes, the same
   d. 1.111   e. 1.111; yes, the same
41a. .3085   b. .2684   c. .2148
   d. .0062   e. About 0
43a. 1.58   b. .63   c. .39
45a. .0778   b. .9544
47. .9641
49. .9836
51. .2776
53a. .7620   b. .0091   c. About 0
55a. For population: mean = 3, σ = 1.58
   b. 5,4 5,2 5,1 4,5 4,2 4,1 2,5 2,4 2,1 1,5 1,4 1,2
   c. 4.5 3.5 3 4.5 3 2.5 3.5 3 1.5 3 2.5 1.5
   d. Mean = 3, yes
   e. SD = .9129
   f. Using the correction factor, σ = .9129; yes

CHAPTER 8

   7. $\bar{x}$ = 16
   9. 11.17 to 12.83
11a. 10.91 to 13.09   b. 11.3 to 12.7
   c. Higher confidence yields a wider interval.
13. 1,891.75 to 2,008.25. It's 98% likely that the interval includes the population mean.
15. 7.54 to 8.66
19. 0 to .106
21a. 0 to .113   b. .01 to .09
   c. A lower confidence level yields a smaller interval.
23. .10 to .22
25. .0077 to .0723
27. .508 to .617
33a. t   b. Normal   c. t   d. Normal
35. 2.75 to 3.16
37. 2,443 to 2,531
39. 8.4% to 10.5%
43a. n = 34   b. n = 87   c. E = .047
45. n = 1,068
47. n = 189
49. n = 19
51a. 13.32 to 14.68   b. 122.74 to 133.26
   c. .508 to .732   d. 1.795 to 1.805
53. 15.0 to 18.6 minutes
55. 89.85 to 100.15
57. $29,070 to $34,490

59. $n = 62, n = 151$
61. .2595 to .3905

CHAPTER 9

9a. $H_0: p \le .02$ $H_1: p > .02$
 b. $H_0: \mu = 7$ $H_1: \mu \ne 7$
 c. $H_0: \mu \ge 600$ $H_1: \mu < 600$
 d. $H_0: \mu = 21$ $H_1: \mu \ne 21$
 e. $H_0: \mu \le 5$ $H_1: \mu > 5$
 f. $H_0: p = .10$ $H_1: p \ne .10$
15. Type II
19. No
23. No
27. If the z value is more than 2.33, reject the null hypothesis that $\mu = 30$ (one-tailed test). Since $z = 10$, reject the null hypothesis. The p-value is approximately .0000.
29. Reject the null hypothesis that $\mu = 3.2$ if z is outside the range, -2.575 to $+2.575$ (two-tailed test). Since $z = 7.5$, reject the hypothesis that $\mu = 3.2$. The p-value is approximately .0000.
31a. $H_0: \mu \ge 45,000$; $H_1: \mu < 45,000$
 b. Reject the H_0 if $t < -2.518$
 c. Reject
 d. Type I
 e. .0007
33. $H_0: \mu \ge 19$; $H_1: \mu < 19$. Reject the H_0 if $t < -1.3836$. $s = .9$. $t = -.74$ Fail to reject.
37. $H_0: p \le .12$ $H_1: p > .12$
39. Reject the null hypothesis that $p = .089$ if z is less than -2.33 (one-tailed test). Since $z = -3.44$, reject the null hypothesis.
41. When one fails to reject the H_0
51. $z = 1.2$; fail to reject; $\beta = .77$
55. $z = .51$; fail to reject; $\beta = .6950$
57. Yes
61. $n = 54$
63. $n = 569$
69. .0228
71a. Normal   b. t   c. t
 d. Binomial   e. Binomial
75. Reject H_0 if $z < -2.05$ Since $z = -7.89$, reject.
77. Reject H_0 if $z > 2.33$ Since $z = .883$, fail to reject.
79. Reject H_0 if $z > 1.28$ Since $z = 1.52$, reject.
81. Since $z = -1.6$, fail to reject.
83. Since $z = -.6$, fail to reject.

85. Since $z = -1.35$, fail to reject.
87. Since $z = 1.41$, fail to reject.
89. Since $z = 2.12$, reject.
91a. $\beta = .48$, power $= .52$ b. $\beta = .61$, power $= .39$
93a. $\beta = .6293$ b. $\beta = .7486$

CHAPTER 10

7. Normal
9a. Yes   b. Yes   c. No   d. Yes   e. 6.5
  f. Reject H_0 if $z < -1.96$ or $z > 1.96$ g. -4.62 h. Reject
11. Reject H_0 if $z < -1.28$. Calculated $z = -4.76$. Reject; females are earning significantly less than males.
13. Reject H_0 if $z < -2.575$ or $z > 2.575$. Calculated $z = .99$. Fail to reject; the average mileages using the two types of gas are not significantly different.
15. t
17a. Yes   b. Yes   c. Yes   d. t
  e. For the sample:

	A	B
$\bar{x}$	37.1	40.8
s	2.41	2.48

  so s(pooled) $= 2.43$
  f. $df = 11$ g. 1.35   h. Reject H_0 if $t < -2.201$ or $t > 2.201$
  i. $t = -2.82$, reject; the populations have different means.
19a. $H_0: \mu_1 - \mu_2 = 0$ $H_1: \mu_1 - \mu_2 \neq 0$
  b. t distribution
  c. Reject H_0 if $t < -2.02$ or $t > 2.02$
  d. Since $t = -5.59$, reject; sedans get better mileage than station wagons.
21a. $H_0: \mu_1 - \mu_2 = 0, H_1: \mu_1 - \mu_2 \neq 0$
  b. Reject H_0 if $t < -2.048$ or $t > 2.048$ Since $t = 3.24$, reject; battery 1 lasts longer than battery 2
23a. $H_0: \mu_1 - \mu_2 \geq 0, H_1: \mu_1 - \mu_2 < 0$ b. t distribution with $n - 1 = 7$ df
  c. Reject H_0 if $t < -1.895$ d. Since $t = -.98$, fail to reject
  e. There hasn't been a significant change during the new ad campaign.
25a. $H_0: \mu_1 - \mu_2 = 0, H_1: \mu_1 - \mu_2 \neq 0$ b. t distribution with df $= 11$
  c. Reject H_0 if $t < -1.796$ or $t > 1.796$ d. Since $t = -.48$, fail to reject
  e. The two commercials are the same.
31. 0.
33a. $H_0: p_1 - p_2 = 0, H_1: p_1 - p_2 \neq 0$ b. Normal   c. .0257
  d. Reject H_0 if $z < -2.575$ or $z > 2.575$ e. Since $z = -2.335$, reject
  f. Idaho and Oregon are the same with regard to preference for the wine.
35. Since the calculated $z = 1.2$, fail to reject. The data don't support the conclusion that small cars have more rollovers than large cars.

39. $H_0: \mu_1 - \mu_2 = 0$, $H_1: \mu_1 - \mu_2 \neq 0$. Normal.
Reject H_0 if $z < -1.645$ or $z > 1.645$. Since $z = -2.89$, reject.
Conclude different average heights

41a. $H_0: \mu_1 - \mu_2 \leq 0$, $H_1: \mu_1 - \mu_2 > 0$ b. t distribution for 10 *df*
c. Reject H_0 if $t < -1.812$ or $t > 1.812$ d. Since $t = 5.78$, reject
e. Sample supports the notion that the L cars have a lower impact force.

43a. $H_0: \mu_1 - \mu_2 = 0$, $H_1: \mu_1 - \mu_2 \neq 0$ b. Normal
c. Reject H_0 if $z < -1.96$ or $z > 1.96$ d. Since $z = -5.7$, reject
e. Conclude that one store is selling more per customer.

45a. t table $= \pm 2.228$ and $t = -5.04$ so reject H_0.
b. t table $= \pm 2.01$ (interpolated) and $t = 9.7$ so reject H_0.
c. t table $= \pm 2.045$ and $t = 3.33$ so reject H_0.

47a. $H_0: p_1 - p_2 = 0$, $H_1: p_1 - p_2 \neq 0$ b. Normal
c. Reject H_0 if $z < -1.645$ or $z > 1.645$ d. Since $z = -.5$, fail to reject
e. The death rates are the same.

49a. $H_0: p_1 - p_2 = 0$, $H_1: p_1 - p_2 \neq 0$ b. Normal
c. Reject H_0 if $z < -1.645$ or $z > 1.645$ d. Since $z = .69$, fail to reject
e. The percentage of towns with negative balance sheets hasn't changed
significantly since 1991.

51a. $H_0: \mu_1 - \mu_2 \leq 0$, $H_1: \mu_1 - \mu_2 > 0$ b. Normal
c. Reject H_0 if $z > 2.064$ d. Since $t = 2.55$, reject
e. Claim seems correct

CHAPTER 11

1. Qualitative

7a. Proximity and payment status are independent. Proximity and payment status
are dependent.
b. df $= (r - 1)(c - 1) = (2 - 1)(2 - 1) = 1$
c. Reject H_0 if $\chi^2 > 5.412$

	Expected		
	Paid	Over	Total
1 =	67.5	102.5	170
2 =	67.5	102.5	170
Total	135	205	340

Critical chi square value: 5.0200.
Computed chi square value: 2.7642.
Fail to reject the null; proximity and payment status are independent.

9a. Part quality and production shift are independent. Part quality and production
shift are dependent.
b. df $= (r - 1)(c - 1) = (3 - 1)(2 - 1) = 2$
c. Reject H_0 if $\chi^2 > 5.99$

	Expected		
	Def	Good	Total
1 =	69.958	723.042	793
2 =	53.637	554.363	608
3 =	37.405	386.595	424
Total	161	1664	1825

Critical chi square value: 5.9900.
Computed chi square value: 25.1696.
Reject the null; part quality and production shift are dependent.

11a. Age and sports preference are independent. Age and sports preference are dependent.
   b. $df = (r - 1)(c - 1) = (4 - 1)(4 - 1) = 9$
   c. Reject H_0 if $\chi^2 > 14.68$
   Critical chi square value: 14.68
   Computed chi square value: 173.80
   Reject the null; age and sports preference are dependent.

17. $df = k - 1 - c = 4 - 1 - 0 = 3$

21a. H_0: The population from which the accounts-having-errors data came is Poisson distributed. H_1: The population from which the accounts-having-errors data came isn't Poisson distributed.
   b. $df = k - 1 - c = 5 - 1 - 1 = 3$
   c. Reject H_0 if $\chi^2 > 7.18$

Frequency	Poisson prob. for $\mu = 1.4$	f_e (Prob. x 400)	f_o	$\frac{(f_o - f_e)^2}{f_e}$
0	.2466	98.6	102	.12
1	.3452	138.1	140	.03
2	.2417	96.7	75	4.87
3	.1128	45.1	52	1.06
4+	.0537	21.5	31	4.20
		Sum: 400		10.28

Reject the null; the population from which the accounts-having-errors data came isn't Poisson distributed.

23a. H_0: The population from which the data on number of service calls received came is Poisson distributed.
   H_1: The population from which the data on number of service calls received came isn't Poisson distributed.
   b. $df = k - 1 - c = 5 - 1 - 1 = 3$
   c. Reject H_0 if $\chi^2 > 7.81$

Frequency	Poisson prob. for $\mu = 1.4$	f_e (Prob. x 400)	f_o	$\frac{(f_o - f_e)^2}{f_e}$
0	.3012	60.2	45	3.84
1	.3614	72.3	99	9.86
2	.2169	43.4	32	2.99
3	.0867	17.3	19	.17
4+	.0338	6.8	5	.48
		Sum: 400		17.34

Reject the null; the population from which the data on number of service calls received came isn't Poisson distributed.

27a. Income level and whether a person will vote yes for the aquifer protection area are independent. Income level and whether a person will vote yes for the aquifer protection area are dependent.

b. $df = (r - 1)(c - 1) = (3 - 1)(4 - 1) = 6$

c. Reject H_0 if $\chi^2 > 12.59$

	Expected			
	Yes	No	Un	Total
1 =	181.474	43.736	19.790	245
2 =	406.650	98.004	44.346	549
3 =	251.842	60.695	27.464	340
4 =	77.034	18.565	8.401	104
Total	917	221	100	1238

Critical chi square value: 12.5900
Computed chi square value: 33.6369

Reject the null; income level and whether a person will vote yes for the aquifer protection area are dependent.

29a. Type of advertising and sales are independent. Type of advertising and sales are dependent.

b. $df = (r - 1)(c - 1) = (3 - 1)(2 - 1) = 2$

c. Reject H_0 if $\chi^2 > 4.61$

	Expected		
	Inc	Sta	Total
1 =	15.423	18.577	34
2 =	14.062	16.938	31
3 =	14.515	17.485	32
Total	44	53	97

Critical chi square value: 4.6100
Computed chi square value: 1.3751

Fail to reject the null; type of advertising and sales are independent.

33a. Type of postage and response rate are independent. Type of postage and response rate are dependent.

b. $df = (r - 1)(c - 1) = (2 - 1)(2 - 1) = 1$

c. Reject H_0 if $\chi^2 > 6.63$

	Expected		
	Meter	Stamp	Total
1 =	762.5	762.5	1,525
2 =	1,237.5	1,237.5	2,475
Total	2,000	2,000	4,000

Critical chi square value: 6.6300
Computed chi square value: 0.6624

Fail to reject the null; type of postage and response rate are independent.

35a. H_0: The population from which the service-to-users data came is Poisson distributed. H_1: The population from which the service-to-users data came isn't Poisson distributed.

b. df $= k - 1 - c = 6 - 1 - 1 = 4$

c. At the .05 significance level, reject H_0 if $\chi^2 > 9.49$

$$\bar{x} = \frac{466}{365} = 1.276$$

Frequency	Poisson prob. for $\mu = 1.3$	f_e (Prob. x 365)	f_o	$\frac{(f_o - f_e)^2}{f_e}$
0	.2725	99.5	117	3.08
1	.3543	129.3	128	.01
2	.2303	84.1	63	5.29
3	.0998	36.4	30	1.13
4+	.0431	15.7	27	8.13
		Sum:	365	17.64

Reject the null; the population from which the service-to-users data came isn't Poisson distributed.

37a. Rider status and proximity to bus stop are independent. Rider status and proximity to bus stop are dependent.

b. df $= (r - 1)(c - 1) = (5 - 1)(2 - 1) = 5$.

c. Tested at the .05 level, reject H_0 if $\chi^2 > 11.07$.

	Expected		
	Riders	Nonriders	Total
1 =	176.708	257.292	434
2 =	159.200	231.800	391
3 =	67.996	99.004	167
4 =	68.810	100.190	169
5 =	16.286	23.714	40
Total	489.000	712	1,201

Critical chi square value: 9.4900
Computed chi square value: 19.4346

Reject the null; rider status and proximity to bus stop are dependent. The memo should indicate the surprising finding that nonriders are more likely to live closer to a bus stop than riders.

39a. H_0: The population of jelly doughnuts is normally distributed.
H_1: The population of jelly doughnuts isn't normally distributed. df $= k - 1 - c = 5 - 1 - 2 = 2$ Reject H_0 if $\chi^2 > 5.99$ $\bar{x} = 39.94, s = 3.97$

Jelly doughnuts	x	z	Area	f_e
30–32	32	−2.00	.0228	2
33–35	35	−1.25	.0828	8
36–38	38	−0.50	.2029	20
39–41	41	0.25	.2902	29
42–44	44	1.00	.2426	24

Jelly doughnuts	x	z	Area	f_e
45–47	47	1.75	.1186	12
48–50	50	2.50	.0401	4
			1.0000	99

Jelly doughnuts	f_o	f_e	$\dfrac{(f_o - f_e)^2}{f_e}$
30–35	12	10	.40
36–38	26	20	1.80
39–41	27	29	.14
42–44	19	24	1.04
45–50	16	16	.00
	100	99	3.38

Fail to reject the null; the population of jelly doughnuts is normally distributed.

41. Use x^2 goodness-of-fit test, reject H_0 because $27.82 > 12.59$.

Chapter 12

3a. H_0: $\sigma^2 \leq 16{,}000{,}000$ H_1: $\sigma^2 > 16{,}000{,}000$ b. df $= n - 1 = 12 - 1 = 11$

c. Reject the H_0 if $\chi^2 > 22.618$

d. $\chi^2 = \dfrac{(n-1)s^2}{\sigma^2} = \dfrac{(12-1)4{,}112^2}{4{,}000^2} = 11.62$

Fail to reject the null: $\sigma^2 = 16{,}000{,}000$

7. H_0: $\sigma_1^2 - \sigma_2^2 \leq 0$
H_1: $\sigma_1^2 - \sigma_2^2 > 0$

9a. H_0: $\sigma_1^2 - \sigma_2^2 \leq 0$ H_1: $\sigma_1^2 - \sigma_2^2 > 0$

b. $df_n = n - 1 = 20 - 1 = 19$
$df_d = n - 1 = 20 - 1 = 19$

c. Reject the H_0 if $F > 2.21$

d. $F = \dfrac{s_1^2}{s_2^2} = \dfrac{.002^2}{.0015^2} = 1.78$

Fail to reject the null; the variability of diameters of ball bearings is the same for the two machines.

25. $\bar{x}_a = 4$, $\bar{x}_b = 4$, $\bar{x}_c = 6$, $\bar{x}_d = 4.5$, $\bar{\bar{x}} = 4.625$

Source of variance	SS	df	Estimate σ^2	F ratio
Between:	10.750	3	3.583	.683
Within:	63	12	5.250	
Totals:	73.750	15		

27a. H_0: $\mu_1 = \mu_2 = \mu_3$ H_1: not equal   b. $df_b = 2$ $df_w = 12$

c. Reject H_0 if $F > 6.93$

d.

Source of variance	SS	df	Estimate σ^2	F ratio
Between:	496.54	2	248.27	8.94
Within:	333.20	12	27.77	
Totals:	829.74	14		

e. Reject the null; the number of defectives differs for the three contractors.
f. No. He needs to compare the group means.

33a.

Source of variance	SS	df	Estimate σ^2	F ratio
Rows	5.1	3	1.7	1.63
Columns	18.1	2	9.1	8.72
Interaction	17.4	6	2.9	2.78
Within:	37.6	36	1.044	
Totals:	78.2	47		

b. 4   *c.* 3   *d.* 4
e. There's no interaction. There's no difference between row means. There's a difference between column means.

35a. H_0: no interaction present
H_1: interaction present
H_0: machine means are equal
H_1: machine means aren't equal
H_0: operator means are equal
H_1: operator means aren't equal

b. $\bar{x}_a = 11.17$, $\bar{x}_b = 21$, $\bar{x}_c = 12$
$\bar{x}_1 = 15.17$, $\bar{x}_2 = 15$, $\bar{x}_3 = 14$, $\bar{\bar{x}} = 14.72$

Source of variance	SS	df	Estimate σ^2	F ratio
Rows	4.778	2	2.39	.368
Columns	356.778	2	178.39	27.444
Interaction	19.556	4	4.89	.752
Within:	58.500	9	6.50	
Totals:	439.611	17		

c. There's no interaction. There's no difference between machines. There's a difference between operators.
d. The memo should emphasize the determination of which operators are different.

39. Fail to reject the H_0 because 8.4 isn't greater than 9.49.

41a.

Source of variance	SS	df	Estimate σ^2	F ratio
Between:	14,398	3	4,799.3	18.3
Within:	5,256	20	262.8	
Totals:	19,654	23		

b. Four groups   *c.* Tabled $F = 3.10$
d. Calculated $F = 18.3$ *e.* Reject the null

43a. $H_0: \sigma_1^2 - \sigma_2^2 \leq 0; \quad H_1: \sigma_1^2 - \sigma_1^2 > 0.$

   b. $df_n = n - 1 = 30 - 1 = 29$
     $df_d = n - 1 = 30 - 1 = 29$

   c. Reject the H_0 if $F > 1.90$

   d. $F = \dfrac{s_1^2}{s_2^2} = \dfrac{.93^2}{.68^2} = 1.87$

   Fail to reject the null; the variability of the stocks is the same.

45a.

Source of variance	SS	df	Estimate σ^2	F ratio
Between:	695.8	2	347.9	64.4
Within:	129.6	24	5.4	
Totals:	825.4	26		

   b. Three groups   c. Tabled $F = 5.61$
   d. Calculated $F = 64.4$ e. Reject the null

47a. $\bar{x}_1 = 87.44, \quad \bar{x}_2 = 55.89, \quad \bar{x}_3 = 129.89, \quad \bar{\bar{x}} = 91.07$

Source of variance	SS	df	Estimate σ^2	F ratio
Between:	5,494.9	2	2,747.4	2.12
Within:	31,165.1	24	1,298.5	
Totals:	36,660	26		

Critical $F = 3.4$, so fail to reject null hypothesis. There's no difference in the mean amounts charged on the three credit cards.

49. $\bar{x}_1 = 13.33, \quad \bar{x}_2 = 16.5, \quad \bar{x}_3 = 24.5, \quad \bar{\bar{x}} = 18.11$

Source of variance	SS	df	Estimate σ^2	F ratio
Between:	397.4	2	198.7	13.06
Within:	228.3	15	15.2	
Totals:	625.8	17		

Critical $F = 6.36$, so reject null hypothesis. The three shifts produce different mean rates of defective units.

51. $\bar{x}_b = 12.75, \quad \bar{x}_p = 13.42, \quad \bar{x}_a = 9.25, \quad \bar{\bar{x}} = 11.81$
   $\bar{x}_1 = 14.56, \quad \bar{x}_2 = 13.11, \quad \bar{x}_3 = 11.22, \quad \bar{x}_4 = 8.33$

Source of variance	SS	df	Estimate σ^2	F ratio
Rows:	194.97	3	64.99	24.12
Columns:	120.22	2	60.11	22.319
Interaction:	31.78	6	5.30	1.976
Within:	64.67	24	2.69	
Totals:	411.64	35		

Critical F value (Int.): 2.51; fail to reject null hypothesis

Critical F value (Row): 3.01; reject null hypothesis
Critical F value (Col.): 3.4; reject null hypothesis

53. $\bar{x}_a = 77$, $\bar{x}_b = 76.25$, $\bar{x}_c = 76.75$
$\bar{x}_n = 76.5$, $\bar{x}_e = 76.83$, $\bar{\bar{x}} = 76.67$

Source of variance	Sum of squares	Degrees of freedom	Mean squared	Computed F value
Rows:	0.333	1	0.333	0.018
Columns:	1.167	2	0.583	0.031
Inter:	20.167	2	10.083	0.535
Error:	113.000	6	18.833	
Totals:	134.667	11		

Critical F value (Row): 5.99; fail to reject null hypothesis.
Critical F value (Int.): 5.14; fail to reject null hypothesis.
Critical F value (Col.): 5.14; fail to reject null hypothesis.

CHAPTER 13

7. SPC
13. .0026
15a. LCL = 26.4   UCL = 33.6   Process in control   b. Process potentially out of control
21. Process in control
23. Process potentially out of control
25a. $\bar{x}$ chart   b. $\bar{x} = 22.88$ LCL = 21.57,   UCL = 24.20.   Process in control.
31. Process in control
33. Process potentially out of control
35a. R chart
    $\bar{R} = 2.722$
    LCL = 0   UCL = 5.456
  b. Process in control
41a. LCL = 0   UCL = .102   b. LCL = 0   UCL = .072
  c. LCL = .001   UCL = .059
43a. CL = .07   LCL = .026   UCL = .114
  b. Zone C: .055 to .085
    Zone B: .041 to .055 and .085 to .099
    Zone A: .026 to .041 and .099 to .114
  c. Process potentially out of control
45a. p chart   b. c chart   c. p chart
  d. c chart   e. c chart
47a. CL = 55.33   LCL = 33.02   UCL = 77.65
  b. Zone C: 47.89 to 62.77
    Zone B: 40.46 to 47.89 and 62.77 to 70.21
    Zone A: 33.02 to 40.46 and 70.21 to 77.65
  c. Process potentially out of control

65*a.* Process in control   *b.* Process potentially out of control
67*a.* H_0: $\mu \geq 20$; H_1: $\mu < 20$ *b.* Reject H_0 if $z < -1.645$
   c. Example:

μ	β	$1 - \beta$
19.7	.7939	.2061
19.4	.5000	.5000
19.0	.1357	.8643

   e. $\bar{x} = .19$ $z = -2.74$ Reject H_0
71*a.* $n = 31$ (one-tailed test)
   b. Example:

μ	β	$1 - \beta$
5.30	.8238	.1762
5.55	.5000	.5000
5.80	.1762	.8238

73*a.* *p* chart
      CL = .03467   LCL = 21.57   UCL = 24.20
   b. Process potentially out of control
75*a.* *c* chart
      CL = 1.55   LCL = 0   UCL = 5.285
   b. Process potentially out of control

CHAPTER 14

9. H_0: $\rho = 0$; H_1: $\rho \neq 0$
   Reject H_0 if $t < -1.98$ or $t > 1.98$ (using df = 120)

$$s_r = \sqrt{\frac{1 - r^2}{n - 2}} = \sqrt{\frac{1 - (.38)^2}{400 - 2}} = \sqrt{\frac{.86}{398}} = \sqrt{.00216} = .0465$$

$$t = \frac{r}{s_r} = \frac{.38}{.0465} = 8.17$$

   Reject the null; the two variables are linearly related.
11*b.* Positive   *c.* $r = .483$
   e. H_0: $\rho = 0$; H_1: $\rho > 0$
   Reject H_0 if $t > 1.895$

$$s_r = \sqrt{\frac{1 - r^2}{n - 2}} = \sqrt{\frac{1 - (.483)^2}{9 - 2}} = \sqrt{\frac{.767}{7}} = \sqrt{.11} = .332$$

$$t = \frac{r}{s_r} = \frac{.483}{.332} = 1.455$$

   Fail to reject the null; minutes spent and account size aren't linearly related.
17. Yes. $\hat{y} = 12.1656 + 3.3758x$

19a. For every unit increase in GNP, AT&T earnings per share increase by an average amount of .05

b. When the GNP is 0, AT&T earnings per share equal .058

21b. Positive   c. $r = .95$

d. $H_0: \rho = 0$; $H_1: \rho \neq 0$

Reject H_0 if $t < -1.833$ or $t > 1.833$

$t = 9.151$

Reject the null; feet of shelf space and number of books sold are linearly related.

e. Yes   f. $\hat{y} = 32.4576 + 36.4053x$

g. $\hat{y} = 32.4576 + 36.4053(4) = 178.0779$

29. $\hat{y} = 208.20 + 70.918(10) = 917.4$

Prediction interval: 627.6 to 1,207.2

Confidence interval: 797.8 to 1,036.9

31b. $\hat{y} = .1774 + .0833x$

c. $\hat{y} = .1774 + .0833(19) = 1.7598$

$e = y - \hat{y} = 1.3 - 1.76 = -.46$

d. Standard error estimate: .9338

e. Each time the checkout time is estimated using amount of purchases, the prediction is typically off by .93 minutes.

f. $\hat{y} = .1774 + .0833(75) = 6.423$

g. 5.607 to 7.240   h. 4.596 to 8.250

33. $r^2 = 1 - \dfrac{s_{y \cdot x}^2}{s_y^2} = 1 - \dfrac{6^2}{20^2} = 1 - .09 = .91$

35a. When the price of unleaded gas increases by one unit, sales decrease by an average of 5,000 gallons.

b. $\hat{y} = 100 - 5(.95) = 95,230$

37b. $r = .9846$

c. Reject H_0 if $t < -2.306$ or $t > 2.306$

$t = 15.9352$

Reject the null; catalogs distributed and mail orders received are linearly related.

d. $\hat{y} = 11.95 + 1.77x$ e. 1,770   f. $r^2 = .9695$

g. Using knowledge of the linear relationship between catalogs distributed and mail orders received (.9846), we can explain 96.95% of the mail orders received variable variance.

41b. $\hat{y} = 75.4856 + .0449x$

c. The residual analysis is

Number	y-actual	y-pred	Residual
1	98	126	16.8600
2	94	141	12.1869
3	93	108	12.6678
4	84	121	3.0844
5	84	68	5.4628
6	78	111	-2.4668
7	77	159	-5.6209
8	77	117	-3.7361

Number	y-actual	y-pred	Residual
9	75	141	-6.8131
10	74	164	-8.8453
11	71	95	-8.7488
12	65	79	-14.0308

d. Sum of squares error: 1,082.31
e. Sum of squares total: 1,101.67
f. $r^2 = .0176$
g. $H_0: \rho^2 = 0; \quad H_1: \rho^2 > 0$
   Reject H_0 if $F > 4.96$

$$F = \frac{SSR/(k-1)}{SSE/(n-k)} = \frac{19.4/(2-1)}{1,082.31/(12-2)} = \frac{19.4}{108.231} = .179$$

   Fail to reject the null; the regression equation isn't explaining a significant percentage of the wins variable variance.

49. $r = 1.0$.
51b. $\hat{y} = 1.4539 + 2.0526x$
   c. $\hat{y} = 1.4539 + 2.0526(10) = 21.9799$
53. $H_0: \beta \geq 0; \quad H_1: \beta < 0$
   $df = n - 2 = 26 - 2 = 24$
   Reject H_0 if $t < -1.711$

$$t = \frac{b}{s_b} = \frac{-.6}{2.3} = -.261$$

   Fail to reject the null; the two variables aren't linearly related.
55b. $r = .9562$
   c. The null and alternative hypotheses are
      $H_0: \rho = 0; \quad H_1: \rho \neq 0$
      $df = n - 2 = 13 - 2 = 11$
      The decision rule is: If the sample t statistic is less than -2.2 or greater than 2.2, reject the null hypothesis. (Reject H_0 if $t < -2.2$ or $t > 2.2$.)
      The standard error of r is

$$s_r = \sqrt{\frac{1-r^2}{n-2}} = \sqrt{\frac{1-(.9562)^2}{13-2}} = \sqrt{.0078} = .088$$

      The t statistic is

$$t = \frac{r - \rho}{s_r} = \frac{.9562 - 0}{.088} = 10.87$$

      The calculated t statistic (10.87) is greater than the tabled t value (2.2) so the null hypothesis is rejected. It's concluded that there's a linear relationship between miles and minutes.
   d. $\hat{y} = 3.9095 + 2.2736x$ e. 2.27 minutes   f. $r^2 = .9143$
   g. Using knowledge of the linear relationship between miles and minutes (.9562), we can explain 91.43% of the amount of time variable variance.

h.

Number	y-actual	y-pred	Residual
1	28	28.9186	−0.9186
2	27	26.6451	0.3549
3	35	38.0129	−3.0129
4	15	19.8244	−4.8244
5	8	8.4566	−0.4566
6	14	15.2773	−1.2773
7	20	22.0980	−2.0980
8	29	24.3715	4.6285
9	13	13.0037	−0.0037
10	16	10.7302	5.2698
11	40	35.7393	4.2607
12	9	10.7302	−1.7302
13	31	31.1922	−0.1922

i. Sum of squares error: 109.9414   *j.* Sum of squares total: 1,282.9231
k. $H_0: \rho^2 = 0$; $H_1: \rho^2 > 0$
Reject H_0 if $F > 4.84$

$$F = \frac{SSR/(k-1)}{SSE/(n-k)} = \frac{1{,}172.98/(2-1)}{109.94/(13-2)} = \frac{1{,}172.98}{9.99} = 117.42$$

Reject the null; the regression equation is explaining a significant percentage of the time to make a delivery variable variance.
l. $\hat{y} = 3.9095 + 2.2736(10) = 26.2$ minutes   *m.* 20.285 to 32.115
57. $\hat{y} = 3.24 + .39x$
    $r^2 = .61898$
    Computed $t = 4.03$
59a. $r = .92$ *b.* Yes, $t = 5.276$ *d.* $\hat{y} = 2.753 + .0042x$

CHAPTER 15

5a. Variables 2 and 3 are.   *b.* No
 c. Variables 2 and 3.
7a. Because the correlations for the bottom half would be exactly the same as those for the top half.
 b. Variables 5 and 6. Variables 2 and 4 are possibilities.
 c. Negative
 d. Variable 5 $(r_{15} = .81)^2 = .66$ or 66%
 e. Variables 5 and 6.
 f. Variables 2, 4, and 5. Variables 2, 4, and 6.
13. $\hat{y} = 4.72 + 13(40) - 4.2(20) = 440.72$
15a. $\hat{y} = -622.313 + .067x_2 + .127x_3$ *b.* .127 minutes
 c.

	y-actual	y-pred	Residual
1	576	588.1050	−12.1050
2	497	503.0244	−6.0244
3	789	741.4278	47.5722

c.

	y-actual	y-pred	Residual
4	862	863.2562	−1.2562
5	361	346.6572	14.3428
6	688	721.2757	−33.2757
7	532	541.2541	−9.2541

d. Standard error estimate: 31.0086

e. Each time a prediction is made using the multiple regression equation in part *a*, the estimate is typically off by about $31.

f. $\hat{y} = -622.313 + 2.398(150) + 9.914(100) = 728.8$

g. 633.25 to 824.356   h. 687.33 to 770.27

i. The correlation matrix shows potential for multicollinearity. The $R^2 = .98$ is good but Mario should obtain a larger sample.

19a. $R^2 = 1 - \dfrac{SSE}{SST} = 1 - \dfrac{424.81}{2,873.46} = 1 - .148 = .852$

b. df $= n - k = 22 - 4 = 18$

c. Yes, if no multicollinearity exists between the variables.

21a. Both variables are good potential predictor variables and multicollinearity shouldn't be a problem.

b. Reject the H_0 if $t > 1.703$

$$t = \frac{b_2}{s_{b2}} = \frac{.13589}{.04855} = 2.8 \qquad \text{Reject the null}$$

$$t = \frac{b_3}{s_{b3}} = \frac{.81245}{.19568} = 4.15 \qquad \text{Reject the null}$$

Both variables are making a contribution.

c. When the high temperature increases by one degree, holding traffic count constant, pop sales increase by an average of .81 quart bottles.

d. $\hat{y} = -31.85 + .13589(900) + .81245(70) = 147.3$ bottles.

e. $s_{y\cdot x} = \sqrt{\dfrac{3,125.61}{30 - 3}} = \sqrt{115.76} = 10.76$

f. $r^2 = 1 - \dfrac{SSE}{SST} = 1 - \dfrac{3,125.61}{15,271.15} = 1 - .205 = .795$

g. Reject the H_0 if $F > 5.57$

$$F = \frac{SSR/(k-1)}{SSE/(n-k)} = \frac{12,145.54/(3-1)}{3,125.61/(30-3)} = \frac{6,072.77}{115.76} = 52.46$$

h. No

i. This is a good equation that could only be made better by adding a new predictor variable.

23.

	y	x_2	x_3
y	1	−.864	.891
x_2		1	−.655
x_3			1

a. Both variables are good potential predictor variables and multicollinearity shouldn't be a problem.

b. Reject the H_0 if $t < -2.365$ or $t > 2.365$

Variable	β-coeff	Beta	t value
X3	0.006	0.571	4.377
X2	-0.008	-0.490	-3.756

Reject the null for both variables.

c. $\hat{y} = 16.406 - .0082x_2 + .0059x_3$

d. When the selling price increases by \$1, holding advertising expenditures constant, sales decrease by an average of .0082 units. When advertising expenditures increase by \$1, holding the selling price constant, sales increase by an average of .0059 units.

e. $R^2 = .932$ f. No

g. $\hat{y} = 16.406 - .0082(1500) + .0059(1000) = 10.006$

27a. The curvilinear model is a good model.   b. 43.97

33. $\hat{y} = 6.95 - 1.1x_2 - .467x_3 + 1.3x_4$
   $R^2 = .7106$

Source of variance	SS	df	Estimate σ^2	F ratio
Between:	18.61	3	6.203	16.37
Within:	7.57	20	.379	
Totals:	26.18	23		

35a. $\hat{y} = 9.667 + .833x_2 - 1.667x_3$ b. $\hat{y} = 9.667 + .833(1) - 1.667(0) = 10.5$

c. $\hat{y} = 9.667 + .833(0) - 1.667(1) = 8$ d. $\hat{y} = 9.667 + .833(0) - 1.667(0) = 9.667$

e.

Source of variance	SS	df	Estimate σ^2	F ratio
Between:	19.44	2	9.72	4.19
Within:	34.83	15	2.32	
Totals:	54.28	17		

Reject H_0 if $F > 3.68$
Reject the null; there are significant differences in the hourly wages of bus drivers.

37a. Variable 2. $r_{12} = -.87$ b. Variable 3. $r_{13} = .78$ and $r_{23} = -.43$
c. Variables 2 and 3

39a. View: $r_{12} = .86$ b. Area: $r_{15} = .57$ $r_{25} = .38$
c. View and area

49. $\hat{y} = 7.81 + 1.5(2) - 8.46(1.4) + 10.68(3.5) = 36.35$

51. $H_0: \rho^2 = 0$; $H_1: \rho^2 > 0$
   Reject H_0 if $F > 3.71$ $F = 189.04 \div 3.79 = 49.88$ Reject the null; the

regression equation explains a significant percentage of the miles per gallon variable variance.

53b. $\hat{y} = 7.319 - .0457x$.

  c. H_0: $\beta = 0$; H_1: $\beta \neq 0$.
Reject H_0 if $t < -2.3$ or $t > 2.3$.
Since the computed t value is $-.47$, fail to reject the null hypothesis. The linear equation isn't a good model.

  d. $\hat{y} = -18.633 + 1.347x - .017x^2$.

  e. H_0: $\beta_2 = 0$; H_1: $\beta_2 \neq 0$
Reject H_0 if $t < -2.365$ or $t > 2.365$
Since the computed t value is 1.861, fail to reject the null hypothesis. The linear effect isn't significant.
H_0: $\beta_3 = 0$; H_1: $\beta_3 \neq 0$
Reject H_0 if $t < -2.365$ or $t > 2.365$
Since the computed t value is -1.938, fail to reject the null hypothesis. The curvilinear effect isn't significant.

Variable	b coefficient	Beta	t
AGE	1.347	4.817	1.861
AGE2	−0.017	−5.014	−1.938

  f. The model isn't valid.

55. Answer to Exercise 47 in Chapter 12:

Source of variance	SS	df	Estimated σ^2	F ratio
Between	5,494.9	2	2,747.4	2.12
Within	31,165.1	24	1,298.5	
Total	36,660	26		

Critical F value = 3.4; fail to reject the null hypothesis. There's no difference in the mean amounts charged on the three credit cards.

57a. $\hat{y} = -69.1 + 0.0044(\text{Use}) + 31.7(\text{Charge})$ *b.* $\hat{y} = -69.1 + 0.0044(14,000) + 31.7(4.50) = 135.15$

  c. The model is very accurate, explaining 98.4% of the revenue variance.

59a. H_0: $\beta_2 = 0$; $\beta_3 = 0$; $\beta_4 = 0$; $\beta_5 = 0$
H_1: $\beta_2 \neq 0$; $\beta_3 \neq 0$; $\beta_4 \neq 0$; $\beta_5 \neq 0$
Tested at the .05 significance level:
$df = n - k = 30 - 5 = 25$
Reject H_0 if $t < -2.06$ or $t > 2.06$.
Computed t values:
Sales: $t = .350$
Assets: $t = -.667$
Equity: $t = 1.142$
Profits: $t = 2.710$

Reject the null hypothesis for the profits as a percentage of equity variable. None of the rest of the variables explain much variance.

b. Yes. There's a multicollinearity problem when sales, assets, and equity are used as predictor variables.

c. $\hat{y} = 1.082 + .139(\text{Profits})$ is the only valid regression equation. It only explains 17.5% of the earnings per share variance.

61a. $\hat{y} = 20.021 + 9.358(\text{Permits})$ b. $\hat{y} = 10.131 + 8.496(\text{Permits}) + 65.531(\text{Season})$

c. The simple regression equation

Variable	b coefficient	Beta	t
PERM	8.496	.858	8.865
SEAS	64.531	.164	1.694

d. Quarter 1: $\hat{y} = 20.021 + 9.358(19) = 197.823$
Quarter 2: $\hat{y} = 20.021 + 9.358(13) = 141.675$

e. Yes. The observations don't constitute a random sample.

CHAPTER 16

5. $1,289.73(2.847) = 3,671.86$

7. Multiply the number of sick days by the cost per day for each quarter to get the new value series. Divide each of these values by the value in the last quarter base period (25,010), then multiply by 100 to get the value indexes:

99.0   115.5   93.9   100.0

9. Divide each data value by the value for the base period, January 1993 (3,921.8), then multiply by 100:

1992			1993		
	June	95.5		Jan.	100.0
	July	96.3		Feb.	100.6
	Aug.	97.0		March	101.6
	Sept.	97.4		April	102.0
	Oct.	99.4		May	102.5
	Nov.	99.0		June	103.2
	Dec.	100.4		July	103.8

11.
Jan	100.0
Feb	69.1
March	90.7
April	99.5
May	96.0
June	91.9

17.
Jan	124.25
Feb	124.20
March	123.45
April	123.10

19. Jan   281,631
    Feb   233,139
    March   280,624
    April   295,097

21a. Nov   3,231.44
     Dec   2,429.85
     Jan   2,119.36
     Feb   1,809.84
     March   2,545.15
     April   2,154.87

29a. 1,600   b. 85   c. 3,385
31b. The linear model is best.   c. $\hat{Y} = 212 + 25X$ d. 25
  e. 612; 637   f. Compare 621 and 637 to 566 and 623
  g. Inflation and population growth
37a. No   b. Both are important
  c. Trend estimate for 1992:
     $\hat{Y} = -1.29 + .571(21) = 10.701$
     Cyclical for 1991:
     $\hat{Y} = -.7395 + .4904(20) = 10.13$
     $C = Y/\hat{Y}(100) = 11.63/10.13 = 114.88$
     $Y(1992) = TC = 10.701(1.148) = 12.285$

39.

Year	Cyclical
1980	99.717
1981	96.667
1982	96.791
1983	98.200
1984	105.517
1985	102.858
1986	102.909
1987	99.474
1988	99.455
1989	97.350

47. Average 100
49. 64.3   Eliminate the lowest (64.3) and the highest (92.4).
    80.1   Average the remaining indexes.
    82.4
    85.9 $(80.1 + 82.4 + 85.9 + 88.2)/4 = 336.6/4 = 84.15$
    88.2
    92.4
51. 65.4   Eliminate the lowest (65.4) and the highest (76.8).
    66.9   Average the remaining indexes.
    70.0
    72.6 $(66.9 + 70.0 + 72.6)/3 = 209.5/3 = 69.83$

76.8

69.83(.98) = 68.43

Y = TS = 800(.6843) = 547.44

53. (1,200/1,195)(96.9) = 97.3

55a.

Jan	3,000	Jul	3,600
Feb	3,750	Aug	3,900
Mar	4,750	Sep	5,250
Apr	5,500	Oct	5,800
May	5,350	Nov	6,450
Jun	5,050	Dec	7,600

b. 3,500/3,000 = 1.167

60,000(1.167) = 70,020

c. 70,020/12 = 5,835

5,835(1.10) = 6,418.50
5,835(1.07) = 6,243.45
5,835(1.01) = 5,893.35
            ─────────
            18,555.30

57.

Quarter	
1	94.96
2	103.32
3	100.11
4	102.15

67.

Sep	106.4
Oct	104.9
Nov	102.7
Dec	100.5
Jan	100.0
Feb	102.5
Mar	101.9

69.

1980	102.2
1985	102.1
1986	99.7
1987	100.3
1988	101.7
1989	100.0

73. Top and middle management

77a. $\hat{Y} = 250 - 2.455X$ b. 2.455   c. Inflation and population growth
e. Lot of fluctuation   g. Cyclical   h. 195.67

79. $\hat{Y} = 908.84 - 4.33X$

1980	100.0
1981	110.9
1982	121.3

1983	86.4
1984	93.3
1985	94.7
1986	91.0
1987	78.7
1988	89.9
1989	111.3
1990	122.9

81*a.* $\hat{Y} = 1499 + 3.177X$

No seasonality and some cyclical variation.

83*a.* $\hat{Y} = 395 + 2.229X$

Jan.	89.0	July	102.2
Feb.	109.6	Aug.	105.6
March	103.4	Sept.	99.2
April	108.3	Oct.	110.8
May	99.0	Nov.	78.7
June	100.4	Dec.	93.8

b. Seasonal and cyclical   *c.* Yes

CHAPTER 17

5. a, b, and d
7. Exponential smoothing
9. Naive
11*a.* $\Sigma e_t = 2.75$; $\Sigma|e_t| = 8.53$; $\Sigma e_t^2 = 8.83$; $\Sigma|e_t|/Y_t = 85.6$; $\Sigma e_t/Y_t = 21.2$
   b. MAD $= 8.53/11 = .78$ *c.* MSE $= 8.83/11 = .80$ *d.* MAPE $= 85.6/11 =$
   7.78   *e.* MPE $= 21.2/11 = 1.93$ *f.* Jan. 1993 $= 12.14$

13*a.*

Period	Actual	Predicted	Error	% error
6	11.08	10.04	1.04	9.39%
7	11.51	10.40	1.11	9.63%
8	10.99	10.71	0.28	2.53%
9	10.78	10.90	−0.12	1.09%
10	10.55	11.00	−0.45	4.25%
11	10.82	10.98	−0.16	1.50%
12	9.96	10.93	−0.97	9.74%

Mean squared error (MSE) $= 0.51$
Mean absolute percentage error (MAPE) $= 5.45\%$
Mean percentage error (MPE) or bias $= 0.71\%$

b.

Period	Actual	Predicted	Error	% error
4	10.28	9.76	0.52	5.03%
5	10.63	10.10	0.53	4.99%
6	11.08	10.32	0.76	6.83%

Period	Actual	Predicted	Error	% error
7	11.51	10.66	0.85	7.36%
8	10.99	11.07	−0.08	0.76%
9	10.78	11.19	−0.41	3.83%
10	10.55	11.09	−0.54	5.15%
11	10.82	10.77	0.05	0.43%
12	9.96	10.72	−0.76	7.60%

Mean squared error (MSE) $\quad = 0.32$
Mean absolute percentage error (MAPE) $= 4.66\%$
Mean percentage error (MPE) or bias $\quad = 0.81\%$

c. 5 month—MAD = .69 $\qquad$ 3 month—MAD = .56
d. 5 month—MSE = .51 $\qquad$ 3 month—MSE = .32
e. 5 month—MAPE = 5.45% $\qquad$ 3 month—MAPE = 4.66%
f. 5 month—MPE = .71% $\qquad$ 3 month—MPE = .81%
g. Three-month moving average forecast = 10.44

15.

Period	Y-actual	Y-pred
1	205	205.0
2	251	205.0
3	304	214.2
4	284	232.2
5	352	242.5
6	300	264.4
7	241	271.5
8	284	265.4
9	312	269.1
10	289	277.7
11	385	280.0
12	256	301.0

Demand for January 1993 = 292.0
Mean square error: $\quad$ 3,855.7

17. Exponential smoothing using $\alpha = .75$ was best.
MSE = 7.26, MAPE = 9.95%
Forecast for first quarter 1992 = 29.97

21a. 2.1 $\quad$ b. 1.2 $\quad$ c. 4.0
d. $Y_{20} = 1.2 + 2.1(20) + 4(0) - 2(1) + .8(0) = 41.2$
e. $Y_{22} = 1.2 + 2.1(22) + 4(0) - 2(0) + .8(0) = 47.2$

23. $\hat{Y} = 49.2 - 29.5S_1 - 30.2S_2 - 17.8S_3$.
$R^2 = 70.3\%$.
Second quarter 1992 = 19.03
Third quarter 1992 = 31.43
Fourth quarter 1992 = 49.23

27. a and b are stationary

29a. Trend $\quad$ b. Random $\quad$ c. Seasonal $\quad$ d. Trend

31a. $r_1 = .942$; $\quad r_2 = .873$ $\quad$ b. $r_1 = .633$

33. $0 \pm .196$
35a. $r_1 = .822,$ $r_2 = .623,$ $r_3 = .431,$ $r_4 = .309,$
    $r_5 = .220,$ $r_6 = .130,$ $r_7 = .067,$ $r_8 = .069,$
    $r_9 = .082,$ $r_{10} = .060,$ $r_{11} = -.027,$ $r_{12} = -.133$
  b. No
  c. $r_1 = .496, r_2 = .168, r_3 = -.096, r_4 = -.074,$
    $r_5 = -.217, r_6 = -.238, r_7 = -.399, r_8 = -.172,$
    $r_9 = -.002, r_{10} = .278, r_{11} = .263, r_{12} = .250$
  d. Pattern
39. Durbin-Watson
41. Positive autocorrelation
47. Positive autocorrelation
53. Overestimating
55. Box-Jenkins
65b. 1.307   c. 2.78   d. 17.08%
  e. 17.08%   g. 13.25
67a. Trend   b. Seasonal   c. Pattern in data
69a. 264.4; MAPE = 36.4%   b. 5-month: 264.7; MAPE = 24.6%
  c. 261.2; MAPE = 33.9%
75. $\alpha = .05$; reject H_0 if D.W. < 1.19. Best model: $\hat{y} = -69.1 + .0044$ (use)
    $+ 31.7$ (charge)
    D.W. $= .85$; reject the null and conclude that serial correlation is a problem.

CHAPTER 18

5.

Prob.	Dem.	Stock (payoffs in hundreds)			
		20	30	40	50
.20	20	6	4.50	3.00	1.50
.25	25	6	6.75	5.25	3.75
.20	30	6	9.00	7.50	6.00
.15	35	6	9.00	9.75	8.25
.10	40	6	9.00	12.00	10.50
.05	45	6	9.00	12.00	12.75
.05	50	6	9.00	12.00	15.00

7a. $5 per hundred ($.05)   b. $2 per hundred ($.02)   c. $9.05
  d. Stock 300 since the expected payoffs, in order, are
    5, 8.25, 9.05, 8.10, 6.45
  e. EVPI = 11.75 − 9.05 = 2.70
9. The expected profits, in millions, are
  Build 25,000: .05
  Build 40,000: .40
  Build 55,000: .25
  So if the objective is to maximize expected profits, a 40,000-capacity plant
  should be built.
17. .682

19*b.* Large: 24.3; medium: 24.9; expand: 26.6.
 c. Expand the present plant; expand again if much larger or somewhat larger
  demand results.
 d. A conservative approach suggests expanding the present plant since less money
  would be needed.

21*a.* EMV = $380,000

23*a.*

		Class size (payoffs: in hundreds)					
P	Dem.	10	11	12	13	14	15
.10	10	10	8	6	4	2	0
.10	11	10	11	9	7	5	3
.20	12	10	11	12	10	8	6
.25	13	10	11	12	13	11	9
.30	14	10	11	12	13	14	12
.05	15	10	11	12	13	14	15

b. The EMVs are, in order, 10, 10.7, 11.1, 10.9, 9.95, and 8.1 so the optimum class
 size is 12.
c. 12.7 − 11.1 = 1.6

25*a.* .625.

27*a.*

		Stock (payoffs: in hundreds)					
P	Dem.	500	750	1,000	1,250	1,500	1,750
.15	500	125	112.5	100	87.5	75	62.5
.25	750	125	187.5	175	162.5	150	137.5
.25	1000	125	187.5	250	237.5	225	212.5
.20	1250	125	187.5	250	312.5	300	287.5
.10	1500	125	187.5	250	312.5	375	362.5
.05	1750	125	187.5	250	312.5	375	437.5

b. The EMVs, in order, are 125, 176.3, 208.8, 222.5, 221.4, and 212.6 so 1,250 units
 should be stocked.
c. EVPI = 250.1 − 222.5 = 27.6
d. A higher marginal loss would result in fewer than 1,250 units stocked to
 maximize expected profits.
e. A higher marginal profit would increase the optimum stocking level above
 1,250.

33*a.* The EMV for both projects is $9,500 so the choice would lead to indifference.
 b. Venture A would be preferred by a conservative company while Venture B would
  be favored by an aggressive, risk-seeking company.

35*b.* EMVs: A: 2.34; B: 14.8; C: 12.2.
 So the first choice is B. Then choose branch 2 of B since its payoff (14.8) is
 higher than the other two choices (10 and 5.25).
 c. EMV = 14.8
 d. The attractiveness of large payoffs and the negative aspect of negative amounts
  might affect the final decision.

Chapter 19

5. Parametric tests are more powerful.

7. The one-sample mean test of Chapter 9.

9. $H = 6$ and $L = 10$, so $z = 1$; fail to reject the null hypothesis. Neither high nor low pressures are favored.

11. The normal approximation to the binomial is similar.

13. $r = 15$, $\mu = 16$, $\sigma = 2.60$, and $z = -.38$. Fail to reject the null hypothesis of a random string.

15. The small sample t test is similar.

17. Sum of ranks for A is 192, $U = 183$, $\mu = 127.5$, $\sigma = 26.5$, so $z = 2.09$. At $\alpha = .05$, critical z values are ± 1.96, so the null hypothesis is rejected. B is a better seller than A.

19. The Spearman test is similar to the Pearson test used for quantitative data.

21. Sum of $d^2 = 76$, so $r = .095$ and $t = .23$. Fail to reject the null hypothesis of zero population correlation.

23. One-sample sign test: $n = 26$ and $X(U) = 10$; $z = -1.18$. Fail to reject the null hypothesis of equal overfills and underfills.

25. Sum of squared rank differences $= 150$ so $r = .476$, a moderate correlation.

27. U test: Sum of ranks for Regular $= 101$, $U = 121$, $\mu = 72$, and $\sigma = 17.3$. So $z = 2.83$ and table z for one-tailed test at $.05 = 1.645$ so the null hypothesis is rejected. Free days increase sales.

29. Runs test: runs $= 16$, $\mu = 20.3$, $\sigma = 2.93$, and $z = -1.47$. Since table $z = \pm 1.96$ (.05), fail to reject the null hypothesis of randomness.

31. One sample runs test: plus signs $= 13$ and $z = 1.89$. Since table z (one-tailed, $\alpha = .10) = 1.28$, the null hypothesis of equal preference is rejected. Purple-power is preferred.

33. Sum of squared ranks $= 78$ so $r = .07$. $t = .17$ and since table t (df $= 6$, two-tailed, $\alpha = .10$) is ± 1.943, fail to reject the null hypothesis of no population correlation. Men and women react differently to the commercials.

35. U test: $U = 256$, $\mu = 200$, $\sigma = 37.0$, and $z = 1.51$. Since table z (two-tailed, $.10) = \pm 1.645$, fail to reject the null hypothesis of equal tire lifetimes.

37. One-sample sign test: remove unchanged value and $n = 8$. Plus $= 6$ so $z = 1.41$. Table z (one-tailed, $.10) = 1.28$ and null hypothesis is rejected. There has been a significant increase in ratings after the program.

39. Sum of squared differences in ranks $= 192$ and $r = -.17$. $t = -.49$ and table t (two-tailed, df $= 8$, $\alpha = .05) = \pm 2.306$ so fail to reject the null hypothesis. There's no correlation between service and rating in the population.

APPENDIX E   STATISTICAL TABLES

TABLE E.1   Table of Random Numbers

75421	11182	31304	08036	86922	77941	88944	30226	60766	90951
06692	19591	14171	04356	06744	46546	99184	97684	43285	86345
66065	12379	70386	09035	90126	74677	39885	84335	09442	21772
01098	06343	88773	94702	07203	60936	54445	12423	64560	99694
93526	56837	42025	45578	95193	97695	53146	51370	79913	83145
85129	31088	36253	40011	62078	72245	58783	47555	55681	45450
74312	81501	94303	30800	60660	69979	57625	00050	69795	15120
67348	11345	13361	40573	75687	78415	42407	97830	98069	98605
29241	77892	67728	60876	53046	75840	18933	18108	73509	76958
04366	94984	95131	22993	17240	63185	54786	31607	50705	61581
54205	61584	99698	74013	88263	96563	18003	77390	05762	40975
52801	44366	19745	74219	20982	91400	50685	56541	68392	96624
02573	59494	26362	40769	39340	19677	16923	04761	65952	03630
15896	32426	64984	99029	58073	28814	44849	39871	00825	29966
26032	33340	54573	55786	75383	14546	37499	43894	86358	19706
41349	18921	50835	65861	79521	38319	33999	74851	97319	17221
31246	35797	89051	36319	38137	11101	02808	36771	63163	00816
55704	87671	81967	18984	94617	89097	91625	49172	07106	06218
09107	53117	75664	25300	98186	29702	73632	77044	08238	08097
53779	05917	99367	58743	33981	66547	45685	11168	81086	29458
05252	99475	70537	29636	46984	49231	73571	64092	26162	26361
92966	81458	79792	39399	39278	20247	45367	76937	64563	73930
68109	88529	70116	11782	24198	68334	83184	26202	49315	38471
53118	70359	68973	95173	29213	29969	00445	24846	50957	80443
60924	44136	71034	80642	62977	93957	21006	66422	96753	69814
11151	59784	77446	64703	22038	40357	57749	62349	88018	20160
32731	14203	36222	13436	16935	26412	09878	27931	54679	35275
04037	48341	95595	26036	57521	16245	71204	44232	09527	49083
75807	89169	30622	23911	73689	50718	33796	30145	97763	75437
93509	65893	82351	54938	26829	04823	71697	46159	43465	99159
93528	38008	53069	29029	36617	09019	95758	52955	75018	83253
10603	93078	11673	36373	71957	89710	15378	52022	57934	86236
99155	30214	58351	16606	08569	19665	22531	58753	22759	90501
97268	87653	40124	51615	27365	26827	70255	23368	78952	05515
93564	66965	91850	25093	53517	39997	17521	57074	76743	11610
06959	27612	66188	19351	17367	84340	00247	49881	01997	33756
13172	61241	53558	59919	15082	75692	43138	22677	55844	70034
03690	57173	38889	03032	69496	42566	23096	43416	78732	12420
38005	70085	74744	32644	88440	12489	39538	64712	92792	51310
28758	45596	59049	79799	68763	49827	57854	76334	99237	11388
84260	58136	31250	88953	04929	06903	21175	42463	15227	15205
77800	77252	68397	37935	53941	59771	92875	37004	57044	18210
99505	24764	22807	54083	90303	43362	71223	96233	88058	03268
53803	68932	38510	87838	68543	73671	57403	50077	63351	55781
68379	47885	33501	10666	74222	81999	16699	51745	84672	11640
30033	45809	69655	31679	56931	40579	53867	22586	00794	67305
73888	69685	91050	60898	06171	01165	04192	03700	27979	76516
50935	51867	76172	52543	38383	43396	67725	68868	15571	78654
04689	09839	31801	18560	21328	87664	08203	82426	23946	82792
65860	84568	88383	49927	52267	63736	01964	86914	14949	55467

Source: Robert D. Mason and Douglas A. Lind, *Statistical Techniques in Business and Economics*, 7th ed. (Homewood, Ill.: Richard D. Irwin, 1990), p. 855.

TABLE E.2 Binomial Probability Distribution

$n = 1$
PROBABILITY

x	0.05	0.10	0.20	0.30	0.40	0.50	0.60	0.70	0.80	0.90	0.95
0	0.950	0.900	0.800	0.700	0.600	0.500	0.400	0.300	0.200	0.100	0.050
1	0.050	0.100	0.200	0.300	0.400	0.500	0.600	0.700	0.800	0.900	0.950

$n = 2$
PROBABILITY

x	0.05	0.10	0.20	0.30	0.40	0.50	0.60	0.70	0.80	0.90	0.95
0	0.903	0.810	0.640	0.490	0.360	0.250	0.160	0.090	0.040	0.010	0.003
1	0.095	0.180	0.320	0.420	0.480	0.500	0.480	0.420	0.320	0.180	0.095
2	0.003	0.010	0.040	0.090	0.160	0.250	0.360	0.490	0.640	0.810	0.903

$n = 3$
PROBABILITY

x	0.05	0.10	0.20	0.30	0.40	0.50	0.60	0.70	0.80	0.90	0.95
0	0.857	0.729	0.512	0.343	0.216	0.125	0.064	0.027	0.008	0.001	0.000
1	0.135	0.243	0.384	0.441	0.432	0.375	0.288	0.189	0.096	0.027	0.007
2	0.007	0.027	0.096	0.189	0.288	0.375	0.432	0.441	0.384	0.243	0.135
3	0.000	0.001	0.008	0.027	0.064	0.125	0.216	0.343	0.512	0.729	0.857

$n = 4$
PROBABILITY

x	0.05	0.10	0.20	0.30	0.40	0.50	0.60	0.70	0.80	0.90	0.95
0	0.815	0.656	0.410	0.240	0.130	0.063	0.026	0.008	0.002	0.000	0.000
1	0.171	0.292	0.410	0.412	0.346	0.250	0.154	0.076	0.026	0.004	0.000
2	0.014	0.049	0.154	0.265	0.346	0.375	0.346	0.265	0.154	0.049	0.014
3	0.000	0.004	0.026	0.076	0.154	0.250	0.346	0.412	0.410	0.292	0.171
4	0.000	0.000	0.002	0.008	0.026	0.063	0.130	0.240	0.410	0.656	0.815

$n = 5$
PROBABILITY

x	0.05	0.10	0.20	0.30	0.40	0.50	0.60	0.70	0.80	0.90	0.95
0	0.774	0.590	0.328	0.168	0.078	0.031	0.010	0.002	0.000	0.000	0.000
1	0.204	0.328	0.410	0.360	0.259	0.156	0.077	0.028	0.006	0.000	0.000
2	0.021	0.073	0.205	0.309	0.346	0.313	0.230	0.132	0.051	0.008	0.001
3	0.001	0.008	0.051	0.132	0.230	0.313	0.346	0.309	0.205	0.073	0.021
4	0.000	0.000	0.006	0.028	0.077	0.156	0.259	0.360	0.410	0.328	0.204
5	0.000	0.000	0.000	0.002	0.010	0.031	0.078	0.168	0.328	0.590	0.774

TABLE E.2 (continued)

$n = 6$
PROBABILITY

x	0.05	0.10	0.20	0.30	0.40	0.50	0.60	0.70	0.80	0.90	0.95
0	0.735	0.531	0.262	0.118	0.047	0.016	0.004	0.001	0.000	0.000	0.000
1	0.232	0.354	0.393	0.303	0.187	0.094	0.037	0.010	0.002	0.000	0.000
2	0.031	0.098	0.246	0.324	0.311	0.234	0.138	0.060	0.015	0.001	0.000
3	0.002	0.015	0.082	0.185	0.276	0.313	0.276	0.185	0.082	0.015	0.002
4	0.000	0.001	0.015	0.060	0.138	0.234	0.311	0.324	0.246	0.098	0.031
5	0.000	0.000	0.002	0.010	0.037	0.094	0.187	0.303	0.393	0.354	0.232
6	0.000	0.000	0.000	0.001	0.004	0.016	0.047	0.118	0.262	0.531	0.735

$n = 7$
PROBABILITY

x	0.05	0.10	0.20	0.30	0.40	0.50	0.60	0.70	0.80	0.90	0.95
0	0.698	0.478	0.210	0.082	0.028	0.008	0.002	0.000	0.000	0.000	0.000
1	0.257	0.372	0.367	0.247	0.131	0.055	0.017	0.004	0.000	0.000	0.000
2	0.041	0.124	0.275	0.318	0.261	0.164	0.077	0.025	0.004	0.000	0.000
3	0.004	0.023	0.115	0.227	0.290	0.273	0.194	0.097	0.029	0.003	0.000
4	0.000	0.003	0.029	0.097	0.194	0.273	0.290	0.227	0.115	0.023	0.004
5	0.000	0.000	0.004	0.025	0.077	0.164	0.261	0.318	0.275	0.124	0.041
6	0.000	0.000	0.000	0.004	0.017	0.055	0.131	0.247	0.367	0.372	0.257
7	0.000	0.000	0.000	0.000	0.002	0.008	0.028	0.082	0.210	0.478	0.698

$n = 8$
PROBABILITY

x	0.05	0.10	0.20	0.30	0.40	0.50	0.60	0.70	0.80	0.90	0.95
0	0.663	0.430	0.168	0.058	0.017	0.004	0.001	0.000	0.000	0.000	0.000
1	0.279	0.383	0.336	0.198	0.090	0.031	0.008	0.001	0.000	0.000	0.000
2	0.051	0.149	0.294	0.296	0.209	0.109	0.041	0.010	0.001	0.000	0.000
3	0.005	0.033	0.147	0.254	0.279	0.219	0.124	0.047	0.009	0.000	0.000
4	0.000	0.005	0.046	0.136	0.232	0.273	0.232	0.136	0.046	0.005	0.000
5	0.000	0.000	0.009	0.047	0.124	0.219	0.279	0.254	0.147	0.033	0.005
6	0.000	0.000	0.001	0.010	0.041	0.109	0.209	0.296	0.294	0.149	0.051
7	0.000	0.000	0.000	0.001	0.008	0.031	0.090	0.198	0.336	0.383	0.279
8	0.000	0.000	0.000	0.000	0.001	0.004	0.017	0.058	0.168	0.430	0.663

$n = 9$
PROBABILITY

x	0.05	0.10	0.20	0.30	0.40	0.50	0.60	0.70	0.80	0.90	0.95
0	0.630	0.387	0.134	0.040	0.010	0.002	0.000	0.000	0.000	0.000	0.000
1	0.299	0.387	0.302	0.156	0.060	0.018	0.004	0.000	0.000	0.000	0.000
2	0.063	0.172	0.302	0.267	0.161	0.070	0.021	0.004	0.000	0.000	0.000
3	0.008	0.045	0.176	0.267	0.251	0.164	0.074	0.021	0.003	0.000	0.000
4	0.001	0.007	0.066	0.172	0.251	0.246	0.167	0.074	0.017	0.001	0.000
5	0.000	0.001	0.017	0.074	0.167	0.246	0.251	0.172	0.066	0.007	0.001
6	0.000	0.000	0.003	0.021	0.074	0.164	0.251	0.267	0.176	0.045	0.008
7	0.000	0.000	0.000	0.004	0.021	0.070	0.161	0.267	0.302	0.172	0.063
8	0.000	0.000	0.000	0.000	0.004	0.018	0.060	0.156	0.302	0.387	0.299
9	0.000	0.000	0.000	0.000	0.000	0.002	0.010	0.040	0.134	0.387	0.630

TABLE E.2 (continued)

n = 10
PROBABILITY

x	0.05	0.10	0.20	0.30	0.40	0.50	0.60	0.70	0.80	0.90	0.95
0	0.599	0.349	0.107	0.028	0.006	0.001	0.000	0.000	0.000	0.000	0.000
1	0.315	0.387	0.268	0.121	0.040	0.010	0.002	0.000	0.000	0.000	0.000
2	0.075	0.194	0.302	0.233	0.121	0.044	0.011	0.001	0.000	0.000	0.000
3	0.010	0.057	0.201	0.267	0.215	0.117	0.042	0.009	0.001	0.000	0.000
4	0.001	0.011	0.088	0.200	0.251	0.205	0.111	0.037	0.006	0.000	0.000
5	0.000	0.001	0.026	0.103	0.201	0.246	0.201	0.103	0.026	0.001	0.000
6	0.000	0.000	0.006	0.037	0.111	0.205	0.251	0.200	0.088	0.011	0.001
7	0.000	0.000	0.001	0.009	0.042	0.117	0.215	0.267	0.201	0.057	0.010
8	0.000	0.000	0.000	0.001	0.011	0.044	0.121	0.233	0.302	0.194	0.075
9	0.000	0.000	0.000	0.000	0.002	0.010	0.040	0.121	0.268	0.387	0.315
10	0.000	0.000	0.000	0.000	0.000	0.001	0.006	0.028	0.107	0.349	0.599

n = 11
PROBABILITY

x	0.05	0.10	0.20	0.30	0.40	0.50	0.60	0.70	0.80	0.90	0.95
0	0.569	0.314	0.086	0.020	0.004	0.000	0.000	0.000	0.000	0.000	0.000
1	0.329	0.384	0.236	0.093	0.027	0.005	0.001	0.000	0.000	0.000	0.000
2	0.087	0.213	0.295	0.200	0.089	0.027	0.005	0.001	0.000	0.000	0.000
3	0.014	0.071	0.221	0.257	0.177	0.081	0.023	0.004	0.000	0.000	0.000
4	0.001	0.016	0.111	0.220	0.236	0.161	0.070	0.017	0.002	0.000	0.000
5	0.000	0.002	0.039	0.132	0.221	0.226	0.147	0.057	0.010	0.000	0.000
6	0.000	0.000	0.010	0.057	0.147	0.226	0.221	0.132	0.039	0.002	0.000
7	0.000	0.000	0.002	0.017	0.070	0.161	0.236	0.220	0.111	0.016	0.001
8	0.000	0.000	0.000	0.004	0.023	0.081	0.177	0.257	0.221	0.071	0.014
9	0.000	0.000	0.000	0.001	0.005	0.027	0.089	0.200	0.295	0.213	0.087
10	0.000	0.000	0.000	0.000	0.001	0.005	0.027	0.093	0.236	0.384	0.329
11	0.000	0.000	0.000	0.000	0.000	0.000	0.004	0.020	0.086	0.314	0.569

n = 12
PROBABILITY

x	0.05	0.10	0.20	0.30	0.40	0.50	0.60	0.70	0.80	0.90	0.95
0	0.540	0.282	0.069	0.014	0.002	0.000	0.000	0.000	0.000	0.000	0.000
1	0.341	0.377	0.206	0.071	0.017	0.003	0.000	0.000	0.000	0.000	0.000
2	0.099	0.230	0.283	0.168	0.064	0.016	0.002	0.000	0.000	0.000	0.000
3	0.017	0.085	0.236	0.240	0.142	0.054	0.012	0.001	0.000	0.000	0.000
4	0.002	0.021	0.133	0.231	0.213	0.121	0.042	0.008	0.001	0.000	0.000
5	0.000	0.004	0.053	0.158	0.227	0.193	0.101	0.029	0.003	0.000	0.000
6	0.000	0.000	0.016	0.079	0.177	0.226	0.177	0.079	0.016	0.000	0.000
7	0.000	0.000	0.003	0.029	0.101	0.193	0.227	0.158	0.053	0.004	0.000
8	0.000	0.000	0.001	0.008	0.042	0.121	0.213	0.231	0.133	0.021	0.002
9	0.000	0.000	0.000	0.001	0.012	0.054	0.142	0.240	0.236	0.085	0.017
10	0.000	0.000	0.000	0.000	0.002	0.016	0.064	0.168	0.283	0.230	0.099
11	0.000	0.000	0.000	0.000	0.000	0.003	0.017	0.071	0.206	0.377	0.341
12	0.000	0.000	0.000	0.000	0.000	0.000	0.002	0.014	0.069	0.282	0.540

TABLE E.2 (continued)

n = 13
PROBABILITY

x	0.05	0.10	0.20	0.30	0.40	0.50	0.60	0.70	0.80	0.90	0.95
0	0.513	0.254	0.055	0.010	0.001	0.000	0.000	0.000	0.000	0.000	0.000
1	0.351	0.367	0.179	0.054	0.011	0.002	0.000	0.000	0.000	0.000	0.000
2	0.111	0.245	0.268	0.139	0.045	0.010	0.001	0.000	0.000	0.000	0.000
3	0.021	0.100	0.246	0.218	0.111	0.035	0.006	0.001	0.000	0.000	0.000
4	0.003	0.028	0.154	0.234	0.184	0.087	0.024	0.003	0.000	0.000	0.000
5	0.000	0.006	0.069	0.180	0.221	0.157	0.066	0.014	0.001	0.000	0.000
6	0.000	0.001	0.023	0.103	0.197	0.209	0.131	0.044	0.006	0.000	0.000
7	0.000	0.000	0.006	0.044	0.131	0.209	0.197	0.103	0.023	0.001	0.000
8	0.000	0.000	0.001	0.014	0.066	0.157	0.221	0.180	0.069	0.006	0.000
9	0.000	0.000	0.000	0.003	0.024	0.087	0.184	0.234	0.154	0.028	0.003
10	0.000	0.000	0.000	0.001	0.006	0.035	0.111	0.218	0.246	0.100	0.021
11	0.000	0.000	0.000	0.000	0.001	0.010	0.045	0.139	0.268	0.245	0.111
12	0.000	0.000	0.000	0.000	0.000	0.002	0.011	0.054	0.179	0.367	0.351
13	0.000	0.000	0.000	0.000	0.000	0.000	0.001	0.010	0.055	0.254	0.513

n = 14
PROBABILITY

x	0.05	0.10	0.20	0.30	0.40	0.50	0.60	0.70	0.80	0.90	0.95
0	0.488	0.229	0.044	0.007	0.001	0.000	0.000	0.000	0.000	0.000	0.000
1	0.359	0.356	0.154	0.041	0.007	0.001	0.000	0.000	0.000	0.000	0.000
2	0.123	0.257	0.250	0.113	0.032	0.006	0.001	0.000	0.000	0.000	0.000
3	0.026	0.114	0.250	0.194	0.085	0.022	0.003	0.000	0.000	0.000	0.000
4	0.004	0.035	0.172	0.229	0.155	0.061	0.014	0.001	0.000	0.000	0.000
5	0.000	0.008	0.086	0.196	0.207	0.122	0.041	0.007	0.000	0.000	0.000
6	0.000	0.001	0.032	0.126	0.207	0.183	0.092	0.023	0.002	0.000	0.000
7	0.000	0.000	0.009	0.062	0.157	0.209	0.157	0.062	0.009	0.000	0.000
8	0.000	0.000	0.002	0.023	0.092	0.183	0.207	0.126	0.032	0.001	0.000
9	0.000	0.000	0.000	0.007	0.041	0.122	0.207	0.196	0.086	0.008	0.000
10	0.000	0.000	0.000	0.001	0.014	0.061	0.155	0.229	0.172	0.035	0.004
11	0.000	0.000	0.000	0.000	0.003	0.022	0.085	0.194	0.250	0.114	0.026
12	0.000	0.000	0.000	0.000	0.001	0.006	0.032	0.113	0.250	0.257	0.123
13	0.000	0.000	0.000	0.000	0.000	0.001	0.007	0.041	0.154	0.356	0.359
14	0.000	0.000	0.000	0.000	0.000	0.000	0.001	0.007	0.044	0.229	0.488

TABLE E.2 (continued)

n = 15
PROBABILITY

x	0.05	0.10	0.20	0.30	0.40	0.50	0.60	0.70	0.80	0.90	0.95
0	0.463	0.206	0.035	0.005	0.000	0.000	0.000	0.000	0.000	0.000	0.000
1	0.366	0.343	0.132	0.031	0.005	0.000	0.000	0.000	0.000	0.000	0.000
2	0.135	0.267	0.231	0.092	0.022	0.003	0.000	0.000	0.000	0.000	0.000
3	0.031	0.129	0.250	0.170	0.063	0.014	0.002	0.000	0.000	0.000	0.000
4	0.005	0.043	0.188	0.219	0.127	0.042	0.007	0.001	0.000	0.000	0.000
5	0.001	0.010	0.103	0.206	0.186	0.092	0.024	0.003	0.000	0.000	0.000
6	0.000	0.002	0.043	0.147	0.207	0.153	0.061	0.012	0.001	0.000	0.000
7	0.000	0.000	0.014	0.081	0.177	0.196	0.118	0.035	0.003	0.000	0.000
8	0.000	0.000	0.003	0.035	0.118	0.196	0.177	0.081	0.014	0.000	0.000
9	0.000	0.000	0.001	0.012	0.061	0.153	0.207	0.147	0.043	0.002	0.000
10	0.000	0.000	0.000	0.003	0.024	0.092	0.186	0.206	0.103	0.010	0.001
11	0.000	0.000	0.000	0.001	0.007	0.042	0.127	0.219	0.188	0.043	0.005
12	0.000	0.000	0.000	0.000	0.002	0.014	0.063	0.170	0.250	0.129	0.031
13	0.000	0.000	0.000	0.000	0.000	0.003	0.022	0.092	0.231	0.267	0.135
14	0.000	0.000	0.000	0.000	0.000	0.000	0.005	0.031	0.132	0.343	0.366
15	0.000	0.000	0.000	0.000	0.000	0.000	0.000	0.005	0.035	0.206	0.463

n = 16
PROBABILITY

x	0.05	0.10	0.20	0.30	0.40	0.50	0.60	0.70	0.80	0.90	0.95
0	0.440	0.185	0.028	0.003	0.000	0.000	0.000	0.000	0.000	0.000	0.000
1	0.371	0.329	0.113	0.023	0.003	0.000	0.000	0.000	0.000	0.000	0.000
2	0.146	0.275	0.211	0.073	0.015	0.002	0.000	0.000	0.000	0.000	0.000
3	0.036	0.142	0.246	0.146	0.047	0.009	0.001	0.000	0.000	0.000	0.000
4	0.006	0.051	0.200	0.204	0.101	0.028	0.004	0.000	0.000	0.000	0.000
5	0.001	0.014	0.120	0.210	0.162	0.067	0.014	0.001	0.000	0.000	0.000
6	0.000	0.003	0.055	0.165	0.198	0.122	0.039	0.006	0.000	0.000	0.000
7	0.000	0.000	0.020	0.101	0.189	0.175	0.084	0.019	0.001	0.000	0.000
8	0.000	0.000	0.006	0.049	0.142	0.196	0.142	0.049	0.006	0.000	0.000
9	0.000	0.000	0.001	0.019	0.084	0.175	0.189	0.101	0.020	0.000	0.000
10	0.000	0.000	0.000	0.006	0.039	0.122	0.198	0.165	0.055	0.003	0.000
11	0.000	0.000	0.000	0.001	0.014	0.067	0.162	0.210	0.120	0.014	0.001
12	0.000	0.000	0.000	0.000	0.004	0.028	0.101	0.204	0.200	0.051	0.006
13	0.000	0.000	0.000	0.000	0.001	0.009	0.047	0.146	0.246	0.142	0.036
14	0.000	0.000	0.000	0.000	0.000	0.002	0.015	0.073	0.211	0.275	0.146
15	0.000	0.000	0.000	0.000	0.000	0.000	0.003	0.023	0.113	0.329	0.371
16	0.000	0.000	0.000	0.000	0.000	0.000	0.000	0.003	0.028	0.185	0.440

TABLE E.2 (continued)

n = 17
PROBABILITY

x	0.05	0.10	0.20	0.30	0.40	0.50	0.60	0.70	0.80	0.90	0.95
0	0.418	0.167	0.023	0.002	0.000	0.000	0.000	0.000	0.000	0.000	0.000
1	0.374	0.315	0.096	0.017	0.002	0.000	0.000	0.000	0.000	0.000	0.000
2	0.158	0.280	0.191	0.058	0.010	0.001	0.000	0.000	0.000	0.000	0.000
3	0.041	0.156	0.239	0.125	0.034	0.005	0.000	0.000	0.000	0.000	0.000
4	0.008	0.060	0.209	0.187	0.080	0.018	0.002	0.000	0.000	0.000	0.000
5	0.001	0.017	0.136	0.208	0.138	0.047	0.008	0.001	0.000	0.000	0.000
6	0.000	0.004	0.068	0.178	0.184	0.094	0.024	0.003	0.000	0.000	0.000
7	0.000	0.001	0.027	0.120	0.193	0.148	0.057	0.009	0.000	0.000	0.000
8	0.000	0.000	0.008	0.064	0.161	0.185	0.107	0.028	0.002	0.000	0.000
9	0.000	0.000	0.002	0.028	0.107	0.185	0.161	0.064	0.008	0.000	0.000
10	0.000	0.000	0.000	0.009	0.057	0.148	0.193	0.120	0.027	0.001	0.000
11	0.000	0.000	0.000	0.003	0.024	0.094	0.184	0.178	0.068	0.004	0.000
12	0.000	0.000	0.000	0.001	0.008	0.047	0.138	0.208	0.136	0.017	0.001
13	0.000	0.000	0.000	0.000	0.002	0.018	0.080	0.187	0.209	0.060	0.008
14	0.000	0.000	0.000	0.000	0.000	0.005	0.034	0.125	0.239	0.156	0.041
15	0.000	0.000	0.000	0.000	0.000	0.001	0.010	0.058	0.191	0.280	0.158
16	0.000	0.000	0.000	0.000	0.000	0.000	0.002	0.017	0.096	0.315	0.374
17	0.000	0.000	0.000	0.000	0.000	0.000	0.000	0.002	0.023	0.167	0.418

n = 18
PROBABILITY

x	0.05	0.10	0.20	0.30	0.40	0.50	0.60	0.70	0.80	0.90	0.95
0	0.397	0.150	0.018	0.002	0.000	0.000	0.000	0.000	0.000	0.000	0.000
1	0.376	0.300	0.081	0.013	0.001	0.000	0.000	0.000	0.000	0.000	0.000
2	0.168	0.284	0.172	0.046	0.007	0.001	0.000	0.000	0.000	0.000	0.000
3	0.047	0.168	0.230	0.105	0.025	0.003	0.000	0.000	0.000	0.000	0.000
4	0.009	0.070	0.215	0.168	0.061	0.012	0.001	0.000	0.000	0.000	0.000
5	0.001	0.022	0.151	0.202	0.115	0.033	0.004	0.000	0.000	0.000	0.000
6	0.000	0.005	0.082	0.187	0.166	0.071	0.015	0.001	0.000	0.000	0.000
7	0.000	0.001	0.035	0.138	0.189	0.121	0.037	0.005	0.000	0.000	0.000
8	0.000	0.000	0.012	0.081	0.173	0.167	0.077	0.015	0.001	0.000	0.000
9	0.000	0.000	0.003	0.039	0.128	0.185	0.128	0.039	0.003	0.000	0.000
10	0.000	0.000	0.001	0.015	0.077	0.167	0.173	0.081	0.012	0.000	0.000
11	0.000	0.000	0.000	0.005	0.037	0.121	0.189	0.138	0.035	0.001	0.000
12	0.000	0.000	0.000	0.001	0.015	0.071	0.166	0.187	0.082	0.005	0.000
13	0.000	0.000	0.000	0.000	0.004	0.033	0.115	0.202	0.151	0.022	0.001
14	0.000	0.000	0.000	0.000	0.001	0.012	0.061	0.168	0.215	0.070	0.009
15	0.000	0.000	0.000	0.000	0.000	0.003	0.025	0.105	0.230	0.168	0.047
16	0.000	0.000	0.000	0.000	0.000	0.001	0.007	0.046	0.172	0.284	0.168
17	0.000	0.000	0.000	0.000	0.000	0.000	0.001	0.013	0.081	0.300	0.376
18	0.000	0.000	0.000	0.000	0.000	0.000	0.000	0.002	0.018	0.150	0.397

TABLE E.2   (concluded)

n = 19
PROBABILITY

x	0.05	0.10	0.20	0.30	0.40	0.50	0.60	0.70	0.80	0.90	0.95
0	0.377	0.135	0.014	0.001	0.000	0.000	0.000	0.000	0.000	0.000	0.000
1	0.377	0.285	0.068	0.009	0.001	0.000	0.000	0.000	0.000	0.000	0.000
2	0.179	0.285	0.154	0.036	0.005	0.000	0.000	0.000	0.000	0.000	0.000
3	0.053	0.180	0.218	0.087	0.017	0.002	0.000	0.000	0.000	0.000	0.000
4	0.011	0.080	0.218	0.149	0.047	0.007	0.001	0.000	0.000	0.000	0.000
5	0.002	0.027	0.164	0.192	0.093	0.022	0.002	0.000	0.000	0.000	0.000
6	0.000	0.007	0.095	0.192	0.145	0.052	0.008	0.001	0.000	0.000	0.000
7	0.000	0.001	0.044	0.153	0.180	0.096	0.024	0.002	0.000	0.000	0.000
8	0.000	0.000	0.017	0.098	0.180	0.144	0.053	0.008	0.000	0.000	0.000
9	0.000	0.000	0.005	0.051	0.146	0.176	0.098	0.022	0.001	0.000	0.000
10	0.000	0.000	0.001	0.022	0.098	0.176	0.146	0.051	0.005	0.000	0.000
11	0.000	0.000	0.000	0.008	0.053	0.144	0.180	0.098	0.017	0.000	0.000
12	0.000	0.000	0.000	0.002	0.024	0.096	0.180	0.153	0.044	0.001	0.000
13	0.000	0.000	0.000	0.001	0.008	0.052	0.145	0.192	0.095	0.007	0.000
14	0.000	0.000	0.000	0.000	0.002	0.022	0.093	0.192	0.164	0.027	0.002
15	0.000	0.000	0.000	0.000	0.001	0.007	0.047	0.149	0.218	0.080	0.011
16	0.000	0.000	0.000	0.000	0.000	0.002	0.017	0.087	0.218	0.180	0.053
17	0.000	0.000	0.000	0.000	0.000	0.000	0.005	0.036	0.154	0.285	0.179
18	0.000	0.000	0.000	0.000	0.000	0.000	0.001	0.009	0.068	0.285	0.377
19	0.000	0.000	0.000	0.000	0.000	0.000	0.000	0.001	0.014	0.135	0.377

n = 20
PROBABILITY

x	0.05	0.10	0.20	0.30	0.40	0.50	0.60	0.70	0.80	0.90	0.95
0	0.358	0.122	0.012	0.001	0.000	0.000	0.000	0.000	0.000	0.000	0.000
1	0.377	0.270	0.058	0.007	0.000	0.000	0.000	0.000	0.000	0.000	0.000
2	0.189	0.285	0.137	0.028	0.003	0.000	0.000	0.000	0.000	0.000	0.000
3	0.060	0.190	0.205	0.072	0.012	0.001	0.000	0.000	0.000	0.000	0.000
4	0.013	0.090	0.218	0.130	0.035	0.005	0.000	0.000	0.000	0.000	0.000
5	0.002	0.032	0.175	0.179	0.075	0.015	0.001	0.000	0.000	0.000	0.000
6	0.000	0.009	0.109	0.192	0.124	0.037	0.005	0.000	0.000	0.000	0.000
7	0.000	0.002	0.055	0.164	0.166	0.074	0.015	0.001	0.000	0.000	0.000
8	0.000	0.000	0.022	0.114	0.180	0.120	0.035	0.004	0.000	0.000	0.000
9	0.000	0.000	0.007	0.065	0.160	0.160	0.071	0.012	0.000	0.000	0.000
10	0.000	0.000	0.002	0.031	0.117	0.176	0.117	0.031	0.002	0.000	0.000
11	0.000	0.000	0.000	0.012	0.071	0.160	0.160	0.065	0.007	0.000	0.000
12	0.000	0.000	0.000	0.004	0.035	0.120	0.180	0.114	0.022	0.000	0.000
13	0.000	0.000	0.000	0.001	0.015	0.074	0.166	0.164	0.055	0.002	0.000
14	0.000	0.000	0.000	0.000	0.005	0.037	0.124	0.192	0.109	0.009	0.000
15	0.000	0.000	0.000	0.000	0.001	0.015	0.075	0.179	0.175	0.032	0.002
16	0.000	0.000	0.000	0.000	0.000	0.005	0.035	0.130	0.218	0.090	0.013
17	0.000	0.000	0.000	0.000	0.000	0.001	0.012	0.072	0.205	0.190	0.060
18	0.000	0.000	0.000	0.000	0.000	0.000	0.003	0.028	0.137	0.285	0.189
19	0.000	0.000	0.000	0.000	0.000	0.000	0.000	0.007	0.058	0.270	0.377
20	0.000	0.000	0.000	0.000	0.000	0.000	0.000	0.001	0.012	0.122	0.358

Source: Goldstein Software, Inc. for the program Goldspread Statistical, which was used to generate this table.

TABLE E.3   Cumulative Binomial Probability Distribution

$n = 1$
PROBABILITY

x	0.1	0.2	0.3	0.4	0.5	0.6	0.7	0.8	0.9
0	0.900	0.800	0.700	0.600	0.500	0.400	0.300	0.200	0.100
1	1.000	1.000	1.000	1.000	1.000	1.000	1.000	1.000	1.000

$n = 2$
PROBABILITY

x	0.1	0.2	0.3	0.4	0.5	0.6	0.7	0.8	0.9
0	0.810	0.640	0.490	0.360	0.250	0.160	0.090	0.040	0.010
1	0.990	0.960	0.910	0.840	0.750	0.640	0.510	0.360	0.190
2	1.000	1.000	1.000	1.000	1.000	1.000	1.000	1.000	1.000

$n = 3$
PROBABILITY

x	0.1	0.2	0.3	0.4	0.5	0.6	0.7	0.8	0.9
0	0.729	0.512	0.343	0.216	0.125	0.064	0.027	0.008	0.001
1	0.972	0.896	0.784	0.648	0.500	0.352	0.216	0.104	0.028
2	0.999	0.992	0.973	0.936	0.875	0.784	0.657	0.488	0.271
3	1.000	1.000	1.000	1.000	1.000	1.000	1.000	1.000	1.000

$n = 4$
PROBABILITY

x	0.1	0.2	0.3	0.4	0.5	0.6	0.7	0.8	0.9
0	0.656	0.410	0.240	0.130	0.063	0.026	0.008	0.002	0.000
1	0.948	0.819	0.652	0.475	0.313	0.179	0.084	0.027	0.004
2	0.996	0.973	0.916	0.821	0.688	0.525	0.348	0.181	0.052
3	1.000	0.998	0.992	0.974	0.938	0.870	0.760	0.590	0.344
4	1.000	1.000	1.000	1.000	1.000	1.000	1.000	1.000	1.000

$n = 5$
PROBABILITY

x	0.1	0.2	0.3	0.4	0.5	0.6	0.7	0.8	0.9
0	0.590	0.328	0.168	0.078	0.031	0.010	0.002	0.000	0.000
1	0.919	0.737	0.528	0.337	0.188	0.087	0.031	0.007	0.000
2	0.991	0.942	0.837	0.683	0.500	0.317	0.163	0.058	0.009
3	1.000	0.993	0.969	0.913	0.813	0.663	0.472	0.263	0.081
4	1.000	1.000	0.998	0.990	0.969	0.922	0.832	0.672	0.410
5	1.000	1.000	1.000	1.000	1.000	1.000	1.000	1.000	1.000

TABLE E.3 (continued)

n = 6
PROBABILITY

x	0.1	0.2	0.3	0.4	0.5	0.6	0.7	0.8	0.9
0	0.531	0.262	0.118	0.047	0.016	0.004	0.001	0.000	0.000
1	0.886	0.655	0.420	0.233	0.109	0.041	0.011	0.002	0.000
2	0.984	0.901	0.744	0.544	0.344	0.179	0.070	0.017	0.001
3	0.999	0.983	0.930	0.821	0.656	0.456	0.256	0.099	0.016
4	1.000	0.998	0.989	0.959	0.891	0.767	0.580	0.345	0.114
5	1.000	1.000	0.999	0.996	0.984	0.953	0.882	0.738	0.469
6	1.000	1.000	1.000	1.000	1.000	1.000	1.000	1.000	1.000

n = 7
PROBABILITY

x	0.1	0.2	0.3	0.4	0.5	0.6	0.7	0.8	0.9
0	0.478	0.210	0.082	0.028	0.008	0.002	0.000	0.000	0.000
1	0.850	0.577	0.329	0.159	0.063	0.019	0.004	0.000	0.000
2	0.974	0.852	0.647	0.420	0.227	0.096	0.029	0.005	0.000
3	0.997	0.967	0.874	0.710	0.500	0.290	0.126	0.033	0.003
4	1.000	0.995	0.971	0.904	0.773	0.580	0.353	0.148	0.026
5	1.000	1.000	0.996	0.981	0.938	0.841	0.671	0.423	0.150
6	1.000	1.000	1.000	0.998	0.992	0.972	0.918	0.790	0.522
7	1.000	1.000	1.000	1.000	1.000	1.000	1.000	1.000	1.000

n = 8
PROBABILITY

x	0.1	0.2	0.3	0.4	0.5	0.6	0.7	0.8	0.9
0	0.430	0.168	0.058	0.017	0.004	0.001	0.000	0.000	0.000
1	0.813	0.503	0.255	0.106	0.035	0.009	0.001	0.000	0.000
2	0.962	0.797	0.552	0.315	0.145	0.050	0.011	0.001	0.000
3	0.995	0.944	0.806	0.594	0.363	0.174	0.058	0.010	0.000
4	1.000	0.990	0.942	0.826	0.637	0.406	0.194	0.056	0.005
5	1.000	0.999	0.989	0.950	0.855	0.685	0.448	0.203	0.038
6	1.000	1.000	0.999	0.991	0.965	0.894	0.745	0.497	0.187
7	1.000	1.000	1.000	0.999	0.996	0.983	0.942	0.832	0.570
8	1.000	1.000	1.000	1.000	1.000	1.000	1.000	1.000	1.000

n = 9
PROBABILITY

x	0.1	0.2	0.3	0.4	0.5	0.6	0.7	0.8	0.9
0	0.387	0.134	0.040	0.010	0.002	0.000	0.000	0.000	0.000
1	0.775	0.436	0.196	0.071	0.020	0.004	0.000	0.000	0.000
2	0.947	0.738	0.463	0.232	0.090	0.025	0.004	0.000	0.000
3	0.992	0.914	0.730	0.483	0.254	0.099	0.025	0.003	0.000
4	0.999	0.980	0.901	0.733	0.500	0.267	0.099	0.020	0.001
5	1.000	0.997	0.975	0.901	0.746	0.517	0.270	0.086	0.008
6	1.000	1.000	0.996	0.975	0.910	0.768	0.537	0.262	0.053
7	1.000	1.000	1.000	0.996	0.980	0.929	0.804	0.564	0.225
8	1.000	1.000	1.000	1.000	0.998	0.990	0.960	0.866	0.613
9	1.000	1.000	1.000	1.000	1.000	1.000	1.000	1.000	1.000

TABLE E.3   (continued)

n = 10
PROBABILITY

x	0.1	0.2	0.3	0.4	0.5	0.6	0.7	0.8	0.9
0	0.349	0.107	0.028	0.006	0.001	0.000	0.000	0.000	0.000
1	0.736	0.376	0.149	0.046	0.011	0.002	0.000	0.000	0.000
2	0.930	0.678	0.383	0.167	0.055	0.012	0.002	0.000	0.000
3	0.987	0.879	0.650	0.382	0.172	0.055	0.011	0.001	0.000
4	0.998	0.967	0.850	0.633	0.377	0.166	0.047	0.006	0.000
5	1.000	0.994	0.953	0.834	0.623	0.367	0.150	0.033	0.002
6	1.000	0.999	0.989	0.945	0.828	0.618	0.350	0.121	0.013
7	1.000	1.000	0.998	0.988	0.945	0.833	0.617	0.322	0.070
8	1.000	1.000	1.000	0.998	0.989	0.954	0.851	0.624	0.264
9	1.000	1.000	1.000	1.000	0.999	0.994	0.972	0.893	0.651
10	1.000	1.000	1.000	1.000	1.000	1.000	1.000	1.000	1.000

n = 11
PROBABILITY

x	0.1	0.2	0.3	0.4	0.5	0.6	0.7	0.8	0.9
0	0.314	0.086	0.020	0.004	0.000	0.000	0.000	0.000	0.000
1	0.697	0.322	0.113	0.030	0.006	0.001	0.000	0.000	0.000
2	0.910	0.617	0.313	0.119	0.033	0.006	0.001	0.000	0.000
3	0.981	0.839	0.570	0.296	0.113	0.029	0.004	0.000	0.000
4	0.997	0.950	0.790	0.533	0.274	0.099	0.022	0.002	0.000
5	1.000	0.988	0.922	0.753	0.500	0.247	0.078	0.012	0.000
6	1.000	0.998	0.978	0.901	0.726	0.467	0.210	0.050	0.003
7	1.000	1.000	0.996	0.971	0.887	0.704	0.430	0.161	0.019
8	1.000	1.000	0.999	0.994	0.967	0.881	0.687	0.383	0.090
9	1.000	1.000	1.000	0.999	0.994	0.970	0.887	0.678	0.303
10	1.000	1.000	1.000	1.000	1.000	0.996	0.980	0.914	0.686
11	1.000	1.000	1.000	1.000	1.000	1.000	1.000	1.000	1.000

n = 12
PROBABILITY

x	0.1	0.2	0.3	0.4	0.5	0.6	0.7	0.8	0.9
0	0.282	0.069	0.014	0.002	0.000	0.000	0.000	0.000	0.000
1	0.659	0.275	0.085	0.020	0.003	0.000	0.000	0.000	0.000
2	0.889	0.558	0.253	0.083	0.019	0.003	0.000	0.000	0.000
3	0.974	0.795	0.493	0.225	0.073	0.015	0.002	0.000	0.000
4	0.996	0.927	0.724	0.438	0.194	0.057	0.009	0.001	0.000
5	0.999	0.981	0.882	0.665	0.387	0.158	0.039	0.004	0.000
6	1.000	0.996	0.961	0.842	0.613	0.335	0.118	0.019	0.001
7	1.000	0.999	0.991	0.943	0.806	0.562	0.276	0.073	0.004
8	1.000	1.000	0.998	0.985	0.927	0.775	0.507	0.205	0.026
9	1.000	1.000	1.000	0.997	0.981	0.917	0.747	0.442	0.111
10	1.000	1.000	1.000	1.000	0.997	0.980	0.915	0.725	0.341
11	1.000	1.000	1.000	1.000	1.000	0.998	0.986	0.931	0.718
12	1.000	1.000	1.000	1.000	1.000	1.000	1.000	1.000	1.000

TABLE E.3   (continued)

$n = 13$
PROBABILITY

x	0.1	0.2	0.3	0.4	0.5	0.6	0.7	0.8	0.9
0	0.254	0.055	0.010	0.001	0.000	0.000	0.000	0.000	0.000
1	0.621	0.234	0.064	0.013	0.002	0.000	0.000	0.000	0.000
2	0.866	0.502	0.202	0.058	0.011	0.001	0.000	0.000	0.000
3	0.966	0.747	0.421	0.169	0.046	0.008	0.001	0.000	0.000
4	0.994	0.901	0.654	0.353	0.133	0.032	0.004	0.000	0.000
5	0.999	0.970	0.835	0.574	0.291	0.098	0.018	0.001	0.000
6	1.000	0.993	0.938	0.771	0.500	0.229	0.062	0.007	0.000
7	1.000	0.999	0.982	0.902	0.709	0.426	0.165	0.030	0.001
8	1.000	1.000	0.996	0.968	0.867	0.647	0.346	0.099	0.006
9	1.000	1.000	0.999	0.992	0.954	0.831	0.579	0.253	0.034
10	1.000	1.000	1.000	0.999	0.989	0.942	0.798	0.498	0.134
11	1.000	1.000	1.000	1.000	0.998	0.987	0.936	0.766	0.379
12	1.000	1.000	1.000	1.000	1.000	0.999	0.990	0.945	0.746
13	1.000	1.000	1.000	1.000	1.000	1.000	1.000	1.000	1.000

$n = 14$
PROBABILITY

x	0.1	0.2	0.3	0.4	0.5	0.6	0.7	0.8	0.9
0	0.229	0.044	0.007	0.001	0.000	0.000	0.000	0.000	0.000
1	0.585	0.198	0.047	0.008	0.001	0.000	0.000	0.000	0.000
2	0.842	0.448	0.161	0.040	0.006	0.001	0.000	0.000	0.000
3	0.956	0.698	0.355	0.124	0.029	0.004	0.000	0.000	0.000
4	0.991	0.870	0.584	0.279	0.090	0.018	0.002	0.000	0.000
5	0.999	0.956	0.781	0.486	0.212	0.058	0.008	0.000	0.000
6	1.000	0.988	0.907	0.692	0.395	0.150	0.031	0.002	0.000
7	1.000	0.998	0.969	0.850	0.605	0.308	0.093	0.012	0.000
8	1.000	1.000	0.992	0.942	0.788	0.514	0.219	0.044	0.001
9	1.000	1.000	0.998	0.982	0.910	0.721	0.416	0.130	0.009
10	1.000	1.000	1.000	0.996	0.971	0.876	0.645	0.302	0.044
11	1.000	1.000	1.000	0.999	0.994	0.960	0.839	0.552	0.158
12	1.000	1.000	1.000	1.000	0.999	0.992	0.953	0.802	0.415
13	1.000	1.000	1.000	1.000	1.000	0.999	0.993	0.956	0.771
14	1.000	1.000	1.000	1.000	1.000	1.000	1.000	1.000	1.000

TABLE E.3   (continued)

n = 15
PROBABILITY

x	0.1	0.2	0.3	0.4	0.5	0.6	0.7	0.8	0.9
0	0.206	0.035	0.005	0.000	0.000	0.000	0.000	0.000	0.000
1	0.549	0.167	0.035	0.005	0.000	0.000	0.000	0.000	0.000
2	0.816	0.398	0.127	0.027	0.004	0.000	0.000	0.000	0.000
3	0.944	0.648	0.297	0.091	0.018	0.002	0.000	0.000	0.000
4	0.987	0.836	0.515	0.217	0.059	0.009	0.001	0.000	0.000
5	0.998	0.939	0.722	0.403	0.151	0.034	0.004	0.000	0.000
6	1.000	0.982	0.869	0.610	0.304	0.095	0.015	0.001	0.000
7	1.000	0.996	0.950	0.787	0.500	0.213	0.050	0.004	0.000
8	1.000	0.999	0.985	0.905	0.696	0.390	0.131	0.018	0.000
9	1.000	1.000	0.996	0.966	0.849	0.597	0.278	0.061	0.002
10	1.000	1.000	0.999	0.991	0.941	0.783	0.485	0.164	0.013
11	1.000	1.000	1.000	0.998	0.982	0.909	0.703	0.352	0.056
12	1.000	1.000	1.000	1.000	0.996	0.973	0.873	0.602	0.184
13	1.000	1.000	1.000	1.000	1.000	0.995	0.965	0.833	0.451
14	1.000	1.000	1.000	1.000	1.000	1.000	0.995	0.965	0.794
15	1.000	1.000	1.000	1.000	1.000	1.000	1.000	1.000	1.000

n = 16
PROBABILITY

x	0.1	0.2	0.3	0.4	0.5	0.6	0.7	0.8	0.9
0	0.185	0.028	0.003	0.000	0.000	0.000	0.000	0.000	0.000
1	0.515	0.141	0.026	0.003	0.000	0.000	0.000	0.000	0.000
2	0.789	0.352	0.099	0.018	0.002	0.000	0.000	0.000	0.000
3	0.932	0.598	0.246	0.065	0.011	0.001	0.000	0.000	0.000
4	0.983	0.798	0.450	0.167	0.038	0.005	0.000	0.000	0.000
5	0.997	0.918	0.660	0.329	0.105	0.019	0.002	0.000	0.000
6	0.999	0.973	0.825	0.527	0.227	0.058	0.007	0.000	0.000
7	1.000	0.993	0.926	0.716	0.402	0.142	0.026	0.001	0.000
8	1.000	0.999	0.974	0.858	0.598	0.284	0.074	0.007	0.000
9	1.000	1.000	0.993	0.942	0.773	0.473	0.175	0.027	0.001
10	1.000	1.000	0.998	0.981	0.895	0.671	0.340	0.082	0.003
11	1.000	1.000	1.000	0.995	0.962	0.833	0.550	0.202	0.017
12	1.000	1.000	1.000	0.999	0.989	0.935	0.754	0.402	0.068
13	1.000	1.000	1.000	1.000	0.998	0.982	0.901	0.648	0.211
14	1.000	1.000	1.000	1.000	1.000	0.997	0.974	0.859	0.485
15	1.000	1.000	1.000	1.000	1.000	1.000	0.997	0.972	0.815
16	1.000	1.000	1.000	1.000	1.000	1.000	1.000	1.000	1.000

TABLE E.3 (concluded)

$n = 17$
PROBABILITY

x	0.1	0.2	0.3	0.4	0.5	0.6	0.7	0.8	0.9
0	0.167	0.023	0.002	0.000	0.000	0.000	0.000	0.000	0.000
1	0.482	0.118	0.019	0.002	0.000	0.000	0.000	0.000	0.000
2	0.762	0.310	0.077	0.012	0.001	0.000	0.000	0.000	0.000
3	0.917	0.549	0.202	0.046	0.006	0.000	0.000	0.000	0.000
4	0.978	0.758	0.389	0.126	0.025	0.003	0.000	0.000	0.000
5	0.995	0.894	0.597	0.264	0.072	0.011	0.001	0.000	0.000
6	0.999	0.962	0.775	0.448	0.166	0.035	0.003	0.000	0.000
7	1.000	0.989	0.895	0.641	0.315	0.092	0.013	0.000	0.000
8	1.000	0.997	0.960	0.801	0.500	0.199	0.040	0.003	0.000
9	1.000	1.000	0.987	0.908	0.685	0.359	0.105	0.011	0.000
10	1.000	1.000	0.997	0.965	0.834	0.552	0.225	0.038	0.001
11	1.000	1.000	0.999	0.989	0.928	0.736	0.403	0.106	0.005
12	1.000	1.000	1.000	0.997	0.975	0.874	0.611	0.242	0.022
13	1.000	1.000	1.000	1.000	0.994	0.954	0.798	0.451	0.083
14	1.000	1.000	1.000	1.000	0.999	0.988	0.923	0.690	0.238
15	1.000	1.000	1.000	1.000	1.000	0.998	0.981	0.882	0.518
16	1.000	1.000	1.000	1.000	1.000	1.000	0.998	0.977	0.833
17	1.000	1.000	1.000	1.000	1.000	1.000	1.000	1.000	1.000

$n = 18$
PROBABILITY

x	0.1	0.2	0.3	0.4	0.5	0.6	0.7	0.8	0.9
0	0.150	0.018	0.002	0.000	0.000	0.000	0.000	0.000	0.000
1	0.450	0.099	0.014	0.001	0.000	0.000	0.000	0.000	0.000
2	0.734	0.271	0.060	0.008	0.001	0.000	0.000	0.000	0.000
3	0.902	0.501	0.165	0.033	0.004	0.000	0.000	0.000	0.000
4	0.972	0.716	0.333	0.094	0.015	0.001	0.000	0.000	0.000
5	0.994	0.867	0.534	0.209	0.048	0.006	0.000	0.000	0.000
6	0.999	0.949	0.722	0.374	0.119	0.020	0.001	0.000	0.000
7	1.000	0.984	0.859	0.563	0.240	0.058	0.006	0.000	0.000
8	1.000	0.996	0.940	0.737	0.407	0.135	0.021	0.001	0.000
9	1.000	0.999	0.979	0.865	0.593	0.263	0.060	0.004	0.000
10	1.000	1.000	0.994	0.942	0.760	0.437	0.141	0.016	0.000
11	1.000	1.000	0.999	0.980	0.881	0.626	0.278	0.051	0.001
12	1.000	1.000	1.000	0.994	0.952	0.791	0.466	0.133	0.006
13	1.000	1.000	1.000	0.999	0.985	0.906	0.667	0.284	0.028
14	1.000	1.000	1.000	1.000	0.996	0.967	0.835	0.499	0.098
15	1.000	1.000	1.000	1.000	0.999	0.992	0.940	0.729	0.266
16	1.000	1.000	1.000	1.000	1.000	0.999	0.986	0.901	0.550
17	1.000	1.000	1.000	1.000	1.000	1.000	0.998	0.982	0.850
18	1.000	1.000	1.000	1.000	1.000	1.000	1.000	1.000	1.000

Source: Goldstein Software, Inc. for the program Goldspread Statistical, which was used to generate this table.

TABLE E.4   Poisson Probabilities

x	0.1	0.2	0.3	0.4	0.5	μ 0.6	0.7	0.8	0.9	1.0
0	.9048	.8187	.7408	.6703	.6065	.5488	.4966	.4493	.4066	.3679
1	.0905	.1637	.2222	.2681	.3033	.3293	.3476	.3595	.3659	.3679
2	.0045	.0164	.0333	.0536	.0758	.0988	.1217	.1438	.1647	.1839
3	.0002	.0011	.0033	.0072	.0126	.0198	.0284	.3083	.0494	.0613
4	.0000	.0001	.0002	.0007	.0016	.0030	.0050	.0077	.0111	.0153
5	.0000	.0000	.0000	.0001	.0002	.0004	.0007	.0012	.0020	.0031
6	.0000	.0000	.0000	.0000	.0000	.0000	.0001	.0002	.0003	.0005
7	.0000	.0000	.0000	.0000	.0000	.0000	.0000	.0000	.0000	.0001

x	1.1	1.2	1.3	1.4	1.5	μ 1.6	1.7	1.8	1.9	2.0
0	.3329	.3012	.2725	.2466	.2231	.2019	.1827	.1653	.1496	.1353
1	.3662	.3614	.3543	.3452	.3347	.3230	.3106	.2975	.2842	.2707
2	.2014	.2169	.2303	.2417	.2510	.2584	.2640	.2678	.2700	.2707
3	.0738	.0867	.0998	.1128	.1255	.1378	.1496	.1607	.1710	.1804
4	.0203	.0260	.0324	.0395	.0471	.0551	.0636	.0723	.0812	.0902
5	.0045	.0062	.0084	.0111	.0141	.0176	.0216	.0260	.0309	.0361
6	.0008	.0012	.0018	.0026	.0035	.0047	.0061	.0078	.0098	.0120
7	.0001	.0002	.0003	.0005	.0008	.0011	.0015	.0020	.0027	.0034
8	.0000	.0000	.0001	.0001	.0001	.0002	.0003	.0005	.0006	.0009
9	.0000	.0000	.0000	.0000	.0000	.0000	.0001	.0001	.0001	.0002

x	2.1	2.2	2.3	2.4	2.5	μ 2.6	2.7	2.8	2.9	3.0
0	.1225	.1108	.1003	.0907	.0821	.0743	.0672	.0608	.0550	.0498
1	.2572	.2438	.2306	.2177	.2052	.1931	.1815	.1703	.1596	.1494
2	.2700	.2681	.2652	.2613	.2565	.2510	.2450	.2384	.2314	.2240
3	.1890	.1966	.2033	.2090	.2138	.2176	.2205	.2225	.2237	.2240
4	.0992	.1082	.1169	.1254	.1336	.1414	.1488	.1557	.1622	.1680
5	.0417	.0476	.0538	.0602	.0668	.0735	.0804	.0872	.0940	.1008
6	.0146	.0174	.0206	.0241	.0278	.0319	.0362	.0407	.0455	.0504
7	.0044	.0055	.0068	.0083	.0099	.0118	.0139	.0163	.0188	.0216
8	.0011	.0015	.0019	.0025	.0031	.0038	.0047	.0057	.0068	.0081
9	.0003	.0004	.0005	.0007	.0009	.0011	.0014	.0018	.0022	.0027
10	.0001	.0001	.0001	.0002	.0002	.0003	.0004	.0005	.0006	.0008
11	.0000	.0000	.0000	.0000	.0000	.0001	.0001	.0001	.0002	.0002
12	.0000	.0000	.0000	.0000	.0000	.0000	.0000	.0000	.0000	.0001

x	3.1	3.2	3.3	3.4	3.5	μ 3.6	3.7	3.8	3.9	4.0
0	.0450	.0408	.0369	.0334	.0302	.0273	.0247	.0224	.0202	.0183
1	.1397	.1304	.1217	.1135	.1057	.0984	.0915	.0850	.0789	.0733
2	.2165	.2087	.2008	.1929	.1850	.1771	.1692	.1615	.1539	.1465
3	.2237	.2226	.2209	.2186	.2158	.2125	.2087	.2046	.2001	.1954
4	.1734	.1781	.1823	.1858	.1888	.1912	.1931	.1944	.1951	.1954
5	.1075	.1140	.1203	.1264	.1322	.1377	.1429	.1477	.1522	.1563
6	.0555	.0608	.0662	.0716	.0771	.0826	.0881	.0936	.0989	.1042
7	.0246	.0278	.0312	.0348	.0385	.0425	.0466	.0508	.0551	.0595
8	.0095	.0111	.0129	.0148	.0169	.0191	.0215	.0241	.0269	.0298
9	.0033	.0040	.0047	.0056	.0066	.0076	.0089	.0102	.0116	.0132
10	.0010	.0013	.0016	.0019	.0023	.0028	.0033	.0039	.0045	.0053
11	.0003	.0004	.0005	.0006	.0007	.0009	.0011	.0013	.0016	.0019
12	.0001	.0001	.0001	.0002	.0002	.0003	.0003	.0004	.0005	.0006
13	.0000	.0000	.0000	.0000	.0001	.0001	.0001	.0001	.0002	.0002
14	.0000	.0000	.0000	.0000	.0000	.0000	.0000	.0000	.0000	.0001

TABLE E.4 (continued)

x	μ 4.1	4.2	4.3	4.4	4.5	4.6	4.7	4.8	4.9	5.0
0	.0166	.0150	.0136	.0123	.0111	.0101	.0091	.0082	.0074	.0067
1	.0679	.0630	.0583	.0540	.0500	.0462	.0427	.0395	.0365	.0337
2	.1393	.1323	.1254	.1188	.1125	.1063	.1005	.0948	.0894	.0842
3	.1904	.1852	.1798	.1743	.1687	.1631	.1574	.1517	.1460	.1404
4	.1951	.1944	.1933	.1917	.1898	.1875	.1849	.1820	.1789	.1755
5	.1600	.1633	.1662	.1687	.1708	.1725	.1738	.1747	.1753	.1755
6	.1093	.1143	.1191	.1237	.1281	.1323	.1362	.1398	.1432	.1462
7	.0640	.0686	.0732	.0778	.0824	.0869	.0914	.0959	.1002	.1044
8	.0328	.0360	.0393	.0428	.0463	.0500	.0537	.0575	.0614	.0653
9	.0150	.0168	.0188	.0209	.0232	.0255	.0280	.0307	.0334	.0363
10	.0061	.0071	.0081	.0092	.0104	.0118	.0132	.0147	.0164	.0181
11	.0023	.0027	.0032	.0037	.0043	.0049	.0056	.0064	.0073	.0082
12	.0008	.0009	.0011	.0014	.0016	.0019	.0022	.0026	.0030	.0034
13	.0002	.0003	.0004	.0005	.0006	.0007	.0008	.0009	.0011	.0013
14	.0001	.0001	.0001	.0001	.0002	.0002	.0003	.0003	.0004	.0005
15	.0000	.0000	.0000	.0000	.0001	.0001	.0001	.0001	.0001	.0002

x	μ 5.1	5.2	5.3	5.4	5.5	5.6	5.7	5.8	5.9	6.0
0	.0061	.0055	.0050	.0045	.0041	.0037	.0033	.0030	.0027	.0025
1	.0311	.0287	.0265	.0244	.0225	.0207	.0191	.0176	.0162	.0149
2	.0793	.0746	.0701	.0659	.0618	.0580	.0544	.0509	.0477	.0446
3	.1348	.1293	.1239	.1185	.1133	.1082	.1033	.0985	.0938	.0892
4	.1719	.1681	.1641	.1600	.1558	.1515	.1472	.1428	.1383	.1339
5	.1753	.1748	.1740	.1728	.1714	.1697	.1678	.1656	.1632	.1606
6	.1490	.1515	.1537	.1555	.1571	.1584	.1594	.1601	.1605	.1606
7	.1086	.1125	.1163	.1200	.1234	.1267	.1298	.1326	.1353	.1377
8	.0692	.0731	.0771	.0810	.0849	.0887	.0925	.0962	.0998	.1033
9	.0392	.0423	.0454	.0486	.0519	.0552	.0586	.0620	.0654	.0688
10	.0200	.0220	.0241	.0262	.0285	.0309	.0334	.0359	.0386	.0413
11	.0093	.0104	.0116	.0129	.0143	.0157	.0173	.0190	.0207	.0225
12	.0039	.0045	.0051	.0058	.0065	.0073	.0082	.0092	.0102	.0113
13	.0015	.0018	.0021	.0024	.0028	.0032	.0036	.0041	.0046	.0052
14	.0006	.0007	.0008	.0009	.0011	.0013	.0015	.0017	.0019	.0022
15	.0002	.0002	.0003	.0003	.0004	.0005	.0006	.0007	.0008	.0009
16	.0001	.0001	.0001	.0001	.0001	.0002	.0002	.0002	.0003	.0003
17	.0000	.0000	.0000	.0000	.0000	.0001	.0001	.0001	.0001	.0001

TABLE E.4 (continued)

					μ					
x	6.1	6.2	6.3	6.4	6.5	6.6	6.7	6.8	6.9	7.0
0	.0022	.0020	.0018	.0017	.0015	.0014	.0012	.0011	.0010	.0009
1	.0137	.0126	.0116	.0106	.0098	.0090	.0082	.0076	.0070	.0064
2	.0417	.0390	.0364	.0340	.0318	.0296	.0276	.0258	.0240	.0223
3	.0848	.0806	.0765	.0726	.0688	.0652	.0617	.0584	.0552	.0521
4	.1294	.1249	.1205	.1162	.1118	.1076	.1034	.0992	.0952	.0912
5	.1579	.1549	.1519	.1487	.1454	.1420	.1385	.1349	.1314	.1277
6	.1605	.1601	.1595	.1586	.1575	.1562	.1546	.1529	.1511	.1490
7	.1399	.1418	.1435	.1450	.1462	.1472	.1480	.1486	.1489	.1490
8	.1066	.1099	.1130	.1160	.1188	.1215	.1240	.1263	.1284	.1304
9	.0723	.0757	.0791	.0825	.0858	.0891	.0923	.0954	.0985	.1014
10	.0441	.0469	.0498	.0528	.0558	.0588	.0618	.0649	.0679	.0710
11	.0245	.0265	.0285	.0307	.0330	.0353	.0377	.0401	.0426	.0452
12	.0124	.0137	.0150	.0164	.0179	.0194	.0210	.0227	.0245	.0264
13	.0058	.0065	.0073	.0081	.0089	.0098	.0108	.0119	.0130	.0142
14	.0025	.0029	.0033	.0037	.0041	.0046	.0052	.0058	.0064	.0071
15	.0010	.0012	.0014	.0016	.0018	.0020	.0023	.0026	.0029	.0033
16	.0004	.0005	.0005	.0006	.0007	.0008	.0010	.0011	.0013	.0014
17	.0001	.0002	.0002	.0002	.0003	.0003	.0004	.0004	.0005	.0006
18	.0000	.0001	.0001	.0001	.0001	.0001	.0001	.0002	.0002	.0002
19	.0000	.0000	.0000	.0000	.0000	.0000	.0000	.0001	.0001	.0001

					μ					
x	7.1	7.2	7.3	7.4	7.5	7.6	7.7	7.8	7.9	8.0
0	.0008	.0007	.0007	.0006	.0006	.0005	.0005	.0004	.0004	.0003
1	.0059	.0054	.0049	.0045	.0041	.0038	.0035	.0032	.0029	.0027
2	.0208	.0194	.0180	.0167	.0156	.0145	.0134	.0125	.0116	.0107
3	.0492	.0464	.0438	.0413	.0389	.0366	.0345	.0324	.0305	.0286
4	.0874	.0836	.0799	.0764	.0729	.0696	.0663	.0632	.0602	.0573
5	.1241	.1204	.1167	.1130	.1094	.1057	.1021	.0986	.0951	.0916
6	.1468	.1445	.1420	.1394	.1367	.1339	.1311	.1282	.1252	.1221
7	.1489	.1486	.1481	.1474	.1465	.1454	.1442	.1428	.1413	.1396
8	.1321	.1337	.1351	.1363	.1373	.1382	.1388	.1392	.1395	.1396
9	.1042	.1070	.1096	.1121	.1144	.1167	.1187	.1207	.1224	.1241
10	.0740	.0770	.0800	.0829	.0858	.0887	.0914	.0941	.0967	.0993
11	.0478	.0504	.0531	.0558	.0585	.0613	.0640	.0667	.0695	.0722
12	.0283	.0303	.0323	.0344	.0366	.0388	.0411	.0434	.0457	.0481
13	.0154	.0168	.0181	.0196	.0211	.0227	.0243	.0260	.0278	.0296
14	.0078	.0086	.0095	.0104	.0113	.0123	.0134	.0145	.0157	.0169
15	.0037	.0041	.0046	.0051	.0057	.0062	.0069	.0075	.0083	.0090
16	.0016	.0019	.0021	.0024	.0026	.0030	.0033	.0037	.0041	.0045
17	.0007	.0008	.0009	.0010	.0012	.0013	.0015	.0017	.0019	.0021
18	.0003	.0003	.0004	.0004	.0005	.0006	.0006	.0007	.0008	.0009
19	.0001	.0001	.0001	.0002	.0002	.0002	.0003	.0003	.0003	.0004
20	.0000	.0000	.0001	.0001	.0001	.0001	.0001	.0001	.0001	.0002
21	.0000	.0000	.0000	.0000	.0000	.0000	.0000	.0000	.0001	.0001

TABLE E.4 (concluded)

x	8.1	8.2	8.3	8.4	8.5	8.6	8.7	8.8	8.9	9.0
					μ					
0	.0003	.0003	.0002	.0002	.0002	.0002	.0002	.0002	.0001	.0001
1	.0025	.0023	.0021	.0019	.0017	.0016	.0014	.0013	.0012	.0011
2	.0100	.0092	.0086	.0079	.0074	.0068	.0063	.0058	.0054	.0050
3	.0269	.0252	.0237	.0222	.0208	.0195	.0183	.0171	.0160	.0150
4	.0544	.0517	.0491	.0466	.0443	.0420	.0398	.0377	.0357	.0337
5	.0882	.0849	.0816	.0784	.0752	.0722	.0692	.0663	.0635	.0607
6	.1191	.1160	.1128	.1097	.1066	.1034	.1003	.0972	.0941	.0911
7	.1378	.1358	.1338	.1317	.1294	.1271	.1247	.1222	.1197	.1171
8	.1395	.1392	.1388	.1382	.1375	.1366	.1356	.1344	.1332	.1318
9	.1256	.1269	.1280	.1290	.1299	.1306	.1311	.1315	.1317	.1318
10	.1017	.1040	.1063	.1084	.1104	.1123	.1140	.1157	.1172	.1186
11	.0749	.0776	.0802	.0828	.0853	.0878	.0902	.0925	.0948	.0970
12	.0505	.0530	.0555	.0579	.0604	.0629	.0654	.0679	.0703	.0728
13	.0315	.0334	.0354	.0374	.0395	.0416	.0438	.0459	.0481	.0504
14	.0182	.0196	.0210	.0225	.0240	.0256	.0272	.0289	.0306	.0324
15	.0098	.0107	.0116	.0126	.0136	.0147	.0158	.0169	.0182	.0194
16	.0050	.0055	.0060	.0066	.0072	.0079	.0086	.0093	.0101	.0109
17	.0024	.0026	.0029	.0033	.0036	.0040	.0044	.0048	.0053	.0058
18	.0011	.0012	.0014	.0015	.0017	.0019	.0021	.0024	.0026	.0029
19	.0005	.0005	.0006	.0007	.0008	.0009	.0010	.0011	.0012	.0014
20	.0002	.0002	.0002	.0003	.0003	.0004	.0004	.0005	.0005	.0006
21	.0001	.0001	.0001	.0001	.0001	.0002	.0002	.0002	.0002	.0003
22	.0000	.0000	.0000	.0000	.0001	.0001	.0001	.0001	.0001	.0001

x	9.1	9.2	9.3	9.4	9.5	9.6	9.7	9.8	9.9	10
					μ					
0	.0001	.0001	.0001	.0001	.0001	.0001	.0001	.0001	.0001	.0000
1	.0010	.0009	.0009	.0008	.0007	.0007	.0006	.0005	.0005	.0005
2	.0046	.0043	.0040	.0037	.0034	.0031	.0029	.0027	.0025	.0023
3	.0140	.0131	.0123	.0115	.0107	.0100	.0093	.0087	.0081	.0076
4	.0319	.0302	.0285	.0269	.0254	.0240	.0226	.0213	.0201	.0189
5	.0581	.0555	.0530	.0506	.0483	.0460	.0439	.0418	.0398	.0378
6	.0881	.0851	.0822	.0793	.0764	.0736	.0709	.0682	.0656	.0631
7	.1145	.1118	.1091	.1064	.1037	.1010	.0982	.0955	.0928	.0901
8	.1302	.1286	.1269	.1251	.1232	.1212	.1191	.1170	.1148	.1126
9	.1317	.1315	.1311	.1306	.1300	.1293	.1284	.1274	.1263	.1251
10	.1198	.1210	.1219	.1228	.1235	.1241	.1245	.1249	.1250	.1251
11	.0991	.1012	.1031	.1049	.1067	.1083	.1098	.1112	.1125	.1137
12	.0752	.0776	.0799	.0822	.0844	.0866	.0888	.0908	.0928	.0948
13	.0526	.0549	.0572	.0594	.0617	.0640	.0662	.0685	.0707	.0729
14	.0342	.0361	.0380	.0399	.0419	.0439	.0459	.0479	.0500	.0521
15	.0208	.0221	.0235	.0250	.0265	.0281	.0297	.0313	.0330	.0347
16	.0118	.0127	.0137	.0147	.0157	.0168	.0180	.0192	.0204	.0217
17	.0063	.0069	.0075	.0081	.0088	.0095	.0103	.0111	.0119	.0128
18	.0032	.0035	.0039	.0042	.0046	.0051	.0055	.0060	.0065	.0071
19	.0015	.0017	.0019	.0021	.0023	.0026	.0028	.0031	.0034	.0037
20	.0007	.0008	.0009	.0010	.0011	.0012	.0014	.0015	.0017	.0019
21	.0003	.0003	.0004	.0004	.0005	.0006	.0006	.0007	.0008	.0009
22	.0001	.0001	.0002	.0002	.0002	.0002	.0003	.0003	.0004	.0004
23	.0000	.0001	.0001	.0001	.0001	.0001	.0001	.0001	.0002	.0002
24	.0000	.0000	.0000	.0000	.0000	.0000	.0000	.0001	.0001	.0001

Source: Adapted from Howard Gitlow, Shelly Gitlow, Alan Oppenheim, and Rosa Oppenheim, *Tools and Methods for the Improvement of Quality* (Homewood, Ill.: Richard D. Irwin, 1989), pp. 584–87.

TABLE E.5   Cumulative Poisson Table

x	μ .10	.20	.30	.40	.50	.60	.70	.80	.90
0	.9048	.8187	.7408	.6703	.6065	.5488	.4966	.4493	.4066
1	.9953	.9825	.9631	.9384	.9098	.8781	.8442	.8088	.7725
2	.9998	.9989	.9964	.9921	.9856	.9769	.9659	.9526	.9371
3	1.0000	.9999	.9997	.9992	.9982	.9966	.9942	.9909	.9865
4		1.0000	1.0000	.9999	.9998	.9996	.9992	.9986	.9977
5					1.0000	1.0000	.9999	.9998	.9997
6					1.0000	1.0000	1.0000	1.0000	1.0000

x	μ 1.0	1.1	1.2	1.3	1.4	1.5	1.6	1.7	1.8	1.9
0	.3679	.3329	.3012	.2725	.2466	.2231	.2019	.1827	.1653	.1496
1	.7358	.6990	.6626	.6268	.5918	.5578	.5249	.4932	.4628	.4337
2	.9197	.9004	.8795	.8571	.8335	.8088	.7834	.7572	.7306	.7037
3	.9810	.9743	.9662	.9569	.9463	.9344	.9212	.9068	.8913	.8747
4	.9963	.9946	.9923	.9893	.9857	.9814	.9763	.9704	.9636	.9559
5	.9994	.9990	.9985	.9978	.9968	.9955	.9940	.9920	.9896	.9868
6	.9999	.9999	.9997	.9996	.9994	.9991	.9987	.9981	.9974	.9966
7	1.0000	1.0000	1.0000	.9999	.9999	.9998	.9997	.9996	.9994	.9992
8	1.0000	1.0000	1.0000	1.0000	1.0000	1.0000	1.0000	.9999	.9999	.9998
9	1.0000	1.0000	1.0000	1.0000	1.0000	1.0000	1.0000	1.0000	1.0000	1.0000

x	μ 2.0	2.1	2.2	2.3	2.4	2.5	2.6	2.7	2.8	2.9
0	.1353	.1225	.1108	.1003	.0907	.0821	.0743	.0672	.0608	.0550
1	.4060	.3796	.3546	.3309	.3084	.2873*	.2674	.2487	.2311	.2146
2	.6767	.6496	.6227	.5960	.5697	.5438	.5184	.4936	.4695	.4460
3	.8571	.8386	.8194	.7993	.7787	.7576	.7360	.7141	.6919	.6696
4	.9473	.9379	.9275	.9162	.9041	.8912	.8774	.8629	.8477	.8318
5	.9834	.9796	.9751	.9700	.9643	.9580	.9510	.9433	.9349	.9258
6	.9955	.9941	.9925	.9906	.9884	.9858	.9828	.9794	.9756	.9713
7	.9989	.9985	.9980	.9974	.9967	.9958	.9947	.9934	.9919	.9901
8	.9998	.9997	.9995	.9994	.9991	.9989	.9985	.9981	.9976	.9969
9	1.0000	.9999	.9999	.9999	.9998	.9997	.9996	.9995	.9993	.9991
10	1.0000	1.0000	1.0000	1.0000	1.0000	.9999	.9999	.9999	.9998	.9998
11	1.0000	1.0000	1.0000	1.0000	1.0000	1.0000	1.0000	1.0000	1.0000	.9999
12	1.0000	1.0000	1.0000	1.0000	1.0000	1.0000	1.0000	1.0000	1.0000	1.0000

Table E.5 (continued)

x	3.0	3.1	3.2	3.3	3.4	3.5	3.6	3.7	3.8	3.9
0	.0498	.0450	.0408	.0369	.0334	.0302	.0273	.0247	.0224	.0202
1	.1991	.1847	.1712	.1586	.1468	.1359	.1257	.1162	.1074	.0992
2	.4232	.4012	.3799	.3594	.3397	.3208	.3027	.2854	.2689	.2531
3	.6472	.6248	.6025	.5803	.5584	.5366	.5152	.4942	.4735	.4532
4	.8153	.7982	.7806	.7626	.7442	.7254	.7064	.6872	.6678	.6484
5	.9161	.9057	.8946	.8829	.8705	.8576	.8441	.8301	.8156	.8006
6	.9665	.9612	.9554	.9490	.9421	.9347	.9267	.9182	.9091	.8995
7	.9881	.9858	.9832	.9802	.9769	.9733	.9692	.9648	.9599	.9546
8	.9962	.9953	.9943	.9931	.9917	.9901	.9883	.9863	.9840	.9815
9	.9989	.9986	.9982	.9978	.9973	.9967	.9960	.9952	.9942	.9931
10	.9997	.9996	.9995	.9994	.9992	.9990	.9987	.9984	.9981	.9977
11	.9999	.9999	.9999	.9998	.9998	.9997	.9996	.9995	.9994	.9993
12	1.0000	1.0000	1.0000	1.0000	.9999	.9999	.9999	.9999	.9998	.9998
13	1.0000	1.0000	1.0000	1.0000	1.0000	1.0000	1.0000	1.0000	1.0000	.9999
14	1.0000	1.0000	1.0000	1.0000	1.0000	1.0000	1.0000	1.0000	1.0000	1.0000

μ

x	4.0	4.2	4.4	4.6	4.8	5.0	5.2	5.4	5.6	5.8
0	.0183	.0150	.0123	.0101	.0082	.0067	.0055	.0045	.0037	.0030
1	.0916	.0780	.0663	.0563	.0477	.0404	.0342	.0289	.0244	.0206
2	.2381	.2102	.1851	.1626	.1425	.1247	.1088	.0948	.0824	.0715
3	.4335	.3954	.3594	.3257	.2942	.2650	.2381	.2133	.1906	.1700
4	.6288	.5898	.5512	.5132	.4763	.4405	.4061	.3733	.3421	.3127
5	.7851	.7531	.7199	.6858	.6510	.6160	.5809	.5461	.5119	.4783
6	.8893	.8675	.8436	.8180	.7908	.7622	.7324	.7017	.6703	.6384
7	.9489	.9361	.9214	.9049	.8867	.8666	.8449	.8217	.7970	.7710
8	.9786	.9721	.9642	.9549	.9442	.9319	.9181	.9026	.8857	.8672
9	.9919	.9889	.9851	.9805	.9749	.9682	.9603	.9512	.9409	.9292
10	.9972	.9959	.9943	.9922	.9896	.9863	.9823	.9775	.9718	.9651
11	.9991	.9986	.9980	.9971	.9960	.9945	.9927	.9904	.9875	.9840
12	.9997	.9996	.9993	.9990	.9986	.9980	.9972	.9962	.9949	.9932
13	.9999	.9999	.9998	.9997	.9995	.9993	.9990	.9986	.9980	.9973
14	1.0000	1.0000	.9999	.9999	.9999	.9998	.9997	.9995	.9993	.9990
15	1.0000	1.0000	1.0000	1.0000	1.0000	.9999	.9999	.9998	.9998	.9996
16	1.0000	1.0000	1.0000	1.0000	1.0000	1.0000	1.0000	.9999	.9999	.9999
17	1.0000	1.0000	1.0000	1.0000	1.0000	1.0000	1.0000	1.0000	1.0000	1.0000

TABLE E.5 (continued)

					μ					
x	6.0	6.2	6.4	6.6	6.8	7.0	7.2	7.4	7.6	7.8
0	.0025	.0020	.0017	.0014	.0011	.0009	.0007	.0006	.0005	.0004
1	.0174	.0146	.0123	.0103	.0087	.0073	.0061	.0051	.0043	.0036
2	.0620	.0536	.0463	.0400	.0344	.0296	.0255	.0219	.0188	.0161
3	.1512	.1342	.1189	.1052	.0928	.0818	.0719	.0632	.0554	.0485
4	.2851	.2592	.2351	.2127	.1920	.1730	.1555	.1395	.1249	.1117
5	.4457	.4141	.3837	.3547	.3270	.3007	.2759	.2526	.2307	.2103
6	.6063	.5742	.5423	.5108	.4799	.4497	.4204	.3920	.3646	.3384
7	.7440	.7160	.6873	.6581	.6285	.5987	.5689	.5393	.5100	.4812
8	.8472	.8259	.8033	.7796	.7548	.7291	.7027	.6757	.6482	.6204
9	.9161	.9016	.8858	.8686	.8502	.8305	.8096	.7877	.7649	.7411
10	.9574	.9486	.9386	.9274	.9151	.9015	.8867	.8707	.8535	.8352
11	.9799	.9750	.9693	.9627	.9552	.9466	.9371	.9265	.9148	.9020
12	.9912	.9887	.9857	.9821	.9779	.9730	.9673	.9609	.9536	.9454
13	.9964	.9952	.9937	.9920	.9898	.9872	.9841	.9805	.9762	.9714
14	.9986	.9981	.9974	.9966	.9956	.9943	.9927	.9908	.9886	.9859
15	.9995	.9993	.9990	.9986	.9982	.9976	.9969	.9959	.9948	.9934
16	.9998	.9997	.9996	.9995	.9993	.9990	.9987	.9983	.9978	.9971
17	.9999	.9999	.9999	.9998	.9997	.9996	.9995	.9993	.9991	.9988
18	1.0000	1.0000	1.0000	.9999	.9999	.9999	.9998	.9997	.9996	.9995
19	1.0000	1.0000	1.0000	1.0000	1.0000	1.0000	.9999	.9999	.9999	.9998
20	1.0000	1.0000	1.0000	1.0000	1.0000	1.0000	1.0000	1.0000	1.0000	.9999
21	1.0000	1.0000	1.0000	1.0000	1.0000	1.0000	1.0000	1.0000	1.0000	1.0000

TABLE E.5   (concluded)

			μ		
x	8.0	8.5	9.0	9.5	10.0
0	.0003	.0002	.0001	.0001	.0000
1	.0030	.0019	.0012	.0008	.0005
2	.0138	.0093	.0062	.0042	.0028
3	.0424	.0301	.0212	.0149	.0103
4	.0996	.0744	.0550	.0403	.0293
5	.1912	.1496	.1157	.0885	.0671
6	.3134	.2562	.2068	.1649	.1301
7	.4530	.3856	.3239	.2687	.2202
8	.5925	.5231	.4557	.3918	.3328
9	.7166	.6530	.5874	.5218	.4579
10	.8159	.7634	.7060	.6453	.5830
11	.8881	.8487	.8030	.7520	.6968
12	.9362	.9091	.8758	.8364	.7916
13	.9658	.9486	.9261	.8981	.8645
14	.9827	.9726	.9585	.9400	.9165
15	.9918	.9862	.9780	.9665	.9513
16	.9963	.9934	.9889	.9823	.9730
17	.9984	.9970	.9947	.9911	.9857
18	.9993	.9987	.9976	.9957	.9928
19	.9997	.9995	.9989	.9980	.9965
20	.9999	.9998	.9996	.9991	.9984
21	1.0000	.9999	.9998	.9996	.9993
22	1.0000	1.0000	.9999	.9999	.9997
23	1.0000	1.0000	1.0000	.9999	.9999
24	1.0000	1.0000	1.0000	1.0000	1.0000
25	1.0000	1.0000	1.0000	1.0000	1.0000
26	1.0000	1.0000	1.0000	1.0000	1.0000
27	1.0000	1.0000	1.0000	1.0000	1.0000

= ≠   if α=.02   2 tailed   z= 2.33
≥ <   α=.05   1 tail   z= 1.645
       α=.10   2 tail   z= 1.645

TABLE E.6   Areas of the Standard Normal Distribution

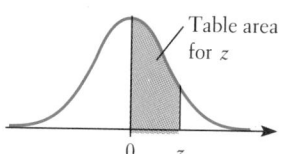

Table area for z

The table areas are probabilities that the standard normal random variable is between 0 and z.

z	Second Decimal Place in z									
	0.00	0.01	0.02	0.03	0.04	0.05	0.06	0.07	0.08	0.09
0.0	0.0000	0.0040	0.0080	0.0120	0.0160	0.0199	0.0239	0.0279	0.0319	0.0359
0.1	0.0398	0.0438	0.0478	0.0517	0.0557	0.0596	0.0636	0.0675	0.0714	0.0753
0.2	0.0793	0.0832	0.0871	0.0910	0.0948	0.0987	0.1026	0.1064	0.1103	0.1141
0.3	0.1179	0.1217	0.1255	0.1293	0.1331	0.1368	0.1406	0.1443	0.1480	0.1517
0.4	0.1554	0.1591	0.1628	0.1664	0.1700	0.1736	0.1772	0.1808	0.1844	0.1879
0.5	0.1915	0.1950	0.1985	0.2019	0.2054	0.2088	0.2123	0.2157	0.2190	0.2224
0.6	0.2257	0.2291	0.2324	0.2357	0.2389	0.2422	0.2454	0.2486	0.2517	0.2549
0.7	0.2580	0.2611	0.2642	0.2673	0.2704	0.2734	0.2764	0.2794	0.2823	0.2852
0.8	0.2881	0.2910	0.2939	0.2967	0.2995	0.3023	0.3051	0.3078	0.3106	0.3133
0.9	0.3159	0.3186	0.3212	0.3238	0.3264	0.3289	0.3315	0.3340	0.3365	0.3389
1.0	0.3413	0.3438	0.3461	0.3485	0.3508	0.3531	0.3554	0.3577	0.3599	0.3621
1.1	0.3643	0.3665	0.3686	0.3708	0.3729	0.3749	0.3770	0.3790	0.3810	0.3830
1.2	0.3849	0.3869	0.3888	0.3907	0.3925	0.3944	0.3962	0.3980	0.3997	0.4015
1.3	0.4032	0.4049	0.4066	0.4082	0.4099	0.4115	0.4131	0.4147	0.4162	0.4177
1.4	0.4192	0.4207	0.4222	0.4236	0.4251	0.4265	0.4279	0.4292	0.4306	0.4319
1.5	0.4332	0.4345	0.4357	0.4370	0.4382	0.4394	0.4406	0.4418	0.4429	0.4441
1.6	0.4452	0.4463	0.4474	0.4484	0.4495	0.4505	0.4515	0.4525	0.4535	0.4545
1.7	0.4554	0.4564	0.4573	0.4582	0.4591	0.4599	0.4608	0.4616	0.4625	0.4633
1.8	0.4641	0.4649	0.4656	0.4664	0.4671	0.4678	0.4686	0.4693	0.4699	0.4706
1.9	0.4713	0.4719	0.4726	0.4732	0.4738	0.4744	0.4750	0.4756	0.4761	0.4767
2.0	0.4772	0.4778	0.4783	0.4788	0.4793	0.4798	0.4803	0.4808	0.4812	0.4817
2.1	0.4821	0.4826	0.4830	0.4834	0.4838	0.4842	0.4846	0.4850	0.4854	0.4857
2.2	0.4861	0.4864	0.4868	0.4871	0.4875	0.4878	0.4881	0.4884	0.4887	0.4890
2.3	0.4893	0.4896	0.4898	0.4901	0.4904	0.4906	0.4909	0.4911	0.4913	0.4916
2.4	0.4918	0.4920	0.4922	0.4925	0.4927	0.4929	0.4931	0.4932	0.4934	0.4936
2.5	0.4938	0.4940	0.4941	0.4943	0.4945	0.4946	0.4948	0.4949	0.4951	0.4952
2.6	0.4953	0.4955	0.4956	0.4957	0.4959	0.4960	0.4961	0.4962	0.4963	0.4964
2.7	0.4965	0.4966	0.4967	0.4968	0.4969	0.4970	0.4971	0.4972	0.4973	0.4974
2.8	0.4974	0.4975	0.4976	0.4977	0.4977	0.4978	0.4979	0.4979	0.4980	0.4981
2.9	0.4981	0.4982	0.4982	0.4983	0.4984	0.4984	0.4985	0.4985	0.4986	0.4986
3.0	0.4987	0.4987	0.4987	0.4988	0.4988	0.4989	0.4989	0.4989	0.4990	0.4990
3.1	0.4990	0.4991	0.4991	0.4991	0.4992	0.4992	0.4992	0.4992	0.4993	0.4993
3.2	0.4993	0.4993	0.4994	0.4994	0.4994	0.4994	0.4994	0.4995	0.4995	0.4995
3.3	0.4995	0.4995	0.4995	0.4996	0.4996	0.4996	0.4996	0.4996	0.4996	0.4997
3.4	0.4997	0.4997	0.4997	0.4997	0.4997	0.4997	0.4997	0.4997	0.4997	0.4998
3.5	0.4998									
4.0	0.49997									
4.5	0.499997									
5.0	0.4999997									
6.0	0.499999999									

Source: Amir D. Aczel, *Complete Business Statistics* (Homewood, Ill.: Richard D. Irwin, 1989), p. 1018.

TABLE E.7   Student *t*-Distribution

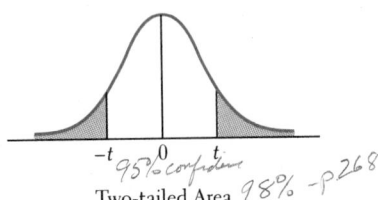

$-t$ 0 t
95% confidence
Two-tailed Area   98% - p 268

df	.20	.10	.05	.02	.01	.001
1	3.078	6.314	12.706	31.821	63.657	636.619
2	1.886	2.920	4.303	6.965	9.925	31.598
3	1.638	2.353	3.182	4.541	5.841	12.941
4	1.533	2.132	2.776	3.747	4.604	8.610
5	1.476	2.015	2.571	3.365	4.032	6.859
6	1.440	1.943	2.447	3.143	3.707	5.959
7	1.415	1.895	2.365	2.998	3.499	5.405
8	1.397	1.860	2.306	2.896	3.355	5.041
9	1.383	1.833	2.262	2.821	3.250	4.781
10	1.372	1.812	2.228	2.764	3.169	4.587
11	1.363	1.796	2.201	2.718	3.106	4.437
12	1.356	1.782	2.179	2.681	3.055	4.318
13	1.350	1.771	2.160	2.650	3.012	4.221
14	1.345	1.761	2.145	2.624	2.977	4.140
15	1.341	1.753	2.131	2.602	2.947	4.073
16	1.337	1.746	2.120	2.583	2.921	4.015
17	1.333	1.740	2.110	2.567	2.898	3.965
18	1.330	1.734	2.101	2.552	2.878	3.922
19	1.328	1.729	2.093	2.539	2.681	3.883
20	1.325	1.725	2.086	2.528	2.845	3.850
21	1.323	1.721	2.080	2.518	2.831	3.819
22	1.321	1.717	2.074	2.508	2.819	3.792
23	1.319	1.714	2.069	2.500	2.807	3.767
24	1.318	1.711	2.064	2.492	2.797	3.745
25	1.316	1.708	2.060	2.485	2.787	3.725
26	1.315	1.706	2.056	2.479	2.779	3.707
27	1.314	1.703	2.052	2.473	2.771	3.690
28	1.313	1.701	2.048	2.467	2.763	3.674
29	1.311	1.699	2.045	2.462	2.756	3.659
30	1.310	1.697	2.042	2.457	2.750	3.646
40	1.303	1.684	2.021	2.423	2.704	3.551
60	1.296	1.671	2.000	2.390	2.660	3.460
120	1.289	1.658	1.980	2.358	2.617	3.373
∞	1.282	1.645	1.960	2.326	2.576	3.291

	.10	.05	.025	.01	.005	.0005

One-tailed Area

Source: Goldstein Software, Inc. for the program Goldspread Statistical, which was used to generate this table.

TABLE E.8 Critical Values of Chi-Square

This table contains the values of χ^2 that correspond to a specific right-tail area and specific numbers of degrees of freedom df.

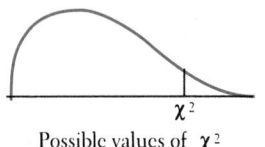

Possible values of χ^2

DEGREES OF FREEDOM df	RIGHT-TAIL AREA			
	0.10	0.05	0.02	0.01
1	2.706	3.841	5.412	6.635
2	4.605	5.991	7.824	9.210
3	6.251	7.815	9.837	11.345
4	7.779	9.488	11.668	13.277
5	9.236	11.070	13.388	15.086
6	10.645	12.592	15.033	16.812
7	12.017	14.067	16.622	18.475
8	13.362	15.507	18.168	20.090
9	14.684	16.919	19.679	21.666
10	15.987	18.307	21.161	23.209
11	17.275	19.675	22.618	24.725
12	18.549	21.026	24.054	26.217
13	19.812	22.362	25.472	27.688
14	21.064	23.685	26.873	29.141
15	22.307	24.996	28.259	30.578
16	23.542	26.296	29.633	32.000
17	24.769	27.587	30.995	33.409
18	25.989	28.869	32.346	34.805
19	27.204	30.144	33.687	36.191
20	28.412	31.410	35.020	37.566
21	29.615	32.671	36.343	38.932
22	30.813	33.924	37.659	40.289
23	32.007	35.172	38.968	41.638
24	33.196	36.415	40.270	42.980
25	34.382	37.652	41.566	44.314
26	35.563	38.885	42.856	45.642
27	36.741	40.113	44.140	46.963
28	37.916	41.337	45.419	48.278
29	39.087	42.557	46.693	49.588
30	40.256	43.773	47.962	50.892

Source: Robert D. Mason and Douglas A. Lind, *Statistical Techniques in Business and Economics*, 7th ed. (Homewood, Ill.: Richard D. Irwin, 1990), p. 860.

TABLE E.9   The F Distribution for $\alpha = 0.05$ and $\alpha = 0.01$ (Bold) for Many Possible Degrees of Freedom

Numerator Degrees of Freedom (k_1)

Denominator Degrees of Freedom (k_2)	α	1	2	3	4	5	6	7	8	9	10	11	12	14	16	20	24	30	40	50	75	100	200	500	∞
1	.05	161	200	216	225	230	234	237	239	241	242	243	244	245	246	248	249	250	251	252	253	253	254	254	254
	.01	**4,052**	**5,000**	**5,403**	**5,625**	**5,764**	**5,859**	**5,928**	**5,981**	**6,022**	**6,056**	**6,083**	**6,106**	**6,143**	**6,170**	**6,209**	**6,235**	**6,261**	**6,287**	**6,303**	**6,324**	**6,334**	**6,350**	**6,360**	**6,366**
2	.05	18.51	19.00	19.16	19.25	19.30	19.33	19.35	19.37	19.38	19.40	19.40	19.41	19.42	19.43	19.45	19.45	19.46	19.47	19.48	19.48	19.49	19.49	19.49	19.50
	.01	**98.50**	**99.00**	**99.17**	**99.25**	**99.30**	**99.33**	**99.36**	**99.37**	**99.39**	**99.40**	**99.41**	**99.42**	**99.43**	**99.44**	**99.45**	**99.46**	**99.47**	**99.47**	**99.48**	**99.49**	**99.49**	**99.49**	**99.50**	**99.50**
3	.05	10.13	9.55	9.28	9.12	9.01	8.94	8.89	8.85	8.81	8.79	8.76	8.74	8.71	8.69	8.66	8.64	8.62	8.59	8.58	8.56	8.55	8.54	8.53	8.53
	.01	**34.12**	**30.82**	**29.46**	**28.71**	**28.24**	**27.91**	**27.67**	**27.49**	**27.35**	**27.23**	**27.13**	**27.05**	**26.92**	**26.83**	**26.69**	**26.60**	**26.50**	**26.41**	**26.35**	**26.28**	**26.24**	**26.18**	**26.15**	**26.13**
4	.05	7.71	6.94	6.59	6.39	6.26	6.16	6.09	6.04	6.00	5.96	5.94	5.91	5.87	5.84	5.80	5.77	5.75	5.72	5.70	5.68	5.66	5.65	5.64	5.63
	.01	**21.20**	**18.00**	**16.69**	**15.98**	**15.52**	**15.21**	**14.98**	**14.80**	**14.66**	**14.55**	**14.45**	**14.37**	**14.25**	**14.15**	**14.02**	**13.93**	**13.84**	**13.75**	**13.69**	**13.61**	**13.58**	**13.52**	**13.49**	**13.46**
5	.05	6.61	5.79	5.41	5.19	5.05	4.95	4.88	4.82	4.77	4.74	4.70	4.68	4.64	4.60	4.56	4.53	4.50	4.46	4.44	4.42	4.41	4.39	4.37	4.37
	.01	**16.26**	**13.27**	**12.06**	**11.39**	**10.97**	**10.67**	**10.46**	**10.29**	**10.16**	**10.05**	**9.96**	**9.89**	**9.77**	**9.68**	**9.55**	**9.47**	**9.38**	**9.29**	**9.24**	**9.17**	**9.13**	**9.08**	**9.04**	**9.02**
6	.05	5.99	5.14	4.76	4.53	4.39	4.28	4.21	4.15	4.10	4.06	4.03	4.00	3.96	3.92	3.87	3.84	3.81	3.77	3.75	3.73	3.71	3.69	3.68	3.67
	.01	**13.75**	**10.92**	**9.78**	**9.15**	**8.75**	**8.47**	**8.26**	**8.10**	**7.98**	**7.87**	**7.79**	**7.72**	**7.60**	**7.52**	**7.40**	**7.31**	**7.23**	**7.14**	**7.09**	**7.02**	**6.99**	**6.93**	**6.90**	**6.88**
7	.05	5.59	4.74	4.35	4.12	3.97	3.87	3.79	3.73	3.68	3.64	3.60	3.57	3.53	3.49	3.44	3.41	3.38	3.34	3.32	3.29	3.27	3.25	3.24	3.23
	.01	**12.25**	**9.55**	**8.45**	**7.85**	**7.46**	**7.19**	**6.99**	**6.84**	**6.72**	**6.62**	**6.54**	**6.47**	**6.36**	**6.28**	**6.16**	**6.07**	**5.99**	**5.91**	**5.86**	**5.79**	**5.75**	**5.70**	**5.67**	**5.65**
8	.05	5.32	4.46	4.07	3.84	3.69	3.58	3.50	3.44	3.39	3.35	3.31	3.28	3.24	3.20	3.15	3.12	3.08	3.04	3.02	2.99	2.97	2.95	2.94	2.93
	.01	**11.26**	**8.65**	**7.59**	**7.01**	**6.63**	**6.37**	**6.18**	**6.03**	**5.91**	**5.81**	**5.73**	**5.67**	**5.56**	**5.48**	**5.36**	**5.28**	**5.20**	**5.12**	**5.07**	**5.00**	**4.96**	**4.91**	**4.88**	**4.86**
9	.05	5.12	4.26	3.86	3.63	3.48	3.37	3.29	3.23	3.18	3.14	3.10	3.07	3.03	2.99	2.94	2.90	2.86	2.83	2.80	2.77	2.76	2.73	2.72	2.71
	.01	**10.56**	**8.02**	**6.99**	**6.42**	**6.06**	**5.80**	**5.61**	**5.47**	**5.35**	**5.26**	**5.18**	**5.11**	**5.01**	**4.92**	**4.81**	**4.73**	**4.65**	**4.57**	**4.52**	**4.45**	**4.41**	**4.36**	**4.33**	**4.31**
10	.05	4.96	4.10	3.71	3.48	3.33	3.22	3.14	3.07	3.02	2.98	2.94	2.91	2.86	2.83	2.77	2.74	2.70	2.66	2.64	2.60	2.59	2.56	2.55	2.54
	.01	**10.04**	**7.56**	**6.55**	**5.99**	**5.64**	**5.39**	**5.20**	**5.06**	**4.94**	**4.85**	**4.77**	**4.71**	**4.60**	**4.52**	**4.41**	**4.33**	**4.25**	**4.17**	**4.12**	**4.05**	**4.01**	**3.96**	**3.93**	**3.91**
11	.05	4.84	3.98	3.59	3.36	3.20	3.09	3.01	2.95	2.90	2.85	2.82	2.79	2.74	2.70	2.65	2.61	2.57	2.53	2.51	2.47	2.46	2.43	2.42	2.40
	.01	**9.65**	**7.21**	**6.22**	**5.67**	**5.32**	**5.07**	**4.89**	**4.74**	**4.63**	**4.54**	**4.46**	**4.40**	**4.29**	**4.21**	**4.10**	**4.02**	**3.94**	**3.86**	**3.81**	**3.74**	**3.71**	**3.66**	**3.62**	**3.60**
12	.05	4.75	3.89	3.49	3.26	3.11	3.00	2.91	2.85	2.80	2.75	2.72	2.69	2.64	2.60	2.54	2.51	2.47	2.43	2.40	2.37	2.35	2.32	2.31	2.30
	.01	**9.33**	**6.93**	**5.95**	**5.41**	**5.06**	**4.82**	**4.64**	**4.50**	**4.39**	**4.30**	**4.22**	**4.16**	**4.05**	**3.97**	**3.86**	**3.78**	**3.70**	**3.62**	**3.57**	**3.50**	**3.47**	**3.41**	**3.38**	**3.36**
13	.05	4.67	3.81	3.41	3.18	3.03	2.92	2.83	2.77	2.71	2.67	2.63	2.60	2.55	2.51	2.46	2.42	2.38	2.34	2.31	2.28	2.26	2.23	2.22	2.21
	.01	**9.07**	**6.70**	**5.74**	**5.21**	**4.86**	**4.62**	**4.44**	**4.30**	**4.19**	**4.10**	**4.02**	**3.96**	**3.86**	**3.78**	**3.66**	**3.59**	**3.51**	**3.43**	**3.38**	**3.31**	**3.27**	**3.22**	**3.19**	**3.17**

Numerator Degrees of Freedom (k_1)

Denom. k_2	1	2	3	4	5	6	7	8	9	10	11	12	14	16	20	24	30	40	50	75	100	200	500	∞
14	4.60	3.74	3.34	3.11	2.96	2.85	2.76	2.70	2.65	2.60	2.57	2.53	2.48	2.44	2.39	2.35	2.31	2.27	2.24	2.21	2.19	2.16	2.14	2.13
	8.86	**6.51**	**5.56**	**5.04**	**4.69**	**4.46**	**4.28**	**4.14**	**4.03**	**3.94**	**3.86**	**3.80**	**3.70**	**3.62**	**3.51**	**3.43**	**3.35**	**3.27**	**3.22**	**3.15**	**3.11**	**3.06**	**3.03**	**3.00**
15	4.54	3.68	3.29	3.06	2.90	2.79	2.71	2.64	2.59	2.54	2.51	2.48	2.42	2.38	2.33	2.29	2.25	2.20	2.18	2.14	2.12	2.10	2.08	2.07
	8.68	**6.36**	**5.42**	**4.89**	**4.56**	**4.32**	**4.14**	**4.00**	**3.89**	**3.80**	**3.73**	**3.67**	**3.56**	**3.49**	**3.37**	**3.29**	**3.21**	**3.13**	**3.08**	**3.01**	**2.98**	**2.92**	**2.89**	**2.87**
16	4.49	3.63	3.24	3.01	2.85	2.74	2.66	2.59	2.54	2.49	2.46	2.42	2.37	2.33	2.28	2.24	2.19	2.15	2.12	2.09	2.07	2.04	2.02	2.01
	8.53	**6.23**	**5.29**	**4.77**	**4.44**	**4.20**	**4.03**	**3.89**	**3.78**	**3.69**	**3.62**	**3.55**	**3.45**	**3.37**	**3.26**	**3.18**	**3.10**	**3.02**	**2.97**	**2.90**	**2.86**	**2.81**	**2.78**	**2.75**
17	4.45	3.59	3.20	2.96	2.81	2.70	2.61	2.55	2.49	2.45	2.41	2.38	2.33	2.29	2.23	2.19	2.15	2.10	2.08	2.04	2.02	1.99	1.97	1.96
	8.40	**6.11**	**5.18**	**4.67**	**4.34**	**4.10**	**3.93**	**3.79**	**3.68**	**3.59**	**3.52**	**3.46**	**3.35**	**3.27**	**3.16**	**3.08**	**3.00**	**2.92**	**2.87**	**2.80**	**2.76**	**2.71**	**2.68**	**2.65**
18	4.41	3.55	3.16	2.93	2.77	2.66	2.58	2.51	2.46	2.41	2.37	2.34	2.29	2.25	2.19	2.15	2.11	2.06	2.04	2.00	1.98	1.95	1.93	1.92
	8.29	**6.01**	**5.09**	**4.58**	**4.25**	**4.01**	**3.84**	**3.71**	**3.60**	**3.51**	**3.43**	**3.37**	**3.27**	**3.19**	**3.08**	**3.00**	**2.92**	**2.84**	**2.78**	**2.71**	**2.68**	**2.62**	**2.59**	**2.57**
19	4.38	3.52	3.13	2.90	2.74	2.63	2.54	2.48	2.42	2.38	2.34	2.31	2.26	2.21	2.16	2.11	2.07	2.03	2.00	1.96	1.94	1.91	1.89	1.88
	8.18	**5.93**	**5.01**	**4.50**	**4.17**	**3.94**	**3.77**	**3.63**	**3.52**	**3.43**	**3.36**	**3.30**	**3.19**	**3.12**	**3.00**	**2.92**	**2.84**	**2.76**	**2.71**	**2.64**	**2.60**	**2.55**	**2.51**	**2.49**
20	4.35	3.49	3.10	2.87	2.71	2.60	2.51	2.45	2.39	2.35	2.31	2.28	2.22	2.18	2.12	2.08	2.04	1.99	1.97	1.93	1.91	1.88	1.86	1.84
	8.10	**5.85**	**4.94**	**4.43**	**4.10**	**3.87**	**3.70**	**3.56**	**3.46**	**3.37**	**3.29**	**3.23**	**3.13**	**3.05**	**2.94**	**2.86**	**2.78**	**2.69**	**2.64**	**2.57**	**2.54**	**2.48**	**2.44**	**2.42**
21	4.32	3.47	3.07	2.84	2.68	2.57	2.49	2.42	2.37	2.32	2.28	2.25	2.20	2.16	2.10	2.05	2.01	1.96	1.94	1.90	1.88	1.84	1.83	1.81
	8.02	**5.78**	**4.87**	**4.37**	**4.04**	**3.81**	**3.64**	**3.51**	**3.40**	**3.31**	**3.24**	**3.17**	**3.07**	**2.99**	**2.88**	**2.80**	**2.72**	**2.64**	**2.58**	**2.51**	**2.48**	**2.42**	**2.38**	**2.36**
22	4.30	3.44	3.05	2.82	2.66	2.55	2.46	2.40	2.34	2.30	2.26	2.23	2.17	2.13	2.07	2.03	1.98	1.94	1.91	1.87	1.85	1.82	1.80	1.78
	7.95	**5.72**	**4.82**	**4.31**	**3.99**	**3.76**	**3.59**	**3.45**	**3.35**	**3.26**	**3.18**	**3.12**	**3.02**	**2.94**	**2.83**	**2.75**	**2.67**	**2.58**	**2.53**	**2.46**	**2.42**	**2.36**	**2.33**	**2.31**
23	4.28	3.42	3.03	2.80	2.64	2.53	2.44	2.37	2.32	2.27	2.24	2.20	2.15	2.11	2.05	2.01	1.96	1.91	1.88	1.84	1.82	1.79	1.77	1.76
	7.88	**5.66**	**4.76**	**4.26**	**3.94**	**3.71**	**3.54**	**3.41**	**3.30**	**3.21**	**3.14**	**3.07**	**2.97**	**2.89**	**2.78**	**2.70**	**2.62**	**2.54**	**2.48**	**2.41**	**2.37**	**2.32**	**2.28**	**2.26**
24	4.26	3.40	3.01	2.78	2.62	2.51	2.42	2.36	2.30	2.25	2.22	2.18	2.13	2.09	2.03	1.98	1.94	1.89	1.86	1.82	1.80	1.77	1.75	1.73
	7.82	**5.61**	**4.72**	**4.22**	**3.90**	**3.67**	**3.50**	**3.36**	**3.26**	**3.17**	**3.09**	**3.03**	**2.93**	**2.85**	**2.74**	**2.66**	**2.58**	**2.49**	**2.44**	**2.37**	**2.33**	**2.27**	**2.24**	**2.21**
25	4.24	3.39	2.99	2.76	2.60	2.49	2.40	2.34	2.28	2.24	2.20	2.16	2.11	2.07	2.01	1.96	1.92	1.87	1.84	1.80	1.78	1.75	1.73	1.71
	7.77	**5.57**	**4.68**	**4.18**	**3.85**	**3.63**	**3.46**	**3.32**	**3.22**	**3.13**	**3.06**	**2.99**	**2.89**	**2.81**	**2.70**	**2.62**	**2.54**	**2.45**	**2.40**	**2.33**	**2.29**	**2.23**	**2.19**	**2.17**
26	4.23	3.37	2.98	2.74	2.59	2.47	2.39	2.32	2.27	2.22	2.18	2.15	2.09	2.05	1.99	1.95	1.90	1.85	1.82	1.78	1.76	1.73	1.71	1.69
	7.72	**5.53**	**4.64**	**4.14**	**3.82**	**3.59**	**3.42**	**3.29**	**3.18**	**3.09**	**3.02**	**2.96**	**2.86**	**2.78**	**2.66**	**2.58**	**2.50**	**2.42**	**2.36**	**2.29**	**2.25**	**2.19**	**2.16**	**2.13**

Numerator Degrees of Freedom (k_1)

Denominator Degrees of Freedom (k_2)	1	2	3	4	5	6	7	8	9	10	11	12	14	16	20	24	30	40	50	75	100	200	500	∞
27	4.21 **7.68**	3.35 **5.49**	2.96 **4.60**	2.73 **4.11**	2.57 **3.78**	2.46 **3.56**	2.37 **3.39**	2.31 **3.26**	2.25 **3.15**	2.20 **3.06**	2.17 **2.99**	2.13 **2.93**	2.08 **2.82**	2.04 **2.75**	1.97 **2.63**	1.93 **2.55**	1.88 **2.47**	1.84 **2.38**	1.81 **2.33**	1.76 **2.26**	1.74 **2.22**	1.71 **2.16**	1.69 **2.12**	1.67 **2.10**
28	4.20 **7.64**	3.34 **5.45**	2.95 **4.57**	2.71 **4.07**	2.56 **3.75**	2.45 **3.53**	2.36 **3.36**	2.29 **3.23**	2.24 **3.12**	2.19 **3.03**	2.15 **2.96**	2.12 **2.90**	2.06 **2.79**	2.02 **2.72**	1.96 **2.60**	1.91 **2.52**	1.87 **2.44**	1.82 **2.35**	1.79 **2.30**	1.75 **2.23**	1.73 **2.19**	1.69 **2.13**	1.67 **2.09**	1.65 **2.06**
29	4.18 **7.60**	3.33 **5.42**	2.93 **4.54**	2.70 **4.04**	2.55 **3.73**	2.43 **3.50**	2.35 **3.33**	2.28 **3.20**	2.22 **3.09**	2.18 **3.00**	2.14 **2.93**	2.10 **2.87**	2.05 **2.77**	2.01 **2.69**	1.94 **2.57**	1.90 **2.49**	1.85 **2.41**	1.81 **2.33**	1.77 **2.27**	1.73 **2.20**	1.71 **2.16**	1.67 **2.10**	1.65 **2.06**	1.64 **2.03**
30	4.17 **7.56**	3.32 **5.39**	2.92 **4.51**	2.69 **4.02**	2.53 **3.70**	2.42 **3.47**	2.33 **3.30**	2.27 **3.17**	2.21 **3.07**	2.16 **2.98**	2.13 **2.91**	2.09 **2.84**	2.04 **2.74**	1.99 **2.66**	1.93 **2.55**	1.89 **2.47**	1.84 **2.39**	1.79 **2.30**	1.76 **2.25**	1.72 **2.17**	1.70 **2.13**	1.66 **2.07**	1.64 **2.03**	1.62 **2.01**
32	4.15 **7.50**	3.29 **5.34**	2.90 **4.46**	2.67 **3.97**	2.51 **3.65**	2.40 **3.43**	2.31 **3.26**	2.24 **3.13**	2.19 **3.02**	2.14 **2.93**	2.10 **2.86**	2.07 **2.80**	2.01 **2.70**	1.97 **2.62**	1.91 **2.50**	1.86 **2.42**	1.82 **2.34**	1.77 **2.25**	1.74 **2.20**	1.69 **2.12**	1.67 **2.08**	1.63 **2.02**	1.61 **1.98**	1.59 **1.96**
34	4.13 **7.44**	3.28 **5.29**	2.88 **4.42**	2.65 **3.93**	2.49 **3.61**	2.38 **3.39**	2.29 **3.22**	2.23 **3.09**	2.17 **2.98**	2.12 **2.89**	2.08 **2.82**	2.05 **2.76**	1.99 **2.66**	1.95 **2.58**	1.89 **2.46**	1.84 **2.38**	1.80 **2.30**	1.75 **2.21**	1.71 **2.16**	1.67 **2.08**	1.65 **2.04**	1.61 **1.98**	1.59 **1.94**	1.57 **1.91**
36	4.11 **7.40**	3.26 **5.25**	2.87 **4.38**	2.63 **3.89**	2.48 **3.57**	2.36 **3.35**	2.28 **3.18**	2.21 **3.05**	2.15 **2.95**	2.11 **2.86**	2.07 **2.79**	2.03 **2.72**	1.98 **2.62**	1.93 **2.54**	1.87 **2.43**	1.82 **2.35**	1.78 **2.26**	1.73 **2.18**	1.69 **2.12**	1.65 **2.04**	1.62 **2.00**	1.59 **1.94**	1.56 **1.90**	1.55 **1.87**
38	4.10 **7.35**	3.24 **5.21**	2.85 **4.34**	2.62 **3.86**	2.46 **3.54**	2.35 **3.32**	2.26 **3.15**	2.19 **3.02**	2.14 **2.92**	2.09 **2.83**	2.05 **2.75**	2.02 **2.69**	1.96 **2.59**	1.92 **2.51**	1.85 **2.40**	1.81 **2.32**	1.76 **2.23**	1.71 **2.14**	1.68 **2.09**	1.63 **2.01**	1.61 **1.97**	1.57 **1.90**	1.54 **1.86**	1.53 **1.84**
40	4.08 **7.31**	3.23 **5.18**	2.84 **4.31**	2.61 **3.83**	2.45 **3.51**	2.34 **3.29**	2.25 **3.12**	2.18 **2.99**	2.12 **2.89**	2.08 **2.80**	2.04 **2.73**	2.00 **2.66**	1.95 **2.56**	1.90 **2.48**	1.84 **2.37**	1.79 **2.29**	1.74 **2.20**	1.69 **2.11**	1.66 **2.06**	1.61 **1.98**	1.59 **1.94**	1.55 **1.87**	1.53 **1.83**	1.51 **1.81**
42	4.07 **7.28**	3.22 **5.15**	2.83 **4.29**	2.59 **3.80**	2.44 **3.49**	2.32 **3.27**	2.24 **3.10**	2.17 **2.97**	2.11 **2.86**	2.06 **2.78**	2.03 **2.70**	1.99 **2.64**	1.94 **2.54**	1.89 **2.46**	1.83 **2.34**	1.78 **2.26**	1.73 **2.18**	1.68 **2.09**	1.65 **2.03**	1.60 **1.95**	1.57 **1.91**	1.53 **1.85**	1.51 **1.80**	1.49 **1.78**
44	4.06 **7.25**	3.21 **5.12**	2.82 **4.26**	2.58 **3.78**	2.43 **3.47**	2.31 **3.24**	2.23 **3.08**	2.16 **2.95**	2.10 **2.84**	2.05 **2.75**	2.01 **2.68**	1.98 **2.62**	1.92 **2.52**	1.88 **2.44**	1.81 **2.32**	1.77 **2.24**	1.72 **2.15**	1.67 **2.07**	1.63 **2.01**	1.59 **1.93**	1.56 **1.89**	1.52 **1.82**	1.49 **1.78**	1.48 **1.75**
46	4.05 **7.22**	3.20 **5.10**	2.81 **4.24**	2.57 **3.76**	2.42 **3.44**	2.30 **3.22**	2.22 **3.06**	2.15 **2.93**	2.09 **2.82**	2.04 **2.73**	2.00 **2.66**	1.97 **2.60**	1.91 **2.50**	1.87 **2.42**	1.80 **2.30**	1.76 **2.22**	1.71 **2.13**	1.65 **2.04**	1.62 **1.99**	1.57 **1.91**	1.55 **1.86**	1.51 **1.80**	1.48 **1.76**	1.46 **1.73**
48	4.04 **7.19**	3.19 **5.08**	2.80 **4.22**	2.57 **3.74**	2.41 **3.43**	2.29 **3.20**	2.21 **3.04**	2.14 **2.91**	2.08 **2.80**	2.03 **2.71**	1.99 **2.64**	1.96 **2.58**	1.90 **2.48**	1.86 **2.40**	1.79 **2.28**	1.75 **2.20**	1.70 **2.12**	1.64 **2.02**	1.61 **1.97**	1.56 **1.89**	1.54 **1.84**	1.49 **1.78**	1.47 **1.73**	1.45 **1.70**

Numerator Degrees of Freedom (k_1)

Denominator Degrees of Freedom (k_2)	1	2	3	4	5	6	7	8	9	10	11	12	14	16	20	24	30	40	50	75	100	200	500	∞
50	4.03 / 7.17	3.18 / 5.06	2.79 / 4.20	2.56 / 3.72	2.40 / 3.41	2.29 / 3.19	2.20 / 3.02	2.13 / 2.89	2.07 / 2.78	2.03 / 2.70	1.99 / 2.63	1.95 / 2.56	1.89 / 2.46	1.85 / 2.38	1.78 / 2.27	1.74 / 2.18	1.69 / 2.10	1.63 / 2.01	1.60 / 1.95	1.55 / 1.87	1.52 / 1.82	1.48 / 1.76	1.46 / 1.71	1.44 / 1.68
55	4.02 / 7.12	3.16 / 5.01	2.77 / 4.16	2.54 / 3.68	2.38 / 3.37	2.27 / 3.15	2.18 / 2.98	2.11 / 2.85	2.06 / 2.75	2.01 / 2.66	1.97 / 2.59	1.93 / 2.53	1.88 / 2.42	1.83 / 2.34	1.76 / 2.23	1.72 / 2.15	1.67 / 2.06	1.61 / 1.97	1.58 / 1.91	1.53 / 1.83	1.50 / 1.78	1.46 / 1.71	1.43 / 1.67	1.41 / 1.64
60	4.00 / 7.08	3.15 / 4.98	2.76 / 4.13	2.53 / 3.65	2.37 / 3.34	2.25 / 3.12	2.17 / 2.95	2.10 / 2.82	2.04 / 2.72	1.99 / 2.63	1.95 / 2.56	1.92 / 2.50	1.86 / 2.39	1.82 / 2.31	1.75 / 2.20	1.70 / 2.12	1.65 / 2.03	1.59 / 1.94	1.56 / 1.88	1.51 / 1.79	1.48 / 1.75	1.44 / 1.68	1.41 / 1.63	1.39 / 1.60
65	3.99 / 7.04	3.14 / 4.95	2.75 / 4.10	2.51 / 3.62	2.36 / 3.31	2.24 / 3.09	2.15 / 2.93	2.08 / 2.80	2.03 / 2.69	1.98 / 2.61	1.94 / 2.53	1.90 / 2.47	1.85 / 2.37	1.80 / 2.29	1.73 / 2.17	1.69 / 2.09	1.63 / 2.00	1.58 / 1.91	1.54 / 1.85	1.49 / 1.77	1.46 / 1.72	1.42 / 1.65	1.39 / 1.60	1.37 / 1.57
70	3.98 / 7.01	3.13 / 4.92	2.74 / 4.07	2.50 / 3.60	2.35 / 3.29	2.23 / 3.07	2.14 / 2.91	2.07 / 2.78	2.02 / 2.67	1.97 / 2.59	1.93 / 2.51	1.89 / 2.45	1.84 / 2.35	1.79 / 2.27	1.72 / 2.15	1.67 / 2.07	1.62 / 1.98	1.57 / 1.89	1.53 / 1.83	1.48 / 1.74	1.45 / 1.70	1.40 / 1.62	1.37 / 1.57	1.35 / 1.54
80	3.96 / 6.96	3.11 / 4.88	2.72 / 4.04	2.49 / 3.56	2.33 / 3.26	2.21 / 3.04	2.13 / 2.87	2.06 / 2.74	2.00 / 2.64	1.95 / 2.55	1.91 / 2.48	1.88 / 2.42	1.82 / 2.31	1.77 / 2.23	1.70 / 2.12	1.65 / 2.03	1.60 / 1.94	1.54 / 1.85	1.51 / 1.79	1.45 / 1.70	1.43 / 1.65	1.38 / 1.58	1.35 / 1.53	1.33 / 1.50
100	3.94 / 6.90	3.09 / 4.82	2.70 / 3.98	2.46 / 3.51	2.31 / 3.21	2.19 / 2.99	2.10 / 2.82	2.03 / 2.69	1.97 / 2.59	1.93 / 2.50	1.89 / 2.43	1.85 / 2.37	1.79 / 2.27	1.75 / 2.19	1.68 / 2.07	1.63 / 1.98	1.57 / 1.89	1.52 / 1.80	1.48 / 1.74	1.42 / 1.65	1.39 / 1.60	1.34 / 1.52	1.31 / 1.47	1.28 / 1.43
125	3.92 / 6.84	3.07 / 4.78	2.68 / 3.94	2.44 / 3.47	2.29 / 3.17	2.17 / 2.95	2.08 / 2.79	2.01 / 2.66	1.96 / 2.55	1.91 / 2.47	1.87 / 2.39	1.83 / 2.33	1.77 / 2.23	1.73 / 2.15	1.66 / 2.03	1.60 / 1.94	1.55 / 1.85	1.49 / 1.76	1.45 / 1.69	1.40 / 1.60	1.36 / 1.55	1.31 / 1.47	1.27 / 1.41	1.25 / 1.37
150	3.90 / 6.81	3.06 / 4.75	2.66 / 3.91	2.43 / 3.45	2.27 / 3.14	2.16 / 2.92	2.07 / 2.76	2.00 / 2.63	1.94 / 2.53	1.89 / 2.44	1.85 / 2.37	1.82 / 2.31	1.76 / 2.20	1.71 / 2.12	1.64 / 2.00	1.59 / 1.92	1.54 / 1.83	1.48 / 1.73	1.44 / 1.66	1.38 / 1.57	1.34 / 1.52	1.29 / 1.43	1.25 / 1.38	1.22 / 1.33
200	3.89 / 6.76	3.04 / 4.71	2.65 / 3.88	2.42 / 3.41	2.26 / 3.11	2.14 / 2.89	2.06 / 2.73	1.98 / 2.60	1.93 / 2.50	1.88 / 2.41	1.84 / 2.34	1.80 / 2.27	1.74 / 2.17	1.69 / 2.09	1.62 / 1.97	1.57 / 1.89	1.52 / 1.79	1.46 / 1.69	1.41 / 1.63	1.35 / 1.53	1.32 / 1.48	1.26 / 1.39	1.22 / 1.33	1.19 / 1.28
400	3.86 / 6.70	3.02 / 4.66	2.63 / 3.83	2.39 / 3.37	2.24 / 3.06	2.12 / 2.85	2.03 / 2.68	1.96 / 2.56	1.90 / 2.45	1.85 / 2.37	1.81 / 2.29	1.78 / 2.23	1.72 / 2.13	1.67 / 2.05	1.60 / 1.92	1.54 / 1.84	1.49 / 1.75	1.42 / 1.64	1.38 / 1.58	1.32 / 1.48	1.28 / 1.42	1.22 / 1.32	1.17 / 1.25	1.13 / 1.19
1000	3.85 / 6.66	3.00 / 4.63	2.61 / 3.80	2.38 / 3.34	2.22 / 3.04	2.11 / 2.82	2.02 / 2.66	1.95 / 2.53	1.89 / 2.43	1.84 / 2.34	1.80 / 2.27	1.76 / 2.20	1.70 / 2.10	1.65 / 2.02	1.58 / 1.90	1.53 / 1.81	1.47 / 1.72	1.41 / 1.61	1.36 / 1.54	1.30 / 1.44	1.26 / 1.38	1.19 / 1.28	1.13 / 1.19	1.08 / 1.12
∞	3.84 / 6.63	3.00 / 4.61	2.60 / 3.78	2.37 / 3.32	2.21 / 3.02	2.10 / 2.80	2.01 / 2.64	1.94 / 2.51	1.88 / 2.41	1.83 / 2.32	1.79 / 2.25	1.75 / 2.18	1.69 / 2.08	1.64 / 2.00	1.57 / 1.88	1.52 / 1.79	1.46 / 1.70	1.39 / 1.59	1.35 / 1.52	1.28 / 1.42	1.24 / 1.36	1.17 / 1.25	1.11 / 1.18	1.00 / 1.00

TABLE E.10 Critical Values of the Durbin-Watson Test Statistic for $\alpha = 0.01$

	k = 1		k = 2		k = 3		k = 4		k = 5	
n	d_L	d_U	d_L	d_U	d_L	d_U	d_L	d_U	d_L	d_U
15	0.81	1.07	0.70	1.25	0.59	1.46	0.49	1.70	0.39	1.96
16	0.84	1.09	0.74	1.25	0.63	1.44	0.53	1.66	0.44	1.90
17	0.87	1.10	0.77	1.25	0.67	1.43	0.57	1.63	0.48	1.85
18	0.90	1.12	0.80	1.26	0.71	1.42	0.61	1.60	0.52	1.80
19	0.93	1.13	0.83	1.26	0.74	1.41	0.65	1.58	0.56	1.77
20	0.95	1.15	0.86	1.27	0.77	1.41	0.68	1.57	0.60	1.74
21	0.97	1.16	0.89	1.27	0.80	1.41	0.72	1.55	0.63	1.71
22	1.00	1.17	0.91	1.28	0.83	1.40	0.75	1.54	0.66	1.69
23	1.02	1.19	0.94	1.29	0.86	1.40	0.77	1.53	0.70	1.67
24	1.05	1.20	0.96	1.30	0.88	1.41	0.80	1.53	0.72	1.66
25	1.05	1.21	0.98	1.30	0.90	1.41	0.83	1.52	0.75	1.65
26	1.07	1.22	1.00	1.31	0.93	1.41	0.85	1.52	0.78	1.64
27	1.09	1.23	1.02	1.32	0.95	1.41	0.88	1.51	0.81	1.63
28	1.10	1.24	1.04	1.32	0.97	1.41	0.90	1.51	0.83	1.62
29	1.12	1.25	1.05	1.33	0.99	1.42	0.92	1.51	0.85	1.61
30	1.13	1.26	1.07	1.34	1.01	1.42	0.94	1.51	0.88	1.61
31	1.15	1.27	1.08	1.34	1.02	1.42	0.96	1.51	0.90	1.60
32	1.16	1.28	1.10	1.35	1.04	1.43	0.98	1.51	0.92	1.60
33	1.17	1.29	1.11	1.36	1.05	1.43	1.00	1.51	0.94	1.59
34	1.18	1.30	1.13	1.36	1.07	1.43	1.01	1.51	0.95	1.59
35	1.19	1.31	1.14	1.37	1.08	1.44	1.03	1.51	0.97	1.59
36	1.21	1.32	1.15	1.38	1.10	1.44	1.04	1.51	0.99	1.59
37	1.22	1.32	1.16	1.38	1.11	1.45	1.06	1.51	1.00	1.59
38	1.23	1.33	1.18	1.39	1.12	1.45	1.07	1.52	1.02	1.58
39	1.24	1.34	1.19	1.39	1.14	1.45	1.09	1.52	1.03	1.58
40	1.25	1.34	1.20	1.40	1.15	1.46	1.10	1.52	1.05	1.58
45	1.29	1.38	1.24	1.42	1.20	1.48	1.16	1.53	1.11	1.58
50	1.32	1.40	1.28	1.45	1.24	1.49	1.20	1.54	1.16	1.59
55	1.36	1.43	1.32	1.47	1.28	1.51	1.25	1.55	1.21	1.59
60	1.38	1.45	1.35	1.48	1.32	1.52	1.28	1.56	1.25	1.60
65	1.41	1.47	1.38	1.50	1.35	1.53	1.31	1.57	1.28	1.61
70	1.43	1.49	1.40	1.52	1.37	1.55	1.34	1.58	1.31	1.61
75	1.45	1.50	1.42	1.53	1.39	1.56	1.37	1.59	1.34	1.62
80	1.47	1.52	1.44	1.54	1.42	1.57	1.39	1.60	1.36	1.62
85	1.48	1.53	1.46	1.55	1.43	1.58	1.41	1.60	1.39	1.63
90	1.50	1.54	1.47	1.56	1.45	1.59	1.43	1.61	1.41	1.64
95	1.51	1.55	1.49	1.57	1.47	1.60	1.45	1.62	1.42	1.64
100	1.52	1.56	1.50	1.58	1.48	1.60	1.46	1.63	1.44	1.65

TABLE E.10   Critical Values of the Durbin-Watson Test Statistic for $\alpha = 0.05$

	$k = 1$		$k = 2$		$k = 3$		$k = 4$		$k = 5$	
n	d_L	d_U	d_L	d_U	d_L	d_U	d_L	d_U	d_L	d_U
15	1.08	1.36	0.95	1.54	0.82	1.75	0.69	1.97	0.56	2.21
16	1.10	1.37	0.98	1.54	0.86	1.73	0.74	1.93	0.62	2.15
17	1.13	1.38	1.02	1.54	0.90	1.71	0.78	1.90	0.67	2.10
18	1.16	1.39	1.05	1.53	0.93	1.69	0.82	1.87	0.71	2.06
19	1.18	1.40	1.08	1.53	0.97	1.68	0.86	1.85	0.75	2.02
20	1.20	1.41	1.10	1.54	1.00	1.68	0.90	1.83	0.79	1.99
21	1.22	1.42	1.13	1.54	1.03	1.67	0.93	1.81	0.83	1.96
22	1.24	1.43	1.15	1.54	1.05	1.66	0.96	1.80	0.86	1.94
23	1.26	1.44	1.17	1.54	1.08	1.66	0.99	1.79	0.90	1.92
24	1.27	1.45	1.19	1.55	1.10	1.66	1.01	1.78	0.93	1.90
25	1.29	1.45	1.21	1.55	1.12	1.66	1.04	1.77	0.95	1.89
26	1.30	1.46	1.22	1.55	1.14	1.65	1.06	1.76	0.98	1.88
27	1.32	1.47	1.24	1.56	1.16	1.65	1.08	1.76	1.01	1.86
28	1.33	1.48	1.26	1.56	1.18	1.65	1.10	1.75	1.03	1.85
29	1.34	1.48	1.27	1.56	1.20	1.65	1.12	1.74	1.05	1.84
30	1.35	1.49	1.28	1.57	1.21	1.65	1.14	1.74	1.07	1.83
31	1.36	1.50	1.30	1.57	1.23	1.65	1.16	1.74	1.09	1.83
32	1.37	1.50	1.31	1.57	1.24	1.65	1.18	1.73	1.11	1.82
33	1.38	1.51	1.32	1.58	1.26	1.65	1.19	1.73	1.13	1.81
34	1.39	1.51	1.33	1.58	1.27	1.65	1.21	1.73	1.15	1.81
35	1.40	1.52	1.34	1.58	1.28	1.65	1.22	1.73	1.16	1.80
36	1.41	1.52	1.35	1.59	1.29	1.65	1.24	1.73	1.18	1.80
37	1.42	1.53	1.36	1.59	1.31	1.66	1.25	1.72	1.19	1.80
38	1.43	1.54	1.37	1.59	1.32	1.66	1.26	1.72	1.21	1.79
39	1.43	1.54	1.38	1.60	1.33	1.66	1.27	1.72	1.22	1.79
40	1.44	1.54	1.39	1.60	1.34	1.66	1.29	1.72	1.23	1.79
45	1.48	1.57	1.43	1.62	1.38	1.67	1.34	1.72	1.29	1.78
50	1.50	1.59	1.46	1.63	1.42	1.67	1.38	1.72	1.34	1.77
55	1.53	1.60	1.49	1.64	1.45	1.68	1.41	1.72	1.38	1.77
60	1.55	1.62	1.51	1.65	1.48	1.69	1.44	1.73	1.41	1.77
65	1.57	1.63	1.54	1.66	1.50	1.70	1.47	1.73	1.44	1.77
70	1.58	1.64	1.55	1.67	1.52	1.70	1.49	1.74	1.46	1.77
75	1.60	1.65	1.57	1.68	1.54	1.71	1.51	1.74	1.49	1.77
80	1.61	1.66	1.59	1.69	1.56	1.72	1.53	1.74	1.51	1.77
85	1.62	1.67	1.60	1.70	1.57	1.72	1.55	1.75	1.52	1.77
90	1.63	1.68	1.61	1.70	1.59	1.73	1.57	1.75	1.54	1.78
95	1.64	1.69	1.62	1.71	1.60	1.73	1.58	1.75	1.56	1.78
100	1.65	1.69	1.63	1.72	1.61	1.74	1.59	1.76	1.57	1.78

Source: Reproduced by permission from J. Durbin and G. S. Watson, "Testing for Serial Correlation in Least Squares Regression, II," *Biometrika* 38 (1951), pp. 159–78, as found in Amir D. Aczel, *Complete Business Statistics* (Homewood, Ill.: Richard D. Irwin, 1989), pp. 1036–37.

INDEX

· ·

Areas of the Standard Normal Distribution

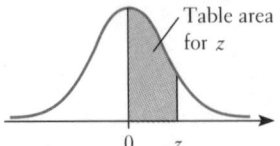

Table area
for z

The table areas are probabilities that the standard normal random variable is between 0 and z.

z	0.00	0.01	0.02	0.03	0.04	0.05	0.06	0.07	0.08	0.09
					Second Decimal Place in z					
0.0	0.0000	0.0040	0.0080	0.0120	0.0160	0.0199	0.0239	0.0279	0.0319	0.0359
0.1	0.0398	0.0438	0.0478	0.0517	0.0557	0.0596	0.0636	0.0675	0.0714	0.0753
0.2	0.0793	0.0832	0.0871	0.0910	0.0948	0.0987	0.1026	0.1064	0.1103	0.1141
0.3	0.1179	0.1217	0.1255	0.1293	0.1331	0.1368	0.1406	0.1443	0.1480	0.1517
0.4	0.1554	0.1591	0.1628	0.1664	0.1700	0.1736	0.1772	0.1808	0.1844	0.1879
0.5	0.1915	0.1950	0.1985	0.2019	0.2054	0.2088	0.2123	0.2157	0.2190	0.2224
0.6	0.2257	0.2291	0.2324	0.2357	0.2389	0.2422	0.2454	0.2486	0.2517	0.2549
0.7	0.2580	0.2611	0.2642	0.2673	0.2704	0.2734	0.2764	0.2794	0.2823	0.2852
0.8	0.2881	0.2910	0.2939	0.2967	0.2995	0.3023	0.3051	0.3078	0.3106	0.3133
0.9	0.3159	0.3186	0.3212	0.3238	0.3264	0.3289	0.3315	0.3340	0.3365	0.3389
1.0	0.3413	0.3438	0.3461	0.3485	0.3508	0.3531	0.3554	0.3577	0.3599	0.3621
1.1	0.3643	0.3665	0.3686	0.3708	0.3729	0.3749	0.3770	0.3790	0.3810	0.3830
1.2	0.3849	0.3869	0.3888	0.3907	0.3925	0.3944	0.3962	0.3980	0.3997	0.4015
1.3	0.4032	0.4049	0.4066	0.4082	0.4099	0.4115	0.4131	0.4147	0.4162	0.4177
1.4	0.4192	0.4207	0.4222	0.4236	0.4251	0.4265	0.4279	0.4292	0.4306	0.4319
1.5	0.4332	0.4345	0.4357	0.4370	0.4382	0.4394	0.4406	0.4418	0.4429	0.4441
1.6	0.4452	0.4463	0.4474	0.4484	0.4495	0.4505	0.4515	0.4525	0.4535	0.4545
1.7	0.4554	0.4564	0.4573	0.4582	0.4591	0.4599	0.4608	0.4616	0.4625	0.4633
1.8	0.4641	0.4649	0.4656	0.4664	0.4671	0.4678	0.4686	0.4693	0.4699	0.4706
1.9	0.4713	0.4719	0.4726	0.4732	0.4738	0.4744	0.4750	0.4756	0.4761	0.4767
2.0	0.4772	0.4778	0.4783	0.4788	0.4793	0.4798	0.4803	0.4808	0.4812	0.4817
2.1	0.4821	0.4826	0.4830	0.4834	0.4838	0.4842	0.4846	0.4850	0.4854	0.4857
2.2	0.4861	0.4864	0.4868	0.4871	0.4875	0.4878	0.4881	0.4884	0.4887	0.4890
2.3	0.4893	0.4896	0.4898	0.4901	0.4904	0.4906	0.4909	0.4911	0.4913	0.4916
2.4	0.4918	0.4920	0.4922	0.4925	0.4927	0.4929	0.4931	0.4932	0.4934	0.4936
2.5	0.4938	0.4940	0.4941	0.4943	0.4945	0.4946	0.4948	0.4949	0.4951	0.4952
2.6	0.4953	0.4955	0.4956	0.4957	0.4959	0.4960	0.4961	0.4962	0.4963	0.4964
2.7	0.4965	0.4966	0.4967	0.4968	0.4969	0.4970	0.4971	0.4972	0.4973	0.4974
2.8	0.4974	0.4975	0.4976	0.4977	0.4977	0.4978	0.4979	0.4979	0.4980	0.4981
2.9	0.4981	0.4982	0.4982	0.4983	0.4984	0.4984	0.4985	0.4985	0.4986	0.4986
3.0	0.4987	0.4987	0.4987	0.4988	0.4988	0.4989	0.4989	0.4989	0.4990	0.4990
3.1	0.4990	0.4991	0.4991	0.4991	0.4992	0.4992	0.4992	0.4992	0.4993	0.4993
3.2	0.4993	0.4993	0.4994	0.4994	0.4994	0.4994	0.4994	0.4995	0.4995	0.4995
3.3	0.4995	0.4995	0.4995	0.4996	0.4996	0.4996	0.4996	0.4996	0.4996	0.4997
3.4	0.4997	0.4997	0.4997	0.4997	0.4997	0.4997	0.4997	0.4997	0.4997	0.4998
3.5	0.4998									
4.0	0.49997									
4.5	0.499997									
5.0	0.4999997									
6.0	0.499999999									